THE CULTURE OF CITIES

Westport: Greenwood Press,   0313227462

BOOKS BY LEWIS MUMFORD

THE CULTURE
OF CITIES

LEWIS MUMFORD

GREENWOOD PRESS, PUBLISHERS
WESTPORT, CONNECTICUT

Library of Congress Cataloging in Publication Data

Mumford, Lewis, 1895–
   The culture of cities.

   Reprint of the ed. published by Harcourt, Brace,
Jovanovich, New York.
   Bibliography: p.
   Includes index.
   1. Cities and towns. 2. City planning. 3. Reg-
ional planning. I. Title.
[HT151.M78 1981]   307.7'6   80-23130
ISBN 0-313-22746-2 (lib. bdg.)

First published, 1938; this is a reprint of the paperback re-
issue, 1970.

Reprinted by arrangement with Harcourt Brace Jovanovich,
Inc.

Reprinted in 1981 by Greenwood Press
A division of Congressional Information Service, Inc.
88 Post Road West, Westport, Connecticut 06881

Printed in the United States of America

P

In order to keep this title in print and available to the academic community, this edition
was produced using digital reprint technology in a relatively short print run. This would
not have been attainable using traditional methods. Although the cover has been changed
from its original appearance, the text remains the same and all materials and methods
used still conform to the highest book-making standards.

As far back as 1915, under the stimulus of Patrick Geddes, I began to collect the materials that have gone into this book. Like my hitherto published papers and books on architecture, community planning, housing, and regional development, the present study rests primarily on first-hand surveys, conducted in many different regions: beginning with a close study of my own city and region—New York and its immediate hinterland. It both attempts to explore in a more unified way a field hitherto worked on divergent lines by specialists, and to establish, for the purpose of communal action, the basic principles upon which our human environment—buildings, neighborhoods, cities, regions—may be renovated. Certain aspects of life, those ordinarily treated under the head of ethics, religion, and education, remain to be dealt with at another time. Even at the risk of an occasional repetition of thought, I have had to parallel in this volume parts of Technics and Civilization; but it should be plain that the two works, while independent, are complementary: each seeks to explore what the modern world may hold for mankind once men of good will have learned to subdue the barbarous mechanisms and the mechanized barbarisms that now threaten the very existence of civilization. **L. M.**

PREFACE TO THE
1970 EDITION

When 'The Culture of Cities' appeared a generation ago, the literature of cities was still extremely meager. Despite the work of Marcel Poëte and Pierre Lavedan, the urban historians, Max Weber, the sociologist, and my own master, Patrick Geddes, most of the current thinking about cities proceeded without sufficient insight into their nature, their function, their purpose, their historic role, or their potential future. The brief Introduction that opened 'The Culture of Cities' put the whole process of urban development in a fresh perspective; and the chapters that followed were so far in advance of current thinking that I have no hesitation in reprinting them without altering a word —though further observation and experience have called for various minor revisions I have made in later works.

From the outset, 'The Culture of Cities' was widely hailed as an outstanding interpretation and a worthy successor to its earlier companion volume, 'Technics and Civilization.' But despite a certain measure of popular success, the book exerted little influence in the United States. To many urban planners, administrators, and academic specialists, its constructive proposals seemed too remote from 'practical' financial and political requirements to be acceptable; and even some of my onetime co-workers and friends regarded my picture of the increasing demoralization and disintegration of Megalopolis as farfetched and unduly pessimistic.

But elsewhere in the world, as it turned out, 'The Culture of Cities' proved to be a timely and encouraging contribution; and during the next two decades, while hope was still "too like despair for prudence to smother," it exerted a marked influence. The very parts of the book that offended the American specialists in planning and housing made sense to the peoples of Britain and the occupied countries of Europe, whose cities, from Warsaw to London, were being reduced to rubble. They had no difficulty in envisaging Necropolis, the City of the Dead: it was already there. They knew all too well that something had gone wrong with civilization itself: the mounting disasters from 1914 on had prepared their minds for the constructive changes that would be necessary to rebuild their world on a sounder human foundation.

In some countries, notably Britain, 'The Culture of Cities' served as a guidebook to reconstruction and renewal. Despite its high price, the first English edition sold out promptly; and half a generation ago, in a poll of municipal officials in Britain, it was still chosen, almost unanimously, as the one book essential for a planner's education. Not the least service performed by this work was to re-enforce the policy for handling urban growth, not by endless suburban extensions, or heavier internal congestion, but by building New Towns: the method advocated and demonstrated by Sir Ebenezer Howard and his associates in the successful building of two garden cities. These proposals, for long dismissed as 'romantic' or 'old-fashioned'—and even now strangely denounced by Jane Jacobs as an effort to destroy the city—were, so far from being backward, half a century ahead of their time, for Howard's 'Garden Cities of Tomorrow' had been published in 1898.

If 'The Culture of Cities' encouraged and stimulated many people in Britain, it had an even more extraordinary, if more limited, effect upon the younger planners of the continent. (The one exception here was France, whose leading urban propagandist, Le Corbusier, had set the fashion for those extravagant high-rise structures that have conformed so admirably to the bureaucratic and technocratic—above all, financial—requirement of the dominant pecuniary-power economy.) Though only a few copies of the American or English editions had trickled into the occupied countries before 1939, they had an effect out of all proportion to their numbers. Summarized in translations, the book, I am happy to report, was used in underground schools of planning in Poland, the Netherlands, and even in Greece. The one copy available in Poland, Matthew Nowicki told me, was actually taken by a prisoner to Auschwitz, and miraculously survived, like its possessor, to return to Warsaw. Similarly, in Finland, a copy of the Swedish edition—brought back, I believe by Alvar Aalto—was presented to the Prime Minister as offering valuable proposals for Finland's housing and planning after the war.

But soon after the war ended, in the letdown that too often follows an all-out collective effort, the tide turned against such a radical approach to urban and regional rehabilitation. Though the ideas put forward in 'The Culture of Cities' continued to have an indirect effect upon the design of the British New Towns from 1947 onward, and had a direct effect upon the rebuilding of Coventry, not least its Shopping Center, more fashionable thought, extrapolating past tendencies, turned toward further metropolitan concentration, with high-rise building for residences as well as offices, with ruthless, socially destructive modes of 'urban renewal,' with the reckless dispersal of population by means of multi-laned expressways that daily poured pollution-laden streams of traffic into the city, turning even the proud boulevards of Paris into mere parking lots. In short, Le Corbusier's bureaucratic concept of the modern metropolis—artfully disguised as *'la ville radieuse'*—temporarily won out.

As a result, by the mid-nineteen-fifties, a professor of urban planning did not hesitate to dismiss 'The Culture of Cities' as a 'Museum Piece.' In 'The Urban Prospect' I have paid my respects to the reigning authorities in urban planning, the technocrats and bureaucrats, the statisticians and mathematical modellers who turned their backs upon the ecological and cultural realities of the city in the hope of transferring all its essential activities to the computer; and I will not trouble to repeat those disrespectful compliments. Enough to say that I only wish I had written more such 'Museum Pieces'; for the very parts of 'The Culture of Cities' that were rejected as obsolete or irrelevant—the chapters on megalopolitan disintegration, on The Politics of Regional Development, and on the Social Basis of the New Urban Order, like my earlier descriptions of environmental pollution—were precisely those that had grown immensely in significance. At least the younger generation has now caught up with me.

Meanwhile, my own thinking did not halt at the point I had reached in 1938. As a professor of City and Regional Planning at the University of Pennsylvania during the nineteen-fifties, I found it necessary to cover the entire span of urban history; and I accordingly expanded the historic chapters of 'The Culture of Cities' into the wider panorama of 'The City in History': a book whose measure has still to be taken. In conceiving that new work, I intended to follow it with an equally exhaustive account of the contemporary urban prospects: a generous expansion of the second half of the present volume. But since there is no immediate likelihood of my completing such a book, there is all the more reason for bringing out the present volume in its original form; for it is in these final chapters that the ecological foundations for a balanced urban environment were laid down. For those who wish to pursue this line of thinking further, I would suggest the final chapters of 'The Pentagon of Power' (1971).

LEWIS MUMFORD

Spring 1970

CONTENTS

CONTENTS

ILLUSTRATIONS

NOTE: *Illustrations and captions are an integral part of the book: but designed to be consulted separately without breaking the flow of the text. References to them in the index are denoted by the plate number, enclosed in brackets.*

THE CULTURE OF CITIES

INTRODUCTION

The city, as one finds it in history, is the point of maximum concentration for the power and culture of a community. It is the place where the diffused rays of many separate beams of life fall into focus, with gains in both social effectiveness and significance. The city is the form and symbol of an integrated social relationship: it is the seat of the temple, the market, the hall of justice, the academy of learning. Here in the city the goods of civilization are multiplied and manifolded; here is where human experience is transformed into viable signs, symbols, patterns of conduct, systems of order. Here is where the issues of civilization are focused: here, too, ritual passes on occasion into the active drama of a fully differentiated and self-conscious society.

Cities are a product of the earth. They reflect the peasant's cunning in dominating the earth; technically they but carry further his skill in turning the soil to productive uses, in enfolding his cattle for safety, in regulating the waters that moisten his fields, in providing storage bins and barns for his crops. Cities are emblems of that settled life which began with permanent agriculture: a life conducted with the aid of permanent shelters, permanent utilities like orchards, vineyards, and irrigation works, and permanent buildings for protection and storage.

Every phase of life in the countryside contributes to the existence of cities. What the shepherd, the woodman, and the miner know, becomes transformed and "etherealized" through the city into durable elements in the human heritage: the textiles and butter of one, the moats and dams and wooden pipes and lathes of another, the metals and jewels of the third, are finally converted into instruments of urban living: underpinning the city's economic existence, contribut-

3

ing art and wisdom to its daily routine. Within the city the essence of each type of soil and labor and economic goal is concentrated: thus arise greater possibilities for interchange and for new combinations not given in the isolation of their original habitats.

Cities are a product of time. They are the molds in which men's lifetimes have cooled and congealed, giving lasting shape, by way of art, to moments that would otherwise vanish with the living and leave no means of renewal or wider participation behind them. In the city, time becomes visible: buildings and monuments and public ways, more open than the written record, more subject to the gaze of many men than the scattered artifacts of the countryside, leave an imprint upon the minds even of the ignorant or the indifferent. Through the material fact of preservation, time challenges time, time clashes with time: habits and values carry over beyond the living group, streaking with different strata of time the character of any single generation. Layer upon layer, past times preserve themselves in the city until life itself is finally threatened with suffocation: then, in sheer defense, modern man invents the museum.

By the diversity of its time-structures, the city in part escapes the tyranny of a single present, and the monotony of a future that consists in repeating only a single beat heard in the past. Through its complex orchestration of time and space, no less than through the social division of labor, life in the city takes on the character of a symphony: specialized human aptitudes, specialized instruments, give rise to sonorous results which, neither in volume nor in quality, could be achieved by any single piece.

Cities arise out of man's social needs and multiply both their modes and their methods of expression. In the city remote forces and influences intermingle with the local: their conflicts are no less significant than their harmonies. And here, through the concentration of the means of intercourse in the market and the meeting place, alternative modes of living present themselves: the deeply rutted ways of the village cease to be coercive and the ancestral goals cease to be all-sufficient: strange men and women, strange interests, and stranger gods loosen the traditional ties of blood and neighborhood. A sailing ship, a caravan, stopping at the city, may bring a new dye for wool, a new glaze for the potter's dish, a new system of signs for long distance communication, or a new thought about human destiny.

In the urban milieu, mechanical shocks produce social results; and social needs may take shape in contrivances and inventions which will lead industries and governments into new channels of experiment. Now the need for a common fortified spot for shelter against predatory attack draws the inhabitants of the indigenous village into a hillside fortification: through the compulsive mingling for defense, the possibilities for more regular intercourse and wider co-operation arise. That fact helps transform the nest of villages into a unified city, with its higher ceiling of achievement and its wider horizons. Now the collective sharing of experience, and the stimulus of rational criticism, turn the rites of the village festival into the more powerful imaginative forms of the tragic drama: experience is deepened, as well as more widely circulated, through this process. Or again, on another plane, the goldsmith's passive repository for valuables becomes, through the pressure of urban needs and the opportunities of the market, the dynamic agent of capitalism, the bank, lending money as well as keeping it, putting capital into circulation, finally dominating the processes of trade and production.

The city is a fact in nature, like a cave, a run of mackerel or an ant-heap. But it is also a conscious work of art, and it holds within its communal framework many simpler and more personal forms of art. Mind *takes form* in the city; and in turn, urban forms condition mind. For space, no less than time, is artfully reorganized in cities: in boundary lines and silhouettes, in the fixing of horizontal planes and vertical peaks, in utilizing or denying the natural site, the city records the attitude of a culture and an epoch to the fundamental facts of its existence. The dome and the spire, the open avenue and the closed court, tell the story, not merely of different physical accommodations, but of essentially different conceptions of man's destiny. The city is both a physical utility for collective living and a symbol of those collective purposes and unanimities that arise under such favoring circumstance. With language itself, it remains man's greatest work of art.

Through its concrete, visible command over space the city lends itself, not only to the practical offices of production, but to the daily communion of its citizens: this constant effect of the city, as a col lective work of art, was expressed in a classic manner by Thomas Mann in his address to his fellow-townsmen of Lübeck on the cele-bration of the anniversary of Lübeck's foundation. When the city ceases to be a symbol of art and order, it acts in a negative fashion: it expresses and helps to make more universal the fact of disintegra-tion. In the close quarters of the city, perversities and evils spread more quickly; and in the stones of the city, these anti-social facts become embedded: it is not the triumphs of urban living that awaken the prophetic wrath of a Jeremiah, a Savonarola, a Rousseau, or a Ruskin.

What transforms the passive agricultural regime of the village into the active institutions of the city? The difference is not merely one of magnitude, density of population, or economic resources. For the active agent is any factor that extends the area of local inter-course, that engenders the need for combination and co-operation, communication and communion; and that so creates a common un-derlying pattern of conduct, and a common set of physical structures, for the different family and occupational groups that constitute a city. These opportunities and activities superimpose upon primary groups, based upon traditional acceptances and daily face-to-face contact, the more active associations, the more specialized functions, and the more purposive interests of secondary groups: in the latter the purpose is not given, but chosen: the membership and the activi-ties are selective: the group itself becomes specialized and differen-tiated.

Historically, the increase of population, through the change from hunting to agriculture, may have abetted this change; the widening of trade routes and the diversification of occupations likewise helped. But the nature of the city is not to be found simply in its economic base: the city is primarily a social emergent. The mark of the city is its purposive social complexity. It represents the maximum pos-sibility of humanizing the natural environment and of naturalizing the human heritage: it gives a cultural shape to the first, and it ex-ternalizes, in permanent collective forms, the second.

"The central and significant fact about the city," as Geddes and Branford pointed out, "is that the city . . . functions as the spe-cialized organ of social transmission. It accumulates and embodies

the heritage of a region, and combines in some measure and kind
with the cultural heritage of larger units, national, racial, religious,
human. On one side is the individuality of the city—the sign manual
of its regional life and record. On the other are the marks of the
civilization, in which each particular city is a constituent element."

Today a great many things stand in the way of grasping the rôle
of the city and of transforming this basic means of communal existence. During the last few centuries the strenuous mechanical organization of industry, and the setting up of tyrannous political states,
have blinded most men to the importance of facts that do not easily
fit into the general pattern of mechanical conquest, capitalistic forms
of exploitation, and power politics. Habitually, people treat the
realities of personality and association and city as abstractions, while
they treat confused pragmatic abstractions such as money, credit,
political sovereignty, as if they were concrete realities that had an
existence independent of human conventions.

Looking back over the course of Western Civilization since the
fifteenth century, it is fairly plain that mechanical integration and
social disruption have gone on side by side. Our capacity for effective physical organization has enormously increased; but our ability
to create a harmonious counterpoise to these external linkages by
means of co-operative and civic associations on both a regional and
a world-wide basis, like the Christian Church in the Middle Ages, has
not kept pace with these mechanical triumphs. By one of those mischievous turns, from which history is rarely free, it was precisely
during this period of flowing physical energies, social disintegration,
and bewildered political experiment that the populations of the
world as a whole began mightily to increase, and the cities of the
Western World began to grow at an inordinate rate. Forms of social
life that the wisest no longer understood, the more ignorant were
prepared to build. Or rather: the ignorant were completely unpre-
pared, but that did not prevent the building.

The result was not a temporary confusion and an occasional lapse
in efficiency. What followed was a crystallization of chaos: disorder
hardened uncouthly in metropolitan slum and industrial factory districts; and the exodus into the dormitory suburbs and factory spores
that surrounded the growing cities merely widened the area of social

derangement. The mechanized physical shell took precedence in every growing town over the civic nucleus: men became dissociated as citizens in the very process of coming together in imposing economic organizations. Even industry, which was supposedly served by this planless building and random physical organization, lost seriously in efficiency: it failed to produce a new urban form that served directly its complicated processes. As for the growing urban populations, they lacked the most elementary facilities for urban living, even sunlight and fresh air, to say nothing of the means to a more vivid social life. The new cities grew up without the benefit of coherent social knowledge or orderly social effort: they lacked the useful urban folkways of the Middle Ages or the confident esthetic command of the Baroque period: indeed, a seventeenth century Dutch peasant, in his little village, knew more about the art of living in communities than a nineteenth century municipal councilor in London or Berlin. Statesmen who did not hesitate to weld together a diversity of regional interests into national states, or who wove together an empire that girdled the planet, failed to produce even a rough draft of a decent neighborhood.

In every department, form disintegrated: except in its heritage from the past, the city vanished as an embodiment of collective art and technics. And where, as in North America, the loss was not alleviated by the continued presence of great monuments from the past and persistent habits of social living, the result was a raw, dissolute environment, and a narrow, constricted, and baffled social life. Even in Germany and the Low Countries, where the traditions of urban life had lingered on from the Middle Ages, the most colossal blunders were committed in the most ordinary tasks of urban planning and building. As the pace of urbanization increased, the circle of devastation widened.

Today we face not only the original social disruption. We likewise face the accumulated physical and social results of that disruption: ravaged landscapes, disorderly urban districts, pockets of disease, patches of blight, mile upon mile of standardized slums, worming into the outlying areas of big cities, and fusing with their ineffectual suburbs. In short: a general miscarriage and defeat of civilized effort. So far have our achievements fallen short of our needs that even a hundred years of persistent reform in England, the first country to suffer heavily from disurbanization, have only in the last decade begun to leave an imprint. True: here and there patches of good building and coherent social form exist: new nodes of integration can be detected, and since 1920 these patches have been spreading. But the main results of more than a century of misbuilding and malformation, dissociation and disorganization still hold. Whether the observer focuses his gaze on the physical structure of communal living or upon the social processes that must be embodied and expressed, the report remains the same.

Today we begin to see that the improvement of cities is no matter for small one-sided reforms: the task of city design involves the vaster task of rebuilding our civilization. We must alter the parasitic and predatory modes of life that now play so large a part, and we must create region by region, continent by continent, an effective symbiosis, or co-operative living together. The problem is to co-ordinate, on the basis of more essential human values than the will-to-power and the will-to-profits, a host of social functions and processes that we have hitherto misused in the building of cities and polities, or of which we have never rationally taken advantage.

Unfortunately, the fashionable political philosophies of the past century are of but small help in defining this new task: they dealt with legal abstractions, like Individual and State, with cultural abstractions, like Humanity, the Nation, the Folk, or with bare economic abstractions like the Capitalist Class or the Proletariat—while life as it was lived in the concrete, in regions and cities and villages, in wheatland and cornland and vineland, in the mine, the quarry, the fishery, was conceived as but a shadow of the prevailing myths and arrogant fantasies of the ruling classes—or the often no less shadowy fantasies of those who challenged them.

Here and there one notes, of course, valiant exceptions both in theory and in action. Le Play and Reclus in France, W. H. Riehl in Germany, Kropotkin in Russia, Howard in England, Grundtvig in Denmark, Geddes in Scotland, began half a century ago to lay the ideological basis for a new order. The insights of these men may prove as important for the new biotechnic regime, based on the deliberate culture of life, as the formulations of Leonardo, Galileo,

Newton, and Descartes were for the more limited mechanical order upon which the past triumphs of our machine civilization were founded. In the piecemeal improvement of cities, the work of sanitarians like Chadwick and Richardson, community designers like Olmsted, far-seeing architects, like Parker and Wright, laid the concrete basis for a collective environment in which the needs of reproduction and nurture and psychological development and the social processes themselves would be adequately served.

Now the dominant urban environment of the past century has been mainly a narrow by-product of the machine ideology. And the greater part of it has already been made obsolete by the rapid advance of the biological arts and sciences, and by the steady penetration of sociological thought into every department. We have now reached a point where these fresh accumulations of historical insight and scientific knowledge are ready to flow over into social life, to mold anew the forms of cities, to assist in the transformation of both the instruments and the goals of our civilization. Profound changes, which will affect the distribution and increase of population, the efficiency of industry, and the quality of Western Culture, have already become visible. To form an accurate estimate of these new potentialities and to suggest their direction into channels of human welfare, is one of the major offices of the contemporary student of cities. Ultimately, such studies, forecasts, and imaginative projects must bear directly upon the life of every human being in our civilization.

What is the city? How has it functioned in the Western World since the tenth century, when the renewal of cities began, and in particular, what changes have come about in its physical and social composition during the last century? What factors have conditioned the size of cities, the extent of their growth, the type of order manifested in street plan and in building, their manner of nucleation, the composition of their economic and social classes, their physical manner of existence and their cultural style? By what political processes of federation or amalgamation, co-operative union or centralization, have cities existed; and what new units of administration does the present age suggest? Have we yet found an adequate urban form to harness all the complex technical and social forces in our civilization; and if a new order is discernible, what are its main outlines?

What are the relations between city and region? And what steps are necessary in order to ·redefine and reconstruct the region itself, as a collective human habitation? What, in short, are the possibilities for creating form and order and design in our present civilization?

These are some of the questions I shall pose in the following study. Wherever possible, I shall utilize for answer concrete contemporary examples: a procedure that is all the easier because the germs and embryonic forms of the new order are by now, for the greater part, in existence. But where this is impossible, I shall seek to uncover the essential principle upon whose basis a viable answer or solution may be predicted.

Today our world faces a crisis: a crisis which, if its consequences are as grave as now seems, may not fully be resolved for another century. If the destructive forces in civilization gain ascendancy, our new urban culture will be stricken in every part. Our cities, blasted and deserted, will be cemeteries for the dead: cold lairs given over to less destructive beasts than man. But we may avert that fate: perhaps only in facing such a desperate challenge can the necessary creative forces be effectually welded together. Instead of clinging to the sardonic funeral towers of metropolitan finance, ours to march out to newly plowed fields, to create fresh patterns of political action, to alter for human purposes the perverse mechanisms of our economic regime, to conceive and to germinate fresh forms of human culture.

Instead of accepting the stale cult of death that the fascists have erected, as the proper crown for the servility and the brutality that are the pillars of their states, we must erect a cult of life: life in action, as the farmer or the mechanic knows it: life in expression, as the artist knows it: life as the lover feels it and the parent practices it: life as it is known to men of good will who meditate in the cloister, experiment in the laboratory, or plan intelligently in the factory or the government office.

Nothing is permanent: certainly not the frozen images of barbarous power with which fascism now confronts us. Those images may easily be smashed by an external shock, cracked as ignominiously as fallen Dagon, the massive idol of the heathen: or they may be melted, eventually, by the internal warmth of normal men and women. Nothing endures except life: the capacity for birth, growth, and daily renewal. As life becomes insurgent once more in our civilization, conquering the reckless thrust of barbarism, the culture of cities will be both instrument and goal.

CHAPTER I.

PROTECTION AND THE MEDIEVAL TOWN

1: Stripping Off the Medieval Myth

Before one approaches the medieval town one must strip off the false wrappings in which successive generations have swathed this portion of the European past. The Middle Ages were defamed during the early Renascence for vices that actually belonged to their defamers: history offers many instances of the "transferred reproach." Thus the earlier inhabitants of historic cities were vilified for demolishing precious Roman monuments that were not in fact destroyed until the very period that professed to value them, the age of the new humanists.

Let us depart, to begin with, from the notion that the period from the tenth to the sixteenth century was a compound of ignorance, filth, brutality, and superstition; for such a description does not altogether fit the life of Europe as a whole even during the worst parts of the Dark Ages, which still felt the civilizing influences of Celtic monasticism and the resolute order and economy of Charles the Great. This view of the Middle Ages is partly a product of the eighteenth century "Gothic Romances," with their lurid pictures of torture chambers, cobwebs, mystery, and madness. No doubt such elements existed; but they no more characterized the civilization as a whole than the existence of armed gangsters and organized rackets and fascist pirates entirely characterizes our present civilization. One must not magnify the black spots in the past nor minimize those in our own day.

One must of course equally set aside the charming tapestry of the Middle Ages, composed by Pugin, Ruskin, Morris, and similar writers: they often treated intentions as if they were facts and ideals as if they were realizations. Above all, this version forgets that if the Middle Ages were governed by bold warriors and patient craftsmen, it was likewise a period of embryonic capitalist enterprise and audacious technical improvements: eager merchants, adventurous entrepreneurs, canny inventors: a period that invented the mechanical clock, made radical improvements in mining, sailing, and military attack, and learned to cast iron and manufacture glass spectacles and utilize physical energy on a scale never before achieved by any other civilization.

Our Middle Ages is far richer in detail than the earlier versions; and as respects the management of industry and the building of cities one finds even more to commend than did the most ardent early advocates of Catholic piety. There is a social kinship between our own age and the age of the guilds that parallels the relation I pointed out in Technics and Civilization between the eotechnic and the neotechnic complexes. And in the domain of cities, we have tardily begun to realize that our hard-earned discoveries in the art of laying out towns, especially in the *hygienic* laying out of towns, merely recapitulate, in terms of our own social needs, the commonplaces of sound medieval practice. Does this seem topsy-turvy? On the contrary: it was the myth that was baseless.

2: The Need for Protection

Between the date that symbolizes the fall of Rome and the eleventh century, when the cities of the West awakened to a new life, lies a period that is hard to describe but important to understand. It was out of the incurable misery and terror of this age that certain special attitudes toward life grew up which powerfully affected the development of all the dominant social institutions of the West—particularly the city. Five centuries of violence, paralysis, and uncertainty had created in the European heart a profound desire for security. When every chance might prove a mischance, when every moment might be one's last moment, the need for protection rose above every other concern, and to find a safe haven was about the most one asked from life.

In Italy and France the old ways, it is true, had never entirely disappeared: hence the pagan undercurrents in that life: hence the

twelfth century Renascence, so much more vital, both as continuation and as rebirth, than that which was to follow. But a disorganization and diminishment of the forces of civilization did characterize this period: the worst effects became visible only around the
ninth century. Slavery, which had taken root in Roman agriculture,
was introduced on a wide scale by the conquering barbarians; and
the population, never far from famine, actually decreased. Military
terrorism and its parasitic economy led to a devolution of the city:
people left these stony wastes because they were driven to accept life
at a subsistence level. Even when they remained in the neighborhood
of an old city, like Mainz or Trier, it was no longer a meaningful
part of their active life: only the shell remained. Its stones served as
caves in the rock might have served—bare hiding places for those
fleeing from the wrath to come.

If the Saracen encirclement of the Mediterranean hastened the
passage from the uniform organization on the old imperial lines to a
feudal economy of local production, barter, and consumption, under
special local customs and local laws, the final blow was given at the
other end of Europe by the invasions of the Norsemen in the ninth
century. The final blow—and the first move toward recovery. These
Norse raids were conducted in small boats that pierced the heart of
the countryside between Brittany and the Elbe: no district was immune to their sacking, burning, slaying. The terror of these visitations must have created a new community of interest between the
feudal lord and his dependents; but it also showed the technical inferiority of the local war-band in opposing attacks carried on by
more audacious, perhaps more highly specialized, opponents.

Sheer necessity led to the rediscovery of an important fact. In the
crude state of Western military technics in the ninth century, the
strength and security of a fortified stronghold, perched on some impregnable rock, could be secured even for the relatively helpless
people of the lowlands provided they built a wooden palisade or a
stone wall around their village. Such a wall, particularly when surrounded by a moat, kept the attacker out, and made his weapons
ineffective. In terror of the invaders, the inhabitants of Mainz, for
example, restored at last their dilapidated Roman wall. Under com-
missions from the German emperor, Henry I, walls were built even

around monasteries and nunneries to guard them from attack. And in Italy, too, walls were built again at the end of the ninth century in order to repel the Hungarians and other invaders.

This discovery, fortunately, proved to be double-edged. If the wall could protect the town from outside invasions more successfully than the feudal war-band, could it not also protect the community from the invasions and usurpations of these greedy and arrogant "protectors"? By means of the wall, any village could become another stronghold: people would flock to that island of peace, as originally they had submitted in desperation to the feudal gang-leaders or had given up the hopes of domesticity to find protection in a monastery or a nunnery. Life in the open country, even under the shadow of a castle, ceased to be as attractive as life behind the urban wall. Stockades, such as one still sees in Lucas Cranach's woodcut of the siege of Wolfenbüttel in 1542, were a cheap price to pay for such collective security of life and property, such regularity in trade and work, such peace in thought and worship.

Note the sequence. First the cowering countryside, with its local production and mainly local barter: social life gathered in little villages or in "suburbs," as the agricultural settlements that nestled under the castle's walls were called. Then a deliberate physical reconstruction of the environment: the wall: protection made permanent and regular. In this security from outside raids and impositions, local craftsmen and peasants and fishermen, under privileges wrung from their local lord, came together for a regular weekly or fortnightly market: presently they sought permanent quarters for themselves in a spot that combined so many advantages in living. It is significant to note that, as Hegel points out, the *new* quarter of Regensburg, in the eleventh century—as distinguished from the royal and the clerical quarters—is that of the merchants. As social life became more solid and compact, this industrial and merchants' quarter, the suburb, became the town center; and the seats of feudal and ecclesiastical power tended to become more suburban.

This urban movement was a chequered one. It marched under various banners, issued out of different circumstances, and produced diverse results. Sometimes urbanization was deliberately promoted by the feudal lords; often it was opposed by them, particularly by

the princes of the Church, above all, when the rights of political and economic independence were claimed by the new townsmen. In some countries, as in England and France, municipal freedom was promoted by a temporary coalition with the central power, as a means of weakening the feudal nobles who challenged the king's dominion. But, opposed or helped, the population flowed into these protected centers, built and rebuilt them, and in a few centuries created perhaps the highest type of urban civilization that had been known in Europe since the fifth century in Greece.

3: The "Increase of Population and Wealth"

The revival of trade is often taken, even by eminent scholars like Pirenne, as the direct cause of the city-building and civilizing activities that took place in the eleventh century. But the fact is that this urban renascence and its characteristic agents date from the previous century: their locus is not the isolated market, but the monastery.

Up to the time of the Norse invasions, the monasteries had served as a secure haven amid all the stormy uncertainties of life. In fact, the monastery had during this period performed the functions of the city in transmitting, if not greatly enlarging, the social heritage. Thanks to the knowledge the Benedictines preserved, sometimes even of Roman agricultural practice, it was many levels above the state of the surrounding countryside. Here the arts of building flourished and the technics of glass manufacture and decoration were carried on; above all, it was here that the written record was preserved and manifolded. In facing the new conditions of life in the ninth century, the monasteries were not in the least backward. The nunnery of Gernrode in Germany was called Kloster und Burg; and this meant something more than that the place was fortified.

A regular market worked to the advantage of the feudal lord or monastic proprietor. Considerably before the grand revival of trade in the eleventh century one finds under Otto II (973-983) that permission was given to the Widow Imma, who was founding a cloister in Kärnten, to provide a market and a mint and to draw taxes therefrom: typical characteristics of the new urban foundations. In the time of Otto, according to Hegel, most of the market privileges were granted to religious proprietors rather than to temporal lords. These markets, under the supervision of the monastery, were probably older than the walls which later provided security of a more material order; for as early as 833 Lewis the Pious in Germany gave a monastery permission to erect a mint for a market that was already in existence. The market peace, symbolized by the market cross that stood in the market-place, could not be broken without suffering heavy penalties. Finally, under this royal aegis, a special market law, applying to fairs and markets, with a special court having jurisdiction over traders, came into existence. The various forms of security offered by religion, by jurisprudence, and by standard economic practice entered into the foundation of medieval towns.

The revival of trade in the eleventh century, then, was not the critical fact that laid the foundation of the new medieval type of city: many actual foundations antedated that fact. Commercial zeal was rather a symptom of a far more inclusive revival that was taking place in Western Civilization; not least, it was a mark of the new sense of security that the walled town itself had most potently helped to bring into existence. If trade is one symptom, the political unification of Normandy, Flanders, Aquitaine, and Brandenburg is another; and the land reclamations and forest clearance of the monastic orders, such as the Cistercians (founded in 1098), is a third. The confusion scholars have fallen into here derives partly from the fact that they read present motives back into past situations, and partly because they have not distinguished carefully between local, regional, and international markets. Local merchants, as distinguished from craftsmen who sell their own goods, could have played only an insignificant part in the eleventh century revival.

In general, the early trade revival on semi-capitalistic lines was confined to the luxury wares that entered into international commerce. This was incapable of fostering the growth of towns until the towns themselves had come into existence. Moreover, the special international market was the Great Fair, held usually once a year: there merchants from all parts of Europe would come together. But this type of merchant, with his caravan and his armed guards and his special treaties for political protection moved from place to place: he was a glorified peddler, more like the Yankee merchant captain of the early nineteenth century than like an urban business man. To fancy that these wandering international traders were re· sponsible for the original growth of the medieval town is to put the cart before the horse.

It was rather a revival of the protected towns that helped the reopening of the regional and international trade routes, and led to the inter-European circulation of surplus commodities, particularly those of little bulk, wine from the Rhine, spices and silks from the East, armor from Lombardy, woolen goods from Flanders, leather from Pomerania, across the footways and waterways of Europe. Cities formed stepping stones in this march of goods: from Byzantium to Venice, from Venice to Augsburg, from Augsburg over the Rhine—and so, too, from Baltic cities, down to the Mediterranean.

The great fairs of the Middle Ages no doubt laid the foundation for the international capitalism of the sixteenth century, localized earlier in Florence and Augsburg, and later in Antwerp and Amsterdam, before it finally crossed in the eighteenth century to London. No less than the Crusades, the Fairs furthered the interchange of regional modes and patterns of life. But if the cultural importance of international trade was high, its economic importance—particularly as a source of urban growth—has been grossly exaggerated for the early Middle Ages. The fact is that even at a later period than the eleventh century the merchants with their retainers accounted, according to von Below, for only a small part of the town's population: far smaller than today. For the *producers* in the early medieval town composed about four-fifths of the inhabitants, as compared with two-fifths in the modern city.

Once the food supply was enlarged, once urban settlements became secure, commerce did serve as a powerful stimulus to growth: above all because it was necessary to pay for luxuries in money. As the demand for finery grew, and as more money was needed for the equipment of the feudal soldiery, the feudal lords had a special incentive to transform their holdings into urban areas which brought in a large return in cash rent. Urban rents may not have exclusively provided the funds for capitalist enterprise, but capitalist enterprise certainly stimulated the desire for urban rents. This gave the feudal landlord an ambivalent attitude toward the city. As power ceased to

[TOP] Verona: colonized by the Romans in 89 B.C.; leading city in the Lombard League in the twelfth century. Embanked rivers were no less important than hillside sites or the more elaborate canals, moats, and walls that surrounded other medieval cities for protection. Note the Campanile standing in isolation among the lower buildings. The erection of these bell-towers in the thirteenth century helped synchronize the activities of the townsmen and peasants within earshot of the new tower clocks. (*Photograph: Ewing Galloway*)

[MIDDLE LEFT] Dinkelsbühl. Blocked vista and irregular, upward pointing silhouette: gabled roof, tower, and spire worked in esthetic harmony. The tracery of ironwork in the standard and shield of the foreground was a fine feature of civic art, especially notable in South Germany. Arms, symbols, emblems, denoting the status and function of a class or an occupation were commonplaces in civic ritual, a connecting link between costume and architecture. Signs and signboards, with symbols and images rather than words and numbers, occupied an important place in the streets through the eighteenth century, when Watteau did not disdain to paint them. The harness maker's horse and the cigar stores Indian remained in American towns and villages through the whole nineteenth century. The transformation of the medieval sign into the blatant advertisement of the nineteenth century hoarding marks the degradation of civic art as effectually as the similar change from the modest uniform tombstone slab to the ostentatious competition of monument and mausoleum in the nineteenth century cemetery. (*Photograph: Ewing Galloway*)

[MIDDLE RIGHT] Rothenburg-an-der-Tauber: another typical profile, irregular but harmonious, following the contour of the land, with the more significant buildings thrusting against the sky. Organic planning and building, not for show but for defense, civic association, the expression of common values. This contemporary photograph closely coincides, in the various types of building and their arrangement, with many woodcuts in the Nürnberg Chronicle. (*Photograph: Ewing Galloway*)

[BOTTOM] Segovia. The hill-site as a means of defense: likewise the domination of the gigantic cathedral over the lesser buildings of the secular life. The bounding wall of the old city is still visible in the foreground; and as in Verona, the buildings show the typical low-pitched Mediterranean roof; but the principle of social organization and visual composition nevertheless closely resembles that of the northern cities: the same irregular silhouette, the same variety within a common pattern, the same crescendo movement in vertical space—contrasting with the horizontal movement of baroque planning—from the secular to the sacred, from the individual to the collective: counterpart of the hierarchical order of Heaven. (*Photograph: Ewing Galloway*)

[TOP LEFT] The great Marienkirche (Lady Church) above the supporting roof-tops of the burgher city. While the chaster Cathedral was the home of the clericals, the Marienkirche was built by the bourgeoisie, an emblem of their riches and power in the days when leadership in the Hanseatic League belonged to Lübeck. Religious art was one of the great export products of this city; hence one local museum contains chiefly replicas of the indigenous altar pieces and carvings.

[TOP RIGHT] Surviving fragment of the town wall and the gate that opens to the Landstrasse, banked with ancient linden trees, which leads to the fishing village and summer resort of Travemünde. (See Buddenbrooks by Thomas Mann.) The beauty of the surviving gates repeats the salute of the Seven Towers as one approaches Lübeck across the flat surrounding landscape.

[MIDDLE] Town Hall and Market Square, with the Marienkirche on the left. While the buildings of the foreground, right, belong to later periods, the town hall and church are survivals of the great period of Backstein Gothik. The touch of Venice in the design of the Town Hall may well not be an accident in a town once justly famous for its St Mark's Bread, or marzipan.

[MIDDLE INSERT] Typical late medieval burgher houses: office and temporary warehouse as well as residence. Garden spaces in rear, which belonged to the more modest houses of the thirteenth century, have been overbuilt: sometimes with summer wings whose windows opened more directly on the garden. Kitchen and offices on lower two floors: parlors on upper floors, often with a glass-enclosed chamber separating the elders from the young folks at dances and parties. Spacious quarters but bad ventilation; big windows but no direct contact with the sun: physiologically, a lowering of the cruder but more healthy early standards of accommodation. Note formal resemblance between these dwellings and the warehouses: partly due to lack of differentiation, partly because they belong organically to the same order. (*Photograph: Catherine Bauer*)

[BOTTOM LEFT] Heilige Geist Hospital: a medieval foundation for the aged: still in use as the old men and women sunning themselves in front prove. Each pensioner has a cubicle within the great nave. The design is closer to that of a late medieval hospital for the diseased than is the more domestic sort of foundation for the aged still found in England and the Low Countries.

[BOTTOM RIGHT] Salt warehouses along the Trave: highly important in the days when salt fish for the fast days of the Church played a unique part in international trade: indeed, the migration of the herring from the Baltic to the North Sea in the early fifteenth century was a decisive factor in the decay of the Hansa towns and the rise of Amsterdam and Norwich. Rivertowns like Rouen and Lübeck were in the early centuries in a better position for navigation and defense than towns nearer the open ocean. (*Photograph: Catherine Bauer*) be represented in his mind in purely military terms, he was tempted to part with a modicum of control over his individual tenants and dependents in order to have their responsible collective contribution in the form of cash payments: demands the land-bound serf could not meet. This was an important secondary stimulus to the building of towns.

Capitalism itself, however, was a disruptive rather than an integrating force in the internal life of the medieval city. It supplanted the old protective economy, based on status, mollified by religious precept, by a trading economy based on individual enterprise and the lust for gain: the economic history of the town is largely a story of the transformation of a group of protected producers living in a state of relative equality, into a small group of privileged merchants for whom the rest of the population ultimately toils. This change was already over the horizon when Chaucer wrote his wistful economium on the Former Age, when "ther lay no profit, ther was no richesse." By providing a nest in which the cuckoo bird of capitalism could lay her eggs, the walled town made it possible for her own offspring to be crowded out by the boisterous newcomer it harbored.

Beneath the revival of industry that took place between the eleventh and the thirteenth century was a fact of more fundamental economic importance: the immense extension of arable land and the application to the land of more adequate methods of husbandry. Wooded areas in Germany, a wilderness in the ninth century, gave way to plowland; the Low Countries, which had supported only a handful of dejected fishermen, were taken over and transformed into one of the richest productive soils in Europe. As early as 1150 the first polders, land reclaimed from marsh or sea by means of dykes were created in Flanders. (Agricultural irrigation was practiced in Milan as early as 1179.) The breeding of horses, the invention of an improved harness and the use of the iron horseshoe, the spread of querns, water mills, and windmills—these improvements endowed the new communities with relatively vast sources of power. This not merely transformed mining and metallurgy: it removed the need for servile labor and added to the surplus of human energies that had always existed in the more favored regions.

In the course of three centuries the Europe we know today was opened or re-opened for settlement: a feat exactly comparable to the opening up of the American continent between the seventeenth and the twentieth century. Indeed, one may regard the American conquest as a continuation of the original process on a new soil, for the colonization of New England, at all events, was on medieval urban lines, as that of Virginia and South Carolina was on the typical feudal pattern.

This vast extension of the agricultural base and this enormous increase in power in turn made possible the increase of population. According to Boissonade, the region between the Rhine and the Moselle increased its population tenfold between the tenth and the thirteenth century. The English counties, which had numbered 1,200,000 souls in 1086 reached a total of 2,355,000 toward 1340. The birthrate was perhaps higher; the number of people who survived was certainly greater; and this fact was not confined to the newly exploited territories of the North. Italy had made such progress in its agricultural economy as to number at least ten million souls in the fourteenth century. Better established and more favorably situated with respect to the higher civilizations of the East, Italy was the leader in both the material and the spiritual revival. In the thirteenth century Venice was a magnificently organized municipality; and Venice and Milan each then had probably over 100,000 people.

The Germanic cities, with perhaps the exception of the old Roman bordertown of Wien, averaged a much lower population; but there was no lack of energy in the German colonization movement, or in the process of urbanization. For in the course of four centuries 2500 cities were founded; and the municipal framework then laid out lasted substantially until the nineteenth century: the very outlines of municipal territory often remained, though in the meanwhile the town had filled them up. During the peak years of the movement not merely did the number of cities multiply, but the rate of urban population growth, as far as it can be estimated, was roughly comparable to that recorded in the nineteenth century. At the end of the twelfth century, for example, Paris had about 100,000 inhabitants; and at the end of the thirteenth century something like 240,000. In 1280 Florence had 45,000 inhabitants, and in 1339 around 90,000.

Trade, industrial production, mechanization, organization—all these facts helped expand the life of the cities. But they do not account for the feeding of the hungry mouths. People do not live on coins, even if the local mint has the exclusive privilege of coining them; nor do they live on air, even though "city air makes people free" as the saying went. The thriving life of these towns had its origin in the agricultural improvement of the countryside: an improvement that was spotty, and vitiated ultimately by the reckless deforestation that accompanied it, but sufficient to create unheard-of stores of energy: even the dismal colonization lands in Pomerania could send their honey and wax and hides back to the more industrial towns of the West. This agricultural improvement was duly transported into the city in the gardens, the cultivated spaces, and the common fields within the city itself. For except for a few congested centers, the town of the Middle Ages was not merely *in* the country but *of* the country: food was grown within the walls, as well as on the terraces, or in the orchards and fields, outside.

4: Lordly Scadders and Medieval New Edens

If the new methods of military protection accounted for the popularity of cities as places for residence and productive work, a special set of economic motives nevertheless existed which accounts for the headway this movement made. The liberation of towns was a step toward the efficient ordering of economic life: the replacement of barter by money, and of life-service by urban piecework or seasonal hire: in short, the transition, to use Maine's old distinction, from status to contract. The eighteenth century myth of the social contract was a rationalization of the political basis of the medieval town, whose survival in Geneva Rousseau knew. For the corporate town was in fact based upon a social contract between the landed proprietor and the settlers or inhabitants.

The cities movement, from the tenth century on, is a tale of old urban settlements becoming more or less self-governing cities, and of new settlements being made under the auspices of the feudal lord, endowed with privileges and rights that served to attract permanent groups of craftsmen and traders. The city charter was a social contract; the free city had legal as well as military security, and to live in the corporate town for a year and a day removed the obligations of serfdom. Hence the medieval city became a selective environment, gathering to itself the more skilled, the more adventurous, the more upstanding—probably therefore the more intelligent—part of the rural population.

Political interest in tnis period usually centers on the struggle for power between the urban bourgeoisie and its overlords. This tends to neglect the part that feudalism itself had in encouraging the growth of cities. Many of the conflicts in the old centers came from attempts to drive a hard bargain with the new citizens, rather than from absolute resistance to granting any privileges whatever. For towns were founded on a great scale throughout Europe, particularly on the borderlands, by the great proprietors: even in the old centers the habit of bequeathing land to a church or a monastery put the Church in control of large areas of urban land. Many of the new towns were frontier posts, as in Gascony and Wales; and they resembled such later foundations in America in that they served as a means of making a fresh start.

On the political side, I shall quote Tout, whose study of medieval town planning was a landmark in English in this field. "The political necessity for town making arose earlier than the economic need. In the humble beginnings of the new towns of the Middle Ages, military considerations are always paramount. A strong ruler conquered a district adjacent to his old dominions, or wished to defend his frontier against a neighboring enemy. He built rude fortresses, and encouraged his subjects to live in them, so that they might undertake the responsibility of their permanent defense." But since the serf, after all, had a permanent claim to the land he was tied to, it needed some extra bait to move him two or three hundred miles away: for the first time he had bargaining power, and the proprietor was forced to meet the demands of the new settler half-way.

By fighting, by bargaining, by outright purchase, or by some combination of these means, the towns won the right to hold a regular market, the right to be subject to a special market law, the right to coin money and establish weights and measures, the right of the citizens to be tried in their local courts and to bear arms in their own defense. All of these rights might or might not lead to complete local self-government, as in the great Hansa towns; but at all events it endowed the local community with many of the marks of what is now called in pious legal phrase a sovereign state. In general, membership in the urban community, even in such an insignificant little town as Lorris in France (which got no general right of self-government), meant freedom from forced payments and from military service, as well as freedom to sell one's possessions and go elsewhere. Citizenship gave its possessor mobility of person: indispensable for the rise of a trading class.

When a feudal lord desired to equip an army, join the Crusades, or indulge the new luxuries that seeped into Europe after the Crusades, he had only one economic source of wealth: his land. Under feudal custom he might not usually alienate the land or sell it off; but by dividing it up, by encouraging the growth of towns and founding new centers, he could increase his annual rents. Even though, with the customary long leases, rents might rise slowly for the original proprietor, his heirs would nevertheless in the course of time claim the unearned increment of the city's growth and prosperity. The same desire for "ready money" eventually took hold of the religious orders which, by gift and inheritance, steadily came into possession of ever larger urban domains. One must not forget that even in London down to the twentieth century a few feudal proprietors, the Duke of Bedford, the Duke of Westminster, and the Crown, had title to the most heavily exploited areas. In Germanic law land was placed in a special category that set it apart from buildings or personal property.

Almost as important as the actual rent in cities were special sources of urban income in which the proprietor of the land had a share: tolls at the bridges and the local market, customs imports and fines from courts, all of which multiplied as the town itself increased in population. Originally, in a pioneer town, it might be necessary to remit taxes to the newcomer provided he built a house: tax exemption to promote housing is a very old dodge. But later, such enticements could be omitted: houses might be at a premium. As with all speculative enterprises, some towns might more than justify the landlord's hopes; and others, like many of the fortified towns (bastides) in Southern France, might remain economically as well as socially torpid. But town building itself was one of the major industrial enter-prises of the early Middle Ages. Villages that succeeded in achiev-ing the necessary privileges might hope to have their urban status confirmed by productive enterprise, trade, and cultural wealth.

Now we can understand feudalism's ambivalent attitude toward this movement. The free city was a new source of wealth, but the challenging self-confidence and independence of the people who ral-lied to the Commune was a threat to the entire feudal scheme. The town concentrated man-power and economic power and the weapons of defense; but it drained off man-power from the countryside, leav-ing a greater share of the oafs and dullards behind: eventually the urban need for labor power would undermine the institution of serf-dom. In Italy, the opportunities for civil life attracted the nobles to the town; in the countries of Northern Europe, this class usually held aloof, clinging to the boar hunt and the "brittling of the deer," the open air life, and the smoky manorial hall, remaining themselves more akin to the peasants they oppressed than to the townsmen they freed. As urban occupations step by step drove out the rural ones that had at first been pursued in the city with almost equal vigor, the an-tagonism widened between town and country. The city was an ex-clusive society; and every townsman was, in relation to the country-folk, something of a snob, with such snobbery as only the upstart and the *nouveau riche* can achieve. This fact was eventually to contribute toward the undoing of urban freedom and self-government.

5: Domination of the Church

The ideas and institutions of medieval civilization concern us here only as they affected the structure of cities and the development of the organs of their cultural life. But unless one understands these ideas, the purely physical shell must remain blank.

In Western Europe, after the fall of the Roman Empire, the one powerful and universal institution was the Church. Membership in that association was a constant source of life and well-being; and to be cut off from its communion was so great a punishment that, until the sixteenth century, even kings trembled before it. The funda-mental political divisions of society, surviving all other ties and al-legiances, were the parish and the diocese; the most universal form

of taxation was the tithe, which went to the support of the great establishment of Rome. No small part of the economic life was devoted
to the glorification of God, the support of the clergy and of those
who waited on the clergy, and to the construction and maintenance
of ecclesiastical buildings—cathedrals, churches, monasteries, hospitals, schools. By itself, the local church would often be a "museum
of Christian faith," as well as a house of worship: the presence of
a saintly hermit walled up in his cell near its doors, or even the
bones and relics of such a saint, would be an attraction to the pious.
Churches and monasteries that possessed such relics became the goal
of a pilgrimage: the bones of Thomas à Becket at Canterbury, the
Chalice Well at Glastonbury, where Joseph of Arimathea was supposed to have dropped the Holy Grail—these things drew men to
cities no less than the possibility of trade.

In the early Middle Ages, even business and religion were in organic relationship: so much so that business would copy the institutions of religion in the organization of its trading posts: the Hansa
settlements were plainly fashioned on monastic lines, and exacted the
same sort of narrow devotion. But at the end of the Middle Ages—
and this is one of the signs of the end—even pious matters have a
worldly tinge: one seeks security, no longer in the depths of the
Church, but in a shrewd loan, backed by a note, and ultimately
vouched for by the armed might of the state. "Faith" gives way to
"credit."   •

Perhaps the most important civic effect of this other-worldly religion, with its enfolding protection, its abstentions, its withdrawals,
was that it universalized the cloister. Medieval culture, constantly
"in retreat," had its *claustrum,* where the inner life could flourish.
One withdrew at night: one withdrew on Sundays and on fast days:
so long as the medieval complex was intact, a constant stream of
disillusioned worldly men turned from the market place and the
battlefield to seek the quiet contemplative round of the monastery.
The ineffectiveness and costliness of artificial forms of illumination
even prolonged the withdrawal of the night: and winter served, so to
say, as the cloistered period of the year. This universal concentration
on the inner life had its compensatory effect on the imagination: the
vulgar daylight perceptions were illumined by the impassioned hal

lucinations and visions of dream: the figures of the inner eye were as real as those that fell peripherally on the retina. And though protestantism in the sixteenth century brought in a distrust of the wanton eye, it preserved for private use the habits of the cloister: prayer and inner communion.

Today, as we shall see later, our architecture has passed from the cave to the garden, from the monument to the dwelling house. But in throwing open our buildings to the daylight and the outdoors, we will forget, at our peril, the co-ordinate need for quiet, for darkness, for inner privacy, for retreat. The cloister in both its public and private form is a constant element in the life of men in cities. Without formal opportunities for isolation and contemplation, opportunities that require enclosed space, free from prying eyes and extraneous stimuli and secular interruptions, even the most externalized and extraverted life must eventually suffer. The home without such cells is but a barracks: the city that does not possess them is but a camp. In the medieval city the spirit had organized shelters and accepted forms of escape from worldly importunity. Today, the degradation of the inner life is symbolized by the fact that the only place sacred from interruption is the private toilet.

6: The Service of the Guild

The unattached person during the Middle Ages was one either condemned to exile or doomed to death: if alive, he immediately sought to attach himself, at least to a band of robbers. To exist, one had to belong to an association: a household, a manor, a monastery, a guild; there was no security except in association, and no freedom that did not recognize the obligations of a corporate life. One lived and died in the style of one's class and corporation.

Outside the Church, the most universal representative of corporate life was the guild. When one first encounters the guild in England in Anglo-Saxon times, it is primarily a religious fraternity under the patronage of a saint, meeting for brotherly comfort and cheer, insuring its members against the dire accidents of life and providing a decent burial. It had features not unlike those of the later English friendly society, or the Society of Freemasons, Elks, or Odd Fellows. The guild never lost this religious color: it was a brotherhood adapted to specific economic tasks but not wholly engrossed in them: the brothers ate and drank together on regular occasions: they formulated regulations for the conduct of their craft: they planned and paid for and enacted their parts in their mystery plays, for the edification of their fellow-townsmen: and they built chapels, endowed chantries, and founded schools.

Such unions and brotherhoods had existed among the urban craftsmen of the Roman empire; they lingered on in Byzantium; and though the connection remains obscure, perhaps the memory of them, like the memory of a far remoter event, Alexander's spectacular conquests, remained alive in popular myth, if not practice, during the Dark Ages. In Germany, among the first guilds of which there are records, apart from burial associations, are those of the weavers of Mainz in 1099, and the fishermen of Worms in 1106. If the growth of the merchant guild in general anticipated by half a century or so the growth of the craft guilds, it must be remembered that, except in international trade, the line between craftsmen and merchants was not closely drawn till the fourteenth century in the northern part of Europe. So that, during this period, craftsmen were, according to Gross, admitted to the merchant guilds and probably constituted the majority of the members.

The merchant guild was a general body, organizing and controlling the economic life of the town as a whole: regulating conditions of sale, protecting the consumer from extortion and the honest craftsman from unfair competition, protecting the traders of the town from the disorganization of their market by outside influences. The craft guild, on the other hand, was an association of masters working up their products and banded together to regulate production and establish standards of workmanship. In time, each of these institutions found its physical expression in the city: at first in modest houses or rented rooms, later in special guild halls and market halls that sometimes vied in magnificence with the town hall or the Cathedral. Ashley notes that the cost of these buildings was "one of the circumstances which led to and seemed to justify the demand for heavy entrance fees": this in turn led to the restriction of membership to the more wealthy members of the community. Not the first or last

time in which the pomp of a great architectural shell has destroyed
the creature who burdened himself with its creation.

Note the difference between the medieval community and that of
the modern city. In industry, since the eighteenth century, it is the
organization of the economic process that has taken definite corporate form in the factory, the business corporation, the chain store.
Political associations, such as the Chamber of Commerce, the Manufacturer's Association, and the Trade Union for long had no integral
part in the economic organization: they sprang up at the edges, included only a part of the population concerned, appeared belatedly;
and in no case, not even that of the trade union, did they cover any
large part of the cultural life of their members. In the medieval
town, the actual organization of industry was simple: the primary
fact was association. It was in fulfillment of its social purposes that
the Guild became a health and old-age insurance society, a dramatic
society, an educational society.

Once the economic motive isolated itself and became the all-
engrossing end of the guild's activities, the institution decayed: a
patriciate of wealthy masters rose within it to hand on their privileges
to their sons and to work together to the exclusion and disadvantage
of the poorer craftsmen and the growing proletariat. By the time the
religious dissensions of the sixteenth century broke up the religious
brotherhood itself, its co-operative economic nature had already been
seriously undermined. The fat people were battening upon the lean
people. In fact, the guild rises and falls with the medieval city: the
guilds are the city in its economic aspect, and the city is the guilds
in their social and political aspect.

The center of the municipality's activities was the town hall. In
the beginning, according to Dehio, the town hall was a free-standing
building in the market-place, usually of two stories, containing two
halls, that on the lower floor being originally used for the finer wares
that needed protection from the weather, not afforded by the booths
that lined the market-place itself. The upper room would be used for
the meeting of the mayor and the council, for the administration of
justice, for the reception of ambassadors, and for periodic feasts and
drinking bouts. The remains of the latter, incidentally, linger on in
modern London, along with the ghost of the old Livery Companies,

in the famous feast at the Guildhall that follows the annual election of the new Lord Mayor, and the Lord Mayor's parade.

In the town hall, too, toward the close of the Middle Ages, the leading families, drawn chiefly from the wealthier circle of the wholesale merchants, might—to the envy of the rest of the population—hold their dances and routs. It became, in fact, a sort of collective palace for the patriciate: hence it was often called a "theatrum" or playhouse. Here marriages would be celebrated with due pomp: a provision that has survived, with genuflections toward democracy, down to the present day: note the acknowledgment of the older order in the two special marriage chambers, first and second class, in the new Hilversum Town Hall in Holland. Thomas Mann, in Buddenbrooks, has given us a last faltering glimpse of that old life.

By membership in the municipality one escaped feudal dues: one assumed burgher responsibilities. Not merely was military service imposed on males who were not officers of the church, but the police force of the town was selected by rotation from among the burghers: the duty of watch and ward. In modern times, we have such service only for war or some sudden disaster: but in the medieval city it struck much closer home, and it is a serious question whether the leaving of such functions of protection to the care of a professional police has not weakened the sense of civic responsibility and done away with an effective means of education. To patrol one's city at night: to know its dark alleys under the moon, or with no light at all except one's lantern, to enjoy the companionship of the watch— was this not an early practical example of William James's Moral Equivalent of War: more useful, more humane, than any national scheme of military training? In assuming the policeman's duty of regulating traffic at crossings during the hours when children are going to and from school, the American school child is perhaps recovering some of that sense of responsibility which disappeared in the eighteenth century with the final collapse of the medieval municipality.

Here, as in most other departments, there existed great differences between the conditions in the eleventh century, still bare and constricted and precarious, and those in the sixteenth century, when wealth had poured into the city and heaped up. At the beginning the city was striving as a social unit to establish its existence: the very insecurity promoted neighborly effort and even solidarity between the various ranks and occupations. They needed each other, and voluntary groups of neighbors formed, as Schevill has emphasized, very much as they would form today under pressure in a small New England village. When the privileges had been won, and when great disparities in riches appeared between the "successful" and the "unsuccessful," when wealth as well as station was inherited, then the walls between the classes became more important than the protective barrier that had once made the city one.

At the close of the Middle Ages wealthy individuals began to endow schools, build asylums for the aged and the orphaned, taking over functions once performed by the guild, precisely as the new despots were taking over for the country as a whole the political privileges of the free cities. But when one attempts to generalize the period as a whole, one may still echo Gross, deeply though he was imbued with a Victorian distrust of the closed corporation and the protective policies of the guild "Exclusive of the inhabitants of the privileged *sokes,* the . . . population was more homogeneous than that of towns existing at present; there were in the former fewer class distinctions, more equality of wealth, and more harmony of interests than in the latter." These are the words of one who was no admirer of the medieval economic system: they therefore carry double weight.

The social activities of the town shrank as the new capitalistic economy grew up. Outside the Church, only one institution survived from the old guilds and even increased its power and influence: perhaps the most important single institution in the medieval town. With an instinctive recognition of its importance, the name of this institution was originally the common term for all guilds in the twelfth century: universitas. Like other forms of craft guild, the aim of the university was to prepare for the practice of a vocation and to regulate the conditions under which its members performed their work. Each of the great schools that originally formed the university, jurisprudence, medicine, and theology, was professional in character: the general humanistic education that began to come in with the Renascence college, particularly in England, was an upper class graft on the original tree.

Beginning with Bologna in 1100, Paris in 1150, Cambridge in 1229, and Salamanca in 1243, the university lay down the basis of a co-operative organization of knowledge on an inter-regional basis: scholars flocked to these centers from every part of Europe, and in turn, the masters studied and taught at distant centers. The combination of scientific knowledge, political knowledge, and sacred knowledge, which the university offered in its faculties, had no exact parallel in any other culture. The germs of the university doubtless were latent in the Library-School at Alexandria or in the lecture system of the Roman municipalities: but in the university the organization of knowledge was elevated into an enduring system, which did not depend for its continuance upon any single group of texts: the system of knowledge was more important than the thing known. In the university the functions of storage, dissemination, and creative addition were adequately performed. As the cloister of the monastery might be termed a passive university, so the university might be called an active cloister: it made explicit, concrete, and systematic one of the enduring functions of the city: withdrawal from immediate practical responsibility and the critical reappraisal and renewal of the cultural heritage.

Here was a social invention of the first order: for this alone the medieval corporation would be important. And the very independence of the university from the standards of the market and the city, fostered the special sort of authority it exercised: the authority of verifiable truth, ratified by the methods of philosophic dialectic, factual scholarship, and scientific method, as these have been developed from period to period. The vices of such an organization may be many; and its services during the intervening centuries have not been of uniform value, for the university shares to this day the exclusiveness and the professional conservatism of the guild system, and it has sometimes put a brake upon discovery and creation, so that the major contributions to knowledge have often been made outside its walls. Nevertheless, the enlargement and transmission of the social heritage would have been inconceivable, during the last three centuries, without the agency of the university. As the Church ceased to be the repository of modern values, the university gradually took over the office. The university has become for the modern city what the Cathedral was for the predominantly religious culture of the Middle Ages.

7: Medieval Domesticity

In most aspects of medieval life, the closed corporation prevailed: even the city originally was so restricted. But compared to modern life, the medieval urban family was no private unit: it included, as part of the normal household, not only relatives by blood but a group of industrial workers as well as domestics whose relationship was that of secondary members of the family. Young men from the upper classes got their knowledge of the world by serving as attendants in a noble family; while apprentices and journeymen lived as members of the master craftsman's family. If marriage was perhaps deferred longer for men than today, the advantages of home life were not entirely lacking, even for the bachelor.

The workshop was a family: likewise the merchant's counting house. The members ate together at the same table, worked in the same rooms, slept in the same dormitory, joined in the family prayers, participated in the common amusements. Chastity and virginity were the ideal states; but even the prostitutes formed guilds, and in Hamburg, Wien, and Augsburg, for example, the brothels were under municipal protection. When one remembers that syphilis did not make its definite appearance, at least in malignant form, until the late fifteenth century, even prostitution constituted a smaller threat to domestic health and well-being than it did in the following centuries.

The intimate union of domesticity and labor, surviving now in the city only in petty shops or in the household of an artist, dictated the major arrangements within the dwelling house itself. Naturally, between the rude huts and stone enclosures of the tenth and eleventh centuries, and the elaborate merchant houses that were built from the thirteenth to the sixteenth century there was a difference as great as that between the seventeenth century dwelling and a New York apartment house today. Let us attempt, nevertheless, to single out the common factors in this development.

[TOP LEFT] Sixteenth century market-place: Antwerp. Primitive use of light for civic celebration. Contrast the occasional extravagances and festivities of the medieval order, to celebrate the arrival of an emperor, the birthday of a saint, the victory of an army, with the permanent order of illumination used in Broadway or Piccadilly Circus. Note the size and scale of the Town Hall, symbol of the relative importance of civic authority in the towns of the lowlands: the Cloth Hall at Ypres shows the equivalent might and majesty of the textile guilds. Where feudal or royal power dominated, as in Edinburgh or Durham, the castle would bulk largest. In London, however, with its small guildhall and big Tower the symbolism is not quite so accurate.

[TOP RIGHT] Children at play in the open spaces of a Dutch city: rolling hoops, whipping tops, walking on stilts, flying kites. The wiping out of the playfields and archery butts of the medieval order was one of the prime sins of overcrowding in the big capitals and other overcrowded towns. The paling fence in the background is a reminder of the frequent use of wood even in the Low Countries, where most of it was imported from the Baltic forests.

[MIDDLE] Tournament in München, with the Cathedral on the left. The survival of feudal practices in the medieval town: due partly to the usually continued maintenance of the castle by the lord and his retainers. Such spectacles, in contrast with the guilds' plays and pageants, were primarily aristocratic. The market-place had many uses: it served as agora, acropolis, theater and stadium all in one. The print is dated 1568.

[BOTTOM] Florence. Holy procession, winding about the streets and market places, finally to enter the Cathedral for the culminating ceremony. The slow irregular order of the procession contrasts with the brisk mechanical order of the march: the difference between them is that between two civilizations, and this fact is recorded in the whole design of the city. In the medieval city, of the less geometric type of plan, the tortuous and the unexpected, infinite variety without spatial progression, are characteristics of design. In the later baroque city visual axes and straight lines are urban counterparts of mechanical movement toward a fixed goal: the street to the right of the Campanile shows the new mutation. In the present procession note the relative absence of lookers-on: ritual, like drama in the medieval city, is arranged for participants, who both see and do.

[UPPER LEFT] Fuggerei in Augsburg: sixteenth century housing foundation for the deserving poor: often built by the richer guilds, in this case the gift of an individual capitalist, Jacob Fugger. The houses are two rooms deep, well-lighted, built in parallel rows: an early example of Zeilenbau. The Fuggerei forms a unified neighborhood unit with a handsome little chapel of its own. Water is still piped only to the fountains. Housing standards here compare favorably with those of present day in all but the best workers' housing.

[UPPER RIGHT] High Street in Stamford, Lincolnshire: good vernacular tradition of sixteenth and seventeenth century: strong, clean, light and spacious: the wide windows across the whole front are typical of this period: see the Antwerp market-place on Plate 3.

[MIDDLE LEFT] Magdalen College, Oxford: built 1474-81. Open type of planning around quadrangle, as in many monasteries, housing foundations, and as in the various Inns of Court in London. Such islands, enclosed by walls and buildings, sometimes entered by a court from the street, expressed that need for solitude, protection, sanctuary, which was a formative factor in medieval culture: a type of order that was foreign to the unbalanced extraverted life of the Renascence. But in organic adaptation to modern needs, a not dissimilar type of planning, with each function rationally ordered in appropriate zones surrounded by open spaces, has come in with the twentieth century: see Plates 27 to 32.

[MIDDLE RIGHT] Market-place in Bremen: late sixteenth century buildings still excellently preserved. The temporary structures of the periodic market had its equivalent in the temporary structures used for tournaments, plays, festivals. Contrary to the usual idée fixe of the Middle Ages, the early part of this period was more fluid and mobile than the present age, with its vast mass of fixed utilities, frozen as capital investments.

[BOTTOM LEFT] The Shambles in York: row of shops with overhanging fronts. The open shop front demanded protection against the inclement weather: hence the narrow street, the deliberately broken pattern of streets—to break the force of the wind—and even perhaps the overhangs, which served partly as protective arcade where complete arcades were not provided.

[BOTTOM MIDDLE] Medieval town garden. The checkerboard layout was typical of medieval garden plans: they contradict the notion of medieval order as necessarily capricious or irregular. Bathing pools were not uncommon and gardens within the walls were universal. see Plate 15.

[BOTTOM RIGHT] Spire of the Cathedral at Ulm. Though not erected till the nineteenth century the design of this lofty structure was made when the rest of the Cathedral was built: its final embodiment marks that essential continuity with their medieval past, so characteristic of German cities.

Houses were usually built in rows around the perimeter of their rear gardens: sometimes in large blocks they formed inner courts, with a private green, reached through a single gateway on the street. Free-standing houses, unduly exposed to the elements, wasteful of the land on each side, were relatively scarce: even farmhouses would form part of a solid block that included the stables, barns, granaries. The materials for the houses came out of the local soil and they varied with the region: now wattle and daub, now stone or brick. Their type depended upon economic factors, and the wider use of half timber and stucco after the fourteenth century arose partly out of the need for building cheap houses for the rising proletariat. The earliest houses would have small window openings, with shutters to keep out the weather; the later, permanent windows of oiled cloth or paper. In the fifteenth century glass, hitherto used mainly for public buildings, became more frequent: at first only in the upper part of the window. The glass would be heavy, irregular, feebly transparent; and the leads that held it would further reduce the amount of light. By the sixteenth century, however, glass had become cheap and fashionable. The popular saying in England about Hardwick Hall—"more glass than wall"—was equally true of the burgher houses. In North Germany and England a broad bank of window would extend across the whole house at each story, front and rear, thus making up in effect for the tendency to deepen the house. The effort of governments in the eighteenth century to raise revenue by means of window taxes partly arrested this popular development: an atrocious stupidity. Result: the sixteenth century house is often closer to modern requirements for light and air than the common run of Victorian mansions.

Heating arrangements steadily improved. This fact, plus the increased use of distilled liquors, as fortification against inclement weather, partly accounts for the outburst of human energy in the North: winter gradually ceased to be a period of stupefied hibernation. The open hearth in the middle of the floor, scarcely as effective as the arrangements in an Indian tepee, gave way to the fireplace and the chimney. Fireproofing went along with this development; for originally, lacking proper materials, the poorer burghers were tempted to experiment with wooden chimneys: an unduly optimistic practice repeated in the early settlement of New England. In 1276 Lübeck passed an ordinance enforcing the use of fireproof roofing and the fireproof party wall; and in London, after the severe fire of 1189, special privileges were given to people building in stone and tile; while in 1212 thatched roofs were ordered to be whitewashed, the better to resist fire.

As for the plan of the house, it varied with the region and the century; yet certain features remained common. Viollet-le-Duc has shown us the ground plan of a French house, with a shop on the ground floor connected by an open gallery with the kitchen in the rear. The two formed a court, where the well occupied a corner. There was a chimney in the kitchen and in the living room or *grande salle* above the shop: from the latter there is access to the dormitories above. Heyne's plan of an old house in Nürnberg is not essentially different; but, as in the surviving houses from the seventeenth century, there are more interior rooms, a kitchen and a smaller room on the ground floor, a heatable room above the kitchen, and a number of chambers, with a toilet on the second floor directly above that on the first.

The only form of modern hallway was the open gallery: this was a common feature in houses not built around a closed court. It survived in the design of inns, where a means of circulation was specially necessary, and the internal hall, because of the absence of artificial light, was not an attractive solution. The main outlines of this type of house lasted right down through the seventeenth century, even later. But as one went downward in the economic scale, arrangements would be less differentiated and the space more constricted: the one room apartment, still common among the poor in many countries, possibly had its origin in the more industrialized cities of the late Middle Ages.

The fact that the burgher house served as workshop, store, and counting house prevented any zoning between these functions. The competition for space between the domestic and the working quarters, as business grew and the scale of production expanded, was also perhaps responsible for encroachment over the original back gardens by sheds, storage bins, and special workshops. Mass production and the concentration of looms in great sheds was known in

Flanders in the fourteenth century, and operations like fulling, mill-
ing, glassmaking, and iron-making required a more isolated type of
workshop: in these industries came the earliest break between living
and working. But at first the family pattern dominated industry, just
as it dominated the organization of the Benedictine monastery. Survivals of this regime lingered on in every European city: the habit
of "living in" long retained by London drapers, with the men and
the women divided into dormitories, was a typical holdover from the
Middle Ages.

In the disposition and specialization of rooms in the Middle Ages
the ways of the aristocracy filtered down but slowly to the rest of the
population. Comforts that were enjoyed by lords and ladies alone
in the thirteenth century did not become popular customs until the
seventeenth or even the nineteenth century. The first radical change,
which was to destroy the form of the medieval dwelling house, was
the development of a sense of privacy. This meant, in effect, withdrawal at will from the common life and the common interests of
one's associates. Privacy in sleep: privacy in eating: privacy in
religious and social ritual: finally privacy in thought. In 1362
Langland, in Piers Plowman, chided the tendency of the Lord and
Lady to withdraw from the common hall for private meals and for
private entertainment. He must have foreseen the end of that reciprocal social relation between the stationary upper and lower ranks
of the feudal regime: a relation that had mitigated its oppressions.
The desire for privacy marked the beginning of that new alignment
of classes which was to usher in the merciless class-competition and
individual self-assertion of a later day. In the castles of the period
one notes the existence, not merely of a private bedroom for the
noble owners: one also notes the private toilet, perched over the
moat: the first hint of the twentieth century arrangement for a private
toilet. (Monasteries, however, had long had collective latrines in
separate buildings.)

The separation of the kitchen from the dining room is not characteristic, probably, of the majority of the population in any country
today. It had taken place in the monastery because of the scale of
the preparations, and it was copied eventually in the manorial hall
and the fine town house. But the common quarters offered this in-

centive to social living: they alone were usually heated. That the medieval house was cold in winter perhaps accounts for the development of inner rooms, insulated from the outer walls by air. Yet the cold could not have been unendurable, or else people in the Middle Ages would have worn nightdresses, instead of "going to their naked bed," as numberless illustrations depict them. Privacy in bed came first in Italy, among the upper classes; but the desire for it developed slowly; even in the seventeenth century maidservants often slept in trundle beds at the foot of that of their master and mistress.

Until the curtained bed was invented, sexual intercourse must have taken place for the most part under cover, and whether the bed was curtained or not, in darkness. Privacy in bed preceded the private bedroom; for even in seventeenth century engravings of upper middle class life, and in France, a country of refinement, the bed still often occupies part of the living room. Under these circumstances, the erotic ritual must have been short and almost secretive, with little preliminary stirring through eye or voice or free movement: it had its intense seasons, especially spring; but the late medieval astrological calendars, which depict this awakening, show the lovers having intercourse in the open with their clothes on. In short, erotic passion was more attractive in the garden and the wood, despite stubble or prickly stems or insects, than it was in the house, on a mattress whose stale straw or down was never quite free from musty dampness. For lovers in the medieval house the winter months must have been a large wet blanket. An endless succession of pregnancies punctuated the married lives of all but barren women, and brought many of them to early graves. No wonder virginity figured as the ideal state.

To sum up the medieval dwelling house, one may say that it was characterized by lack of differentiated space and differentiated function. In the cities, however, this lack of internal differentiation was offset by a completer development of domestic functions in public institutions. Though the house might lack a private bake-oven, there was a public one in the baker's or the cook-shop. Though it might lack a private bathroom, there was a municipal bath-house. Though it might lack facilities for isolating and nursing a diseased member, there were numerous public hospitals. And though lovers might lack a private bedroom, they could "lie between the acres of the rye," just outside the city's walls. Plainly, the medieval house had scarcely an inkling of the two important domestic requirements of the present day: privacy and comfort. And the tendency in the late Middle Ages to deepen the house, chiefly under pressure of rising ground rents, progressively deprived those who worked most steadily indoors, the mother, the domestics, the children, of the necessary air and light which dwellers in much cruder country hovels could have. Mark this paradox of "prosperity." As long as conditions were rude—when people lived in the open, pissed freely in the garden or the street, bought and sold outdoors, opened their shutters and let in full sunlight—the defects of the house were far less serious than they were under a more refined regime.

It was no lack of care and concern for children that made the infant mortality records so black, so far as we may estimate them: the cradle, the hobby horse, and even the toddler, for the child who had not yet learned to walk, are depicted in sixteenth century prints: these cherubs were treated with love. But the domestic environment became increasingly defective; and such diseases as are spread through either contact or respiration must have had a maximum opportunity for sweeping through the family in the late medieval house. The urban dwelling was indeed perhaps the weakest link in medieval sanitary arrangements; for in other respects, the standards were far more adequate than most Victorian commentators—and those who blindly repeat their mistakes—believed.

8: Hygiene and Sanitation

What gave the early medieval town a sound basis for health was the fact that, though surrounded with a wall, it was still part of the open country. Until the fourteenth century, these two types of environment were scarcely differentiated. The village had not been devoted purely to agriculture since handicraft, at the time of the English Domesday Book, had flourished there; nor were the towns, for centuries to come, wholly industrial: a good part of the population had private gardens and practiced rural occupations, just as they did in the typical small American town up to about 1870. At harvest time, the population of the town would swarm out into the country, as the slum dwellers of the East End still migrate to Kent for the hop-picking. One has only to read the household recipes of the Goodman of Paris, who was of the well-to-do merchant order, to see how the more prosperous burghers kept a leg firmly planted in each world. Near the city, the fowler and the rabbit hunter could go after game. Fitz-Stephens noted that the citizens of London had the right of hunting in Middlesex, Herefordshire, the Chiltern Hundreds, and part of Kent. And in the streams by the city, fishing was diligently pursued: not merely on the coast but inland. Augsburg, for example, was noted for its trout; until 1643 many of the city officials took their pay in trout.

This strong rural influence can be marked on the early city plans; all but a handful of medieval towns were closer to what we should now call a village or a small country town than a city: "greatness" did not mean a big population or a spreading territory. In the original towns, with the exception of a few that kept to original Roman foundations or were constricted by topographical obstacles, ample gardens spread in the rear of the houses. The size of the medieval houseblock was not standardized; but in general a hundred-foot depth was common and a fifty-foot width was not unusual. Since it was customary to build row houses, for cheapness, for compactness, and above all, perhaps, for maximum protection against cold, this would mean that in some cities houses originally would show their long side to the street, as they still do at Grantham, for example, in England: a type of planning that did not come back till the development of modern workers' housing estates in England. Gardens and orchards, sometimes fields and pastures, existed within the city, as well as in the "suburb" outside: endless illustrations and plans as late as the seventeenth century prove how universal these open spaces were. Goethe describes such a fine rear-garden, so favorable to a genial family life, in his Dichtung und Wahrheit. Medieval people were used to outdoor living: they had shooting grounds and bowling grounds and tossed the ball and kicked the football and ran races and practiced archery. When the open spaces filled up, Botero notes, Francis I provided a meadow near the river for the scholars of the University of Paris. The spirit of this hearty informal play is carried on, even today, in the merriest of all urban parks, the Jardin du Luxembourg.

In sum: as far as usable open spaces go, the medieval city had at its foundation and through most of its existence a far higher standard for the mass of the population than *any later form of town,* down to the first romantic suburbs of the nineteenth century.

To form a notion of medieval standards of open space in building one must turn to such surviving semi-public buildings as the Inns of Court in London, the colleges at Oxford or Cambridge, or to the Homes for the Aged, such as one still finds in Holland. One must not look at the narrow streets between the houses without remembering the open green, or the neatly chequered gardens, that usually stretched behind. I lay emphasis on the rural character of the medieval town for two reasons: first, because a false notion about its dinginess and overcrowding has grown up, which has no foundation at all in most cities except the notorious fact of *post*-medieval overcrowding; and second, because the existence of these open spaces shows that sanitary arrangements were not necessarily as offensive as they have been pictured, nor vile smells as uniformly ubiquitous. How the original open spaces got built over one may learn in a typical instance from Stow. The Parish church of St. Mary Bow needed room in the churchyard for the burial of the dead, but was by the middle of the fifteenth century hemmed in with houses. John Rotham, in his will, gave a certain garden in Hosier's Lane to be a churchyard. After a hundred years the overcrowded capital could not even afford open spaces for the dead: so this plot was built on. Garden: graveyard: houseplot: finally, in the seventeenth century, the back-garden might be built over, too—and the resultant insanitary mass would then be regarded by the hopeful nineteenth century investigator as "typical medieval" overcrowding.

Up to a generation ago American country towns existed in which neither the streets nor the privies were much more advanced, technically, than they were in the early Middle Ages. But they were neither as foul nor as dangerous to health as might be fancied, just because of the openness of their layout. The point is that crude sanitation is not necessarily bad sanitation: indeed, a medieval farmhouse, in which the common dung pile served as domestic privy,

was not as inimical to health, probably, as the pre-Pasteur town of
the nineteenth century, blessed with refined water closets—and a
water supply drawn from the same river into which the sewage of
the town above was emptied. There is no proof that visitations of the
plague were much worse in the medieval town than in the American
or European town of the first half of the nineteenth century; nor is
there sufficient proof that poor sanitary arrangements alone were
responsible for the origin or the virulence of medieval epidemics.
Consider the death rate from influenza in 1918 in countries entirely
outside the war-zone, or from poliomyelitis in its recurrent waves
today. If the medieval expectation of life was low, a defective diet,
especially a defective winter diet, must perhaps take as large a share
of the blame as the defective disposal of fecal matter.

As the cities increased in size and density of population, their
rural base was undermined and new sanitary difficulties arose out
of the very fact of density. Not alone the density of the living but
the congestion of the dead, who were buried for convenience and
piety, not outside the city's walls, but in the vaults or graveyards
of the parish churches. By the seventeenth century the overcrowded
conditions here constituted a serious sanitary menace, through seepage into the water supply; and in a few cosmopolitan centers, like
Paris or London, this may have been true at an earlier date. But in
the twelfth and thirteenth centuries, these breeding places for disease
were no more congested than the city itself. And as early as the
sixteenth century special provisions were made toward sanitary
control and decency in the matter of excrement: thus Stow mentions
an ordinance which commands that "no man shall bury any dung
or goung within the liberties of the city" nor "carry any ordure till
after nine-o'clock in the night," that is, after bedtime.

On these matters, as Professor Thorndike points out, evidence
favorable to many medieval cities is indisputable. He quotes Bruni's
eulogy of Florence in which Bruni remarks that "some towns are so
dirty that whatever filth is made during the night is placed in the
morning before men's eyes to be trodden underfoot, 'than which it is
impossible to imagine anything fouler. For even if there are thousands there, inexhaustible wealth, infinite multitude of people, yet
will I condemn so foul a city and never think much of it.' " Simi-

larly, Leland, a later observer, in his journeys about England makes special mention of the dirt whenever he comes across it: it is rare enough to deserve comment. As long as the open spaces and gardens remained, as long as the countryside was easily accessible to the dung-farmer, the normal smells of the medieval town were not more offensive than those of the farmyard; nor were the evils overwhelming.

What applies to human excreta applies also to garbage. Leftovers were eaten by the dogs, the chickens, and the pigs, which acted as general town scavengers. The ban on pigs and the general introduction of paving comes in about the same time: by the sixteenth century, in well-managed towns that had made provisions for street cleaning, there was also a ban upon keeping pigs in any part of the town, even in the gardens behind the houses. But in the early days the pig was an active member of the local Board of Health. Like a great many medieval institutions the pig lingered on in more backward centers till the middle of the nineteenth century: in Manchester, for example, and in New York, the great world emporium.

Non-edible waste was doubtless harder to dispose of: ashes, tannery offal, the scourings of wool: but certainly there was less of it than in the modern city: tins, iron, broken glass and paper did not form such gigantic heaps. Here again, a few overgrown centers doubtless polluted their streams even in the Middle Ages; but big towns like Paris and London were quite exceptional places; and in the run of medieval towns the damage was insignificant. In the main, the waste materials were organic ones, which decomposed and mingled with the earth; and in these flimsy nests of buildings, particularly in the earlier centuries, there would be outbreaks of fire, famous in the annals of almost every town, which subjected whole streets and quarters to the most powerful of germicidal agents. It was the plating of the medieval town in imperishable materials and the heaping up of the living in smaller quarters, with more meager open spaces, that created the filthy conditions that met the eye in the seventeenth and eighteenth centuries. The worst conditions prevailed when the city had lost its natural rural base, and had not yet created an adequate mechanical substitute.

Two other matters closely connected with hygiene remain to be discussed: the bath and the drinking water supply. Even as early as the thirteenth century the private bath made its appearance: sometimes with a dressing room, as we learn from a sixteenth century Nürnberg merchant's household book. In 1417, indeed, hot baths in private houses were specially authorized by the City of London. If anything were needed to establish the medieval attitude toward cleanliness the ritual of the public bath should be sufficient. Bathhouses were characteristic institutions in every city, and they could be found in every quarter: complaint was even made by Guarinonius that children and young girls from ten to eighteen years of age ran shamelessly naked through the streets to the bathing establishment. Bathing was a family enjoyment. These bath-houses would sometimes be run by private individuals; more usually, perhaps, by the municipality. In Riga as early as the thirteenth century bath-houses are mentioned, according to von Below; in the fourteenth century there were 7 such houses in Würzburg; and at the end of the Middle Ages there were 11 in Ulm, 12 in Nürnberg, 15 in Frankfurt-am-Main, 17 in Augsburg, and 29 in Wien. Frankfurt had 29 bath-house keepers as early as 1387. So widespread was bathing in the Middle Ages that the bath even spread as a custom back into the country districts, whose inhabitants had been reproached by the writers of the early Fabliaux as filthy swine. What is essentially the medieval bath lingers in the Russian or Finnish village today.

Bathing in the open, in a pool in the garden or by a stream in the summer time of course remained in practice. Public baths however were for sweating and steaming and thorough cleanliness: it was customary to take such a purging of the epidermis at least every fortnight. In time, the bath-house came to serve again as it had in Roman times; it was a place where people met for sociability, as Dürer plainly shows in one of his prints, a place where people gossiped and ate food, as well as attended to the more serious business of being cupped for pains or inflammatory conditions. As family life in the late medieval town deteriorated, the bath-houses became the resort of loose women, looking for game, and of lecherous men, looking for sensual gratification: so that the medieval word for bath-house, namely, stew, comes down to us in English as a synonym for brothel: indeed, it is so used as early as Piers Plowman.

The provision of drinking water was also a collective function of the town. First the guarding of a brook or spring: the provision of a fountain in the public square and of other fountains in the local quarters: sometimes within the block, sometimes on the street. As numbers increased, it was necessary to find new sources and distribute old ones over a wider territory. In 1236 a patent for a leaden conduit to convey water from Tyborne Brook to the City of London was granted; pipes were laid in Zittau in 1374; and in Breslau in 1479 water was pumped from the river and conducted by pipes through the city—probably such wooden pipes as are illustrated in Bauer's De Re Metallica, and were used, on Manhattan Island for example, down to the nineteenth century. As late as the fifteenth century the provision of water conduits in London was a matter for private philanthropy, like hospitals or almshouses.

The author of the Maison Rustique warns his readers against the use of lead pipes: the dangers of lead poisoning had presumably been noted. As with baths, the piping of water to fountains, whence it was distributed by hand to the houses, was not as convenient as the private water supply that began to trickle in, all too literally, in the seventeenth century. But to offset this, it satisfied two important functions that tended to disappear with the reign of greater mechanical efficiency—art, in the shape of the handsome fountains that decorated the squares and public places of the medieval city, and sociability, the occasion for meeting and gossiping as people waited their turn around the village pump. The pump, no less than the taproom, served as local newspaper for the quarter.

The diffused local water supply of the medieval town was, finally, a source of strength in defense. When, in the seventeenth century, the growing cities were forced to seek outside their fortifications for water, they put themselves at the mercy of an army that could command the open country. But in the big cities, the population grew more rapidly than the technical means and the capital necessary to capture sufficient water for its inhabitants: this partly accounts for the loss of cleanly habits and for the water famines that overtook the seventeenth century capitals, and made the later development of the industrial town so vile.

In its remedial measures for health, the medieval town was far in advance of its contemptuous Victorian successor. The holy orders founded hospitals in almost every town: there would be at least two in most German towns, one for lepers and one for other types of disease, according to Heil; while in "big" cities, such as Breslau, with its 30,000 population in the fifteenth century, there would be as many as fifteen, or one for every two thousand inhabitants. Plainly cases that in more recent times would have been treated at home must at this earlier period have had systematic hospital care: a fact which mitigated the lack of domestic facilities.

Municipal physicians made their appearance in the fourteenth century: in Konstanz as early as 1312. In Venice a permanent health magistracy was created in 1485, to which in 1556 inspection and enforcement machinery were added which long served as a model to the rest of Europe. Contagious diseases, incidentally, were usually isolated outside city walls: the value of isolation wards, with separate toilets, had long been established by the better-equipped monasteries. The establishment of quarantine, for people passing in and out of cities from foreign parts, was one of the major innovations of medieval medicine. Much as travelers hated it, it was based on sound empiric observation, and the gradual eradication of leprosy in Europe, thanks to the same policy of isolation, was nothing less than a triumph.

In the main, then, the medieval town was not merely a vital social environment: it was likewise adequate, at least to a greater degree than one would gather from its decayed remains, on the biological side. There were smoky rooms to endure; but there was also perfume in the garden behind the burgher's house: the fragrant flowers and the savory herbs were widely cultivated. There was the smell of the barnyard in the street, diminishing in the sixteenth century, except for the growing presence of horses: but there would also be the odor of flowering orchards in the spring, or the scent of the new mown hay, floating across the fields in early summer. Though cockneys may wrinkle their noses at this combination of odors, no lover of the country will be put off by the smell of horse-dung or cow-dung, even though mingled occasionally with that of human excrement: is the reek of gasoline exhaust, the sour smell of a subway crowd, the pervasive odor of a garbage dump, or the chlorinated rankness of a

public lavatory more gratifying? Even in the matter of smells, sweetness is not entirely on the side of the modern city.

As for the eye and ear, there is no doubt where the balance of advantage goes: the majority of medieval towns were infinitely superior
to those erected during the last century. One awoke in the medieval
town to the crowing of the cock, the chirping of birds nesting under
the eaves, or to the tolling of the hours in the monastery on the outskirts, perhaps to the chime of bells in the new bell-tower. Song rose
easily on the lips, from the plain chant of the monks to the refrains
of the ballad singer in the market place, or that of the apprentice
and the house-maid at work. As late as the seventeenth century, the
ability to hold a part in a domestic choral song was rated by Pepys
as an indispensable quality in a new maid. There were work songs,
distinct for each craft, often composed to the rhythmic tapping or
hammering of the craftsman himself. Fitz-Stephens reported in the
twelfth century that the sound of the water mill was a pleasant one
amid the green fields of London. At night there would be complete
silence, but for the stirring of animals and the calling of the hours
by the town watch. Deep sleep was possible in the medieval town,
untainted by either human or mechanical noises.

If the ear was stirred, the eye was even more deeply delighted.
The craftsman who had walked through the fields and woods on
holiday, came back to his stone-carving or his wood-working with a
rich harvest of impressions to be transferred to his work. The buildings, so far from being "quaint," were as bright and clean as a
medieval illumination, often covered with whitewash, so that all
the colors of the image makers in paint or glass or polychromed
wood would dance on the walls, even as the shadows quivered like
sprays of lilac on the façades of the more richly carved buildings.
(Patina and picturesqueness were the results of time's oxidation:
not original attributes of the architecture.) Common men thought
and felt in images, far more than in the verbal abstractions used by
scholars: esthetic discipline might lack a name, but its fruit were
everywhere visible. Did not the citizens of Florence vote as to the
type of column that was to be used on the Cathedral? Image makers
carved statues, painted triptychs, decorated the walls of the cathedral, the guild hall, the town hall, the burgher's house: color and

design were everywhere the normal accompaniment of the practical daily tasks. There was visual excitement in the array of goods in the open market: velvets and brocades, copper and shining steel, tooled leather and brilliant glass, to say nothing of foods arranged in their panniers under the open sky. Wander around the survivals of these medieval markets today. Whether they be as drab as the Jews' Market in Whitechapel, or as spacious as that on the Plain Palais at Geneva, they still have some of the excitement of their medieval prototypes.

This daily education of the senses is the elemental groundwork of all higher forms of education: when it exists in daily life, a community may spare itself the burden of arranging courses in art appreciation. Where such an environment is lacking, even the purely rational and signific processes are half-starved: verbal mastery cannot make up for sensory malnutrition. If this is a key, as Mme. Montessori discovered, to the first stages of a child's education, it continues to be true even at a later period: the city has a more constant effect than the formal school. Life flourishes in this dilation of the senses: without it, the beat of the pulse is slower, the tone of the muscles is lower, the posture lacks confidence, the finer discriminations of eye and touch are lacking, perhaps the will-to-live itself is defeated. To starve the eye, the ear, the skin, is just as much to court death as to withhold food from the stomach. Though diet was often meager in the Middle Ages, though the religious often imposed abstentions upon themselves in fasts and penances, even the most ascetic could not wholly close his eye to beauty: the town itself was an omnipresent work of art; and the very clothes of its citizens on festival days were like a flower garden in bloom.

9: Principles of Medieval Town Planning

The layout of the medieval town followed the same general patterns as the village. There were street villages and street towns: there were crossroads villages and crossroads towns; there were circular villages and circular towns; and finally, there were irregularly accreted villages and towns of the same apparently aimless and accidental pattern.

The common mistake of supposing that the last type is typically medieval rests upon a misreading of the facts; while the corresponding belief, uttered by Spengler, that the rectangular city pattern is purely a product of the final stage of the hardening of culture into civilization, or a special example of soulless mechanization particularly marked by the appearance of the American city, is even more willfully fallacious.

At the very beginning of the Middle Ages one discovers the regular, geometrical type of plan, with the rectangle as the basis of subdivision: even the monastery of St. Gall in the ninth century exhibited in its ground plan and disposition of buildings the use of straight lines and right angles. This order preceded both military colonization and the development of capitalistic forms of regularity. In general, one may say that a geometric layout is more characteristic of freshly founded towns, and that the irregular layouts, with blocks of different dimensions, with varied perimeters, were a product of slower growth and less systematic settlement. But the distinction does not always hold.

Sometimes the use of the rectangular block unit is coupled with a rectangular outline for the city as a whole: see Montpazier in Southern France. Sometimes this pattern exists within a circular bounding wall; and sometimes, as in Montségur, a rectangular unit is intelligently modified so as to adapt it to the contours and natural boundaries of the site. Rectangular platting has been subject to a vast amount of superficial interpretation, particularly by writers who fail to note that the pattern may in fact be as rural in origin as the windings of the most capricious cowpath. In all probability, the layout of fields in rectangular strips or plots is a product of plow culture on land of low relief: indeed the Etruscan priest used to define the boundaries of the rectangular Etruscan town by means of a plow. Or still earlier, the rectangular town may have grown out of the use of piles and long horizontal wooden beams in lake villages.

Confusion has arisen here because of a failure to grasp the difference, familiar to students of biology, between homologous and analogous forms. A similar form does not necessarily have a similar significance in a different culture; and so, too, similar functions may have quite different forms. Thus the rectangle meant one thing to an Etruscan priest, another to Hippodamus, the planner of the Piraeus, a third to the Roman legionary, spading up his camp for the night, and a fourth to the City Plan Commissioners of New York in 1811. To the first, the rectangle might symbolize cosmic law: to the last it simply meant the maximum possibilities for real estate speculation.

There is indeed a certain ground for thinking of medieval plans as more irregular than most modern plans: this was because uneven sites were more frequently utilized, since they had advantages in fortification and defense. Medieval builders had no *a priori* love for symmetry as such: it was simpler to follow nature's contours than to attempt to grade them down or even them up. Internal traffic for wheeled vehicles made no demands for regular streets; as long as water came from wells and springs, a steep rocky site might be as satisfactory as a low-lying one. (Note how the drumlins of Boston were occupied and platted long before the Back Bay Fens were drained and captured for residence.) Indeed, it is by its persistent power of adaptation to site and to practical needs that the medieval town presented such multiform examples of individuality: the planner made use of the irregular, the accidental, the unexpected; and by the same token, he was not averse to symmetry and regularity when, as in the frontier towns, the plan could be laid out in a single step on fresh land. Many of the surviving irregularities on medieval plans are due to streams that have been covered over, trees that have been cut down, old balks that once defined rural fields.

Whether adaptive or geometrical, of slow growth or quick development, on an old Roman foundation, like Köln or on an entirely new site like Lübeck or Salisbury, the determining elements in the medieval town are the bounding wall, and the central open space where the principal church is usually located, and where the town hall, the guild hall, the market and the inns, finally cluster. The wall, with its outside moat, both defines and symbolizes the town: it made it an island. To retreat, to wall off a secure place, to interpose armor between the naked flesh and the sword, or a dogma between doubt and the harsh facts of life—all these actions were conceived and performed in the same style. This was not a world of wide horizons, shadowy borderlands, clouds and mist, uncharted seas and giddy distances. It was a world of sharp definitions: what could not be paced and measured, defined and classified, immediately dropped into the realm of the mythological. Walls of custom bounded the economic classes and kept them in their place: virtue was white: vice was black. To be unclassed, unbounded, was essentially to be defenseless. Philosophical nominalism, which challenged the objective reality of classes, was as destructive to the medieval conception of the world as cannonballs proved to be to the old palisades and walls of the city: no wonder the Church bristled at the heresy.

Though the wall existed for military defense and the main ways of the city were usually planned to facilitate rallying to the main gates, the psychological import of the wall must not be forgotten. One was either in or out of the city; one belonged or one did not belong. When the town gates were locked at sundown, and the portcullis was drawn, the city was insulated from the outside world. As in a ship, the wall helped create a feeling of unity between the inhabitants: in a siege or a famine the morality of the shipwreck— share-and-share-alike—developed easily. But the wall also served to build up a fatal sense of insularity: all the more because of the absence of roads and quick means of communication between cities.

Usually near the center of the city, both for practical reasons of assembly and for symbolic reasons, was the principal church or cathedral: here the main routes might converge, although they rarely crossed or attempted to form a continuous route: the market place was not a device for attracting or pumping out fast-moving traffic. In the shadow of the church, sometimes hugging its walls for protection, the regular market takes place: this square forms an agora and an acropolis in one. Sometimes the chief buildings in the market place form conspicuous islands, with access on all sides; sometimes they are directly attached to the neighboring houses: but it is highly unusual to find them surrounded on four sides by a wide open plaza, as the "improvers" of the nineteenth century transformed them.

The central position of the church or cathedral is the key to the layout of the medieval city: within its narrow area its towers, or the shadows they throw, are visible from every point, and the difference in size between its towering walls and the little houses that huddle at the base is a symbol of the relation between sacred and profane affairs. When one finds the market square spreading beside the Cathedral one must not be tempted to assign to these institutions the same values they have today: it was the first that was occasional, and the second whose services were regular. The market place grows up by the church because it is there that the citizens most frequently assemble. It was in the church, in the early days, that the city's treasury was stored; and it was in the church, sometimes behind the High Altar, that deeds were deposited for safekeeping; because of its central location, in quarter or city, the arms might even be kept in the church. In fact, one must think of the early church as what one would now call in America a community center building: not too holy to serve as a dining hall for great public festivals.

The scale of the market place is not directly determined by either the height of the main buildings or the size of the city: it is rather adapted to marketing and public ceremony, for it is on the porch of the cathedral that the miracle plays were enacted: it was within the square that the guilds set up their stages for the performance of their mystery plays; it was here that great tourneys would be held. It was not merely acropolis but amphitheater. Often one market place will open into another subordinate square, connected by a narrow passage: Parma is an example. Except in the church, where grandeur and height were important symbolic attributes, the medieval planner tended to keep to human dimensions. Almshouses would be founded for seven or ten men; and instead of building one large hospital, it was commoner to provide a small one for every two or three thousand people: similarly Coulton reckons that there was one parish church for every hundred families. In London in the twelfth century, according to Fitz-Stephens, there were 13 conventual and 126 smaller churches. The habit of erecting such buildings continued long after the social need had exhausted itself: note the church-building that went on in the City of London under Wren. This decentralization of the essential social functions of the city not merely prevented overcrowding and needless circulation: it kept the whole town in scale. Here the physical form confirmed the social fact, and the social fact gave significance to the physical form. The loss of this fine sense of scale, which one notes in the over-sized burgher houses of the

North, or the crazy towered urban fortresses in Italy, was symptomatic of social pathology.

The street occupied in medieval city planning a quite different place than in an age of locomotion. Except in the country, we inevitably think of houses being built along a line of predetermined streets. But on the less regular medieval sites it would be the other way about: groups of trades or groups of institutional buildings would form self-contained quarters or "islands." Within these "islands," and often outside, as part of the connecting urban tissue, the streets were essentially footways: marks of the daily comings and goings of the inhabitants. "Islands" formed by the castle, the monasteries, or the specialized industrial section of the technically more advanced towns were characteristic features: they had their counterpart in the little internal "islands" one encounters in the Northern countries in the housing foundations for the aged or the poor. The Fuggerei in Augsburg is the most handsomely built survival of this mode, although the Dutch and English foundations of the same period surpass it in spaciousness.

In the early medieval city, the street was a line of communication rather than a means of transportation: the unpaved streets were more like the courtyard of a farm. The streets were sometimes narrow and the turns and closures frequent: there was a difference in breadth between the main streets and the subordinate ones. When the street was narrow and twisting, or when it came to a dead end, the plan broke the force of the winter's wind and reduced the area of the mud: the overhang of the houses not merely gave extra space to the inhabitants above but furnished a partly covered way to the pedestrian. Sometimes the building was constructed to form an arcaded walk, as in the street leading up to das Goldene Dachl in Innsbruck: protection against summer sun or winter sleet. One must not forget how important this physical protection against the weather was: for the stalls and booths of the handicraftsmen and merchants were not generally put behind glass until the seventeenth century: the greater part of the citizen's active life was spent outdoors. The closed narrow street and the exposed shop were complementary: not till glass closed the second could new conceptions of town planning open up the first.

Some three centuries before wheeled vehicles became common the street lost its rural underfooting. Paving for the pedestrian came in as early as 1184 in Paris, 1235 in Florence, and 1310 in Lübeck; while by the end of the fourteenth century, even in England, Langland could use the figure "as common as the pavement to every man that walketh." Often these early efforts applied only to a single important street; and the movement spread so slowly that it did not reach Landshut in Bavaria till 1494, although that other great technical innovation, window-glass, was used by South Bavarian farmers, according to Heyne, in the thirteenth century. The provision and care of paving reminds one of another feature about the management of the medieval town: for here again it was association that was put on a public basis, while physical organization was, more often than not, on a private basis. Certainly this applies to paving, lighting, and the piped water supply. By the sixteenth century the first two were usually mandatory; but they were carried out by the private householder for his particular private property. The cleaning of streets likewise for long remained a private concern: a custom that lingered through the nineteenth century in London in the institution of the crossing sweeper. (Medieval practice still applies to the building and maintenance of sidewalks.) Under the paving act that prevailed in Northampton in 1431, the municipal authorities had the power to order the owners of the property to have and keep in repair the street in front of their houses and adjoining their property; but "no property owner was compelled to extend the pavement into the street above 30 feet, so it became the duty of the town to pave the market and similar wide places."

As the physical utilities of the town became more complicated, the need for more detailed municipal regulations and for more zealous and far-sighted municipal enterprise became greater. The growth of population gradually centered political attention more and more upon the mechanical means of existence, and the institutions bound up with common interests and feelings, with the common ideology, became more feeble, if they did not disappear. This change was closely associated with those larger transformations that marked the growth of a technical and capitalistic culture. Finally, in the nineteenth century, the physical organs and activities became the main determinants of plan, and the social life of the city was squeezed, as it were, into the accidental apertures left open by railroad extension and real estate speculation.

10: Control of Growth and Expansion

How did the medieval town grow? To what extent did it grow? These questions bring us face to face with important aspects of both the polity and the culture, as well as the physical necessities, of medieval life.

As long as the simple wooden palisade or masonry wall sufficed for military protection, the wall was no real obstacle to town extension. Technically, it was a simple matter to tear down the wall and extend the city's boundaries once the inner spaces had been filled up. Florence, for example, enlarged her wall circuit for the second time in 1172, and not more than a century later built a third circuit that enclosed a still greater area. This was common practice in the growing towns up to the sixteenth century. But even at its widest, no medieval town usually extended more than half a mile from its center. The "historic mile" of Edinburgh stretched between the extreme limits of castle-top and the Holyrood Abbey on the outskirts.

The limitations on the medieval town's growth were rather of a different nature: limitations of water supply and local produce: limitations by municipal ordinance and by guild regulations which prevented the uncontrolled settlement of outsiders: limitations of transport and communications which were overcome only in the advanced eotechnic cities that had waterways instead of roadways for traffic, such as Venice. For practical reasons alone, the limitations on horizontal expansion were speedily reached. In the early centuries of city development, between the eleventh and the fourteenth, as in the seventeenth in New England, the surplus population was cared for by building new cities, sometimes close by, but nevertheless an independent and self-sufficient unit. The medieval city did not break through its walls and stretch over the countryside in an amorphous blob.

Contrary to the common impression, however, medieval urbanism was far from static. Not merely were thousands of new urban foundations made during the early Middle Ages; but settled towns that found themselves physically hampered or inconveniently located moved to other sites: Lübeck changed its site in order to better the means of trade and defense, and Old Sarum was abandoned and Salisbury created with a ready expenditure of energy for which there are few modern parallels outside devastated areas. How far the actual layout was the work of an official city architect it is difficult to determine. But toward the end of the Middle Ages the municipal buildings would be designed by such an official; and by that time the city architect was often a man in the top rank of his profession, like Elias Holl in Augsburg. Order in private building, too, came through his supervision.

But population growth was not governed by the covetousness of the real estate speculator: even colonization towns did not increase indefinitely in population. The general pattern of town growth was that of small cities, distributed widely over the landscape: Reclus, indeed, discovered that the villages and towns of France could be plotted with amazing regularity on the pattern of a day's walk back and forth between them. This urban pattern corresponded to the economic one: facilities for shipping food were extremely limited —Francis Bacon died as a result of making one of the first experiments with cold storage—and power, whether obtained through wind mills or water mills or sailing ships, was similarly distributed. While internally, the importance of the Church and its accessory institutions limited the growth of the town almost as much as the provisional definition of the wall itself: its buildings served as cohesive nucleus.

At all events, the facts are plain. The typical medieval town ranged in size from three or four hundred, which was frequently the size of a fully privileged municipality in Germany, to forty thousand, which was the size of London in the fourteenth century: the hundred thousand achieved earlier by Paris and Venice was highly exceptional. Toward the close of the period, Nürnberg, a thriving place, had in 1450 about twenty thousand inhabitants, while Basel had around eight thousand. Even on the fine soils of the lowlands, supported by the technically advanced and capitalistically exploited textile industries, the same thing holds: in 1412 Ypres had only 10,736 inhabitants, and Louvain and Brussels, in the middle of the same century, had between 25,000 and 40,000. As for Germany, town life was concentrated in some 150 large cities, of which the largest did not have more than 35,000 inhabitants. All these statistics, it is true, date from the century after the Black Death, which in some provinces carried off half the population; but even if one doubles the figures the towns themselves, in terms of modern population massings, were numerically small. In Italy alone, partly because of the early rise of capitalism there, do these figures have to be increased. The phenomena of overcrowding and overbuilding—as well as indefinite suburban expansion—did not come in until the capacity for building *new* cities had, for reasons to be discussed in the next chapter, greatly diminished.

11: The Stage and the Drama

Every culture has its characteristic drama. It chooses from the sum total of human possibilities certain acts and interests, certain processes and values, and endows them with special significance: provides them with a setting: organizes rites and ceremonies: excludes from the circle of dramatic response a thousand other daily acts which, though they remain part of the "real" world, are not active agents in the drama itself. The stage on which this drama is enacted, with the most skilled actors and a full supporting company and specially designed scenery, is the city: it is here that it reaches its highest pitch of intensity.

Between the underlying facts of life and the drama of a culture there is something of the same relation that exists between daily events and the dreamwork of a sleeper, who transposes and magnifies certain fragments of actuality in relation to the trends and conflicts in his inner life. Actual life provides the material for both dream and culture: but both are warped by the pressure of fear, power, ancient traumas, or newly awakened desires. The practical, day-to-day occupations tell much about a culture; but until one has located and envisaged its essential drama, it is impossible to affix to the actors and the scenery the values that they actually had for their participants and spectators. In one culture a rose is purely a botanical species: in another, it has greater significance as an allegorical symbol of passion.

What was the essential drama of the medieval culture? It took place within the Church; it concerned the passage of sinning man through an evil and painful world, from which he might emerge through repentance into heaven, or sink through hardness of heart or confirmed mischief into hell. The earth itself was but a mean stopping place, a wayside tavern of ill fame, on the way to these other worlds. But nothing that concerned this drama was mean: on the contrary, the Church, founded through an act of God, brought into the world constant reminders of the grace and beauty that was to come: though art and music might tempt men from a higher life, they also indicated its possibility, indeed its immanence. Life was a succession of significant episodes in man's pilgrimage to heaven: for each great moment the Church had its sacrament or its celebration. Beneath the active drama was the constant chant of prayer: in solitude or in company, men communed with God and praised him. It was in such moments, only in such moments, that one truly lived.

Whatever else the medieval city was, in its busy turbulent life, it was above all things a stage for the ceremonies of the Church. Just as in an industrial age, the imagination soars to its highest level in a railroad station or bridge, in medieval culture practical achievement reached its peak in the service of a great symbol. Men who had little to eat gave part of that little to say prayers and masses, light candles, and build a mighty fabric, in which legend, allegory, and knowledge crystallized in nave and altar, screen and wall-painting. On isolated occasions of great religious exaltation, such as Henry Adams described in Mt. Saint Michel and Chartres, they might even carry the very stones that were needed to the site, rich and poor alike. The sin of pride might enter into the building of such monuments: Eugene O'Neill did well to interpret Marco Polo as a medieval Babbitt, and there was more than a touch of vainglory in the famous announcement of the burghers of Florence when they laid their plans for their Cathedral. But pride was not pettiness: luxury and art were not sordid concessions to an otherwise foreign culture. The Duomo in Florence *is* a great building; and it was in the construction of such buildings that the ordinary energies of the medieval community were lifted to a higher potential.

No sedentary student, viewing this architecture in pictures, no superficial observer, taking up a position and attempting to plot out axes and formal relationship, is in a state to penetrate this urban setting even in its purely esthetic aspect. For the key to the visible city lies in the procession, above all, in the great religious procession that winds about the streets and places before it finally debouches into the church or the cathedral for the great ceremony itself. Here is no static architecture. The masses suddenly expand and vanish, as one appoaches them or draws away: a dozen paces may alter the relation of the foreground and background, or the lower and upper range of the line of vision. The silhouettes of the buildings, with their steep gables, their sharp roof lines, their pinnacles, their towers, ripple and flow, break and solidify, rise and fall, with no less vitality than the structures themselves. As in a fine piece of sculpture, the silhouettes are often inexhaustible in their variety: the outlines vary no less constantly than the relations of the planes.

Within the general medieval pattern, deep changes in feeling took place. Radically different life experiences separate the confident sobriety of the great Romanesque buildings, as solid as a fortress, from the humanism of the magnificent Lady Churches that defied the dogma of the wall with the heresy of the fragile window and the flying buttress; or again, from the sickly, over-ripe estheticism of the fifteenth century, which embroidered its buildings because it lacked the patience and the honesty and the courage to put its soul into the weaving of the fabric. But through all these changes, the setting itself possessed vitality: it incorporated these successive moments of the spirit without losing form. The towers of the churches raised the eyes to heaven: their masses rose, in hierarchic rank, over all the lesser symbols of earthly wealth and power: through their stained glass windows the light burst in aureoles of splendid color. From almost any part of the city, the admonitory fingers of the spires, archangelic swords, tipped with gold, were visible: if hidden for a moment, they would suddenly appear as the roofs parted, with the force of a blast of trumpets.

The lines of the subordinate buildings did not necessarily run upward: horizontal banks of windows are common in the houses and horizontal string courses often separate the parts of a church tower, in England no less than in Italy. In the Palace of the Doges in Venice, begun in 1422, there is already, perhaps, a touch of bureaucratic discipline. But the movement of the eye is up and down, if only because the blocked vista is a characteristic of medieval planning and design. The eye blocked, it moves upward. The body blocked in movement, it changes its position and goes on in another direction. So one walked about the streets: so one joined in a guild pageant, or in a religious procession, turning and winding till one reached the portals of the church. Let us look at a medieval procession through the eyes of a late contemporary who left behind a precious picture of the occasion. The time is early sixteenth century: the place is Antwerp: the witness is Albrecht Dürer.

"On Sunday after Our Dear Lady's Assumption, I saw the Great Procession from the Church of Our Lady at Antwerp, when the whole town of every craft and rank was assembled, each dressed in his best according to his rank. And all ranks and guilds had their signs, by which they might be known. In the intervals, great costly pole-candles were borne, and three long old Frankish trumpets of silver. There were also in the German fashion many pipers and drummers. All the instruments were loudly and noisily blown and beaten.

"I saw the Procession pass along the street, the people being arranged in rows, each man some distance from his neighbor, but the rows close behind the other. There were the Goldsmiths, the Painters, the Masons, the Broderers, the Sculptors, the Joiners, the Carpenters, the Sailors, the Fishermen, the Butchers, the Leatherers, the Clothmakers, the Bakers, the Tailors, the Cordwainers—indeed, workmen of all kinds, and many craftsmen and dealers who work for their livelihood. Likewise the shopkeepers and merchants and their assistants of all kinds were there. After these came the shooters with guns, bows, and crossbows, and the horsemen and foot-soldiers also. Then followed the watch of the Lord Magistrates. Then came a fine troop all in red, nobly and splendidly clad. Before them, however, went all the religious orders and the members of some foundations, very devoutly, all in their different robes.

"A very large company of widows also took part in the procession. They support themselves with their own hands and observe a special rule. They were all dressed from head to foot in white linen garments made expressly for the occasion, very sorrowful to see. Among them I saw some very stately persons. Last of all came the Chapter of Our Lady's Church, with all their clergy, scholars, and treasurers. Twenty persons bore the image of the Virgin Mary with the Lord Jesus, adorned in the costliest manner, to the honor of the Lord God.

"In this procession very many delightful things were shown, most splendidly got up. Wagons were drawn along with masques upon ships and other structures. Behind them came the Company of the Prophets in their order, and scenes from the New Testament, such as the Annunciation, the Three Holy Kings riding on great camels, and on other rare beasts, very well arranged. . . . From the beginning to end, the Procession lasted more than two hours before it was gone past our house."

Note the vast number of people arrayed in this procession. As in the church itself, the spectators were also communicants and participants: they engaged in the spectacle, watching it from within, not from without: or rather, feeling it from within, acting in unison, not dismembered beings, reduced to a single specialized rôle. Prayer, mass, pageant, life-ceremony, baptism, marriage, or funeral—the city itself was stage for these separate scenes of the drama, and the citizen himself was actor. Once the unity of this social order was broken, everything about it was set in confusion: the great Church itself became a sect, and the city became a battleground for conflicting cultures, dissonant ways of life.

12: What Overthrew the Medieval City?

As the nineteenth century idea of unceasing change and progress raises for us today the problem of stabilization and equilibrium, so the medieval idea of protection raised, from the fourteenth century onward, the problem of how life and growth and movement were to take place in a world governed by the ideas of safety and salvation. Must the armor be removed? Must the wall be torn down? Or did this civilization have the capacity to arrive, without disintegration, at a wider synthesis?

About the ensuing facts, there is little occasion for dispute. After the sixteenth century, the medieval city tended to become a mere shell: the better the shell was preserved, the less life was left in it. Its creative day was over. That is the history of Carcassonne, Bruges, Chipping Camden, or Braunschweig. Where the external form was rapidly altered by pressure of population and new measures of economic enterprise, the inner spirit was transformed, too. In the first series of examples the body retained its shape because the new currents of life had drifted elsewhere. But the old shape did not express the new life: so the city became in effect a museum of the past, and its inhabitants, if not curators, had only a mean restricted part to play in the new culture. Such puddles of medieval life, sometimes dried up, sometimes rank with decay, are still scattered over Europe.

The protected economy of the medieval city was capable of being maintained by one fact alone: the superiority of the city over the barbarous, insecure life of the open country. So great were its advantages in the way of training men for orderly economic effort, fostering skill by every variety of emulation and gain, that industry for long was not tempted to seek the low wages of the country, or accept the low standards and the clumsy technical equipment of the rural craftsman. Municipal restrictions might be onerous to the more speculative enterprisers; but they were easier to endure than feudal restrictions, and since they rested on rational common consent, they were less capricious. Even the nobility appreciated these urban advantages: life and the goods of life at least had the spice of variety in the city.

By the sixteenth century the disparity between city and country, politically speaking, had been partly removed. Improvements in transport by water had lessened the distance between city and countryside; and since feudal dues had been converted into money payments in many regions, people could remain in the open country or go back and forth without falling into the status of serfs or liegemen. One evidence of this equalization is the number of dialogues gentlemen wrote in the sixteenth century weighing the advantages of the two environments: the two modes were at last near enough to be compared.

This new parity was abetted by the fact that security was gradually being established in the open country through the rise of a central authority in the newly consolidated states. When the kings put down the warring nobles, industry could prosper outside organized municipalities: protected by the symbolic might of the law, industry might spring up in a non-enfranchised village, beyond the pale of any older municipal government. Merchants with capital enough to purchase raw materials and the instruments of production—knitting machines for instance—could farm their work out in the countryside, paying subsistence wages instead of town rates, escaping regulations as to employment made by the guilds, cutting under the urban standard of living, and in general playing the devil with the regulated market. Under this regime, infant labor came in.

Moreover, toward the close of the Middle Ages the mining industries and the glass industries played a far larger part than they had played at the beginning. These industries, in the nature of the case, were usually placed outside the limits of the earlier settlements; and from the first they had taken on most of the features of later capitalistic industry, for the same reasons that were decisive later: the machinery of production was too expensive to be purchased by a single man or worked by a family unit; and the methods themselves required the hiring and organization of whole gangs who were usually employed as wage laborers, and who could be hired only by an employer with enough capital to tide them over between the season of production and the moment when sales were finally made. Proportionately, a larger part of the industrial population came to get its livelihood outside the incorporated municipalities: even if these industries gave rise to urban settlements, they remained competitors with the guild-protected centers.

The old monopolies had been achieved by the co-operative action of the burghers for the benefit of the town. From the sixteenth century on the new monopolies issued in England and France were not town monopolies but trade monopolies: they worked for the benefit of the privileged individuals who controlled the trade, no matter where they were scattered. For these producing monopolies, the whole country was a province; and their promoters, like Sir Richard Maunsell, the English glass manufacturer, were either drawn from the nobility or speedily elevated to it. Big industry, investment banking, and wholesale trade were not on a single town basis. Even within the incorporated municipalities the old guilds and corporations crumbled, first in Italy, then elsewhere, before the attack of financially more powerful groups that often usurped the very function of town government through their ability to hire mercenaries.

The growing importance of international commerce from the fifteenth century on took advantage of weaknesses that were inherent in the craft guild and the walled town. The first weakness is that they were both on a purely local basis: to exercise monopolistic control within their walls it was essential that they should be able to govern the realm outside, too: this meant harmony with the countryside plus a federal union of cities. Now and then the guilds of one town might help those of another, as the guilds in the neighborhood of Colmar supported the Colmar guild of bakers on a ten year strike. But on the whole, the guild was able to exercise its authority only over those who actually came to practice within the walls of the town. Once the lanes of travel opened and the countryside became safe, the towns were helpless.

As an organization of crafts, the guild had one further weakness: it was incapable of meeting the new situation that had sprung up in industry—as incapable as the craft unions of the American Federation of Labor were of organizing the motor industry. Jurisdictional disputes between the crafts took place: this divided their energy and caused them to fight against their own fellows instead of against the big merchants who were becoming more powerful and more bent on exploiting both the little masters and the proletariat. As the guilds grew more exclusive, the excluded turned to the non-protected industries. In addition, many new types of worker, unskilled, but of increasing weight in the new industrial routine, dockers, porters, navvies, were not brought into the guild organization. This growing class helped depress the standard of living and began to constitute that casual labor reserve upon which capitalistic industry was to cast its own characteristic form of organization.

Still another factor was the extension of the class war. The medieval system, based on a hierarchy of social rank, of course knew no economic equality: there were vast gaps between rich and poor, master and beggar. But in the earlier part of the period, when urban land was fairly evenly divided and the means of production were largely individual tools, the mobility of the skilled journeymen partly insured him against victimization. In those days there was far less of a spread between upper and lower ranks: they had a common city, a common culture, a common religious faith.

In the textile industry of Flanders and Northern Italy, the characteristic breach between workers and masters appeared as early as the thirteenth century: the newly introduced spinning wheel and draw-loom exercised an influence comparable to that of the spinning jenny and the power loom five centuries later. In Köln the weavers temporarily succeeded in overthrowing the patriciate in 1370-71. But the odds were against the guilds; their victories were brief. While they operated on a local basis, their opponents, through family marriages and alliances and international contacts, were united on a European basis. Hence the ruling classes could bring many forms of pressure and authority to bear at a single point.

Apart from the weaknesses of the guilds, the defect of the medieval urban policy was that it had never—outside certain regions in Italy —embraced a sufficient area of countryside. It was an island in a hostile sea. Ecologically speaking, the city and countryside are a single unit; if one can do without the other, it is the country, not the city, the farmer, not the burgher. The triumphs of art and invention in the city had made it doubly contemptuous of its rural neighbors; the countryman was treated as a dependent, or what was worse, a foreigner. Cities attempted to solve the problem of a common union by forcing their peasant neighbors into a state of subjection. In Italy they denied the peasants the privileges of citizenship; and in Germany the Bannmeilenrecht compelled the nearby peasants to supply the city with both food and the necessities of industry. Instead of creating allies in the open country, who could have helped strike at the roots of feudal power, they created a sullen wall of enemies.

The power of the feudal aristocracies and the princely dynasties, though challenged, was never successfully displaced over any considerable period by any combination of cities in Europe. When the cities joined the king, in order to lessen the impositions of the nobles or ecclesiastics, they succeeded only in displacing a local tyrant by a more ubiquitous one: presently they found themselves the subjects of the state they had helped create. The essential difficulty was that the political unit, the economic unit, and the religious unit were not in symmetrical relationship, and were not unified in any common frame-work other than the dynastic state. Power, privilege, ancient custom had made the political map of Europe a crazy quilt of conflicting jurisdictions and disparate allegiances and meaningless particu-larisms.

Various attempts at confederation were made, indeed, between re-lated cities. In addition to the enterprising and relatively enduring union of Hansa cities, there was a League of Swabian Cities in 1376 and a Rhenish League in 1381, while England had the Union of Cinque Ports. In Italy, during the same century, Lombardy, the Romagna, Tuscany, Umbria, and the Marches were partitioned be-tween 80 city states, or, as Toynbee puts it, in one half of Italy in A.D. 1300 there were more self-governing states than could be counted in the whole world in 1933. The unifications that took place during the next two centuries reduced these Italian self-governing municipalities to ten political units: but that change was accom-panied by a loss of freedom, autonomy, and power.

It was in Switzerland and Holland that the problem of the federal unification of the corporate towns and the countryside was actually solved without undermining the political integrity of the urban unit; and it is to the Swiss and Dutch cities that one must turn for perhaps the most successful examples of the transition from the medieval to the modern order. That the Swiss achieved unity without despotism or submission to the arbitrary forms of centralized authority shows that the feat was technically possible: moreover, it gives color to the notion that it was humanly practicable on a wide European basis, since the three language groups in Switzerland, with their mountain barriers to transportation and intercourse, gave the country almost as many obstacles to unity as the most diverse territories of Europe as a whole. The proof was genuine, but the example was not infectious: actual life in other regions took a different political course.

Now territorial unification and internal peace and freedom of movement were all highly necessary conditions for the new system of capitalistic industry. Centralized power developed in states like England and France, with at least the passive connivance of the underlying corporations and communities, because of the tangible benefits that flowed from the establishment of the king's peace, the king's justice, the king's protection that insured travel on the king's highway. From the standpoint of trade, transportation, and travel, conditions had actually been worsening since the twelfth century. Along the Rhine, for example, there had been only nineteen toll stations toward the end of that century: in the thirteenth twenty-five more were added, and in the fourteenth another twenty: so that by the *end* of the Middle Ages the total was something over sixty: the stoppages and the burdensome fees might occur as often as every six miles.

Road tolls, bridge tolls, river tolls, town tolls—these economic exactions had been multiplying precisely at the moment when the routes of trade were lengthening and when the constant flow of goods was becoming more important to a stable economic market. In addition, the lack of uniform coinage, combined with the dubious inflationary policies of this or that needy ruler or town, offered another handicap to commerce. Except in the provinces mentioned, the cities of Europe were too insular, too parochial-minded, too jealous of their special privileges to solve the problems by common measures. External conformity, enforced by the military power of the state, stepped in to perform the task where co-operative methods were not tried, or were given but a partial grudging trial and had failed. And inept self-government, leading to bankruptcy, often provided an opportunity for the central authority to step in and set matters straight—at the sacrifice of urban liberties, as in France.

We who live in a world consumed by a similar folly, now embracing the planet rather than the continent of Europe, can without any sense of ironic superiority understand this fatal impasse. The medieval corporations, plainly, sought to solve within the walls of the town problems that could be solved only by breaking down the walls and deliberately pooling their sovereignty and their control in a wider unity. Every aspect of European life was involved in this reorientation: it was not simply a question, as Dante thought, of putting a Pope or an Emperor at the head of the temporal realm. Forerunner in so many political departments of the National State, the medieval town proved the impossibility of meeting the situation by purely local adjustments. The island-states of today are cracking into chaos for similar reasons—still pursuing the same obstinate methods, still aiming at a delusive autarchy.

Only one institution was perhaps capable of transcending this narrow parochialism and these futile monopolistic efforts: that was the universal Church. But the diminishing universalism of the Church itself was organically a phase of the disease that undermined medieval culture: another negative sign of the new capitalistic organization of society, which was creating a new spiritual power, physical science, a new order of dedicated men, the bureaucrats and commercial enterprisers, and a new hierarchy of values, based on the supremacy of the physical world and material goods. From the thirteenth century on the Church, if it did not lose immediately in spiritual authority, had gained in worldly estate—and that is one of the surest ways of undermining spiritual authority. Poor people resented the rich ecclesiastics: there was often more ascetic renunciation in the counting house than in the monastery.

Had the Church remained economically disinterested, it could perhaps have joined forces with the cities and provided a framework for their union. But though the Dominican and Franciscan orders arose in the thirteenth century and quickly made their way, preaching and building, into the city, the Church itself remained rooted in the feudal mold of the past. When it transcended that mold it was to succumb to the very forces and the very ways of life that its essential teachings condemned. By the sixteenth century, the authority of the Church was seriously undermined from within. Corruption had become a constant stench in Rome, and the very blessing of the Church, the indulgence, was farmed out on a share basis to the leading investment banker of the time, Jacob Fugger.

If the international religious order was incapable of preserving the medieval regime by renewal from within, protestantism, which rested on a national basis and issued in a state-supported Church, was even less capable of serving the needs of cities. The protestant doctrine of justification by Faith and the doctrine of Divine Election came in with credit finance and the rise of the self-perpetuating urban patriciate: the visibly elect, the manipulators of intangible values. With the coming of protestantism the old fellowship in the city weakened: cleavages in matters of faith increased the forces of eco·

nomic disruption and further destroyed the possibilities of creating a united front. The validity of the universal Church was denied; the reality of the group was denied; only the individual counted on earth as in heaven: nominalism or social atomism. This common débâcle was summed up in the caustic lines of Robert Crowley, writing in the sixteenth century:

> And this is a city
>   In name but in deed
> It is a pack of people
>   That seek after meed [gain].
> For officers and all
>   Do seek their own gain
> But for the wealth of the Commons
>   Not one taketh pain.
> And hell without order
>   I may it well call
> Where every man is for himself
>   And no man for all.

What Langland had predicted in the fourteenth century in his long harangue on the wiles and perversities of Lady Meed had in two centuries finally come to pass throughout European society. The city had almost ceased to be a common enterprise for the common good; and neither the local authority of the municipal corporation, nor the universal authority of the Church, was sufficient to direct for the benefit of the commonwealth the new forces that were making headway throughout European civilization.

There is little more to be said about the medieval city. Its economic and its social basis had disintegrated, and its organic pattern of life had been broken up. Slowly, the form itself became dilapidated, and even when it continued to stand, its walls enclosed a hollow shell, harboring institutions that were also hollow shells. It is only, as it were, by holding the shell quietly to one's ear, as with a sea-shell, that one can catch in the ensuing pause the dim roar of the old life that was once lived, with dramatic conviction and solemn purpose, within its walls.

CHAPTER II.   COURT, PARADE, AND CAPITAL

1: The Afterglow of the Middle Ages

Human institutions do not die like biological organisms. Fragments of culture continue to live long after the society that originally sustained them has passed away: often long after they have ceased to be a rational response to a situation or the expression of a need. The culture of the medieval period was still active during the Renascence: the remains of the medieval city were ubiquitous. Some institutions renewed themselves by adopting the manners of their time: monasticism took on a new life in the military organization of the Society of Jesus: while other institutions, like the university, hibernated.

In the countryside there was no real interruption between gothic building and neo-gothic building. The English provincial builder carried into the eighteenth century traditional modes of construction that educated gentlemen, ignorant of the life outside their circle, were beginning to revive *as decoration* and amusement, in the fashion of Sir Horace Walpole. Even in the New World the older medieval laws of the market remained in force in the towns.

Is Wren's Tom Tower at Oxford gothic or neo-gothic? One can assign equally good reasons for calling it either. A good part of the new building of the seventeenth century, practically all of the renascence building before this century, took place on medieval street plans, within the walls of essentially medieval cities, erected by crafts and guilds that were still organized on medieval lines. There are churches like the Oratoire in Paris which combine medieval constructional forms with renascence columns and "gothic" buttresses: the counterpart in stone of Rabelais' combination of the medieval monastery and the new country house in his description of the Abbey of Thelema. These are significant symbols. No verbal generalization, still less such pat terms as "Renascence" or "Baroque" or "Neoclassic," can do justice to all the varieties and gradations of form that mark the transition period. No two cities exhibit quite the same combination of architectural characteristics.

The fact is that only a handful of people in any age are its true contemporaries. Only sluggishly do the mass of people respond to the currents that are sweeping through the ruling classes or the intellectual élite; if this is mainly true even today, it was more so before universal literacy had quickened the pace of communication. What historians are tempted to characterize as the traits of an age indicates quite as much about their own standpoint and frame of reference as it does about the objective facts. For the purpose of clarity one should perhaps adopt for sociology a parallel set of terms to the Mendelian classification of biological traits into dominants and recessives; and one should add two other useful categories: survivals and mutations. In Rome before Constantine the Christian Church was a mutation: within the city one would scarcely be aware of its presence: living in crypts and catacombs on the outskirts, it hid even its physical presence. In the medieval city the Church was a dominant: no part of life could fail to record its existence and its influence. In the great seventeenth century capitals, the Church had become a recessive: still an imposing visible presence, but no longer a unifying and dynamic social force. In the metropolis today the Church is a survival: its power rests upon numbers, wealth, *material* organization, not upon its capacity to give its stamp to the daily activities of men: it claims much, but except by repetition and rote, it contributes little to the active spiritual life of the city.

What "characterizes" an age? Mainly, the dominants and recessives, for they bear the active inheritance of the past and they focus the successful forces of the present. But the survivals often occupy a larger part of the visible scene than either the dominants or the recessives: they modify these new elements, sometimes they retard their introduction, sometimes they achieve fresh power by submitting themselves to the process of renovation. Survivals of ancient, pre-Christian religions, belief in sympathetic magic, belief in wizardry, still linger in various strata of the modern mind, immune to the germicidal action of positive science: they are, in effect, an automatic provision against a too narrow basis of continuity in the social heritage. Was it not partly through the stimulus of magical dream books, like that of Artemidorus Daldianus, that Dr. Sigmund Freud made his profound psychological discoveries on the function of dreams? As for the fresh mutations, often isolated, feeble, struggling for bare existence, they usually can have but little contemporary effect: their influence may be as limited as was Leonardo's astonishing technical perspective and inventive ingenuity in the fifteenth century—thinking that would have been magnified many diameters had it appeared in the more genial milieu of the early nineteenth century.

Between the fifteenth and the eighteenth century a new complex of cultural traits took shape in Europe. Both the form and the contents of urban life were in consequence transformed. The new pattern of existence sprang out of a new economy, that of mercantilist capitalism, a new political framework, that of a centralized despotism or oligarchy, usually focused in a national state, and a new ideological form, that of mechanism, whose lines were first laid down in the monastery and the army. But until the seventeenth century all these changes were sporadic and tentative: they were restricted to a minority: they were effective only in patches: they were in an embryonic state, receiving nourishment from an older society, from which they were soon to emerge with a lusty squawk.

In order to understand the discipline and order of the post-medieval city, one must penetrate more fully into the disintegration of the medieval synthesis. And here after one has made due allowance for the choices of men and for the immanent development of institutions, one must perhaps give greatest weight to an overpowering accident: the devastation caused by the Black Death in the fourteenth century. For the real Renascence in European life, the great age of city building and intellectual triumph, had begun two centuries before that event, and had achieved its symbolic apotheosis in the work of an Aquinas, an Albertus Magnus, a Dante, a Giotto.

The so-called Renascence that followed in the fifteenth century was rather in the nature of an illusory belief on the part of its contemporaries: they mistook the brilliant spray of the falling rocket for the energy that had originally lifted it into the air. Thorndike has indeed properly raised the question as to whether there was not a general falling off in civilization and scientific productiveness after the twelfth and thirteenth centuries. He cites the contrast in Petrarch's mind between the happy, confident days of his youth, "when there was no need to close the town gates after dark or keep the walls in repair," when Petrarch was able to wander alone at night in the mountains near Avignon, and the conditions in his old age, when this once-peaceful landscape had become infested with robbers and wolves.

Meanwhile, the plague had intervened: a breach in continuity, a lowering of vitality had followed, like that which comes after an exhausting war. Social disorders resulted: the spread of war and military despotisms, the suppression of academic freedom at the universities, and the studied subordination of the spiritual powers in the interest of temporal authority: a parallel to what is going on in Germany, Italy, and various other parts of Europe again today. The transformation of the universities from international associations of scholars to nationalistic organizations, servile to the new rulers, impervious to "dangerous thoughts" went on steadily.

Within a few centuries, every department of social life showed signs of profound debility or decay. In the fifteenth century, according to von Below, there was the beginning of organized gambling in houses provided by the municipality. And the same tendencies appeared in the Church; not merely the buying of offices and the sale of blessings, but the general recrudescence of superstition. Belief in witchcraft, rejected by St. Boniface in the eighth century and treated as a crime by the laws of Charlemagne, was given the final sanction of the Church in 1484. And it was in the seventeenth century, marked by the appearance of Galileo and Newton and the exact methods of physical science, that the persecution of witches became popular. Indeed, some of the most vicious offenders in this respect were the new scientists and scientific philosophers themselves: people like Glanvill who in almost the same breath were predicting the triumph of science and the complete transformation of the physical world by technics.

From medieval universality to baroque uniformity: from medieval localism to baroque centralism: from the absolutism of God and the Catholic Church to the absolutism of the temporal sovereign and the National State—there is a passage of four or five centuries between these phenomena. Let us not obscure the essential nature of this change by referring solely to its esthetic accompaniments: the unearthing and measurement of classic monuments, the discovery of Plato and Vitruvius, the worship of the Five Orders in architecture. These facts give only a superficial clue to what was happening. The underlying tendencies of the new order did not become visible until every aspect of life had departed from the medieval whole and re-united under a new sign. This did not occur until the seventeenth century. It was then that the intuitions of precursors like Alberti were finally expressed in the baroque style of life, the baroque plan, the baroque garden, and the baroque city.

Because all these tendencies were finally brought to a head in the baroque city, I have chosen to use this term—originally contemptuous —as one of social description, not of limited architectural reference. The concept of the baroque, as it shaped itself in the seventeenth century, is particularly useful because it holds in itself the two contradictory elements of the age. First: the mathematical and mercantile and methodical side, expressed to perfection in its rigorous street plans, its formal city layouts, and in its geometrically ordered landscape designs. And at the same time, in the painting and sculpture of the period, it embraces the sensuous, rebellious, anti-classical, anti-mechanical side, expressed in its clothes and its sexual life and its religious fanaticism and its crazy statecraft. Between the sixteenth and the nineteenth century these two elements existed together: sometimes acting separately, sometimes held in tension within a larger whole.

In this respect, one may regard the early Renascence forms, in their purity, as proto-baroque, and the neo-classic forms, from Versailles to St. Petersburg, as "late" baroque: while even the careless uncontrolled romanticism of the gothic revivalists might be considered, paradoxically, as a phase of baroque caprice. None of this makes sense if one thinks of the baroque as a single moment in the development of architectural style. But the widening of the term has gone on steadily during the last generation; and a certain original vagueness and contradictoriness in the epithet adds sanction to this special use. In terms of the city, the renascence forms are the mutation, baroque forms are the dominants, and neo-classic forms are the survivals in this complex cultural transformation.

2: Territory and City

From the beginning of the Middle Ages two powers had been jockeying for leadership in Western Europe: one was royal, the other municipal. Even in the great days of the Free Cities there were parts of Europe where the royal power had consolidated more swiftly and had kept the cities themselves in a state of feudal vassalage: England, Aquitaine, Sicily, Austria. Where royal and imperial power was weakest, as in Northern Italy, the city achieved its fullest independence as a political entity. But even where it was strong, as in Aragon, royal power was far from absolute: witness the oath sworn by the subjects of the King of Aragon: "We, who are as good as you, swear to you, who are not better than we, to accept you as our king and sovereign lord, provided that you observe all our liberties and laws; but if not, then not."

The consolidation of dispersed feudal estates and the creation of continuous fields of political administration within a clearly defined frame was important for the welfare of the communities concerned. The real question was whether this consolidation was to be undertaken on behalf of a small privileged class, or whether it was to be achieved through a free union of cities and regions. Unfortunately the cities themselves, as we have seen, were not immune to the temptations of a predatory and parasitic life, made possible by the command of military weapons: they undertook exploitation by force both in home territories and in more distant imperialistic ventures: alternately repeating the political mistakes of the Spartans and the Athenians.

The more powerful cities often sought to conquer their weaker neighbors, if for no better purpose than to suppress a rival market: and in times of war, from the end of the twelfth century on, they would in Italy transfer a great measure of executive power to a spe-

cial officer, the Podesta, who in the emergency was released from the bondage of law.

In short, to achieve despotic power over their neighbors, the cities consented to the loss of their own internal freedom: what is more, they lost the moral case against other forms of despotism. As I have already pointed out, the only part of Europe where the civic corporations and the territorial state were unified without loss of civic liberty was the Swiss Cantonal Confederation.

In the early Middle Ages, the great feudal lords had succeeded in feeding their retainers, collecting their rents, and securing a modicum of peace and order in their domains only by being in continual movement from one estate to another. The court was a mobile camp: vigilance and movement were the price of power. This held for kings as well as lesser nobles. The royal ministers, the royal judges, the whole apparatus of government and fiscal control, was essentially a mobile one: authority was maintained by personal supervision. During the fourteenth century in the great monarchies of England and France, this process came to an actual halt. The records of the courts, the rolls, the registers, the archives, the correspondence, not to mention the officials themselves, had become too numerous and bulky to move. As population and territory increased in size, direct personal supervision became impossible: impersonal administration and delegated authority became necessary.

Though the popular movement for parliamentary control did not maintain itself very successfully except in England, the modern state began to shape itself in the fourteenth century. Its marks are a permanent bureaucracy, permanent courts of justice, permanent archives and records, and permanent buildings, more or less centrally located, for conducting the official business. The process was well described by Tout. "By Henry II's reign," Tout observes, "the English king had centralized so much authority under his immediate jurisdiction that all men of substance had frequent occasion to seek justice or to request favors at court." This movement, or rather, this *settlement*, took place first in financial administration, which had its special seat at Westminster: it was gradually extended to all the other offices of State. And the process itself was a reciprocal one: the centralization of authority necessitated the creation of the capital

city, while the capital city, commanding the main routes of trade
and military movement, was a powerful contribution to the unification of the state.

Mark that the capital city had a social as well as a political rôle
to play. In the capital, provincial habits, customs, and dialects were
melted down and recast in the image of the royal court: the so-called
national image, national by prescription rather than in origin. Centuries were needed to effect a unification even in such extra-personal
activities as the regulation of weights and measures: it was not until
1665 that Colbert proposed to "bring the whole of his majesty's
kingdom within the same statutes and within the same system of
weights and measures." Even security of life and property did not
follow very swiftly in every corner of the new national realm: as late
as 1553 in the Guides des Chemins de France there were notations
in the open spaces between towns of "brigandage" or "Dangerous
Forest."

The consolidation of power in the political capital was accompanied by a loss of power and initiative in the local centers: national
prestige meant the death of local municipal freedom. The national
territory itself became the connecting link between diverse groups,
corporations, cities: the nation was an all-embracing society one
entered at birth. The new theorists of law, as Gierke pointed out,
were driven to deny that local communities and corporate bodies had
an existence of their own: the family was the sole group, outside the
state, whose existence was looked upon as self-validated, the only
group that did not need the gracious permission of the sovereign to
exercise its natural functions.

Once political power had been thus consolidated, economic privileges were obtained by individuals, not from the city, but from the
prince; and they could be exercised, as a rule, anywhere in the
realm. After the sixteenth century, accordingly, the cities that increased most rapidly in population and area and wealth were those
that harbored a royal court: the fountainhead of economic power.
About a dozen towns quickly reached a size not attained in the Middle
Ages even by a bare handful: presently London had 250,000 inhabitants, Naples 240,000, Milan over 200,000, Palermo and Rome,
100,000, Lisbon, port of a great monarchy, over 100,000; similarly

Seville, Antwerp, and Amsterdam; while Paris in 1594 had 180,000.

As the great states of the modern world took shape, the capitals continued to monopolize population. In the eighteenth century the cities with over 200,000 included Moscow, Wien, St. Petersburg, and Palermo, while already in the 100,000 class were Warsaw, Berlin, and Copenhagen. Toward the end of the eighteenth century Naples had 433,930 inhabitants, Paris around 670,000, and London over 800,000; while the trading cities like Bristol and Norwich, or the industrial cities like Leeds, Manchester, Iserlohn and Paderborn for the most part remained small in size: that is, with less than fifty thousand inhabitants. The trading town of Hamburg and the industrial town of Lyons, both with secure medieval foundations and a continuing economic life, are the main exceptions; for they both had over 100,000 inhabitants at the beginning of the nineteenth century; but up to then they did not represent the dominant forms of political and financial power.

In contrast to the medieval regime, power and population were no longer disconnected, scattered, decentralized. Only in the Germanic countries did the older type of municipal economy effectively linger on; and the growth of Brandenburg-Prussia in the seventeenth century changed the shape of things even there. The state grew at the expense of the component parts: the capital city grew out of all proportion to the provincial cities, and in no small measure at their expense. Though natural capitals were usually situated at points of special advantage for trade and military defense—these being elements that entered originally into their selection—the baroque rulers brought all the powers of the state to bear to confirm these advantages. Where a natural center was lacking, they imitated at a distance Peter the Great's colossal willfulness in the founding of St. Petersburg.

In short, the multiplication of cities ceased; city building was no longer, for a rising class of small craftsmen and merchants, a means of achieving freedom and security. It was rather a means of consolidating political power in a single center directly under the royal eye and preventing such a challenge to the central authority from arising elsewhere, in scattered centers, more difficult to control. The age of free cities, with their widely diffused culture and their rela-

tively democratic modes of association, gave way to the age of absolute cities: a few centers that grew inordinately, leaving other towns
either to accept stagnation or to stultify themselves in hopeless gestures of imitation.

Law, order, uniformity—all these are special products of the
baroque capital: but the law exists to confirm the status and secure
the position of the privileged classes, the order is a mechanical order,
based not upon blood or neighborhood or kindred purposes and affections but upon subjection to the ruling prince; and as for the uniformity—it is the uniformity of the bureaucrat, with his pigeonholes, his
dossiers, his red tape, his numerous devices for regulating and systematizing the collection of taxes. The external means of enforcing
this pattern of life lies in the army; its economic arm is mercantile
capitalist policy; and its most typical institutions are the standing
army, the bourse, the bureaucracy, and the court. There is an underlying harmony that pervades all these institutions: between them
they create a new form for social life—the baroque city.

3: Instruments of Coercion

In the growth of the modern state, capitalism and technics and
warfare play a decisive part; but it is impossible to assign a prior
rôle to one or the other. Each developed through internal causes and
in response to a common milieu; and the state developed along with
them.

How did the modern doctrines of absolute political power arise?
Why did the political despot emerge so easily out of the concentrations of economic capital and political authority that took place in
the fourteenth century Italian city, with more than one guild, more
than one family, contending for the position? How did the fashion
of despotism, creating big despots like the Tudors and midget despots
like the minor rulers of German states, spread over Europe—despots
who have their counterparts, sometimes their origins, in the new business men and financiers? There is another name for this growing
belief in absolute power: one might call it the illusion of gunpowder.

The old saw that gunpowder brought about the ruin of feudalism
is far from being true. Although feudal independence could not resist the centralization of power in national monarchies, gunpowder

had the effect of giving the feudal aristocrats a new lease on life, rescuing them from the pressure of the walled towns; for gunpowder increased the range, power, and mobility of the professional soldiers —and arms was the age-old profession of the feudal leader. In a very real sense, however, the introduction of gunpowder early in the fourteenth century—that century which undermined so many medieval institutions—sounded the death knell of the free cities.

Up to this time security had rested mainly on a very simple technical device: the moat and the wall: sufficient defense against raiding warriors who carried no heavy instruments of assault. A well-fortified city was virtually impregnable: even as late as Macchiavelli's day he remarked that the "cities of Germany . . . are fortified in such a manner that . . . to reduce them would be tedious and difficult, for they all have the necessary moats and bastions, sufficient artillery, and always keep in the public storehouses food and drink and fuel for one year."

Down to the fifteenth century, defense had the upper hand over assault. Alberti's advanced treatise on city planning, published posthumously, did not reckon with cannon, and the new art of fortification played but a minor rôle. Indeed, artillery was so imperfect and was used with so little skill at first that, as Guicciardini remarks, the besieging of towns was slow and uncertain; and until the French invasion of Italy under Charles VIII, with an unprecendented number of troops, 60,000, and with iron cannonballs instead of stone, all moving at a hitherto unheard-of speed—until this happened cities were on equal terms, or rather more than equal terms, with the attacking parties. Thereafter, conditions were reversed: while a non-explosive stone or iron ball, which the defender's cannon could employ, did but little harm when dropped among companies of men, it could do great damage when used in assault for breaking open a wall or dropping through a roof. The new artillery of the late fifteenth century made cities vulnerable.

In the attempt to equalize military conditions, the towns from this point on were compelled to abandon their old system of simple walls, defended for the most part by a citizen soldiery. They were forced to hire soldiers, so that they might sally forth and engage the enemy in open battle; and after the successful defense of Milan by Prospero

Colonna in 1521 they were forced to adopt the new methods of fortification that had been worked out there by the Italian military engineers. These new fortifications were far more elaborate than the old
walls: they had outworks, salients, bastions, in starlike formations
which permitted both the artillery and the armed infantry to rake the
ranks of the attacking forces, from whatever side they might approach. By bringing the muskets of the defenders to the outmost positions they could theoretically put the city itself, whose circumference would be many hundred yards behind, beyond the reach of the
enemy's most powerful gun. For two centuries these ingenious defenses seemed to promise security: but like so many other forms of
military protection, they cast a dreadful social burden upon the
protected population, and were ultimately responsible, in many cities,
for those vile conditions for which the medieval town has been so
often reproached.

Instead of the simple masonry wall, which an ordinary house
mason might plan or build, it was necessary now to create a complicated system of defense that called for great engineering knowledge
and a vast expenditure of money. These fortifications, difficult to
build, were even more difficult to alter except at a prohibitive cost.
The old walls could be extended to include a suburb: they did not
handicap natural growth and adaptation. But the new fortifications
prevented lateral expansion. In the sixteenth and seventeenth century cities, fortification must have had the same effect upon finances
that the building of subways so often has had on the modern metropolis: they put an intolerable burden on the municipality and exposed
it to the exorbitant aid of the financier.

Even under a centralized regime, as in France, the inhabitants of
Metz offered their services gratis, so that they might accomplish at
an expenditure of 25,000 livres work that would otherwise have cost
50,000: a voluntary effort to escape heavy financial impositions.
Despite the frequent use of forced labor in France, the social cost
was no slight one. Unproductive capital expenditures, diverting
energy from the production of consumable goods, drain a people's
resources even when the cost is not expressed in terms of money.
Perhaps one of the great advantages of the English towns after the
sixteenth century, which aided England in the race for commercial

supremacy, was that they alone were free from this tax on their resources.

No less disastrous than the financial costs of construction were the direct results upon the population itself. While the old-fashioned city was divided into blocks and squares and then surrounded by a wall, the newly fortified city was planned as fortification, and the city was fitted into this straight-jacket. Whether old or new, its opportunities for expansion were over. New growth could take place only vertically; and no prudent burgher would build his house outside the walls in a possible no man's land. Administrators like Richelieu indeed ordered every building razed in the territory surrounding a fortified town: the city lay, as Paris did until but the other day, in the midst of a waste of non-building land, subject to artillery fire.

Not alone did the new fortifications remove the suburbs and gardens and orchards too far from the city to be reached conveniently except by the wealthier classes who could afford horses: open spaces within were rapidly built over as population was driven from the outlying land by fear and disaster, or by pressure of enclosure and land-monopoly. This new congestion led to the destruction of medieval standards of building space even in some of the cities that kept their medieval form and had preserved them longest. Overcrowding had in fact begun in the capital cities even before the seventeenth century: Stow notes in London that stone buildings were being replaced by wooden-framed ones to save space taken up by the heavier stone walls, and four and five story buildings were taking the place of two story ones. (The change from masonry to steel cage construction took place in the late nineteenth century American city for the same reason.) But in the seventeenth century these practices became universal: the systematic building of high tenements began— five or six stories high in old Geneva or in Paris, sometimes ten or twelve in Edinburgh.

This pressure of competition for space forced up land values in the political capitals. High land values, as in Berlin from the time of Frederick the Great on, hardened into a bad pattern for housing: overcrowding of the land, absence of play areas for children, lack of light, air, interior accommodation: high rents. Slum housing for a large part of the population, not simply for beggars, thieves, casual laborers and other outcasts, became the characteristic mode of the growing seventeenth century city. The existence of those slums defiled the high esthetic principles of the architects and builders in the same way that the frequent use of the corridors in Versailles as common urinals defiled the exorbitant esthetic pretensions of that court.

By the sixteenth century the practices of the Italian engineers dominated city building. Dürer's treatise on urban fortification gives only scant attention to the city proper; and in most of the other books and plans on the subject the city is treated as a mere appendage to the military form: it is, so to say, the "unoccupied" space that is left. Leonardo da Vinci, like Palladio, dealt in his notebooks with the city proper, suggested the separation of pedestrian ways from heavy traffic arteries, and went so far as to urge upon the Duke of Milan the standardized mass production of workers' houses. But despite these pregnant suggestions, his contributions to the art of city building remain poor and meager compared with his extraordinary zeal in improving the art of fortification and assault. It is easy to see where both opportunity and creative energy lay.

Eventually the new movement reached its summit in the types of fortification devised in the seventeenth century under the great engineer, Vauban—a method so complete that it required a new arm of the army, also systematized by Vauban, the miners and sappers, to overthrow it. Although the art of fortification had entailed endless sacrifices, it collapsed soon after it had evolved this final form. The new spy glass improved the fire of artillery; and the increased mobility of supplies, through canals and roads and the organization of a responsible commissariat, gave an impetus to the mobile army: meanwhile the territorial state itself had become the "City" that was to be defended.

4: War as City-Builder

The intensive development of the art of fortification shifted the emphasis in building from architecture to engineering, from esthetic design to material calculations of weight, number, and position: prelude to the wider technics of the machine. But especially it altered the urban picture from the short-range world of the medieval city, with its walking distances, its closed vistas, its patchwork space, to

the long-range world of baroque politics, with its long-distance gun-
fire and its wheeled vehicles and its increasing desire to conquer
space and make itself felt at a distance.

A good part of the new tactics of life sprang from an impulse toward destruction: long-range destruction. Christian piety and capitalist cupidity combined to thrust the new conquistadors across the
seas to plunder India, Mexico, and Peru; while the new type of
fortification, the new type of army, the new type of industrial workshop, best exemplified in the vast arsenals and arms factories, con-
spired to upset the relatively co-operative ways of the protected
town. Protection gave way to ruthless exploitation: instead of security, men sought adventurous expansion and conquest. And the proletariat at home was subject to a form of government no less ruthless
and autocratic than that which ground the barbaric civilizations of
North and South America into pulp.

War hastened all these transformations; it set the pace for every
other institution. The new standing armies, vast and powerful and
awe-inspiring in peace time no less than in war, transformed war
itself from a spasmodic to a continuous activity. The need for more
costly sinews of war put the cities into the hands of usurious
oligarchies that financed the ruler's mischievous policies, lived sumptuously on the profits and loot, and sought to entrench their positions
by backing the ensuing despotism. In an economic crisis the guns
of the hired solidiery could be turned, at the first signs of revolt,
upon the miserable subjects. (The English escaped the baroque
pattern earlier than other countries by turning tables on their Stuart
despot.)

In the Middle Ages the soldier had been forced to share his power
with the craftsman, the merchant, the priest: now, in the politics of
the absolute states, all law had in effect become martial law. Whoever could finance the army and the arsenal was capable of becoming master of the city. Shooting simplified the art of government: it
was a quick way of ending an embarrassing argument. Instead of
accepting the ordinary accommodations that ensure the healthy expression of diversities of temperament and interest and belief, the
ruling classes could dispense with such give-and-take methods: their
vocabulary recognized only "take." The gun, the cannon, the stand-

ing army helped produce a race of rulers who recognized no other law than that of their own will and caprice—that fine race of des· pots, sometimes imbecile, sometimes talented, who elevated the suspicions and delusions of the paranoid state into a political ritual. Their totalitarian imitators today, with no smaller delusions but with greater capacities for destruction, now threaten the very existence of world civilization.

The transformation of the art of war gave the baroque rulers a powerful advantage over the real corporations and groups that con· stitute a community. It did more than any other single force to alter the constitution of the city. Power became synonymous with numbers. "The greatness of a city," Botero observed, "is said to be, not the largeness of the site or the circuit of the walls, but the multitude and number of inhabitants and their power." The army, recruited for permanent warfare, became a new factor in the state and in the life of the capital city. In Paris and Berlin, and other lesser centers, these standing armies created a demand for special forms of housing, since soldiers could not be permanently quartered on the population without provoking a sense of grievance: witness the result of such an attempt in the British colonies of North America. The army barracks have almost the same place in the baroque order that the monastery had in the medieval one; and the Parade Grounds—the new Champ de Mars in Paris, for instance—were as conspicuous in the new cities as Mars himself was in Renascence painting. Turning out the guard, drilling, parading, became one of the great mass spectacles for the increasingly servile populace: the blare of the bugle, the tattoo of the drum, were as characteristic a sound for this new phase of urban life as the tolling of the bells had been for the medieval town. The laying out of great *Viae Triumphales*, avenues where a victorious army could march with the maximum effect upon the spectator, was an inevitable step in the replanning of the new capi- tals: notably in Paris and Berlin.

Along with the barracks and drill grounds, which occupy such large sites in the big capitals, go the arsenals. In the sixteenth cen- tury an extraordinary number of such buildings were erected. By 1540 Francis I had erected eleven arsenals and magazines: this went on, at a keener or slower pace, in all the other capitals. Soldiers, as Sombart has pointed out, are pure consumers, even as in action they are negative producers. Their demand for dwelling quarters was accompanied by a demand for provisions and drink and clothes on a similar scale. Hence the ranks of public houses and the army of tailors around the barracks quarters; indeed, a second standing army of shopkeepers, tailors, publicans, and whores springs up—the more miserable members of which owe their plight, perhaps, to the effect of the never-ending succession of military conflicts that agitated Europe and reached a climax in the eighteenth century. (See Sorokin's able statistical summary.)

Do not underestimate the presence of a garrison as a city-building agent. In 1740 the military population of Berlin numbered 21,309 out of a total of about 90,000 people: almost a quarter. The presence of this mass of mechanized and obedience-conditioned human beings necessarily touched every other aspect of life. The army supplied the model in its discipline for other forms of political coercion: people got into the habit of accepting the aggressive bark of the drill sergeant and the arrogant brutal manners of the upper classes: they were copied by the new industrialists, who governed their factories like absolute despots. Hutton in his history of Birmingham relates how the lord of the manor in "1728 . . . seized a public building called the Leather-Hall and converted it to his private uses. . . . The constable summoned the inhabitants to vindicate their rights, but none appearing, the Lord smiled at their supineness and kept the property." Beneath the superficial polish of baroque upper class manners there is the constant threat of an ugly, coercive discipline. These two qualities thread through every aspect of its life, even its luxury and folly.

5: The Ideology of Power

The two arms of this new system are the army and the bureaucracy: they are the temporal and spiritual support of a centralized despotism. Both agents owed no small part of their influence to a larger and more pervasive power, that of capitalist industry and finance. One must remember, with Max Weber, that the rational administration of taxation was an accomplishment of the Italian cities in the period *after* the loss of their freedom. The new Italian oli-

garchy was the first political power to order its finances in accordance with the principles of mercantile bookkeeping—and presently
the fine Italian hand of the tax-expert and financial administrator
could be observed in every European capital.

The change from a life economy to a money economy greatly
widened the resources of the state. The monopoly of rent, the booty
from piracy and brigandage, the loot of conquest, the monopoly
of special privileges in production and sale through patents granted
by the state, the application of this last system to technical inventions
—all these resources swelled the coffers of the sovereign. To increase
the boundaries of the state was to increase the taxable population: to
increase the population of the capital city was to increase the rent of
land. Both forms of increase could be translated ultimately into
terms of money pouring into the central exchequer. Not merely did
the royal governments become capitalistic in their workings, founding industries of their own, in arms, porcelain, tapestry: but they
sought, under the notion of a "favorable balance of trade," to create
a system of exploitation in which every sovereign state would receive
more in exchange, in measure of gold, than what it had given.

Capitalism in its turn became militaristic: it relied on the arms
of the state when it could no longer bargain to advantage without
them: the foundations of later colonial exploitation and imperialism.
Above all, the development of capitalism brought into every department secular habits of thought and matter-of-fact methods of appraisal: this was the warp, exact, orderly, superficially efficient, upon
which the complicated and effulgent patterns of baroque life were
worked out. The new merchant and banking classes emphasized
method, order, routine, power, mobility, all the habits that tended to
increase effective practical command. Jacob Fugger the Elder even
had a specially designed traveling set made for himself, containing
a compact, efficiently organized dining service: nothing was left to
chance. The uniformity of the die that stamped the coin at the
National Mint became a symbol of these emergent qualities in the
new order. Interests that were later sublimated and widened in physical science first disclosed themselves in the counting house: the
merchant's emphasis upon mathematics and literacy—both so necessary to long-distance trade through paid agents acting on written

instructions—became the fundamental ingredient in the new education of the grammar schools. It was not by accident that Newton, the physicist, became master of the mint, or that the merchants of London helped found the Royal Society and conducted experiments in physics. These mechanical disciplines were in effect interchangeable.

Behind the immediate interests of the new capitalism, with its abstract love of money and power, a change in the entire conceptual framework took place. And first: a new conception of space. It was one of the great triumphs of the baroque mind to organize space, make it continuous, reduce it to measure and order, to extend the limits of magnitude, embracing the extremely distant and the extremely minute; finally, to associate space with motion.

These changes were first formulated by the painters and architects, beginning with Alberti, Brunelleschi, and Uccello. While the Flemish realists, working in the medium of the advanced spinning industries, had accurate perceptions of space, it remained for the Italians of the fifteenth century to organize space on mathematical lines, within two planes, the foreground-frame, and that of the horizon line. They not merely correlated distance with intensity of color and quality of light, but with the movement of bodies through the projected third dimension. This putting together of hitherto unrelated lines and solids within the rectangular baroque frame—as distinguished from the often irregular boundaries of a medieval painting—was contemporary with the political consolidation of territory into the coherent frame of the state. But the development of the straight line and the uniform building line, as a means of expressing uniform motion, took place at least a century before the building of actual façades on visually limitless avenues.

Similarly, the study of perspective demolished the bounding wall, lengthened the distance toward the horizon, and centered attention on the receding planes, long before the wall was abolished as a fea-ture of town planning. This was an esthetic preface to the grand avenues of baroque design, which at most have an obelisk, an arch, or a single building to terminate the converging rays of the cornice lines and the pavement edges. The long approach and the vista into space—those typical marks of the baroque plan—were first discovered by the painter. The act of passage is more important than the object reached: there is keener interest in the foreground of the Farnese Palace than in the gawky façade that caps the hill. The new Renascence window is definitely a picture frame, and the Renascence painting is an imaginary window which, in the city, makes one forget the dull courtyard that an actual opening would reveal.

If the earlier painters demonstrated Cartesian mathematics before Descartes, on their system of co-ordinates, the general sense of time likewise became more mathematical. From the sixteenth century on the domestic clock was widespread in upper-class households. But whereas baroque space invited movement, travel, conquest by speed —witness the early sail wagons and velocipedes—baroque time lacked dimensions: it was a moment-to-moment continuum. Time expressed itself, not as cumulative and continuous, but as disjunctive: it ceased to be life-time. The social mode of baroque time is fashion, which changes every year; and in the world of fashion a new sin was invented—that of being out of date. Its practical instrument was the newspaper, which deals with scattered, logically incoherent "events" from day to day: no underlying connection except contemporaneity. If in spatial forms repeating patterns take on a new meaning—columns on the façades of buildings, ranks of men on parade—in time the emphasis rests on novelty. As for the archaeological cult of the past, it was plainly not a recovery of history but a denial of history. Real history cannot be recovered.

The abstractions of money, spatial perspective, and mechanical time provided the enclosing frame of the new life. Experience was progressively reduced to just those elements that were capable of being split off from the whole and measured separately: conventional counters took the place of organisms. What was real was that part of experience which left no murky residues; and anything that could not be expressed in terms of visual sensations and mechanical order was not worth expressing. In art, perspective and anatomy; in morals, the systematic casuistry of the Jesuits; in architecture, the fixed proportions of the Five Orders, and in city building, the elaborate geometrical plan. These are the new forms.

Do not misunderstand me. The age of abstract analysis was an age of brilliant intellectual clarification. The new system of dealing with mathematically analyzable fragments instead of with wholes gave the first intelligible collective means of approaching such wholes: as useful an instrument of order as double-entry bookkeeping in commerce. In the natural sciences, the method of abstraction led to the discovery of units that could be investigated completely *just because* they were dismembered and fragmentary. The gain in the power of systematic thought and in the accurate prediction of physical events was to justify itself in the nineteenth century in a series of mighty advances in technics.

But in society the habit of thinking in terms of abstractions worked out disastrously. The new order established in the physical sciences was far too limited to describe or interpret social facts, and until the nineteenth century even the legitimate development of statistical analysis played little part in sociological thought. Real men and women, real corporations and cities, were treated in law and government as if they were imaginary bodies; whilst presumptuous fictions, like Divine Right, Absolute Rule, the State, Sovereignty, were treated as if they were realities. Freed from his sense of dependence upon corporation and neighborhood, the "emancipated individual" was dissociated and delocalized: an atom of power, ruthlessly seeking whatever power can command. With the quest for financial and political power, the notion of limits disappeared—limits on numbers, limits on wealth, limits on population growth, limits on urban expansion: on the contrary, quantitative expansion became predominant. The merchant cannot be too rich; the state cannot possess too much territory; the city cannot become too big.

Botero, contemporary with this development, noted its implications. "The founders of cities," he said, "considering that laws and civil discipline could not be easily conserved and kept where a mighty multitude of people swarmed (for multitudes do breed and bring confusion) they limited the number of citizens beyond which they supposed the form and order of government they sought to hold within their cities could not else be maintained. But the Romans, supposing power (without which, a city cannot long be maintained) consisteth for the most part in the multitude of people, endeavored all the ways and means they might to make their country great."

In the desire for more subjects—that is, for more cannon-fodder, more milch-cows for taxation and rent—the desires of the Prince coincided with those of the capitalists who were looking for larger and more concentrated markets. Power politics and power economics reinforced each other. Cities grew: rents rose: taxes increased. None of these results was accidental.

6: Movement and the Avenue

Since I am dealing with an age of abstractions, I purpose to follow its style. I shall treat of the part before I discuss the whole. First the avenue: then the separate institutions and buildings: only after that the city, as an esthetic if not a complete social unit.

The avenue is the most important symbol and the main fact about the baroque city. Not always was it possible to design a whole new city in the baroque mode; but in the layout of half a dozen new avenues, or in a new quarter, its character could be re-defined. In the linear evolution of the city plan, the movement of wheeled vehicles played a critical part; and the general geometrizing of space, so characteristic of the period, would have been altogether functionless had it not facilitated the movement of traffic and transport, at the same time that it served as an expression of the dominant sense of life. It was during the sixteenth century that carts and wagons came into more general use within cities. This was partly the result of technical improvements that replaced the old-fashioned solid wheel with one built of separate parts, hub, rim, spoke, and added a fifth wheel, to facilitate turning.

The introduction of wheeled vehicles was resisted, precisely as that of the railroad was resisted three centuries later. Plainly the streets of the medieval city were not adapted either in size or in articulation to such traffic. In England, Thomas tells us, vigorous protests were made, and it was asserted that if brewer's carts were permitted in the streets the pavement could not be maintained; while in France, parliament begged the king in 1563 to prohibit vehicles from the streets of Paris—and the same impulse even showed itself once more in the eighteenth century. Nevertheless, the new spirit in society was on the side of rapid transportation. The hastening of movement and the conquest of space, the feverish desire to "get somewhere," were manifestations of the pervasive will-to-power.

"The world," as Stow remarked when the fashion was taking hold in London, "runs on wheels." Mass, velocity, and time were categories of social effort before Newton's law was formulated.

Movement in a straight line along an avenue was not merely an economy but a special pleasure: it brought into the city the stimulus and exhilaration of swift motion, which hitherto only the horseman had known galloping over the fields or through the hunting forest. It was possible to increase this pleasure esthetically by the regular setting of buildings, with regular façades and even cornices, whose horizontal lines tended toward the same vanishing point as that toward which the carriage itself was rolling. In walking, the eye courts variety, but above this gait, movement demands repetition of the units that are to be seen: it is only so that the individual part, as it flashes by, can be recovered and pieced together. What would be monotony for a fixed position or even in a procession, becomes a necessary counterpoise to the pace of fast-moving horses.

In emphasizing the demands of wheeled traffic, which became urgent in the seventeenth century, I do not wish to neglect a characteristic need that disclosed itself at an even earlier period: the need of avenues for military movement. Alberti, who is in every sense the chief theoretical exponent of the baroque city, distinguished between main and subordinate streets. The first he called—and the name is important—*viae militares,* or military streets: he required that these should be straight. Anyone who has ever led a company of men through an irregularly planned city knows the difficulty of conducting them in martial order through its windings and twistings, particularly when the streets themselves are ungraded: inevitably, the individual falls out of alignment and the ranks present a disorderly appearance. To achieve the maximum effect on parade, the maximum appearance of order and power, it is necessary to provide a body of soldiers either with an open square or a long unbroken avenue.

The new town planners had the needs of the army constantly in mind: Palladio seconded Alberti. In addition to observing that the ways will be short and convenient if planned in a straight line, and so large that horses and coaches be no hindrance to each other when they meet, Palladio says that "the ways will be more convenient if they are made everywhere equal; that is to say, that there be no place in them where armies may not easily march." This uniform over-sized street, which was to become such a blight in the development of neighborhoods in new cities, and which was to add so greatly to the expenses, had purely a military basis.

Palladio's further definition of the military avenue is equally sig-nificant: he distinguished them from the non-military kind by point-ing out that they pass through the midst of the city and lead from one city to another, and that they "serve for the common use of all passengers for carriages to drive or armies to march." Accordingly Palladio dealt with the military streets alone because non-military streets ought to be regulated according to the same principle as mili-tary ways, and the more alike they are the *"more commendable they will be."* In view of the importance of the army to the ruling classes, it is no wonder that military traffic was the determining factor in the new city plan, from the first mutation in Alberti to the final survival in the laying down of Haussmann's boulevards in Paris.

The esthetic effect of the regular ranks and the straight line of soldiers is increased by the regularity of the avenue: the unswerving line of march greatly contributes to the display of power, and a regi-ment moving thus gives the impression that it would break through a solid wall without losing a beat. That, of course, is exactly the be-lief that the soldier and the Prince desire to inculcate in the popu-lace: it helps keep them in order without coming to an actual trial of strength, which always carries the bare possibility that the army might be worsted. Moreover, on irregular streets, poorly paved, with plenty of loose cobblestones and places of concealment, the spon-taneous formations of untrained people have an advantage over a drilled soldiery: soldiers cannot fire around corners, nor can they protect themselves from bricks heaved from chimney tops immedi-ately overhead: they need space to manoeuvre in. Were not the ancient medieval streets of Paris one of the last refuges of urban liberties? No wonder that Napoleon III sanctioned the breaking through of narrow streets and cul-de-sacs and the razing of whole quarters to provide wide boulevards: this was the best possible pro-tection against assault from within. To rule merely by coercion, without affectionate consent, one must have the appropriate urban background.

In the new city, or in the formal additions made to old centers, the building forms a setting for the avenue, and the avenue is essentially a parade ground: a place where spectators may gather, on the sidewalks or in the windows, to review the evolutions and exercises and triumphal marches of the army—and be duly awed and intimidated. The buildings stand on each side, stiff and uniform, like soldiers at attention: the uniformed soldiers march down the avenue, erect, formalized, repetitive: a classic building in motion. The spectator remains fixed: life marches before him, without his leave, without his assistance: he may use his eyes, but if he wishes to open his mouth or leave his place, he had better ask for permission first.

In the medieval town the upper classes and the lower classes had jostled together on the street, in the market-place, as they did in the cathedral: the rich might ride on horseback, but they must wait for the poor man with his bundle or the blind beggar groping with his stick to get out of the way. Now, with the development of the wide avenue, the dissociation of the upper and the lower classes achieves form in the city itself. The rich drive: the poor walk. The rich roll along the axis of the grand avenue: the poor are off-center, in the gutter: and eventually a special strip is provided for the ordinary pedestrian, the sidewalk. The rich stare, the poor gape: insolence battens on servility. The daily parade of the powerful becomes one of the principal dramas of the baroque city: a vicarious life of dash and glitter and expense is thus offered to the butcher's boy with a basket on his head, to the retired merchant out for a stroll, to the fashionable housewife, shopping for bargains and novelties, to the idle mob of hangers-on in all degrees of shabby gentility and downright misery—corresponding to the clients of imperial Rome.

"Mind the carriages!" cried Mercier in his eighteenth century Tableau de Paris. "Here comes the black-coated physician in his chariot, the dancing master in his *cabriolet,* the fencing master in his *diable*—and the Prince behind six horses at the gallop as if he were in the open country. . . . The threatening wheels of the overbearing rich drive as rapidly as ever over stones stained with the blood of their unhappy victims." Do not fancy the danger was exaggerated: in France the stage-coach, introduced in the seventeenth century, killed more people annually than the railroad that followed

it. This increase in the tempo of life, this rapid motion, these superficial excitements and dangers, were the psychological sweetening of
the bitter pill of autocratic political discipline. In the baroque city
one might say, "The carriages move swiftly," just as people say in
present-day fascist Italy, "The trains run on time."

There was only one desirable station in this despotism; it was that
of the rich. It was for them that the avenue was made and the pavement smoothed out and springs and cushions added to the wheeled
vehicle: it was to protect them that the soldiers marched. To keep a
horse and carriage was an indispensable mark of commercial and
social success; to keep a whole stable was a sign of affluence. In the
eighteenth century the stables and mews crept into the less savory
quarters of the capitals, behind the wide avenues and the sumptuous
squares, carrying there the faint healthy smell of straw and manure.
If the fowls no longer cackled at dawn, the restless stomp of a high-
bred horse might be heard at night from rear windows: the man on
horseback had taken possession of the city.

7: The Shopping Parade

The military parade had its feminine counterpart in the capital:
the shopping parade. The ritual of conspicuous waste took up an
ever larger share of the time and effort of living: competitive spending affected every class; for "the same flourishing pride has dictated
new methods of living to the people, and while the poorest citizens
strive to live like the rich, the rich like the gentry, the gentry like
the nobility, and the nobility strive to outshine one another, no wonder that all the sumptuary trades increase." In the baroque period
the medieval sumptuary laws, governing the dress and expenditure
of each class according to tradition, began to fall into disrepute, even
when they were not actually lifted from the statute books. Luxury,
instead of distinguishing special public festivals and celebrations,
became a daily commodity. Competitive luxury. To spend *more* was
more important than to spend *enough*.

The old open market, while it did not disappear from the cities
of the Western World, henceforth restricted itself largely to provisions: it was only in the poorer quarters, like the Jews' market in
Whitechapel, that one could still pick up a dress, a pair of trousers,

or a stove from an open cart; though in Paris, more tenacious of medieval habits than would appear on the surface, the nineteenth century department stores were compelled to open up street-stands, at least in the lower middle class neighborhoods. Market squares where people gathered no longer had a place in the new urban layout: the circles and stars of the new plans, with their jam of wheeled traffic, had no place for chaffering or cheapening.

The open air shop, the outlet for the workroom in the rear, tended to disappear, too: the new type of shop took shape behind glass windows, greatly enlarged to cover the whole front and serve as a center of display. No effort was spared to decorate the interior smartly, particularly in the more modish commodities. To fit up a pastry-cook's shop with plate glass windows and pier glasses and glass lanterns and twenty-five sconces for candles and six large silver salvers, and to paint the ceiling and carve the columns and gild the lanterns took a pretty sum. It is a modern custom, observes Daniel Defoe in The Compleat English Tradesman, to "have tradesmen lay out two-thirds of their fortune in fitting up their shops. . . . 'Tis a small matter to lay out two or three, nay five hundred pounds."

The display market for goods already made, rather than produced on the order system, had already come into existence: from the seventeenth century on, it gradually encroached into one line after another, hastening the tempo of sale and placing a premium upon the visual enticement of the buyer. The special market day lingered on in rural neighborhoods; but in the commercial town every day tended to be market day. Buying and selling became not merely an incidental traffic in the conveyance of goods from producer to consumer: it became one of the principal preoccupations of all classes. "Marketing" rested on the basis of domestic needs: "shopping" was a less urgent, a more frivolous, occupation. Shopping furnished excitement: it afforded a special occasion for the lady of the house to dress up, to sally forth, to exhibit her own person.

"I have heard," said Defoe, still obviously shocked by the practice, "that some ladies, and these, too, persons of good note, have taken their coaches and spent a whole afternoon in Ludgate Street or Covent Garden, only to divert themselves in going from one mercer's shop to another, to look upon their fine silks and to rattle

II: THE BAROQUE CITY   [5] THE MECHANICAL AND THE SENSUOUS

Baroque order was heralded by a series of great mathematical and mechanical conquests: the conquest of space through the use of the magnetic compass at sea, the rediscovery of the Greek conception of the earth as sphere, the projection of accurate maps through the use of co-ordinates for latitude and longitude, the development of trigonometry, the invention of the telescope with its lengthening of visual distance, and the discovery of the mechanical laws of perspective. Mechanization of time: mechanization of space: mechanization of power.

[TOP] New market-place: transitional between the medieval market and the avenue market and open circle of later planning. Uniform roof line: symmetrical placement of buildings, duplication of churches and towers on each side of the avenue of approach: a perfect example of the order theoretically laid down by Alberti and, later, Palladio.

[FIRST LEFT] Regimentation of space extended even to park design after Le Nôtre: the sacrifice of the autonomy of living forms to visual order: Procrustes at play. The public use of open spaces for promenade was possible in the medieval city only on the walls. This new vehicle of recreation and ceremony is a courtly product. Contrast it with the romantic Victorian park, refuge of the solitary individual, spoiled even by signs of human occupation. The two poles are the parade ground and the wild forest. Fill in the parade ground with uniform rows of trees in military formation and you have the formal park: thin out the forest irregularly and you have the romantic park. The nineteenth century endeavored to combine philanthropy (crowds) with naturalism (privacy). Today we must plan the entire region with special zones and structures appropriately set off to fulfill each personal and communal function.

[FIRST RIGHT] Renascence ceiling: same order of design as the new city plan, with a central open circle, converging lines for traffic, and irregular house-blocks: see Plate 8.

[SECOND] Early royal art gallery for easel-paintings: removable art, no longer designed for a specific social context.

[BOTTOM LEFT] Counterbalancing of the mechanical by the sensuous: politeness, graceful movement, artful relaxation: the claim of Venus against Mars. See Sombart's Luxus und Kapitalismus.

[BOTTOM RIGHT] Baroque bedroom. The same artist, in this series of prints on the five senses, has depicted the bed also in the dining room. Privacy and specialized functions came in slowly. Closed doors and open fires in the bedroom yielded new erotic variations: including the visual pleasure of nakedness.

[TOP] Tuileries esplanade: swift movement, with the aid of horsepower, was one of the privileges of the rich and great: cavalcades dash along the straight avenues between Versailles and Paris. Note the six-horse coach, as well as the mounted men. "Four companies of the French Guard and two of the Swiss Guard parade every day in the court of the minister between the two railings, and when the king issues forth in his carriage to go to Paris or Fontainebleau the spectacle is magnificent." (Taine.) Public coaches, proposed by Pascal, were introduced in Paris in the mid-seventeenth century, and in 1650 Nicolas Sauvage at the Hotel de Fiacre in the Rue St Martin first offered wagons and horses for hire: beginnings of modern urban transportation. But streets long remained badly paved; good roads awaited Telford and Macadam; hence water transportation kept its importance. As late as 1803 London had 3000 wherries on the water, as against 1000 hackney coaches and 400 sedan chairs.

[MIDDLE LEFT] Ball, Versailles: diffusion of eroticism in luxury, and sustenance of the will-to-power in a success outwardly spectacular and imposing. *Courtliness:* slow gestures and dignified movements: emphasis of separation from the spontaneity and uncouthness of the "lower classes." *Courtesy:* the mollification of privilege: imagination and reciprocity in the smaller acts of life. *Courtship:* the labyrinthine approach to sexual union: the difference between a hunter's approach to an animal and the butcher's.

[MIDDLE RIGHT] Teatro San Carlo at Naples: model of many of the great theaters and opera houses that followed. The theater dominated this period: architecture became scene painting. Upper class life was an effort to put on a good show: the elect had speaking parts. From the sixteenth century on theater buildings were erected in Italy: one of the first was the Teatro Olimpico at Vicenza, designed by Palladio and erected by Scamozzi in 1584. The transplantation of the theater from the Church to the Court, and the settlement of the wandering players' troupes in a permanent abode, were characteristic urban developments: even the popular theater in England was under the patronage of the nobility.

[BOTTOM] Ranelagh Gardens, London. One of a series of popular pleasure resorts that lasted as such into the nineteenth century. After temporary banishment they reappeared in the newer guise of the later nineteenth century amusement park, itself partly an outgrowth of the International Fairs. In the earliest type, court forms predominated: see the description of Sir Roger de Coverley's visit to Vauxhall Gardens in the Spectator Papers. The specialized pleasure resort is the urban form of this baroque mutation: Bath, Baden-Baden, Monte Carlo, Saratoga.

and banter the shopkeepers, having not so much as the least occa·
sion, much less intention, to buy anything."

As the permanent market took form both producer and consumer
tended to become more anonymous: it was the middleman who made
a name for himself by anticipating the idiosyncrasies of the buyer
or by manipulating his taste and judgment. To avoid striking in the
dark, a new patron and purchaser assumed control of the market:
Dame Fashion. Again I must quote the invaluable Defoe: "Every
tailor invents fashions, the mercer studies new patterns, the weavers
weave them into beautiful and gay figures, and stores himself with
a vast variety to allure the fancy; the coachmaker contrives new
machines, chairs, Berlins, flies, etc., all to prompt the whimsies and
unaccountable pride of the gentry. . . . The upholder [upholsterer]
does the like in furniture, till he draws the gay ladies to such an
excess of Folly that they must have their houses new furnished every
year; everything that has been longer than a year must be called old,
and to have their fine lodgings seen by a person of any figure above
twice over, looks ordinary and mean."

Money was supreme: the customs of the market were not confined
to the shops. Vicomte d'Avenel, whose history of property gives invaluable documentation of goods and prices, has put the matter well.
"It was in the past, under the ancient regime, from the end of the
Middle Ages to the Revolution, when force did not exercise a great
place and when public opinion counted for little, that money ruled
in France. Almost everything could be bought, power and honors,
civil and military employment, and the nobility itself, whose titles
were inseparable from the ground upon which they rested. It was
necessary to be rich to become somebody, and if the favor of a prince
occasionally distinguished a poor man, it would at the same stroke
make him rich, since riches were the ordinary consequence of
power."

Life, even aristocratic life, expressed itself most easily in terms of
trade and money. In a moral homily of the sixteenth century on
serving men, note the figure of the very opening passage: "In this
Bourse or Exchange of Human Affairs, which consisteth (as it were)
altogether in merchandise, buying and selling, it is very meet that
there should be all manner conditions and callings . . . summoned

on forfeiture of ten pounds on Issues to appear, with money and ware always ready, to maintain the mundane market." Life was like that. By hook or crook, by trade or theft or public corruption or financial enterprise, one got hold of money: "rapine, avarice, expense" made life "mean handiwork of craftsman, cook, or groom." Wordsworth's sonnet was a compact indictment.

In the great capital cities, too large for people to know their neighbors, the standards of the market came generally to prevail. People sought by overt display to make a decisive impression as to their station in life, their taste, their prosperity: every individual, every class, put on a front. Fashion is, so to say, the uniform of the day, and well-to-do people wore this uniform in the home or the street with the same discipline as the soldier on his military parade. Venice had set the pace in dictating personal fashions, thanks to the charm of her courtesans; Paris took up these duties in the seventeenth century; and thereafter each national capital served as pattern for the rest of the country. Part of the economic use of the capital city, from the standpoint of the great factors and importers, *was to discredit local goods, which varied in pattern, in color, in stuff, in texture, in decoration, in accordance with local tradition, and give circulation to those in use at the capital. Slippery metropolitan styles undermined the sobrieties of craftsmanship, even as they annulled the traditional preferences, or idiosyncrasies, of maker and customer.*

Some hint of this state had already become plain in the sixteenth century; for Stow is at pains to "answer the accusation of those men, which charge *London* with the loss and decay of many (or most) of the ancient cities, corporate towns, and markets within this realm. . . . As for retailers thereof, and handicraftsmen, it is no marvel if they abandon country towns and resort to London; for not only the court, which is nowadays much greater and more gallant than in former times . . . but also by occasion thereof the gentlemen of all shires do fly and flock to the city, the younger sort of them to see and show vanity, and the elder to save the cost and charge of hospitality and house-keeping." Fashion competition, which was the life of baroque trade (and remains its chief bequest to later capitalism), was also largely the death of the customary in-

dustries of the provincial towns. Eventually they were forced to produce for the anonymous distant market or lose their industries entirely. The effect of this is observable in our irregional system of
production and distribution down to the present day. Economists
often tend to confuse it with the natural effects of regional specialization.

In this economy, the centralization of the baroque capital, which
involved costly wastes in transport, became a special virtue. "The
magnitude of the city of London adds very considerably to the Inland
Trade, for as the City is the center of our trade, so all the manufactures are brought hither, and hence circulated again to all the country. . . ." "How many thousands," Defoe exclaims again in another
place, "I might say how many hundreds of thousands of men and
horses are employed in the carrying and re-carrying to and from
London the growth of England and the importations of foreign countries; and how many of these would stand still and want business
. . . if this great city was divided into fifteen cities . . . and they
were situated in so many different places remote from one another,
where the countryside within 20 or 30 miles round would be sufficient for them and able to supply them, and where every port would
import its own goods from abroad."

This last passage is a succinct explanation of the difference between the medieval urban economy and the baroque state economy:
no better could be offered. But in terms of social energetics and cultural life, what Defoe took for a eulogy is actually a damning indictment.

The military capital as an agent for enforcing uniformity and
standardization, in the annual uniforms of fashion no less than in
the uniforms of the soldiery, was a necessary contribution to the
mechanical standardization that made possible the further mechanization of the whole process of production. And just as in the regular
façade of the new palaces at St. Petersburg one sees, beneath the
ornament, the bare skeleton of the paleotechnic factory, so, in the
formal elegances of the baroque city plan, one already sees the
dreary mechanical subdivision of the industrial town. Note that the
critical changes took place first in the form of play, show, luxury:
this was the specific baroque contribution.

One last remote outcome of the tendencies I have been discussing must be noted: the evolution of the fashion parade into a specialized type of city. While spas and watering places where people went for reasons of health had never fallen out of existence, in the eighteenth century these old resorts took on new life as people began to flock to them for a new reason: fashionable display. The parade (Corso) became not merely the core but the very reason for existence of a new kind of city: Bath, Margate, Brighton, Ostend, later Baden-Baden, Carlsbad, Travemunde, the Riviera, Saratoga Springs. Here were places where people of fashion met: met in order to exhibit themselves at the proper season, sometimes under the pretext of seeking health, but also to enjoy life, untainted by any visible connection with trade and industry, occupations that were already filling the capital with obnoxious sights, sounds, and smells. Here all the typical baroque pleasures were available: particularly gambling, dress, flirtation, music, sometimes the theater. These new cities were in effect minor courts, ruled by a self-elected prince, specialist in dress and manners, despot of fashion—the dandy. A whole town would grow up around this parade, eventually, and business would crowd in again once more and take precedence over courtliness; so that Atlantic City, for example, a typical latter-day vulgarization of the baroque mode of life, is in detail an extension of Broadway, Fifth Avenue, Market Street, no more restful than the first, scarcely more maritime in character than the last.

8: The New Divinity

The breakup of the medieval church set free the "ions" that were re-polarized in the baroque city. One may seize the process in a concrete figure, if one considers how each element in the old structure was appropriated by a special institution, sect, or group. Follow the dismemberment: the protestants captured the preacher's rostrum and made it the core of their new chapels, where no graven image competed with the speaker's face, and no rich ceremonial distracted attention from his urgent voice. The aristocracy commanded the painter and the architect: art was carried away to special halls and galleries, and to make the process easier, the new easel picture took the place of the wall fresco. Angels and saints became Bacchuses

and Graces: first secular faces of popes, courtiers, business men surround the Holy Image: finally they displace it. The choir, which once
chanted hymns to God, was removed to the concert hall or to a bal-
cony of the ballroom: the religious festival became the court
masque, to celebrate a mundane birthday or a wedding; while the
drama, leaving the porches of the church, where the clergy and
guildsmen had once enacted their mysteries and moralities, was
turned over to professional actors under the patronage of the nobility: their first raffish quarters are on the outskirts of the city.
The chapter-house, with its complement of at least formally celibate
clergy, became the aristocratic men's club of the nineteenth century:
exclusive, monastic, even if ostentatiously sybaritic: the Carlton, the
Reform, and their imitators.

Finally the nave, the bare assembly place, became the bourse. Do
not fancy that the latter is a wild imaginary parallel: in the seventeenth century the brokers plied their trade in the nave of St. Paul's,
and the money changers all but drove the representatives of Christ
from the temple—till at last the stench became too great for even a
venal church to endure. Wren's unused plan for the reconstruction
of London after the fire handsomely recognized this new order of
life. He did not give the dominating site to St. Paul's: he planned the
new avenues so as to give this honor to the Royal Stock Exchange.

This analytical decomposition of the church gave each institution
a special opportunity to flourish in its own right. On the positive side,
this was another witness to the visual clarification and the intelligent
specialization of functions that characterized baroque order. All these
institutions had become detached from the church because fresh life
and growth were stifled there: there would have been no Shakespeare
if the Church had kept control of the drama, and no great Rembrandt
portraits if he had continued to paint the staple group portraits of
the complacent worthies of the Guild. But these various fragments of
art and culture were dispersed with respect to the population as a
whole: dispersed and put out of their reach. It was only in the court
of the Prince that the parts were united again to form a new whole
for the exclusive benefit of those who wielded power.

We have seen what became of the medieval cathedral. But what
became of its God? Here the transformation can be recorded only

in terms of blasphemy. The absolute ruler by divine right usurped the place of the Deity and claimed his honors; he might even call himself Le Roi Soleil, superstitiously arrogating to himself the myth of a Pharaoh or an Alexander. In the new cult, the part of the Virgin Mary, most powerful intercessor at the throne of heaven, was taken by the king's mistress. The powers and principalities of the new Heaven, indispensable to its regimen, were the courtiers who crowded around the throne of the Monarch and proclaimed his glory. The parallel was not absent from even pious minds in the seventeenth century. "Whoever," said La Bruyère, "considers that the king's countenance is the courtier's supreme felicity, that he passes his life looking at it and within sight of it, will comprehend to some extent how to see God constitutes the glory and the happiness of the saints."

Learned flunkies wrote treatises to prove the despot's direct connection with heaven, to uphold his omnipotence, to admonish obedience to his divine commands. When their rationalizations fell short of his own exorbitant claims he might even, like James I of England, take a hand in writing the necessary eulogium himself. "The prince," according to Castiglione, who wrote the classic treatise on the Courtier, "ought to be very generous and splendid, and give to all men without reserve, because God, as the saying runs, is the treasurer of generous princes." Fortune's cornucopia must indeed be inexhaustible at the rate it was drained at court: Avenel reports that one of the great ballets at Versailles, in which one hundred and fifty people took part, came to a hundred thousand francs.

This demand for unlimited funds infected every rank in society; and it was the key to the economic policies of the absolute state. When taxation did not supply sufficient means for the prince and his favorites, he resorted to pillage: distant kingdoms in the case of Philip of Spain, or nearer monasteries for Henry VIII: when these did not suffice, he robbed the poor man of his pennies in order to bestow gold on those already rich. Hence the whole policy of licenses and patents: one needed a special permission, to be obtained at a price, even to build a house.

The growth of a bureaucracy to superintend these exactions and further the distribution of privilege added to the burden on the community: the Circumlocution Office was a convenient means of taking

care of retainers and their younger sons: from St. Petersburg to
Whitehall it was an inevitable appanage of upper class society.
"Never was bureaucracy carried to such a point of exaggeration,
extravagance, and tiresomeness," wrote Mercier. "Never did business
so drag since the creation of this army of clerks who are in business
what footmen are in service. References, regulations, registrations,
formalities of all kinds have multiplied with such profusion and so
little discernment."

It finally came down to this: a whole country was run for the
benefit of a few dozen families, or a few hundred, who owned a good
share of the land—almost half in France in the eighteenth century—
and who battened on the unearned increments from industry, trade,
and urban rents.

9: Position of the Palace

City building, in the formal sense, was an embodiment of the
prevalent drama and thema that shaped itself in the court: it was, in
effect, a collective embellishment of the life and gestures of the palace. The palace faced two ways. From the urban side came rent,
tribute, taxes, control of the army and control of the organs of the
state; from the countryside came the well-built, well-exercised, well-
fed, well-sexed men and women who formed the body of the court
and who received honors, emoluments, and the perquisites the king
magnanimously bestowed. Power and pleasure, a dry abstract order
and an effulgent sensuality, were the two poles of this life. Mars and
Venus were the presiding deities, until Vulcan finally cast his cunning iron net of utilitarianism over their concupiscent forms.

The court was a world in itself; but a world in which all the harsh
realities of life were shown in a diminishing glass, and all its frivoli-
ties magnified. Pleasure was a duty, idleness a service, and honest
work the lowest form of degradation. To become real in the baroque
court, it was necessary that an object or a function should bear the
marks of exquisite uselessness. The most powerful waterwheels of
the seventeenth century and the great hydraulic pumps that counted
among its chief technical advances were used merely to work the
fountains in the Gardens of Versailles. Fischer von Erlach's steam
pump, the first used in Austria, was not applied to a mine but in the

gardens of the Belvedere Palace in Wien; and that significant agent of production, the automatic power-machine, achieved its first great success applied to buttons (the stamping machine), to ribbons (the narrow automatic loom), and to army uniforms (the first sewing machine).

The ritual of the court was an attempt to confirm the make-believe of absolute power by a special drama. I know no better picture of the environment, no more fulsome demonstration of its narcotic illusions, than the panegyric uttered by Nicholas Breton:

"Oh, the gallant life of the Court, where so many are the choices of contentment, as if on earth it were the Paradise of the World: the majesty of the sovereign, the wisdom of the Council, the honour of the Lords, the beauty of the Ladies, the care of the officers, the courtesy of the gentlemen, the divine services of the morning and evening, the witty, learned, noble, and pleasant discourses all day, the variety of wits and the depth of judgements, the dainty fare, sweetly dressed and neatly served, the delicate wines and rare fruits, with excellent music and adorable voices, masques, and plays, dancing and riding; diversity of games, delightful to the gamester's purposes; and riddles, questions, and answers; poems, histories, and strange inventions of wit, to startle the brain of good understanding; rich apparel, precious jewels, fine proportions, and high spirits, princely coaches, stately horses, royal buildings and rare architecture, sweet creatures and civil pleasure; and in the course of love such carriage of content as sets the spirit in the lap of pleasure, that if I should talk of the praise of it all day, I should be short of the worth of it at night."

One need not underscore the counter-accents of actuality: the lees in the wine, the inane conversation that passed for wit, the unwanted babies that got past the barriers of the fashionable contraceptives known from the sixteenth century on to the upper classes of France and Italy. There was still enough plausibility in the picture even when the sour notes were accounted for. The motto written over the door of Rabelais' Abbey of Thelema was: Do as You Please. Over the palace gates there was an extra proviso: As Long as It Pleases the Prince. One must however add one fact that is too often left out of the conception of this ceremonious and sensuous baroque life. Its

ritual was so tedious that it veritably bored people to distraction.
The daily routine of Prince and courtier was comparable to that of
a Ford worker in an assembly plant: every detail of it laid out and
fixed, as much for the sovereign as for his entourage. From the moment the Prince's eyes opened to the last moment when his mistress
left his bedchamber, he was, so to say, on the assembly line.

Perhaps this pervasive tedium accounts not only for the effortful
frivolity, but for the element of sheer vagrant mischief, like the outbreak of schoolboys who have been kept under too strict confinement,
in baroque state policy. Much of the intricate plotting and counter-
plotting was the work of bored virtuosos of diplomacy who liked
nothing better than to prolong the game itself. Surely the eternal
standing, waiting, bowing, scraping—of which Taine has given an
unforgettable picture in his description of the ancient regime—must
have run against the grain of well-fed men and women. Small wonder that spectacular amusements played such a large part in their
lives.

Unfortunately, the very distractions of the court became duties.
The performance of leisure imposed new sacrifices. The dinner party,
the ball, the formal visit, as worked out by the aristocracy and by
those who, after the seventeenth century, aped them, gave satisfaction
only to those for whom form is more important than content. No
small part of the life described in Vanity Fair and The Red and the
Black, at one end of the nineteenth century, and by Proust at the
other end, consisted of visiting and "paying court": formalities.
Proust noted that it was at the time of Louis XIV that a serious
change had come about in the life of the aristocracy, which had once
had active responsibilities, grave duties, serious interests: the only
questions treated with moral earnestness were those which concerned
manners. As in so many other departments of life the baroque court
here anticipated the ritual and the psychal reaction of the twentieth
century metropolis. A similar grind: a similar boredom: a similar
attempt to take refuge in "distractions" from the tyrannical oppression that had become a routine and from the routine that had become
an overwhelming oppression.

10: Influence of the Palace on the City

One detects the influence of the baroque court upon the city in nearly every aspect of its life—it is even the parent of many of the new institutions that were later claimed by democracy for its own. There is no parallel type of intercourse between the castle and the market-place in the medieval city; if anything, the influence moved in the reverse direction: the feudal aristocracy became urbane.

Thanks to aristocratic patronage, the theater took its modern form in London, Paris, and the minor cities: the special hall in which the audience is seated according to rank and ability to pay, and in which, from their fixed positions, they become the passive spectators of a drama which is seen, as it were, through the transparent show· window, revealed by an opened curtain. Thanks to the princely de· sire to bring home loot from foreign conquests and to acquire by purchase or patronage what could not be obtained by arms, the great collections of art that form the Vatican Museum, the Louvre, and the National Gallery were first started. And at the very moment that music was being driven out of the home—as the result no doubt of the growing distance in education, manners, and taste between the master of the house and his menials—it achieved an independent existence in the baroque orchestra: therewith the concert hall makes its appearance.

One by one these new institutions mark their existence on the new city plan. Now a national theater in Naples, now a concert hall in Wien, now a museum and gallery in London. Sometimes they come under private auspices: sometimes with royal or municipal support; but always in the image originally stamped by the court. Perhaps the first baroque feature to be opened to the public and duly incorpo· rated in the city was the park: the new equivalent of the smaller pleasure grounds and playing fields of the medieval city. The broad landscape park, preserved in the heart of the city, remains perhaps the greatest single contribution that the baroque period of city build· ing made to modern urban existence. But even here the spirit of the age asserted itself. When the Crown planned Regent's Park in Lon· don the park itself was appreciated as a device for increasing the ground values of the neighboring properties held by the Crown.

It was on the side of pleasure and recreation that the influence of the court was most potent. The pleasure garden, such as Ranelagh Gardens in London in the seventeenth century, and Vauxhall and Cremorne Gardens in the eighteenth, was an attempt to supply the pleasures of the palace to the commonalty at a reasonable price per head: the French equivalent was the Bal Masque and the German parallel the more domestic and *ordentlich* Beer Garden. These pleasure gardens were popular in the baroque period, and remained so in New York, which took them over, down to the Civil War. They consisted in a large central building where dances and routs could be held, and where great feasts could be given; and of gardens and woods where people might roam on a fine night, eating, drinking, flirting, love-making, watching fireworks or lantern displays. Swings and roundabouts made their appearance here; likewise, at the beginning of the nineteenth century, the aristocratic love of speed came out in the more popular promenade aérienne, or chute-the-chutes. In time, the older elegant features of baroque taste disappeared; beginning first, perhaps, in the great international fairs more rowdy forms of amusement, more dangerous distractions—like the Ferris Wheel —came to the front: only the tawdry glitter remained in a Coney Island. But the point of origin is as plain as the downward path.

If the pleasure garden grew on one stem of baroque life, the museum—originally the very consummation of the acquisitive life— grew on the other stem. At first the museum proceeded from the motive of scientific curiosity, as in Aristotle's collections; and after the Alexandrian age of learning the "museum" was reduced to the collections of saints' relics—a bone, a tooth, a phial of blood—in the medieval churches. But museum collections in the modern sense began with the collections of coins and inscriptions that took form as early as the fifteenth century in Italy: these anticipated by a few years the natural history collections of a von Netteshyn, a Paracelsus or an Agricola. Indeed, the writings of the latter were instrumental in causing the Elector Augustus of Saxony to form the collections that have since developed into the museums of Dresden.

In every part of Europe this random search for curiosities and wonders and specimens took place: a primitive "collection economy" of the mind. Acquisition for acquisition's sake was the very spirit of the age: the curiosity parade of the museum was a sort of learned counterpart to the shopping parade: in its earliest form, it was mainly another example of vain display. In the transformation of these cabinets of curiosities, these cabinets of coins, these cabinets of etchings into independent public edifices, the court and the aristocracy played a leading part. But the opening of the British Museum in 1759, after Sir Hans Sloane's bequest was a landmark in *popular* culture; for when display ceased to be merely a private gratification of the possessor it had the possibility of becoming a means of public education.

Half-way between pleasure and curiosity stands one last bequest of the court: the zoological garden. The keeping of wild animals, especially the more exotic ones from foreign parts, was an attribute of kings even in the Middle Ages: they would sometimes be used in processions, like the animals in the traveling circus of the nineteenth century. The extension of these collections of living animals, the provision of permanent quarters and exhibition grounds for them, took place as part of the same movement of an acquisitive and scientific culture as created the museum. Like the museum, they furnished a suitable destination for the explorer's and hunter's trophies. Here was a fresh contribution to the city: a symbol of that feral state which man too easily forfeits when he seeks the comforting presence of his own kind in the city. The playful antics of the monkey, the imperturbability of the hippopotamus, the gay sleek motions of the sealions—all these things, if they did not bring the citizen in touch with nature, at least had a relaxing effect upon overstretched urban ego: they gave a common pleasure to the adult and the child. Even such moth-eaten baroque relics as the dancing bear or the organ grinder's monkey often served as the one touch of animal gaiety between the drab walls of the nineteenth century street. Is it by accident that these vestigial emblems of court life were usually presided over by an Italian?

11: Bedroom and Salon

If the influence of the court was effective in the city at large, it was no less so in the household: at all events, in the houses of the middle classes and their economic superiors. Here the habits of the court, both for good and bad, prevailed. For bad in that a new domestic despotism grew up, which had its source in the vast number of disfranchised people who crowded into the capitals to sell their services for a pittance. The good side was the esthetic improvement in manners, perhaps not altogether unaffected by the increased knowledge of the bland and perfect forms of Chinese civilization; and above all, the spread of privacy within the home: a fact which gave rise to a new code of sexual manners, embroidering the preliminaries of sexual intercourse, and tending to lengthen the period of amatory youth for both sexes. The very word courtship, for that preliminary play which includes the display of wit and charm as well as physical passion, shows how much our erotic life owes to the practice of the court: it is a late sixteenth century coinage.

The change in the constitution of the household manifested itself in various ways. First, by the gradual divorce of the home, henceforth a place for eating, for entertaining, and in a secondary way for rearing children, from the workplace. The three functions of producing, selling, and consuming were now separated in three different institutions, three different sets of buildings, three distinct parts of the city. Transportation to and from the place of work was first of all a privilege of the rich merchants in the big cities: it was only in the nineteenth century that it filtered down to the other classes in the city, and, instead of being a privilege, became a grievous burden. As the result of the household's becoming exclusively a consumer's organization, the housewife lost her touch with the affairs of the outside world: she became either a specialist in domesticity or a specialist in sex, something of a drudge, something of a courtesan, more often perhaps a little of both. Therewith the "private house" comes into existence: *private from business*. And every part came increasingly to share this privacy.

This growth of domesticity partly signified the weakening of public interest among the middle class citizens, especially among the excluded religious sects. Among the middle classes, there was a natural tendency to substitute private life for public affairs. Deprived of his liberties, unable often even to vote for his municipal officers or take part in the official business of his town unless appointed by the Prince, it was natural that the citizen's interest should shift, or become more restricted. If he were a member of a banned religious sect, as many among the merchant classes were, the incentive was even greater. To use a Victorian catchword: the middle classes began to keep themselves *to* themselves.

To make up for lack of effective domestic work, a new type of housework was invented that took up the slack and enriched the ritual of conspicuous consumption. I mean the care of furniture. The fixtures of the medieval household were equipment: chairs to sit on, beds to sleep in: icons to pray before: so much and no more. Furniture is really a re-invention of the baroque period: for by furniture one means useless or super-refined equipment, delicate vases to dust, inlays and precious woods to polish, metal work to keep shiny, curtains to be shaken and cleaned, bric-a-brac and curios to be washed. Display outstripped use; and the care of furniture commanded time that once went to the weaving of tapestries, the embroidery of garments, the making of useful household preserves, perfumes, and simples. These new burdens were inflicted upon housewives and domestics at the very moment that the form of the house itself had changed, multiplying the number of private chambers to be supplied with wood, coal, water, and raising the height of dwellings from two flights of stairs to five, one below ground.

Up to the seventeenth century, at least in the North, building and heating had hardly advanced far enough to permit the arrangement of a series of private rooms in the dwelling. But now a separation of functions took place within the house as well as within the city as a whole. Space became specialized, room by room. In England, following the pattern of the great houses, the kitchen was broken off from the scullery, where the dirty work was done; and the various social functions of the kitchen were taken over by the living room and the parlor. The dining room was separated from the bedroom; and though in the seventeenth century a lady's bedroom still served as a reception room for her guests, whether or not the bed stood in an alcove, in the eighteenth a special room for meeting and conversation, the drawing room, the salon, came into existence. And the rooms no longer opened into each other: they were grouped along the corridor, like houses on a street. The need for privacy produced this special organ for public circulation.

[TOP] Courtyard of the Royal Exchange, London. The rise of the international Bourse in the sixteenth century signalized the change from a goods economy to a money economy, in which trading took place without actual sight of or contact with the goods that were bought and exchanged. The newspaper, beginning with such international reports as those sent back to the House of Fugger, was a necessary accompaniment of this new institution: for international prices were affected by wars, temporary monopolies, gluts, and shortages; and those who got the first news of these events could profit by them. A good part of every metropolitan newspaper is still devoted to financial items.

[MIDDLE LEFT] Interior of Bank of England. Transformation of the goldsmith's depositary into the modern bank is such a complex social phenomenon that the process of banking is still overlaid with magical prescriptions that have nothing to do with the essential relationships. Ideally, the bank is a responsible agency for allocating the collective potential energies of a community into a multitude of nicely inter-related channels where the conversion into kinetic energy and human productivity may take place with a minimum loss. But the conception of banking as a private function of speculators and profiteers has overlaid the necessity of creating responsible publicly controlled bodies performing such collective services. Speculation and abstemiousness, luxurious display and miserly hoarding, economic service and capitalist incantation went hand in hand: an ambivalence reflected in the architecture of the city.

[MIDDLE RIGHT] An early Parisian department store: display shopping and ready-made goods for sale. The Female Tatler (London, 1709) observed that "the shops are perfect guilded theaters." With the increasing size of the city and the increasing distance of the hinterland from which it draws goods, the middleman enters the scene as a go-between for the buyer and seller: carting, water-transportation, warehousing, jobbing, credit purchase all become specialized institutions with specialized buildings. The convenience of having wide assortments of goods available at any time is immense: hence buying and selling become daily occupations: urban hand-to-mouth living, as contrasted with the countryman's long-range seasonal foresight. But the price paid for this convenience is also huge: sometimes destitution for the producer, sometimes bankruptcy for the middleman: eventually higher prices for the consumer.

[BOTTOM] The shopping promenade, with the wide, glass-enclosed shop front, with its goods attractively on display, but protected against the sun and rain. The combination of shopping with wheeled traffic, the tendency to transform every avenue into a shopping avenue, instead of concentrating purchase in market squares, is a characteristic bequest of the mercantile city: an element of de-building and disorganization. It introduced confusion into the domestic quarters and, as the streets lengthened, uselessly multiplied the amount of competitive commercial space, without regard to service or even to profit.

[TOP LEFT] Place de la Concorde, facing the Madeleine through the Rue Royale. A place dedicated solely to wheeled traffic and vistas: but a barrier to safe pedestrian movement, and without a concourse of vehicles, a little empty. The agoraphobia of the Middle Ages here gives way to a claustrophobia, characteristic bequest of a period of restless movement and exploration: the feeling is purer in such later plans as this than in earlier places like the Place des Victoires, which still record the drag of surviving medieval forms. (*Photograph: Ewing Galloway*)

[TOP RIGHT] Arc de Triomphe: the baroque avenue in action: a theater for marching men and spectators. The Place de l'Etoile with its radiating avenues is an admirable emplacement for artillery to command the approach of threatening mobs—and was so intended. Compare this two-dimensional circle, with its formal movement of traffic, with the clover-leaf pattern of the modern motor roads, designed functionally for the movement of cross-traffic in various directions, without friction or stoppages, by means of viaduct and underpass. (*Photograph: Ewing Galloway*)

[MIDDLE LEFT] Rue de Rivoli: partly built under Napoleon I and extended by Haussmann under Napoleon III. Effective city planning, because the street and the arcaded buildings that line one side were conceived as a unit; a contrast to the notion of arbitrarily laying out blocks and quarters for unknown (therefore speculative) purposes. (*Photograph: Ewing Galloway*)

[MIDDLE RIGHT] Diagonal avenues, lined with trees. Here the irregular block shapes are fairly well-managed; but the determination of their size, contour, and orientation by the external needs of traffic is foreign to the functional method of laying out residential neighborhoods. Throughout the Renascence, straightness was a laudatory description of a street or avenue: straightness and breadth. To the street as the theater of swift traffic many other essential urban needs were sacrificed from the seventeenth century on: the curved street, the dead-end, the cul-de-sac, were reviled as old-fashioned or obstructive. The tree-lined boulevard was the highest expression of baroque street planning: forerunner, in the Avenue du Bois de Boulogne, of the universal parkway. (*Photograph: Ewing Galloway*)

[BOTTOM LEFT] Place Royale, now Place des Vosges: built in 1605. With the Place Vendôme the masterpiece of early formal planning: even though the elevation is marred by the awkward Mansard roofs.

[BOTTOM RIGHT] Middle class street in Zürich: typical baroque survival in modest scale, characteristic of a wide variety of cities from Boston and Baltimore to Geneva and München. Order, decency, good manners. Drab and depressing in the old Brownstone section of New York or the duller parts of South Kensington and Pimlico, but usually a happy contrast to the romantic suburb.

Privacy was the new luxury of the well-to-do; only gradually did the servants and the shopkeepers' assistants and the industrial workers have a trace of it. Even in the fine houses of the nineteenth century, the domestics often slept in the kitchen or in a bunk adjacent to it, or in dormitories. Now, privacy had been reserved, in the medieval period, for solitaries, for holy persons who sought refuge from the sins and distractions of the outside world: only lords and ladies might dream of it otherwise. In the seventeenth century it went with the satisfaction of the individual ego. The lady's chamber became a boudoir, literally a sulking place; the gentleman had his office or his library, equally inviolate; and in Paris he might even have his own bedroom, too. For the first time not merely a curtain but a door separated each individual member of the household from every other member.

Privacy, mirrors, heated rooms: these things transformed full-blown love-making from a seasonal to a year-round occupation: another example of baroque regularity. In the heated room, the body need not cower under a blanket: visual erethism added to the effect of tactile stimuli: the pleasure of the naked body, symbolized by Titian and Rubens and Fragonard, was part of that dilation of the senses which accompanied the more generous dietary, the freer use of wines and strong liquors, the more extravagant dresses and perfumes of the period. Flirtation and courtship created those movements of suspense and uncertainty, of blandishment and withdrawal, that serve as safeguards against satiety: a counterpoise to the regimentation of habit. These lusty men and women were never so much at home as when they were in bed. Ladies received callers in bed; statesmen dictated their correspondence in bed; an undercurrent of erotic interest thus permeated the household, sometimes bawdy, sometimes brutal, sometimes romantic, sometimes tender—every shade from the bedroom of Juliet to that in which Joseph Andrews almost lost his virtue. The private needs of the bedroom even penetrated the garden: the summer house, the temple of love, or the more aristocratic maze, composed of high box hedges: places remote from the prying eyes and admonitory footsteps of even the servants.

Meanwhile other technical changes haltingly entered the dwelling house. The invention of the water-closet by Sir John Harrington in

1596 made an important sanitary improvement in the house; but the fashion did not spread fast; for even the interior dry privy was introduced into France in the eighteenth century as an English novelty; while the Palace of Versailles, built regardless of expense, did not have even the conveniences of a medieval castle: portable commodes on wheels were used. Before the invention of the trap and the ventilating stack for the water-closet, the backing up of sewer gas into the dwelling house almost counterbalanced the advantages of the new improvement: witness the British concern during the nineteenth century with "bad drains." With the eotechnic device of the water-closet came another practice directly derived from the Chinese: the use of toilet paper: more important for domestic hygiene than the wallpaper that came in more or less simultaneously.

With all its luxurious display, the baroque city will not bear close inspection in the matter of hygienic and sanitary standards: the typical medieval town was more salubrious. Much though the body was now celebrated in poesy and painting, or systematically investigated in physiology, the people of the period neglected to clean it as thoroughly as the preceding culture had done. Perhaps because of the dangers of syphilis, the medieval bath had begun to fall out of use in the sixteenth century: even among the Jews, who might have been expected in their ghettos to preserve medieval habits so thoroughly in harmony with Mosaic sanitation, the ritual bath that used to take place in the Synagogue—the Mikveh—was given up during the Renascence. The new Baptists might insist upon total immersion; but one experience seems to have lasted them a lifetime.

Perhaps the rising price of hot water had something to do with this lapse, among the common people at least: it would follow upon the scarcity of wood fuel in the immediate neighborhood of the bigger cities. But the fact itself is beyond doubt. In 1387 there were 29 bathmen in Frankfort; in 1530, none. In the seventeenth century, after a breach, the bath was re-introduced as a foreign importation, a luxury, a means of renovating the body after a debauch: the so-called Turkish or Russian bath. But almost immediately these baths became pleasure haunts and houses of assignation: bagnio again meant brothel. Dirt diseases, such as smallpox, flourished in this period; and with the crowding up of the cities the volume of

water that had been sufficient when the mains were installed in the
sixteenth century proved altogether inadequate. Since these mains
were often neither renewed nor extended, the inhabitants of the town
would have a much smaller quantity of water per capita in the
eighteenth century than they had had two or three centuries before.
When the bathroom finally made its way into the house in the nineteenth century, to the chants of mechanical progress that then arose,
only a belated antiquary might possibly recognize that Johann Andreae had assigned such a room *to each three room apartment* in his
ideal city, Christianopolis, and that such rooms had been common,
in the better burgher houses in Germany, in the Middle Ages.

12: The Muddle of Speculative Overcrowding

When one speaks of the new standard of domesticity, one refers
only to the middle and upper class dwellings. Even here the new
comforts, the new luxury of privacy, the new sensuous ornateness,
came in but slowly. The change was marked more rapidly in decoration, from wooden ceilings to plaster ceilings, from paneled walls
to papered walls, from heavy overwrought oak furniture to the more
delicate mahoganies and maples, from gothic motifs to classic motifs,
than in the more essential parts of the structure. The change of scale,
the new sense of spaciousness, the raising of the ceiling in northern
climates—a deliberate innovation by Vanbrugh—gradually produced an internal order that corresponded to the new baroque avenues outside.

But this expansion of upper class quarters was at the expense of
lower class dwellings: if one opened up, the other became more constricted. Overcrowding and land speculation were the canker worms
that ate into the heart of the lovely baroque flower: with them goes
that rise of land values which was to solidify the consequent physical
depression and give it a permanent form. Some of the baroque
princes themselves were not unaware of the dangers of overcrowding; for the movement had begun in the capital cities as early as the
fifteenth century: in Piers Plowman one finds the observation that if
landlords sold honestly they would not build so high; and Robert
Crowley wrote a vigorous poem about the rent raisers.

The stoppage of building congestion in the city, however, would

have been possible only if the forces that were thrusting people into the city had been controlled at the source: if rural economic conditions had been improved, if provincial industry had been placed on a parity with that in the capital, if new cities had been founded and old ones put in repair and extended, if the upper classes had been deprived of their monopoly of land and other privileges, and if taxation had been adjusted so as to lop off the unearned increment from congestion. Unfortunately, the expropriation of the peasant and the depression of the urban worker went hand in hand. Competition for space by poor unprotected immigrants had the same effect on seventeenth century Paris as on eighteenth century Manchester, and nineteenth century Liverpool and New York: the ground rents rose and the living quarters worsened. A hectare of land in Paris was in the thirteenth century worth 2600 francs, according to Avenel: in the twentieth century a hectare in the same district was worth 1,297,000 francs. Who benefited by this rise? Not the occupants. Whose incomes kept pace with it? Not those of the workers.

"The worker of the Middle Ages, who had an annual income of a thousand francs, could pay without difficulty for a little house from one hundred to two hundred francs a year: his situation became still better when rents went immensely lower in the fifteenth century by reason of the abundance of empty dwellings, while wages had gone up 1200 francs. But at the moment when the journeyman did not, from 1550 to the end of the eighteenth century, earn any more than 675 francs per year, and when the poorest Parisian houses rented for 350 francs, one perceives why it was necessary for him to give up living under a separate roof." With appropriate variations this condition held throughout Europe. From the standpoint of the working classes, the period after the middle of the sixteenth century was one of increasing exploitation, and with regard to their quarters, one of increasing dilapidation and constriction.

The contrast between the new residence quarters of the rich and the decaying medieval quarters, now overbuilt and crowded, or the even more wretched new accommodations, was marked in every city where the two were placed side by side: Paris, London, Edinburgh, Berlin. To understand this servility and depression, one must realize that before the humanitarian conscience of the nineteenth century had begun to alter social attitudes, destitution had been accepted as the normal lot in life for a considerable part of the population. In the seventeenth and eighteenth centuries, it has been estimated that as much as a quarter of the urban population consisted of casuals and beggars. In a memorandum dated 1684 the Chief of Police in Paris referred to the "frightful misery that afflicts the greater part of the population of this great city." Between forty and sixty-five thousand were reduced to outright beggary.

The groundwork of a large servile proletariat was a necessary feature of the blaze and pomp of baroque life. For just as even kings were reduced to using plaster and gilt for ornament when the supply of marble and more costly decoration came too high, so gentlemen who wished to have a great retinue in attendance were forced to draw upon the poor and the starving, since for all their boast of riches, they did not have enough money to pay their menials in competition with a healthy labor market. Without a surplus of casuals, there would have been a general scarcity, and service would not have been so cheap. Lackeys and flunkeys and domestic servants of all kinds, if not uprooted from the country, were drawn from the horde of people that had swarmed into the metropolis. Some of them rose into service, where they were provided with a uniform, a more or less sufficient supply of food, occasional opportunities for pilfering, and security of employment during good behavior. In these respects, army service and domestic service had many points in common. The rest begged and cadged and seized odd jobs, they sank further into thieving, pimping, pickpocketing and prostitution, and they ended up in the gutters of Gin Lane or the gallows of Tyburn. I have taken these examples from London: Wien, Madrid, Naples or Berlin would have served equally well.

Given this large proletariat at the mercy of the market, there went on a steady downward movement in housing accommodations for the mass of people, who could no longer afford a cottage of their own or had a chance to board in the house of their master, but rented a shakedown where they could. Overbuilding of land and over-occupation of houses caused grievous sanitary difficulties in London, for example, as early as the sixteenth century. For about fifty years, from 1582 to 1632, there were frequent references to those evils and half-hearted attempts to correct them. After this upper class greed and lower class necessity largely took their course.

The Lords of the Council in 1583 found that overcrowded buildings had greatly increased the danger of pestilence and riot. Attention was drawn to the congestion that resulted from dividing up single houses meant to house a single family: a practice that was to become almost universal in every growing town during the next three centuries. In 1593 an act of Parliament observed that "great mischiefs daily grow and increase by reason of pestering the houses with diverse families, harboring of inmates, and converting great houses into several tenements, and exacting the erecting of new buildings in London and Westminster."

Almost needless to say, these proclamations and edicts went for nothing: the poultices soothed the doctor's conscience; they could not cure the patient's ache. In so far as the efforts to prohibit building were successful, without removing the causes of congestion, they only intensified the existing evils. But ground rents went up as living conditions went down: public vices could be capitalized as private benefits. The Old Soldiers' Homes, which the military capitals began to boast in the seventeenth century, might be palatial, like that Wren created in Chelsea: the new workers' homes were designedly hovels.

The transformation of the older houses into clotted tenements, where a whole family could be cooped into a single room, was not sufficient to accommodate the increased population. New quarters must be built which would accept these depressed conditions as a standard. According to Roger North's autobiography, speculative building began on a large scale in London with Dr. Barbone's ventures, after the Great Fire of 1666. The decrease in housing quarters then gave him a favorable opportunity. "He was the inventor of this new method of building by casting of ground into streets and small houses, and selling the ground to workmen by so much per front foot, and what he could not sell, built himself. This had made ground rents high for the sake of mortgaging, and others, following his steps, have refined and improved upon it, and made a superfoetation of houses round London."

For the rotten perfection of this system we may thank the seventeenth century; but it awaited the introduction of the steam engine and the large scale factory for this method of building to become standardized practice more or less throughout the Western World; often in worse forms, rarely in better ones. As land values rose, building heights rose, too, in cities where land monopoly or topographic obstacles lessened the amount of available building space. The more congested the land, the higher the income; the higher the income, the higher the capitalizable value of the land. London was saved from the worst results of this vicious circle by the fact that so much of the land was in feudal holdings on long-term leases; but when Frederick the Great departed from Germanic custom and put the land on a Roman basis, with the same status as the structure, he opened the way for that untrammeled realty speculation which corrupted the planning and block-layout of Berlin down to the formation of the German republic in 1918.

In short, congestion brought financial reward: slum properties often earned much higher returns than investments in more respectable parts of the town. The transformation of the poverty of the East End into the riches of the West End was the supreme magic of baroque finance: wealth out of illth. It played a major part in that over-expansion and over-concentration which, by the time of Cobbett, had made his epithet, The Wen, an accurate description of every capital city.

13: The Baroque Plan

Except for overseas colonization, the chief new cities built from the sixteenth to the nineteenth century were the "Residenzstädte," places selected for the permanent home of the Prince and his court. Mannheim, Karlsruhe, and Potsdam belong to this group. The town extensions that took place on the new lines were usually done in capital cities, like Naples or München, or in towns like Edinburgh and Nancy where the new bourgeoisie had achieved almost aristocratic pretensions. The new plan distinguished itself from the older medieval accretions by the use of straight lines, regular block units, and as far as possible uniform dimensions; and the new order is symbolized in the roundpoint with its radiating streets and avenues, cutting impartially through old tangles or new gridirons.

The prototype of the asterisk type of avenue plan was, as one would expect from a hunting aristocracy, the royal hunting park itself. Here the long lanes, cut through the trees, enabled the hunters to rally at a central point and go galloping off in every direction. Hunting, and the breakneck riding that accompanies it, remains to this day the privileged sport of the aristocracy in every country. The central meeting point, the roundpoint or *place* of the new plan, was originally the seat of the hunting lodge. When the plan for Versailles was laid down, the palace itself was set on the site of the old hunting lodge where Louis XIV had first wooed his mistress, Madame de la Vallière. The palace at Karlsruhe was likewise on the site of a hunting lodge. But in the plan, this meeting place had a different context: the palace gathered to itself the new avenues of the city as the ruler himself gathered together the political power that had once been dispersed among a multitude of groups and corporations. All the main avenues would lead to the palace. And when one raised one's eyes in the street, the palace, as often as not, would close the vista.

In France, this type of plan was extremely popular: in fact, it left its marks in the suburban districts of Garches and Meudon. But it was imitated over as wide an area as Western Civilization itself— places as far apart as Samarkand and Washington. The plan of Samarkand, as it stood at the end of the nineteenth century, was indeed classic in every respect. There was a citadel, and to the east the old city spread out. Raying out from the citadel were the streets and boulevards of the new town, moving westward. Is it by accident that these boulevards terminated, north and south, in a barracks and a military hospital?

For the asterisk plan there was however another parallel point of origin. In the early starlike schemes of fortification, the city proper became a regular polygon, usually eight-sided; and the main streets were either divided in the form of a cross, or placed so as to converge in the center from each of the angles of the octagon. When the fortification lost its efficacy, the main effect of this pattern was to make the city, or the quarter, a sector of the original spiderweb, with the other avenues radiating out into the park or the open country.

The scheme of central places, dominated by monuments, flanked symmetrically by public buildings, and avenues spreading out from this center, profoundly altered every dimension of planning. For the avenue now became definitely the horizontal frame of the terminal buildings: though these edifices might be capped by a dome, the main effect of the planning was to increase the importance of the regulating horizontal lines. Not merely did the domes of the central buildings seem to float: the principal buildings themselves, when set apart by broad avenues, likewise floated in space: if the medieval town was conducive to claustrophobia, the absolute city had just the other effect—that of promoting agoraphobia. The repetitive motifs, the use of a small stock of classic forms, only added to the sense of visual emptiness in the new street pictures. Only by tying the park and the alley of trees very close to the urban street picture could a certain bleakness in the architecture be avoided: the Avenue de l'Observatoire and the Champs Elysées have a warm quality that was not altogether forgotten in the nineteenth century Parisian boulevard.

But, as I have hinted before, the city was sacrificed to the avenue in the new plan. The uniform avenue brought traffic and confusion into parts of the city that had been quiet and self-contained, and it tended to stretch the market out along the lines of traffic, instead of providing local points of neighborhood concentration. Moreover, the avenue determined the size and the shape of the block; and the needs of domesticity were consistently subordinated to the ostentatious demands of wheeled traffic.

It is possible to represent the new method of platting and laying out towns by a geometrical symbol: a circle like Freudenstadt, an octagon, like Villa Nuova, a partial star like Karlsruhe or Mannheim. What does this mean? It means that the abstract figure determines the social contents: the institutions of the community no longer generate the plan and modify it in accordance with the special needs of living. If the topography is irregular, the land must be evened out, at whatever absurd cost in materials and manpower, merely in order to make the plan work. So difficult, however, is this that most baroque city building took place on level sites. Not alone did this add to the expense of city development: but the increase of wheeled vehicles also added expense by entailing the use of a heavier type of paving: the widening and lengthening of these avenues further multiplied the costs.

Now, the function of geometry in planning is to clarify and guide. Like every other type of useful abstraction, it must be conditioned by facts and give way to facts when the latter point to some aspect of life that has escaped the formula. Up to a point, the mathematical approach of the absolutist planner had a value in normalizing the procedure of laying out quarters, blocks, and individual plots. In a period where changes were rapid and where custom could no longer be sufficient guide, such an approach might be helpful, at least expedient. Unfortunately, baroque planners were too confident about the type of order they imposed: they had no place even in their three-dimensional planning for the factor of time, and, in turn, they gave themselves no time to study the topographic peculiarities of the place. Having gone to the monuments of Greece and Rome for their original inspiration, these classically trained minds had no sense of time as a process of development. All those changes and adaptations that are inevitable with further growth, they left out of their purview: hence their plans were too symmetrical, their order too exclusive and rigid, to allow as a rule for the needs of further generations. A baroque plan was a geometric achievement: it must be laid out and built up at a stroke: if possible under the guidance of an architectural despot. Since to alter this type of plan, to introduce fresh elements, is to spoil its symmetry, even the superficial esthetic contents of the plan could be preserved only by severe administrative regulations. Where these were maintained, as in Paris, order might be preserved on the surface for many generations.

As long as a single proprietor or builder carried out the planning and building of a new quarter within a limited time it might have great consistency and elegance: witness Bath, Nancy, Potsdam. But when the plan existed only in patches, as in London, or when the execution of a good part of it was left for future action, as in Washington, the result might be a disorder that could hardly be distinguished from what would have existed without the plan: witness the sordid slum that is still Pennsylvania Avenue. While these new planners devoted themselves most zealously to the creation of settings for public buildings, our present age finds most to admire in the more intimate marks of formal design: the Place des Vosges (originally the Place Royale) in Paris, 1612; the Place Vendôme, 1708; the parts of Nancy built between 1705 and 1763, the parts of Bath built between 1763 and 1767, the squares of eighteenth century Bloomsbury and Mayfair, or those of nineteenth century Belgravia.

Here was the new order at its best. Its ingredients were exceedingly simple, and owed very little to the spurious cult of the past. A common square, oval, or circle, with a railed park in the center whose trees and shrubberies formed a green enclosure for the approaching street. Common building materials throughout: brick, stucco, or stone bound in the same color the whole façade. A common roof-line with a point of accent, in the form of a pediment, at the point required in the design, not by the demand of some individual wishing to be more conspicuous than his neighbors. These qualities of design were based upon a common financial standing, a common social status, and a common standard of taste.

But one must not look too closely, even in upper class quarters, behind the handsome classic front. Observe the backs of the fine houses in Charlotte Square, Edinburgh: they are barracks. Follow the alleys that lead off the grand avenues: you will find a slum.

Definitely, such order was class planning: it symbolized the common front of the possessing classes. This point was admirably illustrated in a sixteenth century dialogue between a countryman and a city man. The former extols the advantages of the country and the sociable life he enjoyed there with his honest neighbors—"graziers, butchers, farmers, drovers, carpenters, carvers, taylors, and such like men, very good and honest companions." His opponent answers: "And so I think, but not for you, being a gentleman." "What," exclaims the countryman, "would you have me live alone and solitary. That were worse than to be dead." To which the gentleman of the town replies: "Nay, neither, for if you did for the most live in court and city among the better sort, you would ever find company there, *fit for your estate and condition.*"

14: Architectural Forms

Between the sixteenth and the nineteenth centuries there are three formal styles: each bears the marks of a special phase in social and economic development. They succeed each other and intermingle, these new modes of building: hints of the last stage were already present in the sixteenth century.

The first phase is that which is usually tagged as early Renascence. The serene eye-opening of the fifteenth century: the unearthing of statues and monuments, in a state of mingled ecstasy and awe: the quest leading to the horizon and the arched sky above it. The symbol of this first stage is the round arch: every object, from a lady's mirror to a new monument will bear this sign. While the new standardization may be expressed in repeating patterns of column and window, the new regularity and uniformity is only carried on at first for a short distance in the street picture. One may discover a Renascence square, a street, a place: but one looks in vain for a Renascence avenue or a Renascence city: so far they existed only in the mind.

Then the pace of life quickened and the turbulent forces of religious criticism and economic adventure and mechanical invention set up new pressures and counter pressures. The invention of printing gave to the processes of standardization the authority of the printed word and the mechanically copied drawing and plan: book knowledge assumed greater authority than craft-experience, and literacy presently became an indispensable mark of good building. To know the classic forms described in the newly printed work of Vitruvius, to keep in touch with the printed prescriptions of an Alberti, a Vignola, a Palladio, became more important than to understand the needs and the processes of life of one's contemporaries. The courts encouraged this cult and the more practical groups in the city were powerless to oppose it: only the homes of the people and their workshops continued to be built, for the greater part, in the vernacular manner. At the same time other elements of standardization appeared besides the printed word: uniformed armies, uniform codes and laws, uniform coinages. As if in contradiction, a new lawlessness appeared, too: in religion the authority of the individual conscience, against the institutions of the Church; in government, the will of the prince, against local laws and hitherto inviolable customs; in private life, an unbridled sensuality that, for the upper classes, recognized no limits to eating, drinking, and sexual intercourse except animal exhaustion. The machine and the sensual life,

reformation and license, fanaticism and frivolity, equally characterized the new order that became uppermost in the seventeenth century.

On one hand, a more pedantic study of the Five Orders and a more
faithful effort to geometrize life: the street vista was lengthened
and the house type standardized on the façade. On the other hand,
more defiant caprice in dealing with this mass of organized pedantry:
the classic forms were used merely as the skeleton for more voluptu-
ous corporeal members: the columns of the churches writhed like
the body of an African dancer, and the interiors of the churches
might be transformed into ballrooms by the mere expedient of removing the altar. The broken pediment and the spiral symbolize this
new phase. Ornament became more profuse and the interiors were
strewn with life and the representations of life: sea shells of glitter-
ing gold and cornucopias and garlands of flowers and flying cherubs
and the warm fragrant bodies of men and women in love, as conceived by a Fragonard, a Watteau, a Greuze. The strong solemn reds
and blues of the old rose windows of the cathedrals became the
frivolous blues and pinks and whites of the new baroque interior:
in the rococo churches, heaven became visible in gilt and plaster: a
materialization of the vulgar dream of St. John of Patmos.

In one sense, this second phase of the Renascence represented a
falling away from the limpid purity of the early moment: just as
current spasms of religiosity were but a tawdry substitute for the
integral faith of the twelfth century church. This fact gave to the
first use of the word baroque, as Croce has properly contended, the
derogatory meaning of something bombastic and weakly florid. But
this new architecture symbolized the growing divisions and contradictions in the whole life of European culture. If it pushed the abstractions of mechanism too far in one direction, in its one-sided
craving for power, it pushed the anti-mechanical animus too far in
another. Often the same building or the same street picture would
express both elements. Perhaps the sorriest symbol of all is the type
of steeple that became common in the seventeenth century: this old
medieval symbol that had pointed to heaven came back in a sort of
caricature: height was achieved by superimposing one set of columns
above another, till the thin pedantic mass was crowned by a minia-
ture temple of love.

But the most representative symbol of baroque design in both its weakest and its most creative phase is the seventeenth century formal garden or park. This is a formal composition in space, in which the natural growths and efflorescences become merely subordinate patterns in a geometrical design: mere carpet and wall paper, artfully pieced together out of nature's foreign materials. The clipped alley, in which the trees are turned into a smooth green wall: the clipped hedge: the deformation of life in the interests of an external pattern of order—here was something at once magnificent and preposterous, as if Procrustes had been given the inspiration of Raphael.

Finally, the awakening moment of the early Renascence and the tormented conscience of the Reformation and Counter-Reformation, was replaced by the frigid correctness of old age. With the seventeenth century came the age of academies, and formal correctness took precedence over the inner content and the irresistible creativeness of a living art. The codification of architectural design was a natural effort to preserve a common front at a moment when the real interests and activities of people were becoming more divided, more disparate, more filled with internal contradictions. The publication of the Architectura by De Vriese in 1557 was a prelude to a movement that was to dominate architecture in the eighteenth century and issue forth into crazy copybook simulacra in the nineteenth. Under this precedent, measurement and imitation take the place of intelligent design.

Beginning early in the Prado and in Versailles, this phase of architecture creeps like a numbing frost over the more vital forms, either withering them into black shrunken stems, or casting its own cold glaze over the once-animated form. This phase achieved most authority and, architecturally speaking, counts for least: ultimately it produced, at many removes, those monuments, too dead even to be incorrect, that crowned the new civic centers in the United States after 1900: the corpse-like classicism of the New York Public Library, the Lincoln Memorial, the Supreme Court Building, or the new government office buildings in the Washington Triangle.

This final frigidity was pre-figured in many early Renascence discussions and projects; but it took a couple of centuries before social regimentation had removed the last touches of vitality. It is associated with the lifeless plans, in which convenience is sacrificed to axial grouping, in which abstract symmetry dictates the shape and arrangement of rooms and the pattern of the windows, in which—in the city—churches may be built on each side of a plaza merely in order to achieve visual balance. Later this type of planning became commonplace: witness the planning of governmental Berlin in the eighteenth century.

The last phase of the baroque is an age of paper patterns, paper plans, paper constitutions: even warfare was taken over by the academy and conducted according to accepted rules of strategy. Although Ruskin's reasons were often bad, and his failure to perceive the creative moments in the new architecture was unfortunate, his instincts about the Renascence and classic modes of building were, on the whole, correct. There was something sinister in this new order: if it sacrificed the craft autonomy of the worker to the vanity of the architect, it equally sacrificed the uses of life to the formalities of plan and elevation.

The seventeenth century feeling for outward unity was perhaps best summed up by Descartes, who is one of the most representative thinkers of the period, not least because he was a soldier as well as a mathematical philosopher. "It is observable," said Descartes, "that the buildings which a single architect has planned and executed are generally more elegant and more commodious than those which several have attempted to improve. . . . Thus, also, those ancient cities which from being at first only villages have become, in the course of time, large towns, are usually but ill laid out compared with the regularly constructed towns which a professional architect has freely planned on an open plain; so that although the several buildings of the former may often equal or surpass in beauty those of the latter, yet when one observes their indiscriminate juxtaposition, there a large and here a small, and the consequent crookedness and irregularity of the streets, one is disposed to allege that chance, rather than any human will guided by reason, must have led to such an arrangement. And if we consider that nevertheless there have been at all times certain officers whose duty was to see that private buildings contributed to public ornament, the difficulty of reaching high perfection with but the materials of others to operate on will be readily acknowledged."

There could be no sharper contrast between the two orders of thinking, the organic and the mechanical, than here: the first springs out of the total situation, the other simplifies the facts of life for the sake of an artful system of concepts, more dear to the mind than life itself. One works co-operatively with "the materials of others," perhaps guiding them, but first acknowledging their existence and understanding their purpose: the other, that of the baroque despot, insisting upon *his* law, *his* order, *his* society, is imposed by a single mind working under his command. For those on the inside of baroque life, the courtier and the financier, this formal order was in effect organic: it represented the values they had created for themselves as a class. For those outside, it was a denial of reality and a form of oppression.

To understand the final limitations of the baroque plan, one must ask what provisions were made for the civic nucleus? In the neighborhood, none: the local market and the school are not given special positions and sites on the plan: nor does the local park within the big square serve even as a minor playground except for the children of those who have legal access to the square. But in the city as a whole, there is a civic nucleus, in subordinate relation to the Prince's palace; and the theory of this nucleus was admirably set forth by Palladio. "To return to the principal squares, to those that ought to be joined the Prince's palace, or that for the meeting of the states, as the country is either a monarchy or a republic. The exchequer or the public treasury, where the money and treasure of the public is lodged, ought to join them likewise, as well as prisons. These latter were anciently of three sorts; one for such as were debauched or immodest . . . and which we now assign to fools or mad-folks; another was for Debtors . . . and the third was for traitors or wicked persons."

The palace: the exchequer: the prison: the mad-house—what four buildings could more completely sum up the new order, or symbolize the features of its political life? It was by combinations of one or another of these institutions that the baroque community was built; and it was on variants of one or another of their plans and forms that the streets and town-planning extensions and new cities of the period were built.

Truth is that something vital had been forgotten in the culture of the baroque gentleman; and it was naturally missing from the cities he conceived and executed. What was this element—religion? Not in externals, for in sheer mass of building the Church continued to occupy an undiminished place in the city. What was lacking in this scheme was suitable provision for work. No interest in labor as such: hence no suitable provision for the workplaces of industry, or even for the counting houses of the merchant, on the city plan. Special industrial buildings were indeed beginning to dot the eotechnic city: the dwelling house, even with the aid of sheds, could not assimilate the processes of big industry. Brewers, founders, dyers, fullers, tanners, weavers with establishments that brought together a hundred looms or more—all these crafts demanded a special place in the city. As for watermills and windmills, they had become essential to the industrial existence of the town after the twelfth century: their masses formed an ever more obtrusive part of the new street picture and the new skyline. Docks and storage sheds were hardly less important.

What part did architectural theory or urban design have in the evolution of these structures? Practically none: they were not covered in the formal plan or the cult of the Five Orders. Evelyn, who did so much to promote reforestation, was in advance of his culture in this department: he proposed to remove every industry requiring large fires from the heart of London to the district between Greenwich and Woolwich, and prevent similar buildings from being erected near the city in future. Tallow melting and butchering and soap-boiling were not to be carried on within the city, either: co-ordinately he suggested laying all the lower grounds on the outskirts into fields, separated by thick plantations of fragrant shrubs, to improve the air of the city. But these were the suggestions of an extremely able and far-sighted man: one may examine a score of ideal baroque city plans without finding that the planner had the faintest notion of the part played by industry in cities. The most characteristic mark of baroque planning was the effort to keep industry out of sight: zoning for the eye. Ledoux's early nineteenth century attempt to monumentalize industrial buildings was a belated exception.

Occasionally, the engineer would attempt to apply to his industrial buildings the same formula he employed on public monuments: Smeaton's lighthouses and Rennie's Waterloo Bridge are examples. But such tags of ornament could not conceal the fact that the principle for an effective synthesis was lacking. Hence the most gracious forms of baroque planning took place in those parts of the environment where these contradictions and incompatibilities did not wreck the surface order: above all in the country house and the great country estate. Outside the court, the *life* of this period expressed itself, as *dis*-order: muddy boots of reality walking over the elegant carpets.

15: What Saved the Olympians

For the mass of people in the baroque city, the result of its political absolutism, its mercantile enterprise, and its ruthless system of taxation was deterioration of environment and a depression of the standard of life. But the Olympians themselves were saved: so long as they spent part of the time on their grand estates in the country, and so long as the city itself was not invaded too heavily by machine industry, with its dirt and its congestion of neighboring quarters, their environment was a salubrious one. They had order, and they had space: they alone. Just as capitalistic enterprise itself was partly a protest against the stale privilege and staler routine of the guilds; so the cult of luxury was a protest against making a special virtue of poverty and abstention: miserliness and middle-class thrift.

So, too, the open order of baroque planning was an effort to counteract, not the original defects of the medieval city, but the defects that had accreted with time, through an accumulation of vested interests and the failure to replan drastically when occasion demanded: still more perhaps, the niggardly overbuilding of open spaces practiced after the sixteenth century by the new urban bourgeoisie. Even the classic order of architecture can be explained partly as an attempt to wipe off the meaningless dribble of ornament that characterized the flamboyant gothic of the fifteenth century. The esthetic purity of the baroque plan was forced; its type of order was limited: but it marked, within its limits, an attempt to make a

[TOP] Royal Crescent at Bath: one of the culminating points of eighteenth century upper class planning. Formal order and coherence of a palatial sort,
achieved by the collective pooling of resources by the individual occupants, by
the unified control of the land, and by a comprehensive design executed by a
single mind that controls and orders all the elements: possible only when there
is a consensus in society: a common point of view and common values. The
relation of buildings and open spaces here shows a closer kinship to modern
esthetic and social conceptions than does the more typical urban plan of Covent
Garden, below. Here is standardization and uniformity, of the strictest sort,
without the usual connotations of dreariness. (*Photograph: Aerofilms*)

[FIRST LEFT] Street view of another circle at Bath: the architectural form is
nearer the quiet eighteenth century English vernacular than to the somewhat
more pretentious classic façades of the Royal Crescent. The crowded servants'
quarters under the roof remind one, however, of the class exploitation and servility that accompanied this regime. (*Photograph: Carl Feiss*)

[SECOND LEFT] The class front in the new town of Edinburgh: like Karlsruhe,
Nancy, and Bath one of the great examples of coherent upper class town planning made possible by unified ownership of large parcels of land and centralized, co-ordinated design and building: conditions which disappeared in the
nineteenth century, only to be recovered in the publicly aided housing projects
of today. Later exigencies broke the roof line and spoiled the esthetic effect of
this example: the irregularity, so inevitable in medieval façades, is mere disorder in the baroque street picture.

[BOTTOM LEFT] Rear of a handsome façade in Edinburgh: barracks architecture,
facing a catwalk: typical indifference to rear views characteristic of scene painting. An architecture of fronts. Beautiful silks: costly perfumes: dirty bodies.
Elegance and smallpox. Out of sight, out of mind. Modern functional planning
distinguishes itself from this purely visual conception of the plan by dealing
honestly and competently with every side, abolishing the gross distinction between front and rear, seen and obscene, and creating structures that are harmonious in every dimension: planning for the human organism as a whole.

[MIDDLE RIGHT] Arcade in Covent Garden: the Renascence theme in its purity.
(*From London; the Unique City, by S. E. Rasmussen: New York, 1937. By permission of the Macmillan Company, Publishers.*)

[BOTTOM RIGHT] Plan of Covent Garden in the eighteenth century: except for the
axial approach of Russell Street, the disposition and scale of this square is
closer to late medieval Italian than to more absolutist concepts of baroque order.
But note overcrowding of the surrounding blocks and courts: notably the airless
buildings bounded by Maiden Lane and Half Moon Streets. Broad Court, lower
right, is a typical late medieval form.

The mastery of water and soil, the building up of polderland by means of dykes and canals, the utilization of windmills for keeping the land below sea level from flooding, the multiplication of windmills as prime movers, gave the Netherlands their pre-eminence in the seventeenth century: mastery of the practical life in every aspect of agriculture and industry. Their continued eminence in horticulture, their fine craftsmanship in wood and pottery, the complete electrification of railroads and farmhouses no less than cities, has again given these communities a leadership, rivaled only by the Scandinavian countries, in the essential arts of modern civilization. Though the bigger Dutch cities suffered the characteristic paleotechnic blight—so badly that special probationary quarters are sometimes used when removing Dutch slum dwellers to improved dwellings—they retained an architectural and civic tradition capable of renewal. Hence the essential continuity between the Amsterdam of the seventeenth century (*top and middle left*) and a modern housing development like that of Oud in Rotterdam (*top right*), to take the least traditional modern work as a test. Note again the kinship between modern housing and the early seventeenth century Home for the Aged at The Hague with its spacious windows (*third right*). The air view of Naarden (*bottom*) shows the late medieval city in a state of marvelous preservation. The outlines of the fortifications admirably illustrate the baroque military engineer's art; the conversion of these bastions and salients into parks is a classic example of swords unexpectedly beaten into plowshares, to the great hygienic advantage of the town. But see how the Dutch highway engineers, with an indifference to beauty and efficiency still too common in their profession, have stupidly pushed the main motor road into the center of Naarden, instead of by-passing it. The generous open spaces behind the houses accentuate the comeliness of detail, as well as that which characterizes the whole. An excellent urban environment, almost a garden city, greenbelt and all. The Wieringermeer village (*second right*) in the Zuyder Zee development is another example of continuity: but with that tendency to overaccent the traditional that the historical-minded townsman often too readily shows when dealing with the peasant or farmer: a habit of mind that overlooks the fact that the latter is often as eager to exchange his traditional dwelling for a better modern one as he is to exchange the pump for running water, or horsepower for electricity if he can get it: a fact particularly notable in Holland.

fresh start and to think out the necessities of life as they appeared to a contemporary. In its clarity and precision there was something vital: an urgent challenge to the complacent Struldbrugs of the medieval order.

But what saved the Olympians was not their faked classical gestures or their despotic order: what saved them was their new sense of space, and their deliberate effort to bring the country back for their personal use into the town. With the garden and the park, with the morning canter on horseback, with their fencing and dueling, with their visits and their courtship in spacious rooms, with their dances and their theaters, they developed a routine of life that kept their youth, at least, at a high level of biological well-being: their bodies responded to command. Apart from their necessity for turning the performance of leisure into a work routine, they had created in their urban quarters a balanced environment for life. They had what the Germans call Lebensraum, living space, or what one might dub colloquially "space to turn around in." Hence in a period when the landed aristocracy was forced to meet the competition of a new race of industrialists and financiers the aristocracy created for themselves a city in which they could propagate their customs and their biological issue by reason of their all-round fitness. Life for people in other quarters of the city, for the puritan who frowned on the drama and the dance, for the businessman who was suspicious of frivolity and idleness, for the drudge tied to some minute mechanical occupation, was at lower key than in the quarters of the Olympians.

This effort to span life in all its dimensions, this delight in sensuous extravagance, in the body's appetites, in all that the ear, the eye, and the touch could make their own, was an essentially different attitude from that which had governed the Middle Ages. If it had developed first in the cinquecento artists and scholars and courtiers, it had now at last by the eighteenth century created its form in the city. These things were to have revolutionary implications. After the French Revolution, the city began one by one to absorb the institutions of the court and the aristocracy: the common man began to feel, in the words of an old American popular song, "What's good enough for Rockie is good enough for me." The successful industrialist first imitated the aristocracy: then whole bodies of people began to demand similar privileges for the city at large. What is called the rise of democracy is, as far as the city is concerned, the diffusion of baroque privilege: so that by the twentieth century even the most reluctant of upper class housing reformers might admit that the poor were entitled to the privilege of privacy. But by this time the possibilities of modern life could no longer be effectively conceived in terms of the baroque environment.

16: Fulfillment and Renewal

The best examples of a culture are not always the most characteristic ones; for what is most typical is what is most time-bound and limited. Dekker and Chapman are characteristic of Elizabethan London, while Shakespeare, though he shared this milieu, transcended it at a hundred points. This is likewise true of the culture of cities. In the sixteenth and seventeenth centuries certain fresh city forms came into existence; they were characteristic of neither medieval nor baroque civilization. And these types, which are not "transitional" since they led only in their own direction, have more significance for us today than do the classic specimens of the period.

If one takes Amsterdam as the most important example of a city that effected the transition without losing form, that is not to disparage the vitality of other Dutch cities. It is rather to show, by taking the hardest example, that the rapid commercial expansion and the physical growth of the post-medieval city need not have raised insuperable obstacles to order. Throughout its main period of expansion, Amsterdam did not lose its unity; and though its medieval quarter finally decayed, the city as a whole did not deteriorate, except for a brief period in the nineteenth century.

The original form of Amsterdam was an irregular one. With great foresight the planners of the sixteenth century laid out in advance a series of canals and long, shallow building blocks that rounded out the shape of the city and provided effective water connection with the harbor. They created a unified organism, not an abstract geometrical figure. In the new large-windowed houses the builders produced a domestic form that remained stable until the growth of the nineteenth century proletariat turned the speculative builder to the laying out of hideous tenements. The combination of tree-lined water courses and unified block fronts had an irresistible charm: all the more because in Holland the canal brings the country into the heart of the city, in canal boats laden with vegetables and flowers. The pretentious water courses before Nymphenburg or Versailles are, by comparison, empty settings for a mere costume play: historical but inane.

The technical development of the Dutch city was based on the marvelous control of water, not merely for communication and transport but for the sculpture of the landscape, established by the Dutch engineers. Their influence, like that of the advanced horticulturists with their glass houses, was felt throughout Europe: the Dutch farm and the Dutch garden became patterns for a progressive balanced agriculture. And this command of water was felt within the city as well as on the polders: it gave the Dutch town not merely a clean façade and a frame of verdure but a super-clean interior, such as could be established, with the aid of sand or holystone and sea water, on the most shipshape of vessels. The big windows of the seventeenth century small house in Holland, repeated today alike in the architecture of the radical Oud and that of the conservative Granpré-Molière, brought into the house an amount of sunlight and fresh air that corresponded to that which Johann Andreae pictured in his Utopia. Hooch's paintings preserve the very color and light in these dwellings. In general, the layout and amenities of the Dutch brick cottage of this period were not merely in advance of its contemporary upper class housing: they are still above the level that has so far been reached by a good share of modern housing.

No less outside the baroque frame was another phenomenon of the seventeenth century: the New England village. The center of the village was an open common, dominated by the meeting house and the town hall. These three institutions served as a rallying point for the community, the common for military drill as well as for the pasturing of cattle. Around the central area were set the separate houses, sometimes a single line on a block, with deep rear gardens, large enough for a small orchard as well as a vegetable plot. Tall elm trees on each side of the road furnished shade from the torrid summer sun and partial windbreaks against the winter wind—a perfect unison of man and nature. At a time when the medieval city was being encysted, when people swarmed behind massive fortifications, here in America a more open type was being kept in existence, surrounded, like so many early medieval towns, by a simple wooden stockade.

In the seventeenth century the great capitals had begun to absorb population with no effort at limitation. But the New England town during this period ceased to grow beyond the possibility of socializing and assimilating its members: when near crowding, a new congregation would move off under a special pastor, erect a new meeting house, form a new village, lay out fresh fields. Hiving off to new centers discouraged congestion in the old ones; and the further act of dividing the land among the members of the community in terms of family need, as well as wealth and rank, gave a rough equality to the members, or at least guaranteed them a basic minimum of existence. Each family had its rights in the common lands; each family had fields on the outskirts as well as gardens near their homes; each male had the duty of participating in the political affairs of the town through the town-meeting. A democratic polity—and the most healthy and comely of urban environments: a typical contrast to the despotic order of the dominant baroque city. To describe it is almost to define everything that the absolute order was not.

While the cities of Europe were decaying or being transformed into a more mechanical pattern, the countryside was undergoing improvement and rejuvenation. The finest stone villages in the Cotswolds in England—Burford and Bybury for example—date in their final stone form from the period that must otherwise be described as one of decay. The gradual disappearance of the three-field system and the unification of scattered strips into larger parcels created the more unified landscape of post-medieval Europe, with its broad division of fields, sometimes with definite boundary marks and hedges, sometimes in the older open forms, as in some parts of Bavaria and Switzerland. The wild forest became the park: the feudal village, stimulated by the fresh infusion of hand-industry escaping from the closely regulated towns, got almost its first opportunity to command goods from the outside world. So the grace and solidity that were departing from the medieval town took up residence in the new villages; and it is from these surviving villages in England, Holland, France, and Germany today that one can get one's best notions of the layout of the older towns, now hopelessly confused in their formations with the debris of half a dozen different cultural epochs.

These practical common-sense advances in city development were burked by the prevailing ideology; for "progressive" ideas gave authority and economic power to the big city. The ruin of the balanced region, with a multitude of small cities and villages connected by a network of canals and roads, and amply supplied with water and wind power, has been little noted in political history. I have pointed out in Technics and Civilization how the earlier invention of a more efficient prime mover, Fourneyron's water turbine and the turbine windmill, might perhaps have provided the coal mine and the iron mine with serious technical competitors, based on a further development of eotechnic methods. With the co-ordinate development of science, this might easily have led directly into the present neotechnic phase of industry. While it is useless to linger over these vanished possibilities, one would be blind to ignore the fact that they once existed. For no one can know this period and its urban culture who is not conscious of the strange eddies and countercurrents that ruffle the stream of actual events.

Today one looks with a fresh eye on these mutations: the Dutch city and the seventeenth century New England village. As in the penetrating psychology of a Spinoza or a Rembrandt we find a spirit more akin to our own than in the sharp mechanical analysis of a Descartes or the more typical portraiture of court painters like Van Dyck, so in these urban forms we find an early experimental anticipation of patterns for a living environment, like those we must eventually create, in terms of our own culture, for a whole civilization. For the Dutch town architects and the preachers and governors of New England, had a far more significant understanding of the life of men in cities than did the baroque princes: their synthesis was a more inclusive one, and in terms of real life, it is Louis XIV and Le Nôtre whom we must now consider the provincials. Versailles was essentially a spoiled child's toy, precisely as what Spengler worshipfully calls high dynastic politics was, realistically considered, only child's play: adult infantilism disguised as national statesmanship and architectural magnificence. The planners who have reclaimed the Zuyder Zee, the architects who have built a multitude of well-knit modern communities over the face of that great garden which is Holland, follow a sturdier tradition.

CHAPTER III.

THE INSENSATE
INDUSTRIAL TOWN

1: The Displacement of Population

The despotic impulse has been scarcely less tenacious in its hold upon society than the medieval ideology. Armies, governments, capitalistic enterprises, still show the characteristic animus and form of this order. Is it strange that governmental planning was usually conceived in the baroque image throughout the world? It was the characteristic style of bureaucrats: true pigeonhole architecture. And certain typically baroque institutions, like the hotel, which had its origin in Rome in the sixteenth century, did not achieve complete form until the nineteenth.

If in Paris or in Wien the style still retained a little of its old vitality—as in Garnier's Opera House, for example, or in the more chaste Renascence arcades of the Rue de Rivoli—that was only because so little had changed in these cities in the underlying social and economic relationships. Despite its many functional weaknesses, the baroque in its classic mode was destined to remain during the nineteenth century the image of order. Almost all the city planning or building that was esthetically worth attention before the middle of the nineteenth century was along classic lines: the work of Schinkel in Berlin, of the brothers Adam in London and Edinburgh, or that of L'Enfant, Bulfinch, Jefferson, Ramée, and Latrobe in America.

Meanwhile the solidarity of the upper classes was visibly breaking down; the court was becoming supernumerary. In every quarter, the principles of aristocratic education and culture were being displaced by a single-minded devotion to pecuniary success. The new industrialists and bankers, intent on making money and extending their powers through their canny initiatives, had no use for habits of life that did not give them a direct edge over their competitors. Uncouth people, rich speculators who had made a lucky gamble, ruthless factory organizers who had pushed their way to the top, ambitious men, avaricious men, the Napoleons of the factory and the counting house, people as innocent of the principles of humane self-control as a diapered baby, pushed themselves into the established ranks.

The baroque dream of power and luxury had at least human outlets, human goals: the tangible pleasures of the hunt, the dinner table, the bed were constantly in view. The new dream of human destiny, as the utilitarians projected it, had little place for even sensual delights: it rested on a doctrine of productive avarice and physiological denial; and it took the form of a wholesale disparagement of the needs of life.

Yet the triumph of the iron discipline of the machine was not complete. The repressive regimentation that entered the new factories was counterbalanced by the tremendous release from restrictive regulations of all kinds that attended the free movements of peoples over the face of the earth. Within the state there were similar contradictions. The French Revolution looked like a triumph of popular democracy over aristocratic privilege: at least a victory of the middle classes. But it was this revolution that created that hitherto unheard-of engine of destruction, the National Army, and introduced recruitment by popular conscription: it gave the rulers of the state a power that the most absolute princes had rarely dared to exercise.

The cities of the nineteenth century embodied with utmost fidelity all the confusions and contradictions of the period of transition. Those centers in which the new energies and the new discipline of society were most completely focused showed the greatest departures from the best norms: between 1820 and 1900 the chaos of the great cities is like that of a battlefield, proportionate to the very extent of their equipment and the strength of the forces employed. In the new provinces of city building, one must now keep one's eyes on the bankers and the industrialists and the mechanical inventors. They were responsible for most of what was good and almost all that was bad. In their own image, they created a new type of city: that which Dickens, in Hard Times, called Coketown. In a greater or less degree, every city in the Western World was stamped with the characteristics of Coketown.

The political base of this new type of urban aggregation rested on three main pillars: the abolition of the guilds and the creation of a state of permanent insecurity for the working classes: the establishment of the open market for labor and for the sale of goods: the maintenance of foreign dependencies as source of raw materials, necessary to the new industries, and as a ready market to absorb the surplus of mechanized industry. Its economic foundations were the exploitation of the coal mine, the vastly increased production of iron, and the use of a steady, reliable—if highly inefficient—source of mechanical power: the steam engine.

Actually, these technical advances depended socially upon the invention of new forms of corporate organization and administration. The joint stock company, the limited liability investment, the delegation of administrative authority under divided ownership, and control of the process by budget and audit were all matters of co-operative political technique whose success was not due to the genius of any particular individual or group of individuals. This holds true, too, of the mechanical organization of factories, which greatly augmented the efficiency of production. But the basis of this system, in the ideology of the time, was thought to be the atomic individual: to guard his property, to protect his rights, to ensure his freedom of choice and freedom of enterprise, was the whole duty of government.

This myth of the untrammeled individual was in fact the democratization of the baroque conception of the despotic Prince: now every enterprising man sought to be a despot in his own right: emotional despots like the romantic poets: practical despots like the businessmen. Adam Smith indeed had a comprehensive theory of political society: he had a correct conception of the economic basis of the city and valid insight into the non-profit-making economic functions. But his interest gave way, in practice, to the aggressive desire to increase the wealth of individuals: that was the be-all and the end-all of the new Malthusian struggle for existence.

Perhaps the most gigantic fact in the whole urban transition was the displacement of population that took place over the whole planet. For this movement and resettlement was accompanied by another fact of colossal import: the astounding rise in the rate of population increase.

In 1800 England had a population of a little over nine million, Germany had some twenty-four million, France about twenty-seven million, and the United States not much over five million. By 1930, their population in round numbers had risen to respectively forty-five million, sixty-six million, forty-two million, and one hundred twenty-three million. This increase affected industrially backward countries like Russia, with a predominantly rural population and a high rate of births and deaths, quite as much as it affected progressive countries that were predominantly mechanized and de-ruralized. The general increase in numbers was accompanied by a drawing of the surplus into cities, and an immense magnification of the bigger centers. Urbanization increased in almost direct proportion to industrialization: in England and in New England it finally came about that almost eighty per cent of the entire population was living in centers with more than twenty-five hundred population.

Into the newly opened lands of the planet, originally peopled by military camps, trading posts, religious missions, small agricultural settlements, there came an inundation of immigrants from countries suffering from political oppression and economic poverty. This movement of people, this colonization of territory, had two forms: land pioneering and industry pioneering. The first filled the sparsely occupied regions of America, Africa, Australia, of Siberia and, later, Manchuria: the second brought the overplus into the new industrial villages and towns. In most cases, these types came in successive waves.

During the eighteenth and nineteenth centuries, the people of Western Europe re-initiated a process that had gone on in the tenth and eleventh centuries. They opened up millions of acres of new land, whose surplus of furs, hides, timber, metals and cereals they could send back to Europe. In the New World, in particular, the suppressed land hunger of the European, whose land had been carefully controlled by the feudal landlord or the Crown, who felt more and more constricted as the local population rose above its medieval level—this suppressed land hunger led irresistibly to colonization.

Impoverished, sometimes starving men, were willing to forego all the advantages of a socialized and settled life in order to have the elementary privilege of having enough food to eat and enough land to produce most of it. Sometimes they never actually reached their goal, but rotted away in the big seaports into which they were dumped, without the means of going further. But the goal itself was plain. Land meant security. Land meant power and independence. Land might even mean individual riches, when sufficient settlers crowded together to form cities. Lured by these possibilities thousands of families began to explore new geographic provinces, test new soils and new modes of agriculture, acquire new habits of working and living.

This land migration in turn helped to bring to the European system of agriculture the resources of hitherto untapped parts of the world: particularly a whole series of new energy crops, maize and potato—and that instrument of relaxation and social ceremony, the tobacco plant. Moreover the thrusting open of tropical and subtropical lands added a further energy crop now supplied to Europe for the first time on a grand scale—cane-sugar. A surplus of grain had already made possible the distillation of liquors in the seventeenth and eighteenth centuries: whiskey, cognac, and the poor man's drink, gin, supplemented the imperfect fireplaces and stoves with an internal application of warmth: potent if treacherous aids in facing all manner of rough weather. And with the cultivation of the wheatlands of the New World, wheaten flour began to come again into common use, instead of the barley and oaten flour which had, in so many parts of Europe, become the staple ingredient for bread.

Plainly this enormous increase in the food supply was what made possible the increase of population. And the external colonization in new rural territories thus helped to create that surplus of men and women and children which went toward the internal colonization of the new industrial towns and commercial emporia. Villages expanded into towns; towns became metropolises. The number of urban centers multiplied; the number of cities with populations above five hundred thousand increased, too. Extraordinary changes of scale took place in the masses of buildings and the areas they covered:

vast structures were erected almost overnight. Men built in haste, and had hardly time to repent of their mistakes before they tore down their original structures and built again, just as heedlessly. The newcomers, babies or immigrants, could not wait for new quarters: they crowded into whatever was offered. It was a period of vast urban improvisation: makeshift piled upon makeshift.

Mark that the rapid growth of cities was no mere New World phenomenon. Indeed, the rate of city growth was swifter in Germany after 1870, when the paleotechnic revolution was in full swing there, than in new countries like the United States: this despite the fact that the United States was steadily receiving immigrants. Though the nineteenth century was the first to rival the early Middle Ages in large-scale land colonization and settlement, the premises upon which these enterprises were conducted were far more primitive than those of the eleventh century. Colonization by communities, except in the case of little idealistic groups, the most successful of which were the Mormons, was no longer the rule. Every man was for himself; and the Devil, if he did not take the hindmost, at least reserved for himself the privilege of building the cities.

A blight that had its origin in England's dark Satanic mills, as William Blake called them, laid its diseased fingers on the new cities and stultified the further development of the old ones. Here was a chance to build on a firm foundation and make a fresh start: such a chance as democracy had claimed for itself in political government. Almost everywhere that chance was fumbled. In an age of rapid technical progress the city, as a *social* unit, lay outside the circle of invention. Except for utilities such as gas mains, water pipes, and sanitary equipment, often belatedly introduced, often slipshod and inadequate, the industrial city could claim no important improvements over the seventeenth century town. Indeed, the most wealthy and "progressive" metropolises often denied themselves elementary necessities of life like light and air that even backward villages still possessed. Until 1838 neither Manchester nor Birmingham even functioned politically as incorporated boroughs: they were man-heaps, machine-warrens, not organs of human association.

2: Mechanization and *Abbau*

Before we inquire how this vast flood of people found urban accommodation, let us examine the assumptions and attitudes that people brought to the new task of city building.

The leading philosophy of life was the offspring of two entirely dissimilar types of experience. One was the rigorous concept of mathematical order derived from the study of the motions of the heavenly bodies: the highest pattern of mechanical regularity. The other was the physical process of breaking up, pulverizing, calcining, smelting, which the alchemists, working with the mechanically advanced mine workers of the late Middle Ages, had turned from a mere mechanical process into the routine of scientific investigation. As formulated by the new philosophers of nature, neither this mathematical order nor the systematic analysis of matter had any place for organisms or societies: neither institutional patterns nor esthetic patterns derived from the external analysis of the "physical world." The machine alone could embody this order.

Art, religion, personal culture, the building of cities, all felt the results of this systematic indifference to organic events and organic patterns. So far as these disciplines remained true to themselves, they tended to lose an essential connection with the social complex; whilst people who were in harmony with that complex, who expressed it, who profited by it, forfeited some of the attributes of men. In this new environment, only machines could be quite at home; for they express order, purpose, regularity, without the mechanically irrelevant need for love, or sympathy, or beauty.

So immersed are we, even at this late date, in the surviving medium of paleotechnic beliefs that we are not sufficiently conscious of their profound abnormality. Few of us correctly evaluate the destructive imagery that the mine carried into every department of activity, sanctioning the anti-vital and the anti-organic. Before the nineteenth century the mine had, quantitatively speaking, only a subordinate part in man's industrial life. By the middle of the century it had come to underlie every part of it. And the spread of mining was accompanied by a general loss of form throughout society: a degradation of the landscape and a no less palpable disordering of the communal environment.

Agriculture creates a balance between wild nature and man's social needs. It restores deliberately what man subtracts from the earth; while the plowed field, the trim orchard, the serried vineyard, the vegetables, the grains, the flowers, are all examples of disciplined purpose, orderly growth, and beautiful form. The process of mining, on the other hand, is destructive: the immediate product of the mine is disorganized and inorganic; and what is once taken out of the quarry or the pithead cannot be replaced. Add to this the fact that continued occupation in agriculture brings cumulative improvements to the landscape and a finer adaptation of it to human needs; while mines as a rule pass quickly from riches to exhaustion, from exhaustion to desertion, within at most a few generations: they are the very image of human discontinuity, here today and gone tomorrow, now feverish with gain, now drained and exhausted.

From the eighteen-thirties on, the environment of the mine, once restricted to the original site, was universalized by the railroad. Wherever the iron rails went, the mine and its debris went with them. Whereas the canals of the eotechnic phase, with their locks and bridges and toll-houses, with their trim banks and their gliding barges, had brought a new element of beauty into the rural landscape, the railroads of the paleotechnic phase made huge gashes: the cuts and embankments for the greater part long remained unplanted, and the wound in the earth was unhealed. The rushing locomotives brought noise, smoke, grit, into the hearts of the towns: more than one superb urban site, like Prince's Gardens in Edinburgh, was desecrated by the invasion of the railroad. And the factories that grew up alongside the railroad sidings mirrored the slatternly environment of the railroad itself. If it was in the mining town that the characteristic process of *Abbau*—mining or un-building—was seen at its purest, it was by means of the railroad that this process was extended by the third quarter of the nineteenth century to almost every industrial community.

The process of un-building, as Wheeler pointed out, is not unknown in the world of organisms. In un-building, a more advanced form of life loses its complex character; there is an evolution downward, toward simpler and less finely integrated organisms. "There is," observed Wheeler, "an evolution by atrophy as well as by increasing complication, and both processes may be going on simultaneously and at varying rates in the same organism." This held precisely true of paleotechnic society: it showed itself clearly in the organization of urban communities. A process of up-building, with increasing differentiation, integration, and social accommodation of the individual parts in relation to the whole was going on: an articulation within an ever-widening environment was taking place within the factory, and indeed within the entire economic order. Food-chains and production-chains of an extremely complicated nature were being formed throughout the planet: ice traveled from Boston to Calcutta and tea journeyed from China to Ireland, whilst machinery from Birmingham and Manchester found its way to the remotest corners of the earth. A universal postal service, fast locomotion, and almost instantaneous communication by telegraph and cable synchronized the activities of vast masses of men who had hitherto lacked the most rudimentary facilities for co-ordinating their tasks.

But at the same time, an *Abbau*, or un-building, was taking place, often at quite as rapid a rate, in other parts of the environment: forests were slaughtered, soils were mined, whole animal species, such as the beaver, the bison, the wild pigeon, were practically wiped out, while the sperm whales and right whales were seriously decimated. Therewith the natural balance of organisms within their ecological regions was upset, and a lower and simpler biological order—sometimes marked by the complete extermination of the prevalent forms of life—followed the Western man's ruthless exploitation of nature for the sake of his temporary and petty profit-economy.

Above all, this un-building took place in the urban environment. The loss of form and the loss of effective social institutions for transmitting and enlarging the social heritage can indeed be seen at their worst in the mining towns that sprang up during this period: the oil towns, the coal towns, the gold towns, the copper towns, the diamond towns, that began their existence in a "rush," like the tropismic flight of moths toward strong light, and that collapsed, again and again, into empty hulks, or continued in existence as production centers without evolving for themselves any of the other attributes that make life in close communities valuable to man. To this day, these towns remain, despite precious efforts at philanthropy, among the darkest and most benighted parts of the world; their inhabitants, often cut off from physical contact with the rest of the world because of their mountainous terrain, cut off likewise by poverty and cramped desires, are even in free countries the most feudally organized part of the population: here the company town, with its mean power of exploitation and tyranny, has flourished.

Physically, life is at a minimum in these mining areas; and socially, outside the fellowship of work, in an occupation still so dangerous that it calls for heroic efforts and no less heroic sacrifices for one's comrades, these towns are even more destitute. The mining spore, the factory spore, the undifferentiated industrial district— these are the lowest contemporary forms of even semi-permanent organized life. Towns that have been formed by the physical expansion and coalescence of these spores remain, for the most part, areas of barbarism. Exceptions exist: the physical rehabilitation of the Ruhr district and its comprehensive planning as a region for living as well as working, presents a civilized contrast to the usual blight and affliction; but it happens that this Rhineland is one of the oldest continuously occupied industrial centers in the world: its culture dates back to Roman days.

As long as the idolum of the machine remained uppermost, the two processes of up-building and un-building went on together. The *Abbau* reached its lowest point in England around 1840; and at a somewhat later date in other countries. I shall confine most of my observations to England. Here the non-city achieved its classic form; and it was here that the most decisive reactions against un-building first took place.

3: The Postulates of Utilitarianism

In so far as there was any conscious political regulation of the growth and development of cities during the paleotechnic period it was done in accord with the postulates of utilitarianism. The most fundamental of these postulates was a notion that the utilitarians had taken over, in apparent innocence, from the theologians: the notion that a divine providence ruled over economic activity and ensured, so long as man did not presumptuously interfere, the maximum good through the dispersed and unregulated efforts of every individual. Another way of putting it is that they regarded industry as an internally self-regulating system that achieved a harmonious balance through the individual pursuit of pecuniary gain. The nontheological name for this pre-ordained harmony was laissez-faire. The protestant's right of private judgment became the systematic calculus of society.

The historic justification for laissez-faire needs no demonstration now: it was an attempt to break through the network of stale privileges and franchises and trade regulations that the absolute state had imposed upon the decayed economic fabric and dwindling social morality of the medieval town. The new enterprisers had good reason to distrust the public spirit of a venal court or the social efficiency of the Circumlocution Offices of the growing taxation-bureaucracy. Hence the utilitarians sought to reduce governmental functions to a minimum: they wished to have a free hand in making investments, in building up industries, in buying land, in hiring workers. Unfortunately, the pre-ordained harmony of the economic order turned out to be a superstition: the scramble for power remained a scramble, and individual competition for ever-greater profits led the more successful to the practice of monopoly.

In practice, the political equality that was slowly introduced into the Western polities from 1789 onward, and the freedom of initiative that was demanded by the industrialists were contradictory claims. To achieve political equality and personal freedom, strong economic limitations were necessary. In countries where the experiment at equality was made without attempting to rectify annually the effects of the law of rent, the result was a stultification of the original purpose. In the United States, for example, the free bestowal of land upon settlers in 160 acre tracts under the Homestead Law did not lay the basis of a free polity: within a generation the unequal properties of the soil, the unequal talents of the users, had resulted in gross social inequalities. Without systematically removing the fundamental disparities that grew out of the private monopoly of land, the inheritance of large fortunes, the monopoly of patents, the only effect of laissez-faire was to supplement the old privileged class with a new one.

The freedom demanded by the utilitarians was in reality freedom for unrestricted profits and unlimited aggrandizement. Profits and rents were to be limited only by what the traffic would bear: decent customary rents, and a just price, were out of the question. Wages, too, were limited in their downward leveling only by the endurance of the poor: theoretically they should drop to the lowest amount of food and shelter necessary to return the laborer to his job. The ruling classes wished to preserve individual initiative and freedom of contract (that is, social helplessness) for the workers: their right to accept starvation wages was held sacred. They themselves, however, maintained an almost unbroken class front on any issue that concerned their pocketbooks as a class; and they never scrupled to act collectively when it was a question of beating down the working classes.

This theological belief in pre-ordained harmony had, however, an important result upon the organization of the paleotechnic town. It created the natural expectation that the whole enterprise should be conducted by private individuals, with a minimum amount of interference on the part of local or national governments. The location of factories, the building of quarters for the workers, even the supply of water and the collection of garbage, should be done exclusively by private enterprise seeking for private profit. Free competition was supposed to choose the correct location, provide the correct time-sequence in development, and create out of a thousand uncoordinated efforts a coherent social pattern.

Laissez-faire, even more than absolutism, destroyed the notion of a co-operative polity and a common plan: did not the utilitarian expect the *effects* of plan to appear from the unrestricted operation of random private interests? By giving rein to chaos, reason and order were to emerge: indeed rational planning, by preventing automatic adjustments, could only interfere with the higher workings of a divine economic providence. The test of social success was not the consequences to society in good homes and healthy lives and a friendly environment: the sole test was the pecuniary reward that flowed to the enterpriser. If his rewards shrank, the enterprise was "unwise" and its automatic cessation must follow, by bankruptcy if not by choice: if they increased, the enterprise was blessed, and would expand. We shall presently follow the results of this mystical doctrine as it worked out in the housing of the town laborer.

The main point to note now is that these doctrines undermined such municipal authority as had survived, and they discredited the city itself as anything more than a "fortuitous concourse of atoms" —as the physics of the time described the universe—held together temporarily by motives of self-seeking and private profit. Even in the eighteenth century, before either the French Revolution or the paleotechnic revolution had been consummated, it had become the fashion to discredit municipal authorities and to sneer at local interests. In the newly organized states, even those based on republican principles, only matters of national moment, organized by political parties, counted in men's hopes or dreams.

The time of the Enlightenment, as W. H. Riehl sharply said, was a period when people yearned for humanity and had no heart for their own people; when they philosophized about the state and forgot the community. "No period was more impoverished than the eighteenth century in the development of a common community spirit; the medieval community was dissolved and the modern was not yet ready. . . . In the satirical literature of the time, whoever wanted to portray a blockhead represented him as a Burgomaster, and if he wished to describe a meeting of Jackasses, he described a meeting of Town Councillors."

This contempt for the civic business of the local community, this scorn for the old agents of the common weal, this childish belief in the industrialist as the divinely appointed agent of a Higher Power, prepared the way for the complete un-building of the city. The brakes of tradition and custom were lifted from the exploitation of land; there was no limit to congestion, no limit to rent-raising: there was no standard of order or decency or beauty to dictate the division and layout and building up of urban structures. Only one controlling agent remained: profit.

Urban growth had indeed begun, from industrial and commercial causes, even before the paleotechnic revolution was well started. In 1685 Manchester had about six thousand people; in 1760 between thirty and forty-five thousand. Birmingham had four thousand at the first date and almost thirty thousand in 1760. But once the concentration of factories abetted the growth of towns, the increase in numbers became overwhelming. Since the increase produced extraordinary opportunities for profit making, there was nothing in the current traditions of society to curb this growth; or rather, there was everything to promote it. Wherever the land could be broken up into individual parcels, and exploited by competing individuals, wherever, that is, the population could increase freely, the lid was off. Every norm was disregarded: every limitation pushed aside. "The roof was the limit," and business succeeded in raising the roof.

Note one more point. In their relation to the land, the new industrial interests were two-faced. Historically the new oligarchy of big enterprisers, bankers, and industrialists were in opposition to those whose wealth rested mainly on the soil. But despite loud professions of laissez-faire, the new industrial interests sought their own special kinds of monopoly, through patents, trade marks, special subsidies, tariffs, and exclusive rights of exploitation in colonial markets: above all, they needed the privilege of calling upon the soldiery of the state to defend their property and their persons in case of an uprising on the part of the workers—an event they actively dreaded with a fear that grew out of their own capacity for terrorism and injustice, rather than an objective appraisal of the workers' talents for revenge. Even the great philosopher of this regime, Herbert Spencer, whose theoretic individualism had so far advanced toward anarchy that he tended to reject public enterprise even in street paving or sewage disposal, nevertheless firmly upheld the function of the state as policeman.

By allowing the landlord to exploit urban land monopoly the industrialist not merely assented to a sort of equilibrium of privilege: he also favored himself as a potential owner of land, and logically carried out, not his fictitious doctrine of "free enterprise," but his actual policy of a limited monopoly framed so as to favor the more aggressive members of his own class. Hence the weakness of Henry George's effort in Progress and Poverty (1879) to dissociate business enterprise from landlordism. In a society where pecuniary values were uppermost and where no social motives were permitted to stand in the way of financial aggrandizement, such distinctions could gain no hold upon the industrial interests. The displacement of privilege in land could only come through the initiative of the community as a whole, with an enlightened and militant working class as the spearhead. In this respect, Thomas Spence was a greater realist than a Henry George or a Theodor Hertzka.

4: The Technics of Agglomeration

In the first stage of the factory system in England, water power was all-important: hence the woolen industry tended to spread through the valleys of Yorkshire, where such power was abundant. Even in the Manchester region the cotton manufacturers were often attracted at first to the open country by cheap land for their huge plants, a docile working population, and easy access to power: so, too, in New England.

It took the better part of a century before all the agents of agglomeration were developed in equal degree: before the advantages offered industry in the towns counterbalanced the lure of independent organization in separate factory villages, sufficient to make the former the prevailing mode. Once these agents played into each other's hands, the attractive power of the city became irresistible; and the cities came to absorb an ever larger share of the natural increase in population.

By the end of the eighteenth century most of the necessary conditions were satisfied in London, Paris, and Berlin: hence the ability to pile people into these throbbing centers was limited now only by the human tolerance for an obnoxious environment. Unfortunately, on this score, human beings show qualities that remarkably resemble those of the pig: give swine a clean sty on hard ground with plenty of sunlight, and they will keep it remarkably clean: put them in the midst of muck and putrescence underground, and they will accommodate themselves to these conditions. When starvation and homelessness are the alternatives, there is apparently no horror to which defeated men and women will not adapt themselves and endure.

Apart from the incentive of profit, industry itself, from the beginning of the nineteenth century onward, became an active factor in urban agglomeration. Eotechnic industry had, in the nature of things, been decentralized: wind power and water power caused its spread along the coast lines and rapid-flowing rivers; the unit of production was necessarily limited in size, and only in a minor degree was there any advantage in the concentration of a *single* industry or plant. Despite occasional large munitions factories and textile plants, the small workshop was the typical unit.

The use of Watt's steam engine as a prime mover in the seventeen-eighties changed all this. Steam worked most efficiently in big concentrated units, with the parts of the plant no more than a quarter of a mile from the power-center: every spinning machine or loom had to tap power from the belts and shafts worked by the central steam engine. The more units within a given area, the more efficient was the source of power: hence the tendency toward giantism in textile factories, which covered a large area and were usually five stories high. Big factories, such as those developed in Manchester from the eighteen-twenties onward—repeated in New Bedford and Fall River—could utilize the latest instruments of power production, whereas the smaller factories were at a technical disadvantage. A single factory might employ two hundred and fifty hands. A dozen such factories, with all the accessory instruments and services, were already the nucleus of a considerable town.

In their attempts to produce machined goods at low prices for consumption in the world market, the manufacturers cut costs at every point in order to increase profits. The most obvious place to begin this paring was in the wages of the workers. In the eighteenth century, as Robert Owen noted, even the most enlightened manufacturers made unsparing use of child labor and pauper labor: but when the ages of child workers were legally regulated and the supply diminished, it became necessary to tap other sources. To have the necessary surplus of workers, to meet the extra demands in the busy seasons, it was important for industry to settle near a great center of population, for in a country village the support of the idle might fall directly upon the manufacturer himself. It was the fluctuating rhythm of the market, its spurts and cessations, that made the large urban center so important to industry. For it was on an underlayer of irregular labor, fitfully employed, insufficiently paid, that the new capitalists managed to depress wages and meet any sudden demand in production. Size, in other words, took the place of an efficiently organized labor market. Topographical agglomeration was a substitute for a well-timed and nicely regulated mode of production.

If the steam factory, producing for the world market, was the first factor that tended to increase the area of urban congestion, the new railroad transportation system, after 1830, greatly abetted it. Power was concentrated on the coal fields. Where coal could be mined or stored or obtained by cheap means of transportation, industry could produce regularly throughout the year without stoppages through seasonal failure of power. In a business system based upon time-contracts and time-payments, this regularity was highly important. Coal and iron exercised a gravitational pull on many subsidiary and accessory industries: first by means of the canal, and after 1830, through the new railroads. A direct connection with the mining areas was a prime condition of urban concentration: to this day the chief commodity carried by railroads is coal for heat and power.

The dirt roads, the sail-power, the horse-power of the eotechnic transportation system had favored a dispersal of population: within the region, there were many points of equal advantage. But the relative weakness of the steam locomotive, which could not easily climb a grade steeper than two feet in a hundred, tended to concentrate the new industrial centers on the coalbeds and in the connecting valleys: the Lille district in France, the Merseburg and Ruhr districts in Germany, the Black Country of England, the Allegheny-Great Lakes region and the Eastern Coastal Plain region in the United States.

Port cities, because of their overseas connections, played an equal part in this assemblage. They became the termini or junction towns of the main lines, and they served likewise, by this fact, to concentrate more narrowly the routes of ocean travel, so that a few great ports, like Liverpool, London, New York, Antwerp, and Hamburg gathered to themselves a disproportionate share of traffic and burdened themselves with an extra source of population congestion. With the steady increase in the size and draft of ships, these disparities grew: smaller ports lost their trade to the big ports where the channels were deep, the railroad connections many, and where the concentration of commercial enterprise made it possible to make the necessary investments in dredges, docks, cranes, warehouses and similar facilities. (Liverpool's exceptionally far-sighted public provision of docks, markets, and warehouses in the eighteenth century gave it a unique place.) In short: numbers begot numbers; and concentration, once well started, tended to pile up in ever-increasing ratios, claiming increase by inertia where it could no longer promise more effective economic performance. Industry prospered in the big metropolises into which raw materials, unemployed workers, and unemployed capital were automatically drifting: both technics and capitalism during the nineteenth century promoted urban congestion.

Population growth, then, during the paleotechnic regime, showed two characteristic patterns: a general massing on the coal areas, where the new heavy industries, iron and coal mining, smelting, cutlery, hardware production, glass manufacture, and machine building flourished. And in addition a partly derivative thickening of population along the new railroad lines, with a definite clotting in the new industrial centers along the great trunk lines and a further massing in the greater junction towns and export terminals. Along with this went a thinning out of population and a running down of activities in the back country: the falling off of local mines, quarries, and furnaces, and the diminishing use of highways, canals, small factories, local mills.

Most of the great political and commercial capitals of the baroque period, at least in the Northern countries, shared in this growth. Not merely did they usually occupy geographically strategic positions: they had special resources of exploitation through their intimacy with the agents of political power and through the central banks and bourses that controlled the flow of investments. Moreover, they had the further advantage of having gathered, for centuries, a vast reserve of miserable people at the margin of subsistence: what was euphemistically called the Labor Supply. The fact that almost every great capital became *ipso facto* a great industrial center served to give a further push to the policy of urban aggrandizement and congestion.

5: Factory and Slum

The two main elements in the new urban complex were the factory and the slum. By themselves they constituted what was called the town: a word that describes merely the fact that more than twenty-five hundred people are gathered in an area that can be designated for postal communication with a proper name. Such urban masses could and did expand a hundred times without acquiring more than a shadow of the institutions that characterize a city in the sociological sense—that is, a place in which the social heritage is concentrated, and in which the possibilities of continuous social intercourse and interaction raise to a higher potential the activities of men.

The factory became the nucleus of the new urban organism. Every other detail of life was subordinate to it. Even the utilities, such as the water supply and the minimum of governmental buildings that were necessary to a town's existence often, if they had not been built by an earlier generation, entered belatedly: an afterthought. It was not merely art and religion that were treated by the utilitarian as mere embellishments: intelligent political administration was in the same category.

The factory usually claimed the best sites: mainly, in the cotton industry, the chemical industries, and the iron industries, the sites near a waterfront; for large quantities of water were needed now in the processes of production, supplying the steam boilers, cooling hot surfaces, making the necessary chemical solutions and dyes. Above all, the river or canal had still another important function: it was the cheapest and most convenient dumping ground for all soluble or semi-soluble forms of waste. The transformation of the rivers into open sewers was a characteristic feat of the paleotechnic economy. Result: poisoning of the aquatic life: destruction of food: befouling of water so it was unfit to bathe in.

For generations, the members of every "progressive" urban community were forced to pay for the sordid convenience of the manufacturer, who often, it happened, consigned precious by-products to the river, for lack of the scientific knowledge or the empirical skill to use them. If the river was a liquid dumpheap, great mounds of

ashes, slag, rubbish, rusty iron, and even garbage blocked the horizon
with their vision of misplaced and unusable matter. The rapidity of
production was in part matched by the rapidity of consumption, and
before a conservative policy of scrap utilization became profitable,
the formless or deteriorated end-products were cast back over the
surface of the landscape. One might almost measure the "prosperity"
of the paleotechnic community by the size of its scrapheaps and junk-
piles.

The testimony that substantiates this picture is voluminous; indeed, it is still open for inspection in the older industrial cities of
the Western World, despite herculean efforts to cleanse the environment. Let me however quote from an early observer, Hugh Miller,
the author of Old Red Sandstone: a man thoroughly in harmony with
his age, but not insensitive to the actual qualities of the new environment. He is speaking of Manchester in 1862. "Nothing seems more
characteristic of the great manufacturing city, though disagreeably
so, than the river Irwell, which runs through the place. . . . The
hapless river—a pretty enough stream a few miles up, with trees
overhanging its banks and fringes of green sedge set thick along its
edges—loses caste as it gets among the mills and print works. There
are myriads of dirty things given it to wash, and while wagonloads
of poisons from dye houses and bleachyards throw into it to carry
away, steam boilers discharge into it their seething contents, and
drains and sewers their fetid impurities; till at length it rolls on—
here between tall dingy walls, there under precipices of red sandstone—considerably less a river than a flood of liquid manure."

Note the environmental effect of the *massing* of industries that the
new regime tended to make universal. A single factory chimney, a
single blast furnace, a single dye works may easily have its effluvia
absorbed by the surrounding landscape: twenty of them in a narrow
area effectively pollute the air or water beyond remedy. So that the
unavoidably dirty industries became through urban concentration far
more formidable than they were when they had existed on a smaller
scale and were more widely dispersed about the countryside. At the
same time clean industries, such as the making of blankets, which
still goes on at Witney in England, with bleaching and shrinking
conducted out in the open air of a charming countryside, became

impossible under the old rural methods in the new centers: chlorine took the place of sunlight, and for the healthful outdoor work that often accompanied the older processes of manufacture, with changes of scene as well as process to renew the spirit of the worker, came the dull drudgery of work within a dirty building hemmed in by other dirty buildings. Such losses cannot be measured in pecuniary terms; and we have no calculus for figuring out how much the gains in production must be offset by the palpable sacrifice of life and a living environment.

While factories were usually set near the rivers, or the railroad lines that paralleled the rivers (except where a level terrain invited diffusion), no authority was exercised to concentrate factories in a particular area, to segregate the more noxious or noisy industries that should be placed far from human habitations, or to zone for purely domestic purposes the appropriate adjacent areas. Factories were permitted to exist wherever the owner happened to have bought enough land to build on: "free competition" alone determined location, without thought of the possibility of functional planning; and the jumbling together of industrial, commercial, and domestic functions went on steadily in industrial cities.

In areas with a rough topography, such as the valleys of the Allegheny plateau, a certain amount of natural zoning might take place, since only the river bottoms would afford enough space for a big mill to spread. Otherwise living quarters were often placed within the leftover spaces between the factories and sheds and the railroad yards. To pay attention to such matters as dirt, noise, vibration, was accounted an effeminate delicacy. Workers' houses, often those of the middle classes too, would be built smack up against a steel works, a dye plant, a gas works, or a railroad cutting. They would be built often enough on land filled in with ashes and broken glass and rubbish, where even the grass could not take root; they might be on the edge of a dump or a vast permanent pile of coal and slag: day in and day out the stench of the refuse, the murky outpouring of chimneys, the noise of hammering or of whirring machinery, accompanied household routine.

So widespread was this deterioration of environment, so hardened have people in big cities become to it in the course of a century, that even the richer classes, who can presumably afford the best, to this day often indifferently embrace the worst. By continued extensions over their backyards, some of the finest houses off Fifth Avenue are built almost back-to-back: dark, dingy quarters, fit for disciples of Midas. One of the most fashionable residence districts in New York is situated plump between a huge gas works and an electric power station; the South Side of Chicago, once lined with sumptuous mansions, is close to the sickening effluvia of the monster-stockyards; while potentially the finest residential quarters in London, Westminster and Chelsea Reach, are befouled by the factories that have long been permitted to occupy the Lambeth and Battersea shores. Small wonder the rich have failed to understand the housing problem: they never discovered their own.

As for housing itself, the alternatives were simple. In the industrial towns that grew up on older foundations, the workers were first accommodated by turning old one-family houses into rent barracks. In these made-over houses, each separate room now would enclose a whole family: from Dublin and Glasgow to Bombay, the standard of one room per family long held. Bed overcrowding, with three to eight people of different ages sleeping on the same pallet, often aggravated room overcrowding in such human sties. This type of overcrowding, as we have seen, had been going on in the big capitals since the sixteenth century; and by the beginning of the nineteenth, according to Dr. Willan, who wrote a book then on the diseases of London, it had produced an incredible state of physical defilement among the poor. The other type of dwelling offered to the working class was, essentially, a standardization of these degraded conditions; but it had this further defect—the plans of the new houses and the materials of construction usually had none of the original decency of the older burgher houses: they were jerry-built from the ground up.

In both the old and the new quarters a pitch of foulness and filth was reached that the lowest serf's cottage scarcely achieved in medieval Europe. It is almost impossible to enumerate objectively the bare details of this housing without being suspected of perverse exaggeration. But those who speak glibly of urban improvements during this period, or of the alleged rise in the standards of living, fight shy of the actual facts: they generously impute to the town as a whole benefits which only the more favored middle class minority enjoyed; and they read into the original conditions those improvements which three generations of active legislation and massive sanitary engineering have finally brought about.

In England, to begin with, thousands of the new worker's dwellings, in towns like Birmingham and Bradford, were built back to back. (They still exist.) Two rooms out of four on each floor therefore had no direct daylight or ventilation. There were no open spaces except the bare passages between these doubled rows. While in the sixteenth century it was an offense in many English towns to throw rubbish into the streets, in these early paleotechnic towns this was the regular method of disposal. The rubbish remained there, no matter how vile and filthy, "until the accumulation induced someone to carry it away for manure." Of the latter, there was naturally no lack in the crowded new quarters of the town. The privies, foul beyond description, were usually in the cellars; it was a common practice to have pigsties under the houses, too, and pigs roamed the streets once more, as they had not done for centuries in the larger towns. There was even a dire lack of toilets: the Report on the State of Large Towns and Populous Districts (1845) states that "in one part of Manchester in 1843-44 the wants of upward 7000 inhabitants were supplied by 33 necessaries only—that is, one toilet to every 212 people."

Even at such a low level of design, even with such foul accompaniments, not enough houses were built in many cities; and then far worse conditions prevailed. Cellars were used as dwelling places. In Liverpool, one-sixth of the population lived in "underground cellars," and most of the other port cities were not far behind: London and New York were close rivals to Liverpool: *even in the present decade there were 20,000 basement dwellings in London medically marked as unfit for human occupation.* This dirt and congestion, bad in themselves, brought other pests: the rats that carried bubonic plague, the bedbugs that infested the beds and tormented sleep, the lice that spread typhus, the flies that visited impartially the cellar privy and the infant's milk. Moreover the combination of dark rooms and dank walls formed an almost ideal breeding medium for bacteria, especially since the overcrowded rooms afforded the maximum possibilities of transmission through breath and touch.

If the absence of plumbing and municipal sanitation created frightful stenches in these new urban quarters, and if the spread of exposed excrement, together with seepage into local wells, meant a corresponding spread of typhoid, the lack of water was even more sinister. It removed the very possibility of domestic cleanliness or personal hygiene. Even in the big capital cities, where some of the old municipal traditions still lingered, no adequate provision for water was made in the new areas. In 1809, when London's population was about a million, water was available over the greater part of the city only in the basements of houses. In some quarters, water could be turned on for only three days in a week. And though iron pipes made their appearance in 1746, they were not extensively used until a special act in England in 1817 required that all new mains be built of iron after ten years.

In the new industrial towns, the most elementary traditions of municipal service were absent. Whole quarters were sometimes without water even from local wells. On occasion, the poor would go from house to house in the middle class sections, begging for water as they might beg for bread during a famine. With this lack of water for drinking and washing, it is no wonder that the filth accumulated. Open drains represented, despite their foulness, comparative municipal affluence. And if families were thus treated, one need scarcely turn to the documents to find out how the single workers fared: the flotsam and jetsam of casual labor. Deserted houses of uncertain title were used as lodging houses, fifteen or twenty people in a single room. In Manchester, according to the police statistics of 1841, there were some 109 lodging houses where people of both sexes slept indiscriminately; and there were 91 mendicant lodging houses. "Playfair told the Health of Towns Commission in 1842 that in all Lancashire there was only one town, Preston, with a public park, and only one, Liverpool, with public baths."

This depression of living quarters was well-nigh universal among the workers in the new industrial towns, once the paleotechnic regime was fully established. Local conditions sometimes permitted an escape from the extremes of foulness I have been describing: the housing of the millworkers at Manchester, New Hampshire, were for example of a better order; and in the more rural industrial towns of America, particularly in the Middle West, there was at least a little free elbow room and garden space for the workers. But wherever one looks, the improvement was but one of degree: the *type* had definitely changed for the worse.

Not merely were the new cities as a whole bleak and ugly, environments hostile to human life even at its most elementary physiological level, but the standardized overcrowding of the poor was repeated in middle class dwellings and in the barracks of the soldiers, classes which were not being directly exploited for the sake of profit. Mrs. Peel cites a sumptuous mid-Victorian mansion in which the kitchen, pantry, servant's hall, housekeeper's room, butler's and footmen's bedrooms were all placed in the cellar: two rooms in front and two rooms in the rear looked onto a deep back basement: all the others were "lighted" and "ventilated" by panes of glass high up in the ceiling. Corresponding forms of degraded housing were worked out in Berlin, Wien, New York, and Paris during the middle of the nineteenth century. The new apartment houses of the middle classes backed upon deep, airless courts that had all the characteristics of cellars even when they were technically above ground.

To judge by popular oratory, these defects were narrow in range, and, in any event, have been wiped out during the past century through the onward march of science and humanitarian legislation. Unfortunately, popular orators—and even historians and economists who supposedly deal with the same set of facts—have not formed the habit of making firsthand surveys of the environment: hence they ignore the fact that great clots of typically paleotechnic housing exist in only slightly modified form throughout the Western World today: even back-to-back houses and cellar-lodgings. These clots not merely include most of the worker's dwellings built before 1900; they include a great part of what has been done since, though they show improvements in sanitation. The surviving mass of housing that was built between 1830 and 1910 does not represent *even the hygienic standards of its own day;* and it is far below a standard framed in terms of present-day knowledge of sanitation, hygiene, and child care—to say nothing of domestic felicity.

"Slum, semi-slum, and super-slum—to this has come the evolution of cities." These mordant words of Patrick Geddes apply inexorably to the new environment. Even the most revolutionary of contemporary critics lacked genuine standards of building and living: they had no notion how far the environment of the upper classes themselves had become impoverished. Thus Friedrich Engels not merely opposed all "palliative" measures to provide better housing for the working classes: he seems to have held the innocent notion that the problem would be solved eventually for the proletariat by a revolutionary seizure of the commodious quarters occupied by the bourgeoisie. This notion, quantitatively considered, was fatuously optimistic; socially speaking, it merely urged as a revolutionary measure a process that had gone on in the older towns as the richer classes moved out of their original quarters and divided them up for working class occupation. But above all the suggestion was extremely naïve because it did not perceive that the standards embodied in the more pretentious residences were *below* those which were desirable for human life. In other words, even this revolutionary critic was apparently unaware of the fact that the upper class quarters were, more often than not, intolerable super-slums. The necessity for increasing the amount of housing, for expanding the space, for multiplying the equipment, for providing communal facilities, was far more revolutionary in its demands than any trifling expropriation of the quarters occupied by the rich would be. The former notion was merely an impotent gesture of revenge: the latter demanded a revolutionary reconstruction of the entire social environment—such a reconstruction as we are on the brink of today.

6: Houses of Ill-Fame

Let us look more closely at these new houses of the working classes. Each country, each region, had its own special pattern: tall tenements in Glasgow, Edinburgh, Paris, Berlin, Hamburg, or two story buildings, with four, five, sometimes six rooms in London, Brooklyn, Philadelphia, Chicago: vast wooden firetraps called three-deckers in New England, or narrow brick row houses, still clinging to an older Georgian row pattern, in Baltimore. But they are united by certain common characteristics. Block after block repeats the same formation: there are the same dreary streets, the same bleak alleys, the same absence of open spaces for children's play and gardens; the same lack of coherence and individuality to the local neighborhood. The windows are usually narrow; the interior light insufficient; no effort is made to orient the street pattern with respect to sunlight and winds. The painful grayish cleanliness of the more respectable quarters, where the better-paid artisans or clerks live, perhaps in a row, perhaps semi-detached, with a soiled pocket-handkerchief of grass before their houses, or a tree in the narrow courtyard in the rear—this respectability is almost as depressing as the outright slatternliness of the poorer quarters: more so indeed, because the latter often at least have a touch of color and life, a Punch-and-Judy show in the street, the chatter of the market stalls, the noisy camaraderie of the public house or bistro; in short, the more public and friendly life that is lived on the poorer streets.

The age of invention and mass production scarcely touched the worker's house or its utilities. Iron piping came in; likewise the improved water closet; eventually the gas light and the gas stove, the stationary bathtub with attached water pipes and fixed outlets; a collective water system with running water available for every house, and a collective sewage system. All these improvements slowly became available to the middle and upper economic groups after 1830; within a generation of their introduction they indeed became middle class necessities. But at no point during the paleotechnic phase were these improvements made available to the mass of the population. The problem for the builder was to achieve a modicum of decency *without* these new expensive utilities. This problem remained soluble only in terms of a primitive rural environment. Thus the original division of Muncie, Indiana, the Middletown of Robert Lynd's survey, had houses eight to a block, each on a lot sixty-two and a half feet wide and a hundred and twenty-five feet deep. This certainly provided better conditions for the poorer workers than what followed when rising land values crowded the houses and narrowed the garden space and the play space, and one out of four houses still lacked running water. In general, the congestion of the industrial town increased the difficulties in the way of good housing, and added to the cost of overcoming these difficulties.

As for the furnishing of the interiors, Gaskell's picture of the housing of the working classes in England strikes the lowest level; but the sordor continued, despite minor improvements, in the century that followed. The effects of pecuniary poverty were in fact aggravated by a general falling off in taste, which accentuated the impoverishment of the environment, by offering to the poor barbarous wall paper, meretricious bric-a-brac and framed oleograph pictures, and furniture derived from the worst examples of stuffy middle class taste: the dregs of the dregs.

In China a friend of mine reports seeing a miner, bent with toil, tenderly fondling a stalk of delphinium as he walked along the road; but in the Western World, down to the twentieth century, when the allotment garden began to have its civilizing effect, the same instinct for fresh vital form was destined to feed on the deliberate monstrosities that the manufacturer offered to the working classes under the guise of fashion and art. Even religious relics, in Catholic communities, reached an esthetic level so low as almost to be a profanation. In time, the taste for ugliness became ingrained: the worker was not willing to move from his older quarters unless he could carry a little of its familiar filth, confusion, noise, and overcrowding with him. Every move toward a better environment encountered that resistance: a real obstacle to decentralization.

A few such houses, a few such lapses into ugliness, would have been a blot; but perhaps every period could show a certain number of houses of this description. Now, however, whole quarters and cities, acres, square miles, provinces, were filled with such dwellings, which mocked every boast of material success that the "Century of Progress" uttered. In these new warrens, a race of defectives was created. Poverty and the environment of poverty produced organic modifications: rickets in children, due to the absence of sunlight, malformations of the bony structure and organs, defective functioning of the endocrines, through a vile diet; skin diseases for lack of the elementary hygiene of water; smallpox, typhoid, scarlet fever, septic sore throat, through dirt and excrement; tuberculosis, encouraged by a combination of bad diet, lack of sunshine, and room overcrowding, to say nothing of the occupational diseases, also partly environmental. Presently the recruiting sergeant was not able to use the children of this regime even as cannon-fodder: the medical discovery of England's mistreatment of her workers, during the Boer War and the World War, did perhaps as much as any one other factor to promote better housing.

The crude results of all these conditions may be followed in the mortality tables for adults, in the disease rates for urban workers compared with agricultural workers, in the expectations of life enjoyed by the various occupational classes. Above all, perhaps, the most sensitive barometer of the fitness of the social environment for human life is the infant mortality tables.

Wherever the comparison was made between country and city, between middle class quarters and poor quarters, between a low density district and a high density district, the higher rate usually fell in the latter class. Had other factors remained the same, urbanization by itself would have been sufficient to lop off part of the potential gains in vitality. Farm laborers, though they remained throughout the nineteenth century a depressed class in England, showed a much longer expectation of life than the higher grades of town mechanics, even after municipal sanitation and medical care had been introduced. Indeed, it was only by a continual influx of new life from the country that the paleotechnic city could survive at all: the new towns were established in the mass by immigrants. In 1851, out of 3,336,000 people of twenty years and upward, inhabiting London and 61 other English and Welsh towns, only 1,337,000 had been born in the town of their residence.

As for the infant mortality rate, the record is even more disgraceful. In New York City, for example, the mortality rate for infants in 1810 was between 120 and 145 per thousand live births; it rose to 180 per thousand by 1850, 220 in 1860, and 240 in 1870. This was accompanied by a steady depression in living conditions: for after 1835 the overcrowding was standardized in the newly built tenement houses. These recent calculations corroborate what is known about the infant mortality rate in England during the same period: there the rise took place after 1820 and fell most heavily on the towns. There are doubtless other factors responsible for these retrograde tendencies; but the new towns, as an expression of the entire social complex, conditioning hygiene, diet, working conditions, wages, child care, education, had an important part to play in the result.

There has been much unwarranted congratulation over improve·ments in urban health under industrialism because those who be·lieved that progress automatically occurred in every department of life during the nineteenth century refused to face the harsh facts. They did not let themselves make comparative studies between town and country, between the mechanized and the unmechanized; and they assisted further in creating confusion by using crude mortality tables, not corrected according to age and sex groups, and not there·fore allowing for the heavier distribution of adults in the cities and the larger incidence of children and old people in the countryside. These statistics made town mortality rates look more favorable than they really were on close actuarial analysis. To this day scarcely the beginnings have been made toward a satisfactory analysis of births and deaths, health and disease, in relation to environment. By lumping urban and rural rates together in a "national" figure the relatively poorer showings of the "prosperous" industrialized and urbanized areas have been concealed.

Similar misleading analyses continue to be made, even today. Thus Mabel Buer has attempted to vindicate the industrial revolu·tion from the charge of creating urban blight by making a study of the changes in the death rate that took place *before* 1815—that is, before the overcrowding and bad sanitation and general urbanization of the population had produced their characteristic devitalizing re·sults. There is no need to cast doubt upon this earlier improvement any more than one need forget the steady *general* drop in the death rate throughout the nineteenth century. But it fails to wipe out the equally indisputable fact of later deterioration.

Instead of giving credit for the early advance to the industrial revolution, one should give due credit to quite another department—the increase of the food supply, which provided a better diet and helped raise resistance to disease. Still another factor may have had a part: the wider use of soap made possible through the increased amount of available fats. The use of soap in personal hygiene may have extended from the washing of the nipples of the nursing mother to the child in her care: finally it passed by example from the femi·

nine to the masculine half of society. This increased use of soap is not easily measurable in trade schedules; for soap was originally a commercial monopoly, and as such, a luxury article: ordinary soap was produced and consumed within the household. The spread of the soap-and-water habit might well account for the lowering of infant mortality rates before the nineteenth century; even as the dearth of water and soap might account in part for the deplorable infant death rates of the paleotechnic town.

Mark this: hygienic poverty was widespread. Lack of sunlight, lack of pure water, lack of untainted air, lack of a mixed diet—these lacks were so common that they amounted to a chronic starvation among the greater part of the population. Even the more prosperous classes succumbed; sometimes prided themselves on their vital deficiencies. Herbert Spencer, who was a nonconformist even to his own creed of utilitarianism, was forced to preach the gospel of play and physical relaxation to his contemporaries; and in his Essays on Education he went so far as to make a special plea to parents to permit their children to *eat fruit*. The mischief was universal. Only those relics of an older culture, the country clergyman, the landed aristocrat, the artist, had enough sense to flee the paleotechnic environment, as the ladies and gentlemen of Boccaccio's Decameron fled from the plague in Florence. Doing so, they had their reward: not riches perhaps, but length of days. Do you doubt it? Consult the life insurance tables.

7: Resistance to Barbarism

That people remained in any degree human in this depauperate and devitalized environment was a triumph. That the working classes could raise families and keep their children from utter physical and moral debasement was a tribute to their heroic fiber. On a moral level, the standard of the paleotechnic town often remained high. If Catholicism, Baptism, Wesleyanism, perhaps made the worker oblivious to his actual environment, too patient toward oppression, too content with his mean station in life, they nevertheless prevented him from sinking spiritually to the level of his physical surroundings.

It is partly to this poor remnant of the old Temple City, embodied now in sheet-iron chapels and tawdry red-brick churches, designed in debased gothic—it is to this fragment that one must attribute some of the saving grace that kept it from outright barbarism. From the older gospel of Christianity, but still more from the new social gospel first preached as a political doctrine during the French Revolution and later elaborated as an economic creed in socialism, came important compensations. The first was a survival; the second a mutation. In the slums and working class quarters a new hope was born. From the depths of the proletariat came the dream of a more friendly social order and a more humane way of life than a mechanistic capitalism had made possible.

Out of the friendly societies, a surviving bequest of the guilds, the new trade unions began to spring up. Around the table of a public house, that vestigial club of the workingman, a more purposive sociability was born. Here plans were made for banding against the employers; here projects for universalizing the ballot, for raising wages and shortening hours, for regulating the general conditions of industry and eventually taking command of the state were first hazily argued and inchoately formed. In some half-used building, a bare room, like that of a dissenter's chapel, would become the meeting place for those who were struggling for some modicum of economic security: trade union headquarters. The bleak walls, lighted by a bluish gas flame, the room itself reached by a rickety flight of stairs and a dusty passage, did not provoke a feeling of confidence and power. Two generations must pass before the Maison du Peuple in Brussels and other cities would serve as social centers for the working classes. Still: the early unionists did not make the mistake of confusing a beautiful building with a strong union: the spirit was firm though the shell was weak.

Similarly, a group of Rochdale weavers pooled their pennies to purchase tea outside the retail system: thus they founded the cooperative movement without a modicum of help from the classes above: an attempt to eliminate the sacred motive of private profit. This movement, in less than a century, came to rival in power and size and capital—as it was to surpass immensely in moral significance—the greatest capitalistic corporations of the world: clear proof of the absurdity of the contention that without opportunities for unlimited profits and unlimited individual aggrandizement the

talent and skill necessary to run great collective enterprises cannot
be summoned forth.

Rochdale weavers: Lancashire cotton spinners, who, though starving thereby, stuck to the anti-slavery cause; resolute trade unionists:
decent workers in every paleotechnic town throughout the Western
World—their sturdy examples modify one part of our just indictment of the environment. All the outer evils remained real: the brutality, the exploitation, the befoulment and the depression. These
things were persistently inimical to life at its best, cramping it, frit-
tering away its energies, robbing it of gaiety and sweetness. But despite these grave handicaps, the spirit of the working classes, who
suffered most acutely, was not overwhelmed: again and again these
heroic men and women displaced circumstances and rose superior to
the motives that governed their rulers, even as they rose superior to
the stultifying environment that capitalism had provided for men
and masters alike. Perhaps as compensation, the most debased urban
environments sometimes stimulated the most valiant efforts at change.
Were not the miners, more than once, the leaders in revolutionary
unionism—and in Europe did they not provide out of their own
membership great choral societies?

In fact, the slum offered the worker compensations that the new
villa quarter did not possess. There is snobbery in the grand salon
of the ocean steamer, but not in the storm-tossed lifeboat. When
people are shorn of all expectation of worldly goods and worldly
success, they find their neighbors: reduced to a bare crust, Lazarus
finds it easier to share the scrap with his neighbor than Dives does
the surplusage of his banquet. The Circe of capitalism might transform the workers' dwellings into pigsties; she could not metamor-
phose all their inhabitants into swine. Thrust into this cruel environment, the workers of Europe, after enduring much, threw off their
passive rôle: they took the first steps forward toward a new order
of co-operative endeavor, out of which the city, as a conserver of the
human heritage, could again arise. It needed, perhaps, this last exas-
perated contact with the paleotechnic hell to give mankind, in desperate revulsion, a fresh vision of heaven. At all events the vision
slowly took form.

8: The Minimum of Life

From the standpoint of theoretic capitalist economics there was no housing problem in the paleotechnic town. Even the meanest paid worker could be housed at a profit, in strict accordance with his income, provided no outside standards based on health and safety were introduced to mar the free play of economic forces. If the result was a slum, that fact was a justification of the slum, not a condemnation of the profit system.

Unfortunately, this method of housing was not a permanently satisfactory one. Sooner or later, the question of standards upset the pure equation of supply and demand. Diseases could not be segregated: the laundress or the milkman might introduce typhoid fever into the most exclusive quarters of the city. Sheer self-protection demanded that the upper classes should concern themselves with the housing of the poor. So the first public attacks on the evils of housing came from the heads of the health departments in London and New York. The health officers pointed out that poverty, malnutrition, and bad housing were correlates of crime and disease.

By the middle of the nineteenth century, the housing problem was discovered, if not rigorously defined. In the industrial towns there was usually a chronic shortage of living quarters for the lower paid workers; and the quality of the accommodations offered was below the minimum current standards.

The attempt to remedy this situation took various forms. Philanthropists like the American merchant, Peabody, and Prince Albert, formed in London philanthropic associations to promote better housing for the poor and during the next half century they built an experimental series of working-class homes. This example was followed in other metropolises. Beginning in 1851 in England, through the initiative of Lord Shaftesbury, an attempt was made to establish minimum standards of sanitation: the decent repair of workers' houses and the provision of a minimum of paving, water, open spaces, and sewer drainage in the new quarters, was ultimately enforced by law. Private initiative, like that of Ruskin's disciple, Octavia Hill, working strictly within the lines of capitalism, attempted to show that with the proper upkeep and supervision of slum quarters, the conditions of backward properties could be improved to the common advantage of owner and renter. As early as 1851 the Netherlands permitted communes to expropriate land for housing purposes; and in 1873 the city of Amsterdam provided sites and furnished funds to an association formed to construct sanitary dwellings for workingmen. Finally, beginning in Belgium in the eighties, an effort was made to supply money at lower rates of interest to special societies dedicated to the provision of good workers' dwellings.

All these experimental initiatives had a certain educational value; they proved that something better could be done. Unfortunately, neither the second nor the third built new quarters; while in England local authorities were very reluctant to make use of their new powers to declare insanitary buildings vacant, or tear them down. As for the Model Housing Associations, their propaganda was better than their performance.

In England, for example, the Metropolitan Association for Improving the Dwellings of the Industrial Poor—a title that says much—was founded in 1842. By 1851 they had succeeded in building a model tenement, which won a prize in the Crystal Palace Exposition. When compared with the quarters that had been built for workers up to this time, these dwellings were palatial. Judged by reasonable human standards, they were extremely cramped. Worst of all: the improvements embodied in these model dwellings, privacy, sanitary devices, and water, added to the cost of the structure.

Here at the beginning the reformers knocked their heads against an inexorable fact: a fact that still makes adequate housing within the framework of unregulated private capitalism all but impossible. James Hole, a contemporary writer on housing, recognized the crux of the difficulty when he wrote that the worker "cannot have wide streets and proper conveniences for his house without paying for these advantages, and the cost has been frequently brought forward as an objection to such improvements; and, in fact, to all proposals for raising the standard of workingmen's dwellings, either by legal restriction or by the building of better houses when undertaken as a measure of philanthropic enterprise." Those reasons and those ob· jections still linger on today.

The point cannot be gainsaid. Higher standards *do* mean higher costs. There were only two ways of meeting these increased costs: one was to raise the wage level for the lower income groups; the other was to provide a public subsidy out of taxes to make up for the difference between what the worker's family can afford, and what he must pay in order to have better accommodations in new quarters. Thus the two family houses built by this London association cost about 450 pounds; and the rent of from three shillings sixpence per week to four shillings was at the time within the reach only of regularly employed skilled artisans: it did not touch the problem of housing the great mass of underpaid workers. In order to offset these costs, the reformers—wishing to do something—were forced to whittle down the necessary improvements.

From the beginning, the usual panaceas were offered: above all, that which has been resurrected again today, namely, mass production and mechanization of the process of building. In designing the Langbourn buildings for Mr. Alderman Waterlow the architect had the joinery made to uniform size and pattern and attempted to effect a saving through building the walls of artificial stone, consisting of clinkers and Portland cement. Had the method effected any real economies, the example might have spread; *but even in the relatively simple dwellings of the early Victorian period, without the mechanized utilities of our present age, the advantages of such economies in the shell of the fabric were unexpectedly small.*

Result: model tenements were forced to lower earlier standards of good housing. It was only by comparison with contemporary slums that they could be thought of as improvements. In London, after 1850, model dwellings were six story tenements, as contrasted with the usual two and three story buildings in the older quarters of the East End: models of congestion. In establishing these new barracks for the poor, the reformers sought to conserve their properties by an extra-legal series of regulations: regulations that were posted on the walls, enforced by inspection, re-enforced by the penalty of expulsion.

In other words, they suppressed some of the worst features of capitalistic housing by methods which, if applied to the old quarters, would often have made them more agreeable for human habitation than what the reformers themselves could show. By such prudent management these model structures sometimes accumulated a surplus profit, above the six per cent to which they restricted themselves. But even with speculative profits eliminated, the provision of new sanitary facilities and conveniences resulted in higher rents. Hence these model quarters were usually occupied by classes economically above the level of those for whom the dwellings were originally intended.

The net result of model tenement building and remedial legislation aiming at higher standards, was to give the sanction of law, philanthropy, and municipal effort to a low grade urban environment. Doolittle, Bernard Shaw's Dustman in Pygmalion, might well prefer the unsupervised licentiousness of his original slum to the sordid respectability of the new quarters. Such minimum standards, finally, had the effect sometimes of calling the attention of builders and land exploiters to possibilities they had guilelessly passed by: the new minima upset the more generous provisions that often continued to prevail through local custom. Schumacher points out that this took place in Germany; and there is little doubt that it was also a consequence of "housing reform"—particularly after New York City's model law—in America.

Perhaps here we have a key to the essential human achievement of the new urban culture: it worked out a minimum of life. There have been periods in the past that exhibited greater animal ferocity, gashing or burning the flesh of people who had sinned against the prevailing moral code or theological beliefs. But the nineteenth century, smugly conscious of its new humanitarian principles, converted such outright brutalities into a slow quiet process of attrition and inanition. A minimum of schooling: a minimum of rest: a minimum of cleanliness: a minimum of shelter. A gray pall of negative virtue hung over the urban improvements of the period, and its highest boast was the expansion of these minimum conditions and these negative gains.

The quintessence of this minimum life was achieved in the prison. Indeed, one might without much exaggeration say that housing reform was preceded by prison reform, as John Howard preceded Shaftesbury; and the prisons embodied most of the negative improvements that were introduced for the benefit of free citizens of the non-

criminal classes, in the factories and tenements. The factory maintained the coercion of the prison: the enforced silence, the repetitive
routine, the lockstep, the constant surveillance of the foreman or
jailer: often enough a formidable prison wall would be around the
structure, too; and the new housing quarters, with their closely calculated number of cubic feet of air and square feet of window space,
cut off from sight of grass and flowers by the dusty paved courts and
the dustier streets, could not have been more adequately designed if
the sole object of the building were punishment.

The speculative spread of the industrial town meant the growth
and spread of a dreary prison environment. The reward an honest
man got for a faithful day's labor was not measurably different from
that which a more erring member of society got as punishment: indeed, the "freedom" of the first was another name for anxiety and
insecurity and fearful humiliation. A minimum of life: malnutrition
at every level. When, according to Olmsted, the teachers in the
Ragged Schools of New York took their pupils for a holiday in the
country they "found it quite impossible to prevail upon them to refrain from completely ravishing the private gardens of the benevo-
lent gentlemen who have offered them entertainment." Was it a wonder? The children were starved. Indeed, half the anti-social symptoms that broke out in the new towns, the brawls, the pervasive
drunkenness, the love of violence, were not special signs of inner
depravity: they were blind reactions to the environment: a step
higher, perhaps, than complete submission to its degradation.

9: Paleotechnic Drama

In the routine of Coketown's life, what respite existed from the
monotony of subdivided occupations: from the warped, one-sided
attempt to drive human energies into a single channel: mechanical
production: financial gain? After his weekly spree in the tavern or
the brothel, the worker returned to the factory or the mine more
cheated, more defeated, more empty of life, than ever. Dickens reduced the facts of paleotechnic life to the simple terms of a schoolboy's primer; but his observation holds a great measure of truth:
Dombey loses his wife, Gradgrind betrays his son and daughter, be-

cause these hard utilitarian rationalists overlooked the need for spontaneous joy and human understanding.

Nevertheless, one or two elements of drama still remained in the industrial town. The main drama revolved around the factory: its actors were the masters and the leaders of labor, and the workmen themselves took part, now as actors, now as passive chorus. It was in the lockout and the strike, those double-edged weapons, each of which cuts sharply into the hand that wields it, that the inert weight of impersonal forces and passive adjustments suddenly became lightened by a deed. The drama was a grim one, and, in the picket line, or by the factory gate, the action might become deadly: while behind the scenes, in the silent heroism of the workers' homes, there was often sacrifice on the level of high tragedy. The stakes might seem sordid, at best trivial: half an hour less of work, a few shillings more per week, the restoration of a dismissed comrade, the willingness to meet and bargain: but for the workers those little matters meant life and death. And this was the major tragedy: the workers' utmost success still meant only such life as might exist within the paleotechnic prison. Without the possibility of the strike, however, the filth, the monotony, the starvation, the anxiety, would have been unbearable: and the strike alone brought the possibility—and therewith the necessity—of a comradeship that could break through the mechanical partitions of the factory. An alternative to Mr. Stiggins' Grand Junction Ebenezer Temperance Association.

With the polis itself gone in the industrial non-city, politics became supreme. The ghost of the old civic unity now spread over national and imperial territory by the device of representative government and universal suffrage: the lure of the ballot led men to concentrate their political interests upon abstract issues, and parliaments attempted to solve by purely legal formulae matters that demanded concrete experiment and the co-operation of engineers, architects, administrators, artists. Most successful in fostering the political drama, then, were such issues of war and peace as lent themselves to the machinations of the politician: a good war, in Afghanistan or the Soudan, might save a bad peace. Thumb through the old files of the Illustrated London News. In the most turbulent years you will look in vain for scenes of strikes and demonstrations: instead, you will be filled with images of the far-flung British armies and the exotic places in which they conducted their missionary and military operations.

The ancient medieval civic pomp, which had lingered in Leeds, for example, till the middle of the eighteenth century, according to the Webbs, disappeared: by the middle of the nineteenth century the pageantry of the Lord Mayor's parade in London had become so dull and threadbare that it prompted the ridicule of Mr. Punch. But in the bleak industrial towns *national* politics became drama, battle, sport: its orators were the chief actors, its protagonists were the greatest prize-fighters, its parliamentary leaders were the leading generals, and its election bouts, with their speeches and their torchlight parades and their hysterical mass enthusiasms, were the principal occasions for emotional release: more universal even than the revival meeting. Politics in fact in the industrial city took the place that the motion pictures and the football and cricket matches do under a later regime. In every such center the political auditorium became the chief civic institution: Exeter Hall, Albert Hall, Madison Square Garden, the endless Mechanics' Halls. Sonorous oratory served the double function of stimulant and anesthetic: exciting the populace and making it oblivious to its actual environment. In the ranks of the Trade Union movement itself mere political windbags rose to leadership: men who commanded crowds in order to sate their narcissism: copious in emotion, diffident, fumbling in action. Such actors threw in the shade the type of personality whose grasp of the practical life and whose administrative skill would have equipped him to run the industry on behalf of the workers: the latter kind of organizer either remained frustrate, or deserted to the capitalist camp, where his talents were more readily recognized and given freer play. This migration of the proletarian élite into the commercial or political bureaucracy was a weakness that only the co-operative movement, apparently, knew how to cope with.

The final word on this systematized exploitation of wind and verbiage was written, not by Lenin or Mussolini, but by William Morris in News from Nowhere. In his Utopia the only use he could find for the old Houses of Parliament at Westminster was as a storage place for dung. Genuine democracy needed more persistent

organs of association, and more specialized competence, than the talkers whose wiles governed political parties could muster. Even today those organs, that competence, have still to be locked together in an effective reciprocal arrangement, in which the principle of rational criticism and consent will be combined with the acceptance of the authority that science and functional ability must in the nature of things wield.

10: The Non-Plan of the Non-City

The standardization of the factory-slum was the chief urban achievement of the nineteenth century. Wherever the steam engine, the factory, and the railroad went, an impoverished environment usually went with them. To make this development easier, it was necessary to have an appropriate type of urban layout. Fortunately the mechanical city plan had been invented before the machine-conditioned town itself had come into existence.

If the layout of the town has no relation to social activities and needs other than those of the surveyor, the real-estate speculator, and the jerry-builder, the simplest means of organizing it topographically is by means of rectangular blocks: blocks of identical size, separated by streets and avenues of standard widths. This plan offers the engineer none of those special problems that irregular parcels with curved boundary lines present. An office boy can figure out the number of square feet involved in a street opening, or in a sale; and a lawyer's clerk can write a description of the necessary deed of sale, merely by copying a standard document. With a T-square and a triangle, finally, the municipal engineer, without the slightest training as either an architect or a sociologist, could "plan" a metropolis. The neatness of the mechanical drawing, as in the plan of 1811 for New York, would obscure the extent of the eventual civic folly.

This rectangular type of plan is often referred to as a particularly American contribution to city planning; but like so many "American" innovations, it had its origin in the Old World; and if it is more conspicuous in American cities, this is merely because other types of planning were, after the nineteenth century, less influential. From the seventeenth century on the extension of old towns, Stuttgart and Berlin, for example, took place by the addition of regular rectangular blocks. Such a mechanical extension could proceed into an in definite future, toward an ever-receding horizon; and once the boundaries of walls and fortifications were let down, either figuratively or by actual demolition, cities began to grow by a process of indefinite accretion. The essential urban unit was no longer the quarter: it was the block, projected as a function of a traffic artery.

From the standpoint of the new real-estate speculators, this type of plan was perfect. Each lot, being of uniform shape, became a unit, like a coin, capable of ready appraisal and exchange. Such block platting provided the maximum number of valuable corner lots, with double exposures; and it permitted "plans" to be made for unlimited future development without foresight or responsibility. Being conceived as a purely physical agglomeration of buildings, the town planned on rectangular lines could sprawl in any direction, limited only by gross physical obstacles and the means of transportation. Every street might be a traffic street; every section might be a business section. Indeed, to permit the progressive intensification of land use, with a corresponding rise in rent and realty values, was the prime virtue, from the capitalist standpoint, of this inorganic type of plan. So deeply ingrained has this point of view become that in the zoning plans made by allegedly competent authorities in the United States, something like sixteen per cent of the urban area has usually been allotted to industry, although the needs of actual business, as Bartholomew shows, are amply covered by an average use of under five per cent.

Even from the most limited physical point of view, most of these rectangular plans were highly inefficient. By usually failing to discriminate sufficiently in the first instance between traffic arteries and residential streets, the first were not made wide enough and the second were usually too wide, thus throwing the cost of excessive paving and over-lengthy utilities lines upon residential districts that could ill afford them. (The refined meanness of the English by-law street was an exception; but even here, as Unwin was brilliantly to demonstrate in Nothing Gained by Overcrowding, money was thrown into excessive street acreage that could have been spent to better purpose on internal parks and play areas.) By paying no attention to topography the municipal engineer opened the way for fat pieces of "honest" municipal jobbery in the grading and filling of streets. On steep hilly sites, like that of San Francisco, the rectangular plan, by failing to respect the contour levels of the hillside, placed a constant tax on the time and energy of its inhabitants, and inflicted on them and their heirs a daily economic loss, measurable in tons of coal and gallons of gasoline wasted, to say nothing of undoing the major esthetic possibilities of a hill-site that is intelligently platted.

Although the absence of the short-cuts provided on the diagonal baroque plan has also been held a point against the checkerboard plan, one must admit that the wasteful and unusable plots formed by diagonal avenues at their point of concentration probably even up accounts. What was more serious, in causing waste and confusion, was the platting of checkerboards within the highway net created by old roads: the irregular direction of the latter would often create a crazy pattern of streets which the municipal engineer never brought together: Brooklyn offers many examples. The indifference to geographic contours, in the application of the formal gridiron to the land-surface, was nothing short of sublime: the engineer's streets often swept through swamps, embraced dump-heaps, accepted piles of slag and waste, climbed cliffs, and ended up a quarter of a mile beyond the low water mark of the waterfront.

In the layout no thought was given either to the direction of the prevailing winds, the placing of industrial districts, the salubrity of the underlying foundations, or any of the other vital factors involved in the proper utilization of a site. Hence there was no functional differentiation on the plan between the industrial, the commercial, the civic, and the residential quarters. In a street map, all these parts looked alike, although their requirements for traffic alone, no less than for efficient work, were different. *This means that in reality no section was suitably planned for its specific function.* As a result, industry and business were encouraged—until zoning ordinances were tardily introduced at a much later stage of development—to spread everywhere. External regularity: internal disruption.

Since the main purpose of the inorganic gridiron plan was speculation and sale, it succeeded admirably on its own premises. The first step in the development of the town or the new quarter was the platting of the streets: the next step was the division of the blocks into building lots and their early sale in individual parcels to the private owner or builder. Once the land had been hopelessly broken up into separate lots under separate ownership, it was practically impossible to make a socially co-ordinated development for a single block, to say nothing of a whole quarter. When land was needed for any public purpose, the buying out of the owners became one of the great handicaps to good public management: a process that lent itself in many cities, not only to tedious delays, but to various forms of blackmail and graft. (The Lex Adickes, which permitted the assemblage of parcels and the pro-rata distribution on a better plan to the individual owners, did not come in, even in Germany, until 1902, And the much earlier principle of excess condemnation which permits the municipality to condemn more land for a public purpose than it actually needs, in order to have control over the surrounding development, likewise was used with great diffidence.)

As for an expression of the permanent social functions of the city in the new type of plan, it was utterly lacking. Although civic centers might sometimes be provided in new towns, as they were in the early nineteenth century in the plans for Cincinnati, St. Louis, and Chicago, by the time the gambling fever had risen these municipal sites would be sold to pay for their street extension and street paving. When the need arose for sites for city halls and law courts and municipal administration buildings, for schools and universities and parks and playgrounds, the appropriate parcels of land would have been already in individual ownership, sometimes already built upon. Even if these tracts could then be purchased, the cost of assemblage or condemnation, the cost of demolition, the cost of the original and now useless structures, all raised the total cost; while the size and shape of the new parcel and the disposition of the surrounding streets might be altogether inappropriate to its functional use. It is only when special sites are located and delimited before building has taken place, as in the medieval bastides, that the rectangular plan affords a possibility for intelligent social adaptation. This implies a degree of civic co-ordination that the municipal engineer cannot, by himself, practice.

The reckless extension of the paleotechnic town was accompanied by the progressive destruction of open spaces; and as the periphery widened, the open country became ever more remote from the center. The filling up of small brooks and streams, the covering over of the canals, the building up of vacant lots, demanded that equivalent spaces be restored for the use of growing children within the city. But the very growth of the city increased land values; so that plots that could easily have been afforded for playgrounds and playing fields, if planned for the original development, rose so high in price that their acquisition became excessively costly, if not prohibitive. No serious public recognition of even the need for public playgrounds came, however, until after 1870, and the movement itself did not begin to make headway until the twentieth century. Hence a peculiar function of the paleotechnic street: it was forced to take the place of the back-garden of the medieval town or the open place of the baroque order. Thus this paved area, adapted primarily to wheeled traffic, became also park, promenade, and playground: a grim park, a dusty promenade, a dangerous playground.

Even where overcrowding of the land did not exist—for example in many of the towns of Midland America—the broad street was taken as a peculiar symbol of progress; so that it was laid out with an amplitude that bore no functional relation to its present or potential use. The value of such street planning was largely decorative: it was a symbol of *possible* traffic, *possible* commercial opportunity, *possible* conversion into more intensive uses: it thus provided an extra excuse for the fantastic land values that were sometimes optimistically tagged onto the abutting properties. The surviving civic traditions of New England were not better shown than in the fact that towns like Pittsfield and New Bedford, though submitting to industrialization, kept conservatively to narrow streets—thirty to sixty feet in width—and thereby eased the burden of taxes on the adjacent houses and gardens. They thus kept some of the advantages that a new generation of planners was to re-discover in the platting of the modern industrial garden village at the end of the nineteenth century.

All over the Western World during the nineteenth century new cities were founded and old ones extended themselves along the lines I have just described. The first sign of a boom would be the extension of skeleton streets, consisting of curbstones, and standpipes for the water system. The multiplication of these streets unnecessarily widened the city and added to the amount of expensive pavement, expensive sewers and water mains, permitted growth to take place in the most costly fashion possible, by scattered individual houses, instead of by compact settlements, and increased the unnecessary burden of man-hours spent in transportation. The better all these facilities were from the technical standpoint, the worse they often proved in terms of social values: money was being spent prematurely, sometimes spent on the wrong functions, usually in the wrong order.

The pecuniary values derived from urban growth were roughly in proportion to the size of the city, the importance of its commercial life, and the density of its population. Did not the financiers and industrialists who governed the nineteenth century towns regard growth as the very essence of civic success? Each new city made a chart of its increase in population and predicted its future as a great metropolis of its region. At the beginning of its growth, the citizens of Toledo, Ohio, proved statistically to their own satisfaction that by the end of the nineteenth century it would be greater than Chicago or New York. This belief in unlimited growth was pervasive. People gambled on such growth, and then tried to put a bottom under their hopes by deliberately attracting business and industry and population away from competing towns: sometimes by gifts of land, even factory buildings, without ever demanding that the manufacturers who settled in the town guarantee a wage level high enough to keep the new workers from being a public liability. New York, indeed, not only built the Erie Canal to ensure her connection with the hinterland but managed later, through securing differential freight rates worked out at the expense of other towns, to maintain her monopoly of the oceanic and continental traffic routes.

The rectangular street and block system, projectable indefinitely toward the horizon, was the universal expression of capitalistic fantasies. The abstract street-net, with its lots selling and renting by the front-foot, became the dominant expression of the city. The hope for a steady rise in the unearned increment was at its lowest in the meaner factory towns: it achieved its maximum of feverish excitement in the great commercial and political centers. So far from expressing utilitarian interests (other than profit) these plans carried the system of absolutist abstractions even farther away from reality. Paleotechnic planning had the mechanical regularity of the baroque without its coherence: the despotic restrictions without the esthetic mastery and the visual compensations. Even when a great piece of planning was undertaken, as in the conversion of the old wall around Köln into a boulevard, the bordering houses would, stylistically speaking, present a picture of dull esthetic caprice: so-called individuality.

The ultimate unit in this rectangular street platting, the atom of mechanical design, was the individual rectangular plot into which each block was divided. Rarely, in big cities, was the width of this plot greater than twenty feet; often, as in parts of Baltimore, it was only fifteen or twelve: but the depth might be a hundred or a hundred and twenty-five feet. As long as row houses were two rooms deep, this platting was tolerable; but as soon as the need for more dwelling space grew, the natural line of expansion was not laterally, to embrace a second costly plot, but backward, to eat up the backyard areas and to increase thereby the sunless interior space. Bad enough for individual houses: worse when the same system of lot-units constricted the building of multiple-family houses or office buildings.

The desire to utilize every square foot of rentable space possessed the owner, even when he was building for his own use, and not for sheer pecuniary exploitation; and in its search for profits it often over-reached itself, for an overcrowded plan does not necessarily bring the maximum financial return. Cumbrous, uneconomic plans, with a maximum amount of wasteful corridor space and dark ill-ventilated rooms, characterized the two-family houses, the three deckers, the higher tenements. And the habit of letting the shape of the individual lot determine the plan and layout of the house dominated the imagination of the architect: he lost the ability to design freely in more comprehensive units, built for common living and not for individual division, individual ownership, individual sale. The individual rectangular lot was his sole determinant. It needed the social criticism of the present generation, backed by detailed cost analysis, to compel the architect to think in terms of light, insolation, open space, communal grouping; and even today, so deeply embedded is the pecuniary order of thinking, it is hard for the architect fully to embrace his freedom.

In short: as practical urban design, the dominant method of planning was simply a bad dream. Millions of people are still living in the midst of blighted areas, destitute of civic comeliness, paying bitter tribute day by day to the collective hallucinations that governed the layout of the paleotechnic town.

11: A Close-up of Coketown

One may grant that at the tempo at which industrialism was introduced into the Western World, the problem of building adequate cities was almost insoluble. The premises which made these operations possible also limited their human success. How build a coherent city out of the efforts of a thousand competing individualists who knew no law but their own sweet will? How integrate new mechanical functions in a new type of plan that could be laid out and speedily developed—if the very essence of such integration depended upon the firm control of public authorities who often did not exist, or who, when they did exist, exercised no powers except those specifically granted by the state, which put individual property rights at the top. How provide a multitude of new utilities and services for workers who could not afford to rent any but the most destitute types of shelter? How create a good physical plan for social functions that themselves remained abortive? It was small wonder that almost the only examples of good planning were on traditional lines: planning flourished better in historic cities, under the guidance of a surviving baroque bureaucracy (as in Paris and München) than in those newer centers where a fresh start could, theoretically, have been made.

Cities that still contained vital residues of medieval tradition, like Ulm, sometimes managed, through the slow tempo of their growth and a bold policy of large-scale municipal land ownership, to effect the transition with relatively little loss. Where industry came in explosively, however, as in Nürnberg, the results were as vile as in towns that had no historic shell whatever. And in the New World, towns were built as late as 1906 (Gary, Indiana) with no regard for any physical features except the location of the industrial plant. The very century that boasted its mechanical conquests and its scientific prescience left its social processes to chance, as if the scientific habit of mind had exhausted itself upon machines, and was not capable of advancing further. The torrent of energy that was tapped from the coal beds ran downhill with the least possible improvement of the environment: the mill-villages, the factory agglomerations, were socially more crude than the feudal villages of the Middle Ages.

The new urban emergent, the coal-agglomeration, which Patrick Geddes called the conurbation, was neither isolated in the country nor attached to a historic core. It spread in a mass of relatively even density over scores and sometimes hundreds of square miles. There were no real centers in this urban massing: no institutions capable of uniting its members into an active city life. Only the sects, the fragments, the social debris of old institutions remained, left like the flotsam of a great river after the flood has receded: a no-man's land of social life. These new cities not merely failed for the most part to produce art, science, or culture: they failed at first even to import them from older centers. When a surplus was locally created, it was promptly drained off elsewhere: the rentiers and financiers employed it upon personal luxuries, or upon philanthropies, like that of Carnegie's Music Hall in New York, which often benefited the capital cities long before any similar bequests were made to the region from which the riches were originally drawn.

Approach more closely the paleotechnic town: examine it with eye, ear, nose, skin. The ordinary observer, because of the growing contrast with the emerging neotechnic environment, can at last see what only poets like Hugo or Ruskin or Morris saw a hundred years ago: a reality which the philistines, tangled in their utilitarian web of dreams, alternately denied as a sentimental exaggeration or greeted with enthusiasm as an indisputable mark of "progress."

Night spread over the coal-town: its prevailing color was black. Black clouds of smoke rolled out of the factory chimneys, and the railroad yards, which often cut clean into the town, mangling the very organism, spread soot and cinders everywhere. The invention of artificial illuminating gas was an indispensable aid to this spread: Murdock's invention dates back to the end of the eighteenth century, and during the next generation its use widened, first in factories, then in homes, first in big cities, later in small centers; for without its aid work would frequently have been stopped by smoke and fog. The manufacture of illuminating gas within the confines of the towns became a characteristic new feature: the huge gas tanks reared their bulk over the urban landscape, great structures, on the scale of a cathedral: indeed, their tracery of iron, against an occasional clear lemon-green sky at sunrise, was one of the most pleasant esthetic elements in the new order.

Such structures were not necessarily evil; indeed, with sufficient care in their segregation they might have been handsome. What was atrocious was the fact that, like every other building in the new towns, they were dumped almost at random; the leakage of escaping gas scented the so-called gas-house districts, and not surprisingly these districts frequently became among the most degraded sections of the city. Towering above the town, polluting its air, the gas tanks symbolized the dominance of "practical" interests over life-needs.

Night had already come into the pottery districts in the eighteenth century through the use of cheap salt glazes; now it closed in everywhere, in Sheffield and Birmingham, in Pittsburgh and Lille. In this new environment black clothes were only a protective coloration, not a form of mourning; the black stovepipe hat was almost a functional design. The oil and smudge of soft coal spat everywhere; even those who washed their hands left a rim of undissolved grease around the side of the washbowl. Add to these constant smudges on flesh and clothing the finely divided particles of iron from the grinding and sharpening operations, the unused chlorine from the soda works, the clouds of acrid dust from the cement plant, the various by-products of other chemical industries: these things smarted the eyes, rasped the throat and lungs, lowered the general tone, even when they did not produce on contact any definite disease. As for the reek of coal itself, it is perhaps not a disagreeable one: man with his long savage past has become fond of musty odors: so perhaps its chief misdemeanor was that it supplanted, and made people insensitive to, other smells.

Under such conditions, one must have all one's senses blunted in order to be happy; and first of all, one must lose one's taste. This loss of taste had an effect upon diet: even well-to-do people began to eat canned goods and stale foods, when fresh ones were available, because they could no longer tell the difference. The loss of elementary taste-discrimination extended to other departments than food: color-discrimination became feeble, too: the darker tones, the soberer colors, the dingier mixtures, were preferred to pure bright colors, and both the Pre-Raphaelites and the Impressionist painters were reviled by the bourgeoisie because their pure colors were thought "unnatural" and "inartistic." If an occasional touch of bright color was left, it was only in the signs on the hoardings—for Coleman's mustard or Reckitt's blue—paper surfaces that remained cheerful because they frequently had to be changed.

Dark, colorless, acrid, evil-smelling, this new environment was. All these qualities lowered human efficiency and required extra compensation in washing and bathing and sanitation—or at the last extreme, in medical treatment. The cash expenditure on cleaning alone was no small expenditure in the paleotechnic town, at least after the need for cleanliness itself was acknowledged. Take one item alone from a typical paleotechnic survival: Pittsburgh today. Its smoke pollution began early, for a print in 1849 shows it in full blast. Today the annual cost of keeping Pittsburgh cleaned has been estimated at $1,500,000 for extra laundry work, $750,000 for extra general cleaning, and $60,000 for extra curtain cleaning. This estimate, some $2,310,000 per year, does not include losses due to the corrosion of buildings or the increased costs of painting woodwork, nor yet the extra costs of lighting during periods of smog. So much for pecuniary losses. But what of the incalculable losses through disease, through ill-health, through all the forms of psychological deterioration from apathy to outright neurosis? The fact that such losses do not lend themselves to objective measurement does not make them non-existent.

Indifference to these forms of devitalization during the paleotechnic period rested mainly on invincible ignorance. In Technics and Civilization I quoted the indignation and surprise of a leading apologist for this civilization, Ure, over the testimony offered by the acute physicians called before Sadler's Factory Investigation Committee. These physicians referred to the experiments made by Dr.

Edwards of Paris upon the growth of tadpoles, proving that sunlight
was essential to their development. From this they concluded—we
now know with complete justification—that it was equally necessary
to the growth of children. Ure's proud answer was that the gas
lighting of factories was a sufficient substitute for the sun. So contemptuous were these utilitarians of nature and well-tried human custom that they brought up more than one generation upon a devitalized diet, based purely on the consumption of calories. That diet has
been modified during the last twenty years by a fresh budget of
scientific knowledge. Unfortunately, the paleotechnic environment is
less amenable to correction; and it still casts its blight over tens of
millions of people.

Next to dirt, the new towns boasted another distinction, equally
appalling to the senses. The baneful effects of this blight have been
recognized only in recent years, thanks to advances in technics not
unconnected with that typical neotechnic invention, the telephone. I
refer to noise. Let me quote an ear-witness account of Birmingham
in the middle of the nineteenth century.

"In no town in the world are the mechanical arts more noisy:
hammerings incessantly on the anvil; there is an unending clang of
engines; flame rustles, water hisses, steam roars, and from time to
time, hoarse and hollow, rises the thunder of the proofing house
[where firearms are tested]. The people live in an atmosphere vibrating with clamor; and it would seem as if their amusement had caught
the general tone, and become noisy, like their inventions." The indifference to clang and racket was typical. Did not the manufacturers
of England keep Watt from reducing the noise made by his recipro-
cating engine because they wanted auricular evidence of its power?

Today, numerous experiments have established the fact that noise
can produce profound physiological changes: music can keep down
the bacteria count in milk; and by the same token definite ailments,
like stomach ulcers, seem to be aggravated by the strain of living,
say, within sound of an elevated railroad. The diminishment of working efficiency through noise has likewise been clearly established.
Unfortunately, the paleotechnic environment seemed specially designed to create a maximum amount of noise: the early hoot of the
factory whistle, the shriek of the locomotive, the clank and urge of

the old-fashioned steam engine, the wheeze and screech of the shafts and belting, the click and whirr of the loom, the pounding of the drop hammer, the mutter and snuffle of the conveyor, the shouts of the workers who worked and lived amid this varied clamor—all these sounds abetted the general assault on the senses.

When reckoning up the vital efficiency of the country as compared with the city, or the medieval town as opposed to the paleotechnic town, one must not forget this important factor in health. Nor have recent improvements in certain departments, the use of rubber heels and rubber tires, for instance, lessened the strength of the indictment. The noise of the gasoline driven motor cars and trucks in a busy city, as they start up, change gears, acquire speed, is a sign of their deplorable technical immaturity. Had the energy that has been put into styling hoods gone into the design of a silent engine, the neotechnic city would not be as backward as its paleotechnic predecessor in the matter of noise.

Recent experiments with sound in Chicago show that if one grades noise by percentages up to 100 per cent which is the sound— like an artillery cannonade—that would drive one mad if continued over an extended period, the countryside has only from eight to ten per cent noise, the suburbs fifteen, the residential districts of the city twenty-five per cent, commercial districts thirty per cent and industrial districts thirty-five. These broad lines would doubtless hold almost anywhere during the last century and a half, though perhaps the upper limits were higher. One must remember, too, that the paleotechnic towns made no effort to separate factories from workers' homes; so that in many towns noise was omnipresent, in the day and often in the night.

Considering this new urban area on its lowest physical terms, without reference to its social facilities or its culture, it is plain that never before in recorded history had such vast masses of people lived in such a savagely deteriorated environment. The galley slaves of the Orient, the wretched prisoners in the Athenian silver mines, the depressed proletariat in the insulae of Rome—these classes had known, no doubt, a similar foulness; but never was human blight so widespread; never before had it so universally been accepted as normal —normal and inevitable. The point becomes all the more appalling

[TOP] Coketown, alias Smokeover, alias Mechanicsville, alias Manchester, Leeds, Birmingham, Merseburg, Essen, Elberfeld, Lille, Roubaix, Newark, Pittsburgh, or Youngstown. Here, Preston: a cotton town in England. The factory units in the center, and the gas tanks on the right pre-empt the space: by the inefficient utilization of coal in the steam engine and domestic earth, the smoke of the chimneys covers the landscape, blotting out the sun, rasping the lungs. Rows of workers' houses crowd close under the shadows of the factories and scatter into the distance: no zoning, no open spaces except the railroad yards in the distance or the mean streets, with their meanly standardized and wretchedly planned dwellings: no parks, no gardens, no playgrounds. The poor mechanical order of foreground violated, even on its own terms, by the disorder of the background. (*Photograph: Ewing Galloway, Aerofilms*)

[MIDDLE LEFT] Railroad yards and steel plants in Cleveland, Ohio. The railroad and the industrial plant controlled paleotechnic urban development, even the surface order of rectangular planning was frequently disrupted by their superior claims. Smoke pollution was constant; noise and dirt ubiquitous. The railroad, so far from being used to zone heavy industries in the open country, away from the areas of residence, brought them into the heart of the town, until land values rose high enough to compel a partial removal of ironworks and chemical plants to the outskirts. Paleotechnic filth, disorder, and poverty remain as a widespread survival in towns, big and little, throughout the world: witness Boston and Washington no less than Chicago and Detroit. (*Photograph: Ewing Galloway*)

[MIDDLE RIGHT] Steel and armaments: the big Krupp works at Essen. In the foreground, close to the mills, are the workers' houses. Contrast this formation with that of the neotechnic order shown on Plate 29. While armament manufacture, like mining, often provided the worst conditions of housing to begin with, the example of Godin at Guise and Krupp at Essen showed the possibility of a different order of domestic building under industrialism.

[BOTTOM] Another type of paleotechnic disorder: Hanley, a pottery town, which came to life in the eighteenth century with the introduction of the Chinese technique of making porcelain and the rise of great industrial fabricators and designers, above all Wedgwood. One of the Five Towns so lovingly described by Arnold Bennett, himself a product of them, in An Old Wives' Tale and Clayhanger. Pottery kilns placed next to dwellings, as if there were no difference between a furnace, a kiln, and a domestic workshop. The mass production of pottery for eating vessels and wash-bowls, toilet bowls, and urinals was a genuine triumph of the paleotechnic period: but as with so many of its short-sighted achievements, the means often defied and partly annulled the end. (*Photograph: Ewing Galloway*)

[TOP LEFT] Manchester Cotton Factory: a great working unit formed about the steam engine and its connected shafting. In such factories the typical paleotechnic inventions were quickly introduced, such as gas-lighting to overcome inadequate interior lighting even by day, and elevators, more than a generation before their use in office buildings or residences. Schinkel, viewing these factories, felt that they were prophetic of the new architecture: not observing that the architecture was already in existence in the superior vernacular forms that prevailed in England between 1780 and 1830.

[TOP RIGHT] London market: continuation of the busy huckstering of the medieval town. Like the Halles in Paris, this building shows current technical innovations: slender iron posts, sheet iron and glass roof. Growth and concentration of the food market was an inevitable accompaniment of paleotechnic city agglomeration: but only a few cities, like Baltimore, continued the tradition of the large, centralized neighborhood market. (See Zola's Le Ventre de Paris.)

[SECOND LEFT] Celebration of the opening of a railroad in the forties. Section by section the railroad extended its environment from mountain top to port, quickening the tempo of life, binding together distant communities, widening the market, and developing trunk lines and express routes at the expense of older forms of transportation. Its main freight was and still is coal.

[THIRD LEFT] Rally of the striking Gas Workers' Union in the eighteen-eighties: a typical act of the supreme paleotechnic drama—the struggle between the haves and the have-nots for money and power and security. So great was the terror of the working classes on the part of their exploiters that, as the Hammonds document, army barracks were deliberately scattered over the industrial towns in England: an army of occupation. Similar building of militia armories, in heavily defensive buildings, took place in the United States after the seventies.

[SECOND RIGHT] London slum, drawn from life by Gustave Doré for Harper's Weekly. A hell of depression and misery and hopeless degradation. Foul odors, vermin, vile food, drunkenness and promiscuity were the chief by-products of its depauperate and crowded existence: crime and disease were but the inevitable psychological and physiological responses.

[BOTTOM] Peace meeting in Exeter Hall. Sweetness, light, pious hopes, and unrelieved futility: the impossibility of a doctrine of Peace and Progress based upon the struggle for existence, bitter economic competition, and the survival of the fittest—i.e., the more rapacious and brutal types. Oratory largely took the place of the more personal drama of the theater during the Victorian period: issues, questions, problems, matters to be talked about, debated, framed in resolutions, and voted on occupied attention: a habit that placed a premium upon the eloquent verbalists and flouted the different procedures of the artist, scientist, and engineer, with their technique of planning and design and experiment.

when one realizes, not only the absolute unfitness of this environment for human life, but its extraordinary quantitative multiplication. In 1850 there were but six towns with over one hundred thousand population in the United States, and but five in Germany. By 1900 there were thirty-six such places in the United States and thirty-three in Germany.

12: The Old Curiosity Shop

We have followed in detail the process of decomposition and unbuilding in the new industrial and commercial city: we have watched a bleak ideology and a coarse practical routine deface the landscape, undermine the body, desiccate the spirit. If our gaze has been narrowed to the factory and the slum, it is because they were the new dominants, and because quantitatively they occupied so large a space.

The survivals of the past, including many useful ones, capable of being re-conditioned for life at a higher level than the buildings that replaced them, were swept away in almost every growing city during the nineteenth century in a fever and a fury of demolition. Old open spaces were built over, and old buildings were hastily destroyed: trim medieval market-places became dusty plazas, and quiet, well-insulated residential quarters became opened up to traffic, through the systematic widening and straightening of old streets. A factory, a new block of offices, a railroad yard, had the right of way over the finest monuments of the past. One cannot object to such replacement when the new is in any sense the equivalent of the old. But in many cases the new building was a tawdry makeshift, thrusting its way into the picture, not because it better expressed the vital social needs of the new day, but because it offered some callous philistine the opportunity for speculative gain.

The same disintegration took place in every other part of the city's culture: it is effectively symbolized in the new architectural forms.

There was, indeed, a moment in the development of form when in England it seemed as if a new synthesis might be created. Between 1780 and 1830, owing to the strong vernacular impulses that persisted, it seemed as if the false alternatives of classicism and romanticism would be thrown off. Middle class houses were built in this period that might—had they become universal forms—have met halfway the best of Manchester's factories. Schinkel, when he visited Manchester, had an intuition that in these new buildings the source of a new form could be found: had he looked at the squares and row houses of Bloomsbury he would have found their direct equivalent. And the design that accompanied Robert Owen's proposed factory colony even suggested how these simple, common-sense forms might have been worked out in terms of workers' housing: his plan is still sounder than a great many more elaborate housing developments that have been put up in England during the last generation.

In all these various initiatives there was an early anticipation of an effective synthesis of modern materials, modern methods of construction, and modern needs: symbols of positive science and cooperative effort. Soane in England showed it in some of his work; so did Schinkel in Berlin; but the proof of its soundness is that the same spirit appeared, perhaps even more clearly, in the work of anonymous builders and designers, in bold and beautiful forms. This mutation—although real—was swamped in the proliferation of fashionable architectural weeds: noxious weeds like the filthy factory slums, sentimental weeds like the cottages and churches of the gothic revival, weeds transported from arid areas, like the brittle classic structures that became schools, banks, court houses, government offices. By the middle of the nineteenth century the mutations were so far lost that when Philip Webb designed the Red House for William Morris, he went back to the vernacular form of the late seventeenth century, romanticized further by ogive patterns in the brickwork: a type of house with relatively small windows—instead of beginning at the point where the best domestic building of a generation earlier had left off.

Not merely was there a break in form. The movement toward synthesis was further handicapped by the earlier disruption of symbols. Almost all the leading architects in Europe, from Wren onward, exhibited this disruption. Who would guess that the Schinkel who projected the clean design for a department store in Berlin also designed extremely romantic gothic churches, while he dreamed in his paintings of buildings even more deeply saturated with wild mysticism and mysterious gloom? Such a gap between building and faery, between architecture as the flesh and bones of civilization and architecture as stylistic fancy dress, had been opened up indeed by the architects of the Renascence. But they at least had the justification of believing for the moment that their fancy dress was reality: they read the old texts: they aped the old gestures: they looked upon themselves as continuators of a more noble manner of life, once lived by the Greeks and the Romans. In this respect, most of the new classicists, the new medievalists, the eclectics, were humbugs: they made no attempt to reduce the distance between their background and their life. Though the medievalists might affect piety and preach a return to the Middle Ages, their efforts were as half-hearted and their buildings were as sterile as the Renascence forms they derided.

In short, the gothic revival, from first to last, from Horace Walpole to Pugin, from Scott to Ralph Adams Cram, remained the work of a sect. Even when it sought to embrace every element in civilization, its premises were antagonistic to that mission: it rejected the best along with the worst. As in religion, the architectural sects multiplied throughout the nineteenth century: so that, by the middle of the period, the hope for a common form based upon the prevalence of some narrow set of historic types was doubly lost. Though once Ruskin foolishly suggested that salvation lay in going back to a single style, that of the thirteenth century in Lombardy, his own historic interpetations proved, if they proved anything, that this was as impossible as the suggestion that the novels of Dickens and Reade should be cast in the mold of The Divine Comedy or The Song of Roland.

The age demanded new forms, for new functions had come into life, and a multitude of new associations and organizations, a new kind of civic ritual, had grown up in the city—along with a new attitude toward the universe and a new feeling for nature. None of these demands could be framed or satisfied in the old forms: none of these new feelings could be symbolized in a Roman column or in a gothic vault. When the architects of the period resurrected old symbols, they felt the plutonian touch of this new society: in spirit, if not in material, they turned to iron. Only in their plans—as Dr. Behrendt has shown in relation to Persius—did they advance to contemporary ground. Byzantine cottages and Swiss chalets, Italian villas and Moorish palaces, began to fill the Victorian landscape in the villa quarters around the British and the American cities. Germany, more insulated before 1870, attempted with sentimental clumsiness to recapture architectural "Bilder aus der deutschen Vergangenheit."

By the third quarter of the nineteenth century, the disruption had become complete. A single avenue might contain, as the result of a decade's building, souvenirs from cultures millennia apart and from regions at the remotest ends of the earth, now modified with cast-iron ornament or "original" embellishments, now copied with photographic lifelessness. Under this impulse every city, in proportion to the available wealth and historical scholarship, tended to become an Old Curiosity Shop: a junkheap of discarded styles, cut off completely from the culture that had given them a rational meaning.

What was the result of this cultural rag-picking? Variety? No: the solidification of chaos: an order no less mechanical in its unexpected façades and its reproductive ornament than the meanest bye-law street of identical houses. Every avenue was designed in accordance with the most inexorable of laws—the law of chance. The street picture lost all consistence: it was a jumble of competing styles, carried out in no common material, ordered to no common visual end. The ground plan might be that of a rectangular plot in a rectangular block; but even that fact did not make for order, since a large building might be placed alongside a shabby cramped building, and a church might be dwarfed by a nearby warehouse. The actual design of the façade and the evolution of the interior as often as not denied the limited surface order. Individualistic style competition—mistakenly looked upon as a sign of a quite different state, individuality—took the place of that collective mastery of form which characterizes a vital culture.

Meanwhile, the only contemporary style that manifested vitality, that of the mechanical age itself, was carefully kept out of the architect's training. Even the engineer, seeking confirmation from the esthete, bashfully hid his clean forms under melancholy iron foliage. And as if the architectural picture itself was not sufficiently chaotic, a crisscross of telegraph wires, trolley poles, railroad bridges, elevated structures, and competitive advertisements completed the visual disorder.

This collapse of form was of course as visible in the interiors of buildings as on the streets. Within the home it was associated with the proliferation of ugly sub-baroque decoration and with the cult of comfort. Shall we say that this hard-bitten age sacrificed all the older esthetic pleasures of ear and eye to the pleasures of tactile relaxation? Instead of beauty, a new quality was demanded—comfort. Ottomans, ranged with pillows, to meet each cushion of flesh with a softer cushion of horse-hair or down: super-upholstered chairs, stuffed and over-stuffed. There is some reason to think that the Victorian middle classes, who could afford warm bedrooms, nevertheless made love by preference beneath blankets, under cover of darkness: thus reducing sexual intercourse to purely tactile terms.

Bare was a term of reproach in Victorian decoration. One of Conan Doyle's early characters almost goes insane because placed in a bare, white-washed room, and Tolstoy was regarded as a saint by his disciples because his bedroom was in the Victorian sense "unfurnished." Just as nakedness of the body caused a flutter of shocked reproof, even when exhibited in statues, so naked architectural forms not merely seemed "harsh": they seemed indecent. The change took place early: note the "carpenter-gothic" details with which even the excellent Downing improved the severe and excellent farmhouse architecture of the early nineteenth century. And as the outer environment in the paleotechnic town became more bleak, the domestic interiors filled up and spilled over with ornament: every square foot of the wall must be covered with pictures, bad reproductions, if not originals: every square foot of floor must be covered with carpets, which caught and held the dust and prolonged the menial duties of those who were supposed to keep them clean: every shelf must be crowded with vases, knick-knacks, souvenirs, shells from the seashore, minerals from distant mountains, sandalwood boxes from India, lacquered trays from China, cloisonné from Japan. Double and triple layers of hangings obscured the light and filtered out a little dirt from the street, but in turn became dirty: table covers, with tassels or embroidery, and covers upon the table covers, and doilies upon those, formed another rampart of decoration. Wax flowers under glass cases, or a left-over ormolu clock: dried flowers in the fireplace in summer: immortelles in a wreath around the portrait of a deceased member of the family—dust and desiccation, fancywork and ornament: in short, the art of the what-not.

In this pursuit of interior decoration the middle class dwelling, like the city outside, became an old curiosity shop; and though up to the eighties the Victorians often avoided historicism, and made their furniture in shapes whose incredible ugliness was the product of an active, if appalling, imagination, after this a reviving cult of the antique completed the parallel. As for the worker's dwellings, imitating all these fashions in the only forms open to the worker's purse, they were little better than a rubbish heap. But no matter how sordid the room, it would not be bare: I have lived in a Bloomsbury lodging house in which every vase on the mantel-shelf was broken, and had thus lost the only value it ever possessed esthetically: that of being whole. The cult of the formless, it would seem, could go no further than it did in decoration. It prevailed over the whole period that began around 1830; its worst inroads were marked by the atrocities duly celebrated in the Great Exhibition of 1851 in London, and of 1876 in Philadelphia; and it did not receive its first sharp check until the eighties, when the esthetic movement took shape under Whistler, William Morris and their varied collaborators. Comfort was associated with ugly superfluity: misplaced art: purposeless manufacture: decorative dirt.

And as form broke up, formlessness itself was theoretically systematized: the age made a virtue of necessity. For the spirit of romanticism, as it took shape in the eighteenth century ruin and the informal landscape, or in the nineteenth century Jardin Anglais, was essentially a denial of the importance of form: more than that, it was a justification of the processes of decomposition. Shrinking from the problem of orderly collective control, people overvalued the wild, the irregular, the unrestricted—forgetting the fact that the wilderness itself could not continue to exist, on the edge of the paleotechnic environment, without eventually invoking bold administrative supervision by the community over the land and the land-uses. For nature to be untouched and unspoiled, men must collectively determine the appropriate means of exploitation and refrain from opening up to competitive ownership that which should be sequestered for the large common good.

"Beauty alone," observed Sir Uvedale Price, one of the chief exponents of romantic design, "has hitherto been aimed at." Beauty, in the romantic mind, meant a certain utilitarian order and purposefulness: the new planners set their minds in another direction and sought to preserve—and if necessary to introduce—the rough, the unexpected, the decayed, the disorganized, the dilapidated. They preferred deformed trees to those that were well-grown, rocky landscapes to lush, nourishing meadows, and the more scraggly conifers to rounded symmetrical trees like the horse-chestnut and the maple. What they sought was not a livable landscape but a picturesque landscape. And the same animus that they displayed toward nature had a part in their conception of architecture: hence their fake abbeys, their newly built ruins, such as the crazy castle of Pichelsberg near Potsdam, done in the English fashion.

In a sense, this worship of national history recognized something that the classic architects with their static forms tended to overlook—the dynamic quality of time, the effect of duration upon form. But unfortunately the romantics centered their interest in the last process in the cycle of growth—the stage of decay and death. They should have been primitives and have begun, so to say, with a live baby: but in fact they were decadents and began with a corpse.

In fine, this cult of the picturesque was a disguised form of laissez-faire—applied wholesale to the environment. The accidental, the unforeseen, and the perverse became new values. Whatever could not be reduced to an orderly pattern, whatever denied man's collective control and defied his organization and avoided the human measure, was exalted.

While this cult had its origin in the landscape painting of the seventeenth century, as the very word picturesque indicates, it was carried to a logical conclusion in the paintings of Turner, the contemporary of Watt and Bentham and Stephenson. For Turner pushed the belief in formlessness, symbolically, to its final state: all the solid realities of the earth, buildings, trees, men, were dissolved in his atmospheric effects of mist and cloud. Given a sufficiently heavy blanket of fog, the new industrial environment itself became, as it were, disembodied. Turner seized that fact and turned it to creative uses. Behind the curtain of atmospheric effects, architecture disappeared: a castle on a bold headland became an amiable blur; so did a factory or a railroad viaduct by a foul river. The general effect was to make man's most strenuous efforts at disciplined expression seem unimportant or insignificant. To be successful, from this point of view, buildings must fall into ruin, and orderly plans must miscarry.

In this manner, romanticism was anti-communal and anti-architectural, for all its tendency to exalt the institutional order of the Middle Ages. Lawlessness was the only rule it recognized and the wilderness was its only proper home. As a counterpoise to a sessile routine and a humdrum institutional life, there was a need, no doubt, for this new expression of the spirit. But applied to urban buildings, such an animus turned the city into a mechanical jungle, which was in fact the urban counterpart of the landscape park, as developed theoretically in the writings of a Repton, a Gilpin, a Price, a Downing—little though these romantics might have been prepared to recognize their saturnine urban offspring. The unexpected, the disorderly, the dilapidated, prevailed to such an extent in the cities of the nineteenth century, both new and old, that the very precision and articulateness of a good mechanical order, which at very least one might reasonably have expected to emerge in the new civilization, were lost. As an expression of a machine culture, or as an environment planned intelligently for mechanized production, the new cities were defective. Much of the "new" architecture of the last twenty years, with its one-sided glorification of the factory as a *standard* of form, must be recognized as an extremely belated attempt to build the utilitarian city.

13: The Triumph of Iron

There was however one department of building that occasionally showed something better than picturesque sprawl or dead standardized ugliness: that which was based upon the use of iron. Here, if anywhere, the paleotechnic period excelled; and here it found its first approach to a coherent form, in the planning and building of its great iron structures.

Inevitably, when the utilitarians thought of forms for their new

industrial fabrics, they thought either of converting iron into natural materials, or natural materials into iron. The first impulse was
silly: the imitations in cheap woods and metals of the grain of a
fine natural wood was a typical triumph of cheap romantic decoration, like the translation of stucco into marble in the baroque period:
Schinkel actually brought this perversity back to Germany from
England. But the other impulse was honest enough, given the new
necessities of life and the new powers of the machine. In discussing
the architecture of the new Smithsonian Institution, Robert Dale
Owen predicted that the time would come when iron would be commonly used in all sorts of buildings. Long before, Faustus Verantius
in the sixteenth century had suggested that iron might be used for
walls and for the roofs of big buildings, like churches.

At last these predictions and hopes were fulfilled. Toward the end
of the eighteenth century the first iron bridge in the Western World
—China had long known them—was built over the Severn. And early
in the nineteenth century iron was used to frame the roof of the
Central Markets in Paris; for iron's great quality in spanning space,
its strength in cross section both under compression and tension, gave
it a special place in such structures. The first original step in the application of iron to building, however, came toward the end of the
eighteenth century in England: the erection of glass and iron conservatories. Such hot-houses were an eotechnic invention: Albertus
Magnus, who had a reputation in the thirteenth century for being
a magician, showed flowers growing in mid-winter to one of his
visitors—presumably in a glass hot-house. And these conservatories,
either as an annex to the house or a special feature of the garden,
had become common in the great country houses of France and
England.

This effort finally crystallized—and the symbolism is appropriate
in every respect—in the design of the Crystal Palace in London by
Joseph Paxton, the engineer, who had achieved his reputation as a
builder of hot-houses. The great Crystal Palace in Hyde Park
sheltered the Industrial Exhibition of 1851, the first such exhibition
to be conducted on an international scale. Both as a technical feat
and as an imaginative application of modern design to modern materials, the Crystal Palace was perhaps the foremost contribution to

building that had been made since the development of the ogive and the flying buttress. For the heavy forms of masonry it substituted the relative lightness of the iron skeleton; for the solid masses and enclosures of the old-fashioned supporting walls, the new design substituted open space bounded by mere filaments of glass. What was spacious became more spacious by interposing only the lines of construction between the eye and the landscape or sky without.

In the thirteenth century cathedrals, in the sixteenth century mansions and town houses, in the early nineteenth century dwellings in England, people had not been afraid of such broad surfaces of glass. Now, however, they cowered a little before the possibilities that their mechanical triumphs had opened up to them. When the time came to translate Paxton's daring initiatives into other buildings in the city, the result was a disappointment. James Buckingham, most energetic of Victorian utopian writers, might imagine a new city whose avenues would be covered by iron and glass arcades: such arcades might even be built here and there as an annex to the shopping parade, from Naples to Westminster. But there was no real congruence between this imaginative architectural form and the new environment.

Need I stress the reason? Glass is of all possible building materials the one that most requires a clean atmosphere. Its smooth surface does not absorb dirt and grime, but permits it visibly to accumulate, and in the act of accumulation it loses its own best qualities. Glass could be at its best in the eotechnic Dutch town, woven around canals, with plenty of water and little smoke: but in the paleotechnic town it was in downright contradiction to the rest of the environment: however cheap its original cost, the upkeep in cleaning was prohibitive. Even the brightest of iron and glass department stores, such as the Bon Marché in Paris, speedily looked a little dingy.

Ironically enough, the Victorian blindness to the visible environment exhibited its opacities most profoundly in the use of glass. For the only type of building in which Paxton's construction was repeatedly used was the dirtiest spot in town; the railroad station: the last place where glass could be used with profit. Most of the train-halls of the new stations were great sheds of glass and iron. From the St. Pancras Station in London, built as early as 1866, to the later

stations like that at Frankfort-am-Main or Hamburg, these structures were often, in the abstract, very handsome—especially those
built after the great Hall of Machines in the Paris Exposition of
1889 had achieved something like a perfect engineering and architectural solution of the problem of spanning the space.

But the actual effect of the glass sheds was to keep the smoke and
effluvia of the locomotives from being dissipated at once into the
surrounding air: hence they produced the maximum concentration
of choking gases and dust, to welcome the stranger or speed the
parting guest. Meanwhile the glass covering became almost as
opaque to the sun's rays as it would have been if solid iron or brick
had been used instead. In short, the misuse was ludicrous. Small
wonder that these new types of construction awaited for fuller use
the technological improvements that produced the neotechnic phase:
electricity, the distillation of coal, smokeless cities.

The cheapening of steel through the utilization of the Bessemer
process nevertheless had a direct effect upon architecture. Form
coalesced swiftly in the decade of the eighties, particularly in the
hands of the bold architects who dominated the scene in Chicago.
As a result of competition for central sites within a limited building
area in American cities—a competition originally intensified by the
inadequacy of surface transportation and the lack of instantaneous
oral communication over a distance—the architects of the United
States, uncontrolled by Old World building heights and municipal
regulations, had from the eighteen-sixties onward been pushing up
the height of masonry constructions at the instance of the ground
landlord. In order to go higher, the supporting wall had to be thickened inordinately at the base; and this took away rentable space. A
new material, a different method, were needed.

In the eighteen-forties a New York engineer, James Bogardus, had
introduced iron members as supporting columns and had greatly
opened the face of commercial buildings. Now iron was added for the
horizontal beams; and since iron rapidly loses strength under heat,
the metal members were surrounded by a fire-resistant material.
When these various parts were articulated together, as was first done
theoretically by Leroy Buffington and practically by Major Jenney
in Chicago, first in the Home Insurance Building (1885) and com-

pletely in the Leiter Building (1889), an entirely new type of construction appeared: the iron cage and the curtain wall. This translated into colossal paleotechnic forms the vernacular frame and clapboard construction of the old American farmhouse. The outer wall became a mere boundary of the interior space, as in the Crystal Palace itself; instead of the building's being a shell, it became essentially a skeleton—a skeleton with internal organs for equalizing the temperature and for circulation, with a tough external skin.

This invention greatly simplified difficult constructions; and the more positive architectural talents of the time, like Louis Sullivan, were quick to take advantage of it and to further its logical development. Unfortunately, like so many Janus-headed inventions, it was the antisocial features of this new method that were exploited. The system of construction was used to squeeze the last drop of rent out of a site by overcrowding the land, putting a thousand people on a spot that had hitherto accommodated but a hundred. Result: intensified land speculation, site-crowding, increased traffic congestion— frequently lack of daylight and decent working space within the new buildings. Likewise a constant tendency to pyramid land values and structures, recapitalizing the original values on the basis of prospective congestion, and using the advance in values as an excuse for perpetrating further congestion. Finally, an urban form, towering against the skies, in which the actual living demands of men and women were subordinated at every step to pecuniary considerations.

From a purely esthetic standpoint, the early Chicago skyscraper was a triumph. Essentially it has been unsurpassed by later designs: it must be put alongside the early Manchester cotton mills, the Crystal Palace, the Brooklyn Bridge, and its immediate contemporary, the Eiffel Tower. *These were expressions of the power and order that were inherent in the new mechanical complex.* They were structures purposefully designed to assist the organization of productive machinery, to exhibit goods to large crowds in a well-ventilated building, to enable traffic to pass over a wide body of water, or to serve as a signpost of technological achievement itself: rational means toward rational ends. Such triumphs had little effect upon the ordering of the rest of the environment. In this utilitarian age, the truly mechanical remained an exception; and half-baked compromises in form, the not-yet mechanical, the sentimentalized mechanical, the less-than-adequate mechanical, continued to prevail.

Yet all these forms had a preparatory meaning: a meaning that was to come forth once more with the opening of the neotechnic phase in industry. The Crystal Palace prepared the way for the synthetic materials and the clean surfaces used in neotechnic urban architecture: the Eiffel Tower prepared the way for the electric power pole and the radio transmission tower: the skyscrapers made possible, through their experimental organization, a new type of building with flexible interiors, adjustable from generation to generation to new demands of life. While from the tops of tall steel towers, almost as high as the Eiffel Tower itself, the populace became aware—as from the Ferris wheel and chute-the-chutes of the amusement park—of the new angle of vision of the approaching airplane, soaring and diving through space. Within the common industrial scheme, a new order, an appropriate form, was slowly coalescing at last.

14: Far from the Madding Crowd

Those who valued paleotechnic civilization were inclined to be contemptuous of the countryside; whereas those who were sensitive to rural sights and sounds and who enjoyed rural occupations, fled, when they could, from the blackened walls of Coketown.

Throughout this period the impulse to escape, although it could not cure the diseases of industrialism, took special forms that momentarily counteracted the compulsions of the day's routine and its defilements. For the belligerent, there was war and piracy, for the ambitious, there was colonization in new lands, for the powerful, the planning of parks and landscapes, for the reflective, rambling, musing, botanizing in rural retreats. For the rising middle classes of the nineteenth century the romantic retreat took the form of building villas and suburbs, where the spreading agglomeration of Coketown could be temporarily kept at bay. In the city, Mars and Vulcan had become friends. Venus, neglected, sought the consolations of domesticity in a distant suburb.

The impulse toward suburban living perhaps came directly from the more temporary escape of the watering place or the summer resort. Mr. Van Wyck Brooks has pointed out that in the discovery of almost every important summer resort in America, artists and writers, people who gauged life by other standards than the pragmatic one, were mainly responsible: sensitive to the environment, they served like the hazel wand to indicate the places where the springs of life were still flowing. Unfortunately, the effect of these recreation centers was too limited: even the chosen few who visited them returned eventually to the city to dissipate their vigor and lust of life in its smoky streets. Some more permanent form for the exodus was needed: the answer was the middle class romantic suburb.

In embryo, the modern suburb already existed in the sixteenth century: quite different in function and purpose from the so-called suburb around the medieval town, which often served rather for summer residence and recreation. There is an allusion to the new type in The English Courtier. "The manner of most gentlemen and noblemen also is to house themselves (if they possibly may) in the suburbs of the city, because most commonly, the air there being somewhat at large, the place is healthy, and through the distance from the body of the town, the noise is not much; and so consequently quiet. Also for commodity we find many lodgings, both spacious and roomethy, with gardens and orchards very delectable. So with good government we have as little cause to fear infection there as in the very country; our water is excellent and much better than you have any, on ground and fields most pleasant."

That briefly sums up most of the advantages of the new suburb: pure air and water, quiet, space, rural beauty. As the crowding became more universal during the next three centuries, the demand to get away became more imperious: if one did not leave on one's own initiative the doctor's orders would prescribe it. Soame Jenyns remarked in 1795 that tradesmen's wives who felt suffocated by the smoke of London must have their villas at Clapham; and though this tendency developed more slowly in the pure industrial city, which often knew no alternative possibility, it characterized most of the mixed towns with their infiltration of a rural aristocracy and leisured people. At first, the possibilities of suburban living were limited to those who could afford a horse and carriage of their own, or who could make the daily journey to town by public coach. But by the eighteen-twenties in London—later of course elsewhere—a

[TOP] Tenements in Farringdon Road, London: characteristic of model housing for the working classes in the big cities, whether undertaken on old slum properties or in new areas. An effort to circumvent high land values by overcrowding the land, instead of reducing the living place per family as in less-organized slums. The economies in building cost, sometimes put forward in support of high buildings for urban housing, are offset by higher costs of upkeep when paid specialized services supplant self-service.

[SECOND RIGHT] One of the model houses for the working classes exhibited in the Great Exhibition of 1851. Four flats in a unit equipped with an external stairs. Each had a lobby, a living room with a heating cupboard (150 square feet); scullery with sink, rack, dustshaft, ventilator, meatsafe, coalbin; three bedrooms with external ventilation (one of 150 square feet and two of 50 square feet), and a water closet flushed from a cistern. Hollow brick construction. In terms of mid-nineteenth century standards a superior type: but also an expensive one: which accounts for the relative lack of emulation. Hence the usual alternative was the drab ill-designed "model tenements." The White buildings in Brooklyn were a notable exception before the present generation: though cramped internally they had a *Laubengang* arrangement of apartments and were ranged on the perimeter of a good-sized court.

[THIRD RIGHT] Collins plant at Collinsville, Conn. Axes and edged tools: founded 1828. Early industrialists prided themselves on the superior advantage of such plants located in the countryside; apologists for the factory system alleged that most of the evils imputed to the system were due to urban overcrowding. Industrial villages like Collinsville were typical of New England before 1875, and extended through Ohio into Wisconsin. American factory towns like Syracuse, Rochester, Grand Rapids, to say nothing of Muncie, Indiana (see the Lynds' Middletown) often preserved the cottage system of housing and tree-lined streets: sometimes even the garden plots and the opportunities for hunting and fishing of the simpler agricultural town. But social life in such factory centers remained destitute: often the physical environment, as in the chain of brass towns in the valleys around Waterbury, would be miserably deteriorated.

[BOTTOM] Proposed model industrial village. Here church and school are duly provided for; but the only available open spaces within the neighborhood are the streets: a backward step from the Fuggerei three centuries before.

[LEFT] Portion of Central Park, New York, designed by Olmsted and Vaux: consummate example of romantic planning: deliberate separation of pedestrian paths, carriage drives, and crosstown traffic thoroughfares: a mutation that anticipated the organization of the modern city. By placing houses on these winding roads and paths, set behind a front garden, one arrives (with a few minor changes) at the plan of the romantic nineteenth century suburb or town-extension.

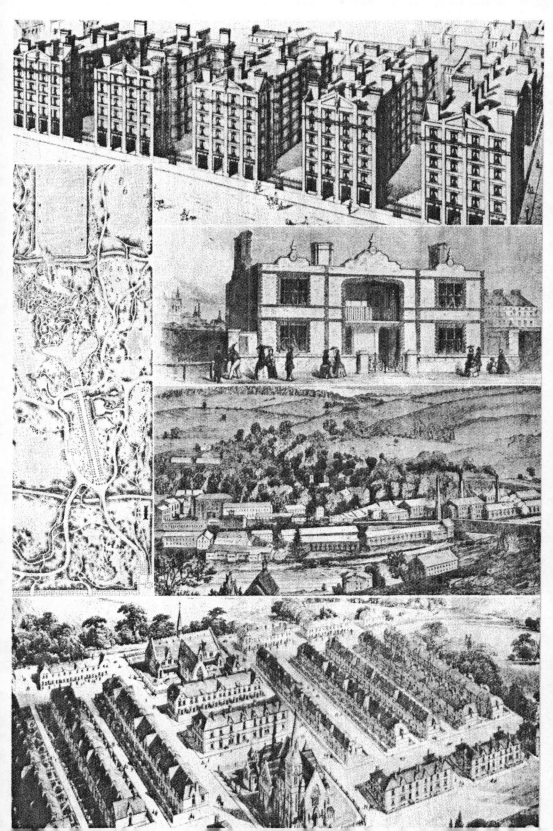

IV: THE INDUSTRIAL CITY   [14] THE PROMISE OF IRON AND GLASS

[TOP LEFT] Rear of the palace at Potsdam. Utilization of glass in hot-houses and shelters was first a royal luxury: it here creates a structure close to the modern factory in lightness and openness and flexibility of internal space. The spread of the hot-house to horticulture is reinforced by the spread of hot-house principles to other types of building. While the hot-house is a primitive form for using solar light and heat, technically more adroit forms for heating and power production are obviously on their way: forms that will demand that unobstructed spread to the sun which characterizes a well-designed and well-oriented modern community—in contrast to the costly artificial horrors of so-called super-cities, as projected by paleotechnic and megalopolitan architects and planners.

[TOP RIGHT] Maison du Peuple in Brussels: the more democratic equivalent of the Settlement House. Designed by Horta: able example of L'Art Nouveau, with a grasp of functional relationships and expression, to say nothing of technical delicacy, sometimes lacking in the more formal cubistic designs that followed. Hull House (1892) and the Whitechapel Art Gallery (1899) show a similar vigor of expression: they were the mutations in the megalopolitan scheme that were to have deep significance for modern types of community design and organization.

[MIDDLE] Crystal Palace: the design of a hot-house builder, Joseph Paxton. This glass and iron structure heralded an epoch. (*Photograph: Ewing Galloway*)

[BOTTOM LEFT] Domestic use of glass in large windows characterized vernacular building from the sixteenth century on. Particularly in England between 1780 and 1830 the row house demonstrated a freedom and a clean adroitness that links it with contemporary building—plain walls, large windows, rational plans and elevations: houses in which domestic ease and comfort were not sacrificed to show. Mirrors and glass walls altered the character of both house and occupants.

[BOTTOM RIGHT] Glasgow Art School (1898) designed by the Scotch architect, Mackintosh. It points to the continued relation between the painter's studio of the nineteenth century and the new expressions of life in architecture. The painters of the nineteenth century led the exodus away from the town into a more vital environment: Fontainebleau, Barbizon, Arles, Worpswede. Their residences and working quarters, with their wide studio windows, brought light and sun into the heart of the living room; while the palettes and forms of the impressionists reinforced the hygienists' demands for light, air, sunlight, nakedness.

new environment was taking shape on the outskirts: Barnes, St. John's Wood, Hampstead, later Bedford Park.

At first the street pattern of these new villa districts remained regular. The houses, even if externally given over to neo-gothic caprice were the usual spacious houses with regular, often square ground plans and high-ceilinged rooms: pseudo-Greek temples with an altar in every room but no god. Following romantic principles, house and plot pattern and garden changed: the street avoided straight lines, even when no curves were given by nature; when the cult of naturalism finally invaded German town planning toward the end of the nineteenth century contour levels of even the minor sort were treated as definitive guiding lines for the sake of the irregularity they produced: an exaggerated rebuke to the engineer's habit of forgetting them completely.

But after allowance is made for these lapses, the fact remains that the suburb served as an experimental seedbed for the new domestic architecture. It was in the suburban house that Richardson made his decisive advance toward a new architecture, and after him, Frank Lloyd Wright; it was in the suburb that Sitte effectively applied his post-baroque doctrines of the discontinuous street, and thus made one of the first systematic efforts to insulate the new domestic quarters from through-traffic. By economizing on paving, curbing, wide road-ways, and similar extravagant utilities, the suburb often created a far better residential scheme than the city: the money thus saved could go directly into trees, gardens, open spaces. Simple natural forms were less expensive than mechanical substitutes: no small discovery in an age that believed that iron piping was cheaper than privet hedges, or paper flowers, made in sweatshops, more commendable than those grown in the earth.

But the very popularity of this move to escape partly robbed it of its success. Land values went up on the outskirts of every town, sometimes in sound agricultural territory, in expectation of suburban developments. By the time the impulse reached the lower middle classes and the manual workers, the form of the suburb had changed, too, into a derisive caricature: rows of cramped cottages, with a grass rug in the front, a minor drying green and catwalk in the rear—half an hour or more away from the place of work. Even for the well-to-do the growth of a suburban neighborhood usually meant a progressive intensification of use: a change in site values: eventually a further change in use toward completer coverage of the land. As the city crept nearer the suburb, its purity and solitude vanished, along with its ample gardens: finally it would be swallowed up, as Chelsea and Hammersmith and Hampstead, suburbs all, were swallowed up, in the growth of London.

Two points should be noted about this new type of community. First it was a segregated community, not merely set apart topographically from the central areas of a city: but its occupants were laterally segregated from other economic classes. Except for a small detail of tradesmen and handymen, the suburb was a one-class community: it boasted, in fact, of its "exclusiveness"—which means, sociologically speaking, of the fact that it was not and could not become a city. Further, suburban living encouraged a complete segregation of consumption from production: there was no visible connecting link, except the iron rails that led to the city, between the barbarous industries that manufactured the goods and the romantic suburban homes, remote from the grime and the sweat, where these things were consumed.

In the industrial town, poor men demonstrated: beggars held out their hands in the street: the eye, if it were not carefully averted, would behold a slum, or at least a slum-child, on a five minute walk in any direction. In the suburb, the illusion of an innocent world could be preserved, without encountering these inconvenient reminders of social brutality. Here domesticity could flourish, forgetful of the exploitation upon which so much of it was based. Here individuality could prosper, oblivious to the pervasive regimentation beyond its curving roadways and naturalistic gardens.

In short, the romantic suburb was a collective attempt to live a private life: an effort to make the apparatus of Coketown tolerable to the possessing classes by enabling them to profit by its goods and avoid its evils, to have the best of both worlds. Women and children first is a sound motto; and the instincts that prompted this exodus by the middle classes were sound; life was actually in danger in the new factory slum, and the merest counsel of prudence was to flee— flee with all one's goods, as Lot and his household had fled before the sultry hell of Sodom and Gomorrah. But unfortunately this sound motto did not apply to the women and children of the working classes, despite many pious hopes vouchsafed in the middle of the nineteenth century that cheap fares and special workers' trains would at once solve the housing problem of the poor and permit everyone to spend part of his day in a rural environment.

In a sense, the suburb was woman's special contribution to the new urban complex: for the suburb alone met the needs of child-bearing and child-rearing. Untainted by thoughts of child labor, foul air, prostitution, the home achieved a new spaciousness: the long Victorian novel and the strong Victorian parent were both largely by-products of the suburban fireside. As the sense of privacy increased, the suburbanites copied the romantic Byrons and Lamartines. They made a virtue of idiosyncrasy. If a private retreat, why not a private religion, why not a private architecture? Dickens caricatured these private crotchets in his picture of the Old 'Un, Mr. Wemmick's father, in Great Expectations: with his castellated house and his moat and drawbridge and sunset salute. But it was impossible really to caricature an impulse that had, from the beginning, a constant air of unreality.

The desire for privacy, for exclusiveness, for an environment of snobbish isolation—these things are drawn from the same root. The fact was that the collective economic methods of paleotechnic civilization and the common social life did not bear looking at. The individuality of the suburban cottage, now expressing itself in painful excrescences of "original" ornament, or again in no less painful imitation of historic styles—this "individuality" was in effect a confession that the proud philistines of the period had neither the intellectual penetration to analyze their condition nor the courage and the imagination to transform it. The suburb was a pharisaic way of passing by on the other side: leaving the civic organism itself in the gutter.

So much for the weakness of this movement. One must realize nonetheless that like so many other impulses of romanticism it was a healthy reaction, to be condemned, not for what it did, but for what it omitted to do. After all the suburb was a first semi-collective attempt to create for the middle classes, if not for the whole community, a biological environment on an urban basis. That was a rational purpose. These new houses were more spacious as a rule and more open to the sun than the dingy rows that lined the streets of the town; and this new setting, with its trees and lawns and gardens, was more sweet to the eye and ear and nose than were the city's pavements. In these open spaces, with their nearby fields and streams, children could play and gambol again, as even the children of the wealthiest had but little chance to do in the big centers. In the suburb there was space for gardening and caring for children: for playing at lawn tennis, croquet, or at bowls: puttering around the carpenter's workbench. In short, the suburb was nearer to providing a balanced round of activities—outside daily work—than the paleotechnic city. If not as healthy as the countryside proper, the suburb would still be healthier than the congested city, once its water supply and its sewage disposal were taken in hand.

In creating a better biological environment, however, the builders of the suburb failed to take account of the need for a more adequate social environment. On the contrary, the suburb usually fell off from even the low standards of Coketown: it started a de-politizing process that has been steadily spreading as the suburb itself has been spreading throughout our civilization. The suburb was a "Teilstadt," a specialized urban fragment: just as much so as the meanest coal town, iron town, cotton town. Hence it lacked the necessary elements for extensive social co-operation, for creative intercourse, for an expansion of the social heritage as a whole. Consuming much, it produced little, created less. The stimulus of variety, the shock and jostle and challenge of different groups, were largely absent from its life. For the inhabitants of the suburb lived divided lives. Their purses were in the central city; their domestic affections were concentrated one or two hours away, in the villa. Neither side of their lives could be wholly active, wholly efficient. The necessary routine, with its daily shuttling between home and workplace, between nest and market, undermined life at both extremes. *Spatial concentration has an essential part to play in psychological focus—and that above all was lacking in this new regime.*

Hence a final paradox: the most lasting benefits in the suburban pattern of development came from a handful of industrialists who worked within the heart of the paleotechnic scheme and who—some·times quite literally—stuck to their guns. Godin at Guise, Krupp at Essen, Salt at Saltaire, Cadbury at Bourneville, Lever at Port Sun·light, all heralded at the beginning of the nineteenth century by the hardheaded fanaticism of Robert Owen—these men made a sound contribution to urban life. They accepted the vital principles of romanticism, the delight in nature, the concern for children, the interest in healthy rural sports, as a basis for a new type of community development. But they did not forget the factory: they united the domestic and the industrial scheme in the same general frame. In this handful of exemplary developments, the foundation for a new attack upon the problems of housing and city development were finally laid: they paved the way for the new biotechnic conception of a balanced urban environment—what was first called the Garden City.

15: The Woodlanders

If the so-called working class suburb was merely a peripheral slum or semi-slum rather than a central one, a new element neverthe·less entered the city, at about the same time, which improved the environment. The new landscape park. In a sense, this was merely a remodeling of the baroque park which, as a setting for the royal palace, had remained in the capital cities of Europe. Under pressure of democratic and humanitarian demands, these parks had been thrown open to the inhabitants. But in the nineteenth century the nature of the park was altered: its mission was, as Olmsted said of Central Park, to provide for the masses of the city a brief equiva·lent of a visit to the countryside. The designers recognized the need of the saving opposite within the city. This was the more positive side of romantic disorder.

In what form do these new pastoral spaces first appear? To achieve peace and quiet, to insulate oneself from the noisy lanes of traffic, one must—do not laugh!—visit the dead. Mount Auburn Cemetery in Boston was one of the first of the new landscaped areas, spread out in ample acres, which was designed to resuscitate the living as well as solemnly to enfold the deceased. In this crazy utilitarian world, it was the dear departed who enjoyed most fully a good en·

vironment; while the dark caves of houses were more like catacombs than homes for the living. Life came back to the town by way of the graveyard; just as in more than one city the removal of tombstones served to turn the churchyard into a necessary breathing space for congested quarters. This is not the first time in recorded history, from the days of the Egyptian tomb-builders onward, when the dead were abundantly supplied with the necessaries of life that were denied to the quick.

In the main, the great capitals, still under the sway of baroque standards, still profiting by the regular seasonal migration of the county families, were more receptive to the idea of the landscape park than were the purely industrial towns. London and New York responded to the idea sooner than Pittsburgh and Leeds. In the capitals, indeed, there was this further stimulus: the avenues were becoming too congested for the fashionable display of equipages, which were an important part of the surviving baroque ritual, and the country had become too inaccessible to aristocratic horseback riders. It was necessary to set aside special areas where the merchant princes and their wives could drive. To achieve their own special privileges, they had to secure municipal support for such open greens.

The leaders in this whole movement to re-ruralize the town were the Americans Downing and Olmsted: the latter one of the vital artists of the nineteenth century. He took the capricious naturalism of the earlier lovers of dead trees and broken branches, and the meaningless irregularities of the Jardin Anglais, and created new harmonies, based upon a closer study of the lay of the land and of native plant formations. He was not afraid to use the commonest wild flowers and native shrubs in his planting; and he followed the contour lines in the laying out of paths and roads. These naturalistic plans accordingly saved expense on grading, filling, and vain architectural embellishment; and his native plants had a better chance of surviving without excessive labor than had the exotics of an earlier school of design. But his plans were animated by technical intelligence and civic foresight. He was the first planner to see the necessity—in his extremely original design for Central Park—of deliberately separating pedestrian traffic from wheeled traffic by creating underpasses and overpasses that permitted them to operate as sepa-

rate systems. This bold scheme anticipated by more than two generations the rational layout of the modern town, as first comprehensively
set down by Messrs. Henry Wright and Clarence Stein at Radburn,
New Jersey: a major contribution.

By 1870 Olmsted had carried his thinking about parks beyond his
original conception of the big landscape park, lying in the midst of
the growing city. He saw that even better tracts of land might be
destroyed on the outskirts, and that by the time the urban mass had
reached these outlying areas they might be just as badly needed.
Hence he outlined the conception of the complete *park system*. This
system began with the individual square for local promenade and
meeting, and the individual playground for active recreation. Such
grounds were connected up by strips of roadway, greensward, and
rows of trees, called parkways: elongated versions of the strip common of New England—already embodied in the Avenue des Champs
Elysées. Accordingly, by increasing passages of open space, it led
into such neighboring wild landscapes—like that of the Palisades in
New York or Middlesex Fells in Boston—as might and should be
preserved. Olmsted's disciple, Charles Eliot, Jr., saw the further
necessity of using the riverside and sea-coast areas, no less than the
pastoral or mountain landscape so dear to the older romantic planner; and had Eliot's timely warning been carried into political action,
by creating permanent park strips and footpaths along the beaches
and promontories of Massachusetts and Maine, that splendid coast
would not have been turned into the dissolute landscape-slum so much
of it has now become.

This conception of a *continuous* environment of public greens and
open spaces as an essential element in urban planning—and not an
afterthought or a mere embellishment—was an important contribution to sound contemporary city design: in a more systematic and
highly developed form it must still govern every rational conspectus
of the new city. Neither the medieval town nor the baroque town had
such continuous areas: indeed, the notion of the country and the
city as being continuously inter-related and inter-penetrating was
foreign to the earlier conception of urban organization.

Unfortunately, the attempt to thrust park areas into a paleotechnic
street-net met with countless obstructions. Though experience proved

again and again that, even upon purely commercial terms, these new open areas paid for themselves by raising the land values along adjacent properties, the commercial interests tended nevertheless jealously to oppose the removal from speculative action of such large tracts of land. Meanwhile, the premature platting of streets and the speculation in building lots, which went on in every growing center, made it difficult to get hold of the necessary land. The failure to make the park system central to planning resulted in a certain belatedness in every program for parks and playgrounds: by the time the need had become pressing enough to demand action, the price tended to be prohibitive. Smaller towns here had an advantage over bigger ones, though too frequently they failed to seize it.

Still, the landscape park and the park system were real social mutations in urban form: perhaps the only ones of importance, outside the plan of the romantic suburb, that the period could point to. In Europe, by a happy sort of revenge, the old baroque fortifications, which had done so much to cause congestion, were torn down and replaced by parks: these formed the lovely rings and starlike green salients around a Bremen, a Lübeck, a Wien, a Cracow, a Köln. The immediate platting of big landscape parks helped break up the clotted urban massing of the great metropolis and softened the rigors of life for its inhabitants: and the best of these parks, such as Prospect Park in Brooklyn, count among the proudest works of art of this century. Eventually, the idea and the example touched even the sordid milieu of the pure industrial towns, creating a guilty conscience, if not a fresh will-to-order. By 1890 the typical paleotect had begun to lose a little of his pride and self-confidence in the insensate environment he had helped create.

16: Reaction

One may well close this picture of paleotechnic urban form with a quotation from John Storer, in his essay on Our Cities, published in 1870. "It may be doubted whether, among the arts yet to be discovered, or at least perfected, among the almost uninvestigated sciences to be shaped into form, worked out in theory, and harder still, in practice by the strong men of the future, should not be included the art and science of city life. . . . To mould the vast congeries of life massed around a given center, say ten miles around Charing Cross, for instance, into a systematic organism, so as to give the most good possible to every one of the vast human family therein contained, is a matter difficult of achievement, and one admitting a vast improvement over all former precedents."

The statement was admirable. And after fully canvassing the defects of the paleotechnic town, one must balance up accounts by admitting that nothing one can say today is more rigorous or more penetrating than the criticisms of a sanitarian like Chadwick or Richardson or Simon, of a political reformer like Shaftesbury or Buckingham or Bellamy, of a prophet like Ruskin or Morris, of a creative geotect like Olmsted. For the first people to discover what was wrong with these vast, inconsequential urban clottings, and the first to take vigorous steps to rectify the manifold evils, were the more intelligent, public-spirited members of this society. They attended to first things first. It was the leader of Victorian estheticism, John Ruskin, who begged the industrial leaders not to worry about art until they had provided for the inhabitants of their towns clean air and pure water and easy access to the country. "When you know how to build cities, and how to rule them," he observed in Munera Pulveris, "you will be able to breathe in their streets, and the 'excursion' will be the afternoon's walk or game in the fields round them."

And even on the social side of existence, the towns had begun during the early part of the nineteenth century to make a great contribution. For this century, which is so often falsely called the age of individualism, in reflection of the callous public morals of the rich, was in essence an age full of associational experiments: closer to the spirit of Fourier than its smug leaders imagined. If the physical organization of the new urban areas was entirely inadequate, one must remember, nevertheless, that within the interstices of these towns, new organs for social co-operation and social thought were defining themselves: the trade union, the scientific society, the consumers' co-operative society, the public library: means whereby the military-capitalistic regime could be eventually transformed into a social commonwealth.

CHAPTER IV.
RISE AND FALL
OF MEGALOPOLIS

1: The New Coalition

The story of every city can be read through a succession of deposits: the sedimentary strata of history. While certain forms and phases of development are successive in time, they become, through the very agency of the civic process, cumulative in space. The point of maximum accumulation, the focus of past achievements and present activities, is the metropolis. The emergence of the big city from the multitude of regional cities that characterized the Middle Ages is so obvious a fact that certain economic historians have described the change as that from a town economy to a metropolitan economy. The characterization is mainly sound, but is the fact a permanent one? Will life continue to ebb out of the villages and country towns and regional centers? Will urban life come to mean the further concentration of power in a few metropolises whose ramifying suburban dormitories will finally swallow the rural hinterland?

Many analyses of contemporary city growth have taken this development to be a final one. Vast plans have been drawn up in various metropolises for continuing this process, and for absorbing a greater population: even in countries whose rate of population increase has been steadily diminishing, the continuance of metropolitan aggrandizement has been taken for granted. Unhappily for these hopes and plans even the blind drift of contemporary forces does not promise a continuance of this process: it is self-limiting. Meanwhile the disabilities and burdens of metropolitan development have been heaping up. Already, one can detect a new economic and social pattern: a step beyond the metropolitan economy.

So far from representing adequately the forces of modern civilization, the metropolis is one of the biggest obstacles to their fruitful human use. In what ways is this true? How has it come about? And what alternatives lie before us? Those questions I purpose to answer.

Thorstein Veblen made us familiar with the conflict that is latent between mechanical enterprise and commercial enterprise: between the old-fashioned industrialist, whose fun was in the day's work, and whose pecuniary gains were testimonials of success after the event, and the new kind of financier, growing out of the banker and speculator, for whom pecuniary gain was the be-all and end-all of existence. Up to a point this distinction is a genuine one. It is reflected in the environments they have helped to create. One may distinguish roughly between producing cities and consuming cities: between the Five Towns, Pittsburgh, Lyons, Turin, Essen, on one hand, and London, New York, Paris, Berlin, Rome, and their subsidiary pleasure resorts, on the other.

During the paleotechnic period, when great fortunes were being made in steel and coal and oil and machinery, money would be amassed in the back country, at the expense of local resources and the local population, and then spent, if not completely dispersed, in cities far remote. The very means of luxurious expenditure were often wanting in the industrial towns. Beginning in the third quarter of the nineteenth century, the center of gravity shifted from the producing towns to the capital cities: free competition, which was the dominant catchword of the early nineteenth century, if never the universal practice, gave way to the effort to achieve practical monopoly or quasi-monopoly.

This movement broke down the partition between the various classes in society that had hitherto been relatively isolated. A coalition of land, industry, finance, and officialdom was formed in almost every country in order to effect the maximum amount of pecuniary exploitation. The agents of power, the aristocracy, the political bureaucracy, and the army began to direct "national interests" toward the service of the industrialist: they sought raw materials and markets capable of absorbing his excess production: hence the partition of Africa, Asia, and similar "backward" sections of the world. The industrialist, in turn, abandoning his naïve belief in laissez-faire and free enterprise, came to rely upon his imperialistic allies to help stabilize industry and to give it monopoly advantages: hence protective tariffs, subsidies, export subventions.

This coalition of economic interests was in good part responsible for the continuous increase of population in the great capitals during the nineteenth century, and for the building up of new metropolitan centers. The overgrown city, instead of appearing as an isolated phenomenon, an emblem of purely political concentration, became the dominant type: Coketown, the pure industrial city, was the recessive form after 1890.

Even in the most secluded provincial town, the pattern of institutional life was a metropolitan one: the shibboleths of power-politics, the orgiastic urges of nationalism, the acceptance of both the commercial and the cultural trade-marks of the metropolis became well-nigh universal. England, whose utilitarians had turned the green country of Shakespeare into the Black Country of Dickens, proceeded during the nineteenth century to paint the rest of the map red. In successive waves of belligerent exploitation, other countries followed suit. The colors of life, ebbing from the insensate milieu of the industrial town, flowed back into the metropolis in the gay uniforms of the Guards and Cuirassiers.

The basis for metropolitan agglomeration lay in the tremendous increase of population that took place during the nineteenth century. Peoples of European stock multiplied from about two hundred million during the Napoleonic Wars to about six hundred million at the outbreak of the World War. This stock, which accounted for only about one-sixth of the population of the earth in Malthus' day, rose to about a third of it in a little over a century. In 1800 not a city in the Western World had over a million in population: London, the biggest, had only 959,310, while Paris had a little more than half a million, and Wien about half of that. By 1850 London had over two millions and Paris over a million inhabitants: they were still without serious rivals. But by 1900 eleven metropolises with more than a million inhabitants had come into existence, including Berlin, Chicago, New York, Philadelphia, Moscow, St. Petersburg, Wien, Tokyo, and Calcutta. Thirty years later, as a result of this feverish concentration of capital and the military and mechanical means of exploitation, there were twenty-seven cities with more than

a million population, headed by New York and grading down to Birmingham, including metropolises on every continent, even Australia.
The rise of cities with a population of over a hundred thousand was
equally marked: likewise the spread of vast suburban rings around
the central districts of all these cities. Nearly one-half of the population of the United States at the time of the 1930 census lived within
a radius of from twenty to fifty miles of cities with over a hundred
thousand inhabitants. The mere alteration of scale and extent resulted
in qualitative changes in these centers.

2: The Tentacular Bureaucracy

What forces furthered this process of urban agglomeration? What
made the metropolis the image of social hope and economic enterprise, even for those parts of the world whose dear ways of life were
sapped and undermined by the extension of "la ville tentaculaire"?

The means of agglomeration were the continental railroad lines
and the worldwide lanes of ocean commerce: means which brought
an endless flow of raw materials and foods into the metropolis: all
roads led to the capital. But the civic force was the centralization of
the organs of administration in the great capitals, and the growing
dependence of every type of enterprise, political, educational, economic, upon the process of administration itself.

Once the means of instantaneous communication were available,
there was a fresh incentive to concentrate the organs of administration: production could be controlled, the shipment of goods routed,
orders given and canceled, credits extended and the exchanges of
goods and drafts cleared, on a single spot. Remote control, first embodied in the separation of staff and line in the army, spread to business operations. With the manufacture of the typewriter in the seventies, and the coincident spread of high speed stenography, more and
more business could be conducted on paper. Mechanical means of
communication: mechanical means of making and manifolding the
permanent record: mechanical systems of audit and control—all
these devices aided the rise of a vast commercial bureaucracy, capable of selling in ever remoter territories.

The word bureaucracy had indeed become a discouraging by-word
for inefficiency by the middle of the nineteenth century: Dickens

needed no special powers of invention to create Sir Tite Barnacle and the Circumlocution Office. Everyone experienced, throughout the financial and political world, the difficulty of getting things done by direct action. The simplest civil act required legal sanctions, documents, verifications. From the searching of a deed up to the establishment of civil rights in marriage, no one could move without the aid of special functionaries. Lawyers, who knew the prescribed forms and technicalities, formed a large part of the growing professional population: their services were needed in the observance, and even more in the tactful breach, of the law.

In all this development, the political bureaucracy served as a special target for chronic disparagement: it was supposed to have a monopoly of roundabout methods and a finicking attention to form. But the businessman's self-righteous indignation about the monstrous growth of political bureaucracy was extremely humorless. Such an attitude overlooked the fact that the *greatest development of bureaucracy during the last century took place within the realm of business itself:* this development put to shame the punier additions to the governmental bureaucracy. Plainly, no great corporate enterprise with a worldwide network of agents, correspondents, market outlets, factories, and investors could exist without relying upon the services of an army of patient clerkly routineers in the metropolis: stenographers, filing clerks, and bookkeepers, office managers, sales managers, and their varied assistants, right up to the fifth vice-president whose name or o.k. sets the final seal of responsibility upon an action. The housing of this bureaucracy in office buildings and tenements and residential suburbs constituted one of the major tasks of metropolitan expansion: their transportation back and forth to work, within a limited time-span, raised one of the difficult technical problems that confronted the city planner and the engineer.

Not merely did the bureaucracy itself require office space and living space: but the by-products of its routine came to occupy an increasing share of the new quarters: files, vaults, places for live storage and dead storage, parade grounds and cemeteries of documents, where the records of business were alphabetically kept, with an eye to the possibility of future exploitation, future reference, future lawsuits, future contracts. This age found its form in a new type of office building: a sort of human filing case, whose occupants spent their days in the circumspect care of paper: numbering, ticketing, assorting, routing, recording, manifolding, filing, to the end that the commodities and services thus controlled could be sold to the profit of the absentee owners of the corporation.

A new trinity dominated the metropolitan scene: finance, insurance, advertising. By means of these agents, the metropolis extended its rule over subordinate regions, both within its own political territory and in outlying domains: directly or indirectly, they expedited the flow of tribute back into the big centers. Economic enterprise, political power, social authority, once divided over the length and breadth of the land, now concentrated in the seven Romes. To obtain money, one must go to the metropolis: to exercise influence, one must achieve a prominent financial position in the metropolis. Here and there a lone wolf, like Henry Ford, would temporarily remain outside the system. But such isolation would be largely an illusion: mark how Ford himself, who once manufactured a car adapted to popular needs and rural life, finally succumbed to the lure of metropolitan style in the outer design of his car.

Monopoly capitalism: credit finance: pecuniary prestige—these are the three sides of the metropolitan pyramid. Whatever goes on in the big city ultimately traces back to one or another of these elements. The metropolis is the natural reservoir of capital under this economic phase; for its banks, its brokerage offices, its stock exchanges, serve as a collecting point for the savings of the surrounding country, and in the case of world capitals, for the surplus capital of foreign investors. Investors and manufacturers both gravitate to the metropolis: the more constant the need for credit capital, the more important for the borrower to be close to the big banks that can advance it.

The concentration of financial power in national or semi-national banks, like the Banks of England and France, or in the hands of politically irresponsible private bankers, like the Houses of Rothschild and Morgan, is a characteristic feature of this regime. As Balzac clearly saw at the very beginning of this concentration, the banker was supreme: directly or indirectly, he manipulated the puppets that appeared on the political stage: he contributed to the funds

of the political parties, and his sanction was as necessary to the suc·
cess of a political policy or an industrial invention as his veto was
fatal.

But mortgages on metropolitan real estate, whose values are
"secured" by the continued prosperity and growth of the metropolis,
become a mainstay of savings banks and insurance companies. In
order to protect their investments, these institutions must combat any
attempt to lessen congestion; for this would also deflate the values
that are based on congestion. Note how the program for slum replacement and suburban re-settlement mapped out by the Roosevelt
administration in 1933 was undermined by the fact that the administration created at the same time another agency whose sole purpose
was to keep intact the existing structure of mortgages and interest
rates: a policy that made it impossible to scale down sufficiently the
grotesque burden of urban land values and urban debt.

In the medieval order, the fatalities and insecurities of life were
offset by the organization of guilds and friendly societies. In the
metropolitan regime, these services are performed by special financial corporations: insurance companies. Fire, flood, sickness, disability, accident, and death are all covered by one or another form
of insurance. In the calculations made to ascertain the rates of insurance, the first advances in statistical sociology took place; and in
intensive work toward health maintenance and disease prevention,
great organizations like the Metropolitan Life Insurance Company
have demonstrated the cash value of improvement in these departments by education and medical aid.

Unfortunately, within the current metropolitan scheme, insurance
is an attempt to achieve security by piling together at one point the
maximum number of risks. In the short run, the insurance company
may be solvent: in the long run, it becomes itself one of the elements
contributing to the bankruptcy of the regime as a whole. By their
control of vast capital resources, the insurance companies become the
effective landlords of distant farming lands, as well as of metropolitan real estate. Remote farms in Arkansas and Iowa, rubber
plantations in Brazil and power plants in Africa—these and a hundred other rural domains become directly tributary to the big city
through the agency of finance. So long as the productive mechanism

is in working order, the flow is continuous: but a drought, a dust-storm, an earthquake, a glut of commodities, or a war will seriously shake the fabric; and the existence of these implacable metropolitan claims may then stand in the way of rational political adjustment.

Hence the necessity for completing the process of metropolitan monopoly and concentrating the control even further. To prevent aggressive rivalry on the part of sub-metropolises and their provinces one final step is necessary: the effective monopoly of advertising, news, publicity, periodical literature. These four departments have diverse points of origin and represent various initial interests; but historically, they have been loosely tied together since the beginning, and within the metropolitan framework they finally coalesce. They work to a single end: to give the stamp of authenticity and value to the style of life that emanates from the metropolis. They establish the national brand: they attempt to control the national market: they create a picture of a unified, homogeneous, completely standardized population that bears, in fact, no relation to the actual regional sub-stratum—although in the course of time it partly succeeds in producing the thing it has imagined.

In all these efforts, the stage, the motion picture screen, the radio, no less than the newspaper and the printed book, concentrate upon fixing the national appetite upon just those products that the metropolis can sell at a profit. Similarly, they create an image of a valuable life that can be satisfied only by a ruthless concentration of human interest upon pecuniary standards and pecuniary results: the clothes of the metropolis, the jewels of the metropolis, the dull expensive life of Park Avenue and the Kurfürstendamm, Piccadilly and the Champs Elysées, become the goals of vulgar ambition.

Advertisement becomes the "spiritual power" of this new regime: ostentatiously or covertly, the greater part of the literature produced with the imprint of the metropolis is advertisement: an effort to establish the universal prestige of the metropolis, if not of this or that special product. Such methods, such standards, infect the older emblems of the spiritual power, the Church and the University: these institutions imitatively create huge ornate buildings, also in the spirit of advertisement, and are tempted grossly to copy the methods of the financier on whom they more and more rely. Example: the employment of commercial fund-raisers by various religious bodies and institutions to acquire capital for buildings and other purposes. Such a concordat between the ecclesiastical and the financial powers has many parallels in the modern metropolis.

Where the organs of finance and publicity are concentrated, the possessing classes are likewise brought together; for the ritual of their life, as lived in public for the benefit of the illustrated newspapers and the newsreels, is an essential part of the pecuniary lure. The concentration of the rich is a typical metropolitan phenomenon: the wealth that they accumulate in the metropolis goes into private foibles and public philanthropies, when it does not return to commerce in the form of further investments. The princely ritual of conspicuous expenditure, no longer confined to the royal court, gives rise to the special luxury industries of the metropolis: dress, food, adornment. Because of the universal nature of metropolitan standards, the exotic fashions of the rich are presently copied and reproduced on a mass scale for the benefit of the entire populace. As for the more altruistic modes of expenditure, some, like hospitals, are inherited from the past: some, like research foundations, are peculiar to the metropolitan economy itself: here, too, the millionaire of the new regime takes the place of the absolute prince.

In the second and third generations of money-making, philanthropy itself becomes a business of high repute. Just as about two hundred corporations control about half the industrial capital in America, so do a relatively small group from the financial classes control the organs of culture in the metropolis and in a good part of the outlying territories. When new lines of activity are to be promoted in the arts and sciences, it is inevitably to the swollen purses of the metropolis that the promoters direct themselves: here, more often than not, the new foundation settles. Thus a multitude of associations of national and international scope naturally have their headquarters in New York, London, or Paris: charitable organizations, religious foundations, scientific and educational institutes. Here patrons and clients come together: here competitive patronage increases the opportunity for special interests to find support. A disproportionate share of power and influence and wealth has been drained away from the hinterland: in order to recapture any of these things, it is necessary for the provincial to leave his home and fight for a place in the metropolis.

A third condition abets the agglomeration of population. Victor Branford suggested that the growth of imperial bureaucracies, coming as a result of political centralization in war, was the characteristic agent that transformed the industrial town or caused it to yield in power and influence and numbers to the metropolis. War is the forcing-house of bureaucracy: in America, the Civil War and the World War, in Europe, the Napoleonic Wars, the Franco-Prussian War, the Russo-Japanese War, and again the World War. The fact is that imperialism and financialism go hand in hand: exploitation, whether external or internal, requires protection: the protection of the flag, the protection of the military forces that march under the flag. As the population is heaped further into great centers, they must rely more fully upon distant sources of supply: to widen the base of supplies and to protect the "life-line" that connects the source with the voracious mouth of the imperial metropolis, become the functions of the army and the navy.

Whereas the agricultural base of the village is the local fields, and the base of the regional city is the local region, the base of the metropolis may be outside the political unit of which it is a member. In so far as it dominates those distant sources of goods and those distant markets, the growth of the capital can proceed indefinitely. Such an increase as London showed in a century, from one million to six million people, is unprecedented, so far as history offers any records for comparison; and it was dependent upon the worldwide transportation system and the worldwide system of capital investment and market-interchange that London had so vigorously helped to invent and knit together.

Beneath these tendencies toward centralization of power and agglomeration of people lies another economic fact. This is the increase of ground-rents that follows inevitably from such growth. In the metropolis the rent of land, no longer fixed by custom, no longer stabilized by slowness in change of use, rises by leaps and bounds. Parcels change rapidly from hand to hand, with successive increases in value, until they have "ripened" sufficiently to permit the fullest value to be plucked by the last owner who holds it just before its actual use. Under capitalism, the rise of land values attendant upon congestion is by itself sufficient motive for—and justification of—the whole process.

Do not fancy that this increase of values is incidental. On the contrary, strenuous efforts are made to ensure it. In Cobbett's day, he complained about the effect of the funding system upon the over-building of London: the gathering of rentiers into the capital was a powerful factor in its expansion. But there are other means of effecting this end: railroad systems are deliberately designed to compel passengers and goods to pass through the metropolis before going elsewhere: each great capital sits like a spider in the midst of its transportation web. In America, in addition, as Thompson points out, the rate structure is not based upon the actual cost of service: the charges are arbitrarily equalized in such a fashion as to give a subsidy to the big cities at the expense of the rival towns that are perhaps more conveniently located—even though the cost of handling freight in big cities is, by reason of their very congestion, disproportionately high.

By itself, the big city becomes the prestige symbol for the whole civilization. Life in all the subordinate regions is sacrificed to its temples of pleasure and towers of pecuniary aspiration, as life in the Valley of the Nile was sacrificed to the theocratic cult of the tomb-builders. So much for the economist's naïve myth that the gigantic metropolis is what it is merely because of its tangible economic benefits or the natural superiority of its geographic situation.

3: Shapeless Giantism

Circle over London, Berlin, New York, or Chicago in an airplane, or view the cities schematically by means of an urban map and block-plan. What is the shape of the city and how does it define itself? As the eye stretches toward the hazy periphery one can pick out no definite shape, except that formed by nature: a banked river or a lake-front: one beholds rather a shapeless mass, here bulging or ridged with buildings, there broken by a patch of green or the separate geometric shapes of a gas tank or a series of freight sheds. The growth of a great city is amoeboid: failing to divide its social chromosomes and split up into new cells, the big city continues to grow by breaking through the edges and accepting its sprawl and shapelessness as an inevitable by-product of its physical immensity.

Here the city has absorbed villages and little towns and reduced them to place names, like Manhattanville and Harlem in New York; there it has left the organs of local government and the vestiges of an independent civic life, as in Chelsea and Kensington in London; but it has nevertheless enveloped those urban areas in its physical organization. In this all-devouring growth, the outskirts during the last generation have grown faster than the center: in America, at twice the rate of the metropolis proper, and almost six times the rate of the non-metropolitan parts of the United States. Physically incoherent, socially disparate, these new metropolitan districts are at best statistical collections. Here and there in the mass one may partly trace the outline of a city: but the mass itself is not a city, in a functional sense, any more than the immediate countryside that surrounds it is a rural area.

What was purely a visual perspective in the baroque city becomes in the later metropolis a more pragmatic perspective of profits through urban extensions. In the upward extension of the city the same tendencies prevail: to increase urban heights and distances and numbers has now a direct financial motive.

Sometimes the shapelessness of the metropolitan aggregate is further expressed by the irregular blocks and the aimless inconsecutive streets, or the wild jumble of structures that have been superimposed on a regular pattern of streets: that is San Francisco, Chicago, Detroit, London. Sometimes there are large patches of orderly, consecutive growth: that is Paris, Berlin, Madrid, Buenos Aires. But the difference between one type of order and another is a difference in the *degree* of sprawl, confusion, de-building. As one moves out of the central district the vast enveloping aimlessness of this growth becomes overwhelming. No human eye can take in this metropolitan mass at a glance. No single gathering place except the totality of its streets can hold all its citizens. No human mind can comprehend more than a fragment of the complex and minutely specialized activities of its citizens. There is a special name for power when it is con-centrated on such a scale: it is called impotence.

4: Means of Congestion

Contrary to popular belief the growth of great cities preceded the decisive technical advances of the last two centuries. But the metro-politan phase became universal only when the technical means of congestion had become adequate—and their use profitable to those who manufactured or employed them. The modern metropolis, how-ever, is an outstanding example of a peculiar cultural lag within the realm of technics itself: namely, the continuation by advanced neo-technic means of the forms and ends of paleotechnic civilization. The machines and utilities that will lend themselves to decentralization in a life-centered order, here become a means either to increase the congestion or afford some slight palliation: at a price.

The most characteristic technical achievements of the big city are those that further congestion; and the first of these is the canaliza-tion of water, its storage in vast reservoirs, its transmission through vast mains, tubular rivers, from the open country to the heart of the city. With reason New York prided itself on leading the way here: the Croton system, opened in 1842, was both a handsome piece of engineering and an intelligent means of combating some of the worst effects of urban overcrowding. The provision of pure, municipally supervised drinking water lowered the incidence of typhoid epi-demics and helped offset the rising death rate in other departments: accordingly, the seizure and purification of an abundance of water has become a main line of municipal strategy. In closely settled areas, or in areas of limited catchment, this brings the growing me-tropolis into conflict with other cities and other political divisions: the fight between Arizona and California over the diversion of water to Los Angeles became a bitter one: the very living of the farmers of Arizona was threatened by the city's expansion.

Not merely does running water become a necessity of metro-politan life: the bathroom reappears with it. This improvement comes to the mass of workers but slowly; but the facilities for clean-liness have now become accepted as a necessary part of the metro-politan standard of life: the bathtub becomes a permanent fixture,

[TOP LEFT] Grenoble. Natural circular plan. Irregular blocks dictated by topography and original circular wall.

[BOTTOM LEFT] Torino. Rigorous geometrical plan with blocks of almost uniform size. Varied size of squares and their placing indicates higher order of design than nineteenth century gridiron plans.

[MIDDLE LEFT] Delft. Irregular rectangular plan: natural adaptation to flat site, but with diagonal canal giving access to market square.

[TOP RIGHT] Nice. Acropolis type, like Athens, Geneva, Edinburgh. Fortified hill site and original settlement below: a true *Burg*. Typical Baroque town extension.

[BOTTOM RIGHT] Köln. Mixed type: regular Roman subdivision at center with irregular blocks of different sizes and shapes as later accretions.

Superficial observers often regard plans like those of Torino or the newer parts of Nice as the only authentic examples of urban order: while cities that have grown more slowly, with piecemeal changes and modifications, are looked upon as disorderly or even planless. But the more subtle organization of time and space, represented here by Grenoble and post-Roman Köln, has its own kind of order: the tactics of life, in all its manifestations, will include both types: the formal and the adaptive, the mechanical and the vital.

In the first type, the plan is preconceived on the lines of some regulating figure, like a circle or square, and the site and its structures are made to conform to the dominant idea. In the adaptive plan, the given conditions of soil and site are accepted and followed, with such reconstructions as convenience and necessity may dictate: the functions of life are not fitted into the mind's pattern but into nature's. The resulting order may be predominantly geometrical, as in Delft, or irregular, as in Grenoble. Note ample gardens within.

When the topographic outlines are bold and decisive, economy rests on willing conformity with the earth's contours. For lack of such acceptance, the "regular" plans of cities like San Francisco are not merely frightfully extravagant but badly adapted to meet the actual conditions imposed. Given the appropriate social conditions and the appropriate site, a formal plan may be genuinely organic: Wren's plan for London was a true expression of capitalism and mechanism, though it failed to reckon with survivals, and so came to nothing. The weakness of adaptive planning is that it sometimes gives more weight to the external factors of history and geography than they deserve: when the occasion arises, man can and should move mountains, cutting through natural obstacles opposing the inertia of tradition. Geometric planning tends to give too simple or arbitrary a form to complicated human functions: the procrustean fallacy: it boldly controls future needs without understanding them or being able to anticipate them. True organic planning embraces both elements, adaptation and formal order, timeliness and timelessness, functional adjustment and abstract clarity and coherence of design. Amsterdam is a classic example.

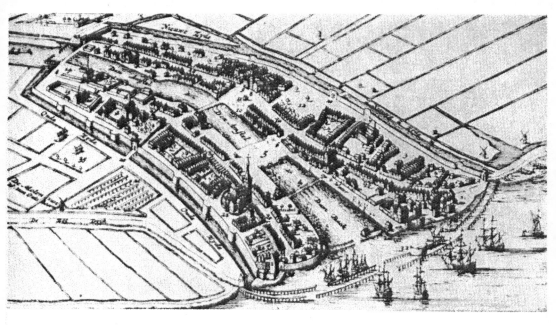

V: ELEMENTS OF PLAN [16 and 17] AMSTERDAM—ORGANIC PLANNING

[ABOVE] Stage One: The fishing and shipping town on the Amstel: a site not dissimilar to that of Geneva or Zürich. Banking and bridging of Amstel already begun. Harbor partly developed.

[BELOW] Stage Three: Development of large regular houseblocks on right of old city in adaptation to new facilities of water transportation: somewhat unfortunate continuation of field divisions and their orientation in smaller houseblocks.

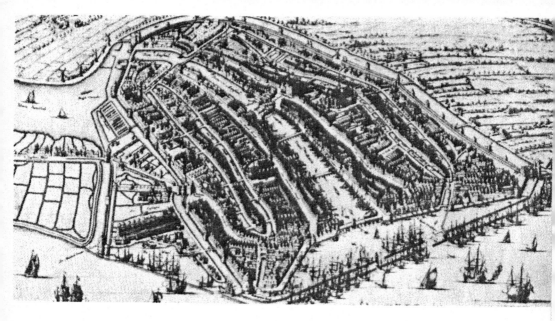

[ABOVE] Stage Two: Utilization of original protective canal as a means of urban transportation: multiplication of water avenues of the city: increase of port facilities on new land to left.

[BELOW] Stage Four: Partial regularity of newer parts of city rounded out by what becomes a semi-circular web of canals. The resultant plan, though geometrical, is a magnificent adaptation to economic and social opportunities: what townplanner could have plotted this result at stage one?

NETTE AFTEKENING VAN D'OUDE EN NIEUWE   ROOJINGH DER STADT AMST

and presently the provision of hot water as well as cold water seems desirable. Such a level of bodily hygiene had never been reached before even among the upper classes: the pace of its introduction was undoubtedly quickened by the necessity for overcoming the disagreeable or dangerous effects of metropolitan living. As the installation of the bathroom becomes more elaborate, the cost of building per dwelling increases: hence an increasing constriction in room space sets in among the middle classes, who are the first to espouse frequent washing and bathing as necessities. A characteristic process: overt relief of the effects of congestion: *indirect increase of congestion itself*.

This flood of water cleanses the Augean metropolitan stable: so far well. For such cities as are exposed to military attack, however, it increases the precariousness of their existence in times of war. Not merely must the distant water supply be guarded against pollution; but the dams and pumping stations and viaducts must be guarded against bombing from the air. More than ever the water supply remains the key to permanent residence in cities; and since the very growth of the city blots out wells and defiles minor streams, there are no decentralized substitute sources worth speaking of. If the system as a whole does not work, the city will collapse. Should an enemy disorganize the water supply of the metropolis for as much as three days, the result would be a far more horrible loss of life than the worst conceivable vomit of poison gas from the skies.

The next important agent of congestion is the transportation system. In the early stages of metropolitan growth, this was met by the use of horse-drawn vehicles; and since the main metropolitan areas were laid out before 1900, it means that the entire street and avenue system had been designed for the use of carriages and wagons. As traffic increases, the elaboration of utilities follows: first macadam surfaces; later the wooden block; then asphalt. To keep these ways clean and clear, a public street-cleaning service must be supported: eventually, in the Northern cities, the cost of snow removal, in order to ensure regular transportation of goods and food, must be added, too.

An increase in transportation facilities, however, does not lessen congestion in the streets. Even with horse-drawn vehicles there were serious traffic difficulties in the first half of the nineteenth century: New York then experimented with creating a pedestrian's bridge over Broadway. Avenues must be widened: new avenues, more palatial in scale, must be broken through in order to make the necessary shortcuts and connections: sometimes solid blocks of buildings must be swept away. The extension of Seventh Avenue and the widening of Varick Street in New York cost over six million dollars a mile: the Wacker Drive in Chicago cost twenty-two million dollars a mile, while the double decking of Michigan Avenue cost sixteen million dollars a mile. These terrific costs put a serious curb on the wide reconstruction of the metropolis.

Where such improvements are financed, at least in part, by taxes and assessments against the properties benefited, they tend to produce a rise in rents, which in turn becomes capitalized in the form of higher land values. Result: more intensive uses, and in time the congestion thus produced results in a further traffic congestion that nullifies the improvement. No one has in fact suggested a means of providing these additional facilities for transportation without having precisely this effect upon taxes, upon land values, and upon occupancy. The burden of costs may be shifted; but the amount remains.

What holds of the street system holds even more of the mechanical transportation systems by subway and elevated railroad. Technically, these, too, are the pride and delight of the metropolis. With the coming of electric traction in the nineties large scale congestion became popular by multiplying tracks and trolleys on the surface of the town, and by building cuts and tunnels for sub-surface transportation. The architecture of the new stations, from the Paris Metro to Professor Grenander's handsome buildings in Berlin, or those of Adams, Holden and Pearson in London, are among the highest architectural achievements of the metropolis.

The result of all these assiduous attempts mechanically to mobilize and disperse, night and morning, the inhabitants of the metropolis is nevertheless plain: one and all, they have intensified the pattern of congestion. And the difference between the actual costs of transportation and the fares paid—about three cents in New York on every five cent fare—constitutes a public subsidy to the real estate speculator. Though such transportation systems open up new areas on the outskirts of the city, they but thicken the crowding at the center. Except for the Inner Circle Railway in London, metropolitan subway lines have been almost uniformly built so as to throw an *increasing* load of passengers into the central district. In the middle of the nineteen-twenties, as many as two million people came into Manhattan from the outlying boroughs and territories in a single day; and a good part of this traffic took place within the span of an hour and a half, morning and night.

Note the effect of all these new utilities as they cross and criss-cross, through and over and under the city. Beneath the visible city an invisible city grows apace: a buried city of water pipes and sewers and gas mains and electric cables and steam pipes and telephone wires and vast cellars where heat and electricity are produced for the buildings above: a city of ramifying subways and ominous tunnels in which the entire population spends no inconsiderable part of the day.

This underground city, growing step by step, followed the main outlines of the street-net on the surface. Because each property owner is a law unto himself, no attempt was made to work out a collective policy and a coherent plan which would enable this dual city growth to take place in an economic fashion. The necessary utility mains, which might have been carried through the cellars of buildings, are carried in the public territory occupied by the street: not merely is the cost of outside connections high, but no repair or change can be made in these utilities without periodically mangling the street and blocking the traffic.

Here is a paradox that runs through contemporary metropolitan civilization: the existence of a rational collective organization of the physical means of life without the necessary organs of collective association and responsible social control. The result is that even in terms of purely mechanical efficiency the system is an extremely wasteful one.

In addition to these main public means of congestion, the metropolises of the Western World worked out a series of private means: vertical transportation by means of the elevator. Elevators were first used in this fashion in the early Manchester cotton factories; one of the first elevators to be run by steam power was that in the tower of the New York Crystal Palace in 1853, and shortly after the Civil War the first elevator was used in a New York apartment house. The example spread rapidly to the office building: it became the principal means, along with the steel-framed building, of increasing plot congestion. Until the first heights of building and setback ordinances were passed in New York in 1916, any individual owner was at liberty to overcrowd a site to a limit set only by the safety of the foundations and the superstructure. This vicious pattern has now become a symbol of material progress. For no reason at all, more than one recent housing project, in Rotterdam, in Paris, in Lyons, in Moscow, has copied these forms of metropolitan congestion. Even with the generous open spaces provided at Drancy, the achievement is as senseless as it is financially extravagant.

The result of such methods upon the transportation system was to increase the normal congestion by adding special pools and clots. The city plan worked out for New York in 1811, for example, was on the basis of four-story buildings. On those terms the street widths were adequate. In areas where buildings sixteen stories or more high came into existence, there was not enough land to provide sufficient streets alone, *without building sites*, on the previous scale. Fortunately for circulation, the *average* number of stories in New York remains today, despite skyscraper building, less than the number of Berlin or Paris.

The notion that vertical transportation relieves horizontal congestion is one of those desperate rationalizations that are sometimes put forward on behalf of a losing cause. Not merely does it promote an intensified use of the abutting streets and transportation lines: but it creates secondary forms of congestion within the building during the periods of maximum movement, at morning, noon, and night: hence further delays and stoppages.

5: The Costs of Costiveness

The facts of metropolitan congestion are undeniable. One reads them abstractly on the density maps and the transportation traffic maps: one participates in them in the clamor and the confusion of the streets: one encounters them in the constant stoppages of movement as one follows the traffic lights from one part of the city to the other; one becomes physically oppressed with the concrete fact of congestion in the crowded office elevator or in the even more tightly jammed subway train, rank with the odor of human bodies on a summer's evening. Congestion appears in the form of impeded movement and cramped space: lack of office room, lack of house-room: the universal presence of crowds. Such form as the metropolis achieves is crowd form: the procession on the Boardwalk at Coney Island, or the body of spectators in the boxing arena or the football stadium. To escape from these congested quarters requires skill and patience: *Watch your step! . . . What's your hurry?* Even the motor car, which originally carried with it the promise of swift movement and free command of space, becomes reduced, by the fact of congestion, to the limp of a faltering pedestrian. Confusion: constriction: costiveness—these are the typical by-products of metropolitan congestion. Those who seek to escape to larger quarters in the suburbs only serve to increase for those who remain the difficulty of getting beyond the spreading confines of the city.

Consider the costs of metropolitan congestion. We shall find that they are rising to a point that makes congestion financially unendurable, even if it were humanly tolerable.

The purely physical limits to metropolitan congestion are set mainly by three facts: the available amount of water, the point at which one metropolis begins to melt into a rival metropolis, and finally, the cost of mechanized transportation when the outskirts are too far from the center. But long before the first two points are reached, other serious handicaps enter.

First: the demand for water. As the metropolis absorbs more inhabitants, it must eat further back into its hinterland for water. In addition to the Croton system, New York was compelled to build the even grander Catskills system, tapping a source a hundred miles away. In less than twenty years, the need for a new source became evident: the city now reaches back for the waters of the Susquehanna River, claimed equally by the states of Pennsylvania and New Jersey. Each additional mile of tunnel and pipe, each additional reservoir, adds to the unit cost.

When the Regional Plan for New York made a study of the water system, it found that the cost of water during the decade of 1920 was between $35 and $65 per year per head. If the rate of growth then prevailing kept up, the cost by 1965 would reach $69 per inhabitant: in other words, a family of four would have, on a pro-rata basis, to pay $276 for water alone. This is almost as much as a good third of them can afford for the rent of their urban dwellings. The further increase of the use of water for industrial purposes, for bathing, and for air-conditioning will aggravate the need and raise the cost higher. Indeed, the latest toy of metropolitan engineering, air-conditioning, makes such huge demands for water that, if popularly adopted, it would almost be enough in itself to wreck municipal finances. Only its high upkeep per unit will forestall its collective collapse.

The cost of all the necessary transportation systems in a big city is equally massive: certain factors elude exact calculation. The initial capital cost, particularly for the underground systems, with their difficult tunneling and boring, is necessarily high: but this is only a part of the total expenses. Year by year one must add the cost of coal consumed in hauling around live human bodies: above all, one must add on the human cost, the physiological wear and tear, the psychological boredom and harassment and depression brought about by this daily shuttling between dormitory and workplace. Consider the number of man-hours reckoned in multiples of a million stupidly expended in the daily transportation of the human body: minutes and hours which, at the peak of traffic, cannot even be utilized in achieving the trivial anesthesia of the daily newspaper. Add to this the depression of the uncomfortable journey, the exposure to infectious diseases in the overcrowded car, the disturbance to the gastro-intestinal functions caused by the strain and anxiety of having to reach the office or factory on time.

Emerson said that life was a matter of having good days; but it is a matter of having good minutes, too. Who shall say what compensations are not necessary to the metropolitan worker to make up for the strain and the depression of the twenty, forty, sixty minutes he spends each night and morning passing through these metropolitan man-sewers. A walk to work, as much as a mile each way, is at most seasons a tonic, particularly for the sedentary worker, who plays such a part even in the typical metropolitan industries: at the typewriter, the linotype machine, the sewing machine. In the subway, even more than in the water system and the sewage disposal system, one encounters a characteristic form of metropolitan waste: namely, *a vast expenditure of time, energy, money, human vitality upon an activity that has flatly no value in itself:* an activity whose main use is to uphold the crowd-prestige of the metropolis and increase the pecuniary values garnered by the ground landlords and the financiers.

The organized decentralization of industry and the building up of a series of sub-centers within what is now the metropolitan region would obviate a good part of metropolitan transportation. But this is impossible; for while congestion originally provided the excuse for the subway, the subway becomes the further excuse for congestion. An enlightened administrator like Mayor La Guardia may observe that he could do more effective improvement in a city with a million inhabitants than in one with five million; but that is not the metropolitan consensus. For congestion becomes frozen in the form of a price-pyramid: land rents and mortgages. Any attempt to reorganize the metropolis on rational lines threatens the stability of that pyramid: it would mean a collapse of values in the central area: a deflation of its putative claims on future wealth. For this reason almost every bank, every insurance company, every individual landowner, ultimately every savings bank depositor, has, as F. L. Ackerman has pointed out, a *stake in congestion.* The whole structure of our present pecuniary values and prestige values assumes the indefinite continuance of this metropolitan pattern.

All these hopes, however, are gigantic bubbles. During the last century, the costs of mechanical utilities necessary for a congested metropolitan existence have been steadily mounting. Hence, despite the fabulous riches that heap up in the metropolis, the municipality itself is constantly threatened with an expenditure out of all proportion to its income or its benefits. Failing to attack the problem of planning on the social and economic side, where alone effective control is possible, the metropolis fumbles with mechanical palliatives. The policy of living beyond its income, in the hope of making it up by further increases in population, which will bring in areas of taxation, is a chronic one in the metropolis: a habit imitated even by

smaller cities with metropolitan pretensions. In America only an occasional city like Milwaukee is sufficiently free from these financial
standards to show anything like solvency without piling up grievous
social deficiencies. Actually, every new group of underpaid workers
is a municipal liability: an extra tax on the budget.

And here finally is a new source of congestion. Each new utility
requires a special corps of workers to build it and operate it, and a
further increment of other workers to supply them with goods and
services. Once the metropolis has reached a certain point of concentration, it tends to gather up population like a snowball rolling down
hill: for the existence of an expanding market of consumers draws
into the metropolitan area other industries, eager to take advantage
of the concentrated market—and once again there is a demand for
new transit routes, new municipal services, new housing. When the
high costs of these municipal services no longer leave a profit for
the enterpriser, the municipality itself assumes the burden: one
might call this socialism by default. This change to collective ownership and the absence of profit does not improve the actual situation—
in which vast sums of money are being expended to maintain a physical organization that should be decentralized and a structure of
values that should be deflated.

And mark this: not merely does the cost of mechanical utilities
rise directly with the size of the city: the cost of other municipal
services rise, too. What is the social cost of robbery and other forms
of crime? Robberies occur seven times as often in cities of over
250,000 population as in centers of 10,000: 189 people are known
to the police per ten thousand in the bigger centers, as compared
with 94 in smaller centers. This means more courts, more prisons,
more policemen, more costly devices for maintaining what is hopefully called law and order.

Some of these costs of congestion must be borne directly by the
citizens. Other costs are passed on in the form of higher prices for
metropolitan products, even for products that are merely controlled
financially by groups in the big center. But a large part of the burden
is paid for in the form of deteriorated domestic quarters and poorer
opportunities for living. The richest inhabitant of New York can
afford a smaller patch of garden than the meanest inhabitant of many

a country town: similarly the latter has often within sight and sound a refreshing environment that money cannot buy within the overgrown city. Sooner or later these costs and these deteriorations must be faced. When once such costly success is reduced to rational terms, the case for congestion is gone.

6: The Blighted Area

One must view the swift development of the metropolis from an ideal position in time and watch the transition that takes place over a period of a century. First the back gardens and the breathing spaces disappear, since the land is becoming too dear for such open areas: then the original residential areas are eaten into from within, as if by termites, as the original inhabitants move out and are replaced by lower economic strata: then these overcrowded quarters, serving as an area of transition between the commercial center and the better dormitory areas become in their disorder and their misery special breeding points for disease and crime: see the careful investigations of the Chicago sociologists. But every area in the metropolis tends to be a transitional area; and because of the very instability and uncertainty as to future uses, each area tends to go through a period in which the necessary repairs and renewals are not made. Since stability of uses and values means, from the commercial standpoint, a state little better than death, there is no motive in the existing economic regime sufficient to combat the habits that make for deterioration and blight.

The assumption upon which all this building is based is that population must continue to increase and values must vault skyward. The facts are that population may decrease, that values may go down, and that deterioration may be permanent. One can behold this contradiction at work in the zoning plans that have been popular in America during the last generation, following the example set by New York in 1916. Not merely do these zoning plans turn over to business and industrial uses from four to twenty times the area that could possibly be required at any future date, but they generously make provision for more intensive uses, when these are demanded by a sufficient number of owners, even though such uses would upset the general pattern that the city must rationally attempt to set up.

Moreover, none of these zoning ordinances suggest any practicable plan for deflating land values, thus permitting a change backward from a business to a residential use or from a tenement district to a park—although it is plain that sound adaptations to new needs must work both ways. The popular assumption is that values change in only one direction: upward.

But when blight sets in the opposite process happens. The inhabitants or the owners of buildings can no longer pay their share of municipal taxes; the street-cleaning department tends to overlook the more run-down neighborhoods, where the need for public hygiene is often worst, and even the fire inspectors and sanitary inspectors become lax: the repairs needed to keep blighted properties up to standard would do away with what little profits may remain in the investment, and so, by indifference or collusion or bribery, the city officials permit the blight to deepen. Roofs leak; plaster cracks on the walls; toilets fall into disrepair; pools of water gather in the cellar; the little patches of green, that once served as playgrounds, disappear, covered over with cinders, torn paper, discarded boxes, twisted bedsprings and broken iron. What may have been once a street of fine mansions—such as Euclid Avenue, Cleveland, or parts of the South Side in Chicago—is converted into low quarters, boarding houses and tenements, usually crowded, often filthy. The last stage is depopulation: deserted houses, in ruins: no rents: no taxes: a vast economic and civic liability.

The alternative to this form of progressive urban corrosion is the *standardization of blight.* The new-law tenement districts of the Bronx, the nearer one-family house districts of Queens, the sordid streets of Brixton or Clapham Junction, the tenements of Berlin and Hamburg and Paris built before the first World War—the difference between these structures and the blight that is produced by the piecemeal conversion of old structure is the difference between officially regulated prostitution, in segregated districts, and that which takes place at random. The most that is achieved in areas of regulated blight is an outward order and decency: but the content remains the same.

The fact is that these migrations of population and these alterations of use are inevitable consequences of metropolitan development under a capitalist system of production. For the rotten conditions near the center of the metropolis cause a flow into the outlying areas, to what seem by contrast better quarters. When these become built up, covered over, and run down, when their surrounding open spaces disappear by reason of the very movement they have attracted, those who can afford to jump once more beyond the pale of blight. But high land values tend to draw heavy industries that need more land to spread on toward the periphery of the metropolis: so the pressure at the center forms a new circle of blight; and rim developments are often as foul as those in the central area. Paris and London perhaps show these tendencies to a lesser degree than New York, Chicago and Philadelphia: but it is visible, through change of fashion or pressure of commercial competition, around the Place des Vosges or Berkeley Square.

Many observers of cities, as well as political administrators, tend to look upon the existence of blighted areas as an accidental fact in the modern city's development. On the contrary, the congestion of population at the center and the effort to compensate for instability by adding to the existing population, gives a large part of the building a purely transitory character: it is assumed that people will move in and out, that small businesses will eat into residential areas, that every residential street will be, potentially at least, a traffic and trading street, and that small stores and shops may, at some unpredictable point in space and time, be replaced by a department store or an office building. To plan a residential area so that it could only with great difficulty and wholesale changes be converted into any other kind of area is foreign to the metropolitan municipal engineer's mind. In this matter, a new order was instituted in London after 1910, in Amsterdam after 1920, and in other big cities at still later dates: but it has yet to become a dominant one, even in London, where re-building has been pushed most vigorously.

The blighted area may be defined as an area which is chronically unable to pay its share of the municipal services essential to its existence, and unable by reason of its economic status to pay for its own internal renovation and repair. All working class neighborhoods are by sheer poverty in a state of blight because, in the more outlying areas, the cost of the utilities that connect them with the center has risen steadily without any coeval rise in the income or economic privileges of the inhabitants; while in the center only intensive congestion of the foulest sort will "pay its way."

7: The Acceptance of Depletion

In the original urban formation, the central institutions of the city bear a direct relation to its whole population. Even when organized in quarters, with separate parish churches and subordinate markets, the central institutions are within walking distance. As the city increases in size, however, these central institutions occupy a relatively less important place in the active life of the citizens. (Observing this, the General Assembly of Massachusetts in the seventeenth century ordered that no one should live more than half a mile from his Common, lest he fail in his civic obligations.) In the metropolis, institutions that originally served 100,000 people fail to meet the needs of ten times that number. Even if the city only doubled in size, such institutes would fail merely by reason of internal congestion.

Now, the fact is that metropolitan expansion is accompanied by a permanent lag in building up the necessary communal institutions in the outlying sections: this, in fact, is one of the typical features of the sordid blighted areas: neglect by absence or by disuse. In such depressed quarters one may sometimes wander about for half a mile in any direction without finding a school, a public library, a playground, a firehouse, even a motion picture theater or a church: when one exists, it will be a makeshift.

In fact, just the opposite tendency exists: there is an increasing dearth of facilities. In other words, the Central District is the only part of the metropolis that really functions with anything like full efficiency, and it functions with respect to the needs of only a minority of the total population. Such an arrangement may satisfy the special interests of minorities: the music lover in the metropolis, for example, will have his desires sated in a fashion that the provincial center—*under a metropolitan economy*—can rarely afford. But as far as the diffusion of the highest metropolitan standards among every part of the population goes, the outcome is a mockery. The cultural standard is little higher than the housing standard: slum-level.

What is called the "growth" of the metropolis is in fact the constant recruitment of a proletariat, capable of accommodating itself to an environment without adequate natural or cultural resources: people who do without pure air, who do without sound sleep, who do without a cheerful garden or playing space, who do without the very sight of the sky and the sunlight, who do without free motion, spontaneous play, or a robust sexual life. The so-called blighted areas of the metropolis are essentially *"do without"* areas. If you wish the sight of urban beauty while living in these areas, you must ride in a bus a couple of miles: if you wish a touch of nature, you must travel in a crowded train to the outskirts of the city. Lacking the means to get out, you succumb: chronic starvation produces lack of appetite. Eventually, you may live and die without even recognizing the loss.

The same rule—"growth by civic depletion"—holds true for the provision of hospitals and playing fields and concert halls and colleges. These institutions often increase in size in order to measure up to megalopolitan standards; but what is true for biological organisms holds true, it would appear, for social bodies: effective growth requires cell-division, not merely a swelling of the original nucleus. A parish church in a village of five hundred might hold a hundred people, perhaps a crowded two hundred at one time. A hall that holds three thousand people might be adequate for a town with fifty thousand inhabitants; but it certainly cannot do justice to a city that holds a dozen times that number. The streets alone can hold such crowds: and unlike the medieval city, the metropolis is too huge to give a direct sense of unity to those who gather on the streets for a great celebration: no one can see or know what takes place in the city at large without listening to the radio and consulting the newspaper.

Moreover, beyond a certain point, even mechanical devices demand a limitation in size. With the use of loud speakers, the visible presence of a speaker is futile in an arena so large that most of the members of the audience are too far away to observe his expression or even follow his gestures. One of the reasons that passive sports, which put the emphasis upon the spectator, occupy such a large place in metropolitan routine is that the choice is one between vicarious exercise or none at all. Forty-five thousand people may attend a baseball game: but not even Chicago could boast the twenty-five hundred diamonds that would be necessary if each spectator claimed the right to play.

When institutions are planned rationally for convenience and for functional use, the metropolitan pattern does not suffice. To achieve a functional relationship, the unit has to be scaled to actual working capacity: reproduction rather than growth is what is required, while the effect of unified growth can be achieved through the orderly integration of the separate units. Where inorganic expansion of mechanical facilities takes place, a chronic deficiency results. The size of the building or the institution becomes a mere mask for this deficiency. Fifty thousand people gathered in a single place can do fewer things together than twenty-five groups of two thousand: their chief function is limited to *being* there and saying Hurrah! or Heil! at the right moment. That is why dictators love crowds and seek to provide bigger arenas and auditoriums for them: the bigger the crowd, the emptier their function.

Just as the great financial achievements of the metropolitan economy are based in part upon the monopoly of territories and raw materials, upon the exploitation of a growing urban proletariat, upon the transformation of the independent farmer into the tenant farmer, so its great achievements in urban growth are based upon the acceptance of blighted and sub-standard areas within the city: areas that are suburban, not because they are close to the countryside, but because they are below the current norms of civilization.

The very giantism of the metropolis leads to a depletion of its environment. On the surface, the massing of two or three million people within a relatively small central area should promote social intercourse; but except in the slums, where misery enforces a sort of neighborliness, there is a greater field for collective action in a village, for the ordinary man and woman, than there is in the most congested area. Complexity of organization does not necessarily mean richness and effectiveness of association: the mechanical principle of efficiency, which governs the first, as in a well-articulated factory, may actually obstruct the second: it is, in fact, where mechanical organization is *defective*, as in the queue waiting for a bus, that intercourse and association spontaneously awaken.

Beyond a certain point, density even obstructs association: if friendship requires a degree of isolated communion, so does neighborliness. There is less chance of knowing your neighbors on a block with a thousand people than on one that holds a hundred; for all association, even that in primary groups, has a selective aspect: it rests on the existence of recognizable faces and repeatable opportunities. Distance has an effect similar to density in breaking down associated life.

Neither the telephone nor the radio has diminished the importance of spatial nearness for all primary forms of intercourse. People who live in Oak Park and the South Side, in East Boston and Arlington, are nominally members of the same metropolitan complex: but for practical purposes they are sundered more effectively than if they were separated by three times these distances in the open country. Consider the difficulty of keeping the members of a trade union actively concerned in the affairs of their union, when, in order to attend to these affairs in the evening, they must either make the journey back again to the city from the dormitory where they live, at a great waste of time, sometimes with unendurable further fatigue, or they must remain in the center, at the cost of a meal which, even at its simplest, must be reckoned with seriously in a narrow budget. Small wonder that apathy sets in; or, to put it in its best light, that domesticity takes precedence over an effective political life.

At all events, in every metropolitan association, a social club, a museum, a trade union, a professional society, it is notorious that a small group tends to dominate its activities—usually composed of those who, either by topographical advantage, or by command of special means of transportation, are able to remain working at the center without undue sacrifice.

It is impossible here to go into all the perversions and miscarriages of civic functions because of the physical spread and the congestion and mis-planning of the mass city: hospitals placed on noisy dusty thoroughfares: overgrown schools so separated from the open country or even from parks that a bus-ride is necessary to introduce the pupils to the most rudimentary connections with living creatures and living plants: the emotional depression that follows the transition from a symphony concert to a crowded subway train: the discouragement to study when a student must travel an hour and a half each day on a subway train between his home and his high school.

The physical drain, the emotional defeat, of these cramped quarters, these dingy streets, the tear and noise of transit—these are but the most obvious results of megalopolitan growth: many of them cast a shadow upon the prosperous and the successful as well as upon the submerged members of the proletariat. For what the metropolis gives with one hand, it takes back with the other: one climbs its golden tree with such difficulty that, even if one succeeds in plucking the fruit, one can no longer enjoy it: the most successful of megalopolitans, wishing for life in his limbs, must take refuge in a country estate, or forego its advantages for Florida, Africa, the Riviera.

8: Defacement of Nature

Meanwhile, the urban agglomeration produces a similar depletion in the natural environment. Nature, except in a surviving landscape park, is scarcely to be found near the metropolis: if at all, one must look overhead, at the clouds, the sun, the moon, when they appear through the jutting towers and building blocks. The blare of light in the evening sky blots out half the stars overhead: the rush of sewage into the surrounding waters converts rivers into open sewers, drives away the more delicate feeders among the fish, and infects the bathers in the waters with typhoid: through the greater part of the nineteenth century typhoid was an endemic disease in big cities, brought in with the food supply, the shellfish, if not absorbed directly from the colon bacilli in the bathing or drinking water.

If the metropolis attempts to counteract these evils, it can do so only at a vast outlay: stations where the water is filtered and chlorinated, plants where the sewage is reduced and converted into fertilizer bring additional items of expense to the budget. If some isolated beauty in nature is preserved as a park, like the Bear Mountain Park, outside New York, it will be at a distance that requires half a morning to reach, even from the center of the city. When one arrives there one will find that a multitude of other people, equally eager to escape the metropolis, have by their presence created another metropolis—if not a wilderness-slum. One will see nature through the interstices of their bodies.

Indeed, the only successful metropolitan recreation grounds are those that accept the fact of overcrowding and give it appropriate form: a Wannseebad in Berlin, or a Jones Beach on Long Island: a vast stretch of waterfront domed by a vaster sky, well-organized, efficiently policed, with thousands of automobiles drawn up in ranks, giant pavilions, scores of assiduous life-guards on spidery towers, thousands of bathers basking in the sun and watching each other. A great mass spectacle: perhaps the nearest approach to genuine life, life esthetically intensified and ordered, that the metropolis offers.

As the pavement spreads, nature is pushed farther away: the whole routine divorces itself more completely from the soil, from the visible presence of life and growth and decay, birth and death: the slaughterhouse and the cemetery are equally remote, and their processes are equally hidden. The ecstatic greeting of life, the tragic celebration of death, linger on merely as mumbled forms in the surviving churches. The rhythm of the seasons disappears, or rather, it is no longer associated with natural events, except in print. Millions of people grow up in this metropolitan milieu who know no other environment than the city streets: people to whom the magic of life is represented, not by the miracles of birth and growth, but by placing a coin in a slot and drawing out a piece of candy or a prize. This divorce from nature has serious physiological dangers that the utmost scruples of medical care scarcely rectify. For all its boasted medical research, for all its real triumphs in lessening the incidence of disease and prolonging life, the city must bow to the countryside in the essentials of health: almost universally the expectation of life is greater in the latter, and the effect of deteriorative diseases is less.

But how find the country? The depletion of the metropolis does not stop at the legal boundaries of the metropolis: urban blight leads to rural blight. Since 1910 or thereabouts, the highways of motor traffic have begun to spread out from every metropolis in ever thickening and multiplying streams: these highways carry with them the environment of the metropolis: the paved highway, the filling station, the roadside slum, the ribbon development of houses, the roadhouse and cabaret. The farther and faster one travels, the more the life that accompanies one remains like that one has left behind. The same standardization of ugliness: the same mechanical substitutes: the same cockney indifference to nature: the same flippant attitude: the same celluloid pleasures and canned noise. A row of bungalows in the open country alongside an express highway is a metropolitan fact: so are the little heaps of week-end cabins by lake or stream or oceanside. Their density and concentration may not be greater than that of a rural village: but in their mode of life, their amusements, their frame of social reference, they are entirely metropolitan: hardly better or worse for being fifty miles away from the center.

Under this regime, every environment bears the same taint: its abiding picture of life is colored by the same newspapers, the same magazines, the same moving pictures, the same radio. Dependent upon the metropolitan markets for current cash, the outlying farming regions, mining centers, and industrial areas are all under the sway of metropolitan interests. What is not metropolitan is either the original bequest of nature, often neglected, misused, rundown, or a relic of an historical past when the community once showed an autonomous and autochthonous life. But the rural regions and the provincial towns taste only the metropolitan skimmed milk: the cream has been mechanically separated for the benefit of the big city. The provincial town now faces a poverty, or at least an impecuniousness, that is without the vicarious enjoyments of the metropolis, and without the residue of philanthropies, trusts, foundations, which provide the hospitals and libraries and institutions of learning in the big city: residual pledges of a better life.

The inhabitants of these rural areas, indeed, are taught to despise their local history, to avoid their local language and their regional accents, in favor of the colorless language of metropolitan journalism: their local cooking reflects the gastronomic subterfuges of the suburban woman's magazines; their songs and dances, if they survive, are elbowed off the dance floor: at best are given an audition at a metropolitan cabaret or radio station, where they are driven to an early death by universal repetition. The whole moral of this metropolitan regime is that one does not live, truly live, unless one lives in the metropolis or copies closely, abjectly, its ways. Expensive ways: ways that may be turned into monetary profits for the benefits of those who have a capital stake in the regime and who live in the light of its reflected glory. This moral is implanted by education, driven home by advertisement, spread by propaganda: *life means metropolitan life.* Not merely is the exodus to the city hastened, but the domination of the surviving countryside is assured: the same hand, as it were, writes the songs and lays down the terms for the mortgage.

In short: to scorn one's roots in one's own region and admiringly to pluck the paper flowers manufactured and sold by the metropolis becomes the whole duty of man. Though the physical radius of the metropolis may be only twenty or thirty miles, its effective radius is much greater: its blight is carried in the air, like the spores of a mold. The outcome is a world whose immense potential variety, first fully disclosed to man during the nineteenth century, has been sacrificed to a low metropolitan standardization. A rootless world, removed from the sources of life: a Plutonian world, in which living forms become frozen into metal: cities expanding to no purpose, cutting off the very trunk of their regional existence, defiling their own nest, reaching into the sky after the moon: more paper profits, more vicarious substitutes for life. Under this regime more and more power gets into hands of fewer and fewer people, ever further and further away from reality.

9: The Paper Dream City

When one examines the state of the metropolis one discovers a curious hallucination: the notion that its size, power, mechanical equipment and riches have effected a corresponding improvement in the life of its inhabitants. What is the mechanism of this error? We shall find it in the pseudo-environment of paper.

To believe that civilization has reached a culmination in the modern metropolis one must avert one's eyes from the concrete facts of metropolitan routine. And that is precisely what the metropolitan schools himself to do: he lives, not in the real world, but in a shadow world projected around him at every moment by means of paper and celluloid: a world in which he is insulated by glass, rubber, cellophane, from the mortifications of living. When the metropolitan lives most keenly, he lives by means of paper. The classic caricature of this tendency was given by Samuel Butler. When he took his man, Alfred, a perfect cockney, to the peaks of the High Alps to show him the overpowering landscape, Alfred gave the scene a bored glance and said: "And now, if you please, Sir, I should like to lie down on the grass here and have a read of Tit-Bits."

The swish and crackle of paper is the underlying sound of the metropolis: more important to the inner content of its existence than the whining rhythm of its machines. What is visible and real in this world is only what has been transferred to paper. The essential gossip of the metropolis is no longer that of people meeting face to face on the crossroads, at the dinner table, in the market-place: a few dozen people writing in the newspapers, a dozen more broadcasting over the radio, provide the daily interpretation of movements and happenings. The principle of concentrated propaganda and irresponsible dictatorship is written over the popular intellectual activities of the metropolis: in its evaluations, no less than in its deliberate suppressions. It is a short step from a yellow journal proprietor, skillfully manufacturing the day's news, to a propaganda ministry in a war government or a fascist dictatorship. Was it not from the commercial advertisers that political governments perhaps learned not to argue about the merits of their actions, but to keep on asserting with forceful insolence whatever they wanted the public to believe?

All the major activities of the metropolis are directly connected with paper; and printing and packaging are among its principal industries. The activities pursued in the offices of the metropolis are directly connected with paper: the tabulating machines, the journals, the ledgers, the card-catalogs, the deeds, the contracts, the mortgages: so, too, the prospectus, the advertisement, the magazine, the newspaper. As early as the eighteenth century Mercier had observed this metropolitan form of the White Plague. Modern methods of manifolding have not lessened the disease: they have only changed easygoing slipshod ways, that often sufficed, for forms of exact record that are economically out of all proportion to the intrinsic importance of the matter recorded. What was a mere trickle in Mercier's day has now become a ravaging flood of paper.

As the day's routine proceeds the pile of paper mounts higher: the trashbaskets are filled and emptied and filled again. The ticker tape exudes its quotations of stocks and its reports of news; the students in the schools and universities fill their notebooks, digest and disgorge the contents of books, as the silkworm feeds on mulberry leaves and manufactures its cocoon, unraveling themselves on examination day. Buildings rise recklessly, often in disregard of ultimate profits, in order to provide an excuse for paper capitalizations and paper rents. In the theater, in literature, in music, in business, reputations are made—on paper. The scholar with his degrees and publications, the actress with her newspaper clippings, and the financier with his shares and voting proxies, measure their power and importance by the amount of paper they can command. No wonder the anarchists once invented the grim phrase: "Incinerate the documents!" That would ruin this whole world quicker than universal flood and earthquake.

The event in the newsreel, the drama on the motion picture screen, the disembodied speech of the radio announcer: this is the "eye of the world" and the "voice of experience" and the "march of time." The words and actions of men are more and more framed for their effect on paper: or they are posed, with a view to historical reproduction, in the photograph and the motion picture. That life is an occasion for living, and not a pretext for supplying items to newspapers or spectacles for crowds of otherwise vacant bystanders —these notions do not occur to the metropolitan mind. For the denizens of this world are at home only in the ghost city of paper: they live in a world of "knowledge about," as William James would have said, and they daily drift farther away from the healthy discipline of first-hand "acquaintance with."

Hence the importance of statistics. The principal achievements that quicken the metropolitan mind are quantitative ones: record-breaking in some fashion or another. Size competition is indeed the very mode of metropolitan expansion: a forty-story building is *ipso facto* a more important building than a two-story one, and a

university teaching ten thousand students is similarly more important than one teaching ten hundred. If these were not axioms in
the metropolitan mind it might be a prey to occasional doubts about
its own importance. To lop a quarter of a second off the running of
a mile, to sit on a flagpole three days longer than a rival, to graduate
so many hundred more bachelors of art a year, to build a building
ten stories higher than the nearest rival—these are typical metropolitan records—important only on paper. Metropolitans flout the
wise Biblical story of the king who insisted on counting his army.

This metropolitan world, then, is a world where flesh and blood
is less real than paper and ink and celluloid. It is a world where the
great masses of people, unable to have direct contact with more satis-
fying means of living, take life vicariously, as readers, spectators,
passive observers: a world where people watch shadow-heroes and
heroines in order to forget their own clumsiness or coldness in love,
where they behold brutal men crushing out life in a strike riot, a
wrestling ring or a military assault, while they lack the nerve even
to resist the petty tyranny of their immediate boss: where they
hysterically cheer the flag of their political state, and in their neighborhood, their trades union, their church, fail to perform the most
elementary duties of citizenship.

Living thus, year in and year out, at second hand, remote from
the nature that is outside them and no less remote from the nature
within, handicapped as lovers and as parents by the routine of the
metropolis and by the constant specter of insecurity and death that
hovers over its bold towers and shadowed streets—living thus the
mass of inhabitants remain in a state bordering on the pathological.
They become the victims of phantasms, fears, obsessions, which bind
them to ancestral patterns of behavior. At the very point where super-
mechanization takes hold of economic production and social intercourse, a treacherous superstition, a savage irrationality, reappear
in the metropolis. But these reversionary modes of behavior, though
they are speedily rationalized in pseudo-philosophies, do not remain
on paper: they seek an outlet. The sadistic gangster, the bestial
fascist, the homicidal vigilante, the law-offending policeman burst
volcanically through the crust of metropolitan life. They challenge
the dream city with an even lower order of "reality."

10: The Acquisitiveness of a Sick Metropolis

Over many precarious millenniums man's acquisitiveness has stood him in good stead. Where nature's terms were hard the very restriction over the food supply and production placed a natural limit on his tendency to gather and hoard: there was safety in nature's niggardliness. His habits were as innocent as the bee's or the squirrel's.

Capitalism made a special virtue of this tendency to store up food and seed: only instead of vital goods, it substituted money, and so far from hoarding money, like the miser, it sent it forth in order to multiply itself in "gainful employment." Buying and selling ceased to be agents of consumption: they were important as mechanisms of profit. Consumption was confined, beyond the immediate wants of the body, to those who commanded capital, acquired profits, and were ready to consume with voracity. Once such attitudes became respectable, any scheme that kept human wants stationary or that encouraged a wantless life—the bias of a St. Francis or a Thoreau—became a blasphemous rejection of the new gods. For a wantless life means a marketless productive system: whereas stability in investment for profit demanded the concoction of fresh wants and the continuous expansion of the market.

The expansion of the market has been one of the most characteristic attributes of the metropolitan regime: it is involved in the whole scheme of substituting vicarious satisfactions for direct ones, and money goods for life experiences. By the eighteenth century the public markets and producers' shops of the medieval town were being converted into specialized shops under continuous operation. Even at this early date in Paris, in the reign of Louis XV, a banker named Kromm founded a department store with some two or three hundred employees. In 1844 a modern department store, the Ville de France, opened in Paris with a hundred and fifty employees on its staff.

If the vitality of an institution may be gauged by its architecture, the department store was one of the most vital institutions in this metropolitan regime. One of the first large buildings to employ iron columns instead of a masonry wall was the A. T. Stewart department store in New York; while Schinkel's design for a Berlin department

Political capitals: emblems of worldwide exploitation. Here political and financial power is concentrated: here the forces that parade as "national history"—a minor fragment of the total life of peoples and cities and regions—take shape. But the day of these dinosaur cities is over: their burdens outweigh their benefits. The orderly breakup of their unwieldy structures, and the reconstitution of their power and culture on a federal basis is one of the major tasks of urbanism.

[TOP] London, facing the Thames, with the relatively new Kingsway cutting through the partial order of Bloomsbury from Southampton Row, terminating in Bush House and the crescent of Aldwych. An imperial avenue, naturally lined with business offices of overseas corporations. Beautiful survivals of an older London however remain: the spacious quadrangles of the Temple by the Thames on the left, and the orderly building and gracious verdure of the Bloomsbury Squares of the foreground mingle with the irregular clottings of buildings in the uncontrolled spaces between. (*Photograph: Ewing Galloway, Aerofilms*)

[MIDDLE LEFT] Berlin: the formidable barracks city on the Spree: combination of Preussentum and Spekulantentum: also Junker arrogance and Slavonic servility. Imposing order in its public buildings and systematic foulness in its old rear court tenements. Its brief renascence as a more humane type of city coincided with the life-span of the German republic, with its temporary release from military preoccupations. The parks and housing communities created between 1920 and 1932, especially developments like Britz, Zehlendorf, and Siemensstadt, set a new standard in collective planning toward beauty and efficiency: a happy humane contrast with the grandiose triumphal ways and mass-squares planned by the later National Socialist regime. (*Photograph: Ewing Galloway*)

[MIDDLE RIGHT] Madrid: perched like a spider in the midst of a transportation web: originally a symbol of irregional unification, in defiance of the Basques, Catalans, Andalusians: transformed through the brutal Fascist uprising of 1936 into a symbol of Federal unity and democratic hope. The heroic resistance of Madrid's population to the systematic massacre of women and children conducted by the Fascists is a proof of those enduring human qualities that neither metropolitanism nor fascism can permanently wipe out: symbol of human vitality, human nobility, human sacrifice, capable of creating a new civilization. (*Photograph: Ewing Galloway*)

[BOTTOM] Rome: approach to St. Peter's seen from the Cathedral itself: pointing toward the Tiber, but suddenly cut short in its attempt to impose order by the historic tangle of buildings that blocks the connection. The memory of imperial destiny, the visible reminder of a splendid past—with a certain amnesia as to the causes of its downfall—recurs in the dreams of a Dante, a Rienzi, a Mussolini: it even seizes an alien race in the nineteenth century concept of the Pax Britannica. (*Photograph: Ewing Galloway*)

[TOP LEFT] Beginning of the typical metropolitan day: descent into Hades: in this instance the Paris Metro, with Art Nouveau decoration in iron that marks the neotechnic phase of subway building: the first underground being a coal-smudged inferno built in London in 1860. Underground quarters become part of the normal environment of the metropolis: repeated in effect even above ground. (*Photograph: Ewing Galloway*)

[SECOND LEFT] New York: Orpheus and Eurydice in the Kingdom of Pluto. The photograph is unavoidably idyllic: an actual subway crush effectually prevents the use of a camera. Rushing beneath geological strata, rivers, tall buildings, avenues, the fortunate travelers who have seats struggle to assimilate the day's dispersed events recorded in the newspaper. For those who stand, the subway becomes a cloister: a place of enforced inactivity and contemplation: if you will, a traveling prison. The acceptance of this environment, as a necessity of daily life, is perhaps no more singular than the acceptance of a day that includes no glimpse of the sun, no taste of the wind, no smell of earth or growing things, no free play of the muscles, no spontaneous pleasure not planned for a week in advance and recorded on a memorandum pad: in short, that day without an hour given to sauntering, which so amazed and horrified Henry Thoreau. Hence the need for synthetic stimuli. (*Photograph: Ewing Galloway*)

[MIDDLE RIGHT] London. Alternatives: a crowded bus, creeping through congested streets, spreading petrol fumes and the more deadly odorless carbon monoxide: or a railroad journey, over a longer distance, from a suburb, to the "City," over whose confusion hangs the dome of St. Paul's. (*Photograph: Ewing Galloway*)

[BOTTOM] Leipziger Strasse, Berlin: showing trolley cars and commercial buildings. The central district with its quick tempo, its strained concentration upon pecuniary affairs. Not as chaotic as an American metropolis, with its indiscriminate congestion: but scarcely less obsolete from the standpoint of working efficiency. (*Photograph: Ewing Galloway*)

[TOP RIGHT] Well-to-do suburb of London: Wimbledon. The development of a central district devoted to business, finance, and the accessory industries has its typical by-product: the dormitory suburb. The rapid growth of metropolitan districts in the twentieth century has been mainly a suburban growth: migration (encouraged by land speculators) to cheaper land, open spaces, temporarily more decent living conditions. In the obsolete mono-nucleated type of city this decentralization and dispersal of the main functions of urban living merely increases the extent of the waste and human wear-and-tear. In its ideal form, with large houses, spacious lawns and gardens, tree-bordered streets, the suburb is an upper class luxury. The great mass of the population, lured out to the periphery of the metropolis, get no closer to Wimbledon than the Long Island example shown on Plate 21: a mockery of the free standing house, the individual garden. (*Photograph: Aerofilms*)

store in the eighteen-thirties, though never executed, was far ahead
of the labored traditionalism of Messel's overpraised Wertheim store
in Berlin. Finally, one of the best utilitarian buildings of the early
twentieth century, a radical departure in design, was the Schlesinger
and Meyer Building (now Carson, Pirie, and Scott) in Chicago.

Now, the department store is the spender's paradise. For a long
while luxury spending, with its made-to-order goods, remained in
small specialized shops: this holds even today on New Bond Street,
the Rue de la Paix, and Madison Avenue. Below this level of expense, the department store has flourished; for it offers the buyer
the greatest possible number of wares under one roof: it diversifies
the temptations to buy at the same time as it concentrates the opportunity: sometimes it even adds to the normal routine of spending and
sampling the vehement competition of the bargain counter. As the
household industries disappeared from the metropolitan dwelling,
and as household routines became more simplified, not less by the
reduction of domestic space than by labor-saving devices, middle
class mothers and daughters needed a fresh occupation. They found
it in shopping: counter-shopping and window-shopping. On a Satur-
day night in an industrial town the flow of people through the main
shopping street is the principal form of recreation and drama. The
ultimate symbol of this acquisitive life was that final product of
the metropolitan regime: the five-and-ten-cent store, which opened
up this typical bourgeois excitement even to the very poor.

Each practical manifestation of a culture tends to leave a shadow-
self in the mind: this may be the result of the economic institution
itself, or it may issue out of the same cultural complex that created
it. A whole series of such parallels exist in the spiritual life of the
metropolis: one may accept them, without committing oneself to
a purely materialist interpretation of culture. What is the big metropolitan university but a megalopolis of learning, a great cartel
formed by the financial unification of a diversity of foundations and
schools. With its jumble of buildings, its mechanical methods of
intercourse, its mass production of students, its intellectual bookkeeping by points and credits, the overswollen university is the exact
counterpart of the metropolitan life for which it prepares its students
from all over the land. The universities of Chicago, Berlin, and

London have been built up during the last fifty years in the faithful image of the city that surrounds them: the same technical adroitness, the same aggressive emphasis on physical equipment, the same waste of substance in material organization, and finally, the same innocence of cultural values that are embodied, not in statistical achievements, but in a mode of feeling, thinking, acting.

Similarly the department store, as Mr. Lee Simonson has pointed out, has its exact counterpart in the big metropolitan museum. Culture and knowledge are regarded from this standpoint mainly as a means of acquisitions and display. Historically the contents of the art museum derive from the palace and the country house: displays of loot that mark either ostentatious purchase or the military conquest of foreign lands. (The form of the natural history museum is still largely that of the trophy room of the country house, where the hunter displays his horns, pelts, and skeletons.) In time, genuine esthetic and scientific interests develop in these institutions; but the trustees of the museums are more interested in abstract acquisition and honorific display than in matters of truth, taste, and value. Physical size serves again as a *substitute* for organization, as in the labor market: mechanical expansion is confused with significance.

No doubt the big museum may serve a rational function: but the popular interest in it is a by-product of the search for pecuniary profits that characterizes even the remoter provinces of this pecuniary metropolitan culture. By the patronage of the museums, the ruling metropolitan oligarchy of financiers and officeholders establish their own claims to culture: more than that, they fix their own standards of taste, morals, and learning as that of their civilization—thus maintaining and stabilizing the favored pattern of acquisitive living. Even when the patron is the municipality, the same ingrained habits prevail: the worth of the museum will be gauged by the size of its collections and the number of people who visit it. Consider the monstrous installation of the Pergamon altar in Berlin: a vulgar triumph.

Patrons and public alike, these *nouveaux riches* of the metropolis are culture-shoppers. They tend to transform the chief institutions of learning into vast department stores of the arts and sciences, where everything is ticketed and labeled, where bargain attractions are offered, where the turnover of goods is more important than the ultimate satisfactions of the purchaser. The growing bewilderment of the student and spectator, the patent sterility of his acquired knowledge and taste—none of these facts interferes with the tendency toward expansion. In the sciences, outside the museum, a systematic rationale has been laid down since the seventeenth century. But this fundamental order cannot be detected in the badly organized and feebly related collections of the great museums: on the contrary, the total impression is that of chaos, modified by good intentions and incidental patches of order. This chaos reflects accurately, not so much the state of science or historical research, as the disorganized contents of the metropolis itself.

Is there a single metropolitan museum of art or natural history in the world that could not profit enormously by being decentralized, with each unit reduced to a modicum of its present size, and completely reorganized? That the museum is a valuable type of cultural enterprise I have no doubt: in the final chapter of this book I shall, indeed, sketch out briefly its place in a genuine civic economy. But at present all its valid purposes are corrupted by the fact that its standards are, frankly, those of the department store: the lure of many unrelated articles and their random purchase, all under one roof. Around the art museum, an antique art market grows up, abetted by the instincts of the rich, for whom rarity has a market value apart from any other token of value: a rare wood carving is no less valuable than a rare postage stamp. When the supply of genuine antiques dwindles, copies are forged—or new reputations among modern artists are manufactured to take the place of the old. Sometimes the forgeries are consummately executed and deceive the experts who examine them: but their worth hangs, not on their esthetic merit, but on their genuineness: if that is demolished, they become worthless. To acquire goods without having contributed an iota of thought or energy to their production is the mark of metropolitan success. To acquire knowledge and taste without a single first-hand experience, such as that possessed by the artist and the craftsman and the woodsman and the hunter and the scientist is the mark of cultural acquisition as fostered, for the greater part, by the metropolitan museum.

Here, as elsewhere in the metropolis, there are counter-initiatives that throw a more favorable light over the picture, such as the redoubtable work done by the school extension department of the American Museum of Natural History in Manhattan, and similar attempts to decentralize and re-focus the museum's resources in other institutions. But the main outlines still hold. Aimless acquisition: reckless expansion: progressive disorganization—these are the dominating facts, and they bring their own nemesis.

11: Routine and Relaxation

Economically, the metropolis may be described as the urban embodiment of the international fair. Its routine is subordinate to the exhibition and sale of goods. But the fair has two sides: business and pleasure; and as business takes on a more abstract form, with greater stress on monetary manipulation, regularity, mechanism, mathematical discipline, the need for compensatory relief becomes greater. The traditional pleasures of the fair—jugglers, acrobats, gamblers, sideshows, sexual license of all sorts—cease to be sporadic: they too become part of the metropolitan routine. The metropolis itself may be described as a World's Fair in continuous operation.

Even in earlier days, fairs served in something the same fashion as national conventions and congresses do today: they provided suitable opportunities for relaxation from the strict observance of family ties, local customs, respectable ways. Indeed, the old St. James's Fair in London was closed by one of the most lascivious monarchs of England, Charles II, because of the excess of bawdy entertainment; while in great Nizhni Novgorod, at the end of the nineteenth century, the poorer prostitutes conducted their rites in public under the open sky: shouting their wares to the passer-by. In the metropolis the usual excess of unmarried males helps further to build up a whole fabric of institutions based upon the commercial exploitation of sexual interests: whore-houses, dance halls, burlesque shows and girl shows, houses of assignation and hotels that serve the casual couple.

These elements of the fair all become systematized, standardized, commercialized. Every step in relaxation from spontaneous horseplay to drunkenness, from flirtation with music to a sexual orgy, is conducted with a view toward producing a maximum profit for the enterpriser. Saturnalia charges what the traffic will bear. Bawdiness, no longer the goatlike outburst of animal spirits after the abstentions and rigors of the winter, becomes in itself a jaded, night-in-night-out part of metropolitan routine: it measures its titillations and charges accordingly. And since the overt code of Western society has no place for such compensatory outbursts or moral holidays, an additional air of furtiveness hangs over these enterprises, even when they have official sanction. Thus is formed a tie-up with the under-world of racketeers and criminals which introduces new elements of degradation into gambling and promiscuous sexual intercourse: connections between the "respectable classes" and the underworld, by way of pleasure, amusement, and sexual release, that tend to undermine the morale of the body politic.

With respect to these relaxations, the big city has the same advantage that international fairs once had: its very bigness makes it an admirable hiding place. Within its endless streets, the metropolis provides shelter from prying eyes: here the drunkenness that would be a public spectacle becomes a private foible: here the liaison that might disrupt a provincial family can be consummated with a minimum of exposure. A man and a woman incur less danger from gossip by going to bed together in a metropolitan hotel than they would if they merely dined together in the restaurant of a small provincial town.

Indeed, the advantages of the metropolis as a hiding place—an advantage that illicit lovers share with more violent breakers of law and convention—is not the least of its attractions to the visitors who swarm in from other parts of the country. If one has anything to conceal, the place to conceal it is among a million other people. The anonymity of the big city, its impersonality, is a positive encouragement to a-social or anti-social actions. Hence a professional form of surveillance, by an organized police, must take the place of neighborly scrutiny and pressure: a city of strangers lacks any other form of stabilizing check. The transformation of the town guard into the professional police, which first took place in Paris in the seventeenth century, marks one of the critical changes from a town economy to a metropolitan economy. There is perhaps a moral in the fact that the Greek equivalent for policeman means citizen.

The a-social character of metropolitan routine can in fact be partly deduced from the relative cost of police service in cities of different size. In American cities with a million or more people, the cost of police is sixty cents per inhabitant per year: in cities with from three hundred to six hundred thousand it is forty cents; in cities between one hundred and three hundred thousand, it is only twenty cents, while cities with thirty thousand people or under pay only ten cents. Doubtless the bigger cities get more in the way of service: but they need it. In the United States, except in cases of rape and manslaughter, the number of police cases per thousand forms an ascending curve in direct relationship to the size of cities.

Among the specialized pleasures of the metropolis, those connected with nutrition or its surrogates play no small part: oral erethism, stimulation through food and drink, has a place in metropolitan routine that was once reserved for special feasts and celebrations. The restaurants, the cafés, the saloons and pubs, are necessarily ubiquitous; and their trade is intensified by the fact that the home itself plays a smaller part in furnishing such stimuli. To speak of the metropolis in the loftier economic ranks is to speak of the Hermitage, the Adlon, Maxim's, the Ritz, the Colony Club: places where the reputations built up in finance, law, or the theater are put on parade. A certain psychological intensity goes into these expenditures on food and drink; for good eating and drinking are the ultimate justifications of the metropolitan's day: stuffing, gourmandizing, sipping, he achieves a momentary euphoria that obscures the eventual physiological derangement. Balzac's incarnation of the antique collector and the gourmandizer in the single figure of Cousin Pons was a master-stroke.

12. The Poison of Vicarious Vitality

In cheaper substitute forms, all these activities are pursued by the masses; and they are enjoyed vicariously, at least, in the motion pictures, the illustrated papers, the fashion advertisements. But the crowds, as such, have their own forms of mass enjoyment: it is for them that the lights twinkle on the avenues outside the theaters and restaurants and cabarets they cannot afford to enter: it is to them that the advertiser appeals in a myriad of colored bulbs, tempting them to drink this whisky, ride in this motor car, or to renew their fading vitality with "pilules pinks pour personnes pâles."

By day, the crowd has its special parades: the passage of a potentate through the city: the carefully arranged reception to a general who has redeemed for civilization a barbarous country whose inhabitants cannot defend themselves with poison gas: the return of a girl who has swum the English Channel. And they greet these ambitious nonentities in the appropriate metropolitan fashion: not with flowers, as Lindbergh was greeted in still rural Mexico City, but by emptying on the head of the illustrious hero the contents of their waste-paper baskets, swirling festoons of ticker tape, or, when exhausted of the normal supply of paper, with ribbons of toilet paper: the ultimate mark of metropolitan approbation: Bravo!

The arrangement of such spectacles is an important contribution to metropolitan equilibrium, as the classes that rule the city almost instinctively understand: it is, so to say, the vulgarization of the prestige values of monopoly. Without such shows the bitter actualities of poverty and impotence might for the mass of metropolitans be almost unendurable: these spectacles help counteract the inferior sense of manliness and womanliness that develops under stress of mechanization, and they break down, likewise, through mass participation, that sense of loneliness which haunts the atomic individual in the big city. (See Jules Romains' keen depiction of The Lonely in Men of Good Will.)

Life comes back to the metropolis in the intercourse in spontaneous groups for which the great mass spectacles serve as occasion. Boxing matches, wrestling bouts, feats of dull endurance like bicycle races and dance marathons, spectacular exhibitions of derring-do like rodeos, or motor races and air races. All these exaggerations of strength, skill, daring, are necessary to stir the basic animal needs from their costive torpidity. Doing so, they promote at least the lowest form of sociality: the basic tie in this amorphous metropolitan body: gregariousness. What was once called the herd instinct is in fact the *residual* sociality of the metropolitan crowd. The stadium, where the great crowds assemble for these various spectacles, is,

like the police force, one of the special stigmata of the metropolitan regime: here, if anywhere, is its essential drama: *spectacular* achievement and *spectacular* death.

In most of these performances an inverted sense of life is promoted through the presence of fear and the nearness to death. The maiming of the sacrificial victims is one of the high points in the spectacle, precisely as in the gladiatorial bouts of ancient Rome, or in the ritualistic murders of the Aztecs. Without death or the threat of death, the populace feels itself cheated: so that the more peaceful games, like baseball and horse-racing, must be spiced by gambling if they are to equal the excitement of a rodeo or a motor race. Not merely are those who actually see these morbid spectacles aware of them: by means of the newspaper, the radio, the newsreel, the most sadistic exhibitions are inflicted upon those who are humane enough still to loathe them with an honest human hate.

There is little doubt however as to the value of these spectacles from the standpoint of the exploiting groups: they tend to make people indifferent to the values of life. Satiated with milder forms of brutality, the spectator demands bloodier satisfactions. If games do not provide them sufficiently, he will manufacture occasions: note the zestful terrorism practiced by the bourgeoisie under the guise of restoring law and order in a labor conflict: note the prompt effort on the part of police to turn peaceful struggles for power into occasions for violence. The tameness of the metropolitan routine must have its compensatory mobilizations of ferocity.

Perhaps the best psychological interpretation of this regime has been given by John Ruskin: I must quote it in full, for the intervening years have only underlined and more fully substantiated his analysis of the metropolitan mind in Arrows of the Chace.

"What thought can enough comprehend the contrast between such [human] life, and that in streets where summer and winter are only alternations of heat and cold; where snow never fell white nor sunshine clear; where the ground is only a pavement and the sky no more than the glass roof of an arcade; where the utmost power of a storm is to choke the gutters and the finest magic of spring, to change mud into dust: where—chief and most fatal difference of state—there is no interest or occupation for any of the inhabitants but the routine of counter or desk within doors, and the effort to pass each other without collision outside; so that from morning to evening the only possible variation of the monotony of the hours, and lightening of the penalty of existence must be some kind of mischief, limited, unless by more than ordinary godsend of fatality, to the fall of a horse or the slitting of a pocket.

"I said that under these laws of inanition, the craving of the human heart for some kind of excitement could be supplied from *one* source only. It might have been thought by any other than a sternly tentative philosopher, that the denial of their natural food to human feelings would have provoked a reactionary desire for it; and that the dreariness of the street would have been gilded by dreams of pastoral felicity. Experience has shown the fact to be otherwise; the thoroughly trained Londoner can enjoy no other excitement than that to which he has been accustomed, but as for *that* in continually more ardent or more virulent concentration; and the ultimate power of fiction to entertain him is by varying to his fancy the modes, and defining for his dullness the horrors of death. In the single novel of Bleak House there are nine deaths . . . carefully wrought out or worked up to: one by assassination, Mr. Tulkinghorn; one by starvation with phthisis, Joe; one by chagrin, Richard; one by spontaneous combustion, Mr. Krock; one by sorrow, Lady Dedlock's lover; one by remorse, Lady Dedlock; one by insanity, Miss Flite; one by paralysis, Sir Leicester. It is the fact that all these deaths, but one, are of inoffensive, or at least, in the world's estimate, respectable persons; and that they are all grotesquely either violent or miserable, purporting thus to illustrate the modern theory that the appointed destiny of a large average of our population is to die like rats in a drain, either by trap or poison."

Have we not here a clue to that sadism of the imagination which still characterizes such a large part of the novels, the moving pictures, the dramas, the daily newspaper accounts of murder and violence? This sadism has helped harden the metropolitan world into a dull acceptance of the use of poison gas in civil riots or the massacre of unprotected citizens in time of war: fulsome totalitarian murder.

Let us sum up these diversions. To counteract an intolerable pre-

occupation with arithmetical abstractions and mechanical instruments, an almost equally abstract interest in the stomach and the
sexual organs, divorced from their organic relations. To counteract
boredom and isolation, mass spectacles: to make up for biological
inferiority, a series of collective games and exhibitions, based on
withering specializations of the body. In short, the metropolis is
rank with forms of *negative vitality*. Nature and human nature,
violated in this environment, come back in destructive forms: drugs,
anodynes, aphrodisiacs, hypnotics, sedatives, are a necessary accompaniment of this exacerbated state, strenuous efforts to recover
the normal equilibrium of the healthy body and the healthy mind:
salvation by aspirin. James Joyce, in Ulysses, projected this phan-
tasmal state: he showed the mind of Leopold Bloom regurgitating
the contents of the newspaper and the advertisement, living in a
hell of unfulfilled desires, vague wishes, enfeebling anxieties, morbid
compulsions, and dreary vacuities: a dissociated mind in a disintegrated city: perhaps the *normal* mind of the world metropolis.

In this mangled state, the impulse to live departs from apparently
healthy personalities, as it might depart from someone who had been
crushed under the wheels of a locomotive. The impulse to die sup-
plants it. And just as the will-to-live can triumph over all but catastrophic accidents or derangements to the physical organism, so the
will-to-die can eat cancerously into the personality, until the body
itself, no matter how outwardly healthy, is tainted and finally is
consumed by the malady.

Is it any wonder that Dr. Sigmund Freud found a death wish at
the seat of human activity? The analysis does not lack justification,
provided one remembers it is a historic phenomenon, time-condi-
tioned, place-conditioned, culture-conditioned. The scene is Megalopolis: in Freud's case, Wien; and the time is the period of imperial
and financial collapse, in a structure already cracking before the
first World War. At this particular moment, the death wish appears
as a collective impulse: an effort to save life from further defeats,
from more unbearable indignities, through suicide. Evil and sinister
though this impulse may be, in terms of the life-values a genuine
culture embodies, it is one degree better, perhaps, than extinction
by slow paralysis.

13: A Brief Outline of Hell

Behold the present moment in Western Civilization. Examine the economic state of the metropolis during the last century and note how its infirmities have piled up.

The main economic problem for the metropolitan regime, even on its own premises, is to reduce its tendency to swing violently from prosperity to bankruptcy. To overcome this manic-depressive economic cycle without flattening out into a stable economic regime that would curb the further acquisition of wealth by the minority, presents, however, an inherent contradiction. For the metropolis is by its very nature in a state of permanent unbalance: its proletariat lacks good housing and an adequate diet, to say nothing of other opportunities, even during the most flatulent periods of prosperity. Hence its financiers and statesmen seek to prevent the pyramid of values from falling by broadening the base. American motor car manufacturers, choked at home, seek outlets in Europe: Japanese cotton mills seek buyers in India and Africa: surplus capital, unable to find investment markets at home or lured abroad by the less modest returns offered, exposes itself to forces beyond its control.

These new centers of economic gravity often fall within the base of another state or people. Conflicts result, sometimes with the states or peoples themselves. To command new areas for raw materials, to conquer new markets, to ensure the safety of new investment areas, to collect tribute from unsafe or irregular investments, to seize territory from weaker peoples, every state must devote itself to the expansion of its army and navy. Once the territory is partitioned, the states that were slow to join the scramble look enviously upon those in possession: they demand their share in the loot, their portion of the real or illusory benefits; and their threats constitute a further menace to this unstable order.

So far from improving conditions, imperialistic expansion only complicates the disorder: it increases the insecurity of the home areas, and it drains away economic vitality by concentrating production upon the materials of war and all its accessory equipment. To maintain the armed forces in a state of ready aggression, the proletariat must be further exploited and taxed: even the rich, to keep their wealth at all, must part with a share of it. The sense of insecurity thus produced tempts every class to keep its savings in a liquid form; and this in turn discourages long term investments at low interest rates, upon which improved production and far-sighted expenditures in consumptive equipment, such as housing and municipal utilities, depends.

Meanwhile, psychological tensions increase: belligerent impulses demand expression. The simple love of country and home and soil, a love that needs neither reasons nor justifications, is turned by the official apologists of the state into the demented cult of "patriotism": coercive group unanimity: blind support of the rulers of the state: maudlin national egoism: an imbecile willingness to commit collective atrocities for the sake of "national glory."

The buildings of the imperial metropolis serve as an appropriate background for these war-ceremonies and reinforce these pretensions. From Washington to Tokyo, from Berlin to Rome, the architecture of imperialism is a monotonous reflection of the military-bureaucratic mind. They exhibit the extravagance of the financial *arriviste,* without a touch of creative warmth: the dull façades of endless columns, the heavy armor of stone in which they are usually encrusted, their pompous emphasis of their historic predecessor, Rome, the solemn tomb-like quality of their offices and halls mark that failure in life-efficiency which is characteristic of this regime. And the quarters of the bureaucracy are planned with so little discretion that a few bombs strategically dropped from the air might paralyze the major government services for weeks at a time: except for the building of occasional vaults and underground chambers, this war-regime has not in the matter of planning and building and layout mastered the most elementary demands of war-protection.

But the growing war-bureaucracy presents an outward front of power: power as expressed in wide avenues, endless vistas of useless columns, and huge stadiums fit for martial exercises and games: the element of feeling, completely lacking in the stereotypes of architectural form, is provided by the crowds on the street: the children assembled for the singing of vainglorious national anthems, the crowds marching in parades, or the mob that assembles in the public square to behold, at a discreet distance, the leader of the state. This is the crowd whose simple hates, fueled by propaganda, transfers to foreign devils the unconscious hatred it dare not express for the classes that exploit it, or the unconscious contempt each member feels for his own thwarted self. Essential to this metropolitan regime are these passive atoms: metropolitan barbarians: a million cowards upon whose blank minds the leader writes: Bravery. A million scattered, bewildered individuals whom the rulers cajole, bully, and terrorize into a state of unity.

What follows? External conflicts pile upon internal contradictions. Psychologically, a violent paranoia, with pronounced delusions of grandeur, takes hold of the ruling classes: the alternative is something like collective dementia praecox: suspicion, hatred, isolation, desire to inflict destruction, appear in extreme forms. These psychological states are deliberately fostered by a positive cult of irrationality: intellectual disintegration is expressed in wishful systems of anthropology, sociology, and philosophy, which hold in contempt the most elementary obligations to respect fact or to establish new truths by the discipline of objective verification. The inactivity of despair alternates with national delusions of persecution, followed by attempts to inflict damage upon the putative persecutors. Read the tirades of hate that accompanied the first World War, from the *Hassgesang* of the Germans to the *Hang the Kaiser* campaign conducted by the righteous Lloyd George. Recall the extravagant hatreds expressed by the Italian fascists for the "sanctionist" powers: that is, for a major part of the civilized world. These exhibitions plainly belong to the domain of collective psychopathology.

Imperialism, pretending to conquer the wilderness and civilize the natives of backward areas of the planet, actually helps the wilderness creep in on civilization. It was so in the Roman era and it is so again today: only today the Romes have multiplied and the whole surface of the earth is now endangered. A regiment of eight-year-old children, learning the first formations of military drill, represents a lower state of savagery than that of the most ferocious cannibals: those who drill them are rejecting the birthright of civilization, and are thus more reprehensible than those who have never reached civilization. And truly it has been said: *one can not forgive them, for*

they know what they do, even as they know what they do when they bomb defenseless cities and torpedo defenseless ships.

This systematic barbarism spreads like a cancer through the healthy tissue of urban life: the war capital, through its organs of indoctrination, makes every subordinate province war-minded. The actual conflict, when it finally takes place, is a mere bursting of a vast pus-bag of vulgar pretense and power. But the intervening period, although sometimes fantastically referred to as "peace," is equally a state of war: the passive war of war-propaganda, war-indoctrination, war-rehearsal: a preliminary maneuvering for position.

The metropolis, which is the focus of these war forces, thus comes to represent the maximum possible assault upon the processes of civilization. Observe one of the concrete results: periodic preparation for defense against an attack by air: the materialization of a skillfully evoked nightmare.

The sirens sound. School-children, factory hands, housewives, office workers, one and all don their gas masks. Whirring planes overhead lay down a blanket of protective smoke. Cellars open to receive their refugees. Red Cross stations to succor the stricken and the wounded are opened at improvised shelters: underground vaults yawn to receive the gold and securities of the banks: masked men in asbestos suits attempt to gather up the fallen incendiary bombs. Presently the anti-aircraft guns sputter. Fear vomits: poison crawls through the pores. Whether the attack is arranged or real, it produces similar psychological effects. Plainly, terrors more devastating and demoralizing than any known in the ancient jungle or cave have been re-introduced into modern urban existence. Panting, choking, spluttering, cringing, hating, the dweller in Megalopolis dies, by anticipation, a thousand deaths. Fear is thus fixed into routine: the constant anxiety over war produces by itself a collective psychosis comparable to that which active warfare might develop. Waves of fear and hatred rise in the metropolis and spread by means of the newspaper and the newsreel and the radio program to the most distant provinces.

Here is the final contradiction in metropolitan civilization. The city arose as a special kind of environment, favorable to co-operative

[TOP] Faery palaces and cloud-capped towers of Lower Manhattan, seen from Governors Island. Visually speaking, a miraculous mountain of buildings: the zenith of romantic architecture. To work in a skyscraper, even in the dingiest tower on an airless shaft, is a manifestation of metropolitan power, to have an office of one's own on an upper floor, blessed with sunlight and the view of the ferryboats gliding up and down the Harbor, is one of the highest emoluments of metropolitan success. (*Photograph: Ewing Galloway*)

[SECOND LEFT] The dream deepens; night falls. The great offices where a million people go through a million similar motions, day in and day out, adding, subtracting, multiplying, ticketing, labeling, checking, dictating and taking dictation, begging and borrowing, giving orders and carrying them out: high pressure bureaucracy. Great loft buildings where, to the whirr of machines, the latest fashion in women's clothes is speeded into production or the latest newspaper drops off the presses. Honeycombs of light, filled with temporarily neuter insects—in a hive that boasts ever fewer fertile queens. (*Photograph: Ewing Galloway*)

[SECOND RIGHT] The White Way: here the occasional blaze of the old-fashioned festival becomes the routine of commercial enticement: a stimulus for those seeking adventure and beauty, at so much per head, in the shops, cabarets, theaters, hotels. But these constant stimuli need constant stepping up of intensification: the alternative is satiety and boredom. Hence the demand for novelties. The need for irregular stimuli becomes the great problem of metropolitan culture in every phase: counterbalance to the compulsive automatisms and too-even regularities of metropolitan existence. The need is probably increased by the achievement of an artificial environment, with constant heating and air-conditioning and lighting: uniformities that raise physiological problems to organisms whose eyesight, muscle-tone, and nervous reactions demand a wider span of variation. Further physiological research may well upset many of the assumptions upon which metropolitan improvements in lighting and heating, for example, have been based—once variation is included in defining optimum conditions. (*Photograph: Ewing Galloway*)

[BOTTOM] The Sleeper Awakes: morning light. The dream city is still visible above the roofs of the tenements; but these massed dwellings show the power and glory of metropolitan life in true perspective: here are the homes of the sustaining proletariat, the local equivalent of the mean steel towns and oil towns, the depressed farming areas and manufacturing areas, through whose efforts the dividends are piled higher for the fractional portion of the entire population that effectively rules this metropolitan regime. (*Photograph: Ewing Galloway*)

[MIDDLE] Midtown District of New York: solidified chaos. Proof that under a financial economy the gestures of zoning, height-restriction, setbacks are futile: these skyscraper offices and factories have almost all been built since "restrictions" were placed upon overcrowding the land. Under the prevailing zoning ordinance, with no new building over 600 feet in height, the permitted capacity of the residential districts of New York, according to the New York City Housing Authority, would be approximately 77,000,000, while the commercial districts would provide for a working population of 344,000,000. Isolated skyscrapers, like the fine McGraw-Hill building (second skyscraper left-center) claim enough light and air for themselves, even if they rob their neighbors and help overcrowd local traffic; but even in Rockefeller Center the excessive land value frustrated, by its absurd demand for density, the first attempt at a rational plan. Subways, tunnels, double-decked streets, express highways, so far from relieving congestion, only intensify the economic need for it: hence the relief is but temporary, though the burden imposed is permanent. Warnings of complete traffic blockage and of the "menace of decentralization" are annually uttered by so-called traffic experts. But no real remedy exists that does not involve a deflation of values, a draining off of population, and a complete rebuilding of the entire metropolitan structure at a far lower density. (*Photograph: Ewing Galloway*)

[UPPER LEFT] Pattern of congestion in what is hopefully called a suburb: not the worst. The difference between this and other forms of metropolitan housing congestion requires micrometer measurements. (*Photograph: Ewing Galloway*)

[UPPER RIGHT] Self-defilement of the bourgeoisie: not a lower but an upper class slum immediately off the most expensive part of Fifth Avenue: characteristic of the reckless building over of back garden areas in both private houses and apartment houses. Dark, dismal, airless quarters: unfit for permanent habitation. Air conditioning is only a partial remedy for these subway dwellings: the lack of sunlight and a gracious environment—to say nothing of quarters fit for children—cannot be remedied without razing these super-slums. If this is what private initiative and ample means does for the rich, it is plain that they need public aid and more limited incomes.

[BOTTOM LEFT] Coney Island Beach on a summer day. The ritual is called recreation: prefaced and concluded usually by half an hour or more spent in a stifling subway. Pollution of beaches through sewage and garbage results in a closing off of bathing privileges or invokes the need for costly measures of relief: sewage and garbage disposal plants. (*Photograph: Ewing Galloway*)

[BOTTOM RIGHT] Grand Central Station, New York: an entrance to the city, partly put out of commission as a station by the overload of high buildings in its neighborhood. (*Photograph: Ewing Galloway*) association, favorable to nurture and education, because it was a *protected* environment. It was a collective utility that ensured order and regularity in the comings and goings of men, that diminished the force of nature's random onslaughts, and reduced the menace of wild animals and the more predatory tribes of men. Permanent settlement meant not only continuity but security. In the city, as in the agricultural villages, domestic functions and co-operative actions prevailed over the more predatory and destructive modes of life; man thus made himself the greatest of the domesticated animals.

A humane life, a civic life, is one that restricts the fear-producing elements and reduces fear to a prudent provision against the common mischances of existence. Only in a well-wrought domesticated environment, protected against disaster and the gnawing anticipations of disaster, can the higher activities for long flourish: solicitude for the young, tenderness for the aged, an underlying co-operation between rival groups and interests, prolonged and systematic thought directed toward truth, free expression in the arts, and creative release, under the discipline of humane standards, in the arts of living: in short, a mode of life in which man's biological and social needs are artfully wrought into a many-threaded and variegated cultural pattern.

Concentrated upon war, the metropolitan regime opposes these domestic and civic functions: it subordinates life to organized destruction, and it must therefore regiment, limit, and constrict every exhibition of real life and culture. Result: the paralysis of all the higher activities of society: truth shorn or defaced to fit the needs of propaganda: the organs of co-operation stiffened into a reflex system of obedience: the order of the drill sergeant and the bureaucrat. Such a regime may reach unheard-of heights in external co-ordination and discipline, and those who endure it may make superb soldiers and juicy cannonfodder; but it is for the same reason deeply antagonistic to every valuable manifestation of life.

Plainly, a civilization that terminates in a cult of barbarism has disintegrated as civilization; and the war-metropolis, as an expression of these institutions, is an anti-civilizing agent: a *non*-city. To assume that this process can go on indefinitely is to betray an ignorance of social facts: decay at last halts itself. While the tasks of building, co-operation, and integration are never finished, un-building may be completed in a few generations. The chief question now before the Western World today is whether disintegration must be complete before a fresh start is made.

14: Phenomena of the End

While the continuance of the metropolitan economy is curbed by the destructive forces it piles up and releases, a more local set of conditions operates with more direct impact upon metropolitan expansion. In addition to its military vulnerability, the metropolis is economically weakened by the fact of growth; and there comes at long last a time when it cannot evade or pass on elsewhere the burden of its own magnified expenses.

As long as the economic system works smoothly, the metropolis may ignore the costs of congestion: when things begin to go ill, when bankruptcy threatens, when inflation devaluates the claims of metro-politan creditors on the rest of the country, even the food supply may be endangered. And how quickly the ornate central offices empty: how inessential the giddy restaurants and the fifteen-room apartments suddenly become! Even the museums may close their doors, as their panicky patrons withdraw funds. Let the disorganization continue, so that the metropolis can neither command the necessary force of arms and law and common assent, nor furnish a modicum of goods in return for the country's products, and the metropolis may be starved out: the drift outward may begin. These are not hypothetical alarms. Conditions in Central Europe and in Soviet Russia after the first World War presented almost unbearable difficulties to the harassed and starving metropolises, while out in the countryside, in many regions, the peasant remained relatively secure and well-fed.

Even without the disorganization of war, similar circumstances, of almost catastrophic dimensions, may arise: consider the state of the big cities in the United States, between 1930 and 1935. The National Resources Committee, in the 1937 report on Our Cities makes this pertinent observation: "Insecurity of the urban worker, his lack of reserve resources, and the impersonality and mobility of urban life combine to make the problems of dependency more acute and more widespread in cities than in rural areas. . . . One-fifth of all the employable persons on relief in 1935 were located in the ten largest cities, and consisted mainly of unskilled workmen." Without the mobilization of national funds for public works projects and local relief, the demoralization of the great metropolises would have been appalling.

Apart from the latent hostility of the exploited countryside, nourishing grievances against the big city because of the low prices it gets in the market, and the high rate of interest it must pay on its loans, there are internal elements that place a limit to metropolitanism. The very cost of doing business in the big city is magnified by high land values, by expensive delays in transportation, by the high expense of storage: all these costs increase with congestion, and eventually they become prohibitive. The congestion of traffic alone in New York City during the nineteen-twenties was estimated by the Russell Sage Survey to involve a loss of $500,000 a day, or $150,-000,000 per year. And still it thickens: still it forms tedious snarls: finally the very *hope* of movement collapses.

In recreation, a different sort of inefficiency exists: instead of an overplus of physical equipment, there is a serious lack of sufficient space for play, and for lack of play areas, the toll of children killed or maimed on the streets rises. According to very conservative estimates, there should be a minimum of one acre of recreation space for every three hundred persons: many cities are able to afford more. Such a standard has been met in our generation in America by regional cities like Kansas City (400,000 inhabitants), Portland, Oregon (300,000), and Indianapolis (360,000): but in New York City there was but one acre of space to 1234 inhabitants.

Meanwhile, other expenses pile up: other breakdowns become chronic. The passenger transportation system, for example. The subways of great cities may serve as bomb-proof shelters during air raids; otherwise they are mainly obstacles to that conceivable decentralization of the metropolis which would reduce the burden of congestion by building up sub-centers of industry, business, and residence. As the lines extend, the costs increase: this means either higher fares for the worker, or higher taxes for the city as a whole.

Here, then, is the choice: a breakdown of functions through neglect, or a financial breakdown through the increased expense of adequate service and repair. I have already cited the increased costs of police service in the bigger cities. The same relationship holds for municipal expenditures upon health: three times as much is spent per capita in cities with over a million inhabitants as in cities with from thirty to fifty thousand inhabitants: yet the *latter* present, on the whole, more favorable vital statistics.

In short, one may say definitely that beyond a certain point, which varies with regional conditions and culture, urban growth penalizes itself. Too large a part of the capital outlays and annual income of the city must be spent in devices for increasing congestion and mechanically relieving its worst results.

The present economic scheme of the big city depends upon the expectation of a stable income from an investment, public and private, that becomes ever more speculative, unstable, and insecure. The growth of such a city means an increase of insecurity: to ensure such growth, to subsidize it, to attempt to freeze this obsolete structure in the effort to maintain the financial values that have been attached to it is to exhibit an ungovernable antagonism to prudence and good sense. Metropolitan bankers, with their own narrow interests in view, may encourage such uneconomic folly: did they not in the decade before the depression ingenuously overcalculate the capacity of the metropolis to absorb new skyscrapers and hotels? But a similar optimism as to the city's capacity to absorb tunnels, bridges, double-decked streets, widened avenues, and underground transit systems is now unpardonable. That process cannot continue indefinitely.

There are perhaps parallels to all these weaknesses in many smaller cities: but the reason should be plain: they, too, worked under the canons of metropolitan finance and imitated the most blatant defects of the metropolis. Note, for example, Cincinnati's almost completed but never opened subway.

The cold facts upon which these conclusions are based are set forth, with statistical substantiation, in a ten volume report: that by the Russell Sage Foundation for the Regional Plan of New York. The authority is unimpeachable: not least because the report naïvely and wholeheartedly accepted the premises of metropolitan finance and diligently endeavored to show on what terms the New York agglomeration could be increased from a population of ten million in 1930 to between twenty and twenty-nine million in 1965. What holds for New York holds with appropriate modifications for other metropolises and sub-metropolises. The end of their reckless expansion is near.

But there is one final limitation on metropolitan growth: more stringent than the rising cost of utilities or the unbearable municipal burden of blighted areas. I mean the cutting off of the supply of inhabitants at the source. In almost every country except Russia a tapering off process has begun for the population as a whole. Despite dictatorial threats, despite special rewards and bounties for large families, despite attempts to limit the supply of convenient contraceptives, the movement goes on. Hence the flood of people who imperiously demanded urban accommodation during the nineteenth century has spent its original force. Throughout the world, if this movement keeps up, the metropolitan economy will have to adjust itself to the fact of a relatively stable population and a relatively fixed market: an end to its hitherto boundless financial increments.

This movement toward the stabilization of numbers may, if intelligently directed, result in great human gains. It affords a breathing space for reorganization, and it will enable population to be planned and distributed in accordance with regional resources. But the finer this adjustment is, the less part can the metropolis play in it: for under conditions now prevailing, no big metropolis reproduces its own population through births: indeed, in the United States, only three cities with over a hundred thousand population have a reproductive index of over 1.0. *This fact alone reduces to complete nullity the notion that the metropolitan population pattern is a permanent one, or that it could, if dominant, maintain itself over any considerable period.* Without steady immigration, its population must sink. The biological norm of city growth, that is, the degree of concentration beyond which the community fails in reproducing the full quota of its members, is between twenty-five and fifty thousand. As we even out the economic and cultural differences between the rural and the urban environments, this tentatively fixes an upper limit for the size of the biotechnic city. With cities of such size forming the dominant element in the urban pattern, no country need utilize its hinterland as mere breeding ground.

No single element is perhaps sufficient to bring about an immediate breakdown in the metropolitan regime. But in actual life, these high costs, these economic disorganizations, these retrograde tendencies do not appear as isolated events: they come together and reinforce each other: abetted by a series of catastrophes, both immanent and imminent, they may easily mean the end of the entire civilization. Such a breakup has happened many times in history before. What we have been witnessing, during the last thousand years, is a cycle that societies in the past have never successfully smoothed out or short-circuited: a cycle from which even the most stable of civilizations—even that of the Chinese—has not been able completely to escape. Let us examine this movement: it may give us a clue as to the possibilities of achieving a comprehensive social and political reconstruction: a benign instead of a catastrophic outcome.

15: Cycle of Growth and Decay

During the last generation there have been numerous attempts to summarize the course of city development and to correlate this with the rise and fall of civilizations. One of the best-known of these interpretations is that of Oswald Spengler in the book euphemistically translated as The Decline of the West. He traced the development of the community from "culture" to "civilization": from its beginnings as the living expression of a people, harmoniously interacting upon a certain soil and swayed by a common feeling toward life and the earth and the universe, not yet formulated as philosophic vision, to the final stage, that which he called civilization, with its hard mechanistic organization of men and goods and ideas: rootless, spiritless, ultimately lifeless and hopeless: concentrated in a few world capitals that were no longer related to the land, where the malleable and changeable forms of earlier cultures were made over into dead stereotypes.

According to Spengler's early scheme, the process of mastery, which begins with agriculture, ends with a predominance of the machine: a contrivance in which there is for him something infernal, inimical to life. The business man and the engineer and the industrialist displace the artist and the peasant. But mechanism, tied to a ruthless scheme of exploitation, leads into savagery: Spengler ac-

knowledged that fact and in his later formulations he even boasted
of man's being a carnivore in order to justify the conclusion that the
men of our time must heartily embrace savagery: submit to the lash
of a Caesar and take part in his brutal machinations. There is of
course a serious contradiction between Spengler's romantic belief
in the predatory carnivore and the historic facts of rural domestication and urbane culture; but one may pardon Spengler's barbarous
solecisms if only because he was one of the first in our generation to
grasp the critical significance of the city in the development of
culture.

A later interpretation of this cycle of development and deterioration is that of Arnold J. Toynbee, in his monumental survey, A Study
of History. Toynbee's study is more profound than Spengler's, is
based on a much richer grasp of historic facts, and does not neglect
empirical evidence for the sake of preserving intact a literary figure.
Unfortunately, Toynbee's theory of the development of civilization
does not embrace the special function of the city, as both the instrument and the symbol of this process; and although he rediscovers
the function of the cloister, in his conception of withdrawal-and-re-
turn as necessary for the process of renewal, he does not connect this
with the process of urban development itself. Hence Toynbee is weak
precisely at the point where Spengler is strongest: though his division
of the component cultures into societies, and his schematic cycle of
development rest on a closer reading of the historical evidence.

The most significant summary of all, from the point of view developed in this book, is likewise the earliest: that put forward by
Patrick Geddes a generation ago in his outline of the six stages of
city development, from polis to nekropolis. Like a true disciple, I
have modified Geddes's scheme, something in the way that I modified his analysis of the paleotechnic and the neotechnic phases of the
machine. Thus I propose to insert an earlier stage that he left out
of the picture, and I have combined two of his later stages, those of
Parasitopolis and Patholopolis into a single stage, since there is no
observable time-interval between them. These modifications, made
after his death, too late for his sanction, have the merit of placing
the first three stages of the cycle on the rising curve, and the last

three on the descending side; and this, I believe, is more in line with his essential views than his own original diagram.

First Stage: Eopolis. Rise of the village community. Development of permanent habitation and permanent external organs of association through the domestication of plants and the ensurance of a balanced food supply by the domestication of animals. Cultivation of the hard grains and legumes: also deliberate tree and vine culture: plentiful supply of proteins, vegetable fats, and fermented liquors. Surplus production in agriculture smooths over seasonal and cyclical irregularities and ensures an orderly routine of life: security and continuity. Permanent utilities for storage: translation of kinetic energy into potential energy (food storage) brings vast increase in power, economic and cultural.

Differentiation of the permanent dwelling house, and regular outlines of the village through systematic layout and orderly apportionment of land: pile villages, plains villages, etc. Important technical advances, especially in development of utensils and agricultural tools: basketwork, pottery, hoe, beginnings of systematic mining and tool-working: dawn of metallurgy. Fire as symbol of advance: hearth and altar. Oral transmission of tradition through occupational groups and through close companionship of senescents and youths. Association on basis of blood and neighborhood: predominance of primary groups. Culture continuous with life but limited by arbitrary restriction of experience (tabus), fear of departure from magical formulae, submissive respect for ancestral wisdom as transmitted by priesthood, and lack of stimulating intercourse with other cultures. First crude differentiation of villages on basis of topographic facts, local resources, indigenous occupations: mining villages, fishing villages, agricultural villages.

Arising probably in neolithic culture, the village remains the most enduring of collective forms. Its life underlies all subsequent transformations of civilization; and although villages that continue as such never climb more than part of the cycle upward and never participate except by adaptive infiltration in the advances made in the city, they likewise tend to escape the worst defects of decay. The agricultural village, not the market, is the prototype of the city: its utilities for protection, storage, and life-maintenance are the essential nucleus of the city: they become "etherealized" in culture-forms, at the same time as they are finally given concrete expression in the form of collective art: altar becomes temple: planting and harvest rituals become drama and theater, granary bin and cellar are village prototypes of library, archive, museum and vault. The village remains the essential root from which fresh urban shoots from time to time thrust upward: its form and content persist long after more differentiated urban types have flourished and disappeared. Hence the truth in the boast of the little village near Edinburgh:

> *Musselburgh was a borough when Edinburgh was none,*
> *And Musselburgh will be a borough when Edinburgh is gone.*

Second Stage: Polis. An association of villages or blood-groups having a common site that lends itself to defense against depredation: a common deity with a common shrine or temple, usually on or near the defensive site: a common meeting place where the special products and skills of the larger community may be interchanged in periodical markets. Rise in industrial productivity through the more systematic division of labor and the partial specialization of functions: development of trades and crafts: surplus of manufactured goods as well as surplus of food. Beginnings of mechanization: stamping, molding, casting, in the early river-civilizations, the water-mill, the paved road, the general use of wheeled vehicles in Graeco-Roman civilization: special instruments of power and precision in addition to the above in modern civilization in its eotechnic phase.

Free energy: free time: release from incessant preoccupation with physical survival. Opportunity for further nurture of the family, for education, for the cultivation of the body in military and athletic exercise, for the discipline of the mind in contemplation and dialectics and science, and for the practice of the humane arts. Systematic medicine and health-culture. Further development of social division of labor through multiplication of purposive associations and organizations. Differentiation of theoretic from empiric knowledge: beginnings of mathematics, astronomy, philosophy: increased scope of a special class, immune to obligations of practical labor, devoted to preserving and extending the cultural heritage. Erection of special buildings that collectively embody new cultural and politi·

cal functions: temple, stadium, theater, guildhall, cathedral. Rise of
the school, as the organ for systematically transmitting elements of
social heritage to the young; and further differentiation of the cloister
from the school: grove, shaded walk, porch, cloister, study, studio,
laboratory. Civic unity and common vision of life symbolized in
Temple or Cathedral. Increase of cultural storage by means of sculptured figures, painted images, monuments, books.

Preservation of rural occupations and rural customs, including
the practice of piety toward ancestors and ancestral rites: the polis
remains a collection of families; family organization tends to prevail in industry no less than in agriculture; and seasonal and other
migrations between village and polis preserve and renew rural connections. Dependence upon the local region for water, building materials, food, and main industrial resources. Transformation of
structures in impermanent materials into more durable ones: refinement of architectural detail: formal modifications of shrines and important buildings so as to reflect collective sentiments about life and
the universe. Pervasiveness of esthetic and moral culture through all
ranks of society: expression of a differentiated but still homogeneous
way of life.

Third Stage: Metropolis. Within the region one city emerges from
the less differentiated groups of villages and country towns. Taking
advantage of a strategic location, a larger supply of potable water, a
more defensible site, better land for agriculture, easier command of
land routes or water routes, a safer harbor—usually with a number
of these advantages coming together—one city succeeds in attracting larger numbers of inhabitants: it becomes the metropolis or
"mother-city." In heaping up these advantages, the command of
transportation routes probably marks the critical change: compare
the Hittites with the Egyptians, or the land-locked Spartans with the
adventurous, mobile, water-borne Athenians.

With a surplus of regional products, a specialized trade develops
with other regions. This brings to the growing metropolis the necessary food supply, which can no longer be raised in the immediate
vicinity, along with a host of stimulating goods from other regions:
special fabrics, special forms, even esthetic patterns, unused by the
traditional industries of the local region. Cross-fertilization of cul-

ture takes place: stimulus to fresh invention: stimulus to departures from routine. Long distance trading and long distance administra-tion help further invention and create a necessity for abstract sym-bols: pictorial signs, numerical tables, alphabets. A foreign popula-tion of traders and students enters the metropolis: unabsorbed as citizens at first, since blood and neighborhood may still count, they bring the shock of fresh habits and ideas: challenges to old ways. Further specialization of economic and social functions: the special-ized workshop: the specialized trading class: subdivisions of these. Large-scale development of library and university as storehouse and powerhouse of ideas. Development of more effective organs of cen-tralized administration, apart from primitive courts and assemblies. Agriculture tends to be secondary to manufacture: manufacture in turn becomes an instrument of trade. Rivalry between patricians of the soil and new trades and industrialists of the metropolis: splitting off of landless workers, selling their labor, with no prospect of rise in economic rank. Also migration of an élite within the polity.

Religion, literature, the drama reach the stage of self-conscious criticism and expression: the systematic-rational grows at the ex-pense of organic and instinctive modes of expression. Every part of the environment and the culture is deliberately remolded: written law supplements custom and common law, written language helps to shape the labile dialects of the surrounding regions and gives them a common medium of secondary intercourse: rational inquiry chal-lenges customary acceptance. The representatives of religion, phi-losophy, and science, no longer united as a single priestly hierarchy, pursue separate paths: the gap between sacred knowledge and sec-ular knowledge, between empiricism and theory, between deed and idea, tends to widen; but out of these oppositions and likenesses, out of these hostilities and wider friendships, new syntheses come forth. A similar refocusing takes place in every other department of life: emancipation from fixed patterns and stereotyped routine. Fusion of the instinctive, the imaginative, and the rational in great philoso-phies and works of art: maximum release of cultural energy: Pla-tonic Athens: Dantean Florence: Shakespearean London: Emersonian Boston.

Signs of weakness appear beneath the surface. Increasing failure to absorb and integrate disparate cultural elements: beginnings of an individualism that tends to disrupt old social bonds without creating new order on a higher plane. Professionalizing of war, already differentiated as a culture-trait, acquires new energy through increasing technical equipment, and new impetus from economic rivalry. Opening up of a grave breach between the owners of the machinery of production and the workers, whether slave or free: beginning of the class struggle in active form. Fixation on pecuniary symbols of gain, as the growing class of merchants and bankers begin to exercise greater influence.

Fourth Stage: Megalopolis. Beginning of the decline. The city under the influence of a capitalistic mythos concentrates upon bigness and power. The owners of the instruments of production and distribution subordinate every other fact in life to the achievement of riches and the display of wealth. Physical conquest by military means: financial domination by trade and legal processes: loans, mortgages, speculative enterprises. The agricultural base extends: the lines of supply become more tenuous: the impulse to aggressive enterprise and enterprising aggression grows as the lust for power diminishes the attraction of all other attributes of life: as the moral sense becomes more callous and the will-to-culture increasingly impotent. Standardization, largely in pecuniary terms, of the cultural products themselves in art, literature, architecture, and language. Mechanical reproduction takes the place of original art: bigness takes the place of form: voluminousness takes the place of significance. Triumph of mechanism in every department: passivity: manual helplessness: bureaucratism: failure of direct action.

Megalopolis ushers in an age of cultural aggrandizement: scholarship and science by tabulation: sterile research: elaborate fact-finding apparatus and refined technic with no reference to rational intellectual purpose or ultimate possibilities of social use: Alexandrianism. Belief in abstract quantity in every department of life: the biggest monuments, the highest buildings, the most expensive materials, the largest food supply, the greatest number of worshipers, the biggest population. Education becomes quantitative: domination of the cram-machine and the encyclopedia, and domination of megalopolis as concrete encyclopedia: all-containing. Knowledge divorced from life: industry divorced from life-utility: life itself compart-mentalized, dis-specialized, finally disorganized and enfeebled. Representatives: Alexandria, third century B.C.; Rome, second century A.D.; Byzantium, tenth century; Paris, eighteenth century; New York, early twentieth century.

Over-investment in the material apparatus of bigness. Diversion of energy from the biological and social ends of life to the preparatory physical means. Outright exploitation of the proletariat and increasing conflict between organized workers and the master classes. Occasional attempts at insurance by philanthropy on the part of the possessing classes: justice in homeopathic doses. Occasional outbursts of savage repression on the part of frightened bourgeoisie, employing basest elements in the city. As conflict intensifies rise of a coalition between landed oligarchy, trained in combat, and a megalopolitan rabble of speculators, enterprisers, and financiers who furnish the sinews of war and profit by all the occasions for class-suppression, price-lifting, and looting that it gives. The city as a means of association, as a haven of culture, becomes a means of dissociation and a growing threat to real culture. Smaller cities are drawn into the megalopolitan network: they practice imitatively the megalopolitan vices, and even sink to lower levels because of lack of higher institutions of learning and culture that still persist in bigger centers. The threat of widespread barbarism arises. Now follow, with cumulative force and increasing volume, the remaining downward movements of the cycle.

Fifth Stage: Tyrannopolis. Extensions of parasitism throughout the economic and social scene: the function of spending paralyzes all the higher activities of culture and no act of culture can be justified that does not involve display and expense. Politics becomes competition for the exploitation of the municipal and state exchequer by this or that class or group. Extirpation of organs of communal and civic life other than "state." Caesarism. Development of predatory means as a substitute for trade and give-and-take: naked exploitation of colonies and hinterland: intensification of the cycles of commercial depression, following overexpansion of industry and dubious speculative enterprise, heightened by wars and war-preparations. Failure of the economic and political rulers to maintain the bare decencies of administration: place-hunting, privilege-seeking, bonus-collecting, favor-currying, nepotism, grafting, tribute-exacting become rife both in government *and* business. Widespread moral apathy and failure of civic responsibility: each group, each individual, takes what it can get away with. Widening of the gap between producing classes and spending classes. Multiplication of a *Lumpenproletariat* demanding its share of bread and shows. Overstress of mass-sports. Parasitic love of sinecures in every department of life. Demand for "protection money" made by armed thugs and debased soldiery: organized looting, organized blackmail are "normal" accompaniments of business and municipal enterprise. Domination of respectable people who behave like criminals and of criminals whose activities do not debar them from respectability.

Imperialistic wars, internal and external, result in starvation, epidemics of disease, demoralization of life: uncertainty hangs over every prospect of the future: armed protection increases all the hazards of life. Municipal and state bankruptcy. Drain of local taxes to service increasing load of local debt. Necessity to appeal to the state for further aid in periods of economic disorganization: loss of autonomy. Drain of national taxes to support the growing military establishment of the state. This burden penalizes the remnants of honest industry and agriculture, and further disrupts the supply of elementary material goods. Decrease in agricultural production by soil-mining and erosion, through falling off in acreage, through the withholding of crops from the city by resentful husbandmen. Decline in rate of population-increase through birth control, abortion, mass slaughter, and suicide: eventual absolute decline in numbers. General loss of nerve. Attempt to create order by external military means: rise of gangster-dictators (Hitler, Mussolini) with active consent of the bourgeoisie and systematic terrorism by pretorian guards. Recrudescence of superstition and deliberate cult of savagery: barbarian invasions from within and without. Beginnings of megalopolitan exodus. Material deficiencies and lapses of cultural continuity: repression and censorship. Cessation of productive work in the arts and sciences.

Sixth and Final Stage: Nekropolis. War and famine and disease rack both city and countryside. The physical towns become mere shells. Those who remain in them are unable to carry on the old municipal services or maintain the old civic life: what remains of that life is at best a clumsy caricature. The names persist; the reality vanishes. The monuments and books no longer convey meaning; the old routine of life involves too much effort to carry on: the streets fall into disrepair and grass grows in the cracks of the pavement: the viaducts break down, the water mains become empty; the rich shops, once looted, remain empty of goods by reason of the failure of trade or production. Relapse into the more primitive rural occupations. The historic culture survives, if at all, in the provinces and the remote villages, which share the collapse but are not completely carried down by it or submerged in the debris. First the megalopolis becomes a lair: then its occupants are either hunted out by some warrior band, seeking the last remnants of conquest in gold or women or random luxuries, or they gradually fall away of their own accord. The living forms of the ancient city become a tomb for dying: sand sweeps over the ruins: so Babylon, Nineveh, Rome. In short, Nekropolis, the city of the dead: flesh turned to ashes: life turned into a meaningless pillar of salt.

16: Possibilities of Renewal

History is full of burying grounds: the dead forms and deserted shards of communities that had not learned the art of living in harmonious relations with nature and with other communities. The end stage, over which Spengler gloated, is an undeniable reality that has overtaken many civilizations: dead-food for the vulturelike imagination.

But one must not, like a Spengler or a Sorokin, make the mistake of identifying the *logical* stages of a process, as discovered and systematized by intellectual analysis, with the living reality. For in real life, in real cultures, history does not present a solid laminated block of uniform dimensions that one may break down into smaller blocks, each unified within itself to form part of a consistent whole. End-processes often occur in the middle of a culture; accidental mischances and injuries may bring to the middle-aged the normal deteriorations of senescence. Likewise early processes or rejuvenating reactions may be noted in the final phases of the most mechanized civilization. In short, time as experience and duration upsets this logical order, which is based chiefly on time as an attribute of spatial movement. Mutations arise in human communities from unexpected sources: the social heritage makes society much less of a unity than we are compelled to conceive it, by the nature of language, when we interrupt the complex stream of actual life in order to take account of it in thought. Out of these mutations, a new social dominant may arrive: veritably a saving remnant.

To take the simplest point of all: the final stage in civilization is often reached at an intermediate point in urban development. Witness fourteenth century Rome. It exhibited most of the characteristics of a Nekropolis, including a loss, not alone of the single title to papal supremacy, but of a good part of its population. Yet, after that nadir had been reached, a renewal took place: two centuries later its ruins stimulate Brunelleschi and its new buildings offer a challenge to the genius of Michelangelo. The other point to remember is that civilization is not, even in its utmost megalopolitan phase, confined to the world-cities alone. Though they cast their shadows over the farthest territories, neither their governments nor their armies nor their culture institutes can embrace with any degree of thoroughness the provinces they lay claim to: part of their dominion is mere bluff and pretense, unchallengeable until actually challenged.

Even in the ultimate stage of Tyrannopolis, the tyranny is only partly effective: Krilov contrives to tell his satirical fables and Epictetus, the slave, thinks his own thoughts and preserves autonomy within his soul. At this stage there still remain regions and cities and villages with other memories, other backgrounds, other hopes: though in shackles to the external dictatorship, they remain essentially withdrawn. In the heyday of the megalopolitan economy, such regional centers remain partly outside the cycle: some failure of enterprise, some lack of opportunity, or some sturdier sense of life-values keeps them from sharing the delusive growth and splendor of the metropolis.

When, through the processes of decay and destruction hastened by Tyrannopolis, the great cities sink into ruin, these other centers, though they may stagger from the blow, will nevertheless continue to live: indeed, they may live more intensely once the incubus of the

big city and its tyrannous system of political and financial administration is removed. Marseilles and some of the other towns of Provence had such a function after the disintegration of the old Roman
civilization in Italy: this fact, along with their closer contact with
Byzantium and the Arabic possessions, played a significant part,
no doubt, in that brilliant outburst of Provençal culture in the early
Middle Ages. On the other hand, to face the blacker side of the picture, the reverse process may happen: a process that doubly demands
our watchful care today: that is, a deteriorative phase of culture
may prolong its existence by capturing the fresh energies of a
younger growth. In this fashion, Byzantium reached up to paralyze
the "young" culture of sixteenth century Russia; and in similar
fashion, again, the Tyrannopolis of the Czars in Russia, which exhibited many of the symptoms of the end-process by the close of the
nineteenth century, has left its cruel mark on the fresh beginnings
made by the Soviet regime: furthering that aimless centralization
and that rigid bureaucratism and that habit of systematic repression
of valid differences which leaves no place for young initiative, or for
those forms of co-operation which, to be wholehearted, must be
voluntary.

In other words, the life course of cities is essentially different
from that of most higher organisms. Cities exhibit the phenomena of
broken growth, of partial death, of self-regeneration. Cities and city
cultures may have sudden beginnings from remote gestations; and
they are capable of prolongations as *physical organizations* through
the life-spans of more than one culture: witness Damascus, most
ancient of surviving towns, already venerable in St. Paul's day. It is
only as parable rather than as scientific statement that one may talk
of the spring or winter of a civilization as if the cycle had a climatic
inevitability, or of the birth and death of a culture-phase, as if any
contemporary observer could confidently recognize either the birth-
cry or the death-rattle.

Cities can take on new life by a transplantion of tissues from
healthy communities in other regions or civilizations: a few hundred
people, like the Huguenots in Scotland or Germany, or the Jews in
almost every civilization, may have a profoundly stimulating effect.
Today, the dispersal of the élite from Germany and Italy and in some

degree from Russia may be one of the elements that will compensate for the growing elements of barbarism within those countries. And these transplanted tissues need not even be in the form of living people: the collective organs of culture, signs, symbols, forms, the abstract and etherealized essences, may likewise exercise a decisive effect: witness the powerful influence of Roman monuments and Greek literature in temporarily supplementing the spent energies of the Middle Ages. All that is necessary is that the organism which receives these new tissues shall be in a state of readiness.

In short: the roots of a culture are deep. If the crown is blighted by disease, it may still put forth new shoots at the base; and in time these shoots may flourish and provide a new trunk and crown. All these are of course figures of speech: but they are means of counteracting and truing up analogies that are even more abstract, figures that are even more fanciful: the curve of a cycle, the succession of the seasons. Social life has its own laws and rhythms: much remains hidden or irrational: much escapes empiric observation and still more escapes statistical analysis. All one can say with any surety is this: when a city has reached the megalopolitan stage, it is plainly on the downward path: it needs a terrific exertion of social force to overcome the inertia, to alter the direction of movement, to resist the immanent processes of disintegration. But while there is life, there is the possibility of counter-movement, fresh growth. Only when the big city has finally become wasteland must the locus of life be elsewhere.

17: Signs of Salvage

The boast of the metropolis is that it is a world city, and the boast is not altogether a vain one. Thirty centers of world-contact, temporary concentration points for travelers and observers, for administrators and motivators, for students and scholars and technicians, would not be too many to serve a culture as complicated and many-sided as that which we now possess. Most of the existing world cities have become over-congested because they did have real advantages in international communication: they were the meeting-points of transcontinental and trans-oceanic highways: often they possessed a superior inheritance of culture institutes, reaching back into a unique historic past. These advantages would remain even if the present mass-agglomerations of people were reduced to a cluster of inter-related cities, no one of which would have over fifty thousand people, nor the cluster have more than a million: What was once present only in an urban *point*, is now available throughout a whole region.

But the world city in order to function as such requires a world order. A world in disorder can find no use for such a city, except to make it a center of political aggression and financial aggrandize-ment, incapable of performing the essential functions of a city even for its own teeming population. Any effective effort to reconstitute the metropolis demands something more than local traffic plans or local building regulations: as Benton MacKaye has said, to diminish the congestion of traffic at Times Square it may be necessary to re-route the export of wheat from the hinterland; and what is true for traffic holds for the other functions of the city. Most metropolitan planning has involved the use of seven local maids with seven mops to hold back the sea.

Any effort to reconstitute the metropolis, in other words, must go *against* the basic pattern of the metropolitan economy. It must work against population increase, against multiplying the mechanical facilities for congestion, against the expansion of the continuous urban area, against unmanageable bigness and irrational "great-ness." The proof that this alone provides a suitable occasion for the relief of metropolitan difficulties lies in the experience of the last twenty-five years.

Almost all the decisive improvements that have taken place in Wien, London, Berlin, and New York have been put through during the periods when the metropolitan financial system was in a state of collapse. It was in the midst of the dreadful period of inflation that Berlin captured a sufficient amount of outlying land to build great parks and housing communities and control the development of pri-vate land areas. Not till the collapse came could Berlin afford to take the steps that a small regional city like Ulm had been able to take a generation before. So, too, it was in the period of most dire need that Wien gathered in local taxes the funds necessary to float the great housing developments that were done under the socialist government of the municipality after the war: more improvement in a dozen years than capitalism and "prosperity" had achieved in a dozen decades. And it was in the midst of the great depression that began in 1930 that the city of New York, *through the utter bankruptcy of numerous landholders,* obtained a sufficient number of small plots to serve as local playgrounds: it was similarly as a by-product of the effort to increase employment through Public Works that the city obtained sufficient funds from the National Government to build two great colleges and to carry through a comprehensive program of park rehabilitation. Life-values came back to the city only after financial values had been deflated. From the standpoint of decent metropolitan living one might well speak of the "menace of prosperity."

In laying down the foundations for a new regional order, based on the culture of life, the metropolis nevertheless has a proud part to play. At present the world cities, through the very fact of monopoly, contain many of the best elements in man's heritage. Here the keenest criticism of the metropolitan regime has come forth; and it is here that the need for decentralization has been felt and intelligent plans for it worked out. Given the concentration of power and activity in the big city, the courage to attack large tasks, the ability to assemble, transport, and organize vast quantities of men and materials have grown up, too. Energy that has so far been mobilized here to produce congestion can also be utilized toward the rebuilding of the metropolis and the founding of a biotechnic regime. The biological renewal of modern life, through the cult of hygiene and the systematic pursuit of games and sports, is a product of the metropolis: so, too, the first redefinition of the social nucleus of the modern city, in the embryonic form of the Settlement House, the People's Palace, and the Community Center.

The settlement house, in fact, was the first effective effort, not merely to overcome the barbarism of the submerged areas of the metropolis, but to establish in its random neighborhoods an appropriate social nucleus which could serve as a meeting-point for its social and educational activities. Young clergymen and earnest young women, a Canon Barnett, a Jane Addams, instead of traveling to remote parts of the world to carry the gospel, began in the eighties to settle in the slums: they found people as benighted as the Fiji cannibals, and in many ways just as innocent of contemporary Western culture. These denizens of Whitechapel and the South Side were out-casts: without hope, without pride: victims not merely of exploita-tion but of what William Morris called the damned wantlessness of the poor.

The colonization of the slums by means of the Settlement House was an important event: not merely did it give the slum dweller him-self his first glimpse of art, literature, drama, music, play: not merely did it provide a place for clubs and social groups to meet. Something else happened. The success of the Settlement House called attention to the fact that more prosperous neighborhoods were in fact equally devoid of the elementary organs of association: civically speaking, every middle-class neighborhood was a non-entity, too. It was, then, precisely out of the most degrading poverty and the most disorganized environment that the new conception of an organized urban neighborhood, with a central building adapted to a varied round of communal activities, took shape. This conception is fundamental to the best housing and community building that have been done during the past generation: it will probably remain, even though the name disappear and the institution be modified, the most fundamental cultural contribution of the metropolis to the new order.

To cast off the dead form of the metropolitan order, and to con-centrate its surviving energies upon the social utilization of its real goods, within the greater regional framework, is perhaps the most pressing task of our civilization: the issues of war and peace, social-ization or disorganization, culture or barbarism, rest in good part on our success in handling this problem. Already, the *symbols* of the new order have appeared. In new buildings, new schools, a new pro-gram of living, fresh mutations, have disclosed themselves: in the biological and the sociological sciences, the positive foundations for this order have been laid: an order more comprehensive than Marx conceived, and more profound in its demands and readjustments than a merely economic revolution. The next step lies in contriving the political organization appropriate to this new task, and in work-ing out, in concrete detail, the effective economic means.

Before either of these steps can be taken, however, we must have a clearer visual picture of the actual changes that have occurred and of the new possibilities that have emerged. The dynamics of social change require an actual situation in time: a series of processes that can be hastened or retarded, energized or depleted: groups of people interacting with their place and their form of work, with other groups, with their social heritage: and a collective framework of interests and goals which, while slowly changing themselves, serve to concentrate and direct the intermediate social process. When all the other elements in social change are duly taken into account, the definition of the new framework itself becomes, not a piece of uto-pian wishfulness, but a decisive element in the whole process.

Periods of rapid social crystallization—as in Rome at the time of St. Augustine, or England in the time of Bentham—are periods when the community acquires, through critical inquiry and self-conscious re-orientation, a firm collective insight into its own purposes and a passionate faith in the possibility of a new attitude and a profound societal change: further command of the social processes follows. While the rational definition of the ideal framework does not alone effect the necessary transition, it is an important element in changing the direction of the blind process, and in hastening the necessary social adaptations. The strongest social organizations and social pressures, without such well-defined goals, dissipate their energies in uneasy random efforts occasioned by passing opportunities. No goal, then no direction: no underlying plan, no consensus, then no effective practical action. If society is paralyzed today, it is not for lack of means but for lack of purpose.

CHAPTER V.   THE REGIONAL FRAMEWORK
OF CIVILIZATION

1: New Patterns of Life and Thought

What has been called the triumph of urbanization has been very largely the systematic frustration of those social and co-operative endeavors which modern collective thought has made possible. Metropolitan civilization, with its resourceful technical ingenuity, its delicately articulated physical organization, has failed through its very structure to distribute the benefits that it potentially commands. *Starvation in the midst of plenty* applies to its social life no less than to its inequitable system of distribution.

But the human failure of metropolitan civilization has awakened compensatory reactions; and profound changes have been going on in life and thought which will alter the idolum out of which this civilization has grown. Society as a whole, fortunately, tends to act more wisely than its individual members. It retains areas of experience and reserves of force that the narrower vision of a single party, group, or generation does not encompass.

The orientation of thought toward the realities of organic life, something that in the eighteenth century went no further than the intuitions of the poet or the naturalist, had by the end of the nineteenth century become so pervasive that it entered even into the hitherto lifeless realm of mechanics: the telephone, the phonograph, the motion picture, the airplane, sprang out of an interest in the functions of organisms and could not have developed without a scientific knowledge of their processes. Steadily, for the past generation, a transformation has been going on in every department of thought: a re-location of interest from mechanism to organism, a change from a world in which material bodies and mechanical motion alone were real to a world in which invisible rays and emanations, in which human projections and dreams, are as real as any immediately visible or external phenomenon—as real and on occasion more important.

Nineteenth century industry had been mainly concerned, in its paleotechnic phase, with the inorganic processes of factory, steel mill, and mine. The first significant revelation of experimental biological knowledge to industry came through Pasteur's researches on the diseases of silkworms, and the rôle of ferments in wines. That knowledge, which was to lay the foundation for modern hygiene and medicine, did not go into circulation until the eighteen-seventies. It needed the triumphant demonstrations of medicine in the ensuing decades to give authority to a new world-view, which accords to the organism and the world of life the priority that had been accorded, from the seventeenth century on, to the machine and to a universe whose cold mechanical perfection was described by physics and astronomy.

The leading ideas of this organic order may be briefly summed up.

First: the primacy of life, and of autonomous but perpetually inter-related organisms as vehicles of life. Each organism has its own line of growth, that of its species, its own curve of development, its own span of variations, its own pattern of existence. To maintain its life-shape the organism must constantly alter it and renew itself by entering into active relations with the rest of the environment. Even the most sessile and sleepy forms of life must seize energy in order to maintain their equilibrium: thus the organism changes, by no matter what infinitesimal amounts, the balance of the environment; and the failure to act and re-act means either the temporary suspension of life or its final end. Not merely is the organism implicated in its environment in space: it is also implicated in time, through the biological phenomena of inheritance and memory; and in human societies it is even more consciously implicated through the necessity of assimilating a complicated social heritage which forms, as it were, a second environment.

Human beings and groups are the outcomes of an historic complex, their inheritance, and they move toward a conditioned but uncertain destination, their future. The assimilation of the past and the making of the future are the two ever-present poles of existence in a human community. In so far as Aristotle appreciated the future, as potentiality and possibility, he was more truly a sociologist than those thinkers of the past century whose minds, even when dealing with society, have stopped short with time-categories that completely suffice only for elementary mechanics.

The autonomy of the organism, so characteristic of its growth, renewal, and repair, does not lead to isolation in either time or space. On the contrary, every living creature is part of the general web of life: only as life exists in all its processes and realities, from the action of the bacteria upward, can any particular unit of it continue to exist. As our knowledge of the organism has grown, the importance of the environment as a co-operative factor in its development has become clearer; and its bearing upon the development of human societies has become plainer, too. If there are favorable habitats and favorable forms of association for animals and plants, as ecology demonstrates, why not for men? If each particular natural environment has its own balance, is there not perhaps an equivalent of this in culture? Organisms, their functions, their environments: people, their occupations, their workplaces and living-places, form inter-related and definable wholes.

Such questions as yet can evoke only tentative answers; but they provide a new starting point for investigation. And from the negative processes, the destruction and deterioration of the environment through man's misuse, much has already been learned: Marsh's classic treatise on the Earth and Man was followed by the highly intelligent surveys of natural resources, in terms of potential human use, by Major Powell and Raphael Pumpelly, and the later conservationists, from Van Hise to MacKaye. Beginning with Kropotkin's Mutual Aid the study of human ecology has taken a more positive turn: witness Huntington's studies of civilization and climate, the urban investigations of the Chicago school of sociologists, and above all, Patrick Geddes's lifelong effort to develop a sociology on the basis of biology, and a social art on the positive foundation of our biological, psychological and sociological knowledge. In the doctrines of emergents, organisms, and wholes, particularly as set forth in Lloyd Morgan and Whitehead, lie the outline of an appropriate metaphysics.

In emphasizing the importance of this new orientation toward the living and the organic, I expressly rule out false biological analogies between societies and organisms: Herbert Spencer and others pushed these to the point of absurdity. Such analogies sometimes provide useful suggestions, suggestions no less practical than those derived— with equally little realism—from the machine. But the point is that our knowledge directs attention to parallel processes, parallel conditions and reactions; and it gives rise to related pictures of the natural and the cultural environments, considered as wholes, within which man finds his life and being and drama.

So long as the machine was uppermost, people thought quantitatively in terms of expansion, extension, progress, mechanical multiplication, power. With the organism uppermost we begin to think qualitatively in terms of growth, norms, shapes, inter-relationships, implications, associations, and societies. We realize that the aim of the social process is not to make men more powerful, but to make them more completely developed, more human, more capable of carrying on the specifically human attributes of culture—neither snarling carnivores nor insensate robots. Once established, the vital and social order must subsume the mechanical one, and dominate it: in practice as well as in thought. In social terms, this means a re-orientation not only from mechanism to organism, but from despotism to symbiotic association, from capitalism and fascism to co-operation and basic communism.

There is one further important consequence of this recognition of the organic: that is, the disappearance of the boundary walls between the inner and the outer, the conscious and the unconscious, the external and the internal environment. With man there is no outer environment available except through the medium of society—that medium which supplies nourishment to the growing baby, equips it with the signs of language and the symbols of association, prepares it by cultural habituation to eat this food and reject that poison, to believe this truth and turn aside from that error. In order for the outer environment to function effectively, man must face it, seize it,

assimilate it: and when that is done, it is no longer an *outer* environment.

Within its figure on the web of life, each organism is by nature
selective: it extracts from the total environment, its potential field of
action, just those elements that can be taken in and that promote
growth or security. When it makes bad selections its life is impaired;
and when it goes on making them, it ultimately dies. As man's scale
of cultural development rises, nature becomes a more active element
in his culture, and his culture, in turn, becomes second nature. Thus
an ever greater part is played by deliberate selection, and by the
collective reconstruction of the environment in terms of man's needs,
desires, and purposes. The house, for example, has its origin in the
nest and the cave; but in what animal exigencies is there anything
to be compared to the burial tomb or the monument? Just as man
himself is the most triumphant example of man's domestication of
animals, so society is the result of man's long experiment in refining
the processes of animal association. One might almost define the city
as the structure through which domestication and association were
purposively united.

The time has come to express more fully this re-orientation toward
life and organism. In the present chapter I shall attempt to outline
the broader requirements of a life-conditioned environment: first,
in the barest terms of "air, water, and places"; and then in terms of
the economic and political pattern that is already present, like the
buds of spring, in the wintry thicket of metropolitan civilization.
Within this emerging regional framework, we shall more easily
find the place and form of the new urban community that has also
begun to emerge.

2: The Regional Outlook

Man's conscious relation to the earth underwent a profound change
in Western Europe in the fifteenth century. The desire to conquer
space and explore the unknown upset his more sedentary habits and
gave him fresh excuses for motion which undermined his close vege-
tative relationship to his native soil. But collectively, the great era of
exploration and colonization, which opened in the sixteenth century,
introduced a period of terrestrial neglect. In the act of seizing all

the habitable parts of the earth, the colonists of Africa and the Americas systematically misused and neglected their possession: first, perhaps, out of ignorance, but no less because, even when better knowledge existed, an imperious government, a rapacious economic corporation or individual, would set no bounds to greed or to momentary needs. Where industries developed, where towns spread, land values rose—and the land lost most of its value.

Today the period of exploration has come to an end, and our attitude toward the earth is undergoing another profound change: a by-product of our increased knowledge of the sources of life, and our critical examination of human history. We can no longer leave soils and landscapes and agricultural possibilities out of our calculations in considering the future of either industries or cities. For the era of the callous pioneer, who laid waste to a particular area, looted its natural resources, and moved on, is over: there is no place left to move. We have reached the end of our journey, and in the main, we must retrace our steps, and, region by region, learn to do intelligently and co-operatively what we hitherto did in such disregard of the elementary decencies of life. The grasp of the region as a dynamic social reality is a first step toward a constructive policy of planning, housing, and urban renewal.

In different countries, this consciousness of the underlying geographic conditions and earth-relations has taken different forms. In France, the home of regionalism as a deliberate movement, regionalism has meant first of all a protest against the excessive centralization that took place in politics and culture: it has led to the reconstitution of the provincial universities and to the active development of regions such as the French Alps, around Grenoble. In Denmark, regionalism meant the recapture of the native heritage of the ballads and the folk-literature, the founding of Folk High Schools in the countryside, and the growth of the co-operative movement— and scientific agronomy and breeding—in agriculture; in Czecho-Slovakia, it has meant the founding of an independent political state.

These movements are not unrelated; behind them are certain common ideas. At a period when the uniformities of the machine civilization were being overstressed, regionalism served to emphasize compensatory organic elements: above all, those differences that arise out of geographic, historic, and cultural peculiarities. In its recognition of the region as a basic configuration in human life; in its acceptance of natural diversities as well as natural associations and uniformities; in its recognition of the region as a permanent sphere of cultural influences and as a center of economic activities, as well as an implicit geographic fact—here lies the vital common element in the regionalist movement. So far from being archaic and reactionary, regionalism belongs to the future.

3: The Region as a Geographic Unit

Walking through the countryside in the United States, one may find in the midst of an open field or at the corner of a woodlot a granite post, with the name of one state on one side of it, and that of the adjoining state on the other side. Similar monuments exist at every national frontier, although the population in the transitional zone may be almost as similar to the casual eye as the inhabitants of New York and Connecticut.

Political boundaries of the "imaginary" kind have a hard-and-fast character: that is their convenience. They define the limits of certain man-made conventions and obligations, like constitutions and codes of law. The creation of such boundaries is part of man's efforts to create a more orderly social world: a world of uniform and predictable events. Indeed, the notion of giving some sort of spatial continuity to behavior patterns, instead of permitting them to change in form from one local district to another, with endless quirks and confusing variations, is one of the great political changes that separates the modern world of states from the spatially inconsecutive and muddled allegiances of the feudal world.

Underlying all our political conventions, however, is the basic fact of the earth itself; and the question is how far these political unifications correspond effectively to those provided by nature and other aspects of human culture. The formal partition of the landscape antedated, for the most part, modern geographic knowledge: it was the empirical work of statesmen and lawgivers who believed, for the most part, that differences between peoples or regions were man-made, and could be wiped out by an act of the legislature. Even the

[22] OUTLINES FOR REGIONAL PLANNING

New York State, while not a complete region, needs only to be rounded out by the inclusion of Northern New Jersey, and that part of Connecticut which swings over from a point opposite the central part of Long Island. Otherwise it has the major requirements for a human region: individuality and coherence, the possibilities of a balanced and partly self-sustaining agricultural and economic life, a diversity of resources and a variety of habitats from the partly primeval Adirondack mountains down to the coves, sand-dunes, and beaches of Long Island, with its mild climate, its early growing season, its duck-ponds, and its rich aquatic life. The original national traditions, those of the Dutch, the English, and the French Huguenots, have been variegated with later cultural strains; but from the beginning the international importance of the port of New York, to say nothing of the place occupied by Buffalo in grain shipments, has given New York a cosmopolitan standard: its typical sons, like Washington Irving, James Fenimore Cooper, Samuel Morse, and Herman Melville, were as much at home in Europe as in their own country, while its Whitman uttered his salute to the world and received the world's response before his fellow-countryman had measured his grand dimensions. The geological surveys instituted by the University of the State of New York in the forties were not merely a milestone in science: they were, in specialized form, a fragment of those publicly aided regional surveys whose making is the effective prelude to rational programs and plans. Its agricultural wealth lies not merely in its dairy regions, with their large surpluses of milk and cheese, but in the grape culture of the Mohawk Valley, where some of the finest American wines are made, and in apple orchards whose excellent apples have ironically often been pushed out of the metropolitan market in favor of insipid varieties that have traveled many thousand miles: another example of the metropolitan habit of carrying coals to Newcastle. In its power policies, its conservation policies, its setting aside of large areas for state parks and its buying-up of sub-marginal lands, New York State has demonstrated that steady movement toward rational socialization which a democratic political life makes possible: a movement that will be accelerated when the schools and universities of the state accept even more fully than now their responsibility for working out policies, laying down programs, and projecting plans. Through its initiatives in housing and regional planning, beginning with the setting up of the New York State Housing and Regional Planning Commission in 1923, with Clarence S. Stein as Chairman, New York laid the foundations for much of the work that has been done during the present decade throughout the country: both in public housing and in regional development.

[TOP] Three important phases in the development of the State of New York, as outlined by Henry Wright in the report of the first Housing and Regional Planning Commission (1926). The first period reached its fruition between 1840 and 1880. Mainly an eotechnic economy, based upon the use of local forests, local water mills for sawing wood and grinding grain and running machinery, with small factories situated in mainly agricultural villages and country towns. The second period was one of industrial and financial concentration; it probably reached its apex between 1910 and 1920, although the inordinate growth of Buffalo and still more New York continued by inertia, even after the main supply of immigrants from Europe had been cut off. In the third phase a new pattern of population distribution emerges, based upon new technical facilities and revised social aims: if its promise is seized, it means the substitution of a biotechnic for a pecuniary economy. Neither the congestion of the paleotechnic period nor the undiscriminating diffusion of the eotechnic period with its exploratory colonization: instead, the broadening out of the valley belts, as locus for settlement, rather than congesting already crowded centers along the railroad *line,* the utilization of a hitherto neglected area by Lake Ontario is pointed to by scientific study of climatic and soil maps; similar studies suggest the zoning of the state as a whole into major utilization areas. The planning of electric power and motor highways and housing developments so as to further a new type of balanced development is here plainly indicated. The partial socialization of hydro-electric power and the reservation of great parks have already taken place. The period of re-settlement and community building now opens before us. Instead of encouraging the further building up of metropolitan areas, already overburdened, a rational policy demands a systematic urban re-settlement in Greenbelt Towns, with a minimum expenditure on the elaborate mechanical means of congestion, and a sane provision of opportunities for *living.*

[BOTTOM LEFT] Regionalism as conceived by the administrator. The division is based upon considerations that are now superior to the old-fashioned divisions between the states; but the respect for the underlying geographic and cultural realities is subordinated to the administrator's convenience, and many of these proposed regional divisions are as arbitrary as the older historic lines. A first essay in a complex re-ordering of political realities that will require at least a generation of re-statement and criticism before the inevitable order will emerge.

[BOTTOM RIGHT] While the metropolitan area is not a region, since it is, by its nature, in a state of permanent unbalance, no region can be defined as a geographic, economic, and cultural complex without respect to the essential relationships between city and country. Since in most cases the metropolis has achieved the maximum growth because it possesses a maximum number of advantages, and so is a natural meeting point, the outline of a region is partly determined by the range of influence exerted by its natural capital. McKenzie's use of the sphere of newspaper circulation as a criterion of this influence is arbitrary; its convenience for measurement cannot make up for the absence of other data and criteria; but the resulting outline of regional units is closer to geographic and sociological realities than the administrative areas shown above.

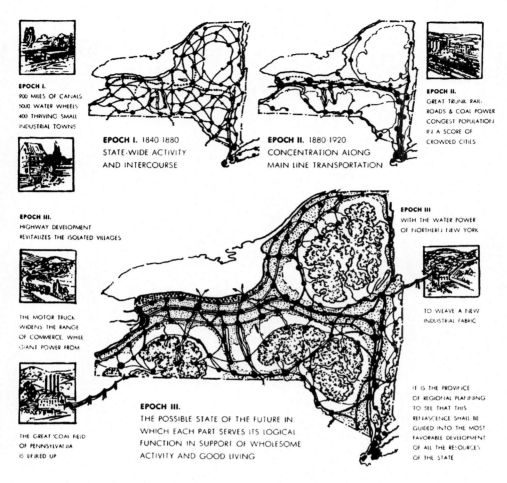

EPOCH I.
900 MILES OF CANALS
5000 WATER WHEELS
400 THRIVING SMALL
INDUSTRIAL TOWNS

EPOCH I. 1840-1880
STATE-WIDE ACTIVITY
AND INTERCOURSE

EPOCH II. 1880-1920
CONCENTRATION ALONG
MAIN LINE TRANSPORTATION

EPOCH II.
GREAT TRUNK RAIL-
ROADS & COAL POWER
CONGEST POPULATION
IN A SCORE OF
CROWDED CITIES

EPOCH III.
HIGHWAY DEVELOPMENT
REVITALIZES THE ISOLATED VILLAGES

THE MOTOR TRUCK
WIDENS THE RANGE
OF COMMERCE, WHILE
GIANT POWER FROM

THE GREAT COAL FIELD
OF PENNSYLVANIA
IS LINKED UP

EPOCH III
WITH THE WATER POWER
OF NORTHERN NEW YORK

TO WEAVE A NEW
INDUSTRIAL FABRIC

IT IS THE PROVINCE
OF REGIONAL PLANNING
TO SEE THAT THIS
RENASCENCE SHALL BE
GUIDED INTO THE MOST
FAVORABLE DEVELOPMENT
OF ALL THE RESOURCES
OF THE STATE

EPOCH III.
THE POSSIBLE STATE OF THE FUTURE IN
WHICH EACH PART SERVES ITS LOGICAL
FUNCTION IN SUPPORT OF WHOLESOME
ACTIVITY AND GOOD LIVING

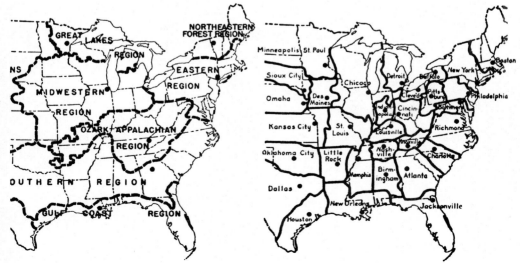

new democratic states, in defining the limits of territorial sovereignty, followed the arbitrary patterns of the absolute rulers and princelings of the baroque period. As in the delimitation of the political departments of France during the French Revolution, administrators usually chose to ignore natural regions, with their historic complexes and their customary privileges. They could not dissociate the older organic pattern from the feudal and ecclesiastical order that had grown up with it: antagonistic to the privileges of the latter, they sought to displace the reality of the first.

In general, during the nineteenth century, functional geographic associations and functional boundaries were disregarded. States were set up, municipalities were created, administrative districts bounded, new areas of authority outlined, with little concern for the geographic constants and for the underlying community relations founded upon them. Rivers, which are channels of unification for the communities on both sides, were even favored as boundary lines: what was solely a military obstacle was treated as an actual division. Little effort was made to create harmonious regional units that would give equal expression to the needs of the countryside and the needs of cities.

Up to a point, these arbitrary units of administration worked better than the facts warranted. The reason should be plain. In many cases any sort of boundary, defining the limits of obligation and interest, is better than no boundary at all: even an artificial association is more efficient than aimless, unorganized juxtaposition. But these new political units forced many institutions into molds that did not fit them, and they ceased to exercise effective control over organizations—like the great industrial corporations—that were set up on a continental or a worldwide basis; while the growth of the metropolis under the financial and imperial regime made it often form a homogeneous urban unit over areas under diverse and conflicting administrative authorities. After much strain and frustration, the weaknesses of these abstract divisions at last became apparent: meanwhile, the human geographer and the sociologist have opened our eyes to the fundamental geographic facts; and we can now define the regional complex, not in terms solely of men's wishes, but in terms woven into objective reality.

In what sense does the region exist as a geographic unit; and what conditions does it lay down for human occupation?

One may define a region by working upward from the smallest unit of human habitation, in terms of functions, activities, and interests; or by working downward, mainly in terms of land mass, climate, and physical interactions. The geographer divides the world into five great habitable land-masses. But one has only to examine these masses closely to see that while the differences between them are many, they are no greater than the differences that exist within them, among their subordinate areas. Each mass divides into provinces, regions, and sub-regions: these units form complexes that are more or less differentiated in pattern. Their geologic structure, soil, situation, climate, vegetation, and animal life differentiate them from other complexes.

As soon as one adds man to the picture the difference between areas becomes multifarious and subtle: for laws, manners, customs, the patterns of communal living, the forms of architecture, the village types and city types, the transformation of the original landscape into the humanly modified landscape of agriculture, with its orderly patterns and deliberate culture—all these are fresh factors of differentiation, marking off one region from another. In regions of long settlement indeed the aboriginal characteristics of the environment have been profoundly modified by man's occupation: many of the most valuable food-plants used in Western agriculture, for example, are exotics. As social conditions vie with natural conditions in establishing the regional character it becomes easier to define even the boundaries of the region in terms of the spheres of attraction, the dominant cities, rather than in terms of purely physical barriers, like the swamps and forests that originally bounded the counties of South England.

Now, the more thoroughly one is acquainted with the social and geographic facts in any area, the more keenly one becomes aware that unity and differentiation go hand in hand. When one searches for unity, the human race is obviously one. When one looks for differences one discovers not only national types and regional types, one discovers likewise important differences between a Florentine and a Neapolitan, between a Glasgow man and an Edinburgh man, even differences in language, accent, gesture, feeling between villages that are but a day's walk apart. Finally, one reaches the primordial unit of individuality and realizes that no two identical finger prints of different persons have yet been discovered. Unity does not annul difference; and difference does not undermine a dynamic unity.

There are accordingly two kinds of unity which one must clearly distinguish: unity by suppression, in which a single pattern of life is universalized, and that of unity by inclusion, in which a multitude of different patterns either find their common elements, or become elements in a more complex configuration that includes them. Unity by suppression is achieved by de-building organic relations and by the reduction of the complicated facts of life to a simpler system: such method is ingrained in all the generalizing processes of thought, and when such procrustean likeness and uniformity and unison is sought by the political administrator, the violence that he does to reality is not perhaps sufficiently noticed for the reason that the method itself grows out of one of the inherent limitations of thought—a limitation that sacrifices accuracy and comprehensiveness to the practical needs of the moment. Although one may treat a human being as an arbitrary numerical unit, one of a thousand that is born on a given day, one of ten thousand taxpayers in a certain income bracket, one does not eliminate him as a complex social reality. This is likewise true of regional units. De-building, in order to widen the scheme of life invoked by the metropolis and the governing state, ends in impoverishment: like a financial system in which the currency and the credit no longer summon up, on demand, the food and machinery and services which alone can give reality to the counters by which they are manipulated.

In general, one may say that geographic differences are primordial, while social differentiations, including those derived from urban association, are emergent: one is foundation, the other pinnacle. Merely by examining the geographic base one cannot tell what the social emergent will be; for, precisely because it *is* an emergent, precisely because it necessarily contains elements from other geographic regions and other cultures and other layers of historic experience, it is a new configuration, not given in the geographic complex itself. But geographic conditions nevertheless place the possibilities of cultural development within certain limits: the skills of the Eskimo are of no use in the tropical jungle.

Each regional complex then is marked by three special qualities. The first is its specific geographic character: certain common properties of soil, climate, vegetation, agriculture and technical exploitation.

Take the State of Ohio. The greater part of the state is glaciated; the land is fertile; and a network of small communities distributes the population fairly evenly over the whole area, with here and there a further concentration in cities like Toledo and Cleveland in the north and Cincinnati in the south. With its fertile fields, its vast nursery gardens of peonies, its tree-lined villages, the northern parts of Ohio present a physiognomy that curiously combines that of New England with that of Holland. On the surface, it is like a handsome Dutch landscape with all its dimensions magnified: the brick highways even underline the likeness. At the same time the villages themselves, often founded by New Englanders, have a closer relation to the agricultural type of settlement in New England than to the close urban pattern of the Netherlands, where land was more precious. But the formal political boundary does not define this regional complex: it is an historic emergent that now calls for understanding and further political and cultural expression. One of the main tasks of regionalism is to see and develop further the geographic and social realities that underlie a multitude of more or less empty formal differentiations. Often the latter are based on traditions, political interests, or institutions that no longer prevail.

Next, a region is characterized by the existence of a balance, a state of dynamic equilibrium, between its various parts: when any large alteration is made in one section of the environment, corresponding or compensating changes must be made, as a rule, in every other part. When man upsets the natural balance by introducing a new creature, as the jack rabbit was introduced into Australia, when he plows up the grassland in semi-arid areas in order to make an evanescent profit out of farming wheat, or when he removes the forest cover wholesale—he sets up a whole train of consequences that disrupt the complicated fabric upon which permanent human settlement is based: soil erosion, floods, insect pests, blights of various kinds, may follow such upsets.

One creature indeed man cannot help introducing—himself. And perhaps the chief problem of human settlement has been to adapt the planet to man's many new needs without completely disrupting the balance of nature. Favorable adaptations of the environment, like the systematic adaptation of the Nile floodlands to permanent agriculture, are the foundations for a great release in energy and a durable human culture. Each region has its own configuration: its own special partnerships and associations, its own favored resources, and its own equally characteristic dearths or impoverishments. These resources vary with the culture of the community itself. As the cultural heritage increases, a larger part of the environment becomes useful and meaningful: *the natural conditions of a region, so far from being nullified by the increase of culture and technical skill, are actually magnified.* The hunter knows the forest only as a home for game; but for modern man the forest is also a source of lumber, a protection against soil erosion, a recreation area, and a field for scientific observation.

Hence the popular notion that modern technology has lessened the importance of the natural habitat is precisely the opposite of the truth: likewise the notion that "regional differences fade out as isolation disappears." On a sandy spit like Cape Cod, for instance, there will be originally only fishermen and primitive agriculturists: growers of corn, diggers of clams, pickers of cranberries in the bogs. Later, the same area, because of the availability of wood and sand, may nourish a glass industry, such as the ancient one at Sandwich; and at still a further stage, it may support an institute of scientific research at one end of the peninsula and a colony of artists at the other: each group revealing new resources in the environment. Meanwhile, a fresh succession of newcomers deposited on the original Indian layer—English, Portuguese, French-Canadian, Negro—increases the specific individuality of this particular regional complex. So far from disappearing with isolation, regional differences become more marked, as each new occupation, each new social interest, brings out a hitherto undiscovered color that modifies the common pattern. *Primitive* regional differences may diminish with intercultural contact: but *emergent* differences become more profound, unless the region itself is disabled by the metropolitan effort to wipe out every other mode of life except that which reflects its own image. This is a sociological fact of universal bearing.

From the human standpoint, the essential point about balance is that it involves the utilization of a variety of ecological groupings and a variety of human responses: balance and variety are the two concepts, in fact, which help one to define a region of cultural settlement. Likeness of interest and singleness of response are only one side of the regional pattern: used as a basis for communal organization such criteria would create one-sided, specialized regions in a state of imbalance and cultural impoverishment. What is no less important than the feeling of identity is the fact of variety: the meeting and mingling of diverse types, the "etherealization" and interchange of diverse environments, is essential to a sound regional life.

In conceiving a region, then, it is necessary to take an area large enough to embrace a sufficient range of interests, and small enough to keep these interests in focus and to make them a subject of direct collective concern. In older regions of settlement, the interplay of geography and history has produced such human areas: even if they have lost some of their attributes, the essential shell remains: a memory if not a fact. In newer parts of the earth it is important to understand, by intensive investigation, all the factors that lend themselves to scientific description, in order finally to build the complex earth-form, not discoverable in nature: the balanced human region. Take away the notions of variety and balance, however, and the very notion of the region becomes a mere spatial expression—applicable to any of the 108 different administrative divisions of the United States, for example, as made by this or that government department in Washington. Our task is to replace the primeval balance that exists in a region with organisms in a state of nature, by a richer environment, a more subtle and many-weighted balance, of human groups and communities in a state of high culture. The sort of regional planning that seeks some simple arbitrary pattern, more closely fitted to the convenience of the political or industrial administrator is regional in name only. Unfortunately the tendency to call any large-scale administrative unit a region—now a fashionable name—is one from which even the admirable Report on Regional Factors in National Planning is not free.

Finally, one comes to a third characteristic of natural regions. Unlike the old-fashioned political areas they have not—except in the case of isolated islands, oases, or high mountain areas—any definite physical boundaries. The region may be defined and delimited in thought; but this is largely a practical convenience: even the purely physical characteristics often grade into each other, with intermediate zones that belong partly to one, partly to the other area. As soon as the human communities are considered, the region becomes even more plainly a system of inter-relationships that overflow and become shadowy at the margins.

This means that all boundaries in black and white are, in one degree or another, arbitrary. Reality implies a certain looseness and vagueness, a certain failure of definition. To define human areas, one must seek, not the periphery alone but the center. Fawcett wisely took the regional capital as a means of defining his sub-regions in England; and in human culture generally, the urban spheres of attraction become geographic facts of utmost importance: for the urban center tends to focus the flow of energies, men, and goods that passes through a region, concentrating them, dispersing them, diverting them, re-routing them, in short, exerting a close and controlling influence over the development of region as a dynamic reality. Indeed, the bare physiographic area itself receives some of its contour through the operation of human needs and human processes: wherever man found even the primeval wilderness, up to the days of the airplane, his own footprints accompanied him, and participated in the definition. Nature provides the materials. Conceptually and concretely, man designs the structure. The region, no less than the city, is a collective work of art. That is why it requires the actions of men, as well as the specialized knowledge of geographer and sociologist, to define it.

4: The City as a Geographic Fact

Consider the city itself as an expression of regional individuality. Even in its most highly developed stages, the city is, among other things, an earth form. It is put together out of wood, stone, clay, asphaltum, glass. Its shape is conditioned by topography and the nature of the land; and the special requisites of the site alter with the needs of defense and industry and transportation. The numerical size of an urban settlement, before routes of trade have been secured, depends directly upon the agricultural capacities of the surrounding soils, combined with the yield of the nearest fisheries. And the possibility of reaching out into other regions for sustenance depends upon its situation. The most obdurate form of local control is that of the drinking water supply: one cannot even pitch camp conveniently for a night without water.

In the river, the region provides the first natural routes of transportation, which man later modifies into irrigation systems for his crops and transportation canals for his commerce. As the river is the easiest route to travel over, it has remained in existence longest as a utility: even the new railroad usually clung to its banks. Small wonder that the Nile and the Euphrates and the Hoang-Ho and the Donau and the Rhine were the roadbeds of their civilization. The river is a unifying agent, drawing together in its stream of transportation materials gathered from each side of its course, depositing its burden of goods and culture at the terminal cities, as the river itself deposits its silt at the delta. Ocean transportation on the land-locked seas was long a secondary form of transport; and it is only by degrees that cities have established themselves—though rarely without the aid of an oasis spring—on land routes and have planted themselves with success in unwatered parts of the hinterland.

Few cultures, unless isolated by insuperable barriers and numbed into submission by exceptional rigors of climate, have ever practiced anything like complete self-subsistence, or autarchy. Inter-regional transport is one of the pillars of urban life: it multiplies contacts, social relations, products; and by the very diversity of the resources it brings together contributes to the specific pattern of the city's life. The clogging of the main routes of transportation, such as the stop·

page of oriental trade through the Bosporus after the Turkish con·
quest of Byzantium may vitiate the life of a city which, like Venice,
lies at the other end of the route. On the other hand, the multiplication of trade routes may pour into a single center a larger population than it can handle competently: witness the uneasy sprawl of
Hamburg and London.

No less important is climate. The climatic belt in which cities have
flourished is a broad one: it is roughly coincident with the distribution of the hard grains, whose suitability for permanent storage probably contributed greatly to that stability and continuity out of which
city life could grow. One may speak of rye cities, wheat cities, maize
cities, rice cities. The city is, in effect, a means of overcoming partly
the effect of climatic conditioning and direct topographic control:
hence their wide range in temperature and height from Angkor to
Helsinki, from Rotterdam to Mexico City or Lassa. City life takes
one form in the Mediterranean area, where the mild climate decreases the need for protective shelter and increases the opportunity
for public life in the open. It takes another form in the North, where
the words "chimney" or "roof" are sufficient to indicate a dwelling
house. Climate does not so much limit the existence of cities as indi-
vidualize the type of urban adaptation. Each city has its characteristic play of weather, set off against its special landscape: the fog of
London, the stinging wind of Edinburgh, the luxuriant warmth of
palm-lined Los Angeles, the dramatic patches of sunlight in the
gloomy skies of Berlin, set in the midst of its pine-barrens.

One further influence of climate: its effects upon habits of eating
and drinking. Perhaps cities first developed in the warm valleys of
Asia Minor and Northern Africa not merely because the food supply
had increased but because a larger population could subsist on a
sparser diet than was necessary in the North. As one goes north-
ward, both the production of food and the eating of it become a
more engrossing daily occupation; and whereas the temperate
Greek regarded the habit of drinking undiluted wine as a barbarism,
the northern city dweller, battling with the dank winds, chilled by
the sloshy underfooting, depressed by the eternal dullness of the sky,
drinks much and often: not content with wine neat, he spices it, dis-
tills it, turns it into firewater.

Food and drink, no less than climate, add to the individuality of a city; and they affect the port and gesture and manners and alertness of the inhabitants. The bouillabaisse of Marseilles, the fried cakes of Amsterdam, the baked beans of Boston and the hot puddings of London, the cheeses of Rouen and the spaghetti of Naples—on all these climate, vegetation, regional occupations and regional needs, have left their mark. The quickening of European intellectual life in the urban coffee houses of the seventeenth century, and the befuddlement of the proletariat through cheap gin and brandy in the nineteenth, are capital events in the human culture of cities.

Diet, too, plays a part in differentiating castes in a city: not alone the lean diet of holiness and the fat diet of assertive sensuality, but the meatless diet of the peasant, as contrasted with the epicurean carnivorousness of the stout bourgeois, whose refined path of conduct never leads him, if he can help it, to the door of the slaughterhouse. Diet and drink, moreover, play a real if little examined rôle in the erotic ritual, particularly in the manner and duration of sexual intercourse: there is even evidence at hand now to indicate its effect upon procreation. The tendency of an urban diet to be mixed, *inter*-regional in origin, not limited to traditional materials or recipes, is of course characteristic of most other cultural aspects of city life. And like them, it serves to unite the citizens in a common cult: in no profane allusion one may say that every urban table is a communion table.

Because of its close, if not abject, dependence upon local building materials and local qualities of site, the city epitomizes the surrounding country and gives a special character to the natural setting. At no moment in its existence is the divorce between the man-made environment and the earth complete. The red sandstone of Strasbourg, the yellow clay of London, the red brick of Bremen, the gray limestone of post-medieval Paris, the brown sandstone of old Frankfort-am-Main—the very bricks and stones symbolize that underlying partnership between man and nature which is accepted and furthered, even while it is transformed, in the structure of the city.

The immediate geological foundations remain an important attribute of urban individuality; they seep into the consciousness in all sorts of indirect ways. The very infant at play, digging in the earth of his dooryard, is conscious of the ubiquitous sand if he lives in Rotterdam, of the oily shale if in Pittsburgh, or of the tantalizing gleam of mica in the schist of Manhattan. And as cities develop, external conditions become internal influences, while internal impulses work themselves out in new forms and patterns born of the playful necessities or earnest choices of the human imagination. Just as the climate and food give a peculiar gleam or sallowness to the skin, so the "internal" influences of a region—a religion, a scientific technique, an educational doctrine—will eventually alter the shape and distribution of its buildings.

If the earth acts upon the city in such immediate ways, the indirect processes are even more numerous and potent. Above all, each trade and industry tends, as nothing else in the city's life does, to maximize the environment: to concentrate within a limited area, the widest sweep of resources, products, processes, and modes of life. This phenomenon is so constant and so universal that it tends to escape notice; yet it is one of the most essential features of urban existence. A handful of people, settled in a village, with a personal range of movement limited to a day's walk, can, even in a state of intense awareness, embrace only a limited environment: their knowledge of life, however intense, will be confined to what their meadows and forests and immediate neighbors disclose to them.

The city, on the other hand, may cover a visible terrain more cramped than that of the village and its fields. But its invisible regional base, embraced through the raw materials that reach it, the technical methods that are acclimatized in its workshops, the personal and regional idiosyncrasies that are poured into it through its immigrants—its regional base is much broader. Because it extracts only the essence of the surrounding regions, because so much of life comes to it in physically dismembered or sublimated (symbolic) forms, the city embodies the region, and indeed the whole outside world, more fully than any other single fragment of landscape could do.

In the city, the environment takes on a more social form: indeed, through the media of the vocations, groups, and personalities so closely mobilized here, one part of the environment can react upon another part of the environment to produce results that would be impossible through direct intercourse and interaction. Once this transmutation has taken place within the city, the abstract or sym-bolic products, no less than the concrete ones, can be transported back to other parts of the earth.

Trade and industry have, therefore, a social significance within the city that they do not possess in more primitive and one-sided envi-ronments: the richer the urban pattern, the more significant, in gen-eral, become the subordinate processes: and the greater the possi-bility for socially valuable mutations and inventions of more uni-versal application. While over-devotion to the subsidiary economic processes and their pecuniary evaluations may produce an insensate culture, devoid of further significance, one cannot doubt the enliven-ing effects of the more complicated processes of production, crea-tion, and interchange: it distinguishes urban culture from village culture.

In the very act of lending to economic aims the full cultural equip-ment of the city, the city also gives the stimulus of wider economic and regional experiences to its specific cultural processes. By maxi-mizing, by intensifying, the environment, the city vastly increases the possibilities of fruitful inter-regional intercourse. It is for this reason that the complete disappearance of the city is unthinkable, so long as civilization remains intact—although the fundamental forms of the city are all subject to radical alteration. Disurbanization and gen-eral dispersal would ruin the countryside no less than the urban centers.

The complex effect of the region upon the city, and of the city in turn upon the groups and individuals within it, has been very sen-sitively interpreted by Marcel Proust in the second volume of the Remembrance of Times Past. Let me quote the passage:

"Last of all, and even more general than the family heritage, was the rich layer imposed by the native province from which they de-rived their voices, and of which indeed their intonations smacked. Between that province and the temperament of the little girl who dic-tated these inflections, I caught a charming dialogue. A dialogue, not in any sense a discord. It would not have been possible to separate the girl herself and her native place. She was herself; she was it also. Moreover, this reaction of locally procured materials on the genius who utilizes them and to whose work their reaction imparts an added freshness, does not make the work any less individual, and whether it be that of an architect, a cabinet maker, or a composer, it reflects no less minutely the most subtle shades of the artist's personality, because he has been compelled to work in the millstone of Senlis or the red sandstone of Strasbourg, has respected the knots peculiar to the ash-tree, has borne in mind, when writing his score, the resources, the limitations, the volume of sound, the possibilities of flute or alto voice."

Note that this play of the local, individualized environment upon the community does not counteract the more universal forces that are also at work. For the very existence of universal forms and ideas within the city indicates, not merely the valiant effort of the human mind to create a viable abstract order, good for all times and places, but it also indicates the human desire to share experience; since the higher the degree of uniqueness, the smaller are the possibilities of finding a similar response in the bosom of one's neighbor. The local and the intense must be balanced off against the universal and the wide-spreading: the first must become more broadly *intelligible*, the second must become more narrowly *applicable*. Universals that cannot take root are of the same order as roots from whose stems no flower issues and no seeds disseminate themselves.

No region can ignore universal forces: the city, above all, is an instrument for capturing them and transmitting them more effectively. The spread of a universal religion, such as Buddhism or Christianity or Communism, or the conquest of a universal system of technics, like that now based on Western science, depends not merely upon the original power of the transformer but upon the delicacy and fine tuning of the regional receptors: both must be adequate. One has only to compare the original production per man hour in a British cotton factory with that in a Russian or Indian one or an English bricklayer's production with that of an American, to see how local habits of life modify the universal pattern and produce different quantitative as well as different qualitative results.

Only the careless eye will fail to detect deep cultural modifications from region to region, from city to city: quite as marked as the differences in the appearance of the common sparrow of Texas compared with the same species in New England. Beneath the Catholicism of Naples still lurk the forms of Venus and Diana: beneath the Protestantism of Germany, the violent gods and heroes of the Nibelungen tales still assert themselves. The region, then, is the warp upon which the fabric of communal life is woven. Even when the coarse geographic threads are unnoticed, their quality and number and closeness will affect the weaving of the ultimate cloth. The variety of these natural influences, the complexity and individuality of their assembled character in the city, are in fact a perpetual guarantee against man's inveterate tendency toward over-simplification: by this means he escapes that mechanization and falsification of the living reality which Bergson has correctly interpreted as a constant vice of human thought. Communities may wisely strive for uniformity, for certainty and fixity, for universality of pattern: indeed, unless they strove for these things the most precious human achievements would not be possible. But only upon this condition: that they shall never finally succeed.

5: The Earth as Home

Civilizations have risen and fallen without apparently perceiving the full import of their relations with the earth. For soil exhaustion and mineral exhaustion have been felt locally in other periods of history without stirring the rulers of the threatened communities to take effective measures against these dangers.

From the standpoint of earth-culture, modern civilization achieved its highest form, perhaps, in the Dutch communities of the eotechnic period, when the usual habits of wastage and degradation were reversed. Though Holland set an example to the rest of the world in the resourceful exploitation of her terrain, the example was largely ignored. The rapid spread of mankind to new countries, where the resources seemed boundless, encouraged a more primitive type of farming: lands were planted for a single crop, like cotton; and the farmers moved on to new areas when the older territories gave signs of exhaustion. Nomadic agriculture and nomadic forestry literally cut the ground from under the feet of countries like the United States. By the middle of the nineteenth century the process had gone so far in the Appalachian area that it awakened the consciousness of keen observers, like G. P. Marsh, to the universal aspects of the situation.

Viewing the result of this destruction from the standpoint of human habitability, Henry Thoreau suggested that every community in America should have, as part of its permanent domain, a portion of the wilderness, kept free for the citizens from all the encroachments of civilization, like the Royal Hunting Parks in England. A short while after this a movement was started to reserve through the Federal Government certain areas whose striking natural beauty should remain unscarred by permanent human settlement. The founding of the Yellowstone National Park in 1872, the first of a series of such reservations in the United States, was a capital event in regional culture. It was the first public recognition of the need for the primeval wilderness as a background for a civilized life, and of the value of the natural environment for other purposes than reckless financial exploitation. Utilitarian needs, such as the planting of the forests of England under Sir John Evelyn, in order to ensure a supply of timber for the British Navy, had hitherto governed the reservation of wild areas; and the state forests of Europe are one of the oldest forms of socialized ownership and activity. But although the forestry movement was, happily, to produce similar reservations in America, the United States National Parks were the first recognition of landscape as a communal resource.

Marsh and Thoreau were primarily concerned with the threatened extinction of the primeval wilderness and the impoverishments and dangers that might arise from the destruction of the forest cover. But other observers in the nineteenth century noted evils equally threatening in other provinces: Stanley Jevons pointed out that at the rate the coal beds were being exploited in the paleotechnic period, the supply of coal would give out within a century or two unless new resources were discovered or more thrifty ways introduced. While new deposits were in fact discovered and improved methods of coal-burning reduced the actual consumption per horsepower, the prediction held true in general: for mineral resources, especially energy resources like coal and petroleum and lignite are irreplaceable once consumed. This is almost equally true of the more precious metals

VII: THE REGIONAL COMPLEX
[23] AGENTS OF REGIONAL DEVELOPMENT

The Tennessee Valley project, with its fundamental policy of public conservation of power resources, land, forest, soil and stream, in the public interest, is an indication of a new approach to the problems of regional development: an advance in certain ways over those already initiated in New York and Wisconsin. The river valley has the advantage of bringing into a common regional frame a diversified unit: this is essential to an effective civic and social life, and has been overlooked in many schemes of regional development that are erected on the basis of purely homogeneous resources or interests. Regional unity is partly an emergent: a cultural product: a result of co-operative political and economic action. Upland areas, from the Alps to Norway, from the Cascade Range to the Appalachians, are scenes for neotechnic planning with electric power and decentralized industry. In the Tennessee Valley and kindred areas, like the Upper Connecticut Valley, a basis can be laid, not merely for a more efficient industrial order, but for a new social order and a new type of urban environment, provided the requisite political courage and social imagination are collectively brought to bear.

[UPPER LEFT] High tension standards, marching across a rough terrain: expressive of the freedom of location that electric power, in contrast to old-fashioned uses of coal and water, carries with it. (*Photograph: Ewing Galloway*)

[UPPER RIGHT] Dam and spillway at Norris, Tennessee: power house below: the order and beauty of modern geotechnics. White coal: smokeless cities. (*Photograph: Tennessee Valley Authority*)

[MIDDLE] Upland area in Tennessee: potentially the scene of a more intensive settlement that will conserve rather than blot out the natural foundations for a good and durable social life. Sun, wind, cloud, earth, grass, forest, farm, garden—these are constants in human life that only shriveled imaginations would displace by mechanical substitutes: but the finer utilizations of these gifts of nature are themselves a product of a higher type of scientific and technical organization. Airplanes and electric lights are but beginnings: the sun-accumulator and the solar engine are already in embryonic existence: we await, among other things, an efficient electric accumulator, light and powerful, to displace the gasoline-driven engine, and a localized domestic method of sewage disposal which will convert sewage into fertilizer. Domestic hothouses capable of supplying fresh vegetables and fruits throughout the year should soon be available where power and fuel are cheap: these things promise a diminishment of wheeled transportation except for travel and association. (*Photograph: Tennessee Valley Authority*)

[BOTTOM] Top of the Norris Dam, facing the wild park area that has been set aside for recreation. (*Photograph: Tennessee Valley Authority*)

[TOP] Handsome interior of co-operative store in the new town of Norris, Tenn.:
the unification of the modern retail market, partly expressed in metropolitan-
financial terms in the chain store, is brought to its culmination in the co-operative store: elimination of wasteful duplications, ruinous competitive salesmanship, ballyhoo, and profit for absentee investors: such co-operatives are characteristic of the new housing throughout Europe: expressions of the same order.
As goods become standardized and stabilized, in terms of biological need and
tested performance and fair price, there will be a general curtailment of competitive retail selling. More products of the bulkier and more expensive sort will
be available for critical inspection and buying by sample or by catalog in the
special regional centers: more products, too, will be bought on the basis of
tested knowledge, such as is now offered by the Consumers' Union. The big department stores and the big mail order houses have already been reorganizing
their services on a regional basis, with warehouses and salesrooms in outlying
areas. (*Photograph: Tennessee Valley Authority*)

[SECOND LEFT] Spillway of the Norris Dam: the reinforced concrete of Monnier's
original bird-baths here utilized to harness a mighty current of water: a superb
form, expressing the highest energy of the technical imagination: a form that
recalls in its austere beauty Worringer's comparison of Egypt and America.
(*Photograph: Tennessee Valley Authority*)

[SECOND RIGHT] Roadway atop Norris Dam: the use of elemental geometric forms,
the slim metal column and the glass lighting globe reflects the spirit of the rest
of the construction: no false monumentalism, no spurious allusions to other
esthetic orders or other cultures. (*Photograph: Tennessee Valley Authority*)

[THIRD] Individual dwelling houses at Norris. A let-down: little of the order and
imagination expressed in the Tennessee Valley Project itself or in the dams,
reservoirs, construction works, and power plants, has been embodied in either
the plan of the town or the architectural elements—with the exception of the
interior of the co-operative store. These houses affect the weakly traditional—
and in fact betray the living tradition. (*Photograph: Tennessee Valley Authority*)

[BOTTOM] Row of small houses at Neubühl, a co-operatively built community near
Zürich. Example of modern design entirely in harmony with the order expressed
in the Norris hydro-electric works, and more fully adapted to current habits of
living than the sentimental fakes beloved of the suburban realty speculator and
his imitators. Wide windows like these encourage the constant use of growing
plants throughout the year as interior ornament: sunbaths for infants are possible behind them. The spontaneous building of sunrooms in rural America, in
opposition to reactionary architectural precedent, is a sign that only a few
American architects have as yet adequately interpreted the essential needs of
their countrymen.

and rare-earths upon which so much of modern technology now depends: nickel, vanadium, tungsten, tantalum, manganese.

None of the original warnings about the need for dealing thriftily with natural resources was without point. The recovery of scrap metals has become an important business today; and the supply of metals has now become a sort of revolving capital fund, from which only a small part need be lost, from generation to generation, through wastage and wear. Like the general culture of the environment, this new trend must have important effects: for it *diminishes the rôle of the mine* and reduces the importance of the extractive occupations in the general economy. As the population of a country tends toward stability, the capital fund of minerals—unless drawn upon by outside areas or upset by some sudden shift in demand— will reach a point where it no longer needs to be augmented by mining, except for a small annual deficit. This day is being hastened by the more refined metallurgy and machine technics of the neotechnic regime, with its finer calculations, its dislike of superfluous bulk, and its use of other sources of power than coal.

Mark the result. Under paleotechnic methods of industry, the opening up of new mines and the settlement of the mining areas were characteristic marks of progress. Under the neotechnic complex just the opposite holds: the closing up of the mines and the diminishment of the mining process are the signs of technical advance.

What is happening to the coal industry and the railroad through the competition of petroleum will happen in the petroleum industry, too, as soon as new kinetic sources of power, such as the solar engine, supplement the present water-power resources. This further advance needs chiefly the perfection of an economic utility for the storage of electric energy. All these improvements indicate a revolutionary displacement. They are part of that change from the inorganic to the organic, from the destructive to the conservative utilization of land and energy that marks the transition from the paleotechnic to the neotechnic period, and will further mark the change from a purely mechanical ideology and method to a biotechnic one: technics based on the culture of life. Special energy crops, grown under the new scientific agronomy, may eventually further this transformation. And the psychological effect of this change must not be underestimated: the closing up of the mining industries, with their speculative animus, their gambling, their recklessness of human life, their indifference to beauty and order will produce results not confined to the mining areas alone.

The conservation movement, as it has been called in America, has perhaps been most beneficial in promoting a more economic use of raw materials. It has been less effective in creating an appropriate use of the region as a whole as a habitat for human living. For while it is to the interest of an industry to save raw materials instead of losing them to the dump pile, befouling rivers with them, or puffing them into the air, the pattern of outright individual land ownership makes it difficult to zone land areas for permanent uses that will best accord with the solid needs and interests of the community. But if the conservation of a single resource is important, the conservation of the region, as an economic and social whole, is even more important. If individual land ownership works against the best utilization of the land as a human resource, it is not the environment that must be sacrificed but the principle of unrestricted individual ownership.

Now land, like the people who live on it, is "given." It is only in a capitalistic civilization that people have come lightly to believe that land may be bought and sold, divided up, monopolized, and speculated in like any other commodity. Feudal land ownership knew no such levity: the feudal lord was a steward of the land: his rents and fees were fixed by custom: the meanest serf had a right to certain portions of the land, and if he could not leave it, neither could the land leave him. What is important in a sound scheme of land-utilization is not individual ownership but security of tenure: this is what makes possible continuity of use, encourages permanent improvements, permits long range investment of effort. The public control of land for the benefit of the region and the city as a whole is the outstanding problem for modern statesmanship: a problem toward whose solution even the legal nationalization of the land would be only a subordinate step.

The history of the division of the public lands originally possessed by the Federal Government of the United States shows that putative individual ownership and permanent tenure are contradictions. Ownership, where capital is needed to work the land, and where, in a bad season the farmer or owner comes under the sway of the money-lender, results in excessive *in*security. Even the temporary absence of a mortgage does not throw off this menace; and the increase of tenant farming in the United States, par excellence the home of the independent individual farmer, is a sure sign of social and economic insecurity, leading eventually to unthrifty forms of use.

Today, despite a constitutional propensity to guard the "rights of property," the community is the residuary legatee of the land in a very peculiar manner: it may take possession of real property without further ado as compensation for the non-payment of taxes over a certain period. In this passive sense, the communal interest in land is recognized. But to have permanent tenure in land under modern conditions and to ensure a measure of security to the individual worker or occupant, the community must be prepared to assume the active responsibilities of ownership: increasingly the land must be owned by the community, and placed in the trusteeship of appropriate municipal and regional authorities.

By owning the land, the community will dispense with the economically inert (that is, privileged or piratical) rôle of the private landlord: it will then be able to collect in the form of rent all those values that derive directly from social organization. Since regional communities are more permanent bodies than individual families or business organizations, they can undertake improvements of the land that the individual cannot wait for or hope to profit by. When population and industrial uses are stable, this system secures stability for the user: when the population is shifting, and new uses of the land are introduced, the divorce of public ownership from occupancy permits the most flexible type of adjustment, whilst it avoids the grave evil of absentee ownership and administration. As long as individual ownership is regarded as sacred, the most important needs of the community may be balked, and its most vital plans may be mangled: nothing can be done, even under the law of eminent domain, without more or less paying the landlord's price. By means of communal ownership, the land can be functionally apportioned with respect to the needs of communal life: planning may thus deal, not with the whims of individual owners, but with the stable needs of the community.

Regional planning is essentially the effort to apply scientific knowledge and stable standards of judgment, justified by rational human values, to the exploitation of the earth. Such knowledge was deliberately flouted in the opening up of the dry lands which have become the dust-bowl of America, and the commonwealth has paid dearly for that sacrifice to the demands of the individual farmer and speculator. No community can afford such luxuries of ignorance: the function of science is to reduce the area of such costly mistakes and finally wipe them out. Without the decisive control that rests with collective ownership, in the hands of responsible public administrators, working for the common good, regional planning is an all but impossible task: at best it must confine itself to weak admonitions, partial prohibitions, various forms of negative action: at most it can say what shall not be done, but it has little power to command the forces of positive action.

The common ownership of land would put the division and supervision of the land in the hands of the appropriate local and regional authorities, who would map out areas of cultivation, areas of mining, areas of urban settlement, as they now map out areas for public parks. On this basis, a stable social adjustment could be worked out for every part of the region, and for every type of resource and activity. This common ownership is not an objective in itself: it is merely a means toward creating a system of dressing and keeping the land as it must be dressed and kept for an advanced civilization. Something can indeed be done by education and public regulation where the obsolete system of private ownership and control is preserved; but infinitely more can and must be done by active authorities, capable not merely of suggestion but decisive action, capable of looking ahead over half a century or more, and borrowing funds on the basis of such long term action. A useful step toward this system of common ownership consists in a broadly applied scheme of land zoning: such as that provided in the current English law which "sterilizes" against change of use without public permission all existing rural areas, or like that worked out, again, under the ample administrative authority of Dr. Schmidt, with a special planning body, in the Ruhr district before 1933. A partial step in the same direction—restricting marginal lands against inappropriate uses—has been made in Wisconsin. But these are only preliminary steps. No intelligent community can avoid the further socialization of land once it discards the policy of furthering individual ownership for the sake of pecuniary gain.

One must not evade the fundamental issue. Modern civilization will not be able to use its collective energies and collective wisdom for the benefit of its members until the land goes back to the community from which it was originally derived and becomes part of the common stock. This should be particularly easy in the United States; for here there are no immemorial privileges of ownership and residence, no ancient titles that run back before the memory or written record of man; and here the greater part of the continent was still *public land* up to a century ago. Had there been sufficient wisdom and foresight, and had not the *mores* of capitalism and the short-sighted urge of the land-hungry worked against it, all this land might have remained in the hands of the Federal Government, as a permanent possession of the country as a whole.

What one proposes now is that a bad land policy, which confused stable occupation and security of tenure with the irrelevant concept of individual ownership, should be obliterated. In its stead, one proposes a sound land policy which shall vest ownership in the community, and guarantee tenure, for definitely assigned periods, to those who work the land thriftily and pay their communal taxes. This policy can be put into effect piecemeal, by permitting cities to buy up land necessary for their development and to hold it permanently: an indispensable aid in four-dimensional planning. It can be furthered by the state's buying up marginal agricultural lands, as in New York State, in order to turn them back into forest—or by the setting of great recreation areas, such as the Adirondack State Park in New York. But for regional planning on a grand scale to begin, the policy must apply to the holding of all land; and until this is effected planning can achieve only part of its potential results.

The difficulties in the method of piecemeal purchase should be plain. As one passes from waste areas and sub-agricultural lands to areas where land values have been steadily boosted as the result of intensive settlement and extensive improvements the possibility of purchase on a sufficient scale diminishes. No community is rich enough to redeem its own land as a whole at the prices asked by the present owners. Hence, except in Soviet Russia, where a revolutionary change in ownership took place, the most important steps in making the earth a permanent and satisfactory human home are halted by a small privileged class, upheld in turn by a much larger group who mistakenly hold exclusive land-ownership to be a symbol of power and independence. *But regional planning cannot be confined merely to backward areas;* hence the problem must be eventually faced and a new social policy of leasehold possession worked out, under forms which will combine individual security and collective interests. The alternative consists in public regulations so broad and drastic as to turn the individual proprietor into a mere trustee or steward. An ownership so limited—though perhaps useful in effecting a transition—is bound, however, to awaken the owner's resentful protest scarcely less than a scheme for outright expropriation with drastically limited compensation. The latter, in the form of pensions, seems to me preferable—though in the United States it would demand a social interpretation of the words "due process."

6: The Landscape: A Cultural Resource

Originating in the spectacle of waste and defilement, the conservation movement has tended to have a negative influence: it has sought to isolate wilderness areas from encroachment and it has endeavored to diminish waste and prevent damage. The present task of regional planning is a more positive one: it seeks to bring the earth as a whole up to the highest pitch of perfection and appropriate use—not merely preserving the primeval, but extending the range of the garden, and introducing the deliberate culture of the landscape into every part of the open country. Olmsted began his career as a park planner by giving advice to his farmer-neighbors on the layout of their house and grounds: it is time that park planning went back into the open country, from which, in the eighteenth century, it originated. The parking and landscaping of highways, such as the remarkable system in Westchester County, New York, is a first step toward these more universal forms of collective gardening and cultivation. The rapid extension of such arteries and recreation grounds around the great metropolises in America is an earnest of a deeper transformation.

Our planners in the past have had a tendency to single out the more striking forms of landscape. This was an inevitable heritage from the romantic movement, which attached itself to the "picturesque" and loathed more orderly and cultivated forms of beauty. There has been no comparable movement to cultivate other types of landscape and bring them up to a high pitch of esthetic delight. So it happens that in most parts of America the early canal systems have been permitted to lapse: the waterways have either been turned into open sewers or have been allowed to fall into a state of ragged disrepair, only finally to be covered up, as in New Jersey, by express highways. And the fault is not solely an American one. There have been similar sacrifices in Holland, due to the systematically insensate education of the old type of civil engineer. Have there not even been proposals to fill up the canals of Amsterdam in order to make them swift motor highways? A proposal to sacrifice for the sake of speed and noise, one of the most beautiful urban environments created by man.

If the culture of the environment had yet entered deeply into our consciousness, our esthetic appreciations would not stop short with stupendous geological formations like the Grand Canyon of Arizona: we should have an equal regard for every nook and corner of the earth, and we should not be indifferent to the fate of less romantic areas. Though the old canals no longer serve industrial uses in most parts of America, they have grand possibilities for recreation: they should, in fact, become the backbone of a regional park system, for swimming, boating, ice-skating, and ice-boat racing, to say nought of being specially stocked for fishing. So much so, that where these canals have not been left over from the eotechnic economy, they should be deliberately built, as is now being done along the Delaware River in Pennsylvania. Especially in the flatter regions of the Middle West, bereft of natural recreation areas, a system of lordly water courses, banked with grass, lined with trees, dotted with groves for picnicking and camping, should be built for the whole region, supplementing and rounding out the natural water drainage: no longer the mere half-mile water courses of the baroque park.

The reservation of coastal areas as wildernesses is equally important. For though we owe much to the romantic love of high mountains and mysterious forests, modern man finds other parts of nature equally attractive: the pine barren, the savannah, the rocky coast, the moorland, the sandy spit, no less than the more overwhelming species of scenery: the bayberry, the sweetfern, the shrub-oak, and the low blueberry can touch his spirit as they outline the contours of a headland no less than the mightiest pines. As for the ocean itself, it is the least spoiled of all primeval wildernesses, except where it is tainted by the adjoining land and the offal of its population. The recapture of the coastal wilderness has become an important element in every sound scheme of regional planning: South England feels the need as well as Long Island. The reservation of the Everglades in Florida, and of forest and heath in Marthas Vineyard, are welcome signs. Similarly, the creation of a "Cape Hatteras National Seashore" by Congress in 1937 sets an important precedent within the national domain.

Each type of environment, then, has its special interest for man, its special economic capacities—above all, its special uses as a social habitat. The cultivated landscape of the plain with its soft meadows, its human definitions and landmarks, its meandering rivers and its quiet pauses of lake and marsh, is no less capable of enriching the spirit than the hanging valleys of the Tyrol, where the sun does not rise over the ice peaks until eleven o'clock in the morning. In the second milieu man's principal care must be to step lightly and leave as small an account of himself as possible: part of the value of the primeval environment lies in maintaining an extreme contrast with the region of close settlement. In the high forests he may erect a chain of cabins and a trail: but he will not, if his sense of place-possibility is disciplined and acute, provide for hotels, motor caravans, main highways, or the other impedimenta of civilization. If our modern culture, with all its resources and wealth, cannot afford the final luxury of such unused spots, it is poor indeed.

While during the eighteenth century the Western European sharpened his sense of place-possibility and discovered some of the joys that the cultivated Chinese had so long known, there was a violent movement in the other direction: in the act of pioneering, the European peasant and townsmen often lost some of that intuitive feeling for the environment that they had preserved by inertia in their original habitat. Instead of co-operating with nature in the new lands, they raped nature, eager for quick returns; and in the very act of violating her, rejected her best gifts and rejected the possibility of having permanent intercourse with her. Therein lies the vast irony of man's proud "Conquest of Nature" during the nineteenth century.

This rape took many forms: with respect to the landscape among the earliest was the building of funicular railways to the top of inaccessible Alpine spots, whose very glory demanded for full appreciation a pitting of man's energies against the difficulties of the ascent. One of the latest violations takes the form, in the United States, of motor roads that lead into the heart of a wilderness and concentrate urban populations in big recreation halls, playgrounds, and hotels that might better have been placed at the very doors of the metropolis. In the eastern part of the United States, the so-called skyline drives along the crest of the lonely Appalachians combine extravagant expenditure with a complete debauchery of the specific character and use of the mountain wilderness.

This form of desecration, in the act of making nature accessible, removes all that is valuable from the enjoyment of those who seek solitude and a renewed sense of the primeval. Both these spiritual needs increase in importance as man rises in the scale of civilization and is no longer harried by the crude enmities of nature: they are indispensable correctives to the mechanical rigors and the compulsive collective disciplines and the omnipresent crowds of modern life. Man must not merely have the privilege of selecting a type of environment in contrast to that which embraces his daily routine: each environment should exercise its own type of selective control: choosing its men.

The principle of democracy does not mean that every type of environment should be equally available to every type of person; and that every part of the natural scene should be as open to dense occupation as the concert hall of a great metropolis. This vulgarization of activities that are by their essential nature restricted and isolated would blot out the natural varieties of the habitat and make the whole world over into a single metropolitan image. In the end, it would mean that one must be content with only one type of life, and to accept only one type of environment: that of the metropolis—a degradation in both the geological and the human sense.

Such perversions of the cult of nature and the principles of democracy as are marked by the skyline drive and similar types of metropolitan invasion are carried to the final level of complete caricature in the exploitation of the great caves of Virginia. To increase accessibility, these caves are reached by elevators: they are lighted theatrically with different colors that play over the stalactites and the stalagmites as they might play over the body of a dancer in a cabaret. This series of mechanical "improvements" transforms a precious experience of darkness and mystery and danger, never to be forgotten by anyone who has explored a natural cave, into something that is on the exact level of a spectacle at Coney Island: indeed, the urban type of spectacle has the advantage of being less of a fake and more easy to reach.

A culture so innocent of genuine human and esthetic values as to encourage such exploitation will obviously stop at nothing. Hence it is under the seal of a non-metropolitan culture, still only in its embryonic phase, that genuine regional planning works: some of its worst enemies will long be those who espouse "nature" for purely metropolitan ends: profitable jobs, publicity, lavish expenditure for engineering and public works.

In sum, man cannot achieve a high level of economic life or culture in an environment whose resources he has plundered and defaced. And if even an economic system demands a balance between energy income and outgo, human culture demands a still greater degree of discrimination and care in the use of the environment: a more active sense of place-possibility, a more delicately poised equilibrium between the landscape and the modes of human occupation. To turn a forest into a metropolitan slum is an even more serious barbarism than would be the turning of a metropolitan area back into its primeval field or forest. Each type of landscape has its special meaning to civilized man. Astronomy, geology, biology, landscape painting, poetry, send man out to face nature in another mood from that of his ancestors. And it is precisely because our culture has reached a higher stage of development that we can no longer be satisfied with the impoverished conceptions of the environment that have hitherto satisfied the urban ego. We respect, as never before, the infinite variety of nature, and wish for the sake of both wealth and health to preserve it to the utmost degree. The greater number of natural resources man makes use of, the finer are the distinctions he makes between one part and another of his habitat.

The task of regional planning, as concerns both the earth and cities, is to make the region ready to sustain the richest types of human culture and the fullest span of human life, offering a home to every type of character and disposition and human mood: creating and preserving objective fields of response to man's deeper subjective needs. It is precisely those of us who recognize the value of mechanization and standardization and universalization who must be most alert to the need for providing an equal place for the complementary set of activities—the wild, the various, the spontaneous, the natural as opposed to the human, the lonely as opposed to the collective. A habitat planned so as to form a continuous background to a delicately graded scale of human feelings and values is the prime requisite of a cultivated life. Where that is lacking, men will fumble uneasily with substitutes, or starve.

7: The Economic Region

There are, as Benton MacKaye has noted, three types of economic region. The first is mainly self-sufficing and therefore in economic balance. Few regions today exhibit such a balance in its original simplicity: our wants and our technics have brought into existence a whole series of complicating factors.

The second type is the wholly specialized region: a part of the earth that, no matter what its potential variety, has devoted itself to the production of a limited series of commodities. Mining regions, particularly in the areas developed during the eighteenth and nineteenth centuries, are examples of such one-sided economic units. To create any sort of human equilibrium in such regions, the exports of the special products must be balanced by a great diversity of imports. This will partly counteract the environmental impoverishment: but only partly. Those activities and skills and experiences that arise out of the more varied use of the region will still be lacking. Under capitalist economics there is still a further weakness: only a fraction of the population in such an area will receive an income sufficient to import the ingredients necessary to a more rounded culture. And when an industry "gives out"—as certain textile plants gave out in New England, as coal mines gave out in Durham and Wales in England, the population is stranded.

The third type of economic region is that which has usually characterized advanced cultures: it is partly self-sufficing and partly specialized. It contains within its area a varied and representative range of resources; and out of its specialized products and individualized skills it obtains from other regions the elements that are needed for a many-sided human culture. Agricultural areas tend to the first type of balance: they limit their requirements and learn to do without many exotic products. Specialized industries tend to the second type: their achievement corresponds to that of the one-sided specialist, who eventually loses command of his own subject by the poverty of his life and thought outside the province of his specialization. Culture regions need the third type of economic base.

During the nineteenth century the tendency toward economic balance and variety within a given region was disparaged by the popular schools of economics. It was assumed, on the basis of England's exploitation of paleotechnic industry, that balance was to be achieved only on a planetary basis, through an international division of labor: such a scheme would have made permanent England's supremacy in utilizing coal and steam power for the mass production of textiles, cutlery, pottery, and other machine-made goods. The rest of the world was supposed to be content with the modest task of supplying some of the raw materials and consuming the products in return for their agricultural surplus. The region considered as a theater for human activity occupied no place in this scheme. Only its lop-sided potentialities for specialized production mattered.

One need not here go into the defects of this one-sided regime. Sufficient to say that it treated the region as a whole as a mine from which certain special materials were to be extracted, and it produced a one-sided, monotonous, socially crude life in its main industrial centers and factory villages. With the export of machines and technical knowledge to other countries, it was only a matter of time be-

fore each province, each region, would take over for itself the special processes of machine industry. The very fact that industrialism
became worldwide in its applications has kept it from developing
along the lines expected by the Manchester economists: that of international specialization for a single world market. Regions once
treated as mere sources have become manufacturing centers in their
own right. In America the Southern states not merely produce cotton
but weave it; while the shoe industry, once centralized in Brockton
and Lynn, has now created independent centers in the Middle West,
nearer to both the sources of supply and the local markets. As this
diffusion continues to take place, the balance of population must
likewise alter: internally, by fostering a variety of occupations
within any given region, and in hitherto predominantly agricultural
regions it will give mechanical industries and urban communities a
parity in the regional economy.

Metropolitan finance with its attempt to put over national labels
and trademarks, and to limit consumption to nationally advertised
products, dominated largely by metropolitan bankers and investors,
naturally opposes this tendency toward regional decentralization. To
this end it buys up local plants and welds them into single financial
organizations governed by a centralized bureaucracy. But in the very
act of establishing such wide controls it finally awakens counter-
forces. The protest of the local merchant against the chain-store has
already been recorded in the United States in State legislation: however ill-advised the restriction, the need for a different pattern of
control and operation is a genuine one.

Moreover, the increasing concentration of metropolitan finance
makes it necessary to invent a technique for decentralized management: this shifts responsibility for daily decisions to the point where
production takes place, and therefore allows a place for the development of greater autonomy. And the further specialization of production tends in the same direction: the building of a whole plant in
order to produce a single unit like a carburetor, a storage battery or
a bearing has done away with the need for heaping subordinate
plants in a single narrow district. Finally, the closer accountancy of
costs by metropolitan finance has revealed the necessity for reducing
the overhead expenses: not merely administrative costs, but rent,

taxes, transportation charges. All this works against the one-sided concentration of industry into a few limited industrial areas: it favors regional decentralization and regional diversity of occupation.

Up to the present generation, financial canons have worked against the more rational exploitation of resources and the more regional layout of industries and cities. In an effort to force a "national" market, against the natural regional affiliations and standards, an enormous amount of energy has been thrown into sales organizations, into advertising, into fashion-publicity, which might have been better used to raise the purchasing power of labor and to assist in a reorganization on regional lines of the essential means of produc tion. All these wastes are paid for, not merely in money, but in con fusion of mind and social deterioration. The questions what is "economic" and what is "profitable" belong to two different orders of thought: so far the latter, with its indifference to social values and consumptive needs, has been the almost exclusive determinant of the economic pattern of the region.

Professor J. Russell Smith, the economic geographer, has discussed the matter in the following words: "Perhaps this regional specialization of manufacture, like the regional specialization of agriculture, has gone too far. There are signs that it has. We may yet have a renewal of manufacture for local needs as we are already having of agriculture for local needs. Two comparatively new industrial factors make this possible. One is the widespread distribution of electric power in town, village, and home. . . . The second factor is standardization. These two factors make it possible to manufacture many small things in small villages, possibly even in the farm-home. It may become easier to transport the man's raw materials and his produce than his food. This may shift some of the manufacturing from Boston, Worcester, Detroit or Chicago to farms and villages in food-producing sections of New York State, Michigan, Manitoba, Saskatchewan, or the Rocky Mountain valleys. . . . It is possible that we are at the beginning of an era of the partial redistribution of manufacturing over the land where food production and climate and commercial access are good."

Kropotkin made similar observations and drew the same deductions a generation ago. What was bold prophecy when he first published Fields, Factories, and Workshops has now become a definite movement, as the technical means of economic regionalism and the social impulses that gave it direction have converged. For the other side of the industrialization of agriculture, which has been so rapidly going on alike under capitalism, co-operation, and socialism, is the ruralization of industry.

The possibility of creating economically balanced regions rests upon permanent geographic factors. These constants have in turn been reinforced by new inventions and fresh acquisitions of scientific knowledge which abet, rather than oppose, the tendency toward regional integration. Most of these favorable factors derive from what I described in Technics and Civilization as the neotechnic complex: a system of industry based upon the mobility of power, the use of electricity and a diversity of prime movers, upon the employment of light metals and precious elements, upon the maximum application of systematic scientific knowledge in the exploitation of resources and the organization of work: finally, upon the growing importance of the biological and social sciences even within realms hitherto occupied almost exclusively by the physical sciences and the purely mechanical arts.

Not the least effect of the neotechnic regime is the transformation of agriculture from a backward industry into an advanced one. Whereas the first technical improvements in agriculture were derived from the paleotechnic interest in machines considered as devices for labor saving and mass production, a good part of the recent improvements have been based upon chemical and biological knowledge: they have increased the absolute yields per acre. Among the earliest of these advances was the discovery of the rôle of fertilizers and crop rotation in maintaining the nutritional qualities of the soil: hence a tendency to displace single-crop farming, which characterized so much pioneer agriculture during the nineteenth century, by mixed crops. This means not only more conservative use of the soil: it means a more varied local food supply.

During the last generation the whole field of improvement has widened: soil regeneration through the use of nitrogen-producing crops has come: likewise the improvement of plant and animal strains, selective breeding toward potency of growth; the utilization of chemical wastes for soil enrichment; finally the intensification of crop yield, both as to time and space, through the cultivation of plants in specially prepared tanks, with scientific mixture of plant food, complete control of light and heat, and elimination of insect pests and blights. All these advances have, in one way or another, equalized agricultural advantages over greater areas and removed the incentives toward one-sided specialization.

Modern agronomy preaches the wisdom of reducing the area of soil cultivated and intensifying the method of cultivation. Even if every crop does not lend itself economically to artificial cultivation, the area needed for active farming is diminishing, and the area opened up to permanent tree culture and to purely spectacular horticulture is potentially increasing. So the pattern of agriculture originally set by the Dutch in the seventeenth century will come back again in new forms, just as the seventeenth century Dutch urban pattern is coming back again with appropriate modifications: that early mutation will probably become the new dominant.

Our modern knowledge of diet, with its stress upon the importance of fresh foods and the succulent leafy vegetables, reinforces this agricultural tendency. Already it has vastly lowered in the United States the per capita acreage devoted to wheat and corn. A *local* supply of fresh vegetables and fruits in every season will presently become the mark of biotechnic agriculture: for with the spread of electrical energy and the contraction of the agricultural acreage there is no reason why the major part of the supply should not come from the local region. Most of the machines and utilities needed by modern agriculture are collective in character and they employ electric power in increasing amounts. Moreover, for their effective use they need adequate technical training and constant revision in the light of fresh scientific knowledge: all this implies the effective inter-relation of agriculture with the city. Hence the need, even purely from the standpoint of agriculture itself, for a closer pattern of settlement within rural areas, and for a regional distribution of all the modern instruments of culture and co-operation.

To speak of agricultural areas, industrial areas, urban areas, will be to refer to an increasingly moribund division of labor. Rural regions will attract industry, foster a co-operative way of life, promote biotechnic urbanism; while industry must, for the sake of life-efficiency, seek a wider rural basis. Each village nucleus will thus be the embryo of a modern city, not the discouraged, depauperate fragment of an indifferent metropolis.

8: Power as Region-Builder

The same tendencies against overspecialization and overconcentration are at work in industry. Specialization within the industrial plant, with a vast capital outlay for machines designed for a single purpose, followed the fashionable pattern of the successful textile industries of the early nineteenth century: the formula at first seemed applicable to every part of the industrial process. But both experience and analysis have shown, during the last generation, that such specialization may be a serious liability: for one product whose outlines remain as firmly fixed as woven cloth, there are a score of others that have been subject to radical alterations; and it is necessary to keep the industrial plant flexible and adaptable. Small units, capable of diversified production and quick adaptation, are more economic than large units: they frequently justify themselves, likewise, by superior management, since the larger the organization the greater the amount of effort that must go into its supervision—and the supervision of the supervisor. The costly transformation of the Ford plant when it abandoned its early model and started to turn out a new type of car was a significant turning point: its moral has not been lost.

Up to the present, at least in the United States, this topographic decentralization of industry has been promoted chiefly for reasons of financial economy: often on dubious or anti-social grounds, as in the effort of the silk industry to escape unionization, or in the attempt to make profit out of a low standard of living among the workers, as in the cotton mills of the South.

Plainly, however, the new agents of power, communication, and transportation work to like effect in both industry and agriculture: they give equal service to city and country: a critical distinction between the neotechnic and the paleotechnic regime. Under modern conditions, an electric power plant may perhaps be gigantic in order to increase the operating efficiency or take advantage of a big head of water: but by means of long distance interconnecting transmission systems or grids, the power itself may be produced in many centers and made available over a wide area, with a balanced load and little idle plant. No longer is the river, the coal bed, or the railroad line the sole effective power area. In other words, power production no longer demands local concentration, either within the plant or within the manufacturing area. And the unity that was once achieved by the centralization of production in a single plant can now be achieved by plan, time-schedules, and other forms of administrative and technical co-ordination. Indeed, as the timing of the productive process becomes finer, the size of the efficient plant tends to diminish; since part of this size is due to the stoppages which tend to pile up material at various points.

But it is not power alone that has brought with it the possibility of a new industrial, and therefore an essentially different urban, structure. The same holds for systems of transportation and communication. The motor car has decentralized transportation as radically as the transformer and the motor have decentralized the applications of electric energy. Instead of the *train*, which increases in economy up to a point with the number of cars attached, we have begun to employ, since 1910, the motor car, the motor bus, the motor truck: a more flexibly used individual unit, which can start or stop, take the highroad or the branch road, at its own convenience, without waiting for other cars. And instead of the railroad *line*, which tended to centralize transportation along the main arteries, and which was more or less confined to the water level routes, at grades of two per cent or less, the motor car has brought into existence the new highway *network*. Thus the motor car can penetrate the hinterland in a more effective and economic fashion than the railroad could: for economy in railroading depends upon loading the tracks to maximum capacity and confining transportation, as much as possible, to the main routes. Moreover, the motor car can climb steep grades and penetrate hilly country with a freedom unknown to the railroad; and it makes an effective connecting link with the airplane field and the airplane, the latest means of fast cross-country transportation. The usefulness of the airplane has up to now been greatly lessened in congested metropolitan centers through the fact that it takes as much time to journey five or ten miles from the airport on the outskirts of the city as it does to cover fifty or a hundred miles in the air.

The motor car has potentially opened up new frontiers of human settlement, even as the airplane has extended the outposts of civilization to the very poles. For the uplands, which motors reach so easily, are the seat of the fast-running young rivers and waterfalls, the new sources of power; and by means of motor car and hydro-electric plants areas that have hitherto been remote and uncultivated can now support well-balanced industrial communities. The salubrious climate of these uplands, with their varied sports of field and forest and stream, make them, in many parts of the world, ideal centers for all-year living. In the nineteenth century many of these regions were the recreation grounds of the bourgeoisie: tomorrow they may become the favored seats of living for an enfranchised working class. Norway, the French and the Swiss Alps, the Tennessee Valley, the Columbia Valley, all begin to show the energizing and civilizing results of these new forms of industrial energy, and the new types of human equipment that may be installed for living and working. Here again, to achieve the characteristic benefits of the new systems of transportation, an open pattern of settlement must be maintained: the greater the congestion, the lower the working efficiency of the new transportation system.

With these new means of transportation and power-generation, special local advantages, once concentrated in a circumscribed center, a mere point, can be distributed throughout a whole region. Even under the metropolitan regime itself the unit is no longer the central district but an area with a radius of from ten to sixty miles of the center. To complete this, the telegraph, the telephone, the radio, the teletypewriter, and television apparatus have likewise arisen out of the neotechnic complex. The effect of all these instruments is to *enlarge the sphere of activity at the same time that they diminish the need for physical movement and close settlement.* Plants or offices that are two hundred miles apart today may be in closer effective communication than when they were two miles apart a hundred years ago. Yet most of the concentration of administrative units and industrial units assumes that obsolete century-old conditions still prevail. The important thing that has happened is that the geographic region has become potentially the unit that the metropolis was under the past economic regime: it needs to be linked up, interlaced, and settled with a view to the new opportunities and the new conditions of life. With a fuller exploitation of the region as an economic unit, the need for costly cross-haulage and duplex movements of like commodities will be lessened.

Now that advanced technical processes lend themselves to the decentralization of production, the means of living can be once more produced in an environment fit for living: an environment that lends itself not only to production, but to a higher standard of consumption and more vivid creative activities. Under a regime of economic regionalism, industries would be varied and balanced locally in order to secure a varied and balanced life: likewise the multiform, many-threaded cultural heritage that goes with such a life. Extra-regional production and consumption, instead of stopping at national frontiers, would move, as they increasingly did during the nineteenth century, in worldwide channels of trade. Such a regime might require, for effective control, two systems of currency: a regional system and a foreign exchange system, in order to establish some sort of parity between disparate areas during the long, difficult period of transition. The experience of various European countries since the war, particularly that of Soviet Russia and Nazi Germany, show that the administrative obstacles, while serious, are not overwhelming.

Economic regionalism, I emphasize, cannot aim at either economic or cultural self-sufficiency: no region is rich enough or varied enough to supply all the ingredients of our present civilization: the dream of autarchy is merely a military dodge for putting a population in a state of mind appropriate to war. What regionalism does aim at is a more even development of local resources: a development that does not gauge success purely by the limited financial profits obtained through a one-sided specialization.

Neither does economic regionalism mean bare industrial decentralization. Such a tendency has been latent from the beginning of the paleotechnic revolution, with manufacturers seeking to utilize the cheap sites and cheap labor of the open country; and it is still taking place in patches for this same reason. The point is that centralization and decentralization are qualitatively empty terms: merely directions of movement. The question for regionalism is what sort of life, at any particular point in a region, such movements produce. A scattered development of subsistence farms, economically connected with a sweated industry, is no less undesirable a growth than the utmost congestion of a megalopolitan proletariat.

Under the new pattern, it is necessary not only to break up old centers of congestion but to create new centers of industrial and civic life, and to re-invigorate, with new plans and activities, such older towns and villages as are favorably situated and lend themselves to such renewal. But in so far as the new unit of economic and cultural life is the balanced region, rather than the vast amorphous metropolitan district, the needed movement, at the moment, is that which will result in a further emptying out of the central district, and a courageous re-building of life in what used to be, from the standpoint of the metropolis, merely the hinterland. Any point in the new region may be the locus of its maximum culture.

Economic balance is not a speculative concept. In the more simple eotechnic phase of industry it actually existed. The very difficulties of inter-regional transport made it necessary for the local community to rely chiefly upon its immediate resources, and to restrict haulage to exotic commodities of relatively limited bulk, unless they could travel by water.

During the first two hundred years of the seaboard settlement in America, the economic resources were used for the most part with thrift and intelligence, and industries and communities were in a state of balance. Out of this even-handed exploitation of regional possibilities an integrated regional life arose which came to its consummation, economically speaking, around 1850 in New York and slightly earlier, perhaps, in New England. Local mines, quarries, waterfalls, forests, fields, orchards, were woven together by a ramifying system of canals and highroads: this formed the basis of a multitude of settlements, no one of which, outside New York, achieved a disproportionate size. Small colleges and universities, together with lecture lyceums, were widely distributed: they served as nodes of cultural growth. A similar state had existed during the earlier part of the eotechnic period in Europe: the basis of its great cultural efflorescence: and in many regions it continued right down to the nineteenth century.

The problem for the regional planner and administrator is to effect a similar type of economic balance in terms of the more complicated modern industries, more lengthy production-chains, and more varied consumptive needs of today; for the self-sufficient life of a cruder agricultural regime is no longer possible, except in terms of gross cultural indigence. Certain Southern agrarians may fondly dream of such a life; but the more honest of them will also arbitrarily limit culture to the purely literary interests and language-skills of the ante-bellum regime: a pious renunciation of the modern heritage. In other words, they accept cultural impoverishment.

But in order to make economic planning possible, the field of planning cannot be confined to industries and services alone. No survey, however exact in all its preliminary methods, can arrive at sound results so long as the most important variables lie outside the province of the particular industry for which a production plan is made. Energy flow, production flow, goods flow must be directed finally into channels of human use. This means that at some point there must be a means of determining, for a given region and period, the norm of consumption in terms of food, clothing, shelter, recreation, education, and culture. The standards set for production must not only include private consumption but public works—houses and highways, parks and gardens, cities and civic institutes and all the interconnecting tissue that finally compose an organic region. Only when the whole has been plotted out can the individual function be directed with efficiency. Lacking such plans, there is a constant hiatus between productive energies and human fulfillments: the wheel turns rapidly, but the squirrel remains within his cage.

CHAPTER VI.

THE POLITICS OF REGIONAL DEVELOPMENT

1: Regionalism and Politics

The re-animation and re-building of regions, as deliberate works of collective art, is the grand task of politics for the opening genera· tion. It raises anew, in a form that now has fuller human significance, the fundamental questions of human inter-relationship across the ethnic, ideological, and cultural boundaries that have been carried over from the past. And as the new tasks of region-building imply shifts in the population, migration into more favored areas, and the building up or reconstruction of a multitude of new urban complexes, the politics of regional development become of critical importance. Not merely must we define and express the region: we must work out, by deliberate experiment, the areas for inter-regional co-operation and for super-regional authority. In displacing the functions of the power-state by those of the service-state we must also transform the structure of the existing organizations. The task calls for imaginative audacity and moral vision: how much so, one may discover by considering the methods of political co-ordination that grew up in our recent past.

The process of political unification has taken place, throughout the world, in fairly generous disregard of geographic and economic realities. And the result is that political areas, economic areas, and cultural areas do not exist in concentric relationship: overlappings, duplications, conflicts, and blank spaces characterize our territorial relationships. Though the sovereignty of the state is supposed to polarize all these relationships it actually adds to the confusion, since it often attempts to displace in the interests of "unity" more natural allegiances. In general, political unification has meant de-regionalization: this is equally true in federal states, like the United States, and in unitary states like France. As the powers of the central government have waxed and its territory increased, the powers of the local regions and cities have waned: earliest perhaps in France, latest in Germany. Finally, each state has tended to reach the pathological condition wittily described by the French critic: apoplexy at the center and paralysis at the extremities.

In creating the semblance of political unity between diverse regions and communities, the idea of the nation has been an important one: a term inherently so vague and so contradictory that it must always be taken in a mystic sense, as meaning whatever the ruling classes hold it convenient to mean at the moment. Sometimes language is the key to nationhood: sometimes a common political territory: sometimes common institutions: sometimes all of these together. But a common language does not make the English and the Americans a single nation, and a common territory does not make the Germans and the Czechs in Czecho-Slovakia a single nation: so in any scientific sense the concept is worthless. Viewed realistically, however, "nationalism" is an attempt to make the laws and customs and beliefs of a single region or city do duty for the varied expressions of a multitude of other regions. To the extent that such a unity does not grow out of spontaneous allegiances and natural affiliations it must constantly be held together by deliberate effort: indoctrination in the school, propaganda in the press, restrictive laws, extirpation of rival dialects and languages, either by mockery or mandate, suppression of the customs and privileges of minorities.

The national state, fortunately, never achieves anything like the omnicompetence and omnipotence it aspires to. Only in times of war, when frontiers are closed, when the movement of men and goods and ideas across "national" boundaries can be blocked, when a pervading sense of fear sanctions the extirpation of differences, does the national state conform to its ideal pattern. All the great national states, and the empires formed around a national core, are at bottom war-states: their politics is war-politics; and the all-absorbing preoccupation of its governing classes lies in collective preparation for armed assault. The final caricature of this tendency is National Socialist Germany today, with its fatuous racial mythology (taken over from the descendants of Abraham), its operatic religion, and its cult of brutality: all focused on war.

In the so-called national state there is only an accidental correspondence between the outlines of the state and the departments of state administration on one hand, and the nature of the component regions on the other. Rival forces, rival authorities, rival centers of culture are suppressed under a centralized system of government: witness the fate of the provincial centers of France between 1600 and 1900, and observe what is happening in Germany, the ancient home of municipal freedom, today. The suppression of regional characteristics, in the interests of national unity, is systematically carried on by the modern state; and in this effort the political agents are powerfully abetted by the financial forces of the metropolis, seeking to impose uniform standards in order to guarantee their own control of the "national market."

But at the very moment, in the middle of the nineteenth century, when the repressive forces of nationalism seemed about to achieve an unqualified victory, they met a fresh challenge. It was in 1854 that the Félibrigistes first met in order to restore the language and the autonomous cultural life of Provence: that marked the conscious beginning of a regionalist movement that has grown slowly but steadily ever since. The Bretons and Provençals in France, the Czechs and Slovaks in the old Austro-Hungarian Empire, the Irish, Welsh, and Scotch in Great Britain, the Basques and Catalans in Spain, the Flemings and Walloons in Belgium—these and similar groups have asserted their claims to an autonomous regional life. If the movement took no hold on Germany during this period, it was only because that country, before the advent of the Nazis, was the outstanding example of an historic federalism which roughly satisfied the needs of regional and cultural autonomy: it needed only a political re-definition of the constituent regions, including a division of Prussia, to make Germany a world example of economic and cultural regionalism.

The rise of regional groups raised the specter of national disunity: a fatal image to states immersed in war or preparation for war. National systems of education have therefore attempted to break down whatever regional consciousness has survived: history is national history, and the focus of events is always the national capital, not the local city. Even more, metropolitan fashions and metropolitan propaganda, spread through magazines and newspapers, have sought to make the whole movement for regional autonomy seem, if not actually traitorous, a little ridiculous. Since the rulers of the state have refused to give regionalism a status in the existing structure of the political community, they have to some extent forced the movement toward autonomy to assume a recalcitrant and back-ward-looking air. Regionalism has been identified with sectionalism or separatism; and even the regionalists themselves have often laid too great stress upon the formation of fractional sovereign states, as if the evils of over-centralization and the superstitions of Austinian sovereignty were to be diminished by multiplying the opportunities for petty despotism.

At the very beginning of the regionalist movement, intelligent observers like Auguste Comte and still later, Le Play, not merely observed that it was bound to take place, because it satisfied the ultimate conditions of political existence: but Comte indeed predicted that within a century or so there would be a hundred and sixty such regional entities in Europe. Though that prediction has not been completely fulfilled, the fact is that there are now a greater number of states than there were in the middle of the nineteenth century; and what is more important, perhaps, a greater number of national languages are now in existence than were on the tongues of men a century ago. Political consolidation, in indifference to regional real-ities, has met with unexpected obstacles: under the even whitewash of "national unity" the colors of the underlying geographic, eco-nomic, and cultural realities are beginning to show through. Not the least important sign of this new regime is the recognition ac-corded under Lenin in Soviet Russia to the principle of cultural autonomy.

The fact is that real communities and real regions do not fit into the frontiers and the ideological pattern of the national state. The state is usually too big to define a single region, with its political, economic, and social elements in symmetrical relationships, and it is too small to include a whole society, like that of Western Europe or the North American Continent, which must ultimately become the sphere of a larger system of co-operative administration. The limits of functional authority, such as is involved in the organization of a continental railroad system or the steel industry, cannot rest effectively within the fortuitous boundaries of the state: the larger relationships need a larger framework of authority, and the more intimate relationships require a narrower field of effort. This is no less true of art and science and religion, which are by nature part of the common stock, not of a region, a province, or a state, but of a whole society. There is no way short of tyrannical repression in which the interests of a scholar, a man of letters, or a member of the Catholic Church can be kept within the boundaries of the national state. Real interests, real functions, real intercourse flow across such frontiers: while the effective organs of concentration are not the national states (which means in practice the exclusive pre-eminence of the national capital) but the regional city and the region. The local polarization of loyalties, for all sane political uses, does not involve the building of cultural Maginot lines.

"One of the main reasons for getting rid of power politics," an eminent political theorist of Oxford has said, "is to enable the world to get back to natural political groupings; and natural groupings mean smaller areas and smaller groups." Branford and Geddes, in Our Social Inheritance, have summarized the situation with equal perspicuity: "Does it not rather seem," they say, "as if something were wrong with this whole theory and practice of modern organization into great centralized states with their megalopolitan rivalry? Must we not seek some better mode of adjusting our human lives, if we would plough in peace and reap in safety? If uni-centralization be obviously intolerable, and septem-centralization [in the seven great national capitals] be so unstable and thus unpractical, must we not look . . . to the decentralization of these, as the true road to European peace and re-unity?"

At no point have the realities of social existence coincided with the claims, the demands, and the pretenses of the power-state: its politics can be successfully driven home, momentarily, only at the point of a bayonet. If this fact was true at the beginning of the baroque attempt to centralize power, it is even more massively true today, when worldwide transportation, travel, and communication, a worldwide system of intercourse through printed books and phono-graph records and moving pictures, have given to the most important activities of society a frame of reference that no longer can be restricted to the so-called national territories.

On one hand the state, as at present organized, tends to obliterate the intimacy of primary communities, organized on a basis of active daily association and face-to-face intercourse. And on the other hand, it often viciously obstructs the organization and control of activities on a continental and finally a worldwide scale. This applies to the allocation of limited resources, the passage of goods and people, the migration of individuals and families, and the exploitation of un-settled or extra-national territories. Power politics, as practiced in the past by Great Britain, France, Russia and the United States, and as threatened even more menacingly today by Italy, Germany, and Japan, works merely to add to the area of un-building and de-civilization.

Yet our inability to devise at once the appropriate structure for our civilization should be no cause for permanent discouragement. Most of the forces that work benignly toward the co-operation and communion of peoples are young: most of the forces that work against such intercourse are old, and are deeply ingrained in insti-tutional habits and in organizations. Our failure even to contrive a breathing space in bellicose effort—if one makes the very partial and dubious exception of the nineteenth century—is partly due to the inertia of historic burdens.

Too hastily we have attempted to achieve a more beneficent align-ment in culture, while retaining those power states whose existence perpetuates the habits of territorial conquest and class exploitation. One might as well turn over to a band of inveterate thieves the un-supervised guardianship of a public fund. The territorial extent of control, as implied in the original outline of the Society of Nations, could not counterbalance the inherent antagonism, on the part of its member-states, to any form of co-operation that implied a diminu-tion of their prestige and power. Such an attempt was plainly fore-doomed to failure; and as long ago as 1919 intelligent observers pointed out these grounds for believing that failure must ensue. What

has taken place since has merely confirmed the realism of that elementary analysis.

But in the reorganization of the political community, as in the
remoralization of modern society, which must go along with it, a
generation is a small span of time: too short to hope for effective
changes. Our present discouragement at the results of the last generation's effort is premature by at least a century or two. In the
meanwhile, it is highly important to recognize the basic regional
and economic realities that have been ignored by the mythology of
the national state, with its egoistic schemes of conquest, dominion,
and belligerent assertion.

No effort to improve the structure of communities and cities will
be effective without re-defining the areas of territorial association in
consonance with the objective geographic, economic, and social facts.
And meanwhile, too, no effective change can be worked in the regional unit on the basis of past historic situations: what one seeks is
not the ancient structure, but the emerging one: a structure that will
include not only the geographic constants but the social variables, as
these are redefined and projected from generation to generation.
What we have to conceive and work out is a federal system of government which shall be based upon a progressive integration of region
with region, of province with province, of continent with continent:
each part loose enough and flexible enough to adjust to the continuing
changes in local and transregional life. Once such a structure has
been outlined, it will tend to make effective that concentric regroup-
ing of political, economic, and cultural functions, whose absence
is today a severe handicap to co-operative effort.

For the false stability of the national state, purchased by tyranny
and suppression or sheer obliviousness to local characteristics, we
must substitute the dynamic stability of a body politic in a state of
tension and readjustment, in which no issues need ever pile up to
the point where they will cause a morbid mobilization of violence
and ill-will. Such a federal system must be conceived in the spirit
of Blake's great dictum: One law for the lion and the ox is oppression.

Still another important principle must be embodied in the reconstitution of regions: that of social relativity. Here politics has

still to recognize and express the deep change that has taken place in our entire world picture. In the Middle Ages, man naïvely regarded himself as the center of the universe; and Europeans regarded themselves as occupying a conspicuously central and favored position among the civilizations of the world—of which they were pathetically ignorant. This general view expressed itself politically in the hierarchical organization of society: a social pyramid of classes, whose apex was the pope or king: later a pyramid of communities whose apex and central point was the capital city. The baroque sense of time and space altered this picture in certain details; but it carried out completely, within the boundaries of the rising states, the hierarchic organization of medieval theory. And by turns one state or another succeeded to a central position within the European polity: while within that state the capital city concentrated the power and culture of the whole country.

In the light of our new world picture, these views are obsolete and the maintenance of such a system of relationships is absurd. From the standpoint of relativity, no one state can claim pre-eminence, and no one position within the community is central. Every unit and every activity, no matter how small, no matter how apparently insignificant, has a fundamental importance for itself, and ultimately for the whole body politic. Thanks to our system of instantaneous communication, any center may become, for a particular purpose or function, the center of the region: any particular region may become the center of the world. For certain types of surgical operation one must go, not to great New York, but to little Rochester, Minnesota; just as for a certain quality of intellectual culture one must still go to the universities of Oxford or Poitiers, not London or Paris.

Authority under the emerging regime of political relativity is a matter of functional competence, not a matter of mere bulk or spatial advantage: neither size, position, nor physical power—nor a monopoly of all these qualities—by itself determines the importance of a city or a community. For cultural individualities are incommensurable: proportionately, the smaller countries, like Belgium, Holland, Denmark, Sweden, and Norway, have contributed far more to the development of modern life than colossi like England and

[TOP] Suburban house by Frank Lloyd Wright. Following the handsome indigenous adaptations in wooden cottage architecture introduced in New England by H. H. Richardson, Wright began in the nineties on a fresh foundation. Here a whole century of suburban experiment culminated in an organic union of garden and house. In re-discovering the long strip window, in throwing aside obsolete forms, in adapting the form of the house freely to the new requirements of living, in embodying the middle western sense of hospitality and public friendliness, Wright likewise dramatized the new sense of space, breaking down the wall between the inner and outer environment and achieving freedom without sacrifice of order. Wright's work was the first symbol of the new order.

[SECOND ROW] Elements in the Japanese house. The Japanese capacity for elimination, their sense of exquisite purity and esthetic rigor embodied in the tea room and the tea ceremony, their ingenious wood and paper technics, have been at work on the western mind since the middle of the nineteenth century: first by way of the Japanese print. Their use of sliding wall and sliding window, their control of both exterior and interior space by these means, and their utilization of the wall itself—rather than the cubby-hole closet—for storage and utility offer pregnant suggestions which the western architect has still to translate effectively into modern technical forms. This is civilization's partial compensation for the humorless barbarism of Japan's military caste.

[THIRD] Design for an Institute of Heliotherapy by Tony Garnier: an advanced project for the treatment of tuberculosis whose excellent form antedates Le Corbusier and the Cubists by half a generation. The indebtedness of modern architecture to the hospital has been insufficiently recognized: unbroken walls, doors without moldings, spotless interiors, partly derive from the post-Listerian hospital. These advantages are now often counterbalanced in the institutions themselves by a false idea of "hominess" which does not place sufficient trust in the healing qualities of light, color, order, visual repose.

[BOTTOM LEFT] Modern American kitchen: a well-organized laboratory for the preparation of food: compact, efficient, it ceases in itself to be a living room but encourages the use of adjoining space as a dining area, since the forms used are congruent with good modern furnishings. Modern form, indeed, begins to flow back from the kitchen and the bathroom, the two great biotechnic utilities of the modern dwelling—which completely distinguish it from other cultures—into the remaining rooms of the house. (*Photograph: Ewing Galloway*)

[BOTTOM RIGHT] Cage and exhibition house for primates in a modern zoo: Regent's Park, London. The circular wall opens to the sunlight in fine weather but can be closed completely: it thus adapts itself to the season and to the life needs of the inmates. (*Photograph: Museum of Modern Art*)

[TOP LEFT] New York Public Library. Actual working facilities as a storage place for books and manuscripts and as a workplace for scholars and writers and readers seriously marred by the sacrifice of space, convenience, and efficiency to solidity and monumentality. Overcrowded within a decade of its opening. Light, air, space, and silence—the Benedictine luxuries, according to Dom Butler—were all forfeited in this inept design. (*Photograph: Ewing Galloway*)

[TOP RIGHT] London Underground Station: the excellent achievement of an administration whose posters have done more for public art than many more pretentious efforts at mural design. (*Photograph: Museum of Modern Art*)

[MIDDLE LEFT] New offices for the bureaucracy at Washington: a monument of irregional and irrational planning. Closed courts that trap the summer sun without taking advantage of summer breezes, window area sacrificed to classic massiveness, grotesque waste of money on tedious stone columns that further diminish light and air. Nowhere a clear indication of the purpose of the building or the location of departments. This unified building project might have set a masterly precedent for rational business building in every city: unfortunately, it was organized esthetically for an obsolete baroque street picture, characteristic of a despotic order. (*Photograph: Ewing Galloway*)

[MIDDLE RIGHT] Court at Sunnyside Gardens, Long Island, with common green in the center (F. L. Ackerman, Architect). Comprehensive and orderly design of a new order: the open court at right angles to the street or road is characteristic of *Zeilenbau* block organization. Sunnyside Gardens, in its combination of technical and social initiative, continued the work of the housing experiments begun in the Federal war housing projects: its demonstration of rational neighborhood planning and community development paved the way for the large-scale public housing movement that was taken up in Washington in 1932. The disintegration of the Sunnyside community during the economic crisis was a mark, not of any essential mistakes in design, but of the inevitable *insecurity of all individual home ownership,* even the non-speculative type fostered by co-operatives or limited dividend corporations, under our present financial structure. Only publicly owned housing can remedy this. (*Photograph: B. J. Lubschez*)

[BOTTOM LEFT] Palace of the Soviets in Moscow: a project whose archaic grandiosity recalls the Russia of Peter the Great rather than Lenin's comradely republic of free workers: the same kind of thinking shown here that characterizes the swaggering skyscraper blunders of American businessmen. But see Plate 27 for a different picture of the USSR. (*Photograph: Sovfoto*)

[BOTTOM RIGHT] Philadelphia Hosiery Workers' Union Apartments: not merely a symbol of the new order of planning and living, but likewise a token of the importance of the trade union movement and the co-operatives in focusing the *demand* for housing.

Germany. This fact was recognized, very wisely, in the original constitution of the United States, which allotted as many senators to tiny Rhode Island as to the vast state of Pennsylvania; and it is capable of further application. In the days of Goethe, Weimar exercised more cultural authority than centralized Berlin; and with the redistribution of physical energy, political power, and cultural interest that is now incipient, the principle of social relativity will be incorporated in both the regional and the urban pattern. No longer will a single center monopolize advantage, or substitute its activities for those of the whole.

2: The Process of Regionalization

Neither the regional nor the cosmopolitan organization of society is so remote or so chimerical as the exponents of financial and political centralization persuade themselves. For so ingrained are international processes in modern society that it is only by deliberate efforts that they can be starved or rooted out. Without constant interference on the part of the existing states, the industrial and scientific organizations of the modern world would, like the Rockefeller, Guggenheim, and Carnegie Foundations, overpass local lines.

Indeed, until the World War awakened reversionary tendencies, these new forms of organization had already gone far. The world before 1914 was a place in which men traveled in civilized countries without passports or special permission: where within the world capitals the broader allegiances of European society were replacing the more parochial limitations of nationalism. Similarly, the regional pattern of life was breaking through, once more, the imposed or self-imposed national uniformities. So far from going against the grain of modern culture, both regionalism and internationalism were working with the grain: it was the more traditional forms of bellicose etatism that worked against it; for even finance, if irregular, was nevertheless cosmopolitan.

The great opposition to a regional and cosmopolitan organization of political society comes from the psychological complexes that have been deliberately built up around the ideas of national sovereignty and centralized government. A large, so far unbreakable chunk of irrationality serves not merely as a handicap to co-operation, but as a justification of national antagonisms. Men have been encouraged to project upon their nation or the state godlike attributes of wisdom and power they would never claim in their right minds for themselves as identifiable individuals. Symbols like Fatherland, King, Il Duce, the Old Flag, serve to unite in compulsive automatic behavior people who might, in relation to the everyday realities of the common life, exercise rational judgment and good sense.

To nullify these atavistic emotional clusters and break up these formidable reflexes, a more humanized system of allegiances must be built up.

Here the historic development of the regionalist movement itself provides a helpful example: it reminds us that the course of development is not directly from scientific truth and rational judgment to social application and acceptance: the process begins rather with a dynamic emotional urge, springing out of a sense of frustration on one hand and a renewed vision of life on the other. Only at a later stage does the movement achieve a rationale: a systematic scientific and economic basis. Regionalism, as one of the French observers of the movement has pointed out, tends to pass through a regular cycle. It begins with a revival of poetry and language: it ends with plans for the economic invigoration of regional agriculture and industry, with proposals for a more autonomous political life, with an effort to build up local centers of learning and culture. This cycle of development seems to be so common that one might examine it in India as well as in Catalonia; but in the spirit of the regionalist, I prefer to draw my illustrations from an example closer at hand: the United States.

If France is the oldest exponent of conscious cultural regionalism, one might take the United States as an example of the latent, unconscious cultural processes, working out to much the same end. Before the Civil War there had come forth in the United States a number of culturally differentiated sections. Each had its characteristic polity and art and way of life. New England, Tidewater and Piedmont Virginia, South Carolina, Kentucky, Louisiana, had distinct and special traditions, even though the state boundaries did not always coincide with the regional complex. In New England and New York the poetic cycle of regionalism had begun, not a little aided by the original federal constitution of the states. Hawthorne, Emerson, Thoreau, were New Englanders first, and "Americans" only for the sake of that wider unity—so necessary to a flourishing local life—that might equally have been worldwide as American. Although Whitman and Melville, in distinction to the New Englanders, tended to emphasize their identity with "These States" taken as a whole, one may see in that very concern the influence of the brisk cosmopolitan port of New York, the Empire City, already bidding for the financial leadership of the continent.

The cycle of prose and the cycle of practical action were disturbed by the Civil War, by the Western migration of farmers that followed the generous public distribution of land under the Homestead Act, and by the great influx of non-English-speaking immigrants. In this babble of tongues, in this flux of industrial enterprise, in this drift and shift of population, regional affiliations were lost: the new trusts, the oil trust, the steel trust, and the packing trust, utilized the older division of states merely in order to protect their enterprises from national regulation. But in the writings of Liberty Hyde Bailey in the East, and of Frederick Jackson Turner in the Middle West, the cycle of prose was not altogether neglected: indeed, Bailey was one of the great leaders in that revitalizing, and, as it were, re-ruralizing of thought that took place under the surface of the mechanical exploitation of the nineteenth century. The work of the state colleges, with their rising schools of agriculture, carried on in detailed surveys and in practical experiments tasks that were being undertaken on a wider scale by the United States Department of Agriculture. Indeed, the county soil surveys of the latter department, though highly specialized reports on geological data, had in them also the germs of those broader land utilization surveys which are one of the characteristic instruments of regional planning. The unit-area was an arbitrary one; but the method itself was capable of being pushed further.

During the last decade or so the regional pattern, broken by the Civil War with its excessive emphasis upon the unifying and centralizing tendencies of the power state, has been pieced together again. During the last generation, there has been opportunity for the newer groups to make permanent homes for themselves and to be assimilated into the landscape. To some extent this latter tendency has followed the original pattern of their homeland: California has selectively attracted Italians to its fruit-growing regions, while the hard winters of Minnesota have beckoned to the already acclimated Swedes and Norwegians.

These mingled strands of linguistic and cultural inheritance from the older countries lend their colors to the newer regional patterns that are emerging. So it happens that the cycle of poetry and the cycle of prose have revived: not least in the South, where the negative notion of sectionalism, a term of reproach invented by Northerners, has given way to the more positive interpretations of regionalism: some of the clearest and most enlightened expressions of the regional political philosophy are those that have issued from Professor Howard Odum and his colleagues at Chapel Hill, N. C.

The poetic consciousness of the regional setting and its cultural implications has come in the emergence of a group of poets and painters with distinct regional characteristics: artists conscious of their local identity and their local idiom even when their themes are not of a local nature. Carl Sandburg, Vachel Lindsay, Sherwood Anderson, Theodore Dreiser, Sinclair Lewis and Willa Cather in the Middle West have been followed by painters like Thomas Benton from Missouri and a rising school in Illinois. Ellen Glasgow, Julia Peterkin, and John Gould Fletcher in the South, together with later writers like John Crowe Ransom, are forerunners of that recasting of the cultural consciousness of the region which, at third and fourth remove, often plays such an active part in the political and economic movements of a later generation. Similar developments have taken place in many other places: notably Oklahoma, Nebraska, Montana, and New Mexico.

The same tendencies have appeared in other areas: the intuitions of the poets have been abetted by a fresh group of historians, anthropologists, economists, and geographers who have begun to delve more deeply into the materials of their local regions. Much that has been glozed over or neglected in our concern for superficially national interests and national attitudes, is in the act of being recovered and re-valued. Instead of unification by suppression of diversities we are now approaching a time when we may have a more effective unity through their representation and integration.

As for New England, it has never entirely lost its consciousness of being a regional entity. Even when the agricultural life was ebbing from it, during the period after the Civil War, some of its old vitality and individuality was embodied in the literary school of Sarah Orne Jewett and her successors. Winslow Homer and Albert Pinkham Ryder, to say nothing of George Fuller, perpetuated its heroic images of life in noble paintings, perhaps the finest that any artist has yet achieved in America, while at still a later stage, Robert Frost and E. A. Robinson preserved, in their several individualities, the essence of the old New England culture. New England, too, either fostered or harbored a new group of scientists and planners who were to embody the new interests of geotechnics, or earth-molding: G. P. Marsh, first of the conservationists, Shaler, the geologist, Charles Eliot, II, who carried Olmsted's conception of the landscape park into the wilder parts of the landscape, and Benton MacKaye, the founder of the Appalachian Trail, who has been one of the foremost philosophers and theoretic exponents of regional planning in our generation.

During the last fifteen years practical activity on regional lines has widened. The landmarks are many: the launching of the conservation movement by President Theodore Roosevelt in 1908, the masterly outline regional plan for the State of New York, published in 1926, the power and conservation projects undertaken on a great scale by President F. D. Roosevelt, in an effort to stay soil wastage and to achieve flood control. The interest in regions as foci of human activity has been growing. All these are important developments. The initiative taken in the Tennessee Valley, which treats as a unified area for power development a whole series of disunited county and state authorities, offers a strong precedent for kindred projects in other great units, such as the Columbia River Valley and the Connecticut Valley. These initiatives have not yet altered the focus of political life: indeed many of them are handicapped by the fact that they continue to operate through a tangle of irrelevant boundaries and jurisdictions: but at least they have made a departure. They should be pushed further, in sub-regional as well as inter-regional areas.

No less significant of the same general tendency to recognize the underlying geographic and economic realities are the new units of administration that have appeared. The division of the country as a whole into broad inter-regional provinces, for Federal Farm Loan Banks, for the Federal Reserve Banks, and for the administration of a unified railroad system during the war, indicated the first faint emergence of a new type of federal system. Within single local areas under conflicting political jurisdiction the organization of the Palisades Interstate Park Commission for New York and New Jersey, and the New York-New Jersey Port of New York Authority point equally to a more realistic and rational mode of administration.

If these new super-regional authorities and divisions are not to turn into another crazy-quilt of overlapping or inconsecutive areas, they should be based upon the geographic and cultural constants of the constituent regions. Plainly, there are provinces, that is, inter-regional areas, where the administrative authority must transcend the boundaries of the national state: the Great Lakes-St. Lawrence waterway is one. (In Europe, incidentally, the electrification project of the upper Rhine Valley is another, while, under any rational system of government, the coal-and-iron areas of Lorraine and the Saar Basin would be a third.)

While regions should become the basic units of political and economic life, the inter-relation of regions within the province, of provinces within the "country," is no less important: for both conflicts and co-operations must take place over these wider areas. But the reconstitution of regions will not automatically solve a community's problems: on the contrary, it will raise new problems; for, as A. E. once remarked, no country can marry any particular solution and live happily ever afterwards. The advantage of creating a sound basis for economic and social activities, is that the new problems will have greater significance; they will embody more important issues and lead to more fruitful results. Ideally, these inter-regional areas of jurisdiction and control and taxation—functions implied in the political definition of sovereignty—should be worked out by collective experiment. Such a method, however, is limited by various irrational factors. These form an obstacle even in countries like the United States and Canada, which have no military frontiers and no belligerent ambitions: hence temporarily the unit of *inter*-regional control must remain the existing political state.

Here, however, a distinction must be drawn between the dual functions of the state, as they have defined themselves during the last century, and even more during the last two generations. On one hand is the power state, that creation of the baroque imagination: a territorial unit, based on military force, devoted mainly to the protection of the powers, properties, and privileges of the ruling classes. Even in its earliest developments such a state performed certain important service functions: it maintained internal peace and order, protected the traveler on the king's highway, dispensed justice between individuals and corporate groups. One may say, however, that the power state supplied services for the common weal chiefly for the sake of enhancing its own power: the welfare of communities and regions was a secondary matter.

Out of this power state a different type of organization has grown up: a service state: the outcome of the effort, through democratic pressure, to reapportion the existing balance of power within the "nation," to equalize the privileges of different regions and groups, and to distribute the benefits of human culture. This type of activity derived originally from the necessity to regulate the hours of labor and the conditions of employment, first of all in England, in order to do away with the most hideous forms of exploitation: its activities extended to the regulation of housing and the provision of funds for the local improvement of housing: and even earlier, beginning in Prussia, it had taken over the function of education. In the United States, the activities of the Department of the Interior and the Department of Agriculture and the Department of Commerce, the Forest Service, the Parks Service, the Children's Bureau, are examples of the service state.

Though these two aspects of super-regional organization operate within the same general framework, they perform different functions and work to different ends. Perhaps the most critical problem for human society today is that of diminishing the rôle of the power state and undermining both its pretenses and its ultimately militaristic forms of authority. At the same time, we must look to a steady enlargement of the rôle of the service state, for, in contrast to the earlier form of the state, this emerging type expands its power for the sake of increasing its services, and these inter-regional and super-regional services are the essential complements of every form of local and regional activity. Our main problem is to constitute the service state so that it can operate, not as the arbitrary ruler and dictator of regional life, but as the willing agent of that life in all those functions which transcend the immediate limits of local control and regulation. Eventually one may look forward to the time when co-operation between service states, without regard to so-called national boundaries, will take place within an even larger framework: a step that is dimly foreshadowed in the Labor and Health Offices established by the League of Nations at Geneva.

While the power state, on its own premises, is jealous and intolerant of any subordinate groups or corporations or regional associations that claim autonomous functions, the service state, to perform its services effectually, must accept these realities of communal life at full value. Its own functions, indeed, are seriously handicapped if the regional units of initiative, administration, and control are paralyzed, or have failed, through some original deficiency, to develop. Professor Burgess, as far back as 1886, foresaw that the arbitrary constitution of the separate states in the United States would have a diminishing validity; he looked forward to an enlargement of national functions and the increase of independent "municipal" activity. If today one substitutes the term region for municipality, as being an exact equivalent under modern technological conditions, one may well accept the prophecy of this acute political scientist.

Plainly, therefore, the change from the power state to the service state cannot be effectually accomplished within the existing structure of the "nation" or "empire": there must be a drastic revision of the method as well as the area of control. But on the other hand mere inertia, mere legalistic bickering over state's rights or local privileges, mere attempts to substitute a more parochial past for the claims of a wider future will not succeed in restoring the political authority or the cultural life of a region or a group of regions. The right to challenge the power state can come only to those who are ready to utilize fully the equally wide sovereignty of the service state

in order to build up a more humanly satisfactory type of organization.

Regionalism must not make the mistake of the medieval municipalities: it must not fancy that it can control within its local area
alone economic and political forces that lie outside the scope of
any single area. As a positive political and cultural doctrine, regionalism implies an inter-regional framework: ultimately a world culture on every plane. Regionalism belongs, therefore, not to a sentimental past but to a more realistic future: a future that will diminish the sphere of the irrational in public life, and rise above the
obsessive mythologies and the life-defeating mechanisms of the
power state.

3: The Postulates of Regionalism

One can scarcely over-rate the significance of a sound political
pattern; or do justice to the mischief that has been caused by arbitrary systems of control and fictitious centers of allegiance. Part of
the difficulty that confronts the world today is due to the fact that
our political behavior has been conditioned by crazy dreams and
baseless beliefs that have no relation to reality: beliefs in the supremacy of the Anglo-Saxon race or the Nordic lineage, carried to
its last grotesque folly in the belief in a wholly imaginary "Aryan"
race: the desire to assume the White Man's Burden (now also the
Yellow Man's Burden), to paint the map red, to find a place in the
sun, to fill out the national boundaries, to establish a "safe" frontier.

All these attitudes and shibboleths place political behavior outside the realm of rational thought. They are the symptoms of a
power politics that has taken on a definitely pathological character.
In opposition to this wanton mythology, the regionalist points to
the following facts:

First: During the last three hundred years the populations of the
earth have, willy-nilly, become inter-related and unified: warfare,
famine, disease, the negative unifiers, have their repercussions in
the daily existence of even remote communities, while the organizing
forces of science and technics and instantaneous communication have
given a common ideological background to culturally and geograph-

ically sundered areas. Isolation is a delusion, and willful isolation is a morbid intensification of this condition.

Second: Rationally defined, the locus of human communities is the region. The region is the unit-area formed by common aboriginal conditions of geologic structure, soil, surface relief, drainage, climate, vegetation and animal life: reformed and partly re-defined through the settlement of man, the domestication and acclimatization of new species, the nucleation of communities in villages and cities, the re-working of the landscape, and the control over land, power, climate, and movement provided by the state of technics.

In other words, the region, as a unit of geographic individuation, is given: as a unit of cultural individuation it is partly the deliberate expression of human will and purpose. The poles of these two aspects of regional life are the raw physiographic region and the city: they express the extremes of natural and human control. The human region, in brief, is a complex of geographic, economic, and cultural elements. Not found as a finished product in nature, not solely the creation of human will and fantasy, the region, like its corresponding artifact, the city, is a collective work of art. One must not confuse the region, which is a highly complex human fact, with arbitrary areas carved out to serve some single interest, such as government or economic exploitation. The country within fifty miles of a metropolitan center is not a region just because it is a convenience for a metropolitan advertising agency or newspaper or planning board to call it so. The discovery of the rough outlines and elementary components of the region is a task for the sciences: the utilization of the region in all its varied potentialities as a theater of collective action is a task for democratic politics. The new regional disciplines complicate the task of finding and expressing political form; for they weaken faith in arbitrary simplifications: but in recompense, they promise a more durable pattern.

Third: The boundaries between regions are not sharp but graded: even when nature sets up relatively sharp frontiers, like seacoasts, the facts of human intercourse ordinarily break down these supposedly hard-and-fast boundaries, reducing or entirely overcoming physical obstacles. At the present stage in civilization man tends more and more to inter-regional and worldwide intercourse and association. To oppose this tendency, in the interests of military security, is to further barbarism. The facts of regional integration and inter-regional intercourse must be expressed through the technique of modern political administration, as well as through rational under-standing: communities must consciously educate themselves up to these conditions and needs. The parochial mind, stultifying in the village, has become a menace through carrying its suspicions and fears and naïve hatreds into the governance of the power state.

Fourth: Human institutions and relationships change in the course of relatively brief years or generations, whereas the basic geographic realities alter only over centuries or aeons. Hence it is important to keep the political and cultural pattern in a state of effective re-adjustment, within the more fixed lines laid down by the primordial region. But it is no less important to recognize, with Professor Roland Dixon, that "there is some reason . . . to believe that very often the strength of a culture, its virility and energy, and even its vitality, depends in no small measure on the tenacity of its environmental fibre, as does its richness and brilliance on the number and variety of exotic traits it contains." A rational system of political govern-ment must give a place to these two complementary conditions of culture. *A migration of the élite, from region to region, is a neces-sary stimulus to regional culture:* the higher cultural equivalent to that one-sided attraction toward the megalopolis which so fatally de-pleted the regions of their most precious human elements.

Fifth: No existing state or administrative lines are sacred or un-alterable. The political map of the world has always been in a state of constant flux; and it would be absurd to imagine that the tempo-rary forms achieved during an era of extreme instability and rapid transition were permanent ones. Many of the existing boundary lines, whether within or around a country, are but a few generations old; at most only a few centuries; and what has been created by man in the past can be re-defined and re-created in the interests of a more effective communal life.

Hence local administrative boundaries or national boundaries that interrupt the more fundamental configurations of regions, or the grouping of regions into inter-regional areas or provinces, must be progressively diminished: eventually wiped out. This means the devolution of political power and the building up of local centers of initiative and control: but it also means the closer interlinkage of regions through the service state, and the building up of areas of co-operation far beyond the frontiers of the national state.

Now, in most countries, with the exception of those smaller states which embrace only one or two regions, neither the state boundaries nor the local administrative units are based upon the fundamental economic and cultural facts. Result: a failure of focus within the local area: a distraction of interests and a confusion of effort. These conditions lead ultimately to a lapse or deterioration in the common life. The effective re-definition of regional areas—a scientific re-mapping of these areas and a political and cultural *re-willing* of them—is one of the essential preliminary tasks toward building up a co-operative and serviceable civilization. For as a man can have no fruitful traffic with the world around him, until he has a firm core of personality, so the region cannot engage in the necessary interchanges and intercourse with other regions until it possesses an integrated life, on its own solid foundations.

This means that the cultural reconstitution of the region is an essential part of the political and administrative task. Our most rational plans await the emotive pressure of human purposes, human desires, human urges: the most admirable mechanism is inert until its engines are fueled by these means. And it is because regionalism actually has its basis in spontaneous human motivations, that one may look forward, confidently, to its wider conquests of rationality. In that great federation of regions and peoples which compose the Soviet Republics of Russia, the first step toward this regional redefinition has already been taken; and projects for similar readjustments have been current in France, Spain, and Great Britain for more than a generation, while a similar rebirth of regional consciousness will, in all probability, be one of the stimulating reactions to the National Socialist scheme of compulsory unification in Germany. Finally, in the United States, the work of the National Resources Committee and various State Planning Boards has opened the way toward a broad reconsideration of the essential problems in community building, regional design, and government.

Fortunately, the notion of the inviolable frontier is now dead

even in a military sense: the airplane has robbed it of actuality.
Railroads can be halted at frontiers; ships are confined to landing
in ports and can be halted at ports; but man's latest invention, the
airplane, laughs at these restrictions. For the first time in history
every region, every city, is open to attack—open and relatively helpless. The longer the frontier, the greater the opening; the bigger
the national capital, the more exposed to assault. *The task of modern
civilization is to live in a wall-less world.* At present the nations
are like people fleeing from a rainstorm who take refuge behind the
walls of a ruin, forgetting that the roof itself has fallen down, and
no matter how close they huddle to the wall, they will be drenched
from overhead. There is no alternative: no system of bombproof
shelters, no generosity in supplying gas masks, no mobilization of
fire-fighting apparatus, will avail as defense: the only possible answer is the certainty of equal aggression *by the same means.* In cold
realistic terms this implies that if we cannot create a wall-less world
our civilization will die: it will die by inanition, through the terrified
expenditure upon "protection," or it will die by common extermination, aggravated by neurotic fury, the first time an autarchic state
attempts to overcome its self-imposed sense of enclosure by committing an aggression upon an equal.

The fact is that planning and co-operative enterprise must take
the place occupied by political boundaries and purely legal codes
in creating an orderly polity and an ordered economic life. Our
present tariff barriers, which may be called supplementary military
walls, in so far as they are not thievish efforts to enrich a special
group of manufacturers at the expense of the whole community, are
efforts to achieve, by altogether inadequate means, the effects of a
planned system of production and distribution. Now the great worldwide commodities, such as wheat, cotton, and rubber, commodities
which are necessarily grown for an inter-regional market, must be
planned and rationed eventually by a world authority. The fact that
attempts to do this have again and again broken down during the
present state of economic anarchy, does not lessen the necessity nor
should it blind us to the need for trying again under better auspices.
Once a basic production was established; once the surplus was rationed, the social effects of a tariff would be created without

walling off intercourse and without arbitrarily raising prices. Our walls are feeble, indeed disastrous, military measures to evade the necessity for altering an economic system based upon priority of property rights and profit-opportunities: while imperialism is the bastard effort to create an international framework for modern production on the basis of conquest, robbery, and class exploitation. Both these efforts are inimical to civilization.

We have still to create the adequate political framework for Western Civilization: a political framework which will recognize both the universalizing forces and the differentiating forces that are at work.

At the same time, we must create a groundwork, in city, in region, in province, for the differentiating forces that are so necessary to such a worldwide system: a foundation which will accept the differentiation of local tongues and dialects, which will foster, instead of trying to extirpate or standardize, the living speech, with its slang, its colloquialisms, its local variants, its color both in form and in pronunciation: local literatures, local forms of art and culture, from cooking to painting, from the platting and carving of the landscape to the variants on universal forms in engineering and architecture.

Originating in this or that region, a local force will rise to universality: co-operation will spread throughout the world from the little town of Rochdale, or the technique of psychoanalysis will penetrate every culture, once it has taken shape in Zürich and in Wien. Such inter-regional influence and intercourse must be made possible on a far greater scale than during the liberal era of the nineteenth century. Old persecution complexes and old fears of being poisoned by cultural food offered by a strange hand must be completely expunged. For make no mistake: the creation of a more orderly world, more susceptible to reason, more adequately founded on reality, awaits a re-orientation of the human ego: it demands a more effective psychological insight and a broader collective discipline.

4: Regional Planning: A New Task

The orderly development of the region and its finer articulation with other regions is the task of regional planning.

Planning involves the co-ordination of human activities in time

[FIRST LEFT] Factory for light industry in Detroit, Mich. Type of industrial unit that need not be placed in a separate zone, but which may often, was with the Spirella corset factory at Letchworth, be integrated in a predominantly residential development. Old-fashioned stereotyped zoning plans, still popular in America, would not permit such organic planning, any more than they would permit apartment houses in one-family blocks: so much the worse for this system of zoning.

[FIRST RIGHT] Apostolic Church designed by Oud for the Kiefhoek development at Rotterdam: a masterpiece of great esthetic purity and delight: a monument of the non-monumental.

[SECOND LEFT] Public Garden in Essen. Spacious formal order that owes none of its charm to mere holdovers of renascence gardening. The intelligent indigenous landscaping of Jones Beach, L. I., would serve equally well as an example of the new design if only the architecture belonged to the same order.

[SECOND RIGHT] Department store in Prague: latest product of a long development that began in Paris, was carried on in the Art Nouveau buildings of Paris and San Francisco, and further developed by Mendelsohn in Chemnitz and Dudok in Rotterdam.

[THIRD LEFT] Three-story apartment building in Warsaw: fine example of the spacious new vernacular that does not have to climb thirty stories into the air to be assured of its modernism.

[THIRD RIGHT] Part of the Town Hall at Hilversum, near Amsterdam: a handsome public building effectively designed as part of a living- landscape, without invoking the now incongruous formalities of the baroque planners. No building or community development can be considered a satisfactory example of biotechnic design unless it includes open spaces and gardens as an integral part of its plan: this applies to every part of the urban environment.

[FOURTH LEFT] Modern school by Richard Neutra in California. Note removable outside wall: the easy transition of the class from indoor to outdoor activities: the opportunity to study and play in the open air. Note, too, that the amount of sun indoors can likewise be controlled, since too much may be as undesirable in the tropical climate of the south as too little. Schools of this type are common in Switzerland: Zürich has made notable public provision for small nursery units in its new housing developments.

[FOURTH RIGHT] South Russia: modern street with dwellings at right angles to the line of traffic: spacious, verdure-lined, composed: visually at least one of the better examples of modern housing in Russia, where imitations of American congestion, as in certain quarters in Moscow, too often compete with a disagreeably arid and over-systematized type of German rationalism. (*Sovfoto*)

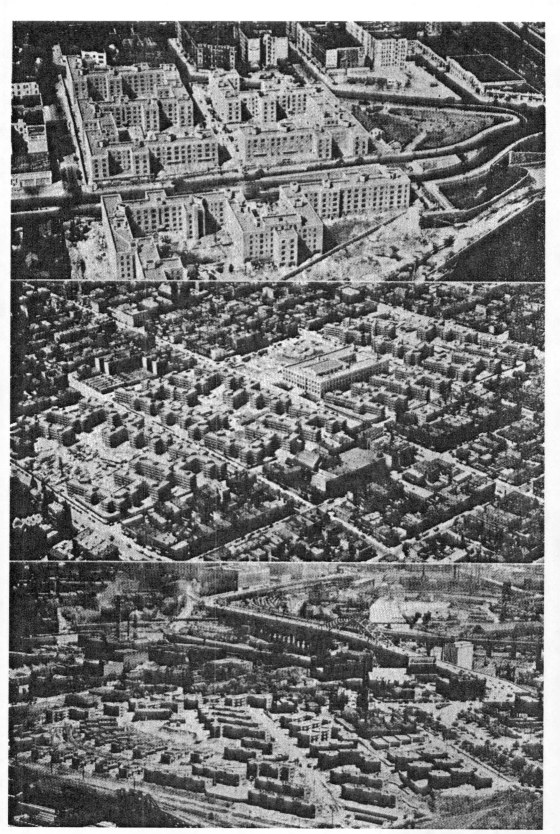

Government aid in housing, first through restrictive legislation, then through slum improvement programs, then through loans at low interest rates and finally through actual supervision and building, has grown steadily for almost a century. Beginning in England in the 1850's the housing movement reached the United States in the form of philanthropic organizations for model housing, and not till 1917 did the government take more positive measures. War-housing, such as in Bridgeport (Black Rock) and in Yorkship Village, set a new standard in community development; but this precedent was neglected both during the period of housing shortage, 1918-1924, and during the miserable speculative boom that followed. Government housing received a new impetus in 1932, after President Hoover's Housing Conference, in the offer of Federal funds for limited dividend housing projects. In 1933 the aid to housing under the Public Works Administration was greatly extended: not sufficiently to meet the actual need for slum clearance and the re-building of blighted areas, but at least enough to make an admirable beginning. The triumph of the Public Works Administration has been to demonstrate superior methods of comprehensive planning and design, to show the advantage of large-scale operations and unified technical direction, to prove the desirability of planned housing, not for individuals, but for communities, with communal facilities provided as part of the original design. No urban community can afford the costly luxury of unco-ordinated and insecure private enterprise: for economy in the long run, it must plan and build its own housing as it now plans and builds its own waterworks and parks.

[TOP] Harlem Houses, New York. Handsomely designed apartments for Negroes, overlooking the Harlem River. Note approach through triangular park, right, the playground on the river front, the spacious open courts with ample light and air. Contrast with the legally permissible congestion and darkness of the "improved" new law tenements of 1901 in the background. In essentials of plan and arrangement, these quarters are superior to any comparable area of residential apartments in the city. (*Photograph: Public Works Administration*)

[MIDDLE] Ten Eyck Houses, Williamsburg district, Brooklyn. A blighted area, partly cleared and redeemed. The school in the center, though admirably placed and new, is an old-fashioned type that contrasts unfavorably with the apartments. Note the closing up of wasteful streets in the replanning of this area into superblocks: also the orientation of the houses for maximum sunlight, a typical modern innovation here somewhat marred by the introduction of wings at right angles to the main exposure. (*Photograph: Public Works Administration*)

[BOTTOM] Lakeview Terrace, Cleveland. Good plan, well-adapted to site, with combination of apartment house and smaller dwellings. Note the placement of the dwellings at right angles to the roads, the skillful use of contours on the left, the abandonment of useless and costly streets, the ample interior playground. (*Photograph: Public Works Administration*) and space, on the basis of known facts about place, work, and people. It involves the modification and re-location of various elements in the total environment for the purpose of increasing their service to the community; and it calls for the building of appropriate structures—dwellings, industrial plants, markets, water works, dams, bridges, villages, cities—to house the activities of a community and to assist the performance of all its needful functions in a timely and orderly fashion.

Regional planning is the conscious direction and collective integration of all those activities which rest upon the use of the earth as site, as resource, as structure, as theater. To the extent that such activities are focused within definite regions, consciously delimited and utilized, the opportunities for effective co-ordination are increased. Hence regional planning is a further stage in the more specialized or isolated processes of agriculture planning, industry planning, or city planning.

In every society there is some sort of spontaneous co-ordination of functions based upon tradition. But this sort of empirical "planning," though not altogether ineffective in a stable society working under long-tried conditions with well-established conventions and duties, was cancelled out by the changes that took place during the last three centuries. The growth of population, the multiplication of inventions, the rise of hitherto unknown needs and the employment of uncertain techniques, the acceleration of change itself—all these conditions turned empirical and spontaneous co-ordination into helpless mockeries. For lack of conscious plan, the empire of muddle arose: a maximum opportunity for social conflict and cross-purposes and duplication of effort, and a minimum means of achieving collective order. Planful order came only in patches through the work of the military strategist, the geographer, the architect, the engineer, and the competent industrial organizer. The chief opportunities to plan fell only to organizations that had the advantage of size and monopoly: the Bell Telephone System, for example, in the United States.

Each industry, each institution, each area, each civic entity, has need under modern conditions for a plan of activity and for a procedure in development. The more effective such an organization, the more certainly does plan play such a part in directing its internal activities. But all these separate instances of planning suffer from two things: a lack of understanding of the social meaning of the plan, and a failure to achieve co-ordination with other organizations, by dove-tailing, under a common authority, into a broader scheme for regional and inter-regional planning. Even organizations that attempt a maximum of scientific planning within their own walls tend to resist the need for this wider kind of co-ordination. Behind this skepticism and this hostility to plan lie certain presuppositions and prejudices that need to be thoroughly aired.

What is a plan? To the Oblomovs of the world a plan is a dodge for evading the realities of life and for avoiding the responsibilities of action. To them a plan is a purely fictitious contrivance, a series of propositions drawn up in graphic form on paper, which serve as a surrogate for reality. Such two-dimensional plans were the bane of architecture, when they became separated from the processes of building, and were elaborated by learned esthetes who had little direct knowledge of the technical processes of construction. Often, in the act of making such a plan, the object is forgotten: the paper design, elegant, symmetrical, unspotted by sordid considerations of cost, availability of materials, suitability to purpose, ignores important environmental facts. The paper landscape gardener forgets the drainage of the land and the adaptation of his flora to the climate: the paper architect plays with elegant decoration and achieves a formal balance on the façade and forgets to put the dining room near enough to the kitchen to keep the food from getting cold in service; the paper engineer—this is an actual case—designs an irrigation project with admirable skill in hydraulics, only to discover, after the water works have been built, that the soil is unfit for cultivation.

All such "plans" are inefficient and embarrassing when they are carried out: they are at their best when they are still on the drafting board. Too often, as in so many beautiful city planning and zoning schemes in the United States, they are piously docketed in the appropriate file, and something radically different is done from day to day by the powers that be. Planning, in the sense of making idle pictures and diagrams, of covering all the tough knots of reality with coats of esthetic paint, of making the wish a substitute for the thought, has justly earned the derision of hard-headed, intelligent people. Similarly, attempts to impose a limited order of reality upon the future actions of men—as in grandiose mappings of the New York of the future, a century in advance by the "practical" city plan commissioners of 1811—are often more mischievous in their fake order than the purely empirical provision for the day's needs would be.

In contrast, genuine planning is an attempt, not arbitrarily to displace reality, but to clarify it and to grasp firmly all the elements necessary to bring the geographic and economic facts in harmony with human purposes. Regional planning involves four stages. The first stage is that of survey. This means disclosing, by first-hand visual exploration and by systematic fact-gathering, all the relevant data on the regional complex. Since even the geographic constants have been altered in one degree or another by time-processes, the historic side of the survey is as necessary as the elementary topographic mapping.

The orderly arrangement and graphic presentation of these data, through maps, statistical charts, and photographs, are important aids in clearing the mind of confusion, partial observation, and misleading generalizations formed on the basis of insufficient evidence. Charles Booth and his associates in London, Patrick Geddes and his colleagues in Edinburgh, were perhaps the first to undertake a thoroughgoing civic survey as a preliminary to town planning and municipal action. Booth was the more exhaustive in his detailed, house-to-house canvass of living conditions in London: Geddes was the more broad-visioned, in that he included, as matters of first importance, the geographic setting, the climatic and meteorological facts, the economic processes, the historic heritage. Between them, long before industrial analysis had reached this systematic stage, they created a pattern for orderly diagnosis and treatment of civic conditions. As an ecological sociologist, Geddes made the necessary passage from the civic survey to the regional survey; and at various removes his example has been widely followed: note the surveys of various industrial areas, by Abercrombie and others in England.

The second stage in planning is the critical outline of needs and activities in terms of social ideals and purposes. Unfortunately, this is the element of planning that has been least developed. Within the still dominant economic system, the main purpose of plan would be to increase the pecuniary rewards to the owners of industry and in some faint degree perhaps to the workers therein. These pecuniary canons have tended to remain, under slight disguise, the accepted warrant of planning: hence the usual emphasis upon the means of transportation, the provision of fresh commercial opportunities, and the desirability of national self-sufficiency in times of war. Under such canons of planning, housing and community building would enter belatedly, if at all.

Planning, however, is a selective process: it demands evaluation and choice. Though the values that are to issue from effective regional planning must ultimately harmonize with actuality, they do not automatically derive from the immediate situation: they may, on the contrary, deliberately work against it. It is naïve to think that geographers, sociologists, or engineers can by themselves formulate the social needs and purposes that underlie a good regional plan: the work of the philosopher, the educator, the artist, the common man, is no less essential; and unless they are actively brought into the process of planning, as both critics and creators, the values that will be imported into the plan, when it is finally made, will be merely those that have been carried over from past situations and past needs, without critical revision: old dominants, not fresh emergents.

Planning will take one form in a country where the desire for bellicose achievement and conquest is uppermost: it will take still another where education and the nurture of life is the main aim of collective endeavor. Whether the resources of a region are utilized to build military airplane bases, strategic mobilization highways, and ammunition dumps, or to build schools, playgrounds, and parks is something that is not answered purely by geographic or technical data.

Not merely does planning, then, require a visualization of resources and activities and processes, by means of the regional survey: it demands a critical formulation—and revision—of current values.

One of the main difficulties in the way of applying the advanced collective technical processes and instrumentalities of thought to the

creation of a better commonwealth has been due to the dissipation
of values that has taken place during the last century. Though the
common instruments of production have increased the human basis
for association, the breakup of coherent value-systems has undermined the possibilities for unified action. And in addition, the values
of Orthodox Christianity, of Protestantism, of individualistic humanism, of capitalism, of humanitarianism and libertarianism, have
been weakened, not merely through conflict, but through internal
erosion. One may confidently prophesy the emergence of a new system of values, which will displace the debris of these dying systems:
a system shared, if not yet successfully formulated, by most men of
good-will today. But until this system has been defined, it will be
easier to expand or diminish the amount of social energy than to
alter its direction. In detail, however, a process of revaluation has
been going on generally for over a century: its most profound outcome has been the belief that the opportunities for the fullest manifestation of life belong, not to an exclusive minority, but to every
citizen, up to the limits of his capacities. What Christianity expressed
in terms of Heaven, a humanistic socialism expressed in terms of
daily living.

The third stage in planning is that of imaginative reconstruction
and projection. On the basis of known facts, observed trends, estimated needs, critically formulated purposes, a new picture of regional
life is now developed. In this picture a host of dispersed projects—
the dredging of a river here, the extension of a library service, the
shifting of an industry to a better location—are for the first time set
down in a fashion that discloses their essential spatial and temporal
inter-relationships. On this plan, blank spots, weaknesses, unused resources, disclose themselves and new means of repairing such handicaps perhaps suggest themselves: similarly, new opportunities, hitherto overlooked, become visible. No better picture of the integrating effect of plan can be offered than that made by Henry Wright's
sketch plan for New York: it is all the more significant because he
did not overlook the historic succession.

Here plan finally appears in the accepted sense of the word. For
a good part of these projects can be graphically drawn up. Such
plans, however, are instrumental, not final: what is planned is not

simply a location or an area: what is planned is an activity-in-an-area, or an area-through-an-activity. Such planning draws attention to the fact that the old question as to whether society is to be organized on territorial lines or on an economic and functional basis is almost meaningless. For a territorial society, such as a city or a regional authority, is not describable merely in terms of the area it governs; and similarly, a steel industry, owning or operating a multitude of mines, furnaces, sheds, railroads, cannot be described purely in terms of its corporate organization or the legal-political relations of workers, managers, stockholders, and consumers. The fact is that all associations and organizations are carried on through physical structures that exist in space, and that are geographically conditioned: only imaginary societies can do without a parcel of earth for site and the physical means of coming together. Regional planning is industrial planning in its place aspect: industrial planning is regional planning in its resource-activity-product aspect. This would be a truism were it not for the fact that the very word "plan" connotes in many minds merely the more static aspects of regional development: the mapping of the terrain and the disposition of forces, but not the movements of the troops or the issue of the battle.

At this stage of planning, the disciplined play of the creative imagination is extremely important; but unfortunately civilization has as yet presented little scope for the collective planner. In small compass, nevertheless, one may observe a parallel process at work: landscape architects like Olmsted and Eliot in America, architects like H. H. Richardson and Louis Sullivan, thrust deep roots into their civilization and had, in an extraordinary degree, the capacity to understand and express its new wants. In this stage of planning new combinations of old elements, and fresh additions from new sources, make their appearance. The re-modeling of the earth and its cities is still only at a germinal stage: only in isolated works of technics, like a power dam or a great highway, does one begin to feel the thrust and sweep of the new creative imagination: but plainly, the day of passive acquiescence to the given environment, the day of sleepy oblivion to this source of life and culture, is drawing to an end. Here lies a new field for intense creative activity.

Now these three main aspects of planning—survey, evaluation, and the plan proper—are only preliminary: a final stage must follow, which involves the intelligent absorption of the plan by the community and its translation into action through the appropriate political and economic agencies.

In this stage, the plan undergoes a readaptation as it encounters the traditions, the conventions, the resistances, and sometimes the unexpected opportunities of actual life. No plan can automatically foresee all contingencies: moreover, it loses some of its efficacy as plan if it sacrifices, at the beginning, the clarity of the ideal by timidly anticipating all the qualifications and reductions that ideals are subject to in the course of their translation. Nor can a plan, as such, provide for its own fulfillment: to emerge as a reorganizing agent, it must help conjure up and re-educate the very groups and personalities that will bring it to fruition. Weak plans, which hesitate to leave solid ground at all, are often far less effective than overbold ones that awaken the popular imagination: such success as totalitarian states have shown in their collective planning has perhaps been due to their willingness to cleave at a blow the Gordian knot of historic resistances.

No architect or engineer is skilled enough to be able to detail, with specific instructions, every act in such a simple job as that of building a house or installing a machine: on the contrary, he must rely upon the autonomous skill and comprehension of even the unskilled laborer. Plan, then, is not a substitute for intelligent choice, decision, or invention on the part of those who must execute it in detail: it rather assumes the existence of these qualities and organizes the milieu in which they can most effectively work. What is true in individual constructions is even more true in the complicated co-ordinations of society. Regional plans are instruments of communal education; and without that education, they can look forward only to partial achievement. Failing intelligent participation and understanding, at every stage in the process, from the smallest unit up, regional plans must remain inert. Hence the need for positive organs of assimilation. Regional plans must provide in their very constitution the means of future adjustments. The plan that does not leave the way open to change is scarcely less disorderly than the aimless empiricism that rejects plan. Renewal: flexibility: adjustment: these are essential attributes of all organic plans.

If the problem of planning is more complex today than ever before the means, too, have become more adequate. A community that is technically capable of inventing calculating machines for the solution of abstruse mathematical problems, and that can send talking images through space, cannot plead lack of ability when it comes to applying a more complex technique of thought and administrative procedure to its social needs. Part of the dislocation from which economic life suffers is due to the fact that our mechanical equipment has been more quickly invented and improved and scrapped than our means of social control. Except in a few matters like bookkeeping and the permanent record and limited liability organization, our vast industrial mechanisms have been built up empirically without sufficient attention to the psychology of human organization. We have isolated mechanical factors and learned to deal with them in a fruitful systematic manner; but we have still to invent that wider system of order which will assist in the transformation of our social relations: one of its symbols is the regional plan itself.

5: Survey and Plan as Communal Education

The party politics of the nineteenth century was as remote from the thick tissue of actual life as were its pecuniary canons of success. A voter might loyally cast his vote every election without touching on a single issue that concerned his immediate life, without an intimate knowledge of a single phase of political administration, from taxes to the school system, and without affecting for the better a single aspect of his working life or his daily environment. The system "worked" in an atmosphere of windy ignorance.

The new totalitarian states profess to regard the liberal politics of the nineteenth century with scorn; but in fact they carry on the same traditions in an even more costly way, with the further disadvantage that their political wind must be kept at high pressure in order to divert attention from the human sterility of the power state's achievements. The fascists go through the forms of voting without having the privilege of even casting a negative vote; they go through the forms of sounding out public opinion without daring to hear more

than one side: even more than the most imperialist states of the nineteenth century they endeavor to wipe out local differences, local preferences, local pressures. The totalitarian state has but two important
functions: to prepare for war and to keep power in the hands of the
governing party. This is not in the least a new form of politics: it is
merely the old form, shamelessly reduced to its naked reality.

The fascist state may be defined as the war dictatorship of the
power state frozen into a permanent form: opinion governed by war
censorship, action governed by military coercion, all law converted,
openly or implicitly, into martial law. In a sense, any fool can govern
such a community; but only a fool would mistake such a process for
government.

None of the attributes of an advanced civilization can be maintained in a permanently cowed and servile population: the delicate
initiatives, the fine co-operations, the deeper loyalties toward truth
and rational judgment upon which our civilization depends cannot be
preserved in governments that know no law, even in the spiritual life,
except the whim of the dictator or the command of the party. If the
totalitarian state still shows the surface characteristics, here and
there, of our common civilization it is only because it still lives on
the going energies of the more civilized generation that preceded it;
so far as fascism succeeds, these energies will wane, and barbarism
will progressively rise to the surface, whether hastened by war or
not. Such peoples will sink to the level of ancient Sparta—at whose
very "bravery" the ancient world sometimes smiled. Toynbee's interpretation of this possibility in the third volume of A Study of History is extremely suggestive.

The real alternative to the empty political patterns of the nineteenth century lies, not in totalitarianism, but in just the opposite of
this: the restoration of the human scale in government, the multiplication of the units of autonomous service, the widening of the co-
operative processes of government, the general reduction of the area
of arbitrary compulsion, the restoration of the processes of persua-
sion and rational agreement. Political life, instead of being the
monopoly of remote specialists, must become as constant a process
in daily living as the housewife's visit to the grocer or the butcher,
and more frequent than the man's visit to the barber. If the leisure

that man has been promised by the machine counts for anything, it must count for the extension of the privilege of being an active political animal. For every phase of group activity, industrial, professional, educational, has its political aspect: each activity raises special problems of power, organization, control, and discipline—problems that cry for intelligent and orderly solutions.

The opposite of tyrannical compulsion is not unconditional "freedom" but the systematic practice of rational discipline through education and co-operative service: through education the curve of the individual career may be ultimately harmonized with that of the community, not by a mere restriction of response to that desired by a governing despot, but by a widening of personal scope and opportunity, in those spheres of rational understanding and administrative action which are properly the concern of the citizen and the polity. That human conduct is full of irrational residues does not lessen this need: for what is true of human beings in the mass is equally true of self-elected rulers and leaders: in any case, the problem is to increase the area of rational judgments and rational political activity, and to divert or sublimate those forces which are inimical to co-operation. To the extent that political power becomes rationally conditioned and successfully diffused by education, the individual citizen will be reluctant to sacrifice his own initiatives and his own judgments to the terroristic monopoly of dictatorship. The impotence of the many is the power of the few—and vice-versa.

Where shall this return to political realities begin? Where better than in the region? All rational politics must begin with the concrete facts of regional life, not as they appear to the specialist, but as they appear first of all to those who live within the region. Our educational systems are only beginning to make use of the local community and the region as a locus of exploratory activities: but before the resources and activities of a region are treated as abstract subjects they should be understood and felt and lived through as concrete experiences. Beginning with the crawling of an infant in his home, the systematic contact with the environment should broaden out until it includes the furthest horizon of mountain top and sea: in a bout of sailing, fishing, hunting, quarrying or mining every child should have a firsthand acquaintance with the primitive substratum of economic

life: the geography and geology of the textbook should be annota·
tions to these experiences, not substitutes. So, too, with work in the
garden, the vegetable patch, the hayfield and the grain field: here is
the very substance of regional life, and no system of education, no
urban environment, can be considered even remotely satisfactory
that does not include these experiences as a vital element. Child
labor, as Karl Marx pointed out, will be an essential part in all education once the element of exploitation is removed from it.

The next step toward a rational political life—note how different
this process is from the military automatisms of the fascist—is the
hitching of these concrete experiences to local surveys, more systematically undertaken. The soil survey, the climatic survey, the geological survey, the industrial survey, the historic survey, on the basis
of the immediate local environment, are the next important instruments of education: this is a process of grasping in detail and as a
whole what has hitherto been taken in through passive observation in
city and countryside. All these local surveys, taken together, become
the focus for a more general regional survey. Already such surveys
have come to play an important part in English education: indeed the
land utilization survey, completed recently in England, was carried
out through the co-operation of the school children in every locality.

Such surveys, if made by specialist investigators alone, would be
politically inert: made through the active participation of school children, at an appropriate point in adolescent development, they become a central core in a functional education for political life. It is
in the local community and the immediate region, small enough to
be grasped from a tower, a hilltop, or an airplane, to be explored in
every part before youth has arrived at the period of political responsibility, that a beginning can be made toward the detailed resorption
of government—an alternative to that half-world of vague wishes,
idle dreams, empty slogans, pretentious mythologies in which the
power politics of the past has flourished. The scientific approach, the
method of intellectual co-operation, embodied in the regional survey,
are moralizing forces, and it is only when science becomes an integral
part of daily experience, not a mere coating of superficial habit over
a deep layer of uncriticized authority, that the foundations for a
common collective discipline can be laid.

Most of our educational routine, as built up during the past century, has reflected the dominant political and economic institutions: it has substituted mere paper counters for reality. The elimination of concrete views and concrete experiences has reduced rather than widened the sphere of effective education: finally, we arrived at the age of extreme specialization, the present age, when the amount of specialized knowledge, often accurate, often extremely refined, has far outstripped our capacity to make use of it as part of a consistent whole. The remedy for this is not to be found in any mechanical combination of specialisms: we might digest the contents of an encyclopedia without achieving anything more in the nature of unity than a headache. The cure lies rather in starting from the common whole—a region, its activities, its people, its configuration, its total life—and relating each further achievement in specialized knowledge to this cluster of images and experiences.

Here and there this organic approach to knowledge, as one with life, and to life as a constant function of knowledge, has been made in education: beginning at the lowest stage in the new nursery school. But the fact is that education, instead of rising above this unifying attitude, must keep it at every later stage, along with the element of deliberate play and art.

What is needed for political life is not mere factual knowledge: for this by itself is inert: what is needed are those esthetic and mythic impulses which open up new activities and carve out new forms for construction and contemplation. When the landscape as a whole comes to mean to the community and the individual citizen what the single garden does to the individual lover of flowers, the regional survey will not merely be a mode of assimilating scientific knowledge: it will be a dynamic preparation for further activity. The Boston Metropolitan Park System of Boston, one of the most varied and comprehensive in the world, owes its existence to just such regional surveys as practiced by Charles Eliot in his schoolboy rambles about the region. The Appalachian trail, again, owes not a little to the extra-curricular activities of Benton MacKaye, making as a mere youngster a systematic exploration of the environment of Shirley Center.

Once this more realistic type of education becomes universal, instead of being pieced into the more conventional system, we will create a whole generation that will look upon every aspect of the region, the community, and their personal lives as subject to the same processes: exploration, scientific observation, imaginative reconstruction, and finally, transformation by art, by technical improvement, and by personal discipline. Instead of an external doctrinal unity, imposed by propaganda or authoritarian prescription, such a community will have a unity of background and a unity of approach that will not need external threats in order to preserve the necessary state of inner cohesion. Science has given us the building stones of an orderly world. We need the further utilization of science, through the regional survey, regional exploration, and regional reconstruction if we are to increase the area of political rationality and human control. Visual synthesis provides a foundation for unified creative activity.

Once the human scale is overpassed, once the concrete fact disappears from view, knowledge becomes remote, abstract, and overwhelming: a lifetime's effort will not provide sufficient grasp of the environment. The more people who are thrust together in a limited area, without organic relationships, without a means of achieving an autonomous education or preserving autonomous political activities in their working and living relations, the more must they become subject to external routine and manipulation. The resorption of scientific knowledge and the resorption of government must go hand in hand. We must create in every region people who will be accustomed, from school onward, to humanist attitudes, co-operative methods, rational controls. These people will know in detail where they live and how they live: they will be united by a common feeling for their landscape, their literature and language, their local ways, and out of their own self-respect they will have a sympathetic understanding with other regions and different local peculiarities. They will be actively interested in the form and culture of their locality, which means their community and their own personalities. Such people will contribute to our land-planning, our industry planning, and our community planning the authority of their own understanding, and the pressure of their own desires. Without them, planning is a barren externalism.

At present, we have inferior forms of life because our metro-politanized populations throughout the world are both witless and wantless: true cannon-fodder, potential serfs for a new totalitarian feudalism, people whose imaginative lives are satiated by shadows, people whose voices are dimmed by loud-speakers, people whose will is capable of response only under mass stimuli and mass pressures, people whose personalities, instead of being represented by an integer, can be represented as but a fraction—one one-millionth of a voting crowd, a war-crowd, a drill-crowd.

The task of regional survey, then, is to educate citizens: to give them the tools of action, to make ready a background for action, and to suggest socially significant tasks to serve as goals for action. Ultimately, this becomes the essential duty of every vital school, every responsible university. In this concrete sense—and not in any vague hope—education is the alternative to irrational and arbitrary compulsion. The opposite of this is the reduction of education to drill and cram, and the reduction of the body politic to a corpse that is galvanically brought to some semblance of life by the application of external stimuli from the center. Such a state may create "heroes": it can never create a wide society of true personalities, men and women who have learned the arts of personal and communal living, who neither renounce the will-to-order nor seek to create it on a single monotonous pattern. Without such a broader cultural foundation, regional planning can have but a minor political significance. Once the cultural base is achieved, however, regional planning becomes one of the essential attributes of a progressive civilization; and every effective economy it introduces tends to further the capacity for association and to widen the field of significant action.

6: Conditions of Urban Re-building

Many things that were done hastily in the nineteenth century, because there was in a sense no time to think, now have to be done over again. The division of the exploitable areas of the world between the existing powers of Europe, on a basis that lacked reason and justice, has become an intolerable anachronism: the empires that were founded on the notion that such a division was permanent must be dissolved, unless civilization itself is to be dissolved. On the way to that end the belligerent outlines and routines of the national state itself must be softened by systematic inter-regional co-operation: if neither of these things can be done so long as screaming tyrannies of the totalitarian states threaten more democratic and civilized modes of life, it will come after they have been liquidated: the men of good will outnumber the homicidal barbarians, and one day, it has been promised, peace will come to all men of good will.

One of the major tasks of the twentieth century is the re-settlement of the planet. The past three centuries have been centuries of random exploration. The pressure of population, rising first in Europe, and then in the Orient through forces originating in Europe, has pumped into the areas of low population-pressure millions of immigrants: to find a parallel for this movement one would perhaps have to go back to the desiccation of the grasslands of Central Asia, which thrust the Hun into the heart of Europe. Here again, unfortunately, the flow of population was spontaneous and unguided by sufficient knowledge; and much of the work of settlement must be done over again.

In North America, this need has already been recognized: farm lands that should have been left in forest are returning to forest; grassland that should have been left to the grazing of cattle, instead of being plowed for wheat, will return to grass again; grazing land in the West has been put back, through the Taylor Act, under close Federal control. Population that spread with no more social direction than the surface tension which gives definition to an ink blot, must be re-grouped and nucleated in a fashion that will make possible a co-operative civilized life. Industries that flowed into the centers of congestion in order to take advantage of cheap labor, must now flow out into new centers, where a better life is possible for the workers: conscious scientific intelligence must determine the new loci of industrial advantage, and organize industries and communities in such a fashion that neither the labor supply itself, nor the organized protection of the workers against exploitation, will rest on the mere congestion of population in crowded cities. Industries that during the nineteenth century naturally gravitated to the coal mine, the railroad line, or the cluttered seaport, must now be put in more advantageous areas, where the new sources of power and new modes of transport may be used to fuller advantage.

But although the decadent metropolitan form cannot long remain a dominant, the sources of urbanization nevertheless persist. The chief source is the increasing efficiency of agriculture. With mechanization of the main processes of plowing, harrowing, reaping, binding, threshing, milking, sorting, an even smaller number of people is capable of doing the original work; and with improvements in agronomy, through seed-selection, new stocks, and increased knowledge of the biochemistry of plant growth, both the number of people and the area engaged in agricultural production will be smaller: this will release a larger number of men and women for non-agricultural work. Hence the need for building urban communities remains, even though the population of a country as a whole approaches stability.

The danger is that this process of re-settlement and continued urbanization will continue, through inertia, in the forms that prevailed in the past. Most of our plans for urban development have been static: they have taken past habits, past technical methods, past legal codes, past financial opportunities, and past social attitudes as the sole elements that will condition future development. On this basis, it is easy to prove that, if the metropolis has increased in population in the past, it will continue to in future. Those who hold these views regard any other possibility as unthinkable—by which they mean, in reality, that they are incapable of further thought.

But apart from the fact that history is full of reverses in existing trends—above all in such tricky matters as urban increases in population—such plans for the future leave out of account all those elements that exist in the present only as imagination, desire, dream, and project: the latent social forces which materialize in each generation in unexpected forms. The incalculable element in every scheme for urban and regional planning is not what men have and are accustomed to: but what they want, and are ready, when the want has been organized and dramatized, to reach for. Without taking advantage of the directive force of the imagination, releasing elements not given, or not dominant, in a present situation, planning must remain a belated mopping up after the forces of life have spilled over:

never catching up with its opportunities, committed to drifting with the current, never tacking to catch a breeze.

Plans that do not rise out of real situations, plans that ignore existing institutions, are of course futile: mere utopias of escape. But plans that neglect to formulate the potential creative forces, even though they are perhaps feeble at the moment of formulation, are equally futile, no matter how copiously they are ballasted with statistics and quasi-scientific demonstration: they lend all their authority to an order that is already, by definition, past.

The difference between these two types of planning was well-exemplified in the difference between Henry Wright's Report on Regional Planning for New York State, in 1926, and the voluminous report on the Metropolitan District of New York by Thomas Adams and his associates during the same decade. Wright's report dealt not only with past facts but with new social and economic emergents: as a result the work of Wright and his associates laid a foundation for the regional planning movement throughout the United States. The Russell Sage report, on the other hand, was obsolete even at the moment of its original formulation, to say nothing of its final summary: a compendious handbook on how not to approach the future, and of what not to do. Adams's report committed the city to a continuance of its past mistakes: Henry Wright's report showed, in the existing situation, the latent possibilities for a new order: not a passive continuation but a re-integration.

Do not ignore the difference between these two orders of thinking: it underlies the approach to the whole problem of urban re-settlement and re-building that now confronts the Western World.

This problem has two sides to it: one is the building up of new centers on lines that embody current improvements in architecture, planning, and social insight; the other side is the re-building of existing centers, great and small, cutting out morbid tissue, restoring functional relationships that have lapsed, giving them, in the process of renewal, a parity with the newer communities. If the planning bodies accept the existing structures of finance and administration as sound, indeed as indispensable—because they have been bequeathed by the past—no important changes can be made in any part of the urban environment: planning will be little better than the application of plasters to the sore spots of civic life, or of beauty patches upon its diseased complexion.

The real opportunity for urban and regional development lies in the fact that the existing pattern of economic life cannot remain stable. The accretion of the debt structure in the great metropolises, the toppling pyramid of land values, make economic life precarious and effective social planning an impossibility. Hence the real need is to deflate this burdensome structure as a deliberate public policy and to set up a responsible public body capable of directing the flow of investment into social channels and to liquidate with the least possible hiatus the present speculative structure. Only with this radical alteration in objectives and methods will it be possible to build up through public aid and initiative alternative centers which will attract industry and population, on the basis of their own essential superiority of life. As the drift out of the overgrown cities begins, the opportunity for their re-planning will come. Need I recall again that the vast increase of the number of playgrounds in Manhattan was not a result of financial prosperity: it was the outcome of deflation, failure to pay taxes, bankruptcy, and loss of population.

Existing cities must eventually participate in the re-urbanization of the modern environment: but before they can become regional cities, capable of sustaining a well-balanced environment for their now miserably housed masses, the metropolitan regime as a whole must be progressively liquidated. In the process of urban development, social values and financial values are in decisive conflict: pecuniary canons of success have produced an environment destructive to life, and similarly, biotechnic standards of achievement must produce a system of values destructive to metropolitan finance. Our whole program of re-urbanization and housing demands a definite choice. That choice may not be revolutionary in the sense of implying a complete break and an overpowering catastrophe: but it is revolutionary in the sense that when, by steady pressure and day-to-day movement, it has achieved its end, the metropolis and the insidious pecuniary values of metropolitan life will be obliterated, and a new set of working institutions, more consonant with a humane scheme of values, will have taken its place. Planners who are not aware of these implications are sociologically too unsophisticated to be trusted with important functions: instead of helping to define an adequate public policy, they can only obfuscate the issues and sabotage a sound social program.

7: The New Method of City Development—Garden Cities

The above issues were first defined during the nineteenth century. Three groups of men had an influence upon our later conception of population grouping and civic design; and a fourth group has still to achieve widespread acceptance.

The earliest contributor to the housing movement was Robert Owen: an original if somewhat fanatical mind, the first manufacturer who, out of his own success as an enterpriser, deliberately set his face against the barbarizing social results of the new machine industry: a process he had observed at firsthand as an agent of a well-meaning owner, and as a working industrialist himself. Owen proposed, in order to enable the new industrial workers to rise out of the squalid state in which they lived under the new factory system, to build small balanced communities in the open country. The educational and social facilities needed by these new settlements, as well as adequate houses, would be a charge on production, no less than the wages of the workers.

In the orderly community for which Owen furnished plans, one finds the first attempt, apart from the literature of utopias, to define the nucleus, or basic cell, of city growth in relation to the new form of industrial organization that had grown up in the mechanized and power-driven factory. Owen's design was not merely radically better than any other urban pattern in the early nineteenth century: it had the advantage over the new upper class squares of Edinburgh or London in that it provided, as part of the plan itself, some of the essential features of social life. On the whole Owen's original essay even compares favorably with the better work done in the twentieth century, after more than a generation of intensive experiment: for one thing, his designs were not marred by a weak feeling for the quaint and the picturesque, and for another he was not afraid to give the community the convenience and compactness of a city.

Owen's combination of vision and practical experience gave a special influence to his doctrine: his hopes and feelings were a yeasty ferment that continued to work through the nineteenth century. He had his coadjutors and successors: Fourier's idea of a harmonic society had a richer psychological basis than Owen's somewhat arid rationalism, and Fourier's scheme for phalansteries—though sometimes fantastic and irrelevant—nevertheless contributed imaginative details to the conception of a rational civic economy. The phalanstery built by Godin, the steel manufacturer, at Guise in France was a direct outcome of Fourier's ideas: one of the first efforts at collective workers' housing *and* community building. Sheer necessity often caused the industrialist to build houses for his workers, when his plant was situated in the open country: this gave an opportunity for fresh initiative, and the work of Sir Titus Salt at Saltaire, in the eighteen-fifties, paved the way for later settlements such as those of Krupp at Essen, Cadbury at Bourneville, and Lever at Port Sunlight. In terms of open suburban living, the last two initiatives had an important immediate effect upon the design of middle class suburbs with generous allotments of open spaces: but the improvements they instituted, their good planning and their low density, kept them from having any decisive influence upon low cost workers' housing done by the speculator and the jerrybuilder.

In one important way these new communities differed from middle class suburban settlements: they were directly related to industry; they made provision for the social life of the workers; they tended to form a small civic whole. The weaknesses of such beneficent effort was that they existed mainly, if not entirely, at the initiative of the "enlightened employer," and they were sometimes tyrannical in the underlying financial and administrative arrangements—so much so that in the case of Pullman, Illinois, the irate beneficiaries rebelled. Despite weaknesses in social organization the new industrial garden villages were, on the whole, the best working class quarters that had been built since the charitable foundations of the sixteenth century—if one excepts, perhaps, the small towns and villages set up in New England, Pennsylvania, and parts of Ohio before the middle of the nineteenth century. If they did nothing else, they dissociated the processes of industry from the idea of human degradation in a filthy environment: a useful dissociation.

Meanwhile, the spectacle of colonization and city building was not lost on the more acute observers of the nineteenth century—however foreign the idea of the city was to its scheme of abstract thought. An English observer, Wakefield, published a book in which he advocated a more systematic application of the art of colonization in new lands; and another Englishman, James Silk Buckingham, exercised his imagination in the construction of an ideal city, Victoria, which had the distinction of being limited in population, and of accepting the social services that had sprung up through voluntary associations in the new industrial towns as essential elements in the new order of urban existence. Finally, Henry George, viewing the process of settlement in the Far West, observed how the congestion of population automatically raised land values: thus, so long as land remained in private hands, it imposed a tax upon all those who either directly or derivatively were forced to use expensive land. The more advanced the machine industry, the more complicated the transportation net, the more dense the population, the higher the private tax in the form of rent.

By the end of the nineteenth century, all these plans, dreams, and initiatives were still in circulation: their actual effect upon society, however, was practically nil. At this point a benign Englishman, unfettered by those forms of specialized competence that paralyze creative thought, published a book called To-morrow, re-issued in later editions as The Garden City. In this book the views of Thomas Spence and Henry George, those of Owen and Fourier and Wakefield and Buckingham, were fused into a new and by now thoroughly original conception: that of the garden city, or the balanced urban environment.

Howard started from the basic fact in nineteenth century urbanization: population was increasing, and it was being drawn toward the existing centers of industry, particularly to the already overcrowded metropolises. New quarters had to be provided every year for factories and for factory workers. Why should this colonization go on automatically in centers that were so dismally congested, already clotted with foul slums? Why should there not be a deliberate attempt to create new cities out of the surplus? Every new increment of population was, in effect, a fresh opportunity to reverse those tendencies which were making life in cities more prohibitive in cost and more unsatisfactory in the social result.

Here Howard seized on a point where the individual industrialist, with his philanthropic plans for decentralized industrial villages, or model towns, was weak, and where the more vulpine industrialist, who sometimes escaped to little centers in order to enjoy the benefits of sweated labor, was positively anti-social. Howard recognized the human limitations of what is called in America the Company Town —the town organized and controlled, if not entirely owned, by a single industry. Such a method of "decentralization" left everyone but the industrialist himself poorer; it removed the possibility of alternative industries or modes of living from the workers; and it naturally aroused the opposition of organized labor in the better-graded industries. The problem of organizing good industrial cities was something more, for Howard, than the problem of selecting good industrial sites or finding cheap land.

But Howard showed his keen social imagination in still another way: his vision was bi-focal: he saw the countryside as well as the city, and he observed that the rural areas were fast becoming depopulated because they had ceased, from the standpoint of economic and social opportunity, to be attractive. The young, the adventurous, the intelligent were drawn off to the big cities because, in so far as there was any life in this new civilization, it was focused in these centers. The depopulation of the country and the overpopulation of the city were aspects of a single set of facts: the problem of bettering life at both poles was a single one. Hitherto the movement into the cities had aimlessly piled up great dormitory areas, remote from the essential social institutions of the city, and no less remote from the recreational advantages of the country: pools of urban and suburban squalor. As for industry, it generally followed the lines of least resistance: even when it wished better quarters for its workers it usually lacked the resources to build them: a large, easily accessible labor market was essential. So the country became poorer in human resources; and the cities did not show any commensurate gains in civic improvement.

Howard proposed to rectify this condition: if colonization could be more wisely directed in foreign areas, as Wakefield taught, and as the settlement of New Zealand and Utah had demonstrated, why should not the internal colonization of a country be equally deliberate? Why leave to chance something that was by nature subject to social control, since, once the elementary urban services were introduced in the nineteenth century, nothing could be effectively done except with direct municipal aid? What was wrong was not that the late nineteenth century city was unplanned: but that it was belatedly and badly planned, and the control of its existence was too largely in the hands of private land speculators and private transportation companies, seeking their own profits, not the common good. New industrial sites were to be spotted and allocated to their appropriate use; new housing quarters were to be built: why should these functions not be undertaken in the name of civilization and civic life?

If new cities were deliberately founded, as reservoirs are formed in flood areas, the uncontrolled flood of population which plunged so devastatingly into the metropolis would be abated: there would be a chance to build a new type of civilization. The new type of regional center would combine the hygienic advantages of the open suburbs with the social advantages of the big city, would give an equal place in its scheme to the urban and the rural possibilities of modern life: in short, it would be a balanced environment. To this new urban nucleus—new, that is, to the nineteenth century—Howard gave the title of the Garden City. "Town and country," said Howard, "must be married, and out of this union will spring a new hope, a new life, a new civilization." Without using the concept of the region, Howard's contribution was to see the problem of city building and housing as a regional one.

The name "garden city" was quickly appropriated by groups and interests that had no conception of Howard's statesmanlike proposals: it has even in our day been treated by Thomas Sharp as a scapegoat for the open type of planning characteristic of suburbs since the Middle Ages. So it is important that we recognize what was essential and original in Howard's new concept. The first point to be noted is that the land in the garden city is not parceled out into individual ownership: it must be held by the common authority under which it is developed: such increments as may arise through the growth of the garden city must be reserved for the community.

Not merely did Howard seek to eliminate the private landlord: he eliminated the temptation to increase density in order to raise land values. He likewise did away with instability through irrational or speculative changes in land use.

The second important characteristic is controlled growth and limited population. The outward limit of urban development was set by Howard's proposal to surround every garden city by a permanent reserve of open country: to be used either for agriculture or recreation. This agricultural belt was not merely to serve as a green wall against the encroachment of other communities: it was to provide opportunity for local production of food, with a good market close at hand. Once the area and plan and density of such a plan were determined, its upward limit of growth was set. Howard put this figure at about thirty thousand; but that was a shot in the dark: the main point was the notion that a modern city, no less than a medieval town, must be planned to the human scale and must have a definite size, form, boundary. It was no longer to be a mere sprawl of houses along an indeterminate avenue that moved toward infinity and ended suddenly in a swamp. Howard conceived the notion of promoting urban growth up to the point of maximum service to the social and economic life of the center: further growth could take place, not by overcrowding or spreading, as in existing cities, but in the foundation of a new garden city on the same lines.

The third notion that Howard introduced as an important attribute of the garden city, no less important than its human scale, was that of functional balance. In its regional relations, there was to be a balance between town and country; in its internal development, there was to be a balance between home, industry, and market, between political, social, and recreational functions. By providing in his scheme for a balanced environment, with a full equipment of social services, Howard offset the disadvantages of one-sided schemes of decentralization.

Howard, in other words, not merely avoided the weaknesses of the specialized dormitory suburb and the specialized company town: he also eliminated the possibility of deterioration through success— unlimited agglomeration. Howard may be said to be the first modern thinker about cities who had a sound sociological conception of the dynamics of rational urban growth.

In his plans for relieving metropolitan congestion, for limiting peripheral expansion, and for creating new urban nuclei, Howard had been anticipated centuries before by Leonardo da Vinci: on what remote sands can that bold pioneer's footprints not be found? Leonardo had proposed to the Duke of Milan that he be permitted to build ten cities of thirty thousand inhabitants each in order to "separate this great congregation of people who herd together like goats on top of another, filling every place with foul odor and sowing seeds of pestilence and death." It is interesting to note that Leonardo's proposal for garden cities came to fruition in the same decade as his experiments with mechanical flight: he had in fact projected two of the main inventions of the new economy. But Howard's garden city was as great an advance over Leonardo's dreams as Wright's airplane was over his Great Bird; for one thing, the social milieu was ready, and for another, the new invention worked.

Howard's scheme was first broached in 1898. Letchworth, the first fully equipped garden city to be built after Howard's outline, was founded in 1904 by a specially organized public utility association. Both events occurred, if not before the main neotechnic inventions were made, at all events before they had gone fully into circulation: when Howard proposed this civic method of decentralization no one could yet estimate the concrete support that was to be offered to his general scheme by the development of the electric transmission grid, the motor car and the motor road and the use of motor vehicles for transporting goods, to say nothing of the universal reception of the telephone and radio and phonograph and motion picture. Only a few original minds of the period, notably Peter Kropotkin and Patrick Geddes, had seized upon the implications of all these inventions for our civilization as a whole.

Howard's outline for a garden city, which was a rational suggestion in 1898, nevertheless was compelled to encounter the blind counterdrift of paleotechnic industry, still empirical in organization, still indifferent to plan, still even more indifferent to the effects of a congested environment on health and working capacity. A generation ago, the garden cities movement was an uphill movement be-

cause the concentration of industries was still economically profitable: hence the garden city encountered technical as well as financial resistance from industries that were still mainly equipped to use
steam power. After 1910, however, the currents of industry and administration both reversed their direction. For one thing, the decentralization of power and transportation became technically as feasible
as it had been in the days of the windmill, the water mill, and the
canal; and the decentralization of administration likewise became
possible through the wide use of the telephone, and more refined
mechanical means of audit and control. Urban development continued on the old mass pattern, no longer because of objective mechanical or economic advantages, but because the financial order had
crystallized its pecuniary structure in obsolete buildings, obsolete
equipment, and obsolete, technically over-developed cities.

Letchworth, the first garden city, was a demonstration project undertaken by a private association. Its supporters were drawn from
those bourgeois groups that were well disposed to social experiment,
that were content to receive a limited return on their investment, and
that for a long time even forewent the payment of interest on their
debt. Because of the need for attracting industries to the new center,
it grew slowly: but the growth was healthy and solid; and it was
achieved without an essential sacrifice of the original principles.
While other settlements, namely Hampstead Garden Suburb, had
physical qualities of plan that equaled, perhaps surpassed, Letchworth, they were purely middle class developments: because of its
success in incorporating industries and in building workers' houses,
the garden city became a focal point in the mind of social-minded
planners and administrators throughout the world.

After 1920, however, the conditions for the success of the garden
city became more favorable: for now the garden city was no longer
an isolated biological sport: it was the concrete embodiment of neotechnic processes, as applied to city development. Wherever enlightened control made possible the building of large scale developments,
Howard's conception became a potent influence: Hilversum in Holland, the new satellite communities built under Ernst May in Frankfurt-am-Main, the new town of Radburn in New Jersey, embodied to
a greater or lesser degree Howard's principles.

The public policy that Howard advocated, however, long awaited the support that can come only through a broad policy of regional development. Hence the industrial re-settlement of England after 1925, which resulted in the industrial building up of the southern counties around London, was a wantonly lost opportunity: a deplorable failure in civic statesmanship. Though thousands of working class houses were built in this district for the accommodation of the new workers, the work was done under the direction of existing boroughs and counties, and the opportunity for laying out new cities, as wholes, was neglected: Becontree, the most vast of the new working class suburbs, was even deprived of the possibility of taking advantage of the new Ford Motor works nearby, because those who settled there were by legal and administrative mandate exiles from the London slums, not new workers.

Accordingly an important step was taken in the United States when the Suburban Resettlement Bureau was called into existence in 1934 for the purpose of setting up a number of demonstration garden sites, appropriately called greenbelt towns, throughout the country. Like so many other good policies pursued under the administration of President Franklin D. Roosevelt, it lacked the advantage of consistent executive support and it failed to gather to itself the co-operation of the local communities affected: eventually the bureau itself was dismantled at the very moment when, through trial and error, it had begun to promise effective action. But the scope and intention of these projects, as demonstrated by those that were actually built, gave them a significance that mere housing estates, planned in already built-up areas, often on inadequate or mangled sites, did not possess. Perhaps the most critical failure of all, characteristic of the stultifying division that exists in practice between regional planning, housing, and city building, lies in the fact that no attempt was made to plan greenbelt towns for the area in which a great project in socialized planning was being carried out: namely, the Tennessee Valley.

Similar opportunities for co-ordinated large scale-planning have presented themselves in the new industrial development of Soviet Russia; but here the pattern has been defeated, in part, through haste, and through a tendency toward giantism left over as a burdensome heritage from the time of Peter the Great. Perhaps the closest approach to civic and industrial and agricultural planning, on a human scale, is that which the Dutch have embodied in their reclamation of land from the Zuyder Zee; but although Holland is preeminent in urban culture, the Dutch have not yet given the Zuyder Zee development the stamp of the best modern communities around Amsterdam or The Hague.

The slowness of the garden city in taking root is due to the fact that it is, so to speak, the native form only for a co-operative and socially planned society: one in which agriculture is on a parity with industry, and in which the necessary social basis in land ownership and land control is lodged in the community. To be built successfully, the garden city should be the product of a regional authority, with a wider scope of action than the municipality, and with greater local concentration than a centralized bureau operating from Washington, London, or Paris. The garden city can take form, in other words, only when our political and economic institutions are directed toward regional rehabilitation. What is important to recognize is that these new principles of urban development, as demonstrated by Sir Ebenezer Howard and his associates, are universal ones: they point toward balanced urban communities within balanced regions: on one hand, a wider diffusion of the instruments and processes of a high human culture, and on the other the infusion into the city of the life-sustaining environment and life-directed interests of the countryside.

CHAPTER VII.   SOCIAL BASIS OF THE
NEW URBAN ORDER

1: Architecture as Symbol

"The problems of bettering life and its environment are not separate ones, as political and other mechanically educated minds constantly think, and as religious ones have also too much come to believe. Nor is it, as politicians especially think—now with mistaken hope, or again with unnecessary discouragement—a matter of moving great numbers and masses before anything can be done. It is not a matter of area and wealth. It is at bottom an experimental problem, that of starting a re-adaptation." These words of Geddes and Branford have been verified during the last twenty years. In the housing of families and the building of communities a re-adaptation has started; and against the very grain of capitalist finance, over active protest and passive sabotage and dull indifference, the housing movement has continued to grow.

The symbol of this new adaptation is a common architectural form, and new types of communal layout. So far these growths have been sporadic: they have taken place, for the most part, on the outskirts of great cities, London, Amsterdam, Paris, Berlin, Wien; and they still bear some of the defects of their origin. But the movement toward better housing, not for isolated fortunate individuals, but for a whole community, is one that has been going on for a century; and it has now reached a point where the positive results have awakened desire and emulation. In this approaching transformation of our cities lies the justification of Patrick Geddes's prophetic words, in 1905, in describing the transition from the paleotechnic to the neotechnic phase of modern industry: "As the former period may be characterized by the predominance of the relatively unskilled workman and the skilled, so this next incipient age by the development of the chief workman proper, the literal *architektos* or architect; and by his companion, the rustic improver, gardener, and forester, farmer, irrigator, and their correspondingly evolved types of civil engineer."

In the transformation of the environment, architecture has a peculiar part to play. This arises not merely because buildings constitute such a large part of man's daily surroundings; but because architecture reflects and focuses such a wide variety of social facts: the character and resources of the natural environment, the state of the industrial arts and the empirical tradition and experimental knowledge that go into their application, the processes of social organization and association, and the beliefs and world-outlooks of a whole society. In an age of social disintegration and unrelated specialism, like the passing one, architecture loses most of its essential character: in an age of synthesis and construction, it steps forward once more as the essential commanding art.

And precisely because architectural form crystallizes, becomes visible, is subject to the test of constant use, it endows with special significance the impulses and ideas that shape it: it externalizes the living beliefs, and in doing so, reveals latent relationships. With the help of his orderly accurate plans, the architect brings together a multitude of crafts, skills, and arts, creating in the act of building that species of intelligent co-operation which we seek on a wider scale in society: the very notion of planning owes more to this art than to any other, except perhaps the co-ordinate art of the engineer.

The architect confronts human needs and desires with the obdurate facts of site, materials, space, costs: in turn, he molds the environment closer to the human dream. And in a social sense, architecture is more advanced than any purely mechanical technique because good building has always embodied, as an essential element in both design and operation, the understanding and expression of organic human purposes. In the state of building at any period one may discover, in legible script, the complicated processes and changes that are taking place within civilization itself. In a period of integration, such as we are now again on the brink of, architecture becomes a guide to order in every other department of activity.

Architecturally speaking, the nineteenth century was a period of disintegration. Buildings outwardly without roots in their landscape or affiliations with their society appeared in the midst of the growing cities. Such buildings were the work of individual architects, responsible only for their individual building: producing work that was bound to be swallowed up in the disorderly urban mass produced by the speculative builder, the ground landlord, and the industrial corporation, operating solely under the principles of laissez-faire. This original architectural Babel became more confused as foreign travel and wide archaeological research combined with a lack of creative impulse to encourage either dead imitation or a feeble eclecticism.

Originally the architects of the Renascence had turned to the dead for inspiration: as if the breath of life could come from the tomb. No one could doubt the improvements in farming that followed when Columella's treatise on farming began to influence progressive agricultural practice. No one could doubt the stimulus to mechanical invention that arose from the reprinting of Hero of Alexandria's experiments with the steam engine. But there was a vast difference between such experimental selection and lifeless imitation; in architecture, after Brunelleschi, what was taken over was not the process, capable of modification and complete alteration as new needs arose, but the external form: the dead stereotype of another culture. Note how post-sixteenth century architecture, instead of organizing the banked window further as a constructional form, relapsed into the more primitive system of the hole left gaping in the solid masonry wall: a loss both in terms of technical facility and livability; for the overhead glare of the tall rectangular window in turn resulted in a need for curtains to cut off some of the irritating light, while that entering in the lower part of the window was optically useless.

This period from the sixteenth century to the twentieth witnesses the fatal lack of connection between architecture and the dominant social sources of order. The proof that architecture in the social sense was dead lies in the series of dusty revivals that took place. People sought, in Roman forms, Greek forms, neo-gothic forms, finally in Romanesque and even Byzantine forms, some quick and easy route to a real society and a living culture: lacking the soil and the plants that could produce a beautiful efflorescence, they fash-

ioned for themselves paper flowers. As drawn on paper, or photo-
graphed, who could tell the difference between the living and the
dead? Unconsciously seeking the bread of social life, the architect
offered decorated stones: empty symbols of a non-existent society.
Meanwhile, the germs of a living order existed alike in building, in
technics, and in the culture of the landscape; but the confused minds
and irresolute purposes of the directing classes did not find it easy
to accept these beginnings. The common Victorian justification for
the new industrial buildings was not that they were good art, but that
a progressive industrial civilization had no need for art.

Viewed on the surface, the battle of the styles that was carried on
between the early baroque architects and the traditional medieval
builder, or between the neo-classicists of the nineteenth century and
the neo-medievalists, was trivial; for both schools were united in this
respect: they had lost their connections with a common social milieu.
Meanwhile society itself was losing all sense of a common order: its
forms were capricious because its values were uncertain and it had
yielded to a belief in purely quantitative achievement: fine architecture had become a matter of size and expense, while common
building, divorced from human standards, became cheap, niggardly,
cramped.

As if to add an ironic touch to this social disorganization, the field
was marked out roughly between the two great schools. After the
opening of the nineteenth century, the classic style claimed the government offices, the courts of justice, the police stations, the banks,
the art museums; while the gothic style claimed the school, the university, the town hall, the church, the natural history museum. There
would, of course, be occasional compromises and modifications in
this program. Survivals that stubbornly refused to acknowledge their
death, mistaking mumification for vitality, combined with mutations
that shrank from the struggles of birth—such was architecture during most of the nineteenth century in those reaches of the community
where it still had any significance. Even the most penetrating of
critics was confused: Ruskin had the courage to admire the Ashmo-
lean Museum at Oxford.

Yet, from the beginning of the nineteenth century on, a succession
of thinkers and planners appeared who knew that a more funda-

mental attack must be made on the whole problem of form. With those who went into form from the standpoint of community planning, beginning with Robert Owen, I have dealt in another section. Here we are concerned with the architects who realized that society itself was the main source of architectural form, and that only in terms of living functions could living form be created. There were many forerunners in this movement: but perhaps the most important figure of all was William Morris; for Morris, with Philip Webb, created the famous Red House in 1851, where Morris was to spend the early part of his married life. Here an attempt was made to discard ornamental tags and go back to essentials: honest materials, well-wrought: plain brick walls: a roof of heavy slates: every detail as straightforward and sensible as in a seventeenth century English farmhouse.

Heretofore architectural monuments had alone been the center of appreciation and the accepted source of style: the Pantheon, the Maison Carrée, the palace of Diocletian at Spalato, the Cathedral of Strasbourg, St. Mark's in Venice. These monumental buildings, crystallizations of a whole social order, were mistakenly seized as starting points for architectural design. In the middle of the nineteenth century this error had been carried so far that little cottages cowered behind massive Greek pediments, and the student of architecture began his apprenticeship with a study of the decorative elements in classic monumental forms; while he had so little training in matter-of-fact design that he would leave his atelier, proud of his skill in handling pencil or brush, and ignorant of the first motions in handling a trowel or a plumb-line; capable of designing a Hall of Justice but without the capacity to design an honest dog-kennel, to say nothing of a human dwelling.

By making the dwelling house a *point of departure* for the new movement in architecture, William Morris symbolically achieved a genuine revolution. The doctrines he laid down with respect to its design were fundamental ones: implicit in them, as he himself realized in his development as a revolutionary socialist, was the conception of a new social order, oriented not toward mechanization and profits, but toward humanization, welfare, and service. Little though Morris liked the machine—little though he had *reason* to like it in its defective early manifestations—he had achieved an attitude toward form and society that was capable of utilizing and directing the real advances that were being made in the organization of men and materials and the impersonal forces of nature. If the factory was the nucleus of the paleotechnic community, the house was to become the nucleus of the biotechnic age: his instincts here served him well.

"Believe me," William Morris wrote, "if we want art to begin at home, as it must, we must clear our houses of troublesome superfluities that are forever in our way; conventional comforts that are no real comforts, and do but make work for servants and doctors; if you want the golden rule that will fit everybody, this is it: have nothing in your house that you do not know to be useful or believe to be beautiful." This clearing away of the historic debris, this stripping to the skin, was the first essential mark of the new architecture, as it was, in effect, for the new view of life and cosmic relations that was introduced by the systematic sciences. In building: the open window, the blank wall, the unlittered floor: nothing for show and nothing that cannot be shown.

The next great impulse toward coherent form came from the American master builder, H. H. Richardson. Starting work after the American Civil War, Richardson at first used the current eclectic symbols, and finally established a reputation for himself by his bold handling of monumental forms: so far, an obstacle to genuine achievement. But as Richardson entered more deeply into the problems of his age, and became familiar with its social and economic forces, he turned to the design of an office building, a warehouse, a railroad station, a public library: he found himself on new ground. Richardson discarded, step by step, the archaic touches and the hampering symbols: he worked with the fundamental forms of masonry, organizing the elements solely with a view to the practical and visual expression of the function to be encompassed: he carried the lesson Webb and Morris had worked out in the dwelling house into every aspect of building. Though it was only in his latest buildings that Richardson finally came face to face with the possibility of new form, organically based on the technical resources and social principles of the new society, he achieved a sort of preliminary integration in terms of masonry. He proved that the ugliness of utilitarian forms had not been due to their origins nor their uses but to the inferior quality of mind applied to their development. Organically conceived, a railroad station had no less capacity for beauty than a medieval fortress or a bridge; and a dwelling house in wood might be better related to human needs than a costly palace.

Richardson's work was confirmed at a later period in Europe by the advances of kindred architects: Berlage's handsome bourse in Amsterdam is a parallel example of great force and merit; and Richardson laid the foundation for the work of another group of architects, Adler and Sullivan, and Frank Lloyd Wright in Chicago, who carried the theme farther. Sullivan's task was to formulate, in social terms, the order that was implicit in Richardson's last work: he took up, perhaps unconsciously, perhaps quite independently, the rule laid down by the American sculptor, Horatio Greenough—form follows function. And Sullivan sought, on this basis, to create an architecture in which the fundamental principles formulated for one type of building would hold for other types—a rule so broad that it would admit of no exceptions. Such a rule must have its foundations, not only in the architect's mind, but in the political institutions, the working order, the social attitudes of his community. To formulate it in fact, and to translate it from fantasy to concrete reality, the architect needs the active co-operation of his contemporaries; and no one had better reason than Sullivan to appreciate the failure of energies and the paralysis of imagination that follows when the architect is either at odds with his community, or is forced to degrade his best energies in order to conform to the limitations of his clients. Taken together, Sullivan's buildings do not have that unity his doctrine demands.

It remained for Frank Lloyd Wright, working again in the same medium as Morris, the dwelling house, to effect a synthesis of nature, the machine, and human activities and purposes. Wright increased the size of the window opening and restored the horizontal window bank, which had been lost, except for a sporadic revival or two, since the seventeenth century. By altering the layout of the house and keeping it low, and close to the soil of the prairie, he made a fundamental change in the relation of the house and the land, and introduced the garden almost into the heart of the living room. Outside and inside became aspects of a single unity, as in the human organism: the house-in-nature, nature-in-the-house. Although Wright showed special gifts in using natural materials and in adapting his designs to the local landscape, he used, likewise with masterly facility, the modern constructional methods and the new utilities provided by the machine: he treated the machine as a collaborating agent of human purpose, not merely as the cheapener of costs and the purveyor of spurious imitations that it had been during the formative period of Morris's thought.

In his respect for the soil, the site, the climate, the environing region, Wright was in advance, not merely of his eclectic contemporaries, but of those metropolitanized interpreters of the "modern" who followed almost a generation later: his "prairie architecture," like his later "desert architecture" was true regional form. Wright, indeed, depolarized regionalism from its connection with the historic and the archaic: he oriented it toward the living present, which contains both the past and the future; and he brought together in his new building forms the special and the universal, the local and the worldwide. It is not by accident that Wright's prairie architecture took deepest hold in Holland, a country not without geographic parallels to the prairie and Great Lakes areas, though built to a different scale. He created, not a mechanical form to be copied, as the clichés of the classicist were copied in the eighteenth century, and those of Le Corbusier during the last decade: he created an organic form, to be adapted and modified, precisely because the principles upon which it was based were universal.

Wright's architecture was therefore, to an unusual degree, a prophetic synthesis: a microcosm of the new biotechnic economy. This synthesis antedated in its individual forms the best work done on similar lines in Europe: antedated it by a generation. Unfortunately, Wright's early work had the weakness of being conceived in response to demand within the communal pattern of the romantic suburb: an individual free-standing house for the well-to-do bourgeois family. Except for one abortive, over-ingenious effort at group housing, which accepted far too high a level of density, Wright did not pass on to the more fundamental problem of communal integration until he developed, during the present decade, the plans and models and

projects of Broadacre City. That failure to incorporate the communal into the personal was perhaps responsible for the small extent
of his influence in the actual housing movement, even after 1920.

All these architects were, in effect, the representatives of a society
that had not yet appeared. Their contributions were like delicate
seedlings, carefully nurtured, and well-grown in March, before the
blanket of snow has lifted from the garden where they are to be
transplanted: often they died before the weather had taken a favorable change or the season had advanced sufficiently. The best of their
buildings even when they were brought into the open were lost in
weedy patches of speculative enterprise and industrial disorder: deprived even of their main esthetic effect through the lack of a background built on the same principles. Thus Wright's magnificent
Larkin Administration Building rises like some enigmatic temple in
the midst of a black industrial desert—contradicting but not sup-
pressing the ugliness and disorder around it.

These architects, then, share a place with the romantic poets, like
Blake and Whitman, who wrote for a non-existent democracy, and
with romantic individualists in all the other arts who were attempting to embody in their own personalities and in their own work something that could not be brought into secure existence without the political and social co-operation of a sympathetic community. In the
main, these romantics were prophets of life: but of a life and order
to come. What the artist created was but a sample, a small working
model, which must be thrown as it were into mass production before
the existence of the new pattern could be guaranteed and its full
meaning for society realized.

In almost every country, similar innovators appeared and the first
essays toward new form were made. Voysey, Mackintosh, Baillie-
Scott, Lutyens, Unwin, and Parker in England: Van de Velde in Belgium: Wagner, Hoffmann, and Loos in Austria: Behrens, Poelzig,
Schumacher in Germany, Berlage in Holland, Tony Garnier and
the Perrets in France. And in each country, with the possible exception of America, the new movement in life first registered itself in
the arts and crafts, in printing, in textiles, in pottery, in furniture,
before it became generalized and socialized as architectural and
communal form. Being more closely connected with machine technics

than the inherited handicrafts of building, it was perhaps natural that these subordinate departments of design should be influenced first. Perhaps another reason lies in the fact that the most fundamental change involved at first was a change in attitude and interest: a refocusing of the social objectives. The desire for sunlight and open air appeared symbolically in the painting of the impressionists more than a generation before it became widespread in the community: almost two generations before it was embodied formally in architecture. Does not the mind tend to project in a more facile medium, that which responds quickest to the artist's impression, what can be embodied only through long painful processes of trial and error, and co-operative discipline, in the structure of the community? One has reason to respect such symbols—except when they are treated as fetiches and accepted as substitutes for the life which they postulate.

From the eighties onward there was no lack of vigorous and intelligently conceived individual buildings; but at first the esthetic conception prevailed over the more comprehensive social conception, which includes the esthetic as but one of its ingredients. One sees the danger of a purely esthetic formulation of the problem in the rise of the new style toward the end of the nineteenth century: the style called Art Nouveau in France and Jugendstil in Germany. The two main technical examples of this form were embodied in printing and in jewelry; and in the latter department, indeed, one is conscious of the benign influence of woman, never wholly at ease in the power-world of the machine, turning instinctively to the symbols of life: flowers and fruit and her own naked body. L'Art Nouveau was an early attempt to incorporate biological symbolism in the arts. In architecture, it disdained straight lines and rigid geometric surfaces: it cultivated wavy lines, lines of growth and free movement: the designer turned electroliers into sprays of metallic flowers, and a simple balustrade railing into a descending foam of metallic waves. The first marks of this type of floral ornament were to be found in the old iron bridges, and before its expression in the furniture of Bing at the Paris Fair of 1900 it had left its marks on the base of the Eiffel Tower.

In the actual handling of its materials, chiefly metal and glass, L'Art Nouveau showed many examples of brilliant architectural design, some of which was more decisively functional than that of later schools which paid greater verbal respect to the principle of function. What was weak in l'Art Nouveau was in fact not its constructive execution but its formal symbolism: its reliance upon extraneous ornament for an expression of its purposes. It was indeed high time that the living was expressed in architecture: this precisely was a necessary mark of the new biotechnic age that was dawning, an age effectively distinguished by the radical contributions of scientists like Pasteur in bio-chemistry, Geddes in bio-sociology, and artists like Rodin—if one may conclude the verbal parallel—in bio-sculpture.

But "living" in architecture means in adequate relation to life. It does not mean an imitation in stone or metal of the external appearance of organic form: houses with mushroom roofs or rooms shaped like the corolla of a flower. It was not flowered wallpaper that was needed in the modern house, but space and sunlight and temperature conditions under which living plants could grow: not pliant and moving lines in the furniture, but furniture that responded adequately to the anatomical form and physiological needs of the body: chairs that furthered good posture and gave repose, beds that favored sexual intercourse and permitted deep slumber. In short: a physical environment that responded sensitively to the vital and personal needs of the occupants.

Symbolically, the Art Nouveau architects were right in exhibiting and glorifying life: practically, they were mistaken, because in their art they exerted most of their zeal to provide only a formal counterfeit: mere ornamental forms. The problem for the new age was to create a new type of living environment: to enable people to live in cities without losing the fellowship of nature, and to group together for the sake of specialized social activities without losing the means of good health and the decent nurture of children. None of these needs could be satisfied by mere ornament, no matter how whimsically imaginative, or how vitally fluent that ornament might be. Architecture required structural forms which were organically at one with life: flexible, adaptable, renewable.

For this reason the reaction against l'Art Nouveau in Europe, which took shape in the cubist movement in painting, and in the con·

structivist movement in architecture, pointed form once more in the right direction. (The movement had never really taken hold in America, and Wright's early work needed no such admonition.) Contrary to l'Art Nouveau, the symbolism of cubism was mistaken: it glorified the machine as an unmitigated benefactor of mankind, in strange innocence of all the social horrors that had accompanied capitalist exploitation; it placed an excessive emphasis upon formal geometrical shapes, particularly the rectangle and the cube which do not characterize real machines; and it proposed to turn the dwelling house into a machine, without explaining why mechanism should exercise such a one-sided control over life. But cubism was the necessary corrective of the dogma of the wavy line which, in pursuing the external forms of life, forgot the objective conditions: the form of a bowl, as conditioned by the potter's wheel: the form of a room, as conditioned by the economic placement of beams, posts, windows.

Instead of disguising the forms of modern construction under a load of decoration, the cubists sought to dramatize them. The cubists went out of their way to use concrete, to exhibit cantilever construction, to raise the house above the ground on steel columns. And instead of seeking to display the egoistic touch of the individual architect, they sought after an anonymous method of design and a collective formula. Structurally speaking cubism performed an important work of purification: it divorced itself from capitalist canons of reputability and expense, and it cleared the ground for a fresh start. In its keen appreciation of the products of the machine (led by artists like Marcel Duchamp), it pointed toward more conspicuous efforts to achieve clean forms within other branches of industry than architecture.

Although cubism had at the beginning a certain bias against living forms, the fact is that the machine itself is a product and an instrument of life: the more perfect it becomes, the more it simulates the automatisms and self-regulating devices of real organisms and the more finely it mimics the eye, the ear, the voice, the memory. In the attempt to use the machine adequately and create a more universal order, the collective interests of cubism inevitably led toward the formulation, in modern terms, of a theory of the city.

Under the leadership of Le Corbusier the cubists ceased to con-cern themselves alone with the isolated architectural product: they passed on to the urban environment as a whole, and sought to place the entire process of building and re-building on a fresh foundation.

Le Corbusier himself began with the stale nineteenth century no-tion of the city so often explored in the time-romances of Mr. H. G. Wells: *la ville mécanique.* His early schemes explore a series of blind alleys: the skyscraper city, the traffic city, finally the grotesque combination of the two in a curving viaduct whose supports were to be filled with apartment houses. But by a steady process of re-formulation he has drawn closer to the biotechnic notion of *la ville radieuse:* a marked ideological improvement, and his plan for Nemours is one of the best rational layouts that has yet appeared. Thus life re-enters the picture, not in the form of extraneous orna-ment, but in the demand for air, sunlight, gardens, parks, play-grounds, recreation fields, and all the various forms of social equip-ment that are necessary for the stimulating life of the city: informal places of meeting and relaxation, like the café, and formal places of purposive education, like the museum and the university. In the orientation of architecture toward life and the processes of life the architect began with the decoration of the house: he ends with the city.

In their attempt actively to incorporate the machine into architec-ture the cubists were sometimes misled by a static and external con-ception of the machine; but unconsciously they were recognizing the direct tribute that the mechanical arts owed to improvements that were first made in the culture of living things, particularly in horti-culture. The first evolved pattern of the new architecture appeared in the glass hothouse: the Crystal Palace in London was but the monumental embodiment of this mutation. Just as the Crystal Palace was the work of an engineer in the service of horticulture, so, by reverse process, the new system of ferro-concrete construction was the invention of the gardener, Monnier, seeking to build more effi-cient bird baths and fountain basins for his gardens.

The new improvements in domestic heating, too, were originally the conception of gardeners. One of the first persons to suggest steam heating was Sir Hugh Platt, who had the notion of conveying heat from a steam boiler on a kitchen stove through pipes to growing plants in order to keep them at a temperate heat, no matter what the conditions of the weather outside. In 1745 Platt's suggestion was improved by Sir William Cook, who published a diagram for heating all the rooms in the house from the kitchen fire. The full importance of these inventions was grasped for the first time by Paxton himself. In a letter to the Illustrated London News (July 5, 1851) he sketched out the design of a Crystal Sanitorium: not merely to give patients the benefit of extra oxygen from the growing plants, but for the sake of sunlight and room wherein to exercise in all weather. To make this possible, he suggested the installation of apparatus to provide filtered and heated air: the first proposal for complete air-conditioning—not as a mere remedy against baneful gases, as in mines or in the British House of Parliament, but as a positive aid to health.

Thus the new methods of construction, the new materials, and the new means of regulating the air of a building in order to adapt it more perfectly to the needs of living occupants *came directly from the biotechnics of gardening.* These changes were to prove more important to human welfare than the symbolic incorporation of floral shapes by means of carved ornaments and curved trusses.

Taken together, modern form, modern architecture, modern communities are prophetic emergents of a biotechnic society: a society whose productive system and consumptive demands will be directed toward the maximum possible nurture, under ever more adequate material conditions, of the human group, and the maximum possible culture of the human personality. What has so far been accomplished is but a taste of the more thoroughgoing order that is to come. So far, architecture and community planning have aided experimentally in the clarification of this order: but further re-valuations of doctrine and belief, further accretions of positive knowledge, will in turn alter profoundly the new communities we are in process of building. Throughout the world, a consensus is gradually being established among men of good will and effective competence. Let us then attempt to seek further the social basis of modern form, and to establish even more definitively its underlying principles.

2: Principles of Modern Form—Economy

Perhaps the main guiding principle of modern architecture is economy: economy of material, economy of means, economy of expression. And the reason why economy occupies the very center of our thought is that it is a sign of orderly understanding and perfect control—like the cut of a diver's body through the air, hitting the water without a splash.

Let us begin with the most elementary statement of economy: modern means of construction. Under past systems of architecture the actual strength and mass of a structure was determined by empiric practice: if a tower fell down, its foundations were too feeble or its top too heavy: a bad guess. Not merely is there a considerable range of difference between the strength of various natural materials; but there existed no reliable means for working out the tensile and compression strengths of various types of members: indeed, in some of their temples the Greeks, eager to reinforce their stones, carved channels for iron rods that actually weakened the structure.

During the last half century the creation of new manufactured building materials, like steel and reinforced concrete, with determinable strengths, determinable coefficients of expansion, radically altered the problem of building: it decreased the need for large solid members that built up into great sculptural masses. To use the least possible amount of material compatible with safety has become a mark of fine calculation and intelligent architectural insight: to be oversized, or overweight, is a sign of technical uncouthness, even if not immediately apparent to the eye. Building codes, framed according to the canons of guesswork, with an absurd margin of over-safety, do not generally recognize this change: but building codes, throughout the world, are overdue for revision.

The very interest in economy has given a special sanction to the lighter materials, which are easier to transport and usually easier to erect: the metal framework, the glass or composite surface to serve as sheath for the inner space, the flexible partition, have taken the place of clumsier and more static members. The esthetic attitude that goes with these new materials was very well put by J. J. P. Oud, the Dutch architect, one of the most able exponents of the new form:

"In place of the natural charm of walls and roofs of rough materials, unstable in their plasticity and uncertainly patined; in place of windows cut into small panes, nebulously glazed and irregularly colored; a new architecture will offer us the definite values of artificial materials, surfaces polished and finished, the scintillation of steel and the brilliance of paint, the transparent openness of large windows of plate glass. . . . Architectural evolution will lead us toward a style that will appear liberated from matter, although it is joined to it more completely than ever."

The entire functional development of architecture from the fifteenth century on, as Meyer remarked, is a response to the demand: "More light!" This development has thrown the structural emphasis from the supporting wall or column to the interior skeleton, from the enclosing *mass* to the bounding surface, from architectural form as the sculpture of solids to architectural form as the definition and articulation of voids. The age of crustacean building has given way to the age of vertebrates, and the wall, no longer a protective shell, has become a skin. Other organic changes within buildings have necessarily followed this development: a specialization of parts, a finer articulation of the various members, a system for maintaining a standard interior temperature and for renovating the air, which may be compared, roughly, with the action of heart and lungs in the body—while similarly the organization of the functions of ingestion (light, air, water, coal, gas, electricity) and that of excretion (inorganic and organic waste) has modified the nature of practically every structure.

The building is no longer a passive shell: it is a functioning organization in which the primitive aspect of shelter, as embodied in the original cave, and of symbol, as embodied in the monument, have become secondary attributes of more complicated processes. Some of these functions have indeed been provided for in other systems of architecture: they reached a high point in the eotechnic wood-and-water culture of the Japanese. But now their range has been extended through new forms of industrial fabrication, and their integration and expression, in fresh form, had become imperative.

To resist the use of these new materials and forms of construction is to resist the possibilities of order today. Not merely must one reject the decadent style-mongering of the suburban bourgeoisie, not merely must one throw over the obsolete grandiosities of height or expanse beloved by the conceited dictators of finance or government: one must reject, as still fundamentally inadequate, those more sensible stereotypes of traditional architecture embodied in the otherwise sound and generously planned cottages built by governmental agents, for example, in numerous English housing estates. Modern life has more to offer than these sober compromises and collective timidities would indicate. We do not glue feathers on the wings of airplanes because men have always associated flight with the forms of birds; and there is no reason why, to pay respect to traditional notions of domesticity, we should resort to similar practices in the building of houses—as if what architecture had now to offer the housewife were not something infinitely more attractive to her than slate roofs and roughly smeared stucco walls. The eighteenth century American farmhouse was a gracious traditional form: its fine lines and just proportions, which owed none of their charm to ornamental superfluity, derived from the same technics and culture that built its water mills and its wooden ships. Such harmony between the various parts of the environment is what architecture today requires, worked out in terms of contemporary order.

Even when, for the sake of harmony with the natural surroundings, natural materials may be appropriately used, the modern principle of economy will dictate that they be used in their modern technical form, not in more traditional shapes inherited from an incongruent past: not heavy half-timbers and ponderous oak paneling, for example, but sawed beams and light plywood paneling.

What is true of materials and construction is naturally also true of plan. Here, too, economy must prevail. A modern plan is successful only when it embraces every human need appropriate to the structure without waste of space, duplication, clumsy and inefficient means of circulation. This principle of economy is socially the opposite of the ancient canon of conspicuous waste. For the latter principle, in the interest of pecuniary and caste distinctions, emphasized the rôle of superfluity: rooms were scaled, not to their specific human uses, but solely for the purpose of impressing the spectator, no matter how difficult they might be to heat, or how oppressive they might feel to the individual occupant. Rooms were often duplicated on the plan, too, on either side of an axis, merely for the sake of achieving a formal balance for the eye of the observer outside. So, too, decoration would overlay the structural form: the product of the woodturner was marked with bulges, beads, indentations, which collected dust: the oak paneling was carved in floral or heraldic designs, and the ceiling was plastered with complicated geometric figures. Wherever a clear space remained, it was filled with some product of handicraft or *virtu*, partly because the craftsman himself delighted in such fantasies, even more because the patron took pleasure in sheer excess. Beauty? Perhaps. Show? Decidedly. A barn, a kitchen, a fortress might be built according to the canons of economy; but not works that symbolized social station or social function.

If economy today derives partly from the finer scientific calculations and the complicated inventions that enter into modern building —*inventions whose cost must be offset in other departments*—it has a social and esthetic basis as well. The social principle underlying the canon of economy rests on the fact that there is no modern utility or machine that we do not conceive as universal in its application. We do not have one type of electric light for the rich and another for the poor; we do not have one type of telephone, carved out of some ornate and precious material for the rich, and another type made of inferior materials, for peasants and clerks. All these instruments have an objective standard of performance, determinable by experiment: they are the products of a collective economy and are meant to fit into a collective whole. One's economic position may entitle one to a greater or smaller quantity, but the quality is fixed.

With respect to the fundamental goods of modern life, a basic equality has been partly established, and more and more goods and services are coming into line: this principle has even made its way into realms like clothes where class differences were once duly established by law, and where conspicuous differential waste for long went unchallenged. Such equalization rests in good part on the economies of mass production or on the no less important economies, as in municipal utilities, of collective distribution based on a social monopoly. Mass production itself demands, esthetically, an emphasis upon the generic, the standardized: upon forms freed from irregularity, superfluity,, and imaginative caprice. *In order to make collective production and distribution possible on a scale that will embrace a whole society, economy must be a regulating principle in all design: for it is only by saving on the means and instrumentalities of life that a community can command the necessary abundance at the higher levels of art, science, education, and expression.* Economy, which in an earlier culture signified niggardliness, now provides the means for collective largesse. Holding to this principle means having enough to go round.

There is, however, an additional esthetic basis for economy in modern architecture. It lies in the fact that we live in a far more complicated world than that of the primitive craftsman and peasant: even the most limited person today in our urban communities is played upon by forces and stimuli so numerous, so insistent, so diverting, that he can achieve internal peace only by stripping to the essentials the visual environment. When there were no textbooks of natural history, no museums, no scientific abstracts, no illustrated papers and magazines, it might be amusing and instructive to have the animals in Noah's ark carved on a cathedral: then, truly, in Hugo's phrase, the cathedral was the stone book of mankind. But such decoration today is for the most part a distraction, at best a stale repetition of something that exists in more adequate form in treatises on biology and in museums of science. We demand that our modern environment become more legible, and above all, more serene. The clean surface, the candid revelation of function, the plain conspicuous lettering or symbolism of a sign or a building— these are the conditions that redefine our sense of beauty in urban structures.

To appreciate art and sculpture, as emotional experiences, we must detach them from the function of building: their permanent, non-detachable place has disappeared with the stone forms and the solid walls and stable relations which gave them their functional setting in other cultures. Much of the current demand for murals today is esthetically and socially atavistic: the mural that goes with the modern building is the poster: a form that can be duplicated, broadcast, and frequently renewed. The London Underground has been a more intelligent patron of modern art than more pompous public bodies—such as the United States Post Office—that choose to work in terms of an obsolete social situation.

The true symbol of the modern age in architecture is the *absence* of visible symbols: we no longer seek on the surface that which we can obtain effectively only through penetration and participation in the function of a structure. As our sense of the invisible forces at work in the actual environment increases—not merely our sense of physical processes below the threshold of common observation, but psychological and social processes too—as this sense increases we will tend to ask architecture itself to assume a lower degree of visibility: spectator's architecture, show architecture, will give way to a more thoroughgoing sense of form, not so conspicuous perhaps on the surface, but capable of giving intellectual and emotional stimulus at every step in its revelation.

Carried out imaginatively, the principle of economy becomes a positive pleasure in building: a sign of right relationship with life. Ships show this sense of economy, from modern sailing craft to the ocean liner: so do a great variety of machines; so, for the greater part, do dams and power-stations and factories. Perhaps one of the finest examples, not merely of utilitarian accomplishment but of positive esthetic impulse, is the modern American kitchen, even in houses that frequently contradict all its good features in every other room. Such economy is the moral flower of that long discipline of the spirit which Western man has undertaken during the last millennium under the forms of monasticism, capitalism, militarism, and mechanism: forms in which life was denied, rather than enhanced, for the ulterior purpose of holiness or power. Today, as we slough off the skin of old social habits, economy is at last ready to flow out of these life-constraining departments into a more balanced, a less sterile, human habitat.

3: The Rôle of Hygiene

Hygiene and sanitation were not unknown in other civilizations: what community could have survived the ordeal of close permanent quarters without a certain respect for their laws? But in our new biotechnic economy hygiene occupies a commanding place: not merely does it mean public defenses against disease: it means taking positive steps to make the whole environment favorable to health, animal joy, and length of days.

As long as the body was dualistically separated from mind, its systematic care might be slighted. But the new scientific conception of the organism that grew up in the nineteenth century reunited the physiological and the psychological processes: thus the care of the body became once more a moral and an esthetic discipline. By his researches in bacteriology Pasteur altered the conception of both the external and the internal environment of organisms; and with the progress of medicine, physicians turned attention from the noting of symptoms to the analysis of causes, from a one-sided readjustment of the organism through medication or surgery, to a many-sided readjustment that includes diet, habitation, regimen, social and psychological relations.

Partly, the nineteenth century interest in hygiene and sanitation was an automatic reaction: compensation against the miserably insanitary conditions, the devitalized diet, the constant state of ill-health and enfeeblement, in which the denizens of the nineteenth century towns lived. Advances in the biological sciences, in turn, threw into relief the misdemeanors of the new environment: its lack of sunlight and ultra-violet rays, its frequently infected public water supply, its wholesale materialization of conditions favorable to organic dissipation, physiological maladjustment, and disease.

Modern hygiene has established the fact that most of our cities, not least those big ones built mainly during the last fifty years, are biologically speaking life-inimical or life-destructive environments. When their crude rates for death and disease, of which boast is so often made, are subjected to critical analysis and correction for age-distribution, statistics prove that at almost every stage in life, the rural area with poor medical facilities and a crude system of sanitation is nevertheless decisively superior as an environment of life to the urban area, though the latter be equipped with all the latest services in medicine and sanitation. Moreover, there is an equally significant correlation between size and health: in general the bigger the city the poorer its showing. And there is an equally important correlation between biological fertility and the urban environment: not merely does the city reproduce at a lower rate than the country, but the bigger the city the lower the rate of reproduction. The highest expectations of life go with a country environment and the less industrialized occupations. (See Warren Thompson and the Report of the National Resources Committee on Cities.)

The effect of this biological knowledge, and the fresh interests that have developed with it, is further to shift the center of gravity from the world of the mine and the factory, to the world of the farmstead and the garden. The drift to the suburbs, which has been one of the most conspicuous features of the growth of cities during the past half century, was one response to the more constant concern with health and education that has characterized the life of the middle classes. The cult of cleanliness, upon which modern hygiene fundamentally depends, had its origins, as I have already pointed out, before the nineteenth century: it owes much to the Dutch cities of the seventeenth century, with their plentiful water supplies, their large house windows showing relentlessly every particle of dust in the interior, their tiled floors: the scrubbing and scouring and shining of the Dutch housewife became proverbial. But cleanliness got new reinforcements from medicine after 1870: instead of being a delicate upper class taste, scarcely popular even in aristocratic circles in the eighteenth century, it became a universal necessity. As a result, the farmer milking a cow today takes sanitary precautions which a London surgeon did not trouble to take before performing a major operation, until Lister taught him better. Hygiene magnified the importance of the water supply: not merely demanding purity, but increasing steadily the quantity necessary, as the habits of bathing and washing spread in widening circles from one economic group to another.

At last the paleotechnic indifference to darkness and dirt was exposed as a monstrous barbarism. Frequent hand washing and body washing, to say nothing of clothes washing, made the provision of running water an imperative element in house-planning or community-building. Whereas bathrooms were frequently not provided even for the finest houses early in the nineteenth century, by the end of the century the standard of a separate bathtub for every family—and if possible a separate bathroom—became a minimum ideal, if not an actual achievement, in every rational housing program. In lieu of this, large public bath-houses and public wash-houses were provided for the neighborhood.

With increasing rigor and effectiveness these hygienic requirements extended to the disposal of human excrement, garbage, and waste. The water-closet, invented by Sir John Harrington in 1596, was not perfected until 1778 when the inventive Bramah took a hand in its design. In the course of a century the installation of water-closets in urban houses rose rapidly: by the end of the nineteenth century the standard of one water-closet for every family became the most imperative sanitary precaution for close-built communities throughout the Western World. These individual improvements in the hygienic equipment of dwellings made a radical alteration in costs: together with instruments for lighting and heating the dwelling, refrigerating its food, and bringing it into contact with the outside world through telephone and radio, the new mechanical inventions accounted for an increasing proportion of the cost and upkeep of the structure: the shell cost relatively less, but the "internal organs" multiplied and the costs rose with them.

All these individual changes, moreover, had important collective consequences: they introduced the habit of municipal socialization as a normal accompaniment to improved mechanical service. The rationale of this development should be plain. The collective utilities necessary for the functioning of buildings and cities are in the main natural monopolies. Water had become too much a matter of public concern in big cities to be left to the supply of individual water companies, selling their product only to those who could afford to pay for the services, and continuing in business only so long as the company could show a profit. It became important to distribute pure water, for the sake of health, whether or not a particular family wanted it or could afford it. Such matters could no longer be left to whim. These facts held equally true of the systems for disposing of garbage, waste, and sewage.

In smaller centers private companies might be left with the privilege of maintaining these services, or they might even be left to the individual until some notorious outbreak of disease occurred through carelessness: but in the bigger cities, socialization was the price of safety; and so, despite the theoretic claims of laissez-faire, the nine-teenth century became, as the Webbs properly pointed out, the cen-tury of municipal socialism. Each individual improvement within the building demanded its collectively owned and operated utility: water mains, water reservoirs, pumping stations: garbage wagons and rubbish wagons, incinerators and dumps: sewage mains, sewage reduction plants, sewage farms. Through this effective and wide-spread socialization, the general death rate and infant mortality tended to fall, after the eighteen-seventies: and the social investment of municipal capital in these utilities enormously rose.

And incidentally, the nature of the city itself changed, under pres-sure of these new utilities, just as radically as the nature of the new building: a greater share of its essential services was organized in underground systems: no less important than the visible structures and streets. As with the dwelling house, the potential improvements were partly frustrated through imaginative failure in revising the plan, layout, and structural requirements of the city. Even the theoretic formulation of the needs and opportunities of this more complex urban structure seriously lagged until 1920: in the minds of planners pictorial compositions were uppermost: only to be dis-placed, in the interests of the "practical," by equally half-baked avenue extensions and traffic plans and multiple streets.

From the establishment of personal cleanliness, new standards of hygiene spread to the dwelling house itself, and eventually to other parts of the environment. In 1877 Downes and Blunt established the bactericidal properties of light: the popularization of the camera, during the ensuing decades, likewise tended to make people photo-sensitive: but although architects like Richardson, Mackintosh and Wright sensitively recorded this change, the constant importance of natural light as an accompaniment and accessory of all living func-tions except sleep was slow to be recognized. Here again patho-logical conditions called attention to the more normal human uses: the importance of sunlight and fresh air in treating tuberculosis played a strong part, and the discovery of the rôle of ultra-violet rays in promoting growth was scarcely less critical. An interior accessible to light and air, above all in winter days in the upper latitudes, became a new requirement of good building design: this means shallow rooms, shallow buildings, careful orientation with respect to sunlight and prevailing winds.

Further scientific inquiry into the process of ventilation disclosed other facts of hygienic importance: the need for regulating temperature, humidity, and circulation of air toward appropriate optimums in both summer and winter. The New York State Commission on Ventilation discovered, for example, that the output of work fell 15 per cent when the temperature of the workroom was raised from 68 to 75 degrees, and that it was reduced by 37 per cent when the temperature was raised to 85 degrees. Similarly, the likelihood of incubating colds seems to be increased in temperatures above 68 degrees. The factors are so complicated that only in a rough way can ideal conditions as yet be laid down; but the possibility of discovering optimum conditions, adjusted to regional peculiarities of weather and climate, lies in no very remote future.

These things, at all events, are plain: air must stir, sunlight must penetrate, dirt must be eliminated, waste must be removed. From the furnishing of the room to the layout of the neighborhood, these requirements must be reflected in every detail. The closed court, the symbol of medieval protection, is not a modern form: the glass window that cannot be thrown wide to the sun is not a modern form, even though it be hung in a steel frame and opened automatically: floor coverings and window coverings that cannot be freely washed and sunned are not hygienically acceptable.

Only to a small degree are these various hygienic requirements met in the great bulk of urban buildings; and structures built after the eighteenth century are frequently much worse offenders against the decencies of hygiene than those erected before. Even many buildings of superficially modern design, with wide window openings or air-conditioning equipment, are in their plan and spacing far inferior to earlier examples. To achieve sunlight, air, health, in close urban quarters is usually beyond the skill of any individual architect: it involves a considerable knowledge of physiography, climatology, and astronomy, ordinarily not within the conventional province of the architect or the municipal engineer: good form is a collective product and requires collective collaboration in its production. No continuing cleanliness is possible in a city that harbors paleotechnic industries whose smoke and chemical effluvia have not been eliminated. Merely in order to provide daily sunbaths for growing infants, it is imperative to move the black industries outside a town and erect a permanent barrier of green open space between them and the rest of the community.

The point to be noted is that if the principles of hygiene are valid and important, they must be applied, not alone in the hospital or the home, but also in every other part of the environment. The factories and offices and stores in which the greater part of every urban population spends half its waking hours must be planned for a maximum living and working efficiency. Who can pretend that with all our advances in purely constructional technique any corresponding advances have been made here over a wide area? Individual factories on the outskirts of cities have sometimes achieved good form: say the Van Nelle Factory near Rotterdam. But the overbuilding and overcrowding of land, which has marked the development of office buildings in almost every city has added to the lethal qualities of bureaucratic routine: the dead airless space in these buildings is serious handicap to the work of the staff.

Here the need is obvious: the minimum standards for light and air and density that have been worked out for schools should apply equally to any and all business structures. If this does not fit in with the existing scheme of financial values, these values must be deflated. Instead of regarding the purely monumental swaggering of the skyscraper as the emblem of modern construction, every new office quarter must be planned with shallow buildings, duly oriented for light, spaced in such a fashion that the height shall never be greater than the space between the buildings to the front and the rear. Zoning ordinances that were constructed with due regard for positive scientific knowledge would establish these standards; whereas the metetricious height and setback regulations first introduced into the United States by the municipality of New York had no relation to these standards: their sole use was to establish the legal principle of control. On the principle here outlined, skyscrapers might still be built; but never without a sufficient area of open land to remove the possibility of congestion and blight—and incidentally the possibility of profit from congestion.

Hygiene demands, finally, that the quality of air, even when freed from noxious fumes and smoke, must be improved by the simplest means of renovation: open spaces filled with verdure and shrubbery, which not merely tend to equalize the temperature and freshen the air, but which provide the necessary relaxation for body and mind. Gardens are for delight, and delight by itself is an important factor in the maintenance of health. The dull and the dejected are more susceptible to infection than those who are in tone; and the worst months for health in the temperate zones are the shrouded months of winter, the indoor months, when only the more adventurous of city folk seek the open field and the waterside.

From the standpoint of hygiene, parks and gardens are not luxuries for the fortunate minority: they are essential if the city is to become a permanent habitat for man. The city that adequately commands the resources of modern civilization is not the city of stretched wharves and ships bringing goods from the ends of the earth: it is not the city of skyscraping towers that darken and congest the streets: it is not the city of the widest concrete roadways, the longest double-decked automobile drives, and the most overcrowded subways—it is the city in which every quarter is ribboned with gardens and parks. The Schrebergärten movement, which has been such a sanative influence in the congested German metropolises, giving the tenement dweller a small cultivation patch on the unused land of the outskirts, is but a first step toward ruralizing the urban environment. What the baroque planner gave to the palace and the upper class residential quarter alone, we now conceive as essential for every part of the city.

4: The Prolongation of Youth

England's early pre-eminence in the Black Industries has sometimes concealed the fact that she also led the revolt against this foul regime. This was not merely true of the English cult of nature, so pervasive, so devoted: but in the fact that games and sports, from the early nineteenth century on, came to occupy a greater share of everyone's leisure. Whether Waterloo was won on the playing fields of Eton is doubtful; most of her soldiers on that field had never gone to Eton: but the discipline of sport has not merely taught lessons

in government and co-operative give-and-take that have been useful
for political life: the relaxation of sport has contributed to that
prolongation of youth which is perhaps the most significant biological trait of modern civilization. Is it not perhaps one of the reasons, along with a fuller dietary, a more careful sanitation, a more
prudent physical regimen, for the astounding prolongation of life
during the last century? Retarding maturity, we have increased the
span of senescence.

By keeping girls and boys in a state of healthy distraction, by
spreading more widely the preparation for professional service, modern society, particularly among the higher economic classes, has post-
poned the period of family responsibility. By making contraceptives available, it has helped put off childbearing to the desirable
period of maturity. Whereas the women of many savage tribes or
primitive agricultural regimes are old at twenty-five, through early
responsibility and premature child-bearing, a well-bred modern
woman remains active and wide-awake and sexually attractive well
into her very belated senescence. Though this effect is slightly less
noticeable among males, it nevertheless is equally real: look at the
bearded sombre faces of the typical Victorian youths, and compare
them with the fresh, biologically youthful faces of much older men
today. Sport, play, and diminished sexual anxiety probably make
the difference.

The cult of sport and the more suave care of the physical body
proceeded from the country house and the English public school, set
near a playing field. Only belatedly did they make their way into the
heart of the city. In America, the first public playgrounds date back
to 1871. No less significant than the provision of special urban places
for children's play is the provision of special recreation grounds
serving equally the adult: the public tennis court, the golf course,
to say nothing of the general dedication of beaches to the more ancient pastime of bathing.

Our whole conception of a well-balanced environment has been
altered by this cult of the body. In its specialized metropolitan
forms, with its vast gladiatorial arenas for the professional exhibition
of wrestlers and prize fighters, it has inevitably taken a degraded
form; and the multiplication of such great stadia with their mass

spectacles is not necessarily desirable. But special provision for the play of children must be made in each housing quarter, and in each neighborhood, if it is to fulfill its function as a biotechnic environ- ment: a provision in which relatively few cities have as yet caught up with needs, and in which many otherwise well-meaning efforts at better housing have likewise fallen short.

While the passing age prided itself upon its vast congeries of hospitals, from that at Edinburgh in the nineteenth century to such overpowering structures as the new Medical Centers, in New York, the mark of the biotechnic period will be the number of playgrounds, swimming pools, and beaches a city can afford. Here, admittedly, the great metropolises have taken the leadership in creating collective facilities for sport and play: the great stadium at Frankfurt-am- Main is an example. Such recreation and exercise was the privilege of the aristocratic minority in Athens: today these opportunities are open to every well-administered community: promising that physical dilation and pride which will increase the joy, the confidence, and the self-respect of the participants. Whereas in the tawdry commercial "playland" of an Indiana industrial town one might read over its portals the dismaying puritanic injunction—"Play Hard so that you may Work Hard"—over the playgrounds of the new age one may write with better sense, remembering the close association be- tween the Athenian palestra and the academy, the motto of another Indiana town—"Work, Study, Play." Youth takes sport seriously and achieves discipline; maturity takes sport playfully, and achieves youth.

5: Bi-polar Domesticity

The reduction of the household to a biological unit has been one of the most consequential steps in the whole process of urbanization. It is closely tied to two conditions which distinguish a biotechnic culture from cultures in which the nurture of life was an incidental by-product of existence. The first of these is the growing care of the child: an appreciation of childhood as a valuable phase of life in itself, not as an ordeal that is hastily to be passed through in order to attain the more blissful state of adult responsibility and autonomy. In modern times, the cult of the child began with Rousseau: out of his own sinister guilts and conflicts with respect to procreation he achieved a fresh view of the relationship: in its essentials, his views were fundamentally sound, from his preachment to mothers—Nurse your infants!—on to his conception that a life of activity in a simple natural environment was the best accompaniment to a child's normal growth. Up to this point, children had been little men and little women. Slowly, they came to achieve a life of their own in an environment that was—in families where choice was economically permitted—more and more molded to their activities.

This growing intensity of interest in the life of children was increased, no doubt, by the practice of birth control, which reduced the possibility of replacement, and made the individual child more precious to the parent, as well as the object of more concentrated attention and tender care. Birth control, indeed, has had a dual effect upon the family relation: it has introduced an element of deliberate choice in a situation where a capricious Providence had hitherto prevailed, it has given childbearing itself the special moral value which only objects of free choice have, and it has introduced the possibility of a more rational ordering of the individual phases of life—lengthening the period of erotic experiment and permitting parenthood to take place at the period of fullest physiological capacity.

At the same time, of course, contraception has vastly increased the erotic possibilities of marriage itself, as well as opening a door to bi-lateral erotic relationships outside marriage: there is no comparison whatever between a married pair of the sixteenth century, whose sexual life would normally be interrupted by a series of pregnancies right up to the menopause, and a married pair in the twentieth century: the difference is as great as that between the blessed Thomas More's conception of the sexual act, which he compared to the voiding of urine, and that of Havelock Ellis. Erotic courtship and the fullness of erotic expression are no longer wholly accidental and uncertain delights: still less are they confined to lubricious specialists in sex: they occupy an ever more abundant part of the daily life of healthy men and women. Despite its bludgeoning absolutisms, its vicious wars, the twentieth century may yet be known as the age of sexual efflorescence. In paradoxical fashion, domesticity and eroticism, once enemies as far apart as Antony's Octavia and his Cleopatra, have now advanced together.

These facts have an important bearing upon the place of the dwelling in the urban economy, and upon the internal design of the structure itself. For one thing, the child is no less entitled to space than the adult: he must have shelves and cupboards for his toys, room for play and movement, a place for quiet retreat and study, other than his bed. No housing standard is adequate that provides only cubicles or dressing rooms for the child, or forces him into the constant company of adults. The dwelling must be so arranged, so spaced, that the routine of physical care and the overseeing of activities shall demand the least wasteful sacrifice on the part of the mother: architects, even the best of them, still have much to learn in the proper arrangement of kitchen, living room, playroom, and garden.

At the same time, every part of the dwelling must be arranged equally with an eye to sexual privacy and untrammeled courtship. Private bedrooms alone are not enough: soundproof partitions are equally important, and in communal units soundproof floors. One of the reasons that the poor are so inept at using contraceptives is that the sanest and simplest devices a woman may use still require, if sexual joy is not to be changed into a sordid mockery, such facilities as go only with a well-equipped bathroom. Sexual intercourse must not forever be doomed, except for the luxuriously rich, to take place only, like burglary, under cover of darkness, in that part of the day when the energies are fast ebbing away: but before it can occur at any other times many weaknesses in house design will have to be rectified. Even at some little extra cost in corridor space the architect must eventually learn in house and in apartment design to separate the children's wing from the adult's wing.

And this restriction works both ways: for as children draw on toward maturity, they need, no less than their parents, inviolate apartments in which their hot discussions, their high confidences, their first essays in courtship, may take place. For lack of such space in America, a whole generation of girls and boys has grown up, cramped in the vulgar promiscuities of the automobile, from which they are too often graduated proudly into the no less shabby intimacies of the roadhouse or the overnight cabin: carrying into their erotic life the taint of something that is harried, esthetically embarrassing and emotionally disintegrating. The home, the garden, the park, must be planned for lovers and for love-making: that is an essential aspect of an environment designed for human growth. Love-making and home-making, eroticism and domesticity, sexual delight and the assiduous nurture of children—these are among the highest human goals of genuine biotechnic planning. Everything from the distribution of open spaces to the heights of windows is affected by this program; and the sooner the architect and planner faces these facts of contemporary life and evaluates them intelligently, the quicker will he throw off the clichés of old-fashioned design, and the sooner will he realize that a great many of the economies in plan that have recently been effected have been purchased at too high a price. Good design means going back to fundamentals: a child at work in a stable and reassuring world: a pair of lovers at play in a room where the scent of lilacs may creep through the window, or the shrill piping of crickets be heard in the garden below.

6: The Death of the Monument

One of the most important attributes of a vital urban environment is one that has rarely been achieved in past civilizations: the capacity for renewal. Against the fixed shell and the static monument, the new architecture places its faith in the powers of social adaptation and reproduction. The sign of the older order of architecture, in almost every culture, was the House of the Dead: in modern culture, it is the dwelling house, or House of the Living, renewable generation by generation.

The human impulse to create everlasting monuments springs perhaps out of the desire of the living to perpetuate themselves: to overcome the flux and evanescence of all living forms. To achieve this in terms of biology only one means is possible: organic reproduction. All the classic civilizations, above all that of the Chinese, have regarded the begetting of children as a sacred duty. Renewal through reproduction is the vulgar means of ensuring continuity: this and the transmission of the social heritage through memory, imitation and the written record. But there is still another means, springing not out of life and its renewing impulses, but out of death: a desire to wall out life, to exclude the action of time, to remove the taint of biological processes, to exclude the active care of other generations by a process of architectural mummification. The primitive burial mounds, the big stones of the Salisbury Plains or Brittany, the Pyramids and Sphinxes of Egypt, the grandiose gestures of a Sargon or an Ozymandias, of a Louis XIV or a Peter the Great: these represent that respect for death which is essentially a fear of life.

Ordinary men and women must be content to fix their image in their children. But the eminent and the powerful do not have sufficient faith in these powers of renewal: in their vanity, they seek a petrified immortality: they write their boasts upon tombstones; they incorporate their deeds in obelisks; they place their hopes of remembrance in solid stones joined to other solid stones, dedicated to their subjects or their heirs forever, forgetful of the fact that stones that are deserted by the living are even more helpless than life that remains unprotected and unpreserved by stones.

More or less, the ancient examples of these priestly and kingly cults have been taken over by civic communities: they, too, tended to sacrifice life to the monument. In general, one may say that the classic civilizations of the world, up to our own, have been oriented toward death and fixity: the immobilization of life. A Heraclitus might observe that all things flow, a Lucretius might see that man is a part of the eternally changing cycle of nature, but the aim of civilization was permanence: its highest achievement in cities was the static grandeur of a Pantheon or a Temple. The more shaky the institution, the more solid the monument: repeatedly civilization has exemplified Patrick Geddes's dictum, that the perfection of the architectural form does not come till the institution sheltered by it is on the point of passing away.

Thanks to this cult, permanence comes in the structures of the city: but death comes with it: the burial ground encroaches on the city and the city, with its mass of dead buildings, duly armored in stone, becomes a burial ground. The temple prepares for death, the monument consecrates it, the sacrificial altar sanctifies it, the learning of the schools rehearses it, the burial vault or the cemetery completes it. These beliefs and habits become pervasive: they eat into urban routine. Records of state, the tables of the law, the correspondence of political functionaries, the decisions of the courts—over all these activities a dead hand, a petrified hand, rules. The very permanence of stone and brick, which enable them to defy time, cause them also ultimately to defy life. Stone gives a false sense of continuity, and a deceptive assurance of life: the shell seems to pledge continuity by the fact that it continues to exist, outwardly unaffected by the passage of events. But the fact is that exterior form can only confirm an inner life: it is not a substitute. All living beliefs, all living desires and ideas, must be perpetually renewed, from generation to generation: re-thought, re-considered, re-willed, re-built, if they are to endure. The blight of ancient Rome upon the imagination of Italy in the ensuing ages bears witness to the congealing strength of the monument: each generation mounts guard on a cemetery, and repeats the password of its dusty challenge.

So long as men where wholly oriented toward death and the timeless, the monument had a meaning: no sacrifice was too great to produce it. Just as a poor Christian family today will spend half a year's income to celebrate fitly the death of one of its members, money that it would find impossible to spare for the birth or education of a child, so the civilizations of the past have sacrificed a good part of their life, their income, their ideologic energy to the monument. For us today, beholding the world with eyes awakened by a Buffon, a Goethe, a Darwin, a profound change has come about in our biological conception of death and immortality: a change that robs monumentalism of its main meaning. Biologically speaking, death is an episode in life's renewal: the terminus of a radical maladaptation. A theoretic immortality may exist for lower forms of life, like the amoeba: it is absent in the higher organisms. Continuity for us exists, not in the individual soul as such, but in the germ plasm and the social heritage, through which we are united to all mankind and to all nature. Renewal comes through the sacrifice of the parent to the child, of the having-lived to the living and the yet-to-live.

Instead of being oriented, then, toward death and fixity, we are

By decree of the Consiglio Maggiore of Venice, in 1291, the glass furnaces at Castello were removed to Murano in order to free the city of industries that were either a nuisance or unhealthy: the pattern formed by the separate island, like this zoning ordinance itself, curiously anticipates the open order of modern urban planning. But modern zoning schemes, not least in America, are chiefly attempts to standardize and stabilize pecuniary values. City development, however, cannot forever be left to individual enterprise: it must be placed, as in Holland, under competent regional and local authorities, who are empowered to purchase land, to design and build and operate new communities—or who may delegate these functions to organizations that will work under their direction. *Functional zoning means a federal organization of a city's internal functions as well as a federal organization of cities within the region.*

[UPPER LEFT] Modern port facilities: Bremerhaven. Adequate arrangement of railroad yards, warehouses, docks, and means of access by water. (*Photograph: Ewing Galloway*)

[UPPER RIGHT] Modern industrial plant: lifted out of the entangling street pattern, surrounded by open land: a well-defined zone appropriately designed for its special needs. Discontinuous zoning of quarters, rather than continuous aggregation along corridor avenues, is characteristic of the new urban plan: each function placed in a specially designed environment and deliberately separated from the flow of traffic except for access. The creation of such zones is impossible in piecemeal planning by unco-ordinated individuals: it demands community planning and building. (*Photograph: Ewing Galloway*)

[MIDDLE] Modern English steelworks with housing for workers in the foreground. Contrast with the paleotechnic developments shown on Plate 11. This new type of plan made possible by the change from the competitive muddle of Victorian enterprise to the orderly public housing program, with state aid and state supervision of standards, put through by public authorities. In this change, England has, especially since 1920, led the world: thus turning the disorderly Black Country with its dark satanic mills into a Green Country. The plan itself, like many similar English examples, is unfortunately mediocre: local streets are too wide, orientation for sunlight is disregarded, the corridor avenue is retained; but the separation of the industrial zone, the agricultural zone, and the domestic zone is admirably clarified. (*Photograph: Aerofilms, Ewing Galloway*)

[BOTTOM] Public Works Administration Housing in Chicago. A sample of biotechnic order in the midst of metropolitan congestion and blight: when trees have grown, this new section will have the comeliness of one of the big quadrangles at Welwyn (see Plate 30). Developments like these will counteract the costly drift to the suburbs and will restore life to many old centers. (*Photograph: U. S. Public Works Administration*)

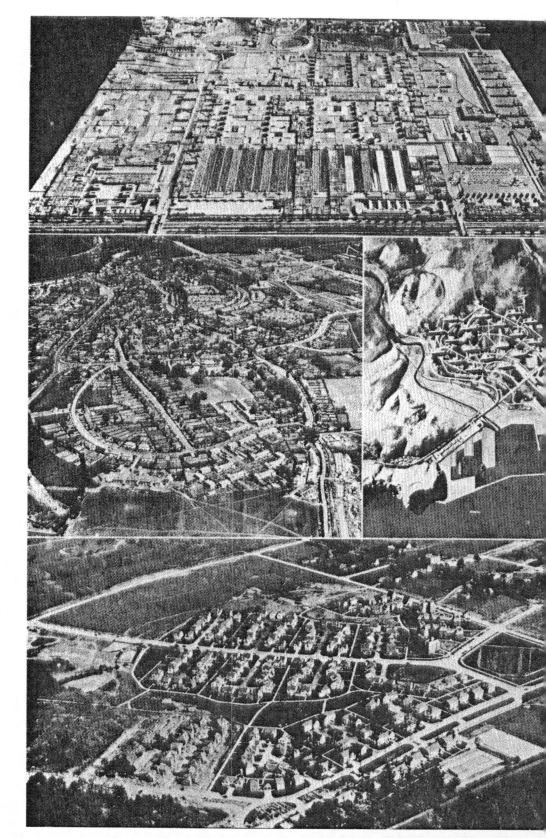

[TOP] Model of Broadacre City, designed by Frank Lloyd Wright. Extreme of decentralized planning: each family has a minimum of one acre of land: the scale of the whole city implies the universal pursuit of agriculture and the universal ownership and use of the motor car. Rectangular section as a design unit is characteristically regional in both historic and topographic sense. Underlying scheme a logical deduction from the premise that the technical means of occasional mobilization now takes the place for special purposes of mobilization by contiguity. Apart from the burden of providing such scattered housing units with necessary collective utilities, this plan makes no provision for the spontaneous association in primary groups—a handicap to mothers and children—nor does it sufficiently allow for close daily contacts as an indispensable element in group life. Broadacre City, then, is partly an overcompensated protest against the reckless and indiscriminate congestion of the metropolis. But its skeletal assumptions are sound. See Wright: The Disappearing City.

[MIDDLE LEFT] Welwyn, England: the second garden city, founded by Ebenezer Howard after the success of Letchworth (1904) was assured. It profited not merely by the government-aided provision of workers' houses but also by the southward migration of industry after 1925: a fact which permitted it in short order to become a balanced town with a strong industrial section: a mixed community. The use of cul-de-sacs and quadrangles is typically English: but the corridor avenue is not consistently abandoned, and the design lacks clarity. Housing through garden cities has now been undertaken by the municipality of Manchester in Wythenshawe, a new town designed by Barry Parker for 100,000 inhabitants, with a permanent agricultural belt of 1,000 acres, and one acre of open space to 50 people. Shopping districts in Wythenshawe are placed at the juncture of four neighborhood units. (*Photograph: Aerofilms*)

[MIDDLE RIGHT] While Le Corbusier's earlier mechanocentric plans for monumental skyscraper cities, with multiple streets, were essentially backward-looking, and his vermicular viaduct roadtown project was the aberration of an overingenious mind, his latest plan (with H. Breuillot) for the little town of Nemours in North Africa, shows that combination of social concentration and openness which is one of the marks of the new urban order.

[BOTTOM] Radburn, N. J. (H. Wright and C. S. Stein, town planners). Here was the first town built anywhere that consistently abandoned the corridor avenue lined with houses, that divorced the functions of domestic living from the noise and traffic of the street, and that provided a continuous belt of park space within the residential super-blocks, instead of placing the park on the outskirts. Each superblock was planned in relation to a school, a playground, and a swimming pool: open spaces were treated as part of the original cost of the development. By means of footpaths with underpasses and bridges one can walk from one part of the community to another without encountering a motor car.

oriented to the cycle of life, with its never-ending process of birth and growth and renewal and death: a process we can neither halt nor limit by ideological fixations or cunning inventions. The very stones of the ancient tombs are no longer for us true symbols of eternity: we know their secret processes and detect their faltering character: we see their civilizations, too, through the perspective of time, perspectives that reveal the feebleness of their boasted power and the frailty of their monuments. The forms that past cultures have chosen for immortality seem to us as essentially childish as the rag doll to which the infant playfully attributes life. Time is a bomb that splits the most august temple open, if indeed the wanton savagery of men does not anticipate death's weapon.

Now, the forms and patterns of past ages die slowly: the idea of fixity has itself been slow to resist change. The architectural embodiment of older notions of survival has persisted, despite the challenge of the modern world picture. The truth is, however, that the notion of material survival by means of the monument no longer represents the impulses of our civilization, and in fact it defies our closest convictions. These Valhallas and Lincoln Memorials, these Victor Emmanuel Monuments and Vimy Ridge Memorials, these "Eternal Lights" that go out when the electric power station breaks down or the bulb blows out—how many buildings of the last century, that pretend to be august and monumental, have a touch of the modern spirit in them? They are all the hollow echoes of an expiring breath, rattling ironically in the busy streets of our cities, heaps of stone, which either curb and confine the work of the living, like the New York Public Library, or are completely irrelevant to our beliefs and demands. The notion of a modern monument is veritably a contradiction in terms: if it is a monument it is not modern, and if it is modern, it cannot be a monument.

This is not to say that a hospital or a power station or an air beacon may not be treated as a memorial to a person or an event; nor is it to deny that a contemporary structure might not easily last two hundred years, or even two thousand: that is not the point. What will make the hospital or the air beacon a good memorial is the fact that it has been well designed for the succor of those who are ill, or for the guidance of men piloting airplanes: not the fact that it has taken form out of a metaphysical belief in fixity and immortality and the positive celebration of death. The gulf between these world views is immense. He who lives sincerely in one world cannot honestly encompass the other.

In most past civilizations the activities of the living were not real until they could be transposed into terms of death. In our emerging civilization death is meaningless until it can be transposed into terms of the living. In the recent Christian culture life was a probational period of preparation for death and the far more significant and important state of after-life: for us, death is a making way for life, and all the fixed and memorial processes, the written record, the painting, the sculptured stone, the photograph, the recorded voice, are offerings to the living—to be accepted, not out of duty to the dead, but out of loyalty to other remoter generations who will also be capable of deriving life from these symbols.

The death of the monument was intuitively forecast by more than one spirit during the last century. For the fact is that this architectural change has implications that go far beyond the conception of individual tombs, memorials, or public buildings: it affects the character of our culture as a whole and the very texture of urban life. Why, for example, should each generation go on living in the quarters that were built by its ancestors? These quarters, even if not soiled and battered, were planned for other uses, other habits, other modes of living: often they were mere makeshifts for the very purpose they were supposed to serve in their own day: the best under existing limitations that now no longer hold.

It was Nathaniel Hawthorne who asked this question: he put it into the mouth of the young photographer in The House of the Seven Gables and repeated it elsewhere. It is only now, perhaps, that we can plumb its full significance. The pastoral nomad spared himself the sacrifice of the living to the dead monument until he copied the ways of men in cities: he traveled light. Civilization today, for different reasons, with different ends in view, must follow this example of the nomad: it must not merely travel light but settle light: it must be ready, not for merely physical movement in space, but for adaptation to new conditions of life, new industrial processes, new cultural advantages. Our cities must not be monuments, but self-renewing organisms: the dominating image should not be the cemetery, where the dead must not be disturbed, but the field, meadow, and park-land, with its durable cover of trees, its light boundary lines, its changing crops for which the fields are plowed every year.

7: Flexibility and Renewal

Today, our distrust of the monument cannot end with the purely symbolic structures of religion and government; for the machines and utilities that have helped foster the dense occupancy of cities often take on a monumental character. Indeed, the Roman roads and aqueducts and sewers have survived at least as well as the Tomb of Hadrian and the Arch of Constantine, and the modern metropolis builds subways and new traffic arteries with something of the sublime collective indifference to earthly realities with which the burghers of the Middle Ages built cathedrals.

The more the energies of a community become immobilized in ponderous material structures, the less ready is it to adjust itself to new emergencies and to take advantage of new possibilities. A two-story building with shallow foundations may be easily torn down, if a different type of structure is needed. But a twenty story building has a deep foundation, elaborate mechanical equipment, an expentive superstructure: it is not easily demolished as a physical structure, still less easily as a credit structure, no matter how short its period of amortization. If such a building should be replaced by a smaller building, or by no building at all, the original capital investment will stand in the way of such rational adaptation.

Every part of the community's shell and equipment presents the same dilemma. The wholesale investment in electric street railways in the eighteen-nineties certainly retarded the development of automobile transportation a generation later: the over-investment in subways in big cities has made a stubborn enforcement of the pattern of congestion almost a condition of municipal solvency. And it is very easily possible that our present gigantic investments in sewage disposal systems, including special treatment stations and sewage farms, may retard the introduction of more simple apparatus that will liquefy and transform sewage close to the point of origin: one of those inventions long overdue.

It follows that every proposal to elaborate the physical shell of the community should be critically examined, and social alternatives to the mechanical means proposed should be canvassed, or the possibility of simpler and lighter mechanical equipment—decentralized rather than centralized, small rather than big—should be examined. Very often there is a live choice between mechanization and socialization: a choice that capitalism naturally prefers to be oblivious to, since its profits spring out of the production and sale of mechanical utilities: the more gigantic, the more numerous, the more profitable. So deeply ingrained is the pecuniary order that even a socialized republic like the USSR more than once has adopted capitalist methods, even superstitions, under socialist slogans.

Our older cities, planned as monuments, with heavy capital investments duly incorporated under capitalism in the toppling structure of mortgages and land values, are incapable of adjustment to fresh needs and fresh demands. Their assets are, as the saying is, frozen: from the standpoint of life they are preposterous and paralyzing deficits: obstacles to a flexible method of meeting new situations by means of appropriate structures. One of the most impressive advantages the small city has over the overgrown metropolis consists in the fact that it does not stagger under such a burden of capital outlays in non-productive utilities. The economy of settling light does not merely consist in a lower scale of investment and lower overhead: its value derives from the greater readiness to take advantage of fresh improvements. Small cities, where people continued to cycle or walk to work, were better prepared to take advantage of motor transportation than cities that had invested heavily in trolley cars, elevateds, and subways. Under a biotechnic regime we shall attempt to get by socialized planning what we have hitherto sought to achieve exclusively by means of costly mechanical equipment. Toynbee calls the process of culture, as a community assumes command over the environment and the physical means of life, "etherealization." In the development of a new type of living environment one may put this concept in a negative mode: de-materialization: a reduction of physical structures to their absolute functional minimum.

The deflation of our mechanical monuments, then, is no less imperative than the deflation of our symbolic monuments. For the biotechnic age will be progressively marked by a simplification of mechanical equipment. Our present overload of mechanical utilities in the dwelling house, the skyscraper, and the city, particularly marked in American cities, is a symptom of our inability to think and plan and act in terms of the total situation: we shrink back into the narrow utilitarian ideology of the machine. The fact is that the so-called Machine Age has treated machines as ornaments: it has invented the vacuum cleaner when it should have done away with the rug: it has retained the steam-heater to produce sub-tropical heat at great expense, when it should have invented better forms of permanent insulation, to do away with the extravagant heating of cold walls and windows: it has retained the private garage as an ornament to the free-standing house, when it should have used the art of community planning to group houses and garages into a more livable environment. Similarly, the advantage of new utilities such as the private automatic refrigerator and the private oil-burning automatic furnace are only half-used because they demand, for complete economy, a more economical pattern of streets, which will dispense with the old need for public access to private dwellings on the road.

If the machine were not in effect a monument, if it were not a symbol of our mechanocentric religion, such irrational expenditures could not be explained. It remains only to note that mechanolatry is a bastard religion: half its glories mock the very mechanical and scientific principles it superficially seeks to enthrone. As a monument the machine is subject to the same ironic deflation that applies to all other attempts to wall out life. In the past, what have been called the triumphs of civilization have often turned out to be studious collections of encumbrances, which finally stifle the possibilities of movement and resilient reaction, and lead ultimately to urban downfall.

Here again one meets the lesson already noted in the section on Economy. We have created for the communities of the past cumbrous physical shells: what we need in future is not so much a shell as a living environment, an organic body capable of circulation and repair and renewal in every organ, member, and tissue. The protective function of the city, which is the utilitarian side of these metaphysical concepts of fixity and permanence, has been overdone. For living creatures, the only real protection comes through growth and renewal and reproduction: processes that are precisely the opposite of petrification. The real offense in the doing over of Regent Street, London, for example, was not the wiping away of Nash's serene façades, but their replacement with flatulent buildings that are hideous to the modern eye, and far less in keeping with modern needs than Nash's buildings. An American traveler has explained the rich architectural tradition of the contemporary inhabitants of Bali as due in part to the fact that they build their buildings with an exceedingly impermanent volcanic stone, which lasts only about fifteen years: hence they have to renew their structures frequently and recarve the stone. This continued demand for art keeps alive a fine tradition in the decorative arts. In modern life glass and synthetic materials, now coming into fuller use in the work of the new pioneers, are valid symbols of this more vital and more enlightened social sense.

Unfortunately, the real promise of this development has been frustrated from two directions. The older schools of architecture have clung to obsolete monumental forms, and manufacturers seeking to exploit fresh materials have been tempted, again and again, to give them the superficial earmarks of earlier technical processes. From the standpoint of capitalist enterprise, on the other hand, there has been a systematic misdirection of effort during the last decade in the effort to contrive free-standing, individual, manufactured houses, which could be put on the market in the same fashion as the automobile. By concentrating on the purely technical element of improved pre-fabrication, the manufacturers of these individual structures have overlooked the critical fact that modern communal services and collective utilities have made the cost of free-standing houses prohibitive, except in the isolation of the open country: they have sought economy in the shell alone, without availing themselves of further economies that rest upon community planning and community building.

When one stresses the factor of *renewability* one does not overlook the fact that effective design involves the discovery of architectural constants that do not have to be renewed from generation to generation: to discover and establish these constants is one of the main tasks of the modern planner. In every art there are forms so implicit in the process, so harmonious with the function, that they are, for practical purposes, "eternal": the safety pin has changed little in form since the later bronze age: the number of silhouettes possible for a bowl or a pitcher that will pour effectively is limited —and so on. Renewability in architecture does not mean designing buildings that must collapse in fifteen years: still less does it mean making pre-fabricated houses whose superficial shape will undergo as many ephemeral and foolish style-changes as the motor car, merely in order to quicken the pace of style-obsolescence and keep the industry profitably occupied. Renewability means the design of buildings in such materials, and by such technical methods, that they may be easily made over, section by section, structure by structure, even neighborhood by neighborhood.

Is this not the great justification of the steel-framed building? For the internal skeleton can be fixed, in terms of sunlight and open spaces and density, while the internal and external partitions, which determine the character of exposure, the size of the rooms, the diverse functional requirements, can all be freely recast, as need requires. Mies van der Rohe made an important essay in this type of construction in one of his Berlin apartment houses, built in such a way that the number and size of the rooms could be changed at will: the late Raymond Hood, in much more conventional fashion, drew the plans for a similar type of building; and although the architectural constants usually have no scientific validity, the precedent for this type of planning was of course set long before in the American office building. Mr. Clarence Stein has shown the application of the same principle to the design of a modern art museum with a thoroughly flexible interior. Essentially, these methods are capable of extension to almost every type of structure, except those specialized for industrial purposes; and even here, in the light industries, with their relatively mobile equipment, the same set of constants— and a wide range of variables—can be worked out.

Does this mean that the modern city is to be renewed every generation? Does this mean that it will "grow" indefinitely and spread indefinitely? Does this mean that the processes of demolition and destruction, so violent in the nineteenth century, will continue on their way, destroying every vestige of the past? Yes to the first question: no to the second and third.

The extent of renewal will depend upon the proportion of variables to constants. Most of the urban quarters built during the last hundred years must undergo profound reconstruction: this is a work which, if systematically carried on, might well occupy a good part of the energies of the next two generations: a work of undoing and redoing. But the outburst of mechanical invention during the nineteenth century, with the rapid alteration of old methods of work and old ways of life and the great shift of population, undoubtedly has made the present generation exaggerate the number of social variables and to forget the constants. Purposive change tends to crystallize once it has achieved its goal: once instantaneous communication at a distance has been achieved, for example, no *faster* mode of communication can be established.

One of the great advantages of mechanical standardization is to increase the number of constants in the environment; and this is equally true of the advance of scientific knowledge. It is extremely unlikely that medical science will suddenly discover that dark and airless buildings are preferable to light and airy ones, or that a cultivated landscape is more inimical to life than a crowded, dusty street. Once we establish constants in our urban planning, a certain kind of variation and change that was common during the last century—changes toward higher densities and overbuilding—will no longer take place.

Some of these constants were achieved by other periods, and were permitted to lapse, through a failure to maintain real standards of life. Quarters built with even an approximation to the standards that are already visible in terms of modern science, quarters like the Place Vendôme in Paris or the Fuggerei in Augsburg, or Gray's Inn in London, have a far greater degree of permanence than the great mass of recent building. As we design our cities for permanent living, not for impermanent financial exploitation, we shall discover, no doubt, a whole series of biological and social constants that will vary little from generation to generation; or at all events, such variation as is necessary will take place within, not in opposition to, the permanent form.

8: The Mission of the Museum

All this is another way of saying that the city itself, as a living environment, must not be condemned to serve the specialized purposes of the museum. If the city is to escape being a confused rubbish heap, the function of preservation and storage must be taken over by the museum. The very meaning of the museum of art and social history is that it is able to detach the memorials of life from the culture that originally supported them. By confining the function of preservation to the museum, we thus release space in the rest of the city for the fresh uses of the living. Where the fragments of a local culture are to be preserved, one of the best means of effecting this is perhaps by the use of an historic building, such as the Taft Museum in Cincinnati, the Behnhaus and the St. Annen Kloster in Lübeck, the Musée de Cluny in Paris, and the historical museums of Edinburgh and London.

The museum gives us a means of coping with the past, of having significant intercourse with other periods and other modes of life, without confining our own activities to the molds created by the past. Starting as a chance accumulation of relics and "valuables," half safety-deposit vault, half show-room, the art museum has in the course of its development gradually discovered its special function: that of selectively preserving the memorials of culture. Here at last is a genuine means of escaping the monument. What cannot be kept in existence in material form, we may now measure, photograph in still and moving pictures, record in sound, and summarize in books and papers. We may—and should—do all these things while the life is still present, so that we shall have, filed away for future reference, not merely a fragment of the original shell, but a working knowledge of the physiology of the building or work of art.

As far as works of pure art go, this detachment may become complete. What makes a work of art eternal in the human sense is not the details it carries over from the dead past, but what it signifies against the background of our own experience. It follows that while the social history museum necessarily seeks to preserve and enshrine the background, the museum of art, properly speaking, should forego any such attempt. One does not need a medieval house to appreciate a picture by Roger van der Weyden or Breughel, because, even if we had the house, we could not see either the environment or the picture through medieval eyes. On the contrary: the more complete the detachment and the more effectively we can screen a symbol from what it meant to another generation, the more swift and final is our own response.

Not unfortunately it is in a sense by our misinterpretations of the past that the past lives again: true understanding would leave the past precisely where it originally was: it is by its "otherness" that the past enriches the present with hints, suggestions, meanings that had no existence in its own day. For a work of art is not a monument: if it has a life at all, it exists as a contemporary fact: a fact of esthetics, a fact of religion, a fact of philosophy. A museum that is properly designed, with ample facilities for storage and preservation as well as for show, serves to enlarge the circle of contemporary experience. But our intercourse with the past is selective: it cannot be otherwise. The encyclopedic culture of the metropolis attempts to preserve everything and show everything; it mistakes acquisition for appreciation, a knowledge of names and incidents for esthetic intuition, and mechanical imitation for cultural intercourse.

Such a culture turns the museum into a second metropolis: like the big city, it aims merely at bigness, and results in purposeless congestion and intellectual bewilderment. On the mere laws of chance something of value must accumulate in the debris, by reason of its extent. But in museums that grew out of a balanced regional culture, not out of an acquisitive pattern of life, each generation would have the opportunity to be in selective control of the past. Each city would have its special museum of civic history: each community within the larger urban cluster would have its type museum of natural history and human culture, portraying in compact and coherent form the actual environment: from the infinitely remote stars to the infinitesimal particles of protoplasm or energy: the place: the work: the people in all their ecological relations. Under such a mode of distribution, a great part of the collections might be centrally stored, so that there would be a wider and more systematic circulation of objects: but the outlet and place of exhibition would not be a confused, overgrown building. Even in the clumsy organization of the big

capitals today there is a tendency in this direction: but any thoroughgoing application of these principles awaits the co-ordinate development of integrated neighborhood communities and integrated cities.

9: The Undifferentiated Background

Another significant social change has come about during the last
three centuries; but it has only been partly consummated, and its
expression in architecture has not been fully appraised. This is the
transference of interest from caste to personality: the lifting of the
naïve moral mask, and its replacement by a more complex tissue of
individuality. The death of the monument has its counterpart in the
disappearance of the uniform.

Although the English and French revolutions left a mark on every
Western community, they were only partly able to remove the older
foundations of caste and status. The process of social de-stratification
took place most thoroughly in the countries of the New World,
particularly in the United States, where under the pressure of conquering the wilderness and seizing a vast territory, the old habits
of life, the old gradations, the old subserviences were replaced by
a more fluid sense of the personality. Not "Where have you come
from?" but "What can you do?" was the question asked: not "What
is your social *position?*" but "What is your business [function]?"

Under this new freedom, a virile type of personality emerged
within a few generations, a type understood and celebrated by
Emerson, Thoreau, Hawthorne, and Whitman. In the new lands,
men were socially equal, politically equal: this meant that differences were no longer merely historic congealments but psychological facts.

Backward and barbarous though this pioneer culture was in many
ways, it achieved a practical revaluation of the personality which
carried into daily living an animus that only the deepest psy-
chologists, such as Shakespeare, had succeeded in achieving in a
caste society. The naked man, the individuated man, divorced from
his background of caste, *taken on his merits,* rose up from the hitherto
stratified mass: his character, his conditions, his feelings were no
longer conditioned by his economic class: a shiftless farmer, brought
up in this new social environment, became a great military leader;

a rail-splitter became a statesman; a sailor became a profound tragic writer; a pencil maker became a philosopher. In contrast to the inhabitants of the more established European societies, the typical pioneer American was a mere jack-of-all-trades: but another way of expressing it is that he was no longer a caste-limited man. If the doctrines of the class struggle were slow to make headway in America, it was because to the average American of the old stock classes were no longer social realities. Equal opportunity to have access to the soil meant unlimited differentiation: it was only with the closing of the frontier and the hemming in of opportunity that social stratification fully set in.

The expansion of educational opportunity during the last century and the collective promise of leisure offered by the machine has reopened, on a higher level, the crude opportunities for social equality that the frontier environment provided. For the modern man, caste is not a permanent attribute of personality: and the personality itself, instead of being a static unit, with a single fatal shape which it bears till eternity, is a function of its habits and responses; a complex if coherent resultant of its manifold associations and linkages. Occupation and regional background may tinge the personality with certain unmistakable colors: but the generic and human, with their vast range of opportunity and choice, provide endless shades and combinations.

Wherever a modern sense of the human personality has penetrated, the external uniform disappears, except as a functional accommodation to climate or work: the internal uniform disappears at the same moment. One cannot automatically derive the conduct of the individual from the pattern of his caste, nor does the individual feel himself fully represented within the area of his purely occupational interests: he preserves, as it were, the standing of the amateur. This attitude springs not only out of a new social milieu but out of a profounder understanding of human aptitude and motive; since however the psychological evaluation and control of conduct is still in its infancy, the modern sense of the personality is still unexpressed—except perhaps in America, where it exists as a holdover of the pioneer experience.

Indeed, part of the world at this moment is in a regressive state:

the automatic compulsions of war-discipline have, in fascist states, re-created the image of the caste-ridden, uniformed individual, with no center of his own, and no life except that prescribed by the rulers of the state. A world of heroes and villains: a world of black shirts and brown shirts and blue shirts: a world in which personality ceases to have existence or value save in the anarchic despotism of the leaders—little men, magnified by martial law and public bullying into the external dimensions of greatness.

The uniform, in both its physical and metaphoric senses, is nevertheless an atavism: a degrading effort to ignore our deeper knowledge of the personality and to limit the effects of science upon human behavior. So long as a man could be fully characterized by his rank or station: so long as he was, in a complete and unified sense, a knight or a burgher or a serf, a pagan or a Christian, a Protestant or a Catholic, so long as these distinctions were primary and clean-cut, the character of his background played an important part in defining his position in society. His costume, often limited by sumptuary laws, was a kind of background: his background in turn was a kind of costume. In the parlor, in the dining room, in the garden, he attempted to impose his personality through his background: deliberately or unconsciously he would display how rich he was, how ancient his family lineage was, how mighty his caste was in the community: these things seemed important.

In such a society, the key to architecture was the class-differentiated decoration: the human personality was, so to say, a mere figure on the carpet. The presence and quality of curtains, say, in a middle class household established its claim to respectability: the quantity of bric-a-brac or linen had a similar effect: and to live in certain American towns on the wrong side of the railroad track was to suffer social ostracism from those on the right side. The one unforgivable sin from the standpoint of caste was the bare room—that is, the room that did not at once establish the owner's place in society; and as costume, through the vulgarization of textiles and furs, defied sumptuary laws and blurred the lines of class cleavage a little, the domestic background became even more important. Without a duly established background, the class-limited personality felt insecure: the quality of his character rested then upon mere performance, not upon the visible tokens of landed property, stocks, bonds, mortgages, upon emblems of acquisitive taste and acquisitive interest.

All these habits linger; but a fresh sense of the personality, in all its immense and fascinating complexity, has been awakened by modern psychology. Much as our modern attitude toward time and death differs from that which prevailed in the past, the modern attitude toward background and foreground differs even more; and the essential innovation of modern architecture is, in effect, to abolish the background and to concentrate attention on the foreground. Gone are the visible signs of riches, travel, and "cultural appreciation": the patterned wallpaper, the curious designs on rugs and carpets, the involved shapes of vases, bowls, tables, each object calling attention to itself, crying to be singled out, competing for attention with the occupants of the room.

Good design today follows the fashion first set in theater decorations by Appia: it concentrates attention upon the *action* and *function* in the foreground, and it does not permit attention to be diverted from the actors to the scenic background. It is the face, the voice, the gesture, the thought, that shall tell the story about the owner's personality: not what he has acquired by way of material goods: not by this fashion and that fancy applied to his material equipment. The more generic the background, the less obtrusive its effect, the more subtly will it tell its story—and the more effectively the actual human presence will count in the picture.

Not merely does the modern sense of the personality demand that the foreground should be focused sharply, and the background retreat: if the background is emphasized, one suspects weakness. The desire for external grandeur, the desire for meretricious luxury or display—what do these things point to except a sense of psychological inferiority or insecurity: a failure to express adequate social relationships. As a sexually unattractive man may attempt to salvage his failure as a lover by showering his wife or his mistress with gifts, so the socially inept personality must attempt to take refuge in the material background, to bolster up his sense of insecurity by taste for antiques or an eager adaptation of the latest trick of fashion.

Whether in doing so he identifies himself with his traditional caste, like a merchant of the seventeenth century, or attempts to "express

In plan the most important new element in the garden city is the lateral wall of agricultural or park land that surrounds and defines the community. Fol· lowing the private initiative of Radburn, the U. S. Resettlement Administration, formed by the Federal Government in 1934, sought to combine housing with the building up of complete communities in areas favorable to sustained industrial and commercial employment. These projects were a step beyond Public Works housing: they recognized the possibility of creating an entirely superior type of urban organization by making a fresh start, instead of being confined to areas from which slums had been razed, already equipped with superfluous streets and utilities, as well as burdened by high land values. Numerous projects were planned; but only three were in process of building when this excellent initiative was capriciously discarded. Greenbelt, Maryland, here shown was the first to reach partial completion: Greendale, near Milwaukee, and Greenhills near Cincinnati exhibit similar principles with different types of plan. Great Britain and other countries had made the mistake, after 1919, of promoting housing without using the opportunity to re-centralize industry and population in complete and well-balanced garden cities. In the Greenbelt towns the United States seemed about to overcome this critical defect in its new governmentally financed housing. This enlightened policy should be resumed.

[TOP] General Layout of Greenbelt, Md. The plan was conditioned by a horse-shoe-shaped plateau. Full advantage was taken of wooded areas and existing trees. While not oriented consistently for maximum sunlight, the rows are rationally ordered within superblocks: a major economy. Note the by-passing of major highways, another characteristic of advanced planning. (*Photograph: Resettlement Administration*)

[MIDDLE] Type of house at Greenbelt. Straightforward design, with concrete blocks and bricks: open outlook and ample garden space. The schools and the community stores are carried through in the same manner: a vast advance over the second-hand picturesqueness of the better American suburb. Urbanity and openness—rather than the bogus rustic and the pseudo-historical—are the key to the new order of design. (*Photograph: Resettlement Administration*)

[BOTTOM] Airplane view of section of Greenbelt, while still under construction. Much more compact than the scatter-building (Streubau) of the nineteenth century suburb; much more open than the traditional types of city design. Shows the great benefits obtainable only through comprehensive design, large scale planning, scientific appraisal of needs, and unified land-ownership and large-scale building operations. Communities of this order were first projected by Robert Owen: they have now become a universal indication of biotechnic city design. (*Photograph: Resettlement Administration*)

IX: CITY AND REGION
[32] FRANKFURT-RÖMERSTADT: BIOTECHNIC ORDER

One of the earliest applications, beginning 1926, of modern methods of planning and building communities: so far probably the best. Parallel rows of houses in long blocks unbroken by traffic streets: narrow roads bordered with verdure for local service: large open spaces, with ample lawns, flower beds, and dining terraces behind the houses. The curving unit in the middle of the air-view is a four story high apartment block and retail business center, equally accessible from both ends of the community: the utilization of low and high units in this scheme gave opportunities for strong rhythms and accents, as in the two apartment units that stand out by the curving ramparts in the top picture. The varying orientation of houses was determined, not by sunlight exposure alone, but by other equally important elements—the lay of the land and the grand view across the Nidda Valley, permanently zoned for agricultural uses. If this development does not show the rigorous economies and stereotyped formulae of some later German schemes, it shows the artists' freedom of design which will be more and more possible in future as our communities turn their economic production to social ends: to plan economically for the future means, not cramping the work to the niggardly possibilities of today, but anticipating the higher standard of living well within our collective grasp—with its call for space and beauty rather than mere economy. To plan on low levels, on the basis of standardized and universally accepted poverty, is to plan for defeat: high standards of space are the best safeguard against obsolescence. The low-lying land beneath the parapet (*top photograph*) shows the individual cultivation gardens with their trim, collectively built, tool sheds: part of the green belt that sets off this community on two sides. The urbanity of the street picture, full of color and subtle variation, is far more stimulating than the mediocre suburbanism of more conventional contemporary schemes.

Here is an urban nucleus that meets the need for concentration (social advantage), for openness (hygienic and biological advantage), and for collective order and beauty: an environment in which the varied needs of the individual and the common life are effectively reconciled. But Römerstadt is only a sample: the widespread building of such units requires equally positive changes in industry, in economic standards, in political organization, and in culture: changes for which the older political parties and programs have only confused, partial, and contradictory formulations. The building of new communities, on a scale commensurate with social need, awaits the wider foundation, in every department, of a biotechnic culture. These new forms are prophetic of a new civilization: a civilization now in the same embryonic state that capitalism and mechanism were in the seventeenth century. Our generation faces the alternative of courageously going forward toward this civilization—or of relapsing into barbarism, marked by the muddled timidities of a disintegrating capitalism, and that neurotic substitute for an integrated order, fascism. . . . Forward!

his personality" in the romantic assumption of some form of architectural fancy dress, dissociated from his real environment, the
effort remains massively inept. The background is a mask, and we
see behind the mask—even as we see behind the puerile uniforms
and decorations and struttings of the totalitarian dictatorships—a
large confession of weakness and impotence in respect to the realities
of social life. We mark the subterfuges, the distortions, the evasions of
reality. The cult of the antique in furniture and decoration, the cult
of the exotic, the attempt to take over the time-bound vestiges of
other periods—what were these fading efforts but concrete utopias
of escape: the desire to establish little dream islands in the steely
sea of reality.

Today the seat of human individuality has altered. The garden, the
flower, the sculpture, the painting, the beautiful costume, the human
body and the human face, belong to the foreground: direct servants
of the personality, not badges of class and pecuniary position. *And
as the background becomes more standardized,* so that it no longer
applies to a single caste but a whole community, no longer to a
single community but a whole civilization, *so will the foreground
become more individuated.* Here we have in architectural taste that
necessity for combining the intimate and the individualized, which
we find in the region, with the generic and universalized, which we
shall find only in the widening of the processes of culture to our
whole planet. The common ground will thus become broader. But
immediate taste and psychological appraisal will become more refined, as the foreground becomes the main center of interest: a psychological foreground, freed from the factitious standardizations
of class, money, social rank. On this basis, within this setting, real
groups and real personalities will have the freedom to emerge, to
coalesce, to function, and to dissolve again.

10: Individuation and Socialization

What we have been discussing, in this new conception of architectural form, is in fact the concrete examples of sociality and individuality: both modes are undergoing radical changes. In the past,
each of these attitudes stood for a whole theory of society: they
came before us as social and political philosophies, clustered around

the dogmas of private property and individual liberty that had taken shape in the eighteenth century. They were looked upon as alternatives. Individualism was a theory that believed in the existence of atomic individuals as a primary fact. It held that these individuals had an inherent right to possess property and enjoy personal protection under the laws; and that no laws abrogating that species of personal freedom founded upon private property were valid. Socialism, in all its diverse manifestations, regarded the community as a primary fact, and it treated the welfare of the community as more important than the claims of any atomic individual to special protection or sustenance.

In actual practice, both these doctrines, during the last century, presented a sinister aspect. Masquerading under the noble slogans of the rights of man, pretending to continue its old war on despotic power, individualism established itself as the claim of small groups of privileged people to exploit the work of other men on the basis of a monopoly, partial or complete, of land, capital, credit, and the machinery of production. For the single despotism of the king, it substituted a multitude of petty, and not so petty, despots: industrialists, financiers, robber barons. "Socialism," on the other hand, has meant in practice the unlimited capacity of the government and the armed forces of the state to impose obedience and co-operation upon its subjects in times of war: pushed to its extreme, it becomes the state-deification of fascism and the unity of war-dictatorship. "Individualism" rested on the doctrine of the "free market" in which price exercises the functions of an almighty Providence: "socialism" rested on the doctrine of the closed frontier, in which every human activity within, thought itself, is subjected to state monopoly. The inequalities of the first and the uniformities of the second were equally oppressive to a good society.

In the senses in which individualism and socialism have gained currency, both are mythological distortions of the underlying facts of community life: the processes of individuation and socialization. In actuality, these terms are alternatives only in the sense that north and south are alternatives. They indicate directions of motion, without giving any descriptive reference to the goal to be reached. No

human society is conceivable in which, to some degree, both tendencies did not play an active part.

As concerns origins, the social theory is largely correct: society
exists as a fact in nature, and without an underlying symbiosis no
single member could survive. The more primitive the state of existence, the greater the influence of brute compulsion and irrational but
coercive tabu. The separation of the individual from the generic is
a social fact that occurs only in those socialized animals that have
some extra-organic means of inheritance; otherwise individuality is
a matter of accident and latent tendency. Only through a specific
social heritage, beginning with the art of language, can individuation
arise. The individual, left to himself, is not a source. Left to himself,
indeed, he would starve, go mad.

As concerns emergents, however, the theory of individuation is a
fact. When the apparatus of socialization becomes more adequate,
through language, through the written word, through the division of
labor, through the development of cities, special forms arise in the
hitherto less differentiated mass. Each group, each community, each
vocation, each habitat creates new patterns of individuality: by their
interaction in the close medium of the city, they provide endless per-
mutations and combinations in all its members. The common environment provides an underlying unity: the city itself may become the
cohesive symbol of that unity: but within that common environment
all the differentiations of a true culture arise with a wealth of example hitherto unexplored. Through intermixture of stocks and races
in the city, the biological inheritance, in turn, combines with the
equally complicated facts of social inheritance: these facts are individuated from moment to moment as personal experience. For practical purposes one often forgets the fact of individuation; but by intercourse with a de-individuated person, whose full human inheritance has been ideologically castrated, one realizes the difference between the deadened oneness of totalitarian doctrine and the vital
and many faceted product of a genuine community, in which social
conflicts and cultural intermixtures play an active part.

Both individuation and socialization must be respected in the design of cities and their separate structures. Unfortunately, working
under the false mythology of individualism, our modern capitalist

societies have in the past assigned values to "individual effort" in precisely those departments where standardized practices and socialized controls are necessary. The right of an individual property owner to obtain by purchase or inheritance a parcel of land, and to use it entirely at his own pleasure under minor legal regulation, has been treated as sacrosanct; and the gains that have followed the collective procedures of science, the collective discoveries of technics, have been permitted to go, like ground rents, to lucky or rapacious individuals, when they should in fact have been kept in trust for the community. In a similar way, laissez-faire principles encouraged the individual prospecting for industrial sites, the individual parceling of ground, the individual owning and building of houses: although all of these are in essence collective functions which are preparatory to true individuation. Indeed, individuation cannot enter in a cultural sense until a good part of our activities are reduced to a mechanized or socialized routine: only by multiplying the functions of the spinal cord, making them automatic, can the higher functions of the brain be released. This is the essential truth underlying Aristotle's otherwise barbarous remark that a good polity must rest on slavery.

Under an equally mythological sort of socialization, whether undertaken in the interest of a ruling financial class or the power state, the reverse of this tendency has been practiced. The state attempts to impose uniformity and "socialization" in matters of education, intellectual culture, and political judgment where, within the common pattern of the civilization (which "enforces" itself) a wide span of individuations should be encouraged. Contrary to the prevailing doctrine, no special measures should be taken, other than the common processes of discovering and systematizing truth, to extirpate obsolete religions, discarded scientific doctrines, idiosyncrasies and aberrant beliefs: since it is sometimes by unexpected combinations in our social inheritance, or unorthodox re-interpretations of past beliefs, that important mutations are made. The tendencies making for human uniformity are indeed so deep, so abiding, that it is only by providing for free play in individuation that we can avoid the sessile habits, the dangerous encystments, of past civilizations.

Every community must attempt in its structure to reconcile stability and adaptation, standardization and flexibility, socialization and individuation. None of these qualities is a terminal point or objective: they are directions of movement and change. Good planning is an attempt to keep the whole environment in a state of dynamic equilibrium, in which freedom does not mean empty chaos, and in which discipline does not mean an even more vacuous death.

The great aristocracies of the past knew that the labor of a thousand serfs, the accumulations of vast congeries of buildings, with all the necessary land for their support, might not be too extravagant a price to pay for the culture of a truly enlightened and disciplined individual: in the long run, the millions would profit. But because of the social inequality and the bitter injustice of these arrangements, such aristocracies but rarely produced a Plato. Today, with our vast accession of energies, with our abundant collective resources, we have the opportunity of upholding these principles, not for the sake of an oligarchy, but for the welfare of every member of the community. The base must be generic, equalized, standardized, communal: the emergent must be specific, unstandardized, individual, aristocratic: differentiated groups, differentiated individuals, differentiated regional and civic communities.

11: From a Money-Economy to Life-Economy

In the pecuniary economy that developed during the last five hundred years, there was only one criterion of effort: profit. If more profit could be obtained by baking stones than by baking bread, stones would be baked, even though in fact people were starving. Scarcity and surplus, demand and supply, had reality not in relation to men's actual wants, but in relation to the market. Wants that could not be expressed in terms of the market remained unfulfilled, unless they were satisfied through an institutional life brought over from another period. Money was the symbol of power, and power was the chief end of man.

Under a pecuniary economy wants that can be expressed in terms of a demand in the market kept on expanding: this was marked first by an increase in the variety of goods offered, and second by an increase in the amount created through mechanized production. In order to make the highly specialized division of labor possible, in an anonymous and undirected production for a world market, it was necessary that wants should keep on increasing: likewise that the rate of consumption should be hastened: by this means alone could production be geared higher and profits increased, or at least kept secure. Saturation of the market, with new production limited to legitimate replacements, would decrease the opportunities for profit and undermine the existence of the over-expanded plant: stability meant, in terms of profit, frustration: contraction meant bankruptcy.

Under this pecuniary economy, the civic and domestic needs of the greater part of the population have never been satisfied through the ordinary processes of the market. Calicoes, knives, and watches might be cheaper, as they entered the channels of international trade and displaced increasingly the local products, by a price competition which often concealed the eventual inferiority of the goods: but the low wage levels which entered into the production of these cheapened goods made it impossible for any large mass of workers to make an adequate demand for dwellings and for the community equipment that goes with urban living.

This held true in the eighteenth and nineteenth centuries, with results that I have described in detail in earlier chapters: but the point is that it holds equally true today. *Without doubt the prime obstacle to urban decentralization is that a unit that consists of workers, without the middle class and rich groups that exist in a big city, is unable to support even the elementary civic equipment,* of roads, sewers, fire department, police service, and schools. At present it is only by remaining in metropolitan areas, where the taxes derived from the well-to-do districts can be partly applied to the working class quarters, that the worker can obtain even a modicum of the facilities for a good life.

This fact was discovered by the planners of Radburn, N. J., in attempting a rational organization of its municipal life and it was further demonstrated by Mr. Clarence Stein in a study made for the Resettlement Administration. It has been amply substantiated by the London County Council's efforts at municipal decentralization: Becontree, for example.

What effect did machine production, corporate economy, special-

ized division of labor, and concentration of output on a blind market of buyers have upon the provision of dwelling houses? Here again
the total inadequacy of a pecuniary economy to satisfy the essential
biological and social needs of a community has been completely
demonstrated. As the standards of housing have risen, the opportunities for profit through their sale or rent have dropped. In a capitalist economy, this means that production has gone into other
channels. Result: a quantitative shortage in dwelling space has been
chronic in highly industrialized countries like England ever since
the beginning of the nineteenth century, and in the more overcrowded
industrial centers, like London, since the sixteenth century.

In order to make it possible for capital to enter this field at all, the
qualitative standards have kept consistently below the level of decency available under the existing technology. The dwelling house,
far more than the farm, has been the backward point of modern
technics. Wage levels and incomes have borne simply no relation
to the requirements for a decent dwelling. The failure of the pecuniary economy in this department is abysmal: all the more because
rent is the largest single item in a family budget: rising from ten or
fifteen per cent among the working classes of Holland to between
twenty and thirty per cent for those in other countries. Rents that
occupy more than twenty per cent of the total, especially on the lower
income levels, mean a sharp curtailment of vital necessities at other
points in the budget.

The failure of decent housing to obtain capital through competition in the market has led to widespread attempts to foster home-
ownership among the workers: under the guise of offering security,
those who have fostered this movement, including government
agencies, have sought to burden the worker with the risks: risks
whose returns are not sufficient to attract the necessary capital from
the more wary. This diversion of the worker's meager budget to housing not merely undermines his standard of life: it lessens his freedom of movement and, during a financial crisis or a local shutdown
often results in the complete loss of his entire investment—and the
roof over his head as well.

Needless to say, this is no solution of the housing problem: even
apart from the fact that the building of individual houses is techni-

cally an extremely wasteful process. Except for the income groups well on the comfort level, the building of houses for profit has been carried on throughout the Western World only by debasements of design: systematic overcrowding of the land, and overpopulation of the interior quarters on the part of those who must eventually rent them. And so long as pecuniary canons remain uppermost, there is no prospect for a change.

What do all these facts signify? They signify that some of the most essential items in the construction and equipment of cities can not be produced, on any terms, under a pecuniary economy; and that houses in particular can be built only by ignoring the positive standards, based on scientific data, that are appropriate in an advanced civilization. This discovery has been slowly sinking into the minds of thoughtful people for the last century; and in the realm of both city development and housing it has resulted in a series of measures that cannot be sanctioned in terms of private gain and pecuniary aggrandizement.

Housing, in fact, is the focal point in that change from a pecuniary to a biotechnic economy which has been slowly developing throughout the Western World, and which received a great impetus in the decade that followed the first World War. The older type of industrialism chose to meet the inadequacy of income to a genuine standard of life by maintaining low wage levels as long as possible and ignoring the possible existence of a positive standard of life. Whatever the worker could get along on, whatever a landlord could demand, in the main determined the rental levels and the standard of accommodation: even during periods of relative prosperity for the worker, housing remained a third choice in his expenditures. In Middletown the Lynds discovered workers who owned automobiles of the latest model, whilst they bred their families in houses that lacked even bare sanitary conveniences. Even the worker, guided by advertising, sales talk, and emulation, followed fashions.

Under the biotechnic economy, these conditions are reversed. Instead of wages and income directing market demand, vital demand determines the level of income and directs production into socially useful channels. First we must erect a standard of living. In terms of housing, the minimum standards are set by objective criteria of air, water, sunlight, heat, privacy, and so forth, and further modified by those social provisions which tradition and current investigation prove to be necessary for the nurture of children and the education of responsible citizens. At any given period, in any given region, these standards should set a minimum level for wages: industries that cannot meet such a level must be looked upon as economically inefficient and socially defective: to be abolished or taken over by the community.

Where such standards have been set to a greater or less degree in publicly aided housing one of two things must happen: either incomes in industry will rise to the necessary level, or the state will tax the larger incomes and make the re-apportionment directly in the form of subsidies to the housing: money lent at low interest rates, subsidies to rents to make up the difference between the cost of the house and the worker's ability to pay, or outright grants. In the governmental housing that has been undertaken so widely through Europe, beginning with the first efforts in England and Belgium after the middle of the nineteenth century, one or all of these methods have been used. Inevitably. Had the capitalist discovered for himself a way to supply decent housing to a depauperate or indigent population at a profit to himself he would have followed it.

Now, in a pecuniary economy, production for sale and profit dominates: the surplus over current need goes back, apart from minimum expenditures for private display and public services, into further mechanical production. In a biotechnic economy, on the other hand, consumption and service must take precedence. Production must be directed, in greater amounts, into channels where a surplus of energy is made available, either for direct use in life, as house, as city, as regional habitat, or for storage against future vital uses. The benefits of automatic machinery, the economies of finely organized production, the displacement of labor, the surplusage of modern agriculture all mean—if they mean any human benefit—this release of energy for the direct service of life. Whereas under a pecuniary economy profit came through the expanded rôle of the machine, the biotechnic economy will be marked by a general contraction of the machine and, with balanced regional economies, a diminution of the importance of the world market: now to be reserved for surpluses and specialties.

But consumption itself, under a biotechnic economy, is not consumption anyhow, in any quantities, toward any purposes. Capitalism had no need to inquire into the quality or end of consumption: indeed its most ardent advocates during the period of intellectual formulation even defended the adulteration of foods and drugs in the competitive market, on the ground that to erect a standard of purity would be to do away with free competition. Under a biotechnic economy consumption is directed toward the conservation and enhancement of life: a matter where qualitative standards are imperative. One uses the word life in no vague sense: one means the birth and nurture of children, the preservation of human health and wellbeing, the culture of the human personality, and the perfection of the natural and civic environment as the theater of all these activities. Here are substantial goals for consumption not envisaged in the abstract doctrine of increasing wants operating within an ever-expanding circle of new inventions and multiplying productive mechanisms.

Against the wasteful duplication of mechanical equipment, the aimless productivity, the random expansiveness of production under pecuniary canons of success, a biotechnic economy erects rational goals: the best possible environment for human nurture and culture: the primacy of consumptive and creative activities over the instrumental processes: the denial of "success" embodied in the destructive facilities of war and the mounting certificates of debt which mark the prevalence of a pecuniary economy. But to normalize consumption is to erect a standard that *no single class*, whatever its expenditures, *possesses today*. That standard cannot be set down in terms of any arbitrary sum of money, like the five thousand dollars a year suggested by Bellamy: for it involves the use of a complicated civic equipment whose individual appropriation is beyond the scope of even wealthy individuals. And indeed, the higher the vital standard, the less can it be expressed adequately in terms of money, and the more remote it is from the operations of the market. Vital standards must be expressed in terms of leisure and health and biological activity and esthetic pleasure and social opportunity: that is, in terms of goods and environmental improvements in which machine production and all the devious and indirect processes that subserve such production have but a subordinate part.

In putting a vital standard first, we thereby make the dwelling house, the school, and the city the concrete, all-engrossing end of industrial and agricultural production. *The aim is not more goods for more people to buy, but more opportunities for them to live: hence only such increases in goods as are instrumental to "the best life possible."* Under such an economic order, communal choices become more important than individual choices, and more and more of the activities of the citizen's life are released from pecuniary constraint.

Until such standards are erected, planned production is merely a wishful abstraction, and none of the preparatory incidents of current production, however resourceful in a technical sense, can contribute more than a modicum of their possible benefits to the community. Fortunately, our civilization as a whole is now at a point technically where it is feasible to give the population as a whole that basis in good breeding and good nurture which has hitherto been the exclusive possession of aristocracies.

This, then, is the meaning of the change that has been slowly taking place in our civilization since the third quarter of the nineteenth century. The increase of collectivism, the rising of municipal and governmental housing, the expansion of co-operative consumers' and producers' associations, the destruction of slums and the building of superior types of community for the workers—all these are signs of the new biotechnic orientation. This change is so deep, so pervasive, that it can be witnessed even in places where the profit system, which is its antithesis, has reached a pinnacle. One can behold it, for example, in the budget of a great municipality like New York, which annually spends more on education than even on transportation or street cleaning; one may watch it at work in a country like England, which has been tearing down slums and planting new communities whose tiled roofs are deeply embedded in green trees and greensward. One saw it on a grand scale in Germany when, in five quick years after 1925, before the suicidal impulses of Nazism got the upper hand, one beheld in every department of life the outlines of a new human culture: a complete conception of the good life which put pre-Nazi Germany at the very forefront of modern civilization.

Whereas the pecuniary economy expanded the rôle of the machine, the biotechnic economy enlarges the rôle of the professional services: a greater proportion of the income and free energy go into the support of the artist, the scientist, the architect and technician, the teacher and physician, the singer, the musician, the actor. This shift has been going on steadily during the last generation: the tendency is statistically demonstrable. But its significance has not been generally grasped: for its result must be the transfer of interest from the subordinate mechanical arts to the direct arts of life. And it brings with it another possibility, indeed another necessity: the universal rebuilding of cities for the sake not merely of better conditions of living, but of a more purposive creation and utilization of the social heritage: such a life as men have occasionally had a glimpse of in Jerusalem, Athens, Florence, or Concord.

12: Modern Housing by Communities

As I have already pointed out, the dwelling house occupies a peculiarly central place in the biotechnic economy. About ninety per cent of the structures in any urban community are houses; so, from the standpoint of practice, an adequate insight into the task of housing today is essential to the development of cities. The socialized provision of housing, in integrated neighborhood units, is the economic foundation for the biotechnic city.

Today, even the finest urban dwellings of the last century are, for the greater part, obsolete. They were conceived in terms of a limited and now outworn mode of living; few of them, even by drastic renovation, can encompass our modern demands. As mere shelters they are sometimes sufficient; but as a frame for living, they are absurd. All our new needs—our desire to avoid unnecessary menial labor, our more conscientious and efficient child care, our recognition of play as an essential part of life from childhood onward, our acceptance of the need for quiet and privacy—all these create a demand for a different type of dwelling and a different communal form. In many ways, we have already crossed the threshold of a new age; but our housing remains behind, clinging to dreams that no longer satisfy, making a parade of sickly archaic tastes, attempting to meet conditions that no longer exist and failing to take advantage of conditions that do exist and promise far more by way of human reward. Even much of the new housing done by both public bodies and private builders exhibits only a stuccoed modernity over an obsolete form.

The new approach to housing is distinguished by the fact that it no longer looks for a satisfactory dwelling house in terms of a single factor—good planning, an isolated advance in technical design, a more socialized system of exploiting the land. For the dwelling is in reality a very complex adaptation to an exceedingly complicated set of requirements; and it is quite unlikely that any simplified solution, expressible in purely mechanical terms, will satisfy all the necessary conditions. What is important is to treat the geographic, economic, social, technical, and personal requirements on a single plane. Twentieth century technics cannot be fitted into laissez-faire economics and seventeenth century taste. Improvements must be made co-ordinately all along the line, and the most spectacular advance is no advance at all until it is integrated. To conceive of a pre-fabricated house designed in a civic and environmental vacuum is to conceive of something that is, by definition, half-baked, scamped, and inadequate.

What is a modern dwelling? The new home is primarily a biological institution; and the house is a specialized structure devoted to the functions of reproduction, nutrition, and nurture. To expand the definition a little, the dwelling house is a building arranged in such a fashion that meals may be easily prepared and served, that the processes of hygiene and sanitation may be facilitated, that rest and sleep may be enjoyed without disturbance from the outside world, that sexual intercourse may take place with privacy and a minimum of distraction at all times in the year, and that the care of the young may be carried on under favorable conditions of companionship and supervision.

None of these functions, needless to say, is restricted to the dwelling house. But the house, with its special utilities, is peculiarly adapted to perform all of them in unison with the necessary co-operative help of the members of the household. Add to these primarily physiological requirements the provision of space for social intercourse and play and study, and the definition of the modern dwelling is complete. Certain functions, domestic in origin, require more ample space or special facilities; these should be taken out of the house even further than they are today: childbirth and infectious illnesses, weddings and funerals, need their communal buildings.

What remains is an irreducible minimum. With the return of entertainment to the house, through the phonograph, the radio and the motion picture—with the near-prospect of television—*the modern house has gained in recreational facilities what it lost through the disappearance of many of the earlier household industries.* The radio and the telephone, moreover, have made the house no less a center of communication than was the old market-place. So if certain functions have diminished, others have gained; while our growing concentration upon biological functions in general has increased the importance of this institution in relation to all competitive activities.

As a well-distributed leisure takes the place of hopeless unemployment, it is probable that more time will be spent within the environs of the house in future than during the passing transition from the mixed household to the single family group. Now more than ever, the intelligent design of the domestic environment has become a matter of critical importance: it demands a sensitive, well-balanced judgment, capable of distinguishing between primary and accessory needs.

Now, in order to provide for the essential biological functions of the dwelling house, we must ruthlessly cut down on many conventional requirements. We must abandon, not merely the old-fashioned desire for "ornament" and conspicuous waste; but we must also shave down the modern desire for ornament in the form of wasteful mechanical gadgets. As Henry Wright, again, was the first to demonstrate clearly, the simple walls and roof and foundations of a century ago has long ceased to constitute the structural reality of the modern house. Most of what was added to the structure, before 1750, was by way of ornament. After this time a succession of mechanical utilities pushed into the house: the heating stove, running water, the bathroom, the kitchen range and the gas lamp, the water closet, the central heating plant and the icebox, electric light, gas and electric ranges, automatic systems of refrigeration and heating, aerials for radios, garages for motor cars; finally, in the present decade, Palladio's original suggestions for air conditioning have been converted into a costly mechanical fact.

These new utilities and machines changed the nature of the dwelling house in two important ways. They broke down its self-sufficient isolation and linked it up, with specially built roads, water mains, sewer pipes, gas pipes, electric wires, telephone lines with other parts of the urban environment: the house functioned as an element in a collective unit, and the efficiency of the individual cell was now conditioned on the efficiency and economy of the whole. Well-equipped houses, without appropriately modified community plans, could achieve only a small part of their mechanical promise.

All these improvements, furthermore, added to the total cost of the house; for whereas the bare structure constituted originally about ninety per cent of the cost, today this structure constitutes but twenty per cent; and even the total cost of the fully equipped dwelling, with all machines and utilities installed, represents from forty-five to sixty-five per cent of the final cost of the dwelling. A reduction of the interest rate by two per cent gives a far more decisive saving than either cheese-paring or pre-fabrication can promise.

If one assumes a stationary family budget it would follow that for each economic group a far greater proportion would have to be spent on housing in 1940 than in 1740. Or if one assumes that the proportional relationship between housing, clothes, food, and other necessaries of life remains fixed, then the total income of the family would have to expand greatly in order to cover the rise in the expenditure. The alternative is deficient accommodations: lack of space, lack of equipment. Up to the present, for the greater part of the population, modern communities have contented themselves with deficient accommodations.

One must grant that many mechanical improvements have still to be made: in general, the internal equipment of the dwelling has not yet been scientifically reorganized. The co-ordination of all the mechanical utilities in a central stack, as proposed by Buckminster Fuller, has now been adopted by various manufacturers of pre-fabricated units in America; and it is no doubt capable of being pushed further: an advance in economy as well as in mechanical efficiency. But though every such gain must be avidly seized, the act of rationalization does not solve the problem of cost that results from the multiplication of utilities and services: nor will it be solved by the further pre-fabrication of floors, roofs, and walls, although each and all of these steps may be decisive improvements. The reason is plain: the external shell of the house is by now the least important part of its total cost: and one might cut the cost of the shell radically without reducing the total cost of land, equipment, improvements, finance, *and* structure by more than a relatively small per cent. The real justification for advances in pre-fabrication is that the eventual product will be a better one than the old clumsy masonry shells: it will be capable of expansion and renewal and adaptation in a fashion that more antique forms are not.

In the modernization of the dwelling during the last century most of our mechanical improvements have remained half-baked. Hence what has been gained in internal convenience—warm rooms in winter, running water, diminished demand for domestic service—has so far been partly forfeited through decrease of spaciousness. Every solution of the housing problem that does not confront the facts I have just spread out is meretricious. The modern house, because of its nature, cannot be a low-cost house: the analogy with the economies of the automobile through mass production is extremely deceptive, and the building of trailer-dwellings, recently started in the United States, has fully demonstrated this fact. It is a false solution to build a dwelling so small that the psychological harmony of family life is sacrificed to economy of space. It is a false solution to economize by doing without a cellar, since either an underground storeroom, or an overground storeroom that will cost approximately as much, is a necessary convenience of family life: storage has a part in every economic process. It is no solution to cover so much of the land, because it is high in price, that neither the open spaces nor the sunlight are sufficient. It is as much a false solution to provide all the mechanical utilities that modern life demands and to fail to supply usable space of good quality as it would be to produce a bare eighteenth century shell and not to equip it with any of these mechanical aids: the latter house would be cheap—but it could not satisfy modern requirements for urban living.

Finally, it is a false solution to suggest, as Fuller and others have done, that a more mobile type of dwelling will solve our difficulties. This proposal assumes that it is possible to escape permanently the cost of social services, schools, hospitals, libraries, government, roads, by moving outside areas where these services are supplied, or by moving away when asked to pay one's share toward their upkeep. As a means of recreation, a way of returning to an irresponsible gypsy life, camping here, moving there, the mobile house or trailer may be as delightful to those who have the proper temperament as life in a houseboat, the aquatic form of the mobile house. But such a house is either temporarily parasitic upon the nearest permanent community, or it must lack those necessary social and cultural attachments without which one sinks to the level of a bargeman: the proposal otherwise idiotically assumes that a "self-sufficient" structure is capable of supplying a self-sufficient life. This does not actually hold even for sanitation.

Such a "solution" is doubly regressive because it attempts to de-communalize the house and break down every last vestige of associative and corporative life: whereas the deepest need of modern life is to re-integrate the organs of association by forming new civic wholes. In short, this mechanical escapism, as embodied in the trailer and the trailer camp, is one of those ludicrous examples of ideological miscegenation of which the modern world is full: the neurotic offspring of romanticism and mechanism: the housing problem solved by reducing it to the provision of bare shelter and doing away with those communal relations which spring up only through close association and permanent settlement.

The reason for the widespread backwardness of housing throughout our civilization is that no fundamental change is possible except by means of a communal redistribution of income. The slum is the outward expression of physical impoverishment: slum demolition is poverty demolition, or it is nothing. And by the same token, the building of houses fit for the nurture of human beings is dependent upon making production and distribution directly subservient to bio-technic standards of consumption, available for the whole community. Any real effort to provide housing must attack this central economic problem.

Hence the importance for community housing of an active trade-union and co-operative movement: the first to push wages upward, claim a larger share of the total product, and create an effective political demand for government-aided housing: the second to organize and administer the units built, focusing and interpreting the consumer's demand, acting as mediator between the official agencies and professional services and the eventual occupants: in some cases, as in pre-Nazi Frankfurt, administering the housing itself. The *educational* services of these organizations are no less important than their political functions.

13: The School as Community Nucleus

The most important fact about group life today is not the pervasiveness of the machine through our mechanical devices for manifolding, recording, and transmitting its signs and symbols: the significant point is that the heritage so transmitted becomes progressively functionless and meaningless, unless it is accompanied by a reawakening of purposive group life. For a city, in order to act the part of a city, is a field for the interaction of "temporal and spiritual powers," as Comte would have said: it is a concentrated socialized environment, where administrators and energizers, assimilators and creators, may react upon each other in a common sphere. A community that does not plan and build the necessary structures for the common life will remain under a perpetual weight and handicap: its buildings may tower against the skies, but its actual social stature may be smaller measured by effective accomplishment than a decent country town.

The church was the essential social nucleus of the medieval city. All its adjacent institutions were dominated by the church: at no point in one's daily routine could one forget its purposes or escape its ministrations. In the baroque city the palace was a similar nucleus: theater and concert hall and art gallery were part of its show: shopping parade and military parade were subservient to its mode of existence: industry itself was dependent upon the palace for privilege as well as patronage. In the paleotechnic economy, the same part was played by the factory; while in the metropolis the market in all its various forms, from the ribbon of stores on the traffic arteries to the banks and stock exchanges and brokers' offices, played a controlling part in the city's design, or designlessness. Each new dominant re-crystallized, in a new pattern, with different tensions, different ponderables, every other institution in the city.

What are the new dominants in the opening biotechnic economy? They are not far to seek: the dwelling house and the school, with all their specialized communal aids, constitute the essential nucleus of the new community. And as the new region is the city writ large—a statement that is not to be taken as mere metaphor—we shall find in every well-organized and well-developed region the corresponding institutions, no longer serving a class, a minority group, but acting as organs of the whole community.

In older cities, the domestic neighborhood, even when formed on the basis of some original village, had no physical identity: it is only verbally that it detached itself from the larger urban area with which it coalesced. Suburbs, indeed, usually began their existence with visible marks of unity and isolation; but except in the case of remote and fortunate ones, they would eventually be swallowed up in the spreading mass of the city. In the new city, a neighborhood has visible definition. Its size is determined by the convenient walking distance for children between the farthest house and the school and playground in which a major part of their activities are focused. Its pattern is determined by the need of isolating school and home from the noise of traffic and its dangers: so main traffic arteries of any sort must never run through a neighborhood: they may exist at its boundaries, separated for both safety and amenity by a broad parkway: whatever traffic filters into the neighborhood must be that which directly subserves it, moving at a pace that respects the rights of the footwalker. Even country villages today often lack this element of safety and freedom from anxiety.

While the school has become a universal institution, and the main symbol of the educational process, the instruments of modern education are continuous with life itself: no mere building can fully house them, and the notion of making education "economical" or "comprehensive" by creating megalopolitan buildings holding from 1500 to 3000 pupils, and then expanding the scale of the neighborhood so that it can bestow a sufficient number of children on these buildings may be dismissed as a typical megalopolitan perversion. A neighborhood should be an area within the scope and interest of a preadolescent child: such that daily life can have unity and significance for him, as a representation of the larger social whole: and accordingly a special effort should be made in the design of neighborhoods to incorporate in them those light industries which directly subserve neighborhood life. There should be a compact, orderly industrial zone containing not only a garage and filling station, but likewise a laundry and a bakery: perhaps even a small electrically powered plant such as a wood-working shop or a garment factory: examples of the industrial process which the child at school may not merely inspect and understand, but also, perhaps, take part in as an educational experience. The direct observance of all kinds of industrial processes in the open workshops of Athens no doubt gave to Plato and his fellow citizens that visual acuteness and that intelligent grasp of the processes of existence which accounts for the extraordinary production of able minds in a town that certainly never harbored more than three hundred thousand people. If in addition a neighborhood could provide a place for other types of activity—such as a plant nursery or a painter's studio—the educational value of the equipment would be highly increased.

The class education of the past and the narrow vocational education of the passing order are both antagonistic to the biotechnic concept of education as the extension and refinement and integration of human experience in all its manifold aspects. The cultivation of the senses, by visual and tactile explorations of the environment, the intensification and communal refinement of feelings in the group activities of sport, in the theater, where the spectator and actor may interchange parts, in the civic festival and religious ritual, above all in the relations of friends, lovers, mates—this is the essential *business* of life, and all other business is trivial except as a preparation and an underpinning to these experiences. The active routine and the orderly duties of workshop, factory, farm, and office are likewise essential contributions to this education: but so far from education's being ordered merely to prepare the pupil for assuming the economic responsibilities of maturity, it is no less important to order industry so that it will contribute to the maturing educational needs of its members. The real question at every step is not simply what one does, but what one makes of it. The workaday economic relations become significant only as they contribute to the better ordering of life itself; and as we pass from the regime of specialization to the balanced industrial and personal economy, more effort must be made to develop the flexible and many-sided personality of the amateur, rather than the vocationally narrowed capacities of the specialist.

In America, partly by shaking off the caste system, partly by accepting the challenge of the frontier, we achieved this type of living education before the full onset of the machine: we have now to recover it in a world that has need both for the machine and for the high discipline of science. But such a new integration cannot be worked out merely with the aid of a specialized institutional routine: the best of schools must remain poor in certain essentials even in relation to the poorest of cities. *Under the new biotechnic economy, the city becomes again, as it has often been in the past, the chief instrument of education:* the wider school of the young and the university of the adult; whilst the factory, the meeting hall, the political committee, the scientific society become, as it were, *auxiliaries* of the school. And under such conditions an important result must follow: the processes and activities of the school will tend to set a mold for the social process as a whole.

The training of the young is a major preoccupation of all societies; and the school was one of the earliest differentiated institutions in the city: but in earlier cultures, the fixed pattern and limited possibilities of adulthood were usually taken as given, and the process of education was essentially one of pouring life into a predetermined mold. Since the eighteenth century, however, the molds have been broken: the period of education and the period of experiment, instead of being limited to youth, must now range over every phase of life: only the grave brings the process to an end. Under the impulse of psychological thought and revolutionary political hopes, directed toward the rational improvement of society, the school has, from the eighteenth century onward, tended to assume a more critical place in the whole political order: from Rousseau and Fichte to Dewey and Croce, pedagogy and politics have gone hand in hand, and the main interest of public education has been to effectuate, through collective means and processes, a better political society.

With the growth of specialized machine industry, the educational opportunities of the extra-school environment, in the confused, amorphous cities that this regime has produced, have become more limited. And the systematic technics of the modern factory or office, while it promotes a rationalization of the process itself, de-rationalizes—that is, makes automatic and non-reflective—the conduct of those in charge of the operation. What happens in the economic world happens also in the play-world: the listener to the radio, the spectator at the motion picture, tends to be passive and machine-conditioned. The results have become familiar: a growth of irrational conduct in the very midst of a meticulous mechanized order and a decrease of what Mannheim distinguishes as *substantial rationality.*

In order to prevent this hiatus from becoming greater, the humanizing and rationalizing elements in human conduct must be more fully incorporated in the organization of both school and city; while the automatic and compulsive processes, already as pronounced in the factory and the bureau as on the military drill ground, must be reduced and narrowed. This means, among other things, the introduction of small units, scaled to direct activity and participation, in every phase of organization: giantism must be challenged and made to prove itself not merely as mechanically adequate but as *humanly assimilable.*

We need, in every part of the city, units in which intelligent and co-operative behavior can take the place of mass regulations, mass decisions, mass actions, imposed by ever remoter leaders and administrators. Small groups: small classes: small communities: institutions framed to the human scale, are essential to purposive behavior in modern society. Very stupidly we have overlooked the way in which large units limit opportunity all along the line: not merely by physical friction of space, or the burden of a vast mechanical and administrative overhead, but also by diminishing opportunities for people with special capacities. Thus Sir Raymond Unwin has pointed out that twenty communities with a population of fifty thousand people would not merely be more adequately governed, probably, than one city that contained a million: it would, for example, give an opportunity for twenty mayors or city managers against one in the big center. This rule holds true in every other part of society. We demand the impossible in the way of direction and specialized service from a few people, and we fail to demand the possible from those who are better equipped to handle adequately a smaller job. With our overgrown institutions, overgrown colleges, overgrown corporations, overgrown cities, is it any wonder that we easily become the victims of propaganda machines, routineers, and dictators?

From the nineteenth century on the criteria of life began to penetrate the school, and the school became the essential instrument in effective orientation of society toward whatever ends its members and its ruling classes conceived. The most progressive school of the early nineteenth century was called a children's garden; and that of the twentieth century is called a nursery school: both of them are far removed from the older way of treating children as little adults. The school, indeed, in the modern sense, may be defined as an environment modified for biological and social development: an environment especially concerned with growth, which no longer treats the processes of growth as accidental intrusions on an ideal pattern.

Under the paleotechnic and metropolitan regime, the school had the duty of making the population responsive to print, skilled in arithmetic, and docile to external stimuli. Today the school has another task: that of making the community as a whole capable of controlling its destinies: capable of disciplining and making over every aspect of its activities, the practical and the instrumental, the personal and the communal. A large order: it puts the school in the central position occupied by the Church in medieval Christendom.

From the drill school to the organic school: from the child school to the child-adult school: from a desiccated environment to a living environment: from closed issues and mechanical indoctrination to open inquiry and co-operative discipline as a normal process of living: that is one series of steps. From the part-time school, confined to a *building*, to the full-time school taking stock of and taking part in the whole life of the neighborhood, the city, the region: from an education whose truths and values are in good part denied by the actual environment and the social practice of the community to an education that is integral with the demands and possibilities of life and that shirks no needed effort to make over reality in conformity with purpose and ideal: here is another series of steps that mark the path of modern education.

A great distance as yet separates the new from the old: no community has as yet fully traversed it; for it is not merely a matter of a new program, a new kind of building, a new attitude on the part of student and teacher and parent: it is a matter of re-harmonizing the practical and the educational needs of the community through a drastic re-building of the entire structure. If the new school is the essential social nucleus, which bears the social heritage, the surrounding cell itself, its shape, its size, its structure, its special components, are no less essential to the process of development.

The institutions that are accessory, as it were, to the school are the public library and reading room, public workshops, studios, and laboratories, and public dance-halls and little theaters. In America both the settlement house and the school itself have demonstrated how these various activities may be effectively grouped, often in a single building, for service to the whole population at every age level. Here again, *what distinguishes the biotechnic community is not the introduction of any essentially new institutions so much as their adequate organization and incorporation as an elemental, indispensable part of the whole.* Most neighborhoods, even where public housing has been achieved, lack more than the most rudimentary physical facilities for a good social life.

It is no criticism of these proposals to urge that they are beyond the financial resources of our existing communities, on anything like the scale contemplated. That is equally true of good housing: both points may be freely granted. In an industrial system devoted solely to producing saleable goods for the market, we have not produced anything like the surplus necessary for well-balanced consumptive and creative activities. That is an elemental truth of the present economic regime. Neglect, disease, crime, illth are in one way or another signs of this environmental deficiency and economic anemia.

So far I have been talking about the essential civic nucleus of the neighborhood. These institutions must be enlarged in order to embrace a city; and there must be further buildings and organizations on a regional scale. But although the ascent to the region implies differences in scale, size, specialization, and opportunity, the fact is that all the facilities that are needed within the larger frame must exist, as active ingredients, in the life of the smallest and simplest unit. The great university, museum, laboratory, serving an élite drawn from every part of the world, will have its counterpart in the local community. And at the same time, the breaking up of overgrown megalopolitan institutions through the multiplication of local units—as in the Metropolitan Museum and the Colleges of the City of New York—is a needful step toward urban integration.

The important thing is to recognize the nature of the civic nucleus, and the necessity of a civic economy. Industry must be planned to put domestic and civic needs first, and industrial enterprise directed into such channels as will produce that surplus of energies out of which will come the equipment and structures, efficient equipment, handsome structures, needful to urban existence. A well-directed economy will reduce the number of manual workers and robots, will lessen the enterprise directed toward competitive salesmanship and advertising, will eliminate wanton wastes and stoppages: and it will multiply by manyfold the present supply of doctors, teachers, administrators, artists, scientists, and scholars.

A biotechnic economy demands that those interests and activities that directly subserve life shall come first; and that those which are instrumental to life, the extraction of raw materials, the preparation and processing of foods, the transformation of raw materials into all their thousand useful forms, shall be put second. The quantity, the direction, and the flow of the latter are to be determined, not by the standards of the market, but by the higher needs of man, as confirmed from year to year, from generation to generation by the desires of the many and the wisdom of the competent. "Recreation, education, welfare, and health are the most rapidly growing urban public services," observed the National Resources Committee in its report on cities (1937). As our cities become the object of broader planning and design, these activities will occupy a growing share in the total budget of every community; and their effective embodiment will be the first task of architect and community planner and administrator.

14: The Social Concept of the City

Much recent housing and city planning has been handicapped because those who have undertaken the work have had no clear notion of the social functions of the city. They sought to derive these functions from a cursory survey of the activities and interests of the contemporary urban scene. And they did not, apparently, suspect that there might be gross deficiencies, misdirected efforts, mistaken expenditures, here that would not be set straight by merely building sanitary tenements or widening narrow streets.

The city as a purely physical fact has been subject to numerous investigations. But what is the city as a social institution? The earlier answers to these questions, in Aristotle, Plato, and the Utopian writers from Sir Thomas More to Robert Owen, have been on the whole more satisfactory than those of the more systematic sociologists: most contemporary treatises on "urban sociology" in America throw no important light upon the problem.

One of the soundest definitions of the city was that framed by John Stow, an honest observer of Elizabethan London, who said: "Men are congregated into cities and commonwealths for honesty and utility's sake, these shortly be the commodities that do come by cities, commonalties, and corporations. First, men by this nearness of conversation are withdrawn from barbarous feritie and force, to certain mildness of manners, and to humanity and justice, whereby they are contented to give and take right, to and from their equals and inferiors, and to hear and obey their heads and superiors. Also the doctrine of God is more fitly delivered, and the discipline thereof more aptly to be executed, in peopled towns than abroad, by reason of the facility of common and often assembling; and consequently such inhabitants be better managed in order, and better instructed in wisdom. . . . Good behavior is yet called *urbanitas* because it is rather found in cities than elsewhere. In sum, by often hearing, men be better persuaded in religion, and for that they live in the eyes of others, they be by example the more easily trained to justice, and by shame-fastness restrained from injury.

"And whereas commonwealths and kingdoms cannot have, next after God, any surer foundation than the love and good will of one man towards another, that also is closely bred and maintained in cities, where men by mutual society and companying together, do grow to alliances, commonalties, and corporations."

It is with no hope of adding much to the essential insight of this description of the urban process that I would sum up the sociological concept of the city in the following terms:

The city is a related collection of primary groups and purposive associations: the first, like family and neighborhood, are common to all communities, while the second are especially characteristic of city life. These varied groups support themselves through economic organizations that are likewise of a more or less corporate, or at least publicly regulated, character; and they are all housed in permanent structures, within a relatively limited area. The essential physical means of a city's existence are the fixed site, the durable shelter, the permanent facilities for assembly, interchange, and storage; the essential social means are the social division of labor, which serves not merely the economic life but the cultural processes.

The city in its complete sense, then, is a geographic plexus, an economic organization, an institutional process, a theater of social action, and an esthetic symbol of collective unity. On one hand it is a physical frame for the commonplace domestic and economic activities; on the other, it is a consciously dramatic setting for the more significant actions and the more sublimated urges of a human culture. The city fosters art and *is* art; the city creates the theater and *is* the theater. It is in the city, the city as theater, that man's more purposive activities are formulated and worked out, through conflicting and co-operating personalities, events, groups, into more significant culminations.

Without the social drama that comes into existence through the focusing and intensification of group activity there is not a single function performed in the city that could not be performed—and has not in fact been performed—in the open country. The physical organization of the city may deflate this drama or make it frustrate; or it may, through the deliberate efforts of art, politics, and education, make the drama more richly significant, as a stage-set, well-designed, intensifies and underlines the gestures of the actors and the action of the play. It is not for nothing that men have dwelt so often on the beauty or the ugliness of cities: these attributes condition men's social activities. And if there is a deep reluctance, on the part of the true city dweller, to leave his cramped quarters for the physically more benign environment of a suburb—even a model garden suburb!—his instincts are partly justified: in its various and many-sided life, in its very opportunities for social disharmony and conflict, the city creates drama; the suburb lacks it.

One may describe the city, in its social aspect, as a special framework directed toward the creation of differentiated opportunities for a common life and a significant collective drama. As indirect forms of association, with the aid of signs and symbols and specialized organizations, supplement direct face-to-face intercourse, the personalities of the citizens themselves become many-faceted: they reflect their specialized interests, their more intensively trained aptitudes, their finer discriminations and selections: the personality no longer presents a more or less unbroken traditional face to reality as a whole. Here lies the possibility of personal disintegration; and here lies the need for re-integration through wider participation in a concrete and visible collective whole. What men cannot imagine as a vague formless society, they can live through and experience as citizens in a city. Their unified plans and buildings become a symbol of their social relatedness; and when the physical environment itself becomes disordered and incoherent, the social functions that it harbors become more difficult to express.

Before man can become fully humanized, the social man must break up into a thousand parts: so that each grain of aptitude, each streak of intelligence, each fiber of special interest, may take a deeper color by mingling with other grains, streaks, and fibers of the same nature. The undifferentiated common bond of primary association is weakened by these specialized associations; but the cable of civilization itself becomes stronger through such multiform twisting into a more complex and many-colored strand. From simple con-

sciousness of kind in the tribe or family to the developed consciousness of kind that goes with special associations and differentiated
groups: from habit to choice: from a fixed mold to a dynamic equilibrium of forces, from taking life as it comes to comprehending it
and redesigning it—that is the path of both human and civic development. This transfer of emphasis from the uniformities and common acceptances of the primary group to the critical choices, the purposive associations, and the rational ends of the secondary group is
one of the main functions of the city. The city is in fact the physical
form of the highest and most complex types of associative life.

One further conclusion follows from this concept of the city:
social facts are primary, and the physical organization of a city, its
industries and its markets, its lines of communication and traffic,
must be subservient to its social needs. Whereas in the development
of the city during the last century we expanded the physical plant
recklessly and treated the essential social nucleus, the organs of
government and education and social service, as mere afterthoughts,
today we must treat the social nucleus as the essential element in
every valid city plan: the spotting and inter-relationship of schools,
libraries, theaters, community centers, is the first task in defining the
urban neighborhood and laying down the outlines of an integrated
city.

If this is the correct interpretation of the nature of the city, a good
part of the work that has been done under the name of city planning
must be discounted and discredited: it has no more to do with the
essential functions of living in cities than the work of the scene shifter
and property man have to do with the development of Hamlet. This
is not to deny its use: for scene shifters have their use: but it is to
cast a doubt upon its sufficiency. The planning of cities by those who
have hitherto called themselves city planners is like having the play
itself written by the property man, or mistaking the stage directions
for the lines of the actors.

Though our conception of the physical structure of cities during
the last century has been inadequate even in purely physical terms,
like the movement of people and the service of industries, people
have been even more wantonly inept in their conception of the social
structure and the social activities of cities. With their eyes on the

purely material changes that are so necessary, even those who have striven most earnestly for improvement have been content to build mere buildings. But buildings do not make a city; and the adequate planning of buildings is only a part of the necessary social schema.

From the standpoint of city design, the sociological theory of groups has a direct bearing upon plan. One of the difficulties in the way of political association is that we have not provided it with the necessary physical organs of existence: we have failed to provide the necessary sites, the necessary buildings, the necessary halls, rooms, meeting places: hence in big cities the saloon and the shabby district headquarters, open only to the more sedulous party members, have served. As for industries, the political opportunities for association have been even scantier: in how many factory districts are there well-equipped halls of sufficient size in which the workers can meet?

On this point one may well quote the Webbs. "We do not think it is usually understood," they observe, "how greatly the efficiency of trade unionism may be increased, and its very character raised to the height of a service of public utility, merely by the provision of structural accommodation equal in dignity to that of a government department, in which all the several unions in each locality may be worthily housed together."

The town meeting of the New England political system had reality because it had dimensions and members: the citizens met face to face in a special building, the town hall: they saw and heard their fellow citizens, and they discussed problems relating to a unit immediately within their grasp and vision. But the peoples of the Western World have sought to live under an abstract and disembodied political democracy without giving its local units any other official organ than the polling booth. We have hitherto lacked the energy or the insight to provide the necessary meeting halls, committee rooms, permanent offices. We have still to organize neighborhoods and corporate organizations as if the political functions of the community were important ones. In the conglomerate masses we have called cities, it is no wonder that political life, as a concrete exercise of duties and functions, has given way to various subtle parasitisms and diversions. And contrariwise, in new communities that have been planned as social units, with visible coherence in the architecture, with a sufficient number of local meeting rooms for group activities, as in Sunnyside Gardens, L. I., a robust political life, with effective collective action and a sense of renewed public responsibility, has swiftly grown up.

The moral should be plain: we must design whole social units: we must design *cities:* and in the order of design the arrangement of the essential social institutes, their adequate provision and servicing, is a key to the rest of the structure. It is on the purely instrumental physical services that we must practice the most stringent economy, even parsimony; it is on the political and educational services that we must spend with a lavish hand. This means a new order of design and a different type of designer: it means that that emphasis will shift progressively from the stage-set to the drama, and that the handling of the social activities and relationships will engage the fuller attention of the planner. In time, this will have the effect of reducing the instrumental arts of town planning to fairly stable routine, while a greater amount of energy and economic support will be set free for the expressive arts: painting and sculpture, drama and music, will again have greater importance than sanitation and sewage and the studious habits of antisepsis.

The elemental unit of planning, then, is no longer the house or the houseblock: the elemental unit is the city, because it is only in terms of this more complex social formation that any particular type of activity or building has significance. And the aim of such planning is not the efficiency of industry by itself, or the diminution of disease by itself, or the spreading of culture by itself: the aim is the adequate dramatization of communal life: the widening of the domain of human significance so that, ultimately, no act, no routine, no gesture will be devoid of human value, or will fail to contribute to the reciprocal support of citizen and community. When this drama is sharply focused and adequately staged, every part of life feels an uprush of social energy: eating, working, mating, sleeping are not less than they were before, but far more: life has, despite its broken moments, the poise and unity of a collective work of art. To create that background, to achieve that insight, to enliven each individual capacity through articulation in an intelligible and esthet ically stimulating whole, is the essence of the art of building cities. And less than that is not enough.

15: Contrapuntal Organization

One more point about the social nature of cities. Reformers and renovators, whose work usually is prompted by some raucous failure in the social machinery, are tempted to oversimplify in the opposite direction: they seek a harmony too absolute, an order whose translation into actual life would stultify the very purpose it seeks to achieve. The student of utopias knows the weakness that lies in perfectionism: for that weakness has now been made manifest in the new totalitarian states, where the dreams of a Plato, a Cabet, a Bellamy have at many removes taken shape. What is lacking in such dreams is not a sense of the practical: what is lacking is a realization of the essential human need for disharmony and conflict, elements whose acceptance and resolution are indispensable to psychological growth.

When we seek a more co-operative order in the design of cities, therefore, we are seeking an order in which more significant kinds of conflict, more complex and intellectually stimulating kinds of disharmony, may take place: in short, we seek a contrapuntal order. Hence the need for plans and buildings that shall not remain frozen against the assault of change, the rivalry of new ideas. One can easily imagine, for instance, a new cult of family life, growing up in the face of some decimating catastrophe, which would necessitate a swift revision in plans for housing and city development: a generous urge toward procreation might clash in policy with the view of the prudent, bent on preserving a barely achieved equilibrium. Such conflicts may occur on every level; and the struggle they provoke is no less essential to the good life than the most affable co-operation. Hence the positive need for variety in urban life: varied groups: varied personalities: varied activities.

Communities that are so small that the essential differences between people and groups must be prudently glozed over, or so large that they cannot intermingle and clash without violent disorder, fail to provide the best environment for the development of human character. Fellowship is a good; and the Lynds do well to recognize it as

an attribute of Middletown: a representative attribute, characteristic of other parts of the world than the small towns of the American
midland. But good-fellowship is not the whole duty of social man;
and some of the highest products of the spirit have been achieved,
not out of small contentments, but out of great frustration, antagonism, disappointment, bitterness: Koheleth and Isaiah, Euripides and
Shakespeare, Dante and Machiavelli, offer testimony to the higher
disharmonies possible in Jerusalem and Athens and Florence and
London. Psychological growth is more important than somatic satisfaction; and in designing cities we must provide an environment
broad enough and rich enough never to degenerate into a "model
community."

It was perhaps his understanding of this vitalizing challenge of
dissonance that caused Patrick Geddes to be more interested in the
renewal of historic cities than in the fresh building of model garden
communities; and despite the difficulties of overcoming the vested
interests that oppose urban renovation in existing centers, it is precisely here, perhaps, that we shall find the necessary stimulus to
create the best type of community design: witness Amsterdam, witness the magnificent achievements in Frankfurt and Berlin before
Nazism came in. Enough, then, to show that the city, if it is to function effectively, cannot be a segregated environment: the city with
a single class, with a single social stratum, with a single type of
industrial activity, offers fewer possibilities for the higher forms of
human achievement than a many-sided urban environment. (As elsewhere, this holds equally true for the region.) If metropolitan districts have grown at the expense of smaller towns during the last
generation it is partly because, *under a metropolitan economy*, this
dramatically viable many-sidedness is to be found only in metropolitan areas.

16: Principles of Urban Order

In giving this sociological answer to the question: What is a city?
one has likewise provided the clue to a number of important other
questions. Above all, one has the criterion for a clear decision as to
what is the desirable size of a city—or may a city perhaps continue
to grow until a single continuous urban area might cover half the

American continent, with the rest of the world tributary to this mass? From the standpoint of the purely physical organization of urban utilities—which is almost the only matter upon which metropolitan planners in the past have concentrated—this latter process might indeed go on indefinitely. But if the city is a theater of social activity, and if its needs are defined by the opportunities it offers to differentiated social groups, acting through a specific nucleus of civic institutes and associations, definite limitations on size follow from this fact. Without such limitations the community lacks social focus.

Plato defined the desirable size of a city as 5000: this was the number of people who could hear the voice of a single orator and so participate in the active political life of his day. In our time, new technical facilities have altered many social functions: but the principle of limitation is still imperative. In one of Le Corbusier's early schemes for an ideal city, he chose three million as the number to be accommodated: the number was roughly the size of the urban aggregate of Paris, but that hardly explains why it should have been taken as a norm for a more rational type of city development. If the size of an urban unit, however, is a function of its productive organization and its opportunities for active social intercourse and culture, certain definite facts emerge as to adequate ratio of population to the process to be served. Thus, at the present level of culture in America, a million people are needed to support a university. Many factors may enter which will change the size of both the university and the population base; nevertheless one can say provisionally that if a million people are needed to provide a sufficient number of students for a university, then two million people should have two universities. One can also say that, other things being equal, five million people will not provide a more effective university than one million people would. The alternative to recognizing these ratios is to keep on overcrowding and overbuilding a few existing institutions, thereby limiting, rather than expanding, their genuine educational facilities.

What is important is not an absolute figure as to population or area: although in certain aspects of life, such as the size of city that is capable of reproducing itself through natural fertility, one can already lay down such limits. What is more important is to *express size always as a function of the social relationships to be served.* There is an optimum numerical size, beyond which each further increment of inhabitants creates difficulties out of all proportion to the benefits. There is also an optimum area of expansion, beyond which further urban growth tends to paralyze rather than to further important social relationships. Rapid means of transportation have given a regional area, with a radius of from forty to a hundred miles, the unity that London and Hampstead had before the coming of the underground railroad. But the activities of small children are still bounded by a walking distance of about a quarter of a mile; and for men to congregate freely and frequently in neighborhoods the maximum distance means nothing, although it may properly define the area served for a selective minority by a university, a central reference library, or a completely equipped hospital.

The area of potential urban settlement has been vastly increased by the motor car and the airplane; but the necessity for solid contiguous growth, for the purposes of intercourse, has in turn been lessened by the telephone and the radio. In the Middle Ages a distance of less than half a mile from the city's center usually defined its utmost limits. The block-by-block accretion of the big city, along its corridor avenues, is in all important respects a denial of the vastly improved type of urban grouping that our fresh inventions have brought in. For all occasional types of intercourse, the region is the unit of social life: but the region cannot function effectively, as a well-knit unit, if the entire area is densely filled with people—since their very presence will clog its arteries of traffic and congest its social facilities.

Limitations on size, density, and area are absolutely necessary to effective social intercourse; and they are therefore the most important instruments of rational economic and civic planning. The unwillingness in the past to establish such limits has been due mainly to two facts: the assumption that all upward changes in magnitude were signs of progress and automatically "good for business," and the belief that such limitations were essentially arbitrary, in that they proposed to "decrease economic opportunity"—that is, opportunity

SOCIAL BASIS OF THE NEW URBAN ORDER 489

for profiting by congestion—and to halt the inevitable course of change. Both these objections are superstitious.

Limitations on height are now common in American cities; drastic limitations on density are the rule in all municipal housing estates in England: that which could not be done has *been* done. Such limitations do not obviously limit the population itself: they merely give the planner and administrator the opportunity to multiply the number of centers in which the population is housed, instead of permitting a few existing centers to aggrandize themselves on a monopolistic pattern.

These limitations are necessary to break up the functionless, overgrown urban masses of the past. Under this mode of design, the planner proposes to replace the "mono-nucleated city," as Professor Warren Thompson has called it, with a new type of "polynucleated city," in which a cluster of communities, adequately spaced and bounded, shall do duty for the badly organized mass city. Twenty such cities, in a region whose environment and whose resources were adequately planned, would have all the benefits of a metropolis that held a million people, without its ponderous disabilities: its capital frozen into unprofitable utilities, and its land values congealed at levels that stand in the way of effective adaptation to new needs.

Mark the change already in process today. The neotechnic sources of power, transport, and communication do not follow the old highway network at all. Giant power strides over the hills, ignoring the limitations of wheeled vehicles; the airplane, even more liberated, flies over swamps and mountains, and terminates its journey, not on an avenue, but in a field. Even the highway for fast motor transportation abandons the pattern of the horse-and-buggy era. The new highways, like those of New Jersey and Westchester, to mention only examples drawn locally, are based more or less on a system definitively formulated by Benton MacKaye in his various papers on the Townless Highway. The most complete plans form an independent highway network, isolated both from the adjacent countryside and the towns that they bypass: as free from communal encroachments as the railroad system. In such a network no single center will, like the metropolis of old, become the focal point of all regional advantages: on the contrary, *the whole region becomes open for settle-ment.*

Even without intelligent public control, the likelihood is that within the next generation this diffusion and decentralization of urban facilities will go even farther. The Townless Highway begets the Highwayless Town in which the needs of close and continuous human association on all levels will be uppermost. This is just the opposite of the earlier mechanocentric scheme of Roadtown, as pictured by Edgar Chambless and the Spanish projectors of the Linear City. For the highwayless town is based upon the notion of effective zoning of functions through initial public design, rather than by blind legal ordinances. It is a town in which the various functional parts of the structure are isolated topographically as urban zones, appropriately designed for their specific use: with no attempt to provide a uniform plan of the same general pattern for the industrial, the commercial, the domestic, and the civic parts.

The first systematic sketch of this type of town was made by Messrs. Wright and Stein in their design for Radburn in 1929; a new type of plan that was repeated on a limited scale—and apparently in complete independence—by planners in Köln and Hamburg at about the same time. Because of restrictions on design that favored a conventional type of suburban house and stale architectural forms, the implications of this new type of planning were not carried very far in Radburn. But in outline the main relationships are clear: the differentiation of foot traffic from wheeled traffic in independent systems, the insulation of residence quarters from through roads; the discontinuous street pattern; the polarization of social life in specially grouped civic nuclei, beginning in the neighborhood with the school and the playground and the swimming pool.

Through these convergent efforts, the principles of the polynucleated city have been well established. Such plans must result in a fuller opportunity for the primary group, with all its habits of frequent direct meeting and face-to-face intercourse: they must also result in a more complicated pattern and a more comprehensive life for the region, for this geographic area can only now, for the first time, be treated as an instantaneous whole for all the functions of social existence. Instead of trusting to the mere massing of population to produce the necessary social concentration and social drama, we must now seek these results through deliberate community planning and closer regional linkages. The words are jargon; but the importance of their meaning should not be missed.

One might call this new method of designing city and region in working partnership the principle of unity by apportioned distribution rather than unity by centralization: the latter means physical spreading and control from a dominant center, whereas the first means functional *spotting*. Any one part of such a complex may become, for a special purpose, the center of the region. But instead of existing merely as a specialized unit, it is part of both a smaller unit, the local community or "city" in the old-fashioned connotation, and of a larger unit, the region—and finally of even greater groupings with wider ramifications: provinces and inter-regional areas.

The working library in any neighborhood should be, for whoever is capable of using it, the sum of all the separate libraries: this principle has already been wisely incorporated in the development of the branch library system in America, and, even more, in the relation of the greater libraries that serve the scholarly community to the Library of Congress. So, too, with every other item of equipment: every service grades upward in functional and topographic specialization, from the smallest residential quarter to the planet considered as man's home.

What is important in this emerging conception is not expressed in the notion of satellite cities—not even of satellite garden cities. For, as the very word indicates, it assumes that one particular city will retain planetary proportions; whereas, from the standpoint of social relativity and social integration, one must conceive that each unit, though ranging in size from five thousand to fifty thousand, will have equal "valence" in the regional scheme. Before the metropolis can achieve a healthy, orderly life, it must boldly re-build its own internal structure as well as its outlying areas on similar lines. And for any particular function, the largest city in the group will often be subordinate to a smaller unit: what is significant is not the quantity of inhabitants but the quality of service.

These new possibilities in city life come to us not merely through better technical organization but through acuter sociological understanding. To embody them in plans and programs and to dramatize the activities themselves in appropriate individual and urban structures, form the task of the coming generation.

To describe the modern community one would have to explore in detail the potentialities of life for modern man. In brief, the care of those whose labors and plans create the solid structure of the community's life must be to unite culture in all its forms: culture as the care of the earth: culture as the disciplined seizure and use of energy toward the economic satisfaction of man's wants: culture as the nurture of the body, as the begetting and bearing of children, as the cultivation of each human being's fullest capacities as a sentient, feeling, thinking, acting personality: culture as the transformation of power into polity, of experience into science and philosophy, of life into the unity and significance of art: of the whole into that tissue of values that men are willing to die for rather than forswear—religion. The culture of cities is ultimately the culture of life in its higher social manifestations. Plainly, to carry this study farther, to follow through its implications for the personality and the community, demands another book. But the outlines, I trust, are by now evident and easy to trace out.

The cycle of the machine is now coming to an end. Mankind has learned much in the hard discipline and the shrewd, unflinching grasp of practical possibilities that the machine has provided during the last three centuries: but we can no more continue to live in the world of the machine than we could live successfully on the barren surface of the moon. Man is at last in a position to transcend the machine, and to create a new biological and social environment, in which the highest possibilities of human existence will be realized, not for the strong and the lucky alone, but for all co-operating and understanding groups, associations, and communities.

"Men come together in cities," said Aristotle, "in order to live: they remain together in order to live the good life." Only fragments of this purpose are fulfilled in the modern world; but a new pattern of the good life is emerging, partly by pressure from within, partly by reaction against the disordered environment, the wry, dehumanized purposes, the ugly barbarisms that still prevail in the world at large.

Already, in the architecture and layout of the new community, one sees the knowledge and discipline that the machine has provided turned to more vital conquests, more human consummations. Already, in imagination and plan, we have transcended the sinister limitations of the existing metropolitan environment. We have much to unbuild, and much more to build: but the foundations are ready: the machines are set in place and the tools are bright and keen: the architects, the engineers, and the workmen are assembled. None of us may live to see the complete building, and perhaps in the nature of things the building can never be completed: but some of us will see the flag or the fir tree that the workers will plant aloft in ancient ritual when they cap the topmost story.

GLOSSARY

Certain terms, originally coined by Patrick Geddes a generation ago, have been freely used in The Culture of Cities. For the convenience of those who have not read Technics and Civilization, in which they are more fully defined, the following definitions are provided.

EOTECHNIC. Refers to the dawn age of modern technics: an economy based upon the use of wind, water and wood as power, with wood as the principal material for construction. Dominant in Western Europe from the tenth to the eighteenth century. Marked by improvements in navigation, glass-making, and the textile industries, from the thirteenth century on: by widespread canal-building and increased utilization of power and power-machines in the later phase.

PALEOTECHNIC. Refers to the coal and iron economy, which existed as a mutation in the eotechnic period (blast furnace and primitive railway) but began in the eighteenth century to displace the eotechnic complex, and became a dominant between 1850 and 1890. Key inventions: steam engine, railroad, steamship, Bessemer converter, various automatic devices in spinning and weaving. Up to the last quarter of the nineteenth century the eotechnic economy remained as a recessive.

NEOTECHNIC. Refers to the new economy, which began to emerge in the eighties, based on the use of electricity, the lighter metals, like aluminum and copper, and rare metals and earths, like tungsten, platinum, thorium, et al. Vast improvements in utilization of power, reaching its highest point in the water-turbine. Destructive distillation of coal: complete utilization of scrap and by-products. Growing perfection and automatism in all machinery. Key inventions: electric transformer, electric motor, electric light, and electric communication by telegraph, telephone, and radio: likewise vulcanized rubber and internal combustion engine. At the present time, the eotechnic complex is a survival, the paleotechnic is recessive, and the neotechnic is a dominant.

BIOTECHNIC. Refers to an emergent economy, already separating out more clearly from the neotechnic (purely mechanical) complex, and pointing to a civilization in which the biological sciences will be freely applied to technology, and in which technology itself will be oriented toward the culture of life. The key inventions, on the mechanical side, are the airplane, the phonograph, the motion picture, and modern contracep-

495

tives, all derived directly, in part, from a study of living organisms. The application of bacteriology to medicine and sanitation, and of physiology to nutrition and daily regimen, are further marks of this order: parallel applications in psychology for the discipline of human behavior in every department are plainly indicated. In the biotechnic order the biological and social arts become dominant: agriculture, medicine, and education take precedence over engineering. Improvements, instead of depending solely upon mechanical manipulations of matter and energy will rest upon a more organic utilization of the entire environment, in response to the needs of organisms and groups considered in their multifold relations: physical, biological, social; economic, esthetic, psychological.

BIBLIOGRAPHY

1: Introduction

This bibliography contains mainly two types of book: the kind that will enable the reader to deepen and widen his knowledge of the subject, and that which, though not covering specifically the field of the present volume, has been drawn upon for special documentation.

Most of the primary sources come under the second head; but, while utilizing and including these texts, I do not depart from the conviction that a work of synthesis must rest mainly upon facts already gathered and critically digested by the relevant specialists: in other words, upon what, from the standpoint of scholarship, must be classed as secondary sources. Those who are suspicious of this foundation show a distaste for the function of interpretation rather than a rationally grounded distrust of the method. All general views are of course open to corrections, both as to fact and as to interpretation; and I cordially welcome such aid.

The main weakness, perhaps, with respect to material in a work like the present one is not its partial reliance upon secondary sources, but the unfortunate absence of monographs on many important subjects. This lack shows a failure of spontaneous interest or systematic direction in many of the fields covered by this book. There is, for example, no good comparative history of municipal government and administration, so far as I am aware; nor has it occurred to anyone, apparently, to write a history of municipal institutions which would trace the function and organization of each separate element in the civic heritage. Such a book indeed perhaps awaits the writing of preliminary monographs upon the historic development of the town council, the water supply, sanitation, public assemblies, and civic institutes, and so forth, on a scale comparable to the existing study of, say, the Museum. The lack of detailed knowledge on the place and duties and earliest appearances of the City Architect points to but one of many fields that needs to be turned over. The absence of detailed critical analyses of even the bare statistics of health, disease, and mortality in city and country is scandalous: meaningless non-comparable units, like nations, are utilized for such statistics, thus avoiding a concrete approach to important facts about the environment. Sociological studies, corresponding to biological ones, on the embryology, morphology, and physiology of cities await a new corps of investigators: present historic and geographic surveys are still largely in the fact-finding stage: deficient in analytic grasp. A series of interpretative studies of important cities, pushing even more systematically along the lines laid down in Poëte's monumental study of Paris, is badly needed. Most histories, even of cities, are pre-civic and pre-sociological.

Fortunately, the most important original sources for the student of cities are not written or printed documents: they are the cities themselves, and the chief use of a literature, perhaps, is to provide clues and answers for the problems raised by a field study of the urban environment. There is no way of abbreviating this first-hand exploration of the environment and the first-hand experience that comes from living and working in cities: indeed, it is partly for lack of it that so many sociological analyses of the city have been so far from satisfactory.

While the study of particular cities, through books and documents as well as personal survey, is indispensable to the serious student, I have found it impossible within the limits of this bibliography to include more than a few outstanding books: notably Davidsohn's Florence and Poëte's Paris. The fact is that the list of books dealing with even a minor town would often prove larger than the present bibliography. Each student should compile his own bibliography for the city where he lives, or for the place that most keenly attracts his interest.

2: Civic and Regional Background

Up to now there have been few general treatises on cities in any language: indeed the lack of important historic and sociological investigations on cities as such is equaled only by a similar neglect in the field of agriculture and the cultivation of the landscape. These areas have lain outside the major spheres of scholarly and practical interest during the last few centuries, during which scholarship often exhausted itself upon trivial pursuits, more easily pursued in the seclusion of the study or the vault of archives.

Because of a persistent civic tradition brought down fairly intact from the Middle Ages, these weaknesses have not been as marked in the literature of Germany as in that of other countries. From Nitsch and Wilda, Maurer, and Riehl, through Below and Bücher, down to the writers of the last two decades, there has been a fairly exhaustive geographical, historical, and even sociological interpretation of the German city: a study marked by a concentration which, though admirable, has the defect of its qualities—provincialism.

While the more recent sociological interpretation of Sombart, Weber, and Tönnies has not been wholly adequate on the civic side, they have at least kept the concept of the city alive: even during that process of centralization and de-regionalizing that followed the Franco-Prussian war and the complete ascendancy of Berlin: indeed, German civic tradition will possibly survive the drastic unifications and docile automatisms of the National Socialists. The civic initiatives of the great burgomasters of Ulm and Frankfurt during the latter part of the nineteenth century, as well as the revival of architecture, probably gave an extra stimulus to the scholarly interest in the past, as well as direct aid to the work of urban reconstruction. Though German cities show some of the worst examples of capitalistic land exploitation, the basis for the great urban renewal that took place under the Republic between 1924 and 1932 was firmly laid.

If Germany is perhaps foremost in urban historic scholarship, France has to its credit the best work on the geographic foundations of cities. Though Le Play, with his rural and primitive preoccupations, did not push his analysis as far as the city—resting content with the family as the fundamental social unit—the work of Comte and Reclus and Le Play, as well as a later school of geographers headed by Vidal de la Blache and Brunhes, supplied the scientific foundations of the regionalist movement—and contributed to the recognition of the individuality of cities and regions. The monumental works of Lavedan and Poëte are of first importance: no serious student of the subject can do without them.

3: British Initiatives

In the English literature of cities, one finds a gap of a century between Adam Smith, perhaps the last of the classic economists who understood the social function of the city and the economic rôle of the political functions and first of a new order of economists, represented by Ashley. Except as a mere political area, the city had no place in the utilitarian tradition; and the first great revival of interest in the city came from another quarter: that of art. Unlike the German Romanticists, the English school had been mainly hostile to cities, or at least indifferent to them, though one of Wordsworth's noblest sonnets was inspired by the view from Westminster Bridge. But the love for Gothic architecture finally spread to its urban surroundings; and in the writings of Ruskin, particularly in the Stones of Venice, the city as a social organism received its first analysis, retrospective but realistic. The treatment was minute and fragmentary: the focus of architectural analysis was the stones, rather than the pattern of the whole. But Ruskin, so often treated contemptuously as a superficial esthete, was one of the first to preach a return to fundamentals in the design of cities: mark his demand in Munera Pulveris and elsewhere for fresh air and clean water as elemental pre-requisites for urban art.

In the eighties Charles Booth, following Mayhew's journalistic studies, began his monumental survey of London: during the same decade Patrick

Geddes, starting as a biologist, began to bring together the diverse sociological traditions of Comte and Le Play: the work of these two men was decisive in supplying both a mode of investigation and a comprehensive diagnostic toward planning and development. Geddes brought together the geographic and the historic sides of the survey: more than that, he united the hitherto quite separate interests of the scholarly investigators of the actual urban environment and the practical aims of the sanitarian, the housing reformer, the municipal engineer, and the town planner, who had sought to make piecemeal changes in that environment without often understanding it as either a social or a structural whole. Geddes's interest in the city as a biologist, a sociologist, and a philosopher, and his practical example as an organizer of civic pageants and cities exhibitions, no less than as planner, was undoubtedly the greatest single factor in the civic and regional revival that has taken place in the British Commonwealth, touching places as distant as India where Geddes, between 1914 and 1924, planned some fifty cities. One must not however forget the initiatives of great English industrialists like Salt, Cadbury, Lever, and Rowntree, the pioneer work of important architects like Webb, Baillie-Scott, Mackintosh, Parker, and Unwin, the statesmanlike leadership of John Burns, nor yet the decisive contribution of Ebenezer Howard.

None of Geddes's thinking about cities was ever adequately embodied in a monograph or a book. His Cities in Evolution is his most viable work on the subject, while his Report on Indore, in two volumes, is the fullest published embodiment of his method, his point of view, and his sociological insight. Some of his cities lectures were taken down stenographically, and typescript copies, made and preserved through the fine initiative of his colleague, Mr. John Ross, are preserved in the Outlook Tower in Edinburgh. The work of Geddes, and that of his brilliant colleague, Victor Branford, if it has lacked a sufficient number of continuators, has nevertheless had a wide influence: Herbertson's work on regional geography was a direct result: so too the numerous admirable regional surveys from that of Doncaster onwards.

4: The American School: Sociological Approach

In America, there is a long interval between Henry Carey and the Chicago school of urban sociologists, which begins properly with Charles Zueblin, who in turn had been deeply stimulated by the work of Geddes at the Outlook Tower in Edinburgh. The intermediate link is perhaps Charles Horton Cooley, on the theoretic analysis of groups and communities, and the influence of Olmsted and Charles Mulford Robinson on the practical side, particularly in the Middle West, where so much of their work was done. During the last decade there has been a considerable ripening of this fruit. The tying up of urban sociology with the preliminary biological discipline of ecology has been a helpful one: note also the contributing influence of Wheeler's bio-sociological studies. American sociologists as a whole, however, have too often left the city, and likewise the village, out of account: even the ethnologists, so given to field studies, have ignored the specific pattern of the habitat: dealing with material objects like canoes or weapons or methods of making fire, but not with the camp or village as another type of collective artifact.

One of the great sins of urban sociology in America, apart from the injudicious use of irrelevant statistics, has been a failure to utilize the geographic disciplines: most conspicuous perhaps in the Lynds' otherwise admirable study of Middletown: least so in Carpenter's The Sociology of City Life. Another great lack has been an absence of comparative knowledge of cities both in time and in space: hence a tendency to limit urban studies to the American city, to the *contemporary* American city, and—final provincialism—to the contemporary *metropolitan* form, as if it were in a sociological sense a final one. Hence a failure to enrich the background of the administrator and the planner. Another weakness American sociologists share pretty generally with their colleagues in other countries: an almost chronic inability to grasp the elementary Aristotelian distinction between the conditions of city life and its purposes and emergents: which results, unfortunately, in a further inability to ask interesting questions about the specifically human and cultural attributes of cities. Hence a tendency to concentrate upon population statistics, police regulations, and methods of sewage disposal: hence a serious failure to deal competently or exhaustively with institutions, social complexes, and social-esthetic structures as such, in terms of their function and meaning as integral parts of the urban habitat.

Much valuable work has been done by Park, Burgess, Wirth, Ogburn, and others: but it is doubtful if urban sociology will be able to proceed much farther without making fundamental alterations in its frame of reference. Cultural ecology must not merely adopt the methods of plant or animal ecology: it must advance further by studying that involved interplay between the physical environment and the conditioned functions of life on one hand, and the social milieu and the released functions—in which choice, desire, fantasy, and purpose play a part—on the other.

5: The Eutopians

Some of the most important works on cities lie outside the period treated in this book, or are radically different in method and scope from the more systematic treatises that have so far been considered. In Western literature, Plato and Aristotle, as one might expect, said not only the first word on the subject but often the last; for one may look in vain for a better mythological

account of the rôle of the division of labor in human society—and its mis-
application as well—than in the opening dialogue of Plato's Republic. Aristotle's Politics is likewise still serviceable: all the more because his concept
of the future as potentiality is more valid for organisms and groups than
the more external statistical conception of future events that now is fashionable: hence the special province of eutopias in his political philosophy.

This great tradition was re-opened by the utopian writers, beginning with
Thomas More; and in a sense all the utopians, from More and Andreae
down to Fourier, Bellamy, and Herzl, have been better sociologists than
more influential abstract thinkers like Machiavelli and Spencer, just because the utopians had a place in their scheme for the city, as the concrete
embodiment of community. Among pre-sociological writers one must say a
special word for Raleigh, Botero, and above all, Stow.

6: Imaginative Literature

One whole class of books, and not the least important, is almost unrepre-
sented in the following list: that is, works of the imagination. Unlike the old-
fashioned historian, I have not left out these works of fiction because of the
curious illusion that they are not documents or do not refer to facts: for the
facts of the imagination belong to the real world no less than sticks and
stones do. There is, indeed, no better clue to what people see and feel and do
than what finds its way into contemporary poems, plays and stories: they
have a sort of veracity which court records, account books, and newspaper
clippings do not possess: for they contain, in an excellent state of preservation, the living man and so much of his environment as he could respond
to and express.

No: the fact is that here, as in the graphic and plastic arts, one is merely
embarrassed by the wealth of documentation. If the reader has not at least
read his Boccaccio and Chaucer, he does not know the medieval city; if he
does not know Mann's Buddenbrooks or Proust's Combray, he will not
appreciate how much of that city survived into the nineteenth century.
For a documentation of the paleotechnic town Nicholas Nickleby and
Hard Times are as important as Engels and Chadwick: at a later stage,
Zola and Arnold Bennett are no less significant; and for extensive grasp
as well as detailed insight into the modern city Balzac is incomparable.

To neglect this vast wealth of sources under the impression that one was
being rigorous or scientific would merely betray the fact that one's science
and metaphysics still belonged to the seventeenth century. I will go farther:
no one knows the life of cities as a social fact who has not drawn upon the
plays and novels produced by men who have lived in cities and described
the existence of their inhabitants: and this is particularly true since the seventeenth century, when the social novel itself came into existence as the sub-

jective precursor of a systematic objective sociology. The London of Defoe, Fielding, Thackeray, Dickens, Meredith and Wells (particularly Tono-Bungay and the New Machiavelli), the cathedral towns of Anthony Trollope, the St. Petersburg and Moscow of Tolstoi, the French cities of Stendhal, Balzac, Hugo, the Chicago of Dreiser and the Midland cities of Sinclair Lewis, to say nothing of the Boston and New York of William Dean Howells —all such imaginative works are important enrichments of the experience of the student of cities. And if I may single out a contemporary work of fiction for its deliberate and extraordinary grasp of every phase of the urban scene, I would specially commend M. Jules Romains' great panorama: Men of Good Will.

7: Cultural Interpretation

Among the cultural interpreters who have dealt with cities, there are two whose work stands out particularly in relation to the present book. For direct example and influence, the most important is W. H. Riehl, whose classic Natural History of the German People, published in the middle of the nineteenth century—and unfashionable because at once belated and too "advanced"—has been strangely neglected, even in Germany. My debt to Riehl, which I acknowledged in Sticks and Stones in 1924, is one that I wish more people shared. The other writer is Oswald Spengler, whose Decline of the West, that strange rubbish heap of atavistic notions and arresting insights, sentimental perversities and intuitive profundities, was one of the first historical interpretations to put the city in the center of the stage once more.

8: Theory and Practice of Regionalism

On the subject of regionalism and regional development, including conservation, there is a succession of classic studies whose influence, though immediately negligible, has had a cumulative importance: among them note G. P. Marsh's Man and Nature, N. S. Shaler's Man and the Earth, Van Hise's The Conservation of Natural Resources and Benton and MacKaye's The New Exploration.

One of the most brilliant expositions of potential changes in man's relation to agriculture and industry was Kropotkin's Fields, Factories, and Workshops: the work of a scientist who continues to grow in importance as a penetrating thinker no less than a humane personality. While Marx's ideology was mainly a paleotechnic one, Kropotkin had by the end of the nineteenth century emerged from that narrow mold to the conception of a neotechnic life-economy: his anarchist communism, which is now indigenous only in Spain, may prove to be the necessary corrective of the sterile bureaucratization to which Marxism has so easily lent its doctrines, both in its Stalinist and Trotskyist forms.

In developing the concept of regionalism itself, the reader will find many useful suggestions in Geddes and Branford; but apart from the French school already mentioned, the most significant work so far is embodied in two public documents: Henry Wright's Report on a Plan for the State of New York, published in 1926 under the Housing and Regional Planning Commission, with Clarence S. Stein as Chairman; and the report of Professor John Gaus and his associates for the National Resources Board on Regional Factors in National Planning. Both reports are approaches to the problem of delimiting and developing the human habitat: reconnaissance of fresh territory. Not closed solutions but new openings. In spirit and outlook, The National Being, by George Russell (A.E.) is closer to the central doctrines of regionalism than many treatises which make free use of the name.

The new school of American regionalists that has taken root especially in the South—I would call attention particularly to the work of Odum, Moore, and Vance—has transformed Turner's descriptive interpretation of sectionalism in American life into a dynamic doctrine of social development. Odum and Moore's new book on American Regionalism, which I have had the privilege of reading in manuscript, is an outstanding effort to unify a diversity of regional approaches.

9: Planning and Development

So far I have been dealing mainly with the historical and sociological literature. It remains to say a word about the field of planning in its many aspects. The literature of city development is an ancient one that goes back to Hippodamus, who according to Aristotle also projected a utopia: indeed, there has been a steady connection between the practical city of everyday life and the projection of utopias: from Alberti to Robert Owen, and from Owen to Howard and Le Corbusier, the ideal plans of one generation have become the practical realizations of the next.

On the actual planning of cities, the esthetic emphasis has long been overstressed: within this field the best books are those of Sitte, Brinckmann and Zucker. Lavedan's Histoire de l'Urbanisme and Poëte's excellent Introduction à l'Urbanisme are outstanding works. The best comparative introduction is Werner Hegemann's two volume summary of the International Cities Exhibitions in Berlin and Düsseldorf, 1910-1912. A more recent survey of similar territory, that of Bruno Schwan, is useful but indifferently done. In English, Unwin's Town Planning in Practice was of first importance at the time of its original publication; but its re-edition in 1932, without sufficient attempt to deal with later developments and theories of planning, relegates it to a somewhat historical position. Schultze-Naumburg's study of landscape and cities and architectural forms in his monumental work, Kulturarbeiten, is more or less oriented to the past: otherwise it is a model of the sort of work that should be undertaken in every region. For further visual background see Creutzburg's superb album of illustrations: Kulturland-schaften der Erde.

Many technical advances have been made in city planning during the last generation. One of the most important was embodied in a little pamphlet, Unwin's Nothing Gained by Overcrowding, which demonstrated the extravagance of past attempts at congestion, which wasted in expensive streets what was saved on building land. I am familiar with no work which has made an effective critical analysis of all these changes and improvements: on matters like orientation, Zeilenbau, cul-de-sacs, high and low buildings, dogmatic positions have been taken, or attacked, with little real critical insight: the nearest approach is the somewhat tangential one of Henry Wright's Re-Housing Urban America. By far the most important book toward advancing the new concept of the city was undoubtedly Ebenezer Howard's The Garden City, first published in 1898 as Tomorrow. Le Corbusier's original contribution on The City of Tomorrow was almost as economically innocent and as mechanocentric as the puerile fulminations of New York's skyscraper architects during the nineteen-twenties: but his later book, La Ville Radieuse, indicates an advance. In formal opposition to Le Corbusier one must place Frank Lloyd Wright's The Disappearing City: it represents the extreme possibility of decentralization under modern technical conditions. Most of the current technical books on city planning are attempts to codify past practices or to make small adaptations to new exigencies: their prescriptions must be taken with reserve: "good for this day only."

10: Housing and Architecture

In the smaller unit, the housing estate and the neighborhood community, there has been greater opportunity for unified practice than in cities as a whole. See Catherine Bauer's admirable Modern Housing, which is particularly good in its esthetic analysis, and which shows many plans and photographs of actual developments. A careful perusal of Henry Wright's Re-Housing Urban America is perhaps the best possible introduction on the planning side. Since the notions of coherence and contemporaneity have, from the standpoint of the present book, a particular part to play in all contemporary design, let me call attention to two books which deal directly with the esthetic and social problem of form: H. R. Hitchcock's Modern Architecture and Walter Curt Behrendt's Modern Building. Monographs on F. L. Wright, Gropius, Oud, Le Corbusier, and others should of course be consulted.

11: Importance of Survey

The chief documents about cities are secondary to the city itself as document. That demonstration owes much to Ruskin, though in the meanwhile the archaeologists, from Schliemann on, have shown how much of the past may be recovered without benefit of the written record. Even the original landscape is often preserved in the stones, like the brooks of London, long covered up or filled, but still persisting in streets or in place names. A keen reader of cities is aware of geology and climate as soon as he enters the city: the site selected, the conformation of the streets, the area of window openings, the houses preserved, the ruins left behind, all tell their story: while the traffic in the streets, on the river, in the port, the movements and gestures of the inhabitants, add their tale to the public document of the city itself.

The first survey of a city should be cursory and random: taking in what one sees and what happens in no particular order, with no desire to anticipate or to take pre-determined routes or to make "short cuts" which in fact serve to cut short the possibilities of fresh experience. One should first float passively in a sea of impressions. When this first process of saturation has finished, one should take every opportunity to become part of the city, even in minor ways: purchases in shops and markets, visits to homes if introductions or chance acquaintances make them possible, above all, some definite work, if that presents itself. Only after a general immersion in the urban scene, should one attempt to explore it systematically from the center outward, and from its periphery in the open country back to the core. Here camera, sketch-pad, and notebook may be used with profit. At this point one may usefully bring in guides and local histories, not to carry in one's pocket, like a plan or a map, but to consult before and after the journey or ramble. But Wordsworth's injunction should be remembered, all the more because it goes against the grain of purposive intellectual activity and our usual pragmatic sense: "Think you, . . . that nothing of itself will come, but we must still be seeking?" A wise passiveness is an important counterpart to intense activity: and research can never dispense with the need for contemplation.

12: Museums and Guides

The detailed knowledge of at least one city is indispensable to the student of cities: detailed and many-sided, amplified and expanded over the course of the years. To concentrate one's studies, once they have the benefit of a grounding in visual survey and first-hand experience, the student should consult local museums. Those at London, Hamburg, Ulm, Augsburg, Edinburgh, and Paris I have found very rewarding; but they can be matched in many other cities: even in America cities like New York, Baltimore, Salem, have a rich quota of material. Most civic collections, unfortunately, are badly assorted and often meaningless from the standpoint of urbanism: overladen with curiosities and antiques. Even when they use models and maps, the exhibits are usually arranged by people in whom a purely antiquarian interest as to fact is superior to a social and cultural interest in the processes of urban life. Much must still be done in the re-assortment and re-selection of city museum collections: much will doubtless be done in future as people of less limited interests appear in the Board of Directors and among the museum curators: for a good city museum would be an indispensable part of an intelligent city planning department.

As to guides, the factual surveys of Baedeker, Muirhead, Grieben and others are of course indispensable: in America the new series of guides gotten out by the Federal Writers' Projects, under the Works Progress Administration, and handsomely illustrated, are superior to the older type of guide in the richness of their sociological and historical material, and in efforts at regional interpretation: this is particularly true of the New England Guides so far published. Their one weakness so far is in a lack of city plans and layouts. As for the latter, modern works, even European, leave much to be desired: city plans are usually so small that the plan is crowded, and except for the general layout and disposition of the most important buildings, they are not very helpful to the student. Every city should have available maps like those of the British Ordnance Survey on a scale of one foot equals a mile, so that the occupation of the land could be surveyed in detail, supplemented by airplane views. Airplane mapping itself will make this possible; and the decennial, or better lustral, record of changes in the city should be part of its orderly record. Where such maps are available, the student will do well to make use of them. Among the Encyclopedias both Brockhaus and Meyer have excellent small scale city maps.

13: Photographs and Motion Pictures

One further aid to the student should be noted: the motion picture. The newsreels often afford interesting, if all too brief, glimpses of cities in action in every part of the globe; and now and again in a dramatic picture, something of the flavor of a city is well projected. Thus La Kermesse Heroique has an exceptionally fine background, quite veraciously portrayed, of a late medieval city of the Lowlands: though the play is a farce, there is a heavy underpainting of reality which goes beyond the costumes. Pabst's Kameradschaft, a moving drama of the mine workers of Germany and France, has all the dimensions of the fierce paleotechnic environment; and no one will ever forget the harbor of Odessa who has seen the great Soviet film of the S.S. Potemkin, nor the heroic face of Madrid after a view of the areas the Fascists have devastated in Joris Iven's film. These are but samples: a more adult art of the motion picture would, without resorting to the perfunctory and dreary travelogue, doubtless have much richer offerings in this department.

For certain cities there are photographic collections, private and public.

of great interest. The documentations of Paris by Atget and of New York by Alfred Stieglitz are pre-eminent here; while the illustrated sections of the newspapers supplement them from day to day—often with striking prints. In America the Federal Arts Projects of the W.P.A. have contributed a treasury of important photographs. The collections of commercial photographers are likewise useful: particularly in the records of the present generation. For an earlier period the lithographs and etchings and engravings, upon which I have drawn freely for illustration, are rich in historic detail: some of the important books containing these prints are listed in the bibliography. So much for the highlights. The following list, though selective, pretty well covers the ground. Wherever possible, however, I have left out periodical publications: the student will find the necessary references in special bibliographies to which I call attention, and in, of course, the Index to Periodicals.

14: List of Books

Abercrombie, Patrick: *Town and Country Planning.* New York: 1933.
    Brief introductory sketch (Home University Series) dealing with the various historic and contemporary aspects of the subject. Limited appreciation of the real advances made during the last fifteen years.

Abercrombie, Patrick, and Brereton, B. F.: *Bristol and Bath Regional Planning Scheme.* Liverpool: 1930.
    One of a series of studies—see those of Sheffield, East Kent, Deeside, Oxfordshire—done by Abercrombie in collaboration with various other people. Intelligent, well-rounded, with an appreciation of the intimacies of regional planning, the beauty of landscape and the variety of local life, often lacking in similar American studies. Recommended.

Ackerman, Frederick L., and Ballard, W. F. D.: *A Note on Site and Unit Planning.* New York City Housing Authority: 1937.

Ackermann, Rudolph: *The Microcosm of London.* 3 vols. London: 1808.
    Select Views of London. London: 1816.

Adams, Henry: *Mont-Saint-Michel and Chartres.* Boston: 1913.

Adams, Thomas: *Outline of Town and City Planning; A Review of Past Efforts and Modern Aims.* New York: 1935.
    Chiefly English examples and precedents.
    Regional Plan of New York and Its Environs.
    Vol. II: *The Building of the City.*
    See *Regional Survey of New York and Its Environs.*

Addams, Jane: *The Spirit of Youth in the City Streets.* New York: 1909.
    Twenty Years at Hull House. New York: 1910.

Addison, Christopher: *The Betrayal of the Slums.* London: 1922.
    By the Minister of Health who helped initiate England's great post-war housing program.

Addy, Sidney Oldall: *The Evolution of the English House*. London: 1889.
(See Lloyd.)

Adshead, S. D.: *Town Planning and Town Development*. New York: un-
dated.

Aldridge, Henry R.: *The National Housing Manual*. London: 1923.

Allee, Warder Clyde: *Animal Aggregations: A Study in General Sociology*.
Chicago: 1931.
Animal Life and Social Growth. Baltimore: 1932.

Allen, George Cyril: *The Industrial Development of Birmingham and the
Black Country: 1860-1927*. Illustrated. London: 1929.
Valuable paleotechnic data.

Allen, John W.: *A History of Political Thought in the Sixteenth Century*.
London: 1928.

Alverdes, Friedrich: *Social Life in the Animal World*. New York: 1927.

American Society of Planning Officials: *Planning Bibliography*, April 1935.
(Strictly land-use planning.)

Anderson, Nels, and Lindeman, Eduard C.: *Urban Sociology; An Introduction to the Study of Urban Communities*. New York: 1928.
Study of the physical and psychological basis of the modern city. Main frame of
reference is a narrow one.

Anderson, William: *The Units of Government in the United States. Public
Administration Service, No. 42*. Chicago: 1934.

Andreae, Johann Valentin: *Christianopolis*. Trans. by F. E. Held. New York:
1916.
A late-medieval Utopia, particularly interesting for its sidelights on actual conditions.

Annals of the American Academy of Political and Social Science:
Housing and Town Planning: January 1914.
Current Developments in Housing: March 1937.

Aristotle: *Politics*.
The Politics still repays close reading: for methodology as well as civic insight.

Armstrong, P. C., and Robinson, F. E. M.: *City and Country; a Study in
Fundamental Economics*. Toronto: 1934.
Unimportant.

Aronovici, Carol: *Housing and the Housing Problem*. Chicago: 1920.

Aronovici, Carol (editor): *America Can't Have Housing*. New York: 1934.
Short contributions by various authorities.

Ashbee, C. R.: *Where the Great City Stands*. London: 1917.
By an architect who was one of the leaders of the post-Morris arts and crafts
movement.

Ashley, W. J.: *An Introduction to English Economic History and Theory*.
2 vols. Fourth Edition. London: 1913-14.

One of the earliest, and still one of the best summaries in English on medieval guilds and cities.

Ashley, W. J.: *Surveys; Historic and Economic.* London: 1900.
Discerning discussion of the medieval town and its institutions in reviews of Flach, von Below, Pirenne, Maitland, et al., by one of the best of the English economic historians.

Atterbury, Grosvenor: *The Economic Production of Workingmen's Houses.* New York: 1931. (In *Buildings; Their Uses and the Spaces About Them. Regional Survey of New York and Its Environs,* Vol. 6.)
Record of early twentieth-century attempts to simplify construction of the shell. See James Hole for Victorian precursors.

Avenel, Georges d': *L'Évolution des Moyens de Transport.* Paris: 1919.

Histoire Economique de la Propriété, des Salaires, des Denrées et de tous les Prix en Général Depuis l'An 1200 Jusqu'en l'An 1800. 7 vols. in 6. Paris: 1894-1926.
An incomparable work of exhaustive scholarship: indispensable. (See especially Vol. VI, Book V, Chapters 5 and 6.)

Histoire de la Fortune Française; la Fortune Privée à travers sept siècles. Paris: 1927.
(See Chapters 9 and 10 on Prix et Loyers des Maisons.)

Le Mécanisme de la Vie Moderne. 4 vols. Paris: 1900-03.
(See Vol. III: *La Maison Parisienne.*)

Richelieu et la Monarchie Absolue. 4 vols. 2nd ed. Paris: 1895.

Baer, C. H.: *Deutsche Wohn und Festräume aus sechs Jahrhunderten.* Stuttgart: 1912.

Bailey, Liberty Hyde: *The Holy Earth.* New York: 1915.

Universal Service. New York: 1918.
Background books on essential regionalism by a great agriculturist who was also a poet.

Balzac, Honoré de: *La Comédie Humaine.*

Le Père Goriot. Paris: 1835.

Le Cousin Pons. Paris: 1847.
Two fine examples from *Scènes de la Vie Parisienne.* It was not for nothing, as Brunetière pointed out, that Balzac was a contemporary of Auguste Comte.

Barde, Charles. See Rey, A. A.

Barker, Mabel: *Education for a State of Peacedom Through Regional Study.* In *A Conference on Regional Surveys.* London: 1915.

L'Utilisation du Milieu Géographique pour l'Education. Montpellier: 1926.
Valuable exposition of the applications of Regional Survey to education as first carried out under Geddes in Edinburgh. (See Geddes.)

Barker, Mabel (editor): *Exploration; Regional Survey.* London: 1938.
Pocket size notebook, interleaved for notes, with schedule of points and questions for regional surveyors. May be obtained from The Le Play Society, 1 Gordon Square, London, W.C. 1. (See also Fagg and Hutchins.)

Barnes, Harry: *The Slum; Its Story and Solution.* London: 1931.

Barnett, Mrs. Henrietta Octavia (Rowland): *Canon Barnett.* London: 1918.
First-hand account of the first Settlement House.

Bartels, Adolph: *Der Bauer in der Deutschen Vergangenheit.* Second Edition. Jena: 1924.
Historic illustrations.

Bartholomew, Harland: *Urban Land Uses; An Aid to Scientific Zoning Practice.* In *Harvard City Planning Studies.* IV. Cambridge: 1932.

Bassett, Edward M.: *Zoning . . . during the first twenty years.* New York: 1936.

Batsford, B. T.: *Amsterdam.* In Batsford's *Pictorial Guide Series.* London: 1936.

Bauer, Catherine: *Modern Housing.* New York: 1934.
By far the best recent survey: main stress on European example, particularly brilliant on the planning and architectural side. Good bibliography.

Bauer, Catherine, and Stein, Clarence S.: *Store Building and Neighborhood Shopping Centers.* In *The Architectural Record:* Feb. 1934.
Important: demonstrates vicious economic mischief of over-building and bad design.

Beaufoy, Samuel Leslie: *Six Aspects of Town Planning.* London: 1932.

Bechtel, Heinrich: *Wirtschaftsstil des Deutschen Spätmittelalters.* München: 1930.
Valuable.

Beeson, E. W.: *Port Sunlight; The Model Village of England.* New York: 1911.
Entirely photographs.

Behrendt, Walter Curt: *Die einheitliche Blockfront als Raumelement im Stadtbau; Ein Beitrag zur Stadtbaukunst der Gegenwart.* Illustrated. Berlin: 1911.

Die Holländische Stadt. Berlin: 1928.
Rich in insight and illustrations.

Der Kampf um den Stil im Kunstgewerbe und in der Architektur. Stuttgart: 1920.
Historical and critical interpretation of the modern attempt to achieve form in the industrial arts and architecture. Wide European and American reference, on the social as well as the esthetic foundations.

Der Sieg des Neuen Baustils. Stuttgart: 1927.

Modern Building; Its Nature, Problems and Forms. New York: 1937.
Excellent critical interpretation.

Bellamy, Edward: *Looking Backward: 2000-1887.* First Edition. Boston: 1888. New Edition. Boston: 1931.
Partial anticipations of neotechnic urban organization (mechanical).

Beloch, J.: *Antike und Moderne Groszstädte.* In *Zeitschrift für Sozialwissenschaften.* Breslau: 1898.

Below, Georg Anton Hugo von: *Das ältere Deutsche Städtewesen und Bürger-tum.* (In *Monographien zur Weltgeschichte,* Vol. VI.) Bielefeld: 1898.
Die Enstehung des modernen Kapitalismus und die Hauptstädte. In *Schmollers Jahrbuch.* Vol. 43, pt. 1. München: 1919.
Keen criticism of Sombart's position in his second edition.
Mittelalterliche Stadtwirtschaft und gegenwärtige Kriegswirtschaft. In *Kriegswirtschaftliche Zeitfragen.* Vol. 10. Tübingen: 1917.
Aus Sozial- und Wirtschaftsgeschichte; Gedächtnisschrift für Georg von Below. Stuttgart: 1928.
(See Essays by Häpke and Schneider.)
Territorium und Stadt. In *Historische Bibliothek.* Bd. 11. München: 1900.
Der Ursprung der deutschen Stadtverfassung. Düsseldorf: 1892.
Below's contributions to the legal and historic foundations of the modern city are important.

Bemis, A. F.: *The Evolving House.* 3 vols. Cambridge: 1933-36.
Vol. I. *A History of the Home* (In Collaboration with John Burchard II).
Vol. II. *The Economics of Shelter.*
Vol. III. *Rational Design.*
The first work on this subject with any pretenses to completeness. Unfortunately, the treatment of the house as an isolated detachable unit, without reference to community, leads to emphasis on only one type, and to the ignoring of important historic material. Vol. II useful for its data on cost, but, like Vol. I, inadequate in its treatment of the communal complex. (See Wright, Henry: Re-Housing Urban America.)

Benians, Sylvia Mary: *From Renaissance to Revolution.* London: 1923.

Benson, Edwin: *Life in a Medieval City: Illustrated by York in the XV Century.* London: 1920.
Compact Summary. (See Green, A. S.)

Berlage, H. P.: *L'Art et la Société.* Brussels: 1914.

Bernan, Walter (pseudonym, see Robert Meikleham).

Berty, A., and Legrand, H.: *Topographie Historique de Vieux Paris.* 6 vols. 1866-97.

Besant, Walter: *Westminster.* London: 1895.
Short historic summary. See many other volumes by same author on various aspects of London.

Bird, Charles S., Jr., Chairman: *Town Planning for Small Communities.* Walpole Town Planning Committee, Walpole, Mass. (National Municipal League Series.) New York: 1917.

Black, Russell V., and Black, Mary Hedges: *Planning for the Small American City.* Chicago: 1933.

Blanchard, Raoul: *Une Methode de Géographie Urbaine.* In *La Vie Urbaine.* October 12, 1922.

Boardman, Philip L.: *Esquisse de l'Œuvre éducatrice de Patrick Geddes.* Montpellier: 1936.
Interesting doctor's thesis on Geddes's educational ideas. See Barker, Mabel.

Boissonnade, Prosper Marie: *Life and Work in Medieval Europe: Fifth to Fifteenth Centuries.* New York: 1927.

Bookwalter, John: *Rural Versus Urban; Their Conflict and Its Causes: a Study of the Conditions Affecting Their Natural and Artificial Relations.* New York: 1911.

Booth, Charles: *Life and Labor in London.* Seventeen vols. Begun 1889. London: 1902.
A monumental survey, exhaustive in details, but as difficult to grasp as a whole as the city it describes.

Botero, Giovanni: *A Treatise Concerning the Causes of the Magnificence and Greatness of Cities.* Trans. London: 1606.
Revealing.

Botkin, Benjamin Albert, editor: *Folk-Say; a Regional Miscellany.* Norman, Oklahoma: 1929-32.
Miscellany of contemporary material by and about the folk, by one of the leaders of the new cultural regionalism of the Middle West.

Brandt, Jürgen: *Landesplanung.* In *Deutscher Verein für Wohnungsreform: Schriften.* Berlin: 1929.

Branford, Benchara: *A New Chapter in the Science of Government.* London: 1919.

Branford, Victor. *The Drift to Revolution.* London: 1919.
One of the *Papers for the Present* that Branford edited. Brilliant.
Interpretations and Forecasts: A Study of Survivals and Tendencies in Contemporary Society. New York: 1914.
On the Calculation of National Resources. In *Journal of Royal Statistical Society.* Sept. 30, 1901.
Science and Sanctity. London: 1923.
Branford's most important book: uneven, but full of penetrating sociological insights.
Sociological View of Westminster. In *Sociological Review:* July 1930.

Branford, Victor (editor): *The Coal Crisis and the Future: A Study of Social Disorders and Their Treatment.* London: 1926.
Coal—Ways to Reconstruction. London: 1926.

Branford, Victor, and Geddes, Patrick: *The Coming Polity.* London: 1917.
Our Social Inheritance. London: 1919.
Branford's chapter on Westminster full of insight.

Bredius, Abraham, and others: *Amsterdam in de Zeventiende Eeuw.* 3 vols. 's Gravenhage: 1897-1904.

Breton, Nicholas: *The Court and the Country*. London: 1618 (see Hazlett, W. C.).

Briggs, Martin S.: *Rusticus; or the Future of the Countryside*. London: 1927.

Brinckmann, A. E.: *Deutsche Stadtbaukunst in der Vergangenheit*. Second revised edition. Frankfurt-am-Main: 1921.
Excellent discussion of esthetic elements of city building with many admirable German examples.

Plastik und Raum; als Grundformen künstlicher Gestaltung. München: 1922.

Platz und Monument. Berlin: 1908.

Stadtbaukunst des achtzehnten Jahrhunderts. Berlin: 1914.

Brooks, Evelyn C., and Brooks, L. M.: *A Decade of Planning Literature*. In *Social Forces*: Mar. 1934.

Brun, L. Charles: *Le Régionalisme*. Paris: 1911.
Good.

Brunhes, Jean: *Human Geography*. Trans. New York: 1920.
Excellent.

Bryan, P. W.: *Man's Adaptation of Nature*. New York: 1934.
Good summary. Unfortunately already out of print.

Bücher, Karl: *Die Bevölkerung von Frankfurt am Main in XIV. und XV. Jahrhundert*. Tübingen: 1886.
Occupational statistics, as well as general ones. Important as an introduction to early municipal statistics in general.

Die Entstehung der Wirtschaft. 2 vols. Tübingen: 1919-20.

Die Grosstadt; Vorträge und Aufsätze zur Städteausstellung. Dresden: 1903.

Buckingham, James Silk: *National Evils and Practical Remedies*. London: 1849.
Contains plans for a model town.

Buer, Mabel Craven: *Health, Wealth & Population in the Early Days of the Industrial Revolution*. London: 1926.
False picture of medieval sanitation, and misleading in interpretation of later paleotechnic industry, but useful on its own ground.

Burchard II, John: See Bemis and Burchard: *Evolving House*.

Burckhardt, Jacob: *The Civilization of the Renaissance in Italy*. Translated from Fifteenth Edition. New York: 1929.
Still suggestive, though no longer an adequate total view of the period.

Burgess, E. W. (editor): *The Urban Community*. Chicago: 1926.
See also Park, Robert E.

Butler, Edward Cuthbert: *Benedictine Monachism*. London: 1919.

Cacheux, Emile: *Habitations Ouvrières*. Laval: 1882.

Cacheux, Emile: *Etat des Habitations Ouvrières à la Fin du XIXe Siècle.* Paris: 1891.
Highly useful documentation of evils and remedies.

Cadoux, G.: *La Vie des Grandes Capitales; Études Comparatives sur Londres—Paris—Berlin—Vienne—Rome.* 2nd ed. Paris: 1913.
On water and transportation.

Campbell, Argyll, and Hill, Leonard: *Health and Environment.* London: 1925 (IV, V).
So far one of the best books on a subject still insufficiently explored, though Hippocrates was aware of its importance. See Sydenstricker.

Carden, Robert Walter: *The City of Genoa.* London: 1908.

Carne, Elizabeth T.: *Country Towns; and the Place They Fill in Modern Civilization.* London: 1868.

Carpenter, Niles: *The Sociology of City Life.* New York: 1931.
A comprehensive text book of city life, limited historically by the fact that its main reference is to Rome. Also draws too heavily upon the limited area of contemporary American cities, while its few references to the medieval city are misleading. Nevertheless relatively satisfactory. See Anderson and Lindemann; also Gist and Halbert.

Carr-Saunders, A. M.: *The Population Problem; A Study in Human Evolution.* Oxford: 1922.

Carr-Saunders, A. M., and Jones, D. C.: *The Social Structure of England and Wales.* London: 1927.

Castiglione, Baldessare: *The Book of the Courtier.* Venice: 1528. Trans. New York: 1901.

Cerdá, Ildefonso: *Teoría General de la Urbanización.* Madrid: 1867.

Chadwick, Edwin: *Report on the Sanitary Condition of the Labouring Population of Great Britain.* London: 1842.
A classic summary of paleotechnic horrors.

Chadwick, Edwin (ed. Richardson, B. W.): *The Health of Nations.* 2 vols. London: 1887.
Summaries and extracts of Chadwick's numerous papers.

Chambless, Edgar: *Roadtown.* New York: 1910.
An attempt "to lay the modern skyscraper on its side" and run the elevators and pipes in continuous line across country. What was valid in Chambless' proposal was later embodied in Zeilenbau schemes *divorced* from the corridor avenue. The scheme has been independently revived recently in England. A classic example of the non-sociological approach. See also Kern.

Chancellor, Edwin Beresford: *The Pleasure Haunts of London During Four Centuries.* New York: 1925.
Full of valuable data.

Chapman, Harry: *Town and Regional Development: A Guide to the Town and Country Planning Act, 1932.* London: 1933.

Chase, Stuart: *The Nemesis of American Business.* New York: 1931.
See chapter on The Future of the Great City.

Chase, Stuart: *Rich Land Poor Land; A Study of Waste in the Natural Re-sources of America.* New York: 1936.
Recommended. See also Sears.

Cheney, Sheldon: *New World Architecture.* New York: 1930.

Chroniken der deutschen Städte vom 14. bis ins 16. Jahrhundert. Lübeck. 5 vols. Transcription of Original Chronicles, edited by Historical Commission of Royal Academy of Science, München. Leipzig: 1884-1911.
There are equally voluminous chronicles for other cities.

Clapham, John Harold: *An Economic History of Modern Britain.* 2 vols. Cambridge: 1930-32.
Comprehensive: with an underlying desire to offset the long tale of horrors that contemporary documents—and later interpreters like the Hammonds—reveal. Useful as a corrective to black one-sided accounts: but itself one-sided in its studious optimism.

Clark, Frederick P., and Woodruff, Joseph T.: *Progress Report to the National Resources Board on the Making of a Plan for New England.* Boston: 1934.

Clark, Victor Selden: *History of Manufactures in the United States (1607-1928).* 3 vols. New York: 1929.

Clarke, Maude Violet: *The Medieval City State; An Essay on Tyranny and Federation in the Later Middle Ages.* London: 1926.
Useful study in a field that will repay further efforts in scholarly analysis.

Cleveland, Frederick A., and others: *Modern Scientific Knowledge of Nature, Man, and Society.* New York: 1929.
(See Chapter by L. L. Bernard.)

Cobden-Sanderson, T. J., and others: *Art and Life; and the Building and Decoration of Cities.* London: 1897.
Excellent expression of original Arts and Crafts movement, which had a strong influence on Unwin and the Garden City. See Lethaby.

Cohen-Portheim, Paul: *The Spirit of London.* London: 1935.
Admirably done portrait of contemporary London. See Rasmussen.

Commelin, Caparus: *Beschrijvinge van Amsterdam.* 2 vols. Amsterdam: 1693-94.

Committee on Community Planning of American Institute of Architects: *Reports.* New York: 1924, 5, 6, 7.
Attempts by group of leading American architects, including Stein, Wright, Ackerman, Bigger, to redefine the position of the architect in relation to community and city planning.

Considérant, Victor P.: *Description du Phalanstère et Considerations Sociales sur l'Architectonique.* Paris: 1848.

Conway, William Martin: *Literary Remains of Albrecht Dürer.* Cambridge: 1889.

Cooley, C. H.: *Social Organization.* New York: 1909.

Cooley, C. H.: *Human Nature and the Social Order*. Revised Ed. New York: 1922.
  Important books by perhaps the wisest of American Sociologists.

Corey, Lewis: *Land Speculation*. In *Encyclopedia of Social Sciences*.

Cornish, Vaughan: *The Great Capitals*. London: 1923.
  Interesting essays in historical geography, with minor emphasis upon the physical shell.

  National Parks, and the Heritage of Scenery. London: 1930.
  Pleas for esthetic conservation of the landscape.

  The Scenery of England; a Study of Harmonious Grouping in Town and Country. London: 1932.

Cosgrove, John Joseph: *History of Sanitation*. Pittsburgh: 1909.
  Faute de mieux. The subject should long ago have been thoroughly canvassed by historians. See Feldhaus, Thorndyke, and Van der Bent.

Coulanges, Numa Denis Fustel de: *La Cité Antique*. 8 Ed. Paris: Trans. Boston: 1874.

Coulton, George Gordon: *Art and the Reformation*. New York: 1928.

  The Medieval Village. Cambridge: 1925.
  Does not deal with layout or physical character.

Cowper, Joseph M. (editor): *The Select Works of Robert Crowley*. London: 1872.

Creutzburg, Nikolaus: *Kultur im Spiegel der Landschaft; Das Bild der Erde in seiner Gestaltung durch den Menschen; Ein Bilderatlas*. Leipzig: 1930.
  Magnificent picture book which should be part of every planner's background.

Crowley, Robert: See Cowper.

Crozet, R.: *Une Ville Neuve du XVIe Siècle; Vitry-le-François*. In *La Vie Urbaine*. August and October 1923.

Cunningham, William: *An Essay on Western Civilization in Its Economic Aspects*. 2 vols. New York: 1913.

Davidge, W. R., and Warren, Herbert (editors): *Decentralisation of Population and Industry; a New Principle in Town Planning*. London: 1930.
  Excellent re-statement in terms of modern needs and opportunities of Howard's original garden city thesis, by various eminent British authorities.

  The Growth of English Industry and Commerce During the Early and Middle Ages. 3 vols. First Ed. Cambridge: 1882.
  Classic study with important references to village and town life.

Davidsohn, Robert: *Geschichte von Florenz*. 4 vols. in 8. Berlin: 1896-1927.
  An exhaustive study.

Defoe, Daniel: *The Complete English Tradesman*. Fourth Ed. London: 1738.
  Also 2 vols. London: 1726-32.
  Invaluable. Sombart draws on it.

De Forest, Robert Weeks and Veiller, Lawrence: *The Tenement House Problem*. 2 vols. New York: 1903.

Study of the rise of the tenement in New York City and the movement for reform. For more comprehensive later study see Ford, James.

Defries, Amelia: *The Interpreter Geddes*. London: 1927.
Not a satisfactory exposition of the man and his thought; but with some recorded flashes.

Dehio, Georg Gottfried: *Geschichte der Deutschen Kunst*. 4 vols. of text and 4 vols. of plates. Leipzig: 1919-1934.
Deals thoroughly with individual works of art and architecture; but is now somewhat dated by the absence of reference to the social complex and the collective form that condition the individual structure.

Delano, Frederic A.: *A Proposed Housing Policy*. In *American City*: Jan. 1937.

Dickens, Charles: *Hard Times*. London: 1854.
Classic picture of the paleotechnic town, with archetypal characters of Gradgrind, Bounderby, and M'Choakumchild.
Sketches by Boz. London: 1836.
Here and in his later sketches Dickens left many invaluable impressions of London. See Mayhew.

Diedrichs, Eugen: *Deutsches Leben in der Vergangenheit in Bildern; Ein Atlas mit 1760 Nachbildungen*. 2 vols. Jena: 1908.
Graphic history of German social life: immensely rewarding to those who can read images as well as letters.

Dieffenbacher, J.: *Deutsches Leben im 12. und 13. Jahrhundert*. In *Sammlung Göschen*. Leipzig: 1907.

Dikansky, Mikhail: *La Ville Moderne*. Paris: 1927.
Considers the city solely from the standpoint of physical circulation.

Dixon, Roland B.: *The Building of Cultures*. New York: 1928.

Dodd, George: *Days at the Factories; or, the Manufacturing Industry of Great Britain Described; Series I: London*. London: 1843.

Dominian, Leon: *The Frontiers of Language and Nationality in Europe*. New York: 1917.

Dopsch, Alfons: *The Economic and Social Foundations of European Civilization*. Wien: 1923-4. Trans. New York: 1937.
Reinterpretation of so-called Dark Ages, emphasizing element of continuity.

Dorau, Herbert B., and Hinman, A. G.: *Urban Land Economics*. New York: 1928.
Comprehensive but conventional. See Hurd.

Douglass, Harlan Paul: *The Little Town; Especially in Its Rural Relationships*. New York: 1919.
The Suburban Trend. New York: 1925.

Dubash, Peshoton S. G.: *Hygiene of Town Planning and Vegetation*. London: 1919.

Dublin, Louis I.: *Health and Wealth*. New York: 1928.

Du Camp, Maxime: *Paris; ses Organes, ses Fonctions et sa Vie; Dans la Seconde Moitié du 19e Siècle*. Sixth Ed. 6 vols. Paris: 1875.
One of the few comprehensive but not exhaustive works on civic institutions— ecclesiastical institutions are for example omitted—made all the more valuable by excellent historic introductions.

Duffus, Robert: *Mastering a Metropolis; Planning the Future of the New York Region*. New York: 1930.
Summary, in the most favorable light possible, of the proposals made by the Regional Plan of New York group. See Mumford.

Dulac, Albert, and Renard, Georges: *L'Evolution Industrielle et Agricole depuis Cinquante Ans*. Paris: 1912.

Dürer, Albrecht: *Unterricht zur Befestigung der Städte, Schlösser und Flecken*. First Ed.: 1527. Also Berlin: 1840; Paris: 1870.

Dykstra, C. A., and others: See National Resources Board.

Eastlake, Charles Locke: *Hints on Household Taste*. London: 1869.
The lawgiver of taste in the mid-Victorian home, whose dreadful incised decoration left its scar on both wood and stone: all in an effort to practice "simplicity, honesty, and propriety."

Eberstadt, Rudolph: *Handbuch des Wohnungswesen und der Wohnungsfrage*. 2 Ed. Jena: 1910. 4 Ed. Jena: 1920.
A comprehensive digest.

Die Spekulation im neuzeitlichen Städtebau. Jena: 1907.
Reply to economists who justified the "free market" in land.

Neue Studien über Städtebau und Wohnungswesen.

Vol. I. *Städtebau und Wohnungswesen in Belgien. Wiener Wohnverhältnisse*. Jena: 1912.

Vol. II. *Städtebau und Wohnungswesen in Holland*. Jena: 1914.

Vol. III. *Die Kleinwohnungen und das Städtebauliche System in Brüssel und Antwerpen*. Jena: 1919.
Important discussion of old and new housing types, with valuable plans of late medieval housing foundations for the indigent.

Elton, Charles: *Animal Ecology*. New York: 1927.

Encyclopédie, ou Dictionnaire Raisonné des Sciences, des Arts et des Métiers. Recueil de planches. 33 vols. Paris: 1751-77.
The city as such is neglected: a significant omission. But the illustrations of urban life, particularly on the industrial side, are important.

Engels, Friedrich: *The Condition of the Working-Class in England in 1844*. Leipzig: 1845. Trans. London: 1887.
Terrible but incontrovertible picture. For more favorable side see Clapham.

Zur Wohnungsfrage. Three pamphlets in one. Leipzig: 1872. Trans. London: 1935.
A curious argument against housing reform, still occasionally repeated by loyal Marxians. Rests on unsound assumption that what the rich possess is good, and that there are enough quarters to go around if "shared."

Engerand, Fernand: *Les Amusements des Villes d'Eaux à Travers les Ages.*
Paris: 1936.
Useful description of spas, baths, and watering resorts.

*English Courtier, The, and the Countrey Gentleman: Of Civil and Uncivil
Life.* London: 1586.
In Inedited Tracts.

Enock, Charles Reginald: *Can We Set the World in Order? The Need for a
Constructive World Culture; an Appeal for the Development and
Practice of a Science of Corporate Life; a New Science of Geography
and Industry Planning.* London: 1916.
A pioneering effort: note the date.

Espinas, Georges: *La Vie Urbaine de Douai au Moyen Age.* 4 vols. Paris:
1913.
The last two volumes present the historic evidence and documents.

Estienne, Charles, and Liébault, John: *Maison Rustique, or the Countrey
Farme.* London: 1616.

Evans, Frederick Noble: *Town Improvement.* New York: 1919.

Evelyn, John: *Fumifugium; or the Inconvenience of the Aer and Smoake of
London Dissipated.* London: 1661. Reprinted London: 1933.
Early zoning proposals: with a view to removing a nuisance that has persisted in
London since the early Middle Ages.

Fagg, Christopher C., and Hutchins, C. E.: *Introduction to Regional Sur-
veying.* Cambridge: 1930.
Particularly good on the side of natural science. Excellent illustration of Geddes's
ideal type valley section. Recommended.

Falke, Jakob von: *Art in the House.* Trans. from third German Ed. Boston:
1879.

Falke, Otto von, and Schnitz, H. (editors): *Deutsche Möbel vom Mittelalter
bis zum Anfang des 19 Jahrhunderts.* 3 vols. Stuttgart: 1923-4.

Farquharson, Alexander, and Branford, Sybella: *An Introduction to Regional Surveys.* London: 1924.

Fassett, Charles M.: *Assets of the Ideal City.* New York: 1922.
On the lines of Zueblin's American Municipal Progress.

Faure, Jean-Pierre: *Alger Capitale.* Paris: 1936.
Essay on the methods and tasks of modern townplanning with a bias in favor of
vertical circulation.

Fawcett, Charles Bungay: *Provinces of England; a Study of Some Geographical Aspects of Devolution.* London: 1919.
In Geddes and Branford's Making of the Future Series.

Federal Writers' Projects: Massachusetts; a Guide to Its Places and People.
Boston: 1937.

Vermont; a Guide to the Green Mountain State. Boston: 1937.

Washington; City and Capitol. Washington: 1937.
Three of a series of guidebooks done under the Works Progress Administration
which should do much to promote an adequate regional and historical conscious-

ness in the American citizen. Other volumes in this American Guide Series to follow.

Feldhaus, Franz Maria, and Siegfried, Karl: *Das blaue Badewannenbuch.* Schwarzenberg: 1932.
Origins of the bath-tub.

Feltham, John: *The Picture of London for 1803.* London: 1803.
The Picture of London for 1817. London: 1817.

Ferriss, Hugh: *The Metropolis of Tomorrow.* New York: 1929.
Actually the metropolis of yesterday: the infantile paper city erected by the megalo-politan business men and skyscraper architects of the nineteen twenties—a morbid dream enlarged and universalized by this able draughtsman.

Filene, Edward Albert: *The Way Out.* New York: 1924.
Plea for decentralization by a far-sighted merchant.

Fischer, Theodor: *Sechs Vorträge über Stadtbaukunst.* München: 1922.

Fisher, F. J.: *The Development of the London Food Market; 1540-1640.* In *Economic History Review:* April 1935.

Fletcher, Joseph S.: *Memorials of a Yorkshire Parish.* London: 1917.

Fleure, Herbert John: *Human Geography of Western Europe; a Study in Appreciation.* London: 1918.

Fleure, Herbert John, and Pelham, R. A. (editors): *Eastern Carpathian Studies; Roumania.* London: 1936.
Good example of regional reconnaissance survey, made by a Le Play Society group. See Barker.

Follett, Mary Parker: *Creative Experience.* New York: 1924.

Ford, James, and others: *Slums and Housing; with Special Reference to New York City; History; Conditions; Policy.* 2 vols. Cambridge, Mass.: 1936.
Does New York too much honor: what is needed is a more comprehensive history of the modern slum with international reference: small cities included.

Fourier, François Marie Charles: *Le Nouveau Monde Industriel et Sociétaire.* 1 vol. Paris: 1829. 2 vols. Paris: 1840.
A book whose wide influence has not yet been adequately estimated or understood.

Frank, Josef: *Architektur als Symbol.* Wien: 1931.

Frank, Waldo: *City Block.* Darien: 1922. Reprint. New York: 1932.
Novelist's fine interpretation of an urban milieu: New York.

Frankfurt, Das Neue; Internationale Monatsschrift für die Probleme kultureller Neugestaltung.
Supported by the city of Frankfurt during the period of its post-war renascence, this magazine did for city and regional planning what Die Form did for architec-ture and the industrial arts: expressions of a new creative spirit which made Germany, between 1925 and 1932, assume a world-leadership in the embodiment of the new culture.

Franklin, Alfred Louis Auguste: *La Vie Privée d'Autrefois; Arts et Métiers,*

Modes, Mœurs, Usages des Parisiens du XIIe au XVIIIe Siècle. 27 vols. Paris: 1887-1902.
Highly useful.

Freeman, Edward Augustus: *Exeter.* In *Historic Towns Series.* London: 1886.
More history *in* a city than of a city.

Freeman, Edward, and Hunt, W., Editors: *Historic Towns Series.* 11 vols. London: 1889-1893.
One of the early stirrings of the cities movement, with parallel manifestations in Germany, Holland, and the United States.

Frey, Dagobert: *Architecture of the Renaissance from Brunelleschi to Michel Angelo.* The Hague: 1925.
Gotik und Renaissance als Grundlagen der modernen Weltanschauung. Augsburg: 1929.
Penetrating.

Friedell, Egon: *A Cultural History of the Modern Age.* 3 vols. München: 1927-31. New York: 1930-1932.

Galpin, Charles Josiah: *Social Anatomy of the Rural Community.* In *University of Wisconsin Bulletin No. 34.*
Rural Relations of the Villages and the Small City. In *University of Wisconsin Bulletin No. 411.*

Gantner, Joseph: *Die Schweizer Stadt.* München: 1925.
Grundformen der Europäischen Stadt. Wien: 1928.
Worthy, but somewhat formal, attempt to establish the historic filiation of modern urban forms.

Ganzenmüller, Wilhelm: *Das Naturgefühl im Mittelalter.* Leipzig: 1914.

Garnier, Charles, and Ammann, A.: *L'Habitation Humaine.* Paris: 1892.
By a "historian who knew little architecture and an architect who knew little history." (Preface.) Emphasis of course on isolated house; but a step beyond Violette-le-Duc's *The Habitations of Man in All Ages.*

Gaus, John: See National Resources Board: *Regional Factors in National Planning.*

Geddes, Patrick: *City Development; a Study of Parks, Gardens, and Culture Institutes.* Edinburgh: 1904.
Report to the Carnegie Trustees on the development of Dunfermline.
City Deterioration and the Need of City Survey. In *Annals of the American Academy of Political and Social Science.* July 1909.
Cities; Being an Introduction to the Study of Civics. University of London Extension Lectures Syllabus. London: 1907.
Cities in Evolution. London: 1915.
Most popular and available of Geddes's writings on cities; made up chiefly of scattered papers, but with a unified point of view.
Country and Town in Development, Deterioration, and Renewal. University of London Extension Lectures Syllabus. London: copy without date.
Talks from My Outlook Tower. In *Survey Graphic:* Feb. 1, April 1, 1925.

Geddes, Patrick: *Town Planning in Patiala State and City*. Lucknow: 1922.

Town Planning Toward City Development; a Report to the Durbar of Indore. Two vols. Indore: 1918.
> Between 1914 and 1924 Geddes made or revised plans for some fifty cities in India and Palestine. The Report on Indore is the completest expression of his town-planning methods and his sociology and philosophy: Vol. II, which deals with the cultural foundations of the city, is particularly recommended.

The Civic Survey of Edinburgh. Edinburgh: 1911.
> From the nineties onward Geddes was a tireless advocate of city surveys as preliminary to intelligent town-planning and city design; and this little pamphlet indicates how much one who knows his subject can put in small compass.

Civics as Applied Sociology. In *Sociological Papers*. London: 1905.

A Suggested Plan for a Civic Museum. In *Sociological Papers*. London: 1906.

Geddes, Patrick, and Branford, Victor: Seen Branford.

Geddes, Patrick, and Mears, F. C.: *Cities and Town Planning Exhibition: Guidebook and Outline Catalog*. Belfast: 1911.
> Refers to Geddes's original and unique collection that was sunk during the first World War; his later collection, still probably intact, would serve as a foundation for a civic museum.

Geddes, Patrick, and Slater, Gilbert: *Ideas at War*. London: 1917.

Geddes, Patrick, and Thomson, J. A.: *Life; Outlines of General Biology*. 2 vols. New York: 1931.
> The chapters on the social applications of biology—along with his systematized charting of life and society—are by Geddes: the best summary of his thought available in print, though it does small justice to his demonic insight and his extraordinary intellectual reach.

Geisler, Walter: *Die Deutsche Stadt; Ein Beitrag zur Morphologie der Kulturlandschaft*. Stuttgart: 1924.

George, Henry: *Progress and Poverty*. New York: 1879.
> Economics of urban land increment and monopoly: weak in its positive proposals to remove monopoly without removing incentives to monopoly.

George, Mary Dorothy: *English Social Life in the 18th Century; illustrated from contemporary sources*. London: 1923.

London Life in the XVIIIth Century. New York: 1925. London: 1925.
> Good.

Gerard, P. (C. E.): *How to Build a City: Designed for the consideration of founders of towns, architects, civil engineers, sanitary organizations, municipal authorities, builders, and especially the managers of the various railroads to the Pacific*. Philadelphia: 1872.

Gerlach, Walther: *Die Entstehungszeit der Stadtbefestigungen in Deutschland; Ein Beitrag zur Mittelalterlichen Verfassungsgeschichte*. In *Leipziger Historische Abhandlungen*. Vol. XXXIV. Leipzig: 1913.
> Analysis of various concepts of city and village in German Middle Ages.

Gierke, Otto: *Natural Law and the Theory of Society; 1500 to 1800.* 2 vols. Trans. Cambridge: 1934.

Political Theories of the Middle Age. Trans. Cambridge: 1900.
From *Das Deutsche Genossenschaftsrecht:* one of the best early statements of the modern sociological theory of groups. See Cooley and MacIver.

Gilpin, William: *Forest Scenery.* First Edition, London: 1791; Second Edition (Revised): 1794.

Giry, A.: *Histoire de la Ville de Saint Omer.* Paris: 1877.
Important source of data on "advanced liberties" of medieval town.

Giry, A., and Réville, A.: *Emancipation of the Medieval Towns.* Trans. in *Historical Miscellany.* New York: 1907.

Gist, Noel Pitts, and Halbert, L. A.: *Urban Society.* New York: 1935.
Textbook.

Gleichen-Russwurm, Alexander von, Editor: *Kultur- und Sittengeschichte aller Zeiten und Völker.* 24 vols. in 12. Hamburg: 1929.
Valuable for its many illustrations.

Glotz, Gustave: *The Greek City; and Its Institutions.* Paris: 1928. Trans. New York: 1930.

Godfrey, Hollis: *The Health of the City.* Boston: 1910.
A fair early treatment of air, waste, noise and housing.

Goethe, Johann Wolfgang von: *Dichtung und Wahrheit.* Trans. London: 1848.
See the many admirable passages on medieval urban survivals.

Gomme, George Laurence: *The Village Community; with Special Reference to the Origin and Form of its Survivals in Britain.* New York: 1890.

Gooch, R. F.: *Regionalism in France.* New York: 1931.

Goodrich, Carter, and others: *Migration and Economic Opportunity; the Report of the Study of Population Distribution.* Philadelphia: 1936.
Careful study of the difficulties besetting decentralization of industry and population under the present capitalist regime. See Pratt.

Gotch, John Alfred: *Growth of the English House, 1100-1800.* London: 1909. Rev. Ed. London: 1928.

Gould, Elgin R. L.: *The Housing of the Working People; A Special Report of U. S. Committee of Labor.* Washington: 1895.

Gras, Norman S. B.: *History of Agriculture in Europe and America.* New York: 1925.
One of the few books available on a topic whose history has received even less attention than that of cities. A subject that awaits the new cultural historian. A co-ordinate history of the modification of landscape forms is also badly needed. See Meitzen and Prothero.

Industrial Evolution. Cambridge, Mass.: 1930.

An Introduction to Economic History. New York: 1922.
Follows the general line of Bücher; but leaves the impression that metropolitanism is a final stage.

Gras, Norman S. B.: *Regionalism and Nationalism.* In *Foreign Affairs.* April 1929.

Green, Alice Stopford: *Town Life in the Fifteenth Century.* 2 vols. London: 1894.
Classic.

Gregorovius, Ferdinand Adolf: *History of the City of Rome in the Middle Ages.* 8 vols. Stuttgart: 1859-1872. Trans. 13 vols. London: 1894-1902.

Grisebach, August: *Die alte deutsche Stadt in ihrer Stammeseigenart.* Berlin: 1930.
Richly illustrated; particularly with a varied lot of house-types.

Gropius, Walter: *The New Architecture and the Bauhaus.* London: 1935.

Gross, Charles: *The Gild Merchant; a Contribution to British Municipal History.* 2 vols. Oxford: 1890.
A fine work in which the conclusions in Vol. I are backed by a second volume of citations from original sources.

Grosstadt, Die. *Vorträge und Aufsätze zur Städteausstellung.* Dresden: 1903.
Includes essays by Bücher and Ratzel and Simmel—the latter on *The Big City and the Spiritual Life.*

Guicciardini, Francesco: *Counsels and Reflections.* London: 1890.
Classic contemporary revelation of Baroque wisdom on the plane of morals and politics.

Hamlin, Talbot Faulkner: *The American Spirit in Architecture.* New Haven: 1926.
Amply illustrated.

Hammarstrand, Nils: *Cities Old and New.* In *Journal of the American Institute of Architects.* New York: 1926.
Well-digested summary of early town planning from classic times onward.

Hammond, John Lawrence and Barbara: *The Skilled Labourer (1760-1832).* London: 1917.
The Town Labourer (1760-1832). New York: 1919.
The Village Labourer (1760-1832). London: 1911.
Graphic and well-documented studies: indispensable for an understanding of the paleotechnic town.

Hardy, Charles Oscar: *The Housing Program of the City of Vienna.* Washington: 1934.

Hardy, Marcel E.: *The Geography of Plants.* Oxford: 1920.

Hassert, Kurt: *Die Städte; geographisch betrachtet.* In *Aus Natur und Geisteswelt.* Leipzig: 1907.
Small but masterly study.

Havemeyer, Loomis (editor): *Conservation of Our Natural Resources.* New York: 1930.

Haverfield, Francis J.: *Ancient Townplanning.* Oxford: 1913.
Limited notion of plan; now superseded by Poëte and others.

Hazlitt, William Carew, Editor: *Inedited Tracts; Illustrating the Manners,*

Opinions and Occupations of Englishmen during the Sixteenth and Seventeenth Centuries. Containing Civil and Uncivil Life; The Court and the Country; The Serving Man's Comfort. London: 1868.

Head, George: *A Home Tour through the Manufacturing Districts of England in the Summer of 1835.* London: 1836.

Heckscher, Eli F.: *Mercantilism.* 2 vols. London: 1935.

Hegel, Karl: *Die Entstehung des Deutschen Städtewesens.* Leipzig: 1898.
Origins of the city and city government in medieval Germany. See also Preuss.

Hegemann, Werner: *City Planning, Housing; Historical and Sociological.* 2 vols. New York: 1936-7.
Muddled.

Der Städtebau, Nach den Ergebnissen der Allgemeinen Städtebau-Ausstellung. 2 vols. Berlin: 1911-13.
Superb piece of documentation and systematic survey. Still valuable: far more so than any other work of the author.

Das steinerne Berlin: Geschichte der grössten Mietskasernenstadt in der Welt. Berlin: 1930.

Hegemann, Werner, and Peets, Elbert: *The American Vitruvius; Civic Art.* New York: 1922.
The title properly betrays the retrospective tendencies and the esthetic approach of this monumental compendium. Now badly dated.

Heilig, Wilhelm: *Stadt und Landbaukunde.* Berlin: 1935.
Illustrations of organic forms of older village and city growth. Like most such books now issuing from Nazi Germany, it is flagrantly unfair to the good work done before 1933.

Held, F. E.: See Andreae.

Helm, William Henry: *Homes of the Past; a Sketch of Domestic Buildings and Life in England from the Norman to the Georgian Age.* New York: 1921.

Herbertson, A. J. and F. D.: *Man and His Work; an Introduction to Human Geography.* London: 1917.
Herbertson's study of the major natural regions laid the foundation for later work by Fennemann and others.

Herzl, Theodor: *Altneuland.*
A modern utopia, too little known even to Zionists, which ranks almost with Howard's Tomorrow.

Heyne, Moritz: *Das Deutsche Wohnungswesen von den ältesten geschichtlichen Zeiten bis zum 16. Jahrhundert.* Vol. I in *Fünf Bücher Deutscher Hausaltertümer.* Leipzig: 1899.
Valuable.

Hilbersheimer, Ludwig: *Grosstadtarchitektur.* Stuttgart: 1927.
Analysis of the possibilities of more rational architectural order possible in the big city: particularly good in suggestions for office and business sections. Contrast to American skyscraper projects.

Hill, Leonard: See Campbell.

Hintze, Hedwig (Guggenheimer): *Regionalism*. In *Encyclopedia of the Social Sciences*. New York: 1930.
Perhaps the best brief summary in any language, except for the section on America, where the facts are scanty and the interpretation painfully inadequate.

Hirth, Georg: *Das Deutsche Zimmer*. 2 vols. München: 1899.
Kulturgeschichtliches Bilderbuch aus drei Jahrhunderten. 6 vols. 2 Ed. Leipzig: 1899-1901.
Pictorial documentation of modern cultural history mainly from prints. Indispensable.

Historic Towns Series: See Freeman, E. A.

Hitchcock, Henry-Russell: *The Architecture of H. H. Richardson and His Times*. New York: 1936.
Rounds out Mrs. van Rensselaer's original account of this great proto-modern who paved the way for Sullivan. For fine appreciation of Richardson see Sullivan's Kindergarten Chats: effectual refutation of the depreciation by Hegemann in City Planning, Housing.
Modern Architecture; Romanticism and Reintegration. New York: 1929.
Valuable pioneer study; mainly esthetic in focus. See also Behrendt and Pevsner.

Hitchcock, Henry-Russell, and Johnson, Phillip: *Modern Architecture*. New York: 1932.

Hobhouse, Christopher: *1851 and the Crystal Palace*. London: 1937.
Complete first-hand documentation is accessible to those who have access to files of *Illustrated London News*.

Hobson, John A.: *Wealth and Life; a Study in Values*. London: 1929.
Ruskin's essential economic doctrine, re-stated by an able modern economist.

Hodgson, Francis: *Venice in the Thirteenth and Fourteenth Centuries (1204-1400)*. London: 1910.

Hoepfner, Karl A.: *Grundbegriffe des Städtebaues*. 2 vols. Berlin: 1921-28.
In part already dated by newer conceptions of open order.

Hoffbauer, Theodore J. H.: *Paris à Travers les Ages; Aspects successifs des monuments et quartiers historiques de Paris depuis le XIIIe siècle jusqu'à nos jours. Fidèlement restitués d'apres les documents authentiques*. 2 vols. Paris: 1875-1882.
Illustrations excellent. Contributions by authorities like LaCroix and Franklin. See Poëte.

Hole, James: *The Homes of the Working Classes; with Suggestions for Their Improvement*. London: 1866.
Good statement of the capitalist dilemma by an advocate of model housing who saw the difficulties. Contains important data on contemporary experiments.

Holland, William King: See Middle West Utilities.

Hoover, Herbert: See President's Research Committee and President's Conference.

Hough, Walter: *Fire as an Agent in Human Culture*. In *Smithsonian Institution Bulletin 139*. Washington: 1926.

Housing America. (By the Editors of *Fortune.*) New York: 1932.
America's lacks and deficiencies in Housing competently revealed: but anything like a positive program vitiated by the authors' naïve belief that the private manu-facturer could solve the crucial economic difficulties by building individual pre-fabricated houses.

Housing Conference, President Hoover's: See President's Conference.

Howard, Ebenezer: *Garden Cities of Tomorrow.* London: 1902. (First edi-tion published as *Tomorrow.* London: 1898.)
A close study of this classic is important for every serious student of housing, city planning, or regional development. Sir Ebenezer was originally a court stenog-rapher: so much for specialization. His book has had consequences more far-reaching than the two English cities that have issued out of it.

Hubbard, Theodora, and Henry Vincent: *Our Cities Today and Tomorrow.* Cambridge, Mass.: 1929.

Hugenberg, Alfred: *Die neue Stadt.* Berlin: 1935.
Worthless.

Hughes, Thomas, and Lamborn, E. A. G.: *Towns and Town Planning, An-cient and Modern.* Oxford: 1923.
Useful short introduction.

Hughes, W. R.: *New Town; a Proposal in Agricultural, Industrial, Educa-tional, Civic, and Social Reconstruction.* London: 1919.

Hugo, Victor: *Notre Dame de Paris.* Paris: 1831.
The sociological approach to the past owes more to the novelists like Scott and Hugo than to the professed historians and sociologists.

Huizinga, Johann: *The Waning of the Middle Ages.* Trans. New York: 1924.
Splended in its revelation of the complexities and contradictions of the medieval idolum.

Hunt, Wray: *The Growth and Development of the English Town.* London: 1931.
Elementary text in the *Simple Guide Series.*

Hunt, W.: See Freeman, E. A.

Huntington, Ellsworth: *The Human Habitat.* New York: 1927.
Perhaps the soundest if not the most original of the author's numerous studies.

Civilization and Climate. New Haven: 1915. Revised Edition: 1933.
An original thesis on the relation of climate and weather to human productivity: somewhat vitiated by parochial assumptions as to what constitutes civilization.

Hurd, Richard Melanchthon: *Principles of City Land Values.* First Ed. New York: 1903. Fourth Ed. New York: 1924.
Deservedly of high repute in a field where till recently it stood almost alone. Many illustrations of early stages of growth in American cities. By a business man who really understood his business.

Hürlimann, Martin: *Deutschland; Landschaft und Baukunst.* Berlin: 1931.

Berlin; Berichte und Bilder. Berlin: 1934.

Das Mittelmeer; Landschaft, Baukunst und Volksleben im Kreise des Mittelländischen Meeres. Berlin: 1937.

Hürlimann, Martin: *La France;* with an introduction by Paul Valéry. Paris: 1927.
Selection from a larger list of sumptuously designed and illustrated books on cities and landscapes, done by the same author. While the illustrations are mainly selected with an eye to beauty, rather than all-round truth, the books fill a serious gap.

Hussey, Christopher: *The Picturesque.* New York: 1927.

Hutchings, G. E.: See Fagg.

Hutton, William: *The History of Birmingham.* Fourth Ed. London: 1819.
A Journey from Birmingham to London. Birmingham: 1785.

International Housing Association: *Slum Clearance and Reconditioning of Insanitary Dwellings.* Two vols. in one. Stuttgart: 1935.
One of a series of volumes published by this association in German, French, and English, of importance to students of Housing.

James, Harlean: *Land Planning in the United States.* New York: 1926.

James, Herman G.: *Municipal Functions.* New York: 1917.

Janssen, Johannes: *History of the German People at the Close of the Middle Ages.* 8 vols. Freiburg: 1881-1894. Trans. 17 vols. London: 1895-1925.
Still useful.

Jean-Desthieux, François: *L'Evolution Régionaliste du Félibrige au Fedéralisme.* Paris: 1918.
Complete account of history of regionalist movement in France. See Gooch.

Jeanneret-Gris, Charles Edouard: See Le Corbusier.

Jennings, Hilda: *Bryn Mawr: A Study of a Distressed Area.* London: 1934.
Based on a social survey of an area in the South Wales coalfield.

Joerg, W. L. G.: *Geography and National Land Planning.* In *Geographical Review.* April 1935.

Joerg, W. L. G., and Mackintosh, W. A. (editors): *Canadian Frontiers of Settlement.* 9 vols. Toronto: 1934-36.

Jones, David Caradog (editor): *The Social Survey of Merseyside.* 2 vols. London: 1934.
Factual study; maps but no photographs.

Jones, Thomas Jesse: *The Sociology of a New York City Block.* New York: 1904.

Kampffmeyer, Hans: *Die Gartenstadtbewegung.* Leipzig: 1909.
By a gallant spirit who left his mark on the German housing movement, and who fortunately died in 1932 before the humiliating arrival of National Socialism.

Kehr, Cyrus: *A Nation Plan.* Washington: 1920.
A pioneering work in its field. Uncritical on certain matters like national unification, and limited by concentration on purely physical side of planning. See MacKaye, Benton.

Keir, Malcolm: *Economic Factors in the Location of Manufacturing Industries.* In *Annals of the American Academy of Political and Social Science.* Philadelphia: 1921.

Kellogg, Paul U. (editor): *The Pittsburgh Survey.* 6 vols. New York: 1909-1914.
> Monumental survey of a representative industrial city: an overhauling not unlike the later Middletown, but with more emphasis on the social workers' point of view and specific interests. Lacking on the civic and urban side, it is nevertheless one of the outstanding demonstrations of the survey method.

Kern, Robert: *The Supercity; a Planned Physical Equipment for City Life.* Washington: 1924.
> A variant on Chambless's Roadtown: much better thought out; but with something of the same innocence as to the relation of physical utilities and social purposes.

King, W.: *Chronicles of Three Free Cities.* London: 1914.

Kohl, Johann Georg: *Der Verkehr und die Ansiedlungen der Menschen in Ihrer Abhängigkeit von der Gestaltung der Erdoberfläche.* 2 Ed. Leipzig: 1850.
> Sombart pokes fun at this work; but its emphasis on transportation as one of the critical factors in city development is not unsound.

Kropotkin, Piotr: *Fields, Factories, and Workshops; or Industry Combined with Agriculture, and Brainwork with Manual Work.* First Ed. Boston: 1899. Revised Ed. London: 1919.
> Sociological and economic intelligence of the first order, founded on Kropotkin's specialized competence as a geographer and his generous social passion as a leader in communist anarchism. Able analysis and penetrating interpretation.

Mutual Aid. London: 1904.
> Pioneer work on symbiosis in sociology: one of the first attempts to redress the one-sided Darwinian emphasis upon the more predatory aspects of life. Note chapter on Mutual Aid in the Medieval City.

Kuczynski, Robert R.: *Population Movements.* Oxford: 1936.

Kulischer, A. M. and Y. M.: *Kriegs- und Wanderzüge; Weltgeschichte als Völkerbewegung.* Berlin: 1932.
> Attempt to interpret world history in the light of migrations.

Kulischer, Josef M.: *Allgemeine Wirtschaftsgeschichte.* 2 vols. München: 1928-29.
> Excellent bibliographies.

Lanciani, Rodolfo Amedeo: *Golden Days of Renaissance in Rome.* Boston: 1906.

Larwood, Jacob (pseudonym for H. D. J. van Schevichaven): *The Story of the London Parks.* London: 1881.

Laski, Harold Joseph: *The Problem of Administrative Areas.* In *Smith College Studies in History.* Northampton: 1918.

Laski, Harold Joseph (editor): *A Century of Municipal Progress; 1835-1935.* London: 1935.
> Useful.

Lavedan, Pierre: *Qu'est-ce que l'Urbanisme? Introduction à l'Histoire de l'Urbanisme.* Paris: 1926.

An introduction to the documents, plans, and other sources for a history of urbanism, rather than to the subject itself. More for the specialist than the general student.

Lavedan, Pierre: *Histoire de l'Urbanisme*. Vol. I. Antiquité, Moyen Age. Paris: 1926.
First rate. Fully documented with plans and illustrations. Second volume on *l'Épaque Classique* has long been promised.

Géographie des Villes. Paris: 1936.
Good beginning in comparative morphology, but with insufficient institutional reference.

Lavisse, Ernest: *Histoire de France Contemporaine depuis la Revolution jusqu'à la Paix de 1919*. 10 vols. Paris: 1920-22.
Exhaustive; illustrations good, too.

Le Corbusier: *Vers une Architecture nouvelle*. Paris: 1923. Trans. *Towards a New Architecture*. New York: 1930.
A book whose literary influence made the author the dominating architect of Europe. Essentially a combination of classic formalism and the machine, with an esthetic derived from cubist painting, Le Corbusier's thought produced a needed clarification: turning attention from problems of decoration to those of construction. At first puritanic in its austerity, the author's architecture became, in his more elaborate houses, a baroque played with machine forms. Unfortunately Le Corbusier's formulas have lent themselves to academic imitation: sometimes by himself.

Urbanisme. Paris: 1924. Trans. *The City of the Future*. New York: 1930.
Defense of standardization, mass-production, the machine. Suggestions for an elaborately mechanical metropolis, with widely spaced skyscrapers and multiple-decked traffic ways: closer to a genuine order than the gaudy projects of the New York skyscraper architects of the same period: but innocent of economic limitations, and superficial in its grasp of social factors.

Précisions. Paris: 1930.
The gist of Le Corbusier's South American lectures, with even more fanciful schemes for skyscraper roadtown.

La Ville Radieuse; Collection de l'Equipement de la Civilisation Machiniste. Boulogne: 1934.
Most mature of Le Corbusier's works; symptomatic of a transformation from purely mechanical ideology to the more biotechnic outlook. Recommended.

Legrand, Jacques G., and Landon, C. P.: *Description de Paris et de ses Edifices*. 2 vols. Paris: 1806-1809.

Leinert, Martin: *Die Sozialgeschichte der Grosstadt*. Hamburg: 1925.

Le Play, Frédéric: *Les Ouvriers Européens*. 6 vols. 2 Ed. Tours: 1877-79.
L'Esquisse d'une Division Provinciale de la France.
One of the early attempts to suggest reconstitution of the old regions of France.

Lethaby, William Richard: *Form in Civilization*. London: 1922.
Wise reflections on the social problem of modern form. See Behrendt and Ozenfant.

Levainville, J.: *Caen; Notes sur L'Evolution de la Fonction Urbaine*. In *La Vie Urbaine*: August, October 1923.

Lewis, Nelson P.: *The Planning of the Modern City*. New York: 1916.

Lewis, Sinclair: *Babbitt*. New York: 1922.
The novelist's complement of Middletown.

Lichtenberg, Reinhold, Freiherr von: *Haus, Dorf, Stadt; Eine Entwicklungs-geschichte des antiken Städtebildes*. Leipzig: 1909.

Lindeman, Eduard C.: See Anderson, Nels. *Wealth and Culture; A Study of One Hundred Foundations and Community Trusts and Their Operations*. New York: 1936.

Lippmann, Walter: *Public Opinion*. New York: 1922.

Lipson, Ephraim: *The Economic History of England*. 3 vols. New York: 1929-31.

Lloyd, Nathaniel: *A History of the English House; from Primitive Times to the Victorian Period*. London: 1931.
Excellent.

Lloyd, Thomas Alwyn: *Planning in Town and Country*. London: 1935.

Loftie, William J.: *A History of London*. 2 vols. London: 1883.

Lohmann, Karl B.: *Principles of City Planning*. New York: 1931.
Summary of current American practices rather than principles.
Regional Planning. Ann Arbor: 1936.
Synopsis of the subject.

London County Council: *Housing Estates; Statistics for the Year 1929-30*. London: 1930.
Housing of the Working Classes in London. London: 1913.
London Housing. London: 1937.
Records of a Herculean accomplishment in slum-razing and community housing.

London School of Economics and Social Science: *New Survey of London Life and Labor*. 9 vols. London: 1930-35.
A compendious survey that seeks in effect to bring Booth up to date.

London Society, The: *London of the Future*. Edited by Sir Aston Webb. New York: 1921.

Lynd, Robert S. and Helen M.: *Middletown*. New York: 1929.
An able survey, though weak on the geographic side and lacking in comparative cultural reference. See Kellogg, P. U.
Middletown in Transition; a Study in Cultural Conflicts. New York: 1937.
Less exhaustive but perhaps more penetrating than the first study.

Mächler, Martin: *Demodynamik*. Berlin: 1933.

MacIver, Robert M.: *Community*. London: 1917.
Society; Its Structure and Changes. New York: 1931.

MacKaye, Benton: *Employment and Natural Resources*. Washington: 1918.
The New Exploration; a Philosophy of Regional Planning. New York: 1928.

Important not merely for point of view but for suggestions of method. MacKaye, originally a forester, and the founder of the Appalachian Trail, is a regionalist in the great tradition of Thoreau, Marsh, and Shaler.

MacKaye, Benton, and Mumford, Lewis: *Townless Highways for the Motorist.* In *Harper's Magazine:* August 1931.

Regional Planning. In *Encyclopedia Britannica.* 14 Edition.

Mackenzie, Findlay, Editor: *Planned Society; Yesterday, Today and Tomorrow.* New York: 1937.
A symposium by thirty-five economists, sociologists, and statesmen. Many important papers and full bibliography.

Maclear, Anne Bush: *Early New England Towns.* In *Studies in History, Economics, and Public Law.* New York: 1908.

Maitland, Frederick William: *Township and Borough.* Cambridge: 1898.

Mann, Thomas: *Lübeck als geistige Lebensform.* Lübeck: 1926.
Summary of spiritual and cultural influence of a great city upon its greatest son.

Mannheim, Karl: *Ideology and Utopia.* Bonn: 1929. Trans. New York: 1936.

Marsh, George P.: *Man and Nature; or, Physical Geography as Modified by Human Action.* New York: 1864.
A masterpiece of geographic thought, at long last being re-discovered by the geographers. Laid the foundation for the conservation of natural resources, particularly forests.

Marshall, T. H.: *The Population of England and Wales from the Industrial Revolution to the World War.* In the *Economic History Review.* April 1935.
Judicious survey.

Martin, Alfred von: *Deutsches Badewesen in vergangenen Tagen.* Jena: 1906.
Soziologie der Renaissance. Stuttgart: 1932.

Matchoss, Conrad (editor): *Technik-Geschichte.* Volume on Roads and Road-making in *Beiträge zur Geschichte der Technik und Industrie.* Vol. 23. Berlin: 1934.

Maunier, René: *Essais sur les Groupements Sociaux.* Paris: 1929.
L'Origine et la Fonction Economique des Villes; Etude de Morphologie Sociale. Paris: 1910.
Important less for what it establishes than for what it attempts.

Mayhew, Henry: *London Labor and the London Poor.* 4 vols. London: 1861-62.
Journalistic but full of interesting material.

Mazel, Henri: *La Synergie Sociale.* Paris: 1896.

McKenzie, Roderick D.: *The Metropolitan Community.* New York: 1933.

McLachlan, Norman W.: *Noise.* London: 1935.

McNamara, Katherine: *Bibliography of Planning; 1928-1935.* Cambridge, Mass.: 1936.

Meakin, Budgett: *Model Factories and Villages.* London: 1905.

Meikleham, Robert: *On the History and Art of Warming and Ventilating Rooms and Buildings.* 2 vols. London: 1845.
Important: a rare book in a poorly explored field. Needs an even more exhaustive successor.

Mercier, Louis Sebastien: *The Picture of Paris; Before and After the Revolution.* Paris: 1781-88. Trans. London: 1929.

Memoirs of the Year 2500. Trans. Liverpool: 1802.
Utopia interesting for historic sidelights.

Merian, Matthaeus: *Topographia Bohemiae, Moraviae et Silesiae.* Frankfurt-am-Main: 1650.

Topographia Germaniae. Frankfurt-am-Main: 1642. Reprinted in small format. München: 1935.
Handsome woodcuts of cities, with curious and sometimes historically informative data. One of the great sources of knowledge as to the state of the late medieval town. Hill and church tower took the place of the airplane for the artist. See Blaeu, Munster.

Metz, Friedrich: *Die Hauptstaedte.* Berlin: 1930.

Meuriot, Paul: *Du Concept de Ville Autrefois et Aujourd'hui.* In *La Vie Urbaine.* Paris: 1919.

Des Aglomerations Urbaines dans l'Europe Contemporaraine; Essai sur les Causes, les Conditions, les Conséquences de leur Développement. Paris: 1898.
Statistical study of urban concentration in the nineteenth century with special reference to France.

Meyer, Alfred Gotthold: *Eisenbauten.* Esslingen: 1907.
Important study of development of use of iron in building: good historically and technically.

Middle West Utilities Company: *America's New Frontier.* Chicago: 1929.
Interesting study of possibilities of economic regionalism.

Migge, Leberecht: *Deutsche Binnenkolonisation; Sachgrundlagen des Siedlungswesens.* Berlin: 1926.
A rural approach to the problem of resettlement. Not to be confused with later experiments with low-grade "Randsiedlungen" in Germany.

Die wachsende Siedlung. Stuttgart: 1932.
Suggestions for biotechnic housing in rural environment, with a house designed for growth of the family, and the land adapted for cultivation.

Miller, Hugh: *First Impressions of England and Its People.* New York: 1875.

Mirabilia Romae; Indulgentie et Reliquie ad Urbis Rome in Latino. Rome: c. 1495.
First modern guide book.

Molmenti, Pompeo G.: *Venice, Its Individual Growth from the Earliest Beginning to the Fall of the Republic.* 6 vols. Trans. Chicago: 1906-8.

Montesquieu, Baron de (Charles de Secondat): *The Spirit of the Laws.* Two vols. Geneva: 1749. Translated. Rev. ed. New York: 1899.
One of the first modern attempts to link geography and politics.

Moore, Charles: *Daniel H. Burnham; Architect; Planner of Cities.* 2 vols. Boston: 1921.
Biography of one of the great exponents of imperialist city design.

Moore, Harry E.: *What is Regionalism.* In *Southern Policy Papers No. 10.* Chapel Hill, N. C.: 1937.
(See also Odum, Howard.)

Morris, William: *News from Nowhere.* London: 1891.
Though as dreamlike as Hudson's *A Crystal Age,* the theme of this utopia is like some fantastic arcadian prelude to our biotechnic economy: much closer to the new idolum than Bellamy or Wells, although Morris speaks with an accent more foreign to our thinking.

Architecture, Industry, and Wealth. London: 1902.

Hopes and Fears for Art. Boston: 1882.
Samples from one of the great critical and constructive minds of the nineteenth century, whose thoughts on architecture and social life are still important.

Mukerjee, Radhakamal: *Regional Sociology.* New York: 1926.
Good conspectus.

Ecological Contributions to Sociology. In *Sociological Review.* October 1930.

Müller, Emile: *Habitations Ouvrières et Agricoles.* Paris: 1856.

Müller, Emile, and Cacheux, Emile: *Les Habitations Ouvrières en Tous Pays.* First Ed. Paris: 1879. Second Ed. Paris: 1903.
Exhaustive survey of model housing schemes for the working classes; the second edition shows many plans exhibited at the Paris Exposition of 1900. See Hole, James.

Mumford, Lewis: *The Story of Utopias.* New York: 1922.

Sticks and Stones; a Study of American Architecture and Civilization. New York: 1924.
The first historic treatment of this subject in English; but the one-sided views of the influence of the machine expressed in the later chapters were modified in *The Brown Decades* and in *Technics and Civilization.*

The Brown Decades; a Study of the Arts in America; 1865-1895. New York: 1931.
Exasperatingly superficial.

American Dwelling House. In *American Mercury.* October 1929.

The City. In *Civilization in the United States, by Thirty Americans.* New York: 1922.
Better than its date might indicate.

The Intolerable City. In *Harper's Magazine.* February 1926.

Housing. In *Modern Architecture,* edited by Hitchcock, Henry-Russell and Johnson, Phillip. New York: 1932.

Machinery and the Modern Style. In *New Republic.* August 3, 1921.

Mumford, Lewis: *Mass Production and the Modern House.* In *Architectural Record.* January-February 1930.

The Metropolitan Milieu. In *America and Alfred Stieglitz,* edited by Norman, D., Frank, W., Rosenfeld, P., and Mumford, L. New York: 1934.
Study of interplay of geographic and cultural influences in a great city, focused through a single personality. Recommended.

Plan of New York. In *New Republic.* June 15 and 22, 1932.
Painstaking and detailed criticism of defects of The Regional Survey and Plan of New York (which see).

The Fourth Migration. In *Survey Graphic.* May 1925.

Technics and Civilization. New York: 1934.
Study of the machine in its social, cultural, and economic aspects. Complementary in scope and theme to the present volume.

Mumford, Lewis (editor): *Regional Planning Number, Survey Graphic:* May 1925.

Munro, William Bennett: *Municipal Administration.* New York: 1934.
American practice.

Municipal Government and Administration. New York: 1923.

The Government of American Cities. New York: 1913.

The Government of European Cities. New York: 1909. Revised. New York: 1927.

Munster, Sebastian: *Cosmographia.* Basel: 1552.
Valuable.

Murray, David: *Museums; Their History and Their Use.* 3 vols. Glasgow: 1904.
Definitive.

Museum of Modern Art, The, of New York: *Modern Architecture.* New York: 1932.

Nash, Elizabeth Gee: *The Hansa.* London: 1929.

National Association of Housing Officials: *A Housing Program for the United States.* Chicago: 1934.

National Planning Board (U. S.): *Final Report; 1933-4.* Section Two: *A Plan for Planning.* Washington: 1934.

National Resources Board (U. S.): *State Planning; a Review of Activities and Progress.* Washington: 1935.
Compact informative survey of state-planning activities in various states. But neglects to note the first systematic introduction of State Planning, that of the New York State Housing and Regional Planning Commission (which see).

Regional Factors in National Planning. Washington: 1936.
A public document of unusual excellence: the best discussion of the problems of administration and planning, with reference to regional realities, that has appeared. Occasionally confuses the concept of the specialized planning area with the reality of a regional complex, by using the adjective regional to cover both.

Regional Planning; New England. Washington: 1936.

Our Cities; Their Rôle in the National Economy. Washington: 1937.
Good study despite a weakness on the historic side and a tendency to overlook or

straddle economic and social questions closely bound up with the maintenance of dominant pecuniary economy.

Neutra, Richard J.: *Amerika.* In *Neues Bauen in der Welt* Series. Wien: 1930.

New Survey of London Life and London Labor. See London School of Economics.

New York State Housing and Regional Planning Commission: *Final Report.* Albany: 1926.
With Clarence S. Stein as Chairman, Henry Wright as Planning Adviser and George Gove as Director, the commission made a series of important investigations, culminating in the above report. Wright's contribution here was the regional parallel to Howard's Garden City; and the above report is a benchmark of regionalism in American politics. See also MacKaye, Wright, Stein.

New York State Planning Board: *A Graphic Compendium of Planning Studies.* Albany: 1935.
State Planning for New York. Albany: 1935.

Nolen, John: *City Planning.* New York: 1929.
New Towns for Old. Boston: 1927.
Nolen understood possibilities of the small town.

Oberhummer, Eugen: *Der Stadtplan; Seine Entwicklung und geographische Bedeutung.* Berlin: 1907.
Examples largely from older cities.

Obermeyer, Henry: *Stop That Smoke!* New York: 1933.
Popular study of the smoke nuisance and problem of its abatement.

Odum, Howard W.: *Southern Regions of the United States.* Chapel Hill, N. C.: 1936.
Able analysis of regions and regional problems by the leading sociologist of the New South.

Odum, Howard W., and Moore, Harry E.: *American Regionalism.* New York: 1938.
Effective outline of various approaches to contemporary regionalism in the United States. Critical and compendious.

Ogburn, William Fielding: *Social Characteristics of Cities.* Chicago: 1937.
Useful analysis of the census returns with cities grouped according to size.

Olmsted, Frederick Law: *Public Parks and the Enlargement of Towns.* Cambridge, Mass.: 1870.
One of the earliest and best expositions of comprehensive park planning.

Olmsted, Frederick Law, Jr., and Kimball, Theodora: *Frederick Law Olmsted, Landscape Architect; 1822-1903.* 2 vols. New York: 1928.
Professional papers and significant biographic data.

Oppenheimer, Franz: *Stadt und Bürgerschaft; Die Neuzeit.* In *Oppenheimers System der Soziologie,* vol. 4, part 3.

Ostwald, Hans: *Berlin und die Berlinerin: Eine Kultur- und Sittengeschichte* Berlin: 1911.
Well illustrated with contemporary prints.

Ottokar, Nicola: *The Medieval City-Communes*. Privately printed. Florence: 1933.

Owen, Robert: *A New View of Society*. London: 1813.

Ozenfant, Amédée: *Foundations of Modern Art*. Paris: 1928. Trans. New York: 1931.
Good: not least on architecture.

Palladio, Andrea: *The Architecture of Palladio in Four Books*. Venice: 1581. Trans. London: 1742.
Indispensable clues to the baroque plan.

Park, Robert E., Burgess, E. W., and McKenzie, R. D.: *The City;* with a Bibliography by Louis Wirth. Chicago: 1925.
Papers relating to the city as an ecological formation.

Pasquet, D.: *Londres et les Ouvriers de Londres*. Paris: 1914.
Good.

Paul-Boncour, Joseph: *Le Féderalisme Economique: Etude sur les Rapports de l'Individu et les Groupements Professionels*. Paris: 1900.
A discussion, historic, economic, political, on the growth of associations and their political rule.

Pearson, Sidney Vere: *The Growth and Distribution of Population*. London: 1935.
Discursive and unfortunately not adequate.

Peel, J.: *Topographia Galliae*. Amsterdam: 1660-1663.

Peets, Elbert: *Haussmann*. In *Town Planning Review*. June 1927.
Current Town Planning in Washington. In *Town Planning Review*. December 1931.
(See also Hegemann.)

Penstone, M. M.: *Town Study; Suggestions for a Course of Lessons Preliminary to the Study of Civics*. London: 1910.
For schools; English illustrations.

Perret, Jacques: *Des Fortifications et Artifices*. Frankfurt-am-Main: 1602.
Demonstrates how completely the town was sacrificed as an entity to artillery defense. City plans show possibilities of quadrangular and irregular semi-open plan.

Perry, Clarence: *The Neighborhood Unit*. In *Regional Survey of New York*. Vol. 7. *Neighborhood and Community Planning*. New York: 1929.

Person, Harlow Stafford: *On the Technique of Planning*. In *Bulletin of the Taylor Society*. November 1934.

Peterson, Arthur Everett, and Edwards, George W.: *New York as an Eighteenth Century Municipality*. 2 vols. New York: 1917.
Medieval survivals in the New World.

Petrie, William Flinders: *The Revolutions of Civilization*. London: 1911.

Pevsner, Nikolaus: *Pioneers of the Modern Movement; from William Morris to Walter Gropius*. London: 1936.

Well-illustrated and replete with useful historic data; not always satisfactory in interpretation. See Behrendt.

Pica, Agnoldomenico: *Nuova Architettura Italiana.* Milano: 1936.
Comprehensive and well-illustrated study of modern Italian architecture, with the text only in Italian. Architecture and engineering under Fascism, even more than under Nazism, is a proof of the unity of *organization* in Western culture, even though the gap has widened during the last fifteen years as to the means and ends of *association.* See Sartoris.

Pidoux, Joseph: See Rey, A. A.

Pinder, Wilhelm: *Deutscher Barock; die grossen Baumeister des 18. Jahrhunderts.* Leipzig: 1929.

Pirenne, Henri: *Medieval Cities; Their Origins and the Revival of Trade.* Princeton: 1925.
Historical and political account of the medieval city with special emphasis upon Flanders. Holds view of urban origins exactly opposite to Sombart's.

Plato: *The Republic*
Timaeus
Critias
The Laws
The *Republic* still has more effective sociology, albeit in mythic form, than most textbooks of sociology, allegedly scientific.

Platz, Gustav Adolf: *Die Baukunst der neuesten Zeit.* Berlin: 1927. Second Edition. Berlin: 1930.
Undue emphasis on European, especially German, architecture. See Sartoris.

Poëte, Marcel: *Comment s'est formé Paris.* Paris: 1925.
A tiny book full of a lifetime's knowledge. See below.
Introduction à l'Urbanisme; l'Evolution des Villes; la Leçon de l'Antiquité. Paris: 1929.
Admirable introduction. First third analyses the social, economic and geographic components of the city plan; the remaining part is a specific study of the city in ancient civilization, Egyptian, Mesopotamian, and Greco-Roman. The approach is organic and historical.
Une Vie de Cité; Paris de sa Naissance à nos Jours. 3 vols. text; 1 vol. illustrations. Paris: 1924-1931.
A monumental work of the first order.

Pound, Arthur: *The Golden Earth; the Story of Manhattan's Landed Wealth.* New York: 1935.

Powell, Lyman P. (editor): *Historic Towns of New England.* New York: 1898.
Historic Towns of the Middle States. New York: 1899.
Historic Towns of Southern States. New York: 1900.

Pratt, Edward Ewing: *Industrial Causes of Congestion of Population in New York City.* New York: 1911.
Good in its day; and still better than some later studies.

President's Conference on Home Building and Home Ownership. Washington, D. C.: 1931.
  Important: paved the way for President Roosevelt's public housing policy.

President's Research Committee on Social Trends: *Recent Social Trends in the United States.* 2 vols. New York: 1933.
  Useful data; some of it available in expanded monographs: see McKenzie.

Preuss, Hugo: *Die Entwicklung des Deutschen Städtewesens.* Vol. I. Leipzig: 1906.
  Excellent.

Price, Uvedale: *Essays on the Picturesque as Compared with the Sublime and the Beautiful.* 3 vols. London: 1810.

Pückler-Muskau, Hermann L. H. von: *Tour in England, Ireland, and France; 1826-1829.* Philadelphia: 1833.

Purdom, Charles B.: *Building of Satellite Towns.* London: 1926.
  Town Theory and Practice. London: 1921.
  The Garden City. London: 1923.
  Well-digested books by one who had participated in, as well as observed, the building of the English garden cities.

Quennell, Marjorie and C. H. G.: *History of Everyday Things in England.* 3 vols. London: 1930-34.
  For children; but until a more adult work comes forth on the same topic it must serve all ages.

Raleigh, Walter: *Observations Concerning the Causes of the Magnificencie and Opulency of Cities.* In *Works.* Vol. II. London: 1751.
  Not devoid of interest.

Rasmussen, Steen Eiler: *London: The Unique City.* New York: 1937.
  Beautiful interpretation of the life and architectural forms of the most lovable of great capitals by an enthusiastic Dane who knows his subject well. Well-illustrated.

Ratzel, Friedrich: *Studies in Political Areas.* In *American Journal of Sociology.* November 1897.

Regional Survey of New York and Its Environs. 8 vols. New York: 1927-31.
  Vol. 1. Haig, R. M., and McCrea, R. C.: *Major Economic Factors in Metropolitan Growth and Arrangement.* 1927.
    Uses argument in favor of economic advantages of city as automatic justification of congested urban areas of metropolitan pattern.
  Vol. 2. Adams, Thomas, and others: *Population, Land Values, and Government.*
  Vol. 3. Lewis, H. M., and Goodrich, E. P.: *Highway Traffic.*
  Vol. 4. Lewis, H. M.: *Transit and Transportation.*
  Vol. 5. Hammer, L. F., and others: *Public Recreation.*
    Sets extremely low standards.
  Vol. 6. Bassett, E. M., and Williams, F. B.: *Buildings, Their Uses, and the Spaces About Them.*

Regional Survey of New York and Its Environs. Vol. 7. *Neighborhood and Community Planning.*

Vol. 8. Lewis, H. M.: *Physical Conditions and Public Services.*

Regional Plan. Vol. 1. *The Graphic Regional Plan;* Vol. 2. *The Building of the City.*

In all, a mass of exhaustive statistical data (much highly useful), well-meaning half-truths, and contradictory plans and prescriptions, dignified by almost ten years of labor, a million dollars in expenses, and ten monumental volumes. The premises upon which the survey was conducted were sociologically unsound: continued population growth up to 1965 was treated as axiomatic and the economic stability of the metropolitan regime was taken for granted. The real task of transforming the inner area of the metropolis was shirked and the duty to prepare to receive larger increments of population in the immediate outlying areas was not even subjected to skeptical inquiry. For exhaustive criticism see articles by Mumford in the New Republic, June 15 and 22, 1932.

Renard, Georges François: *Guilds in the Middle Ages.* Trans. London: 1919.

Renard, G. F., and Weulersse, G.: *Life and Work in Modern Europe; Fifteenth to Eighteenth Centuries.* London: 1926.

Valuable.

Rey, A. Augustin, Pidoux, J., and Barde, C.: *La Science des Plans des Villes.* Lausanne: 1928.

Pioneers on the subject of orientation for sunlight. Most of the dogmatic prescriptions on the subject current in advanced architectural circles in the nineteen-thirties ignored the facts of meteorology, on the naïve assumption that East-West exposures gave maximum sunlight. A subject upon which close regional study is highly necessary, since a solution must include not merely sunlight, but winds, seasonal exposure, physiological need, and working habits.

Richardson, Benjamin Ward: *Hygeia; A City of Health.* London: 1876.

Though in his program of hospitalization Richardson is still in advance of contemporary communities, some of his most advanced prescriptions are now below standard.

Riehl, Wilhelm Heinrich: *Die Naturgeschichte des Volkes als Grundlage einer deutschen Social-Politik.* Vol. I. *Land und Leute;* Vol. II. *Die bürgerliche Gesellschaft;* Vol. III. *Die Familie;* Vol. IV. *Wanderbuch* (als zweiter Theil zu *Land und Leute*). Sixth Ed. Stuttgart: 1866-82.

Important work by a great cultural historian of the same rank as De Sanctis in Italy: also neglected. See especially chapters on the city in Vols. I and IV, and on the house in Vol. III.

Culturstudien aus drei Jahrhunderten. Stuttgart: 1859.

See essays on Das landschaftliche Auge and the Augsburger Studien.

Robinson, Charles Mulford: *The Call of the City.* New York: 1908.

City Planning. New York: 1916.

The Improvement of Towns and Cities. New York: 1901.

Essays by a mid-American who did much to popularize the notion of civic beauty.

Rogers, J.-E. Thorold: *Six Centuries of Work and Wages.* New York: 1884. London: 1884.

Romains, Jules: *Men of Good-Will.* Paris: 1932-current. Trans. New York: 1933-current.

A masterpiece in urban description and interpretation: a series that caps a great tradition that stems back to Stendhal, Balzac, Hugo, and Zola.

Rostovtsev, Mikhail, and others: *Urban Land Economics*. Ann Arbor: 1922.
Note especially Rostovtsev on cities in the Ancient World and Dr. Mary Shine's *Urban Land in the Middle Ages*.

Rouse, Edward Clive: *The Old Towns of England*. New York: 1936.
A good book in the invaluable English Countryside Series.

Ruhr District Settlement Association: *Die Tätigkeit des Siedlungsverbandes Ruhrkohlenbezirk*. Essen: 1926.
Brief exposition of the scope of this great regional planning scheme as developed under Dr. Schmidt.

Ruskin, John: *Unto This Last*. London: 1862.
Munera Pulveris. London: 1872.
Ruskin was the first economist to express the realities of energy income and living standards in relation to production. His grasp of the consummatory and creative functions, neglected by the money economists, makes him—despite frequent solecisms—the fundamental economist of the biotechnic order.
The Stones of Venice. 2 vols. London: 1851.
Social interpretation of architecture and architectural interpretation of societies both have their essential beginnings here.

Russell, George William (A.E.): *Cooperation and Nationality*. Dublin: 1912.
The National Being. Dublin: 1916.
Though not boasting the obvious clichés of regionalism this is a real contribution: an expression of that Ireland, now vanished, which was both regional and interregional in its culture, before relapsing into its present sterile parochialism.

Salaman, Malcolm C.: *London; Past and Present*. London: 1916.
A Studio book, well-illustrated.

Sand, René: *Health and Human Progress; An Essay in Sociological Medicine*. Trans. London: 1935.
Good bibliography. See also Campbell and Hill.

Sander, Paul: *Geschichte des Deutschen Städtewesens*. In *Bonner Wissenschaftliche Untersuchungen*. Heft 6. Bonn: 1922.

Sartoris, Alfredo: *Gli Elementi dell' Archittetura Funzionale*. Milano: 1935.

Schedel, Hartmann: *Das Buch der Chroniker*. Nürnberg: 1493.
Richly illustrated by woodcuts of cities done by Michael Wohlgemuth. The technique is rough and the factual accuracy dubious: one stock cut, for example, is used over and over again to represent various cities.

Scheffler, Karl: *Die Architektur der Grosstadt*. Berlin: 1913.
Good study.
Der Neue Mensch. Berlin: 1935.
Not without insight; but a little disappointing.
Holland. Leipzig: 1930.
Fine picture of the land, its cities, its art.

Schevill, Ferdinand: *History of Florence; from the Founding of the City through the Renaissance*. New York: 1936.

Excellent within its own particular frame; but somewhat lacking on the specifically civic side.

Schevill, Ferdinand: *Siena: The Story of a Medieval Commune.* New York:
1909.

Schlesinger, Arthur Meier: *The Rise of the City; 1878-1898.* New York:
1933.
American history with a view to various urban manifestations; but, as usual with
historians of the passing generation, without grasp of the city as organic whole.

Schmidt, Friedrich Christian: *Der Bürgerliche Baumeister.* 4 vols. in 6.
Gotha: 1790-99.
Historic interest alone.

Schmoller, G.: *Deutsches Städtewesen in Älterer Zeit. In Bonner Staatswis-
senschaftliche Untersuchungen.* Heft 5. Bonn: 1922.

Schott, Sigmund: *Die Grosstädtischen Agglomerationen des Deutschen
Reichs; 1787-1910.* Breslau: 1912.
Statistical analyses.

Schultz, Alwin: *Das häusliche Leben der Europäischen Kulturvölker vom
Mittelalter bis zur zweiten Hälfte des XVIII. Jahrhunderts.* München:
1903.

Schultze-Naumburg, Paul: *Kulturarbeiten.* München: 1916.
Vol. 1. *Hausbau.* Vol. 2. *Gärten.* Vol. 3. *Dörfer und Kolonien.* Vol. 4.
Städtebau. Vol. 5. *Kleinbürgerhäuser.*
Die Gestaltung der Landschaft durch den Menschen: Vol. 7. Part I.
Wege und Strassen, Part 2. *Die Pflanzenwelt und ihre Bedeutung im
Landschaftsbilde;* Vol. 8. Part 3. *Der Geologische Aufbau der Land-
schaft und die Nutzbarmachung der Mineralien,* Part 4. *Die Wasser-
wirtschaft;* Vol. IX. Part 5. *Industrie,* Part 6. *Siedelungen.*
A work of fundamental importance upon the artful and orderly transformation
of the environment by man. While the standpoint of the author is traditional and
somewhat backward looking, this series of books is one of the great monuments
of its generation: not less representative because the author was also an advocate
of dress reform.
Die Kultur des weiblichen Körpers als Grundlage der Frauenkleidung.
Jena: 1901.
One of the first books to use for other than "artistic" purposes photographs of
naked girls: the comparison between the natural bodies and the monstrosities
produced by fashionable deformation was a powerful element in dress reform.
The relation between architectural style and costume is a theme that still awaits
the right critic.

Schulze, Konrad Werner: *Stadt und Land als organischer Lebensraum.* Stuttgart: 1932.

Schumacher, Fritz: *Strömungen in deutscher Baukunst seit 1800.* Leipzig:
1935.
Valuable study of the various movements in modern architecture with particular
reference to Germany, by an architect who left his mark on every phase of modern
Hamburg before 1933.

Schumacher, Fritz: *Darstellungen des soziologischen Zustandes im Ham-burgisch-Preussischen Landesplanungsgebiet.* Hamburg: 1931.

Wesen und Organisation der Landesplanung im Hamburgisch-Preussischen Planungsgebiet. Hamburg: 1932.
> Two of a series of reports on land planning in the Hamburg area which shows how much can be done with a small personnel and modest means, provided the director has a consistent point of view and a firm grasp of social relationships. (Compare with Regional Survey of New York.)

Das Werden einer Wohnstadt; Bilder vom neuen Hamburg. Hamburg: 1932.

Schumacher, Fritz, and Arntz, W.: *Köln.* München: 1923.

Schwan, Bruno (editor): *Town Planning and Housing Throughout the World.* Berlin: 1935.
> Essays by "leading authorities." Translations usually execrable. Not to be com pared to Hegemann, but the best available reference work now.

Scott, Jesup W.: *Future Great City of the World in the Central Plain of North America.* Toledo: 1868.

Scott, Mackay Hugh Baillie-: *Houses and Gardens.* London: 1916.
> Well-illustrated book which shows how high a level the best English architects had reached in their free interpretation of modern needs before the curiously hollow recession into Georgian good taste.

Sears, Paul Bigelow: *Deserts on the March.* Norman, Okla.: 1935.
> Admirable presentation of the durable ecological relationships that govern man's exploitation of the earth.

Sennett, Alfred Richard: *Garden Cities in Theory and Practice.* 2 vols. London: 1905.
> A history and criticism of the garden city, with some interesting early suggestions on the advantages of rationalization.

Shaler, Nathaniel Southgate: *Man and the Earth.* New York: 1905.
> (See also Marsh, George Perkins.)

Sharp, Thomas: *Town and Countryside; Some Aspects of Urban and Rural Development.* New York: 1933.
> Vigorous argumentative book on the principles of urban and rural planning, some-what marred by a perverse animus against the garden city, as if open building and "Streubau" were one.

Sidgwick, Henry: *Development of European Polity.* London: 1903.
> Early study of the rôle of the city in politics.

Simmel, Georg: *The Great City and Cultural Life.* In *Die Grosstadt.* Dresden: 1903.

Simon, John: *Reports Relating to the Sanitary Condition of the City of London.* London: 1854.
> Important documentation.

English Sanitary Institutions; Reviewed in Their Course of Development and in Some of Their Political and Social Relations. London: 1890.
> Exhaustive and excellent.

Sinclair, Robert: *Metropolitan Man; the Future of the English.* London: 1937.
Interpretive study, with ample factual and documentary substantiation of the glory and horror of big city life for John Citizen.

Sismondi, Jean Charles Leonard: *History of the Italian Republics in the Middle Ages.* Trans. and condensed. New York: 1895.
First published in 16 vols. in 1815.

Sitte, Camillo: *Der Städtebau nach seinen künstlerischen Grundsätzen.* Wien: 1899. Fifth Ed. 1922.
Keen analysis of city forms from the esthetic and social point of view: the first real understanding of the method of layout in the medieval city, particularly in the squares with their frequently asymmetrical arrangement. While Sitte's appreciation of the functional significance of irregular or adaptive planning led to caricatures by his followers, his own work was usually intelligent and sound.

Smith, Adam: *An Inquiry into the Nature and Causes of the Wealth of Nations.* 2 vols. London: 1776.
Chapters I and III in Book III show that Smith had a fundamental understanding of the political economy in its fullest sense, including the economy of cities and public works. The dropping out of this view from the later economists was symptomatic.

Stadt, Die Neue.
Continuation of *Das Neue Frankfurt* (which see).

Smith, Joseph Russell: *North America.* New York: 1925.
Fine example of contemporary regional geography.

Sölch, Johann: *Die Frage der zukünftigen Verteilung der Menschheit.* In *Geografiska Annaler:* 1929.

Sombart, Werner: *Krieg und Kapitalismus.* München: 1913.
Luxus und Kapitalismus. München: 1913.
Both these books throw much light on the baroque city.
Der Moderne Kapitalismus. Four vols. München: 1902-1927.
See vol. 2, Second Part, on Ursprung und Wesen der modernen Stadt, for his theory of the city: also Chapter 25, vol. 3 (first half) for relation of population movements and city building. Sombart, like Bücher, Schmoller, and Weber, has much to say about the city; and his notion of the city as primarily a group of consumers, though perhaps historically misleading in its overemphasis of the rôle of the clerical and landed classes, as if all cities were Residenzstädte, is logically correct—as opposed to the usual emphasis upon the market and the function of exchange as primary.
Der Begriff der Stadt und das Wesen der Städtebildung. In *Brauns Archiv.* Vol. 4. 1907.
Die Entstehung der Städte im Mittelalter. In *Rivista di Scienza.* Vol. 3. 1907.
Städtische Siedelung. In *Handwörterbuch der Soziologie.* Stuttgart: 1931.

Speckels, Daniel: *Architectura von Vestungen.* 1608.

Speed, John: *England, Wales, Scotland and Ireland.* London (?): 1627.

Spengler, Oswald: *Der Untergang des Abendlandes.* München: 1920. Trans. 2 vols. New York: 1928.

Important because of emphasis upon the rôle of the city as a formative factor in culture. Has also occasional flashes of profound architectural insight, though usually not without some intermixture of those strange residual barbarisms which disgraced part of German thought even before they had been crystallized by the National Socialists into a system.

Starkey, Thomas: *England in the Reign of Henry VIII; a Dialogue between Cardinal Pole and Thomas Lupset.* Written between 1536-38. London: 1878.

Stein, Clarence S.: *An Outline for Community Housing Procedure.* In *The Architectural Forum.* 1932.

Housing in the United States. Under *Social Architecture* in *Encyclopedia Britannica.* 14 Ed.

Stein, Clarence S., and Bauer, C. K.: *Store Building and Neighborhood Shopping Centers.* In *Architectural Record.* February 1934.

Stephenson, Carl: *Borough and Town; a Study of Urban Origins in England.* Cambridge, Mass.: 1933.
Important. Valuable summary of existing theories of medieval urban origins and well-directed employment of topographic evidence.

Stokes, I. N. P.: *Iconography of Manhattan.* 6 vols. New York: 1915-28.

Storer, John: *Our Cities; Their Present Position and Requirements.* London: 1870.

Stow, John: *A Survay of London; Conteyning the Originall, Antiquity, Increase, Modern Estate, and Description of that City, etc.* First Edition. London: 1598. 2 Edition: 1603. (Reprinted in Everyman Series.) 6 Ed. revised and edited by John Strype. 2 vols. London: 1754-5.
All in all, one of the great classics in urban historiography.

Strieder, Jakob: *Studien zur Geschichte kapitalistischer Organisationsformen; Monopole, Kartelle und Aktiengesellschaften im Mittelalter und zu Beginn der Neuzeit.* München: 1914. 2 Ed. enlarged: 1925.
See especially the chapter on church, state, and early capitalism.

Stuebben, Josef: *Der Städtebau.* Berlin: 1890.

Sullivan, Louis Henry: *Kindergarten Chats.* Washington: 1934.
Reflections on contemporary architecture and civilization by the great leader of the Chicago school.

Survey Graphic: *Regional Planning Number.* May 1925.
First general exposition in the United States of the aims of modern regionalism and regional planning. Contributions by members of the Regional Planning Association of America (not to be confused with that of New York), including Stein, Ackerman, Bing, MacKaye, Wright, and Chase.

Sydenstricker, Edgar: *Health and Environment.* New York: 1933.
Good.

Taine, Hippolyte Adolphe: *The Philosophy of Art in the Netherlands.* Paris: 1869. Trans. New York: 1873.

The Ancient Regime. In *The Origins of Contemporary France.* New York: 1896.

Tait, James: *Mediaeval Manchester and the Beginnings of Lancashire*. Manchester: 1904.

Tappan, Henry P.: *The Growth of Cities*. New York: 1855.

Taut, Bruno: *Die Neue Wohnung*. Leipzig: 1924. Fourth Ed. enlarged: 1926.

Taylor, E. A.: *Paris; Past and Present*. London: 1915.
Studio book. Well-illustrated.

Taylor, Graham Romeyn: *Satellite Cities: a Study of Industrial Suburbs*. New York: 1915.
An early study of the internal decentralization of the metropolis through the building of an industrial rim for the heavy industries.

Taylor, Thomas Griffith: *Environment and Nation; Geographical Factors in the Cultural and Political History of Europe*. Chicago: 1936.

Taylor, William Cooke-: *Factories and the Factory System; from Parliamentary Documents and Personal Examination*. London: 1844.

Notes of a Tour in the Manufacturing Districts of Lancashire in a Series of Letters to His Grace the Archbishop of Dublin. London: 1842.

Tennessee Valley Authority; 1933-1937. Washington: 1937.
Well-organized presentation of aims and achievements.

Terpenning, Walter A.: *Village and Open Country Neighborhoods*. New York: 1931.
First-hand study of importance to planners.

Thackrah, Charles Turner: *The Effects of the Principal Arts, Trades, and Professions, and of Civic States and Habits of Living, on Health and Longevity with a Particular Reference to the Trades and Manufactures of Leeds*. London: 1831.

Thomas, James Henry: *Town Government in the Sixteenth Century*. London: 1933.
Recommended. Based on a study of a group of English towns.

Thompson, John Giffen: *Urbanization; Its Effects on Government and Society*. New York: 1927.
Unimportant.

Thompson, Tracy E.: *Location of Manufactures: 1899-1929; a Study of the Tendencies Toward Concentration and Toward Dispersion of Manufactures in the United States*. Bureau of Census. Washington: 1933.

Thompson, Warren S.: *Population Problems*. New York: 1930.
American sociological scholarship at its best. Wide in range, exhaustive, and intelligent. Ablest treatment of population, particularly in relation to city growth, to date.

Thomson, Robert Ellis: *The History of the Dwelling House and Its Future*. Philadelphia: 1914.
An early attempt based on insufficient data: the subject still waits its master.

Thoreau, Henry David: *Walden*. Boston: 1854.

Thoreau, Henry David: *Cape Cod*. Boston: 1865.
Fundamental classics in regionalism.

Thorndike, E. L., and Woodyard, Ella: *Individual Differences in American Cities*. In *American Journal of Sociology*. September 1937.
Attempt to apply general scheme worked out for individuals to differences between cities.

Thorndike, Lynn: *Sanitation, Baths, and Street-cleaning in the Middle Ages and Renaissance*. Reprinted from *Speculum*. Cambridge, Mass.: 1928.
Important judgment of an undisputed authority: should wipe away ignorance and misinterpretation in a field where popular American scholarship, even now, remains deficient.

Tout, Thomas Frederick: *The Collected Papers of Thomas F. Tout; with a Memoir and Bibliography*. Manchester: 1934.
See especially the chapters on Medieval Town Planning and on the origin of the English bureaucracy. While Tout's survey of the new towns and bastides opened new ground his contribution is weakened by the fact that he held a restricted notion as to what constitutes plan.

Town Planning Review, The. Liverpool: 1911- current.
Invaluable.

Toynbee, Arnold Joseph: *A Study of History*. 3 vols. London: 1934.
A monumental attempt to interpret the development of cultures. Very good in its analysis of the general environment; but so far inadequate because of failure to recognize the critical importance of the city and the cloister in the development of both institutional forms and personality.

Traill, Henry D.: *Social England*. 6 vols. London: 1909.

Turner, Frederick Jackson: *The Significance of Sections in the United States*. New York: 1932.
Turner, while retaining the concept of sectionalism, is in fact the first American historian to appreciate the underlying and perduring influences of regionalism in a country whose uniformities and likenesses have too often been taken for granted.

United States Housing Corporation: *War Emergency Construction; Housing War Workers*. Washington: 1920.
Report of one of the too easily forgotten government war-housing efforts during the first World War: a precedent and example for the work undertaken again fifteen years later.

Unwin, Raymond: *Nothing Gained by Overcrowding*. London: 1918.
First published in the early nineteen hundreds, this exposition of the economic futility of overcrowding has become a classic. Sir Raymond was the first person to demonstrate the relation between frontage and street-and-utilities costs: a discovery that led logically to the cul-de-sac building of England, the Zeilenbau developments of Germany, and the superblocks as developed under Henry Wright's analysis in America.

Town Planning in Practice; An Introduction to the Art of Designing Cities and Suburbs. First Edition. London: 1909.
Admirable introduction to the principles of the new town planning as developed up to 1910. Unfortunately the later 1932 edition makes no effort to digest recent revisions in both theory and practice.

Vance, Rupert B.: *Human Geography of the South; a Study in Regional Resources and Human Adequacy*. Chapel Hill, N. C.: 1935.

Important contribution to American regionalist thought. Fairly exhaustive bibliography.

Van der Bent, T. J.: *The Problem of Hygiene in Man's Dwellings*. New York: 1920.

Van Hise, Charles Richard: *Conservation of Natural Resources*. New York: 1910.
Classic.

Van Hise, Charles Richard, and Havemeyer, Loomis: *Conservation of Our Natural Resources*. New York: 1930.

Vaughan, Robert: *The Age of Great Cities*. London: 1842.

Vidal de la Blache, Paul Marie Joseph: *Principles of Human Geography*. Trans. New York: 1926.

Villes d'art Célèbres, Les. 76 vols. Paris: 1906-1936.
Mainly useful for pictorial documentation. See also Hürlimann.

Violet-le-Duc, Eugene Emmanuel: *Maisons*. In *Dictionnaire Raisonné de l'Architecture Française du XIe au XVIe Siècle*. Vol. 6. Paris: 1863.
Habitations of Man in All Ages. Trans. London: 1876.
Now sadly outmoded.

Vogel, F. R.: *Das Amerikanische Haus*. Berlin: 1910.

Voigt, A. H., and Goldner, P.: *Kleinhaus und Mietskaserne*. Berlin: 1905.
Defense of speculation in land and speculative building. Eberstadt called it a "catechism for speculatordom."

Vossler, Karl: *Medieval Culture*. Trans. 2 vols. New York: 1929.
Completest exposition of the medieval world picture: in relation to Dante, but all-inclusive.

Wagner, Otto: *Die Grosstadt: Eine Studie*. Wien: 1911.

Wakefield, Edward Gibbon: *A View of the Art of Colonization*. London: 1849. Reprinted. Oxford: 1914.
Influenced Howard.

Walker, Charles Rumford: *The American City*. New York: 1937.
The "biography" of an American city of the northwest, particularly as revealed in the crisis of the 1934 strike.

Wallace, Alfred Russel: *Social Environment and Moral Progress*. New York: 1913.

Ware, Caroline Farrar: *Greenwich Village, 1920-1930*. Boston: 1935.

Waugh, Frank Albert: *Country Planning*. New York: 1924.

Webb, Sidney and Beatrice: *English Local Government from the Revolution to the Municipal Corporation Act. The Story of the King's High way*. New York: 1913.
The Manor and the Borough. Part 1 and 2. New York: 1908.
Soviet Communism; a New Civilisation? 2 vols. New York: 1936.

Webber, Adna Ferrin: *The Growth of Cities in the Nineteenth Century; a Study in Statistics.* New York: 1899.
Important: All the more so because it has not tempted emulation.

Weber, Adolf: *Die Grosstadt; und ihre sozialen Probleme.* Leipzig: 1908.

Weber, Alfred: *Theory of the Location of Industries.* Chicago: 1929.
Attempt to work out theoretical distribution in terms of costs of transportation and labor, working regionally, and agglomerative factors within industry.

Weber, Max: *Wirtschaft und Gesellschaft.* 2 vols. 2nd Ed. Tübingen: 1925. (*Grundriss der Sozialökonomie.* Abt. 3.)
Second part of Vol. I has chapter on the city.

Weeden, William B.: *Economic and Social History of New England, 1620-1789.* 2 vols. Boston: 1890.

Wells, Herbert George: *Anticipations.* London: 1902.
Tono Bungay. London: 1909.
New Machiavelli. London: 1911.
A Modern Utopia. London: 1905.

Wheeler, William Morton: *Emergent Evolution and the Development of Societies.* New York: 1928.
Brief but important discussion of the doctrine of emergence, as applied to societies.

Whitaker, Charles Harris. *The Joke About Housing.* Boston: 1920.
From Ramses to Rockefeller. New York: 1934.
A social interpretation of architecture by a distinguished critic whose work as editor of the Journal of the American Institute of Architects put the housing and community planning movement in the United States on new foundations.

Whitaker, Joe Russell, and Parkins, A. E.: *Our Natural Resources and Their Conservation.* New York: 1936.

Whitney, Milton: *Soil and Civilization; A Modern Concept of the Soil and the Historical Development of Agriculture.* New York: 1925.
Dynamic conception of rôle of soil: useful corrective of one-sided quantitative conception in Willcox's *Re-Shaping Agriculture.*

Wickham, Archdale Kenneth: *The Villages of England.* London: 1932.

Wiebeking, Karl Friederich: *Architecture Civile.* 7 vols. München: 1827-31.

Wiese, Leopold von: *Ländliche Siedlungen.* In *Handwörterbuch der Soziologie.* Stuttgart: 1931.

Wijdeveld, H. Th., Editor: *Wendingen; Frank Lloyd Wright.* Santpoort, Holland: 1925.
Completest monograph on Wright's work in English.

Willcox, Oswin William: *Re-Shaping Agriculture.* New York: 1934.
Agrobiologist's interpretation of modern possibilities of selective plant breeding and intensive cultivation. (See Kropotkin.)

Williams, Frank Backus: *The Law of City Planning and Zoning.* New York: 1922.

Williams-Ellis, Clough: *England and the Octopus.* London: 1928.

Winslow, E. A. and C.: *Factory Sanitation and Efficiency*. In *Smithsonian Institution Annual Report:* 1910-11.

Wirth, Louis: *Localism, Regionalism, and Centralization*. In *American Journal of Sociology*. January 1937.

Wolf, Paul: *Städtebau: Das Formproblem der Stadt in Vergangenheit und Zukunft*. Leipzig: 1919.

Wood, Edith Elmer: *The Housing of the Unskilled Wage Earner*. New York: 1919.

Housing Progress in Western Europe. New York: 1923.

Recent Trends in American Housing. New York: 1931.

Slums and Blighted Areas in the United States. In *Housing Division Bulletin No. 1*. Washington: 1935.
Careful studies by an able student and earnest advocate of good housing.

Woods, Robert Archey: *The Neighborhood in Nation-Building*. Boston: 1923.

Woolston, Howard: *The Urban Habit of Mind*. In *American Journal of Sociology*. March 1912.

World Economic Planning; the Necessity for Planned Adjustment of Productive Capacity and Standards of Living. The Hague: 1932.

Wright, Frank Lloyd: *Modern Architecture*. Princeton: 1931.
Brilliant exposition of the principles of organic form by the most original and resourceful living exponent in architecture. Wright, the arch-antagonist of Le Corbusier, expressed the nature of the new biotechnic form from his earliest work onward: using the machine but not dominated by it.

The Disappearing City. New York: 1932.
Brief exposition of a possible type of urban organization in which agriculture would be the fundamental occupation and an acre the minimum area occupied by a family. One of a number of possible lines of development on biotechnic lines: the extreme of decentralized living.

Wright, Frank Lloyd, and Brownell, Baker: *Architecture and Modern Life*. New York: 1932.
Discussion of this great architect's underlying ideas, motifs, purposes.

Wright, Henry: *Re-Housing Urban America*. New York: 1935.
Comprehensive survey by a gifted technician and planner: a fine humane intelligence who left a deep mark on the entire movement for housing and regional planning. See also New York State Housing and Regional Planning Commission's Final Report: mainly the work of Henry Wright.

Yearbook of Design and Industries Association: The Face of the Land. London: 1930.
Illustrations of good and bad culture of the landscape.

Young, George Malcolm, Editor: *Early Victorian England; 1830-1865*. 2 vols. New York: 1934.

Zeiller, Martin: *Topographia Franconiae*. Frankfurt-am-Main: 1648.

Topographia Helvetiae, Rhaetiae et Valesaiae. Frankfurt-am-Main: 1654.
Another great illustrated travel book, invaluable for its woodcuts of medieval survivals. See Merian.

Zimmerman, Erich W.: *World Resources and Industries; a Functional Appraisal of the Availability of Agricultural and Industrial Resources.* New York: 1933.
Except for lack of material on the important precious metals, this work is thorough and well-conceived. Recommended.

Zimmern, Alfred E.: *The Greek Commonwealth.* Oxford: 1911. 5 Ed., revised. Oxford: 1931.
A magnificent survey of the Greek polis.
Nationality and Government. London: 1918.

Zimmern, Helen: *The Hansa Towns.* New York: 1889.
Good.

Zola, Emile: *Paris. Rome. Lourdes.* Trans. New York: 1898.
Conceived as a trilogy in which the cities themselves are in effect characters. Zola bridges the gap between Balzac and Romains.

Zorbaugh, Harvey Warren: *Goldcoast and Slum.* Chicago: 1929.

Zucker, Paul: *Entwicklung des Stadtbildes; die Stadt als Form.* Wien: 1929.
Valuable. Good bibliography of older literature and pictorial documentation.

Zueblin, Charles: *American Municipal Progress.* New York: 1916.

ACKNOWLEDGMENTS

Even more than in Technics and Civilization, my chief intellectual debt is to my master, Patrick Geddes.

To take over Geddes's contributions in block, however, would be to betray their organic nature. Not mimicry and automatic acceptance, but a vital assimilation, was what Geddes sought; for to him thinking was a function of living, not a sequestered sort of play. While I have sometimes utilized Geddes's bold summaries and short cuts, I have never felt bound to respect the mere letter of his teaching, nor to give its details the same emphasis that they had in his own schemata. Many disciples slay or betray their masters while they are still alive, perhaps *because* they are still alive. By waiting till Geddes's death before embarking on these systematic works I perhaps avoided that sad necessity.

But on the subject of cities there were few areas where Geddes was not master: he was not merely a profound sociological observer but a practicing townplanner. There were not many departments that Geddes did not at one time or another cover; little that he did not, if only by a passing flicker of epigram, illuminate. On the literature of cities I have had the advantage of perhaps assimilating a larger amount of material than was available to Geddes during the formative period of his thinking, before 1910; and I have had the good fortune, thanks to contemporary advances in architecture, community planning, and politics, to be able to trace out further certain lines of development about which he was necessarily a little vague, for lack of concrete example: for instance, the nature of biotechnic architecture. But my debt nevertheless remains a large and inclusive one.

Along with Geddes, I owe more than a passing tribute to his colleague, Victor Branford. Sharing quarters with Branford in Le Play House in 1920, walking and talking with him, in Westminster and Chelsea, in the New Forest and Glastonbury and Oxford and Hastings, gave me not a little of my civic education. If the illustrations in the present book have any special pith, they owe much to what I learned, against the very grain of my bookish education, directly from Branford's example.

To my colleagues in the Regional Planning Association of America I owe a debt I can scarcely describe in detail: I am consoled by the Greek proverb which Socrates dwells on in The Republic, that friends hold everything in common. But I cannot omit recording my original obligation to Charles Harris Whitaker, the brilliant editor of the Journal of the American Institute of Architects, who brought us all together; nor fail to express my gratitude for the constant inspiration and example and help of Clarence S. Stein and Benton MacKaye. Not least, I must pay special tribute to the late Henry Wright, whose gallant spirit and unflinching sincerity left a deep mark upon all of us, for his adventurous mind touched nothing in the realm of his professional interests that it did not radioactively transform. To another member of this group, Catherine Bauer, the book owes its present form: her challenging criticisms of the original draft, finished in 1931, helped turn the work from a compact restatement of past views into what I trust has proved a more penetrating and wide-ranging study.

In many matters covered in The Culture of Cities the writer's voice (outside his immediate circle) was a lone one between 1920 and 1930. The Regional Planning Number of the Survey Graphic was almost abandoned in 1924 because the editors, though sympathetic, were not convinced that the subject was in the realm of fact and possibility. If the world has caught up with—and perhaps gone beyond—our original formulation of the tasks of regional reconstruction and city-development, the fact itself is a welcome one. And since practical administrators have already moved far toward establishing new regional and civic conceptions, I have sought, with a confidence borrowed from the events themselves, to map even more boldly the next moves.

For their critical suggestions on the manuscript, in one draft or another, I owe my hearty thanks to a group of self-sacrificing friends: Charles Ascher, Walter Curt Behrendt, Lee Simonson, and Clarence Stein. In a study trip in 1932, on a fellowship from the John Simon Guggenheim Memorial Foundation, I was the recipient of manifold courtesies from municipal officials all over Europe: my obligations here, as well as to friendly scholars and administrators in the various fields I have touched, are too numerous for mention without the possibility of invidious neglect. Finally, the ability to carry this book to completion, with further travel and pictorial illustration, above all time for research and meditation, was made possible by a grant from the Carnegie Corporation of New York; and I herewith place on record my warm thanks for their ready interest and aid.—L. M.

INDEX

NOTE: The numbers in brackets [ ] indicate illustrations as distinguished from the main body of text.

EDITION

5

ORTHOPEDIC IMAGING

A PRACTICAL APPROACH

Adam Greenspan, MD, FACR

Professor Emeritus of Radiology and Orthopedic Surgery
University of California, Davis School of Medicine
Former Director, Section of Musculoskeletal Imaging
Department of Radiology, University of California Davis Medical Center
Sacramento, California
Consultant, Shriners Hospital for Children
Sacramento, California

Foreword by

Lynne S. Steinbach, MD, FACR

Professor of Radiology and Orthopedic Surgery
Director, Musculoskeletal Imaging
Department of Radiology, University of California,
San Francisco, California

Wolters Kluwer | Lippincott Williams & Wilkins
Health
Philadelphia · Baltimore · New York · London
Buenos Aires · Hong Kong · Sydney · Tokyo

Acquisitions Editor: Charles W. Mitchell
Product Manager: Ryan Shaw
Vendor Manager: Alicia Jackson
Senior Manufacturing Manager: Benjamin Rivera
Senior Marketing Manager: Angela Panetta
Design Coordinator: Holly McLaughlin
Production Service: SPi Technologies

Fifth Edition

© 2011 by LIPPINCOTT WILLIAMS & WILKINS, a WOLTERS KLUWER business

Two Commerce Square
2001 Market Street
Philadelphia, PA 19103 USA
LWW.com

Library of Congress Cataloging-in-Publication Data
Greenspan, Adam.
   Orthopedic imaging : a practical approach / Adam Greenspan ; foreword by Lynne S. Steinbach. — 5th ed.
      p. ; cm.
   Includes bibliographical references and index.
   ISBN 978-1-45111-090-6 (hardback)
   1. Radiography in orthopedics. 2. Musculoskeletal system—Imaging. 3. Musculoskeletal system—
Diseases—Diagnosis. I. Title.
   [DNLM: 1. Bone Diseases—diagnosis. 2. Bone and Bones—radiography. 3. Diagnostic Imaging—methods.
4. Joint Diseases—diagnosis. WE 225 G815o 2011]
   RD734.5.R33G74   2011
   616.7′07548—dc22

                                                                                                2010019448

To my wife Barbara, my children Michael, Samantha, and Luddy, and my grandchildren Anna and Sydney, who light up my life; and to the memory of my mother Eugenia and my father Bernard, a brilliant physician, who taught me my ABC's of the medical profession and made me aware of the beauty of the medical practice.

Foreword

Rejoice!!! The fifth edition of Adam Greenspan's *Orthopedic Imaging: A Practical Approach* is here. It is a pleasure to evaluate and comment on this esteemed work.

The author is known internationally to be a well-liked and respected musculoskeletal radiologist, who is a Fellow of the American College of Radiology and has been a longtime member of the International Skeletal Society. Dr. Greenspan has drawn upon his vast experience in the field, which began at the Hospital for Joint Diseases/Orthopedic Institute in New York and led him to the University of California, Davis School of Medicine, where he has been a Professor of Radiology for over 23 years.

This popular icon of musculoskeletal imaging textbooks has been expanded and extensively revised since its last edition, published 6 years ago. It includes the use of the newest imaging modalities, while remaining as a single volume. There is a wide-ranging look at musculoskeletal imaging that includes MRI, CT, three-dimensional imaging, nuclear medicine imaging (scintigraphy), PET, ultrasound, and radiographs. Procedures that are commonly performed by musculoskeletal radiologists—arthrography, percutaneous image-guided biopsy, and radiofrequency ablation—are also covered. Imaging guidelines are stressed throughout the text. Whenever appropriate, therapeutic approaches, pathology, and cytogenetics for musculoskeletal diseases are mentioned. Of note, the text of this book is fully searchable online, bringing the book into the new century and making access very convenient for the reader.

As would be expected from Dr. Greenspan, this book is both comprehensive and extremely well organized. All aspects of musculoskeletal imaging are addressed: trauma, sports medicine, arthritis, congenital and developmental anomalies including variety of dysplasias, metabolic, endocrine, and systemic diseases, infections, and neoplasms of the musculoskeletal system including spine. The writing is clear and precise, providing practical information. A differential diagnosis for each disorder is enumerated. The "Suggested Readings" section includes classical source references as well as current citations on the subject. Each chapter ends with a set of Practical Points which summarize the important concepts. A number of unique topics pepper the book, including the role of the orthopedic radiologist, choice of imaging modality, anatomic-radiologic considerations, bone formation and growth, and similar subjects, forming a foundation for understanding the practical aspect of musculoskeletal imaging.

The tables and charts have been updated, while all of the figures are of excellent quality, making it easier to organize and remember the information. The many diagrams appeal to readers of all backgrounds and specialties. All these visuals are unique and provide more clarity to the underlying concepts, making classification easier to understand and retain. Full color is used throughout the book, enhancing its attraction to all readers.

This book will appeal to a wide audience in the medical field. In addition to radiologists and orthopedic surgeons in practice and in training, also rheumatologists, radiology technologists, primary care physicians, physical therapists, and physiatrists will covet the information herein. This work will be used by medical students, especially those in radiology and orthopedic clerkships, enticing them into pursuing this fascinating and attractive field of medicine.

It is a great honor and privilege to write this Foreword for the book of my good friend. Thank you so much, Adam, for letting me have the opportunity to expound upon one of my all-time favorite textbooks.

Lynne Steinbach, MD, FACR
Professor of Radiology and Orthopedic Surgery
University of California, San Francisco, California

Preface to the First Edition

Orthopedic Radiology: A Practical Approach was written to facilitate the complex process of diagnostic investigation in a broad range of orthopedic disorders. Its underlying concept is threefold: to provide a basic understanding of the currently available imaging modalities used to diagnose many commonly encountered disorders of bones and joints, to help in the choice of the most effective radiologic technique with a view to minimizing the cost of examination as well as the exposure of patients to radiation, and to emphasize the need for providing the orthopedic surgeon with the information required to choose the right therapy. It does not attempt to compete in size and scope with other books on the same subject. Many uncommon entities have been excluded, as have the exact instructions for performing procedures. Likewise, the nature of the volume does not allow inclusion of every detail of a given disorder or full discussion of controversial aspects. These matters are left to the reader's further study of the literature and the many standard and specialized textbooks compiled in the "References and Further Reading" section at the end of the volume.

As its subtitle states, *Orthopedic Radiology* strives to provide its primary audience, medical students and residents in radiology and orthopedics, with a practical approach to its subject. To this end, crucial information within the text of each chapter has been tabulated in a section entitled "Practical Points to Remember" at the end of the chapter. Numerous original schematic diagrams and tables have been developed, detailing, for example, classifications of fractures, the morphologic features of arthritic and neoplastic disorders, and the positioning of patients for the various standard and special radiographic projections, as well as the most effective radiologic techniques for demonstrating abnormalities. Radiographic reproductions, many of which are accompanied by explanatory, labeled line drawings, have been specially prepared to provide high-quality examples of the classic presentations of a wide spectrum of orthopedic disorders. Moreover, most figure captions are written in a case-study format, which, combined with a system of diagnostic notations (explained in Chapter 1) following each legend, is meant to impart an appreciation of the process of radiologic investigations. Although its aim is to teach, *Orthopedic Radiology* should also serve as a convenient reference for physicians interested in bone and joint disorders and those customarily employing radiologic studies in their everyday practice.

Adam Greenspan, MD, FACR

Preface

With each year bringing further technologic advances in musculoskeletal imaging and increasingly wider applications of CT (particularly its three-dimensional variant), PET, MRI, and US to the diagnosis and evaluation of osseous, joint, and soft tissue abnormalities, the time was right to launch a new edition of this text. Like each of the previous versions, this fifth edition of *Orthopedic Imaging: A Practical Approach* has many changes, additions, and improvements.

Principal among these changes is a new design, one incorporating full color. The use of color has added clarity to the text and tables, as well as information of value to the schematics. Many line drawings have been deleted and substituted with indicator arrows with the aim of better delineating the abnormalities. In terms of text, discussion on a variety of conditions was updated and some outdated material deleted. The "Suggested Readings" sections found in each chapter have been significantly trimmed, to include only the classic papers and the most current references. Further, great attention and care were directed toward selecting the most representative images in each section and summarizing important facts in the end-of-chapter "Practical Points to Remember" feature, which comprises clinical pearls and key points.

Because of recent progress in the cytogenetics and molecular genetics of a range of diseases, especially congenital and developmental anomalies and some bone tumors, this diagnostic component was introduced where relevant. Almost every chapter contains new sections and illustrations, and the differential diagnosis of many musculoskeletal disorders has been emphasized. Although the text focuses mainly on diagnostic imaging, some of the latest therapeutic approaches to many conditions (e.g., the arthritides) were also included.

Despite the additions, the single-volume format, so prized by many readers, has once again been retained. And as before, also this edition particularly stresses the mastery of conventional radiography while recognizing the proper application of more advanced imaging techniques such as CT and MRI. The goal was to present an up-to-date approach to the effective and cost-efficient use of available imaging techniques in the clinical evaluation of specific musculoskeletal abnormalities. Every effort has been made to provide a book with concise, readable text and clear illustrations—hence its usefulness to a broad spectrum of radiologists, orthopedic surgeons, rheumatologists, and other physicians interested in the application of imaging techniques to the musculoskeletal system.

Adam Greenspan, MD, FACR

Acknowledgments

I would like to express my thanks to many individuals from Lippincott Williams & Wilkins/Wolters Kluwer Health who guided me in the preparation of this book but particularly to Brian Brown, former Executive Editor, and Charley Mitchell, the current Executive Editor, for supervision over this work; to Holly McLaughlin for beautiful design; and to Rajshri Walia, who managed the creating and colorization of the drawings. A special note of acknowledgment goes to Ryan Shaw, the Product Manager and Developmental Editor, for many editorial advices, enduring and attentive review of the manuscript, meaningful suggestions, and for accommodation of my constant last-minute changes and additions to the text. I also would like to thank Julie A. Ostoich-Prather, Senior Photographer from the Department of Radiology, University of California, Davis Medical Center, for help in creating some digital illustrations. I am grateful to Lynne S. Steinbach, MD, FACR, Professor of Radiology and Orthopedic Surgery from the University of California, San Francisco, for writing the Foreword for this book. Again, I am indebted to all authors who have given permission to reproduce selective illustrations from their books and publications. They are separately acknowledged on the credit page at the end of this book. Finally, I would like to thank G. Biju Kumar, the Project Manager from SPi Technologies, for supervision and help during the final composition of this text.

As with the previous editions, this project could not have been successfully completed without the prudent and dutiful efforts of the many individuals acknowledged here.

Contents

PART III ARTHRITIDES 429

PART V INFECTIONS 787

PART VI METABOLIC AND ENDOCRINE DISORDERS 821

PART VII CONGENITAL AND DEVELOPMENTAL ANOMALIES 881

INTRODUCTION TO ORTHOPEDIC IMAGING

CHAPTER 1

The Role of the Orthopedic Radiologist

Spectacular progress has been made and continues to be made in the field of radiologic imaging. The introduction and constant improvements of new imaging modalities—computed tomography (CT) and its spiral (helical) and 3D variants, 64-channel multidetector row CT (MDCT), high resolution flat-panel volume computed tomography (fpVCT), 3D CT-angiography, digital (computed) radiography (DR or CR) and its variants: digital subtraction radiography (DSR) and digital subtraction angiography (DSA), 3D ultrasound (US), radionuclide angiography and perfusion scintigraphy, positron emission tomography (PET), PET-CT, and PET-MRI, single-photon emission computerized tomography (SPECT), magnetic resonance imaging (MRI) and its 3D variant, 3D MRI/CT fusion imaging, MR-arthrography (MRa), and MR-angiography (MRA). Among others—have expanded the armamentarium of the radiologist, facilitating the sometimes difficult process of diagnosis. These new technologic developments have also brought disadvantages. They have contributed to a dramatic increase in the cost of medical care and have often led clinicians, trying to keep up with new imaging modalities, to order too many frequently unnecessary radiologic examinations.

This situation has served to emphasize the crucial importance of the role of the orthopedic radiologist and the place of conventional radiography. The radiologist must not only comply with prerequisites for various examinations but also, more importantly, screen them to choose only those procedures that will lead to the correct diagnosis and proper evaluation of a given disorder. To this end, radiologists should bear in mind the following objectives in the performance of their role:

1. To *diagnose an unknown disorder*, preferably by using standard projections along with the special views and techniques obtainable in conventional radiography before using the more sophisticated modalities now available.
2. To perform examinations in the *proper sequence* and to know what should be performed *next* in the radiologic investigation.
3. To demonstrate the determining *imaging features of a known disorder*, the *distribution* of a lesion in the skeleton, and its *location* in the bone.
4. To monitor the *progress of therapy* and possible *complications*.
5. To be aware of what *specific information* is important to the orthopedic surgeon.
6. To recognize the *limits of noninvasive radiologic investigation* and to know when to *proceed with invasive techniques*.

7. To recognize lesions that require biopsy and those that do not (the "don't touch" lesions).
8. To assume a more active role in therapeutic management, such as performing an embolization procedure, delivering chemotherapeutic material by means of selective catheterization, or performing (usually CT-guided) radiofrequency thermal ablation of osseous lesions (such as osteoid osteoma).

The radiologic diagnosis of many bone and joint disorders cannot be made solely on the basis of particular recognizable radiographic patterns. Clinical data, such as the patient's age, gender, symptoms, history, and laboratory findings, are also important to the radiologist in correctly interpreting an imaging study. Occasionally, clinical information is so typical of a certain disorder that it alone may suffice as the basis for diagnosis. Bone pain in a young person that is characteristically most severe at night and is promptly relieved by salicylates, for example, is so highly suggestive of osteoid osteoma that often the radiologist's only task is finding the lesion. However, in many cases clinical data do not suffice and may even be misleading.

When presented with a patient, the cause of whose symptom is *unknown* (Fig. 1.1) or *suspected* on the basis of clinical data (Fig. 1.2), the radiologist should avoid, as a point of departure in the examination, the more technologically advanced imaging modalities in favor of making a diagnosis, whenever possible, on the basis of simple conventional radiographs. This approach is essential not only to maintain cost-effectiveness but also to decrease the amount of radiation to which a patient is exposed. Proceeding first with conventional technique also has a firm basis in the chemistry and physiology of bone. The calcium apatite crystal, one of the mineral constituents of bone, is an intrinsic contrast agent that gives skeletal radiology a great advantage over other radiologic subspecialties and makes information on bone production and destruction readily available through conventional radiography. Simple observation of changes in the shape or density of normal bone, for example in the vertebrae, can be a deciding factor in arriving at a specific diagnosis (Figs. 1.3 and 1.4).

To aid the radiologist in the analysis of radiographic patterns and signs, some of which may be pathognomonic and others nonspecific, a number of options within the confines of conventional radiography are available. Certain *ways of positioning the patient* when radiographs are obtained allow the radiologist the opportunity to evaluate

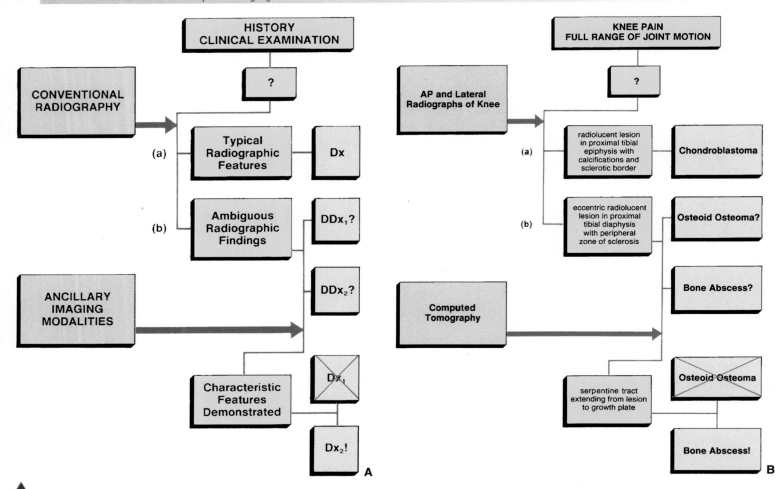

FIGURE 1.1   Cause of symptoms unknown. (A,B) The patient's history and the results of the clinical examination, supplied to the radiologist by the referring physician, are not sufficient to form a diagnosis (*?*). On the basis of conventional radiographic studies, (a) the diagnosis is established (*Dx*), or (b) the studies may suggest the differential possibilities (*DDx*). In the latter case, ancillary imaging techniques, such as arthrography, scintigraphy, CT, or MRI, among others, are called on to confirm or exclude one of the options.

otherwise hidden anatomic sites and to more suitably demonstrate a particular abnormality. The frog-lateral projection of the hip, for example, is better than the anteroposterior view for imaging the signs of suspected osteonecrosis (ON) of the femoral head by more readily demonstrating the crescent sign, the early radiographic feature of this condition (see Figs. 4.59 and 4.60B). The frog-lateral view is also extremely helpful in the early diagnosis of slipped femoral capital epiphysis (see Fig. 32.30B). Likewise, the application of *special techniques* can help to identify a lesion that is difficult to detect on routine radiographs. Fractures of complex structures such as the elbow, wrist, ankle, and foot are not always demonstrated on the standard projections. Because of the overlap of bones on the lateral view of the elbow, for example, detecting a nondisplaced or minimally displaced fracture of the radial head occasionally requires a special 45-degree angle view (called the radial head–capitellum view) that projects the radial head free of adjacent structures, making an otherwise obscure lesion evident (see Figs. 6.12 and 6.28). Stress radiographic views are similarly useful, particularly in evaluating tears of various ligaments of the knee and ankle joints (see Figs. 9.16, 9.74B, 10.10, and 10.11).

An accurate diagnosis depends on the radiologist's acute observations and careful analysis, in light of clinical information, of the radiographic findings regarding the size, shape, configuration, and density of a lesion; its location within the bone; and its distribution in the skeletal system. Until the conventional approach with its range of options fails to provide the radiographic findings necessary for correct diagnosis and

precise evaluation of an abnormality, the radiologist need not turn to more costly procedures.

Knowing the *proper sequence* of procedures in radiologic investigation depends, to a great extent, on the pertinent clinical information provided by the referring physician. The choice of modality or modalities for imaging a lesion or investigating a pathologic process is dictated by the clinical presentation as well as by the equipment availability, physician expertise, cost, and individual patient restrictions. Knowing *where to begin* and *what to do next*, as rudimentary as it may sound, is of paramount importance in reaching a precise diagnosis by the shortest possible route, with the least expense and detriment to the patient. Redundant studies should be avoided. For example, if a patient presents with arthritis and if clinician is interested in demonstrating the distribution of "silent" sites of the disorder, the radiologist should not begin by obtaining radiographs of every joint (a so-called joint survey). It is instead more sensible to perform a skeletal scintigraphy and, afterward, to order radiographs of only those areas that show increased uptake of radiopharmaceutical. A simple radionuclide bone scan rather than a broad-ranging bone survey is also a reasonable starting point for investigating other possible sites of involvement when a lesion is detected in a single bone and is suspected of representing part of a multifocal or systemic disorder, such as polyostotic fibrous dysplasia or metastatic disease. Similarly, if a patient is suspected of having osteoid osteoma around the hip joint and standard radiography has not demonstrated the nidus, a radionuclide bone scan should be performed next to determine the site of the lesion. This should be followed up

FIGURE 1.2   **Cause of symptoms suspected. (A,B)** From the ▶ information supplied by the referring physician, the radiologist may suspect the diagnosis (*Dx?*) and proceed with conventional radiographic studies. The results of the examination may confirm the suspected diagnosis (*Dx!*), reveal an additional abnormality (*Dx! + Dx₂*) or an unsuspected complication (*Dx! + Dx꜀*), or exclude the suspected diagnosis and confirm a different one (*Dx̶₁, Dx₂*). The studies may also show inconclusive evidence of the original suspected diagnosis, in which case ancillary imaging modalities, such as scintigraphy, CT, or MRI, among others, are used.

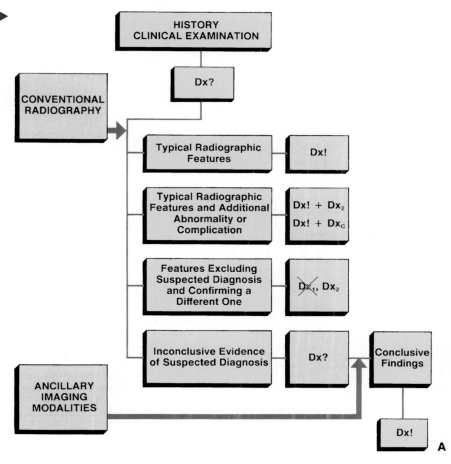

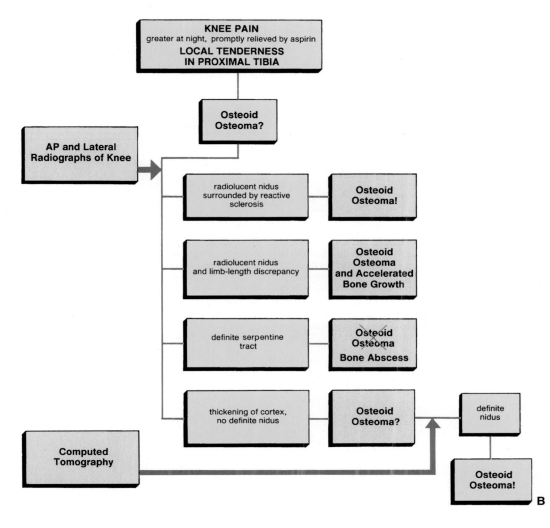

Trauma

acute

chronic

buckling of end plate—
compression fracture

anterior wedging—
compression fracture

localized defect in
end plate—Schmorl node

localized separation
of anterior corner—
limbus vertebra

Arthritides

squaring of body—
ankylosing spondylitis

Tumor-Like Lesion

flattened vertebra
(vertebra plana)—
Langerhans cell histiocytosis
(eosinophilic granuloma)

Metabolic

biconcavity of body
(fish-mouth vertebra)—
osteoporosis

Congenital

central anterior
beaking—Morquio disease

lower anterior
beaking—Hurler
syndrome (gargoylism)

hemivertebra

Developmental

anterior wedging of
body and wavy outline
of end plates—
Scheuermann disease

step-like central
depression of end plate—
sickle-cell disease

scalloping of
posterior border—
neurofibromatosis

FIGURE 1.3 **Shape and contour of bone.** Observation of changes in the shape and contour of a vertebral body on conventional radiographs may disclose critical information leading to a correct diagnosis.

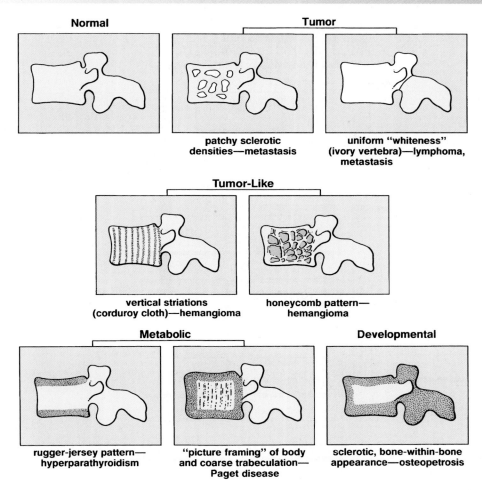

Normal

Tumor

patchy sclerotic densities—metastasis

uniform "whiteness" (ivory vertebra)—lymphoma, metastasis

Tumor-Like

vertical striations (corduroy cloth)—hemangioma

honeycomb pattern— hemangioma

Metabolic

Developmental

rugger-jersey pattern— hyperparathyroidism

"picture framing" of body and coarse trabeculation— Paget disease

sclerotic, bone-within-bone appearance—osteopetrosis

▲

FIGURE 1.4 **Density and texture of bone.** Changes in the density and texture of a vertebral body on conventional radiographs may offer useful data for arriving at a diagnosis.

by CT for more precise localization of a nidus in the bone. However, if the routine examination demonstrates the nidus, scintigraphy can be omitted from the sequence of examination. At this point, only CT scan is required to determine the lesion's exact location in the bone and to obtain specific measurements of the nidus (Fig. 1.5; see also Fig. 17.10). If ON of the femoral head is suspected and the radiographs are normal, MRI should be ordered as the next diagnostic procedure, because it is a more sensitive modality than CT, or scintigraphy. The text that follows presents many similar situations in which the proper sequence of imaging modalities may dramatically shorten the diagnostic investigation.

Reaching a correct diagnosis does not end the process of radiologic investigation, because the course of treatment often depends on the *identification of distinguishing features of a particular disorder* (Fig. 1.6). For example, the diagnosis of Ewing sarcoma by conventional radiography is only the beginning of a radiologic workup of the patient. The *crucial features* of this tumor must be identified, such as intraosseous and soft-tissue extension (by CT or MRI) and the vascularity of the lesion (by conventional arteriography or magnetic resonance angiography [MRA]). Similarly, a diagnosis of osteosarcoma must be followed by determination of the exact extent of the lesion in the bone and the status of bone marrow in the vicinity of the tumor. This can be accomplished by precise measurement of bone marrow density using Hounsfield numbers during CT examination (see Fig. 2.14) or by using MR images with or without contrast enhancement. Diagnosing Paget disease may be an important achievement in the investigation of an unknown disorder, but even more important is the further search for an answer to

a crucial question: Is there any sign of malignant transformation? (see Fig. 29.19). *Localization* of a lesion in the skeleton or in a particular bone can frequently be more important than diagnosis itself. The best example of this is, again, the precise localization of the nidus of osteoid osteoma because incomplete resection of this lesion invariably results in recurrence. Determining the *distribution of a lesion* in the skeleton is helpful in planning the treatment of various arthritides and the management of a patient with metastatic disease. Scintigraphy is an invaluable technique in this respect.

Many of the most important questions put to the radiologist by the orthopedic surgeon concern monitoring the *progress of treatment* and the appearance of possible *complications*. At the stage when the diagnosis is already established, the fate of the lesion, and consequently the patient, must be established. Comparison of earlier radiographic examinations with present findings plays a crucial role at this stage because it may disclose the dynamics of specific conditions (see Fig. 16.6). Likewise, in monitoring the progress of healing fractures, study of the diagnostic sequence of radiographs complemented by CT should decide questionable cases. Ancillary imaging techniques such as scintigraphy, CT, PET-CT, and MRI play an essential role in evaluating one of the most serious complications of benign tumors and tumor-like lesions—malignant transformation that may occur in enchondroma, osteochondroma, fibrous dysplasia, or Paget disease.

Providing the orthopedic surgeon with *specific information* is also an important function of the radiologist at the time when a diagnosis is being established. If, for example, osteochondritis dissecans is diagnosed, the decision on the choice of therapy requires information on the

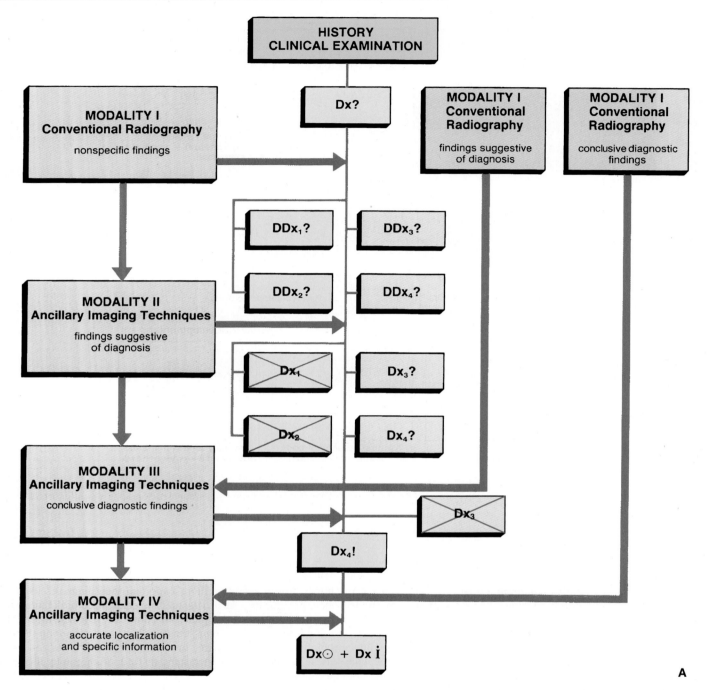

FIGURE 1.5   **Sequence of imaging modalities. (A,B)** A diagnosis is suspected (*Dx?*) on the basis of a patient's history and the results of the clinical examination. The radiologist suggests the proper sequence of imaging modalities, eliminating various disorders in the process and narrowing the differential possibilities to arrive at one correct diagnosis (*Dx!*). An accurate localization (*DxO*) and specific information pertinent to the correct diagnosis (*Dxi*) are also provided.

status of the articular cartilage covering the lesion. This information is obtainable by contrast arthrography, alone or combined with CT, or by MRI (see Figs. 6.40 to 6.42). If the cartilage is intact, conservative treatment should be contemplated; if it is damaged, surgical intervention is the more likely course of treatment. Similarly, in contributing to the plan of treatment of anterior dislocation in the shoulder joint, the radiologist should be aware of the importance to the surgeon of information about the status of the cartilaginous labrum of the glenoid (see Figs. 5.50, 5.52 and 5.53) and the possible presence of osteochondral bodies in the joint. These features must be confirmed or excluded by arthrography combined with tomography (arthrotomography), CT (computed arthrotomography), or MRI (Fig. 1.7).

Recognizing *the limits of noninvasive radiologic investigation* and knowing when to proceed with *invasive techniques* are as important to arriving at a diagnosis and precise evaluation of a condition as any of

the points already mentioned. This situation is best illustrated in the case of tumors and tumor-like bone lesions. Many tumor-like lesions have distinctive radiographic presentations that lead to unquestionable diagnoses on conventional studies. In such cases, invasive procedures such as biopsy are not indicated. This is particularly true of a group of definitely benign conditions commonly called "don't touch" lesions (see Fig. 16.52 and Table 16.10). The name "don't touch" speaks for itself. Conditions such as a bone island (enostosis), posttraumatic juxtacortical myositis ossificans, and a periosteal desmoid are unquestionably benign lesions whose determining features can, with certainty, be demonstrated with the appropriate noninvasive techniques without the need for histopathologic confirmation. Obtaining a biopsy of such lesions may in fact lead to mistakes in diagnosis and treatment. The histologic appearance of a periosteal desmoid, for example, may exhibit aggressive features resembling a malignant tumor; in inexperienced

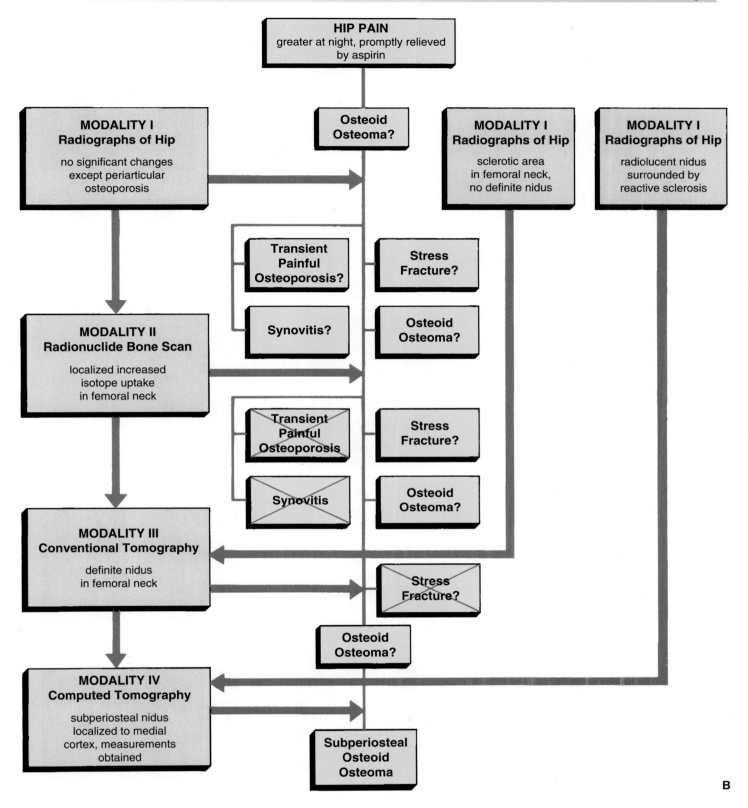

FIGURE 1.5 *(Continued).*

hands, this can lead to inappropriate treatment. However, there are times when the radiologist faces the situation in which a battery of conventional and advanced noninvasive techniques has yielded equivocal information. At this point, there is no shame in saying, "I don't know what it is, but I know a biopsy should be performed" (Fig. 1.8). Fluoroscopy-guided or CT-guided percutaneous biopsy can be performed by the radiologist in the radiology suite, eliminating the use of costly operating-room time and personnel. Occasionally, the radiologist may also assume a more active role in therapeutic management by performing an embolization procedure under image intensification or with CT guidance, or performing radiofrequency thermal ablation of bone lesion. This more interventional role for the radiologist may shorten the length of a patient's hospitalization and be more cost-effective. Information hidden in the radiologic image, whether it is conventional radiography, scintigraphy, ultrasonography, CT, MRI, or other modality, can be effectively extracted by knowing the sensitivity of applied technique, spatial resolution, contrast resolution, and distortion among other factors. But at the same time radiologist should never forget the drawbacks of some techniques, such as radiation exposure to the patient or high cost of imaging procedures (Fig. 1.9). Choosing logical

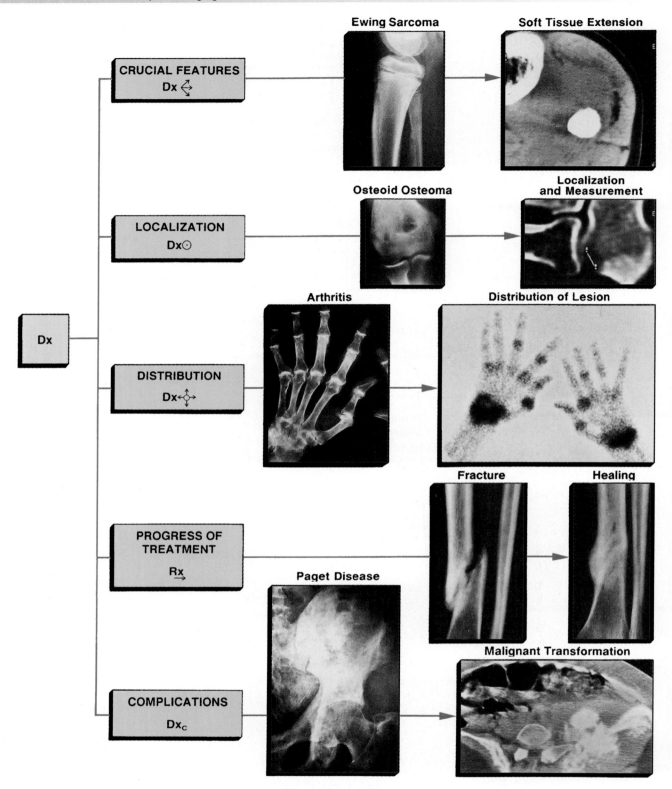

▲

FIGURE 1.6   **Distinguishing features of lesion, progress of treatment, and complications.** The diagnosis is known (*Dx*). The clinician is interested in demonstrating (1) the crucial features of the lesion (*Dx↔*), that is, its character, extent, stage, and other pertinent data; (2) the location of the lesion in the bone (*Dx*O); (3) the distribution of the lesion in the skeleton (*Dx↔*); (4) the progress of treatment (*Rx*); and (5) the emergence of any complications (*Dx*$_c$).

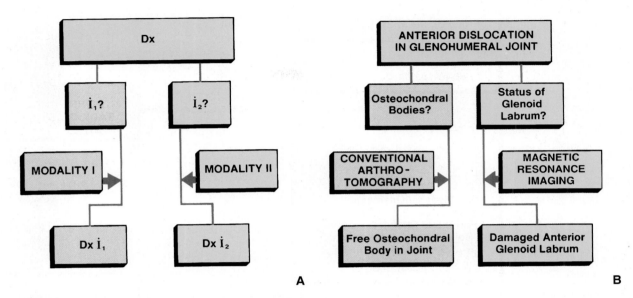

FIGURE 1.7 Specific information. (A,B) The diagnosis is known (*Dx*). The radiologist should be aware of the specific information (*i*), for example, regarding the features (*i₁?*) or extent (*i₂?*) of a lesion, which is required by the orthopedic surgeon in planning treatment. The information may also concern the distribution of a lesion and its localization, the progress of treatment, or the emergence of complications. Application of the best radiologic modality for demonstrating the required information is one of the radiologist's primary functions. The modalities may vary depending on the specific information needed.

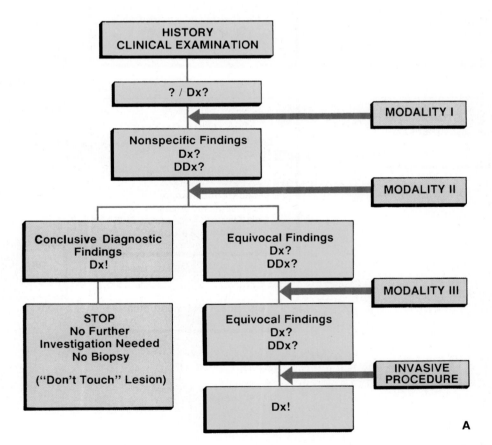

FIGURE 1.8 Noninvasive versus invasive procedures. (A,B) The diagnosis is unknown (*?*) or suspected (*Dx?*). Noninvasive radiologic procedures may yield sufficient data to make an unquestionable diagnosis. No further investigation is required, nor is biopsy indicated, particularly if the diagnosis is that of a definitely benign condition commonly called a "don't touch" lesion. However, noninvasive procedures may yield equivocal information at each step in the examination. At this point, proceeding to an invasive procedure such as biopsy is indicated.

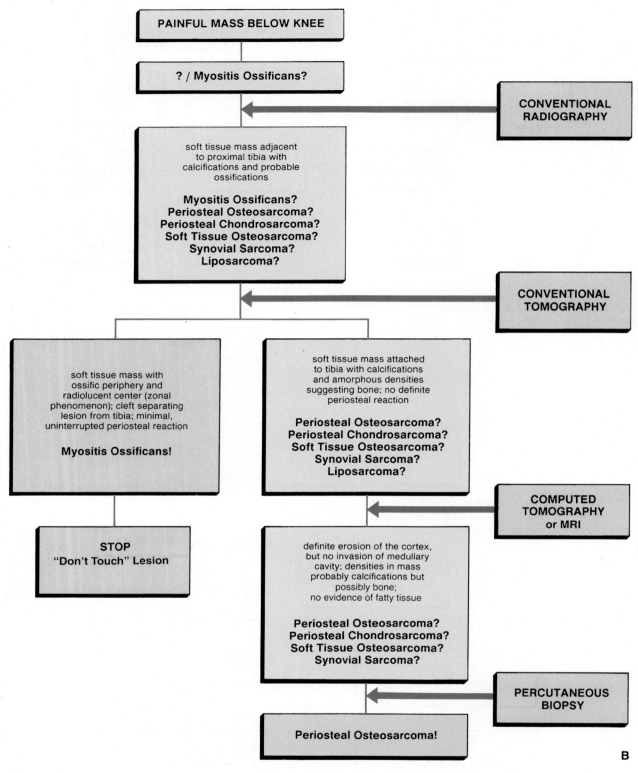

PAINFUL MASS BELOW KNEE

? / Myositis Ossificans?

CONVENTIONAL RADIOGRAPHY

soft tissue mass adjacent
to proximal tibia with
calcifications and probable
ossifications

**Myositis Ossificans?
Periosteal Osteosarcoma?
Periosteal Chondrosarcoma?
Soft Tissue Osteosarcoma?
Synovial Sarcoma?
Liposarcoma?**

CONVENTIONAL TOMOGRAPHY

soft tissue mass with
ossific periphery and
radiolucent center (zonal
phenomenon); cleft separating
lesion from tibia; minimal,
uninterrupted periosteal reaction

Myositis Ossificans!

soft tissue mass attached
to tibia with calcifications
and amorphous densities
suggesting bone; no definite
periosteal reaction

**Periosteal Osteosarcoma?
Periosteal Chondrosarcoma?
Soft Tissue Osteosarcoma?
Synovial Sarcoma?
Liposarcoma?**

COMPUTED TOMOGRAPHY or MRI

STOP
"Don't Touch" Lesion

definite erosion of the cortex,
but no invasion of medullary
cavity; densities in mass
probably calcifications but
possibly bone;
no evidence of fatty tissue

**Periosteal Osteosarcoma?
Periosteal Chondrosarcoma?
Soft Tissue Osteosarcoma?
Synovial Sarcoma?**

PERCUTANEOUS BIOPSY

Periosteal Osteosarcoma!

B

▲
FIGURE 1.8   *(Continued)*.

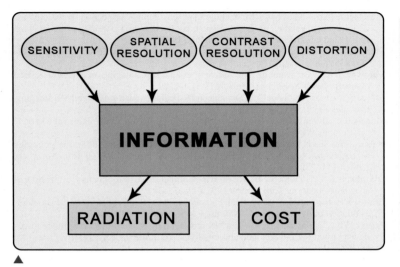

▲
FIGURE 1.9   **Information.** Crucial factors determining the usefulness of information concealed in the radiologic image.

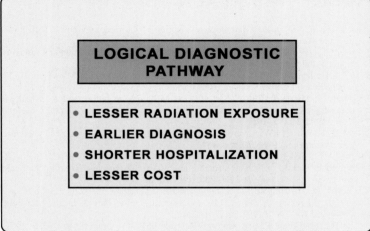

▲
FIGURE 1.10   **Logical diagnostic pathway.** Benefits of a sensible approach to the diagnostic investigation.

diagnostic imaging pathway would not only benefit the patient, but also will reduce the cost of radiologic studies and cost of treatment (Fig. 1.10). Therefore, it is mandatory for musculoskeletal radiologist to develop a strategic course of action in pursuing his or her goal to make the correct diagnosis. Radiologist must take into consideration the effectiveness of imaging modalities, their safety, required time to complete the examination, as well as the cost of investigation (Fig. 1.11A). The effectiveness will depend upon the use of imaging techniques in proper sequence, and knowledge of which of these techniques is better to demonstrate the lesion, its localization and distribution in the skeleton, and which is the best to monitor the progress of treatment or emergence of possible complications (Fig. 1.11B). In summary, to sufficiently manage the diagnosis and treatment of patients with conditions affecting the musculoskeletal system, the radiologist and the referring physician should be aware of the range of radiologic modalities and their proper uses. This will increase the precision of

diagnostic radiologic investigation and reduce the amount of radiation to which a patient is exposed and the cost of hospitalization. The obligation of the radiologist is to:

- Use the conventional radiographic methods, with knowledge of the capabilities and effectiveness of the various techniques, before resorting to more advanced modalities.
- Follow a logical sequence of imaging modalities in diagnostic investigation.
- Be as noninvasive as possible at the start, but use invasive techniques if they will shorten the diagnostic pathway.
- Improve communication between the radiologist and the orthopedic surgeon by using the same language and by knowing what the surgeon needs to know about the lesion.
- Provide knowledge to referring physicians about indications, advantages, disadvantages, risks, contraindications, and limitations of the various imaging techniques.

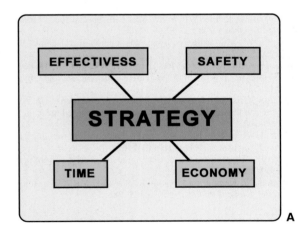

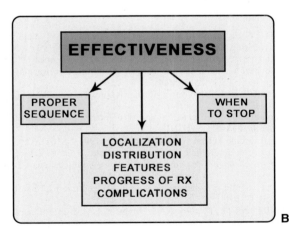

▲
FIGURE 1.11   **Imaging strategy.** Strategic elements (**A,B**) of analytic quest for correct radiologic diagnosis.

SUGGESTED READINGS

Blackmore CC, Magid DJ. Methologic evaluation of the radiology cost-effectiveness literature. *Radiology* 1997;203:87–91.

Bolus NE, George R, Washington J, Newcomer BR. PET/MRI: the blended-modality choice of the future? *J Nucl Med Tech* 2009;37:63–71.

Brink JA, Heiken JP, Wang G, McEnery KW, Schlueter FJ, Vannier MW. Helical CT: principles and technical considerations. *Radiographics* 1994;14:887–893.

Brossmann J, Muhle C, Büll CC, et al. Cine MR imaging before and after realignment surgery for patellar maltracking—comparison with axial radiographs. *Skeletal Radiol* 1995;24:191–196.

Cascade PN, Webster EW, Kazerooni EA. Ineffective use of radiology: the hidden cost. *Am J Roentgenol* 1998;170:561–564.

Cheung AC, Bredella MA, Al Khalaf M, Grasruck M, Leidecker C, Gupta R. Reproducibility of trabecular structure analysis using flat-panel volume computed tomography. *Skeletal Radiol* 2009;38:1003–1008.

Cohen MD. Determining cost of imaging services. *Radiology* 2001;220:563–565.

Collier BD, Fogelman I, Brown ML. Bone scintigraphy: Part 2. Orthopedic bone scanning. *J Nucl Med* 1993;34:2241–2246.

Collier BD, Hellman RS, Krasnow AZ. Bone SPECT. *Semin Nucl Med* 1987; 17:247–266.

Conway WF, Totty WG, McEnery KW. CT and MR imaging of the hip. *Radiology* 1996;198:297–307.

Delfaut EM, Beltran J, Johnson G, Rousseau J, Marchandise X, Cotten A. Fat suppression in MR imaging: techniques and pitfalls. *Radiographics* 1999;19:373–382

Deutsch AL, Mink JH. Magnetic resonance imaging of musculoskeletal injuries. *Radiol Clin North Am* 1989;27:983–1002.

Fishman EK, Magid D, Ney DR, et al. Three-dimensional imaging. *Radiology* 1991;181:321–337.

Fishman EK, Wyatt SH, Bluemke DA, Urban BA. Spiral CT of musculoskeletal pathology: preliminary observations. *Skeletal Radiol* 1993;22:253–256.

Foley WD, Wilson CR. Digital orthopedic radiography: vascular and nonvascular. In: Galasko CSB, Isherwood I, eds. *Imaging techniques in orthopedics*. London, UK: Springer-Verlag; 1989:145–158.

Gates GF. SPECT bone scanning of the spine. *Semin Nucl Med* 1998;28:78–94.

Genant HK, Wu CY, van Kuijk C, Nevitt MC. Vertebral fracture assessment using a semiquantitative technique. *J Bone Miner Res* 1993;8:1137–1148.

Gibson DJ. Technology: the key to controlling health care cost in the future. *Am J Roentgenol* 1994;163:1289–1293.

Hamper UM, Trapanotto V, Sheth S, Dejong MR, Caskey CI. Three-dimensional US: preliminary clinical experience. *Radiology* 1994;191:397–401.

Heiken JP, Brink JA, Vannier MW. Spiral (helical) CT. *Radiology* 1993;189:647–656.

Holder LE. Bone scintigraphy in skeletal trauma. *Radiol Clin North Am* 1993; 31:739–781.

Holder LE. Clinical radionuclide bone imaging. *Radiology* 1990;176:607–614.

Jackson DW. The cost of diagnostic imaging: on our radar for 2009. *Orthop Today* 2009;29:3.

Johnson RP. The role of the bone imaging in orthopedic practice. *Semin Nucl Med* 1997;27:386–389.

Kaplan PA, Matamoros A Jr, Anderson JC. Sonography of the musculoskeletal system. *Am J Roentgenology* 1990;155:237–245.

Kumar R, Guinto FC Jr, Madewell JE, Swischuk L, David R. The vertebral body: radiographic configurations in various congenital and acquired disorders. *Radiographics* 1988;8:455–485.

Kuszyk BS, Heath DG, Bliss DF, Fishman EK. Skeletal 3-D CT: advantages of volume rendering over surface rendering. *Skeletal Radiol* 1996;25:207–214.

Levin DC, Spettell CM, Rao VM, Sunshine J, Bansal S, Busheé GR. Impact of MR imaging on nationwide health care costs and comparison with other imaging procedures. *Am J Roentgenol* 1998;170:557–560.

Loehr SP, Pope TL Jr, Martin DF, et al. Three-dimensional MRI of the glenoid labrum. *Skeletal Radiol* 1995;24:117–121.

Magid D, Fishman EK, Sponseller PD, Griffin PP. 2D and 3D computed tomography of the pediatric hip. *Radiographics* 1988;8:901–933.

Manaster BJ. Imaging of the musculoskeletal system. *Acad Radiol* 1995;2:S164–S166.

Margulis AR. Introduction to the algorithmic approach to radiology. In: Eisenberg RL, Amberg JR, eds. *Critical diagnostic pathways in radiology*. Philadelphia: JB Lippincott; 1981.

McDougall IR, Rieser RP. Scintigraphic techniques in musculoskeletal trauma. *Radiol Clin North Am* 1989;27:1003–1011.

McEnery KW, Wilson AJ, Pilgram TK, Murphy WA Jr, Marushack MM. Fractures of the tibial plateau: value of spiral CT coronal plane reconstructions for detecting displacement in vitro. *Am J Roentgenol* 1994;163:1177–1181.

Meschan I, Farrer-Meschan RM. Radiographic positioning, projection, pathology and definition of special terms. In: Meschan I, ed. *Roentgen signs in diagnostic imaging*, vol. 4, 2nd ed. Philadelphia: WB Saunders; 1987.

Mezrich R. A contrarian view of X-ray doses: it ain't necessarily so. *Appl Radiol* 2006;35:6–8.

Mirowitz SA. Fast scanning and fat-suppression MR imaging of musculoskeletal disorders. *Am J Roentgenol* 1993;161:1147–1157.

Moore SG, Bisset GS, Siegel MJ, Donaldson JS. Pediatric musculoskeletal MR imaging. *Radiology* 1991;179:345–360.

Murray IPC, Dixon J. The role of single photon emission computed tomography in bone scintigraphy. *Skeletal Radiol* 1989;18:493–505.

Nelson SW. Some important diagnostic and technical fundamentals in the radiology of trauma, with particular emphasis on skeletal trauma. *Radiol Clin North Am* 1966;4:241–259.

O'Sullivan GS, Goodman SB, Jones HH. Computerized tomographic evaluation of acetabular anatomy. *Clin Orthop* 1992;277:175–181.

Palmer WE, Brown JH, Rosenthal DI. Fat-suppressed MR arthrography of the shoulder: evaluation of the rotator cuff. *Radiology* 1993;188:683–687.

Palmer WE, Caslowitz PL, Chew FS. MR arthrography of the shoulder: normal intraarticular structures and common abnormalities. *Am J Roentgenol* 1995;164:141–146.

Peterfy CG, Roberts T, Genant HK. Dedicated extremity MR imaging: an emerging technology. *Radiol Clin North Am* 1997;35:1–20.

Petersilge CA. Current concepts of MR arthrography of the hip. *Semin US CT MR* 1997;18:291–301.

Pettersson H, Resnick D. Musculoskeletal imaging. *Radiology* 1998;208:561–562.

Pitt MJ, Speer DP. Radiologic reporting of skeletal trauma. *Radiol Clin North Am* 1990;28:247–256.

Pretorius ES, Scott WW Jr, Fishman EK. Acute trauma to the shoulder: role of spiral computed tomographic imaging. *Emergency Radiol* 1995;2:13–17.

Richardson ML, Frank MS, Stern EJ. Digital image manipulation: what constitutes acceptable alteration of a radiologic image? *Am J Roentgenol* 1995;164:228–229.

Rogers LF. From the editor's notebook. Imaging literacy: a laudable goal in the education of medical students. *Am J Roentgenol* 2003;180:1201.

Rubin DA, Kneeland JB. MR imaging of the musculoskeletal system: technical considerations for enhancing image quality and diagnostic yield. *Am J Roentgenol* 1994;163:1155–1163.

Ruwe PA, McCarthy S. Cost-effectiveness of magnetic resonance imaging. In: Mink JH, Reicher MA, Crues JW, Deutsch AL, eds. *MR imaging of the knee*, 2nd ed. New York: Raven Press; 1993:463–466.

Ryan PJ, Fogelman I. The bone scan: where are we now? *Semin Nucl Med* 1995;25:76–91.

Saini S, Seltzer SE, Bramson RT, et al. Technical cost of radiologic examinations: analysis across imaging modalities. *Radiology* 2000;216:269–272.

Seibert JA, Shelton DK, Moore EH. Computed radiography x-ray exposure trends. *Acad Radiol* 1996;3:313–318.

Sheppard S. Basic concepts in magnetic resonance angiography. *Radiol Clin North Am* 1995;33:91–113.

Siegel E. Primum non-nocere: a call for re-evaluation of radiation doses used in CT. *Appl Radiol* 2006;35:6–8.

Slone RM, Heare MM, Vander Griend RA, Montgomery WJ. Orthopedic fixation devices. *Radiographics* 1991;11:823–847.

Smith RC, Constable RT, Reinhold C, McCauley T, Lange RC, McCarthy S. Fast spin-echo STIR imaging. *J Comput Assist Tomogr* 1994;18:209–213.

Steinbach LS, Palmer WE, Schweitzer ME. Special focus session—MR arthrography. *Radiographics* 2002;22:1223–1246.

Stoller DW. MR arthrography of the glenohumeral joint. *Radiol Clin North Am* 1997;35:97–116.

Swan JS, Grist TM, Sproat IA, Heiner JP, Wiersma SR, Heisey SM. Musculoskeletal neoplasms: preoperative evaluation with MR angiography. *Radiology* 1995;194:519–524.

Swan JS, Grist TM, Weber DM, Sproat IA, Wojtowycz M. MR angiography of the pelvis with variable velocity encoding and a phased-array coil. *Radiology* 1994;190:363–369.

Thrall JH, Aubrey O. Hampton lecture. Directions in radiology for the next millenium. *Am J Roengenol* 1998;171:1459–1462.

Udupa JK. Three-dimensional imaging techniques: a current perspective. *Acad Radiol* 1995;2:335–340.

Yamanaka Y, Kamogawa J, Katagi R, et al. 3-D MRI/CT fusion imaging of the lumbar spine. *Skeletal Radiol* 2010; 39:285–288.

Imaging Techniques in Orthopedics

Choice of Imaging Modality

In this chapter, the principles and limitations of current imaging techniques are described. Understanding the basis of the imaging modalities available to diagnose many commonly encountered disorders of the bones and joints is of utmost importance. It may help determine the most effective radiologic technique, minimizing the cost of examination and the exposure of patients to radiation. To this end, it is important to choose the modality appropriate for specific types of orthopedic abnormalities and, when using conventional techniques (namely, "plain" radiography), to be familiar with the views and the techniques that best demonstrate the abnormality. It is important to reemphasize that conventional radiography remains the most effective means of demonstrating bone and joint abnormalities.

The use of radiologic techniques differs in evaluating the presence, type, and extent of various bone, joint, and soft-tissue abnormalities. Therefore, the radiologist and the orthopedic surgeon must know the indications for use of each technique, the limitations of a particular modality, and the appropriate imaging approaches for abnormalities at specific sites. The question, "What modality should I use for this particular problem?" is frequently asked by radiologists and orthopedic surgeons alike, and although numerous algorithms are available to evaluate various problems at different anatomic sites, the answer cannot always be clearly stated. The choice of techniques for imaging bone and soft-tissue abnormalities is dictated not only by clinical presentation but also by equipment availability, expertise, and cost. Restrictions may also be imposed by the needs of individual patients. For example, allergy to ionic or nonionic iodinated contrast agents may preclude the use of arthrography; the presence of a pacemaker would preclude the use of magnetic resonance imaging (MRI); physiologic states, such as pregnancy, preclude the use of ionized radiation, favoring, for instance, the use of ultrasound (US). Time and cost consideration should discourage redundant studies.

No matter what ancillary technique is used, conventional radiograph should be available for comparison. Most of the time, the choice of imaging technique is dictated by the type of suspected abnormality. For instance, if osteonecrosis is suspected after obtaining conventional radiographs, the next examination should be MRI, which detects necrotic changes in bone long before radiographs, computed tomography (CT), or scintigraphy becomes positive. In the evaluation of internal derangement of the knee, conventional radiographs should be obtained first and, if the abnormality is not obvious, should again be followed up by MRI, because this modality provides exquisite contrast resolution of the bone marrow,

articular cartilage, ligaments, menisci, and soft tissues. MRI and magnetic resonance arthrography (MRa) are currently the most effective procedures for the evaluation of rotator cuff abnormalities, particularly when a partial or complete tear is suspected. Although ultrasonography can also detect a rotator cuff tear, its low sensitivity (68%) and low specificity (75% to 84%) make it a less definitive diagnostic procedure. In evaluating a painful wrist, conventional radiographs should precede the use of more advanced techniques, such as CT-arthrography or MRI. If a tear of triangular fibrocartilage complex, a tear of intercarpal ligaments, or a carpal tunnel syndrome is suspected, MRI is preferred because it provides a high-contrast difference among muscles, tendons, ligaments, and nerves. Similarly, if osteonecrosis of carpal bones is suspected and the conventional radiographs are normal, MRI would be the method of choice to demonstrate this abnormality. In the evaluation of fractures and fracture healing of carpal bones, CT is the procedure of choice, preferred over MRI, because of the high degree of spatial resolution. In diagnosing bone tumors, conventional radiography is still the gold standard for diagnostic purposes. However, to evaluate the intraosseous and soft-tissue extension of tumor, it should be followed by either CT scan or MRI, with the latter modality being more accurate. To evaluate the results of radiotherapy and chemotherapy of malignant tumors, dynamic MRI using gadopentetate dimeglumine (gadolinium-DTPA—Gd-DTPA) as a contrast enhancement is far superior to scintigraphy, CT, or even "plain" MRI.

Imaging Techniques

Conventional Radiography

The most frequently used modality for the evaluation of bone and joint disorders, and particularly traumatic conditions, is conventional radiography. The radiologist should obtain at least two views of the bone involved, at 90-degree angles to each other, with each view including two adjacent joints (see Fig. 4.1). This decreases the risk of missing an associated fracture, subluxation, and/or dislocation at a site remote from the apparent primary injury. In children, it is frequently necessary to obtain a radiograph of the normal unaffected limb for comparison. Usually, the standard radiography comprises the anteroposterior and lateral views; occasionally, oblique and special views are necessary, particularly in evaluating complex structures, such as the elbow, wrist, ankle, and pelvis. A weight-bearing view may be of value for a dynamic evaluation of the joint space under the weight of the body (see Fig. 13.16). Special projections, such as those described in the following chapters, may, at times, be required to demonstrate an abnormality of the bone or joint to further advantage.

Magnification Radiography

Magnification radiography is occasionally used to enhance bony details not well appreciated on the standard radiographic projections and to maximize the diagnostic information obtainable from a radiographic image. This technique involves a small focal-spot radiographic tube, a special screen–film system, and increased object-to-film distance, resulting in a geometric enlargement that yields magnified images of the bones and joints with greater sharpness and greater bony detail. This technique is particularly effective in demonstrating early changes in some arthritides (see Fig. 12.7) as well as in various metabolic disorders (see Fig. 26.9B). Occasionally, it may be useful in demonstrating subtle fracture lines otherwise not seen on routine projections.

Stress Views

Stress views are important in evaluating ligamentous tears and joint stability. In the hand, abduction–stress film of the thumb may be obtained when a gamekeeper's thumb, resulting from a disruption of the ulnar collateral ligament of the first metacarpophalangeal joint, is suspected (see Fig. 7.103B). In the lower extremity, stress views of the knee and ankle joints are occasionally obtained. The evaluation of knee instability caused by ligament injuries may require the use of this technique in cases of a suspected tear of the medial collateral ligament and, less frequently, in evaluating an insufficiency of the anterior and posterior cruciate ligaments. The evaluation of ankle ligaments also may require stress radiography. Inversion (adduction) and anterior–draw stress films are the most frequently obtained stress views (see Figs. 4.4, 10.10, and 10.11).

Scanogram

The scanogram is the most widely used method for limb-length measurement. This technique requires a slit-beam diaphragm with a 1/16-in. opening attached to the radiographic tube and a long film cassette. The radiographic tube moves in the long axis of the radiographic table. During an exposure, the tube traverses the whole length of the film, scanning the entire extremity. This technique allows the x-ray beam to intersect the bone ends perpendicularly; therefore, comparative limb lengths can be measured. When a motorized radiographic tube is not available, a modified technique may be used with three separate exposures over the hip joints, knees, and ankles. In this technique, an opaque tape measure is placed longitudinally down the center of the radiographic table. Occasionally, an orthoroentgenogram is obtained. For this technique, the patient is positioned supine with the lower limbs on a 3-ft–long cassette and a long ruler at one side. A single exposure is made, centered at the knees to include the entire length of both limbs and the ruler.

Fluoroscopy and Videotaping

Fluoroscopy is a fundamental diagnostic tool for many radiologic procedures, including arthrography, tenography, bursography, arteriography, and percutaneous bone or soft-tissue biopsy. Fluoroscopy combined with videotaping is useful in evaluating the kinematics of joints. Because of the high dose of radiation, however, it is only occasionally used, such as in evaluating the movement of various joints or to detect transient subluxation (i.e., carpal instability) (see Fig. 7.85). Occasionally, it is used after fractures in follow-up examinations of the healing process to evaluate the solidity of the bony union. Fluoroscopy is still used in conjunction with myelography, where it is important to observe the movement of the contrast column in the subarachnoid space; in arthrography, to check the proper placement of the needle and to monitor the flow of the contrast agent; and intraoperatively, to assess the reduction of a fracture or placement of hardware.

Digital Radiography

Digital (computed) radiography (DR) is the name given to the process of digital image acquisition using an x-ray detector comprising a photostimulable phosphor imaging plate and an image reader–writer that processes the latent image information for subsequent brightness scaling and laser printing on film (Fig. 2.1). The system works on the principle of photostimulated luminescence. When the screen absorbs x-rays, the x-ray energy is converted to light energy by the process of fluorescence, with the intensity of light being proportional to the energy absorbed by the phosphor. The stimulated light is used to create a digital image (a computed radiograph).

◀ FIGURE 2.1 **Digital radiography.** Digital radiograph of the hand without **(A)** and with **(B)** edge enhancement. The bone details and the soft tissues are better appreciated than on the standard radiographs.

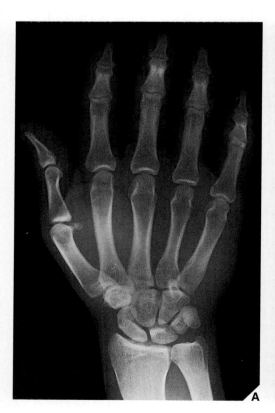

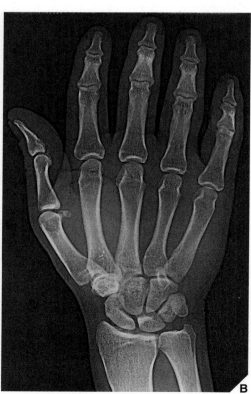

A   **B**

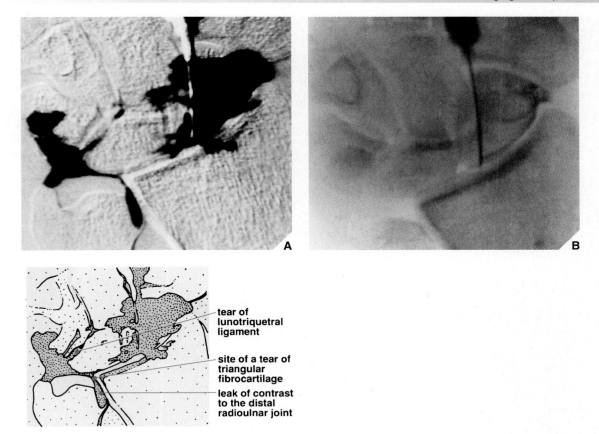

tear of
lunotriquetral
ligament

site of a tear of
triangular
fibrocartilage

leak of contrast
to the distal
radioulnar joint

FIGURE 2.2   Digital subtraction arthrography. Digital subtraction arthrogram demonstrates tears of the lunotriquetral ligament and the triangular fibrocartilage complex. **(A)** This image was obtained by subtracting the digitally acquired preinjection image **(B)** from postinjection film. (Courtesy of Dr. B. J. Manaster, Salt Lake City, Utah.)

A major advantage of computed radiography over conventional film/screen radiography is that once acquired, the digital image data are readily manipulated to produce alternative renderings. Potential advantages of digitization include contrast and brightness optimization by the manipulation of window width and level settings, as well as a variety of image-processing capabilities, quantitation of image information, and facilitation of examination storage and retrieval. In addition, energy subtraction imaging (also called dual-energy subtraction) may be acquired. Two images, acquired either sequentially or simultaneously with different filtration, are used to reconstruct a soft-tissue–only image or a bone-only image.

In digital subtraction radiography, a video processor and a digital disk are added to a fluoroscopy imaging complex to provide online viewing of subtraction images. This technique is most widely used in the evaluation of the vascular system, but it may also be used in conjunction with arthrography to evaluate various joints. The use of high-performance video cameras with low-noise characteristics allows single video frames of precontrast and postcontrast images to be used for subtraction. Spatial resolution can be maximized using a combination of geometric magnification, electric magnification, and a small anode–target distance. The subtraction technique removes surrounding anatomic structures and thus isolates the opacified vessel or joint, making it more conspicuous.

Nonvascular DR may be used to evaluate various bone abnormalities and, in conjunction with contrast injection, a procedure called digital subtraction arthrography (Fig. 2.2); to evaluate subtle abnormalities of the joints, such as tears of the triangular fibrocartilage or intercarpal ligaments in the wrist; or to evaluate the stability of prosthesis replacement. DR offers the potential advantages of improved image quality, contrast sensitivity, and exposure latitude, and it provides efficient storage, retrieval, and transmission of radiographic image data. Digital images may be displayed on the film or on a video monitor. A significant advantage of image digitization is the ability to produce data with low noise and a wide dynamic range suitable for window-level analysis in a manner comparable to that used in a CT scanner.

Digital subtraction angiography (DSA), the most frequently used variant of DR, can be used in the evaluation of trauma, bone and soft-tissue tumors, and in general evaluation of the vascular system. In trauma to the extremity, DSA is effectively used to evaluate arterial occlusion, pseudoaneurysms, arteriovenous fistulas, and transection of the arteries (Fig. 2.3). Some advantages of DSA over conventional film techniques are that its images can be studied rapidly and multiple repeated projections can be obtained. Bone subtraction is useful in clearly delineating the vascular structures. In the evaluation of bone and soft-tissue tumors, DSA is an effective tool for mapping tumor vascularity.

Tomography

Tomography is a body-section radiography that permits more accurate visualization of lesions too small to be noted on conventional radiographs or demonstrates anatomic detail obscured by overlying structures. It uses continuous motion of the radiographic tube and film cassette in opposite directions throughout the exposure, with the fulcrum of the motion located in the plane of interest. By blurring structures above and below the area being examined, the object to be studied is sharply outlined on a single plane of focus. The focal plane may vary in thickness according to the distance the x-ray tube travels; the longer the distance (or arc) traveled by the tube, the thinner the section in focus. Newly developed tomographic units can localize the image more precisely and have aided greatly in the ability to detect lesions as small as approximately 1 mm.

The simplest tomographic movement is linear, with the radiographic tube and film cassette moving on a straight line in opposite directions. This linear movement has little application in the study of bones because it creates streaks that often interfere with radiologic interpretations. Resolution of the plane of focus is much clearer when there is more uniform blurring of undesired structures. This requires a multidirectional movement, such as in zonography or in circular

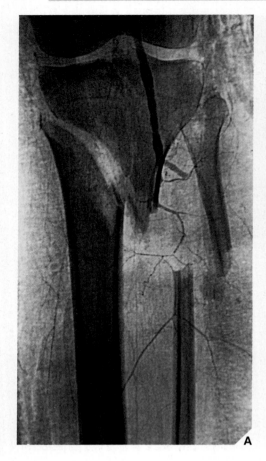
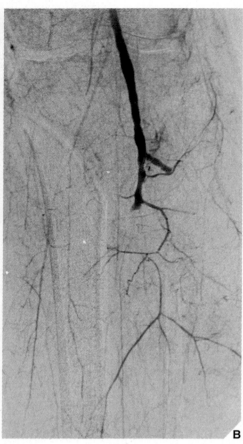

A   B

FIGURE 2.3 **Digital subtraction angiography.** Digital radiograph **(A)** and digital subtraction angiogram **(B)** of a 23-year-old man who sustained fractures of the proximal tibia and fibula show disruption of the distal segment of the popliteal artery.

tomography, in which the radiographic tube makes one circular motion at a preset angle of inclination. More complex multidirectional hypocycloidal or trispiral movements increase the distance of excursion of the tube and create a varying angle of projection of the x-ray beam during the exposure. These complex movements are more advantageous because they produce even greater blurring and yield the sharpest images. Trispiral tomography used to be an important radiographic technique in the diagnosis and management of a variety of bone and joint problems (see Figs. 7.48 and 7.54B). Currently it has been, however, almost completely replaced by CT.

Computed Tomography

CT is a radiologic modality containing an x-ray source, detectors, and a computer data-processing system. The essential components of a CT system include a circular scanning gantry, which houses the x-ray tube and image sensors, a table for the patient, an x-ray generator, and a computerized data-processing unit. The patient lies on the table and is placed inside the gantry. The x-ray tube is rotated 360 degrees around the patient while the computer collects the data and formulates an axial image, or "slice." Each cross-sectional slice represents a thickness between 0.1 and 1.5 cm of body tissue.

The newest CT scanners use a rotating fan of x-ray beams, a fixed ring of detectors, and predetector collimator. A highly collimated x-ray beam is transmitted through the area being imaged. The tissues absorb the x-ray beam to various degrees depending on the atomic number and density of the specific tissue. The remaining, unabsorbed (unattenuated) beam passes through the tissues and is detected and processed by the computer. The CT computer software converts the x-ray beam attenuations of the tissue into a CT number (Hounsfield units) by comparing it with the attenuation of water. The attenuation of water is designated as 0 (zero) H, the attenuation of air is designated as −1,000 H, and the attenuation of normal cortical bone is +1,000 H. Routinely, axial sections are obtained; however, computer

reconstruction (reformation) in multiple planes may be obtained if desired.

The introduction of spiral (helical) scanning was a further improvement of CT. This technique, referred to as volume-acquisition CT, has made possible a data-gathering system using a continuous rotation of the x-ray source and the detectors. It allows the rapid acquisition of volumes of CT data and renders the ability to reformat the images at any predetermined intervals ranging from 0.5 to 10.0 mm. Unlike standard CT, in which up to a maximum of 12 scans could be obtained per minute, helical CT acquires all data in 24 or 32 seconds, generating up to 92 sections. This technology has markedly reduced scan times and has eliminated interscan delay, and hence interscan motion. It also has decreased the motion artifacts, improved the definition of scanned structures, and markedly facilitated the ability to obtain three-dimensional (3D) reconstructions generated from multiple overlapping transaxial images acquired in a single breath hold. Spiral CT allows data to be acquired during the phase of maximum contrast enhancement, thus optimizing the detection of a lesion. The data volume may be viewed either as conventional transaxial images or as multiplanar and 3D reformations.

CT is indispensable in the evaluation of many traumatic conditions and various bone and soft-tissue tumors because of its cross-sectional imaging capability. In trauma, CT is extremely useful to define the presence and extent of a fracture or dislocation; to evaluate various intraarticular abnormalities, such as damage to the articular cartilage or the presence of noncalcified and calcified osteocartilaginous bodies; and to evaluate adjacent soft tissues. CT is of particular importance in the detection of small bony fragments displaced into the joints after trauma, in the detection of small displaced fragments of the fractured vertebral body, and in the assessment of a concomitant injury to the cord or thecal sac. The advantage of CT over conventional radiography is its ability to provide excellent contrast resolution, accurately measure the tissue attenuation coefficient, and obtain direct transaxial images (Fig. 2.4; see also Figs. 11.24C, 11.35B, and 11.61B). A further

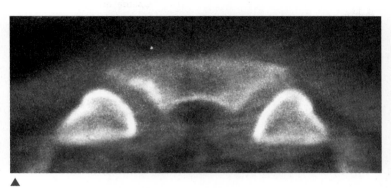

FIGURE 2.4 **CT transaxial imaging.** In this direct transaxial image, the sterno-clavicular joints are well depicted.

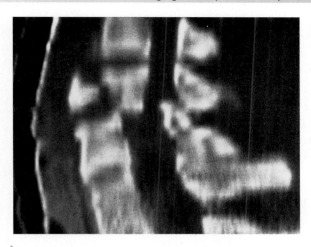

FIGURE 2.5 **CT reconstruction imaging.** Sagittal CT reformatted image demonstrates the flexion tear-drop fracture of C5. It also effectively shows the malalignment of the vertebral bodies and narrowing of the spinal canal. (From Greenspan A, 1992, with permission.)

advantage is its ability—through data obtained from thin, contiguous sections—to image the bone in the coronal, sagittal, and oblique planes using reformation technique. This multiplanar reconstruction is particularly helpful in evaluating the vertebral alignment (Fig. 2.5), demonstrating horizontally oriented fractures of the vertebral body; in evaluating complex fractures of the pelvis, hip (Fig. 2.6), and knee (Fig. 2.7); or in evaluating calcaneus abnormalities, of the sacrum and sacroiliac joints, sternum and sternoclavicular joints, temporomandibular joints, and wrist. Modern CT scanners use collimated fan beams directed only at the tissue layer undergoing investigation. The newest advances in sophisticated software enable 3D reconstruction, which is helpful in analyzing regions with complex anatomy, such as the face, pelvis,

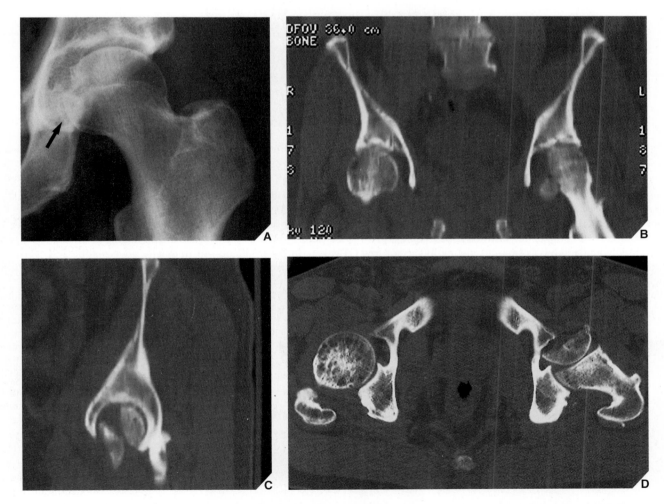

FIGURE 2.6 **CT multiplanar imaging.** A 62-year-old man sustained a posterior dislocation of the left femoral head. After reduction of dislocation, the antero-posterior radiograph of the left hip **(A)** showed increased medial joint space and distortion of the medial aspect of the femoral head (*arrow*). To evaluate the hip joint further, CT was performed. Coronal **(B)** and sagittal **(C)** reformatted images showed unsuspected fracture of the femoral head, and axial image **(D)** demonstrated a 180-degree rotation of the fractured fragment.

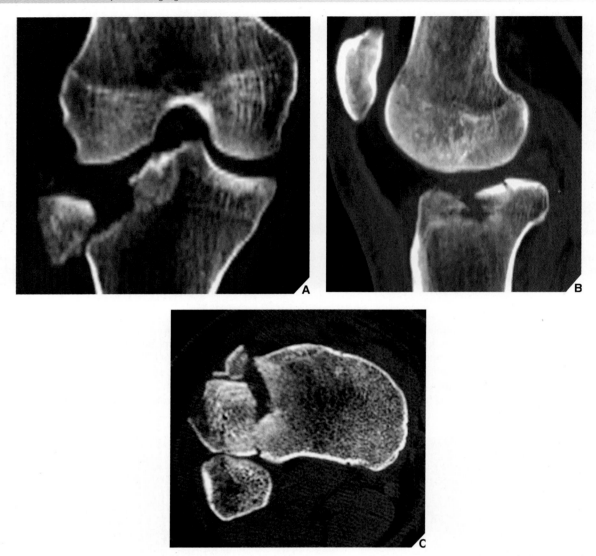

▲
FIGURE 2.7 CT multiplanar imaging. Coronal **(A)**, sagittal **(B)**, and axial **(C)** CT images of the knee show the details of a complex fracture of the lateral tibial plateau.

vertebral column, foot, ankle, and wrist (Figs. 2.8 to 2.11). New computer systems now permit the creation of plastic models of the area of interest based on 3D images. These models facilitate operative planning and allow rehearsal surgery of complex reconstructive procedures.

Most recently, with the advent of 64-channel multidetector row CT (MDCT), images can be generated with subsecond gantry rotation times yielding high-resolution volume data sets, and at the same time minimizing the radiation dose to the patient. Even more advanced is high-resolution flat-panel volume CT (fpVCT), which uses digital flat-panel detectors

and provides volumetric coverage as well as ultra-high spatial resolution in two-dimensional (2D) and 3D projections. Furthermore, it reduces metal and beam hardening artifacts. In addition to the above-listed features, fpVCT also allows dynamic imaging of time-varying processes.

In the evaluation of traumatic abnormalities, 3D CT-angiography is effectively used to determine the presence or absence of injury to the vessels near the fractured bones (Figs. 2.12 and 2.13).

CT plays a significant role in the evaluation of bone and soft-tissue tumors because of its superior contrast resolution and its ability to

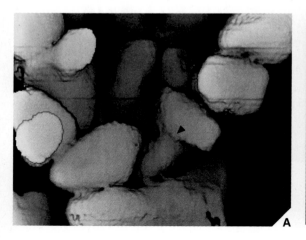

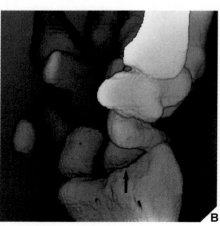

◀ **FIGURE 2.8** CT 3D imaging. Anteroposterior **(A)** and oblique **(B)** 3D CT reformation of the wrist demonstrates a fracture through the waist of the scaphoid bone (*arrow head*), complicated by osteonecrosis of the proximal fragment (*arrow*).

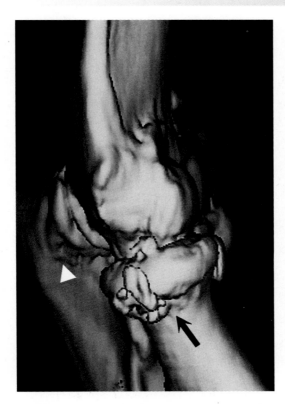

▲
FIGURE 2.9   CT 3D imaging. 3D CT reformation of the elbow shows a fracture of the neck of the radius (*arrow*) and a fracture of the olecranon process (*arrowhead*).

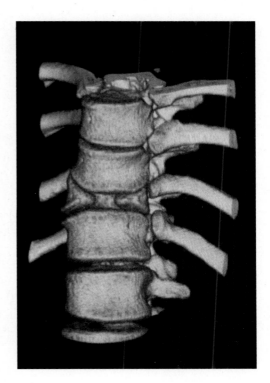

▲
FIGURE 2.11   CT 3D imaging. 3D CT reformation of the thoracic spine shows sagittal cleft with an anterior defect of T11, a typical appearance of congenital butterfly vertebra.

measure the tissue attenuation coefficient accurately. Although CT, by itself, is rarely helpful in making a specific diagnosis, it can precisely evaluate the extent of the bone lesion and may demonstrate a break through the cortex and the involvement of surrounding soft tissues. Moreover, CT is very helpful in delineating a tumor in bones having

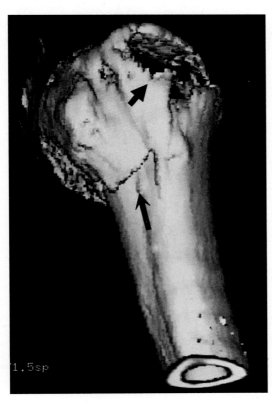

▲
FIGURE 2.10   CT 3D imaging. A fracture of the surgical neck of the humerus (long *arrow*) and a displaced fracture of the greater tubercle (*short arrow*) are well demonstrated.

complex anatomic structures, such as the scapula, pelvis, and sacrum, which may be difficult to image fully with conventional radiographic techniques. CT examination is crucial to determine the extent and spread of a tumor in the bone if limb salvage is contemplated, so that a safe margin of resection can be planned (Fig. 2.14). It can effectively demonstrate the intraosseous extension of a tumor and its extraosseous involvement of soft tissues such as muscles and neurovascular bundles. It is also useful for monitoring the results of treatment, evaluating for the recurrence of a resected tumor, and demonstrating the effect of nonsurgical treatment such as radiation therapy and chemotherapy.

Occasionally, iodinated contrast agents may be used intravenously to enhance the CT images. A contrast agent directly alters image contrast by increasing the x-ray attenuation, thus displaying increased brightness in the CT images. It can aid in identifying a suspected soft-tissue mass when initial CT results are unremarkable, or it can assess the vascularity of the soft-tissue or bone tumor.

CT has a crucial role in bone mineral analysis. The ability of CT to measure the attenuation coefficients of each pixel provides a basis for accurate quantitative bone mineral analysis in cancellous and cortical bones. Quantitative CT (QCT) is a method for measuring the lumbar spine mineral content in which the average density values of a region of interest are referenced to that of calibration material scanned at the same time as the patient. Measurements are performed on a CT scanner using a mineral standard for simultaneous calibration and a computed radiograph (scout view) for localization (see Fig. 26.12). The evaluation of bone mass measurement provides valuable insight into improving the evaluation and treatment of osteoporosis and other metabolic bone disorders.

CT is also a very important modality for successful aspiration or biopsy of bone or soft-tissue lesions, because it provides visible guidance for precise placement of the instrument within the lesion (Fig. 2.15).

Some disadvantages of CT include the so-called average volume effect, which results from a lack of homogeneity in the composition of the small volume of tissue. In particular, the measurement of Hounsfield units results in average values for the different components of the tissue. This partial volume effect becomes particularly important when normal

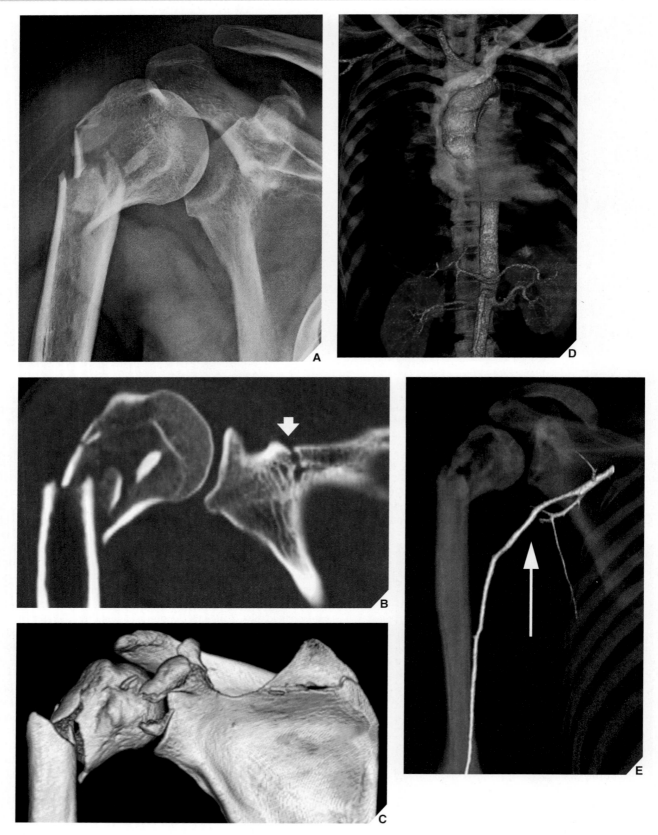

▲
FIGURE 2.12   3D CT-angiography. A 52-year-old man was hit by a car and sustained a chest and right shoulder injury. **(A)** Conventional radiograph of the right shoulder demonstrates a fracture of the proximal humerus. **(B)** Coronal reformatted CT image shows more details of the comminuted displaced fracture of the humerus and, in addition, shows a fracture of the scapular crest (*arrow*). Both these fractures are effectively shown on 3D CT reconstruction image **(C)**. Because an injury to the vascular structures of the chest and right shoulder was clinically suspected, 3D CT-angiography was performed. **(D)** The great vessels of the chest were intact. **(E)** Anterior view of the right shoulder and arm shows the displacement of intact axillary and proximal brachial arteries (*arrow*) due to a large soft-tissue hematoma.

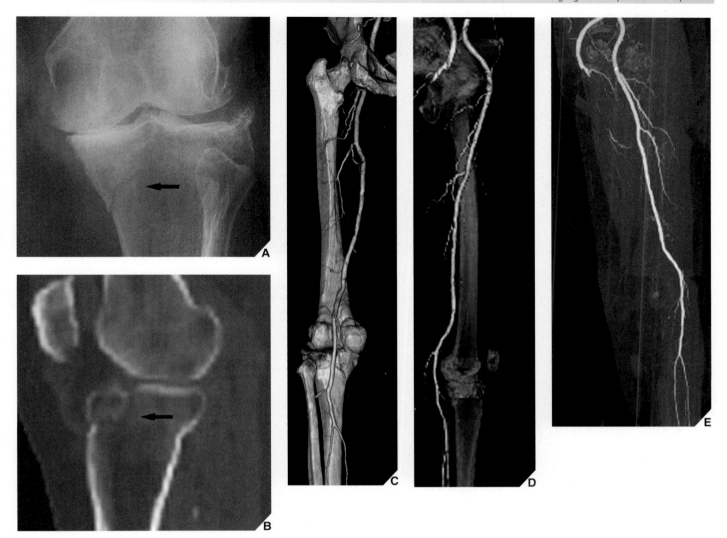

▲
FIGURE 2.13 **3D CT-angiography.** A 68-year-old man was injured in a car accident. **(A)** Anteroposterior radiograph of the left knee and **(B)** sagittal reformatted CT image show a fracture of the medial tibial plateau (*arrows*). Note also advanced osteoarthritis of the knee joint. Because an injury to the popliteal vessels was clinically suspected, 3D CT-angiography was performed. **(C)** Posterior and **(D)** lateral views show intact femoral and popliteal arteries, confirmed on the frontal subtracted vascular image **(E)**.

and pathologic processes interface within a section under investigation. The other disadvantage of CT is poor tissue characterization. Despite the ability of CT to discriminate among some differences in density, a simple analysis of attenuation values does not permit precise histologic characterization. Moreover, any movement of the patient will produce artifacts that degrade the image quality. Similarly, an area that contains metal (e.g., prosthesis or various rods and screws) will produce significant artifacts, although recently several different acquisition and reconstruction parameters have been developed to significantly reduce artifacts related to the metallic implants. Finally, the radiation dose may occasionally be high, particularly when contiguous and overlapping sections are obtained during examination.

Arthrography

Arthrography is the introduction of a contrast agent ("positive" contrast—iodide solution, "negative" contrast—air, or a combination of both) into the joint space. Despite the evolution of newer diagnostic imaging modalities, such as CT and MRI, arthrography has retained its importance in daily radiologic practice. The growing popularity of arthrography has been partially caused by advances in its techniques and interpretation. The fact that it is not a technically difficult procedure and is much simpler to interpret than US, CT, or MRI makes it very desirable for evaluating various articulations. Although virtually every joint can be injected with contrast, the examination, at the present time, is most frequently performed in the shoulder, wrist, and ankle. It is important to obtain preliminary films prior to any arthrographic procedure, because contrast may obscure some joint abnormalities (i.e., osteochondral body) that can be easily detected on conventional radiographs. Arthrography is particularly effective in demonstrating rotator cuff tear (Fig. 2.16; see also Figs. 5.60 and 5.61) and adhesive capsulitis in the shoulder (see Fig. 5.77) and osteochondritis dissecans, osteochondral bodies, and subtle abnormalities of the articular cartilage in the elbow joint (see Fig. 6.42). In the wrist, arthrography retains its value in diagnosing triangular fibrocartilage complex abnormalities (Fig. 2.17, see also Fig. 7.29). The introduction of the three-compartment injection technique and the combination of arthrographic wrist examination with digital subtraction arthrography (see Fig. 2.2) and postarthrographic CT and MRI examinations have made this modality very effective when evaluating a painful wrist.

Although arthrography of the knee has been almost completely replaced by MRI, it still may be used to demonstrate injuries to the soft-tissue structures, such as the joint capsule, menisci, and various ligaments (see Fig. 9.64). It also provides important information on the status of the articular cartilage, particularly when a subtle chondral or osteochondral fracture is suspected, or when the presence or absence of osteochondral bodies (i.e., in osteochondritis dissecans) must be confirmed (see Figs. 9.53C and 9.54).

In the examination of any of the joints, arthrography can be combined with the digitization of image (digital subtraction arthrography) (see Fig. 2.2), with CT (CT-arthrography) (Fig. 2.18), or with MRI (MRa) (Fig. 2.19), thus providing additional information.

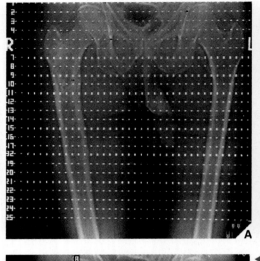

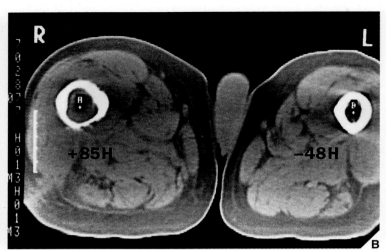

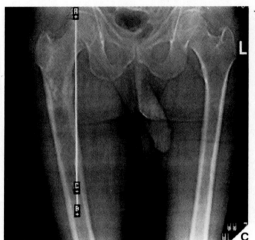

◄ FIGURE 2.14 **CT measurement of Hounsfield values.** CT evaluation of intraosseous extension of chondrosarcoma is an important part of the radiologic workup of a patient if limb salvage is contemplated. **(A)** Several contiguous axial sections, preferably 1 cm in thickness, of affected and nonaffected limbs are obtained. **(B)** Hounsfield values of the bone marrow are measured to determine the distal extent of tumor in the medullary cavity. A value of +85H indicates the presence of tumor; a value of −48H is normal for fatty marrow. **(C)** The linear measurement is obtained from the proximal articular end of the bone *A* to the point located 5 cm distally to the tumor margin *B*. Point *C* corresponds to the most distal axial section that still shows tumor in the marrow. (From Greenspan A, 1989, with permission.)

There are relatively few absolute contraindications to arthrography. Even hypersensitivity to iodine is a relative contraindication because, in this case, a single contrast study using only air can be performed.

Tenography and Bursography

Occasionally, to evaluate the integrity of a tendon, contrast material is injected into the tendon sheath. This procedure is known as a tenogram (see Figs. 10.13 and 10.72). Since the introduction of newer diagnostic modalities, such as CT and MRI, this procedure is seldom performed. It has relatively limited clinical application, mainly being used to evaluate traumatic or inflammatory conditions of the tendons (such as peroneus longus and brevis, tibialis anterior and posterior, and flexor digitorum longus) of the lower extremity and in the upper extremity to outline the synovial sheaths within the carpal tunnel.

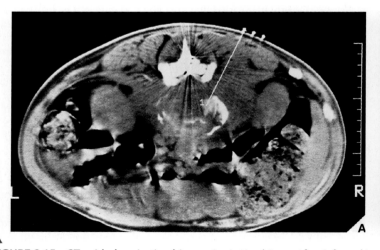

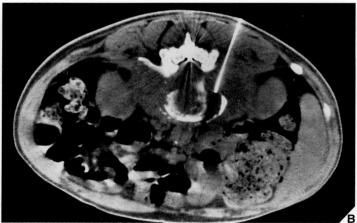

▲ FIGURE 2.15 **CT-guided aspiration biopsy.** Aspiration biopsy of an infected intervertebral disk is performed under CT guidance. **(A)** Measurement is obtained from the skin surface to the area of interest (intervertebral disk). **(B)** The needle is advanced under CT guidance and placed at the site of the partially destroyed disk.

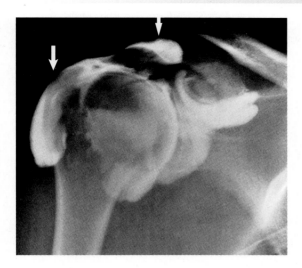

▲
FIGURE 2.16 Shoulder arthrogram. After an injection of contrast into the glenohumeral joint, there is filling of subacromial–subdeltoid bursae complex (*arrows*), indicating rotator cuff tear.

Bursography involves the injection of contrast agents into various bursae. This procedure, in general, has been abandoned, and only occasionally is the subacromial–subdeltoid bursae complex directly injected with a contrast agent to demonstrate partial tears of the rotator cuff.

Angiography

The use of a contrast material injected directly into selective branches of the arterial and venous circulation has aided greatly in assessing the involvement of the circulatory system in various conditions and has provided a precise method for defining local pathology. With *arteriography*, a contrast agent is injected into the arteries and films are made, usually in rapid sequence. With *venography*, a contrast material is injected into the veins. Both procedures are frequently used in the evaluation of trauma, particularly if a concomitant injury to the vascular system is suspected (see Figs. 2.3 and 4.14).

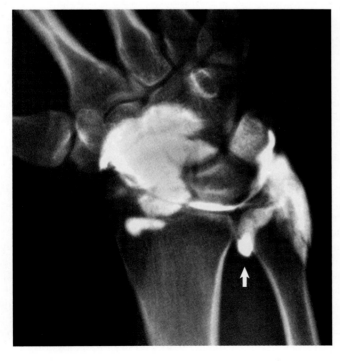

▲
FIGURE 2.17 Wrist arthrogram. After an injection of contrast into the radiocarpal joint, there is filling of distal radioulnar joint (*arrow*), indicating a tear of the triangular fibrocartilage complex.

In the evaluation of tumors, arteriography is used mainly to map out bone lesions, demonstrate the vascularity of the lesion, and assess the extent of disease. It is also used to demonstrate the vascular supply of a tumor and to locate vessels suitable for preoperative intraarterial chemotherapy. It is very useful in demonstrating the area suitable for open biopsy, because the most vascular parts of a tumor contain the most aggressive component of the lesion. Occasionally, arteriography can be used to demonstrate abnormal tumor vessels, corroborating findings with radiography and tomography (see Fig. 16.16B). Arteriography is often extremely helpful in planning for limb-salvage procedures, because it demonstrates the regional vascular anatomy and thus permits a plan to be made for the tumor resection. It is also sometimes used to outline the major vessels before the resection of a benign lesion (see Fig. 16.17). It can also be combined with an interventional procedure, such as the embolization of hypervascular tumors, before further treatment (see Fig. 16.18).

Myelography

During this procedure, water-soluble contrast agents are injected into the subarachnoid space, mixing freely with the cerebrospinal fluid to produce a column of opacified fluid with a higher specific gravity than the nonopacified fluid. Tilting the patient will allow the opacified fluid to run up or down the thecal sac under the influence of gravity (see Figs. 11.17 and 11.51). The puncture usually is performed in the lumbar area at the L2-3 or L3-4 levels. For the examination of the cervical segment, a C1-2 puncture is performed (see Fig. 11.17A). Myelographic examination has been almost completely replaced by high-resolution CT and high-quality MRI.

Diskography

Diskography is an injection of a contrast material into the nucleus pulposus. Although this is a controversial procedure that has been abandoned by many investigators, under tightly restricted indications

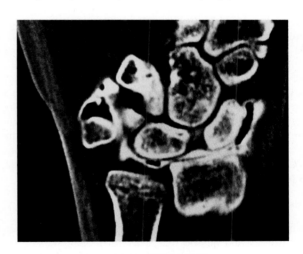

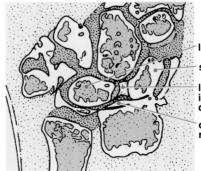

lunate

scaphoid

leak of contrast
into midcarpal
compartment

contrast in
radiocarpal joint

▲
FIGURE 2.18 CT-arthrography. Coronal CT arthrogram of the wrist demonstrates a subtle leak of contrast from the radiocarpal joint through a tear in the scapholunate ligament, a finding not detected on routine arthrographic examination of the wrist.

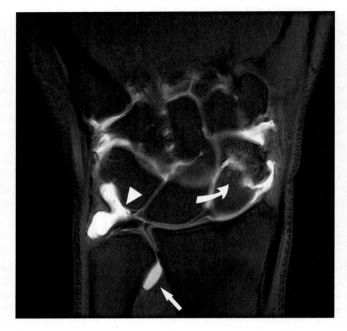

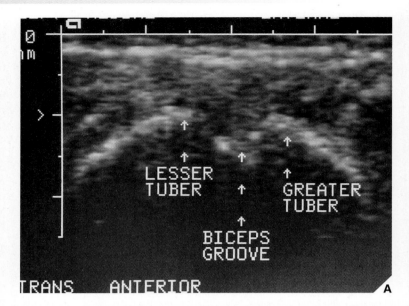

FIGURE 2.19   **MR-arthrography.** Coronal T1-weighted fat-saturated MR image obtained after an injection of contrast into the radiocarpal joint shows opacification of the distal radioulnar joint (*arrow*), diagnostic of a tear of the triangular fibrocartilage complex. In addition noted is a tear of the lunotriquetral ligament (*arrow head*), and leak of contrast into the ununited fracture of the scaphoid (*curved arrow*).

and immaculate technique, a diskogram can yield valuable information. Diskography is a valuable aid to determine the source of a patient's low back pain. It is not purely an imaging technique, because the symptoms produced during the test (pain during the injection or pain provocation) are considered to have even greater diagnostic value than the obtained radiographs. It should always be combined with CT examination (so-called CT-diskogram) (see Figs. 11.52 and 11.53). According to the official position statement on diskography by the Executive Committee of the North American Spine Society in 1988, this procedure "is indicated in the evaluation of patients with unremitting spinal pain, with or without extremity pain, of greater than four months duration, when the pain has been unresponsive to all appropriate methods of conservative therapy." According to the same statement, before a diskogram is performed, the patient should have undergone an investigation with other modalities (such as CT, MRI, and myelography) and the surgical correction of the patient's problem should be anticipated.

Ultrasound

Over the past several years, US has made an enormous impact in the field of radiology and has become a useful tool in skeletal imaging. It has several inherent advantages. It is relatively inexpensive, allows comparisons with the opposite normal side, uses no ionizing radiation, and can be performed at bedside or in the operating room. It is a noninvasive modality, relying on the interaction of propagated sound waves with tissue interfaces in the body. Whenever the directed pulsing of sound waves encounters an interface between tissues of different acoustic impedance, reflection or refraction occurs. The sound waves reflected back to the US transducer are recorded and converted into images.

Various types of US scanning are available. Most modern US equipment displays dynamic information in "real time," similar to information that is provided by fluoroscopy. With real-time sonography, the images may be obtained in any scan plane by simply moving the transducer. Thus, imaging may include transverse or longitudinal images and any obliquity can also be produced. Modern probe technology has extended usefulness of US in orthopedic radiology (Fig. 2.20). Higher-frequency transducers of 7.5 and 10 MHz have excellent spatial resolution and are ideal for imaging the appendicular skeleton.

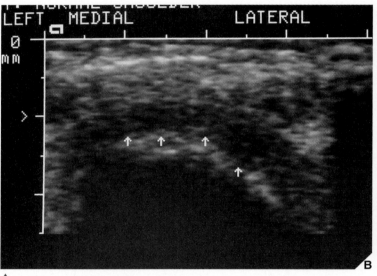

FIGURE 2.20   **US of the shoulder. (A)** The bony landmarks (lesser and greater tuberosities, bicipital tendon groove) and **(B)** tendinous structures, such as supraspinatous tendon (*arrows*), are well outlined.

Applications of US in orthopedics include an evaluation of the rotator cuff, injuries to various tendons (e.g., the Achilles tendon), Osgood-Schlatter disease, and, occasionally, soft-tissue tumors (such as hemangioma).

The most effective application, however, is in the evaluation of the infant hip, for which US has become the imaging modality of choice. Contributing factors are the cartilaginous composition of the hip, US's real-time capability for studying motion and stress, absence of ionizing radiation, and relative cost effectiveness. The newest development in this area is the introduction of 3D US for the evaluation of developmental dysplasia of the hip. 3D sonography provides functional utility in the evaluation of the joint in the added sagittal plane (section image) and craniocaudal projection (revolving spatial image). This technique permits excellent demonstration of the femoral head–acetabulum relationship and femoral head containment (see Figs. 32.16 and 32.17). The important advantage of this technique is not only the acquisition of images in real time but also subsequent reconstruction and viewing at a workstation, allowing further manipulation of the volume image. This permits the extraction of usable measurements and enhancement of the anatomic information obtained from the images.

US has recently been applied to certain areas in rheumatic disorders, particularly to detect intraarticular and periarticular fluid collection, and

FIGURE 2.21   US of the popliteal fossa. A 45-year-old
woman with rheumatoid arthritis presented with pain
in the back of the knee radiating to the leg. Clinically,
deep vein thrombosis (DVT) was suspected and US
was performed. The study was negative for DVT but
demonstrated a large fluid-filled Baker cyst (*arrow*).
The *arrow heads* point to the patent popliteal vein.

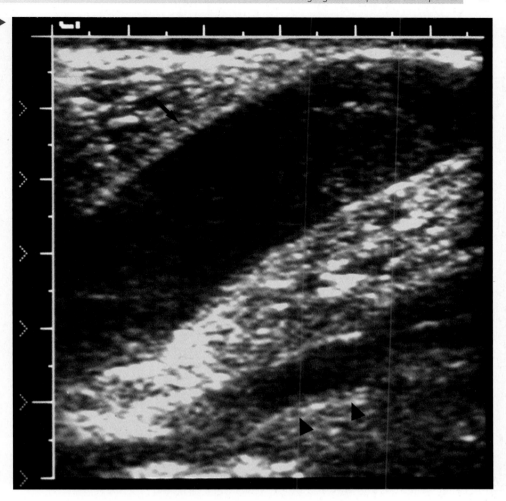

to the differentiation of popliteal fossa masses (e.g., aneurysm versus
Baker cyst versus hypertrophied synovium) (Fig. 2.21).

More recent US techniques such as Doppler US or color-flow
imaging, which expresses motion from moving red blood cells in color,
have found limited applications in orthopedic radiology. This modality is used mainly to detect arterial narrowing and venous thrombosis
(Figs. 2.22 and 2.23). However, there have been a limited number of
reports regarding the use of this technology in detecting complications
of benign soft-tissue masses (such as a Baker cyst; Fig. 2.24) or in
detecting tumor vascularity within malignant soft-tissue tumors.

Scintigraphy (Radionuclide Bone Scan)

Scintigraphy is a modality that detects the distribution in the body of a
radioactive agent injected into the vascular system. After an intravenous
injection of a radiopharmaceutical agent, the patient is placed under a
scintillation camera, which detects the distribution of radioactivity in the
body by measuring the interaction of gamma rays emitted from the body
with sodium iodide crystals in the head of the camera. The photoscans
are obtained in multiple projections and may include either the entire
body or selected parts.

One major advantage of skeletal scintigraphy over all other imaging
techniques is its ability to image the entire skeleton at once (Fig. 2.25).
As Johnson remarked, it provides a "metabolic picture" anatomically
localizing a lesion by assessing its metabolic activity compared with
adjacent normal bone. A bone scan may confirm the presence of the
disease, demonstrate the distribution of the lesion, and help evaluate the
pathologic process. Indications for skeletal scintigraphy include traumatic conditions, tumors (primary and metastatic), various arthritides,
infections, and metabolic bone diseases. The detected abnormality may
consist of either decreased uptake of a bone-seeking radiopharmaceutical agent (e.g., in the early stage of osteonecrosis) or increased uptake

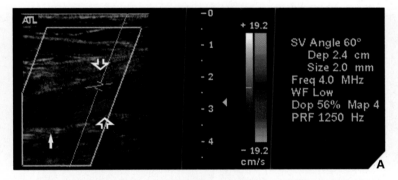

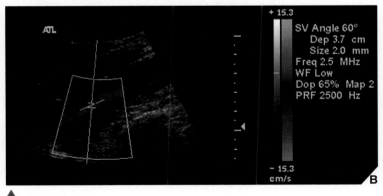

FIGURE 2.22   US of deep vein thrombosis. A 76-year-old man presented
with a history of a chronic pain in the left lower extremity. (**A**) Color Doppler
image of the popliteal fossa shows hypoechoic area in the popliteal vein (*arrow*)
representing an intraluminal thrombus. More proximally noted is diminished
blood flow around the blood clot (*open arrows*). (**B**) A normal color Doppler
US of the same region is shown for comparison.

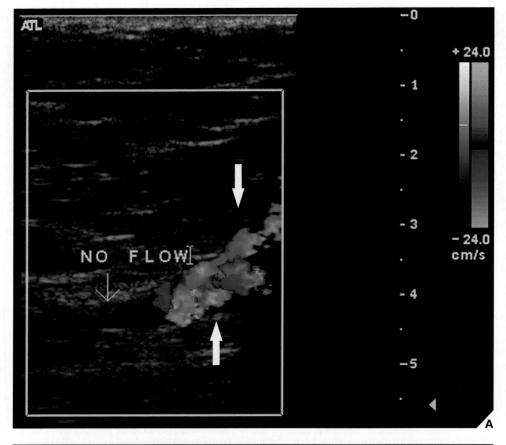

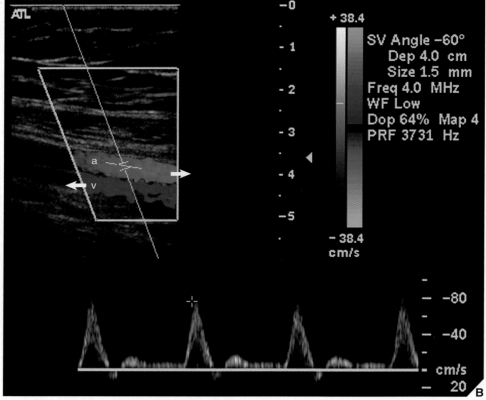

FIGURE 2.23   US of arterial occlusion. A 67-year-old woman presented with a history of claudication worse with exercise. **(A)** Color Doppler image shows complete occlusion of superficial femoral artery. Stream turbulence (*thick white arrows*) is compatible with hemodynamically significant stenosis or occlusion. **(B)** A normal color and pulsed Doppler image is shown for comparison. The *arrows* indicate the direction of blood flow in a vein (*v*) and artery (*a*).

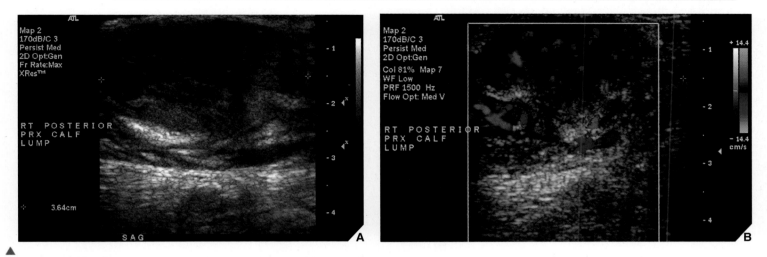

FIGURE 2.24   US of the popliteal fossa. A 41-year-old woman presented with painful mass in the popliteal region. Color-flow US shows portion of intact Baker cyst with hyperechoic heterogeneous fluid collection **(A)** and the site of chronic rupture associated with internal debris, secondary inflammatory changes, and hypervascularity **(B)**.

(such as in the case of fractures, neoplasms, a focus of osteomyelitis, etc.). Some structures under normal conditions may show increased activity (such as sacroiliac joints or normal growth plates).

Scintigraphy is a very sensitive imaging modality; however, it is not very specific, and frequently it is impossible to distinguish various processes that can cause increased uptake. Occasionally, however, the bone scan may yield very specific information and even suggest diagnosis, for instance, in multiple myeloma or osteoid osteoma. In the search for myeloma, scintigraphy can distinguish between similar-looking bony metastases because in most myeloma cases, no significant increase in the uptake of the radiopharmaceutical agent occurs; however, in skeletal metastasis, invariably the uptake of the tracer is significantly elevated. In the case of osteoid osteoma, the typical bone scan may demonstrate the so-called double density sign—greater increased uptake in the center, related to the nidus of the lesion, and lesser increased uptake at the periphery, related to the reactive sclerosis surrounding the nidus (Fig. 2.26).

Radionuclide bone scan is an indicator of mineral turnover. Because there is usually an enhanced deposition of bone-seeking radiopharmaceuticals in areas of bone undergoing change and repair, a bone scan is useful

in localizing tumors and tumor-like lesions in the skeleton. This is particularly helpful in such conditions as fibrous dysplasia, Langerhans cell histiocytosis, and metastatic cancer, in which more than one lesion is encountered, and some may represent a "silent" site of disorder. It also plays an important role in localizing small lesions, such as osteoid osteoma, which may not always be seen on radiographs. In most instances, radionuclide bone scan cannot distinguish benign lesions from malignant tumors, because increased blood flow with consequently increased isotope deposition and osteoblastic activity will take place in both conditions.

In traumatic conditions, scintigraphy is extremely helpful in the early diagnosis of stress fractures. These fractures may not be seen on conventional radiographs or even on tomographic studies. Scintigraphy is often used to differentiate tibial stress fractures from shin splints. In an acute stress fracture, hyperperfusion and hyperemia are typically present, and delayed images demonstrate band-like or fusiform uptake in the lesion. Conversely, shin splints are characterized by normal angiographic and blood pool phases with delayed images revealing longitudinally oriented linear areas of increased uptake. Radionuclide bone imaging also has value in diagnosing fractures of the osteopenic bones in elderly patients when routine radiographic examinations may appear normal.

FIGURE 2.25   (A,B,C) Radionuclide bone ▶ **scan.** Scintigraphy obtained in a patient with renal disease and secondary hyperparathyroidism demonstrates several abnormalities: left hydronephrosis secondary to urinary obstruction, resorptive changes of the distal ends of both clavicles, and periarticular soft-tissue calcifications around both shoulders.

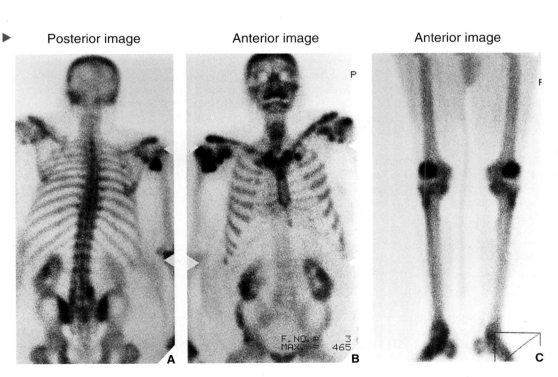

Posterior image

Anterior image

Anterior image

FIGURE 2.26 Osteoid osteoma—diagnosis by scintigraphy. ▶
A 4-year-old girl had symptoms suggesting a diagnosis of osteoid
osteoma; however, a radiograph (**A**) failed to demonstrate the
nidus. Scintigraphic examination (**B**) demonstrates a characteristic "double density" sign: more increased uptake in the center
(*arrow*) is related to the nidus of osteoid osteoma, whereas less
increased uptake at the periphery (*arrow heads*) denotes reactive sclerosis.

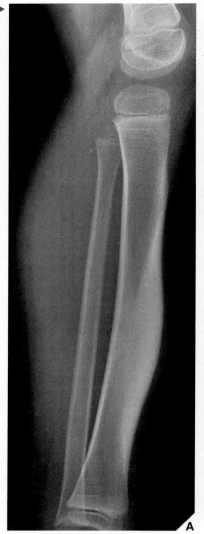

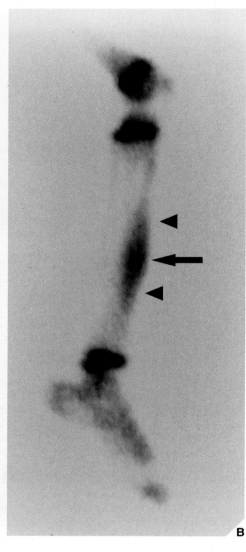

In metabolic bone disorders, bone scintigraphy is helpful, for instance, in establishing the extent of skeletal involvement in Paget disease (see Fig. 26.10) and assessing response to treatment. Although it is of no value for patients with generalized osteoporosis, it may occasionally be helpful in differentiating osteoporosis from osteomalacia and multiple vertebral fractures resulting from osteoporosis from those occurring in metastatic carcinoma. Radionuclide bone scan has also been reported to be useful in the diagnosis of reflex sympathetic dystrophy syndrome.

Skeletal scintigraphy is frequently used in the evaluation of infections. In particular, technetium-99m (99mTc) methylene diphosphonate (MDP) and indium-111 (111In) are highly sensitive in detecting early and occult osteomyelitis. In chronic osteomyelitis, imaging with gallium-67 (67Ga) citrate is more accurate in detecting the response or lack of response to treatment than 99mTc–phosphate bone imaging. For detecting recurrent active infection in patients with chronic osteomyelitis, 111In appears to be the radiopharmaceutical agent of choice. It must be stressed, however, that because the 111In-labeled leukocytes also accumulate in active bone marrow, the sensitivity for the detection of chronic osteomyelitis is reduced. To improve the diagnostic ability of this technique, combined 99mTc–sulfur colloid bone marrow/111In-labeled leukocyte study has been advocated. The three- or four-phase technique using technetium phosphate tracers can be effectively used to distinguish between soft-tissue infections (cellulitis) and osseous infections (osteomyelitis).

The use of 99mTc hexamethylpropylene-amine-oxime (HMPAO)–labeled leukocytes for diagnosing infectious processes has recently been advocated. The kinetics and normal distribution of such leukocytes are similar to those of 111In-labeled white cells. The superior resolution and count density of 99mTc, however, gives this technique an advantage over the use of 111In-labeled leukocytes.

In neoplastic conditions, the detection of skeletal metastasis is probably the most common indication for skeletal scintigraphy. It also is used frequently to determine the extent of a lesion or the presence of so-called skipped lesions or intraosseous metastases. It is not, however, the method of choice to determine the extent of the lesion in bone. It is important to stress that scintigraphy alone cannot diagnose the type of tumor; however, it may be useful to detect and localize some primary tumors as well as multifocal lesions (such as multicentric osteosarcoma).

99mTc MDP scans are used primarily to determine whether a lesion is monostotic or polyostotic. Such a study is therefore essential in staging a bone tumor. It is important to remember that although the degree of abnormal uptake may be related to the aggressiveness of the lesion, this does not correlate well with histologic grade. 67Ga may show uptake in a soft-tissue sarcoma and may help to differentiate a sarcoma from a benign soft-tissue lesion.

Although a bone scan may demonstrate the extent of the primary malignant tumor in bone, it is not as accurate as CT or MRI. It may be useful in the detection of a local recurrence of the tumor and occasionally indicates the response or lack of response to treatment (in the case of radiotherapy or chemotherapy).

In the evaluation of arthritides, a bone scan is extremely helpful in demonstrating the distribution of the lesion in the skeleton and has completely replaced the previously used radiographic joint survey (see Fig. 12.13A). Scintigraphy can determine the distribution of arthritic changes, not only in large and small joints but also in areas usually not detected by standard radiography, such as the sternomanubrial and temporomandibular joints, among others.

With the development of single-photon emission tomography (SPET) and single-photon emission CT (SPECT), diagnostic precision in evaluating bone and joint abnormalities has increased tremendously. Instrumentation efficacy for SPECT is improving with the introduction of multiple crystal detectors, fan beam and cone beam collimators, the detection of a greater fraction of photons, and improved algorithms. In comparison with planar images, SPECT provides increased contrast resolution using a tomographic mode similar to conventional tomography, which eliminates noise from the tissue outside the plane of imaging (Fig. 2.27). It provides not only qualitative information on the uptake of bone-seeking radiopharmaceuticals but also quantitative data.

The principal benefit of SPECT is the improvement of lesion detection and anatomic localization, hence producing a better diagnostic sensitivity. Bone SPECT has proved particularly useful in the detection of lesions in large and complex anatomic structures, in which it allows the removal of overlying and underlying activity from areas of interest. The widest applications have been found in imaging of the spine, pelvis, knees, and ankles. Using SPECT imaging in the spine, for example, lesions can be localized to different parts of the vertebra (i.e., vertebral body, pedicle, articular process, lamina, pars interarticularis, spinous, and transverse process). In the knee, SPECT imaging has proved to be effective in the detection of meniscal tears.

Several bone-seeking tracers are available for scintigraphic imaging. Those that are most frequently used are as follows.

Diphosphonates

In recent years, there has been remarkable progress in the development of new gamma-emitting diagnostic agents for radionuclide imaging. The radiopharmaceuticals currently in use in bone scanning include the organic diphosphonates, ethylene diphosphonates (HEPD), MDPs, and methane hydroxydiphosphonates (HNDP), all labeled with ^{99m}Tc, a pure gamma-emitter with a 6-hour half-life. MDP is more frequently used, particularly in adults, typically in a dose that provides 15 mCi (555 MBq) of ^{99m}Tc. After an intravenous injection of the radiopharmaceutical agent, approximately 50% of the dose localizes in bone. The remainder circulates freely in the body and eventually is excreted by the kidneys. A gamma camera can then be used in a procedure known as four-phase isotope bone scan. The first phase, the *radionuclide angiogram*, is the first minute after the injection when the serial images obtained every 2 seconds demonstrate the radioactive tracer in the major blood vessels. In the second phase, the *blood pool scan*, which lasts from 1 to 3 minutes after the injection, the isotope is detected in the vascular system and in the extracellular space in the soft tissues before being taken up by the bone. The third phase, or *static bone scan*, usually occurs 2 to 3 hours after the injection and discloses the radiopharmaceutical agent in the bone. This phase may be divided into two stages. In the first stage, the isotope diffuses passively through the bone capillaries. In the second stage, the radionuclide

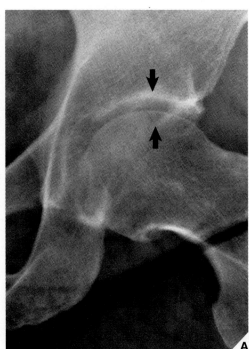

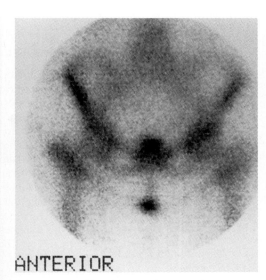

ANTERIOR

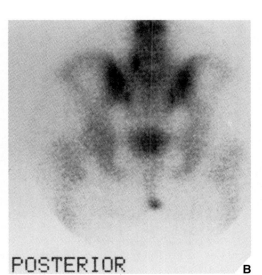

POSTERIOR

B

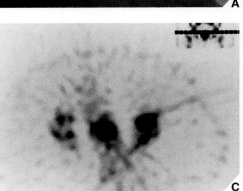

A

C

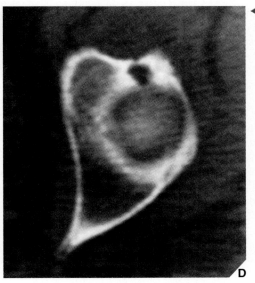

D

◄ FIGURE 2.27 **Effectiveness of SPECT imaging.** A 46-year-old woman presented with left hip pain for several months. **(A)** A radiograph demonstrated only minimal degenerative changes of the hip joint. A small radiolucent area in the superior portion of the acetabulum (*arrows*) raised some concerns about the diagnosis. **(B)** Conventional radionuclide bone scan in anterior and posterior projections demonstrated a slight increase in the uptake of the tracer localized to the left hip joint. **(C)** SPECT examination was performed. On the tomographic cut at the level of the acetabulae (*inset*), there is an area of increased activity localized to the anterosuperior aspect of the left acetabulum and focal areas of activity related to osteophytes of the femoral head. **(D)** CT examination showed a large degenerative cyst (geode) in the acetabulum in the area corresponding to abnormal uptake of a tracer on SPECT section.

is concentrated in the bone. The most intense localization occurs in the first and second phases in areas with increased blood flow, and in the third phase, in areas with increased osteogenic activity, increased calcium metabolism, and active bone turnover. The fourth phase is a 24-hour *static image*.

Gallium 67

^{67}Ga citrate is frequently used to diagnose infectious and inflammatory processes in bones and joints. Although the target site of gallium localization is soft tissue, gallium localizes also to some extent in bones, because it is incorporated into the calcium hydroxyapatite crystal as a calcium analog, and in the bone marrow, because of its behavior as an iron analog. Gallium accumulates in regions of infection because of an association with bacterial and cellular debris as well as leukocytes. Because white blood cells migrate to the foci of inflammation and infection, some of the gallium is transported intracellularly to these sites. The sensitivity of ^{67}Ga for abscess detection varies from 58% to 100% and the specificity varies from 75% to 99%. The images are usually obtained 6 and 24 hours after the injection of 5 mCi (185 MBq) of this radiopharmaceutical agent. These images are extremely accurate in following the response to therapy of chronic osteomyelitis and infectious arthritis. In particular, changing activity of ^{67}Ga uptake parallels the patient's clinical course in septic arthritis more closely than the images obtained after the injection of technetium-labeled diphosphonate. Over the past few years, there has been a considerable change in the role of gallium imaging in infection. Once the mainstay of radionuclide imaging for infection, gallium scanning has now been supplanted by labeled leukocyte imaging. The ^{67}Ga citrate scan, however, enhances and complements the diagnostic value of the ^{99m}Tc MDP scan. In conjunction with the latter, gallium scintigraphy has been used to improve the specificity of technetium imaging. For example, sequential technetium–gallium imaging is superior to technetium MDP scintigraphy alone in distinguishing cellulitis from osteomyelitis and in precise localization of infectious foci.

In neoplastic conditions, gallium scan is used to differentiate a sarcoma from a benign soft-tissue lesion.

Indium

The diagnostic advantage of ^{111}In oxine–labeled white blood cells over other bone-seeking radiopharmaceuticals in detecting inflammatory abnormalities in the skeletal system has recently been advocated. Because ^{111}In leukocytes are not usually incorporated into areas of increased bone turnover, indium imaging presumably reflects inflammatory activity only, and early experience has shown it to be specific in detecting abscesses or acute infectious processes, including osteomyelitis and septic arthritis. The sensitivity varies from 75% to 90% and the specificity, as recently reported, is approximately 91%. False-negative results are often seen in patients with chronic infections in which there is reduced inflow of circulating leukocytes. False-positive results are seen in patients who have an inflammatory process without infection (such as rheumatoid arthritis mistaken for septic arthritis).

Nanocolloid

Very small particles of ^{99m}Tc-labeled colloid of human serum albumin were tried as a bone marrow imaging agent. Approximately 86% of these particles are 30 nm or smaller, and the remainder are between 30 and 80 nm. This nanocolloid has a sensitivity for the detection of osteomyelitis in the extremities equal to that of indium-labeled leukocytes. The clinical value of this method has not been yet determined.

Immunoglobulins

Recently, radiolabeled human polyclonal IgG has been used as an agent for imaging infection. This labeled immunoglobulin is thought to bind to Fc receptors expressed by cells (macrophages, polymorphonuclear leukocytes, and lymphocytes) involved in the inflammatory response. In a study of 128 patients, polyclonal IgG yielded a sensitivity of 91% and a specificity of 100%. Polyclonal immunoglobulins have a number of advantages, such as availability in kit form and the fact that they do not require in vivo labeling.

Chemotactic Peptides

The same investigators who developed ^{111}In-labeled IgG are also pioneering the use of radiolabeled chemotactic peptides for infection imaging. These are small peptides that are produced by bacteria. They bind to high-affinity receptors on the cell membrane of polymorphonuclear leukocytes and mononuclear phagocytes, stimulating chemotaxis. Rather than using the native peptide, synthetic analogs are created that allow radiolabeling. The small size of ^{111}In-labeled chemotactic peptides allows the component to pass quickly through the vascular walls and enter the site of infection.

Iodine

^{125}I is used in a radionuclide technique known as single-photon absorptiometry (SPA) to determine bone mineral density at peripheral bone sites such as finger and radius. This method measures primarily the density of the cortical bone.

Gadolinium

^{153}Gd is a radionuclide source used in a technique known as dual-photon absorptiometry (DPA), which is also used to calculate bone mineral density. This technique permits the measurement of central sites of bone such as the spine and the hip. ^{153}Gd produces photons at two energy levels, and the images are generated on a whole-body rectilinear scanner. The measurements are obtained for compact and trabecular bones.

Positron Emission Tomography, PET-CT, and PET-MRI

Positron emission tomography (PET) is a diagnostic imaging technique that allows the identification of biochemical and physiologic alterations in the body and assesses the level of metabolic activity and perfusion in various organ systems. The process produces biologic images based on the detection of gamma rays that are emitted by a radioactive substance, such as ^{18}F-labeled 2-fluoro-2-deoxyglucose (^{18}FDG). PET differs from other single-photon radionuclide scans in its ability to correct for tissue attenuation signal loss and its relatively uniform spatial resolution. One of the main applications of this technique is in oncology, including the detection of primary and metastatic tumors and recurrences of the tumors after treatment. Only recently has PET scanning been found to be useful in the diagnosis, treatment, and follow-up of musculoskeletal neoplasms (Figs. 2.28 to 2.30). Although some promising results have been reported in using this technique, the detection of bone marrow involvement is still controversial, because physiologic bone marrow uptake and diffuse uptake in reactive changes in bone marrow (such as after chemotherapy) can be observed on FDG PET images. Recently, a significant progress has been made in the application of PET scanning in diagnosing infections associated with metallic implants in patients with traumatic conditions.

PET-CT combines in a single gantry system a PET and CT, allowing a sequential acquisition of images derived from both systems at the same time, and thus combining them into a single superimposed image. The advantage of this fusion image is clear: the functional images obtained with PET that depict the spatial distribution of metabolic and biochemical activities in the tissues are precisely correlated with anatomic images obtained with CT (Fig. 2.31). Two- and three-dimensional image reformation may be rendered as a function of a common software and control system.

PET-MRI is a newest hybrid technology with capability of instantaneous fusion of anatomic and functional data that allows an integrated scanning for simultaneous PET and MRI. In order to avoid the interference of magnetic field on PET performance, the traditional PET detectors based on scintillators coupled to photomultiplier tubes were substituted with the avalanche photodiodes and silicon photomultipliers. This technique combines the strength of MRI, including lack of ionizing radiation and high-resolution as well as high-contrast morphologic imaging of soft tissues and osseous structures, with high sensitivity of PET and its ability to obtain functional images depicting metabolic and biochemical activity in the tissues as in PET-CT. Although still an experimental

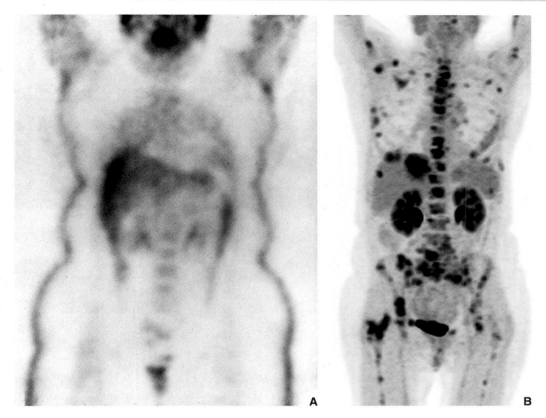

▲
FIGURE 2.28 **Positron emission tomography. (A)** A normal whole-body PET scan of a 62-year-old woman suspected of having skeletal metastases caused by recently treated breast carcinoma. **(B)** A 65-year-old woman diagnosed with stage IV adenocarcinoma of the lungs developed widespread skeletal and internal organs metastases, as revealed on this PET scan.

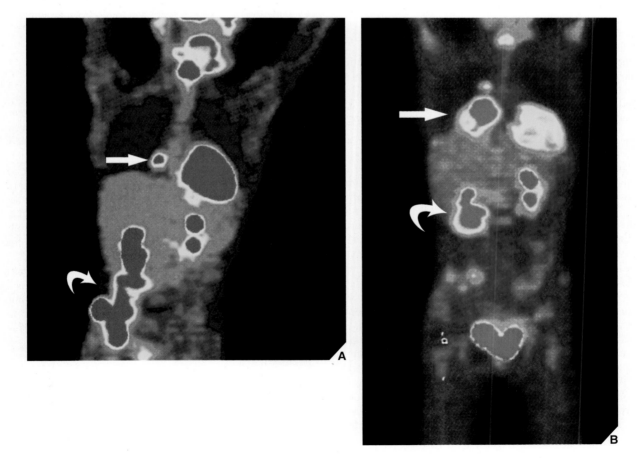

▲
FIGURE 2.29 **Positron emission tomography. (A)** A whole-body PET scan of a 9-year-old girl with Ewing sarcoma of the right ilium shows hypermetabolic tumor in the bone (*curved arrow*) and a metastatic lung nodule (*arrow*). **(B)** After several months of chemotherapy, the primary iliac bone tumor has markedly decreased in size (*curved arrow*), but metastatic lung lesion has enlarged (*arrow*). (Courtesy of Drs. Frieda Feldman and Ronald van Heertum, New York.)

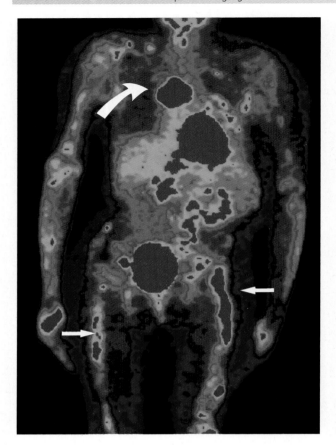

▲
FIGURE 2.30 **Positron emission tomography.** A whole-body PET scan of a 37-year-old woman with fibrous dysplasia shows multiple skeletal deformities. The *arrows* point to the lesions in proximal femora, and the *curved arrow* points to a large hypermetabolic focus in the sternum. (Courtesy of Drs. Frieda Feldman and Ronald van Heertum, New York.)

technique, at the time of this printing, the limited clinical applications yielded encouraging results particularly in the field of evaluation of the progress of treatment of some of the inflammatory arthritides (John Hunter, MD and Stanley Naguwa, MD, UC Davis Medical Center, Sacramento, California, unpublished data and personal communications).

Magnetic Resonance Imaging

MRI is based on the reemission of an absorbed radio frequency (rf) signal while the patient is in a strong magnetic field. An external magnetic field is usually generated by a magnet with field strengths of 0.2 to 3.0 tesla (T). The system includes a magnet, rf coils (transmitter and receiver), gradient coils, and a computer display unit with digital storage facilities. The physical principles of MRI cannot be discussed here in detail because of space limitations; only a brief overview will be given.

The ability of MRI to image body parts depends on the intrinsic spin of atomic nuclei with an odd number of protons and/or neutrons (e.g., hydrogen), thus generating a magnetic moment. Atomic nuclei of tissues placed within the main magnetic field from the usual random alignment of their magnetic poles tend to align along the direction of that field. The application of rf pulses causes the nuclei to absorb energy and induces resonance of particular sets of nuclei, which causes their orientation to the magnetic field. The required frequency of the pulse is determined by the strength of the magnetic field and the particular nucleus undergoing investigation. When the rf field is removed, the energy absorbed during the transition from a high- to low-energy state is subsequently released, and this can be recorded as an electrical signal that provides the data from which digital images are derived. Signal intensity refers to the strength of the radio wave that a tissue emits after excitation. The strength of this radio wave determines the degree of brightness of the imaged structures. A bright (white) area in an image is said to demonstrate high signal

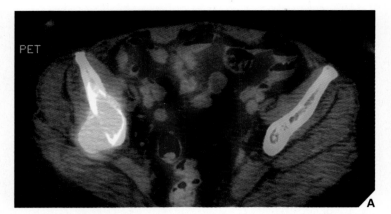

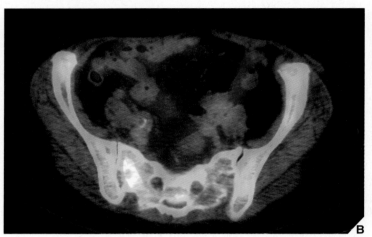

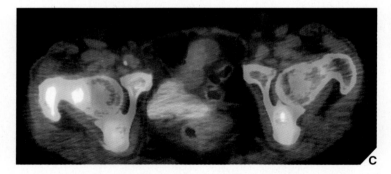

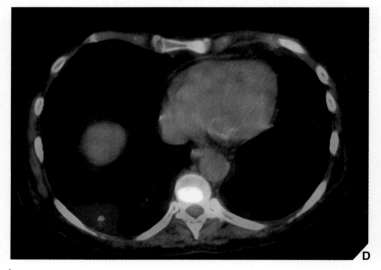

▲
FIGURE 2.31 **PET-CT.** A 60-year-old woman with breast carcinoma underwent a PET-CT scanning. The axial fused PET/CT images revealed several hypermetabolic foci of skeletal metastases including right ilium (**A**), sacrum (**B**), right femur and both acetabulae (**C**), and thoracic vertebrae (**D**).

intensity, whereas a dark (black) area is said to demonstrate a low signal intensity. The intensity of a given tissue is a function of the concentration of hydrogen atoms (protons) resonating within the imaged volume and of the longitudinal and transverse relaxation times, which, in turn, depend on the biophysical state of the tissue's water molecules.

Two relaxation times are described, termed T1 and T2. The T1 relaxation time (longitudinal) is used to describe the return of protons back to equilibrium after the application and removal of the rf pulse. T2 relaxation time (transverse) is used to describe the associated loss of coherence or phase between individual protons immediately after the application of the rf pulse. A variety of rf pulse sequences can be used to enhance the differences in T1 and T2, thus providing the necessary image contrast. The most commonly used sequences are spin echo (SE), partial saturation recovery (PSR), inversion recovery (IR), chemical selective suppression (CHESS), and fast scan (FS) technique. SE short repetition times (TR) (800 msec or less) and short echo delay times (TE) (40 msec or less) pulse sequences (or T1) provide good anatomic detail. Long TR (2,000 msec or more) and long TE (60 msec or more) pulse sequences (or T2), however, provide good contrast, sufficient for the evaluation of pathologic processes. Intermediate TR (1,000 msec or more) and short TE (30 msec or less) sequences are known as proton or spin density images. They represent a mixture of T1 and T2 weighting, and although they provide good anatomic details, the tissue contrast is somewhat impaired. IR sequences can be combined with multiplanar imaging to shorten scan time. With a short inversion time (TI), in the range of 100 to 150 msec, the effects of prolonged T1 and T2 relaxation times are cumulative and the signal from fat is suppressed. This technique, called short time IR (STIR), has been useful for evaluating bone tumors. CHESS is a sequence also used for fat signal suppression. In this sequence, the chemical shift artifacts are removed and the high-intensity fat signal is suppressed; thus, the effective dynamic range of signal intensities is increased and contrast depiction of anatomic details is improved.

Fat suppression technique is commonly used in MRI to detect adipose tissue or suppress the signal from adipose tissue. There are three methods to achieve this goal: frequency-selective (chemical) fat saturation, inversion–recovery imaging, and opposed-phase imaging (Table 2.1). The selection of one of these methods depends on the purpose of fat suppression, whether it is used to enhance the contrast or to characterize the tissue and the amount of fat in the tissue under investigation. *Fat saturation* methods are usually chosen for the suppression of signal from large amounts of adipose tissue and to provide a good contrast resolution. This technique can be used with any imaging sequence. It is useful to visualize small anatomic details, for example, in postcontrast MRa. *Inversion–recovery* method (such as STIR sequence) allows homogeneous and global fat suppression; however, the generated images have low signal-to-noise ratio, and this technique is not only specific for fat. *Opposed-phase* method is recommended for the demonstration of lesions that contain only small amounts of fat. The inability of this technique to detect small tumors embedded in adipose tissue is the main disadvantage.

Recently, fat suppression techniques have been combined with 3D gradient echo imaging, resulting in superior delineation of articular cartilage. The main indication for fat suppression is the assessment of small amounts of bone marrow edema in the subchondral bone, often accompanying osteochondral pathology such as in osteochondral fractures, osteochondritis dissecans, or osteonecrosis.

Fast imaging techniques have become increasingly popular because of a number of advantages compared with much slower SE imaging. In particular, so-called gradient recalled echo (GRE) pulse sequences using variable flip angles (5 to 90 degrees) have gained rapid acceptance in orthopedic imaging, because they represent the most effective means of performing fast MRI. The major advantage is the shortening of imaging time, because the low flip angle rf pulses destroy only a small part of the longitudinal magnetization in each pulse cycle. In general, gradient echo imaging can be performed using either a 2D technique or a 3D so-called volume technique. There are several different types of GRE methods in clinical use. Each of these methods relies on using a reduced flip angle to enhance signal with short TR. These techniques are known by a variety of acronyms such as FLASH (fast low-angle shot), FISP (fast imaging with steady procession), GRASS (gradient-recalled acquisition in the steady state), and MPGR (multiplanar gradient recalled). Gradient echo sequences are particularly useful in imaging tendons, ligaments, articular cartilage, and loose bodies in the joint. The drawback of this technique is the so-called susceptibility effect, which results in artificial signal loss at the interface between tissues of different magnetic properties. This factor limits the use of gradient echo sequences when imaging patients with metallic hardware.

In most examinations, at least two orthogonal planes should be obtained (axial and either coronal or sagittal), and on many occasions, all three planes are necessary. For adequate MRI, surface coils are necessary, because they provide improved spatial resolution. Most surface coils are designed specifically for different areas of the body, such as the knee, shoulder, wrist, and temporomandibular joints. Recently introduced an eight-channel phased-array extremity coil tremendously increased the quality of MR image (see Figs. 7.30 and 7.31B).

Currently, the use of MRI in orthopedic radiology is mainly confined to four areas: trauma, arthritides, tumors, and infections. The musculoskeletal system is ideally suited for the evaluation by MRI because different tissues display different signal intensities on T1- and T2-weighted images. The images displayed may have a low signal intensity, intermediate signal intensity, or high signal intensity. *Low signal intensity* may be subdivided into signal void (black) and signal lower than that of normal muscle (dark). *Intermediate signal intensity* may be subdivided into signal equal to that of normal muscle and signal higher than that of muscle but lower than that of subcutaneous fat (bright). *High signal intensity* may be subdivided into signal equal to that of normal

TABLE 2.1 **Fat Suppression Techniques**

Methods	Advantages	Disadvantages
Frequency-selective (chemical) fat saturation	Lipid-specific Signal in nonfat tissue unaffected Excellent imaging of small anatomic detail Can be used with any imaging sequence	Occasionally inadequate fat suppression Water signal may be suppressed Heterogeneities in areas of sharp variations in anatomic structures Increased imaging time
Inversion recovery (STIR)	Excellent contrast resolution Very good for tumor detection Can be used with low-field-strength magnets	Low signal-to-noise ratio Tissue with a short T1 and long T1 may produce the same signal intensity Signal from mucoid tissue, hemorrhage, and proteinaceous fluid may be suppressed
Opposed-phase	Ability to demonstrate small amounts of lipid tissue Simple, fast, and available on every MR imaging system	Fat signal only partially suppressed Suppresses water signal Difficult to detect small tumors imbedded in fat In postgadolinium studies, contrast material may be undetected

subcutaneous fat (bright) and signal higher than that of subcutaneous fat (extremely bright). High signal intensity of fat planes and differences in the signal intensity of various structures allow the separation of the different tissue components including muscles, tendons, ligaments, vessels, nerves, hyaline cartilage, fibrocartilage, cortical bone, and trabecular bone (Fig. 2.32). For instance, fat and yellow (fatty) bone marrow display high signal intensity on T1-weighted images and intermediate signal on T2-weighted images; hematomas (acute or subacute) display relatively high signal intensity on T1 and T2 sequences. Cortical bone, air, ligaments, tendons, and fibrocartilage display low signal intensity on T1- and T2-weighted images; muscle, nerves, and hyaline cartilage display intermediate signal intensity on T1- and T2-weighted images. Red (hematopoietic) marrow displays low signal on T1-weighted images and low-to-intermediate signal on T2-weighted images. Fluid displays intermediate signal on T1-weighted images and high signal on T2-weighted images. Most tumors display low-to-intermediate signal intensity on T1-weighted images and high signal intensity on T2-weighted images. Lipomas display high signal intensity on T1-weighted images and intermediate signal on T2-weighted images (Table 2.2).

Traumatic conditions of the bones and soft tissues are particularly well suited to the diagnosis and evaluation by MRI. Some abnormalities, such as bone contusions or trabecular microfractures, not seen on radiography and CT are well demonstrated by this technique (Fig. 2.33). Occult fractures, which can be missed on conventional x-ray films, become obvious on MRI (Fig. 2.34).

More recently, MRI proved to be successful in the diagnosis and evaluation of athletic pubalgia and so-called sports hernia, depicting abnormalities of pubic symphysis, of rectus abdominis insertional injury,

and hip adductors tendon injury. The newest reports also revealed that MRI was effective in the diagnosis and evaluation of acute and subacute denervation of skeletal muscles.

Occasionally, MR images may be enhanced by an intravenous injection of Gd-DTPA, known as gadolinium, a paramagnetic compound that demonstrates increased signal intensity on T1-weighted images. The mechanism by which gadolinium produces enhancement in MRI is fundamentally different from the mechanism of contrast enhancement in CT. Unlike iodine in CT, gadolinium itself produces no MRI signal. Instead, it acts by shortening the T1 and T2 relaxation times of tissues into which it extravasates, resulting in an increase in signal intensity on T1-weighted (short TR/TE) imaging sequences.

MRa has become popular in recent years. The diagnostic accuracy of this technique may exceed that of conventional MRI because the intraarticular structures are better demonstrated if they are separated by means of capsular distention. Such distention can be achieved with an intraarticular injection of a contrast material such as diluted gadopentetate dimeglumine (gadolinium) or saline. Most commonly, a mixture of sterile saline, iodinated contrast agent, 1% lidocaine (or Xylocaine), and Gd-DTPA is injected into the joint under fluoroscopic guidance. The generated images are very similar to those obtained of the joint with pre-existing joint fluid (joint effusion). In clinical practice, MRa is predominantly used in the evaluation of shoulder abnormalities, such as internal derangement, glenohumeral joint instability, rotator cuff disorders, or articular cartilage and cartilaginous labrum abnormalities (Fig. 2.35). This technique is equally effective in the evaluation of the fibrocartilaginous labrum of the acetabulum. In particular, femoroacetabular impingement (FAI) syndrome can be accurately diagnosed with MRa, especially

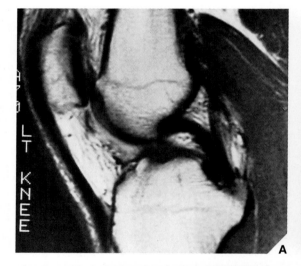

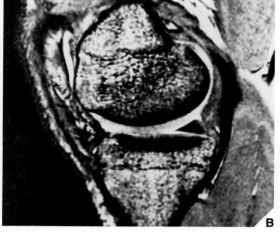

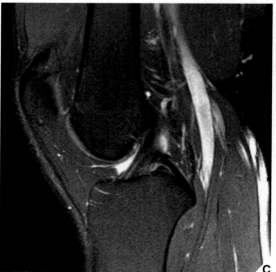

◀ **FIGURE 2.32 MRI of the knee. (A)** Sagittal spin echo T1-weighted image (SE; TR 600/TE 20 msec), **(B)** sagittal MPGR T2*-weighted image (flip angle 30 degrees, TR 35/TE 15 msec), and **(C)** sagittal proton density-weighted fat-saturated image (TR 3300/TE 40) demonstrate various anatomic structures clearly depicted because of variations in signal intensity of bone, articular cartilage, fibrocartilage, ligaments, muscles, and fat.

TABLE 2.2 **MRI Signal Intensities of Various Tissues**

Tissue	Image	
	T1 weighted	*T2 weighted*
Hematoma, hemorrhage (acute, subacute)	Intermediate/high	High
Hematoma, hemorrhage (chronic)	Low	Low
Fat, fatty marrow	High	Intermediate
Muscle, nerves, hyaline cartilage	Intermediate	Intermediate
Cortical bone, tendons, ligaments, fibrocartilage, scar tissue	Low	Low
Hyaline cartilage	Intermediate	Intermediate
Red (hematopoietic) marrow	Low	Intermediate
Air	Low	Low
Fluid	Intermediate	High
Proteinaceous fluid	High	High
Tumors (generally)	Intermediate to low	High
Lipoma	High	Intermediate
Hemangioma	Intermediate (slightly higher than muscle)	High

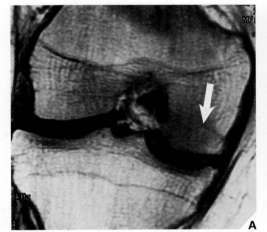
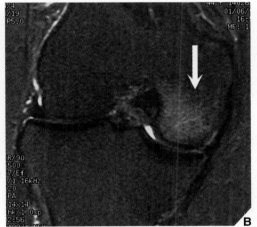

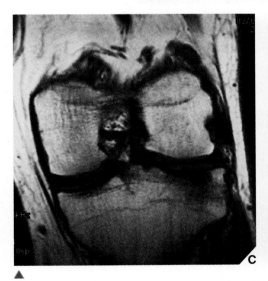
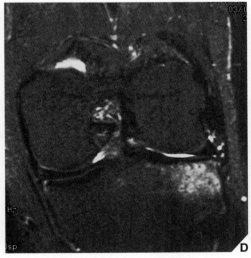
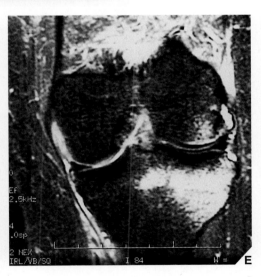

FIGURE 2.33 Bone contusion (trabecular injury). (A) Coronal T1-weighted MRI of a 44-year-old woman who sustained an injury to her right knee shows an area of low signal intensity in the medial femoral condyle (*arrow*). **(B)** On the fast spin-echo IR (FSE-IR) image, the trabecular injury becomes more conspicuous as a focus of high signal intensity against the low-intensity background of suppressed marrow fat (*arrow*). In another patient, a 35-year-old man, T1-weighted **(C)** and FSE-IR **(D)** coronal MR images show a trabecular injury to the lateral aspect of tibial plateau of the left knee. In a 29-year-old woman, T2-weighted IR with fat saturation coronal MRI **(E)** shows a trabecular injury to the lateral femoral condyle and lateral aspect of the proximal tibia.

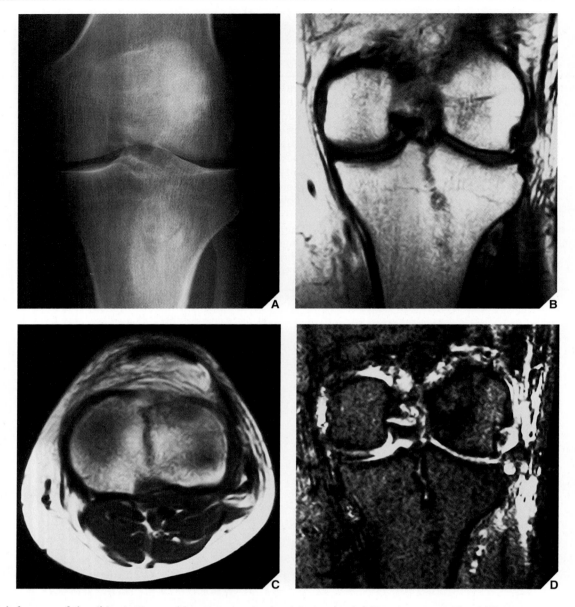

FIGURE 2.34 **Occult fracture of the tibia.** A 47-year-old woman sustained an injury to her left knee in a car accident. **(A)** Anteroposterior radiograph shows sclerotic area in the proximal tibia, but no definite fracture is apparent. **(B)** Coronal and **(C)** axial T1-weighted MR images demonstrate a vertical fracture line extending into the tibial spines. **(D)** A T2-weighted IR coronal MRI, in addition to the fracture line, shows the tears of the lateral meniscus and lateral collateral ligament, extensive soft-tissue edema and hemorrhage, and joint fluid.

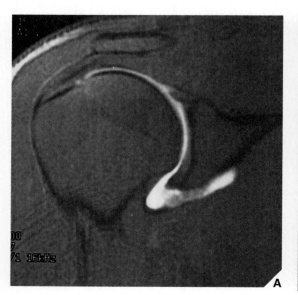

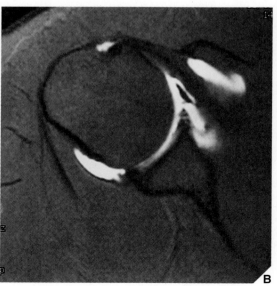

◀ FIGURE 2.35 **Glenoid labrum tear.** Magnetic resonance arthrogram of a 26-year-old man who sustained an injury to his right shoulder shows several abnormalities. **(A)** A coronal T1-weighted MR image with fat saturation shows a tear of the inferior cartilaginous labrum of the glenoid. **(B)** An axial T1-weighted MR image with fat saturation shows tears of the anterior and posterior cartilaginous labra associated with stripping of the anterior joint capsule.

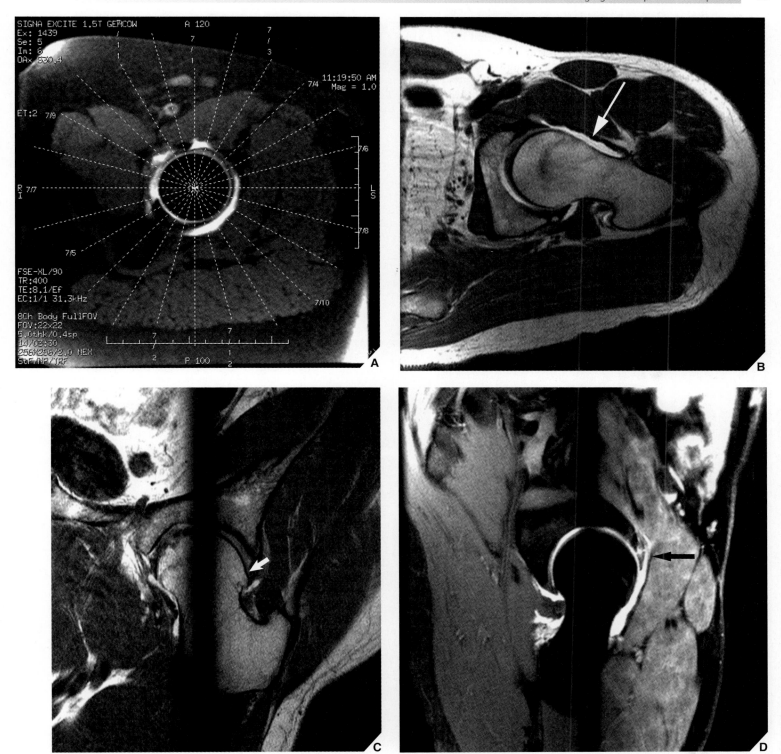

FIGURE 2.36   Radial MR-arthrogram of a hip. A 28-year-old man presented with a left hip and groin pain for several months. Conventional radiographs (not shown here) were highly suggestive of a cam-type femoroacetabular impingement syndrome, confirmed on radial MRa. **(A)** Prescription of the radial plane images off the oblique axial *en face* image of the acetabulum. **(B)** Transverse oblique FSE T1-weighted MR image obtained through the center of the femoral neck shows nonspherical shape of the femoral head and excessive bone formation at the anterosuperior aspect of the head–neck junction (*arrow*). **(C)** The radial reformatted proton density-weighted MR image shows a prominent osteophyte (*arrow*). **(D)** Oblique axial proton density-weighted fat-suppressed radial image shows a tear of the superior acetabular labrum (*arrow*).

when combined with radial reconstruction sequences (Fig. 2.36). The advantages of radial acquisitions are avoidance of partial volume averaging and the elimination of distorted anatomic details.

Indirect MRa is a procedure in which an intravenous injection of gadolinium is administered before MRI examination of the joint. This technique, like MRa, may improve the detection of rotator cuff tears, labral pathology, and adhesive capsulitis.

The newest improvement in the evaluation of articular cartilage of the knee is the introduction of so-called vastly undersampled isotropic projection steady-state free precession (VIPR-SSFP) imaging pulse sequence that combines a balanced SSFP technique with a 3D radial multiplanar image acquisition. In addition to providing important clinical information regarding the cartilage, this technique is also effective in the evaluation of the ligaments, menisci, and osseous structures of the knee in symptomatic patients.

Magnetic resonance angiography (MRA) is a technique that helps to visualize blood vessels (Figs. 2.37 to 2.39). Unlike conventional contrast angiography, it does not visualize the blood volume itself but rather depicts a property of blood flow. One of its advantages is that after a 3D MRA data set is collected, one may choose any number of viewing directions. This feature also eliminates vascular overlapping. Numerous pulse sequences have been proposed to produce angiographic contrast. Some rely on the rapid inflow of relaxed blood into the region in which the stationary tissue is saturated. These methods are called time-of-flight (TOF) or flow-related enhancement (FRE). Others, which rely on the velocity-dependent change of phase of moving blood in the presence of a magnetic field gradient, are called the phase-contrast methods. Some methods involve the subtraction of flow-dephased images from flow-compensated images. Applications of MRA in orthopedic radiology include the evaluation of the vascular structures in patients with trauma to the extremities and the assessment of vascularity of musculoskeletal neoplasms.

Although MRI has many advantages, disadvantages exist as well. These include the typical contraindications of scanning patients with cardiac pacemakers, cerebral aneurysm clips, and claustrophobia. The presence of metallic objects, such as ferromagnetic surgical clips, causes focal loss of signal with or without distortion of image. Metallic objects create "holes" in the image, but ferromagnetic objects cause more distortion. Similar to CT, an average volume effect may be observed in MR images, causing occasional pitfalls in interpretation.

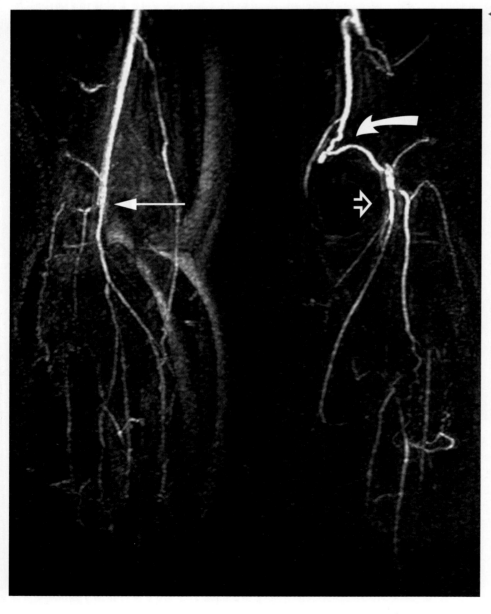

◀ FIGURE 2.37 **MRA of arterial occlusion.** A 67-year-old woman presented with a history of intermittent pain in both lower limbs exaggerated by walking. MRI of the lower extremities obtained after an intravenous injection of contrast (gadolinium) shows significant narrowing of the right popliteal artery *(arrow)* and a complete occlusion of the left popliteal artery *(curved arrow)* with collateral circulation and reconstitution of the short distal segment at the level of popliteal fossa *(open arrow)*.

FIGURE 2.38 MRA—normal findings. A 27-year-old woman was diagnosed with mixed connective tissue disease. Because vasculitis and femoral artery occlusion were also clinically suspected, she underwent MRA. Coronal MR images of the knees **(A)** showed medullary bone infarction in the distal femora; however, MR-angiogram **(B)** demonstrated no abnormalities of the vessels.

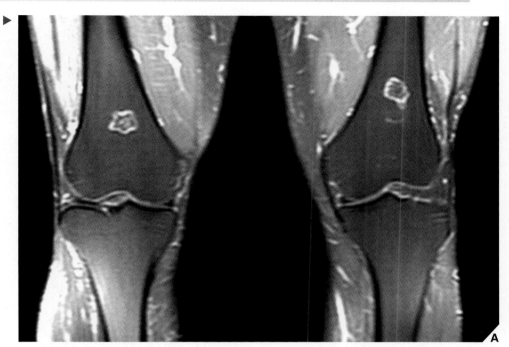

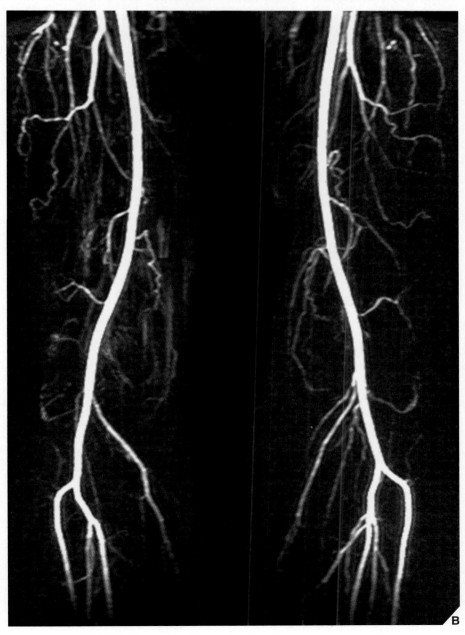

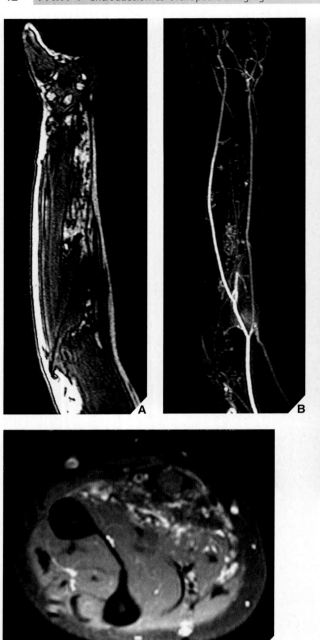

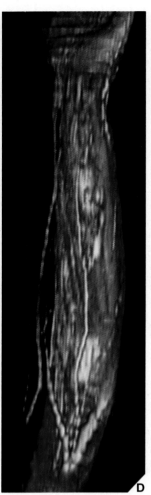

◀ **FIGURE 2.39   3D MR-angiography.** A 35-year-old woman presented with a history of swelling of the left forearm. Dynamic contrast MRI including arterial, venous, and delayed phases (**A,B,C**) shows multiple enhancing vascular spaces and areas of contrast puddling, as well as large draining veins that empty into the antecubital artery. (**D**) 3D color volume MRA image shows simultaneous opacification of veins and arteries of the forearm, diagnostic of arteriovenous malformation.

SUGGESTED READINGS

Abdel-Dayem HM. The role of nuclear medicine in primary bone and soft tissue tumors. *Semin Nucl Med* 1997;27:355–363.

Adam G, Drobnitzky M, Nolte-Ernsting CCA, Günther RW. Optimizing joint imaging: MR imaging techniques. *Eur Radiol* 1996;6:882–889.

Alazraki NP. Radionuclide imaging in the evaluation of infectious and inflammatory disease. *Radiol Clin North Am* 1993;31:783–794.

Alley MT, Shifrin RY, Pelc NJ, Herfkens RJ. Ultrafast contrast-enhanced three-dimensional MR angiography: state of the art. *Radiographics* 1998;18:273–285.

Allman K, Schafer O, Hauer M, et al. Indirect MR arthrography of the unexercised glenohumeral joint in patients with rotator cuff tears. *Invest Radiol* 1999;34:435–440.

Al Sheikh W, Sfakianakis GN, Mnaymneh W, et al. Subacute and chronic bone infections: diagnosis using In-111, Ga-67, and Tc-99 m MDP bone scintigraphy, and radiography. *Radiology* 1985;155:501–506.

Anderson MW, Greenspan A. State of the art: stress fractures. *Radiology* 1996;199:1–12.

Aoki J, Watanabe H, Shinozaki T, et al. FDG PET of primary benign and malignant bone tumors: standardized uptake value in 52 lesions. *Radiology* 2001;219:774–777.

Aoki J, Watanabe H, Shinozaki T, et al. FDG-PET for preoperative differential diagnosis between benign and malignant soft tissue masses. *Skeletal Radiol* 2003;32:133–138.

Arndt WF III, Truax AL, Barnett FM, Simmons GE, Brown DC. MR diagnosis of bone contusions of the knee: comparison of coronal T2-weighted fast spin-echo with fat saturation and fast spin-echo STIR images with conventional STIR images. *Am J Roentgenol* 1996;166:119–124.

Becker W, Goldenberg DM, Wolf F. The use of monoclonal antibodies and antibody fragments in the imaging of infectious lesions. *Semin Nucl Med* 1994;24:142–153.

Beltran J, Bencardino J, Mellado J, Rosenberg ZS, Irish RD. MR arthrography of the shoulder: variants and pitfalls. *Radiographics* 1997;17:1403–1412.

Bianchi S, Martinoli C, Abdelwahab IF. Ultrasound of tendon tears. Part 1: general considerations and upper extremity. *Skeletal Radiol* 2005; 34:500–512.

Brandt TD, Cardone BW, Grant TH, Post M, Weiss CA. Rotator cuff sonography: a reassessment. *Radiology* 1989;173:323–327.

Breyer RJ III, Mulligan ME, Smith SE, Line BR, Badros AZ. Comparison of imaging with FDG PET/CT with other imaging modalities in myeloma. *Skeletal Radiol* 2006;35:632–640.

Buckwalter KA, Braunstein EM. Digital skeletal radiography. *Am J Roentgenol* 1992;158:1071–1080.

Buckwalter KA, Rydberg J, Kopecky KK, Crow K, Yang EL. Musculoskeletal imaging with multislice CT: Pictorial Essay. *Am J Roentgenol* 2001;176:979–986.

Catana C, Procissi D, Wu Y, et al. Simultaneous *in vivo* positron emission tomography and magnetic resonance imaging. *Proc Natl Acad Sci USA* 2008;105:3705–3710.

Chhem RK, Cardinal E, Cho KH. Skeletal and superficial soft tissues. In: McGahan JP, Goldberg BB, eds. *Diagnostic ultrasound. A logical approach.* Philadelphia: Lippincott-Raven Publishers; 1998:1115–1134.

Datz FL. Indium-111-labeled leukocytes for the detection of infection: current status. *Semin Nucl Med* 1994;24:92–109.

Datz FL, Morton KA. New radiopharmaceuticals for detecting infection. *Invest Radiol* 1993;28:356–365.

Delfaut EM, Beltran J, Johnson G, Rousseal J, Marchandise X, Cotten A. Fat suppression in MR imaging: techniques and pitfalls. *Radiographics* 1999;19:373–382.

Delpassand ES, Garcia JR, Bhadkamkar V, Podoloff DA. Value of SPECT imaging of the thoracolumbar spine in cancer patients. *Clin Nucl Med* 1995;20:1047–1051.

Dewhirst MW, Sostman HD, Leopold KA, et al. Soft-tissue sarcomas: MR imaging and MR spectroscopy for prognosis and therapy monitoring. *Radiology* 1990;174:847–853.

Disler DG, Recht MP, McCauley TR. MR imaging of articular cartilage. *Skeletal Radiol* 2000;29:367–377.

Erlemann R, Reiser MF, Peters PE, et al. Musculoskeletal neoplasms: static and dynamic Gd-DTPA-enhanced MR imaging. *Radiology* 1989;171:767–773.

Erlemann R, Sciuk J, Bosse A, et al. Response of osteosarcoma and Ewing sarcoma to preoperative chemotherapy: assessment with dynamic and static MR imaging and skeletal scintigraphy. *Radiology* 1990;175:791–796.

Errico TJ. The role of diskography in the 1980s. *Radiology* 1989;162:285–286.

Even-Sapir E, Martin RH, Barnes DC, Pringle CR, Iles SE, Mitchell MJ. Role of SPECT in differentiating malignant from benign lesions in the lower thoracic and lumbar vertebrae. *Radiology* 1993;187:193–198.

Fayad LM, Corl F, Fishman EK. Pediatric skeletal trauma: use of multiplanar reformatted and three-dimentional 64-row multidetector CT in the emergency department. *Radiographics* 2009; 29:135–150.

Farooki S, Seeger LL. Magnetic resonance imaging in the evaluation of ligament injuries. *Skeletal Radiol* 1999;28:61–74.

Feldman F, van Heertum R, Manos C. [18]FDG PET scanning of benign and malignant musculoskeletal lesions. *Skeletal Radiol* 2003;32:201–208.

Ferrucci JT. Imaging algorithms for radiologic diagnosis. In: Traveras JM, Ferrucci JT, eds. *Radiology—diagnosis, imaging, intervention,* vol. 1. Philadelphia: JB Lippincott; 1990:1–79.

Fishman EK. Spiral CT evaluation of the musculoskeletal system. In: Fishman EK, Jeffrey RB Jr, eds. *Spiral CT. Principles, techniques, and clinical applications.* Philadelphia: Lippincott-Raven; 1998:273–298.

Fishman EK, Wyatt SH, Bluemke DA, Urban BA. Spiral CT of musculoskeletal pathology: preliminary observations. *Skeletal Radiol* 1993;22:253–256.

Flannigan B, Kursunoglu-Brahme S, Snyder S, Karzel R, Del Pizzo W, Resnick D. MR arthrography of the shoulder: comparison with conventional MR imaging. *Am J Roentgenol* 1990;155:829–832.

Fogelman I, Ryan PJ. Bone scanning in Paget's disease. In: Collier BD Jr, Fogelman I, Rosenthal L, eds. *Skeletal nuclear medicine.* St. Louis: Mosby; 1996:171–181.

Foley WD, Wilson CR. Digital orthopedic radiography: vascular and nonvascular. In: Galasko CSB, Isherwood I, eds. *Imaging techniques in orthopedics.* London: Springer-Verlag; 1989:145–158.

Fox IM, Zeiger L. Tc-99m-HMPAO leukocyte scintigraphy for the diagnosis of osteomyelitis in diabetic foot infections. *J Foot Ankle Surg* 1993;32:591–594.

Freiberger RH, Pavlov H. Knee arthrography. *Radiology* 1988;166:489–492.

Genant HK, Doi K, Mall JC, Sickles EA. Direct radiographic magnification for skeletal radiology: an assessment of image quality and clinical application. *Radiology* 1977;123:47–55.

Gerscovich EO, Cronan MS, Greenspan A, Jain K, McGahan JP. Developmental dysplasia of the hip (DDH): three-dimensional ultrasound evaluation. *Proceedings of the 4th Congress of the International Society for Musculoskeletal Sonography (ISMUS),* Madrid, Spain, 1998:71–74.

Gerscovich EO, Greenspan A, Cronan MS, Karol LA, McGahan JP. Three-dimensional sonographic evaluation of developmental dysplasia of the hip: preliminary findings. *Radiology* 1994;190:407–410.

Goodman PC, Jeffrey RB Jr, Brant-Zawadzki M. Digital subtraction angiography in extremity trauma. *Radiology* 1984;153:61–64.

Greenspan A. Tumors of cartilage origin. *Orthop Clin North Am* 1989; 20:347–366.

Greenspan A. Imaging modalities in orthopaedics. In: Chapman MW, ed. *Chapman's orthopaedic surgery.* 3rd ed. Philadelphia: Lippincott-Williams & Wilkins; 2001:53–74.

Greenspan A, Norman A. The radial head-capitellum view: useful technique in elbow trauma. *Am J Roentgenol* 1982;138:1186–1188.

Greenspan A, Stadalnik RC. A musculoskeletal radiologist's view of nuclear medicine. *Semin Nucl Med* 1997;27:372–385.

Guhlmann A, Brecht Krauss D, Suger G, et al. Fluorine-18-FDG PET and technetium-99m antigranulocyte antibody scintigraphy in chronic osteomyelitis. *J Nucl Med* 1998;39:2145–2152.

Gupta R, Grasruck M, Suess C, et al. Ultra-high resolution flat-panel volume CT: fundamental principles, design architecture, and system characterization. *Eur Radiol* 2006;16:1191–1205.

Harned EM, Mitchell DG, Burk DJ, Vinitski S, Rifkin MD. Bone marrow findings on magnetic resonance images of the knee: accentuation by fat suppression. *Magn Reson Imaging* 1990;8:27–31.

Harvey D. PET/MRI: new fusion. *Radiology Today* 2008;9:20–21.

Heiken JP, Brink JA, Vannier MW. Spiral (helical) CT. *Radiology* 1993;189:647–656.

Helgason JW, Chandnani VP, Yu JS. MR arthrography: a review of current technique and applications. *Am J Roentgenol* 1997;168:1473–1480.

Hodler J. Technical errors in MR arthrography. *Skeletal Radiol* 2008;37:9–18.

Hodler J, Fretz CJ, Terrier F, Gerber C. Rotator cuff tears: correlation of sonographic and surgical findings. *Radiology* 1988;169:791–794.

Holder LE. Bone scintigraphy in skeletal trauma. *Radiol Clin North Am* 1993;31:739–781.

Holl N, Enchaniz-Laguna A, Bierry G, et al. Diffusion-weighted MRI of denervated muscle: a clinical and experimental study. *Skeletal Radiol* 2008;247:797–807.

Hu H, He HD, Foley WD, Fox SH. Four multidetector-row helical CT: image quality and volume coverage speed. *Radiology* 2000;215:55–62.

Hunter JC, Blatz DJ, Escobedo EM. SLAP lesions of the glenoid labrum: CT arthrographic and arthroscopic correlation. *Radiology* 1992;184:513–518.

Johnson RP. The role of bone imaging in orthopedic practice. *Semin Nucl Med* 1997;27:386–389.

Jung H-S, Jee W-H, McCauley TR, Ha K-Y, Choi K-H. Discrimination of metastatic from acute osteoporotic compression spinal fractures with MR imaging. *Radiographics* 2003;23:179–187.

Kapelov SR, Teresi LM, Bradley WG, et al. Bone contusions of the knee: increased lesion detection with fast spin echo imaging with spectroscopic fat saturation. *Radiology* 1993;189:901–904.

Kaplan PA, Matamoros A Jr, Anderson JC. Sonography of the musculoskeletal system. *Am J Roentgenol* 1990;155:237–245.

Kertesz JL, Anderson SW, Murakami AM, Pieroni S, Rhea JT, Soto JA. Detection of vascular injuries in patients with blunt pelvic trauma by using 64-channel multidetector CT. *Radiographics* 2009;29:154–164.

Kijowski R, Blankenbaker DG, Klaers JL, Shinki K, De Smet AA, Block WF. Vastly undersampled isotropic projection steady-state free precession imaging of the knee: diagnostic performance compared with conventional MR. *Radiology* 2009;251:185–194.

King AD, Peters AM, Stuttle AWJ, Lavender JP. Imaging of bone infection with labelled white cells: role of contemporaneous bone marrow imaging. *Eur J Nucl Med* 1990;17:148–151.

König H, Sieper J, Wolf KJ. Rheumatoid arthritis: evaluation of hypervascular and fibrous pannus with dynamic MR imaging enhanced with Gd-DTPA. *Radiology* 1990;176:473–477.

Krinsky G, Rofsky NM, Weinreb JC. Nonspecificity of short inversion time inversion recovery (STIR) as a technique of fat suppression: pitfalls in image interpretation. *Am J Roentgenol* 1996;166:523–526.

Kuszyk BS, Heath DG, Bliss DF, Fishman EK. Skeletal 3-D CT: advantages of volume rendering over surface rendering. *Skeletal Radiol* 1996;25:207–214.

Lang P, Steiger P, Faulkner K, Glüer C, Genant HK. Osteoporosis: current techniques and recent developments in quantitative bone densitometry. *Radiol Clin North Am* 1991;29:49–76.

Lee M-J, Kim S, Lee S-A, et al. Overcoming artifacts from metallic orthopedic implants at high-field-strength MR imaging and multidetector CT. *Radiographics* 2007;27:791–803.

Levinsohn EM, Palmer AK, Coren AB, Zinberg E. Wrist arthrography: the value of the three compartment injection technique. *Skeletal Radiol* 1987;16:539–544.

Love C, Din AS, Tomas MB, Kalapparambath TP, Palestro CJ. Radionuclide bone imaging: an illustrative review. *Radiographics* 2003;23:341–358.

Lund PJ, Nisbet JK, Valencia FG, Ruth JT. Current sonographic applications in orthopedics. *Am J Roentgenol* 1996;166:889–895.

Mao J, Yan H. Fat tissue and fat suppression. *Magn Reson Imaging* 1993;11:385–393.

McCollough CH, Zink FE. Performance evaluation of a multi-slice CT system. *Med Phys* 1999;26:2223–2230.

Meuli RA, Wedeeen VJ, Geller SC, et al. MR gated subtraction angiography: evaluation of lower extremities. *Radiology* 1986;159:411–418.

Murphey MD, Quale JL, Martin NL, Bramble JM, Cook LT, D Wyer SJ III. Computed radiography in musculoskeletal imaging: state of the art. *Am J Roentgenol* 1992;158:19–27.

Murray IPC, Dixon J. The role of single photon emission computed tomography in bone scintigraphy. *Skeletal Radiol* 1989;18:493–505.

Negendank WG, Crowley MG, Ryan JR, Keller NA, Evelhoch JL. Bone and soft-tissue lesions: diagnosis with combined H-1 MR imaging and P-31 MR spectroscopy. *Radiology* 1989;173:181–188.

Omar IM, Zoga AC, Kavanagh EC, et al. Athletic pubalgia and "sports hernia": optimal MR imaging technique and findings. *Radiographics* 2008;28:1415–1438.

Palestro CJ, Torres MA. Radionuclide imaging in orthopedic infections. *Semin Nucl Med* 1997; 27:334–345.

Palestro CJ, Love C, Tronco GG, Tomas MB, Rini JN. Combined labeled leukocyte and technetium 99m sulfur colloid bone marrow imaging for diagnosing musculoskeletal infections. *Radiographics* 2006;26:859–870.

Palestro CJ, Roumanas P, Swyer AJ, Kim CK, Goldsmith SJ. Diagnosis of musculoskeletal infection using combined In-111 labeled leukocyte and Tc-99m SC marrow imaging. *Clin Nucl Med* 1992;17:269–273.

Palmer WE, Caslowitz PL, Chew FS. MR arthrography of the shoulder: normal intraarticular structures and common abnormalities. *Am J Roentgenol* 1995;164:141–146.

Peh WC, Cassar-Pullicino VN. Magnetic resonance arthrography: current status. *Clin Radiol* 1999;54:575–587.

Petersein J, Saini S. Fast MR imaging: technical strategies. *Am J Roentgenol* 1995;165:1105–1109.

Pettersson H, Resnick D. Musculoskeletal imaging. *Radiology* 1998;208:561–562.

Pugh DG, Winkler TN. Scanography of leg-length measurement: an easy satisfactory method. *Radiology* 1966;87:130–133.

Reichardt B, Sarwar A, Bartling SH, et al. Musculoskeletal applications of flat-panel volume CT. *Skeletal Radiol* 2008;37:1069–1076.

Rubin DA. MR imaging of the knee menisci. *Radiol Clin North Am* 1997;35:21–44.

Rubin RH, Fischman AJ, Needleman NM, et al. Radiolabeled, nonspecific, polyclonal human immunoglobulin in the detection of focal inflammation by scintigraphy: comparison with gallium-67 citrate and technetium-99m labeled albumin. *J Nucl Med* 1989;30:385–389.

Saloner DA, Anderson CM, Lee RE. Magnetic resonance angiography. In: Higgins CB, Hricak H, Helms CA, eds. *Magnetic resonance imaging of the body.* 2nd ed. New York: Raven Press; 1992:679–718.

Savelli G, Maffioli L, Maccauro M, De Deckere E, Bombardieri E. Bone scintigraphy and the added value of SPECT (single photon emission tomography) in detecting skeletal lesions. *Q J Nucl Med* 2001;45:27–37.

Schauwecker DS. The scintigraphic diagnosis of osteomyelitis. *Am J Roentgenol* 1992;158:9–18.

Sciuk J, Brandau W, Vollet B, et al. Comparison of technetium 99m polyclonal human immunoglobin and technetium 99m monoclonal antibodies for imaging chronic osteomyelitis: first clinical results. *Eur J Nucl Med* 1991;18:401–407.

Shreve PD, Anzai Y, Whal RL. Pitfalls in oncologic diagnosis with FDG PET imaging: physiologic and benign variants. *Radiographics* 1999;19:61–77.

Sorsdahl OA, Goodhart GL, Williams HT, Hanna LJ, Rodriguez J. Quantitative bone gallium scintigraphy in osteomyelitis. *Skeletal Radiol* 1993;22:239–242.

Sostman HD, Charles HC, Rockwell S, et al. Soft-tissue sarcomas: detection of metabolic heterogeneity with P-31 MR spectroscopy. *Radiology* 1990;176:837–843.

Steinbach LS, Palmer WE, Schweitzer ME. Special focus session. MR arthrography. *Radiographics* 2002;22:1223–1246.

Stumpe KD, Dazzi H, Schaffner A, von Schulthess GK. Infection imaging using whole-body FDG-PET. *Eur J Nucl Med* 2000;27:822–832.

Sundaram M, McLeod RA. MR imaging of tumor and tumorlike lesions of bones and soft tissues. *Am J Roentgenol* 1990;155:817–824.

Swan JS, Grist TM, Sproat IA, Heiner JP, Wiersma SR, Heisey DM. Musculoskeletal neoplasms: preoperative evaluation with MR angiography. *Radiology* 1995;194:519–524.

Tian R, Su M, Tian Y, et al. Dual-time point PET/CT with F-18 FDG for the differentiation of malignant and benign bone lesions. *Skeletal Radiol* 2009;38:451–458.

Yagei B, Manisals M, Yilmaz E, Ekin A, Ozaksoy D, Kovanlikaya I. Indirect MR arthrography of the shoulder in detection of rotator cuff ruptures. *Eur Radiol* 2001;11:258–262.

Yoon LS, Palmer WE, Kassarjian A. Evaluation of radial-sequence imaging in detecting acetabular labral tears at hip MR arthrography. *Skeletal Radiol* 2007;36:1029–1033.

Zoga AC, Kavanagh EC, Omar IM, et al. Athletic pubalgia and the "sport hernia": MR imaging findings. *Radiology* 2008;247:797–807.

Bone Formation and Growth

The skeleton is made of cortical and cancellous bones, which are highly specialized forms of connective tissue. Each type of bony tissue has the same basic histologic structure (Fig. 3.1), but the cortical component has a solid, compact architecture interrupted only by narrow canals containing blood vessels (haversian systems), while the cancellous component consists of trabeculae separated by fatty or hematopoietic marrow. A bone is a rigid calcified material and grows by the addition of new tissues to existing surfaces. The removal of unwanted bones, called *simultaneous remodeling*, is also a necessary component of skeletal growth. Unlike most tissues, a bone grows only by apposition on the surface of an already existing substrate, such as a bone or calcified cartilage. Cartilages, however, grow by interstitial cellular proliferation and matrix formation.

A normal bone is formed through a combination of two processes: *endochondral (enchondral) ossification* and *intramembranous (membranous) ossification*. In general, the spongiosa develops by endochondral ossification and the cortex by intramembranous ossification. Once formed, a living bone is never metabolically at rest. Beginning in the fetal period, it constantly remodels and reappropriates its minerals along lines of mechanical stress. This process continues throughout life, accelerating during infancy and adolescence. The factors controlling bone formation and resorption are still not well understood, but one fact is clear: bone formation and bone resorption are exquisitely balanced, coupled processes that result in net bone formation equaling net bone resorption.

Most of the skeleton is formed by endochondral ossification (Fig. 3.2), a highly organized process that transforms a cartilage to a bone and contributes mainly to increasing the bone length. Endochondral ossification is responsible for the formation of all tubular and flat bones, vertebrae, the base of the skull, the ethmoid, and the medial and lateral ends of the clavicle. For example, at approximately 7 weeks of embryonic life, cartilage cells (chondroblasts and chondrocytes) produce a hyaline cartilage model of the long tubular bones from the condensed mesenchymal aggregate. The mechanisms leading to the calcification of the cartilaginous matrix are not completely understood, but it is generally believed that the promoters of calcification are small membrane-bound vesicles known as matrix vesicles, which are present in the interstitial matrix between the cells. At approximately the 9th week, peripheral capillaries penetrate the model, inducing the formation of osteoblasts. Osseous tissue is then deposited on the spicules of the calcified cartilage matrix that remain after osteoclastic resorption, thereby transforming the primary spongiosa into the secondary spongiosa.

As this process moves rapidly toward the epiphyseal ends of the cartilage model, a loose network of bony trabeculae containing cores of calcified cartilage is left behind, creating a well-defined line of advance. This line represents the growth plate (physis) (Fig. 3.3) and the adjacent metaphysis to which the secondary spongiosa moves as it is formed. The many trabeculae of the secondary spongiosa that are resorbed soon after

FIGURE 3.1 **Composition of bone.** A bone consists ▶ of extracellular matter and cellular component.

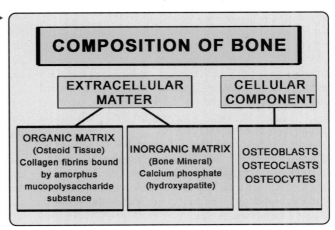

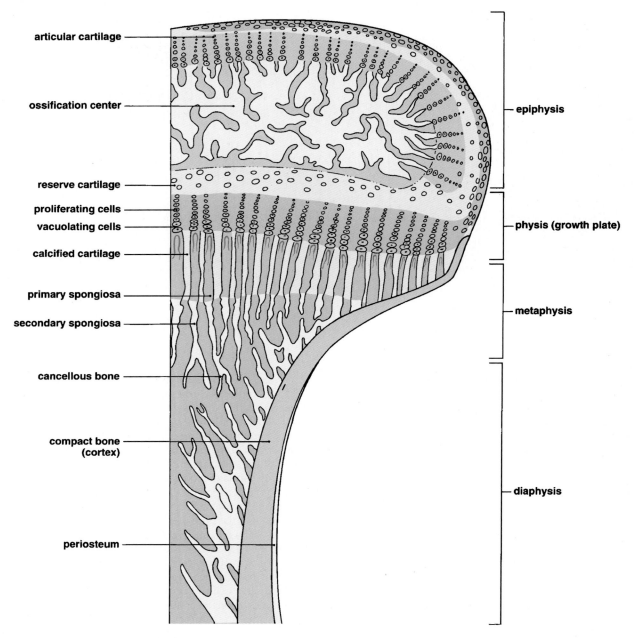

articular cartilage

ossification center

reserve cartilage

proliferating cells

vacuolating cells

calcified cartilage

primary spongiosa

secondary spongiosa

cancellous bone

compact bone
(cortex)

periosteum

epiphysis

physis (growth plate)

metaphysis

diaphysis

▲
FIGURE 3.2   Endochondral bone formation. This process occurs at the ossification center, growth plate, and metaphysis. (Modified from Rubin P, 1964, with permission.)

being formed become the marrow cavity, while other trabeculae enlarge and thicken through the apposition of a new bone, although these too eventually undergo resorption and remodeling. Others extend toward the shaft and become incorporated into the developing cortex of the bone, which is formed by intramembranous ossification. At the ends of tubular bones, a similar process is initiated, creating a secondary ossification center in the epiphysis. This nucleus increases in size by the process of maturation and calcification of the cartilage surrounding the secondary center. The peripheral margin of epiphysis termed acrophysis is formed of zones of cell hypertrophy, degeneration, calcification, and ossification, similar to that of the growth plate. Endochondral bone formation is not normally observed after growth plate closure.

In intramembranous ossification, a bone is formed directly without an intervening cartilaginous stage (Fig. 3.4). Initially, condensed mesenchymal cells differentiate into osteoprogenitor cells, which then differentiate into fibroblasts that produce collagen and fibrous connective tissues and osteoblasts that produce osteoid. Beginning at approximately the 9th week of fetal life, the fibrous membrane produced by the fibroblasts forms a periosteal collar and is replaced with osteoid by the action of the osteoblasts.

Bones formed by this process include the frontal, parietal, and temporal bones and their squamae; bones of the upper face as well as the tympanic parts of the temporal bone; and the vomer and the medial pterygoid.

Intramembranous ossification also contributes to the appositional formation of periosteal bones around the shafts of the tubular bones, thus forming the cortex of the long and flat bones. This type of bone formation increases the bone width. In addition to the periosteal envelope on the outer surface of a bone, intramembranous ossification is active in the endosteal envelope covering the inner surface of the cortex and in the haversian envelope at the internal surface of all intracortical canals. These three envelopes are sites of potent cellular activity involving resorption and formation of bones throughout life.

It is interesting to note that the mandible and middle portions of the clavicle are formed by a process that shares features of endochondral and intramembranous ossification. These bones are preformed in cartilage in embryonic life, but they do not undergo endochondral ossification in the conventional manner. Instead, the cartilage model simply serves as a surface for the deposition of bone by connective tissues. Eventually, the cartilage is resorbed and the bones become fully ossified.

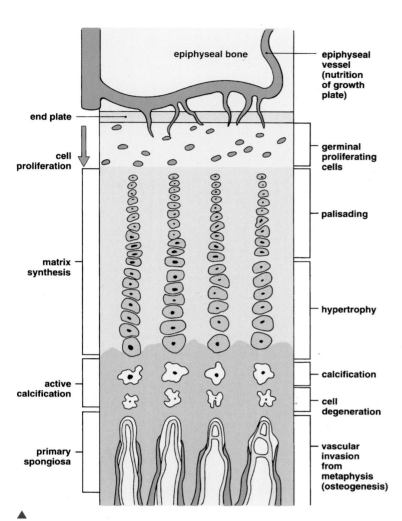

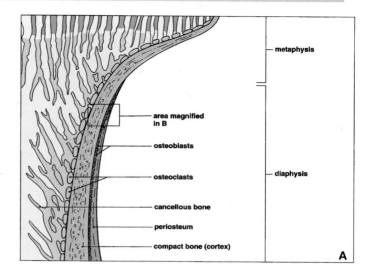

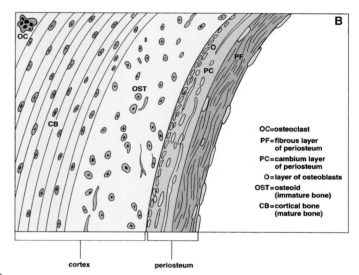

▲
FIGURE 3.3 **Schematic representation of the growth plate.** Growth plate during active bone growth. At the top of the diagram, the epiphyseal vessels are supplying nutrition to the germinal proliferating cells. Further down, the cells begin to palisade into vertical columns, and as they approach the metaphysis, the cells undergo hypertrophy and the matrix calcifies. The calcified matrix is then invaded by blood vessels, and the primary spongiosa forms. (Modified from Bullough PG, 1992, with permission.)

▲
FIGURE 3.4 **Schematic representation of intramembranous ossification.** **(A,B)** Intramembranous bone formation at the junction of the periosteum and the cortex. Subperiosteal bone formation progresses from an immature (woven) to a more mature bone.

SUGGESTED READINGS

Anderson HC. Mechanism of mineral formation in bone. *Lab Invest* 1989;60:320–330.

Aoki J, Yamamoto I, Hino M, et al. Reactive endosteal bone formation. *Skeletal Radiol* 1987;16:545–551.

Bernard GW, Pease DC. An electron microscopic study of initial intramembranous osteogenesis. *Am J Anat* 1969;125:271–290.

Brighton CT. Longitudinal bone growth: the growth plate and its dysfunction. In: Griffin PP, ed. *Instructional course lectures*, vol. 36. Chicago: American Academy of Orthopedic Surgery; 1987:3–25.

Buckwalter JA, Cooper RR. Bone structure and function. In: Griffin PP, ed. *Instructional course lectures*, vol. 36. Chicago: American Academy Orthopedic Surgery; 1987:27–48.

Bullough PG. *Atlas of orthopedic pathology with clinical and radiologic correlations*, 2nd ed. New York: Gower Medical Publishing; 1992:1.2–1.35.

Canalis E, McCarthy T, Centrella M. Growth factors and the regulation of bone remodeling. *J Clin Invest* 1988;81:277–281.

Iannotti JP. Growth plate physiology and pathology. *Orthop Clin North Am* 1990; 21:1–17.

Jaffe HL. *Metabolic, degenerative and inflammatory diseases of bones and joints.* Philadelphia: Lea & Febiger; 1972.

Kirkpatrick JA Jr. Bone and joint growth—normal and in disease. *Clin Rheum Dis* 1981;7:671–688.

Lee WR, Marshall JH, Sissons HA. Calcium accretion and bone formation in dogs. *J Bone Joint Surg Br* 1965;47B:157–180.

Oestreich AE. The acrophysis: a unifying concept for enchondral bone growth and its disorders. *Skeletal Radiol* 2003;32:121–127.

Oestreich AE, Crawford AH. *Atlas of pediatric orthopedic radiology.* Stuttgart: Thieme; 1985:17–18.

Posner AS. The mineral of bone. *Clin Orthop* 1985;200:87–99.

Raisz LG, Kream BE. Regulation of bone formation. *N Engl J Med* 1983;309:83–89.

Reddi AH, Anderson WA. Collagenous bone matrix-induced endochondral ossification and hemopoiesis. *J Cell Biol* 1976;69:557–572.

Reed MH. Normal and abnormal development. In: Reed MH, ed. *Pediatric skeletal radiology.* Baltimore: Williams & Wilkins; 1992:349–392.

Resnick D, Manolagas SC, Niwayama G. Histogenesis, anatomy, and physiology of bone. In: Resnick D, ed. *Bone and joint imaging.* Philadelphia: WB Saunders; 1989:16–28.

Rubin P. *Dynamic Classification of bone dysplasias.* Chicago: Year Book Medical Publishers; 1964:1–23.

Sissons HA. The growth of bone. In: *The biochemistry and physiology of bone*, vol. 3, 2nd ed. New York: Academic Press; 1971.

Sissons HA. Structure and growth of bones and joints. In: Taveras JM, Ferrucci JT, eds. *Radiology, diagnosis-imaging-intervention*, vol. 5. Philadelphia: JB Lippincott; 1986:1–11.

Warshawsky H. Embryology and development of the skeletal system. In: Cruess RL, ed. *The musculoskeletal system. Embryology, biochemistry, physiology.* New York: Churchill Livingstone; 1982.

TRAUMA

Radiologic Evaluation of Trauma

Radiologic Imaging Modalities

The radiologic modalities used in analyzing an injury to the musculoskeletal system are as follows:

1. Conventional radiography, including routine views (specific for various body parts), special views, and stress views
2. Digital radiography, including digital subtraction arthrography (DSa) and angiography (DSA)
3. Fluoroscopy, alone or combined with videotaping
4. Computed tomography (CT)
5. Arthrography, tenography, and bursography
6. Myelography and diskography
7. Angiography (arteriography and venography)
8. Scintigraphy (radionuclide bone scan)
9. Magnetic resonance imaging (MRI).

Radiography and Fluoroscopy

In most instances, radiographs obtained in two orthogonal projections, usually the anteroposterior and lateral, at 90 degrees to each other are sufficient (Fig. 4.1). Occasionally, oblique and special views are necessary, particularly in evaluating fractures of complex structures such as the pelvis, elbow, wrist, and ankle (Figs. 4.2 and 4.3). Stress views are important in evaluating ligamentous tears and joint stability (Fig. 4.4).

Fluoroscopy and videotaping are useful in evaluating the kinematics of joints and fragments. It is also valuable in monitoring the progress of healing.

Computed Tomography

CT is essential in the evaluation of complex fractures, particularly of the spine, pelvis, and scapula, although this modality is useful in the assessment of any fracture near or extending into the joint (Figs. 4.5 to 4.7; see also Figs. 7.13B and 7.14B). The advantage of CT over conventional radiography is its ability to provide excellent contrast resolution and accurate measurement of the tissue attenuation coefficient. The use of sagittal, coronal, and multiplanar reformation (see Figs. 9.29B,C and 9.31A,B) as well as reconstruction to create the 3D CT images (Fig. 4.8; see also Figs. 2.8 to 2.10) provides an added advantage over other imaging modalities.

Scintigraphy

Radionuclide bone scanning can detect occult fractures or fractures too subtle to be seen on conventional radiographs (Fig. 4.9). This technique is also effective in the differentiation of tibial stress fractures from shin splints. Scintigraphy occasionally aids in making a differential diagnosis of old-versus-recent fractures and in detecting such complications as early-stage osteonecrosis. However, bone scans seldom provide new information about the status of fracture healing and, in particular, static bone scans fail to separate normally healing fractures from delayed healing fractures or those that result in nonunion. Also, a bone scan cannot indicate the point at which clinical union is established. Scintigraphy is, however, helpful in distinguishing noninfected fractures from infected ones. With osteomyelitis, scanning, using gallium citrate (^{67}Ga) and indium-labeled white blood cells (^{111}In), demonstrates a significant increase in the uptake of the tracer. Because ^{67}Ga is also actively taken up at the site of a normally healing fracture, but significantly less than that encountered with ^{99m}Tc (technetium) scanning agents, the combination of ^{67}Ga and ^{99m}Tc methylene diphosphonate (MDP) has been suggested, using the ratio of uptake of ^{67}Ga to ^{99m}Tc to determine whether the fracture is infected. The ratio of ^{67}Ga to ^{99m}Tc MDP should be higher in infected fractures than in noninfected fractures. It is very difficult to differentiate pseudoarthrosis from infection at the fracture site. Standard ^{99m}Tc and ^{67}Ga bone scans are not helpful, because both may be positive for both conditions. In these instances, ^{111}In white blood cell scanning combined with ^{99m}Tc MDP scanning appears to be the best method for determining if a fractured or traumatized bone is infected. For more information regarding recent trials of evaluating infected fractures with new radionuclide agents including immunoglobulins, see Chapter 2.

Arthrography

Arthrography is still occasionally used in the evaluation of injuries to articular cartilage, menisci, joint capsules, tendons, and ligaments (Figs. 4.10 and 4.11), although, in general, it has been replaced by MRI and MR arthrography. Although virtually every joint can be injected with a contrast agent, the examination is most frequently performed in the knee, shoulder, ankle, and elbow articulations.

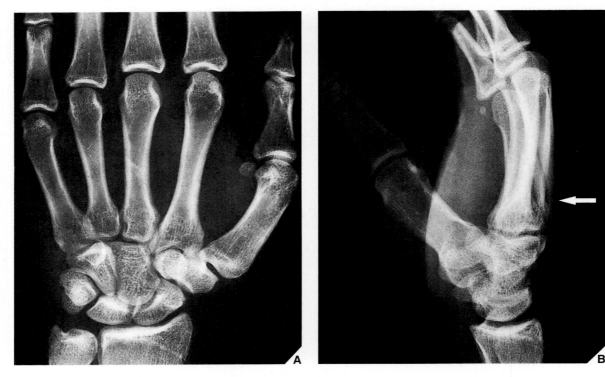

FIGURE 4.1   **Fracture of the metacarpal bone. (A)** Dorsovolar (posteroanterior) view of the hand does not demonstrate a fracture. **(B)** The lateral view reveals a fracture of the third metacarpal bone (*arrow*).

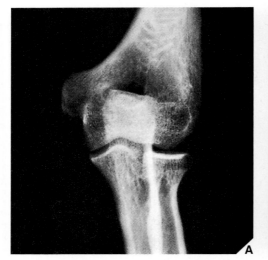

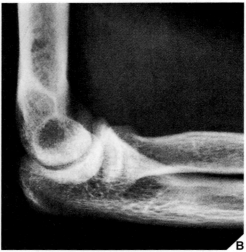

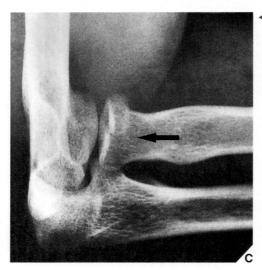

◄ FIGURE 4.2   **Fracture of the radial head.** A patient presented with elbow pain after a fall. Anteroposterior **(A)** and lateral **(B)** views are normal; however, the radial head and coronoid processes are not well demonstrated because of a bony overlap. A special 45-degree angle view of the elbow **(C)** is used to project the radial head ventrad, free of the overlap of other bones. A short, intraarticular fracture of the radial head is now clearly visible (*arrow*).

FIGURE 4.3 **Fracture of the scapula. (A)** Antero-posterior radiograph of the left shoulder shows a fracture of the clavicle. An injury to the scapula is not well demonstrated. **(B)** A special "Y" view of the scapula clearly shows the fracture (*arrow*).

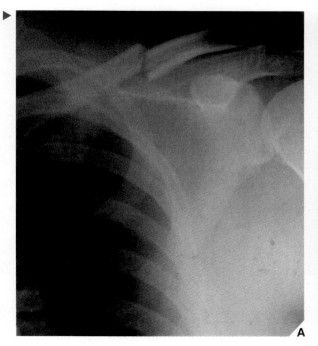
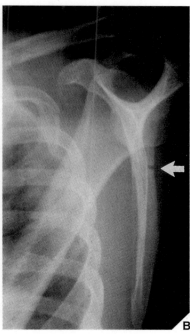

FIGURE 4.4 **Tear of the lateral collateral ligament.** In most ankle injuries, if a ligamentous tear is suspected, then conventional films may be supplemented by stress views. The standard anteroposterior radiograph of this ankle **(A)** is not remarkable. The same view after the application of adduction (inversion) stress **(B)** shows a widening of the lateral compartment of the tibiotalar (ankle) joint, indicating a tear of the lateral collateral ligament.

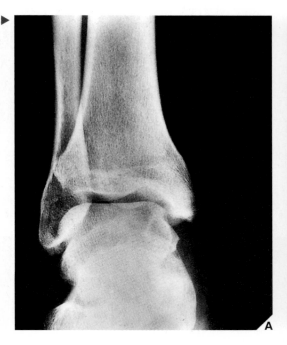
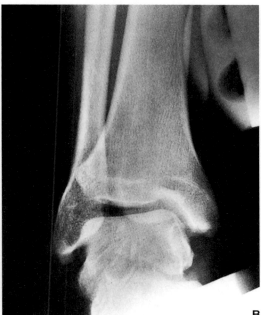

FIGURE 4.5 **Fracture of the vertebra.** Conventional radiographs of the cervical spine (not shown here) were suggestive but not conclusive of a fracture of C7 vertebral body, which is, however, clearly demonstrated on this axial CT image.

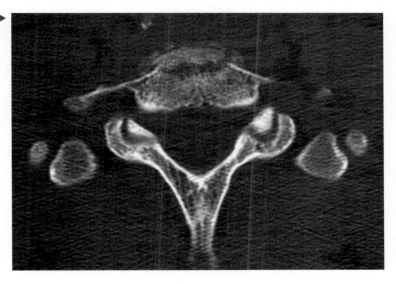

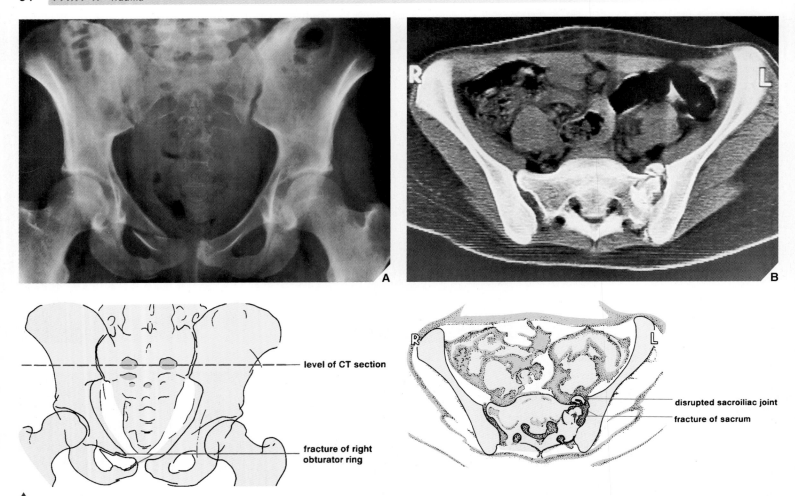

FIGURE 4.6   Fracture of the sacrum. (A) Standard anteroposterior view of the pelvis shows obvious fractures of the right obturator ring. **(B)** CT section demonstrates an unsuspected fracture of the sacrum and disruption of the left sacroiliac joint.

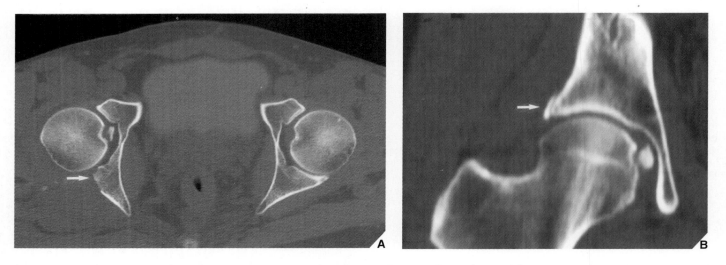

FIGURE 4.7   Fracture of the acetabulum. (A) Axial and **(B)** coronal CT reformatted images show a fractured fragment, unsuspected on conventional radiographs, displaced into the right hip joint. The *arrows* point to the fracture of the posterior column of the right acetabulum.

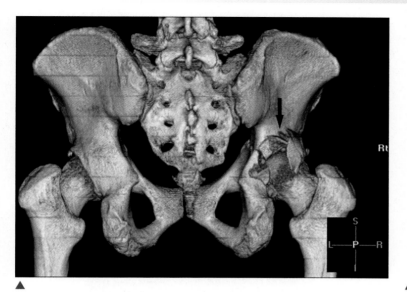

FIGURE 4.8 **Fracture of the acetabulum.** 3D CT reconstructed image shows distinctive features of a fracture of the posterior wall of the right acetabulum (*arrow*).

FIGURE 4.10 **Tear of the medial meniscus.** In this patient, double-contrast arthrography of the knee shows a horizontal cleavage tear in the posterior horn of the medial meniscus (*arrow*).

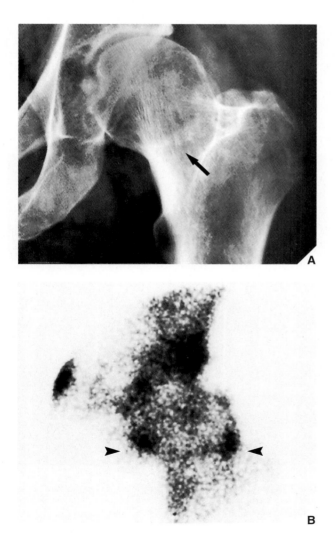

FIGURE 4.9 **Fracture of the femoral neck. (A)** Anteroposterior view of the left hip reveals a band of increased density (*arrow*), suggesting a fracture of the femoral neck. **(B)** A bone scan performed after the administration of 15 mCi (555 MBq) of ⁹⁹mTC-labeled MDP shows increased uptake of isotope in the region of the femoral neck (*arrow* heads), confirming the fracture.

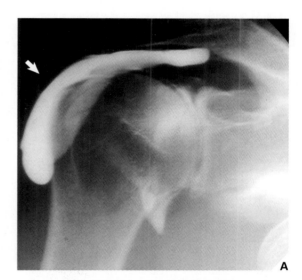

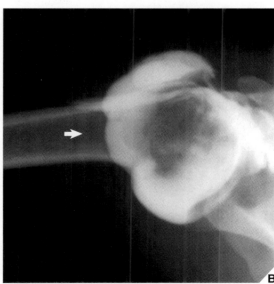

FIGURE 4.11 **Tear of the rotator cuff.** Anteroposterior **(A)** and axillary **(B)** radiographs obtained after single-contrast arthrogram of the right shoulder was performed show a leak of contrast into the subacromial–subdeltoid bursae complex (*arrows*) diagnostic of a full-thickness tear of the supraspinatus tendon.

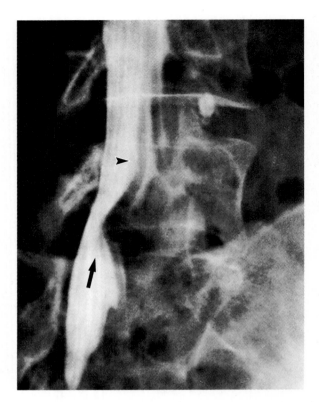

▲
FIGURE 4.12 **Herniation of the lumbar disk.** A patient strained his back by lifting a heavy object. An oblique view of the lower lumbosacral spine after an injection of metrizamide contrast into the subarachnoid space shows an extradural pressure defect on the thecal sac at the L5-S1 intervertebral space (*arrow*) characteristic of disk herniation. Note the markedly swollen, displaced nerve root (*arrow head*).

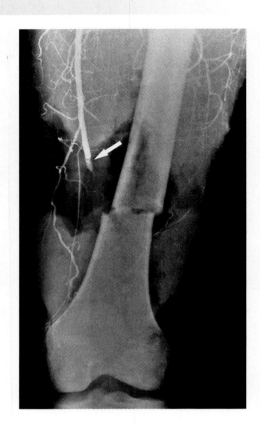

▲
FIGURE 4.14 **Tear of the femoral artery.** A femoral arteriogram was performed to rule out damage to vascular structures by a fractured femur. Transverse fracture of the distal femur resulted in transsection of the superficial femoral artery (*arrow*).

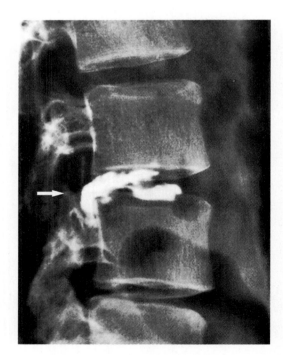

▲
FIGURE 4.13 **Rupture of the annulus fibrosus and disk herniation.** A spinal needle was placed in the center of the nucleus pulposus and a few milliliters of metrizamide were injected. The leak of contrast into the extradural space (*arrow*) indicates a tear of the annulus fibrosus and posterior disk herniation.

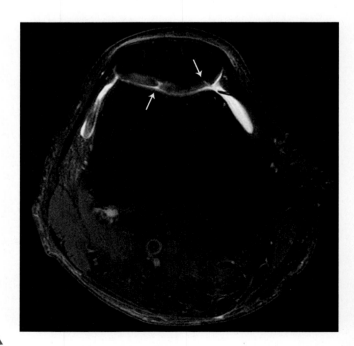

▲
FIGURE 4.15 **Chondral defects.** Axial proton density–weighted fat-saturated MRI of the knee demonstrates subtle defects in the articular cartilage of the right patella (*arrows*).

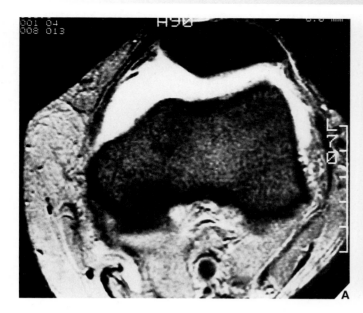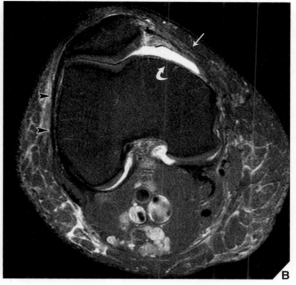

FIGURE 4.16   Joint effusion and a tear of the patellar retinaculum. (A) A 64-year-old man sustained an injury to the left knee. Axial MRI (multiplanar gradient recalled, TR 500/TE 15 msec, flip angle 30 degrees) shows high signal intensity of a posttraumatic effusion. (B) A 33-year-old woman injured her right knee in a ski accident. Axial proton density–weighted fat-suppressed MRI shows a tear of the medial retinaculum of the patella (*arrow*). The lateral retinaculum is intact (*arrow heads*). A *curved arrow* points to posttraumatic joint effusion.

Tenography and Bursography

As already stated in Chapter 2, these procedures at the present time are seldom performed, being replaced by MRI. Tenography used to be done to evaluate the integrity of a tendon, such as peroneus longus and brevis, tibialis anterior and posterior, and flexor digitorum longus. Bursography of the subacromial–subdeltoid bursae complex occasionally demonstrated a partial or full-thickness tear of the rotator cuff.

Myelography and Diskography

Myelography, either alone or in conjunction with CT scan, is used to evaluate certain traumatic conditions of the spine (Fig. 4.12). If a disk abnormality is suspected and a myelographic study is not diagnostic, diskography may yield information required for further patient management (Fig. 4.13).

Angiography

Angiography is indicated if a concomitant injury to the vascular system is suspected (Fig. 4.14). Digital subtraction angiography (DSA) is preferred because subtraction of the overlying bones results in a clear delineation of vascular structures (see Fig. 2.3).

Magnetic Resonance Imaging

MRI plays a leading role in the evaluation of trauma to bone, cartilage, and soft tissue. MRI evaluation of trauma to the knee, particularly abnormalities of the menisci and ligaments, has a high negative predictive value. MRI can be used to screen patients before surgery, so that unnecessary arthroscopies are avoided. MRI is probably the only imaging modality that can demonstrate so-called bone contusions (see Fig. 2.33). These abnormalities consist of posttraumatic marrow change resulting from a combination of hemorrhage, edema, and microtrabecular injury. Meniscal injuries, such as bucket-handle tears, tears of the free edge, and peripheral detachments, can be accurately diagnosed. Other subtle abnormalities of various structures and posttraumatic joint effusion can also be well visualized (Figs. 4.15 and 4.16). Similarly, the medial and lateral collateral ligaments, anterior and posterior cruciate ligaments, and tendons around the knee joint can be well demonstrated (see Figs. 9.13 to 9.15) and abnormalities of these structures can be diagnosed with high accuracy. In the shoulder, impingement syndrome and complete and incomplete rotator cuff tears may be effectively diagnosed most of the time

(Fig. 4.17). Traumatic lesions of the tendons (such as biceps tendon rupture), traumatic joint effusions, and hematomas are easily diagnosed with MRI. Likewise, this modality is effective to diagnose a tear of the cartilaginous labrum. The changes of osteonecrosis at various sites, particularly in its early stage, may be detected by MRI when other modalities, such as conventional radiography and even radionuclide bone scan, may be normal. MRI of the ankle and foot has been used among others in diagnosing tendon ruptures and posttraumatic osteonecrosis of the talus. In the wrist and hand, MRI has been successfully used in the early diagnosis of posttraumatic osteonecrosis of the scaphoid and Kienböck disease. MRI is strongly advocated as the technique of choice in the evaluation of abnormalities of the triangular fibrocartilage complex, although arthrography, particularly in conjunction with digital imaging and CT, is also a very effective modality.

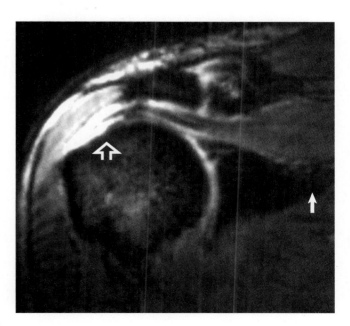

FIGURE 4.17   Tear of the rotator cuff. A 60-year-old man presented with right shoulder pain. Oblique coronal T2-weighted fat-suppressed MRI (SE; TR 2000/TE 80 msec) demonstrates a full-thickness rotator cuff tear. The supraspinatus muscle is retracted medially (*arrow*) and no tendon tissue is present in the subacromial space (*open arrow*).

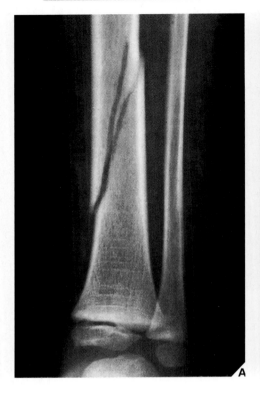

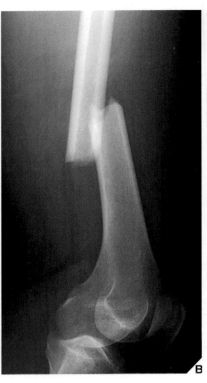

◀ **FIGURE 4.18** **A complete fracture. (A)** The continuity of the bone (tibia) is disrupted and there is a *narrow* gap between the bone fragments. **(B)** A complete fracture of the femur in an adult patient.

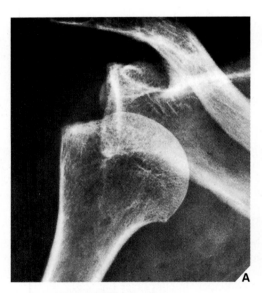

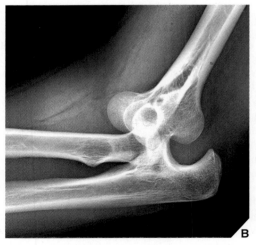

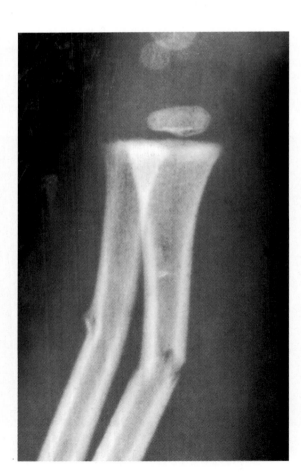

▲

FIGURE 4.19 **An incomplete (greenstick) fracture.** The ulna is bent and there is a fracture line extending only through the posterior cortex. In the fracture of the radius, some trabeculae remain intact.

▲

FIGURE 4.20 **Dislocation. (A)** Typical anterior dislocation of the humeral head. The articular surface of the humerus loses contact with the articular surface of the glenoid. **(B)** Typical posterior dislocation in the elbow joint.

**IMAGING
ADJACENT JOINTS**

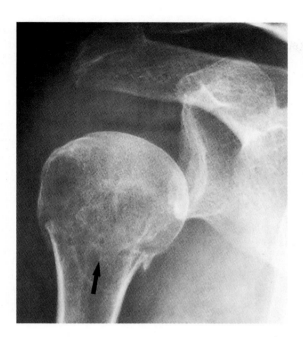

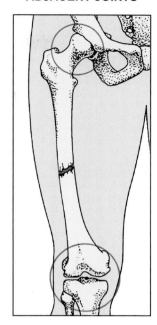

▲
FIGURE 4.21 **Subluxation.** There is malalignment of the head of the humerus and the glenoid fossa, but some articular contact remains. Note the associated fracture of the surgical neck of the humerus (*arrow*).

▲
FIGURE 4.22 **Adjacent joints.** The radiograph of a suspected fracture of the femoral shaft should include the hip and knee articulations.

The greatest use of MRI is for evaluating trauma of the spine, the spinal cord, the thecal sac, and nerve roots, as well as for evaluating disk herniation (see Fig. 11.97). MRI is also useful in the evaluation of spinal ligament injuries. The demonstration of the relationship of vertebral fragments to the spinal cord with direct sagittal imaging is extremely helpful, particularly to evaluate injuries in the cervical and thoracic areas.

Fractures and Dislocations

Fractures and dislocations are among the most common traumatic conditions encountered by radiologists. By definition, a *fracture* is a complete disruption in the continuity of a bone (Fig. 4.18). If only some of the bony trabeculae are completely severed while others are bent or remain intact, the fracture is incomplete (Fig. 4.19). A *dislocation* is a complete disruption of a joint; articular surfaces are no longer in contact (Fig. 4.20). A *subluxation*, however, is a minor disruption of a joint in which some articular contact remains (Fig. 4.21). Proper radiologic evaluation of these conditions contributes greatly to successful treatment by the orthopedic surgeon.

In dealing with trauma, the radiologist has two main tasks:
1. Diagnosing and evaluating the type of fracture or dislocation
2. Monitoring the results of treatment and looking for possible complications

Diagnosis

The important radiographic principle in diagnosing skeletal trauma is to obtain at least two views of the bone involved, with each view including two joints adjacent to the injured bone (Fig. 4.22). In so doing, the radiologist eliminates the risk of missing an associated fracture, subluxation, and/or dislocation at a site remote from the apparent primary injury. In children, it is frequently necessary to obtain a radiograph of the normal, unaffected limb for comparison.

Radiographic Evaluation of Fractures
The complete radiographic evaluation of fractures should include the following elements: (a) the anatomic *site* and *extent* of a fracture

(Fig. 4.23); (b) the *type* of fracture, whether it is incomplete, as seen predominantly in children, or complete (Fig. 4.24); (c) the *alignment* of the fragments with regard to displacement, angulation, rotation, foreshortening, or distraction (Fig. 4.25); (d) the *direction* of the fracture line in relation to the longitudinal axis of the bone (Fig. 4.26); (e) the presence of *special features* such as impaction, depression, or compression (Fig. 4.27); (f) the presence of *associated abnormalities* such as a fracture with concomitant dislocation or diastasis (Fig. 4.28); and (g) *special types* of fractures that may occur as the result of abnormal stress or secondary to pathologic processes in the bone (Fig. 4.29). The distinction between an *open* (or *compound*) fracture, one in which the fractured bone communicates with the outside environment through an

SITE AND EXTENT OF FRACTURE

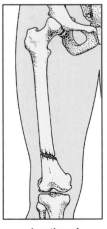

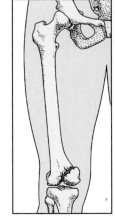

junction of middle and distal thirds of femur   supracondylar   intra-articular

▲
FIGURE 4.23 **Site and extent.** Factors in the radiographic evaluation of a fracture: the anatomic site and extent.

TYPE OF FRACTURE

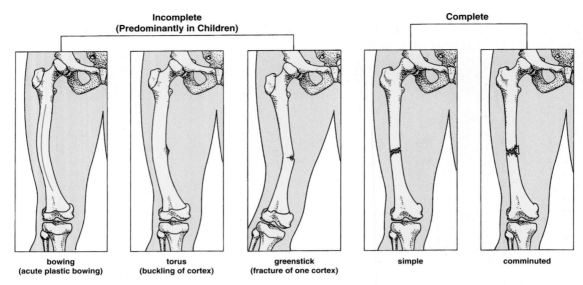

| Incomplete (Predominantly in Children) | | | Complete | |

bowing
(acute plastic bowing)

torus
(buckling of cortex)

greenstick
(fracture of one cortex)

simple

comminuted

▲
FIGURE 4.24   **Incomplete and complete fractures.** Factors in the radiographic evaluation of a fracture: the type of fracture, incomplete or complete.

ALIGNMENT OF FRAGMENTS

◀ FIGURE 4.25   **Alignment.** Factors in the radiographic evaluation of a fracture: the alignment of the fragments.

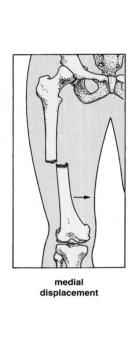 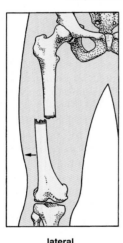 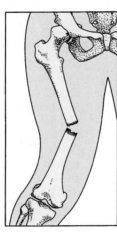 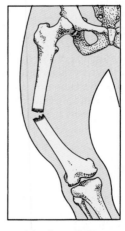

medial
displacement

lateral
displacement

medial angulation
(or lateral
angulation of
distal fragment—
valgus configuration)

lateral angulation
(or medial
angulation of
distal fragment—
varus configuration)

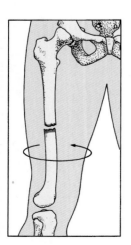 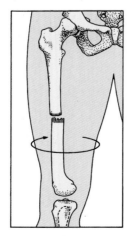 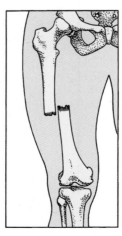 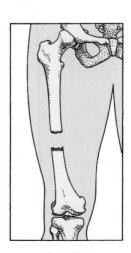

internal rotation

external rotation

overriding with
foreshortening
(bayonet apposition)

distraction

DIRECTION OF FRACTURE LINE

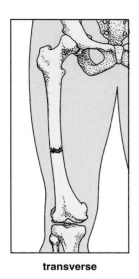 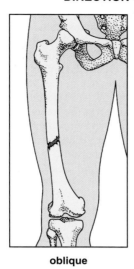 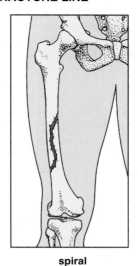 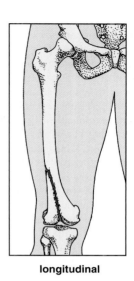

transverse   oblique   spiral   longitudinal

▲ FIGURE 4.26 **Direction.** Factors in the radiographic evaluation of a fracture: the direction of the fracture line.

SPECIAL FEATURES

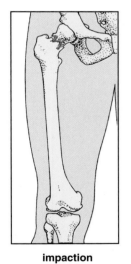 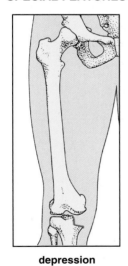 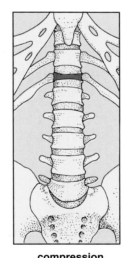

impaction   depression   compression

▲ FIGURE 4.27 **Special features.** Factors in the radiographic evaluation of a fracture: special features.

ASSOCIATED ABNORMALITIES

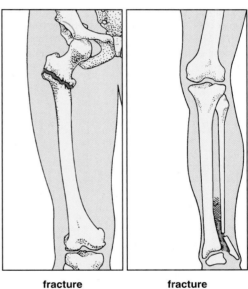

fracture with associated dislocation   fracture with associated diastasis

▲ FIGURE 4.28 **Associated abnormalities.** Factors in the radiographic evaluation of a fracture: associated abnormalities.

FIGURE 4.29 **Special types.** Factors ▶ in the radiographic evaluation of a fracture: special types of fractures.

SPECIAL TYPES OF FRACTURES

Stress   Pathologic

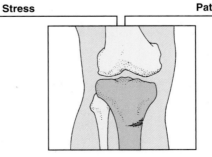 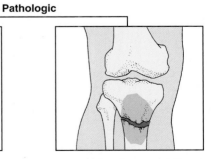

fatigue (normal bone, abnormal stress — e.g., jogging)   insufficiency (abnormal bone – e.g., osteoporotic; normal stress – e.g., walking)   secondary to pre-existing abnormality (usually bone tumor)

open wound, and a *closed* (or *simple*) fracture, one that does not produce an open wound in the skin, should preferably be made by clinical rather than radiographic examination.

In children, the radiographic evaluation of fractures, particularly of the ends of tubular bones, should also take into consideration the involvement of the growth plate (physis). Localization of the fracture line has implications with respect to the mechanism of injury and possible complications. A useful classification of injuries affecting the physis, metaphysis, epiphysis, or all of these structures has been proposed by Salter and Harris (types I to V) and has been expanded by Rang (type VI) and Ogden (types VII to IX) to include four additional types of fractures (Fig. 4.30). Although the injuries described by Rang and Ogden do not directly involve the growth plate, the sequelae of such trauma affect the physis in the same way as the direct injuries described by Salter and Harris. In type VI, which involves only the peripheral region of the growth plate, the injury may not always be associated with a fracture. It may result from a localized contusion, trauma-induced infection, or severe burn. Type VII injury consists of a purely transepiphyseal fracture that, if the epiphysis is not completely ossified, may not even be detectable on the conventional radiograph. Type VIII injury involving the metaphyseal region may be complicated by damage to the blood vessels supplying the growth plate, and in type IX, an injury to the periosteum may interfere with the membranous mechanism of bone formation. All such trauma, but particularly types IV and V (see Fig. 4.72), may lead to growth disturbance with consequent limb-length discrepancy.

Indirect Signs as Diagnostic Clues

Although the diagnosis of most fractures can be made from conventional radiographs, some subtle, nondisplaced, and hairline fractures may not be apparent at the time of injury. In such instances, certain indirect signs of fracture provide useful diagnostic clues.

Soft-Tissue Swelling. Skeletal trauma is always associated with an injury to the soft tissues, and in almost all cases of acute fracture, there is some radiographic evidence of soft-tissue swelling at the fracture site (Fig. 4.31A). The absence of soft-tissue swelling, however, virtually excludes the possibility of an acute fracture (Fig. 4.31B).

Obliteration or Displacement of Fat Stripes. Subtle fractures, particularly in the distal radius, carpal scaphoid, trapezium, and base of the first metacarpal, result in obliteration or displacement of fascial planes. On the lateral view of the wrist, one can detect a radiolucent stripe representing a collection of fat between the pronator quadratus (quadratipronator) and the tendons of the flexor digitorum profundus. A fracture of the distal radius results in a change in the appearance of the *pronator quadratus fat stripe*, which may be anteriorly (volarly) displaced, blurred, or obliterated (MacEwan sign) (Fig. 4.32).

Terry and Ramin have pointed out the usefulness of recognizing the *scaphoid fat stripe*, which is usually visible as a thin radiolucent line paralleling the lateral surface of the scaphoid bone between the radial collateral ligament and the synovial sheath of the abductor pollicis longus and the extensor pollicis brevis. In most fractures of the carpal scaphoid, radial styloid, trapezium, or base of the first metacarpal, the scaphoid fat stripe is obliterated or displaced. This finding is most apparent on the dorsovolar view of the wrist (Fig. 4.33).

Periosteal and Endosteal Reaction. The fracture line may not be visible, but the periosteal or endosteal response may be the first radiographic sign of a fracture (Fig. 4.34).

Joint Effusion. This finding, which results in the radiographic appearance of the fat-pad sign, is particularly useful in diagnosing elbow injuries. The posterior (dorsal) fat pad lies deep in the olecranon fossa and is not visible in the lateral projection. The anterior (ventral) fat pad

INVOLVEMENT OF THE GROWTH PLATE

Salter-Harris Classification

I	II	III	IV	V

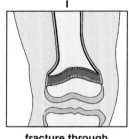 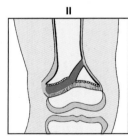 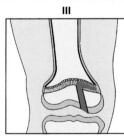 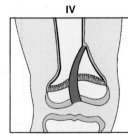 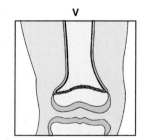

fracture through growth plate	fracture through growth plate and metaphysis	fracture through growth plate and epiphysis	fracture through growth plate, metaphysis, and epiphysis	compression fracture through growth plate

Rang and Ogden Additions to Salter-Harris

VI	VII	VIII	IX

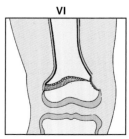 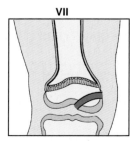 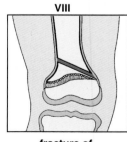 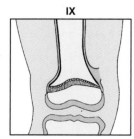

trauma to perichondrium with tethering of growth plate (peripheral bridge)	trauma to epiphysis (chondral or osteochondral fracture)	fracture of metaphysis	avulsion injury to periosteum

▲

FIGURE 4.30   **Classification of the growth plate injuries.** The Salter-Harris classification of injuries involving the growth plate (physis) together with Rang and Ogden additions.

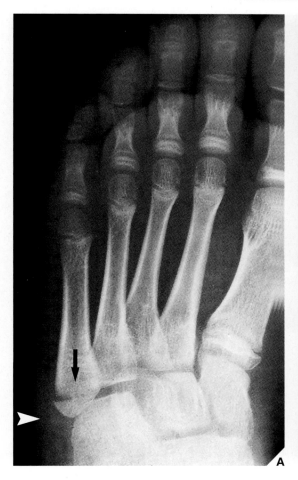
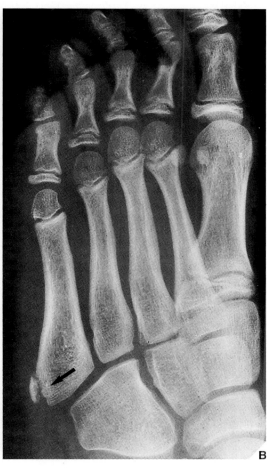

FIGURE 4.31 **Fracture versus ossification center. (A)** Dorsoplantar view of the foot reveals prominent soft-tissue swelling localized in the lateral aspect (*arrow head*). The radiolucent line at the base of the fifth metatarsal indicates a fracture (*arrow*). **(B)** A similar radiolucent line (*arrow*) separates a bone fragment from the base of the fifth metatarsal in another patient who was suspected of sustaining a fracture of this bone. Note the complete lack of soft-tissue swelling. The finding represents a secondary ossification center, not a fracture.

FIGURE 4.32 **Pronator quadratus fat stripe. (A)** The fascial plane of the pronator quadratus is demonstrated on the volar aspect of the distal forearm as a radiolucent stripe. **(B)** With a fracture of the distal radius, the fat stripe is blurred and volarly displaced (*arrow*) secondary to local edema and periosteal hemorrhage. A *short black arrow* points to the subtle nondisplaced fracture of the distal radius.

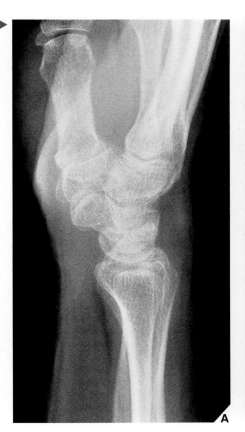
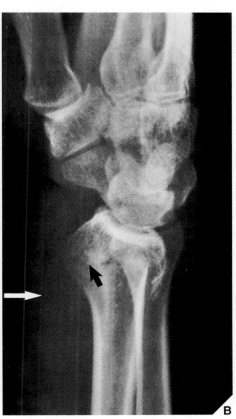

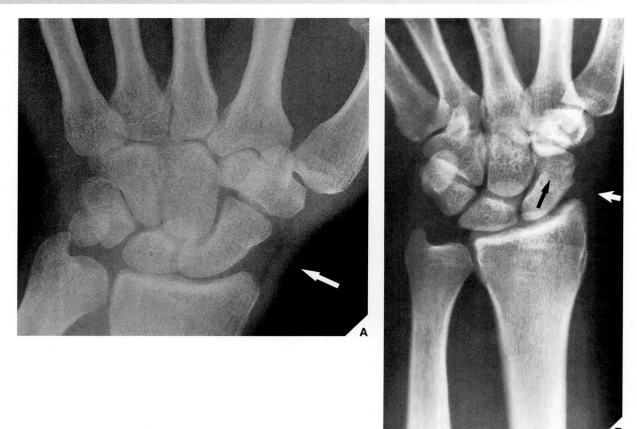

▲

FIGURE 4.33 **Scaphoid fat stripe. (A)** Normal scaphoid fat stripe (*arrow*). **(B)** A subtle fracture of the scaphoid (*arrow*) resulted in obliteration and radial displacement of the fat stripe (*white arrow*).

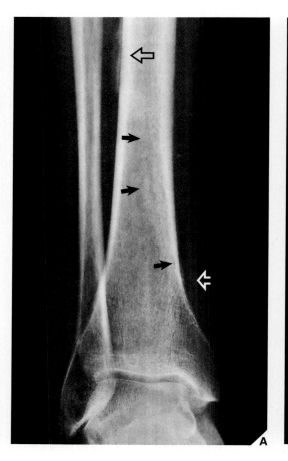 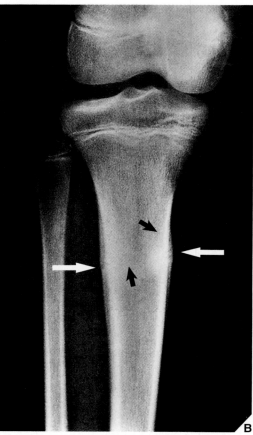

◀ FIGURE 4.34 **Secondary signs of a fracture. (A)** A 49-year-old woman sustained an injury to the lower leg. Anteroposterior radiograph shows periosteal new bone at the medial cortex of the distal third of the tibia just above the malleolus and more proximally at the lateral aspect (*open arrows*). This indirect sign of a fracture represents an early stage of external callus formation. The actual hairline spiral fracture line is barely discernible (*black arrows*). **(B)** An example of periosteal callus formation at the medial and lateral cortices of the proximal tibial diaphysis (*arrows*). A transverse band of increased density, visible in the medullary portion of the bone (*black arrows*), represents endosteal callus. The fracture line is practically invisible. These features are commonly seen in a stress fracture.

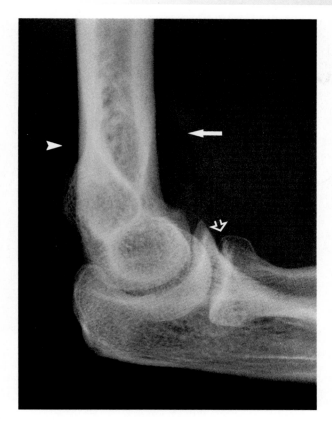

▲
FIGURE 4.35 **Fracture of the radial head.** Lateral view of the elbow shows a positive fat-pad sign. The anterior fat pad is markedly elevated (*arrow*) and the posterior fat pad (*arrow head*) is clearly visible in this patient. There is a subtle, nondisplaced fracture of the radial head (*open arrow*).

occupies the shallower anterior coronoid and radial fossae and is usually seen as a flat radiolucent strip ventrad to the anterior cortex of the humerus. Distention of the articular capsule by synovial or hemorrhagic fluid causes the posterior fat pad to become visible and also displaces the anterior fat pad, yielding the *fat-pad sign* (Fig. 4.35). When there is a history of elbow trauma and the fat-pad sign is positive, there is usually an associated fracture and every effort should be made to demonstrate it. Even if the fracture line is not demonstrated on multiple films, the patient should be treated for fracture.

Intracapsular Fat–Fluid Level. If a fracture involves the articular end of a bone (particularly a long bone such as the tibia, humerus, or femur), blood and bone-marrow fat enter the joint (lipohemarthrosis) and produce a characteristic layering of these two substances on the radiograph: the fat–blood interface, or *FBI sign* (Fig. 4.36). A CT or MRI study can also demonstrate this phenomenon (Figs. 4.37 and 4.38). When the fracture line cannot be demonstrated, the diagnosis should be made on the strength of this sign alone.

Double Cortical Line. This finding indicates a subtle but depressed fracture. The actual fracture line may not be apparent, but the double contour of the cortex reflects impaction (Fig. 4.39).

Buckling of the Cortex. Known as the *torus fracture*, this may be the only sign of a tubular bone fracture in children (Fig. 4.40). This finding is sometimes identified more easily on the lateral than on the frontal projection.

Irregular Metaphyseal Corners. This sign, which is secondary to small avulsion fractures of the metaphysis, indicates a subtle injury to the bone caused by a rapid rotary force exerted on the ligaments' insertion. As a result, small fragments of bone are separated from the metaphysis. These *corner fractures* are often present in infants and children who sustain skeletal trauma, and they should be looked for particularly if battered child syndrome, also known as "shaken baby syndrome" or parent–infant trauma syndrome (PITS), is suspected (Fig. 4.41).

Radiographic Evaluation of Dislocations

Dislocations are more obvious than fractures on conventional radiographs and, consequently, are more easily diagnosed (Fig. 4.42). Some display such a characteristic appearance on frontal projection (anteroposterior view) that this single examination suffices (Fig. 4.42C). However, the same principle of obtaining at least two projections oriented at 90 degrees to each other should apply. Supplemental radiographs are occasionally necessary, and in some instances, CT is required for the exact evaluation of a dislocation.

Monitoring the Results of Treatment

Radiography plays the leading role in monitoring the progress of fracture healing and in detecting any posttraumatic complications. Follow-up radiographs should be taken at regular intervals to evaluate the stage and possible associated complications of fracture healing and other complications that may follow a fracture or dislocation. If radiographs are ambiguous in this respect, CT is the next technique to apply.

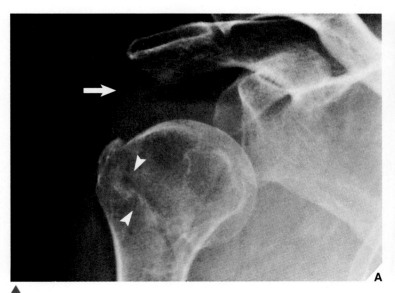
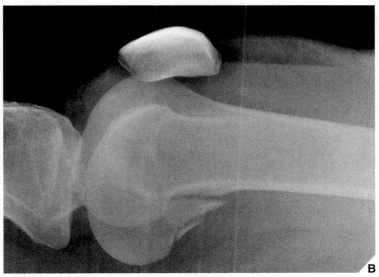

▲
FIGURE 4.36 **Fat–blood interface sign. (A)** Erect anteroposterior view of the shoulder demonstrates the fat–fluid level in the joint (*arrow*), an example of the FBI sign. The fracture line extends from the humeral neck cephalad to the greater tuberosity (*arrow heads*). To demonstrate the FBI sign, the cassette should be positioned perpendicular to the expected fat–fluid level with the central ray directed horizontally. For example, in the shoulder, an upright radiograph (patient standing or sitting) should be obtained. In the knee **(B)**, the patient must be supine and a cross-table lateral view should be performed.

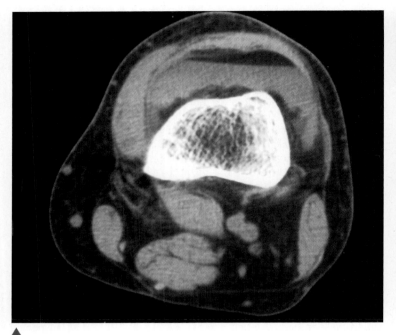

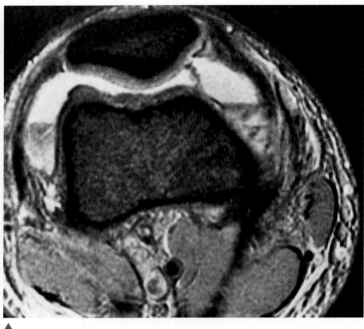

▲
FIGURE 4.37   **FBI sign on CT.** Axial CT section through the knee joint shows an FBI sign in a patient with tibial plateau fracture (not seen on this image).

▲
FIGURE 4.38   **FBI sign on MRI.** Axial MR image of the knee with the patient in the supine position demonstrates an FBI sign secondary to differential layering of fat mixed with fluid (high signal intensity) and blood (intermediate signal intensity). Note the heterogeneous appearance of blood caused by partial clotting.

Fracture Healing and Complications

The healing of a fracture can be divided into three phases: inflammatory (reactive), reparative, and remodeling. The *inflammatory phase* is characterized by vasodilatation, serum exudation, and infiltration by inflammatory cells. It lasts about two to seven days. The *reparative phase* is characterized by the formation of periosteal and endosteal (medullary) calluses by the periosteal and bone marrow osteoblasts. Mesenchymal cell proliferation and differentiation are accompanied by intense vascular proliferation. The resulting osteoblasts produce collagen at a high rate. This phase lasts about a month. The *remodeling phase* is characterized by both modeling and remodeling at the site of

a fracture to restore the original contours of the bone and its optimal internal structure. The endosteal and periosteal calluses are removed, and the woven immature bone is replaced by a secondary lamellar (cortical or trabecular) bone. If the fracture, particularly in the growing skeleton, has healed with incorrect angulation (malunion), this may be corrected by selectively removing bone from the convex side of the cortex by the process of osteoclastic resorption and adding bone to the concave side by the process of osteoblastic apposition. This phase may last from about three months to one year, or even longer.

Fracture healing depends on many factors: the patient's age, the site and type of fracture, the position of the fragments, the status of the blood

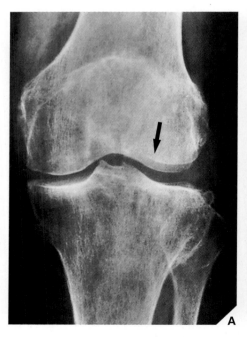

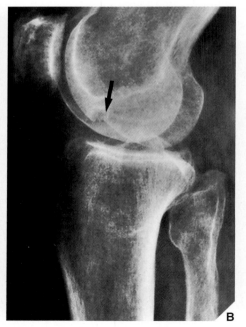

▲
FIGURE 4.39   **Fracture of the femur. (A)** On the anteroposterior view of the knee, the fracture line is not apparent, but a depressed articular cortex of the lateral femoral condyle projects proximally to the normal subchondral line of the intact segment, producing a double cortical line (*arrow*). **(B)** Lateral radiograph confirms the presence of a depressed fracture of the femoral condyle (*arrow*).

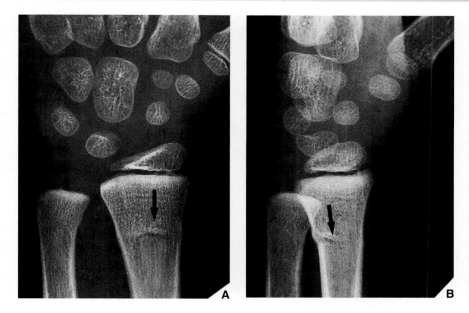

▲
FIGURE 4.40   Torus fracture. Posteroanterior **(A)** and lateral **(B)** radiographs of the distal forearm demonstrate buckling of the dorsal cortex of the diaphysis of the distal radius (*arrows*). This represents an incomplete torus fracture. Note that the lateral view is more revealing.

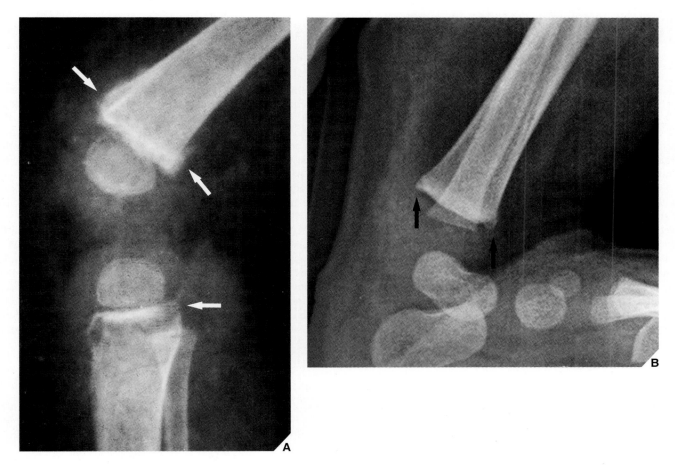

▲
FIGURE 4.41   Battered child syndrome. (A) Lateral view of the knee reveals irregular outlines of the metaphyses of the distal femur and the proximal tibia and subtle corner fractures (*arrows*) characteristic of the battered child syndrome. **(B)** In another infant, metaphyseal corner fractures are identified in the distal tibia (*arrows*).

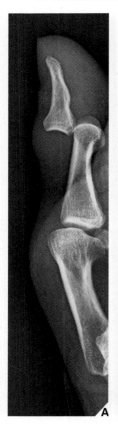

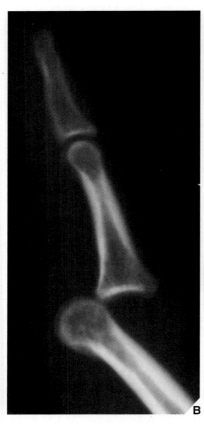

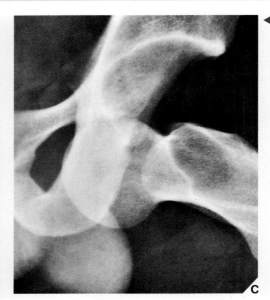

FIGURE 4.42   Dislocations. (A) Lateral radiograph of the thumb shows a dislocation in the interphalangeal joint. (B) Lateral radiograph shows a dislocation in the proximal interphalangeal joint of the index finger. (C) Anteroposterior radiograph of the left hip shows a typical anterior dislocation of the femoral head. The clue to this diagnosis is the presence of abduction and external rotation of the femur and the position of the femoral head, which is medial and inferior to the acetabulum.

supply, the quality of immobilization or fixation, and the presence or absence of associated abnormalities such as infection or osteonecrosis (Table 4.1). An average healing time of some fractures is depicted in Table 4.2. Most fractures heal by some combination of endosteal and periosteal callus. Provided that blood supply is adequate, undisplaced fractures and anatomically reduced fractures immobilized with adequate compression heal by *primary union*. In this type of healing, the fracture line becomes obliterated by endosteal (internal) callus. Displaced fractures, that is, those that are not anatomically aligned or with a gap between fragments, heal by *secondary union*. This type of healing is achieved mainly by excessive periosteal (external) callus, which undergoes full ossification through the stages of granulation tissue, fibrous tissue, fibrocartilage, woven bone, and compact bone. For the radiologist evaluating follow-up radiographs, the primary indication of bone repair is radiographic evidence of periosteal (external) and endosteal (internal) callus formation (Fig. 4.43). This process, however, may not be radiographically apparent in the early stage of healing. Periosteal response may not be visible on radiographs at sites where there is an

anatomic lack of periosteum, for example, in the intracapsular portion of the femoral neck. Likewise, radiographs may not demonstrate endosteal callus formation, because the callus contains only fibrous tissue and cartilage, which are radiolucent. At this early stage of healing, a fracture may be *clinically united*, that is, show no evidence of motion under stress, yet radiographically, the radiolucent band between the fragments may persist (Fig. 4.44A). As the primary temporarily radiolucent callus is gradually converted by the process of endochondral ossification to more mature lamellar bone, it is seen on the film as a dense bridge (Fig. 4.44B). This constitutes *radiographic union*.

Although conventional radiographs are frequently sufficient to evaluate the progress of fracture healing, routine studies must, at times, be supplemented by CT. This modality with multiplanar reformation proves to be a good method to assess fracture healing. It is, in particular, effective in patients with remaining metallic hardware and those who had multiple surgical procedures including bone grafting. CT with reformation in the coronal and sagittal planes supplemented with 3D reconstruction aids surgical planning by providing a more detailed assessment of

TABLE 4.1   **Factors Influencing Fracture Healing**

Promoting	Retarding
Good immobilization	Motion
Growth hormone	Corticosteroids
Thyroid hormone	Anticoagulants
Calcitonin	Anemia
Insulin	Radiation
Vitamins A and D	Poor blood supply
Hyaluronidase	Infection
Electric currents	Osteoporosis
Oxygen	Osteonecrosis
Physical exercise	Comminution
Young age	Old age

TABLE 4.2   **Fracture Healing**

Bone	Average Healing Time (Weeks)
Metacarpal	4–6
Metatarsal	4–8
Distal radius (extraarticular)	6–8
Distal radius (intraarticular)	6–10
Humeral shaft	12
Femoral shaft	12
Radius and ulnar shaft	16
Tibial shaft	16–24
Femoral neck	24

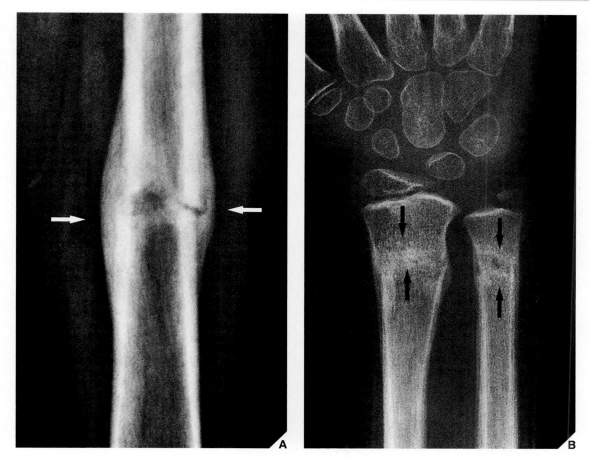

▲
FIGURE 4.43   **Fracture healing. (A)** Anteroposterior radiograph of the femur shows a fracture healing predominantly by periosteal callus formation (*arrows*). There is no radiographic evidence of endosteal callus, and the fracture line is still visible. **(B)** Posteroanterior radiograph of the distal forearm demonstrates healing fractures of the radius and ulna. The fracture lines are almost completely obliterated secondary to the formation of endosteal callus (*arrows*). Note also the minimal amount of periosteal callus.

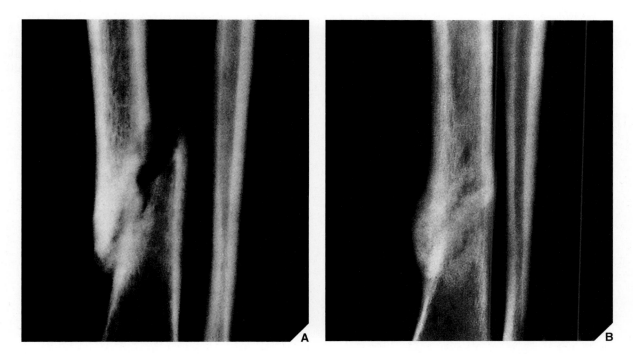

▲
FIGURE 4.44   **Clinical versus radiographic union.** A 30-year-old woman sustained a fracture of the distal third of the tibia. **(A)** After 3 months of immobilization, the plaster cast was removed. The radiograph shows a unilateral periosteal callus from the medial aspect, but the fracture line is still clearly visible. Clinically, however, this fracture was fully united and the patient was allowed to bear weight without a cast. **(B)** One and a half months later, there is evidence of a dense bridge of periosteal and endosteal callus, indicating radiographic union.

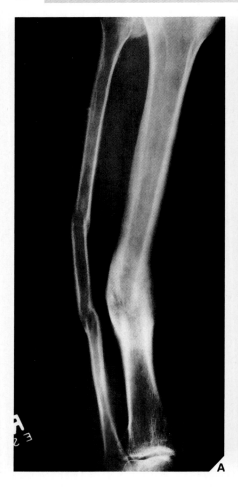
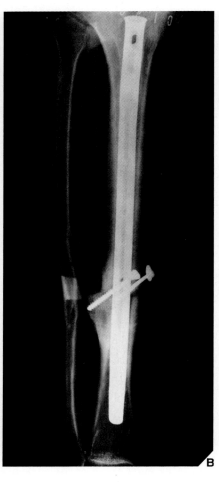

◄ **FIGURE 4.45** **Malunion. (A)** Anteroposterior radiograph of the leg demonstrates angular malunion. The fracture of the tibia and the segmental fracture of the fibula are solidly united. The distal part of the tibia, however, shows rotation and anterior angulation, and the fractures of the fibula have joined in a bowing deformity. **(B)** The malunion was surgically treated by double osteotomy and internal fixation of the tibia with an intramedullary rod to correct the longitudinal alignment and restore the anatomic axis.

malalignment and angular deformities, the magnitude of the gap in the bone, and the integrity of the adjacent weight-bearing joints.

In addition to monitoring the progress of callus formation, the radiologist should be aware of radiographic evidence of associated complications of the healing process. These complications are delayed union, nonunion, and malunion. Of the three, *malunion* is the most apparent radiographically and is characterized by a union of the bone fragments in a faulty and unacceptable position (Fig. 4.45); surgical intervention is usually the preferred method of treatment in this case.

Delayed union refers to a fracture that does not unite within a reasonable amount of time (16 to 24 weeks), depending on the patient's age and the fracture site. *Nonunion*, however, applies to a fracture that simply fails to unite (Fig. 4.46). Some of the causes of nonunion are listed in Table 4.3. A *pseudoarthrosis* is a variant of nonunion in which there is formation of a false joint cavity with a synovial-like capsule and even synovial fluid at the fracture site; however, some physicians refer to any fracture that fails to heal within 9 months as a pseudoarthrosis and use the term as a synonym for nonunion. Radiographically, nonunion is

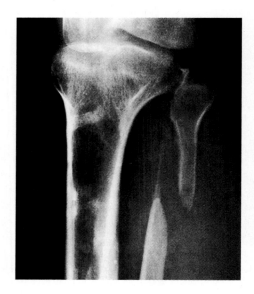

▲
FIGURE 4.46 **Nonunion.** A fracture of the proximal fibula failed to unite. Note the gap between the fragments, the complete lack of callus formation, and the rounding of the fragment edges.

TABLE 4.3 **Causes of Nonunion**

  I. ***Excess motion (inadequate immobilization)***
 II. ***Gap between fragments***
   A. Soft-tissue interposition
   B. Distraction by traction or hardware
   C. Malposition, overriding, or displacement of fragments
   D. Loss of bone substance

III. ***Loss of blood supply***
   A. Damage to nutrient vessels
   B. Excessive stripping or injury to periosteum and muscle
   C. Free fragments, severe comminution
   D. Avascularity caused by hardware placement
   E. Osteonecrosis

IV. ***Infection***
   A. Osteomyelitis
   B. Extensive necrosis of fracture margins (gap)
   C. Bone death (sequestrum)
   D. Osteolysis (gap)
   E. Loosening of implants (motion)

Modified from Rosen H, 1993, with permission.

TYPES OF NONUNION

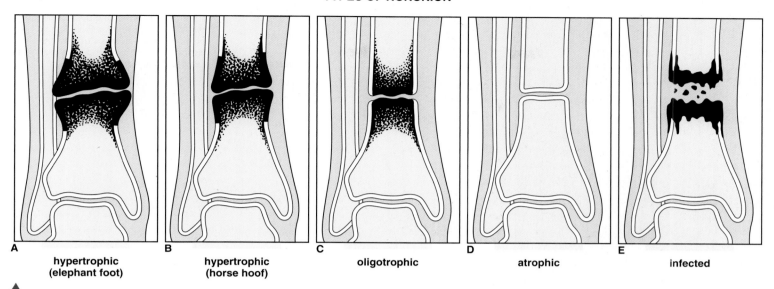

A hypertrophic (elephant foot)	**B** hypertrophic (horse hoof)	**C** oligotrophic	**D** atrophic	**E** infected

FIGURE 4.47   **Complications of a fracture.** Types of nonunion: reactive **(A–C)**; nonreactive **(D)**; infected **(E)**.

characterized by rounded edges; smoothness and sclerosis (eburnation) of the fragment ends, which are separated by a gap; and motion between the fragments (demonstrated under fluoroscopy or on consecutive stress films). To provide adequate evaluation of healing failure, the radiologist needs to distinguish between the three types of nonunion: reactive, nonreactive, and infected (Fig. 4.47).

Reactive (Hypertrophic and Oligotrophic) Nonunion. Radiographically, this type of nonunion is characterized by exuberant bone reaction and resultant flaring and sclerosis of bone ends, the

elephant-foot or horse-hoof type (Fig. 4.48). The sclerotic areas do not represent dead bones but the apposition of well-vascularized new bones. Radionuclide bone scan shows a marked increase of isotope uptake at the fracture site. This type of nonunited fracture is usually treated by intramedullary nailing or compression plating.

Nonreactive (Atrophic) Nonunion. With this type of nonunion, the radiograph shows an absence of bone reaction at the fragment ends, and the blood supply is generally very scanty (Fig. 4.49). A bone scan shows either minimal or no isotope uptake. In addition to stable internal fixation, such fractures often require extensive decortication and bone grafting.

Infected Nonunion. Radiographic presentation of infected nonunion depends on the infection's activity. Old, *inactive* osteomyelitis shows irregular thickening of the cortex, well-organized periosteal reaction, and reactive sclerosis of cancellous bone (Fig. 4.50), whereas the *active*

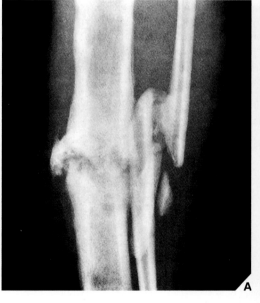

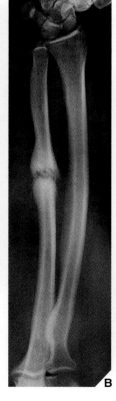

FIGURE 4.48   **Reactive nonunion. (A)** In hypertrophic nonunion, seen here in the shafts of the tibia and fibula, there is flaring of the bone ends, marked sclerosis, and periosteal response, but no evidence of endosteal callus formation. The gap between the bone fragments persists. **(B)** Similar hypertrophic nonunion is present in the shaft of the ulna.

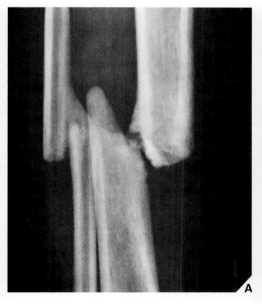

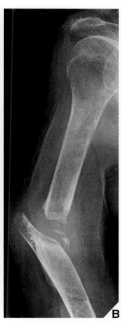

FIGURE 4.49   **Nonreactive nonunion. (A)** In atrophic nonunion, seen here at the junction of the middle and distal thirds of the tibia, there is a gap between the fragments, rounding of the edges, and an almost complete lack of bone reaction. Note the malunited fracture of the fibula. **(B)** Atrophic nonunion of the fracture of the right humerus.

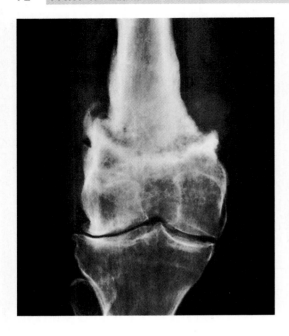

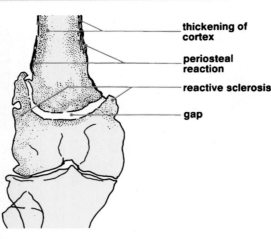

thickening of
cortex

periosteal
reaction

reactive sclerosis

gap

◀ FIGURE 4.50 **Infected nonunion.** Non-union of the fractured distal shaft of the femur with evidence of old, inactive osteomyelitis shows irregular thickening of the cortex, reactive sclerosis of the medullary portion of the bone, and well-organized periosteal reaction.

form shows soft-tissue swelling, destruction of the cortex and cancellous bone associated with periosteal new bone formation, and sequestration (Fig. 4.51). Treatment of infected nonunion depends on the stage of osteomyelitis. Decortication and bone grafting combined with compression plating are used if nonunion is accompanied by inactive osteomyelitis. Treatment of active osteomyelitis involves the application of antibiotics and sequestrectomy, usually followed by bone grafting and intramedullary stabilization. Different procedures are individually tailored, depending on the anatomic site and various general and local factors.

Other Complications of Fractures and Dislocations

In addition to the possible complications associated with the process of fracture healing, the radiologist may encounter complications that are not related to that process. Radiographic evidence of the presence of such complications may not show up on immediate follow-up examination, because they may occur weeks, months, or even years after the trauma and sometimes in a location distant from the original site of injury. Consequently, in dealing with patients presenting with a history of fracture or dislocation, radiologists should direct their investigation to areas where these associated complications may occur and should be aware of their radiologic characteristics and appearance.

Disuse Osteoporosis. Mild or moderate osteoporosis, which can be generally defined as a decrease in bone mass, frequently occurs after a fracture or dislocation as a result of disuse of the extremity caused by pain and immobilization in the plaster cast. Other terms often used to describe this condition are demineralization, deossification, bone atrophy, and osteopenia. The latter term is generally accepted as the best description of the nature of this complication. Radiographically, it is identified by radiolucent areas of decreased bone density secondary to thinning of the cortex and atrophy of the bone trabeculae. It may accompany united as well as nonunited fractures (Fig. 4.52).

Reflex Sympathetic Dystrophy Syndrome. Known also as posttraumatic painful osteoporosis, complex regional pain syndrome (CRPS), or Sudeck atrophy, reflex sympathetic dystrophy syndrome (RSDS), a severe form of osteoporosis, may occur subsequent to a fracture or even a milder form of injury. It has also been reported as resulting from neurologic or vascular abnormalities unrelated to trauma. Clinically, the patient presents with a painful, tender extremity with hyperesthesia, diffuse soft-tissue swelling, joint stiffness, vasomotor instability, and dystrophic skin changes. Three stages have been identified. The initial (or acute) inflammatory stage lasts from 1 to 7 weeks and is characterized by diffuse regional pain, inflammation, edema, and hypothermia or

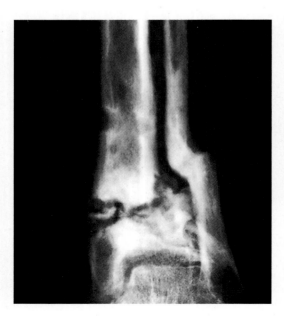

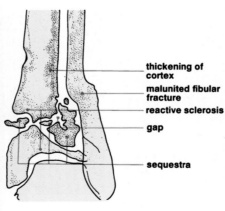

thickening of
cortex

malunited fibular
fracture

reactive sclerosis

gap

sequestra

◀ FIGURE 4.51 **Infected nonunion.** A radiograph of a nonunited fracture in the distal shaft of the tibia with associated active osteomyelitis shows thickening of the cortex, sclerosis of the cancellous bone, a gap between the bony fragments, and several sequestra.

FIGURE 4.52 **Disuse osteoporosis. (A)** An ▶
oblique radiograph of the ankle shows a
completely united fracture of the distal fibula
(*arrow*). Disuse juxta-articular osteoporosis
is evident from the thinning of the cortices
associated with decreased bone density.
(B) Anteroposterior radiograph of the knee
shows a nonunited fracture of the tibial
plateau, with a moderate degree of disuse
osteoporosis.

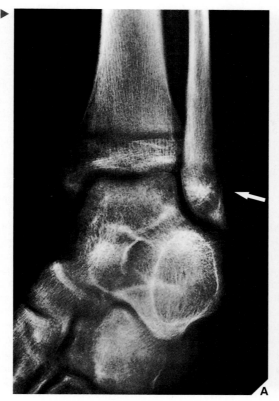
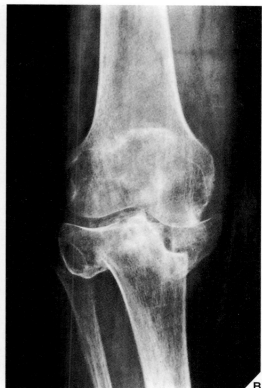

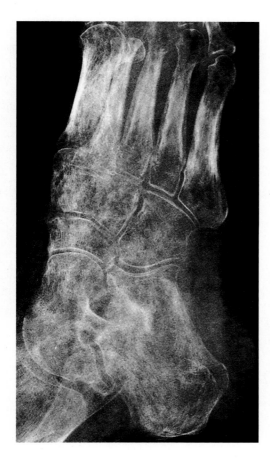

hyperthermia. In the second (or dystrophic) stage, which lasts from 3
to 24 months, the clinical findings include pain on exercise, increased
sensitivity of the skin to pressure and temperature changes, and skin and
muscle atrophy. In the final (or atrophic) stage, irreversible scleroderma-
like skin changes and aponeurotic and tendinous retraction may occur.
On the radiograph, RSDS is characterized by soft-tissue swelling and
severe, patchy osteoporosis that progresses rapidly (Fig. 4.53). Three-
phase technetium bone scan characteristically shows increased blood
flow, blood pool, and periarticular increased uptake in the affected areas.
These findings are seen in approximately 60% of affected patients.

Volkmann Ischemic Contracture. Developing usually after
supracondylar fracture of the humerus, Volkmann contracture is
caused by ischemia of the muscles followed by fibrosis. Clinically, it
is characterized as the "five Ps" syndrome—pulselessness, pain, pallor,
paresthesia, and paralysis. Radiographic examination usually reveals
flexion–contracture in the wrist and in the interphalangeal joints of the
fingers and hyperextension (or, rarely, flexion) of the metacarpophalangeal
joints associated with soft-tissue atrophy (Fig. 4.54).

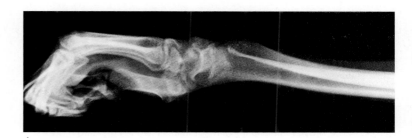

FIGURE 4.53 Sudeck atrophy. A 35-year-old man sustained fractures of the
tibia and fibula, which eventually healed. Subsequently, however, he reported
weakness, stiffness, and pain in his foot. Radiographic examination showed
changes typical of RSDS in the foot: rapidly progressive, patchy osteoporosis
associated with marked soft-tissue swelling.

FIGURE 4.54 Volkmann contracture. Having sustained a supracondylar fracture of the humerus that united, a 23-year-old man presented with symptoms
typical of Volkmann ischemic contracture. The lateral view of the distal forearm
including the wrist and hand shows flexion–contracture in the metacarpophalangeal and the interphalangeal joints, together with a marked degree of soft-
tissue atrophy.

Posttraumatic Myositis Ossificans. Occasionally after a fracture, dislocation, or even minor trauma to the soft tissues, an enlarging, painful mass develops at the site of injury. The characteristic feature of this lesion includes the clearly recognizable pattern of its evolution, which correlates well with the lapse of time after the trauma. Thus, by the 3rd or 4th week, calcifications and ossifications in the mass begin to develop (Fig. 4.55A,B), and by the 6th to 8th week, the periphery of the mass shows definite, well-organized cortical bone (Fig. 4.55C,D). The important radiographic hallmark of this complication is the presence of the so-called zonal phenomenon. On the radiograph, this phenomenon is characterized by a radiolucent area in the center of the lesion, indicating the formation of an immature bone, and by a dense zone of mature ossification at the periphery (myositis ossificans circumscripta). In addition, a thin radiolucent cleft separates the ossific mass from the adjacent cortex (Fig. 4.56). These important features help differentiate this condition from juxtacortical osteosarcoma, which may, at times, appear very similar. It must be stressed, however, that occasionally the focus of myositis ossificans may adhere and fuse with the cortex, mimicking parosteal osteosarcoma on radiographs. In these cases, CT may provide additional information, such as the presence of the zonal phenomenon characteristic of myositis ossificans (Fig. 4.57).

The MRI appearance of myositis ossificans depends on the stage of maturation of the lesion. In the early stage, T1-weighted sequences usually show a mass that lacks definable borders with homogeneous intermediate signal intensity, slightly higher than that of adjacent muscle. T2-weighted images show the lesion to be of high signal intensity. After an intravenous injection of gadopentetate dimeglumine, T1-weighted images show a well-defined peripheral rim of contrast enhancement, but the center of the lesion does not enhance. The more mature lesions show intermediate signal intensity on T1-weighted sequences isointense with adjacent muscle, surrounded by a rim of low signal intensity, which corresponds to peripheral bone maturation. On T2 weighting, the lesion is generally of high signal intensity but may appear inhomogeneous. The rim of low signal is seen at the periphery. Sometimes, the focus of myositis ossificans (whether immature or mature) may contain a fatty component, giving the lesion a high-intensity signal on T1-weighted images (Fig. 4.58).

Osteonecrosis (Ischemic or Avascular Necrosis). Osteonecrosis, the cellular death of bone tissue, occurs after a fracture or dislocation when the bone is deprived of a sufficient supply of arterial blood. However, it is important to recognize that this condition may also develop as a result of factors unrelated to mechanical trauma. Regardless of cause, the pathomechanism of osteonecrosis includes intraluminal vascular obstruction, vascular compression, or disruption of a blood vessel. Among the reported causes of osteonecrosis (other than a fracture or dislocation) are the following:

1. *Embolization of arteries.* This may occur in a variety of conditions. It is seen, for example, in certain hemoglobinopathies, such as sickle cell disease, in which arteries are occluded by abnormal red blood cells; in decompression states of dysbaric conditions, such as caisson disease, in which embolization by nitrogen bubbles occurs; or in chronic alcoholism and pancreatitis, when fat particles embolize arteries.

2. *Vasculitis.* Inflammation of the blood vessels may lead to interruption of the supply of arterial blood to the bone, as seen in collagen disorders such as systemic lupus erythematosus (SLE).

3. *Abnormal accumulation of cells.* In Gaucher disease, which is characterized by the abnormal accumulation of lipid-containing histiocytes in the bone marrow, or after steroid therapy, which can lead to an increase of fat cells, sinusoidal blood flow may be compromised, resulting in a deprivation of blood supply to the bone.

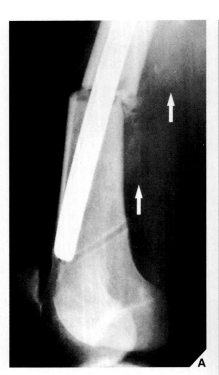

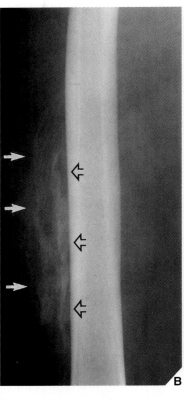

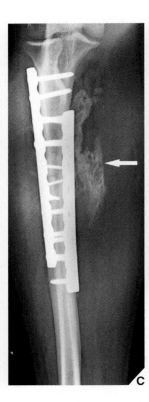

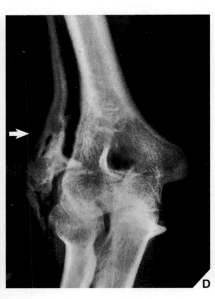

▲ FIGURE 4.55 **Posttraumatic myositis ossificans. (A)** A 20-year-old man sustained a transverse fracture at the junction of the middle and distal thirds of the femur. The fracture was treated by open reduction and internal fixation with an intramedullary rod. On the lateral view, obtained 3.5 weeks after the injury, an immature focus of myositis ossificans with poorly defined densities in the soft-tissue mass is evident adjacent to the posterior cortex of the femur (*arrows*). **(B)** Maturation of myositis ossificans in a 28-year-old woman who sustained an injury to the thigh 5 weeks before this radiograph was obtained. Note the formation of peripheral ossification (*arrows*) and the presence of a radiolucent cleft (*open arrows*). **(C)** A mature focus of myositis ossificans (*arrow*) at the site of the fractures of the proximal radius and ulna, status post open reduction and internal fixation in a 29-year-old woman. **(D)** This radiograph of a 27-year-old man who 1 year previously had sustained a fracture–dislocation in the elbow, which healed, shows a well-organized, mature focus of myositis ossificans circumscripta. Note the well-developed cortex at the periphery of the osseous mass (*arrow*) and the radiolucent gap separating the lesion from the cortex of the humerus.

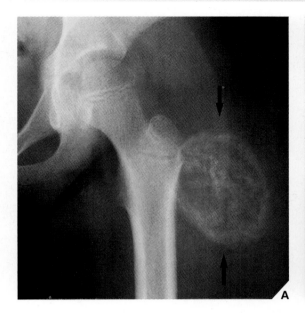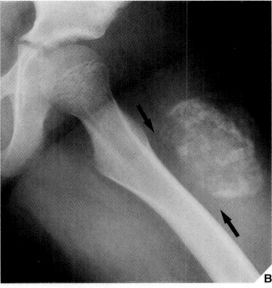

▲

FIGURE 4.56   Posttraumatic myositis ossificans. A 7-year-old boy presented with a history of trauma 6 weeks before this radiographic examination. The anteroposterior radiograph of the left hip **(A)** demonstrates a lesion that exhibits features of zonal phenomenon characteristic of juxtacortical myositis ossificans (*arrows*). On the frog-lateral projection **(B)**, note the cleft (*arrows*) separating the ossific mass from the posterolateral cortex.

FIGURE 4.57   Posttraumatic myositis ossificans. A 52-year-old man sustained an injury to the lateral aspect of the left thigh 6 months previously. He was concerned about a hard mass he had palpated. **(A)** The radiograph shows an ossific mass adherent to the lateral cortex of the left femur (*arrow*). **(B)** CT scan demonstrates the classic zonal phenomenon of myositis ossificans. Note the radiolucent center surrounded by mature cortex.

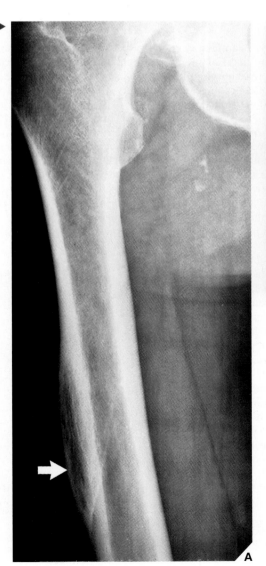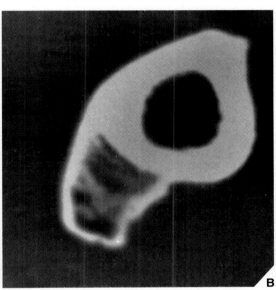

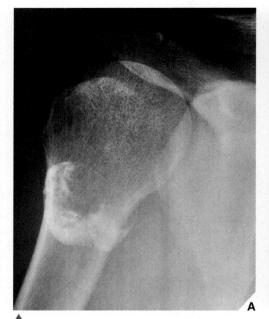
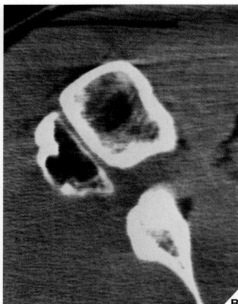
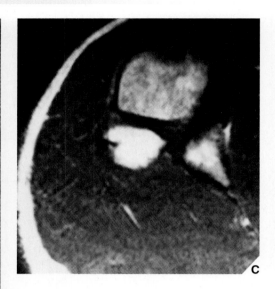

FIGURE 4.58   Posttraumatic myositis ossificans. A 41-year-old man presented with a palpable mass over the posterolateral aspect of the proximal right humerus. **(A)** Conventional anteroposterior radiograph of the right shoulder shows calcifications and ossifications overlaying the proximal humerus. **(B)** CT section demonstrates the zoning phenomenon typical of myositis ossificans. The center of the lesion shows a low-attenuation area caused by fatty changes. The cleft separates the mass from the cortex. **(C)** Axial T1-weighted (SE; TR 600/TE 20 msec) MRI shows the center of the lesion to be of high signal intensity, whereas the periphery exhibits low-to-intermediate signal.

4. *Elevated intraosseous pressure.* This theory, championed by Hungerford and Lennox, suggests that any physiologic or pathologic process that results in increased pressure within the femoral head (which is essentially a sphere of cancellous bone, marrow, and fat surrounded by a cortical shell) may compromise the blood flow and lead to osteonecrosis.

5. *Inhibition of angiogenesis.* Osteonecrosis may result from compromise of normal angiogenesis that occurs consistently in bone tissue. This new hypothesis was recently introduced by Smith et al. It is supported by the fact that a number of drugs and mediators, including glucocorticoids, interferons, and other endogenously produced cytokines, inhibit angiogenesis. A similar effect was observed in the angiographic studies of the femoral head after the administration of steroids.

6. *Mechanical stress.* This causative factor was occasionally attributed to nontraumatic osteonecrosis of the femoral head. The weight-bearing segment of the femoral head is the anterior–superior quadrant and, therefore, is under a large mechanical strain. Occlusion of the vessels in this region of the femoral head might be the result of cartilage breakdown secondary to excessive mechanical stress. Support for this hypothesis stems from experiments on rats by Iwasaki et al. and Suhiro et al.

7. *Radiation exposure.* Exposure to radiation may result in damage to the vascularity of a bone.

8. *Idiopathic.* Often, no definite cause can be established, as in the case of spontaneous osteonecrosis that predominantly affects the medial femoral condyle or in the case of certain osteochondroses such as Legg-Calvé-Perthes disease involving the femoral head or Freiberg disease affecting the head of the second metatarsal.

Diseases or conditions associated with or leading to osteonecrosis are listed in Table 4.4.

After trauma, osteonecrosis occurs most commonly in the femoral head, the carpal scaphoid, and the humeral head because of the precarious supply of blood to these bones.

Osteonecrosis of the femoral head is a frequent complication after an intracapsular fracture of the femoral neck (60% to 75%), dislocation in the hip joint (25%), and slipped capital femoral epiphysis (15% to 40%). In its very early stages, radiographs may appear completely normal; however, radionuclide bone scan may show first decreased and later increased isotope uptake at the site of the lesion, which is a very valuable indication of abnormality. The earliest radiographic sign of this complication is the presence of a radiolucent crescent, which may be seen as early as 4 weeks after the initial injury. This phenomenon, as Norman and Bullough have pointed out, is secondary to the subchondral structural collapse of the necrotic segment and is visible as a narrow radiolucent line parallel to the articular surface of the bone. Radiographically, the sign is most easily demonstrated on the frog-lateral view of the hip (Figs. 4.59 and 4.60). Because the necrotic process most of the time does not affect the articular cartilage, the width of the joint space (i.e., the radiographic joint space: the width of the articular cartilage of adjoining bones plus the actual joint cavity)

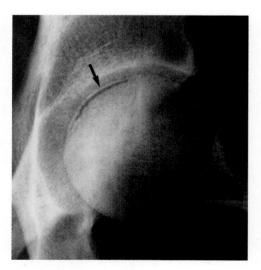

FIGURE 4.59   Osteonecrosis of the femoral head. The frog-lateral view of the left hip shows the crescent sign (*arrow*) in a 45-year-old woman who sustained a hip dislocation 5 weeks earlier.

TABLE 4.4 **Diseases or Conditions Associated with or Leading to Osteonecrosis**

Trauma
  Fracture of femoral neck
  Dislocation of the femoral head
  Proximal femoral epiphysiolysis
  Slipped capital femoral epiphysis
  Epiphyseal compression
  Fracture of talus
  Fracture of scaphoid
  Kienböck disease
  Vascular injury
  Burns
  Radiation exposure
Hemoglobinopathies
  Sickle cell disease
  Hb S/C hemoglobinopathy
  Hb S/thalassemia
  Polycythemia
Congenital and Developmental Conditions
  Congenital dysplasia of the hip
  Ehlers-Danlos syndrome
  Hereditary dysostosis
  Legg-Calvé-Perthes disease
  Fabry disease
Local Infiltrative Lesions
  Gaucher disease
  Neoplastic conditions
  Lymphoproliferative disorders

Metabolic Conditions
  Hypercortisolism
  Corticosteroid medications
  Cushing disease
  Gout and hyperuricemia
  Hyperlipidemia
  Hyperparathyroidism
Dysbaric Disorders
  Caisson disease
Infectious and Inflammatory Conditions
  Osteomyelitis
  Pancreatitis
  Giant cell arteritis
  Systemic lupus erythematosus
  Thrombophlebitis
  Acquired immunodeficiency syndrome
  Meningococcemia
Miscellaneous Factors
  Alcohol consumption
  Cigarette smoking
  Chronic renal failure
  Hemodialysis
  Intravascular coagulation
  Organ transplantation
  Pregnancy
  Idiopathic

is preserved. Preservation of the joint space helps to differentiate this condition from osteoarthritis. In its later stage, osteonecrosis can be readily identified on the anteroposterior view of the hip by a flattening of the articular surface and the dense appearance of the femoral head (Fig. 4.61). The density is secondary to the compression of bony trabeculae after a microfracture of the nonviable bone, calcification of the detritic marrow, and repair of the necrotic area by the deposition of a new bone, the so-called creeping substitution. CT examination frequently helps to delineate the details of this condition. Ficat and Arlet proposed a classification system of osteonecrosis of the femoral head consisting of four stages, based on radiographic, hemodynamic, and symptomatic criteria (Table 4.5).

A significant breakthrough in identifying osteonecrosis in patients who had normal bone scan and normal conventional radiographs was achieved with MRI. Currently, this modality is considered the most sensitive and specific for the diagnosis and evaluation of osteonecrosis. Its characteristic MRI appearance consists of a circumscribed ovoid area (Fig. 4.62A) or crescent-shaped rim (Fig. 4.62B,C) of low signal in a subchondral location. This rim corresponds to the interface of repair between ischemic and normal bone consisting mainly of sclerosis and fibrosis. On T2-weighted images, a second inner rim of high signal has been observed (the double-line sign) (Fig. 4.62D). It is believed that this appearance represents fibrovascular tissue in the reparative zone. Many authors hypothesize that this finding is pathognomonic

FIGURE 4.60 **Osteonecrosis of the femoral head.** ▶ **(A)** A 41-year-old man presented with a history of traumatic dislocation in the left hip joint. On frontal projection, the increased density of the femoral head suggests osteonecrosis, but a definite diagnosis cannot be made. **(B)** The frog-lateral view demonstrates a thin radiolucent line parallel to the articular surface of the femoral head (*arrow*). This represents the crescent sign, a radiographic hallmark of osteonecrosis.

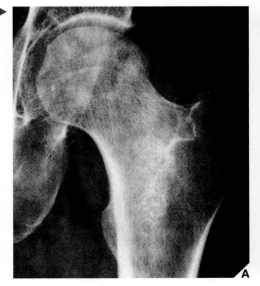
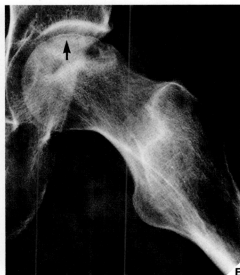

TABLE 4.5   Osteonecrosis of Femoral Head: Correlation of Clinical Symptoms and Radiologic Findings with Histopathologic Changes Based on Ficat and Arlet Classification

Stage	Clinical Symptoms	Radiographic Findings	Scintigraphy	Pathologic Changes	Biopsy
1	None	Normal	Normal	Infarction of weight-bearing segments	Necrotic marrow, osteoblasts
2	Mild pain	Increased density of femoral head, normal joint space	Increased uptake	Spontaneous repair	New bone deposition
3	Mild-to-moderate pain	Loss of sphericity and collapse of the femoral head, crescent sign	Increased uptake	Subchondral fracture with collapse, impaction, and fragmentation of the necrotic segment	Dead bone trabeculae and dead marrow cells on both sides of the fracture line
4	Moderate pain, assistive devices needed	Joint space narrowing, acetabular changes	Increased uptake	Osteoarthritis	Degenerative changes in articular cartilage

Modified from Chang CC, Greenspan A, Gershwin ME, 1993, with permission.

for osteonecrosis. Other authors have played down the importance of this finding, claiming that it may be largely artifactual, representing the so-called chemical shift.

Several reports have established the diagnostic sensitivity of MRI in the early stages of osteonecrosis, when radiographic changes are not yet apparent or are nonspecific. MRI has been shown to have 97% sensitivity in differentiating osteonecrotic femoral head from normal femoral head and 85% sensitivity in differentiating osteonecrotic femoral head from other disorders of the femoral head, with an overall sensitivity of 91%. MRI appears to be a better predictive test for subsequent femoral head collapse than radionuclide bone scan. The narrow band-like area of low signal intensity that traverses the femoral head in midcoronal sections present on MRI was a significant indicator of subsequent collapses.

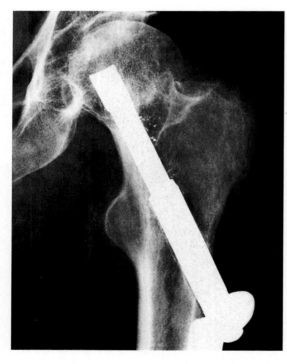

▲
FIGURE 4.61   Osteonecrosis of the femoral head. A 56-year-old woman sustained an intracapsular fracture of the left femoral neck, which healed after surgical treatment by open reduction and internal fixation. The anteroposterior view shows a Smith-Peterson nail inserted into the femoral neck and head. The fracture line is obliterated. The dense (sclerotic) appearance of the femoral head indicates the development of osteonecrosis.

MRI is indispensable in the accurate staging of osteonecrosis, because it reflects the size of the lesion and roughly the stage of the disease. Mitchell and colleagues have described a classification system of osteonecrosis based on alterations in the central region of MR signal intensity in the osteonecrotic focus (Table 4.6). In early stages (class A or fat-like), there is preservation of a normal fat signal, except at the sclerotic reactive margin surrounding the lesion, that manifests as a central region of high signal intensity on short spin-echo (SE) TR/TE images (T1 weighted) and intermediate signal intensity on long TR/TE images (T2 weighted). Later, when there is sufficient inflammation or vascular engorgement, or if a subacute hemorrhage is present (class B or blood-like), a high signal intensity is noted on short and long TR/TE images. This signal is similar to that of a subacute hemorrhage. If there is enough inflammation, hyperemia, and fibrosis present to replace the fat content of the femoral head (class C or fluid-like), a low-intensity signal with short TR/TE and a high-intensity signal with long TR/TE are seen. Finally, in advanced stages, where fibrosis and sclerosis predominate (class D or fibrous-like), a low signal intensity is present on both short and long TR/TE images (Table 4.6 and Figs. 4.63 to 4.66). MRI findings correlate well with histologic changes. The central region of high signal intensity corresponds to necrosis of the bone and marrow. The low signal of the peripheral band corresponds to the sclerotic margin of reactive tissue at the interface between necrotic and viable bones. As Seiler and coworkers have pointed out, MRI evaluation of osteonecrosis of the femoral head has several advantages: It is noninvasive, does not require ionizing radiation, provides multiplanar images, reflects physiologic changes in the bone marrow, provides excellent resolution of surrounding soft tissues, and makes it possible to evaluate the contralateral femoral head simultaneously.

Osteonecrosis of the carpal scaphoid is a complication commonly seen in 10% to 15% of cases of carpal scaphoid fracture, increasing in incidence to 30% to 40% if there is nonunion. Necrosis generally involves the proximal bone fragment but the distal fragment, although rarely, may also be affected. Evidence of this complication most frequently becomes apparent approximately 4 to 6 months after an injury, when radiographic examination shows an increased bone density. Although it is most often diagnosed on conventional radiographs, tomographic study (Fig. 4.67), CT (Fig. 4.68), and MRI are indicated when radiographic findings are equivocal.

Only exceptionally a scaphoid bone may become osteonecrotic in the absence of a fracture. This abnormality is known as Preiser disease.

Osteonecrosis may also develop in the humeral head after a fracture of the humeral neck (Fig. 4.69), but this complication is infrequently seen. A majority of osteonecrosis of the humeral head is either idiopathic or related to connective tissue disorders or treatment with steroids (Fig. 4.70).

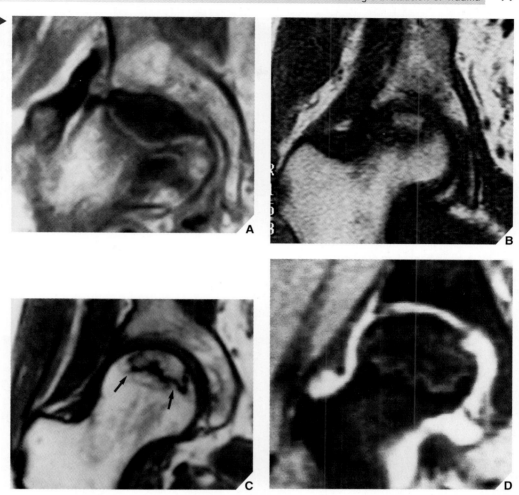

FIGURE 4.62 Osteonecrosis of the femoral head demonstrated by MRI. (A) Coronal T1-weighted (SE; TR 650/TE 25 msec) image shows an ovoid area of decreased signal in the subchondral location. **(B)** Coronal T1-weighted (SE; TR 500/TE 25 msec) image shows a crescent-shaped rim of decreased signal at the weight-bearing segment of the femoral head. **(C)** Coronal T1-weighted (SE; TR 650/TE 25 msec) image shows osteonecrotic segment separated from normal bone by low-intensity serpentine border (*arrows*). **(D)** Coronal T2-weighted gradient-echo (multiplanar gradient recalled, TR 500/TE 15 msec, flip angle 15 degrees) image shows the characteristic "double-line" sign for osteonecrosis. Note also the high signal of joint fluid.

Injury to Major Blood Vessels. A relatively infrequent complication of a fracture or dislocation, an injury to the major blood vessels occurs when bone fragments lacerate or completely transect an artery (see Figs. 2.3 and 4.14) or a vein, resulting in bleeding, the formation of hematoma, arteriovenous fistula, or a pseudoaneurysm (Fig. 4.71). To demonstrate this abnormality, angiography may be performed (see Fig. 2.3). This technique is invaluable in visualizing the site of laceration, ascertaining the exact extent of vascular damage, and assessing the status of collateral circulation. It may also be combined with an interventional procedure, such as embolization to control hemorrhage. At the present time, more often CT-angiography is performed (see Figs. 2.12D,E and 2.13C–E)

Growth Disturbance. A common complication of Salter-Harris type IV and V fractures involving the physis, growth disturbance may result from an injury to the growth plate by the formation of an osseous bridge between the epiphysis and the metaphysis. As a result of this tethering of the growth plate, localized cessation of bone growth occurs. If the entire physis in a single long bone stops growing, a limb-length discrepancy will result (Fig. 4.72A). If only one growth plate at the articulations of parallel bones (the radius and ulna or the tibia and fibula) is damaged and ceases to grow, the uninjured bone continues to grow at the normal rate, leading to overgrowth and consequent joint deformity (Fig. 4.72B).

Posttraumatic Arthritis. If a fracture line extends into the joint, the articular surface may become irregular. Such incongruity in the articular surfaces results in abnormal stresses that lead to precocious degenerative changes recognized on the radiograph by narrowing of the joint space, subchondral sclerosis, and formation of marginal osteophytes (Fig. 4.73). A similar complication may also be seen after a dislocation (Fig. 4.74).

TABLE 4.6 Correlation of MRI Findings with Histologic Changes

Class	MRI Findings	Appearance	Histology
A	Normal fat signal except at the sclerotic margin surrounding the lesion	Fat-like	Premature conversion to fatty marrow within the femoral neck or intertrochanteric region
B	High signal intensity of the inner border and low signal intensity of the surrounding rim	Blood-like	Bone resorption and replacement by vascular granulation tissue
C	Diffusely decreased signal on T1 and high signal on T2 weighting	Fluid-like	Bone marrow edema
D	Decreased signal on T1- and T2-weighted images	Fibrous	Sclerosis from reinforcement of existing trabeculae at the margin of a live bone (i.e., repair tissue interface)

Modified from Chang CC, Greenspan A, Gershwin ME, 1993, with permission.

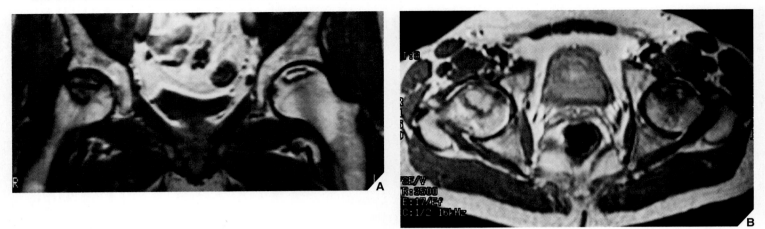

▲

FIGURE 4.63 **MRI staging of osteonecrosis (class A). (A)** Coronal T1-weighted (SE; TR 600/TE 20 msec) image shows the preservation of a normal bright signal of fat within the lesion, surrounded by a low–signal intensity reactive margin in both femoral heads. **(B)** Axial T2-weighted (fast SE; TR 3500/TE 17 msec/Ef) image shows intermediate signal within an osteonecrotic segment, analogous to fat.

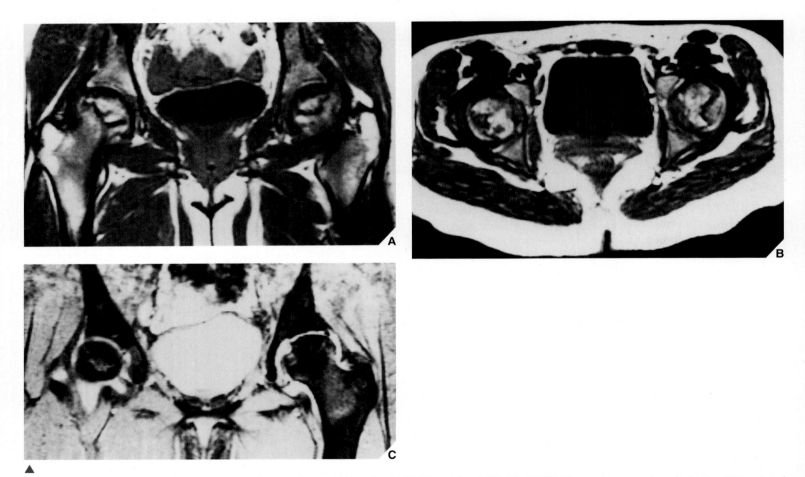

▲

FIGURE 4.64 **MRI staging of osteonecrosis (class B).** Coronal **(A)** and axial **(B)** T1-weighted (SE; TR 600/TE 20 msec) images show high signal intensity of osteonecrotic segment surrounded by a sclerotic margin. **(C)** Coronal T2*-weighted gradient-echo (multiplanar gradient recalled, TR 500/TE 15 msec, flip angle 15 degrees) image shows high signal in the central portion of the femoral heads.

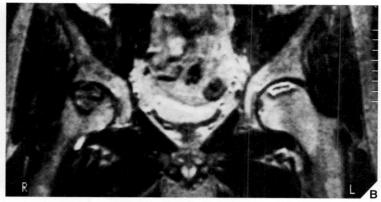

FIGURE 4.65   **MRI staging of osteonecrosis (class C). (A)** Axial T1-weighted (SE; TR 600/TE 20 msec) image shows areas of low signal intensity in both femoral heads. **(B)** Coronal T2-weighted (SE; TR 2000/TE 80 msec) image shows a high–signal intensity area (more pronounced in the left femoral head) surrounded by a low-signal margin.

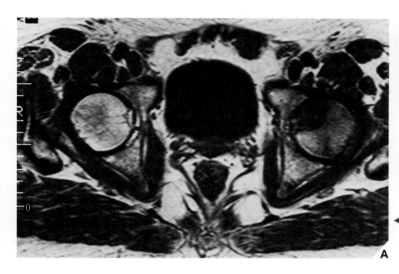

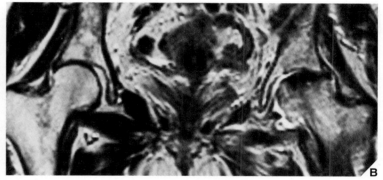

◀ FIGURE 4.66   **MRI staging of osteonecrosis (class D). (A)** Axial T1-weighted (SE; TR 600/TE 20 msec) and **(B)** coronal T2-weighted (fast SE; TR 3000/TE 136 msec/Ef) images demonstrate a sclerotic lesion of late-stage osteonecrosis of the left femoral head that shows low signal intensity on both sequences.

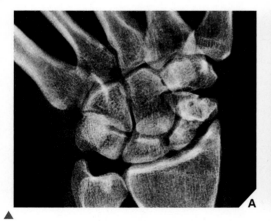
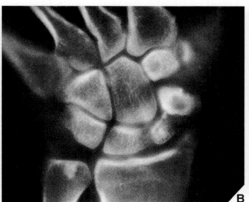
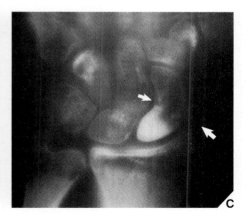

FIGURE 4.67   **Osteonecrosis of the scaphoid. (A)** Radiograph of the wrist demonstrates a fracture of the carpal scaphoid; however, it is unclear whether the fracture is complicated by osteonecrosis. **(B)** Trispiral tomogram clearly shows nonunion and the presence of osteonecrosis of the distal fragment, together with cystic degeneration. The dense spot in the articular end of the ulna represents a bone island. **(C)** In another patient, trispiral tomogram shows ununited fracture of the scaphoid (*arrows*) and osteonecrosis of the proximal fragment.

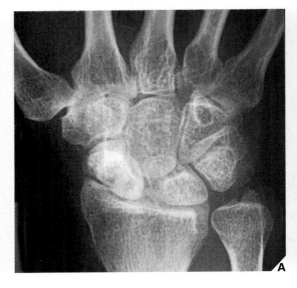

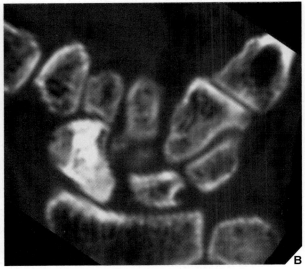

◀ **FIGURE 4.68   CT of scaphoid osteonecrosis.** A 52-year-old woman sustained a fracture of the scaphoid bone, treated conservatively in a cast. **(A)** Conventional radiograph shows sclerotic changes in the scaphoid, which may be due to healing process or osteonecrosis. **(B)** Coronal reformatted CT shows an incompletely healed fracture of the scaphoid complicated by osteonecrosis.

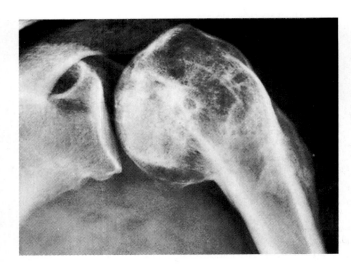

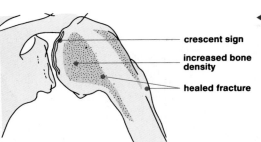

◀ **FIGURE 4.69   Osteonecrosis of the humeral head.** Six months after sustaining a fracture of the left humeral neck that united, a 62-year-old man developed osteonecrosis of the humeral head, evident on the radiograph from the increased bone density and the collapse of the subchondral segment.

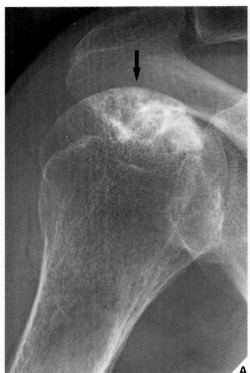

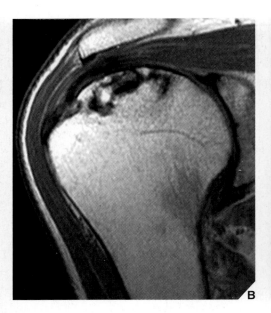

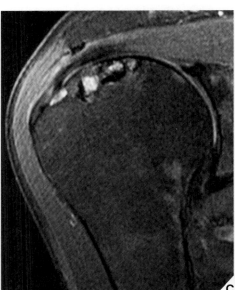

◀ **FIGURE 4.70   Osteonecrosis of the humeral head.** A 58-year-old woman presented with right shoulder pain for several weeks after an apparent dislocation in the glenohumeral joint, which was spontaneously reduced. She also gives a history of SLE treated with corticosteroids. **(A)** Radiograph of the right shoulder shows a classic appearance of osteonecrosis of the humeral head (*arrow*), a diagnosis that was confirmed on **(B)** coronal proton-density and **(C)** coronal proton-density fat-suppressed MR images. Osteonecrosis was more likely secondary to SLE and the treatment with steroids rather than due to traumatic event.

FIGURE 4.71 Pseudoaneurysm of the popliteal artery. A 30-year-old woman with Gaucher disease and a total hip replacement as a result of osteonecrosis of the femoral head sustained a transverse fracture of the left femoral shaft through the acrylic cement just distal to the stem of the prosthesis. A femoral arteriogram revealed a pseudoaneurysm of the popliteal artery resulting from an injury to the vessel by the fractured bone fragment and the acrylic cement. (From Baker ND, 1981, with permission.)

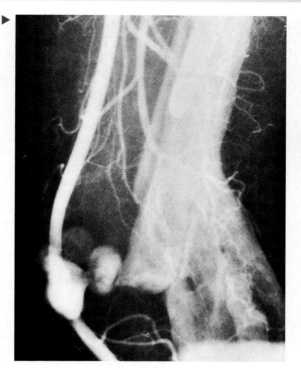
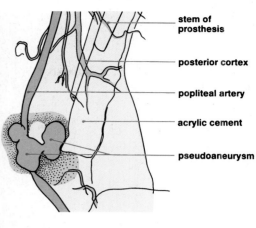

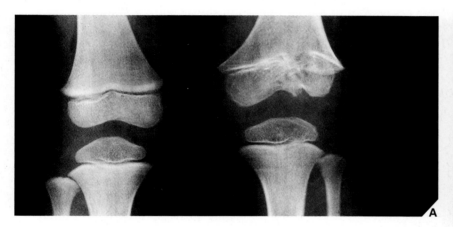
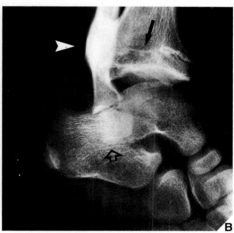

FIGURE 4.72 Growth disturbance. (A) A 3-year-old boy sustained a fracture of the left distal femur that extended through the growth plate. As a result, the bone at this end prematurely ceased to grow. Anteroposterior radiograph of both knees shows a discrepancy in the length of the femora associated with deformity of the distal epiphysis of the left femur secondary to tethering of the growth plate. **(B)** A 5-year-old girl sustained a Salter-Harris type V fracture of the distal tibia. On the lateral view, a joint deformity is evident as a result of the fusion of the physis of the tibia (*arrow*) and overgrowth of the distal fibula (*open arrow*). Note also the posttraumatic synostosis of these two bones (*arrow head*).

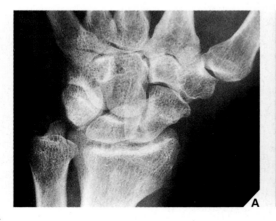
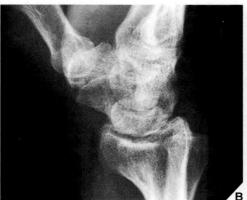
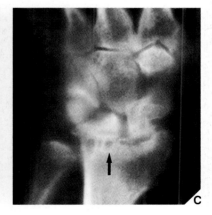

FIGURE 4.73 Posttraumatic osteoarthritis. Dorsovolar **(A)** and lateral **(B)** views of the wrist of a 57-year-old man who had sustained an intraarticular fracture of the distal radius demonstrate residual deformity of this bone and narrowing of the radiocarpal articulation. Trispiral tomogram **(C)** shows, in addition, the multiple subchondral degenerative cysts (*arrow*) often seen in posttraumatic arthritis.

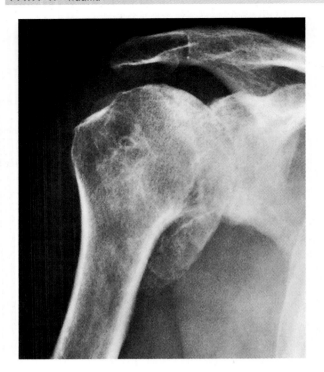

▲
FIGURE 4.74 **Posttraumatic osteoarthritis.** The anteroposterior radiograph of the right shoulder of a 78-year-old man who presented with a history of several previous dislocations in that joint demonstrates the advanced osteoarthritis resulting from repeated trauma to the articular surfaces of the humeral head and glenoid.

Stress Fractures

A bone is a dynamic tissue that requires stress for normal development. *Stress* is the force or absolute load applied to a bone that may arise from weight-bearing or muscular actions. The force may be of an axial, bending, or torsional nature, and the resulting change in shape of the bone is referred to as *strain*. *Tensile* forces are produced along the convex side of a bone, while *compressive* forces occur along its concave margin. According to Wolff's law, intermittent forces applied to a bone stimulate remodeling of its architecture to withstand the new mechanical environment optimally. Stresses related to daily activities stimulate the remodeling process that, in a cortical bone, occurs at the level of the osteon, the basic unit of bone structure. The exact mechanism that activates this process is not known, but some evidence suggests that it may be related to the development of microfractures (Fig. 4.75A). Osteoclastic resorption leading to the formation of small resorption areas at the site of microfractures is the initial response to increased stresses; peak bone loss occurs after approximately 3 weeks. These resorption cavities are subsequently filled with lamellar bone, but if bone formation is slow, then the consequent imbalance between bone resorption and bone formation results in weakening of the bone. Periosteal proliferation, endosteal proliferation, or both may produce a new bone at the sites of stress in an apparent attempt to buttress the temporarily weakened cortex. Stresses in a cancellous bone may result in partial or complete trabecular microfractures (Fig. 4.75B). Microcallus is produced along the complete fractures, and these thickened trabeculae probably account for the sclerosis seen on radiographs when stress injuries occur in a cancellous bone. Although microdamage is a physiologic phenomenon, it becomes pathologic when its production greatly exceeds repair. If the inciting

PATHOMECHANISM OF STRESS FRACTURE

A. Cortex

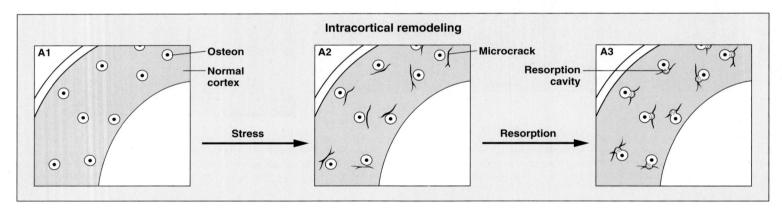

B. Cancellous bone

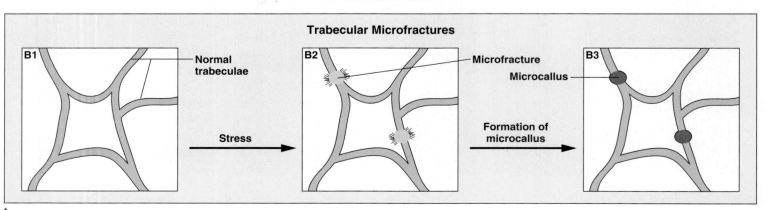

▲
FIGURE 4.75 **Pathomechanism of a stress fracture. (A)** Intracortical remodeling. **(B)** Trabecular microfractures.

activity is not curtailed, repair mechanisms are overwhelmed, which results in the accumulation of microdamage and subsequent fatigue fracture of a trabecular or cortical bone (see Figs. 4.29 and 4.34B).

Diagnostic imaging has acquired a pivotal role in the assessment of stress injuries to bone because clinical evaluation alone is not definitive. If classic radiographic findings are present, then the diagnosis is straightforward. However, because the underlying pathophysiology is a continuing process rather than a single event, imaging findings are extremely variable and depend on such factors as the type of inciting activity, the bone involved, and the timing of the imaging procedure.

Conventional radiographs play an important role in the workup of a suspected stress fracture and should be the first imaging study obtained. Unfortunately, initial radiographs are often normal, which is not surprising given the degree of microscopic remodeling that occurs in the early stages of stress injury. The sensitivity of early radiographs can be as low as 15%, and follow-up radiographs will demonstrate diagnostic findings in only 50% of cases. The time that elapses between the manifestation of initial symptoms and the detection of radiographic findings ranges from 1 week to several months, and cessation of physical activity may prevent the development of any radiographic findings.

Initial changes in the cortical bone include subtle ill definition of the cortex (gray cortex sign) (Fig. 4.76) or faint intracortical radiolucent striations, which are presumably related to the osteoclastic tunneling found early in the remodeling process. These changes may be easily overlooked until periosteal new bone formation and/or endosteal thickening develops in an apparent attempt to buttress the temporarily weakened cortex. As damage increases, a true fracture line may appear (Fig. 4.77). These injuries typically involve the shaft of a long bone and are common in the anterior or posterior cortex of the tibia and in the medial cortex of the femur.

Stress injuries in cancellous bones are notoriously difficult to detect. Subtle blurring of trabecular margins and faint sclerotic radiopaque areas may be seen secondary to peritrabecular callus, but a 50% change in bone opacity is required for these changes to be radiographically detectable (Fig. 4.78). With progression of the pathologic process, a readily apparent sclerotic band is seen (Fig. 4.79).

Radionuclide bone scanning has become the gold standard for evaluating stress fractures owing in large part to its ability to demonstrate subtle changes in bone metabolism long before radiography can. The most widely used radiopharmaceuticals for imaging of a stress injury are the ^{99m}Tc phosphate analogs; these are taken up at sites of bone turnover, probably by means of chemiadsorption to the surface of the bone.

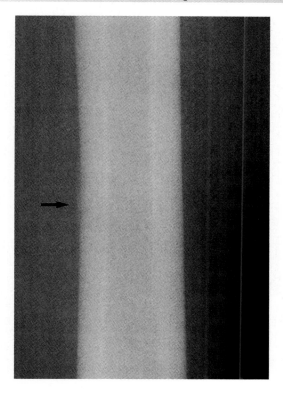

▲
FIGURE 4.76 **Stress fracture.** The earliest radiographic changes of a stress fracture include "gray cortex" sign consisting of a subtle ill-defined cortical margin (*arrow*). Compare with a normal definition of the contralateral cortex.

The degree of uptake depends primarily on the rate of bone turnover and local blood flow, and abnormal uptake may be seen within 6 to 72 hours of injury. The sensitivity of scintigraphy approaches 100%, because only a few false-negative scans have been reported. The classic scintigraphic findings of a stress fracture include a focally intense, fusiform area of cortical uptake or a transverse band of increased activity (Fig. 4.80). However, the spectrum of findings associated with bone stress is broad, which again reflects the underlying pathophysiologic continuum. Despite its high sensitivity, the specificity of scintigraphy is slightly lower than that of radiography because other conditions such as tumors, infections,

FIGURE 4.77 **Stress fracture.** With ▶ progression of the pathologic process, a cortical fracture becomes visible **(A)**. This finding may be enhanced with a trispiral tomography **(B)**.

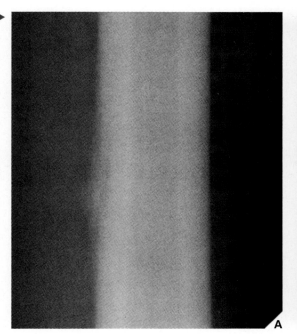

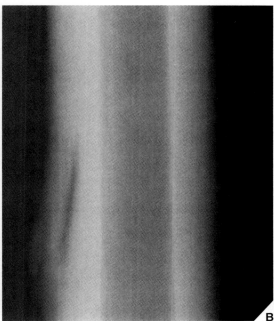

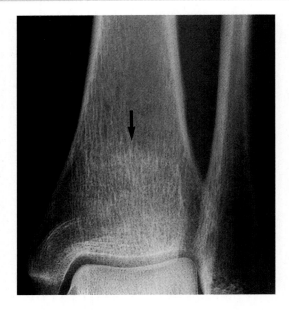

▲
FIGURE 4.78 **Stress fracture.** The earliest radiographic changes of a stress fracture in cancellous bone include subtle blurring of the trabecular margins associated with faint sclerotic areas (*arrow*).

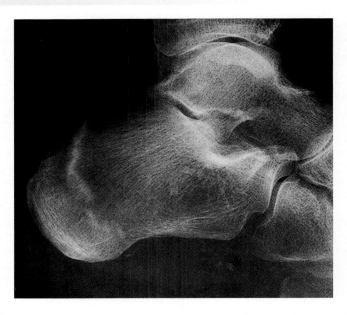

▲
FIGURE 4.79 **Stress fracture.** Typical appearance of a stress fracture in the calcaneus: a vertical band of sclerosis in the posterior aspect of the bone is characteristic of this injury.

bone infarctions, and shin splints or periostitis can produce a positive scan. In these instances, augmentation of scintigraphy with CT or MRI can be helpful in further diagnostic workup.

CT has a limited role in the diagnosis of stress injuries. It is less sensitive than scintigraphy and radiography in the diagnosis of stress fractures but can be quite useful for better defining an abnormality discovered with another modality (Fig. 4.81). It is well suited to delineate a fracture line in a location not well demonstrated on conventional radiography. Longitudinal stress fractures of the tibia occur less frequently than the more typical transverse or oblique varieties, but these may account for up to 10% of tibial stress fractures. These are especially difficult to detect with radiography because of their vertical orientation, and CT has played an important role in their diagnosis.

MRI is extremely sensitive in the detection of pathophysiologic changes associated with stress injuries, and it is even more specific than radionuclide scanning. Typical findings in early stress reactions include

areas of low signal intensity in the marrow on T1-weighted images that increase in signal intensity with T2 weighting. Fat saturation techniques, such as inversion-recovery (IR) or fast spin-echo (FSE) T2-weighted imaging with frequency-selective fat saturation, are especially useful for identifying these injuries. The increased water content of the associated medullary edema or hemorrhage results in high signal intensity against the dark background of suppressed fat such that these sequences should maximize sensitivity. On T2-weighted images of more advanced lesions, low-intensity bands, contiguous with the cortex, have been seen within the marrow edema; these presumably represent fracture lines (Fig. 4.82). The multiplanar capability of MRI provides a further advantage by allowing for optimal demonstration of the fracture line. In some cases, increased signal intensity has also been observed in juxtacortical and subperiosteal locations. MRI has been advocated as a problem-solving modality, such as in a patient with negative or confusing bone scan. It may secure the diagnosis if the fracture line is identified.

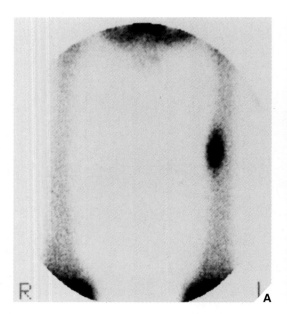
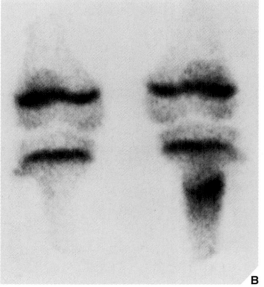

▲
FIGURE 4.80 **Scintigraphic presentation of a stress fracture. (A)** Fusiform area of increased uptake in the medial cortex of the left femur. **(B)** A transverse band of increased uptake in the proximal diaphysis of the left tibia.

FIGURE 4.81   CT of the stress fracture. A stress fracture in the tibia (*arrow*) demonstrated by CT. The *curved arrow* points to the nutrient foramen.

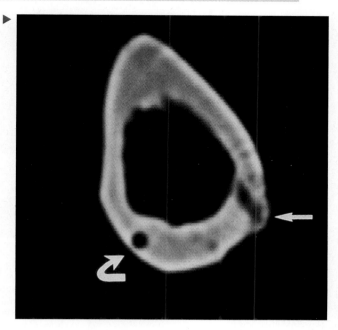

Injury to Soft Tissues

Under normal physiologic circumstances, soft tissues such as muscles, tendons, ligaments, articular menisci, and intervertebral disks are only faintly outlined or not visible at all on conventional radiographs. As a result, only rarely, as in such traumatic conditions as myositis ossificans (see previous discussion) or certain tears of ligaments and tendons, does conventional radiography suffice to demonstrate trauma to the soft tissues (Fig. 4.83). Adequate evaluation of an injury to these structures and of the progress of treatment, consequently, requires supplemental studies, which may include stress radiography, arthrography, tenography, bursography, myelography, CT, and MRI.

MRI, in particular, is considered to be the best imaging modality for evaluating traumatic soft-tissue injuries. Differences in signal intensity enable abnormalities of the various structures (muscles, tendons, ligaments, fascias, vessels, and nerves) to be effectively demonstrated. Posttraumatic tenosynovitis, joint effusion, and soft-tissue hematomas are also seen well on MR images. Tears of various ligaments and tendons can be accurately diagnosed; for instance, when evaluating tendon injuries, MRI provides information regarding the location of the tear (whether it is within the tendon, at the tendon insertion, or at the musculotendinous interface), the size of the gap between both tendon ends, the size of the hematoma at the rupture site, and the presence of any inflammatory component (Fig. 4.84).

MRI is invaluable in identifying various injuries to the muscles that may occur during traumatic hip dislocation (Figs. 4.85 and 4.86). Normal skeletal muscle exhibits an intermediate or slightly prolonged T1 relaxation time and a short T2 relaxation time relative to other soft tissues. When muscles are injured, MRI can effectively delineate the variable degrees of strain, contusion, tear, or hematoma and permits the quantification of these injuries. Acute muscle strain gives rise to increased T2 signal intensity, reflecting tissue edema. When an acute muscle tear occurs, muscle shape and architecture appear altered, and the signal within the muscle shows an abnormal increase because of intramuscular hemorrhage and edema.

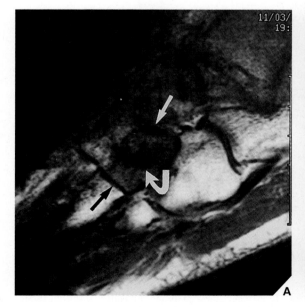
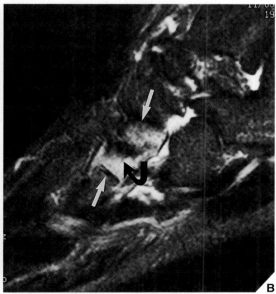

FIGURE 4.82   MRI of the stress fracture. (A) Sagittal T1-weighted image shows a diffusely decreased signal in the lateral cuneiform (*arrows*) and a band of signal void in the center of the bone (*curved arrow*). **(B)** Sagittal FSE inversion recovery MR image shows increased signal in the cuneiform bone (*arrows*) representing changes due to edema and hemorrhage. The stress fracture remains of low signal intensity (*curved arrow*).

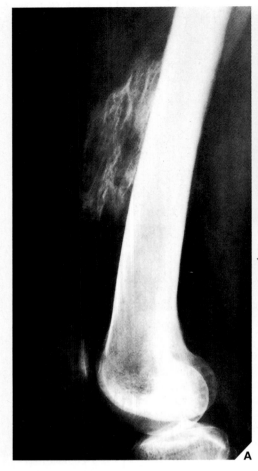

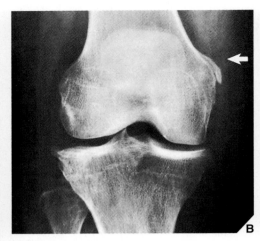

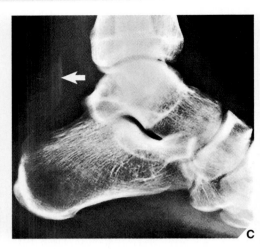

FIGURE 4.83   **Soft-tissue injury. (A)** A common complication of trauma to the muscular structures, myositis ossificans, is characterized by the formation of a bone in the injured muscle. This condition is apparent on conventional radiography. **(B)** The calcification of the medial collateral ligament of the knee, known as Pellegrini-Stieda lesion (*arrow*), represents the sequela of traumatic tear of this ligament. **(C)** In certain instances, the tear of a tendon may be diagnosed on radiography. The lateral radiograph of the ankle shows the typical appearance of a torn Achilles tendon (*arrow*).

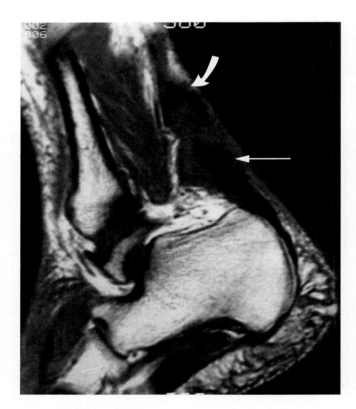

FIGURE 4.84   **Tear of the Achilles tendon.** Sagittal MRI of the ankle (SE; TR 2000/TE 20 msec) shows a discontinuity of the Achilles tendon near its insertion to the calcaneus (*arrow*). An inflammatory mass is seen at the rupture site (*curved arrow*). (From Beltran J, 1990, with permission.)

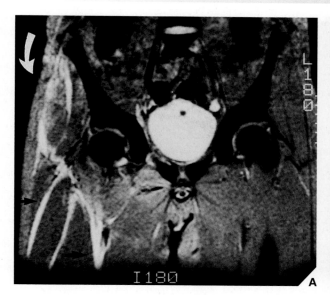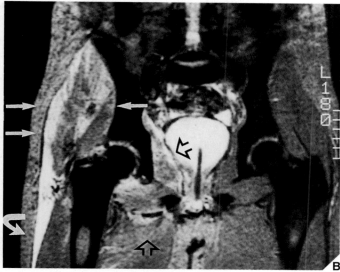

FIGURE 4.85 MRI of a soft-tissue injury. A 14-year-old boy presented with posterior dislocation of the right femoral head. After the dislocation was reduced, MRI was performed to assess the injury to the soft tissues. **(A)** Coronal T2*-weighted (multiplanar gradient recalled, TR 500/TE 15 msec, flip angle 15 degrees) sequence shows markedly increased signal surrounding the vastus lateralis and intermedius muscles (*straight arrows*). Note also the injury involving the medial fascial compartment and gluteal region muscles (*curved arrow*). **(B)** More posterior coronal section demonstrates increased signal in the gluteus medius and minimus muscles (*straight white arrows*) and the tensor fasciae latae (*curved arrow*). There is also an injury of the obturator internus, obturator externus, and adductor brevis and magnus muscles (*open arrows*). (From Laorr A et al., 1995, with permission.)

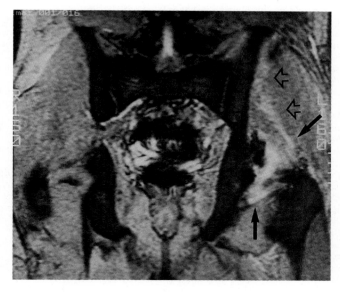

FIGURE 4.86 MRI of a soft-tissue injury. In another patient, a 20-year-old man who sustained posterior dislocation in the left hip, a coronal T2*-weighted (multiplanar gradient recalled; TR 550/TE 15 msec, flip angle 15 degrees) MRI shows disruption and increased signal in the region of the superior and inferior gemelli muscles (*arrows*). There is also an injury to the gluteal muscles (*open arrows*). (From Laorr A et al., 1995, with permission.)

PRACTICAL POINTS TO REMEMBER

[1] When dealing with suspected fractures and dislocations, obtain radiographs in at least two projections at 90 degrees to each other.

[2] To eliminate the risk of missing an associated injury, include the adjacent joints on the film.

[3] When a fracture is suspected, look for associated abnormalities such as
- soft-tissue swelling
- obliteration or displacement of fat stripes
- periosteal and endosteal reaction
- joint effusion

- intracapsular fat–fluid level
- double cortical line
- buckling of the cortex
- irregular metaphyseal corners.

[4] When reporting a fracture, describe
- the site and extent
- the type
- the direction of the fracture line
- the alignment of the fragments
- the presence of impaction, depression, or compression
- the presence of associated abnormalities
- whether the fracture is a special type
- whether the growth plate is involved (in which case, the Salter-Harris classification, together with Rang and Ogden additions, provides a useful method of precise evaluation of the injury).

[5] When a fracture fails to heal, distinguish between the three types of nonunion:
- reactive (hypertrophic and oligotrophic)
- nonreactive (atrophic)
- infected.

[6] In patients presenting with a history of skeletal trauma, be aware of such possible complications as
- disuse osteoporosis (mild or moderate)
- reflex sympathetic dystrophy syndrome (RSDS)
- Volkmann ischemic contracture
- posttraumatic myositis ossificans (the hallmarks of which are the clearly defined pattern of its evolution, the radiographic presence of the zonal phenomenon, and a radiolucent cleft)
- osteonecrosis (the earliest signs may be demonstrated by MRI or later may manifest as an increased uptake of a tracer on scintigraphy; the radiographic hallmark is the radiolucent crescent sign)
- injury to vessels (best demonstrated by DSA)
- growth disturbance
- posttraumatic arthritis.

[7] Regarding juxtacortical myositis ossificans, remember that its MRI appearance depends on the stage of maturation of the lesion:
- in the early stage, T1-weighted images will show a mass of intermediate signal intensity, whereas on T2-weighted images, the lesion will be of high signal intensity

- in the mature stage, T1- and T2-weighted images will demonstrate a peripheral rim of low signal intensity corresponding to bone maturation
- the fatty component of the lesion will image as high signal intensity on T1 weighting and as intermediate signal on T2 weighting.

[8] Osteonecrosis can be best staged with MRI. Four classes of osteonecrosis (fat-like, blood-like, fluid-like, and fibrous) correlate well with histopathologic changes in the bone.

[9] Stress fractures should be viewed as the endpoint of a spectrum along which a bone responds to a changing mechanical environment, ranging from excessive remodeling to a frank fracture. In imaging these injuries, be aware that
- initial radiographs are often normal
- the first radiographic abnormality to look for is a subtle poor definition of the cortex (gray cortex sign)
- radionuclide bone scan is highly sensitive and frequently shows a characteristic fusiform area or transverse band of increased activity
- MRI may show a typical finding of an area of low signal intensity in the bone marrow on T1 weighting that becomes of high signal on T2-weighted images, frequently showing a central low-signal band presumably representing the fracture line.

[10] When dealing with an injury to soft tissues, consider using supplemental imaging modalities, including
- stress radiography
- arthrography
- tenography and bursography
- computed tomography
- magnetic resonance imaging.

[11] MRI is an invaluable technique for identifying various injuries to the muscles, tendons, and ligaments. This modality can effectively delineate the variable degrees of strain, contusion, tear, or hematoma and permits the quantification of these injuries.

SUGGESTED READINGS

Adelberg JS, Smith GH. Corticosteroid-induced avascular necrosis of the talus. *J Foot Surg* 1991;30:66–69.

Allard JC, Porter G, Ryerson RW. Occult posttraumatic avascular necrosis of hip revealed by MRI. *Magn Reson Imaging* 1992;10:155–159.

Anderson MW, Greenspan A. State of the art: stress fractures. *Radiology* 1996;199:1–12.

Arger PH, Oberkircher PE, Miller WT. Lipohemarthrosis. *Am J Roentgenol* 1974;121:97–100.

Arndt WF III, Truax AL, Barnett FM, Simmons GE, Brown DC. MR diagnosis of bone contusions of the knee: comparison of coronal T2-weighted fast spin-echo with fat saturation and fast spin-echo STIR images with conventional STIR images. *Am J Roentgenol* 1996;166:119–124.

Assouline-Dayan Y, Chang C, Greenspan A, Shoenfeld Y, Gershwin ME. Pathogenesis and natural history of osteonecrosis. *Semin Arthritis Rheum* 2002;32:94–124.

Athanasian G, Wickiewicz T. Osteonecrosis of the femoral condyle after arthroscopic reconstruction of a cruciate ligament. *J Bone Joint Surg Am* 1995;77A:1418–1421.

Baker ND. Pseudoaneurysm—a complication of fracture through cement after total hip replacement. *Orthop Rev* 1981;10:110–111.

Bassett LW, Grover JS, Seeger LL. Magnetic resonance imaging of knee trauma. *Skeletal Radiol* 1990;19:401–405.

Beltran J. *MRI: Musculoskeletal system.* Philadelphia: JB Lippincott; 1990.

Beltran J, Burk JM, Herman LJ, et al. Avasacular necrosis of the femoral head: early MRI detection and radiological correlation. *Magn Reson Imaging* 1987;5:531–542.

Beltran J, Herman LJ, Burk JM, et al. Femoral head avascular necrosis: MR imaging with clinical-pathologic and radionuclide correlation. *Radiology* 1988;166:215–220.

Blum GM, Crues JV, Sheehan W. MR of occult bony trauma: the missing link. *Appl Radiol* 1993;22:15–21.

Bohrer SP. The fat pad sign following elbow trauma. Its usefulness and reliability in suspecting "invisible" fractures. *Clin Radiol* 1970;21:90–94.

Borden S. Traumatic bowing of the forearm in children. *J Bone Joint Surg Am* 1974;56A:611–616.

Caffey J. *Pediatric X-ray diagnosis,* vol. 2, 2nd ed. Chicago: Year Book Medical Publishers; 1973.

Chadwick DJ, Bentley G. The classification and prognosis of epiphyseal injuries. *Injury* 1987;18:157–168.

Chan WP, Liu Y-J, Huang G-S, Jiang C-C, Huang S, Chang Y-C. MRI of joint fluid in femoral head osteonecrosis. *Skeletal Radiol* 2002;31:624–630.

Chang CC, Greenspan A, Gershwin ME. Osteonecrosis: current perspectives on pathogenesis and treatment. *Semin Arthritis Rheum* 1993;23:47–69.

Coleman BG, Kressel HY, Dalinka MK, Schiebler ML, Burk DL, Cohen EK. Radiographically negative avascular necrosis: detection with MR imaging. *Radiology* 1988;168:525–528.

Colwell CW, Robinson C. Osteonecrosis of the femoral head in patients with inflammatory arthritis on asthma receiving corticosteroid therapy. *Orthopedics* 1996;19:941–946.

Cushner FO, Friedman RJ. Osteonecrosis of the femoral head. *Orthop Rev* 1988;17:29–34.

Daffner RH, Pavlov H. Stress fractures: current concepts. *Am J Roentgenol* 1992;159:245–252.

Davidson JK. Dysbaric disorders. Aseptic bone necrosis in tunnel workers and divers. *Clin Rheumatol* 1989;3:1–23.

Davidson JK, Briggs JD. Osteonecrosis and fracture following renal transplantation. *Clin Radiol* 1985;36:27–35.

DeSmet AA. Magnetic resonance findings in skeletal muscle tears. *Skeletal Radiol* 1993;22:479–484.

DeSmet AA, Fisher DR, Heiner JP, Keene JS. Magnetic resonance imaging of muscle tears. *Skeletal Radiol* 1990;19:283–286.

DeSmet AA, Norris MA, Fisher DR. Magnetic resonance imaging of myositis ossificans: analysis of seven cases. *Skeletal Radiol* 1992;21:503–507.

Deutsch AL, Mink JH. Magnetic resonance imaging of musculoskeletal injuries. *Radiol Clin North Am* 1989;27:983–1002.

Deutsch AL, Mink JH, Waxman AD. Occult fractures of the proximal femur: MR imaging. *Radiology* 1989;170:113–116.

Drery P, Sartoris DJ. Osteonecrosis in the foot. *J Foot Surg* 1991;30:477–483.

Eisenberg RL. *Atlas of signs in radiology.* Philadelphia: JB Lippincott; 1984.

Ferlic OC, Morin P. Idiopathic avascular necrosis of the scaphoid—Preiser's disease? *J Hand Surg* 1989;14:13–16.

Ficat RP. Treatment of avascular necrosis of the femoral head. In: Hungerford DS, ed. *The hip: Proceedings of the Eleventh Open Meeting of The Hip Society.* St. Louis: CV Mosby; 1983:279–295.

Ficat RP. Idiopathic bone necrosis of the femoral head: early diagnosis and treatment. *J Bone Joint Surg Br* 1985;67B:3–9.

Ficat RP, Arlet J. Ischemia and necrosis of bone. In: Hungerford DS, ed. *Ischemia and necrosis of bone.* Baltimore: Williams & Wilkins; 1980:196.

Ficat RP, Arlet J. Treatment of bone ischemia and necrosis. In: Hungerford DS, ed. *Ischemia and necrosis of bone.* Baltimore: Williams & Wilkins; 1980:171–182.

Frostick SP, Wallace WP. Osteonecrosis of the humeral head. *Clin Rheumatol* 1989;3:651–657.

Genant HK, Kozin F, Bekerman C, McCarty DJ, Sims J. The reflect sympathetic dystrophy syndrome. *Radiology* 1975;117:21–32.

Haajanen J, Saarinen O, Laasonen L, Kuhl back B, Edgren J, Slatis P. Steroid treatment and aseptic necrosis of the femoral head in renal transplant recipients. *Transplant Proc* 1984;16:1316–1319.

Hendrix RW, Rogers LF. Diagnostic imaging of fracture complications. *Radiol Clin North Am* 1989;27:1023–1033.

Herrmann LG, Reineke HG, Caldwell JA. Post-traumatic painful osteoporosis: a clinical and roentgenological entity. *Am J Roentgenol* 1942;47:353–361.

Holt G, Helms CA, Steinbach L, Neumann C, Munk PL, Genart HK. Magnetic resonance imaging of the shoulder: rationale and current applications. *Skeletal Radiol* 1990;19:5–14.

Hungerford DS, Lennox DW. The importance of increased intraoseous pressure in the development of osteonecrosis of the femoral head: implications for treatment. *Orthop Clin North Am* 1985;16:635–654.

Hungerford DS, Zizic TM. Alcoholism associated ischemic necrosis of the femoral head. *Clin Orthop* 1978;130:144–153.

Iannotti JP. Growth plate physiology and pathology. *Orthop Clin North Am* 1990; 21:1–17.

Imhof H, Breitenseher M, Trattnig S, et al. Imaging of avascular necrosis of bone. *Eur Radiol* 1997;7:180–186.

Iwasaki K, Hirano T, Sagara K, Nishimura Y. Idiopathic necrosis of the femoral epiphyseal nucleus in rats. *Clin Orthop* 1992;277:31–40.

Jaramillo D, Hoffer FA, Shapiro F, Rand F. MR imaging of fractures of the growth plate. *Am J Roentgenol* 1990;155:1261–1265.

Jelinek JS, Kransdorf MJ. MR imaging of soft-tissue masses. Mass-like lesions that simulate neoplasms. *Magn Reson Imaging Clin N Am* 1995;3:727–741.

Jergesen HE, Khan AS. The natural history of untreated asymptomatic hips in patients who have nontraumatic osteonecrosis. *J Bone J Surg Am* 1997;79A:359–363.

Johnston RM, Jones WW. Fractures through human growth plates. *Orthop Trans* 1980;4:295.

Jones DA. Volkmann's ischemia. *Surg Clin North Am* 1970;50:329–342.

Jones G. Radiological appearance of disuse osteoporosis. *Clin Radiol* 1969;20: 345–353.

Jones JP, Engleman GP, Najarian JS. Systemic fat embolism after renal transplantation and treatment with corticosteroids. *N Engl J Med* 1965;273:1453–1458.

Kay NRM, Park WM, Bark MB. The relationship between pregnancy and femoral head necrosis. *Br J Radiol* 1972;45:828–831.

Khanna A, Yoon T, Mont M, Hungerford D, Bluemke D. Femoral head osteonecrosis: detection and grading by using a rapid MR imaging protocol. *Radiology* 2000;217:188–192.

Kleinmann P. *Diagnostic Imaging of Child Abuse.* St. Louis: Mosby; 1998.

Koch E, Hofer HO, Sialer G, Marincek B, von Schulthess GK. Failure of MR imaging to detect reflex sympathetic dystrophy of the extremities. *Am J Roentgenol* 1991;156:113–115.

Koo K-H, Ahn I-O, Kim R, et al. Bone marrow edema and associated pain in early stage osteonecrosis of the femoral head: prospective study with serial MR images. *Radiology* 1999;213:715–722.

Kozin F. Reflex sympathetic dystrophy syndrome: a review. *Clin Exp Rheumatol* 1992;10:401–409.

Kransdorf MJ, Meis JM, Jelinek JS. Myositis ossificans: MR appearance with radiologic-pathologic correlation. *Am J Roentgenol* 1991;157:1243–1248.

Kuhlman JE, Fishman EK, Magid D, Scott WW Jr, Brooker AF, Siegelman SS. Fracture nonunion: CT assessment with multiplanar reconstruction. *Radiology* 1988;167:483–488.

Lafforgue P, Dahan P, Chagnaud C, Acquaviva P-C. Early-stage avascular necrosis of the femoral head: MR imaging for prognosis in 31 cases with at least 2 years of follow-up. *Radiology* 1993;187:199–204.

Lang P, Jergesen HE, Moseley ME, Chafetz NI, Genant HK. Avascular necrosis of the femoral head: high-field-strength MR imaging with histologic correlation. *Radiology* 1988;169:517–524.

Langevitz P, Baskila O. Osteonecrosis in patients receiving dialysis: report of two cases and review of the literature. *J Rheumatol* 1990;17:402–406.

Laorr A, Greenspan A, Anderson MW, Moehring HD, McKinley T. Traumatic hip dislocation: early MRI findings. *Skeletal Radiol* 1995;24:239–245.

Laurin NR, Powe JE, Pavlosky WF, Driedger AA. Multimodality imaging of early heterotopic bone formation. *J Can Assoc Radiol* 1990;41:93–95.

Lonergan GJ, Baker AM, Morey MK, Boos SC. From the archives of the AFIP. Child abuse: radiologic-pathologic correlation. *Radiographics* 2003;33:811–845.

Lotke PA, Geker ML. Osteonecrosis of the knee. *J Bone Joint Surg Am* 1988;70A:470–473.

MacEwan DW. Changes due to trauma in the fat plane overlying the pronator quadratus muscle. A radiologic sign. *Radiology* 1964;82:879–886.

Mankin HJ. Nontraumatic necrosis of bone (osteonecrosis). *N Engl J Med* 1992;326:1473–1479.

Marcus NO, Enneking WF. The silent hip in idiopathic aseptic necrosis. *J Bone Joint Surg Am* 1973;55A:1351–1366.

Markisz JA, Knowles RJR, Altchek DW, Schneider R, Whalen JP, Cahill PT. Segmental patterns of avascular necrosis of the femoral heads: early detection with MR imaging. *Radiology* 1987;162:717–720.

Martin JS, Marsh JL. Current classification of fractures. Rationale and utility. *Radiol Clin North Am* 1997;35:491–506.

Mazet R Jr, Hohl M. Fractures of the carpal navicular. *J Bone Joint Surg Am* 1963;45A:82–112.

McDougall IR, Rieser RP. Scintigraphic techniques in musculoskeletal trauma. *Radiol Clin North Am* 1989;27:1003–1011.

Merten DF, Carpenter BLM. Radiologic imaging of inflicted injury in the child abuse syndrome. *Ped Clin North Am* 1990;37:815–837.

Mink JH, Deutsch AL. Occult cartilage and bone injuries of the knee: detection, classification, and assessment with MR imaging. *Radiology* 1989;170:823–829.

Mirzai R, Chang C, Greenspan A, Gershwin ME. Avascular necrosis. *Comp Ther* 1998;24:251–255.

Mirzai A, Chang CC, Greenspan A, Gershwin ME. The pathogenesis of osteonecrosis and the relationship to corticosteroids. *J Asthma* 1999;36:77–95.

Mitchell DG, Joseph PM, Fallon M, et al. Chemical-shift MR imaging of the femoral head: an in vitro study of normal hips and hips with avascular necrosis. *Am J Roentgenol* 1987;148:1159–1164.

Mitchell DG, Kressel HY, Arger PH, Palinka M, Spritzer CE, Steinberg ME. Avascular necrosis of the femoral head: morphologic assessment by MR imaging, with CT correlation. *Radiology* 1986;161:739–742.

Mitchell DG, Kundel JL, Steinberg MF. Avascular necrosis of the hip: comparison of MR, CT and scintigraphy. *Am J Roentgenol* 1986;147:67–71.

Mitchell DG, Rao VM, Dalinka MK, et al. Femoral head avascular necrosis: correlation of MR imaging, radiographic staging, radionuclide imaging, and clinical findings. *Radiology* 1987;162:709–715.

Moran MC. Osteonecrosis of the hip in sickle cell hemoglobinopathy. *Am J Orthop* 1995;24:18–24.

Müller ME, Allgower M, Schneider R, Willenegger H. *Manual of internal fixation, techniques recommended by the AO Group*. 2nd ed. Berlin, Germany: Springer-Verlag; 1979.

Naimark A, Miller K, Segal D, Kossoff J. Nonunion. *Skeletal Radiol* 1981;6:21–25.

Nelson SW. Some important diagnostic and technical fundamentals in the radiology of trauma, with particular emphasis on skeletal trauma. *Radiol Clin North Am* 1966;4:241–259.

Norell H-G. Roentgenologic visualization of the extracapsular fat. Its importance in the diagnosis of traumatic injuries to the elbow. *Acta Radiol* 1954;42:205–210.

Norman A, Bullough P. The radiolucent crescent line—an early diagnostic sign of avascular necrosis of the femoral head. *Bull Hosp J Dis* 1963;24:99–104.

Norman A, Dorfman HD. Juxtacortical circumscribed myositis ossificans: evolution and radiographic features. *Radiology* 1970;96:301–306.

Nuovo MA, Norman A, Chumas J, Ackerman LV. Myositis ossificans with atypical clinical, radiographic, or pathologic findings: a review of 23 cases. *Skeletal Radiol* 1992;21:87–101.

Ogden JA. Injury to the growth mechanisms of the immature skeleton. *Skeletal Radiol* 1981;6:237–247.

Ogden JA. Skeletal growth mechanism injury patterns. *J Pediatr Orthop* 1982;2:371–377.

Ohzono K, Saito M. The fate of nontraumatic avascular necrosis of the femoral head: a radiologic classification to formulate prognosis. *Clin Orthop* 1992;277:73–78.

Ono K, Tohjima T. Risk factors of avascular necrosis of the femoral head in patients with systemic lupus erythematosus under high-dose corticosteroid therapy. *Clin Orthop* 1992;277:89–97.

Pappas JN. The musculoskeletal crescent sign. *Radiology* 2000;217:213–214.

Patton RW, Evans DIK. Silent avascular necrosis of the femoral head in haemophilia. *J Bone Joint Surg Br* 1988;70B:737–739.

Petrini F, Amoroso L, Carotti L, Cerioni M, Ravasi E, Lanza R. Myositis ossificans circumscripta: computerized tomography and magnetic resonance findings. *Radiol Med* 1995;90:492–494.

Rang M. *The growth plate and its disorders*. Baltimore: Williams & Wilkins; 1969.

Riley PM, Weiner DS. Hazards of internal fixation in the treatment of slipped capital femoral epiphysis. *J Bone Joint Surg Br* 1990;72B:854–858.

Rockwood CA Jr, Green DP. *Fractures in adults*, vol. 1. Philadelphia: JB Lippincott; 1984.

Rockwood CA Jr, Wilkins KE, King RE. *Fractures in children*, vol. 3. Philadelphia: JB Lippincott; 1984.

Rogers LF. The radiography of epiphyseal injuries. *Radiology* 1970;96:289–299.

Rogers LF. *Radiology of skeletal trauma*. New York: Churchill Livingstone; 1992.

Rogers LF, Poznanski AK. State of the art. Imaging of epiphyseal injuries. *Radiology* 1994;191:297–308.

Rosen H. Treatment of nonunions: general principles. In: Chapman MW, ed. *Operative orthopaedics*. 2nd ed. Philadelphia: JB Lippincott; 1993:749–769.

Salter RB. *Textbook of disorders and injuries of the musculoskeletal system*. Baltimore: Williams & Wilkins; 1970.

Salter RB, Harris WR. Injuries involving the epiphyseal plate. *J Bone Joint Surg Am* 1963;45A:587–622.

Sclamberg J, Sonin AH, Sclamberg E, D'Sonza N. Acute plastic bowing deformation of the forearm in an adult. *Am J Roentgenol* 1998;170:1259–1260.

Seiler JG III, Christie MJ, Homra L. Correlation of the findings of magnetic resonance imaging with those of bone biopsy in patients who have stage I or II ischemic necrosis of the femoral head. *J Bone Joint Surg Am* 1989;71A:28–32.

Shellock FG, Mink J, Deutsch AL. MR imaging of muscle injuries. *Appl Radiol* 1994;23:11–16.

Shimizu K, Moriya H, Akita T, Sakamoto M, Suguro T. Prediction of collapse with magnetic resonance imaging of avascular necrosis of the femoral head. *J Bone Joint Surg Am* 1994;76A:215–223.

Shinoda S, Hasegawa Y, Kawasaki S, Tagawa N, Iwata H. Magnetic resonance imaging of osteonecrosis in divers: comparison with plain radiographs. *Skeletal Radiol* 1997;26:354–359.

Shirkhoda A, Armin A-R, Bis KG, Makris J, Irwin RB, Shetty AN. MR imaging of myositis ossificans: variable patterns at different stages. *J Magn Reson Imaging* 1995;5:287–292.

Smith DW. Is avascular necrosis of the femoral head the result of inhibition of angiogenesis? *Med Hypotheses* 1997;49:497–500.

Steinbach LS, Fleckenstein JL, Mink JH. MRI techniques and practical applications. Magnetic resonance imaging of muscle injuries. *Orthopedics* 1994;17:991–999.

Stevens K, Tao C, Lee S-V, et al. Subchondral fractures in osteonecrosis of the femoral head: comparison of radiography, CT, and MR imaging. *Am J Roentgenol* 2003;180:363–368.

Stoller DW, Maloney WJ, Glick JM. The hip. In: Stoller DW, ed. *Magnetic resonance imaging in orthopaedics and rheumatology*. Philadelphia: Lippincott Raven; 1997:93–202.

Suehiro M, Hirano T, Mihara K, Shindo H. Etiologic factors in femoral head osteonecrosis in growing rats. *J Orthop Sci* 2000;5:52–56.

Sugimoto H, Okubu RS, Ohsawa T. Chemical shift and the double-line sign in MRI of early femoral avascular necrosis. *J Comput Assist Tomogr* 1992;16:727–730.

Szabo RM, Greenspan A. Diagnosis and clinical findings of Keinböck's disease. *Hand Clin* 1993;9:399–407.

Takatori Y, Kokubo T, Ninomiya S, Nakamura S, Movimoto S, Kusuba I. Avascular necrosis of the femoral head: natural history and magnetic resonance imaging. *J Bone Joint Surg Br* 1993;75B:217–221.

Terry DW Jr, Ramin JE. The navicular fat stripe: a useful roentgen feature for evaluating wrist trauma. *Am J Roentgenol* 1975;124:25–28.

Tervonen O, Snoep G, Stuart MJ, Ehman RL. Traumatic trabecular lesions observed on MR imaging of the knee. *Acta Radiol* 1991;32:389–392.

Thickman D, Axel L, Kressel HY, et al. Magnetic resonance imaging of avascular necrosis of the femoral head. *Skeletal Radiol* 1986;15:133–140.

Thometz JG, Lamdan R. Osteonecrosis of the femoral head after intramedullary nailing of a fracture of the femoral shaft in an adolescent. *J Bone Joint Surg Am* 1995;77A:1423–1426.

Trueta J. Nonunion of fractures. *Clin Orthop* 1965;43:23–35.

Trumble TE. Avascular necrosis after scaphoid fracture: a correlation of magnetic resonance imaging and histology. *J Hand Surg Am* 1990;15:557–564.

Vande Berg B, Malghem J, Labaisse MA, Noel H, Maldague B. Avascular necrosis of the hip: comparison of contrast-enhanced and nonenhanced MR imaging with histologic correlation. *Radiology* 1992;182:445–450.

Weissman BNW, Sledge CB. *Orthopedic radiology*. Philadelphia: WB Saunders; 1986:1–69.

Wenzel WW. The FBI sign. *Rocky Mount Med J* 1972;69:71–72.

Williams ES, Khreisat S, Ell PJ, King JD. Bone imaging and skeletal radiology in dysbaric osteonecrosis. *Clin Radiol* 1987;38:589–592.

Williams M, Laredo J-D, Setbon S, et al. Unusual longitudinal stress fractures of the femoral diaphysis: report of five cases. *Skeletal Radiol* 1999;27:81–85.

Zurlo JV. The double-line sign. *Radiology* 1999;212:541–542.

Upper Limb I
Shoulder Girdle

Shoulder Girdle

Trauma to the shoulder girdle is common throughout life, but the site of injury varies with age. In children and adolescents, fracture of the clavicle sustained during play or athletic activities is a frequent type of skeletal injury. Dislocations of the shoulder and acromioclavicular separation are often seen in the third and fourth decades of life, whereas fracture of the proximal humerus is commonly encountered in the elderly. Most of these traumatic conditions can be diagnosed on the basis of history and clinical examination, with radiographs obtained mainly to define the exact site, type, and extent of the injury. At times, however, as in posterior dislocation in the glenohumeral joint, for example, which is the most commonly missed diagnosis in shoulder trauma, only radiographic examination performed in the proper projections may reveal the abnormality.

Anatomic–Radiologic Considerations

The shoulder girdle consists of osseous components—proximal humerus, scapula, and clavicle, forming the glenohumeral and acromioclavicular joints (Fig. 5.1)—and various muscles, ligaments, and tendons reinforcing the joint capsule (Fig. 5.2). The joint capsule inserts along the anatomic neck of the humerus and along the neck of the glenoid. In front, it is reinforced by three glenohumeral ligaments (GHLs) (the superior, middle, and inferior), which converge from the humerus to be attached by the long head of the biceps tendon to the supraglenoid tubercle. The other important ligaments are the acromioclavicular, coracoacromial, and the coracoclavicular (including trapezoid and conoid portions) (see Fig. 5.2A).

The essential muscles are those that form the rotator cuff (Fig. 5.3). The term rotator cuff is used to describe the group of muscles that envelop the glenohumeral joint, holding the head of the humerus firmly in the glenoid fossa. They consist of the subscapularis anteriorly, the infraspinatus posterosuperiorly, the teres minor posteriorly, and the supraspinatus superiorly (mnemonic SITS). The subscapularis muscle inserts on the lesser tuberosity anteriorly. The insertions of the supraspinatus, infraspinatus, and teres minor muscles are on the greater tuberosity, posteriorly. The supraspinatus tendon covers the superior aspect of the humeral head, inserting on the superior facet of the greater tuberosity. The infraspinatus tendon covers the superior and posterior aspects of the humeral head and inserts on the middle facet, located distal and more posterior to the superior facet. The teres minor is lower in

position and inserts on the posteroinferior facet of the greater tuberosity (Fig. 5.3B). In addition, the long head of the biceps with its tendon, which in its intracapsular portion runs through the joint, and the triceps muscle, inserting on the infraglenoid tubercle inferiorly, provide additional support to the glenohumeral joint.

Most trauma to the shoulder area can be sufficiently evaluated on radiographs obtained in the *anteroposterior* projection with the arm in the *neutral* position (Fig. 5.4A) or with the arm *internally* or *externally rotated* to visualize different aspects of the humeral head. The one limitation of these views is that the humeral head is seen overlapping the glenoid, thereby obscuring the glenohumeral joint space (Fig. 5.4B). Eliminating the overlap can be accomplished by rotating the patient approximately 40 degrees toward the affected side. This special posterior oblique view, known as the *Grashey projection*, permits the glenoid to be seen in profile (Fig. 5.5) and is thus particularly effective in demonstrating suspected posterior dislocation. Obliteration of the normally clear space between the humeral head and the glenoid margin on this view confirms the diagnosis (see Figs. 5.54 and 5.56).

Other special views have proved to be useful in evaluating suspected trauma to various aspects of the shoulder. A superoinferior view of the shoulder, known as the *axillary* projection, is helpful in determining the exact relationship of the humeral head and the glenoid fossa (Fig. 5.6), as well as in detecting anterior or posterior dislocation. This view, however, may at times be difficult to obtain, particularly if the patient is unable to abduct the arm, in which case a variant of the axillary projection known as the *West Point* view may be similarly effective. In addition to all the benefits of the axillary projection, the West Point view effectively demonstrates the anteroinferior rim of the glenoid (Fig. 5.7). Another useful variant of the axillary projection is the *Lawrence* view. The importance of this projection lies in the fact that it does not require full abduction of the arm, because it can be compensated for by angulation of the radiographic tube (Fig. 5.8). Suspected trauma to the proximal humerus, which can be demonstrated on the anteroposterior or the transscapular projection (see Fig. 5.12), may require the *transthoracic lateral* view for sufficient evaluation (Fig. 5.9). Because this projection provides a true lateral view of the proximal humerus, it is particularly valuable in determining the degree of displacement or angulation of the osseous fragments (see Fig. 5.28B). When trauma to the bicipital groove is suspected, a *tangent* radiograph of this structure is required (Fig. 5.10). Injury to the acromioclavicular articulation is usually evaluated on the anteroposterior view obtained with a 15-degree cephalad tilt of the radiographic tube (Fig. 5.11). Stress views in this projection, for which weights are

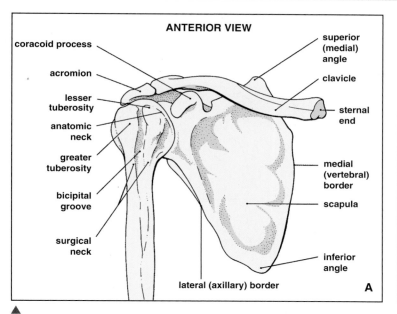

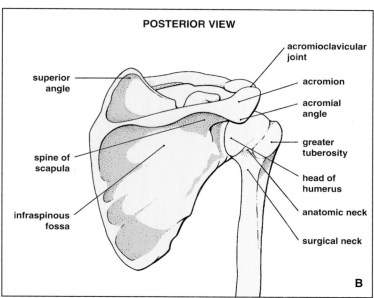

FIGURE 5.1 Osseous structures of the shoulder. Anterior **(A)** and posterior **(B)** views of the osseous components of the shoulder girdle.

strapped to the patient's forearms, are often mandatory, especially in suspected occult acromioclavicular subluxation (see Fig. 5.78). Fracture of the scapula may require a *transscapular* (or *Y*) view for sufficient evaluation (Fig. 5.12). Fracture of the acromion can be adequately evaluated on the shoulder *outlet* view. This projection is obtained similarly to the Y view of the shoulder girdle; however, the central beam is directed toward the superior aspect of the humeral head and is angled approximately 10 to 15 degrees caudad (Fig. 5.13). This view is also effective in demonstration of morphologic types of the acromion (Fig. 5.14; see also Fig. 5.24).

Ancillary imaging techniques are usually used to evaluate injury to the cartilage and soft tissues of the shoulder. The most frequently used modalities are arthrography and magnetic resonance imaging (MRI). Arthrog-

raphy can be performed using a single- or double-contrast technique (Fig. 5.15). In cases of suspected tear of the rotator cuff, for example, a single-contrast arthrogram may reveal abnormal communication between the glenohumeral joint cavity and the subacromial–subdeltoid bursae complex, which is diagnostic of this abnormality (see Fig. 5.60C). Although it is difficult to prescribe for which conditions a single- as opposed to a double-contrast study should be chosen, the latter may be better suited to demonstrate abnormalities of the articular cartilage and capsule, as well as the presence of osteochondral bodies in the joint. A double-contrast study, however, is always indicated when arthrography is to be combined with CT scan (computed arthrotomography) for evaluating suspected abnormalities of the fibrocartilaginous glenoid labrum (Fig. 5.16). The effectiveness of this combination lies in the fact that the injected air outlines the

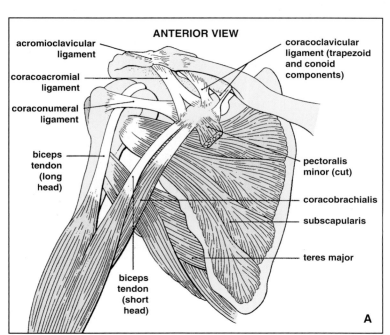

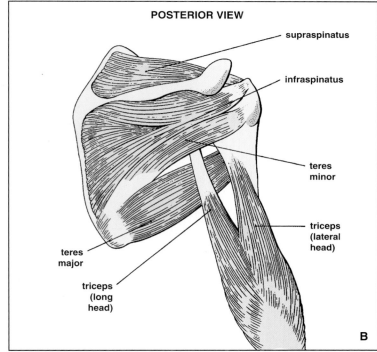

FIGURE 5.2 Muscles, ligaments, and tendons of the shoulder. Anterior **(A)** and posterior **(B)** views of the muscles, ligaments, and tendons of the shoulder girdle. (Modified from Middleton WD, Lawson TL, 1989, with permission.)

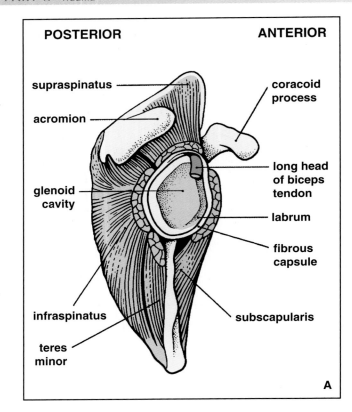

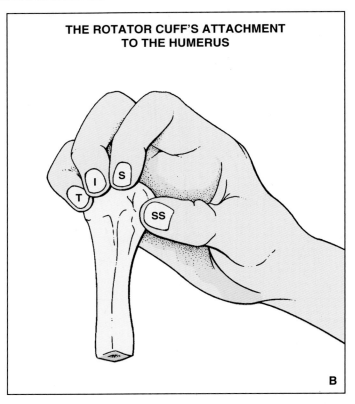

▲
FIGURE 5.3   Rotator cuff. (A) Schematic of the glenoid fossa (with the humerus removed) shows the location of the muscles of the rotator cuff and the intracapsular portion of the long head of the biceps tendon. **(B)** Four muscles form the "rotator cuff": subscapularis (*SS*), supraspinatus (*S*), infraspinatus (*I*), and teres minor (*T*). They envelop the joint, blend with the capsule, and grasp their four points of attachment to the humerus, as does the hand in the figure, thus maintaining the integrity of the joint. (Modified from Anderson JE, 1983, with permission.)

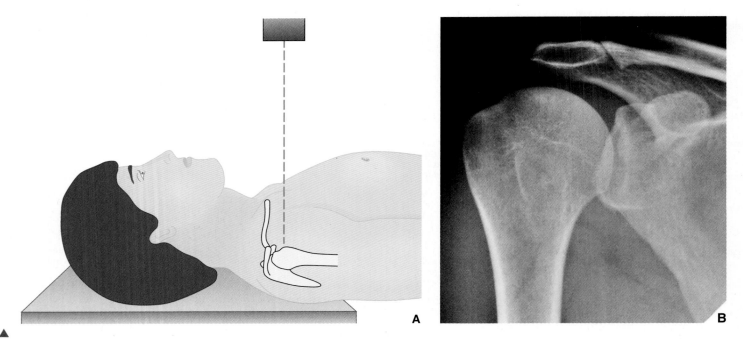

▲
FIGURE 5.4   Anteroposterior view. (A) For the standard anteroposterior projection of the shoulder, the patient may be either supine, as shown here, or erect; the arm of the affected side is fully extended in the neutral position. The central beam is directed toward the humeral head. **(B)** On the radiograph obtained in this projection, the humeral head is seen overlapping the glenoid fossa. The glenohumeral joint is not well demonstrated.

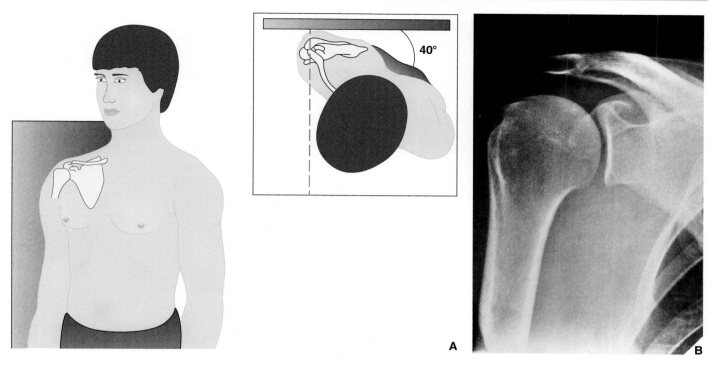

FIGURE 5.5   Grashey view. **(A)** For the anteroposterior view of the shoulder that demonstrates the glenoid in profile (Grashey projection), the patient may be either erect, as shown here, or supine. He or she is rotated approximately 40 degrees toward the side of the suspected injury, and the central beam is directed toward the glenohumeral joint. **(B)** The radiograph in this projection (posterior oblique view) shows the glenoid in true profile. Note that the glenohumeral joint space is now clearly visible.

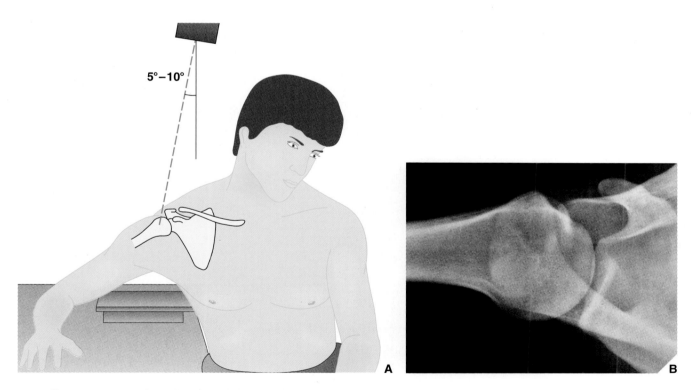

FIGURE 5.6   Axillary view. **(A)** For the axillary view of the shoulder, the patient is seated at the side of the radiographic table, with the arm abducted so that the axilla is positioned over the film cassette. The radiographic tube is angled approximately 5 to 10 degrees toward the elbow, and the central beam is directed through the shoulder joint. **(B)** The film in this projection demonstrates the exact relationship of the humeral head and the glenoid.

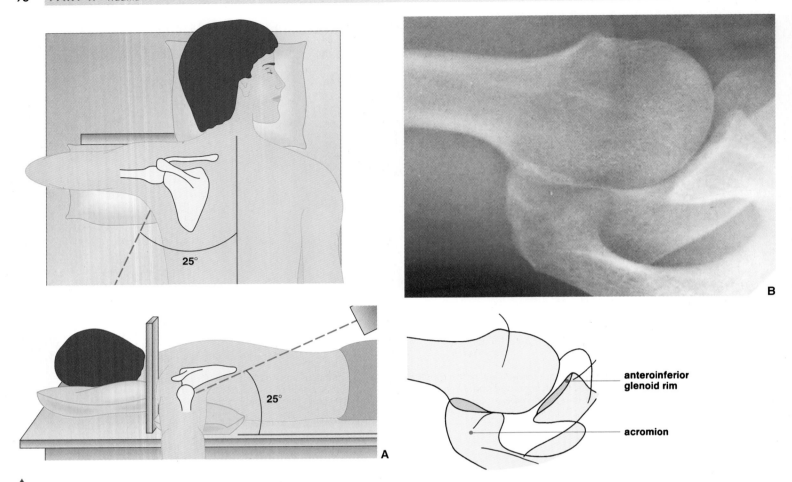

FIGURE 5.7   **West Point view. (A)** For the West Point view of the shoulder, the patient lies prone on the radiographic table, with a pillow placed under the affected shoulder to raise it approximately 8 cm. The film cassette is positioned against the superior aspect of the shoulder. The radiographic tube is angled toward the axilla at 25 degrees to the patient's midline and 25 degrees to the table's surface. **(B)** On the radiograph in this projection, the relationship of the humeral head and the glenoid can be as sufficiently evaluated as on the axillary view, but the anteroinferior glenoid rim, which is seen tangentially, is better visualized.

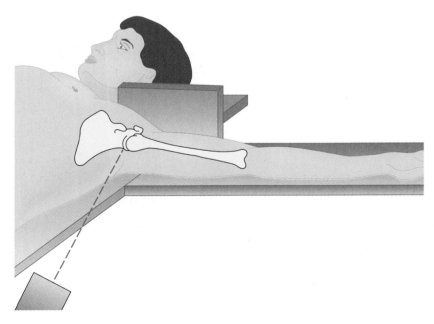

FIGURE 5.8   **Lawrence view.** For the Lawrence variant of the axillary view of the shoulder, the patient lies supine on the radiographic table, with the affected arm abducted up to 90 degrees. The film cassette is positioned against the superior aspect of the shoulder with the medial end against the neck, which places the midportion of the cassette level with the surgical neck of the humerus. The radiographic tube is at the level of the ipsilateral hip and is angled medially toward the axilla. The amount of angulation depends on the degree of abduction of the arm: Less abduction requires increased medial angulation. The central beam is directed horizontally slightly superior to the midportion of the axilla. The Lawrence view demonstrates the same structures as the standard axillary view.

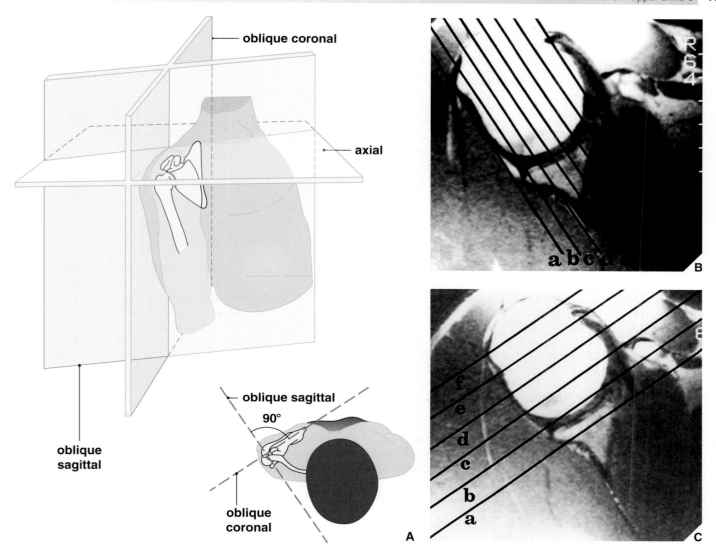

FIGURE 5.17 **MRI of the shoulder. (A)** Standard planes of MRI sections of the shoulder. **(B)** Oblique coronal sections are obtained parallel to the long axis of the supraspinatus muscle. **(C)** Oblique sagittal sections are obtained perpendicular to the coronal sections. (From Beltran J, 1990, with permission.)

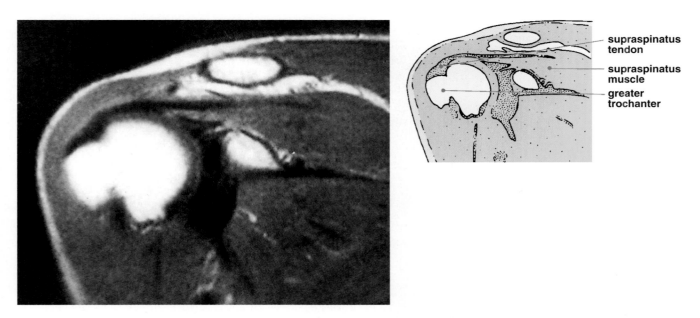

FIGURE 5.18 **MRI of the shoulder.** T1-weighted oblique coronal image of the right shoulder demonstrates a normal supraspinatus muscle and tendon attaching to the greater tuberosity of the humerus. (From Holt RG et al., 1990, with permission.)

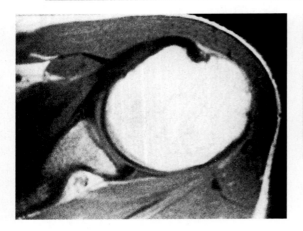

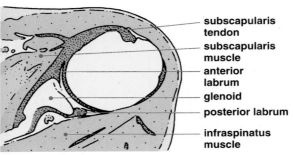

subscapularis tendon

subscapularis muscle

anterior labrum

glenoid

posterior labrum

infraspinatus muscle

◀ FIGURE 5.19   MRI of the shoulder. T1-weighted axial image of the left shoulder demonstrates a normal subscapularis muscle and tendon and the infraspinatus muscle.

the oblique coronal sections (Fig. 5.23). There are numerous imaging variations of the morphology of the cartilaginous labrum. The most common shape is triangular as illustrated in Figure 5.22. The second most common shape is round. The other morphologic variations include the flat labrum and the cleaved or notched labrum. On rare occasions, the anterior and posterior labrum may be absent. Furthermore, there are appearances resembling labral tears, such as undercutting of the labrum by hyaline cartilage, sublabral holes or recesses, and Buford complexes (see Fig. 5.74).

The sagittal images are useful in demonstration of morphologic variations of the acromion. Three types of acromion have been identified by Bigliani and coworkers. Type I shows a flat undersurface, type II a curved undersurface, type III a hooked undersurface, and type IV a convex undersurface (Figs. 5.24 and 5.25). Type III acromion is considered to be associated with tears of the rotator cuff proximal to the site of insertion of the supraspinatus tendon to the greater tuberosity of the humerus. Sagittal images also effectively demonstrate the muscles of the rotator cuff and their tendons (Fig. 5.26).

In the past decade, direct MR arthrography (MRa) using injection of contrast solution into the shoulder joint gained worldwide acceptance. This technique is particularly effective for demonstrating labral–ligamentous abnormalities and distinguishing partial-thickness from full-thickness tears of the rotator cuff. A variety of concentrations and mixtures of solutions are used by different radiologists. In our institution, we follow the recommendation reported by Steinbach and colleagues. We add 0.8 mL of gadopentetate dimeglumine (gadolinium with strength 287 mg/mL) to 100 mL of normal saline solution. Subsequently, we mix 10 mL of this solution with 5 mL of 60% meglumine diatrizoate (iodinated contrast) and 5 mL of 1% lidocaine, which gives a final gadolinium dilution ratio of 1:250. From 12 to 15 mL of this mixture is then injected into the shoulder joint using fluoroscopic guidance in a similar fashion as for conventional shoulder arthrography (see Fig. 5.15). Multiple pre-exercise and postexercise radiographic spot images are obtained in neutral position and in external and internal rotation of the arm. Subsequently, without delay, the patient undergoes MRI examination using similar scanning planes as for a conventional MR study. If glenoid labrum abnormalities are suspected, additional sequences are obtained in so-called ABER (abduction and external rotation) position.

During evaluation of MRI of the shoulder, it is helpful to use a checklist as provided in Table 5.1.

TYPES OF ANTERIOR CAPSULAR INSERTION

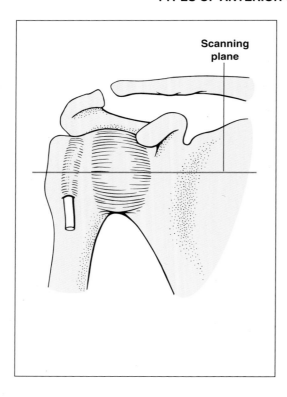

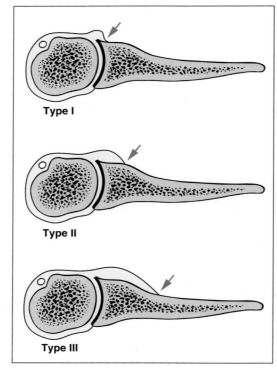

Type I

Type II

Type III

◀ FIGURE 5.20   Capsule of the shoulder joint. Three types of anterior capsular insertion to the scapula.

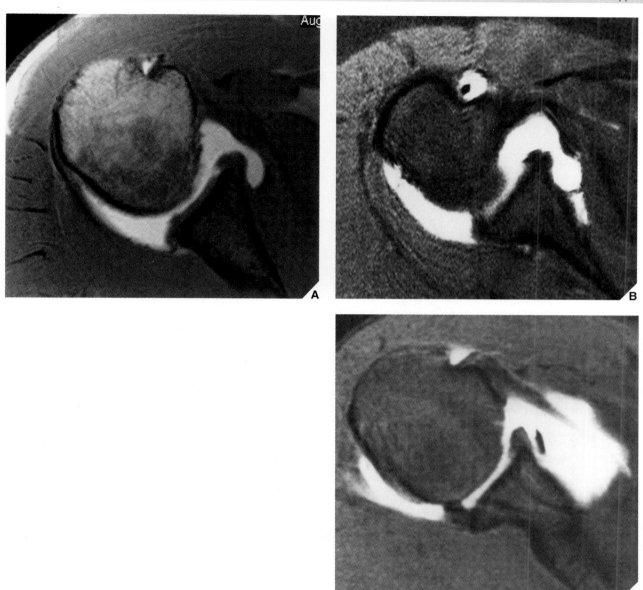

▲
FIGURE 5.21 Capsular insertion to glenoid margin. (A) Axial T1-weighted image after intraarticular injection of gadolinium shows type I of anterior capsular insertion. **(B)** Axial fast spin-echo image with fat saturation and intraarticular gadolinium shows type II of anterior capsular insertion. **(C)** Axial T1-weighted image with fat saturation and intraarticular gadolinium shows type III of anterior capsular insertion.

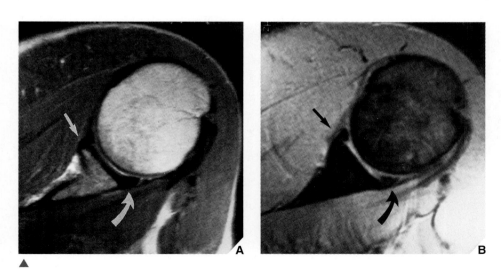

▲
FIGURE 5.22 Fibrocartilaginous labrum of the glenoid. (A) Axial T1-weighted and **(B)** axial T2-weighted (multiplanar gradient-recalled [MPGR]) MR images show anterior (*arrows*) and posterior (*curved arrows*) labra as small triangles of low signal intensity.

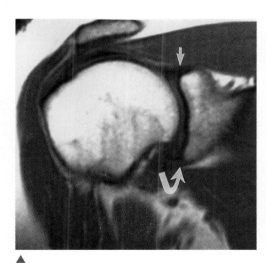

▲
FIGURE 5.23 Fibrocartilaginous labrum. Oblique coronal T1-weighted MRI shows a superior (*arrow*) and inferior (*curved arrow*) labra.

BIGLIANI CLASSIFICATION OF ACROMIAL MORPHOLOGY

A.
Schematic Representation of
MRI Appearance

B.
Anatomical Specimen

Post.   Ant.

Type 1
(flat)

Type 2
(smoothly
curved)

Type 3
(hooked)

Type 4
(convex
under
surface)

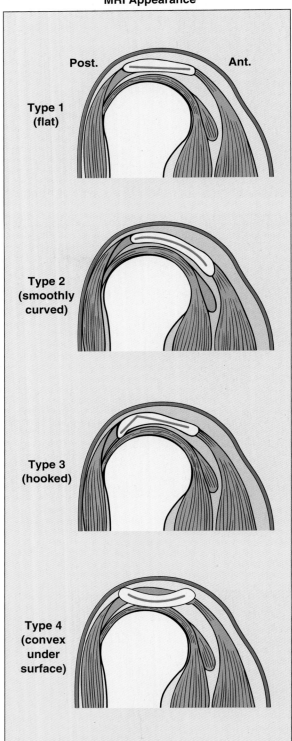

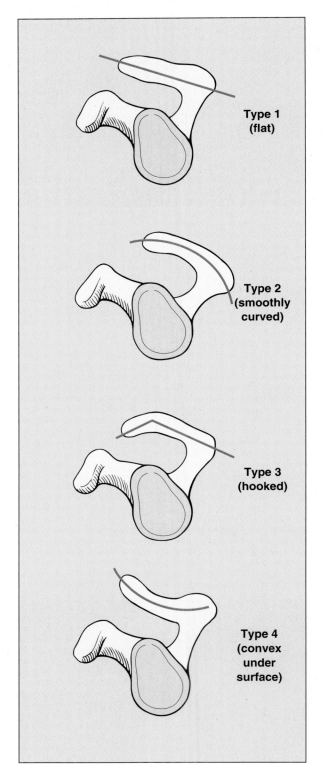

Type 1
(flat)

Type 2
(smoothly
curved)

Type 3
(hooked)

Type 4
(convex
under
surface)

FIGURE 5.24   Variations of the acromial morphology. Schematic representation of morphologic variations of the acromion. **(A)** MRI appearance on oblique sagittal sections. **(B)** Appearance on anatomical specimen.

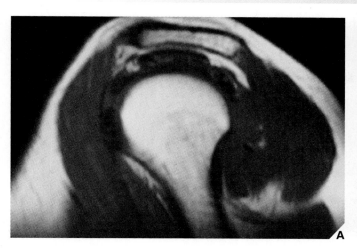
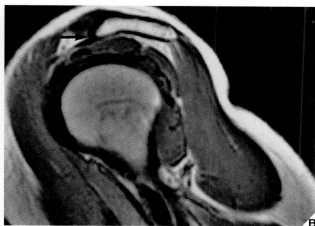

FIGURE 5.25   **Morphologic variations of the acromion. (A)** In the sagittal oblique plane, type II acromion shows a mild curved undersurface. **(B)** Type III acromion demonstrates a hooked undersurface (*arrow*).

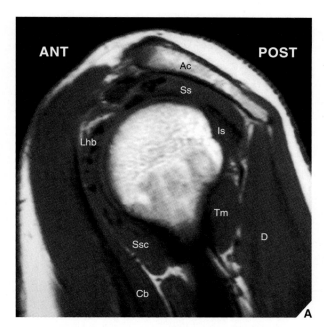

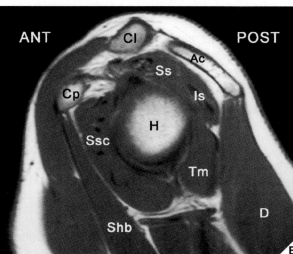

FIGURE 5.26   **Muscles and their tendons of the shoulder girdle as visualized on sagittal MRI. (A)** Lateral section, **(B)** medial section. H, Humeral head; Ac, acromion; Cl, clavicle; Cp, coracoid process; D, deltoid; Ss, supraspinatus; Is, infraspinatus; Ssc, subscapularis; Tm, teres minor; Shb, short head of the biceps; Lhb, long head of the biceps; Cb, coracobrachialis.

TABLE 5.1   **Checklist for Evaluation of MRI and MRa of the Shoulder**

Osseous Structures
   Humeral head (c, s, a)
   Glenoid (c, s, a)
   Acromion (c, s)
   Clavicle (c, s)
   Coracoacromial arch (s)

Cartilaginous Structures
   Articular cartilage (c, s, a)
   Fibrocartilaginous labrum, anterior, posterior, superior, inferior (c, a)

Joints
   Glenohumeral (c, a)
   Acromioclavicular (c)

Capsule
   Attachement (a)
   Laxity (a)

Muscles and Their Tendons
   Supraspinatus (c, s, a)
   Infraspinatus (c, s, a)
   Teres minor (c, s)
   Subscapularis (s, a)
   Biceps—long head (c, s, a)
   Deltoid (c, a)

Ligaments
   Superior glenohumeral (s, a)
   Middle glenohumeral (s, a)
   Inferior glenohumeral (s, a)
   Coracohumeral (c)
   Coracoclavicular—conoid and trapezoid (s)
   Coracoacromial (s)
   Acromioclavicular (c)

Bursae
   Subacromial (c)
   Subdeltoid (c)

Other Structures
   Rotator interval—space between supraspinatus and subscapularis (s)
   Quadrilateral space (s, a)
   Suprascapular notch (c, a)
   Spinoglenoid notch (c, a)

The best imaging planes for visualization of listed structures are given in parenthesis; c, coronal; s, sagittal; a, axial

TABLE 5.2 **Standard and Special Radiographic Projections for Evaluating Injury to the Shoulder Girdle**

Projection	Demonstration
Anteroposterior	
Arm in neutral position	Fracture of
	Humeral head and neck
	Clavicle
	Scapula
	Anterior dislocation
	Bankart lesion
Erect	Fat–blood interface (FBI sign)
Arm in internal rotation	Hill-Sacks lesion
Arm in external rotation	Compression fracture of humeral head (trough line impaction) secondary to posterior dislocation
40-degree posterior oblique (Grashey)	Glenohumeral joint space
	Glenoid in profile
	Posterior dislocation
15-degree cephalad tilt of radiographi tube	Acromioclavicular joint
	Acromioclavicular separation
	Fracture of clavicle
Stress	Occult acromioclavicular subluxation
	Acromioclavicular separation
Axillary	Relationship of humeral head and glenoid fossa
	Anterior and posterior dislocations
	Compression fractures secondary to anterior and posterior dislocations
	Fractures of
	Proximal humerus
	Scapula
West Point	Same structures and conditions as axillary projection
	Anteroinferior rim of glenoid
Lateral Transthoracic	Relationship of humeral head and glenoid fossa
	Fractures of proximal humerus
Tangent (humeral head)	Bicipital groove
Transscapular (Y)	Relationship of humeral head and glenoid fossa
	Fractures of
	Proximal humerus
	Body of scapula
	Coracoid process
	Acromion
Oblique (outlet)	Coracoacromial arch
	Rotator cuff outlet

For a summary of the foregoing discussion in tabular form, see Tables 5.2 and 5.3 and Figure 5.27.

Injury to the Shoulder Girdle

Fractures About the Shoulder

Fractures of the Proximal Humerus. Fractures of the upper humerus involving the head, the neck, and the proximal shaft usually result either from a direct blow to the humerus or, as is more often seen in elderly patients, from a fall on the outstretched arm. Nondisplaced fractures are the most common, representing approximately 85% of all such proximal humeral injuries.

The anteroposterior projection is usually sufficient to demonstrate the abnormality, but the transthoracic lateral or the transscapular (or Y) projection may be required to provide a fuller evaluation, particularly of the degree of displacement or angulation of the osseous fragments (Fig. 5.28). The erect anteroposterior radiograph may demonstrate the presence of fat and blood within the joint capsule (the FBI sign of lipohemarthrosis; see Fig. 4.36A), indicating intraarticular extension of the fracture.

Traditional classifications of trauma to the proximal humerus, according to the level of the fracture or the mechanism of injury, have been inadequate to identify the various types of displaced fractures. The four-segment classification described by Neer in 1970 was complex and difficult to follow. He later modified this classification and simplified divisions to various groups. Classification of a displacement pattern depends on two main factors: the number of displaced segments and the key segment displaced. Fractures of the proximal humerus occur between one or all of four major segments: the articular segment (at the level of the anatomic neck), the greater tuberosity, the lesser tuberosity, and the humeral shaft (at the level of the surgical neck). One-part fracture occurs when there is minimal or no displacement between the segments. In two-part fractures, only one segment is displaced. In three-part fractures, two segments are displaced and one tuberosity remains in continuity with the humeral head. In four-part fractures, three segments are displaced, including both tuberosities. Two-part, three-part, and four-part fractures may or may not be associated with dislocation, either anterior or posterior. The involvement of the articular surface is classified separately into

TABLE 5.3 Ancillary Imaging Techniques for Evaluating Injury to the Shoulder Girdle

Technique	Demonstration	Technique	Demonstration
Tomography (almost completely replaced by CT)	Position of fragments and extension of fracture line in complex fractures Healing process: Nonunion Secondary infection	*Ultrasound* (US)	Rotator cuff tear
Computed Tomography (CT)	Relationship of humeral head and glenoid fossa Multiple fragments in complex fractures (particularly of scapula) Intraarticular displacement of bony fragments in fractures	*Arthrography* Single- or double-contrast	Complete rotator cuff tear Partial rotator cuff tear Abnormalities of articular cartilage and joint capsule* Synovial abnormalities* Adhesive capsulitis Osteochondral bodies in joint* Abnormalities of bicipital tendon*† Intraarticular portion of bicipital tendon*†
Magnetic Resonance Imaging (MRI)	Impingement syndrome Partial and complete rotator cuff tear‡ Biceps tendon rupture Glenoid labrum tears‡ Glenohumeral instability Traumatic joint effusion Subtle synovial abnormalities‡	Double-contrast combined with CT	Inferior surface of rotator cuff*† All of the above and in addition: Abnormalities of cartilaginous glenoid labrum Osteochondral bodies in joint Subtle synovial abnormalities

*These conditions are usually best demonstrated using double-contrast arthrography.

†These features are best demonstrated on erect films.

‡These abnormalties are best demostraed on MRa.

two groups: the anterior fracture–dislocation, termed by Neer "head splitting," and posterior fracture–dislocation, termed "impression" (Fig. 5.29).

One-part fracture may involve any or all of the anatomic segments of the proximal humerus. There is no or minimal (less than 1 cm) displacement and no or minimal (less than 45 degrees) angulation; the fragments are being held together by the rotator cuff, the joint capsule, and the intact periosteum.

Two-part fracture indicates that only one segment is displaced in relation to the three that remain undisplaced. It may involve the anatomic neck, surgical neck, greater tuberosity, or lesser tuberosity. The two-part fracture involving the anatomic neck of the humerus with displacement of the articular end may be associated with tear of the rotator cuff, and complications such as malunion or osteonecrosis may later develop. In two-part fractures involving the surgical neck of the humerus with displacement or angulation of the shaft, three types may be seen: impacted, unimpacted, and comminuted. These fractures may be associated with either anterior or posterior dislocation. With anterior dislocation, the fracture invariably involves the greater tuberosity; with posterior dislocation, the fracture invariably involves the lesser tuberosity.

Three-part fracture may involve either greater tuberosity or lesser tuberosity and may be associated with anterior or posterior dislocation. Two segments are displaced in relation to two other segments that are not displaced.

Four-part fracture involves the greater and lesser tuberosity in addition to the fracture of the surgical neck, and four major segments are displaced (Fig. 5.30). This may be associated with anterior or posterior dislocation. The four-part fracture is usually associated with impairment of the blood supply to the humeral head, and osteonecrosis of the humeral head is a frequent complication.

Fractures of the Clavicle. A common injury in infancy during delivery, in adolescence caused by a direct blow or fall, and in adulthood as the result of a motor vehicle accident is a fracture of the clavicle, which can be divided into three types according to the anatomic segment involved (Fig. 5.31). The most common site of injury is the middle third of the clavicle, representing 80% of all clavicular fractures. Fractures of the distal (lateral) third (15%) and the proximal (medial) third (5%) are less commonly seen. If displacement is present, the proximal fragment is usually elevated and the distal fragment is displaced medially and caudally. Fractures of the distal third of the clavicle have been classified by Neer into three types (Fig. 5.31B). Type I consists of a fracture without significant displacement and with intact ligaments (Fig. 5.32). Type II fractures are displaced and located between two ligaments: the coracoclavicular ligament, which is detached from the medial segment, and the trapezoid ligament, which remains attached to the distal segment. Type III fracture involves the articular surface, but the ligaments remain intact. The anteroposterior projection of the shoulder usually allows sufficient evaluation of any type of clavicular fracture (Fig. 5.33), but the same projection obtained with 15-degree cephalad angulation of the radiographic tube may also be useful, particularly in fractures of the middle third of the clavicle. Occasionally, if the diagnosis is in doubt, or if the fracture cannot be well demonstrated on conventional radiography, then trispiral tomography (Fig. 5.34) or CT (Figs. 5.35 and 5.36) might be more effective.

Fractures of the Scapula. Invariably resulting from direct trauma, frequently sustained in motor vehicle accidents or falls from heights, fractures of the scapula, which constitute approximately 1% of all fractures, 3% of shoulder girdle injuries, and 5% of all shoulder fractures, are classified according to their anatomic locations (Fig. 5.37). Because of their intraarticular extension, fractures of the glenoid rim

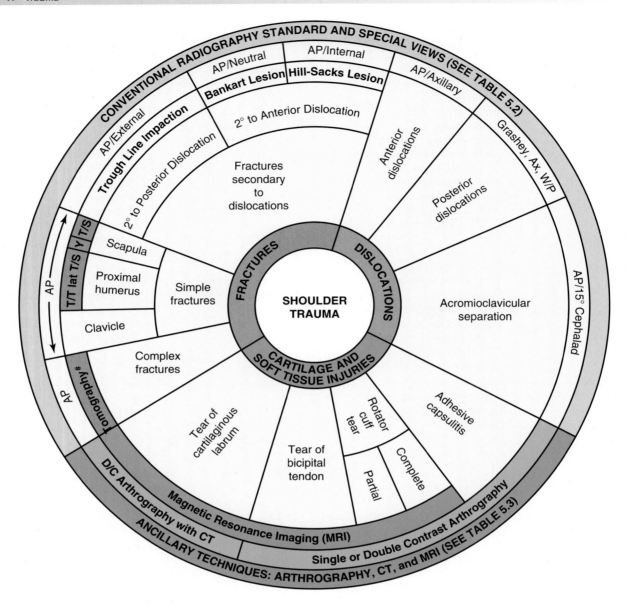

FIGURE 5.27 Spectrum of radiologic imaging techniques for evaluating injury to the shoulder girdle*
The radiographic projections or radiologic techniques indicated throughout the diagram are only those most effective in demonstrating the respective traumatic conditions.
#Almost completely replaced by CT.

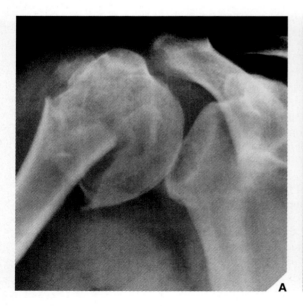

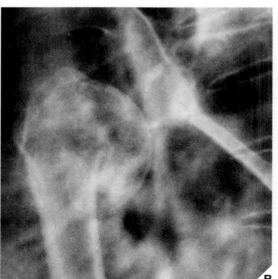

◀ **FIGURE 5.28** **Fracture of the proximal humerus.** A 60-year-old man fell on a staircase and injured his right arm. **(A)** Anteroposterior radiograph of the shoulder demonstrates a comminuted fracture through the surgical neck of the humerus. The greater tuberosity is fractured, too, but is not significantly displaced. To assess the degree of displacement of the various fragments better the transthoracic lateral view **(B)** was obtained. It demonstrates slight anterior angulation of the humeral head, which in addition is inferiorly subluxed—a finding not well appreciated on the anteroposterior projection.

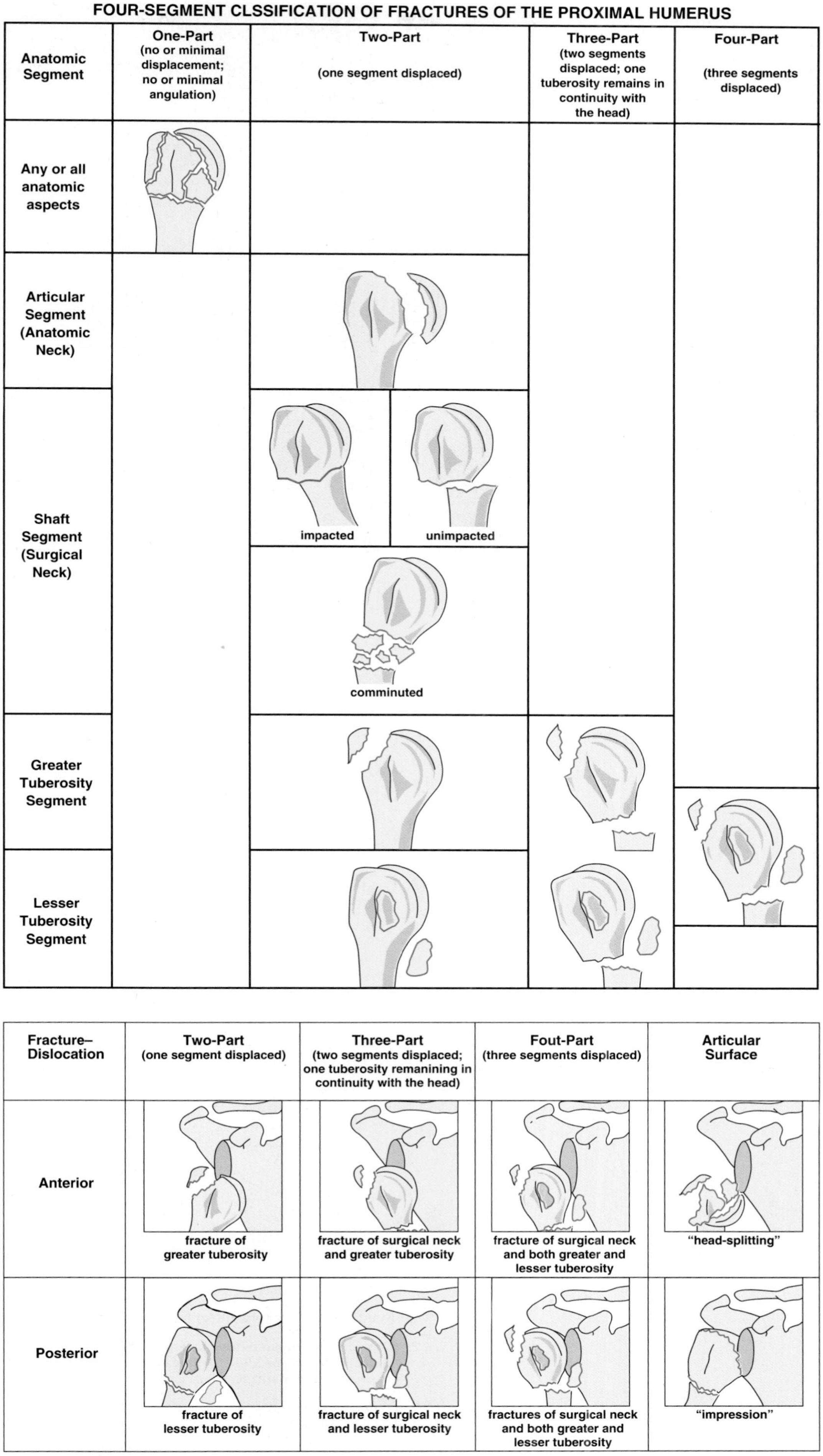

FIGURE 5.29 **Neer classification.** Fractures of the proximal humerus based on the presence or absence of displacement of the four major fragments that may result from fracture. (Modified from Neer CS II, 1975, with permission.)

FOUR-SEGMENT CLSSIFICATION OF FRACTURES OF THE PROXIMAL HUMERUS

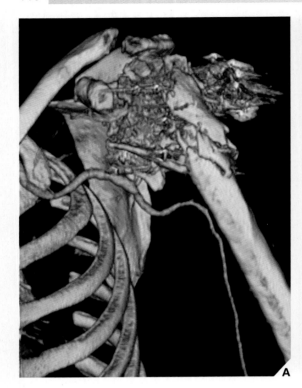
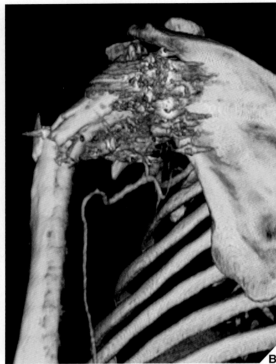

FIGURE 5.30 3D CT of four-part fracture of the proximal humerus. 3D CT reconstructed images of the left shoulder viewed from the anterior (**A**) and posterior (**B**) sides show a complex markedly comminuted displaced and angulated gunshot wound fracture of the humeral head extending into the surgical neck and proximal shaft of the humerus. Note inferior displacement of the axillary artery due to a large soft-tissue hematoma.

TYPES OF CLAVICLE FRACTURES

FIGURE 5.31 Classification of the fractures of the clavicle.

A. Classification According to Involvement of the Anatomic Segment

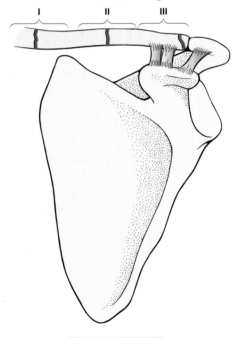

B. Neer Classification of Fractures of the Distal Clavicle

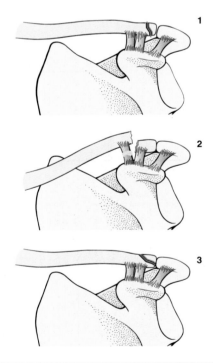

I. Proximal third

II. Middle third

III. Distal third

1. Nondisplaced fracture, intact ligaments

2. Displaced interligamentous fracture; conoid ligament torn, trapezoid ligament remains attached to the distal segment

3. Fracture extends to articular surface, ligaments intact

FIGURE 5.32   **Fracture of the acromial end of the clavicle.** Type I fracture of ▶
the distal third clavicle. There is no displacement of the fractured fragment.

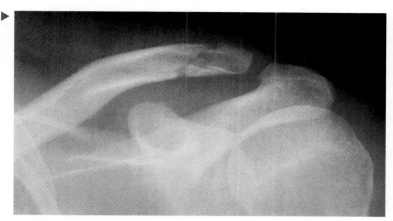

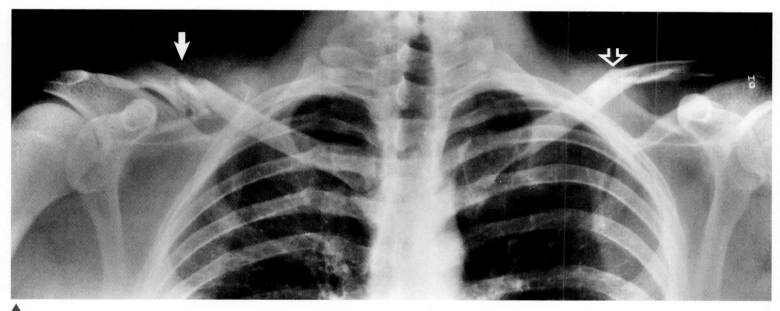

▲
FIGURE 5.33   **Fracture of both clavicles.** A 22-year-old man sustained multiple traumas in a motorcycle accident. Anteroposterior view of both shoulders demonstrates a comminuted fracture of the middle third of the right clavicle (*arrow*) and a simple fracture of the middle third of the left clavicle (*open arrow*).

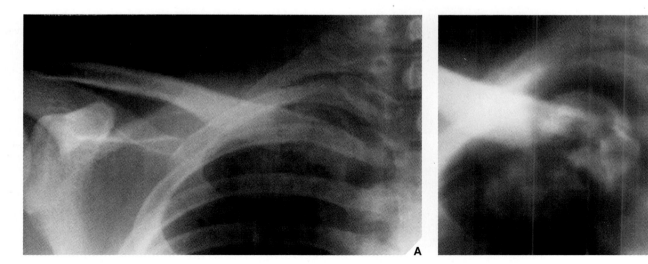

▲
FIGURE 5.34   **Fracture of the sternal end of the clavicle.** A 32-year-old woman was injured in a car accident and presented with pain localized to the medial aspect of the right clavicle for the past 3 weeks. **(A)** Anteroposterior radiograph shows questionable lesion of the medial end of the clavicle; however, the abnormality is not well demonstrated. **(B)** A trispiral tomogram clearly shows healing fracture of the medial clavicle.

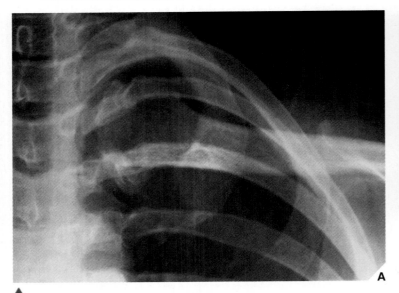

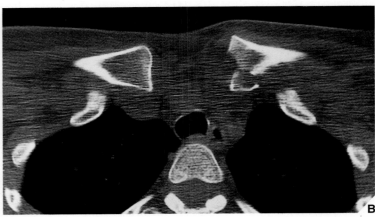

FIGURE 5.35 **Fracture of the sternal end of the clavicle.** A 21-year-old man was assaulted and sustained a direct injury to the left medial clavicle. **(A)** Anteroposterior radiograph is suggestive of a fracture of the medial end of the clavicle, but the fracture line is not well demonstrated. **(B)** CT section shows a fracture of the sternal end of the clavicle and associated soft-tissue swelling.

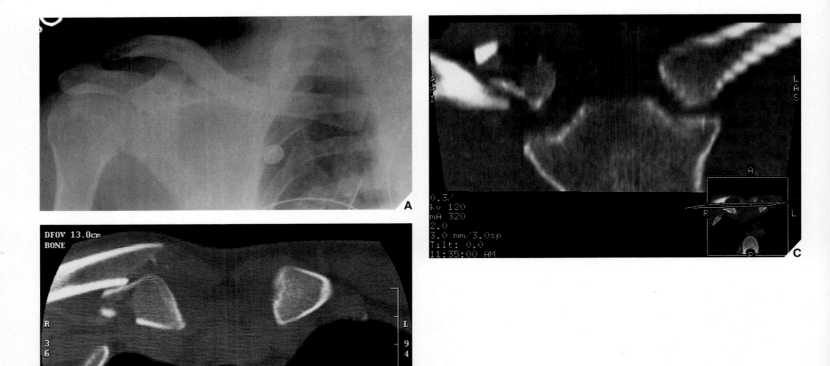

FIGURE 5.36 **Fracture of the sternal end of the clavicle.** A 34-year-old woman was severely injured in a car accident. **(A)** Anteroposterior radiograph of the right shoulder and upper chest shows multiple rib fractures. The medial portion of the clavicle is not adequately visualized. Axial CT scan **(B)** and coronal reformatted image **(C)** show a comminuted fracture of the sternal end of the right clavicle with anterior displacement and overriding of the fragments.

TYPES OF SCAPULA FRACTURES

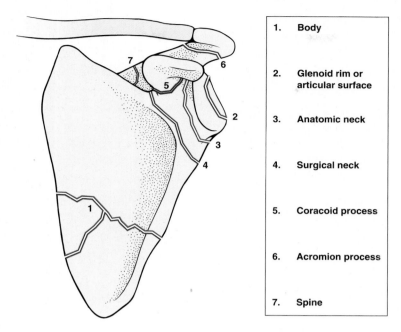

1.	Body
2.	Glenoid rim or articular surface
3.	Anatomic neck
4.	Surgical neck
5.	Coracoid process
6.	Acromion process
7.	Spine

FIGURE 5.37   Fractures of the scapula. Classification of the fractures of the scapula according to anatomic location.

and glenoid fossa are particularly important. They comprise 10% of all fractures of the scapula; however, fewer than 10% are significantly displaced. Fractures of the *glenoid rim* are subclassified into those involving the anterior portion and those affecting the posterior segment. Fractures of the *glenoid fossa* are subclassified into injuries involving the inferior segment; transverse disruption of the fossa extending into the vicinity of the suprascapular notch and the coracoid process; central fossa fractures extending across the entire scapula; and combination of the aforementioned fractures, frequently comminuted and displaced (Fig. 5.38).

Scapular fractures may occasionally be evaluated on the anteroposterior view of the shoulder (Fig. 5.39). More commonly, the transscapular (or Y) view may be required, particularly in cases of comminution, because this projection better demonstrates displacement of the fragments (Fig. 5.40). CT scan may also effectively demonstrate the displacement of various segments (Fig. 5.41), and 3D CT reformatted image may help to visualize the spatial orientation of displaced osseous fragments (Fig. 5.42). Complications, such as injury to the axillary artery or the brachial plexus, are rare.

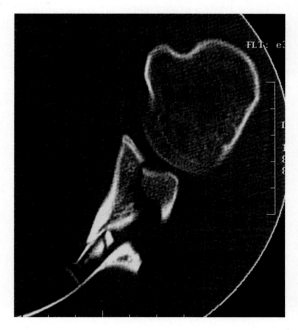

FIGURE 5.38   Comminuted fracture of the glenoid. Axial CT section through the shoulder joint shows a comminuted, displaced fracture of the glenoid fossa extending across the entire scapula.

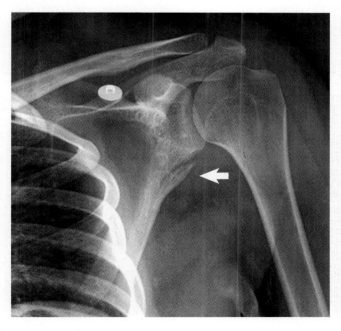

FIGURE 5.39   Fracture of the scapula. Minimally displaced subglenoid fracture of the scapula (*arrow*) is well demonstrated on this anteroposterior radiograph of the left shoulder.

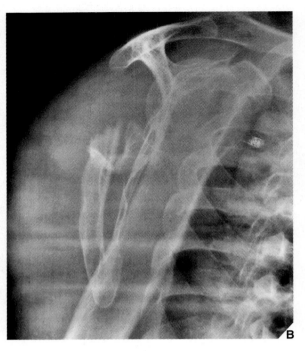

FIGURE 5.40 **Fracture of the scapula.** A 52-year-old man was injured in a motorcycle accident. **(A)** On the anteroposterior view of the right shoulder, a comminuted fracture of the scapula is evident. Displacement of the fragments, however, cannot be evaluated. **(B)** Transscapular (Y) view demonstrates lateral displacement of the body of the scapula.

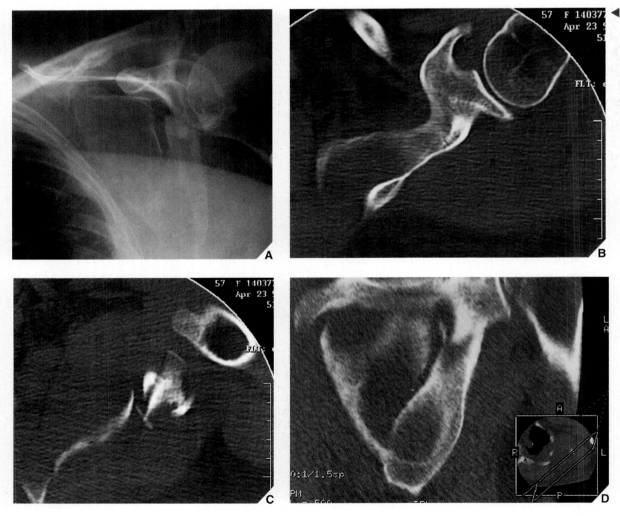

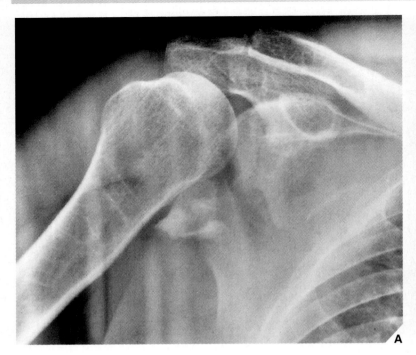

◄ FIGURE 5.41 **Fracture of the scapula.** A 57-year-old woman sustained an injury to the left shoulder in a motorcycle accident. **(A)** Anteroposterior radiograph shows a comminuted fracture of the left scapula. The glenohumeral joint cannot be properly assessed on this study. Two axial CT sections, one at the level of glenohumeral joint **(B)** and the other at the level of body of the scapula **(C)**, and reformatted coronal image **(D)** show to better advantage the configuration of various displaced fragments, as well as an intact glenohumeral joint.

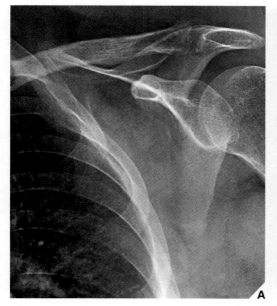

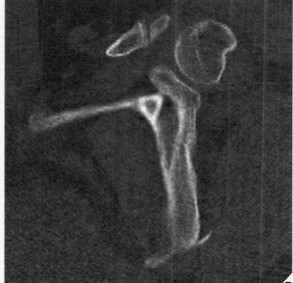

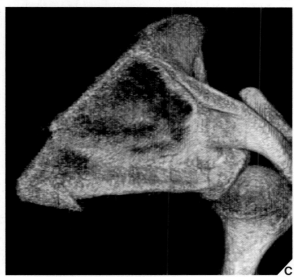

FIGURE 5.42 CT and 3D CT of the fracture of the ▶ scapula. **(A)** On this anteroposterior radiograph of the left shoulder, fracture of the scapula is bearly visible. **(B)** Coronal reformatted CT image and **(C)** 3D CT effectively demonstrate the details of this injury.

Dislocations in the Glenohumeral Joint

Anterior Dislocation. Displacement of the humeral head anterior to the glenoid fossa, which usually results from indirect force applied to the arm—a combination of abduction, extension, and external rotation—accounts for approximately 96% of cases of glenohumeral dislocation. It is readily diagnosed on the anteroposterior view of the shoulder (Fig. 5.43), although the Y view is effective as well (Fig. 5.44). CT is equally effective in demonstrating anterior dislocation (Fig. 5.45).

At the time of dislocation, the humeral head strikes the inferior margin of the glenoid, and this may result in compression fracture of one or both of these structures. Fracture most frequently occurs in the posterolateral aspect of the humeral head at the junction with the neck, producing a "hatchet" defect called the *Hill-Sachs lesion*; it is best demonstrated on the anteroposterior projection of the shoulder with the arm internally rotated (Fig. 5.46). Hills-Sachs lesion can also be imaged with CT (Fig. 5.47) or MR (Fig. 5.48). When using the latter modality, either coronal oblique (Fig. 5.48A) or axial (Fig. 5.48B) image reveals this abnormality. Fracture of the anterior aspect of the inferior rim of the glenoid, known as the *Bankart lesion*, is less commonly seen. It may occur secondary to the anterior movement of the humeral head in dislocation and is readily demonstrated on the anteroposterior radiograph (Fig. 5.49), by CT (Fig. 5.50) or by MRI (Fig. 5.51). When the site of the Bankart lesion is in the cartilaginous labrum, which at

times may be detached, it may only be revealed by either computed arthrotomography (see Fig. 5.16) or MRI (Figs. 5.52 and 5.53). The presence of either of these abnormalities is virtually diagnostic of previous anterior dislocation.

Posterior Dislocation. This type of dislocation, which is much less commonly seen—accounting for only 2% to 3% of dislocations in the glenohumeral joint—results from either direct force, such as a blow to the anterior aspect of the shoulder, or indirect force applied to the arm combining adduction, flexion, and internal rotation. Posterior dislocation caused by indirect force most often occurs secondary to accidental electric shock or convulsive seizures. In this type of dislocation, the humeral head lies posterior to the glenoid fossa and usually impacts on the posterior rim of the glenoid.

Making a correct diagnosis is often problematic, because the abnormality can easily be overlooked on the standard anteroposterior film of the shoulder, where the overlapping humeral head and glenoid fossa may be interpreted as normal. It is imperative when dealing with suspected posterior dislocation to demonstrate radiographically the glenoid fossa in profile. This can be performed on the anteroposterior projection by rotating the patient 40 degrees toward the affected side (see Fig. 5.5). Normally, the glenohumeral joint space is clear on this view. Obliteration of the space because of overlap of the humeral head with the glenoid is diagnostic of posterior dislocation (Fig. 5.54).

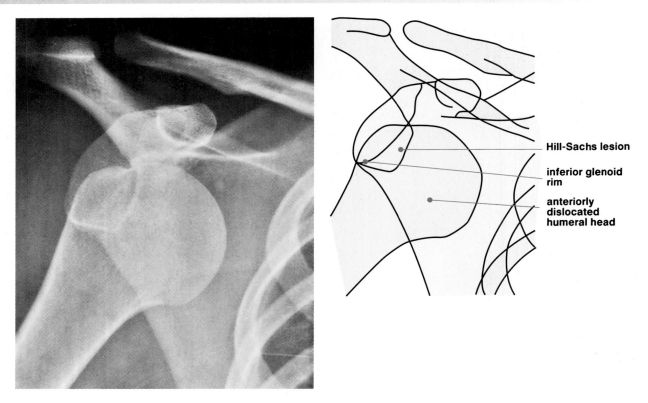

Hill-Sachs lesion

inferior glenoid rim

anteriorly dislocated humeral head

▲
FIGURE 5.43 **Anterior shoulder dislocation.** Anteroposterior film of the shoulder shows the typical appearance of anterior dislocation. The humeral head lies beneath the inferior rim of the glenoid.

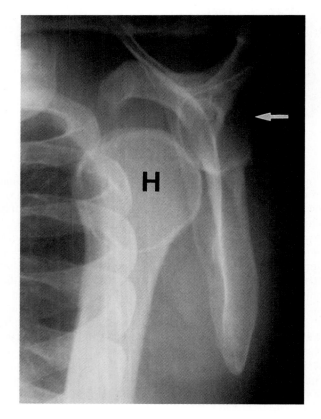

▲
FIGURE 5.44 **Anterior shoulder dislocation.** A dislocation is well demonstrated on this transscapular (or Y) projection of the shoulder girdle. An *arrow* is pointing to the empty glenoid fossa. The humeral head (*H*) is medially and anteriorly displaced.

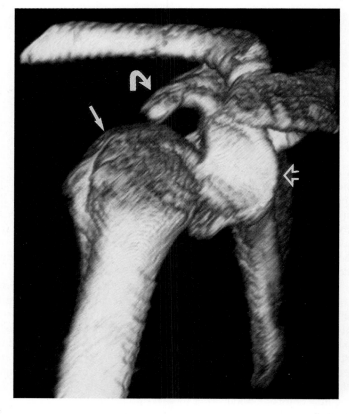

▲
FIGURE 5.45 **Anterior shoulder dislocation.** A 3D shaded surface display CT reconstructed image (side view) demonstrates anterior dislocation of the humeral head (*arrow*). *Open arrow* points to the empty glenoid fossa, and a *curved arrow* points to the coracoid process.

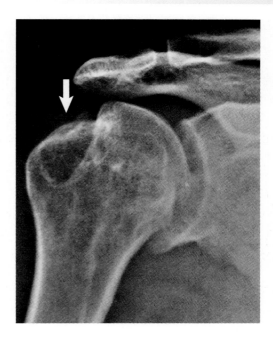

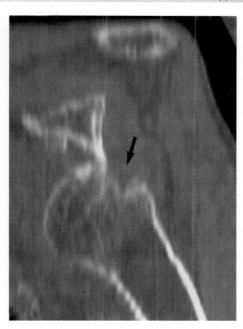

▲
FIGURE 5.46 Hill-Sachs lesion. Anteroposterior view of the shoulder with the arm internally rotated demonstrates a "hatchet" defect, known as the Hill-Sachs lesion, on the posterolateral aspect of the humeral head (*arrow*).

▲
FIGURE 5.47 CT of Hill-Sachs lesion. Coronal CT reformatted image shows anterior dislocation in the shoulder joint. The *arrow* points to the Hill-Sachs lesion.

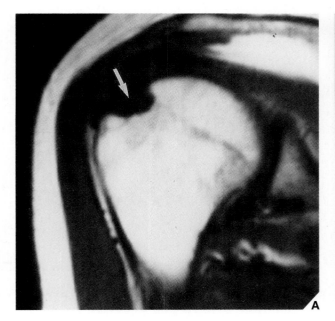

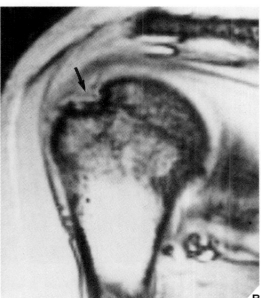

FIGURE 5.48 MRI of Hill-Sachs lesion. A 56-year-old woman ▶ sustained an anterior shoulder dislocation that has been successfully reduced. A postreduction MRI was performed. Coronal oblique T1-weighted image (**A**) and gradient-echo MPGR sequence (**B**) show compression fracture at the posterolateral aspect of the humeral head (*arrows*). The Hill-Sachs compression is also well demonstrated on the axial gradient-echo MPGR image (**C**) as a flattening of the posterolateral aspect of the humeral head (*open arrow*).

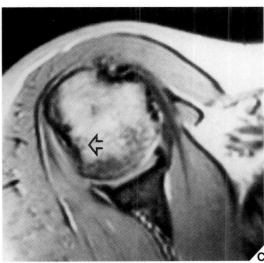

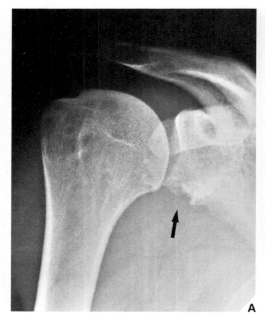

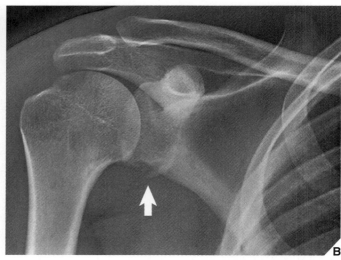

◀ **FIGURE 5.49** **Bankart lesion.** **(A)** Grashey view of the shoulder shows compression fracture of the anterior aspect of the inferior portion of the glenoid, known as the Bankart lesion (*arrow*). **(B)** In another patient, the anteroposterior radiograph of the right shoulder clearly demonstrates the Bankart lesion (*arrow*).

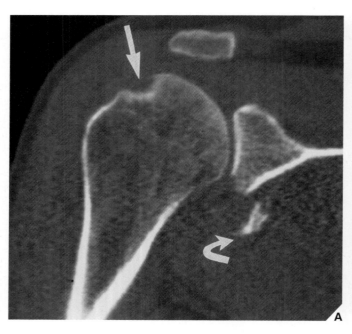

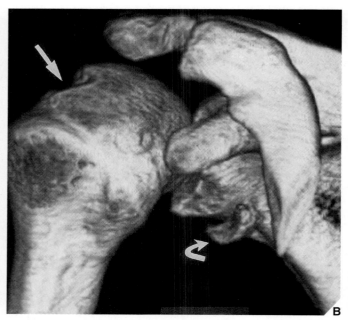

▲ **FIGURE 5.50** **CT of Hill-Sachs and Bankart lesions. (A)** Coronal CT reformatted image and **(B)** 3D CT show Hill-Sachs (*arrow*) and Bankart (*curved arrow*) lesions in a 42-year-old woman with reduced anterior shoulder dislocation.

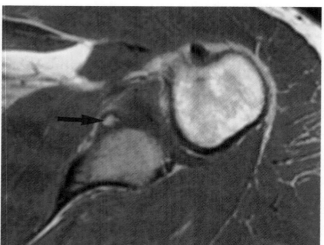

◀ **FIGURE 5.51** **MRI demonstration of osseous Bankart lesion.** T1-weighted axial image shows a high signal of bone fragment adjacent to the anterior glenoid (*arrow*), representing an osseous Bankart lesion.

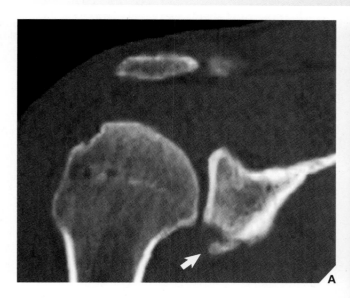

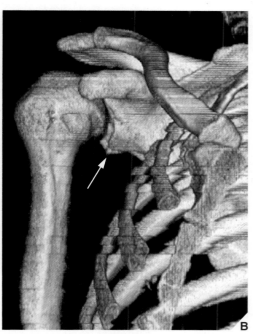

FIGURE 5.52 **CT and MRI demonstration of osseous and cartilaginous Bankart lesion. (A)** Coronal reformatted CT image and **(B)** 3D CT of the right shoulder show only osseous Bankart lesion (*arrows*). **(C)** Axial T1-weighted fat-suppressed MR arthrographic image clearly demonstrate the cartilaginous Bankart lesion (*open arrow*).

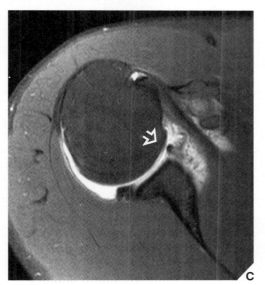

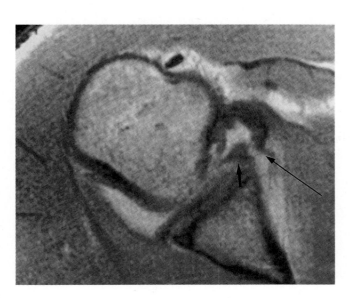

FIGURE 5.53 **MRI demonstration of cartilaginous Bankart lesion.** Proton density-weighted axial MR image shows a detachment of the anteroinferior labrum (*short arrow*), and a tear of the inferior glenohumeral ligament (IGHL) (*long arrow*).

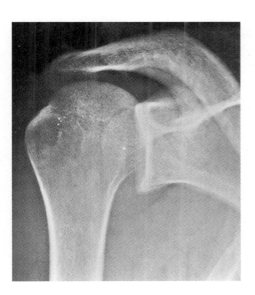

FIGURE 5.54 **Posterior shoulder dislocation.** On the anteroposterior projection of the shoulder obtained by rotating the patient 40 degrees toward the affected side (Grashey view), overlap of the medially displaced humeral head with the glenoid is virtually diagnostic of posterior dislocation.

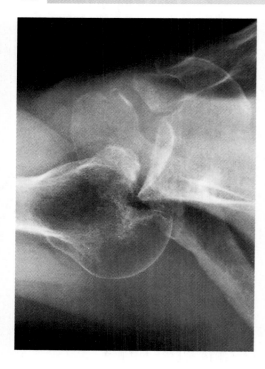

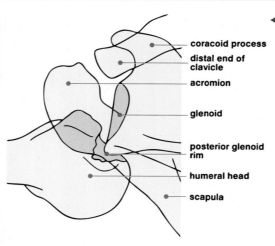

coracoid process

distal end of clavicle

acromion

glenoid

posterior glenoid rim

humeral head

scapula

◄ FIGURE 5.55 Posterior shoulder dislocation. Axillary projection of the shoulder demonstrates posterior dislocation. Note the associated compression fracture of the anteromedial aspect of the humeral head.

Diagnosis can also be made on the axillary projection, although limited abduction of the arm may make it impossible to obtain this view (Fig. 5.55).

Compression fracture of the anteromedial aspect of the humeral head, known as trough line impaction (*trough sign*), commonly occurs in posterior dislocation secondary to the impaction of the humeral head on the posterior glenoid rim. This sign refers to a vertical or archlike line within the cortex of the humeral head that projects parallel and lateral to the articular end of this bone. The anteroposterior view of the shoulder with the arm externally rotated readily demonstrates this type of fracture (Fig. 5.56); it is also identifiable on the axillary projection (see Fig. 5.55).

Inferior Dislocation. Also known as *luxatio erecta humeri*, this is the rarest dislocation in the shoulder joint accounting for only 1%. The mechanism of this injury consists of either application of a direct axial force to a fully abducted arm, or a severe hyperabduction of arm, resulting in the impingement of humeral head against the acromion. Rotator cuff tear and fracture of the greater tuberosity of the humerus are frequently associated abnormalities. The anteroposterior radiograph of the shoulder easily shows this dislocation (Fig. 5.57). Recently described

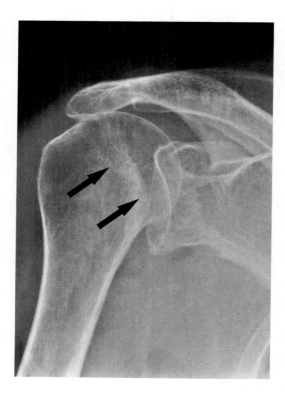

▲ FIGURE 5.56 Posterior shoulder dislocation. Anteroposterior view of the shoulder demonstrates posterior dislocation in the glenohumeral joint. Note the trough line impaction on the anteromedial aspect of the humeral head (*arrows*).

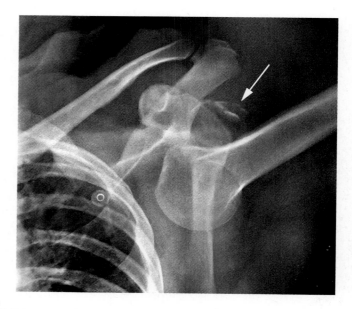

▲ FIGURE 5.57 Inferior shoulder dislocation. Anteroposterior radiograph of the left shoulder shows classic appearance of luxatio erecta humeri. Note that the humeral head faces inferiorly and it is located below the rim of the glenoid. An *arrow* points to associated fracture of the glenoid.

MRI findings include injury to the glenoid labrum, and injury to both the anterior and posterior bands of the inferior glenohumeral ligament.

Complications. Dislocations in the glenohumeral joint may result in complications such as recurrent dislocations, posttraumatic arthritis, and injury to the axillary nerve and axillary artery.

Impingement Syndrome

Impingement syndrome of the shoulder refers to a condition in which the supraspinatus tendon and subacromial bursa are chronically entrapped between the humeral head inferiorly and either the anterior acromion itself, spurs of the anterior acromion or acromioclavicular joint, or the coracoacromial ligament superiorly (coracoacromial arch). Early diagnosis and treatment of impingement syndrome are critical to prevent the progression of this condition and improve shoulder function. Frequently, however, clinical signs and symptoms are nonspecific, and the diagnosis is often delayed until a full-thickness defect in the rotator cuff has developed. Only rarely can it be definitely diagnosed based on the clinical findings, characterized by severe pain during abduction and external rotation of the arm. More reliable are radiographic findings associated with this syndrome, including subacromial proliferation of bone, spurring at the inferior aspect of the acromion, and degenerative changes of the humeral tuberosities at the insertion of the rotator cuff.

Neer described three progressive stages of impingement syndrome apparent clinically and at surgery. Stage I consists of edema and hemorrhage and is reversible with conservative therapy. It typically occurs in young individuals engaged in sport activities requiring excessive use of the arm above the head (i.e., swimming). Stage II implies fibrosis and thickening of the subacromial soft tissue, rotator cuff tendinitis, and sometimes a partial tear of the rotator cuff. It is manifested clinically by recurrent pain and is often seen in patients 25 to 40 years old. Stage III represents complete rupture of the rotator cuff and is associated with progressive disability. It is usually seen in patients older than 40 years old. Arthrography aids little in the early diagnosis of impingement syndrome, and other ancillary imaging techniques are also unsatisfactory for demonstration of the lesion in the early stages. Because of its high soft-tissue contrast resolution and multiplanar imaging capabilities, MRI is the only technique that can accurately image the early changes of this condition, in particular bursal thickening and effusion (subacromial bursitis), edema, and inflammatory changes of the rotator cuff and its tendons (Fig. 5.58).

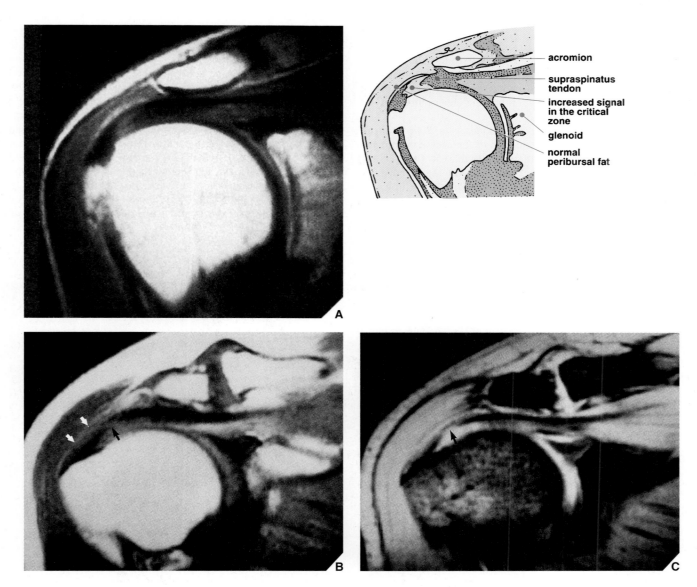

▲
FIGURE 5.58   Impingement syndrome. (A) Oblique coronal T1-weighted MR image of early stage of the impingement syndrome. There is slightly increased signal in the critical zone of the supraspinatus tendon. Peribursal fat demarcating the subacromial subdeltoid bursa complex is still intact. (From Holt RG et al., 1990, with permission.) **(B)** Oblique coronal T1-weighted MR image of stage II impingement syndrome shows a focus of intermediate signal (*black arrow*) of the supraspinatus tendon. The subacromial–subdeltoid fat line is still preserved (*white arrows*). **(C)** Oblique coronal T2*-weighted (MPGR) image of stage II impingement syndrome demonstrate high-signal-intensity attenuation of the inferior surface of the supraspinatus tendon (*black arrow*), representing a partial tear.

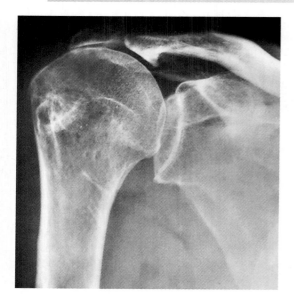

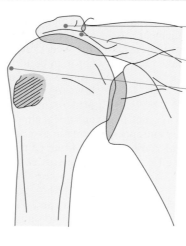

eroded inferior
aspect of
acromion

narrowed
acromiohumeral
space

flattening of
greater tuberosity

◀ FIGURE 5.59 **Chronic rotator cuff tear.** The characteristics of chronic rotator cuff tear are identifiable on the anteroposterior radiograph of the shoulder.

Rotator Cuff Tear

The rotator cuff of the shoulder, a musculotendinous structure about the joint capsule, consists of four intrinsic muscles: the subscapularis, the supraspinatus, the infraspinatus, and the teres minor (see Fig. 5.3). The tendinous portions of the cuff, which converge and fuse to form an envelope covering the humeral head, insert into the anatomic neck and tuberosities of the humerus. Tears usually occur in the supraspinatus portion of the cuff, approximately 1 cm from the insertion into the greater tuberosity of the humerus (known as a critical zone).

Injury to the rotator cuff may occur secondary to dislocation in the glenohumeral joint or to sudden abduction of the arm against resistance. It is most commonly seen in patients older than 50 years of age because of normal degenerative changes in the cuff that predispose this structure to rupture after even minor shoulder injuries. Clinically, patients characteristically present with pain in the shoulder and inability to abduct the arm.

Although radiographs of the shoulder are usually insufficient to demonstrate the tear, certain radiographic features characteristic of chronic rotator cuff tear may be present on the anteroposterior view. These include (a) narrowing of the acromiohumeral space to less than 6 mm; (b) erosion of the inferior aspect of the acromion secondary to cephalad migration of the humeral head; and (c) flattening and atrophy of the greater tuberosity of the humeral head caused by the absence of traction stress by the rotator cuff (Fig. 5.59). Although these findings are usually diagnostic of chronic tear, contrast arthrography may be performed to confirm or exclude the suspected diagnosis. As the intact rotator cuff normally separates the subacromial–subdeltoid bursae complex from the joint cavity, only the glenohumeral joint, the axillary recess, the bursa subscapularis, and the bicipital tendon sheath should opacify on arthrographic examination (Fig. 5.60A; see also Fig. 5.15B). Opacification of the subacromial–subdeltoid bursae is diagnostic of rotator cuff tear (Fig. 5.60B,C). Occasionally, contrast is seen only in the substance

Intact Rotator Cuff

Complete Rotator Cuff Tear

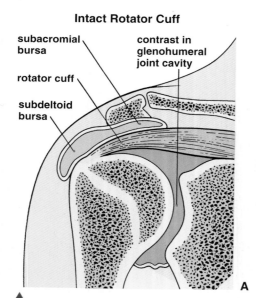

subacromial
bursa

contrast in
glenohumeral
joint cavity

rotator cuff

subdeltoid
bursa

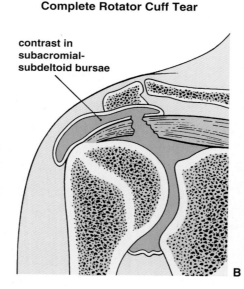

contrast in
subacromial-
subdeltoid bursae

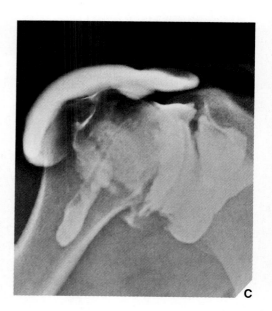

A   **B**   **C**

FIGURE 5.60   **Arthrography of the shoulder joint.** The intact rotator cuff (**A**) does not allow communication between the glenohumeral joint cavity and the subacromial–subdeltoid bursae complex. When arthrography is performed for suspected tear of the cuff, opacification of the bursae (**B,C**) indicates abnormal communication between them and the joint cavity, confirming the diagnosis.

FIGURE 5.61 **Partial tear of the rotator** ▶
cuff. This injury **(A)** allows tracking of contrast
into the substance of the cuff (*arrow*) **(B)**,
whereas the subacromial–subdeltoid bursae
remain free of contrast.

Partial Rotator Cuff Tear

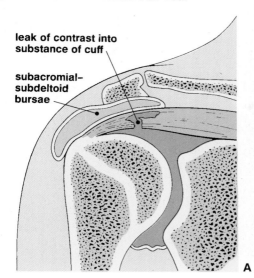

leak of contrast into
substance of cuff

subacromial–
subdeltoid
bursae

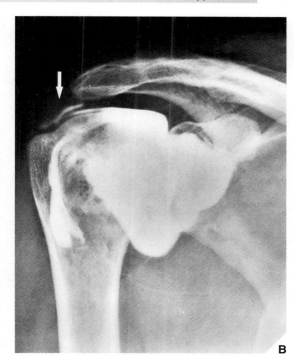

of the rotator cuff, whereas the subacromial–subdeltoid bursae complex remains unopacified, indicating a partial tear of the cuff (Fig. 5.61).

Although arthrography of the shoulder remains the effective technique for evaluating a suspected rotator-cuff tear, MRI is being used more frequently as a noninvasive method to diagnose such a tear. The advantage of MRI over arthrography is not only that it is a noninvasive technique but also that it allows visualization of the osseous and periarticular soft tissue of the shoulder in the coronal, sagittal, axial, and oblique planes. It has proved to be highly sensitive (75% to 92%) and accurate (84% to 94%) for diagnosing full-thickness rotator cuff disruption. Moreover, there is excellent correlation between preoperative assessment of the size of rotator cuff tears by MRI and the measurement at surgery.

Visualization of the rotator cuff is optimal when the images are obtained in all three planes: oblique coronal, oblique sagittal, and axial. The MRI findings for rotator cuff tear consist of focal discontinuity of the supraspinatus tendon, tendon and muscle retraction, abnormally increased signal within the tendon, and the presence of fluid in the subacromial–subdeltoid bursa complex (Figs. 5.62 to 5.65).

It must be noted, however, that the complex MRI appearance of the rotator cuff can occasionally be confounding in the diagnosis of a tear; experience and total knowledge of normal anatomy are required for correct interpretation. Large tears are well visualized on MR images as areas of discontinuity and irregularity of the rotator cuff tendons, with joint fluid tracking through the cuff defect into the subacromial–subdeltoid bursa complex. With complete rotator cuff tears and retraction of the tendons, the corresponding muscle belly assumes a distorted globular shape that is easily recognized. Chronic tears may result in atrophy of the cuff musculature, manifested on T1-weighted images by a decrease in muscle size and bulk, and by infiltration of the muscle by a band of high-signal-intensity fat. Partial tears may be seen as various

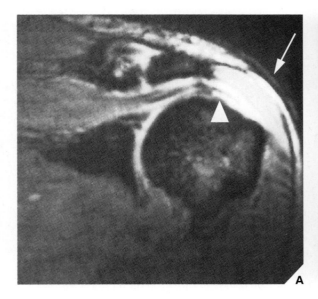

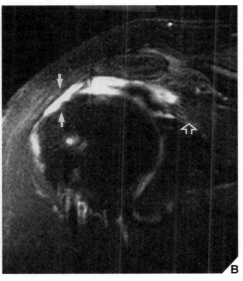

▲
FIGURE 5.62 **Full-thickness tear of the supraspinatus tendon. (A)** Oblique coronal MR image of the left shoulder (MPGR T2*-weighted) demonstrates interruption of the supraspinatus tendon (*arrow head*) and fluid in the subacromial–subdeltoid bursae complex (*arrow*), diagnostic of complete rotator cuff tear. (From Holt RG et al., 1990, with permission.) **(B)** Oblique coronal T2-weighted fat-suppressed MR image of the right shoulder shows a full-thickness tear of the supraspinatus tendon (*arrows*) and medial retraction of the supraspinatus muscle (*open arrow*).

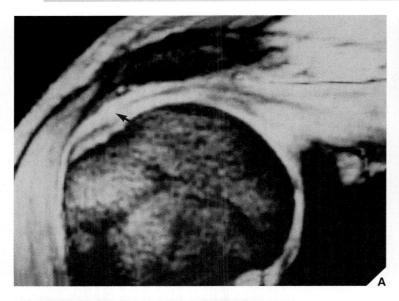

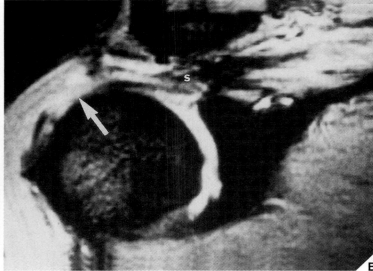

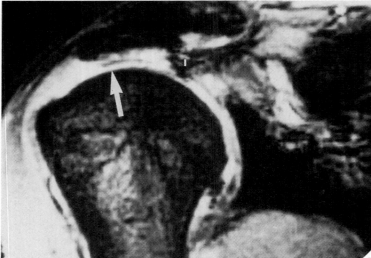

FIGURE 5.63 **Rotator cuff tear.** **(A)** T2*-weighted (MPGR) coronal image shows complete rotator cuff tear with direct communication of fluid between the glenohumeral joint and the subacromial–subdeltoid bursa complex (*arrow*). **(B)** and **(C)** T2*-weighted (MPGR) coronal oblique images show massive rotator cuff tear (*arrows*) with disruption of the supraspinatus (*S*) and infraspinatus (*I*) tendons anteriorly and posteriorly.

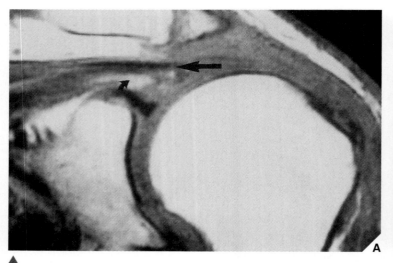

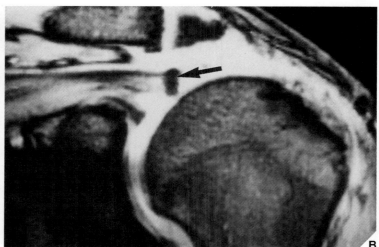

FIGURE 5.64 **Rotator cuff tear.** **(A)** T1-weighted and **(B)** T2*-weighted coronal oblique images show a complete supraspinatus tendon tear with proximal retraction of tendon edge to level of the acromioclavicular joint (*straight arrows*). Mild fatty atrophy of the supraspinatus muscle (*small curved arrow*) is present.

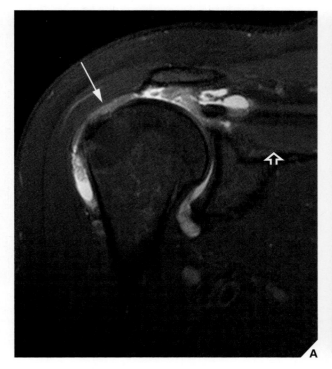

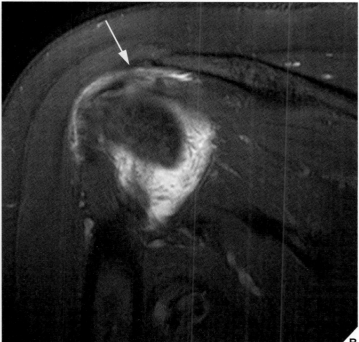

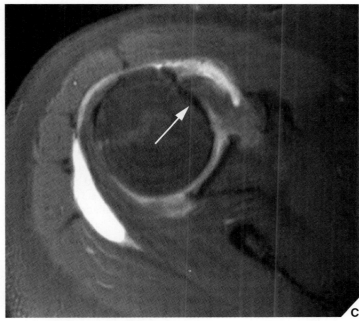

FIGURE 5.65 **Massive rotator cuff tear. (A)** Coronal proton density-weighted fat-suppressed MR arthrographic image of the right shoulder shows a full-thickness tear of the supraspinatus tendon (*arrow*). The supraspinatus muscle is medially retracted (*open arrow*). **(B)** More posterior section shows a tear of the infraspinatus tendon (*arrow*). **(C)** Axial sequence shows a tear of the subscapularis tendon (*arrow*).

foci of high signal within the homogeneous low signal intensity of the tendon or as irregularity or thinning of the tendon. Obliteration of the subacromial–subdeltoid fat line on T2-weighted images is a sensitive indicator of rotator cuff tears, and increased signal in the same region on T2-weighted sequences corresponds to the leakage of joint fluid into the subacromial–subdeltoid bursae complex.

MRI provides the surgeon with critical information regarding size and location of a tear, the specific tendons involved, the degree of musculature atrophy and tendon retraction, and the quality of the torn edges. Such information is invaluable for assessing the feasibility of surgery and the type of necessary repair.

Injury to the Cartilaginous Labrum

Bankart Lesion. Injury to the anterior–inferior cartilaginous labrum, which is usually associated with an avulsion of the inferior glenohumeral ligament (IGHL) from the anterior–inferior glenoid rim, occurs during anterior dislocation in the glenohumeral joint. It may affect only a fibrocartilaginous portion of the glenoid, or it may be associated with a fracture of the anterior aspect of the inferior bony rim of the glenoid (see Figs. 5.49 to 5.53).

POLPSA Lesion. The POLPSA lesion, recently reported as the posterior labrocapsular periosteal sleeve avulsion, consists of avulsion of the attachment of the glenohumeral capsule and the periosteum to which it is attached sustained during posterior shoulder dislocation. Unlike the Bankart lesion, the posterior glenoid labrum is intact, although it is detached from the osseous glenoid.

ALPSA Lesion. The ALPSA lesion is similar to the Bankart lesion. It is an avulsion injury of the anterior labroligamentous periosteal sleeve sustained during anterior dislocation in glenohumeral joint; however, the anterior scapular periosteum does not rupture as it does in the classic Bankart lesion. This results in medial displacement of the labroligamentous structures that also rotate inferiorly on the scapular neck. ALPSA lesion is best seen on axial MRI (Fig. 5.66).

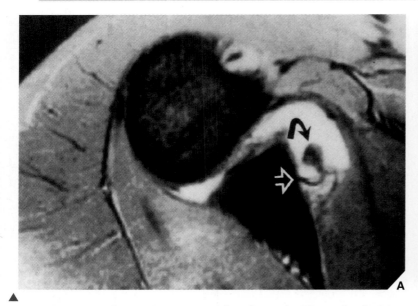
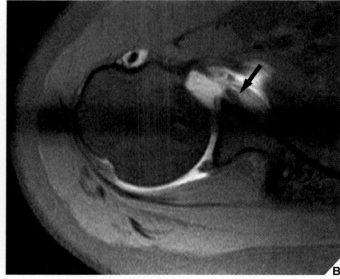

FIGURE 5.66   MRI of ALPSA lesion. (A) Axial gradient-echo T2*-weighted MR image shows avulsion of the anterior cartilaginous labrum (*curved arrow*), but the anterior scapular periosteum, although stripped from the bone, remains attached to the labrum (*open arrow*). (B) In another patient, T1-weighted fat-suppressed radial arthrographic image shows medial displacement of the torn anterior labrum and intact periosteal sleeve (*arrow*).

Perthes Lesion. Perthes lesion, originally described by the German surgeon Perthes in 1905, is very similar to ALPSA lesion. The scapular periosteum is intact; however, it is stripped medially causing incomplete avulsion of the anterior glenoid labrum. Because avulsed cartilaginous labrum is either not displaced or minimally displaced, conventional MRI may not detect this abnormality. The most effective technique to diagnose this lesion is MRa with patient's arm in abduction and external rotation (so-called ABER position) (Fig. 5.67).

SLAP Lesion. Injury to the superior portion of the cartilaginous glenoid labrum, on either side of the attachment of the long head of the biceps tendon into the labrum at the superior glenoid tubercle, is referred to as SLAP lesion (a superior labral, anterior, and posterior tear) and results from a sudden forced abduction of the arm. It is usually sustained in athletic activities such as tennis, volleyball, or baseball,

although occasionally the mechanism of this injury may be a fall on the outstretched arm with the shoulder in abduction and slight forward flexion at the time of impact. SLAP lesions have been classified into four types. Type I is the least common (10%) and consists of a degenerative frayed irregular appearance of the superior portion of the cartilaginous labrum. In this type of injury, the labrum remains firmly attached to the glenoid rim. Type II is the most common (40%) and consists of separation of the superior portion of the cartilaginous labrum to the level of the middle glenohumeral ligament (MGHL), as well as separation of the tendon of the long head of the biceps from the glenoid rim. Type III (30%) consists of a bucket-handle tear of the superior portion of the labrum; however, the attachment site of the tendon of the long head of the biceps is intact. Type IV (15%) consists of the bucket-handle tear of the superior labrum extending into the biceps tendon. Several additional

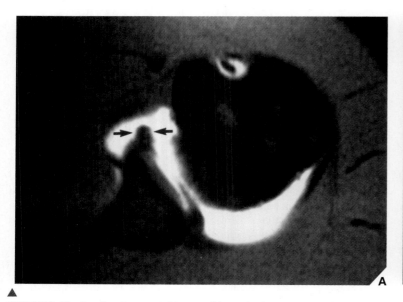
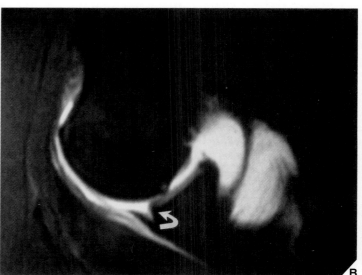

FIGURE 5.67   Perthes lesion. A 32-year-old man had anterior shoulder instability after fall on outstretched hand. (A) Axial T1-weighted MR arthrogram with fat saturation shows thickened anterior labrum (*arrows*), but no tear is demonstrated. (B) Oblique axial T1-weighted MR arthrogram obtained in ABER (abduction–external rotation) position shows detachment of the anterior labrum from the glenoid (*curved arrow*). (Courtesy of Dr. T.K. Wischer, Basel, Switzerland. Reprinted from Wischer TK, et al., 2002, with permission.)

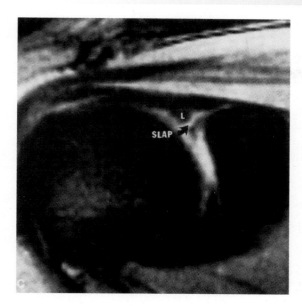

FIGURE 5.68 MRI of SLAP lesion. A coronal oblique T2*-weighted MRI shows a type II SLAP lesion involving anterior superior glenoid labrum (*L*). Note linear high intensity signal extending across the base of the labrum (*arrow*).

the humeral head strikes against the adjacent articular cartilage of the glenoid. The lesion consists of a superficial tear of the anteroinferior portion of the labrum and is always associated with an inferior flap tear but without evidence of anterior glenohumeral joint instability on physical examination. The deep fibers of the IGHL remain attached to the labrum and glenoid rim. A GLAD lesion is effectively diagnosed on MRa. The findings include a nondisplaced tear of the anteroinferior labrum with an adjacent chondral injury, which can range from a cartilaginous flap tear to a depressed lesion of the articular cartilage (Figs. 5.72 and 5.73).

GLOM Lesion. GLOM lesion or GLOM sign (glenolabral ovoid mass) represents an avulsion of a portion of the anterior labrum seen on axial MR image.

Buford Complex. A congenital variant of absence of the anterior superior labrum and marked thickening of the MGHL that can mimic a labral tear has been termed the Buford complex (Fig. 5.74). MRI appearance of this complex should be differentiated from other normal anatomic variants, such as an isolated detachment of the anterior superior labrum (also known as sublabral foramen or sublabral hole), undercutting of articular cartilage between the labrum and the glenoid cortex, or the presence of a synovial recess (sulcus) interposed between the glenoid rim and the cartilaginous labrum.

types of SLAP lesion have recently been described; however, as Helms et al. pointed out, from the practical point of view it is only important to determine whether a SLAP lesion consists of a partial-thickness or full-thickness (bucket-handle) tear of the superior labrum, whether the labrum is completely separated from the glenoid, and if the biceps tendon is torn at its labral anchor. MRI findings of SLAP lesion include linear increased signal intensity in the superior portion of the cartilaginous labrum on T2-weighted sequences (Fig. 5.68); on MRa contrast extends into a detached superior portion of the labrum (Figs. 5.69 to 5.71).

GLAD Lesion. Injury to the anteroinferior portion of the cartilaginous glenoid labrum associated with glenolabral articular disruption is referred to as a GLAD lesion. The usual mechanism of this injury is a fall on an outstretched arm in abduction and external rotation resulting in the forced adduction injury to the shoulder where

Injury to the GHLs

There are three GHLs located within the anterior portion of the glenohumeral joint that contribute to anterior shoulder stability. The IGHL is the thickest structure and extends from the glenoid labrum to the anatomic neck of the humerus. The MGHL originates at the superior portion of the anterior labrum, and attaches to the base of the lesser tuberosity of the humerus. The superior glenohumeral ligament (SGHL) originates from the superior–anterior labrum and attaches distally to the superior aspect of the lesser tuberosity of the humerus. All of these ligaments may be injured during a traumatic event to the shoulder joint; however, the IGHL, the most important stabilizer of the glenohumeral joint, is most commonly traumatized.

HAGL Lesion. Avulsion of the IGHL from the anatomic neck of the humerus is referred to as a HAGL lesion. It may be caused by shoulder dislocation, and is often associated with a tear of the subscapularis tendon. This abnormality can be seen on axial, oblique coronal, or sagittal MR images or on MRa (Figs. 5.75 and 5.76).

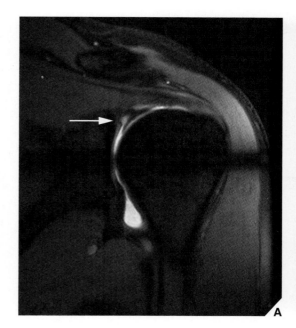
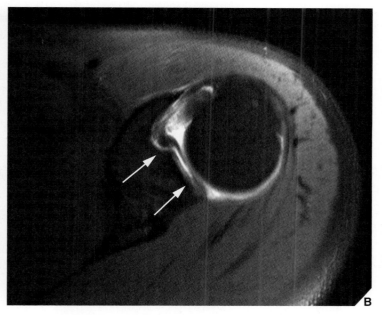

FIGURE 5.69 MRI of SLAP lesion. (A) Coronal T1-weighted fat-suppressed radial arthrographic MR image of the left shoulder shows a full-thickness tear of the superior labrum (*arrow*). **(B)** Axial sequence shows a bucket-handle tear of the glenoid labrum extending from the anterior to the posterior aspect (*arrows*).

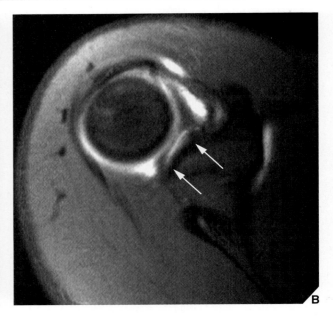

▲ **FIGURE 5.70** **MRI of SLAP lesion. (A)** Coronal T1-weighted fat-suppressed radial arthrographic MR image of the right shoulder shows a full-thickness tear of the superior labrum affecting the labral anchor of the long head of the biceps tendon (*arrow*). **(B)** Axial sequence shows contrast tracking into the tear between the labrum and the glenoid from the anterior to the posterior aspect (*arrows*).

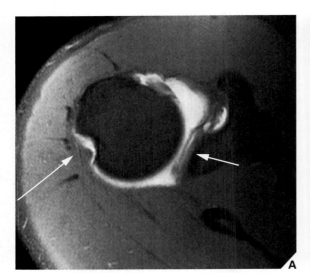

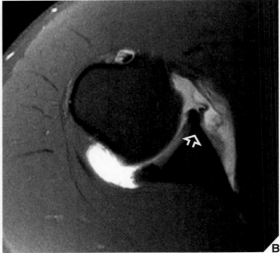

◀ **FIGURE 5.71** **MRI of SLAP lesion.** **(A,B)** Axial proton density-weighted fat-suppressed arthrographic MR images show an extensive tear of the posterosuperior aspect of the glenoid labrum (*arrow*), extending anteriorly through the torn MGHL (*open arrow*). The *long arrow* points to the Hill-Sachs lesion.

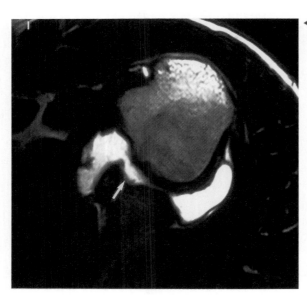

◀ **FIGURE 5.72** **MRI of GLAD lesion.** Axial T2-weighted MR arthrographic image of the left shoulder shows a nondisplaced tear of the anteroinferior labrum associated with an osteochondral defect (*arrow*) in a 21-year-old professional ice-hockey player who sustained anterior shoulder dislocation. (Courtesy of Dr. J. Tehranzadeh, Orange, California.)

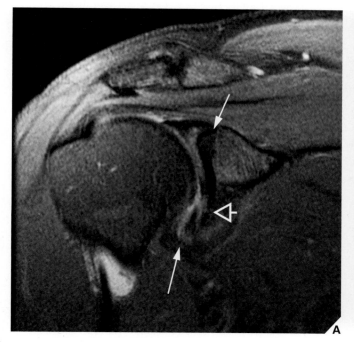
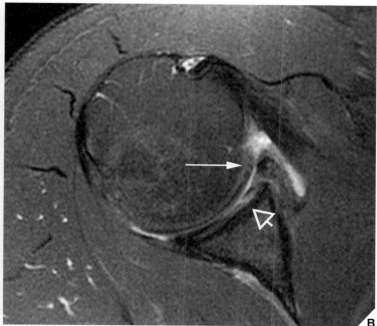

A

B

FIGURE 5.73 **MRI of GLAD lesion. (A)** Coronal T2-weighted fat-suppressed MR image of the right shoulder shows a tear of the anterior aspect of the superior and inferior glenoid labrum (*arrows*) associated with articular chondral defect (*open arrow*), findings confirmed on the axial section (**B**).

BHAGL Lesion. Bony humeral avulsion of the glenohumeral ligament (BHAGL) is similar to HAGL, but it is associated with avulsion of a bone fragment from the humerus.

Miscellaneous Abnormalities

Adhesive Capsulitis. Adhesive capsulitis, also referred to as "frozen shoulder," usually results from posttraumatic adhesive inflammation between the joint capsule and the peripheral articular cartilage of the shoulder. Clinically, it is characterized by progressive shoulder pain, stiffness, and limitation of passive and active motion in the shoulder joint.

Four stages of this condition have been initially described by Neviaser, and later, based on arthroscopic criteria, modified by the same author. *Stage I* is characterized by pain with passive and active motion accompanied by limitation of forward flexion, abduction, and internal and external rotation; however, examination under anaesthesia shows normal or only minimal loss of range of motion (ROM). Arthroscopic examination shows diffuse glenohumeral synovitis, but normal underlying capsule. Pathologic examination shows hypertrophic synovitis, and occasional inflammatory cell infiltrates. *Stage II* is characterized

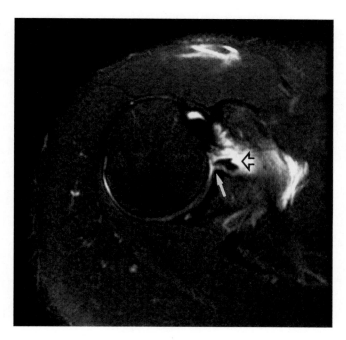

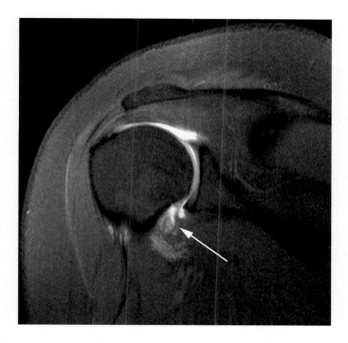

FIGURE 5.74 **MRI of Buford complex.** MR arthrogram shows an absent anterior superior glenoid labrum (*arrow*) and markedly thickened MGHL (*open arrow*), characteristic features of the Buford complex. This congenital variant can mimic a labral tear. (Courtesy of Dr. L. Steinbach, San Francisco, California.)

FIGURE 5.75 **MRI of HAGL lesion.** Coronal proton density-weighted fat-suppressed MR image shows evulsion of the IGHL from the humerus (*arrow*).

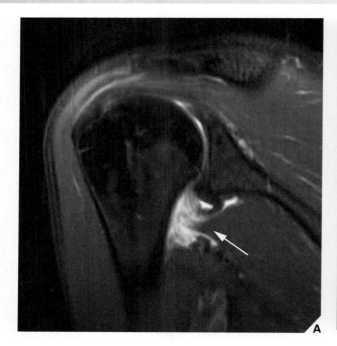
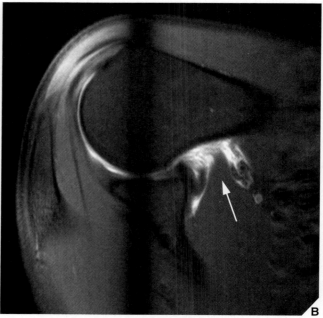

FIGURE 5.76 **MRI of HAGL lesion. (A)** Coronal proton density-weighted fat-suppressed arthrographic image of the right shoulder and **(B)** T1-weighted fat-suppressed radial image shows complete disruption of the humeral attachement of the IGHL (*arrows*).

by pain with passive and active motion and limitation of ROM as in stage I, but examination under anaesthesia shows no change in ROM compared with that when patient is awake. Arthroscopy shows diffuse, hypertrophic synovitis and capsular thickening. Pathology shows hypertrophic, hypervascular synovitis with subsynovial scars and fibroplasia. *Stage III* is characterized by minimal pain, but significant limitation of ROM, and no change on examination under anaesthesia. Arthroscopy demonstrates lack of hypervascularity, but remnants of fibrotic synovium, and significantly diminished capsular volume. Pathology reveals "burned out" atrophic synovitis and dense scar formation within the joint capsule. *Stage IV* is characterized by minimal pain and progressive improvement in ROM.

Because radiography, which may only reveal disuse periarticular osteoporosis secondary to this condition, is insufficient to make a diagnosis, single- or double-contrast arthrography is the technique of choice when this abnormality is suspected. The arthrogram usually reveals decreased capacity of the joint capsule, or even complete obliteration of the axillary and subscapular recesses, findings diagnostic of this condition (Fig. 5.77).

Recently, the use of MRI has been advocated to diagnose adhesive capsulitis of the shoulder. Emig et al. reported that thickening of the capsule and synovium at the level of the axillary pouch greater than 4 mm detected on MR studies may be a useful criterion for the diagnosis of this condition.

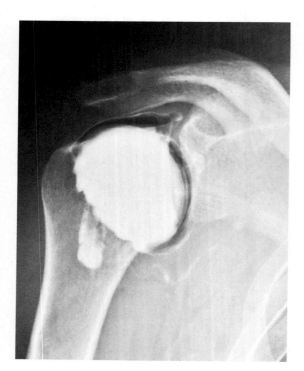
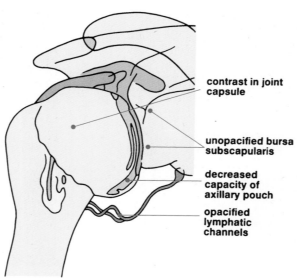

contrast in joint capsule

unopacified bursa subscapularis

decreased capacity of axillary pouch

opacified lymphatic channels

◄ **FIGURE 5.77 Adhesive capsulitis.** Double-contrast arthrogram of the shoulder demonstrates the characteristic findings of frozen shoulder. The capacity of the axillary pouch is markedly decreased and the subscapularis recess remains unopacified, whereas the lymphatic channels are filled with contrast secondary to increased intracapsular pressure.

Acromioclavicular Separation. Injuries to the acromioclavicular joint, which are commonly sustained during athletic activities by individuals between the ages of 15 and 40 years, often result in acromioclavicular separation (dislocation). Various forces may cause injury to the acromioclavicular joint. The most common is a downward blow to the lateral aspect of the shoulder that drives the acromion inferiorly (caudad); others are traction on the arm pulling the shoulder away from the chest wall and a fall on the outstretched hand or on the flexed elbow with the arm flexed forward 90 degrees.

Whatever the mechanism of injury, the degree of damage to the acromioclavicular and coracoclavicular ligaments varies with the severity of the applied force and ranges from *mild sprain* of the acromioclavicular ligament to *moderate sprain* involving tear of the acromioclavicular ligament and sprain of the coracoclavicular ligament, to *severe sprain* characterized by tear of the coracoclavicular ligament, with consequent dislocation in the acromioclavicular joint (Table 5.4). It is important to bear in mind, as Rockwood and Green have pointed out, that the major deformity seen in this type of injury is not elevation of the clavicle, but rather downward displacement of the scapula and upper extremity (Fig. 5.78), although some degree of cephalad displacement of the distal end of the clavicle may accompany this type of injury. The clinical symptoms also vary with the severity of the injury; patients may present with symptoms ranging from tenderness, swelling, and slight limitation of motion in the joint to complete inability to abduct the arm.

Suspected acromioclavicular dislocation is readily evaluated on the anteroposterior projection of the shoulder obtained with a 15-degree cephalad angulation of the radiographic tube (see Fig. 5.11). Often it is necessary to obtain a stress view in this projection by strapping a 5- to 10-lb weight to each forearm. A comparison study of the opposite shoulder is invariably helpful.

Radiographic studies can also be supplemented by quantitating acromioclavicular separation on the basis of the normal relations of the

TABLE 5.4 Grades of Acromioclavicular Separation

Grade	Radiographic Characteristics
I (mild sprain)	Minimal widening of acromioclavicular joint space, which normally measures 0.3–0.8 cm Coracoclavicular distance within normal range of 1.0–1.3 cm
II (moderate sprain)	Widening of acromioclavicular joint space to 1.0–1.5 cm Increase of 25%–50% in coracoclavicular distance
III (severe sprain)	Marked widening of acromioclavicular joint space to 1.5 cm or more and of coracoclavicular distance by 50% or more Dislocation in acromioclavicular joint Apparent cephalad displacement of distal end of clavicle

coracoid process, the clavicle, and the acromion (Fig. 5.79). Normally, the distance between the coracoid process and the inferior aspect of the clavicle, known as the coracoclavicular distance, ranges from 1.0 to 1.3 cm; the joint space at the articulation of the clavicle with the acromion measures 0.3 to 0.8 cm. The degree of widening at these points helps to determine the severity of the injury. An increase, for example, of 0.5 cm in the coracoclavicular distance or a widening of the distance by 50% or more compared with that in the opposite shoulder is characteristic of grade III acromioclavicular separation (Fig. 5.80).

Recently, Antonio and colleagues introduced MRI classification of acromioclavicular joint injury. In *type I injury*, there is a sprain of the acromioclavicular ligament, but the coracoclavicular ligaments are intact. MRI shows nonspecific findings. In *type II injury*, there is evidence of rupture of the acromioclavicular ligament, but the coracoclavicular ligament is only sprained. MRI shows edema of the coracoclavicular ligament and continuity of its fibers. Acromial end of the clavicle and acromion may show marrow edema. Oblique sagittal MR images are most effective to demonstrate this abnormality. In *type III injury*, there

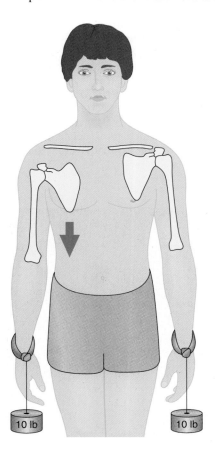

▲
FIGURE 5.78 **Acromioclavicular separation.** The major deformity seen in acromioclavicular separation is the downward displacement of the scapula and upper extremity, whereas the position of the clavicle in the affected side remains the same relative to the clavicle in the unaffected side. (Modified from Rockwood CA Jr, Green DP, 1975, with permission.)

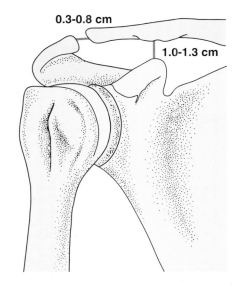

▲
FIGURE 5.79 **Normal measurements.** Schematic diagram shows the normal relation of the coracoid process to the inferior aspect of the clavicle and the normal width of the joint space at the acromioclavicular articulation.

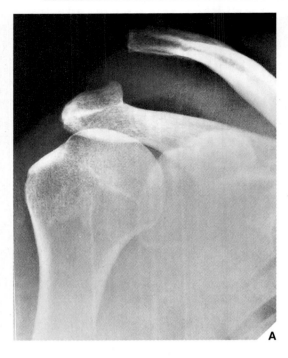

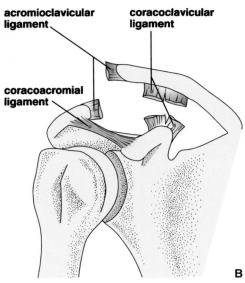

◄ FIGURE 5.80   Acromioclavicular dislocation.
(A) Anteroposterior view of shoulder shows
apparent cephalad displacement of the distal
end of the clavicle and the widening of the
acromioclavicular joint and the coracoclavicular
distance. The marked deformities seen here,
which are characteristic of grade III acromioclavicular separation (severe sprain), are the
result of tear of the coracoclavicular and acromioclavicular ligaments with consequent dislocation in the acromioclavicular joint (B).

is complete acromioclavicular joint dislocation and the coracoclavicular ligament is ruptured. The deltoid and trapezius muscles may be detached from the distal end of the clavicle. Oblique coronal and sagittal MR images are most effective to diagnose this injury. In *type IV injury*, the acromial end of the clavicle is posteriorly dislocated and the scapula is displaced anteroinferiorly. The most effective MR image to detect this type of injury is in axial orientation. In *type V injury*, the findings are similar to type III, but more severe. The trapezius and deltoid muscle attachments on the clavicle and acromion are completely stripped, and the scapula droops inferiorly. The acromial end of the clavicle is displaced cephalad. Coronal, oblique sagittal, and axial MR images well demonstrate this injury. In the rarest, *type VI injury*, the acromial end of the clavicle is displaced inferiorly toward the acromion and coracoid processes.

Sternoclavicular Dislocation. This injury occurs after a fall onto the shoulder. It may be either anterior or posterior. In the anterior dislocation, which is more common, the medial (sternal) end of the clavicle is displaced in front of manubrium. The posterior (retrosternal) dislocation may create more problems because displaced clavicle may impinge on the vital organs such as the great vessels, the nerves in the superior mediastinum, the trachea, or the esophagus. Not infrequently the posterior dislocation is associated with a fracture. Conventional radiography is usually not effective in the demonstration of this injury, although so-called serendipity view introduced by Rockwood occasionally may be helpful (Fig. 5.81). On this projection, if dislocation is anterior, the affected clavicle will project higher, if dislocation is posterior, it will project lower in relation to the unaffected contralateral clavicle. However, the most effective imaging modality for demonstrating the sterno-clavicular joints is CT and 3D CT (Fig. 5.82).

Posttraumatic Osteolysis of the Distal Clavicle. After injury to the shoulder, such as sprain of the acromioclavicular joint, resorption of the distal (acromial) end of the clavicle may occasionally occur. The osteolytic process, which is associated with mild-to-moderate pain, usually begins within 2 months after the injury. The initial

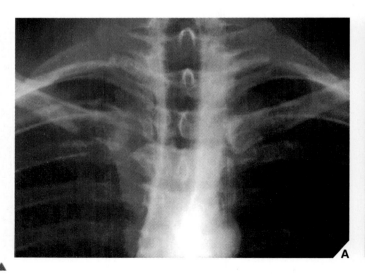

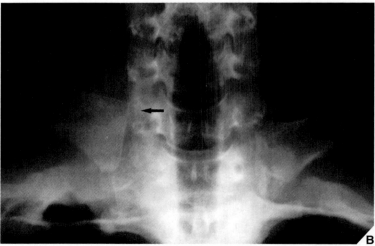

▲ **FIGURE 5.81   Sternoclavicular dislocation. (A)** Anteroposterior radiograph of sternoclavicular joints shows no obvious abnormalities. **(B)** The serendipity view, which is obtained with the patient supine on the radiographic table and the central beam centered over manubrium sterni but directed cephalad with 40-degree angulation of the x-ray tube, shows that the sternal end of the right clavicle projects superiorly in relation to the contralateral clavicle (*arrow*), a feature diagnostic of anterior dislocation.

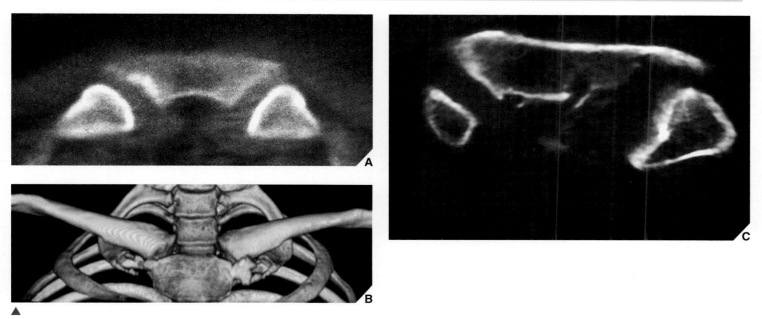

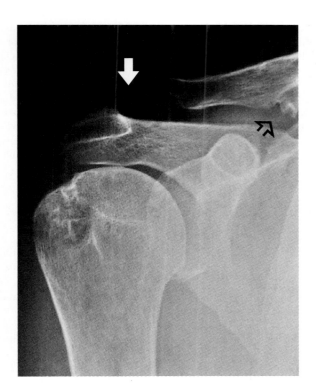

FIGURE 5.82 Sternoclavicular dislocation. (A) Axial CT scan and **(B)** 3D shaded surface display CT reconstructed image shows normal appearance of the sternoclavicular joints. **(C)** Axial CT shows fracture/posterior dislocation in the left sternoclavicular joint. (**C,** courtesy of Dr. Ronald W. Hendrix, Chicago, Illinois.)

radiographic findings consist of soft-tissue swelling and periarticular osteoporosis associated with slightly irregular outline of acromial end of the clavicle (Fig. 5.83). In its late stage, resorption of the distal end of the clavicle results in marked widening of the acromioclavicular joint (Fig. 5.84.)

Suprascapular Nerve Syndrome. The suprascapular nerve runs within the spinoglenoid and suprascapular notches of the scapula. It is a mixed motor and sensory nerve that provides motor fibers to the supraspinatus and infraspinatus muscles and carries pain fibers from the glenohumeral and acromioclavicular joints. A rarely diagnosed

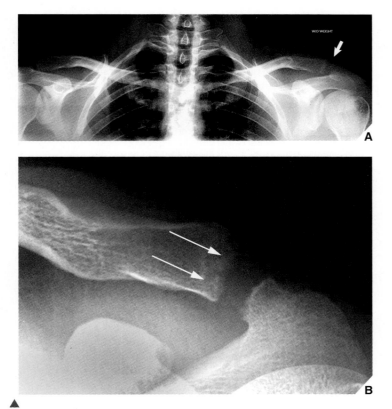

FIGURE 5.83 Posttraumatic osteolysis—early findings. (A) Anteroposterior radiograph of both clavicles shows slight widening of the left acromioclavicular joint (*arrow*). **(B)** A coned-down view of the left acromioclavicular joint shows periarticular osteoporosis and irregular contour of acromial end of the clavicle associated with small radiolucent foci (*arrows*).

FIGURE 5.84 Posttraumatic osteolysis. A 50-year-old man who 5 months previously had injured the right shoulder in a fall presented with symptoms of pain while playing tennis. Anteroposterior view of the shoulder shows marked widening of the acromioclavicular joint (*arrow*) secondary to resorption of the distal end of the clavicle—radiographic features typical of posttraumatic osteolysis. Note also the posttraumatic ossification at the attachment of the coracoclavicular ligament (*open arrow*).

PATHWAY OF THE SUPRASCAPULAR NERVE

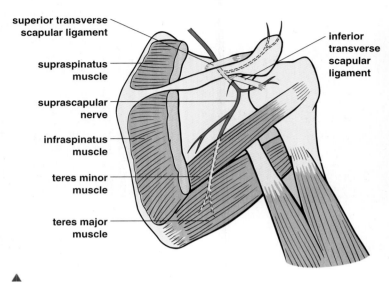

superior transverse
scapular ligament

inferior
transverse
scapular
ligament

supraspinatus
muscle

suprascapular
nerve

infraspinatus
muscle

teres minor
muscle

teres major
muscle

▲
FIGURE 5.85 **Suprascapular nerve.** Pathway of the suprascapular nerve as seen from the posterior aspect of the right scapula.

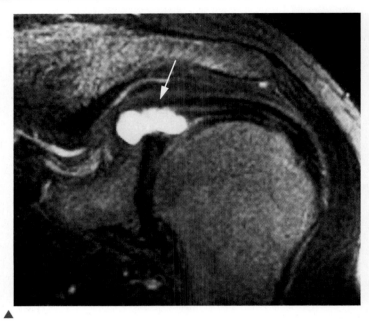

▲
FIGURE 5.86 **Ganglion of the spinoglenoid notch.** Coronal T2-weighted MR image of the left shoulder shows a bright lobulated mass (*arrow*) located within the spinoglenoid notch of scapula, causing a suprascapular nerve syndrome in this 50-year-old man. (Reprinted from Gerscovich EO, Greenspan A, 1993, with permission.)

clinical entity, a suprascapular nerve syndrome results from entrapment or compromise of this nerve at some point in its path (Fig. 5.85). Most patients report nonspecific pain in the shoulder, neck, anterior chest, or in a combination in these anatomic sites. Later severe weakness and atrophy of the supraspinatus and infraspinatus muscles may occur. A variety of causes of injury or entrapment of the suprascapular nerve have been reported, including fracture of the scapula or humerus, anterior shoulder dislocation, thickening of the transverse scapular ligament, rotator cuff tendonitis, and various malignant and benign tumors. Of the latter, the most commonly encountered mass is a ganglion located in the spinoglenoid notch (Fig 5.86). The most effective technique to diagnose suprascapular nerve syndrome is MRI. This modality can distinguish different etiologic factors responsible for the syndrome and provide anatomic information and demonstrate atrophy of the spinatus muscles. It also can exclude other causes of a shoulder pain, such as rotator cuff tear.

PRACTICAL POINTS TO REMEMBER

[1] Fractures of the proximal humerus may be evaluated on the anteroposterior, transscapular, and transthoracic lateral projections. The latter view:
  - provides a true lateral image of the proximal humerus
  - allows sufficient evaluation of the degree of displacement or angulation of the fragments.
[2] Four-segment Neer classification based on the presence or absence of displacement of the four major fragments is a practical and effective way to evaluate the fractures of the proximal humerus.
[3] Fractures of the scapula, particularly if comminuted and displaced, are best evaluated on the transscapular (or Y) projection. If the diagnosis is in doubt, or the fracture cannot be well demonstrated on conventional radiography, CT should be performed.
[4] Neer classification of fractures of the acromial end of the clavicle is based on the site and direction of the fracture line and integrity of the ligaments.

[5] For precise evaluation of the shoulder joint and better demonstration of the glenohumeral articulation, the anteroposterior projection obtained with the patient rotated approximately 40 degrees toward the affected side (Grashey view):
  - eliminates the overlap of the humeral head and the glenoid fossa
  - allows visualization of the glenohumeral joint space and the glenoid in profile.
[6] The Hill-Sachs lesion, which is best demonstrated on the anteroposterior projection obtained with the arm internally rotated, and the Bankart lesion are virtually diagnostic of previous anterior dislocation.
[7] Compression fracture (trough line sign) of the anteromedial aspect of the humeral head is a common sequela of posterior dislocation. The anteroposterior projection obtained with the arm externally rotated readily demonstrates this finding.
[8] MRI characteristics of impingement syndrome include:
  - cystic and sclerotic changes in the greater tuberosity
  - perimuscular and peritendinous edema
  - thickening of subacromial bursa (or effusion)
  - thinning of the supraspinatus tendon
  - increased signal intensity in the tendon (on T2 weighting)
  - subacromial spur.
[9] Rotator cuff tear may effectively be evaluated by contrast arthrography. Opacification of the subacromial–subdeltoid bursae complex is diagnostic of this injury.
[10] MRI characteristics of rotator cuff tear include:
  - discontinuity of the rotator cuff tendons
  - high signal within the tendon structure (on T2-weighted images)
  - retraction of the musculotendinous junction of spinatus muscles
  - atrophy of the supraspinatus muscle and infiltration by fat
  - obliteration of the subacromial–subdeltoid fat line (on T1-weighted images)
  - fluid in the subacromial–subdeltoid bursae complex.
[11] Oblique sagittal MR images are useful to demonstrate four types of acromion: Type 1, flat; type 2, smoothly curved; type 3, hooked; type 4, convex undersurface.

[12] Axial MR images are useful to demonstrate three types of anterior capsular insertion to the scapula.

[13] ABER position of the arm (abduction and external rotation) is effective to evaluate subtle abnormalities of cartilaginous labrum and labral ligmentous complex during MRa.

[14] Acromioclavicular separation is best demonstrated on the stress anteroposterior projection obtained with a 15-degree cephalad angulation of the radiographic tube and weights strapped to the patient's forearms. The radiographic characteristics of this condition include:
- width of the acromioclavicular joint space
- width of the coracoclavicular distance
- presence or absence of apparent cephalad displacement of the distal end of the clavicle.

[15] Suprascapular nerve syndrome results from the entrapment of this nerve caused by a variety of pathologic processes including fracture of the scapula or humerus, anterior shoulder dislocation, rotator cuff tendonitis, and benign or maligmant tumors. MRI is the ideal technique to diagnose this syndrome.

SUGGESTED READINGS

Anderson JE. *Grant's atlas of anatomy*. 8th ed. Baltimore: Williams & Wilkins; 1983.

Antonio GE, Cho JH, Chung CB, Trudell DJ, Resnick D. MR imaging appearance and classification of acromioclavicular joint injury. *Am J Roentgenol* 2003;180:1103–1110.

Arger PH, Oberkircher PE, Miller WT. Lipohemarthrosis. *Am J Roentgenol* 1974;121:97–100.

Bailey RW. Acute and recurrent dislocation of the shoulder. *J Bone Joint Surg Am* 1967;49A:767–773.

Bankart A. The pathology and treatment of recurrent dislocation of the shoulder joint. *Br J Surg* 1938;26:23–29.

Beltran J. *MRI musculoskeletal system*. Philadelphia: JB Lippincott; 1990:3.2–3.22; 4.2–4.11.

Beltran J, Bencardino J, Mellado J, Rosenberg ZS, Irish RD. MR arthrography of the shoulder: variants and pitfalls. *Radiographics* 1997;17:1403–1412.

Beltran J, Gray LA, Bools JC, Zuelzer W, Weis LD, Unverferth LJ. Rotator cuff lesions of the shoulder: evaluation by direct sagittal CT arthrography. *Radiology* 1986;160:161–165.

Beltran J, Rosenberg ZS, Chandnani VP, Cuomo F, Beltran S, Rokito A. Glenohumeral instability: evaluation with MR arthrography. *Radiographics* 1997;17:657–673.

Bencardino JT, Beltran J, Rosenberg ZS, et al. Superior labrum anterior-posterior lesions: diagnosis with MR arthrography of the shoulder. *Radiology* 2000;214:267–271.

Bergin D, Schweitzer ME. Indirect magnetic resonance arthrography. *Skeletal Radiol* 2003;10:551–558.

Berquist TH. *Imaging of sports injuries*. Gaithersburg: Aspen Publication; 1992:265–301.

Bigliani LU, Morrison DS, April EW. The morphology of the acromion and its relationship to rotator cuff tears [abstract]. *Orthop Trans* 1986;10:228.

Bigliani LU, Ticker JB, Flatlow EL, Soslowsky LJ, Mow VC. The relationship of acromial architecture to rotator cuff disease. *Clin Sports Med* 1991;10:823–838.

Braunstein EM, O'Connor G. Double-contrast arthrotomography of the shoulder. *J Bone Joint Surg Am* 1982;64A:192–195.

Brenner ML, Morrison WB, Carrino JA, et al. Direct MR arthrography of the shoulder: is exercise prior to imaging beneficial or detrimental? *Radiology* 2000;215:491–496.

Bright AS, Torpey B, Magid D, Codd T, McFarland EG. Reliability of radiographic evaluation for acromial morphology. *Skeletal Radiol* 1997;26:718–721.

Brossman J, Stäbler A, Preidler KW, Trudell D, Resnick D. Sternoclavicular joint: MR imaging-anatomic correlation. *Radiology* 1996;198:193–198.

Burk DL Jr, Karasick D, Mitchell DG, Rifkin MD. MR imaging of the shoulder: correlation with plain radiography. *Am J Roentgenol* 1990;154:549–553.

Carrino JA, McCauley TR, Katz LD, Smith RC, Lange RC. Rotator cuff: evaluation with fast spin-echo versus conventional spin-echo MR imaging. *Radiology* 1997;202:533–539.

Carroll KW, Helms CA. Magnetic resonance imaging of the shoulder: a review of potential sources of diagnostic errors. *Skeletal Radiol* 2002;31:373–383.

Carroll KW, Helms CA, Otte MT, Moellken SMC, Fritz R. Enlarged spinoglenoid notch veins causing suprascapular nerve compression. *Skeletal Radiol* 2003;32:72–77.

Cartland JP, Crues JV III, Stauffer A, Nottage W, Ryu RKN. MR imaging in the evaluation of SLAP injuries of the shoulder: findings in 10 patients. *Am J Roentgenol* 1992;159:787–792.

Chandnani VP, Yeager TD, DeBerardino T, et al. Glenoid labral tears: prospective evaluation with MR imaging, MR arthrography, and CT arthrography. *Am J Roentgenol* 1993;161:1229–1235.

Chung CB, Dwek JR, Feng S, Resnick D. MR arthrography of the glenohumeral joint: a tailored approach. *Am J Roentgenol* 2001;177:217–219.

Cisternino SJ, Rogers LF, Stufflebam BC, Kruglik CG. The trough line: a radiographic sign of posterior shoulder dislocation. *Am J Roentgenol* 1978;130:951–954.

Clark JM, Harryman DT. Tendons, ligaments, and capsule of the rotator cuff. *J Bone Joint Surg Am* 1992;74A:713–725.

Cone RO, Resnick D, Danzig L. Shoulder impingement syndrome: radiographic evaluation. *Radiology* 1984;150:29–33.

Cvitanic O, Tirman PFJ, Feller JF, Bost FW, Minter J, Carroll KW. Using abduction and external rotation of the shoulder to increase the sensitivity of MR arthrography in revealing tears of the anterior glenoid labrum. *Am J Roentgenol* 1997;169:837–844.

Davies AM. Review: the current role of computed tomographic arthrography of the shoulder. *Clin Radiol* 1991;44:369–375.

Dépelteau H, Bureau NJ, Cardinal E, Aubin B, Brassard P. Arthrography of the shoulder: a simple fluoroscopically guided approach for targeting the rotator cuff interval. *Am J Roentgenology* 2004;182:329–332.

Deutsch AL, Resnick D, Mink JH, et al. Computed and conventional arthrotomography of the glenohumeral joint: normal anatomy and clinical experience. *Radiology* 1984;153:603–609.

Emig EW, Schweitzer ME, Karasick D, Lubowitz J. Adhesive capsulitis of the shoulder: MR diagnosis. *Am J Roentgenol* 1995;164:1457–1459.

Epstein RE, Schweitzer ME, Frieman BG, Fenlin JM Jr, Mitchell DG. Hooked acromion: prevalence on MR images of painful shoulders. *Radiology* 1993;187:479–481.

Erickson SJ, Cox IH, Hyde JS, Carrera GF, Strandt JA, Estkowski LD. Effect of tendon orientation on MR imaging signal intensity: a manifestation of the "magic angle" phenomenon. *Radiology* 1991;181:389–392.

Erickson SJ, Fitzgerald SW, Quinn SF, Carrera GF, Black KP, Lawson TL. Long bicipital tendon of the shoulder: normal anatomy and pathologic findings on MR imaging. *Am J Roentgenol* 1992;158:1091–1096.

Farin PU, Jaroma H. Acute traumatic tears of the rotator cuff: value of sonography. *Radiology* 1995;197:269–273.

Farley TE, Neumann CH, Steinbach LS, Jahnke AJ, Petersen SS. Full-thickness tears of the rotator cuff of the shoulder: diagnosis with MR imaging. *Am J Roentgenol* 1992;158:347–351.

Farooki S, Seeger LL. MR imaging of sports injuries of the shoulder. *Semin Musculoskel Radiol* 1997;1:51–63.

Flannigan B, Kursunoglu-Brahme S, Snyder S, Karzel R, Del Pizzo W, Resnick D. MR arthrography of the shoulder: comparison with conventional MR imaging. *Am J Roentgenol* 1990;155:829–832.

Fritz RC, Helms CA, Steinbach LS, Genant HK. Suprascapular nerve entrapment: evaluation with MR imaging. *Radiology* 1992;182:437–444.

Garneau RA, Renfrew DL, Moore TE, el-Khoury GY, Nepola JV, Lemke JH. Glenoid labrum: evaluation with MR imaging. *Radiology* 1991;179:519–522.

Gerscovich EO, Greenspan A. Magnetic resonance imaging in the diagnosis of suprascapular nerve syndrome. *Can Assoc Radiol J* 1993;44:307–309.

Gobezie R, Warner JJP. SLAP lesion: what is it…really? *Skeletal Radiol* 2007;36:379.

Goldman AB. Double contrast shoulder arthrography. In: Freiberger RH, Kaye JJ, eds. *Arthrography*. New York: Appleton-Century-Crofts; 1979:165–188.

Gor DM. The trough line sign. *Radiology* 2002;224:485–486.

Goss TP. The scapula: coracoid, acromial and avulsion fractures. *Am J Orthop* 1996;25:106–115.

Goss TP. Fractures of the scapula. In: Moehring HD, Greenspan A, eds. *Fractures—diagnosis and treatment*. New York: McGraw-Hill; 2000:207–216.

Graichen H, Bonel H, Stammberger T, et al. Three-dimensional analysis of the width of the subacromial space in healthy subjects and patients with impingement syndrome. *Am J Roentgenol* 1999;172:1081–1086.

Griffith JF, Antonio GE, Tong CWC, Ming CK. Anterior shoulder dislocation: quantification of glenoid bone loss with CT. *Am J Roentgenol* 2003;180:1423–1430.

Guntern DV, Pfirrmann CWA, Schmid MR, et al. Articular cartilage lesions of the glenohumeral joint: diagnostic effectiveness of MR arthrography and prevalence in patients with subacromial impingement syndrome. *Radiology* 2003;226:165–170.

Haygood TM, Langlotz CP, Kneeland JB, Iannotti JP, Williams GR Jr, Dalinka MK. Categorization of acromial shape: interobserver variability with MR imaging and conventional radiography. *Am J Roentgenol* 1994;162:1377–1382.

Helms CA, Major NM, Anderson MW, et al. *Musculoskeletal MRI*. 2nd ed. Philadelphia: Saunders-Elsevier 2009;177–221.

Hannafin JA, Chiaia TA. Adhesive capsulitis: a treatment approach. *Clin Orthop* 2000;372:95–109.

Hendrix RW. Imaging of fractures of the shoulder girdle and upper extremities. In: Moehring HD, Greenspan A, eds. *Fractures—diagnosis and treatment*. New York: McGraw-Hill; 2000:33–46.

Herzog RJ. Magnetic resonance imaging of the shoulder. *J Bone Joint Surg Am* 1997;79A:934–953.

Hill HA, Sachs MD. The grooved defect of the humeral head. A frequently unrecognized complication of dislocations of the shoulder joint. *Radiology* 1940;35:690–700.

Hodler J, Kursunoglu-Brahme S, Snyder SJ, et al. Rotator cuff disease: assessment with MR arthrography versus standard MR imaging in 36 patients with arthroscopic confirmation. *Radiology* 1992;182:431–436.

Holt RG, Helms CA, Steinbach L, Neumann C, Munk PL, Genant HK. Magnetic resonance imaging of the shoulder: rationale and current applications. *Skeletal Radiol* 1990;19:5–14.

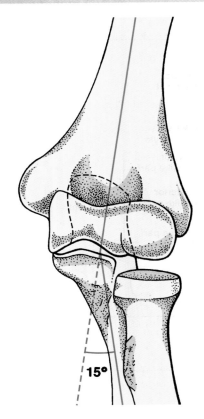

▲
FIGURE 6.5   **Carrying angle.** The angle formed by the longitudinal axes of the distal humerus and the proximal ulna constitutes the carrying angle of the forearm. Normally, there is a valgus angle of 15 degrees.

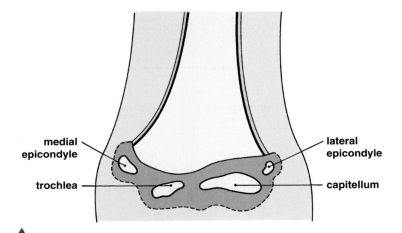

▲
FIGURE 6.6   **Ossification centers of the distal humerus.** The secondary centers of ossification of the distal humerus usually appear in the following order: the capitellum at 1 to 2 years of age, the medial epicondyle at 4 years of age, the trochlea at 8 years of age, and the lateral epicondyle at 10 years of age.

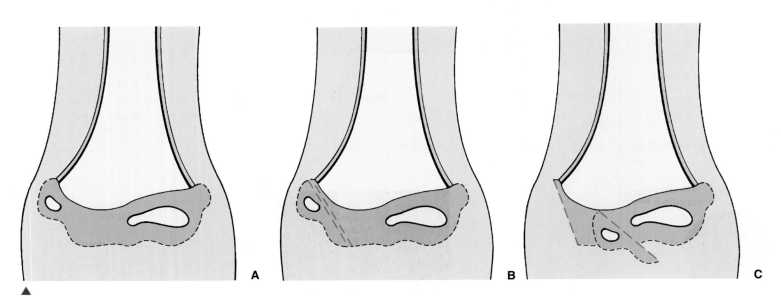

▲
FIGURE 6.7   **Fracture of the medial epicondyle.** Displacement of the ossification center of the medial epicondyle secondary to fracture (**A**) and (**B**) may mimic the normal appearance of the ossification center of the trochlea (**C**). The orange areas represent unossified cartilage which is not visualized on the radiographs.

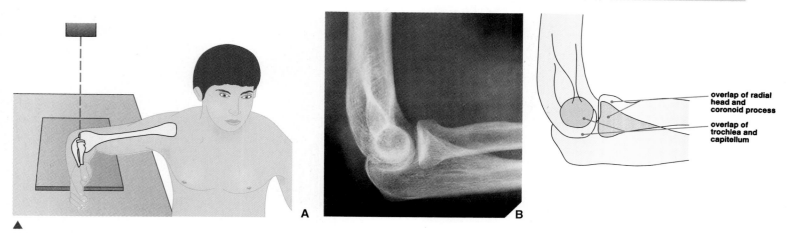

▲
FIGURE 6.8 **Lateral view.** (**A**) For the lateral projection of the elbow, the forearm rests on its ulnar side on the radiographic cassette, with the joint flexed 90 degrees, the thumb pointing upward, and the fingers slightly flexed. The central beam is directed vertically toward the radial head. (**B**) The film in this projection demonstrates the distal shaft of the humerus, the supracondylar ridge, the olecranon process, and the anterior aspect of the radial head. The articular surface and posterior aspect of the radial head are not well demonstrated on this view because of overlap by the coronoid process. The capitellum is also obscured by the overlapping trochlea.

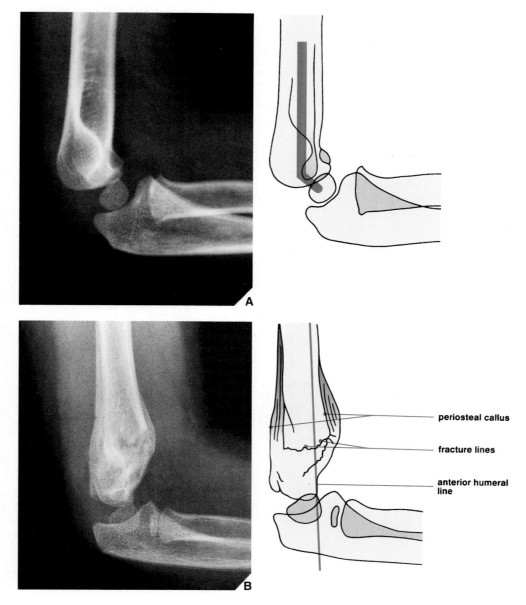

▲
FIGURE 6.9 **Supracondylar fracture.** (**A**) Lateral radiograph of the elbow joint in a 3-year-old child shows the normal hockey-stick appearance of the distal humerus. (**B**) Loss of this configuration, as seen in this radiograph in a 3.5-year-old girl who sustained trauma to the elbow 4 weeks before this examination, serves as an important landmark in recognizing supracondylar fracture of the distal humerus. Note also that the anterior humeral line falls anterior to the capitellum, indicating an extension injury (see Fig. 6.10).

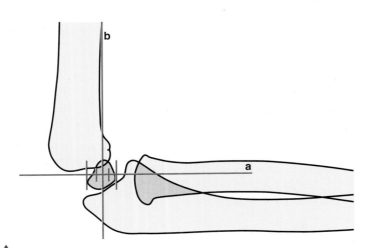

▲
FIGURE 6.10 **Landmarks of the elbow joint.** In children, the normal position of the capitellum relative to the distal humerus and the proximal radius is determined by the portions of the capitellum intersected by two lines: Line (*a*) coincident with the longitudinal axis of the proximal radius passes through the center of the capitellum and line (*b*) parallel to the anterior cortex of the distal humerus intersects the middle third of the capitellum. Disruption of this relation indicates the possible presence of an abnormality (see Figs. 6.9B and 6.25B).

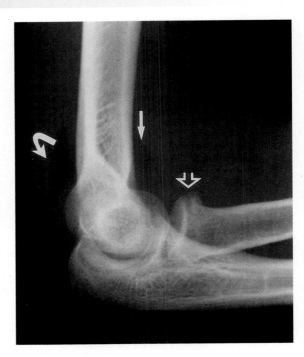

▲
FIGURE 6.11 **Fat-pad sign.** Lateral radiograph of the elbow joint shows positive anterior (*arrow*) and posterior (*curved arrow*) fat-pad sign. *Open arrow* points to the subtle fracture of the radial head.

patient's age, a displacement of the normal positions of the fat pads of the elbow also provides a useful diagnostic clue to the presence of a fracture. Normally, the posterior fat pad, which lies deep in the olecranon fossa, is not visible on the lateral view. When it becomes visible and the anterior fat pad appears displaced—the positive fat-pad sign (Fig. 6.11; see Fig. 4.35)—demonstration of the fracture line should be undertaken.

The *radial head–capitellum* view is a variant of the lateral projection, which was introduced by the author in 1982. As it overcomes the major limitation of the standard lateral view by projecting the radial head ventrad, free of overlap by the coronoid process, it has proved to be a particularly effective technique. In addition to the radial head, it also clearly demonstrates the capitellum, the coronoid process, the humeroradial and humeroulnar articulations (Fig. 6.12), and subtle fractures of

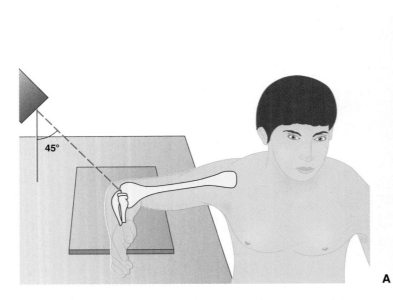

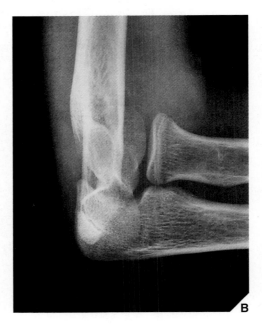

A   B

▲
FIGURE 6.12 **Radial head–capitellum view.** (**A**). For the radial head–capitellum projection of the elbow, the patient is seated at the side of the radiographic table, with the forearm resting on its ulnar side, the elbow joint flexed 90 degrees, and the thumb pointing upward. The central beam is directed toward the radial head at a 45-degree angle to the forearm. (**B**) The film in this projection shows the radial head projected ventrad, free of overlap by the coronoid process, which is also well demonstrated. This projection is also effective in evaluating the capitellum and the humeroradial and humeroulnar articulations.

these structures that may be obscure on other projections (see Figs. 6.27, 6.28, and 6.34).

Other modalities may also be necessary for sufficient evaluation of an injury to the elbow. Single-contrast or, preferably, double-contrast arthrography, combined (in the past) with tomography (*arthrotomography*) and presently with computed tomography (CT), has proved effective in visualizing subtle chondral fractures, osteochondritis dissecans, synovial and capsular abnormalities, and osteochondral bodies in the joint. In general, indications for elbow arthrography include detection of the presence, size, and number of intraarticular osteochondral bodies; determination of whether calcifications around the elbow joint are intraarticular or extraarticular; evaluation of the articular cartilage; evaluation of juxta-articular cysts if they are communicating with the joint; evaluation of the joint capacity; and evaluation of various synovial and capsular abnormalities. Single-contrast arthrography is preferable when evaluating synovial abnormalities and intraarticular osteochondral

bodies, because double contrast may result in air bubbles in the joint. Double-contrast arthrography, however, provides more detailed information; in particular, the articular surface and synovial lining are better delineated and the small details can be better visualized (Fig. 6.13). In the past, in conjunction with elbow arthrography, conventional tomography was used in a procedure called arthrotomography (Fig. 6.14); however, currently it has been substituted by CT examination (CT-arthrography) (Fig. 6.15).

Axial CT images of the extended elbow are occasionally effective in demonstrating traumatic abnormalities. They are, however, difficult to obtain in the traumatized patient, and except for the visualization of the proximal radioulnar joint and ulnatrochlear articulation, they are not frequently used. Occasionally, these sections can demonstrate osteochondral fractures of the radial head and assess the integrity of the proximal radioulnar joint. However, Franklin and colleagues noted that axial CT images of the flexed elbow (so-called coronal

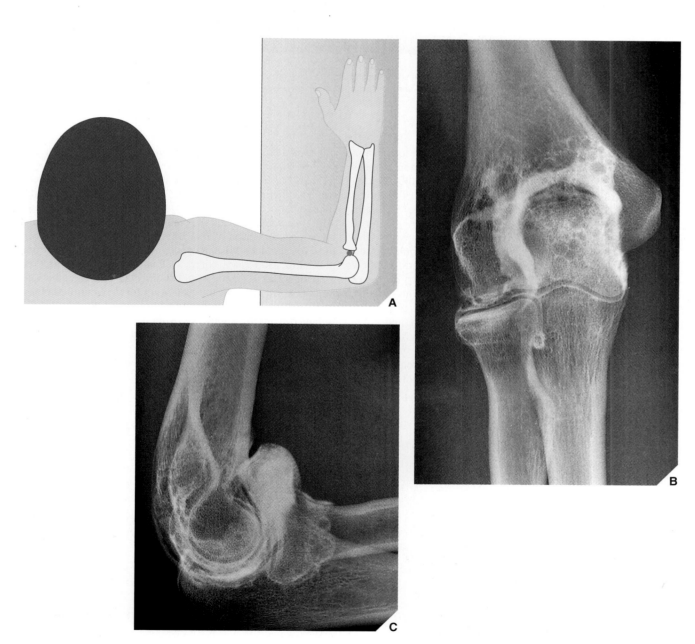

FIGURE 6.13 Arthrography of the elbow joint. (A) For arthrographic examination of the elbow, the patient's forearm is positioned prone on the radiographic table, with the joint flexed 90 degrees and the fingers lying flat. The joint is entered from the lateral aspect between the radial head and the capitellum, and under fluoroscopic control, 2 mL of positive contrast agent (60% diatrizoate meglumine) and 8 to 10 mL of room air are injected into the radiocapitellar joint. (The *red dot* marks the point of needle entrance.) Conventional radiographs or tomograms may then be obtained in the standard projections (see Figs. 6.14 and 6.42). **(B,C)** On the elbow arthrogram, one can distinguish anterior, posterior, and annular recesses of the joint capsule. The articular cartilage of the radial head and capitellum is also well demonstrated.

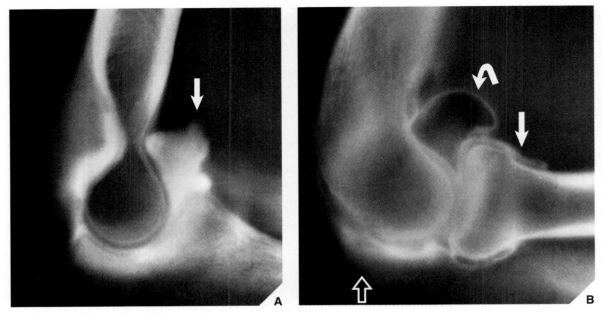

FIGURE 6.14 **Arthrotomography of the elbow joint.** A trispiral section through the ulnar–trochlear articulation (**A**) demonstrates the coronoid recess (*arrow*) and through the radiocapitellar articulation (**B**) demonstrates the annular (periradial) (*arrow*), anterior (*curved arrow*), and posterior (*open arrow*) recesses of the joint capsule.

sections) provide an ideal plane for the evaluation of the olecranon fossa and the space between the trochlea and the olecranon process posteriorly, as well as the radius and the capitellum, and the trochlea and the coronoid process anteriorly. Axial scans through the flexed elbow also allow additional demonstration of the proximal radius in its long axis.

Magnetic resonance imaging (MRI) examination effectively demonstrates traumatic abnormalities of the elbow joint and surrounding soft tissues. Axial, sagittal, and coronal planes are routinely used for elbow imaging. The axial plane is ideal to display the anatomic relationship of the proximal radioulnar joint and the head of the radius. Various tendons, muscles, annular ligament, and neurovascular bundles are also effectively imaged. On coronal images, the trochlea, capitellum, and radial head are well demonstrated, as well as the various tendons, ligaments, and muscles around the elbow (Fig. 6.16A). On the sagittal images, the ulnatrochlear and radiocapitellar articulations are well seen, and the biceps, triceps, and brachialis muscle groups are well demonstrated in

their long axis. The biceps tendon and anconeus muscles are also well imaged (Fig. 6.16B,C).

MR arthrography (MRa) is occasionally performed, mainly to evaluate synovial abnormalities and integrity of the joint capsule and ligaments. In addition, subtle intraarticular loose bodies can be detected with this technique, and the stability of osteochondral fracture or osteochondritis dissecans of the capitellum can be assessed. Similar to one used for shoulder MRa, a concentration of gadolinium mixed with normal saline, iodinated contrast agent, and lidocaine is prepared and a total of up to 10 mL of fluid is injected into the elbow joint. Lateral approach, identical to the technique for conventional elbow arthrography (see Fig. 6.13), is preferred. Coronal, sagittal, and axial images are obtained using fat-suppressed spin echo sequences (Fig. 6.17). During the evaluation of MRI of the elbow, it is helpful to use a checklist as provided in Table 6.1.

For a summary of the preceding discussion in tabular form, see Tables 6.2 and 6.3 and Figure 6.18.

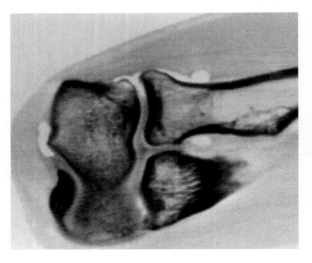

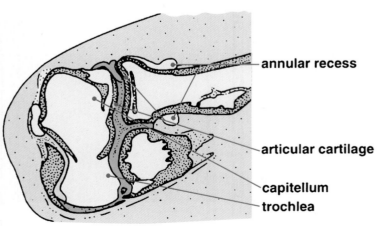

annular recess

articular cartilage

capitellum
trochlea

FIGURE 6.15 **CT-arthrography of the elbow.** Postarthrography coronal CT scan of the elbow joint clearly demonstrates the annular recess and the outline of the lateral extension of the joint capsule. The articular cartilage is also well demonstrated.

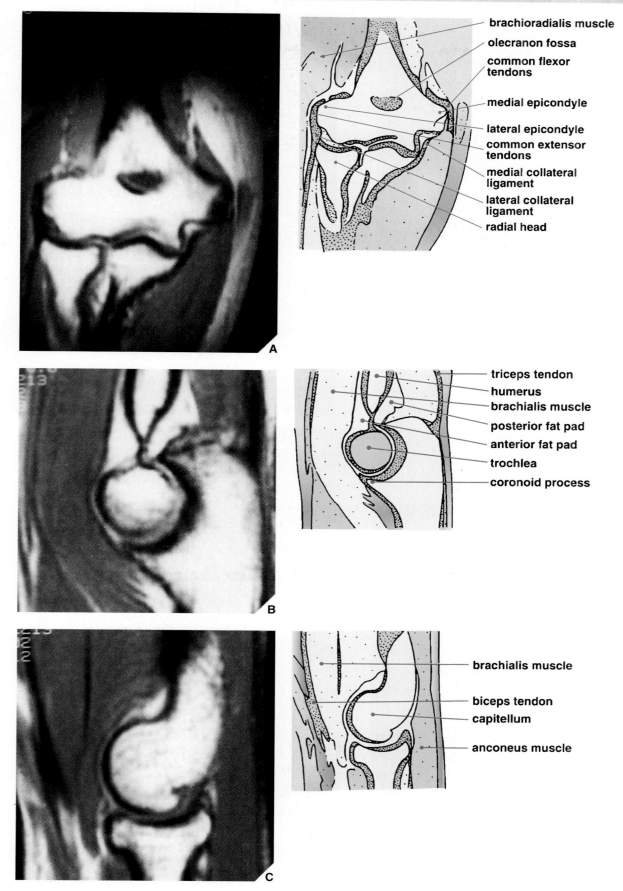

FIGURE 6.16 **Normal MRI anatomy of the elbow joint.** On the coronal section (**A**), note the anatomic relationship of bony, muscular, and tendinous structures. On the sagittal sections (**B**) and (**C**), the muscular structures (brachialis muscle, anconeus muscle), tendons (triceps tendon, biceps tendon), and bones (distal humerus, olecranon process, and radial head) are well demonstrated. (From Beltran J, 1990, with permission.)

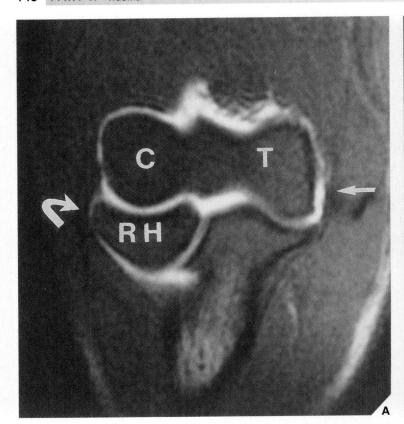

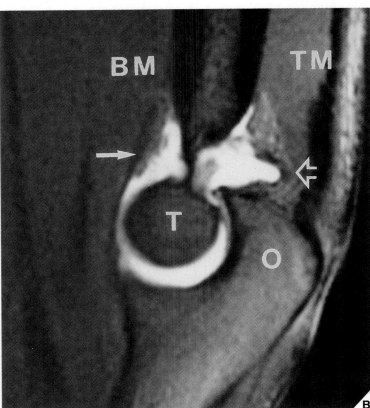

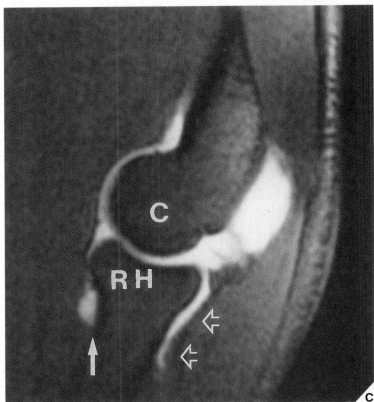

▲
FIGURE 6.17   **MRa of the elbow.** (**A**) Coronal T1-weighted fat-suppressed image shows the anterior band of the ulnar collateral ligament (*arrow*) and the radial collateral ligament (*curved arrow*). The joint is outlined by a bright contrast agent. C, capitellum; T, trochlea; RH, radial head. (**B**) Sagittal T1-weighted fat-suppressed image obtained through the medial part of the elbow joint shows anterior (*arrow*) and posterior (*open arrow*) recesses. T, trochlea; O, olecranon; BM, brachialis muscle; TM, triceps muscle. (**C**) Sagittal T1-weighted fat-suppressed image obtained through the lateral part of the elbow joint shows attachment of the joint capsule to the proximal radius (*arrow*) and its posterior extent (*open arrows*). C, capitellum; RH, radial head.

TABLE 6.1 Checklist for Evaluation of MRI and MRa of the Elbow

Osseous Structures
Medial epicondyle of the humerus (c, s, a)
Lateral epicondyle of the humerus (c, s, a)
Trochlea (c, s)
Capitellum (c, s)
Radial head (c, s)
Radial neck (c, s)
Coronoid process (s)
Olecranon (s)

Cartilaginous Structures
Articular cartilage (c, s, a)

Joints
Radiocapitellar (c, s)
Ulnatrochlear (c, s)
Proximal radioulnar (c, s, a)

Muscles and Their Tendons
Biceps (s, a)
Triceps (s, a)
Anconeus (s, a)
Brachioradialis (c, s, a)
Extensor carpi radialis—brevis, longus (c, a)

Muscles and Their Tendons (continued)
Extensor carpi ulnaris (c, a)
Extensor digitorum (c, a)
Flexor carpi ulnaris (c, a)
Flexor carpi radialis (c, a)
Flexor digitorum—superficialis, profundus (c, a)
Pronator teres (c, a)
Supinator (c, a)
Conjoined extensor–supinator tendon (c, a)
Palmaris longus (a)

Ligaments
Ulnar (medial) collateral—anterior, posterior, transverse (c)
Radial (lateral) collateral, including annular (a, c)

Bursae
Bicipitoradial (a)
Interosseous (a)

Other Structures
Ulnar nerve (a)
Median nerve (a)
Radial nerve (a)

The best imaging planes for visualization of listed structures are given in parenthesis; c, coronal; s, sagittal; a, axial.

TABLE 6.2 Standard and Special Radiographic Projections for Evaluating Injury to the Elbow

Projection	Demonstration
Anteroposterior	Supracondylar, transcondylar, and intercondylar fractures of the distal humerus
	Fractures of
	Medial and lateral epicondyles
	Lateral aspect of capitellum
	Medial aspect of trochlea
	Lateral aspect of radial head
	Valgus and varus deformities
	Secondary ossification centers of distal humerus
Lateral	Supracondylar fracture of the distal humerus
	Fractures of
	Anterior aspect of radial head
	Olecranon process
	Complex dislocations in elbow joint
	Dislocation of radial head
	Fat-pad sign
External Oblique	Fractures of
	Lateral epicondyle
	Radial head
Internal Oblique	Fractures of
	Medial epicondyle
	Coronoid process
Radial Head–Capitellum	Fractures of
	Radial head
	Capitellum
	Coronoid process
	Abnormalities of humeroradial and humeroulnar articulations

TABLE 6.3 Ancillary Imaging Techniques for Evaluating Injury to the Elbow

Technique	Demonstration
Tomography (presently replaced by CT)	Complex fractures about the elbow joint, particularly to assess the position of fragments in comminution
	Healing process:
	Nonunion
	Secondary infection
Arthrography (single or double contrast)	Subtle abnormalities of articular cartilage
	Capsular ruptures
	Synovial abnormalities
	Chondral and osteochondral fractures
	Osteochondritis dissecans
	Osteochondral bodies in joint
Computed Tomography (CT) (alone or combined with double-contrast arthrography)	Same as for arthrography
Magnetic Resonance Imaging (MRI) and Magnetic Resonance Arthrography (MRa)	Abnormalities of the ligaments*, tendons, and muscles
	Capsular ruptures*
	Joint effusion
	Synovial cysts*
	Hematomas
	Subtle abnormalities of bones (e.g., bone contusion)
	Osteochondritis dissecans*
	Epiphyseal fractures (in children)

*These abnormalities are best demonstrated on MRa.

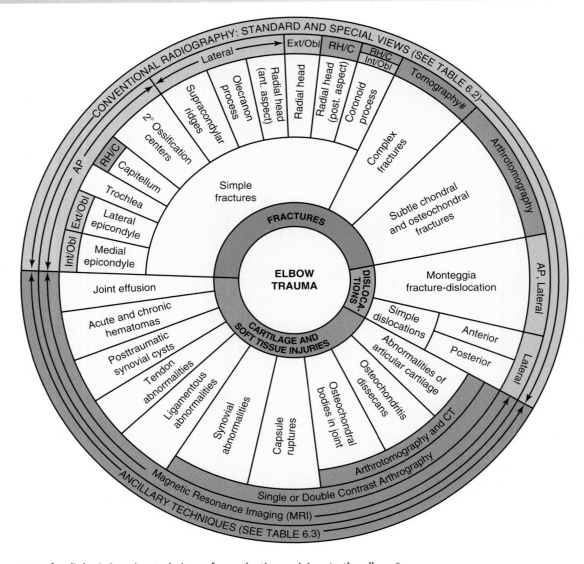

FIGURE 6.18　Spectrum of radiologic imaging techniques for evaluating an injury to the elbow.*

*The radiographic projections or radiologic techniques indicated throughout the diagram are only those that are the most effective in demonstrating the respective traumatic conditions.

#Almost completely replaced by CT.

Injury to the Elbow

Fractures about the Elbow

Fractures of the Distal Humerus. Because the nomenclature of the various structures of the distal humerus used in different anatomy and surgery textbooks is not uniform, confusion has arisen regarding the classification of fractures of the distal humerus. To clarify the picture, a simplified anatomic division of the distal humerus is shown in Figure 6.19. The significance of the distinction between the articular and the extraarticular parts of the distal humerus lies in its importance to diagnosis, treatment, and prognosis. For example, as Rockwood and Green contended, a fracture involving only the articular portion of the distal humerus usually results in a loss of motion, but not a loss of stability, whereas a fracture of an entire condyle—that is, both articular and extraarticular portions—usually leads to restriction of motion and instability.

Based on the structure involved, fractures of the distal humerus can be classified as supracondylar, transcondylar, and intercondylar as well as fractures of the medial and the lateral epicondyles, the capitellum, and the trochlea. The Müller classification is recommended, because it is a practical one based on a distinction between intraarticular and extraarticular fractures (Fig. 6.20). Usually, such injuries pose no diagnostic problems in adults and are readily evaluated on the anteroposterior and lateral projections of the elbow (Figs. 6.21 and 6.22). In the past, tomographic examination was usually performed to localize comminuted fragments. Currently, CT is the modality of choice for this purpose (Fig 6.23).

In children, the diagnosis may be problematic because of the presence of the secondary centers of ossification and their variability. Nevertheless, the anteroposterior and lateral projections usually suffice to demonstrate the abnormality, although the fracture line is occasionally more difficult to evaluate on the anteroposterior than on the lateral view. In children between the ages of 3 and 10 years, supracondylar fracture is the most common type of elbow fracture. Extension injury, caused by a fall on the outstretched hand with the elbow hyperextended, is present in 95% of such cases, and characteristically the distal fragment is posteriorly displaced (Fig. 6.24). In the flexion type of injury caused by a fall on the flexed elbow, which occurs in only 5% of cases of supracondylar fracture, the distal fragment is anteriorly and upwardly displaced. Identifying supracondylar fracture on the lateral projection is usually facilitated by recognition of the loss of the normal hockey-stick appearance of the distal humerus and displacement of the capitellum relative to the line of the anterior cortex of the humerus (see Figs. 6.9 and 6.10). A positive fat-pad sign is invariably present (Fig. 6.25).

Whatever the age of the patient, it is important in a fracture of the distal humerus to demonstrate and evaluate fully the type of injury, the extension of the fracture line, and the degree of displacement, because the method of treatment varies accordingly. When difficulties in interpretation of the type of fracture and the degree of displacement arise, it may be helpful to obtain films of the contralateral normal elbow for comparison.

Complications. The most serious complications of supracondylar fracture are Volkmann ischemic contracture (see Fig. 4.54) and malunion.

FIGURE 6.19 Anatomic structures of the distal humerus. ▶
A simplified anatomic division of the structures of the distal
humerus.

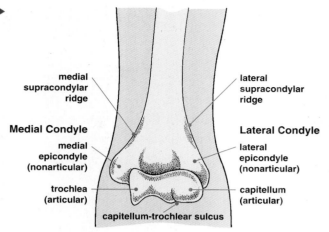

medial
supracondylar
ridge

lateral
supracondylar
ridge

Medial Condyle

Lateral Condyle

medial
epicondyle
(nonarticular)

lateral
epicondyle
(nonarticular)

trochlea
(articular)

capitellum
(articular)

capitellum-trochlear sulcus

FIGURE 6.20 Fractures of the distal humerus. ▶
Classification of fractures of the distal humerus on
the basis of extraarticular and intraarticular extension. (Modified from Müller ME et al., 1979.)

FRACTURES OF THE DISTAL HUMERUS

Extra-articular—Epicondylar, Supracondylar

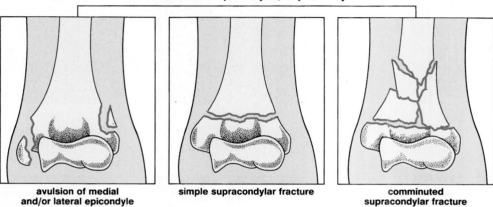

avulsion of medial
and/or lateral epicondyle

simple supracondylar fracture

comminuted
supracondylar fracture

Intra-articular—Transcondylar

fracture of trochlea

fracture of capitellum

Intra-articular—Bicondylar, Intercondylar

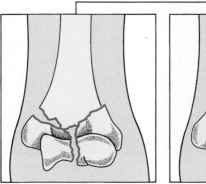

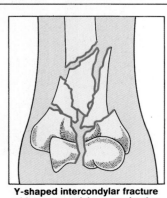

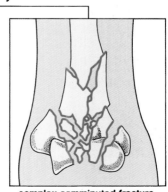

Y-shaped bicondylar fracture

Y-shaped intercondylar fracture
with supracondylar comminution

complex comminuted fracture

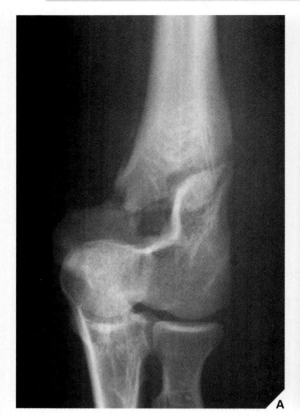
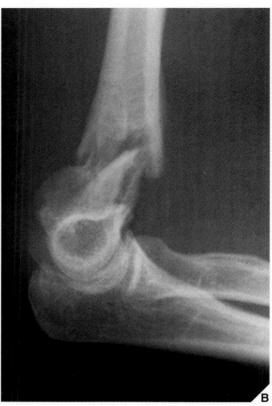

�— FIGURE 6.21 **Supracondylar fracture.** A 27-year-old man fell from the ladder onto his outstretched arm. Anteroposterior (**A**) and lateral (**B**) radiographs show a simple supracondylar fracture of the humerus with posterior displacement of the distal fragment.

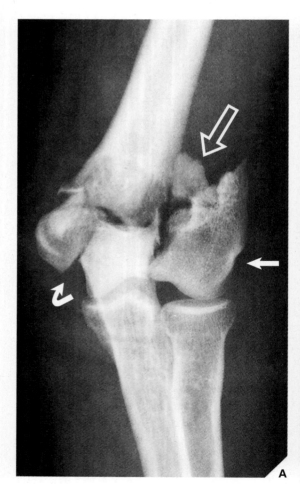
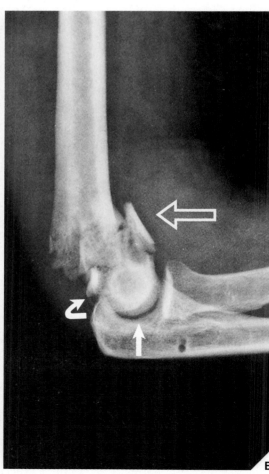

�— FIGURE 6.22 **Fracture of the distal humerus.** A 25-year-old man sustained a complex intraarticular fracture of the distal humerus in a motorcycle accident. Anteroposterior (**A**) and lateral (**B**) views clearly demonstrate the extension of the fracture lines and the position of the various fragments. The capitellum is separated, laterally displaced, and subluxed (*arrow*); the lateral supracondylar ridge is avulsed and anterolaterally displaced (*open arrow*), and the medial epicondyle is externally rotated and medially displaced (*curved arrow*).

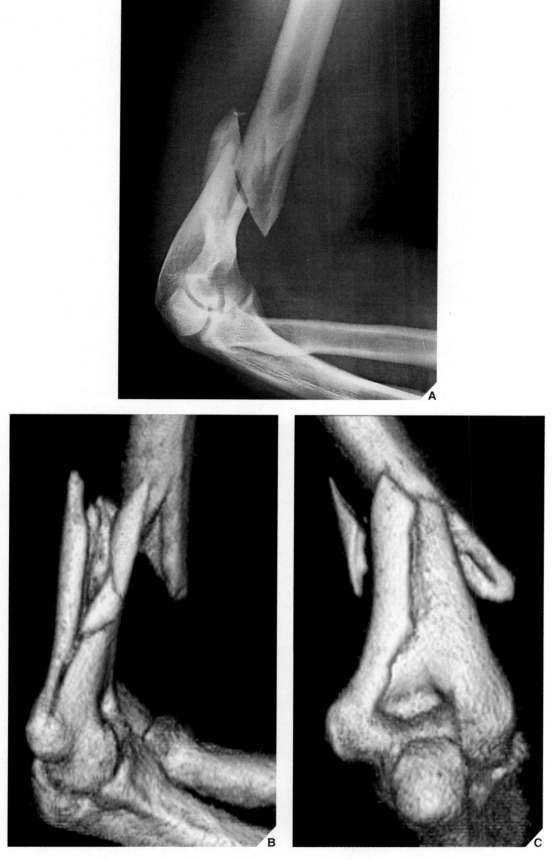

FIGURE 6.23   **3D CT of a fracture of the distal humerus.** (**A**) A conventional radiograph shows a comminuted supracondylar fracture of the humerus. (**B**) and (**C**) 3D CT–reconstructed images demonstrate the details of this injury, including displacement, angulation, and spatial orientation of various fragments.

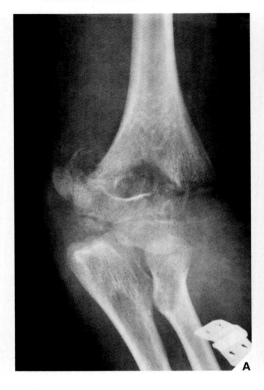

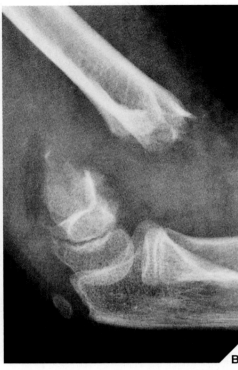

◀ FIGURE 6.24 **Displaced supracondylar fracture.** A 9-year-old boy fell off his bicycle onto his outstretched hand. Anteroposterior (**A**) and lateral (**B**) views of the elbow show supracondylar fracture of the distal humerus with posteromedial displacement of the distal fragment. Note the increase in the valgus angle of the forearm on the anteroposterior view.

The latter commonly results in a varus deformity of the elbow, known as cubitus varus.

Fractures of the Radial Head. A fracture of the radial head is a common injury that results, in most cases, from a fall on the outstretched arm and, only rarely, from a direct blow to the lateral aspect of the elbow.

Radial head fractures have been classified by Mason into three types: type I, undisplaced fractures; type II, marginal fractures with displacement (including impaction, depression, and angulation); and type III, comminuted fractures involving the entire head. Later, DeLee, Green, and Wilkins suggested adding type IV, fractures of the radial head in association with elbow dislocation (Fig. 6.26). All these fractures can be adequately demonstrated on the anteroposterior and lateral radiographs of the elbow. However, because nondisplaced or minimally displaced fractures may go undetected on these projections, the radial head–capitellum view should be included in the routine radiographic examination to detect occult injuries and to evaluate the degree of displacement (Figs. 6.27 and 6.28). Determination of the exact extension of the fracture line (i.e., whether it is extraarticular or intraarticular) and the degree of displacement is crucial to deciding the course of treatment. CT examination plays an important role in this assessment (Fig. 6.29), although MRI may be helpful in confirming the presence of a fracture not clearly shown on routine radiographs (Fig. 6.30). Nondisplaced or minimally displaced fractures are usually treated conservatively by the use of splints or casts, until healing allows active mobilization of the elbow. However, a cleavage fracture of the radial articular surface involving one third or one half of the head with displacement greater than 3 to 4 mm usually indicates the need for open reduction and internal fixation; this is particularly true in younger individuals. Excision of the radial head is the procedure of choice when comminution and displacement of the radial head are present (Fig. 6.31).

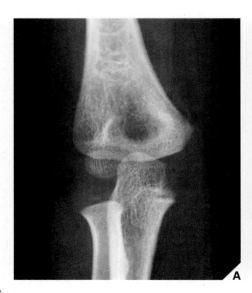

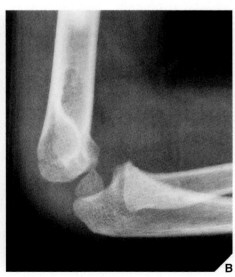

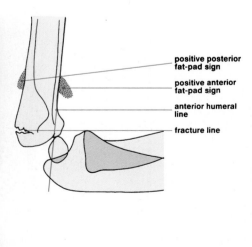

positive posterior fat-pad sign

positive anterior fat-pad sign

anterior humeral line

fracture line

▲
FIGURE 6.25 **Nondisplaced supracondylar fracture.** A 3-year-old girl fell on the street. On the anteroposterior view (**A**), the fracture line is practically invisible, whereas on the lateral view (**B**), it is more obvious. There is a positive posterior fat-pad sign, and the anterior fat pad is also clearly displaced. Note that the anterior humeral line intersects the posterior third of the capitellum, indicating slight anterior angulation of the distal fragment.

FIGURE 6.26 Mason classification of fractures ▶
of the radial head.

**MASON CLASSIFICATION OF FRACTURES
OF THE RADIAL HEAD**

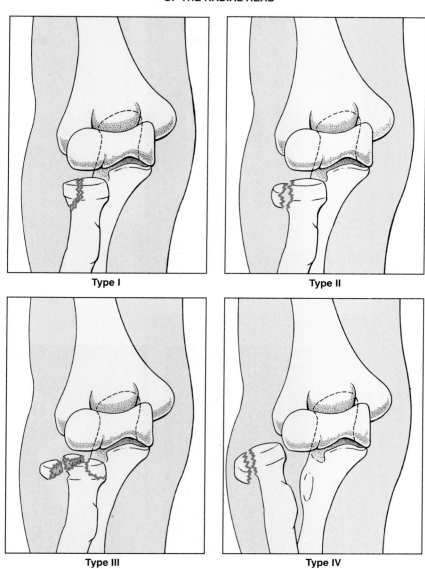

Type I

Type II

Type III

Type IV

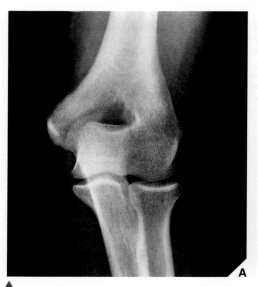

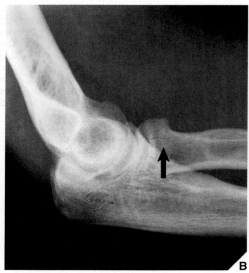

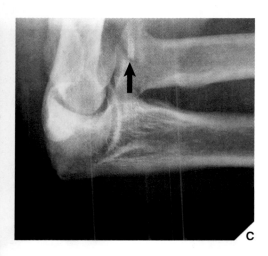

FIGURE 6.27   Fracture of the radial head. Anteroposterior (**A**) and lateral (**B**) films of the elbow show what appears to be a nondisplaced fracture of the radial head (*arrow*). On the radial head–capitellum view (**C**), however, intraarticular extension of the fracture line and 4-mm depression of the subchondral fragment are clearly demonstrated (*arrow*). (From Greenspan A, Norman A, 1983, with permission.)

ESSEX-LOPRESTI FRACTURE–DISLOCATION

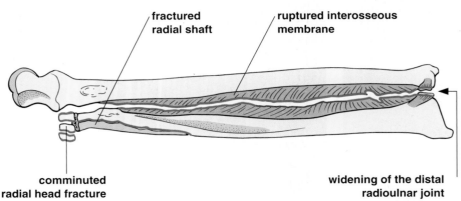

fractured
radial shaft

ruptured interosseous
membrane

comminuted
radial head fracture

widening of the distal
radioulnar joint

◀ FIGURE 6.32   **Essex-Lopresti fracture–dislocation.** The crucial elements of this injury comprise a comminuted fracture of
the radial head, ruptured interosseous membrane, and dislocation in the distal radioulnar joint.

Essex-Lopresti Fracture–Dislocation. This complex injury comprises a comminuted fracture of the radial head and neck with or without distal extension of fracture line, tear of the interosseous membrane of the forearm, and dislocation in the distal radioulnar joint (Fig. 6.32). This is an unstable injury that, because of bipolar loss of radial support at both sites (elbow and wrist), requires unique and tailored treatment. In most patients, interfragmentary fixation of a radial head fracture is performed, or, in cases of severe comminution, silastic or metallic radial head prosthesis may be indicated to maintain length and stability. Chronic Essex-Lopresti injury with irreducible proximal migration of the radius may require ulnar shortening to restore neutral ulnar variance.

Fracture of the Coronoid Process. Rarely occurring as an isolated injury, a fracture of the coronoid process is most often associated with posterior dislocation in the elbow joint (Fig. 6.33). It is, therefore, important in cases of elbow injury to exclude the possibility of a fracture of the coronoid process, because if undiagnosed, it may fail to unite, leading to instability and recurrent subluxation in the joint. The anteroposterior and lateral projections are usually insufficient to evaluate the coronoid process because of overlap of structures on these views. The demonstration of an injury can be made on the radial head–capitellum projection (Fig. 6.34) and, occasionally, on the internal oblique view; however, the best technique to show the coronoid process fracture is CT (Fig. 6.35).

Fracture of the Olecranon. Olecranon fractures usually result from a direct fall on the flexed elbow, and this mechanism frequently produces comminution and marked displacement of the major fragments. An indirect mechanism, such as a fall on the outstretched arm, produces an oblique or transverse fracture with minimal displacement. The fracture is usually well demonstrated on a lateral projection of the elbow.

A number of classifications have been developed to evaluate an olecranon fracture. Colton classified olecranon fractures as undisplaced and displaced, the latter group being subdivided into avulsion fractures, oblique and transverse fractures, comminuted fractures, and fracture–dislocations.

Another practical classification has been developed by Horne and Tanzer, who classified these fractures by their location apparent on the lateral radiographs (Fig. 6.36). Type I fractures are subdivided into two groups: (*A*) oblique, extraarticular fractures of the olecranon tip and (*B*) transverse intraarticular fractures originating on the proximal third of the articular surface of olecranon fossa (Fig. 6.37). Type II fractures are transverse or oblique fractures originating on the middle third of the articular surface of olecranon fossa. These fractures also are subdivided into two groups: (*A*) single fracture line and (*B*) two fracture lines, one proximal (transverse or oblique) and the second, more distal, extending posteriorly (Fig. 6.38). Type III fractures involve the distal third of the olecranon fossa and may be either transverse or oblique (Fig. 6.39). Most fractures are type II.

As far as treatment is concerned, nondisplaced fractures are usually treated conservatively, whereas displaced fractures are most often treated by open reduction and internal fixation.

Osteochondritis Dissecans of the Capitellum

This condition, also occasionally referred to as Panner disease, is considered to be related to trauma, namely, to repeated exogenous injuries to the elbow. However, some investigators contend that Panner disease is an osteochondrosis of the capitellum and affects children (predominantly boys) between the ages of 7 and 12 years, whereas osteochondritis dissecans of the capitellum is a separate entity, affects boys between the ages of 12 and 15 years, and occurs at a time when the epiphysis of the capitellum is almost completely ossified. Regardless of age, valgus strain of the elbow in throwing sports such as baseball and football has been implicated as one causative factor. Apparently during the throwing

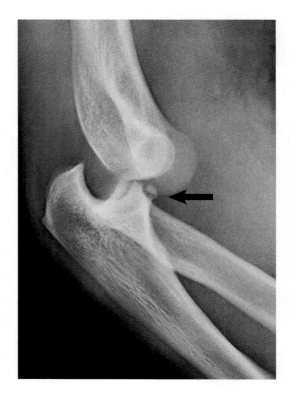

▲
FIGURE 6.33   **Fracture of the coronoid process.** This injury (*arrow*) commonly occurs during a posterior dislocation in the elbow joint.

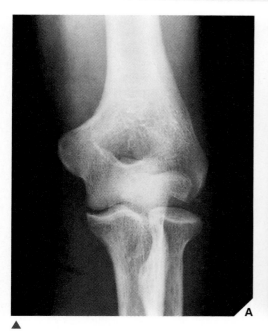
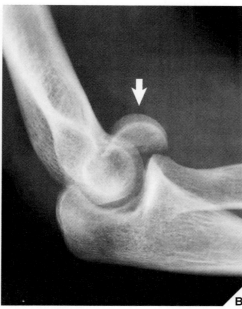
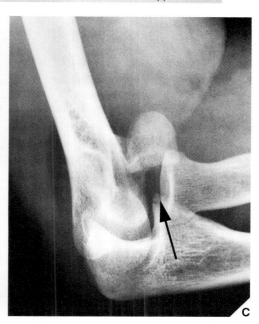

▲
FIGURE 6.34   Fractures of the capitellum and the coronoid process. While playing ice hockey, a 37-year-old man injured his right elbow in a fall. The initial anteroposterior (**A**) and lateral (**B**) radiographs show a fracture of the capitellum with anterior rotation and displacement. Note the typical "half-moon" appearance of the displaced capitellum on the lateral view (*arrow*). On the radial head–capitellum film (**C**), an unsuspected, nondisplaced fracture of the coronoid process is evident (*long arrow*). (**B** and **C** from Greenspan A, Norman A, 1982, with permission.)

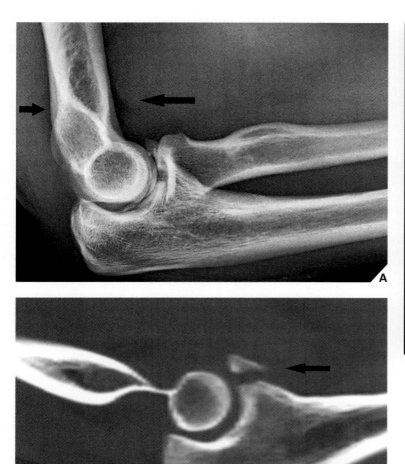
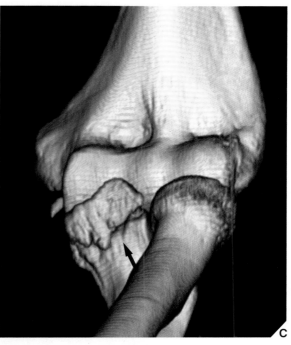

▲
FIGURE 6.35   CT and 3D CT of a fracture of the coronoid process. (**A**) Lateral radiograph of the elbow shows a positive posterior and anterior fat-pad sign (*arrows*), but a fracture of the coronoid process is not well demonstrated. (**B**) Sagittal reformatted CT image and (**C**) 3D CT–reconstructed image in shaded surface display are diagnostic for this injury (*arrows*).

CLASSIFICATION OF OLECRANON FRACTURES

Type I

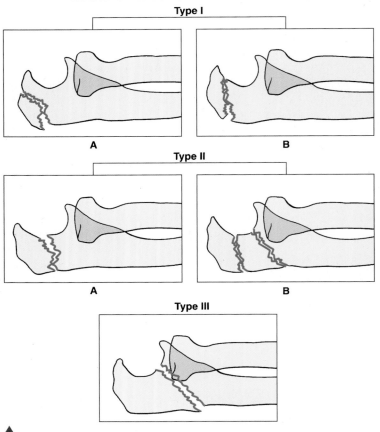

A   B

Type II

A   B

Type III

FIGURE 6.36   Classification of olecranon fractures. (Modified from Horne JG, Tanzer TL, 1981, with permission.)

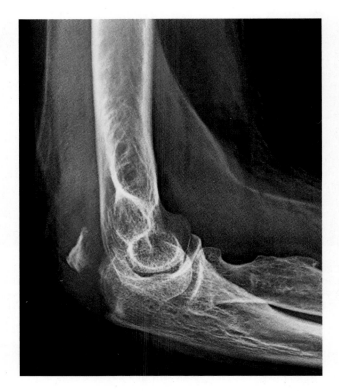

FIGURE 6.37   Olecranon fracture. A 76-year-old woman sustained a type I A olecranon fracture after a fall on the stairs.

motion, the capitellum is subjected to compression and to shear forces. It most frequently affects the right elbow in right-handed children and adolescents, the majority of whom are males.

In the early stage of the disease, anteroposterior and lateral films may show no significant abnormality (Fig. 6.40A,B); the only radiographic sign of early-stage Panner disease may become apparent on the radial head–capitellum view with the finding of subtle flattening of the capitellum (Fig. 6.40C). As the condition progresses, the lesion, consisting of a detached segment of subchondral bone with overlying cartilage, gradually separates from its bed in the capitellum. Before separation, the

lesion is called "in situ"; after separation, the osteochondral fragment becomes a "loose" body in the joint (Fig. 6.41). Because sometimes more than one fragment is discharged into the joint, osteochondritis dissecans may be mistaken for idiopathic synovial (osteo)chondromatosis, a nontraumatic condition that is a form of synovial metaplasia. In this condition, multiple cartilaginous bodies that are regular in outline and usually uniform in size are seen in the joint (see Fig. 23.2).

In the past, one of the radiologic procedures for evaluating osteochondritis dissecans was arthrotomography, which localized the defect in the cartilaginous surface of the capitellum and distinguished

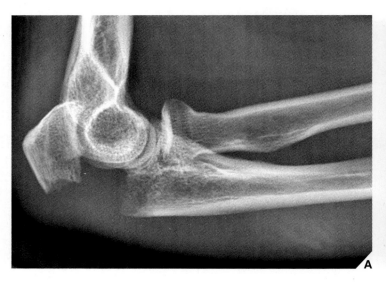

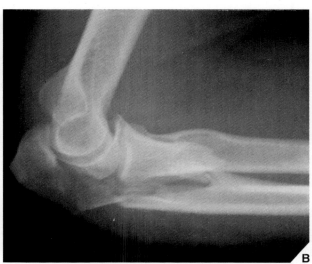

FIGURE 6.38   Olecranon fracture. (A) A 50-year-old woman fell from a ladder and sustained a type II A displaced olecranon fracture, well demonstrated on this lateral radiograph. **(B)** A 41-year-old man fell on his flexed elbow and sustained a type II B comminuted olecranon fracture.

FIGURE 6.39   **Olecranon fracture. (A)** A 52-year-old woman fell on her outstretched arm and sustained a type III olecranon fracture, effectively demonstrated on the lateral view of the elbow. Note the transverse orientation of the fracture line (*open arrow*) and the positive anterior and posterior fat-pad sign (*arrows*). **(B)** A variant of type III olecranon fracture, where a fracture line is oblique in orientation.

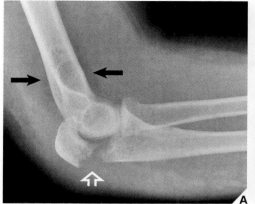
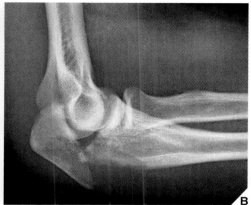

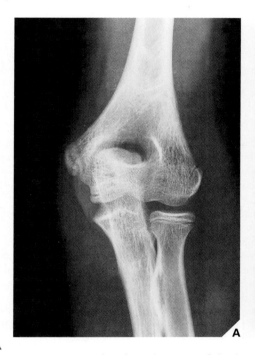
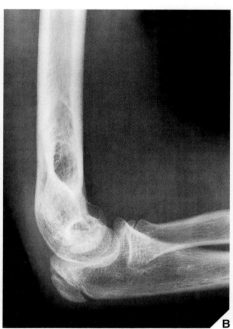
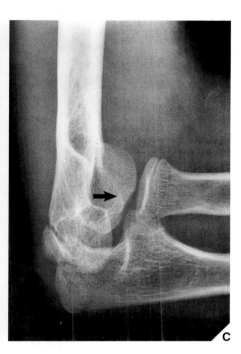

FIGURE 6.40   **Osteochondritis dissecans of the capitellum.** A 13-year-old boy who was very active in little league baseball reported pain in his right elbow for several months. Anteroposterior **(A)** and lateral **(B)** radiographs of the elbow demonstrate no abnormalities. On the radial head–capitellum view **(C)**, subtle flattening of the capitellum (*arrow*) may indicate early-stage osteochondritis dissecans. (From Greenspan A, Norman A, 1982, with permission.)

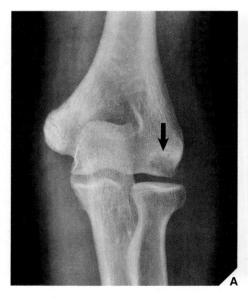
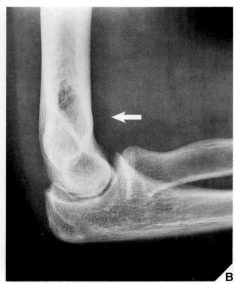
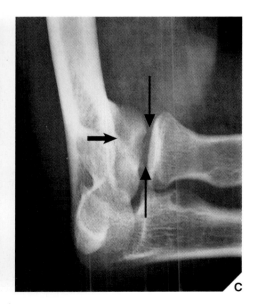

FIGURE 6.41   **Osteochondritis dissecans of the capitellum.** A 15-year-old boy, an active baseball player, reported pain in his right elbow for several months. The anteroposterior view of the elbow **(A)** reveals a radiolucent defect in the capitellum (*arrow*) suggesting osteochondritis dissecans; the lateral view **(B)** shows only positive anterior fat-pad sign (*arrow*). The radial head–capitellum projection **(C)** demonstrates not only the full extent of the lesion in the capitellum (*arrow*) but also the osteochondral bodies in the joint (*thin arrows*)—a sign of advanced-stage osteochondritis dissecans. (From Greenspan A et al., 1984, with permission.)

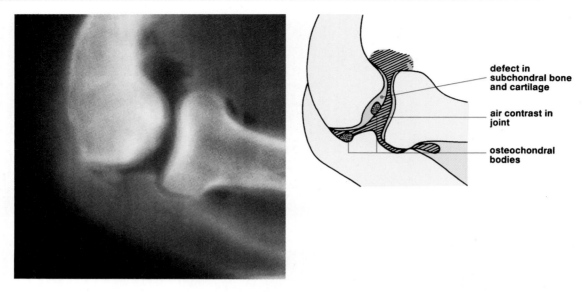

▲
FIGURE 6.42 **Arthrotomography of osteochondritis dissecans of the capitellum.** Lateral arthrotomogram of the elbow demonstrates defects in the subchondral segment of the capitellum and in the overlying cartilage. Loose osteochondral bodies are present, one located posteriorly in the ulnar–trochlear compartment and the other anteriorly in the radiocapitellar compartment. The findings represent advanced-stage osteochondritis dissecans.

an in situ lesion from the more advanced stage of the disease (Fig. 6.42). This information is crucial for the orthopedic surgeon, because the in situ lesion may be treated conservatively, whereas surgical intervention may be required if the osteochondral fragment has been partially separated from its bed or discharged into the joint. At the present time, CT-arthrography almost completely replaced arthrotomography, although MRI is also effective to demonstrate the lesion (Fig. 6.43) and to provide information about its stability (Fig. 6.44). Type I lesions are intact (in situ), with no fragment displacement; type II lesions are slightly displaced, and the articular surface is damaged; type III lesions show detachment of the osteochondral fragment (Fig. 6.45).

Dislocations in the Elbow Joint

Simple Dislocations. The standard method of classifying elbow dislocations is based on the direction of displacement of the radius and the ulna in relation to the distal humerus. Three main types of dislocation can be distinguished as those affecting (A) both the radius and the ulna,

which may be dislocated posteriorly, anteriorly, medially, or laterally (or in a manner combining posterior or anterior with medial or lateral displacement); (B) the ulna only, which may be anteriorly or posteriorly displaced; and (C) the radius only, which may be anteriorly, posteriorly, or laterally dislocated.

Posterior and posterolateral dislocations of the radius and the ulna are, by far, the most common types. They account for 80% to 90% of all dislocations in the joint (Fig. 6.46). Isolated dislocation of the radial head, however, is a rare occurrence; it is more commonly associated with a fracture of the ulna (see "Monteggia Fracture–Dislocation"). Dislocations are easily diagnosed on the standard anteroposterior and lateral radiographs of the elbow.

The presence of a dislocation should signal the possibility of an associated fracture of the ulna, which may be overlooked when radiographic examination is focused only on the elbow. For this reason, if a dislocation in the elbow joint is suspected, it is mandatory to include the entire forearm on the anteroposterior and lateral films; conversely,

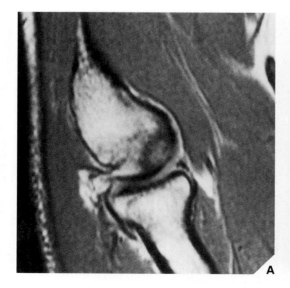
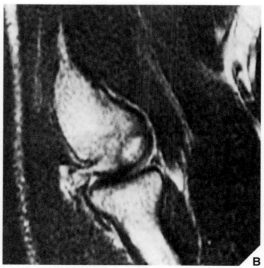

▲
FIGURE 6.43 **MRI of osteochondritis dissecans of the capitellum.** A 16-year-old baseball player presented with pain in the right elbow for 6 months. The two MR sagittal sections (SE sequences; TR 2000/TE 20 msec, TR 2000/TE 80 msec) demonstrate an area of intermediate signal intensity on proton-weighted image (**A**) and high signal intensity on T2-weighted image surrounded by a band of low signal intensity (**B**). The articular cartilage is intact. The findings are typical for in situ lesion of osteochondritis dissecans. (From Beltran J, 1990, with permission.)

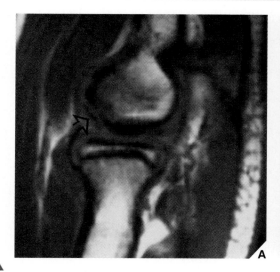
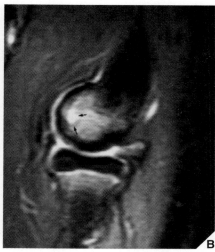
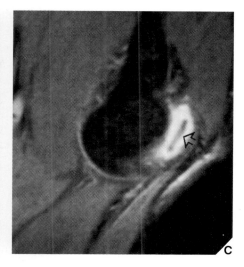

FIGURE 6.44 MRI of osteochondritis dissecans of the capitellum. (A) A sagittal T1-weighted MR image shows a linear focus of decreased signal (*open arrow*) at the anterior aspect of the capitellum. **(B)** A sagittal STIR image shows generalized increased signal surrounding a well-defined cystic-appearing focus (*arrows*) in the anterior aspect of the capitellum, consistent with osteochondritis dissecans. **(C)** A sagittal T2*-weighted gradient-echo image reveals a displaced osteochondral body (*open arrow*).

FIGURE 6.45 MRI of osteochondritis dissecans of the capitellum. A 16-year-old boy with chronic pain in the elbow underwent MR arthrography. **(A)** Coronal and **(B)** sagittal fat-saturation T1-weighted (SE; TR 650/TE 17 msec) MR arthrogram demonstrates osteochondritis dissecans of the capitellum with completely separated, loose osteochondral body (*arrows*) (type III lesion).

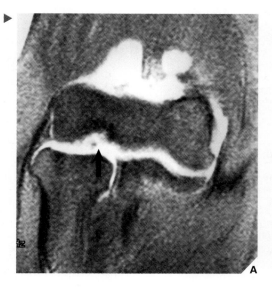
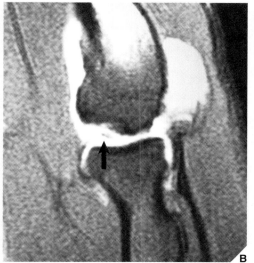

FIGURE 6.46 Elbow dislocation. (A) Anteroposterior and **(B)** lateral radiographs show the most common type of dislocation in the elbow joint—both the radius and the ulna are posteriorly and laterally displaced.

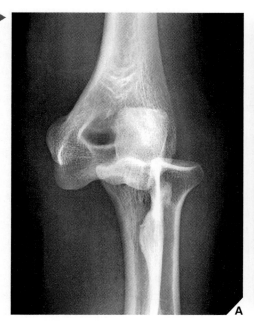
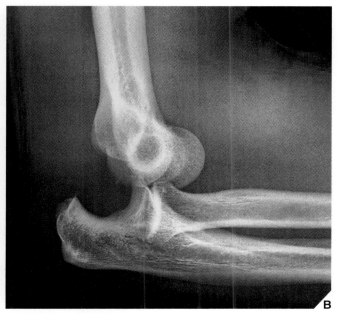

BADO CLASSIFICATION OF MONTEGGIA FRACTURE-DISLOCATION

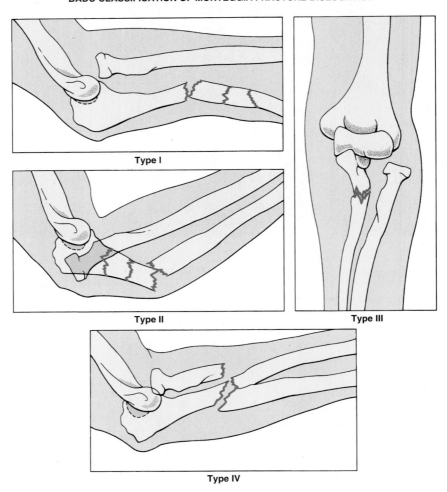

Type I

Type II

Type III

Type IV

▲

FIGURE 6.47 **Monteggia fracture–dislocation.** The Bado classification of Monteggia fracture–dislocation is based on the four types of abnormalities usually resulting from forced pronation of the forearm. These may occur during a fall or as a result of a direct blow to the posterior aspect of the ulna.

in cases of suspected ulnar fracture, radiographs should include the elbow joint. From a practical point of view, it is important, particularly in adults, to obtain two separate films, one centered over the elbow joint and the other over the site of the suspected fracture of the ulna. Care should be taken to center the films properly, because a dislocation of the radial head can easily be missed on improperly centered films.

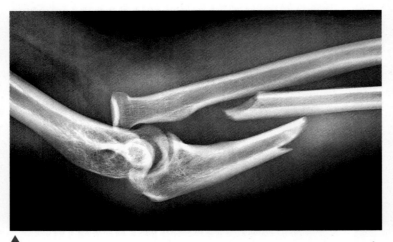

▲

FIGURE 6.48 **Monteggia fracture–dislocation.** Lateral radiograph of the elbow joint and proximal third of the forearm shows type I Monteggia fracture–dislocation; the anteriorly angulated fracture is at the proximal third of the ulna, associated with anterior dislocation of the radial head.

Monteggia Fracture–Dislocation. The association of a fracture of the ulna with a dislocation of the radial head is known by the eponym Monteggia fracture–dislocation. It usually results from forced pronation of the forearm during a fall or a direct blow to the posterior aspect of the ulna. The anteroposterior and lateral projections are sufficient to provide a full evaluation of these abnormalities.

Four types of this abnormality have been described (Fig. 6.47), but the features of the classic description are most commonly (in 60% to 70% of cases) seen: a fracture at the junction of the proximal and middle thirds of the ulna, with anterior angulation associated with anterior dislocation of the radial head (type I) (Fig.6.48). It is identifiable on physical examination by marked pain and tenderness about the elbow and displacement of the radial head into the antecubital fossa. The other types, which Bado has described, are as follows:

Type II: A fracture of the proximal ulna with posterior angulation and posterior or posterolateral dislocation of the radial head.

Type III: A fracture of the proximal ulna with lateral or anterolateral dislocation of the radial head (Fig. 6.49); the variant of type III is an injury showing a comminution of ulnar fracture (Fig. 6.50). Type II and type III injuries account for approximately 30% to 40% of Monteggia fractures.

Type IV: Fractures of the proximal ends of the radius and the ulna, with anterior dislocation of the radial head (this is the least common type).

Injury to the Soft Tissues

Lateral Epicondylitis (Tennis Elbow). Lateral epicondylitis, first described by Runge in 1878, affects approximately 3% of adults,

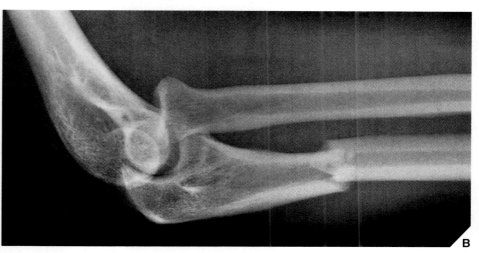

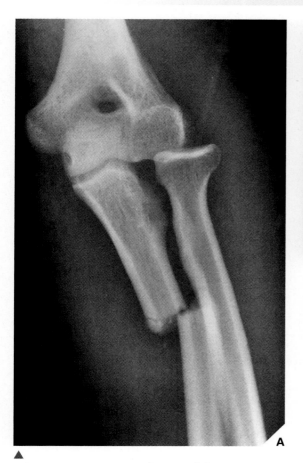

FIGURE 6.49 **Monteggia fracture–dislocation.** Anteroposterior (**A**) and lateral (**B**) radiographs of the elbow that include the proximal third of the forearm demonstrate the typical appearance of type III Monteggia fracture–dislocation; the fracture is at the proximal third of the ulna, associated with anterolateral dislocation of the radial head.

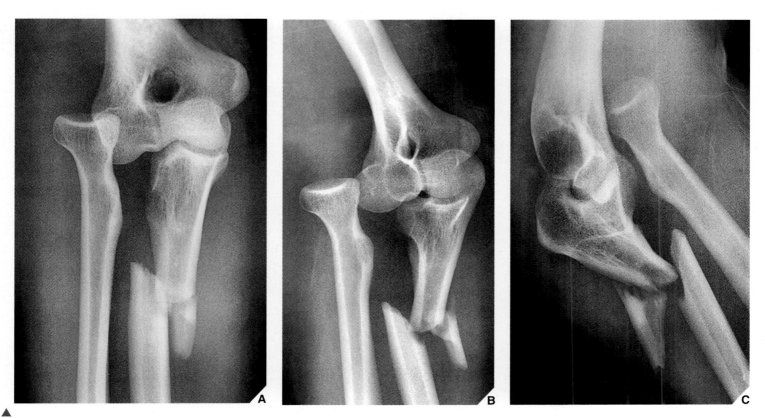

FIGURE 6.50 **Monteggia fracture–dislocation.** Anteroposterior (**A**), external oblique (**B**), and lateral (**C**) radiographs of the elbow joint show a variant of type III injury, where the fracture of the ulna is comminuted.

usually between the ages of 35 and 55. The symptoms include pain of insidious onset, aggravated by activity, at the lateral aspect of the elbow joint. This condition is often diagnosed in tennis players, golfers, and carpenters. The pathomechanism of this abnormality is based on repetitive stress on muscles and tendons adjacent to the lateral aspect of the distal humerus, particularly during excessive pronation and supination of the forearm when the wrist is extended. This results in mucoid degeneration and reactive granulation of the common extensor tendon, primarily the extensor carpi radialis brevis tendon, leading to avascularity and calcification of the tendon at its insertion on the lateral epicondyle.

Conventional radiographs are frequently normal, although soft-tissue swelling and calcification can sometimes be observed adjacent to the lateral epicondyle. MRI is useful for the assessment of damage to the tendons and the evaluation of associated abnormalities of the ligaments (Fig. 6.51). Not uncommonly, MRI may show avulsion of the extensor carpi radialis brevis tendon from the lateral epicondyle and associated bone marrow edema. In some patients, MRI demonstrates increased signal within the anconeus muscle.

Medial Epicondylitis (Golfer's Elbow). This condition affects the origin of tendons of the muscles flexor carpi radialis and pronator teres (common flexor tendon) at the attachment to the medial epicondyle of the humerus, and it is caused by overload of these structures. It is seen mainly in athletes such as golfers, tennis and racquetball players, baseball pitchers, javelin throwers, and occasionally in swimmers. The clinical symptoms include pain at the medial aspect of the elbow exacerbated by flexion of the wrist and pronation of the forearm. The diagnosis is made on the clinical basis but can be confirmed by MRI, which demonstrates thickening of the origin of the common flexor tendon associated with increased signal intensity on T2-weighted sequences and occasionally discontinuity of the fibers of the tendon when there is a complete rupture.

Rupture of the Biceps Tendon. A tear of the distal biceps tendon, which may be either partial or complete, is uncommon, and the reported incidence accounts for about 5% of all biceps tendon injuries. It occurs usually in men between the ages of 40 and 50 years, and in most cases, the dominant arm is affected. A rupture of the tendon is the result of a single traumatic event when a sudden extension force is applied to the arm with elbow flexed to 90 degrees and forearm in supination. The site of a rupture is invariably at the attachment of the tendon into the radial tuberosity. The patients present with an acute onset of pain and swelling

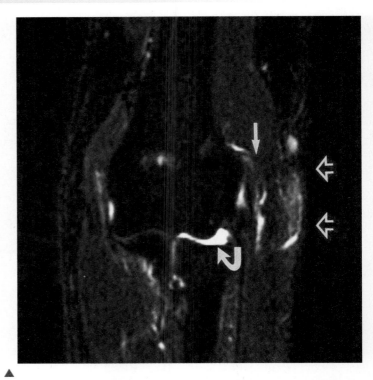

▲ **FIGURE 6.51 Lateral epicondylitis.** A 46-year-old woman presented with chronic pain at the lateral aspect of the elbow. A coronal T2-weighted fat-suppressed MRI shows partial tearing of fibers of the extensor tendons from epicondylar attachment (*arrow*) and soft-tissue edema (*open arrows*). The *curved arrow* points to the joint effusion. (Courtesy of Dr. A. Gentili, San Diego, California.)

in the antecubital fossa and local tenderness on palpation in this region. The most effective technique to demonstrate this injury is MRI. Partial tears exhibit focal or diffuse alteration of signal intensity and size of the tendon. A full-thickness tear results in a gap within the tendon structure or proximal retraction of the distal part of the tendon and the biceps muscle. The best imaging planes for the demonstration of this abnormality are sagittal and axial (Fig. 6.52), although some investigators recommend

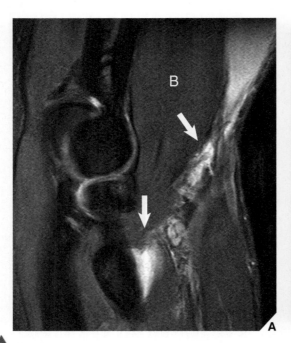

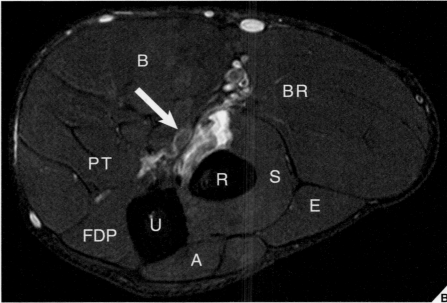

▲ **FIGURE 6.52 MRI of a tear of the biceps tendon. (A)** A 32-year-old man injured his right elbow in wrestling competition. **(A)** Sagittal and **(B)** axial proton density–weighted fat-suppressed MR images show a complete tear of the distal biceps tendon (*arrows*). R, radius; U, ulna; B, brachialis; BR, brachioradialis; PT, pronator teres; FDP, flexor digitorum profundus; S, supinator; E, extensor carpi ulnaris; A, anconeus.

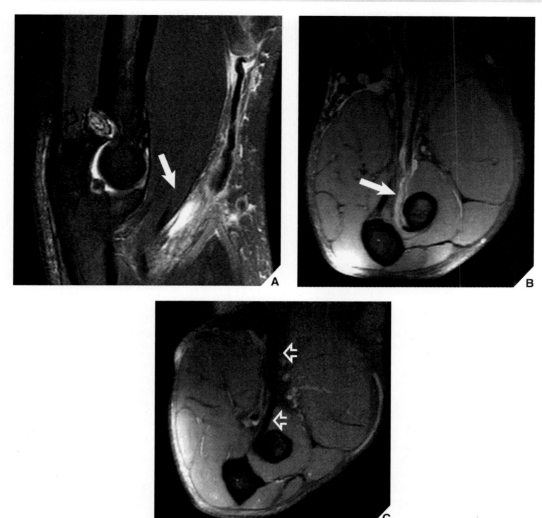

FIGURE 6.53 **MRI of a tear of the biceps tendon.** (**A**) Sagittal T2-weighted fat-suppressed and (**B**) modified coronal proton density–weighted fat-suppressed images of the elbow show a complete rupture of the distal biceps tendon (*arrows*). The *curved arrow* points to joint effusion, and *open arrows* point to the incidental finding of intraarticular osteochondral bodies. (**C**) Normal appearance of distal biceps tendon on modified coronal MR proton density–weighted fat-suppressed image is shown for comparison.

to obtain the MRI-modified coronal sections with the arm in abduction, elbow in flexion, and forearm in supination. The images in this position clearly demonstrate the distal part of bicipital tendon from its musculotendinous junction to insertion into the radial tuberosity (Fig. 6.53).

Rupture of the Triceps Tendon. The rupture of this structure is the least common of all tendon tears, constituting approximately 2% of all tendon injuries and less than 1% of all upper extremity tendon ruptures. The mechanism of this injury is usually a direct blow to the tendon's attachment at the posterior aspect of the olecranon process of the ulna and, less commonly, after a fall on the outstretched hand. As with the ruptures of other tendons, MRI provides the best diagnostic evaluation. Imaging in axial and sagittal planes is most effective, showing discontinuity of the fibers and proximal retraction of the triceps muscle.

Tears of the Radial (Lateral) Collateral Ligament Complex (RCLC). The RCLC consists of the radial collateral ligament, the annular ligament, the accessory collateral ligament, and the posterolateral (lateral ulnar) collateral ligament. The first three ligaments provide lateral stability of the elbow joint and prevent varus deformation. The latter ligament provides posterolateral stabilization of the joint. Chronic repetitive microtrauma that results in varus stress may lead to a sprain or to disruption of the RCLC, both of which can be diagnosed with MRI. A sprain appears as a thinning or thickening of the ligament associated with high signal intensity within or adjacent to this structure. A complete tear manifests as a discontinuation of the fibers or a defect in the ligament. These abnormalities may also be seen in association with lateral epicondylitis (see previous).

Tears of the Ulnar (Medial) Collateral Ligament Complex (UCLC). The UCLC consists of the anterior, posterior, and transverse ligaments. These ligaments provide medial stability to the elbow joint and prevent valgus deformation. The most important of the three bands is the anterior portion, which originates on the inferior aspect of the medial epicondyle and inserts on the medial edge of the coronoid process at the sublime tubercle. UCLC injury commonly occurs in athletes, particularly in baseball pitchers and, less commonly, in javelin throwers, handball players, arm wrestlers, and tennis players. MRI findings include abnormal signal and interruption of the continuity of the fibers or defect in the ligament (in a complete rupture) or thickening of the ligament and foci of calcification or ossification (in a chronic injury).

MRa can distinguish between partial and complete tears of the ulnar collateral ligament. Recently, DeSmet and colleagues have recommended the use of dynamic sonography with valgus stress to assess an injury to the ulnar collateral ligament in baseball pitchers. This technique uniquely demonstrates the medial joint laxity and instability when measurements of the degree of joint widening during valgus stress of the elbow are obtained.

PRACTICAL POINTS TO REMEMBER

[1] On the anteroposterior projection of the elbow:
- observe the normal 15-degree valgus carrying angle formed between the arm and the forearm
- (in the child) recognize the four secondary ossification centers of the distal humerus and the age at which they appear: capitellum at 1 to 2 years, medial epicondyle at 4 years, trochlea at 8 years, and lateral epicondyle at 10 years.

[2] On the lateral view of the elbow:
- note the normal angular (hockey-stick) appearance of the distal humerus; the angle measures approximately 140 degrees; loss of this angle occurs in supracondylar fracture:
- evaluate the position of the capitellum relative to the longitudinal axis of the proximal radius and the anterior humeral line
- pay attention to the presence or absence of the fat-pad sign; if this sign is positive in a patient with an elbow injury, then a fracture should always be considered.

[3] The radial head–capitellum projection is very useful in evaluating elbow trauma and should always be obtained as part of a routine study.

[4] Arthrotomography used to be an effective technique in selected cases of elbow injury. The procedure helped to visualize
- subtle chondral and osteochondral fractures
- osteochondritis dissecans
- synovial and capsular abnormalities
- osteochondral bodies in the joint.

[5] MRa of the elbow joint is useful to evaluate synovial abnormalities and the integrity of the joint capsule and ligaments and to detect intraarticular loose bodies.

[6] Supracondylar fracture of the distal humerus (usually of the extension type) is very common in children. The lateral film showing loss of the hockey-stick appearance of the distal humerus is diagnostic. If the lateral projection is equivocal, then obtain a film of the contralateral (normal) elbow for comparison.

[7] A fracture of the radial head is common in adults. It is important to demonstrate:
- the type of fracture
- the extension of the fracture line
- the degree of articular displacement.

This information determines whether a conservative or a surgical course of treatment is indicated.

[8] A fracture of the coronoid process is usually occult and is most often associated with the posterior dislocation in the elbow joint. If unrecognized, it may fail to unite, leading to recurrent subluxation or dislocation in the joint. The radial head–capitellum view is best suited to demonstrate it.

[9] Fractures of the olecranon are best demonstrated on the lateral view. They are classified into three types, according to the origin of the fracture line at the articular surface of the olecranon fossa.

[10] The orthopedic management of osteochondritis dissecans requires demonstrating the status of the articular cartilage of the capitellum and determining the stability of the osteochondral fragment. MRI or MRa is the procedure of choice.

[11] In every case of ulnar fracture, look for associated dislocation of the radial head; conversely, in every case of dislocation, look for a fracture of the ulna (Monteggia fracture–dislocation). Proper radiographic technique for imaging these often-missed injuries requires, in adults, obtaining two separate films that include the elbow joint and the forearm: one centered over the joint and the other over the midforearm. In children, a single film that includes the elbow joint and the entire forearm suffices.

[12] Essex-Lopresti fracture–dislocation is a complex, unstable injury that comprises a comminuted fracture of the radial head and neck, tear of the interosseous membrane of the forearm, and dislocation in the distal radioulnar joint.

[13] Lateral epicondylitis (or tennis elbow) is most effectively evaluated with MRI. This technique may show avulsion of the extensor carpi radialis brevis tendon from the lateral epicondyle and associated bone marrow edema.

[14] Medial epicondylitis (or golfer's elbow), a condition affecting the origin of the common flexor tendon at its attachment to the medial epicondyle of the humerus, shows on MRI thickening and increased signal of the affected tendons and discontinuity of the fibers with a complete rupture.

[15] A rupture of the distal biceps tendon at its attachment to the radial tuberosity is an uncommon injury, most effectively demonstrated using MRI in sagittal and axial imaging planes.

SUGGESTED READINGS

Anderson SE, Otsuka N, Steinbach LS. MR imaging of pediatric elbow trauma. *Semin Musculoskeletal Radiol* 1998;2:185–198.

Awaya H, Schweitzer ME, Feng SA, et al. Elbow synovial fold syndrome: MR imaging findings. *Am J Roentgenol* 2001;177:1377–1381.

Bado JL. The Monteggia lesion. Springfield, IL: CC Thomas; 1962.

Beltran J, Rosenberg ZS. MR imaging of pediatric elbow fractures. *MRI Clin North Am* 1997;5:567–578.

Berquist T. Elbow and forearm. In: Berquist T, ed. *MRI of the musculoskeletal system*, 3rd ed. Philadelphia: Lippincott–Raven Publishers; 1996:609–672.

Bledsoe RC, Izenstark JL. Displacement of fat pads in disease and injury of the elbow: a new radiographic sign. *Radiology* 1959;73:717–724.

Bohrer SP. The fat pad sign following elbow trauma: its usefulness and reliability in suspecting "invisible" fractures. *Clin Radiol* 1970;21:90–94.

Boyd H, McLeod A. Tennis elbow. *J Bone Joint Surg [Am]* 1973;55-A:1183–1187.

Brodeur AE, Silberstein MJ, Graviss ER. *Radiology of the pediatric elbow*. Boston: Hall Medical; 1981.

Bunnell DH, Fisher DA, Bassett LW, Gold RH, Ellman H. Elbow joint: normal anatomy on MR images. *Radiology* 1987;165:527–531.

Carrino JA, Morrison WB, Zou KH, Steffen RT, Snearly WN, Murray PM. Noncontrast MR imaging and MR arthrography of the ulnar collateral ligament of the elbow: prospective evaluation of two-dimensional pulse sequences for detection of complete tears. *Skeletal Radiol* 2001;30:625–632.

Coel M, Yamada CY, Ko J. MR imaging of patients with lateral epicondylitis of the elbow (tennis elbow): importance of increased signal of the anconeus muscle. *Am J Roentgenol* 1993;161:1019–1021.

Colton CL. Fractures of the olecranon in adults: classification and management. *Injury* 1973;5:121–129.

Cotten A, Boutin RD, Resnick D. Normal anatomy of the elbow on conventional MR imaging and MR arthrography. *Semin Musculoskeletal Radiol* 1998;2:133–140.

Daniels DL, Mallisee TA, Erickson SJ, Boynton MD, Carrera GF. Radiologic-anatomic correlations. The elbow joint: osseous and ligamentous structures. *Radiographics* 1998;18:229–236.

De Smet AA, Winter TC, Best TM, Bernhardt DT. Dynamic sonography with valgus stress to assess elbow ulnar collateral ligament injury in baseball pitchers. *Skeletal Radiol* 2002;31:671–676.

Eto RT, Anderson PW, Harley JD. Elbow arthrography with the application of tomography. *Radiology* 1975;115:283–288.

Falchook FS, Zlatkin MB, Erbacher GE, Moulton. JS, Bisset GS, Murphy BJ. Rupture of the distal biceps tendon: evaluation with MR imaging. *Radiology* 1994;190:659–663.

Fowles JV, Sliman N, Kassab MT. The Monteggia lesion in children. Fracture of the ulna and dislocation of the radial head. *J Bone Joint Surg [Am]* 1983;65A:1276–1282.

Franklin PD, Dunlop RW, Whitelaw G, Jacques E Jr, Blickman JG, Shapiro JH. Computed tomography of the normal and traumatized elbow. *J Comput Assist Tomogr* 1988;12:817–823.

Fritz RC. Magnetic resonance imaging of the elbow. *Semin Roentgenol* 1995;30:241–264.

Fritz RC. The elbow. In: Deutsch AL, Mink JH, eds. *MRI of the musculoskeletal system. A teaching file*, 2nd ed. Philadelphia: Lippincott–Raven Publishers; 1997:77–148.

Fritz RC, Steinbach LS, Tirman PF, Martinez S. MR imaging of the elbow: an update. *Radiol Clin North Am* 1997;35:117–144.

Gaary E, Potter HG, Altchek DW. Medial elbow pain in the throwing athlete: MR imaging evaluation. *Am J Roentgenol* 1997;168:795–800.

Greenspan A, Norman A. The radial head-capitellum view: useful technique in elbow trauma. *Am J Roentgenol* 1982;138:1186–1188.

Greenspan A, Norman A, Rosen H. Radial head-capitellum view in elbow trauma: clinical application and radiographic-anatomic correlation. *Am J Roentgenol* 1984;143:355–359.

Holtz P, Erickson SJ, Holmquist K. MR imaging of the elbow: technical considerations. *Semin Musculoskeletal Radiol* 1998;2:121–131.

Horne JG, Tanzer TL. Olecranon fractures: a review of 100 cases. *J Trauma* 1981;21: 469–472.

Janarv PM, Hesser U, Hirsch G. Osteochondral lesions in the radiocapitellar joint in the skeletally immature: radiographic, MRI, and arthroscopic findings in 13 consecutive cases. *J Pediatr Orthop* 1997;17:311–314.

Kijowski R, Tuite M, Sanford M. Magnetic resonance of the elbow. Part I: Normal anatomy, imaging technique, and osseous abnormalities. *Skeletal Radiol* 2004;33: 685–697.

Kijowski R, Tuite M, Sanford M. Magnetic resonance of the elbow. Part II: Abnormalities of the ligaments, tendons, and nerves. *Skeletal Radiol* 2005;34:1–18.

Mirowitz SA, London SL. Ulnar collateral ligament injury in baseball pitchers: MR imaging evaluation. *Radiology* 1992;185:573–576.

Morrey BF. Anatomy of the elbow joint. In: Morrey BF, ed. *The elbow and its disorders*, 2nd ed. Philadelphia: WB Saunders; 1993:16–52.

Müller ME, Allgower M, Schneider R, Willenegger H. *Manual of internal fixation, techniques recommended by the AO Group*, 2nd ed. Berlin, Germany: Springer-Verlag; 1979.

Murphy BJ. MR imaging of the elbow. *Radiology* 1992;184:525–529.

Murphy WA, Siegel MJ. Elbow fat pads with new signs and extended differential diagnosis. *Radiology* 1977;124:659–665.

Nelson SW. Some important diagnostic and technical fundamentals in the radiology of trauma, with particular emphasis on skeletal trauma. *Radiol Clin North Am* 1966;4:241–259.

Norell HG. Roentgenologic visualization of the extracapsular fat. Its importance in the diagnosis of traumatic injuries to the elbow. *Acta Radiol* 1954;42:205–210.

Peiss J, Adam G, Cassser R, Vohahn R, Gunther RW. Gadopentetate-dimeglumine-enhanced MR imaging of osteonecrosis and osteochondritis dissecans of the elbow: initial experience. *Skeletal Radiol* 1995;24:17–20.

Reckling FW, Peltier LF. Riccardo Galeazzi and Galeazzi's fracture. *Surgery* 1965;58:453–459.

Rogers LF. Fractures and dislocations of the elbow. *Semin Roentgenol* 1978;13: 97–107.

Rogers LF, Malave S Jr, White H, Tachdjian MO. Plastic bowing, torus and greenstick supracondylar fractures of the humerus: radiographic clues to obscure fractures of the elbow in children. *Radiology* 1978;128:145–150.

Rosenberg ZS, Beltran J, Cheung Y, Broker M. MR imaging of the elbow: normal variant and potential diagnostic pitfalls of the trochlear groove and cubital tunnel. *Am J Roentgenol* 1995;164:415–418.

Rosenberg ZS, Bencardino J, Beltran J. MRI of normal variants and interpretation pitfalls of the elbow. *Semin Musculoskeletal Radiol* 1998;2:141–153.

Schwartz ML, Al-Zahrani S, Morwessel RM, Andrews JR. Ulnar collateral ligament injury in the throwing athlete: evaluation with saline-enhanced MR arthrography. *Radiology* 1995;197:297–299.

Sharma SC, Singh R, Goel T, Singh H. Missed diagnosis of triceps tendon rupture: a case report and review of literature. *J Orthop Surg* 2005;13:307–309.

Singson RD, Feldman F, Rosenberg ZS. Elbow joint: assessment with double-contrast CT arthrography. *Radiology* 1986;160:167–173.

Smith FM. Children's elbow injuries: fractures and dislocations. *Clin Orthop* 1967;50: 7–30.

Sonin AH, Tutton SM, Fitzgerald SW, Peduto AJ. MR imaging of the adult elbow. *Radiographics* 1996;16:1323–1336.

Steinbach LS, Palmer WE, Schweitzer ME. Special focus session. MR arthrography. *Radiographics* 2002;22:1223–1246.

Steinbach LS, Schwartz ML. Elbow arthrography. *Radiol Clin North Am* 1998;36: 635–649.

Stoller DW. The elbow. In: Stoller DW, ed. *Magnetic resonance imaging in orthopedics and sports medicine*. Philadelphia: JB Lippincott; 1993:633–682.

Stoller DW, Genant HK. The joints. In: Moss AA, Gamsu G, Genant HK, eds. *Computed tomography of the body with magnetic resonance imaging*, 2nd ed. Philadelphia: WB Saunders; 1992:435–475.

Takahara M, Ogino T, Takagi M, Tsuchida H, Orui H, Nambu T. Natural progression of osteochondritis dissecans of the humeral capitellum: initial observations. *Radiology* 2000;216:207–212.

Tehranzadeh J, Kerr R, Amster J. Magnetic resonance imaging of tendon and ligament abnormalities. Part 1. Spine and upper extremities. *Skeletal Radiol* 1992;21:1–9.

Weston WJ. Elbow arthrography. In: Dalinka MK, ed. *Arthrography*. New York: Springer-Verlag; 1980.

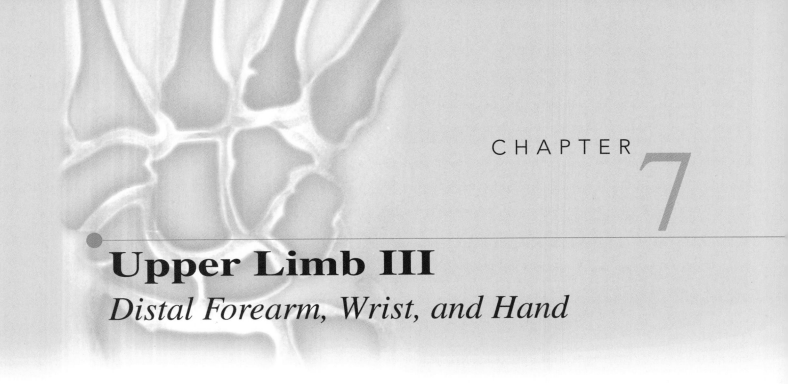

Upper Limb III
Distal Forearm, Wrist, and Hand

Distal Forearm

An injury to the distal forearm, caused predominantly (90% of cases) by a fall on the outstretched hand, is common throughout life but is most common in the elderly. The type of injury usually sustained is a fracture of the distal radius or ulna, the incidence of which substantially exceeds that of a dislocation in the distal radioulnar and radiocarpal articulations. Although history and physical examination usually provide important information regarding the type of injury, radiographs are indispensable in determining the exact site and extent; in several types of fractures, only adequate radiographic examination can lead to a correct diagnosis.

Anatomic–Radiologic Considerations

Radiographs obtained in the posteroanterior and lateral projections are usually sufficient to evaluate most injuries to the distal forearm (Figs. 7.1 and 7.2). On each of these views, it is important to appreciate the normal anatomic relations of the radius and the ulna for a complete evaluation of trauma.

The posteroanterior view of the distal forearm reveals anatomic variations in the length of the radius and the ulna, known as *ulnar variance* or *Hulten variance*. As a rule, the radial styloid process exceeds the length of the articular end of the ulna by 9 to 12 mm. At the site of articulation with the lunate, however, the articular surfaces of the radius and the ulna are on the same level, yielding *neutral ulnar variance* (Fig. 7.3). Occasionally, the ulna projects more proximally—*negative ulnar variance* (or ulna minus variant)—or more distally—*positive ulnar variance* (or ulna plus variant) (Fig. 7.4). Wrist position is an important determinant of ulnar variance. The generally accepted standard position is a posteroanterior view obtained with the wrist flat on the radiographic table, neutral forearm rotation, and with the elbow flexed 90 degrees and the shoulder abducted 90 degrees. The posteroanterior radiograph also reveals an important anatomic feature of the radius known as the *radial angle* (also called the *ulnar slant* of the articular surface of the radius), which normally ranges from 15 to 25 degrees (Fig. 7.5).

The lateral view of the distal forearm demonstrates another significant feature, the *volar tilt* of the articular surface of the radius (known variously as the *dorsal angle*, *palmar facing*, or *palmar inclination*). The tilt normally ranges from 10 to 25 degrees (Fig. 7.6).

Both these measurements have practical importance to the orthopedic surgeon in assessing the displacement and the position of fragments after a fracture of the distal radius. They can also help the surgeon to decide between closed and open reduction as well as assist in follow-up examinations.

Ancillary imaging techniques are occasionally required for evaluating trauma to the distal forearm and wrist. Arthrographic examination (Fig. 7.7) may need to be performed in cases of suspected injury to the triangular fibrocartilage complex (TFCC), which consists of the triangular fibrocartilage (articular disk), the meniscus homolog, the dorsal and volar radioulnar ligaments, and the ulnar collateral ligament (Fig. 7.8). Because the radiocarpal cavity into which contrast is injected normally does not communicate with the distal radioulnar joint, opacification of this compartment indicates a tear of the triangular fibrocartilage (see Fig. 7.29). In a small percentage of cases, a false-positive result may be caused by a normal anatomic variant allowing communication between the radiocarpal compartment and the distal radioulnar joint.

For a summary in tabular form of the standard radiographic projections and ancillary imaging techniques used to evaluate trauma to the distal forearm, see Tables 7.1 and 7.2.

Injury to the Distal Forearm

Fractures of the Distal Radius
Colles Fracture. The most frequently encountered injury to the distal forearm, *Colles fracture*, usually results from a fall on the outstretched hand with the forearm pronated in dorsiflexion. It is most commonly seen in adults older than the age of 50 years and more often in women than in men. In the classic description of this injury, known in the European literature as the *Pouteau fracture*, the fracture line is extraarticular, usually occurring approximately 2 to 3 cm from the articular surface of the distal radius. In many cases, the distal fragment is radially and dorsally displaced and shows dorsal angulation, although other variants in the alignment of fragments may also be seen (Fig. 7.9). Commonly, there is an associated fracture of the ulnar styloid process. It should be noted that some authors (e.g., Frykman) include intraarticular extension of the fracture line, as well as an associated fracture of the distal end of the ulna, under this eponym (Fig. 7.10, Table 7.3).

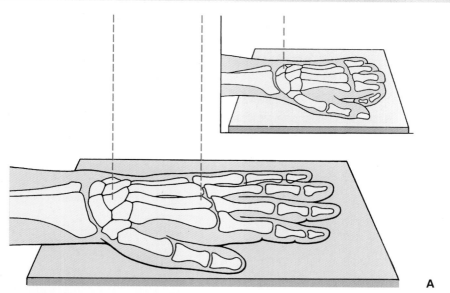

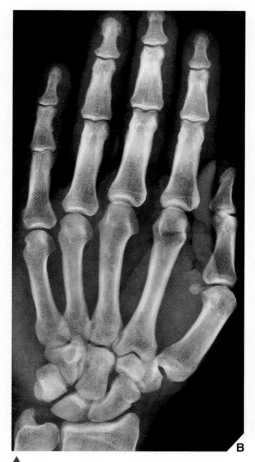

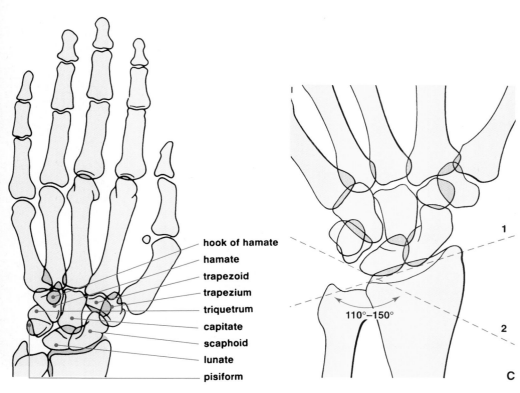

hook of hamate
hamate
trapezoid
trapezium
triquetrum
capitate
scaphoid
lunate
pisiform

110°–150°

FIGURE 7.1 Dorsovolar (posteroanterior) view of the distal forearm, wrist, and hand. For the purpose of classification, a distinction is made between traumatic conditions involving the distal forearm, the wrist, and the hand. From a radiologic perspective, however, the positioning of the limb for posteroanterior and lateral films of the wrist area (i.e., the distal forearm and the carpus) and the hand is essentially the same. (**A**) For the posteroanterior (dorsovolar) view of the wrist and the hand, patients are seated with the arm fully extended on the radiographic table. The portion of the limb from the distal third of the forearm to the fingertips rests prone on the film cassette. Whether the wrist area or the hand is the focus of evaluation, the hand usually lies flat (palm down), with the fingers slightly spread. The point toward which the central beam is directed, however, varies. For the wrist, the beam is directed toward the center of the carpus; for the hand, the beam is directed toward the head of the third metacarpal bone. For better demonstration of the wrist area, the patient's fingers may be flexed to cause the carpus to lie flat on the film cassette (*inset*). (**B**) On the radiograph obtained in this projection, the distal radius and the ulna, as well as the carpal and metacarpal bones and phalanges, are well demonstrated. The thumb, however, is seen in an oblique projection; the bases of the second to fifth metacarpals partially overlap. In the wrist, there is also overlap of the pisiform and the triquetrum, as well as the trapezium and trapezoid bones. (**C**) On this projection, a carpal angle can be determined. It is formed by two tangents, the first drawn against the proximal borders of the scaphoid and lunate (*1*) and the second drawn against the proximal borders of the triquetrum and lunate (*2*). The angle measures normally between 110 and 150 degrees, showing considerable deviation with age, sex, and race.

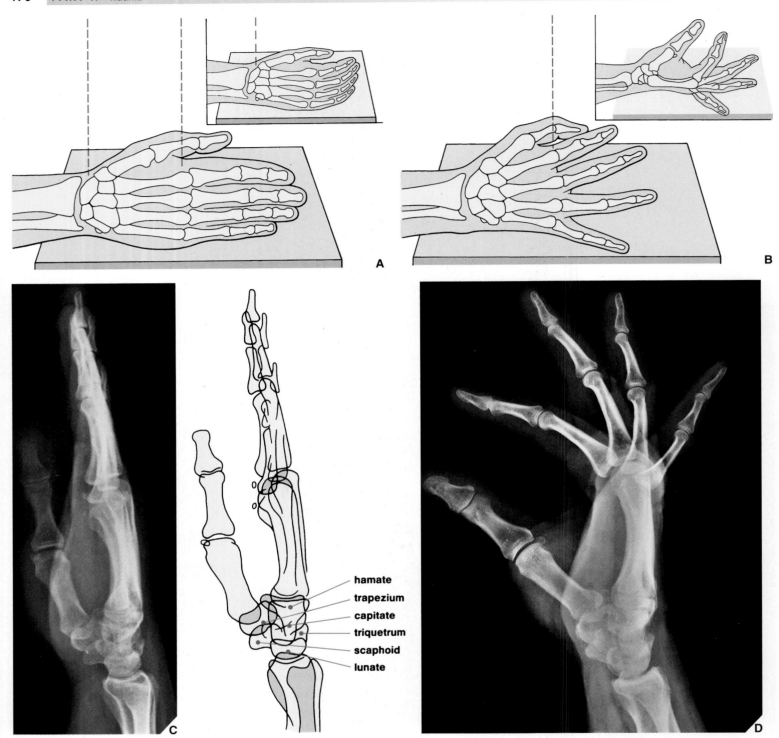

hamate
trapezium
capitate
triquetrum
scaphoid
lunate

FIGURE 7.2 **Lateral view of the wrist and hand.** (**A**) For the lateral projection of the wrist area and the hand, the patient's arm is fully extended and resting on its ulnar side. The fingers may be fully extended or, preferably, slightly flexed (*inset*), with the thumb slightly in front of the fingers. For the evaluation of the wrist area, the central beam is directed toward the center of the carpus, while for the hand, it is directed toward the head of the second metacarpal (**B**). On the radiograph obtained in this projection (**C**), the distal radius and the ulna overlap, but the relation of the longitudinal axes of the capitate, the lunate, and the radius can sufficiently be evaluated (see Fig. 7.80). Although the metacarpals and the phalanges also overlap, dorsal or volar displacement of a fracture of these bones can easily be detected (see Fig. 4.1). The thumb is imaged in true dorsovolar projection. A more effective way of imaging the fingers in the lateral projection is to have the patient spread the fingers in a fan-like manner, with the ulnar side of the fifth phalanx resting on the film cassette. The central beam is directed toward the heads of the metacarpals. (**D**) On the film in this projection, the overlap of the phalanges commonly seen on the standard lateral view is eliminated. The interphalangeal joints can readily be evaluated.

FIGURE 7.3 **Neutral ulnar variance.** (**A**) As a rule, ▶ the radial styloid process rises 9 to 12 mm above the articular surface of the distal ulna. This distance is also known as the radial length. (**B**) At the site of articulation with the lunate, the articular surfaces of the radius and the ulna are on the same level.

9–12mm

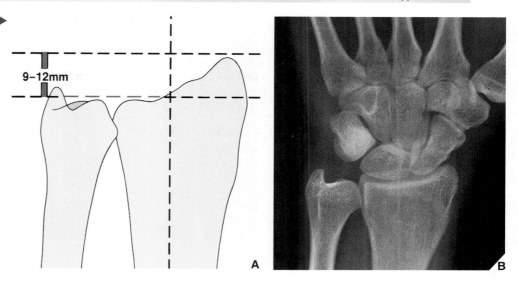

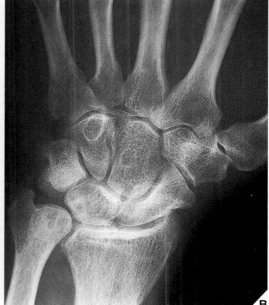

A

B

FIGURE 7.4 **Negative and positive** ▶ **ulnar variance.** (**A**) Negative ulnar variance. The articular surface of the ulna projects 5 mm proximal to the site of radiolunate articulation. (**B**) Positive ulnar variance. The articular surface of the ulna projects 8 mm distal to the site of radiolunate articulation.

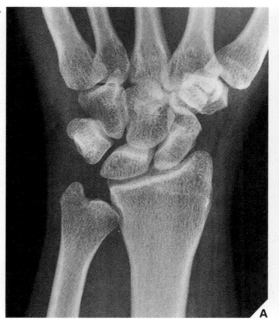

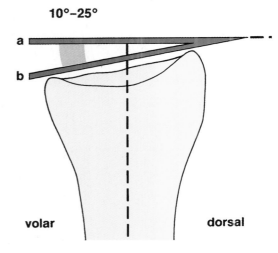

A

B

15°–25°

b

a

10°–25°

a

b

volar   dorsal

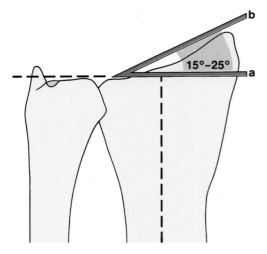

▲ FIGURE 7.5 **Ulnar slant.** The ulnar slant of the articular surface of the radius is determined, with the wrist in the neutral position, by the angle formed by two lines: one perpendicular to the long axis of the radius at the level of the radioulnar articular surface (*a*) and a tangent connecting the radial styloid process and the ulnar aspect of the radius (*b*).

▲ FIGURE 7.6 **Palmar inclination.** The palmar inclination of the radial articular surface is determined by measuring the angle formed by a line perpendicular to the long axis of the radius at the level of the styloid process (*a*) and a tangent connecting the dorsal and volar aspects of the radial articular surface (*b*).

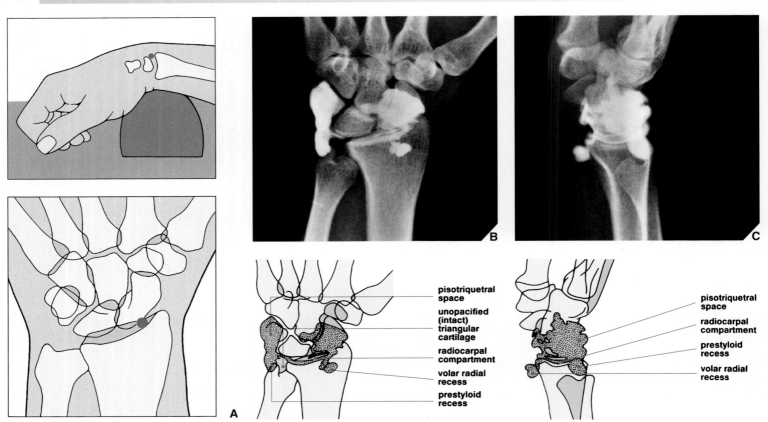

▲
FIGURE 7.7 **Arthrography of the wrist. (A)** For arthrographic examination of the radiocarpal joint, the wrist is positioned prone on a radiolucent sponge to open the joint for needle insertion. Under fluoroscopic control, the joint is entered using a 22-gauge needle at a point lateral to the scapholunate ligament. (The *red dot* marks the site of puncture.) Two or three milliliters of contrast (60% diatrizoate meglumine) is injected, and posteroanterior (dorsovolar), lateral, and oblique films are obtained. Posteroanterior **(B)** and lateral **(C)** views show the contrast filling the radiocarpal compartment, the prestyloid and volar radial recesses, and the pisotriquetral space. Intact triangular fibrocartilage does not allow the contrast to enter the distal radioulnar joint, and intact intercarpal ligaments prevent a leak of contrast into the intercarpal articulations.

TRIANGULAR FIBROCARTILAGE COMPLEX
(TFCC)

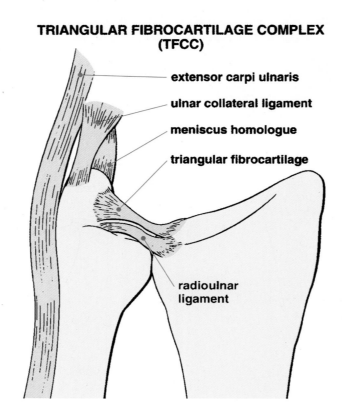

- extensor carpi ulnaris
- ulnar collateral ligament
- meniscus homologue
- triangular fibrocartilage
- radioulnar ligament

▲
FIGURE 7.8 **Triangular fibrocartilage complex.** The TFCC includes the triangular fibrocartilage, radioulnar ligament, ulnocarpal ligament, extensor carpi ulnaris tendon and tendon sheath, and meniscus homolog. It is located between the distal ulna and the proximal carpal row, stabilizes the distal radioulnar joint, and functions as a cushion of compressing axial forces. The triangular fibrocartilage attaches medially to the fovea of the ulna and laterally to the lunate fossa of the radius.

TABLE 7.1 Standard Radiographic Projections for Evaluating Injury to the Distal Forearm

Projection	Demonstration
Posteroanterior	Ulnar variance
	Carpal angle
	Radial angle
	Distal radioulnar joint
	Colles fracture
	Hutchinson fracture
	Galeazzi fracture–dislocation
Lateral	Palmar facing of radius
	Pronator quadratus fat stripe
	Colles fracture
	Smith fracture
	Barton fracture
	Galeazzi fracture–dislocation

Radiographs in the posteroanterior and lateral projections are usually sufficient to demonstrate Colles fracture. The complete evaluation on both views should take note of the status of the radial angle and the palmar inclination as well as the degree of foreshortening of the radius secondary to impaction or bayonet-type displacement (Figs. 7.11 and 7.12). Computed tomography (CT) scanning may provide additional information concerning the exact position of displaced fragments (Figs. 7.13 to 7.15).

Complications. At the time of fracture, a concomitant injury to the median and ulnar nerves may occur. A lack of stability of the fragments during healing may result in a loss of reduction, but delayed union and nonunion are very rarely seen. As a sequela, posttraumatic arthritis may develop in the radiocarpal articulation.

Barton and Hutchinson Fractures. Both these fractures are intraarticular fractures of the distal radius. The classic *Barton fracture* affects the dorsal margin of the distal radius and extends into the radiocarpal articulation (Fig. 7.16); occasionally, there may also be an associated dislocation in the joint. When the fracture involves the volar margin of the distal radius with an intraarticular extension, it is known as a

reverse (or *volar*) *Barton fracture* (Fig. 7.17). Because in both variants the fracture line is oriented in the coronal plane, it is best demonstrated on the lateral or oblique projections.

The *Hutchinson fracture* (also known as chauffeur's fracture—a name derived from the era of hand-cranked automobiles when direct trauma to the radial side of the wrist was often sustained from recoil of the crank) involves the radial (lateral) margin of the distal radius, extending through the radial styloid process into the radiocarpal articulation. Because of the sagittal orientation of the fracture line, the posteroanterior view is better suited to diagnose this type of injury (Fig. 7.18).

Smith Fracture. Usually resulting from a fall on the back of the hand or a direct blow to the dorsum of the hand in palmar flexion, a Smith fracture consists of a fracture of the distal radius, which sometimes extends into the radiocarpal joint, with volar displacement and angulation of the distal fragment (Fig. 7.19). Because the deformity in this fracture is the opposite of that seen in a Colles injury, it is often referred to as a reverse Colles fracture; it is, however, much less common than Colles. There are three types of Smith fracture, defined on the basis of the obliquity of the fracture line (Fig. 7.20), which is best assessed on the lateral projection. Types II and III are usually unstable and may require surgical intervention.

Galeazzi Fracture–Dislocation. This abnormality, which may result indirectly from a fall on the outstretched hand combined with marked pronation of the forearm or directly from a blow to the dorsolateral aspect of the wrist, consists of a fracture of the distal third of the radius, sometimes extending into the radiocarpal articulation and an associated dislocation in the distal radioulnar joint. Characteristically, the proximal end of the distal fragment is dorsally displaced, commonly with dorsal angulation at the fracture site; the ulna is dorsally and ulnarly (medially) dislocated (Fig.7.21). On rare occasion, the distal fragment of the radius is volarly (anteriorly) displaced in relation to the proximal fragment and medially angulated (Fig. 7.22). Two types of Galeazzi injury have been identified. In type I, the fracture of the radius is extraarticular in the distal third of the bone (see Figs. 7.21 and 7.22). In type II, the radius fracture is usually comminuted and extends into the radiocarpal joint (Fig. 7.23).

Posteroanterior and lateral radiographs are routinely obtained when this injury is suspected, but the lateral view clearly reveals its nature and extent (see Figs. 7.21B, 7.22C, and 7.23B).

TABLE 7.2 Ancillary Imaging Techniques for Evaluating Injury to the Distal Forearm

Technique	Demonstration
Arthrography	Radiocarpal articulation
	Tear of TFCC
Arteriography	Concomitant injury to the arteries of the forearm
Radionuclide imaging (scintigraphy, bone scan)	Subtle fractures of the radius and the ulna
Computed tomography	Depression, displacement, and spatial orientation of fracture fragments of the radius and the ulna
	Fracture healing and complications of healing
	Soft-tissue injury (muscles)
Magnetic resonance imaging and MR arthrography	Soft-tissue injury (muscles, tendons, ligaments)
	Subtle fractures and bone contusion of the radius and the ulna
	Tear of TFCC
	Injury to the interosseous membrane
	Abnormalities of various tendons, ligaments, and muscles

Piedmont Fracture. An isolated fracture of the radius at the junction of the middle and distal thirds without an associated disruption of the distal radioulnar joint is known as the Piedmont fracture (Fig. 7.24A). This injury is also called "fracture of necessity," because open reduction and internal fixation are necessary to achieve an acceptable functional result (Fig. 7.24B). If this fracture is treated conservatively with closed reduction and cast application, then the interosseous space may be compromised because of muscle action, resulting in the loss of pronation and supination after the bone union is completed.

Essex-Lopresti Fracture–Dislocation. This fracture, which affects the radial head and is associated with a tear of the interosseous membrane of the forearm and dislocation in the distal radioulnar joint, was discussed in Chapter 6.

Ulnar Impingement Syndrome. Ulnar impingement syndrome is caused by a short distal ulna that impinges on the distal radius proximal to the sigmoid notch. A short ulna may represent a congenital anomaly, such as negative ulnar variance, or may be the result of premature fusion of the distal ulnar growth plate secondary to previous trauma. In most cases, however, it is caused by surgical procedures that involve a resection of the distal ulna secondary to trauma, rheumatoid arthritis, or correction of a Madelung deformity. The clinical symptoms of the ulnar impingement syndrome consist of ulnar-sided wrist pain and limitation of motion in the radiocarpal joint. In addition, patients experience discomfort during pronation and supination of the forearm. On radiography, the characteristic changes of this abnormality include a short ulna and scalloping of the medial aspect of the distal radius, in cases of negative ulnar variance (Fig. 7.25) or premature

COLLES FRACTURE: VARIANTS IN ALIGNMENT OF FRAGMENTS

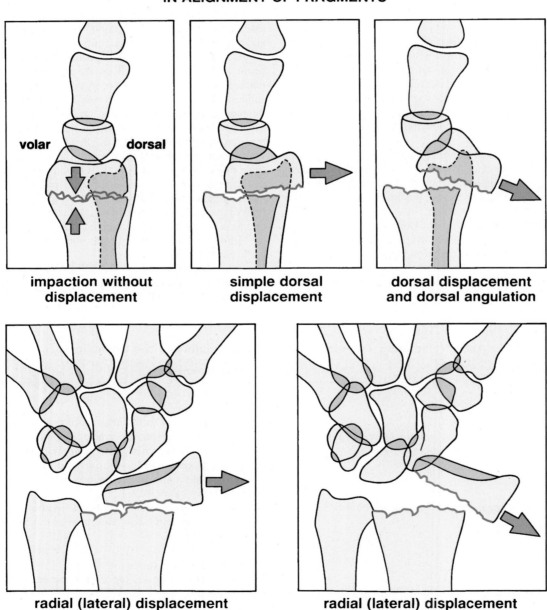

impaction without displacement

simple dorsal displacement

dorsal displacement and dorsal angulation

radial (lateral) displacement

radial (lateral) displacement and radial angulation

FIGURE 7.9 **Colles fracture.** Five variants of displacement and angulation of the distal fragment in Colles fracture. Some of these patterns may occur in combinations, yielding a complex deformity.

DISTAL RADIUS FRACTURES
(Frykman Classification)

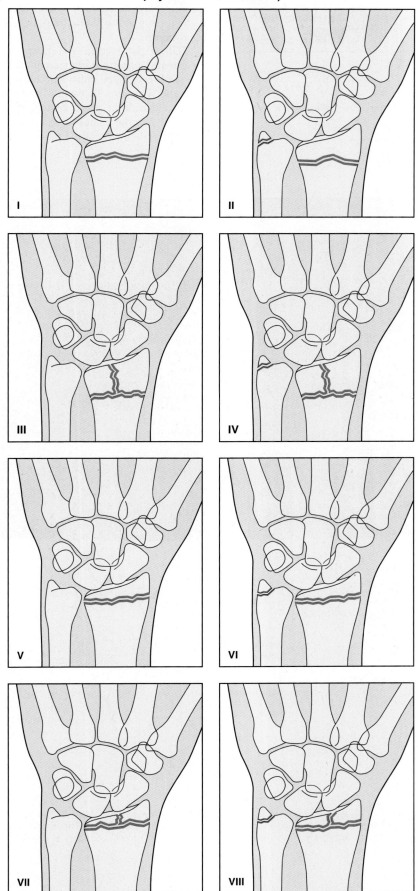

▲
FIGURE 7.10 **Distal radius fractures.** Frykman classification of distal radius fractures according to the location of fracture line (intraarticular vs. extraarticular) and association of distal ulna fracture.

TABLE 7.3 **Frykman Classification of Distal Radius Fractures**

Radius Fracture	Distal Ulna Fracture	
Location	Absent	Present
Extraarticular	I	II
Intraarticular (radiocarpal joint)	III	IV
Intraarticular (radioulnar joint)	V	VI
Intraarticular (radiocarpal and radioulnar joints)	VII	VIII

fusion of the distal ulnar growth plate, or radial scalloping and radioulnar convergence, in cases of distal ulnar resection. Before these findings become obvious on conventional radiologic studies, magnetic resonance imaging (MRI) may be helpful in early recognition of this condition.

Ulnar Impaction Syndrome. Also known as the ulnolunate abutment syndrome or ulnocarpal loading, the ulnar impaction syndrome is a well-recognized entity clinically characterized by ulnar-sided wrist pain and limitation of motion in the radiocarpal joint. It is frequently associated with the positive ulnar variance. The pathologic mechanism of this syndrome is linked to altered and increased forces transmitted across the ulnar side of the wrist, leading to a compression of the distal

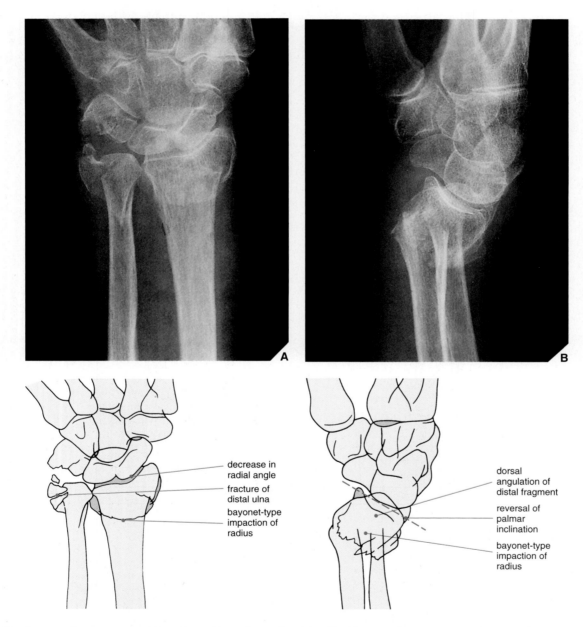

▲
FIGURE 7.11 **Colles fracture.** Posteroanterior (**A**) and lateral (**B**) radiographs of the distal forearm demonstrate the features of Colles fracture. On the posteroanterior projection, a decrease in the radial angle and an associated fracture of the distal ulna are evident. The lateral view reveals the dorsal angulation of the distal radius as well as a reversal of the palmar inclination. On both views, the radius is foreshortened secondary to bayonet-type displacement. The fracture line does not extend to the joint (Frykman type II).

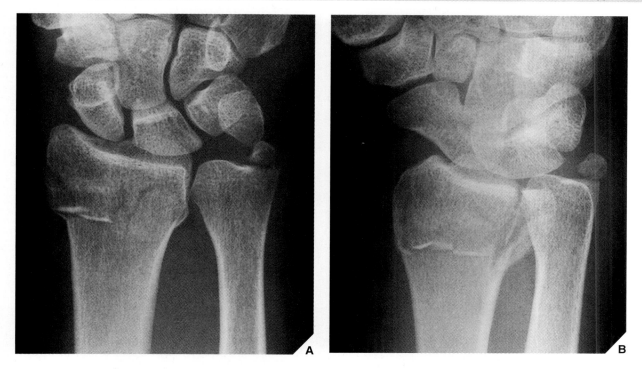

▲
FIGURE 7.12 **Intraarticular fracture of the distal radius.** Posteroanterior (**A**) and oblique (**B**) radiographs of the distal forearm show Frykman type VI fracture. The fracture line extends into the distal radioulnar joint, and, in addition, there is a fracture of the ulnar styloid.

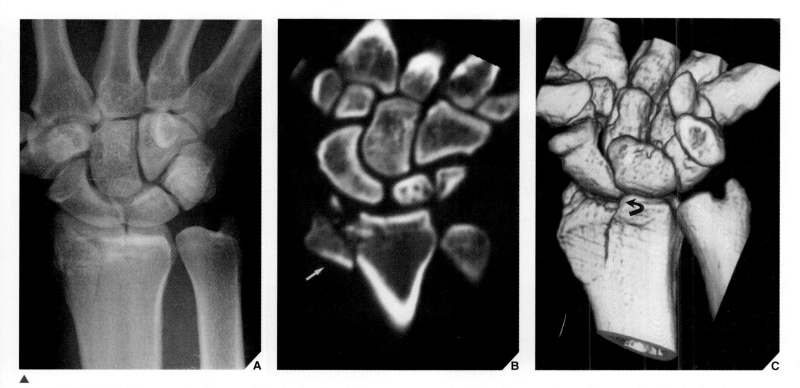

▲
FIGURE 7.13 **CT of an intraarticular fracture of the distal radius.** (**A**) Posteroanterior radiograph of the wrist shows a fracture of the distal radius that appears to be nondisplaced. (**B**) Coronal reformatted and (**C**) 3D reconstructed CT images not only confirm the intraarticular extension of the fracture but also demonstrate displacement (*arrow*) and depression (*curved arrow*) of the fractured fragments. Because the distal radioulnar joint is spared and the ulna is intact, this injury represents Frykman type III fracture.

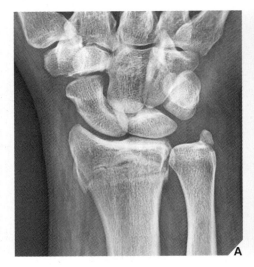

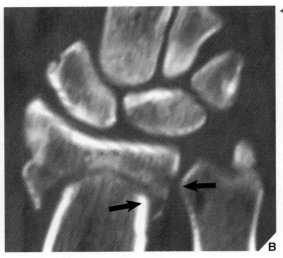

◀ **FIGURE 7.14** **CT of an intraarticular fracture of the distal radius.** (**A**) Posteroanterior radiograph of the wrist shows a fracture of the distal radius, but it is unclear if the fracture is extraarticular or intraarticular. In addition, there is a fracture of the styloid process of ulna. (**B**) Coronal reformatted CT image confirms that the fracture line extends into the distal radio-ulnar joint (*arrows*), but the radiocarpal joint is spared, thus rendering the diagnosis of Frykman type VI fracture.

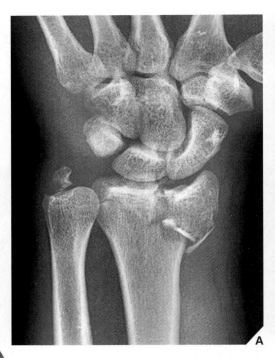

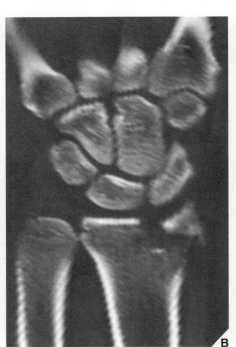

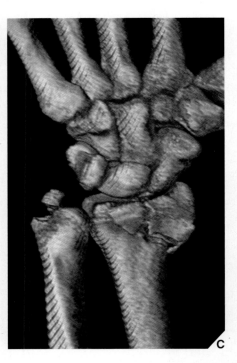

▲ **FIGURE 7.15** **CT of an intraarticular fracture of the distal radius.** (**A**) Posteroanterior radiograph of the wrist shows an intraarticular fracture of the distal radius and a fracture of the ulnar styloid. (**B**) Coronal reformatted and (**C**) 3D reconstructed CT images clearly show an extension of the fracture lines into both the radiocarpal and the distal radioulnar joint compartments, confirming Frykman type VIII fracture.

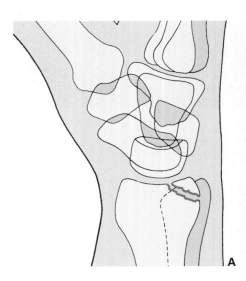

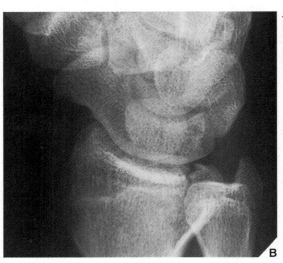

◀ **FIGURE 7.16** **Barton fracture.** Schematic (**A**) and oblique radiograph (**B**) show the typical appearance of Barton fracture. The fracture line in the coronal plane extends from the dorsal margin of the distal radius into the radiocarpal articulation.

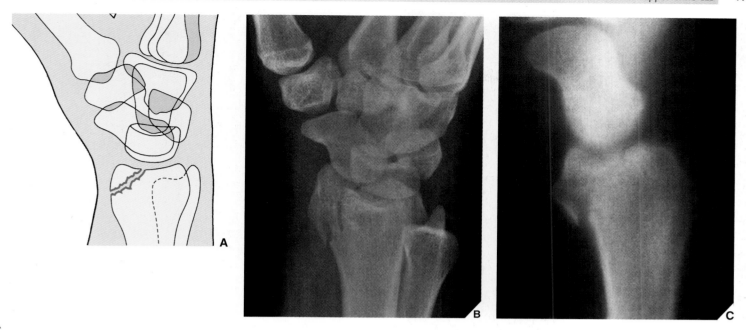

▲
FIGURE 7.17   Reverse Barton fracture. Schematic (**A**), oblique radiograph (**B**), and lateral trispiral tomogram (**C**) show the reverse (or volar) Barton fracture; the fracture line is also oriented in the coronal plane but extends from the volar margin of the radial styloid process into the radiocarpal joint.

FIGURE 7.18   Hutchinson fracture. Schematic ▶ (**A**) and dorsovolar radiographs (**B**) showing classic appearance of Hutchinson fracture. The fracture line in the sagittal plane extends through the radial margin of the radial styloid process into the radiocarpal articulation.

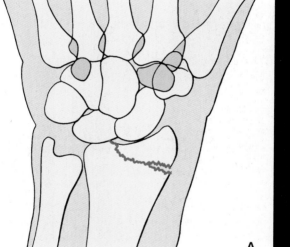

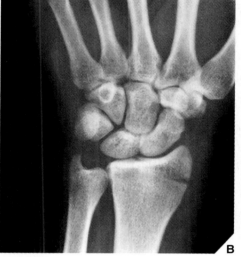

FIGURE 7.19   Smith fracture. Posteroanterior ▶ (**A**) and lateral (**B**) radiographs of the distal forearm show the typical appearance of Smith fracture. Volar displacement of the distal fragment is clearly evident on the lateral view.

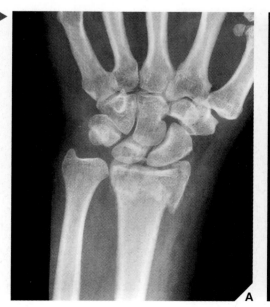

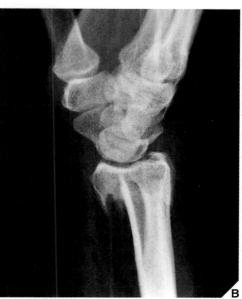

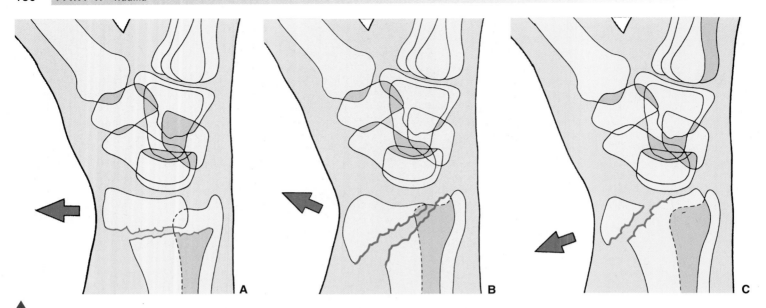

FIGURE 7.20 **Smith fracture.** The three types of Smith fracture are distinguished by the obliquity of the fracture line. Volar displacement of the distal fragment is characteristic of all three types. **(A)** In Smith type I, the fracture line is transverse, extending from the dorsal to the volar cortices of the radius. **(B)** The oblique fracture line in type II extends from the dorsal lip of the distal radius to the volar cortex. **(C)** Type III, which is almost identical to the reverse Barton fracture (see Fig. 7.17), is an intraarticular fracture with an extension to the volar cortex of the distal radius.

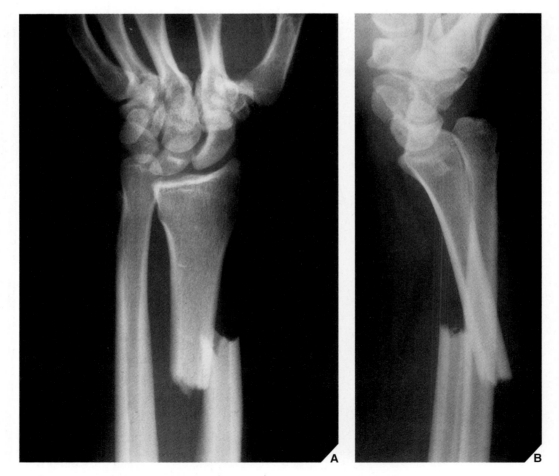

FIGURE 7.21 **Galeazzi fracture–dislocation.** Posteroanterior **(A)** and lateral **(B)** radiographs of the distal forearm show type I Galeazzi fracture–dislocation. The simple fracture of the radius affects the distal third of the bone, and the proximal end of the distal fragment is dorsally displaced and angulated. In addition, there is dislocation in the distal radioulnar joint.

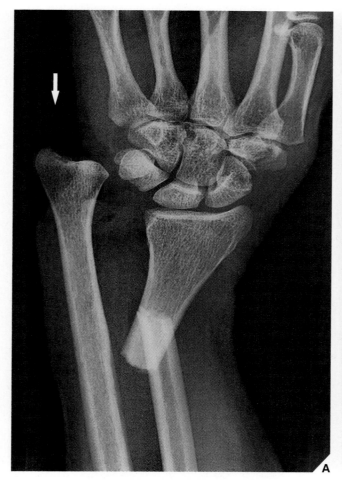

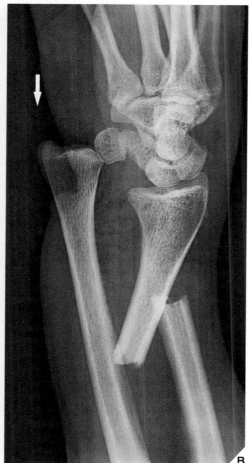

FIGURE 7.22 **Galeazzi fracture–dislocation.** Posteroanterior ▶
(**A**), oblique (**B**), and lateral (**C**) radiographs of the distal forearm
show a variant of type I injury, where the distal fragment of the
radius is volarly displaced and medially angulated. Note that the
distal ulna is protruding through the skin (*arrow*).

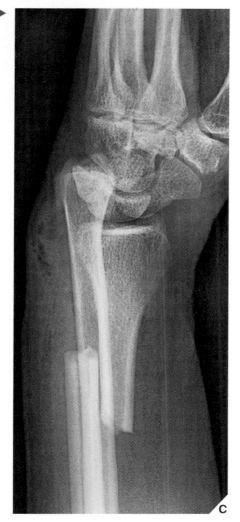

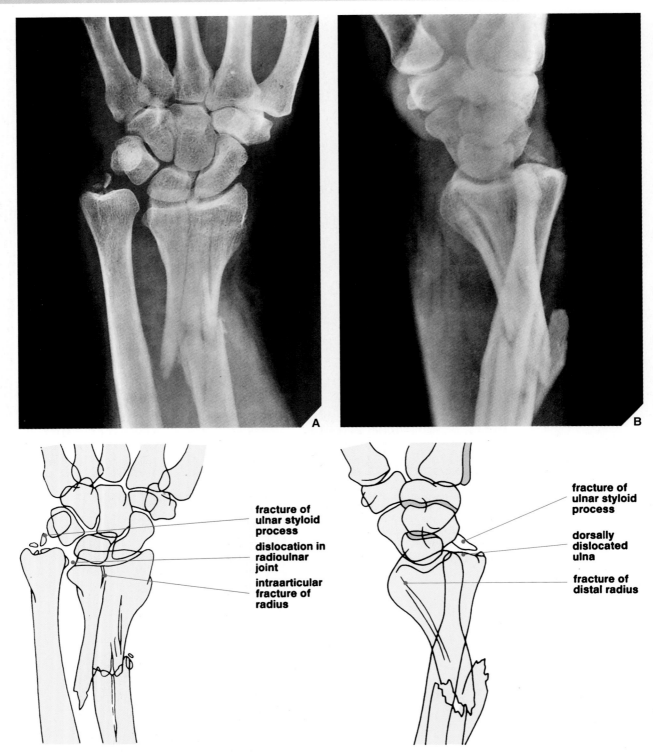

▲

FIGURE 7.23 **Galeazzi fracture–dislocation.** Posteroanterior (**A**) and lateral (**B**) projections of the distal forearm demonstrate the two components of Galeazzi fracture–dislocation type II. The posteroanterior radiograph clearly reveals the fracture of the distal radius, which, in this case, is comminuted, extending into the radiocarpal joint. The distal fragment has a slight lateral angulation. Note also the associated comminuted fracture of the ulnar styloid process and the dislocation in the radioulnar joint. These features are also seen on the lateral projection, but this view provides in addition a better demonstration of the dorsal dislocation of the distal ulna.

FIGURE 7.24 **Piedmont fracture. (A)** Anteroposterior radiograph of the forearm shows a typical appearance of the Piedmont fracture, an isolated fracture at the junction of the middle and distal thirds of the radius, necessitating an open reduction and internal fixation (**B**).

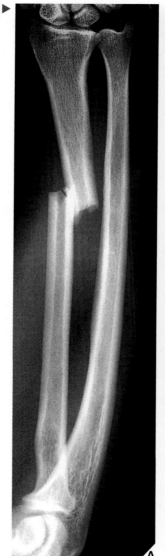
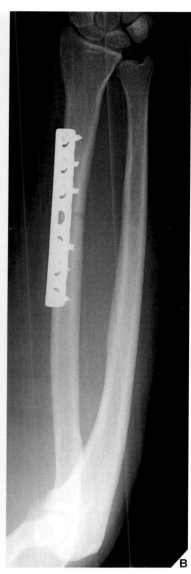

FIGURE 7.25 **Ulnar impingement syndrome.** Posteroanterior radiograph of the wrist shows a negative ulnar variance. The distal ulna impinges on the medial cortex of distal radius.

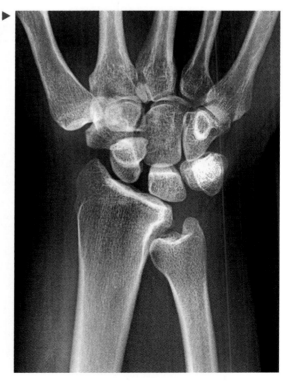

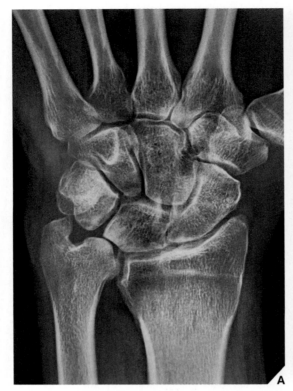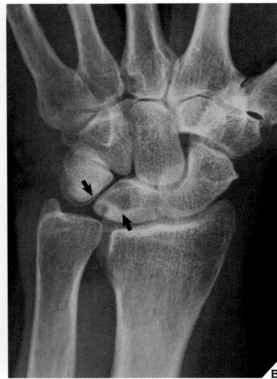

▲
FIGURE 7.26   **Ulnar impaction syndrome.** **(A)** Posteroanterior radiograph of the wrist shows a positive ulnar variance. The ulnolunate interval is significantly decreased, and there is sclerosis of the distal ulna and medial aspect of the lunate. **(B)** In another patient, note the cystic changes in the lunate (*arrows*).

ulna on the medial surface of the lunate bone. This causes the development of degenerative changes in the cartilage covering both bones. In addition, frequent association of the tear of the triangular fibrocartilage has been reported. In cases of excessive ulnar length, dorsal subluxation of the ulna is present compromising supination of the forearm. The conventional radiography shows a positive ulnar variance associated with significantly decreased ulnolunate interval and occasionally foci of sclerosis or cystic changes in the lunate (Fig. 7.26). MRI is the most effective technique for the diagnosis of this syndrome and demonstration of pathologic changes in the affected bones and surrounding soft tissues. MRI reveals bone marrow edema of the distal ulna and lunate, subchondral sclerosis and cyst formation, and destruction of the cartilage. Associated abnormalities, such as tears of the triangular fibrocartilage and lunotriquetral ligament, are also well imaged (Figs. 7.27 and 7.28). Treatment of this condition includes TFCC debridement and ulnar shortening.

Injury to the Soft Tissue at the Distal Radioulnar Articulation

One of the most common sequelae of injury to the distal radioulnar articulation is a tear of the TFCC. A tear may occur as the result of fractures such as those described in the preceding sections or independently after an injury to the distal forearm and wrist.

Radiographs in the standard projections are invariably normal regarding the status of the triangular cartilage, particularly if there is no evidence of fracture or dislocation on which to base a suspicion of soft-tissue injury. When it is suspected, however, a single-contrast arthrogram of the wrist can confirm or exclude the diagnosis. Normally, a contrast fills the radiocarpal compartment, the prestyloid and volar radial recesses, and the pisotriquetral space (see Fig. 7.7). The presence of a contrast in the distal radioulnar compartment or at the site of the triangular cartilage indicates a tear (Fig. 7.29).

Until recently, arthrography has been the procedure of choice for the evaluation of TFCC. Currently, it is generally believed that in the diagnosis of TFCC abnormalities, particularly when using eight-channel phased-array extremity coil, MRI approaches and frequently surpasses arthrography in accuracy. The advantage of MRI is its noninvasiveness and ability to image the entire fibrocartilage substance, whereas arthrography is limited to the evaluation of the surface of this structure only. On coronal T1-weighted MR images, the normal TFCC appears as a biconcave band of homogeneous low signal intensity extending across the space between the distal ulna, the medial aspect of distal radius, and the triquetrum and lunate bones (Fig.7.30, see also Fig. 7.8). Tears of the TFCC manifest as discontinuities and fragmentation of this structure. The torn fibrocartilage becomes irregular in contour and is interrupted by high signal intensity areas on T2-weighted images (Fig. 7.31). However, one of the studies published by Haims and colleagues, questions the sensitivity of MRI in diagnosing peripheral tears of the triangular fibrocartilage. In this respect, the authors reported the sensitivity of MRI of only 17%, with a specificity of 79%, and accuracy of 64%.

Wrist and Hand

Considered as a functional unit, the wrist and hand are the most common sites of injury in the skeletal system. Fractures of the metacarpals and phalanges, however, by far predominate in incidence over fractures and dislocations in the carpal bones and joints, which constitute approximately 6% of all such injuries. In most instances, history and physical examination provide valuable information on which to base a suspected diagnosis, but radiographic findings derived from films obtained in at least two projections at 90 degrees to each other (see Fig. 4.1) are essential to determine a specific diagnosis of injury to these sites.

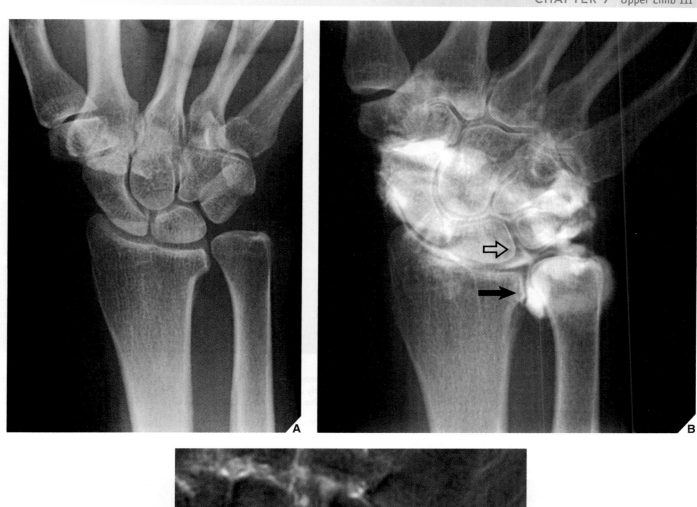

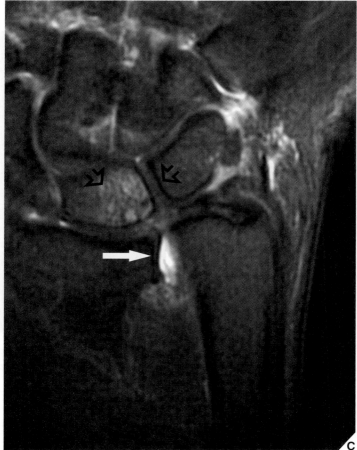

FIGURE 7.27 Arthrography and MRI of the ulnar impaction syndrome. (A) Conventional radiograph of the wrist shows a positive ulnar variance, but there are no other appreciated abnormalities seen. **(B)** Wrist arthrogram shows a tear of the TFCC (*arrow*) and a tear of the lunotriquetral ligament (*open arrow*). **(C)** Coronal T2-weighted fat-suppressed MR arthrographic image shows contrast in the distal radioulnar joint (*arrow*), confirming the diagnosis of a tear of TFCC, and cystic changes and edema of the lunate (*open arrows*), confirming the diagnosis of ulnar impaction syndrome.

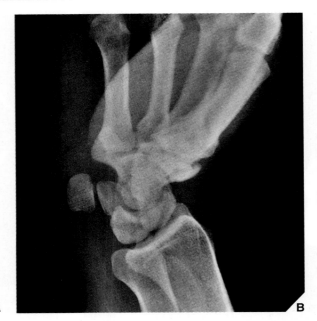

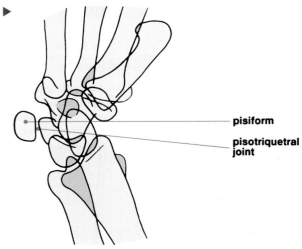

pisiform

pisotriquetral joint

FIGURE 7.33 **Supinated oblique view. (A)** For the supinated oblique view of the wrist, the hand resting on its ulnar side on the film cassette is tilted approximately 30 to 35 degrees toward its dorsal surface. The outstretched fingers are held together, with the thumb slightly abducted. The central beam is directed toward the center of the wrist. **(B)** The radiograph in this projection demonstrates the pisiform bone and the pisotriquetral joint.

detecting subtle fractures and early complications of fracture healing. CT has evolved as a versatile tool and adjunctive procedure for imaging various traumatic abnormalities of the wrist. In many institutions, this technique virtually replaced conventional tomography, because it is easier to perform, is faster, and has a lower radiation dose. After standard axial sections are obtained, reformation images in additional imaging planes can be acquired and 3D reconstruction can be performed (see Fig. 2.8A,B). CT can be combined with arthrography (see Fig. 2.18) or can be enhanced by an intravenous contrast material. It is effective in demonstrating subluxation in the distal radioulnar joint and in evaluating the so-called humpback deformity of the scaphoid, osteonecrosis of the lunate (Kienböck disease), and fractures of the hook of the hamate, among other abnormalities. Axial sections are obtained after positioning the patient prone with the arm extended above the head. Contiguous sections of 1 or 2 mm are acquired, preferably using a spiral (helical) technique. Direct coronal sections can also be obtained with the wrist in maximal volar flexion or dorsal extension.

Arthrography still remains an effective procedure for evaluating the TFCC abnormalities and tears of various intercarpal ligaments. In general, single-contrast arthrography using a positive contrast agent is performed. However, if postarthrographic CT examination is to be performed, double-contrast arthrography using room air is preferable. The introduction of the three-compartment injection technique and combining the arthrographic wrist examination with digital technique and postarthrographic CT examination make this modality very effective in evaluating a painful wrist. A complete arthrographic evaluation of the wrist requires opacification of the midcarpal compartment, radiocarpal compartment, and distal radioulnar joint. These three compartments are normally separated from one another by various interosseous ligaments and, in the case of distal radioulnar joint, by the TFCC (Fig. 7.36). The flow of a contrast from one compartment to another indicates a defect in one of these ligaments. Unidirectional contrast flow through the ligament defects, associated with a small flap acting as a valve, has been reported and may be overlooked if the contrast is injected on only one side of the defect. For this reason, the separate injection of all three compartments is preferable. It has to be stressed, however, that defects in the ligaments may occasionally be found in normal, asymptomatic subjects; therefore, their significance remains uncertain.

More recently, digital subtraction arthrography has been advocated by Resnick and Manaster as an effective way to demonstrate subtle leaks of contrast. The advantages of digital subtraction arthrography include not only shortening of examination time but also a decrease in the concentration of contrast agent and more precise localization of defects in intercarpal ligaments, particularly when the defects are multiple (see Fig. 2.2).

At present, MRI is an imaging modality of choice for the evaluation of the wrist and hand (Fig. 7.37). To achieve optimum quality examination, the use of a dedicated local (surface) radiofrequency coil and limited field of view is recommended. This technique may image not only abnormalities of the soft tissues, including various muscles, tendons, interosseous ligaments, and triangular fibrocartilage, but also osseous abnormalities such as occult fractures and early osteonecrosis, particularly of the lunate and scaphoid. It is also very useful in imaging

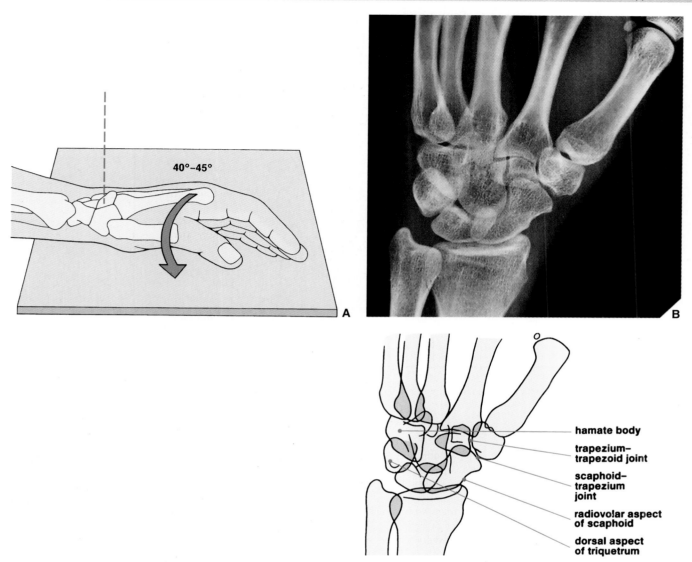

FIGURE 7.34   **Pronated oblique view.** (**A**) For the pronated oblique view of the wrist, the hand resting on its ulnar side on the film cassette is tilted approximately 40 to 45 degrees toward its palmar surface. The slightly flexed fingers are held together, with the thumb in front of them. The central beam is directed toward the center of the carpus. (**B**) The radiograph in this projection demonstrates the dorsal aspect of the triquetrum, the body of the hamate, the radiovolar aspect of the scaphoid, and the scaphoid–trapezium and trapezium–trapezoid articulations.

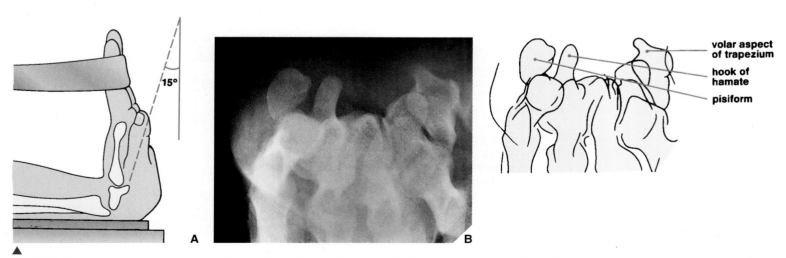

FIGURE 7.35   **Carpal tunnel view.** (**A**) For the carpal tunnel view of the wrist, the hand is maximally dorsiflexed by means of the patient's opposite hand or a strap, with the palmar surface of the wrist resting on the film cassette. The central beam is directed toward the cup of the palm at approximately an angle of 15 degrees. (**B**) The radiograph in this projection demonstrates an axial view of the hook of the hamate as well as the pisiform bone and the volar margin of the trapezium.

CARPAL JOINT COMPARTMENTS

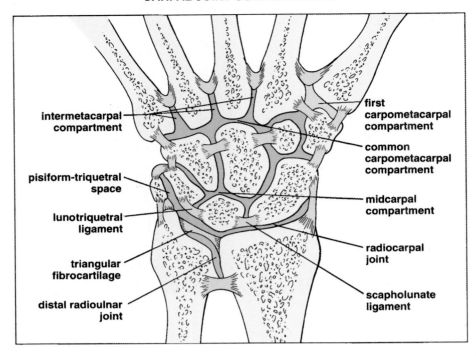

▲
FIGURE 7.36   Compartments of the carpus. Carpal joint compartments are separated from one another by various interosseous ligaments.

the carpal tunnel (Fig. 7.38) and detecting the subtle abnormalities of carpal tunnel syndrome (Fig. 7.39). Commonly, MRI is performed after an intraarticular injection of a contrast agent (diluted gadolinium) into the radiocarpal compartment (see Fig. 7.30).

The coronal plane is the best to demonstrate the interosseous ligaments of the proximal carpal row (scapholunate and lunotriquetral ligaments) and the TFCC. These structures exhibit a low-intensity signal on T1- and T2-weighted sequences (see Fig. 7.37). In this plane, various intrinsic and extrinsic dorsal and volar ligaments of the wrist (Fig. 7.40) are also seen. In the sagittal plane, all flexor and extensor tendons with their respective insertions are clearly depicted, as well as some of the ligaments including the radioscaphocapitate, radiolunotriquetral, and dorsal radiolunate (Fig. 7.41). In the axial plane, various ligaments and tendons are shown in cross sections; their anatomic relationship to the bone structures, arteries, and nerves can be evaluated effectively (Fig. 7.42). This plane is also ideal for imaging of the Guyon canal. This anatomic structure is located on the volar aspect of the wrist, medially to the carpal tunnel, between the pisiform bone and the hook of the hamate (Fig. 7.43). It is bounded by the flexor retinaculum from the dorsal aspect, hypothenar musculature from the medial aspect, and by fascia from the volar aspect. It contains the ulnar vein, ulnar artery, and ulnar nerve.

During the evaluation of MRI of the wrist, it is helpful to use a checklist as provided in Table 7.4.

Ancillary techniques such as stress films and arthrography may also need to be used for the evaluation of disruption or displacement of the ligaments of the hand, particularly in gamekeeper's thumb. For a summary in tabular form of the standard and special radiographic projections, as well as the ancillary techniques used to evaluate trauma to the wrist and hand, see Tables 7.5 and 7.6 and Figure 7.44.

Injury to the Wrist

Fractures of the Carpal Bones

Fracture of the Scaphoid Bone. Fractures of the scaphoid (from the Greek word *skaphos*, meaning *boat*), sometimes called carpal navicular, are the second most common injuries of the upper limb, exceeded in frequency only by fractures of the distal radius, and they constitute 2% of all fractures. Of all fractures and dislocations in the carpus, this fracture

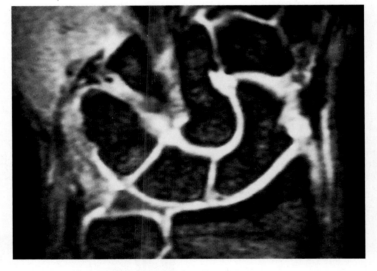

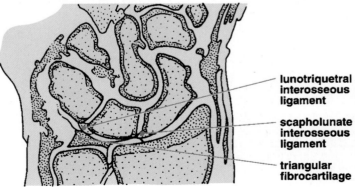

▲
FIGURE 7.37   **MRI of the wrist.** Coronal T2-weighted MR image (gradient-echo pulse sequence) of the wrist demonstrates distal radius and ulna and carpal bones. The proximal interosseous ligaments and the triangular fibrocartilage are clearly delineated. (From Beltran J, 1990, with permission.)

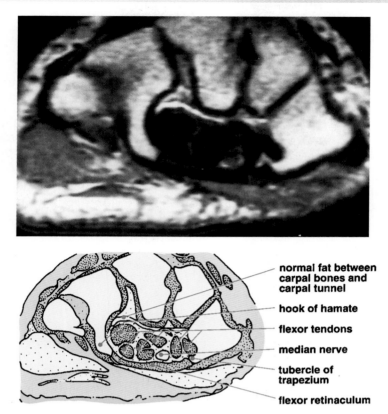

FIGURE 7.38 MRI of the wrist. Proton density–weighted spin-echo axial MR image (TR 2000/TE 20 msec) through the carpal tunnel demonstrates the various structures. Note the median nerve, displaying intermediate signal intensity and flexor retinaculum imaged with low signal intensity. (From Beltran J, 1990, with permission.)

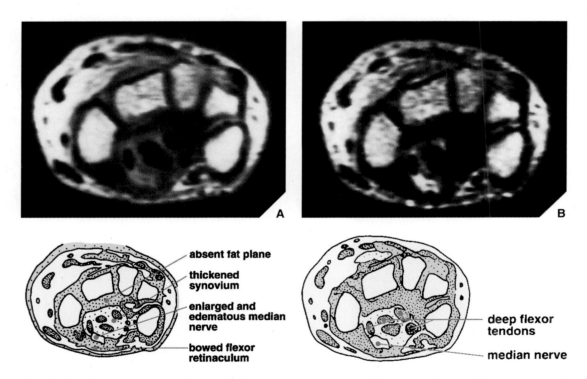

FIGURE 7.39 MRI of carpal tunnel syndrome. A 21-year-old woman with clinically diagnosed carpal tunnel syndrome underwent MRI examination of her right wrist. Proton density–weighted (**A**) and T2-weighted (**B**) axial images demonstrate an increased signal of the median nerve and thickened synovium surrounding the flexor tendons in the carpal tunnel. Note the volar bowing of the flexor retinaculum and the absent fat plane between the deep flexor tendons and the more dorsal radiolunotriquetral ligament. (From Beltran J, 1990, with permission.)

A. Dorsal Ligaments of the Wrist

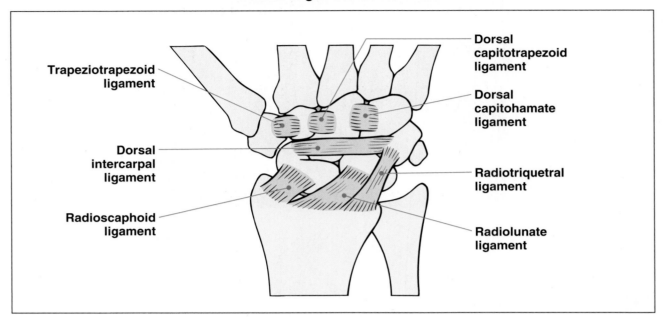

Trapeziotrapezoid ligament

Dorsal capitotrapezoid ligament

Dorsal capitohamate ligament

Dorsal intercarpal ligament

Radioscaphoid ligament

Radiotriquetral ligament

Radiolunate ligament

B. Volar Ligaments of the Wrist

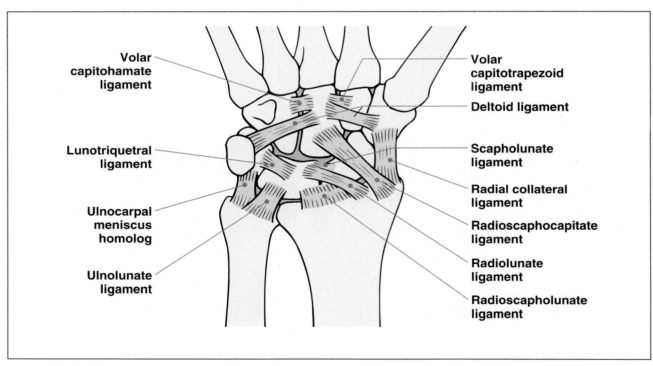

Volar capitohamate ligament

Volar capitotrapezoid ligament

Deltoid ligament

Lunotriquetral ligament

Scapholunate ligament

Ulnocarpal meniscus homolog

Radial collateral ligament

Radioscaphocapitate ligament

Ulnolunate ligament

Radiolunate ligament

Radioscapholunate ligament

▲
FIGURE 7.40   Ligaments of the wrist. A schematic representation of the dorsal (**A**) and volar (**B**) ligaments of the wrist.

is the most common, accounting for 50% to 60% of such injuries. They frequently occur in young adults (ages 15 to 30) after falls on the outstretched palm of the hand. Scaphoid fractures can be classified according to the direction of the fracture line (Fig. 7.45), the degree of stability of the fragments, and the location of the fracture line. From a diagnostic perspective, the latter is a more practical way of classifying fractures of the scaphoid (5% to 10% of which occur in the tuberosity and distal pole, 15% to 20% in the proximal pole, and 70% to 80% in the waist),

because it has prognostic value (Fig. 7.46). Fractures of the tuberosity (extraarticular) and distal pole usually result from a direct trauma and rarely cause any significant clinical problems. Fractures of the waist, if there is no displacement or carpal instability, display a good healing pattern in more than 90% of cases. Fractures involving the proximal pole have a high incidence of nonunion and osteonecrosis.

When a fracture of the scaphoid is suspected, standard radiographs are routinely obtained in the dorsovolar, dorsovolar in ulnar deviation,

FIGURE 7.41 MRI of the wrist. ▶
Sagittal MRI through the wrist
from the midaspect (**A,B**) to the
ulnar aspect (**C,D**). The volar and
dorsal radiolunate components of
the radioscapholunate ligaments
are well demonstrated. The radiolunotriquetral ligament is seen
volar to the capitate–lunate articulation. The radioscaphocapitate
ligament is seen inserting at the
volar and proximal one third of
the capitate bone. (From Beltran
J, 1990, with permission.)

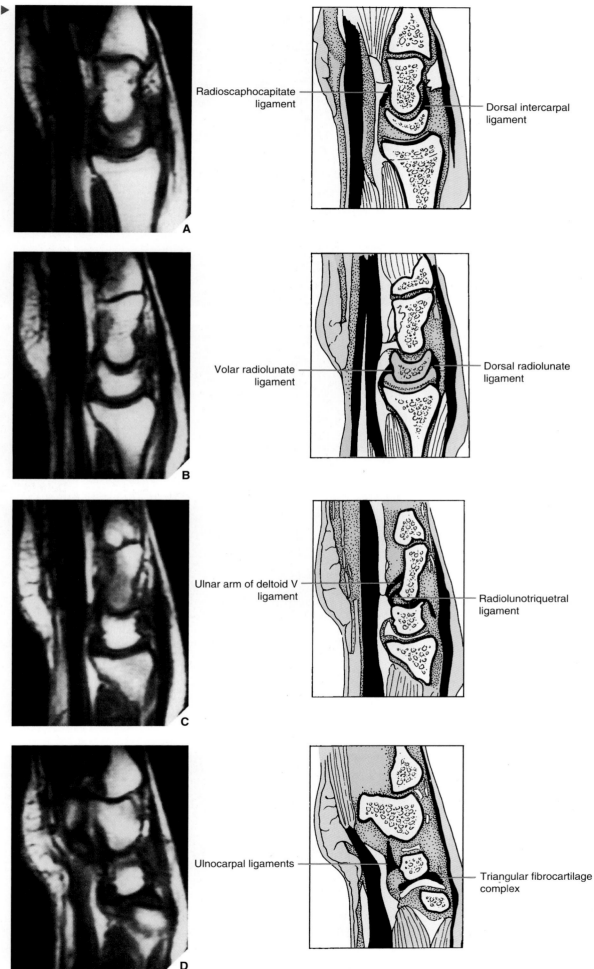

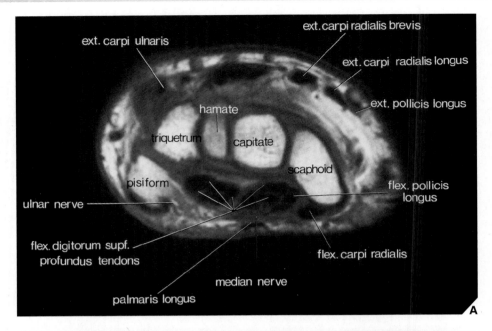

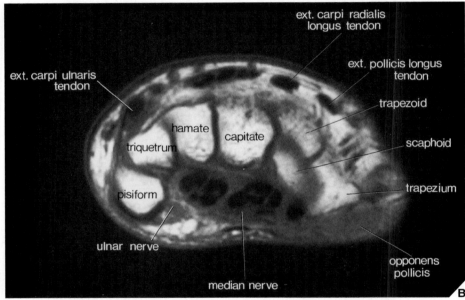

▲
FIGURE 7.42   **MRI of the wrist.** Axial T1-weighted MR images through the proximal (**A**) and distal (**B**) carpus effectively demonstrate various anatomic structures of the wrist.

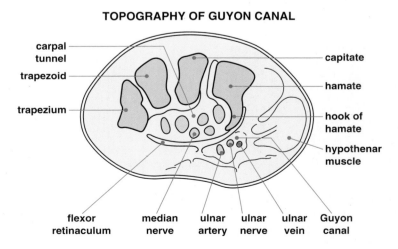

▲
FIGURE 7.43   Location of the Guyon canal within the wrist.

TABLE 7.4 **Checklist for Evaluation of MRI and MRa of the Wrist**

Osseous Structures
  Distal radius, Lister tubercle (c, s, a)
  Distal ulna, styloid process (c, s, a)
  Scaphoid (c, s)
  Lunate (c, s)
  Triquetrum (c, s)
  Pisiform (c)
  Hamate, body, hook (c, s, a)
  Capitate (c, s)
  Trapezium (c)
  Trapezoid (c)

Triangular Fibrocartilage Complex (TFCC)
  TFC proper (c, a)
  Dorsal and volar radioulnar ligaments (c, a)
  Meniscus homolog (c)
  Extensor carpi ulnaris tendon (c, a)
  Ulnar collateral ligament (c)

Ligaments
  Intrinsic
    Scapholunate
      Volar (trapezoid shape) (c)
      Middle (triangle shape) (c)
      Dorsal (band-like) (c)
    Lunotriquetral (c)

Ligaments (continued)
  Extrinsic
    Volar
      Radiocapitate (c,s)
      Radiolunotriquetral (c,s)
      Ulnocapitate (c,a)
      Ulnotriquetral (c,a)
      Ulnolunate (c,a)
    Dorsal
      Radioscaphoid (c)
      Radiolunate (c)
      Radiotriquetral (c)
      Scaphotriquetral (c)
      Intercarpal (c)

Tendons
  Flexors (a)
  Extensors (a)

Nerves
  Median, ulnar (a)

Other Structures
  Carpal tunnel (c)
  Guyon canal (c)
  Ulnar nerve, ulnar artery, ulnar vein

The best imaging planes for visualization of listed structures are given in parenthesis; c, coronal; s, sagittal; a, axial.

TABLE 7.5 **Standard and Special Radiographic Projections for Evaluating Injury to the Wrist and Hand**

Projection	Demonstration	Projection	Demonstration
Dorsovolar	Carpal bones	*Oblique (hand)*	Fractures of
	Three carpal arcs		Metacarpals
	Eye of the hamate		Phalanges
	Scaphoid fat stripe		Boxer's fracture
	Radiocarpal articulation	*Supinated oblique*	Pisotriquetral joint
	Metacarpals	*(wrist)*	Pisiform fractures
	Phalanges	*Pronated oblique (wrist)*	Dorsal aspect of triquetrum and
	Carpometacarpal, metacarpophalangeal,		triquetral fractures
	and interphalangeal joints		Radiovolar aspect of scaphoid
	Scapholunate dissociation:		Articulations between
	Terry-Thomas sign		Scaphoid and trapezium
	Scaphoid signet-ring sign		Trapezium and trapezoid
	Fractures of	*Carpal tunnel*	Volar aspect of trapezium
	Scaphoid		Fractures of
	Capitate		Hook of the hamate
	Lunate		Pisiform
	Hamate (body)	*Abduction–stress*	Gamekeeper's thumb
	Metacarpals	*(thumb)*	
	Phalanges		
	Bennett and Rolando fractures		
In Ulnar Deviation	Scaphoid fractures		
Lateral	Longitudinal axial alignment of third		
	metacarpal, capitate, lunate, and radius		
	Fractures of		
	Triquetrum		
	Metacarpals		
	Phalanges		
	Carpal dislocations:		
	Lunate		
	Perilunate		
	Midcarpal		
	Dislocations of metacarpals and phalanges		

TABLE 7.6   Ancillary Imaging Techniques for Evaluating Injury to the Wrist and Hand

Technique	Demonstration	Technique	Demonstration
Fluoroscopy/Videotaping	Kinematics of wrist and hand Carpal instability Transient carpal subluxations	*Tomography* (usually trispiral) Projections:	
Radionuclide Imaging (scintigraphy, bone scan)	Subtle chondral and osteochondral fractures Fracture healing and complications (e.g., infection, osteonecrosis)	Dorsovolar Lateral Oblique	Fractures of carpal bones, particu- larly scaphoid and lunate Rolando fracture Keinböck disease
Arthrography (single contrast)	Tear of TFCC Intercarpal ligaments Ulnar collateral ligament (gamekeep- er's thumb)	Lateral Carpal tunnel	Fracture healing and complications (e.g., nonunion, osteonecrosis) Fractures of the hook of the hamate
Magnetic Resonance Imaging and MR Arthrography	Same as for arthrography Guyon canal Carpal tunnel syndrome Injury to the soft tissues Subtle fractures Osteonecrosis	*Flexion–extension* *Computed Tomography*	Stability of a scaphoid fracture Humpback deformity of scaphoid Subtle fractures, particularly of the hook of the hamate Fracture healing and complications

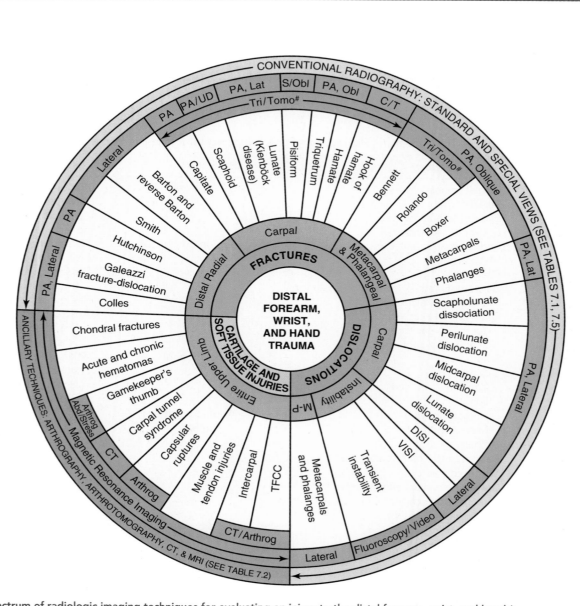

▲ FIGURE 7.44   Spectrum of radiologic imaging techniques for evaluating an injury to the distal forearm, wrist, and hand.*

  *The radiographic projections or radiologic techniques indicated throughout the diagram are only those that are the most effective in demonstrating the respective traumatic conditions.

  #Almost completely replaced by CT.

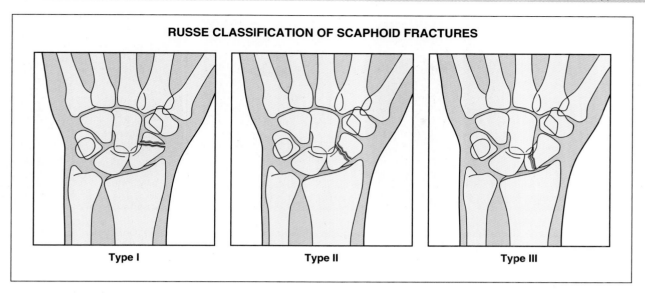

RUSSE CLASSIFICATION OF SCAPHOID FRACTURES

Type I   Type II   Type III

▲ FIGURE 7.45   **Scaphoid fractures.** Russe classified fractures of the scaphoid bone according to the direction of the fracture line.

**CLASSIFICATION OF SCAPHOID FRACTURES
BY LOCATION**

5%–10%

tubercle   distal pole

70%–80%   15%–20%

waist   proximal pole

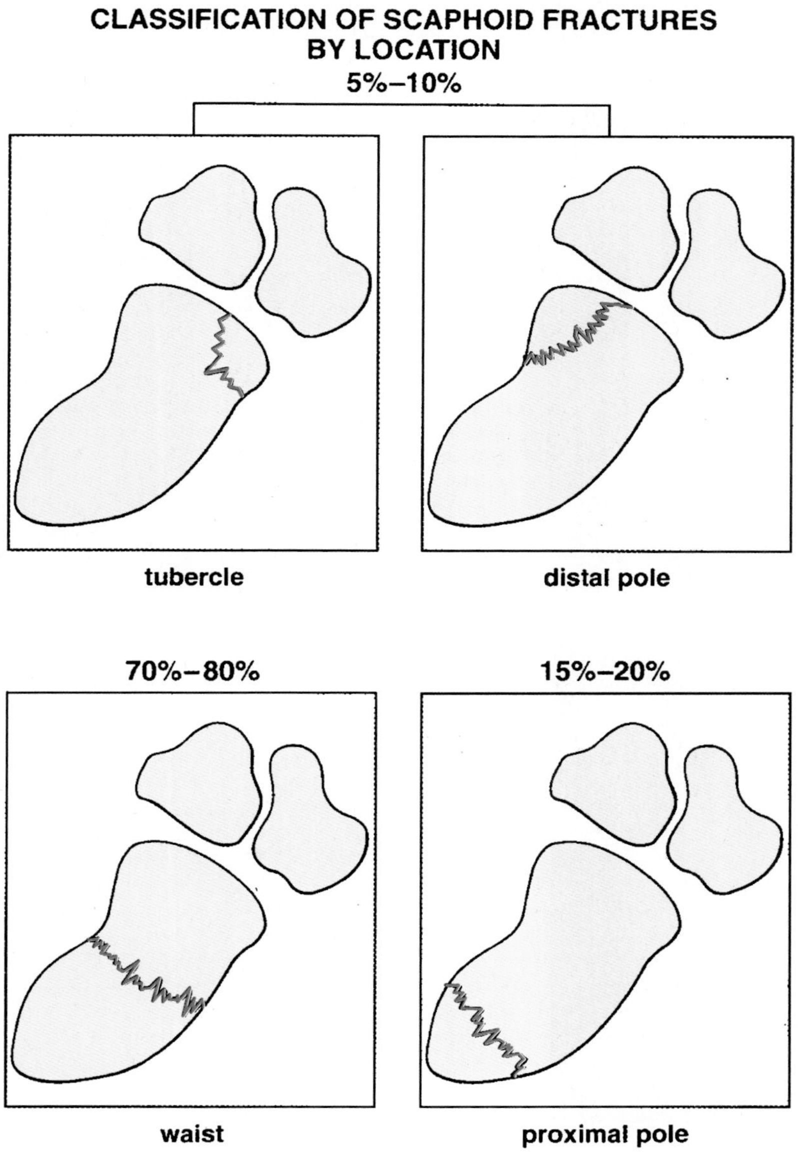

▲ FIGURE 7.46   **Scaphoid fractures.** Classification of scaphoid fractures by the location of the fracture line.

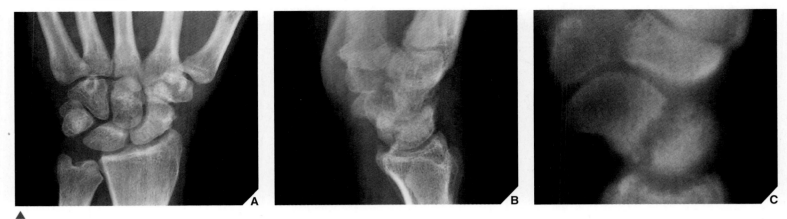

FIGURE 7.47 **Scaphoid fractures.** A 28-year-old man sustained an injury to his left wrist; pain persisted for 3 weeks. Dorsovolar (**A**) and lateral (**B**) films show periarticular osteoporosis, but no fracture line is evident. On a thin-section trispiral tomogram in the lateral projection (**C**), a fracture of the scaphoid becomes apparent.

oblique, and lateral projections, and these conventional studies usually suffice to demonstrate the abnormality. When they failed to do so, in the past, thin-section trispiral tomography has proved very effective (Fig. 7.47). This technique was equally helpful in monitoring the progress of healing of scaphoid fractures and in detecting posttraumatic com-

plications, especially when routine follow-up films were unconvincing (Fig. 7.48). Currently, CT is the technique of choice in this respect (Figs. 7.49 and 7.50; see also Fig. 4.68). In particular, the so-called humpback deformity of the scaphoid after a fracture (in which the proximal fragment dorsiflexes and the distal fragment undergoes palmar flexion,

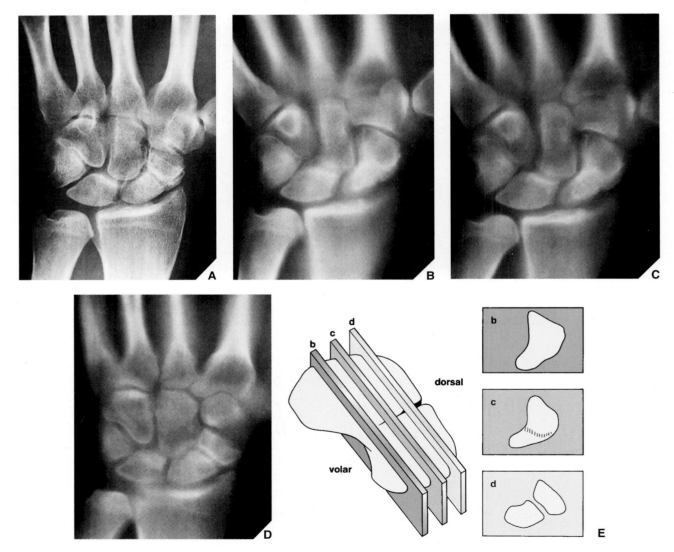

FIGURE 7.48 **Tomography of a healed scaphoid fracture.** On follow-up examination of a 27-year-old man who had undergone a bone grafting procedure for nonunion of a scaphoid fracture, a radiograph in the dorsovolar projection (**A**) suggests persistence of nonunion and graft failure. For a fuller evaluation, trispiral tomography using 1-mm thin sections was performed. The sections from the volar aspect of the bone (**B,C**) demonstrate good union and success of the graft. Although a gap is evident on the dorsal section (**D**), it has no clinical significance, only giving the impression of nonunion. The reason for this is illustrated in the schematic diagram (**E**), in which the planes through the scaphoid (*b, c,* and *d*) correspond to the sections on the tomograms (**B**), (**C**), and (**D**).

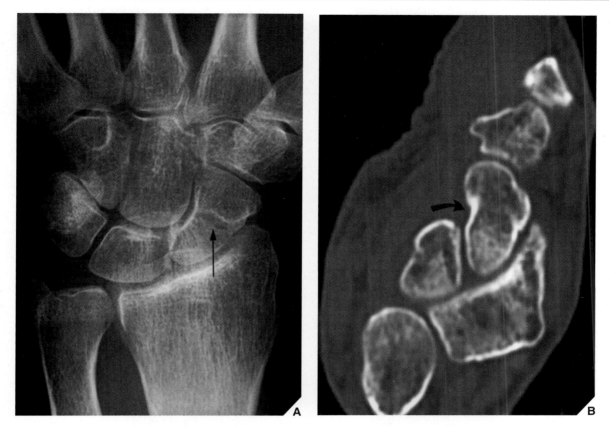

▲
FIGURE 7.49 CT of a healed scaphoid fracture. A 56-year-old man was treated conservatively for a scaphoid fracture with closed reduction and cast application. (**A**) Dorsovolar radiograph of the wrist shows a radiolucent line (*arrow*) suggestive of a nonunion. (**B**) Oblique coronal CT image demonstrates, however, complete union (*curved arrow*).

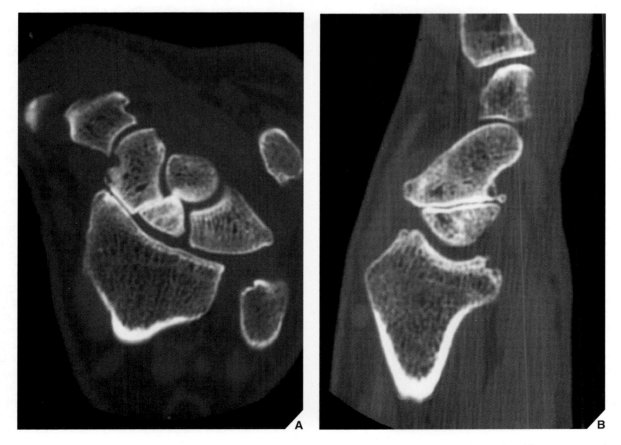

▲
FIGURE 7.50 CT of an ununited scaphoid fracture. Coronal (**A**) and sagittal (**B**) CT images show nonunion of a scaphoid fracture. Note the sclerotic edges and gap between the fractured fragments.

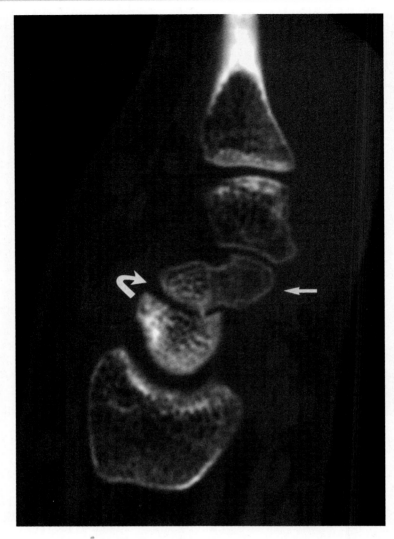

FIGURE 7.51 **Humpback deformity.** A sagittal reformatted CT image shows a humpback deformity of a fractured scaphoid. Note the palmar flexion of the distal fragment (*arrow*) and the dorsal apex angulation (*curved arrow*).

resulting in dorsal apical angulation of the scaphoid) can be well evaluated by this modality (Fig. 7.51). In the past decade, MRI became the technique of choice to diagnose subtle fractures of the carpal bones and to detect various complications, including osteonecrosis. In particular, MRI is very effective in demonstrating a fracture line that is not apparent on conventional radiographs (Fig. 7.52).

Complications. Delayed diagnosis and consequently delayed treatment of a scaphoid fracture may lead to complications such as nonunion, osteonecrosis, and posttraumatic arthritis, the first two of which are the most commonly seen. Although occasionally both fragments of the scaphoid may become necrotic, osteonecrosis usually affects the proximal fragment (see Fig. 7.54) and only rarely the distal pole (Fig. 7.53) because of the good supply of blood to this part of the bone. Osteonecrosis most frequently becomes apparent 3 to 6 months after the injury when the affected fragment shows evidence of increased density. Because conventional radiography may, at times, fail to demonstrate this feature, CT scanning that almost completely replaced conventional tomography is recommended as a valuable aid. Patients with delayed union or nonunion are more prone to osteonecrosis, but healing may sometimes occur despite it (Fig. 7.54). Delayed union and nonunion are usually treated surgically by bone grafting (Fig. 7.55). If this approach fails, then the scaphoid may be excised and replaced by prosthesis (Fig.7.56). One of the more serious complications of chronic nonunion

of scaphoid fracture is the development of scapholunate advanced collapse (SLAC) of the wrist. This condition comprises instability in lunocapitate joint associated with proximal migration of the capitate bone, eventually leading to osteoarthritis of the radiocarpal joint (Fig. 7.57). Treatment of this condition includes proximal row carpectomy and/or limited carpal fusion (so-called four-corner fusion) consisting of arthrodesis of lunate, capitate, hamate, and triquetrum (Fig.7.58). In cases of advanced osteoarthritis, a total wrist arthrodesis using rigid stabilization with a dorsal plate and bone grafting is usually required.

Fracture of the Triquetral Bone. Although a fracture of the triquetrum is not uncommon, it can easily be missed if proper radiographic examination is not performed. In most cases, a triquetral fracture is best demonstrated on the lateral and pronated oblique projections of the wrist. However, as overlapping bones on these views may, at times, obscure the fracture line, tomographic examination in the lateral projection used to be required to confirm the diagnosis. Radionuclide bone scan was also a valuable aid in localizing the site of trauma when a fracture was suspected and routine films were normal (Fig. 7.59). Currently, if a fracture of the triquetral bone is clinically strongly suspected and conventional radiographs are not diagnostic, CT is the technique of choice.

Fracture of the Hamate Bone. An infrequent type of wrist injury—accounting for approximately 2% of all carpal fractures—fracture of the hamate most often results from a direct blow to the volar aspect of the

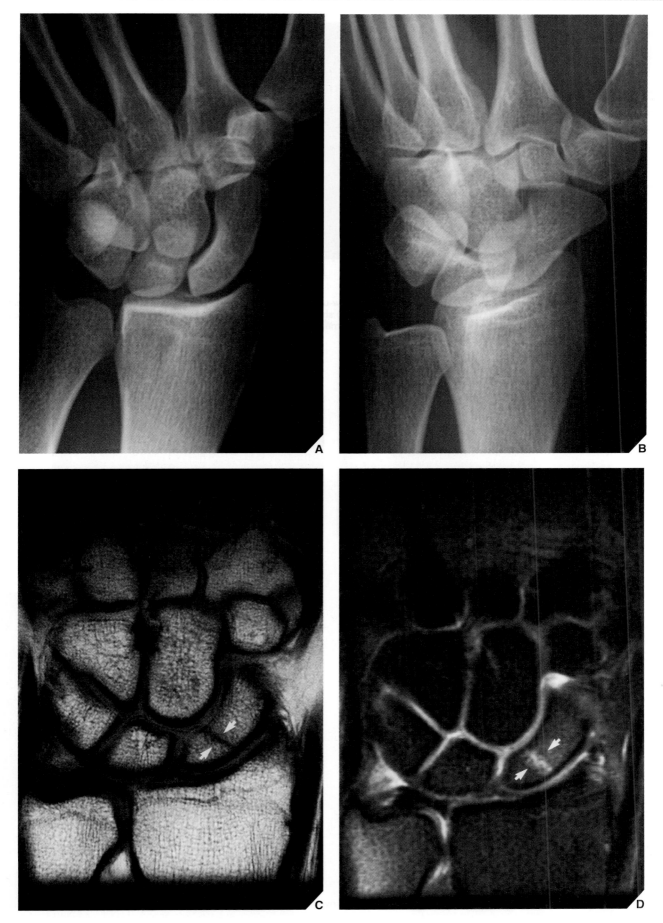

FIGURE 7.52   MRI of a scaphoid fracture. A 27-year-old man fell on ice and presented with snuffbox tenderness. Dorsovolar (**A**) in ulnar deviation and oblique (**B**) radiographs (as well as conventional dorsovolar and lateral views, not shown here) were normal. Coronal T1-weighted (**C**) and coronal fat-suppressed T2-weighted (**D**) MR images show a fracture of the proximal pole of the scaphoid (*arrows*).

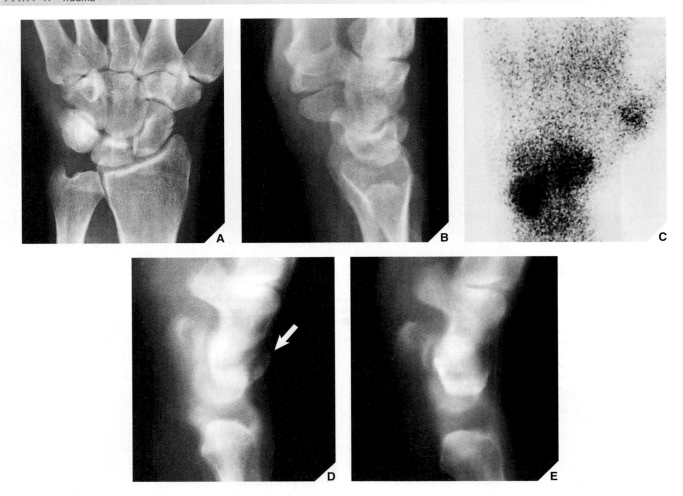

▲
FIGURE 7.59   **Triquetrum fracture.** A 45-year-old man, having fallen on his outstretched hand, presented with localized tenderness on the dorsal aspect of the wrist. Dorsovolar (**A**) and lateral (**B**) radiographs of the wrist are normal. Radionuclide bone scan (**C**), which was performed to localize the possible site of trauma, reveals an increased uptake of the tracer on the ulnar side of the carpus, suggesting a fracture. Tomographic examination in the lateral projection (**D**) unequivocally demonstrates triquetral fracture (*arrow*). The tomographic appearance of the normal triquetrum (**E**) is shown for comparison.

wrist. This is particularly true in fractures of the hook of the hamate (or hamulus), which together with fractures of the hamate body constitute the two groups of hamate injuries. Most hamulus fractures occur in sports activities requiring the use of a racket, club, bat, or similar implement that may cause a direct injury to the palmar aspect of the wrist.

Fractures of the hamate body, which may extend either ulnarly or radially to the hamulus, usually are readily demonstrated on the standard views of the wrist. The lateral and pronated oblique radiographs are preferable, particularly in detecting fractures that may be oriented in the coronal plane (Fig. 7.60).

Fractures of the hamulus, however, are not apparent on routine studies and consequently may go undiagnosed. As an aid to recognizing hamulus fracture on the standard dorsovolar view of the wrist, Norman and colleagues have identified the *eye sign*. The sign derives its name from the dense, oval, cortical ring shadow that is normally seen over the hamate on the dorsovolar projection. This "eye" of the hamate is actually the hook of the hamate seen on end (see Fig. 7.1). Although in most cases the absence or indistinct outline of the cortical shadow or the presence of sclerosis suggests the diagnosis of hamulus fracture, a film of the opposite wrist should be obtained for comparison (Fig. 7.61A,B). Confirmation of the diagnosis and evaluation of the type, site, and extent of the fracture may be made on the carpal tunnel projection (Fig. 7.61C). This view may also be effective when the suspected fracture is distal to the base of the hook and, as a result, the eye of the hamate may still be visible (Fig. 7.62). The carpal tunnel view, however, is not always definitively diagnostic, because the degree of dorsiflexion of the wrist required for this projection (see Fig. 7.35) is often limited because of

pain, particularly in patients with acute or subacute fractures. Limited dorsiflexion may cause the anterior margins of the capitate and the pisiform to overlap and obscure the fracture line (Fig. 7.62B). In such cases, trispiral tomographic studies in the lateral and carpal tunnel projections (Fig. 7.62C,D) were usually diagnostic. At the present time, CT axial sections of the wrist with sagittal reformation are routinely performed

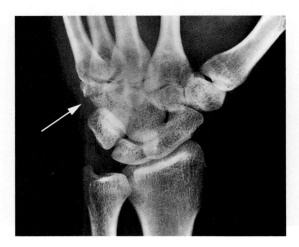

▲
FIGURE 7.60   **Hamate fracture.** On the pronated oblique view of the wrist, a fracture of the hamate body is clearly evident (*arrow*).

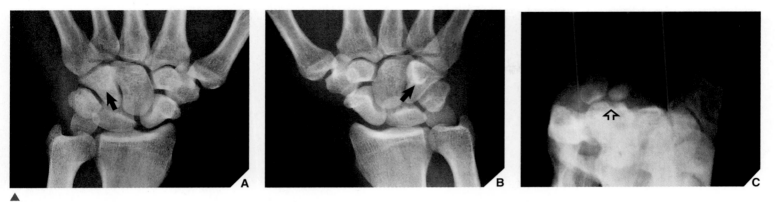

FIGURE 7.61   A fracture of the hook of the hamate. Having injured his right wrist while playing golf, a 36-year-old man presented with symptoms of pain in his palm on pressure, weakness of grasp, and occasional paresthesia of the little finger. The tenderness was limited to the area over the hook of the hamate. On the dorsovolar view of the wrist (**A**), the oval cortical shadow normally seen projecting over the hamate is not visible (*arrow*), suggesting a fracture. On a comparison study of the left wrist (**B**), the "eye" of the hamate is clearly seen (*arrow*). A fracture of the hook of the hamate (*open arrow*), suggested by the disappearance of the cortical shadow of the hamate, is confirmed on the carpal tunnel projection (**C**).

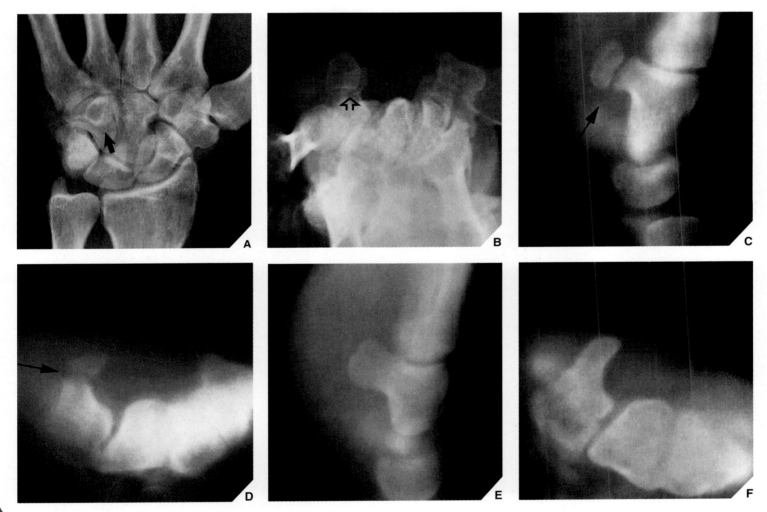

FIGURE 7.62   A fracture of the hook of the hamate. After falling on the palm of his right hand, a 66-year-old man reported pain in the palm, numbness, and weakness in the fingers innervated by the ulnar nerve. No obvious abnormalities are seen on the dorsovolar view of the wrist (**A**); the eye of the hamate is clearly discernible (*arrow*). On the conventional carpal tunnel view (**B**), obtained without the maximum degree of dorsiflexion caused by pain, the pisiform partially overlaps the hamulus. A short radiolucent line is evident, however, at the base of the hamulus (*open arrow*), but the diagnosis of a fracture cannot be made conclusively. Trispiral tomograms in the lateral (**C**) and carpal tunnel (**D**) projections unquestionably demonstrate a fracture of the hook of the hamate distal to the base (*arrows*). The normal appearance of the hamulus on, respectively, the same projections (**E,F**) is shown for comparison. (**A,B,D:** From Greenspan A et al., 1985, with permission.)

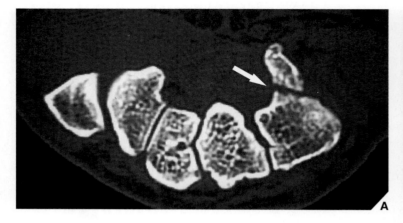

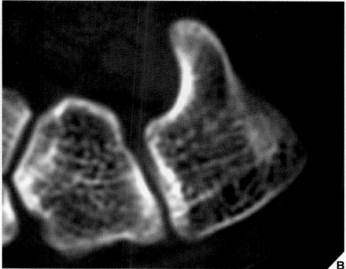

FIGURE 7.63   CT of a fracture of the hook of the hamate. (A) Axial CT image of the wrist shows a fracture of the hook of the hamate (*arrow*). **(B)** Axial CT image of an intact hook is shown for comparison.

(Fig. 7.63). Although MRI is not indicated in the preliminary evaluation of patients with suspected fracture of the hook of the hamate, it can be helpful if the initial conventional radiographs failed to demonstrate this injury (Fig. 7.64).

Fracture of the Pisiform Bone. A fracture of the pisiform is rare. It usually results from a direct injury to the wrist as, for example, from a fall on the outstretched hand or use of the hand as a hammer to strike an object. It may be an isolated injury or may coexist with fractures of other bones. Although this injury may be seen on posteroanterior films of the wrist (Fig. 7.65), radiographs in the supinated oblique and carpal tunnel projections are best suited to demonstrate the abnormality (Fig.7.66).

Fracture of the Capitate Bone. An uncommon type of carpal injury, accounting for only 1% to 3% of carpal fractures, fracture of the capitate usually occurs in association with other injuries to the carpus, particularly a fracture of the scaphoid and perilunate dislocation. It usually results from a fall on the outstretched hand, with hyperdorsiflexion of the hand causing impingement of the bone against the distal radius; it may also result from a direct blow to the wrist. The waist (or neck) of the capitate is the most common site of fracture. The dorsovolar view of the wrist usually demonstrates the abnormality (Fig. 7.67A), although the lateral view may be helpful in determining the rotation or displacement of the fragment. Trispiral tomography was useful in outlining the

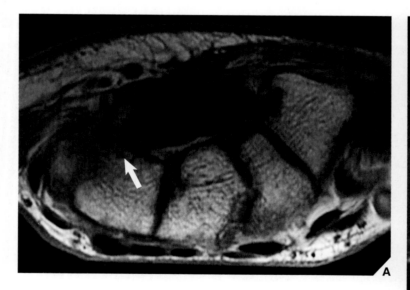

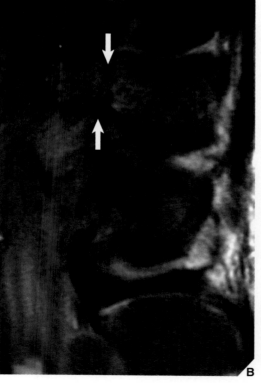

FIGURE 7.64   MRI of a fracture of the hook of the hamate. (A) Axial and **(B)** sagittal proton density–weighted fat-suppressed MR images of the wrist demonstrate a fracture of the hook of the hamate (*arrows*).

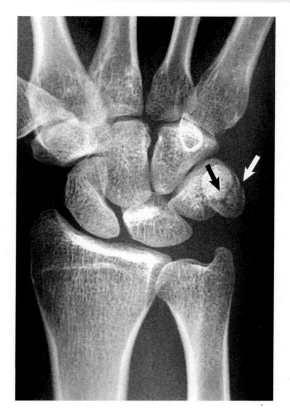

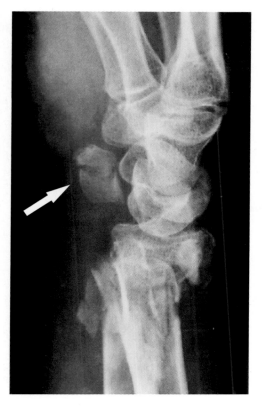

FIGURE 7.65 **Pisiform fracture.** Dorsovolar radiograph of the wrist shows a comminuted fracture of the pisiform bone (*arrows*).

FIGURE 7.66 **Pisiform fracture.** A 66-year-old woman sustained a crush injury to the left wrist in a motor vehicle accident. Conventional radiographs in the dorsovolar, lateral, and oblique projections (not shown here) revealed comminuted fractures of the distal radius and the ulna. To exclude the possibility of associated carpal fractures, especially in view of the severity of the injury seen on the routine studies, a film in the supinated oblique projection was obtained. This view clearly demonstrates, in addition, a fracture of the pisiform (*arrow*).

details of the fracture and determining the stage of healing (Fig. 7.67B), although currently this technique has been replaced by CT.

Fracture of the Lunate Bone. Usually the result of a fall on the dorsiflexed wrist or a strenuous push on the heel of the hand, a fracture of the lunate is a rare type of carpal injury, accounting for less than 3% of all carpal fractures. It is often seen in association with perilunate dislocation but more commonly occurs as a pathologic fracture of necrotic bone secondary to Kienböck disease (see later). The standard views of the wrist, particularly the dorsovolar

and lateral projections, are usually sufficient to demonstrate the abnormality, although CT scanning may also be required for a full evaluation.

Kienböck Disease

Single or repeated trauma to the lunate or dislocation of the bone may impair its blood supply and cause it to become necrotic. However, the development of Kienböck disease, as this form of osteonecrosis affecting the lunate is known, may not be solely attributable to extrinsic trauma.

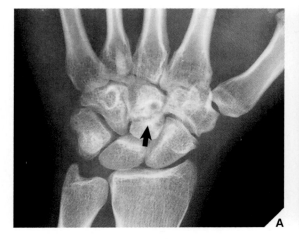

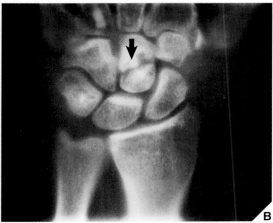

FIGURE 7.67 **Capitate fracture.** A 23-year-old man fell on his outstretched hand. (**A**) Dorsovolar radiograph of the wrist demonstrates a fracture through the neck of the capitate (*arrow*). (**B**) After conservative treatment (3 months of immobilization in a plaster cast), trispiral tomography was performed. On this film, there is clear evidence of lack of union. Note the small necrotic bone fragment (*arrow*), which was not too well demonstrated on the standard projection.

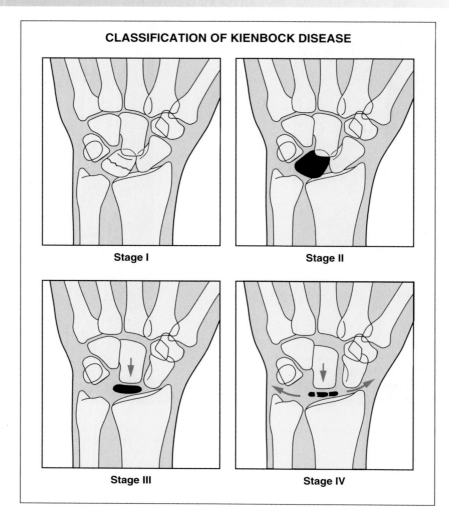

CLASSIFICATION OF KIENBOCK DISEASE

Stage I

Stage II

Stage III

Stage IV

▲
FIGURE 7.68   **The four stages of Kienböck disease.** (Modified from Gelberman RH, Szabo RM, 1993, with permission.)

Whether the natural history begins with a single simple transverse fracture or numerous compression fractures from repeated compressive strains is still the subject of speculation. An interesting but controversial hypothesis links this condition with negative ulnar variance in individuals whose ulna projects more proximally. They may be predisposed to Kienböck disease because of compression of the lunate against the irregular articular surface created by the discrepancy in radial and ulnar lengths.

Once lunate necrosis begins, an established progressive sequence of events is set in motion. This progression is marked by lunate flattening and elongation, proximal migration of the capitate, scapholunate dissociation, and, finally, osteoarthritis of the radiocarpal joint. This series of changes also forms the basis for the classification of Kienböck disease (Fig. 7.68). Clinically, stage I is indistinguishable from a wrist sprain. Wrist radiographs may be completely normal, and only CT may detect a subtle linear fracture. Skeletal scintigraphy may show an increased uptake of a radiopharmaceutical tracer by the lunate. MRI invariably demonstrates the abnormality, displaying decreased signal intensity of lunate on T1-weighted images (Fig. 7.69). As the condition progresses

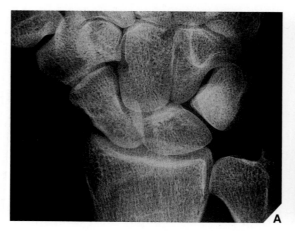

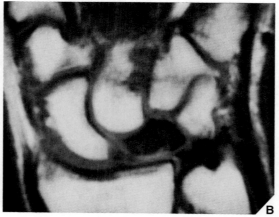

▲
FIGURE 7.69   **Kienböck disease.** A 35-year-old man with wrist pain underwent radiologic investigation for Kienböck disease. **(A)** Conventional dorsovolar radiograph of the left wrist is normal. **(B)** Coronal T1-weighted MRI shows low signal intensity of the lunate consistent with osteonecrosis. (Courtesy of Dr. L. Steinbach, San Francisco, California.)

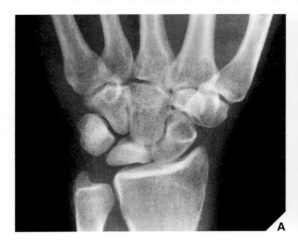

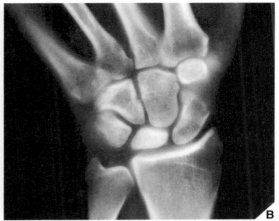

FIGURE 7.70 **Kienböck disease.** Dorsovolar radiograph (**A**) and tomogram (**B**) of the wrist show the dense, flattened appearance of the lunate characteristic of Kienböck disease. Note the presence of negative ulnar variance, a possible predisposing factor in this condition.

(stage II), the conventional radiographs and trispiral tomographic studies in the dorsovolar and lateral projections show increased density of the lunate accompanied by some degree of flattening on the radial side of this bone (Fig. 7.70). The radionuclide bone scan is always positive in this stage. In stage III, the radiographs demonstrate marked decrease in the height of the lunate and proximal migration of the capitate (Fig. 7.71). Necrotic and cystic degeneration may lead to further fragmentation and collapse (Fig. 7.72). Scapholunate dissociation is a prominent feature of this stage. Stage IV is marked by almost complete disintegration of the lunate and the development of radiocarpal osteoarthritis with typical changes of joint space narrowing, osteophyte formation, subchondral sclerosis, and degenerative cysts (Fig. 7.73).

Merely diagnosing Kienböck disease is not sufficient from the orthopedic point of view; rather, it is essential for the radiologist to demonstrate the integrity of the bone. The reason for this is that at an early stage of the disease, in the absence of a fracture or fragmentation, a revascularization procedure aimed at restoring circulation to the lunate may prevent further progression of the necrotic process and eventual collapse of the bone (Fig. 7.74). In the event of a fracture (Fig. 7.75) or fragmentation (Fig. 7.76) of the lunate, which is best diagnosed on CT, alternatives to revascularization—such as silastic arthroplasty or, in the absence of a collapse deformity, ulnar lengthening or radial shortening—would then have to be considered. In some cases, the latter procedures restoring neutral ulnar variance may allow spontaneous healing of a lunate fracture.

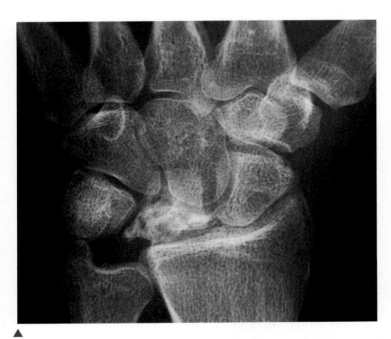

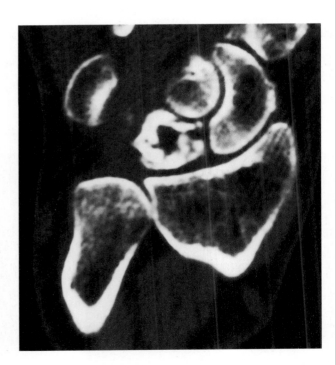

FIGURE 7.71 **Kienböck disease.** A 21-year-old man presented with long-standing wrist pain. A dorsovolar radiograph shows stage III of Kienböck disease. Note the collapse of osteonecrotic lunate and proximal migration of the capitate.

FIGURE 7.72 **Kienböck disease.** Coronal reformatted CT image of the wrist reveals cystic changes of the osteonecrotic lunate associated with a pathologic fracture. (Courtesy of Dr. L. Friedman, Hamilton, Canada.)

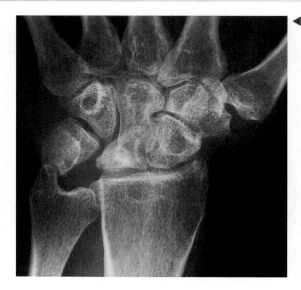

► FIGURE 7.73 **Kienböck disease.** Stage IV of Kienböck disease is marked by fragmentation and collapse of the lunate, proximal migration of the capitate, rotary subluxation of the scaphoid, and osteoarthritis of the radiocarpal joint.

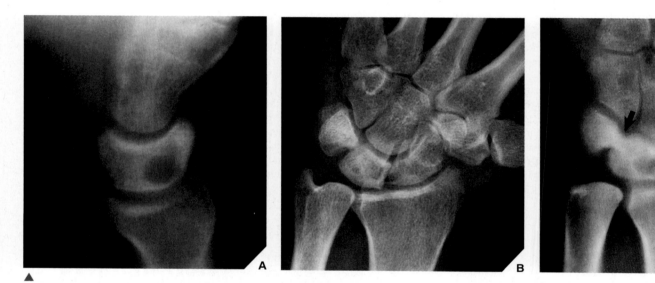

▲ FIGURE 7.74 **Kienböck disease. (A)** Lateral tomogram of the wrist shows the dense appearance of the lunate characteristic of osteonecrosis; there is also clear evidence of cystic degeneration. Because no fracture line is present, the surgeon has the option of performing a revascularization procedure. After triquetrolunate arthrodesis, the dorsovolar view of the wrist in radial deviation **(B)** and a trispiral tomogram **(C)** demonstrate the vascular bone flap (*arrow*) bridging the triquetrum and the lunate.

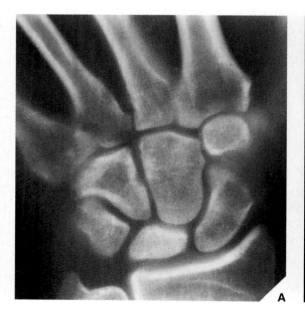

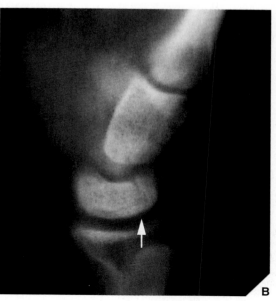

► FIGURE 7.75 **Kienböck disease. (A)** On a trispiral tomogram in the dorsovolar projection with the wrist ulnarly deviated, there is no evidence of lunate fracture. **(B)** The lateral tomographic section, however, shows clear indication of a fracture line (*arrow*).

FIGURE 7.76 Kienböck disease. Dorsovolar (A) and lateral (B) ▶ trispiral tomograms of the wrist demonstrate fragmentation of the lunate seen in advanced Kienböck disease.

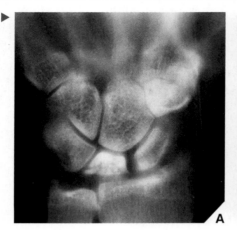
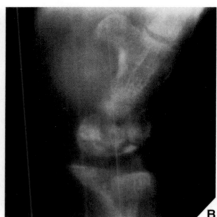

Hamatolunate Impaction Syndrome

Recently described painful condition of the ulnar side of the wrist, hamatolunate impaction syndrome, results from an anatomic variant of the lunate bone that has an "extra" facet articulating with the hamate bone (so-called type II lunate bone). The repeated contact of these two bones when the wrist is in ulnar deviation leads to bone marrow edema, chondromalacia, and, occasionally, erosive changes of the proximal pole of hamate, best demonstrated on MRI (Fig. 7.77).

Dislocations of the Carpal Bones

The most frequent types of dislocation in the wrist are scapholunate dislocation, perilunate dislocation, midcarpal dislocation, and lunate dislocation. To understand better the pattern of dislocation of the carpal bones, Johnson stressed the occurrence of the so-called vulnerable zone, the common site of wrist injuries (Fig. 7.78). Two major types of injury are recognized: the lesser arc and greater arc patterns. A lesser-arc injury involves, in sequential stages, rotary subluxation of the scaphoid, perilunate dislocation, midcarpal dislocation, and lunate dislocation, whereas a greater-arc injury involves a fracture of any of the bones adjacent to the lunate associated with dislocations. The wrist ligaments stabilize the carpus to the distal radius and ulna. The radiocapitate and capitotriquetral ligaments are the prime stabilizers of the distal carpal row. The proximal carpal row is stabilized by the volar radiotriquetral, the dorsal

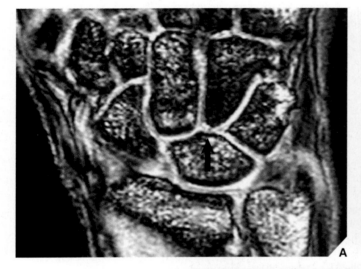
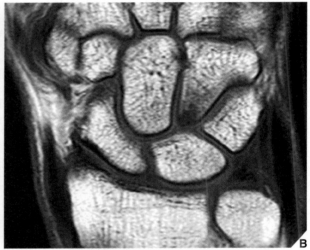
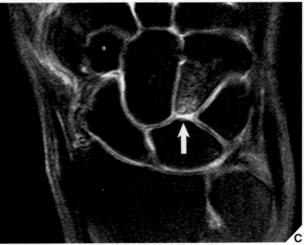

FIGURE 7.77 MRI of the hamatolunate impaction syndrome. (A) Coronal 3D gradient-echo MR image shows a type II lunate articulating with the hamate (*arrow*). Note a decreased signal intensity within the most proximal aspect of the hamate bone. (B) Coronal T1-weighted and (C) coronal T2-weighted fat-suppressed MR images demonstrate the erosion of the cartilage (*arrow*) and edematous changes of the hamate, diagnostic of hamatolunate impaction syndrome.

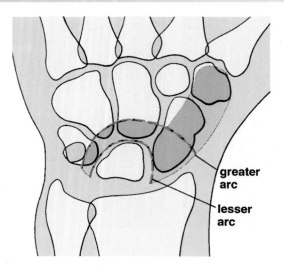

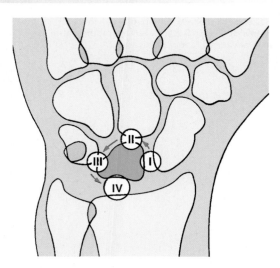

▲
FIGURE 7.78 **Vulnerable zone of the wrist.** The "vulnerable zone" of the carpus is represented by shaded areas. Most fractures, fracture dislocations, and dislocations of the carpal bones occur within it. The lesser arc outlines the "dislocation zone," whereas the greater arc outlines the "fracture–dislocation zone." (Modified from Yeager B, Dalinka M, 1985, with permission.)

▲
FIGURE 7.79 **Injuries of the lesser arc.** Sequential stages of lesser-arc injury. Stage I represents a scapholunate failure that results in a scapholunate dissociation or rotary subluxation of the scaphoid. Stage II represents a capitolunate failure that results in a dislocation of the capitate (perilunate dislocation). Stage III represents a triquetrolunate failure because the articulation between the lunate and the triquetrum is disrupted, leading to a midcarpal dislocation. Stage IV represents a complete lunate disruption, caused by dorsal radiocarpal ligament failure. (Modified from Yeager B, Dalinka M, 1985, with permission.)

radiocarpal, the ulnolunate, the ulnotriquetral, and the ulnar collateral ligaments. The scaphoid is stabilized distally by the radiocapitate and radial collateral ligaments and proximally by the radioscaphoid and scapholunate ligaments (see Fig. 7.40). Mayfield, and later Yeager, Dalinka, and Gilula, stressed the pattern of four sequential stages of lesser-arc injury (Fig. 7.79). Stage I represents a scapholunate dissociation and rotary subluxation of the scaphoid. Stage II represents a dislocation of the capitate known also as perilunate dislocation. Stage III represents a midcarpal dislocation, the result of disruption of articulation between the lunate and the triquetrum. Stage IV represents a complete lunate dislocation. This pattern follows the progression from the least severe injury, *scapholunate dissociation* (rotary subluxation of the scaphoid), in which there is a tear of the radioscaphoid, palmar radiocapitate, and scapholunate ligaments, to a more severe *perilunate dislocation*, in which there is, in addition, a tear of the radiocapitate ligaments, to a still more severe injury, *midcarpal dislocation* (dislocation of the capitate dorsally to the lunate and subluxation, but not complete dislocation, of the lunate), with a tear of the volar and dorsal radiotriquetral and ulnotriquetral ligaments, to the severest injury, *lunate dislocation*, in which there is a tear of the radiolunate fascicle of the dorsal radiocarpal ligament and of the volar ligaments, leaving the lunate entirely without ligamentous attachments.

An appreciation of two important normal relations of the carpal bones—one seen on the lateral view and the other on the dorsovolar view of the wrist—should aid in recognizing the presence of abnormality. The lateral view obtained with the wrist in the neutral position reveals the alignment of the radius, the lunate, the capitate, and the third metacarpal along their longitudinal axes (Fig. 7.80). On the dorsovolar view of the wrist in the neutral position, Gilula has identified three smooth arcs outlining the proximal and distal carpal rows. Arc I joins the proximal articular surfaces of the scaphoid, the lunate, and the triquetrum; arc II outlines the distal concavities of the same bones; arc III is formed by the proximal convexities of the capitate and the hamate (Fig. 7.81). The diagnostic significance of distortion in both these relations is discussed in the sections that follow.

Scapholunate Dissociation. An injury to the scapholunate ligament may result in intercarpal ligament instability that leads to rotary subluxation of the scaphoid, a type of scapholunate dissociation. On the dorsovolar radiograph of the wrist, which alone is sufficient to diagnose this condition, two signs can be seen that indicate its presence.

The first, known in the literature as the *Terry-Thomas sign*, is characterized by a widening of the space between the scaphoid and the

lunate, which normally measures no more than 2 to 3 mm (Fig. 7.82). Occasionally, this finding is not evident on the dorsovolar view of the wrist in the neutral position but becomes apparent when the wrist is ulnarly deviated (Fig. 7.83).

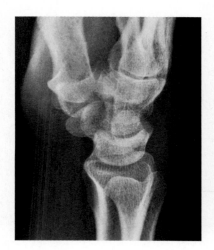

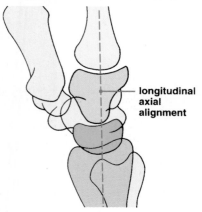

▲
FIGURE 7.80 **Longitudinal axial alignment.** On the lateral radiograph of the wrist, the central axes of the radius, the lunate, the capitate, and the third metacarpal normally form a straight line.

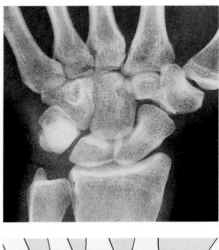

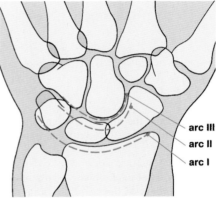

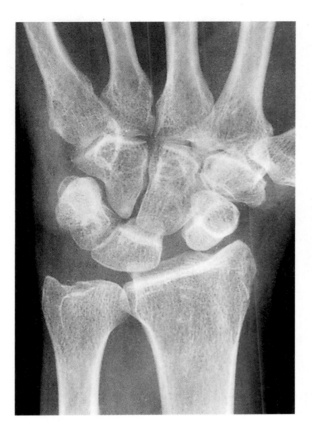

FIGURE 7.81   **Arcs of the carpus.** Three smooth arcs outlining the proximal and distal carpal rows are identifiable on the dorsovolar radiograph of the normal wrist.

FIGURE 7.82   **Terry-Thomas sign.** Dorsovolar radiograph of the wrist shows an abnormally wide space between the scaphoid and the lunate—the Terry-Thomas sign—indicating scapholunate dissociation caused by a tear of the scapholunate ligament.

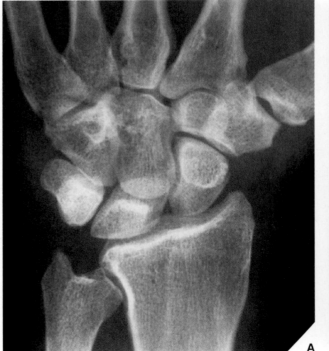

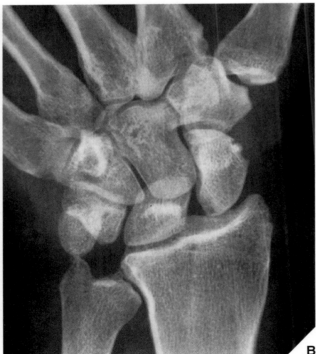

FIGURE 7.83   **Scapholunate dissociation.** (A) On the dorsovolar projection of the wrist in the neutral position, a gap between the scaphoid and the lunate is not well demonstrated. (B) On ulnar deviation, however, the gap becomes apparent, indicating scapholunate dissociation.

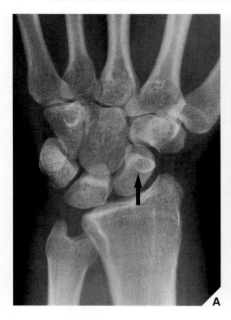
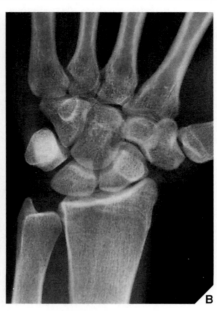

◄ FIGURE 7.84 **Signet-ring sign.** (**A**) On the dorsovolar radiograph of the wrist in the neutral position, rotary subluxation of the scaphoid can be recognized by the cortical ring shadow (*arrow*) that appears projecting over the scaphoid (compare with Fig. 7.81). This phenomenon is caused by the bone's volar tilt and rotation, which cause it to appear foreshortened and its tuberosity to be seen on end. (**B**) A similar picture can be seen on the dorsovolar view of the wrist in radial deviation, but this apparent ring shadow is caused by the normal volar tilt of the scaphoid exaggerated by radial deviation.

The other of these signs, the *signet-ring sign*, receives its name from a cortical ring shadow that is normally *not* seen on the scaphoid on the dorsovolar projection with the wrist in the neutral position (see Fig. 7.81). In rotary subluxation of the scaphoid, however, volar tilt and rotation of the scaphoid cause it to appear foreshortened and the bone's tuberosity to be seen on end, producing the characteristic ring shadow (Fig. 7.84A). To rely on this sign as a diagnostic indicator, dorsovolar films must be obtained with the wrist in the neutral position or in ulnar deviation, because in radial deviation of the wrist, the scaphoid normally tilts volarly, creating a similar radiographic picture (Fig. 7.84B).

When radiographic findings are normal in cases of suspected injury to the intercarpal ligament complex, fluoroscopy combined with videotaping can sometimes contribute to an evaluation of wrist kinematics and to the diagnosis of carpal instability or transient subluxation (Fig. 7.85). An arthrographic examination of the wrist (see Fig. 7.7) is effective when routine radiographic or videofluoroscopic findings are not conclusive. A wrist arthrogram can reveal abnormal communication

between the radiocarpal and the midcarpal compartments that indicates a tear in the scapholunate or lunotriquetral interosseous ligament complex (Figs. 7.86 and 7.87).

MRI may also demonstrate abnormalities of scapholunate and lunotriquetral ligaments. The scapholunate ligament connects the volar, proximal, and dorsal borders of the scaphoid bone to the lunate bone. On MRI, it appears as a structure of low signal intensity. The lunotriquetral ligament connects the volar, proximal, and dorsal borders of the lunate bone to the triquetral bone, also exhibiting low signal intensity. Both ligaments blend almost imperceptibly with the articular cartilages of the joint. The tears of these ligaments are diagnosed on MRI when the single or scattered areas of high signal intensity are identified within the structures or when there is discontinuity of a ligament of low signal intensity traversed by hyperintense fluid (Fig. 7.88). However, according to Schweitzer and colleagues, when MRI results were compared with those of arthrography and arthroscopy, they showed a sensitivity of only 50%, specificity of 86%, and accuracy of 77% for tears of scapholunate

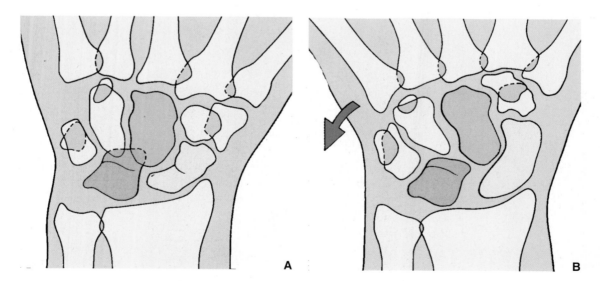

▲ FIGURE 7.85 **Transient subluxation.** Having sustained an injury to the wrist 3 months previously, a patient presented with pain and an audible click on ulnar deviation of the wrist. Routine films in the dorsovolar, dorsovolar in ulnar deviation, and oblique projections were normal. Fluoroscopy combined with videotaping confirmed suspected lunate–capitate instability. On ulnar deviation (the *arrow* indicates the direction of motion), transient scapholunate dissociation and lunate–capitate subluxation became apparent. Schematic diagrams based on the video sequence show the relationship of the carpal bones before (**A**) and after (**B**) the click. In (**B**), note the small gap between the lunate and the capitate caused by transient dorsal subluxation of the capitate.

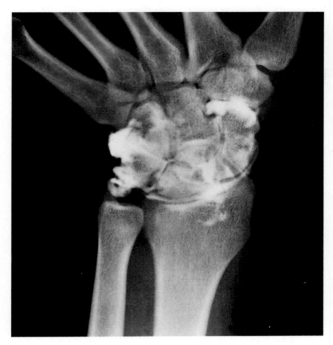

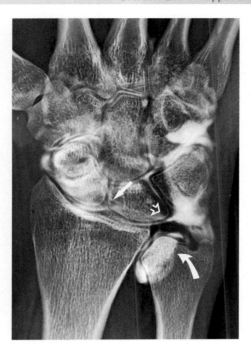

▲
FIGURE 7.86 A tear of the scapholunate ligament. A 21-year-old man injured his right wrist during a wrestling competition. Standard views, including ulnar deviation of the wrist, were unremarkable. Likewise, videofluoroscopic examination did not reveal significant abnormalities. A wrist arthrogram, however, shows a leak of contrast into the midcarpal articulations, indicating a tear in the scapholunate interosseous ligament complex. Note also that the TFCC is intact, because no contrast entered the distal radioulnar joint.

▲
FIGURE 7.87 A tear of the scapholunate and lunotriquetral ligaments. Wrist arthrogram demonstrates tears of the scapholunate (*arrow*) and lunotriquetral (*open arrow*) ligaments. There is also a tear of TFCC (*curved arrow*).

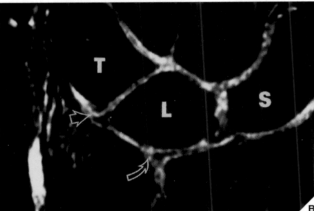

FIGURE 7.88 MRI of a tear of the scapholunate and lunotriquetral ligaments. (**A**) Coronal fat-suppressed T1-weighted image after gadolinium injection to the radiocarpal joint shows a tear of the scapholunate ligament (*arrow*). L, lunate; C, capitate; S, scaphoid. (**B**) Coronal gradient-echo image shows a tear of the lunotriquetral ligament (*arrow*). There is also a tear of the triangular fibrocartilage (*curved arrow*). T, triquetrum; L, lunate; S, scaphoid. (**C**) Coronal T1-weighted fat-suppressed MR arthrographic image of a normal wrist is shown for comparison. *Arrow* points to intact scapholunate ligament, *open arrow* to lunotriquetral ligament, and *curved arrow* to TFCC.

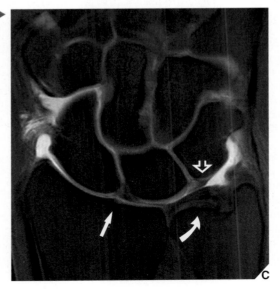

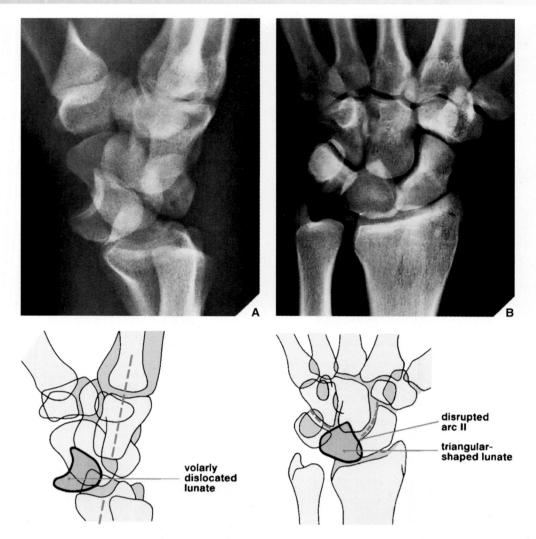

FIGURE 7.89 **Lunate dislocation.** (**A**) On the lateral view of the wrist, lunate dislocation is evident from the break in the longitudinal alignment of the third metacarpal and the capitate over the distal radial surface at the site of the lunate, which is volarly rotated and displaced. (**B**) Dorsovolar projection shows a disrupted arc II at the site of the lunate, indicating malalignment. Note also the triangular appearance of the lunate, a finding virtually pathognomonic of dislocation of this bone.

ligament and 52%, 46%, and 49%, respectively, for lunotriquetral ligament tears. Nonvisualization of the scapholunate ligament was a helpful sign of a tear; however, not seeing the lunotriquetral ligament did not necessarily mean that it was torn.

Lunate and Perilunate Dislocations. Dorsovolar and lateral radiographs of the wrist in the neutral position are usually sufficient to diagnose suspected lunate and perilunate dislocations. As the lateral view clearly demonstrates the normal alignment of the longitudinal axes of the lunate, the capitate, and the third metacarpal over the distal radial surface, a break at any point in this line is pathognomonic of subluxation or dislocation. A lunate dislocation can thus be recognized when its axis is angled away from the distal radial surface, while the capitate remains in its normal alignment (Fig. 7.89A). Similarly, lunate dislocation can also be identified on the dorsovolar projection by the disruption of arc II described by the distal concave surfaces of the scaphoid, the lunate, and the triquetrum as well as the concomitant triangular appearance of the lunate (Fig. 7.89B).

A perilunate dislocation can be recognized on the lateral view of the wrist by the dorsal or volar angulation of the longitudinal axis of the capitate away from its normal central alignment with the lunate and the distal radial surface. The lunate, in this case, remains in articulation with the radius, although there may be some degree of tilt of the lunate because of subluxation associated with perilunate dislocation (Fig. 7.90A). On the dorsovolar view, the overlapping of the proximal and distal carpal rows and a break in arcs II and III at the site of the capitate indicate the presence of a perilunate dislocation (Fig. 7.90B).

Midcarpal Dislocation. This injury is the result of disruption of articulation between the lunate and the triquetrum, secondary to tears of the volar and dorsal radiotriquetral and ulnotriquetral ligaments in addition to the tears of the radiolunotriquetral and lunotriquetral ligaments. Although this abnormality can be diagnosed on the conventional radiography (Fig. 7.91A), CT is usually better suited to demonstrate the position of the lunate, which is volarly subluxed, and the capitate, which is dorsally subluxed (Fig. 7.91B).

Transscaphoid Perilunate Dislocation. When a dislocation of the carpal bones is associated with a fracture, the prefix *trans* indicates which bone is fractured. The most common fracture associated with carpal dislocation is transscaphoid perilunate dislocation. As in the preceding types of carpal dislocations, radiographs in the standard dorsovolar, dorsovolar in ulnar deviation, and lateral projections usually suffice to lead to a firm diagnosis. The normal relations of the carpal bones seen on these views should help to identify the type of abnormality. Although rarely effective in evaluating carpal dislocations, tomographic examination used to be performed when radiographs of the wrist were equivocal as to which carpal bones were dislocated (Fig. 7.92). Other types of associated fractures are less commonly seen (Fig. 7.93).

Scaphoid Dislocation. A dislocation of the scaphoid bone is rare. Two types have been reported: isolated dislocation and dislocation in conjunction with axial carpal disruption. In the former injury, the distal carpal row is normal (Fig. 7.94), whereas in the latter type, there is a disruption of the distal carpal row and proximal migration of the radial half of the carpus (Fig. 7.95). A common factor of this injury is dorsiflexion

FIGURE 7.90 Perilunate dislocation. (**A**) Lateral
radiograph of the wrist demonstrates perilunate dislocation characterized by displacement of the capitate
dorsal to the lunate, which, although slightly volarly
rotated, remains in articulation with the distal radius.
Note the break in the longitudinal alignment of the
third metacarpal and the capitate with the lunate and
the distal radial surface. On the dorsovolar projection
(**B**), perilunate dislocation is evident from the overlapping proximal and distal carpal rows and the resulting
disruption of arcs II and III.

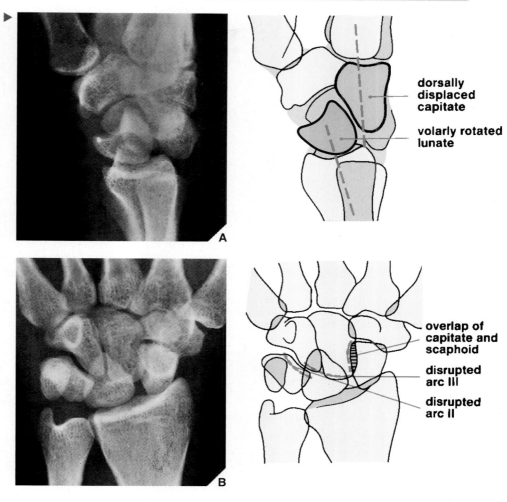

FIGURE 7.91 Midcarpal dislocation. (**A**) Lateral
radiograph of the wrist shows volar subluxation of
the lunate and dorsal subluxation of the capitate,
features of midcarpal dislocation. This injury was
confirmed on the sagittal reformatted CT image
(**B**).

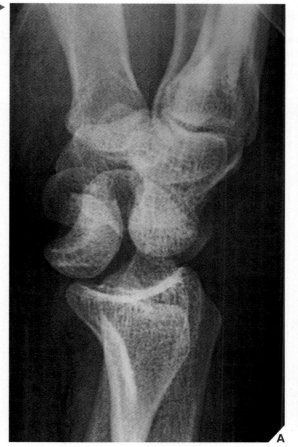
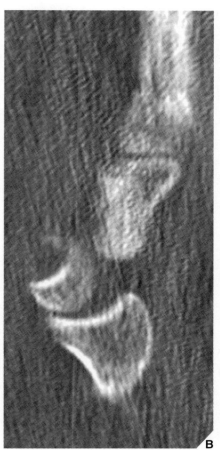

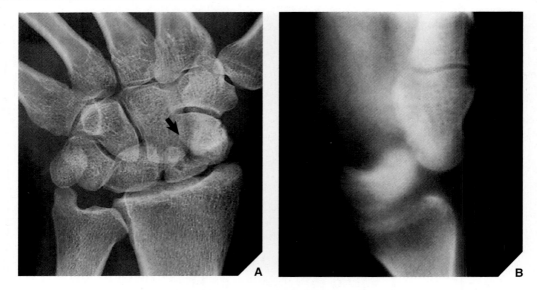

▲
FIGURE 7.92   **Transscaphoid perilunate dislocation. (A)** Dorsovolar radiograph of the wrist in ulnar deviation clearly shows a scaphoid fracture (*arrow*), but the disruptions in the distal carpal arcs are unclear as to the type of dislocation. The lateral view was also inconclusive. **(B)** Lateral tomogram demonstrates that the capitate is displaced dorsal to the lunate, which remains in articulation with the distal radius—the classic appearance of perilunate dislocation.

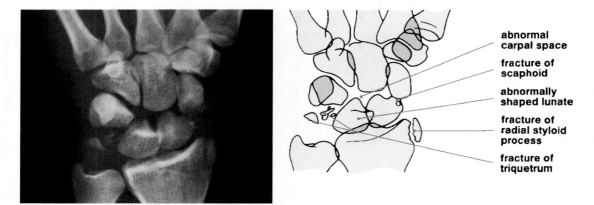

abnormal
carpal space

fracture of
scaphoid

abnormally
shaped lunate

fracture of
radial styloid
process

fracture of
triquetrum

▲
FIGURE 7.93   **Transradial, transscaphoid, transtriquetral lunate dislocation.** Dorsovolar view of the wrist clearly reveals fractures of the radial styloid process, the scaphoid, and the triquetrum. The wide space separating the proximal and the distal carpal rows and the triangular shape of the lunate indicate the possibility of lunate dislocation. Note the disruption in arcs I and II. The lateral view (not shown here) confirmed volar displacement of the lunate and the normal position of the capitate. This abnormality can be described as transradial, transscaphoid, and transtriquetral lunate dislocation.

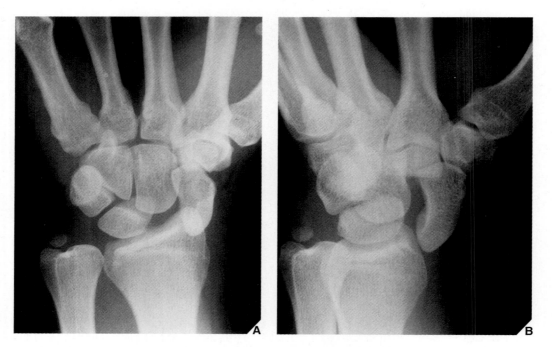

▲
FIGURE 7.94   **Isolated scaphoid dislocation.** Dorsovolar **(A)** and oblique **(B)** radiographs show volar dislocation of the scaphoid. The distal carpal row is not affected and the capitate bone is in anatomic position.

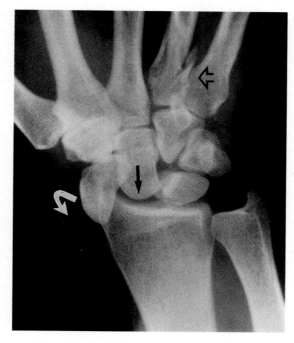

▲
FIGURE 7.95   **Scaphoid dislocation with axial carpal disruption.** Dorsovolar radiograph of the wrist shows radial volar dislocation of the scaphoid bone (*curved arrow*) associated with the proximal migration of the capitate (*arrow*). Note the interruption of the third arc of the carpus (compare with Fig. 7.81). An *open arrow* points to the associated fracture of the fourth metacarpal bone. (Courtesy of Dr. Robert M. Szabo, Sacramento, California.)

and ulnar deviation of the wrist when a sudden force causes a distraction effect on the radial aspect of the wrist, with subsequent ejection of the scaphoid. Isolated dislocations of the scaphoid are generally treated with closed reduction. Dislocations associated with axial carpal disruption mandate open reduction and internal fixation to stabilize the carpus.

Carpal Instability
Various carpal instabilities have been described. The most common include dorsal intercalated segment instability (DISI) and volar intercalated segment instability (VISI).

To explain the carpal instability, Lichtman and colleagues developed the carpal ring theory. The proximal carpal row, which represents the intercalated segment, moves as a unit firmly stabilized by interosseous ligaments. Controlled mobility occurs at the scaphotrapezium (radial link) and triquetrohamate (ulnar link) joints (Fig. 7.96). With a break in the ring, either within bony structures or within ligaments, the proximal carpal row no longer moves as a unit. The lunate will then tilt either dorsally or volarly in response to this uncontrolled mobility, manifested by either DISI or VISI (Fig. 7.97). DISI is the most common deformity.

THE CARPAL RING THEORY

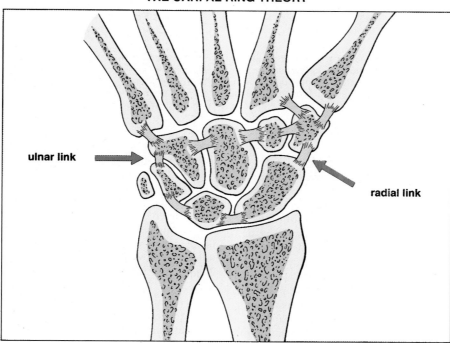

ulnar link

radial link

▲
FIGURE 7.96   **The carpal ring theory.** The proximal carpal row (intercalated segment) moves as a unit firmly stabilized by interosseous ligaments. *Controlled* mobility occurs at the scaphotrapezium (*radial link*) and triquetrohamate (*ulnar link*) joints. A break in the ring, either bony or ligamentous, can produce *uncontrolled* mobility, manifested by either DISI or VISI. (Modified from Lichtman DM et al., 1981, with permission.)

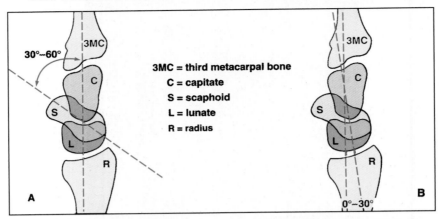

SCAPHOLUNATE ANGLE

CAPITOLUNATE ANGLE

3MC = third metacarpal bone
C = capitate
S = scaphoid
L = lunate
R = radius

in normal wrist the scapholunate
angle is between 30°–60°

in normal wrist the capitolunate
angle is between 0°–30°

DISI AND VISI DEFORMITIES

DISI

Dorsal Intercalated Segment Instability
(Dorsiflexion Carpal Instability)

VISI

Volar Intercalated Segment Instability
(Volarflexion Carpal Instability)

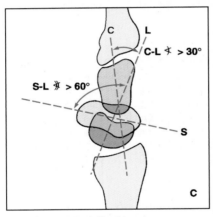

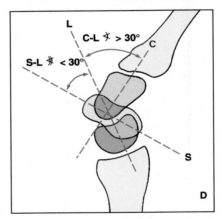

1. dorsal tilt of lunate
2. volar tilt of scaphoid

1. volar tilt of lunate
2. dorsal tilt of capitate

▲
FIGURE 7.97 DISI and VISI. (A) Normal scapholunate angle. The scapholunate angle is formed by the intersection of longitudinal axes of scaphoid and lunate and normally measures from 30 to 60 degrees. (B) Normal capitolunate angle. The capitolunate angle is formed by the intersection of the capitate axis (drawn from the midpoint of its head to the center of its distal articular surface) and the lunate axis (drawn through the center of its proximal and distal poles) and normally measures from 0 to 30 degrees. (C) In DISI, the scapholunate angle measures more than 60 degrees and the capitolunate angle more than 30 degrees. (D) In VISI, the scapholunate angle measures less than 30 degrees, and the capitolunate angle measures much more than 30 degrees. (Modified from Gilula LA, Weeks PM, 1978, with permission.)

It is recognized on the true lateral view of the wrist by dorsal tilt of the lunate, frequently associated with volar (palmar) tilt of the scaphoid (the capitolunate angle measures more than 30 degrees, and the scapholunate angle more than 60 degrees) (Fig. 7.97C). It may be caused by either bony or ligamentous disruption in the ring on the radial side of the wrist. Most commonly, a scaphoid fracture with or without nonunion and scapholunate ligamentous dissociation may be the cause of this deformity. VISI is recognized when a volar tilt of the lunate is noted on the true lateral view frequently accompanied by a dorsal tilt of the capitate (the capitolunate angle measures more than 30 degrees and the scapholunate angle less than 30 degrees) (Fig. 7.97D). It is caused by a break in the ring on the ulnar side of the wrist. Most frequently, it is the ligamentous dissociation and triquetrohamate joint disruption that lead to this deformity. According to McNiesh, when breaks in the ring occur on the radial and ulnar sides as, for instance, in concurrent scapholunate and lunotriquetral ligamentous dissociation, the VISI pattern predominates.

Injury to the Hand

Fractures of the Metacarpal Bones

Bennett and Rolando Fractures. Bennett and Rolando fractures are *intraarticular* fractures that occur at the base of the first metacarpal bone. From the perspective of orthopedic management, it is important to distinguish these from the *extraarticular* types, which are transverse or oblique fractures of the first metacarpal just distal to the carpometacarpal joint (Fig. 7.98). Failure to diagnose and treat properly intraarticular metacarpal fractures may result in protracted pain, stiffness, and posttraumatic arthritis caused by incongruity of articular surfaces.

The *Bennett fracture* is a fracture of the proximal end of the first metacarpal that extends into the first carpometacarpal joint. Usually, a small fragment on the volar aspect of the base of the first metacarpal remains in articulation with the trapezium bone, while the rest of the first metacarpal is dorsally and radially dislocated as the result of pull of the abductor pollicis longus (Fig. 7.99). For this

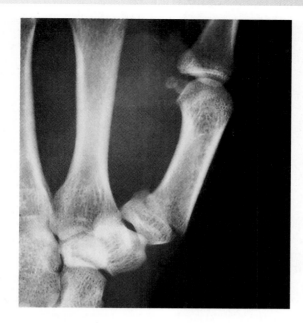

▲
FIGURE 7.98 Extraarticular fracture. An extraarticular fracture at the base of the first metacarpal should not be confused with Bennett and Rolando fractures, which are intraarticular.

reason, the injury should properly be called a fracture–dislocation. The diagnosis and evaluation of the Bennett fracture are readily made on conventional radiographs of the hand in the dorsovolar, oblique, and lateral projections.

The *Rolando fracture* is a comminuted Bennett fracture; the fracture line may have a Y, V, or T configuration (Fig. 7.100). Because there may be multiple fragments, the routine radiographic projections used to diagnose the Bennett fracture occasionally need to be supplemented by CT to localize comminuted fragments and to exclude the possibility of entrapment of a small osseous fragment in the first carpometacarpal joint.

Boxer's Fracture. Boxer's fracture is a fracture of the metacarpal neck with volar angulation of the distal fragment. It may occur in any of the metacarpal bones but is most commonly seen in the fifth metacarpal. The fracture and deformity are sufficiently demonstrated on conventional radiographs of the hand in the dorsovolar and oblique projections (Fig. 7.101). Because comminution frequently accompanies this type of fracture, it is important to determine its extent. Comminution may predispose the fracture after reduction to settle into an angular

deformation. The oblique projection usually suffices to determine the extent of comminution (see Fig. 7.101B).

Injury to the Soft Tissue of the Hand
Gamekeeper's Thumb. Gamekeeper's thumb results from a disruption of the ulnar collateral ligament of the first metacarpophalangeal joint, often accompanied by a fracture of the base of the proximal phalanx. The abnormality is termed "gamekeeper's thumb" because it was originally seen affecting Scottish game wardens who injured the ulnar collateral ligament because of the method they used to kill rabbits. Currently, because it is more frequently seen in skiing accidents, the term "skier's thumb" is applied. This type of injury can also occur in break-dancers (break-dancer's thumb). When ruptured, the torn end of the ulnar collateral ligament can become displaced superficially to the adductor pollicis aponeurosis. This is known as the *Stener lesion*. Standard dorsovolar and oblique radiographs of the thumb usually suffice to demonstrate the associated fracture (Fig. 7.102A,B), but the full evaluation requires an abduction–stress film of the thumb when this

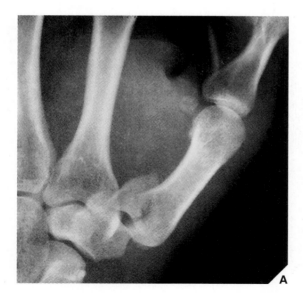

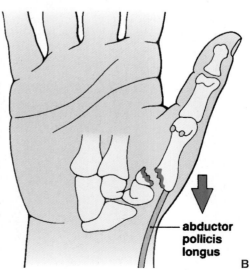

abductor pollicis longus

A   B

▲
FIGURE 7.99 Bennett fracture. A 27-year-old man who was involved in a fistfight presented with pain localized in the right thenar. Dorsovolar radiograph of the hand (**A**) shows the typical appearance of Bennett fracture. A small fragment at the base of the first metacarpal remains in articulation with the trapezium, while the rest of the bone is dorsally and radially dislocated. The accompanying schematic diagram (**B**) shows the pathomechanics of this injury.

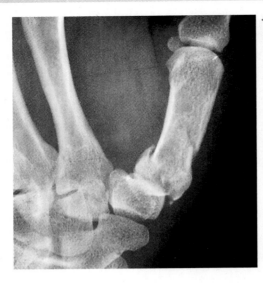

FIGURE 7.100 Rolando fracture. Oblique radiograph of the right hand shows a comminuted intraarticular fracture of the proximal end of the first metacarpal.

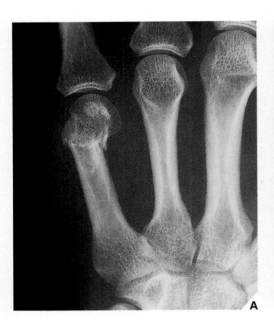

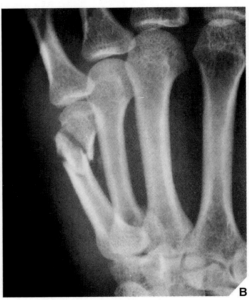

FIGURE 7.101 Boxer's fracture. (A) Dorsovolar radiograph of the right hand demonstrates a fracture of the fifth metacarpal with volar angulation of the distal fragment—a simple boxer's fracture. When comminution is present, it is essential for its prognostic value to demonstrate the extent of fracture lines, because such fractures are frequently unstable. The oblique projection (B) usually suffices to determine the extent of comminution.

A

B

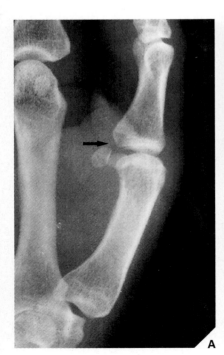

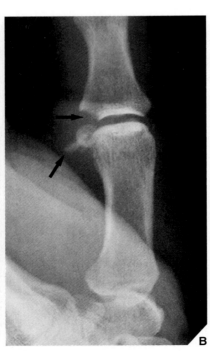

FIGURE 7.102 Gamekeeper's thumb. Having fallen on his hand on the ski slopes, a 38-year-old man presented with pain at the base of his right thumb. Physical examination revealed instability in the first metacarpophalangeal joint. Oblique (A) and dorsovolar (B) radiographs of the right thumb show a fracture of the base of the proximal phalanx (arrows) and local soft-tissue swelling—findings associated with gamekeeper's thumb.

A

B

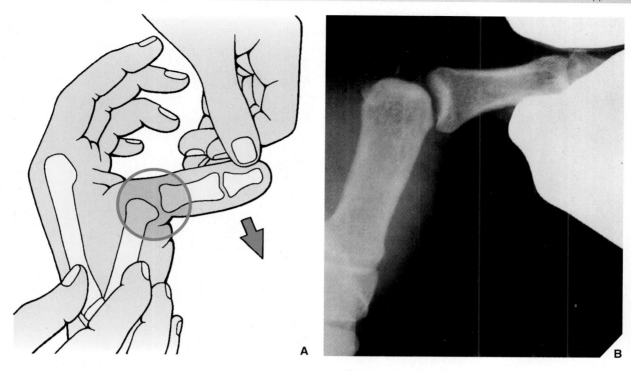

A

B

FIGURE 7.103 **Gamekeeper's thumb.** In another patient, dorsovolar and lateral radiographs of the first phalanx (not shown here) did not show a fracture, but because instability of the first metacarpophalangeal joint was indicated on physical examination (**A**), an abduction–stress film of the thumb was obtained. The stress radiograph (**B**) demonstrates subluxation of the joint by an increase to more than 30 degrees in the angle between the first metacarpal and the proximal phalanx of the thumb, confirming gamekeeper's thumb.

condition is suspected. An increase to more than 30 degrees in the angle between the first metacarpal and the proximal phalanx is a characteristic finding in gamekeeper's thumb, indicating subluxation (Fig. 7.103A,B). Arthrographic examination of the thumb may also be performed to assess disruption, displacement, or entrapment of the ulnar collateral ligament (Fig. 7.104).

Currently, MRI is the procedure of choice to investigate this injury (Fig. 7.105), particularly to detect a displaced tear of the ulnar collateral ligament (Fig. 7.106). Likewise, ultrasound has proved to be a simple, reliable, and cost-effective tool for recognition of the Stener lesion.

FIGURE 7.104 **Gamekeeper's thumb.** An arthrogram ▶ of the first metacarpophalangeal joint demonstrates the characteristic findings in gamekeeper's thumb. The leak of contrast along the ulnar side of the head of the first metacarpal (*arrow*) indicates a tear of the ulnar collateral ligament. (Courtesy of Dr. D. Resnick, San Diego, California.)

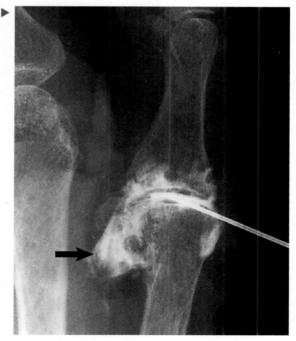

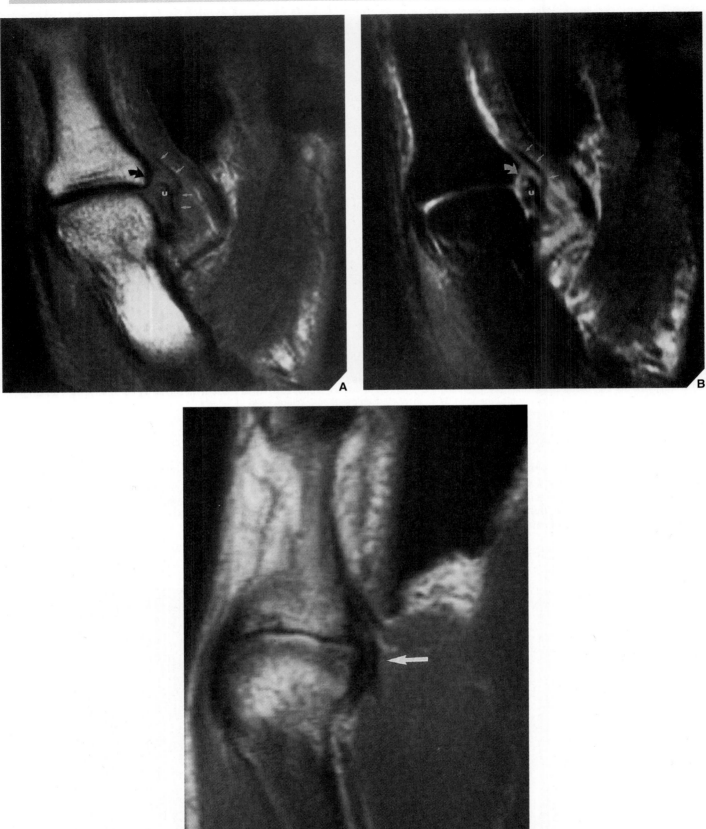

FIGURE 7.105 **MRI of the gamekeeper's thumb.** Coronal T1-weighted (**A**) and coronal STIR (**B**) images show a tear of the ulnar collateral ligament (*u*) of the first metacarpophalangeal joint (*curved arrows*). The torn ligament is not displaced, maintaining its longitudinal orientation (*small arrows*). (**C**) Coronal fat-suppressed T2-weighted image shows a normal appearance of intact ulnar collateral ligament (*arrow*).

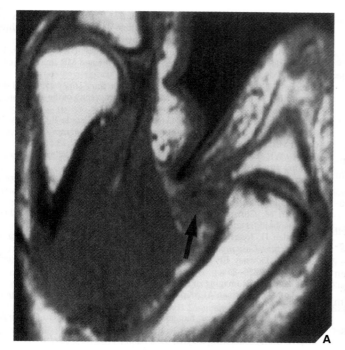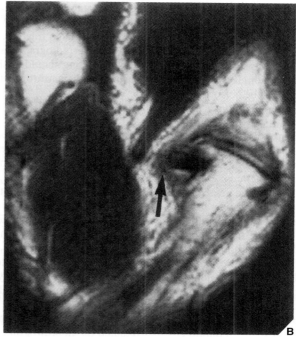

FIGURE 7.106   MRI of the Stener lesion. (A) Coronal T1-weighted MR image shows a disruption of the ulnar collateral ligament (*arrow*). The normal low-intensity signal of this structure is not present. **(B)** Coronal T2-weighted MR image shows displacement of the proximal fragment of this ligament away from the joint and its perpendicular rather than longitudinal orientation (*arrow*), characteristic of the Stener lesion.

PRACTICAL POINTS TO REMEMBER

Distal Forearm

[1] For a full evaluation of trauma on the posteroanterior radiograph of the distal forearm, it is important to recognize:
  • ulnar variance: neutral, negative, and positive
  • the radial angle, which normally ranges from 15 to 25 degrees
  • the radial length.

[2] For a full evaluation of trauma on the lateral radiograph of the distal forearm, it is important to recognize the volar tilt of the articular surface of the radius, which normally ranges from 10 to 25 degrees.

[3] A complete evaluation of the Colles fracture should take into consideration:
  • the degree of foreshortening of the radius
  • the direction of displacement of the distal fragment
  • intraarticular extension of the fracture line
  • associated fracture of the ulna.

[4] Learn to distinguish the Colles fracture from the:
  • Barton fracture, dorsal and volar types, which are best demonstrated on the lateral projection
  • Hutchinson (or chauffeur's) fracture, which is best seen on the posteroanterior view
  • Smith fracture, which is best evaluated on the lateral projection.

[5] Frykman classification of distal radius fractures according to the location of the fracture line (intraarticular versus extraarticular) and association of distal ulna fracture has a practical prognostic value and serves as a guide to orthopedic management.

[6] With the finding of a dislocation in the distal radioulnar articulation, look for an associated fracture of the radius—Galeazzi fracture–dislocation.

[7] Learn to distinguish ulnar impingement syndrome from ulnar impaction (ulnolunate abutment) syndrome. The former is caused by short distal ulna that impinges on the distal radius. The latter, frequently associated with positive ulnar variance, leads to compression of the distal ulna on the medial surface of the lunate bone.

[8] A common sequela of trauma to the distal radioulnar joint, a tear of the TFCC can be confirmed or excluded by a single-contrast arthrogram of the wrist or MRI examination.

Wrist

[1] If clinical history and physical examination are consistent with a scaphoid fracture and routine radiographs appear normal, then either CT or MRI is the next logical step.

[2] CT examination is effective in demonstrating and evaluating the so-called humpback deformity of the scaphoid.

[3] Delayed diagnosis and treatment of a scaphoid fracture may result in nonunion, osteonecrosis, and posttraumatic arthritis.

[4] Triquetral fracture is best diagnosed on the lateral and pronated oblique views of the wrist. If conventional radiographs appear normal, then CT can confirm or exclude the diagnosis.

[5] Fractures of the hamate body are best demonstrated on the lateral and pronated oblique projections.

[6] In a suspected fracture of the hook of the hamate, look for the oval cortical ring shadow projecting over the hamate on the dorsovolar view of the wrist. If this "eye" of the hamate is absent, indistinctly outlined, or sclerotic, then hamulus fracture is highly probable.

[7] A fracture of the pisiform is best demonstrated on the supinated oblique and carpal tunnel projections.

[8] In Kienböck disease, the choice of surgical procedures depends on a demonstration of the integrity of the lunate. MRI may reveal osteonecrosis in the early stages.

[9] Hamatolunate impaction syndrome results from an anatomic variant of the lunate bone that has an "extra" facet articulating with the hamate bone. Repeated contact of these bones leads to bone marrow edema and chondromalacia, best demonstrated on MRI.

[10] Lunate, perilunate, and midcarpal dislocations are readily identified on the lateral radiographs by disruption of the normal central alignment of the longitudinal axes of the capitate and lunate over the distal radial surface:
  • in lunate dislocation, disruption of the alignment occurs at the lunate

Lower Limb I
Pelvic Girdle and Proximal Femur

Pelvic Girdle

Fractures involving the structures of the pelvic girdle, which are usually sustained in motor vehicle accidents or falls from heights, represent only a small percentage of all skeletal injuries. Their importance, however, lies in the significant morbidity and mortality associated with them, which is usually caused by accompanying injury to the major blood vessels, nerves, and lower urinary tract. Because the clinical signs of pelvic trauma may not always be obvious, radiologic examination is essential to establish a correct diagnosis. Fractures of the acetabulum constitute approximately 20% of all pelvic fractures, and they may or may not be associated with dislocation in the hip joint. Fractures of the proximal (upper) femur, occasionally referred to as hip fractures, occur frequently in the elderly, often as a result of minimal injury. They are seen more frequently in women than in men (2:1), with intracapsular fractures of the proximal femur having an even higher female-to-male ratio (5:1).

Anatomic–Radiologic Considerations

The main imaging modalities used in the evaluation of traumatic conditions of the pelvic girdle, acetabulum, and proximal femur include conventional radiography and computed tomography (CT). Other ancillary techniques are also essential for a complete evaluation of concomitant soft-tissue and pelvic–organ injuries: angiography for the pelvic blood vessels and cystourethrography for the lower urinary tract. Radionuclide bone scan and magnetic resonance imaging (MRI) may also be necessary to disclose subtle fractures of the femoral neck and early stages of posttraumatic osteonecrosis of the femoral head.

The standard and special radiographic projections used to evaluate injury to the pelvic girdle and proximal femur include the anteroposterior view of the pelvis, the anterior and posterior oblique views of the pelvis, the anteroposterior view of the hip, and the frog-lateral view of the hip. At times, the groin-lateral or other special projections may also be required.

Most traumatic conditions involving the sacral wings, the iliac bones, the ischium, the pubis, and the femoral head and neck can be evaluated sufficiently on the *anteroposterior* projection of the pelvis and hip (Fig. 8.1). This view also demonstrates an important anatomic relation of the longitudinal axes of the femoral neck and shaft. Normally, the angle formed by these axes ranges from 125 to 135 degrees. This measurement is valuable in determining displacement in femoral

neck fractures. A varus configuration is characterized by a decrease in this angle, and a valgus configuration by an increase in this angle (Fig. 8.2). The anteroposterior view, however, is frequently not sufficient to provide adequate evaluation of the entire sacral bone, the sacroiliac joints, and the acetabulum. Demonstration of the sacroiliac joints requires either a posteroanterior projection, which is obtained to greater advantage with 25 to 30 degrees caudal angulation of the radiographic tube, or an anteroposterior view with 30 to 35 degrees cephalad angulation. The latter projection, known as the *Ferguson* view, is also helpful in more effectively evaluating injury to the sacral bone and the pubic and ischial rami (Fig. 8.3). Oblique projections, known as *Judet* views, are necessary to evaluate the acetabulum. The *anterior* (*internal*) *oblique* projection helps delineate the iliopubic (anterior) column and the posterior lip (rim) of the acetabulum (Fig. 8.4). The *posterior* (*external*) *oblique* projection delineates the ilioischial (posterior) column and the anterior acetabular rim (Fig. 8.5). Of value in demonstrating the structures of the proximal femur and hip, the *frog-lateral* projection allows adequate evaluation of fractures of the femoral head and the greater and the lesser trochanters (Fig. 8.6). Demonstration of the anterior and posterior aspects of the femoral head as well as the anterior rim of the acetabulum may require a *groin-lateral* projection of the hip, which is particularly useful in evaluating anterior or posterior displacement of fragments in proximal femoral fractures and the degree of rotation of the femoral head. This projection, by providing an almost true lateral image of the proximal femur, also demonstrates an important anatomic feature, the angle of anteversion of the femoral neck, which normally ranges from 25 to 30 degrees (Fig. 8.7).

Ancillary imaging techniques play a crucial role in the evaluation of traumatic conditions of the pelvis and acetabulum, providing essential and often otherwise unobtainable information that helps the orthopedic surgeon determine the method of treatment and assess the prognosis of pelvic and acetabular fractures. Because the surgical management of such fractures is based on the stability of the fragments and the presence or absence of intra-articular extension of the fracture line and intra-articular fragments, CT examination is necessary to provide information that is not available from the standard and special projections of conventional radiography (Fig. 8.8; see also Figs. 8.22B,C, and 8.23B–D). In addition to ascertaining the size, number, and position of the major fragments and data about the condition of the weight-bearing parts of the joint and the configuration of the fracture fragments, CT can delineate soft tissue and concomitant injury to soft-tissue structures. However, in

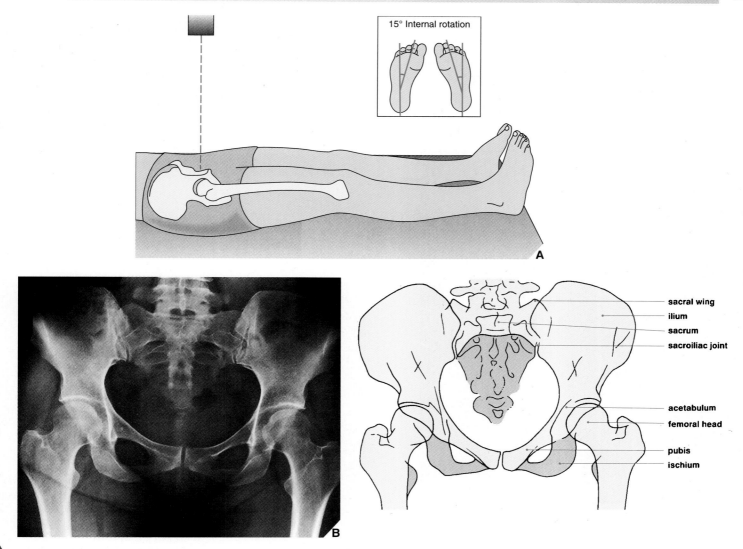

▲
FIGURE 8.1   **Anteroposterior view. (A)** For the anteroposterior view of the pelvis and hip, the patient is supine with the feet in slight (15 degrees) internal rotation (*inset*), which compensates for the normal anteversion of the femoral neck (see Fig. 8.7B), elongating its image. For a view of the entire pelvis, the central beam is directed vertically toward the midportion of the pelvis; for selective examination of either hip joint, it is directed toward the affected femoral head. **(B)** The radiograph in this projection demonstrates the iliac bones, the sacrum, the pubis, and the ischium, as well as the femoral heads and necks and both the greater and the lesser trochanters. The acetabula are partially obscured by the overlying femoral heads, and the sacroiliac joints are seen en face.

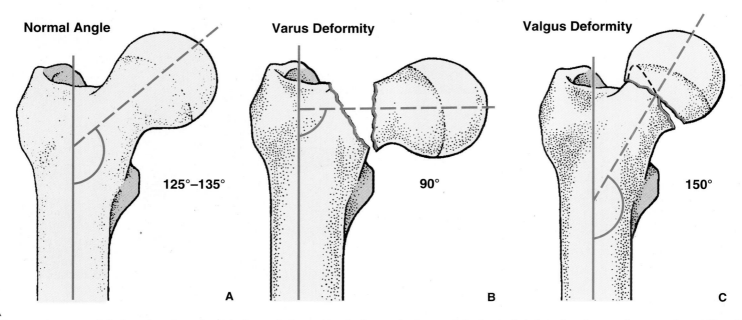

▲
FIGURE 8.2   **Femoral shaft and neck angles. (A)** The angle formed by the longitudinal axes of the femoral shaft and neck normally ranges from 125 to 135 degrees. In the evaluation of displacement in femoral neck fractures, a decrease in this angle **(B)** is known as a varus deformity, while an increase **(C)** characterizes a valgus deformity.

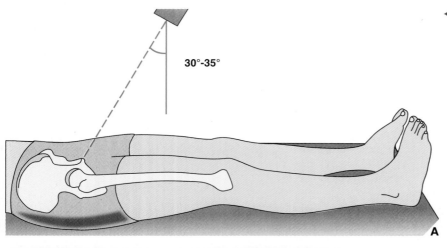

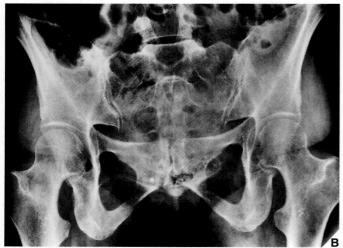

◄ **FIGURE 8.3** Ferguson view. (**A**) For the angled anteroposterior (Ferguson) view of the pelvis, the patient is in the same position as for the standard anteroposterior projection. The radiographic tube, however, is angled approximately 30 to 35 degrees cephalad, and the central beam is directed toward the midportion of the pelvis. (**B**) The radiograph in this projection provides a tangential view of the sacroiliac joints and the sacral bone. The pubic and ischial rami are also well demonstrated.

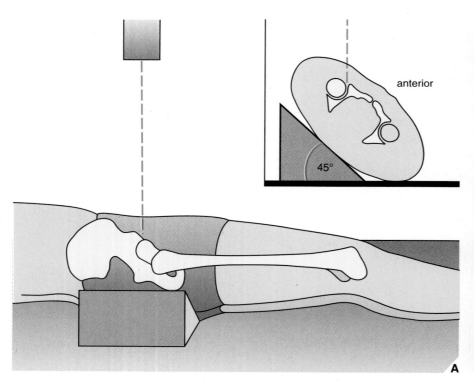

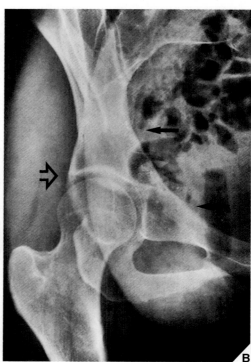

▲ **FIGURE 8.4** Anterior oblique view. (**A**) For the anterior oblique (Judet) view of the pelvis, the patient is supine and anteriorly rotated, with the affected hip elevated 45 degrees (*inset*). The central beam is directed vertically toward the affected hip. (**B**) On the radiograph in this projection, the iliopubic (anterior) column (*arrows*) (see Fig. 8.19) and the posterior lip of the acetabulum (*open arrow*) are well delineated.

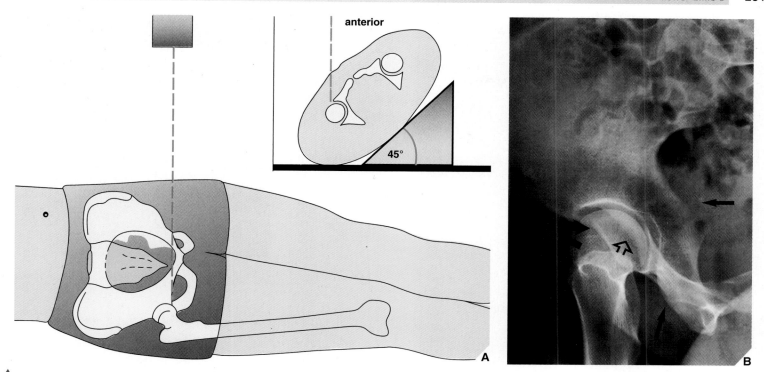

FIGURE 8.5 Posterior oblique view. (**A**) For the posterior oblique (Judet) view of the pelvis, the patient is supine and anteriorly rotated, with the unaffected hip elevated 45 degrees (*inset*). The central beam is directed vertically through the affected hip. (**B**) On the radiograph obtained in this projection, the ilioischial (posterior) column (*arrows*), the posterior acetabular lip (*open arrow*), and the anterior acetabular rim (*curved arrow*) are well demonstrated (see Fig. 8.19).

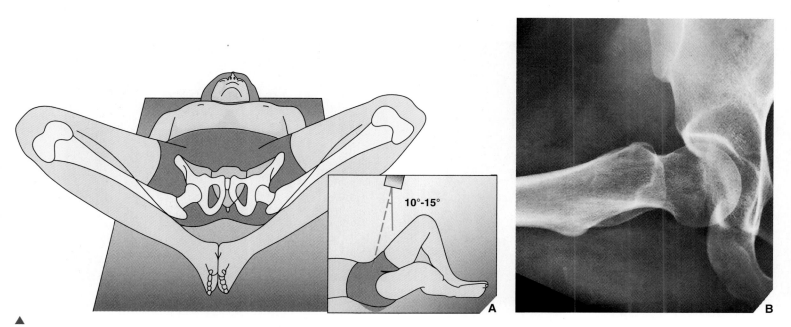

FIGURE 8.6 Frog-lateral view. (**A**) For the frog-lateral view of the proximal femur and hip, the patient is supine with the knees flexed, the soles of the feet together, and the thighs maximally abducted. For simultaneous imaging of both hips, the central beam is directed vertically or with 10 to 15 degrees cephalad angulation to a point slightly above the pubic symphysis (*inset*); for selective examination of one hip, it is directed toward the affected hip joint. (**B**) The radiograph obtained in this projection demonstrates the lateral aspect of the femoral head and both trochanters.

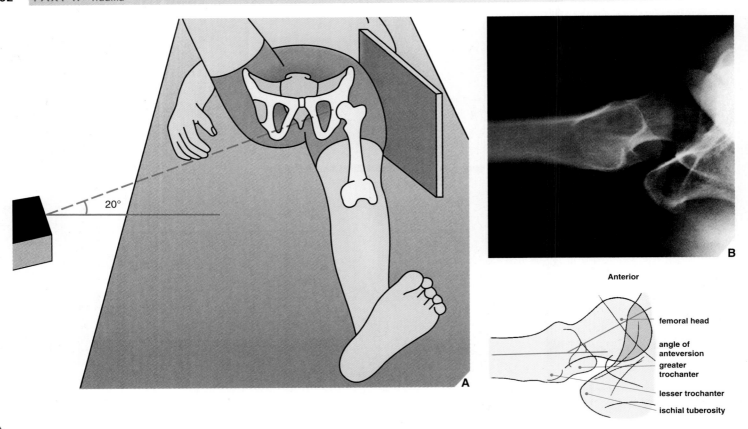

▲
FIGURE 8.7 **Groin-lateral view.** (**A**) For the groin-lateral view of the hip, the patient is supine with the affected extremity extended and the opposite leg elevated and abducted. The cassette is placed against the affected hip on the lateral aspect, and the central beam is directed horizontally toward the groin with approximately 20 degrees cephalad angulation. (**B**) The radiograph obtained in this projection provides almost a true lateral image of the femoral head, thereby allowing evaluation of its anterior and posterior aspects. It also demonstrates the anteversion of the femoral neck, which normally ranges from 25 to 30 degrees.

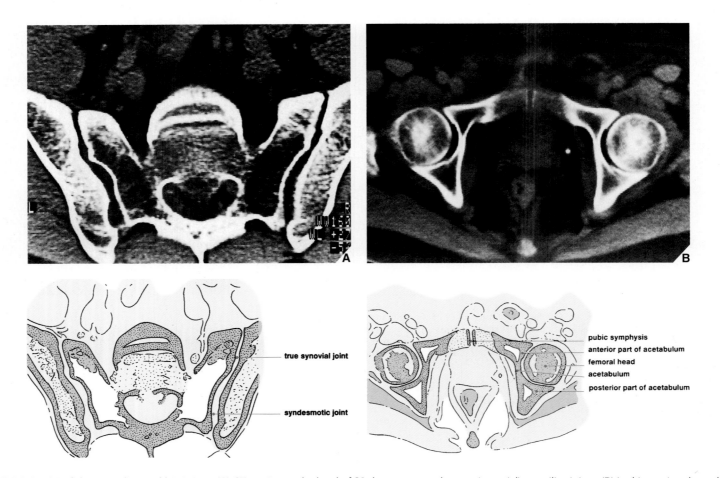

▲
FIGURE 8.8 **CT of the sacroiliac and hip joints.** (**A**) CT section at the level of S2 demonstrates the true (synovial) sacroiliac joints. (**B**) In this section through the hip joints, the relation of the femoral heads to the acetabula can be evaluated sufficiently. The pubic bone and the pubic symphysis are also well delineated.

TABLE 8.1 Standard and Special Radiographic Projections for Evaluating Injury to the Pelvis, Acetabulum, and Proximal Femur

Projection	Demonstration	Projection	Demonstration
Anteroposterior	Angle of femoral neck	*Oblique* (Judet views)	
	Radiographic landmarks (lines) relating to acetabulum:	Anterior (internal)	Iliopubic line
	Iliopubic (iliopectineal)		Fractures of
	Ilioischial		Anterior (iliopubic) column
	Teardrop		Posterior acetabular rim
	Acetabular roof	Posterior (external)	Quadrilateral plate
	Anterior acetabular rim		Fractures of
	Posterior acetabular rim		Posterior (ilioischial) column
	Varus and valgus deformities		Anterior acetabular rim
	Avulsion fractures	*Frog-Lateral*	Fractures of
	Malgaigne fracture		Femoral head and neck
	Fractures of		Greater and lesser trochanters
	Ilium (Duverney)	*Groin-Lateral*	Angle of anteversion of femoral head
	Ischium		
	Pubis		Anterior and posterior cortices of femoral neck
	Sacrum (in some cases)		
	Femoral head and neck		Ischial tuberosity
	Dislocations in hip joint		Rotation and displacement of femoral head in subcapital fractures
With 30–35 degrees cephalad angulation (Ferguson) (or posteroanterior with or without 25–30 degrees caudal angulation)	Fractures of		
	Sacrum		
	Pubis ramus		
	Ischium		
	Injury to sacroiliac joints		

cases of severe injury when immediate surgical intervention is required, obtaining CT scans may be time consuming and impractical. In such cases, conventional radiographs can be obtained more quickly, allowing more rapid recognition of the type of injury. CT is particularly effective in the postsurgical assessment of the alignment of fragments and fracture healing.

MRI offers superior capabilities for evaluating traumatic conditions of the hip. In particular, it has been shown to provide a rapid, precise, and cost-effective diagnosis of radiographically occult hip fractures and may help reveal traumatic lesions such as bone contusions (trabecular microfractures) as the cause of hip pain when the history of trauma is unknown. MRI is also effective in the diagnosis of posttraumatic osteonecrosis of the femoral head and can identify and quantify the muscle injury and joint effusion/hemarthrosis that invariably accompany traumatic anterior and posterior dislocation in the hip joint.

The urinary system is frequently at risk in pelvic fractures. Bladder injuries have been reported in 6% and urethral injuries in 10% of patients with pelvic fractures. The evaluation of such conditions requires contrast examination of the urinary system by means of computed tomography (CT), intravenous urography (IVP), and cystourethrography. Pelvic arteriography and venography may also be required to evaluate injury to the vascular system. In addition to its diagnostic value, arteriography can be combined with an interventional procedure, such as embolization, to control hemorrhage.

For a summary of the preceding discussion in tabular form, see Tables 8.1 and 8.2 and Figure 8.9.

TABLE 8.2 Ancillary Imaging Techniques for Evaluating Injury to the Pelvis, Acetabulum, and Proximal Femur

Technique	Demonstration	Technique	Demonstration
Computed Tomography	Position of fragments and extension of fracture line in complex fractures, particularly of pelvis and acetabulum	*Radionuclide Imaging* (scintigraphy, bone scan)	Occult fractures
			Stress fractures
			Posttraumatic osteonecrosis
	Weight-bearing parts of joints	*Intravenous Urography* (IVP)	Concomitant injury to ureters, urinary bladder, and urethra
	Sacroiliac joints	*Cystourethrography*	
	Intraarticular fragments		
	Soft-tissue injuries	*Angiography* (arteriography, venography)	Injury to vascular system
	Concomitant injury to ureters, urinary bladder, and urethra		
MRI	Soft-tissue injuries		
	Posttraumatic osteonecrosis		
	Occult fractures		
	Bone contusions (trabecular microfractures)		
CT Angiography	Injury to the vascular system		

This system, which corresponds to the more traditional categorization of pelvic fractures into stable and unstable, has practical value in allowing sufficient evaluation of pelvic injuries to be made on the anteroposterior projection in patients requiring immediate surgical intervention when CT scans would be impractical to obtain. It also provides correlations between the type of force delivered to the pelvis and the concomitant ligamentous and pelvic–organ injury that can be expected. In anteroposterior compression-type injuries, for example, the anterior sacroiliac ligaments, the sacrotuberous–sacroiliac ligament complex, and the symphysis ligaments are damaged. This type of injury may also be associated with urethral and urinary bladder rupture and damage to the pelvic blood vessels. In lateral compression injuries, rupture of the posterior sacroiliac ligament and/or the sacrospinous–sacrotuberous ligament complex may result. Injury to the urinary tract may or may not be present. In vertical shear injuries, the ipsilateral posterior and anterior sacroiliac, the sacrospinous–sacrotuberous, and the anterior symphysis ligaments are usually ruptured. Vertical shear injuries are frequently accompanied by damage to the sciatic nerve and pelvic blood vessels, often resulting in massive hemorrhage. The discussion that follows, however, focuses on the more traditional pedagogic categories of pelvic trauma.

Fractures of the Pelvis

Avulsion Fractures. Usually involving the anterosuperior or anteroinferior iliac spine or the ischial tuberosity, avulsion fractures, which are classified as stable fractures (Fig. 8.12, see also Fig. 8.10), most commonly occur in athletes as a result of forcible muscular contraction: the *sartorius muscle* and *tensor fasciae latae* in avulsion of the anterosuperior iliac spine; the *rectus femoris muscle* in avulsion of the anteroinferior iliac spine; the *hip rotators* in avulsion of greater trochanter; the *iliopsoas* in avulsion of the lesser trochanter; the *adductors* and *gracilis* in avulsion of pubic bone; and the *hamstrings* in avulsion of the ischial tuberosity. Most fractures of these structures are apparent on a single anteroposterior radiograph of the pelvis (Fig. 8.13). However, confusion in diagnosis may arise when healing occurs by exuberant callus formation, at which time or after full ossification such fractures may be mistaken for neoplasms. Another entity that may mimic avulsion injury to the pelvis is the so-called pelvic digit, a congenital anomaly characterized by a bony formation in the soft tissue about the pelvic bones (Fig. 8.14).

Malgaigne Fracture. This unstable injury, involving one hemipelvis, most commonly consists of unilateral fractures of the superior and inferior pubic rami and disruption of the ipsilateral sacroiliac joint (see Fig. 8.11). In the variants of this type of injury, the unilateral fractures of the pubic rami may be accompanied by a fracture through the sacral wing near the sacroiliac joint or through the ilium (see Fig. 8.11). Separation of the pubic symphysis may coexist with such injuries, and cephalad or posterior displacement of the entire hemipelvis may occur. The Malgaigne fracture, which is recognized clinically by shortening of the lower extremity, is readily demonstrated on the anteroposterior radiograph of the pelvis (Fig. 8.15).

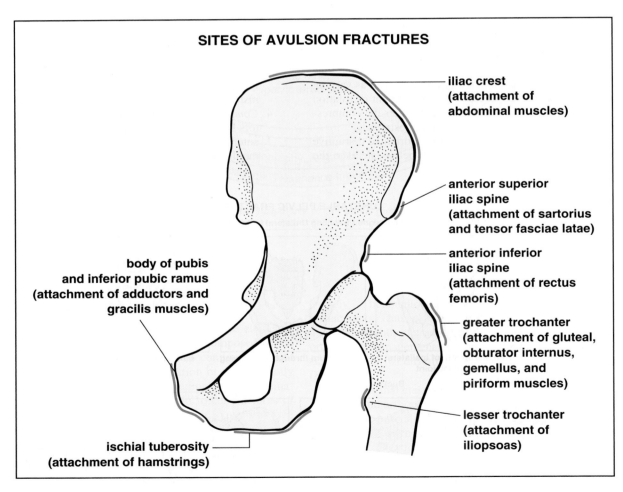

SITES OF AVULSION FRACTURES

iliac crest
(attachment of
abdominal muscles)

anterior superior
iliac spine
(attachment of sartorius
and tensor fasciae latae)

anterior inferior
iliac spine
(attachment of rectus
femoris)

greater trochanter
(attachment of gluteal,
obturator internus,
gemellus, and
piriform muscles)

lesser trochanter
(attachment of
iliopsoas)

body of pubis
and inferior pubic ramus
(attachment of adductors and
gracilis muscles)

ischial tuberosity
(attachment of hamstrings)

FIGURE 8.12   Sites of avulsion fractures.

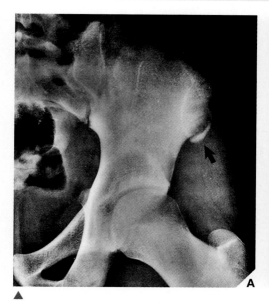
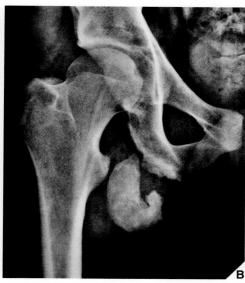
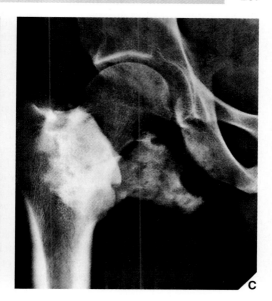

FIGURE 8.13 Avulsion fractures. A 16-year-old boy was injured during an athletic activity. (**A**) Anteroposterior radiograph of the pelvis shows a crescent-shaped fragment adjacent to the lateral aspect of the iliac wing (*arrow*), which represents the avulsed apophysis of the anterosuperior iliac spine. (**B**) Anteroposterior radiograph of the hip in a 26-year-old runner clearly demonstrates avulsion of the ischial tuberosity. (**C**) As a sequela of avulsion of the ischial tuberosity and injury to the soft tissue in the region, a 28-year-old athlete had ossification of the obturator externus muscle.

FIGURE 8.14 Pelvic digit. A rare congenital anomaly, the pelvic digit may occasionally be mistaken for avulsion fracture. (**A**) Anteroposterior view of the left hip shows a finger-like, jointed structure attached to the caudal portion of the left ischium (*arrow*). (**B**) Anteroposterior view of the hip in a 55-year-old man with no history of trauma demonstrates a well-formed digit at the site of the anteroinferior iliac spine (*arrow*). (From Greenspan A, Norman A, 1982, with permission.)

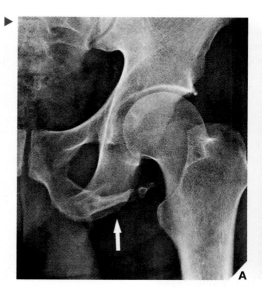
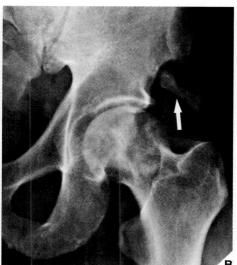

FIGURE 8.15 Malgaigne fracture. A 35-year-old man who was involved in an automobile accident sustained vertical fractures of the left obturator ring (*open arrows*) and fracture of the ipsilateral iliac bone (*arrow*)—a typical Malgaigne injury.

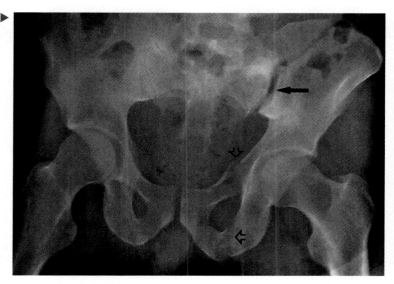

Miscellaneous Pelvic Fractures. Injuries other than the Malgaigne fracture are also easily evaluated on radiographs of the pelvis in the standard and special projections or on CT examination. The *Duverney fracture* is a stable fracture of the wing of the ilium without interruption of the pelvic ring (see Fig. 8.10). The *straddle fracture* (see Fig. 8.11) consists of comminuted fractures of both obturator rings (i.e., all four ischiopubic rami). In one third of patients with this unstable fracture, bladder rupture or urethral injuries occur. The *bucket-handle* or *contralateral double vertical fracture* involves the superior and inferior ischiopubic rami on one side combined with fracture about or disruption of the sacroiliac joint on the opposite side (see Fig. 8.11). *Fractures of the sacrum,* which may be either transversely or vertically oriented (see Fig. 8.10), may occur alone or, more often, in association with other pelvic injuries, such as the so-called *pelvic dislocations.* The latter are characterized by disruption in one or both sacroiliac joints (unilateral or bilateral "dislocation") associated with separation of the pubic symphysis (Fig. 8.16; see also Fig. 8.11). The anteroposterior projection obtained with 30 degrees cephalad angulation or CT is helpful in disclosing sacral fractures, which are frequently overlooked.

Fractures of the Acetabulum

Evaluation of the acetabulum on conventional radiographs may be difficult because of obscuring overlying structures (Fig. 8.17A). If acetabular fracture is suspected, then radiographs in at least four projections should be obtained: the anteroposterior view of the pelvis, the anteroposterior view of the hip, and the anterior and posterior oblique (Judet) views. Radiography may also need to be supplemented by CT, as discussed previously.

As an aid in recognizing the presence of abnormality on the anteroposterior projection of the pelvis and hip, Judet, Judet, and Letournel have identified six lines relating to the acetabulum and its immediately surrounding structures (Fig. 8.17). Fracture of the acetabulum usually distorts these radiographic landmarks, allowing a diagnosis to be made on the anteroposterior projection, but an accurate and complete evaluation of the fracture requires that oblique views be obtained (Fig. 8.18). As mentioned, the anterior (internal) oblique projection demonstrates the iliopubic column and the posterior lip of the acetabulum (see Fig. 8.4), and the posterior (external) oblique view images the ilioischial column

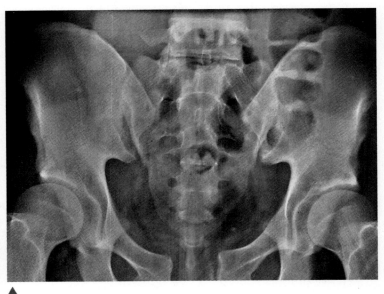

FIGURE 8.16   Sprung pelvis (bilateral dislocation). A 25-year-old man was involved in a motorcycle accident. Anteroposterior view of the pelvis reveals the typical appearance of pelvic "dislocation." The pubic symphysis is disrupted and markedly widened, and there is widening of both sacroiliac joints.

and the anterior rim of the acetabulum (see Fig. 8.5). These projections, together with the division of the pelvic bone into anterior and posterior columns (Fig. 8.19), provide the basis for the traditional classification of acetabular fractures. This classification has been modified by Letournel to include the following types of fractures (Fig. 8.20):

1. Fracture of the iliopubic (anterior) column (rare type of fracture)
2. Fracture of the ilioischial (posterior) column (common type of fracture)
3. Transverse fracture through the acetabulum involving both pelvic columns (common type of fracture)
4. Complex fractures, including T-shaped and stellate fractures, in which the acetabulum is broken into three or more fragment (the most common type of fracture).

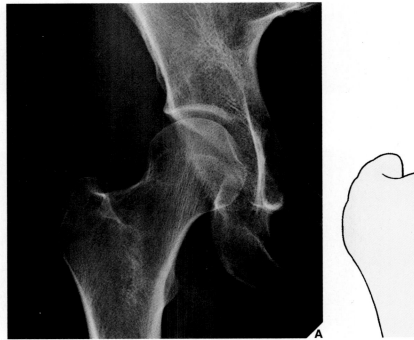
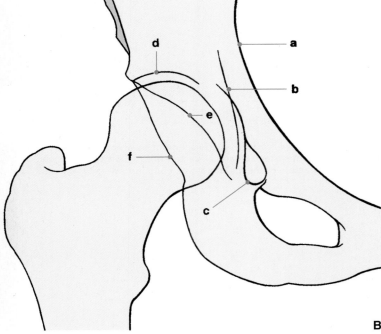

FIGURE 8.17   Radiographic landmarks of the hip. (A,B) On the anteroposterior view of the hip, six lines relating to the acetabulum and its surrounding structures can be distinguished: *a,* iliopubic or iliopectineal (arcuate) line: *b,* ilioischial line, formed by the posterior portion of the quadrilateral plate (surface) of the iliac bone; *c,* teardrop, formed by the medial acetabular wall, the acetabular notch, and the anterior portion of the quadrilateral plate; *d,* roof of the acetabulum; *e,* anterior rim of the acetabulum; and *f,* posterior rim of the acetabulum. Distortion of any of these normal radiographic landmarks indicates the possible presence of abnormality.

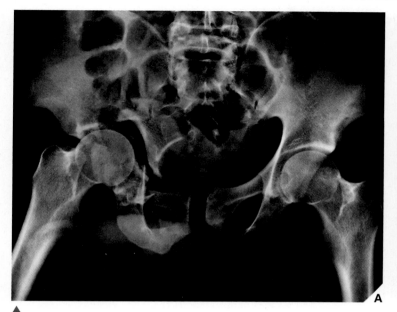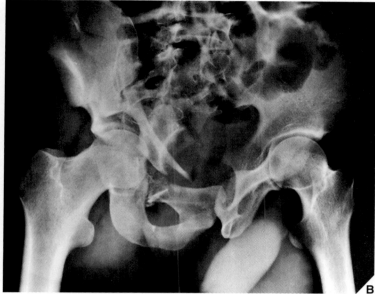

FIGURE 8.18 Acetabular fracture. A 32-year-old drug-addicted subject was hit by a car. (A) Anteroposterior radiograph of the pelvis shows a comminuted fracture of the right acetabulum, fracture of the right ilium, and diastasis of the pubic symphysis. There is also a fracture of the sacrum with diastasis of the left sacroiliac joint. (B) On the anterior oblique projection, the acetabular fracture is seen to involve mainly the anterior pelvic column.

CT plays a leading role in the evaluation of acetabular and pelvic fractures because of its capability of demonstrating the exact position of displaced fragments, which may be trapped within the hip joint, as well as allowing adequate assessment of concomitant soft-tissue injury (Figs. 8.21 to 8.23). It also requires less manipulation of the patient than the standard radiographic views—a fact especially important in patients with multiple injuries.

Injuries of the Acetabular Labrum
The fibrocartilaginous labrum is directly attached to the osseous rim of the acetabulum. It blends with the transverse ligament at the margins of the acetabular notch. Because the labrum is thicker posterosuperiorly and thinner anteroinferiorly, on cross-section it appears as a triangular structure, similar to the labrum of the scapular glenoid. The acetabular labrum can be injured in conjunction with acetabular fracture, hip dislocation, or even minor trauma to the hip joint. In the latter situation, the clinical symptoms include anterior inguinal pain, limitation of motion in the hip joint, painful clicking, transient locking, and "giving way" of the hip. Onset of pain may be linked to sports activities or to twisting or slipping injury. Conventional radiographs, unless obvious fracture or dislocation is present, are invariably normal. The most effective technique for diagnosis of

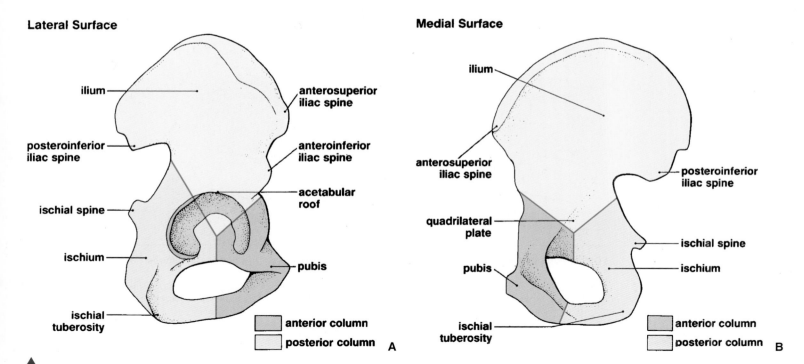

FIGURE 8.19 Columns of the pelvis. Lateral (A) and medial (B) views of the pelvis show the division of the bone into anterior and posterior columns, which provides the basis for the traditional classification of acetabular fractures. (Modified from Judet R et al., 1964, with permission.)

FRACTURES OF THE ACETABULUM

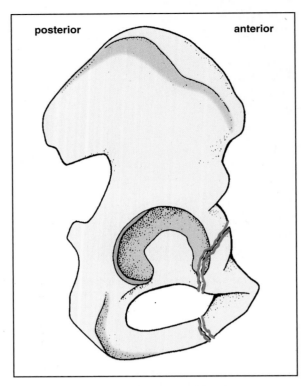

involving anterior (iliopubic) column

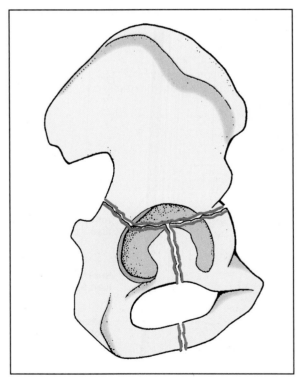

involving posterior (ilioischial) column

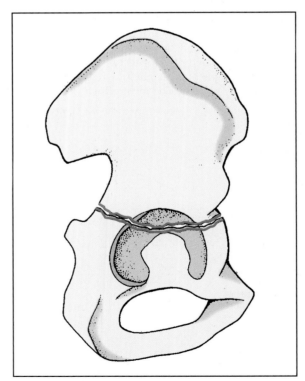

involving both columns (transverse)

complex fractures (T-shaped or stellate)

FIGURE 8.20 Classification of acetabular fractures. In the traditional classification of acetabular fractures, the fracture may involve the anterior column, the posterior column, or both columns. In complex acetabular fractures, both columns are involved and the fracture line may be T shaped or stellate. (Modified from Letournel E, 1980, with permission.)

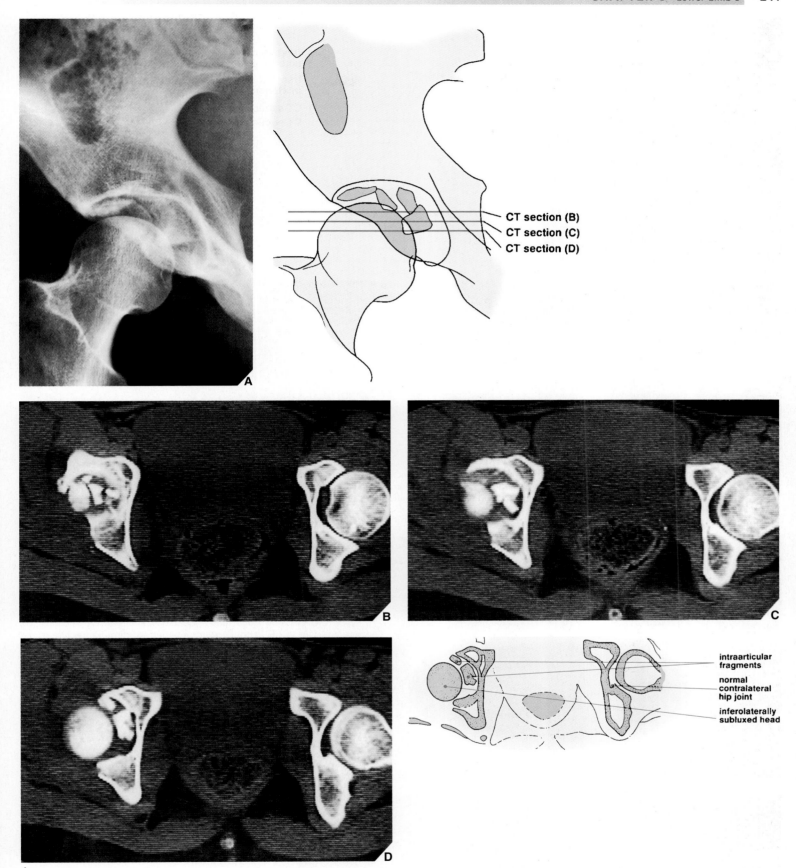

▲
FIGURE 8.21 **CT of the acetabular fracture.** As a result of an automobile accident, a 30-year-old woman sustained an injury that was diagnosed on the standard projections as a fracture of the acetabular roof. (**A**) On the posterior oblique projection, the fracture is shown to be comminuted. CT examination was performed, and sections (**B**), (**C**), and (**D**) show the topographic orientation of the various intraarticular fragments and evidence of infero-lateral subluxation of the femoral head—important information not appreciated on the standard projections.

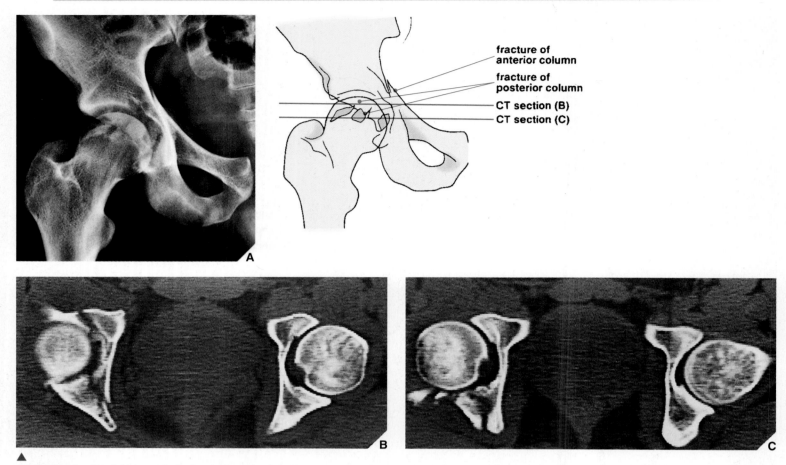

FIGURE 8.22   CT of the acetabular fracture. A 22-year-old man sustained an injury caused by the dashboard during an automobile accident. **(A)** Standard antero-posterior radiograph of the hip shows fractures of the anterior and posterior columns. **(B,C)** On CT examination, demonstration of the exact extent of the fracture lines and the spatial relationships between the fragments provide crucial information for the orthopedic surgeon in planning open reduction and internal fixation.

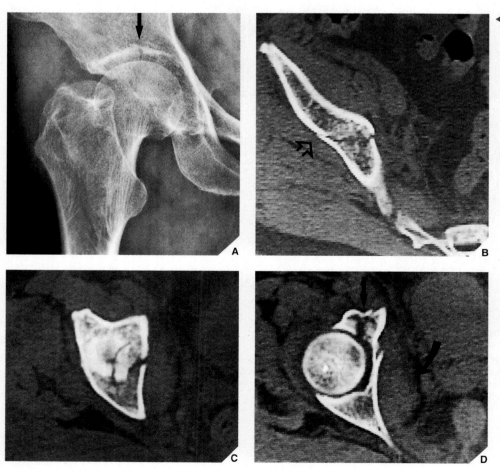

◄ **FIGURE 8.23   CT of the acetabular fracture.** After a fall on the street, a 63-year-old man experienced dis-comfort while walking. **(A)** Standard anteroposterior radiograph of the right hip shows a radiolucent line in the acetabular roof (*arrow*) but no other findings indicative of abnormality. Other views of the pelvis were not obtained because the patient refused. With his consent the next day, multiple CT sections **(B)**, **(C)**, and **(D)** were obtained, confirming fracture of the acetabular roof. They reveal in addition completely unsuspected fractures of the anterior column (*arrow*) and iliac bone (*open arrow*), with marked thickening of the obturator internus muscle (*curved arrow*) second-ary to hemorrhage and edema.

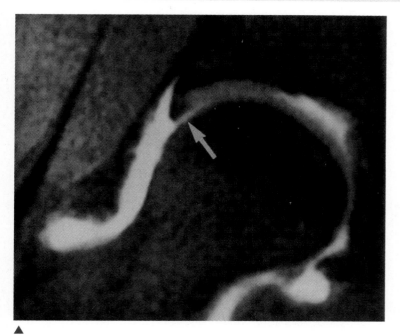

▲
FIGURE 8.24   MRI of normal acetabular labrum. Coronal fat-suppressed T1-weighted MR arthrographic image of the right hip shows a normal appearance of the acetabular labrum (*arrow*). Note the triangular shape, smooth contour, and low signal intensity of this structure. (Reprinted from Steinbach LS, Palmer WE, Schweitzer ME, 2002, with permission).

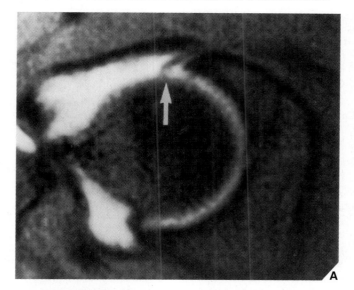

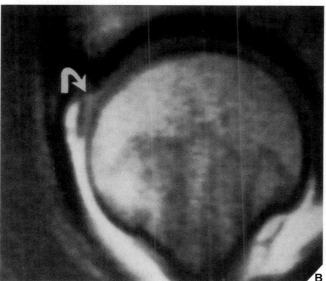

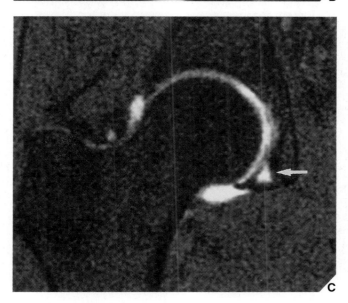

a pathologic labral condition is MR arthrography (MRa). Czerny and colleagues have recently reported a sensitivity of 90% and accuracy of 91% of MRa for the detection of labral tears and detachments. The normal labrum appears on axial and coronal images as a triangular structure with low signal intensity on all imaging sequences (Fig. 8.24). A tear of the labrum is diagnosed either when deformity of its contour is present or when a linear diffuse high signal is present. In the most severe cases, the labrum is detached from the acetabulum (Fig. 8.25). Based on MRa findings that included labral morphology, intralabral signal, presence of tear or labral detachment, and the presence or absence of adjacent perilabral recess, Czerny classified labral tears into the three groups (six subgroups). In general, these groupings take into consideration only either the presence of labrum substance tear or peripheral detachment. Another classification introduced by Lage et al. is based on arthroscopic findings, reflecting morphology of the labrum and functional stability of the tear. Because some investigators found no correlation between these two grading systems, Blankenbaker and colleagues proposed instead to use a description of the labral abnormalities seen at MRa, that can be outlined as follow: (1) *frayed labrum*—irregular margins of the labrum without a discrete tear; (2) *flap tear*—contrast extending into or through the labral substance; (3) *peripheral longitudinal tear*—contrast partially or completely extending between the labral base and acetabulum; and (4) *thickened and distorted labrum*—most likely unstable lesion.

Treatment of labral tears includes arthroscopic resection of the injured labrum or repair of a tear.

Femoroacetabular Impingement Syndrome

This condition results from incongruity of the femoral head and acetabulum, and leads to injury of the fibrocartilaginous labrum and subsequent development of precocious osteoarthritis of the hip joint. Femoroacetabular impingement (FAI) syndrome is discussed in detail in Chapter 13.

During evaluation of MRI and MRa of the hip and pelvis, it is helpful to use the checklist as provided in Table 8.3.

▲
FIGURE 8.25   MRI of torn acetabular labrum. (**A**) Axial fat-suppressed T1-weighted MR arthrographic image shows a torn labrum displaced from the acetabular rim (*arrow*). (**B**) Sagittal T1-weighted MR arthrographic image shows separation of the torn labral fragment from the underlying articular cartilage (*curved arrow*). (**C**) In another patient, coronal fat-suppressed T1-weighted MR arthrographic image shows a tear of the inferior labrum (*arrow*). ([**A**] and [**B**] reprinted from Steinbach LS, Palmer WE, Schweitzer ME, 2002, with permission.).

T A B L E 8.3 **Checklist for Evaluation of MRI and MRa of the Hip and Pelvis**

Osseous Structures Femoral head (c, s, a) Femoral neck (c, a) Greater and lesser trochanters (c, a) Acetabulum (c, a) **Cartilaginous Structures** Articular cartilage (c, a) Fibrocartilaginous labrum (c, s, a) **Joints** Hip (c, s, a) Sacroiliac (c, a) **Muscles and Their Tendons** Gluteus—maximus, medius, minimus (c, a) Adductors—magnus, longus, brevis (c, a) Iliopsoas (c, a) Sartorius (a) Rectus femoris (a) Gracilis (a) Pectineus (a) Tensor fasciae latae (a)	**Muscles and Their Tendons (continued)** Piriformis (a) Obturators—internus, externus (a) Gemelli—superior, inferior (a) Quadratus femoris—vastus lateralis, medialis, intermedius (a) Biceps femoris (c, a) Semimembranosus (c, a) Semitendinosus (c, a) **Ligaments** Iliofemoral (c, a) Pubofemoral (c, a) Ischiofemoral (c, a) Teres (a) **Bursae** Iliopsoas (c, a) Greater trochanteric (c, a) **Other Structures** Pulvinar (a) Sciatic nerve (c, a) Arteries and veins (a)

The best imaging planes for visualization of listed structures are given in parenthesis; c, coronal; s, sagittal; a, axial.

Proximal Femur

Injury to the Proximal Femur

Fractures of the Proximal Femur

When fracture of the proximal femur is suspected, the standard radiographic examination should include at least two projections: the anteroposterior and the frog-lateral views of the hip (see Figs. 8.1 and 8.6); the groin-lateral radiograph of the hip is also frequently required (see Fig. 8.7). For many nondisplaced and displaced fractures, however, a single anteroposterior view of the hip may suffice (Figs. 8.26 and 8.27).

CT or MRI may occasionally be necessary, particularly to determine the type of the fracture and degree of displacement (Figs. 8.28 to 8.31). Radionuclide bone scan may also need to be called on in questionable cases (see Fig. 4.9B).

Traditionally, fractures of the proximal femur (so-called hip fractures) are divided into two groups: (a) *intracapsular fractures* involving the femoral head or neck, which may be capital, subcapital, transcervical, or basicervical and (b) *extracapsular fractures* involving the trochanters, which may be intertrochanteric or subtrochanteric (Fig. 8.32). The significance of this distinction lies in the greater incidence of posttraumatic complications after intracapsular fracture of the

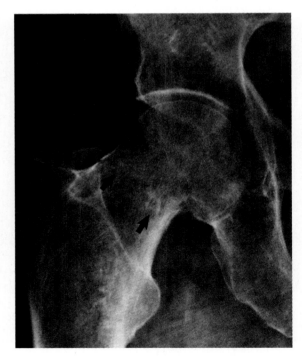

FIGURE 8.26 **Midcervical fracture.** In a fall in her bathroom, an 83-year-old woman sustained a typical nondisplaced midcervical fracture of the femoral neck (*arrows*), as demonstrated on this anteroposterior radiograph of the right hip.

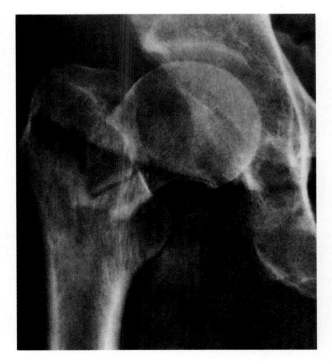

FIGURE 8.27 **Basicervical fracture.** A 37-year-old man fell from a ladder. On the anteroposterior radiograph of the right hip, a displaced basicervical fracture of the femoral neck is evident.

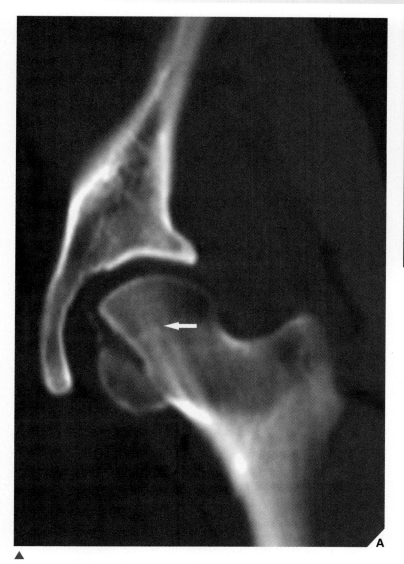
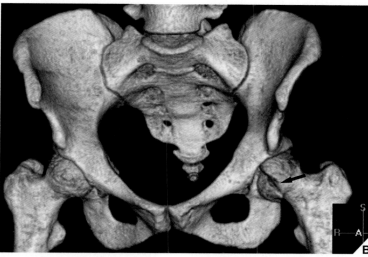

▲
FIGURE 8.28   CT and 3D CT of the fracture of the femoral head. A 20-year-old woman sustained a posterior dislocation of the left hip. The dislocation was successfully relocated. (A) Coronal reformatted CT of the left hip and (B) 3D reconstructed CT image of the pelvis show one of the complications of posterior hip dislocation—a fracture of the femoral head (arrows).

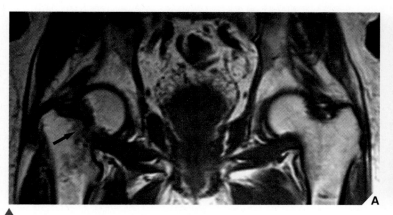
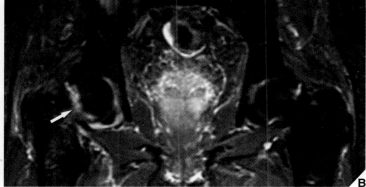

▲
FIGURE 8.29   MRI of the subcapital fracture. A 77-year-old woman presented with right hip pain after a fall on the street. (A) Coronal proton density-weighted and (B) coronal inversion recovery MR images of the pelvis show a subcapital fracture of the right femur (arrows).

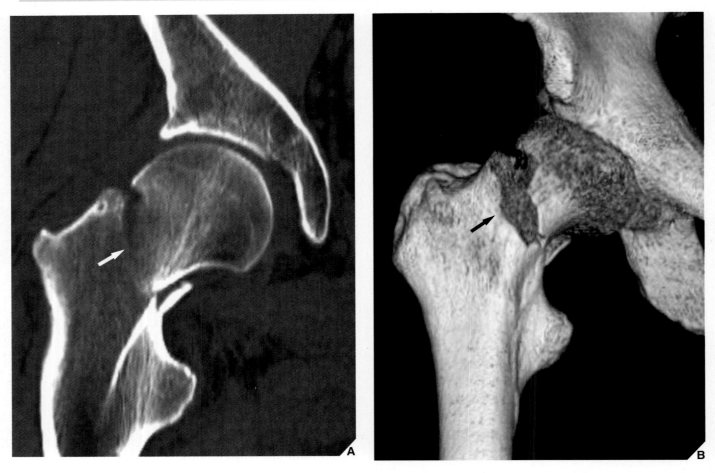

FIGURE 8.30 CT and 3D CT of midcervical fracture. (A) Coronal reformatted CT and (B) 3D reconstructed CT images of the right hip demonstrate a midcervical fracture of the femur (*arrows*).

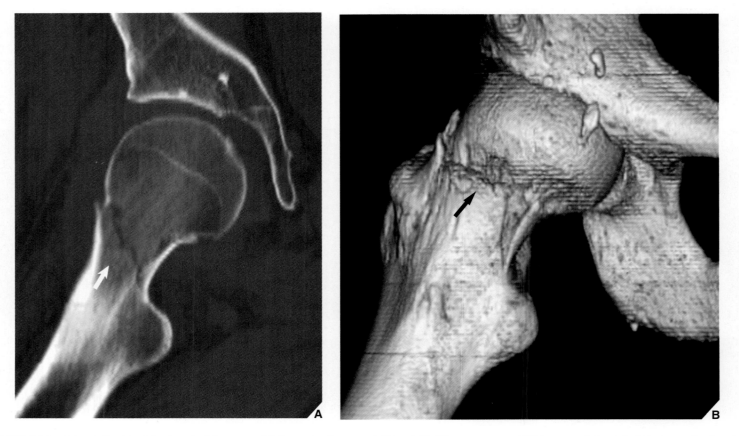

FIGURE 8.31 CT and 3D CT of basicervical fracture. (A) Coronal reformatted CT and (B) 3D reconstructed CT images of the right hip show a basicervical fracture (*arrows*) in this 60-year-old woman who fell from the stairs.

FRACTURES OF THE PROXIMAL FEMUR

Intracapsular

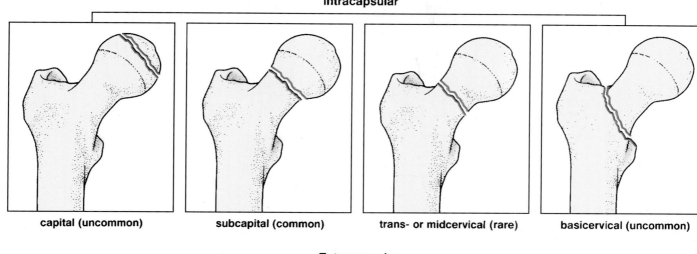

capital (uncommon)   subcapital (common)   trans- or midcervical (rare)   basicervical (uncommon)

Extracapsular

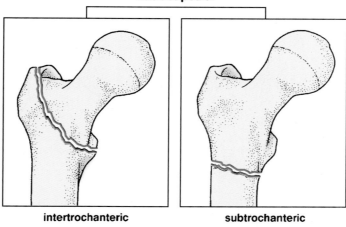

intertrochanteric   subtrochanteric

▲

FIGURE 8.32   Fractures of the proximal femur. Fractures of the proximal femur are traditionally classified as intracapsular and extracapsular.

upper femur. The most common complication, osteonecrosis (ischemic or avascular necrosis), occurs in 15% to 35% of patients sustaining intracapsular fractures, but the percentage varies according to the reported series.

The reason for the high incidence of the development of osteonecrosis after fracture of the femoral neck lies in the nature of the blood supply to the proximal femur. The capsule of the hip joint arises from the acetabulum and attaches to the anterior aspect of the femur along the intertrochanteric line at the base of the femoral neck. Posteriorly, the capsule envelops the femoral head and proximal two thirds of the neck. Most of the blood supply to the femoral head is derived from the circumflex femoral arteries, which form a ring at the base of the neck, sending off branches that ascend subcapsularly along the femoral neck to the femoral head. Only a very small portion of the femoral head is supplied by arteries in the ligamentum teres (ligamentum capitis femoris) (Fig. 8.33). Because of this vascular configuration, intracapsular fractures tend to tear the vessels, interrupting the blood supply and leading eventually to osteonecrosis. The trochanteric region, however, is extracapsular and receives an excellent supply of blood from branches of the circumflex femoral arteries and from muscles that attach around both trochanters. Thus, as a rule, intertrochanteric fractures do not lead to osteonecrosis of the femoral head.

Nonunion is also a common complication following fracture of the femoral neck, occurring in 10% to 44% of patients with such fractures. According to Pauwels, the obliquity of the fracture line determines the

prognosis. The more oblique the fracture line is, the more likely nonunion will occur (Fig. 8.34).

Intracapsular Fractures. Of the many classifications of femoral neck fractures that have been proposed, the Pauwels and Garden classifications are useful from a practical point of view because they take into consideration the stability of the fracture—an important factor in orthopedic management and prognosis.

Pauwels classifies femoral neck fractures according to the degree of angulation of the fracture line from the horizontal plane on the postreduction anteroposterior radiograph, stressing that the closer the fracture line approximates the horizontal, the more stable the fracture and the better the prognosis (see Fig. 8.34). Garden, however, proposed a staging system of femoral neck fractures based on displacement of the femoral head before reduction. Displacement in the Garden system is graded according to the position of the principal (medial) compressive trabeculae (Fig. 8.35). His classification of such fractures is divided into four stages (Fig. 8.36):

Stage I   Incomplete subcapital fracture. In this so-called impacted or abducted fracture, the femoral shaft is externally rotated and the femoral head is in valgus. The medial trabeculae of the femoral head and neck form an angle greater than 180 degrees (Fig. 8.37). This is a stable fracture with a good prognosis.

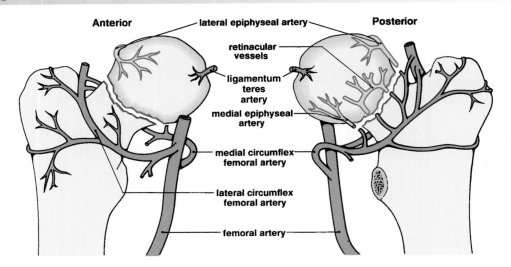

FIGURE 8.33 Blood supply to the proximal femur. The proximal femur is supplied with blood mainly by the circumflex femoral arteries, branches of which ascend subcapsularly along the femoral neck to the femoral head. Intracapsular fracture of the proximal femur may so severely interrupt the blood supply that osteonecrosis results.

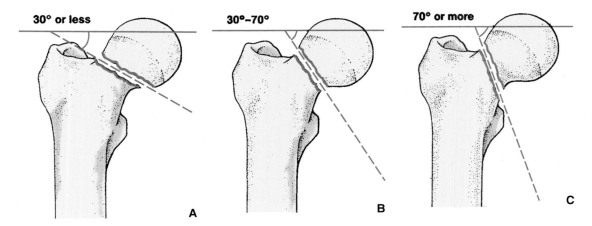

FIGURE 8.34 The Pauwels classification of intracapsular fractures. The classification is based on the obliquity of the fracture line: The more the fracture line approaches the vertical, the less stable is the fracture, and consequently the greater are the chances for nonunion. (Modified from Pauwels F, 1976, with permission.)

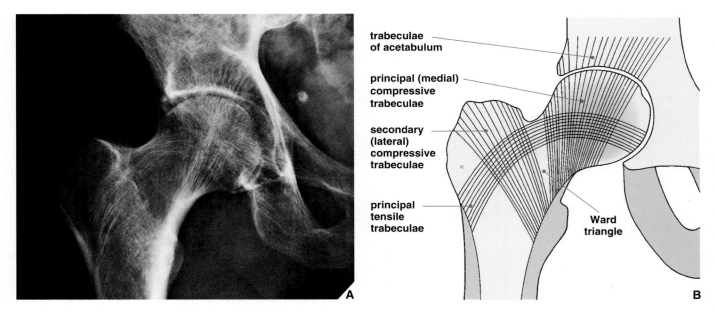

FIGURE 8.35 Trabeculae of the hip. The Garden staging system of femoral neck fractures is based on the three groups of trabeculae that are demonstrable within the femoral head and neck. The principal tensile trabeculae form an arc, extending from the lateral margin of the greater trochanter, through the superior cortex of the neck and across the femoral head, ending at its inferior aspect below the fovea. The principal (medial) compressive trabeculae are vertically oriented, extending from the medial cortex of the neck into the femoral head in a triangular configuration. They are normally aligned with the trabeculae seen in the acetabulum. The secondary (lateral) compressive trabeculae extend from the calcar and lesser trochanter to the greater trochanter in a fan-like pattern. The central area bounded by this trabecular system is known as Ward triangle.

GARDEN STAGING OF SUBCAPITAL FEMORAL FRACTURES

Stage I—Incomplete (Abducted or Impacted)

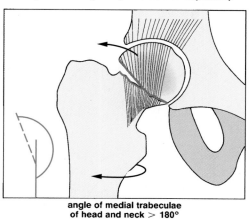

angle of medial trabeculae
of head and neck > 180°

Stage II—Complete, without Displacement

angle of medial trabeculae
of head and neck ≈ 160°

Stage III—Complete, with Partial Displacement

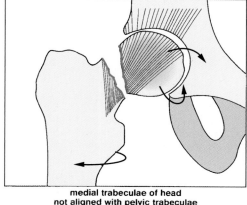

medial trabeculae of head
not aligned with pelvic trabeculae

Stage IV—Complete, with Full Displacement

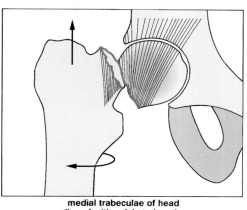

medial trabeculae of head
aligned with pelvic trabeculae

▲
FIGURE 8.36   The Garden classification of subcapital fractures. The Garden staging of subcapital femoral fractures is based on displacement of the femoral head before reduction. Displacement is graded according to the position of the medial compressive trabeculae. (Modified from Garden RS, 1974, with permission.)

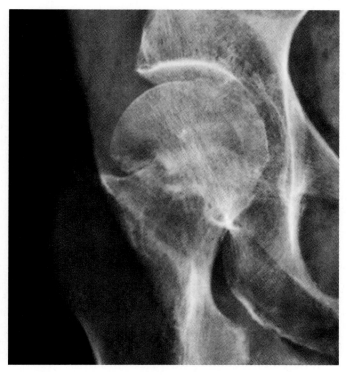

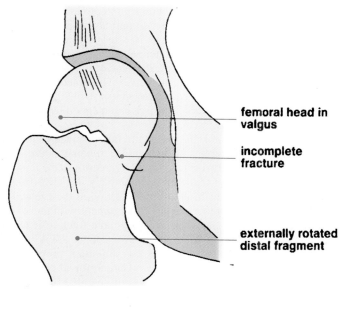

femoral head in
valgus

incomplete
fracture

externally rotated
distal fragment

▲
FIGURE 8.37   Subcapital fracture. After a fall to the floor, a 72-year-old woman sustained a fracture of the right femoral neck. Anteroposterior radiograph demonstrates a subcapital fracture, which appears to be impacted. The femoral head is in valgus, the distal fragment is externally rotated, and the medial trabeculae of the femoral head and neck form an angle greater than 180 degrees. These features characterize a Garden stage I fracture.

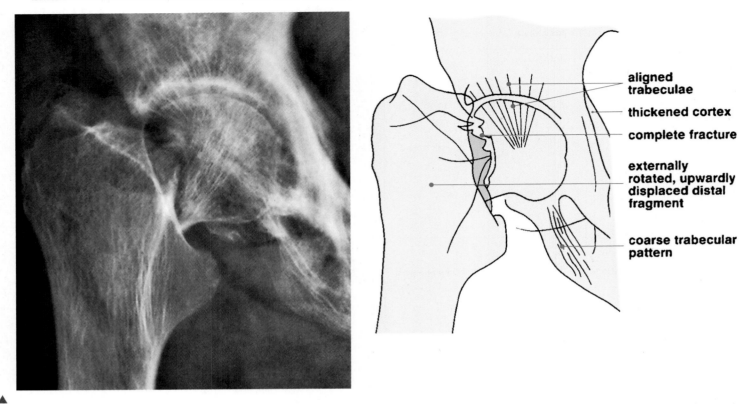

aligned trabeculae

thickened cortex

complete fracture

externally rotated, upwardly displaced distal fragment

coarse trabecular pattern

▲

FIGURE 8.38   **Subcapital fracture.** After a fall on a subway platform, a 77-year-old woman sustained a fracture of the right femoral neck. Anteroposterior radiograph of the hip shows a complete subcapital fracture with full displacement. The head, which is detached from the neck, is in its normal position in the acetabulum. Note the alignment of the trabeculae in the head and acetabulum. The femoral shaft is upwardly displaced and externally rotated. These features identify this injury as a Garden stage IV fracture.

Stage II   Complete subcapital fracture without displacement. In this complete fracture through the neck, the femoral shaft remains in normal alignment with the femoral head, which is not displaced but rather tilted in a varus deformity so that its medial trabeculae do not align with those of the pelvis. The medial trabeculae of the head form an angle of approximately 160 degrees with those of the femoral neck. This is also a stable fracture with a good prognosis.

Stage III   Complete subcapital fracture with partial displacement. In this category, the femoral shaft is externally rotated. The femoral head is medially rotated, abducted, and tilted in a varus deformity. The medial trabeculae of the head are out of alignment with those of the pelvis. This fracture is usually unstable, but it may be converted to a stable fracture by proper reduction. The prognosis is not as good as that for stage I and stage II fractures.

Stage IV   Complete subcapital fracture with full displacement. In this type the femoral shaft, in addition to being externally rotated, is upwardly displaced and lies anterior to the femoral head. Although the head is completely detached from the shaft, it remains in its normal position in the acetabulum. The medial trabeculae are in alignment with those of the pelvis (Fig. 8.38). This is an unstable fracture with a poor prognosis.

This staging of femoral neck fractures has important prognostic value. In following up 80 patients over 1 year, Garden found complete union in all those graded stages I and II, 93% in those graded stage III, and only 57% in those graded stage IV. Osteonecrosis occurred in only 8% of nondisplaced stage I or stage II fractures but in 30% of displaced stage III or IV fractures.

Extracapsular Fractures. Frequently resulting from direct injury in a fall, extracapsular fractures occur in an even older age group than do intracapsular fractures. Most of these fractures are intertrochanteric, the major fracture line extending from the greater to the lesser trochanter, and they are usually comminuted. Radiographic diagnosis can usually be made on a single anteroposterior view of the hip (Fig. 8.39). Rarely, the fracture line may be obscure, requiring oblique projections for its demonstration.

As mentioned, extracapsular fractures of the proximal femur, for which several classifications have been developed, can generally be divided into two major subgroups: intertrochanteric and subtrochanteric. Intertrochanteric fractures can be further subdivided according to the number of fragments or the extension of the fracture line. A simple classification of such fractures has been proposed that considers the number of fragments (Fig. 8.40). The two-part fracture in this system is stable, whereas the four-part and multi-part fractures are unstable. Boyd and Griffin have proposed a classification of intertrochanteric fractures according to the presence or absence of comminution and involvement of the subtrochanteric region (Fig. 8.41). Comminution of the posterior and medial cortices has important prognostic value. If comminuted, the fracture is unstable and may require a displacement osteotomy, a procedure particularly important in the treatment of four-part fractures when both trochanters are involved. If there is no comminution, then the fracture is stable and treatment involves fixation with a compression screw.

Classification introduced by Kyle is very effective from the practical point of view because it is based on the stability of various fractured fragments. Type I and II are stable fractures, and types III, IV, and V—unstable (Fig. 8.42). Stability of the fracture is the crucial information for the orthopedic surgeon, and key to successful treatment. It also permits to render a more accurate prognosis.

Subtrochanteric fractures have been classified by Fielding according to the level of the fracture line and by Zickel according to their level, obliquity, and comminution (Fig. 8.43). An important fact about subtrochanteric fractures is their relatively benign course caused by the good supply of blood and adequate collateral circulation to this region of the femur. The occurrence of osteonecrosis of the femoral head and the incidence of nonunion as a result of intertrochanteric and subtrochanteric fractures are very low. The only serious complication to watch for is postoperative infection.

Dislocations in the Hip Joint

Traumatic dislocation of the femoral head is an uncommon injury resulting from a high-energy force and often accompanied by other

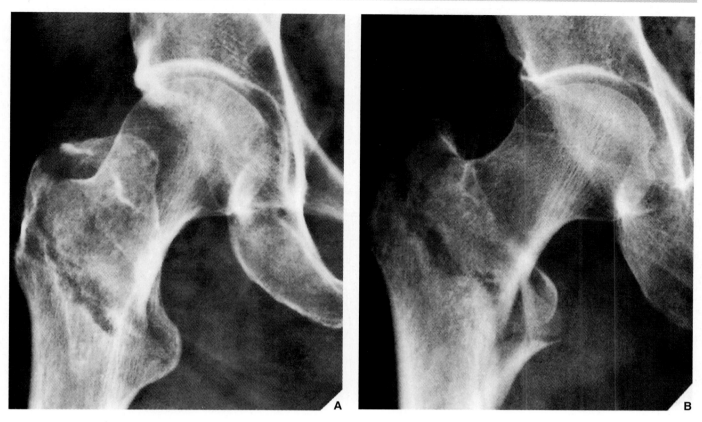

FIGURE 8.39 **Intertrochanteric fracture.** **(A)** Anteroposterior radiograph of the right hip demonstrates a comminuted, three-part intertrochanteric fracture, which can be classified as a Boyd-Griffin type II fracture. **(B)** Anteroposterior projection of the right hip shows a comminuted, multipart intertrochanteric fracture associated with a subtrochanteric component. This fracture can be classified as a Boyd-Griffin type III fracture. (For the Boyd-Griffin classification of intertrochanteric fractures, see Fig. 8.41.)

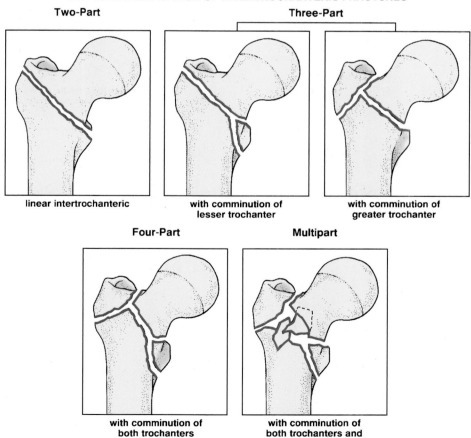

SIMPLE CLASSIFICATION OF INTERTROCHANTERIC FRACTURES

Two-Part

Three-Part

linear intertrochanteric

with comminution of lesser trochanter

with comminution of greater trochanter

Four-Part

Multipart

with comminution of both trochanters

with comminution of both trochanters and intertrochanteric region

FIGURE 8.40 **Classification of intertrochanteric fractures.** The simple classification of intertrochanteric fractures is based on the number of bony fragments.

BOYD–GRIFFIN CLASSIFICATION OF INTERTROCHANTERIC FRACTURES

Type I

linear intertrochanteric

Type II

with comminution
of trochanteric region

Type III

with comminution
associated with
subtrochanteric component

Type IV

oblique fracture of shaft
with extension into
subtrochanteric region

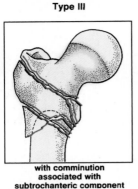

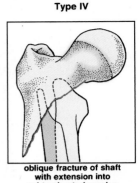

◀ FIGURE 8.41 The Boyd-Griffin classification of intertrochanteric fractures.
This classification is based on the presence or absence of comminution and
the involvement of the subtrochanteric
region. (Modified from Boyd HB, Griffin
LL, 1949, with permission.)

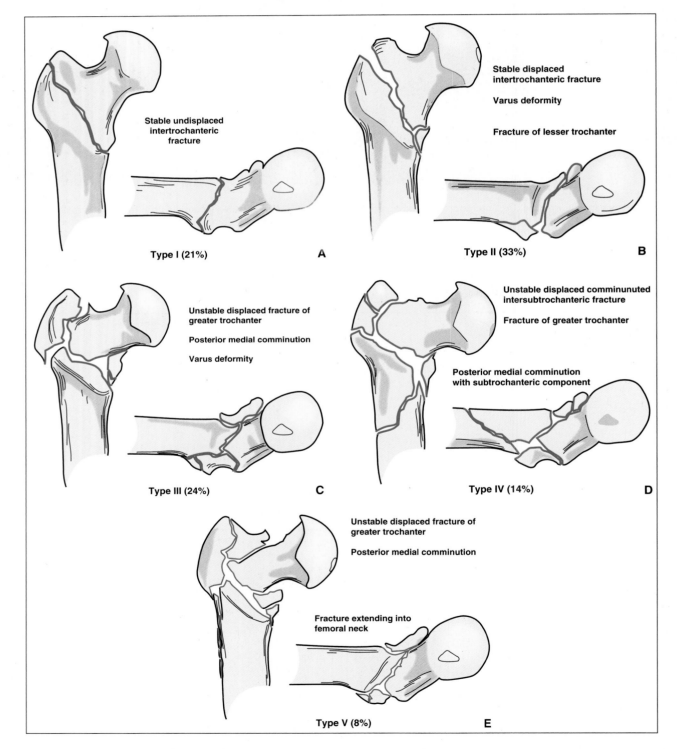

Stable undisplaced
intertrochanteric
fracture

Type I (21%)   A

Stable displaced
intertrochanteric fracture

Varus deformity

Fracture of lesser trochanter

Type II (33%)   B

Unstable displaced fracture of
greater trochanter

Posterior medial comminution

Varus deformity

Type III (24%)   C

Unstable displaced comminunuted
intersubtrochanteric fracture

Fracture of greater trochanter

Posterior medial comminution
with subtrochanteric component

Type IV (14%)   D

Unstable displaced fracture of
greater trochanter

Posterior medial comminution

Fracture extending into
femoral neck

Type V (8%)   E

▲
FIGURE 8.42 **The Kyle classification of intertrochanteric fractures.** This classification is based on stability of the fracture fragments, and permits a more accurate prognosis of this injury (Modified from Moehring HD, Greenspan A, 2000.)

FIELDING AND ZICKEL CLASSIFICATIONS OF SUBTROCHANTERIC FRACTURES

Fielding Classification

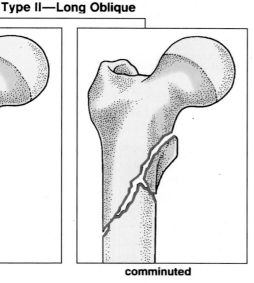

Zickel Classification
Type I—Short Oblique

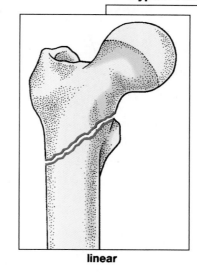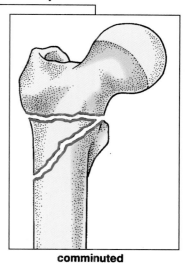

linear   comminuted

Zickel Classification (continued)

Type II—Long Oblique   **Type III—Transverse**

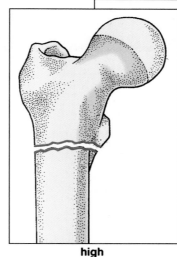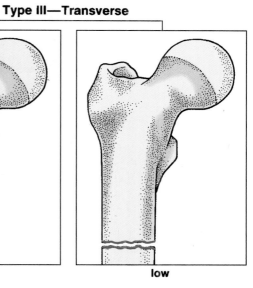

linear   comminuted   high   low

▲
FIGURE 8.43 **Classification of subtrochanteric fractures.** The Fielding classification of subtrochanteric fractures (*top left*) is based on the level of the sub-trochanteric region in which the fracture occurs. Type I fractures, the most common type, occur at the level of the lesser trochanter; type II, within the region 2.5 cm below the lesser trochanter; and type III, the least common type, occurs within the region 2.5 to 5 cm below the lesser trochanter. The Zickel classification of subtrochanteric fractures takes into consideration the level and obliquity of the fracture line as well as the presence or absence of comminution. (Modified from Fielding JW, 1973; Zickel RE, 1976, with permission.)

significant injuries. The injury is caused by a substantial axial force, such as a knee impacting against the dashboard in a motor vehicle accident.

Generally, dislocations in the hip joint can be classified as anterior, posterior, or central (medial). The position of the hip at the moment of impact determines the direction of dislocation: hip flexion, adduction, and internal rotation result in posterior dislocation, and hip abduction and external rotation yield anterior dislocation. Posterior dislocation of the femoral head is far more common than anterior dislocation, which constitutes only 5% to 18% of all hip dislocations. It is also more frequently associated with fractures, particularly involving the posterior acetabular rim; anterior dislocation, in contrast, tends to be simple, without associated fracture. A predisposition to traumatic posterior hip dislocation has been suggested for individuals with retroversion or decreased anteversion of the femoral neck. Similarly, increased femoral neck anteversion may predispose to traumatic anterior hip dislocation. Dislocations are readily identified on radiographs of the hip in the anteroposterior projection. In *anterior dislocation*, which accounts for only 13% of all hip dislocations, the femoral head is displaced into the obturator, pubic, or iliac region. On the anteroposterior film, the femur is abducted and externally rotated and the femoral head lies medial and inferior to the acetabulum (Fig. 8.44). In *posterior dislocation*, which is the most common type of dislocation, the anteroposterior view reveals the femur to be internally rotated and adducted, while the femoral head lies lateral and superior to the acetabulum (Fig. 8.45). *Central dislocation* (or *central protrusio*) is always associated with an acetabular fracture, with the femoral head protruding into the pelvic cavity (Figs. 8.46 and 8.47).

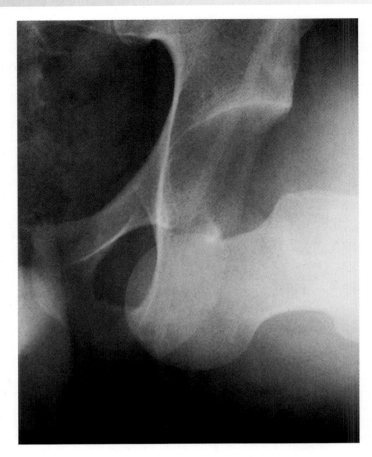

▲
FIGURE 8.44 **Anterior hip dislocation.** A 19-year-old man sustained an anterior hip dislocation. Note on this anteroposterior radiograph a typical position of the femoral head, which lies inferior and medial to the acetabulum.

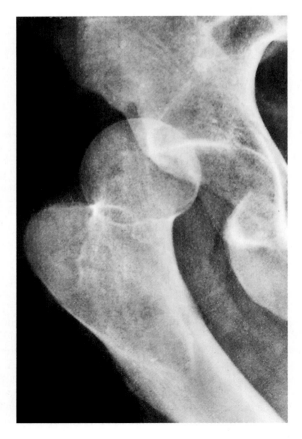

▲
FIGURE 8.45 **Posterior hip dislocation.** A 30-year-old woman sustained a typical posterior hip dislocation in an automobile accident. Note on this anteroposterior projection that the extremity is adducted and the femoral head overlaps the posterior lip of the acetabulum.

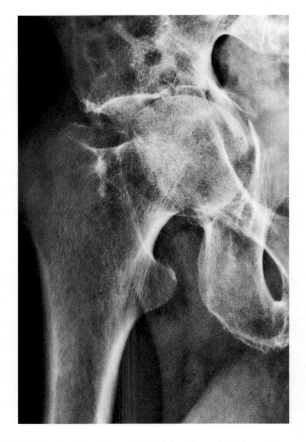

▲
FIGURE 8.46 **Central hip dislocation.** While riding a bicycle, a 43-year-old man was hit by a truck. Anteroposterior radiograph of the right hip shows a typical central dislocation in the hip associated with a comminuted fracture of the medial acetabular wall. Note the protrusion of the femoral head into the pelvic cavity.

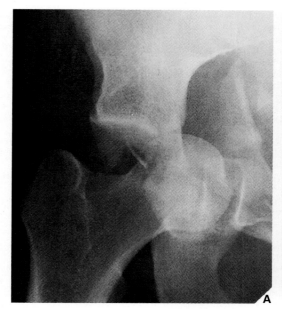 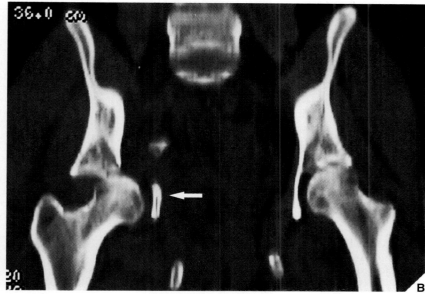

▲
FIGURE 8.47   **Central hip dislocation.** A 22-year-old woman was injured in a car accident. (**A**) Anteroposterior radiograph of the right hip shows a complex acetabular fracture associated with a central displacement of the femoral head. (**B**) A coronal CT reformatted image shows medial displacement of the medial acetabular wall (*arrow*) and central hip dislocation.

Dislocation of the femoral head is often accompanied by significant injuries involving the bone and cartilage, and the muscles and ligaments surrounding the joint. CT has proved indispensable for identifying fractures associated with hip dislocations, and it remains the best means of detecting cortical disruption. MRI has assumed a highly significant role among imaging modalities, especially because of its superior capabilities in comparison with CT in evaluating cancellous bone, cartilage, muscle, ligaments, and intra-articular fluid. MRI can effectively identify and quantify the muscle injury and joint effusion/hemarthrosis that invariably accompany traumatic anterior and posterior dislocation of the hip (see Figs. 4.85 and 4.86). It is also useful for demonstrating bone contusions, which occur commonly in both types of dislocation, as well as the less common sequelae of acute hip dislocation, including cortical infraction, osteochondral fracture, and tear of the acetabular labrum. It may also be helpful in identifying soft-tissue interposition in the joint space. The real importance of performing MRI after hip dislocation is to identify possible complications such as osteonecrosis of the femoral head.

Traumatic hip dislocations are treated with immediate closed reduction, preferably within 6 hours of injury. Such attention is required to lower the risk of osteonecrosis, one of the two main complications related to hip dislocation; the other is posttraumatic osteoarthritis.

A recent study found that osteonecrosis developed in only 4.8% of patients whose hip dislocation was reduced within 6 hours, compared with 58.8% of patients whose reduction occurred more than 6 hours after injury. The early detection of osteonecrosis is critical because the initial period offers the greatest chance of preserving joint function with surgical procedures such as drilling, rotational osteotomy, or core decompression with or without vascularized grafting. Posttraumatic osteoarthritis, with an incidence ranging from 17% to 48.8% in different series, has been attributed to the severity of the initial injury, intra-articular loose bodies, and continued heavy work after injury. Simple dislocations have a better prognosis than those with an associated fracture.

PRACTICAL POINTS TO REMEMBER

Pelvis and Acetabulum

[1] Fractures of the pelvis are important because of the high incidence of concomitant injury to:
- Major blood vessels
- Nerves
- Lower urinary tract.

[2] Pelvic fractures can be classified for the purposes of radiographic diagnosis and orthopedic management:
- Into stable and unstable injuries on the basis of the stability of the fragments
- According to the direction of the force delivered to the pelvis as injuries resulting from anteroposterior compression, lateral compression, vertical shear, or complex pattern.

[3] Fractures of the acetabulum are best demonstrated on the anterior and posterior oblique projections (Judet views).

[4] In acetabular fractures it is important to distinguish between:
- Fractures of the anterior pelvic column
- Fractures of the posterior pelvic column.

[5] CT plays an important role in the evaluation of fractures of both the pelvis and acetabulum because of its capability in demonstrating:
- The exact position and configuration of comminuted fragments
- The presence or absence of intra-articular fragments
- Injury to the soft tissues.

[6] MRI offers superior capabilities for evaluating traumatic conditions of the hip, in particular:
- To diagnose occult fractures and bone contusions (trabecular microfractures)
- To identify and quantify effectively the muscle injury and joint effusion that accompany traumatic hip dislocations.

[7] MRa is effective to evaluate injuries to the acetabular labrum, such as tears and detachments.

[8] IVP and cystourethrography are essential in the evaluation of concomitant injury to the lower urinary system.

Proximal Femur

[1] The importance of distinguishing between intracapsular and extracapsular fractures of the proximal femur (hip fractures) lies in the possible complications. Intracapsular fractures of the femoral neck are associated with a higher incidence of nonunion and osteonecrosis of the femoral head.

[2] The Garden staging of intracapsular fractures of the femoral neck has practical value in determining stability and prognosis.

[3] The Boyd-Griffin classification of intertrochanteric fractures according to the presence or absence of comminution and involvement of the subtrochanteric region has important prognostic value and serves as a guide to operative management.

[4] The Kyle classification is very effective from the practical point of view because it is based on the stability of various fractured fragments, and allows more accurate determination of prognosis of this injury.

[5] Subtrochanteric fractures are classified by:
  • Fielding, according to the level of the fracture line
  • Zickel, according to the level, obliquity, and comminution of the fracture.

[6] MRI is the ideal modality to detect and evaluate early changes of posttraumatic osteonecrosis of the femoral head.

Dislocations in the Hip Joint

[1] Dislocations in the hip joint are classified as anterior, posterior, and central (medial).

[2] Posterior dislocations are more common and are frequently associated with fractures involving the posterior acetabular rim.

[3] Anterior dislocations are rare. On the anteroposterior radiograph, the femur is abducted and externally rotated, and the femoral head lies medial and inferior to the acetabulum.

SUGGESTED READINGS

Aliabadi P, Baker ND, Jaramillo D. Hip arthrography, aspiration, block, and bursography. *Radiol Clin North Am* 1998;36:673–690.

Allard JC, Porter G, Ryerson RW. Occult posttraumatic avascular necrosis of hip revealed by MRI. *Magn Reson Imaging* 1992;10:155–159.

Blankenbaker DG, DeSmet AA, Keene JS, Fine JP. Classification and localization of acetabular tears. *Skeletal Radiol* 2007;36:391–397.

Blundell CM, Parker MJ, Pryor GA, Hopkinson-Woolley J, Bhonsle SS. Assessment of the AO classification of intracapsular fractures of the proximal femur. *J Bone Joint Surg [Br]* 1998;80B:679–683.

Boyd HB, Griffin LL. Classification and treatment of trochanteric fractures. *Arch Surg* 1949;58:853–866.

Brandser E, Marsh JL. Acetabular fractures: easier classification with a systematic approach. *Am J Roentgenol* 1998;171:1217–1228.

Brandser EA, El-Khoury GY, Marsh JL. Acetabular fractures: a systematic approach to classification. *Emerg Radiol* 1995;2:18–28.

Bray TJ. Acetabular fractures: classification and diagnosis. In: Chapman MW, ed. *Operative orthopedics*, vol. 1, 2nd ed. Philadelphia: JB Lippincott; 1993:539–553.

Bray TJ, Templeman DC. Fractures of the femoral neck. In: Chapman MW, ed. *Operative orthopaedics*, vol. 1, 2nd ed. Philadelphia: JB Lippincott; 1993:583–594.

Bucholz RW. The pathological anatomy of Malgaigne fracture-dislocations of the pelvis. *J Bone Joint Surg [Am]* 1981;63A:400–404.

Burgess AR, Tile M. Fractures of the pelvis. In: Rockwood CA Jr, Green DP, Bucholz RW, eds. *Fractures in adults*, vol. 2, 3rd ed. Philadelphia: JB Lippincott; 1991:1399–1479.

Burk DL, Mears DC, Kennedy WH, Cooperstein LA, Herbert DL. Three-dimensional computed tomography of acetabular fractures. *Radiology* 1985;155:183–186.

Combs JA. Hip and pelvis avulsion fractures in adolescents. *Physician Sports Med* 1994;22:41–49.

Conway WF, Totty WG, McEnery KW. CT and MRI imaging of the hip. State of the art. *Radiology* 1996;198:297–307.

Cvitanic O, Henzie G, Skezas N, Lyons J. Minter J. MRI diagnosis of tears of the hip abductor tendons (gluteus medius and gluteus minimus). *Am J Roentgenol* 2004;182:137–143.

Czerny C, Hofmann S, Neuhold A, et al. Lesions of the acetabular labrum: accuracy of MR imaging and MR arthrography in detection and staging. *Radiology* 1996;200:225–230.

Czerny C, Hofmann S, Urban M, et al. MR arthrography of the adult acetabular-labral complex: correlation with surgery and anatomy. *Am J Roentgenol* 1999;173:345–349.

DeLee JC. Fractures and dislocations of the hip. In: Rockwood CA Jr, Green DP, Bucholz RW, eds. *Fractures in adults*, vol. 2, 3rd ed. Philadelphia: JB Lippincott; 1991:1481–1651.

DeSmet AA. Magnetic resonance findings in skeletal muscle tears. *Skeletal Radiol* 1993;22:479–484.

DeSmet AA, Fisher DR, Heiner JP, Keene JS. Magnetic resonance imaging of muscle tears. *Skeletal Radiol* 1990;19:283–286.

Dunn AW, Morris HD. Fractures and dislocations of the pelvis. *J Bone Joint Surg [Am]* 1968;50A:1639–1648.

El-Khoury GY, Daniel WW, Kathol MH. Acute and chronic avulsive injuries. *Radiol Clin North Am* 1997;35:747–766.

Erb RE, Steele JR, Nance EP Jr, Edwards JR. Traumatic anterior dislocation of the hip: spectrum of plain film and CT findings. *Am J Roentgenol* 1995;165:1215–1219.

Fielding JW. Subtrochanteric fractures. *Clin Orthop* 1973;92:86–99.

Fitzgerald RH. Acetabular labrum tears: diagnosis and management. *Clin Orthop* 1995;311:60–68.

Garden RS. The structure and function of the proximal end of the femur. *J Bone Joint Surg [Br]* 1961;43B:576–589.

Garden RS. Low-angle fixation in fractures of the femoral neck. *J Bone Joint Surg [Br]* 1961;43B:647–663.

Garden RS. Reduction and fixation of subcapital fractures of the femur. *Orthop Clin North Am* 1974;5:683–712.

Ghelman B, Freiberger RH. The adult hip. In: Freiberger RH, Kaye JJ, eds. *Arthrography*. New York: Appleton-Century-Crofts; 1979:189–216.

Greenspan A, Norman A. The "pelvic digit"—an unusual developmental anomaly. *Skeletal Radiol* 1982;9:118–122.

Greenspan A, Norman A. The pelvic digit. *Bull Hosp Joint Dis Orthop Inst* 1984;44:72–75.

Guy RL, Butler-Manuel PA, Holder P, Brueton RN. The role of 3-D CT in the assessment of acetabular fractures. *Br J Radiol* 1992;65:384–389.

Haims A, Katz LD, Busconi B. MR arthrography of the hip. *Radiol Clin North Am* 1998;36:691–702.

Hayes CW, Balkissoon AA. Magnetic resonance imaging of the musculoskeletal system. II. The hip. *Clin Orthop* 1996;322:297–309.

Hunter JC, Brandser EA, Tran KA. Pelvic and acetabular trauma. *Radiol Clin North Am* 1997;35:559–590.

Judet R, Judet J, Letournel E. Fractures of the acetabulum: classification and surgical approaches for open reduction—preliminary report. *J Bone Joint Surg [Am]* 1964;46A:1615–1646.

Kricun ME. Fractures of the pelvis. *Orthop Clin North Am* 1990;21:573–590.

Kyle RF, Campbell SJ. Intertrochanteric fractures. In: Chapman MW, ed. *Operative orthopaedics*, vol. 1, 2nd ed. Philadelphia: JB Lippincott; 1993:595–604.

Lage LA, Patel JV, Viller RN. The acetabular labral tear: an arthroscopic classification. *Arthroscopy* 1996;12:269–272.

Laorr A, Greenspan A, Anderson MW, Moehring HD, McKinley T. Traumatic hip dislocation: early MRI findings. *Skeletal Radiol* 1995;24:239–245.

Letournel E. Acetabulum fractures: classification and management. *Clin Orthop* 1980;151:81–106.

Malgaigne JF. The classic-double vertical fractures of the pelvis. *Clin Orthop* 1980;151:8–11.

Martinez CR, DiPasquale TG, Helfet DL, Graham AW, Sanders RW, Ray LD. Evaluation of acetabular fractures with two- and three-dimensional CT. *Radiographics* 1992;12:227–242.

Mears DC. Fracture-dislocation of the pelvic ring. In: Chapman MW, ed. *Operative orthopaedics*, vol. 1, 2nd ed. Philadelphia: Lippincott; 1993:505–538.

Mitchell DG, Rao VM, Dalinka MK, et al. Femoral head avascular necrosis: correlation of MR imaging, radiographic staging, radionuclide imaging, and clinical findings. *Radiology* 1987;162:709–715.

Moehring HD. Hip dislocations and femoral head fractures. In: Chapman MW, ed. *Operative orthopaedics*, vol. 1, 2nd ed. Philadelphia: Lippincott; 1993:571–582.

Moehring HD, Greenspan A, eds. *Fractures – diagnosis and treatment*. New York: McGraw-Hill; 2000:99–105.

Nerubay J. Traumatic anterior dislocation of hip joint with vascular damage. *Clin Orthop* 1976;116:129–132.

Oka M, Monu JUV. Prevalence and patterns of occult hip fractures and mimics revealed by MRI. *Am J Roentgenol* 2004;182:283–288.

Olson SA, Matta JM. Surgical treatment of fractures of the acetabulum. In: Browner BD, Jupiter JB, Levine AM, Trafton PG, eds. *Skeletal trauma*, 2nd ed. Philadelphia: WB Saunders; 1990:1181–1222.

Palmer WE. MR arthrography of the hip. *Semin Musculoskel Radiol* 1998;2:349–361.

Pauwels F. *Biomechanics of the normal and diseased hip*. New York: Springer-Verlag; 1976.

Pennal GF, Tile M, Waddell JP, Garside H. Pelvic disruption: assessment and classification. *Clin Orthop* 1980;151:12–21.

Plotz GM, Brossmann J, von Knoch M, Muhle C, Heller M, Hassenpflug J. Magnetic resonance arthrography of the acetabular labrum: value of radial reconstructions. *Arch Orthop Trauma Surg* 2001;121:450–457.

Potok PS, Hopper KD, Umlauf MJ. Fractures of the acetabulum: imaging, classification, and understanding. *Radiographics* 1995;15:7–23.

Resnik CS, Stackhouse DJ, Shanmuganathan K, Young JWR. Diagnosis of pelvic fractures in patients with acute pelvic trauma. *Am J Roentgenol* 1992;158:109–112.

Richardson P, Young JWR, Porter D. CT detection of cortical fracture of the femoral head associated with posterior hip dislocation. *Am J Roentgenol* 1990;155:93–94.

Rogers LF, Hendrix RW. *Radiology of skeletal trauma,* 2nd ed. New York: Churchill Livingstone; 1992:991–1103.

Schmid MR, Notzli HP, Zanetti M, Wyss TF, Hodler J. Cartilage lesions in the hip: diagnostic effectiveness of MR arthrography. *Radiology* 2003;226:382–386.

Schultz E, Miller TT, Boruchov SD, Schmell EB, Toledano B. Incomplete intertrochanteric fractures: *Radiology* 1999;211:237–240.

Steinbach LS, Palmer WE, Schweitzer ME. Special focus session. MR arthrography. *Radiographics* 2002;22:1223–1246.

Stevens MA, El-Khoury GY, Kathol MH, Brandser EA, Chow S. Imaging features of avulsion injuries. *Radiographics* 1999;19:655–672.

Tehranzadeh J, Vanarthos W, Pais MJ. Osteochondral impaction of the femoral head associated with hip dislocation: CT study in 35 patients. *Am J Roentgenol* 1990;155:1049–1052.

Tile M. *Fractures of the pelvis and acetabulum.* Baltimore: Williams & Wilkins; 1984.

Wiss DA. Subtrochanteric femur fractures. In: Chapman MW, ed. *Operative orthopaedics,* vol. 1, 2nd ed. Philadelphia: JB Lippincott; 1993:605–620.

Yang R-S, Tsuang Y-H, Hang Y-S, Liu T-K. Traumatic dislocation of the hip. *Clin Orthop* 1991;265:218–227.

Yoon LS, Palmer WE, Kassarjian A. Evaluation of radial-sequence imaging in detecting acetabular labral tears at hip MR arthrography. *Skeletal Radiol* 2007;36:1029–1033.

Young JWR, Burgess AR, Brumback RJ, Poka A. Lateral compression fractures of the pelvis: the importance of plain radiographs in the diagnosis and surgical management. *Skeletal Radiol* 1986;15:103–109.

Young JWR, Resnik CS. Fracture of the pelvis: current concepts of classification. *Am J Roentgenol* 1990;155:1169–1175.

Zickel RE. An intramedullary fixation device for the proximal part of the femur. Nine year's experience. *J Bone Joint Surg [Am]* 1976;58A:866–872.

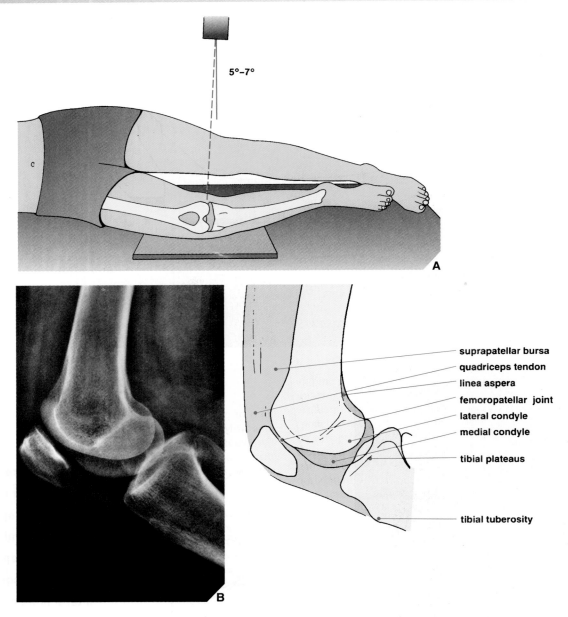

FIGURE 9.2 **Lateral view. (A)** For the lateral view of the knee, the patient is lying flat on the same side as the affected knee, which is flexed approximately 25 to 30 degrees. The central beam is directed vertically toward the medial aspect of the knee joint with an approximately 5- to 7-degree cephalad angulation. **(B)** The film in this projection demonstrates the patella in profile, as well as the femoropatellar joint compartment and a faint outline of the quadriceps tendon. The femoral condyles are seen overlapping, and the tibial plateaus are imaged in profile. Note the slight posterior tilt of the tibial plateaus, which normally measures approximately 10 degrees.

FEMOROPATELLAR RELATIONSHIP ◀ FIGURE 9.3 **Femoropatellar relationship.** The length of the patella and the patellar ligament are approximately equal; normal variability does not exceed 20%.

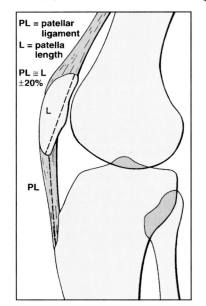

PL = patellar ligament
L = patella length
PL ≅ L ±20%

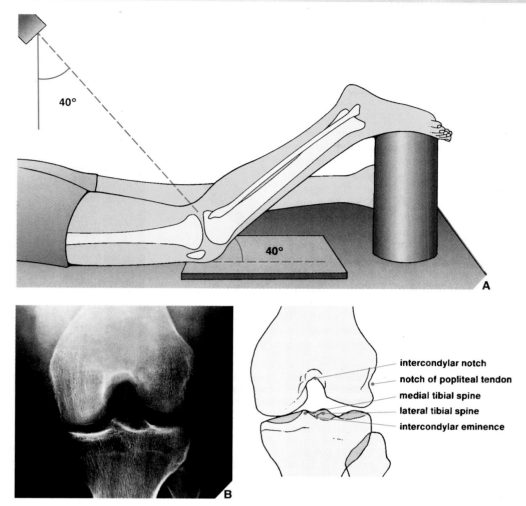

▲
FIGURE 9.4 Tunnel view. (A) For the tunnel (or notch) projection of the knee, the patient is prone with the knee flexed approximately 40 degrees, with the foot supported by a cylindrical sponge. The central beam is directed caudally toward the knee joint at a 40-degree angle from the vertical. **(B)** The radiograph in this projection demonstrates the posterior aspect of the femoral condyles, the intercondylar notch, and the intercondylar eminence of the tibia.

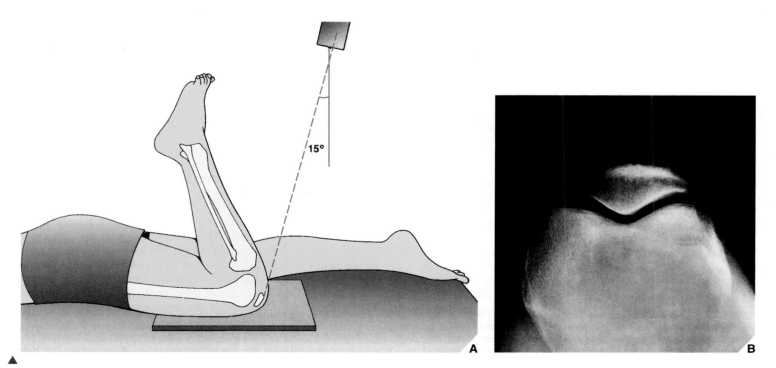

▲
FIGURE 9.5 Sunrise view. (A) For an axial (sunrise) view of the patella, the patient is prone, with the knee flexed 115 degrees. The central beam is directed toward the patella with approximately 15-degree cephalad angulation. **(B)** The radiograph in this projection demonstrates a tangential (axial) view of the patella. Note the deep position of this structure in the intercondylar fossa. The femoropatellar joint compartment is well demonstrated.

TOPOGRAPHY OF THE TIBIAL PLATEAU
Menisci and Ligaments

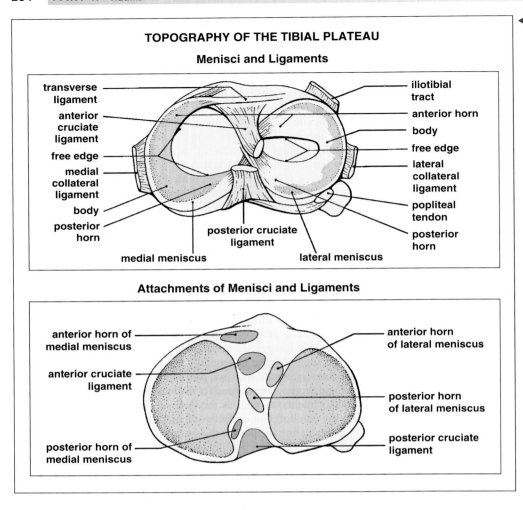

Attachments of Menisci and Ligaments

◄ FIGURE 9.9 **Tibial plateau.** In the topography of the tibial plateau, the medial meniscus is a C-shaped fibrocartilaginous structure with anterior horn attached anteriorly to the intercondylar eminence of the tibia and with posterior horn inserted into the intercondylar area in front of the attachment of the posterior cruciate ligament. The anterior horn of the lateral meniscus, which is an O-shaped structure, is attached in front of the lateral intercondylar tubercle, and the posterior horn inserts medially into the lateral intercondylar tubercle, in front of the attachment of the posterior horn of the medial meniscus.

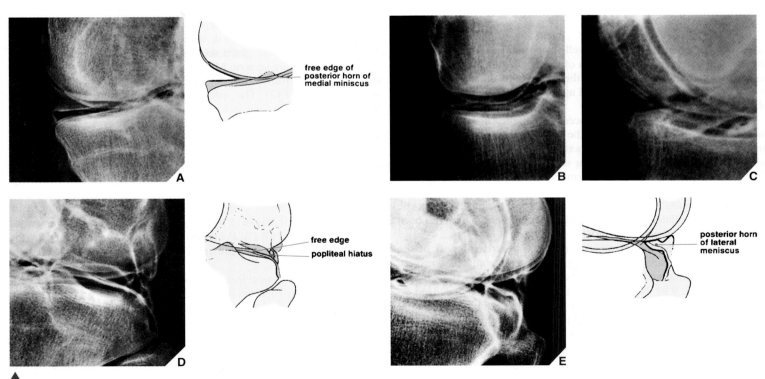

▲ FIGURE 9.10 **Arthrography of the knee.** Multiple spot films obtained during arthrographic examination of the knee demonstrate the normal appearance of the medial (**A,B,C**) and lateral (**D,E**) semilunar cartilages. The contrast-outlined margins of the medial meniscus show its triangular shape. The posterior horn (**A**) is longer than the body (**B**) and the anterior horn (**C**), and the free edge of the meniscus is sharply pointed. Features of the normal lateral meniscus include the gap of the popliteal hiatus, which separates the meniscus from the joint capsule (**D**). The posterior horn reattaches to the capsule more posteriorly (**E**). No contrast should be seen within the substance of any aspect of the menisci.

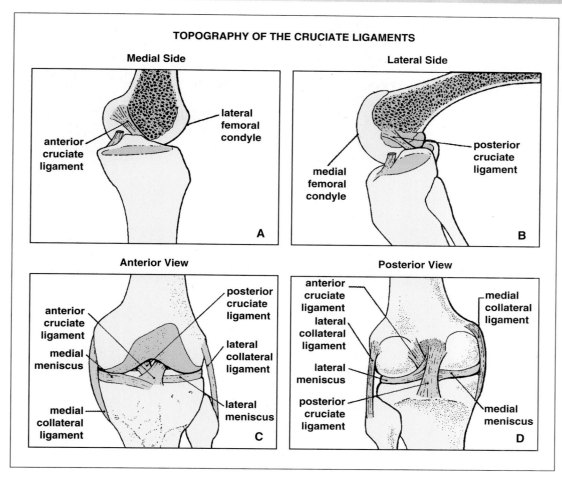

FIGURE 9.11 **The cruciate ligaments.** In the topography of the cruciate ligaments of the knee, the anterior cruciate ligament arises on the medial surface of the lateral femoral condyle at the intercondylar notch (**A**) and attaches on the anterior portion of the intercondylar eminence of the tibia (**C**) (see also Fig. 9.9). The posterior cruciate ligament originates on the lateral surface of the medial femoral condyle within the intercondylar notch (**B**) and inserts on the posterior surface of the intercondylar eminence (**D**) (see also Fig. 9.9). Neither cruciate ligament is attached to the tibial tubercles.

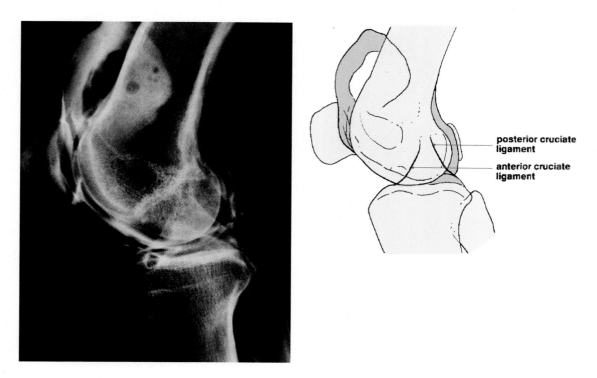

FIGURE 9.12 **Arthrography of the cruciate ligaments.** Double-contrast arthrogram of the knee demonstrates the normal appearance of the cruciate ligaments. Note the angle formed by their projectional intersection and their taut appearance. Each ligament can be traced from its origin in the femur to its insertion in the tibia. The boundaries of the cruciate ligaments are sharply outlined because the contrast medium coats their synovial reflexions. The cruciate ligaments are extrasynovial structures; only the anterior surface of the anterior cruciate ligament and the posterior surface of the posterior cruciate ligament are covered by synovium.

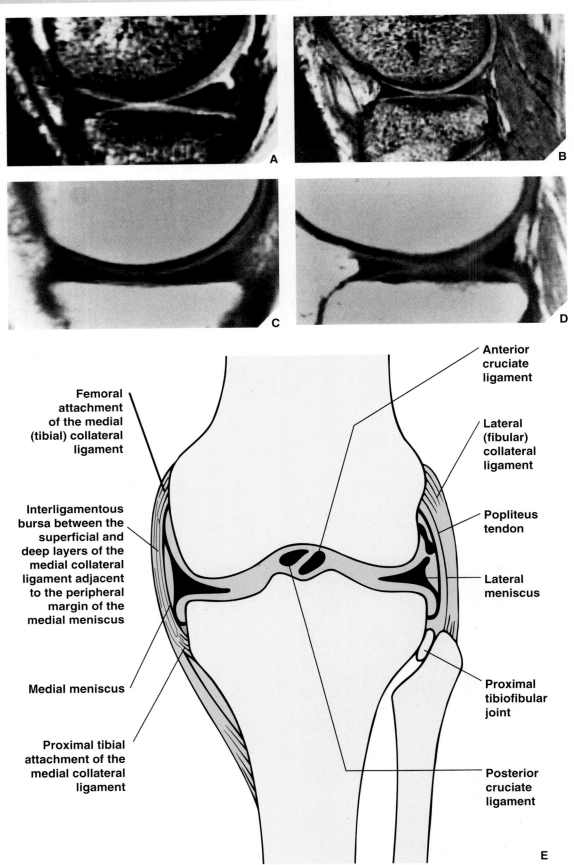

FIGURE 9.13 Appearance of normal menisci on MRI. (A) Anterior and posterior horns of the medial meniscus as seen on sagittal T2*-weighted MPGR sequence (flip angle 30 degrees). **(B)** Anterior and posterior horns of the lateral meniscus as seen on sagittal T2*-weighted MPGR sequence (flip angle 30 degrees). **(C)** Body of the medial meniscus as seen on sagittal spin-echo T1-weighted sequence. **(D)** Anterior and posterior horns of the lateral meniscus as seen on sagittal spin-echo T1-weighted sequence. **(E)** Schematic representation of topography of the medial and lateral menisci and surrounding structures as seen in the midplane of the coronal MRI. (Modified from Firooznia H, Golimbu C, Rafii M, 1994, with permission.)

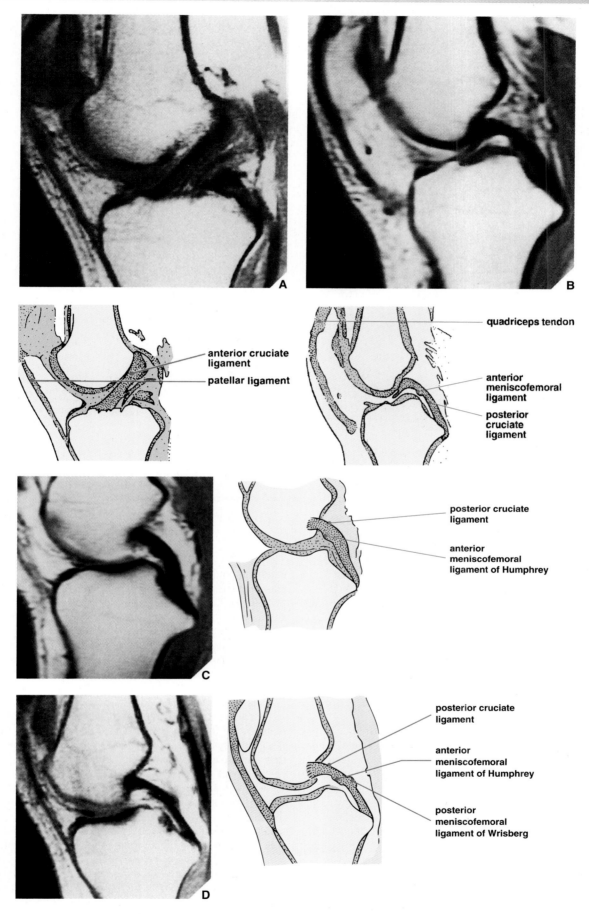

FIGURE 9.14 Cruciate ligaments. Spin-echo sagittal MR images (TR 2000/TE 20 msec) of the normal cruciate ligaments. **(A)** Anterior margin of the anterior cruciate ligament is straight and well defined; the posterior margin is ill defined because of the oblique orientation of the ligament. **(B)** The posterior cruciate ligament is seen in its entirety, in one plane, from the femoral to the tibial attachments. Observe the small bulge anteriorly produced by the anterior meniscofemoral ligament. **(C)** In this sagittal section, the anterior meniscofemoral ligament of Humphrey is very prominent, simulating a loose body or meniscal fragment. **(D)** Here, meniscofemoral ligaments, both anterior (Humphrey) and posterior (Wrisberg), are prominent. (From Beltran J, 1990, with permission.)

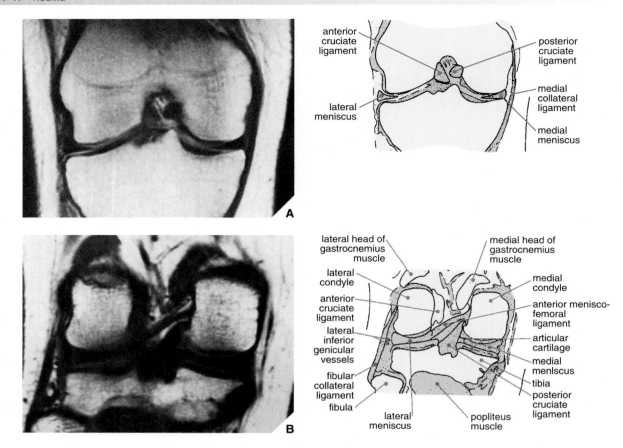

FIGURE 9.15   Collateral ligaments. (A) Spin-echo coronal MR image (TR 2000/TE 20 msec) of the normal medial collateral ligament. The medial collateral ligament is well defined in this section through the intercondylar notch. The insertion of the posterior cruciate ligament in the inner aspect of the medial femoral condyle is well demonstrated. The menisci are seen as small triangles of low signal intensity. **(B)** Spin-echo coronal MR image (TR 2000/TE 20 msec) of the lateral (fibular) collateral ligament. On this posterior section, note the meniscofemoral ligament, which extends from the posterior horn of the lateral meniscus to the inner surface of the medial femoral condyle. The lateral and medial menisci and posterior cruciate ligament are well demonstrated. (From Beltran J, 1990, with permission.)

on the images obtained in the coronal plane. Like the menisci and cruciate ligaments, they also display low signal intensity (Fig. 9.15).

During evaluation of MRI of the knee, it is helpful to use a checklist as provided in Table 9.1.

Evaluation of knee instability caused by ligament injuries may require obtaining stress views. These techniques are most commonly performed in cases of suspected injury to the medial collateral ligament (Fig. 9.16; see also Fig. 9.74). They are less frequently performed during the evaluation of insufficiency of the anterior and posterior cruciate ligaments (Fig. 9.17). These examinations should preferably be performed under local anesthesia.

Arteriography and venography may need to be used in the evaluation of concomitant injury to the vascular system, although recently more often MR angiography is performed for this purpose. CT is effective in the evaluation of tibial plateau fractures, and it is occasionally used to evaluate injury to the cartilage and soft tissues, particularly the menisci and cruciate ligaments. CT used in conjunction with arthrography (computed arthrotomography) is useful in the evaluation of osteochondritis dissecans (see Fig. 9.54C,D) and in detecting nonopaque osteochondral bodies in the knee joint.

For a summary of the preceding discussion in tabular form, see Tables 9.2 and 9.3 and Figure 9.18.

Injury to the Knee

Fractures About the Knee

Fractures of the Distal Femur. Most often sustained in motor vehicle accidents or falls from heights, fractures of the distal femur are classified according to the site and extension of the fracture line as supracondylar, condylar, and intercondylar. Supracondylar fractures can be further classified as nondisplaced, impacted, displaced, and comminuted (Fig. 9.19). These injuries are usually well demonstrated on the standard anteroposterior and lateral radiographs of the knee (Fig. 9.20); however, in rare instances an oblique view of the knee may be needed to evaluate an obliquely oriented fracture line. Tomography used to be required in cases of comminution for a full evaluation of the fracture lines and localization of the fragments (Fig. 9.21), although currently helical CT with multiplanar and 3D reformation has surpassed conventional tomographic technique (Fig. 9.22).

Fractures of the Proximal Tibia. The medial and lateral tibial plateaus are the most common sites of fractures of the proximal tibia. Because they usually result when the knee is struck by a moving vehicle, they are also called "fender" or "bumper" fractures; some, however, may be the result of twisting falls. The Hohl classification gives an overview of six different types of tibial plateau fractures and is useful in correlating the various types of injuries with the applied forces causing them (Fig. 9.23). In the Hohl classification, pure abduction injury results in a nondisplaced split fracture of the lateral tibial plateau (type I) (Fig. 9.24). When axial compression is combined with abduction force, local central depression (type II) and local split depression (type III) fractures occur (Fig. 9.25). Total depression fractures (type IV), which are more commonly seen in the medial tibial plateau because of its anatomic configuration (absence of the fibula), are characterized by the lack of comminution of the articular surface. Type V fractures in the Hohl classification, which are infrequently encountered, are local split fractures without central depression involving the anterior or posterior aspects of the tibial plateau. Comminuted fractures involving both tibial plateaus and having a Y or T configuration (type VI) usually result from vertical

TABLE 9.1 **Checklist for Evaluation of MRI of the Knee**

Osseous Structures
   Femoral condyles (c, s, a)
   Tibial plateau (c, s)
   Gerdy tubercle (s, a)
   Patella (c, s, a)
   Proximal fibula (c, s, a)

Cartilaginous Structures
   Articular cartilage (c, s, a)

Joints
   Femorotibial (c, s)
   Femoropatellar (s, a)

Menisci
   Medial (c, s)
   Lateral (c, s)

Ligaments
   Medial collateral—deep and superficial fibers (c)
   Lateral collateral complex—biceps femoris tendon, lateral collateral
      ligament (LCL) proper,   iliotibial band (c)
   Anterior cruciate—anteromedial and posterolateral bundles (c, s)
   Posterior cruciate (c, s)
   Meniscofemoral—Humphry (anterior) and Wrisberg (posterior) (c, s)
   Transverse (s)
   Patellar ("tendon") (s)
   Patellar retinaculae—medial and lateral (a)
   Arcuate (c, a)
   Popliteofibular (c, s)
   Fabellofibular (c)

Muscles and Their Tendons
   Quadriceps (s, a)
   Popliteus (c, s)
   Plantaris (a)
   Biceps femoris (c)
   Semimembranosus (s, a)
   Semitendinosus (s, a)
   Gracilis (s, a)
   Sartorius (s, a)
   Gastrocnemius (s, a)
   Soleus (s, a)

Bursae
   Popliteal (Baker)—between the tendons of the medial
      head of gastrocnemius and semimembranosus (s, a)
   Prepatellar (s, a)
   Deep infrapatellar (s, a)
   Pes anserinus (c)
   Semimembranosus—tibial collateral ligament (c)

Other Structures
   Synovial plicae (c, a)
   Infrapatellar plica (s)
   Hoffa fat pad (s, a)
   Popliteus hiatus (c)
   Popliteal artery and vein (a)
   Lateral geniculate artery (c)
   Tibial and peroneal nerves (a)

The best imaging planes for visualization of listed structures are given in parenthesis; c, coronal; s, sagittal; a, axial.

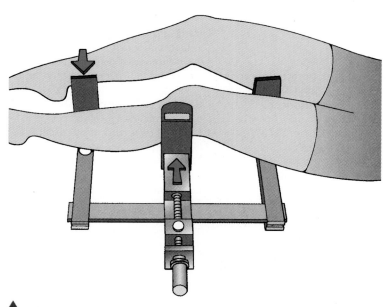

▲
FIGURE 9.16 Valgus stress. For a stress film of the knee evaluating the medial collateral ligament, the patient is supine, with the knee flexed approximately 15 to 20 degrees. The leg is placed in the device, and the pressure plate is applied against the lateral aspect of the knee. (The *arrows* show the direction of the applied stresses.) Films are then obtained in the anteroposterior projection (see Fig. 9.74B).

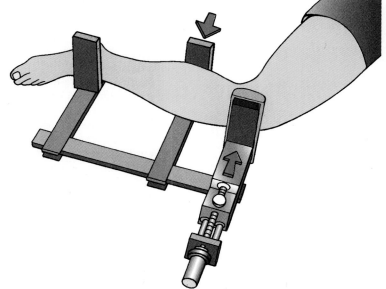

▲
FIGURE 9.17 Anterior-drawer stress. For a stress film of the knee evaluating the anterior cruciate ligament, the patient is placed in the device on his or her side, with the knee flexed 90 degrees. The pressure plate is applied against the anterior aspect of the knee. (The *arrows* show the direction of the applied stresses.) Films are then obtained in the lateral projection.

TABLE 9.2 **Standard and Special Radiographic Projections for Evaluating Injury to the Knee**

Projection	Demonstration	Projection	Demonstration
Anteroposterior	Medial and lateral joint compartments	Lateral (continued)	Sinding-Larsen-Johansson disease*
	Varus and valgus deformities		Osgood-Schlatter disease*
	Fractures of:		Osteochondral fracture
	Medial and lateral femoral condyles		Osteochondritis dissecans (late stage)
	Medial and lateral tibial plateaus		Spontaneous osteonecrosis
	Tibial spines		Joint effusion
	Proximal fibula		Tears of:
	Osteochondral fracture		Quadriceps tendon
	Osteochondritis dissecans (late-stage)		Patellar ligament
	Spontaneous osteonecrosis	Stress	Tears of cruciate ligaments
	Pellegrini-Stieda lesion	Cross-table	FBI sign of lipohemarthrosis
Overpenetrated	Bipartiite or multipartite patella	Tunnel (posteroan-	Posterior aspect of femoral condyles
	Fractures of patella	terior)	Intercondylar notch
Stress	Tear of collateral ligaments		Intercondylar eminence of tibia
Lateral	Femoropatellar joint compartment	Axial (sunrise and	Articular facets of patella†
	Patella in profile	Merchant)	Sulcus angle†
	Suprapatellar bursa		Congruence angle†
	Fractures of:		Fractures of patella
	Distal femur		Subluxation and dislocation of patella†
	Proximal tibia		
	Patella		

*These conditions are best demonstrated using a low-kilovoltage/soft-tissue technique.
†These features are better demonstrated on Merchant axial view.

TABLE 9.3 **Ancillary Imaging Techniques for Evaluating Injury to the Knee**

Technique	Demonstration	Technique	Demonstration
Arthrography (usually double-contrast; occasionally single contrast using air only)	Meniscal tears	Radionuclide Imaging (scintigraphy, bone scan)	Subtle fractures not demonstrated on standard studies
	Injuries to:		Early and late stages of
	Cruciate ligaments		Osteochondritis dissecans
	Medial collateral ligament		Spontaneous osteonecrosis
	Quadriceps tendon	Angiography (arteriography, venography)	Concomitant injury to arteries and veins
	Patellar ligament	Magnetic Resonance Imaging	Same as arthrography, CT, and radionuclide imaging
	Joint capsule		
	Chondral and osteochondral fractures	Magnetic Resonance Arthrography	Residual or recurrent meniscal tears
	Osteochondritis dissecans (early and late stages)		Complications after meniscal surgery
	Osteochondral bodies in joint		Loose intraarticular bodies
	Subtle abnormalities of articular cartilage		Synovial plicae
Computed Tomography and Computed Arthrotomography	Spontaneous osteonecrosis		Stability of osteochondral lesions
	Injuries to:		Tears of collateral ligaments
	Articular cartilage		Tears of cruciate ligaments
	Cruciate ligaments	Magenetic Resonance Angiography	Same as angiography
	Menisci		
	Osteochondral bodies in joint		
	Osteochondritis dissecans		

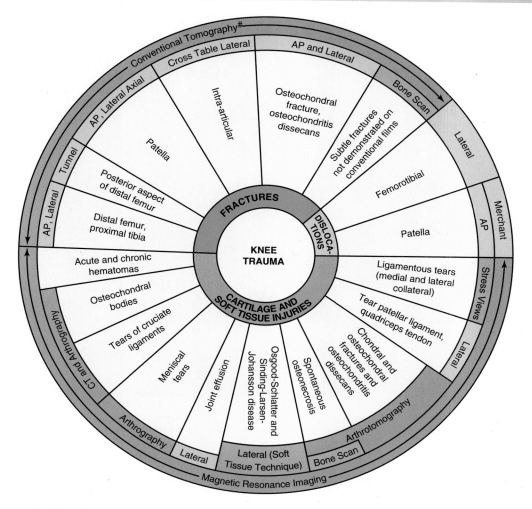

▲
FIGURE 9.18 **Spectrum of radiologic imaging techniques for evaluating injury to the knee.***

The radiographic projections or radiologic techniques indicated throughout the diagram are only those that are the most effective in demonstrating the respective traumatic conditions.

#Almost completely replaced by CT.

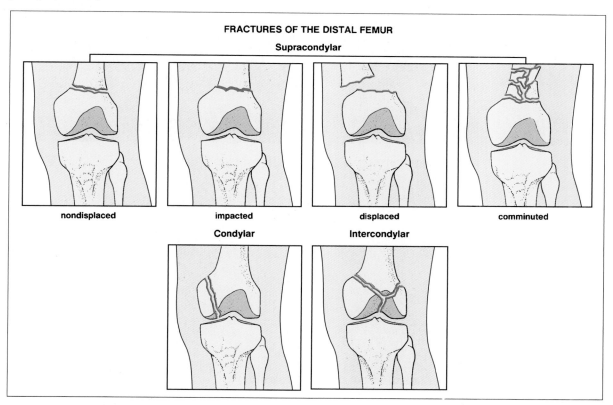

▲
FIGURE 9.19 **Classification of distal femur fractures.** Fractures of the distal femur can be classified according to the site and extension of the injury as supracondylar, condylar, and intercondylar fractures.

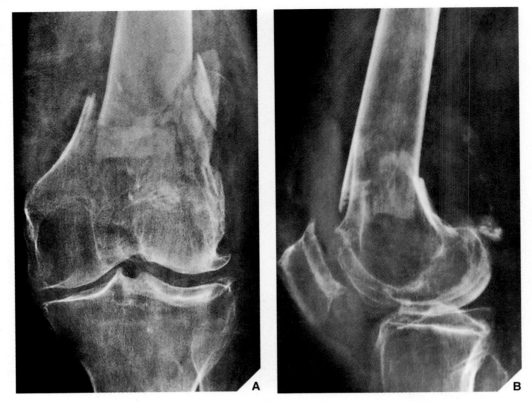

▲
FIGURE 9.20   **Supracondylar fracture.** A 58-year-old man was injured in a motorcycle accident. Anteroposterior (**A**) and lateral (**B**) radiographs of the knee demonstrate a comminuted supracondylar fracture of the distal femur. The extension of the fracture lines and the position of the fragments can be assessed adequately on these standard studies.

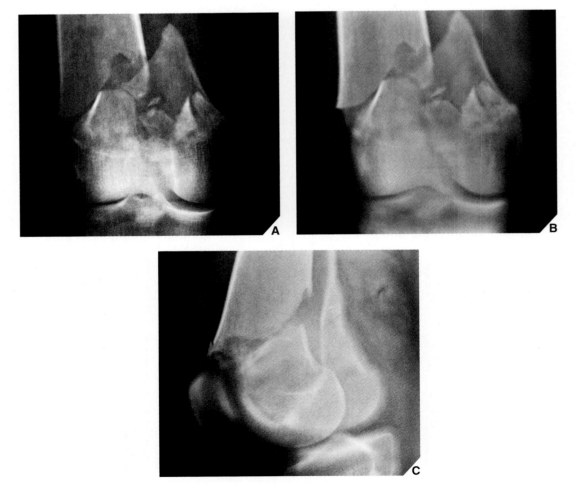

▲
FIGURE 9.21   **Supracondylar fracture.** A 22-year-old racing car driver was injured in an accident on the track. (**A**) Anteroposterior view of the right knee shows a comminuted fracture of the distal femur. Tomography was performed, and sections in the anteroposterior (**B**) and lateral (**C**) projections demonstrate intraarticular extension of the fracture lines, with split of the condyles and posterior displacement of the distal fragments. The multiple comminuted fragments can be localized.

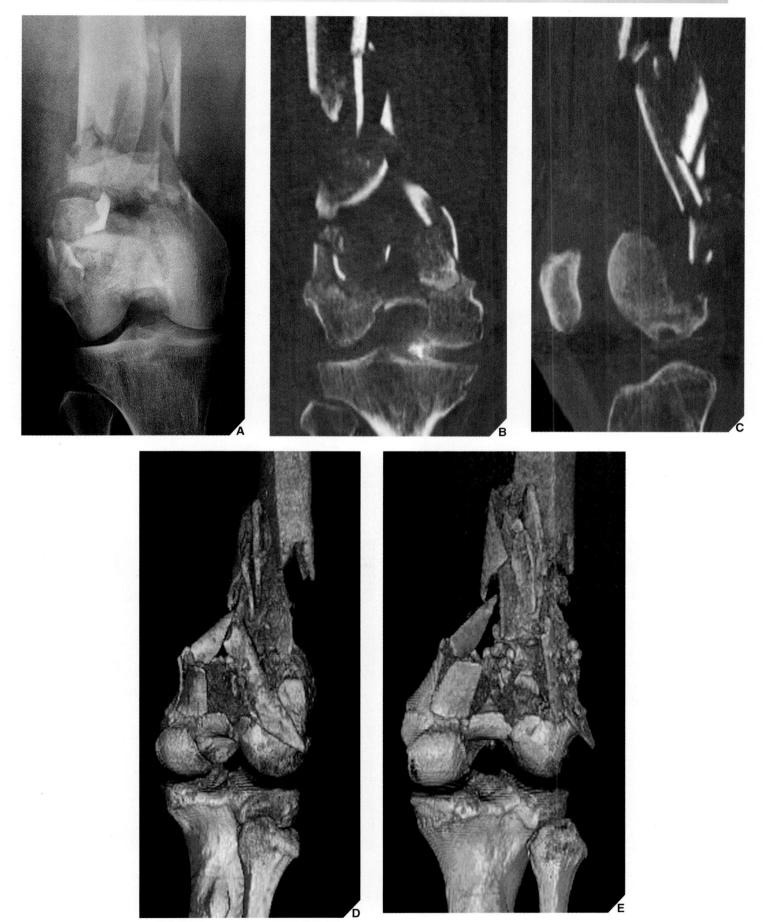

FIGURE 9.22 CT and 3D CT of supracondylar fracture. A 54-year-old woman was injured in a motor vehicle accident. (**A**) Anteroposterior radiograph of the right knee shows markedly comminuted supracondylar fracture of the femur. (**B,C**) Coronal and sagittal reformatted CT images show displacement of various fracture fragments. Three-dimensional CT reconstructed images, (**D**) oblique and (**E**) viewed from the posterior aspect, depict the position and orientation of displaced fracture fragments in more comprehensive fasion.

HOHL CLASSIFICATION OF TIBIAL PLATEAU FRACTURES

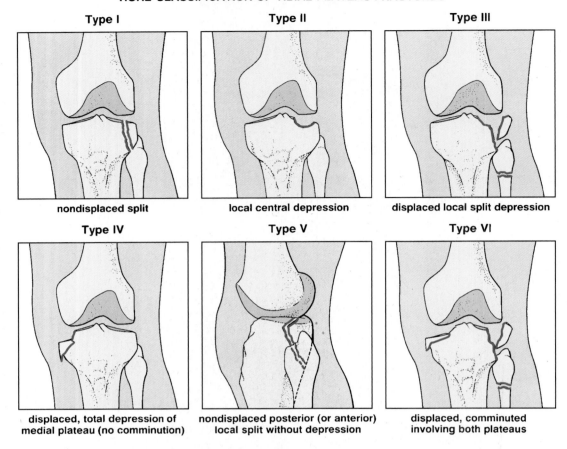

Type I
nondisplaced split

Type II
local central depression

Type III
displaced local split depression

Type IV
displaced, total depression of medial plateau (no comminution)

Type V
nondisplaced posterior (or anterior) local split without depression

Type VI
displaced, comminuted involving both plateaus

▲
FIGURE 9.23   The Hohl classification of fractures of the tibial plateau. (Modified from Hohl M, 1967, with permission.)

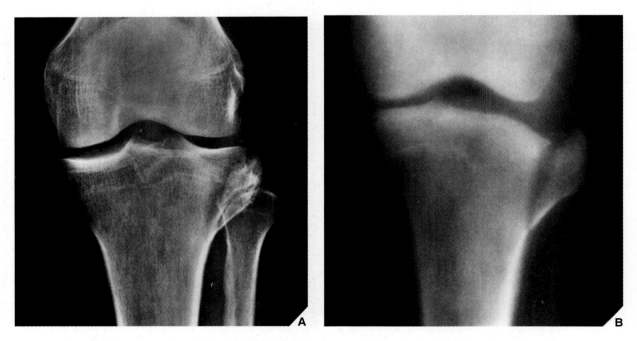

▲
FIGURE 9.24   **Fracture of the tibial plateau.** A 30-year-old man was hit by a car while he was crossing the street. Anteroposterior radiograph (**A**) and tomogram (**B**) show a split fracture of the lateral tibial plateau (Hohl type I).

FIGURE 9.25   **Fracture of the tibial plateau.** Anteroposterior ▶
radiograph of the knee shows the appearance of a tibial plateau
fracture, which is a combination of wedge and central depression fractures involving the lateral tibial condyle (Hohl type III).

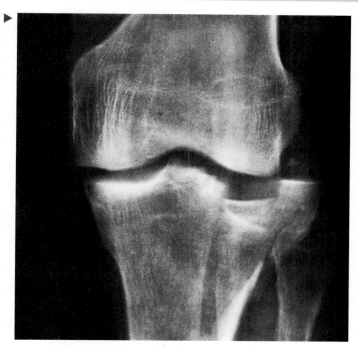

compression, such as a fall on the extended leg (Fig. 9.26). Types III and
VI are frequently associated with fracture of the proximal fibula. In our
institution we use the Schatzker classification of tibial plateau fractures
which, similar to the Hohl classification, arranges tibial plateau fractures
into VI types, but according to involvement of the medial or lateral plateau (Fig. 9.27).

Fractures of the tibial plateau may not be obvious on the routine radiographic examination of the knee, particularly if there is no
depression (Fig. 9.28A,B). In such cases, however, the cross-table lateral
projection often reveals the FBI sign, which indicates the presence of an
intraarticular fracture (Fig. 9.28C). Demonstration of an obscure fracture line may require oblique projections.

The role of CT in evaluation of tibial plateau fractures has been
well established. CT provides optimal visualization of the plateau

depression, defects, and split fragments. It also proved more accurate
than conventional tomography in assessing depressed and split fractures
when they involved the anterior and posterior border of the plateau,
and in demonstrating the extent of fracture comminution. Particularly
useful are reformatted images in various planes and 3D reconstruction
(Figs. 9.29 to 9.31). Recently, Kode and coworkers suggested that MRI
was equivalent or superior to 2D CT reformation for the depiction of tibial plateau fracture configuration (Figs. 9.32 and 9.33). The multiplanar
capabilities of MRI may facilitate 3D perception and, in addition, this
technique permits assessment of the associated injuries to the ligaments
and menisci that are not visible on CT scans (Fig. 9.34).

An important feature of tibial plateau fractures is their association
with injury to ligaments and the menisci. The structures most at risk are
the medial collateral and the anterior cruciate ligaments (see Fig 9.11)

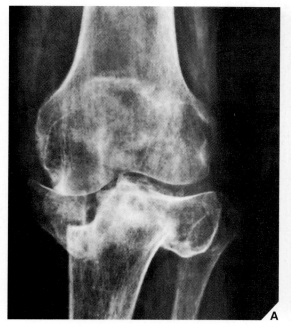

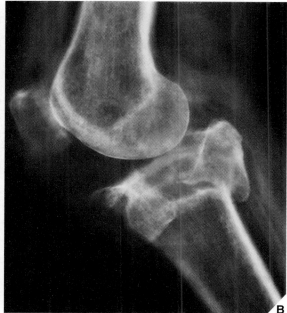

FIGURE 9.26   **Fracture of the tibial plateau.** Anteroposterior radiograph (**A**) and lateral tomogram (**B**) demonstrate the characteristic appearance of the Y-type
bicondylar tibial fracture (Hohl type VI).

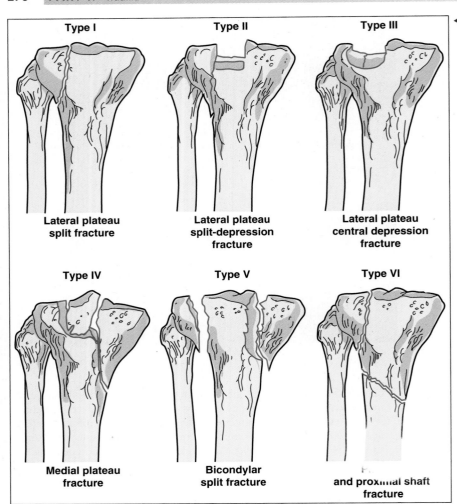

Type I

Lateral plateau
split fracture

Type II

Lateral plateau
split-depression
fracture

Type III

Lateral plateau
central depression
fracture

Type IV

Medial plateau
fracture

Type V

Bicondylar
split fracture

Type VI

and proximal shaft
fracture

◀ FIGURE 9.27 The Schatzker classification of fractures of the tibial plateau. (Modified from Koval, Helfet, 1995, with permission.)

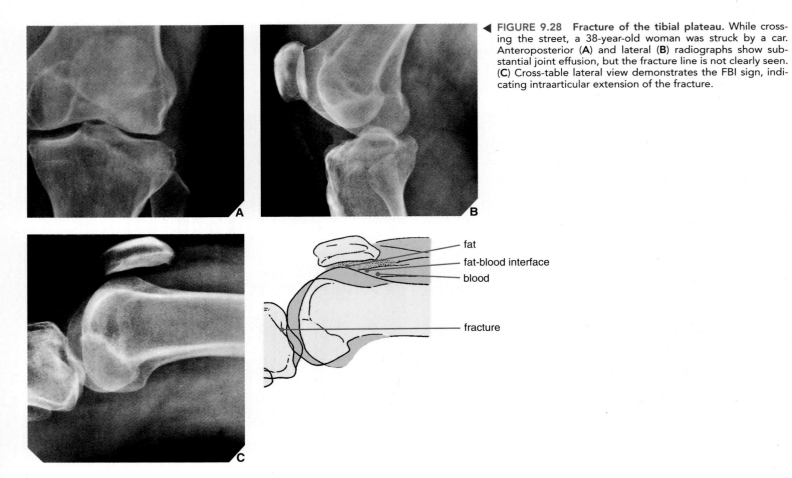

◀ FIGURE 9.28 Fracture of the tibial plateau. While crossing the street, a 38-year-old woman was struck by a car. Anteroposterior (A) and lateral (B) radiographs show substantial joint effusion, but the fracture line is not clearly seen. (C) Cross-table lateral view demonstrates the FBI sign, indicating intraarticular extension of the fracture.

fat
fat-blood interface
blood

fracture

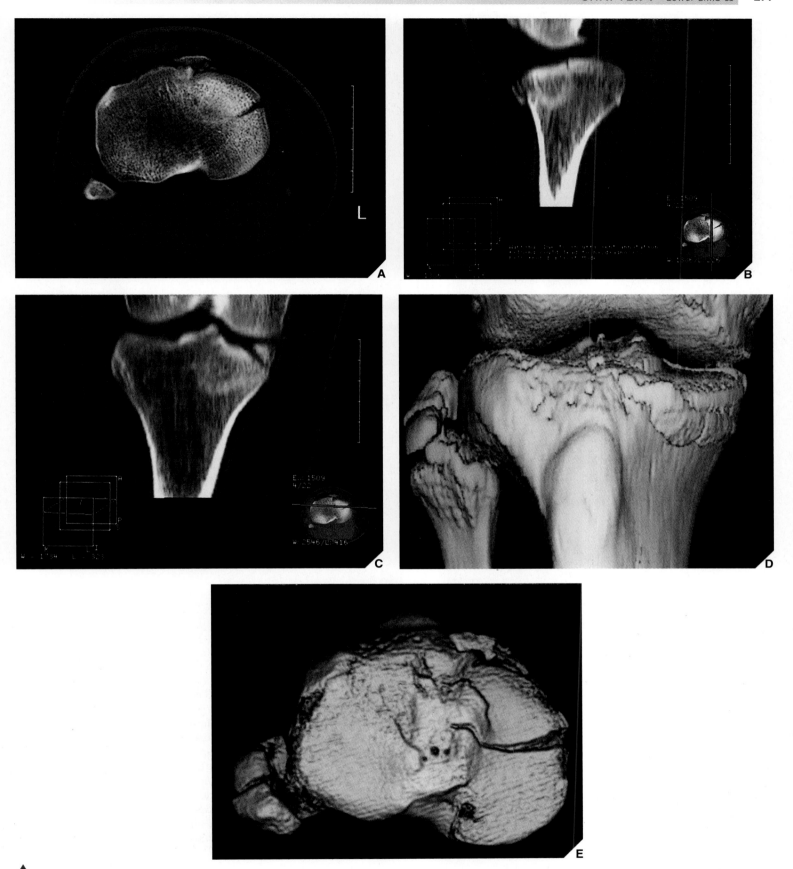

FIGURE 9.29 CT of fracture of the tibial plateau. A 23-year-old man was injured in a motorcycle accident. The conventional radiographs of the right knee showed fracture of the tibial plateau. (**A**) Axial CT section through the proximal tibia shows a comminuted fracture of the medial tibial plateau. (**B**) Sagittal reformatted image shows that the anterior part of the plateau is mainly affected. (**C**) Coronal reformatted image demonstrates comminution and depression. (**D**) Anterior view of the 3D reconstructed image in addition to depression of the medial anterior tibial plateau shows associated fracture of the proximal fibula. (**E**) Bird's eye view of the 3D reconstructed image shows the spatial orientation of the fracture lines.

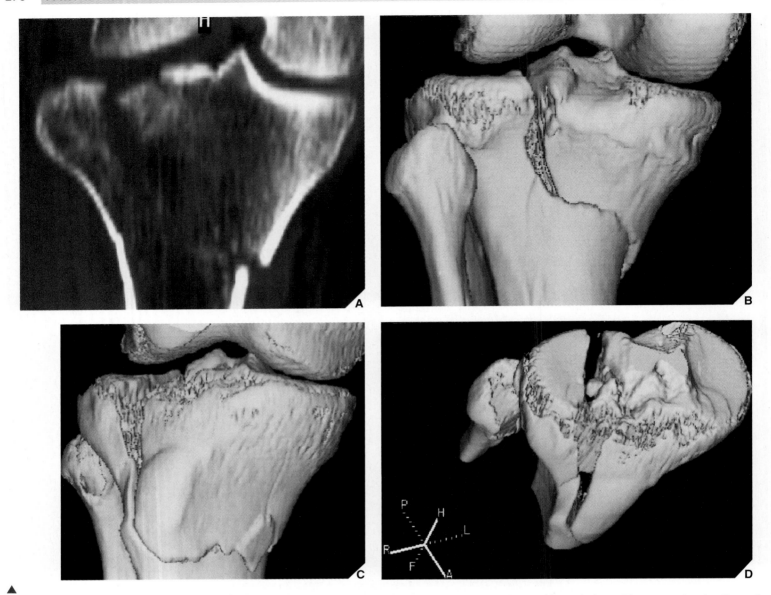

▲
FIGURE 9.30   **CT of fracture of the tibial plateau.** A 22-year-old man fell down from a tall ladder and injured his right knee. The conventional radiographs demonstrated fracture of the tibial plateau. (**A**) Coronal reformatted CT scan shows extension of the lateral tibial plateau fracture into the tibial shaft. (**B**) Posterior view of the 3D reconstruction shows the fracture line, but the interfragmental split is not well demonstrated. (**C**) Anterior view of the 3D reconstruction shows the split better. (**D**) Bird's eye view of the 3D CT scan effectively demonstrates the details of the split and comminution of the tibial plateau.

and the lateral meniscus (see Fig. 9.9), because lateral tibial plateau fractures usually result from valgus stress (Fig. 9.35).

Moreover, damage to the anterior cruciate ligament may be associated with avulsion of the lateral tibial spine or the anterior intercondylar eminence. Stress views and MRI usually reveal these associated abnormalities. If clinical examination and radiologic studies, including stress views, show ligamentous structures to be intact, then nondisplaced fractures of the tibial plateau can be treated conservatively. In depression-type fractures, however, Larson recommends open reduction in patients whose fractures show 8 mm of articular depression. Generally, surgery is indicated for fractures of the tibial plateau showing articular depression of 10 mm or more.

Complications. The most frequent complications of fractures of the distal femur and the proximal tibia are malunion and posttraumatic arthritis.

Segond Fracture. The Segond fracture consists of a small-fragment avulsion fracture from the lateral aspect of the proximal tibia just below the level of the tibial plateau, best demonstrated on anteroposterior radiograph of the knee (Fig. 9.36). The mechanism of this injury is internal rotation of the leg associated with varus stress on a flexed knee that creates tension on the lateral capsule and lateral capsular ligament. This, in turn, causes an avulsion fracture at the insertion of this ligament on the lateral tibial plateau. This injury may be associated with capsular tear, a tear of the anterior cruciate ligament, and lateral meniscus tear, resulting in chronic anterolateral knee instability.

Recently, Hall and Hochman described a reverse Segond-type fracture affecting medial tibial plateau, associated with tears of the posterior cruciate ligament, medial collateral ligament, and medial meniscus. The mechanism of this injury and the constellation of radiographic findings are the reverse of that seen with the classic Segond injury complex. The avulsion fracture of the medial tibial plateau is caused by a valgus stress and external rotation of a flexed knee.

Fractures of the Patella. Fractures of the patella, which may result from a direct blow to the anterior aspect of the knee or from indirect tension forces generated by the quadriceps tendon, constitute approximately 1% of all skeletal injuries. Generally, patellar fractures may be

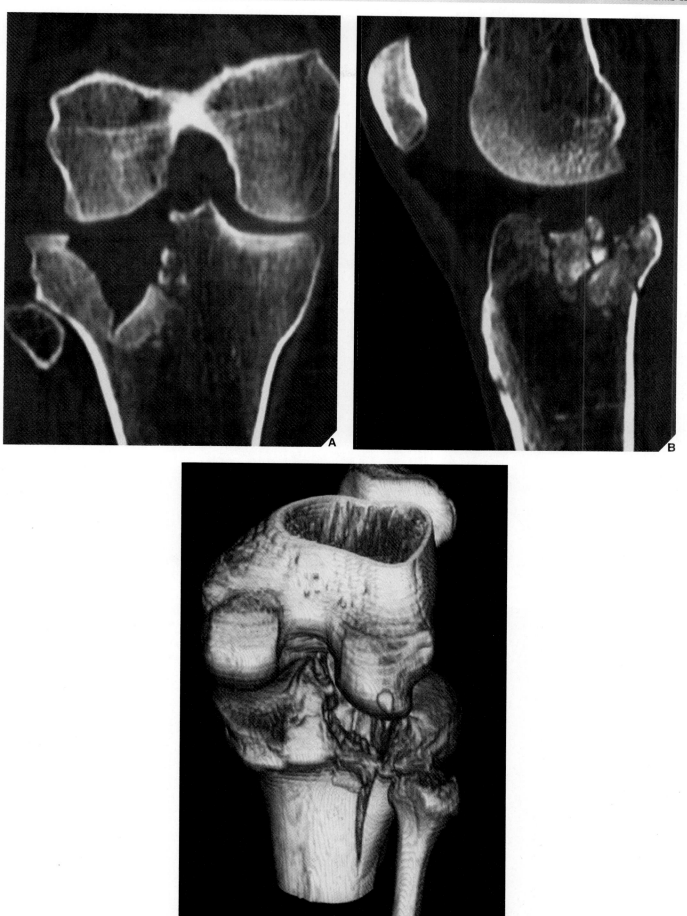

FIGURE 9.31 CT of fracture of the tibial plateau. Coronal (**A**) and sagittal (**B**) CT reformatted images show a Hohl type III (displaced, local spit depression) fracture of the lateral tibial plateau. (**C**) 3D reconstructed image (posterior view) more realistically depicts the features of this injury.

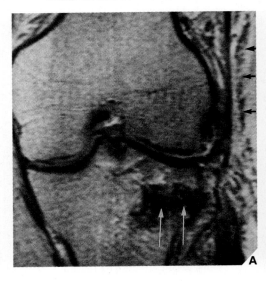
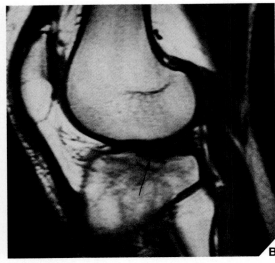

◀ **FIGURE 9.32** **MRI of fracture of the tibial plateau. (A)** T2-weighted (spin-echo, TR 2000/TE 80 msec) coronal image shows a broad-based band of low signal intensity traversing the lateral tibial plateau (*long arrows*). Extensive soft-tissue edema is seen superficial to the iliotibial band (*small arrows*). **(B)** Proton density–weighted (spin-echo, TR 2000/TE 20 msec) sagittal image shows central localized depression of the tibial plateau (*arrow*). The degree of comminution and depression is well depicted.

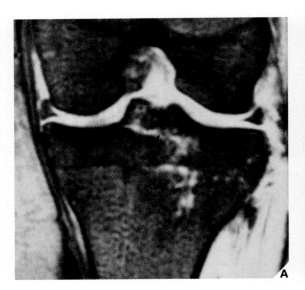
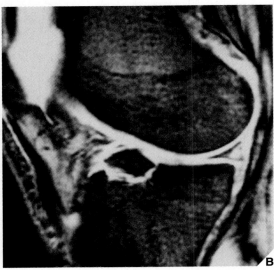

◀ **FIGURE 9.33** **MRI of fracture of the tibial plateau. (A)** Coronal gradient echo (MGPR) image shows a tibial plateau fracture (*arrowheads*). **(B)** Sagittal gradient echo (MGPR) image demonstrates the anterior extension of the fracture and evulsion of the tibial spines (*arrowheads*).

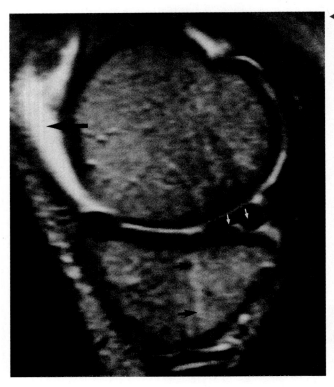

◀ **FIGURE 9.34** **MRI of fracture of the tibial plateau.** Sagittal T2-weighted image shows a fracture of the medial tibial plateau (*small black arrows*) associated with a tear of the posterior horn of the medial meniscus (*white arrows*). Joint effusion (*large black arrow*) demonstrates high signal intensity.

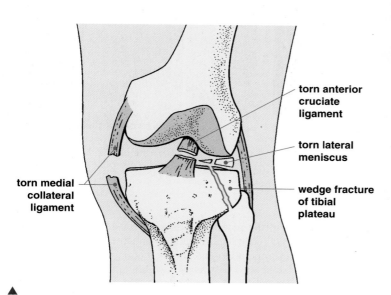

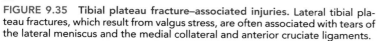

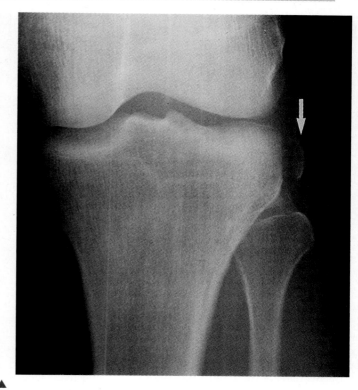

▲
FIGURE 9.35   Tibial plateau fracture–associated injuries. Lateral tibial plateau fractures, which result from valgus stress, are often associated with tears of the lateral meniscus and the medial collateral and anterior cruciate ligaments.

▲
FIGURE 9.36   Segond fracture. A 27-year-old woman sustained an injury to her left knee in a skiing accident. Anteroposterior radiograph shows a small fragment of bone evulsed from the lateral aspect of the tibia (*arrow*), characteristic of Segond fracture.

longitudinal (vertical), transverse, or comminuted (Fig. 9.37). In the most commonly encountered patellar injury, seen in 60% of cases, the fracture line is transverse or slightly oblique, involving the midportion of the patella. In evaluation of such injury, it is important to recognize what has been called the bipartite or multipartite patella. This anomaly represents a developmental variant of the accessory ossification center

or centers of the superolateral margin of the patella and should not be mistaken for a fracture (Fig. 9.38). CT may help distinguish this developmental anomaly from patellar fracture. As an aid to avoid misdiagnosing a bipartite or multipartite patella as a fracture, it is important to keep in mind that the accessory ossification centers are invariably in the upper lateral quadrant of the patella and, if the apparent fragments

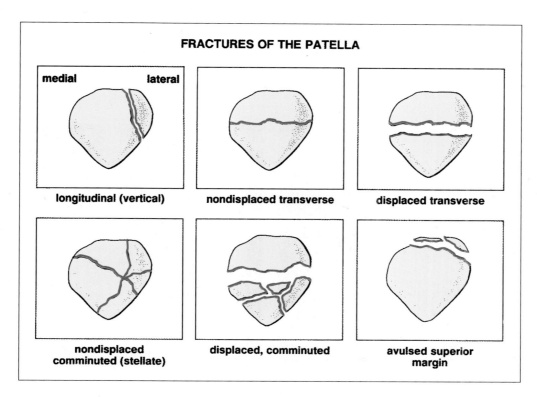

▲
FIGURE 9.37   Classification of patellar fractures. (Modified from Hohl M, Larson RL, 1975, with permission.)

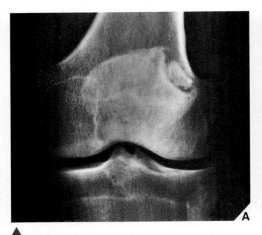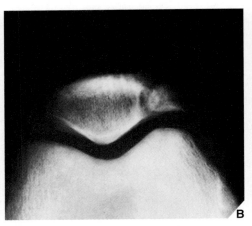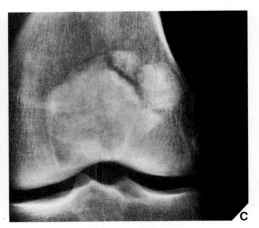

FIGURE 9.38 **Multipartite patella.** Anteroposterior (**A**) and axial (**B**) radiographs demonstrate the typical appearance of a bipartite patella. Note the position of the accessory ossification center at the superolateral margin of the patella. (**C**) A tripartite patella was an incidental finding on this overpenetrated anteroposterior film, which was obtained to exclude the possibility of gouty arthritis.

are put together, they do not form a normal patella. Fracture fragments, however, form a normal patella if they are replaced. Injury to the patella is usually sufficiently demonstrated on the overpenetrated anteroposterior and lateral views of the knee (Fig. 9.39).

Dislocations of the Patella. Dislocations of the patella, which are usually lateral, result from acute injury and are easily diagnosed on the standard projections of the knee. It is much more difficult to diagnose so-called transient dislocation, referred to as the traumatic condition when dislocated patella reduces on its own. Transient dislocation may be associated with hypoplastic trochlear notch of the femur. Although clinical symptoms are helpful, the most accurate diagnostic modality in this respect is MRI. It shows a characteristic pattern of "bone contusion" or trabecular injury on the medial aspect of the patella and anterior lateral femoral condyle (Figs. 9.40 and 9.41). The medial retinaculum is invariably injured, but medial patellar cartilage may or may not show abnormalities. Subluxations of the patella are much more common than true dislocations and usually result from chronic injury. The best radiographic examination for demonstrating patellar subluxation, particularly in subtle cases, is the Merchant axial view (Fig. 9.42).

Sinding-Larsen-Johansson Disease

Sinding-Larsen-Johansson disease is a condition that is seen predominantly in adolescents and is now considered to be related to trauma. It occurs at proximal end of the patellar ligament, where it attaches to the lower pole (apex) of the patella. Sinding-Larsen-Johansson disease is characterized clinically by local pain and tenderness on palpation and radiographically by separation and fragmentation of the lower pole of the patella, associated with soft-tissue swelling and, occasionally, calcifications at the site of the patellar ligament. This condition is believed to be caused by persistent traction at the cartilaginous junction of the patella and patellar ligament. The lateral radiograph, preferably obtained with a low-kilovoltage/soft-tissue technique, is the single most important examination (Fig. 9.43); in combination with a positive clinical examination, it usually establishes the diagnosis.

Osgood-Schlatter Disease

Osgood-Schlatter disease, first described in 1903 by Robert Osgood of Boston and Carl Schlatter of Zurich, occurs three times more frequently in adolescent boys than in adolescent girls, and is characterized by fragmentation of the tibial tuberosity, soft-tissue swelling and thickening at the insertion of the patellar ligament, and inflammation of the deep infrapatellar bursa. In 25% to 33% of all reported cases, the condition is bilateral. As in Sinding-Larsen-Johansson disease, the lateral radiograph, obtained using a soft-tissue technique, is most effective in demonstrating this condition (Fig. 9.44). However, an accurate diagnosis is based on both imaging and clinical findings. Soft-tissue swelling and deep infrapatellar bursitis and/or fibrosis are fundamental diagnostic features. Ultrasound (US) of the tibial tuberosity complex is an effective method

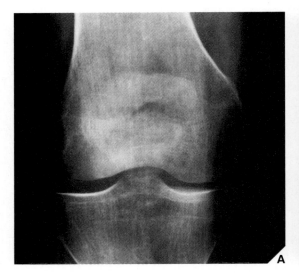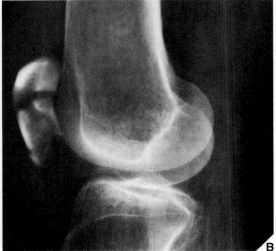

FIGURE 9.39 **Fracture of the patella.** After a fall on the stairs, a 63-year-old man presented with severe pain in the anterior aspect of the right knee. Anteroposterior (**A**) and lateral (**B**) radiographs show the typical appearance of comminuted fracture of the patella.

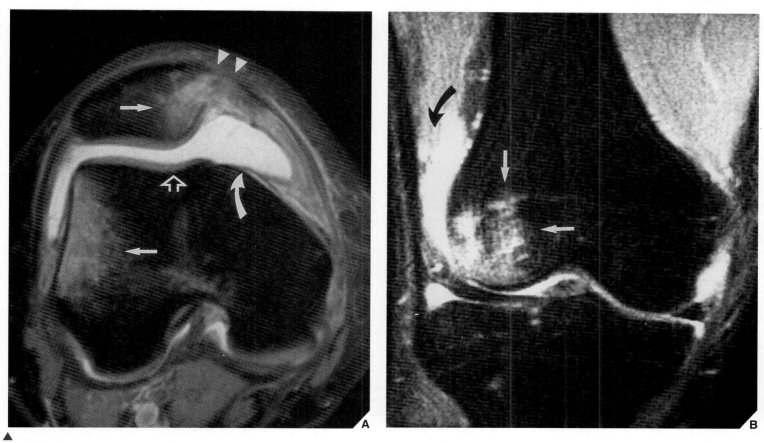

FIGURE 9.40 Transient lateral dislocation of the patella. Axial (**A**) and (**B**) coronal T2-weighted fat-suppressed MR images of a 38-year-old woman show characteristic abnormalities of this injury: "bone contusion" on the medial aspect of the patella and lateral femoral condyle (*arrows*) associated with hypoplastic trochlear notch (*open arrow*) and joint effusion (*curved arrows*). *Arrowheads* are indicating a tear of the medial retinaculum.

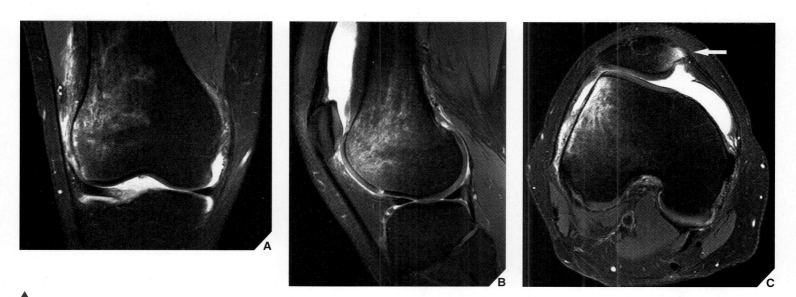

FIGURE 9.41 Transient lateral dislocation of the patella. (**A**) Coronal and (**B**) sagittal proton density–weighted fat-suppressed MR images of the right knee of a 22-year-old woman show a large areas of high signal intensity within anterior aspect of the lateral femoral condyle. Large joint effusion is also present. (**C**) An axial proton density–weighted fat-suppressed image, in addition to bone marrow edema within the lateral femoral condyle, shows a focus of high signal intensity at the medial aspect of the patella (*arrow*), characteristic features of transient dislocation.

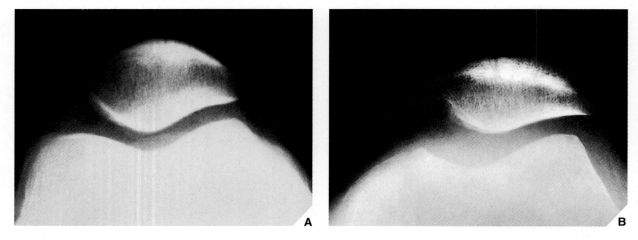

▲
FIGURE 9.42 Subluxation of the patella. A 23-year-old woman experienced occasional knee pain and buckling, particularly while jogging. (**A**) Standard axial (sunrise) view of the patella shows no apparent abnormalities. (**B**) Merchant axial view, however, demonstrates lateral subluxation of the patella. Note the positive congruence angle (see Fig. 9.7).

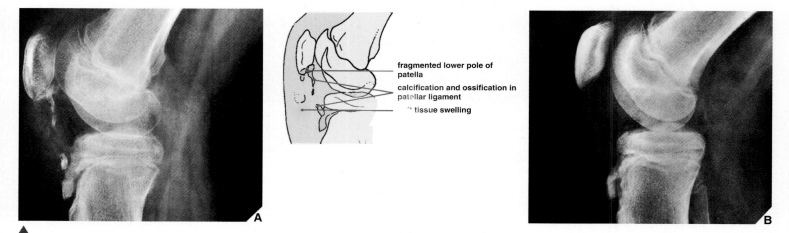

▲
FIGURE 9.43 Sinding-Larsen-Johansson disease. A 13-year-old boy experienced pain and swelling at the site of the patellar ligament. He had no history of acute trauma. (**A**) Lateral radiograph of the right knee shows fragmentation of the lower pole of the patella and significant soft-tissue swelling associated with calcifications and ossifications of the patellar ligament—findings characteristic of Sinding-Larsen-Johansson disease. (**B**) The normal left knee is shown for comparison.

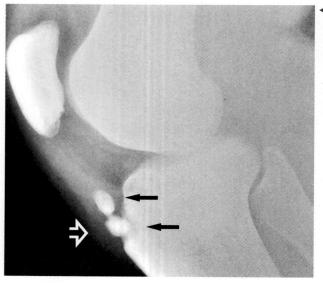

◀ **FIGURE 9.44 Osgood-Schlatter disease.** A 12-year-old boy had severe tenderness over the left tibial tuberosity. The lateral film, obtained with a low-kilovoltage/soft-tissue technique, reveals fragmentation of the tibial tuberosity (*arrows*) in association with soft-tissue swelling (*open arrow*)—characteristic findings in Osgood-Schlatter disease.

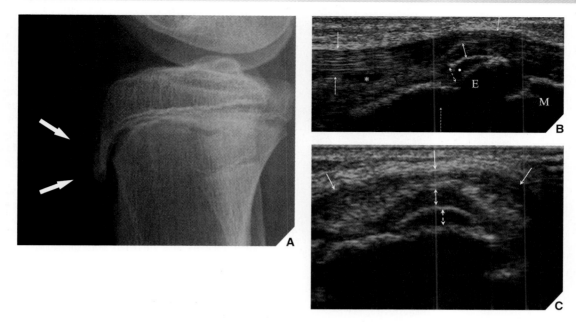

▲
FIGURE 9.45   US of Osgood-Schlatter disease. An 11-year-old boy presented with pain and swelling for several weeks in the region of tibial tuberosity. (**A**) Lateral radiograph shows soft-tissue swelling and small calcifications at the site of ossification center of tibial tuberosity *(arrows)*. (**B**) Longitudinal and (**C**) transverse US images show a fracture and delamination of the cartilaginous portion of ossification center of tibial tuberosity, characteristic of Osgood-Schlatter disease. *Arrows* point to the margins of the patellar ligament; *double solid arrow* indicates the thickness of cartilage between the ossification center and patellar ligament insertion; *double dashed arrow* indicates delamination thickness within the ossification center; *double black arrow* indicates fibrosis within deep infrapatellar bursa; *asterisk*, effusion within deep infrapatellar bursa; *dot*, ossification center; E, epiphysis; M, metaphysis. (Courtesy of Dr. Zbigniew Czyrny, Warsaw, Poland.)

to demonstrate all features of the Osgood-Schlatter disease because it provides excellent visualization of the fine structures of the patellar ligament, the superficial and deep infrapatellar bursae, and the status of the cartilage of the ossification center of the tibial tuberosity (Fig. 9.45). On MRI, as Hayes and Conway pointed out, T1-weighted images shows replacement of the normal high-signal infrapatellar fat with an area of decreased signal adjacent to the patellar ligament insertion. The ligament itself may show focal areas of increased signal, depending on the degree of associated tendinitis (Figs. 9.46 and 9.47).

Occasionally, Sinding-Larsen-Johansson and Osgood-Schlatter diseases may coexist. It is important to remember that the presence of multiple ossification centers in the tibial tuberosity and lower pole of the patella may at times mimic these conditions. However, the absence of soft-tissue swelling in such cases allows the distinction to be made.

Injuries to the Cartilage of the Knee

Osteochondral (or chondral) fracture, osteochondritis dissecans, and spontaneous osteonecrosis are three conditions with similar radiologic

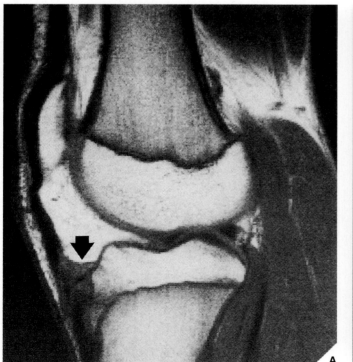

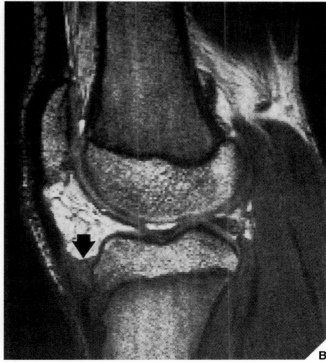

▲
FIGURE 9.46   MRI of Osgood-Schlatter disease. (**A**) T1-weighted (spin-echo, TR 700/TE 20 msec) and (**B**) T2*-weighted sagittal images demonstrate focus of decreased signal within normal sharp V-shaped area formed by the patellar ligament and anterior tibia *(arrow)*.

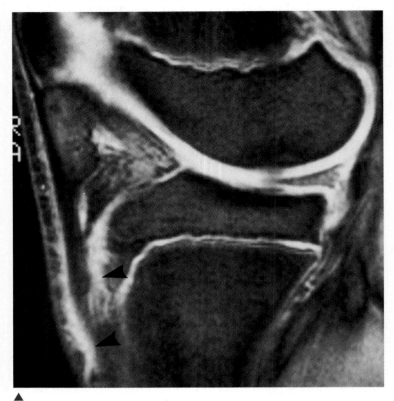

FIGURE 9.47   **MRI of Osgood-Schlatter disease.** A sagittal T2-weighted image of the knee of a 14-year-old boy demonstrates inflammatory changes along the distal patellar ligament (*arrow heads*).

appearances. They are invariably confused with each other, and in many instances the terms are used interchangeably. They represent, however, three separate orthopedic entities, each with a specific cause and each requiring a specific treatment. Usually, history, physical examination, and radiographic presentation can help distinguish these conditions from one another.

Osteochondral (or Chondral) Fracture. Shearing, rotary, or tangentially aligned impaction forces directed to the knee joint may result in acute injury to the articular end of the femur. The resulting fracture may involve cartilage only—chondral fracture—or cartilage and the underlying subchondral segment of bone—osteochondral fracture (Fig. 9.48). These fractures, which may occur in either of the femoral or tibial condyles, the tibial plateau, and the patella, may range in severity

from minimal indentation of the articular surface to displacement of an osteochondral fragment into the joint. Because a chondral fracture involves only articular cartilage, it can be demonstrated either by arthrography or by MRI. An osteochondral fracture, however, may be seen on conventional radiography, particularly if the fragment has been dislodged. The presence of such a fragment in the joint may be indistinguishable from the radiographic appearance of osteochondritis dissecans (see below). However, a clinical history of acute injury sustained in sports-related activities, such as football, soccer, or skiing, and associated with symptoms such as severe pain, local tenderness, and often joint effusion, is invariably helpful in making a distinction between these similar conditions (Fig. 9.49).

Osteochondritis Dissecans. Osteochondritis dissecans is a relatively common condition, seen predominantly in adolescents and young adults and more often in males than in females, and has recently come to be considered a form of osteochondral fracture caused not by acute but by chronic injury. As in acute osteochondral fractures, shearing or rotary forces applied to the articular surface of the femur result in detachment of a fragment of articular cartilage, often together with a segment of subchondral bone.

Aichroth has pointed out that the separated segment is avascular and this feature distinguishes osteochondritis dissecans from acute osteochondral fracture. In a clinical survey of osteochondritis dissecans in 200 patients, he also determined the distribution of the lesion. The most common location was the lateral aspect of the medial femoral condyle, a non–weight-bearing segment; other sites were less commonly affected (Fig. 9.50). The degree of damage to the articular cartilage, as in acute osteochondral fractures, varies from an *in situ* osteochondral body, to an osteocartilaginous flap, to complete detachment of an osteochondral segment (Fig. 9.51).

In the early stages of the disease, conventional radiographs in the standard projections usually show no abnormality. The only positive finding may be joint effusion. In more advanced stages of the disease, a radiolucent line is seen separating the osteochondral body from the femoral condyle (Fig. 9.52). For the orthopedic management of this condition, it is important to evaluate the status of the articular cartilage. Double-contrast arthrography can differentiate an *in situ* lesion from a more advanced lesion, where the osteochondral body is partially or completely detached from its bed (Fig. 9.53). Separation of the fragment mandates surgical intervention. Sometimes, other special techniques may need to be used, such as using only air as a contrast agent combining arthrography with CT to demonstrate the presence and distribution of the osteochondral bodies (Fig. 9.54), or performing MRI examination of the knee (Fig. 9.55). For the latter, T1-weighted and T2-weighted images in coronal and sagittal planes are most

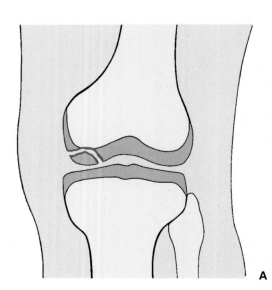
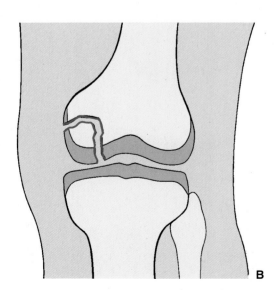

FIGURE 9.48   **Chondral and osteochondral fracture.** A chondral fracture (**A**) affects only the cartilage, whereas an osteochondral fracture (**B**) involves the cartilage and the subchondral segment of bone.

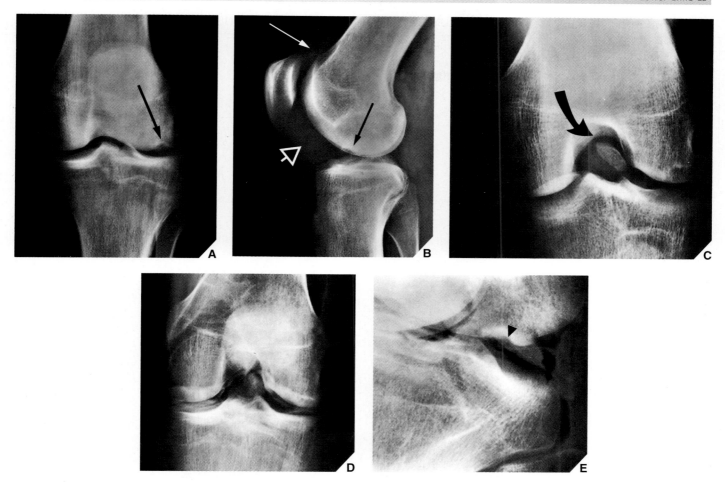

▲

FIGURE 9.49   **Osteochondral fracture.** A 22-year-old man dislocated his left patella in a skiing accident. The dislocation was spontaneously reduced, and he did not seek medical attention. Eight months later, he was seen by an orthopedic surgeon for chronic joint effusion and locking of the knee. The standard radiographic examination in the anteroposterior (**A**), lateral (**B**), and tunnel (**C**) projections reveal joint fluid (*white arrow*), soft-tissue swelling (*open arrow*), a defect in the lateral femoral condyle (*black arrows*), and a large osteochondral body (*curved arrow*), representing an osteochondral fracture, in the area of the intercondylar notch. Double-contrast arthrography (**D**) confirmed the intraarticular osteochondral body and also showed a defect in the articular cartilage covering the posterolateral aspect of the lateral femoral condyle (*arrow head*) (**E**). Note the similarity between this condition and osteochondritis dissecans (see Fig. 9.52).

FIGURE 9.50   **Site of the lesion.** Osteochondritis dissecans most frequently affects the medial femoral condyle, the non–weight-bearing portion (the lateral aspect of the condyle and the intercondylar notch), which is the most common site of the lesion. The lateral femoral condyle is much less commonly involved. (Modified from Aichroth P, 1971, with permission.)   ▶

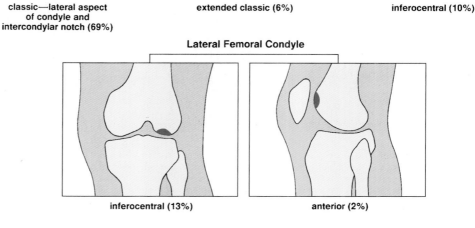

SITES OF LESION OF OSTEOCHONDRITIS DISSECANS

Medial Femoral Condyle

nonweight-bearing | weight-bearing

classic—lateral aspect of condyle and intercondylar notch (69%) | extended classic (6%) | inferocentral (10%)

Lateral Femoral Condyle

inferocentral (13%) | anterior (2%)

SPECTRUM OF OSTEOCHONDRITIS DISSECANS

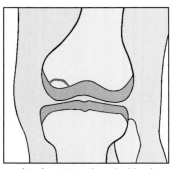
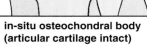

in-situ osteochondral body (articular cartilage intact)

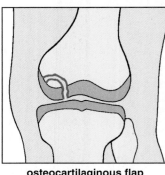
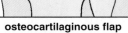

osteocartilaginous flap

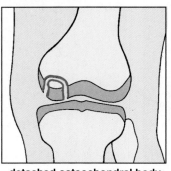

detached osteochondral body

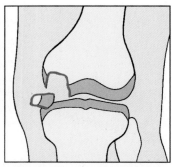

dislodged osteochondral body

▲
FIGURE 9.51   Stages of osteochondritis dissecans. The spectrum of chronic injury to the articular end of the distal femur (osteochondritis dissecans) ranges from an *in situ* lesion to a defect in the subchondral bone associated with a dislodged osteochondral body.

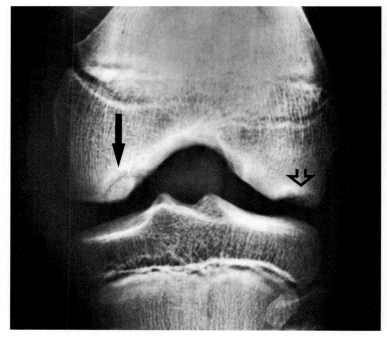

▲
FIGURE 9.52   Osteochondritis dissecans. An 11-year-old boy presented with pain in his right knee for 3 months. Posteroanterior (tunnel) radiograph of the knee shows the typical lesion of osteochondritis dissecans in the medial femoral condyle (*arrow*). A radiolucent line separates the oval *in situ* body from the femoral condyle. Incidentally, the lateral femoral condyle shows an irregular outline of the weight-bearing segment (*open arrow*). This finding represents a developmental variant in ossification and is of no further consequence.

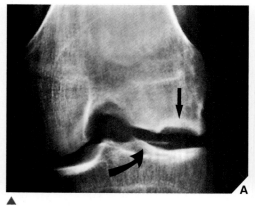
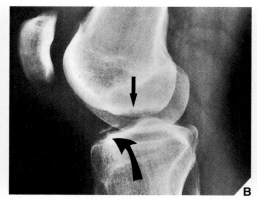
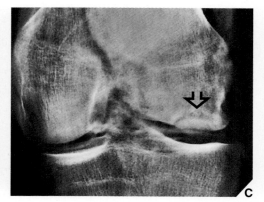

▲
FIGURE 9.53   Arthrography of osteochondritis dissecans. A 23-year-old man presented with chronic pain in the knee for 4 months. He had no history of acute trauma in recent years. Tunnel (**A**) and lateral (**B**) views show a defect in the subchondral bone at the inferocentral aspect of the lateral femoral condyle (*arrows*) and an osteochondral fragment that has been discharged into the joint (*curved arrows*). Arthrography was performed to evaluate the articular cartilage. The arthrogram (**C**) shows contrast filling the subchondral defect (*open arrow*), indicating damage to the articular cartilage.

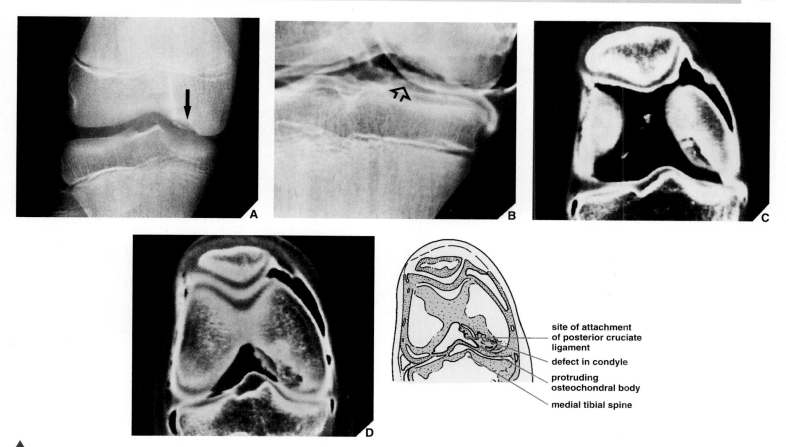

▲

FIGURE 9.54   CT arthrography of osteochondritis dissecans. A 13-year-old boy had pain in his right knee for 8 months. (**A**) Anteroposterior radiograph shows the lesion of osteochondritis dissecans in its classic location, the lateral aspect of the medial femoral condyle (*arrow*). The lesion appears to be still in situ. (**B**) On contrast arthrography, the lesion is shown to be covered by intact articular cartilage from the inferior aspect of the femoral condyle (*open arrow*), but computed arthrotomographic sections (**C**), (**D**) demonstrate that the lesion, located in the anterolateral aspect of the femoral condyle (a portion not protected by articular cartilage), is partial discharged into the joint at the site of the attachment of the posterior cruciate ligament.

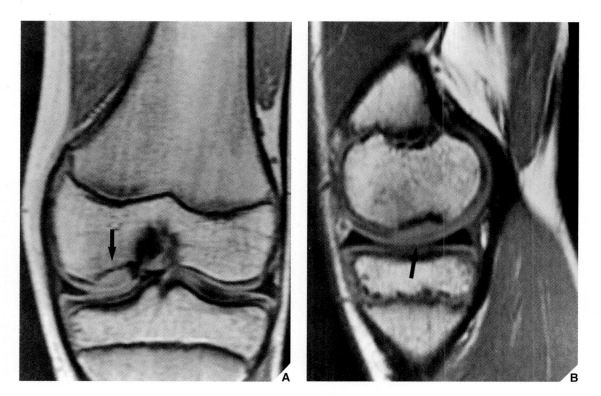

▲

FIGURE 9.55   MRI of osteochondritis dissecans. An 11-year-old boy experienced knee pain for 3 months. (**A**) Coronal proton density–weighted (spin-echo, TR 1800/TE 20 msec) MR image shows osseous fragment well separated from the medial femoral condyle by the low signal intensity line (*arrow*). (**B**) Image in the sagittal plane (spin echo TR 800/TE 20 msec) demonstrates intact articular cartilage overlying the separated fragment (*arrow*), indicating an *in situ* lesion.

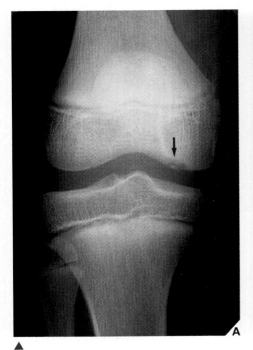
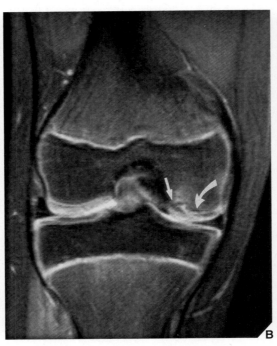
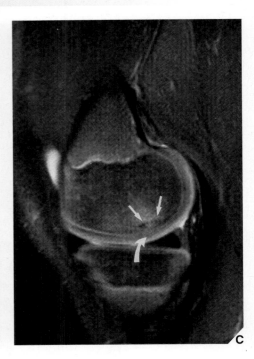

FIGURE 9.56 MRI of osteochondritis dissecans. (A) Anteroposterior radiograph of the right knee shows a lesion of osteochondritis dissecans in the medial femoral condyle (*arrow*). Coronal (**B**) and sagittal (**C**) T2-weighted fat-suppressed MR images demonstrate the osteochondral body being still *in situ* (*arrows*), although the articular cartilage is already damaged (*curved arrows*).

effective. The lesion usually displays intermediate signal intensity on all sequences and is separated by a narrow zone of low signal intensity from the viable bone. The disruption of articular cartilage is best seen on T2 or T2* (gradient echo) images (Fig. 9.56). When osteochondral body is separated from the host bone by a rim of a high signal intensity on T2-weighted images (a phenomenon that denotes a fluid or granulation tissue), it usually signifies loosening or complete detachment of the necrotic fragment (Fig. 9.57).

Occasionally, a small, disk-shaped secondary ossification center is present on the posterior portion of the femoral condyle; this normal variant should not be mistaken for osteochondritis dissecans. Similarly, during normal ossification of the distal femoral epiphysis, developmental changes may appear as irregularities in the outline of the condyle. The appearance of these irregularities, which are usually posteriorly located and hence best seen on the tunnel projection, may mimic osteochondritis

dissecans (see Fig. 9.52). This normal variant is usually seen between the ages of 2 and 12.

Spontaneous Osteonecrosis. Characterized by acute onset of pain, spontaneous osteonecrosis of the knee is a distinct clinicopathologic entity with a predilection for the weight-bearing segment of the medial femoral condyle. It occurs in older adults, frequently in their sixth and seventh decades of life, and should not be mistaken for adult onset of osteochondritis dissecans. Although the cause is obscure, certain factors such as trauma, intraarticular injection of steroids, and possibly tear of the meniscus, as Norman and Baker have pointed out, may play a role in the pathogenesis of this condition.

The earliest radiologic sign of this condition is an increased uptake of isotope on radionuclide bone scan; radiographically, the earliest indication is a minimal degree of flattening of the femoral condyle (Fig. 9.58). Later, usually 1 to 3 months after the sudden onset of

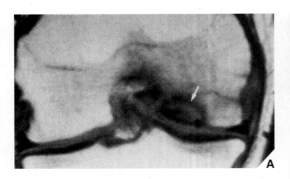
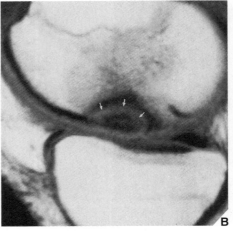
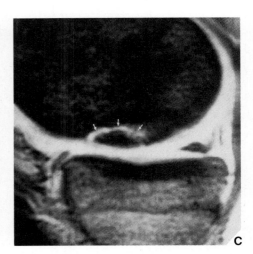

FIGURE 9.57 MRI of osteochondritis dissecans. A loose osteochondral body in the medial femoral condyle is seen on T1-weighted coronal (**A**) and sagittal (**B**) images (*white arrows*). (**C**) On the sagittal T2*-weighted sequence high-signal-intensity fluid (*small arrows*) separates the loose fragment from the viable bone.

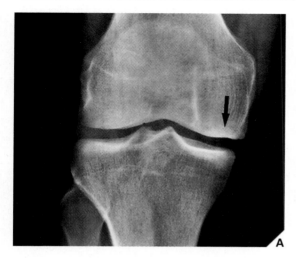
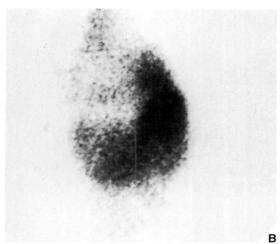

FIGURE 9.58 Spontaneous osteonecrosis. Four weeks before this radiographic examination, a 58-year-old man felt a sharp pain in the right knee when he stepped off a curb. The pain subsided after 1 week but recurred soon afterward. **(A)** Anteroposterior radiograph of the knee shows flattening of the medial aspect of the medial femoral condyle (*arrow*). **(B)** Radionuclide bone scan was performed, and it shows a marked increase in uptake of the tracer in the area of the medial femoral condyle. The features seen in both studies characterize an early stage of spontaneous osteonecrosis.

symptoms, radiographs may show a subchondral focus of radiolucency. As the condition progresses, the lesion may be seen radiographically as a subchondral osteolytic (necrotic) focus surrounded by a sclerotic margin representing a zone of repair (Fig. 9.59). Frequently, these lesions are accompanied by meniscal tears and, for this reason, either contrast arthrography or MRI should always be performed if spontaneous osteonecrosis is suspected (Fig. 9.60). Some authors postulate that the concentration of stress of the torn meniscus on the articular cartilage may result in local ischemia, thus predisposing to the development of osteonecrosis.

Injury to the Soft Tissues about the Knee

Knee Joint Effusion. Normally, the suprapatellar bursa is apparent on a radiograph of the knee in the lateral projection as a thin, radiodense strip just posterior to the quadriceps tendon (Fig. 9.61). In knee joint effusion, which often occurs secondary to injury elsewhere in the knee, the suprapatellar bursa fills with fluid. Distention of the bursa is evident radiographically as an oval density that obliterates the fat space anterior to the femoral cortex (Fig. 9.62). If there is an associated intraarticular fracture of either the distal femur or the proximal tibia, then a cross-table lateral view may demonstrate the FBI sign (see Fig. 9.28C).

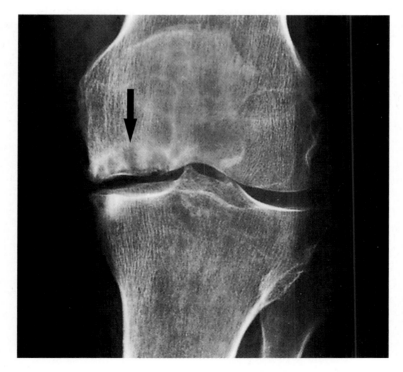

FIGURE 9.59 Spontaneous osteonecrosis. A 74-year-old man stepped off a curb and felt a sharp pain in the left knee. Radiographs obtained on the next day were normal. The pain in the knee subsided after 10 days, but 2 months later joint effusion developed, which was aspirated. He was given a series of three intraarticular injections of steroids (hydrocortisone), after which most of the symptoms subsided. Four months after the initial injury the symptoms recurred, and at this time the standard radiographic examination was repeated. Anteroposterior film shows a large radiolucent defect surrounded by a zone of sclerosis in the weight-bearing segment of the medial femoral condyle (*arrow*). The lesion represents spontaneous osteonecrosis.

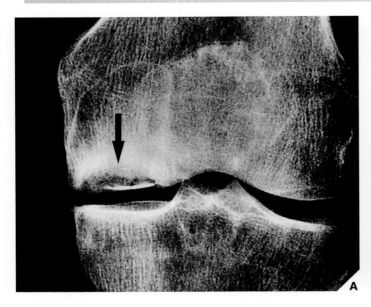
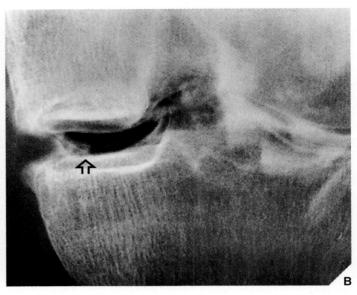

FIGURE 9.60 **Spontaneous osteonecrosis.** A 63-year-old woman missed a step while descending the staircase and felt a sharp pain in the left knee. The radiographic examination performed 3 days later showed only moderate osteoporosis, which was not related to trauma. Three months later she was reexamined for persistent pain and accumulation of fluid in the joint. **(A)** Anteroposterior radiograph of the knee shows spontaneous osteonecrosis in the weight-bearing portion of the medial femoral condyle (*arrow*). Double-contrast arthrography was performed to evaluate any possible injury to the menisci. The arthrogram **(B)** demonstrates a vertical tear of the medial meniscus at the site of the osteonecrotic lesion (*open arrow*).

Meniscal Injury. Similar to the other fibrocartilaginous structures, the menisci of the knee (see Fig. 9.9) are not visible on conventional radiographs. Contrast arthrography may demonstrate these structures, although MRI has become a standard procedure for evaluating the menisci.

Tear of the medial meniscus is a common injury resulting from physical and sports-related activities. Various types of tears may be encountered (Fig. 9.63). The most common type is a vertical tear, which may be simple or bucket-handle; horizontal tears usually occur in an older age group. The patient usually reports pain and locking of the knee. On clinical examination, there is tenderness along the medial joint line.

On arthrography, meniscal tear is recognized as a projection of positive contrast agent or air into the substance of the meniscus or at its periphery (Fig. 9.64). On MRI, the menisci are seen as structures of uniformly low signal intensity. A meniscal tear is identified by the presence of an increased intrameniscal signal that extends to the surface of this structure (Fig. 9.65). A globular or linear focus of increased signal intensity in the meniscus that does not extend to the surface does not represent a tear. The significance of this finding is still unclear. Stoller, Genant, and Beltran believe that these findings represent an area of hyaline or myxoid degeneration within the substance of the meniscus. These abnormalities, known as type I (round focus) and type II (linear area) meniscal lesions

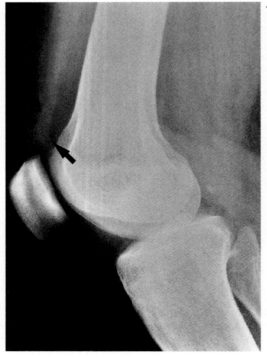

◄ FIGURE 9.61 **Normal appearance of suprapatellar bursa.** The suprapatellar bursa normally appears on the lateral radiograph of the knee as a radiodense strip (*arrow*) just posterior to the quadriceps tendon (*open arrow*).

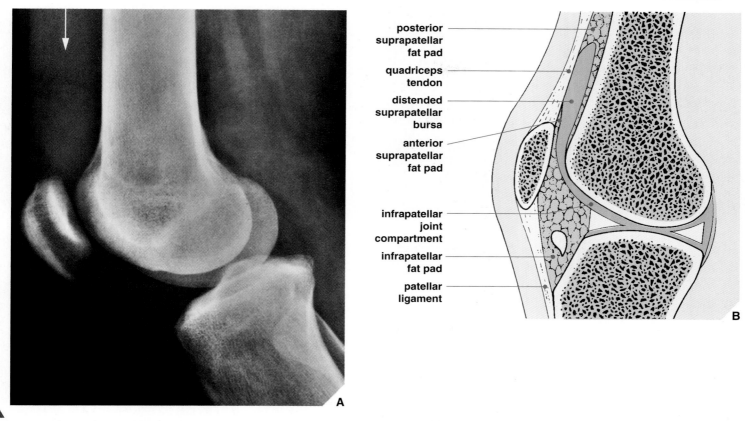

The following labels appear in panel B: posterior suprapatellar fat pad, quadriceps tendon, distended suprapatellar bursa, anterior suprapatellar fat pad, infrapatellar joint compartment, infrapatellar fat pad, patellar ligament.

FIGURE 9.62   (A,B) Knee joint effusion. In knee joint effusion, the suprapatellar bursa distends with fluid, thus obliterating the fat space posterior to the quadriceps tendon (*arrow*). ("**B**" modified from Hall FM, 1975, with permission.)

(Fig. 9.66A,B), are not seen on arthroscopic examination of the knee. The true tears are designated as type III and type IV lesions (Fig. 9.66C; see also Fig. 9.65). Occasionally, meniscal tears may be associated with meniscal or parameniscal cysts (Fig. 9.67).

The sensitivity and specificity of MRI for the diagnosis of meniscal tears are high, ranging from 90% to 95% in most studies. As recently reported by Helms, the use of the fat suppression technique increases the dynamic range of signal in the menisci, rendering meniscal tears more conspicuous. A number of signs related to specific types of meniscal tears have been identified. Among the most accurate secondary signs of the bucket-handle tear of the medial meniscus are absence of two consecutive "bow-tie" appearances of this meniscus on sagittal images and

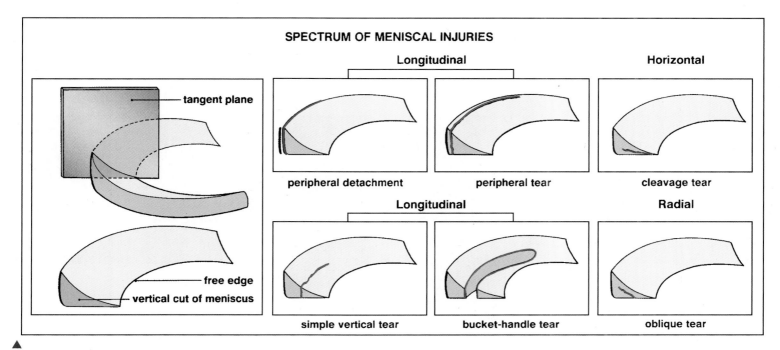

SPECTRUM OF MENISCAL INJURIES

Labels in left panel: tangent plane, free edge, vertical cut of meniscus. Longitudinal: peripheral detachment, peripheral tear. Horizontal: cleavage tear. Longitudinal: simple vertical tear, bucket-handle tear. Radial: oblique tear.

FIGURE 9.63   Spectrum of meniscal injuries. Meniscal injuries can be broadly classified as longitudinal, horizontal, and radial, depending on the plane in which they occur. The left panel represents diagrammatically the radiologic image of the meniscus; the right panel, various tears.

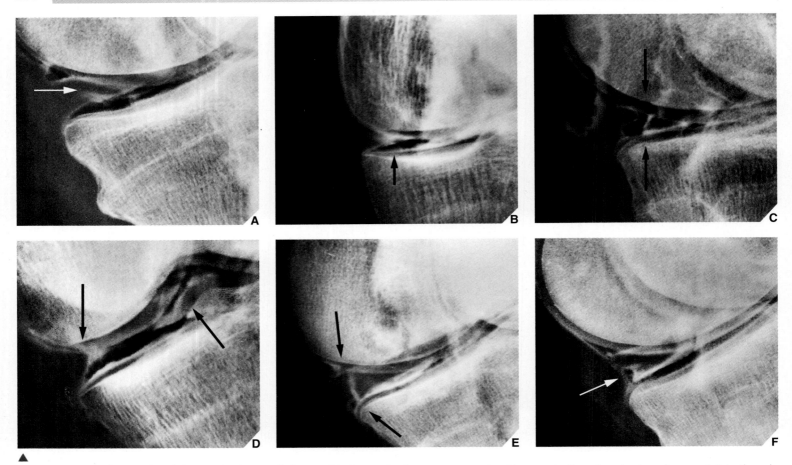

▲
FIGURE 9.64   Arthrography of the meniscal tears. Arthrographically, meniscal tears are recognized by a projection of contrast medium or air into the substance of the structure or at its periphery (*arrows*). The following spot films demonstrate some of the various types of tears that may affect the medial meniscus: (**A**) radial (oblique) tear of the posterior horn; (**B**) horizontal tear of the body; (**C**) bucket-handle tear of the posterior horn; (**D**) bucket-handle tear of the body with displacement of the fragment into the intercondylar notch; (**E**) peripheral tear of the posterior horn; and (**F**) peripheral detachment of the posterior horn.

the so-called double posterior cruciate ligament sign. The normal body of the medial meniscus, which is usually approximately 9 to 12 mm in width, should appear at least on two sections on the peripheral sagittal images as a bow tie. The presence of only a single bow-tie configuration indicates a displaced bucket-handle tear into the middle part of the knee joint. On more central sagittal sections, the displaced part of the meniscus assumes a posterior cruciate ligamentlike configuration, projecting more anteriorly to the posterior cruciate ligament (Fig. 9.68).

Although meniscal tears are best diagnosed on coronal and sagittal MR images, Lee and colleagues pointed out the effectiveness of axial

fat-saturated fast-spin-echo imaging in demonstrating some tears. In particular, vertical tears and displaced meniscal fragments have been clearly demonstrated with this technique (Fig. 9.69).

Tears of the lateral meniscus are less common (see Fig. 9.69). This has been attributed to the greater degree of mobility of the lateral meniscus because of its rather loose peripheral attachment to the synovium and lack of attachment to the fibular (lateral) collateral ligament. Lateral meniscal tears, however, commonly accompany a developmental anomaly, the so-called discoid meniscus, which according to Kaplan is probably related to an abnormal attachment of its posterior horn to

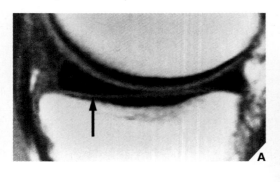

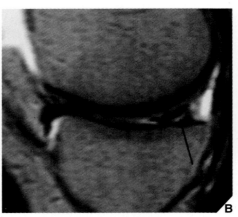

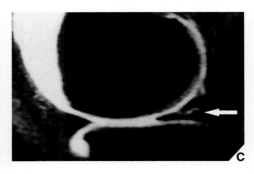

▲
FIGURE 9.65   Tears of the medial meniscus. (**A**) Sagittal spin-echo T1-weighted MR image (SE; TR 700/TE 20 msec) shows a tear of the medial meniscus. Note the high-intensity signal of the tear, which extends into the inferior surface of the meniscus (*arrow*). (**B**) Sagittal T2-weighted MR image (SE; TR 2300/TE 80 msec) shows a tear of the posterior horn of the medial meniscus (*arrow*) extending into the tibial articular surface. (**C**) Sagittal fat-suppressed image obtained after intraarticular administration of a dilute solution of gadopentetate dimeglumine shows a tear of the posterior horn of the medial meniscus (*arrow*).

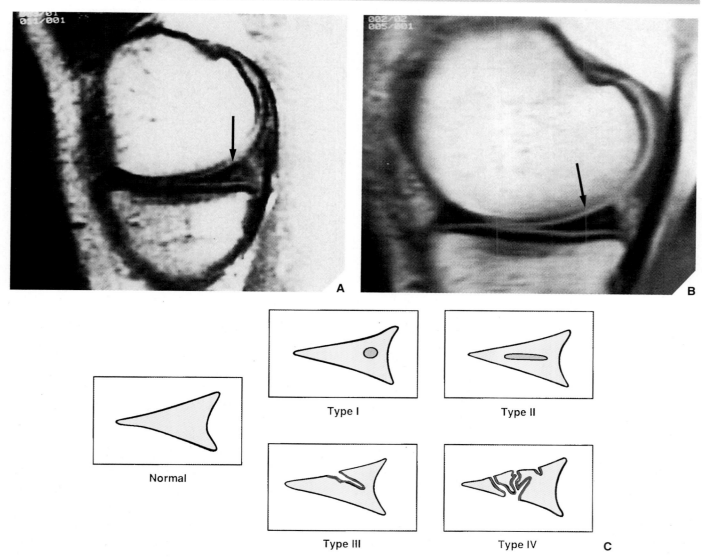

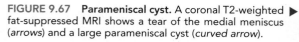

▲
FIGURE 9.66 **Meniscal lesions. (A)** Sagittal spin-echo MR image (SE; TR 2000/TE 20 msec) shows a type I lesion of the posterior horn of the medial meniscus (*arrow*). The intrameniscal round lesion does not extend to the articular surface. **(B)** In a type II lesion of the posterior horn of the medial meniscus (*arrow*), the configuration is linear, and as with a type I, the lesion does not extend into the articular surface. **(C)** Schematic representation of various types of meniscal lesions.

FIGURE 9.67 **Parameniscal cyst.** A coronal T2-weighted ▶ fat-suppressed MRI shows a tear of the medial meniscus (*arrows*) and a large parameniscal cyst (*curved arrow*).

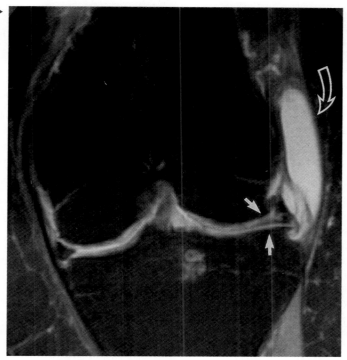

BOW-TIE SIGN

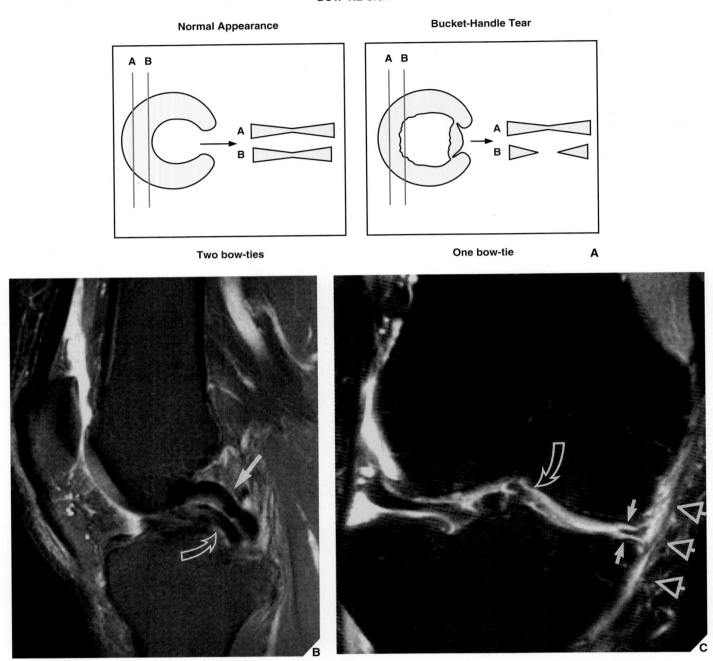

FIGURE 9.68   **Bucket-handle tear of the medial meniscus. (A)** Schematic explanation of absence of the second bow-tie sign of displaced tear. (Modified from Helms CA, 2002, with permission.) **(B)** Sagittal T2-weighted fat-suppressed MRI shows a "double" posterior cruciate ligament sign. An *arrow* points to the normal posterior cruciate ligament and a *curved arrow* points to the displaced fragment of the medial meniscus that assumed configuration of the posterior cruciate ligament. **(C)** Coronal T2-weighted fat-saturated MR image confirms the presence of a bucket-handle tear of the medial meniscus (*arrows*). A curved arrow points to the medially displaced part of the meniscus. Note also a tear of the medial collateral ligament (*arrowheads*).

the tibial plateau and repetitive abnormal movements, with subsequent enlargement and thickening of meniscal tissue. The discoid meniscus is recognized clinically by a loud clicking sound on flexion and extension of the knee joint and radiographically on the anteroposterior radiograph by an abnormally wide lateral joint compartment (Fig. 9.70A). Its arthrographic appearance is characterized by the absence of the normally triangular shape of the structure; the meniscus is thicker and wider and projects more deeply into the joint (Fig. 9.70B). On MRI, the discoid meniscus is similar in appearance to the arthrographic image with a lack of normal triangular shape and deep extension into the interior of the joint. On sagittal images, the normal bow-tie configuration of the body of the lateral meniscus is seen on more than two sections

when the discoid variant is present (Figs. 9.71 and 9.72). Because of its abnormal shape and thickness, the lateral discoid meniscus is prone to tears (Fig. 9.73).

Meniscal tears may also be associated with fractures of the tibial plateau resulting from direct trauma. In this case, both menisci are equally subject to injury.

Ligament and Tendon Injuries.

Tears of the Medial and Lateral Collateral Ligaments. The most common injury to the ligaments of the knee is tear of the tibial (medial) collateral ligament (TCL). It is diagnosed clinically by instability of the medial joint compartment and radiographically on a stress film of the knee by widening of the medial tibiofemoral joint compartment (Fig. 9.74). It

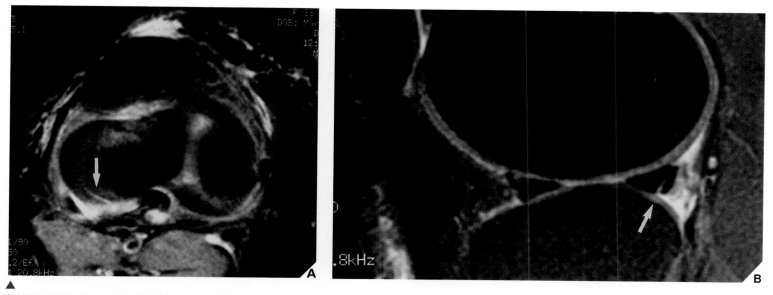

FIGURE 9.69   **Tear of the lateral meniscus. (A)** An axial fast-spin-echo MRI shows a tear of the posterior horn of the lateral meniscus (*arrow*) in a 38-year-old woman. **(B)** A sagittal MR image confirms the presence of a tear (*arrow*).

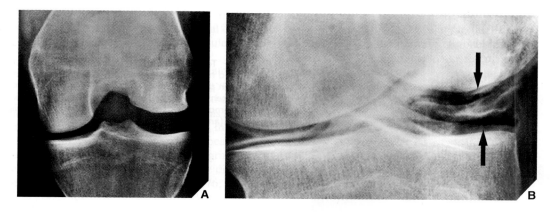

FIGURE 9.70   **Arthrography of discoid meniscus.** A 20-year-old competition ice skater sustained an injury to her left knee. On physical examination, there was a loud click during movement of the knee joint. **(A)** Anteroposterior radiograph of the knee shows an abnormally wide lateral joint compartment. **(B)** Double-contrast arthrogram demonstrates a discoid meniscus (*arrows*). Note the absence of the normal triangular shape of this structure and its extension deep into the interior of the joint. No tear is apparent.

FIGURE 9.71   **MRI of discoid meniscus.** Coronal T1-weighted MR image ▶ shows a discoid lateral meniscus in a 17-year-old boy. Note lack of normal triangular shape of this meniscus (*arrows*) and extension into the interior of the joint (*curved arrow*).

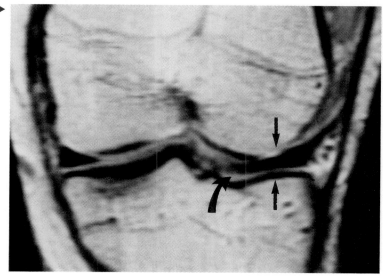

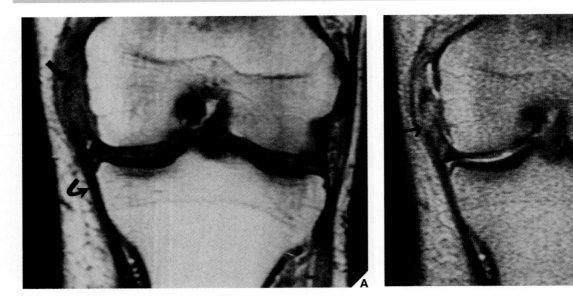

▲
FIGURE 9.78 **Grade 3 medial collateral ligament injury. (A)** A coronal proton density–weighted (SE; TR 2000/TE 20 msec) image shows amorphous structure of intermediate signal intensity replacing the proximal attachment of the medial collateral ligament (*arrow*). The distal part of the ligament is intact (*curved arrow*). **(B)** A coronal T2-weighted (SE; TR 2000/TE 80 msec) image shows mildly increased signal intensity within the region of the proximal segment of the medial collateral ligament, representing a combination of edema and hemorrhage (*arrow*). The underlying ligament cannot be defined.

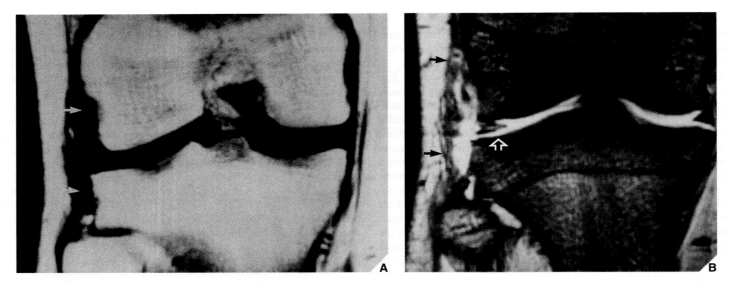

▲
FIGURE 9.79 **Tear of the lateral collateral ligament.** Tear of the lateral collateral ligament (*arrows*) can be seen on **(A)** T1-weighted and **(B)** T2*-weighted coronal images. Note associated tear of the lateral meniscus (*open arrow*).

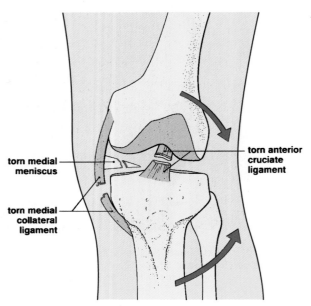

torn medial
meniscus

torn anterior
cruciate
ligament

torn medial
collateral
ligament

◄ FIGURE 9.80 **Triad of meniscoligamentous injury.** The "unhappy O'Donoghue triad" results from valgus stress on the knee joint that causes the medial joint compartment to open. The triad comprises tears of the medial meniscus and the anterior cruciate and the medial collateral ligaments. (Modified from O'Donoghue DH, 1984, with permission.)

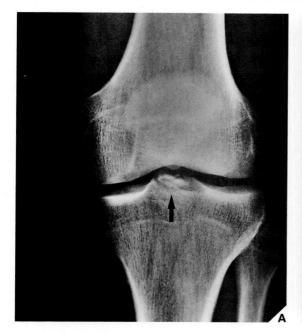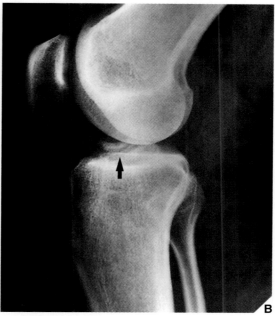

▲
FIGURE 9.81   Tear of the anterior cruciate ligament. Anteroposterior (**A**) and lateral (**B**) radiographs of the knee in a 38-year-old soccer player show avulsion of the tibial eminence (*arrow*), suggesting tear of the anterior cruciate ligament. The diagnosis was confirmed by arthroscopy.

The accuracy of radiographic examinations with respect to injury to the cruciate ligaments has not been completely determined. The standard anteroposterior and lateral radiographs may show a bone fragment, representing the avulsed intercondylar eminence of the tibia, at the site of cruciate insertion (Fig. 9.81). Sometimes, the tear can be diagnosed on double-contrast arthrography, which may demonstrate the posterior cruciate ligament, but not the anterior cruciate ligament—a finding that is regarded as abnormal. This injury is often missed on imaging examinations that include even the use of arthrotomography and CT. The procedure of choice in these circumstances is MRI.

For MR examination of the anterior cruciate ligament (ACL), as Stoller and colleagues advocate, the knee should be placed in 10 to 15degrees of external rotation to orient the ligament with the sagittal imaging plane. Either 3- or 5-mm thin contiguous sections are routinely obtained in axial, sagittal, and coronal planes. A torn anterior cruciate ligament is demonstrated on MR images by the absence or abnormal course of this structure (Fig. 9.82), abnormal signal intensity within the ligamentous substance (Fig. 9.83), or the presence of an edematous focus (Fig. 9.84). The buckling of the posterior cruciate ligament is an indirect sign of anterior cruciate ligament tear. The best plane to demonstrate

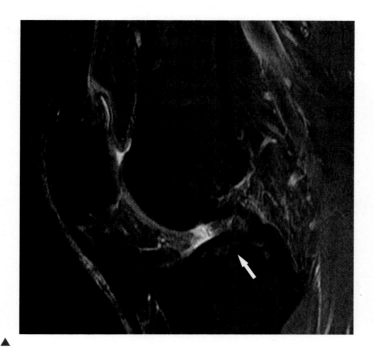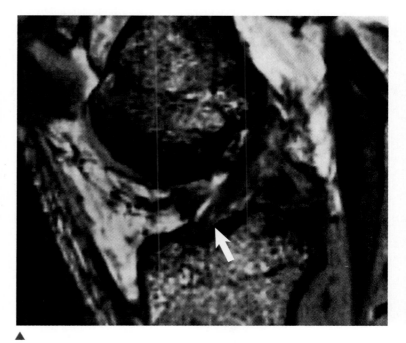

▲
FIGURE 9.82   MRI of tear of the anterior cruciate ligament. A 56-year-old woman twisted her right knee in a fall from the rock. Sagittal proton density–weighted fat-suppressed MR image shows a displaced tear of the ACL (*arrow*).

▲
FIGURE 9.83   MRI of tear of the anterior cruciate ligament. Sagittal spin-echo T2-weighted MR image (SE; TR 2000/TE 80 msec) shows a tear of the anterior cruciate ligament. Only the proximal part of the ligament at the femoral attachment is well seen. The distal half shows lack of normal low signal intensity (*arrow*) caused by swelling and edema (compare with Fig. 9.14A). Arthroscopic examination demonstrated an acute tear of the anterior cruciate ligament at its insertion to the tibia.

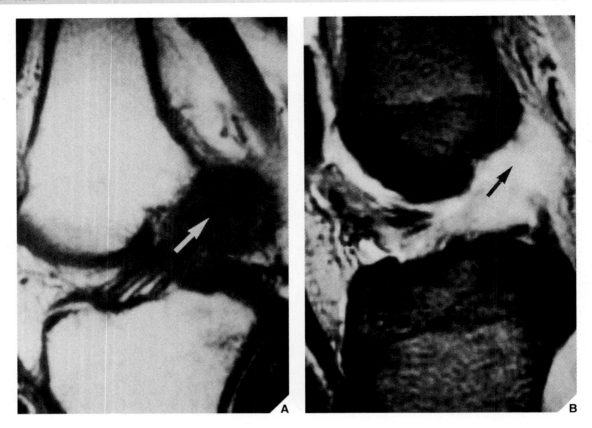

▲
FIGURE 9.84   MRI of tear of the anterior cruciate ligament. (A) Sagittal T1-weighted image shows loss of normal contour of the proximal part of the anterior cruciate ligament (*arrow*). **(B)** Sagittal T2*-weighted image shows hyperintense signal representing hemorrhage within an anterior cruciate ligament at its lateral condylar attachment (*arrow*), characteristic of a ligamentous tear.

these findings is the sagittal plane, and the best pulse sequence is spin-echo T2 weighting or gradient-echo (MPGR) T2* weighting.

Tears of the posterior cruciate ligament are identified on sagittal T1-weighted images by disruption of the integrity of the ligament or by abnormal shape. On T2-weighted images, the tear is demonstrated by the presence of high signal intensity within the ligament, which represents

fluid within the tear (Fig. 9.85). As Bassett and coworkers have pointed out, evulsion of the ligament from its tibial attachment is identified on MR images by bone fracture of the posterior tibial plateau and redundancy of the ligament.

Posterolateral Corner Injuries. The posterolateral corner (PLC) of the knee is a complex unit consisting of several anatomic structures

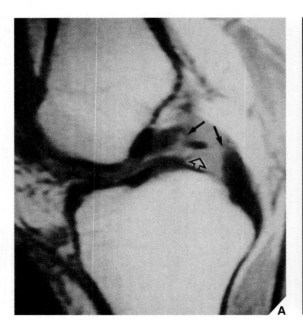

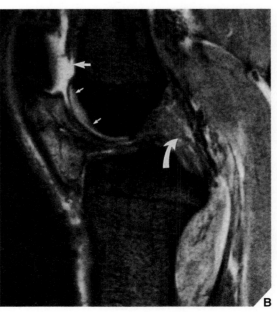

▲
FIGURE 9.85   MRI of tear of the posterior cruciate ligament. (A) Sagittal T1-weighted image shows complete tear of the posterior cruciate ligament. *Open arrow*, area of hemorrhage; *solid arrows*, ligament discontinuity. **(B)** Sagittal T2*-weighted image shows a posterior cruciate ligament tear with edema and hemorrhage (*curved arrow*). The interface between cartilage (*small arrows*) and fluid (*large arrow*) is well demonstrated.

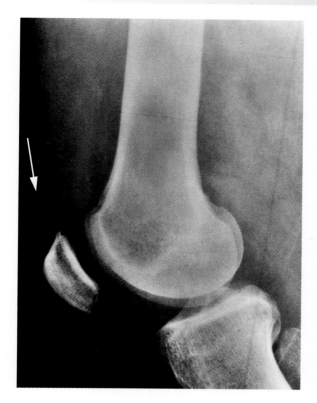

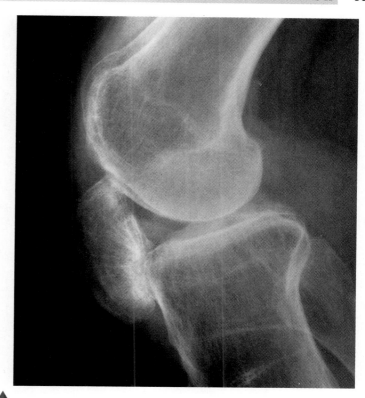

▲

FIGURE 9.86 **Tear of the quadriceps tendon.** A 30-year-old man was injured during a football game. Lateral radiograph of the knee shows lack of definition of the quadriceps tendon (*arrow*) and the presence of a soft-tissue mass in the suprapatellar region—findings characteristic of quadriceps tendon rupture.

▲

FIGURE 9.87 **Tear of the quadriceps tendon.** A lateral radiograph of the knee shows low position of the patella (patella infera, patella baja) secondary to chronic tear of the quadriceps tendon.

responsible for knee joint stabilization. They include popliteal tendon, the lateral collateral ligament, the popliteofibular ligament, and the posterolateral capsule, which is reinforced by the arcuate and fabellofibular ligaments. Trauma to PLC, in addition to tears of the above-listed structures, usually is associated with injuries to the cruciate ligaments, both menisci, and medial collateral ligament. MRI is the technique of choice when the PLC injuries are clinically suspected.

Tears of the Quadriceps Tendon and Patellar Ligament. Although ruptures of the quadriceps tendon usually occur in the elderly, they

may at times be seen in athletes. A lateral radiograph of the knee may show lack of definition of the quadriceps tendon and widening of its anteroposterior diameter secondary to hemorrhage and edema (Fig. 9.86). Occasionally, the lateral film may also show the patella in a lower-than-normal position secondary to an imbalance in forces on the patellar ligamentous attachments (Fig. 9.87); in tear of the patellar ligament, the reverse of this mechanism occurs (Figs. 9.88 and 9.89). MRI is the procedure of choice for demonstrating and evaluating those two types of injury (Figs. 9.90 to 9.92).

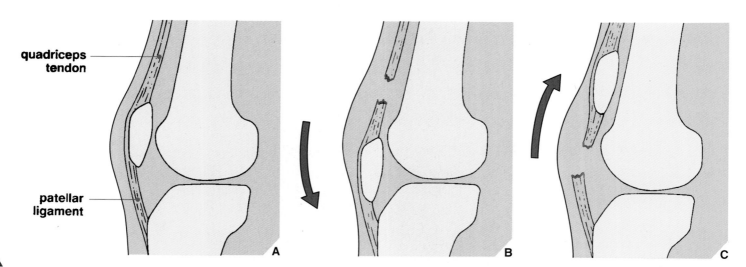

▲

FIGURE 9.88 **Patellar ligamentous-tendinous attachments.** Normally, the balance of forces on the patellar ligamentous-tendinous attachments maintains the patella in position (**A**). Tear of the quadriceps tendon causes downward displacement of the patella (**B**). In tear of the patellar ligament, the reverse mechanism occurs (**C**) (see also Fig. 9.3).

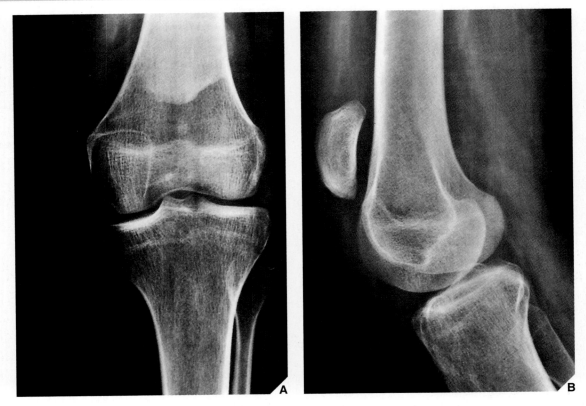

▲
FIGURE 9.89 **Tear of the patellar ligament.** A 38-year-old woman athlete was injured during a running competition. Anteroposterior (**A**) and lateral (**B**) radiographs of the knee demonstrate an abnormally high position of the patella (patella alta), a finding suggesting tear of the patellar ligament. The diagnosis was confirmed on surgical exploration.

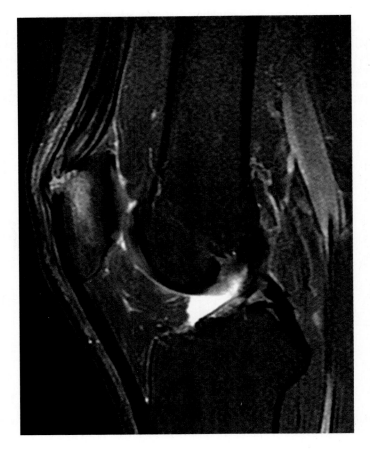

▲
FIGURE 9.90 **MRI of tear of the quadriceps tendon.** A 38-year-old man injured left knee in a ski accident. Sagittal T2-weighted fat-suppressed MR image shows a high-grade partial tear of the quadriceps tendon at its insertion to the patella.

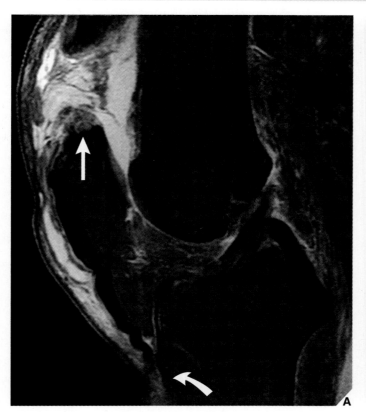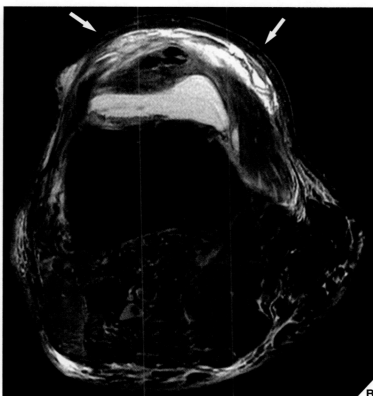

▲

FIGURE 9.91 MRI of tear of the quadriceps tendon. (A) Sagittal T2-weighted and **(B)** axial proton density–weighted fat-suppressed MR images of the knee show a complete, full-thickness tear of the quadriceps tendon (*arrows*). A *curved arrow* points to the associated tear of the patellar ligament.

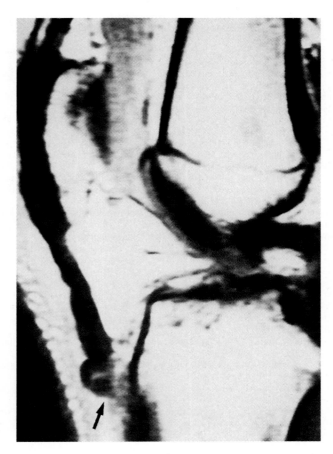

▲

FIGURE 9.92 MRI of tear of patellar ligament. Sagittal spin-echo proton density–weighted MR image (SE; TR 2000/TE 20 msec) demonstrates evulsion of the patellar ligament at the insertion into the tibial tuberosity (*arrow*). (From Beltran J, 1990, with permission.)

PRACTICAL POINTS TO REMEMBER

[1] The posterior aspect of the femoral condyles and the intercondylar notch is best shown on the tunnel projection of the knee.

[2] Merchant axial projection of the patella, rather than the standard sunrise view, is better suited to evaluate:
- the articular facets of the patellofemoral joint
- subtle patellar subluxations.

[3] In arthrographic examination of the menisci, be aware of:
- the popliteal hiatus at the posterior horn of the lateral meniscus, which is a normal feature that may be confused with a tear
- a blind spot involving the posterior portion of the posterior horn of the lateral meniscus, where a tear can be overlooked.

[4] CT is very effective in assessing depressed and split fractures of tibial plateau and in demonstrating the extent of fracture comminution.

[5] MRI is the modality of choice to evaluate soft-tissue injury around the knee, in particular to the menisci and the cruciate and collateral ligaments. It is also the best modality to image posttraumatic joint effusion, acute and chronic hematomas, and other traumatic abnormalities of the muscular, ligamentous, and tendinous structures.

[6] Tibial plateau fractures are often accompanied by meniscal tear and ligament injury, best demonstrated by MRI.

[7] Segond fracture is a small-fragment avulsion fracture from the lateral aspect of the proximal tibia that frequently is associated with a capsular tear, tear of the anterior cruciate ligament, and tear of the lateral meniscus.

[8] The bipartite or multipartite patella may mimic patellar fracture. To avoid misdiagnosing these developmental anomalies as a fracture, remember that:
- the bipartite or multipartite patella is seen at the superolateral margin of the patella
- the apparent comminuted fragments do not form a whole, as they would in patellar fracture.

[9] Sinding-Larsen-Johansson disease is clinically characterized by local pain and tenderness on palpation at the site of lower patella, and radiographically by fragmentation and calcification at the proximal attachement of patellar ligament.

[10] Osgood-Schlatter diseases is a conditions related to trauma. Pain and soft-tissue swelling on clinical examination, and fragmentation of the ossification center of tibial tuberosity and fibrosis and fluid within the deep infrapatellar bursa on imaging studies (conventional radiography, US, and MRI) are fundamental diagnostic features.

[11] Learn to distinguish three conditions that have very similar radiologic presentations:
- osteochondral fracture, which is an acute injury to the articular cartilage and subchondral bone
- osteochondritis dissecans, which is the result of chronic injury
- spontaneous osteonecrosis, which is characterized by acute onset of pain and has been linked to trauma, corticosteroid injections, and meniscal tear.

Contrast arthrography, computed arthrotomography, and MRI are essential techniques in the evaluation of the status of the articular cartilage in each of these conditions.

[12] Tears of the menisci and ligaments of the knee are best demonstrated by MRI. Tears of the medial meniscus are much more common than tears of the lateral semilunar cartilage. The discoid lateral meniscus predisposes this structure to injury.

[13] Bucket-handle tear of the medial meniscus has characteristic MRI appearance:
- on sagittal sections through the body of the medial meniscus, there is only one image of the bow-tie sign
- on more lateral sagittal sections obtained closer to the interior of the knee joint, a double PCL sign may be seen.

[14] Discoid meniscus has characteristic MRI appearance:
- on coronal sections, there is lack of normal triangular shape and deep extension of the meniscus into the interior of the joint
- on sagittal sections through the body of the lateral meniscus, there are more than two images of bow-tie configuration of this structure.

[15] The "unhappy O'Donoghue triad," resulting from valgus stress forces applied to the knee joint, consists of tears of the:
- medial meniscus
- medial collateral ligament
- anterior cruciate ligament.

[16] PLC injuries are considered to be a surgical emergency requiring operative repair without delay. The injured anatomic structures include popliteal tendon, lateral collateral ligament, posterolateral capsule, arcuate ligament, fabellofibular ligament, and popliteofibular ligament.

[17] Transient lateral dislocation of the patella exhibits characteristic appearance on MR: high signal intensity focus on proton density-weighted fat-saturated or T2/IR sequences in the medial aspect of the patella demonstrated on axial images and similar high signal in the anterior aspect of the lateral femoral condyle demonstrated on sagittal and coronal images of the knee. It is invariably associated with a tear of the medial patellar retinaculum.

[18] High position of the patella (patella alta) may indicate a tear of the patellar ligament; low position of the patella (patella infera, patella baja) may indicate a tear of the quadriceps tendon, but MRI is the technique of choice to diagnose these injuries.

SUGGESTED READINGS

Ahlback S, Bauer GCH, Bohne WH. Spontaneous osteonecrosis of the knee. *Arthritis Rheum* 1968;11:705–733.

Aichroth P. Osteochondritis dissecans of the knee: a clinical survey. *J Bone Joint Surg [Br]* 1971;53B:440–447.

Aichroth P. Osteochondral fractures and their relationship to osteochondritis dissecans of the knee. *J Bone Joint Surg [Br]* 1971;53B:448–454.

Anderson MW, Raghavan N, Seidenwurm DJ, Greenspan A, Drake C. Evaluation of meniscal tears: fast spin-echo versus conventional spin-echo magnetic resonance imaging. *Acad Radiol* 1995;2:209–214.

Apley AG. Fractures of the tibial plateau. *Orthop Clin North Am* 1979;10:61–74.

Applegate GR, Flannigan BD, Tolin BS, Fox JM, Del Pizzo W. MR diagnosis of recurrent tears in the knee: value of intraarticular contrast material. *Am J Roentgenol* 1993;161:821–825.

Araki Y, Yamamoto H, Nakamura H, Tsukaguchi I. MR diagnosis of discoid lateral menisci of the knee. *Eur J Radiol* 1994;18:92–95.

Arger PH, Oberkircher PE, Miller WT. Lipohemarthrosis. *Am J Roentgenol* 1974;121:97–100.

Bassett LW, Grover JS, Seeger LL. Magnetic resonance imaging of knee trauma. *Skeletal Radiol* 1990;19:401–405.

Beltran J. *MRI: musculoskeletal system*. Philadelphia: JB Lippincott; 1990.

Berlin RC, Levinsohn EM, Chrisman H. The wrinkled patellar tendon: an indication of abnormality in the extensor mechanism of the knee. *Skeletal Radiol* 1991;20:181–185.

Berquist TH. *Imaging of orthopedic trauma*, 2nd ed. New York: Raven Press; 1991.

Berquist TH. *Magnetic resonance imaging of the musculoskeletal system*. New York: Raven Press; 1990.

Blackburne JS, Peel TE. A new method of measuring patellar height. *J Bone Joint Surg [Br]* 1977;59B:241–242.

Blankenbaker DG, De Smet AA, Smith JD. Usefulness of two indirect MR imaging signs to diagnose lateral meniscal tears. *Am J Roentgenol* 2002;178:579–582.

Bolog N, Hodler J. MR imaging of the posterolateral corner of the knee. *Skeletal Radiol* 2007;36:715–728.

Brandser EA, Riley MA, Berbaum KS, El-Khoury GY, Bennet DL. MR imaging of anterior cruciate ligament injury: independent value of primary and secondary signs. *Am J Roentgenol* 1996;167:121–126.

Brantigan OC, Voshell AF. Ligaments of the knee joint: the relationship of the ligament of Humphry to the ligament of Wrisberg. *J Bone Joint Surg [Br]* 1946B;28:66–67.

Burk DL Jr, Mitchell DG, Rifkin MD, Vinitski S. Recent advances in magnetic resonance imaging of the knee. *Radiol Clin North Am* 1990;28:379–393.

Campos JC, Chung CB, Lektrakul N, et al. Pathogenesis of the Segond fracture: anatomic and MR imaging evidence of an iliotibial tract or anterior band avulsion. *Radiology* 2001;219:381–386.

Capps GW, Hayes CW. Easily missed injuries around the knee. *Radiographics* 1994;14:1191–1210.

Chan WP, Peterfy C, Fritz RC, Genant HK. MR Diagnosis of complete tears of the anterior cruciate ligament of the knee: importance of anterior subluxation of the tibia. *Am J Roentgenol* 1994;162:355–360.

Cheung LP, Li KCP, Hollett MD, Bergman AG, Herfkens RJ. Meniscal tears of the knee: accuracy of detection with fast spin-echo MR imaging and arthroscopic correlation in 293 patients. *Radiology* 1997;203:508–512.

Connolly B, Babyn PS, Wright JG, Thorner PS. Discoid meniscus in children: magnetic resonance imaging characteristics. *Can Assoc Radiol J* 1996;47:347–354.

Coumas JM, Palmer WE. Knee arthrography. Evolution and current status. *Radiol Clin North Am* 1998;36:703–728.

Cross MJ, Waldrop J. The patella index as a guide to the understanding and diagnosis of patello-femoral instability. *Clin Orthop* 1975;110:174–176.

Crues JV III, Stoller DW. The menisci. In: Mink J, Reicher MA, Crues JV III, Deutsch L, eds. *MR Imaging of the Knee*, 2nd ed. New York: Raven: 1993:91–140.

Daffner RH, Riemer BL, Lupetin AR, Dash N. Magnetic resonance imaging in acute tendon rupture. *Skeletal Radiol* 1986;15:619–621.

Dalinka MK. Knee arthrography. In: Dalinka MK, ed. *Arthrography*. New York: Springer-Verlag; 1980:1–88.

De Abreu MR, Chung CB, Trudell D, Resnick D. Meniscofemoral ligaments: patterns of tears and pseudotears of the menisci using cadaveric and clinical material. *Skeletal Radiol* 2007;36:729–735.

DeFlaviis L, Nessi R, Scaglione P, Balconi G, Albisetti W, Derchi LE. Ultrasonic diagnosis of Osgood-Schlatter and Sinding-Larson-Johansson disease of the knee. *Skeletal Radiol* 1989;18:193–197.

Delamarter RB, Hohl M, Hopp E. Ligament injuries associated with tibial plateau fractures. *Clin Orthop* 1990;250:226–233.

De Smet AA, Fisher DR, Graf BK, Lange RH. Osteochondritis dissecans of the knee: value of MR imaging in determining lesion stabilization and presence of articular cartilage defects. *Am J Roentgenol* 1990;155:549–553.

De Smet AA, Ilahi OA, Graf BK. Reassessment of the MR criteria for stability of osteochondritis dissecans in the knee and ankle. *Skeletal Radiol* 1996;25:159–163.

Eqund N. The axial view of the patellofemoral joint. *Acta Radiol Diagn* 1986;27:101–104.

Escobedo EM, Mills WJ, Hunter JC. The "reverse Segond" fracture: association with a tear of the posterior cruciate ligament and medial meniscus. *Am J Roentgenol* 2002;178:979–983.

Ficat RP, Hungerford DS. *Disorders of the patellofemoral joint*. Baltimore: Williams & Wilkins; 1977.

Firooznia H, Golimbu C, Rafii M. MR imaging of the menisci: fundamentals of anatomy and pathology. *Magn Reson Imaging Clin N Am* 1994;2:325–347.

Freiberger RH. Meniscal abnormalities. In: Freiberger RH, Kaye JJ, eds. *Arthrography*. New York: Appleton-Century-Crofts; 1979:55–91.

Freiberger RH. Technique of knee arthrography. In: Freiberger RH, Kaye JJ, eds. *Arthrography*. New York: Appleton-Century-Crofts; 1979:5–30.

Freiberger RH, Pavlov H. Knee arthrography. *Radiology* 1988;166:489–492.

Friedman RL, Jackson DW. Magnetic resonance imaging of the anterior cruciate ligament: current concepts. *Orthopedics* 1996;19:525–532.

Fulkerson JP, Hungerford DS. *Disorders of the patellofemoral joint*, 2nd ed. Baltimore: Williams & Wilkins; 1990.

Gentili A, Seeger LL, Yao L, Do HM. Anterior cruciate ligament tear: indirect signs at MR imaging. *Radiology* 1994;193:835–840.

Goldman AB, Pavlov H, Rubinstein D. The Segond fracture of the proximal tibia: a small avulsion fracture that reflects ligamentous damage. *Am J Roentgenol* 1988;151:1163–1167.

Graf BK, Cook DA, De Smet AA, Keene JS. "Bone bruises" on magnetic resonance imaging evaluation of anterior cruciate ligament injuries. *Am J Sports Med* 1993;21:220–223.

Grelsamer RP, Meadows S. The modified Insall-Salvati ratio for assessment of patellar height. *Clin Orthop* 1992;282:170–176.

Grelsamer RP, Proctor CS, Bazos AN. Evaluation of patellar shape in the sagittal plane: a clinical analysis. *Am J Sports Med* 1994;22:61–66.

Haims AH, Katz LD, Ruwe PA. MR arthrography of the knee. *Semin Musculoskel Radiol* 1998;2:385–395.

Haims AH, Medvecky MJ, Pavlovich R Jr, Katz LD. MR imaging of the anatomy of and injuries to the lateral and posterolateral aspects of the knee. *Am J Roentgenol* 2003;180:647–653.

Hall FJ. Arthrography of the discoid lateral meniscus. *Am J Roentgenol* 1977;128: 993–1002.

Hall FM. Radiographic diagnosis and accuracy in knee joint effusions. *Radiology* 1975;115:49–54.

Hall FM, Hochman MG. Medial Segond-type fracture: cortical avulsion of the medial tibial plateau associated with tears of the posterior cruciate ligament and medial meniscus. *Skeletal Radiol* 1997;26:553–555.

Hall M. Tibial condylar fractures. *J Bone Joint Surg [Am]* 1967;49A:1455–1567.

Harris RD, Hecht HL. Suprapatellar effusions: a new diagnostic sign. *Radiology* 1970;97:1–4.

Heller L, Langman J. The meniscofemoral ligaments of the human knee. *J Bone Joint Surg [Br]* 1964;46B:307–313.

Helms CA. The meniscus: recent advances in MR imaging of the knee. *Am J Roentgenol* 2002;179:1115–1122.

Helms CA, Laorr A, Cannon WD Jr. The absent bow tie sign in bucket-handle tears of the menisci in the knee. *Am J Roentgenol* 1998;170:57–61.

Hohl M. Tibial condylar fractures. *J Bone Joint Surg [Am]* 1967;49A:1455–1467.

Hohl M, Larson RL. Fractures and dislocations of the knee. In: Rockwood CA Jr, Green DP, eds. *Fractures.* Philadelphia: Lippincott; 1975.

Hughston JC, Hergenroeder PT, Courtenay BG. Osteochondritis dissecans of the femoral condyles. *J Bone Joint Surg [Am]* 1984;66A:1340–1348.

Insall J, Salvatti E. Patella position in the normal knee joint. *Radiology* 1971;101:101–104.

Jee W-H, McCauley TR, Kim J-M, et al. Meniscal tear configurations: categorization with MR imaging. *Am J Roentgenol* 2003;180:93–97.

Kaplan PA, Nelson NL, Garvin KL, Brown DE. MR of the knee: the significance of high signal in the meniscus that does not clearly extend to the surface. *Am J Roentgenol* 1991;156:333–336.

Kaye JJ. Anatomy and arthrography of the normal menisci. In: Freiberger RH, Kaye JJ, eds. *Arthrography.* New York: Appleton-Century-Crofts; 1979:31–53.

Kirsch MD, Fitzgerald SW, Friedman H, Rogers LF. Transient patellar dislocation: diagnosis with MR imaging. *Am J Roentgenol* 1993;161:109–113.

Koval JK, Helfet DI. Tibial plateau fractures: evaluation and treatment. *J Am Acad Orthop Surg* 1995;3:86–93.

Krause BL, Williams JP, Catterall A. Natural history of Osgood-Schlatter disease. *J Pediatr Orthop* 1990;10:65–68.

Lancourt JE, Cristini JA. Patella alta and patella infera: their etiological role in patellar dislocation, chondromalacia, and apophysitis of the tibial tubercle. *J Bone Joint Surg [Am]* 1975;57A:1112–1115.

Laurin CA, Levesque HP, Dussault R, Labille H, Peides JP. The abnormal lateral patellofemoral angle. *J Bone Joint Surg [Am]* 1978;60A:55–60.

Lee J, Papakonstantinou O, Brookenthal KR, Trudell D, Resnick DL. Arcuate sign of posterolateral knee injuries: anatomic, radiographic, and MR imaging data related to patterns of injury. *Skeletal Radiol* 2003;32:619–627.

Lee J, Weissman B, Nikpoor N, Aliabodi P, Sosman JL. Lipohemarthrosis of the knee: a review of recent experiences. *Radiology* 1989;173:189–191.

Lee JHE, Singh TT, Bolton G. Axial fat-saturated FSE imaging of the knee: appearance of meniscal tears. *Skeletal Radiol* 2002;31:384–395.

Linden B. The incidence of osteochondritis in the condyles of the femur. *Acta Orthop Scand* 1976;47:6640–667.

Lugo-Olivieri CH, Scott WW Jr, Zerhouni EA. Fluid-fluid levels in injured knees: do they always represent lipohemarthrosis? *Radiology* 1996;198:499–502.

McAnally JL, Southam SL, Mlady GW. New thoughts on the origin of Pellegrini-Stieda: the association of PCL injury and medial femoral epicondylar periosteal stripping. *Skeletal Radiol* 2009;38:193–198.

McKnight A, Southgate J, Price A, Ostlere S. Meniscal tears with displaced fragments: common patterns on magnetic resonance imaging. *Skeletal Radiol* 2010;39:279–283.

Medlar RC, Lynce ED. Sinding-Larsen-Johansson disease. Its etiology and natural history. *J Bone Joint Surg [Am]* 1978;60A:1113–1116.

Mendes LFA, Pretterklieber ML, Cho JH. Pellegrini-Stieda disease: a heterogeneous disorder not synonymous with ossification/calcification of the tibial collateral ligament—anatomic and imaging investigation. *Skeletal Radiol* 2006;35:916–922.

Merchant AC, Mercer RL, Jacobsen RH, Cool CR. Roentgenographic analysis of patello-femoral congruence. *J Bone Joint Surg [Am]* 1974;56A:1391–1396.

Middleton WD, Lawson TL. *Anatomy and MRI of the joints: a multiplanar atlas.* New York: Raven Press; 1989.

Mink JH, Deutsch AL. The knee. In: Mink JH, Deutsch AL, eds. *MRI of the musculoskeletal system: a teaching file.* New York: Raven Press; 1990:251–387.

Nachlas IW, Olpp JL. Para-articular calcification (Pellegrini-Stieda) in affections of the knee. *Surg Gynecol Obstet* 1945;81:206–212.

Nance EP Jr, Kaye JJ. Injuries of the quadriceps mechanism. *Radiology* 1982;142:301–307.

Newberg AH, Seligson D. Patellofemoral joint: 30 degrees, 60 degrees, and 90 degrees views. *Radiology* 1980;137:57–61.

Norman A, Baker ND. Spontaneous osteonecrosis of the knee and medial meniscal tears. *Radiology* 1978;129:653–660.

O'Donoghue DH. *Treatment of Injuries to Athletes,* 4th ed. Philadelphia: Saunders; 1984.

O'Donoghue DH. Surgical treatment of injuries to ligaments of the knee. *JAMA* 1959;169:1423–1431.

O'Donoghue DH. Chondral and osteochondral fractures. *J Trauma* 1966;6:469–481.

Ogden JA, Southwick WO. Osgood-Schlatter's disease and tibial tuberosity development. *Clin Orthop* 1976;116:180–189.

Osgood RB. Lesions of the tibial tubercle occurring during adolescence. *Boston Med Surg J* 1903;148:114–117.

Pavlov H. The cruciate ligaments. In: Freiberger RH, Kaye JJ, eds. *Arthrography.* New York: Appleton-Century-Crofts; 1979:93–107.

Pavlov H, Freiberger RH. An easy method to demonstrate the cruciate ligaments by double-contrast arthrography. *Radiology* 1978;126:817–818.

Pope TL Jr. MR imaging of knee ligaments. In: Weissman BN, ed. *Syllabus: a categorical course in musculoskeletal radiology.* Oak Brook, IL: Radiological Society of North America; 1993:197–210.

Rand JA, Berquist TH. The knee. In: Berquist TH, ed. *Imaging of orthopedic trauma,* 2nd ed. New York: Raven Press; 1991:333–432.

Resnick D. Internal derangements of joints. In: Resnick D, ed. *Diagnosis of bone and joint disorders,* 3rd ed. Philadelphia: WB Saunders; 1995:2899–3228.

Rogers LF. *Radiology of skeletal trauma,* 2nd ed. New York: Churchill Livingstone; 1992:1199–1317.

Rosenberg ZS, Kawelblum M, Cheung YY, Beltran J, Lehman WB, Grant AD. Osgood-Schlatter lesion: fracture or tendinitis? Scintigraphic, CT, and MR imaging features. *Radiology* 1992;185:853–858.

Ruwe PA, McCarthy S. Cost-effectiveness of magnetic resonance imaging. In: Mink JH, Reicher MA, Crues JW, Deutsch AL, ed. *MR imaging of the knee,* 2nd ed. New York: Raven Press; 1993:463–466.

Ryu KN, Kim IS, Kim EJ, et al. MR imaging of tears of discoid lateral menisci. *Am J Roentgenol* 1998;171:963–967.

Sartoris DJ, Kursunoglu S, Pineda C, Kerr R, Pate D, Resnick D. Detection of intra-articular osteochondral bodies in the knee using computed arthrotomography. *Radiology* 1985;155:447–450.

Schatzker J, McBroom R. The tibial plateau fracture: the Toronto experience 1968–1975. *Clin Orthop* 1979;138:94–104.

Schlatter C. Verletzungen des schnabelförmigen Fortsatzes der oberen Tibiaepiphyse. *Beitr Klin Chir* 1903;38:874–887.

Sinding-Larsen MF. A hitherto unknown affection of the patella in children. *Acta Radiol* 1921;1:171–173.

Singson RD, Feldman F, Staron R, Kiernan H. MR imaging of displaced bucket-handle tear of the medial meniscus. *Am J Roentgenol* 1991;156:121–124.

Smillie IS. The congenital discoid meniscus. *J Bone Joint Surg [Br]* 1948;30B:671–682.

Sonin AH, Fitzgerald SW, Friedman H, Hoff FL, Hendrix RW, Rogers LF. Posterior cruciate ligament injury: MR imaging diagnosis and patterns of injury. *Radiology* 1994;190:455–458.

Sonin AH, Fitzgerald SW, Hoff FL, Friedman H, Bresler ME. MR imaging of the posterior cruciate ligament: normal, abnormal, and associated injury patterns. *Radiographics* 1995;15:551–561.

Stark JE, Siegel MJ, Weinberger E, Shaw DW. Discoid menisci in children: MR features. *J Comput Assist Tomogr* 1995;19:608–611.

Stoller DW. *Magnetic resonance imaging in orthopedics and sports medicine.* Philadelphia: JB Lippincott; 1993.

Tung GA, Davis LM, Wiggins ME, Fadale PD. Tears of the anterior cruciate ligament: primary and secondary signs at MR imaging. *Radiology* 1993;188:661–667.

Twaddle BC, Hunter JC, Chapman JR, Simoniah PT, Escobedo EM. MRI in acute knee dislocation: a prospective study of clinical, MRI and surgical findings. *J Bone Joint Surg [Br]* 1996;78B:573–579.

Umans H, Wimpfheimer O, Haramati N, Applbaum YH, Adler M, Bosco J. Diagnosis of partial tears of the anterior cruciate ligament of the knee: value of MR imaging. *Am J Roentgenol* 1995;165:893–897.

Venkatanarasimha N, Kamath A, Mukherjee K, Kamath S. Potential pitfalls of a double PCL sign. *Skeletal Radiol* 2009;38:735–739.

Weber WN, Neumann CH, Barakos JA, Peterson SA, Steinbach LS, Genant HK. Lateral tibial rim (Segond) fractures: MR imaging characteristics. *Radiology* 1991;180:731–734.

Weiss KL, Morehouse HT, Levy IM. Sagittal MR images of the knee: a low-signal band parallel to the posterior cruciate ligament caused by a displaced bucket-handle tear. *Am J Roentgenol* 1991;156:117–119.

Williams JL, Cliff MM, Bonakdarpour A. Spontaneous osteonecrosis of the knee. *Radiology* 1973;107:15–19.

Wright DH, De Smet AA, Norris M. Bucket-handle tears of the medial and lateral menisci of the knee: value of MR imaging in detecting displaced fragments. *Am J Roentgenol* 1995;165:621–625.

Yu JS, Salonen DC, Hodler J, Haghighi P, Trudell D, Resnick D. Posterolateral aspect of the knee: improved MR imaging with a coronal oblique technique. *Radiology* 1996;198:199–204.

CHAPTER 1

Lower Limb III
Ankle and Foot

Ankle and Foot

The ankle is the most frequently injured of all the major weight-bearing joints in the body. Most victims are young adults injured while participating in athletic activities such as running, skiing, and soccer. Ankle structures susceptible to injury include bones, ligaments, tendons, and syndesmoses; ligaments can be damaged in the absence of fractures. When this occurs, damage to ligaments may go unrecognized on conventional radiographs, with the result that the patient is not properly treated.

The type of fracture usually indicates the mechanism of injury determined, as Kleiger has pointed out, by the position of the foot, the direction and intensity of the applied force, and the resistance of the structures making up the joint. The mechanism of injury may in turn serve as an indicator of which ligament structures are damaged.

Although occasionally meticulous history taking and clinical examination can help determine the mechanism of trauma and predict damage to the various structures, radiologic examination is the key to reliable evaluation of the site and extent of injury. There are two basic types of ankle trauma: inversion injuries and eversion injuries. These, however, may be complicated by internal or external rotation, hyperflexion or hyperextension, and vertical compression forces.

Foot injuries are also common and usually result from direct trauma, such as a blow or a fall from a height; only rarely do such injuries result from indirect forces such as abnormal stress or strain of muscles or tendons. Foot fractures, accounting for 10% of all fractures, are more common than dislocations, which usually are associated with fractures, and occur at the midtarsal, tarsometatarsal, and metatarsophalangeal articulations.

Anatomic–Radiologic Considerations

The ankle joint proper consists of the tibiotalar and distal tibiofibular articulations, the latter a syndesmotic joint rather than a true synarthrodial one. In matters of injury, however, one must consider that the ankle joint acts as a unit with other joints of the foot, particularly the talocalcaneal (subtalar) articulation, where application of stress can have great impact on ankle injuries.

The ankle joint is formed by three bones—the distal tibia and fibula and the talus—and three principal sets of ligaments—the medial collateral (deltoid) ligament; the lateral collateral ligament, consisting of the anterior talofibular, posterior talofibular, and calcaneofibular ligaments; and the syndesmotic complex, a fibrous joint between the distal tibia and the fibula (Fig. 10.1). The distal tibiofibular syndesmotic complex, one of the most important anatomic structures in maintaining ankle integrity and stability, consists of three elements: the distal anterior tibiofibular ligament, the distal posterior tibiofibular ligament, and the interosseous membrane.

From the viewpoint of anatomy and kinetics, the foot is divided into three distinct sections: hindfoot, midfoot, and forefoot. The hindfoot, separated from the midfoot by the midtarsal (or Chopart) joint, includes the talus and calcaneus; the midfoot, separated from the forefoot by the tarsometatarsal (Lisfranc) joint, includes the navicular, cuboid, and three cuneiform bones; and the forefoot includes the metatarsals and phalanges (Fig. 10.2). The muscles attached to the tibia and fibula end in tendons proximal to or at the level of the ankle joint. These tendons insert into the foot (Fig. 10.3).

A word about terminology is in order, because the terminology describing motion of the ankle and foot in the literature is not uniform and confusion has been created about the various mechanisms of ankle and foot injuries. Frequently, but incorrectly, the terms adduction, inversion, varus, and supination have been used interchangeably, as have their counterparts abduction, eversion, valgus, and pronation. However, supination and pronation are more appropriately applied to compound motion. *Supination* consists of adduction and inversion of the forefoot (motion in the tarsometatarsal and midtarsal joints) and inversion of the heel, which assumes a varus configuration (motion in subtalar joint), as well as slight plantar flexion of the ankle (tibiotalar) joint. In *pronation*, compound motion consists of abduction and eversion of the forefoot (motion in the tarsometatarsal and midtarsal joints) and eversion of the heel, which assumes a valgus configuration (motion in the subtalar joint), together with slight dorsiflexion (or dorsal extension) of the ankle (Fig. 10.4).

Adduction properly applies to medial deviation of the forefoot, and *abduction* to lateral deviation of the forefoot, both motions occurring in the tarsometatarsal (Lisfranc) joint; *adduction of the heel* refers to inversion of the calcaneus; and *abduction of the heel* refers to eversion of the calcaneus, both motions occurring in the subtalar joint. *Plantar flexion* refers to caudad (downward) foot motion, *dorsiflexion* to cephalad (upward) foot motion—motions occurring in the ankle (tibiotalar) joint. Varus and valgus should not be used to describe motion but should be reserved for the description of ankle or foot position in case of deformity. Occasionally, varus and valgus are used interchangeably with inversion and eversion to describe the applied stress.

PRINCIPAL GROUPS OF ANKLE LIGAMENTS

Medial Collateral (Deltoid) Ligament

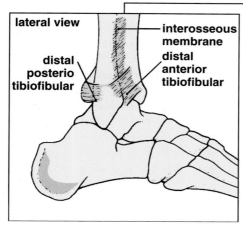

medial view

tibiotalar band

tibionavicular band

tibiocalcaneal band

Lateral Collateral Ligament

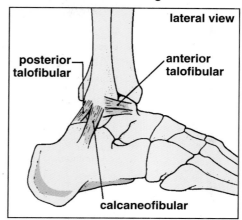

lateral view

posterior talofibular

anterior talofibular

calcaneofibular

Distal Tibiofibular Syndesmotic Complex

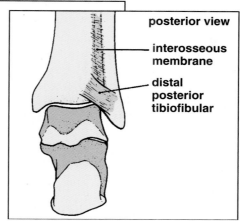

lateral view

interosseous membrane

distal anterior tibiofibular

distal posterio tibiofibular

posterior view

interosseous membrane

distal posterior tibiofibular

▲
FIGURE 10.1 Ligaments of the ankle. Three principal sets of ligaments form the ankle joint: the medial collateral (deltoid) ligament, the lateral collateral ligament, and the distal tibiofibular syndesmotic complex, which is important for maintaining ankle integrity and stability.

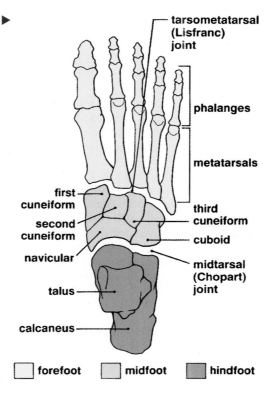

FIGURE 10.2 Anatomic divisions of the foot. The foot can be viewed as comprising three anatomic parts: the hindfoot, midfoot, and forefoot, separated respectively by the midtarsal (Chopart) and tarsometatarsal (Lisfranc) joints. ▶

tarsometatarsal (Lisfranc) joint

phalanges

metatarsals

first cuneiform

second cuneiform

navicular

talus

calcaneus

third cuneiform

cuboid

midtarsal (Chopart) joint

forefoot   midfoot   hindfoot

TENDONS OF THE ANKLE AND FOOT

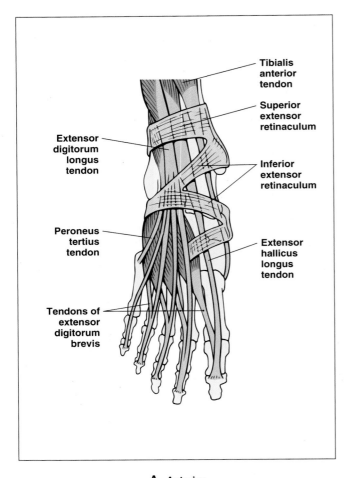

Tibialis anterior tendon

Superior extensor retinaculum

Extensor digitorum longus tendon

Inferior extensor retinaculum

Peroneus tertius tendon

Extensor hallicus longus tendon

Tendons of extensor digitorum brevis

A. Anterior (Dorsal)

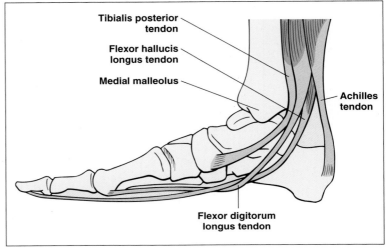

Peroneus longus tendon

Fibula

Superior peroneal retinaculum

Inferior peroneal retinaculum

Peroneus brevis tendon

B. Lateral

Tibialis posterior tendon

Flexor hallucis longus tendon

Medial malleolus

Achilles tendon

Flexor digitorum longus tendon

C. Medial

▲

FIGURE 10.3   Tendons of the ankle and foot. The attachment of various tendons of the ankle and foot are depicted, as viewed from the dorsal aspect (**A**), lateral aspect (**B**), and medial aspect (**C**).

Imaging of the Ankle and Foot

Ankle. The standard radiographic examination of the ankle, as a rule, includes the anteroposterior (including the mortise), lateral, and oblique projections. Stress views are also frequently obtained for evaluating ankle injuries. These may also need to be supplemented with special projections.

On the *anteroposterior* view, the distal tibia and fibula, including the medial and lateral malleoli, are well demonstrated (Fig. 10.5). On this projection, it is important to note that the fibular (lateral) malleolus is longer than the tibial (medial) malleolus. This anatomic feature, important for maintaining ankle stability, is crucial for reconstruction of the fractured ankle joint. Even minimal displacement or shortening of the lateral malleolus allows lateral talar shift to occur and may cause incongruity in the ankle joint, possibly leading to posttraumatic arthritis. A variant of the anteroposterior projection, in which the ankle is internally rotated 10 degrees, is called the mortise view because the ankle mortise is well demonstrated on it (Fig. 10.6).

The *lateral* view is used to evaluate the anterior aspect of the distal tibia and the posterior lip of this bone (the so-called third malleolus) (Fig. 10.7). Some fractures oriented in the coronal plane can be better visualized on this projection.

The *oblique* view of the ankle, best obtained with the foot internally rotated approximately 30 to 35 degrees, is effective in demonstrating the tibiofibular syndesmosis and the talofibular joint (Fig. 10.8). An *external oblique* view may also be required to evaluate the lateral malleolus and the anterior tibial tubercle (Fig. 10.9).

Most ankle ligament injuries require stress radiography, ankle joint arthrography, computed tomography (CT), or magnetic resonance imaging (MRI) (see later) for demonstration and sufficient evaluation. Some, however, can be deduced from the site and extension of fractures on the standard radiographic examination. A thorough knowledge of the skeletal and soft-tissue topographic anatomy of the ankle, together with an understanding of the kinematics and mechanism of ankle injuries, will aid the radiologist in correctly diagnosing traumatic conditions and predicting ligament injuries. With such understanding, the radiologist can even determine the sequence of injury to the various structures.

Some ligament injuries may be diagnosed on the basis of disruption of the ankle mortise and displacement of the talus; others can be deduced from the appearance of fractured bones. For example, fibular fracture above the level of the ankle joint indicates that the distal anterior tibiofibular ligament is torn. Fracture of the fibula above its anterior tubercle strongly suggests that the tibiofibular syndesmosis is completely

FIGURE 10.4 **Motion in the ankle and foot.** ▶
Supination is a compound motion consisting
of adduction and inversion of the forefoot,
together with inversion of the heel and slight
plantar flexion in the ankle joint. In pronation,
the compound motion involves abduction and
eversion of the forefoot with eversion of the
heel and slight dorsiflexion in the ankle joint.

COMPOUND MOTION IN THE ANKLE AND FOOT

Supination

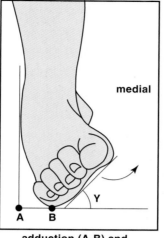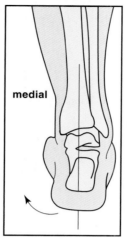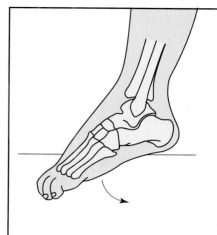

adduction (A-B) and
Inversion (Y)
of forefoot

inversion
(adduction) of heel

plantar flexion

Pronation

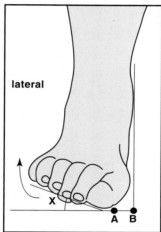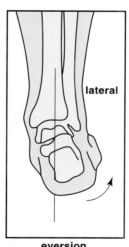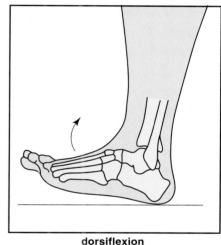

abduction (A-B)
and eversion (X)
of forefoot

eversion
(abduction) of heel

dorsiflexion

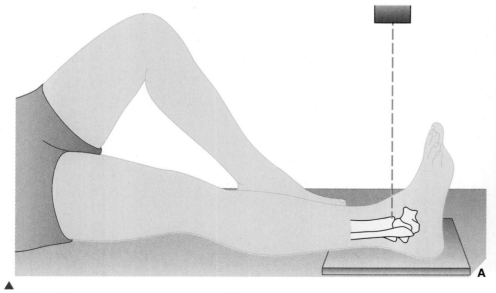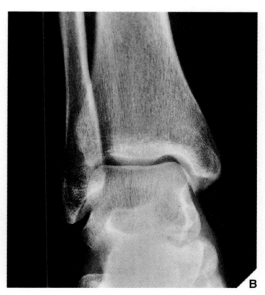

▲
FIGURE 10.5 **Anteroposterior view. (A)** For the anteroposterior view of the ankle, the patient is supine on the radiographic table with the heel resting on the
film cassette. The foot is in neutral position, with the sole perpendicular to the leg and the cassette. The central beam is directed vertically to the ankle joint at the
midpoint between both malleoli. **(B)** The radiograph in this projection demonstrates the distal tibia, particularly the medial malleolus, the body of the talus, and
the tibiotalar joint. Note, however, the overlap of the distal fibula and the lateral aspect of the tibia. The tibiofibular syndesmosis is not clearly demonstrated.

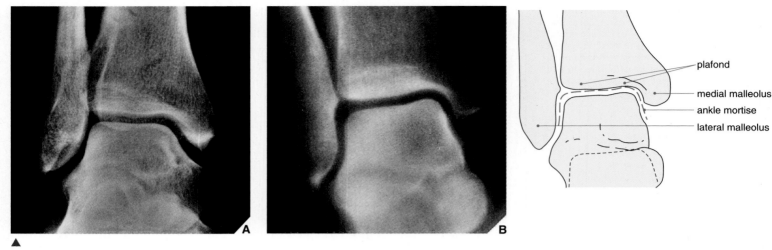

▲
FIGURE 10.6 Mortise view. **(A)** The mortise view, a variant of the anteroposterior projection obtained with 10-degree internal rotation of the ankle, eliminates the overlap of the medial aspect of the distal fibula and the lateral aspect of the talus, so the space between these bones is well demonstrated. **(B)** The ankle mortise, shown here on a tomographic cut through the ankle joint, is formed by the medial malleolus, the articular surface of the distal tibia (the ceiling or plafond), and the lateral malleolus; it is shaped like an inverted U.

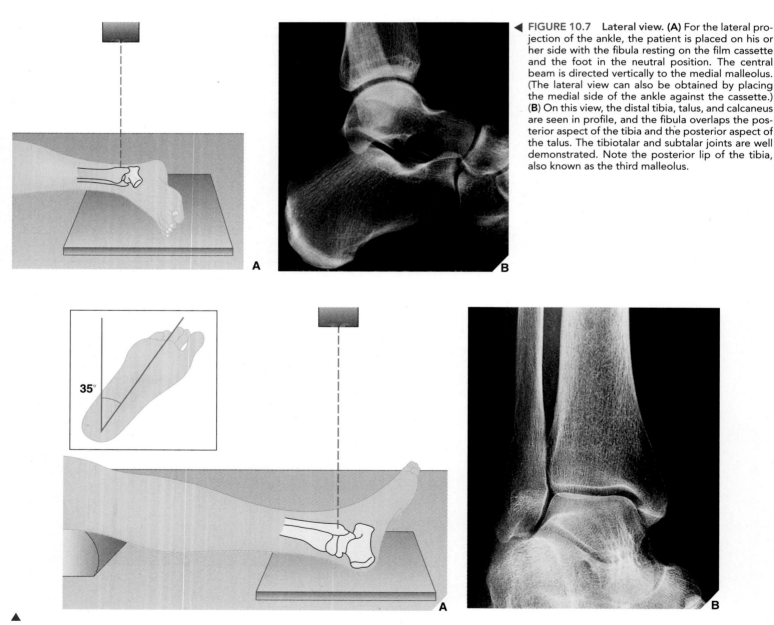

◀ **FIGURE 10.7** Lateral view. **(A)** For the lateral projection of the ankle, the patient is placed on his or her side with the fibula resting on the film cassette and the foot in the neutral position. The central beam is directed vertically to the medial malleolus. (The lateral view can also be obtained by placing the medial side of the ankle against the cassette.) **(B)** On this view, the distal tibia, talus, and calcaneus are seen in profile, and the fibula overlaps the posterior aspect of the tibia and the posterior aspect of the talus. The tibiotalar and subtalar joints are well demonstrated. Note the posterior lip of the tibia, also known as the third malleolus.

▲
FIGURE 10.8 Internal oblique view. **(A)** For the internal oblique view of the ankle, the patient is supine, and the leg and foot are rotated medially approximately 35 degrees (*inset*). The foot is in the neutral position, forming a 90-degree angle with the distal leg. The central beam is directed perpendicular to the lateral malleolus. **(B)** On the radiograph, the medial and lateral malleoli, the tibial plafond, the dome of the talus, the tibiotalar joint, and the tibiofibular syndesmosis are well demonstrated.

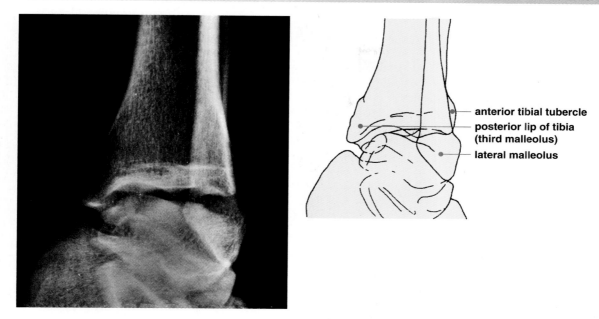

anterior tibial tubercle
posterior lip of tibia
(third malleolus)
lateral malleolus

▲ FIGURE 10.9   **External oblique view.** On the external oblique view, for which the patient is positioned as for the internal oblique view but with the limb rotated laterally approximately 40 to 45 degrees, the lateral malleolus and the anterior tibial tubercle are well demonstrated.

disrupted. Fracture of the fibula above the level of the ankle joint without accompanying fracture of the medial malleolus indicates rupture of the deltoid ligament. Transverse fracture of the medial malleolus indicates that the deltoid ligament is intact. High fracture of the fibula associated with a fracture of the medial malleolus or tear of the tibiofibular ligament, the so-called Maisonneuve fracture (see later), indicates rupture of the interosseous membrane up to the level of the fibular fracture.

When radiographs of the ankle are normal, however, stress views are extremely important in evaluating ligament injuries (see Fig. 4.4). Inversion (adduction) and anterior-draw stress films are most frequently obtained; only rarely is an eversion (abduction)-stress examination required.

On the *inversion-stress* film, obtained in the anteroposterior projection, the degree of talar tilt can be measured by the angle formed by lines drawn along the tibial plafond and the dome of the talus (Fig. 10.10).

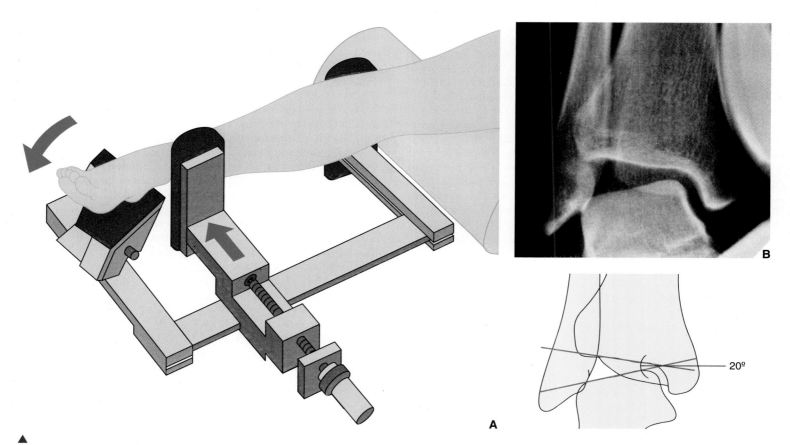

B

20º

A

▲ FIGURE 10.10   **Inversion stress view. (A)** For inversion (adduction)-stress examination of the ankle, the foot is fixed in the device while the patient is supine. The pressure plate, positioned approximately 2 cm above the ankle joint, applies varus stress adducting the heel. (If the examination is painful, 5 to 10 mL of 1% Lidocaine or a similar local anesthetic is injected at the site of maximum pain.) **(B)** On the anteroposterior film, the degree of talar tilt is measured by the angle formed by lines drawn along the tibial plafond and the dome of the talus. The contralateral ankle is subjected to the same procedure for comparison.

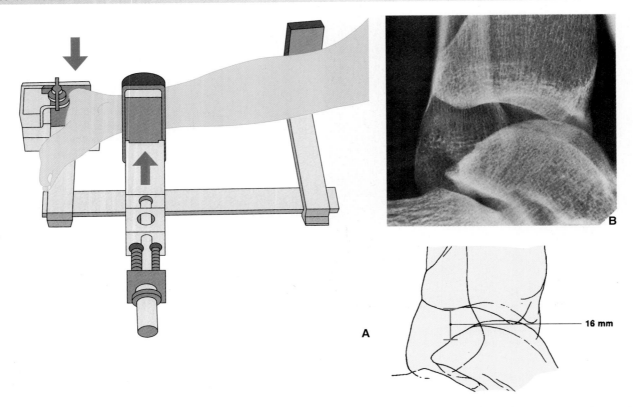

FIGURE 10.11 **Anterior-draw stress view. (A)** For anterior-draw stress examination, the patient is placed on his or her side, with the foot in the device. The pressure plate, positioned anteriorly approximately 2 cm above the ankle, applies posterior stress on the heel. During the examination, the amount of pressure is monitored on a light-emitting diode digital reader. **(B)** On the lateral stress film, the amount of transposition of the talus in relation to the distal tibia can be determined.

This angle helps diagnose tears of the lateral collateral ligament. However, the wide range of normal values for these measurements may make interpretation difficult, and thus comparison studies of the contralateral ankle should be obtained. Even this method is not always accurate; up to 25 degrees of talar tilt has been reported in people with no history of injury, and occasionally there will be a patient whose ankles exhibit considerable variation in measurement. Many authorities advise that with forced inversion, tilt less than 5 degrees is normal, 5 to 15 degrees may be normal or abnormal, 15 to 25 degrees strongly suggests ligament injury, and more than 25 degrees is always abnormal. With forced eversion, talar tilting of more than 10 degrees is probably pathologic.

The *anterior-draw* stress film, obtained in the lateral projection, provides a useful measurement for determining injury to the anterior talofibular ligament (Fig. 10.11). Values of up to 5 mm of separation between the talus and the distal tibia are considered normal; values between 5 and 10 mm may be normal or abnormal, and the opposite ankle should be stressed for comparison. Values above 10 mm always indicate abnormality.

Ancillary imaging techniques are essential to the diagnosis and evaluation of many ankle injuries. CT may be required to determine the position of comminuted fragments in complex fractures, for example, of the distal tibia, talus, and calcaneus. Arthrography (Fig. 10.12) is occasionally used for assessing the integrity of the ligamentous structures in acute trauma, although recently it has been almost completely supplanted by MRI. It is still, however, an effective technique for evaluating the articular cartilage, and detecting and localizing loose osteocartilaginous bodies. It is also helpful in evaluation of chondral and osteochondral fractures and osteochondritis dissecans, which usually affects the dome of the talus. A single-contrast study is usually performed to assess the integrity of the ankle ligaments. For evaluating the articular cartilage, a double-contrast study (combining a positive-contrast agent and air) is more effective.

Ankle tenography is a useful procedure for evaluating tendon tears, particularly tears of the Achilles tendon, peroneus longus and brevis,

tibialis posterior, flexor digitorum longus, and flexor hallucis longus. According to Bleichrodt and colleagues, tenography particularly has proved to be reliable in the diagnosis of injuries of the calcaneofibular ligament, with a sensitivity of 88% and specificity of 87% to 94%. In a procedure similar to that for ankle arthrography, a 22-gauge needle is inserted into the tendon sheath, with the needle tip directed distally, and 15 to 20 mL of contrast medium is injected under fluoroscopic guidance. Films are then obtained in the standard projections (Fig. 10.13). Tear is indicated by the extravasation of contrast agent from the tendon sheath, abrupt termination of the contrast-filled tendon sheath, or leak of contrast into the adjoining articulations (see Figs. 10.69 and 10.72). Recently, this technique has been completely replaced by MRI.

CT is an effective modality to evaluate various ligaments and tendons, because the soft-tissue contrast resolution of CT allows the easy differentiation of these structures from surrounding fat. Specifically, tendon injuries including tendinitis, tenosynovitis, and rupture and dislocation of tendons can be effectively diagnosed. The major limitation in evaluating pathologic conditions of tendons with CT is the inability to scan the tendons in the coronal and sagittal planes. Reformation images, while occasionally helpful, suffer from the lack of spatial resolution and require additional examination time.

For adequate CT of the ankle and foot, proper positioning of the leg in the gantry is essential. In addition, because nomenclature for imaging planes of the feet occasionally creates a problem, it is important to recognize that the coronal, sagittal, and axial planes of the ankle and foot are determined the same way as for the body (Fig. 10.14A). For coronal images, the knees are flexed and the feet are positioned flat against the gantry table. The coronal sections are obtained with the beam directed to the dorsum of the foot. More commonly modified coronal images are obtained by angling the gantry or by using a foot wedge (Fig. 10.14B). A lateral scanogram helps to establish the degree of necessary gantry tilt. Axial images are obtained with the feet perpendicular to the gantry table, great toes together, and the knees fully extended. The beam is directed parallel to the soles of the feet. Sagittal images are usually generated

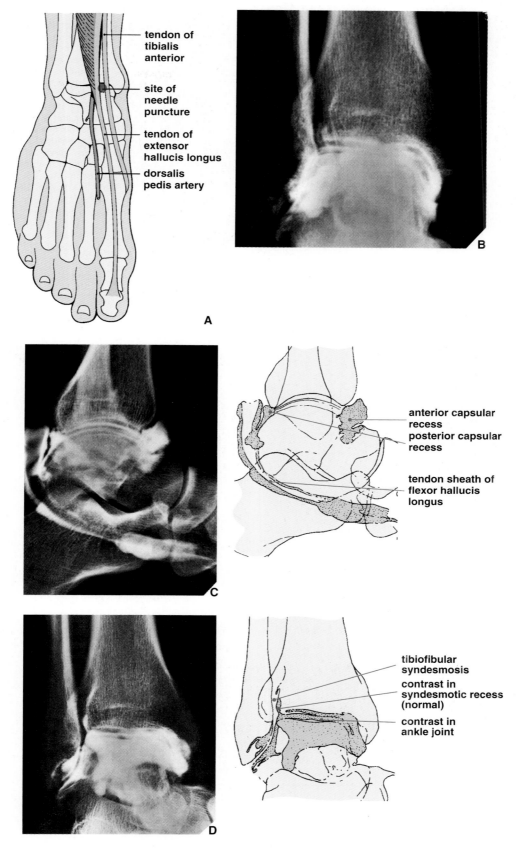

FIGURE 10.12   Arthrography of the ankle joint. (A) For arthrographic examination of the ankle, the patient is supine on the table, with the foot in the neutral position (see Fig. 10.5A). Under fluoroscopic control, the injection site between the tendons of the tibialis anterior and the extensor hallucis longus is marked. Care should be taken to avoid puncturing the dorsalis pedis artery, which should be located by palpation and its site marked on the skin. The needle (preferably 21-gauge) is directed slightly cephalad to avoid the overhanging anterior margin of the tibia. After the joint is entered, approximatley 5 to 7 mL of 60% meglumine diatrizoate or a similar contrast agent is injected for a single-contrast arthrogram. For a double-contrast study, 1 to 2 mL of positive contrast agent and 6 to 8 mL of room air are injected. Films are then obtained in the standard anteroposterior, lateral, and oblique projections. **(B)** The normal anteroposterior view shows contrast agent outlining the ankle joint, coating the articular surface of the talus and extending into the syndesmotic recess, which normally should not exceed 2.5 cm. **(C)** On the lateral view, the anterior and posterior capsular recesses are outlined. Filling of the posterior facet of the subtalar joint represents a normal variant, occurring in approximately 10% of cases (see Fig. 10.61C). In approximately 20% of cases, the tendon sheaths of the flexor hallucis longus and flexor digitorum longus opacify on the medial aspect of the ankle. When this occurs, the full extension of the flexor hallucis longus should be noted as it passes proximal to the groove in the talar tubercle and into the groove beneath the sustentaculum tali. Under normal conditions, no tendon sheath opacification should occur on the lateral side of the ankle. **(D)** Oblique radiograph demonstrates the tibiofibular syndesmosis. No contrast agent should be seen in this area except for normal opacification of the syndesmotic recess.

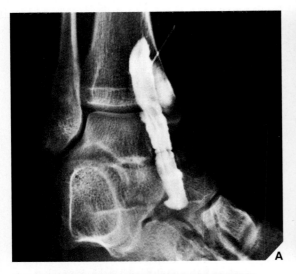

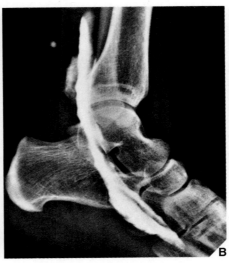

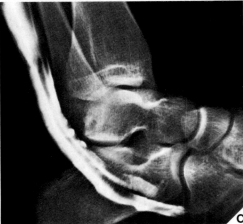

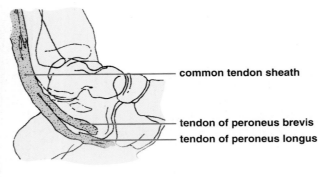

- common tendon sheath
- tendon of peroneus brevis
- tendon of peroneus longus

◀ **FIGURE 10.13** **Ankle tenography.** Tenograms in the oblique (**A**) and lateral (**B**) projections demonstrate the normal appearance of the tendon of the flexor hallucis longus. On the oblique view, note the distal direction of the needle tip at the beginning of the injection. Normally, the tendon of the flexor hallucis longus does not opacify beyond the limit of the Lisfranc joint. (**C**) On the normal tenogram of the peroneus longus and brevis, seen here on the lateral view, note the position of these tendons below the flexor hallucis longus. The tendon of the peroneus brevis is seen normally opacified; the tendon of the peroneus longus passes below it, crossing into the plantar aspect of the foot to its insertion at the base of the first metatarsal bone.

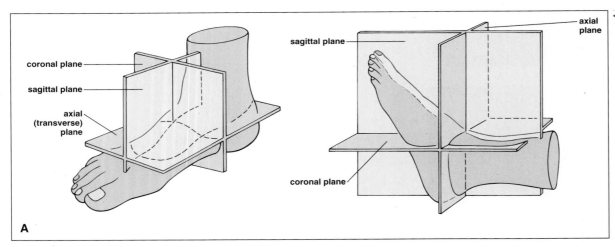

◀ **FIGURE 10.14** **Anatomic and imaging planes. (A)** Anatomic planes of the ankle and foot and **(B)** CT imaging planes.

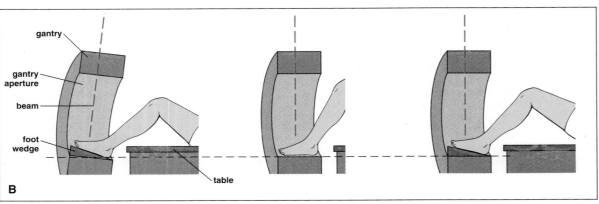

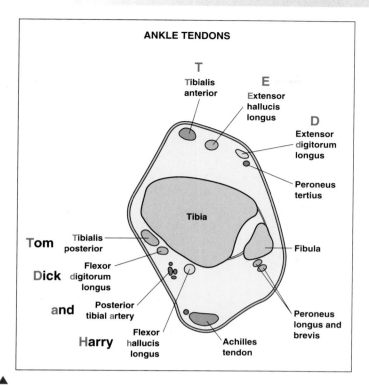

ANKLE TENDONS

FIGURE 10.15 Schematic representation of ankle tendons on axial MRI. (Modified from Helms CA et al., 2009.)

of ankle tendons and ligaments. The tendons show uniformly low signal intensity in all spin-echo pulse sequences, with the exception of the Achilles tendon and tibialis posterior tendon. These two tendons, on long TR sequences, occasionally show small foci of intermediate signal intensity within their substance, particularly near their insertions to the calcaneal tuberosity and the navicular bone, respectively. From a practical point of view, it is helpful to memorize the location and relationship of various tendons seen on axial MR image of the ankle by using the mnemonic phrase, "Tom, Dick, and Harry" for the posteromedial aspect, and "TED" for the anterolateral aspect of the ankle (Fig. 10.15). The ankle ligaments, likewise, demonstrate low signal intensity on MR images, with the exception of the posterior talofibular ligaments, which often appears inhomogeneous, similar to the anterior cruciate ligament of the knee. The anterior and posterior talofibular ligaments can be visualized over their entire length on axial scans with the foot in neutral position (Fig. 10.16), because they are approximately in the same plane of section. The calcaneofibular ligament can be similarly visualized when the foot is in 40-degree plantar flexion. The anterior and posterior tibiofibular ligaments can be demonstrated on the axial images in more proximal sections (Fig. 10.17).

On the sections in the sagittal plane, the tibialis posterior, flexor digitorum longus, and flexor hallucis longus tendons are identified on the medial cuts. The peroneus longus and brevis tendons are seen on the lateral sections (Fig. 10.18). The Achilles tendon is best seen on midline sagittal section (Fig. 10.19). The coronal plane is also effective in the visualization of various ligaments and tendons (Fig. 10.20).

The pathologic conditions of tendons and ligaments are demonstrated by discontinuity of the anatomic structure, the presence of high signal intensity within the tendon substance on T2-weighted images, and inflammatory changes within or around the tendons, which again can be demonstrated by a change in the normal signal intensity.

Foot. Most injuries to the foot can be sufficiently evaluated on the standard radiographic examination of the foot, which includes the anteroposterior, lateral, and oblique projections. Only occasionally are special tangential projections required.

The *anteroposterior* view of the foot adequately demonstrates the metatarsal bones and phalanges (Fig. 10.21) This view reveals an important anatomic feature known as the *first intermetatarsal angle*, which normally ranges from 5 to 10 degrees (Fig. 10.21C). This angle

by using reformation technique, although direct sagittal sections can also be obtained by placing the patient in the lateral decubitus position. Images in all planes are usually acquired using 3- or 5-mm thin contiguous sections. For three-dimensional (3D) reconstruction, 1.5- or 2-mm contiguous sections are required, although 5-mm sections with a 3-mm overlap can also be used.

MRI, with its direct multiplanar capabilities and excellent soft-tissue contrast resolution, has proved to be superior to CT for the evaluation

FIGURE 10.16 MRI of the anterior talofibular ligament. Axial spin-echo MR image (SE; TR 2000/TE 20 msec) through the lateral malleolus and talus demonstrates normal anterior talofibular ligament. (From Beltran J, 1990, with permission.) ▶

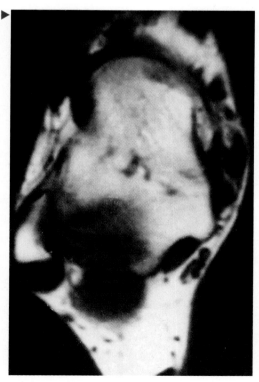

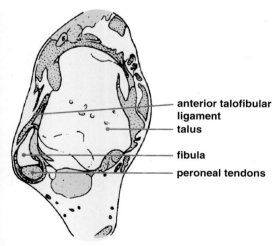

anterior talofibular ligament

talus

fibula

peroneal tendons

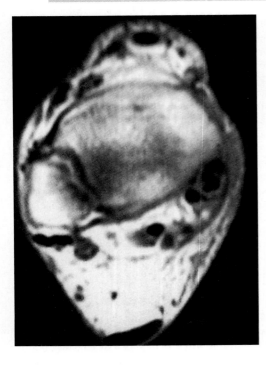

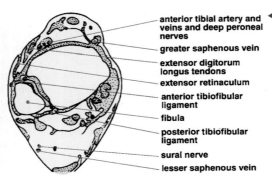

anterior tibial artery and
veins and deep peroneal
nerves

greater saphenous vein

extensor digitorum
longus tendons

extensor retinaculum

anterior tibiofibular
ligament

fibula

posterior tibiofibular
ligament

sural nerve

lesser saphenous vein

◄ FIGURE 10.17   MRI of the anterior and posterior tibiofibular ligaments. Axial spin-echo
MR image (SE; TR 2000/TE 20 msec) shows
normal anterior and posterior tibiofibular ligaments. (From Beltran J, 1990, with permission.)

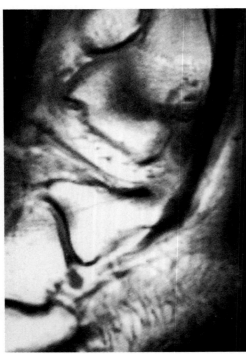

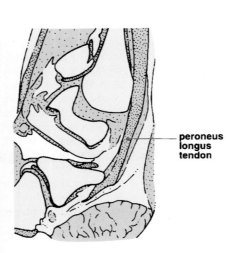

peroneus
longus
tendon

◄ FIGURE 10.18   MRI of the peroneus longus tendon.
Sagittal spin-echo MR image (SE; TR 800/TE 20 msec)
through lateral malleolus shows normal appearance of
peroneus longus as it curves around the lateral malleolus. (From Beltran J, 1990, with permission.)

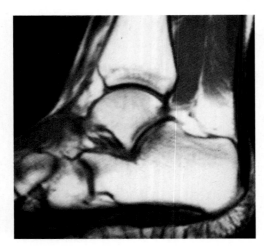

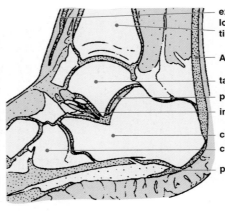

extensor hallucis
longus tendon

tibia

Achilles tendon

talus

posterior subtalar joint

interosseous ligament

calcaneus

cuboid

plantaris fascia

◄ FIGURE 10.19   MRI of the Achilles tendon. Midline sagittal spin-
echo MR image (SE; TR 800/TE 20
msec) demonstrates normal Achilles tendon. Note the uniformly low
signal intensity of the tendon contrasting with the high signal intensity of the anterior fat pad. (From
Beltran J, 1990, with permission.)

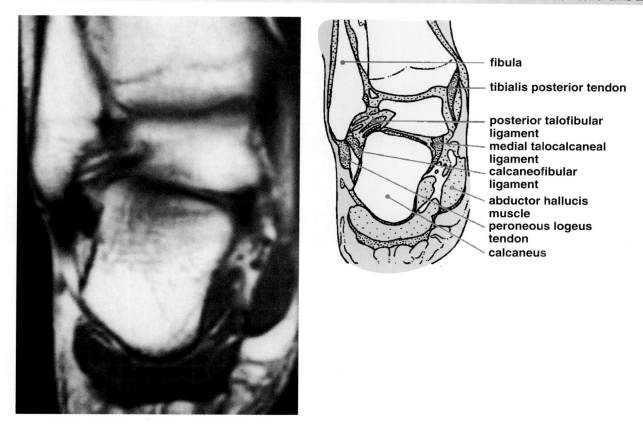

— fibula

— tibialis posterior tendon

— posterior talofibular ligament

— medial talocalcaneal ligament

— calcaneofibular ligament

— abductor hallucis muscle

— peroneous logeus tendon

— calcaneus

▲
FIGURE 10.20   **MRI of the posterior talofibular and calcaneofibular ligaments.** Coronal spin-echo T1-weighted MR image of the ankle shows normal posterior talofibular and calcaneofibular ligaments. (From Beltran J, 1990, with permission.)

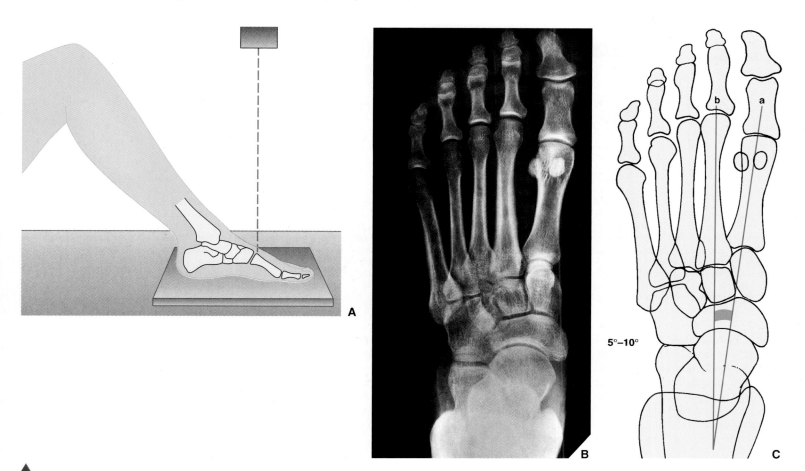

A

B

C

5°–10°

▲
FIGURE 10.21   **Anteroposterior view. (A)** For the anteroposterior (dorsoplantar) view of the foot, the patient is supine, with the knee flexed and the sole placed firmly on the film cassette. The central beam is directed vertically to the base of the first metatarsal bone. **(B)** On the radiograph obtained in this projection, injury to the metatarsal bones and phalanges can be adequately assessed. Note that 75% of the talar head articulates with the navicular bone. (For identification of the bones of the foot, see Fig. 10.2.) **(C)** The first intermetatarsal angle is formed by the intersection of the lines bisecting the shafts of the first (a) and second (b) metatarsals.

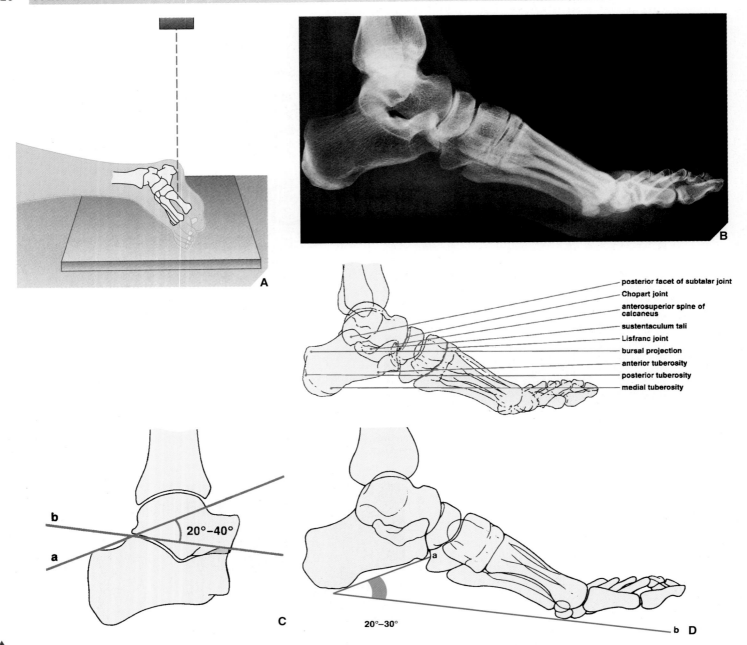

▲
FIGURE 10.22   **Lateral view. (A)** For the lateral view of the foot, the patient lies on his or her side with the knee slightly flexed and the lateral aspect of the foot against the film cassette. The central beam is directed vertically to the midtarsus. **(B)** The lateral radiograph demonstrates the bursal projection, the most prominent feature on the posterior aspect of the calcaneus; the posterior tuberosity where the Achilles tendon inserts; the medial tuberosity on the plantar surface where the plantar fascia inserts; the anterior tuberosity; the anterosuperior spine of the calcaneus; the posterior facet of the subtalar joint; the sustentaculum tali; and the talonavicular and calcaneocuboid articulations. The Chopart and Lisfranc joints are also well visualized. **(C)** The lateral view also allows evaluation of the angular relationship between the talus and the calcaneus—Boehler angle. This feature is determined by the intersection of a line (*a*) drawn from the posterosuperior margin of the calcaneal tuberosity (bursal projection) through the tip of the posterior facet of the subtalar joint, and a second line (*b*) drawn from the tip of the posterior facet through the superior margin of the anterior process of the calcaneus. Normally, this angle ranges between 20 and 40 degrees. **(D)** Calcaneal pitch is described by the intersection of a line drawn tangentially to the inferior surface of the calcaneus and one drawn along the plantar surface of the foot.

is an important factor in the evaluation of forefoot deformities, because it represents a way to quantify the amount of metatarsus primus varus associated with hallux valgus. On the *lateral* projection (Fig. 10.22A,B), *Boehler angle*, an important anatomic relation of the talus and the calcaneus, can be appreciated (Fig. 10.22C). In fractures of the calcaneus, this angle, which normally ranges from 20 to 40 degrees, is decreased because of compression of the superior aspect of the bone (see Fig. 10.73B). This measurement also aids in the evaluation of depression of the posterior facet of the subtalar joint. On the lateral view, calcaneal pitch can also be evaluated. This measurement is an indication of the height of the foot and normally ranges from 20 to 30 degrees (Fig. 10.22D). Higher values indicate a cavus foot deformity. An *oblique* view of the foot is also obtained as part of the standard radiographic examination (Fig. 10.23). Injuries to

the subtalar joint occasionally require special, tangential projections such as the posterior tangential *(Harris-Beath)* view (Fig. 10.24) or oblique tangential *(Broden)* view (Fig. 10.25). A tangential view of the sesamoid bones of the great toe (Fig. 10.26) may also be necessary.

Radiographic evaluation of foot injuries is complicated by the presence of multiple accessory ossicles, which are considered secondary centers of ossification, and the sesamoid bones, which may mimic a fracture (Fig. 10.27A,B); conversely, a chip fracture can be misinterpreted as a mere ossicle (Fig. 10.27C,D). Thus, it is important to recognize these structures on conventional radiographs.

In addition to radiography, ancillary imaging techniques may need to be used in the evaluation of injury to the foot. Radionuclide imaging (bone scan) is a valuable means of detecting stress fractures, common

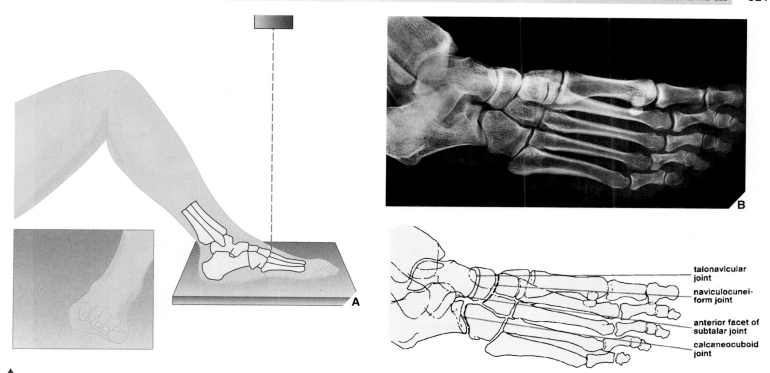

FIGURE 10.23   Oblique view. **(A)** For the oblique view of the foot, the patient is supine on the table with the knee flexed. The lateral border of the foot is elevated about 40 to 45 degrees *(inset)* so that the medial border of the foot is forced against the film cassette. The central beam is directed vertically to the base of the third metatarsal. **(B)** On the oblique radiograph of the foot, the phalanges and metatarsals are well demonstrated, as are the anterior part of the subtalar joint and the talonavicular, naviculocuneiform, and calcaneocuboid joints.

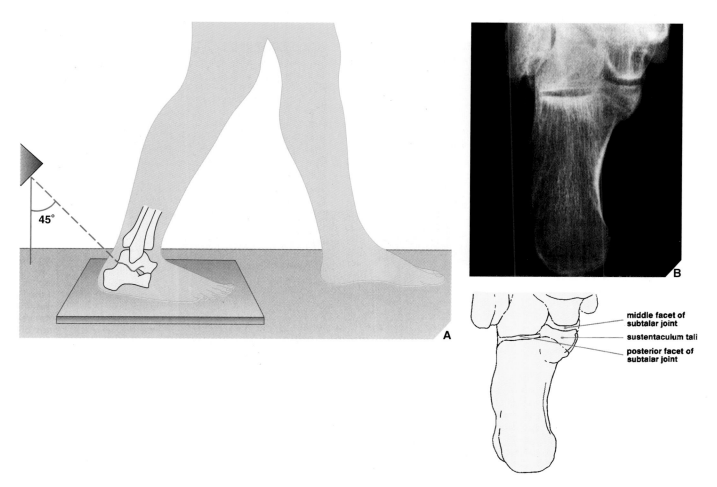

▲
FIGURE 10.24   Harris-Beath view. **(A)** For the posterior tangential (Harris-Beath) view of the foot, the patient is erect, with the sole of the foot flat on the film cassette. The central beam is usually angled 45 degrees toward the midline of the heel, but 35 or 55 degrees of angulation may also be used. **(B)** On the film in this projection, the middle facet of the subtalar joint is seen, oriented horizontally; the sustentaculum tali projects medially. The posterior facet projects laterally and is parallel to the middle facet. The body of the calcaneus is well demonstrated.

TABLE 10.1 Checklist for Evaluation of MRI of the Foot and Ankle

Osseous Structures
Distal tibia (c, s)
Distal fibula (c, s)
Talus (c, s, a)
Calcaneus (c, s, a)
Cuboid (s, a)
Navicular (s, a)
Cuneiform—medial, middle, lateral (c, a)
Sesamoid bones (c, a)
Os naviculare (external tibial ossicle) (a)
Peroneal ossicle (c, s)

Joints and Articular Cartilage
Tibiotalar (c, s)
Chopart (s)
Lisfranc (s)
Subtalar (c, s)

Muscles and Their Tendons
Achilles (s, a)
Tibialis anterior (a)
Tibialis posterior (a)
Peroneus—longus, brevis, tertius (a)
Flexor hallucis longus (s, a)
Flexor hallucis brevis (s, a)
Extensor hallucis longus (s, a)
Extensor hallucis brevis (s, a)
Flexor digitorum—longus, brevis (s, a)
Extensor digitorum—longus, brevis (s, a)
Plantaris (a)
Abductor hallucis (a)
Adductor hallucis (a)

Ligaments
Deltoid
Tibiocalcaneal band (c)
Tibiotalar band—anterior, posterior (c, a)
Tibionavicular band (s, a)
Spring (tibio-spring) (c, a)
Lateral collateral
Posterior talofibular (a)
Anterior talofibular (a)
Calcaneofibular (c)
Distal tibiofibular syndesmosis
Interosseous membrane (c, a)
Posterior tibiofibular (c, a)
Anterior tibiofibular (c, a)
Inferior transverse (a)
Lisfranc (a)

Bursae
Retrocalcaneal (s)
Retro-Achilles (s, a)

Other Structures
Fascia plantaris (s)
Plantar plate (s)
Sinus tarsi (c, s, a)
Tarsal tunnel (c, s, a)
Anterolateral gutter (a)
Kager fat pad (s)
Tibial artery, vein, nerve (a)
Greater saphenous vein (a)

The best imaging planes for visualization of listed structures are given in parenthesis; c, coronal (coronal of ankle, short-axis axial of foot); s, sagittal; a, axial (axial of ankle, long-axis axial of foot).

foot injuries that are not always obvious on the standard radiographic examination. CT is especially effective in assessing complex fractures, particularly of the calcaneus. Tenographic examination may also be required to evaluate injury to the tendons of the foot (see previous text and Figs. 10.13 and 10.69B). MRI is now frequently used to evaluate trauma to the foot. During evaluation of MRI of the ankle and foot, it is helpful to use checklist as provided in Table 10.1.

For a tabular summary of the preceding discussion, see Tables 10.2 and 10.3 and Figure 10.28.

Injury to the Ankle

All ankle injuries can be broadly classified, according to the mechanism of injury, as resulting from inversion (Fig. 10.29) or eversion (Fig. 10.30) stress forces. Inversion injuries are much more common, as O'Donoghue has pointed out, accounting for 85% of all traumatic conditions involving the ankle. These groupings apply to both fractures and injuries to the ligament complexes of the ankle. However, it is in the latter type of injuries that they are particularly helpful in determining and evaluating the specific type of ligament injury, especially in the presence of certain fractures about the ankle.

Fractures About the Ankle Joint

In addition to being classified by mechanism of injury, fractures about the ankle joint can also be classified by the anatomic structure involved (Fig. 10.31) and designated as:

1. *Unimalleolar*, when the fracture involves the medial (tibial) or lateral (fibular) malleolus (Fig. 10.32)
2. *Bimalleolar*, when both malleoli are fractured (Fig. 10.33)

3. *Trimalleolar*, when fractures involve the medial and lateral malleoli as well as the posterior lip (or tubercle) of the distal tibia (the third malleolus) (Fig. 10.34)
4. *Complex fractures*, known also as pilon fractures, when comminuted fractures of the distal tibia and fibula occur (Fig. 10.35).

These fractures, when viewed from the standpoint of pathomechanics, may be either inversion or eversion injuries or a combination of both. The various types of eversion fractures are best known by their eponyms, including the Pott, Maisonneuve, Dupuytren, and Tillaux fractures (see later).

All of the following ankle fractures involving the distal tibia and fibula can be diagnosed on the standard radiographic projections. However, CT may be useful in delineating the extent of the fracture line, and this modality is particularly effective in evaluating lateral displacement in the juvenile Tillaux fracture. To evaluate associated ligament injuries, MRI is the technique of choice.

Fractures of the Distal Tibia. *Pilon (Pylon) Fracture.* Fracture of the distal tibia is called a pilon (pylon) fracture when the comminuted fracture lines extend into the tibiotalar joint (Fig. 10.36; see also Fig. 10.35). These injuries comprise approximately 5% of all lower leg fractures. Most pilon fractures occur during fall from a height, motor vehicle accidents, snow or water skiing accidents, or are caused by a forward fall on a level surface with the foot entrapped. Although the pathomechanics of this injury may be complex, the predominant force is vertical compression. Not infrequently there is associated fracture of the distal fibula, talus, and subluxation in the ankle joint (Fig. 10.37), in addition to severe damage to the soft-tissue sleeve of the distal leg. Pilon fractures are a distinct clinical and radiologic entity and should not be

TABLE 10.2 Standard and Special Radiographic Projections for Evaluating Injury to the Ankle and Foot

Projection	Demonstration	Projection	Demonstration

Anteroposterior (ankle)	Fractures of
	  Distal tibia
	  Distal fibula
	  Medial malleolus
	  Lateral malleolus
	Pilon fractures (extension into
	  tibiotalar joint)
		Lateral (continued)
		(ankle and foot)
			Talus (particularly neck)
			Calcaneus (particularly in coronal plane)
			Posterior facet of subtalar joint
			Sustentaculum tali
			Accessory ossicles
			Cuboid bone

(foot)	Fractures of
	  Distal portion of talus
	  Navicular, cuboid, and cuneiform
	    bones
	  Metatarsals and phalanges (including stress fractures and accessory ossicles)
	Dislocations in
	  Subtalar joint
	    Peritalar (anterior and posterior types)
	    Total talar
	  Tarsometatarsal (Lisfranc) joint
			Dislocations in
			  Subtalar joint
			    Peritalar (anterior and posterior types)
			  Tarsometatarsal (Lisfranc) joint

		Stress (anterior-draw)	Tear of anterior talofibular ligament Ankle instability

With 10 degrees of internal ankle rotation (mortise view)	Same structures and abnormalities as anteroposterior but better demonstration of tibial plafond	*Oblique*
		  Internal
		  External
			Fractures of
			  Medial malleolus
			  Talus
			  Tuberosity of calcaneus
			  Metatarsals
			  Phalanges

Stress (inversion, eversion)	Tear of lateral collateral ligament
	Ankle instability
		Posterior Tangential (Harris-Beath)	Fractures involving
			  Middle and posterior facets of subtalar joint
			  Calcaneus (in axial plane)

Lateral (ankle and foot)	Boehler angle
	Fractures of
	  Distal tibia
	    Anterior aspect
	    Posterior lip (third malleolus)
	  Tibiotalar joint
		Oblique Tangential (Broden)	Fractures involving
			  Posterior facet of subtalar joint
			  Calcaneus
			  Sustentaculum tali

		Axial (sesamoid view)	Fractures of sesamoid bones

TABLE 10.3 Ancillary Imaging Techniques for Evaluating Injury to the Ankle and Foot

Technique	Demonstration	Technique	Demonstration
Radionuclide Imaging (scintigraphy, bone scan)	Stress fractures Healing process	*Computed Tomography*	Complex fractures (particularly of os calcis) Intraarticular extension of fracture line Injuries to tendons (particularly peroneal, tibialis, and Achilles) and ligaments
Arthrography (single-contrast) (double-contrast, usually combined with tomography or CT)	Tears of ligament structures of ankle joint Osteochondral fractures Osteochondritis dissecans of talus Osteochondral bodies in joint		

Tenography	Tears of
	  Achilles tendon
	  Posterior tibialis tendon
	  Peroneal tendons
	  Digitorum longus tendon
		Magnetic Resonance Imaging	Same as arthrography, tenography, and CT

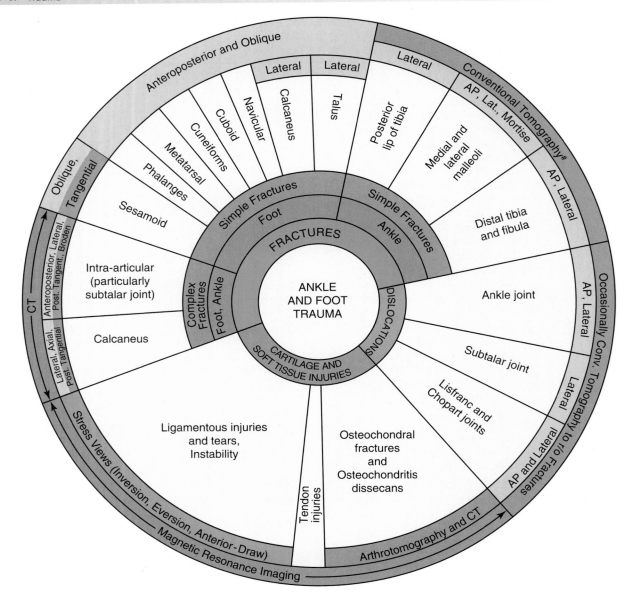

▲
FIGURE 10.28 **Spectrum of radiologic imaging techniques used to evaluate trauma to the ankle and foot.***

The radiographic projections or radiologic techniques indicated throughout the diagram are only those that are the most effective in demonstrating the respective traumatic conditions.

#Replaced almost completely by CT.

confused with trimalleolar fractures. The following features distinguish pilon fractures from the trimalleolar fractures: the presence of profound comminution of the distal tibia; intraarticular extension of tibial fracture through the dome of the plafond; usual association of fracture of the talus; and usual preservation of tibiofibular syndesmosis. This fracture's significance comprises the intraarticular extension of the fracture line and its consequent potential to cause late complications of posttraumatic arthritis, as well as nonunion and malunion.

Müller's widely accepted classification of pilon fractures divides these injuries into three groups, depending on the displacement of the fragments and the incongruity of the joint (Fig. 10.38).

Tillaux Fracture. In 1872, Tillaux described an ankle fracture resulting from abduction and external-rotation injury and consisting of avulsion of the lateral margin of the distal tibia. The fracture line is vertical and extends from the distal articular surface of the tibia upward to the lateral cortex (Figs. 10.39 and 10.40). In children, a similar type

of fracture, referred to as *juvenile Tillaux fracture*, is actually a Salter-Harris type III injury to the distal tibial growth plate (Fig. 10.41; see also Fig. 4.30). This injury probably occurs because the growth plate fuses from medial to lateral, making the medial side stronger than the lateral.

The radiologic evaluation of a Tillaux fracture is critical for establishing whether surgery will be necessary. If the fracture fragment is laterally displaced more than 2 mm or if there is an irregularity of the articular surface of the distal tibia (a step-off), then surgical rather than conservative treatment is indicated. CT is the best method for obtaining this information (Figs. 10.42 and 10.43).

If, instead of avulsion of the lateral margin of the tibia, the medial portion of the fibula becomes detached and the anterior tibiofibular ligament remains intact, then the fracture is called a *Wagstaffe-LeFort fracture* (Fig. 10.44).

Triplanar (Marmor-Lynn) Fracture. Fractures involving the lateral aspect of the distal tibial epiphysis may be complicated by extension of

SPECTRUM OF INVERSION INJURIES ABOUT THE ANKLE JOINT

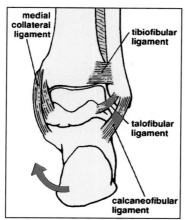
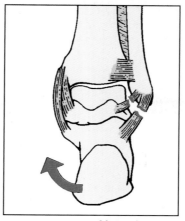
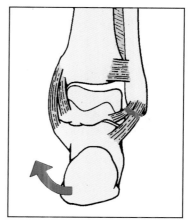

| sprain of lateral collateral ligament | rupture of lateral collateral ligament | avulsion of lateral collateral ligament |

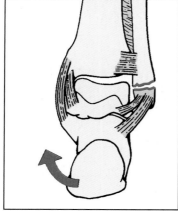
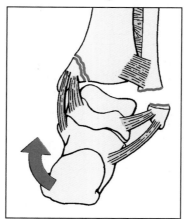
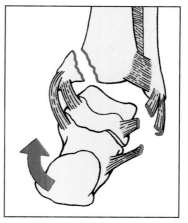

| transverse fracture of lateral malleolus | fractures of medial and lateral malleoli | fracture of medial malleolus with rupture of lateral collateral ligament |

FIGURE 10.29 Inversion injuries. Depending on its severity, an inversion force delivered to the lateral structures of the ankle joint may manifest in a broad spectrum of injuries of the lateral collateral ligament complex, as well as the lateral and medial malleoli. Note, however, that inversion-stress forces do not affect the posterior tibiofibular or medial collateral ligaments. (Modified from Edeiken J, 1978, with permission.)

SPECTRUM OF EVERSION INJURIES ABOUT THE ANKLE JOINT

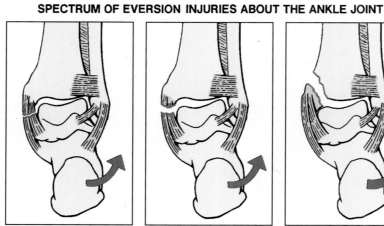
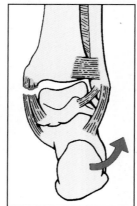
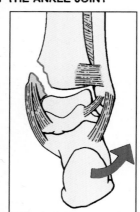

| sprain of deltoid ligament | rupture of deltoid ligament | avulsion of deltoid ligament | fracture of medial malleolus | fracture of lateral malleolus with rupture of deltoid ligament |

FIGURE 10.30 Eversion injuries. Depending on its severity, an eversion force delivered to the medial structures of the ankle joint may manifest in a broad spectrum of injuries of the medial collateral (deltoid) ligament complex, as well as the medial and lateral malleoli. Note, however, that eversion-stress forces do not affect the posterior tibiofibular or lateral collateral ligaments. (Modified from Edeiken J, 1978, with permission.)

CLASSIFICATION OF ANKLE FRACTURES BY ANATOMIC STRUCTURE

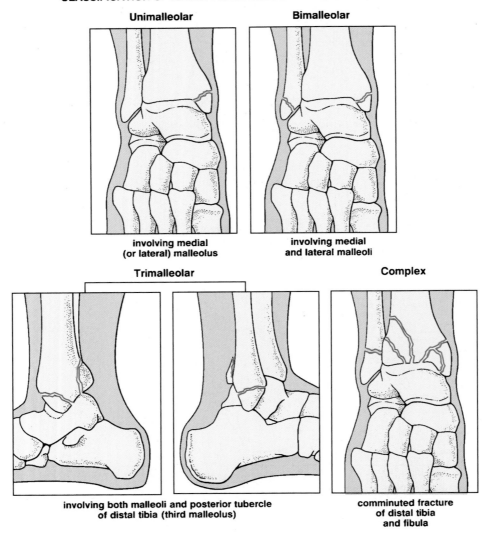

Unimalleolar

involving medial
(or lateral) malleolus

Bimalleolar

involving medial
and lateral malleoli

Trimalleolar

involving both malleoli and posterior tubercle
of distal tibia (third malleolus)

Complex

comminuted fracture
of distal tibia
and fibula

▲
FIGURE 10.31   Classification of ankle fractures. Ankle fractures can be classified according to the anatomic structure as unimalleolar, bimalleolar, trimalleolar, or complex.

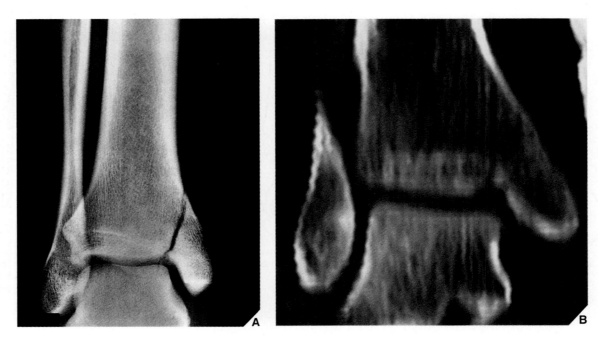

▲
FIGURE 10.32   Unimalleolar fracture. Anteroposterior radiograph of the ankle (**A**) and coronal CT reformatted image (**B**) demonstrate the typical appearance of a unimalleolar fracture involving the medial malleolus.

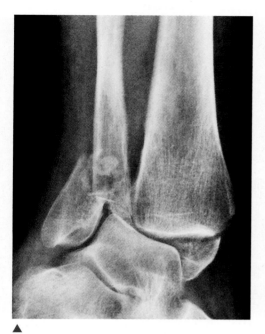

▲ FIGURE 10.33 **Bimalleolar fracture.** Oblique radiograph of the ankle shows a bimalleolar fracture involving the tibial and fibular malleoli.

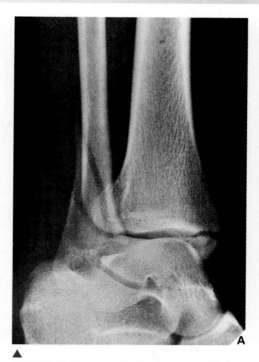

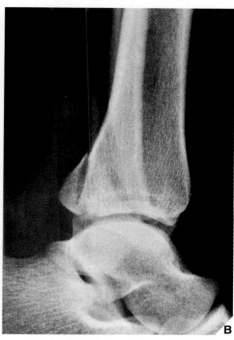

▲ FIGURE 10.34 **Trimalleolar fracture.** Oblique (**A**) and lateral (**B**) radiographs of the ankle show a trimalleolar fracture affecting both malleoli and the posterior lip of the distal tibia. The latter feature is better seen on the lateral view.

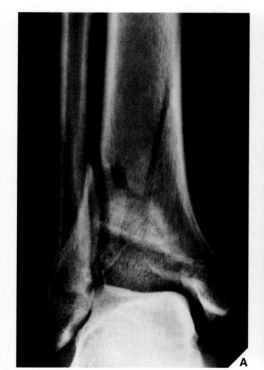

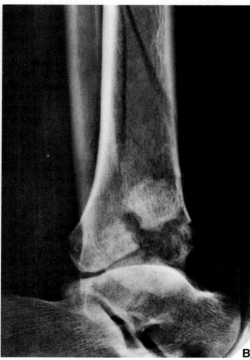

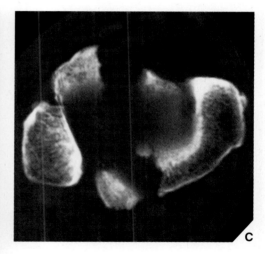

▲ FIGURE 10.35 **Pilon fracture.** Anteroposterior (**A**) and lateral (**B**) radiographs of the ankle demonstrate a complex, comminuted fracture of the distal tibia and fibula in a 30-year-old man who fell from a third-floor window. (**C**) Axial CT section through the tibial plafond shows typical appearance of pilon fracture.

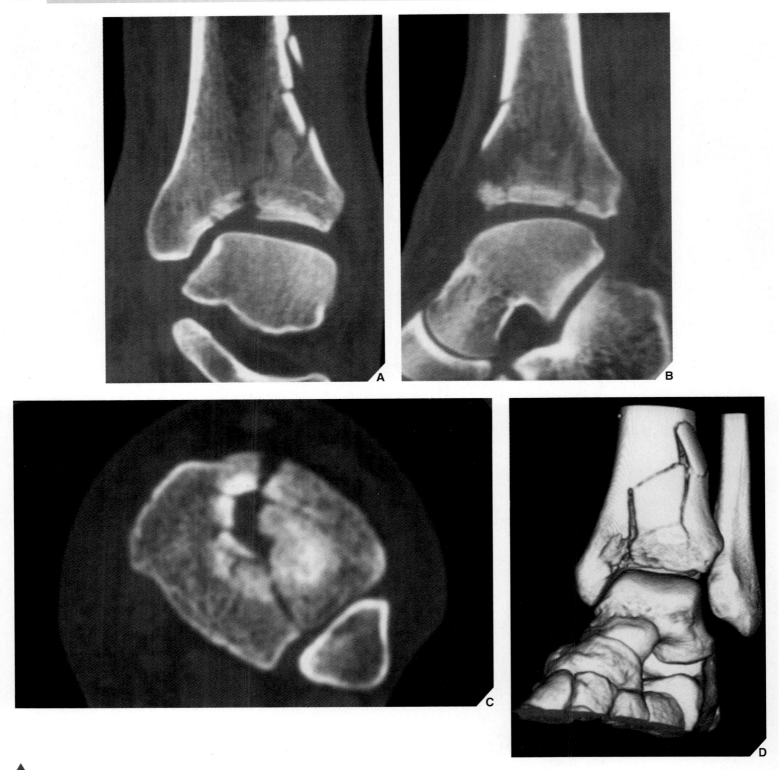

FIGURE 10.36 CT of pilon fracture. Coronal (**A**), sagittal (**B**), axial (**C**), and 3D (**D**) reformatted CT images show characteristic features of pilon fracture in a 30-year-old man who was injured in a motorcycle accident.

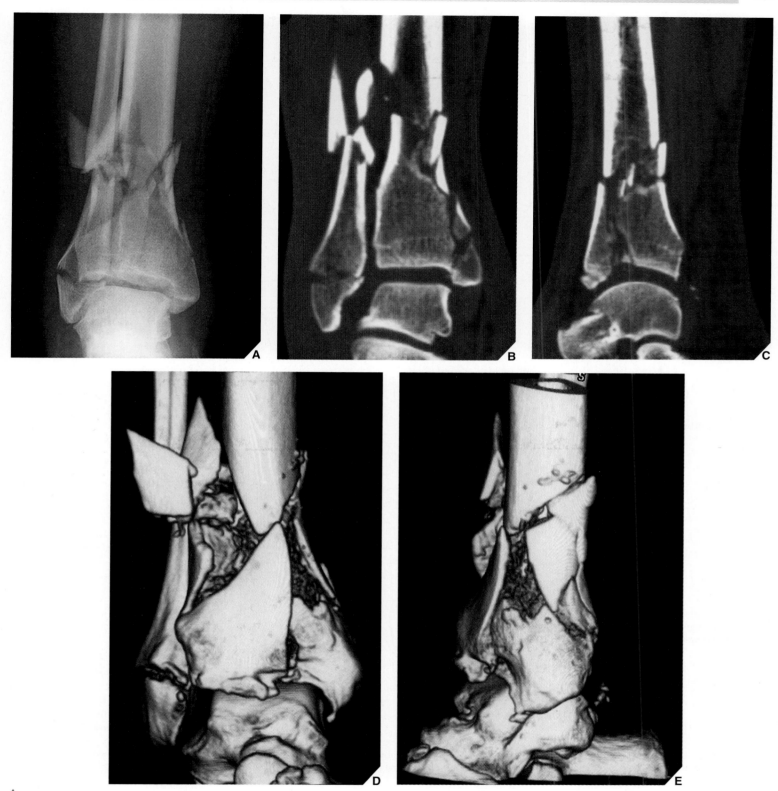

FIGURE 10.37   **Pilon fracture.** A 36-year-old man was injured in a motor vehicle accident and sustained a complex fracture of the distal tibia and fibula. **(A)** Conventional radiograph shows markedly comminuted intraarticular fracture of the distal tibia and segmental fracture of the distal fibula. Coronal **(B)** and sagittal **(C)** CT reformatted images demonstrate the number and direction of displaced fragments. **(D, E)** 3D CT images viewed from anterior and medial directions display spatial orientation of various fractured fragments, thus providing an orthopedic surgeon with a "road map" for successful open reduction and internal fixation of this complex fracture.

MULLER CLASSIFICATION OF PILON FRACTURES

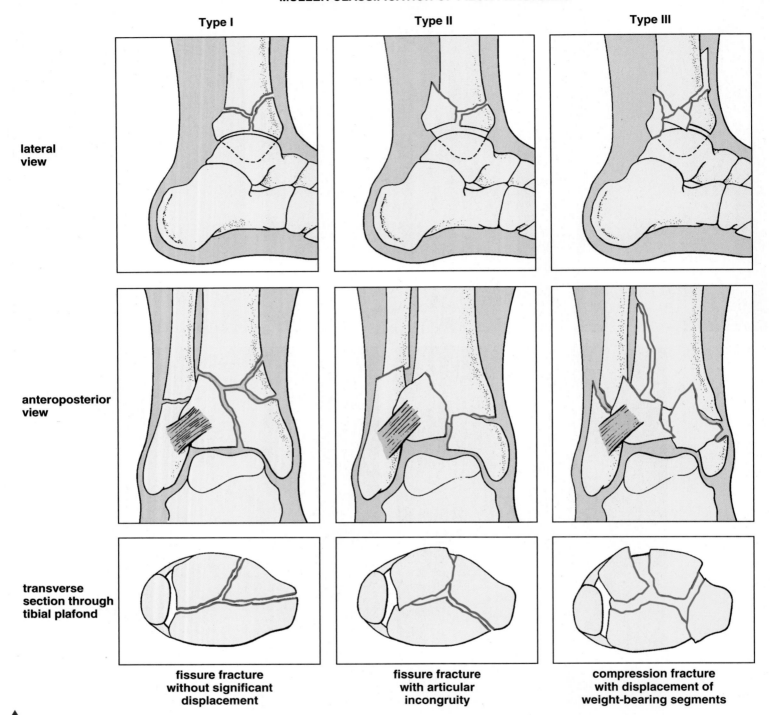

	Type I	Type II	Type III

lateral view

anteroposterior view

transverse section through tibial plafond

fissure fracture without significant displacement

fissure fracture with articular incongruity

compression fracture with displacement of weight-bearing segments

▲

FIGURE 10.38 Classification of pilon fractures. The Müller classification of intraarticular fractures of the distal tibia (pilon fractures) is based on the amount of displacement of the fragments and the consequent degree of incongruity of the joint. (Modified from Müller ME et al., 1979, with permission.)

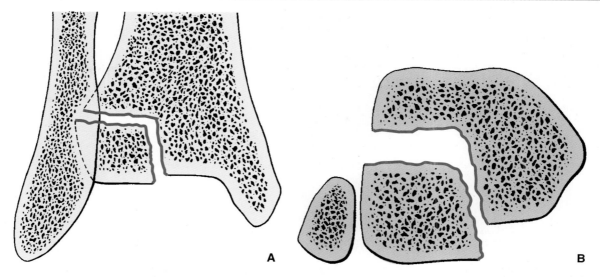

▲ FIGURE 10.39   **Tillaux fracture.** In the classic Tillaux fracture, shown here schematically in coronal (**A**) and transverse (**B**) sections through the distal tibia, the fracture line extends from the distal articular surface of the tibia upward to the lateral cortex.

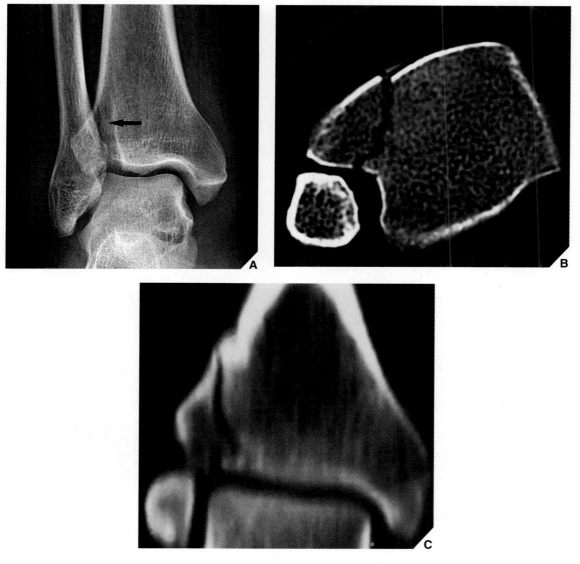

▲ FIGURE 10.40   **CT of Tillaux fracture.** A 39-year-old man sustained a nondisplaced Tillaux fracture, demonstrated on (**A**) anteroposterior radiograph of the ankle (*arrow*), (**B**) axial CT, and (**C**) coronal reformatted CT image.

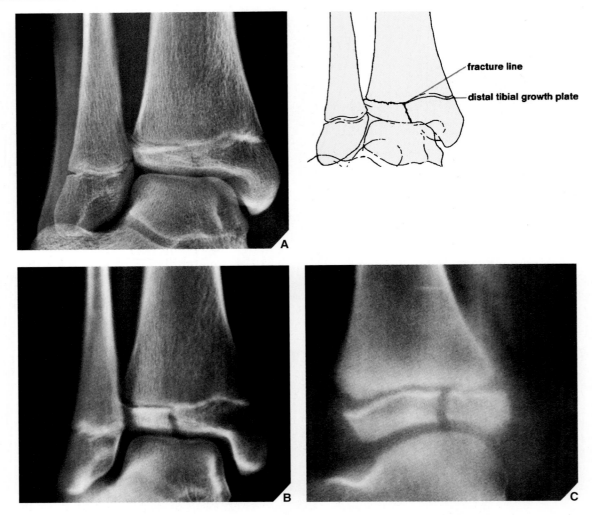

fracture line

distal tibial growth plate

▲
FIGURE 10.41   Juvenile Tillaux fracture. A 13-year-old girl injured her right ankle during a basketball game. Oblique view of the ankle (**A**) and tomographic sections in the oblique (**B**) and lateral (**C**) projections demonstrate a typical Salter-Harris type III injury to the growth plate, also called juvenile Tillaux fracture.

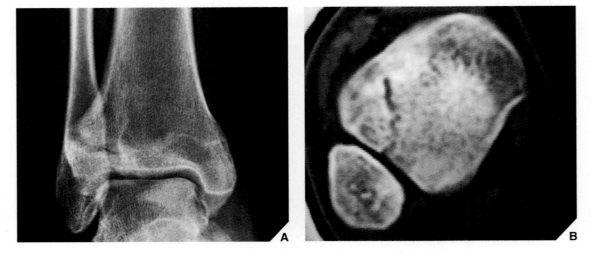

▲
FIGURE 10.42   CT of Tillaux fracture. A 24-year-old woman twisted her ankle while ice-skating. Anteroposterior radiograph (**A**) and CT section (**B**) show a marginal fracture of the lateral aspect of the tibia, a characteristic Tillaux fracture. The minimal amount of displacement seen here would mandate only conservative treatment.

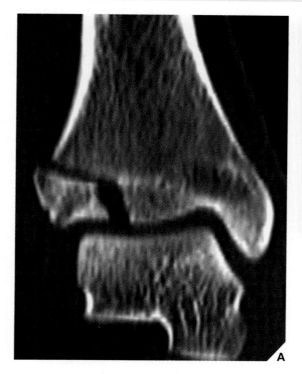
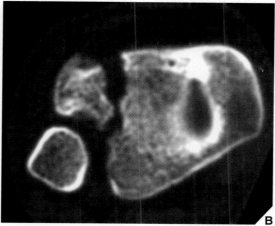

FIGURE 10.43 CT of Tillaux fracture. A 28-year-old woman injured right ankle during ski competition. (**A**) Coronal reformatted and (**B**) axial CT images show a displaced Tillaux fracture that was later treated with open reduction and internal fixation.

the fracture line into two other planes, hence the term *triplanar fracture*. The mechanism of this type of injury is usually plantar flexion and external rotation. The three planes involved are the *sagittal plane*, in which there is a vertical fracture through the epiphysis; the *axial plane*, in which a horizontally oriented fracture extends through the lateral aspect of the growth plate; and the *coronal plane*, in which there is an oblique fracture through the metaphysis into the diaphysis, extending superiorly from the anterior aspect of the growth plate to the posterior cortex of the tibia (Fig. 10.45).

The epiphyseal component of this fracture is best seen on the anteroposterior view, the axial component on both the anteroposterior and lateral views, and the diaphyseal extension on the lateral view. The typical triplanar fracture thus consists of a combination of the juvenile Tillaux fracture and a Salter-Harris type II fracture (Figs. 10.46 and 10.47; see also Figs. 10.40 and 4.30) and should not be mistaken for a Salter-Harris type IV fracture (Fig. 10.48). Occasionally, metadiaphyseal component of the triplanar fracture may cross the growth plate and extend into the epiphysis, thus making the distinction from Salter-Harris

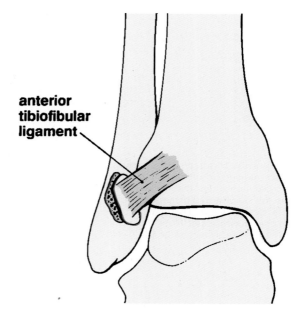

FIGURE 10.44 **Wagstaffe-LeFort fracture.** In the Wagstaffe-LeFort fracture, seen here schematically on the anteroposterior view, the medial portion of the fibula is avulsed at the insertion of the anterior tibiofibular ligament. The ligament, however, remains intact.

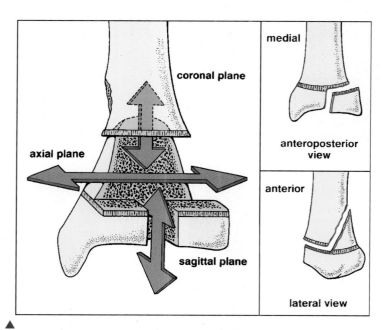

FIGURE 10.45 **Triplanar fracture.** The Marmor-Lynn (or triplanar) fracture comprises a vertical fracture of the epiphysis in the sagittal plane, a horizontally oriented fracture in the axial plane through the lateral aspect of the growth plate, and an oblique fracture through the metaphysis into the diaphysis in the coronal plane, extending superiorly from the anterior aspect of the growth plate to the posterior cortex of the tibia.

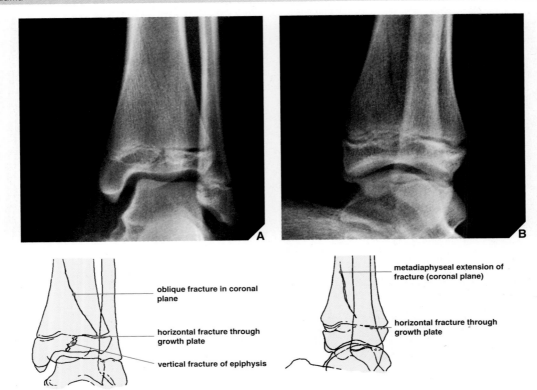

oblique fracture in coronal plane

horizontal fracture through growth plate

vertical fracture of epiphysis

metadiaphyseal extension of fracture (coronal plane)

horizontal fracture through growth plate

▲
FIGURE 10.46   Triplanar fracture. A 12-year-old girl fell on ice and sustained a typical triplanar fracture. **(A)** Anteroposterior radiograph of the left ankle shows a vertical fracture of the epiphysis and horizontal extension through the lateral aspect of the growth plate. The metaphyseal and diaphyseal components of the fracture are barely seen. **(B)** Lateral radiograph clearly demonstrates the posteriorly directed fracture line in the coronal plane, the third component of a triplanar fracture.

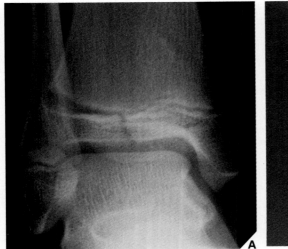

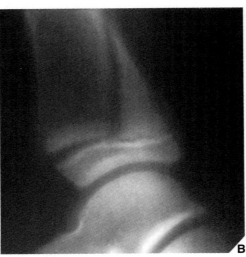

◄ **FIGURE 10.47   Triplanar fracture.** A 13-year-old boy presented with a triplanar fracture. **(A)** Anteroposterior radiograph shows only horizontal and vertical components. **(B)** A trispiral lateral tomogram shows horizontal and oblique components.

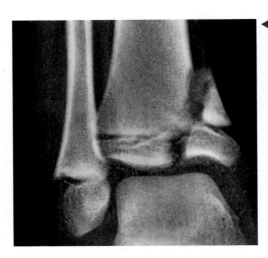

◄ **FIGURE 10.48   Salter-Harris type IV fracture.** Anteroposterior radiograph of the ankle in an 8-year-old boy demonstrates that the fracture line traverses the epiphysis and metaphysis of the distal tibia, but there is no horizontal extension through the growth plate. Note the associated Salter-Harris type I fracture of the distal fibula (see also Fig. 4.30).

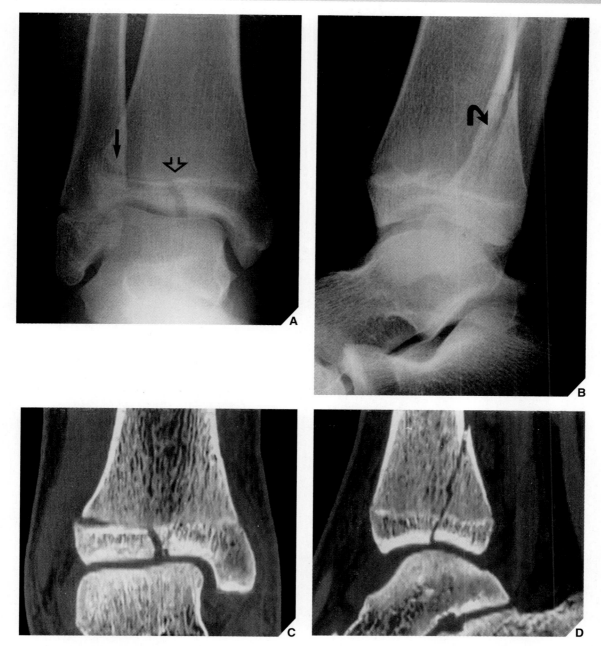

FIGURE 10.49 CT of triplanar fracture. (A) An anteroposterior radiograph shows horizontal (*arrow*) and vertical (*open arrow*) components of this injury. **(B)** Lateral radiograph shows the oblique component (*curved arrow*), but the distal extent of the fracture line is not well demonstrated. The coronal **(C)** and sagittal **(D)** CT reformatted images confirm the diagnosis of triplanar fracture. Note that the obliquely oriented fracture line extends into the epiphysis.

type IV fracture more difficult (Fig. 10.49). CT is an effective technique to demonstrate the details of this injury (Fig. 10.50).

Fractures of the Fibula. *Pott Fracture.* After sustaining a fracture of his own leg, Sir Percivall Pott described in 1769 what he believed to be the most common type of ankle fracture, a fracture of the distal third of the fibula (Fig. 10.51). It is now recognized that this type of fracture usually occurs as a result of the disruption of the tibiofibular syndesmosis. In fact, many authorities believe that the type of fracture Pott described does not exist as a primary fracture.

Dupuytren Fracture. Dupuytren fracture is the name given to a fracture of the fibula occurring 2 to 7 cm above the distal tibiofibular syndesmosis and including disruption of the medial collateral ligament (Fig. 10.52). The associated tear of the syndesmosis leads to ankle instability.

Maisonneuve Fracture. Like the Dupuytren fracture, the Maisonneuve fracture is an eversion-type injury of the fibula. The fracture,

however, occurs in the proximal half of the bone, commonly at the junction of the proximal and middle thirds of the shaft (Fig. 10.53). The tibiofibular syndesmosis is disrupted, and either tear of the tibiofibular ligament or fracture of the medial malleolus is also present (Fig. 10.54). The more proximal the location of the fibular fracture, the more is the damage to the interosseous membrane between the tibia and the fibula, which is always disrupted up to the point of the fibular fracture.

Injury to the Soft Tissues About the Ankle Joint and Foot

As mentioned, all ankle injuries can be grossly classified as resulting from inversion-stress or eversion-stress forces (see Figs. 10.29 and 10.30). However, the forces delivered to the ankle are rarely pure inversion or pure eversion. A combination of forces is usually at work to produce ligament and tendon injuries that may occur secondary to fractures or as primary injuries. Several classifications have been developed to reflect the complexity of these forces. Lauge-Hansen classified ankle injuries based on the mechanism of injury by combining the position of

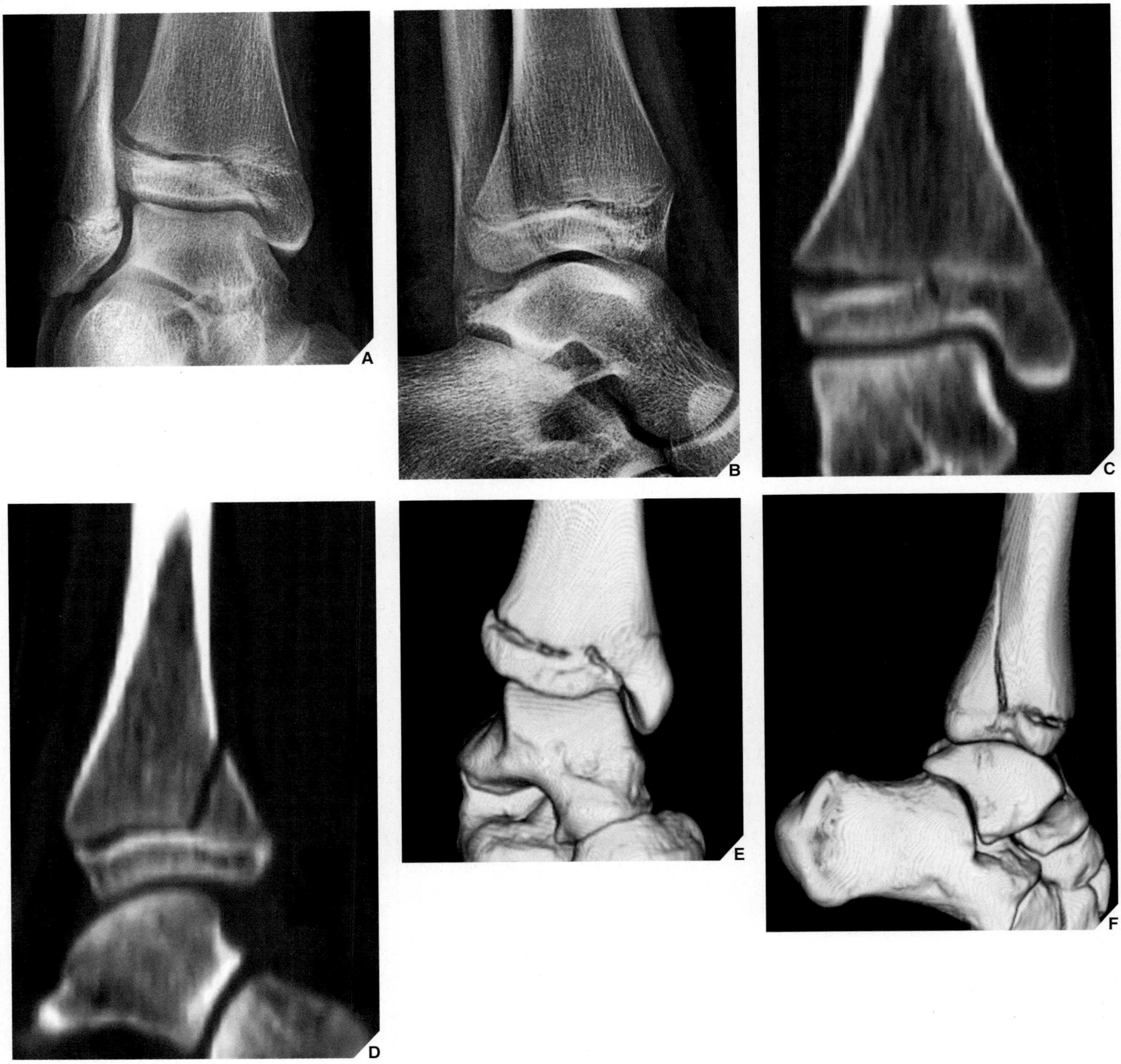

FIGURE 10.50 **CT and 3D CT of triplanar fracture. (A)** Anteroposterior and **(B)** lateral radiographs of the right ankle show all three components of the triplanar fracture that are more vividly demonstrated on **(C)** coronal and **(D)** sagittal reformatted CT images, and on **(E)** and **(F)** 3D CT reconstruction.

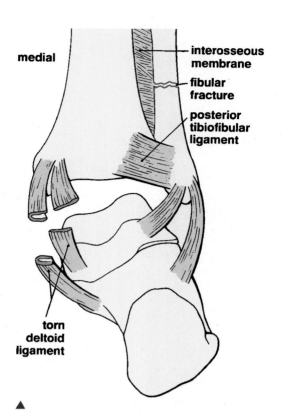

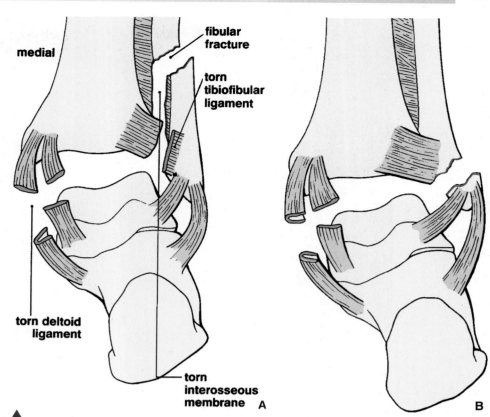

▲ **FIGURE 10.51   Pott fracture.** In the Pott fracture, the fibula is fractured above the intact distal tibiofibular syndesmosis, the deltoid ligament is ruptured, and the talus is subluxed laterally.

▲ **FIGURE 10.52   Dupuytren fracture. (A)** This fracture usually occurs 2 to 7 cm above the distal tibiofibular syndesmosis, with disruption of the medial collateral ligament and, typically, tear of the syndesmosis leading to ankle instability. **(B)** In the low variant, the fracture occurs more distally and the tibiofibular ligament remains intact.

FIGURE 10.53   Maisonneuve fracture. The classic ▶ Maisonneuve fracture commonly occurs at the junction of the middle and distal thirds of the fibula. The tibiofibular syndesmosis is disrupted, and the interosseous membrane is torn up to the level of the fracture. The tibiotalar (medial) joint compartment is widened because of lateral subluxation of the talus.

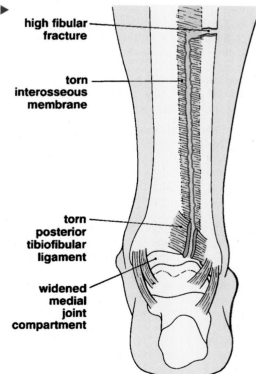

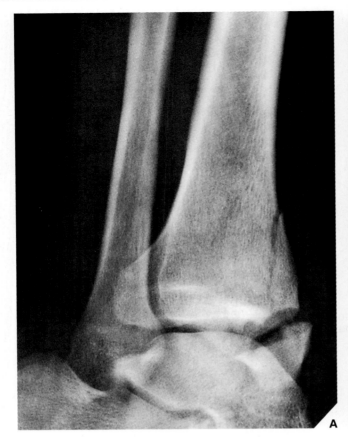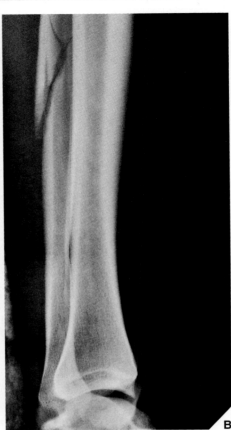

▲
FIGURE 10.54 **Maisonneuve fracture.** A 22-year-old man injured his right ankle in a skiing accident. **(A)** Oblique radiograph of the ankle shows a comminuted fracture of the medial malleolus, with extension into the anterior lip of the tibia. **(B)** On the lateral view, a comminuted fracture of the fibula is apparent. This is a characteristic of a Maisonneuve-type fracture.

the foot (supination or pronation) with the direction of the deforming force vector (external rotation, adduction, or abduction) (Table 10.4). He emphasized the close relationship between bone and ligament injuries, but the complexity of his classification diminishes its value in treatment.

From the practical orthopedic point of view, the Weber classification, based on the level of fibular fracture and therefore on the type of syndesmotic ligament injury, is much more useful (Fig. 10.55):

Stage A   The fibular fracture may be a transverse avulsion fracture at the level of or just distal to the ankle joint. There may be an associated fracture of the medial malleolus. Alternatively, the fibula is intact, but the lateral collateral ligament is disrupted. In either case, the tibiofibular syndesmosis, the interosseous membrane, and the deltoid ligament are intact.

Stage B   There is a spiral fracture of the distal fibula, beginning at the level of the tibiofibular syndesmosis, with partial disruption of mainly the posterior tibiofibular ligament. It may also be associated with an avulsion fracture of the medial malleolus below the level of the ankle joint (Fig. 10.56). Alternatively, the medial malleolus may be intact and the deltoid ligament may be disrupted.

Stage C   Fracture of the fibula occurs at a level higher than the ankle joint, with associated tear of the posterior tibiofibular ligament and resultant lateral talar instability. If the fibular fracture is high (Maisonneuve type), the interosseous membrane is torn to the level of the fracture. There is also an avulsion fracture of the medial malleolus, in which case the deltoid ligament is intact. Alternatively, the medial malleolus is intact, but the deltoid ligament is disrupted (Fig. 10.57).

The likelihood of injury to the distal tibiofibular syndesmosis can be inferred from the nature and level of the fibular fracture: The higher the fibular fracture, the more extensive the damage to the tibiofibular ligaments and, thus, the greater the risk of ankle instability. The greatest value of this classification lies in the fact that it emphasizes the lateral syndesmosis-malleolar complex as an important factor in congruence and stability in the ankle joint.

Tear of the Medial Collateral Ligament. Depending on the severity of the eversion force, injury to the medial collateral ligament ranges from sprain to complete rupture (see Fig. 10.30). Tear may occur either in the body of the ligament or at its attachment to the medial malleolus. Rupture of the medial collateral ligament is typically associated with a tear of the tibiofibular ligament and lateral subluxation of the talus. On clinical examination, soft-tissue swelling is prominent, distal to the tip of the medial malleolus. If the standard radiographic examination of the ankle reveals lateral shift of the talus in the absence of a spiral fracture of the fibula, one must assume that both the tibiofibular and the medial collateral ligaments are torn. Arthrographic examination shows leak of contrast agent beneath the medial malleolus (Fig. 10.58).

Although tears of the ligaments of the ankle can be demonstrated on CT examination, more commonly these injuries are evaluated by MRI. Acute tear of the medial collateral ligament appears as disruption of continuity or absence of the low-intensity ligamentous fibers surrounded by edema or hemorrhage (Fig. 10.59). Chronic or healed ligamentous disruption shows generalized thickening of the ligament.

Tear of the Lateral Collateral Ligament. Inversion-stress forces delivered to the lateral ankle structures may cause a spectrum of injuries to the lateral collateral ligament, ranging from sprain to complete rupture (see Fig. 10.29). The body of the ligament or its attachment to the fibular malleolus may be the site of injury. In the absence of fracture of the fibular malleolus on the standard radiographic examination,

TABLE 10.4 **Lauge-Hansen Classification of Ankle Injuries**

Pronation—Abduction Injuries

Stage I   Rupture of the deltoid ligament or transverse fracture of the medial malleolus

Stage II   Disruption of the distal anterior and posterior tibiofibular ligaments

Stage III   Oblique fracture of the fibula at the level of the joint* (best seen on the anteroposterior projection)

Pronation—Lateral (External) Rotation Injuries

Stage I   Rupture of the deltoid ligament or transverse fracture of the medial malleolus

Stage II   Disruption of the anterior tibiofibular ligament and interosseous membrane

Stage III   Fracture of the fibula usually 6 cm or more above the level of the joint*

Stage IV   Chip fracture of the posterior tibia or rupture of the posterior tibiofibular ligament

Supination—Adduction Injuries

Stage I   Injury to the lateral collateral ligament or transverse fracture of the lateral malleolus below the level of the joint*

Stage II   Steep oblique fracture of the medial malleolus

Supination—Lateral (External) Rotation Injuries

Stage I   Disruption of the anterior tibiofibular ligament

Stage II   Spiral fracture of the distal fibula near the joint* (best seen on the lateral projection)

Stage III   Rupture of the posterior tibiofibular ligament

Stage IV   Transverse fracture of the medial malleolus

*The appearance of the fibular fracture is the key to determining the mechanism of injury.
Modified from Lauge-Hansen N, 1950, with permission.

WEBER CLASSIFICATION OF INJURIES ABOUT THE ANKLE JOINT

Type A

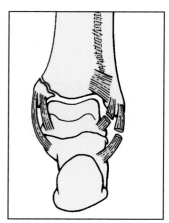

avulsion fibular fracture
at or below joint
level with associated
fracture of
medial malleolus or

intact fibula with
rupture of lateral
collateral ligament

Type B

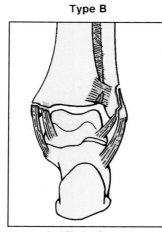
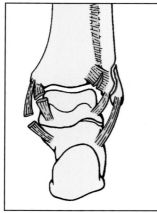

spiral fibular fracture
with partial disruption
of tibiofibular
ligament and avulsion
fracture of
medial malleolus or

intact medial
malleolus with rupture
of deltoid ligament

Type C

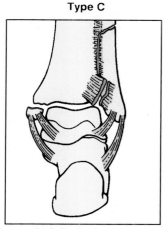
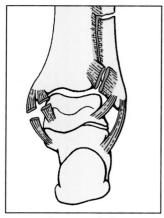

high fibular fracture
with rupture of
tibiofibular ligament and
interosseous membrane
and avulsion fracture
of medial malleolus or

intact medial
malleolus with rupture
of deltoid ligament

FIGURE 10.55 Weber classification. The Weber classification of injuries to the structures about the ankle joint is based on the level at which fibular fracture occurs, as well as the presence or absence of an associated fracture of the medial malleolus. Disruption of the medial and lateral ligament complexes can be deduced from the level of the fibular fracture, as well as that of the medial malleolar fracture. (Modified from Weber BG, 1972, with permission.)

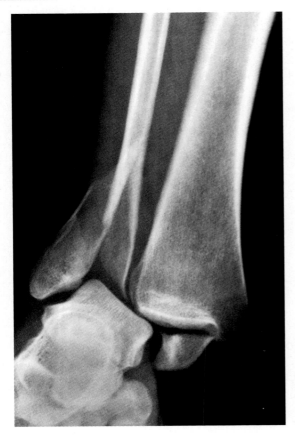

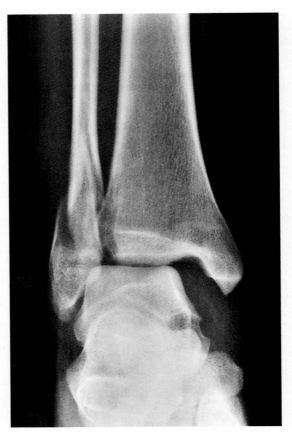

▲
FIGURE 10.56 **Weber type B fracture.** A 24-year-old woman injured her right ankle in a skiing accident. Anteroposterior radiograph of the ankle demonstrates a spiral fracture of the fibula beginning at the level of the tibiofibular syndesmosis with consequent tear of the inferoposterior portion of the syndesmotic complex; the interosseous membrane is intact. The site of the fracture of the medial malleolus suggests that the deltoid ligament may be intact. According to the Weber classification, this is a type B fracture.

▲
FIGURE 10.57 **Weber type C fracture.** A 32-year-old woman stepped into a pothole and injured her right ankle. Anteroposterior view of the ankle demonstrates a fracture of the fibula above the level of the ankle joint, indicating disruption of the interosseous membrane. The intact medial malleolus indicates a tear of the deltoid ligament. This type of fracture is classified as a Weber type C. The risk of ankle mortise instability due to disruption of the medial and lateral ligament complexes gives this type of injury a worse prognosis than type A or B.

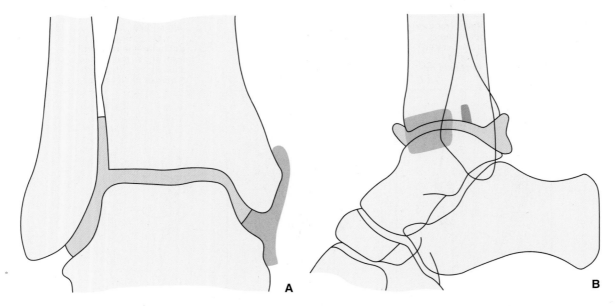

▲
FIGURE 10.58 **Tear of the deltoid ligament. (A,B)** Tear of the deltoid ligament in the absence of fracture is characterized on the arthrogram, represented here schematically, by a leak of contrast beneath the medial malleolus (compare with Fig. 10.12).

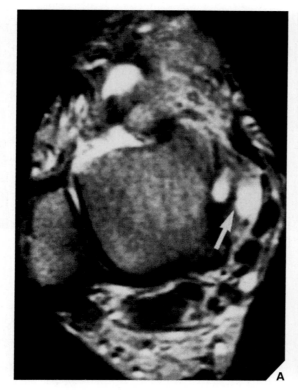
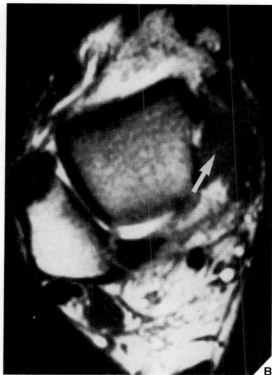

FIGURE 10.59   **MRI of the tear of the deltoid ligament. (A)** An axial T2-weighted image of the right ankle shows a partial tear of the deltoid ligament (*arrow*) with high-signal-intensity hemorrhage in the tibiotalar and tibiocalcaneal fibers. **(B)** An axial T2-weighted image of a normal deltoid ligament that demonstrates low signal intensity of its intact fibers (*arrow*) is shown for comparison.

disruption of the ligament complex can be recognized on the inversion-stress film of the ankle by an increase in talar tilt to 15 degrees or more (see Figs. 10.10B and 10.60A). Arthrographic examination, however, is always diagnostic.

The component ligaments of this complex may also be injured independently. The *anterior talofibular ligament* is the most frequently injured ankle ligament. It can be diagnosed on the inversion-stress film of the ankle (see Fig. 10.10), but arthrographic examination may be required for confirmation (Fig. 10.60). Characteristically, contrast agent is seen to leak anteriorly to the lateral malleolus and laterally alongside it (Fig. 10.61); rupture of the *posterior talofibular ligament* is better appreciated on the lateral view. Rupture of the *calcaneofibular ligament* is invariably associated with tear of the anterior talofibular ligament (Fig. 10.62). The distinguishing arthrographic finding is opacification of the peroneal tendon sheath (Fig. 10.63).

MRI is equally effective in evaluating injury to the lateral collateral ligament. The diagnosis of a tear is based on lack of visualization of the one or more components of this ligament. The tears of the calcaneofibular ligament are best demonstrated in the coronal plane, while the tears of the anterior and posterior talofibular ligaments are best seen on the axial sections (Fig. 10.64).

Tear of the Distal Anterior Tibiofibular Ligament. Commonly associated with other ligament injuries, tear of the anterior tibiofibular ligament may also occur as an isolated injury (Fig. 10.65). Its arthrographic appearance is characterized by leak of contrast agent into the syndesmotic space (Fig. 10.66).

Tendon Ruptures. Most tendon ruptures can be diagnosed by history and clinical examination. For example, tear of the *Achilles tendon*, the most common injury to the soft tissues of the foot, is often indicated by severe tenderness at the tendon's insertion, together with limitation of plantar flexion. Avulsion of this tendon from its calcaneal insertion (Fig. 10.67) can be recognized on the lateral radiograph of the foot obtained with a low-kilovoltage/soft-tissue technique (Fig. 10.68), although tenography (Fig. 10.69) or MRI (Figs. 10.70 and 10.71; see also Fig. 10.19) is confirmatory. Tenography, although rarely performed

at the present time, is also helpful in confirming rupture of the various tendons (Fig. 10.72).

Injury to the Foot

Fractures of the Foot

Fractures of the Calcaneus. Commonly sustained in falls from heights, fractures of the calcaneus are sometimes called "lover's fractures"; in 10% of cases, they are seen bilaterally. According to Cave, fractures of the calcaneus account for 60% of all major tarsal injuries.

In the evaluation of such injuries, it is critical to determine whether the fracture line involves the subtalar joint and, if so, to assess the degree of depression of the posterior facet. Determination of the Boehler angle (see Fig. 10.22C) helps evaluate depression, but CT is usually essential (Fig. 10.73). The CT examination should include coronal and axial sections. Sagittal reformatted images and 3D reconstruction may enhance depiction and characterization of calcaneal fractures (Figs. 10.74 to 10.76) and may be helpful in the assessment of adequacy of postsurgical reduction. In all calcaneal fractures sustained in a fall from a height, a radiograph of the thoracolumbar spine is essential because of the commonly associated finding of compression fracture of one of the vertebral bodies (Fig. 10.77).

Essex-Lopresti classified calcaneal fractures into two main categories: those sparing the subtalar joint (25%) and those extending into it (75%), with the latter subdivided into joint-depression fractures and tongue-type fractures. Rowe and coworkers classified calcaneal fractures into five types (Fig. 10.78):

Type I	Fractures of the tuberosity, sustentaculum tali, or anterior process (21%).
Type II	Beak fractures and avulsion fractures of the Achilles tendon insertion (3.8%).
Type III	Oblique fractures not extending into the subtalar joint (19.5%).
Type IV	Fractures involving the subtalar joint (24.7%).
Type V	Fractures with central depression and varying degrees of comminution (31%).

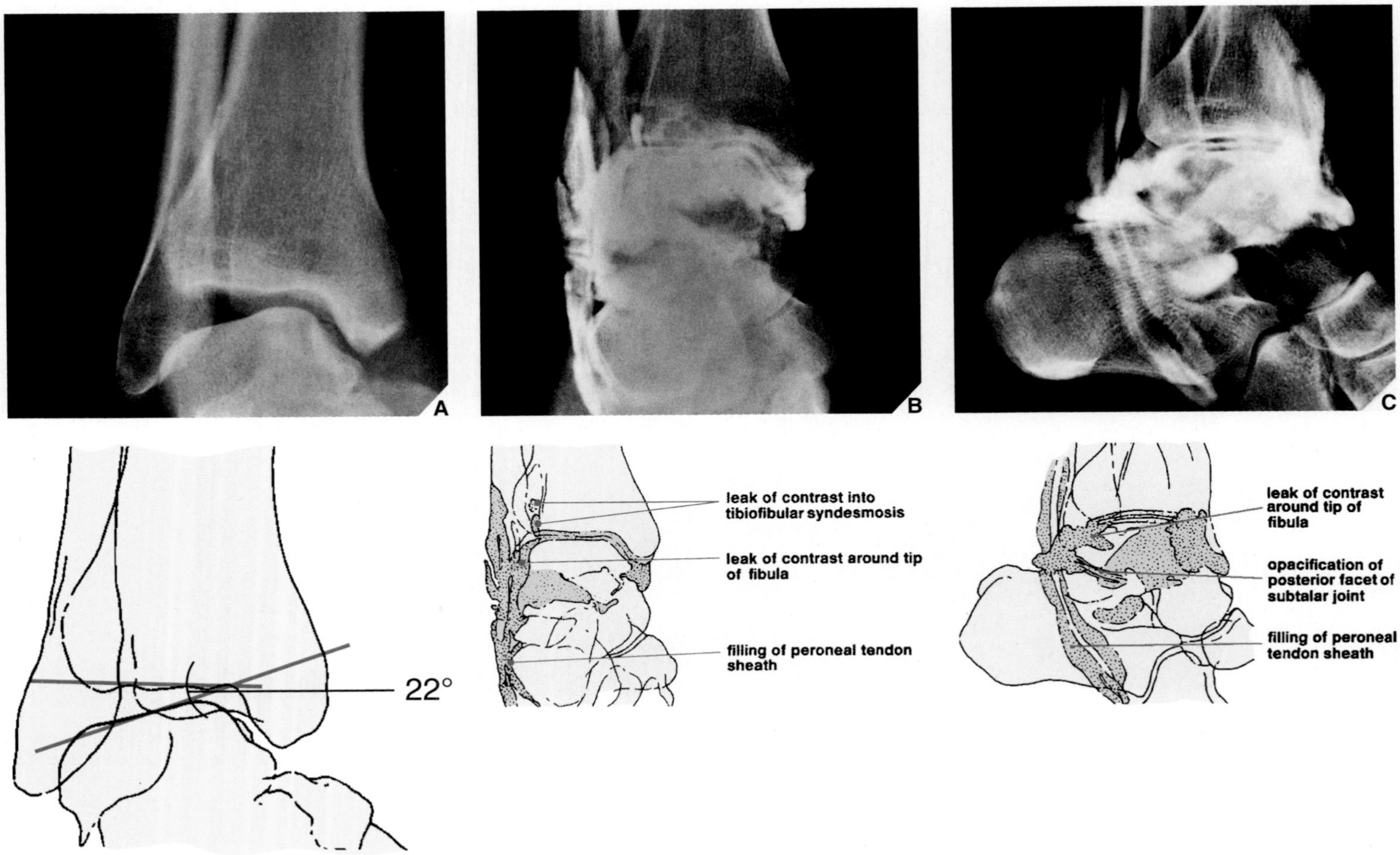

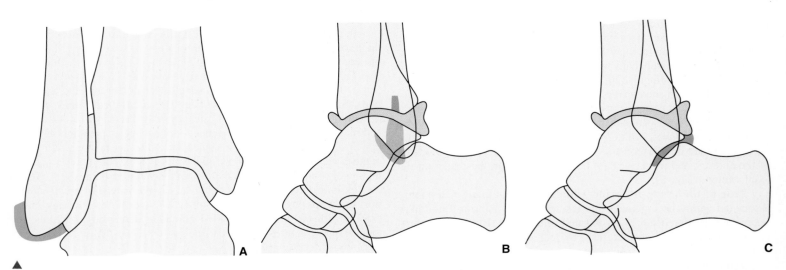

FIGURE 10.60 Multiple tears of the ankle ligaments. A 28-year-old woman injured her ankle in a skiing accident. **(A)** Inversion-stress radiograph shows a talar tilt of 22 degrees, suggesting tear of the lateral collateral ligament complex. Single-contrast arthrograms in the anteroposterior **(B)** and lateral **(C)** projections reveal tears of several ligaments: leakage around the tip of the fibula indicates a tear of the anterior talofibular ligament, filling of the peroneal tendon sheath indicates a tear of the calcaneofibular ligament, and leak of contrast into the tibiofibular syndesmosis indicates a tear of the distal anterior tibiofibular ligament. Filling of the posterior facet of the subtalar joint indicates a tear of the posterior talofibular ligament.

FIGURE 10.61 Tear of the anterior and posterior talofibular ligaments. (A,B) On arthrography, leak of contrast around the tip of the lateral malleolus characterizes a tear of the anterior talofibular ligament. **(C)** Tear of the posterior talofibular ligament can be recognized on the lateral view by opacification of the posterior facet of the subtalar joint. In 10% of cases, however, this finding may represent a normal variant.

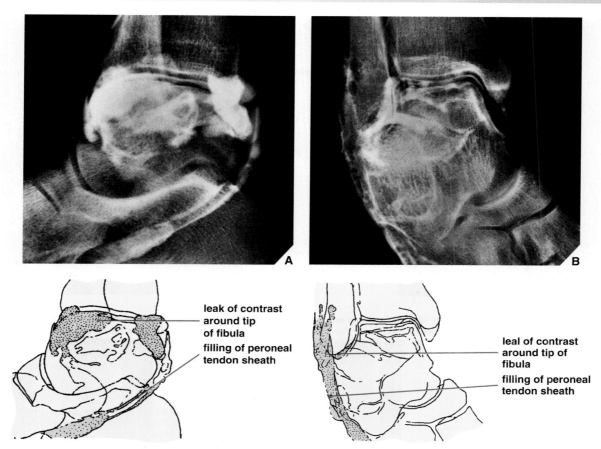

FIGURE 10.62 **Tear of the calcaneofibular and anterior talofibular ligaments.** A 27-year-old man twisted his ankle during a sports activity. Conventional radiographs were normal, and stress views were equivocal. Contrast arthrograms in the lateral (**A**) and oblique (**B**) projections of the ankle show opacification of the peroneal tendon sheath, characteristic of tear of the calcaneofibular ligament. Leak of contrast agent along the fibular malleolus, seen on both views, indicates an associated tear of the anterior talofibular ligament.

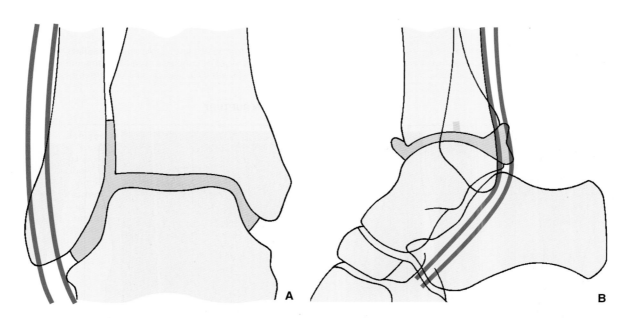

FIGURE 10.63 **Tear of the calcaneofibular ligament. (A,B)** The characteristic arthrographic finding in rupture of the calcaneofibular ligament is opacification of the peroneal tendon sheath.

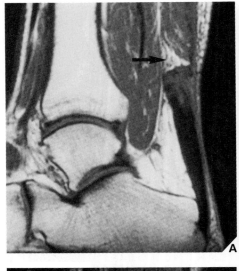

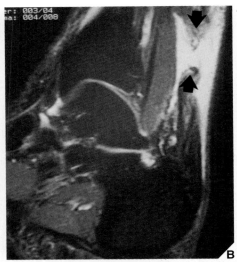

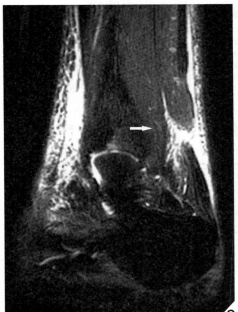

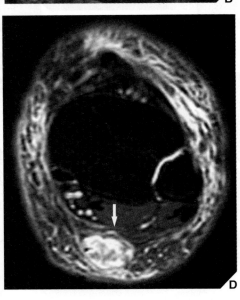

◄ FIGURE 10.71 MRI of the Achilles tendon tear. (A) Sagittal T1-weighted MRI shows a complete rupture of the Achilles tendon near the musculotendinous junction (*arrow*). (B) In another patient, a complete Achilles tendon tear with a large 3-cm gap (*arrows*) is seen on this sagittal STIR MR image. There is massive edema and hemorrhage subcutaneously and deep to the Achilles tendon. Yet in another patient, sagittal inversion recovery (C) and axial T2-weighted fat-suppressed (D) MR images show a complete full-thickness tear of the Achilles tendon (*arrows*).

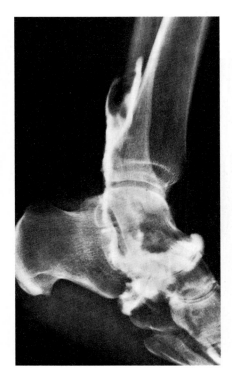

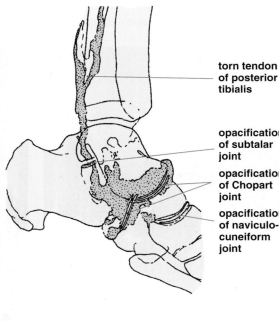

torn tendon
of posterior
tibialis

opacification
of subtalar
joint

opacification
of Chopart
joint

opacification
of naviculo-
cuneiform
joint

◄ FIGURE 10.72 Tenogram of the posterior tibialis muscle tendon tear. A 57-year-old man sustained an eversion injury to the left ankle while playing tennis. On clinical examination, he was diagnosed as having ruptured the tendon of the posterior tibialis muscle. Tenography confirms the clinical findings. Note the abnormal opacification of the subtalar, Chopart, and naviculocuneiform joints.

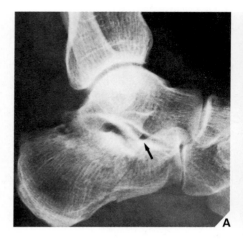
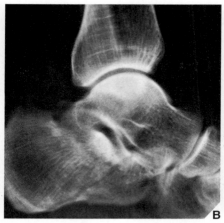
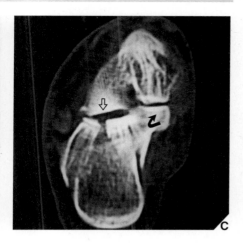

▲
FIGURE 10.73 **Fracture of the calcaneus.** A 54-year-old man fell from a scaffold and sustained a fracture of the left calcaneus. (**A**) Lateral radiograph shows a comminuted fracture of the calcaneus. There is a suggestion of extension of the fracture line into the subtalar joint (*arrow*). (**B**) Tomographic examination in the lateral projection confirms intraarticular extension of the fracture line. The amount of depression of the articular surface, however, cannot be definitely assessed. (**C**) CT section precisely demonstrates the position of the comminuted fragments and depression at the posterior facet of the subtalar joint (*open arrow*). It also shows that the middle facet is intact (*curved arrow*), important information that the conventional and tomographic studies could not provide.

FIGURE 10.74 **CT of the calcaneus fracture.** A 34-year-old man sustained a comminuted fracture of the right calcaneus. (**A**) Coronal CT section shows extension of the fracture line to the subtalar joint. (**B**) Sagittal reformatted CT image shows in addition a fracture of the anterior process of the calcaneus with extension into the anterior facet of subtalar joint (*arrow*). ▶

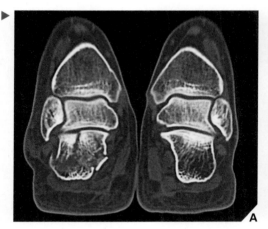
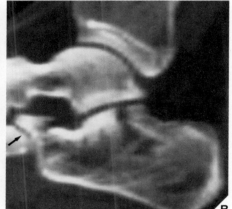

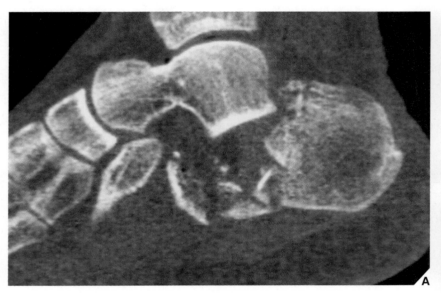
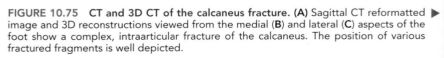

FIGURE 10.75 **CT and 3D CT of the calcaneus fracture.** (**A**) Sagittal CT reformatted ▶
image and 3D reconstructions viewed from the medial (**B**) and lateral (**C**) aspects of the foot show a complex, intraarticular fracture of the calcaneus. The position of various fractured fragments is well depicted.

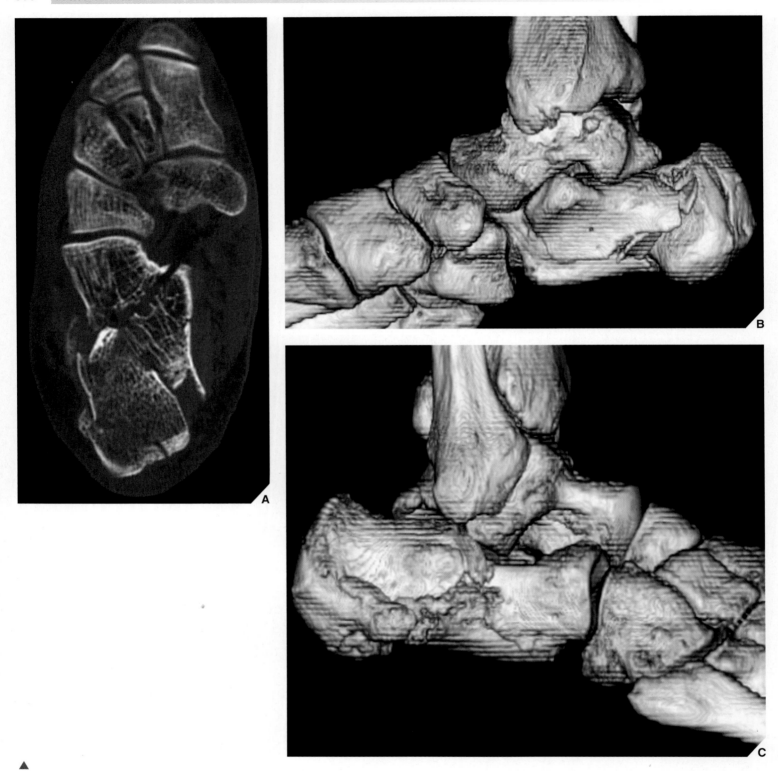

▲
FIGURE 10.76   **CT and 3D CT of the calcaneus fracture. (A)** Axial CT image shows a comminuted fracture of the calcaneus. 3D reconstructed CT images of the foot viewed from the medial **(B)** and lateral **(C)** aspects show the various fracture lines and intraarticular extension to the better advantage.

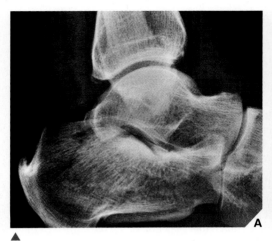
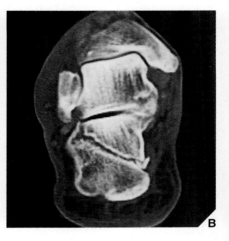
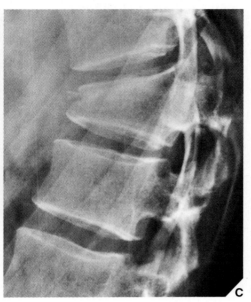

FIGURE 10.77 **Fractures of the calcaneus and the thoracic vertebra.** A 48-year-old man jumped from a second-floor window. (**A**) Lateral radiograph of the ankle demonstrates a comminuted fracture of the calcaneus. (**B**) Coronal CT section demonstrates the position of multiple, small, comminuted fragments and involvement of the sustentaculum tali. (**C**) Lateral radiograph of the thoracolumbar spine shows compression fracture of the T12 vertebral body.

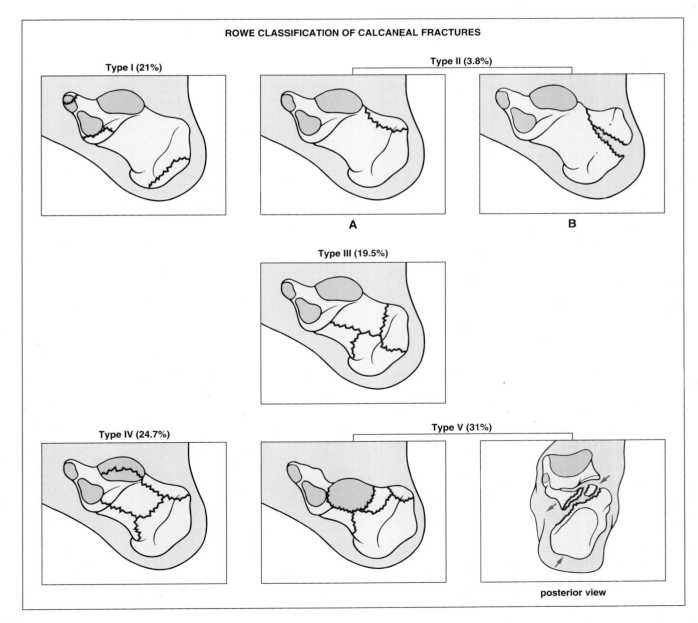

FIGURE 10.78 **The Rowe classification of calcaneal fractures.** Type I (21%)—fractures of the tuberosity, sustentaculum tali, or anterior process; type II (3.8%)—beak fractures (**A**) and avulsion fractures of the Achilles tendon insertion (**B**); type III (19.5%)—oblique fractures not extending into the subtalar joint; type IV (24.7%)—fractures involving the subtalar joint; type V (31%)—fractures with central depression and varying degrees of comminution. (Modified from Rowe CR et al., 1963, with permission.)

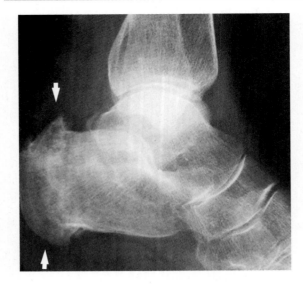

FIGURE 10.79 Stress fracture of the calcaneus. A 75-year-old woman reported pain in the left heel; she had no history of trauma. She walked about a mile to the supermarket every day. Lateral radiograph of the right ankle shows a typical stress fracture of the os calcis (*arrows*).

Stress fractures of the calcaneus occur in joggers and runners but do not spare the older population when bones are weakened by osteoporosis (Fig. 10.79). Like stress fractures in long bones, these fractures are not immediately evident but typically become obvious approximately 10 to 14 days after the precipitating incident. They can be recognized on radiographs by a band of sclerosis, representing formation of endosteal callus. The fracture line is usually oriented either vertically or parallel to the posterior contour of the bone. If stress fractures are suspected but radiographs are normal, a bone scan may validate the diagnosis, although MRI examination is preferred (Fig. 10.80).

Fractures of the Talus. Fractures of the talus are the second most common tarsal bone fractures, after the calcaneus. Fracture may involve the head, neck, body, or posterior process. The neck of the talus is the most vulnerable site, and the vertical fractures are most frequently encountered. Hawkins proposed three types of vertical fractures of the neck of the talus (Fig. 10.81). His classification, based on the damage to the blood supply of the talus, serves as a guide to prognosis for healing of the fracture, incidence of osteonecrosis, and indication for open reduction. Recently, Canale and Kelly modified this classification to include a

fourth, rare type of a displaced fracture with subtalar or tibiotalar dislocation and subluxation or dislocation in the talonavicular joint.

Whether vertical or comminuted, fractures of the talus most often result from forced dorsiflexion of the foot, as may occur in automobile accidents. Accompanying dislocation in the subtalar and talonavicular joints is common. Talar fractures are usually obvious on the standard radiographic projections, although CT is usually required for demonstration and quantification of displacement (Figs. 10.82 and 10.83). MRI may be of value for detecting various complications (Fig. 10.84).

Osteochondritis Dissecans of the Talus. Osteochondritis dissecans should not be confused with osteochondral fracture of the dome of the talus resulting from inversion or eversion injury to the ankle. (The differential diagnosis of osteochondritis dissecans and osteochondral fracture was discussed in detail in Chapter 9.)

Osteochondritis dissecans results from chronic stress and is seen most commonly in athletes and ballet dancers. In the past, the best diagnostic procedures for demonstrating the lesion was arthrotomography (Fig. 10.85), and, at present time, MRI (Fig. 10.86).

Navicular Fractures. Navicular fractures are rare and are usually sustained along with fractures of other bones of the foot. Occasionally, navicular fracture may be caused by a fall from a height. Sangeorzan and colleagues classified navicular fractures into three types based on the orientation of the fracture line and the degree of comminution. Type I fractures pass through the navicular bone in a coronal plane, without associated forefoot angulation. Type II fractures are associated with forefoot angulation and the fracture line runs from the dorsolateral to the plantar-medial aspect of the bone. Type III fractures are comminuted and the forefoot is laterally displaced. Eichenholtz and Levine classified these fractures as cortical avulsion (47%), tuberosity avulsion (24%), and fractures of the body (29%).

Because navicular fractures can be missed on conventional radiography, CT including reformatted imaging is recommended when such fractures are suspected (Fig. 10.87).

Jones Fracture. This avulsion fracture of the base of the fifth metatarsal results from inversion stress placed on the peroneus brevis tendon, which is attached to the fifth metatarsal (Fig. 10.88; see also Fig. 4.31A). From a historical point of view, however, the term "Jones fracture" is used incorrectly, because the original fracture described by Robert Jones in 1902 was one sustained approximately three fourths of 1 inch from the base of the fifth metatarsal (Fig. 10.89). The distinction between a "true" Jones fracture and an avulsion fracture of the base of the fifth metatarsal is also of prognostic value: Avulsion fractures generally heal quickly, while fractures through the proximal metatarsal shaft, because of poor blood supply, have a significant incidence of delayed union and

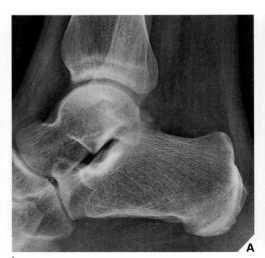
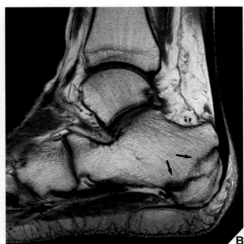
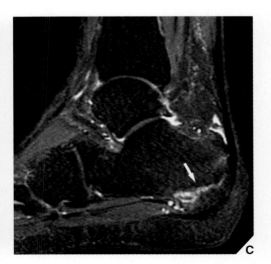

FIGURE 10.80 MRI of stress fracture of the calcaneus. A 30-year-old woman, a marathon runner, presented with a heal pain. (**A**) Lateral radiograph of the ankle was suspicious but not diagnostic for a stress fracture of the calcaneus. This diagnosis was confirmed on (**B**) sagittal proton density-weighted and (**C**) sagittal T2-weighted MR images (*arrows*).

HAWKINS CLASSIFICATION OF TALAR NECK FRACTURES

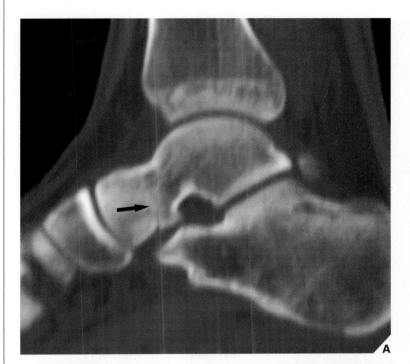

Type I
(11%-21%)

Type II
(40%-42%)

Type III
(23%-47%)

▲
FIGURE 10.81 **The Hawkins classification of vertical talar neck fractures.** Type I fracture shows no displacement of the talus in relation to the subtalar joint. Type II fracture exhibits subluxation or dislocation of the talus in the subtalar joint. Type III fracture is characterized by the displacement of the body of the talus, which is locked behind the sustentaculum tali, so that the fracture surface is pointing laterally.

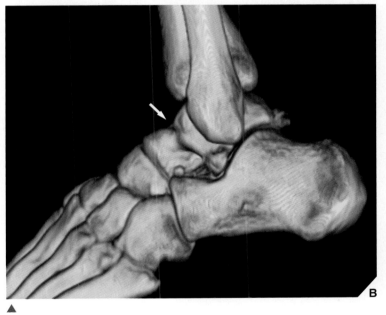

▲
FIGURE 10.82 **CT of fracture of the talus. (A)** Sagittal reformatted CT image of the ankle and **(B)** 3D CT reconstruction in shaded surface display (SSD) show a nondisplaced fracture of the talus (*arrows*).

fibrous union. In children, it is important not to confuse this fracture with the normal (and frequently present) secondary ossification center of the base of the fifth metatarsal (see Fig. 4.31B). The fracture line is transversely oriented, whereas the gap separating the ossification center from the fifth metatarsal is oblique.

Complications

The most common complications of ankle and foot fractures are nonunion and posttraumatic arthritis. Although conventional radiography can usually demonstrate the features of these complications, CT is the better technique for delineating their details.

Dislocations in the Foot

The most common dislocation in the foot occurs in the tarsometatarsal (Lisfranc) joint. In general, however, dislocations are less common than fractures of the ankle and foot. They are occasionally seen as a result of motor vehicle or aircraft accidents, as in dislocation of the talus—the so-called aviator's astragalus. According to Shelton and Pedowitz, aircraft accidents account for 43% of all talar injuries.

Dislocations in the Subtalar Joint. The two major types of subtalar joint dislocations are peritalar dislocation of the foot and total dislocation of the talus.

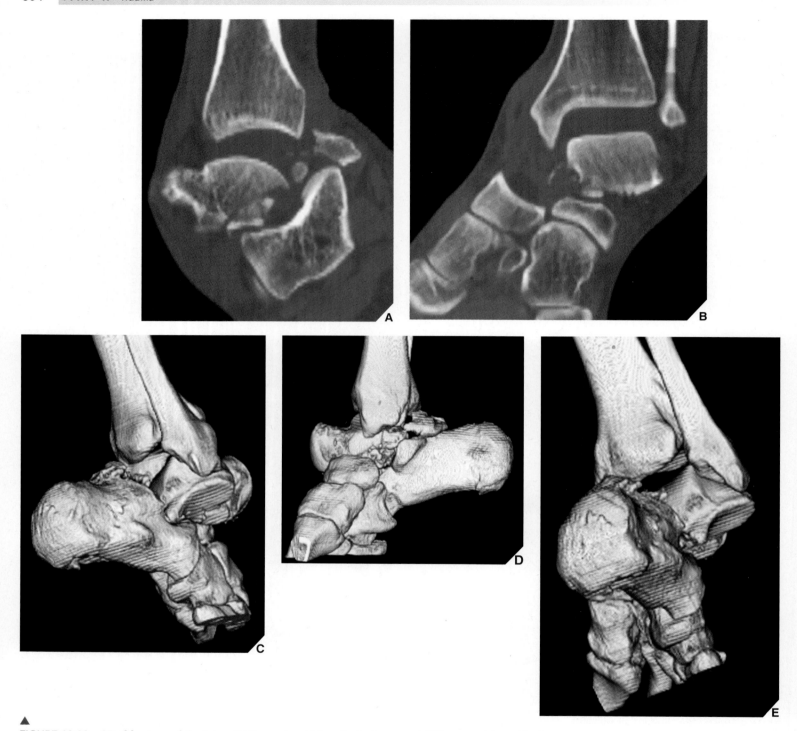

▲
FIGURE 10.83   **CT of fracture of the talus. (A)** Coronal and **(B)** sagittal reformatted CT images of the ankle show a comminuted, displaced fracture of the talus. **(C,D,E)** 3D CT reconstructed images viewed from various angles depict the details of this injury.

Peritalar Dislocation. This type of abnormality involves simultaneous dislocations in the talocalcaneal and talonavicular joints with normal maintenance of the tibiotalar relationship. Often referred to as subtalar or subastragalar dislocation, peritalar dislocation, as Pennal has pointed out, accounts for approximately 15% of all talar injuries and approximately 1% of all dislocations. Patients vary in age from 10 to older than 60 years, but three to ten times more men than women sustain these injuries.

Four subtypes of peritalar dislocation have been identified: medial, lateral, posterior, and anterior. *Medial dislocation* is the most common subtype, resulting from a violent inversion force acting as a fulcrum for the sustentaculum tali to cause initial dislocation of the talonavic-

ular joint, together with rotary subluxation of the talocalcaneal joint. A greater force may cause complete dislocation. The dorsoplantar (anteroposterior) view of the foot is recommended to demonstrate this abnormality. The radiographs should be scrutinized carefully for associated fractures, particularly of both malleoli, the articular margin of the talus, and the navicular and fifth metatarsal bones.

Lateral dislocation is the next most common subtype, accounting for approximately 20% of all peritalar dislocations. At the time of injury, the foot is everted and, with the anterior calcaneal process acting as a fulcrum, the head of the talus is forced out of the talonavicular joint; the calcaneus is dislocated laterally. As in medial dislocation, the dorsoplantar view of the foot is diagnostic.

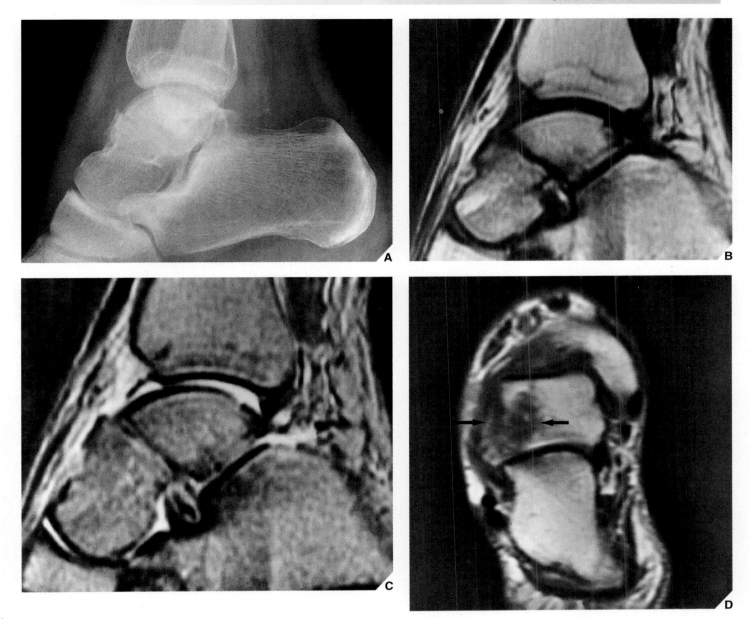

▲
FIGURE 10.84   **MRI of fracture of the talus.** A 41-year-old woman injured her right foot in an automobile accident. (**A**) Lateral radiograph of the ankle demonstrates a vertical fracture of the talus. T1-weighted (**B**) and T2-weighted (**C**) sagittal spin-echo MR images demonstrate lack of union and persistent joint effusion. The axial image (**D**) demonstrates segmental osteonecrosis of the posterolateral part of the talus (*arrows*).

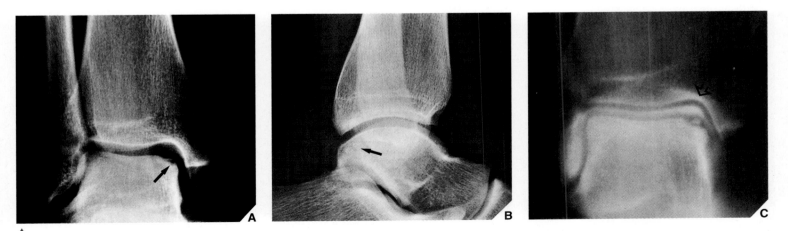

▲
FIGURE 10.85   **Osteochondritis dissecans of the talus.** A 29-year-old man, a professional ballet dancer, reported pain in the ankle over the preceding 8 months. Anteroposterior (**A**) and lateral (**B**) radiographs demonstrate a radiolucent defect in the medial aspect of the dome of the talus and a small osteochondral body within the defect (*arrows*), characteristic findings in osteochondritis dissecans. (**C**) Arthrotomography demonstrates the intact articular cartilage over the lesion (*open arrow*), distinguishing it as an *in situ* lesion.

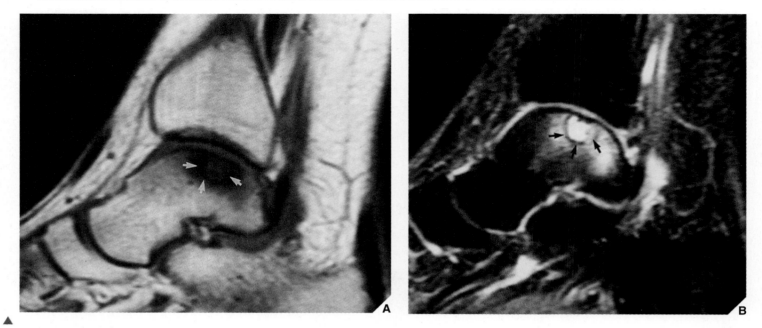

FIGURE 10.86   MRI of osteochondritis dissecans of the talus. (A) A sagittal T1-weighted image shows an area of low signal intensity at the talar dome (*arrows*). **(B)** A sagittal inversion recovery image shows high-signal-intensity lesion of osteochondritis dissecans (*arrows*).

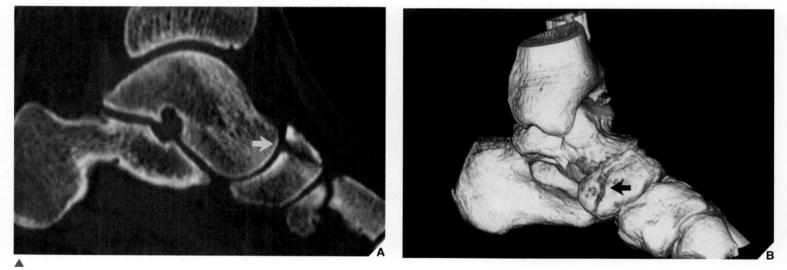

FIGURE 10.87   CT of the navicular fracture. (A) Sagittal CT reformatted image and **(B)** 3D CT reconstruction show a fracture of the navicular bone (*arrows*).

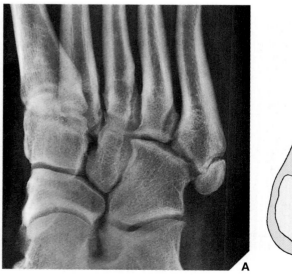

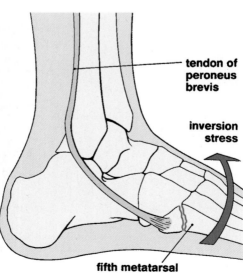

◀ **FIGURE 10.88   Avulsion fracture.** A 28-year-old man stumbled on uneven pavement and sustained an inversion injury of the right foot. **(A)** Oblique radiograph demonstrates a fracture of the base of the fifth metatarsal, frequently but incorrectly interpreted as the Jones fracture. **(B)** Inversion-stress forces on the peroneus brevis tendon cause avulsion fracture of the base of the fifth metatarsal.

tendon of
peroneus
brevis

inversion
stress

fifth metatarsal

JONES FRACTURE

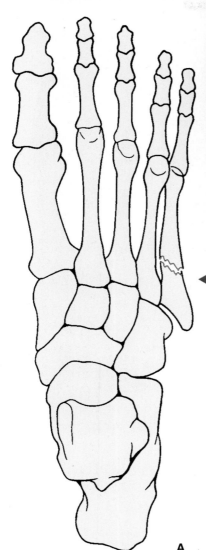

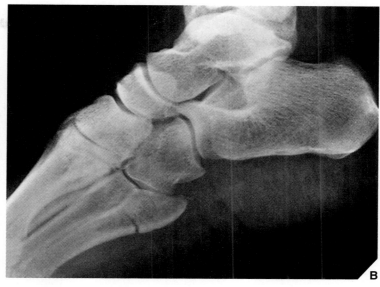

◄ **FIGURE 10.89   Jones fracture. (A)** A "true" Jones fracture is located about an inch distally to the base of the fifth metatarsal. **(B)** A 43-year-old woman, while dancing, twisted her left foot and sustained a "true" Jones fracture of the fifth metatarsal.

A

Posterior and anterior dislocations are the rarest subtypes, occurring as a result of a fall from a height onto the plantar-flexed foot (posterior dislocation) or the dorsiflexed foot (anterior dislocation). In either case, the lateral radiograph of the foot and ankle is best for demonstrating the abnormality (Fig. 10.90).

Total Talar Dislocation. Characterized by complete disruption of both the ankle (tibiotalar) and the subtalar joints, total talar dislocation is the most serious of all talar injuries. It is frequently complicated by osteonecrosis of the astragalus.

Tarsometatarsal Dislocation. Also termed *Lisfranc fracture–dislocation* (named after Napoleonic army field surgeon Jacques Lisfranc de St. Martin), this is the most common dislocation in the foot. It also frequently occurs in association with various types of fractures. Basically, this is a dorsal dislocation, often occurring as the result of a fall from a height or down a flight of stairs or even of stepping off a curb. There are two basic forms of injury: *homolateral*—dislocation of the first to the fifth metatarsal; and *divergent*—lateral displacement of the second to the fifth metatarsals with medial or dorsal shift of the first metatarsal (Fig. 10.91). Associated fractures most often occur at the base of the second metatarsal bone; they may also be seen in the third metatarsal, first or second cuneiform, or navicular bones. The divergent form of tarsometatarsal dislocation is most frequently associated with such fractures. Although these injuries are well demonstrated on the standard views of the foot (Fig. 10.92), ancillary imaging

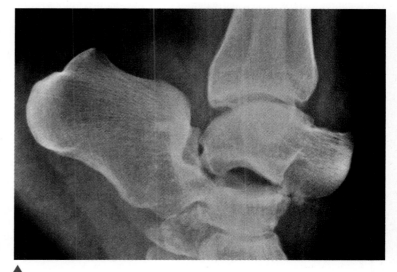

▲
FIGURE 10.90   Peritalar dislocation. A 25-year-old man fell from a ladder and landed on his plantar-flexed left foot. Lateral radiograph demonstrates posterior peritalar dislocation. Note that the talus articulates normally with the tibia, but there are simultaneous dislocations in the talocalcaneal and talonavicular joints. The entire foot (except for the talus) is posteriorly displaced. Associated fractures of the navicular and cuboid bones are evident.

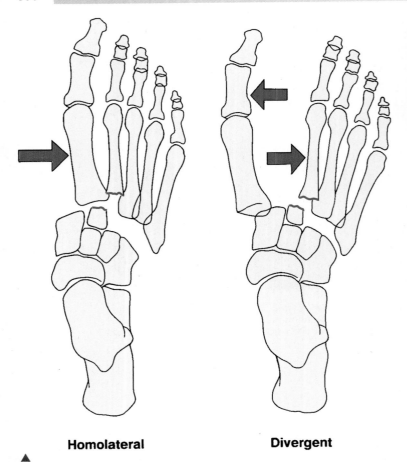

Homolateral   **Divergent**

▲
FIGURE 10.91 Types of the Lisfranc fracture–dislocation. Tarsometatarsal dislocation (Lisfranc fracture–dislocation) may be seen in two variants. In the homolateral form, the first to the fifth metatarsals are dislocated laterally. In the divergent form, the first metatarsal is medially dislocated. Both types are often associated with fracture of the base of the second metatarsal bone.

techniques are frequently required. CT examination demonstrates the details of this injury (Fig. 10.93) and unsuspected additional fractures (Fig. 10.94), and MRI not seen otherwise associated tear of the Lisfranc ligament (Fig. 10.95). The most common complications of ankle and foot fractures are nonunion and posttraumatic arthritis. Although conventional radiography can usually demonstrate the features of these complications, CT is the better technique for delineating their characteristic features.

Tarsal Tunnel Syndrome

The tarsal tunnel is a fibro-osseous structure located in the medial side of the ankle and hindfoot, extending from the medial malleolus to the navicular bone. The roof of the tunnel is formed by the flexor retinaculum, the lateral side is formed by the medial aspect of the talus and sustentaculum tali, and the medial side is bordered by the flexor retinaculum, abductor hallucis muscle, and the medial wall of the calcaneus. The tarsal tunnel contains the posterior tibial nerve, the posterior tibial artery and vein, the posterior tibial tendon, the flexor digitorum longus tendon, and the flexor hallucis longus tendon. The term "tarsal tunnel syndrome" was originally and independently coined by Keck and Lam in 1962. The syndrome is caused by the compression of the posterior tibial nerve or its branches as they pass deep to the flexor retinaculum, either by extrinsic masses or posttraumatic fibrosis. The clinical symptoms include pain, a burning sensation, and paresthesias in the sole of the foot and the toes. MRI is very effective in demonstrating the cause of nerve impingement.

Sinus Tarsi Syndrome

The sinus tarsi (or tarsal sinus) is a cone-shaped space located in the lateral aspect of the foot between the neck of the talus and the anteroposterior surface of the calcaneus. The sinus tarsi contains fat,

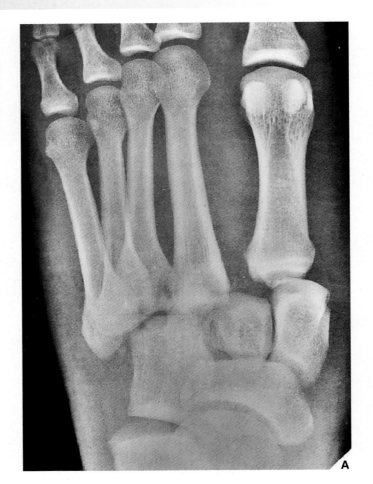

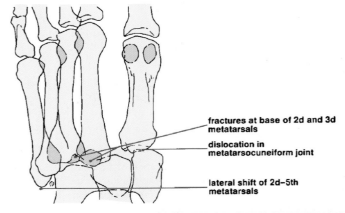

fractures at base of 2d and 3d metatarsals

dislocation in metatarsocuneiform joint

lateral shift of 2d–5th metatarsals

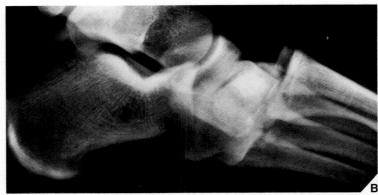

▲
FIGURE 10.92 Divergent Lisfranc fracture–dislocation. A 39-year-old man fell down a flight of stairs. Anteroposterior (**A**) and lateral (**B**) radiographs of the right foot show the divergent type of the Lisfranc fracture–dislocation. There is lateral shift of the second to fifth metatarsals as well as dislocation, and dorsal shift in the first metatarsocuneiform joint, which is better appreciated on the lateral film. Note the fractures at the base of the second and third metatarsals.

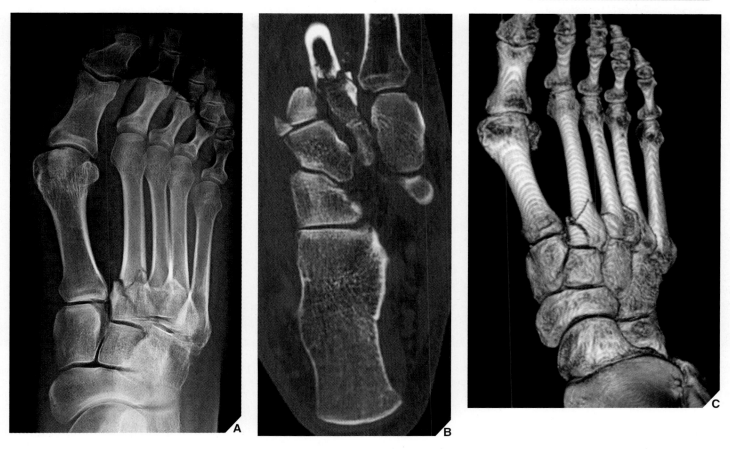

FIGURE 10.93   **CT of the Lisfranc fracture–dislocation.** (A) Anteroposterior radiograph of the left foot shows a typical Lisfranc injury, more accurately displayed on the (B) axial CT image and (C) 3D CT reconstruction.

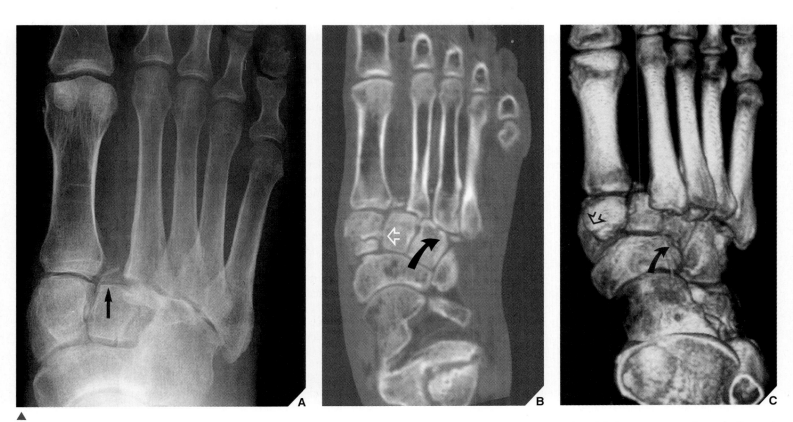

FIGURE 10.94   **CT of the Lisfranc fracture–dislocation.** A 54-year-old man fell down a flight of stairs and injured his left foot. (A) Dorsoplantar radiograph shows typical appearance of divergent Lisfranc fracture–dislocation. A small fractured fragment from the base of the second metatarsal is well-seen (arrow). CT reformatted image in axial (transverse) plane (B), and 3D CT reconstruction (C) demonstrate an unsuspected fracture of the medial (open arrow) and lateral (curved arrow) cuneiform bones.

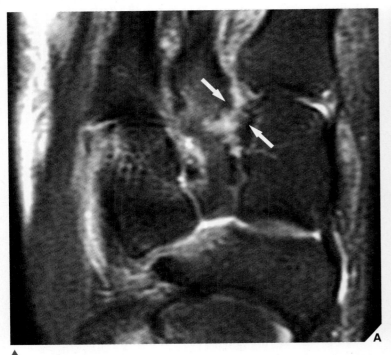 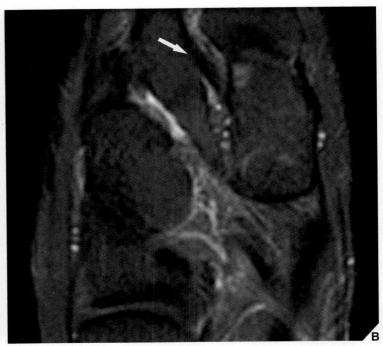

▲
FIGURE 10.95 **MRI of tear of the Lisfranc ligament. (A)** Proton density-weighted fat-suppressed axial MR image shows a tear of the Lisfranc ligament (*arrows*). **(B)** Normal appearance of Lisfranc ligament (*arrow*) is shown for comparison.

talocalcaneal ligaments, interosseous ligaments, portions of the joint capsule of the posterior subtalar joint, and neurovascular structures. The sinus tarsi syndrome is caused by abnormalities of one or more structures contained in the sinus and is characterized by pain in the lateral portion of the foot and a feeling of instability of the hindfoot. Pain relief can be achieved by injection of anesthetic agents into the tarsal sinus. In 70% of reported cases, the causing factor responsible for the sinus tarsi syndrome was trauma, usually involving inversion injury to the foot. MRI may show obliteration of sinus tarsi fat, tear of calcaneofibular and anterior talofibular ligaments, and tear of the posterior tibial tendon.

PRACTICAL POINTS TO REMEMBER

Ankle

[1] There are three principal sets of ligaments around the ankle joint:
- the medial collateral (deltoid) ligament
- the lateral collateral ligament
- the distal tibiofibular syndesmotic complex.

[2] Traumatic conditions of the ankle should be evaluated according to the mechanism that caused the injury, including:
- inversion-stress forces
- eversion-stress forces
- complex stresses combining supination or pronation with rotation, abduction, or adduction.

[3] Inversion-stress forces may manifest in a spectrum of injuries to the lateral collateral ligament, as well as in associated fractures of the distal tip of the fibula and occasionally the medial malleolus.

[4] Eversion-stress forces may manifest in a range of injuries to the medial collateral (deltoid) ligament, as well as fracture of the medial malleolus. Pott, Maisonneuve, and Dupuytren fractures are all eversion injuries.

[5] Pilon fracture is a comminuted fracture of the distal tibia with extension into the tibiotalar joint.

[6] Tillaux fracture consists of avulsion of the lateral margin of distal tibia resulting from abduction and external rotation injury.

[7] Juvenile Tillaux fracture is a Salter-Harris type III injury to the distal tibial growth plate.

[8] Triplanar Marmor-Lynn fracture consists of a vertical fracture through the distal tibial epiphysis (in the sagittal plane), horizontal fracture through the lateral aspect of the distal tibial growth plate (in the axial plane), and oblique fracture through the distal metaphysis extending into the diaphysis (in the coronal plane).

[9] Traumatic conditions of the structures about the ankle joint may not be obvious on the standard radiographic examination when only damage of soft-tissue structures is present. Correct management of such injuries may be much more important to a successful orthopedic outcome than correct management of a simple fracture. For this reason, stress views, arthrographic examination, and MRI are of paramount importance for full evaluation of the extent of damage to the complex structures about the joint.

[10] The ligament structure most important for congruence of the joint and ankle stability is the distal tibiofibular syndesmotic complex.

[11] Lauge-Hansen classification of ankle trauma is based on the mechanism of injury, combining the position of the foot with the direction of deforming force vector.

[12] The Weber classification of ankle fractures—based on the level of fibular fracture—is practical for assessing the risk of future ankle instability because of its emphasis on the lateral syndesmotic–malleolar complex as an important factor in ankle joint stability.

[13] On arthrographic examination of the ligament structures about the ankle and foot:
- leak of contrast around the tip of the fibular malleolus indicates a tear of the anterior talofibular ligament
- opacification of the peroneal tendon sheath suggests a tear of the calcaneofibular ligament
- leak of contrast more than 2.5 cm into the tibiofibular syndesmotic recess indicates a tear of the distal anterior tibiofibular ligament
- leak of contrast beneath the medial malleolus indicates a tear of the deltoid ligament.

[14] Tenography is a useful technique for evaluating tears of the tendons, such as the Achilles tendon, the posterior tibialis tendon, or the peroneal tendon.

[15] MRI is a noninvasive modality capable of demonstrating pathologic conditions of tendons and ligaments by displaying discontinuity of the anatomic structures, the presence of abnormal signal within them, and the presence of inflammatory changes.

Foot

[1] It is important to recognize the multiple accessory ossicles of the foot:
  - the normal appearance of these secondary ossification centers may mimic fractures
  - conversely, an avulsion fracture may be misinterpreted as a normal ossicle.

[2] Harris-Beath and Broden views, tangential projections, are important techniques for evaluating injury to the subtalar joint.

[3] The Boehler angle demonstrates an important anatomic relation of the calcaneus and subtalar joint. It is useful for evaluating compression fracture of the calcaneus, particularly with extension into the subtalar joint.

[4] In fracture of the calcaneus (so-called lover's fracture), look for an associated compression fracture of the vertebral body in the thoracic or lumbar spine.

[5] Hawkins classification of talar neck fractures is based on the damage to the blood supply of the talus and serves as a prognostic guide for healing of the fracture, incidence of osteonecrosis, and indication for open reduction.

[6] In Lisfranc fracture–dislocation in the tarsometatarsal articulation, always look for an associated fracture either
  - at the base of the metatarsals
  - or in the cuneiform bones.

SUGGESTED READINGS

Ala-Ketola L, Puranen J, Koivisto E, Puupera M. Arthrography in the diagnosis of ligament injuries and classification of ankle injuries. *Radiology* 1977;125:63–68.

Arimoto HK, Forrester DM. Classification of ankle fractures: an algorithm. *Am J Roentgenol* 1980;135:1057–1063.

Baker K, Gilula L. The current role of tenography and bursography. *Am J Roentgenol* 1990;154:129–133.

Beltran J. *MRI: musculoskeletal system*. Philadelphia: JB Lippincott; 1990.

Beltran J. MRI techniques and practical applications: magnetic resonance imaging of the ankle and foot. *Orthopedics* 1994;17:1075–1082.

Beltran J, Munchow AM, Khabiri H, Magee DG, McGhee RB, Grossman SB. Ligaments of the lateral aspect of the ankle and sinus tarsi: an MR imaging study. *Radiology* 1990;177:455–458.

Bencardino J, Rosenberg ZS. MR imaging and CT in the assessment of osseous abnormalities of the ankle and foot. *Magn Reson Imaging Clin N Am* 2001;9:567–577.

Berquist TM. Foot, ankle, and calf. In: Berquist TM, ed. *MRI of the musculoskeletal system*. New York: Raven Press; 1990:253–311.

Bone LB. Fractures of the tibial plafond. The pilon fracture. *Orthop Clin North Am* 1987;18:95–104.

Boruta PM, Bishop JO, Braly WG, Tullos HS. Acute lateral ankle ligament injuries: a literature review. *Foot Ankle Int* 1990;11:107–113.

Brown KW, Morrison WB, Schweitzer ME, Parellada JA, Nothnagel H. MRI findings associated with distal tibiofibular syndesmosis injury. *Am J Roentgenol* 2004;182:131–136.

Canale ST, Belding RH. Osteochondral lesions of the talus. *J Bone Joint Surg Am* 1980;62A:97–102.

Canale ST, Kelly FB. Fractures of the neck of the talus. *J Bone Joint Surg Am* 1978;60A:143–156.

Cheung Y, Rosenberg ZS, Magee T, Chinitz L. Normal anatomy and pathologic conditions of ankle tendons: current imaging techniques. *Radiographics* 1992;12:429–444.

Cone RO III, Nguyen V, Flournoy JG, Guerra J Jr. Triplane fracture of the distal tibial epiphysis: radiographic and CT studies. *Radiology* 1984;153:763–767.

Corbett M, Levy A, Abramowitz AJ, Whitelaw GP. A computer tomographic classification system for the displaced intraarticular fracture of the os calcis. *Orthopedics* 1995;18:705–710.

Daffner RH. Ankle trauma. *Radiol Clin North Am* 1990;28:395–421.

De Smet AA, Fisher DR, Burnstein MI, Graf BK, Lange RH. Value of MR imaging in staging osteochondral lesions of the talus (osteochondritis dissecans): results in 14 patients. *Am J Roentgenol* 1990;154:555–558.

DeLee JC. Fractures and dislocations of the foot. In: Mann RA, Coughlin MJ, eds. *Surgery of the foot and ankle*, 6th ed. St. Louis: CV Mosby; 1993:1550–1551.

Dias LS, Giegerich CR. Fractures of the distal tibial epiphysis in adolescence. *J Bone Joint Surg Am* 1983;65A:438–444.

Dias LS, Tachdjian MO. Physeal injuries in the ankle in children: classification. *Clin Orthop* 1978;136:230–233.

Donnelly EF. The Hawkins sign. *Radiology* 1999;210:195–196.

Edeiken J, Cotler JM. Ankle trauma. *Semin Roentgenol* 1978;13:145–155.

Edeiken J, Cotler JM. Ankle. In: Felson B, ed. *Fractures*. New York: Grune & Stratton; 1978.

Edeiken J, Cotler JM. Ankle. In: Felson B, ed. *Roentgenology of fractures and dislocations*. New York: Grune & Stratton; 1978:151.

Eichenholtz S, Levine DB. Fractures of the tarsal navicular bone. *Clin Orthop* 1964;34:142.

Erickson SJ, Quinn SF, Kneeland JB, et al. MR imaging of the tarsal tunnel and related spaces: normal and abnormal findings with anatomic correlation. *Am J Roentgenol* 1990;155:323–328.

Essex-Lopresti P. The mechanism, reduction technique and results in fracture of the os calcis. *Br J Surg* 1982;39:395–419.

Faciszewski T, Burks RT, Manaster BJ. Subtle injuries of the Lisfranc joint. *J Bone Joint Surg Am* 1990;72A:1519–1522.

Farooki S, Yao L, Seeger LL. Anterolateral impingement of the ankle: effectiveness of MR imaging. *Radiology* 1998;207:357–360.

Feldman F, Singson RD, Rosenberg ZS, Berdon WE, Amodio J, Abramson SJ. Distal tibial triplane fractures: diagnosis with CT. *Radiology* 1987;164:429–435.

Finkel JE. Tarsal tunnel syndrome. *Radiol Clin North Am* 1994;2:67–78.

Fordyce AJW, Horn CV. Arthrography in recent injuries of the ligaments of the ankle. *J Bone Joint Surg Br* 1972;54B:116–121.

Freiberger RH. Introducing arthrography. In: Freiberger RH, Kaye JJ, eds. *Arthrography*. New York: Appleton-Century-Crofts; 1979:1–4.

Frost HM, Hanson CA. Technique for testing the drawer sign in the ankle. *Clin Orthop* 1977;123:49–51.

Gallo RA, Kolman BH, Daffner RH, Sciulli RL, Roberts CC, DeMeo PJ. MRI of tibialis anterior tendon rupture. *Skeletal Radiol* 2004;33:102–106.

Geissler WB, Tsao AK, Hughes JL. Fractures and injuries of the ankle. In: Rockwood CA, Green DP, Bucholz RW, Heckman JD, eds. *Rockwood and Green's fractures in adults*, 4th ed. Philadelphia: Lippincott-Raven Publishers; 1996:2236–2242.

Giannestras NJ. *Foot disorders. Medical and surgical management*, 2nd ed. Philadelphia: Lea & Febiger; 1973.

Giannestras NJ, Sammarco GL. Fractures and dislocations of the foot. In: Rockwood CA Jr, Green DP, eds. *Fractures*, vol. 2. Philadelphia: JB Lippincott; 1975.

Goldman AB. *Procedures in skeletal radiology*. New York: Grune & Stratton; 1984:181.

Goss CM, Gray H, eds. *Anatomy of the human body*, 29th ed. Philadelphia: Lea & Febiger; 1973:355–359.

Greenspan A. Imaging of the foot and ankle. *Curr Opin Orthop* 1996;7:61–68.

Greenspan A, Anderson MW. Imaging of the foot and ankle. *Curr Opin Orthop* 1993;4:68–75.

Gross RH. Fractures and dislocations of the foot. In: Rockwood CA, Wilkins KE, Kuig RE, eds. *Fractures in children*, vol. 3. Philadelphia: JB Lippincott; 1984:1043–1103.

Hansen ST. Foot injuries. In: Browner BD, Jupiter JB, Levine AM, Trafton PG, eds. *Skeletal trauma: fractures—dislocations—ligamentous injuries*. Philadelphia: WB Saunders; 1992:1960–1961.

Hawkins LG. Fractures of the lateral process of the talus. *J Bone Joint Surg Am* 1965;47A:1170–1175.

Hawkins LG. Fractures of the neck of the talus. *J Bone Joint Surg Am* 1970;52A:991–1002.

Heckman JD. Fractures and dislocations of the foot. In: Rockwood CA Jr, Green DP, Bucholz RW, Heckman JD, eds. *Rockwood and Green's fractures in adults*, 4th ed. Philadelphia: Lippincott-Raven; 1996:2295–2308.

Helgason JW, Chandnani VP. MR arthrography of the ankle. *Radiol Clin North Am* 1998;36:729–738.

Helms CA, Major NM, Anderson MW, et al. *Musculoskeletal MRI*, 2nd ed. Philadelphia: Saunders/Elsevier; 2009:384–429.

Herring C. Nomenclature for imaging planes of the feet [Letter]. *Am J Roentgenol* 1997;168:277.

Jahss MH. *Disorders of the foot and ankle*, vol. 2, 2nd ed. Philadelphia: WB Saunders; 1991.

Jones R. Fracture of the base of the fifth metatarsal by direct violence. *Ann Surg* 1902;35:697.

Kaye JJ. The ankle. In: Freiberger RH, Kaye JJ, eds. *Arthrography*. New York: Appleton-Century-Crofts; 1979:237–256.

Keck C. The tarsal-tunnel syndrome. *J Bone Joint Surg Am* 1962;44A:180–182.

Khoury NJ, El-Khoury GY, Saltzman CL, Kathol MH. Peroneus longus and brevis tendon tears: MR imaging evaluation. *Radiology* 1996;200:833–841.

Kirch MD, Erickson SJ. Normal magnetic resonance imaging of the ankle and foot. *Radiol Clin North Am* 1994;2:1–22.

Kleiger B. A review of ankle fractures due to lateral strains. *Bull Hosp Joint Dis Orthop Inst* 1968;29:138–186.

Kleiger B. Mechanisms of ankle injury. *Orthop Clin North Am* 1974;5:127–146.

Kleiger B, Mankin HJ. Fracture of the lateral portion of the distal tibial epiphysis. *J Bone Joint Surg Am* 1964;46A:25–32.

Klein MA, Spreitzer AM. MR imaging of the tarsal sinus and canal: normal anatomy, pathologic findings and features of the sinus tarsi syndrome. *Radiology* 1993;226:169–173.

Lau JTC, Daniels TR. Tarsal tunnel syndrome: a review of the literature. *Foot Ankle Int* 1999;20:201–209.

Lauge-Hansen N. Fractures of the ankle. Analytical survey as the basis of new experimental, roentgenological, and clinical investigations. *Arch Surg* 1948;56:259–317.

Lauge-Hansen N. Fractures of the ankle. II. Combined experimental-surgical and experimental-roentgenologic investigations. *Arch Surg* 1950;60:957–985.

Lauge-Hansen N. "Ligamentous" ankle fractures: diagnosis and treatment. *Acta Chir Scand* 1949;97:544–550.

Lee SH, Jacobson J, Trudell D, Resnick D. Ligaments of the ankle: normal anatomy with MR arthrography. *J Comput Assist Tomogr* 1998;22:807–813.

Leitch JM, Cundy PJ, Paterson DC. Three-dimensional imaging of a juvenile Tillaux fracture. *J Pediatr Orthop* 1989;9:602–603.

Lowery RBW. Fractures of the talus and os calcis. *Curr Opin Orthop* 1995;6:25–34.

Lynn MD. The triplane distal tibial epiphyseal fracture. *Clin Orthop* 1972;86:187–190.

Magid D, Michelson JD, Ney DR, Fishman EK. Adult ankle fractures: comparison of plain films and interactive two- and three-dimensional CT scans. *Am J Roentgenol* 1990;154:1017–1023.

Mainwaring BL, Daffner RH, Riemer BL. Pylon fractures of the ankle: a distinct clinical and radiologic entity. *Radiology* 1988;168:215–218.

Marmor L. An unusual fracture of the tibial epiphysis. *Clin Orthop* 1970;73:132–135.

Mast J. Pilon fractures of the tibia. In: Chapman MW, ed. *Operative orthopaedics*, 2nd ed. Philadelphia: JB Lippincott; 1993:711–729.

Meschan I. *Synopsis of roentgen signs.* Philadelphia: WB Saunders; 1962.

Michelson JD. Current concepts review: fractures about the ankle. *J Bone Joint Surg Am* 1995;77A:142–152.

Mink JH. Tendons. In: Deutsch AL, Mink JH, Kerr R, eds. *MRI of the foot and ankle.* Philadelphia: Lippincott-Raven Publishers; 1992:135–172.

Morrey BF, Cass JR, Johnson KA, Berquist TH. Foot and ankle. In: Berquist TH, ed. *Imaging of orthopedic trauma and surgery.* Philadelphia: WB Saunders; 1986: 407–498.

Müller ME, Allgower M, Schneider R, Willenegger H. *Manual of internal fixation techniques recommended by AO Group*, 2nd ed. New York: Springer-Verlag; 1979.

Müller ME, Nazarian S, Koch P. *The AO classification of fractures.* New York: Springer-Verlag; 1979.

Newburg AH. Osteochondral fractures of the dome of the talus. *Br J Radiol* 1979;52: 105–109.

Norman A, Kleiger B, Greenspan A, Finkel JE. Roentgenographic examination of the normal foot and ankle. In: Jahss MM, ed. *Disorders of the foot and ankle. Medical and surgical management*, vol. 1, 2nd ed. Philadelphia: WB Saunders; 1991:64–90.

Oae K, Takao M, Naito K, et al. Injury of the tibiofibular syndesmosis: value of MR imaging for diagnosis. *Radiology* 2003;227:155–161.

Pavlov H. Talo-calcaneonavicular arthrography. In: Freiberger RH, Kaye JJ, eds. *Arthrography.* New York: Appleton-Century-Crofts; 1979:257–260.

Peltier LF. Guillaume Dupuytren and Dupuytren's fracture. *Surgery* 1958;43:868–874.

Peltier LF. Percival Pott and Pott's fracture. *Surgery* 1962;51:280–286.

Peltier LF. Eponymic fractures: Robert Jones and Jones' fracture. *Surgery* 1972;71: 522–526.

Pennal GF. Fractures of the talus. *Clin Orthop* 1963;30:53–63.

Protas JM, Kornblatt BA. Fractures of the lateral margin of the distal tibia. The Tillaux fracture. *Radiology* 1981;138:55–57.

Rijke AM, Jones B, Vierhovt PAM. Stress examination of traumatized lateral ligaments of the ankle. *Clin Orthop* 1986;210:143–151.

Robbins MI, Wilson MG, Sella EJ. MR imaging of the anterior calcaneal process fractures. *Am J Roentgenol* 1999:172:475–479.

Robinson P, White LM. Soft-tissue and osseous impingement syndromes of the ankle: role of imaging in diagnosis and management. *Radiographics* 2002;22: 1457–1471.

Rogers LF. *Radiology of skeletal trauma.* New York: Churchill Livingstone, 1992:1319–1385.

Rosenberg ZS. Normal anatomy of ankle tendons and ligaments: computed tomography and magnetic resonance imaging. In: Taveras JM, Ferrucci JT, eds. *Radiology*, vol. 5. Hagerstown: JB Lippincott; 1989:1–6.

Rowe CR, Sakellarides HT, Freeman PA, Sorbie C. Fracture of the os calcis: a long-term follow-up study of 146 patients. *JAMA* 1963;184:920.

Sangeorzan BJ, Benirschke SK, Mosca V, et al. Displaced intra-articular fractures of the tarsal navicular. *J Bone Joint Surg Am* 1989;71A:1504–1510.

Sarrafian S. *Anatomy of the foot and ankle*, 2nd ed. Philadelphia: JB Lippincott; 1993.

Sartoris DJ, Mink JH, Kerr R. The foot and ankle. In: Mink JH, Deutsch AL, eds. *MRI of the musculoskeletal system: a teaching file.* New York: Raven Press; 1990: 389–450.

Schneck CD, Mesgarzadeh M, Bonakdarpour A. MR imaging of the most commonly injured ankle ligaments. Part II. Ligament injuries. *Radiology* 1992;184:507–512.

Schneck CD, Mesgarzadeh M, Bonakdarpour A, Ross GJ. MR imaging of the most commonly injured ankle ligaments. Part I. Normal anatomy. *Radiology* 1992;184: 499–506.

Schreibman KL, Gilula LA. Ankle tenography. A therapeutic imaging modality. *Radiol Clin North Am* 1998;36:739–756.

Schweitzer ME, Karasick D. MR imaging of disorders of the Achilles tendon. *Am J Roentgenol* 2000;175:613–625.

Staples OS. Ligamentous injuries of the ankle joint. *Clin Orthop* 1965;42:21–35.

Stewart I. Jones' fracture: fracture of the base of the fifth metatarsal. *Clin Orthop* 1960;16:190–198.

Swanson TV. Fractures and dislocations of the talus. In: Chapman MW, ed. *Operative orthopaedics*, 2nd ed. Philadelphia: JB Lippincott; 1993:2143–2145.

Tehranzadeh J, Stuffman E, Ross SDK. Partial Hawkins sign in fractures of the talus: a report of three cases. *Am J Roentgenol* 2003;181:1559–1563.

Teng MMH, Destovet JM, Gilula LA, Resnick D, Hembree JL, Oloff LM. Ankle tenography: a key to unexplained symptomatology. Part I: Normal tenographic anatomy. *Radiology* 1984;151:575–580.

Theodorou DJ, Theodorou SJ, Kakitsubata Y, Botte MJ, Resnick D. Fractures of proximal portion of fifth metatarsal bone: anatomic and imaging evidence of a pathogenesis of avulsion of the plantar aponeurosis and the short peroneal muscle tendon. *Radiology* 2003;226:857–865.

Theodorou DJ, Theodorou SJ, Resnick D. Proximal fifth metatarsal bone: not everything is a Jones' fracture [abstract]. *Radiology* 2001;221(P):667.

Vuori JP, Aro HT. Lisfranc joint injuries: trauma mechanisms and associated injuries. *J Trauma* 1993;35:40–45.

Watson-Jones R. *Fractures and joint injuries*, vols. I, II. St. Louis: Mosby; 1952,1955.

Weber BG. *Die Verletzungen des Oberen Sprunggelenkes.* Stuttgart: Verlag Hans Huber; 1972.

Weber MJ. Ankle fractures and dislocations. In: Chapman MW, ed. *Operative orthopaedics,*. 2nd ed. Philadelphia: JB Lippincott; 1993:731–745.

Wechsler RJ, Schweitzer ME, Karasick D, Deely DM, Glaser JB. Helical CT of talar fractures. *Skeletal Radiol* 1997;26:137–142.

Spine

Fractures of the vertebral column are important not only because of the structures involved but also because of the complications that may arise affecting the spinal cord. Constituting approximately 3% to 6% of all skeletal injuries, fractures of the vertebral column are most commonly encountered in people between the ages of 20 and 50 years, with the majority of cases (80%) being seen in males. Most spinal fractures occur at the thoracic and lumbar levels, but injury to the cervical area has a greater potential risk for spinal cord damage. Automobile accidents, sports-related activities (e.g., diving, skiing), and falls from heights are usually the circumstances in which spinal injuries are sustained.

The spine is composed of 33 vertebrae: 7 cervical, 12 thoracic, 5 lumbar, a sacrum of 5 fused segments, and a coccyx of 4 fused segments. With the exception of the first and second cervical vertebrae (C1 and C2), the vertebral bodies are separated from each other by intervertebral disks.

Cervical Spine

Anatomic–Radiologic Considerations

Structurally, the first and second cervical vertebrae possess anatomic features distinct from those of the remaining five cervical vertebrae (Fig. 11.1). The first cervical vertebra, C1 or atlas, is an osseous ring consisting of anterior and posterior arches connected by two lateral masses. The atlas has no body; its main structures are the lateral masses, also called "articular pillars." The second vertebra, C2 or axis, is a more complex structure whose distinguishing feature is the odontoid process, also known as the "dens" (tooth), projecting cephalad from the anterior surface of the body. The space between the odontoid process and the anterior arch of the atlas, called the "atlantal–dens interval," should not exceed 3 mm in adults, whether the head is flexed or extended. In children younger than age 8 years, this distance has been reported to be as much as 4 mm, particularly in flexion, secondary to greater ligamentous laxity.

The vertebrae C3-7 exhibit identical anatomic features and are more uniform in appearance, consisting of a vertebral body and a posterior neural arch, including the right and left pedicles and laminae, which together with the posterior aspect of the body enclose the spinal canal (Fig. 11.2). Extending caudad and cephalad from the junction of the pedicle and lamina on each side are superior and inferior articular processes, which form the apophyseal joints between the successive vertebrae. Extending

laterally from the pedicle on each side is a transverse process and, in the posterior portion, a spinous process extends from the junction of the laminae in the midline. The vertebra C7, in addition, is distinguished by its long spinous process and large transverse processes.

Radiographic examination of a patient with cervical spine trauma may be difficult and is usually limited to one or two projections; because frequently the patient is unconscious, there are associated injuries, and unnecessary movement risks damage to the cervical cord. The single most valuable projection in these instances is the lateral view, which may be obtained in the standard fashion or with the patient supine, depending on the condition (Fig. 11.3). This projection suffices to demonstrate most traumatic conditions of the cervical spine, including injuries involving the anterior and posterior arches of C1; the odontoid process, which is seen in profile; and the anterior atlantal–dens interval. The bodies and spinous processes of C2-7 are fully visualized, and the intervertebral disk spaces and prevertebral soft tissues can be adequately evaluated. The lateral radiograph may also be obtained in flexion of the neck, which is particularly effective in demonstrating suspected instability at C1-2 by allowing evaluation of the atlanto–odontoid distance; an increase in this distance to more than 3 mm indicates atlantoaxial subluxation. It is of the utmost importance on the lateral projection of the cervical spine that the C7 vertebra be visualized, because this is the most commonly overlooked site of injuries.

The lateral view of the cervical spine, including the lower part of the skull, is extremely important to evaluate the vertical subluxation involving the atlantoaxial articulation and the migration of the odontoid process into the foramen magnum. Several measurements are helpful to determine atlantoaxial impaction or cranial settling resulting in superior migration of the odontoid process (Figs. 11.4 to 11.7).

On the anteroposterior view of the cervical spine (Fig. 11.8), the bodies of the C3-7 vertebrae (and occasionally in young persons, even the C1 and C2 vertebrae) are well demonstrated, as are the uncovertebral (Luschka) joints and the intervertebral disk spaces. The spinous processes are seen almost on end, casting oval shadows resembling teardrops. A variant of the anteroposterior projection known as the open-mouth view (Fig. 11.9) may also be obtained as part of the standard examination. This view provides effective visualization of the structures of the first two cervical vertebrae. The body of C2 is clearly imaged, as are the atlantoaxial joints, the odontoid process, and the lateral spaces between the odontoid process and the articular pillars of C1. If the open-mouth view is difficult to obtain or the odontoid process is not clearly

TOPOGRAPHIC ANATOMY OF THE C-1 AND C-2 VERTEBRAE

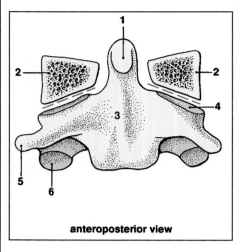

anteroposterior view

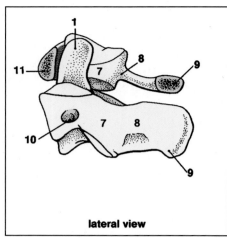

lateral view

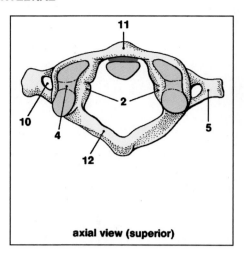

axial view (superior)

☐ atlantoaxial joint
▨ atlantal–dens interval

1 odontoid process of axis (dens)
2 lateral masses of atlas
3 body of axis
4 superior articular facet
5 transverse process
6 inferior articular facet

7 pedicle
8 lamina
9 spinous process
10 transverse foramen
11 anterior arch of atlas
12 posterior arch of atlas

▲
FIGURE 11.1   Topographic anatomy of the C1 and C2 vertebrae.

TOPOGRAPHIC ANATOMY OF THE C-4 AND C-5 VERTEBRAE

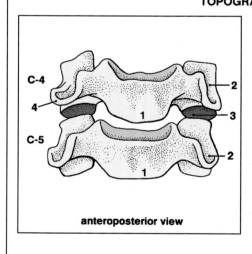

anteroposterior view

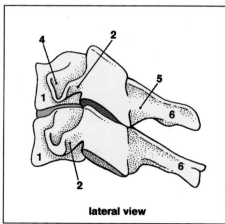

lateral view

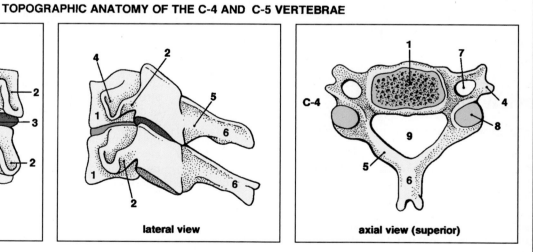

axial view (superior)

▨ intervertebral disk
▨ apophyseal joint

1 vertebral body
2 pedicle
3 inferior articular process
4 transverse process
5 lamina

6 spinous process
7 transverse foramen
8 superior articular process
9 spinal canal

▲
FIGURE 11.2   Topographic anatomy of the C4 and C5 vertebrae, representing the midcervical and lower cervical vertebrae.

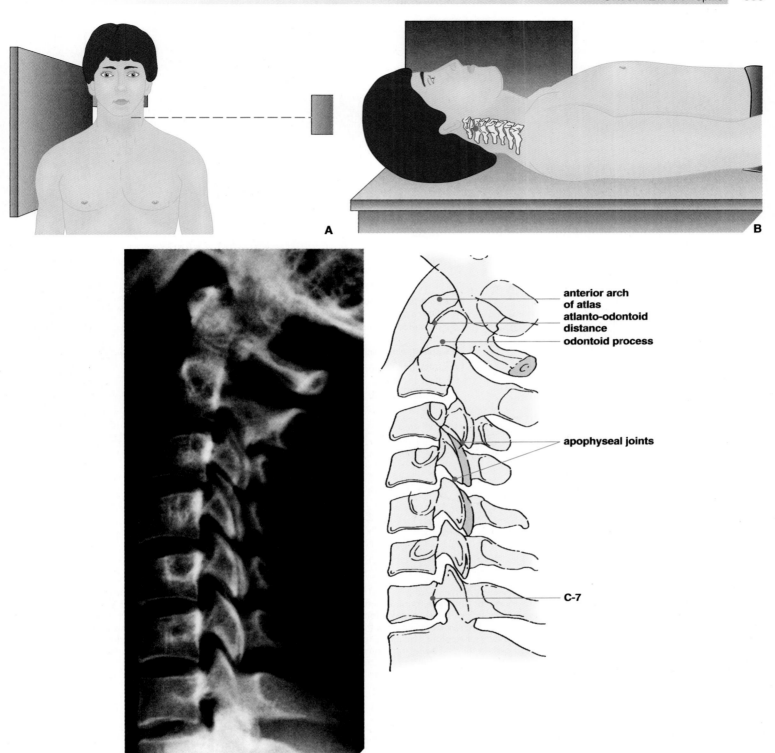

FIGURE 11.3   Lateral view. **(A)** For the erect lateral view of the cervical spine, the patient is standing or seated, with the head straight in the neutral position. The central beam is directed horizontally to the center of the C4 vertebra (at the level of the chin). **(B)** For the cross-table lateral view, the patient is supine on the radiographic table. The radiographic cassette (a grid cassette to obtain a clearer image) is adjusted to the side of the neck, and the central beam is directed horizontally to a point (*red dot*) approximately 2.5 to 3 cm caudal to the mastoid tip. **(C)** The radiograph in this projection clearly shows the vertebral bodies, apophyseal joints, spinous processes, and intervertebral disk spaces. It is mandatory to demonstrate the C7 vertebra. *(Continued)*

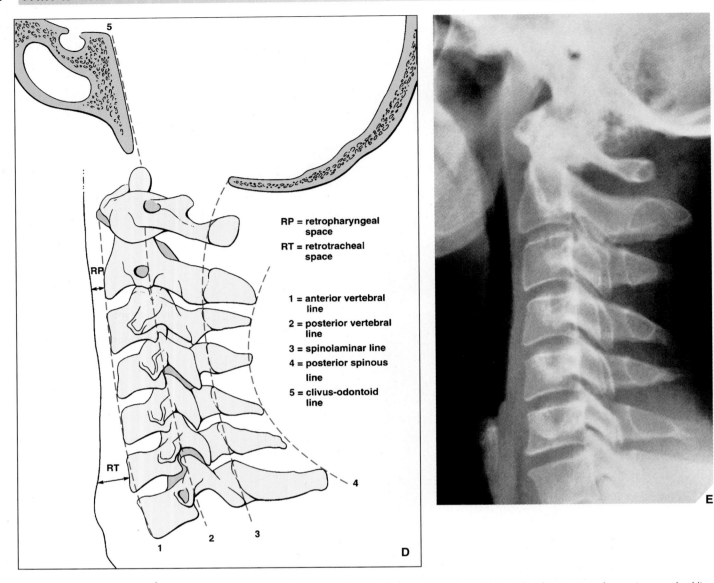

FIGURE 11.3 **Lateral view.** *Continued* **(D)** With this view, the five contour lines of the normal cervical spine can be demonstrated: anterior vertebral line drawn along anterior margins of the vertebral bodies; posterior vertebral line (outlines anterior margin of spinal canal), drawn along posterior margins of the vertebral bodies; spinolaminar line (outlines posterior margin of the spinal canal), drawn along the anterior margins of the bases of the spinous processes at the junction with lamina; posterior spinous line drawn along the tips of the spinous processes from C2-7, which should be running smoothly, without angulation or interruption; and the clivus-odontoid line, drawn from the dorsum sellae along the clivus to the anterior margin of the foramen magnum should point to the tip of the odontoid process at the junction of the anterior and middle thirds. The retropharyngeal space (distance from the posterior pharyngeal wall to the anteroinferior aspect of C2) should measure 7 mm or less; the retrotracheal space (distance from the posterior wall of the trachea to the anteroinferior aspect of C6) should measure no more than 22 mm in adults and 14 mm in children. **(E)** Low-kilovoltage technique demonstrates prevertebral soft tissues to better advantage.

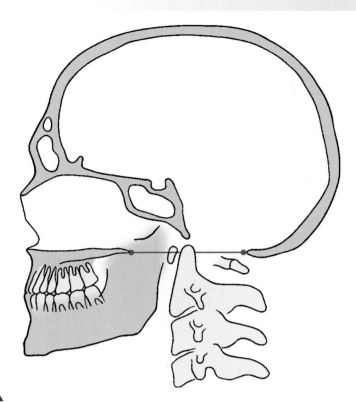

▲

FIGURE 11.4 The Chamberlain line. This line is drawn from the posterior margin of the foramen magnum (opisthion) to the dorsal (posterior) margin of the hard palate. The odontoid process should not project above this line more than 3 mm; a projection of 6.6 mm (±2 SD) above this line strongly indicates cranial settling.

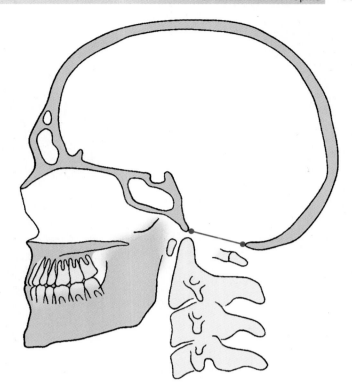

▲

FIGURE 11.5 The McRae line. This line defines the opening of the foramen magnum and connects the anterior margin (basion) with posterior margin (opisthion) of the foramen magnum. The odontoid process should be just below this line or the line may intersect only at the tip of the odontoid process. In addition, a perpendicular line drawn from the apex of the odontoid to this line should intersect it in its ventral quarter.

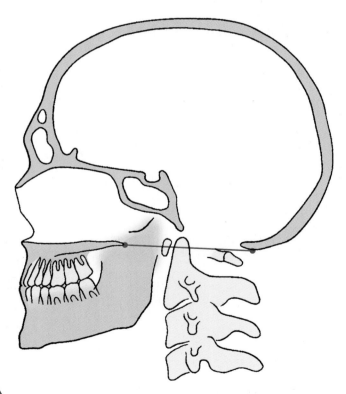

▲

FIGURE 11.6 The McGregor line. This line connects the posterosuperior margin of the hard palate to the most caudal part of the occipital curve of the skull. The tip of the odontoid normally does not extend more than 4.5 mm above the line.

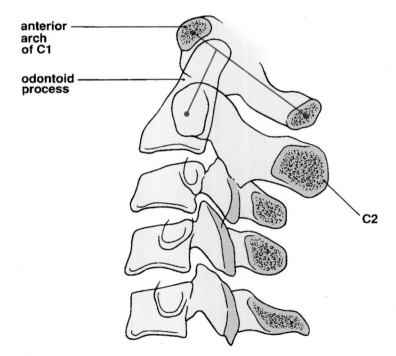

▲

FIGURE 11.7 Ranawat method. Ranawat and associates developed a method for determining the extent of the superior margin of the odontoid process, since the hard palate often is not identifiable on radiographs of the cervical spine. The coronal axis of C1 is determined by connecting the center of the anterior arch of the first cervical vertebra with its posterior ring. The center of the sclerotic ring in C2, representing the pedicles, is marked. The line is drawn along the axis of the odontoid process to the first line. The normal distance between C1 and C2 in men averages 17 mm (±2 mm SD), and in women, 15 mm (±2mm SD). A decrease in this distance indicates cephalad migration of C2.

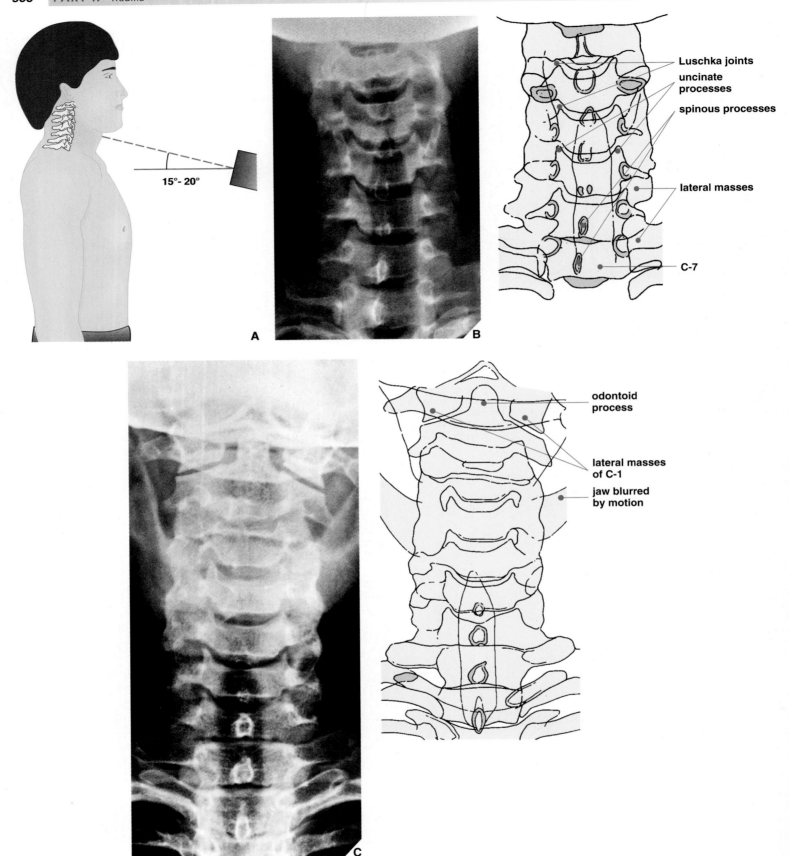

FIGURE 11.8 Anteroposterior view. (A) For the anteroposterior view of the cervical spine, the patient is either erect or supine. The central beam is directed toward the C4 vertebra (at the point of the Adam's apple) at an angle of 15 to 20 degrees cephalad. **(B)** The radiograph in this projection demonstrates the C3-7 vertebral bodies and the intervertebral disk spaces. The spinous processes are seen superimposed on the bodies, resembling teardrops. The C1 and C2 vertebrae are not adequately seen. For their visualization, the patient is instructed to open and close the mouth rapidly. Motion of the mandible blurs this structure, and C1 and C2 become visible **(C).**

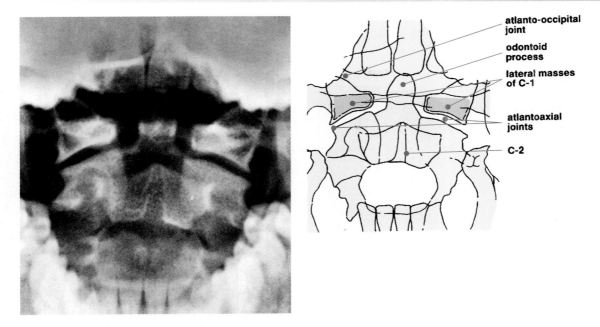

FIGURE 11.9 **Open-mouth view.** For the open-mouth view, the patient is positioned in the same manner as for the supine anteroposterior projection; the head is straight, in the neutral position. With the patient's mouth open as widely as possible, the central beam is directed perpendicular to the midpoint of the open mouth. During the exposure, the patient should softly phonate "ah" to affix the tongue to the floor of the mouth so that its shadow is not projected over C1 and C2. On the radiograph obtained in this projection, the odontoid process, the body of C2, and the lateral masses of the atlas are well demonstrated; the atlantoaxial joints are seen to best advantage.

visualized, particularly its upper half, then the Fuchs view may be helpful (Fig. 11.10). Oblique projections of the cervical spine (Fig. 11.11) are not routinely obtained, although at times they help visualize obscure fractures of the neural arch and abnormalities of the neural foramina and apophyseal joints. Special projections may occasionally be required for sufficient evaluation of the structures of the cervical spine. The pillar view (Fig. 11.12), which may be obtained in the anteroposterior or oblique projection, serves to demonstrate the lateral masses of the cervical vertebrae, and the swimmer's view (Fig. 11.13) may be used for better demonstration of the C7, T1, and T2 vertebrae, which on the standard lateral or oblique projection are obscured by the overlapping clavicle and soft tissues of the shoulder girdle. Fluoroscopy and videotaping are usually of little help in acute injuries because pain may prevent the necessary movement for positioning.

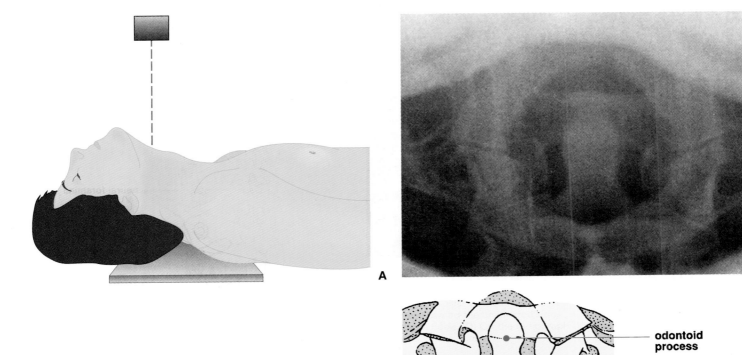

FIGURE 11.10 **Fuchs view.** (A) For the Fuchs views of the odontoid process, the patient is supine on the table, with the neck hyperextended. The central beam is directed vertically to the neck just below the tip of the chin. (B) On the radiograph obtained in this projection, the odontoid, especially its upper half, is clearly visualized.

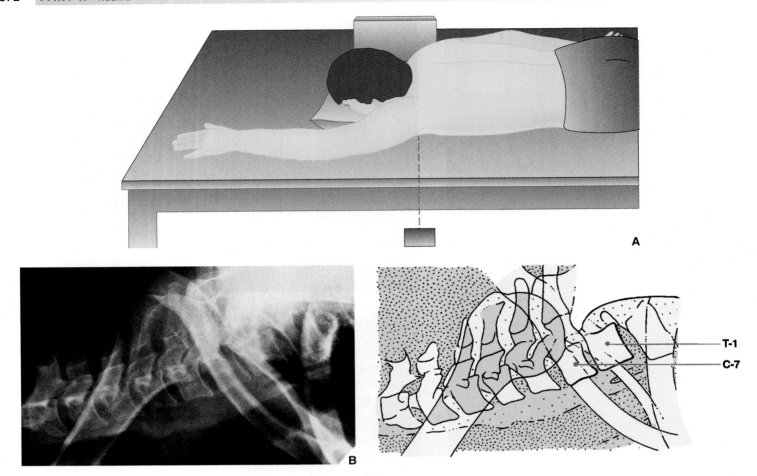

FIGURE 11.13 Swimmer's view. (A) For the swimmer's view of the cervical spine, the patient is placed prone on the table with the left arm abducted 180 degrees and the right arm by the side, as if swimming the crawl. The central beam is directed horizontally toward the left axilla. The radiographic cassette is against the right side of the neck, as for the standard cross-table lateral view. **(B)** The radiograph obtained in this projection provides adequate visualization of the C7, T1, and T2 vertebrae, which would otherwise be obscured by the shoulders.

In order to not overlook an abnormality during evaluation of the conventional radiographs of the cervical spine, systematic approach to the imaging study is of paramount importance. "Job list" such as provided in Figure 11.14 may be of help to methodically analyze the various anatomic structures.

Ancillary imaging techniques play an important role in the evaluation of suspected spinal trauma. Computed tomography (CT) is commonly used modality (Fig. 11.15). In the evaluation of fractures of the odontoid process, for example, CT is particularly helpful. In determining the extent of cervical spine injuries in general, including soft-tissue trauma, this technique provides valuable information regarding the integrity of the spinal canal and the localization of fracture fragments within the canal.

Magnetic resonance imaging (MRI) has become the most effective modality to evaluate vertebral trauma because of the impressive quality of its images and its multiplanar capabilities, which allow the examination of acutely traumatized patients without moving them. In evaluating fractures, MRI is useful not only to determine the relationship of bony fragments that may be displaced in the vertebral canal but also to demonstrate the full extent of injury, especially to the soft tissues and the spinal cord. The effect of the trauma on the spinal cord can be directly imaged, and spinal cord compression can be diagnosed. The superior soft-tissue contrast resolution of MRI can reveal minimal edema and small quantities of hemorrhage within the spinal cord. Injury to ligamentous structures and extradural pathology also may be readily identified. In the cervical spine, 3-mm-thick sagittal sections and 5-mm-thick axial sections are routinely obtained. The most effective are spin-echo T1- and T2- or T2*-weighted images obtained in the sagittal plane. Sagittal MR images permit the evaluation of vertebral body alignment and integrity, along with the size of the spinal canal (Fig. 11.16A). On the parasagittal section, the articular facets are well demonstrated (Fig. 11.16B). More recently, fast scans (fast spin-echo [FSE]) have been advocated for demonstrating injuries in the sagittal and axial planes. These fast gradient-echo pulse sequences have become a popular addition to, or a replacement for, spin-echo T2-weighted sequences. Gradient-echo sequences have short acquisition times and adequate resolution and show a satisfactory "myelographic effect" between cerebrospinal fluid and adjacent structures (Fig. 11.16C,D).

On T1-weighted sagittal images of the cervical spine, the vertebral bodies that contain yellow (or fatty) marrow are imaged as high-signal-intensity structures (see Fig. 11.16A). The intervertebral disks and the cord demonstrate intermediate signal intensity, while cerebrospinal fluid demonstrates low signal intensity.

On T2-weighted sagittal images, the vertebral bodies are imaged with low signal intensity, the intervertebral disks and cerebrospinal fluid demonstrate high signal intensity, and the cord demonstrates intermediate-to-low signal intensity.

On the axial images obtained in T1 weighting, the disk demonstrates intermediate signal intensity, the spinal fluid has low signal intensity, and the cord has high-to-intermediate signal intensity.

On the axial images obtained in T2* weighting, multiplanar gradient recalled (MPGR), the disk is of high signal intensity and the spinal fluid is also of high signal intensity, in contrast to the spinal cord, which images as an intermediate-signal-intensity structure. The bone demonstrates low signal intensity (see Fig. 11.16C,D).

In addition to its imaging capabilities, MR also has, according to some investigators, a prognostic value when attempting to predict the degree of neurologic recovery following trauma.

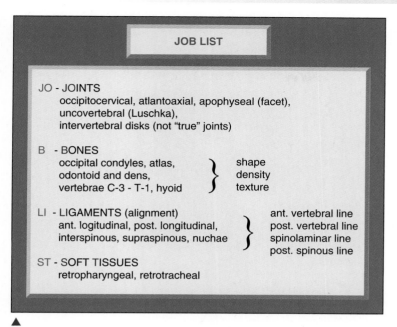

JOB LIST

JO - JOINTS
  occipitocervical, atlantoaxial, apophyseal (facet),
  uncovertebral (Luschka),
  intervertebral disks (not "true" joints)

B - BONES
  occipital condyles, atlas,   } shape
  odontoid and dens,   } density
  vertebrae C-3 - T-1, hyoid   } texture

LI - LIGAMENTS (alignment)
  ant. logitudinal, post. longitudinal,   ant. vertebral line
  interspinous, supraspinous, nuchae   }   post. vertebral line
                                            spinolaminar line
                                            post. spinous line

ST - SOFT TISSUES
  retropharyngeal, retrotracheal

▲
FIGURE 11.14 "JOB LIST" for evaluation of the cervical spine.

It has to be stressed, however, that CT alone or combined with myelography remains the better choice for evaluating vertebral fractures, especially when they are nondisplaced or involve the posterior elements (lateral masses, facets, laminae, spinous processes), largely because of the limitations of spatial resolution of MRI. In addition, imaging the acutely injured patient is difficult. The patient may be unstable or immobilized with either a halo or traction device unsuitable for the magnetic environment. For this reason, radiographs, CT, and myelography continue to play a significant role in the evaluation of the acutely traumatized spine. However, as Hyman and Gorey noted, chronic injury to the spinal cord is most accurately evaluated with MRI.

Since the advent of CT and MRI, myelography alone (Fig. 11.17A–C) is now rarely indicated in the evaluation of cervical injuries; if needed, this examination is usually performed in conjunction with CT (Fig. 11.17D).

For a summary of the preceding discussion in tabular form, see Tables 11.1 to 11.3.

Injury to the Cervical Spine

Traumatic conditions involving the cervical spine are almost always the result of indirect stress forces acting on the head and neck, the position of which at the time of impact determines the site and type of damage. As Daffner stressed, vertebral fractures occur in predictable and reproducible patterns that are related to the type of force applied to the vertebral column. The same force applied to the cervical, thoracic, or lumbar spine will result in injuries that appear quite similar, producing a pattern of recognizable signs that span the spectrum from mild soft-tissue damage to severe skeletal and ligamentous disruption. Daffner termed these patterns "fingerprints" of spinal injury; they depend on the mechanism of injury, which may be an excessive movement in any direction: flexion, extension, rotation, vertical compression, shearing, distraction—or a combination of these.

Of the greatest initial importance in suspected cervical injuries, however, is the question of stability of a fracture or dislocation (Table 11.4). Stability of the vertebral column depends on the integrity of the major skeletal components, the intervertebral disks, the apophyseal joints, and the ligamentous structures. One of the most important factors is the integrity of the ligaments of the spine: the supraspinous and interspinous ligaments, the posterior longitudinal ligament, and the ligamenta flava, which together with the capsule of the apophyseal joints constitute the so-called posterior ligament complex of Holdsworth (Fig. 11.18). Injuries are stable by virtue of intact ligamentous structures; the more severe the damage to these structures, the more liable they are to further displacement, with greater risk of sequelae involving the spinal cord. Radiographic findings that indicate instability, according to Daffner, are displacement of vertebrae, widening of the interspinous or interlaminar

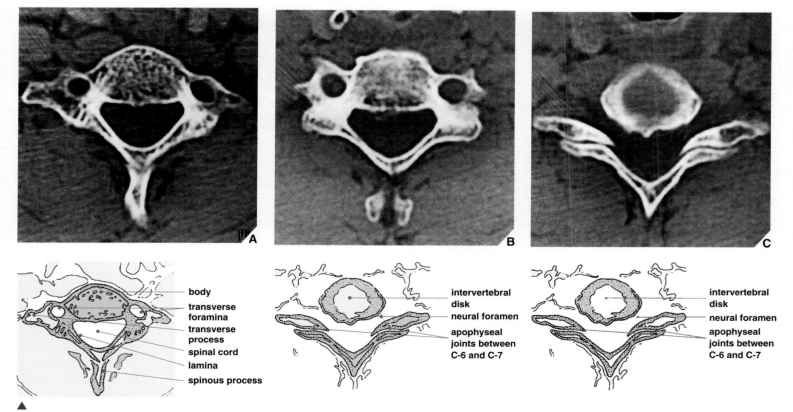

body
transverse foramina
transverse process
spinal cord
lamina
spinous process

intervertebral disk
neural foramen
apophyseal joints between C-6 and C-7

intervertebral disk
neural foramen
apophyseal joints between C-6 and C-7

▲
FIGURE 11.15   **CT of the cervical spine.** CT sections through the body of C6 (**A**), C7 (**B**), and the C6-7 intervertebral space (**C**) show the normal appearance of these structures.

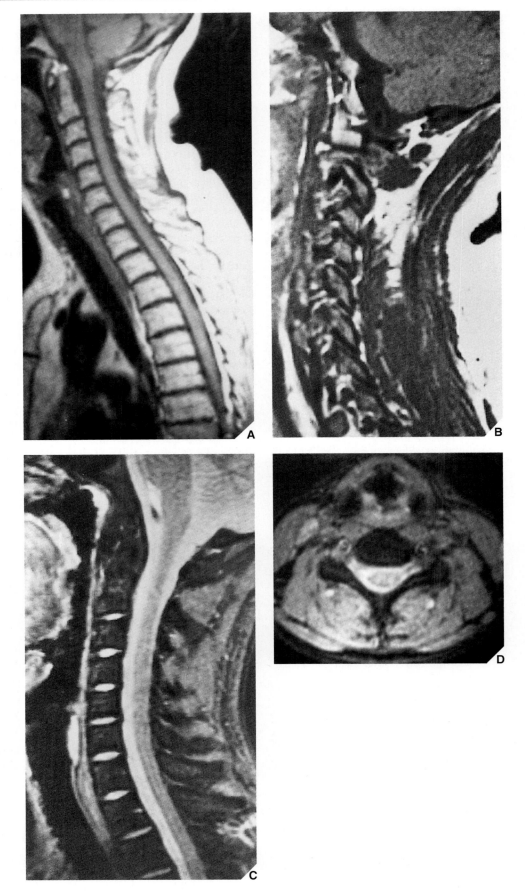

FIGURE 11.16 MRI of normal cervical spine. (A) T1-weighted (TR 800/TE 20 msec) spin-echo sagittal midline section demonstrates anatomic details of the bones and soft tissues. The craniocervical junction is well outlined. The foramen magnum is defined by the fat within the occipital bone and clivus. The anterior and posterior arches of C1 appear as small oval marrow-containing structures at the upper cervical spine. The spinal cord is of an intermediate signal intensity outlined by lower signal of CSF. The intervertebral disks are imaged with low signal intensity. **(B)** Parasagittal section demonstrates the apophyseal joints. **(C)** T2*-weighted MPGR sagittal image shows vertebral bodies and spinous processes to be of low signal intensity. The high water content of the intervertebral disks produces a very high signal similar to that of cerebrospinal fluid. The cord is imaged as an intermediate signal intensity structure. **(D)** Axial section demonstrates neural foramina and nerve roots. The cervical cord is faintly outlined. (From Beltran J, 1990, with permission.)

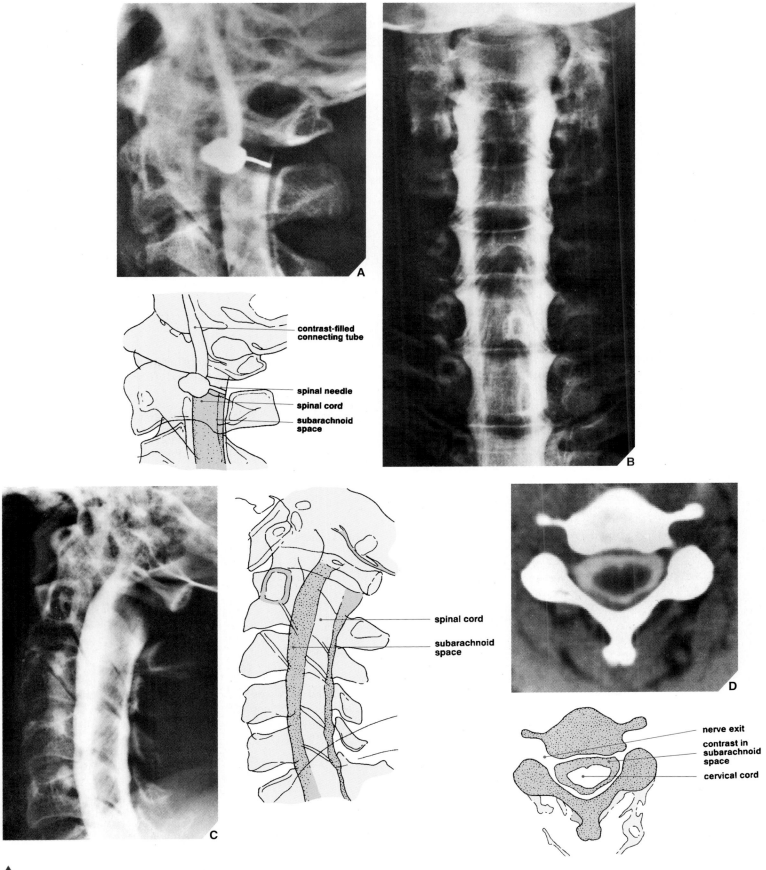

FIGURE 11.17 **Myelography of the cervical spine.** For myelographic examination of the cervical spine, the patient is recumbent on the table, lying on the left side. Using fluoroscopy, the point of entrance of the needle is marked at the C1-2 level, and a 22-gauge needle is inserted vertically, the tip being directed to the dorsal aspect of the subarachnoid space, above the lamina of C2. Free flow of spinal fluid indicates the correct position of the needle. (**A**) Approximately 10 mL of iohexol or iopamidol, water-soluble nonionic iodinated contrast agents, at a concentration of 240 mg iodine per mL, is slowly injected. Radiographs are obtained in the posteroanterior (**B**), cross-table lateral (**C**), and oblique projections. (Oblique projections, however, are obtained not by rotating the patient but by angling the radiographic tube 45 degrees.) If the lower segment of the cervical spine is not satisfactorily demonstrated or if the upper thoracic segment needs to be visualized, a radiograph may also be obtained in the swimmer's position. Myelography demonstrates the thecal sac filled with contrast and the outline of the normal nerve roots and nerve root sleeves. (**D**) CT section at the level C3-4 obtained following myelography demonstrates the normal appearance of contrast in the subarachnoid space.

TABLE 11.1 **Tissue MRI Signal Characteristics**

Signal Intensity	T1 Weighting	T2 Weighting	Gradient Echo (T2*)
Low signal	Cortical bone Vertebral end plates Degenerated disks Osteophytes Spinal vessels Cerebrospinal fluid	Cortical bone Vertebral end plates Ligaments Degenerated disks Osteophytes Spinal vessels Nerve roots	Bone marrow Vertebral bodies Vertebral end plates Ligaments Osteophytes
Intermediate signal	Spinal cord Paraspinal soft tissue Intervertebral disks Nerve roots Osteophytes	Paraspinal soft tissue Osteophytes Spinal cord Facet cartilage Bone marrow Vertebral bodies	Annulus fibrosus Spinal cord Nerve roots
High signal	Epidural venous plexus Hyaline cartilage Epidural and paraspinal fat Bone marrow Vertebral bodies	Intervertebral disks Cerebrospinal fluid	Intervertebral disk Cerebrospinal fluid Facet cartilage Epidural venous plexus Arteries

Modified from Kaiser MC, Ramos L, 1990, with permission.

TABLE 11.2 **Standard and Special Radiographic Projections for Evaluating Injury to the Cervical Spine**

Projection	Demonstration

Anteroposterior	Fractures of the bodies of C3-7
	Abnormalities of the
	  Intervertebral disk spaces
	  Uncovertebral (Luschka) joints

Open-mouth	Fractures of
	  Lateral masses of C1
	  Odontoid process
	  Body of C2
	Jefferson fracture
	Abnormalities of atlantoaxial joints

Fuchs	Fractures of odontoid process

Lateral	Occipitocervical dislocation
	Fractures of
	  Anterior and posterior arches of C1
	  Odontoid process
	  Bodies of C2-7
	  Spinous processes
	Hangman's fracture
	Burst fracture
	Teardrop fracture
	Clay shoveler's fracture
	Simple wedge (compression) fracture
	Unilateral and bilateral locked facets
	Abnormalities of
	  Intervertebral disk spaces
	  Prevertebral soft tissues
	  Atlanto-odontoid space

In flexion	Atlantoaxial subluxation

Oblique	Abnormalities of
	  Intervertebral (neural) foramina
	  Apophyseal joints

Pillar (anteroposterior or oblique)	Fractures of lateral masses (pillars)
Swimmer's	Fractures of C7, T1, and T2

TABLE 11.3 **Ancillary Imaging Techniques for Evaluating Injury to the Cervical, Thoracic, and Lumbar Spine**

Technique	Demonstration

Tomography (almost completely replaced by CT)	Fractures, particularly of the odontoid process
	Localization of displaced fracture fragments
	Progress of treatment
	  Fracture healing
	  Status of spinal fusion

Myelography	Obstruction or compression of the dural (thecal) sac
	Displacement or compression of the spinal cord
	Abnormalities of
	  Spinal nerve root sleeves (sheaths)
	  Subarachnoid space
	Herniated disk

Diskography	Limbus vertebra Schmorl node Herniated disk

Computed Tomography (alone or combined with myelography and/or diskography)	Fractures of the occipital condyles
	Abnormalites of
	  Lateral recesses and neural foramina
	  Spinal cord
	Complex fractures of the vertebrae
	Localization of displaced fracture fragments in spinal canal
	Spondylolysis
	Disk herniation
	Paraspinal soft-tissue injury (e.g., hematoma)
	Progress of treatment
	  Fracture healing
	  Status of spinal fusion

Radionuclide Imaging (scintigraphy, bone scan)	Subtle or obscure fractures Recent versus old fractures Fracture healing
Magnetic Resonance Imaging	Same as myelography and CT combined Annular tears

TABLE 11.4   **Classification of Injuries to the Cervical Spine by Mechanism of Injury and Stability**

Condition	Stability
Flexion Injuries	
Occipitocervical dislocation	Unstable
Subluxation	Stable
Dislocation in facet joints (locked facets)	
Unilateral	Stable
Bilateral	Unstable
Odontoid fractures	
Type I	Stable
Type II	Unstable
Type III	Stable
Wedge (compression) fracture	Stable
Clay shoveler's fracture	Stable
Teardrop fracture	Unstable
Burst fracture	Stable or unstable
Extension Injuries	
Occipitocervical dislocation	Unstable
Fracture of posterior arch of C1	Stable
Hangman's fracture	Unstable
"Extension teardrop" fracture	Stable
Hyperextension fracture–dislocation	Unstable
Compression Injuries	
Occipital condyle fracture (types I, II)	Stable
Jefferson fracture	Unstable
Burst fracture	Stable or unstable
Laminar fracture	Stable
Compression fracture	Stable
Shearing Injuries	
Lateral vertebral compression	Stable
Lateral dislocation	Unstable
Transverse process fracture	Stable
Lateral mass fracture	Stable
Rotation Injuries	
Occipital condyle fracture (type III)	Unstable
Rotary subluxation C1-2	Stable
Fracture–dislocation	Unstable
Facet and pillar fractures	Stable or unstable
Transverse process fracture	Stable
Distraction Injuries	
Occipitocervical dislocation	Unstable
Hangman's fracture	Unstable
Atlantoaxial subluxation	Stable or unstable

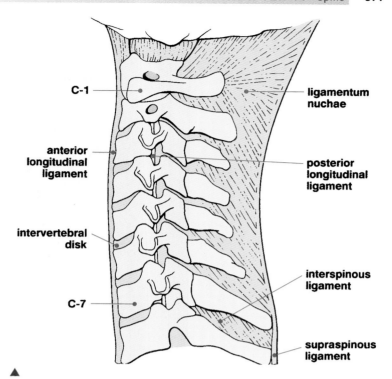

▲ FIGURE 11.18   Anatomy of the principal ligaments of the cervical spine.

spaces, widening of the apophyseal joints, widening and elongation of the vertebral canal manifesting as widening of the interpedicular distance in transverse and vertical planes, and disruption of the posterior vertebral body line. Only one of these features needs to be present to make a radiographic assumption of an unstable injury. These remarks on stability also apply to injuries of the thoracic and lumbar segments.

Recently, Daffner and colleagues modified the classification of cervical vertebral injuries on the basis of CT findings, introducing "major" injuries and "minor" injuries. The former are defined as having either radiographic or CT evidence of instability, with or without associated localized or central neurologic findings. The latter injuries have no radiographic or CT evidence of instability and do not produce or have no potential to cause neurologic findings. According to these authors, cervical injury should be classified as "major" if the following radiographic and CT criteria are present: displacement of more than 2 mm in any plane, widening of the vertebral body in any plane, widening of the interspinous or interlaminar space, widening of the facet joints, disruption of the posterior vertebral body line, widening of the disk space,

vertebral burst, locked or perched facets either unilateral or bilateral, "hanged man" fracture of C2, fracture of the odontoid process, and type III occipital condyle fracture. All other types of fractures are considered to be "minor."

Fractures of the Occipital Condyles

Fractures of the occipital condyles are rare. This injury is often overlooked and is not obvious on the conventional radiography. Instead, the diagnosis requires a high index of suspicion, after which confirmation can easily be obtained by CT with coronal reformation. A classification system of occipital condyle fractures was devised by Anderson and Montesano in 1988 based on fracture morphology, pertinent anatomy, and biomechanics (Fig. 11.19).

Type I is an impacted occipital condyle fracture occurring as the result of axial loading force on the skull, similar to the mechanism for a Jefferson fracture. CT shows comminution of the occipital condyle with minimal or no displacement of fragments into the foramen magnum (Fig. 11.20). Although the ipsilateral alar ligament may be functionally inadequate, spinal stability is ensured by the intact tectorial membrane and contralateral alar ligament.

Type II occipital condyle fracture occurs as a component of a basilar skull fracture. On axial CT sections of the base of the skull, a fracture line can be seen exiting the occipital condyle and entering the foramen magnum. The mechanism of injury is a direct blow to the skull. Stability is maintained by intact alar ligaments and tectorial membrane.

Type III is an avulsion fracture of the medial aspect of occipital condyle by the alar ligament: a small fragment of the condyle is displaced toward the tip of odontoid process (Fig. 11.21). The alar ligaments are primary restraints of occipitocervical rotation and lateral bending. Therefore, the mechanism of injury in this type is rotation, lateral bending, or a combination of the two. After avulsion of the occipital condyle, the contralateral alar ligament and tectorial membrane are loaded. Therefore, this type of occipital condyle fracture is a potentially unstable injury.

Occipitocervical Dislocations

Traumatic occipitocervical dislocations are usually fatal and therefore rarely present a clinical problem. With the improvement in trauma care, which now includes on-site-intubation and immediate resuscitation as

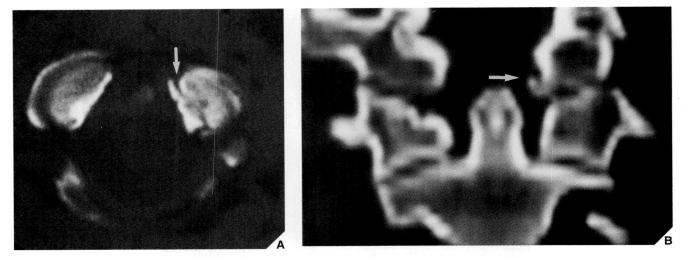

▲
FIGURE 11.21 Fracture of the occipital condyle. A 16-year-old girl was assaulted and sustained a blow injury to the head. Conventional radiographs of the skull and upper cervical spine were interpreted as normal. **(A)** Axial CT section through the base of the skull shows a type III fracture of the occipital condyle (*arrow*). **(B)** Coronal reformatted CT image confirms the presence of an evulsion fracture (*arrow*).

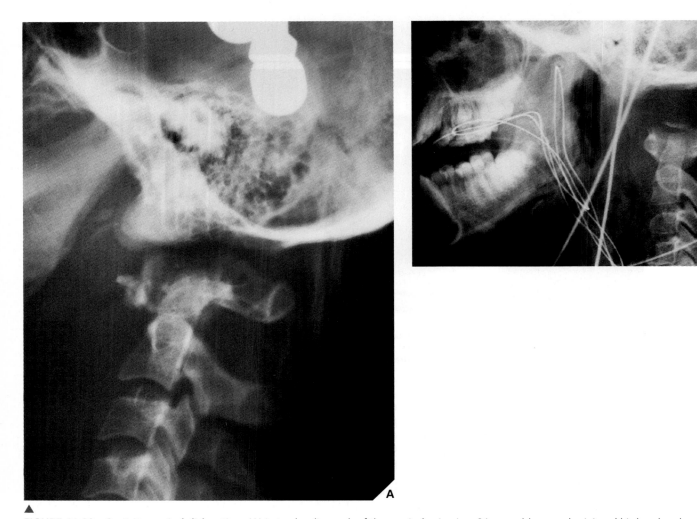

▲
FIGURE 11.22 Occipitocervical dislocation. (A) Lateral radiograph of the cervical spine in a 24-year-old man, who injured his head and neck in a motorcycle accident that resulted in complete quadriplegia, shows type I of occipitocervical dislocation: the occipital condyles are anteriorly displaced in relation to C1 vertebra. (From Greenspan A, Montesano PX, 1993, with permission.) **(B)** In another patient, lateral radiograph demonstrates a type IIA vertical occipitocervical dislocation. (From Chapman MW, 1993, with permission.)

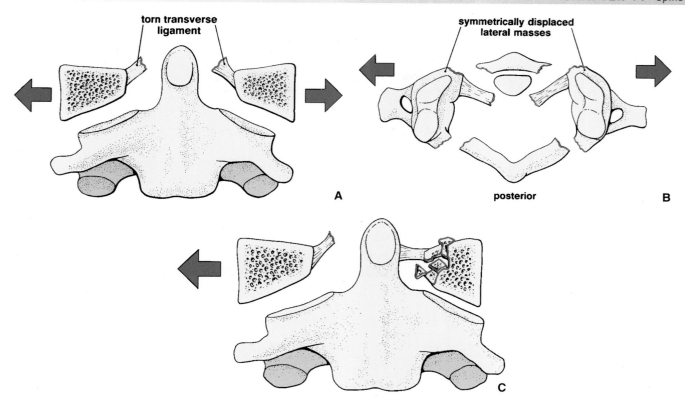

▲
FIGURE 11.23 **Jefferson fracture.** The classic Jefferson fracture, seen here schematically on the anteroposterior (**A**) and axial (**B**) views, exhibits a characteristic symmetric overhang of the lateral masses of C1 over those of C2. Lateral displacement of the articular pillars results in disruption of the transverse ligaments. (**C**) On occasion, only unilateral lateral displacement of an articular pillar may be present.

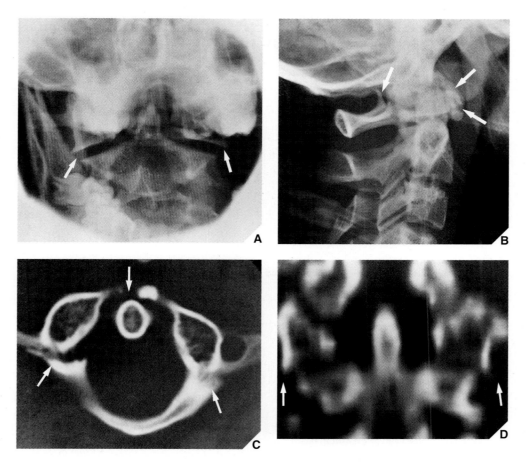

▲
FIGURE 11.24 **Jefferson fracture.** A 19-year-old man sustained a neck injury while being mugged. (**A**) Open-mouth anteroposterior view of the cervical spine shows lateral displacement of the lateral masses of the atlas (*arrows*), suggesting a ring fracture of C1. (**B**) Lateral view demonstrates fracture lines of the posterior and anterior arch of C1 (*arrows*). (**C**) CT section demonstrates two fracture lines of the posterior arch and a fracture of the anterior arch (*arrows*). (**D**) CT coronal reformation confirms lateral displacement of the lateral masses (*arrows*).

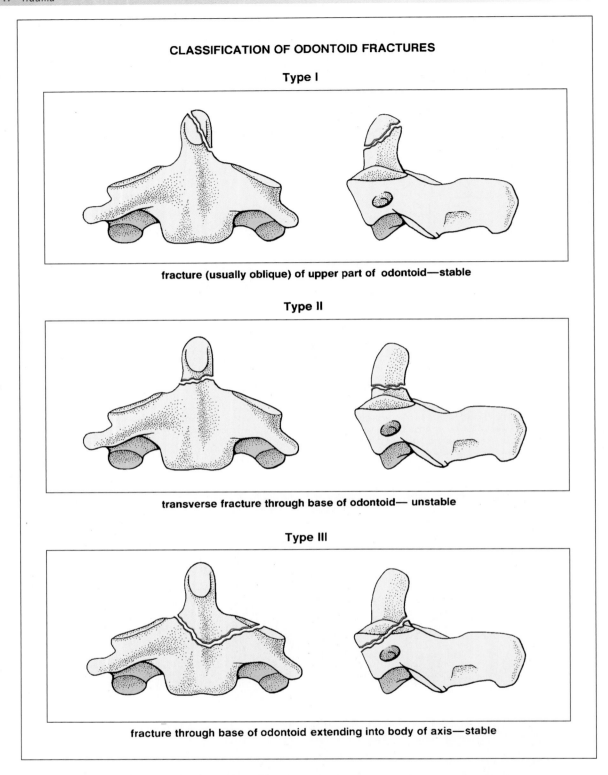

CLASSIFICATION OF ODONTOID FRACTURES

Type I

fracture (usually oblique) of upper part of odontoid—stable

Type II

transverse fracture through base of odontoid— unstable

Type III

fracture through base of odontoid extending into body of axis—stable

▲

FIGURE 11.25   Classification of odontoid fractures. (Modified from Anderson LD, D'Alonzo RT, 1974, with permission.)

ossification center (ossiculum terminale of Bergman) or os odontoideum.

Type II   Transverse fractures through the base of the odontoid are unstable injuries (Fig. 11.26). Conservative treatment has been complicated by nonunion in approximately 35% of cases; therefore, surgical fusion is the usual method of treatment.

Type III   Fractures through the base of the odontoid extending into the body of the axis are stable injuries (see Fig. 11.27). Conservative treatment is usually sufficient.

The best techniques for demonstrating fractures of the dens are the anteroposterior view, including the open-mouth variant, or Fuchs projection, and the lateral projection; thin-section trispiral tomography (at present rarely used) may also prove effective in delineating ambiguous or subtle features (see Figs. 11.26C,D and 11.27C).

CT detection of the dens fractures, particularly type II, may be difficult if the axial sections are obtained parallel to the usually horizontally oriented fracture line. For this reason, it is essential to obtain routinely reformatted images in coronal and sagittal planes (Fig. 11.28).

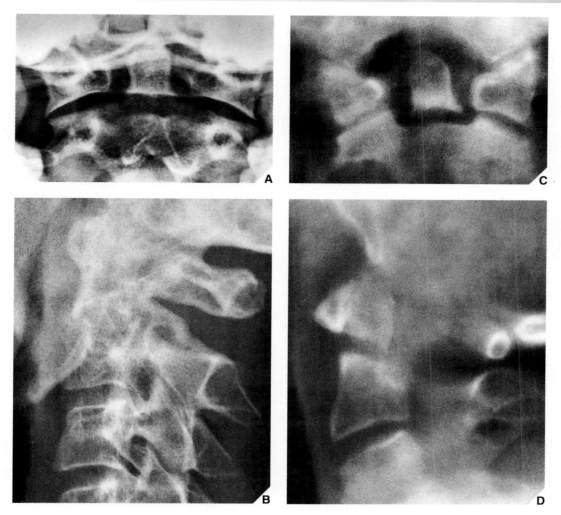

FIGURE 11.26 **Fracture of the odontoid process.** A 62-year-old man sustained a flexion injury of the cervical spine in an automobile accident. Open-mouth anteroposterior (**A**) and lateral (**B**) views demonstrate a fracture line at the base of the odontoid process, but the details of this injury cannot be well appreciated. Thin-section trispiral tomographic sections in the anteroposterior (**C**) and lateral (**D**) projections confirm the fracture at the base of the dens. This is a type II (unstable) fracture.

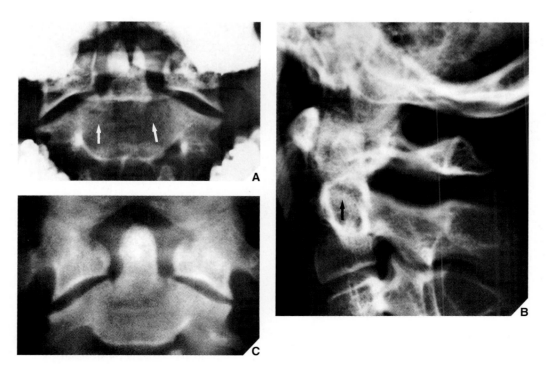

FIGURE 11.27 **Fracture of the odontoid process.** A 24-year-old man fell on his head in a skiing accident. Open-mouth anteroposterior (**A**) and lateral (**B**) radiographs of the cervical spine demonstrate a fracture of the odontoid process extending into the body of C2 (*arrows*)—a type III stable fracture. The diagnosis was confirmed by trispiral tomography in the anteroposterior projection (**C**).

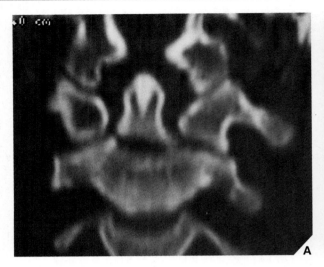
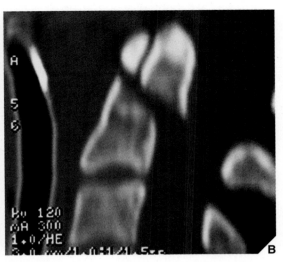

FIGURE 11.28   **Fracture of the odontoid process.** A 50-year-old man sustained a flexion neck injury during a motorcycle accident. The conventional radiographs of the cervical spine suggested odontoid fracture but were not conclusive. Coronal (**A**) and sagittal (**B**) reformatted CT images clearly demonstrate a type II odontoid fracture.

Hangman's Fracture. In 1912, Wood-Jones described the pathomechanism associated with execution by hanging. He found that hyperextension and distraction resulted in bilateral fractures through the pedicles of the axis, with anterior dislocation of the body and subsequent tearing of the spinal cord. A similar fracture, which in fact constitutes traumatic spondylolisthesis of C2, is common in automobile accidents, when the face strikes the windshield before the vertex of the head, forcing the neck into hyperextension. This injury, which accounts for 4% to 7% of all cervical spine fractures and dislocations, may present as simple, nondisplaced fractures through the pedicles of the axis or as

fractures through the arches with anterior subluxation and angulation of C2 onto C3 (Fig. 11.29). The fracture line usually lies anterior to the inferior articular facet of C2 in both variants, but displaced fractures are more often associated with ligament disruption and intervertebral disk injuries. The best projection for demonstrating this injury is the lateral view (Fig. 11.30).

Hangman's fractures (which probably should be correctly called "hanged man" fractures) have been classified into three types (Fig. 11.31). Type I injury is characterized by the fracture through the pedicle of C2 extending between the superior and inferior facets. Type

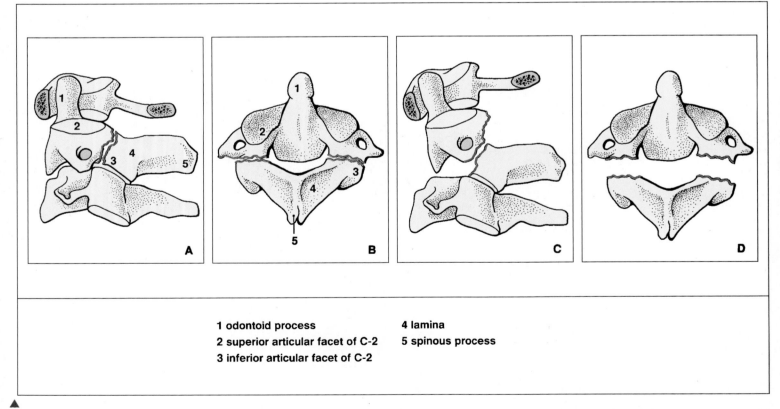

1 odontoid process
2 superior articular facet of C-2
3 inferior articular facet of C-2
4 lamina
5 spinous process

FIGURE 11.29   **Hangman's fracture.** This injury may present as nondisplaced fractures through the arches of C2, as seen here schematically on the lateral (**A**) and axial (**B**) views, or as displaced fractures with anterior angulation (**C**) and (**D**) associated with disruption of ligaments, the intervertebral disk, or articular facets.

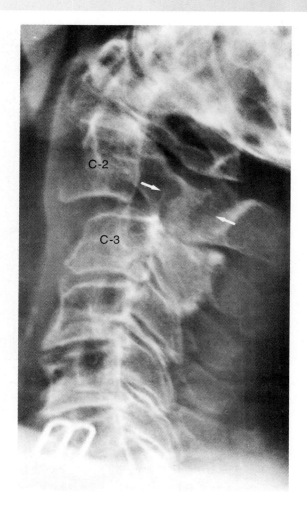

▲

FIGURE 11.30 **Hangman's fracture.** A 62-year-old man sustained a severe hyperextension injury to the cervical spine in an automobile accident. Lateral radiograph shows a fracture through the pedicles of C2 (*arrows*) associated with C2-3 subluxation, a typical finding in hangman's fracture.

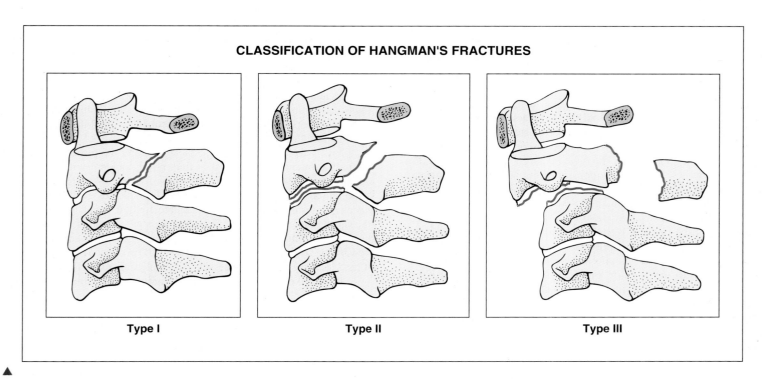

▲

FIGURE 11.31 **Classification of hangman's fractures.** (Modified from Levine AM, Edwards CC, 1985, with permission.)

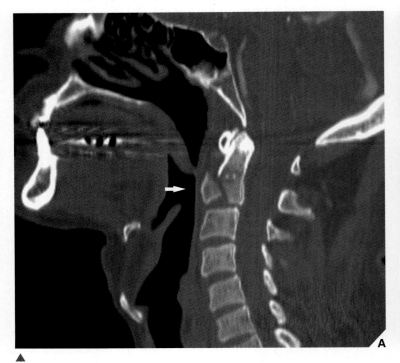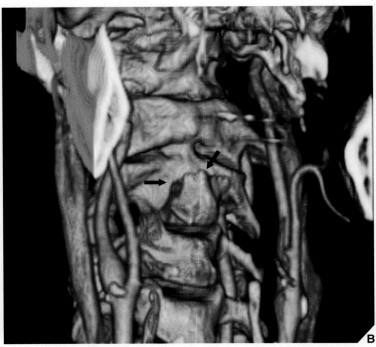

FIGURE 11.32   CT of fracture of the body C2. (A) Sagittal CT reformatted image shows a fracture of the body of C2 vertebra (*arrow*). Because clinically injury to the neck vessels was suspected, 3D CT angiographic study was performed. The 3D reconstructed image **(B)** confirmed the fracture (*arrows*), but the neck arteries were intact.

II injury constitutes a type I fracture with concomitant disruption of intervertebral disk C2-3. Type III injury consists of a type II fracture associated with a C2-3 facet dislocation.

Fracture of the Body of C2. Fracture of the body of C2 (Fig. 11.32) is rare, usually presented as a stable "extension tear drop" injury (see later). It may occasionally be complicated by trauma to the vessels.

Fractures of the Mid and Lower Cervical Spine

Burst Fracture. The mechanism of this fracture is identical to that of Jefferson fractures involving C1, but burst fractures are seen in the lower cervical vertebrae (C3-7). When the nucleus pulposus, which is normally contained within the intervertebral disk, is driven through the fractured vertebral end plate into the vertebral body, the body explodes from within, resulting in a comminuted fracture. Typically, the posterior fragment is posteriorly displaced and may cause injury to the spinal cord. If the posterior ligament complex is not disrupted, a burst fracture is stable. Occasionally, with ligamentous disruption, a burst fracture becomes unstable. Radiographically, it is characterized by a vertical split in the vertebral body, as seen on the anteroposterior view, but the lateral projection better demonstrates the extent of comminution and posterior displacement (Fig. 11.33A). The most revealing modality in the case of burst fracture is CT since it demonstrates the details of fracture of the posterior part of the vertebral body in the axial plane (Fig. 11.33B).

Teardrop Fracture. The most severe and most unstable of injuries of the cervical spine, teardrop fracture, is characterized by posterior displacement of the involved vertebra into the spinal canal, fracture of its posterior elements, and disruption of the soft tissues, including the ligamentum flavum and the spinal cord, at the level of injury. In addition, stress applied to the anterior longitudinal ligament causes it either to rupture or to avulse from the vertebral body, taking along a piece of the anterior surface of the body. This small, triangular or teardrop-shaped fragment is usually anteriorly and inferiorly displaced (Fig. 11.34). Associated spinal cord injury results in the acute anterior cervical cord syndrome, consisting of abrupt quadriplegia and loss of pain and temperature distinction; however, posterior column senses—position, vibration, and motion—are usually preserved.

The lateral view is the best radiographic projection for demonstrating this injury, but CT is superior technique for this purpose (Figs. 11.35 and 11.36). The evaluation of spinal cord compression requires MRI (Fig. 11.37).

It should be kept in mind in the evaluation of this fracture that occasionally a triangular fragment of bone similar in shape and location to that seen in the classic teardrop fracture may be noted in an extension type of injury. This "extension teardrop" fracture, however, is completely different; it is a stable fracture without the potentially dangerous complications of the flexion type of injury, and usually occurs at the level of C2 or C3 (Fig. 11.38, see also Fig. 11.32).

Clay Shoveler's Fracture. This oblique or vertical fracture of the spinous process of C6 or C7 is caused by an acute powerful flexion, such as that produced by shoveling. Deriving its name from its common occurrence in Australian clay miners in the 1930s, clay shoveler's fracture was simultaneously labeled with the same name in Germany, where it was seen among workers building the Autobahn. A direct blow to the cervical spine or indirect trauma to the neck in automobile accidents can result in similar injury.

Clay shoveler's fracture is a stable fracture, the posterior ligament complex remaining intact, and is thus not associated with neurologic damage. The best radiographic projection for demonstrating this injury is the lateral view of the cervical spine (Fig. 11.39A). If C7 cannot be visualized despite good positioning and technique, for example, because of a short, thick neck or wide shoulders, then the swimmer's view should be obtained. This fracture can also be identified on the anteroposterior view by the so-called ghost sign (Fig. 11.39B) produced by displacement of the fractured spinous process. CT is rarely indicated (Fig. 11.40).

Simple Wedge (Compression) Fracture. Resulting from hyperflexion of the cervical spine, a simple wedge fracture generally occurs in the midcervical or lower cervical segment. There is anterior compression (wedging) of the vertebral body, and although the posterior ligament complex is stretched, it remains intact, making this a stable fracture. The lateral projection of the cervical spine adequately demonstrates this injury (Fig. 11.41).

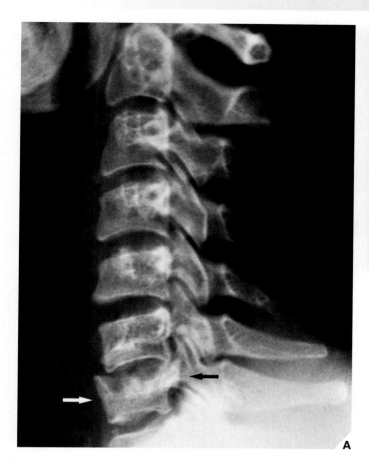
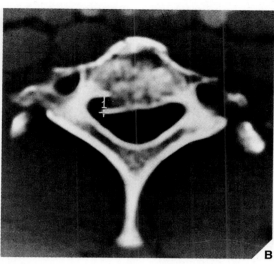

FIGURE 11.33 Burst fracture. A 40-year-old man was ejected from a motorcycle and hit the pavement with the vertex of his head. **(A)** Lateral radiograph of the cervical spine demonstrates a comminuted fracture of the body of C7, involving the anterior and middle columns (*arrows*). **(B)** A CT section confirms the burst fracture. The posterior part of the vertebral body is displaced into the spinal canal.

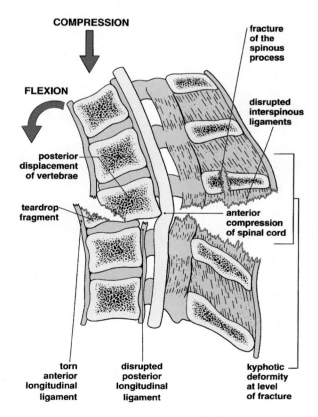

FIGURE 11.34 Teardrop fracture. Teardrop fracture, seen here schematically in a sagittal section of the lower cervical spine, is the most serious and unstable of cervical spine injuries. Disruption of the anterior longitudinal ligament may cause avulsion of a teardrop-shaped fragment of the anterior surface of the body of C5. This fracture is also typified by posterior displacement of the involved vertebra and fracture of its posterior elements. Depending on the severity of the injury, varying degrees of spinal cord damage may result.

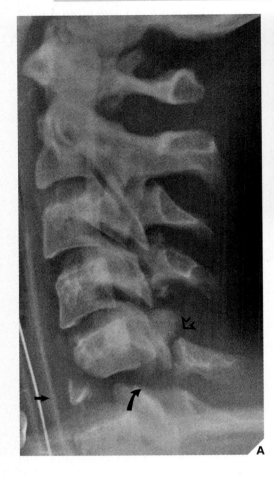

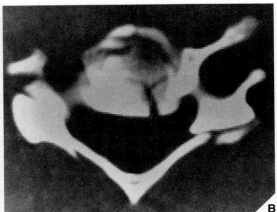

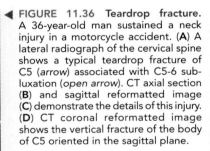

A

B

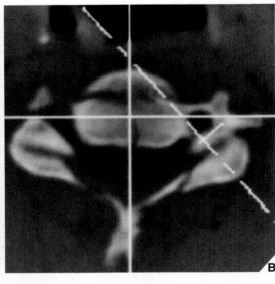

◄ FIGURE 11.35 Teardrop fracture. A 38-year-old man sustained an injury of the neck in a motorcycle accident. (**A**) Lateral radiograph of the cervical spine demonstrates an avulsion fracture of the anteroinferior aspect of the body of C5 (*arrow*) and a fracture of its spinous process (*open arrow*). The lamina of C4 is fractured as well. There is disruption of the facets at the level of C5-6 with marked widening (*curved arrow*). There is posterior displacement of all vertebrae including and above C5. (**B**) Axial CT section demonstrates in addition a markedly comminuted fracture of the body of C5.

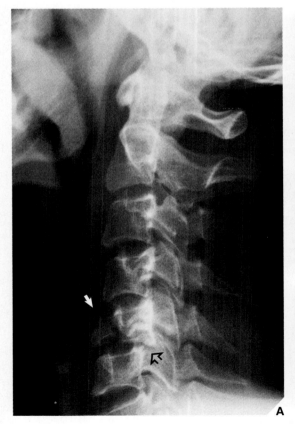

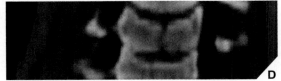

A

B

C

D

◄ FIGURE 11.36 Teardrop fracture. A 36-year-old man sustained a neck injury in a motorcycle accident. (**A**) A lateral radiograph of the cervical spine shows a typical teardrop fracture of C5 (*arrow*) associated with C5-6 subluxation (*open arrow*). CT axial section (**B**) and sagittal reformatted image (**C**) demonstrate the details of this injury. (**D**) CT coronal reformatted image shows the vertical fracture of the body of C5 oriented in the sagittal plane.

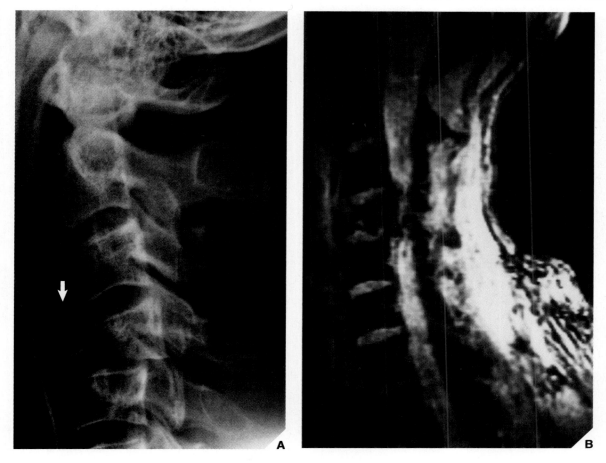

FIGURE 11.37 Teardrop fracture. A 38-year-old man, an unrestrained passenger, was injured in a car accident. (A) A lateral radiograph of the cervical spine shows a teardrop fracture of C4 (*arrow*). (B) A sagittal gradient-echo (MPGR) MR image shows posterior displacement of the C4 vertebral body compromising the spinal canal and almost complete transection of the cervical cord. Extensive high-signal soft-tissue edema and hemorrhage are evident.

FIGURE 11.38 Extension teardrop fracture. A 37-year-old man sustained an extension injury to the cervical spine in a fall. Lateral radiograph of the spine demonstrates an extension teardrop fracture of the vertebral body of C3. Note that, in contrast to a flexion-type injury, there is no subluxation, and the posterior vertebral and spino-laminar lines are not disrupted.

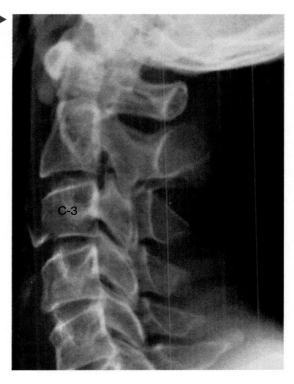

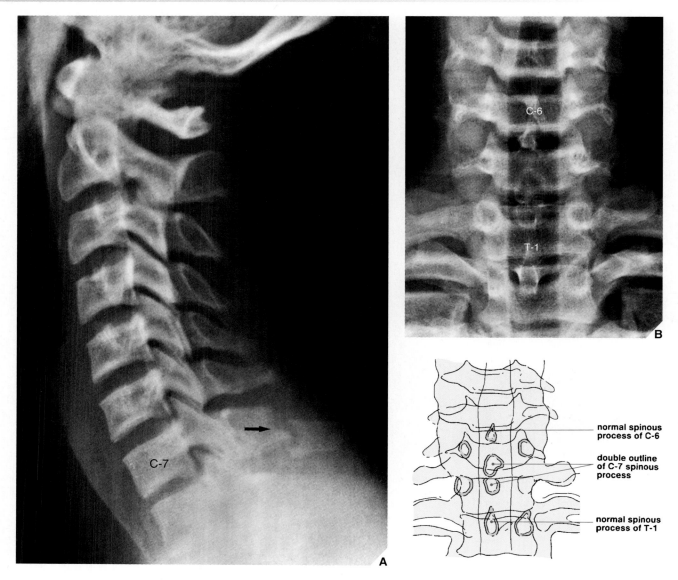

normal spinous process of C-6

double outline of C-7 spinous process

normal spinous process of T-1

FIGURE 11.39 **Clay shoveler's fracture.** A 22-year-old man sustained a neck injury in an automobile accident. (**A**) Lateral radiograph of the cervical spine shows a fracture of the spinous process of C7 (*arrow*), identifying this injury as a clay shoveler's fracture. (**B**) On the anteroposterior view, clay shoveler's fracture can be identified by the appearance of a double spinous process for C7. This ghost sign is secondary to slight caudal displacement of the fractured tip of the spinous process.

Locked Facets

Unilateral Locked Facets. This type of injury is secondary to the flexion-rotation force with subsequent tearing of the joint capsule of one facet and posterior ligamentous complex. In the absence of disk space widening or subluxation, unilateral facet locking is a relatively stable injury. Frequently, however, there is approximately 25% anterior subluxation. These patients are at risk of sustaining nerve root injury or, rarely, a Brown-Sequard type spinal cord injury.

Bilateral Perched Facets. This type of vertebral subluxation occurs as a result of a flexion injury. There is disruption of the posterior ligamentous complex, and the inferior and superior articular processes of the involved vertebrae are in apposition. The shingled appearance of the facet joints is changed to a configuration in which the laminar cortices intersect at one point (Figs. 11.42 and 11.43A). This injury is best diagnosed on the lateral and oblique projections of the cervical spine, or CT with sagittal and oblique reformation.

Bilateral Locked Facets. Bilateral dislocation of the cervical spine in the facet joints is the result of extreme flexion of the head and neck; it is an unstable condition caused by extensive disruption of the posterior

ligament complex. Interlocking of the articular facets is initiated by the forward movement of the inferior articular facet of the upper vertebra over the superior articular facet of the underlying vertebra (Fig. 11.43). This causes the lamina and spinous process of the two adjacent vertebrae to spread apart and the vertebral bodies to sublux. In the later stage of dislocation, the inferior articular facet of the upper vertebra locks in front of the superior articular facet of the lower vertebra, which results in complete anterior dislocation. The configuration of this injury leads to complete disruption of the posterior ligament complex, the posterior longitudinal ligament, the annulus fibrosus, and frequently the anterior longitudinal ligament. It is also associated with a high incidence of cervical spinal cord damage.

The lateral projection of the cervical spine, preferably a crosstable lateral, is sufficient to demonstrate bilaterally locked facets. The key to the correct diagnosis is the presence of malalignment of the affected vertebrae associated with disruption of all lateral cervical spine landmarks (see Fig. 11.3D) and position of the dislocated facets posteriorly and cephalad in relation to the facets of the vertebra above (Fig. 11.43C).

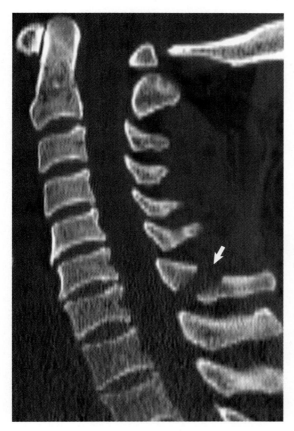

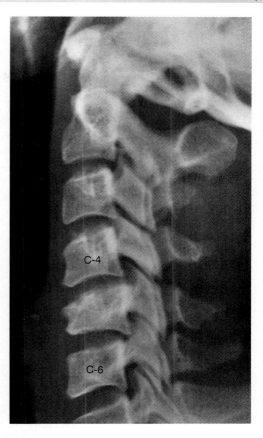

FIGURE 11.40 **CT of the clay shoveler's fracture.** A 33-year-old man injured his neck in wrestling competition. Conventional radiographs were not diagnostic because of excessive neck musculature. Sagittal CT reformatted image of the cervical spine shows a displaced fracture of the spinous process of C7 (*arrow*).

FIGURE 11.41 **Compression (wedge) fracture.** A 30-year-old woman sustained a neck injury in an automobile accident. Lateral radiograph of the cervical spine demonstrates a simple wedge fracture of C5.

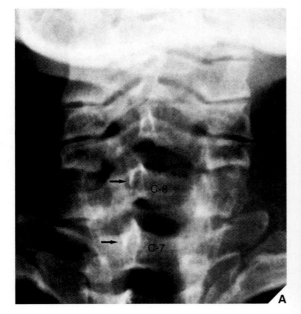

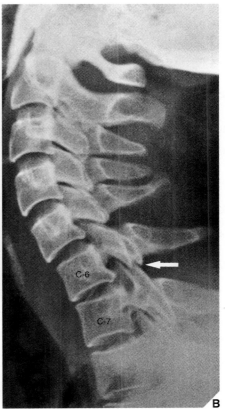

FIGURE 11.42 **Perched facets.** A 34-year-old woman injured her neck in a skiing accident. (**A**) Pillar view of the cervical spine demonstrates bilateral obliteration of the facet joints at the C6-7 level. The joints above appear normal. Displacement of the spinous processess to the right (*arrows*) is the result of rotation. (**B**) Lateral view shows perched facets of vertebrae C6 and C7 (*arrow*).

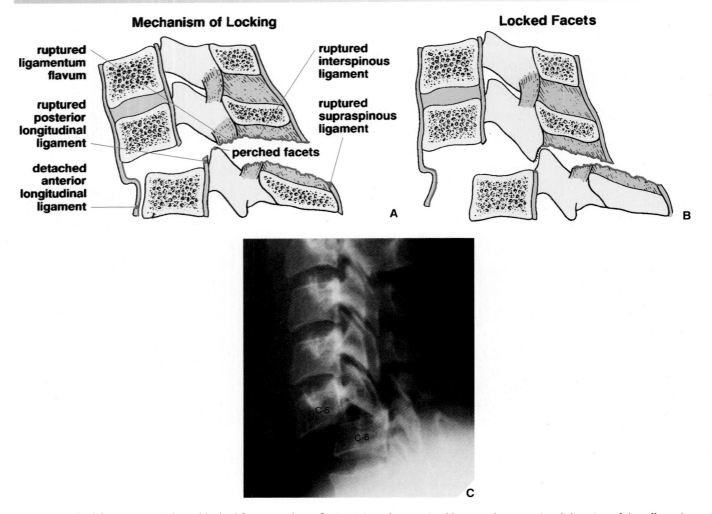

FIGURE 11.43 **Locked facets. (A,B)** Bilateral locked facets is a hyperflexion injury characterized by complete anterior dislocation of the affected vertebra. It is always associated with extensive ligament disruption and carries a great risk of cervical spinal cord damage. **(C)** A 36-year-old man injured his neck in a motor vehicle accident that resulted in quadriplegia. Lateral radiograph of the cervical spine shows bilateral locked facets at the C5-6 level.

Thoracolumbar Spine

Anatomic–Radiologic Considerations

The standard radiographic projections for evaluating an injury to the *thoracic spine* are the anteroposterior (Fig. 11.44) and lateral (Fig. 11.45) views. The lateral projection is obtained using a technique called autotomography, which requires shallow breathing by the patient to blur the structures involved in respiratory motion and give a clear view of the thoracic vertebral column.

As in cervical spine injuries, CT and MRI play leading roles in the evaluation of fractures of the thoracic spine, particularly in defining the extent of injury. Axial CT images provide an exellent means of evaluating not only osseous abnormalities but also soft-tissue injuries, and reformatted sagittal, coronal and 3D reconstructed images, in addition, allow to demonstrate axially oriented fracture lines that can be missed on axial sections. MR images are ideal for evaluating concomitant soft-tissue injury, particularly to the spinal cord and thecal sac.

The standard radiographic examination for evaluating injuries of the *lumbar spine* includes the anteroposterior, lateral, and oblique projections, supplemented by coned-down lateral spot films of the lumbosacral junction (L5-S1). The anteroposterior view is usually sufficient for evaluating traumatic conditions involving the vertebral bodies and transverse processes; the intervertebral disk spaces are also well demonstrated, except for the lowest (L5-S1) (Fig. 11.46). The spinous processes, seen as teardrops, and the articular facets, however, are not well demonstrated

on this projection. A characteristic configuration of the end plates of the L3-5 vertebral bodies can be observed on the anteroposterior projection. Normally, the inferior aspects of these vertebrae form what is called a "Cupid's bow" contour (Fig. 11.47), which is lost in cases of compression fractures affecting this part of the vertebral column.

On the lateral projection of the lumbar spine, the vertebral bodies are seen in profile, and the superior and inferior end plates are well demonstrated (Fig. 11.48). Fractures of the spinous processes can be adequately evaluated on this projection, as can abnormalities involving the intervertebral disk spaces, including L5-S1. As in the cervical spine, an oblique projection of the lumbar spine can be obtained from the patient's anterior or posterior aspect, although the posteroanterior oblique projection is preferable (Fig. 11.49). This view is particularly effective in demonstrating the facet joints (articular facets) and reveals a configuration of the elements of adjoining vertebrae, known as the "Scotty dog" formation (Fig. 11.49C,D), which was first identified by Lachapele.

Ancillary imaging techniques are frequently used in the evaluation of traumatic conditions of the lumbar spine. As in cervical and thoracic injuries, CT provides useful information in assessing the extent of damage in vertebral body fractures and abnormalities involving the intervertebral disks (Fig. 11.50). Moreover, myelography (Fig. 11.51) and diskography (Fig. 11.52) are often required, and they are frequently performed in conjunction with CT examination (Fig. 11.53).

MRI is now frequently used in the evaluation of injury to the thoracic and lumbar spine. In general, the images are obtained using a

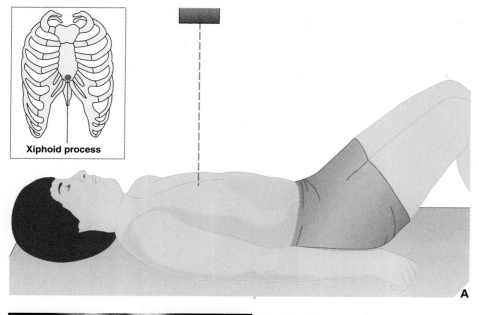

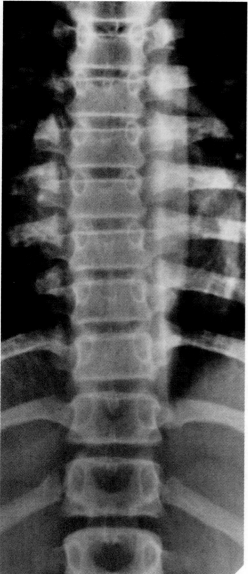

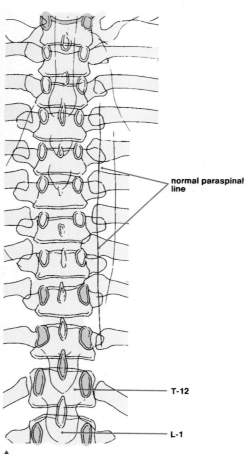

Xiphoid process

normal paraspinal line

T-12

L-1

▲
FIGURE 11.44 **Anteroposterior view of the thoracic spine. (A)** For the anteroposterior view of the thoracic spine, the patient is supine on the table, with the knees flexed to correct the normal thoracic kyphosis. The central beam is directed vertically about 3 cm above the xiphoid process. **(B)** On the radiograph in this projection, the vertebral end plates and pedicles and the intervertebral disk spaces are seen. The height of the vertebrae can be determined, and changes in the paraspinal line can be evaluated.

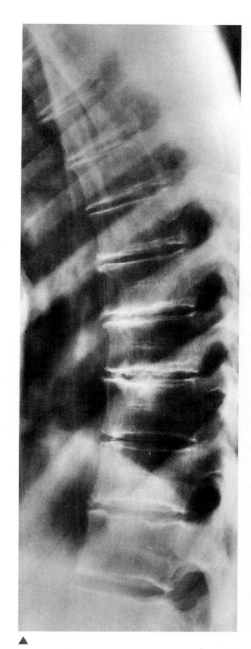

▲
FIGURE 11.45 **Lateral view of the thoracic spine.** For the lateral view of the thoracic spine, the patient is erect with the arms elevated. To eliminate structures that would obscure the bony elements of the thoracic spine, the patient is instructed to breathe shallowly during the exposure. The central beam is directed horizontally to the level of the T6 vertebra with about 10-degree cephalad angulation. The radiograph in this projection demonstrates a lateral image of the vertebral bodies and intervertebral disk spaces.

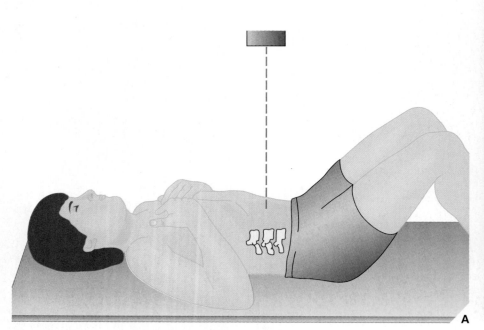

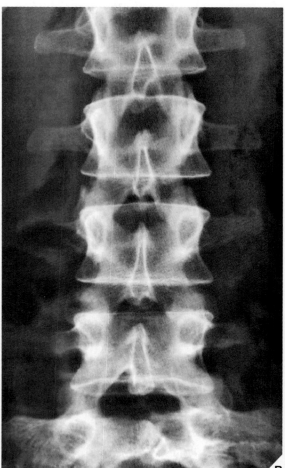

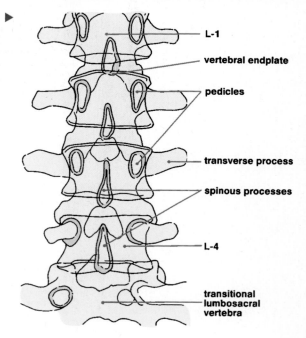

FIGURE 11.46 **Anteroposterior view of the lumbar spine. (A)** For the anteroposterior projection of the lumbar spine, the patient is supine on the table, with the knees flexed to eliminate the normal physiologic lumbar lordosis. The central beam is directed vertically to the center of the abdomen at the level of the iliac crests. **(B)** The radiograph in this projection demonstrates the vertebral bodies, the vertebral end plates, and the transverse processes; the intervertebral disk spaces are also well delineated. The spinous processes are seen en face, appearing as teardrops; the pedicles, also visualized en face, project as oval densities on either side of the bodies.

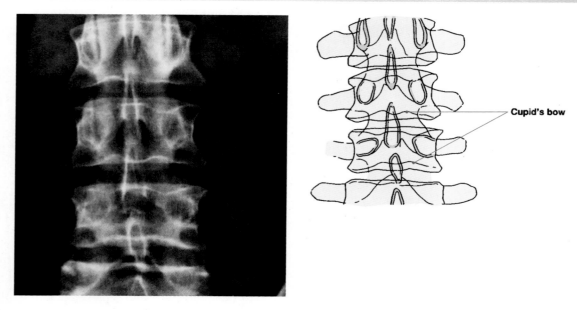

▲
FIGURE 11.47 **Cupid's bow sign.** Anteroposterior coned-down view of the lumbar spine demonstrates a characteristic configuration of the lower aspects of L3 and L4. This "Cupid's bow" contour is lost in cases of compression fracture.

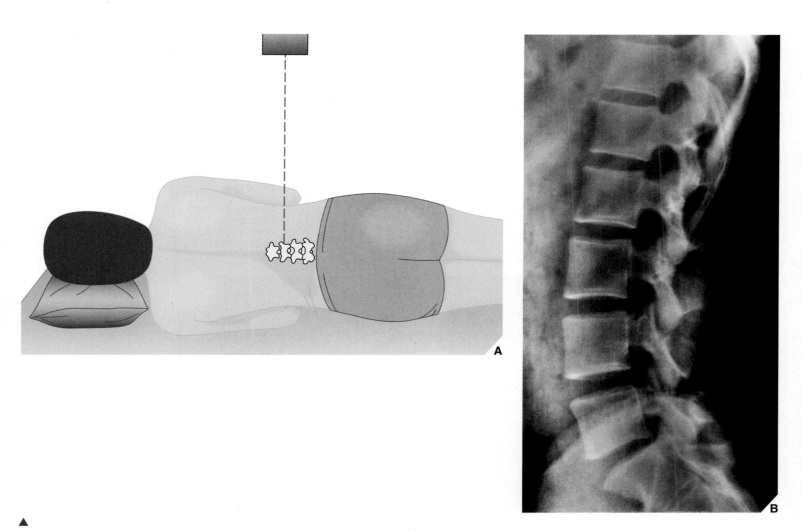

▲
FIGURE 11.48 **Lateral view of the lumbar spine. (A)** For the lateral projection of the lumbar spine, the patient is recumbent on the radiographic table on either the left or right side; the knees and hips are flexed to eliminate the lordotic curve. The central beam is directed vertically to the center of the body of L3, at the level of the patient's waist. **(B)** The lateral radiograph of the lumbar spine allows adequate evaluation of the vertebral bodies, pedicles, and spinous processes, as well as the intervertebral foramina and disk spaces.

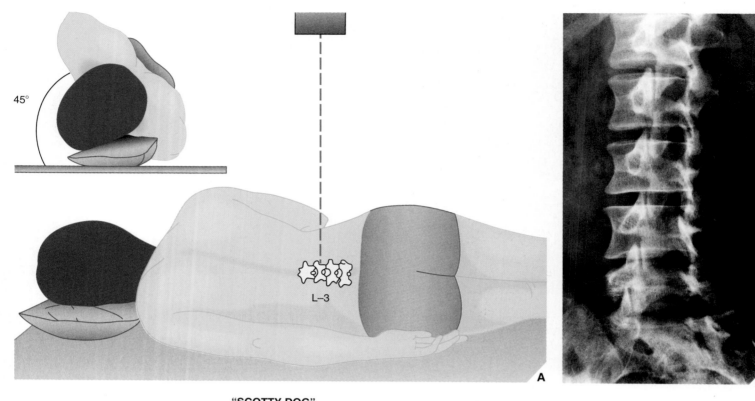

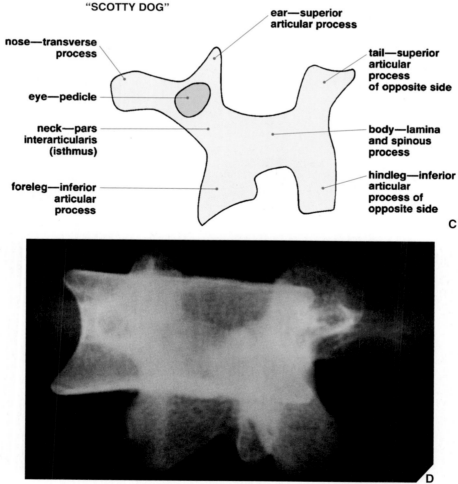

"SCOTTY DOG"

nose—transverse process

ear—superior articular process

eye—pedicle

tail—superior articular process of opposite side

neck—pars interarticularis (isthmus)

body—lamina and spinous process

foreleg—inferior articular process

hindleg—inferior articular process of opposite side

FIGURE 11.49   Oblique view of the lumbar spine. (A) For the posteroanterior oblique projection of the lumbar spine, the patient is recumbent on the table, with the right side rotated 45 degrees to demonstrate the right-sided articular facets. (Elevation of the left side allows demonstration of the left-sided articular facets.) The central beam is directed vertically toward the center of L3. **(B)** The posteroanterior oblique radiograph demonstrates the facet joints, the superior and inferior articular process, the pedicles, and the pars interarticularis. **(C,D)** The oblique film also demonstrates a characteristic configuration of the elements of adjacent lumbar vertebrae known as the "Scotty dog."

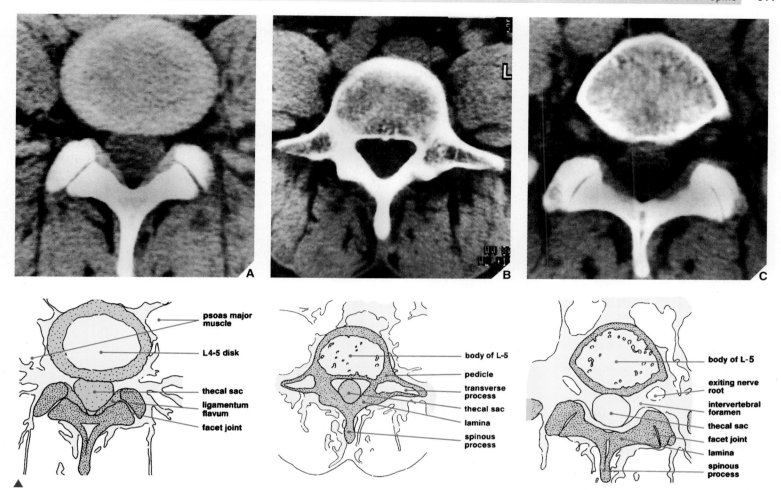

FIGURE 11.50 **CT of the lumbar spine. (A)** CT section through the L4-5 disk space demonstrates the facet joints in full view, as well as the spinous process and laminae of L4. Note the appearance of the ligamentum flavum. **(B)** CT section through upper third of the body of L5 demonstrates an axial view of the pedicles, transverse processes, and laminae, as well as a cross section of the thecal sac and the superior part of the spinous process. **(C)** In a section through the lower third of the body of L5 intervertebral foramina, the caudal part of the body and the spinous process are seen. Note the L5-S1 facet joints.

planar surface coil with its long axis oriented parallel to the spine. The slice thickness used to image the thoracic and lumbar spine in both sagittal and axial planes is usually 5 mm, with a 1-mm gap between slices to reduce the artifactual signal from adjacent slices. Sagittal images of the thoracic and lumbar spine are obtained with T1 and T2 weighting. In the axial plane, T1- and T2*-gradient-recalled echo pulse sequences (MPGR or GRASS) are usually obtained. Similarly to the imaging of the cervical spine, cerebrospinal fluid is visualized with low signal intensity on the sagittal images in T1 weighting, in contrast to the intermediate signal intensity of the spinal cord. The marrow within the vertebral bodies is seen as a high signal intensity, in contrast to the intermediate signal intensity of the intervertebral disks (Fig. 11.54A).

On T2-weighted images, the thoracic cord is visualized as low-to-intermediate signal intensity, in contrast to the high signal intensity of the cerebrospinal fluid. The intervertebral disks demonstrate high signal intensity on both T2- and T2*-(MPGR) weighted images. The vertebral body marrow is imaged as intermediate signal intensity on T2-weighted images and low signal intensity on T2*-weighted MPGR and GRASS images (Fig. 11.54B).

The axial images effectively demonstrate the relation of the intervertebral disk spaces to the thecal sac. On axial T1-weighted images, the vertebral body, pedicles, laminae, transverse, and spinous processes demonstrate high signal intensity, whereas the nucleus pulposus yields intermediate signal intensity, in contrast to the low signal intensity peripherally of the annulus fibrosus. The nerve roots demonstrate low-to-intermediate signal intensity and are in contrast with the high signal intensity of the surrounding fat (Fig. 11.54C). On T2-weighted images,

the nucleus pulposus demonstrates high signal intensity, in contrast to the low signal intensity of the annulus fibrosus. The nerve roots are imaged as low-signal-intensity structures (Fig. 11.54D).

The most recent advances in high-field MRI of the spine (cervical, thoracic, and lumbar), specifically the introduction of 3 Tesla magnets capable of rendering 3D FSE MR images with multiplanar reconstruction, could preclude the routine need for obtaining images in two planes (axial and sagittal), with advantage of decreasing the examination time, and thus decreasing patient discomfort and motion artifacts.

For a summary of the preceding discussion in tabular form, see Tables 11.1, 11.3, and 11.5 and Figure 11.55.

Injury to the Thoracolumbar Spine

Fractures of the Thoracolumbar Spine

Classification. Fractures of the thoracolumbar segment of the spine may involve the vertebral body and arch, as well as the transverse, spinous, and articular processes. They can generally be grouped by the mechanism of injury as compression fractures, burst fractures, distraction fractures (Chance and other seat-belt injuries), and fracture–dislocations.

Because different classifications of thoracolumbar spine fractures have been used in the past by numerous authors, reports concerning the stability or lack of stability of a particular fracture pattern have varied. In 1983, Denis introduced the concept of the three-column spine classification of acute injuries to the thoracic and lumbar segments (Fig. 11.56). The significance of this system is its usefulness in

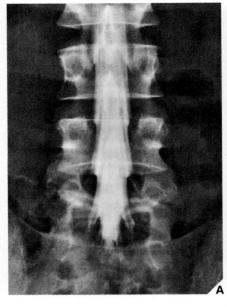

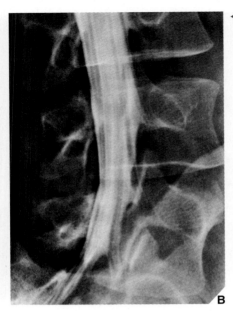

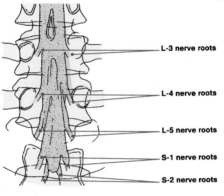

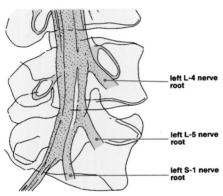

L-3 nerve roots

L-4 nerve roots

L-5 nerve roots

S-1 nerve roots

S-2 nerve roots

left L-4 nerve root

left L-5 nerve root

left S-1 nerve root

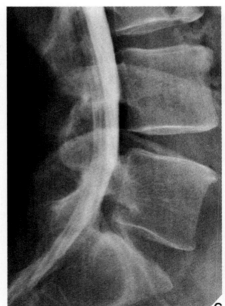

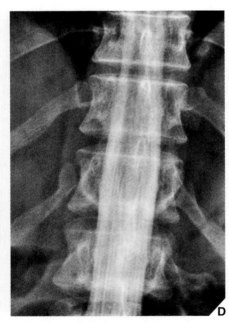

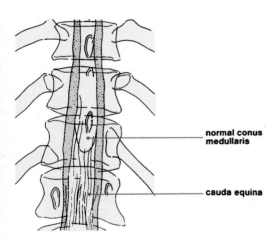

normal conus medullaris

cauda equina

◄ FIGURE 11.51 **Myelography of the lumbar spine.** For myelographic examination of the lumbar spine, the patient is prone on the table. The puncture site, usually at the L3-4 or L2-3 level, is marked under fluoroscopic control. A 22-gauge needle is inserted into the subarachnoid space, and free flow of spinal fluid indicates proper placement. Iohexol or iopamidol (15 mL), in a concentration of 180 mg iodine per mL, is slowly injected, and films are obtained in the posteroanterior (**A**), left and right oblique (**B**), and cross-table lateral (**C**) projections. In these normal studies, contrast is seen outlining the subarachnoid spaces of the thecal sac, as well as the cul-de-sac or most caudal part of the subarachnoid space. The nerve roots appear symmetric on both sides of the contrast column. A linear filling defect represents a nerve root in its contrast-filled sleeve. The length of the root pocket may vary from one patient to another, but in each patient, all roots are approximately equal in length. It is imperative during myelographic examination of the lumbar segment to obtain one spot film of the thoracic segment at the level T10-12 (**D**), because tumors localized in the conus medullaris may mimic the clinical symptoms of a herniated lumbar disk.

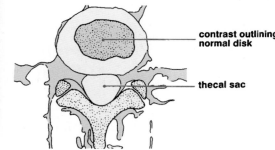

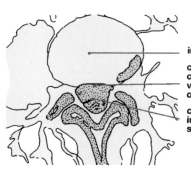

FIGURE 11.52   **Diskography of the lumbar spine.** For diskographic examination of the lumbar spine, the patient is prone on the table, and the level of the injection, depending on the indication, is marked. The needle is inserted into the center of the nucleus pulposus, and about 2 to 3 mL of metrizamide is injected. **(A)** Lateral radiograph of a normal diskogram shows a concentration of contrast medium in the nucleus pulposus outlining the disk; there should be no leak of contrast while the needle is in place. **(B)** CT section through the L3-4 disk space after diskography shows the normal appearance of this structure.

determining the stability of various fractures, based on the site of injury in one or more of the spinal columns or elements:

The *anterior column* comprises the anterior two thirds of the annulus fibrosus and vertebral body, and the anterior longitudinal ligament. The *middle column* includes the posterior longitudinal ligament, and the posterior third of the vertebral body and annulus fibrosus. The *posterior column* consists of the posterior ligament complex, which has been defined by Holdsworth to include the supraspinous and infraspinous ligaments, the capsule of the intervertebral joints, and the ligamentum flavum (or interlaminar ligament), as well as the posterior portion of the neural arch. Generally, one-column fractures are stable and three-column

unstable; two-column fractures may be stable or unstable, depending on the extent of injury (Table 11.6).

Compression Fractures. Usually resulting from anterior or lateral flexion, compression fracture is a failure of the anterior column under compression forces; the middle column remains intact, acting as a hinge, even in severe cases in which there may also be partial failure of the posterior column. The standard radiographic examination of the thoracic and lumbar segments is usually sufficient to demonstrate this injury (Fig. 11.57), although CT or MRI may be required to delineate the extent of the fracture or demonstrate obscure features (Figs. 11.58 and 11.59). The anteroposterior radiograph reveals buckling of

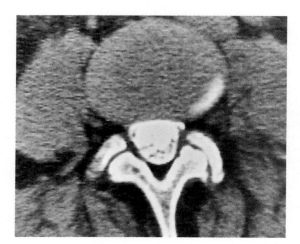

FIGURE 11.53   **CT myelography of the lumbar spine.** CT section obtained after myelography shows the normal appearance of contrast agent in the subarachnoid space. Note that the disk does not encroach on the ventral aspect of the thecal sac.

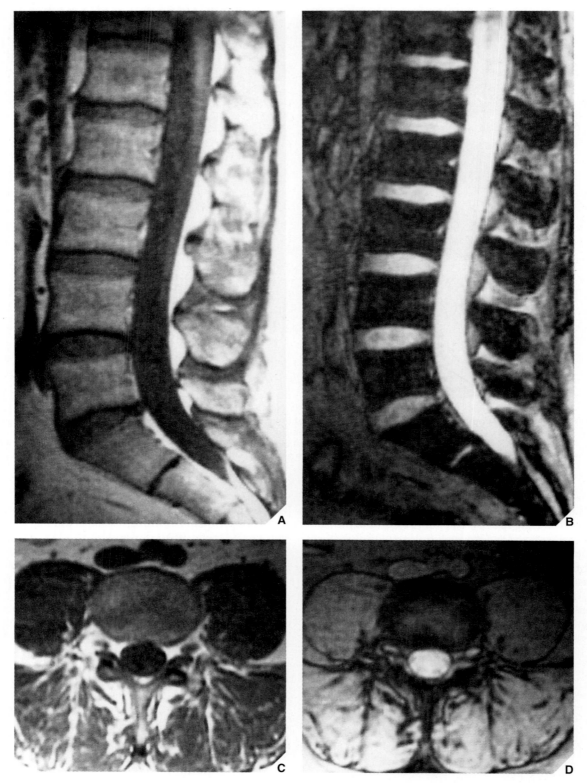

▲
FIGURE 11.54   **MRI appearance of a normal lumbar spine. (A)** On this spin-echo T1-weighted sagittal midline section (TR 800/TE 20 msec), the tip of the conus medullaris is identified at the T12-L1 level, surrounded by low-signal-intensity cerebrospinal fluid. Epidural fat is of a very high signal intensity. It is most clearly seen posteriorly but also some fat is present anteriorly at the lumbosacral junction. Intervertebral disks are of an intermediate signal intensity because of their high water content. The low-signal-intensity lines along the ventral and dorsal aspects of the vertebral body are related to the anterior and posterior longitudinal ligaments and cortical bone of the vertebral bodies. These ligaments also span and cover the anterior and posterior portions of the disks. The thin black line along the inferior end plate and the bright line at the superior portion of each vertebral body are due to a chemical shift artifact. **(B)** Gradient-echo T2-weighted sagittal midline section (MPGR; TR 1000/TE 12 msec, flip angle 22.5 degrees) provides an image with a similar appearance to that of the myelographic technique, because of its very high gray-scale contrast. There is clear delineation of the thecal sac filled with high-signal-intensity cerebrospinal fluid. The posterior longitudinal ligament and dura are silhouetted against the high water signal of the cerebrospinal fluid and the intervertebral disks. The epidural fat is of intermediate-to-low signal intensity and the vertebral bodies are of a very low signal intensity. A high signal intensity of the mid posterior cleft in the vertebral bodies is related to the basivertebral veins. **(C)** On the spin-echo T1-weighted axial section (SE; TR 800/TE 20 msec), the nerve roots are surrounded by high-signal-intensity fat in the neural foramen. The ventral margin of the thecal sac at the disk level is convex outward and the canal is ample in size. The facet joints are well seen as the two low-signal-intensity arcs of the cortical bone. **(D)** Gradient-echo T2-weighted axial section (MPGR; TR 1000/TE 12 msec, flip angle 22.5 degrees) demonstrates low-signal nerve roots of the cauda equina surrounded by high-signal-intensity cerebrospinal fluid. The anterior margin of the thecal sac is well delineated. The individual nerve-root sheaths in the foramen also appear at a somewhat higher signal intensity.

TABLE 11.5 Standard and Special Radiographic Projections for Evaluating Injury to the Thoracic and Lumbar Spine*

Projection	Demonstration	Projection	Demonstration

Anteroposterior	Fractures of
	  Vertebral bodies
	  Vertebral end plates
	  Pedicles
	  Transverse processes
	Fracture–dislocations
	Abnormalities of intervertebral disks
	Paraspinal bulge
	Inverted Napoleon's-hat sign
		Lateral (Continued)
		
		Oblique
			Chance fracture (seat-belt fractures)
			Abnormalities of
			  Intervertebral foramina
			  Intervertebral disk spaces
			Limbus vertebra
			Schmorl node
			Spondylolisthesis
			Spinous-process sign
			Abnormalities of
			  Articular facets
			  Pars interarticularis
			Spondylolysis
			"Scotty dog" configuration

Lateral	Fractures of
	  Vertebral bodies
	  Vertebral end plates
	  Pedicles
	  Spinous processes		

*For the ancillary imaging techniques, see Table 11.3.

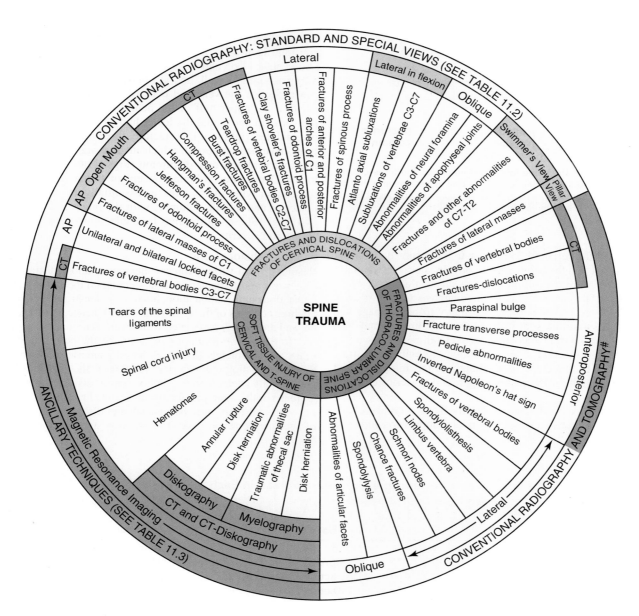

FIGURE 11.55 Spectrum of radiologic imaging techniques for evaluating injury to the spine.*
  *The radiographic projections or radiologic techniques indicated throughout the diagram are only those that are the most effective in demonstrating the respective traumatic conditions.
  #Replaced almost completely by CT.

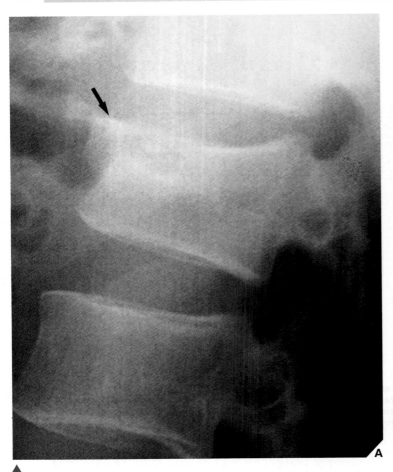
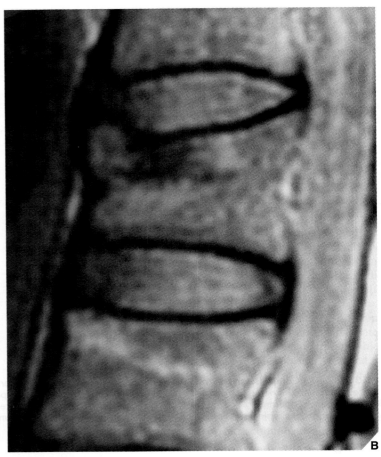

FIGURE 11.59 **MRI of the compression fracture. (A)** Lateral radiograph of the lumbar spine shows compression of the anterosuperior part of the vertebral body of L1 (*arrow*). **(B)** Sagittal proton-density MRI demonstrates a fracture involving only the anterior column, confirming the diagnosis of compression fracture.

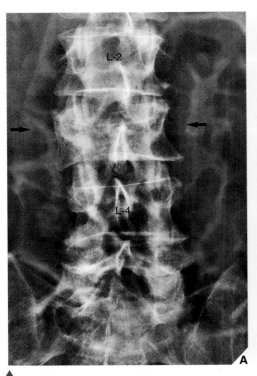
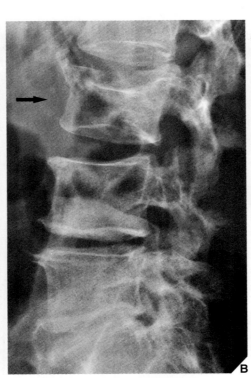
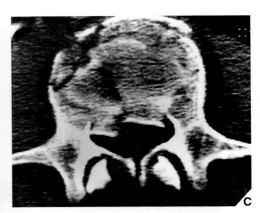

FIGURE 11.60 **Burst fracture.** A 56-year-old merchant seaman fell from a 60-foot-high ladder on a ship. Anteroposterior **(A)** and lateral **(B)** radiographs of the lumbar spine show a burst fracture of the body of L3 (*arrows*). Note widening of the interpediculate distance on the anteroposterior radiograph, the hallmark of burst fracture. The severity of the injury, however, is better appreciated on a CT section **(C)** through the body of L3. There is comminution of the vertebral fracture and displacement of two osseous fragments into the spinal canal, with compression of the thecal sac, indicating involvement of anterior and middle columns.

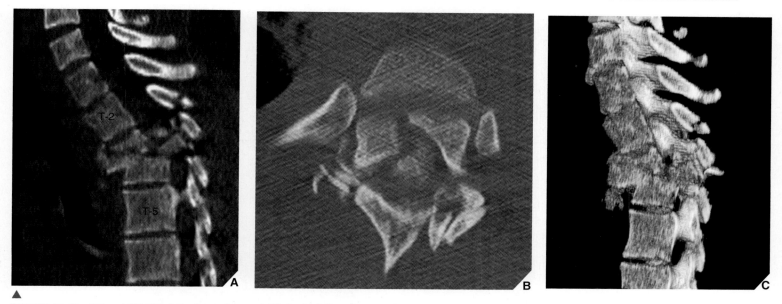

FIGURE 11.61 **CT and 3D CT of the burst fracture. (A)** Sagittal CT reformatted image shows a burst fractures of T3 and T4 vertebrae. **(B)** Axial CT image of T3 shows comminution and displacement of osseous fragments into the spinal canal. **(C)** 3D CT reconstructed image delivers more comprehensive picture of this injury.

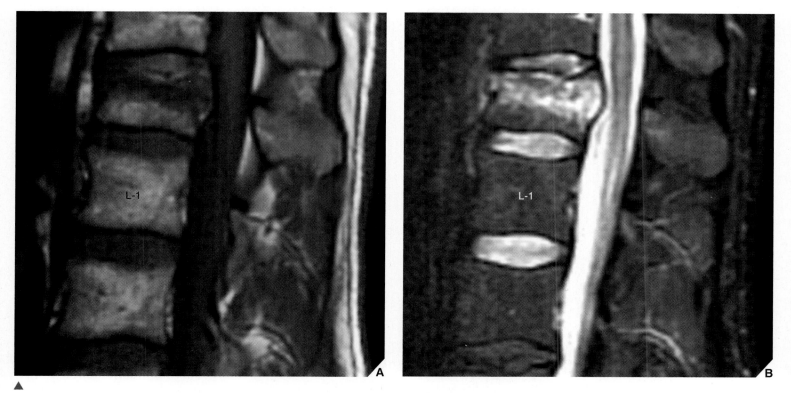

FIGURE 11.62 **MRI of the burst fracture. (A)** Sagittal T1-weighted and **(B)** T2-weighted MR images demonstrate a burst fracture of T12 vertebra. Note compression of the ventral aspect of the thecal sac, but the posterior longitudinal ligament remains intact.

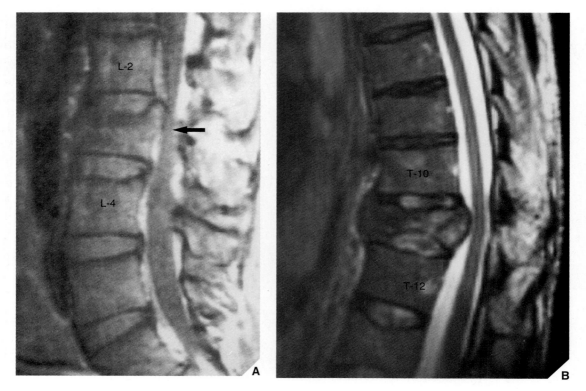

▲

FIGURE 11.63 **MRI of burst fracture. (A)** In a 26-year-old man with a burst fracture of L3, sagittal T1-weighted MR image (SE; TR 800/TE 20 msec) demonstrates posterior displacement of the middle column with compression of the thecal sac (*arrow*). **(B)** A sagittal T2-weighted MR image of a 58-year-old man who fell from the roof of a three-story building shows a typical appearance of a burst fracture of T11. Note compression of the thecal sac.

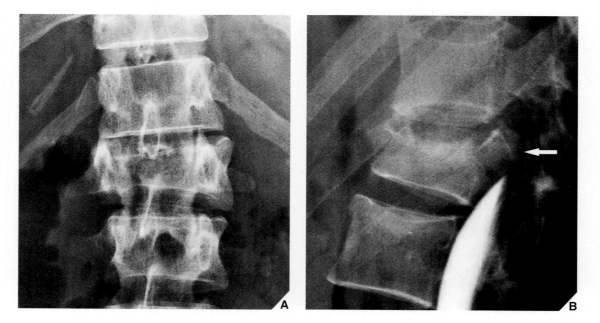

▲

FIGURE 11.64 **Myelography of the burst fracture.** A 28-year-old woman made a parachute jump and landed on her back. Hemiplegia and incontinence developed thereafter. **(A)** Anteroposterior radiograph of the lumbar spine shows a burst fracture of L1. **(B)** Lateral view as part of a myelogram shows complete obstruction of the flow of contrast agent at the level of fracture caused by a small osseous fragment impinging on the thecal sac (*arrow*).

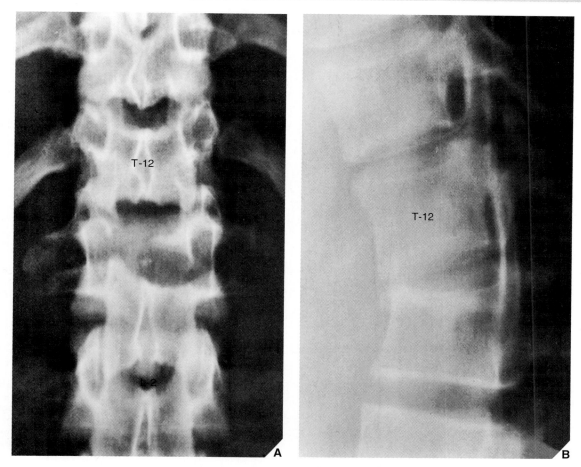

FIGURE 11.65 **Chance fracture.** A 30-year-old woman sustained an injury to the lower back in a car collision; she had been wearing a lap seat belt. Anteroposterior (**A**) and lateral (**B**) tomograms of the lumbar spine show a fracture of the vertebral body of L1 extending into the lamina and spinous process. (Courtesy of Dr. D. Faegenburg, Mineola, New York.)

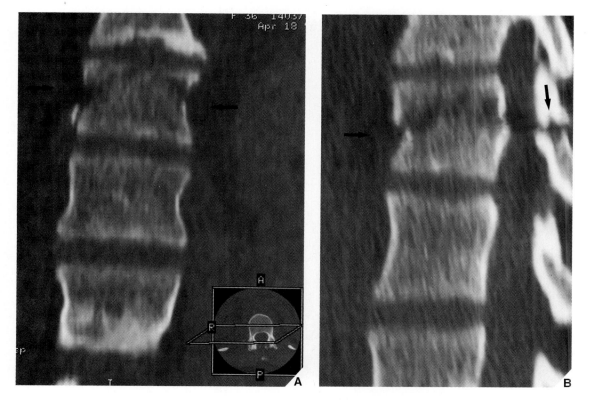

FIGURE 11.66 **CT of the Chance fracture.** A 36-year-old woman was injured in a car accident. She had been wearing a lap seat belt but not a restraining shoulder belt. Reformatted CT images in coronal (**A**) and sagittal (**B**) planes show a typical one-level Chance fracture through the L2 vertebra (*arrows*).

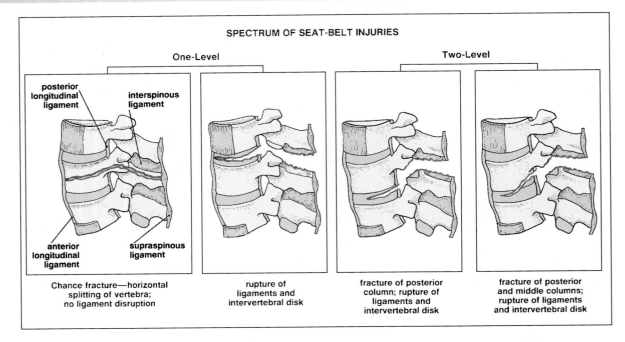

SPECTRUM OF SEAT-BELT INJURIES

One-Level

posterior longitudinal ligament
interspinous ligament

anterior longitudinal ligament
supraspinous ligament

Chance fracture—horizontal splitting of vertebra; no ligament disruption

rupture of ligaments and intervertebral disk

Two-Level

fracture of posterior column; rupture of ligaments and intervertebral disk

fracture of posterior and middle columns; rupture of ligaments and intervertebral disk

FIGURE 11.67 The spectrum of seat-belt injuries involving the lumbar spine.

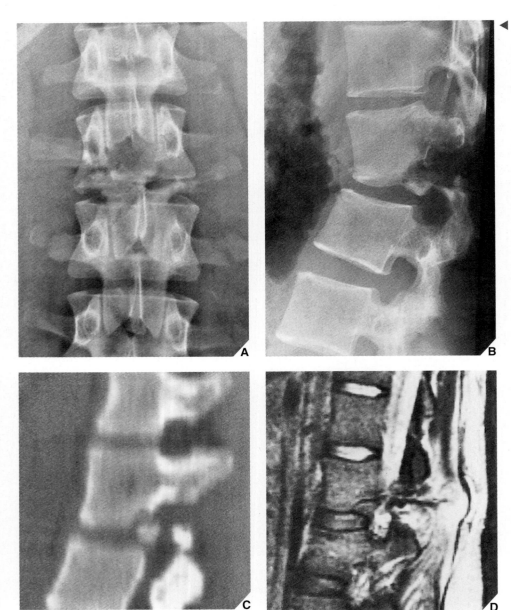

◀ **FIGURE 11.68 Two-level seat-belt injury.** A 21-year-old woman sustained an injury to the lower back in a car accident. (**A**) Anteroposterior radiograph of the lumbar spine demonstrates a horizontal cleft in the L2 vertebral body. Note increased distance between the pedicles of L2 and L3 and fractures of several transverse processes. (**B**) Lateral view shows posterior angulation at the L2-3 level and an oblique fracture extending from the inferoposterior part of the L2 vertebral body to the lamina and posterior elements. (**C**) Sagittal CT reformation demonstrates the fracture of posterior elements to better advantage. (**D**) Parasagittal MR image demonstrates disruption of the posterior ligaments and a large soft-tissue hematoma. The findings are typical of a two-level seat-belt injury.

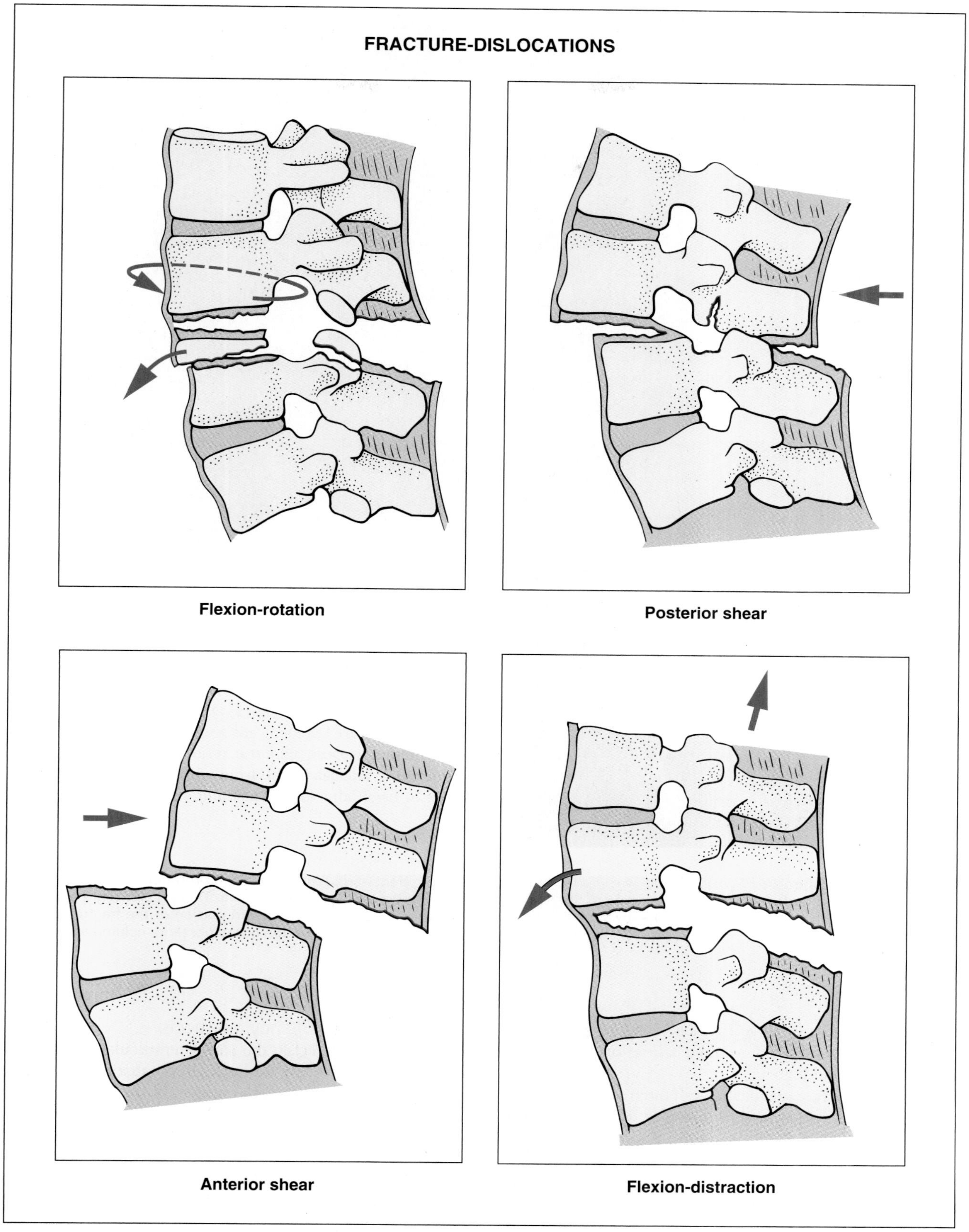

FRACTURE-DISLOCATIONS

Flexion-rotation

Posterior shear

Anterior shear

Flexion-distraction

FIGURE 11.69   Types of fracture–dislocations. Schematic representation of various types of fracture–dislocation of the thoracolumbar spine.

Spondylolisthesis

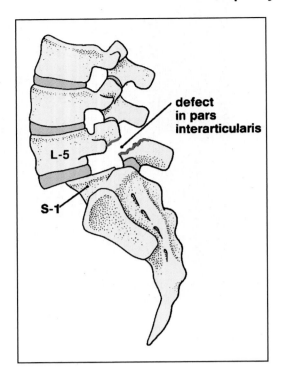

defect
in pars
interarticularis

L-5

S-1

**associated with spondylolysis
(true spondylolisthesis)**

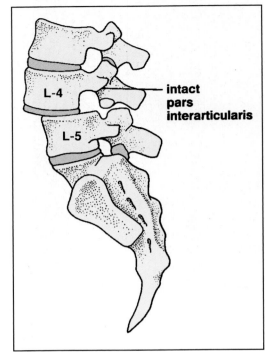

L-4

intact
pars
interarticularis

L-5

**without spondylolysis
(pseudo- or degenerative
spondylolisthesis)**

▲
FIGURE 11.74   **Types of spondylolisthesis.** Spondylolisthesis may occur in association with spondylolysis resulting from a defect in the pars interarticularis, or secondary to degenerative disk disease and degeneration and subluxation of the apophyseal joints (pseudospondylolisthesis).

Spinous-Process Sign

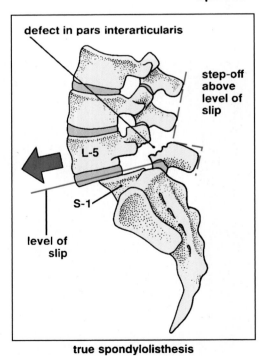

defect in pars interarticularis

step-off
above
level of
slip

L-5

S-1

level of
slip

true spondylolisthesis

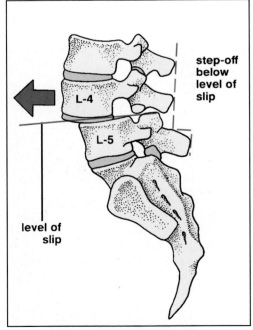

step-off
below
level of
slip

L-4

L-5

level of
slip

pseudospondylolisthesis

▲
FIGURE 11.75   **The spinous-process sign.** The spinous-process sign can help differentiate true spondylolisthesis from pseudospondylolisthesis by the appearance of a step-off in the spinous processes above the level of vertebral slip in the former and below that level in the latter.

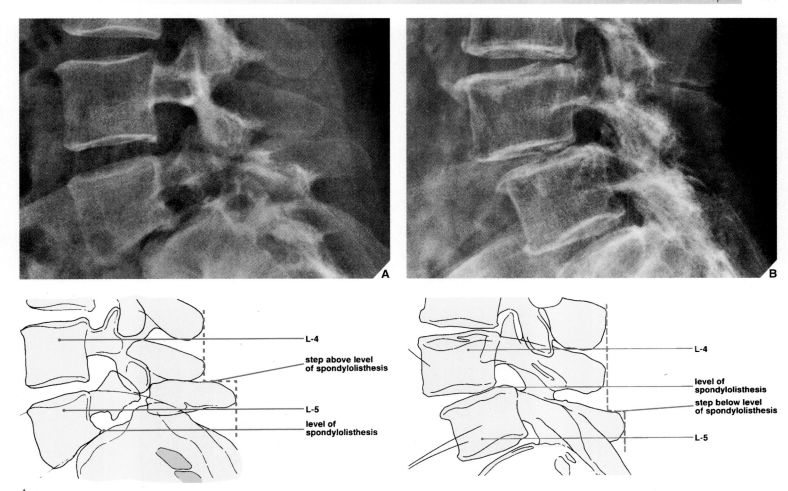

FIGURE 11.76 Spondylolisthesis and "pseudospondylolisthesis." (A) Lateral radiograph of the lumbar spine demonstrates the typical appearance of spondylolisthesis secondary to a defect in the pars interarticularis. Note that the most dorsal aspect of the spinous process of L5 forms a step with that of L4 above the level of slippage of L5. **(B)** In spondylolisthesis without spondylolysis (degenerative spondylolisthesis), a step-off in the spinous processes below the level of vertebral slippage is an identifying feature.

The defect in the pars interarticularis precipitating spondylolisthesis can be demonstrated on the standard oblique projection of the lumbar spine, which in the past used to be supplemented by conventional tomography, and currently by CT (Fig.11.77A–C); myelography on the lateral view may show an extradural defect on the ventral aspect of the thecal sac, similar to that created by disk herniation (Fig. 11.77D). A severe degree of spondylolisthesis at the L5-S1 level can be identified on the anteroposterior view by the ventrocaudal displacement of L5 over the sacrum. This configuration creates curvilinear densities forming what is called the "inverted Napoleon's hat" sign (Figs. 11.78 and 11.79). The simple grading of spondylolisthesis proposed by Meyerding is based on the amount of forward slipping (Fig. 11.80).

Injury to the Diskovertebral Junction

One of the most frequent conditions affecting the diskovertebral junction is herniation of an intervertebral disk. The chief structural unit between adjacent vertebral bodies, the intervertebral disk, comprises a soft central portion, the nucleus pulposus, composed of collagen fibrils and mucoprotein gel, lying eccentrically and somewhat posteriorly, and a firm fibrocartilaginous ring, the annulus fibrosus, surrounding the nucleus pulposus and reinforced by the anterior and posterior longitudinal ligaments. Injury to the intervertebral disk and the disko-vertebral junction can result from acute trauma or from subtle subclinical, often endogenous injury. Depending on the direction of herniation of disk material, a spectrum of injuries of the intervertebral disk and adjacent vertebrae may be seen (Fig. 11.81).

Anterior Disk Herniation. When the normal attachments of the annulus fibrosus to the vertebral rim by Sharpey fibers and to the anterior longitudinal ligament loosen, disk material (nucleus pulposus) herniates anteriorly. Elevation of the anterior longitudinal ligament by herniating material stimulates the formation of peripheral osteophytes, leading to a degenerative condition known as spondylosis deformans (see Chapter 13), which can be demonstrated on the lateral radiograph of the lumbar spine (Fig 11.82A). Anterior herniation can also be demonstrated on diskography (Fig. 11.82B) and MRI.

Intravertebral Disk Herniation. Ventrocaudal disk herniation, as well as ventrocephalad herniation, which is much less commonly seen, produces an abnormality known as limbus vertebra. Herniation of disk material into a vertebral body at the site of attachment of the annulus fibrosus to the body's rim separates a small, triangular fragment of bone, which is commonly mistaken for an acute fracture or infectious spondylitis. Reactive bone sclerosis adjacent to the defect, however, indicates a chronic process. The adjacent disk space is invariably narrowed, and a radiolucent cleft known as the vacuum phenomenon may be seen in the disk space, representing degeneration of the disk (Fig. 11.83). This abnormality, which is invariably asymptomatic, is the product of chronic, endogenous trauma. The characteristic radiographic changes are best seen on the lateral projection of the lumbar spine (see Fig. 11.83); only rarely is conventional tomography or CT indicated to exclude a true vertebral fracture (Fig. 11.84). MRI may be performed to confirm or exclude the concomitant posterior disk herniation (Fig. 11.85, see also Fig. 11.97). Occasionally, more than one vertebra is affected, and although limbus vertebra is usually seen in the lumbar spine, it may also be present in a thoracic vertebra.

Limbus vertebra should not be confused with the secondary ossification centers of the vertebral ring apophysis, which are commonly seen

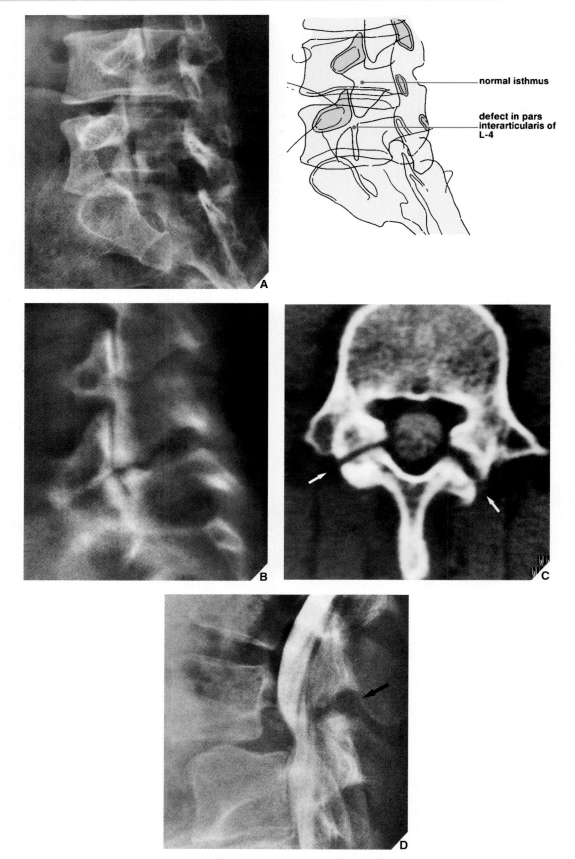

FIGURE 11.77 **Spondylolysis and spondylolisthesis.** Oblique radiograph (**A**) and trispiral tomogram (**B**) of the lumbar spine in a 28-year-old man show a defect in the pars interarticularis (neck of the "Scotty dog") of L4 typical of spondylolysis. (**C**) CT section through the body clearly demonstrates defects in the left and right pars interarticularis (*arrows*). (**D**) Lateral spot film obtained during myelography shows an extradural defect, similar to that of disk herniation, on the ventral aspect of the thecal sac caused by grade 2 spondylolisthesis at L4-5. The defect in the pars interarticularis is also clearly seen (*arrow*).

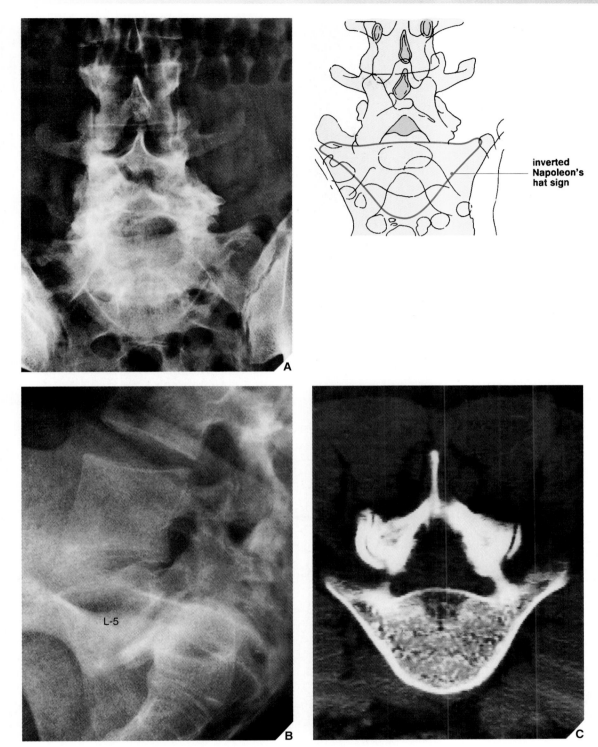

inverted
Napoleon's
hat sign

L-5

FIGURE 11.78 Inverted Napoleon's hat sign. (A) Anteroposterior radiograph of the lumbosacral spine in a 21-year-old man with severe (grade 4) spondylolis-thesis shows curvilinear densities in the sacral area forming an inverted Napoleon's hat. This configuration is caused by a severe degree of slip at the L5-S1 level, as seen on the lateral projection **(B)**. **(C)** The sign is created by imaging the vertebral body in the axial projection, similar to that seen on a CT section of a normal vertebra.

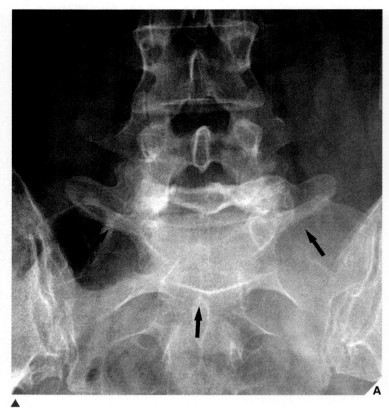
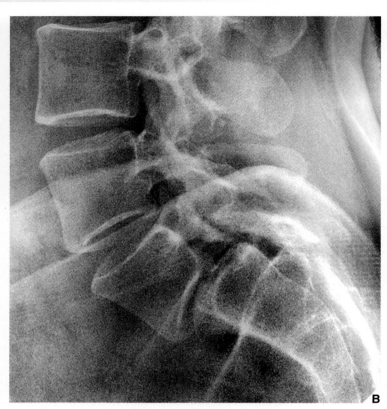

FIGURE 11.79   Inverted Napoleon's hat sign. (A) Anteroposterior radiograph shows an inverted Napoleon's hat sign (*arrows*). **(B)** The lateral radiographs shows spondylolisthesis at L5-S1 level.

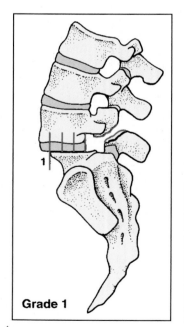
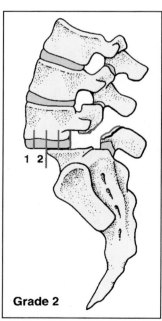
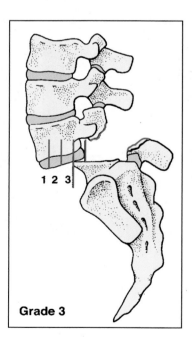
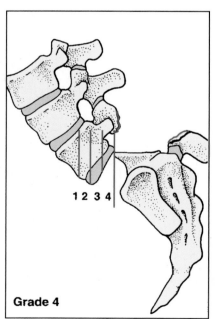

FIGURE 11.80   Grades of spondylolisthesis. The grading of spondylolisthesis, as proposed by Meyerding, is based on the amount of forward displacement of L5 on S1.

SPECTRUM OF INTERVERTEBRAL DISK HERNIATION

Normal

Anterior Herniation

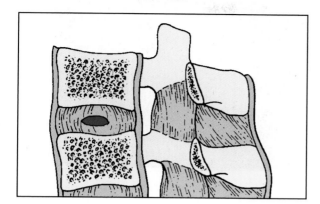

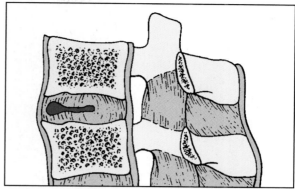

ventrad extrusion leading to elevation of
anterior longitudinal ligament and osteophyte
formation—spondylosis deformans

Intravertebral Herniation

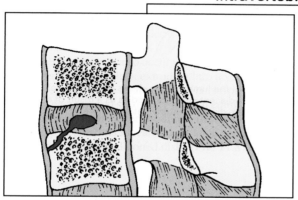

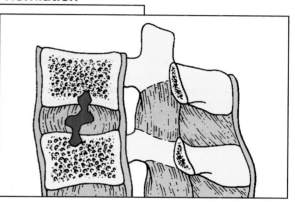

anterocaudad extrusion separating
a triangular fragment from
adjacent vertebra—limbus vertebra

cephalad or caudad extrusion
through end plate into adjacent
vertebra—Schmorl node

Intraspinal Herniation

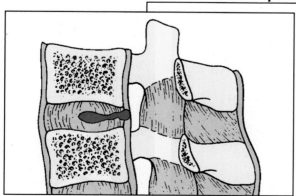

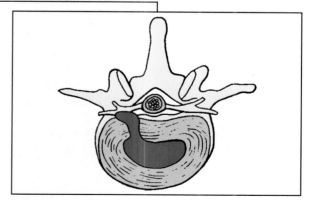

posterior or posterolateral extrusion into spinal canal—herniated disk

▲
FIGURE 11.81 The spectrum of intervertebral disk herniation.

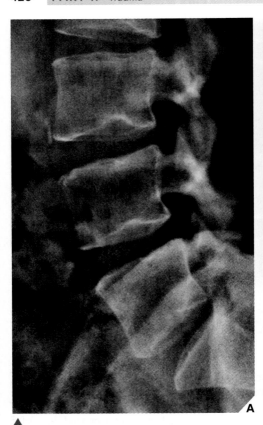
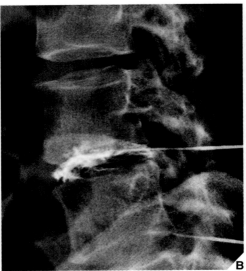
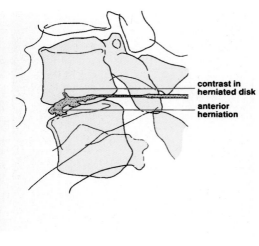

contrast in
herniated disk

anterior
herniation

▲

FIGURE 11.87 **Schmorl nodes. (A)** Lateral radiograph of the lumbar spine in an asymptomatic 77-year-old woman with osteoporosis of the spine shows multiple indentations particularly of the inferior end plates, representing the Schmorl nodes, secondary to intravertebral disk herniation caused by weakening of the vertebral end plates. **(B)** In another patient, a small Schmorl node is demonstrated, on diskography, by opacification of extruded disk material in the body of L4. Some anterior herniation is also evident.

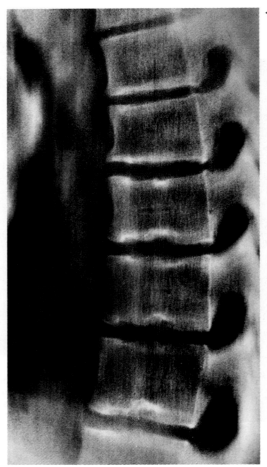

◄ FIGURE 11.88 **Scheuermann disease.** Lateral tomogram of the thoracic spine in a 23-year-old man demonstrates several Schmorl nodes in T5-8 and slight anterior wedging of the vertebral bodies. Note the wavy outline of the superior and inferior end plates and the mild kyphotic curve of the thoracic spine in this patient, an abnormality also called juvenile thoracic kyphosis.

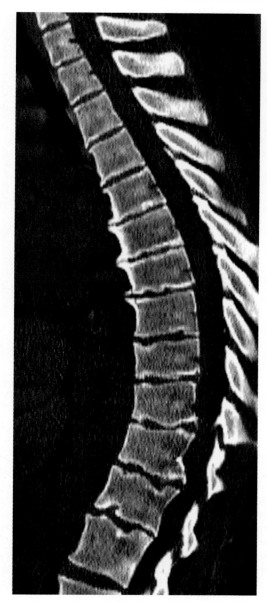

▲
FIGURE 11.89 **CT of Scheuermann disease.** Sagittal reformatted CT image of the thoracic spine shows lower thoracic kyphosis and classic appearance of type I Scheuermann disease in 24-year-old man.

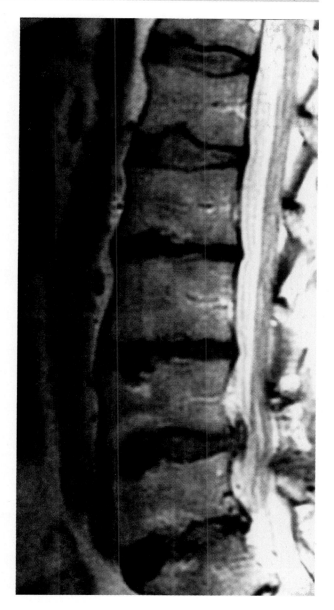

▲
FIGURE 11.90 **MRI of Scheuermann disease.** A 28-year-old man presented with low back pain lasting several months. Sagittal MRI of the lumbar spine demonstrates characteristic features of Scheuermann disease, type II. Note prominent Schmorl nodes involving all five vertebral bodies, decreased height of the vertebral bodies, and narrowing of the intervertebral disk spaces.

asymptomatic, whereas others may experience fatigue and thoracic pain aggravated by physical exertion. Neurologic findings are rare. Although the thoracic spine is predominantly affected (Fig. 11.89), involvement of the lumbar spine has also been reported. This condition is called Scheuermann disease type II (in contrast to type I, which involves the upper thoracic spine), although some investigators prefer the term "juvenile lumbar osteochondrosis." Imaging studies demonstrate changes almost identical to those seen in Scheuermann disease type I, including prominent Schmorl nodes, irregularity of the endplates, and narrowing of the disk spaces (Fig. 11.90). However, anterior vertebral wedging is not a constant feature of this variant.

Posterior and Posterolateral Disk Herniation. Intraspinal herniation or "herniated disk" is the most serious of the three variants of disk-overtebral junction injury. It is most commonly seen in the lumbar spine, particularly L4-5 and L5-S1, although it may be seen in the cervical region. It is commonly associated with clinical symptoms such as sciatic pain and weakening of the lower extremity, especially when herniation in the lumbar segment causes compression on an exiting nerve root or the thecal sac. A predisposing factor in some patients may be the loss of elasticity of the annulus fibrosus caused by degenerative changes, with subsequent rupture of the annulus or even the posterior longitudinal ligament and retropulsion of the nucleus pulposus into the spinal canal. Typically, the patient, usually a young adult man, gives a history of straining his back by lifting a heavy object. The subsequent pain in the lumbar region radiates to the posterior aspect of the thigh and buttock and the lateral aspect of the leg, and is aggravated by coughing and sneezing; sometimes, there is associated paresthesia or numbness in the foot. Physical examination reveals muscular spasm, limitation of forward bending, and restriction of straight-leg raising on the affected side. Various other symptoms and physical findings may be present depending on the level and degree of injury.

The standard radiographic examination in herniated disks is usually normal, and ancillary radiologic techniques including myelography and CT, either alone or in conjunction with one another, as well as

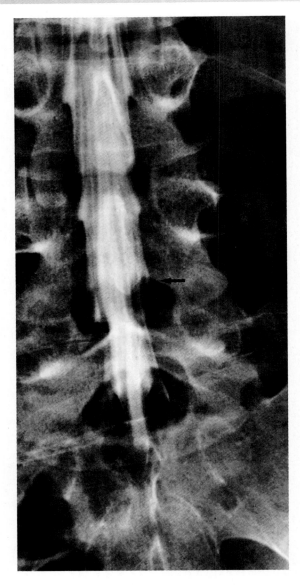

▲
FIGURE 11.91　**Lateral disk herniation.** In lifting a heavy object, a 27-year-old man felt sudden, sharp pain in the lower back radiating to the left lower extremity. The standard radiographs of the lumbosacral spine were normal. Anteroposterior view of a myelogram demonstrates a subtle lack of filling of the left L5 nerve sheath (*arrow*), which at surgery was found to be compressed by a lateral herniation of the L4-5 disk.

diskography, and now MRI, are required to make a diagnosis. The myelographic findings in disk herniation may be very subtle, such as absent opacification of a nerve sheath (Fig. 11.91), or more obvious, such as an extradural pressure defect in the contrast-filled thecal sac (Fig. 11.92). Disk herniation can also be diagnosed on standard CT examination (Fig. 11.93) or on CT sections obtained after myelography (Figs. 11.94 and 11.95) or diskography (Fig. 11.96). The most effective technique, however, is MRI (Fig. 11.97).

The latter imaging modality is being used increasingly for the diagnosis of conditions causing acute low back pain and sciatica. The sensitivity of MRI for the diagnosis of herniated disk and spinal stenosis is equivalent to or better than that of CT, even in combination with myelography and diskography.

Radicular symptoms represent one of the most common reasons why patients are referred for MRI of the spine. MRI is particularly sensitive and is used to detect and characterize disk herniation because it allows for direct evaluation of the internal morphology of the disk. The sagittal imaging plane is more sensitive for defining disk impingement

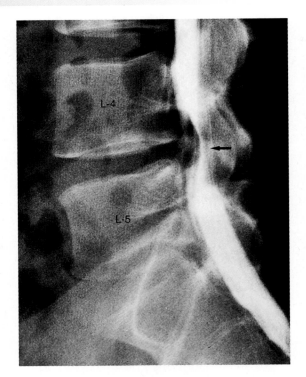

▲
FIGURE 11.92　**Myelography of herniated disk.** Lateral spot film obtained during myelography in a 38-year-old man demonstrates a large posterior herniation of the intervertebral disk at L4-5 (*arrow*).

on the thecal sac, or for demonstrating extruded fragments and showing the relationship to the vertebral bodies and intervertebral disk spaces (Fig. 11.97A). The axial imaging plane can demonstrate the effect of the herniated disk on the exiting nerve roots and thecal sac (Fig. 11.97B). Axial images are also important in evaluating neural foramina and nerve root effacement in cases of lateral and posterolateral disk herniation. Free disk fragments can be easily identified.

The use of T1-weighted images in the axial plane provides excellent contrast between high-signal fat and low-signal thecal sac, nerve roots, and disk fragments. Fast-scan techniques provide increased cerebrospinal fluid signal and allow enhanced contrast between herniated fragments

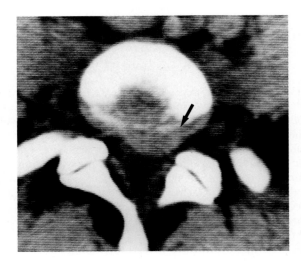

▲
FIGURE 11.93　**CT of herniated disk.** Axial CT section of the lumbar spine at the L5-S1 level demonstrates a large centrolateral disk herniation encroaching on the left intervertebral foramen (arrow).

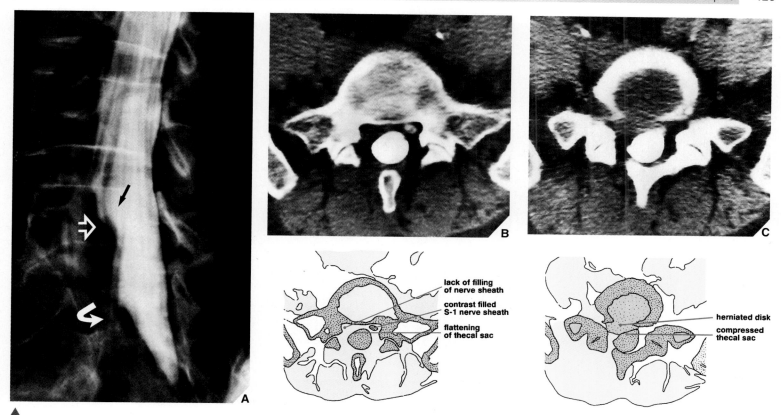

FIGURE 11.94   **CT myelography of herniated disk.** A 47-year-old man presented with severe back pain radiating to the right buttock and leg. (**A**) Spot film in the oblique projection obtained during myelography shows an extradural defect on the right side of the thecal sac at the L5-S1 disk space (*arrow*) involving the right S1 nerve root, which is cut off (*open arrow*). The S2 nerve root is normally outlined (*curved arrow*). CT sections (**B,C**) also obtained during myelography, demonstrate the lack of opacification of the S1 nerve root on the right side and a large herniation of the L5-S1 disk compressing the thecal sac from the right.

and cerebrospinal fluid. Some advantages of MRI in comparison with myelography and CT of lumbar disk disease are evident. MRI is sensitive to the water content of the nucleus pulposus. As the water content of this structure decreases with aging or degeneration, decreased signal appears, particularly on T2-weighted images. In addition, the myelographic effect provided with heavily T2-weighted images and fast-scan techniques allows the visualization of nerve roots within the thecal sac. Anomalies such as conjoint nerve roots, which may simulate a herniated nucleus pulposus on CT studies, can be visualized directly with MRI. It has to be stressed, however, that evaluating patients with radiculopathy and herniated disk is an area in which both MRI and CT can be complementary. When an extradural defect is identified with MRI, it may be difficult to ascertain whether the lesion represents a herniated nucleus pulposus or an osteophyte; in these situations, CT can make the distinction easily, by identifying the increased mineralization within the osteophyte. When the herniated fragment is clearly in continuity with the intervertebral disk and is of the same signal intensity, the diagnosis is suggested by MRI alone.

Annular Tears. Tears or fissures of the annulus fibrosus of lumbar intervertebral disks may occur secondary to trauma and may also be caused by degenerative changes of the disk related to normal aging. According to Munter and associates, these tears represent separations between annular fibers, separations of annular fibers from their vertebral insertions, or breaks through these fibers in any orientation, involving one or more layers of the annular lamellae. Annular tears are found in both symptomatic and asymptomatic individuals. In a cadaver study, Yu and colleagues identified three types of annular tears. Type I is a concentric tear that is characterized by rupture of the transverse fibers connecting adjacent lamellae in the annulus, without disruption of the longitudinal fibers. Type II is a radial tear that represents fissures extending from the periphery of the annulus to the nucleus pulposus associated

with disruption of the longitudinal fibers. Type III is a transverse tear caused by the disruption of Sharpey fibers at the periphery of the annulus fibrosus. Type II and III tears can be seen on T2-weighted MRI as hyperintense foci within the annulus. These tears can also be occasionally demonstrated by CT diskography.

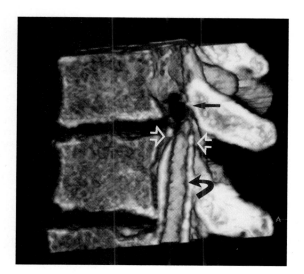

FIGURE 11.95   **3D CT myelography of herniated disk.** A 3D CT reconstructed image in maximum intensity projection (MIP) of the lower thoracic spine was obtained after contrast agent was injected into the thecal sac (CT myelography). There is disk herniation at the level of T7-T8 (*arrow*) associated with complete obstruction of contrast flow (*open arrows*). The *curved arrow* points to the spinal cord.

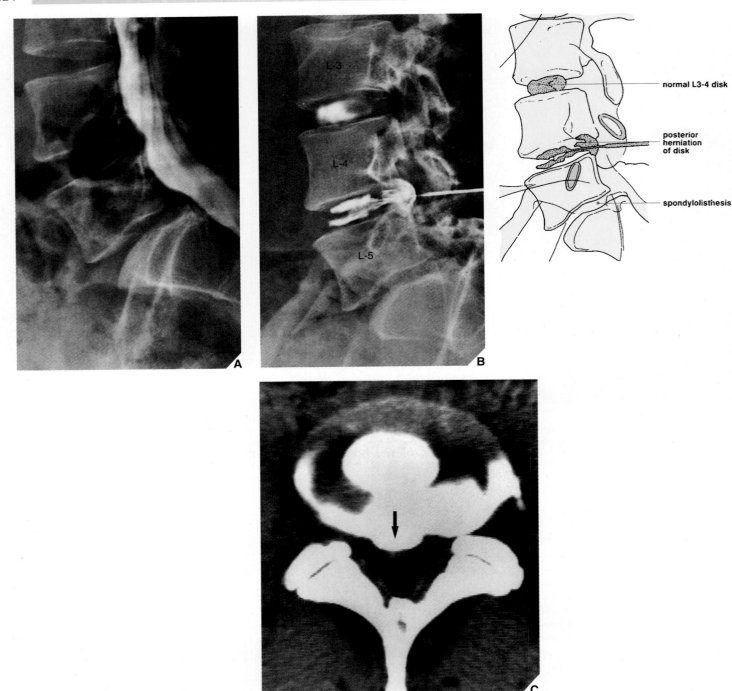

Labels in figure: L-3, L-4, L-5, normal L3-4 disk, posterior herniation of disk, spondylolisthesis, A, B, C

▲
FIGURE 11.96 CT diskography of herniated disk. A 30-year-old male construction worker strained his lower back at work and was admitted to the hospital with severe sciatica. **(A)** Lateral radiograph of the lumbar spine during myelographic examination reveals a slight separation of the ventral aspect of the dural sac from the dorsal aspect of L5 due to grade 1 spondylolisthesis. In addition, there is an extradural pressure defect on the ventral aspect of the dural sac at the L4-5 level and a much smaller defect at the L3-4 disk space. **(B)** A diskogram using metrizamide was performed at the L3-4 and L4-5 levels, the latter demonstrating posterior herniation. **(C)** CT at the L4-5 level following diskography shows posterior protrusion of the opacified disk material (*arrow*).

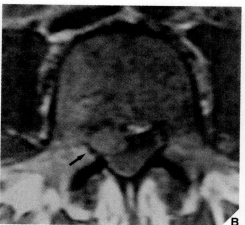

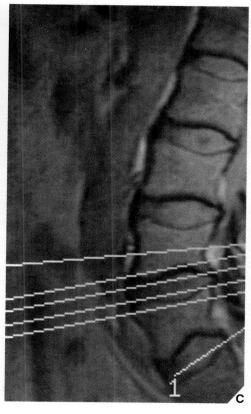

FIGURE 11.97 MRI of herniated disk. A 44-year-old man presented with sciatic pain radiating to the right buttock and thigh. **(A)** Sagittal MRI (SE; TR 1500/TE 20 msec) demonstrates a posterior herniation of disk L4-5 and a bulging disk at L5-S1. **(B)** Axial MRI (SE; TR 1500/TE 30 msec) clearly shows posterolateral disk herniation with marked compression of the thecal sac (*arrow*). **(C)** The levels of the several axial sections obtained at the L4-5 disk space are indicated.

PRACTICAL POINTS TO REMEMBER

Cervical Spine

[1] The single most important projection in the radiographic examination of the cervical spine is the lateral view—either the erect or cross-table lateral.

[2] In the evaluation of injury to the cervical spine, it is mandatory to visualize the C7 vertebra, the site of the most commonly missed fractures. If this cannot be accomplished on the lateral projection, the swimmer's view should be attempted.

[3] CT examination and MRI are useful techniques for evaluating vertebral-column trauma and associated soft-tissue and spinal cord injuries.

[4] Stability of a cervical spine fracture is the most important practical factor in the evaluation of injuries to this region.

[5] Fractures of the occipital condyles are best demonstrated on CT with coronal reformation.

[6] A classification system of three types of occipital condyle fractures devised by Anderson and Montesano is based on fracture morphology, pertinent anatomy, and biomechanics.

[7] Occipitocervical dislocation is effectively demonstrated on the lateral radiographs supplemented with CT reformatted images.

[8] Jefferson fracture—a symmetrical fracture of the anterior and posterior arches of C1—can be diagnosed on the anteroposterior open-mouth view by the lateral displacement of the lateral masses.

[9] In the evaluation of fractures of the odontoid process (dens), note that:
  • type I (an oblique fracture cephalad to the base) and type III (a fracture through the base extending into the body) are stable
  • type II (a transverse fracture through the base) is unstable.

[10] Teardrop fracture, a flexion injury representing a variant of a burst fracture, is the most severe and unstable of cervical spine fractures; it is frequently associated with spinal cord damage.

[11] Extension teardrop fracture, which usually occurs at the level of C2 or C3, is a stable injury without the potentially dangerous complications of the flexion teardrop fracture.

[12] Clay shoveler's fracture, involving the spinous processes of C6 or C7, can be recognized on the anteroposterior projection of the cervical spine by the ghost sign produced by caudal displacement of the fractured spinous process.

[13] In the radiographic evaluation of locked facets, a bow-tie or bat-wing appearance of the dislocated articular pillars on the lateral projection is characteristic.

Thoracolumbar Spine

[1] The three-column spine classification of acute injuries to the thoracic and lumbar segments is a practical approach to defining the stability of various fractures.

[2] Subtle fractures of the thoracic vertebrae can be recognized by a localized bulge in the paraspinal line secondary to edema and hemorrhage.

[3] Chance fracture, known also as a seat-belt fracture, is a horizontal fracture through a lumbar vertebral body with extension into the lamina and spinous process.

[4] Fracture–dislocations of thoracic and lumbar spine, which are unstable injuries, are classified into four types:
  • flexion-rotation injury
  • posteroanterior shear injury
  • anteroposterior shear injury
  • flexion-distraction injury.

[5] Spondylolysis, a defect in the pars interarticularis (neck of the "Scotty dog"), leads to ventral slipping of one vertebra on the vertebra beneath it—spondylolisthesis.

[6] Spondylolisthesis:
  • may be associated with a defect in the pars interarticularis, so-called true spondylolisthesis
  • or exist without an isthmic defect, so-called pseudospondylolisthesis or degenerative spondylolisthesis (associated with degenerative changes in the intervertebral disk and apophyseal joints).

[7] A simple test to distinguish between the two types of spondylolisthesis is the spinous-process sign.

[8] A severe degree of spondylolisthesis at the L5-S1 level can be recognized on the anteroposterior projection by the phenomenon known as the "inverted Napoleon's hat" sign.

[9] An intervertebral disk can herniate anteriorly or anterolaterally, as well as posteriorly, or posterolaterally. Intraosseous herniation into a vertebral body may occur caudad or ventrocaudad, cephalad, or ventrocephalad.

[10] Intravertebral ventrocaudad or ventrocephalad herniation results in the separation of a small, triangular segment of a vertebra. This limbus vertebra should not be mistaken for a fracture.

[11] Posterior disk herniation can be documented by:
  • CT
  • myelography
  • diskography
  • MRI
  • or a combination of these.

[12] As a rule, diskography is performed if the results of CT, myelography, and MRI are equivocal.

SUGGESTED READINGS

Amundsen P, Skalpe IO. Cervical myelography with a watersoluble contrast medium (metrizamide). *Neuroradiology* 1975;8:209–212.

Anderson LD, D'Alonzo RT. Fractures of the odontoid process of the axis. *J Bone Joint Surg [Am]* 1974;56A:1663–1674.

Anderson PA, Montesano PX. Morphology and treatment of occipital condyle fractures. *Spine* 1988;13:731–736.

Anderson PA, Montesano PX. Injuries to the occipitocervical articulation. In: Chapman MW, ed. *Operative orthopaedics*, vol. 4, 2nd ed. Philadelphia: JB Lippincott; 1993:2631–2640.

Anderson PA, Montesano PX. Treatment of sacral fractures and lumbosacral injuries. In: Chapman MW, ed. *Operative orthopaedics*, vol. 4, 2nd ed. Philadelphia: JB Lippincott; 1993:2699–2710.

Beltran J. *MRI: musculoskeletal system.* Philadelphia: JB Lippincott; 1990.

Blacksin MF, Lee HJ. Frequency and significance of fractures of the upper cervical spine detected by CT in patients with severe neck trauma. *Am J Roentgenol* 1995;165:1201–1204.

Boyd WR, Gardiner GA Jr. Metrizamide myelography. *Am J Roentgenol* 1977;129:481–484.

Brandser EA, El-Khoury GY. Thoracic and lumbar spine trauma. *Radiol Clin North Am* 1997;35:533–557.

Brodsky AE, Binder WF. Lumbar discography. Its value in diagnosis and treatment of lumbar disc lesions. *Spine* 1979;4:110–120.

Brown RC, Evans ET. What causes the "eye in the Scotty dog" in the oblique projection of the lumbar spine? *Am J Roentgenol* 1973;118:435–437.

Bryk D, Rosenkranz W. True spondylolisthesis and pseudospondylolisthesis—the spinous process sign. *J Can Assoc Radiol* 1969;20:53–56.

Bucholz RW. Unstble hangman's fractures. *Clin Orthop* 1981;154:119–124.

Bucholz RW, Burkhead WZ. The pathologic anatomy of fatal atlanto-occipital dislocations. *J Bone Joint Surg [Am]* 1979;61A:248–250.

Burke JT, Harris JH. Acute injuries of the axis vertebra. *Skeletal Radiol* 1989;18:335–346.

Cancelmo JJ Jr. Clay shoveler's fracture: a helpful diagnostic sign. *Am J Roentgenol* 1972;115:540–543.

Chance CQ. Note on a type of flexion fracture of the spine. *Br J Radiol* 1948;21:452–453.

Christenson PC. The radiologic study of the normal spine: cervical, thoracic, lumbar, and sacral. *Radiol Clin North Am* 1977;15:133–154.

Clark WM, Gehweiler JA Jr, Laib R. Twelve significant signs of cervical spine trauma. *Skeletal Radiol* 1979;3:201–205.

Collis JS Jr, Gardner WJ. Lumbar discography. An analysis of one thousand cases. *J Neurosurg* 1962;19:452–461.

Daffner RH. Injuries of the thoracolumbar vertebral column. In: Dalinka MK, Kaye JJ, eds. *Radiology in emergency room medicine.* New York: Churchill Livingstone; 1984:317–341.

Daffner RH. *Imaging of vertebral trauma*, 2nd ed. Philadelphia: Lippincott-Raven; 1996.

Daffner RH. Helical CT of the cervical spine for trauma patients: a time study. *Am J Roentgenol* 2001;177:677–679.

Daffner RH, Brown RR, Goldberg AL. A new classification of cervical vertebral injuries: influence of CT. *Skeletal Radiol* 2000;29:125–132.

Daffner RH, Deeb ZL, Rothfus WE. "Fingerprints" of vertebral trauma—a unifying concept based on mechanisms. *Skeletal Radiol* 1986;15:518–525.

Denis F. Three column spine and its significance in the classification of acute thoracolumbar spinal injuries. *Spine* 1983;8:817–831.

Denis F. Spinal instability as defined by the three-column spine concept in acute spinal trauma. *Clin Orthop* 1984;189:65–76.

Dietz GW, Christensen EE. Normal "Cupid's bow" contour of the lower lumbar vertebrae. *Radiology* 1976;121:577–579.

Dullerud R, Johansen JG. CT-discography in patients with sciatica. Comparison with plain CT and MR imaging. *Acta Radiol* 1995;36:497–504.

Epstein BS, Epstein JA, Jones MD. Lumbar spondylolisthesis with isthmic defects. *Radiol Clin North Am* 1977;15:261–273.

Ferguson RL, Allen BL Jr. A mechanistic classification of thoracolumbar spine fractures. *Clin Orthop* 1984;189:77–88.

Firooznia H, Benjamin V, Kricheff II, Rafii M, Golimbu C. CT of lumbar spine disc herniation: correlation with surgical findings. *Am J Roentgenol* 1984;142:587–592.

Freyschmidt J, Brossmann J, Wiens J, Sternberg A. *Freyschmidt's "Koehler/Zimmer" Borderlands of normal and early pathological findings in skeletal radiography*, 5th ed, Stuttgart-New York: Thieme; 2003:671–730.

Fuchs AW. Cervical vertebrae (Part I). *Radiogr Clin Photogr* 1940;16:2–17.

Gabrielsen TO, Maxwell JA. Traumatic atlanto-occipital dislocation. *Am J Roentgenol* 1966;97:624–629.

Gerlock AJ Jr, Kirchner SG, Heller RM, Kaye JJ. *The cervical spine in trauma.* Philadelphia: WB Saunders; 1978.

Gerlock AJ Jr, Mirfakhraee M. Computed tomography and hangman's fractures. *South Med J* 1983;76:727–728.

Greenspan A. CT-discography vs. MRI in intervertebral disk herniation. *Appl Radiol* 1993;22:34–40.

Greenspan A, Amparo EG, Gorczyca D, Montesano PX. Is there a role for diskography in the era of magnetic resonance imaging? Prospective correlation and quantitative analysis of computed tomography-diskography, magnetic resonance imaging, and surgical findings. *J Spinal Disord* 1992;5:26–31.

Guerra J Jr, Garfin SR, Resnick D. Vertebral burst fractures: CT analysis of the retropulsed fragment. *Radiology* 1984;153:769–772.

Gumley G, Taylor TK, Ryan MD. Distraction fractures of the lumbar spine. *J Bone Joint Surg [Br]* 1982;64B:520–525.

Han SY, Witten DM, Mussleman JP. Jefferson fracture of the atlas. Report of six cases. *J Neurosurg* 1976;44:368–371.

Haughton VM. MR imaging of the spine. *Radiology* 1988;166:297–301.

Hayes CW, Conway WF, Walsh JW, Coppage L, Gervin AS. Seat belt injuries: radiologic findings and clinical correlation. *Radiographics* 1991;11:23–36.

Hecht ST, Greenspan A. Digital subtraction lumbar diskography: technical note. *J Spinal Disord* 1993;6:68–70.

Holdsworth F, Chir M. Fractures, dislocations and fracture-dislocations of the spine. *J Bone Joint Surg [Am]* 1970;52A:1534–1551.

Holt EP Jr. The question of lumbar discography. *J Bone Joint Surg [Am]* 1968;50A:720–726.

Hyman RA, Gorey MT. Imaging strategies for MR of the spine. *Radiol Clin North Am* 1988;26:505–533.

Jefferson G. Fractures of the atlas vertebra. Report of four cases, and a review of those previously recorded. *Br J Surg* 1920;7:407–422.

Johansen JG, Orrison WW, Amundsen P. Lateral C1-2 puncture for cervical myelography. Part I: Report of a complication. *Radiology* 1983;146:391–393.

Kaiser MC, Ramos L. *MRI of the spine. A guide to clinical applications.* Stuttgart: Thieme Verlag; 1990.

Kathol MH. Cervical spine trauma. What is new? *Radiol Clin North Am* 1997;35:507–532.

Kim KS, Chen HH, Russell EJ, Rogers LF. Flexion teardrop fracture of the cervical spine: radiographic characteristics. *Am J Roentgenol* 1989;152:319–326.

Kornberg M. Discography and magnetic resonance imaging in the diagnosis of lumbar disc disruption. *Spine* 1989;14:1368–1372.

Kricun R, Kricun ME, Dalinka MK. Advances in spinal imaging. *Radiol Clin North Am* 1990;28:321–339.

Lee C, Woodring JH. Unstable Jefferson variant atlas fractures: an unrecognized cervical injury. *Am J Roentgenol* 1992;158:113–118.

Levine AM, Edwards CC. The management of traumatic spondylolisthesis of the axis. *J Bone Joint Surg [AM]* 1985;67A:217–226.

MacDonald RL, Schwartz ML, Mirich D, Sharkey PW, Nelson WR. Diagnosis of cervical spine injury in motor vehicle crash victims: how many X-rays are enough? *J Trauma* 1990;30:392–397.

Mirvis SE, Young JW, Lim C, Greenberg J. Hangman's fracture: radiologic assessment in 27 cases. *Radiology* 1987;163:713–717.

Modic MT. Degenerative disorders of the spine. In: Modic MT, Masaryk TJ, Ross JS, eds. *Magnetic resonance imaging of the spine*. Chicago: Year Book Medical Publishers; 1989.

Modic MT. Magnetic resonance imaging of the spine. In: Modic MT, Masaryk TJ, Ross JS, eds. *Magnetic resonance imaging of the spine*. Chicago: Year Book Medical Publishers; 1989.

Montesano PX, Benson DR. The thoracocolumbar spine. In: Rockwood CA, Green DP, Bucholz RW, eds. *Rockwood and Green's fractures in adults*, 3rd ed. Philadelphia: JB Lippincott; 1991:1359–1397.

Montesano PX, Benson DR. Thoracolumbar spine fractures. In: Chapman MW, ed. *Operative orthopaedics*, vol. 4, 2nd ed. Philadelphia: JB Lippincott; 1993:2665–2697.

Munter FM, Wasserman BA, Wu H-M, Yousem DM. Serial MR imaging of annular tears in lumbar intervertebral disks. *Am J Neuroradiol* 2002;23:1105–1109.

Myerding HW. Spondylolisthesis. *Surg Gynecol Obstet* 1932;34:371–377.

Newman PH. The etiology of spondylolisthesis. *J Bone Joint Surg [Br]* 1963;45B:39–59.

Nuñez DB Jr, Quencer RM. The role of helical CT in the assessment of cervical spine injuries. *Am J Roentgenol* 1998;171:951–957.

Nuñez DB Jr, Zuluaga A, Fuentes-Bernardo DA, Rivas LA, Becerra JL. Cervical spine trauma: how much more do we learn by routinely using helical CT? *Radiographics* 1996;16:1307–1318.

Orrison WW, Eldevik OP, Sackett JF. Lateral C1-2 puncture for cervical myelography. Part III: Historical, anatomic and technical considerations. *Radiology* 1983;146:401–408.

Raila FA, Aitken AT, Vickers GN. Computed tomography and three-dimensional reconstruction in the evaluation of occipital condyle fracture. *Skeletal Radiol* 1993;22:269–271.

Rogers LF. The roentgenographic appearance of transverse or Chance fractures of the spine: the seat belt fracture. *Am J Roentgenol* 1971;111:844–849.

Rogers LF, Lee C. Cervical spine trauma. In: Dalinka MK, Kaye JJ, eds. *Radiology in emergency room medicine*. New York: Churchill Livingstone; 1984.

Scher AT. Unilateral locked facet in cervical spine injuries. *Am J Roentgenol* 1977;129:45–48.

Scher AT. "Tear-drop" fractures of the cervical spine—radiologic features. *S Afr Med J* 1982;61:355–356.

Schneider RC, Livingston KE, Cave AJE, Hamilton G. "Hangman's fracture" of the cervical spine. *J Neurosurg* 1965;22:141–154.

Slone RM, MacMillan M, Montgomery WJ. Spinal fixation. Part 1. Principles, basic hardware, and fixation techniques for the cervical spine. *Radiographics* 1993;13:341—356.

Slone RM, MacMillan M, Montgomery WJ, Heare M. Spinal fixation. Part 2. Fixation techniques and hardware for the thoracic and lumbosacral spine. *Radiographics* 1993;13:521–543.

Smith GR, Northrop CH, Loop JW. Jumper's fractures: patterns of thoracocolumbar spine injuries associated with vertical plunges. A review of 38 cases. *Radiology* 1977;122:657–663.

Spencer JA, Yeakley JW, Kaufman HH. Fracture of the occipitale condyle. *Neurosurgery* 1984;15:101–103.

Spengler DM. Lumbar disc herniation. In: Chapman MW, ed. *Operative orthopaedics*, vol. 4, 2nd ed. Philadelphia: JB Lippincott; 1993:2735–2744.

Taber KH, Herrick RC, Weathers SW, Kumar AJ, Schomer DF, Hayman LA. Pitfalls and artifacts encountered in clinical MR imaging of the spine. *Radiographics* 1998;18:1499–1521.

Tehranzadeh J. Discography 2000. *Radiol Clin North Am* 1998;36:463–495.

Wiltse LL. Spondylolisthesis: classification and etiology. In: *AAOS Symposium on the Spine*. American Academy of Orthopedic Surgeons. St. Louis: Mosby; 1969:143–167.

Wiltse LL, Winter RB. Terminology and measurement of spondylolisthesis. *J Bone Joint Surg [Am]* 1983;65A:768–772.

Whitley JE, Forsyth HF. Classification of cervical spine injuries. *Am J Roentgenol* 1958;83:633–644.

Woodring JF, Lee C. Limitations of cervical radiography in the evaluation of acute cervical trauma. *J Trauma* 1993;34:32–39.

Yu S, Sether IA, Ho PS, Wagner M, Haughton VM. Tears of the annulus fibrosus: correlation between MR and pathologic findings in cadavers. *Am J Neuroradiol* 1988;9:367–370.

Zanca P, Lodmell EA. Fracture of spinous processes: new sign for the recognition of fractures of cervical and upper dorsal spinous processes. *Radiology* 1951;56:427–429.

ARTHRITIDES

Radiologic Evaluation of the Arthritides

In its general meaning, the term *arthritis* indicates an abnormality of the joint as the result of a degenerative, inflammatory, infectious, or metabolic process (Fig. 12.1). Also included among the arthritides are connective tissue arthropathies, such as those associated with systemic lupus erythematosus (SLE) and scleroderma.

Radiologic Imaging Modalities

Conventional Radiography

The radiologic modalities used to evaluate arthritis are very similar to those used in traumatic conditions involving the bones and joints (see Chapter 4), although there are some modifications. The most important modality for the evaluation of arthritis is conventional radiography. As in the radiographic examination of traumatic conditions, standard films of the involved joint should be obtained in at least two projections at 90 degrees to each other (Fig. 12.2; see also Fig. 4.1). A weight-bearing view may be of value, particularly for a dynamic evaluation of any decrement in the joint space under the weight of the body (Fig. 12.3). Special projections may at times be required to demonstrate destructive changes in the joint to better advantages. The radial head–capitellum view (see Chapter 6), by eliminating overlap of the radial head and coronoid process and by more clearly demonstrating the humeroradial and humeroulnar joints, shows the inflammatory changes in the elbow joint to better advantage (Fig. 12.4). The semisupinated oblique view of the hand and wrist (the so-called Allstate or ball-catcher's view), introduced by Norgaard in 1965, effectively demonstrates the radial aspects of the metacarpal heads and of the base of the proximal phalanges in the hand and the triquetrum and pisiform in the wrist (Fig. 12.5). Because the earliest erosive changes of some inflammatory arthritides begin in these areas, the Norgaard view may provide important information at the early stages of arthritides (Fig. 12.6). It may also demonstrate subtle subluxations in metacarpophalangeal joints frequently seen in SLE.

Magnification Radiography

This technique used to diagnose the very early articular changes of arthritis, which were not well appreciated on standard projections (Fig. 12.7). The method involves a special screen-film system and geometric enlargement that yields magnified images of the bones and joints with greater sharpness and bony detail. Magnification radiography is now completely replaced by digital radiography and cutting-edge technology of PACS (picture archive and communication system) for radiology images, allowing i-site stentor filmless high-resolution image-display format with advanced radiology reading workstations.

Tomography, Computed Tomography, and Arthrography

Among the ancillary imaging techniques, conventional tomography was used in the past, its major purpose being demonstration to better advantage of the degree of joint destruction (Fig. 12.8). Computed tomography (CT) is effective in evaluating degenerative and inflammatory changes of various joints (Fig. 12.9A–C), and in the spine to document spinal stenosis (Fig. 12.9D). In the assessment of spinal stenosis secondary to degenerative changes, CT examination may also be performed after myelography (Fig. 12.10), although myelography alone is often sufficient (Fig. 12.11). Arthrography has some limited application in the evaluation of degenerative (Fig. 12.12), inflammatory, and infectious (see Fig. 25.17B) conditions of the joint.

Scintigraphy

Radionuclide bone scan is much more commonly used than these other techniques, mainly for evaluating the distribution of arthritis in different joints (see Chapter 2). The radiopharmaceuticals currently in use in bone scan include organic diphosphonates—ethylene diphosphonate (HEPD) and methylene diphosphonate (MDP)—labeled with ^{99m}Tc, a gamma emitter with a 6-hour half-life; MDP is more commonly used, typically in a dose that provides 15 mCi (555 MBq) of ^{99m}Tc. After intravenous injection of the radiopharmaceutical, approximately 50% of the dose localizes in bone, with the remainder circulating freely in the body and eventually excreted by the kidneys. A gamma camera can then be used in a procedure known as a three-phase radionuclide bone scan. Scintigraphy can determine the distribution of arthritic changes in large and small joints (Fig. 12.13). It can also distinguish an infected joint from infected periarticular soft tissues (see Fig. 24.9). To distinguish infectious arthritis from other forms of arthritides, ^{111}In-labeled leukocytes and ^{57}Ga scans are employed (see Chapter 2, section on Scintigraphy).

Serial examinations with bone scintigraphy, as Brower and Flemming have pointed out, have also been helpful in evaluating the activity of given arthritis at a particular point in time. Such examinations may differentiate active disease from arthritis in remission.

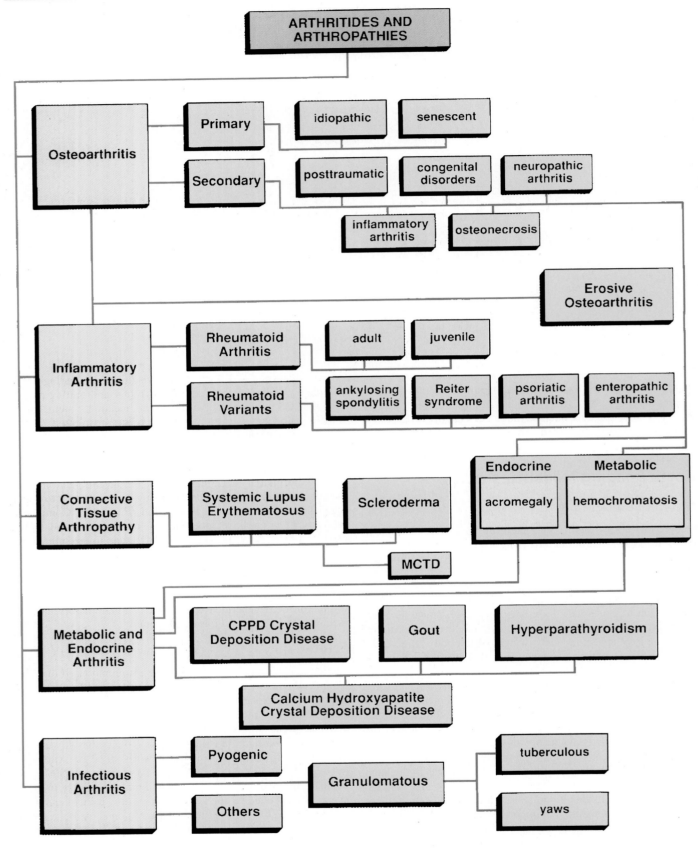

▲
FIGURE 12.1   Classification of the arthritides.

FIGURE 12.2   Osteoarthritis. A 58-year-old woman presented with a history of pain in the left knee. (**A**) Anteroposterior radiograph demonstrates narrowing of the medial femorotibial joint compartment and marginal osteophytes arising from both the medial and lateral femoral condyles—findings typical of osteoarthritis (degenerative joint disease). (**B**) Lateral radiograph demonstrates, in addition, osteophytes at the anterior and posterior aspects of the articular end of the tibia, which are not appreciated on the anteroposterior projection. Involvement of the femoropatellar joint compartment and the presence of synovitis, represented by suprapatellar joint effusion, are also well demonstrated.

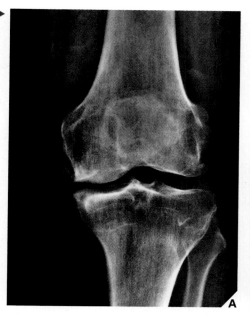
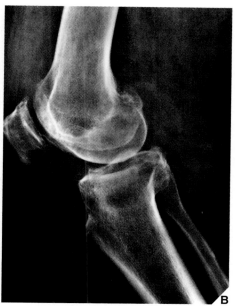

FIGURE 12.3   Osteoarthritis. Weight-bearing anteroposterior film of the left knee of the same patient shown in Figure 12.2 demonstrates collapse of the medial femorotibial compartment under the weight of the body, with a resulting varus configuration of the knee.

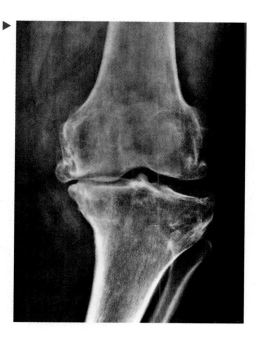

FIGURE 12.4   **Rheumatoid arthritis.** (**A**) Standard lateral radiograph of the elbow of a 48-year-old woman with known rheumatoid arthritis of several years' duration shows destructive changes typical of inflammatory arthritis. (**B**) A special projection known as the radial head-capitellum view (see also Fig. 6.12) demonstrates to better advantage the details of the arthritic process involving the humeroradial and humeroulnar joints. (From Greenspan A, Norman A, 1983, with permission.)

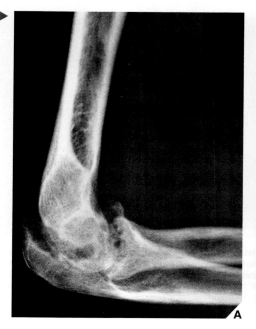
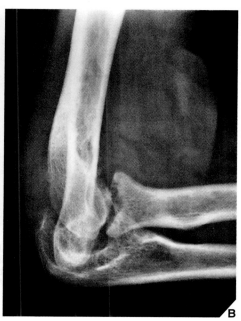

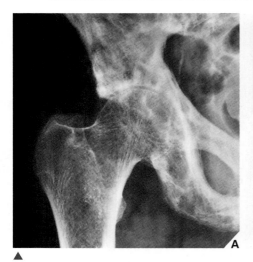
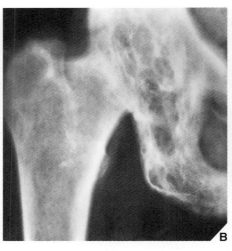
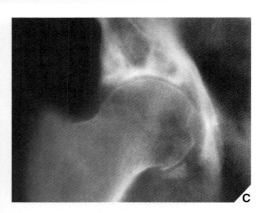

FIGURE 12.8 **Tomography of secondary osteoarthritis in Paget disease.** A 74-year-old woman with Paget disease and secondary degenerative changes in the hip joint was evaluated for a possible total hip arthroplasty. (**A**) Standard anteroposterior view of the right hip shows extensive Paget disease evident in the thickening of the cortex of the pelvic bones, particularly the ischium, and a coarse trabecular pattern. Note the narrowing of the radiographic joint space indicative of osteoarthritis of the hip joint. Conventional tomograms show predominant involvement of the acetabulum (**B**) with preservation of the femoral head (**C**).

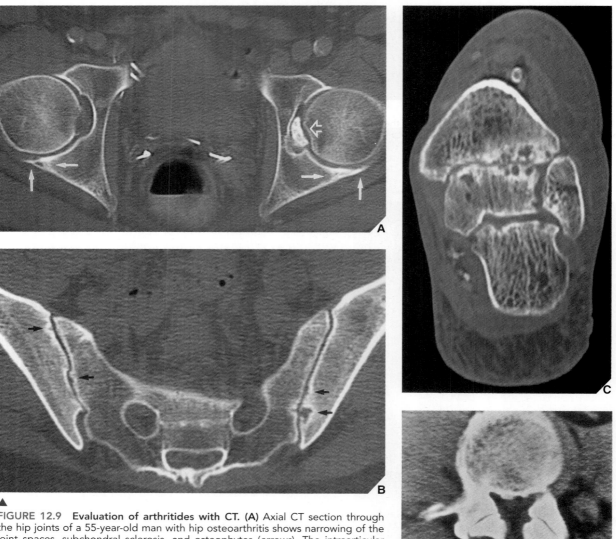

FIGURE 12.9 **Evaluation of arthritides with CT.** (**A**) Axial CT section through the hip joints of a 55-year-old man with hip osteoarthritis shows narrowing of the joint spaces, subchondral sclerosis, and osteophytes (*arrows*). The intraarticular osteochondral body (*open arrow*) was not clearly demonstrated on conventional radiographs. (**B**) Axial CT section through the sacroiliac joints of a 49-year-old man with psoriatic arthritis shows diffuse narrowing of the joints and articular erosions (*arrows*). (**C**) Coronal CT section through the ankle and foot of a 52-year-old woman with rheumatoid arthritis shows erosions of the tibiotalar and subtalar joints. (**D**) CT scan of the lumbar spine in a 66-year-old patient with advanced osteoarthritis of the facet joints shows marked narrowing of the spinal canal secondary to degenerative changes. At 8 mm, the transverse diameter is well below normal.

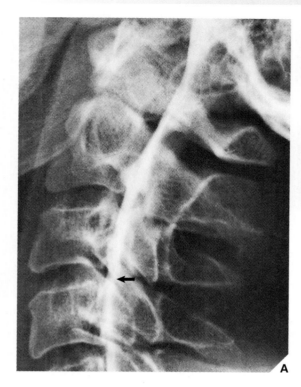

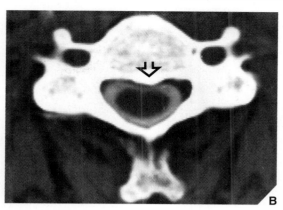

FIGURE 12.10   CT myelography of impingement of the thecal sac. A 56-year-old man reported constant pain in the neck radiating to the left arm; there was also associated weakness and numbness in the left hand. **(A)** Cervical myelogram in the lateral projection shows a small extradural defect on the ventral aspect of the thecal sac at C3-4 (*arrow*). **(B)** CT section obtained after myelography shows impingement of a posterior osteophyte on the thecal sac at the corresponding level (*open arrow*).

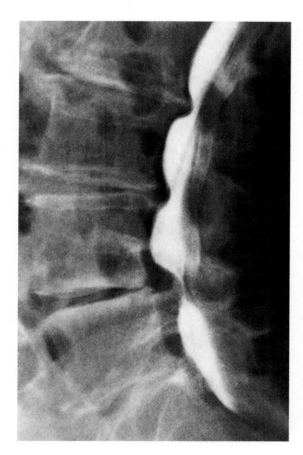

FIGURE 12.11   Myelography of spinal stenosis. Lateral radiograph of the lumbosacral spine obtained after injection of metrizamide into the subarachnoid space shows an "hourglass" configuration of the contrast agent in the thecal sac, a feature characteristic of spinal stenosis. This appearance results from concomitant hypertrophy of the facet joints and posterior bulging of the intervertebral disks.

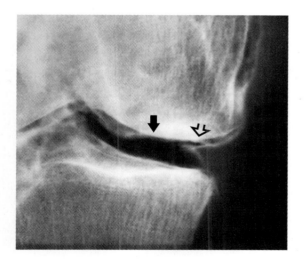

FIGURE 12.12   Arthrography of osteoarthritis. Double-contrast arthrogram in a 62-year-old man with progressive pain localized to the medial femorotibial joint compartment demonstrates destruction of the articular cartilage (*arrow*) and degenerative changes of the free edge of the medial meniscus (*open arrow*), consistent with osteoarthritis.

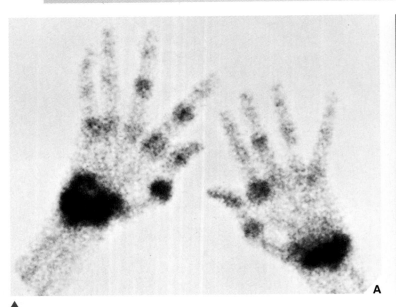
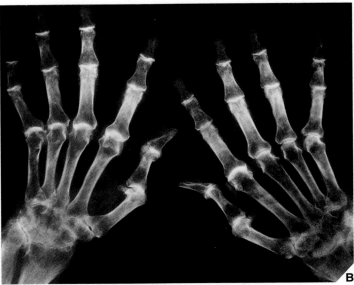

FIGURE 12.13   Scintigraphy of psoriatic arthritis. Radionuclide bone scan (**A**) obtained 2 hours after the intravenous injection of 15 mCi (555 MBq) of ^{99m}Tc-labeled MDP shows an increased uptake of radiopharmaceutical in several joints of the hand and wrist. A conventional radiograph (**B**) of the same patient shows advanced psoriatic arthritis.

Ultrasound

Ultrasound (US) is occasionally used in the evaluation of joint abnormalities. This technique helps to differentiate popliteal fossa masses in patients with rheumatoid arthritis, in whom complications of an arthritic process (such as popliteal cyst or hypertrophied synovium) may be distinguished from conditions not related to arthritis (such as popliteal artery aneurysm) (see Fig. 2.21). It may also effectively diagnose deep vein thrombosis, occasionally seen in patients with rheumatoid arthritis (see Fig. 2.22). At times US may demonstrate bone erosions and inflammatory panus. Recently some investigators have explored the use of power Doppler US in the evaluation of rheumatoid synovitis.

Magnetic Resonance Imaging

Magnetic resonance imaging (MRI) of the joints provides excellent contrast between soft tissues and bone. Articular cartilage, fibrocartilage, cortex, and spongy bone can be distinguished from each other by their specific signal intensities. It is an excellent modality for demonstrating the rheumatoid nodules and synovial abnormalities in patients with rheumatoid arthritis. MRI's ability to contrast the synovium-covered joint from other soft-tissue structures allows for noninvasive delineation of the degree of synovial hypertrophy that accompanies synovitis, previously demonstrable only by means of arthrography or arthroscopy. Because synovitis is often accompanied by joint effusion, this too can be effectively demonstrated by MRI (Fig. 12.14). In particular, when this technique is combined with intravenous administration of gadolinium diethylenetri-amine penta-acetic acid (Gd-DTPA), it is highly effective in differentiation between fluid-filled joints and tendon sheaths from synovitis. Both, fluid and intraarticular synovial tissue exibit an intermediate signal intensity on T1-weighted images and a high signal on T2 weighting. However, gadolinium-enhanced T1-weighted images will show high intensity signal of inflammatory pannus/synovial tissue, whereas fluid will not enhance (Fig. 12.15). MRI is also quite helpful in diagnosing Baker cyst (Fig. 12.16). Although MRI is quite sensitive in detecting joint effusion, it

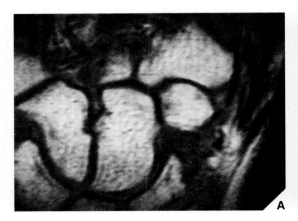
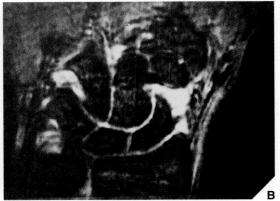

FIGURE 12.14   MRI of rheumatoid arthritis. Conventional radiographs were normal in this patient with known rheumatoid arthritis of the wrist. MRI in the coronal plane using (**A**) spin-echo sequence and (**B**) gradient echo technique demonstrates marginal scaphoid erosions with adjacent fluid and inflammatory panus. Inflammatory fluid is also seen in the radioulnar, midcarpal, radiocarpal, and carpometacarpal joints.

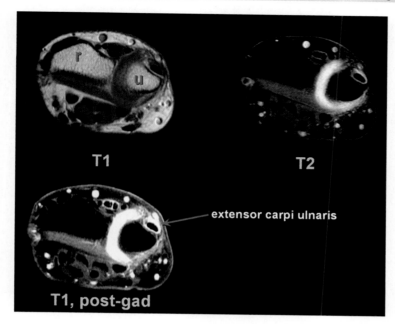

▲
FIGURE 12.15   MRa of rheumatoid arthritis. Axial T1-weighted, T2-weighted, and contrast-enhanced T1-weighted MR images of the wrist of the 28-year-old woman with clinical diagnosis of rheumatoid arthritis show advantage of postgadolinium study for diagnosis of synovitis of the distal radioulnar joint and extensor carpi ulnaris tendon. Although the high signal on T2 weighting may indicate either fluid or inflammatory pannus, the marked enhancement on postgadolinium sequences confirms the presence of the latter, because fluid would not enhance. r, radius; u, ulna.

cannot yet distinguish between inflammatory fluid and noninflammatory fluid. Occasionally, MRI may provide some additional information on osteoarthritis (Figs. 12.17 and 12.18) and hemophilic arthropathy (Figs. 12.19 and 12.20). With the development of more sophisticated orthopedic methods for cartilage repair in osteoarthritis, such as new articular cartilage replacement techniques, including chondrocyte transplantation, osteochondral transplantation, and cartilage growth-stimulating factors, optimized MRI of these interventions for diagnosis and treatment planning in osteoarthritis is essential.

The most promising role of MRI, however, is in the evaluation of the spine. MR images in the sagittal plane are useful for demonstrating hypertrophy of the ligamentum flavum or the vertebral facets, grading the degree of foramina stenosis, and measuring the sagittal diameter of the spinal canal and the spinal cord. MR images in the axial plane facilitate detailed analysis of the facet joints and more accurate measurement of the thickness of the ligamentum flavum and the diameter of the spinal canal. The quality of evaluation of spinal cord abnormalities by MRI in the cervical area in patients with rheumatoid arthritis and of spinal stenosis in patients with advanced degenerative changes of the spine surpasses that obtained with other modalities. MRI is particularly useful in the examination of patients with pain related to disk disease because it can differentiate normal, degenerated, and herniated disks noninvasively (see Chapter 11). In fact, the changes of disk degeneration can be identified by MRI long before they can be detected by conventional radiography or CT.

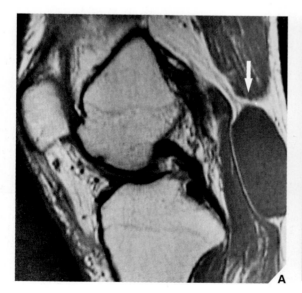
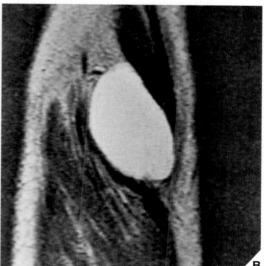

▲
FIGURE 12.16   MRI of the Baker cyst. A 68-year-old woman with rheumatoid arthritis reported pain in the region of the popliteal fossa. The presumptive diagnosis of thrombophlebitis was made. (A) Sagittal MRI (SE; TR 900/TE 20 msec) demonstrates an oval structure in the popliteal fossa displaying intermediate signal intensity (arrow). Also note a small subchondral erosion of the anterior aspect of the medial femoral condyle. (B) Coronal MRI (SE; TR 1800/TE 80 msec) at the level of the popliteal fossa demonstrates a large Baker cyst that displays a high signal intensity caused by fluid content.

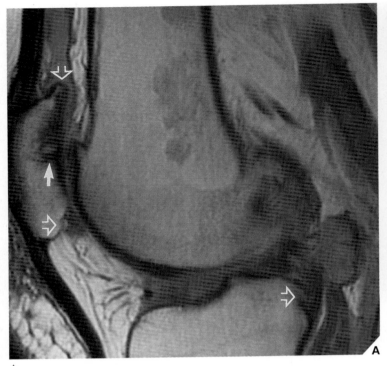

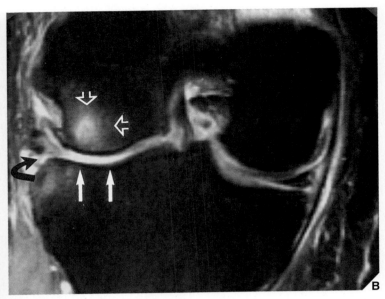

FIGURE 12.17 **MRI of osteoarthritis. (A)** Sagittal proton density-weighted MRI of a 62-year-old woman with osteoarthritis of the right knee shows involvement of the femoropatellar compartment. Note joint space narrowing, subchondral cyst (*arrow*), and osteophytes (*open arrows*). **(B)** Coronal T2-weighted fat-suppressed MR image shows complete destruction of articular cartilage of the lateral joint compartment (*arrows*), subchondral edema (*open arrows*), and degenerative tear of the lateral meniscus (*curved arrow*).

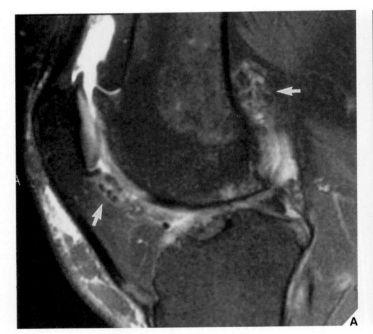

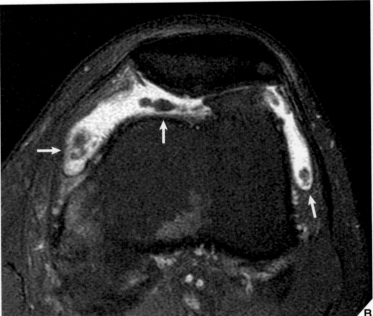

FIGURE 12.18 **MRI of osteoarthritis. (A)** Sagittal and **(B)** axial T2-weighted fat-suppressed MR images of the knee of a 60-year-old man show osteoarthritis complicated by multiple osteochondral bodies (*arrows*).

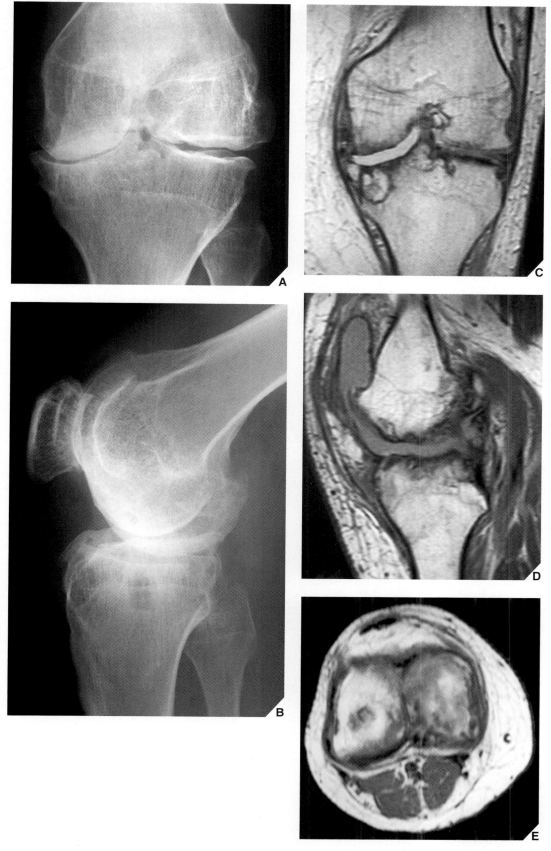

▲

FIGURE 12.19   **MRI of hemophilic arthropathy.** A 29-year-old man with hemophilia and multiple episodes of intraarticular bleeding. (**A**) Anteroposterior and (**B**) lateral radiographs of the left knee demonstrate an advanced stage of hemophilia. Abnormalities include periarticular osteoporosis, irregularity of subchondral bone at the tibial plateau and femoral condyles, narrowing of the radiographic joint space, and erosion of the subchondral bone. (**C**) Coronal MRI (SE; TR 1900/TE 20 msec) demonstrates, in addition, complete destruction of articular cartilage at the medial joint compartment, and a large, subchondral cyst in the proximal tibia, not well appreciated on the radiographic films. (**D**) Sagittal MRI (SE; TR 800/TE 20 msec) demonstrates to better advantage the intraarticular blood in the suprapatellar and infrapatellar bursae, displaying intermediate signal intensity. (**E**) Axial MRI (TR 400/TE 20 msec) shows erosive changes of the articular cartilage of the femoral condyles.

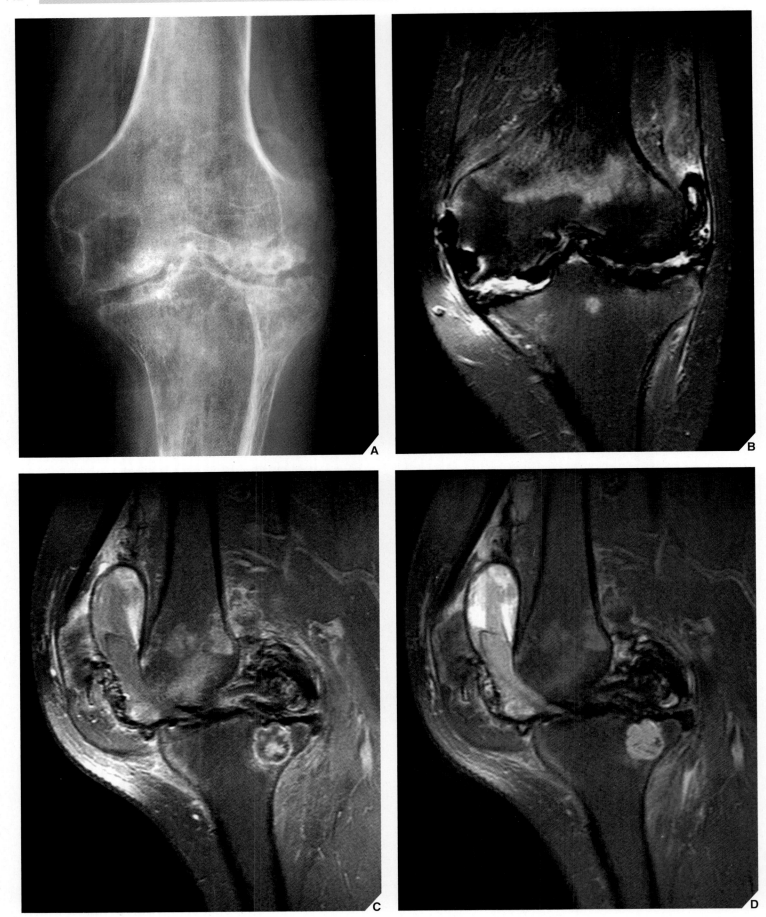

FIGURE 12.20   MRI of hemophilic arthropathy. (A) Anteroposterior radiograph of the left knee, **(B)** coronal proton density-weighted fat-suppressed, **(C)** sagittal T1-weighted contrast-enhanced fat-suppressed, and **(D)** sagittal proton density-weighted fat-suppressed MR images of a 34-year-old man show destructive changes of all three joint compartments. Note heterogeneous appearance of bloody effusion in the joint and suprapatellar bursa.

The Arthritides

Diagnosis

Clinical Information
The accurate diagnosis of specific arthritis depends on many factors; however, the most important is to understand the patterns of symptoms and the mechanism of disease.

The clinical manifestations and laboratory data, in conjunction with the imaging findings, are of significant help in making the diagnosis of a specific arthritic process. The various arthritides, for example, have different frequencies of occurrence between the sexes. Rheumatoid arthritis is much more common in females, and erosive osteoarthritis is seen almost exclusively in middle-aged women. Psoriatic arthritis, Reiter syndrome (currently known as reactive arthritis), and gouty arthritis, however, are more common in males. Clinical symptoms are of further assistance. Patients with Reiter syndrome, for example, usually present with urethritis, conjunctivitis, and mucocutaneous lesions, and those with psoriatic arthritis may present with swelling of a single finger, the so-called sausage digit, as well as changes in the skin and fingernails. Patients with gouty arthritis may exhibit soft-tissue masses, representing chronic tophi, on the dorsal aspect of the hands or feet.

Laboratory data are also essential. Gouty arthritis, for instance, is associated with elevated serum uric acid concentrations, and a synovial fluid examination reveals monosodium urate crystals in leukocytes in the fluid. The synovial fluid of patients with pseudogout, however, contains calcium pyrophosphate crystals. The detection of autoantibodies is another important aid in the diagnostic workup. Rheumatoid factor (RF) is a typical finding in rheumatoid arthritis. Patients lacking the specific antibodies represented by RF are said to have "seronegative" arthritis. Patients with lupus arthritis have a positive lupus erythematosus cell test. Lastly, identification of the antigens of the major histocompatibility complex, particularly human leukocyte–associated antigens HLA-B27 and HLA-DR4, has in recent years become a crucial test in the diagnosis of arthritic disease. It has been reported that 95% of patients with ankylosing spondylitis, 86% of patients with reactive arthritis, and 60% of patients with psoriatic arthropathy test positively for antigen HLA-B27, whereas a majority of those with rheumatoid arthritis exhibit the HLA-DR4 antigen. This is helpful in differentiating certain types of arthritides, as well as distinguishing psoriatic arthritis from rheumatoid arthritis in cases in which the radiographic presentation of these conditions may be very similar.

Imaging Features
The true or diarthrodial joint consists of cartilage covering the articular ends of the bones forming the joint; the articular capsule, which is reinforced by ligamentous structures; and the joint space, which is lined with synovial membrane and filled with synovial fluid (Fig. 12.21). Because of its physicochemical constitution, articular cartilage absorbs only a minimal amount of x-rays, thus appearing radiolucent on a radiographic film. The radiolucent articular cartilage, together with the joint cavity filled with synovial fluid, creates the so-called radiographic joint space.

The abnormality of the joint in arthritis usually consists of destruction of the articular cartilage, which appears on a film as a narrowing of the radiographic joint space, usually accompanied by subchondral erosion; narrowing of the joint is the cardinal sign of arthritis (Fig. 12.22). It should be kept in mind, however, that in some arthritic processes the joint space may not become narrow, appearing instead slightly expanded. This happens, for example, in the early stages of some arthritides, when joint effusion and ligamentous laxity cause distention of the joint with fluid, but the articular cartilage has not yet been destroyed. It may also be seen in rare instances when granulation pannus erodes the subchondral bone without destroying the articular cartilage (Fig. 12.23).

Other radiographic signs specific to different types of arthritis include periarticular soft-tissue swelling, periarticular osteoporosis, and, in the more advanced stages of some arthritides, complete destruction of the joint with subluxation or dislocation and ankylosis (joint fusion) (Fig. 12.24).

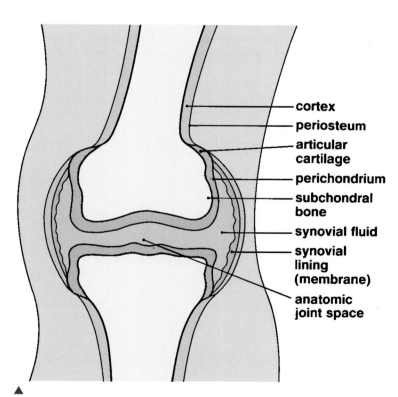

cortex
periosteum
articular cartilage
perichondrium
subchondral bone
synovial fluid
synovial lining (membrane)
anatomic joint space

▲ FIGURE 12.21   The constituent structures of a true or diarthrodial joint.

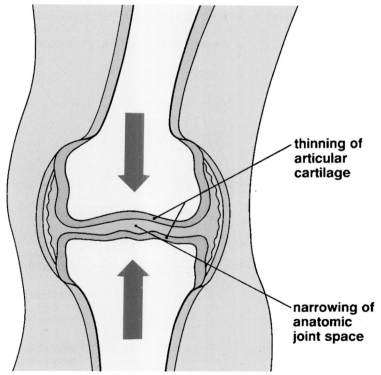

thinning of articular cartilage

narrowing of anatomic joint space

▲ FIGURE 12.22   Narrowing of the joint space. The cardinal sign of an arthritic process is narrowing of the radiographic joint space. Thinning of the articular cartilage reduces the space mechanically.

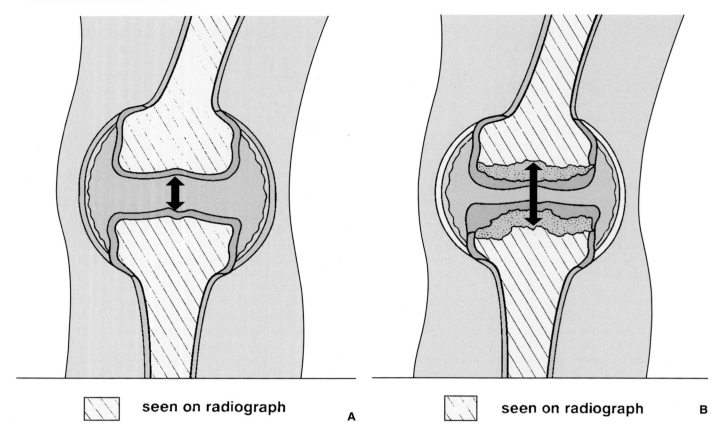

seen on radiograph **A**

seen on radiograph **B**

▲
FIGURE 12.23 **Variations in the width of the joint space.** In the early stage of some arthritides, widening rather than narrowing of the joint space may be seen radiographically. This may be caused by distention of the joint with fluid (**A**) or erosion of the subchondral bone by granulation pannus with some preservation of the articular cartilage (**B**).

The radiographic presentation of arthritis depends on the type and stage of the disease, as well as the site of the original insult characteristic for the various forms of arthritis (Fig. 12.25)—whether it is the articular cartilage, as in osteoarthritis (see Figs. 12.2 and 12.29); the synovial membrane, as in inflammatory arthritis (Fig. 12.26A); the synovial membrane, subchondral bone, and periarticular soft tissues, as in infectious arthritis (see Fig. 25.16); or the synovial membrane, articular cartilage, subchondral bone, and periarticular soft tissues as in some metabolic arthritides (Fig. 12.26B,C).

The radiographic diagnosis of arthritis, as Resnick observed, is based on the evaluation of two fundamental parameters: the *morphology* of the articular lesion and its *distribution* in the skeleton. If these findings are

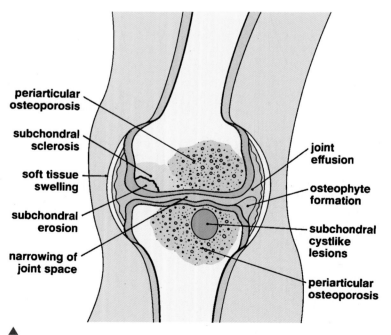

periarticular osteoporosis

subchondral sclerosis

soft tissue swelling

subchondral erosion

narrowing of joint space

joint effusion

osteophyte formation

subchondral cystlike lesions

periarticular osteoporosis

▲
FIGURE 12.24 **Radiographic features of arthritides.** Summary representation of radiographic features seen in the arthritides. Not all of these features are seen in every type of arthritis.

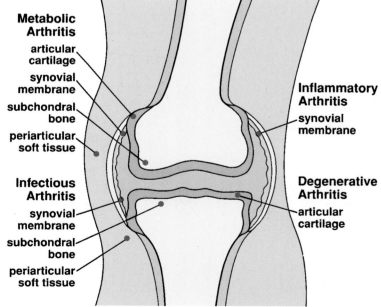

Metabolic Arthritis
articular cartilage
synovial membrane
subchondral bone
periarticular soft tissue

Infectious Arthritis
synovial membrane
subchondral bone
periarticular soft tissue

Inflammatory Arthritis
synovial membrane

Degenerative Arthritis
articular cartilage

▲
FIGURE 12.25 Target sites of various arthritides in a joint.

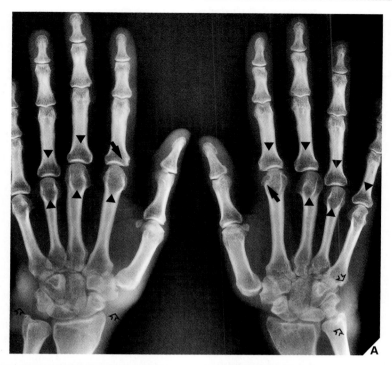

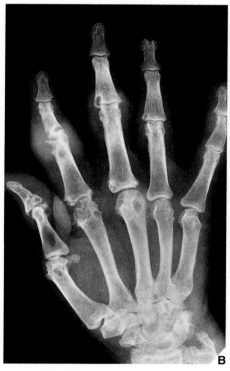

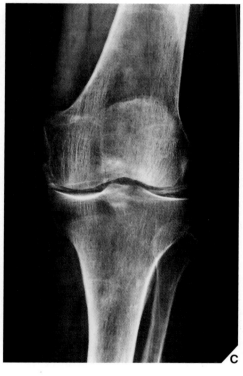

FIGURE 12.26 **Radiographic features of various arthritides. (A)** Early changes of rheumatoid arthritis, as seen in the hands of a 40-year-old woman, present as marginal erosions (*arrows*) in so-called bare areas at the locus of attachment of the capsular synovial lining. Also note the periarticular osteoporosis (*arrow heads*) and soft-tissue swelling, particularly in both wrists (*open arrows*). **(B)** The asymmetric marginal erosions affecting various articulations in the hand of a 38-year-old man with tophaceous gout are characteristic of a metabolic process involving the subchondral bone. Note the preservation of part of the joint and the location of several erosions at some distance from the joint space. **(C)** In calcium pyrophosphate dihydrate (CPPD) crystal deposition arthropathy, seen here in the knee of a 45-year-old woman, there is calcification of the fibrocartilage (semilunar cartilage or menisci) and hyaline cartilage (articular cartilage) in association with narrowing of the medial femorotibial joint compartment. Aspirated fluid from the knee joint yielded CPPD crystals.

combined with the history, physical examination, and relevant laboratory data in a given case, then the accuracy of the diagnosis is markedly improved.

Morphology of the Articular Lesion. The various arthritides exhibit morphologically distinct features, as observed radiographically in the large (Fig. 12.27) and small (Fig. 12.28) joints. In the degenerative form of the disease known as osteoarthritis, thinning of the articular cartilage results in localized narrowing of the joint space; there is also subchondral sclerosis and osteophyte and cyst formation, but generally osteoporosis is absent (Fig. 12.29). Inflammatory arthritides, such as rheumatoid arthritis, are characterized by a diffuse, usually multicompartmental narrowing of the joint space associated with marginal or central erosions, periarticular osteoporosis, and symmetric periarticular soft-tissue swelling; subchondral sclerosis is minimal or absent, and formation of osteophytes is lacking (Fig. 12.30). In a metabolic arthritis such as gout, well-defined bony

RADIOGRAPHIC MORPHOLOGY OF ARTHRITIDES IN A LARGE JOINT

Osteoarthritis

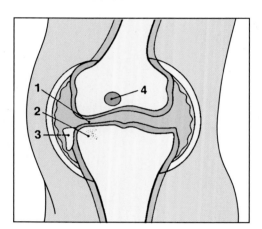

1 localized joint-space narrowing

2 subchondral sclerosis

3 osteophytes

4 cyst or pseudocyst

Inflammatory Arthritis (Rheumatoid Arthritis)

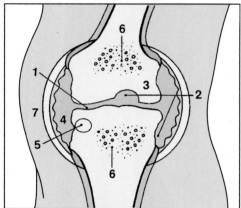

1 diffuse joint-space narrowing

2 marginal or central erosions

3 absent or minimal subchondral sclerosis

4 lack of osteophytes

5 cystic lesions

6 osteoporosis

7 periarticular soft tissue swelling (symmetric, usually fusiform)

Metabolic Arthritis (Gout)

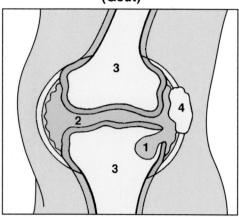

1 marginal erosion with overhanging edge

2 partial preservation of joint space

3 lack of osteoporosis

4 lobulated, asymmetric soft tissue mass

Infectious Arthritis

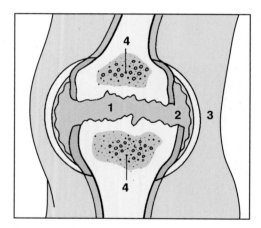

1 destruction of joint space

2 joint effusion

3 soft tissue swelling

4 osteoporosis

Neuropathic Joint

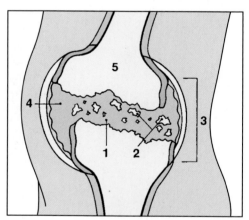

1 destruction of joint with gross disorganization

2 bony debris

3 joint instability

4 joint effusion

5 (usual) lack of osteoporosis

▲

FIGURE 12.27 Morphologic features distinguishing the various arthritides in a large joint.

RADIOGRAPHIC MORPHOLOGY OF ARTHRITIDES IN THE HAND

Osteoarthritis

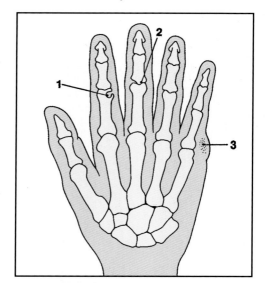

1 Heberden nodes
2 Bouchard nodes
3 joint space narrowing
4 subchondral sclerosis

Erosive Osteoarthritis

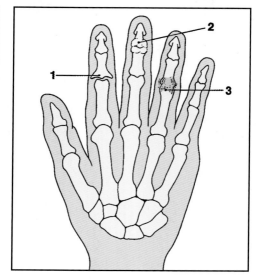

1 gull-wing erosion
2 Heberden nodes (occasionally)
3 interphalangeal ankylosis

Rheumatoid Arthritis

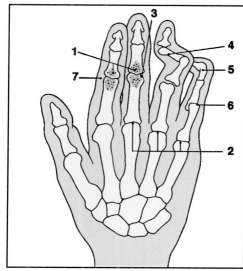

1 periarticular osteoporosis
2 joint space narrowing
3 marginal erosions
4 boutonniére deformity
5 swan-neck deformity
6 subluxations and dislocations
7 soft tissue swelling (symmetric, fusiform)

Gouty Arthritis

1 asymmetric erosion with
  overhanging edge
2 partial preservation of joint space
3 asymmetric soft tissue swelling with
  or without calcifications (tophus)
  (usually at dorsal aspect)

Psoriatic Arthritis

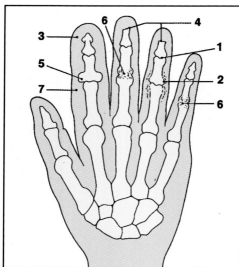

1 joint space narrowing
2 fluffy periostitis
3 "sausage digit" (soft tissue
  swelling of single digit)
4 erosion of terminal tufts
5 "mouse-ear" type of articular erosion
6 interphalangeal ankylosis
7 soft tissue swelling

Lupus Arthritis

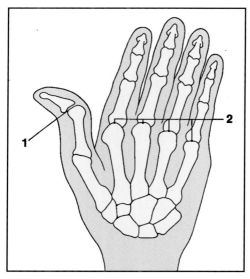

1 hitchhiker's thumb deformity
2 flexible deformities
  (subluxations)

▲
FIGURE 12.28   Morphologic features distinguishing the various arthritides in the small joints of the hand.

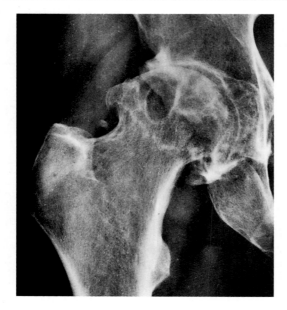

▲

FIGURE 12.29   Osteoarthritis. Conventional radiograph of the hip demonstrates the typical morphologic changes seen in degenerative joint disease (osteoarthritis): focal narrowing of the joint space (here at the weight-bearing segment), subchondral sclerosis, cyst-like lesions, and marginal osteophytes. Note the lack of osteoporosis.

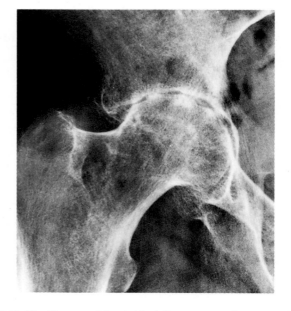

▲

FIGURE 12.30   Rheumatoid arthritis. Inflammatory arthritis, seen here in the hip, is marked by diffuse, uniform narrowing of the joint space, axial migration of the femoral head, marginal and central subchondral erosions, and severe periarticular osteoporosis. Note the almost total absence of reactive subchondral sclerosis and the lack of osteophyte formation.

erosions displaying a so-called overhanging edge are usually associated with preservation of part of the joint space and a localized, asymmetric soft-tissue nodules; osteophyte formation and osteoporosis are absent (Fig. 12.31). Infectious arthritis is characterized by the complete destruction of both articular ends of the bones forming the joint; all communicating joint compartments are invariably involved, with

diffuse osteoporosis, joint effusion, and periarticular soft-tissue swelling (see Fig. 25.17A). Neuropathic arthritis is marked by destruction of the articular surfaces, which leaves bony debris, and a substantial joint effusion; osteoporosis is usually lacking. Depending on the amount of destruction, varying degrees of joint instability are present (Fig. 12.32).

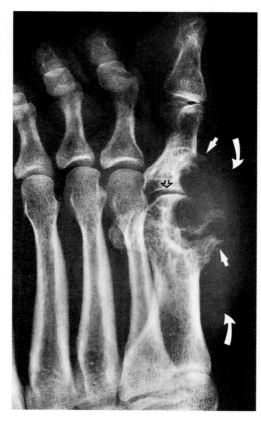

▲

FIGURE 12.31   Gouty arthritis. Asymmetric periarticular erosions that spare part of the joint are typical of gouty arthritis, seen here involving the first metatarsophalangeal joint of the right foot. Note the characteristic overhanging edge at the site of erosion (*arrows*) and the soft-tissue mass representing a tophus (*curved arrows*); osteophytes and osteoporosis are absent, and the joint is partially preserved (*open arrow*).

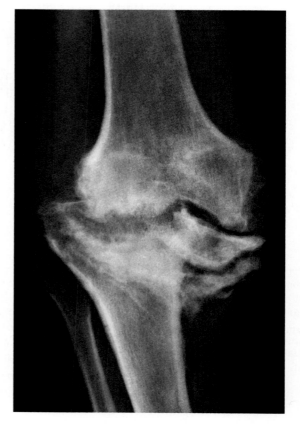

▲

FIGURE 12.32   Neuropathic joint. The neuropathic joint is morphologically identified by gross articular disorganization, multiple bony debris, and joint effusion, as seen here in the knee. Note the lack of osteoporosis. The amount of destruction evident in this case results in severe joint instability.

RADIOGRAPHIC MORPHOLOGY OF ARTHRITIDES IN THE HEEL

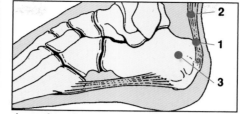

Degenerative Arthritis

traction osteophytes at
1 posterior aspect of os calcis
(insertion of Achilles tendon) and

2 plantar aspect of os calcis
(insertion of fascia plantaris)

3 osteophytes at the posterior
facet of subtalar joint

Rheumatoid Arthritis

1 erosion at posterosuperior
aspect of os calcis
(secondary to retrocalcaneal bursitis)

2 thickening of Achilles tendon

3 focal osteoporosis

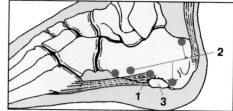

Psoriatic Arthritis, Ankylosing Spondylitis, and Reiter Syndrome

1 fluffy periostitis

2 erosions at posterior aspect of
os calcis above attachment of
Achilles tendon, at attachment
of plantar fascia, and at
plantar surface of os calcis
anterior to aponeurotic attachment

3 broad-based osteophyte

▲
FIGURE 12.33   Arthritic changes in the heel. Morphologic features distinguishing the various arthritides as manifest in arthritic lesions at the heel.

Analysis of the morphologic features of an arthritic lesion at certain sites other than the diarthrodial joints may be of further assistance in differentiating the various arthritides and reaching a correct diagnosis. Two such sites that are frequently affected are the heel (Fig. 12.33) and the spine (see Fig. 12.35). In the heel, degenerative changes are usually manifested by a traction osteophyte at the posterior and plantar aspects of the os calcis (Fig. 12.34A). Rheumatoid arthritis produces erosive changes in the area of the retrocalcaneal bursa secondary to inflammatory rheumatoid bursitis (Fig. 12.34B). Psoriatic arthritis (Fig. 12.34C), Reiter syndrome (Fig. 12.34D), and ankylosing spondylitis all produce a

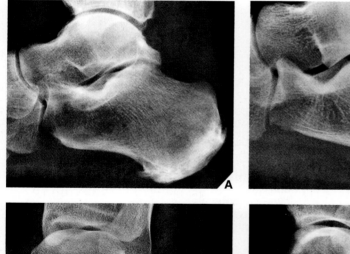

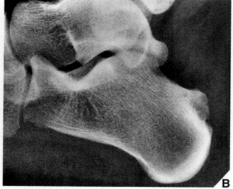

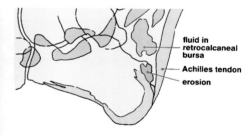

fluid in
retrocalcaneal
bursa

Achilles tendon

erosion

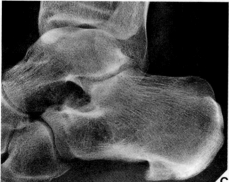

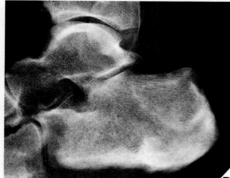

◄ FIGURE 12.34   Arthritic changes in the heel. The morphology of arthritic lesions in the heel can be helpful in differentiating the various arthritides. (A) In the degenerative variant, traction osteophytes (enthesophytes) are evident at the insertions of the Achilles tendon and fascia plantaris on the posterior and plantar aspects of the os calcis. (B) Rheumatoid arthritis typically exhibits retrocalcaneal bursitis and erosion of the posterosuperior aspect of the os calcis at the site of the bursa. Note the fluid-filled retrocalcaneal bursa projecting into the triangular-shaped fat pad anterior to the Achilles tendon. (C) The calcaneus in psoriatic arthritis characteristically shows a coarse, broad-based osteophyte arising from the plantar aspect of the bone at the insertion of the fascia plantaris. Note the "fluffy" outline and bone proliferation along the plantar aspect of the os calcis. (D) In this case of Reiter syndrome, there is erosion of the posterior aspect of the os calcis, bone sclerosis, and a "fluffy" periostitis along its plantar aspect.

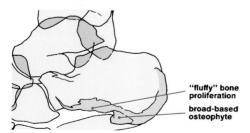

"fluffy" bone
proliferation

broad-based
osteophyte

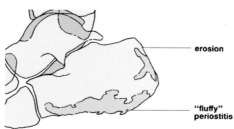

erosion

"fluffy"
periostitis

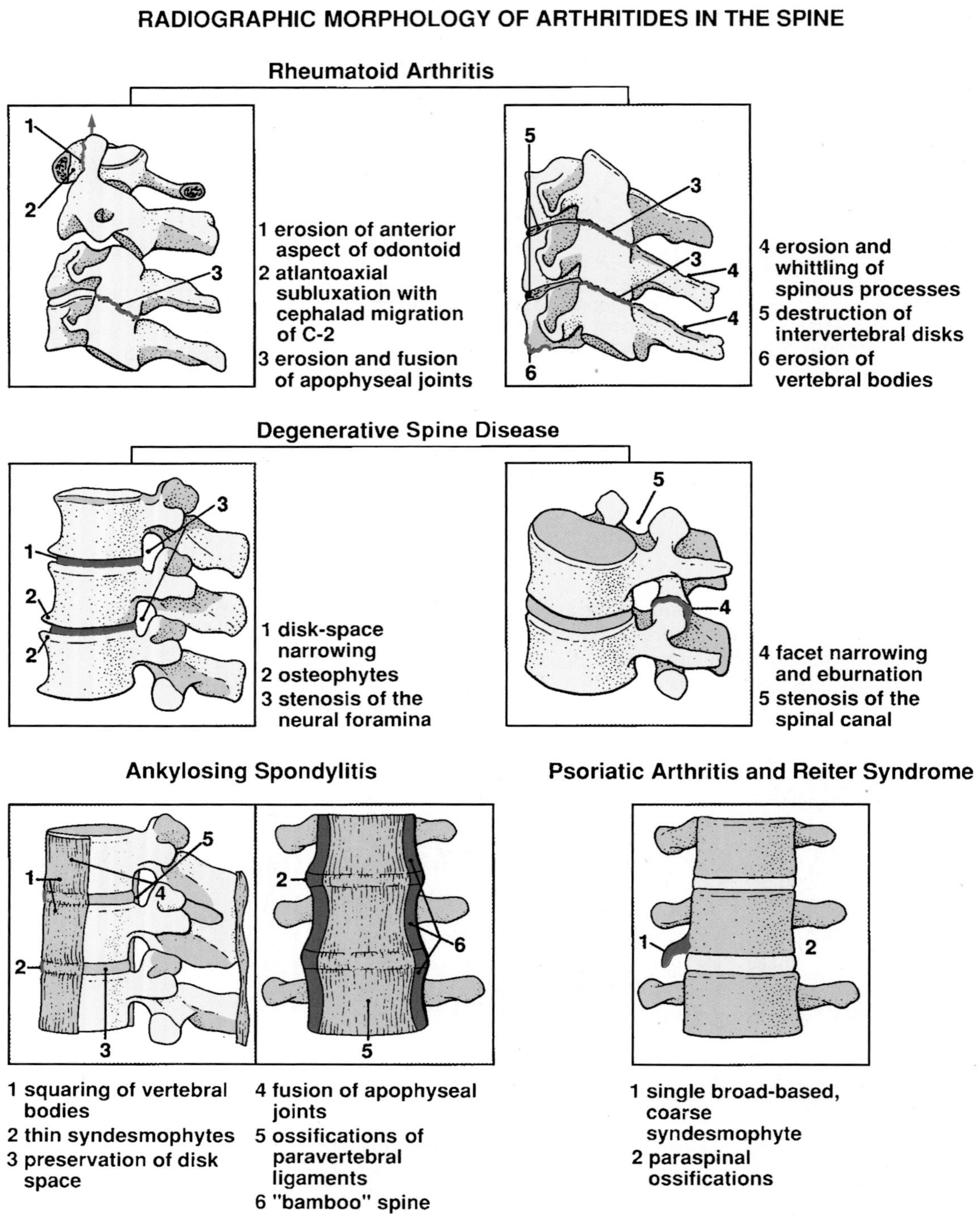

RADIOGRAPHIC MORPHOLOGY OF ARTHRITIDES IN THE SPINE

Rheumatoid Arthritis

1 erosion of anterior aspect of odontoid
2 atlantoaxial subluxation with cephalad migration of C-2
3 erosion and fusion of apophyseal joints

4 erosion and whittling of spinous processes
5 destruction of intervertebral disks
6 erosion of vertebral bodies

Degenerative Spine Disease

1 disk-space narrowing
2 osteophytes
3 stenosis of the neural foramina

4 facet narrowing and eburnation
5 stenosis of the spinal canal

Ankylosing Spondylitis

1 squaring of vertebral bodies
2 thin syndesmophytes
3 preservation of disk space
4 fusion of apophyseal joints
5 ossifications of paravertebral ligaments
6 "bamboo" spine

Psoriatic Arthritis and Reiter Syndrome

1 single broad-based, coarse syndesmophyte
2 paraspinal ossifications

FIGURE 12.35 **Arthritides of the spine.** Morphologic features distinguishing the various arthritides as manifested in the spine.

characteristic "fluffy" periostitis that results in a broad-based osteophyte at the site of attachment of the fascia plantaris on the plantar aspect of the os calcis, associated with erosions of the plantar surface and the posterior aspect of the calcaneus.

Similarly, the morphology of arthritic lesions in the spine offers important indications of the disease process at work (Fig. 12.35). Among the inflammatory arthritides, for instance, rheumatoid arthritis causes a characteristic erosion of the odontoid process (Fig. 12.36). Moreover, as a result of inflammatory pannus and erosion of the transverse ligament between the anterior arch of the atlas and C2, there may be subluxation in the atlantoaxial joint. This is usually manifested by an increase to more than 3 mm in the distance between the arch of the atlas and the

dens, as demonstrated on a lateral view of the cervical spine in flexion (Fig. 12.37). Erosion of the apophyseal joints of the cervical spine, sometimes leading to fusion, is frequently seen in juvenile rheumatoid arthritis (Fig. 12.38).

Arthritic lesions involving other segments of the spine also exhibit distinguishing features that help in differentiating the disease process. Degenerative changes may manifest in the cervical, thoracic, or lumbar (Fig. 12.39) spine by the appearance of marginal osteophytes, narrowing and sclerosis of the apophyseal joints, and narrowing of the disk spaces. In ankylosing spondylitis, there is a characteristic "squaring" of the vertebral bodies, with the formation of delicate syndesmophytes, which differ morphologically from degenerative osteophytes, arising

FIGURE 12.36 Rheumatoid arthritis. Anteroposterior (**A**) ▶ and lateral (**B**) trispiral tomograms of the cervical spine in a 55-year-old woman with a 15-year history of rheumatoid arthritis show erosion of the odontoid process typical for this condition.

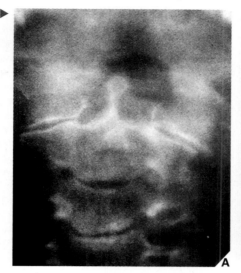
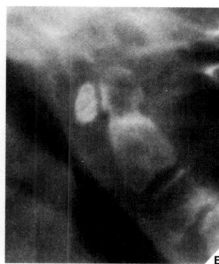

FIGURE 12.37 Rheumatoid arthritis. (**A**) Lateral film ▶ of the cervical spine in flexion in a 68-year-old woman with a long history of rheumatoid arthritis shows a marked increase in the distance between the anterior arch of the atlas and the odontoid process (*arrows*), measuring 12 mm; normally, it should not exceed 3 mm. (**B**) Trispiral tomogram demonstrates the atlan-toaxial subluxation more clearly.

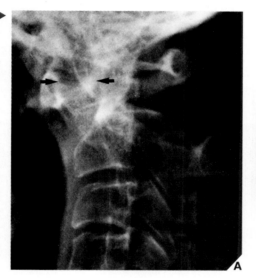
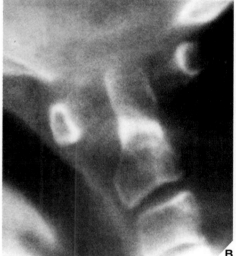

FIGURE 12.38 Juvenile rheumatoid arthritis. ▶ Lateral radiograph of the cervical spine in a 34-year-old woman with juvenile rheumatoid arthritis since age 20 shows the typical involvement of the apo-physeal joints. In this case, there is complete fusion of the joints.

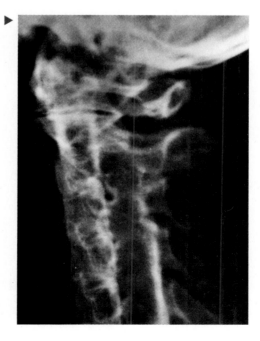

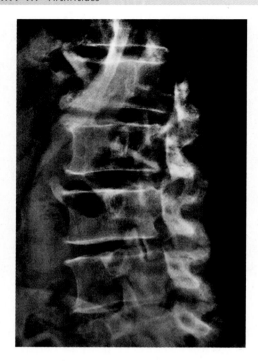

FIGURE 12.39 Degenerative spine disease. Oblique radiograph of the lumbar spine in a 72-year-old woman shows narrowing and eburnation of the articular margins of the facet joints, osteophytosis, and narrowing of the intervertebral disk spaces—a combination of the effects of true facet joint arthritis, spondylosis deformans, and degenerative disk disease.

from the anterior aspects of the vertebral bodies. In the later stages of this condition, inflammation and fusion of the apophyseal joints lead to the appearance of what has been called "bamboo" spine; the sacroiliac joints are also invariably affected (Fig. 12.40). In psoriasis and Reiter syndrome, one can occasionally see a single, coarse osteophyte/syndesmophyte in the lumbar spine, frequently bridging adjacent vertebral bodies, as well as paravertebral ossifications; there are also associated inflammatory changes in the sacroiliac joints (Fig. 12.41).

Distribution of the Articular Lesion. Osteoarthritis tends to have a characteristic distribution in the skeletal system. Typically, the large joints such as the hip and knee and the small joints of the hand and wrist are involved, whereas the shoulder, elbow, and ankle are spared (Fig. 12.42). Inflammatory arthritides, however, have different sites of predilection in the skeleton, depending on the specific variant of the disease. Rheumatoid arthritis, for example, involves most of the large joints such as the hip, knee, elbows, and shoulders. In the hand, it has a characteristic distribution that spares the distal interphalangeal joints (see Fig. 12.42); in the cervical spine, the C1-2 articulation and the apophyseal joints are frequently affected. Juvenile rheumatoid arthritis has a similar pattern of distribution, except that the distal interphalangeal joints of the hand may also be affected. Psoriatic arthritis, in contrast to rheumatoid arthritis, has a predilection for the distal interphalangeal joints, as well as the sacroiliac joints, resembling Reiter syndrome in this respect (see Fig. 12.42). Erosive osteoarthritis, which some investigators consider a variant of osteoarthritis, others a variant of rheumatoid arthritis, and still others a distinct form of arthritis, has a tendency to affect the proximal and distal interphalangeal joints of the hand (see Fig. 12.28).

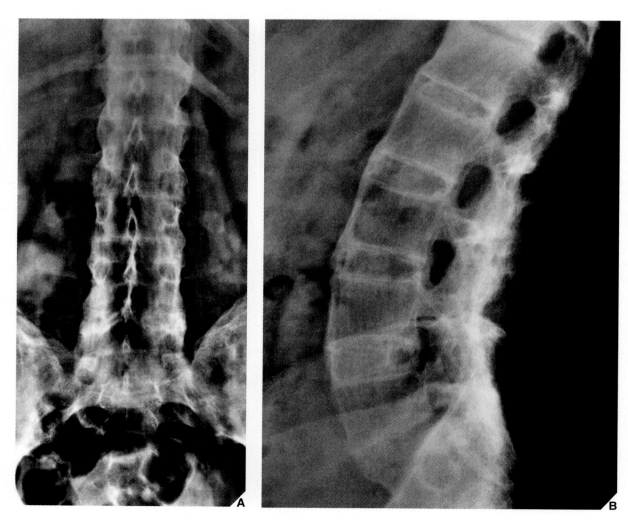

FIGURE 12.40 Ankylosing spondylitis. Anteroposterior (**A**) and lateral (**B**) radiographs of the lumbar spine in a 31-year-old man with advanced ankylosing spondylitis demonstrate the typical appearance of "bamboo spine" secondary to inflammation, ossification, and fusion of the apophyseal joints associated with ossification of the anterior and posterior longitudinal ligaments, as well as the supraspinous and interspinous ligaments. Note also the fusion of the sacroiliac joints.

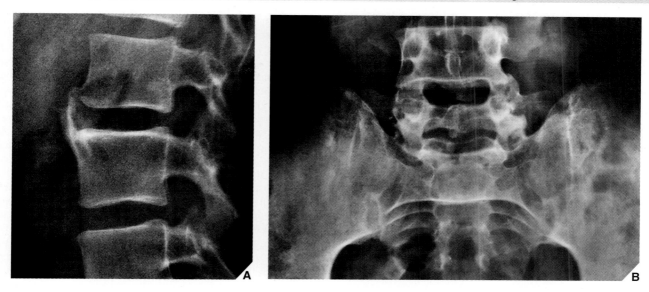

▲
FIGURE 12.41   Reiter syndrome (reactive arthritis). Lateral radiograph (**A**) of the lumbar spine in a 27year old man with Reiter syndrome shows a single, coarse osteophyte/syndesmophyte bridging the bodies of L1 and L2. Anteroposterior radiograph (**B**) of the lumbosacral segment shows the effects of the inflammatory process on the sacroiliac joints (sacroiliitis).

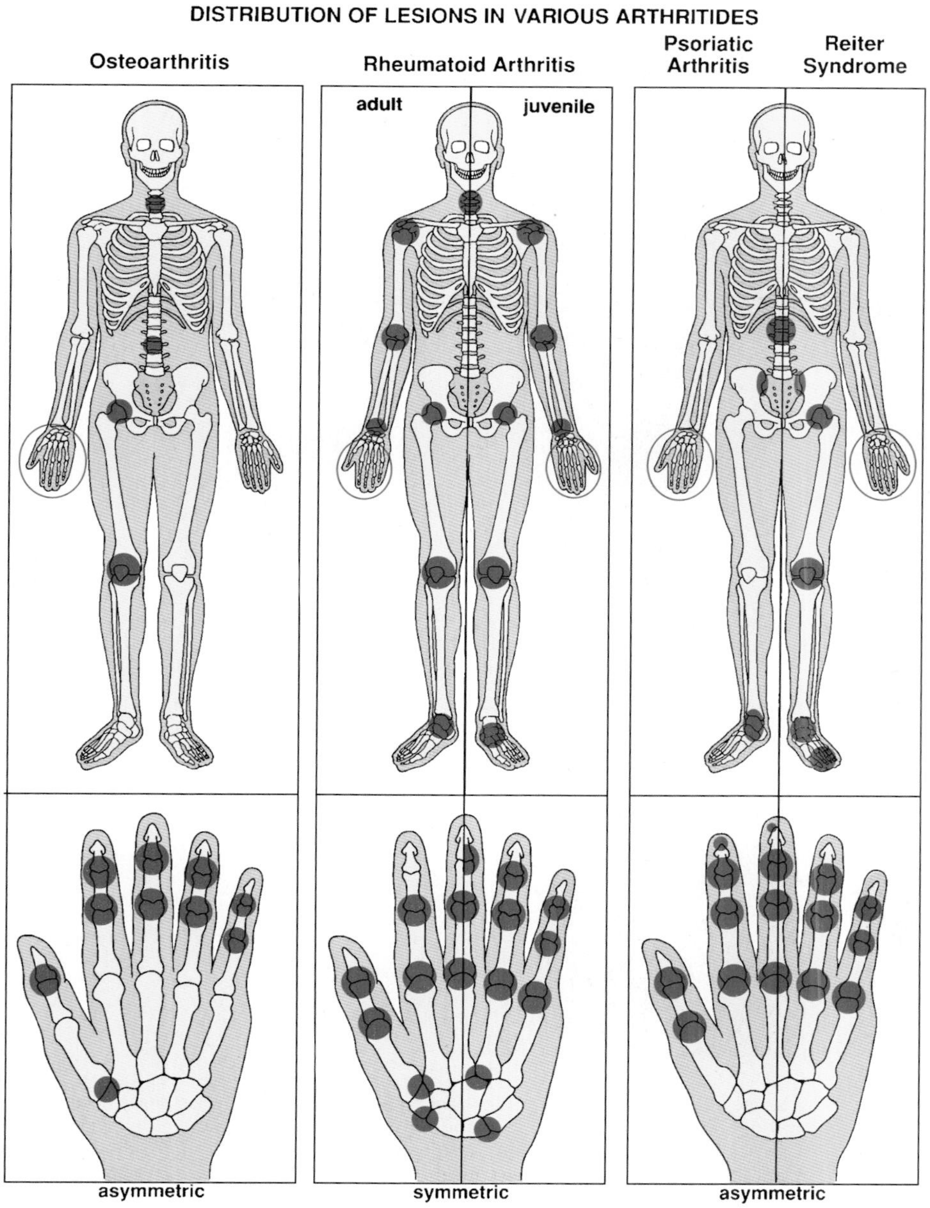

DISTRIBUTION OF LESIONS IN VARIOUS ARTHRITIDES

Osteoarthritis   Rheumatoid Arthritis   Psoriatic   Reiter
                                                        Arthritis   Syndrome

                        adult   juvenile

asymmetric   symmetric   asymmetric

▲
FIGURE 12.42   Distribution of arthritic lesions in the skeleton in various arthritides.

Management

Monitoring the Results of Treatment

Similar modalities as for diagnosis are used for monitoring the results of medical and surgical treatment of arthritis. Because the most effective treatment, particularly when large joints are involved, entails corrective and reconstructive procedures such as femoral or tibial osteotomy or total joint replacement of the hip, knee, or shoulder, the surgeon follows the postsurgical progress of the patient with sequential radiographic examinations. In osteoarthritis of the hip, the corrective procedures most often performed are varus or valgus osteotomies of the proximal femur to improve the congruence of the articular surfaces and redistribute the stress forces over different areas of the joint. Similarly, a high tibial osteotomy is performed to correct severe varus or valgus deformities in osteoarthritis of the knee, particularly in cases of unicompartmental involvement. The radiographic techniques used in monitoring the outcome of these procedures, which in fact represent iatrogenic surgical fractures, are similar to those used in evaluating traumatic fractures. As in traumatic fractures, the radiologist also pays attention to similar features, such as bone union, nonunion, or delayed union (see Chapter 4). In patients in whom total hip arthroplasties are performed, radiographic scrutiny is also essential. At present, three basic types of hip arthroplasty are used in orthopedic practice: unipolar hip hemiarthroplasty, bipolar hip hemiarthroplasty, and total hip arthroplasty. The first two of these are used mainly for patients with fracture of the femoral head and neck, and those with advanced femoral head osteonecrosis. Total hip arthroplasty is commonly used in patients with advanced arthritis of the hip joint. The prosthetic components are usually cemented to the bone with methylmethacrylate, although cementless fixation is now gaining popularity. The latter technique is based on the use of a rough or porous surface on the prosthetic parts that enables ingrowth of the bone. A bioactive coating (i.e., hydroxyapatite) can also be used for the same purpose. Acetabular components usually have a porous coating over the entire surface of the cup, whereas femoral components can be either partially or fully coated. Cementless acetabular components are sometimes reinforced with screws. Occasionally, so-called hybrid arthroplasties are performed with cementless acetabular and cemented femoral components. After total hip replacement using cemented components it is important to evaluate the position of the prosthesis, with particular reference to the degree of inclination of the acetabular component, the position of the stem of the prosthesis (whether it is in valgus, varus, or the neutral position), and the status of the separated and rejoined greater trochanter, among other features (Fig. 12.43). Equally important is the evaluation of cement–bone interface to detect the radiolucent area suggestive of

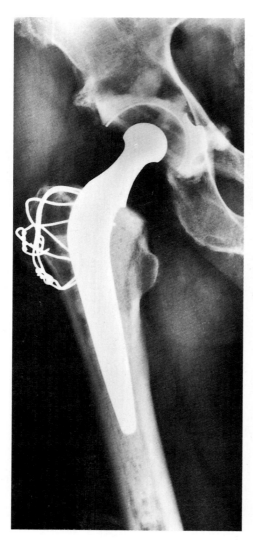
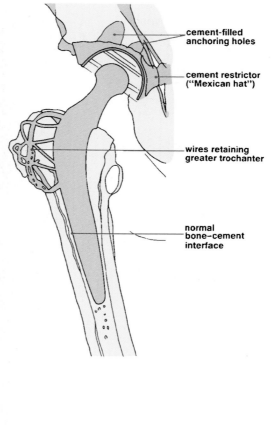

▲
FIGURE 12.43 Cemented total hip arthroplasty. A 69-year-old man underwent total hip replacement because of advanced degenerative joint disease; a Charnley low-friction arthroplasty was performed. On the anteroposterior radiograph of the right hip, one can evaluate all the parts of the prosthesis. Note that the acetabular component is oriented approximately 45 degrees to the horizontal plane and is cemented to the bone with methylmethacrylate previously impregnated with barium sulfate to make it visible radiographically. A wire-mesh cement restrictor ("Mexican hat") prevents significant leakage of methylmethacrylate into the pelvis. The stem of the prosthesis is in the neutral position in the medullary canal of the femur. Note the extent of cement below the distal end of the prosthesis, for secure anchoring. The greater trochanter, which was osteotomized to facilitate exposure of the joint, has been reattached by metallic wires slightly distal and lateral for improved stability. Note the normal appearance of the bone–cement interface.

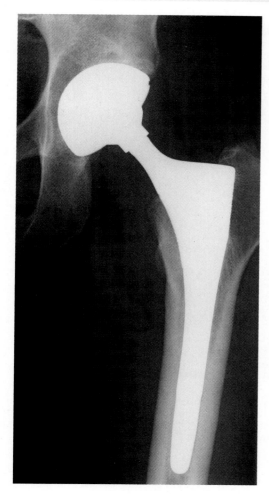

▲
FIGURE 12.44 Cementless total hip arthroplasty. A 48-year-old woman underwent total hip arthroplasty because of advanced osteoarthritis. Note porous-coated acetabular component and partially coated femoral stem. The prosthetic components are in anatomic alignment, the femoral stem is in neutral position, the endocortex is intact, and there are no signs of loosening.

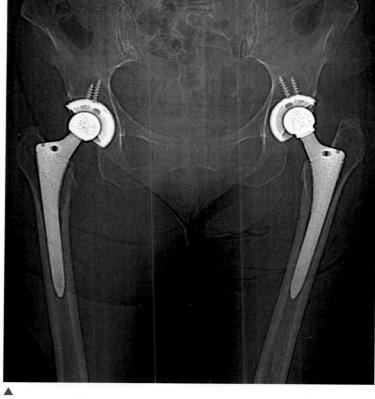

▲
FIGURE 12.45 CT of total hip arthroplasty. A scout CT image of the pelvis shows status post–bilateral total hip arthroplasties using noncemented prostheses. The acetabular components have been reinforced with the rim screws.

prosthesis loosening (see Fig. 12.49). After total hip arthroplasty using noncemented components (Figs. 12.44 and 12.45), radiologic evaluation should focus on the interface between the prosthesis and the bone to detect areas of bone resorption (focal osteolysis) that may indicate loosening of the prosthesis. After a total knee arthroplasty with a condylar type of prothesis, it is important to evaluate the position of the tibial component relative to the tibial shaft, as well as the axial alignment and the status of the methylmethacrylate fixation of the components (Fig. 12.46). After a total shoulder arthroplasty, whether conventional (Fig. 12.47) or the one using reverse Delta shoulder prosthesis (Fig. 12.48), alignment of the prosthetic components and metal–cement and cement–bone interface must be evaluated. With the latter arthroplasty, radiologic evaluation will include in addition the position of the anchoring screws within the scapula, relationship of the humeral component to the scapula, and status of supporting bone. After total ankle arthroplasty, in addition to assessing the position and alignment of the prosthetic parts, attention should be paid to syndesmotic fusion and status of adjacent osseous structures.

Complications of Surgical Treatment

As important as evaluating the outcome of the surgical treatment of arthritic disease is monitoring the complications that may arise from such treatment, especially those after osteotomies and joint-replacement procedures. These complications include thrombophlebitis, hematomas, heterotopic bone formation, the intrapelvic leakage of acrylic cement,

infection, loosening, subluxation or dislocation of a prosthesis, and fracture of a prosthesis.

Thrombophlebitis. A rather frequent complication in the immediate postoperative period, particularly in patients with previous circulatory problems, thrombophlebitis is related to venous stasis and the lack of movement of the surgically treated extremity; sudden pain and swelling of the leg are common clinical findings. The venous soleal plexus in the calf is the most common site of thrombus formation. Radiologically, this complication can be detected by venography, radionuclide scanning, or US. On radionuclide scan, an increased gamma-count rate in an area of the lower extremities following intravenous administration of ^{125}I-labeled fibrinogen suggests adherence of the tracer to a developing clot. US can detect venous thrombosis using compression technique. Lack of compressibility of a vein is thought to be the single most reliable finding in differentiating between thrombosed and normal veins. Other criteria useful in detection of vein thrombosis are the presence of echogenic intraluminal material and enlargement of the vein.

Hematoma. The formation of a hematoma is a common complication of surgery for arthritic disease. However, it usually subsides within a short time, unless it is associated with infection. This complication can be easily detected with MRI.

Leakage of Acrylic Cement. Intrapelvic leakage of methylmethacrylate may lead to vascular and neurologic damage, visceral necrosis, and urinary tract disorders, as a result of the heat of polymerization of the acrylic cement. To prevent an accidental leak, a wire mesh

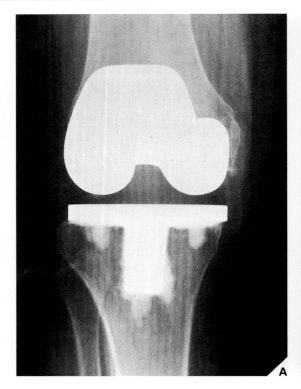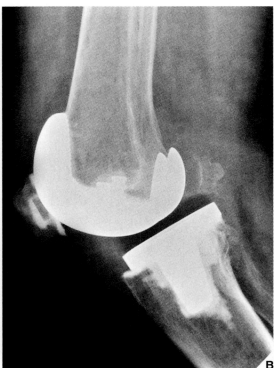

▲
FIGURE 12.46   Cemented total knee arthroplasty. A 62-year-old woman underwent total knee arthroplasty using a nonconstrained three-part cemented condylar prosthesis. **(A)** Anteroposterior radiograph demonstrates that the tibial component is aligned with the surface of the bone, forming a 90-degree angle with the long axis of the tibia. There is no evidence of a radiolucent line at the cement–bone interface. The slight valgus configuration at the knee (approximately 7 degrees) is acceptable. On the lateral projection **(B)**, note the tight adherence of the femoral component of the prosthesis to the bone.

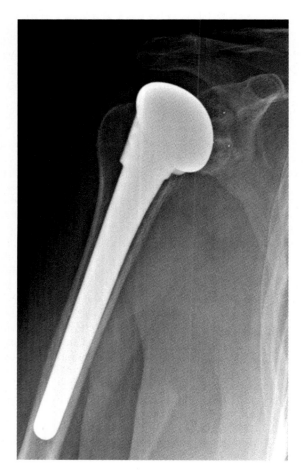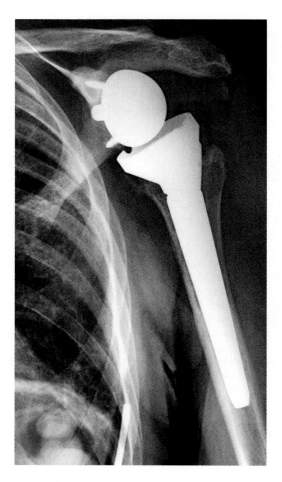

▲
FIGURE 12.47   Total shoulder prosthesis. Anteroposterior radiograph of the right shoulder shows status post–total shoulder arthroplasty with a conventional prosthesis in anatomic alignment.

▲
FIGURE 12.48   Total reversed shoulder prosthesis. Anteroposterior radiograph of the left shoulder shows status post–total shoulder arthroplasty with a Delta reverse shoulder system in anatomic alignment.

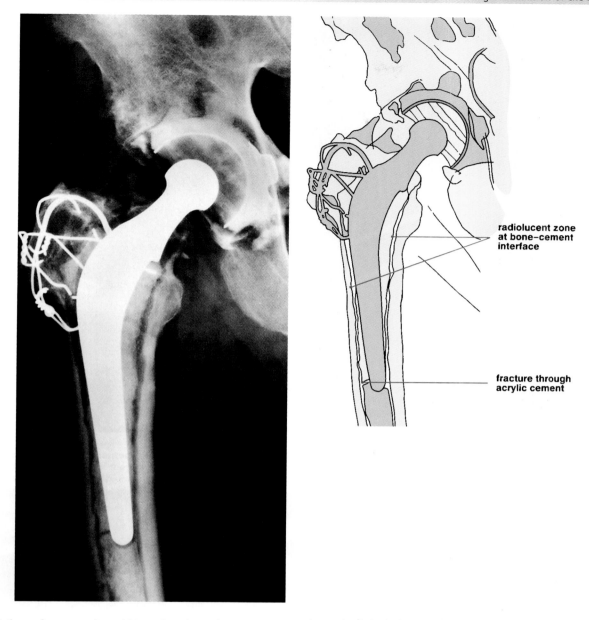

▲
FIGURE 12.49   **Failure of cemented total hip arthroplasty.** Anteroposterior radiograph of the right hip of a 69-year-old woman shows a wide radiolucent zone at the bone–cement interface characteristic of loosening of a Charnley prosthesis. Note the fracture through the acrylic cement at the distal segment of the prosthetic stem.

restrictor ("Mexican hat") is applied around the acetabular anchoring holes of the prosthesis (see Fig. 12.43).

Heterotopic Bone Formation. This is a relatively frequent complication of surgery for arthritic disease in the hip. The amount of new bone that forms in the adjacent soft tissues varies: if extensive, it may interfere with function of the hip joint. Conventional radiography and occasionally CT are sufficient to evaluate this complication.

Infection. Although infection may occur at any time postoperatively, it is usually observed shortly after the joint-replacement procedure. Clinically, it is manifested by pain, elevation of temperature, and discharge from the wound. The radiographic findings in cases of infection include soft-tissue swelling, rarefaction of bone, and, occasionally, a periosteal reaction. Scintigraphy using ^{111}In-oxine–labeled white blood cells has been reported to be very useful in these circumstances.

Loosening of a Prosthesis. Infection after a joint-replacement procedure may result in loosening of a prosthesis, but loosening may also be seen as a late complication resulting from mechanical factors.

The standard radiographic projections are usually sufficient to reveal this development (Figs. 12.50 and 12.51). The most effective technique for demonstrating loosening of a prosthesis, however, is arthrography. The subtraction technique is commonly used to demonstrate the cardinal sign of loosening—the extension of contrast agent into the gap that develops at the interface of the bone and acrylic cement (Fig. 12.51B,C). At times, when even arthrography is inconclusive, traction applied on the examined hip by pulling on the leg can be helpful in demonstrating occult loosening of a prosthesis. A radionuclide bone scan may occasionally be helpful in differentiating mechanical loosening from infectious loosening. Foci of increased activity, representing accumulation of radioisotope, are consistent with mechanical loosening, while diffuse increased activity indicates infection.

Dislocation of a Prosthesis. This complication is easily diagnosed on the lateral view of the knee or anteroposterior view of the hip. Tomography may occasionally be required, particularly if there are difficulties in reducing a dislocation (Fig. 12.52).

- rheumatoid arthritis—atlantoaxial subluxation and erosion of the odontoid process
- juvenile rheumatoid arthritis—fusion of the apophyseal joints of the cervical spine
- psoriatic arthritis and Reiter syndrome—coarse, asymmetric paraspinal ossifications
- ankylosing spondylitis—delicate syndesmophytes.

[11] Certain arthritides show lack of periarticular osteoporosis–osteoarthritis, gouty arthritis, calcium pyrophosphate dihydrate crystal deposition disease, and multicentric reticulohistiocytosis.

[12] Sacroiliitis is commonly seen in ankylosing spondylitis (in which it is bilateral and symmetrical) and in psoriatic arthritis and Reiter syndrome (in which it is either unilateral or bilateral but asymmetric in terms of degree of involvement).

[13] Monitoring the results of treatment of the arthritides involves detecting possible complications of various osteotomies and joint-replacement procedures. These complications include:
- thrombophlebitis
- intrapelvic leakage of methylmethacrylate cement
- heterotopic bone formation
- infection
- loosening, dislocation, and fracture of a prosthesis.

[14] Scintigraphy and contrast arthrography utilizing the subtraction technique are useful in detecting loosening of a prosthesis.

SUGGESTED READINGS

Alazraki NP, Fierer J, Resnick D. The role of gallium and bone scanning in monitoring response to therapy in chronic osteomyelitis. *J Nucl Med* 1978;19:696–697.

Allen AM, Ward WG, Pope Jr TL. Imaging of the total knee arthroplasty. *Radiol Clin North Am* 1995;33:289–303.

Anderson LS, Staple TW. Arthrography of total hip replacement using substraction technique. *Radiology* 1973;109:470–472.

Beabout JW. Radiology of total hip arthroplasty. *Radiol Clin North Am* 1975;13:3–19.

Beltran J. *MRI: musculoskeletal system*. Philadelphia: JB Lippincott; 1990.

Beltran J, Caudill JL, Herman LA, et al. Rheumatoid arthritis: MR imaging manifestations. *Radiology* 1987;165:153–157.

Bianchi S, Martinoli C, Abdelwahab, IF. High-frequency ultrasound examination of the wrist and hand. *Skeletal Radiol* 1999;28:121–129.

Boutry N, Morel M, Flipo R-M, Demondion X, Cotton A. Early rheumatoid arthritis: a review of MRI and sonographic findings. *Am J Roetgenol* 2007;189:1502–1509.

Brower AC, Flemming DJ. *Arthritis in black and white*, 2nd ed. Philadelphia: WB Saunders; 1997.

Datz FL, Morton KA. New radiopharmaceuticals for detecting infection. *Invest Radiol* 1993;28:356–365.

Erickson SJ. High-resolution imaging of the musculoskeletal system. *Radiology* 1997;205:593–618.

Farrant JM, Grainger AJ, O'Connor PJ. Advanced imaging in rheumatoid arthritis. Part 2: erosions. *Skeletal Radiol* 2007;36:381–389.

Farrant JM, O'Connor PJ, Grainger AJ. Advanced imaging in rheumatoid arthritis. Part 1: synovitis. *Skeletal Radiol* 2007;36:269–279.

Forrester DM. Imaging of the sacroiliac joints. *Radiol Clin North Am* 1990;28:1055–1072.

Forrester DM, Brown JC. *The radiology of joint disease*, 3rd ed. Philadelphia: WB Saunders; 1987.

Freiberger RH. Evaluation of hip prostheses by imaging methods. *Semin Roentgenol* 1986;21:20–28.

Gee R, Munk PL, Keogh C, et al. Radiography of the PROSTALAC (prosthesis with antibiotic-loaded acrylic cement) orthopedic implant. *Am J Roentgenol* 2003;180:1701–1706.

Gelman MI, Coleman RE, Stevens PM, Davey BW. Radiography, radionuclide imaging, and arthrography in the evaluation of total hip and knee replacement. *Radiology* 1978;128:677–682.

Genant HK, Doi K, Mall JC, Sickles EA. Direct radiographic magnification for skeletal radiology. *Radiology* 1977;123:47–55.

Grammont PM, Baulot E. Delta shoulder prosthesis for rotator cuff rupture. *Orthopedics* 1993;16:65–68.

Greenspan A, Norman A. Gross hematuria: a complication of intrapelvic cement intrusion in total hip replacement. *Am J Roentgenol* 1978; 130: 327–329.

Greenspan A, Norman A. Radial head-capitellum view in elbow trauma [Letter]. *Am J Roentgenol* 1983;140:1273–1275.

Greenspan A, Norman A. Radial head-capitellum view: an expanded imaging approach to elbow injury. *Radiology* 1987;164:272–274.

Griffiths HJ, Priest D, Kushner D. Total hip replacement and other orthopedic hip procedures. *Radiol Clin North Am* 1995;33:267–287.

Habermann ET. Total joint replacement: an overview. *Semin Roentgenol* 1986;21:7–19.

Insall J, Tria AJ, Scott WN. The total condylar knee prosthesis: the first 5 years. *Clin Orthop* 1979;145:68–77.

Kamishima T, Tanimura K, Henmi M, et al. Power Doppler ultrasound of rheumatoid synovitis: quantification of vascular signal and analysis of intraobserver variability. *Skeletal Radiol* 2009;38:467–472.

Kim S-H, Chung S-K, Bahk Y-W, Park Y-H, Lee S-Y, Son H-S. Whole-body and pinhole bone scintigraphic manifestations of Reiter's syndrome: distribution patterns and early and characteristic signs. *Eur J Nucl Med* 1999;26:163–170.

Kursunoglu-Brahme S, Riccio T, Weissman MH, et al. Rheumatoid knee: role of gadopentetate-enhanced MR imaging. *Radiology* 1990;176:831–835.

Lund PJ, Heikal A, Maricic MJ, Krupinski EA, Williams CS. Ultrasonographic imaging of the hand and wrist in rheumatoid arthritis. *Skeletal Radiol* 1995;24:591–596.

Manaster BJ. Total hip arthroplasty: radiographic evaluation. *Radiographics* 1996;16:645–660.

McAfee JG. Update on radiopharmaceuticals for medical imaging. *Radiology* 1989;171:593–601.

McCauley TR, Disler DG. State of the art. MR imaging of articular cartilage. *Radiology* 1998;209:629–640.

McFarland EG, Sanguanjit P, Tasaki A, Keyurapan E, Fishman EK, Fayad LM. The reverse shoulder prosthesis: a review of imaging features and complications. *Skeletal Radiol* 2006;35:488–496.

Ostergaard M, Ejbjerg B, Szkudlarek M. Imaging in early rheumatoid arthritis: roles of magnetic resonance imaging, ultrasonography, conventional radiography and computed tomography. *Best Pract Res Clin Rheumatol* 2005;19:91–116.

Oudjhane K, Azouz EM, Hughes S, Paquin JD. Computed tomography of the sacroiliac joints in children. *Can Assoc Radiol J* 1993;44:313–314.

Peterfy CG, Genant HK. Emerging applications of magnetic resonance imaging in the evaluation of articular cartilage. *Radiol Clin North Am* 1996;34:195–213.

Peterfy CG, Majumdar S, Lang P, van Dijke CF, Sack K, Genant HK. MR imaging of the arthritic knee: improved discrimination of cartilage, synovia, and effusion with pulsed saturation transfer and fat-suppressed T1-weighted sequences. *Radiology* 1994;191:413–419.

Recht MP, Resnick D. MR imaging of articular cartilage: current status and future directions. *Am J Roentgenol* 1994;163:283–290.

Reynolds PPM, Heron C, Pilcher J, Kiely PDW. Prediction of erosion progression using ultrasound in established rheumatoid arthritis: a 2-year follow-up study. *Skeletal Radiol* 2009;38:473–478.

Roberts CC, Ekelund AL, Renfree KJ, Liu PT, Chew FS. Radiologic assessment of reverse shoulder arthroplasty. *Radiographics* 2007;27:223–235.

Salvati EA, Ghelman B, McLaren T, Wilson PD Jr. Subtraction technique in arthrography for loosening of total hip replacement fixed with radiopaque cement. *Clin Orthop* 1974;101:105–109.

Schneider R, Hood RW, Ranawat CS. Radiologic evaluation of knee arthroplasty. *Orthop Clin North Am* 1982;13:225–244.

Schumacher TM, Genant HK, Kellet MJ, Mall JC, Fye KM. HLA-B27 associated arthropathies. *Radiology* 1978;126:289–297.

Sebes JI, Nasrallah NS, Rabinowitz JG, Masi AT. The relationship between HLA-B27 positive peripheral arthritis and sacroillitis. *Radiology* 1978;126:299–302.

Steinbach L, Hellman D, Petri M, Sims R, Gillespy T, Genant H. Magnetic resonance imaging: a review of rheumatologic applications. *Semin Arthritis Rheum* 1986;16:79–91.

Subramanian G, McAfee JG. A new complex of 99m-Tc for skeletal imaging. *Radiology* 1971;99:192–196.

Taljanovic MS, Jones MD, Hunter TB, et al. Joint arthroplasties and prostheses. *Radiographics* 2003;23:1295–1314.

Tehranzadeh J, Ashikyan O, Anavim A, Tramma S. Enhanced MR imaging of tenosynovitis of hand and wrist in inflammatory arthritis. *Skeletal Radiol* 2006;35:814–822.

Tehranzadeh J, Ashikyan O, Dascalos J. Advanced imaging of early rheumatoid arthritis. *Radiol Clin North Am* 2004;42:89–107.

Weissman BN. Spondyloarthropathies. *Radiol Clin North Am* 1987;25:1235–1262.

Winalski CS, Palmer WE, Rosenthal DI, Weissman BN. Magnetic resonance imaging of rheumatoid arthritis. *Radiol Clin North Am* 1996;34:243–258.

CHAPTER 13

Degenerative Joint Disease

Osteoarthritis

Degenerative joint disease (osteoarthritis, osteoarthrosis) is the most common form of arthritis. In its primary (idiopathic) form, it affects individuals aged 50 and older; in its secondary form, however, osteoarthritis may be seen in a much younger age group. Patients in the latter group have clearly defined underlying conditions leading to the development of degenerative joint disease (see Fig. 12.1).

Some authorities postulate that there are two types of primary degenerative joint disease. The first form is apparently closely related to the aging process ("wear and tear") and represents not a true arthritis but a senescent process of the joint. It characteristically shows limited destruction of the cartilage, slow progression, lack of significant joint deformity, and no restriction of joint function. This process is not affected by gender or race. The second type, a true osteoarthritis, is unrelated to the aging process, although it shows an increased prevalence with age. Marked by progressive destruction of the articular cartilage and reparative processes such as osteophyte formation and subchondral sclerosis, true osteoarthritis progresses rapidly, leading to significant joint deformity. This form may be related to genetic factors, as well as to gender, race, and obesity. It has been shown that osteoarthritis tends to affect women more commonly than men, particularly in the proximal and distal interphalangeal joints and the first carpometacarpal joints. In the population older than 65 years, osteoarthritis affects whites more frequently than African Americans. Obesity is associated with a higher incidence of osteoarthritis in the knees, which may be related to an excessive weight-bearing load on these joints.

Generally, in osteoarthritis the large diarthrodial joints such as the hip or knee and the small joints such as the interphalangeal joints of the hand are most often affected; the spine, however, is just as frequently involved in the degenerative process (Fig. 13.1). The shoulder, elbow, wrist, and ankle are unusual sites for primary osteoarthritis, and if degenerative changes are encountered in these locations, secondary arthritis should be considered. It should be kept in mind, however, that evidence exists for an association between degenerative arthritis in unusual sites and certain occupations. Even primary osteoarthritic changes may develop more rapidly, for example, in the lumbar spine, knees, and elbows of coal miners and in the wrists, elbows, and shoulders of pneumatic drill operators. Degenerative changes are also commonly seen in the ankles and feet of ballet dancers and in the femoropatellar joints of bicyclists.

An overview of the clinical and radiographic hallmarks of degenerative joint disease is presented in Table 13.1.

Osteoarthritis of the Large Joints

The hip and knee joints are the most common sites of osteoarthritis. The severity of radiographic changes does not always correlate with the clinical symptoms, which may vary from stiffness and pain to severe deformities and limitation of joint function.

Osteoarthritis of the Hip

There are four cardinal radiographic features of degenerative joint disease in the hip:

1. Narrowing of the joint space as a result of thinning of the articular cartilage
2. Subchondral sclerosis (eburnation) caused by reparative processes (remodeling)
3. Osteophyte formation (osteophytosis) as a result of reparative processes in sites not subjected to stress (so-called low-stress areas), which are usually marginal (peripheral) in distribution
4. Cyst or pseudocyst formation resulting from bone contusions that lead to microfractures and intrusion of synovial fluid into the altered spongy bone; in the acetabulum, these subchondral cystlike lesions are referred to as *Eggers cysts*.

These hallmarks of degenerative joint disease can be readily demonstrated on the standard projections of the hip (Fig. 13.2). In the past, tomography used to demonstrate the details of the degenerative process; however, its application was not to make a specific diagnosis but rather to confirm or exclude possible complications (see Fig. 12.8). CT scanning may further delineate the characteristic features of osteoarthritis (Fig. 13.3).

As articular cartilage is destroyed and reparative changes develop, evidence emerges of a change in the relation of the femoral head with respect to the acetabulum, known as "migration." Generally, three patterns of femoral head migration can be observed: superior, which may be either superolateral or superomedial; medial; and axial (Fig. 13.4). The most common pattern is superolateral migration; the medial pattern is less common, whereas axial migration is only exceptionally seen. It should be kept in mind, however, that in inflammatory arthritis of the hip, such as rheumatoid arthritis, in which a previous axial migration of the femoral head is commonly associated with acetabular protrusio, degenerative changes might develop as a complication of the

HIGHLIGHTS OF PRIMARY OSTEOARTHRITIS

Morphology

Large Joints

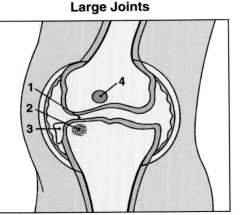

1 localized joint-space narrowing
2 subchondral sclerosis
3 osteophytes
4 cyst or pseudocyst

Small Joints

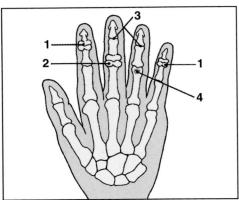

1 Heberden nodes
2 Bouchard nodes
3 joint-space narrowing
4 subchondral sclerosis

Distribution

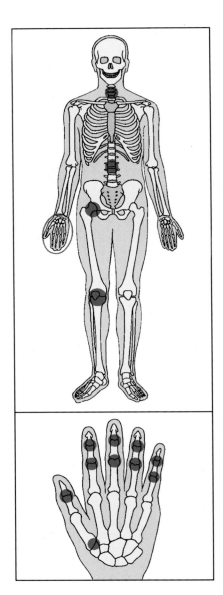

Spine

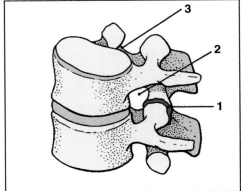

1 facet narrowing and eburnation
2 foraminal stenosis
3 stenosis of spinal canal

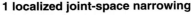

▲
FIGURE 13.1   Highlights of the morphology and distribution of arthritic lesions in primary osteoarthritis.

inflammatory process. Thus, one may see secondary osteoarthritis with axial migration (Fig. 13.5).

Occasionally, the degenerative process in the hip may run a more rapid course. This destructive arthrosis of the hip joint is known as *Postel coxarthropathy*, a condition characterized by rapid chondrolysis that may quickly lead to complete destruction of the hip joint. Originally described by Lequesne, and also by Postel and Kerboull in 1970, this unique hip disorder occurs predominantly in women, with age of onset at 60 to 70 years. In all cases, a rapid clinical course of hip pain is the consistent common symptom. The histologic findings are those of conventional osteoarthritis with severe degenerative changes in the articular cartilage. However, osteophyte formation is absent or minimal. Hypervascularity in the subchondral bone is a common finding. The bone trabeculae are either abnormally thickened or abnormally thinned. Occasionally, one can observe foci of fibrosis,

interstitial edema and hemorrhage in the marrow spaces, focal marrow fat fibrosis, and focal areas of bone resorption. The precise pathogenesis of this condition remains unclear, although direct drug toxicity and the analgesic effects of nonsteroidal anti-inflammatory drugs have been implicated. Some investigators have suggested that intraarticular deposition of hydroxyapatite crystals might lead to joint destruction. Others have proposed subchondral insufficiency fracture of the femoral head as a cause of this arthritis. Because of the rapidity of the process, the radiographic presentation of this condition is marked by very little, if any, reparative changes, mimicking infectious or neuropathic arthritis (Charcot joint) (Fig. 13.6). More recently, Boutry and colleagues reported MRI findings of this form of osteoarthritis. These included joint effusion, a bone marrow edema-like pattern in the femoral head, neck, and acetabulum, femoral head flattening, and cyst-like subchondral defects (Fig. 13.7).

TABLE 13.1 **Clinical and Radiographic Hallmarks of Degenerative Joint Disease**

Type of Arthritis	Site	Crucial Abnormalities	Technique*/Projection
Primary Osteoarthritis (F > M; >50 years)	Hand	Degenerative changes in Proximal interphalangeal joints (Bouchard nodes) Distal interphalangeal joints (Heberden nodes)	Dorsovolar view
	Hip	Narrowing of joint space Subchondral sclerosis Marginal osteophytes Cysts and pseudocysts Superolateral subluxation	Anteroposterior view
	Knee	Same changes as in hip Varus or valgus deformity Degenerative changes in Femoropatellar compartment Patella (tooth sign)	Anteroposterior view Weight-bearing anteroposterior view Lateral view Axial view of patella
	Spine	Degenerative disk disease Narrowing of disk space Degenerative spondylolisthesis Osteophytosis Spondylosis deformans Degenerative changes in apophyseal joints Foraminal stenosis Spinal stenosis	Lateral view Lateral flexion/extension views Anteroposterior and lateral views Anteroposterior and lateral views Oblique views (cervical, lumbar) CT, myelogram, MRI
Secondary Osteoarthritis Posttraumatic	Hip Knee Shoulder, elbow, wrist, ankle (unusual sites)	Similar changes to those in primary osteoarthritis History of previous trauma Younger age	Standard views
FAI syndrome	Hips	Bone formation at the head/neck junction Acetabular crossover sign	MRI/MRa
Slipped capital femoral epiphysis	Hips	Herndon hump Narrowing of joint space Osteophytosis	Anteroposterior and frog-lateral views
Congenital hip dislocation (F > M)	Hips	Signs of acetabular hypoplasia	Anteroposterior and frog-lateral views
Perthes disease (M > F)	Hip	Unilateral or bilateral Osteonecrosis of femoral head Coxa magna Lateral subluxation	Anteroposterior and frog-lateral views
Inflammatory arthritis	Hip Knee	Medial and axial migration of femoral head Periarticular osteoporosis Limited osteophytosis	Standard views
Osteonecrosis	Hip Shoulder	Increased bone density Joint space usually preserved or only slightly narrowed Crescent sign	Anteroposterior views (hip, shoulder) Grashey view (shoulder) Frog-lateral view (hip)
Paget disease (>40 years)	Hips, knees, shoulders	Coarse trabeculations Thickening of cortex	Standard views of affected joints Radionuclide bone scan
Multiple epiphyseal dysplasia	Epiphyses of long bones	Dysplastic changes Narrowing of joint space Osteophytes	Standard views of affected joints
Hemochromatosis	Hands	Degenerative changes in second and third metacarpophalangeal joints with beak-like osteophytes Chondrocalcinosis	Dorsovolar view
Acromegaly	Large joints Hands	Joint spaces widened or only slightly narrowed Enlargement of terminal tufts Beak-like osteophytes in heads of metacarpals	Standard views of affected joint Dorsovolar view

*Radionuclide bone scan is used to determine the distribution of arthritic lesions in the skeleton.

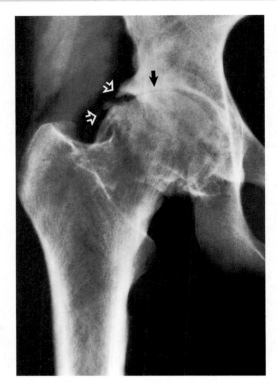

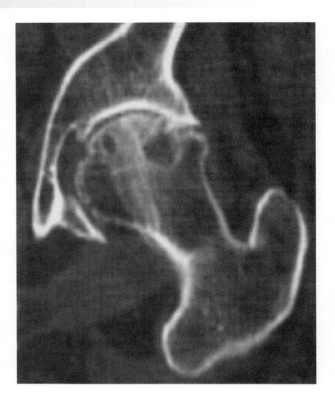

▲
FIGURE 13.2 **Osteoarthritis of the hip joint.** A 51-year-old woman presented with a history of right hip pain for the past 10 years and no previous history suggesting predisposing factors for osteoarthritis. Anteroposterior radiograph of the hip demonstrates the radiographic hallmarks of osteoarthritis: narrowing of the joint space, particularly at the weight-bearing segment (*arrow*); formation of marginal osteophytes (*open arrows*); and subchondral sclerosis. Note the lack of osteoporosis.

▲
FIGURE 13.3 **CT of osteoarthritis of the hip.** Coronal reformatted image shows diminution of the joint space, osteophytes, and subchondral cysts in the femoral head.

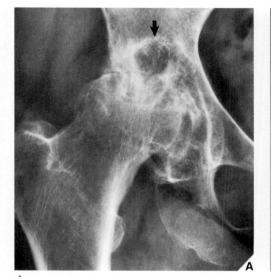
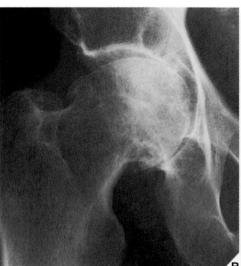
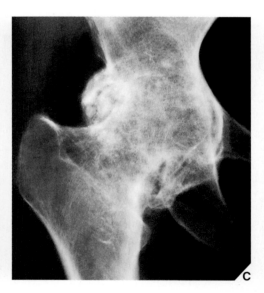

▲
FIGURE 13.4 **Migration of the femoral head.** **(A)** Anteroposterior radiograph of the right hip of a 65-year-old woman with long-standing degenerative joint disease in both hips demonstrates superolateral migration of the femoral head, the most common pattern seen in osteoarthritis of the hip joint. Note the typical Eggers cyst in the acetabulum (*arrow*). **(B)** Medial migration of the femoral head is apparent in this 48-year-old woman with osteoarthritis of the right hip. **(C)** Axial migration of the femoral head is evident in this 57-year-old woman who was suspected of having inflammatory arthritis. Clinical and laboratory investigations, however, led to a diagnosis of idiopathic osteoarthritis, which was confirmed on histopathologic examination after total hip replacement.

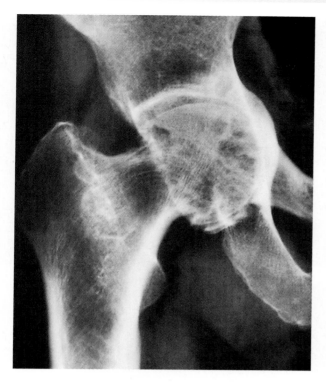

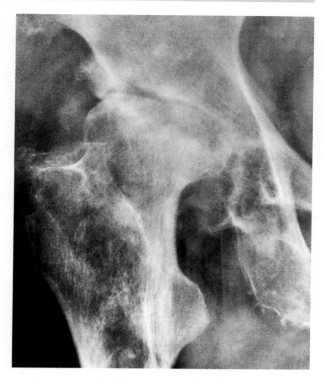

FIGURE 13.5 **Rheumatoid arthritis with superimposed osteoarthritis.** Anteroposterior radiograph of the right hip of a 42-year-old woman with a known history of long-standing rheumatoid arthritis shows the typical changes of inflammatory arthritis, including axial migration of the femoral head and acetabular protrusio. Superimposition of secondary osteoarthritis is evident in subchondral sclerosis and marginal osteophytes.

FIGURE 13.6 **Postel coxarthropathy.** Anteroposterior radiograph of the right hip of a 72-year-old man who had pain in the hip for 4 months shows the typical appearance of Postel coxarthropathy, which often mimics Charcot joint or infectious arthritis. Note the destruction of the articular portion of the femoral head, which is laterally subluxed. The same destructive process has led to widening of the acetabulum.

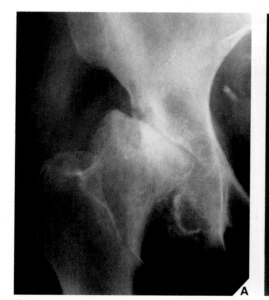

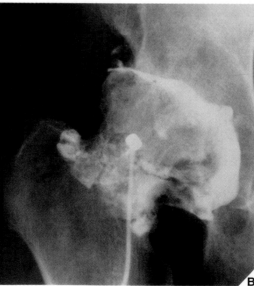

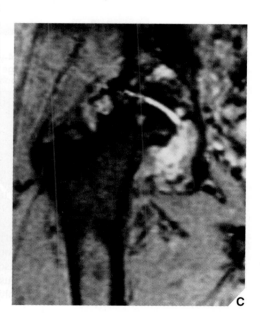

FIGURE 13.7 **Postel coxarthropathy. (A)** Anteroposterior radiograph of the right hip of a 44-year-old man shows destructive changes of the femoral head and acetabulum. **(B)** Aspiration arthrogram, that was performed to rule out infection, shows hypertrophic synovitis. **(C)** A gradient-echo T2*-weighted MRI shows joint effusion, hypertrophied synovium, and subchondral cysts in the acetabulum and femoral head.

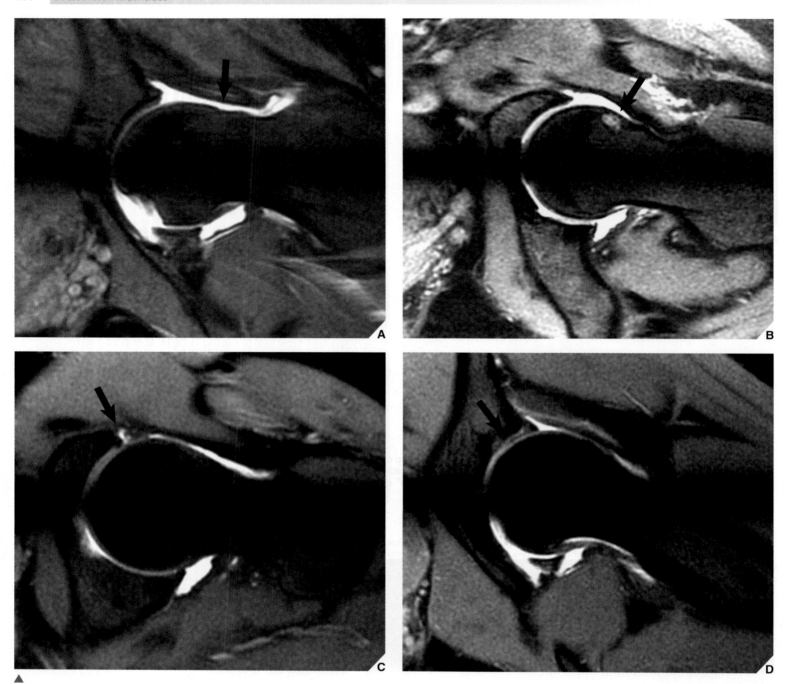

FIGURE 13.11 MR arthrography of cam type FAI. Radial reconstructed MRa images of the hip joint show various characteristic features of this abnormality. **(A)** In a 34-year-old woman—a decreased femoral head/neck offset associated with hypertrophic ossification (*arrow*). **(B)** In a 32-year-old woman—a fibroosseous lesion at the anterosuperior aspect of the femoral head/neck junction (*arrow*). **(C)** In a 38-year-old man—a tear of the superior anterior cartilaginous labrum (*arrow*). **(D)** In a 30-year-old woman—a delamination injury to the acetabular labrum (*arrow*).

lateral projection of anterior acetabulum, which normally should project medially to the posterior acetabulum, "crosses" the posterior acetabular outline (Fig. 13.12). MRI demonstrates acetabular version and depth of the femoral head coverage (Fig. 13.13). To determine the sphericity of the femoral head and the prominence of the anterior femoral head/neck junction, the alpha angle is calculated on the oblique axial CT or oblique axial MR images (Fig. 13.14). Radial reformatted MR images are of particular value in this respect, because they allow optimal visualization of the anterosuperior region of the femoral head/neck junction, where the most significant changes in the alpha angle occur (see Fig. 13.14B). The normal alpha angle should not exceed 50 degrees. The larger the alpha angle, the more pronounced is nonspherical shape of the femoral head, and the greater is predisposition for anterior FAI.

Treatment

In very early stages of osteoarthritis, particularly in the patients with FAI, open or arthroscopic trimming of acetabular rim and/or femoral head may be attempted. In younger patients, labral and acetabular repair and/or osteoplasty with reshaping of femoral head/neck junction contributed to satisfactory results. Occasionally intertrochanteric flexion-valgus osteotomy may also relieve the clinical symptoms. Periacetabular osteotomy is an effective way to reorient the acetabulum in young adults with symptomatic FAI due to acetabular retroversion. Advanced osteoarthritis, whether primary or secondary, is usually treated surgically by total hip arthroplasty using, among the various types available, either a cemented or a noncemented prosthesis. The reader is referred to Chapter 12 for further discussion of management.

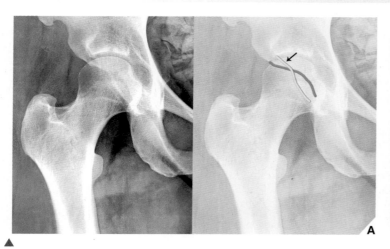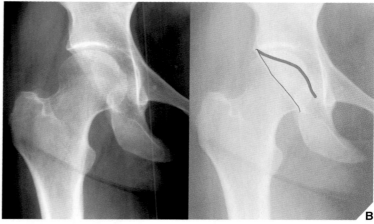

FIGURE 13.12 **Pincer type FAI. (A)** Anteroposterior radiograph of the left hip in a 29-year-old woman shows a cross-over sign. Note that the posterior acetabular rim outline (*yellow line*) projects medially (*arrow*) in relation to the anterior acetabular rim (*red line*), indicative of acetabular retroversion. **(B)** In a normal hip joint, the posterior acetabular rim outline projects laterally to the posterior acetabular rim.

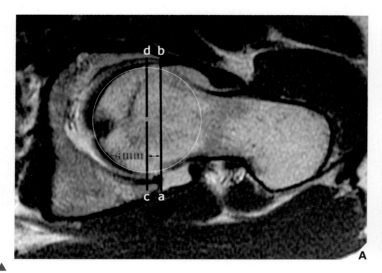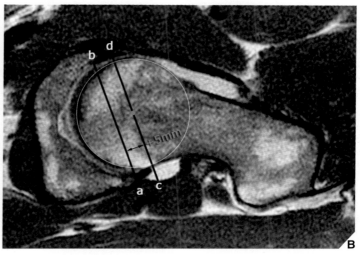

FIGURE 13.13 **MRI of pincer FAI. (A)** Axial oblique T1-weighted MR image shows deeply seated femoral head secondary to acetabular retroversion. Acetabular depth can be quantified by drawing a line (a-b) connecting the posterior and anterior acetabular rims, and a parallel line (c-d) that passes through the center of the femoral head (*red dot*). The distance between these two lines defines the acetabular depth, with the value being positive (+) if the center of the femoral head projects lateral to the line connecting the acetabular rims. Negative values (−) indicate deep seating of the femoral head within the acetabulum. **(B)** Axial oblique MR image of normal hip joint is shown for comparison.

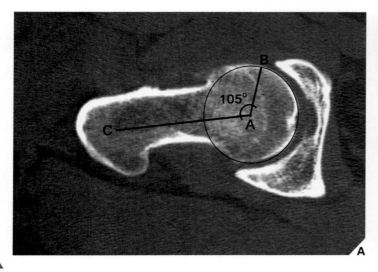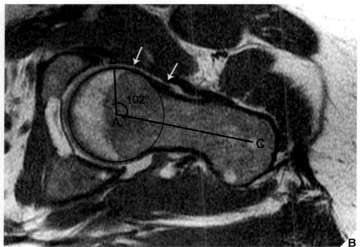

FIGURE 13.14 **Femoroacatabular impingement—calculation of alpha angle.** The alpha angle is formed by the intersection of two lines: line A-B, drawn from the center of the femoral head (A) to the point where peripheral osseous contour of the anterior femoral head intersects the extrapolated circle of the femoral head (B), and the second line A-C, drawn from the center of the femoral head (A) through the longitudinal axis of the femoral neck (C). Normal alpha angle should not exceed 50 degrees. **(A)** Alpha angle calculated on the oblique axial CT image of the right hip in a patient with cam FAI. **(B)** Alpha angle calculated on the oblique axial MR image of the left hip in a patient with cam FAI. The *arrows* point to excessive bone formation at the anterosuperior aspect of the femoral head/neck junction.

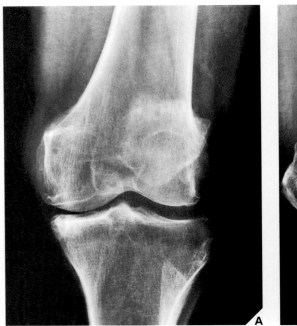
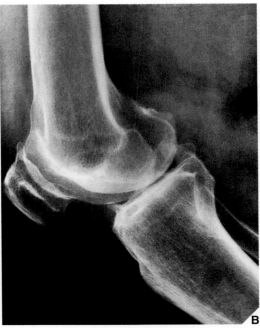

FIGURE 13.15 Osteoarthritis. Anteroposterior (**A**) and lateral (**B**) radiographs of the knee of a 57-year-old woman demonstrate narrowing of the medial femorotibial and femoropatellar compartments, subchondral sclerosis, and osteophytosis, which are the typical features of osteoarthritis. Note that osteophytes that were not obvious on the frontal projection are much better demonstrated on the lateral radiograph.

Osteoarthritis of the Knee

The knee is a complex joint comprising three major compartments—the medial femorotibial, the lateral femorotibial, and the femoropatellar—and each of which may be affected by degenerative changes. The radiographic features of these changes are similar to those seen in osteoarthritis of the hip, including narrowing of the joint space (usually one or two compartments), subchondral sclerosis, osteophytosis, and subchondral cyst (or pseudocyst) formation. The standard anteroposterior and lateral

projections of the knee are sufficient to demonstrate these processes (Fig. 13.15). If the medial joint compartment is affected, the knee may assume a varus configuration, which is best demonstrated on the weight-bearing anteroposterior view (Fig. 13.16A); involvement of the lateral compartment may lead to a valgus configuration (Fig. 13.16B). CT and 3D reconstructed CT images may provide additional information as to the status of osteoarthritic process (Fig. 13.17). A frequent complication of osteoarthritis of the knee is the formation of osteochondral

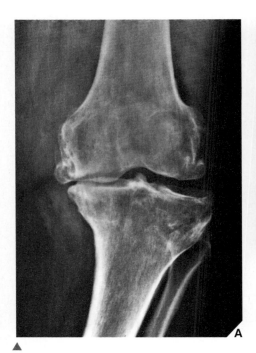
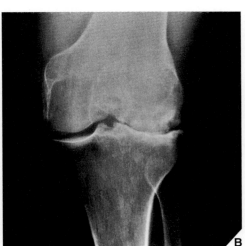
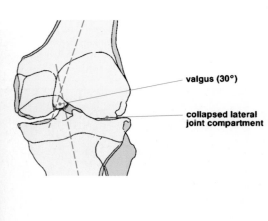

valgus (30°)

collapsed lateral
joint compartment

FIGURE 13.16 Osteoarthritis. (A) Weight-bearing anteroposterior radiograph of the knee of a 58-year-old woman demonstrates advanced osteoarthritis of the medial femorotibial joint compartment, which has led to a varus configuration of the joint. **(B)** Involvement of the lateral femorotibial joint compartment in advanced osteoarthritis as seen on this weight-bearing anteroposterior radiograph of another patient has resulted in a valgus configuration.

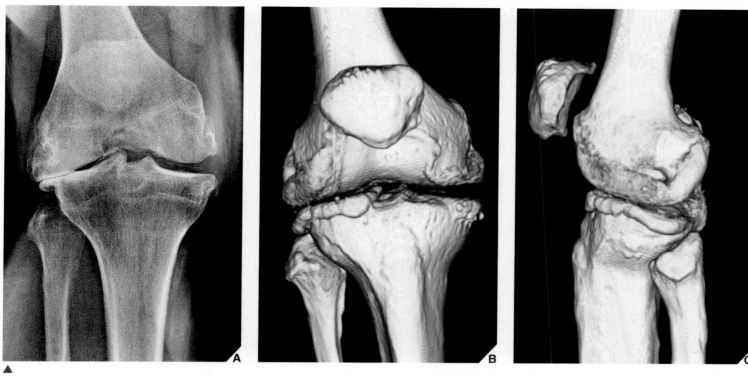

▲
FIGURE 13.17 **3D CT of osteoarthritis. (A)** Radiograph of the right knee of a 58-year-old man shows advanced osteoarthritis. **(B,C)** 3D reconstructed CT images in shaded surface display demonstrate advanced three-compartmental osteoarthritis.

bodies, which can be demonstrated on the standard projections of the knee (Figs. 13.18 and 13.19); however, MRI may also be effective in this respect (Figs. 13.20 to 13.22). The femoropatellar joint compartment is also commonly involved in primary osteoarthritis. The lateral radiograph of the knee and axial view of the patella are the most effective means of visualizing degenerative changes of the femoropatellar compartment (Fig. 13.23).

Often, particularly in individuals past their fifth decade of life, degenerative changes unrelated to femoropatellar osteoarthritis are seen at the insertion of the quadriceps tendon into the base of the patella. These changes are manifest as vertical ridges resembling teeth on an axial view of the patella and have been designated by Greenspan and colleagues as the "tooth" sign (Fig. 13.24A). The dentate structures represent an enthesopathy probably related to stress at the attachment of the quadriceps apparatus, and their nature is clearly demonstrated on the lateral projection (Fig. 13.24B). At times they can be recognized on the anteroposterior radiograph of the knee as well (Fig. 13.24C). MRI also effectively demonstrates these changes (Fig. 13.25).

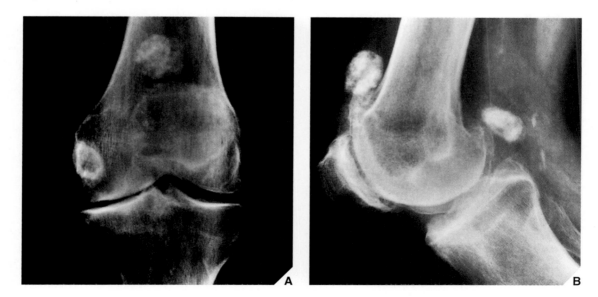

▲
FIGURE 13.18 **Osteoarthritis complicated by osteochondral bodies.** Anteroposterior **(A)** and lateral **(B)** radiographs of the knee of a 66-year-old man with advanced osteoarthritis demonstrate predominant involvement of the medial femorotibial and femoropatellar joint compartments, with formation of two large osteochondral bodies.

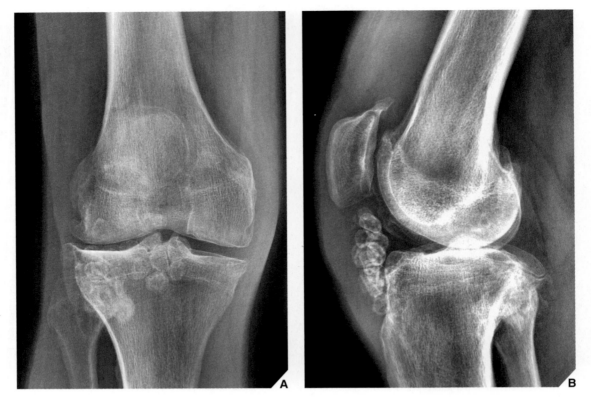

▲
FIGURE 13.19   Osteoarthritis complicated by osteochondral bodies. **(A)** Anteroposterior and **(B)** lateral radiographs of the right knee show osteoarthritis complicated by numerous osteochondral bodies.

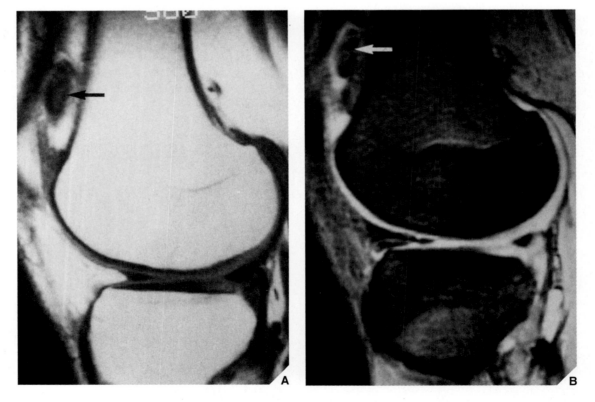

▲
FIGURE 13.20   **MRI of osteochondral body.** A low-signal-intensity osteocartilaginous loose body in suprapatellar bursa is revealed on T1-weighted **(A)** and T2*-weighted **(B)** sagittal MR images of the knee (*arrows*).

FIGURE 13.21 MRI of osteochondral bodies. Sagittal ▶ T2-weighted fat-suppressed MR image of the knee shows several intraarticular osteochondral bodies in this 67-year-old woman with osteoarthritis.

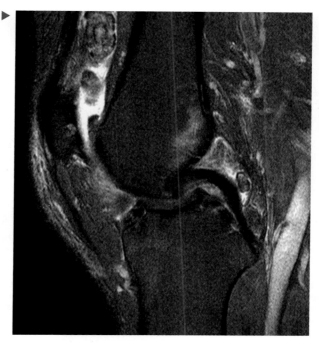

FIGURE 13.22 Baker cyst with osteochondral ▶ bodies. Sagittal T1-weighted (**A**) and T2*-weighted (**B**) MR images show multiple osteochondral loose bodies (*arrows*) in a popliteal (Baker) cyst adjacent to the medial head of gastrocnemius muscle.

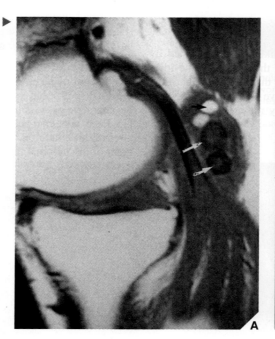
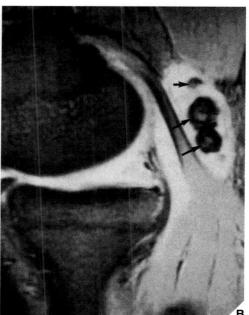

FIGURE 13.23 Femoropatellar osteoar- ▶ thritis. Lateral radiograph of the knee (**A**) and axial radiograph of the patella (**B**) of a 72-year-old woman demonstrate narrowing of the femoropatellar joint compartment and osteophytes formation.

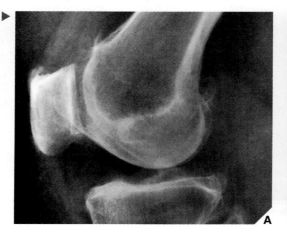
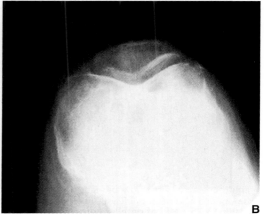

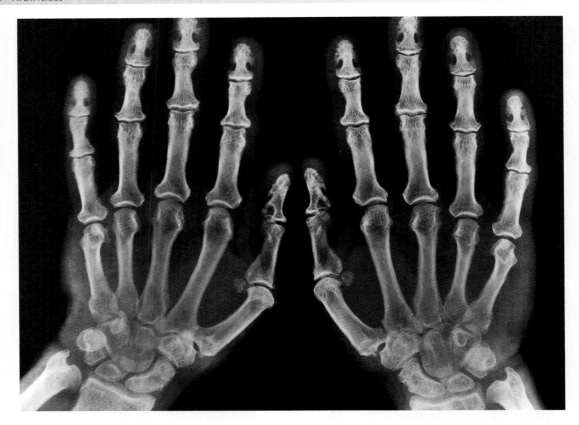

▲
FIGURE 13.29 **Acromegalic osteoarthritis.** Dorsovolar radiograph of both hands of a 42-year-old man with acromegaly shows widening of some and narrowing of other joint spaces, enlargement of the distal tufts and the bases of terminal phalanges, and beak-like osteophytes affecting particularly the heads of the metacarpals. Note the soft tissue prominence and the large sesamoid bones at the first metacarpophalangeal joints. The sesamoid index (derived by multiplying the vertical and horizontal diameters of the sesamoid bone) is 48 in this patient; normally, it should not exceed 20 to 25.

Hemochromatosis. Commonly associated with the development of secondary osteoarthritis in the small joints, hemochromatosis (iron storage disease) is a rare disorder characterized by iron deposition in internal organs, articular cartilage, and synovium. Some investigators believe that the arthropathy seen in this condition differs from typical degenerative joint disease and warrants classification in the group of metabolic arthritides (see Chapter 15).

In the hand, the second and third metacarpophalangeal joints are characteristically affected (Fig. 13.30), although other small joints such as the interphalangeal and carpal articulations may be involved. Degenerative changes may also be seen at the shoulders, knees, hips, and ankles. Loss of the articular space, eburnation, subchondral cyst formation, and osteophytosis are the most prominent radiographic features of hemochromatosis. The changes may occasionally mimic those seen in calcium pyrophosphate dihydrate deposition disease and rheumatoid arthritis.

Osteoarthritis of the Foot
In the foot, the most commonly affected articulation is the metatarsophalangeal joint of the great toe. This condition is known as *hallux rigidus* or *hallux limitus* (Fig. 13.31).

Degenerative Diseases of the Spine

Degenerative changes may involve the spine at the following sites:
1. The synovial joints—atlantoaxial, apophyseal, costovertebral, and sacroiliac—leading to *osteoarthritis* of these structures
2. The intervertebral disks, leading to the condition known as *degenerative disk disease*
3. The vertebral bodies and annulus fibrosus, leading to the condition known as *spondylosis deformans*
4. The fibrous articulations, ligaments, or sites of ligament attachment to the bone (entheses), leading to the condition known as *diffuse idiopathic skeletal hyperostosis* (DISH).

Frequently, all four conditions coexist in the same patient.

Osteoarthritis of the Synovial Joints

Degenerative changes of the vertebral facet joints are very common, particularly in the mid- and lower cervical and the lower lumbar segments. As in the other synovial joints, the characteristic radiographic features include diminution of the joint space, eburnation of subchondral bone, and osteophyte formation, all of which are most easily demonstrated on the oblique projection of the spine (Fig. 13.32). In the cervical spine, osteophytes on the posterior aspect of a vertebral body may encroach on the neural foramina or the thecal sac, causing various neurologic symptoms. In addition to the standard oblique views (Fig. 13.33), conventional tomography (in the past) or computed tomography (at the present time) may demonstrate these changes (Fig. 13.34). Anterior osteophytes, however, are as a rule asymptomatic unless they are unusually prominent. Involvement of the apophyseal joints may exhibit a "vacuum phenomenon" (Fig. 13.35), which in fact represents gas in the joint. This finding is almost pathognomonic for a degenerative process.

As in other diarthrodial joints, degenerative changes of the sacroiliac joints are manifested by narrowing of the joint space, subchondral sclerosis, and osteophytosis (Fig. 13.36). It is important to note in the evaluation of the sacroiliac joints that only the lower half of the radiographic sacroiliac joint space is lined by synovium; the upper portion is a syndesmotic joint (Fig. 13.37).

Degenerative Disk Disease

In degenerative disk disease, the vacuum phenomenon in the disk space is common. These radiolucent collections of gas, principally nitrogen, are related to the negative pressure created by abnormally altered joint or disk spaces.

Other radiographic findings of degenerative disk disease include disk space narrowing and osteophytosis at the marginal borders of the adjacent vertebral bodies (Fig. 13.38). Degenerative disk disease, in

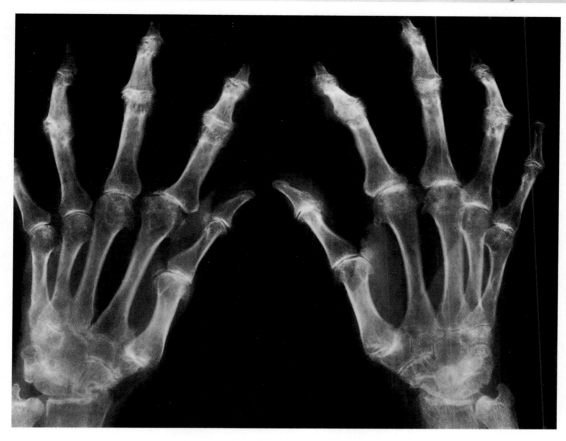

▲ **FIGURE 13.30 Hemochromatosis arthropathy.** Oblique radiographs of both hands of a 53-year-old woman with hemochromatosis show beak-like osteophytes arising from the heads of the second and third metacarpals on the radial aspect of both hands. The interphalangeal, metacarpophalangeal, and carpal articulations are also affected.

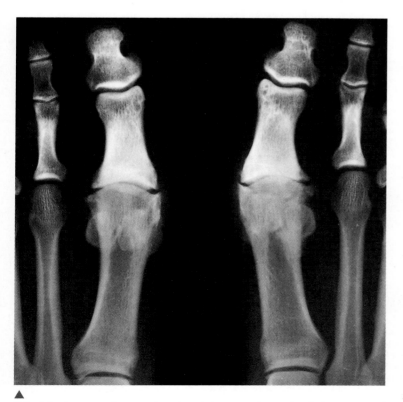

▲ **FIGURE 13.31 Hallux rigidus.** Dorsoplantar radiograph of the great and second toes of the feet of a 33-year-old man shows osteoarthritis of the first metatarsophalangeal joints, which are known as hallux rigidus (hallux limitus). Note the narrowing of the joint space, subchondral sclerosis, and marginal osteophytes.

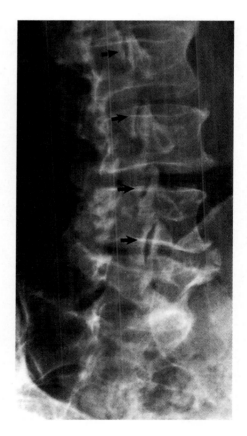

▲ **FIGURE 13.32 Osteoarthritis of the facet joints.** Oblique radiograph of the lumbar spine in a 68-year-old man demonstrates advanced osteoarthritis of the facet joints. Narrowing of the joint spaces, eburnation of the articular margins, and small osteophytes (*arrows*) are similar to the changes seen in osteoarthritis of the large synovial joints.

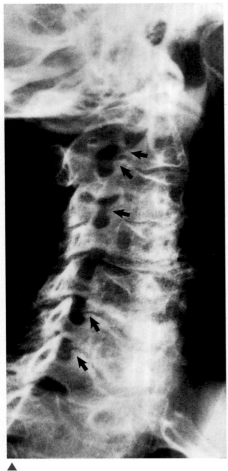

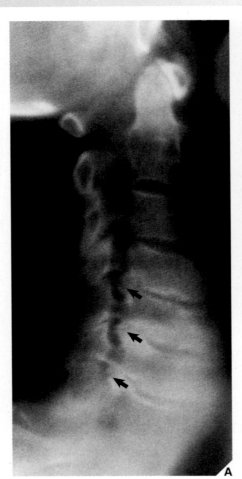

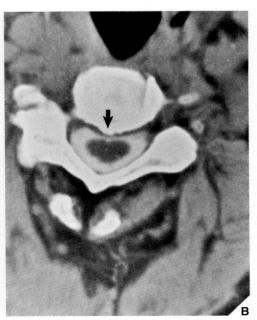

▲

FIGURE 13.33   Encroachment of the neural foramina. Oblique radiograph of the cervical spine in a 72-year-old woman who reported neck pain radiating to both shoulders reveals multiple posterior osteophytes encroaching on numerous neural foramina (*arrows*).

▲

FIGURE 13.34   Encroachment of the neural foramina and the thecal sac. (A) Conventional lateral tomogram of the cervical spine in a 56-year-old man demonstrates encroachment of the neural foramina by posterior osteophytes (*arrows*). **(B)** CT section at the level of C3 obtained during myelography demonstrates a large posterior osteophyte impinging on the thecal sac and compressing the subarachnoid space filled with contrast agent (*arrow*).

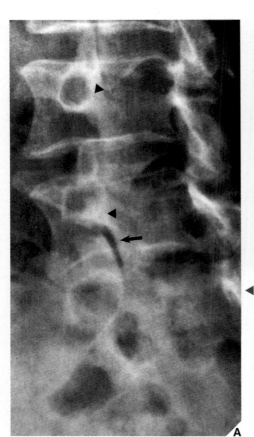

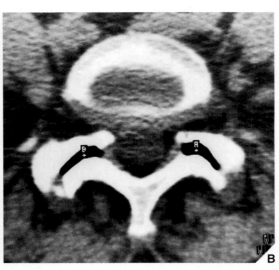

◄ **FIGURE 13.35   Osteoarthritis of the apophyseal joints.** A 56-year-old man with osteoarthritis affecting the apophyseal joints of the lumbar spine. **(A)** Oblique radiograph of the lumbosacral spine demonstrates a vacuum phenomenon of the facet joint L5-S1 (*arrow*) and eburnation of the subarticular bone (*arrow heads*). **(B)** CT section through both facets clearly demonstrates the presence of gas, as confirmed by the Hounsfield values. These units are related to the attenuation coefficient for various tissues in the body and represent absorption values directly related to tissue density. Note also the hypertrophic spur arising from the right facet and encroaching on the spinal canal.

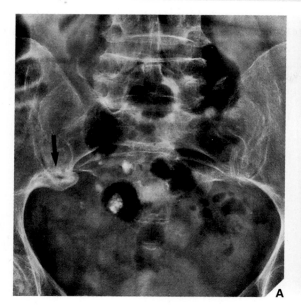 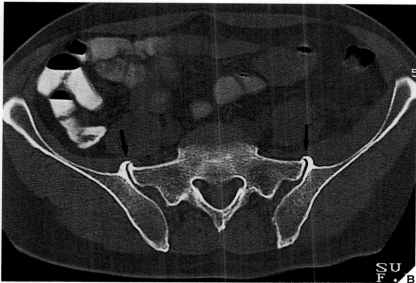

FIGURE 13.36   Osteoarthritis of the sacroiliac joints. (A) Degenerative changes in the sacroiliac joints, seen here affecting predominantly the right sacroiliac joint (arrow) in an 82-year-old woman, are manifested by narrowing of the joint space and osteophytosis. (B) In another patient, a 68-year-old man, osteoarthritis of both sacroiliac joints (arrows) is demonstrated on axial CT image.

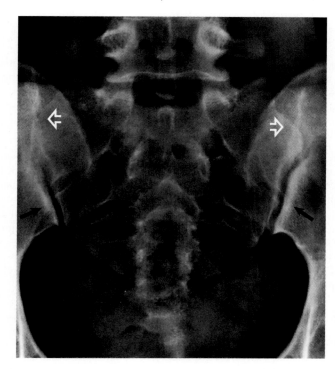

FIGURE 13.37   Sacroiliac joints. The true diarthrodial portion of the sacroiliac joint comprises only approximately 50% of the radiographic joint space (arrows). The upper part is a syndesmotic joint (open arrows).

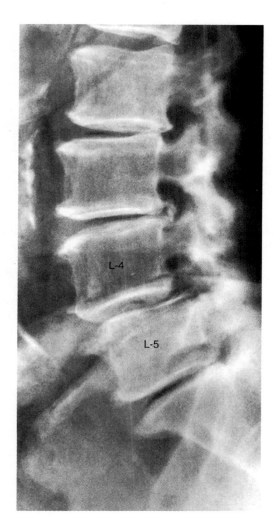

FIGURE 13.38   Degenerative disk disease. Lateral radiograph of the lumbosacral spine in a 66-year-old woman demonstrates advanced degenerative disk disease at multiple levels. Note the radiolucent collections of gas in several disks (the vacuum phenomenon) as well as the narrowing of the disk spaces and marginal osteophytes. Grade 1 degenerative spondylolisthesis is seen at the L4-5 level.

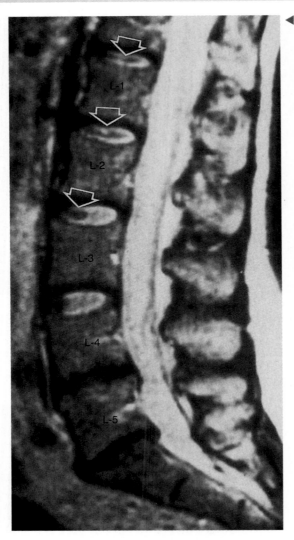

◀ **FIGURE 13.39** **MRI of degenerative disk disease.** Sagittal T2-weighted MR image shows early degenerative changes in the T12-L1, L1-2, and L2-3 intervertebral disks (*open arrows*), more advanced process in the L3-4 disk, and severe degenerative disk disease at L4-5 and L5-S1. At the latter levels, markedly decreased intervertebral spaces and low signal intensity of degenerated disks are seen.

combination with degenerative changes in the apophyseal joints, may lead to degenerative spondylolisthesis (see Figs. 11.75, 11.76B, and 13.38).

MRI is highly effective in demonstrating changes of disk degeneration. Decrease in the water content results in a decreased signal intensity of the nucleus pulposus on T2-weighted images (Fig. 13.39). Frequently, additional characteristic alterations are seen in the end-plates of the vertebral bodies adjacent to the degenerative disk. These abnormalities consist of a focal decreased signal intensity of the marrow on T1-weighted images and increased signal on T2- or T2*-weighted images (Fig. 13.40). According to Modic, these alterations represent subchondral vascularized fibrous tissue associated with end-plate fissuring and disruption (type I). These changes may progress to fatty marrow end-plate conversion (type II) (Fig. 13.41), and later to sclerosis (type III).

Spondylosis Deformans

Spondylosis deformans is a degenerative condition marked by the formation of anterior and lateral osteophytes as a result of anterior and anterolateral disk herniation (see Figs. 11.81 and 11.82). As Schmorl and other investigators have pointed out, the initiating factors in the development of this condition are abnormalities in the peripheral fibers of the annulus fibrosus that result in weakening of the anchorage of the intervertebral disk to the vertebral body at the site where Sharpey fibers attach to the vertebral rim. Unlike degenerative disk disease, the intervertebral spaces in spondylosis deformans are relatively well preserved, with the primary radiographic feature being extensive osteophytosis (Fig. 13.42). These osteophytes must be differentiated from the delicate

syndesmophytes of ankylosing spondylitis, from the large characteristically asymmetric bone excrescences that are seen in psoriatic arthritis and Reiter syndrome involving the lateral aspect of vertebral bodies, and from the flowing, usually anterior, hyperostosis of the DISH syndrome.

Diffuse Idiopathic Skeletal Hyperostosis

DISH, originally described by Forestier and popularized by Resnick, is characterized by flowing ossification along the anterior aspect of the vertebral bodies extending across the disk spaces. It is also associated with hyperostosis at the sites of tendon and ligament attachments to the bone, ligament ossification, and osteophytosis involving the axial and appendicular skeleton. A lateral radiograph of the spine best demonstrates these changes. As in spondylosis deformans, the disk spaces are usually well preserved (Fig. 13.43). It is important to distinguish this condition from the apparently similar "bamboo spine" seen in ankylosing spondylitis (see Fig. 14.35).

Complications of Degenerative Disease of the Spine

Degenerative Spondylolisthesis

One of the most common complications of degenerative disease of the spine, degenerative spondylolisthesis, results from degenerative changes in the disk and apophyseal joints. In this condition, there is anterior displacement of a vertebra onto the one below, which usually is easily recognized on the lateral view of the spine by the spinous-process sign (Fig. 13.44; see also Fig. 11.75). However, on occasion, the displacement

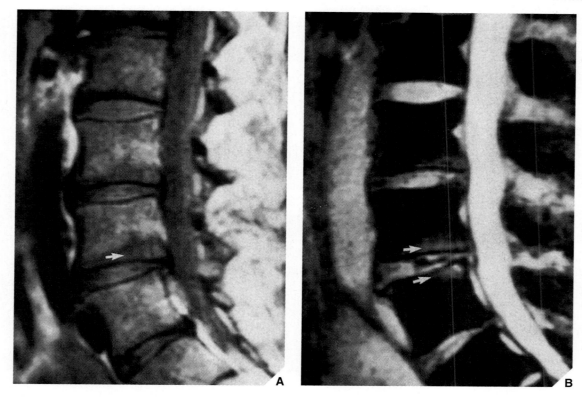

▲
FIGURE 13.40   **MRI of degenerative disk disease.** A type I vertebral end-plate change (*arrows*) demonstrates a focus of low signal intensity in subchondral marrow on a T1-weighted sagittal MRI (**A**) and a high signal intensity on T2* weighting (**B**).

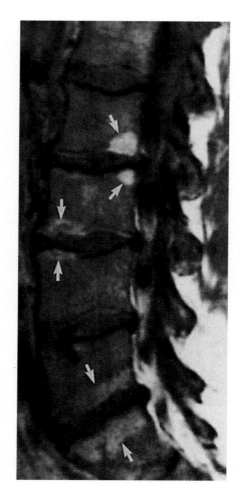

▲
FIGURE 13.41   **MRI of degenerative disk disease.** Type II end-plate changes in degenerative disk disease consisting of focal areas of yellow marrow conversion (*arrows*) are seen on a sagittal T1-weighted MR image.

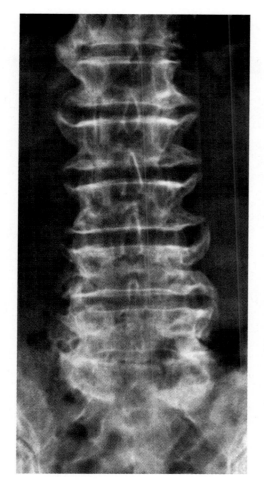

▲
FIGURE 13.42   **Spondylosis deformans.** Anteroposterior radiograph of the lumbosacral spine in a 68-year-old woman exhibits the typical changes of spondylosis deformans. Note the extensive osteophytosis and relatively well-preserved intervertebral disk spaces.

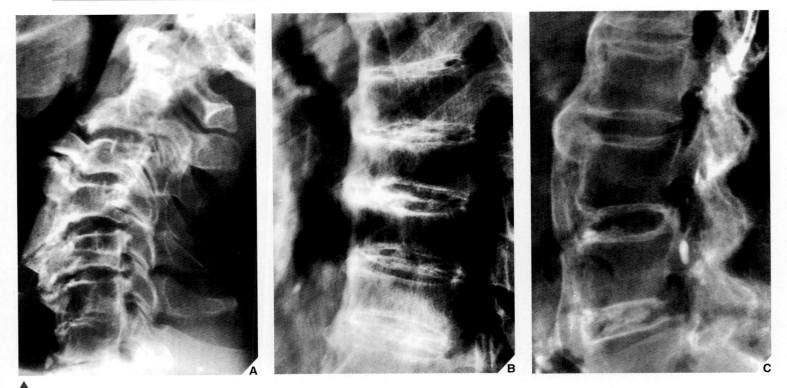

▲
FIGURE 13.43 **Diffuse idiopathic skeletal hyperostosis.** Lateral radiographs of the cervical (**A**), thoracic (**B**), and lumbar (**C**) spine in a 72-year-old man with Forestier disease (DISH) show the characteristic flowing hyperostosis extending across the vertebral disk spaces, which are relatively well preserved.

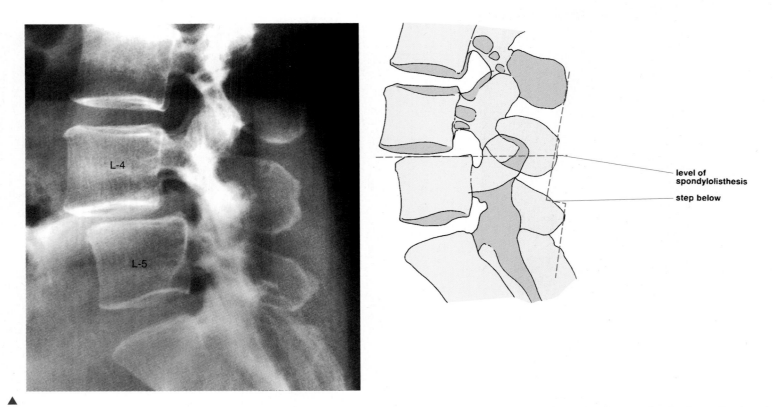

▲
FIGURE 13.44 **Degenerative spondylolisthesis.** A 55-year-old woman with degenerative disk disease at L4-5 and degenerative facet arthritis developed spondylolisthesis, a common complication of this condition. Lateral radiograph of the lumbosacral spine is sufficient to differentiate this condition from spondylolisthesis associated with spondylolysis by the appearance of a step-off of the spinous process at the vertebra below the involved intervertebral space (see Fig. 11.75).

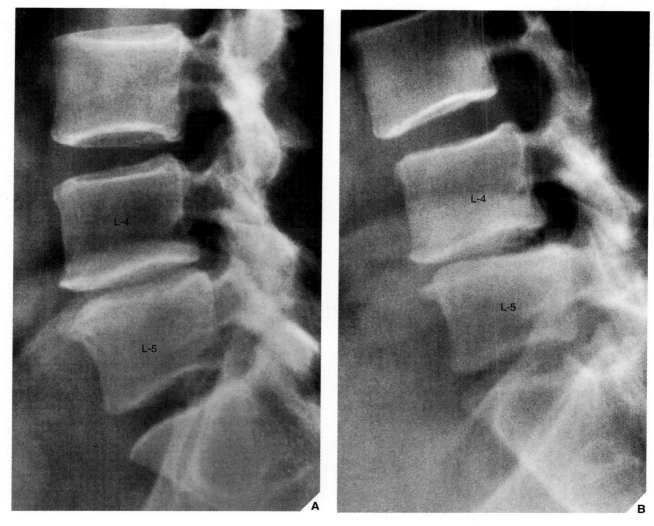

▲
FIGURE 13.45   **Degenerative spondylolisthesis.** A 50-year-old man presented with chronic low back pain. **(A)** Standard lateral radiograph of the lumbosacral spine in the neutral position shows narrowing of the L4-5 disk space, indicating degenerative disk disease. There is no evidence of vertebral list. **(B)** Lateral radiograph in flexion, however, demonstrates grade 1 spondylolisthesis at L4-5.

may not be obvious on the standard lateral film, and radiographs must be obtained while the patient maximally extends and flexes the spine (Fig. 13.45). As Milgram pointed out, the stress applied by forward and backward motion of the spine discloses instability (spondylolisthesis), which may be overlooked on other projections.

Degenerative spondylolisthesis occurs in approximately 4% of patients with degenerative disk disease and affects women more frequently than men. It has a predilection for the L4-5 spinal level. This predilection has been attributed to developmental or acquired alterations in the neural arch that lead to instability and abnormal stress. The stress applied to the vertebra may result in decompensation of the ligaments, hypermobility, instability, and osteoarthritis of adjacent apophyseal joints.

Clinical symptoms associated with degenerative spondylolisthesis include low back pain with or without radiation into the leg, sciatic pain with signs of nerve root compression, and intermittent claudication of the cauda equina. It should be noted, however, that many patients with degenerative spondylolisthesis are asymptomatic.

Radiographic findings of degenerative spondylolisthesis include osteoarthritic changes of the facet joints (joint narrowing, marginal eburnation, and osteophyte formation), anterior slippage of the superior vertebra on the inferior vertebra, and, in many instances, intervertebral

vacuum phenomenon (see Fig. 11.38). Invariably, the affected intervertebral disk space is narrowed. CT may also effectively demonstrate this complication (Fig. 13.46).

The intervertebral vacuum phenomenon associated with degenerative disk disease should not be confused with the intravertebral vacuum cleft sign. This sign appears on radiographs as a transverse, linear, or semilunar radiolucency located within the vertebral body. According to recent reports, this sign represents gas (principally nitrogen) in the fracture line of the vertebral body. Although the pathogenesis of this process is not completely clear, the sign is most suggestive of ischemic necrosis of bone. This phenomenon has been also reported in association with Kümmell disease, a delayed posttraumatic collapse of the vertebral body (Fig. 13.47).

Spinal Stenosis

Spinal stenosis is a much more severe complication of degenerative disease of the spine. In its acquired form, it results from hypertrophy of the structures surrounding the spinal canal, such as the pedicles, laminae, articular processes, and posterior aspect of the vertebral bodies, as well as the ligamentum flavum. These alternations usually are apparent on conventional radiography; however, spinal stenosis can be better

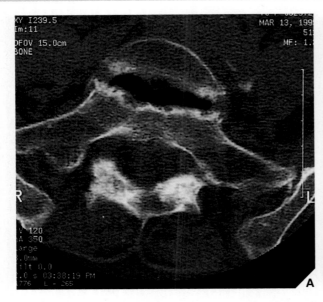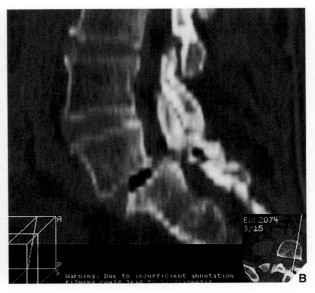

FIGURE 13.46 **Degenerative spondylolisthesis and spinal stenosis. (A)** Axial CT of a 70-year-old woman with chronic low back pain shows the vacuum phenomenon at the disk L5-S1. **(B)** Sagittal reformatted image demonstrates degenerative disk disease at L5-S1 associated with a vacuum phenomenon and spondylolisthesis. There is also evidence of spinal stenosis at the S1 level.

demonstrated by ancillary techniques. Spinal stenosis can be demonstrated by myelography, which can show the impingement of the thecal sac by hypertrophic changes of the posterior parts of the vertebral body and bulging disks, but CT best delineates its details (Fig. 13.48). MRI is also an effective modality in this respect (Fig. 13.49).

Spinal stenosis in the lumbar segment can be divided into three groups on the basis of its anatomic location: stenosis of the spinal canal, stenosis of the subarticular or lateral recesses, and stenosis of the neural foramina.

The causes of stenosis of the central canal are related to hypertrophic changes of osteoarthritis of the apophyseal joints, thickening of the

ligamentum flavum, and osteophytes arising from the vertebral bodies. Bone hypertrophy at the site of the facet joints is a major cause of stenosis of the subarticular or lateral recesses, leading to encroachment on the neural elements in this region. Clinical manifestations of lateral recess syndrome include unilateral or bilateral leg pain, which is initiated or aggravated by long periods of standing or walking. These symptoms are usually relieved entirely by sitting or squatting. The stenosis of the neural foramina is caused by hypertrophic changes and osteophytosis involving the vertebral body and articular process. Moreover, degenerative spondylolisthesis may be associated with distortion of the intervertebral foramen and may lead to compromise of the exiting nerve.

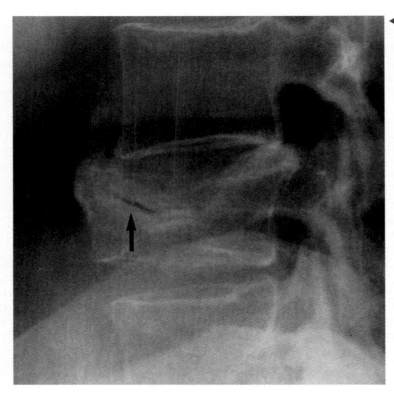

◀ **FIGURE 13.47** **Kümmell disease.** Lateral radiograph of the lumbar spine shows posttraumatic collapse of the vertebral body of L4 associated with intravertebral vacuum cleft sign (*arrow*).

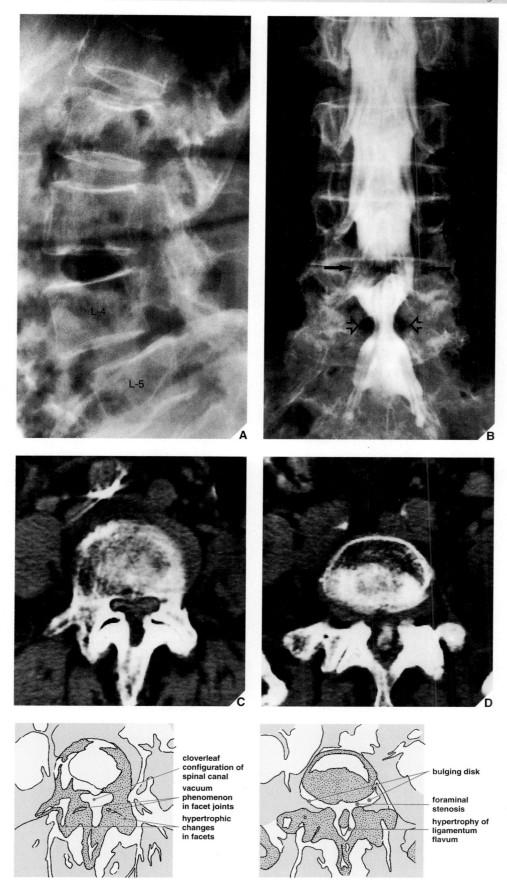

▲
FIGURE 13.48 **Spinal stenosis.** A 71-year-old woman was evaluated for severe low back pain. (**A**) Standard lateral radiograph of the lumbar spine shows degenerative spondylolisthesis at the L4-5 interspace. Note the short appearance of the pedicles. (**B**) Myelogram in the anteroposterior projection also discloses segmental narrowing of the thecal sac; the upper defect is related to spondylolisthesis (*arrows*), the lower to spinal stenosis (*open arrows*). CT sections (**C,D**) demonstrate the details of the abnormalities—severe spinal and foraminal stenosis, hypertrophy of the ligamenta flava, and posterior bulging of the intervertebral disk. Note the cloverleaf configuration of the spinal canal secondary to marked hypertrophy of the facet joints. The vacuum phenomenon in the apophyseal joints is well demonstrated.

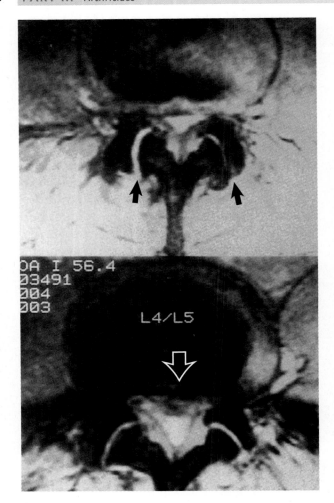

▲
FIGURE 13.49 **MRI of spinal stenosis.** Degenerative changes of the facet joints (*arrows*) and disk bulging (*open arrow*) contributed to central canal stenosis at the L4-5 disk level, as demonstrated here on T2*-weighted axial MR images.

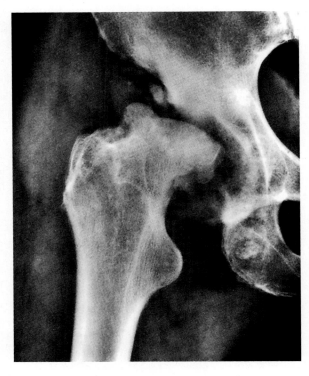

▲
FIGURE 13.50 **Neuropathic joint.** Anteroposterior radiograph of the right hip of a 57-year-old woman with neurosyphilis (tabes dorsalis) shows the typical features of neuropathic (Charcot) joint. There is complete disorganization of the joint, fragmentation, and subluxation. The absence of osteoporosis is a characteristic feature of the neuropathic joint. This condition represents the most severe manifestation of degenerative joint disease.

Neuropathic Arthropathy

This acute or chronic destructive arthritis, also known as Charcot joint, is grouped with other degenerative joint diseases because it exhibits manifestations similar to those seen in other forms of osteoarthritis—destruction of articular cartilage, subchondral sclerosis, and marginal osteophytosis—but in their most severe form. Neuropathic arthropathy comprises a spectrum of destructive processes in the joint associated with neurosensory deficit. Pathognomonic for neuropathic joints are fragmentation of the bone and cartilage, which are discharged as debris into the joint; chronic synovitis with accumulation of varying amounts of fluid in the joint; and joint instability manifested by subluxation and dislocation (Fig. 13.50). Underlying conditions leading to neuropathic joint include, among others, diabetes mellitus, syphilis, leprosy, syringomyelia, congenital indifference to pain, and spina bifida with meningomyelocele (Table 13.2). In diabetic patients, the condition has a greater predilection for the joints of the foot and ankle (Fig. 13.51); in patients with syringomyelia, joints of the upper extremities are more commonly affected (Fig. 13.52). The eponym *Charcot joint* was originally reserved for neuropathic joint in syphilitic patients with tabes dorsalis (Fig. 13.53). Currently, this term applies to any joint displaying features of neuropathic arthropathy, regardless of the causative factor.

TABLE 13.2 **Causes of Neuropathic Arthropathy**

Alcoholism
Amyloidosis
Charcot-Marie-Tooth disease
Congential indifference to pain
Diabetes mellitus
Extrinsic compression of the spinal cord
Familial dysautonomia (Riley-Day syndrome)
Leprosy
Meningomyelocele
Multiple sclerosis
Peripheral nerve tumors
Pernicious anemia
Poliomyelitis
Spinal cord tumors
Steroids (systemic or intraarticular)
Syringomyelia
Tabes dorsalis (syphilis)
Uremia

Modified from Jones EA et al., 2000, with permission.

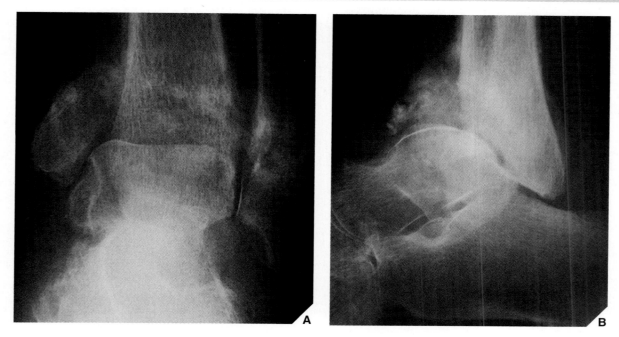

FIGURE 13.51   Neuropathic joint. A 59-year-old woman with long-standing diabetes mellitus presented with neuropathic changes of left ankle joint, demonstrated here on the anteroposterior (**A**) and lateral (**B**) radiographs.

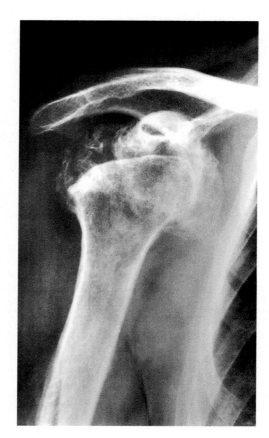

FIGURE 13.52   Neuropathic joint. A 59-year-old woman with syringomyelia developed a neuropathic shoulder joint. Anteroposterior radiograph shows destruction of the joint, bony debris, and subluxation of the humeral head.

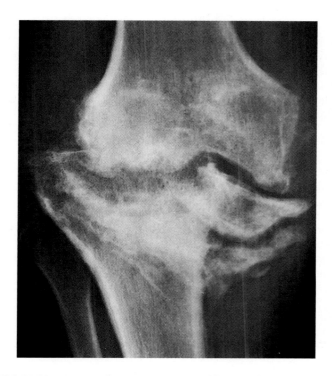

FIGURE 13.53   Neuropathic joint. A 62-year-old man with syphilis presented with a typical neuropathic (Charcot) knee joint.

PRACTICAL POINTS TO REMEMBER

Osteoarthritis

[1] Degenerative joint disease (osteoarthritis, osteoarthrosis, degenerative arthritis) is classified as primary (idiopathic) or secondary; in the latter, there is an underlying predisposing disorder.

[2] The radiographic hallmarks of osteoarthritis are:
- diminution (narrowing) of the joint space
- subchondral sclerosis
- osteophytosis
- cyst or pseudocyst formation
- lack of pronounced osteoporosis.

Osteoarthritis of the Large Joints

[1] In the hip joint, the degenerative process results in migration of the femoral head, most commonly in a superolateral direction.

[2] One of the most common causes of precocious secondary osteoarthritis of the hip joint is FAI syndrome. Two types have been recognized: cam, where abnormality is at the femoral head/neck junction; and pincer, commonly resulting from acetabular retroversion.

[3] Postel coxarthropathy is a rapidly destructive arthrosis of the hip joint, which radiographically can mimic infection or neuropathic joint.

[4] The medial femorotibial and femoropateller compartments of the knee joint are commonly involved in osteoarthritis. Weight-bearing examination may reveal a varus configuration of the knee.

[5] The "tooth" sign of the patella, recognized on an axial view by vertical ridges at the insertion of the quadriceps tendon into the base of the patella, represents a type of degenerative change (enthesopathy) unrelated to femoropatellar osteoarthritis. It is commonly seen after the fifth decade of life.

[6] If the shoulder, elbow, or ankle joints are affected by degenerative joint disease, a diagnosis of secondary rather than primary osteoarthritis should be considered.

Osteoarthritis of the Small Joints

[1] In the hand, the hallmarks of primary degenerative joint disease are:
- Heberden nodes affecting the distal interphalangeal joints
- Bouchard nodes affecting the proximal interphalangeal joints.

[2] The first carpometacarpal articulation is frequently involved in primary degenerative joint disease.

Degenerative Disease of the Spine

[1] In the spine, degenerative changes may be present in four major forms:
- as osteoarthritis of the synovial joints, including the atlantoaxial, apophyseal, costovertebral, and sacroiliac
- as spondylosis deformans, a condition manifested by formation of anterior and lateral marginal osteophytes with preservation of the disk spaces (at least in the early stages)
- as degenerative disk disease, a condition primarily involving the intervertebral disks and manifested by the destruction of these structures, the vacuum phenomenon, and narrowing of the disk spaces
- as diffuse idiopathic skeletal hyperostosis (DISH syndrome or Forestier disease), characterized by flowing ossifications along the anterior aspects of vertebral bodies extending across the disk spaces, relative preservation of the intervertebral disks, and hyperostosis at the sites of tendon and ligament attachment to the bone (enthesopathy).

[2] Two common conditions can complicate degenerative spine disease:
- degenerative spondylolisthesis
- spinal stenosis.

[3] Degenerative spondylolisthesis is marked by anterior (ventral) displacement of a vertebra onto the one below and recognized on the lateral view of the spine by the spinous-process sign.

[4] Spinal stenosis can readily be diagnosed using CT or MRI.

Neuropathic Arthropathy

[1] Neuropathic (Charcot) joint manifests with the same degenerative changes as osteoarthritis, but they are seen in their most severe form. This condition is also marked by:
- fragmentation of the bone and cartilage, filling the joint with debris
- chronic synovitis with joint effusion
- joint instability with subluxation or dislocation.

[2] The underlying conditions leading to neuropathic joint include diabetes mellitus, syphilis, leprosy, syringomyelia, and congenital indifference to pain.

SUGGESTED READINGS

Adamson TC III, Resnik CS, Guerra Jr J, Vint VC, Weisman MH, Resnick D. Hand and wrist arthropathies of hemochromatosis and calcium pyrophosphate deposition disease: distinct radiographic features. *Radiology* 1983;147:377–381.

Bennett GL, Leeson MC, Michael A. Extensive hemosiderin deposition in the medial meniscus of a knee. Its possible relationship to degenerative joint disease. *Clin Orthop* 1988;230:182–185.

Bhalla S, Reinus WR. The linear intravertebral vacuum: a sign of benign vertebral collapse. *Am J Roentgenol* 1998;170:1563–1569.

Blackburn WD Jr, Chivers S, Bernreuter W. Cartilage imaging in osteoarthritis. *Semin Arthritis Rheum* 1996;25:273–281.

Bloem JL, Sartoris DJ, eds. *MRI and CT of the musculoskeletal system. A text-atlas.* Baltimore: Williams & Wilkins; 1992.

Bock GW, Garcia A, Weisman MH, et al. Rapidly destructive hip disease: clinical and imaging abnormalities. *Radiology* 1993;186:461–466.

Bora FW Jr, Miller G. Joint physiology, cartilage metabolism, and the etiology of osteoarthritis. *Hand Clin* 1987;3:325–336.

Boutry N, Paul C, Leroy X, Fredoux D, Migaud H, Cotten A. Rapidly destructive osteoarthritis of the hip: MR imaging findings. *Am J Roentgenol* 2002;179:657–663.

Broderick LS, Turner DA, Renfrew DL, Schnitzer TJ, Huff JP, Harris C. Severity of articular cartilage abnormality in patients with osteoarthritis: evaluation with fast spin-echo MR vs arthroscopy. *Am J Roentgenol* 1994;162:99–103.

Brower AC, Downey EF. Kümmell disease: report of a case with serial radiographs. *Radiology* 1981;141:363–364.

Buckwalter JA, Mankin HG. Articular cartilage. II. Degeneration and osteoarthritis, repair, regeneration, and transplantation. *J Bone Joint Surg [Am]* 1997;79A:612–632.

Buckwalter JA, Mow VC. Cartilage repair in osteoarthritis. In: Moskowitz RW, Howell DS, Goldberg VM, Mankin HJ, eds. *Osteoarthritis*, 2nd ed. Philadelphia: WB Saunders; 1992:71–107.

Bullough PG. The pathology of osteoarthritis. In: Moskowitz RW, Howell DS, Goldberg VM, Mankin HJ, eds. *Osteoarthritis*, 2nd ed. Philadelphia: WB Saunders; 1992:39–69.

Bullough PG, Bansal M. The differential diagnosis of geodes. *Radiol Clin North Am* 1988;26:1165–1184.

Chan WP, Lang P, Stevens MP, et al. Osteoarthritis of the knee: comparison of radiography, CT, and MR imaging to assess extent and severity. *Am J Roentgenol* 1991;157:799–806.

Charcot JM. Sur quelques arthropathies qui paraissent dépendre d'une lesion du cervean ou de la moëlle épindère. *Arch Physiol Norm Pathol* 1868;1:161–178.

Chen L, Boonthathip M, Cardoso F, Clopton P, Resnick D. Acetabulum protrusio and center edge angle: new MR-imaging measurement criteria—a correlative study with measurement derived from conventional radiography. *Skeletal Radiol* 2009;38:123–129.

Chou L, Knight R. Idiopathic avascular necrosis of a vertebral body: a case report and literature review. *Spine* 1997;22:1928–1932.

Cohn EL, Maurer EJ, Dussault RG, Kaplan PA. Plain film evaluation of degenerative disk disease at the lumbosacral junction. *Skeletal Radiol* 1997;26:161–166.

Davis MA. Epidemiology of osteoarthritis. *Clin Geriatr Med* 1988;4:241–255.

Della Torre P, Picuti G, Di Filippo P. Rapidly progressive osteoarthritis of the hip. *Ital J Orthop Traumatol* 1987;13:187–200.

Dieppe P, Cushnaghan J. The natural course and prognosis of osteoarthritis. In: Moskowitz RW, Howell DS, Goldberg VM, Mankin HJ, eds. *Osteoarthritis*, 2nd ed. Philadelphia: WB Saunders; 1992:399–412.

Epstein BS, Epstein JA, Jones MD. Lumbar spinal stenosis. *Radiol Clin North Am* 1977;15:227–239.

Erkintalo MO, Salminen JJ, Alanen AM, Paajanen HEK, Kormano MJ. Development of degenerative changes in the lumbar intervertebral disk: results of a prospective MR imaging study in adolescents with and without low-back pain. *Radiology* 1995;196:529–533.

Fairbank TJ. Knee joint changes after meniscectomy. *J Bone Joint Surg [Br]* 1948;30B:664–670.

Felson DT. The course of osteoarthritis and factors that affect it. *Rheum Dis Clin North Am* 1993;19:607–615.

Forestier J, Rotes Querol J. Senile ankylosing hyperostosis of the spine. *Ann Rheum Dis* 1950;9:321–330.

Ganz R, Parvizi J, Beck M, Leunig M, Notzli H, Siebenrock KA. Femoroacetabular impingement: a cause for osteoarthritis of the hip. *Clin Orthop Relat Res* 2003;417:112–120.

Giori NJ, Trousdale RT. Acetabular retroversion is associated with osteoarthritis of the hip. *Clin Orthop Relat Res* 2003;417:263–269.

Golimbu C, Firooznia H, Rafii M. The intravertebral vacuum sign. *Spine* 1986;11:1040–1043.

Greenspan A, Norman A, Tchang FKM. "Tooth" sign in patellar degenerative disease. *J Bone Joint Surg [Am]* 1977;59A:483–485.

Harrison MH, Schajowicz F, Trueta J. Osteoarthritis of the hip: a study of the nature and evolution of the disease. *J Bone Joint Surg [Br]* 1953;35B:598–629.

Hayward I, Bjorkengren AG, Pathria MN, Zlatkin MB, Sartoris DJ, Resnick D. Patterns of femoral head migration in osteoarthritis of the hip: a reappraisal with CT and pathologic correlation. *Radiology* 1988;166:857–860.

Hill CL, Gale DG, Chaisson CE, et al. Knee effusions, popliteal cysts, and synovial thickening: association with knee pain in osteoarthritis. *J Rheumatol* 2001;28:1330–1337.

Jacobson JA, Girish G, Jiang Y, Sabb BJ. Radiographic evaluation of arthritis: degenerative joint disease and variations. *Radiology* 2008;248:737–747.

Jones EA, Manaster BJ, May DA, Disler DG. Neuropathic osteoarthropathy: diagnostic dilemmas and differential diagnosis. *Radiographics* 2000;20:S279–S293.

Kassarjian A, Yoon LS, Belzile E, Connolly SA, Millis MB, Palmer WE. Triad of MR arthrographic findings in patients with cam-type femoroacetabular impingement. *Radiology* 2005;236:588–592.

Kellgren JH, Moore R. Generalized osteoarthritis and Heberden's nodes. *Br Med J* 1952;1:181–187.

Kerr R, Resnick D, Pineda C, Haghighi P. Osteoarthritis of the glenohumeral joint: a radiologic-pathologic study. *Am J Roentgenol* 1985;144:967–972.

Kirkaldy-Willis WH, Farfan HF. Instability of the lumbar spine. *Clin Orthop* 1982;165:110–123.

Knutsson F. The vacuum phenomenon in the intervertebral discs. *Acta Radiol* 1942;23:173–175.

Kumpan W, Salomonowitz E, Seidl G, Wittich GR. The intervertebral vacuum phenomenon. *Skeletal Radiol* 1986;15:444–447.

Lawrance JAL, Athanasou NA. Rapidly destructive hip disease. *Skeletal Radiol* 1995;24:639–641.

Leach RE, Gregg T, Siber FJ. Weight-bearing radiography in osteoarthritis of the knee. *Radiology* 1970;97:265–268.

Lefkowitz DM, Quencer RM. Vacuum facet phenomenon: a computed tomographic sign of degenerative spondylolisthesis. *Radiology* 1982;144:562.

Leone A, Cassar-Pullicino VN, Guglielmi G, Bonomo L. Degenerative lumbar intervertebral instability: what is it and how does imaging contribute? *Skeletal Radiol* 2009;38:529–533.

Lequesne M. La coxarthrose destructrice rapide. *Rhumatologie* 1970;22:51–63.

Lequesne MG, Laredo J-D. The faux profil (oblique view) of the hip in the standing position. Contribution to the evaluation of osteoarthritis of the adult hip. *Ann Rheum Dis* 1998;57:676–681.

Maldague BE, Noel HM, Malghem JJ. The intravertebral vacuum cleft: a sign of ischemic vertebral collapse. *Radiology* 1978;129:23–29.

Mankin HJ, Brandt KD. Biochemistry and metabolism of articular cartilage in osteoarthritis. In: Moskowitz RW, Howell DS, Goldberg VM. Mankin HJ, eds. *Osteoarthritis*, 2nd ed. Philadelphia: WB Saunders; 1992:109–154.

Martel W, Snarr JW, Horn JR. The metacarpophalangeal joints in interphalangeal osteoarthritis. *Radiology* 1973;108:1–7.

McAfee PC, Ullrich CG, Yuan HA, Cacayorill ED, Lockwood RC. Computed tomography in degenerative lumbar spinal stenosis: the value of multiplanar reconstruction. *Radiographics* 1982;2:529–537.

McCauley TR, Disler DG. Magnetic resonance imaging of articular cartilage of the knee. *J Am Acad Orthop Surg* 2001;9:2–8.

Milgram JE. Recurrent articular spondylolisthesis: common cause of vertebral instabilities, root pain, sciatica, and ultimately spinal stenosis. Early detection and blocking of specific dislocations. *Bull Hosp Joint Dis Orthop Inst* 1986;46:47–51.

Modic MT, Masaryk TJ, Ross JS, Carter JR. Imaging of degenerative disk disease. *Radiology* 1988;168:177–186.

Modic MT, Steinberg PM, Ross JS, Masaryk TJ, Carter JR. Degenerative disk disease: assessment of changes in vertebral body marrow with MR imaging. *Radiology* 1988;166:193–199.

Norman A, Robbins H, Milgram JE. The acute neuropathic arthropathy—a rapid severely disorganizing form of arthritis. *Radiology* 1968;90:1159–1164.

Notzli HP, Wyss TF, Stoecklin CH, Schmid MR, Treiber K, Hodler J. The contour of the femoral head-neck junction as a predictor for the risk of anterior impingement. *J Bone Joint Surg [Br]* 2002;84B:556–560.

Pepper HW, Noonan CD. Radiographic evaluation of total hip arthroplasty. *Radiology* 1973;108:23–29.

Peyron JG. Epidemiologic and etiologic approach of osteoarthritis. *Semin Arthritis Rheum* 1979;8:288–306.

Peyron JG, Altman RD. The epidemiology of osteoarthritis. In: Moskowitz RW, Howell DS, Goldberg VM, Mankin HJ, eds. *Osteoarthritis*, 2nd ed. Philadelphia: WB Saunders; 1992:15–37.

Pfirrmann CWA, Mengiardi B, Dora C, Kalberer F, Zanetti M, Hodler J. Cam and pincer femoroacetabular impingement: characteristic MR arthrographic findings in 50 patients. *Radiology* 2006;240:778–785.

Postel M, Kerboull M. Total prosthetic replacement in rapidly destructive arthrosis of the hip joint. *Clin Orthop* 1970;72:138–144.

Resnick D. Patterns of migration of the femoral head in osteoarthritis of the hip. Roentgenographic-pathologic correlation and comparison with rheumatoid arthritis. *Am J Roentgenol* 1975;124:62–74.

Resnick D. Degenerative diseases of the vertebral column. *Radiology* 1985;156:3–14.

Resnick D, Niwayama G. Entheses and enthesopathy. Anatomical, pathological and radiological correlation. *Radiology* 1983;146:1–9.

Resnick D, Niwayama G. Degenerative disease of extraspinal locations. In: Resnick D, ed. *Diagnosis of bone and joint disorders*, 3rd ed. Philadelphia: WB Saunders; 1995:1263–1371.

Resnick D, Niwayama G. Diffuse idiopathic skeletal hyperostosis (DISH): ankylosing hyperostosis of Forestier and Rotes-Querol. In: Resnick D, ed. *Diagnosis of bone and joint disorders*, 3rd ed. Philadelphia: WB Saunders; 1995:1463–1495.

Resnick D, Niwayama G, Coutts RD. Subchondral cysts (geodes) in arthritic disorders: pathologic and radiographic appearance of the hip joint. *Am J Roentgenol* 1977;128:799–806.

Resnick D, Niwayama G, Goergen TG. Degenerative disease of the sacroiliac joint. *Invest Radiol* 1975;10:608–621.

Resnick D, Shaul SR, Robins JM. Diffuse idiopathic skeletal hyperostosis (DISH). Forestier's disease with extraspinal manifestations. *Radiology* 1975;115:513–524.

Rosenberg ZS, Shankman S, Steiner GC, Kastenbaum DK, Norman A, Lazansky MG. Rapid destructive osteoarthritis: clinical, radiographic, and pathologic features. *Radiology* 1992;182:213–216.

Ross JS, Modic MT, Masaryk TJ, Carter J, Marcus RE, Bohlman H. Assessment of extradural degenerative disease with Gd DTPA-enhanced MR imaging: correlation with surgical and pathologic findings. *Am J Neuroradiol* 1989;10:1243–1249.

Schiebler ML, Grenier N, Fallon M, Camerino V, Zlatkin M, Kressel HY. Normal and degenerated intervertebral disk: in vivo and in vitro MR imaging with histopathologic correlation. *Am J Roentgenol* 1991;157:93–97.

Schmorl G, Junghanns H. *The human spine in health and disease*, 2nd ed. New York: Grune & Stratton; 1971.

Schumacher HR. Articular cartilage in the degenerative arthropathy of hemochromatosis. *Arthritis Rheum* 1982;25:1460–1468.

Sienbenrock KA, Schoeniger R, Ganz R. Anterior femoroacetabular impingement due to acetabular retroversion: treatment with periacetabular osteotomy. *J Bone J Surg [Am]* 2003;85-A:278–286.

Sokoloff L. Pathology and pathogenesis of osteoarthritis. In: Hollander JL, McCarty DJ, eds. *Arthritis and allied conditions*, 8th ed. Philadelphia: Lea & Febiger; 1972:1009–1031.

Stoller DW, Cannon WD Jr, Anderson LJ. The knee. In: *Magnetic resonance imaging in orthopaedics and sports medicine*. Philadelphia: JB Lippincott; 1993:139–372.

Theodorou DJ. The intravertebral vacuum cleft sign. *Radiology* 2001;221:787–788.

Waldschmidt JG, Braunstein EM, Buckwalter KA. Magnetic resonance imaging of osteoarthritis. *Rheum Dis Clin North Am* 1999;25:451–465.

Watt I. Osteoarthritis revisited–again! *Skeletal Radiol* 2009;38:419–423.

Watt I, Dieppe P. Osteoarthritis revisited. *Skeletal Radiol* 1990;19:1–3.

Weber BG. Total hip replacement: rotating versus fixed and metal versus ceramic heads. In: Salvati EA, ed. *The hip. Proceedings of the Ninth Open Scientific Meeting of the Hip Society, 1981*. St. Louis: CV Mosby; 1981:264–275.

TABLE 14.1   Clinical and Imaging Hallmarks of Inflammatory Arthritides

Type of Arthritis	Site	Crucial Abnormalities	Technique*/Projection

Erosive Osteoarthritis (F; middle age)	Hands	Involvement of
		    Proximal interphalangeal joints
		    Distal interphalangeal joints
		Gull-wing deformities associated with
		    erosions
		Heberden nodes
		Joint ankylosis
			Dorsovolar view

Rheumatoid Arthritis (F > M; presence of rheumatoid factor and DRW4)	Hands and wrists	Involvement of
		    Metacarpophalangeal joints
		    Proximal interphalangeal joints
		Central and marginal erosions
		Periarticular osteoporosis
		Joint deformities: swan-neck, boutonnière,
		    main-en-lorgnette, hitchhiker's thumb
		Synovitis
			Dorsovolar view

			Dorsovolar and lateral views
	Hip	Narrowing of joint space Erosions Acetabular protrusion	MRI Anteroposterior and lateral views
	Knee	Narrowing of joint space Erosions Synovial cysts	Anteroposterior and lateral views
	Ankle and foot	Involvement of subtalar joint	MRI Anteroposterior and lateral views
		Erosions of calcaneus	Lateral and Broden views Lateral view (heel)
Juvenile Rheumatoid Arthritis	Hands	Joint ankylosis Periosteal reaction Growth abnormalities	Dorsovolar view (wrist and hand)
	Knees	Growth abnormalities	Anteroposterior and lateral views
	Cervical spine	Fusion of apophyseal joints	Anteroposterior, lateral, and oblique views
		C1-2 subluxation	Lateral view in flexion
Rheumatoid Variants Ankylosing Spondylitis (M > F; young adult; 95% positive for HLA-B27)	Spine	Squaring of vertebral bodies Syndesmophytes "Bamboo" spine Paravertebral ossifications	Anteroposterior and lateral views
	Sacroiliac joints	Inflammatory changes Fusion	Posteroanterior and Ferguson views
	Pelvis	Whiskering of iliac crests and ischial tuberosity	Anteroposterior view
Reiter Syndrome (M > F)	Foot	Involvement of great toe articulations Erosions of calcaneus	Anteroposterior and lateral views
	Spine	Single, coarse syndesmophyte	Anteroposterior and lateral views
	Sacroiliac joints	Unilateral or bilateral but asymmetric involvement	Posteroanterior and Ferguson views Computed tomography
Psoriatic Arthritis (M ≥ F; skin changes; HLA-B27 positive)	Hands	Involvement of distal interphalangeal joints Erosion of terminal tufts Mouse-ear erosions Pencil-in-cup deformities Sausage digit Joint ankylosis Fluffy periosteal reaction	Dorsovolar view
	Foot	Involvement of distal interphalangeal joints Erosions of terminal tufts and calcaneus	Anteroposterior and lateral views (ankle and foot)
	Spine	Single, coarse syndesmophyte	Anteroposterior and lateral views
	Sacroiliac joints	Unilateral or bilateral but asymmetric involvement	Posteroanterior and Ferguson views
Enteropathic Arthropathies	Sacroiliac joints	Symmetric involvement	Posteroanterior and Ferguson views Computed tomography

*Radionuclide bone scan is used to determine the distribution of arthritic lesions in the skeleton.

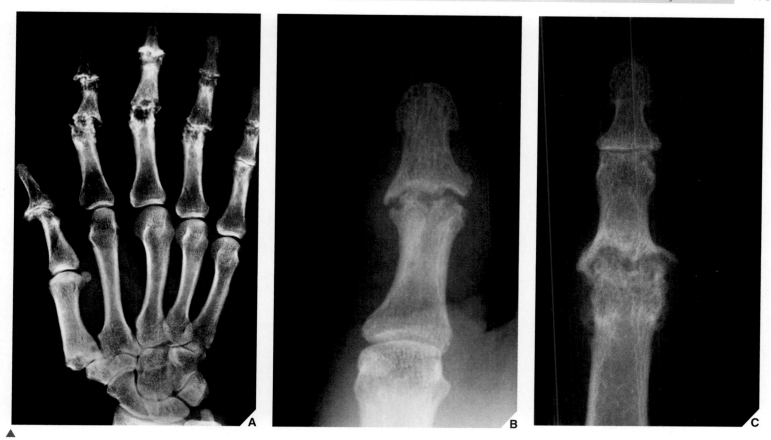

FIGURE 14.2 Erosive osteoarthritis. (A) Dorsovolar film of the left hand of a 48-year-old woman with erosive osteoarthritis shows the typical involvement of the proximal and distal interphalangeal joints. Note the "gull-wing" pattern of articular erosion, a configuration resulting from peripheral bone erosion in the distal side of the joint and central erosion in the proximal side of the joint associated with marginal bone proliferation. **(B)** Dorsovolar radiograph of the left thumb of a 51-year-old woman shows characteristic gull-wing erosion of the interphalangeal joint. Note adjacent fusiform soft-tissue swelling and lack of periarticular osteoporosis. **(C)** In another patient, a 50-year-old woman, gull-wing erosion is accompanied by periosteal reaction and fusiform soft-tissue swelling, very similar to psoriatic arthritis.

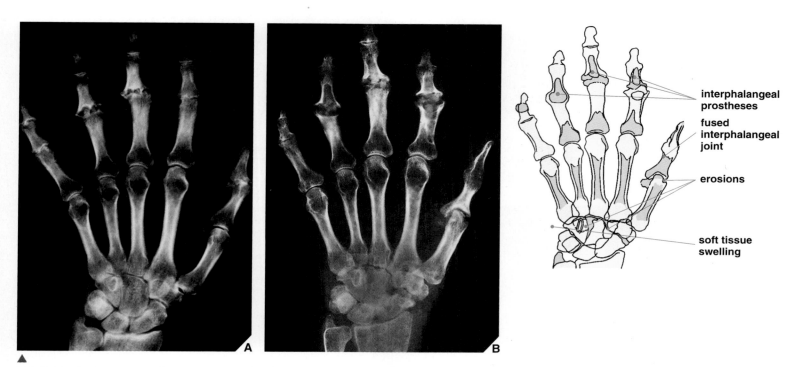

FIGURE 14.3 Progression of erosive osteoarthritis into rheumatoid arthritis. (A) Dorsovolar radiograph of the hand of a 58-year-old woman demonstrates the gull-wing configuration of erosive changes in the proximal interphalangeal joints and the distal interphalangeal joint of the small finger. Because of protracted pain and lack of response to conservative treatment, she underwent joint resection followed by implantation of silicone–rubber prostheses in the proximal interphalangeal joints of the index, middle, and ring fingers, together with fusion of the interphalangeal joint of the thumb and the distal interphalangeal joint of the small finger. Five years after surgery, the classic radiographic features of rheumatoid arthritis developed, involving the wrists **(B)**, elbows, shoulders, hips, and cervical spine. Note the surgical fusion of interphalangeal joints of the thumb and fifth finger, as well as the spontaneous fusion of the distal interphalangeal joints of the index and ring fingers.

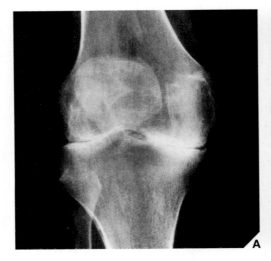
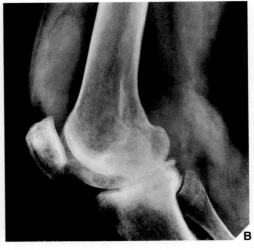

▲
FIGURE 14.4 **Rheumatoid arthritis.** Anteroposterior (**A**) and lateral (**B**) radiographs of the knee of a 52-year-old woman with rheumatoid arthritis affecting several joints show tricompartmental involvement. Note the periarticular osteoporosis, joint effusion, and lack of osteophytosis.

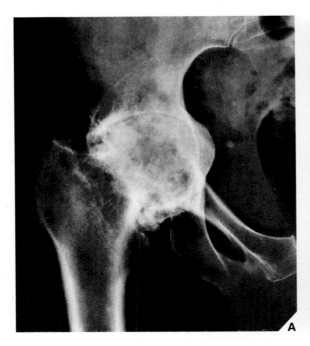
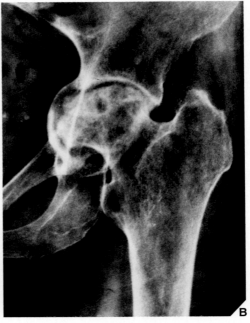

▲
FIGURE 14.5 **Rheumatoid arthritis. (A)** Anteroposterior radiograph of the right hip of a 60-year-old woman with advanced rheumatoid arthritis shows concentric joint space narrowing, with axial migration of the femoral head leading to acetabular protrusion. Some superimposed secondary osteoarthritic changes are also present. **(B)** Anteroposterior radiograph of the left hip of a 64-year-old woman shows erosions of the femoral head and acetabulum, concentric narrowing of the hip joint, and acetabular protrusion.

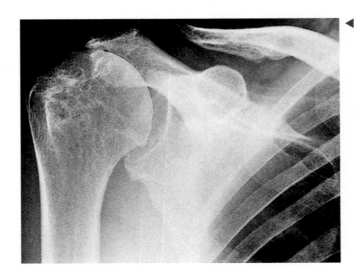

◀ FIGURE 14.6 **Rheumatoid arthritis.** Anteroposterior radiograph of the right shoulder of a 72-year-old man with advanced rheumatoid arthritis shows upward migration of the humeral head secondary to rotator cuff tear, a common complication of rheumatoid changes in the shoulder joint. Note the characteristic tapered erosion of the distal end of the clavicle, erosions of the humeral head, and the substantial degree of periarticular osteoporosis.

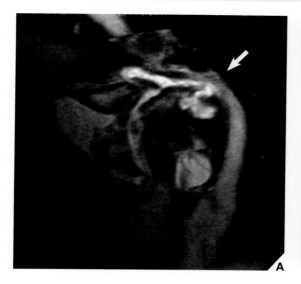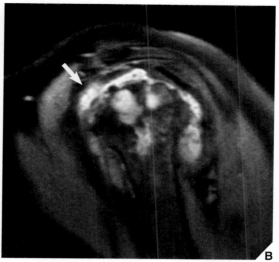

FIGURE 14.7 **MRI of rheumatoid arthritis.** **(A)** Oblique coronal and **(B)** sagittal proton density-weighted fat-suppressed MR images of the left shoulder of a 64-year-old woman show large articular and periarticular erosions, joint space narrowing, joint effusion, and a tear of the supraspinatus tendon (*arrows*), all the features of advanced rheumatoid arthritis.

resorption of the distal end of the clavicle, which assumes a pencil-like appearance, may also be observed. Tear of the rotator cuff in this condition (Fig. 14.7) must be differentiated from the chronic traumatic form of this abnormality (see Fig. 5.62).

Articular Erosions. Erosive destruction of a joint may be central or peripheral in location. As a rule, reparative processes are absent or very minimal; thus, there is no evidence of subchondral sclerosis or osteophytosis (Fig. 14.8), which may be present only if secondary degenerative changes are superimposed on the underlying inflammatory process (see Fig. 13.5).

Synovial Cysts and Pseudocysts. These radiolucent defects are usually seen in close proximity to the joint (Fig. 14.9). They may or may not communicate with the joint space.

Joint Effusion. Fluid can be best demonstrated in the knee joint on the lateral projection (see Fig. 14.4B). Fluid in the other large joints such

as the shoulder, elbow, and hip can be best demonstrated by magnetic resonance imaging (MRI).

Rice bodies. Bearing macroscopic similarity to grains of polished white rise, these small, usually uniform in size intraarticular or intrabursal loose bodies are commonly associated with rheumatoid arthritis, and are thought to represent a complication of chronic inflammatory process. Occasionally, they also may be seen in seronegative inflammatory arthritis, and even in tuberculous arthritis. These particles contain collagen, fibrinogen, fibrin, reticulin, elastin, mononuclear cells, blood cells, and some amorphous material. On radiography (Fig. 14.10), this condition occasionally can be mistaken for synovial chondromatosis (see Chapter 23). On MR T1-weighted images rice bodies exhibit intermediate signal intensity, whereas on T2 weighting they are only slightly hyperintense relative to muscle (Fig. 14.11).

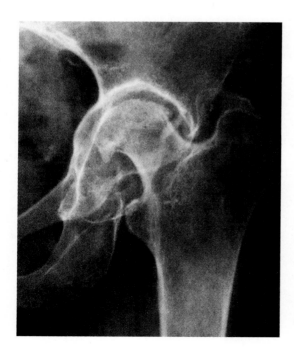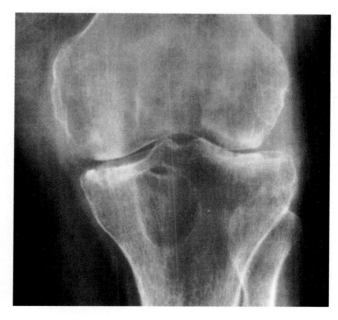

FIGURE 14.8 **Rheumatoid arthritis.** Anteroposterior radiograph of the left hip of a 59-year-old woman with advanced rheumatoid polyarthritis demonstrates the typical erosions of the femoral head and acetabulum. Note the lack of osteophytosis and the only very minimal reactive sclerosis.

FIGURE 14.9 **Rheumatoid cyst.** Anteroposterior radiograph of the left knee of a 35-year-old woman with rheumatoid arthritis shows a large synovial cyst in the proximal tibia. Note also articular erosions and periarticular osteoporosis.

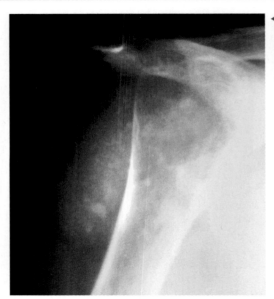

◀ FIGURE 14.10 Rice bodies. Anteroposterior radiograph of the right shoulder of a 60-year-old woman with advanced rheumatoid arthritis demonstrates multiple rice bodies within subacromial-subdeltoid bursae complex.

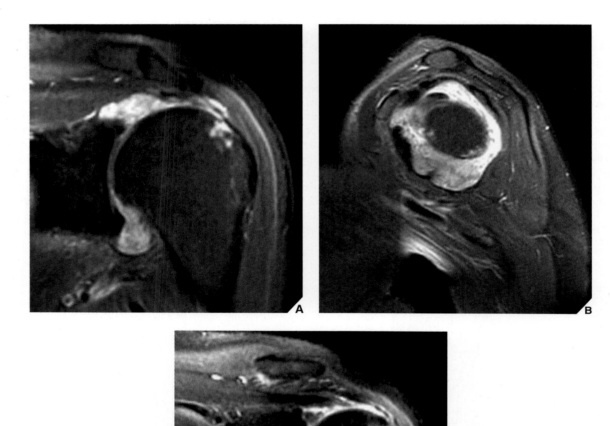

▲

FIGURE 14.11 **MRI of rice bodies. (A)** Oblique coronal proton density-weighted, **(B)** sagittal proton density-weighted, and **(C)** oblique coronal T2-weighted fat-suppressed MR images of the left shoulder of a 66-year-old woman with rheumatoid arthritis show numerous rice bodies within the shoulder joint.

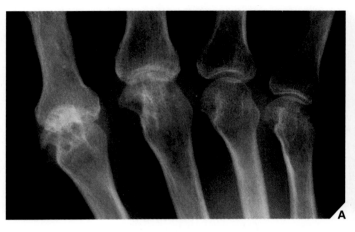
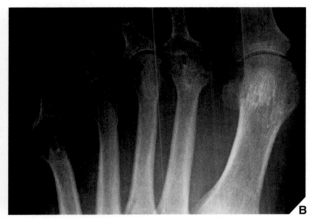

FIGURE 14.12   Rheumatoid arthritis of the small joints. Radiographs of the hand (**A**) and foot (**B**) of a 51-year-old woman with rheumatoid arthritis show typical erosions of the small joints.

Small Joint Involvement

Rheumatoid arthritis characteristically affects the small joints of the wrist, as well as the metacarpophalangeal and proximal interphalangeal joints of the hands and feet (Fig. 14.12). As a rule, the distal interphalangeal joints in the hand are spared, although in advanced stages of the disease even these may be affected. This latter point, however, is controversial, because some investigators believe that if the distal interphalangeal joints are involved, the condition may represent juvenile rheumatoid arthritis or another form of polyarthritis, not classic rheumatoid arthritis.

In addition to the characteristic changes exhibited in large joint involvement, the small joints may also show radiographic features specific for these sites.

Soft-Tissue Swelling. This earliest sign of rheumatoid arthritis usually has a fusiform, symmetric shape. It is periarticular in location and represents a combination of joint effusion, edema, and tenosynovitis.

Marginal Erosions. The earliest articular changes manifest as marginal erosions at so-called bare areas. These are the sites within the

small joints that are not covered by articular cartilage. The most common locations for these erosions are the radial aspects of the second and third metacarpal heads and the radial and ulnar aspects of the bases of the proximal phalanges (Fig. 14.13). Synovial inflammation in the prestyloid recess, a diverticulum of the radiocarpal joint that is intimate with the styloid process of ulna, as Resnick pointed out, produces marginal erosion of the styloid tip.

Joint Deformities. Although not pathognomonic for rheumatoid arthritis, certain deformations such as the *swan-neck deformity* and the *boutonnière deformity* are more often seen in this form of arthritis than in other inflammatory arthritides. The first of these represents hyperextension in the proximal interphalangeal joint and flexion in the distal interphalangeal joint, a configuration resembling a swan's neck (Fig. 14.14). In the boutonnière deformity, the configuration is just the opposite, with flexion in the proximal joint and extension in the distal interphalangeal joint (Fig. 14.15). The word *boutonnière* is French for "buttonhole," the term for this deformity deriving from the configuration of the finger while securing a flower to a lapel. A similar deformation of the thumb is called *hitchhiker's thumb*.

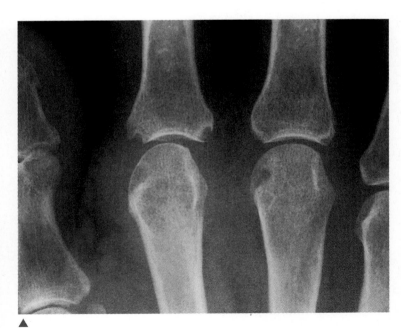

FIGURE 14.13   Rheumatoid arthritis. Typical erosions in the bare areas are seen in this 55-year-old woman with rheumatoid arthritis. Note also periarticular osteoporosis and soft-tissue swelling.

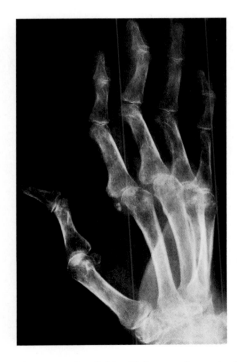

FIGURE 14.14   Rheumatoid arthritis. Oblique radiograph of the hand of a 59-year-old woman shows the swan-neck deformity of the second through fifth fingers. Note the flexion in the distal interphalangeal joints and the extension in the proximal interphalangeal joints, the hallmarks of this abnormality.

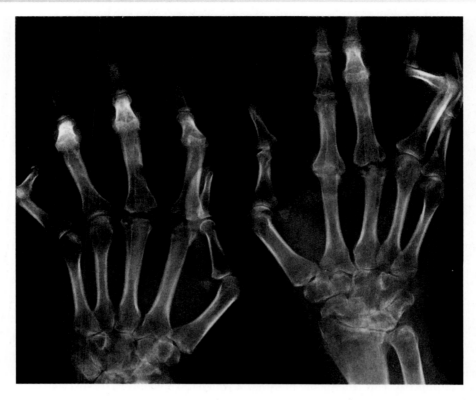

▲
FIGURE 14.15   Rheumatoid arthritis. Dorsovolar radiograph of the hands of a 48-year-old woman with rheumatoid arthritis demonstrates the boutonnière deformity in the small and ring fingers of the right hand and in the ring finger of the left hand.

Moreover, subluxations and dislocations with malalignment of the fingers are common findings in advanced stages of rheumatoid arthritis. Particularly characteristic are ulnar deviation of the fingers in the metacarpophalangeal joints and radial deviation of the wrist in the radiocarpal articulation (Fig. 14.16). In far-advanced stages of rheumatoid arthritis, shortening of several phalanges may be encountered secondary to destructive changes in the joints associated with dislocations in the metacarpophalangeal joints. This deformity appears as a "telescoping" of the fingers, hence its name, *main-en-lorgnette*, from the French name for the telescoping type of opera glass (Fig. 14.17). An abnormally wide space between the lunate and the scaphoid may also be encountered in advanced stages of the disease secondary to erosion and rupture of the scapholunate ligament (Fig. 14.18); this phenomenon resembles the Terry-Thomas sign seen secondary to trauma

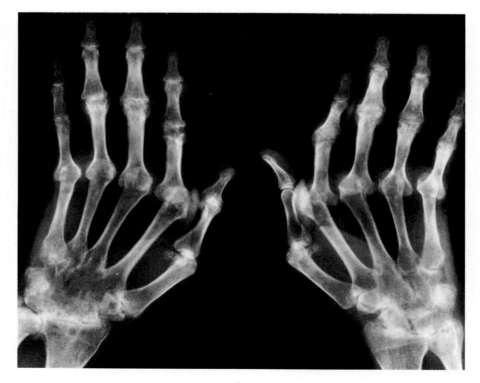

▲
FIGURE 14.16   Rheumatoid arthritis. Dorsovolar projection of both hands of a 51-year-old woman shows subluxation in the metacarpophalangeal joints resulting in ulnar deviation of the fingers and radial deviation in the radiocarpal articulations. Note also ankylosis of the midcarpal articulations of the right hand.

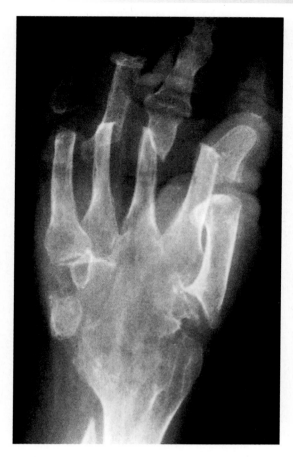

▲
FIGURE 14.17 Rheumatoid arthritis. Dorsovolar view of the right hand of a 54-year-old woman with long-standing advanced rheumatoid arthritis demonstrates the *main-en-lorgnette* deformity. Note the telescoping of the fingers secondary to destructive joint changes and dislocations in the metacarpophalangeal joints. There is also ankylosis of the radiocarpal and intercarpal articulations and "penciling" of the distal ulna.

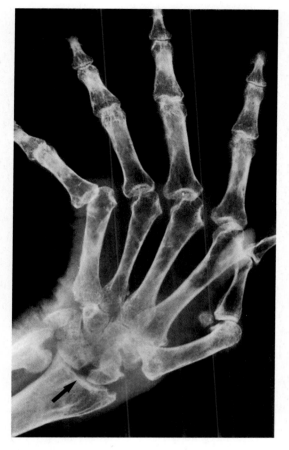

▲
FIGURE 14.18 Rheumatoid arthritis. Dorsovolar view of the hand of a 60-year-old woman shows a gap between the scaphoid and lunate (*arrow*), indicating destruction of the scapholunate ligament. Note also the subluxation in the metacarpophalangeal joints resulting in ulnar deviation of the fingers.

(see Fig. 7.82). Joint deformities are also often seen in the foot; the subtalar joint is frequently affected, and subluxation in the metatarsophalangeal joints often leads to deformities such as hallux valgus and hammertoes.

Joint Ankylosis. A rare finding that may be observed in advanced stages of rheumatoid arthritis is joint ankylosis, which is most commonly encountered in the midcarpal articulations (see Figs. 14.16 and 14.17). Ankylotic changes in the wrist are more common in patients with juvenile rheumatoid arthritis and with so-called seronegative rheumatoid arthritis.

Involvement of the Spine
The thoracic and lumbar segments are affected by rheumatoid arthritis only on rare occasions. The cervical spine, however, is involved in approximately 50% of individuals with this condition (Table 14.2). The most characteristic radiographic features of rheumatoid arthritis in the cervical spine can be observed in the odontoid process, the atlantoaxial joints, and the apophyseal joints. Erosive changes may be encountered in the odontoid process (see Fig. 12.36) and apophyseal joints (Fig. 14.19), whereas subluxation is a common finding in the atlantoaxial joint (see Fig. 12.37), frequently accompanied by vertical translocation of the odontoid process (also known as cranial settling or atlantoaxial impaction) (Figs. 14.20 and 14.21). The most frequent abnormality is laxity of the transverse ligament connecting the odontoid to the atlas. This laxity becomes apparent on the radiograph obtained in the lateral view of the flexed cervical spine, is expressed by subluxation in the atlantoaxial joint (Fig. 14.22), and is frequently accompanied by cephalad migration of the odontoid process. This complication often requires surgical intervention, and the most common procedure to correct this is posterior fusion.

Severe involvement of the apophyseal joints leads to subluxations. In extremely rare cases, in a manner similar to that in juvenile rheumatoid arthritis, the apophyseal joints may ankylose. The other structures occasionally affected by rheumatoid process are the intervertebral disks and adjacent vertebral bodies, which become involved as a result of synovitis extending from the joints of Luschka. Only a small percentage of patients with cervical disease may have cervical myelopathy. MRI is an ideal modality to evaluate spinal cord involvement in these patients (see Fig. 14.21).

TABLE 14.2 **Abnormalities of the Cervical Spine in Rheumatoid Arthritis**

Osteoporosis
Erosion of the odontoid process
Atlantoaxial (C1-2) subluxation
Vertical translation of the odontoid (cranial settling)
Erosions of the apophyseal joints
Fusion of the apophyseal joints
Erosions of the Luschka joints
Disk space narrowing
Erosions and sclerosis of the vertebral body margins
Erosions (whittling) of the spinous processes
Subluxations of the vertebral bodies ("stepladder" or "doorstep" appearance on lateral radiographs)

Modified from Resnick D, Niwayama G, 1995, with permission.

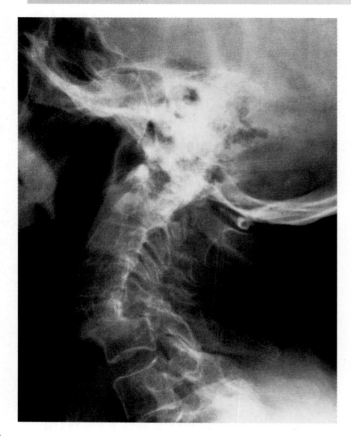

▲
FIGURE 14.19 **Rheumatoid arthritis of the cervical spine.** Lateral radiograph of the cervical spine of a 52-year-old woman with advanced rheumatoid arthritis shows erosive changes of the apophyseal joints. In addition, note osteoporosis, erosion of the odontoid, erosions at the diskovertebral junctions, and whittling of the spinous processes.

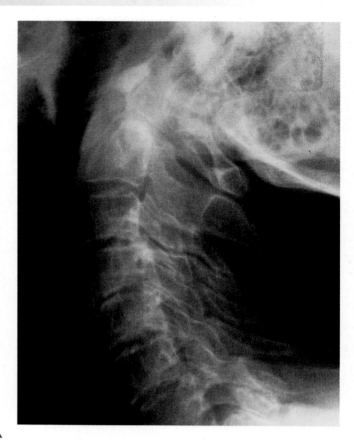

▲
FIGURE 14.20 **Rheumatoid arthritis of the cervical spine.** Lateral radiograph of the cervical spine of a 41-year-old woman with rheumatoid arthritis shows a vertical translocation of the odontoid process (cranial settling). Note also erosive changes at the diskovertebral junctions, erosions of the apophyseal joints, and whittling of the spinous processes.

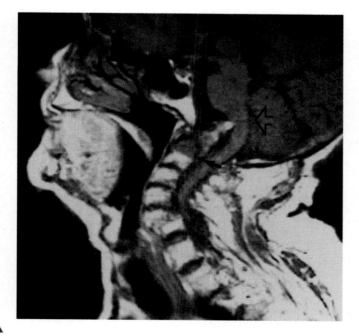

▲
FIGURE 14.21 **MRI of rheumatoid arthritis of the cervical spine.** A 52-year-old woman with advanced rheumatoid arthritis presented with chronic neck pain, weakness of the upper limbs, numbness in both hands, and occasional dyspnea and cardiac arrhythmia. A sagittal spin-echo T1-weighted MR image shows inflammatory pannus eroding odontoid (*arrow*), and cranial settling with cephalad migration of C2 impinging on the medulla oblongata (*open arrow*).

Complications of Rheumatoid Arthritis

The complications of rheumatoid arthritis are related not only to the inflammatory process itself but also to the sequelae of treatment (see the discussion on the complications of treatment in Chapter 12). The large doses of steroids that are commonly prescribed in therapy often lead to the development of generalized osteoporosis. Severe osteoporosis and large bony erosions may in turn precipitate pathologic fracture, a frequent complication. Tear of the rotator cuff may also occur because of erosion by inflammatory pannus in the shoulder joint (see Fig. 14.6). In the knee, a large popliteal (Baker) cyst may complicate rheumatoid arthritic changes (Figs. 14.23 to 14.25); this condition may be misdiagnosed as thrombophlebitis (see Fig. 2.21).

Rheumatoid Nodulosis

A variant of rheumatoid arthritis is rheumatoid nodulosis, which occurs predominantly in men. It is a nonsystemic disorder characterized by the presence of multiple subcutaneous nodules (Fig. 14.26) and a very high rheumatoid factor titer; as a rule, there are no joint abnormalities. Occasionally, small cystic lesions may be present in various bones. Nodules are usually different in size and consistency, and distribution is over the elbows, extensor surfaces of hands and feet, and other pressure points. The most striking feature is the lack of systemic manifestations of rheumatoid arthritis.

On histologic examination, the nodules show typical rheumatoid changes, including central necrosis surrounded by palisading histiocytes and fibroblasts, with an outer layer of connective tissue and chronic inflammatory cells. Only occasionally will the histologic appearance be

FIGURE 14.22 **Rheumatoid arthritis: C1-C2 instability.** Flexion (**A**) and extension (**B**) lateral radiographs demonstrate C1-2 subluxation in a 66-year-old woman with rheumatoid arthritis.

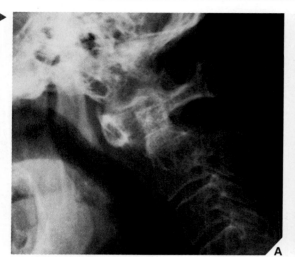
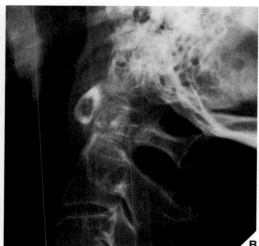

FIGURE 14.23 **Rheumatoid arthritis complicated by a Baker cyst.** A 31-year-old woman with a 2-year history of seropositive rheumatoid arthritis developed swelling of the upper calf and tenderness in the popliteal fossa. A presumptive diagnosis of thrombophlebitis was made, but a venogram failed to corroborate this. This lateral view of a knee arthrogram shows a large popliteal (Baker) cyst dissecting into the medial aspect of the calf. This condition is a well-documented complication in patients with rheumatoid arthritis. (From Greenspan A et al., 1983, with permission.)

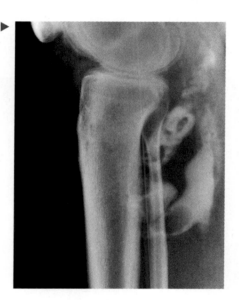

FIGURE 14.24 **CT of a Baker cyst. (A)** Sagittal reformatted and (**B**) axial CT images, obtained after intravenous administration of contrast agent, show a large Baker cyst (*arrows*) in a patient diagnosed with rheumatoid arthritis.

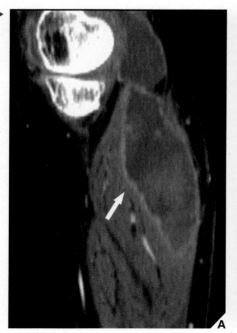
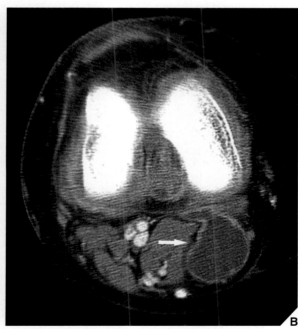

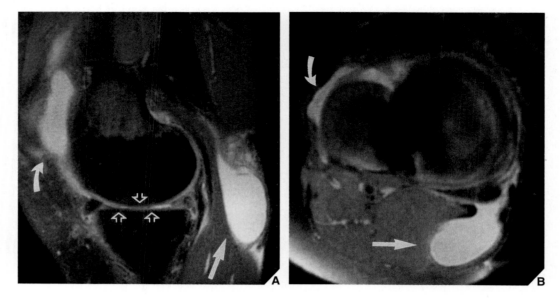

FIGURE 14.25   **Rheumatoid arthritis complicated by a Baker cyst.** A 60-year-old woman with rheumatoid arthritis developed a popliteal cyst. Sagittal (**A**) and axial (**B**) T2-weighted fat-suppressed MR images demonstrate a large Baker cyst (*arrows*). *Open arrows* point to erosive changes of the articular cartilage, *curved arrows* indicate joint effusion.

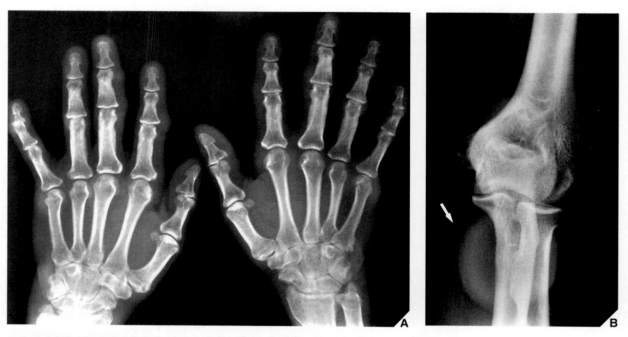

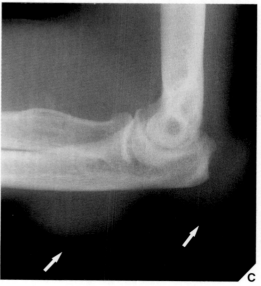

◄ FIGURE 14.26   **Rheumatoid nodulosis.** A 52-year-old man with a 15-year history of polyarthritis presented with large, fluctuant nodules on the dorsal aspect of the hands and elbows. A high titer of rheumatoid factor (1:1,280) was identified in his serum. (**A**) Dorsovolar view of both hands shows several soft-tissue nodules adjacent to joints (*arrows*). Note the lack of joint abnormalities. Anteroposterior (**B**) and lateral (**C**) radiographs of the left elbow demonstrate similar soft-tissue masses at the dorsal aspect of the proximal forearm (*arrows*). The elbow joint is intact. (From Greenspan A et al., 1983, with permission.)

atypical. In these cases, the nodule may contain abundant cholesterol clefts and lipid-loaded macrophages, suggestive of xanthoma or even multicentric reticulohistiocytosis.

Therapy is usually limited to the occasional use of NSAIDs. Nodules that cause local pain because of nerve compression can be surgically removed. Some investigators have reported a decrease in nodule size after the use of penicillamine. These reports are controversial, however, because the regression and even disappearance of rheumatoid nodules may occur without any treatment at all.

In classic rheumatoid arthritis, small-vessel vasculitis is a primary factor in nodule development, and circulating immune complexes used by rheumatoid synovium are responsible for such extraarticular manifestations as vasculitis, polyserositis, and nodules. In rheumatoid nodulosis, however, nodules develop in the absence of active joint disease. Thus, the pathogenesis of rheumatoid nodulosis remains unclear.

A positive family history of rheumatoid arthritis in some patients with rheumatoid nodulosis and the occurrence of familial nodulosis suggest the involvement of hereditary factors. Investigations into tissue typing, particularly the search for DW4/DRW4 antigens, may illustrate the pathogenesis of this rheumatoid variant. The strong male preponderance suggests that androgens may modify disease expression in genetically predisposed individuals. Rheumatoid nodulosis is often misdiagnosed as gout or xanthomatosis. Moreover, it should be kept in mind when evaluating this condition that approximately 20% of patients with classic rheumatoid arthritis have rheumatoid nodules, which are usually located at sites of pressure or stress such as the dorsal aspect of the hands and forearms (Fig. 14.27). Articular involvement in nodular rheumatoid arthritis distinguishes it from rheumatoid nodulosis, which consequently has a better prognosis.

Juvenile Rheumatoid Arthritis

Juvenile rheumatoid arthritis is a group of at least three chronic inflammatory synovial diseases that affect children; girls are more frequently affected than boys. The three defined subtypes are Still disease, polyarticular arthritis, and pauciarticular arthritis. Each of these subgroups has distinct clinical and laboratory findings and different natural histories. There is no pathognomonic laboratory test for any of them, and the diagnosis is based on the clinical spectrum exhibited by a given patient.

Still Disease
Still disease is well-known for sudden onset of spiking fever, lymphadenopathy, and an evanescent salmon-colored skin rash. Patients may exhibit hepatosplenomegaly, fatigue, anorexia, and weight loss. the majority of patients have chronic and recurrent arthralgias. A significant number of patients, depending on the series, may also subsequently have chronic polyarthritis. A poorly understood Still-like disease with fever and arthralgias may develop in some adult patients.

Polyarticular Juvenile Rheumatoid Arthritis
Polyarticular juvenile rheumatoid arthritis consists of inflammation at four or more joints with associated findings of anorexia, weight loss, fatigue, and adenopathy. Growth retardation is common. This disorder also results in the following abnormalities: undergrowth of the mandible, early closure of the growth plates resulting in shortening of metacarpals and metatarsals, and overgrowths of the epiphyses at the knees, hips, and shoulders. A worse prognosis occurs in patients with positive rheumatoid factors.

Juvenile Rheumatoid Arthritis With Pauciarticular Onset
The third subtype of juvenile rheumatoid arthritis has pauciarticular onset, with four or fewer joints involved. Approximately 40% of patients with juvenile rheumatoid arthritis exhibit involvement of fewer than four joints in the first 6 months of the disease. Some of these patients may even present with negative rheumatoid factor whereas others may have positive antigen HLA-B27. Pediatric rheumatologists have attempted to define other subgroups within this pauciarticular subgroup, but, with the exception of HLA-B27-positive children with sacroiliitis, such definitions are broad and clinically dependent on unique systemic features such as iridocyclitis. However, involvement of the sacroiliac joints is not a feature of juvenile rheumatoid arthritis as was thought in the past; rather, it represents juvenile onset of ankylosing spondylitis. Similarly, some investigators believe that patients with pauciarticular arthritis, particularly those with positive histocompatibility antigen HLA-B27, may in fact have atypical ankylosing spondylitis syndrome or spondyloarthropathy; both these conditions are different from rheumatoid arthritis.

Other Types of Juvenile Rheumatoid Arthritis
It is worthwhile to note that two new diagnostic terms currently in use in childhood arthritides—*juvenile chronic arthritis* and *juvenile arthritis*—are not equivalent to each other or to classic juvenile rheumatoid

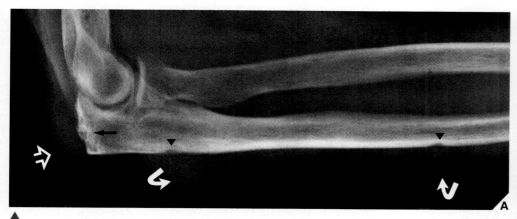

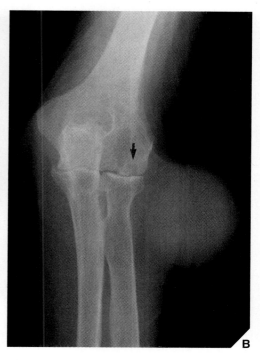

FIGURE 14.27 Rheumatoid nodules. (A) A 39-year-old man with rheumatoid arthritis originally misdiagnosed as gout. Lateral radiograph of the right elbow demonstrates erosions of the olecranon process (*arrow*), olecranon bursitis (*open arrow*), and rheumatoid nodules on the dorsal aspect of the forearm (*curved arrows*). Note the characteristic pit-like cortical erosions at the site of the rheumatoid nodules (*arrow heads*). This presentation of rheumatoid arthritis should not be mistaken for rheumatoid nodulosis. **(B)** A 68-year-old woman with rheumatoid arthritis had a large rheumatoid nodule at the lateral side of the elbow joint. Note erosions at the radiocapitellar joint (*arrow*).

arthritis. These conditions lack any characteristic radiographic features. Much research is needed to gain a better understanding of juvenile rheumatoid arthritis before we will clearly be able to define the number of different diseases involved.

Imaging Features

Juvenile rheumatoid arthritis exhibits many of the features of adult rheumatoid arthritis. However, some additional features that are almost pathognomonic for this condition have been identified.

Periosteal Reaction. This feature is usually seen along the shafts of the proximal phalanges and metacarpals (Fig. 14.28).

Joint Ankylosis. Ankylosis may occur not only in the wrist but also in the interphalangeal articulations (Fig. 14.29). Fusion in the apophyseal joints of the cervical spine is also a characteristic finding (Fig. 14.30).

Growth Abnormalities. Because the onset of juvenile rheumatoid arthritis frequently occurs before completion of skeletal maturation, alterations in growth of the bones is a common finding. The involvement of epiphyseal sites often leads to fusion of the growth plate, with resultant retardation of bone growth (Fig. 14.31); it may also precipitate acceleration of growth caused by stimulation of the growth plates by hyperemia. Enlargement of the epiphysis of the distal femur leads to characteristic overgrowth of the condyles in the knee (Fig. 14.32).

Treatment

Medical. Over the past several years there has been significant change in treatment of rheumatoid arthritis that contributed to major improvement in clinical outcome of patients with this debilitating disease. These encouraging results were mainly achieved through the combination of early treatment with disease-modifying antirheumatic drugs (DMARDs) and introduction of the newer biologic agents. Treatment with DMARDs includes the following medications: methotrexate, sulphasalazine,

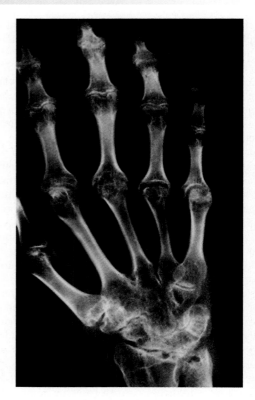

▲
FIGURE 14.29 Juvenile rheumatoid arthritis. Dorsovolar radiograph of the hand of a 25-year-old woman with a 10-year history of juvenile rheumatoid arthritis shows advanced destructive changes in multiple joints of the hand and wrist. Joint ankylosis is evident in several articulations.

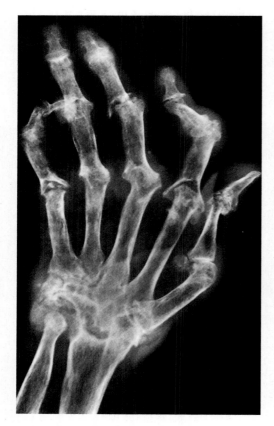

▲
FIGURE 14.28 Juvenile rheumatoid arthritis. Dorsovolar radiograph of the wrist and hand of a 26-year-old woman with a 14-year history of juvenile rheumatoid arthritis shows severe destructive changes in the wrist and in the metacarpophalangeal and proximal interphalangeal articulations. Note the ankylosis of the third and fourth metacarpophalangeal joints and periostitis involving the proximal phalanges and metacarpals.

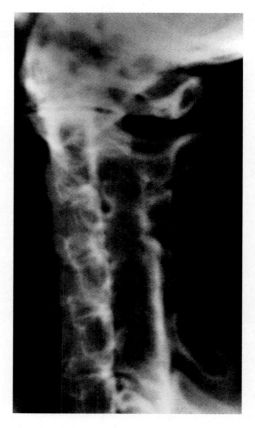

▲
FIGURE 14.30 Juvenile rheumatoid arthritis. Lateral radiograph of the cervical spine in a 25-year-old woman with a 15-year history of polyarthritis shows fusion of the apophyseal joints, a common finding in juvenile rheumatoid arthritis.

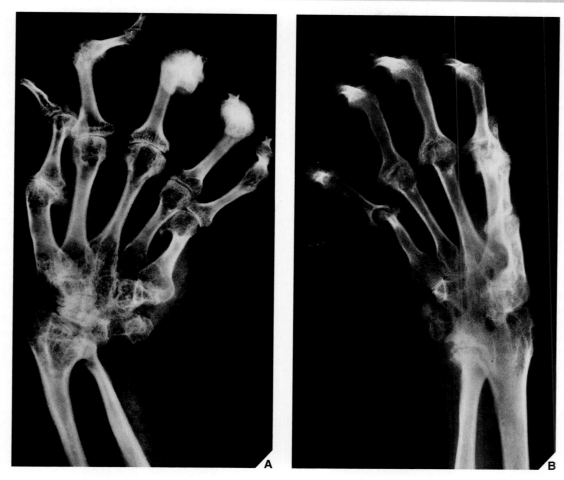

▲
FIGURE 14.31   Juvenile rheumatoid arthritis. (A,B) Dorsovolar radiograph of the hands of a 24-year-old woman with advanced juvenile rheumatoid arthritis, which was diagnosed when she was 7 years old, shows retarded growth of the bones caused by early fusion of the growth plates. Multiple deformities of the digits include hitchhiker's thumb and a boutonnière configuration of the fingers.

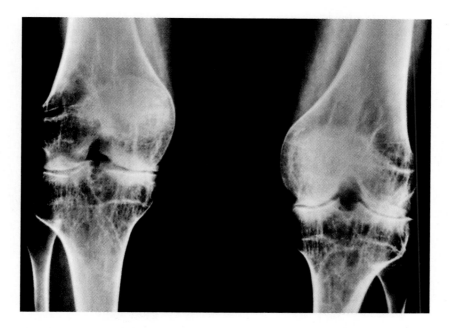

▲
FIGURE 14.32   Juvenile rheumatoid arthritis. Anteroposterior radiograph of both knees of a 20-year-old woman with juvenile rheumatoid arthritis shows overgrowth of the medial condyles, one of the characteristic features of this disorder.

letlunomide, hydroxychloroquine, azathioprine, cyclosporine, etanercept, minocycline, and gold salts. Commonly combinations of DMARDs with or without prednisone are used in patients who do not respond favorably to treatment with only one agent. Newest methods of treatment include the use of biologic agents. They comprise tumor necrosis factor (TNF) blocking agents (so-called anti-TNF agents—infliximab, etanercept, and adalimumab), rituximab (monoclonal antibody against the protein CD 20), abatacept (a fusion protein), and tocilizumab (interleukin-6 receptor–inhibiting monoclonal antibodies).

Surgical. Surgical treatment includes mainly total joint arthroplasties, performed not only on the large joints like hip, knee, shoulder, and elbow, but also replacement of small joints of the hands and feet.

Seronegative Spondyloarthropathies

Ankylosing Spondylitis

Clinical Features
Ankylosing spondylitis, known in the European literature as *Bechterev disease* or *Marie-Strümpell disease*, is a chronic, progressive, inflammatory arthritis principally affecting the synovial joints of the spine and adjacent soft tissues as well as the sacroiliac joints; however, the peripheral joints such as the hips, shoulders, and knees may also be involved. It is seen seven times more frequently in men than in women, and predominantly at a young age. Patients with ankylosing spondylitis

frequently exhibit extraarticular features of disease including iritis, pulmonary fibrosis, cardiac conduction defects, aortic incompetence, spinal cord compression, and amyloidosis. Patients may also have low-grade fever, anorexia, fatigue, and weight loss.

Rheumatoid factor is negative in patients with ankylosing spondylitis, which is the prototype of the seronegative spondyloarthropathies. A high percentage of patients (up to 95%), however, possess histocompatibility antigen HLA-B27. Pathologically, ankylosing spondylitis is a diffuse proliferative synovitis of the diarthrodial joints exhibiting features similar to those seen in rheumatoid arthritis.

Imaging Features
Squaring of the anterior border of the lower thoracic and lumbar vertebrae is one of the earliest radiographic features of ankylosing spondylitis, best demonstrated on the lateral radiograph of the spine (Fig. 14.33). As the condition progresses, syndesmophytes form, bridging the vertebral bodies (Fig. 14.34). The delicate appearance of these excrescences and their vertical rather than horizontal orientation distinguish them from the osteophytes of degenerative spine disease. Paravertebral ossifications are common in ankylosing spondylitis. When the apophyseal joints and vertebral bodies fuse late in the course of the disease, a radiographic hallmark of this condition, the "bamboo" spine, can be observed (Fig. 14.35); the sacroiliac joints are also invariably affected in this process (see Fig. 14.35B). Among conditions affecting vertebral column that should not be mistaken for ankylosing spondylitis is progressive

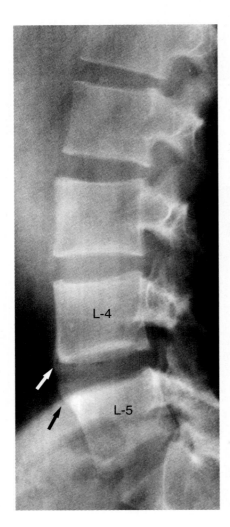

▲ FIGURE 14.33   **Ankylosing spondylitis.** Lateral radiograph of the lumbar spine in a 28-year-old man demonstrates squaring of the vertebral bodies secondary to small osseous erosions at the corners. This finding is an early radiographic feature of ankylosing spondylitis. Note also the formation of syndesmophytes at the L4-5 disk space (*arrows*).

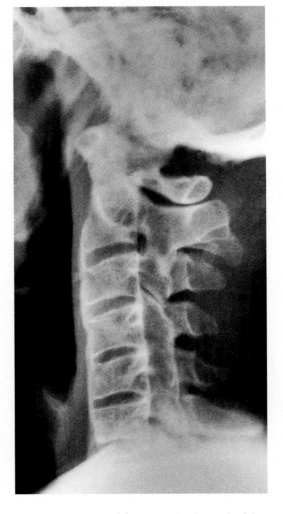

▲ FIGURE 14.34   **Ankylosing spondylitis.** Lateral radiograph of the cervical spine in a 31-year-old man demonstrates delicate syndesmophytes bridging the vertebral bodies, a common feature of ankylosing spondylitis. Note the fusion of several apophyseal joints.

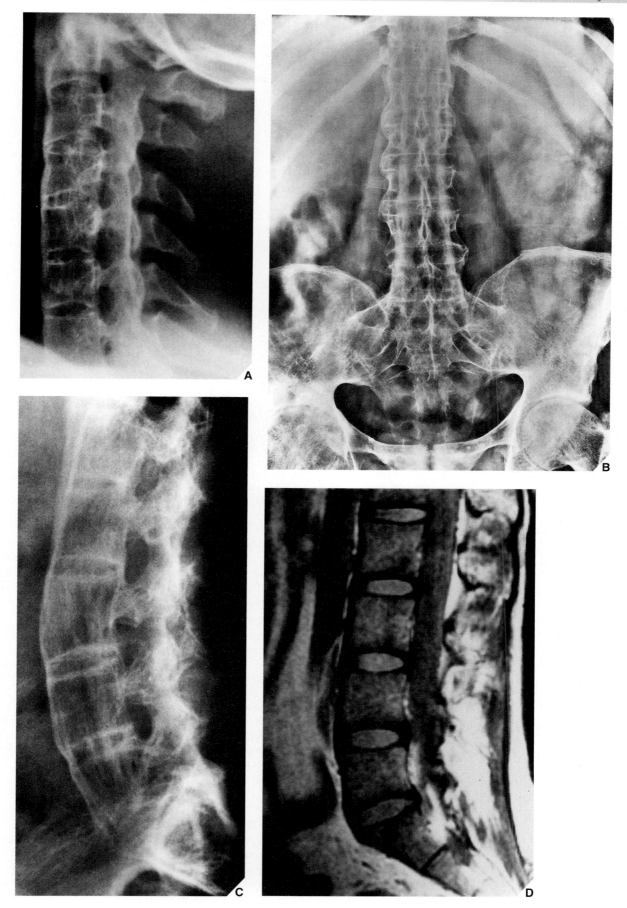

FIGURE 14.35 Ankylosing spondylitis. (A) Lateral radiograph of the cervical spine in a 53-year-old man with advanced ankylosing spondylitis shows anterior syndesmophytes bridging the vertebral bodies and posterior fusion of the apophyseal joints, together with paravertebral ossifications, producing a "bamboo-spine" appearance. The same phenomenon is seen on the anteroposterior **(B)** and lateral **(C)** radiographs of the lumbosacral spine. Note on the anteroposterior view the fusion of the sacroiliac joints and the involvement of both hip joints, which show axial migration of the femoral heads similar to that seen in rheumatoid arthritis. **(D)** Sagittal proton density-weighted MRI shows anterior syndesmophytes, calcification of the posterior longitudinal ligament, and preservation of the intervertebral disks.

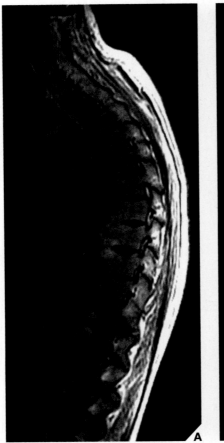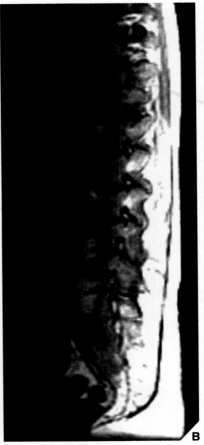

▲
FIGURE 14.36 **Copenhagen syndrome.** Sagittal T1-weighted MR images of the (**A**) thoracic and (**B**) lumbar spine of a 16-year-old girl show fusion of the anterior aspects of the vertebral bodies. Unlike in ankylosing spondylitis, the apophyseal joints are normal.

noninfectious anterior vertebral fusion, so-called *Copenhagen syndrome*. The disease usually presents in early childhood and adolescent age and is characterized by disk-spaces obliteration and anterior osseous ankylosis with fusion of the vertebral bodies (Fig. 14.36).

In the peripheral joints, inflammatory changes may be indistinguishable from those seen in rheumatoid arthritis (see Fig. 14.35B). In the foot, erosions characteristically occur at certain tendinous insertions, particularly in the os calcis (see Fig. 12.30). Involvement of the ischial tuberosities and iliac crests exhibits a lace-like formation of new bone called "whiskering."

Reiter Syndrome (Reactive Arthritis)

Clinical Features

Reiter syndrome, an autoimmune condition that develops in response to an infection in another part of the body, affects five times more males than females and is characterized by arthritis, conjunctivitis, and urethritis. It was first reported in 1916 by the German military physician Hans Conrad Julius Reiter, and in the same year it was described by the French physicians Fiessinger and LeRoy. Reiter syndrome is also well-known for the presence of mucocutaneous rash, keratoderma blenorrhagica. Like ankylosing spondylitis, eye involvement is common and can include conjunctivitis, iritis, uveitis, and episcleritis. Approximately 60% to 80% of patients are positive for HLA-B27. This frequency varies according to the ethnic origin of the patient. Unlike ankylosing spondylitis, Reiter syndrome may exhibit unilateral sacroiliac diseases.

Two types of this syndrome have been identified. First, the sporadic or endemic type, which is common in the United States, is associated with nongonococcal urethritis, prostatitis, or hemorrhagic cystitis, although recently genital infections with *Clamydia trachomatis* have been reported. It occurs almost exclusively in males. In Europe, a

second type has been identified, which is an epidemic form associated with bacillary (*Shigella*) dysentery. It may be seen in women as well. There has been considerable research on the putative role of *Yersinia enterocolitica* in inducing disease, particularly in Scandinavia, where such infections are more prevalent than in North America.

Imaging Features

Radiographically, Reiter syndrome is marked by peripheral and usually asymmetric arthritis, with a predilection for the joints of the lower limb (Fig. 14.37). The foot is the most common site of involvement, particularly the metatarsophalangeal joints and the heels (Fig. 14.37B; see also Figs. 12.33 and 12.34). Periosteal new bone formation is not uncommon. Involvement of the sacroiliac joints, which is frequently encountered, may be either asymmetric (unilateral or bilateral) or symmetric (bilateral) (Fig. 14.38). In the thoracic and lumbar spine, coarse syndesmophytes or paraspinal ossifications may be present, characteristically bridging adjacent vertebrae (Fig. 14.39).

Psoriatic Arthritis

Clinical Features

Psoriasis is a dermatologic disorder that affects approximately 1% to 2% of the population. The macular and papular skin lesions of psoriasis display characteristic focal plaques covered with silvery white scales and are commonly located over extensor surfaces of the extremities. Nail abnormalities, including discoloration, fragmentation, pitting, and onycholysis, may provide an early diagnostic clue. Approximately 10% to 15% of patients with psoriasis develop inflammatory arthritis. Articular disease is more common in patients with moderate or severe skin abnormalities and, according to Wright, severe and mutilating arthropathy is often associated with extensive exfoliative skin abnormalities.

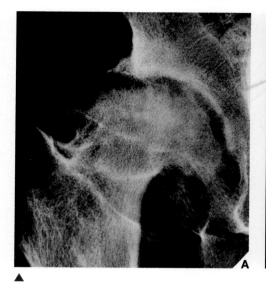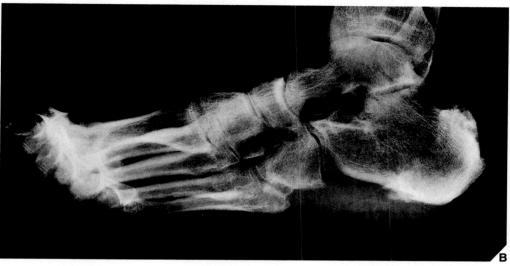

FIGURE 14.37   Reiter syndrome. **(A)** Anteroposterior radiograph of right hip joint of a 39-year-old man with Reiter syndrome shows characteristic changes of inflammatory arthritis. **(B)** Lateral radiograph of the foot of a 28-year-old man with Reiter syndrome demonstrates the "fluffy" periostitis of the os calcis and inflammatory changes of the metatarsophalangeal joints typical of this condition.

The cause of psoriatic arthritis is unknown, and its relationship to rheumatoid arthritis and spondyloarthropathies is still unsettled. The arthritis predominantly affects the distal interphalangeal joints of the hands and feet, although other sites of involvement—the proximal interphalangeal joints as well as the hips, knees, ankles, shoulders, and spine—may also be encountered.

Five specific subgroups of arthritic syndromes have been described in psoriatic arthritis.

Subgroup 1, or classic psoriatic arthritis, includes nail pathology with frequent erosion of the terminal tufts termed acroosteolysis (Fig. 14.40) and involvement of the distal and occasionally proximal interphalangeal joints of the hand and foot (Fig. 14.41). It is important, however, to remember that other conditions may also exhibit acroosteolysis (Table 14.3).

Subgroup 2, well-known for the "opera glass" deformity of the hand, is termed *arthritis mutilans* because of the extensive destruction of the phalanges and metacarpal joints, including the "pencil-in-cup" deformity (Fig. 14.42). Other joints such as hip or elbow (Fig. 14.43) are also frequently affected. Patients with arthritis mutilans often will have sacroiliitis.

Subgroup 3 is characterized by symmetric polyarthritis (Figs. 14.44 and 14.45) and may result in ankylosis of the proximal and distal interphalangeal joints. In this form, psoriatic arthritis is frequently indistinguishable from rheumatoid arthritis (Fig. 14.46).

Subgroup 4 is characterized by oligoarticular arthritis, and in contrast to subgroup 3 the joint involvement is asymmetric, generally including the proximal and distal interphalangeal and metacarpophalangeal articulations (Fig. 14.47). Patients with this oligoarticular arthritis form the most frequent subgroup of psoriatic arthritis and are known for the appearance of sausage-like swelling of digits (Fig. 14.48).

Subgroup 5 is a spondyloarthropathy that has features similar to those of ankylosing spondylitis.

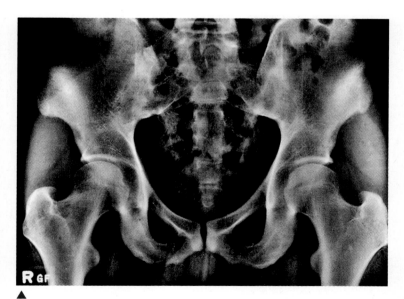

FIGURE 14.38   Reiter syndrome. Anteroposterior radiograph of the pelvis of the patient shown in Figure 14.37B demonstrates symmetric bilateral involvement of the sacroiliac joints.

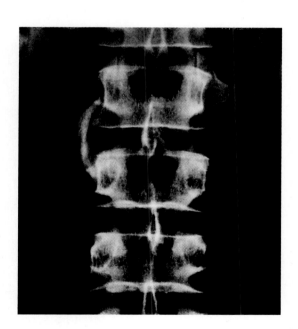

FIGURE 14.39   Reiter syndrome. Anteroposterior radiograph of the lumbar spine of a 23-year-old man with Reiter syndrome demonstrates a paraspinal ossification bridging the L2 and L3 vertebrae.

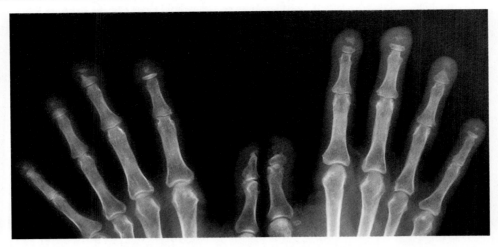

▲
FIGURE 14.40 **Psoriatic arthritis.** A 57-year-old woman with long-standing psoriasis developed resorption of the tufts of the distal phalanges (acroosteolysis) of both hands, typical of this condition.

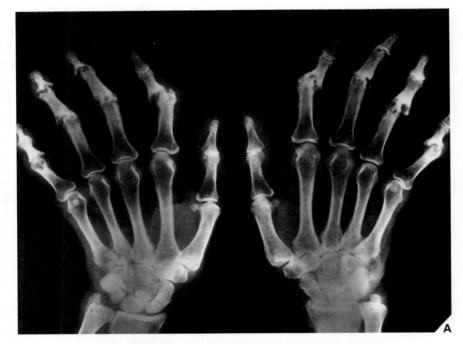

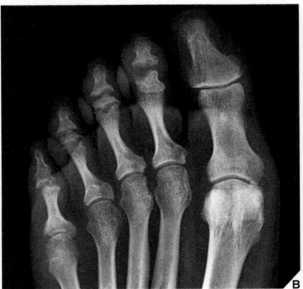

▲
FIGURE 14.41 **Psoriatic arthritis. (A)** Dorsovolar radiograph of both hands of a 55-year-old woman who presented with skin changes typical of psoriasis shows destructive changes in the proximal and distal interphalangeal joints. **(B)** Anteroposterior radiograph of the right foot shows similar erosions of the interphalangeal joints of her toes.

TABLE 14.3 **Most Common Causes of Acroosteolysis**

Trauma
Diabetic gangrene
Psoriasis
Scleroderma
Dermatomyositis
Rheumatoid arthritis
Raynaud disease
Hyperparathyroidism (primary, secondary)
Frostbite
Burn (thermal, electrical)
Congenital (Hajdu-Cheney syndrome)
Leprosy
Gout
Pyknodysostosis
Sarcoidosis
Sjögren syndrome
Polyvinyl chloride
Pachydermoperiostosis
Thromboangiitis obliterans
Syringomyelia

Modified from Reeder MM, Felson B, 1975, with permission.

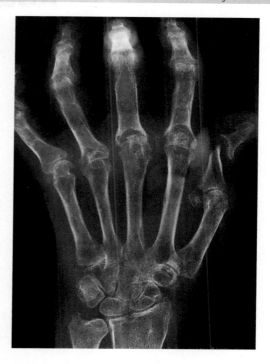

▲
FIGURE 14.42 **Psoriatic arthritis.** Dorsovolar radiograph of the hand of a 57-year-old woman shows the typical presentation of psoriatic polyarthritis. The "pencil-in-cup" deformity in the interphalangeal joint of the thumb is characteristic of this form of psoriasis.

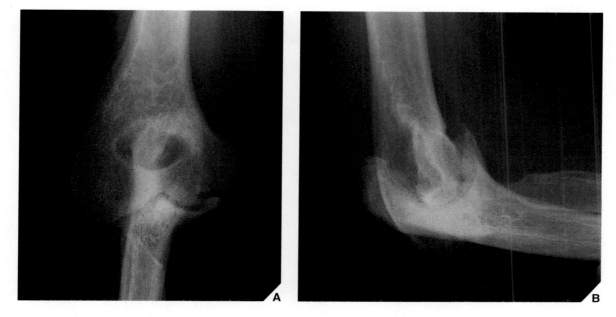

▲
FIGURE 14.43 **Psoriatic arthritis.** A 49-year-old man presented with psoriatic arthritis mutilans. Anteroposterior (**A**) and lateral (**B**) radiographs of the right elbow show extensive articular erosions. Elevated anterior fat pad indicates a joint effusion.

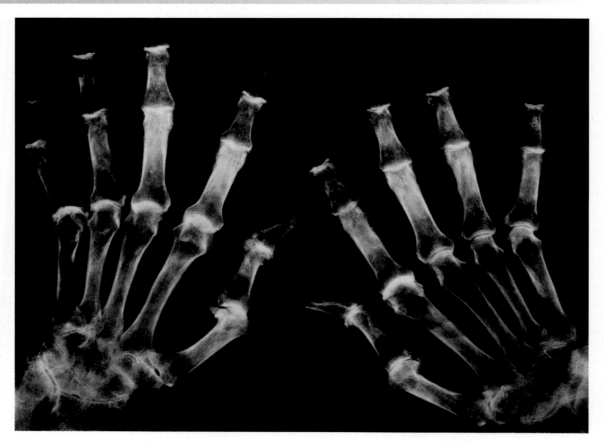

▲
FIGURE 14.44 Psoriatic arthritis. A 75-year-old woman presented with symmetric psoriatic polyarthritis affecting all joints of the hands and wrists. Unlike in adult-onset-type of rheumatoid arthritis the distal interphalangeal joints are also involved.

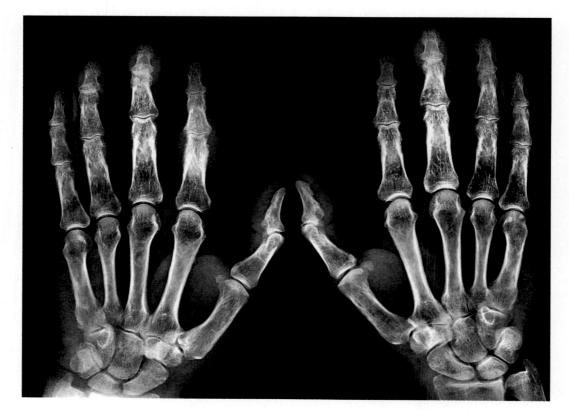

▲
FIGURE 14.45 Psoriatic arthritis. A 65-year-old man presented with psoriatic arthritis affecting symmetrically both hands. Note soft-tissue swelling, articular erosions, and periostitis.

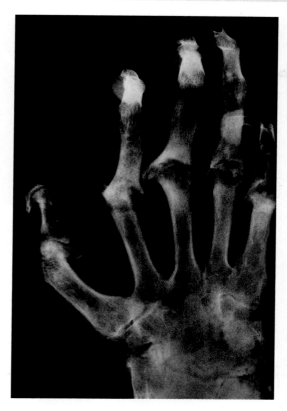

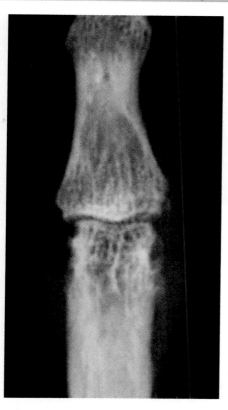

▲ FIGURE 14.46   **Psoriatic arthritis.** Dorsovolar radiograph of the left hand of a 67-year-old man with the polyarthritic form of psoriatic arthritis demonstrates erosions and fusion of multiple joints. The swan-neck deformity of the small finger is similar to that seen in patients with rheumatoid arthritis.

▲ FIGURE 14.47   **Psoriatic arthritis.** A 39-year-old man with psoriasis presented with a painful and swollen middle finger of his right hand. The magnification radiograph shows subtle periarticular erosions, fluffy periosteal reaction, and soft-tissue swelling, features characteristic of oligoarticular psoriatic arthritis.

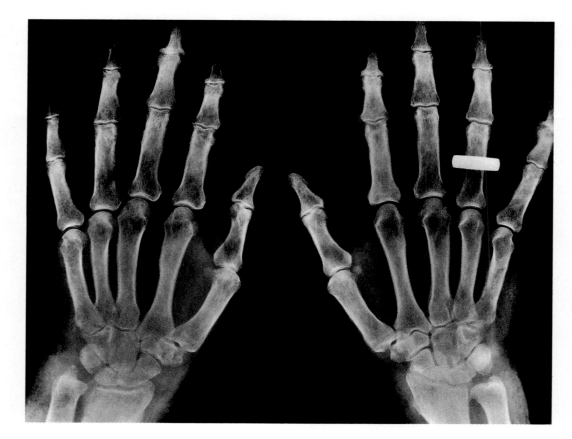

▲ FIGURE 14.48   **Psoriatic arthritis.** Dorsovolar radiograph of the hands of a 33-year-old man with psoriasis and oligoarticular involvement shows destructive changes in the distal interphalangeal joints of the right middle finger and the left index and small fingers. The right middle and left index fingers presented as "sausage digits."

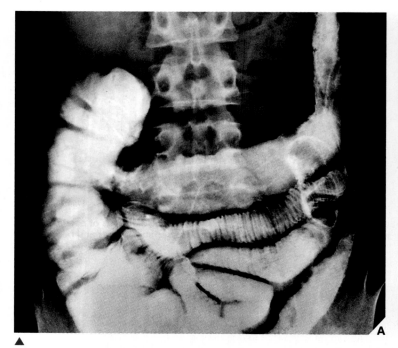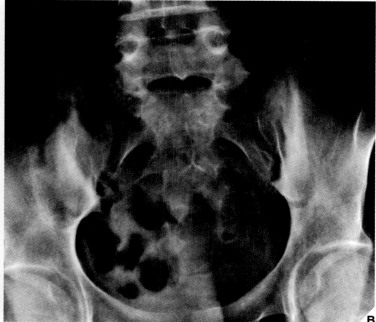

FIGURE 14.54 Ulcerative colitis complicated by sacroiliitis. A 20-year-old woman with known ulcerative colitis developed severe low back pain localized to the sacroiliac joints. **(A)** Barium enema study shows extensive involvement of the transverse and descending colon, consistent with ulcerative colitis. **(B)** Posteroanterior radiograph of the pelvis shows symmetric, bilateral sacroiliitis similar to that seen in ankylosing spondylitis.

Enteropathic Arthropathies

This group comprises arthritides associated with inflammatory intestinal diseases such as ulcerative colitis, regional enteritis (Crohn disease), and intestinal lipodystrophy (Whipple disease), the last of which predominantly affects men in their fourth and fifth decades. The histocompatibility antigen HLA-B27 is present in most patients with enteropathic abnormalities. In all three conditions, the spine and the sacroiliac and peripheral joints may be affected. In the spine, squaring of the vertebral bodies and the formation of syndesmophytes are common features. Sacroiliitis, which is usually bilateral and symmetric, is radiographically indistinguishable from ankylosing spondylitis (Fig. 14.54). In addition, patients may also exhibit a peripheral arthritis, the activity of which generally approximates the activity of the bowel disease.

Finally, it should be noted that arthritis may follow intestinal bypass procedures. The synovitis is polyarticular and symmetric, but radiographically the lesions are nonerosive.

PRACTICAL POINTS TO REMEMBER

Erosive Osteoarthritis

[1] Erosive osteoarthritis, a condition seen predominantly in middle-aged women, combines the clinical manifestations of rheumatoid arthritis with the radiographic features of osteoarthritis.
[2] Erosive osteoarthritis can be recognized by:
   • involvement of the proximal and distal interphalangeal joints
   • a characteristic "gull-wing" configuration of articular erosions. Spontaneous fusion (ankylosis) in the interphalangeal joints may develop.

Rheumatoid Arthritis

[1] Rheumatoid arthritis has a predilection for:
   • the large joints (knees and hips)
   • the small joints in the hand (metacarpophalangeal and proximal interphalangeal)
   • the carpal articulations.
   The distal interphalangeal and sacroiliac joints are usually spared.

[2] The radiographic hallmarks of rheumatoid arthritis include:
   • diffuse, symmetric narrowing of the joint space
   • periarticular osteoporosis
   • fusiform soft-tissue swelling
   • marginal and central articular erosions
   • periarticular synovial cysts
   • subluxations and other joint deformities—swan-neck, boutonnière, hitchhiker's thumb.
[3] In the cervical spine, rheumatoid arthritis is characterized by:
   • erosion of the odontoid process associated with subluxation in the atlantoaxial joints and, frequently, cephalad translocation of C2 (cranial settling)
   • involvement of the apophyseal joints
   • erosions of vertebral bodies
   • destruction of intervertebral disks
   • erosions (whittling) of the spinous processess.
[4] In rheumatoid arthritis:
   • axial or, less frequently, medial migration of the femoral head and acetabular protrusio are characteristic in the hip joint
   • rotator cuff tear is a frequent complication in the shoulder joint
   • the subtalar joint is most often affected in the foot, and a hallux valgus deformity is observed.
[5] Rheumatoid nodulosis, a condition occurring predominantly in men, is a variant of rheumatoid arthritis. It exhibits:
   • a characteristic lack of joint abnormalities
   • multiple subcutaneous nodules
   • a high titer of rheumatoid factor.
[6] Juvenile rheumatoid arthritis displays several characteristic features that are not present in adult-onset disease:
   • a periosteal reaction
   • joint ankylosis, particularly affecting the apophyseal joints of the cervical spine
   • growth abnormalities secondary to involvement of epiphyseal sites.

Other Inflammatory Arthritides

[1] Spondyloarthropathies comprise four distinctive entities: ankylosing spondylitis, psoriatic arthritis, Reiter syndrome, and arthritides associated with inflammatory bowel disease.

[2] Ankylosing spondylitis (Bechterev or Marie-Strümpell disease), a condition seen predominantly in young men, characteristically affects the spine and sacroiliac joints. Histocompatibility antigen HLA-B27 is invariably present in 95% of patients. The radiographic hallmarks of this condition include:
- squaring of the vertebral bodies
- the development of delicate syndesmophytes
- in a later stage of disease, complete fusion of the apophyseal joints and vertebrae, leading to "bamboo" spine.

[3] Reiter syndrome, also known as reactive arthritis, consists of inflammatory arthritis, urethritis, conjunctivitis, and mucocutaneous rash. Its radiographic features include:
- a peripheral, usually asymmetric arthritis that shows a predilection for the lower-limb joints, particularly in the foot
- coarse syndesmophytes and paraspinal ossifications bridging vertebral bodies
- sacroiliitis, which usually is asymmetric.

[4] Psoriatic arthritis has a predilection for the distal interphalangeal joints. Oligoarticular involvement may yield a phenomenon known as "sausage digit." Radiographically, psoriatic arthritis is marked by:
- fluffy periostitis
- "pencil-in-cup" deformity of the joints (arthritis mutilans)
- coarse syndesmophytes and paraspinal ossifications that are indistinguishable from those seen in Reiter syndrome
- involvement of the sacroiliac joints.

[5] Enteropathic arthropathies are associated with:
- ulcerative colitis
- regional enteritis (Crohn disease)
- intestinal lipodystrophy (Whipple disease)
- intestinal bypass procedures.

Characteristically, there is symmetric involvement of the sacroiliac joints.

SUGGESTED READINGS

Adam G, Dammer M, Bohndorf K, Christoph R, Fenke F, Günther RW. Rheumatoid arthritis of the knee: value of gadopentetate dimeglumine-enhanced MR imaging. *Am J Roentgenol* 1991;156:125–129.

Algin O, Gokalp G, Baran B, Ocakoglu G, Yazici Z. Evaluation of sacroiliitis: contrast-enhanced MRI with subtraction technique. *Skeletal Radiol* 2009;38:983–988.

Ansell BM, Wigley RA. Arthritic manifestations in regional enteritis. *Ann Rheum Dis* 1964;23:64–72.

Arnett FC, Bias WB, Stevens MB. Juvenile-onset chronic arthritis. Clinical and roentgenographic features of a unique HLA-B27 subset. *Am J Med* 1980;69:369–376.

Arnett FC, Edworthy SM, Bloch DA, et al. The American Rheumatism Association 1987 revised criteria for the classification of rheumatoid arthritis. *Arthritis Rheum* 1988;31:315–324.

Azouz EM, Duffy CM. Juvenile spondyloarthropathies: clinical manifestations and medical imaging. *Skeletal Radiol* 1995;24:399–408.

Belhorn LR, Hess EV. Erosive osteoarthritis. *Semin Arthritis Rheum* 1993;22:298–306.

Berens DL. Roentgen features of ankylosing spondylitis. *Clin Orthop* 1971;74:20–33.

Björkengren AG, Geborek P, Rydholm U, Holtas S, Petterson H. MR imaging of the knee in acute rheumatoid arthritis: synovial uptake of gadolinium-DOTA. *Am J Roentgenol* 1990;155:329–332.

Björkengren AG, Pathria MN, Sartosis DJ, et al. Carpal alterations in adult-onset Still disease, juvenile chronic arthritis, and adult-onset rheumatoid arthritis: comparative study. *Radiology* 1987;165:545–548.

Bland JH, Brown EW. Seronegative and seropositive rheumatoid arthritis: clinical, radiological and biochemical differences. *Ann Intern Med* 1964;60:88–94.

Boden SD, Dodge LD, Bohlman HH, Rechtine GR. Rheumatoid arthritis of the cervical spine. *J Bone J Surg [Am]* 1993;75A:1282–1297.

Bollow M, Braun J, Biedermann T, et al. Use of contrast-enhanced MR imaging to detect sacroiliitis in children. *Skeletal Radiol* 1998;27:606–616.

Boutin RD, Resnick D. The SAPHO syndrome: an evolving concept for unifying several idiopathic disorders of bone and skin. *Am J Roentgenol* 1998;170:585–591.

Breedveld FC, Algra PR, Vielvoye CJ, Cats A. Magnetic resonance imaging in the evaluation of patients with rheumatoid arthritis and subluxations of the cervical spine. *Arthritis Rheum* 1987;30:624–629.

Brower AC, Allman RM. Pencil pointing: a vascular pattern of deossification. *Radiographics* 1983;3:315–325.

Burgos-Vargas R. Juvenile ankylosing spondylitis. *Rheum Dis Clin North Am* 1992;18:123–142.

Burgos-Vargas R, Vazquez-Mellado J. The early clinical recognition of juvenile-onset ankylosing spondylitis and its differentiation from juvenile rheumatoid arthritis. *Arthritis Rheum* 1995;38:835–844.

Calabro JJ, Gordon RD, Miller KI. Bechterew's syndrome in children: diagnostic criteria. *Scand J Rheumatol* 1980;32(Suppl):45–48.

Cassidy JT, Levinson JE, Bass JC, et al. A study of classification criteria for a diagnosis of juvenile rheumatoid arthritis. *Arthritis Rheum* 1986;29:274–281.

Cassidy JT, Petty RE. Spondyloarthropathies. In: Cassidy JT, Petty RE, eds. *Text book of pediatric rheumatology*, 2nd ed. New York: Churchill Livingstone; 1990:221–259.

Chung C, Coley BD, Martin LC. Rice bodies in juvenile rheumatoid arthritis. *Am J Roentgenol* 1998;170:698–700.

Clark RL, Muhletaler CA, Margulies SI. Colitic arthritis: clinical and radiographic manifestations. *Radiology* 1971;101:585–594.

Cobby M, Cushnaghan J, Creamer P, Dieppe P, Watt I. Erosive osteoarthritis: is it a separate disease entity? *Clin Radiol* 1990;42:258–263.

Dale K, Paus AC, Laires K. A radiographic classification in juvenile rheumatoid arthritis applied to the knee. *Eur Radiol* 1994;4:27–32.

Dihlmann W. Current radiodiagnostic concept of ankylosing spondylitis. *Skeletal Radiol* 1979;4:179–188.

Dixon AS. "Rheumatoid arthritis" with negative serological reaction. *Ann Rheum Dis* 1960;19:209–228.

Eastmond CJ, Woodrow JC. The HLA system and the arthropathies associated with psoriasis. *Ann Rheum Dis* 1977;36:112–121.

Ehrlich GE. Inflammatory osteoarthritis. II. The superimposition of rheumatoid arthritis. *J Chronic Dis* 1972;25:635–643.

Ehrlich GE. Erosive osteoarthritis: presentation, clinical pearls, and therapy. *Curr Rheum Rep* 2001;3:484–488.

El-Khoury GY, Larson RK, Kathol MH, Berbaum KS, Furst DE. Seronegative and seropositive rheumatoid arthritis: radiographic differences. *Radiology* 1988;168:517–520.

el-Noueam KI, Giuliano V, Schweitzer ME, O'Hara BJ. Rheumatoid nodules: MR/pathological correlation. *J Comput Assist Tomogr* 1997;21:796–799.

Fezoulidis I, Neuhold A, Wicke L, Seidl G, Eydokimidis B. Diagnostic imaging of the occipito-cervical junction in patients with rheumatoid arthritis. *Eur J Radiol* 1989;9:5–11.

Forrester DM. Imaging of the sacroiliac joints. *Radiol Clin North Am* 1990;28:1055–1072.

Galvez J, Sola J, Ortuno G, et al. Microscopic rice bodies in rheumatoid synovial fluid sediments. *J Rheum* 1992;19:1851–1858.

Ginsberg MH, Genant HK, Yü TF, McCarty D. Rheumatoid nodulosis: an unusual variant of rheumatoid disease. *Arthritis Rheum* 1975;18:49–58.

Giovagnoni A, Grassi W, Terilli F, et al. MRI of the hand in psoriatic and rheumatical arthritis. *Eur Radiol* 1995;5:590–595.

Gordon DA, Hastings DE. Rheumatoid arthritis: clinical features—early, progressive and late disease. In: Klippel JH, Dieppe PA, eds. *Rheumatology*. St. Louis: CV Mosby; 1994:3.4.1–3.4.14.

Gran JT, Husby G. The epidemiology of ankylosing spondylitis. *Semin Arthritis Rheum* 1993;22:319–334.

Graudal NA, Jurik AG, de Carvalho A, Graudal HK. Radiographic progression in rheumatoid arthritis: a long-term prospective study of 109 patients. *Arthritis Rheum* 1998;41:1470–1480.

Green L, Meyers OL, Gordon W, Briggs B. Arthritis in psoriasis. *Ann Rheum Dis* 1981;40:366–369.

Greenspan A. Erosive osteoarthritis. *Semin Musculoskel Radiol* 2003;7:155–159.

Greenspan A, Baker ND, Norman A. Rheumatoid arthritis simulating other lesions. *Bull Hosp Joint Dis Orthop Inst* 1983;43:70–77.

Hazes JMW, Dijkmans BAC, Hoevers JM, et al. R4 prevalence related to the age at disease onset in female patients with rheumatoid arthritis. *Ann Rheum Dis* 1989;48:406–408.

Helliwell PS, Wright V. Clinical features of psoriatic arthritis. In: Klippel JH, Dieppe PA, eds. *Practical rheumatology*. London, UK: Mosby; 1995:235–242.

Herve-Somma CMP, Sebag GH, Prieur AM, Bonnerot V, Lallemand DP. Juvenile rheumatoid arthritis of the knee: MR evaluation with Gd-DOTA. *Radiology* 1992;182:93–98.

Hoffman GS. Polyarthritis: the differential diagnosis of rheumatoid arthritis. *Semin Arthritis Rheum* 1978;8:115–141.

Hughes RJ, Saifuddin A. Progressive non-infectious anterior vertebral fusion (Copenhagen Syndrome) in three children: features on radiographs and MR imaging. *Skeletal Radiol* 2006;35:397–401.

Kahn MF. Why the "SAPHO" syndrome? *J Rheumatol* 1995; 22: 2017–2019.

Kapasi OA, Ruby LK, Calney K. The psoriatic hand. *J Hand Surg [Am]* 1982;7A:492–497.

Kaye BR, Kaye RL, Bobrove A. Rheumatoid nodules. *Am J Med* 1984;76:279–292.

Keat A. Reiter's syndrome and reactive arthritis in perspective. *N Engl J Med* 1983;309:1606–1615.

Kelly JJ III, Weisiger BB. The arthritis of Whipple's disease. *Arthritis Rheum* 1963;25:615–632.

Kettering JM, Towers JD, Rubin DA. The seronegative spondyloarthropathies. *Semin Roentgenol* 1996;31:220–228.

Khan MA, van der Linden SM. A wider spectrum of spondyloarthropathies. *Semin Arthritis Rheum* 1990;20:107–113.

Klecker R, Weissman BN. Imaging features of psoriatic arthritis and Reiter's syndrome. *Semin Musculoskel Radiol* 2003;7:115–126.

Klenerman L. The foot and ankle in rheumatoid arthritis. *Br J Rheum* 1995;34:443–448.

König H, Sieper J, Wolf K-J. Rheumatoid arthritis: evaluation of hypervascular and fibrous pannus with dynamic MR imaging enhanced with Gd-DTPA. *Radiology* 1990;176:473–477.

Küster W, Lenz W. Morbus Crohn und Colitis ulcerosa. Häufigkeit, familiäres Vorkommen und Schwangerschaftsverlauf. *Ergeb Inn Med Kinderheilkd* 1984;53:103–132.

Laxer RM, Babyn P, Liu P, Silverman ED, Shore A. Magnetic resonance studies of the sacroiliac joints in children with HLA-B27 associated seronegative arthropathies. *J Rheumatol* 1992;19(Suppl 33):123.

Leirisalo M, Skylv G, Kousa M, et al. Follow-up study on patients with Reiter's disease and reactive arthritis with special reference to HLA-B27. *Arthritis Rheum* 1982;25:249–259.

Lindsley CB, Schaller JG. Arthritis associated with inflammatory bowel disease in children. *J Pediatr* 1974;84:16–20.

Lund PJ, Heikal A, Maricic MJ, Krupinski EA, Williams CS. Ultrasonographic imaging of the hand and wrist in rheumatoid arthritis. *Skeletal Radiol* 1995;24:591–596.

Maksymowych WP, Crowther SM, Dhillon SS, et al. Systemic assessment of inflammation by magnetic resonance imaging in the posterior elements of the spine in ankylosing spondylitis. *Arthritis Care Research* 2010;62:4–10.

Mak W, Hunter JC. MRI of early diagnosis of inflammatory arthritis. *J Musculoskeletal Med* 2009;26:478–486.

Marsal L, Winblad S, Wollheim FA. *Yersinia enterocolitica* arthritis in Southern Sweden: a four-year follow-up study. *Br Med J* 1981;283:101–103.

Martel W, Braunstein EM, Borlaza G, Good AE, Griffin PE. Radiologic features of Reiter disease. *Radiology* 1979;132:1–10.

Martel W, Holt JF, Cassidy JT. The roentgenologic manifestations of juvenile rheumatoid arthritis. *Am J Roentgenol* 1962;88:400–423.

Martel W, Snarr JW, Horn JR. Metacarpophalangeal joints in interphalangeal osteoarthritis. *Radiology* 1973;108:1–7.

Martel W, Stuck KJ, Dworin AM, Hylland RG. Erosive osteoarthritis and psoriatic arthritis: a radiologic comparison in the hand, wrist and foot. *Am J Roentgenol* 1980;134:125–135.

McGonagle. The history of erosions in rheumatoid arthritis: are erosions history? *Arthritis Rheum* 2010;62:312–315.

Mutlu H, Silit E, Pekkafali Z, et al. Multiple rice body formation in the subacromial-subdeltoid bursa and knee joint. *Skeletal Radiol* 2004;33:531–533.

Nance EP, Kaye JJ. The rheumatod variants. *Semin Roentgenol* 1982;17:16–24.

Oloff-Solomon J, Oloff LM, Jacobs AM. Rheumatoid nodulosis in the foot: a variant of rheumatoid disease. *J Foot Surg* 1984;23:382–385.

Ostendorf B, Mattes-Gyorgy K, Reichelt DC, et al. Early detection of bony alterations in rheumatoid and erosive arthritis of finger joints with high-resolution single photon emission computed tomography, and differentiation between them. *Skeletal Radiol* 2010;39:55–61.

Paimela L. The radiographic criterion in the 1987 revised criteria for rheumatoid arthritis. *Arthritis Rheum* 1992;35:255–258.

Peterson CC Jr, Silbiger ML. Reiter's syndrome and psoriatic arthritis. Their roentgen spectra and some interesting similarities. *Am J Roentgenol* 1967;101:860–871.

Polster JM, Winalski CS, Sundaram M, et al. Rheumatoid arthritis: evaluation with contrast-enhanced CT with digital bone masking. *Radiology* 2009;252:225–231.

Reiter H. Ueber eine bisher unerkannte Spirochaeteninfektion (Spirochaetosis arthritica). *Dtsch Med Wochenschr* 1916;42:1535–1536.

Resnick D. Rheumatoid arthritis of the wrist: why the ulnar styloid? *Radiology* 1974;112:29–35.

Resnick D. Common disorders of synovium-lined joints: pathogenesis, imaging abnormalities, and complications. *Am J Roentgenol* 1988;151:1079–1093.

Resnick D, Niwayama G. On the nature and significance of bony proliferation in "rheumatoid variant" disorders. *Am J Roentgenol* 1977;129:275–278.

Resnick D, Niwayama G. Rheumatoid arthritis and the seronegative spondyloarthropathies: radiographic and pathologic concepts. In: Resnick D, ed. *Diagnosis of bone and joint disorders*, 3rd ed. Philadelphia: WB Saunders; 1995:807–865.

Reynolds H, Carter SW, Murtagh FR, Silbiger M, Rechtine GR. Cervical rheumatoid arthritis: value of flexion and extension views in imaging. *Radiology* 1987;164:215–218.

Rominger MB, Bernreuter WK, Kenney PJ, Morgan SL, Blackburn WD, Alarcon GS. MR imaging of the hands in early rheumatoid arthritis: preliminary results. *Radiographics* 1993;13:37–46.

Sanders KM, Resnik CS, Owen DS. Erosive arthritis in Cronkhite-Canada syndrome. *Radiology* 1985;156:309–310.

Solomon G, Winchester R. Immunogenetic aspects of inflammatory arthritis. In: Taveras JM, Ferrucci JT, eds. *Radiology—diagnosis, imaging, intervention*, vol. 5. Philadelphia: JB Lippincott; 1986:1–4.

Sommer OJ, Kladosek A, Weiler V, Czembirek H, Boeck M, Stiskal M. Rheumatoid arthritis: a practical guide to state-of-the-art imaging, image interpretation, and clinical implications. *Radiographics* 2005;25:381–398.

Stiskal MA, Neuhold A, Szolar DH, et al. Rheumatoid arthritis of the craniocervical region by MR imaging: detection and characterization. *Am J Roentgenol* 1995;165:585–592.

Sundaram M, Patton JT. Paravertebral ossification in psoriasis and Reiter's disease. *Br J Radiol* 1975;48:628–633.

Swett HA, Jaffe RB, McIff EB. Popliteal cysts: presentation as thrombophlebitis. *Radiology* 1975;115:613–615.

Tehranzadeh J, Ashikyan O, Dascalos J. Magnetic resonance imaging in early detection of rheumatoid arthritis. *Semin Musculoskel Radiol* 2003;7:79–94.

Uhl M, Allmann KH, Ihling C, Hauer MP, Conca W, Langer M. Cartilage destruction in small joints by rheumatoid arthritis: assessment of fat-suppressed three-dimensional gradient-echo MR pulse sequences in vitro. *Skeletal Radiol* 1998;27:677–682.

Van der Kooij SM, Allaart CF, Dijkmans BA, Breedveld FC. Innovative treatment strategies for patients with rheumatoid arthritis. *Curr Opin Rheumatol* 2008;20:287–294.

Villeneuve E, Emery P. Rheumatoid arthritis: what has changed? *Skeletal Radiol* 2009;38:109–112.

Vinson EN, Major NM. MR imaging of ankylosing spondylitis. *Semin Musculoskel Radiol* 2003;7:103–113.

Weissman BN. Spondyloarthropathies. *Radiol Clin North Am* 1987;25:1235–1262.

Weissman BN. Imaging techniques in rheumatoid arthritis. *J Rheumatol Suppl* 1994;42:14–19.

Whitehouse RW, Aslam R, Bukhari M, Groves C, Cassar-Pullicino V. The sesamoid index in psoriatic arthropathy. *Skeletal Radiol* 2005;34:217–220.

Wisnieski JJ, Askari AD. Rheumatoid nodulosis. A relatively benign rheumatoid variant. *Arch Intern Med* 1981;141:615–619.

Wright V. Seronegative polyarthritis: a unified concept. *Arthritis Rheum* 1978;21:619–633.

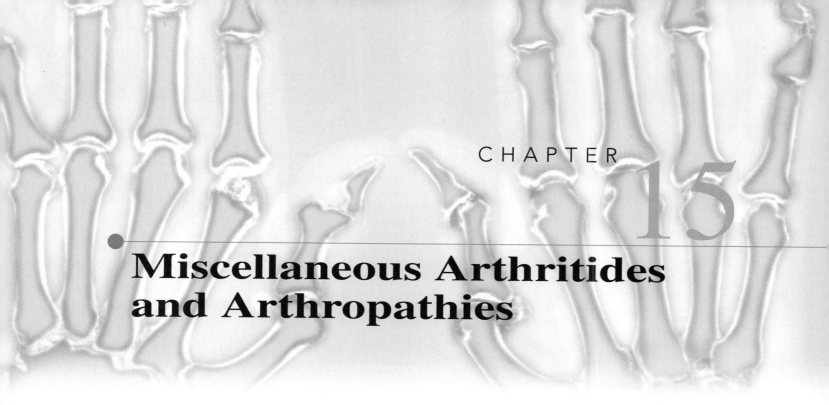

Miscellaneous Arthritides and Arthropathies

Connective Tissue Arthropathies

An overview of the clinical and radiographic hallmarks of the forms of arthritis associated with connective tissue disorders is presented in Table 15.1.

Systemic Lupus Erythematosus

Systemic lupus erythematosus (SLE) is a chronic, inflammatory, connective tissue disorder of unknown cause characterized by significant immunologic abnormalities and involvement of multiple organs. Women, particularly adolescents and young adults, are affected four times as frequently as men. The clinical manifestations of SLE vary according to the distribution and extent of systemic alterations. The most common symptoms are malaise, weakness, fever, anorexia, and weight loss. Consistent and characteristic features of this disease are serologic abnormalities, including a variety of serum autoantibodies to nuclear antigens, which have been historically associated with the presence of lupus erythematosus cells and neutrophilic leukocytes filled with cytoplasmic inclusion bodies.

Antinuclear antibodies are useful in the differential diagnosis of SLE, and changes in the titer of antibodies to DNA are useful in following disease activity. Antinuclear antibodies are a heterogeneous group of antibodies directed against a number of discrete nuclear macromolecular proteins. They represent what has classically been referred to as "autoantibodies," because they are directed against components normally present in all nucleated cells. They generally lack tissue or species specificity; therefore, they will cross-react with nuclei from different sources. The primary sources for study of these antibodies are patients with SLE and related systemic rheumatic diseases. Many studies have centered on defining the specificity of these antibodies and have contributed extensively to our understanding of their immunopathologic role in connective tissue disorders.

The musculoskeletal system is a frequent site of involvement in SLE, and joint abnormalities, exhibited by 90% of patients during the course of the disease, represent a significant part of the clinical and radiologic picture. Arthritic involvement is symmetric, and articular deformities without fixed contractures are a hallmark of this disorder. The hands are the predominant site of involvement. Typically, the conventional radiography discloses malalignments, most commonly at the metacarpophalangeal and proximal interphalangeal joints of the fingers and the first carpometacarpal, metacarpophalangeal, and the interphalangeal joints

of the thumb (Fig. 15.1). These abnormalities may not be apparent on a dorsovolar radiograph because the malalignments are flexible and are corrected by the pressure of the hand against the radiographic cassette (Fig. 15.2). These pathognomonic deformities usually occur secondary to a loss of support from the ligamentous and capsular structures about the joint and, at least in the early stage of disease, are completely reducible. Only very seldom are these abnormalities fixed and/or accompanied by articular erosions (Fig. 15.3).

Some patients present with sclerosis of the distal phalanges (acral sclerosis) (Fig. 15.4) or with resorption of the terminal tufts (acroosteolysis). Osteonecrosis, which is frequently seen, has been attributed to complications of treatment with corticosteroids (Fig. 15.5). However, current investigations suggest the vital role of the inflammatory process (vasculitis) in the development of this complication.

Scleroderma

Scleroderma (progressive systemic sclerosis) is a generalized disorder of unknown cause. It is seen predominantly in young women, usually becoming apparent in their third and fourth decades. Primarily a connective tissue disorder characterized by deposition of collagen and other components of extracellular matrix in the skin and internal organs, it is distinguished by thickening and fibrosis of the skin and subcutaneous tissues, with frequent involvement of the musculoskeletal system. Clinically, many patients develop joint involvement, which is manifesting as arthralgia and arthritis leading to flexion contractions of the fingers. Most patients have the so-called CREST syndrome, which refers to the coexistence of calcinosis, Raynaud phenomenon (episodes of intermittent pallor of the fingers and toes on exposure to cold, secondary to vasoconstriction of the small blood vessels), esophageal abnormalities (dilatation and hypoperistalsis), sclerodactyly, and telangiectasia; 30% to 40% of patients have a positive serologic test for rheumatoid factor and a positive antinuclear antibody (ANA) test.

Radiographically, scleroderma presents with characteristic abnormalities of the bone and soft tissues. The hands usually exhibit atrophy of the soft tissues at the tips of the fingers (Fig. 15.6), resorption of the distal phalanges (acroosteolysis), osteopenia, subcutaneous and periarticular calcifications (Figs. 15.7 and 15.8A), and destructive changes of the small articulations, usually the interphalangeal joints (Fig. 15.9). Soft-tissue calcifications within the upper limbs can occasionally be quite prominent (see Fig. 15.8B). Corroborative findings are seen in the gastrointestinal tract, where dilatation of the esophagus and

TABLE 15.1 **Clinical and Radiographic Hallmarks of Connective Tissue Arthritides (Arthropathies)**

Type of Arthritis	Site	Crucial Abnormalities	Technique/Projection
Systemic Lupus Erythematosus (F > M; young adults; blacks > whites; skin changes: rash)	Hands Hips, ankles, shoulders	Flexible joint contractures Osteonecrosis	Lateral view Standard views of affected joints Scintigraphy Magnetic resonance imaging
Scleroderma (F > M; skin changes: edema, thickening)	Hands	Soft-tissue calcifications Acroosteolysis Tapering of distal phalanges Interphalangeal destructive changes	Dorsovolar and lateral views
	Gastrointestinal tract	Dilatation of esophagus Decreased peristalsis Dilatation of duodenum and small bowel Pseudodiverticulosis of colon	Esophagram Esophagram (cine or video study) Upper gastrointestinal and small bowel series Barium enema
Polymyositis/Dermatomyositis	Upper and lower extremities (proximal parts) Hands	Soft-tissue calcifications Periarticular osteoporosis Erosions and destructive changes in distal interphalangeal articulations	Xeroradiography; digital radiography Dorsovolar and lateral views
Mixed Connective Tissue Disease (overlap of clinical features of SLE, scleroderma, dermatomyositis, and rheumatoid arthritis)	Hands, wrists	Erosions and destructive changes in proximal interphalangeal, metacarpophalangeal, radiocarpal and midcarpal articulations, associated with joint space narrowing Symmetric soft-tissue swelling Soft-tissue atrophy and calcifications	Dorsovolar and lateral views Magnetic resonance imaging Posteroanterior and lateral views
	Chest	Pleural and pericardial effusions	Ultrasound

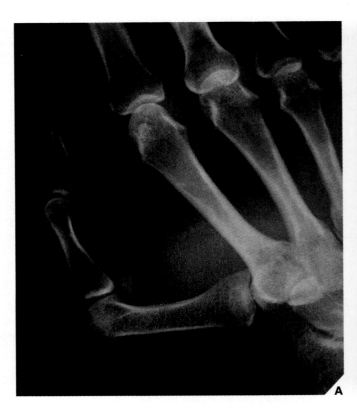 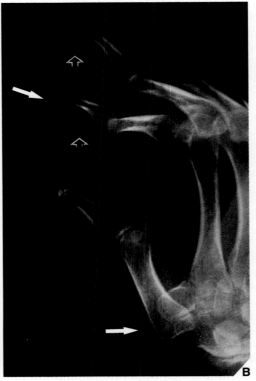

▲ FIGURE 15.1 Systemic lupus erythematosus. **(A)** Typical appearance of the thumb in a 43-year-old woman with SLE. Note subluxations in the first carpometacarpal and metacarpophalangeal joints without articular erosions. **(B)** In anther patient, a 32-year-old woman with SLE, the oblique radiograph of her left hand shows dislocations at the first carpometacarpal joint and distal interphalangeal joint of the index finger (*arrows*), and subluxations in the metacarpophalangeal joints of the index and middle fingers associated with swan-neck deformities (*open arrows*).

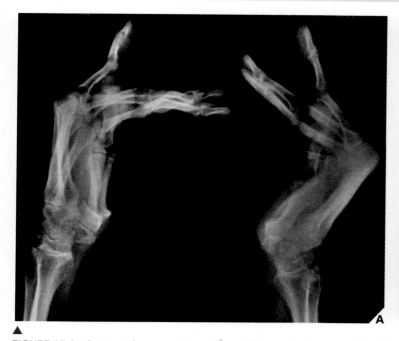
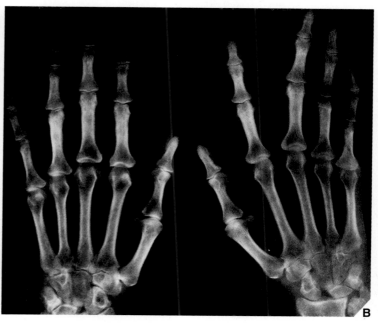

FIGURE 15.2   **Systemic lupus erythematosus. (A)** Lateral radiograph of both hands of a 42-year-old woman with documented SLE for the past 4 years demonstrates flexion deformities in the metacarpophalangeal joints. On the dorsovolar projection **(B)**, the flexion deformities have been corrected by the pressure of the hands against the radiographic cassette.

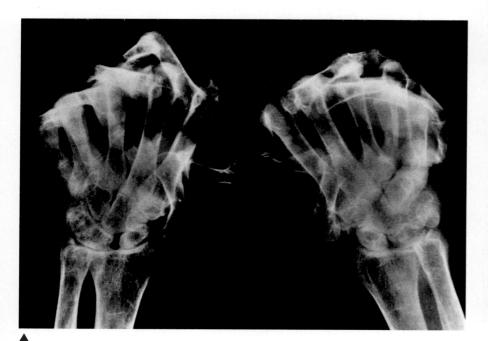

FIGURE 15.3   **Systemic lupus erythematosus.** A 62-year-old woman presented with a 15-year history of SLE. Dorsovolar view of both hands shows severe deformities, subluxations, and articular erosions. Note the advanced osteoporosis secondary to disuse of the extremities and treatment with corticosteroids.

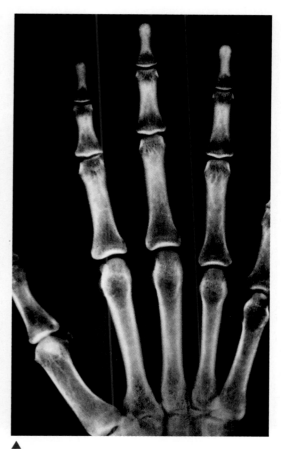

FIGURE 15.4   **Systemic lupus erythematosus.** Dorsovolar film of the hand of a 29-year-old woman with SLE demonstrates sclerosis of the distal phalanges (acral sclerosis). Similar sclerotic changes are also occasionally seen in rheumatoid arthritis and scleroderma.

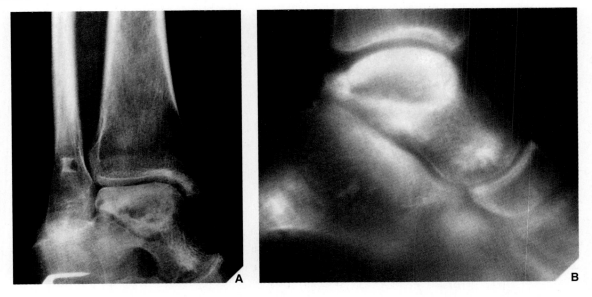

▲
FIGURE 15.5 **SLE complicated by osteonecrosis.** Oblique radiograph (**A**) and lateral tomogram (**B**) of the ankle demonstrate osteonecrosis of the talus in a 26-year-old woman with lupus who was treated with massive doses of steroids.

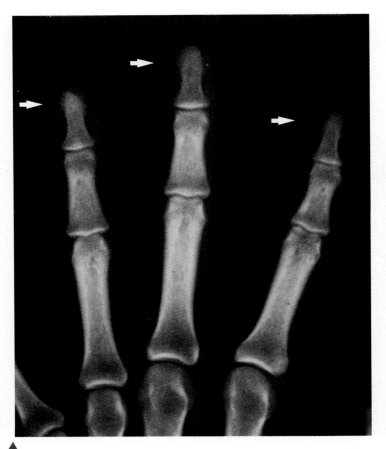

▲
FIGURE 15.6 **Scleroderma.** A 24-year-old woman presented with atrophy of the soft tissues at the distal phalanges of the index, middle, and ring fingers (*arrows*).

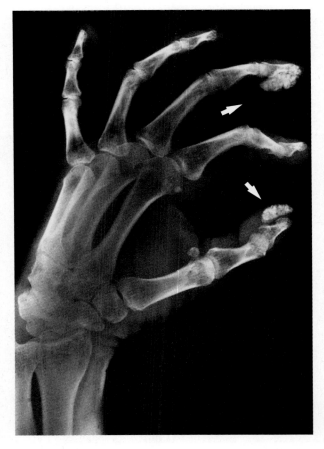

▲
FIGURE 15.7 **Scleroderma.** A 32-year-old woman with progressive systemic sclerosis exhibits soft-tissue calcifications in the distal phalanges of the right hand (*arrows*), a typical feature of this disorder.

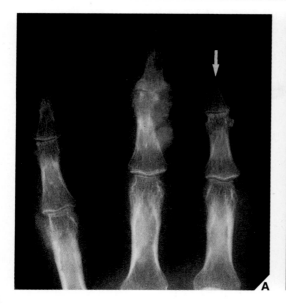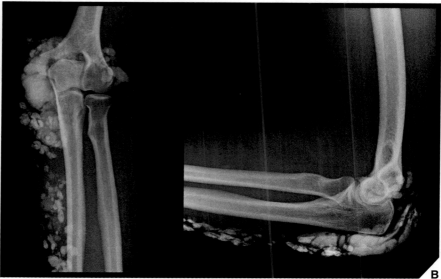

▲
FIGURE 15.8 **Scleroderma. (A)** Dorsovolar radiograph of the fingers of a 44-year-old woman reveals acroosteolysis (*arrow*), soft-tissue calcifications, and destructive changes of the distal interphalangeal joint of the middle finger. **(B)** In another patient, a 46-year-old woman, extensive soft-tissue calcifications are present around the elbow and the forearm.

FIGURE 15.9 **Scleroderma. (A)** Dorsovolar radiograph of the hands of ▶ a 50-year-old man with documented systemic sclerosis shows destructive changes in the distal interphalangeal joints, as well as soft-tissue calcifications and resorption of the tip of the distal phalanx of the left middle finger. **(B)** Dorsovolar radiograph of the hands of a 53-year-old woman with long-standing systemic sclerosis shows acroosteolysis of all distal phalanges. Note also erosions of the first carpometacarpal joints.

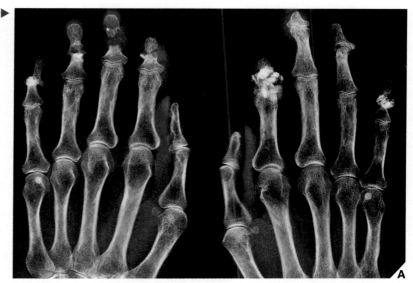

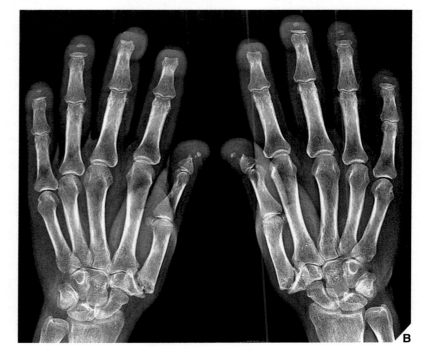

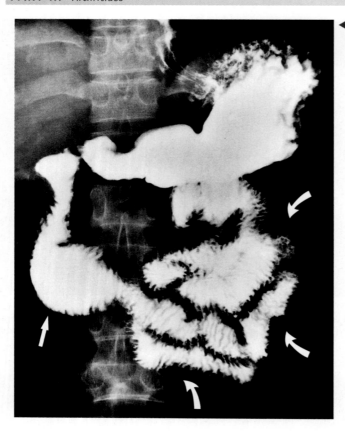

◀ **FIGURE 15.10** **Scleroderma.** Upper gastrointestinal series and small bowel study in the patient shown in Figure 15.9A demonstrate dilatation of the second and third portions of the duodenum (*arrow*) and jejunum (*curved arrows*), with a pseudoobstruction pattern.

small bowel, together with a pseudoobstruction pattern, is characteristic (Fig. 15.10). Pseudodiverticula in the colon are also commonly seen.

Polymyositis and Dermatomyositis

Polymyositis and dermatomyositis are disorders of striated muscle and skin and are characterized by diffuse, nonsuppurative inflammation, as well as degeneration. Early diagnosis and subsequent management of patients with any type of myopathy, including polymyositis and dermatomyositis, can be facilitated by the use of appropriate laboratory tests. The four tests most helpful in evaluating muscle disorders include (1) serum enzymes; (2) urinary creatine and creatinine excretion; (3) electromyogram; and (4) muscle biopsy.

Different serum enzyme determinations have been advocated, but the most valuable tests include serum creatine phosphokinase (CPK), serum aldolase (ALD), serum lactate dehydrogenase (LDH), serum glutamic oxalacetic transaminase (SGOT), and serum glutamic pyruvic transaminase (SGPT). Further, the determination of serum enzyme levels and urinary creatine excretion is helpful for the clinical management of polymyositis and dermatomyositis, because the two tests provide a broader perspective than either test alone.

A positive biopsy may not only demonstrate that the disease process is myopathic, thus enabling the physician to rule out a neurogenic lower motor neuron lesion, but may also identify those patients whose muscle disease is more severe pathologically than was suspected on clinical grounds. This is important with respect to prognosis. With the aid of histochemical and electron microscopic techniques, muscle biopsy will occasionally enable the pathologist to diagnose one of the rare forms of myopathy that can clinically mimic polymyositis. Such diseases include sarcoid myopathy, central core disease, and muscle diseases associated with abnormal mitochondria.

The pathologic changes found on muscle biopsy in polymyositis have been well described. The degree of pathologic change may vary widely; one patient may show only negligible pathologic changes in muscle fibers on biopsy results, whereas another patient presenting similar clinical features may show extensive necrosis and fiber replacement. This variability in histologic findings is probably responsible for the frequent normal muscle biopsy results from patients with otherwise classic polymyositis. The overall rate of positive findings from muscle biopsy in several studies of polymyositis was in the range of 55% to 80%.

Imaging abnormalities in polymyositis and dermatomyositis are divided into two types: those involving soft tissues and those involving joints. The most characteristic soft-tissue abnormality in both conditions is soft-tissue calcifications. The favorite sites of intermuscular calcification are the large muscles in the proximal parts of upper and lower extremities. In addition, subcutaneous calcifications similar to those of scleroderma are seen (Fig. 15.11).

Articular abnormalities are rare. The most frequently reported, however, is periarticular osteoporosis. Destructive joint changes have been reported only occasionally, and primarily in the distal interphalangeal articulations of the hands.

Mixed Connective Tissue Disease

Mixed connective tissue disease (MCTD) was first reported as a distinctive syndrome by Sharp and associates in 1972. This syndrome is characterized by clinical abnormalities that combine the features of SLE, scleroderma, dermatomyositis, and rheumatoid arthritis. The one feature that distinguishes MCTD as a separate entity is a positive serologic test for antibody to the ribonucleoprotein (RNP) component of extractable nuclear antigen (ENA). The typical clinical pattern consists of Raynaud phenomenon, polyarthralgia, swelling of the hands, esophageal hypomotility, inflammatory myopathy, and pulmonary disease. Women constitute approximately 80% of affected patients. Patients with MCTD have prominent joint abnormalities, with typical involvement of the small articulations of the hand, wrist, and foot; large joints such as the knee, elbow, and shoulder may also be affected. The joint deformities mimic those seen in rheumatoid arthritis, but occasionally joint subluxation may be nonerosive, as in SLE. Soft-tissue abnormalities are identical to those encountered in scleroderma (Figs. 15.12 to 15.14).

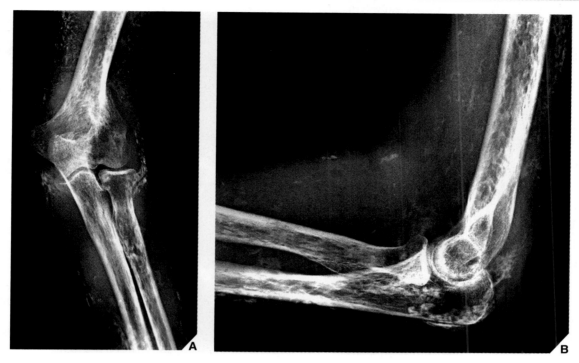

▲
FIGURE 15.11   **Dermatomyositis. (A)** External oblique and **(B)** lateral radiographs of the left elbow of a 64-year-old woman with clinical diagnosis of dermato-myositis show extensive soft-tissue calcifications, characteristic for this disorder. Note also prominent periarticular osteoporosis.

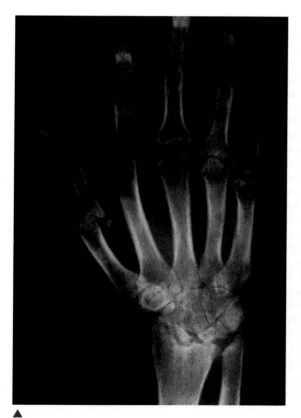

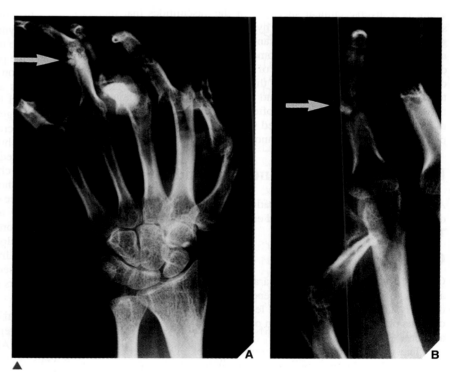

▲
FIGURE 15.12   **Mixed connective tissue disease.** A 44-year-old woman presented with clinical and imaging features of rheumatoid arthritis. In addition, she had clinically documented dermatomyositis. A dorsovolar radiograph of her left hand shows extensive articular erosions at radiocarpal, metacarpophalangeal, and proximal interphalangeal joints, typical for rheumatoid arthritis. The muscle biopsy result was consistent with polymyositis.

▲
FIGURE 15.13   **Mixed connective tissue disease.** A 26-year-old woman presented with swelling of both hands, polyarthralgia, and Raynaud phenomenon. She tested positively for the rheumatoid factors and antinuclear antibodies, and her clinical findings were characteristic for SLE and scleroderma. Oblique radiograph **(A)** of the right hand and coned-down view **(B)** of the thumb and index finger of the left hand show flexion deformities and subluxations in the multiple joints. Deformities of both thumbs are characteristic for SLE, whereas soft-tissue calcifications (*arrows*) are typical for scleroderma. The clinical diagnosis was MCTD.

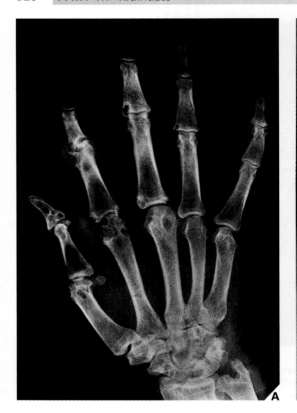
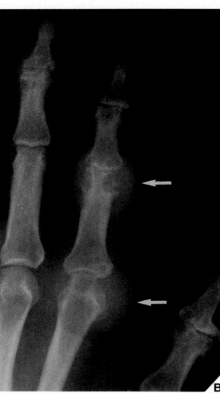

◀ FIGURE 15.15 **Gouty arthritis. (A)** Dorsovolar radiograph of the left hand of a 43-year-old man with tophaceous gout shows multiple sharply marginated periarticular erosions and soft-tissue masses at the proximal interphalangeal joints of the index and middle fingers, representing tophi. **(B)** Dorsovolar radiograph of the fingers of a 70-year-old man with gouty arthritis shows multiple articular and periarticular erosions associated with large tophi (*arrows*).

in location and are later seen to extend into the joint (Fig. 15.15); an "overhanging edge" of erosion is a frequent identifying feature (Figs. 15.16 and 15.17). Occasionally, intraosseous defects are present secondary to the formation of intraosseous tophi (Figs. 15.18 and 15.19). Usually, there is a striking lack of osteoporosis, which helps differentiate this condition from rheumatoid arthritis. The reason for the absence of osteoporosis is that the duration of an acute gouty attack is too short to allow the development of the disuse osteoporosis so often seen in patients with rheumatoid arthritis. If erosion involves the articular end of

the bone and extends into the joint, part of the joint is usually preserved (Fig. 15.20, see also Fig. 15.16). Unlike rheumatoid arthritis, periarticular and articular erosions are asymmetric in distribution (Fig. 15.21). In chronic tophaceous gout, sodium urate deposits in and around the joint are seen, creating a dense mass in the soft tissues called a tophus, which frequently exhibits calcifications (Figs. 15.22 and 15.23, see also Figs. 15.15 and 15.16). Characteristically, tophi are randomly distributed and are usually asymmetric; if they occur in the hands or feet, they are more often seen on the dorsal aspect (Fig. 15.24).

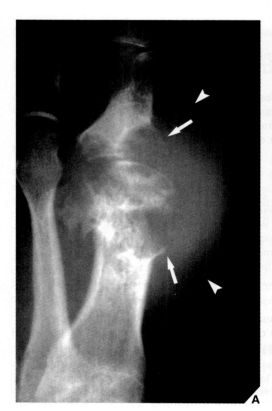
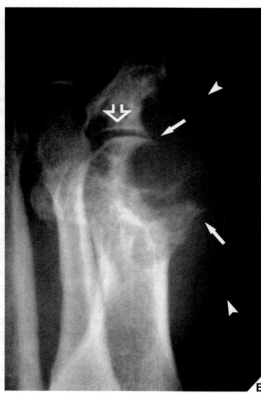

◀ FIGURE 15.16 **Gouty arthritis. (A)** Anteroposterior and **(B)** oblique radiographs of the right great toe of a 58-year-old man with a 3-month history of gout shows the typical involvement of the first metatarsophalangeal joint. Note the characteristic "overhanging edge" of the erosive changes (*arrows*), preservation of the lateral portion of the joint (*open arrow*), and a large tophus (*arrow heads*).

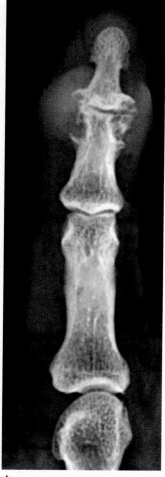

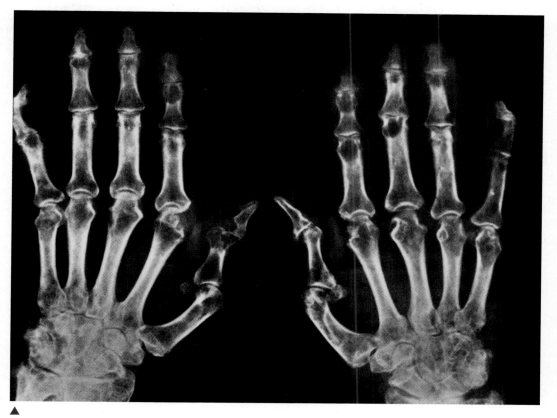

▲
FIGURE 15.17 **Gouty arthritis.** Typical paraarticular erosions in the distal interphalangeal joint of the index finger exhibiting an "overhanging edge" are associated with a large tophus.

▲
FIGURE 15.18 **Gouty arthritis.** Dorsovolar radiograph of both hands of a 60-year-old man with gout shows articular and periarticular erosions. In addition, note the presence of intraosseous defects in the phalanges consistent with intraosseous tophi.

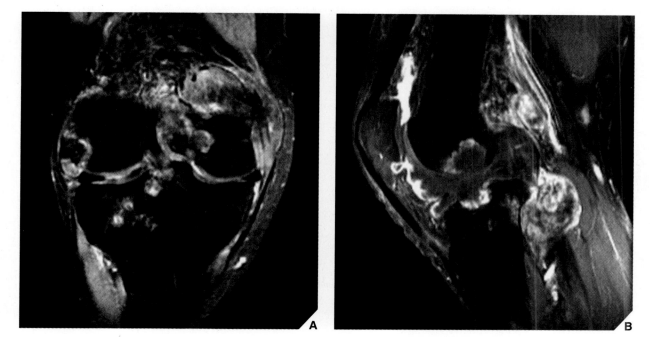

▲
FIGURE 15.19 **MRI of gouty arthritis. (A)** Coronal proton density-weighted fat-suppressed and **(B)** sagittal T1-weighted fat-suppressed contrast enhanced MR images of the right knee of a 53-year-old man show multiple articular and paraarticular erosions associated with intraosseous as well as soft-tissue tophi.

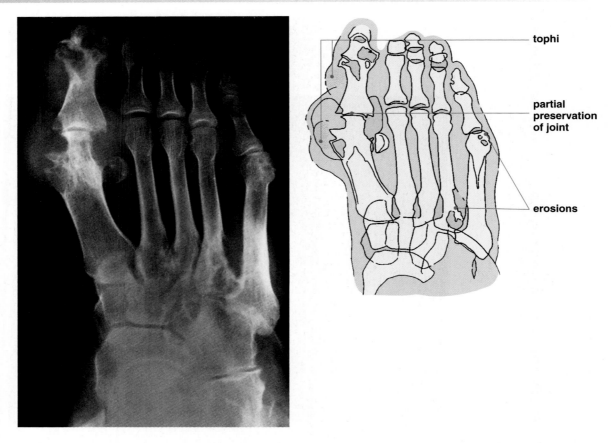

▲
FIGURE 15.20 **Gouty arthritis.** Dorsoplantar radiograph of the left foot of a 62-year-old man with a long history of tophaceous gout shows multiple erosions involving the big and small toes and the base of the fourth and fifth metatarsals. The first metatarsophalangeal joint is partially preserved, a characteristic feature of gouty arthritis. A large soft-tissue mass of the great toe represents a tophus.

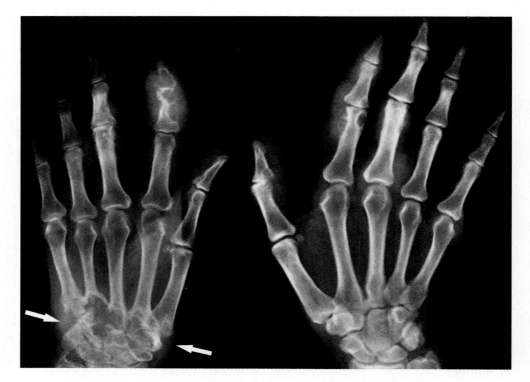

▲
FIGURE 15.21 **Gouty arthritis.** Dorsovolar radiograph of the hands of a 64-year-old woman with gout shows the typical asymmetric distribution of periarticular and articular erosions. Note involvement of the carpometacarpal joints of the right hand (*arrows*), a typical site for gout.

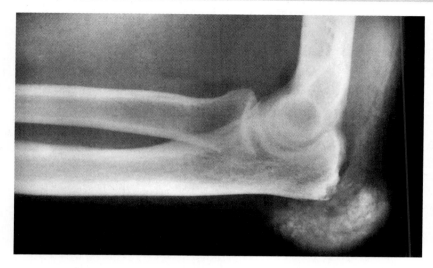

▲
FIGURE 15.22 **Gouty tophus.** Lateral radiograph of the elbow of a 73-year-old man with a 30-year history of gout shows a tophus with dense calcifications adjacent to the olecranon process, which exhibits a small erosion.

CPPD Crystal Deposition Disease

Clinical Features
Resulting from the intraarticular presence of calcium pyrophosphate dihydrate (CPPD) crystals, CPPD crystal deposition disease affects men and women equally; most commonly, patients are middle aged and older. The condition may be asymptomatic, in which case the only radiologic finding may be *chondrocalcinosis* (see later). When symptomatic, it is called *pseudogout*. There is, however, a great deal of confusion about these terms, and they are often misused.

In an effort to explain the relationship between chondrocalcinosis, calcium pyrophosphate arthropathy, and the pseudogout syndrome, Resnick has proposed an integration of these terms under the rubric CPPD crystal deposition disease. *Chondrocalcinosis*, a condition in which calcification of the hyaline (articular) cartilage or fibrocartilage (menisci) occurs, may be seen in other disorders as well, such as gout, hyperparathyroidism, hemochromatosis, hepatolenticular degeneration (Wilson disease), and degenerative joint disease (Table 15.3). *Calcium pyrophosphate arthropathy* refers to CPPD crystal deposition disease affecting the joints and producing structural damage to the articular

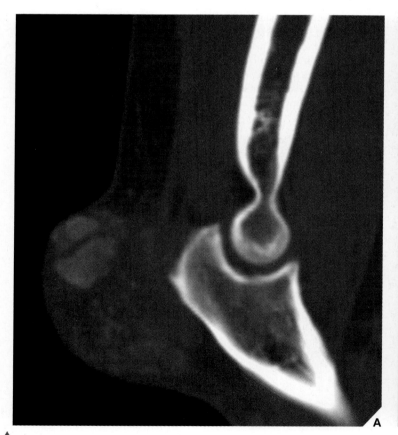
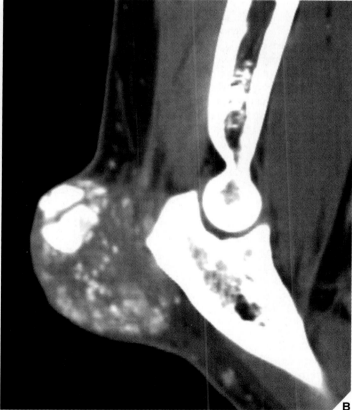

▲
FIGURE 15.23 **CT of gouty tophus.** Sagittal reformatted CT images of the elbow viewed in (**A**) bone and (**B**) soft-tissue window show a large soft-tissue mass with numerous calcifications adjacent to the olecranon process of ulna.

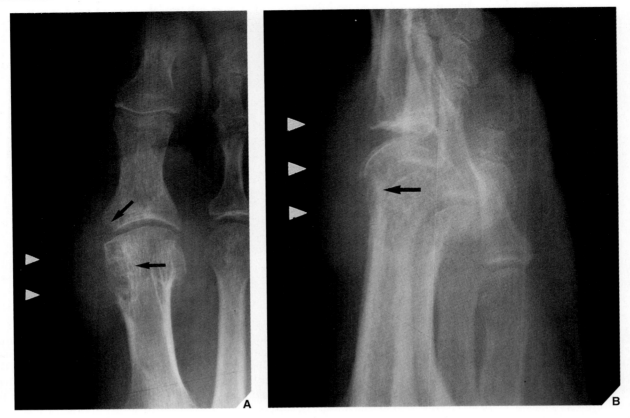

▲
FIGURE 15.24 **Gouty tophus.** Dorsoplantar (**A**) and lateral (**B**) radiographs of the great toe show articular and periarticular erosions (*arrows*) associated with a large tophus on the dorsal aspect of the first metatarsophalangeal joint (*arrow heads*).

cartilage. It displays distinctive radiographic abnormalities such as narrowing of the joint space, subchondral sclerosis, and osteophytosis, similar to osteoarthritis. The *pseudogout syndrome* represents a condition in which symptoms such as acute pain are similar to those seen in gouty arthritis; however, it does not respond to the usual treatment (colchicine) for the latter disease.

Calcium pyrophosphate crystals, the pathogens in pseudogout, range up to 10 μm in length. As in gout, many intracellular crystals are seen during an acute episode. The colors are usually but not always much less intense than urates, that is, they are weakly birefringent. Pyrophosphate crystals are generally chunkier and often show a line down the middle. The most common form of calcium pyrophosphate crystal is a rhomboid. Pyrophosphate crystals are positively birefringent in that they are blue when the longitudinal axis of the crystal is parallel to the slow vibrations axis of the red compensator and yellow when it is perpendicular.

Imaging Features

Radiographically, the arthritic changes encountered in this condition are similar to those seen in osteoarthritis, but the wrist (Fig. 15.25), elbow (Fig. 15.26), shoulder, ankle, and femoropatellar joint compartment (Fig.15.27) are characteristically involved. As mentioned, CPPD crystal

deposition disease is characterized by calcification of the articular cartilage and fibrocartilage; the tendons, ligaments, and joint capsule may exhibit calcifications as well (Figs. 15.28 and 15.29).

Rarely, CPPD deposits can assume the form of bulky tumor-like masses located in the joint and paraarticular soft tissues. In these instances, it may mimic a malignant tumor; hence, this form of CPPD deposition was termed by Sissons and associates, "tumoral calcium pyrophosphate deposition disease." The mineral deposits are associated with a tissue reaction characterized by the presence of histiocytes

TABLE 15.3 **Most Common Causes of Chondrocalcinosis**

Senescent (aging process)	Hyperparathyroidism
Osteoarthritis	Hypophosphatasia
Posttraumatic	Ochronosis
Calcium pyrophosphate arthropathy (CPPD crystal deposition disease)	Oxalosis
	Wilson disease
Gout	Acromegaly
Hemochromatosis	Idiopathic

Modified from Reeder MM, Felson B, 1975, with permission.

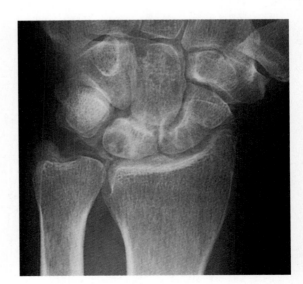

▲
FIGURE 15.25 **CPPD crystal deposition disease.** A 63-year-old man with CPPD crystal deposition disease presented with an acute onset of pain in the wrist. A dorsovolar radiograph shows chondrocalcinosis of the triangular fibrocartilage, cystic changes in the scaphoid and lunate, and narrowing of the radiocarpal joint.

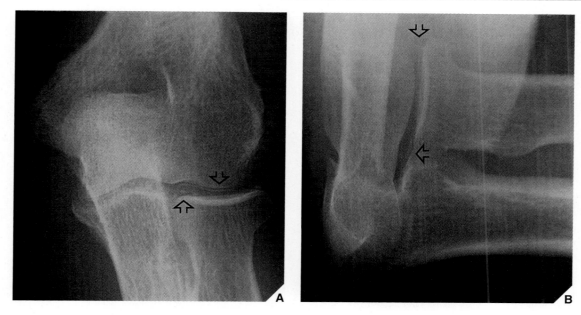

▲
FIGURE 15.26 **CPPD crystal deposition disease. (A)** Anteroposterior and **(B)** radial head–capitellum views of the right elbow of a 52-year-old woman with pseudogout syndrome demonstrate chondrocalcinosis (*open arrows*) but no other alterations of the joint space.

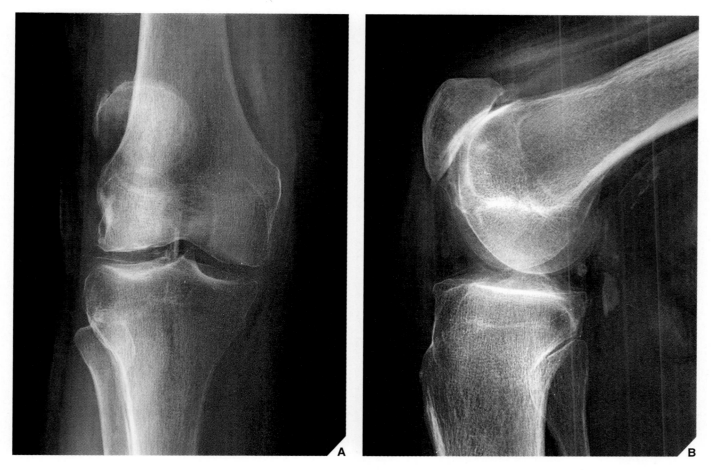

▲
FIGURE 15.27 **CPPD crystal deposition disease. (A)** Anteroposterior and **(B)** lateral radiographs of the right knee of a 58-year-old woman, whose knee joint aspiration revealed CPPD crystals, show chondrocalcinosis and marked narrowing of the femoropatellar joint.

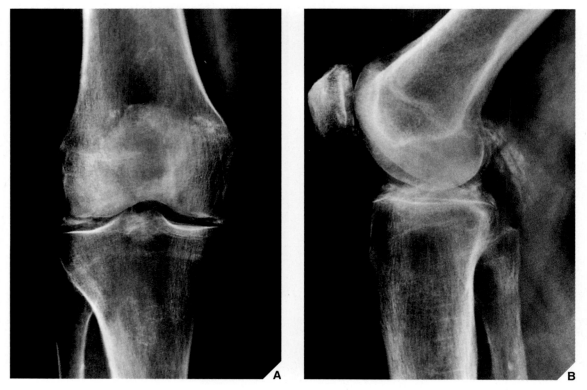

▲
FIGURE 15.28 CPPD crystal deposition disease. A 70-year-old woman presented with acute onset of pain in her right knee and was treated with colchicine for acute gouty arthritis without relief of her pain. Synovial fluid yielded crystals of CPPD. Anteroposterior (**A**) and lateral (**B**) radiographs of the knee demonstrate calcification of the hyaline and fibrocartilage. Capsular calcifications are also apparent, as well as narrowing of the femoropatellar joint compartment, a characteristic feature of CPPD crystal deposition disease.

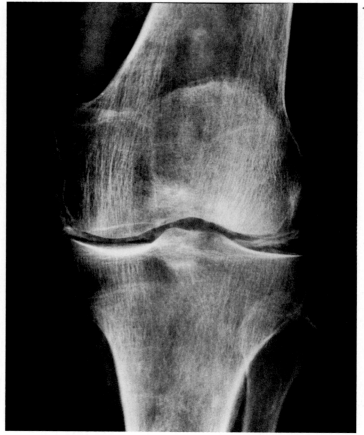

◀ FIGURE 15.29 CPPD crystal deposition disease. A 51-year-old man presented with pain in the left knee. A frontal radiograph shows calcifications of the menisci and articular cartilage. Joint aspiration was diagnostic for CPPD crystal deposition disease.

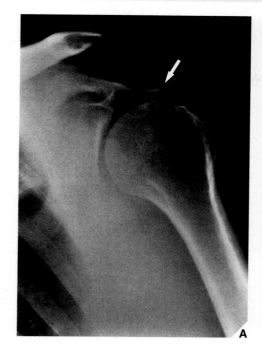 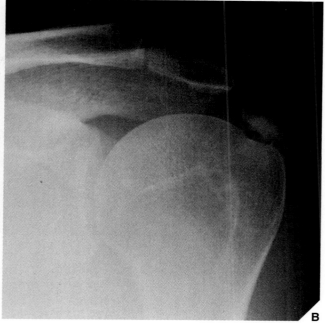

▲
FIGURE 15.30 CHA crystal deposition disease. **(A)** Anteroposterior radiograph of the left shoulder of a 50-year-old woman who had been experiencing pain in this region for several months demonstrates an amorphous, homogenous calcific deposit in the soft tissues at the site of supraspinatus tendon (*arrow*). This finding is typical of CHA crystal deposition disease. **(B)** In another patient, a 38-year-old woman who presented with left shoulder pain, a similar calcific deposit is seen at the site of insertion of the supraspinatus tendon to the greater tuberosity of the humerus.

and multinucleated giant cells, sometimes with bone and cartilage formation. The differential diagnosis should include tumoral calcinosis, a disorder characterized by the presence of single or multiple lobulated cystic masses in the soft tissues, usually near the major joints, containing chalky material consisting of calcium phosphate, calcium carbonate, or hydroxyapatite. The calcified deposits fail to show a crystalline appearance when examined by polarization microscopy. In this condition, the masses are painless and usually occur in children and adolescents, a majority of whom are black.

CHA Crystal Deposition Disease

Resulting from abnormal deposition of calcium hydroxyapatite (CHA) crystals in and around the joints, CHA crystal deposition disease is more common in women and may at times simulate gout or pseudogout syndrome. Acute symptoms include pain, tenderness on palpation, and local swelling and edema. The syndrome may be associated with other disorders, such as scleroderma, dermatomyositis, MCTD, and chronic renal disease, particularly one treated by hemodialysis. Recent investigations suggested a genetic predisposition for this condition. Amor and associates raised the possibility of an inherited defect that might be responsible for the development of CHA crystal deposition disease by demonstrating an increased prevalence of the histocompatibility antigen of HLA-A2 and HLA-BW35 in patients affected by this disorder.

CHA crystals are most frequently deposited in periarticular locations, usually in and around tendons, joint capsule, or bursae. This is the feature that distinguishes the syndrome from CPPD crystal deposition disease, which affects primarily hyaline cartilage and fibrocartilage.

Radiographic features depend on the site of involvement, but usually cloud-like or dense homogeneous calcific deposits are seen around the joint and tendons. The most common location is around the shoulder joint at the site of the supraspinatus tendon (Fig. 15.30).

Hemochromatosis

Hemochromatosis is a rare disorder characterized by iron deposition in various organs, particularly the liver, skin, and pancreas. It may be primary (endogenous or idiopathic), caused by an error in metaboliz-

ing iron, or secondary, caused by iron overload. Idiopathic hemochromatosis may be familial and has been linked with histocompatibility antigens HLA-A3, HLA-B7, and HLA-B14. The secondary form of hemochromatosis is related to iron overload (such as transfusions or dietary intake) and may be associated with alcohol abuse. Hemochromatosis affects men ten times more frequently than women. It is generally diagnosed between the ages of 40 and 60 on the basis of markedly elevated serum iron levels. For confirmation, biopsy of the liver or synovium may be performed. Fifty percent of patients with hemochromatosis will have a slowly progressing arthritis, starting in the small joints of the hands, but eventually the large joints (Fig. 15.31) and intervertebral disks in the cervical and lumbar region may become affected. Some investigators believe that the arthropathy seen in this condition differs from typical degenerative joint disease and warrants classification in the group of metabolic arthritides.

In the hand, the second and third metacarpophalangeal joints are characteristically affected (Fig. 15.32; see also Fig. 13.30), although other small joints such as the interphalangeal and carpal articulations may also be involved. Degenerative changes may also be seen in the shoulders, knees, hips, and ankles. Loss of the articular space, eburnation, subchondral cyst formation, and osteophytosis are the most prominent radiographic features of hemochromatosis. The changes may occasionally mimic those seen in CPPD crystal deposition disease and rheumatoid arthritis.

Alkaptonuria (Ochronosis)

Alkaptonuria is a rare autosomal-recessive inherited disease characterized by the presence of homogentisic acid in the urine that turns black when oxidized. This metabolic abnormality results from the absence of the enzyme homogentisic acid oxidase, which plays a part in the normal degradation process of the aromatic amino acids tyrosine and phenylalanine. As a consequence, there is significant accumulation of homogentisic acid in various organs, with predilection for connective tissues. The genetic defect is mapped to the *HGO* gene located on the arm of chromosome 3q1. The deposition of an abnormal brown-black pigment, a polymer of homogentisic acid, within the intervertebral disks

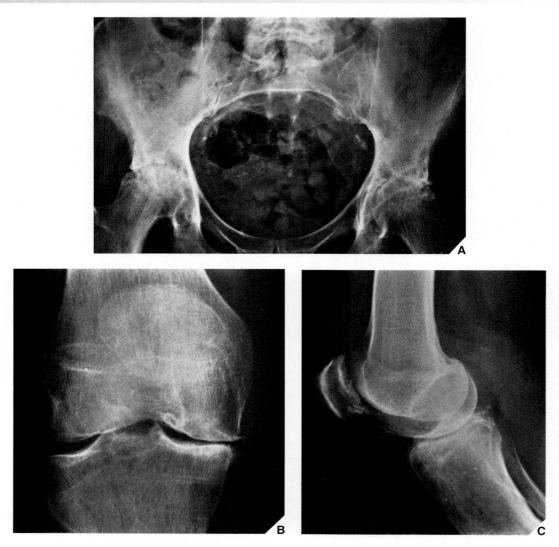

FIGURE 15.31 **Hemochromatosis.** A 67-year-old woman was diagnosed with hemochromatosis arthropathy. (**A**) Anteroposterior radiograph of the pelvis shows advanced arthritis of both hip joints. Severe concentric narrowing of joint space, subchondral sclerosis, and periarticular cysts are typical of hemochromatosis. (**B**) Anteroposterior and (**C**) lateral radiographs of the right knee demonstrate predilection for medial and femoropatellar compartments. Joint space narrowing and marked subarticular sclerosis with small osteophyte formation are characteristic. (From Baker ND, 1986, with permission.)

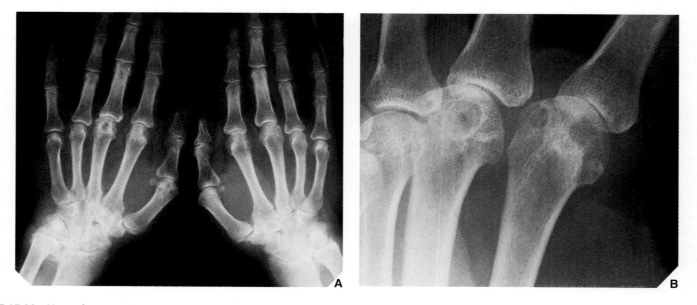

▲
FIGURE 15.32 **Hemochromatosis.** (**A**) A dorsovolar radiograph of both hands of a 45-year-old man shows typical abnormalities of hemochromatosis predominantly affecting wrists and metacarpophalangeal joints. (**B**) A coned-down magnified radiograph of the second and third metacarpophalangeal joints of the right hand demonstrates characteristic involvement of the metacarpal heads.

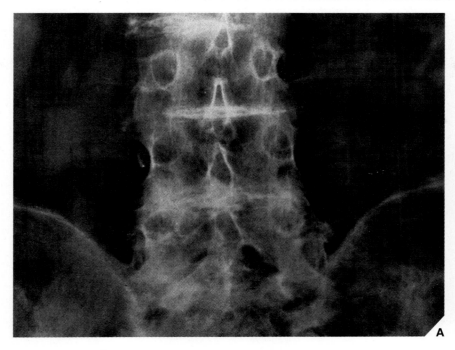
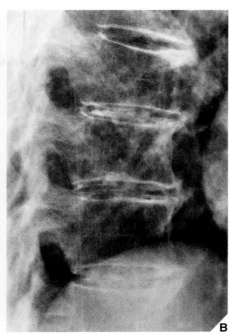

FIGURE 15.33 **Ochronosis.** Anteroposterior radiograph of the lumbar spine (**A**) and lateral (**B**) radiograph of the thoracic spine of a 64-year-old woman with a clinical diagnosis of alkaptonuria demonstrate narrowing of several intervertebral disk spaces associated with marginal anterior osteophytes and moderate osteoporosis. Characteristic calcifications of multiple intervertebral disks are a hallmark of ochronosis. (Courtesy of Dr. J. Tehranzadeh, Orange, California).

and in the articular cartilage is termed ochronosis. This deposition leads to spondylosis and peripheral arthropathy. As a rule, ochronotic arthropathy is a manifestation of long-standing alkaptonuria. The condition affects men and women equally. The clinical signs consist of mild pain and a decreased range of motion in various joints. The radiographic presentation includes dystrophic calcifications, most commonly in the intervertebral disks and the articular cartilage, tendons, and ligaments (Fig. 15.33). Osteoporosis is usually present. Disk spaces are narrowed, with occasional vacuum phenomena. The extraspinal abnormalities are limited to involvement of the sacroiliac joints, the symphysis pubis, and the large peripheral joints, which are likewise narrowed and show periarticular sclerosis with occasional small osteophytes. Tendinous calcifications and ossifications may occur, at times leading to tendon rupture. The radiographic appearance may mimic that of degenerative joint disease or CPPD.

Hyperparathyroidism

Hyperparathyroidism is the result of overactivity of the parathyroid glands, which produce parathormone. Increased production of this hormone is secondary to either hyperplasia of glands or adenoma; only in very rare instances does hyperparathyroidism occur secondary to parathyroid carcinoma. Excessive secretion of parathormone, which acts on the kidneys and bones, leads to disturbances in calcium and phosphorus metabolism, resulting in hypercalcemia, hyperphosphaturia, and hypophosphatemia. Renal excretion of calcium and phosphate is increased, and serum levels of calcium are elevated while those of phosphorous are reduced; serum levels of alkaline phosphatase are also elevated. Most characteristic features of subperiosteal and subchondral bone resorption appear at the margins of certain joints, thus accounting for articular manifestation or "arthropathy" of hyperparathyroidism. This is frequently noted at the acromioclavicular joint, at the sternoclavicular and sacroiliac articulations (Fig. 15.34), at the symphysis pubis, and sometimes at the metacarpophalangeal and interphalangeal joints. The erosions can mimic rheumatoid arthritis, although they are usually asymptomatic, involve more commonly distal interphalangeal joints (Fig. 15.35), and almost invariably are associated with subperiosteal bone resorption, typical for hyperparathyroidism.

The other feature of hyperparathyroidism arthropathy is chondrocalcinosis, which involves calcium deposition in the articular cartilage and fibrocartilage. This finding may mimic degenerative joint disease and CPPD crystal deposition arthropathy. It may be distinguished from the calcification of degenerative joint disease by the absence of arthritic changes in the joint and from CPPD crystal deposition by the presence of osteopenia and other typical features of hyperparathyroidism. A more detailed description of hyperparathyroidism is provided in Part VI: Metabolic and Endocrine Disorders.

Acromegaly

Degenerative joint changes in acromegaly are the result of hypertrophy of articular cartilage, which is not adequately nourished by synovial fluid because of its abnormal thickness.

After initial overgrowth of cartilage, as reflected by widening of the radiographic joint spaces in the hand, particularly at the

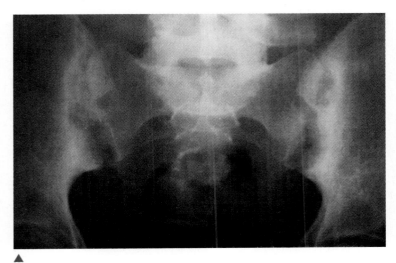

FIGURE 15.34 **Hyperparathyroidism arthropathy.** Subchondral resorption resulted in widening of the sacroiliac joints in this patient with hyperparathyroidism arthropathy.

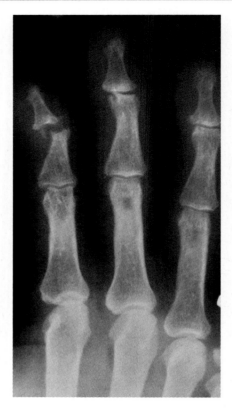

▲
FIGURE 15.35 Hyperparathyroidism arthropathy. Typical hyperparathyroidism arthropathy at the distal interphalangeal joints of the index and middle fingers. Note also beginning of the resorption of the distal tufts (acroosteolysis).

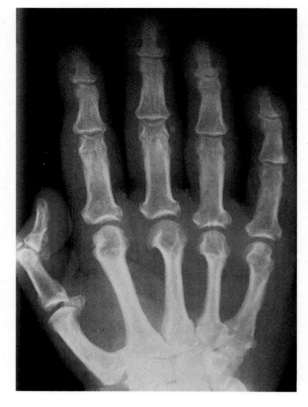

▲
FIGURE 15.36 Acromegalic arthropathy. Characteristic abnormalities in acromegalic hand include prominence of the soft tissue, enlargement of the tufts and bases of the distal phalanges, widening of the metacarpophalangeal joints, and beak-like osteophytes at the radial aspect of the metacarpal heads. Note also markedly enlarged sesamoid bone at the first metacarpophalangeal joint.

metacarpophalangeal joints (Fig. 15.36), a later manifestation of this disorder is thinning of the joint cartilages with osteophyte formation caused by secondary osteoarthritis. Arthritis-like symptoms including pain and stiffness are common, and limitation of joint motion becomes apparent. Besides articulations of the hands, large joints such as the hip, knee, and even shoulder or elbow may be affected. In particular, beak-like osteophytes on the inferior aspect of the humeral head, the lateral aspect of the acetabulum, the superior margin of the symphysis pubis, and radial aspects of the heads of metacarpals are characteristic (see Fig. 13.29).

Miscellaneous Conditions

Amyloidosis

Amyloidosis is a systematic disorder characterized by the infiltration of various organs by a homogeneous eosinophilic material consisting of protein fibers in a ground substance of mucopolysaccharides. Amyloid arthropathy is a sign of acquired idiopathic systemic amyloidosis and is a condition that results in noninflammatory arthropathy. Clinically, it bears a striking resemblance to rheumatoid arthritis, because the joints are stiff and painful and the arthropathy is bilateral and symmetric. There is a predilection for large joints such as the hips, knees, shoulders, and elbows. Subcutaneous nodules are noted over the extensor surfaces of the forearm and dorsum of the hand, often mimicking the rheumatoid nodules. Another characteristic feature is the massive involvement of the soft tissues, giving the patient an almost pathognomonic appearance known as "shoulder-pad sign" or "football player shoulders." Carpal tunnel syndrome is frequently an associated abnormality.

The bone abnormalities and arthropathy associated with deposition of B_2-microglobulin (B_2-MG) amyloid are well-recognized complications of long-term hemodialysis and chronic renal failure. B_2-MG, a low-molecular-weight serum protein, is not filtered by standard dialysis

membranes. It therefore accumulates in the bones, joints, and soft tissues. Clinically, characteristic pain and decreased joint mobility occur in the shoulders, hips, and knees.

Regardless of cause, imaging studies show massive accumulation of amyloid around the joints, and there is invasion of the periarticular tissue, capsule, and joint. Also, deposits can be seen in the synovium. The articular ends of the bone can be destroyed, and both subluxations and pathologic fractures are frequently encountered. In addition, focal osteolytic lesions, particularly in the bones of the upper extremities and in the proximal ends of the femora, can be seen (Fig. 15.37).

Multicentric Reticulohistiocytosis

Multicentric reticulohistiocytosis is a rare systemic disorder of unknown cause seen in adulthood and is characterized by the proliferation of the histiocytes in the skin, the mucosa, the subcutaneous tissue, and the synovium. The disease has been also called lipoid dermatoarthritis, reticulohistiocytoma, lipid rheumatism, giant cell reticulohistiocytosis, giant cell histiocytoma, and giant cell histiocytosis. Women are more frequently affected than men. In approximately 60% to 70% of patients, polyarthralgia is the first manifestation of the disease. Clinical findings, like those of rheumatoid arthritis, consist of soft-tissue swelling, stiffness, and tenderness. Unlike rheumatoid arthritis, however, the distal interphalangeal joints are most frequently affected. Occasionally, the articular lesions may be marked by severe destruction similar to arthritis mutilans of rheumatoid arthritis or psoriatic arthritis (Fig. 15.38). The characteristic absence of significant periarticular osteoporosis distinguishes this disorder from the inflammatory arthritides, and there is also no periosteal new bone formation, which distinguishes it from psoriatic arthritis or juvenile rheumatoid arthritis. Lack of osteophytes and interphalangeal ankylosis, and the presence of soft-tissue nodules and atlantoaxial abnormalities including subluxation and erosion of the odontoid process distinguish this arthropathy from erosive osteoarthritis. At

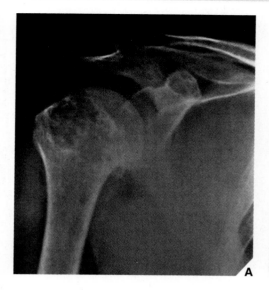
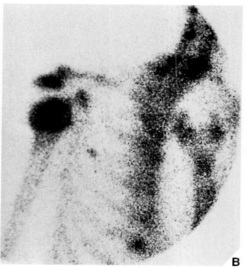

FIGURE 15.37 Amyloidosis. (A) Anteroposterior radiograph of the right shoulder of an 80-year-old man with amyloidosis demonstrates a moderate degree of juxtaarticular osteoporosis, soft-tissue swelling, and a large osteolytic lesion in the humeral head. The glenohumeral joint space is relatively well-preserved. **(B)** Radionuclide bone scan shows an increased uptake of technetium-labeled methylene diphosphonate (MDP) around the shoulder. (Courtesy of Dr. A. Norman, New York)

times, the pattern of bone erosions with sclerotic margins and overhanging edges may mimic those of gout (Fig. 15.39). Unlike gout, however, there is symmetrical distribution of the lesions in the hands and feet and lack of calcification within soft-tissue nodules.

Hemophilia

Hemophilia A is an inherited bleeding disorder characterized by an anomaly of blood coagulation caused by functional deficiency of antihemophilic factor (AHF) VIII. It is inherited as an X-linked recessive trait and essentially occurs only in males, although female carriers transmit the abnormal gene. In hemophilia B, also known as "Christmas disease,"

there is a deficiency of plasma thromboplastin component, factor IX. This disorder may also affect females.

The articular changes in hemophilia most often occur in the first and second decades of life and are secondary to chronic repetitive bleeding into the joints and bones. Repeated episodes of intraarticular bleeding and inflammatory tissue response cause proliferation of synovium and erosion of cartilage and subchondral bone. Usually there is no problem in the clinical recognition of this disorder; however, the changes of hemophilic arthropathy may radiographically mimic those of rheumatoid arthritis, particularly juvenile rheumatoid arthritis (Fig. 15.40). Cartilage destruction, joint space narrowing, and erosions of the articular surfaces are identical to those seen in rheumatoid arthritis

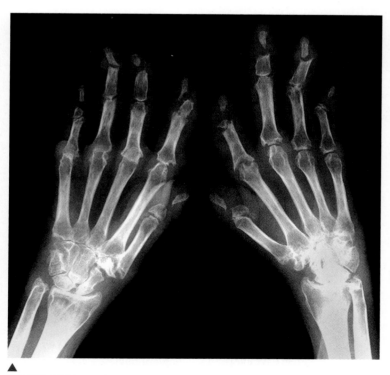

FIGURE 15.38 Multicentric reticulohistiocytosis. Dorsovolar radiograph of both hands of a 57-year-old woman with long-standing polyarthralgia, soft-tissue swelling, and deformities of the fingers, demonstrates severe destruction of multiple carpometacarpal, metacarpophalangeals, and interphalangeals joints similar to those seen in rheumatoid or psoriatic arthritis.

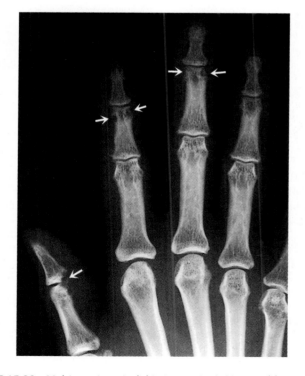

FIGURE 15.39 Multicentric reticulohistiocytosis. A 46-year-old woman with multicentric reticulohistiocytosis. Note sharply marginated erosions at the distal interphalangeal joints (*arrows*) resembling gout.

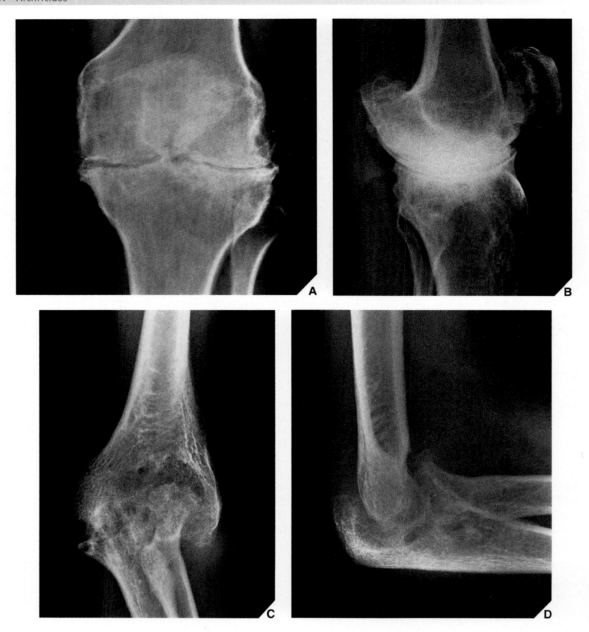

FIGURE 15.40   Hemophilic arthropathy. A 42-year-old man with hemophilia had several intraarticular bleeding episodes in his life. Anteroposterior (**A**) and lateral (**B**) radiographs of his left knee demonstrate advanced hemophilic arthropathy. Note the involvement of all three joint compartments. Similar destructive changes in the left elbow are demonstrated on anteroposterior (**C**) and lateral (**D**) radiographs of this joint.

(Fig. 15.41, see also Figs. 12.19 and 12.20). The knee, ankle, and elbow are the most frequently involved articulations, and this involvement is usually bilateral. In the knee, the radiographic features include periarticular osteoporosis, joint effusion (hemarthrosis), overgrowth of femoral condyles with widening of the intercondylar notch, and squaring of the patella. Frequently, multiple subchondral cysts and articular erosions are evident. In the late stages of disease, the uniform narrowing of the joint space and secondary osteoarthritic changes may be observed. The differential diagnosis from juvenile rheumatoid arthritis is based on evidence that there is no bony ankylosis, no evidence of growth inhibition, and frequent presence of pseudotumors.

Jaccoud Arthritis

Jaccoud arthritis is related to repeated attacks of rheumatic fever and migratory arthralgias. Usually there is complete recovery, but residual stiffness in metacarpophalangeal joints may develop with subsequent attacks. The lesion appears to be periarticular rather than articular, and the changes are caused by mild flexion at the metacarpophalangeal joints with ulnar deviation, most notably in the fourth and fifth fingers, although any finger may be affected. The articular changes are not erosive and patients can physically correct the deformity, particularly in the early course of the disease. The syndrome is rare and not well recognized in the United States.

Arthritis Associated With Acquired Immunodeficiency Syndrome

Recently, an increased prevalence of rheumatologic disorders has been described in patients with human immunodeficiency virus (HIV) infection. Berman and colleagues stated that 71% of patients infected with HIV virus had rheumatic symptoms, including arthralgias, Reiter syndrome, psoriatic arthritis, myositis, vasculitis, and undifferentiated spondyloarthropathy. Solomon and colleagues found that patients with HIV infection demonstrated a 144-fold increase in the prevalence of Reiter syndrome and a 10-fold to 40-fold increase in the prevalence of psoriasis compared

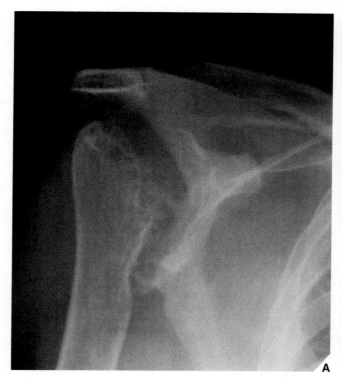
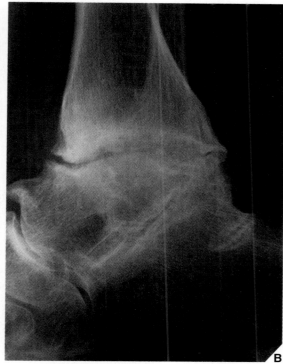

▲ **FIGURE 15.41 Hemophilic arthropathy. (A)** Anteroposterior radiograph of the right shoulder and **(B)** lateral radiograph of the left ankle of a 49-year-old man with hemophilia A show destructive arthropathy of the glenohumeral, ankle, and subtalar joints.

with the general population. It is interesting to note that arthritis was seen during various stages of HIV infection and often preceded clinical manifestations of the acquired immunodeficiency syndrome (AIDS). The arthritis was more severe and was unresponsive to conventional treatment with nonsteroidal antiinflammatory medications. A few hypotheses have been suggested to explain the coexistence of inflammatory arthritis and HIV infection. One is that Reiter syndrome entails an interaction between a genetic predisposition (e.g., HLA-B27 locus) and environmental factors, most often venereal infections. The immune system also plays a role in the pathogenesis of Reiter syndrome. Likewise, the pathogenesis of psoriatic arthritis may entail genetic predisposition (e.g., HLA-B27 or HLA-B38 loci). Because HIV infection is commonly followed by the development of immunodeficiency, it is possible that the altered immune mechanism noted in patients with AIDS triggered the onset of Reiter syndrome or psoriatic arthritis in genetically predisposed patients. The second hypothesis is that HIV-related immunodeficiency causes susceptibility to infection with a variety of bacterial and viral organisms, which in turn trigger the onset of arthritis in a genetically predisposed patient. A third hypothesis is that there may be yet-undiscovered causative factors that predispose an individual to arthritis when exposed to HIV. Finally, the arthritis may reflect the direct action of HIV infection on synovium. As Rosenberg and colleagues have pointed out, radiographic documentation of seronegative arthritis should raise the possibility of HIV-associated arthritis as part of the differential diagnosis, particularly in patients with known risk factors for HIV infection.

Infectious Arthritis

Most infectious arthritides demonstrate a positive radionuclide bone scan, particularly when using indium-labeled white cells as a tracer (see Chapter 2), and they also show a very similar radiographic picture, including joint effusion and destruction of cartilage and subchondral bone with consequent joint space narrowing. However, certain clinical and radiographic features are characteristic of individual infectious processes

as demonstrated at various target sites. In general, however, infectious arthritis is characterized by the complete destruction of both articular ends of the bones forming the joint; all communicating joint compartments are invariably involved, with diffuse osteoporosis, joint effusion, and periarticular soft-tissue swelling. A detailed description of pyogenic arthritis, tuberculous arthritis, fungal arthritis, and other infectious arthritides caused by viruses and spirochetes is provided in Part V: Infections.

PRACTICAL POINTS TO REMEMBER

Connective Tissue Arthropathies

[1] SLE is characterized by flexible joint contractures and malalignments of the metacarpophalangeal and proximal interphalangeal joints. These abnormalities are better demonstrated on the lateral radiographs, because they can easily be reduced during positioning of the hand for the dorsovolar view.

[2] Osteonecrosis is a frequent complication of SLE.

[3] Radiographically, the musculoskeletal abnormalities associated with scleroderma are recognized by:
  • atrophy of the soft tissues, particularly the tips of fingers
  • resorption of the distal phalanges (acroosteolysis)
  • subcutaneous and periarticular calcifications
  • destructive changes in the interphalangeal joints.

[4] In scleroderma, corroborative findings are seen in the gastrointestinal tract, where characteristically there is:
  • dilatation and hypomotility of the esophagus
  • dilatation of the duodenum and small bowel, with a pseudoobstruction pattern
  • pseudodiverticula of the colon.

[5] MCTD is characterized by the clinical and radiologic features that combine the findings of SLE, scleroderma, dermatomyositis, and rheumatoid arthritis.

Metabolic and Endocrine Arthritides

[1] Gout is a metabolic disorder characterized by recurrent episodes of arthritis associated with the presence of monosodium urate monohydrate crystals in the synovial fluid.

[2] Hyperuricemia may result from either increased uric acid production or decreased renal excretion.

[3] Gouty arthritis can be recognized radiographically by:
- sharply marginated periarticular and articular erosions, with an "overhanging edge" phenomenon
- partial preservation of the joint space
- asymmetric joint involvement
- asymmetric distribution of tophi
- the absence of osteoporosis.

[4] CPPD crystal deposition disease consists of three distinct entities:
- chondrocalcinosis
- calcium pyrophosphate arthropathy
- the pseudogout syndrome.

[5] The presence of intraarticular crystals and calcifications of hyaline and fibrocartilage, occasionally associated with painful attacks similar to gout, are characteristic features of CPPD crystal deposition disease.

[6] Chondrocalcinosis may also be seen in other conditions such as gout, hyperparathyroidism, hemochromatosis, ochronosis, oxalosis, Wilson disease, acromegaly, and degenerative joint disease.

[7] CHA crystal deposition disease results from abnormal deposition of mineral crystals in and around the joints. The most common location is around the shoulder joint, at the site of supraspinatus tendon.

[8] Hemochromatosis is a disorder resulting from an error of metabolism of iron or caused by iron overload. The arthropathy starts in the small joints of the hand with characteristic involvement of the heads of second and third metacarpals.

[9] Alkaptonuria (ochronosis) is characterized by narrowing of the intervertebral disk spaces, disk calcification and ossification, involvement of sacroiliac joints and symphysis pubis, and joint space narrowing with periarticular osteosclerosis. The radiographic appearance may occasionally mimic degenerative joint disease or CPPD crystal deposition disease.

[10] Hyperparathyroidism arthropathy results from subperiosteal and subchondral resorption at the site of small joints of the hand. This accounts for articular manifestation of this disorder.

[11] Acromegaly arthropathy is the result of overgrowth of the articular cartilage and secondary degenerative changes (secondary osteoarthritis). The characteristic findings include:
- beak-like osteophytes of the radial aspects of the metacarpal heads
- beak-like osteophytes of the inferior aspects of the humeral heads
- widening of the radiographic joint spaces.

Miscellaneous Arthropathies

[1] Amyloid arthropathy is a noninflammatory symmetric polyarthritis. It may complicate long-term hemodialysis and chronic renal failure. The articular ends of the bone can be destroyed and subluxations and pathologic fractures occur. Focal osteolytic lesions, particularly of the bones of the upper extremities and in the proximal ends of the femora, can be seen.

[2] Multicentric reticulohistiocytosis is characterized by proliferation of histiocytes in the skin, mucosa, subcutaneous tissue, and synovium. This may lead to severe articular destruction, but there is neither periarticular osteoporosis nor periosteal bone formation. The radiographic appearance may simulate gouty, rheumatoid, or psoriatic arthritis.

[3] The articular changes in hemophilia are due to repetitive bleeding into the joints and bone. The radiographic presentation is similar to that of juvenile rheumatoid arthritis. In the bones, pseudotumors are frequently encountered.

[4] Jaccoud arthritis is a poorly defined entity resulting in periarticular stiffness in patients with repeated attacks of rheumatic fever. The articular changes are not erosive.

[5] There is an increased prevalence of rheumatologic disorders in patients with AIDS, particularly Reiter syndrome, psoriatic arthritis, and vasculitis.

[6] Infectious arthritis is characterized by the complete destruction of both articular ends of the bones forming the joint. All communicating joint compartments are invariably involved, with diffuse osteoporosis, joint effusion, and periarticular soft-tissue swelling.

SUGGESTED READINGS

Adamson TC III, Resnik CS, Guerra J Jr, Vint VC, Weisman MH, Resnick D. Hand and wrist arthropathies of hemochromatosis and calcium pyrophosphate deposition disease: distinct radiographic features. *Radiology* 1983;147:377–381.

Amor B, Cherot A. Delbarre F, Nunez Roldan A, Hors J. Hydroxyapatite rheumatism and HLA markers. *J Rheumatol* 1977;4(Suppl 3):101–104.

Arnett FC, Reveille JD, Duvic M. Psoriasis and psoriatic arthritis associated with human immunodeficiency virus infection. *Rheum Dis Clin North Am* 1991;17:59–78.

Baker ND. Hemochromatosis. In: Taveras JM, Ferrucci JT, eds. *Radiology—diagnosis, imaging, intervention*. Philadelphia: JB Lippincott; 1986:1–6.

Baker ND, Jahss MH, Leventhal GH. Unusual involvement of the feet in hemochromatosis. *Foot Ankle* 1984;4:212–215.

Barrow MV, Holubar K. Multicentric reticulohistiocytosis. A review of 33 patients. *Medicine* 1969;48:287–305.

Barthelemy CR, Nakayama DA, Carrera GF, Lightfoot RW Jr, Wortmann RL. Gouty arthritis: a prospective radiographic evaluation of sixty patients. *Skeletal Radiol* 1984;11:1–8.

Beltran J, Marty-Delfaut E, Bencardino J, et al. Chondrocalcinosis of the hyaline cartilage of the knee: MRI manifestations. *Skeletal Radiol* 1998;27:369–374.

Berman A, Espinoza LR, Diaz JD, et al. Rheumatic manifestations of human immunodeficiency virus infections. *Am J Med* 1988;85:59–64.

Bonavita JA, Dalinka MK, Schumacher HR Jr. Hydroxyapatite deposition disease. *Radiology* 1980;134:621–625.

Boskey AL, Vigorita VJ, Sencer O, Stuchin SA, Lane JM. Chemical, microscopic, and ultrastructural characterization of the mineral deposits in tumoral calcinosis. *Clin Orthop* 1983;178:258–269.

Brower AC, Resnick D, Karlin C, Piper S. Unusual articular changes of the hand in scleroderma. *Skeletal Radiol* 1979;4:119–123.

Burke BJ, Escobedo EM, Wilson AJ, Hunter JC. Chondrocalcinosis mimicking a meniscal tear on MR imaging. *Am J Roentgenol* 1998;170:69–70.

Bywaters EGL, Dixon ASJ, Scott JT. Joint lesions of hyperparathyroidism. *Ann Rheum Dis* 1963;22:171–187.

Calabrese LH. The rheumatic manifestations of infection with human immunodeficiency virus. *Semin Arthritis Rheum* 1989;18:225–239.

Campbell SM. Gout: how presentation, diagnosis, and treatment differ in the elderly. *Geriatrics* 1988;43:71–77.

Chen C, Chandnani VP, Kang HS, Resnick D, Sartoris DJ, Haller J. Scapholunate advanced collapse: a common wrist abnormality in calcium pyrophosphate dihydrate crystal deposition disease. *Radiology* 1990;177:459–461.

Chen CKH, Yeh LR, Pan H-B, Yang CF, Lu YC, Resnick D. Intra-articular gouty tophi of the knee: CT and MR imaging in 12 patients. *Skeletal Radiol* 1999;28:75–80.

Chung CB, Mohana-Borges A, Pathria M. Tophaceous gout in an amputation stump in a patient with chronic myelogenous leukemia. *Skeletal Radiol* 2003;32:429–431.

Dalinka MK, Reginato AJ, Golden DA. Calcium deposition diseases. *Semin Roentgenol* 1982;17:39–48.

Escobedo EM, Hunter JC, Zink-Brody GC, Andress DL. Magnetic resonance imaging of dialysis-related amyloidosis of the shoulder and hip. *Skeletal Radiol* 1996;25:41–48.

Fam AG, Topp JR, Stein HB, Little AH. Clinical and roentgenographic aspects of pseudogout: a study of 50 cases and a review. *Can Med Assoc J* 1981;124:545–551.

Gaary E, Gorlin JB, Jaramillo D. Pseudotumor and arthropathy in the knees of a hemophiliac. *Skeletal Radiol* 1996;25:85–87.

Goldman AB, Pavlov H, Bullough P. Case report 137. Primary amyloidosis involving the skeletal system. *Skeletal Radiol* 1981;6:69–74.

Grossman RE, Hensley GT. Bone lesions in primary amyloidosis. *Am J Roentgenol* 1967;101:872–875.

Hayes CW, Conway WF. Calcium hydroxyapatite deposition disease. *Radiographics* 1990;10:1031–1048.

Hirsch JH, Killien FC, Troupin RH. The arthropathy of hemochromatosis. *Radiology* 1976;118:591–596.

Jensen PS. Chondrocalcinosis and other calcifications. *Radiol Clin North Am* 1988;26:1315–1325.

Justesen P, Andersen PE Jr. Radiologic manifestations in alkaptonuria. *Skeletal Radiol* 1984;11:204–208.

Laborde JM, Green DL, Ascari AD, Muir A. Arthritis in hemochromatosis. *J Bone Joint Surg [Am]* 1977;59A:1103–1107.

La Montagna G, Sodano A, Capurro V, Malesci D, Valentini G. The arthropathy of systemic sclerosis: a 12 month prospective clinical and imaging study. *Skeletal Radiol* 2005;34:35–41.

Lawson JP, Steere AC. Lyme arthritis: radiologic findings. *Radiology* 1985; 154:37–43.

Lee DJ, Sartoris DJ. Musculoskeletal manifestations of human immunodeficiency virus infection: review of imaging characteristics. *Radiol Clin North Am* 1994;32:399–411.

Maclachlan J, Gough-Palmer A, Hargunani R, Farrant J, Holloway B. Hemophilia imaging: a review. *Skeletal Radiol* 2009;38:949–957.

Major NM, Tehranzadeh J. Musculoskeletal manifestations of AIDS. *Radiol Clin North Am* 1997;35:1167–1189.

Mannoni A, Selvi E, Lorenzini S, et al. Alkaptonuria, ochronosis, and ochronotic arthropathy. *Sem Arthritis Rheum* 2004;33:239–248.

Martel W. The overhanging margin of bone: a roentgenologic manifestation of gout. *Radiology* 1968;91:755–756.

Martel W, McCarter DK, Solsky MA, et al. Further observation of the arthropathy of calcium pyrophosphate dihydrate crystal deposition disease. *Radiology* 1981;141:1–15.

McCarty DJ. Calcium pyrophosphate dihydrate crystal deposition disease: pseudogout—articular chondrocalcinosis. In: McCarty DJ, ed. *Arthritis and allied conditions: a textbook of rheumatology*, 11th ed. Philadelphia: Lea & Febiger; 1989:1714–1720.

McCarty DJ Jr, Haskin ME. The roentgenographic aspects of pseudogout (articular chondrocalcinosis). An analysis of 20 cases. *Am J Roentgenol* 1963;90:1248–1257.

Melton JW 3rd, Irby R. Multicentric reticulohistiocytosis. *Arthritis Rheum* 1972;15:221–226.

Misra R, Darton K, Jewkes RF, Black CM, Maini RN. Arthritis in scleroderma. *Br J Rheumatol* 1995;34:831–837.

Reeder MM, Felson B. *Gamuts in radiology*. Cincinnati: Audiovisual Radiology of Cincinnati; 1975:D142–143.

Resnik CS, Resnick D. Crystal deposition disease. *Semin Arthritis Rheum* 1983;12:390–403.

Resnick D. Calcium hydroxyapatite crystal deposition disease. In: Resnick D, ed. *Diagnosis of bone and joint disorders*, 3rd ed. Philadelphia: WB Saunders; 1995:1615–1648.

Resnick D. Hemochromatosis and Wilson's disease. In: Resnick D, ed. *Diagnosis of bone and joint disorders*, 3rd ed. Philadelphia: WB Saunders; 1995:1649–1669.

Resnick D. Alkaptonuria. In: Resnick D, ed. *Diagnosis of bone and joint disorders*, 3rd ed. Philadelphia: WB Saunders; 1995:1670–1685.

Resnick D. Bleeding disorders. In: Resnick D, ed. *Diagnosis of bone and joint disorders*, 4th ed. Philadelphia: WB Saunders; 2002;2346–2373.

Resnick D, Niwayama G. *Diagnosis of bone and joint disorders*, 3rd ed. Philadelphia: WB Saunders; 1995:1511–1555.

Resnick D, Niwayama G. Calcium pyrophosphate dihydrate (CPPD) crystal deposition disease. In: Resnick D, ed. *Diagnosis of bone and joint disorders*, 3rd ed. Philadelphia: WB Saunders; 1995:1556–1614.

Resnick D, Niwayama G, Goergen TC, et al. Clinical, radiographic and pathologic abnormalities in calcium pyrophosphate dihydrate crystal deposition disease (CPPD): pseudogout. *Radiology* 1977;122:1–15.

Rosenberg ZS, Norman A, Solomon G. Arthritis associated with HIV infection: radiographic manifestations. *Radiology* 1989;173:171–176.

Ross LV, Ross GJ, Mesgarzadeh M, Edmonds PR, Bonakdarpur A. Hemodialysis-related amyloidomas of bone. *Radiology* 1991;178:263–265.

Sharp GC, Irvin WS, Tan EM, Gould RG, Holman HR. Mixed connective tissue disease—an apparently distinct rheumatic disease syndrome associated with a specific antibody to an extractable nuclear antigen (ENA). *Am J Med* 1972;52:148–159.

Sissons HA, Steiner GC, Bonar F, May F, Rosenberg ZS, Samuels H, Present D. Tumoral calcium pyrophosphate deposition disease. *Skeletal Radiol* 1989;18:79–87.

Steinbach LS, Tehranzadeh J, Fleckenstein J, Vanarthos WJ, Pais MJ. Human immunodeficiency virus infection: musculoskeletal manifestations. *Radiology* 1993;186:833–838.

Steinbach LS, Resnick D. Calcium pyrophosphate dihydrate crystal deposition disease revisited. *Radiology* 1996;200:1–9.

Stoker DJ, Murray RO. Skeletal changes in hemophilia and other bleeding disorders. *Semin Roentgenol* 1974;9:185–193.

Tehranzadeh J, Steinbach LS. *Musculoskeletal manifestations of AIDS*. St. Louis: Warren H. Green; 1994.

Udoff EJ, Genant HK, Kozin F, Ginsberg M. Mixed connective tissue disease: the spectrum of radiographic manifestations. *Radiology* 1977;124:613–618.

Yamada T, Kurohori YN, Kashiwazaki S, Fujibayashi M, Ohkawa T. MRI of multicentric reticulohistiocytosis. *J Comput Assist Tomogr* 1996;20:838–840.

Yang BY, Sartoris DJ, Djukic S, Resnick D, Clopton P. Distribution of calcification in the triangular fibrocartilage region in 181 patients with calcium pyrophosphate dihydrate crystal deposition disease. *Radiology* 1995;196:547–550.

Yu JS, Chung CB, Recht M, Dailiana T, Jurdi R. MR imaging of tophaceous gout. *Am J Roentgenol* 1997;168:523–527.

TUMORS AND TUMOR-LIKE LESIONS

CHAPTER
16

Radiologic Evaluation of Tumors and Tumor-like Lesions

Classification of Tumors and Tumor-like Lesions

Tumors, including tumor-like lesions, can generally be divided into two groups: benign and malignant. The latter group can be further sub-classified into primary malignant tumors, secondary malignant tumors (from the transformation of benign conditions), and metastatic tumors (Fig. 16.1). All of these lesions can be still further classified according to their tissue of origin (Table 16.1). Table 16.2 lists benign conditions that have the potential for malignant transformation.

To understand the terminology applied to tumors and tumor-like lesions of the bone, it is important to redefine certain terms pertinent to lesions and their location in the bone. The term *tumor* generally means *mass*; in common radiologic and orthopedic parlance, however, it is the equivalent of the term *neoplasm*. By definition, a neoplasm, ruled by an uncontrolled process of aberrant cellular and morphologic mechanisms, demonstrates autonomous growth; if in addition it produces local or remote metastases, it is defined as a *malignant neoplasm* or *malignant tumor*. Beyond this (and not dealt with in this chapter) are specific histopathologic criteria for defining a tumor as benign or malignant. It is nevertheless worth mentioning that certain giant cell tumors, despite a "benign" histopathology, may produce distant metastases, and that certain cartilage tumors, despite adhering to a "benign" histopathologic pattern, can behave locally like malignant neoplasms, even though this is detectable only radiologically. Moreover, certain lesions discussed here and termed *tumor-like lesions* are not true neoplasms, but rather have a developmental or inflammatory origin. They are included in this chapter because they display an imaging pattern that is almost indistinguishable from that of true neoplasms. Their cause is, in some cases, still being debated.

Equally important is the redefinition of certain terms pertinent to the location of a lesion in the bone. In the growing skeleton, one can clearly distinguish the epiphysis, growth plate, metaphysis, and diaphysis (Fig. 16.2A), and when lesions are located at these sites they are named accordingly. The greatest confusion is in the use of the term *metaphysis*. The metaphysis is a histologically very thin zone of active bone growth, adjacent to the physis (growth plate). Consequently, for a lesion to be called metaphyseal in location, it must extend into and abut the growth plate. However, it is customary—however incorrect—to use the same term for locating a lesion after skeletal maturity has occurred.

By the time of maturity, the growth plate is scarred, and neither the epiphysis nor metaphysis remains. More proper and less confusing would be a terminology (Fig. 16.2B) such as *articular end of the bone* and *shaft* for locating lesions in the bone whose growth plate has been obliterated and whose metaphysis has ceased to exist. Some other terms used to describe the location of bone lesions are illustrated in Figure 16.3.

Radiologic Imaging Modalities

In general, the imaging of musculoskeletal neoplasms can be considered from three standpoints: detection, diagnosis (and differential diagnosis), and staging (Fig. 16.4). The detection of a bone or a soft-tissue tumor does not always require the expertise of a radiologist. The clinical history and the physical examination are often sufficient to raise the suspicion of a tumor, although radiologic imaging is the most common means of revealing one. The radiologic modalities most often used in analyzing tumors and tumor-like lesions include (a) conventional radiography; (b) angiography (usually arteriography); (c) computed tomography (CT); (d) magnetic resonance imaging (MRI); (e) scintigraphy (radionuclide bone scan); (f) positron emission tomography (PET) and PET-CT; and (g) fluoroscopy-guided or CT-guided percutaneous soft-tissue and bone biopsy.

Conventional Radiography

In most instances, the standard radiographic views specific for the anatomic site under investigation suffice to make a correct diagnosis (Fig. 16.5), which can subsequently be confirmed by biopsy and histopathologic examination. Conventional radiography yields the most useful information about the location and morphology of a lesion, particularly concerning the type of bone destruction, calcifications, ossifications, and periosteal reaction. Moreover, it is important to compare recent radiographic studies with earlier films. This point cannot be emphasized enough. The comparison can reveal not only the nature of a bone lesion (Fig. 16.6) but also its aggressiveness, a critical factor in a diagnostic workup. Chest radiography may also be required in cases of suspected metastasis, the most frequent complication of malignant lesions. This should be done before any treatment of a malignant primary bone tumor because most bone malignancies metastasize to the lung.

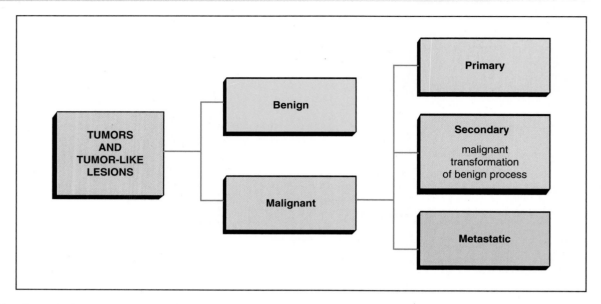

▲

FIGURE 16.1 Classification of tumors and tumor-like lesions.

TABLE 16.1 Classification of Tumors and Tumor-like Lesions by Tissue of Origin

Tissue of Origin	Benign Lesion	Malignant Lesion
Bone forming (osteogenic)	Osteoma	Osteosarcoma (and variants)
	Osteoid osteoma	Juxtacortical osteosarcoma (and variants)
	Osteoblastoma	
Cartilage forming (chondrogenic)	Enchondroma (chondroma)	Chondrosarcoma (central)
	Periosteal (juxtacortical) chondroma	Conventional
	Enchondromatosis (Ollier disease)	Mesenchymal
	Osteochondroma (osteocartilaginous exostosis, solitary or multiple)	Clear cell
		Dedifferentiated
	Chondroblastoma	Chondrosarcoma (peripheral)
	Chondromyxoid fibroma	Periosteal (juxtacortical)
	Fibrocartilaginous mesenchymoma	
Fibrous, osteofibrous, and fibro-histiocytic (fibrogenic)	Fibrous cortical defect (metaphyseal fibrous defect)	Fibrosarcoma
	Nonossifying fibroma	Malignant fibrous histiocytoma
	Benign fibrous histiocytoma	
	Fibrous dysplasia (monostotic and polyostotic)	
	Fibrocartilaginous dysplasia	
	Focal fibrocartilaginous dysplasia of long bones	
	Periosteal desmoid	
	Desmoplastic fibroma	
	Osteofibrous dysplasia (Kempson-Campanacci lesion)	
	Ossifying fibroma (Sissons lesion)	
Vascular	Hemangioma	Angiosarcoma
	Glomus tumor	Hemangioendothelioma
	Cystic angiomatosis	Hemangiopericytoma
Hematopoietic, reticuloendothelial, and lymphatic	Giant cell tumor (osteoclastoma)	Malignant giant cell tumor
	Langerhans cell histiocytosis	Histiocytic lymphoma
	Lymphangioma	Hodgkin lymphoma
		Leukemia
		Myeloma (plasmacytoma)
		Ewing sarcoma
Neural (neurogenic)	Neurofibroma	Malignant schwannoma
	Neurilemoma	Neuroblastoma
		Primitive neuroectodermal tumor (PNET)
Notochordal		Chordoma
Fat (lipogenic)	Lipoma	Liposarcoma
Unknown	Simple bone cyst	Adamantinoma
	Aneurysmal bone cyst	
	Intraosseous ganglion	

TABLE 16.2 **Benign Conditions With Potential for Malignant Transformation**

Benign Lesion	Malignancy
Enchondroma (in the long or flat bones*; in the short, tubular bones almost always as a part of Ollier disease or Maffucci syndrome)	Chondrosarcoma
Osteochondroma	Peripheral chondrosarcoma
Synovial chondromatosis	Chondrosarcoma
Fibrous dysplasia (usually polyostotic, or treated with radiation)	Fibrosarcoma Malignant fibrous histiocytoma Osteosarcoma
Osteofibrous dysplasia† (Kempson-Campanacci lesion)	Adamantinoma
Neurofibroma (in plexiform neurofibromatosis)	Malignant schwannoma Liposarcoma Malignant mesenchymoma
Medullary bone infarct	Fibrosarcoma Malignant fibrous histiocytoma
Osteomyelitis with chronic draining sinus tract (usually more than 15–20 years duration)	Squamous cell carcinoma Fibrosarcoma
Paget disease	Osteosarcoma Chondrosarcoma Fibrosarcoma Malignant fibrous histiocytoma

*Some authorities believe that, at least in some "malignant transformations" of enchondroma to chondrosarcoma, there was in fact from the very beginning a malignant lesion masquerading as benign and not recognized as such.

†Some authorities believe that this is not a true malignant transformation, but rather independent development of malignancy in the benign condition.

Computed Tomography

Although CT by itself is rarely helpful in making a specific diagnosis, it can provide a precise evaluation of the extent of a bone lesion and may demonstrate breakthrough of the cortex and involvement of surrounding

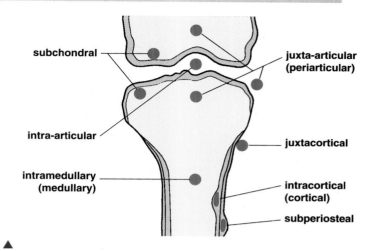

▲
FIGURE 16.3 **Terminology used to describe the location of lesions in the bone.**

soft tissues (Fig. 16.7). CT is moreover very helpful in delineating a bone tumor having a complex anatomic structure. The scapula (Fig. 16.8), pelvis (Fig. 16.9), and sacrum, for example, may be difficult to image fully with conventional radiographic techniques. At times, three-dimensional computed tomography (3D CT)–reconstructed images are used to better and more comprehensively demonstrate the tumors. This technique can be useful, for example, in depicting surface lesions of bone, such as osteochondroma (Fig. 16.10), parosteal osteosarcoma, or juxtacortical chondrosarcoma. CT examination is crucial in determining the extent and spread of a tumor in the bone if limb salvage is contemplated, so that a safe margin of resection can be planned (Fig. 16.11). It can effectively demonstrate the intraosseous extension of a tumor and its extraosseous involvement of soft tissues such as muscles and neurovascular bundles. CT is also useful for monitoring the results of treatment, evaluating for recurrence of a resected tumor, and demonstrating the effect of nonsurgical treatment such as radiation therapy or chemotherapy (Fig. 16.12). It is also helpful in evaluating soft-tissue tumors (Fig. 16.13), which on standard radiographs are indistinguishable from one another (with the exception of lipomas, which usually demonstrate low-density features), blending imperceptibly into the surrounding normal tissue.

Contrast enhancement of CT images aids in the identification of major neurovascular structures and well-vascularized lesions. Evaluating the relationship between the tumor and the surrounding soft tissues

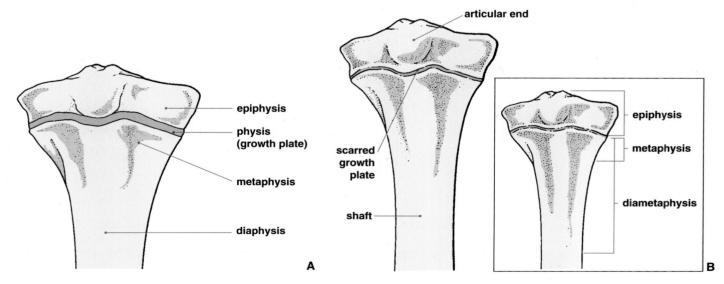

▲
FIGURE 16.2 **Parts of the bone. (A)** In the maturing skeleton, the epiphysis, growth plate, metaphysis, and diaphysis are clearly recognizable areas. **(B)** With skeletal maturity, distinct epiphyseal and metaphyseal zones have ceased to exist. The terminology for describing the location of lesions should alter accordingly. The inset illustrates an alternate terminology.

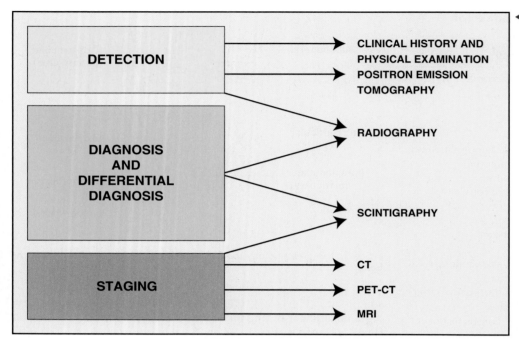

◀ FIGURE 16.4 **Imaging of tumors.** Imaging of musculoskeletal neoplasms can be considered from three aspects: detection, diagnosis and differential diagnosis, and staging. (Modified from Greenspan A et al., 2007.)

and neurovascular structures is particularly important for planning limb-salvage surgery.

PET and PET-CT

Recently, 2-fluoro[fluorine-18]-2-deoxy-D-glucose (F-18 FDG) PET and PET-CT have emerged as very effective metabolic-anatomic imaging techniques for the assessment of variety of neoplastic conditions. The simultaneous detection and precise localization of metabolic and biochemical activities by PET combined with anatomic details obtained by CT into a single superimposed image provides the radiologist with an unique opportunity not only to make a distinction between the normal and pathologic processes, but frequently between the various pathologic disorders as well. Although the most common use of PET/CT is to improve the staging of musculoskeletal tumors

and evaluate their response to therapy and emergence of recurrences, this technique is also a powerful tool for the detection and evaluation of metastatic disease (Fig. 16.14, see also Figs. 2.28B and 2.31) and some primary musculoskeletal tumors (Fig. 16.15, see also Figs. 2.29 and 2.30). In addition, recent trials using dual-time point F-18 FDG PET to distinguish malignant tumors from benign conditions yielded promising results.

Arteriography

Arteriography is used mainly to map out bone lesions and to assess the extent of disease. It is also used to demonstrate the vascular supply of a tumor and to locate vessels suitable for preoperative intra-arterial chemotherapy, as well as to demonstrate the area suitable for open biopsy because the most vascular area of a tumor contains the most aggressive

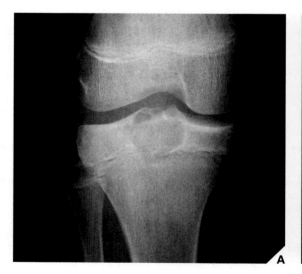
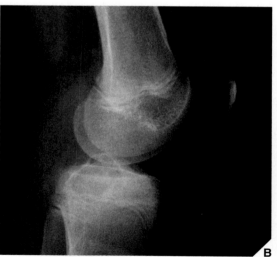

▲
FIGURE 16.5 **Chondroblastoma.** Anteroposterior (**A**) and lateral (**B**) radiographs of the right knee of a 13-year-old girl reveal a radiolucent lesion located eccentrically in the proximal epiphysis of the tibia, with sharply defined borders and a thin, sclerotic margin. Here, the standard projections led to the correct radiographic diagnosis of chondroblastoma.

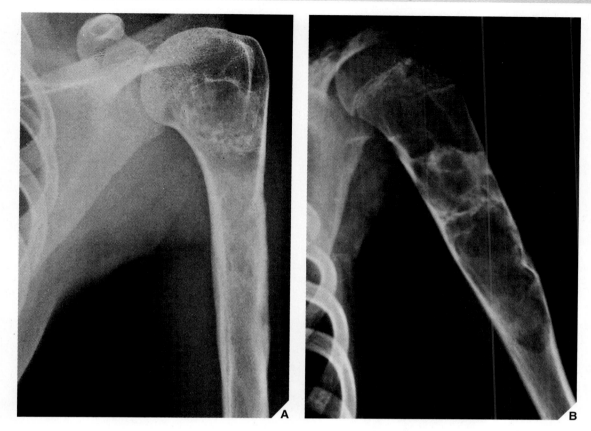

▲
FIGURE 16.6 **Comparison radiography: a simple bone cyst. (A)** Anteroposterior radiograph of the left humerus in a 26-year-old woman with vague pain for 2 months shows an ill-defined lesion in the medullary region, with a periosteal reaction medially and laterally. There appear to be scattered calcifications in the proximal portion of the lesion. The possibility of a cartilage tumor such as chondrosarcoma was considered, but a radiograph taken 17 years earlier **(B)** shows an unquestionably benign lesion (a simple bone cyst) that had been treated by curettage and the application of bone chips. In view of this, the later findings were interpreted as representing a healed bone cyst. The patient's pain was found to be related to muscle strain.

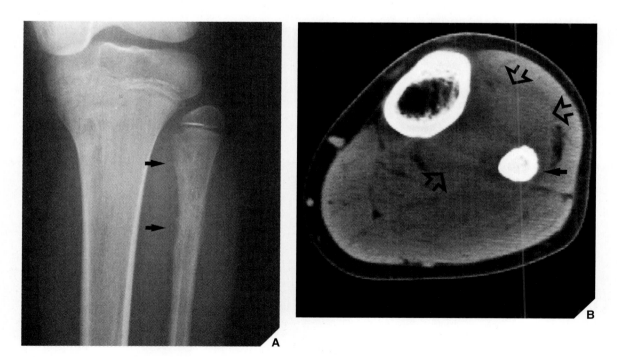

▲
FIGURE 16.7 **Ewing sarcoma. (A)** Anteroposterior radiograph demonstrates a malignant lesion that proved to be Ewing sarcoma in the proximal diaphysis of the left fibula (*arrows*) of a 12-year-old boy. **(B)** On CT examination, there is involvement of the bone marrow (*arrow*) and extension of the tumor into the soft tissues (*open arrows*).

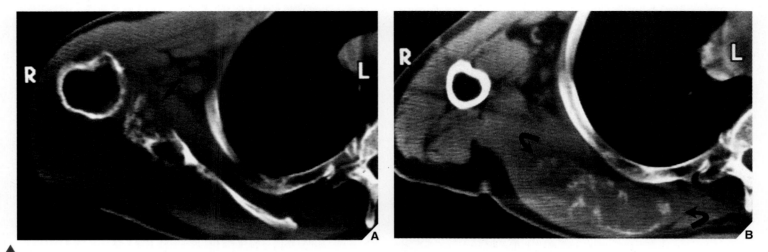

FIGURE 16.8 **Chondrosarcoma.** Standard radiographs were ambiguous in this 70-year-old man with a palpable mass over the right scapula. However, two CT sections demonstrate a destructive lesion of the glenoid portion and body of the scapula (*arrows*) (**A**), with a large soft-tissue mass extending to the rib cage and containing calcifications (*curved arrows*) (**B**).

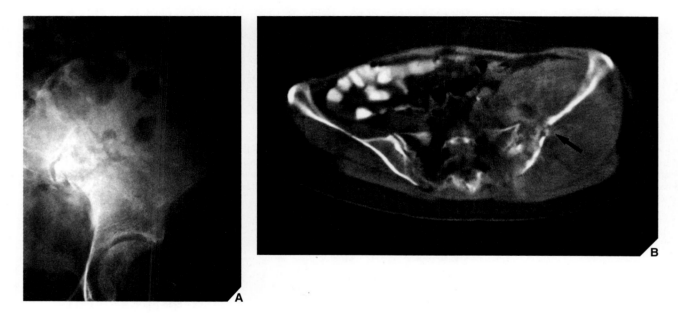

FIGURE 16.9 **Osteosarcoma.** (**A**) Standard anteroposterior radiograph of the pelvis was not sufficient to delineate the full extent of the destructive lesion of the iliac bone in this 66-year-old woman. (**B**) A CT scan, however, showed a pathologic fracture of the ilium (*arrow*) and the full extent of soft-tissue involvement. The high Hounsfield values of the multiple soft-tissue densities suggested bone formation. Enhancement of the CT images with contrast agent showed an increased vascularity of the lesion. Collectively, the CT findings suggested a diagnosis of osteosarcoma that, although unusual for a person of this age, was confirmed by open biopsy.

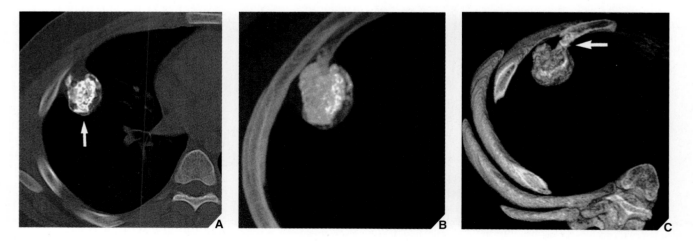

FIGURE 16.10 **Osteochondroma: effectiveness of 3D CT.** (**A**) Conventional CT section through the chest shows an osteochondroma at the site of the antero-lateral portion of the right forth rib (*arrow*). It is difficult to determine if the lesion is sessile or pedunculated. (**B**) 3D CT reconstructed image in maximum intensity projection (MIP) delivers a much more informative image of osteochondroma, and allows one to characterize the internal architecture of the lesion; note typical chondroid matrix of the tumor. (**C**) 3D CT reconstructed image in shaded surface display (SSD) renders better conspicuity of the lesion; the pedicle of osteochon-droma (*arrow*) is now clearly demonstrated. (Reprinted from Greenspan A et al., 2007.)

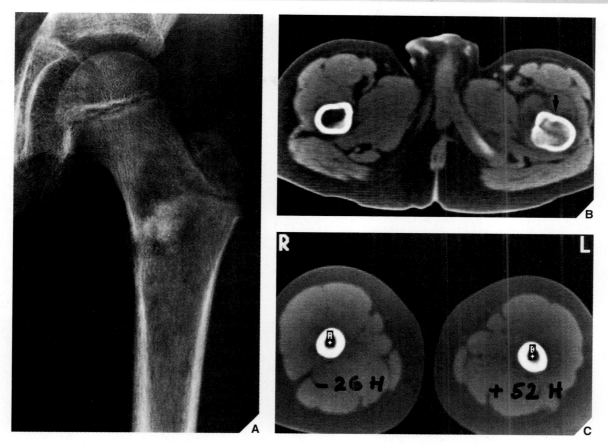

▲

FIGURE 16.11 **Osteosarcoma: effectiveness of CT. (A)** Anteroposterior radiograph of the left proximal femur of a 12-year-old boy demonstrates an osteolytic lesion in the intertrochanteric region, with a poorly defined margin and amorphous densities in the center associated with a periosteal reaction medially—features suggesting osteosarcoma, which was confirmed on open biopsy. Because a limb-salvage procedure was contemplated, a CT scan was performed to determine the extent of marrow infiltration and the required level of bone resection. The most proximal section **(B)** shows obvious gross tumor involvement of the marrow cavity of the left femur (*arrow*). A more distal section **(C)** shows no gross marrow abnormality, but a positive Hounsfield value of 52 units indicates tumor involvement of the marrow, which was not shown on the standard radiographs. By comparison, the section of the right femur shows a normal Hounsfield value of −26 for bone marrow.

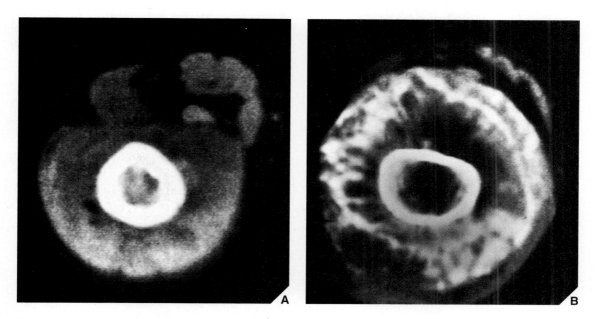

▲

FIGURE 16.12 **Osteosarcoma after chemotherapy.** Before surgery, this 14-year-old girl with an osteosarcoma of the left femur underwent a full course of chemotherapy. **(A)** CT section before the therapy was begun shows involvement of the bone and marrow cavity. Note the soft-tissue extension of the tumor, with nonhomogeneous, amorphous tumor bone formation. After combined treatment with doxorubicin hydrochloride, vincristine, methotrexate, and cisplatin, a repeat CT scan **(B)** shows calcifications and ossifications in the periphery of the lesion, which represents reactive rather than tumor bone and demonstrates the success of chemotherapy. Radical excision of the femur and a subsequent histopathologic examination showed almost complete eradication of malignant cells, confirming the CT findings.

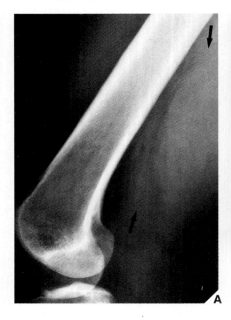

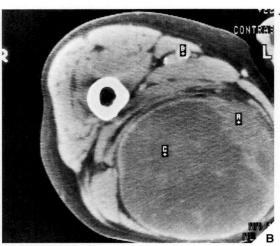

FIGURE 16.13 CT of malignant fibrous histiocytoma (MFH) of the soft tissue. A 56-year-old woman presented with a soft-tissue mass on the posteromedial aspect of the right thigh. (A) Lateral radiograph of the femur demonstrates only a soft-tissue prominence posteriorly (arrows). (B) CT section shows an axial image of the mass, which is contained by a fibrotic capsule. The overlying skin is not infiltrated. Despite the benign appearance, the mass proved on biopsy to be a MFH.

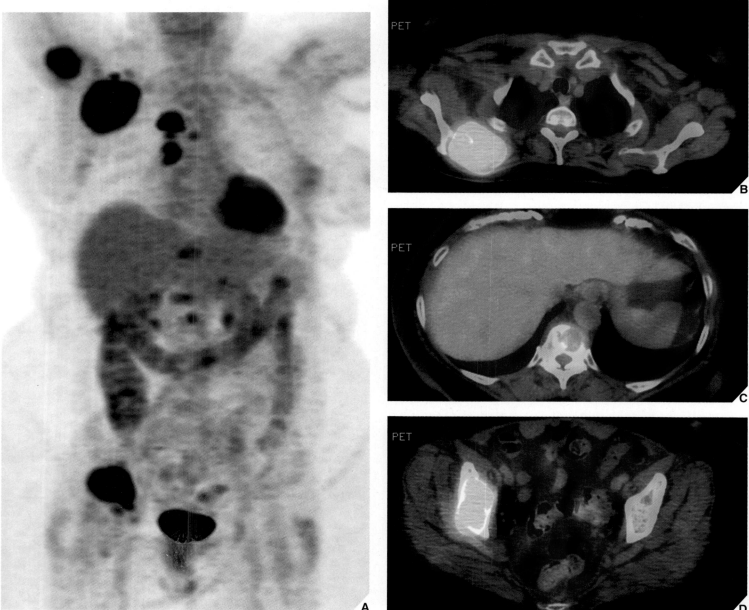

FIGURE 16.14 **PET and PET-CT of metastases.** A 61-year-old woman was diagnosed with lung carcinoma. (A) A whole body PET scan shows several hypermetabolic foci in the internal organs, lymph nodes, and osseous structures, representing metastatic disease. The fused PET-CT images demonstrate metastatic lesions in the right scapula (B), thoracic vertebral body (C), and right ilium (D).

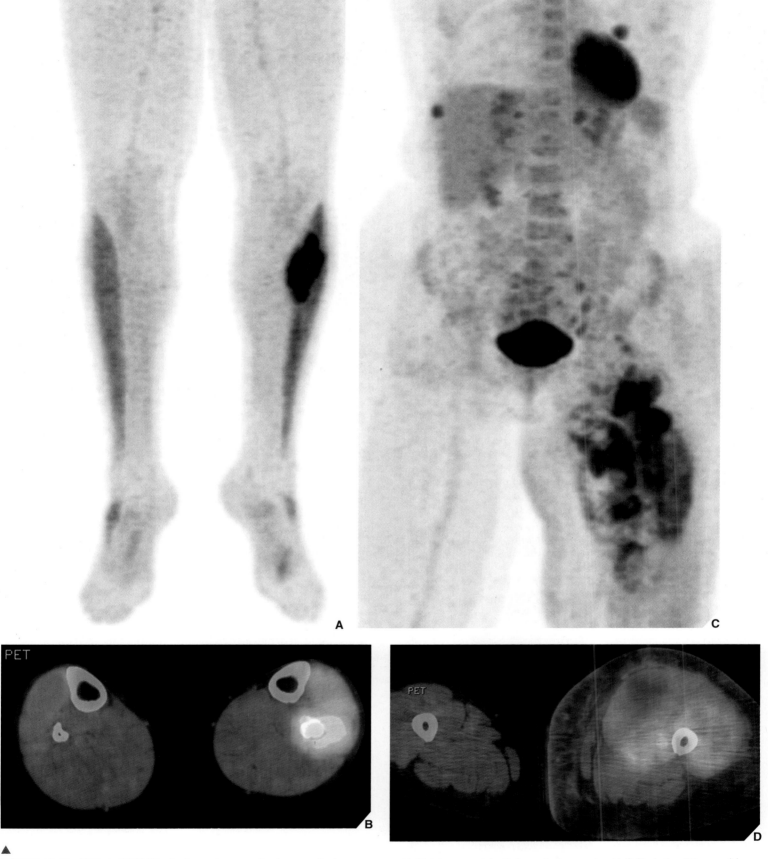

FIGURE 16.15 PET and PET-CT of primary bone and primary soft-tissue tumors. (A,B) A hypermetabolic focus in the proximal left fibula in a 23-year-old man proved to be a Ewing sarcoma. **(C,D)** A hypermetabolic lesion in the vastus lateralis and medialis in the proximal left thigh in a 58-year-old woman was diagnosed on histopathologic examination as MFH of the soft tissues.

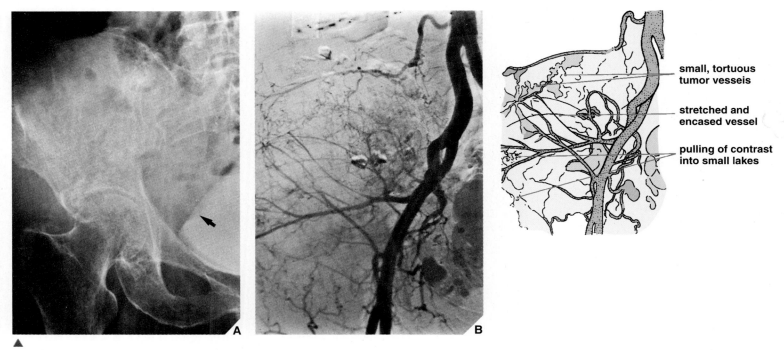

▲
FIGURE 16.16   Arteriography of dedifferentiated chondrosarcoma. (A) Anteroposterior radiograph of the pelvis in a 79-year-old woman with an 8-month history of pain in the right buttock and weight loss demonstrates a poorly defined destructive lesion of the right iliac bone, with multiple small calcifications and a soft-tissue mass extending into the pelvis. Note the effect of the mass on the urinary bladder filled with contrast (*arrow*). A chondrosarcoma was suspected, and a femoral arteriogram was performed as part of the diagnostic workup. **(B)** Subtraction study of an arteriogram demonstrates hypervascularity of the tumor. Note the abnormal tumor vessels, encasement and stretching of some vessels, and "pulling" of contrast medium into small "lakes"—all characteristic signs of a malignant lesion. Biopsy revealed a highly malignant, dedifferentiated chondrosarcoma. In this case, the vascular study corroborated the radiographic findings of a malignant bone tumor.

component. Occasionally, arteriography can be used to demonstrate abnormal tumor vessels, corroborating findings with conventional radiography (Fig. 16.16). Arteriography is often useful in planning for limb-salvage procedures because it demonstrates the regional vascular anatomy and thus permits a plan to be drawn up for the resection procedure. It is also sometimes used to outline the major vessels before resection of a benign tumor (Fig. 16.17), and it can be combined with an interventional procedure, such as embolization of hypervascular tumors, before further treatment (Fig. 16.18). In selected cases, arteriography may help make a differential diagnosis, such as of osteoid osteoma versus a bone abscess.

Myelography

Myelography may be helpful in dealing with tumors that invade the vertebral column and thecal sac (Fig. 16.19), although recently this procedure has been almost completely replaced by MRI.

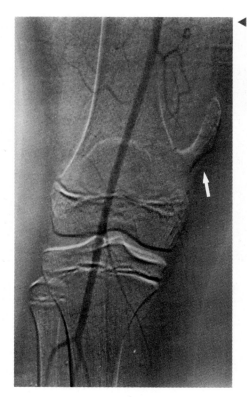

◀ **FIGURE 16.17   Arteriography of osteochondroma.** A 12-year-old boy with osteochondroma of the distal femur (*arrow*) underwent arteriography to demonstrate the relationship of the distal superficial femoral artery to the lesion. This subtraction study shows no major vessels near the planned site of resection at the base of the lesion, important information for surgical planning.

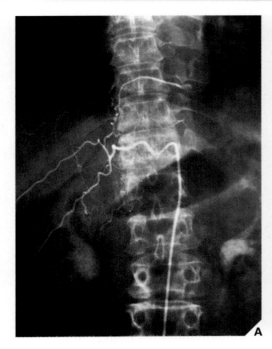
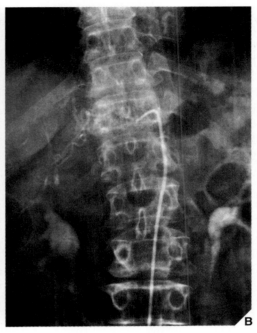

FIGURE 16.18 **Vertebral arteriography and embolization of hemangioma.** A 73-year-old woman presented with a collapsed T11 vertebra, which showed a corduroy-like pattern suggestive of hemangioma. Vertebral angiography was performed. (**A**) Arteriogram of the 11th right intercostal artery outlines a vascular paraspinal mass associated with hemangioma and indicating extension of the lesion into the soft tissues. (**B**) After embolization, the lesion shows a marked decrease in vascularity. Subsequently, the patient underwent decompression laminectomy and anterior fusion at T10-11 using a fibular strut graft.

Magnetic Resonance Imaging

MRI is indispensable in evaluating bone and soft-tissue tumors. Particularly with soft-tissue masses, MRI offers distinct advantages over CT. There is improved visualization of tissue planes surrounding the lesion, for example, and neurovascular involvement can be evaluated without the use of intravenous contrast.

In the evaluation of intraosseous and extraosseous extensions of a tumor, MRI is crucial because it can determine with high accuracy the presence or absence of soft-tissue invasion by a tumor (Fig. 16.20). MRI has often proved to be superior to CT in delineating the extraosseous and intramedullary extent of the tumor and its relationship to surrounding structures (Fig. 16.21). By showing sharper demarcation between normal and abnormal tissue than CT, MRI—particularly in evaluation of the extremities—reliably identifies the spatial boundaries of tumor masses (Fig. 16.22), the encasement and displacement of major neurovascular bundles, and the extent of joint involvement. Spin-echo

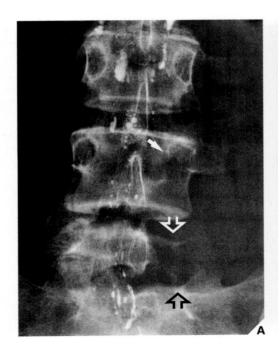
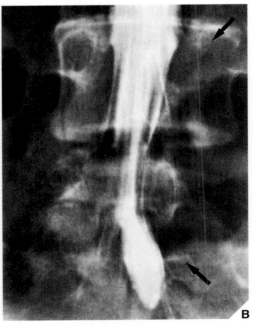

FIGURE 16.19 **Myelography of aneurysmal bone cyst.** Initial radiographic examination of the lumbar spine of this 14-year-old girl with an 18-month history of pain in the lower back and sciatica of the left leg did not disclose any abnormalities; myelography was performed because of suspected herniation of a lumbar disk, but it was inconclusive. A repeat study was requested when the symptoms became more severe after 3 months. (**A**) Posteroanterior radiograph of the lumbosacral spine shows destruction of the left pedicle of L-4 (*arrow*) and the left part of the L5 body (*open arrows*). Note the residual contrast in the subarachnoid space. A repeat myelogram using a water-soluble contrast (metrizamide) shows, on the posteroanterior view (**B**), extradural compression of the thecal sac on the left side with displacement of the nerve roots (*arrows*). Biopsy confirmed the radiographic diagnosis of an aneurysmal bone cyst.

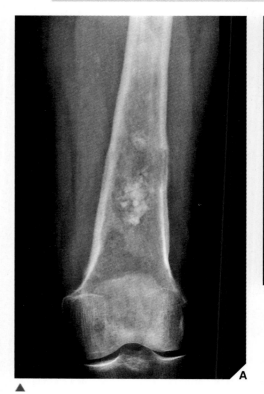

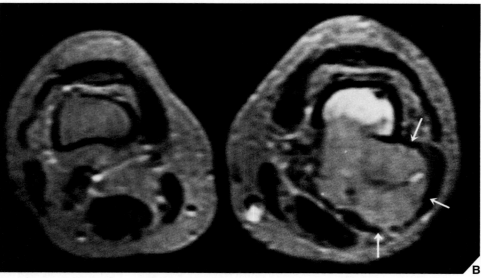

FIGURE 16.20 **MRI of chondrosarcoma (A)** Conventional radiograph of the left femur in anteroposterior projection of a 67-year-old woman with chondrosarcoma demonstrates a tumor in the distal shaft destroying the medullary portion of the bone and breaking through the cortex. The soft-tissue extension cannot be determined. **(B)** Axial T2-weighted MR image (SE; TR 2500/TE 70 msec) demonstrates a tumor infiltrating bone marrow, destroying the posterolateral cortex, and breaking into the soft tissues with the formation of a large mass (*arrows*). Compare with a normal contralateral extremity.

T1-weighted images enhance tumor contrast with bone, bone marrow, and fatty tissue, whereas spin-echo T2-weighted images enhance tumor contrast with muscle and accentuate peritumoral edema. Axial and coronal images have been used in determining the extent of soft-tissue invasion in relation to important vascular structures. However, in comparison with CT, MR images do not clearly demonstrate calcification in the tumor matrix; in fact, large amounts of calcification or ossification may be almost undetectable. Moreover, MRI has been shown to be less satisfactory than CT in the demonstration of cortical destruction. It is important to realize that both MRI and CT have advantages and disadvantages, and circumstances exist in which either can be the preferential or complementary study. But it is even more important that the surgeon

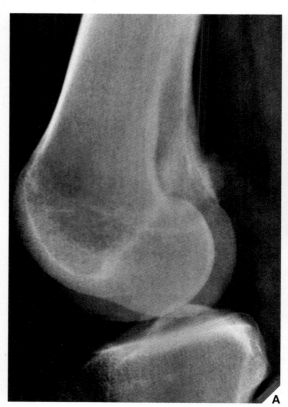

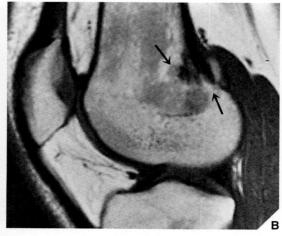

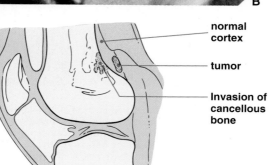

◄ FIGURE 16.21 **MRI of parosteal osteosarcoma. (A)** From this lateral radiograph of the distal femur of a 22-year-old woman with parosteal osteosarcoma, it is difficult to evaluate if the tumor is on the surface of the bone or already infiltrated through the cortex. **(B)** Sagittal T1-weighted MRI (SE; TR 500/TE 20 msec) demonstrates invasion of the cancellous portion of the bone, as represented by an area of low signal intensity (*arrows*).

normal cortex

tumor

Invasion of cancellous bone

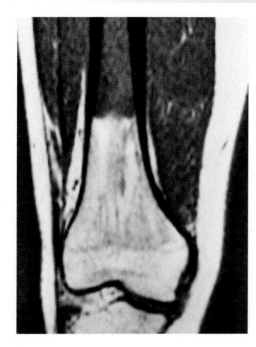

▲
FIGURE 16.22 **MRI of MFH.** Coronal T1-weighted MRI (SE; TR 500/TE 20 msec) demonstrates involvement of the medullary cavity of the right femur in this 16-year-old girl with MFH. Note the excellent demonstration of the interface between normal bone displaying high-signal intensity and a tumor displaying intermediate signal intensity.

tell the radiologist who is performing and interpreting the study what information is needed.

Several investigators have stressed the superior contrast enhancement of MR images using intravenous injection of gadopentetate dimeglumine (gadolinium diethylenetriamine-penta-acetic acid, [Gd-DTPA]). Enhancement was found to give better delineation of the tumor's richly vascularized parts and of the compressed tissue immediately surrounding the tumor. It was also found to assist in the differentiation of intraarticular tumor extension from joint effusion, and, as Erlemann pointed out, improved the differentiation of necrotic tissue from viable areas in various malignant tumors.

According to the recent investigations, MRI may have an additional application in evaluating both the tumor's response to radiation and chemotherapy and any local recurrence. On gadolinium-enhanced T1-weighted images, signal intensity remains low in avascular, necrotic areas of tumor while it increases in viable tissue. Although static MRI was of little value for the assessment of response to the treatment, dynamic MRI using Gd-DTPA as a contrast enhancement, according to Erlemann, had the highest degree of accuracy (85.7%) and was superior to scintigraphy, particularly in patients who were receiving intra-arterial chemotherapy. In general, drug-sensitive tumors display slower uptake of Gd-DTPA after preoperative chemotherapy than do nonresponsive lesions. As Vaupel contended, the rapid uptake of Gd-DTPA by malignant tissues may be due to increased vascularity and more rapid perfusion of the contrast material through an expanded interstitial space. The latest observation by Dewhirst and Kautcher suggests that MR spectroscopy may also be useful in the evaluation of patients undergoing chemotherapy.

It must be stressed, however, that most of the time MRI is not suitable for establishing the precise nature of a bone tumor. In particular, too much faith has been placed in MRI as a method of distinguishing benign lesions from malignant ones. An overlap between the classic characteristics of benign and malignant tumors is often observed. Moreover, some malignant bone tumors can appear misleadingly benign on MR images and, conversely, some benign lesions may exhibit a misleadingly malignant appearance. Attempts to formulate precise criteria for correlating MRI findings with histologic diagnosis have been largely unsuccessful. Tissue characterization on the basis of

MRI signal intensities is still unreliable. Because of the wide spectrum of bone tumor composition and their differing histologic patterns, as well as in tumors of similar histologic diagnosis, signal intensities of histologically different tumors may overlap or there may be variability of signal intensity in histologically similar tumors.

Trials using combined hydrogen-1 MRI and P-31 MR spectroscopy also failed to distinguish most benign lesions from malignant tumors. Despite the use of various criteria, the application of MRI to tissue diagnosis has rarely brought satisfactory results. This is because, in general, the small number of protons in calcified structures renders MRI less effective in diagnosing bone lesions, and hence valuable evidence concerning the production of the tumor matrix can be missed. Moreover, as several investigations have shown, MRI is an imaging modality of low specificity. T1 and T2 measurements are generally of limited value for histologic characterization of musculoskeletal tumors. Quantitative determination of relaxation times has not proved to be clinically valuable in identifying various tumor types, although, as noted by Sundaram, it has proved to be an important technique in the staging of osteosarcoma and chondrosarcoma. T2-weighted images in particular are a crucial factor in delineating extraosseous tumor extension and peritumoral edema, as well as in assessing the involvement of major neurovascular bundles. Necrotic areas change from a low-intensity signal in the T1-weighted image to a very bright, intense signal in the T2-weighted image and can be differentiated from viable, solid tumor tissue. Although MRI cannot predict the histology of bone tumors, as Sundaram pointed out, it is a useful tool for distinguishing round cell tumors and metastases from stress fractures or medullary infarcts in symptomatic patients with normal radiographs, and, according to Baker, it can occasionally differentiate benign from pathologic fracture.

Skeletal Scintigraphy

The radionuclide bone scan is an indicator of mineral turnover, and because there is usually enhanced deposition of bone-seeking radiopharmaceuticals in areas of bone undergoing change and repair, a bone scan is useful in localizing tumors and tumor-like lesions in the skeleton, particularly in such conditions as fibrous dysplasia, Langerhans cell histiocytosis, or metastatic cancer, in which more than one lesion is encountered (Fig. 16.23). It also plays an important role in localizing small lesions such as osteoid osteomas, which may not always be seen on conventional radiographs (see Fig. 17.11B). Although in most instances, a radionuclide bone scan cannot distinguish benign lesions from malignant tumors, because increased blood flow with increased isotope deposition and increased osteoblastic activity takes place in benign and malignant conditions, it is still occasionally capable of making such differentiation in benign lesions that do not absorb the radioactive isotope (Fig. 16.24). The radionuclide bone scan is sometimes also useful for differentiating multiple myeloma, which usually shows no significant uptake of the tracer, from metastatic cancer, which usually does.

Aside from routine radionuclide scans performed using ^{99m}Tc-labeled phosphate compounds, occasionally ^{67}Ga is used for the detection and staging of bone and soft-tissue neoplasms. Gallium is handled by the body much like iron in that the protein transferrin carries it in the plasma, and it also competes for extravascular iron-binding proteins such as lactoferrin. The administered dose for adults ranges from 3 mCi (111 MBq) to 10 mCi (370 MBq) per study. The exact mechanism of tumor uptake of gallium remains unsettled, and its uptake varies with tumor type. In particular, Hodgkin lymphomas and histiocytic lymphomas are prone to significant gallium uptake.

Interventional Procedures

Percutaneous bone and soft-tissue biopsy performed in the radiology department has in recent years gained its place in the diagnostic workup for various neoplastic diseases, including bone tumors. In patients with primary bone neoplasms, it is a helpful diagnostic and evaluative tool,

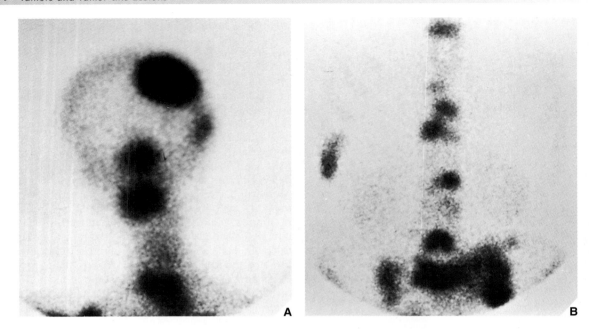

▲
FIGURE 16.23 **Scintigraphy of the metastases.** A radionuclide bone scan was performed on a 68-year-old woman with metastatic breast carcinoma to determine the distribution of metastases. After an intravenous injection of 15 mCi (555 MBq) of ^{99m}Tc diphosphonate, an increased uptake of the radiopharmaceutical agent is seen in the skull and cervical spine (**A**) and lumbar spine and pelvis (**B**), localizing the site of the multiple metastases.

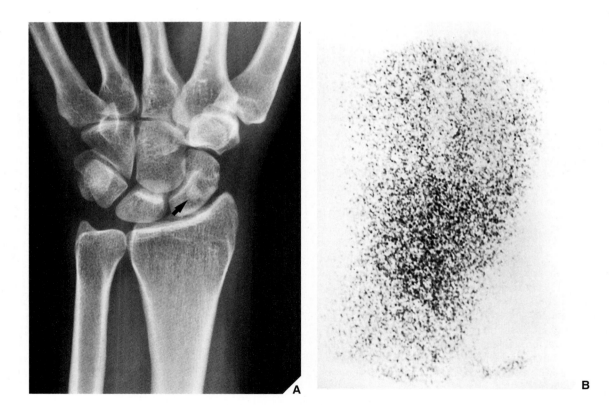

▲
FIGURE 16.24 **Scintigraphy of enostosis.** A 32-year-old woman presented with pain localized in the wrist area. (**A**) Dorsovolar radiograph of the wrist demonstrates a sclerotic round lesion in the scaphoid (*arrow*), and a diagnosis of osteoid osteoma was considered. (**B**) Radionuclide bone scan reveals normal isotope uptake, ruling out osteoid osteoma, which is invariably associated with an increased uptake of radiopharmaceutical. The lesion instead proved to be a bone island (enostosis), an asymptomatic developmental error of endochondral ossification without any consequence to the patient. The pain was unrelated to the island, coming instead from tenosynovitis; it disappeared after the patient was treated for the latter condition.

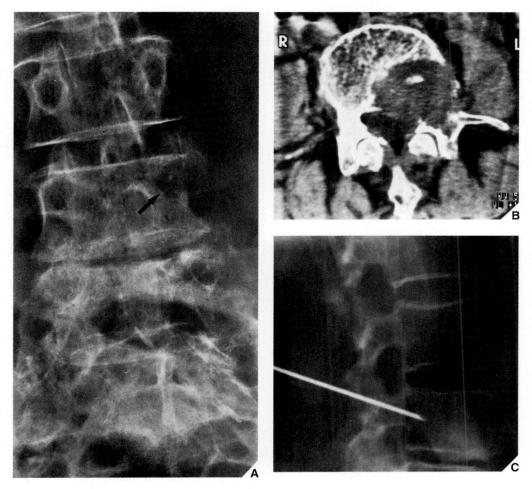

▲
FIGURE 16.25   **Percutaneous bone biopsy. (A)** Anteroposterior radiograph of the lumbar spine in a 67-year-old woman with lower back pain for 4 months demonstrates destruction of the left pedicle of the L4 vertebra (*arrow*). **(B)** CT section shows, in addition, involvement of the vertebral body by the tumor. **(C)** Percutaneous biopsy of the lesion, performed in the radiology suite for the purpose of rapid histopathologic diagnosis, revealed a metastatic adenocarcinoma from the colon.

allowing rapid histologic diagnosis, which is now considered essential, particularly in the planning of a limb-salvage procedure. It also helps assess the effect of chemotherapy and radiation therapy and helps locate the site of the primary tumor in cases of metastatic disease (Fig. 16.25). In addition, percutaneous bone and soft-tissue biopsy performed in the radiology suite is simpler and costs less than a biopsy performed in the operating room.

Tumors and Tumor-like Lesions of the Bone

Diagnosis

Patient age and determination of whether a lesion is solitary or multiple are the starting approaches in the diagnosis of bone tumors (Fig. 16.26).

◀ FIGURE 16.26   **Diagnosis of bone lesion.** Analytic approach to evaluation of the bone neoplasm must include patient age, multiplicity of a lesion, location in the skeleton and in the particular bone, and radiographic morphology.

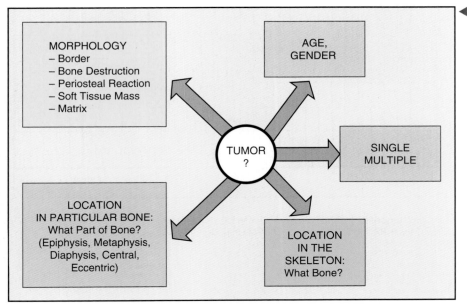

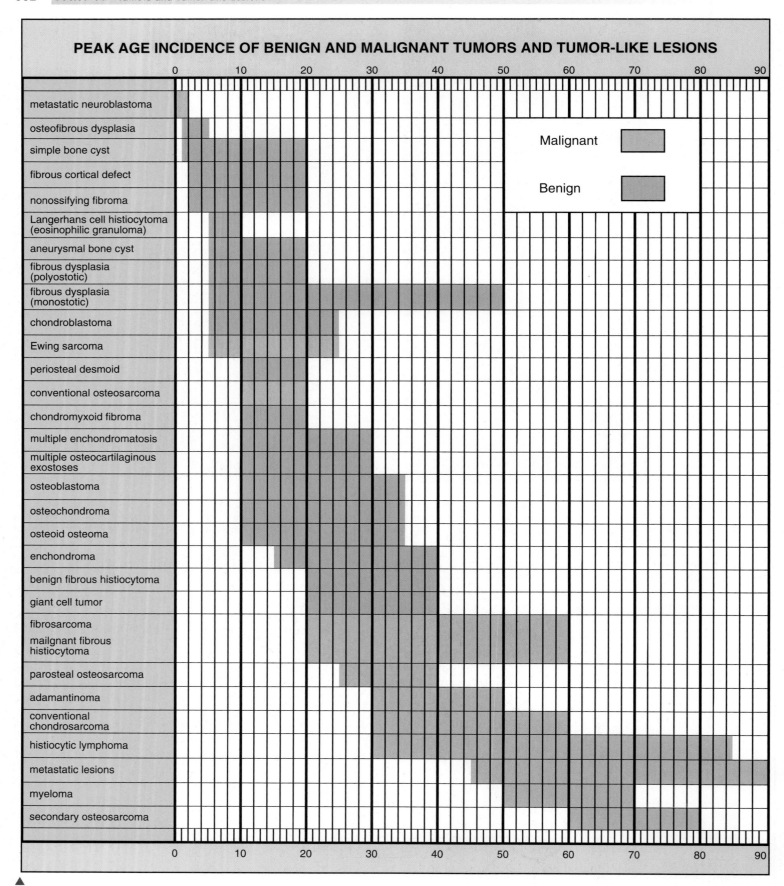

FIGURE 16.27   Peak age incidence of benign and malignant tumors and tumor-like lesions. (Sources: Dahlin DC, 1986; Dorfman HD, Czerniak B, 1998; Fechner RE, Mills SE, 1993; Huvos AG, 1979; Jaffe HL, 1968; Mirra JM, 1989; Moser RP, 1990; Schajowicz F, 1994; Unni KK, 1988; Wilner D, 1982.)

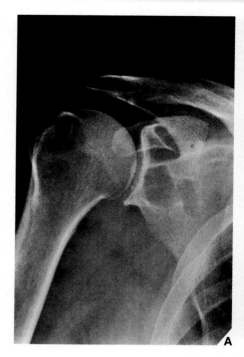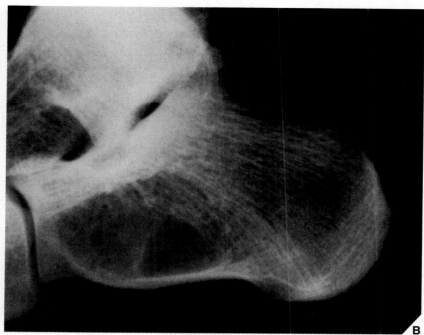

▲
FIGURE 16.28   **Simple bone cyst. (A)** Anteroposterior radiograph of the right shoulder of a 69-year-old man with shoulder pain for 8 months demonstrates a well-defined radiolucent lesion with a sclerotic border in the glenoid portion of the scapula. Because the patient had a history of gout, the lesion was thought to represent an intraosseous tophus. In the differential diagnosis, an intraosseous ganglion and even a cartilage tumor were also considered. An excision biopsy, however, revealed a simple bone cyst, which is very unusual in the glenoid part of the scapula. **(B)** Lateral radiograph of the left hindfoot of a 50-year-old woman shows a radiolucent lesion in the calcaneus proven on the excision biopsy to be a simple bone cyst.

Clinical Information

The age of the patient is probably the single most important item of clinical data in radiographically establishing the diagnosis of a tumor (Fig. 16.27). Certain tumors have a predilection for specific age groups. Aneurysmal bone cysts, for example, rarely occur beyond age 20, and giant cell tumors as a rule are found only after the growth plate is closed. Other lesions may have different radiographic presentations or occur in different locations in patients of different ages. Simple bone cysts, which before skeletal maturity present almost exclusively in the long bones such as the proximal humerus and proximal femur, may appear in other locations (pelvis, scapula, os calcis) and have unconventional radiographic presentations with progressing age (Fig. 16.28).

Also important for clinically differentiating lesions of similar radiographic presentation—such as Langerhans cell histiocytosis (formerly called eosinophilic granuloma), osteomyelitis, and Ewing sarcoma—is the duration of the patient's symptoms. In Langerhans cell histiocytosis, for example, the amount of bone destruction seen radiographically after 1 week of symptoms is usually the same as that seen after 4 to 6 weeks of symptoms in osteomyelitis and 3 to 4 months in Ewing sarcoma.

Occasionally, race may also be an important differential diagnostic factor because certain lesions, such as tumoral calcinosis or bone infarctions, are seen more commonly in blacks than in whites, whereas others, such as Ewing sarcoma, are almost never seen in blacks.

The growth rate of the tumor may be an additional factor in differentiating malignant tumors (usually rapid-growing) from benign tumors (usually slow-growing).

Laboratory data, such as an increased erythrocyte sedimentation rate or an elevated alkaline or acid phosphatase level in the serum, occasionally can be a corroborative factor in diagnosis.

Imaging Modalities

With so many imaging techniques available to diagnose and characterize the bone tumor further, radiologists and clinicians are frequently at a loss as to how to proceed in a given case, what modality to use for this particular problem, in what order of preference to use the modalities,

and when to stop. It is important to keep in mind that the choice of techniques for imaging the bone or soft-tissue tumor should be dictated not only by the clinical presentation and the technique's expected effectiveness but also by equipment availability, expertise, cost, and restrictions applicable to individual patients (e.g., allergy to ionic or nonionic iodinated contrast agents may preclude the use of arthrography; presence of a pacemaker may preclude the use of MRI; or physiologic states such as pregnancy warrant the use of ultrasound over the use of ionized radiation). Some of these problems were discussed in general in Chapters 1 and 2.

Here, I give a general guideline related to the most effective modality for diagnosing and evaluating bone and soft-tissue tumors. In the evaluation of bone tumors, conventional radiography is still the standard diagnostic procedures. No matter what ancillary technique is used, the conventional radiograph should always be available for comparison. Most of the time, the choice of imaging technique is dictated by the type of suspected tumor. For instance, if osteoid osteoma is suspected based on the clinical history (see Fig. 1.5), conventional radiography followed by scintigraphy should be performed first, and after the lesion is localized to the particular bone, CT should be used for more specific localization and for obtaining quantitative information (measurements). However, if a soft-tissue tumor is suspected, MRI is the only technique able to localize and characterize the lesion accurately. Likewise, if radiographs are suggestive of a malignant bone tumor, MRI or CT should be used next to evaluate both the intraosseous extent of the tumor and the extraosseous involvement of the soft tissues.

The use of CT versus MRI is based on the radiographs: If there is no definite evidence of soft-tissue extension, then CT is superior to MRI for detecting subtle cortical erosions and periosteal reaction, while providing at the same time an accurate means of determining the intraosseous extension of the tumor; if, however, the radiographs suggest cortical destruction and soft-tissue mass, then MRI would be the preferred modality because it provides an excellent soft-tissue contrast and can determine the extraosseous extension of the tumor much better than CT.

EVALUATION OF A BONE LESION DISCOVERED ON STANDARD RADIOGRAPHS

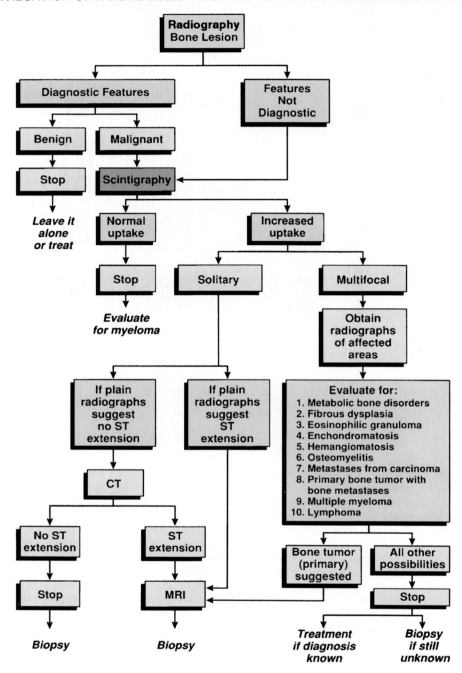

FIGURE 16.29 Algorithm to evaluate and manage a bone lesion discovered on standard radiographs.

In evaluating the results of malignant tumors treated by radiotherapy and chemotherapy, dynamic MRI using Gd-DTPA as a contrast enhancement is much superior to scintigraphy, CT, or even plain-MRI.

Figure 16.29 depicts an algorithm for evaluating a bone lesion discovered on the standard radiographs. Note that the proper order of the various imaging modalities depends on two main factors: whether the radiographic findings are or are not diagnostic for any particular tumor and the lesion's uptake of a tracer on the radionuclide bone scan. Scintigraphy plays a crucial role here, dictating further steps in using the different techniques.

Radiographic Features of Bone Lesions

The radiographic features that help the radiologist diagnose a tumor or tumor-like bone lesion include (a) the site of the lesion (location in the skeleton and in the individual bone); (b) the borders of the lesion (the so-called zone of transition); (c) the type of matrix of the lesion (composition of the tumor tissue); (d) the type of bone destruction; (e) the type of periosteal response to the lesion (periosteal reaction); (f) the nature and extent of soft-tissue involvement; and (g) the single or multiple nature of the lesion (Fig. 16.30).

Site of the Lesion. The site of a bone lesion is an important feature because some tumors have a predilection for specific bones or specific sites in the bone (Table 16.3 and Fig. 16.31). The sites of some lesions are so characteristic that a diagnosis can be suggested on this basis alone, as in the case of parosteal osteosarcoma (Fig. 16.32) or chondroblastoma (see Fig. 16.5). Moreover, certain entities can be readily excluded from the differential diagnosis on the basis of the lesion's location. Thus, for example, the diagnosis of a giant cell tumor should not be made for a

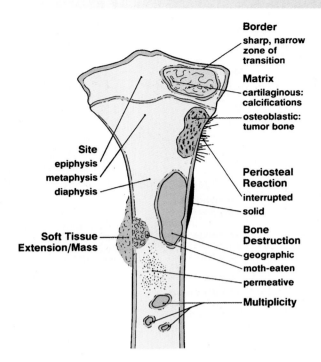

FIGURE 16.30 Radiographic features of tumors and tumor-like lesions of bone.

lesion that does not reach the articular end of the bone, because very few of these tumors develop in sites remote from the joint.

Borders of the Lesion. Evaluation of the borders or margins of a lesion is crucial in determining whether it is slow growing or fast growing (aggressive) (Fig. 16.33). Three types of lesion margins have been described: (a) a margin with sharp demarcation by sclerosis between the peripheral aspect of the tumor and the adjacent host bone (IA margin); (b) a margin with sharp demarcation without sclerosis around the periphery of the lesion (IB margin); and (c) a margin with an ill-defined region (either the entire circumference or only a portion of it) at the interface between lesion and host bone (IC margin). Slow-growing lesions, which are usually benign, have sharply outlined sclerotic borders (a narrow zone of transition) (Fig. 16.34A), whereas malignant or aggressive lesions typically have indistinct borders (a wide zone of transition) with either minimal or no reactive sclerosis (Fig. 16.34B). Some lesions ordinarily lack a sclerotic border (Table 16.4), and some lesions commonly display a sclerotic border (Table 16.5). It must be emphasized that treatment can alter the appearance of malignant bone tumors; after radiation or chemotherapy, they may exhibit significant sclerosis as well as a narrow zone of transition (Fig. 16.35).

Type of Matrix. All bone tumors are composed of characteristic tissue components, the so-called tumor matrix. Only two of these—osteoblastic and cartilaginous tissue—can usually be clearly demonstrated radiographically. If one can identify bone or cartilage within a tumor, one can assume that it is osteoblastic or cartilaginous (Fig. 16.36). The identification of tumor bone within or adjacent to the area of destruction should alert the radiologist to the possibility of osteosarcoma. However, the deposition of new bone may also be the result of a reparative process secondary to bone destruction—so-called reactive sclerosis—rather than production of osteoid or bone by malignant cells. This new tumor bone is often radiographically indistinguishable from reactive bone; however, fluffy, cotton-like, or cloud-like densities within the medullary cavity and in the adjacent soft tissue should suggest the presence of tumorous bone and hence the diagnosis of osteosarcoma (Fig. 16.37).

Cartilage is identified by the presence of typically popcorn-like, punctate, annular, or comma-shaped calcifications (Fig. 16.38). Because cartilage usually grows in lobules, a tumor of cartilaginous origin can often be suggested by lobulated growth. A completely radiolucent

TABLE 16.3 Predilection of Tumors for Specific Sites in the Skeleton

	Skeletal Predilection of Benign Osseous Neoplasms and Tumor-like Lesions	Skeletal Predilection of Malignant Osseous Neoplasms
Axial skeleton	*Skull and facial bones*: Osteoma, osteoblastoma, Langerhans cell histiocytosis, fibrous dysplasia, solitary hemangioma, osteoporosis circumscripta (lytic phase of Paget disease)	*Skull and facial bones*: Mesenchymal chondrosarcoma, multiple myeloma, metastatic neuroblastoma, metastatic carcinoma
	Jaw: Giant cell reparative granuloma, myxoma, ossifying fibroma, desmoplastic fibroma	*Mandible*: Osteosarcoma
	Spine: Aneurysmal bone cyst, osteoblastoma, Langerhans cell histiocytosis, hemangioma	*Spine*: Chordoma, myeloma, metastases
Appendicular skeleton	*Long tubular bones*: Osteoid osteoma, simple bone cyst, aneurysmal bone cyst, osteochondroma, enchondroma, periosteal chondroma, chondroblastoma, chondromyxoid fibroma, nonossifying fibroma, giant cell tumor, osteofibrous dysplasia, desmoplastic fibroma, intraosseous ganglion	*Long tubular bones*: Osteosarcoma (all variants), adamantinoma, malignant fibrous histiocytoma, primary lymphoma, chondrosarcoma, angiosarcoma, fibrosarcoma
	Hands and feet: Giant cell reparative granuloma, florid reactive periostitis, enchondroma, glomus tumor, epidermoid cyst, subungual exostosis, bizarre parosteal osteochondromatous lesion	*Hands and feet*: None
Specific predilections	Simple bone cyst—proximal humerus, proximal femur	Adamantinoma—tibia, fibula
	Osteofibrous dysplasia—tibia, fibula (anterior cortex)	Parosteal osteosarcoma—distal femur (posterior cortex)
	Osteoid osteoma—femur, tibia	Periosteal osteosarcoma—tibia
	Chondromyxoid fibroma—tibia, metaphyses	Clear cell chondrosarcoma—proximal femur and humerus
	Chondroblastoma—epiphyses	Chordoma—sacrum, clivus, C2
	Giant cell tumor—articular ends of femur, tibia, radius	Multiple myeloma—pelvis, spine, skull
	Liposclerosing myxofibrous tumor—intertrochanteric region of femur	

Modified from Fechner RE, Mills SE, 1993, with permission.

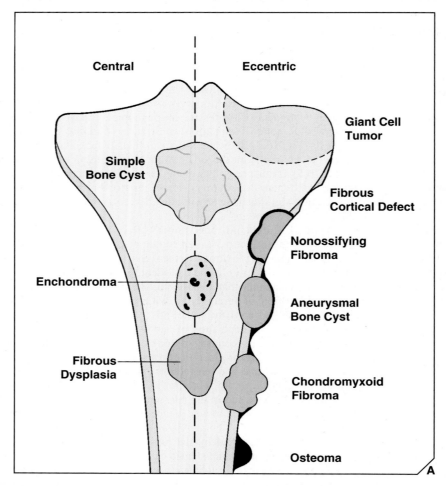

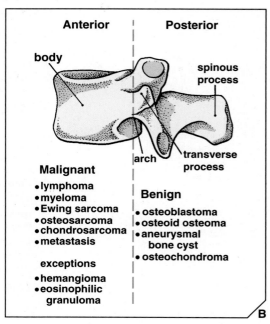

FIGURE 16.31 **Site of the lesion.** **(A)** Eccentric versus central location of the similar-appearing lesions is helpful in differential diagnosis. **(B)** Distribution of various tumors and tumor-like lesions in a vertebra. Malignant lesions are seen predominantly in its anterior part (body), while benign lesions predominate in its posterior elements (neural arch).

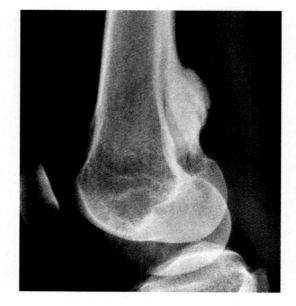

FIGURE 16.32 **Parosteal osteosarcoma.** Parosteal osteosarcoma has a predilection for the posterior aspect of the distal femur.

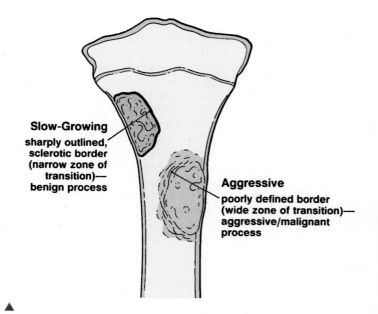

FIGURE 16.33 **Borders of the lesion.** The radiographic features of the borders of a lesion characterize it as either slow growing (and most likely benign) or aggressive (and most likely malignant).

FIGURE 16.34 Borders of the lesion: benign ▶ versus malignant. **(A)** A sclerotic border or narrow zone of transition from normal to abnormal bone typifies a benign lesion, as in this example of nonossifying fibroma (*arrows*). **(B)** A wide zone of transition typifies an aggressive/malignant lesion, in this case a solitary plasmacytoma involving the pubic bone and the supra-acetabular portion of the right ilium (*arrows*).

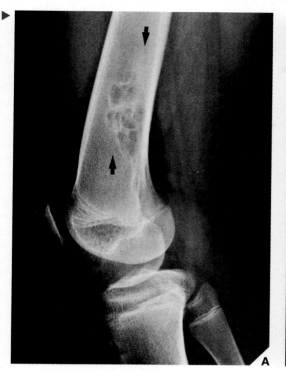
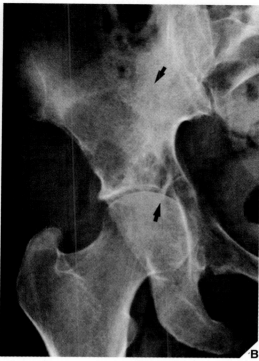

TABLE 16.4 Bone Lesions Usually Lacking a Sclerotic Border	
Benign	**Malignant**
Acute osteomyelitis	Angiosarcoma
Brown tumor of hyperparathyroidism	Fibrosarcoma
	Leiomyosarcoma of bone
Enchondroma in short tubular bone	Leukemia
	Lymphoma
Fibrocartilaginous mesenchymoma	Malignant fibrous histiocytoma
	Metastases from primary tumor in lung, gastrointestinal tract, kidney, breast, or thyroid
Giant cell tumor	
Langerhans cell histiocytosis (sometimes)	Myeloma (plasmacytoma)
Osteolytic phase of Paget disease	Telangiectatic osteosarcoma

TABLE 16.5 Bone Lesions Commonly Displaying a Sclerotic Border	
Benign	**Malignant**
Aneurysmal bone cyst	Chordoma
Benign fibrous histiocytoma	Clear-cell chondrosarcoma
Bone abscess	Conventional chondrosarcoma (sometimes)
Chondroblastoma	
Chondromyxoid fibroma	Low-grade central osteosarcoma
Epidermoid inclusion cyst	Some malignant tumors after treatment with radiation or chemotherapy
Fibrous cortical defect	
Fibrous dysplasia	
Giant cell reparative granuloma	
Intraosseous ganglion	
Intraosseous lipoma	
Medullary bone infarct	
Nonossifying fibroma	
Osteoblastoma	
Osteofibrous dysplasia	
Periosteal chondroma	
Simple bone cyst	

FIGURE 16.35 Osteosarcoma after chemotherapy. After ▶ 3 months of combined therapy with methotrexate, doxorubicin hydrochloride, and vincristine, the anteroposterior radiograph of the knee of this 16-year-old boy with a conventional osteosarcoma of the right tibia reveals reactive sclerosis at the borders of the tumor and a narrow zone of transition, features more often seen in benign lesions. The patient underwent a limb-salvage procedure.

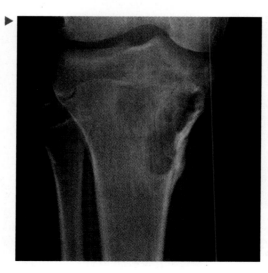

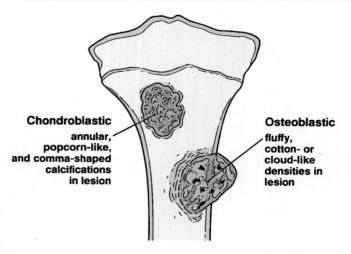

Chondroblastic
annular,
popcorn-like,
and comma-shaped
calcifications
in lesion

Osteoblastic
fluffy,
cotton- or
cloud-like
densities in
lesion

▲
FIGURE 16.36 Tumor matrix. Radiographic features of the matrix of tumors and tumor-like lesions that characterize a lesion as cartilage forming or bone forming.

lesion may be either fibrous or cartilaginous in origin, although hollow structures produced by tumor-like lesions, such as simple bone cysts or intraosseous ganglia, can also present as radiolucent areas (Table 16.6). The list of tumors and pseudotumors that may present as radiodense lesions is provided in Table 16.7.

Type of Bone Destruction. The type of bone destruction caused by a tumor is primarily related to the tumor growth rate. While not pathognomonic for any specific neoplasm, the type of destruction, which can

be described as geographic, moth-eaten, or permeative (Fig. 16.39), may suggest not only a benign or malignant neoplastic process (Fig. 16.40A,B) but also, at times, the histologic type of a tumor, as in the permeative type of bone destruction characteristically produced by the so-called round cell tumors—Ewing sarcoma (Fig. 16.40C) and lymphoma.

Periosteal Response. The periosteal reaction to a neoplastic process in the bone is usually categorized as uninterrupted or interrupted (Fig. 16.41 and Table 16.8). The first type of reaction is marked by solid layers of periosteal density, indicating a long-standing benign process, such as that seen in osteoid osteoma (Fig. 16.42) or osteoblastoma (see Fig. 17.33). Uninterrupted reaction is also seen in nonneoplastic processes, such as Langerhans cell histiocytosis, osteomyelitis, bone abscess (Fig. 16.43), or pachydermoperiostosis, in fractures in the healing stage, or in hypertrophic pulmonary osteoarthropathy (Fig. 16.44). The interrupted type of periosteal reaction suggests malignancy or a highly aggressive nonmalignant process. It may present as a sunburst pattern, a lamellated (onion-skin) pattern, a velvet pattern, or a Codman triangle, and it is commonly seen in malignant primary tumors such as osteosarcoma or Ewing sarcoma (Fig. 16.45).

Soft-Tissue Extension. With few exceptions—such as giant cell tumors, aneurysmal bone cysts, osteoblastomas, or desmoplastic fibromas—benign tumors and tumor-like bone lesions usually do not exhibit soft-tissue extension; thus, almost invariably, a soft-tissue mass indicates an aggressive lesion and one that is in many instances malignant (Fig. 16.46). It should be kept in mind, however, that nonneoplastic conditions such as osteomyelitis also exhibit a soft-tissue component, but the involvement of the soft tissues is usually poorly defined, with obliteration of fatty tissue layers. In malignant processes, however, the tumor mass is sharply defined, extending through the destroyed cortex with preservation of the tissue planes (Fig. 16.47).

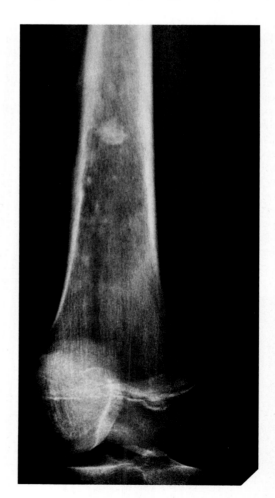

▲
FIGURE 16.37 Osteoblastic matrix. The matrix of a typical osteoblastic lesion, in this case an osteosarcoma, is characterized by the presence of fluffy, cotton-like densities within the medullary cavity of the distal femur.

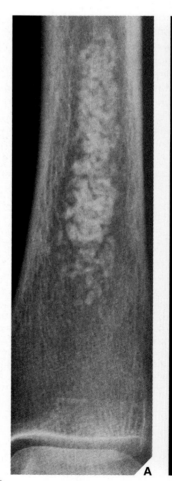
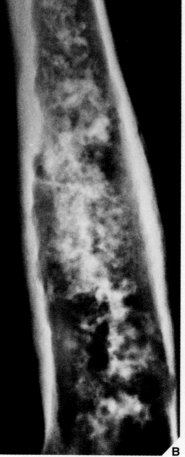

A
B

▲
FIGURE 16.38 Chondroid matrix. The matrix of the typical cartilaginous tumor is characterized by punctate, annular, and popcorn-like calcifications within the radiolucent lesion. **(A)** Enchondroma. **(B)** Chondrosarcoma.

TABLE 16.6 **Tumors and Pseudotumors That May Present as Radiolucent Lesions**

Solid	Cystic
Cartilaginous (enchondroma, chondroblastoma, chondromyxoid fibroma, chondrosarcoma)	Aneurysmal bone cyst
	Bone abscess
	Brown tumor of hyperparathyroidism
Ewing sarcoma	Cystic angiomatosis
Fibrous and histiocytic (nonossifying fibroma, fibrous dysplasia, osteofibrous dysplasia, desmoplastic fibroma, fibrosarcoma, malignant fibrous histiocytoma)	Hemophilic pseudotumor
	Hydatid cyst
	Intraosseous ganglion
	Intraosseous lipoma
Giant cell reparative granuloma	Simple bone cyst
Giant cell tumor	Various bone cysts (synovial, degenerative)
Langerhans cell histiocytosis	Vascular lesions
Lymphoma	
Metastatic (from lung, breast, gastrointestinal tract, kidney, thyroid)	
Myeloma (plasmacytoma)	
Osteoblastic (osteoid osteoma, osteoblastoma, telangiectatic osteosarcoma)	
Paget disease (osteolytic phase—osteoporosis circumscripta)	

TABLE 16.7 **Tumors and Pseudotumors That May Present as Radiodense Lesions**

Benign	Malignant
Bone island	Adamantinoma
Caffey disease	Chondrosarcoma
Calcifying enchondroma	Ewing sarcoma (after chemotherapy)
Condensing osteitis	
Diskogenic vertebral sclerosis	Lymphoma
Healed fibrous cortical defect	Osteoblastic metastasis
Healed nonossifying fibroma	Osteosarcoma, conventional
Healing or healed fracture	Parosteal osteosarcoma
Liposclerosing myxofibrous tumor	
Mastocytosis	
Medullary bone infarct	
Melorheostosis	
Osteoblastoma	
Osteofibrous dysplasia	
Osteoid osteoma	
Osteoma	
Osteonecrosis	
Osteopoikilosis	
Sclerosing hemangioma	

In the case of a bone lesion associated with a soft-tissue mass, it is always helpful to determine which condition arose first. Is the soft-tissue lesion, in other words, an extension of a primary bone tumor or is it itself a primary lesion that has invaded the bone? Although not always applicable, certain imaging criteria may help in deciding this issue (Fig. 16.48). In most instances, for example, a large soft-tissue mass and a smaller bone lesion indicate secondary skeletal involvement. Ewing sarcoma breaks this rule, however. Its destructive primary bone lesion may be small and often accompanied by a large soft-tissue mass. A destructive lesion of bone lacking a periosteal reaction and adjacent to a soft-tissue mass may indicate secondary invasion by a primary soft-tissue tumor, which usually destroys the neighboring periosteum. This contrasts with primary bone lesions, which usually prompt a periosteal reaction when they break through the cortex and extend into adjacent soft tissues. Because these observations are not universally applicable, however, they should be taken only as indicators and not as pathognomonic features.

Multiplicity of Lesions. A multiplicity of malignant lesions usually indicates metastatic disease, multiple myeloma, or lymphoma (Fig. 16.49). Very rarely do primary malignant lesions, such as an osteosarcoma or Ewing sarcoma, present as multifocal disease. Benign lesions, however, tend to involve multiple sites, as in polyostotic fibrous dysplasia (Fig. 16.50), multiple osteochondromas (see Fig. 18.36), enchondromatosis (see Fig. 18.21), Langerhans cell histiocytosis, hemangiomatosis, and fibromatosis.

FIGURE 16.39 **Type of bone destruction.** The radiographic features of the type of bone destruction may suggest a benign or malignant neoplastic process. ▶

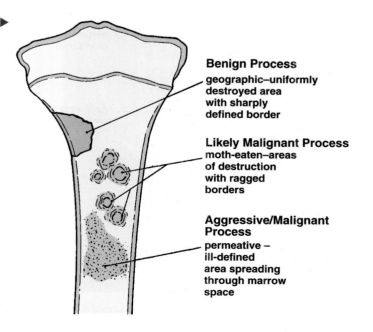

Benign Process
geographic–uniformly destroyed area with sharply defined border

Likely Malignant Process
moth-eaten–areas of destruction with ragged borders

Aggressive/Malignant Process
permeative – ill-defined area spreading through marrow space

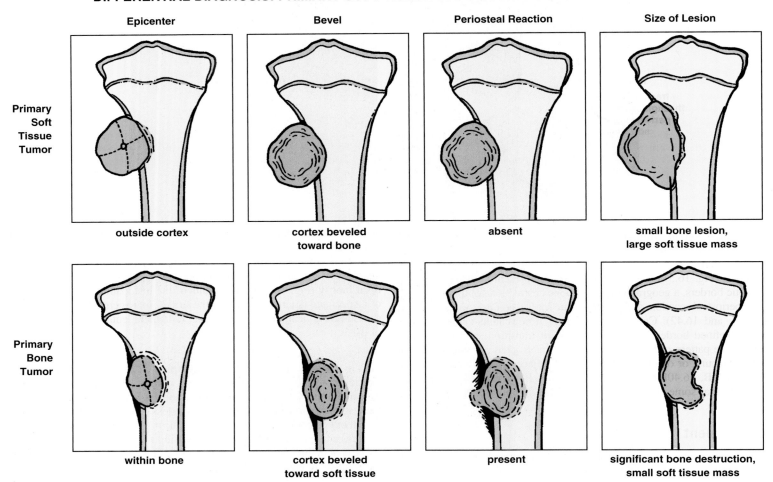

▲
FIGURE 16.48 **Primary soft-tissue tumor versus primary bone tumor.** Certain radiographic features of bone and soft-tissue lesions may help differentiate a primary soft-tissue tumor invading the bone from a primary bone tumor invading soft tissues.

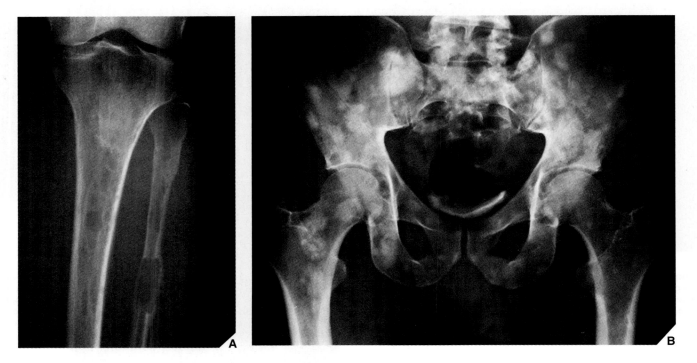

▲
FIGURE 16.49 **Multiplicity of lesion. (A)** Multiple myeloma is characterized by numerous osteolytic lesions. **(B)** Metastatic disease may also present with multiple foci, as seen in this 66-year-old man with carcinoma of the prostate. Note several osteoblastic lesions scattered throughout the pelvis and both femora.

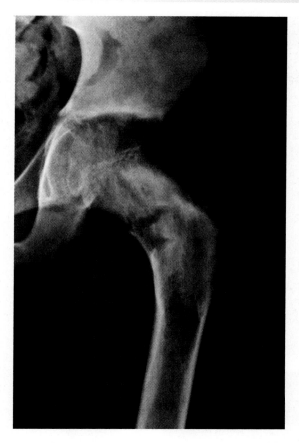

▲
FIGURE 16.50 **Multiplicity of lesion—fibrous dysplasia.** Anteroposterior radiograph of the hip in a 10-year-old boy with polyostotic fibrous dysplasia shows numerous sites of involvement in the left femur and ilium. Scintigraphy (not shown here) demonstrated the involvement of additional sites.

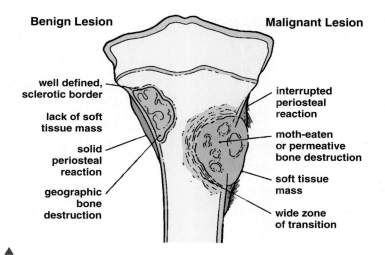

▲
FIGURE 16.51 **Benign versus malignant lesion.** Radiographic features that may help differentiate benign from malignant lesions.

TABLE 16.9 **Benign Lesions With Aggressive Features**

Lesion	Radiographic Presentation
Osteoblastoma (aggressive)	Bone destruction and soft-tissue extension similar to osteosarcoma
Desmoplastic fibroma	Expansive destructive lesion, frequently trabeculated
Periosteal desmoid	Irregular cortical outline, mimics osteosarcoma or Ewing sarcoma
Giant cell tumor	Occasionally aggressive features such as osteolytic bone destruction, cortical penetration, and soft-tissue extension
Aneurysmal bone cyst	Soft-tissue extension, occasionally mimicking malignant tumor (i.e., telangiectatic osteosarcoma)
Osteomyelitis	Bone destruction, aggressive periosteal reaction Occasionally, features resembling osteosarcoma, Ewing sarcoma, or lymphoma
Langerhans cell histiocytosis	Bone destruction, aggressive periosteal reaction Occasionally, features resembling Ewing sarcoma
Pseudotumor of hemophilia	Bone destruction, periosteal reaction occasionally mimics malignant tumor
Myositis ossificans	Features of parosteal or periosteal osteosarcoma, soft-tissue osteosarcoma, or liposarcoma
Brown tumor of hyperparathyroidism	Lytic bone lesion, resembling malignant tumor

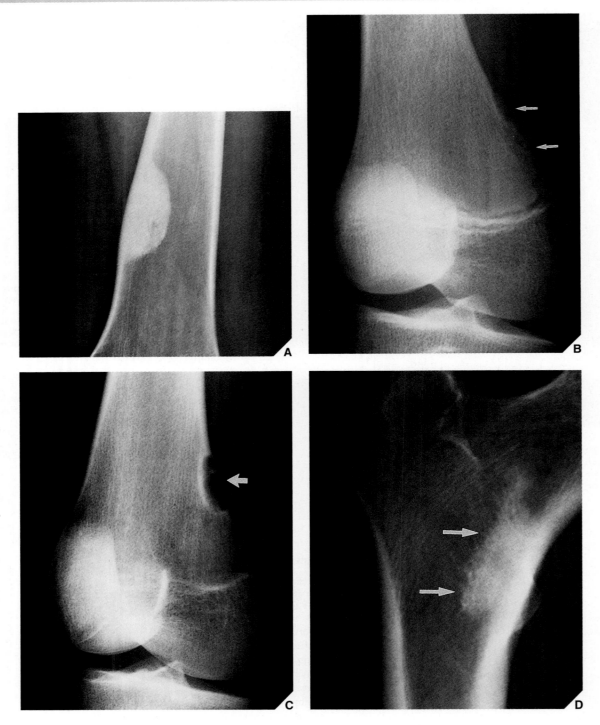

FIGURE 16.52 "Don't touch" lesions. **(A)** A typical benign "don't touch" lesion, in this case a nonossifying fibroma in healing phase, should not be mistaken for a malignant tumor of bone. **(B)** Another "don't touch" lesion, a periosteal (cortical) desmoid (*arrows*) in a typical location at the distal femoral metaphysis, medially. **(C)** A fibrous cortical defect (*arrow*) is an innocent fibrous lesion that never requires biopsy. **(D)** A bone island (*arrows*) should be recognized by a characteristic brush border and not to be mistaken for a sclerotic neoplasm.

TABLE 16.10 "Don't Touch" Lesions That Should Not Undergo Biopsy

Tumors and Tumor-like Lesions	Nonneoplastic Processses
Fibrous cortical defect	Stress fracture
Nonossifying fibroma (healing phase)	Avulsion fracture (healing stage)
Periosteal (cortical) desmoid	Bone infarct
Small, solitary focus of fibrous dysplasia	Bone island (enostosis)
Pseudotumor of hemophilia	Myositis ossificans
Intraosseous ganglion	Degenerative and posttraumatic cysts
Enchondroma in a short, tubular bone	Brown tumor of hyperparathyroidism
Intraosseous hemangioma	Diskogenic vertebral sclerosis

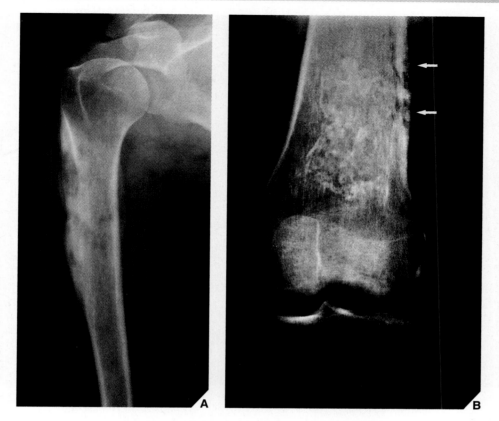

▲
FIGURE 16.53 Ambiguous lesions: chronic osteomyelitis and bone infarction. **(A)** A typical "ambiguous" lesion exhibiting aggressive characteristics requires biopsy. The radiographic differential diagnosis in this case included osteosarcoma, Ewing sarcoma, lymphoma, and bone infection. Biopsy revealed chronic osteomyelitis. **(B)** Although the lesion in the distal femur exhibits all the characteristics of the medullary bone infarct, the lateral cortex shows some permeation and lamellated periosteal reaction (*arrows*), features not ordinarily seen with benign condition. Biopsy revealed MFH arising in bone infarct.

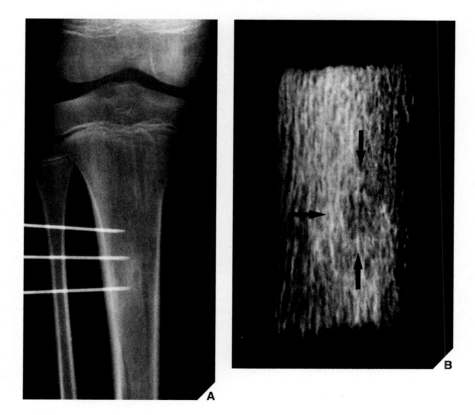

▲
FIGURE 16.54 Osteoid osteoma. **(A)** During surgery for resection of a nidus of osteoid osteoma in the proximal diaphysis of the tibia of a 10-year-old boy, needles are taped into the skin to localize the nidus. **(B)** Radiograph of the resected specimen demonstrates complete excision of the lesion (*arrows*).

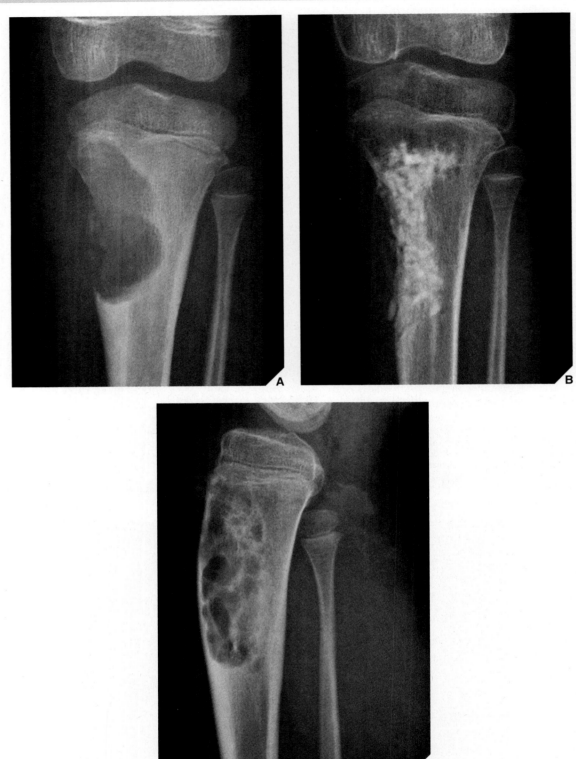

FIGURE 16.55 **Chondromyxoid fibroma.** A 9-year-old boy was treated for a chondromyxoid fibroma, a benign cartilaginous lesion in the proximal left tibia. **(A)** Preoperative film shows a lesion exhibiting a thin sclerotic border with endosteal scalloping, a geographic-type bone destruction, and a solid buttress of periosteal new bone formation at its distal part. **(B)** Postoperative film shows the lesion's cavity packed with bone chips after curettage. **(C)** Two years later, the tumor recurred.

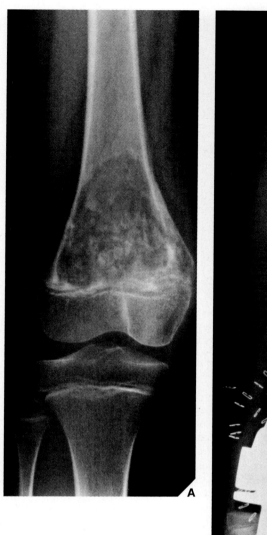

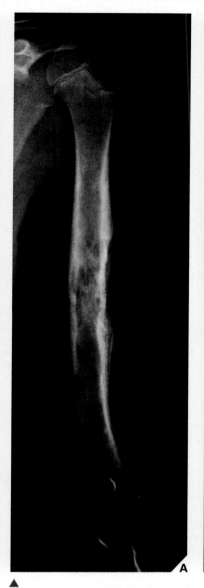
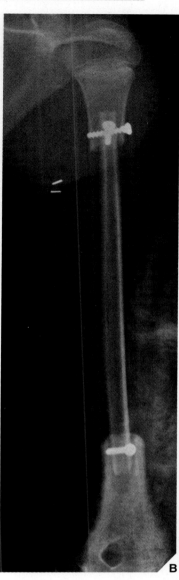

FIGURE 16.56   Osteosarcoma: endoprosthesis. After a course of chemotherapy, an 8-year-old girl with an osteosarcoma of the right femur (**A**) underwent radical resection of the distal three fourths of the femur, with insertion of an expandable and adjustable (LEAP) prosthesis (**B**), which can be lengthened as the child grows (see also Fig. 21.12). (Courtesy of Dr. MM Lewis, Santa Barbara, California.)

FIGURE 16.57   Ewing sarcoma: resection and bone grafting. After a course of radiotherapy and chemotherapy, a 9-year-old girl with a Ewing sarcoma in the diaphysis of the left humerus (**A**) underwent radical resection of the middle segment of the humerus. (**B**) Reconstruction was accomplished with the application of a fibular autograft.

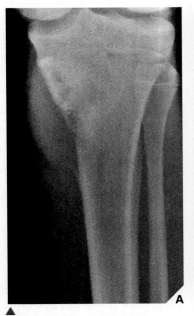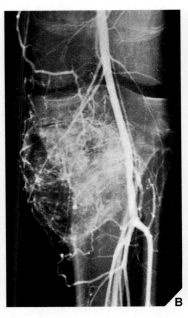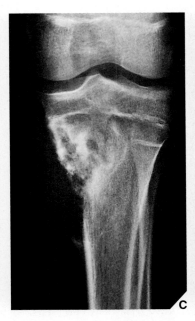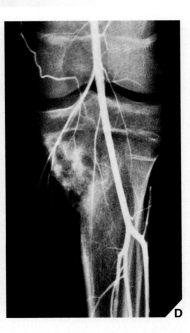

▲
FIGURE 16.58 **Osteosarcoma after chemotherapy. (A)** Anteroposterior radiograph of the proximal left tibia of a 15-year-old boy demonstrates an osteosarcoma in the metaphysis associated with a large soft-tissue mass. **(B)** An arteriogram done prior to treatment shows the soft-tissue mass to be hypervascular. After combination chemotherapy with methotrexate, vincristine, doxorubicin hydrochloride, and cisplatin, a repeated radiograph **(C)** and arteriogram **(D)** show marked reduction of the tumor mass. Subsequently, a wide resection of the proximal tibia was performed, and a metallic spacer similar to the one shown in Figure 16.56B was implanted.

limb-salvage procedures. The effectiveness of chemotherapy is best monitored by a combination of radiography, arteriography (Fig. 16.58), CT (see Fig. 16.12), and MRI. Recurrence or metastatic spread of a tumor can be effectively shown at an early stage on scintigraphy, CT, or MRI.

Complications

Although the most frequent direct complication of malignant bone tumors is metastasis, particularly to the lung, the most serious complication of some benign lesions is their potential for malignant transformation (Fig. 16.59; see also Table 16.2). Moreover, some benign lesions, such as those seen in multiple cartilaginous exostoses

(Fig. 16.60) or enchondromatosis (see Fig. 18.22B), may result in severe growth disturbance. The most common complication of tumors and tumor-like lesions in general, however, is pathologic fracture. Although not a diagnostic feature, this may complicate both benign and malignant lesions. Among lesions with a high potential for fracture are simple bone cysts, large nonossifying fibromas (Fig. 16.61), fibrous dysplasia, and enchondromas (see Fig. 18.4). Occasionally, pathologic fracture is the first sign of a neoplastic process. Other complications, such as pressure erosion of adjacent bone (Fig. 16.62) or compression of adjacent blood vessels or nerves (see Fig. 18.30B), may occur with growth of a lesion beyond the cortex.

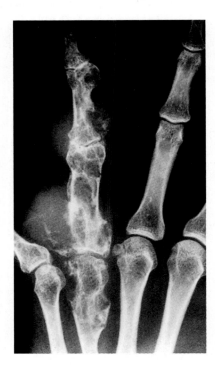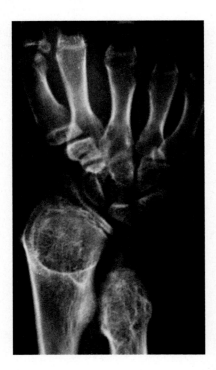

▲
FIGURE 16.59 **Malignant transformation to chondrosarcoma.** An enchondroma at the base of the ring finger of this 32-year-old man with multiple enchondromatosis underwent sarcomatous transformation to a chondrosarcoma.

▲
FIGURE 16.60 **Multiple cartilaginous exostoses: growth disturbance.** Anteroposterior radiograph of the wrist of a 14-year-old boy with multiple cartilaginous exostoses (osteochondromas) shows marked growth disturbance of the distal ends of the radius and ulna.

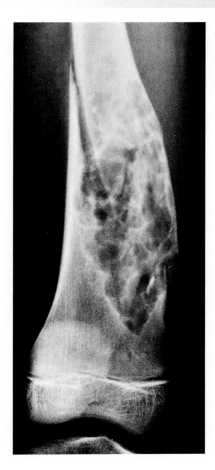

▲
FIGURE 16.61 Nonossifying fibroma complicated by a pathologic fracture. A 9-year-old boy with a giant nonossifying fibroma of the distal diaphysis of the right femur developed a pathologic fracture, a common complication of this lesion.

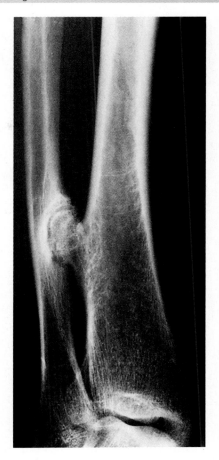

▲
FIGURE 16.62 Osteochondroma eroding the adjacent bone. Extension of a lesion arising from the posterolateral aspect of the distal tibia in a 24-year-old man with an osteochondroma erodes the adjacent fibula.

Soft-Tissue Tumors

Unlike tumors and tumor-like lesions of bone, most soft-tissue tumors (Table 16.11) lack specific radiographic characteristics that might be helpful in their diagnosis. Some findings, however, may point to a particular kind of lesion. For instance, calcified phleboliths in a soft-tissue mass suggest a hemangioma or hemangiomatosis (Fig. 16.63); radiolucency within a mass suggests a lipoma (Fig. 16.64); mottled lucencies within a dense mass, in association with bone formation,

TABLE 16.11 **Most Common Benign and Malignant Soft-tissue Lesions**

Benign	Malignant
Ganglion	Rhabdomyosarcoma
Lipoma	Leiomyosarcoma
Myoma, leiomyoma	Malignant fibrous histiocytoma
Fibroma	Fibrosarcoma
Myxoma	Myxofibrosarcoma
Hemangioma, hemangiomatosis	Malignant schwannoma
	Spindle-cell sarcoma
Lymphangioma	Liposarcoma
Chondroma	Synovial sarcoma
Neurofibroma	Extraskeletal osteosarcoma
Desmoid	Extraskeletal chondrosarcoma
Giant cell tumor of tendon sheath	Hemangioendothelioma
	Kaposi sarcoma
Morton neuroma	Angiosarcoma

suggest liposarcoma (Fig. 16.65); popcorn-like calcifications suggest soft-tissue chondroma or chondrosarcoma; similar calcifications in the vicinity of a joint, particularly when associated with bone destruction, suggest synovial sarcoma; and ill-defined, nonhomogeneous, smudgy bone in a soft-tissue mass may indicate a soft-tissue osteosarcoma (Fig. 16.66). Several investigators implied the efficacy of MRI in the characterization and evaluation of soft-tissue masses; its superiority over CT stems from the lack of ionizing radiation, its capability of multidirectional and multiplanar imaging, and its excellent contrast resolution and accurate anatomic definition of soft-tissue tumors. On T1-weighted pulsing sequences, the majority of soft-tissue masses display low-to-intermediate signal intensity, whereas on T2-weighted images they display high-signal intensity. There are, however, masses that show high-signal intensity on T1 weighting because of blood or fat content, such as lipomas, hemangiomas, and chronic hematomas. One of the fatty tumors that does not show a high signal on T1 weighting is myxoid liposarcoma. At present, however, as Sundaram contended based on MRI results, neither visual characteristics nor signal intensity values permit one to distinguish or predict the histology of soft-tissue masses. Nevertheless, certain criteria are very helpful to predict the benign or malignant nature of the tumor; sharp margination and homogeneity of the mass favor benignity, whereas prominent peritumoral edema and necrosis suggest malignancy. Recently, the application of high-resolution ultrasound including color Doppler ultrasound, power Doppler ultrasound, and spectral wave analysis was advocated for the initial assessment and sonographic-guided core biopsy of ambiguous soft-tissue masses.

The main role of the radiologist is not to make a specific diagnosis, but rather to demonstrate the extent of the lesion and decide whether the lesion is a tumor or pseudotumor (Table 16.12), and in case of malignancy, whether it is a primary soft-tissue tumor invading the bone

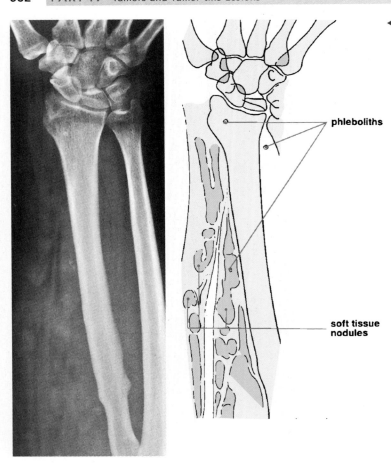

phleboliths

soft tissue
nodules

◄ FIGURE 16.63   **Soft-tissue hemangiomatosis.** Conventional radiograph in a 39-year-old woman with a nodular swelling of the left forearm demonstrates multiple small calcified phleboliths, suggesting the diagnosis of hemangiomatosis.

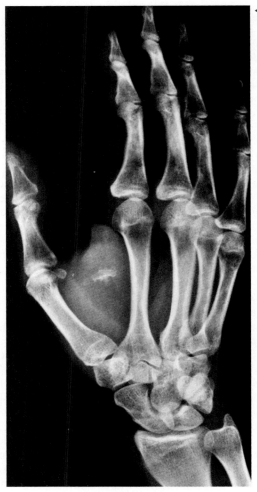

◄ FIGURE 16.64   **Soft-tissue lipoma.** Oblique radiograph of the hand of a 27-year-old woman with a soft-tissue mass in the dorsal aspect shows a radiolucent lesion in the soft tissues adjacent to the radial aspect of the second metacarpal bone. Within the radiolucent area there is evidence of bone formation.

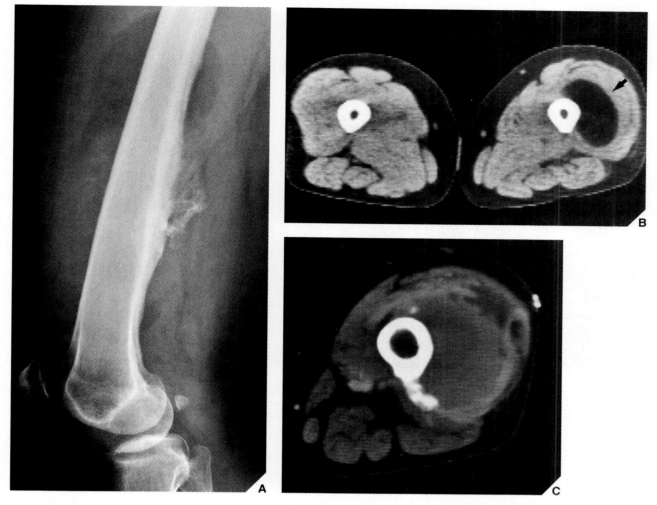

▲
FIGURE 16.65 **Soft-tissue liposarcoma. (A)** Lateral radiograph in a 54-year-old man with a slowly enlarging mass on the posterior aspect of the thigh demonstrates a poorly defined soft-tissue mass with radiolucent areas and bone formation at the site of the posterior cortex of the femur. **(B)** CT section at the level of the radiolucency confirms the presence of fatty tissue (*arrow*). **(C)** A section through the bone formation discloses a denser mass infiltrating surrounding muscular structures.

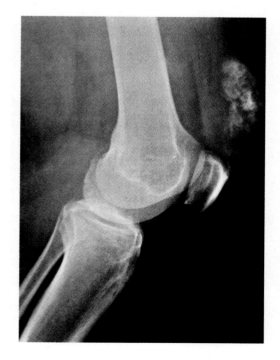

▲
FIGURE 16.66 **Soft-tissue osteosarcoma.** A 51-year-old woman presented with a large suprapatellar soft-tissue mass. Lateral radiograph of the knee demonstrates a mass with ill-defined nonhomogeneous bone formation in the central part of the lesion. (From Greenspan A et al., 1987, with permission.)

or an extracortical extension of a primary bone tumor (see Fig. 16.48). Most often, this is achieved by using arteriography (Fig. 16.67), CT (Fig. 16.68), and MRI (Fig. 16.69). After this, the radiologist's role may become more active, involving fluoroscopy-guided or CT-guided percutaneous biopsy of the lesion. In this respect, arteriography helps select the proper area for biopsy, with the specimen usually taken from the most vascular part of the lesion (Fig. 16.70).

TABLE 16.12 **Most Common Benign Soft-tissue Masses That May Mimic Neoplasms**

Abscess	Myositis ossificans
Amyloidoma	Nodular fasciitis
Calcific myonecrosis	Pigmented villonodular synovitis
Cyst	Pseudoaneurysm
Florid reactive periostitis	Reactive adenopathy
Foreign body granuloma	Rheumatoid nodule
Ganglion	Seroma
Gouty tophus	Synovial cyst
Hematoma	Tumoral calcinosis

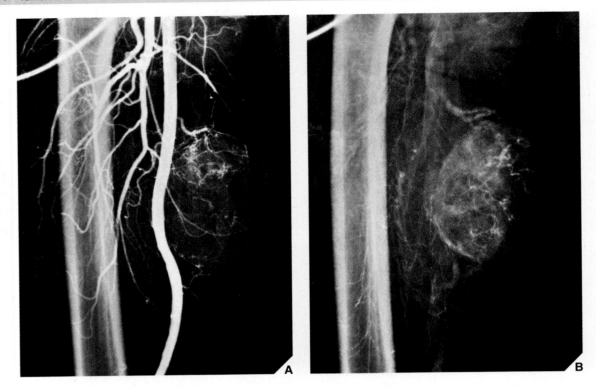

▲
FIGURE 16.67 **Soft-tissue MFH.** Femoral arteriography was performed on a 56-year-old man with a tumor on the medial aspect of the right thigh, which proved to be a MFH of the soft tissues. **(A)** The arterial phase demonstrates the displacement of the superficial femoral artery by the tumor, the extent of the tumor and area of neovascularity, and the accumulation of contrast agent within the tumor. **(B)** The venous phase shows the accumulation of contrast in abnormal vessels and a tumor "stain," as well as the topography of venous structures.

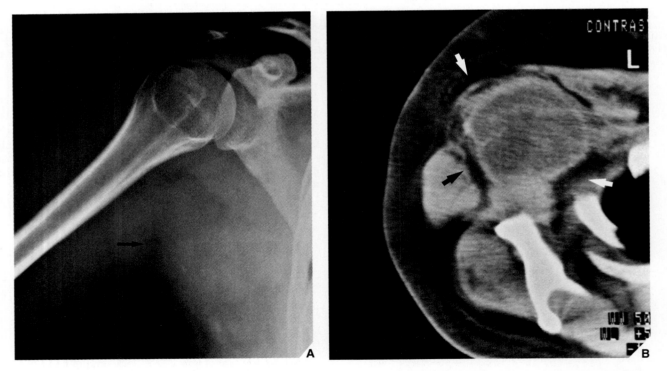

▲
FIGURE 16.68 **Soft-tissue fibrosarcoma. (A)** Anteroposterior radiograph of the shoulder of a 40-year-old woman with a history of an enlarging mass in the right axilla shows an ill-defined mass (*arrows*) adjacent to the lateral border of the scapula. **(B)** CT section with contrast enhancement shows the extent of the mass (*arrows*) and the lack of bone involvement.

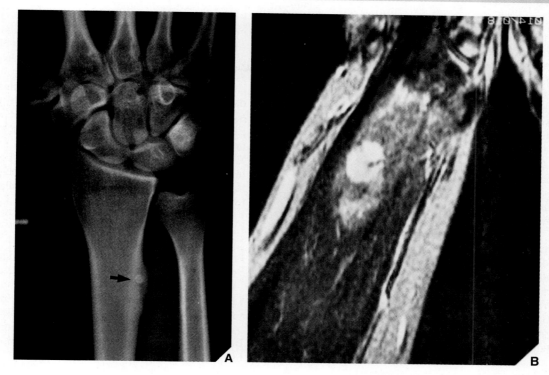

FIGURE 16.69 **Intramuscular hemangioma.** A 34-year-old woman presented with pain in the distal left forearm. (**A**) The radiograph demonstrates periosteal reaction at the ulnar border of the distal radius, associated with a phlebolith (*arrow*). (**B**) Coronal T2-weighted MRI (SE; TR 2000/TE 80 msec) shows a large mass situated in the pronator quadratus muscle of the distal forearm, displaying heterogeneous signal ranging from intermediate to high intensity. (From Greenspan A et al., 1992, with permission.)

FIGURE 16.70 **Parosteal liposarcoma.** Vascular study of the patient shown in Figure 16.65 shows that the lesion consists of two parts: the proximal part is more radiolucent and hypovascular (*arrow*), while the distal part is denser and more hypervascular (*open arrows*). The biopsy specimen on which the diagnosis of liposarcoma was made was obtained from the more vascular segment of the tumor. After radical resection and examination of the entire specimen, the more radiolucent hypovascular area revealed almost no malignant component. Had the biopsy been obtained only from that part of the tumor, the result probably would not have been consistent with the final diagnosis.

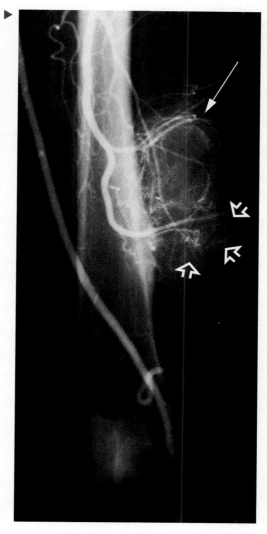

PRACTICAL POINTS TO REMEMBER

[1] The most helpful clinical data concerning patients presenting with suspected bone or soft-tissue lesions are:
- the age of the patient
- the duration of the symptoms
- the growth rate of the tumor.

[2] In the evaluation of tumors or tumor-like bone lesions, several key radiographic features should be sought, including:
- the site of the lesion (the particular bone and site in the bone affected)
- the nature of the border of the lesion (narrow or wide zone of transition)
- the type of matrix (calcified, ossified, or hollow)
- the type of bone destruction (geographic, moth-eaten, or permeative)
- the periosteal reaction (solid or interrupted—sunburst, velvet, lamellated, Codman triangle)
- the presence or absence of soft-tissue extension.

[3] A lytic (radiolucent) lesion located in the epiphysis and showing a narrow zone of transition is most likely a chondroblastoma.

[4] A lytic lesion lacking a sclerotic border and extending into the articular end of a bone after closure of the growth plate is most likely a giant cell tumor. The absence of extension into the articular end of the bone virtually excludes giant cell tumor.

[5] A centrally located lesion having a sclerotic border and abutting the growth plate in the proximal humerus or proximal femur is most likely a simple bone cyst.

[6] A radiolucent lesion located in the lateral aspect of the calcaneus is most likely a simple bone cyst.

[7] An eccentrically located lesion ballooning out from the cortex and seen in a patient below 20 years of age is most likely an aneurysmal bone cyst or a chondromyxoid fibroma. If the patient is 30 or older, these possibilities are remote.

[8] A radiolucent lesion in a short tubular bone is most likely an enchondroma.

[9] A lesion with a sclerotic margin located in the anterior aspect of the tibia in a child is most likely an osteofibrous dysplasia (Kempson-Campanacci lesion). A similar lesion or multiple osteolytic lesions in the tibia in adults most likely represent adamantinoma.

[10] A lesion in the medial aspect of distal femur lying close to the linea aspera and showing cortical irregularity is most likely a periosteal desmoid.

[11] An intramedullary lesion in the posterior aspect of the distal femur having a scalloped, sclerotic margin is most likely a nonossifying fibroma.

[12] A sclerotic, lobulated lesion on the surface of the posterior aspect of distal femur should be considered to represent a parosteal osteosarcoma.

[13] An ill-defined lesion displaying calcifications and located on the anterior aspect of the tibia should raise the possibility of periosteal osteosarcoma.

[14] A lesion in a vertebral body is most often a metastasis, a myeloma, lymphoma, hemangioma, or Langerhans cell histiocytosis.

[15] A lesion in the posterior vertebral arch is most likely an aneurysmal bone cyst, osteoblastoma, or osteoid osteoma.

[16] A lesion most likely represents a benign tumor when it exhibits:
- geographic bone destruction
- a sclerotic margin
- solid, uninterrupted periosteal reaction, or no periosteal response
- no soft-tissue mass.

[17] A lesion most likely represents a malignant tumor when it shows:
- poorly defined margins (a wide zone of transition)
- a moth-eaten or permeative type of bone destruction
- an interrupted periosteal reaction
- a soft-tissue mass.

[18] A lesion most likely represents a cartilage tumor (e.g., enchondroma or chondrosarcoma) when it exhibits:
- lobulation (endosteal scalloping)
- punctate, annular, or comma-like calcifications in the matrix.

[19] An eccentric lesion displaying a solid buttress of periosteal reaction is most likely an aneurysmal bone cyst, chondromyxoid fibroma, or juxtacortical chondroma.

[20] A lesion exhibiting a moth-eaten or permeative type of bone destruction and associated with a large soft-tissue mass without ossifications or calcifications is most likely a Ewing sarcoma. If the patient is younger than age 5 years or is black, Ewing sarcoma is unlikely.

[21] When a soft-tissue mass and a destructive bone lesion coexist, certain radiographic features of the lesion may help differentiate a primary soft-tissue tumor invading bone from a primary bone tumor invading soft tissue:
- the epicenter of the lesion: if outside the bone, then it is probable that it is primary soft tissue; if within it, then it is probable that it is primary bone
- the bevel of cortical destruction: if directed toward the bone, then it is probable that it is primary soft tissue; if toward the soft tissue, then it is probable that it is primary bone
- the absence of periosteal reaction: probable primary soft tissue
- a large soft-tissue mass and a small bone lesion: probable primary soft tissue (with the exception of Ewing sarcoma).

[22] Benign lesions such as fibrous dysplasia, nonossifying fibroma, Langerhans cell histiocytosis, hemangioma, cartilaginous exostoses, and enchondroma tend to be multiple. Multiple malignant lesions, on the other hand, should raise the possibility of metastatic disease, multiple myeloma, and lymphoma.

[23] In the evaluation of soft-tissue lesions, some imaging findings can help suggest a diagnosis. Among these are:
- phleboliths (hemangioma)
- radiolucent areas within the mass (lipoma)
- dense areas dispersed with radiolucencies and ossifications (liposarcoma)
- ill-defined ossifications within the dense mass (osteosarcoma)
- mass near the joint with calcifications (synovial sarcoma)
- popcorn-like calcifications within the mass (chondroma or chondrosarcoma).

[24] MRI features suggesting a benign soft-tissue mass include sharp margination and homogeneity of the lesion, whereas prominent peritumoral edema and necrosis suggest malignant nature.

SUGGESTED READINGS

Aoki J, Wanatabe H, Shinozaki T, et al. FDG PET of primary benign and malignant bone tumors: standardized uptake value in 52 lesions. *Radiology* 2001;219:774–777.

Arata MA, Peterson HA, Dahlin DC. Pathological fractures through nonossifying fibromas: review of the Mayo Clinic experience. *J Bone Joint Surg [Am]* 1981;63A:890–988.

Ayala AG, Zornosa J. Primary bone tumors: percutaneous needle biopsy. *Radiology* 1983;149:675–679.

Barnes G, Gwinn J. Distal irregularities of the femur simulating malignancy. *Am J Roentgenol* 1974;122:180–185.

Berquist TH. Magnetic resonance imaging of musculoskeletal neoplasms. *Clin Orthop* 1989;244:101–118.

Berquist TH. Magnetic resonance imaging of primary skeletal neoplasms. *Radiol Clin North Am* 1993;31:411–424.

Bloem JL. *Radiological staging of primary malignant musculoskeletal tumors. A correlative study of CT, MRI, ^{99m}Tc scintigraphy and angiography.* The Hague, the Netherlands: A. Jongbloed; 1988.

Bloem JL, Reiser MF, Vanel D. Magnetic resonance contrast agents in evaluation of the musculoskeletal system. *Magn Res Q* 1990;6:136–163.

Bloem JL, Taminiau AHM, Eulderink F, Hermans J, Pauwels EK. Radiologic staging of primary bone sarcoma: MR imaging, scintigraphy, angiography, and CT correlated with pathologic examination. *Radiology* 1988;169:805–810.

Bodner G, Schocke MFH, Rachbauer F, et al. Differentiation of malignant and benign musculoskeletal tumors: combined color and power Doppler US and spectral wave analysis. *Radiology* 2002;223:410–416.

Brown KT, Kattapuram SV, Rosenthal DI. Computed tomography analysis of bone tumors: patterns of cortical destruction and soft tissue extension. *Skeletal Radiol* 1986;15:448–451.

Conrad EU III, Enneking WF. Common soft tissue tumors. *Clin Symp* 1990;42:2–32.

Crim JR, Seeger LL, Yao L, Chandnani V, Eckardt JJ. Diagnosis of soft-tissue masses with MR imaging: can benign masses be differentiated from malignant ones? *Radiology* 1992;185:581–586.

Dahlin DC, Unni KK. *Bone tumors: general aspects and data on 8542 cases*, 4th ed. Springfield: Charles C. Thomas; 1986.

Davies MA, Wellings RM. Imaging of bone tumors. *Curr Opin Radiol* 1992;4:32–38.

Dewhirst MW, Sostman HD, Leopold KA, et al. Soft-tissue sarcomas: MR imaging and MR spectroscopy for prognosis and therapy monitoring. Work in progress. *Radiology* 1990;174:847–853.

Dinauer PA, Brixey CJ, Moncur JT, Fanburg-Smith JC, Murphey MD. Pathologic and MR imaging features of benign fibrous soft-tissue tumors in adults. *Radiographics* 2007;27:173–187.

Dorfman HD, Czerniak B. *Bone tumors*. St. Louis: Mosby; 1998:1–33.

Edeiken J, Hodes PJ, Caplan LH. New bone production and periosteal reaction. *Am J Roentgenol* 1966;97:708–718.

Elias DA, White LM, Simpson DJ, et al. Osseous invasion by soft-tissue sarcoma: assessment with MR imaging. *Radiology* 2003; 229:145–152.

Enneking WF. Staging of musculoskeletal neoplasms. *Skeletal Radiol* 1985;13:183–194.

Enneking WF, Spanier SS, Goodman MA. A system for the surgical staging of musculoskeletal sarcoma. *Clin Orthop* 1980;153:106–120.

Enzinger FM, Weiss SW. *Soft tissue tumors*, 3rd ed. St. Louis: Mosby; 1995:3–56.

Erlemann R, Reiser MF, Peters PE, et al. Musculoskeletal neoplasms: static and dynamic Gd-DPTA-enhanced MR imaging. *Radiology* 1989;171:767–773.

Erlemann R, Sciuk J, Bosse A, et al. Response of osteosarcoma and Ewing sarcoma to preoperative chemotherapy: assessment with dynamic and static MR imaging and skeletal scintigraphy. *Radiology* 1990;175:791–796.

Ewing J. A review and classification of bone sarcomas. *Arch Surg* 1922;4:485–533.

Fayad LM, Bluemke DA, Weber KL, Fishman EK. Characterization of pediatric skeletal tumors and tumor-like conditions: specific cross-sectional imaging signs. *Skeletal Radiol* 2006;35:259–268.

Fechner RE, Mills SE. *Tumors of the bones and joints*. Washington, DC: Armed Forces Institute of Pathology; 1993:1–16.

Fletcher DM, Unni KK, Mertens F, eds. *World Health Organization Classification of Tumors: Pathology and Genetics of Tumors of Soft Tissue and Bones*. Lyon, France: IARC Press; 2002.

Frank JA, Ling A, Patronas NJ, et al. Detection of malignant bone tumors: MR imaging vs. scintigraphy. *Am J Roentgenol* 1990;155:1043–1048.

Galasko CS. The pathological basis for skeletal scintigraphy. *J Bone Joint Surg [Br]* 1975;57B:353–359.

Gartner L, Pearce CJ, Saifuddin A. The role of the plain radiographs in the characterisation of soft tissue tumours. *Skeletal Radiol* 2009;38:549–558.

Gaskin CM, Helms CA. Lipomas, lipoma variants, and well-differentiated liposarcomas (atypical lipomas): results of MRI evaluations of 126 consecutive fatty masses. *Am J Roentgenol* 2004;182:733–739.

Gatenby RA, Mulhern CB, Moldofsky PJ. Computed tomography guided thin needle biopsy of small lytic bone lesions. *Skeletal Radiol* 1984;11:289–291.

Gillespy T III, Manfrini M, Ruggieri P, Spanier SS, Pettersson H, Springfield DS. Staging of intraosseous extent of osteosarcoma: correlation of pre-operative CT and MR imaging with pathologic macroslides. *Radiology* 1988;167:765–767.

Gold RH, Bassett LW. Radionuclide evaluation of skeletal metastases: practical considerations. *Skeletal Radiol* 1986;15:1–9.

Golfieri R, Baddeley H, Pringle JS, et al. Primary bone tumors. MR morphologic appearance correlated with pathologic examinations. *Acta Radiol* 1991;32: 290–298.

Greenfield GB, Warren DL, Clark RA. MR imaging of periosteal and cortical changes of bone. *Radiographics* 1991;11:611–623.

Greenspan A. Pragmatic approach to bone tumors. *Semin Orthop* 1991;6:125–133.

Greenspan A. Bone island (enostosis): current concept—a review. *Skeletal Radiol* 1995;24:111–115.

Greenspan A, Jundt G, Remagen W. *Differential diagnosis in orthopaedic oncology*, 2nd ed. Philadelphia: Lippincott Williams & Wilkins; 2007.

Greenspan A, Klein MJ. Radiology and pathology of bone tumors. In: Lewis MM, ed. *Musculoskeletal oncology. A multidisciplinary approach*. Philadelphia: WB Saunders; 1992:13–72.

Greenspan A, McGahan JP, Vogelsang P, Szabo RM. Imaging strategies in the elevation of soft-tissue hemangiomas of the extremities: correlation of the findings of plain radiography, angiography, CT, MRI, and ultrasonography in 12 histologically proven cases. *Skeletal Radiol* 1992;21:11–18.

Greenspan A, Stadalnik RC. Bone island: scintigraphic findings and their clinical application. *Can Assoc Radiol J* 1995;46:368–379.

Greenspan A, Stadalnik RC. Central versus eccentric lesions of long tubular bones. *Semin Nucl Med* 1996;26:201–206.

Greenspan A, Steiner G, Norman A, Lewis MM, Matlen J. Osteosarcoma of the soft tissues of the distal end of the thigh. *Skeletal Radiol* 1987;16:489–492.

Griffin N, Khan N, Thomas JM, Fisher C, Moskovic EC. The radiological manifestations of intramuscular haemangiomas in adults: magnetic resonance imaging, computed tomography and ultrasound appearances. *Skeletal Radiol* 2007;36:1051–1059.

Hamada K, Ueda T, Tomita Y, et al. False positive 18F-FDG PET in an ischial chondroblastoma; an analysis of glucose transporter 1 and hexokinase II expression. *Skeletal Radiol* 2006;35:306–310.

Hanna SL, Fletcher BD, Parham DM, Bugg MR. Muscle edema in musculoskeletal tumors: MR imaging characteristics and clinical significance. *J Magn Reson Imaging* 1991;1:441–449.

Hanna SL, Langston JW, Gronemeyer SA, Fletcher BD. Subtraction technique for contrast-enhanced MR images of musculoskeletal tumors. *Magn Reson Imaging* 1990;8:213–215.

Hayes CW, Conway WF, Sundaram M. Misleading aggressive MR imaging appearance of some benign musculoskeletal lesions. *Radiographics* 1992;12:1119–1134.

Helms C, Munk P. Pseudopermeative skeletal lesions. *Br J Radiol* 1990;63:461–467.

Helms CA. Skeletal "don't touch" lesions. In: Brant WE, Helms CA, eds. *Fundamentals of diagnostic radiology*. Baltimore: Williams & Wilkins; 1994:963–975.

Hermann G, Abdelwahab IF, Miller TT, Klein MJ, Lewis MM. Tumor and tumor-like conditions of the soft tissue: magnetic resonance imaging features differentiating benign from malignant masses. *Br J Radiol* 1992;65:14–20.

Hudson TM. *Radiologic-pathologic correlation of musculoskeletal lesions*. Baltimore: Williams & Wilkins; 1987.

Huvos AG. *Bone tumors. Diagnosis, treatment and prognosis*. Philadelphia: WB Saunders; 1979.

Jaffe HL. *Tumors and tumorous conditions of the bones and joints*. Philadelphia: Lea & Febiger; 1968.

Jelinek JS, Murphey MD, Welker JA, et al. Diagnosis of primary bone tumors with image-guided percutaneous biopsy: experience with 110 tumors. *Radiology* 2002;223:731–737.

Johnson LC. A general theory of bone tumors. *Bull NY Acad Med* 1953;29:164–171.

Kloiber R: Scintigraphy of bone tumors. In: *Current concepts of diagnosis and treatment of bone and soft tissue tumors*. Berlin: Springer-Verlag; 1984:55–60.

Kransdorf MJ. Malignant soft-tissue tumors in a large referral population: distribution of diagnoses by age, sex, and location. *Am J Roentgenol* 1995;164:129–134.

Kransdorf MJ, Bancroft LW, Peterson JJ, Murphey MD, Foster WC, Temple HT. Imaging of fatty tumors: distinction of lipoma and well-differentiated liposarcoma. *Radiology* 2002;224:99–104.

Kransdorf M, Jelinek J, Moser RP Jr, et al. Soft-tissue masses. Diagnosis using MR imaging. *Am J Roentgenol* 1989;153:541–547.

Kransdorf MJ, Murphey MD. *Imaging of soft tissue tumors*. Philadelphia: WB Saunders; 1997.

Kransdorf MJ, Murphey MD. Radiologic evaluation of soft-tissue masses: a current perspective. *Am J Roentgenol* 2000;175:575–587.

Kransdorf MJ, Murphey MD, Sweet DE. Liposclerosing myxofibrous tumor: a radiologic-pathologic-distinct fibro-osseous lesion of bone with a marked predilection for the intertrochanteric region of the femur. *Radiology* 1999;212:693–698.

Kransdorf MJ. Magnetic resonance imaging of musculoskeletal tumors. *Orthopedics* 1994;17:1003–1016.

Kricun ME. Radiographic evaluation of solitary bone lesions. *Orthop Clin North Am* 1983;14:39–64.

Lang P, Honda G, Roberts T, et al. Musculoskeletal neoplasm: perineoplastic edema versus tumor on dynamic postcontrast MR images with spatial mapping of instantaneous enhancement rates. *Radiology* 1995;197:831–839.

Larsson SE, Lorentzon R. The incidence of malignant primary bone tumors in relation to age, sex and site. A study of osteogenic sarcoma, chondrosarcoma, and Ewing's sarcoma diagnosed in Sweden from 1958–1968. *J Bone Joint Surg [Br]* 1974;56B:534–540.

Lewis MM. The use of an expandable and adjustable prosthesis in the treatment of childhood malignant bone tumors of the extremity. *Cancer* 1986;57:499–502.

Lewis MM, Sissons HA, Norman A, Greenspan A. Benign and malignant cartilage tumors. In: Griffin PP, ed. *Instructional course lectures*. Chicago: American Academy of Orthopaedic Surgeons; 1987:87–114.

Lichtenstein L. *Bone tumors*, 5th ed. St. Louis: Mosby; 1977.

Lodwick GS. A systematic approach to the roentgen diagnosis of bone tumors. In: *M.D. Anderson Hospital and Tumor Institute—Clinical Conference on Cancer: Tumors of Bone and Soft Tissue*. Chicago: Year Book; 1965:49–68.

Lodwick GS. Solitary malignant tumors of bone: the application of predictor variables in diagnosis. *Semin Roentgenol* 1966;1:293–313.

Lodwick GS, Wilson AJ, Farrell C, Virtama P, Dittrich F. Determining growth rates of focal lesions of bone from radiographs. *Radiology* 1980;134:577–583.

Lodwick GS, Wilson AJ, Farrell C, Virtama P, Smeltzer FM, Dittrich F. Estimating rate of growth in bone lesions. Observer performance and error. *Radiology* 1980;134: 585–590.

Ma LD, Frassica FJ, McCarthy EF, Bluenke DA, Zerhouni EA. Benign and malignant musculoskeletal masses: MR imaging differentiation with rim-to-center differential enhancement ratios. *Radiology* 1997;202:739–744.

Ma LD, Frassica FJ, Scott WW Jr, Fishman EK, Zerhouni EA. Differentiation of benign and malignant musculoskeletal tumors: potential pitfalls with MR imaging. *Radiographics* 1995;15:349–366.

Madewell JE, Ragsdale BD, Sweet DE. Radiologic and pathologic analysis of solitary bone lesions. Part I: Internal margins. *Radiol Clin North Am* 1981;19:715–748.

Magid D. Two-dimensional and three-dimensional computed tomographic imaging in musculoskeletal tumors. *Radiol Clin North Am* 1993;31:425–447.

McCarthy EF. CT-guided needle biopsies of bone and soft tissue tumors: a pathologist's perspective. *Skeletal Radiol* 2007;36:181–182.

McCarthy EF. Histological grading of primary bone tumors. *Skeletal Radiol* 2009;38:947–948.

McCarville B. The role of positron emission tomography in pediatric musculoskeletal oncology. *Skeletal Radiol* 2006;35:553–554.

McNeil BJ. Value of bone scanning in neoplastic disease. *Semin Nucl Med* 1984; 14:277–286.

Miller TT. Bone tumors and tumorlike conditions: analysis with conventional radiography. *Radiology* 2008;246:662–674.

Mink J. Percutaneous bone biopsy in the patient with known or suspected osseous metastases. *Radiology* 1986;161:191–194.

Mirowitz SA. Fast scanning and fat-suppression MR imaging of musculoskeletal disorders. *Am J Roentgenol* 1993;161:1147–1157.

Mirra JM, Picci P, Gold RH. *Bone tumors: clinical, radiologic and pathologic correlations.* Philadelphia: Lea & Febiger; 1989.

Moore SG, Bisset GS, Siegel MJ, Donaldson JS. Pediatric musculoskeletal MR imaging. *Radiology* 1991;179:345–360.

Moser RP. Cartilaginous tumors of the skeleton. In: *AFIP atlas of radiologic-pathologic correlations.* Fascicle II. St. Louis: Mosby-Year Book; 1990.

Moser RP, Madewell JE. An approach to primary bone tumors. *Radiol Clin North Am* 1987;25:1049–1093.

Moulton JS, Blebea JS, Dunco DM, Braley SE, Bisset GS, Emery KH. MR imaging of soft tissue masses: diagnostic efficacy and value of distinguishing between benign and malignant lesions. *Am J Roentgenol* 1995;164:1191–1199.

Mulder JD, Kroon HM, Schütte HE, Taconis WK. *Radiologic atlas of bone tumors.* Amsterdam, the Netherlands: Elsevier; 1993:9–46.

Mulligan ME, Badros AZ. PET/CT and MR imaging in myeloma. *Skeletal Radiol* 2007;36:5–16.

Munk PL, Lee MJ, Janzen DL, et al. Lipoma and liposarcoma: evaluation using CT and MR imaging. *Am J Roentgenol* 1997;169:589–594.

Murray RO, Jacobson HG. *The radiology of bone diseases,* 2nd ed. New York: Churchill Livingstone; 1977.

Negendank WG, Crowley MG, Ryan JR, Keller NA, Evelhoch JL. Bone and soft-tissue lesions: diagnosis with combined H-1 MR imaging and P-31 MR spectroscopy. *Radiology* 1989;173:181–188.

Nelson MC, Stull MA, Teitelbaum GP, et al. Magnetic resonance imaging of peripheral soft tissue hemangiomas. *Skeletal Radiol* 1990;19:477–482.

Nelson SW. Some fundamentals in the radiologic differential diagnosis of solitary bone lesions. *Semin Roentgenol* 1966;1:244–267.

Norman A, Dorfman HD. Juxtacortical circumscribed myositis ossificans: evolution and radiographic features. *Radiology* 1970;96:301–306.

Norman A, Schiffman M. Simple bone cyst: factors of age dependency. *Radiology* 1977;124:779–782.

Nuovo MA, Norman A, Chumas J, Ackerman LV. Myositis ossificans with atypical clinical, radiographic, or pathologic findings: a review of 23 cases. *Skeletal Radiol* 1992;27:87–101.

Oliveira AM, Nascimento AG. Grading in soft tissue tumors: principles and problems. *Skeletal Radiol* 2001;30:543–559.

Olson P, Everson LI, Griffith HJ. Staging of musculoskeletal tumors. *Radiol Clin North Am* 1994;32:151–162.

Panicek DM, Gatsonis C, Rosenthal DI, et al. CT and MR imaging in the local staging of primary malignant musculoskeletal neoplasms: report of the Radiology Diagnostic Oncology Group. *Radiology* 1997;202:237–246.

Peterson JJ, Kransdorf MJ, Bancroft LW, O'Connor MI. Malignant fatty tumors: classification, clinical course, imaging appearance and treatment. *Skeletal Radiol* 2003;32:493–503.

Pettersson H, Eliasson J, Egund N, et al. Gadolinium-DTPA enhancement of soft tissue tumors in magnetic resonance imaging—preliminary clinical experience in five patients. *Skeletal Radiol* 1988;14:319–323.

Ragsdale BD, Madewell JE, Sweet DE. Radiologic and pathologic analysis of solitary bone lesions. Part II: Periosteal reactions. *Radiol Clin North Am* 1981;19:749–783.

Reinus WR, Wilson AJ. Quantitative analysis of solitary lesions of bone. *Invest Radiol* 1995;30:427–432.

Schajowicz F. *Tumors and tumorlike lesions of bone. Pathology, radiology, and treatment,* 2nd ed. Berlin, Germany: Springer-Verlag; 1994:1–21.

Seeger LL, Widoff BE, Bassett LW, Rosen G, Eckardt JJ. Preoperative evaluation of osteosarcoma: value of gadopentetate dimeglumine-enhanced MR imaging. *Am J Roentgenol* 1991;157:347–351.

Selby S. Metaphyseal cortical defects in the tubular bones of growing children. *J Bone Joint Surg* 1961;43:395–400.

Shin DS, Shon OJ, Han DS, Choi JH, Chun KA, Cho IH. The clinical efficacy of 18F-FDG-PET/CT in benign and malignant musculoskeletal tumors. *Ann Nucl Med* 2008;22:603–609.

Shuman WP, Patten RM, Baron RL, Liddell RM, Conrad EU, Richardson ML. Comparison of STIR and spin-echo MR imaging at 1.5T in 45 suspected extremity tumors: lesion conspicuity and extent. *Radiology* 1991;179:247–252.

Sostman HD, Charles HC, Rockwell S, et al. Soft-tissue sarcomas: detection of metabolic heterogeneity with P-31 MR spectroscopy. *Radiology* 1990;176:837–843.

Spjut HJ, Dorfman HD, Fechner RE, Ackerman LV. Tumors of bone and cartilage. In: *Atlas of tumor pathology,* Fascicle 5. Washington, DC: Armed Forces Institute of Pathology; 1971.

Sundaram M, McLeod R. MR imaging of tumor and tumorlike lesions of bone and soft tissue. *Am J Roentgenol* 1990;155:817–824.

Sweet DE, Madewell JE, Ragsdale BD. Radiologic and pathologic analysis of solitary bone lesions. Part III: Matrix patterns. *Radiol Clin North Am* 1981;19:785–814.

Tateishi U, Yamaguchi U, Seki K, Terauchi T, Arai Y, Kim EE. Bone and soft-tissue sarcoma: preoperative staging with Fluorine 18 fluorodeoxyglucose PET/CT and conventional imaging. *Radiology* 2007;245:839–847.

Trian R, Su M, Trian Y, et al. Dual-time point PET/CT with F-18 FDG for differentiation of malignant and benign bone lesions. *Skeletal Radiol* 2009;38:451–458.

Unni KK, ed. *Bone tumors.* New York: Churchill Livingstone; 1988.

Vanel D, Verstraete KL, Shapeero LG. Primary tumors of the musculoskeletal system. *Radiol Clin North Am* 1997;35:213–237.

Verstraete KL, De Deene Y, Roels H, Dierick A, Uyttendaele D, Kunnen M. Benign and malignant musculoskeletal lesions: dynamic contrast-enhanced MR imaging—parametric "first-pass" images depict tissue vascularization and perfusion. *Radiology* 1994;192:835–843.

Volberg FM Jr, Whalen JP, Krook L, Winchester P. Lamellated periosteal reactions: a radiologic and histologic investigation. *Am J Roentgenol* 1977;128:85–87.

Widmann G, Riedl QA, Schoepf D, et al. State-of-the-art HR-US imaging findings of the most frequent musculoskeletal soft-tissue tumors. *Skeletal Radiol* 2009;38:637–649.

CHAPTER 17

Benign Tumors and Tumor-like Lesions I
Bone-Forming Lesions

Benign Bone-Forming (Osteoblastic) Lesions

Bone-forming neoplasms are characterized by the formation of osteoid or mature bone directly by the tumor cells. They include osteoma, osteoid osteoma, and osteoblastoma.

Osteoma

An osteoma is a slow-growing osteoblastic lesion commonly seen in the outer table of the calvarium and in the frontal and ethmoid sinuses. It is also occasionally encountered in long and short tubular bones, and at these sites, it is known as a parosteal osteoma. The lesion grows on the bone surface and has the radiographic appearance of a dense, ivory-like sclerotic mass attached to the cortex with sharply demarcated borders (Fig. 17.1). Osteomas have been reported in patients from ages 10 to 79 years, with most in the fourth and fifth decades. Men and women are equally affected (Fig. 17.2). Histologically, osteoma is composed primarily of bone, with a mature lamellar architecture consisting of concentric rings as in compact bone or, more commonly, parallel plates as in cancellous bone. An osteoma is an asymptomatic lesion that does not recur if excised surgically. Its importance lies in its similar radiographic presentation to the more aggressive parosteal osteosarcoma (see Fig. 16.32) and its common association with cutaneous and subcutaneous masses and intestinal polyps in the condition known as Gardner syndrome (Fig. 17.3). Intestinal adenomatous polyps, particularly in the colon, may undergo a malignant transformation to carcinoma. The syndrome is a familial, autosomal-dominant disorder, frequently seen in Mormons in Utah.

Differential Diagnosis

The differential diagnosis of solitary parosteal osteoma should include parosteal osteosarcoma, sessile osteochondroma, juxtacortical myositis ossificans, periosteal osteoblastoma, ossified parosteal lipoma, and focus of melorheostosis (Fig. 17.4 and Table 17.1). Among these, parosteal osteosarcoma is the most important entity that needs to be excluded, which may be a difficult task radiographically, because both lesions appear as ivory-like masses attached to the bone's surface. The keys to recognizing osteoma, however, are its usually exquisitely smooth borders and well-circumscribed, intensely homogeneous sclerotic appearance on conventional radiographs. Parosteal osteosarcoma, in contrast, usually appears less dense and homogeneous than osteoma and may show a zone of decreased density at the periphery.

Sessile osteochondroma can usually be identified by its characteristic radiographic features: the cortex of the lesion merges without interruption with the cortex of the host bone, and the cancellous portion is continuous with the host medullary cavity of the adjacent metaphysis or diaphysis (see Fig. 18.26B).

A well-matured focus of myositis ossificans may occasionally mimic parosteal osteoma. The radiographic hallmark of myositis ossificans is the so-called zonal phenomenon, characterized by a radiolucent area in the center of the lesion that indicates immature bone formation and a dense zone of mature ossification at the periphery. Often a thin radiolucent cleft separates the ossific mass from the adjacent cortex. At times, however, a mature lesion may adhere to and fuse with the cortex, thus mimicking a parosteal osteoma. In these instances, computed tomography (CT) may demonstrate the classic zonal phenomenon of the lesion (see Figs. 4.57B and 4.58B).

Periosteal osteoblastoma and ossified parosteal lipoma rarely create a problem in terms of being mistaken for parosteal osteoma. Melorheostosis, a rare form of mixed sclerosing dysplasia, should be recognized on radiography by the characteristic appearance of segmental cortical thickening ("flowing hyperostosis"), often resembling wax dripping down one side of a candle. A typical focus of monostotic melorheostosis usually exhibits both parosteal and endosteal involvement, and the lesion commonly extends into the articular end of the bone, which are features that are almost never present in a parosteal osteoma (see Figs. 33.48 and 33.49).

Osteoid Osteoma

The most important clinical symptom of osteoid osteoma is pain that is more severe at night but is dramatically relieved by salicylates (Aspirin) within approximately 20 to 25 minutes. This typical history holds in more than 75% of cases and serves as an important clue to the diagnosis.

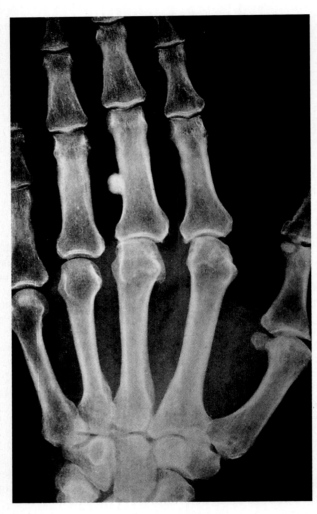

Osteoma

age: 30–50
M = F

■ common sites
■ less common sites

▲
FIGURE 17.1   Parosteal osteoma. Dorsovolar radiograph of the hand demonstrates a parosteal osteoma of the proximal phalanx of the middle finger. A typical ivory-like mass is seen attached to the cortex.

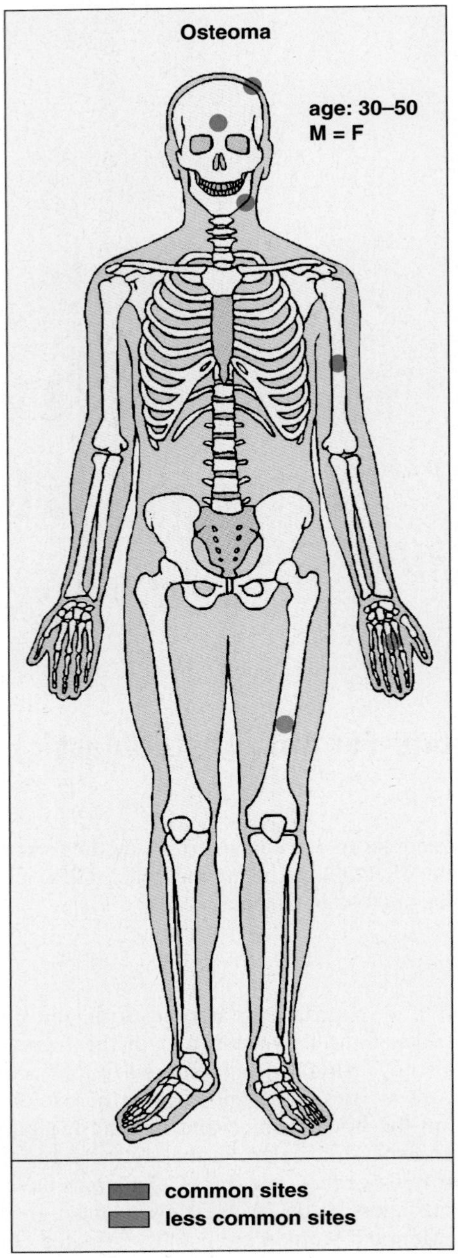

▲
FIGURE 17.2   Osteoma: skeletal sites of predilection, peak age range, and male-to-female ratio.

Osteoid osteoma occurs in the young, usually between the ages of 10 and 35, and its sites of predilection are the long bones, particularly the femur and tibia (Fig. 17.5).

Osteoid osteoma is a benign osteoblastic lesion characterized by a nidus of osteoid tissue, which may be purely radiolucent or have a sclerotic center. The nidus has limited growth potential and usually measures less than 1 cm in diameter. It is often surrounded by a zone of reactive bone formation (Fig. 17.6). Very rarely, an osteoid osteoma may have more than one nidus, in which case it is called a multicentric or multifocal osteoid osteoma (Fig. 17.7). Depending on its location in the particular part of the bone, the lesion can be classified as cortical, medullary (cancellous), or subperiosteal. Osteoid osteomas can be

further subclassified as extracapsular or intracapsular (intraarticular) (Fig. 17.8).

Standard radiographs may demonstrate the lesion, but CT (Fig. 17.9) is required to demonstrate the nidus and localize it precisely. CT has the added advantage of allowing exact measurement of the size of the nidus (Fig. 17.10). Frequently, when the lesion cannot be demonstrated radiographically, a radionuclide bone scan is helpful, because osteoid osteoma invariably shows a marked increase in isotope uptake (Fig. 17.11). This modality can be particularly helpful in cases for which the symptoms are atypical and the initial radiographs appear normal. The use of a three-phase technique is recommended. Radionuclide tracer activity can be observed on both immediate and delayed images (Fig. 17.12).

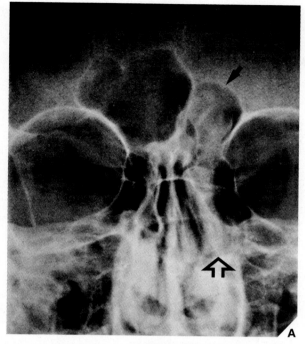

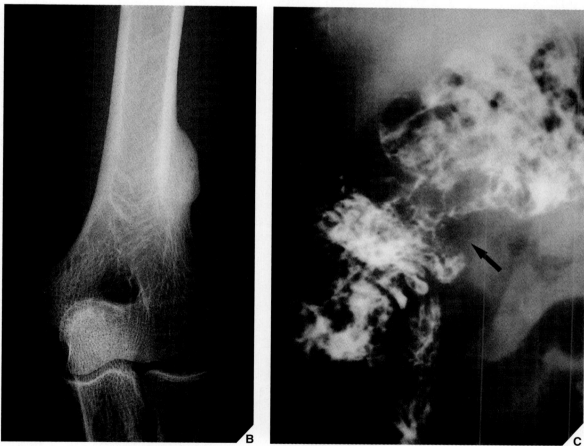

▲

FIGURE 17.3   **Gardner syndrome. (A)** Frontal radiograph of the facial bones of a 36-year-old man shows the typical appearance of osteomas in the left frontal (*arrow*) and ethmoid (*open arrow*) sinuses. The dense, sclerotic masses are sharply demarcated from the surrounding structures by air. **(B)** This patient also had a parosteal osteoma of the distal left humerus, (*arrow*) multiple polyps in the colon, and subcutaneous masses, features of Gardner syndrome. **(C)** Barium enema shows several polyps in the cecum and an apple-core lesion (*arrows*), proved by histologic examination to be adenocarcinoma.

RADIOLOGIC DIFFERENTIAL DIAGNOSIS OF OSTEOMA

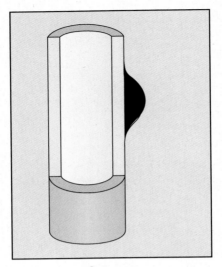

Osteoma

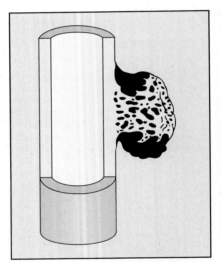

Parosteal Osteosarcoma

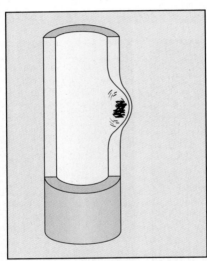

Sessile Osteochondroma

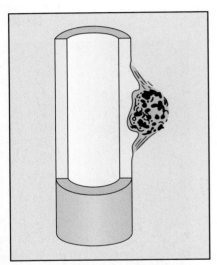

Periosteal Osteoblastoma

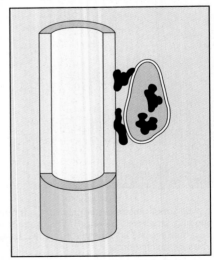

Ossified Parosteal Lipoma

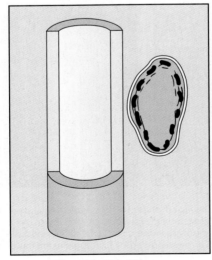

Myositis Ossificans

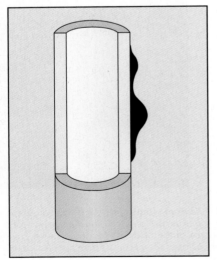

Melorheostosis

▲
FIGURE 17.4 **Differential diagnosis of parosteal osteoma.** Schematic representation of various cortical and juxtacortical lesions having similar appearance to osteoma.

TABLE 17.1 **Differential Diagnosis of Parosteal Osteoma**

Condition (Lesion)	Radiologic Features
Parosteal osteoma	Ivory-like, homogeneously dense sclerotic mass, with sharply demarcated borders, intimately attached to cortex; no cleft between lesion and adjacent cortex
Parosteal osteosarcoma	Ivory-like, frequently lobulated sclerotic mass, homogeneous or heterogeneous in density with more radiolucent areas at periphery; incomplete cleft between lesion and adjacent cortex occasionally present
Sessile osteochondroma	Cortex of host bone merges without interruption with cortex of lesion, and respective cancellous portions of adjacent bone and osteochondroma communicate
Juxtacortical myositis ossificans	Zonal phenomenon: radiolucent area in center of lesion and dense zone of mature ossification at periphery; frequently thin radiolucent cleft separates ossific mass from adjacent cortex
Periosteal osteoblastoma	Round or ovoid heterogeneous in density mass attached to cortex
Ossified parosteal (periosteal) lipoma	Lobulated mass containing irregular ossifications and radiolucent area of fat; hyperostosis of adjacent cortex occasionally present
Melorheostosis (monostotic)	Cortical thickening resembling wax dripping down one side of a candle

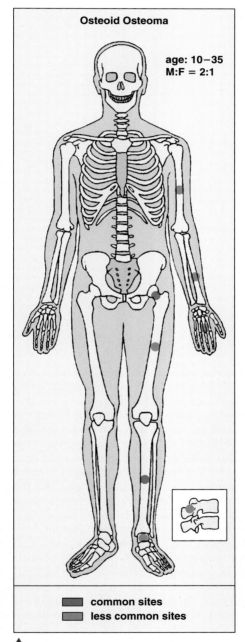

Osteoid Osteoma

age: 10–35
M:F = 2:1

common sites
less common sites

▲
FIGURE 17.5 Skeletal sites of predilection, peak age range, and male-to-female ratio in osteoid osteoma.

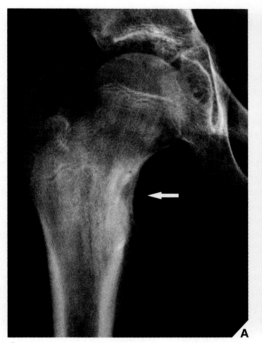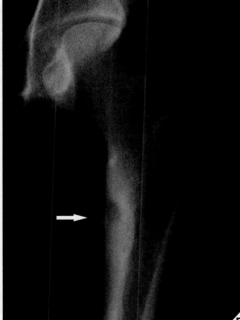

▲
FIGURE 17.6 Osteoid osteoma. **(A)** Anteroposterior radiograph of the right hip of a 12-year-old boy with a history of right groin pain that was more severe at night and was relieved promptly by aspirin shows the typical appearance and location of osteoid osteoma (*arrow*). The radiolucent nidus in the medial aspect of the femoral neck measures 1 cm in diameter and is surrounded by a zone of reactive sclerosis. Note the periarticular osteoporosis that usually accompanies this lesion. **(B)** Purely radiolucent nidus surrounded by a zone of reactive sclerosis (*arrow*) is seen in the medial femoral cortex of an 18-year-old woman.

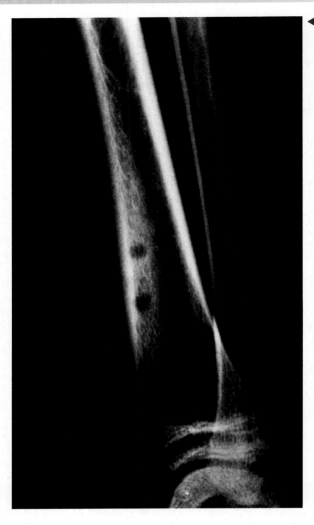

◄ **FIGURE 17.7** **Multifocal osteoid osteoma.** A 17-year-old boy presented with pain in the left lower leg for 3 months. It was promptly relieved by aspirin. Lateral radiograph of the lower leg shows two well-defined radiolucencies within a sclerotic area in the anterior aspect of the distal tibia. A resected specimen showed three nidi of osteoid osteoma, the two most distal of which were fairly close to one another, creating a single radiolucency on the radiograph. (From Greenspan A et al., 1974, with permission.)

If the nidus is demonstrated radiographically, the diagnosis can usually be made with great assurance; only atypical presentations create diagnostic difficulty (Fig. 17.13).

The suitability of magnetic resonance imaging (MRI) for the detection of osteoid osteoma remains unclear, and published reports have shown mixed results. Goldman and associates reported on four cases of intracapsular osteoid osteoma of the femoral neck, in which the lesions were evaluated with bone scintigraphy, CT, and MRI. Although in all cases abnormal findings were apparent in the MR images, the nidi could not be identified prospectively. On the basis of MRI findings of secondary bone marrow edema or synovitis, several incorrect diagnoses were made, which included Ewing sarcoma, osteonecrosis, stress fracture, and juvenile arthritis. In these cases, it is noteworthy that the correct diagnoses were made only after review of the radiographs and thin-section CT studies. Another report by Woods and associates involved three patients with a highly unusual association of osteoid osteoma with a reactive soft-tissue mass. In these cases, MRI studies might have led to confusion of osteoid osteoma with osteomyelitis or a malignant tumor. Moreover, in each case the nidus displayed different signal characteristics. In one case, the intensity of signal was generally low on all pulse sequences, but mild enhancement was seen after administration of gadolinium. In another case, the signal was of intermediate intensity, and administration of gadolinium revealed inhomogeneous enhancement of the nidus. For the third case in which radiographs showed the nidus to be intracortical, MRI could not identify the nidus distinctly.

However, some reports do suggest the effectiveness of MRI for demonstrating the nidus of osteoid osteoma (Figs. 17.14 and 17.15). Bell and colleagues clearly demonstrated an intracortical nidus on MRI that had not been seen on scintigraphy, angiography, or CT scans. In par-

ticular, imaging of osteoid osteoma with dynamic gadolinium-enhanced MR technique demonstrated greater conspicuity in detecting the lesion than with nonenhanced MRI.

Recently, Ebrahim and associates reported sonographic findings in patients with intraarticular osteoid osteoma. Ultrasound images revealed focal cortical irregularity and adjacent focal hypoechoic synovitis at the site of intraarticular lesions. The nidus was hypoechoic with posterior acoustic enhancement, and color Doppler imaging identified a vessel entering a focus of osteoid osteoma. It is noteworthy, however, that the authors concluded that the accuracy of sonography in the diagnosis of intraarticular osteoid osteoma cannot be certain because other intraarticular pathologic conditions, for example, inflammatory synovitis, may have a similar appearance. Therefore, one should seek corroborative features of this lesion using other imaging techniques, such as CT or MRI.

Histologically, the nidus is composed of osteoid or even mineralized immature bone. It is a small, well-circumscribed, and self-limited lesion. Its microtrabeculae and irregular islets of osteoid matrix and bone are surrounded by a richly vascular fibrous stroma in which osteoblastic and osteoclastic activities are often prominent. The perilesional sclerosis is composed of dense bone displaying a variety of maturation patterns.

Differential Diagnosis

It must be emphasized that even when dealing with an apparent cortical osteoid osteoma of classic radiographic appearance, the differential diagnosis should include a stress fracture, a cortical abscess, and an osteosarcoma (Fig. 17.16). In a stress fracture, the radiolucency is usually more linear than in an osteoid osteoma, and it runs perpendicular or at an angle to the cortex rather than parallel to it (Fig. 17.17). A cortical bone abscess may have a similar radiographic appearance to that of osteoid osteoma, but it can usually be differentiated by a linear,

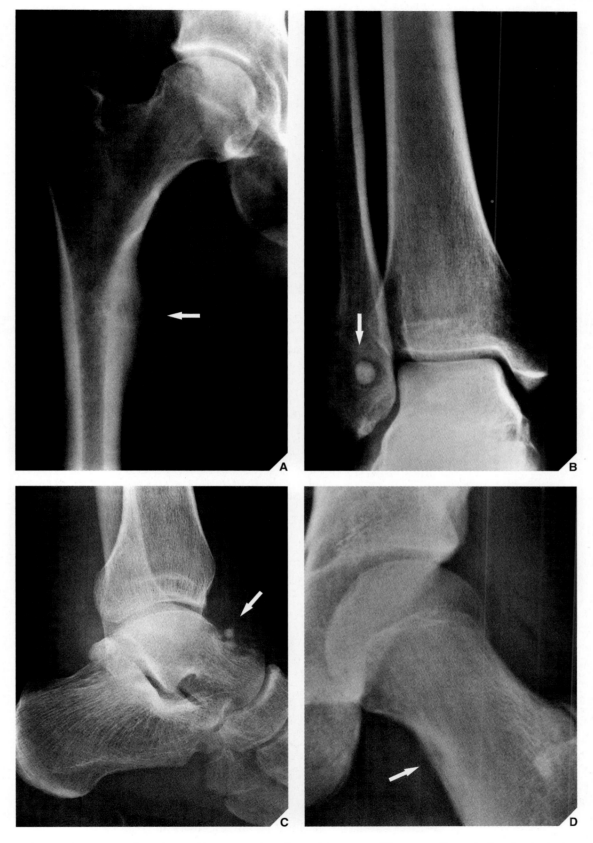

FIGURE 17.8 **Types of osteoid osteoma.** The radiographic presentation of osteoid osteoma differs according to its location in the bone. (**A**) In the cortical type, there is intense reactive sclerosis surrounding the nidus, as seen here in the medial cortex of the femur (*arrow*). (**B**) The medullary variant, as seen here in the distal fibula, exhibits a dense, sclerotic nidus surrounded by a halo of radiolucent osteoid tissue (*arrow*). Note the almost total lack of reactive sclerosis. (**C**) In subperiosteal osteoid osteoma, seen here on the surface of the talar bone (*arrow*), periosteal response is minimal and reactive sclerosis is completely absent. (**D**) In the intracapsular osteoid osteoma, the radiolucent nidus seen here in the medial aspect of the proximal portion of the femoral neck (*arrow*) shows only minimal reactive sclerosis.

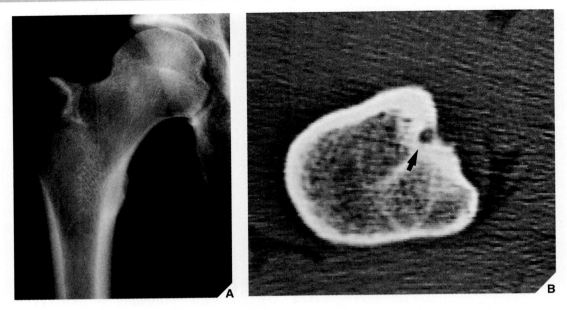

FIGURE 17.9   CT of osteoid osteoma. **(A)** Anteroposterior radiograph of the hip of a 24-year-old man with pain in the right upper thigh shows a lesion in the lesser trochanter, but a diagnosis of osteoid osteoma cannot be made unequivocally. **(B)** CT section, however, clearly demonstrates the nidus (*arrow*).

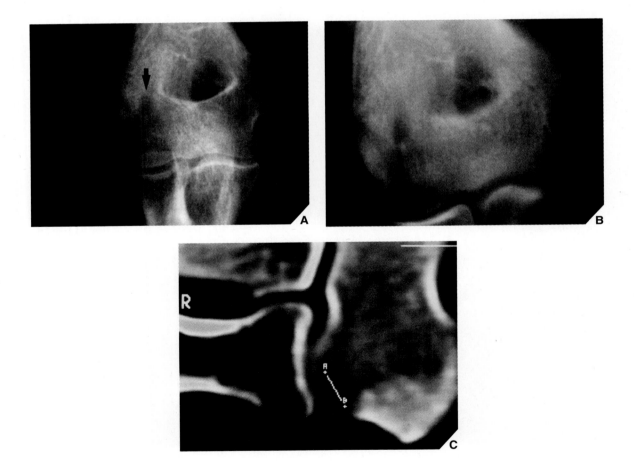

FIGURE 17.10   CT of osteoid osteoma. **(A)** Anteroposterior radiograph of the right elbow of a 31-year-old man with the typical clinical symptoms of osteoid osteoma demonstrates periarticular osteoporosis. There is the suggestion of a lesion in the capitellum (*arrow*). **(B)** Conventional tomogram shows a radiolucent area surrounded by a zone of sclerotic reaction. **(C)** CT section unequivocally demonstrates a subarticular nidus, which measures 6.5 mm.

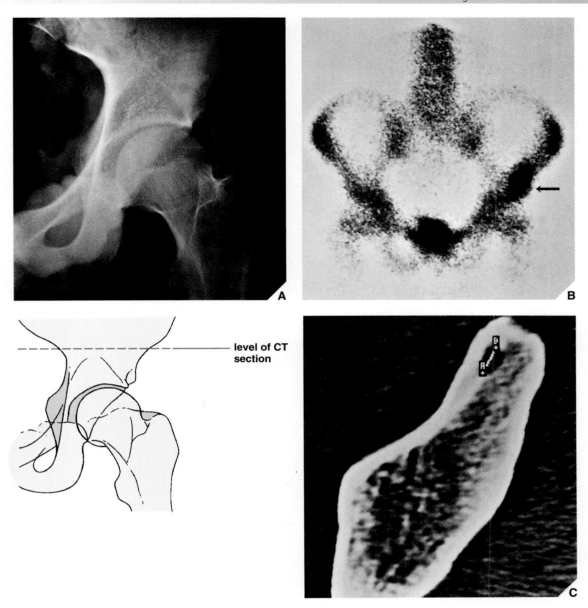

▲
FIGURE 17.11   Scintigraphy and CT of osteoid osteoma. **(A)** Anteroposterior radiograph of the left hip of a 16-year-old boy with a typical history of osteoid osteoma is equivocal, although there is the suggestion of radiolucency in the supraacetabular portion of the ilium. **(B)** Radionuclide bone scan shows an increased uptake of isotope in the supraacetabular portion of the left ilium (*arrow*). **(C)** Subsequent CT scan not only demonstrates the lesion but also allows its measurement (6.8 mm).

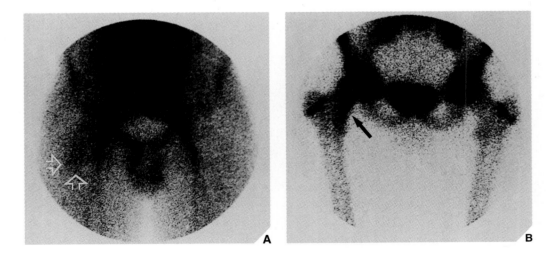

▲
FIGURE 17.12   Scintigraphy of osteoid osteoma. **(A)** In the first phase of a three-phase radionuclide bone scan, 1 minute after intravenous injection of 15 mCi (555 MBq) ^{99m}Tc-labeled methylene diphosphonate (MDP), there is increased activity in the iliac and femoral vessels. Discrete activity in the area of the medial femoral neck (*open arrows*) is related to the nidus of osteoid osteoma. **(B)** In the third phase, 2 hours after injection, there is accumulation of a bone-seeking tracer in the femoral neck lesion (*arrow*). (From Greenspan A, 1993, with permission.)

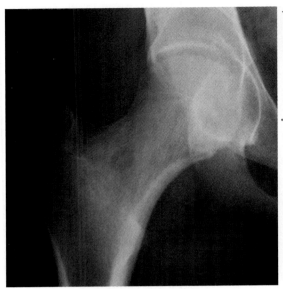

◀ **FIGURE 17.13** **Osteoid osteoma.** An anteroposterior radiograph of the right hip shows a radiolucent lesion in the femoral neck with a faintly outlined central density. There is no evidence of surrounding sclerosis.

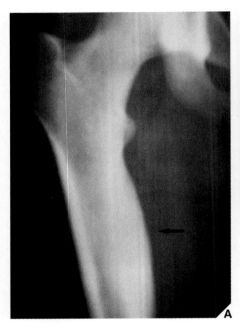
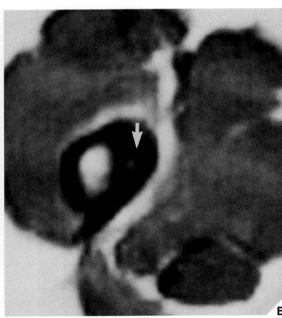

◀ **FIGURE 17.14** **MRI of osteoid osteoma. (A)** Conventional radiograph shows a sclerotic area localized to the medial aspect of proximal femoral shaft (*arrow*). The nidus is not apparent. **(B)** Axial T1-weighted MRI clearly demonstrates the high-intensity nidus (*arrow*) within a low-intensity sclerotic cortex. (Courtesy of Lynne S. Steinbach, M.D., San Francisco, California; from Greenspan A, 1993, with permission.)

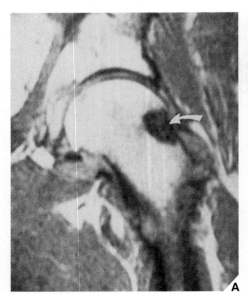
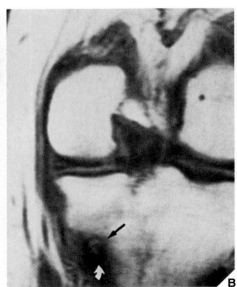

◀ **FIGURE 17.15** **MRI of osteoid osteoma. (A)** Coronal T1-weighted (SE; TR 600/TE 20 msec) MRI shows an osteoid osteoma (*curved arrow*) in the lateral aspect of the neck of the left femur. **(B)** Coronal T1-weighted (SE; TR 600/TE 20 msec) MRI shows an osteoid osteoma in the medial cortex of the left tibia (*arrow*). The *curved arrow* points to the perilesional sclerosis.

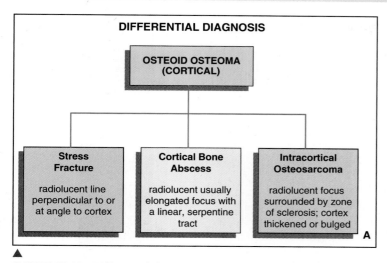

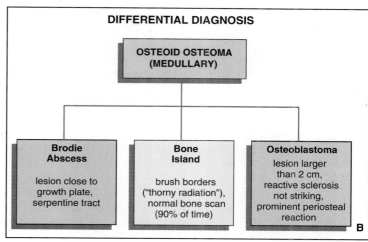

FIGURE 17.16 Differential diagnosis of (A) cortical and (B) medullary osteoid osteoma.

serpentine tract that extends away from the abscess cavity (Fig. 17.18). An intracortical osteosarcoma is a rare bone-forming malignancy that arises solely within the cortex of bone and grossly involves neither the medullary cavity nor the soft tissues. On radiography, it appears as a radiolucent focus within the cortex (femur or tibia), surrounded by zone of sclerosis, and varying in size from 1.0 to 4.2 cm in reported cases. The cortex at the site of the lesion may bulge slightly or may be thickened. Periosteal reaction may or may not be present.

In intramedullary lesions, the differential diagnosis must consider a bone abscess (Brodie abscess), and in a lesion with calcified nidus, a bone island (enostosis). The larger lesions must be also differentiated from osteoblastoma (see Fig. 17.16B). A bone abscess may have a similar radiographic appearance, but one can usually detect a linear, serpentine tract extending from the abscess cavity toward the nearest growth plate (Fig. 17.19). A bone island is characterized on radiography by the lesion's brush borders, which blend with surrounding trabeculae in a pattern likened to "thorny radiation" or pseudopodia (Fig. 17.20). In addition, bone islands usually show no increased activity on radionuclide bone scan. Distinguishing osteoid osteoma from osteoblastoma can be very difficult, if not impossible.

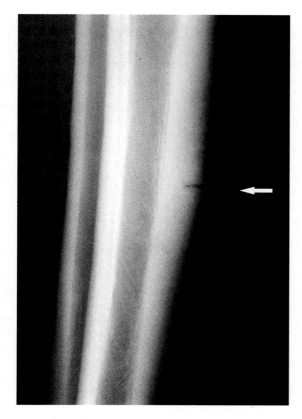

FIGURE 17.17 Stress fracture. Lateral radiograph demonstrates a stress fracture of the tibia (arrow). Note the perpendicular direction of the radiolucency to the long axis of the tibial cortex. In osteoid osteoma, the radiolucent nidus is oriented parallel to the cortex.

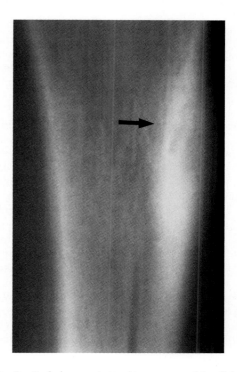

FIGURE 17.18 Cortical abscess. Lateral tomogram of the tibia shows a radiolucent, serpentine tract of a cortical bone abscess (arrow) that was originally misdiagnosed as osteoid osteoma.

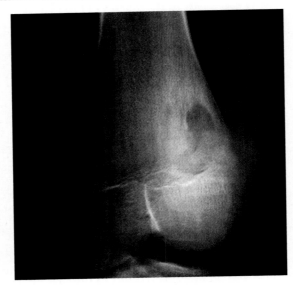

▲
FIGURE 17.19 **Brodie abscess.** In a bone abscess, seen here in the distal femoral metaphysis, a serpentine tract extends from an abscess cavity toward the growth plate. This feature distinguishes the lesion from osteoid osteoma.

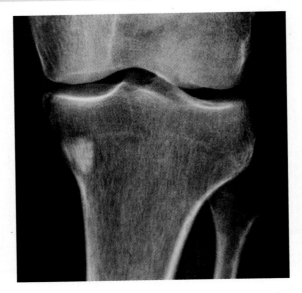

▲
FIGURE 17.20 **Enostosis.** A bone island in the medial aspect of the proximal tibia exhibits the brush borders characteristic of this lesion.

In general, osteoblastoma is larger than osteoid osteoma (usually more than 2 cm in diameter) and exhibits less reactive sclerosis, but the periosteal reaction may be more prominent.

For detailed features of the differential diagnosis of osteoid osteoma, see Table 17.2.

Complications

Osteoid osteoma may be accompanied by a few complications. Accelerated bone growth may occur if the nidus is located near the growth plate, particularly in young children (Fig. 17.21). A vertebral lesion, particularly in the neural arch, may lead to painful scoliosis, with concavity of the curvature directed toward the side of the lesion (Fig. 17.22). An intracapsular lesion may result in arthritis of precocious onset (Fig. 17.23). As observed by Norman and associates, this latter complication may serve as an important diagnostic clue to an osteoid osteoma when a typical history of the condition is elicited from the patient but the nidus is not recognizable radiographically (Fig. 17.24).

TABLE 17.2 Differential Diagnosis of Osteoid Osteoma

Condition (Lesion)	Radiologic Features
Cortical osteoid osteoma	Radiolucent nidus, round or elliptical, surrounded by radiodense reactive sclerosis; solid or laminated (but not interrupted) periosteal reaction; scintigraphy invariably shows increased uptake of radiotracer; "double-density" sign
Medullary osteoid osteoma	Radiolucent (or with central calcification) nidus, without or with only minimal perinidal sclerosis; usually no or only minimal periosteal reaction; scintigraphy—as above
Subperiosteal osteoid osteoma	Radiolucent or sclerotic nidus with or without reactive sclerosis; occasionally shaggy, crescent-like focus of periosteal reaction; scintigraphy—increased uptake of radiotracer
Intracapsular (periarticular) osteoid osteoma	Periarticular osteoporosis; premature onset of osteoarthritis; nidus may or may not be visualized; scintigraphy—as above
Osteoblastoma	Radiolucent lesion more than 2 cm, frequently with central opacities; perilesional sclerosis less intense than in osteoid osteoma; abundant periosteal reaction; scintigraphy—as above
Stress fracture (cortical)	Linear radiolucency runs perpendicular or at an angle to the cortex; scintigraphy—increased uptake of radiotracer
Bone abscess (Brodie)	Irregular in outline radiolucency, usually with a sclerotic rim, commonly associated with serpentine or linear tract; predilection for metaphysis and the ends of tubular bones; scintigraphy—increased uptake of radiotracer; MRI—on T1-weighted image a well-defined low-to-intermediate-signal lesion outlined by a low-intensity rim; on T2-weighted image a very bright homogeneous signal, outlined by a low-signal rim
Bone island (enostosis)	Homogeneously dense, sclerotic focus in cancellous bone with distinctive radiating streaks (thorny radiation) that blend with the trabeculae of the host bone; scintigraphy—usually no increased uptake; MRI—low-intensity signal on T1- and T2-weighted images
Intracortical osteosarcoma	Intracortical radiolucent focus surrounded by zone of sclerosis; occasionally central "fluffy" densities; cortex thickened or bulged; scintigraphy—increased uptake of radiotracer

Treatment

The treatment of osteoid osteoma consists of complete *en bloc* resection of the nidus. The resected specimen and the involved bone should be radiographed promptly (Fig. 17.25) so as to exclude the possibility of incomplete resection, which can lead to recurrence (Fig. 17.26).

A variety of techniques other than *en bloc* excision have been tried, among them intralesional curettage, excision with trephines after surgical exposure, fluoroscopically guided or CT-guided percutaneous extraction, and percutaneous radiofrequency ablation. The latter technique, suggested by Rosenthal and colleagues, is a promising alternative to surgery in selected patients. It is performed through a small radiofrequency electrode that is introduced into the lesion through the biopsy track with CT guidance (Fig. 17.27) to produce thermal necrosis of an approximately 1-cm sphere of tissue.

Osteoblastoma

Osteoblastoma, which accounts for approximately 1% of all primary bone tumors and 3% of all benign bone tumors, is a lesion histologically similar to osteoid osteoma but characterized by a larger size (more than 1.5 cm in diameter and usually more than 2 cm). The age range of its occurrence is also similar to that of osteoid osteoma: 75% of osteoblastomas are found in patients in their first, second, or third decade. Although the long bones are frequently involved, the lesion has a predilection for the vertebral column (Fig. 17.28). Its clinical presentation, however, is different from that of osteoid osteoma. Some patients are asymptomatic, but pain is not as readily relieved by salicylates. Their natural histories also differ. Whereas osteoid osteoma tends toward regression, osteoblastoma tends toward progression and even malignant transformation, although the possibility of the latter event remains controversial. Multifocal osteoblastomas have also been reported. Moreover, toxic osteoblastoma, a rare variant of this tumor, has recently been recognized. It is associated with systemic manifestations, including diffuse periostitis of multiple bones, fever, and weight loss.

Radiography and CT are usually sufficient to demonstrate the lesion and suggest the diagnosis (Figs. 17.29 to 17.31). On those rare occasions when the tumor penetrates the cortex and

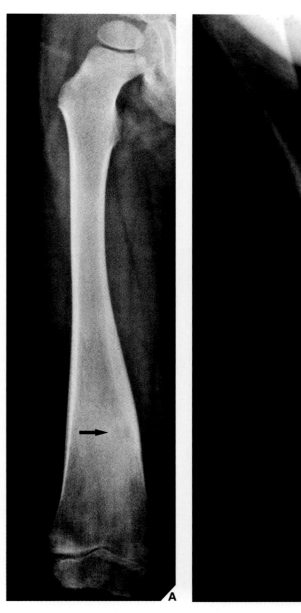

▲
FIGURE 17.21   **Complication of osteoid osteoma. (A)** A 2-year-old boy has been diagnosed with an osteoid osteoma of the distal femoral diaphysis (*arrow*). The proximity of the nidus to the growth plate caused accelerated growth of the bone, with marked widening of the distal femoral diaphysis. **(B)** In another patient, a 7-year-old girl with the lesion in the distal femur, note marked widening of the femoral diaphysis and hypertrophy of the anterior cortex.

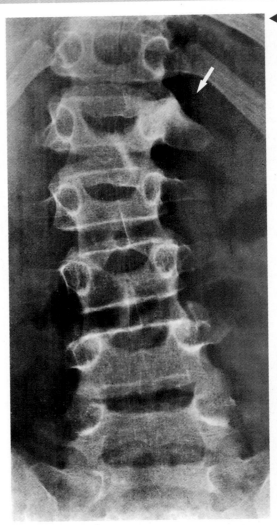

◀ FIGURE 17.22 **Complication of osteoid osteoma.** Anteroposterior radiograph of the spine shows an osteoid osteoma in the left pedicle of L1 (*arrow*) in a 12-year-old boy. Note the shallow-curve scoliosis, with concavity directed toward the lesion.

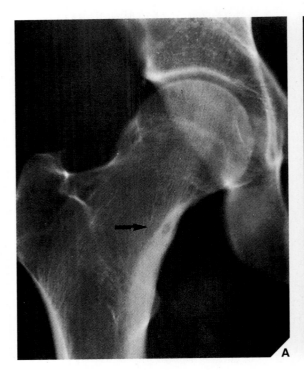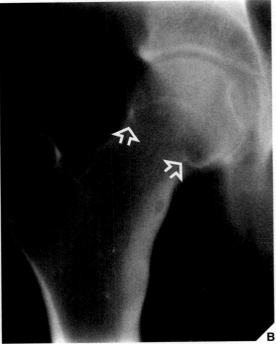

▲ FIGURE 17.23 **Complication of osteoid osteoma. (A)** Anteroposterior radiograph of the right hip demonstrates an intracapsular osteoid osteoma located in the medial aspect of the neck of the right femur (*arrow*) in a 28-year-old man. **(B)** Tomographic cut shows the early changes of osteoarthritis. Note a collar osteophyte (*open arrows*) and slight narrowing of the weight-bearing segment of the hip joint. A radionuclide bone scan showed an increased uptake not only at the site of the lesion but also at the site of the reactive bone formation resulting from the osteoarthritis.

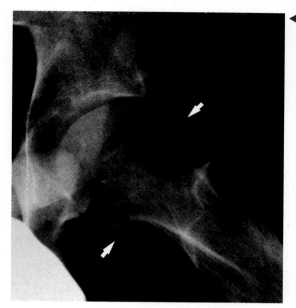

◀ **FIGURE 17.24 Complication of osteoid osteoma.** A 14-year-old boy presented with pain in the left hip for 8 months; it was more severe at night and was relieved by aspirin within 15 to 20 minutes. Several previous radiographic examinations, including computed tomographic scans, had failed to demonstrate the nidus. A frog-lateral view shows evidence of periarticular osteoporosis and early degenerative changes (*arrows*), both presumptive features of osteoid osteoma.

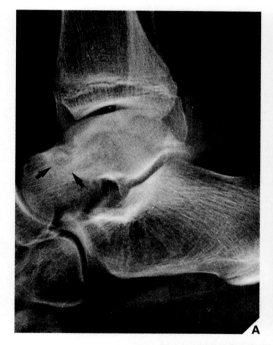

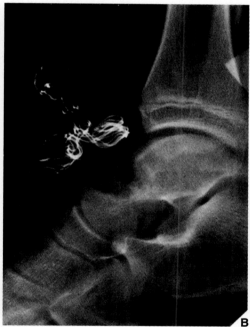

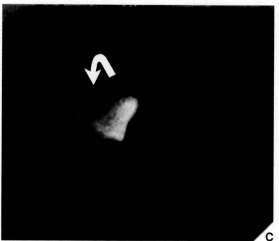

▲

FIGURE 17.25   Surgical treatment of osteoid osteoma. (A) Preoperative lateral radiograph of the ankle of a 13-year-old boy demonstrates the nidus of osteoid osteoma in the talar bone (*arrows*). Intraoperative films demonstrate the area of resection (**B**) and the resected specimen (**C**), confirming that the lesion (*curved arrow*) was totally excised.

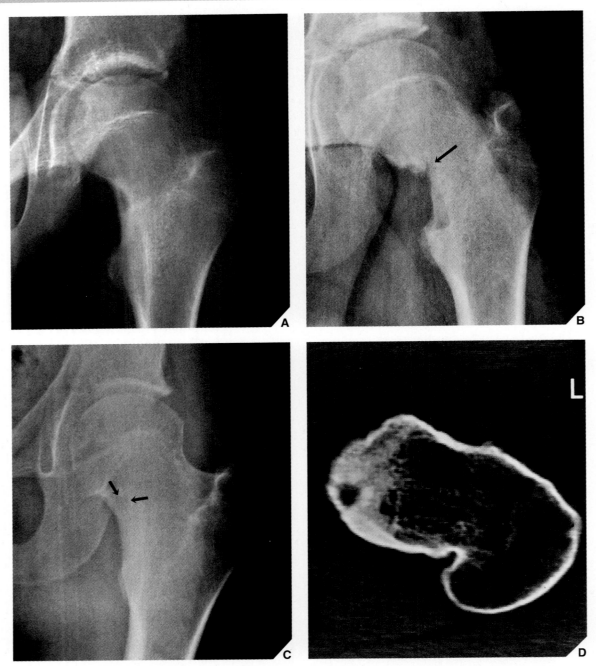

▲
FIGURE 17.26   Recurrence of osteoid osteoma. **(A)** Anteroposterior radiograph of the left hip in a 17-year-old boy with pain in the left groin relieved promptly by salicylates demonstrates a nidus of osteoid osteoma in the medial cortex of the femoral neck. **(B)** The lesion was incompletely resected; note its remnants (*arrow*). Two years later, the symptoms recurred. **(C)** Follow-up radiograph of the left hip shows a radiolucent area in the medial femoral cortex (*arrows*), and a CT section **(D)** demonstrates the nidus.

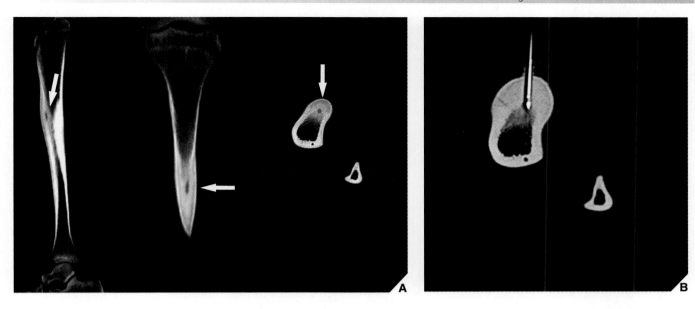

FIGURE 17.27 CT-guided percutaneous radiofrequency ablation of osteoid osteoma. **(A)** Sagittal, coronal, and axial CT images show a lesion in the anterior cortex of tibia (*arrows*). **(B)** Axial CT image obtained during interventional procedure confirms the proper placement of the probe within the nidus of osteoid osteoma.

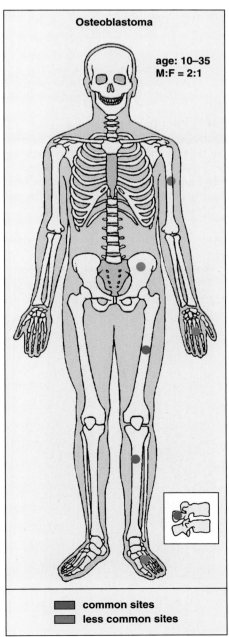

Osteoblastoma

age: 10–35
M:F = 2:1

common sites
less common sites

◀ **FIGURE 17.28** Skeletal sites of predilection, peak age range, and male-to-female ratio in osteoblastoma.

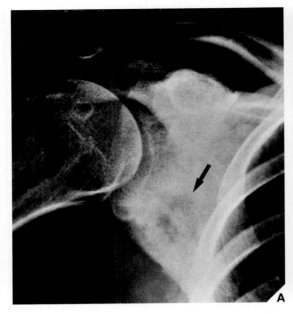
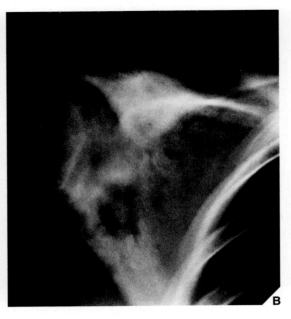

FIGURE 17.29   Osteoblastoma. (A) Anteroposterior radiograph of the right shoulder of a 28-year-old woman shows a faint radiolucent focus in the scapula (*arrow*) surrounded by a sclerotic area, accompanied by shaggy periosteal reaction at the axillary border. **(B)** A conventional tomogram clearly demonstrates a radiolucent nidus with a sclerotic border, resembling an osteoid osteoma. However, the size of this lesion (3 cm × 3 cm) marks it as an osteoblastoma, a diagnosis proved by excision biopsy.

extends into the soft tissues, MRI may demonstrate these features (Fig. 17.32).

Osteoblastoma has four distinctive radiographic presentations:

1. A giant osteoid osteoma. The lesion is usually more than 2 cm in diameter and exhibits less reactive sclerosis and a possibly more prominent periosteal response than does osteoid osteoma (Fig. 17.33).
2. A blow-out expansive lesion similar to an aneurysmal bone cyst with small radiopacities in the center. This pattern is particularly common in lesions involving the spine (Fig. 17.34).

3. An aggressive lesion simulating a malignant tumor (Fig. 17.35).
4. Periosteal lesion that lacks perifocal bone sclerosis but exhibits a thin shell of newly formed periosteal bone (Fig. 17.36).

Differential Diagnosis

Histologic differentiation between osteoid osteoma and osteoblastoma can be very difficult, and in a considerable number of patients it can be impossible. Both are osteoid-producing lesions, but in the typical osteoblastoma the bone trabeculae are broader and longer and seem less densely packed and less coherent than those in osteoid osteoma. Some

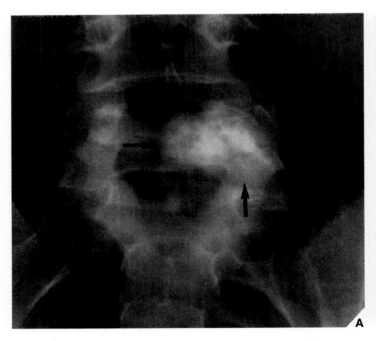
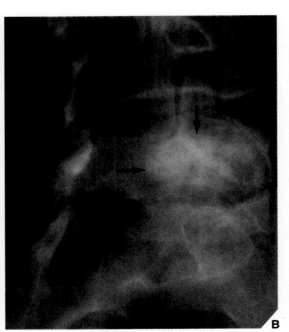

FIGURE 17.30   Osteoblastoma. Anteroposterior **(A)** and oblique **(B)** radiographs of the lumbosacral spine of an 18-year-old man show an expansive lesion in the left pedicle and lamina of L5 (*arrows*).

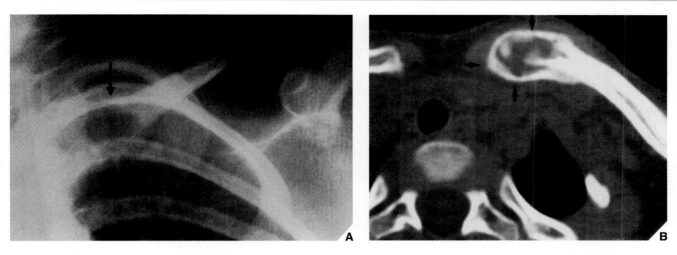

▲
FIGURE 17.31   **CT of osteoblastoma. (A)** Conventional radiograph shows a radiolucent lesion in the sternal end of the left clavicle (*arrow*). (**B**) Axial CT image demonstrates an expansive low-attenuation tumor (*arrows*) with high-attenuation foci of new bone formation. (Reprinted from Greenspan A et al., 2007.)

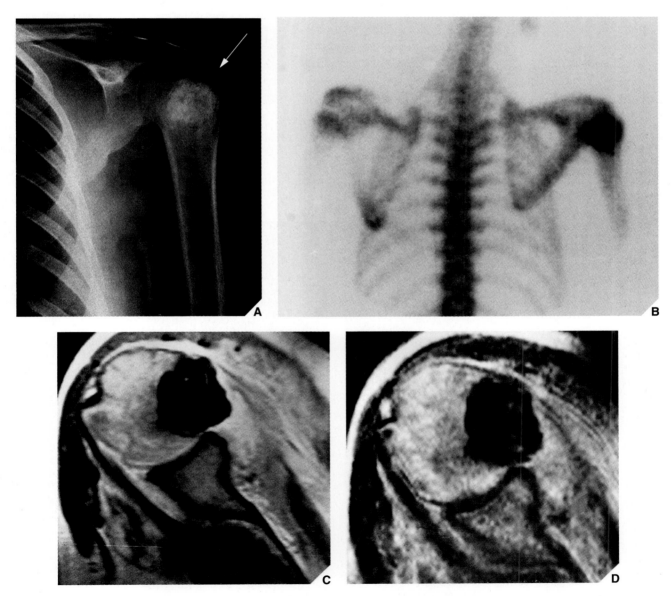

▲
FIGURE 17.32   **Scintigraphy and MRI of osteoblastoma.** A 15-year-old girl presented with pain in her left shoulder. (**A**) Conventional radiograph demonstrates a sharply demarcated sclerotic lesion in the proximal metaphysis of the left humerus abutting the growth plate (*arrow*). (**B**) Radionuclide bone scan obtained after injection of 15 mCi (555 MBq) of ^{99m}Tc-labeled MDP shows an increased uptake of tracer localized to the site of the lesion. (**C**) Axial spin-echo T1-weighted MR image (TR 700/TE 20 msec) demonstrates that the lesion is located posteromedially in the humeral head. The cortex is destroyed and the tumor extends into the soft tissues. (**D**) Axial spin-echo T2-weighted MR image (TR 2200/TE 60 msec) shows that the lesion remains of low signal intensity, indicating osseous matrix. The rim of high-signal intensity adjacent to the posterolateral margin of the tumor reflects peritumoral edema.

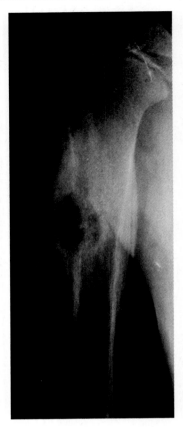

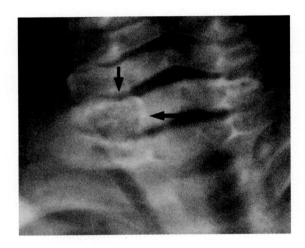

▲
FIGURE 17.33 Osteoblastoma. Osteoblastoma in the proximal humerus of this 8-year-old boy is similar to the lesion of osteoid osteoma. This lesion, however, is larger (2.5 cm in its largest dimension), and there is a more pronounced periosteal response in the medial and lateral humeral cortices. Conversely, the extent of reactive bone surrounding the radiolucent nidus is less than that usually seen in osteoid osteoma. This type of osteoblastoma is frequently called a giant osteoid osteoma.

▲
FIGURE 17.34 Conventional tomography of osteoblastoma. Tomographic section of the cervical spine shows an expanding, blow-out lesion of osteoblastoma, with several small central opacities, in the lamina of C6 (*arrows*).

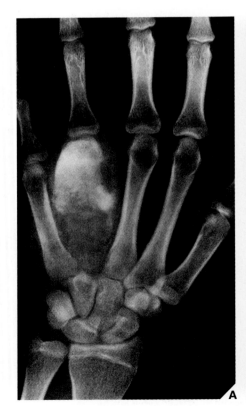

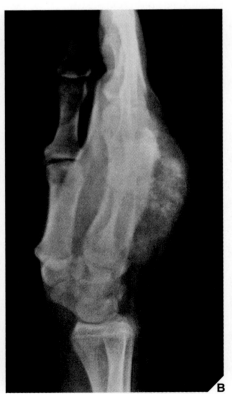

▲
FIGURE 17.35 Aggressive osteoblastoma. Posteroanterior (**A**) and lateral (**B**) radiographs of the hand demonstrate an aggressive osteoblastoma. Note the destruction of the entire fourth metacarpal with massive bone formation, particularly in the distal portion. Although very similar in appearance to osteosarcoma, the lesion still appears to be contained by a shell of periosteal new bone formation.

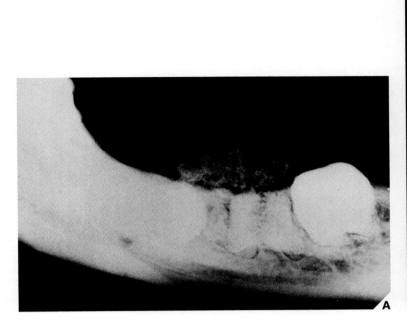
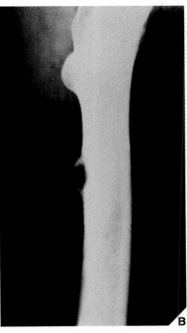

▲ FIGURE 17.36 Periosteal osteoblastoma. **(A)** Periosteal osteoblastoma of the mandible and **(B)** periosteal osteoblastoma of the femur are covered by a thin shell of a new periosteal bone. (Courtesy of Prof. Dr. Wolfgang Remagen, Cologne, Germany.)

authorities believe that because of its striking histologic similarity to osteoid osteoma, osteoblastoma represents a variant of clinical expression of the same pathologic process.

The differential radiologic diagnosis of osteoblastoma should include an osteoid osteoma, a bone abscess, an aneurysmal bone cyst, an enchondroma, and an osteosarcoma (Table 17.3). A bone abscess is usually marked by a serpentine tract (see Fig. 17.19) or it is seen to cross the growth plate (Fig. 17.37), phenomena almost never seen in osteoblastoma. An aneurysmal bone cyst occasionally can assume a similar appearance to osteoblastoma but lacks central radiopacities. An enchondroma will usually display a calcified matrix assuming the form of dots, rings, and arcs. In addition, unless there has been a pathologic fracture,

an enchondroma (see Fig. 18.6), unlike osteoblastoma (Fig. 17.38), does not elicit a periosteal reaction.

Aggressive osteoblastoma should be differentiated from osteosarcoma, for which CT may be helpful. CT may also help in the differential diagnosis of lesions located in complex anatomic regions such as the vertebrae (Fig. 17.39). If there is tumor extension into the thecal sac, MRI may be needed.

Treatment

The treatment for osteoblastoma is similar to that for osteoid osteoma; en bloc resection should be performed. Larger lesions may require additional bone grafting and internal fixation.

TABLE 17.3 Differential Diagnosis of Osteoblastoma

Condition (Lesion)	Radiologic Features
Cortical and medullary osteoid osteoma–like osteoblastoma (giant osteoid osteoma)	Radiolucent lesion, spherical or oval, with well-defined margins; frequent perilesional sclerosis; abundant periosteal reaction; size of the nidus greater than 2 cm
Aneurysmal bone cyst-like expansive osteoblastoma	Blow-out lesion, similar to aneurysmal bone cyst, but with central opacities
Aggressive osteoblastoma (simulating malignant neoplasm)	Ill-defined borders, destruction of the cortex; aggressive-looking periosteal reaction; occasionally soft-tissue extension
Periosteal osteoblastoma	Round or ovoid heterogeneous in density mass attached to cortex, covered by shell of periosteal new bone
Osteoid osteoma	Radiolucent nidus ≤1.5 cm, occasionally with a sclerotic center
Aneurysmal bone cyst	Blow-out, expansive lesion; in long bone buttress of periosteal reaction; thin shell of reactive bone frequently covers the lesion, but may be absent in rapidly growing lesions; soft-tissue extension may be present
Enchondroma	Radiolucent lesion with or without sclerotic border, frequently displaying central calcifications in the form of dots, rings, and arcs
Osteosarcoma	Permeative or moth-eaten bone destruction; wide zone of transition; tumor-bone in form of cloud-like opacities; aggressive periosteal reaction; soft-tissue mass

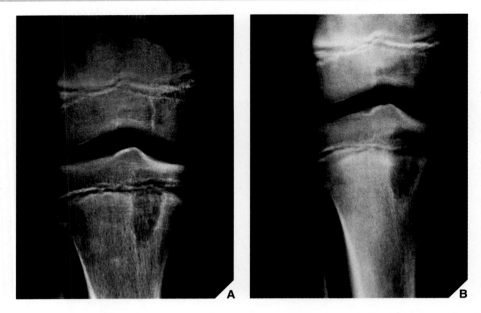

▲
FIGURE 17.37 **Brodie abscess. (A)** Anteroposterior radiograph of the right knee of a 10-year-old boy demonstrates an oval radiolucent lesion abutting and crossing the growth plate of the proximal tibia. Confirmation of extension of the lesion into the epiphysis is shown on an anteroposterior tomographic section **(B)**. The lesion proved to be a bone abscess.

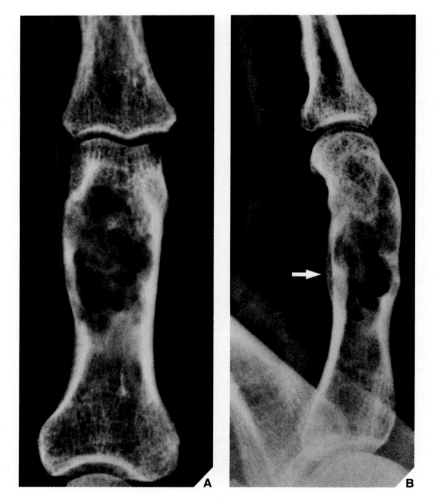

▲
FIGURE 17.38 **Osteoblastoma.** Dorsovolar **(A)** and lateral **(B)** radiographs of the small finger show enchondroma-like osteoblastoma. Note the periosteal reaction (*arrow*) and lack of chondroid matrix, which are typical of enchondroma. Small radiopacities in the center of the lesion represent bone formation, a characteristic feature of osteoblastoma.

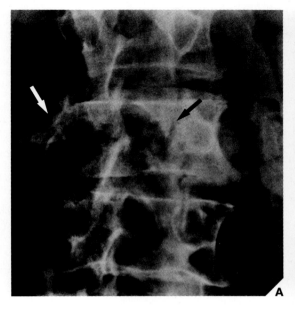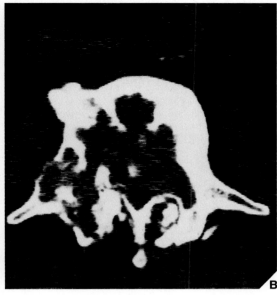

▲
FIGURE 17.39 **Aggressive osteoblastoma.** **(A)** Anteroposterior radiograph of the lumbar spine shows a destructive lytic lesion affecting the right half of the vertebral body of L3 (*arrows*) in a 65-year-old man who presented with insidious onset of pain in the lower back radiating to the right lower extremity. **(B)** CT section demonstrates focal areas of bone formation within the lesion and invasion of the cortex. Subsequent biopsy revealed an aggressive osteoblastoma. (Courtesy of Ibrahim F. Abdelwahab, M.D., New York.)

PRACTICAL POINTS TO REMEMBER

[1] Parosteal osteoma, an asymptomatic bone-forming lesion, may be a part of the Gardner syndrome marked by sebaceous cysts, skin fibromas, desmoid tumors, and intestinal polyposis.

[2] In the differential diagnosis of parosteal osteoma, the most important entity that needs to be excluded is parosteal osteosarcoma.

[3] The most characteristic clinical symptom of osteoid osteoma is pain that is most severe at night and is promptly relieved by salicylates (Aspirin).

[4] In the radiographic evaluation of osteoid osteoma:
- the lesion (nidus) consists of a small radiolucent area, sometimes with a sclerotic center; the dense zone surrounding the nidus represents reactive sclerosis, not a tumor
- the imaging characteristics depend on the location of the lesion: intracortical, intramedullary, subperiosteal, or periarticular (intracapsular)
- the differential diagnoses of osteoid osteoma should include osteoblastoma, stress fracture, bone abscess (Brodie abscess), bone island, and an intracortical osteosarcoma.

[5] The complications of osteoid osteoma include:
- recurrence of the lesion (if not completely resected)
- accelerated growth (if the lesion is close to the growth plate)
- scoliosis
- arthritis of precocious onset (if nidus is intracapsular).

[6] A well-prepared surgical approach to the treatment of osteoid osteoma requires:
- imaging localization of the lesion (by scintigraphy, radiography, conventional tomography, CT)
- verification of total excision of the lesion in vivo (by examination of the host bone) and in vitro (by examination of the resected specimen).

[7] A variety of techniques other than en bloc excision of osteoid osteoma are available, including intralesional curettage, excision with trephines after sugical exposure, percutaneous excision (usually CT-guided), and radiofrequency thermal ablation.

[8] CT-guided radiofrequency thermal ablation of osteoid osteoma is a promising technique and alternative to surgery in selected patients. It is performed through a small radiofrequency electrode that is introduced into the lesion percutaneously to produce thermal necrosis of an approximately 1-cm sphere of tissue.

[9] Osteoblastoma, histologically almost identical with osteoid osteoma, is nevertheless a distinct clinical entity. Its radiographic appearance is characterized by:
- features similar to a giant osteoid osteoma
- a "blow-out" type of expansive lesion with small radiopacities in the center, resembling aneurysmal bone cyst
- a lesion exhibiting aggressive features resembling a malignant tumor (osteosarcoma).

[10] The differential diagnosis of osteoblastoma includes osteoid osteoma, bone abscess, aneurysmal bone cyst, enchondroma, and osteosarcoma.

[11] Unusual presentation of osteoblastoma includes lesion associated with diffuse periostitis and systemic manifestations (so-called toxic osteoblastoma), and lesion in muticentric location (so-called multifocal osteoblastoma).

SUGGESTED READINGS

Adler C-P. Multifocal osteoblastoma of the hand. *Skeletal Radiol* 2000;29:601–604.

Anderson RB, McAlister JA Jr, Wrenn RN. Case report 585. Intracortical osteosarcoma of tibia. *Skeletal Radiol* 1989;18:627–630.

Assoun J, Railhac JJ, Bonnevialle P, et al. Osteoid osteoma: percutaneous resection with CT guidance. *Radiology* 1993;188:541–547.

Assoun J, Richardi G, Railhac JJ, et al. Osteoid osteoma: MR imaging versus CT. *Radiology* 1994;191:217–223.

Atar D, Lehman WB, Grant AD. Tips of the trade: computerized tomography—guided excision of osteoid osteoma. *Orthop Rev* 1992;21:1457–1458.

Azouz EM, Kozlowski K, Marton D, Sprague P, Zerhouni A, Assalah F. Osteoid osteoma and osteoblastoma of the spine in children. Report of 22 cases with brief literature review. *Pediatr Radiol* 1986;16:25–31.

Bauer TW, Zehr RJ, Belhobek GH, Marks KE. Juxta-articular osteoid osteoma. *Am J Surg Pathol* 1991;15:381–387.

Bell RS, O'Conner GD, Waddell JP. Importance of magnetic resonance imaging in osteoid osteoma: a case report. *Can J Surg* 1989;32:276–278.

Bertoni F, Unni KK, Beabout JW, Sim FH. Parosteal osteoma of bones other than of the skull and face. *Cancer* 1995;75:2466–2473.

Bertoni F, Unni KK, McLeod RA, Dahlin DC. Osteosarcoma resembling osteoblastoma. *Cancer* 1985;55:416–426.

Bettelli G, Tigani D, Picci P. Recurring osteoblastoma initially presenting as a typical osteoid osteoma. Report of two cases. *Skeletal Radiol* 1991;20:1–4.

Biebuyck JC, Katz LD, McCauley T. Soft tissue edema in osteoid osteoma. *Skeletal Radiol* 1993;22:37–41.

Bullough PG. *Atlas orthopedic pathology with clinical and radiologic correlations*, 2nd ed. New York: Gower Medical Publishing; 1992.

Byers PD. Solitary benign osteoblastic lesions of bone. Osteoid osteoma and benign osteoblastoma. *Cancer* 1968;22:43–57.

Campanacci M. *Bone and soft tissue tumors*. New York: Springer-Verlag; 1990: 355–373.

Campbell CJ, Papademetriou T, Bonfiglio M. Melorheostosis. A report of the clinical, roentgenographic, and pathological findings in fourteen cases. *J Bone Joint Surg [Am]* 1968;50A:1281–1304.

Carter TR. Osteoid osteoma of the hip: an alternate method of excision. *Orthop Rev* 1990;19:903–905.

Cassar-Pullicino VN, McCall IW, Wan S. Intra-articular osteoid osteoma. *Clin Radiol* 1992;45:153–160.

Chang CH, Piatt ED, Thomas KE, Watne AL. Bone abnormalities in Gardner's syndrome. *Am J Roentgenol* 1968;103:645–652.

Corbett JM, Wilde AH, McCormack LJ, Evarts CM. Intra-articular osteoid osteoma: a diagnostic problem. *Clin Orthop* 1974;98:225–230.

Crim JR, Mirra JM, Eckardt JJ, Seeger LL. Widespread inflammatory response to osteoblastoma: the flare phenomenon. *Radiology* 1990;177:835–836.

Dahlin DC. Osteoma. In: *Bone tumors. General aspects on 8,542 cases*, 4th ed. Springfield: Charles C. Thomas; 1986:84–87, 308–321.

Dahlin DC, Johnson EW Jr. Giant osteoid osteoma. *J Bone Joint Surg [Am]* 1954;36A:559–572.

Dahlin DC, Unni KK. *Bone tumors: general aspects and data on 8,542 cases*, 4th ed. Springfield: Charles C. Thomas; 1987:88–101.

Dale S, Breidahl WH, Baker D, Robbins PD, Sundaram M. Severe toxic osteoblastoma of the humerus associated with diffuse periostitis of multiple bones. *Skeletal Radiol* 2001;30:464–468.

Della Rocca C, Huvos AG. Osteoblastoma: varied histological presentations with a benign clinical course. 55 cases. *Am J Surg Pathol* 1996;20:841–850.

Denis F, Armstrong GW. Scoliogenic osteoblastoma of the posterior end of the rib: a case report. *Spine* 1984;9:74–76.

DeSouza Diaz L, Frost HM. Osteoid osteoma—osteoblastoma. *Cancer* 1974;33: 1075–1081.

Dockerty MB, Ghormley RK, Jackson AE. Osteoid osteoma: clinicopathologic study of 20 cases. *Ann Surg* 1951;133:77–89.

Dolan K, Seibert J, Seibert R. Gardner's syndrome. *Am J Roentgenol* 1973;119: 359–364.

Dorfman HD, Weiss SW. Borderline osteoblastic tumors: problems in the differential diagnosis of aggressive osteoblastoma and low-grade osteosarcoma. *Semin Diagn Pathol* 1984;1:215–234.

Doyle T, King K. Percutaneous removal of osteoid osteomas using CT control. *Clin Radiol* 1989;40:515–517.

Ebrahim FS, Jacobson JA, Lin J, Housner JA, Hayes CW, Resnick D. Intraarticular osteoid osteoma: sonographic findings in three patients with radiographic, CT, and MR imaging correlation. *Am J Roentgenol* 2001;177:1391–1395.

Ehara S, Rosenthal DI, Aoki J, et al. Peritumoral edema in osteoid osteoma on magnetic resonance imaging. *Skeletal Radiol* 1999;28:265–270.

Fechner RE, Mills SE. *Tumors of the bones and joints*. Washington, DC: Armed Forces Institute of Pathology; 1993:25–38.

Fleming RJ, Alpert M, Garcia A. Parosteal lipoma. *Am J Roentgenol* 1962;87: 1075–1084.

Freiberger RH, Loitman BS, Helpern M, Thompson TC. Osteoid osteoma: a report of 80 cases. *Am J Roentgenol* 1959;82:194–205.

Gardner EJ, Plenk HP. Hereditary pattern for multiple osteomas in a family group. *Am J Hum Genet* 1952;4:31–36.

Gardner EJ, Richards RC. Multiple cutaneous and subcutaneous lesions occurring simultaneously with hereditary polyposis and osteomatosis. *Am J Hum Genet* 1953;5:139–147.

Gentry JF, Schechter JJ, Mirra JM. Case report 574. Periosteal osteoblastoma of rib. *Skeletal Radiol* 1989;18:551–555.

Geschickter CF, Copeland MM. Parosteal osteoma of bone: a new entity. *Ann Surg* 1951;133:790–807.

Gil S, Marco SF, Arenas J, et al. Doppler duplex color localization of osteoid osteoma. *Skeletal Radiol* 1999;28:107–110.

Gitelis S, Schajowicz F. Osteoid osteoma and osteoblastoma. *Orthop Clin North Am* 1989;20:313–325.

Glass RB, Poznanski AK, Fisher MR, Shkolnik A, Dias L. MR imaging of osteoid osteoma. *J Comput Assist Tomogr* 1986;10:1065–1067.

Goldberg VM, Jacobs B. Osteoid osteoma of the hip in children. *Clin Orthop* 1975;106:41–47.

Goldman AB, Schneider R, Pavlov H. Osteoid osteomas of the femoral neck: report of four cases evaluated with isotopic bone scanning, CT, and MR imaging. *Radiology* 1993;186:227–232.

Graham HK, Laverick MD, Cosgrove AP, Crone MD. Minimally invasive surgery for osteoid osteoma of the proximal femur. *J Bone Joint Surg [Br]* 1993;75B:115–118.

Greenspan A. Sclerosing bone dysplasias—a target-site approach. *Skeletal Radiol* 1991;20:561–583.

Greenspan A. Benign bone-forming lesions: osteoma, osteoid osteoma, and osteoblastoma. *Skeletal Radiol* 1993;22:485–500.

Greenspan A. Bone island (enostosis): current concept. *Skeletal Radiol* 1995;24: 111–115.

Greenspan A, Elguezabel A, Bryk D. Multifocal osteoid osteoma. A case report and review of the lieterature. *Am J Roentgenol* 1974;121:103–106.

Greenspan A, Jundt G, Remagen W. *Differential diagnosis in orthopaedic oncology*, 2nd ed. Philadelphia: Lippincott Williams & Wilkins; 2007:59–74.

Greenspan A, Stadalnik RC. Bone island: scintigraphic findings and their clinical application. *Can Assoc Radiol J* 1995;46:368–379.

Greenspan A, Steiner G, Knutzon R. Bone island (enostosis): clinical significance and radiologic and pathologic correlations. *Skeletal Radiol* 1991;20:85–90.

Griffith JF, Kumta SM, Chow LTC, Leung PC, Metreweli C. Intracortical osteosarcoma. *Skeletal Radiol* 1998;27:228–232.

Haibach H, Farrell C, Gaines RW. Osteoid osteoma of the spine: surgically correctable cause of painful scoliosis. *Can Med Assoc J* 1986;135:895–899.

Helms CA. Osteoid osteoma: the double density sign. *Clin Orthop* 1987;222:167–173.

Helms CA, Hattner RS, Vogler JB III. Osteoid osteoma: radionuclide diagnosis. *Radiology* 1984;151:779–784.

Jackson RP, Reckling FW, Mants FA. Osteoid osteoma and osteoblastoma. Similar histologic lesions with different natural histories. *Clin Orthop* 1977;128:303–313.

Jacobs P. Parosteal lipoma with hyperostosis. *Clin Radiol* 1972;23:196–198.

Jacobson HG. Dense bone—too much bone: radiological considerations and differential diagnosis. Part I. *Skeletal Radiol* 1985;13:1–20.

Jacobson HG. Dense bone—too much bone: radiological considerations and differential diagnosis. Part II. *Skeletal Radiol* 1985;13:97–113.

Jaffe HL. Osteoid osteoma: a benign osteoblastic tumor composed of osteoid and atypical bone. *Arch Surg* 1935;31:709–728.

Jaffe HL. Osteoid osteoma of bone. *Radiology* 1945;45:319–334.

Jaffe HL. Benign osteoblastoma. *Bull Hosp Joint Dis* 1956;17:141–151.

Jaffe HL, Mayer L. An osteoblastic osteoid tissue-forming tumor of a metacarpal bone. *Arch Surg* 1932;24:550–564.

Keim HA, Reina EG. Osteoid osteoma as a cause of scoliosis. *J Bone Joint Surg [Am]* 1975; 57-A:159–163.

Kenan S, Floman Y, Robin GC, Laufer A. Aggressive osteoblastoma. A case report and review of the literature. *Clin Orthop* 1985;195:294–298.

Klein MH, Shankman S. Osteoid osteoma: radiologic and pathologic correlation. *Skeletal Radiol* 1992;21:23–31.

Kneisl JS, Simon MA. Medical management compared with operative treatment for osteoid osteoma. *J Bone Joint Surg [Am]* 1992;74A:179–185.

Kransdorf MJ, Stull MA, Gilkey FW, Moser RP Jr. Osteoid osteoma. *Radiographics* 1991;11:671–696.

Kricun ME. *Imaging of bone tumors*. Philadelphia: WB Saunders; 1993:121–125, 114–116.

Kroon HM, Schurmans J. Osteoblastoma: clinical and radiologic findings in 98 new cases. *Radiology* 1990;175:783–790.

Kyriakos M. Intracortical osteosarcoma. *Cancer* 1980;46:2525–2533.

Kyriakos M, El-Khoury GY, McDonald DJ, et al. Osteoblastomatosis of bone. A benign, multifocal osteoblastic lesion, distinct from osteoid osteoma and osteoblastoma, radiologically simulating a vascular tumor. *Skeletal Radiol* 2007;36:237–247.

Lawrie TR, Aterman K, Sinclair AM. Painless osteoid osteoma: a report of two cases. *J Bone Joint Surg [Am]* 1970;52A:1357–1363.

Lee DH, Malawer MM. Staging and treatment of primary and persistent (recurrent) osteoid osteoma: evaluation of intraoperative nuclear scanning, tetracycline fluorescence, and tomography. *Clin Orthop* 1992;281:229–238.

Lichtenstein L. Benign osteoblastoma. A category of osteoid- and bone-forming tumors other than classical osteoid osteoma, which may be mistaken for giant-cell tumor or osteogenic sarcoma. *Cancer* 1956;9:1044–1052.

Lichtenstein L. *Bone tumors*, 5th ed. St. Louis: Mosby; 1977:11.

Lichtenstein L, Sawyer WR. Benign osteoblastoma: further observations and report of twenty additional cases. *J Bone Joint Surg [Am]* 1964;46A:755–765.

Liu PT, Chivers FS, Roberts CC, Schultz CJ, Beauchamp CP. Imaging of osteoid osteoma with dynamic gadolinium-enhanced MR imaging. *Radiology* 2003;227:691–700.

Lucas DR, Unni KK, McLeod RA, O'Connor MI, Sim FH. Osteoblastoma: clinico-pathologic study of 306 cases. *Hum Pathol* 1994;25:117–134.

Marinelli A, Giacomini S, Bianchi G, Pellacani A, Bertoni F, Mercuri M. Osteoid osteoma simulating an osteocartilaginous exostosis. *Skeletal Radiol* 2004;33:181–185.

Marsh BW, Bonfiglio M, Brady LP, Enneking WF. Benign osteoblastoma: range of manifestations. *J Bone Joint Surg [Am]* 1975;57A:1–9.

Mazoyer JF, Kohler R, Bossard D. Osteoid osteoma: CT-guided percutaneous treatment. *Radiology* 1991;181:269–271.

McLeod RA, Dahlin DC, Beabout JW. The spectrum of osteoblastoma. *Am J Roentgenol* 1976;126:321–325.

Mirra JM, Dodd L, Johnston W, Frost DB. Case report 700. Primary intracortical osteosarcoma of femur, sclerosing variant, grade 1 to 2 anaplasia. *Skeletal Radiol* 1991;20:613–616.

Mirra JM, Picci P, Gold RH. *Bone tumors: clinical, pathologic, and radiologic correlations*. Philadelphia: Lea & Febiger; 1989:226–248.

Mitchell ML, Ackerman LV. Metastatic and pseudomalignant osteoblastoma: a report of two unusual cases. *Skeletal Radiol* 1986;15:213–218.

Murphey MD, Andrews CL, Flemming DJ, Temple HT, Smith WS, Smirniotopoulos JG. Primary tumors of the spine: radiologic-pathologic correlation. *Radiographics* 1996;16:1131–1158.

Mylona S, Patsoura S, Galani P, et al. Osteoid osteoma in common and in technically challenging locations treated with computed tomography-guided percutaneous radiofrequency ablation . *Skeletal Radiol* 2010;39:443–449.

Nogues P, Marti-Bonmati L, Aparisi F, Saborido MC, Garci J, Dosda R. MR imaging assessment of juxtacortical edema in osteoid osteoma in 28 patients. *Eur Radiol* 1998;8:236–238.

Norman A. Persistence or recurrence of pain: a sign of surgical failure in osteoid osteoma. *Clin Orthop* 1978;130:263–266.

Norman A, Abdelwahab IF, Buyon J, Matzkin E. Osteoid osteoma of the hip stimulating an early onset of osteoarthritis. *Radiology* 1986;158:417–420.

O'Connell JX, Rosenthal DI, Mankin HJ, Rosenberg AE. Solitary osteoma of a long bone. *J Bone Joint Surg [Am]* 1993;75A:1830–1834.

Pettine KA, Klassen RA. Osteoid osteoma and osteoblastoma of the spine. *J Bone Joint Surg [Am]* 1986;68A:354–361.

Picci P, Campanacci M, Mirra JM. Osteoid osteoma. Differential clinicopathologic diagnosis. In: Mirra JM, ed. *Bone tumors. clinical, radiologic, and pathologic correlations*. Philadelphia: Lea & Febiger; 1989:411–414.

Pinto CH, Taminiau AHM, Vanderschueren GM, Hogendoorn PCW, Bloem JL, Obermann WR. Technical considerations in CT-guided radiofrequency thermal ablation of osteoid osteoma: tricks of the trade. *Am J Roentgenol* 2002;179:1633–1642.

Resnick D, Kyriakos M, Greenway G. Tumors and tumor-like lesions of bone: imaging and pathology of specific lesions. In: Resnick D, ed. *Diagnosis of bone and joint disorders*, 3rd ed. Philadelphia: WB Saunders; 1995:3629–3647.

Roger B, Bellin M-F, Wioland M, Grenier P. Osteoid osteoma: CT-guided percutaneous excision confirmed with immediate follow-up scintigraphy in 16 outpatients. *Radiology* 1996;201:239–242.

Rosenthal DI. Percutaneous radiofrequency treatment of osteoid osteomas. *Semin Musculoskelet Radiol* 1997;1:265–272.

Rosenthal DI, Alexander A, Rosenberg AE, Springfield D. Ablation of osteoid osteomas with a percutaneously placed electrode: a new procedure. *Radiology* 1992;183:29–33.

Rosenthal DI, Hornicek FJ, Wolfe MW, Jennings LC, Gebhardt MC, Mankin HJ. Percutaneous radiofrequency coagulation of osteoid osteoma compared with operative treatment. *J Bone Joint Surg [Am]* 1998;80A:815–821.

Rosenthal DI, Springfield DS, Gebhardt MC, Rosenberg AE, Mankin HJ. Osteoid osteoma: percutaneous radiofrequency ablation. *Radiology* 1995;197:451–454.

Sadry F, Hessler C, Garcia J. The potential aggressiveness of sinus osteomas. A report of two cases. *Skeletal Radiol* 1988;17:427–430.

Schai P, Friederich NB, Krüger A, Jundt G, Herbe E, Buess P. Discrete synchronous multifocal osteoid osteoma of the humerus. *Skeletal Radiol* 1996;25:667–670.

Schajowicz F. *Tumors and tumorlike lesions of bone: pathology, radiology and treatment*, 2nd ed. Berlin: Springer-Verlag; 1994:30–32, 48–56, 406–411.

Schajowicz F, Lemos C. Osteoid osteoma and osteoblastoma. Closely related entities of osteoblastic derivation. *Acta Orthop Scand* 1970;41:272–291.

Schajowicz F, Lemos C. Malignant osteoblastoma. *J Bone Joint Surg [Br]* 1976;58B:202–211.

Shaikh MI, Saifuddin A, Pringle J, Natali C, Sherazi Z. Spinal osteoblastoma: CT and MR imaging with pathological correlation. *Skeletal Radiol* 1999;28:33–40.

Sherazi Z, Saifuddin A, Shaikh MI, Natali C, Pringle JAS. Unusual imaging findings in association with spinal osteoblastoma. *Clin Radiol* 1996;51:644–648.

Sim FH, Dahlin DC, Beabout JW. Osteoid-osteoma: diagnostic problems. *J Bone Joint Surg [Am]* 1975;57A:154–159.

Smith FW, Gilday DL. Scintigraphic appearances of osteoid osteoma. *Radiology* 1980;137:191–195.

Spencer MG, Mitchell DB. Growth of a frontal sinus osteoma. *J Laryngol Otol* 1987;101:726–728.

Spjut HJ, Dorfman HD, Fechner RE, Ackerman LV. Tumors of bone and cartilage. In: Firminger HI, ed. *Atlas of tumor pathology*, 2nd series, fascicle 5. Washington, DC: Armed Forces Institute of Pathology; 1971:117–119.

Steinberg GG, Coumas JM, Breen T. Preoperative localization of osteoid osteoma: a new technique that uses CT. *Am J Roentgenol* 1990;155:883–885.

Sundaram M, Falbo S, McDonald D, Janney C. Surface osteomas of the appendicular skeleton. *Am J Roentgenol* 1996;167:1529–1533.

Theologis T, Ostlere S, Gibbons CLMH, Athanasou NA. Toxic osteoblastoma of the scapula. *Skeletal Radiol* 2007;36:253–257.

Thompson GH, Wong KM, Konsens RM, Vibhakars S. Magnetic resonance imaging of an osteoid osteoma of the proximal femur: a potentially confusing appearance. *J Pediatr Orthop* 1990;10:800–804.

Towbin R, Kaye R, Meza MP, Pollock AN, Yaw K, Moreland M. Osteoid osteoma: percutaneous excision using a CT-guided coaxial technique. *Am J Roentgenol* 1995;164:945–949.

Unni KK, *Dahlin's bone tumors: general aspects and data on 11,087 cases*, 5th ed. Philadelphia: Lippincott-Raven Publishers; 1996.

Unni KK, Dahlin DC, Beabout JW, Ivins JC. Parosteal osteogenic sarcoma. *Cancer* 1976;37:2644–2675.

Vanderschueren GM, Taminiau AHM, Obermann WR, Bloem JL. Osteoid osteoma: clinical results with thermocoagulation. *Radiology* 2002;224:82–86.

Verstraete KL, Van der Woude HJ, Hogendoorn PC, De-Deene Y, Kunnen M, Bloem JL. Dynamic contrast-enhanced MR imaging of musculoskeletal tumors: basic principles and clinical applications. *J Magn Reson Imaging* 1996;6:311–321.

Wilner D. *Radiology of bone tumors and allied disorders*. Philadelphia: WB Saunders; 1982:629–638.

Woods ER, Martel W, Mandell SH, Crabbe JP. Reactive soft-tissue mass associated with osteoid osteoma: correlation of MR imaging features with pathologic findings. *Radiology* 1993;186:221–225.

Worland AL, Ryder CT, Johnson AD. Recurrent osteoid osteoma. *J Bone Joint Surg [Am]* 1975;57A:277–278.

Youssef BA, Haddad MC, Zahrani A, et al. Osteoid osteoma and osteoblastoma: MRI appearances and the significance of ring enhancement. *Eur Radiol* 1996;6:291–296.

Benign Tumors and Tumor-like Lesions II
Lesions of Cartilaginous Origin

Benign Chondroblastic Lesions

Diagnosis of a bone lesion as originating from cartilage is usually a simple task for the radiologist. The lesion's radiolucent matrix, scalloped margins, and annular, comma-shaped, or punctate calcifications usually suffice to establish its chondrogenic nature. However, whether a cartilage tumor is benign or malignant is sometimes extremely difficult for the radiologist to determine.

Enchondroma (Chondroma)

Enchondroma is the second most common benign tumor of bone, constituting approximately 10% of all benign bone tumors and representing the most common tumor of the short tubular bones of the hand. This benign lesion is characterized by the formation of mature hyaline cartilage. When it is located centrally in the bone, it is termed an *enchondròma* (Fig. 18.1); if it is extracortical (periosteal) in location, it is called a *chondroma* (periosteal or juxtacortical) (see Figs. 18.10 and 18.11). Although occurring throughout life, enchondromas are usually seen in patients in their second through fourth decades. There is no sex predilection. The short tubular bones of the hand (phalanges and metacarpals) are the most frequent sites of occurrence (Fig. 18.2), although the lesions are also encountered in the long tubular bones (Fig. 18.3). According to recent investigations, enchondromas result from the continued growth of residual benign cartilaginous rests that are displaced from the growth plate. They are often asymptomatic; a pathologic fracture through the tumor (Figs. 18.4 and 18.5) often calls attention to the lesion.

Enchondroma protuberans is a rare variant. It is a lesion that arises in the intramedullary cavity of a long bone and forms a prominent exophytic mass on the cortical surface. This lesion must be distinguished from an osteochondroma or central chondrosarcoma that penetrates the cortex and forms a juxtacortical mass.

In most instances, radiography suffices to demonstrate the lesion. In the short bones, the lesion is often entirely radiolucent (Fig. 18.6), whereas in the long bones it may display visible calcifications. If the calcifications are extensive, enchondromas are called "calcifying" (Fig. 18.7). The lesions can also be recognized by shallow scalloping of the inner (endosteal) cortical margins because the cartilage in general grows in a lobular pattern (see Fig. 18.1).

Computed tomography (CT) and magnetic resonance imaging (MRI) may further delineate the tumor and more precisely localize it in the bone. On spin-echo T1-weighted MR images, enchondromas demonstrate intermediate to low signal intensity, whereas on T2-weighted images they exhibit high signal intensity. The calcifications within the tumor will image as low-signal-intensity structures (Figs. 18.8 and 18.9). It must be stressed, however, that most of the time neither CT nor MRI is suitable for establishing the precise nature of a cartilaginous lesion, nor can CT or MRI distinguish benign from malignant lesions. Despite the use of various criteria, the application of MRI to the tissue diagnosis of cartilaginous lesions has not brought satisfactory results, although preliminary results of recent trials with fast contrast-enhanced MR imaging showed that this technique might assist in differentiation between the benign and malignant cartilaginous tumors.

Skeletal scintigraphy usually reveals mild to moderate increased uptake of the tracer in uncomplicated enchondromas, whereas the presence of a pathologic fracture or malignant transformation is revealed by marked scintigraphic activity.

Intracortical chondroma is a very rare variant of conventional enchondroma. The lesion is located in cortical bone and is surrounded by sclerosis of the medullary bone and periosteal reaction. Some of these lesions may actually represent periosteal chondroma with an atypical radiographic appearance, as reported by Abdelwahab and associates. Intracortical chondroma can occasionally simulate an osteoid osteoma.

Periosteal chondroma is a slow-growing, benign cartilaginous lesion that arises on the surface of a bone in or beneath the periosteum. It occurs in children as well as adults, with no sex predilection. There is usually a history of pain and tenderness, often accompanied by swelling at the site of the lesion, which is most commonly located in the proximal humerus. As the tumor enlarges, it is seen radiographically eroding the cortex in a saucer-like fashion, producing a solid buttress of periosteal new bone (Fig. 18.10). The lesion has a sharp sclerotic inner margin demarcating it from the buttress of periosteal new bone. Scattered calcifications are often seen within the lesion (Fig. 18.11).

CT may show to better advantage the scalloped cortex and matrix calcification (Fig. 18.12). It also may demonstrate the separation of a lesion from the medullary cavity, an important feature

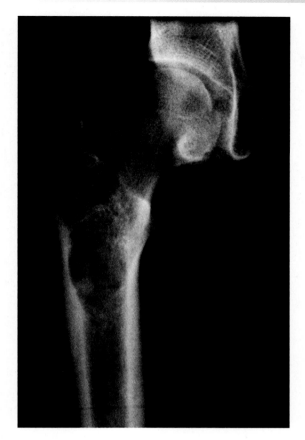

▲
FIGURE 18.1   **Enchondroma.** A radiolucent lesion in the medullary portion of the proximal femur of a 22-year-old man is seen eroding the inner aspect of the lateral cortex. Note scalloped borders and matrix calcification.

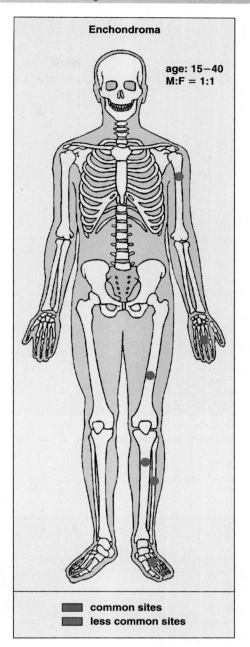

Enchondroma

age: 15–40
M:F = 1:1

■ common sites
■ less common sites

▲
FIGURE 18.3   Skeletal sites of predilection, peak age range, and male-to-female ratio in enchondroma.

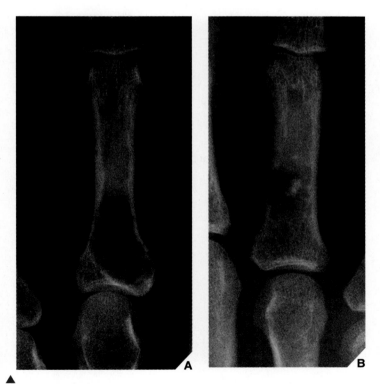

▲
FIGURE 18.2   **Enchondroma. (A)** A radiolucent lesion in the proximal phalanx of the middle finger of a 40-year-old woman, and **(B)** a similar lesion with central calcification in the proximal phalanx of the ring finger of a 42-year-old man are typical examples of enchondroma in the short tubular bones.

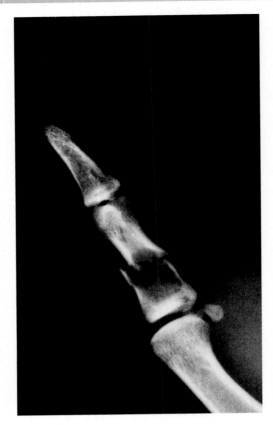

▲
FIGURE 18.4 **Enchondroma.** Radiograph of a 31-year-old man who had injured his left thumb reveals a pathologic fracture through an otherwise asymptomatic lesion.

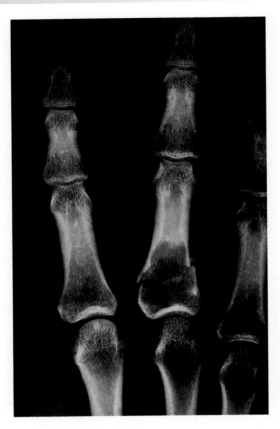

▲
FIGURE 18.5 **Enchondroma.** Pathologic fracture through a large enchondroma is present in the proximal phalanx of the middle finger.

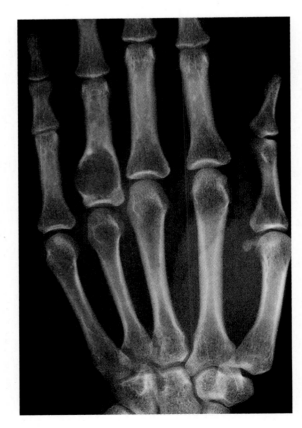

▲
FIGURE 18.6 **Enchondroma.** A typical, purely radiolucent lesion at the base of the proximal phalanx of the ring finger of a 37-year-old woman represents an enchondroma. Note the marked attenuation of the ulnar side of the cortex.

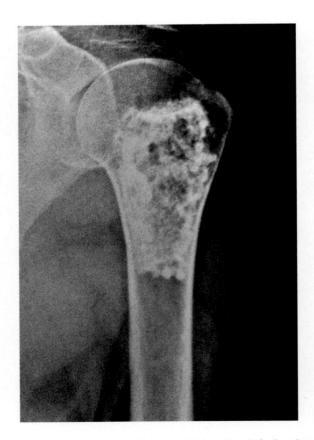

▲
FIGURE 18.7 **Calcifying enchondroma.** In this heavily calcified enchondroma of the proximal humerus of a 58-year-old woman, note the lobular appearance of the lesion and the minimal degree of scalloping of the lateral endocortex.

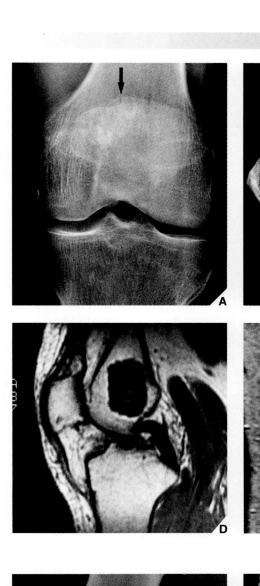
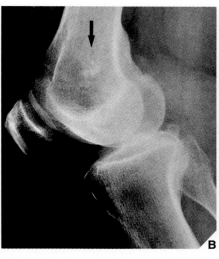
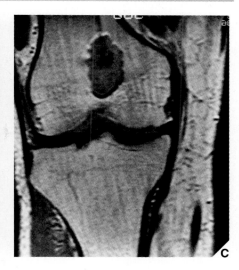
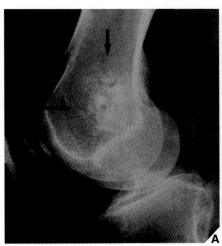
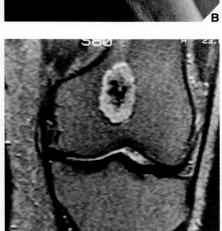

FIGURE 18.8   MRI of enchondroma. Antero-posterior (**A**) and lateral (**B**) radiographs of the left knee of a 61-year-old man demonstrate only a few calcifications in the distal femur (*arrows*). The extent of the lesion cannot be determined. Coronal (**C**) and sagittal (**D**) T1-weighted MR images show a well-circumscribed, lobulated lesion displaying intermediate signal intensity. The darker area in the center represents calcifications. Coronal T2-weighted image (**E**) shows the lesion displaying a mixed-intensity signal: the brighter areas represent cartilaginous tumor and the darker areas calcifications.

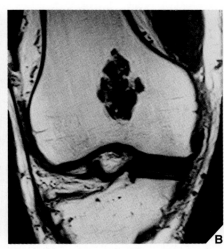
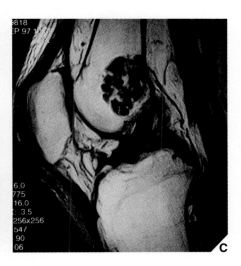
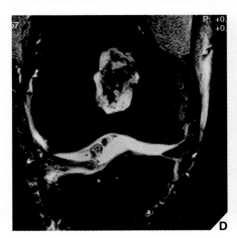
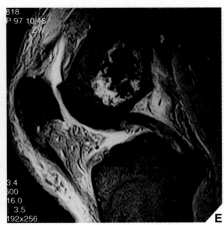

FIGURE 18.9   MRI of enchondroma. (**A**) Lateral radiograph of the knee shows chondroid calcifications in the distal femur (*arrows*). Coronal (**B**) and sagittal (**C**) spin-echo T1-weighted MR images show the lesion being predominantly of low signal intensity. Coronal (**D**) inversion recovery T2-weighted with fat saturation and sagittal (**E**) fast-spin echo T2-weighted images demonstrate the full extent of enchondroma. Calcifications exhibit low signal intensity.

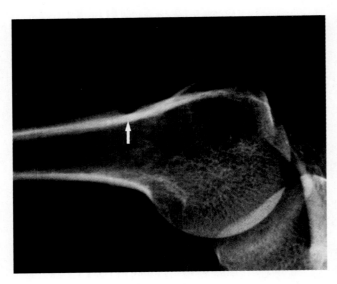

▲
FIGURE 18.10 **Periosteal chondroma.** A radiolucent lesion (*arrow*) is eroding the external surface of the cortex of the proximal humerus of a 24-year-old man.

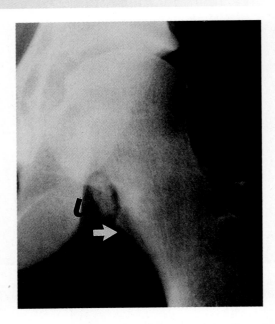

▲
FIGURE 18.11 **Periosteal chondroma.** A periosteal chondroma at the medial aspect of the neck of the left femur eroded the cortex in a saucer-like fashion. The characteristic buttress of a periosteal reaction is seen at the inferior border of the lesion (*arrow*). Note also cluster of calcification in the soft tissue (*curved arrow*).

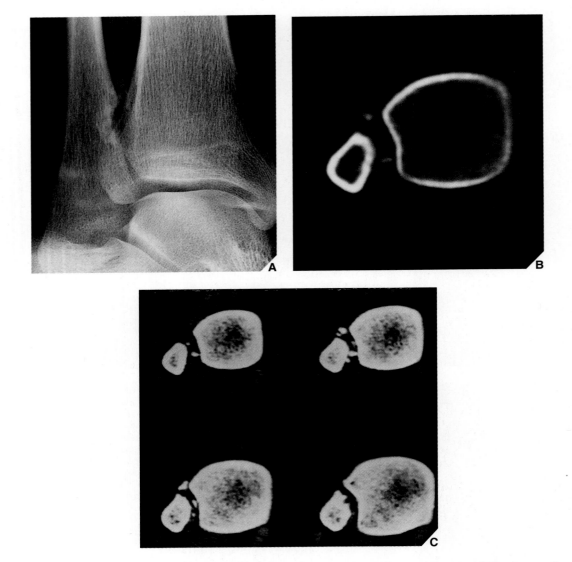

▲
FIGURE 18.12 **CT of periosteal chondroma. (A)** An oblique radiograph of the right ankle shows a lesion containing calcifications eroding the medial cortex of the distal fibula. CT using a bone window (**B**) and a soft-tissue window (**C**) better demonstrates the extent of the lesion and the distribution of the calcifications.

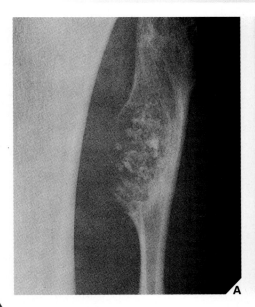
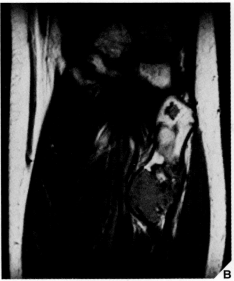
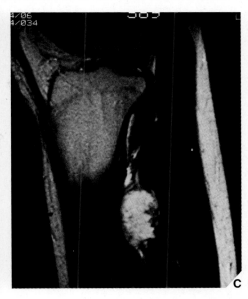

FIGURE 18.13   MRI of periosteal chondroma. (A) A large periosteal chondroma eroded the cortex of the proximal fibula and extended into the medullary cavity. Coronal **(B)** proton-density (SE; TR 2000/TE 19 msec) and sagittal **(C)** T2-weighted (SE; TR 2000/TE 70 msec) MRI show the lesion's extension into the bone marrow.

in differentiation from osteochondroma. MRI findings correspond to radiographic findings, depicting the cartilaginous soft-tissue component. If periosteal chondroma affects the medullary canal, MRI may be useful in depicting the extent of involvement (Fig. 18.13). Fat suppression or enhanced gradient-echo sequences may improve tumor–marrow contrast. The potential pitfall of MRI is marrow edema

mimicking tumor invasion or vice versa. Unlike enchondroma and osteochondroma, periosteal chondroma may continue to grow after skeletal maturation. Some lesions may attain a large size (up to 6 cm) and may resemble osteochondromas (Figs. 18.14 and 18.15). Some lesions may mimic an aneurysmal bone cyst. Very rarely the lesion may encase itself intracortically, thus mimicking other intracortical

FIGURE 18.14   Periosteal chondroma. A large periosteal chondroma (*arrow*) mimics an osteochondroma. Note, however, the periosteal reaction and separation of the tumor from the medullary cavity by a cortex, features that helped in the differentiation from osteochondroma. (Courtesy of Dr. KK Unni, Rochester, Minnesota.)

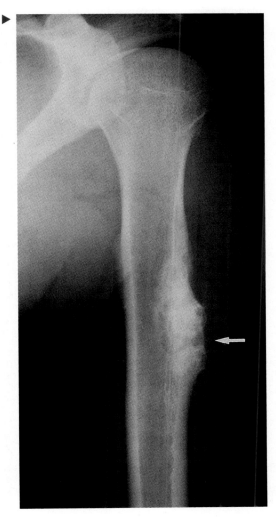

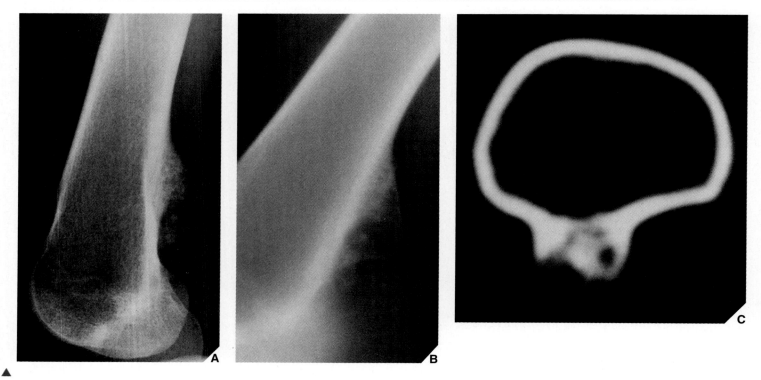

▲

FIGURE 18.15 **Periosteal chondroma. (A)** Lateral radiograph of the distal femur shows a lesion arising from the posterior cortex that resembles an osteochondroma. **(B)** Conventional tomography shows calcifications at the base of the lesion and continuity of the posterior cortex of the femur. **(C)** CT section demonstrates lack of communication between the medullary portion of the femur and the lesion, thus excluding the diagnosis of osteochondroma (**A** and **C** from Greenspan et al., 1993, with permission.)

lesions (such as intracortical angioma, intracortical fibrous dysplasia, or intracortical bone abscess).

Histologically, enchondroma consists of lobules of hyaline cartilage of varying cellularity and is recognized by the features of its intracellular matrix, which has a uniformly translucent appearance and contains relatively little collagen. The tissue is sparsely cellular, and the cells contain small and darkly staining nuclei. The tumor cells are located in rounded spaces known as lacunae. On histologic examination of periosteal chondroma, the findings are identical to those of enchondroma, although the lesion sometimes exhibits higher cellularity, occasionally with atypical cells.

Differential Diagnosis

The main differential diagnosis of enchondroma, particularly in lesions of the long bones, is a medullary bone infarct (Fig. 18.16). At times, the two lesions may be difficult to distinguish from one another, particularly if the enchondroma is small, because both lesions present with similar calcifications. The radiographic features helpful in the differential diagnosis are the lobulation of the inner cortical margins in enchondroma, the annular, punctate, and comma-shaped calcifications in the matrix, and the lack of sclerotic rim that is usually seen in bone infarcts (Fig. 18.17).

The most difficult task for the radiologist is to distinguish a large solitary enchondroma from a slowly growing low-grade chondrosarcoma. One of the most significant findings pointing to a chondrosarcoma in the early stage of development is localized thickening of the cortex (Fig. 18.18). The size of the lesion should also be taken into consideration. Lesions longer than 4 cm (or, according to some investigators, longer than 7 cm) are suggestive of malignancy. In more advanced tumors, destruction of the cortex and the presence of a soft-tissue mass are the hallmarks of malignancy.

Complications

The single most important complication of enchondroma, aside from pathologic fracture (see Fig. 18.4), is its malignant transformation to chondrosarcoma. With solitary enchondromas, this occurs almost

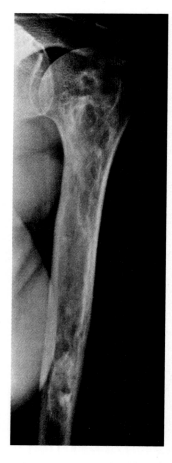

▲

FIGURE 18.16 **Bone infarct.** In a medullary bone infarct, seen here in the proximal humerus of a 36-year-old man with sickle-cell disease, there is no endosteal scalloping of the cortex, and the calcified area is surrounded by a thin, dense sclerotic rim, the hallmark of a bone infarct.

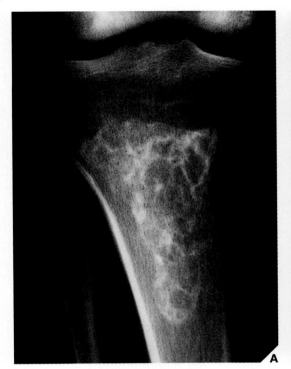
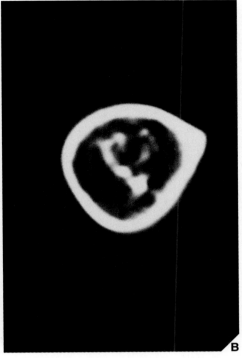

▲
FIGURE 18.17 Bone infarct. **(A)** Conventional radiograph of the proximal tibia shows the typical coarse calcifications of medullary bone infarct. Note the sharply defined peripheral margin separating necrotic from viable bone, and the lack of characteristics for chondroid tumor annular and comma-shaped calcifications. **(B)** In another patient with a bone infarct in the distal femur, a CT section reveals central coarse calcifications and no endosteal scalloping of the cortex.

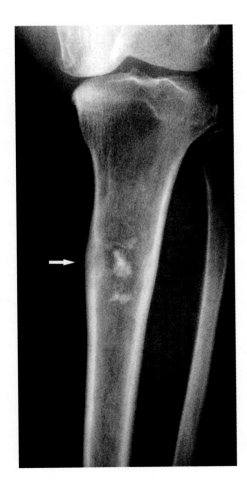

▲
FIGURE 18.18 **Low-grade chondrosarcoma.** A 48-year-old woman presented with pain in the upper leg. A radiograph shows a radiolucent lesion in the proximal tibia with a wide zone of transition and central calcifications. Note focal thickening of the cortex (*arrows*), an important feature that distinguishes chondrosarcoma from similarly appearing enchondroma.

exclusively in a long or flat bone and almost never in a short tubular bone. The radiographic signs of the transformation are thickening of the cortex, destruction of the cortex, and a soft-tissue mass. The development of pain in the absence of fracture at the site of the lesion is an important clinical sign.

Treatment
Curettage of the lesion with the application of bone graft is the most common course of treatment.

Enchondromatosis (Ollier Disease)

Enchondromatosis is a condition marked by multiple enchondromas, generally in the region of the metaphysis and diaphysis (Fig. 18.19). If the skeleton is extensively affected, with predominantly unilateral distribution, the term Ollier disease is applied. The clinical manifestations of multiple enchondromas, such as knobby swellings of the digits or gross disparity in the length of the forearms or legs, are frequently recognized in childhood and adolescence; the disease has a strong preference for one side of the body. The disorder has no hereditary or familial tendency. Some investigators claim that it is not a neoplastic lesion but rather a developmental bone dysplasia.

The pathogenesis of Ollier disease is unknown. There are two hypotheses for the mechanism of enchondroma formation—one attributes formation to ectopic nests of chondroblasts and the other to the failure of chondrocytes and the growth plate to mature.

Conventional radiography is usually sufficient to demonstrate the typical features of enchondromatosis. Characteristically, interference of the lesion with the growth plate causes foreshortening of the limbs. Deformity of the bones is marked by radiolucent masses of cartilage, often in the hand and foot, containing foci of calcification (Fig. 18.20). Enchondromas in this location may be intracortical and periosteal. They sometimes protrude from the shaft of the short or long tubular bone, thus resembling osteochondromas (Fig. 18.21). Linear columns of cartilage in the form of radiolucent streaks extend from the growth plate to the diaphysis, and a fan-like pattern is common in the iliac bones (Fig. 18.22).

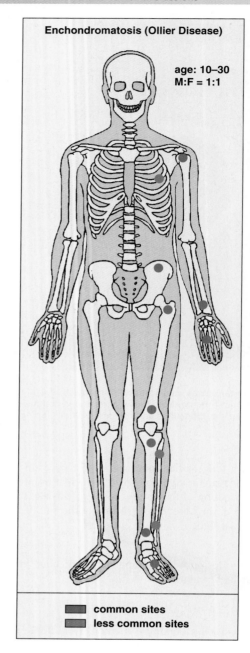

Enchondromatosis (Ollier Disease)

age: 10–30
M:F = 1:1

common sites
less common sites

▲
FIGURE 18.19   Skeletal sites of predilection, peak age range, and male-to-female ratio in enchondromatosis (Ollier disease).

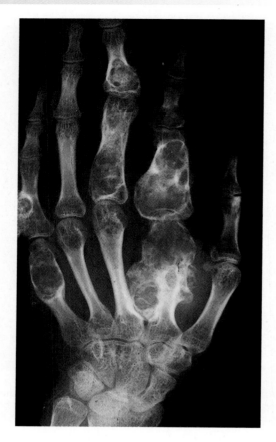

▲
FIGURE 18.20   **Ollier disease.** Large, lobulated cartilaginous masses markedly deform the bones of the hand in this 20-year-old man.

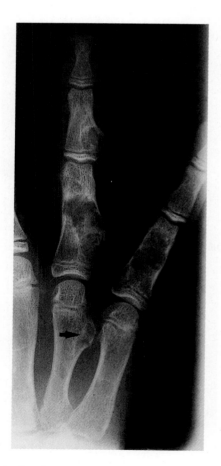

▲
FIGURE 18.21   **Enchondromatosis.** In this 12-year-old boy, the intracortical lesion in the metaphysis of the fourth metacarpal protrudes from the bone (*arrow*), thus resembling an osteochondroma.

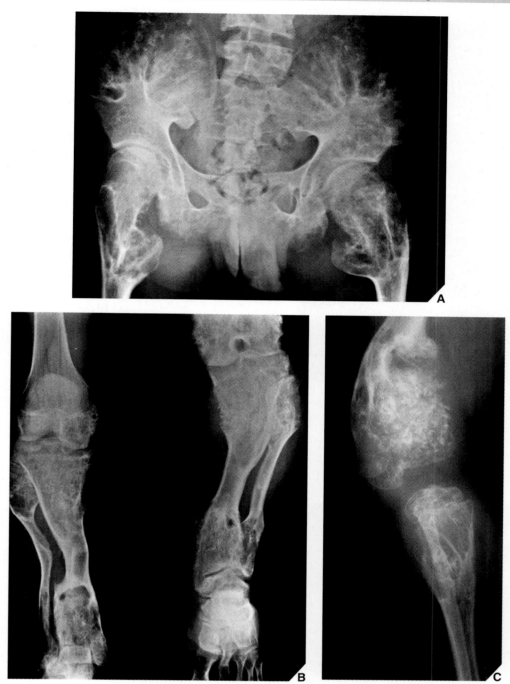

▲
FIGURE 18.22   Ollier disease. The classic features of Ollier disease in a 17-year-old boy are exhibited in extensive involvement of multiple bones. **(A)** Antero-posterior radiograph of the pelvis demonstrates crescent-shaped and ring-like calcifications in tongues of cartilage extending from the iliac crests and proximal femora. **(B)** A radiograph of both legs shows growth stunting and deformities of the tibia and fibula. **(C)** In another patient, a 6-year-old boy with Ollier disease, note extensive involvement of the tibia and distal femur. **(A** from Norman A, Greenspan A, 1982, with permission.)

Histologically, the lesions of enchondromatosis are essentially indistinguishable from those of solitary enchondromas, although on occasion they tend to be more cellular.

Complications

The most frequent and severe complication of Ollier disease is malignant transformation to chondrosarcoma. In contrast to solitary enchondromas, even lesions in the short tubular bones may undergo sarcomatous change (Fig. 18.23). This is particularly true in patients with Maffucci syndrome, a congenital, nonhereditary disorder manifested by enchondromatosis and soft-tissue hemangiomatosis (Fig. 18.24). The hemangiomas are mostly located in the subcutaneous soft tissues. The skeletal lesions in this syndrome show a predilection for involvement of the tubular bones and have the same distribution as those in Ollier disease, with a similarly

strong predilection for one side of the body. Maffucci syndrome is recognized radiographically by multiple calcified phleboliths.

Osteochondroma

Also known as osteocartilaginous exostosis, this lesion is characterized by a cartilage-capped bony projection on the external surface of a bone. It is the most common benign bone lesion, constituting approximately 20% to 50% of all benign bone tumors, and is usually diagnosed in patients before their third decade. Osteochondroma, which has its own growth plate, usually stops growing at skeletal maturity. The most common sites of involvement are the metaphyses of the long bones, particularly in the region around the knee and the proximal humerus (Fig. 18.25). Variants of osteochondroma include subungual exostosis, turret exostosis,

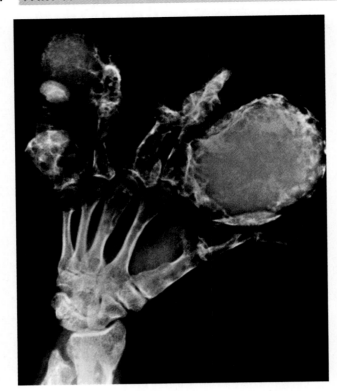

▲
FIGURE 18.23 **Chondrosarcoma in Ollier disease.** In this case of sarcomatous transformation of enchondroma in the hand in a patient with Ollier disease, note the large, lobulated masses of cartilage in all fingers. The lesion of the middle phalanx of the ring finger shows destruction of the cortex and extension into the soft tissues.

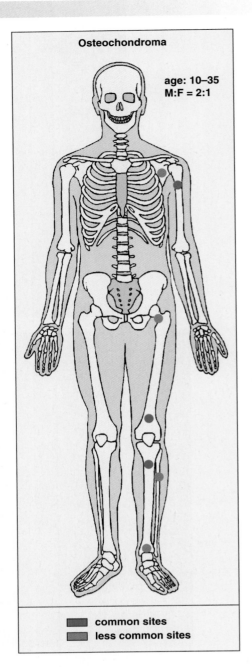

▲
FIGURE 18.25 Skeletal sites of predilection, peak age range, and male-to-female ratio in osteochondroma (osteocartilaginous exostosis).

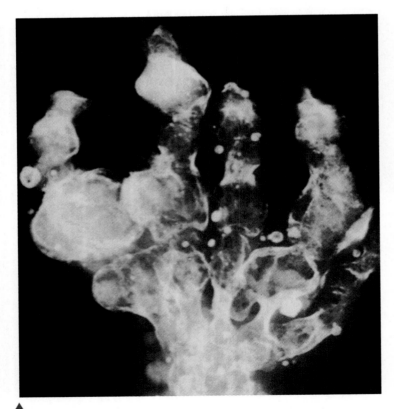

▲
FIGURE 18.24 **Maffucci syndrome.** Radiograph of the hand reveals typical changes of enchondromatosis, accompanied by calcified phleboliths in soft-tissue hemangiomas. (From Bullough PG, 1992, with permission.)

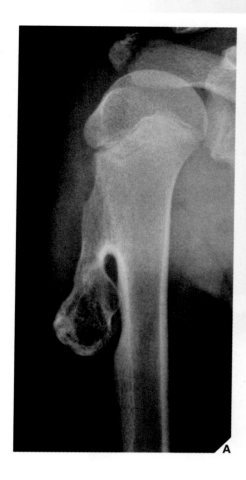

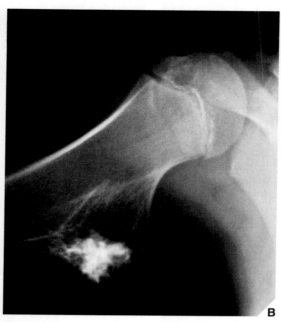

◀ FIGURE 18.26 **Osteochondroma. (A)** The typical pedunculated type of osteochondroma is seen arising near the proximal growth plate of the right humerus in a 13-year-old boy. **(B)** In the typical sessile or broad-based variant, seen here arising from the medial cortex of the proximal diaphysis of the right humerus in a 14-year-old boy, the cortex of the host bone merges without interruption with the cortex of the lesion. The cartilaginous cap is not visible on the conventional radiographs, but dense calcifications in the stalk can be seen.

traction exostosis, bizarre parosteal osteochondromatous proliferation, florid reactive periostitis, and dysplasia epiphysealis hemimelica (also called intraarticular osteochondroma).

The radiographic presentation of osteochondroma is characteristic according to whether the lesion is pedunculated, with a slender pedicle usually directed away from the neighboring growth plate (Fig. 18.26A), or sessile, with a broad base attached to the cortex (Fig. 18.26B). The most important characteristic feature of either type of lesion is uninterrupted merging of the cortex of the host bone with the cortex of the osteochondroma; additionally, the medullary portion of the lesion and the medullary cavity of the adjacent bone communicate. CT scanning can establish unequivocally the lack of cortical interruption

and the continuity of cancellous portions of the lesion and the host bone (Fig. 18.27). These are important features that distinguish this lesion from the occasionally similar looking bone masses of osteoma, periosteal chondroma, juxtacortical osteosarcoma, soft-tissue osteosarcoma, and juxtacortical myositis ossificans (Fig. 18.28). The other characteristic feature of osteochondroma involves calcifications in the chondro-osseous portion of the stalk of the lesion (see Fig. 18.26) and cartilaginous cap. The thickness of the cartilaginous cap ranges from 1 to 3 mm and rarely exceeds 1 cm. On MRI, the cartilaginous cap shows high signal intensity on T2-weighted and gradient-echo sequences. A narrow band of low signal intensity surrounding the cap represents the overlying perichondrium (Fig. 18.29).

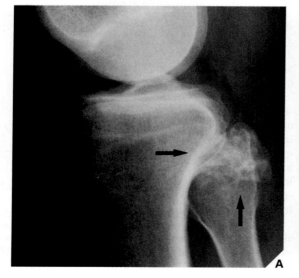

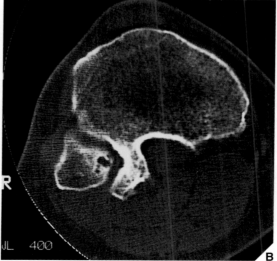

▲ FIGURE 18.27 **CT of osteochondroma. (A)** Lateral radiograph of the knee shows a calcified lesion at the posterior aspect of the proximal tibia (*arrows*). The exact nature of this lesion cannot be ascertained. **(B)** CT clearly establishes the continuity of the cortex, which extends without interruption from the osteochondroma into the tibia. Note also that the medullary portion of the lesion and the tibia communicate.

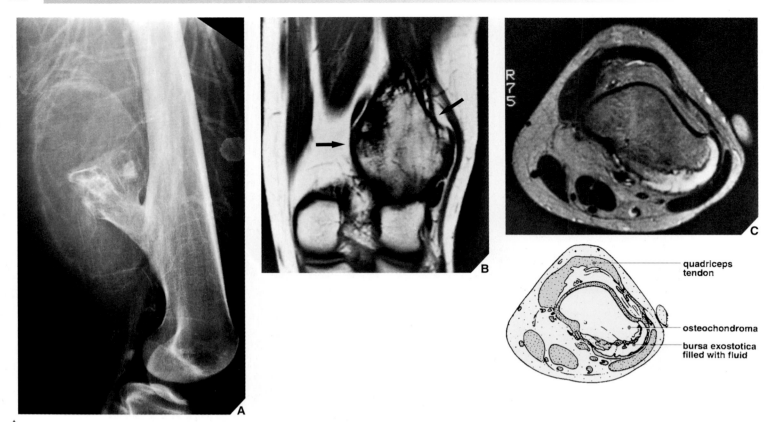

FIGURE 18.32 Bursa exostotica. (A) A 25-year-old man with a known solitary osteochondroma of the distal right femur reported gradually increasing pain. The capillary phase of an arteriogram reveals a huge bursa exostotica. Inflammation of the bursa, with the accumulation of a large amount of fluid (bursitis), was the cause of the patient's symptoms. **(B)** Another patient, a 12-year-old girl, presented with pain in the popliteal fossa. Coronal T1-weighted MR image (SE; TR 650/ TE 25 msec) demonstrates a large osteochondroma arising from the posterolateral aspect of distal femur (*arrows*). **(C)** Axial T2-weighted image (SE; TR 2200/TE 70 msec) demonstrates a bursa exostotica distended with fluid.

whether the calcifications in an osteochondroma are contained within the stalk of the lesion—a clear indication of benignity (see Fig. 18.26). Similarly, CT can demonstrate both dispersed calcifications in the cartilaginous cap and increased thickness of the cap, cardinal signs of

malignant transformation of the lesion, as Norman and Sissons have pointed out (Fig. 18.33).

The unreliability of radionuclide imaging is related to the fact that even benign exostoses exhibit an increased uptake of radiopharmaceutical

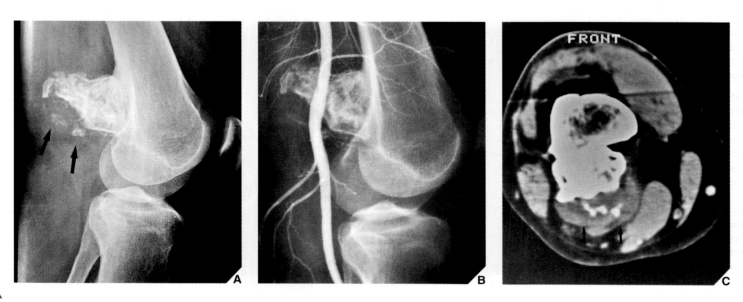

FIGURE 18.33 Transformation of osteochondroma to chondrosarcoma. A 28-year-old man had pain in the popliteal region and also noticed an increase in a mass he had been aware of for 15 years—important clinical information that warranted further investigation to rule out the malignant transformation of an osteochondroma. **(A)** Lateral radiograph of the knee demonstrates a sessile-type osteochondroma arising from the posterior cortex of the distal femur. Note that calcifications are present not only in the stalk of the lesion but also are dispersed in the cartilaginous cap (*arrows*). **(B)** An arteriogram demonstrates displacement of the small vessels, which are draped over the invisible cartilaginous cap. **(C)** CT section confirms the increased thickness of the cartilaginous cap (2.5 cm) and dispersed calcifications within the cap (*arrows*). These imaging features are consistent with a diagnosis of malignant transformation to chondrosarcoma, which was confirmed by histopathologic examination.

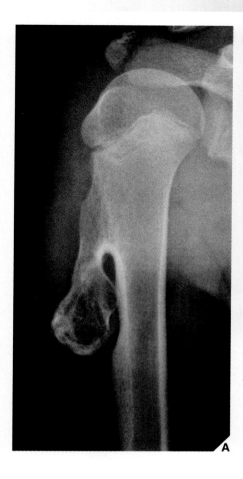

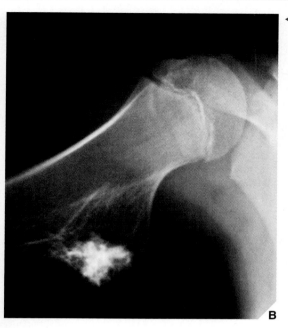

◀ FIGURE 18.26   Osteochondroma. (A) The typical pedunculated type of osteochondroma is seen arising near the proximal growth plate of the right humerus in a 13-year-old boy. (B) In the typical sessile or broad-based variant, seen here arising from the medial cortex of the proximal diaphysis of the right humerus in a 14-year-old boy, the cortex of the host bone merges without interruption with the cortex of the lesion. The cartilaginous cap is not visible on the conventional radiographs, but dense calcifications in the stalk can be seen.

traction exostosis, bizarre parosteal osteochondromatous proliferation, florid reactive periostitis, and dysplasia epiphysealis hemimelica (also called intraarticular osteochondroma).

The radiographic presentation of osteochondroma is characteristic according to whether the lesion is pedunculated, with a slender pedicle usually directed away from the neighboring growth plate (Fig. 18.26A), or sessile, with a broad base attached to the cortex (Fig. 18.26B). The most important characteristic feature of either type of lesion is uninterrupted merging of the cortex of the host bone with the cortex of the osteochondroma; additionally, the medullary portion of the lesion and the medullary cavity of the adjacent bone communicate. CT scanning can establish unequivocally the lack of cortical interruption and the continuity of cancellous portions of the lesion and the host bone (Fig. 18.27). These are important features that distinguish this lesion from the occasionally similar looking bone masses of osteoma, periosteal chondroma, juxtacortical osteosarcoma, soft-tissue osteosarcoma, and juxtacortical myositis ossificans (Fig. 18.28). The other characteristic feature of osteochondroma involves calcifications in the chondro-osseous portion of the stalk of the lesion (see Fig. 18.26) and cartilaginous cap. The thickness of the cartilaginous cap ranges from 1 to 3 mm and rarely exceeds 1 cm. On MRI, the cartilaginous cap shows high signal intensity on T2-weighted and gradient-echo sequences. A narrow band of low signal intensity surrounding the cap represents the overlying perichondrium (Fig. 18.29).

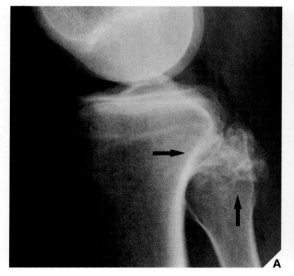

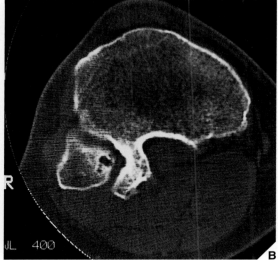

▲ FIGURE 18.27   CT of osteochondroma. (A) Lateral radiograph of the knee shows a calcified lesion at the posterior aspect of the proximal tibia (arrows). The exact nature of this lesion cannot be ascertained. (B) CT clearly establishes the continuity of the cortex, which extends without interruption from the osteochondroma into the tibia. Note also that the medullary portion of the lesion and the tibia communicate.

LESIONS OF SIMILAR APPEARANCE TO OSTEOCHONDROMA

Osteochondroma

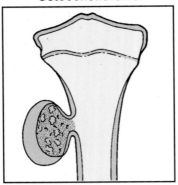

uninterrupted merging of
cortex of host bone
with cortex of lesion

Myositis Ossificans

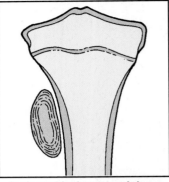

lesion with dense periphery
and lucent center, cleft
separating lesion from cortex

Juxtacortical Osteosarcoma

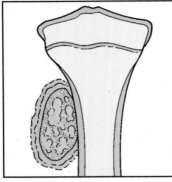

lesion with lucent periphery
and dense center, no cleft

Soft Tissue Osteosarcoma

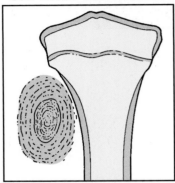

lesion with smudgy
densities in center,
more lucent at periphery

Juxtacortical Osteoma

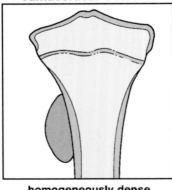

homogeneously dense
(ivory) lesion, no cleft

Periosteal Chondroma

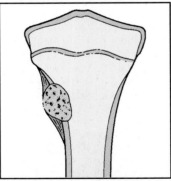

solid buttress of periosteal
reaction, calcifications in
center of lesion

▲
FIGURE 18.28 **Differential diagnosis of osteochondroma.** Radiographic features characterizing lesions similar in appearance to osteochondroma.

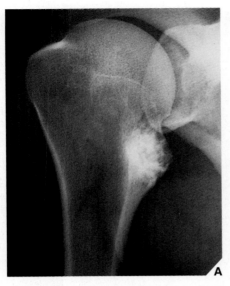

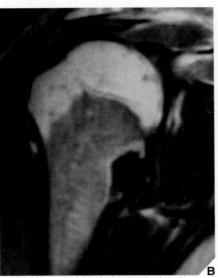

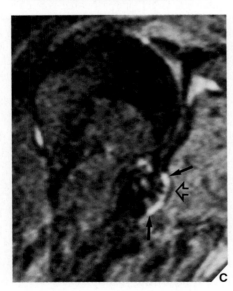

▲
FIGURE 18.29 **MRI of osteochondroma. (A)** Radiograph of the right proximal humerus shows a sessile osteochondroma at the medial aspect of metadiaphysis. **(B)** T1-weighted coronal MRI reveals that the lesion exhibits low signal intensity because of extensive mineralization. **(C)** T2-weighted image shows the thin cartilaginous cap as a band of high signal intensity (*arrows*), covered by a linear area of low signal representing perichondrium (*open arrow*).

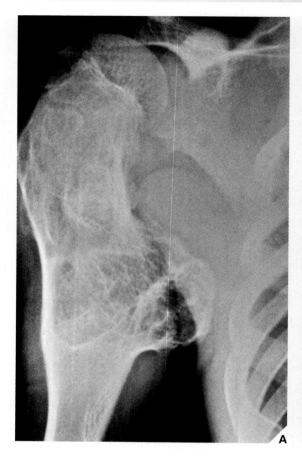
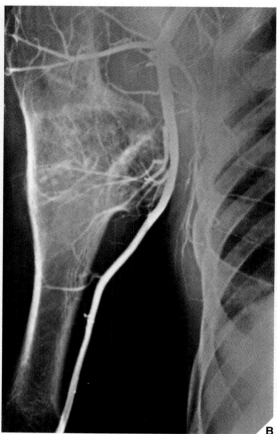

▲
FIGURE 18.30   Complication of osteochondroma. A 14-year-old boy with a known osteochondroma of the right humerus complained of pain and numbness of the hand and fingers. (**A**) Radiograph of the right shoulder demonstrates a sessile-type osteochondroma arising from the medial aspect of the proximal diaphysis of the humerus. (**B**) Arteriography reveals compression and displacement of the brachial artery.

Histologically, the osteochondroma cap is composed of hyaline cartilage arranged similarly to that of a growth plate. A zone of calcification in the chondro-osseous portion of the stalk corresponds to the zone of provisional calcification in the physis. Beneath this zone, there is vascular invasion and replacement of the calcified cartilage by new bone formation, which undergoes maturation and merges with the cancellous bone of the host bone's medullary cavity.

Complications

Osteochondroma may be complicated by a number of secondary abnormalities, including pressure on nerves or blood vessels (Fig. 18.30), pressure on the adjacent bone, with occasional fracture (Fig. 18.31), fracture through the lesion itself, and inflammatory changes of the bursa exostotica ("exostosis bursata") covering the cartilaginous cap (Fig. 18.32).

The least common complication of osteochondroma, seen in solitary lesions in less than 1% of cases, is malignant transformation to chondrosarcoma. Nevertheless, it is important to recognize this complication at an early stage. The chief clinical features suggesting malignant transformation are pain (in the absence of a fracture, bursitis, or pressure on nearby nerves) and a growth spurt or continued growth of the lesion beyond the age of skeletal maturity. Certain imaging features have also been identified that may help in the determination of malignancy (Table 18.1).

The most reliable imaging modalities for evaluating the possible malignant transformation of an osteochondroma are conventional radiography, CT, and MRI; the results of a radionuclide bone scan, which may show increased uptake of radiopharmaceutical at the site of the lesion, may not be reliable. The radiography usually demonstrates

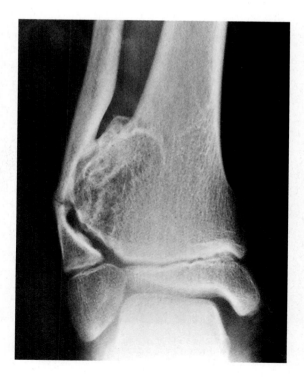

▲
FIGURE 18.31   Complication of osteochondroma. A 9-year-old boy had a sessile osteochondroma of the distal tibia. The lesion produced pressure erosion, and later bowing and attenuation of the fibula, with subsequent fracture of the bone. (From Norman A, Greenspan A, 1982, with permission.)

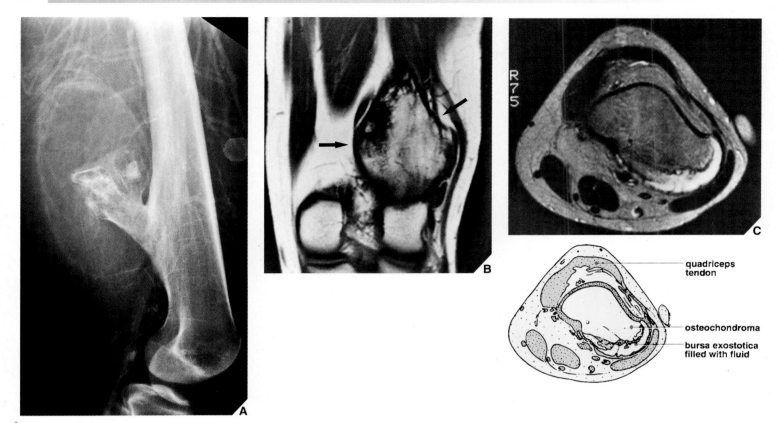

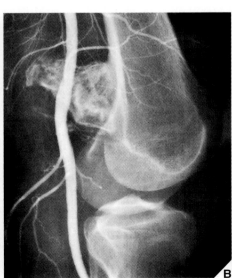

quadriceps
tendon

osteochondroma

bursa exostotica
filled with fluid

▲
FIGURE 18.32   Bursa exostotica. (A) A 25-year-old man with a known solitary osteochondroma of the distal right femur reported gradually increasing pain. The capillary phase of an arteriogram reveals a huge bursa exostotica. Inflammation of the bursa, with the accumulation of a large amount of fluid (bursitis), was the cause of the patient's symptoms. **(B)** Another patient, a 12-year-old girl, presented with pain in the popliteal fossa. Coronal T1-weighted MR image (SE; TR 650/TE 25 msec) demonstrates a large osteochondroma arising from the posterolateral aspect of distal femur (*arrows*). **(C)** Axial T2-weighted image (SE; TR 2200/TE 70 msec) demonstrates a bursa exostotica distended with fluid.

whether the calcifications in an osteochondroma are contained within the stalk of the lesion—a clear indication of benignity (see Fig. 18.26). Similarly, CT can demonstrate both dispersed calcifications in the cartilaginous cap and increased thickness of the cap, cardinal signs of

malignant transformation of the lesion, as Norman and Sissons have pointed out (Fig. 18.33).

The unreliability of radionuclide imaging is related to the fact that even benign exostoses exhibit an increased uptake of radiopharmaceutical

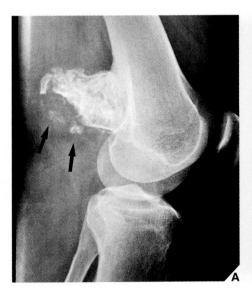

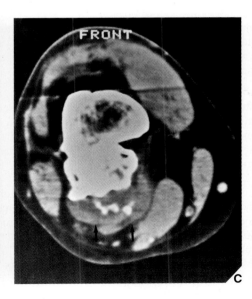

▲
FIGURE 18.33   Transformation of osteochondroma to chondrosarcoma. A 28-year-old man had pain in the popliteal region and also noticed an increase in a mass he had been aware of for 15 years—important clinical information that warranted further investigation to rule out the malignant transformation of an osteochondroma. **(A)** Lateral radiograph of the knee demonstrates a sessile-type osteochondroma arising from the posterior cortex of the distal femur. Note that calcifications are present not only in the stalk of the lesion but also are dispersed in the cartilaginous cap (*arrows*). **(B)** An arteriogram demonstrates displacement of the small vessels, which are draped over the invisible cartilaginous cap. **(C)** CT section confirms the increased thickness of the cartilaginous cap (2.5 cm) and dispersed calcifications within the cap (*arrows*). These imaging features are consistent with a diagnosis of malignant transformation to chondrosarcoma, which was confirmed by histopathologic examination.

TABLE 18.1 **Clinical and Imaging Features Suggesting Malignant Transformation of Osteochondroma**

Clinical Features	Radiologic Findings	Imaging Modality
Pain (in the absence of fracture, bursitis, or pressure on nearby nerves)	Enlargement of the lesion	Conventional radiography (comparison with earlier radiographs)
Growth spurt (after skeletal maturity)	Development of a bulky cartilaginous cap usually 2–3 cm thick	CT, MRI
	Dispersed calcifications in the cartilaginous cap	Radiography, CT, MRI
	Development of a soft-tissue mass with or without calcifications	
	Increased uptake of isotope after closure of growth plate (not always reliable)	Scintigraphy

caused by endochondral ossification. Exostotic chondrosarcoma is also marked by isotope uptake, which is related to active ossification, osteoblastic activity, and hyperemia within the cartilage and bony stalk of the tumor. Thus, although the uptake is more intense in exostotic chondrosarcomas than in benign exostoses, various investigations show that this is not always a reliable feature distinguishing these lesions.

Treatment

Solitary lesions of osteochondroma usually can simply be monitored if they do not cause clinical problems. Surgical resection is indicated if the lesion becomes painful, if there is suspected encroachment on adjacent nerves or blood vessels, if pathologic fracture occurs, or if there is concern about the diagnosis.

Multiple Osteocartilaginous Exostoses

This condition, also known as multiple hereditary osteochondromata, familial osteochondromatosis, or diaphyseal aclasis, is classified by some authorities in the category of bone dysplasias. It is a hereditary, autosomal-dominant disorder with incomplete penetrance in females. Approximately two thirds of affected individuals have a positive family history. The specific genetic defect has been recently identified, with three distinct loci on chromosomes 8, 11, and 19. There is a decided 2:1 male predilection. The knees, ankles, and shoulders are the sites most frequently affected by the development of multiple osteochondromas (Fig. 18.34). The radiographic features are similar to those of single osteochondromas (see Fig. 18.26), but the lesions are more frequently of the sessile type (Figs. 18.35 to 18.37). CT and 3D CT show spatial distribution of the lesions (Fig. 18.38). The histopathologic features of multiple osteochondromas are the same as those of solitary lesions.

Complications

There is a greater incidence of growth disturbance in multiple osteocartilaginous exostoses than in solitary osteochondroma. Growth abnormalities are primarily seen in the forearms (Fig. 18.39) and legs. Malignant transformation to chondrosarcoma is also more common, seen in 5% to 15% of cases, with lesions at the shoulder girdle and around the pelvis at greater risk of undergoing transformation. The clinical and imaging signs of this complication are identical to those in the malignant transformation of a solitary osteochondroma (Fig. 18.40, see also Fig. 18.33 and Table 18.1).

Treatment

Multiple osteochondromas are treated individually. Like solitary lesions, they are likely to recur in younger children, and surgery may be deferred to a later date.

Chondroblastoma

Also known as a Codman tumor, chondroblastoma, representing fewer than 1% of all primary bone tumors, is a benign lesion occurring before skeletal maturity, characteristically presenting in the epiphyses of long

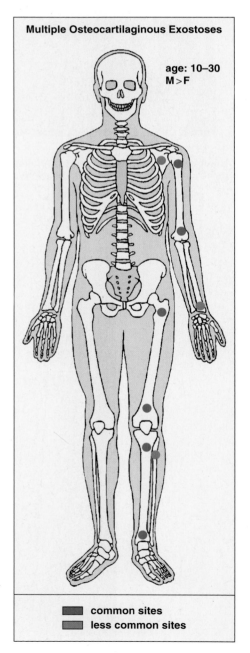

Multiple Osteocartilaginous Exostoses

age: 10–30
M > F

■ common sites
■ less common sites

FIGURE 18.34 Skeletal sites of predilection, peak age range, and male-to-female ratio in multiple osteocartilaginous exostoses (multiple osteochondromata, diaphyseal aclasis).

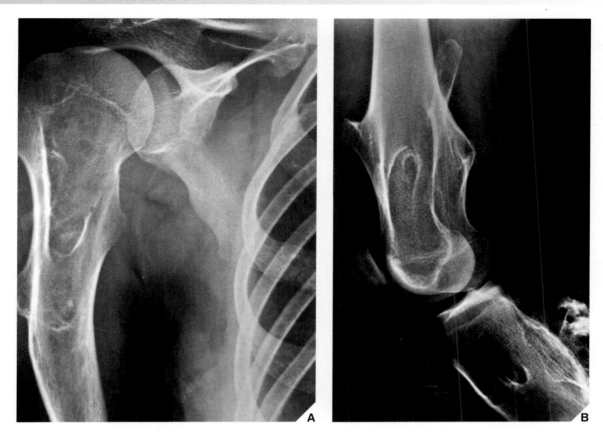

▲
FIGURE 18.35 Hereditary multiple exostoses. (A) Anteroposterior radiograph of the shoulder of a 22-year-old man demonstrates multiple sessile lesions involving the proximal humerus, scapula, and ribs. **(B)** Involvement of the distal femur and proximal tibia is characteristic of this disorder.

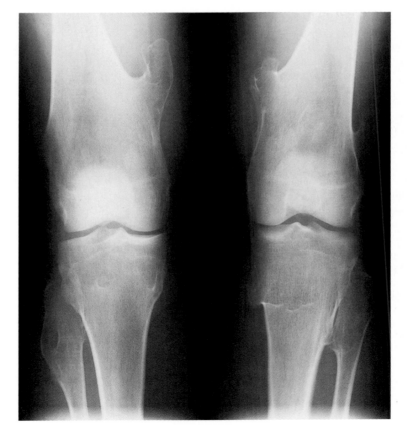

▲
FIGURE 18.36 Hereditary multiple exostoses. An anteroposterior radiograph of both knees of a 17-year-old boy shows numerous sessile and pedunculated osteochondromas.

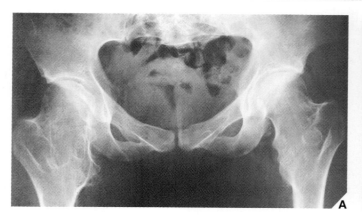

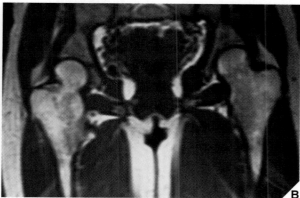

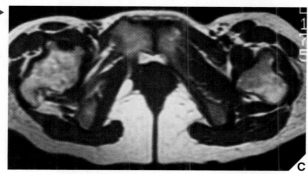

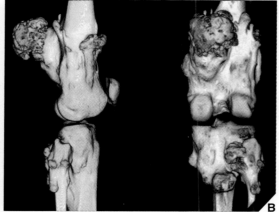

FIGURE 18.37 MRI of hereditary multiple exostoses. (A) Antero-posterior radiograph of the hips shows multiple sessile osteochondromas mainly affecting proximal femora. Some lesions are also present at the pubic bones. Coronal (B) and axial (C) T1-weighted (SE; TR 600/TE 20 msec) MR images demonstrate continuity of the lesions with the medullary portion of the femora. Note also dysplastic changes expressed by abnormal tubulation of the bones.

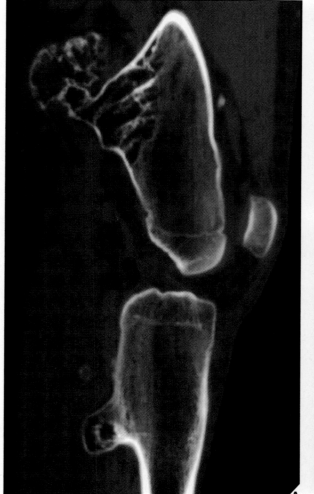

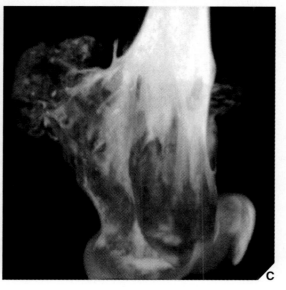

FIGURE 18.38 CT and 3D CT of hereditary multiple exostoses. (A) Sagittal reformatted CT image of the knee shows multiple osteochondromas in the distal femur and proximal tibia. (B) 3D reconstructed CT images in shaded surface display (SSD) show spatial orientation of osteochondromas. (C) 3D reconstructed CT image in maximum intensity projection (MIP) shows internal architecture of one of the lesions. (Reprinted from Greenspan A et al., 2007.)

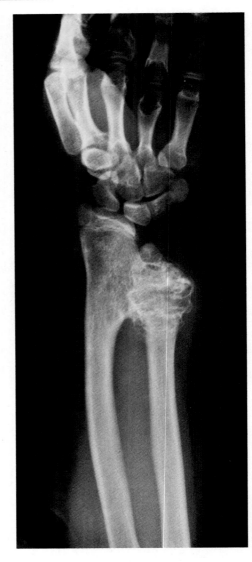

▲
FIGURE 18.39 **Hereditary multiple exostoses: growth disturbance.** Posteroanterior radiograph of the forearm of an 8-year-old boy with multiple osteochondromas shows a growth disturbance in the distal radius and ulna, which is frequently seen as a complication in this disorder.

bones such as the humerus, tibia, and femur (Fig. 18.41). Although secondary involvement of the metaphysis after skeletal maturity is recognized, a predominantly metaphyseal or diaphyseal location is exceedingly rare. Equally unusual is involvement of the vertebra or intracortical location in the long bones. Occasionally the patella, which is considered equivalent to an epiphysis, is affected. Ten percent of chondroblastomas involve the small bones of the hands and feet, with the talus and calcaneus representing the most common sites. Although the lesion is usually seen in growing bones, some cases have been reported after obliteration of the growth plate. Chondroblastoma is usually located eccentrically, shows a sclerotic border, and often demonstrates scattered calcifications of the matrix (25% of cases) (Fig. 18.42). Brower and colleagues noticed a distinctively thick, solid periosteal reaction distal to the lesion in 57% of chondroblastomas in long bones (Fig. 18.43). This most likely represents an inflammatory reaction to the tumor. In most cases, radiography suffices to demonstrate the lesion (Fig. 18.44), but CT scan can help demonstrate the calcifications if they are not visible on the standard radiographs (Fig. 18.45). MRI usually reveals a larger area of involvement than can be seen on radiography, including regional bone marrow and soft-tissue edema (Fig. 18.46).

Histologically, chondroblastoma is composed of nodules of fairly mature cartilage matrix surrounded by a highly cellular tissue containing uniformly large round cells with ovoid nuclei and clear cytoplasm. Multinucleated osteoclast-like giant cells are a frequent finding. The matrix shows characteristic fine calcifications surrounding apposing chondroblasts, having a spatial arrangement resembling the hexagonal configuration of chicken wire.

Treatment and Complications

Chondroblastomas are usually treated by curettage and bone grafting. Only few reported cases have been treated with percutaneous radiofrequency ablation.

In rare cases, pulmonary metastases develop in the absence of any histologic evidence of malignancy in either the primary bone tumor or the pulmonary lesions. Only in exceptional circumstances, pulmonary or widespread metastases led to patient death.

Chondromyxoid Fibroma

Chondromyxoid fibroma is a rare tumor of cartilaginous derivation, characterized by the production of chondroid, fibrous, and myxoid tissues in variable proportions, and accounts for 0.5% of all primary

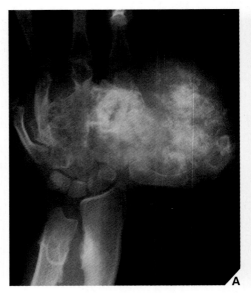
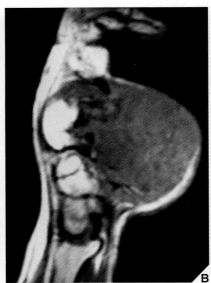
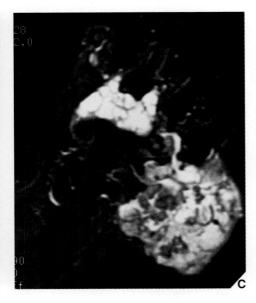

▲
FIGURE 18.40 **Malignant transformation. (A)** Oblique radiograph of the right hand of a 22-year-old man shows multiple osteochondromas. A large soft-tissue mass situated between the index finger and thumb and containing chondroid calcifications indicates malignant transformation to chondrosarcoma. **(B)** Sagittal T1-weighted (SE; TR 600/TE 16 msec) MRI reveals volar extension of a large soft-tissue tumor. **(C)** Coronal inversion recovery (FMPIR/90; TR 4000/TE 64 msec/ Ef) MR image shows malignant lobules of the cartilage invading the bones and soft tissues of the hand.

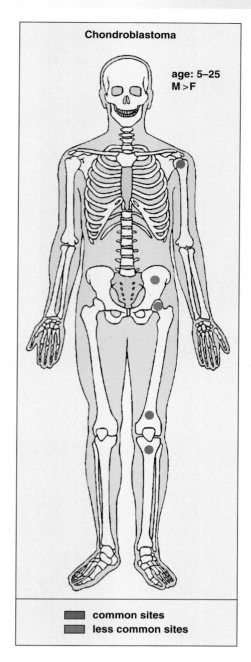

Chondroblastoma

age: 5–25
M > F

common sites
less common sites

FIGURE 18.41 Skeletal sites of predilection, peak age incidence, and male-to-female ratio in chondroblastoma.

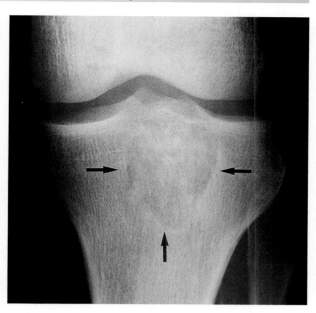

FIGURE 18.42 **Chondroblastoma.** A lesion located in the proximal tibia (*arrows*) of a 17-year-old boy exhibits faint sclerotic border and central calcifications.

intensity on T1-weighted and high signal on T2-weighted sequences (Fig. 18.50).

Pathologically, the most important feature of the lesion is its lobular or pseudolobular arrangement into zones of varying cellularity. The center of the lobule is hypocellular. Within the matrix, loosely arranged spindle-shaped and stellate cells with elongated processes are present. The periphery of the lobule is densely cellular, containing a mixture of mononuclear

bone tumors and 2% of all benign bone tumors. It occurs predominantly in adolescents and young adults (males more than females), most commonly in the patient's second or third decade. It has a predilection for the bones of the lower extremities, with preferred sites in the proximal tibia (32%) and distal femur (17%) (Fig. 18.47). Exceedingly rare, the lesion may be located in the vertebra. Few cases of chondromyxoid fibroma have been reported in juxtacortical location. Its clinical symptoms include local swelling and pain, which are occasionally caused by pressure on adjacent neurovascular structures by a peripherally located mass.

Its characteristic radiographic picture is that of an eccentrically located radiolucent lesion in the bone, with a sclerotic scalloped margin often eroding or ballooning out the cortex (Figs. 18.48 and 18.49). The lesion may range from 1 to 10 cm in size, with an average of 3 to 4 cm. Calcifications are not apparent radiographically, but focal microscopic calcifications have been reported in as many as 27% of cases. Frequently, a buttress of periosteal new bone can be observed. MRI reveals characteristics of most cartilaginous tumors: intermediate to low signal

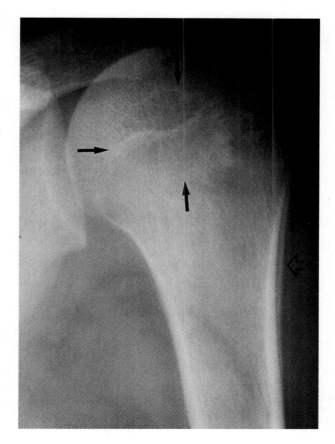

FIGURE 18.43 **Chondroblastoma.** A lesion in the proximal humerus (*arrows*) elicited periosteal reaction along the lateral cortex (*open arrow*).

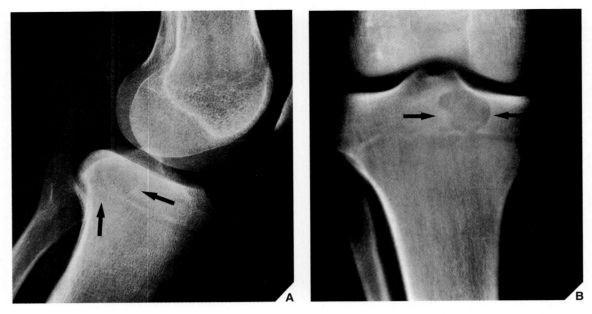

▲
FIGURE 18.44 Chondroblastoma. (A) Lateral radiograph and **(B)** anteroposterior tomogram of the knee show the typical appearance of a chondroblastoma in the proximal epiphysis of the tibia. Note the radiolucent, eccentrically located lesion with a thin, sclerotic margin (*arrows*). There are small, scattered calcifications in the center of the lesion, which are better seen on the tomogram.

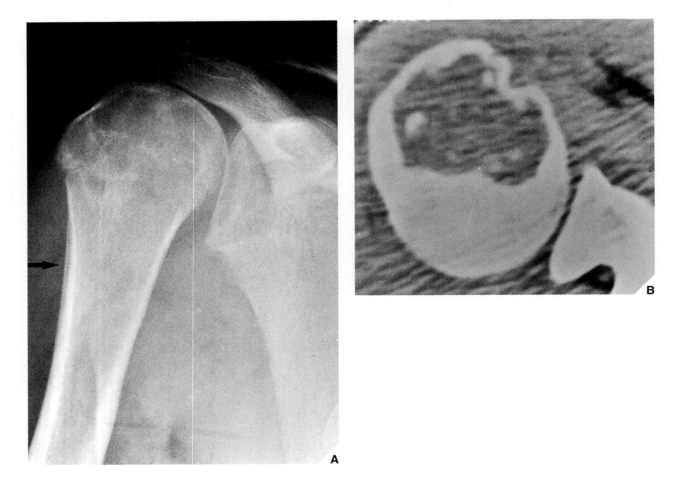

▲
FIGURE 18.45 CT of chondroblastoma. (A) Anteroposterior radiograph of the right shoulder of a 16-year-old boy shows a lesion in the proximal humeral epiphysis, but calcifications tumors are not well demonstrated. Note the well-organized layer of periosteal reaction at the lateral cortex (*arrow*). **(B)** CT section shows the calcifications clearly. The tumor was removed by curettage, and a histopathologic examination confirmed the radiographic diagnosis of chondroblastoma.

spindle-shaped and polyhedral stromal cells with a variable number of multinucleated giant cells.

Differential Diagnosis

Commonly, one can observe a characteristic buttress of periosteal new bone formation (Fig. 18.51), in which case a chondromyxoid fibroma may be radiographically indistinguishable from an aneurysmal bone cyst. In unusual locations such as in short tubular or flat bones, it may mimic a giant cell tumor or desmoplastic fibroma.

Treatment

The treatment of this lesion usually consists of curettage and a bone graft. Recurrences are frequent, with the reported rate between 20% and 80% (see Fig. 16.55).

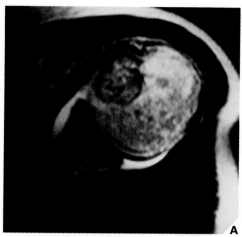

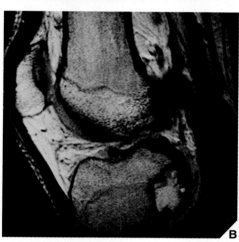

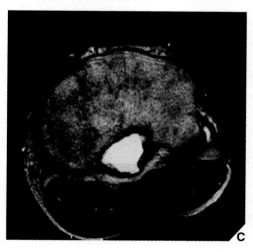

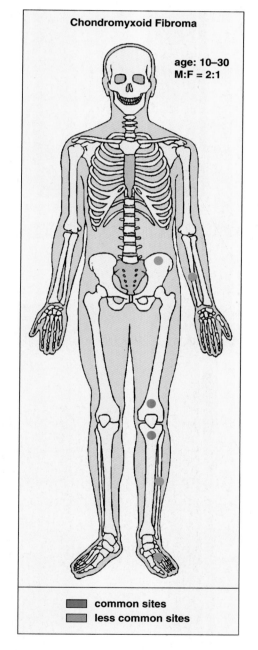

FIGURE 18.47 Skeletal sites of predilection, peak age range, and male-to-female ratio in chondromyxoid fibroma.

FIGURE 18.46 MRI of chondroblastoma. (A) Axial T2-weighted (SE; TR 2000/TE 80 msec) MRI of the shoulder in an 18-year-old man shows sharply marginated lesion with sclerotic border and central calcifications within the left humeral head. Note the small amount of joint effusion and peritumoral edema. In another patient, **(B)** sagittal proton density-weighted (SE; TR 2000/TE 28 msec) and **(C)** axial T2-weighted (SE; TR 2000/TE 80 msec) MR images of the knee show extension of chondroblastoma located in the posterior aspect of proximal tibia into the soft tissues.

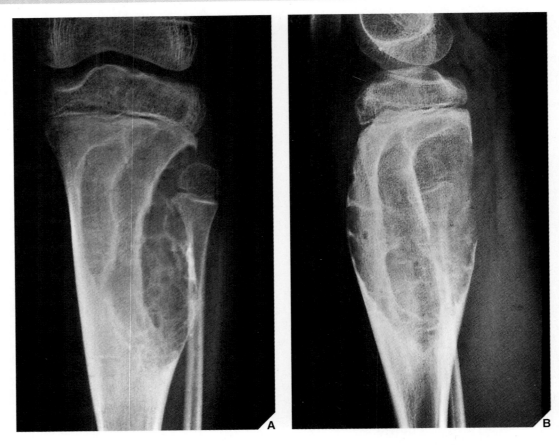

▲
FIGURE 18.48   Chondromyxoid fibroma. Anteroposterior (**A**) and lateral (**B**) radiographs of the left leg of an 8-year-old girl demonstrate a radiolucent lesion extending from the metaphysis into the diaphysis of the tibia, with a geographic type of bone destruction and a sclerotic scalloped border.

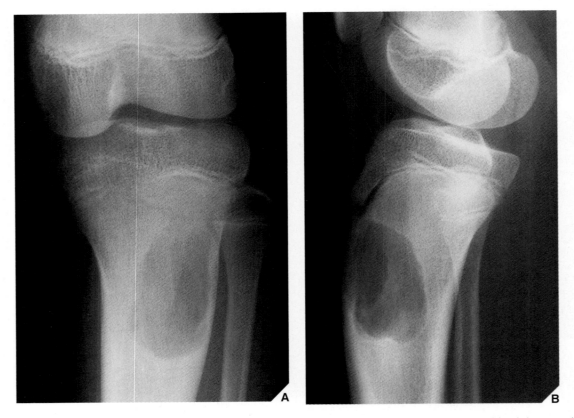

▲
FIGURE 18.49   Chondromyxoid fibroma. Anteroposterior (**A**) and lateral (**B**) radiographs of the left knee of a 12-year-old girl show a radiolucent, slightly lobulated lesion with a thin sclerotic margin in the proximal tibial diaphysis. Note the lack of visible calcifications.

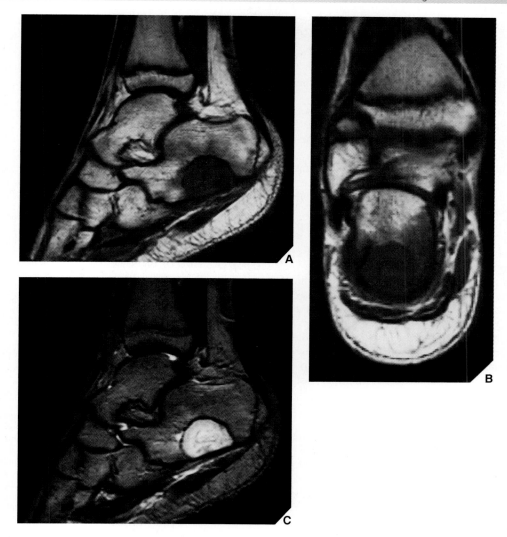

FIGURE 18.50 **MRI of chondromyxoid fibroma. (A)** Sagittal T1-weighted (SE; TR 600/TE 19 msec) MRI in a 10-year-old girl shows a well-demarcated lesion in the plantar aspect of the calcaneus, displaying low signal intensity. **(B)** An axial T1-weighted (SE; TR 600/TE 17 msec) image shows significant amount of peritumoral edema. **(C)** Sagittal T2-weighted (SE; TR 2000/TE 80 msec) MRI shows the lesion displaying high signal intensity. A sclerotic border is imaged as a rim of low signal intensity.

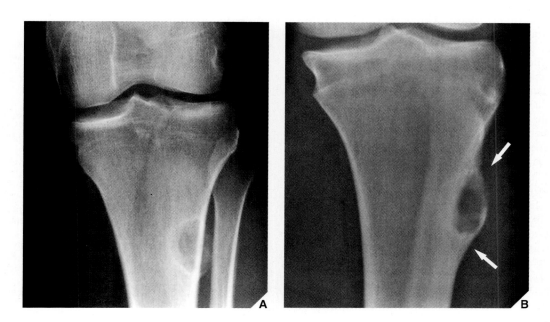

FIGURE 18.51 **Chondromyxoid fibroma resembling an aneurysmal bone cyst. (A)** Anteroposterior radiograph of the knee of an 18-year-old woman shows a lesion in the lateral aspect of the proximal tibia. The tumor balloons out from the cortex and is supported by a solid periosteal buttress resembling that seen in an aneurysmal bone cyst. The periosteal buttress *(arrows)* is better appreciated on a tomographic cut **(B)**.

PRACTICAL POINTS TO REMEMBER

[1] Enchondroma is characterized by the formation of mature hyaline cartilage and is seen:
- most commonly in the short tubular bones of the hand, where the lesion is usually radiolucent
- in the long bones, where scattered calcifications may be seen, resembling a medullary bone infarct.

[2] The characteristic radiographic features of enchondroma include:
- popcorn-like, annular, or punctate calcifications
- a lobulated growth pattern with frequent shallow scalloping of the endosteal cortex.

[3] Important clinical and radiographic features of the malignant transformation of an enchondroma include:
- the development of pain, in the absence of a fracture, in a previously asymptomatic lesion
- thickening or destruction of the cortex
- development of a soft-tissue mass.

[4] Enchondromatosis is a condition marked by multiple enchondromas, commonly in metaphysis and diaphysis. If skeleton is extensively affected and the lesions are distributed unilaterally, the term Ollier disease is applied.

[5] Ollier disease and Maffucci syndrome (an association of Ollier disease with soft-tissue hemangiomatosis) both carry an increased risk for malignant transformation to chondrosarcoma.

[6] In the radiographic evaluation of osteochondroma, the most common benign bone lesion, note that:
- it can be seen as predunculated or sessile (broad-based) variants
- its two important radiographic features are uninterrupted merging of the lesion's cortex with the host bone cortex and continuity of the cancellous portion of the lesion with the medullary cavity of the host bone.

[7] The most important differential diagnoses in suspected osteochondroma include:
- juxtacortical osteoma
- juxtacortical osteosarcoma
- soft-tissue osteosarcoma
- juxtacortical myositis ossificans.

[8] Osteochondroma may be complicated by:
- pressure on adjacent nerves or blood vessels
- pressure on the adjacent bone, frequently leading to fracture
- bursitis exostotica
- malignant transformation to chondrosarcoma.

[9] In the malignant transformation of osteochondroma, imaging signs include:
- enlargement of the lesion
- marked thickening of the cartilaginous cap of the lesion
- dispersion of calcifications into the cartilaginous cap
- development of a soft-tissue mass
- increased isotope uptake by the lesion after skeletal maturity.

[10] Variants of osteochondroma include subungual exostosis, turret exostosis, traction exostosis, bizarre parosteal osteochondromatous proliferation, florid reactive periostitis, and dysplasia epiphysealis hemimelica (Trevor-Fairbank disease).

[11] Multiple osteocartilaginous exostoses, a familial hereditary condition, carries the increased risk of malignant transformation of an osteochondroma to a chondrosarcoma, particularly in the shoulder girdle and pelvis.

[12] Chondroblastoma is characterized radiographically by:
- its eccentric epiphyseal location
- sclerotic margin
- scattered calcifications
- periosteal reaction (>50% cases).

[13] Chondromyxoid fibroma is characterized radiographically by:
- its location close to the growth plate
- its scalloped, sclerotic border
- a buttress of periosteal new bone
- lack of visible calcifications.

It may mimic an aneurysmal bone cyst.

SUGGESTED READINGS

Aoki JA, Sone S, Fujioka F, et al. MR of enchondroma and chondrosarcoma: rings and arcs of Gd-DTPA enhancement. *J Comput Assist Tomogr* 1991;15:1011–1016.

Azouz EM, Greenspan A, Marton D. CT evaluation of primary epiphyseal bone abscesses. *Skeletal Radiol* 1993;22:17–23.

Bandiera S, Bacchini P, Bertoni F. Bizarre parosteal osteochondromatous proliferation of bone. *Skeletal Radiol* 1998;27:154–156.

Bansal M, Goldman AB, DiCarlo EF, McCormack R. Soft tissue chondromas: diagnosis and differential diagnosis. *Skeletal Radiol* 1993;22:309–315.

Beggs IG, Stoker DJ. Chondromyxoid fibroma of bone. *Clin Radiol* 1982;33:671–679.

Berquist TH. Magnetic resonance imaging of primary skeletal neoplasms. *Radiol Clin North Am* 1993;31:411–424.

Björnsson J, Unni KK, Dahlin DC, Beabout JW, Sim FH. Clear-cell chondrosarcoma of bone: observation in 47 cases. *Am J Surg Pathol* 1984;8:223–230.

Bloem JL, Mulder JD. Chondroblastoma: a clinical and radiological study of 104 cases. *Skeletal Radiol* 1985;14:1–9.

Borges AM, Huvos AG, Smith J. Bursa formation and synovial chondrometaplasia associated with osteochondromas. *Am J Clin Pathol* 1981;75:648–653.

Boriani S, Bacchini P, Bertoni F, Campanacci M. Periosteal chondroma. A review of twenty cases. *J Bone Joint Surg [Am]* 1983;65A:205–212.

Braunstein E, Martel W, Weatherbee L. Periosteal bone apposition in chondroblastoma. *Skeletal Radiol* 1979;4:34–36.

Brien EW, Mirra JM, Luck JV Jr. Benign and malignant cartilage tumors of bone and joint: their anatomic and theoretical basis with an emphasis on radiology, pathology, and clinical biology. II. Juxtacortical cartilage tumors. *Skeletal Radiol* 1999;28:1–20.

Brower AC, Moser RP, Gilkey FW, Kransdorf MJ. Chondroblastoma. In: Moser RP, ed. *Cartilaginous tumors of the skeleton. AFIP atlas of radiologic-pathologic correlation*, Fascicle II. Philadelphia: Hanley & Belfus; 1990:74–113.

Brower AC, Moser RP, Kransdorf MJ. The frequency and diagnostic significance of periostitis in chondroblastoma. *Am J Roentgenol* 1990;154:309–314.

Bruder E, Zanetti M, Boos N, von Hochstetter AR. Chondromyxoid fibroma of two thoracic vertebrae. *Skeletal Radiol* 1999;28:286–289.

Bui KL, Ilaslan H, Bauer TW, Lietman SA, Joyce MJ, Sundaram M. Cortical scalloping and cortical penetration by small eccentric chondroid lesions in the long tubular bones: not a sign of malignancy? *Skeletal Radiol* 2009;38:791–796.

Bullough PG. *Atlas of orthopedic pathology*, 2nd ed. New York: Gower; 1992:14.9.

Cannon CP, Nelson SD, Seeger L, Eckardt JJ. Clear cell chondrosarcoma mimicking chondroblastoma in a skeletally immature patient. *Skeletal Radiol* 2002;31:369–372.

Chung EB, Enzinger FM. Chondromas of soft parts. *Cancer* 1978;41:1414–1424.

Codman EA. Epiphyseal chondromatous giant cell tumors of the upper end of the humerus. *Surg Gynecol Obstet* 1931;52:543–548.

Cohen EK, Kressel HY, Frank TS, et al. Hyaline cartilage-origin bone and soft-tissue neoplasms: MR appearance and histologic correlation. *Radiology* 1988;167:477–481.

Collins PS, Han W, Williams LR, Rich N, Lee JF, Villavicencio JL. Maffucci's syndrome (hemangiomatosis osteolytica): a report of four cases. *J Vasc Surg* 1992;16:364–371.

Dahlin DC. Chondromyxoid fibroma of bone, with emphasis on its morphological relationship to benign chondroblastoma. *Cancer* 1956;9:195–203.

Dahlin DC, Ivins JC. Benign chondroblastoma: a study of 125 cases. *Cancer* 1972;30:401–413.

Dahlin DC, Unni KK. *Bone tumors: general aspects and data on 8,542 cases*, 4th ed. Springfield, IL: Charles C. Thomas; 1986:18, 33–51, 227–259.

Davids JR, Glancy GL, Eilert RE. Fracture through the stalk of pedunculated osteochondromas. A report of three cases. *Clin Orthop* 1991;271:258–264.

De Beuckeleer LHL, De Schepper AMA, Ramon F. Magnetic resonance imaging of cartilaginous tumors: retrospective study of 79 patients. *Eur J Radiol* 1995;21:34–40.

De Beuckeleer LHL, De Schepper AMA, Ramon F. Magnetic resonance imaging of cartilaginous tumors: is it useful or necessary? *Skeletal Radiol* 1996;25:137–141.

deSantos LA, Spjut HJ. Periosteal chondroma: a radiographic spectrum. *Skeletal Radiol* 1981;6:15–20.

Dhondt E, Oudenhoven L, Khan S, et al. Nora's lesion, a distinct radiological entity? *Skeletal Radiol* 2006;35:497–502.

El-Khoury GY, Bassett GS. Symptomatic bursa formation with osteochondromas. *Am J Roentgenol* 1979;133:895–898.

Enzinger FM, Weiss SW. Cartilaginous tumors and tumor-like lesions of soft tissue. In: *Soft tissue tumors*, 2nd ed. St. Louis: Mosby; 1988:861.

Epstein DA, Levin EJ. Bone scintigraphy in hereditary multiple exostoses. *Am J Roentgenol* 1978;130:331–333.

Erickson JK, Rosenthal DI, Zaleske DJ, Gebhardt MC, Cates JM. Primary treatment of chondroblastoma with percutaneous radiofrequency heat ablation: report of three cases. *Radiology* 2001;221:463–468.

Fairbank TJ. Dysplasia epiphysealis hemimelica (tarso-epiphyseal aclasis). *J Bone Joint Surg [Br]* 1956;38B:237–257.

Fechner RE, Mills SE. *Tumors of the bones and joint.* Washington, DC: Armed Forces Institute of Pathology; 1993.

Feldman F, Hecht HL, Johnston AD. Chondromyxoid fibroma of bone. *Radiology* 1970;94:249–260.

Flach HZ, Ginai AZ, Oosterhuis JW. Best cases from the AFIP. Maffucci syndrome: radiologic and pathologic findings. *Radiographics* 2001;21:1311–1316.

Flemming DJ, Murphey MD. Enchondroma and chondrosarcoma. *Semin Musculoskelet Radiol* 2000;4:59–71.

Garrison RC, Unni KK, McLeod RA, Pritchard DJ, Dahlin DC. Chondrosarcoma arising in osteochondroma. *Cancer* 1982;49:1890–1897.

Geirnaerdt MJA, Bloem JL, Eulderink F, Hogendoorn PCW, Taminiau AH. Cartilaginous tumors: correlation of gadolinium-enhanced MR imaging and histopathologic findings. *Radiology* 1993;186:813–817.

Geirnaerdt MJA, Hogendoorn PCW, Bloem JJ, Taminiau AHM, van der Woude H-J. Cartilaginous tumors: fast contrast-enhanced MR imaging. *Radiology* 2000; 214:539–546.

Giudici MA, Moser RP Jr, Kransdorf MJ. Cartilaginous bone tumors. *Radiol Clin North Am* 1993;31:237–259.

Gohel VK, Dalinka MK, Edeiken J. Ischemic necrosis of the femoral head simulating chondroblastoma. *Radiology* 1973;107:545–546.

González-Lois C, Garcia-de-la-Torre JP, SantosBriz-Terrón A, Vila J, Manrique-Chico J, Martinez-Tello FJ. Intracapsular and para-articular chondroma adjacent to large joints: report of three cases and review of the literature. *Skeletal Radiol* 2001;30:672–676.

Goodman SB, Bell RS, Fornasier VS, De Demeter D, Bateman JE. Ollier's disease with multiple sarcomatous transformation. *Hum Pathol* 1984;15:91–93.

Green P, Wittaker RP. Benign chondroblastoma. Case report with pulmonary metastasis. *J Bone Joint Surg [Am]* 1975;57A:418–420.

Greenfield GB, Arrington JA. *Imaging of bone tumors. A multimodality approach.* Philadelphia: JB Lippincott; 1995.

Greenspan A. Tumors of cartilage origin. *Orthop Clin North Am* 1989;20:347–366.

Greenspan A, Jundt G, Remagen W. *Differential diagnosis in orthopaedic oncology*, 2nd ed. Philadelphia: Lippincott Williams & Wilkins; 2007.

Greenspan A, Klein MJ. Radiology and pathology of bone tumors. In: Lewis MM, ed. *Musculoskeletal oncology. A multidisciplinary approach.* Philadelphia: WB Saunders; 1992:13–72.

Greenspan A, Unni KK, Matthews J II. Periosteal chondroma masquerading as osteochondroma. *Can Assoc Radiol J* 1993;44:205–210.

Griffiths HJ, Thompson RC Jr, Galloway HR, Everson LI, Suh J-S. Bursitis in association with solitary osteochondromas presenting as mass lesions. *Skeletal Radiol* 1991;20:513–516.

Hau MA, Fox EJ, Rosenberg AE, Mankin HJ. Chondromyxoid fibroma of the metacarpal. *Skeletal Radiol* 2001;30:719–721.

Hayes CW, Conway WF, Sundaram M. Misleading aggressive MR imaging: appearance of some benign musculoskeletal lesions. *Radiographics* 1992;12:1119–1134.

Helliwell TR, O'Connor MA, Ritchie DA, Feldberg L, Stilwell JH, Jane MJ. Bizarre parosteal osteochondromatous proliferation with cortical invasion. *Skeletal Radiol* 2001;30:282–285.

Helms C. Pseudocyst of the humerus. *Am J Roentgenol* 1979;131:287–292.

Hensinger RN, Cowell HR, Ramsey PL, Leopold RG. Familial dysplasia epiphysealis hemimelica associated with chondromas and osteochondromas. Report of a kindred with variable presentations. *J Bone Joint Surg [Am]* 1974;56A:1513–1516.

Hudson TM, Chew FS, Manaster BJ. Scintigraphy of benign exostoses and exostotic chondrosarcoma. *Am J Roentgenol* 1983;140:581–586.

Hudson TM, Spriengfield DS, Spanier SS, Enneking WF, Hamlin DJ. Benign exostoses and exostotic chondrosarcomas: evaluation of cartilage thickness by CT. *Radiology* 1984;152:595–599.

Huvos AG. Chondroblastoma and clear cell chondrosarcoma: In: Huvos AG, ed. *Bone tumors. Diagnosis, treatment and prognosis*, 2nd ed. Philadelphia: WB Saunders; 1991:295–318.

Huvos AG, Higinbotham NL, Marcove RC, O'Leary P. Aggressive chondroblastoma: review of the literature on aggressive behavior and metastases with a report of one new case. *Clin Orthop* 1977;126:266–272.

Ilaslan H, Sundaram M, Unni KK. Vertebral chondroblastoma. *Skeletal Radiol* 2003;32:66–71.

Jaffe HL. Juxtacortical chondroma. *Bull Hosp Joint Dis* 1956;17:20–29.

Jaffe HL, Lichtenstein L. Benign chondroblastoma of bone: reinterpretation of so-called calcifying or chondromatous giant cell tumor. *Am J Pathol* 1942;18:969–991.

Jaffe HL, Lichtenstein L. Chondromyxoid fibroma of bone: a distinctive benign tumor likely to be mistaken especially for chondrosarcoma. *Arch Pathol* 1948;45:541–551.

Janzen L, Logan PM, O'Connell JX, Connel DG, Munk PL. Intramedullary chondroid tumors of bone: correlation of abnormal peritumoral marrow and soft-tissue MRI signal with tumor type. *Skeletal Radiol* 1997;26:100–106.

Kahn S, Taljanovic MS, Speer DP, Graham AR, Dennis PD. Kissing periosteal chondroma and osteochondroma. *Skeletal Radiol* 2002;31:235–239.

Kaim AH, Hügli R, Bonél HM, Jundt G. Chondroblastoma and clear cell chondrosarcoma: radiological and MRI characteristics with histopathological correlation. *Skeletal Radiol* 2002;31:88–95.

Keating RB, Wright PW, Staple TW. Enchondroma protuberans of the rib. *Skeletal Radiol* 1985;13:55–58.

Kettelkamp DB, Campbell CJ, Bonfiglio M. Dysplasia epiphysealis hemimelica. A report of fifteen cases and a review of the literature. *J Bone Joint Surg [Am]* 1966;48A:746–766.

Kricun ME. *Imaging of bone tumors.* Philadelphia: WB Saunders; 1993.

Kricun ME, Kricun R, Haskin ME. Chondroblastoma of the calcaneus: radiographic features with emphasis on location. *Am J Roentgenol* 1977;128:613–616.

Kroon HM, Bloem JL, Holscher HC, van der Woude HJ, Reijnierse M, Taminiau AHM. MR imaging of edema accompanying benign and malignant bone tumors. *Skeletal Radiol* 1994;23:261–269.

Kurt AM, Unni KK, Sim FH, McLeod RA. Chondroblastoma of bone. *Hum Pathol* 1989;20:965–976.

Lang IM, Azouz EM. MRI appearances of dysplasia epiphysealis hemimelica of the knee. *Skeletal Radiol* 1997;26:226–229.

Leffler SG, Chew FS. CT-guided percutaneous biopsy of sclerotic bone lesions: diagnostic yield and accuracy. *Am J Roentgenol* 1999;172:1389–1392.

Lichtenstein L, Hall JE. Periosteal chondroma: a distinctive benign cartilage tumor. *J Bone Joint Surg [Am]* 1952;34A:691–697.

Liu J, Hudkins PG, Swee RG, Unni KK. Bone sarcomas associated with Ollier's disease. *Cancer* 1987;59:1376–1385.

Ly JQ, Beall DP. A rare case of infantile Ollier's disease demonstrating bilaterally symmetric extremity involvement. *Skeletal Radiol* 2003;32:227–230.

Ly JQ, LaGatta LM, Beall DP. Calcaneal chondroblastoma with secondary aneurysmal bone cyst. *Am J Roentgenol* 2004;182:130.

Maffucci A. Di un caso di encondroma el antioma multiplo. Contribuzone alla genesi embrionale dei tumori. *Movimento Med Chir Napoli* 1881;3:399–412.

Mellon CD, Carter JE, Owen DB. Ollier's disease and Maffucci's syndrome: distinct entities or a continuum? *J Neurol* 1988;235:376–378.

Meneses MF, Unni KK, Swee RG. Bizarre parosteal osteochondromatous proliferation of bone (Nora's lesion). *Am J Surg Pathol* 1993;17:691–697.

Mirra JM, Gold R, Downs J, Eckardt JJ. A new histologic approach to the differentiation of enchondroma and chondrosarcoma of the bones: a clinicopathologic analysis of 51 cases. *Clin Orthop* 1987;2:89–107.

Mirra JM, Picci P, Gold RH. *Bone tumors: Clinical, radiologic and pathologic correlations.* Philadelphia: Lea & Febiger; 1989.

Mirra JM, Ulich TR, Eckardt JJ, Bhuta S. "Aggressive" chondroblastoma. Light and ultramicroscopic findings after *en bloc* resection. *Clin Orthop* 1983;178:276–284.

Monda L, Wick MR. S-100 protein immunostaining in the differential diagnosis of chondroblastoma. *Hum Pathol* 1985;16:287–293.

Moser RP, Brockmole DM, Vinh TN, Kransdorf MJ, Aoki J. Chondroblastoma of the patella. *Skeletal Radiol* 1988;17:413–419.

Moser RP, Gilkey FW, Madewell JE. Enchondroma. In: Moser RP, ed. *Cartilaginous tumors of the skeleton. AFIP atlas of radiologic-pathologic correlation*, Fascicle II. Philadelphia: Hanley & Belfus; 1990:8–34.

Mulder JD, Schütte HE, Kroon HM, Taconis WK. *Radiologic atlas of bone tumors.* Amsterdam, the Netherlands: Elsevier; 1993.

Murphey MD, Choi JJ, Kransdorf MJ, Flemming DJ, Gannon FH. Imaging of osteochondroma: variants and complications with radiologic-pathologic correlation. *Radiographics* 2000;20:1407–1434.

Murphey MD, Flemming DJ, Boyea SR, Bojescul JA, Sweet DE, Temple HT. From the archives of the AFIP. Enchondroma versus chondrosarcoma in the appendicular skeleton: differentiation features. *Radiographics* 1998;18:1213–1237.

Nora FE, Dahlin DC, Beabout JW. Bizarre parosteal osteochondromatous proliferation of the hands and feet. *Am J Surg Pathol* 1983;7:245–250.

Norman A, Sissons HA. Radiographic hallmarks of peripheral chondrosarcoma. *Radiology* 1984;151:589–596.

O'Connor PJ, Gibbon WW, Hardy G, Butt WP. Chondromyxoid fibroma of the foot. *Skeletal Radiol* 1996;25:143–148.

Ollier L. De la dyschondroplasie. *Bull Soc Lyon Med* 1899;93:23–24.

Ozkoc G, Gonlusen G, Ozalay M, Kayaselcuk F, Pourbagher A, Tandogan RN. Giant chondroblastoma of the scapula with pulmonary metastases. *Skeletal Radiol* 2006;35:42–48.

Pösl M, Werner M, Amling M, Ritzel H, Delling G. Malignant transformation of chondroblastoma. *Histopathology* 1996;29:477–480.

Ragsdale BD, Sweet DE, Vinh TN. Radiology as gross pathology in evaluating chondroid tumors. *Hum Pathol* 1989;20:930–951.

Rahimi A, Beabout JW, Ivins JC, Dahlin DC. Chondromyxoid fibroma: clinicopathologic study of 75 cases. *Cancer* 1972;30:726–736.

Resnik CS, Levine AM, Aisner SC, Young JW, Dorfman HD. Case report 522. Concurrent adjacent osteochondroma and enchondroma. *Skeletal Radiol* 1989;18:66–69.

Resnick D, Cone RO III. The nature of humeral pseudocyst. *Radiology* 1984;150: 27–28.

Schajowicz F. Cartilage-forming tumors. In: Schajowicz F, ed., *Tumors and tumorlike conditions of bone*. New York: Springer-Verlag; 1994:141–256.

Schajowicz F, Gallardo H. Chondromyxoid fibroma (fibromyxoid chondroma) of bone. *J Bone Joint Surg [Br]* 1971;53B:198–216.

Schajowicz F, McGuire M. Diagnostic difficulties in skeletal pathology. *Clin Orthop* 1989;240:281–308.

Schajowicz F, Sissons HA, Sobin LH. The World Health Organization's histologic classification of bone tumors. A commentary on the second edition. *Cancer* 1995;75:1208–1214.

Spjut HJ, Dorfman HD, Fechner RE, Ackerman LV. Tumors of bone and cartilage. In: *Atlas of Tumor pathology*, Second Series, Fascicle 5. Washington, DC: Armed Forces Institute of Pathology; 1971.

Sun TC, Swee RG, Shives TC, Unni KK. Chondrosarcoma in Maffucci's syndrome. *J Bone Joint Surg [Am]* 1985;67A:1214–1219.

Unger EC, Kessler HB, Kowalyshyn MJ, Lackman RD, Morea GT. MR imaging of Maffucci syndrome. *Am J Roentgenol* 1988;150:351–353.

Unni KK. Chondroma. In: Unni KK, ed. *Dahlin's bone tumors. General aspect and data on 11,087 cases*, 5th ed. Philadelphia: Lippincott–Raven Publishers; 1996:25–45.

Uri DS, Dalinka MK, Kneeland JB. Muscle impingement: MR imaging of a painful complication of osteochondromas. *Skeletal Radiol* 1996;25:689–692.

Varma DGK, Kumar R, Carrasco CH, Guo S-Q, Richli WR. MR imaging of periosteal chondroma. *J Comput Assist Tomogr* 1991;15:1008–1010.

Weatherall PT, Maale GE, Mendelsohn DB, Sherry CS, Erdman WE, Pascoe HR. Chondroblastoma: classic and confusing appearance at MR imaging. *Radiology* 1994;190:467–474.

White PG, Saunders L, Orr W, Friedman L. Chondromyxoid fibroma. *Skeletal Radiol* 1996;25:79–81.

Wilson AJ, Kyriakos M, Ackerman LV. Chondromyxoid fibroma: radiographic appearance in 38 cases and in a review of the literature. *Radiology* 1991;179:513–518. [Erratum, *Radiology* 1991;180:586.]

Yamaguchi T, Dorfman HD. Radiologic and histologic patterns of calcification in chondromyxoid fibroma. *Skeletal Radiol* 1998;27:559–564.

Yamamura S, Sato K, Sugiura H, Iwata H. Inflammatory reaction in chondroblastoma. *Skeletal Radiol* 1996;25:371–376.

Benign Tumors and Tumor-like Lesions III
Fibrous, Fibroosseus, and Fibrohistiocytic Lesions

Fibrous Cortical Defect and Nonossifying Fibroma

Fibrous cortical defects and nonossifying (nonosteogenic) fibromas are the most common fibrous lesions of bone and are predominantly seen in children and adolescents. More common in boys than in girls, they have a predilection for the long bones, particularly the femur and tibia (Fig. 19.1). Some authors prefer the term fibroxanthoma for both lesions, whereas Schajowicz prefers the term histiocytic xanthogranuloma. These lesions are not true neoplasms and are considered by many investigators developmental defects.

Fibrous cortical defect (metaphyseal fibrous defect) is a small asymptomatic lesion found in 30% of normal individuals in the first and second decades of life. The radiolucent lesion is elliptical and confined to the cortex of a long bone near the growth plate; it is demarcated by a thin margin of sclerosis (Figs. 19.2 and 19.3). Most of these lesions disappear spontaneously, but a few may continue to enlarge. When they encroach on the medullary region of a bone, they are designated nonossifying fibroma (Fig. 19.4).With continued growth, these lesions, which are typically located eccentrically in the bone, display a characteristic scalloped sclerotic border (Fig. 19.5).

Occasionally, nonossifying fibroma may involve several bones, in which case the condition is called disseminated nonossifying fibromatosis. Some of the patients with this presentation may exhibit on the skin café-au-lait spots with smooth ("coast of California") borders, similar to those seen in neurofibromatosis. Furthermore, they may develop neurofibromas affecting varius nerves (see Chapter 33). This association is known as Jaffe-Campanacci syndrome (Fig. 19.6).

Skeletal scintigraphy shows a minimal to mild increase in activity. During the healing phase, mild hyperemia may be seen on the blood pool image, and the positive delayed scan reflects the osteoblastic activity. Computed tomography (CT) may demonstrate to better advantage the cortical thinning and medullary involvement (Fig. 19.7) and may delineate early pathological fracture more precisely. Hounsfield attenuation values for nonossifying fibroma are higher than for normal bone marrow.

Magnetic resonance imaging (MRI), usually performed for another reason, shows intermediate to low signal intensity on T1-weighted and intermediate to high signal on T2-weighted sequences (Fig. 19.8). After gadolinium-diethylenetriamine-pentaacetic acid (DTPA) injection, both fibrous cortical defects and nonossifying fibromas invariably exhibit a hyperintense border and signal enhancement (Fig. 19.9). Mineralization of the lesion during healing appears predominantly as low signal intensity on MR images.

Histologically identical, regardless of size, fibrous cortical defect and nonossifying fibroma are composed of spindle and histiocytic cells that have a clear, foamy cytoplasm. In addition, osteoclast-like multinucleated giant cells are present, and varying numbers of inflammatory cells (lymphocytes) and plasma cells are scattered in the background. The cells are often arranged in a storiform pattern, typifying fibrohistiocytic lesions. Some lesions contain an excessive amount of fat within the foam cells, and the term *xanthoma* or *fibroxanthoma* may be applied to such lesions.

Complications and Treatment

Most lesions undergo spontaneous involution (healing) by sclerosis or remodeling (Fig. 19.10). Some larger lesions may be complicated by pathological fracture (Fig. 19.11). Therefore, if a lesion is large, extending across 50% or more of the medullary cavity, then curettage and bone grafting is the treatment of choice.

Benign Fibrous Histiocytoma

The term benign fibrous histiocytoma, although it may be controversial, is useful to subclassify lesions with histologic features similar to those of nonossifying fibroma but having an atypical clinical presentation and an atypical radiographic pattern. This lesion frequently has radiographic features very similar to those of nonossifying fibroma; it is radiolucent, with sharply defined and frequently sclerotic borders, without any mineralization of the matrix (Figs. 19.12 and 19.13). Its differentiation

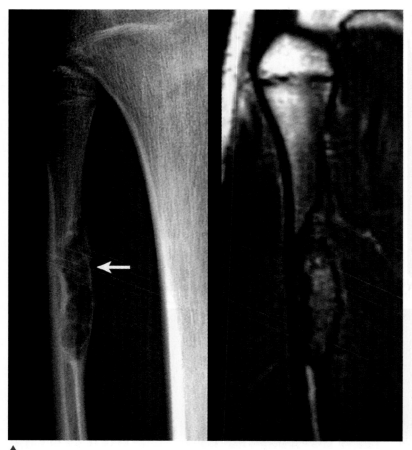

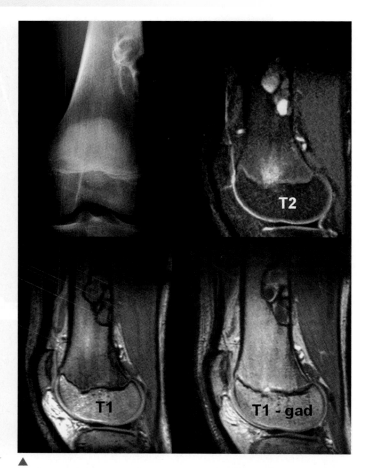

FIGURE 19.8   MRI of nonossifying fibroma. Anteroposterior radiograph of the right fibula of a 14-year-old girl shows an eccentric well-defined radiolucent lesion with sclerotic border. Note thinning of the medial cortex and a pathological fracture (*arrow*). Coronal T1-weighted MRI shows the lesion exhibiting intermediate signal intensity. (Reprinted from Greenspan A et al., 2007.)

FIGURE 19.9   MRI of nonossifying fibroma. Anteroposterior radiograph shows a radiolucent lesion with sclerotic border abutting the posteromedial cortex of the right femur. Sagittal T1-weighted MR image shows predominantly intermediate signal intensity of the lesion. The sclerotic border exhibits low signal intensity. Sagittal T2-weighted image shows that the lesion exhibits heterogeneous but mostly high signal intensity. Sagittal T1-weighted fat-suppressed MRI after intravenous injection of gadolinium shows slight heterogenous enhancement of NOF. (Reprinted from Greenspan A et al., 2007.)

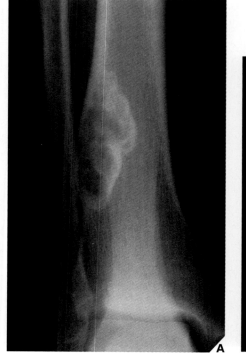

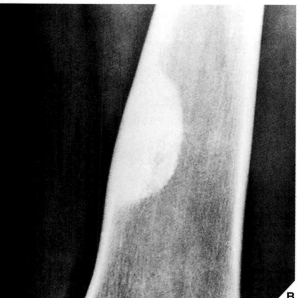

FIGURE 19.10   Healing of nonossifying fibroma. (A) Spontaneous involution of nonossifying fibroma in the distal tibia is characterized by progressive sclerosis of peripheral parts of the lesion. **(B)** A nonossifying fibroma that healed completely may persist as a sclerotic patch. Nonossifying fibromas in this sclerosing phase should not be mistaken for osteoblastic tumors or for sclerosing dysplasia.

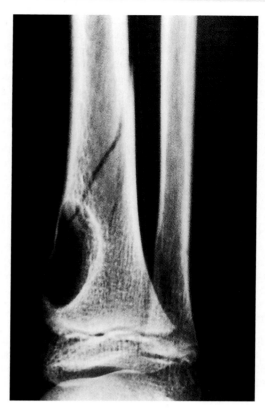

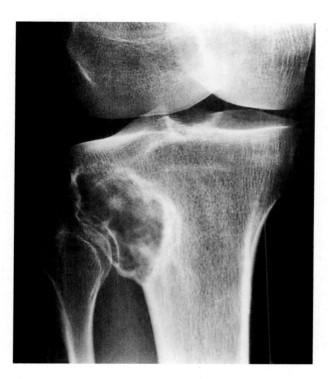

▲
FIGURE 19.11 Complication of nonossifying fibroma. Pathological fracture is a common complication of a large nonossifying fibroma, as seen here in the distal tibia of a 10-year-old boy. Lesions extending halfway or farther into the medullary region of a bone should be treated by curettage and bone grafting.

▲
FIGURE 19.12 Benign fibrous histiocytoma. A 37-year-old man presented with occasional pain in the right knee. Oblique radiograph of the knee demonstrates a lobulated radiolucent lesion with a well-defined sclerotic border, located eccentrically in the proximal tibia. Biopsy revealed benign fibrous histiocytoma.

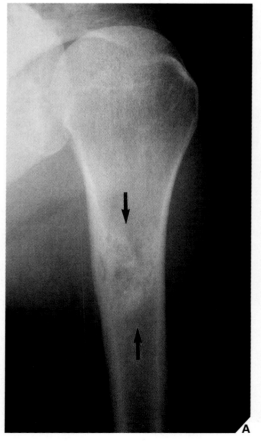

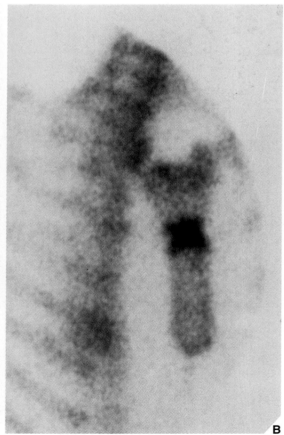

A

B

▲
FIGURE 19.13 Benign fibrous histiocytoma. (A) Anteroposterior radiograph of the left proximal humerus in a 26-year-old woman with chronic arm pain shows eccentric, well-defined, partially sclerotic lesion (*arrows*). **(B)** A radionuclide bone scan demonstrates a focal homogenous increased uptake of radiotracer. Excisional biopsy was consistent with healing benign fibrous histiocytoma.

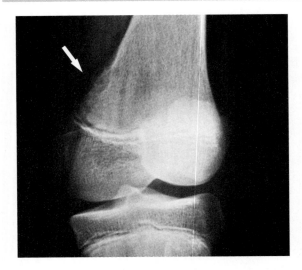

FIGURE 19.14 Periosteal desmoid. Oblique view of the left knee of a 12-year-old boy shows the classic appearance of periosteal desmoid. Note the saucer-like radiolucency eroding the medial border of the distal femoral metaphysis at the linea aspera and producing cortical irregularity (*arrow*). This lesion should not be mistaken for a malignant bone tumor.

from nonossifying fibroma is made on purely clinical grounds, because the histologic features of both lesions are almost identical. Patients presenting with benign fibrous histiocytoma are older (usually older than 25 years) than those with nonossifying fibroma; unlike the latter lesion, benign fibrous histiocytomas may produce symptoms such as pain or discomfort in the involved bone. These lesions also seem to run a more aggressive clinical course and may recur after treatment, which consists of curettage and bone grafting.

Periosteal Desmoid

The periosteal desmoid is a tumor-like fibrous proliferation of the periosteum. It occurs in patients between the ages of 12 and 20 years and has a striking predilection for the posteromedial cortex

of the medial femoral condyle. Many patients have a history of injury, although trauma is not necessarily a predisposing factor. The lesion simulates a fibrous cortical defect, except in the specificity of its location. Occasionally, it may simulate an aggressive and even malignant tumor. Radiographically, the hallmarks of a periosteal desmoid are its radiolucent saucer-shaped appearance, with sclerosis at the base eroding the cortex or producing cortical irregularity (Fig. 19.14). The radionuclide bone scan is usually normal, but sometimes may show a focal increase in activity. CT shows a well-defined lesion, commonly with a sclerotic border (Fig. 19.15). On MRI, the lesion appears hypointense on T1-weighted and hyperintense on T2-weighted images, with a dark rim on both sequences at or near the sites of the bony attachment of the medial head of the gastrocnemius muscle. Periosteal desmoid belongs to the "don't touch" lesions (see Table 16.10), so it should not undergo biopsy. Most lesions disappear spontaneously by the time the patient reaches age 20.

The histologic appearance of the lesion demonstrates fibroblastic spindle cells that produce large amounts of collagen. Large areas of hyalinization and fibrocartilage and small fragments of bone may be scattered within the fibrous tissue.

Differential Diagnosis

Some authorities believe that periosteal desmoid should be differentiated from distal femoral cortical irregularity. This latter abnormality, which presents as cortical roughening just distal to the extension of the linea aspera, is a common finding in boys in the 10- to 15-year age group. Its cause is not settled. Although it was thought to represent an avulsion injury caused by traction of the adductor magnus aponeurosis, Brower and colleagues have shown that this lesion may exist in the area without any muscular or ligamentous attachment. Others consider periosteal desmoid and distal femoral cortical irregularity to be the same entity. Dahlin suggests that the periosteal desmoid is a hypocellular variant of nonossifying fibroma, and Schajowicz classifies it as a periosteal variant of desmoplastic fibroma. Other authors apply a broader definition to periosteal desmoid, considering it essentially a hypocellular variant of fibrous cortical defect. In any event, it is a self-limited benign lesion that requires no treatment, and its characteristic imaging appearance and location should serve as clues to the correct diagnosis.

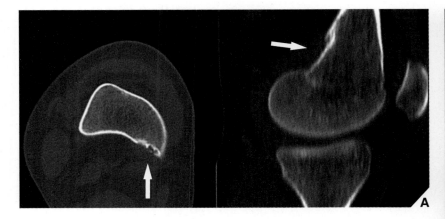
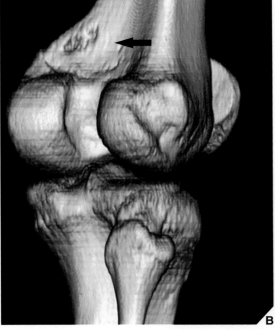

FIGURE 19.15 CT of periosteal desmoid. (A) Axial and sagittal reformatted CT images of the knee of a 17-year-old boy and (B) 3D reconstructed CT image show well-marginated cortical defect in the posteromedial aspect of the distal femur (*arrows*).

Fibrous Dysplasia

Fibrous dysplasia, occasionally termed fibrous osteodystrophy, osteodystrophia fibrosa, or osteitis fibrosa disseminata, is a fibroosseous lesion that some authorities classify among the group of developmental dysplasias. At present time, however, it is considered to be a genetically based sporadic disorder due to mutation in the *GNAS1* gene, the defect that prevents osteoblasts to form a normal lamellar bone. There are two common *GNAS1* mutations associated with fibrous dysplasia, both occuring at codon 201, with argenine being substituted for either cysteine or histidine, R201C and R201H respectively. Most recently reported the third *GNAS1* gene mutation (Q227L) represent only about 5% of the *GNAS1* mutation in this condition. It may affect one bone (monostotic form) or several bones (polyostotic form). Fibrous dysplasia is characterized by the replacement of normal lamellar cancellous bone by an abnormal fibrous tissue that contains small, abnormally arranged trabeculae of immature woven bone formed by metaplasia of the fibrous stroma.

Monostotic Fibrous Dysplasia

Monostotic fibrous dysplasia most commonly affects the femur—particularly the femoral neck—as well as the tibia and ribs (Fig. 19.16). The lesion arises centrally in the bone, usually sparing the epiphysis in children, and it is very rarely seen in the articular end of the bone in adults (Fig. 19.17). As the lesion enlarges, it expands the medullary cavity. The radiographic appearance of monostotic fibrous dysplasia varies, depending on the proportion of osseous-to-fibrous content. Lesions with greater osseous content are more dense and sclerotic, whereas those with greater fibrous content are more radiolucent, with a characteristic ground-glass appearance (Figs. 19.18 and 19.19, see also Fig. 19.16B). One of the lesions that mimics monostotic fibrous dysplasia, particularly when located in the intertrochanteric region of the femur, is the so-called liposclerosing myxofibrous tumor (Fig. 19.20), a benign fibroosseous lesion characterized by a complex mixture of histologic elements that include lipoma, fibroxanthoma, myxoma, myxofibroma, fat necrosis, bone, and cartilage.

Scintigraphy is helpful in determining the activity of fibrous dysplasia (Fig. 19.21) and the potential multicentricity of the lesion. Machida and associates reported that although a high incidence to show similarly increased uptake.

The CT findings parallel those of conventional radiography. CT sections show areas of high attenuation in more sclerotic lesions and a low-attenuation matrix with an amorphous ground-glass texture in lesions with greater fibrous content (Figs. 19.22 and 19.23). The lesion of fibrous dysplasia shows a variety of appearances on MRI caused by the histologic composition of these lesions. Some lesions show a decreased signal on T1 and T2 sequences, and some show intermediate or low signal on T1-weighted but either mixed or high signal on T2-weighted images. The sclerotic rim (rind sign) is invariably imaged as a band of low signal intensity on T1 and T2 sequences.

Pathological fracture of the structurally weakened bone is the most frequent complication of monostotic fibrous dysplasia.

Histologically, fibrous dysplasia presents as an aggregate of moderately dense fibrous connective tissue containing bony trabeculae in haphazard distribution instead of the stress-oriented distribution expected in normal cancellous bone. The trabeculae are curved and branching, with sparse interconnections. Low-power photomicrographs have been likened to "alphabet soup" or Chinese ideographs. They are composed of woven, immature bone and exhibit no evidence of osteoblastic activity ("naked trabeculae"). Occasionally, an area of cartilage formation may be present within the lesion.

Polyostotic Fibrous Dysplasia

Although radiographically similar to the monostotic form, polyostotic fibrous dysplasia is a more aggressive disorder. It also has a different distribution in the skeleton and a striking predilection for one side of the body (Fig. 19.24), a tendency that has been noted in more than 90% of cases. The pelvis is frequently affected, followed by the long bones, skull, and ribs; the proximal end of the femur is a common site of involvement (Fig. 19.25). The lesions generally

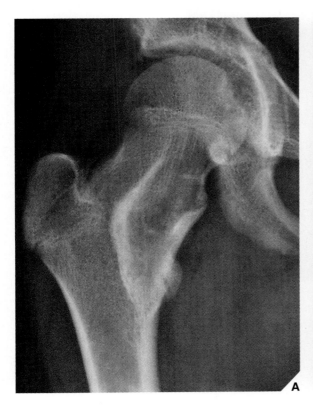
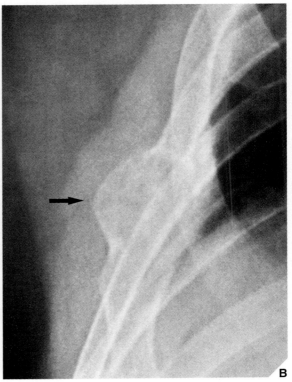

▲ FIGURE 19.16 Monostotic fibrous dysplasia. **(A)** Typically, the focus of fibrous dysplasia is located in the femoral neck, as seen here in a 13-year-old girl. Note a characteristic sclerotic "rind" encapsulating the lesion. **(B)** The rib is a frequent site of fibrous dysplasia. Note the expansive lesion exhibiting a ground-glass appearance (*arrow*).

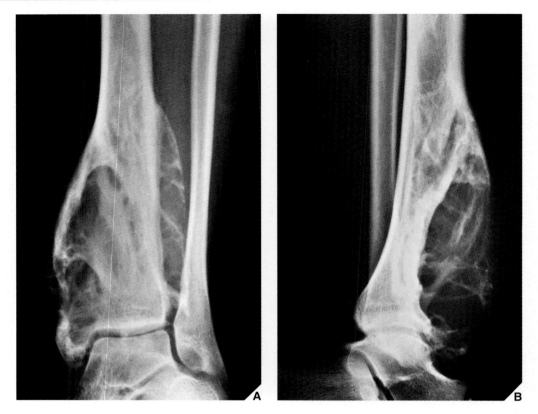

▲
FIGURE 19.17 **Monostotic fibrous dysplasia.** Oblique **(A)** and lateral **(B)** radiographs of the left leg of a 32-year-old woman demonstrate a large, trabeculated radiolucent lesion in the distal tibia. Because of its aggressive features, it was thought to be a desmoplastic fibroma; however, biopsy proved it to be a fibrous dysplasia, a rare lesion at this site in adults.

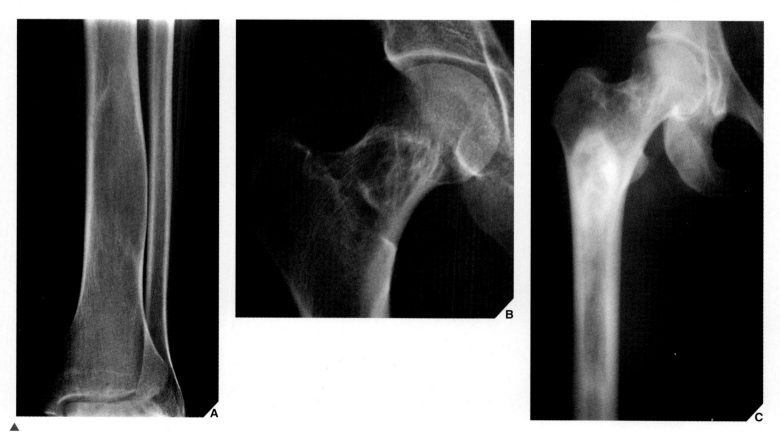

▲
FIGURE 19.18 **Monostotic fibrous dysplasia.** **(A)** Anteroposterior radiograph of the distal leg of a 17-year-old girl shows a monostotic focus of fibrous dysplasia in the diaphysis of the tibia. Observe the slight expansion and thinning of the cortex and the partial loss of trabecular pattern in the cancellous bone, which gives the lesion a ground-glass or smoky appearance. **(B)** The focus of fibrous dysplasia in the femoral neck in this 25-year-old man exhibits a more sclerotic appearance than that seen in **A.** **(C)** Markedly sclerotic lesion of fibrous dysplasia in the proximal right femur of a 30-year-old woman.

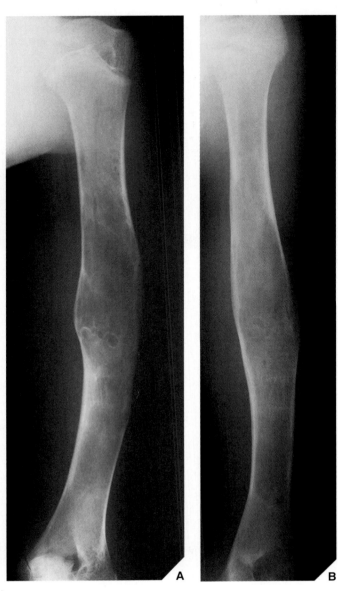

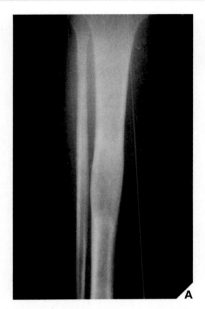

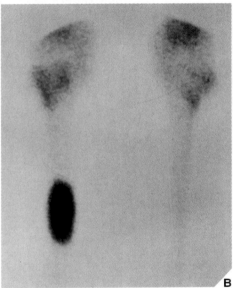

FIGURE 19.19 **Monostotic fibrous dysplasia.** Anteroposterior radiographs of the left humerus in neutral **(A)** and external rotation **(B)** projections of a 13-year-old boy show a radiolucent focus of fibrous dysplasia in the diaphysis of the bone.

FIGURE 19.21 **Scintigraphy of fibrous dysplasia.** A 24-year-old woman presented with mild discomfort in the right leg. **(A)** Anteroposterior radiograph shows a radiolucent lesion in the midshaft of the tibia, with "smoky" appearance associated with thinning of the cortex and slight expansion, characteristic of fibrous dysplasia. **(B)** Radionuclide bone scan shows markedly increased uptake of the radiopharmaceutical tracer indicating an active lesion.

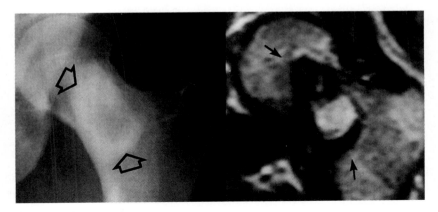

FIGURE 19.20 **Liposclerosing myxoid tumor.** Anteroposterior radiograph of the left hip of a 38-year-old woman presenting with vague hip pain shows a radiolucent lesion with well-defined thick scleroting border in the intertrochanteric region of the femur (*open arrows*). Coronal T2-weighted MR image shows the lesion (*arrows*) to exhibit heterogeneous signal intensity. Peripheral sclerotic "rind" displays signal void. (Reprinted with permission from Kransdorf MJ et al., 1999.)

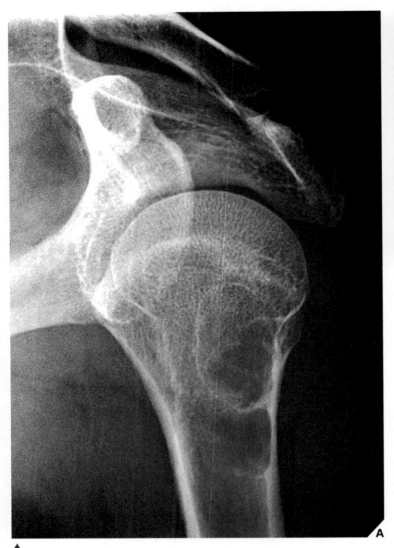
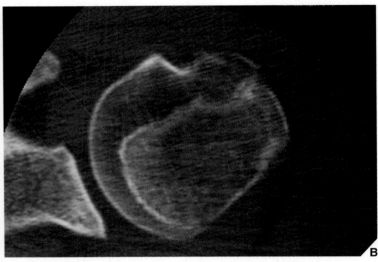

▲
FIGURE 19.22 CT of fibrous dysplasia. (A) Conventional radiograph shows a monostotic focus in the neck and head of the left humerus. **(B)** CT section shows "ground-glass" appearance of the lesion and a sclerotic high-attenuation border.

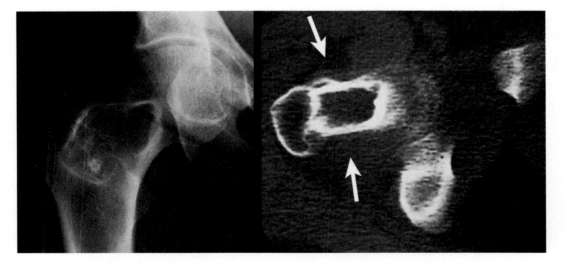

▲
FIGURE 19.23 CT of monostotic fibrous dysplasia. Anteroposterior radiograph of the right hip and axial CT image show a focus of fibrous dysplasia in the neck of the femur exhibiting a typical "rind sign"—thick sclerotic border surrounding a radiolucent/low-attenuation lesion (*arrows*).

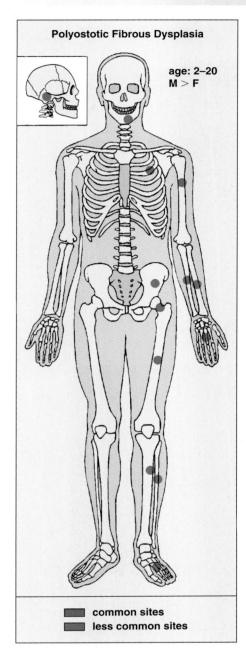

Polyostotic Fibrous Dysplasia

age: 2–20
M > F

common sites
less common sites

▲
FIGURE 19.24 Skeletal sites of predilection, peak age range, and male-to-female ratio in polyostotic fibrous dysplasia, which is usually seen in only one side of the skeleton.

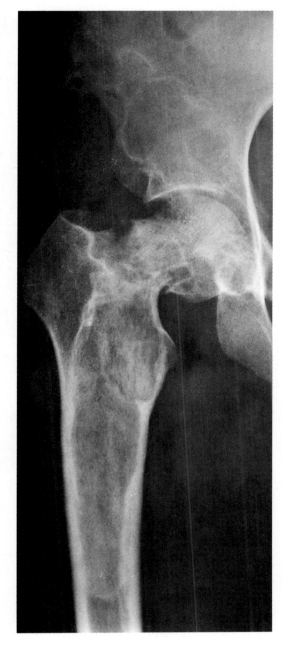

▲
FIGURE 19.25 **Polyostotic fibrous dysplasia.** Anteroposterior radiograph of the right hip of an 18-year-old woman with polyostotic fibrous dysplasia shows unilateral involvement of the ilium and femur. There is a pathological fracture of the femoral neck with a varus deformity.

progress in number and size until the end of skeletal maturation, at which time they become quiescent. In only 5% of cases do they continue to enlarge.

Radiographically, the changes typical of fibrous dysplasia may occur in a limited segment or a major portion of the long bones affected by the polyostotic form of the disease, but as in the monostotic form, the articular ends are usually spared. The cortex, which is generally left intact, is often thinned by the expansive component of the lesion, and the inner cortical margins may show scalloping. The lesion has a well-defined border. Occasionally, as in the monostotic form, the replacement of medullary bone by fibrous tissue leads to a loss of the trabecular pattern, giving the lesions a ground-glass, "milky," or "smoky" appearance (see Fig. 19.18A). More osseous lesions appear dense. The quickest means of determining the distribution of the lesion in the skeleton is radionuclide bone scan, which often discloses unsuspected sites of skeletal involvement (Fig. 19.26).

CT can accurately delineate the extent of bone involvement (Figs. 19.27 and 19.28). Tissue attenuation values, as measured by Hounsfield units, are usually within the 70- to 400-HU range, apparently reflecting the presence of calcium and microscopic ossification throughout the abnormal tissue. As pointed out by Daffner and colleagues, CT is particularly useful to define the extent of craniofacial disease, including impingement on orbital structures (Fig. 19.29). On MRI, fibrous dysplasia exhibits homogeneous, intermediate or moderately low signal intensity on T1-weighted images, whereas on T2 weighting, the signal is bright or mixed. After gadolinium infusion, most lesions show central contrast enhancement and some peripheral rim enhancement (Figs. 19.30 and 19.31). In general, signal intensity on T1- and T2-weighted images and the degree of contrast enhancement on T1-weighted sequences depend on the amount and degree of bone trabeculae, collagen, and cystic and hemorrhagic changes in fibrous dysplasia.

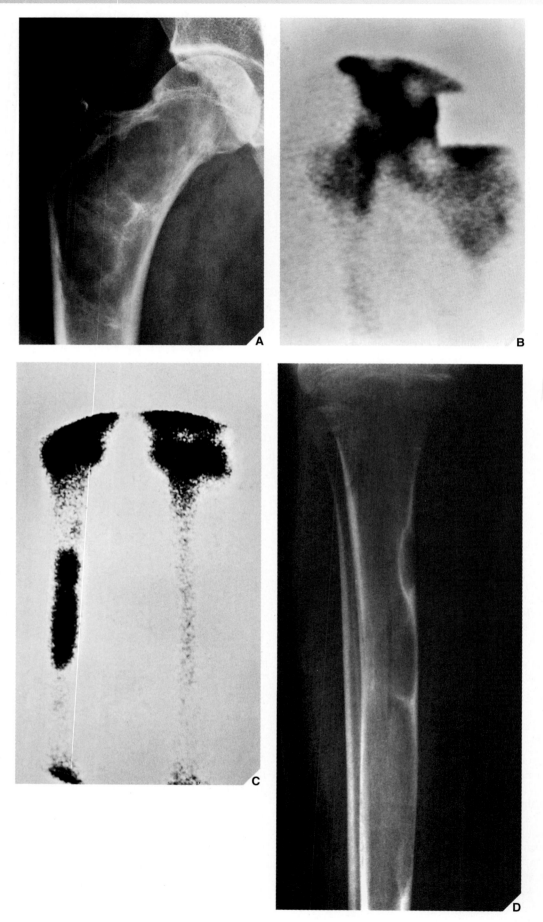

▲
FIGURE 19.26 **Polyostotic fibrous dysplasia.** A 13-year-old girl injured her right hip. **(A)** A radiograph of the hip, obtained to exclude a fracture, demonstrates a silent focus of fibrous dysplasia in the femoral neck. To determine other sites of involvement, a radionuclide bone scan was obtained. In addition to the focus in the femoral neck **(B)**, increased uptake of isotope was demonstrated at various other sites, but predominantly the right leg **(C)**. Subsequent radiograph of the right lower leg in the anteroposterior projection **(D)** confirms the presence of multiple foci of polyostotic fibrous dysplasia.

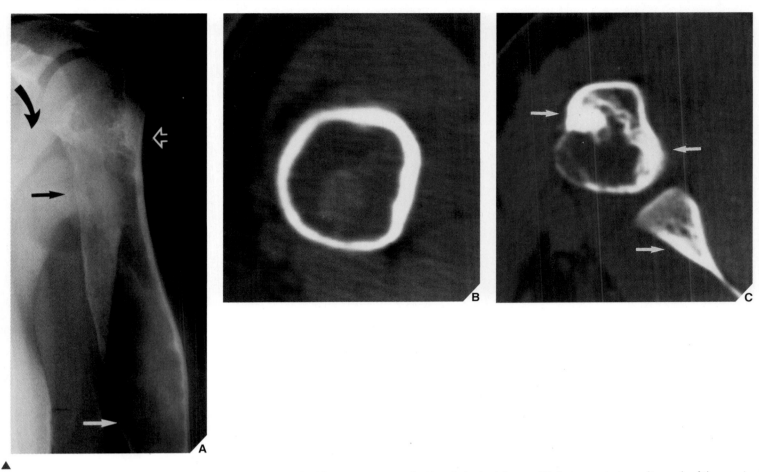

FIGURE 19.27   CT of polyostotic fibrous dysplasia. A 24-year-old woman presented with pain in the left arm. **(A)** Anteroposterior radiograph of the proximal left humerus shows expansive, mostly radiolucent lesion (*arrows*) with focal sclerotic areas at the junction of the head and neck (*open arrow*). The cortex is thinned out. Another sclerotic focus is seen in the scapula (*curved arrow*). **(B)** CT section through the shaft of the humerus shows a low-attenuation lesion with minimal scalloping of the endocortex. **(C)** CT section through the shoulder joint reveals the high-attenuation areas of sclerosis in the humeral head and scapula (*arrows*).

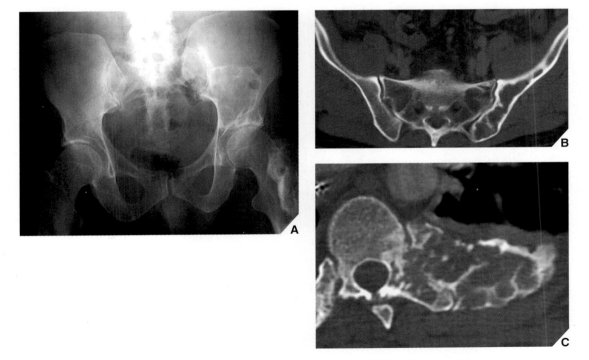

FIGURE 19.28   CT of polyostotic fibrous dysplasia. (A) Anteroposterior radiograph of the pelvis shows multiple lesions in the left ilium and proximal left femur. The involvement of the sacrum is not well demonstrated. **(B)** CT section of the pelvis precisely shows the extent of involvement of the ilium and sacrum. **(C)** Axial CT image of one of the thoracic vertebrae and ribs shows multiloculated appearance of the lesions, expansion of the bone, pseudosepta, thinning of the cortex, and a pathological fracture. (Reprinted from Greenspan A et al., 2007.)

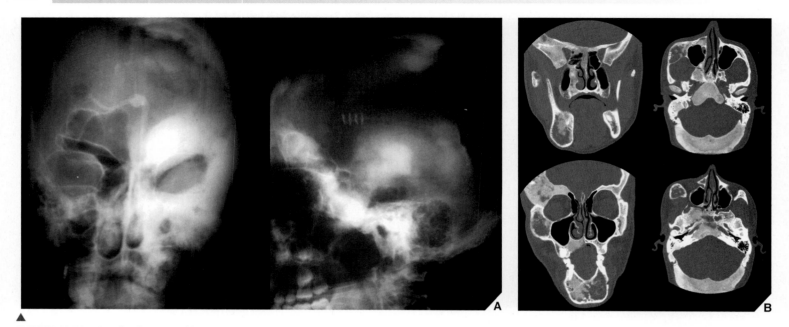

▲ FIGURE 19.29   **CT of polyostotic fibrous dysplasia. (A)** Anteroposterior and lateral radiographs of the skull of the 17-year-old boy show extensive involvement of the skull and the facial bones. **(B)** Several thin CT sections of the facial bones demonstrate the details and distribution of these lesions.

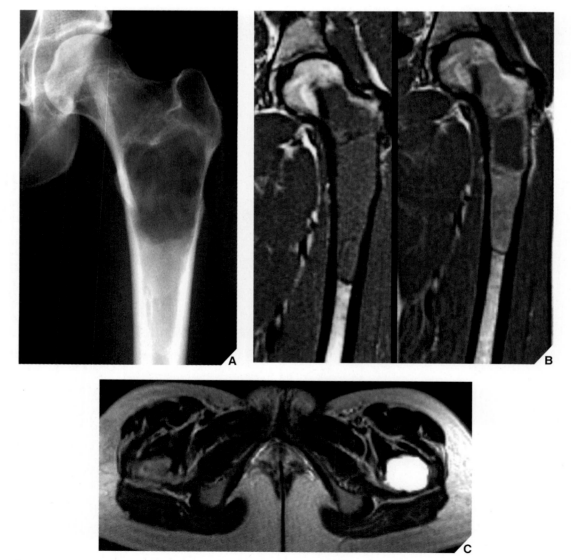

▲ FIGURE 19.30   **MRI of polyostotic fibrous dysplasia. (A)** Anteroposterior radiograph of the proximal left femur of a 23-year-old woman shows a geographic radiolucent lesion in the subtrochanteric region of the bone. **(B)** Coronal MRI shows the full extent of the lesion, which is of intermediate signal intensity on T1-weighted image and exhibit mild enhancement on postcontrast sequence. **(C)** Axial T2-weighted MR image shows the lesion to be of high signal intensity. (Reprinted from Greenspan A et al., 2007.)

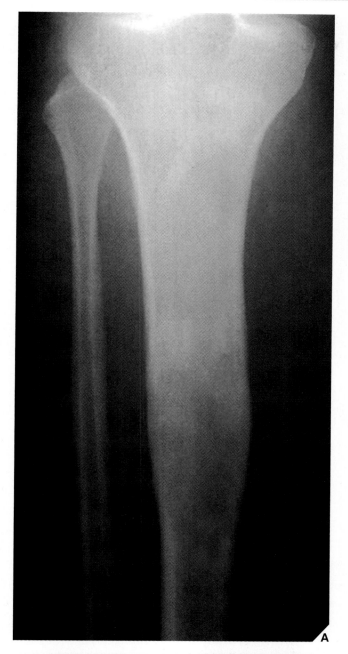

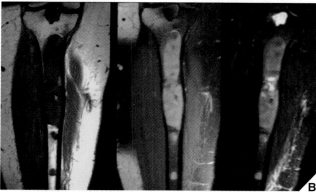

FIGURE 19.31 MRI of polyostotic fibrous dysplasia. (A) Anteroposterior radiograph of the proximal right leg of a 23-year-old woman shows a multifocal long lesion in the proximal tibia exhibiting a "ground-glass" appearance. The bone is mildly expanded; the cortex is thin. **(B)** Coronal T1-weighted, postcontrast fat-suppressed T1-weighted, and T2-weighted images show characteristic features of this lesion: Intermediate signal intensity similar to that of the skeletal muscle on T1 weighting, heterogenous signal on T2 weighting, and slight enhancement after intravenous injection of gadolinium. (Reprinted from Greenspan A et al., 2007.)

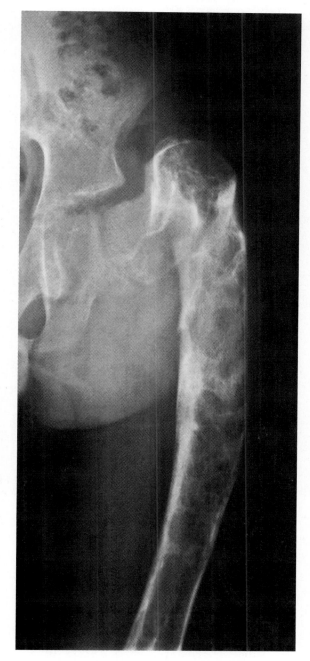

FIGURE 19.32 Polyostotic fibrous dysplasia. A "shepherd's crook" deformity, seen here in the proximal femur in a 12-year-old boy with polyostotic fibrous dysplasia, is often the result of multiple pathological fractures.

The histologic appearance of polyostotic fibrous dysplasia is identical to that of the monostotic form. The presence of small trabeculae of woven bone of various sizes and shapes, scattered within a fibrous tissue without the evidence of osteoblastic activity, is diagnostic for this disorder.

Complications

The most frequent complication of polyostotic fibrous dysplasia is pathological fracture. If fracture occurs at the femoral neck, it commonly leads to a deformity called "shepherd's crook" (Fig. 19.32). Occasionally, accelerated growth of a bone or hypertrophy of a digit may be encountered (Fig. 19.33). Massive cartilage hyperplasia (cartilaginous differentiation) may also be seen in this disorder, resulting in the accumulation of cartilaginous masses in the medullary portion of the affected bone (Figs. 19.34 to 19.36). This condition is commonly referred to as *fibrochondrodysplasia or fibrocartilaginous dysplasia*. However, it should not be confused with so-called *focal fibrocartilaginous dysplasia*

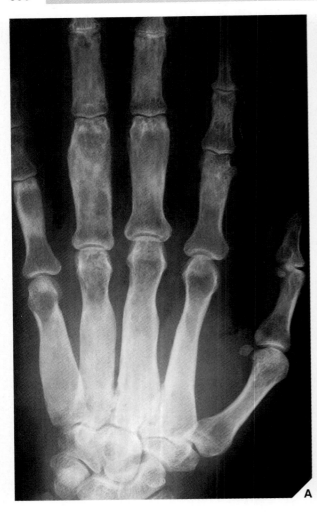

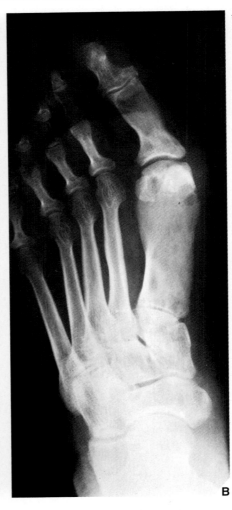

FIGURE 19.33 **Complication of fibrous dysplasia.** Posteroanterior radiograph of the hand **(A)** and dorsoplantar film of the foot **(B)** of a 20-year-old man with polyostotic fibrous dysplasia demonstrate a frequent complication of this condition—accelerated growth of affected bones. In the hand, observe the enlargement of the third and fourth rays, including the metacarpals and phalanges, and in the foot note the hypertrophy of the first metatarsal.

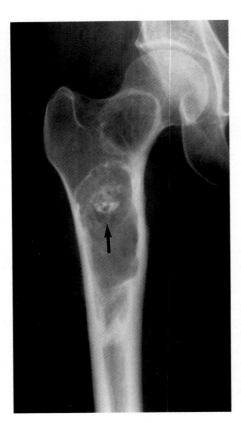

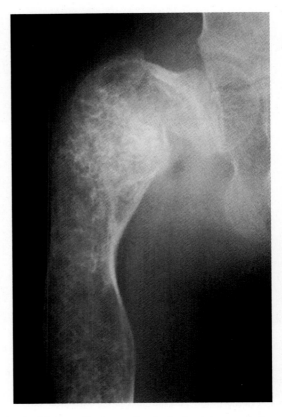

FIGURE 19.34 **Fibrocartilaginous dysplasia.** An anteroposterior radiograph of the right proximal femur in a 20-year-old man with polyostotic fibrous dysplasia shows foci of cartilage formation (*arrow*), identifying this lesion as fibrocartilaginous dysplasia.

FIGURE 19.35 **Fibrocartilaginous dysplasia.** An anteroposterior radiograph of the proximal right femur of a 10-year-old boy with polyostotic fibrous dysplasia exhibits typical appearance of a massive formation of cartilage, known as fibrocartilaginous dysplasia.

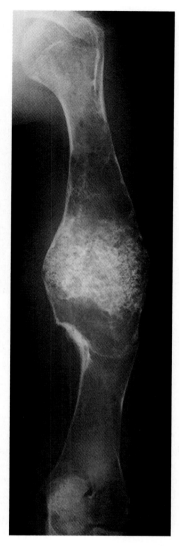

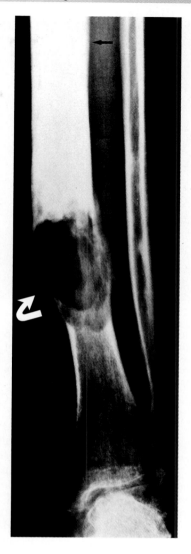

▲
FIGURE 19.36 Fibrocartilaginous dysplasia. An anteroposterior radiograph of the left humerus in a 19-year-old man with polyostotic fibrous dysplasia shows an extensive involvement of almost the entire bone, with cartilage formation in the midportion of the diaphysis.

▲
FIGURE 19.37 Complication of fibrous dysplasia. A 34-year-old man was noted to have a deformity of the left leg at age 5 years. Radiographic examination at that time showed typical involvement of the tibia by fibrous dysplasia, which subsequently was confirmed by biopsy. No treatment was given, and he was asymptomatic for 28 years until acute pain in his left leg developed. Conventional radiograph shows evidence of fibrous dysplasia affecting the proximal shaft of the tibia (*arrows*). A large osteolytic destructive lesion in the distal third of the tibia is also seen encroaching on the dense segment of bone and affecting the medullary portion and the cortex (*curved arrow*). There is a periosteal reaction and a soft-tissue mass. Biopsy revealed transformation of fibrous dysplasia to undifferentiated spindle-cell sarcoma.

of long bones. The latter occurs mainly in children and young adults. Characteristically, it affects the proximal tibia, although other long bones, such as the ulna and femur, may sometimes be involved. The lesion shows a variety of histopathological features, ranging from purely dense fibrous tissue to benign fibrocartilaginous tissue. The sarcomatous transformation of either form of fibrous dysplasia is extremely rare, but it may occur spontaneously (Fig. 19.37) or, more commonly, after radiation therapy (Fig. 19.38).

Associated Disorders

Albright-McCune Syndrome

When polyostotic fibrous dysplasia is associated with endocrine disturbances (premature sexual development, hyperparathyroidism, and other endocrinopathies) and abnormal pigmentation marked by café-au-lait spots of the skin, the disorder is called Albright-McCune syndrome (Fig. 19.39). Overall, this condition almost exclusively affects girls who present with true sexual precocity secondary to acceleration of the normal process of gonadotropin release by the anterior lobe of the pituitary gland. The café-au-lait spots seen in Albright-McCune syndrome have characteristically irregular ragged borders (commonly called "coast of Maine" borders), as opposed to the smoothly marginated ("coast of California") borders of the spots seen in neurofibromatosis.

Mazabraud Syndrome

This syndrome, which is characterized by an association of polyostotic fibrous dysplasia with soft-tissue myxomas (solitary or multiple), was first described by German pathologist F. Henschen in 1926, and later was reemphasized by French physician A. Mazabraud in 1967. Recently Endo and associates reported a rare variant of Mazabraud syndrome—monostotic fibrous dysplasia coexisting with solitary intramuscular myxoma. The cause of Mazabraud syndrome remains unsettled. A variety of pathological mechanisms have been suggested to explain the link between fibrous dysplasia and soft-tissue myxomas. Some investigators have emphasized a common histiogenic origin or a shared abnormality in tissue metabolism. Others have suggested a collaborative developmental error, perhaps related to a genetic predisposition.

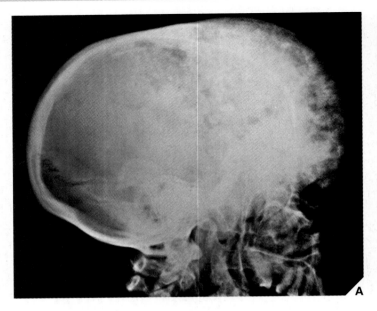
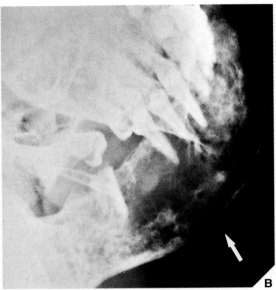

▲ **FIGURE 19.38 Complication of fibrous dysplasia.** Eleven years before this examination, a 35-year-old woman with polyostotic fibrous dysplasia underwent radiation treatment of the mandible. **(A)** Lateral radiograph of the skull demonstrates predominant involvement of the frontal bones with a characteristic expansion of the outer table. The base of the skull, a frequent site of polyostotic fibrous dysplasia, is typically thickened, and the frontal and ethmoid sinuses are obliterated. The maxilla and mandible are also affected. This advanced stage of involvement of the skull and facial bones by polyostotic fibrous dysplasia is frequently termed leontiasis ossea. **(B)** Oblique radiograph shows an expansive lytic lesion in the body of the left mandible, with partial destruction of the cortex (*arrow*). Biopsy revealed an osteosarcoma.

In this syndrome, it is important to recognize the soft-tissue masses as benign myxomas and not to confuse them with malignant soft-tissue tumors that may develop *de novo* (e.g., malignant fibrous histiocytoma, malignant mesenchymoma, or liposarcoma) or those that may be present in cases of malignant transformation of fibrous dysplasia. MR imaging is very helpful, because it reveals typical features of benign myxomas, that is, very sharply defined borders, homogeneous signal intensity before administration of contrast, and a heterogeneous pattern of enhancement after the injection of gadolinium. As pointed out by several investigators, the signal characteristics of myxoma on T1-weighted and T2-weighted sequences are quite similar to those of fluid: low-to-intermediate signal intensity on T1-weighted and high signal intensity on T2-weighted images.

Osteofibrous Dysplasia

Osteofibrous dysplasia (Kempson-Campanacci lesion), called "ossifying fibroma" in the past, is a rare, benign, fibroosseous lesion that occurs predominantly in children, although it may not be discovered until adolescence. It has a decided preference for the tibia, being located with few exceptions in the proximal third or mid segment of the bone and often localized to its anterior cortex. In more than 80% of patients, there is some degree of anterior bowing. Larger lesions may destroy the cortex and invade the medullary cavity.

On radiography, the Kempson-Campanacci lesion exhibits a lobulated sclerotic margin and a striking resemblance to nonossifying fibroma and fibrous dysplasia (Figs. 19.40 to 19.42). MRI features are also similar to those two lesions (Fig. 19.43). Furthermore, osteofibrous dysplasia and fibrous dysplasia, as the similarity in their names might suggest, display a remarkable histopathological similarity. Like a lesion of fibrous dysplasia, osteofibrous dysplasia is composed of a fibrous background containing deformed trabeculae. These trabeculae, however, unlike those of fibrous dysplasia, display woven bone only in the center, being surrounded by an outer zone of lamellar bone with prominent appositional osteoblastic activity ("dressed trabeculae").

This lesion should not be confused with the lesion, also called ossifying fibroma, that is seen almost exclusively in the jaw (mandible) of women in their third and fourth decades, although it is still uncertain whether some of the latter lesions represent an atypical form of fibrous dysplasia. Sissons and colleagues reported two cases of fibroosseous lesions that differed histologically from osteofibrous dysplasia and fibrous dysplasia. They proposed the term *ossifying fibroma* for these, suggesting that the term *osteofibrous dysplasia* continue to be used for lesions of the tibia and fibula (Kempson-Campanacci lesions). To avoid confusion in terminology, the differential features of the various lesions are summarized in Table 19.1.

A relationship of osteofibrous dysplasia with fibrous dysplasia and adamantinoma has been suggested by some investigators. Although this remains a controversial matter, adamantinoma—a malignant tumor—may contain a fibroosseous component that on pathological examination resembles both fibrous and osteofibrous dysplasia. Moreover, in recent years, patients have presented with lesions that contained foci of epithelial tissue corresponding to adamantinoma within areas of osteofibrous dysplasia. Czerniak and associates have termed such lesions "differentiated (regressing) adamantinomas." According to these investigators, features characteristic of differentiated adamantinomas include onset during the first two decades of life, an exclusively intracortical location, uniform predominance of osteofibrous dysplasia, and scattered foci of epithelial elements that are identical to those observed in classic adamantinoma. This suggests that a single disease entity may exhibit a spectrum of manifestations with benign osteofibrous dysplasia at one end of the spectrum and malignant adamantinoma at the other end.

Complications and Treatment

Osteofibrous dysplasia is known to be an aggressive lesion that frequently recurs after local excision. According to some researchers, it may coexist with another very aggressive lesion, adamantinoma (see previous discussion).

Desmoplastic Fibroma

Desmoplastic fibroma (also called intraosseous desmoid tumor) is a rare, locally aggressive tumor that occurs in individuals younger than age 40

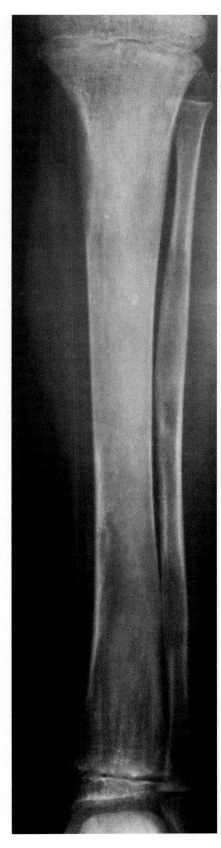

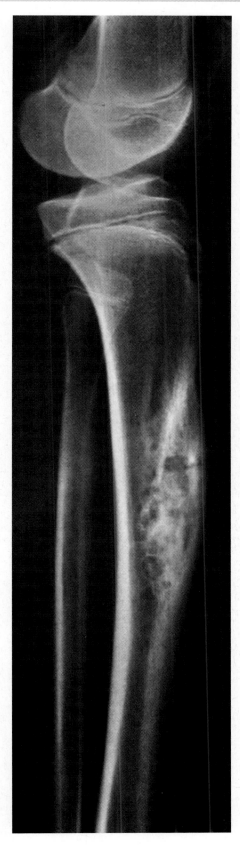

▲
FIGURE 19.39 **Albright-McCune syndrome.** Polyostotic fibrous dysplasia typically affects one side of the skeleton, as seen here in a 5-year-old girl with precocious puberty whose left upper and lower extremities were affected (Albright-McCune syndrome). Radiograph of the lower leg shows expansion of the tibia and fibula associated with thinning of the cortex. Note the ground-glass appearance of the medullary portion of these bones.

▲
FIGURE 19.40 **Osteofibrous dysplasia.** This lesion in the anterior aspect of the right tibia of a 14-year-old girl was originally thought to be a nonossifying fibroma. Although it is similar to a nonossifying fibroma and fibrous dysplasia, its site is typical of osteofibrous dysplasia, which was confirmed by biopsy. Note the characteristic anterior bowing of the tibia.

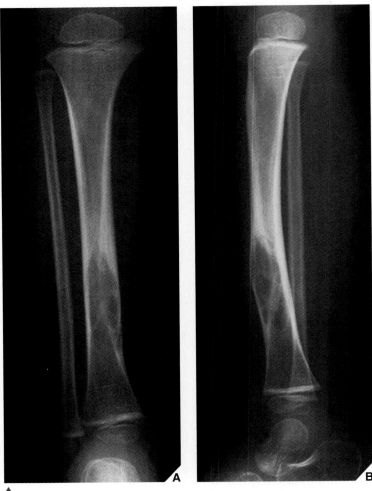

▲
FIGURE 19.41 Osteofibrous dysplasia. Anteroposterior **(A)** and lateral **(B)** radiographs of the right leg in a 2-year-old boy show the lesion in the distal tibia.

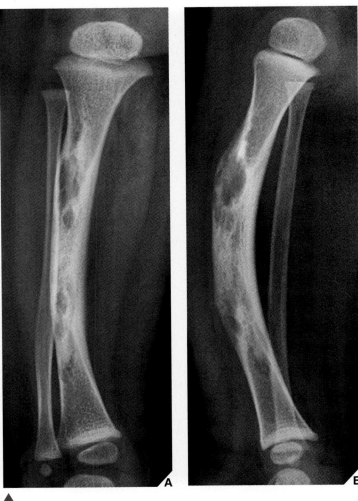

▲
FIGURE 19.42 Osteofibrous dysplasia. (A) Anteroposterior and **(B)** lateral radiographs of the right leg of a 10-month-old girl show extensive involvement of the midtibial diaphysis. Note the characteristic anterior bowing of the tibia.

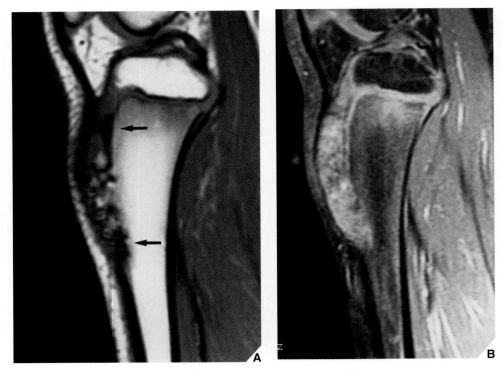

▲
FIGURE 19.43 MRI of osteofibrous dysplasia. (A) Sagittal T1-weighted image shows an oblong lesion involving the anterior cortex of tibia, exhibiting non-homogeneous, mixed signal intensity *(arrows)*. **(B)** Sagittal T1-weighted fat-suppressed sequence after injection of gadolinium shows significant enhancement of the lesion.

TABLE 19.1 **Differential Features of Various Fibroosseous Lesions With Similar Radiographic Appearance**

Sex	Age	Location	Radiographic Appearance	Histopathology
		Fibrous Dysplasia		
M/F	Any age (monostotic) First to third decades (polyostotic)	Femoral neck (frequent) Long bones Pelvis Ends of bones usually spared Polyostotic: unilateral in skeleton	Radiolucent, ground-glass, or smoky lesion Thinning of cortex with endosteal scalloping "Shepherd's crook" deformity Accelerated growth	Woven (nonlamellar) type of bone in loose to dense fibrous stroma; bony trabeculae lacking osteoblastic activity ("naked trabeculae")
		Nonossifying Fibroma		
M/F	First to third decades	Long bones (frequently posterior femur)	Radiolucent, eccentric lesion Scalloped, sclerotic border	Whorled pattern of fibrous tissue containing giant cells, hemosiderin, and lipid-filled histiocytes
		Osteofibrous Dysplasia (Kempson-Campanacci Lesion)		
M/F	First to second decades	Tibia (frequently anterior aspect) Fibula Intracortical (frequent)	Osteolytic, eccentric lesion Scalloped, sclerotic border Anterior bowing of long bone	Woven and mature (lamellar) type of bone surrounded by cellular fibrous spindle-cell growth in whorled or matted pattern; bony trabeculae rimmed by osteoblasts ("dressed trabeculae")
		Ossifying Fibroma of Jaw		
F	Third to fourth decades	Mandible (90%) Maxilla	Expansive radiolucent lesion Sclerotic, well-defined borders	Uniformly cellular fibrous spindle-cell growth with varying amounts of lamellar bone formation and small, round cementum-like bodies
		Ossifying Fibroma (Sissons Lesion)		
M/F	Second decade	Tibia Humerus	Radiolucent lesion Sclerotic border Similar to osteofibrous dysplasia	Fibrous tissue containing rounded and spindle-shaped cells with scant intercellular collagen and small, partially calcified spherules resembling cementum-like bodies of ossifying fibroma of jaw
		Liposclerosing Myxofibrous Tumor		
M/F	Second to seventh decades	Intertrochanteric region of femur	Radiolucent or partially sclerotic lesion with well-defined sclerotic border, occasionally central matrix mineralization	Fibrous or myxofibrous areas with metaplastic curvilinear or circular woven bone ossicles and/or dystrophic mineralization in necrotic fat

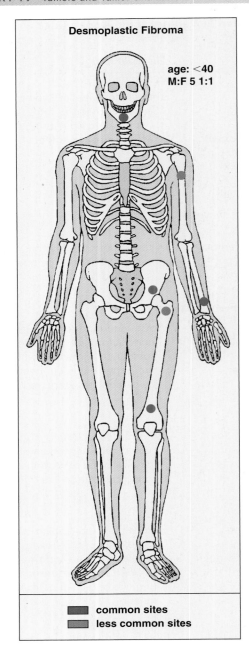

Desmoplastic Fibroma

age: <40
M:F 5 1:1

■ common sites
■ less common sites

▲
FIGURE 19.44 Skeletal sites of predilection, peak age range, and male-to-female ratio in desmoplastic fibroma.

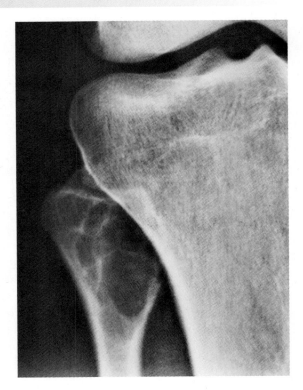

▲
FIGURE 19.45 **Desmoplastic fibroma.** A radiolucent, trabeculated, sharply marginated lesion occupies the proximal end of the right fibula in a 17-year-old girl. Note lack of periosteal reaction.

years, with 50% of all cases occurring in the patient's second decade. It was first described as a distinct entity in 1958 by H. Jaffe. Pain and local swelling are the most common symptoms, but some patients may be asymptomatic. The long bones (femur, tibia, fibula, humerus, and radius), the pelvis, and the mandible are frequent sites of involvement (Fig. 19.44). In the long bones, the lesion occurs in the diaphysis but often extends into the metaphysis. Although the epiphysis is spared, the lesion may extend into the articular end of the bone after closure of the growth plate.

Desmoplastic fibroma has no characteristic radiographic features. The lesion is generally expansive and radiolucent, with sharply defined borders (Fig. 19.45); the cortex of the bone may be thickened or thinned, with no significant periosteal response. Usually a geographic pattern of bone destruction is noted, with narrow zones of transition and nonsclerotic margins (76%). Internal pseudotrabeculation is present in 90% of cases (Fig. 19.46). Pathological fractures through the tumor are rare (9%). Aggressive lesions of this type are marked by bone destruction and invasion of the soft tissues and may simulate malignant bone tumors (Fig. 19.47).

In addition to conventional radiography, radiologic evaluation of desmoplastic fibroma should include bone scintigraphy, CT, and MRI. Radionuclide bone scan shows an increase in the uptake of the radiopharmaceutical agent at the site of the lesion. CT is useful for evaluating cortical breakthrough and tumor extension into the soft tissues. MRI, also helpful in assessing intraosseous and extraosseous extension, can further characterize the tumor (Fig. 19.48; see also Fig. 19.46D). The lesion appears well defined on MR images, exhibiting an intermediate signal intensity on T1 weighting and a heterogeneous pattern on T2 weighting, marked by an area of increased signal intensity mixed with foci of intermediate and low signal intensity. The hypointensity of the signal reflects the dense connective tissue matrix and relative acellularity of the tumor. After intravenous administration of gadolinium contrast, a majority of the lesions demonstrate heterogenous enhancement, with peripheral areas enhancing more intensely than the central portions of the tumor.

Histologically, the lesion is composed of spindle-shaped and occasionally stellate fibroblasts associated with a densely collagenized matrix. Cells are almost always in a smaller proportion to the matrix. The stroma usually contains large, thin-walled vessels similar to those seen in desmoid tumors of soft tissues. Desmoplastic fibroma may be difficult to distinguish from other fibrous tumors, particularly low-grade fibrosarcoma.

Wide excision is the treatment of choice, although the recurrence rate is high even after complete excision of the tumor. Despite this aggressiveness, metastases have never been reported.

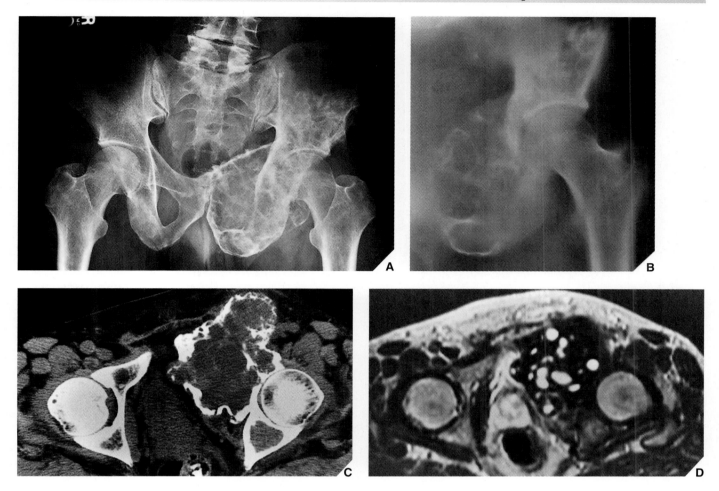

▲
FIGURE 19.46 Desmoplastic fibroma. A 67-year-old man presented with a large pelvic mass. **(A)** Anteroposterior radiograph of the pelvis demonstrates an expansive trabeculated lytic lesion that involves ischium and pubis and extends into the supra-acetabular portion of the ilium. **(B)** Conventional tomography shows the lytic nature of the tumor and its expansive character. The involvement of ilium is better demonstrated. **(C)** CT section of the tumor through the hip joint shows a lobulated appearance and a thick, sclerotic margin. The lesion extends into the pelvic cavity, displacing the urinary bladder. **(D)** Axial spin-echo T2-weighted MR image (TR 2000/TE 80 msec) demonstrates nonhomogeneity of the signal from the tumor: The bulk of the lesion displays low to intermediate signal intensity with central areas of high signal intensity. An incisional biopsy revealed desmoplastic fibroma. (From Greenspan A et al., 1992, with permission.)

FIGURE 19.47 Desmoplastic fibroma. Anteroposterior **(A)** and lateral **(B)** radiographs of the distal forearm in a 31-year-old woman show aggressive destructive lesions involving the radius and ulna, extending into the articular surfaces, complicated by pathological fractures (*arrows*). Histologic study of an excisional biopsy revealed desmoplastic fibroma.

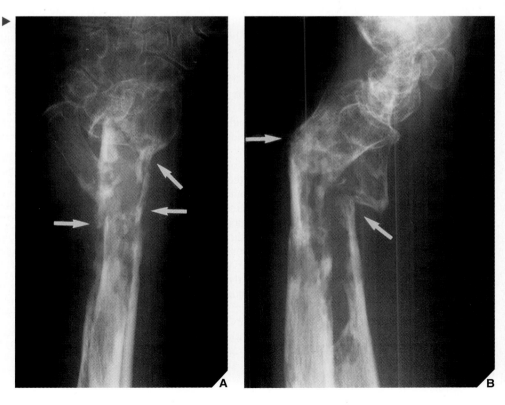

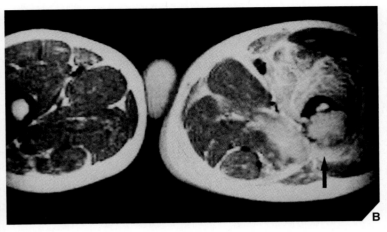

▲
FIGURE 19.48   **MRI of desmoplastic fibroma. (A)** Coronal T1-weighted MRI shows desmoplastic fibroma in the left femoral shaft breaking through the cortex and extending into the soft tissues (*arrows*). **(B)** Axial proton-density MR image demonstrates replacement of the bone marrow by the tumor (*arrow*), soft-tissue involvement, and peritumoral edema. (Courtesy of Prof. Dr. Wolfgang Remagen, Cologne, Germany.)

PRACTICAL POINTS TO REMEMBER

[1] A fibrous cortical defect (metaphyseal fibrous defect) and nonossifying fibroma are closely related lesions of similar histopathological structure. They differ radiologically only in their size.

[2] Most of these lesions disappear spontaneously. With continued growth, they are eccentrically located and display a characteristic scalloped sclerotic border.

[3] Association of disseminated nonossifying fibromatosis with café-au-lait spots is known the Jaffe-Campanacci syndrome.

[4] Benign fibrous histiocytoma has radiographic features similar to those of nonossifying fibroma; however, it affects older patients, may be symptomatic, and runs a more aggressive clinical course (may recur after surgical treatment).

[5] Periosteal desmoid has a characteristic predilection for the posteromedial cortex of the medial femoral condyle. It should not be mistaken for a malignant bone tumor.

[6] Fibrous dysplasia may be monostotic or polyostotic, with the latter having a decided preference for one side of the skeleton. The polyostotic form, if accompanied by precocious puberty and café-au-lait spots (with irregular, ragged, or "coast of Maine" borders), is called Albright-McCune syndrome and is seen predominantly in girls.

[7] Association of polyostotic fibrous dysplasia with intramuscular myxomas is known as the Mazabraud syndrome.

[8] Massive formation of cartilage may be observed in fibrous dysplasia, a condition known as fibrocartilaginous dysplasia. This variant can radiographically resemble a cartilaginous neoplasm, such as chondrosarcoma.

[9] Fibrocartilaginous dysplasia (cartilaginous differentiation in fibrous dysplasia) should not be confused with focal fibrocartilaginous dysplasia of long bones, a condition seen predominantly in children and young adults that characteristically affects the proximal tibia.

[10] The best radiologic technique for evaluating the distribution of fibrous dysplasia is radionuclide bone scan.

[11] Osteofibrous dysplasia, a benign fibroosseous lesion seen in children and adolescents, has a decided predilection for the anterior aspect of the tibia. This lesion may be associated with adamantinoma.

[12] Desmoplastic fibroma, a locally aggressive tumor, is frequently marked by bone destruction and invasion of the soft tissues, thus mimicking a malignant neoplasm.

SUGGESTED READINGS

Albright F, Butler AM, Hampton AO, Smith P. Syndrome characterized by osteitis fibrosa disseminata, areas of pigmentation and endocrine dysfunction with precocious puberty in females. *N Engl J Med* 1937;216:727–731.

Alguacil-Garcia A, Alonso A, Pettigrew NM. Osteofibrous dysplasia (ossifying fibroma) of the tibia and fibula and adamantinoma. *Am J Clin Pathol* 1984;82:470–474.

Bahk W-J, Kang Y-K, Lee A-H, Mirra JM. Desmoid tumor of bone with enchondromatous nodules, mistaken for chondrosarcoma. *Skeletal Radiol* 2003;32:223–226.

Bancroft LW, Kransdorf MJ, Menke DM, O'Connor MI, Foster WC. Intramuscular myxoma: characteristic MR imaging features. *Am J Roentgenol* 2002;178:1255–1259.

Barnes GR Jr, Gwinn JL. Distal irregularities of the femur simulating malignancy. *Am J Roentgenol* 1974;122:180–185.

Bertoni F, Calderoni P, Bacchini P, Campanacci M. Desmoplastic fibroma of bone: a report of six cases. *J Bone Joint Surg [Br]* 1984;66B:265–268.

Bertoni F, Calderoni P, Bacchini P, Sudanese A. Benign fibrous histiocytoma of bone. *J Bone Joint Surg [Am]* 1986;68A:1225–1230.

Bertoni F, Unni KK, McLeod RA, Sim FH. Xanthoma of bone. *Am J Pathol* 1988;90:377–384.

Blau RA, Zwick DL, Westphal RA. Multiple nonossifying fibromas. *J Bone Joint Surg [Am]* 1988;70A:299–304.

Brower AC, Culver JE Jr, Keats TE. Histological nature of the cortical irregularity of the medial posterior distal femoral metaphysis in children. *Radiology* 1971;99:389–392.

Bufkin WJ. The avulsive cortical irregularity. *Am J Roentgenol* 1971;112:487–492.

Bullough PG, Vigorita VJ. *Atlas of orthopaedic pathology with clinical and radiologic correlations*, 2nd ed. New York: Gowen Medical Publishing; 1992.

Cabral CEL, Guedes P, Fonseca T, Rezende JF, Cruz Jr LC, Smith J. Polyostotic fibrous dysplasia associated with intramuscular myxomas: Mazabraud's syndrome. *Skeletal Radiol* 1998;27:278–282.

Caffey J. On fibrous defects in cortical walls of growing tubular bone: their radiologic appearance, structure prevalence, natural course and diagnostic significance. *Adv Pediatr* 1955;7:13–51.

Camilleri AE. Craniofacial fibrous dysplasia. *J Laryngol Otol* 1991;105:662–666.

Campanacci M. Osteofibrous dysplasia of the long bones. A new clinical entity. *Ital J Orthop Traumatol* 1976;2:221–237.

Campanacci M, Laus M. Osteofibrous dysplasia of the tibia and fibula. *J Bone Joint Surg [Am]* 1981;63A:367–375.

Campanacci M, Laus M, Boriani S. Multiple non-ossifying fibromata with extraskeletal anomalies: a new syndrome? *J Bone Joint Surg [Br]* 1983;65-B: 627–632.

Campbell CJ, Hawk T. A variant of fibrous dysplasia (osteofibrous dysplasia). *J Bone Joint Surg [Am]* 1982;64A:231–236.

Choi IH, Kim CJ, Cho T-J, Chung CY, Song KS, Hwang JK, Sohn YJ. Focal fibrocartilaginous dysplasia of long bones: report of eight additional cases and literature review. *J Ped Orthop* 2000;20:421–427.

Clarke BE, Xipell JM, Thomas DP. Benign fibrous histiocytoma of bone. *Am J Surg Pathol* 1985;9:806–815.

Cohen DM, Dahlin DC, Pugh DG. Fibrous dysplasia associated with adamantinoma of the long bones. *Cancer* 1962;15:515–521.

Crim JR, Gold RH, Mirra JM, Eckardt JJ, Bassett LW. Desmoplastic fibroma of bone: radiographic analysis. *Radiology* 1989;172:827–832.

Cunningham BJ, Ackerman LV. Metaphyseal fibrous defects. *J Bone Joint Surg* 1956;38:797–808.

Czerniak B, Rojas-Corona RR, Dorfman HD. Morphologic diversity of long bone adamantinoma. The concept of differentiated (regressing) adamantinoma and its relationship to osteofibrous dysplasia. *Cancer* 1989;64:2319–2334.

Dahlin DC, Unni KK. *Bone tumors: general aspects and data on 8,542 cases*, 4th ed. Springfield, IL: Charles C Thomas, 1986:141–148.

DeSmet A, Travers H, Neff JR. Chondrosarcoma occurring in a patient with polyostotic fibrous dysplasia. *Skeletal Radiol* 1981;7:197–201.

DiCaprio MR, Enneking WF. Fibrous dysplasia. Pathophysiology, evaluation, and treatment. *J Bone Joint Surg* 2005;87:1848–1864.

Dominok GW, Eisengarten W. Benignes fibroeses Histiozytom des Knochens. *Zentralbl Pathol* 1980;124:77–83.

Dorfman HD, Ishida T, Tsuneyoshi M. Exophytic variant of fibrous dysplasia (fibrous dysplasia protuberans). *Hum Pathol* 1994;25:1234–1237.

Endo M, Kawai A, Kobayashi E, et al. Solitary intramuscular myxoma with monostotic fibrous dysplasia as a rare variant of Mazabraud's syndrome. *Skeletal Radiol* 2007;36:523–529.

Evans GA, Park WM. Familial multiple non-osteogenic fibromata. *J Bone Joint Surg [Br]* 1978;60B:416–419.

Flanagan AM, Delaney D, O'Donnell P. Benefits of molecular pathology in the diagnosis of musculoskeletal disease. Part II of a two-part review: bone tumors and metabolic disorders. *Skeletal Radiol* 2010;39:213–224.

Friedland JA, Reinus WR, Fisher AJ, Wilson AJ. Quantitative analysis of the plain radiographic appearance of nonossifying fibroma. *Invest Radiol* 1995;30: 474–479.

Gebhardt MC, Campbell CJ, Schiller AL, Mankin HJ. Desmoplastic fibroma of bone. A report of eight cases and review of the literature. *J Bone Joint Surg [Am]* 1985;67A:732–747.

Greenspan A, Jundt G, Remagen W. *Differential diagnosis in orthopaedic oncology*, 2nd ed. Philadelphia: Lippincott Williams & Wilkins; 2007.

Greenspan A, Unni KK. Case report 787. Desmoplastic fibroma. *Skeletal Radiol* 1993;22:296–299.

Gross ML, Soberman N, Dorfman HD, Seimon LP. Case report 556. Multiple nonossifying fibromas of long bones in a patient with neurofibromatosis. *Skeletal Radiol* 1989;18:389–391.

Hamada T, Ito H, Araki Y, Fujii K, Inoue M, Ishida O. Benign fibrous histiocytoma of the femur: review of three cases. *Skeletal Radiol* 1996;25:25–29.

Henschen F. Fall von Ostitis fibrosa mit multiplen Tumoren in der umgebenden Muskulatur. *Verh Dtsch Ges Pathol* 1926;21:93–97.

Hermann G, Klein M, Abdelwahab IF, Kenan S. Fibrocartilaginous dysplasia. *Skeletal Radiol* 1996;25:509–511.

Hoshi H, Futami S, Ohnishi T, et al. Gallium-67 uptake in fibrous dysplasia of the bone. *Ann Nucl Med* 1990;4:35–38.

Hudson TM, Stiles RG, Monson DK. Fibrous lesions of bone. *Radiol Clin North Am* 1993;31:279–297.

Huvos A. *Bone tumors: diagnosis, treatment and prognosis*, 2nd ed. Philadelphia: WB Saunders; 1991:677–693.

Huvos AG, Higinbotham NL, Miller TR. Bone sarcomas arising in fibrous dysplasia. *J Bone Joint Surg [Am]* 1972;54A:1047–1056.

Inamo Y, Hanawa Y, Kin H, Okuni M. Findings on magnetic resonance imaging of the spine and femur in a case of McCune-Albright syndrome. *Pediatr Radiol* 1993;23:15–18.

Inwards CY, Unni KK, Beabout JW, Sim FH. Desmoplastic fibroma of bone. *Cancer* 1991;68:1978–1983.

Ishida T, Dorfman HD. Massive chondroid differentiation in fibrous dysplasia of bone (fibrocartilaginous dysplasia). *Am J Surg Pathol* 1993;17:924–930.

Iwasko N, Steinbach LS, Disler D, et al. Imaging findings in Mazabraud's syndrome: seven new cases. *Skeletal Radiol* 2002;31:81–87.

Jaffe HL. Fibrous cortical defect and non-ossifying fibroma. In: *Tumors and tumorous conditions of the bones and joints*. Philadelphia: Lea & Febiger; 1958:76–91.

Jaffe HL, Lichtenstein L. Non-osteogenic fibroma of bone. *Am J Pathol* 1942;18: 205–221.

Jee W-H, Choe B-Y, Kang H-S, et al. Nonossifying fibroma: characteristics at MR imaging with pathologic correlation. *Radiology* 1998;209:197–202.

Jee W-H, Choi K-H, Choe B-Y, Park J-M, Shinn K-S. Fibrous dysplasia: MR imaging characteristics with radiopathologic correlations. *Am J Roentgenol* 1996;167: 1523–1527.

Johnson CB, Gilbert EE, Gottlieb LI. Malignant transformation of polyostotic fibrous dysplasia. *South Med J* 1979;72:353–356.

Kahn LB. Adamantinoma, osteofibrous dysplasia and differentiated adamantinoma. *Skeletal Radiol* 2003;32:245–258.

Kaushik S, Smoker WRK, Frable WJ. Malignant transformation of fibrous dysplasia into chondroblastic osteosarcoma. *Skeletal Radiol* 2002;31:103–106.

Keeney GL, Unni KK, Beabout JW, Pritchard DJ. Adamantinoma of long bones. *Cancer* 1989;64:730–737.

Kempson RL. Ossifying fibroma of the long bones. A light and electron microscopic study. *Arch Pathol* 1966;82:218–233.

Khanna M, Delaney D, Tirabosco R, Saifuddin A. Osteofibrous dysplasia, osteofibrous dysplasia-like adamantinoma, and adamantinoma: correlation of radiological imaging features with surgical histology and assessment of the use of radiology in contributing to needle biopsy diagnosis. *Skeletal Radiol* 2008;37:1077–1084.

Kimmelstiel P, Rapp I. Cortical defect due to periosteal desmoids. *Bull Hosp Joint Dis* 1951;12:286–297.

Kransdorf MJ, Murphey MD. Case 12: Mazabraud syndrome. *Radiology* 1999;212: 129–132.

Kransdorf MJ, Murphey MD, Sweet DE. Liposclerosing myxofibrous tumor: a radiologic-pathologic-distinct fibro-osseous lesion of bone with a marked predilection for the intertrochanteric region of the femur. *Radiology* 1999;212:693–698.

Kransdorf MJ, Utz JA, Gilkey FW, Berrey BH. MR appearance of fibroxanthoma. *J Comput Assist Tomogr* 1988;12:612–615.

Kumar R, Madewell JE, Lindell MM, Swischuk LE. Fibrous lesions of bones. *Radiographics* 1990;10:237–256.

Kumar R, Swischuk LE, Madewell JE. Benign cortical defect: site for an avulsion fracture. *Skeletal Radiol* 1986;15:553–555.

Kyriakos M, McDonald DJ, Sundaram M. Fibrous dysplasia with cartilaginous differentiation ("fibrocartilaginous dysplasia"): a review, with an illustrative case followed for 18 years. *Skeletal Radiol* 2004;33:51–62.

Levine SM, Lambiase RE, Petchprapa CN. Cortical lesions of the tibia: characteristic appearances at conventional radiography. *Radiographics* 2003;23:157–177.

Lichtenstein L, Jaffe HL. Fibrous dysplasia of bone. *Arch Pathol* 1942;33:777–816.

Lichtman EA, Klein MJ. Case report 302. Desmoplastic fibroma of the proximal end of the left femur. *Skeletal Radiol* 1985;13:160–163.

Luna A, Martinez S, Bossen E. Magnetic resonance imaging of intramuscular myxoma with histological comparison and a review of the literature. *Skeletal Radiol* 2005;34:19–28.

Markel SF. Ossifying fibroma of long bone. *Am J Clin Pathol* 1978;69:91–97.

Matsuno T. Benign fibrous histiocytoma involving the ends of long bone. *Skeletal Radiol* 1990;19:561–566.

Mazabraud A, Semat P, Roze R. A propos de l'association de fibromyxomes des tissus mous à la dysplasie fibreuse des os. *Presse Med* 1967;75:2223–2228.

Mesiter P, Konrad E, Hohne N. Incidence and histological structure of the storiform pattern in benign and malignant fibrous histiocytomas. *Virchows Arch [A]* 1981;393:93–101.

Mirra JM. Fibrohistiocytic tumors of intramedullary origin. In: Mirra JM, Picci P, Gold RH, eds. *Bone tumors: clinical, pathologic, and radiologic correlations*. Philadelphia: Lea & Febiger; 1989:691–799.

Mirra JM, Gold RH. Fibrous dysplasia. In: Mirra JM, Picci P, Gold RH, eds. *Bone tumors*. Philadelphia: Lea & Febiger; 1989:191–226.

Mirra JM, Gold RH, Rand F. Disseminated nonossifying fibromas in association with café-au-lait spots (Jaffe-Campanacci Syndrome). *Clin Orthop* 1982;168:192–205.

Moser RP Jr, Sweet DE, Haseman DB, Madewell JE. Multiple skeletal fibroxanthomas: radiologic-pathologic correlation of 72 cases. *Skeletal Radiol* 1987;16:353–359.

Mulder JD, Schütte HE, Kroon HM, Taconis WK. *Radiologic atlas of bone tumors*. Amsterdam, the Netherlands: Elsevier; 1993:607–625.

Park Y, Unni KK, McLeod RA, Pritchard DJ. Osteofibrous dysplasia: clinicopathologic study of 80 cases. *Hum Pathol* 1993;24:1339–1347.

Pennes DR, Braunstein EM, Glazer GM. Computed tomography of cortical desmoid. *Skeletal Radiol* 1984;12:40–42.

Rabhan WN, Rosai J. Desmoplastic fibroma. Report of ten cases and review of the literature. *J Bone J Surg [Am]* 1968;50A:487–502.

Ragsdale BD. Polymorphic fibro-osseous lesions of bone: an almost site-specific diagnostic problem of the proximal femur. *Hum Pathol* 1993;24:505–512.

Resnick D, Greenway G. Distal femoral cortical defects, irregularities, and excavations: A critical review of the literature with the addition of histologic and paleopathologic data. *Radiology* 1982;143:345–354.

Riley GM, Greenspan A, Poirier VC. Fibrous dysplasia of a parietal bone. *J Comput Assist Tomogr* 1997;21:41–43.

Ritschl P, Hajek PC, Pechmann U. Fibrous metaphyseal defects. Magnetic resonance imaging appearances. *Skeletal Radiol* 1989;18:253–259.

Ritschl P, Karnel F, Hajek PC. Fibrous metaphyseal defects—determination of their origin and natural history using a radiomorphological study. *Skeletal Radiol* 1988;17:8–15.

Ruggieri P, Sim FH, Bond JA, Unni KK. Malignancies in fibrous dysplasia. *Cancer* 1994;73:1411–1424.

Schajowicz F. Histological typing of bone tumors. *World Health Organization International Histological Classification of Tumors.* Berlin, Germany: Springer-Verlag; 1993.

Schajowicz F. *Tumors and tumorlike lesions of bone. Pathology, radiology, and treatment,* 2nd ed. Berlin, Germany: Springer-Verlag; 1994.

Schajowicz F, Sissons HA, Sobin LH. The World Health Organization's histologic classification of bone tumors. A commentary on the second edition. *Cancer* 1995;75:1208–1214.

Schwartz AM, Ramos RM. Neurofibromatosis and multiple nonossifying fibroma. *Am J Roentgenol* 1980;135:617–619.

Schwartz DT, Alpert M. The malignant transformation of fibrous dysplasia. *Am J Med Sci* 1964;247:1–20.

Selby S. Metaphyseal cortical defects in the tubular bones of growing children. *J Bone Joint Surg [Am]* 1961;43A:395–400.

Shelton III CH, Nimityongskul P, Richardson PH, Brogdon BG. Progressive painful bowing of the right leg. *Acad Radiol* 1995;2:351–353.

Singnurkar A, Phancao JP, Chatha DS, Stern J. The appearance of Mazabraud's syndrome on 18F-FDG PET/CT. *Skeletal Radiol* 2007;36:1085–1089.

Sissons HA, Kancherla PL, Lehman WB. Ossifying fibroma of bone. Report of two cases. *Bull Hosp Joint Dis Orthop Inst* 1983;43:1–14.

Spjut HJ, Dorfman HD, Fechner RE, Ackerman LV. *Tumors of bone pathology. Atlas of tumor pathology,* 2nd series, Fascicle 5. Washington, DC: Armed Forces Institute of Pathology; 1971:249–292.

Springfield DS, Rosenberg AE, Mankin HJ, Mindell ER. Relationship between osteofibrous dysplasia and adamantinoma. *Clin Orthop* 1994;309:234–244.

Steiner GC. Fibrous cortical defect and non-ossifying fibroma of bone: a study of the ultrastructure. *Arch Pathol* 1974;97:205–210.

Sugiura I. Desmoplastic fibroma. Case report and review of the literature. *J Bone Joint Surg [Am]* 1976;58A:126–130.

Sundaram M, McDonald DJ, Merenda G. Intramuscular myxoma: a rare but important association with fibrous dysplasia of bone. *Am J Roentgenol* 1989;153:107–108.

Sweet DE, Vinh TN, Devaney K. Cortical osteofibrous dysplasia of long bone and its relationship to adamantinoma. *Am J Surg Pathol* 1992;16:282–290.

Taconis WK, Schütte HE, van der Heul RO. Desmoplastic fibroma of bone: a report of 18 cases. *Skeletal Radiol* 1994;23:283–288.

Totty WG, Murphy WA, Lee JKT. Soft tissue tumors: MR imaging. *Radiology* 1986;160:135–141.

Ueda Y, Blasius S, Edel G, Wuisman P, Bocker W, Roessner A. Osteofibrous dysplasia of long bones—a reactive process to adamantinomatous tissue. *J Cancer Clin Oncol* 1992;118:152–156.

Unni KK. Fibrous and fibrohistiocytic lesions of bone. *Semin Orthop* 1991;6:177–186.

Unni KK, Dahlin DC, Beabout JW, Ivins JC. Adamantinoma of long bones. *Cancer* 1974;34:1796–1805.

Utz JA, Kransdorf MJ, Jelinek JS, Moser RP, Berrey BH. MR appearance of fibrous dysplasia. *J Comput Assist Tomogr* 1989;13:845–851.

Vanhoenacker FM, Hauben E, De Beuckeleer LH, Willemen D, Van Marck E, De Schepper AM. Desmoplastic fibroma of bone: MRI features. *Skeletal Radiol* 2000;29:171–175.

Weiss SW, Dorfman HD. Adamantinoma of long bones. *Hum Pathol* 1977;8:141–153.

Wold LE. Fibrohistiocytic tumors of bone. In: Unni KK, ed. *Bone tumors.* New York: Churchill Livingstone; 1988:183–197.

Yabut SM, Kenan S, Sissons HA, Lewis MM. Malignant transformation of fibrous dysplasia. *Clin Orthop* 1988;228:281–289.

Yamazaki T, Maruoka S, Takahashi S, et al. MR findings of avulsive cortical irregularity of the distal femur. *Skeletal Radiol* 1995;24:43–46.

Young JWR, Aisner SC, Levine AM, Resnik CS, Dorfman HD. Computed tomography of desmoid tumors of bone: desmoplastic fibroma. *Skeletal Radiol* 1988;17:333–337.

Benign Tumors and Tumor-like Lesions IV

Miscellaneous Lesions

Simple Bone Cyst

The simple bone cyst (SBC), also called a unicameral bone cyst, is a tumor-like lesion of unknown cause, representing approximately 3% of all primary bone lesions. It has been attributed to a local disturbance of bone growth. Although the pathogenesis is still unclear, SBC appears to be reactive or developmental rather than represent a true neoplasm. More common in males than in females, it is ordinarily seen during the first two decades of life. The majority of SBCs are located in the proximal diaphysis of the humerus and femur, especially in patients younger than age 17 years. In older patients, the incidence of bone cysts in atypical sites such as the calcaneus, talus, and ilium increases significantly (Fig. 20.1). The clinical symptoms include pain, swelling, or stiffness at the nearest joint. A pathologic fracture is often the first sign of the lesion. Radiographically, SBC appears as a radiolucent, centrally located, well-circumscribed lesion with sclerotic margins (Figs. 20.2 to 20.5). There is no periosteal reaction, a feature distinguishing a SBC from an aneurysmal bone cyst (ABC), which invariably shows some degree of periosteal response; however, in the presence of pathologic fracture, there is periosteal reaction. Conventional radiography usually suffices to make a diagnosis. Magnetic resonance imaging (MRI) of SBC shows the signal characteristics of fluid: a low-to-intermediate signal on T1-weighted images and a bright, homogeneous signal on T2 weighting (Fig. 20.6).

Histologically, SBC is a diagnosis of exclusion. A surgical curettage yields almost no solid tissue, but the walls of the cavity may show remnants of fibrous tissue or a flattened single-cell lining. The fluid content of the cyst contains elevated levels of alkaline phosphatase.

Complications and Differential Diagnosis

The most common complication of SBC is pathologic fracture, which occurs in approximately 66% of cases (Fig. 20.7). Occasionally, one can identify a piece of fractured cortex in the interior of the lesion—the "fallen fragment" sign—indicating that the lesion is either hollow or fluid filled, as most SBCs are. This sign permits the differentiation of a bone cyst, particularly in a slender bone, such as the fibula (Fig. 20.8), from other radiolucent, radiographically similar lesions containing solid fibrous or cartilaginous tissue, such as fibrous dysplasia, nonossifying fibroma, or enchondroma (Fig. 20.9).

A bone abscess may occasionally mimic a SBC, particularly if located in the proximal humerus or proximal femur, the sites of predilection for SBCs. In such cases, the presence of a periosteal reaction and extension beyond the growth plate are important differentiating features favoring a bone abscess (Fig. 20.10). On rare occasions, an intraosseous ganglion may be mistaken for a SBC (Fig. 20.11).

Treatment

The treatment of SBCs is based on the premise that the induction of osteogenesis results in complete healing of the lesion. The simplest inducement for bone repair is fracture, but this alone is insufficient to obliterate the lesion completely, and SBCs usually do not disappear after spontaneous fracture. The most common treatment is curettage followed by grafting with small pieces of cancellous bone. With this procedure, however, there is a higher rate of recurrence in patients younger than age 10 years. Moreover, this approach may lead to damage to the growth plate, because most solitary bone cysts occur about the physis. Recently, Scaglietti reported treating bone cysts with simple injection of methylprednisolone acetate. In younger patients so treated, complete bone repair occurred more rapidly than in older patients, who sometimes had to be administered several injections.

Aneurysmal Bone Cyst

The term ABC was first used by Jaffe and Lichtenstein to describe two examples of blood-filled cyts in which tissue from the cyst wall contained conspicuous spaces, areas of hemosiderin deposition, giant cells, and occasional bone trabeculae. In a subsequent publication, Jaffe chose the designation ABC as a descriptive term for this lesion to emphasize the blown-out appearance. Although the cause of this lesion is unknown, alterations in local hemodynamics related to venous obstruction or arteriovenous fistula are believed to play an important role. Some investigators believe that the lesion is caused by a trauma. Dahlin and McLeod postulated that it may be similar to and related to other reactive nonneoplastic processes, such as giant-cell reparative granuloma or traumatic reactions observed in periosteum and bone. ABC may arise *de novo* in bone, in which case no recognizable preexisting lesion can be demonstrated in the tissue, or it may be associated with various benign (e.g., giant-cell tumor, osteoblastoma, chondroblastoma, chondromyxoid

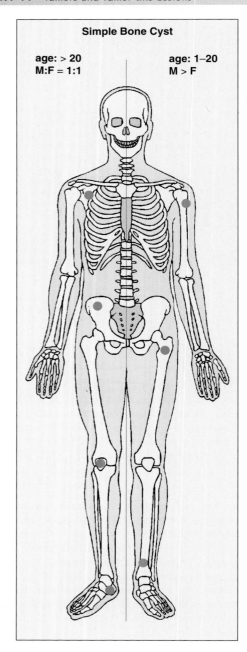

FIGURE 20.1 Skeletal sites of predilection, peak age range, and male-to-female ratio in SBC. The left half of the skeleton shows unusual sites of occurrence seen in an older patient population.

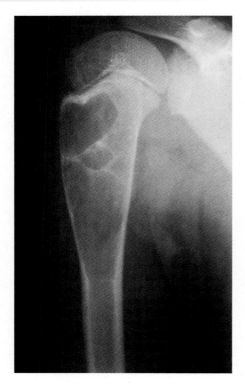

▲
FIGURE 20.2 Simple bone cyst. Anteroposterior radiograph of the right proximal humerus demonstrates the typical appearance of a SBC in a 6-year-old boy. Its location in the metaphysis and the proximal diaphysis of the humerus is also characteristic. The radiolucent lesion is centrally located and shows pseudosepta. Note the slight thinning of the cortex and lack of periosteal reaction.

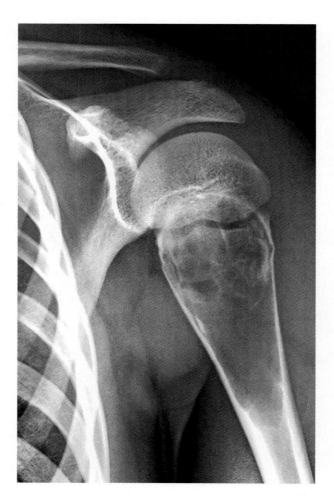

▲
FIGURE 20.3 Simple bone cyst. Anteroposterior radiograph of the left shoulder of a 12-year-old boy shows a centrally located radiolucent lesion in the metadiaphysis of the humerus. The cortex is thin, and there is lack of periosteal reaction.

FIGURE 20.4 **Simple bone cyst.** Anteroposterior radiograph of the ▶
left hip of an 11-year-old girl shows characteristic features of this
lesion. Note the central location, narrow zone of transition, geographic type of bone destruction, pseudotrabeculation, and lack of
periosteal reaction.

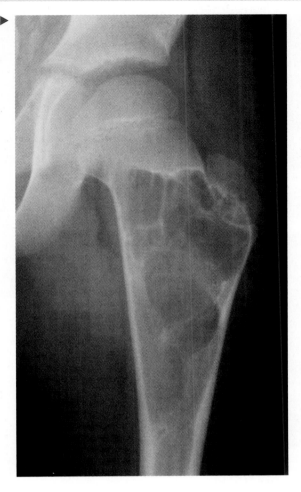

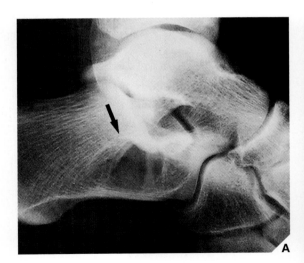

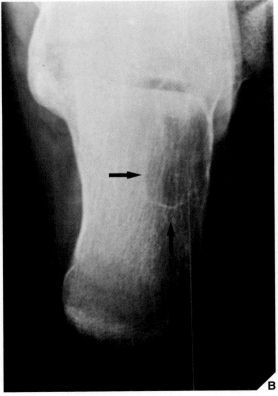

FIGURE 20.5 **Simple bone cyst.** Lateral radiograph of the hindfoot (**A**) and Harris-Beath view of the calcaneus (**B**) in a 32-year-old man show a SBC in the os
calcis (*arrows*). Typically, bone cysts occurring at this site are located in the anterolateral aspect of the bone, as shown here.

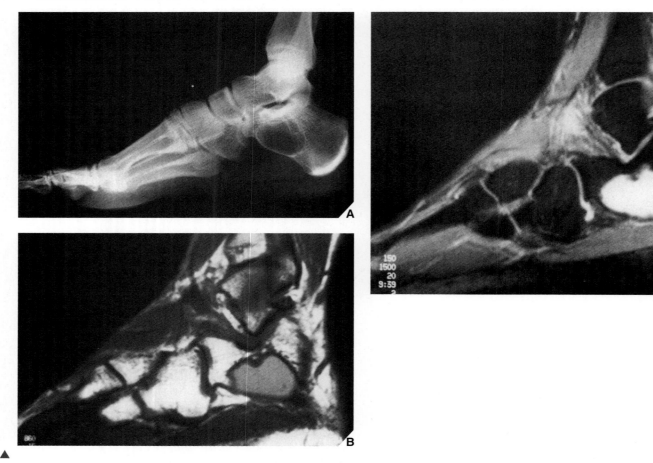

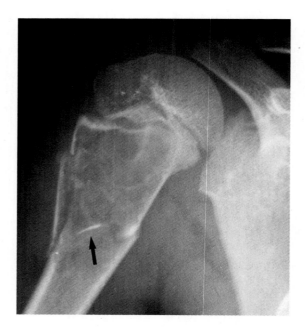

▲
FIGURE 20.6 **MRI of simple bone cyst. (A)** Lateral radiograph of the foot of an 18-year-old man shows a radiolucent lesion in the calcaneus with a slightly sclerotic border. **(B)** Sagittal T1-weighted (SE; TR 850/TE 15 msec) MR image demonstrates homogeneous intermediate signal intensity within the lesion, rimmed by low signal intensity sclerotic margin. **(C)** Sagittal STIR MR image shows that the lesion now is of homogeneous high signal intensity. (From Greenfield GB, Arrington JA, 1995, with permission.)

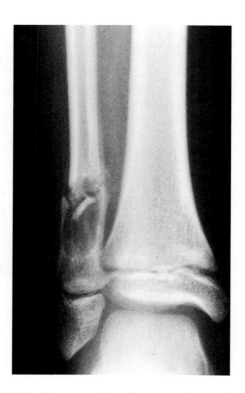

▲
FIGURE 20.7 **SBC with pathologic fracture.** One of the most common complications of SBC is pathologic fracture, as seen here in the proximal humeral metadiaphysis in a 6-year-old boy. The presence of the "fallen fragment" sign (*arrow*) is characteristic of a SBC.

▲
FIGURE 20.8 **Fallen-fragment sign.** Anteroposterior radiograph demonstrates a radiolucent lesion in the distal diaphysis of the right fibula of a 5-year-old boy who sustained mild injury to the lower leg. Note the pathologic fracture through the lesion and the associated periosteal reaction. A radiodense cortical fragment in the center of the lesion represents the "fallen fragment" sign, identifying this lesion as a SBC.

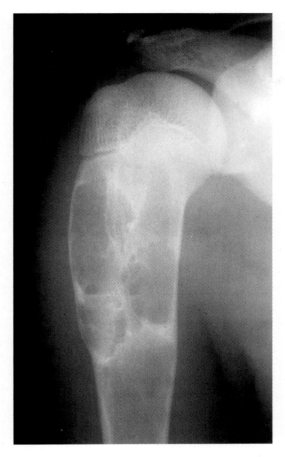

▲
FIGURE 20.9 **Nonossifying fibroma resembling a SBC.** Anteroposterior radiograph of the right shoulder of a 10-year-old boy shows a radiolucent lesion in the metadiaphyseal region of the humerus, slightly eccentric in location, with a narrow zone of transition and a geographic type of bone destruction. The lateral cortex is significantly thinned and bulging. The lesion was believed to be a SBC; however, excisional biopsy revealed a nonossifying fibroma.

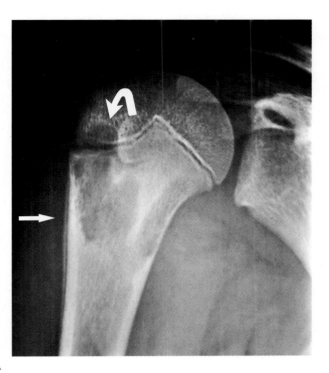

▲
FIGURE 20.10 **Bone abscess.** A bone abscess may mimic a SBC, as seen here in the proximal humerus of a 12-year-old boy. The periosteal reaction (*arrow*) in the absence of pathologic fracture and the extension of the lesion into the epiphysis (*curved arrow*) favor the diagnosis of bone abscess.

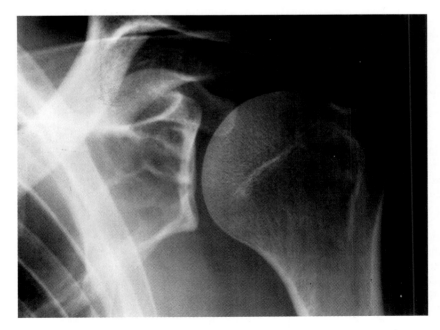

▲
FIGURE 20.11 **Intraosseous ganglion.** An 18-year-old woman presented with left shoulder pain. Anteroposterior radiograph shows a radiolucent, trabeculated lesion in the glenoid, with the appearance of a SBC. Excisional biopsy was consistent with an intraosseous ganglion (see also Fig. 16.28A).

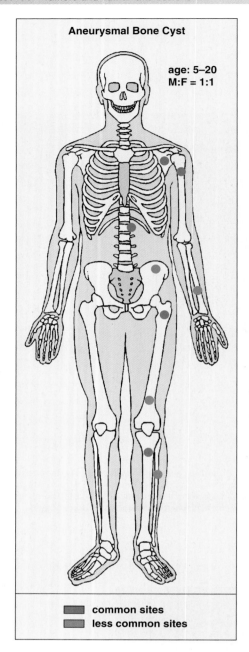

FIGURE 20.12 Skeletal sites of predilection, peak age range, and male-to-female ratio in ABC.

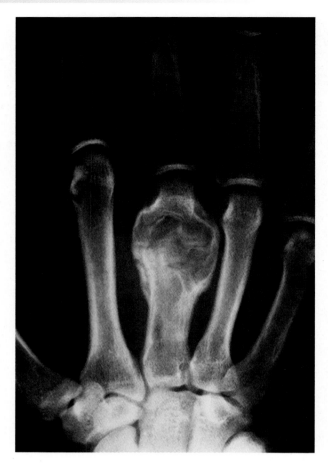

FIGURE 20.13 **Secondary ABC.** A 14-year-old boy had a painless swelling on the dorsum of the left hand. Dorsovolar film of the hand shows an expansive lesion in the distal segment of the third metacarpal. The lesion exhibits a well-organized periosteal reaction; the articular end of the bone is spared. Biopsy revealed an ABC engrafted on a monostotic focus of fibrous dysplasia

fibroma, fibrous dysplasia) and malignant (e.g., osteosarcoma, fibrosarcoma, or chondrosarcoma) lesions. The concept of ABC as a secondary phenomenon occurring in a preexisting lesion has been validated by several researchers. Some investigators, however, regard ABC as a reparative process, probably the result of trauma or tumor-induced anomalous vascular process.

ABC constitutes approximately 6% of the primary lesions of bone and is seen predominantly in children; 90% of these lesions occur in patients younger than age 20 years. The metaphysis of long bones is a frequent site of predilection, although ABCs may sometimes be seen in the diaphysis of a long bone, as well as in flat bones such as the scapula or pelvis and even in the vertebrae (Fig. 20.12). As already stated, these lesions can develop *de novo* or as a result of cystic changes in a preexisting lesion such as a chondroblastoma, osteoblastoma, giant cell tumor (GCT), or fibrous dysplasia (Fig. 20.13). The radiographic hallmark of an ABC is multicystic eccentric expansion (blow-out) of the bone, with a buttress or thin shell of periosteal response (Figs. 20.14 to 20.17). Although conventional radiographs usually suffice for evaluating the

lesion, computed tomography (CT), MRI, and radionuclide bone scan can be of further assistance. CT is particularly helpful in determining the integrity of the cortex (Fig. 20.17B, see also Fig. 20.19B). CT may also show internal ridges described on radiography as trabeculation or septation (Fig. 20.18). Fluid-fluid levels can also be demonstrated by this technique. These fluid levels are believed to represent the sedimentation of red blood cells and serum within the cystic cavities. To demonstrate this phenomenon, the patient must remain motionless for at least 10 minutes before scanning, and imaging must be performed in a plane perpendicular to the fluid levels.

MRI findings are rather characteristic and usually allow a specific diagnosis of ABC. These include a well-defined lesion, often with lobulated contours, cystic cavities with fluid–fluid levels, multiple internal septations, and an intact rim of low-intensity signal surrounding the lesion (Figs. 20.19 to 20.23). This rim has been described as an indicator of a benign process. The wide range of signal intensities within the cyst on T1- and T2-weighted sequences is probably caused by settling of degraded blood products and reflects intracystic hemorrhages of different ages.

Skeletal scintigraphy (see Fig.20.17C) may occasionally be helpful because it reflects the vascular nature of the lesion. Some investigators have reported an increased uptake of radiopharmaceutical in a ring-like pattern around the periphery of ABC. Although this phenomenon is not specific for the lesion (it can also be observed in SBC and in bone infarct), the scintigraphic findings corroborate the radiographic presentation. Hudson, in his experience with 25 patients with ABC who underwent skeletal scintigraphy using technetium-99m methylene diphosphonate (99mTc-MDP) and 99mTc-pyrophosphate, found a correlation between the histopathologic features of the lesion, the amount and type of fluid contained within the cyst, and the scintigraphic pattern or intensity of uptake.

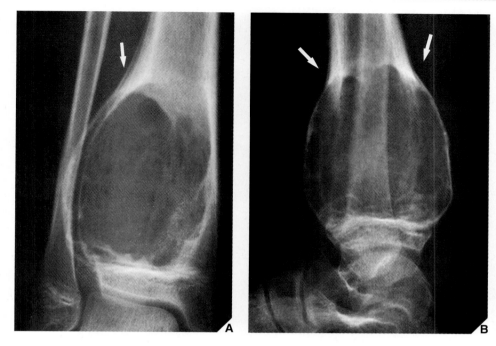

FIGURE 20.14 Aneurysmal bone cyst. Anteroposterior (**A**) and lateral (**B**) radiographs of the lower leg in an 8-year-old girl with a history of ankle pain demonstrate an expansive radiolucent lesion in the metaphysis of the distal tibia, extending into the diaphysis. Note its eccentric location in the bone and the buttress of periosteal response at the proximal aspect of the lesion (*arrows*).

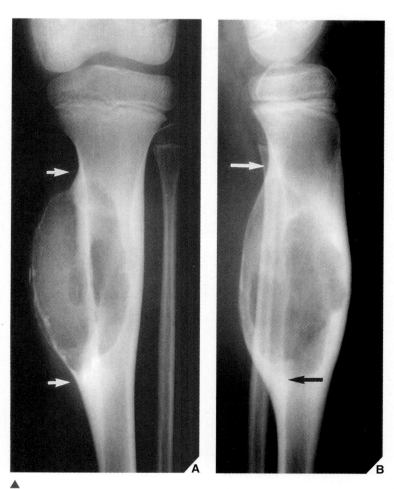

FIGURE 20.15 Aneurysmal bone cyst. Anteroposterior (**A**) and lateral (**B**) radiographs of the left proximal tibia of a 10-year-old girl show characteristic appearance of ABC, including eccentric location, expansive character, and a buttress of solid periosteal reaction proximally and distally (*arrows*).

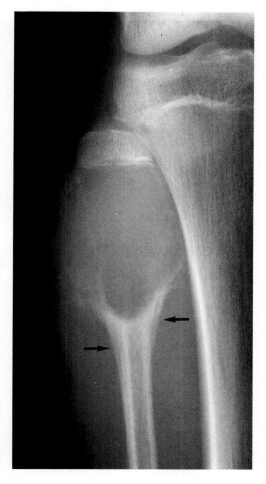

FIGURE 20.16 Aneurysmal bone cyst. A large, radiolucent expansive lesion in the proximal fibula of an 11-year-old girl reveals a buttress of periosteal reaction (*arrows*).

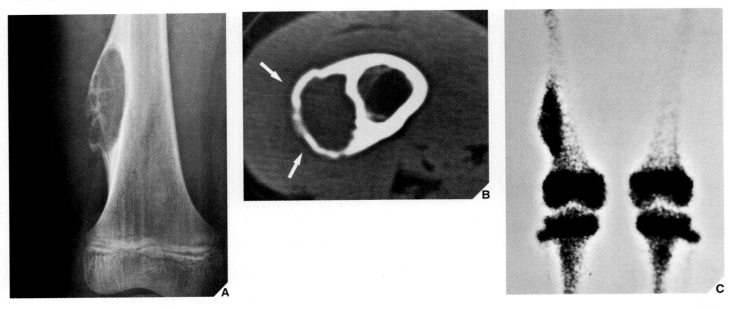

FIGURE 20.17 **Aneurysmal bone cyst. (A)** Radiograph of the distal femur of an 8-year-old boy with a 6-month history of pain in the lower right thigh demonstrates a radiolucent expansive lesion located eccentrically in the femur and buttressed proximally and distally by a solid periosteal reaction, radiographic features consistent with an ABC. **(B)** CT section shows its intracortical location; the lesion balloons out from the lateral aspect of the femur but is contained within a thin uninterrupted shell of periosteal new bone (*arrows*). **(C)** Radionuclide bone scan obtained after injection of 10 mCi (375 MBq) of ^{99m}Tc-labeled diphosphonate demonstrates increased uptake of radiopharmaceutical by the lesion.

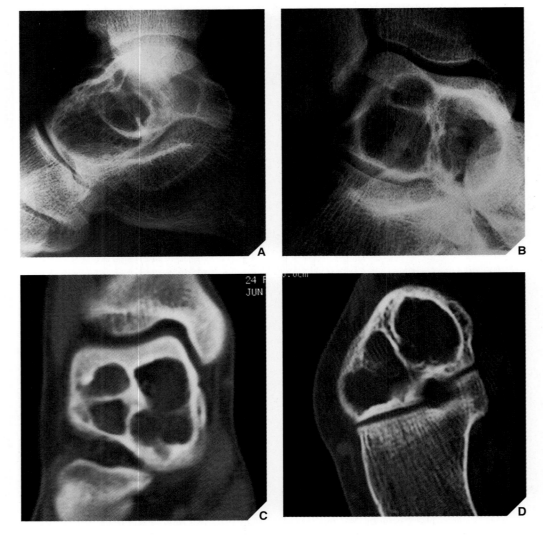

FIGURE 20.18 **CT of aneurysmal bone cyst.** Lateral **(A)** and oblique **(B)** radiographs of the right ankle of a 24-year-old woman show a radiolucent, trabeculated lesion in the talus. Coronal anterior **(C)** and coronal posterior **(D)** CT sections demonstrate the internal ridges of an ABC.

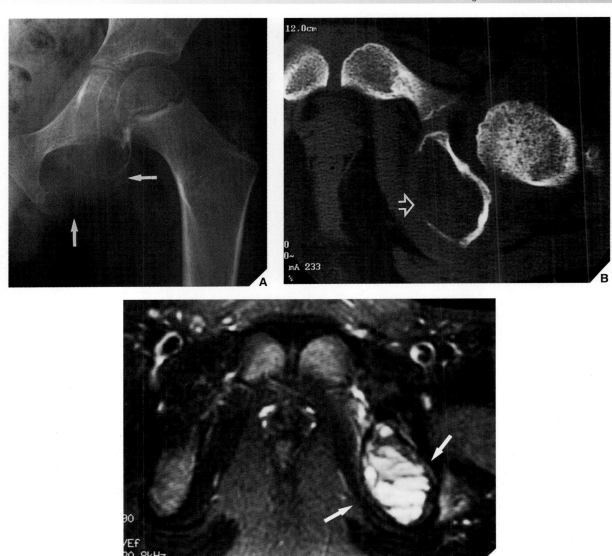

▲
FIGURE 20.19 MRI of aneurysmal bone cyst. (A) Anteroposterior radiograph of the left hip of a 4-year-old girl shows an expansive radiolucent lesion destroying the ischial bone (*arrows*). **(B)** CT section demonstrates that the lesion broke through the medial cortex (*open arrow*). **(C)** Axial T2-weighted MR image shows the lesion to be of high signal intensity (*arrows*). Multiple fluid-fluid levels characteristic of an ABC are well demonstrated.

Histologically, the ABC consists of multiple blood-filled sinusoid spaces alternating with more solid areas. The solid tissue is composed of fibrous elements containing numerous multinucleated giant cells and is richly vascular. The sinusoids have fibrous walls, often containing osteoid tissue or even mature bone. Focal or diffuse collections of hemosiderin or reactive foam cells may be seen in the fibrous septa.

Complications and Differential Diagnosis

The most common complication of an ABC is a pathologic fracture.

The conditions that should always be included in the differential diagnosis at any age are SBC, chondromyxoid fibroma, and GCT, which occurs after skeletal maturity when the lesion extends into the articular end of bone. The most critical points in differentiation of ABC from SBC are that the former is an eccentric, expansive lesion, invariably associated with some degree of periosteal reaction (usually a solid layer or solid buttress). The latter is a centrally located lesion, showing little if any expansion and exhibiting periosteal reaction only when a pathologic fracture has occurred. In thin bones, such as the ulna, fibula, metacarpals, or metatarsals, the characteristic eccentricity of ABC may be lost and, conversely, SBC may demonstrate expansive features (Fig. 20.24). Because the former contains solid tissue whereas SBC is a hollow structure filled with fluid, a fallen fragment sign (if present) is a good differential feature, pointing to the latter diagnosis. Chondromyxoid fibroma may be indistinguishable from ABC because

both lesions are eccentric, expansive, and usually affect the metaphysis, exhibiting a reactive sclerotic rim and the aforementioned solid periosteal reaction (usually in the form of a buttress). CT and MRI are sometimes effective in making this distinction if they identify fluid–fluid levels, a phenomenon that points to the diagnosis of ABC because chondromyxoid fibroma is a solid lesion. In the mature skeleton, GCT may closely mimic ABC, although it usually is not associated with a periosteal reaction and rarely exhibits a zone of reactive sclerosis. Giant cell reparative granuloma (so-called solid aneurysmal bone cyst) may be indistinguishable from the conventional ABC. This lesion, however, unlike true ABC, usually involves the short tubular bones of the hands and feet. The cortex is thin but is characteristically intact. Extension into the surrounding soft tissues is distinctly uncommon, and the periosteal reaction is usually absent (see later). In thinner bones, such as the fibula, metacarpals, or metatarsals, ABC caused by expansive growth may destroy the cortex, mimicking an aggressive tumor such as telangiectatic osteosarcoma. Conversely, it is important to remember that at times a telangiectatic osteosarcoma may masquerade as an ABC. Histopathologic differentiation is critical in these situations.

Treatment

The treatment for ABC consists of surgical removal of the entire lesion. At times, bone grafting to repair the resulting defect may be necessary

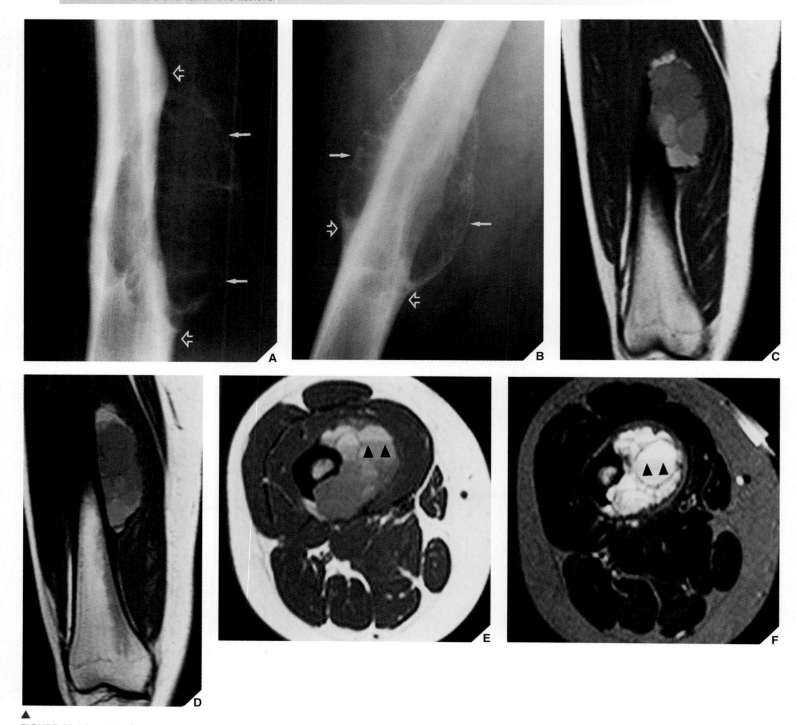

FIGURE 20.20   MRI of aneurysmal bone cyst. Anteroposterior (**A**) and lateral (**B**) radiographs of the midshaft of right femur of a 15-year-old girl show an expansive lesion arising eccentrically from the medial aspect of the bone. Note a thin shell of periosteal bone covering the lesion (*arrows*) and a buttress of periosteal reaction at its proximal and distal extent (*open arrows*), characteristic for ABC. (**C,D**) Coronal T1-weighted (SE; TR 600/TE 20 msec) MR images demonstrate heterogeneity of the lesion and internal septations. Axial T1-weighted (**E**) and T2-weighted (**F**) images show fluid-fluid levels (*arrowheads*).

(Fig. 20.25). Recently, percutaneous injections of Ethiblock, an alcoholic (ethanol) solution of corn protein which has thrombogenic and fibrogenic properties, have been advocated. Recurrence of the lesion, however, is frequent.

Solid Variant of ABC

In 1983, Sanerkin and colleagues described a variant of ABC in which the predominant histology was that of the solid components of a conventional ABC. The histopathologic appearance of this lesion was very similar to that of another condition, reported originally by Jaffe in 1953 and later by Lorenzo and Dorfman in 1980, that represented a nonneoplastic hemorrhagic process in bones, termed *giant cell reparative granuloma*. The terms *solid aneurysmal bone cyst* and *giant cell reparative granuloma* are now being used interchangeably. These lesions are considered reactive and nonneoplastic, although they can lead to a mistaken diagnosis of malignancy. Although these lesions are seen primarily in craniofacial and short tubular bones of the hands and feet, they may also occur in the long bones, such as femur, tibia, and ulna. Radiography reveals that most of these lesions are expansive and eccentric in location, with variably aggressive features. At times, there is a thin shell of periosteal reaction indistinguishable from conventional ABC. MRI findings are variable, but most lesions show intermediate signal intensity on T1-weighted images, with heterogeneous but predominantly high signal intensity on T2 weighting (Fig. 20.26).

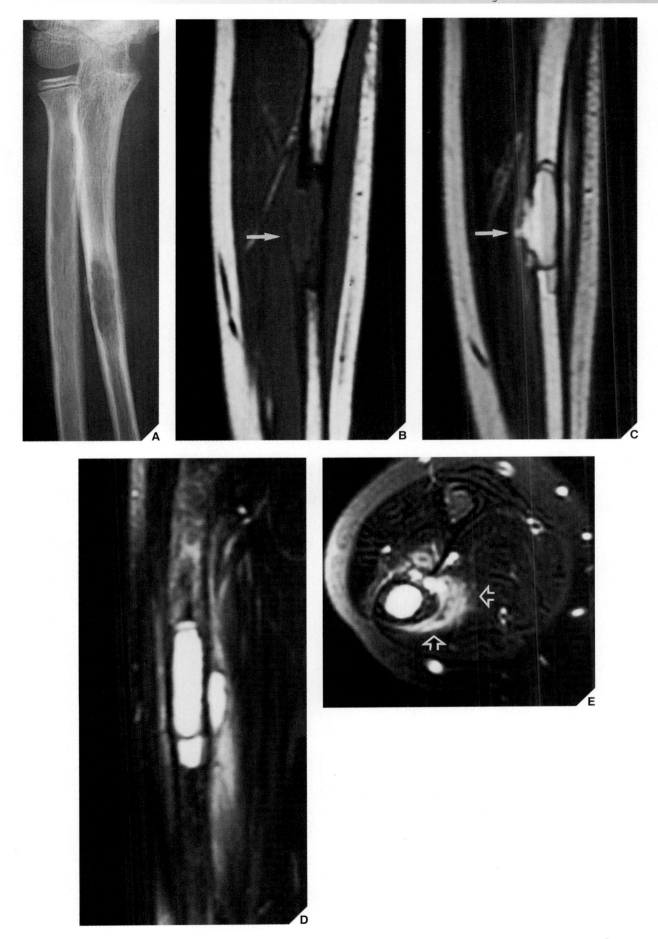

▲
FIGURE 20.21   **MRI of aneurysmal bone cyst. (A)** Radiograph of the right forearm of a 10-year-old boy shows a radiolucent lesion in the middiaphysis of the ulna exhibiting a narrow zone of transition and periosteal reaction. **(B)** Coronal T1-weighted MR image shows expansive lesion of low signal intensity (*arrow*). **(C)** Coronal proton density-weighted MR image shows soft-tissue extension (*arrow*). **(D)** Sagittal T2-weighted image demonstrates high signal of fluid and internal septa. **(E)** Axial T2-weighted image shows cortical breakthrough and soft-tissue extension of the lesion and peritumoral edema (*open arrows*).

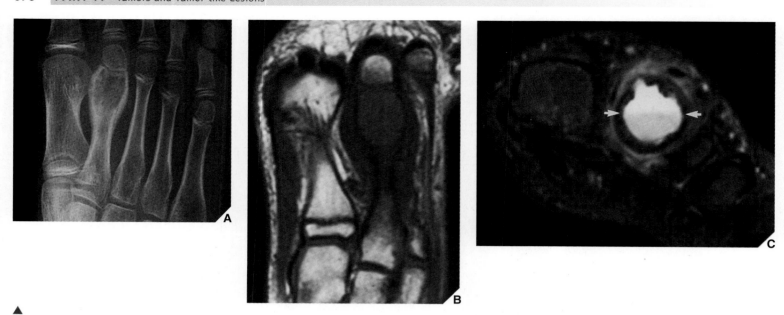

▲
FIGURE 20.22 MRI of aneurysmal bone cyst. A 10-year-old boy presented with left foot pain for the previous 3 weeks. **(A)** Radiograph shows an expansive lesion of the second metatarsal abutting the growth plate, associated with well-organized periosteal reaction. **(B)** Axial T1-weighted (SE; TR 500/TE 17 msec) MR image shows the lesion to exhibit an intermediate to low signal intensity. **(C)** Coronal T2-weighted (FSE; TR 4500/TE 75 msec/Ef) image shows the lesion to become bright. Fluid–fluid level (*arrows*) is a typical finding in an ABC.

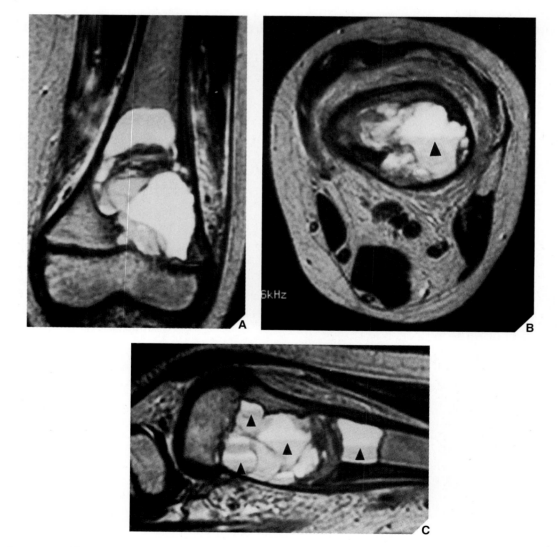

▲
FIGURE 20.23 MRI of aneurysmal bone cyst. (A) Coronal T2-weighted (FSE; TR 2583/TE 110 msec/Ef) MR image of a distal femur in a 5-year-old girl shows a lesion extending into the growth plate that is heterogeneous in appearance. Axial **(B)** and sagittal **(C)** T2-weighted images demonstrate multiple fluid–fluid levels (*arrowheads*).

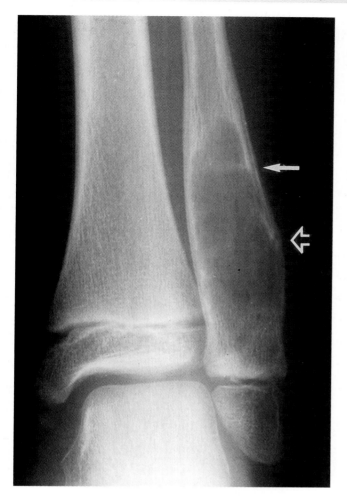

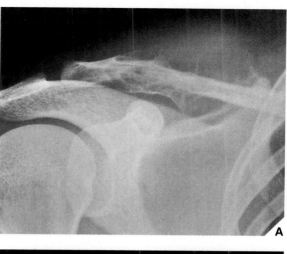

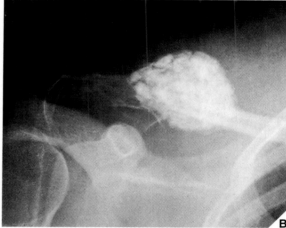

▲
FIGURE 20.24 **SBC mimicking ABC.** A radiolucent expansive lesion in the distal fibula of an 8-year-old girl exhibits periosteal reaction (*arrow*) secondary to a healing pathologic fracture (*open arrow*). Although diagnosis of an ABC was suggested, the excision biopsy was consistent with a SBC.

▲
FIGURE 20.25 **Aneurysmal bone cyst. (A)** Anteroposterior radiograph of the shoulder of a 19-year-old woman shows a lesion in the right clavicle that was diagnosed on biopsy as an ABC. **(B)** The lesion was treated with curettage and the application of cancellous bone chips.

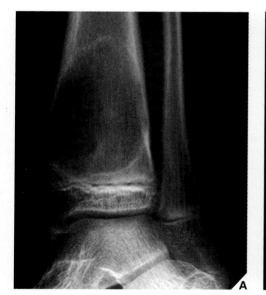

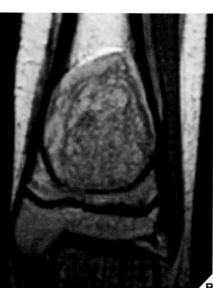

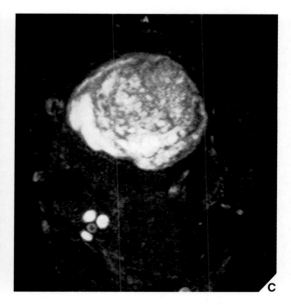

▲
FIGURE 20.26 **Solid variant of ABC. (A)** Oblique radiograph of the left ankle of an 11-year-old girl shows a sharply marginated radiolucent lesion in the meta-diaphysis of the tibia. **(B)** On coronal T1-weighted MR image, the lesion exhibits intermediate heterogeneous signal intensity. **(C)** On axial T2-weighted MRI, the lesion exhibits heterogeneous but predominantly high signal intensity. (Reprinted from Greenspan A et al., 2007.)

The areas of low signal on T2-weighted sequences represent mineralization within the lesion. Histopathologic examination of these lesions reveals fibrous stroma, an admixture of spindle cells, and many multinucleated giant cells. Occasional formation of osteoid and even mature bone trabeculae can be noted. Vascular spaces and hemorrhagic areas are also present. Some of these lesions have a histologic appearance similar to that of the so-called brown tumors of hyperparathyroidism. Treatment of these lesions usually consists of curettage. The recurrence rate, as recently reported from the Rizzoli Institute in Bologna, Italy, is close to 24%, whereas the Mayo Clinic reports approximately 39%.

Giant Cell Tumor

Also known as osteoclastoma, a GCT of bone is an aggressive lesion characterized by richly vascularized tissue containing proliferating mononuclear stromal cells and numerous uniformly distributed giant cells of osteoclast type. It represents approximately 5% to 8.6% of all primary bone tumors and approximately 23% of benign bone tumors; it is the sixth most common primary osseous neoplasm. Sixty percent of these lesions occur in long bones, and almost all are localized to the articular end of the bone. Preferred sites include the proximal tibia, distal femur, distal radius, and proximal humerus (Fig. 20.27). GCTs are seen almost exclusively after skeletal maturity, when the growth plate is obliterated. Most patients are between ages 20 and 40 years, and there is a female predominance of 2:1.

Multifocal GCTs are rare, accounting for less than 1% of all cases of GCT of bone. They occur most commonly in patients with Paget disease. Multiple lesions can be discovered synchronously or metachronously. The preferential locations are skull and facial bones in Paget disease, and small bones of the hands and feet in other patients.

Clinical symptoms in patients with solitary lesions are nonspecific. They include pain (usually reduced by rest), local swelling, and limitation of range of motion in the adjacent joint. When a lesion is located in the spine, neurologic symptoms may be present.

The imaging features of a GCT are characteristic. It is a purely osteolytic, radiolucent lesion with narrow zone of transition lacking sclerotic margins, revealing geographic bone destruction and usually no periosteal reaction (Figs. 20.28 to 20.30). Scintigraphy may show more intense uptake of the tracer around the periphery of the lesion than within the lesion itself, which Hudson calls a "donut configuration," and is presumably caused by hyperemic changes in the bone surrounding the tumor. A soft-tissue mass may also be present, and CT or MRI is usually required for sufficient evaluation (Figs. 20.31 to 20.33). Approximately 5% of GCTs are malignant *de novo*. Having no characteristic imaging features, however, malignant lesions cannot be diagnosed radiologically (Figs. 20.34 and 20.35). It is also well known that benign GCT may evolve into a malignant lesion. Several authors have reported cases of malignant transformation of GCT of bone. In most cases, this transformation occurs after radiation therapy. Only a few cases have been reported of spontaneous malignant transformation after initial surgical therapy. Histologically, the secondary malignancies include malignant fibrous histiocytoma, fibrosarcoma, osteosarcoma, and undifferentiated sarcoma.

Histologically, a GCT is composed of a related dual population of mononuclear stromal cells and multinucleated giant cells. The tumor background contains varying amounts of collagen. Morphologically, the giant cells bear some resemblance to osteoclasts, and they display increased acid phosphatase activity.

Historically, the imaging appearance and staging of GCTs have not accurately reflected the ultimate clinical outcome, but nevertheless several investigators, including Enneking, Campanacci, and Bertoni, have developed staging systems based on imaging and histologic appearance of this tumor. The stage 1 lesion has an indolent radiographic and histologic appearance. The stage 2 lesion demonstrates a more aggressive radiographic appearance, with extensive remodeling

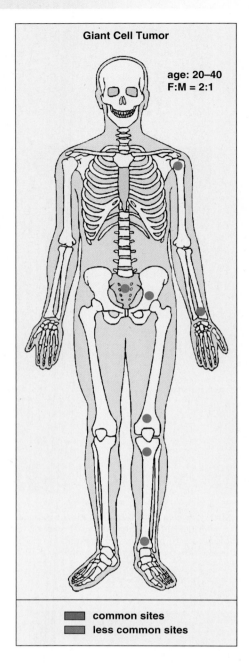

Giant Cell Tumor

age: 20–40
F:M = 2:1

common sites
less common sites

▲
FIGURE 20.27 Skeletal sites of predilection, peak age range, and male-to-female ratio in GCT.

of bone but intact periosteum and a benign histologic pattern. Stage 3 GCT reveals aggressive growth and extension into adjacent soft tissues but remains histologically benign, although distant metastases may occur.

Differential Diagnosis

Various lesions may be mistaken for GCT and, conversely, GCT can mimic other lesions that affect the articular end of a bone. Primary ABC rarely affects the articular end of a bone and occurs in a younger age group. However, after obliteration of the growth plate at skeletal maturity, this lesion may extend into the subarticular region of a long bone, becoming indistinguishable from a GCT. Occasionally, if the fluid–fluid level is demonstrated either on CT or on MRI examination, this feature is more consistent with ABC. However, it should be noted that ABC might sometimes coexist with other lesions, among them the GCT. The so-called solid ABC, or a giant cell reparative granuloma at the articular end, may have the same radiologic characteristics as a conventional GCT. Benign

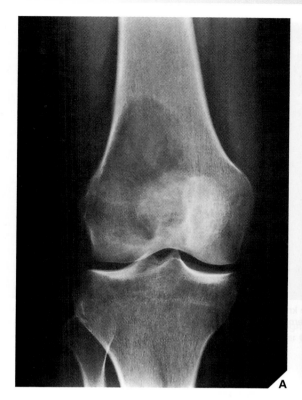
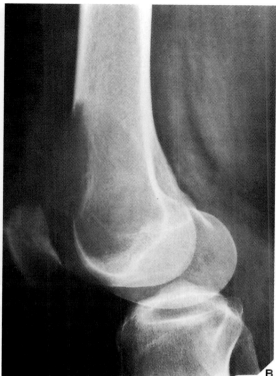

FIGURE 20.28 Giant cell tumor. Anteroposterior (**A**) and lateral (**B**) radiographs of the knee of a 32-year-old man demonstrate a purely osteolytic lesion in the distal end of the femur. Note its eccentric location, the absence of reactive sclerosis, and the extension of the lesion into the articular end of the bone, all characteristic features of GCT.

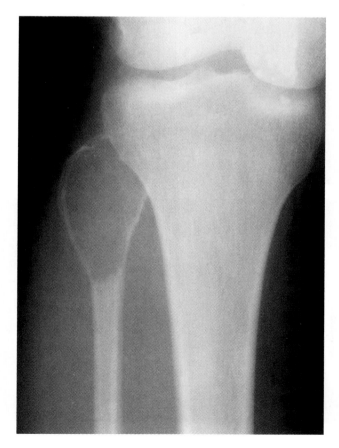
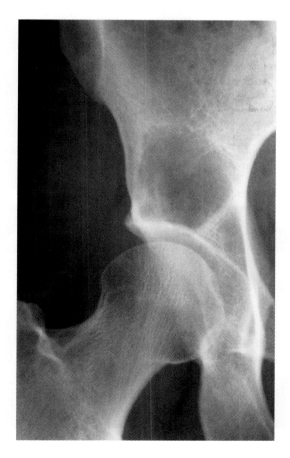

FIGURE 20.29 Giant cell tumor. Anteroposterior radiograph of the right knee in a 28-year-old woman shows an expansive radiolucent lesion in the head of the fibula.

FIGURE 20.30 Giant cell tumor. Anteroposterior radiograph of the right hip in a 31-year-old woman shows a radiolucent lesion in the supraacetabular portion of the ilium, with a narrow zone of transition and a geographic type of bone destruction.

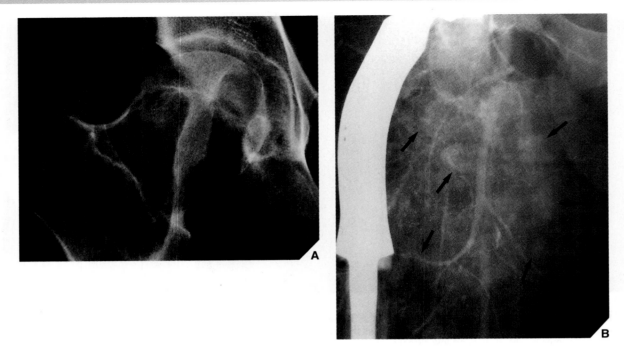

▲
FIGURE 20.35   **Complication of GCT.** A 28-year-old man had a 4-month history of right hip pain. **(A)** Anteroposterior radiograph of the hip shows a destructive radiolucent lesion involving the medial aspect of the femoral head and extending into the femoral neck. Biopsy revealed an ABC. Five months after curettage and packing of the cavity with cancellous bone chips, the lesion recurred. This time the histopathologic examination revealed a benign GCT with an engrafted ABC. The proximal femur was resected and an endoprosthesis was implanted. Eight months after this procedure, the patient was readmitted to the hospital with increased pain and a significant increase in the circumference of the thigh. **(B)** A femoral arteriogram demonstrates multiple soft-tissue nodules (*arrows*), which on biopsy proved to be metastases from the GCT. The patient also had pulmonary metastases.

Fibrocartilaginous Mesenchymoma

Fibrocartilaginous mesenchymoma is an extremely rare tumor composed of two distinct tissues, one benign and cartilaginous, resembling an active growth plate, and the other resembling a low-grade fibrosarcoma. Mirra and associates classify this lesion as desmoid tumor with enchondroma-like nodules. The number of reported cases is probably less than 20, although several unpublished cases may exist. Fibrocar-

tilaginous mesenchymoma has been reported in patients ranging from ages 9 to 23 years (mean age 13 years). Males were more frequently affected. The lesion is usually located in the epiphysis of a long bone, such as the fibula or humerus. The symptoms usually indicate a slow-growing tumor. They consist of slight discomfort and tenderness at the site of the lesion and occasionally a palpable mass.

On radiography, the lesion is radiolucent with scalloped borders, extending to or abutting the growth plate. After skeletal maturity, the

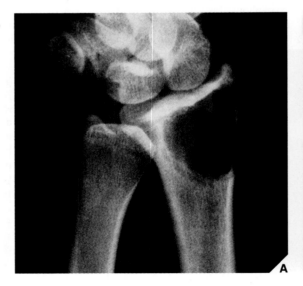

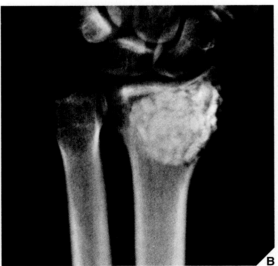

▲
FIGURE 20.36   **Treatment of GCT. (A)** Radiograph of the distal forearm of a 32-year-old woman shows a lytic lesion in the distal radius. **(B)** After extensive curettage, postoperative film shows application of bone chips.

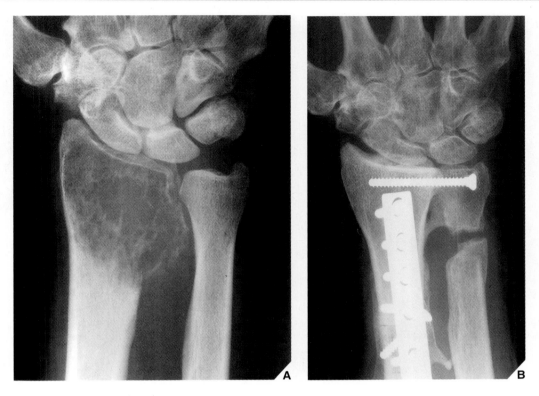

FIGURE 20.37   Treatment of GCT. (A) Dorsovolar radiograph of the left wrist of a 38-year-old woman shows the classic appearance of a GCT of the distal radius. **(B)** Treatment consisted of resection of the distal radius and application of an allograft. In addition, a Suavé-Kapandji procedure was performed, creating a pseudoarthrosis of the distal ulna and fusion of the distal radioulnar joint.

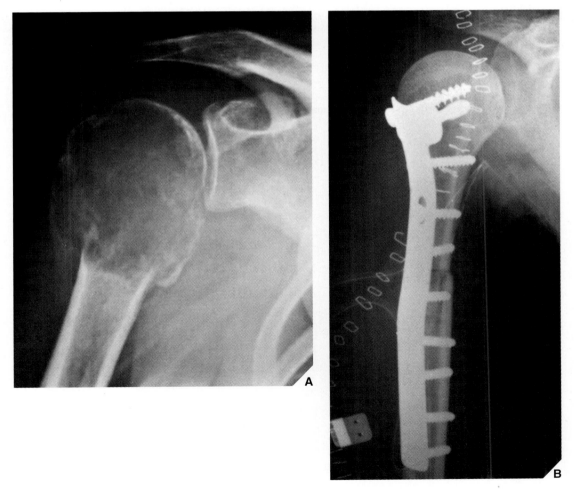

FIGURE 20.38   Treatment of GCT. (A) Anteroposterior radiograph of the right shoulder of a 27-year-old woman shows a GCT affecting almost the entire proximal end of the humerus. **(B)** Wide resection was performed and the humerus was reconstructed by means of allograft.

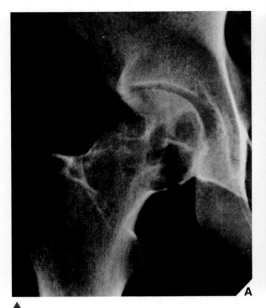
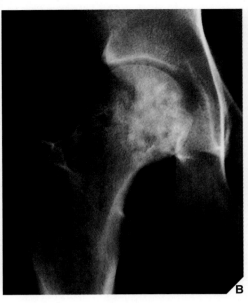
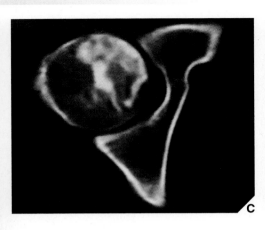

FIGURE 20.39   **Treatment of GCT. (A)** A 27-year-old woman was diagnosed with a GCT in the femoral head. **(B)** Two years after curettage and application of allograft there was no recurrence of the lesion. **(C)** CT demonstrates good incorporation of the graft into the normal bone (compare with Fig. 20.40).

lesion may extend into the articular end of bone (Fig. 20.41). Occasionally, the cortex is expanded and thinned. The cortex may be invaded, and in these cases, the lesion extends into the soft tissues (Fig. 20.42). This can be effectively demonstrated with CT and MRI. Although a periosteal reaction is usually absent, when present it is sparse and of benign appearance. The tumor may contain visible calcifications typical of cartilaginous matrix.

By microscopy, the lesion is composed of a tissue made of intersecting bundles of spindle cells and collagen fibers. The tissue is fairly cellular, the nuclei are plump, and there is evidence of pleomorphism and hyperchromatism, with occasional mitotic figures. Superimposed on this background are well-defined islands of obviously benign cartilage. In its first description, the tumor was named fibrocartilaginous mesenchymoma with low-grade malignancy. However, because metastases have never been observed thus far, the group at the Mayo Clinic later deleted that addition, simply calling it fibrocartilaginous mesenchymoma.

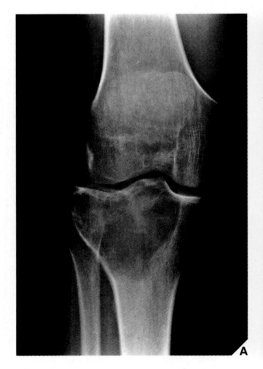
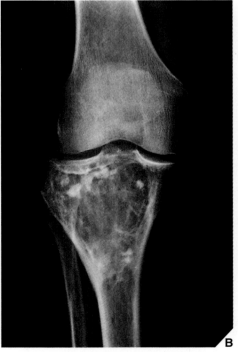

FIGURE 20.40   **Recurrence of GCT.** A 30-year-old woman had a GCT of the proximal end of the right tibia **(A)** and was subsequently treated with curettage and application of cancellous bone chips. Twenty months after surgery, she began to experience progressive knee pain. **(B)** Follow-up radiograph shows that most of the bone chips have been resorbed; the osteolytic foci indicate recurrence of the tumor.

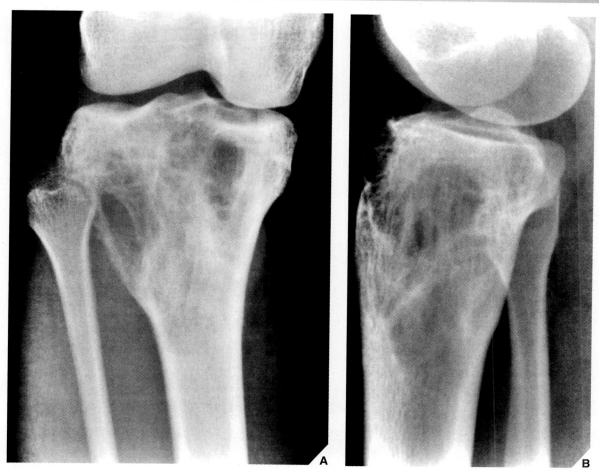

▲ **FIGURE 20.41** **Fibrocartilaginous mesenchymoma.** Anteroposterior (**A**) and lateral (**B**) radiographs of the right knee of a 23-year-old man show a radiolucent trabeculated lesion in the proximal tibia, bulging the anterolateral cortex and extending into the articular end of bone.

Hemangioma

A hemangioma is a benign bone lesion composed of newly formed blood vessels. It comprises approximately 2% of all benign and 0.8% of benign and malignant lesions of the skeletal system. Some investigators consider hemangiomas benign neoplasms; others put them into the category of congenital vascular malformations. They are classified, according to the type of vessels in the lesion, as capillary, cavernous, venous, or mixed.

Capillary hemangiomas are composed of small vessels that consist merely of a flat endothelium, surrounded only by a basal membrane. In bone, they most commonly occur in the vertebral body. *Cavernous hemangiomas* are composed of dilated, blood-filled spaces lined by the same flat endothelium with a basal membrane. Osseous cavernous hemangiomas most commonly involve the calvaria. *Venous hemangiomas* are composed of thick-walled vessels that possess a muscle layer. They frequently contain phleboliths. *Arteriovenous hemangiomas* are characterized by abnormal communications between arteries and veins. These are extremely rare in bone and almost exclusively involve the soft tissues. The biologic classification of vascular anomalies has recently gained renewed attention. Based on a system by Mulliken and Glowacki, who advocate regarding hemangiomas as hamartomas rather than true neoplasms, this classification takes into consideration cellular turnover and histology, as well as natural history

and physical findings. It clearly separates hemangiomas of infancy, with their early proliferative and later involutional stages, from vascular malformations, which are congenital lesions and are characterized as arterial, venous, capillary, lymphatic, or combined. However, epithelioid hemangiomas have been observed that apparently are true tumors.

The incidence of hemangiomas seems to increase with age and is most frequent after middle age. Women are affected twice as often as men. The most common sites are the spine, particularly the thoracic segment, and the skull (Fig. 20.43). In the spine, the lesion typically involves a vertebral body, although it may extend into the pedicle or lamina and, rarely, to the spinous process. Occasionally, multiple vertebrae may be affected. Most hemangiomas of the vertebral column are asymptomatic and discovered incidentally. Symptoms occur when the lesion in an affected vertebra compresses the nerve roots or spinal cord secondary to epidural extension. This neurologic complication is more commonly associated with lesions in the midthoracic spine (Fig. 20.44). Another mechanism considered responsible for compression of the cord, although seen less frequently, is fracture of the involved vertebral body with formation of an associated soft-tissue mass or hematoma.

Hemangioma is typified on imaging studies by the presence of multiloculated lytic foci (Fig. 20.45) or coarse vertical striations. In a vertebral body, this pattern is referred to as a "honeycomb" or "corduroy cloth"

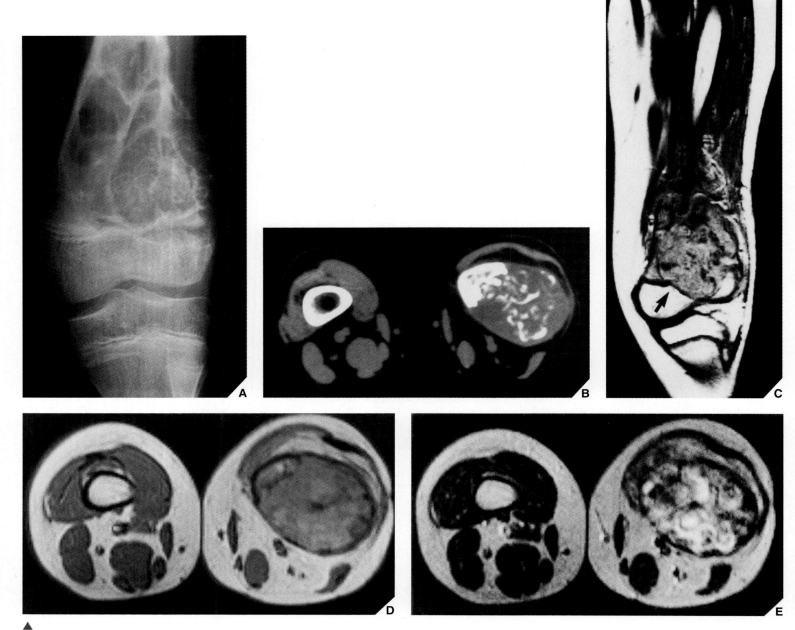

FIGURE 20.42   MRI of fibrocartilaginous mesenchymoma. (A) Oblique radiograph of the left knee of a 14-year-old boy shows an osteolytic trabeculated lesion in the distal femur abutting the growth plate. The lateral cortex is destroyed. **(B)** CT section through the tumor shows destruction of the posterolateral cortex and a large soft-tissue mass containing calcifications. **(C)** Coronal T1-weighted MRI shows heterogeneous signal of the tumor that violated the growth plate and extended into the distal femoral epiphysis (*arrow*). **(D)** Axial T1-weighted MR image shows destruction of the cortex and a large soft-tissue mass of intermediate signal. Calcifications within the mass display low signal intensity. **(E)** On axial T2-weighted MR image, the tumor becomes that of high signal intensity. Pseudoseptation of the mass and its heterogeneous character are well demonstrated. (Courtesy Prof. Dr. Wolfgang Remagen, Cologne, Germany.)

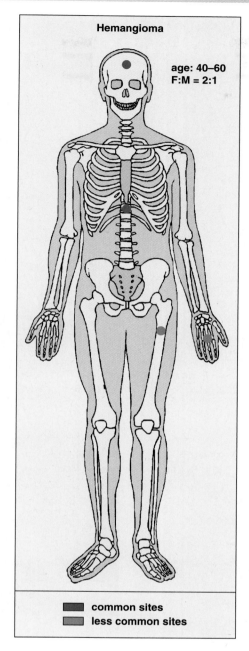

FIGURE 20.43   Skeletal sites of predilection, peak age range, and male-to-female ratio in hemangioma.

pattern, respectively (Fig. 20.46), and in the skull as a "spoke-wheel" configuration. When seen in the spine, this pattern is considered virtually pathognomonic for hemangioma. CT examination characteristically shows the pattern as multiple dots (often referred to as the "polka-dot" appearance), which represent a cross section of reinforced trabeculae (Fig. 20.47). On MRI, T1- and T2-weighted images usually reveal areas of a high-intensity signal that correspond to the vascular components (Fig. 20.48). Areas of trabecular thickening exhibit a low signal intensity regardless of the pulse sequence used. Both CT and MR images obtained after intravenous administration of contrast material demonstrate lesion's enhancement. In the long and short tubular bones, hemangiomas are recognized by a typical lace-like pattern and honeycombing (Fig. 20.49).

On scintigraphy, the appearance of osseous hemangiomas ranges from photopenia to a moderate increase in the uptake of radiopharmaceutical tracer. A recent study of planar images and single-photon emission computed tomography (SPECT) of vertebral hemangiomas and their correlation with MRI showed that in most cases, hemangiomas exhibited normal uptake on planar images. SPECT images were also normal, particularly if the lesions were less than 3 cm in diameter. This study also showed a disparity between SPECT images and MRI: there was no correlation between MRI signal intensity changes and patterns of uptake on bone imaging. Arteriography of the hemangioma is rarely indicated.

Histologically, most hemangiomas consist of simple endothelium-lined channels, morphologically identical with capillary endothelium.

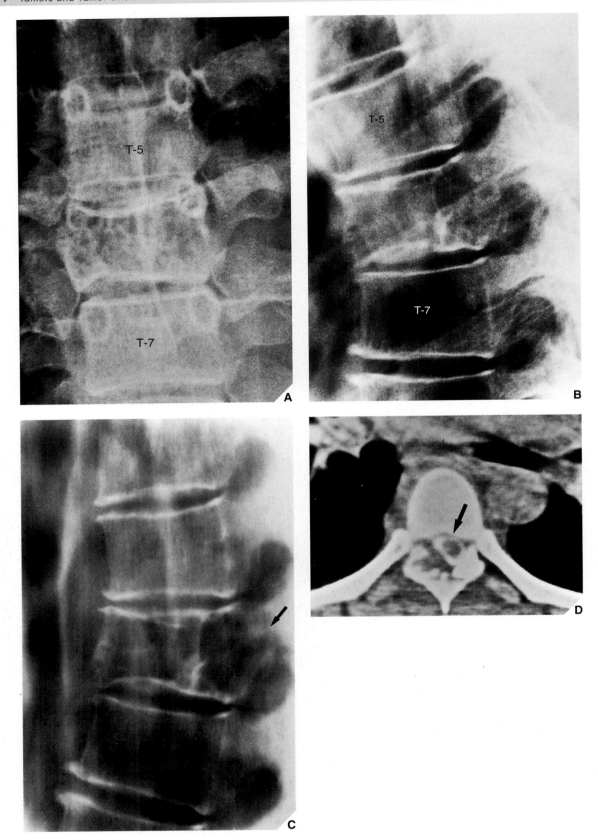

▲

FIGURE 20.44   **Vertebral hemangioma.** A 39-year-old woman presented with back pain and decreased sensation and strength in the right upper extremity. Anteroposterior (**A**) and lateral (**B**) radiographs of the thoracic spine show a radiolucent lesion involving the body of T6 and extending into the pedicle. (**C**) Lateral tomographic cut demonstrates ballooning of the posterior cortex of the vertebra and extension of the lesion into the posterior elements (*arrow*). (**D**) CT shows a soft-tissue mass encroaching on the spinal canal and displacing the spinal cord (*arrow*) (From Greenspan A et al., 1983, with permission).

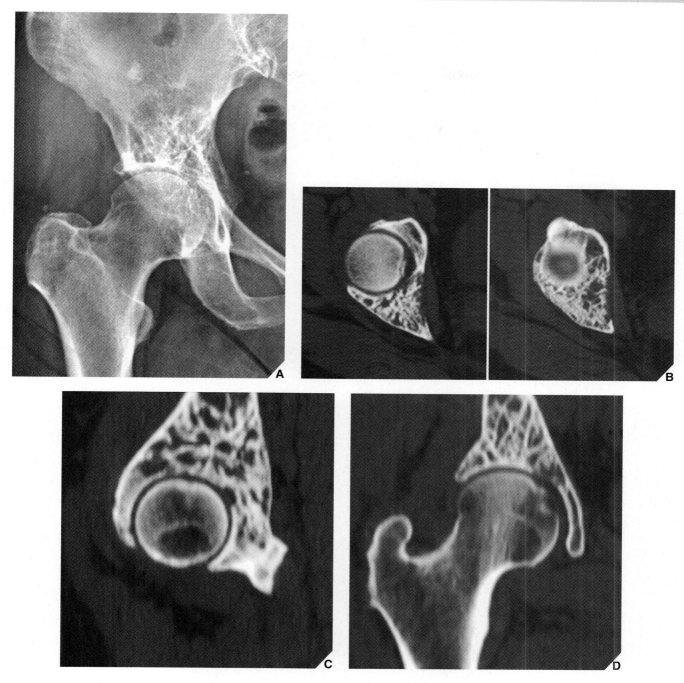

▲
FIGURE 20.45   **Hemangioma of the hip.** A 58-year-old woman presented with right hip pain on-and-off for 1 year. **(A)** Anteroposterior radiograph of the right hip shows mixed radiolucent and sclerotic lesion in the ilium extending into the acetabulum. **(B)** Axial CT sections, and **(C)** sagittal and **(D)** coronal reformatted CT images show a characteristic for hemangioma "honeycomb" pattern.

Some or all of the vascular channels may be enlarged and have a sinusoidal appearance, in which case the lesion is referred to as cavernous type. Occasionally, hemangiomas are composed of larger, thick-walled arteries or veins and resemble arteriovenous malformations of the soft tissues.

Epithelioid hemangioma is a variant of conventional hemangioma. It has been previously described as *angiolymphoid hyperplasia with eosinophilia* and as *histiocytoid hemangioma* because of its morphologic features. Although it most commonly affects skin and subcutaneous tissue, epithelioid hemangioma may also involve bones, with a predilection for the vertebrae. The radiographic features of this lesion include expansive lytic areas with well-defined lobulated borders and

marginal sclerosis. Rarely, the cortex is destroyed, causing formation of new periosteal bone. Histologically, as pointed out by Wenger and Wold, well-formed vessels with open lumina are observed, surrounded by multiple epithelioid endothelial cells with abundant eosinophilic cytoplasm. The vessels are usually of capillary size, and hemorrhage into the surrounding connective tissue may be present. The neighboring stroma may contain an inflammatory infiltrate. Occasionally, the histopathology of this lesion is similar to that of epithelioid hemangioendothelioma.

Diffuse involvement of bones by hemangiomatous lesions is defined as *hemangiomatosis* or *angiomatosis*. Occasionally, the soft tissues are also affected (Fig. 20.50). The imaging presentation of angiomatosis is that of lytic lesions, often with a honeycomb or latticework

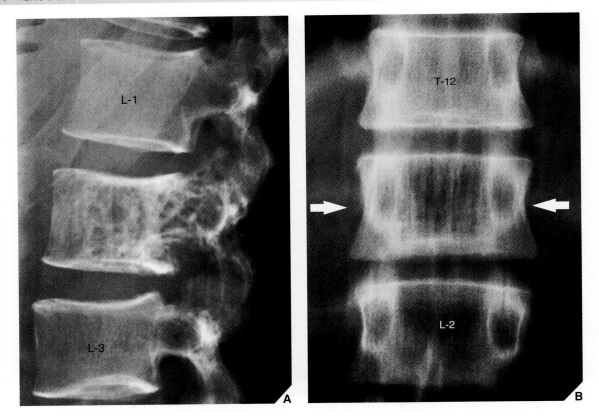

▲
FIGURE 20.46　**Vertebral hemangioma. (A)** Lateral radiograph of the lumbar spine demonstrates a "honeycomb" pattern of hemangioma of L2 vertebra. **(B)** Anteroposterior tomogram in another patient demonstrates vertical striations of hemangioma of L1 vertebra (*arrows*), referred to as a "corduroy cloth" pattern.

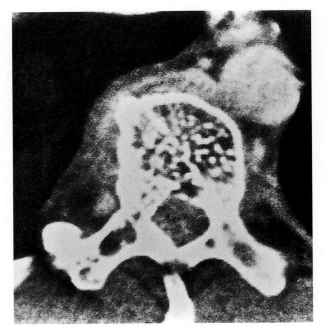

▲
FIGURE 20.47　**CT of vertebral hemangioma.** CT section of a T10 vertebra demonstrates coarse dots that indicate reinforced vertical trabeculae of the cancellous bone, characteristic of hemangioma.

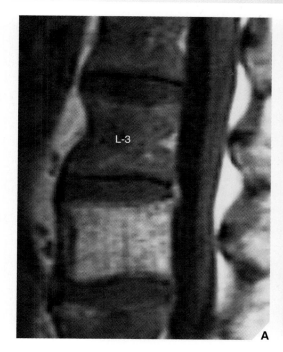
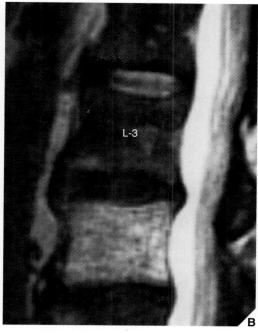

▲
FIGURE 20.48   **MRI of vertebral hemangioma. (A)** Sagittal T1-weighted (SE; TR 517/TE 12 msec) and **(B)** T2-weighted (SE;TR 2000/TE 80 msec) MR images show high signal intensity of hemangioma of L4 vertebra.

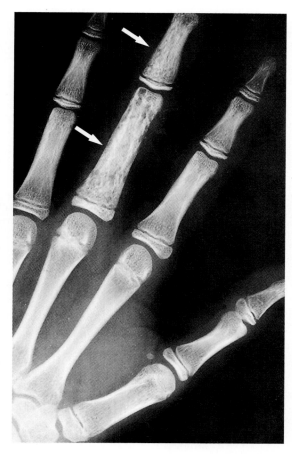

▲
FIGURE 20.49   **Hemangioma of a short tubular bone.** Dorsovolar view of the hand of an 11-year-old girl with hemangioma involving the middle finger shows the lace-like pattern and honeycombing characteristic of this lesion (*arrows*). Overgrowth of the digit, as seen here, is a frequent complication of hemangioma.

("hole-within-hole") appearance. When bone is extensively involved, the term *cystic angiomatosis* is applied. Some other terms used for this condition include diffuse skeletal hemangiomatosis, cystic lymphangiectasia, and hamartous hemolymphangiomatosis. Schajowicz postulated that cystic hemangiomatosis should be distinguished from diffuse angiomatosis because of their different radiologic and macroscopic aspects. This is a rare bone disorder characterized by diffuse cystic lesions of bone, frequently (60% to 70% of cases) associated with visceral involvement. Patients with cystic angiomatosis usually present in the first three decades. There is 2:1 male-to-female predominance. The bones affected are most often those of the axial skeleton, as well as the femur, humerus, tibia, radius, and fibula. The bone-related symptoms are usually secondary to pathologic fractures through the cystic lesions. Most of the symptoms, however, are related to visceral involvement. On radiography, the osseous lesions are usually osteolytic (Fig. 20.51), occasionally with a honeycomb appearance (Fig. 20.52). They are well defined and surrounded by a rim of sclerosis, and they vary in size (Fig. 20.53). Although medullary involvement predominates, cortical invasion, osseous expansion, and periosteal reaction can occur. Rarely, sclerotic lesions may be present, and in these instances, the condition may mimic osteoblastic metastases. On MRI, the lesions usually show intermediate signal intensity on T1-weighted images, and T2-weighted images with fat saturation show a mixture of high, intermediate, and low signal intensities. On histologic examination, cystic angiomatosis is characterized by cavernous angiomatous spaces, indistinguishable from benign hemangioma of bone.

A condition that must be distinguished from angiomatosis is *Gorham disease* of bone, also known as massive osteolysis, disappearing bone disease, and phantom bone disease. This entity is characterized by progressive, localized bone resorption, probably caused by multiple or diffuse cavernous hemangiomas or lymphangiomas of bone or by a combination of both. The radiographic presentation of Gorham disease consists of radiolucent areas in the cancellous bone or concentric destruction of the cortex, giving rise to a sucked-candy appearance. Eventually, the entire medullary cavity and the cortex are destroyed. On histologic examination,

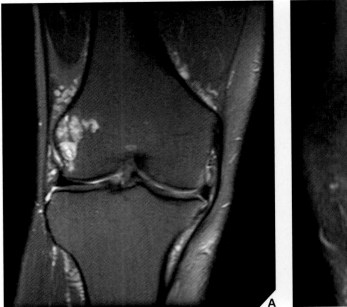
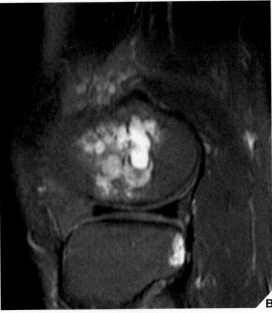

FIGURE 20.50 **Hemangiomatosis of bone and soft tissues.** A 51-year-old man presented with a vague pain and "fullness" of the right knee. **(A)** Coronal and **(B)** sagittal T2-weighted fat-suppressed MR images show high-signal-intensity multiple lesions affecting the osseous and soft-tissue structures of the knee.

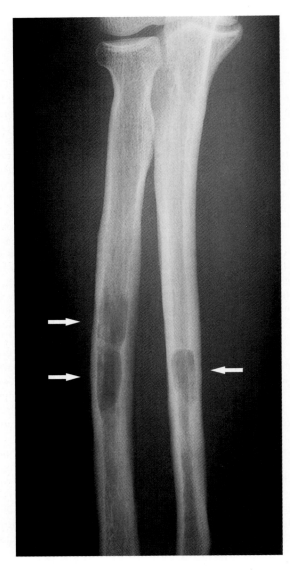

FIGURE 20.51 **Cystic angiomatosis.** Several osteolytic lesions (*arrows*) affect the shafts of the radius and ulna in this 25-year-old man.

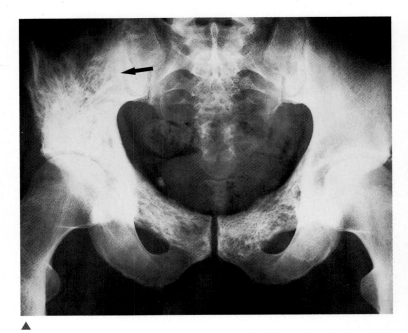

FIGURE 20.52 **Cystic angiomatosis.** A radiograph of the pelvis of a 28-year-old man shows a honeycomb pattern in the right ilium (*arrow*) and both pubic bones.

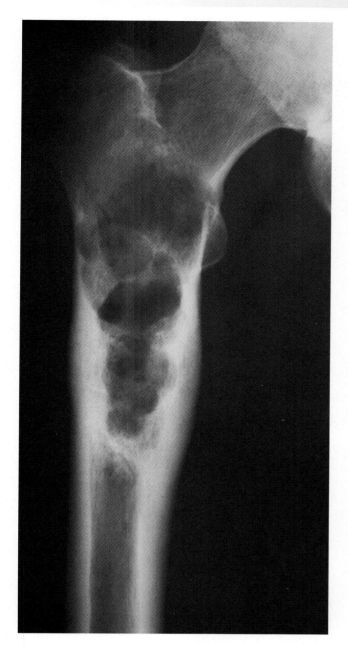

FIGURE 20.53 **Cystic angiomatosis.** Several confluent lesions with peripheral sclerosis and cortical thickening marked cystic angiomatosis in the right femur of a 20-year-old man.

a marked increase is observed in intraosseous capillaries, which form an anastomosing network of endothelium-lined channels that are usually filled with erythrocytes or serum. Although some investigators claim that there is no evidence of osteoclasts in areas of bone resorption, studies by Spieth and coworkers suggest that osteoclastic activity plays a role in the pathogenesis of Gorham disease.

Differential Diagnosis

The differential diagnosis of hemangioma, particularly in the spine, should include Paget disease, Langerhans cell histiocytosis (LCH), myeloma, and metastatic lesions. The characteristic "picture frame" appearance of a vertebra affected by Paget disease (see Fig. 29.5), as well as its larger than normal size, distinguishes it from hemangioma. Myeloma in a vertebra, unlike hemangioma, is purely radiolucent—as are most metastatic lesions—and shows no vertical striations.

Treatment

Asymptomatic hemangiomas do not require treatment. Symptomatic lesions are usually treated with radiation therapy to ablate the venous channels forming the lesions. Embolization, laminectomy, spinal fusion, or a combination of these is also used in treatment (see Fig. 16.18).

Intraosseous Lipoma

Lipomas can be categorized according to their location in the bone as intraosseous, cortical, or parosteal lesions. Intraosseous lipoma is considered to be an extremely rare tumor (with an incidence of less than 1 in 1,000 primary bone tumors). In recent years, an increasing number of reports of intraosseous lipoma have appeared, particularly located in the intertrochanteric and subtrochanteric regions of the femur and in the calcaneus. The tumor has no sex predilection and occurs in a wide range of ages, from 5 to 75 years. It is usually an asymptomatic lesion, found on imaging examinations performed for other reasons. Some investigators report a higher incidence of symptomatic patients; however, even when a patient is symptomatic, the symptoms are not necessarily related to the lesion. In the large series of 61 intraosseous lipomas reported by Milgram, the most common sites were the intertrochanteric and subtrochanteric regions of the femur, followed by the calcaneus, ilium, proximal tibia, and sacrum.

Intraosseous lipoma has a rather characteristic radiographic appearance. It is invariably a nonaggressive radiolucent lesion with sharply defined borders, associated with thinning and bulging of the cortex, particularly in thin bones such as fibula or rib. The central calcifications and ossifications are frequently present (Fig. 20.54). CT may be helpful in the diagnosis of these lesions because the Hounsfield units are consistent with fat. MRI shows the lesion to have a signal similar to subcutaneous fat on T1- and T2-weighted images (Fig. 20.55). A thin circumferential rim of low signal intensity on T1- and T2-weighted images, consistent with reactive sclerosis, is commonly present demarcating the margin of the fatty lesion. After administration of intravenous gadolinium, there is no enhancement of the lesion. MRI is highly effective in demonstrating the exact intraosseous extension of the lesion.

Histologically, intraosseous lipomas are composed of lobules of mature adipose tissue and are characterized by the presence of mature lipocytes, which are slightly larger than nonneoplastic fat cells, in a background of fibroblasts with occasional foci of fat necrosis. A capsule may occasionally encompass all or part of the tumor mass, and in most cases reported, atrophic bone trabeculae are found throughout the lesion.

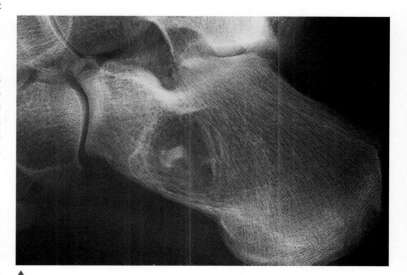

FIGURE 20.54 **Intraosseous lipoma.** Typical appearance of intraosseous lipoma in the calcaneus. Observe sharply marginated radiolucent lesion with central calcification.

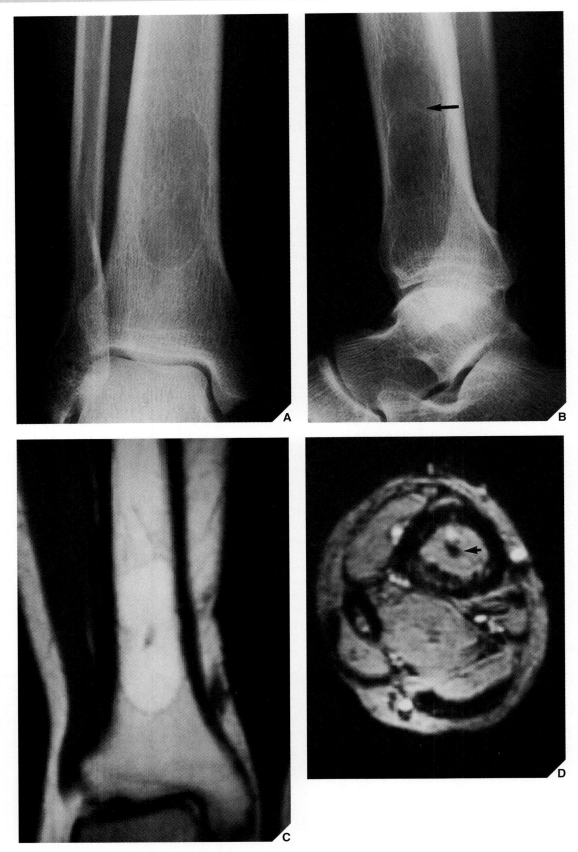

▲
FIGURE 20.55   **Intraosseous lipoma. (A)** Radiograph of the right lower leg in a 42-year-old man shows a radiolucent lesion in the distal tibia sharply delineated by a thin sclerotic margin. **(B)** On the lateral radiograph, there is a suggestion of a faint calcific body in the center of the lesion (*arrow*). **(C)** Coronal T1-weighted (SE; TR 685/TE 20 msec) MRI demonstrates the lesion to be of a high signal intensity paralleling that of subcutaneous fat and thus consistent with intraosseous lipoma. A small focus of low signal is present within the lesion, corresponding to a calcific body seen on the conventional radiography. **(D)** Axial T2-weighted (SE; TR 2000/TE 70 msec) MR image shows that the lesion becomes low in intensity, again paralleling the signal of subcutaneous fat. The central calcification exhibits low signal (*short arrow*).

Nonneoplastic Lesions Simulating Tumors

Some nonneoplastic conditions that may mimic bone tumors include intraosseous ganglion, a "brown tumor" of hyperparathyroidism, LCH, Chester-Erdheim disease, encystified bone infarct, and myositis ossificans.

Intraosseous Ganglion

This lesion of unknown cause is frequently encountered in adults between ages 20 and 60 years. It has a predilection for the articular ends of the long bones, usually the non–weight-bearing segment. Radiographically, it exhibits the characteristic picture of a round or oval radiolucent area located eccentrically in the bone and rimmed by a sclerotic margin (Fig. 20.56). Its appearance is very similar to that of a degenerative cyst, but the adjacent joint does not show any degenerative changes; in most cases, the ganglion, in contrast to a degenerative cyst, does not communicate with the joint cavity. An intraosseous ganglion may also mimic chondroblastoma, osteoblastoma, enchondroma, pigmented villonodular synovitis, or bone abscess (Fig. 20.57).

Brown Tumor of Hyperparathyroidism

Hyperparathyroidism is a condition resulting from the excess secretion of parathormone by overactive parathyroid glands (see Chapter 28). Not infrequently, patients with this disorder present with solitary or multiple lytic lesions, most commonly in the long and short tubular bones; on radiographic examination, the lesions may resemble a tumor (Fig. 20.58). This lesion is called a brown tumor because, in addition to fibrous tissue, it contains decomposing blood, which gives specimens obtained for pathologic examination a brown coloration. The correct diagnosis can be made on radiography by observing associated abnormalities, including a decrease in bone density (osteopenia); subperiosteal bone resorption, which is best seen on the radial aspect of the proximal and middle phalanges of the second and third fingers; a granular "salt-and-pepper" appearance of the cranial vault; resorption of the acromial ends of the clavicles; and soft-tissue calcifications. Because of disturbed calcium and phosphorus metabolism, the serum calcium concentration is usually high (hypercalcemia) and the serum phosphorus concentration low (hypophosphatemia), which are laboratory findings that usually confirm the diagnosis.

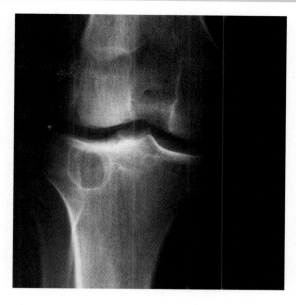

▲ **FIGURE 20.56 Intraosseous ganglion.** A 28-year-old man sustained an injury to the right knee that tore the lateral meniscus. Anteroposterior radiograph of the knee discloses an eccentric radiolucent lesion in the articular end of the proximal tibia. During surgery to remove the meniscus, the lesion was biopsied and histopathologic examination revealed it to be an intraosseous ganglion.

Langerhans Cell Histiocytosis (Eosinophilic Granuloma)

A nonneoplastic condition, eosinophilic granuloma, currently termed LCH, belongs to the group of disorders known as reticuloendothelioses (or histocytoses X, according to Lichtenstein's proposed name), which is a group that includes two other conditions, Hand-Schüller-Christian disease (xanthomatosis) and Letterer-Siwe disease (nonlipid reticulosis). The grouping has gained wide acceptance with the recognition that all three entities represent different clinical manifestations of a single pathologic disorder, characterized by granulomatous proliferation of the reticulum cell.

Although its causes and pathogenesis remain unsettled, LCH is now considered a disorder of immune regulation rather than neoplastic

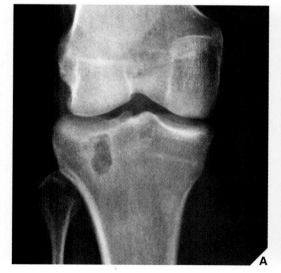
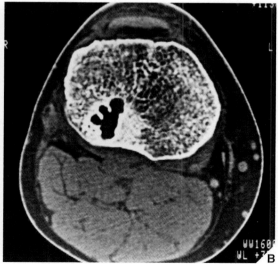

▲ **FIGURE 20.57 Intraosseous ganglion.** A 24-year-old man presented with an 8-week history of pain in the knee. Anteroposterior radiograph of the right knee **(A)** and CT section **(B)** demonstrate an oval radiolucent lesion eccentrically located in the proximal tibia with ramifications, rimmed by a zone of reactive sclerosis. The differential diagnosis included a bone abscess, osteoblastoma, chondroblastoma, and an intraosseous ganglion. Biopsy confirmed an intraosseous ganglion.

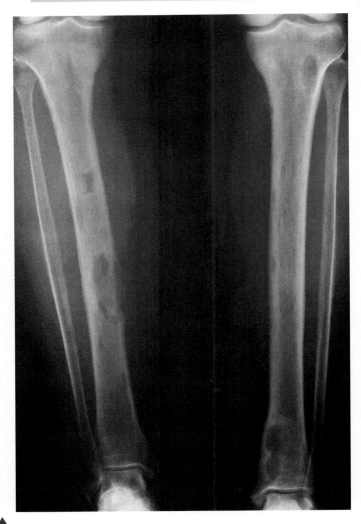

▲ FIGURE 20.58 **Brown tumors of hyperparathyroidism.** Radiograph of the lower legs of a 28-year-old woman with clinically documented hyperparathyroidism shows multiple brown tumors involving both tibiae. This condition can easily be misdiagnosed as multiple myeloma or metastatic disease.

In the long bones, LCH presents as a destructive radiolucent lesion commonly associated with a lamellated periosteal reaction. It may mimic a malignant round cell tumor such as lymphoma or Ewing sarcoma (Fig. 20.63). In its later stages, the lesion becomes more sclerotic, with dispersed radiolucencies (Fig. 20.64). The distribution of the lesion and the detection of silent sites in the skeleton are best ascertained by a radionuclide bone scan; this may also be helpful in differentiating LCH from Ewing sarcoma, which rarely presents with multiple foci.

CT may be useful if conventional radiography inadequately defines the extent of the process, particularly in cases of spine and pelvic involvement. This modality effectively demonstrates periosteal reaction, beveled edges, and reactive sclerosis. There have been isolated reports of the usefulness of MRI in evaluating this condition. The

process. Molecular genetic studies using comparative genomic hybridization (CGH) and loss of heterozygosity (LOH) experiments have revealed chromosomal alterations, with predominant losses affecting chromosomes 1p, 5p, 6q, 9, 16, 17, and 22q in CGH, and highest LOH frequencies on 1p and 17, leading to the hypothesis that loss of tumor suppressor genes located on chromosome 1p may be involved in development and progression of the disease. The term Langerhans cell histiocytosis has been accepted because it has been verified that the primary proliferative element in this disease is the Langerhans cell, a mononuclear cell of the dendritic type that is found in the epidermis but is derived from precursors in the bone marrow. The disorder exhibits a broad spectrum of clinical and imaging abnormalities. It is characterized by an abnormal proliferation of histiocytes in various parts of the reticuloendothelial system such as bone, lungs, central nervous system, skin, and lymph nodes.

LCH may manifest with solitary or with multiple lesions. It is usually seen in children, the common age of occurrence ranging from 1 to 15 years, with a peak incidence from 5 to 10 years. The most frequently affected sites are the skull, ribs, pelvis, spine, and long bones (Fig. 20.59). In the skull, the lytic lesions have a characteristic "punched-out" appearance, with sharply defined borders (Fig. 20.60). In the mandible or maxilla, the radiolucent lesions have the appearance of "floating teeth" (Fig. 20.61). In the spine, collapse of a vertebral body, the so-called vertebra plana, is a characteristic manifestation of the disease (Fig. 20.62). This finding was for a long time mistakenly interpreted as representing osteochondrosis of the vertebra and was called "Calve disease."

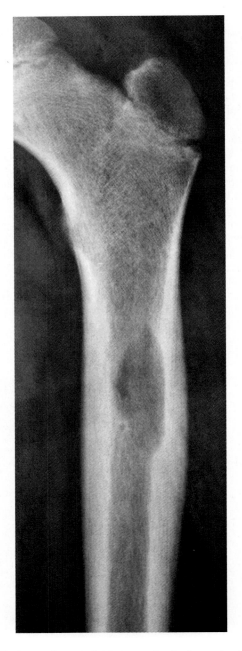

▲ FIGURE 20.59 **Langerhans cell histiocytosis.** Radiograph of the proximal femur of a 3-year-old boy with a limp and tenderness localized to the upper thigh shows an osteolytic lesion in the medullary portion of the bone, without sclerotic changes. There is fusiform thickening of the cortex and a solid periosteal reaction. The patient's age, the location of the lesion, and its radiographic appearance are typical of LCH.

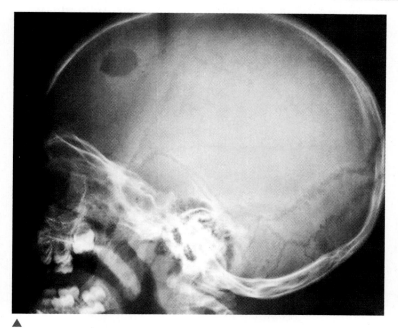

▲
FIGURE 20.60   Langerhans cell histiocytosis. Lateral radiograph of the skull of a 2.5-year-old boy with disseminated disease shows an osteolytic lesion in the frontal bone with a sharply outlined margin, giving it a punched-out appearance. Uneven involvement of the inner and outer tables results in its beveled appearance.

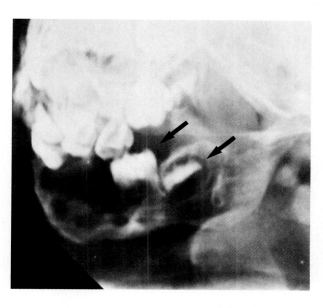

▲
FIGURE 20.61   Langerhans cell histiocytosis. A 3-year-old girl with extensive skeletal involvement had in addition a large destructive lesion in the mandible. Note the characteristic appearance of the floating teeth (*arrows*), which results from destruction of supportive alveolar bone.

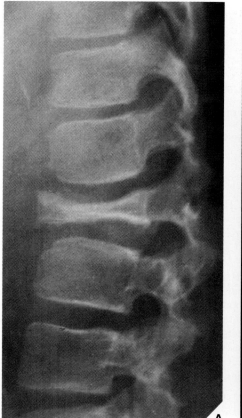

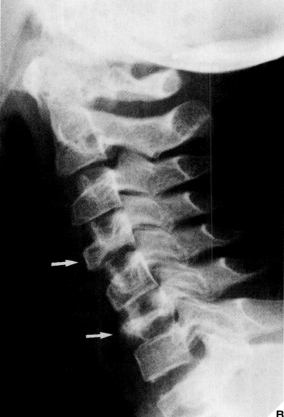

▲
FIGURE 20.62   Langerhans cell histiocytosis. (A) Vertebra plana in LCH represents collapse of a vertebral body secondary to the destruction of bone by a granulomatous lesion. Note the preservation of the adjacent intervertebral disk spaces. **(B)** In another patient, observe compression fractures of the vertebral bodies C4 and C6 (*arrows*).

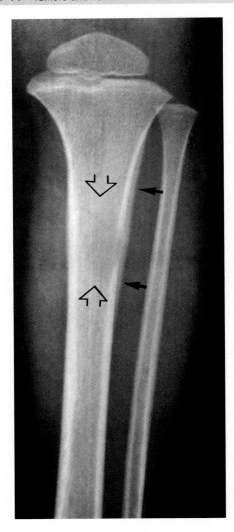

▲
FIGURE 20.63 Langerhans cell histiocytosis. Radiograph of the left lower leg of a 4-year-old boy demonstrates a lesion in the diaphysis of the tibia exhibiting a permeative type of bone destruction (*open arrows*) and a lamellated (onion skin) type of periosteal response (*arrows*) not infrequently seen in osteomyelitis or Ewing sarcoma. The duration of the patient's symptoms (fever and pain for 10 days), however, favored LCH.

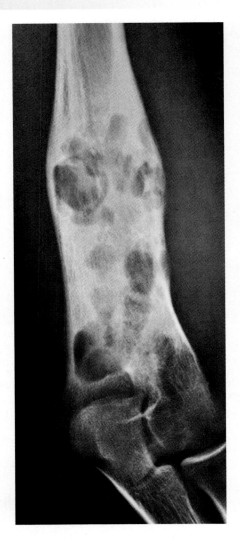

▲
FIGURE 20.64 Langerhans cell histiocytosis. The healing stage of disease, seen here in the distal humerus of a 16-year-old girl, exhibits predominantly sclerotic changes with interspersed radiolucent foci, thickening of the cortex, and a well-organized periosteal reaction. In this stage, the lesion mimics chronic osteomyelitis.

MRI appearance varies and appears to correlate with the radiographic appearance. The MRI manifestations of LCH during the earlier stages are nonspecific and may simulate an aggressive lesion, such as osteomyelitis or Ewing sarcoma, and occasionally benign tumors, such as osteoid osteoma or chondroblastoma. After gadolinium-diethylene triamine pentaacetic acid (DTPA) injection, the lesions show marked enhancement on T1-weighted images (Fig. 20.65). Occasionally, MRI can demonstrate early bone marrow involvement in the absence of radiographic or scintigraphic abnormalities. In some studies, on T1-weighted sequences the lesions were isointense with adjacent structures. In the skull, lesions have been reported to show well-defined high-signal-intensity areas of marrow replacement on T2-weighted sequences. The most recent investigations have shown that the most common MRI appearance of LCH is that of a focal lesion, surrounded by an extensive, ill-defined signal from bone marrow and by soft-tissue reaction with low signal intensity on T2-weighted images, considered to represent bone marrow and soft-tissue edema or the flare phenomenon.

The so-called Langerhans cell sarcoma represents an exceedingly rare but very aggressive form of LCH with multiorgan involvement. It can arise *de novo* or may progress from the conventional disorder.

Histologically, LCH is composed of a variable admixture of two types of cells: eosinophilic leukocytes possessing bilobate nuclei and coarse eosinophilic cytoplasmic granules and histiocytes, identical with the Langerhans histiocytes seen in the skin.

Infantile myofibromatosis is a condition that can be mistaken for LCH. It is a nodular myofibroblastic lesion of unknown cause that occurs in either a solitary (more commonly) or a multicentric form. In addition to bones, the dermis, subcutis, muscle, and viscera (heart, lungs, gastrointestinal tract) may be affected. Infantile myofibromatosis usually affects children younger than age 2 years. On radiography, radiolucent areas with or without sclerotic border are identified in the long bones, facial bones, and calvaria. MRI shows the lesions to be of low signal intensity on T1- and high signal intensity on T2-weighted sequences.

Chester-Erdheim Disease (Lipogranulomatosis)

Also known as Erdheim-Chester disease, this disseminated process of unknown cause affects the musculoskeletal system and various organs including heart, lungs, and skin. The clinical symptoms include bone pain, abdominal pain, shortness of breath, neurologic dysfunction, exophthalmos, fever, and generalized weakness. The imaging findings are characteristic. Radiographs show extensive medullary sclerosis

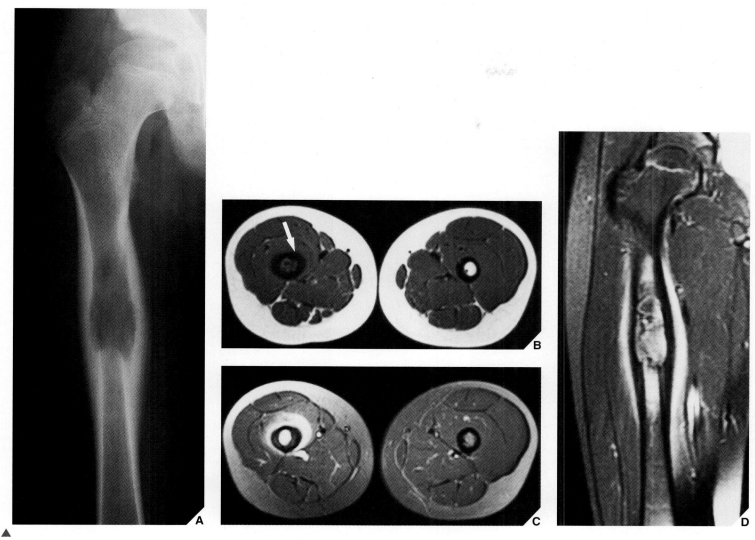

FIGURE 20.65 **MRI of Langerhans cell histiocytosis. (A)** Anteroposterior radiograph of the right femur of a 13-year-old boy shows a radiolucent lesion in the proximal femoral diaphysis associated with a lamellated periosteal reaction. **(B)** Axial T1-weighted (SE; TR 600/TE 14 msec) MR image demonstrates the lesion to be of low signal intensity. The cortex is markedly thickened (*arrow*). **(C)** Axial T2-weighted MR image shows high signal intensity of granuloma and perilesional edema. **(D)** Coronal fat-suppressed T1-weighted (SE; TR 500/TE 15 msec) MR image obtained after intravenous injection of gadolinium shows marked enhancement of the lesion and the soft tissues adjacent to the thickened femoral cortex.

and cortical thickening affecting predominantly the long bones, with sparing of the articular ends. The axial skeleton is usually not affected. MRI demonstrates decreased signal on T1-weighted images and increased signal on T2 weighting. The condition may mimic lymphoma and metastatic disease. Histologically, there is evidence of a dense infiltrate of lipid-laden foamy macrophages associated with cholesterol crystals, scattered giant cells, chronic inflammatory cells, and various amounts of fibrosis. Occasionally, Langerhans cells may be present, which raised the hypothesis of possible association of this disorder with LCH.

Medullary Bone Infarct

Radiographically, a medullary bone infarct presents with calcifications in the marrow cavity, usually surrounded by a well-defined hyalinized fibrotic or sclerotic border (see Figs. 18.16 and 18.17); occasionally, this presentation may be mistaken for a cartilage tumor such as an enchondroma. In the rare instances when a cyst develops in an infarcted segment of a long or flat bone, that is, an encystified bone infarct, it is visualized radiographically as an expanding radiolucent lesion associated with thinning of the surrounding cortex. Usually, the cyst cavity is

sharply outlined and the lesion is demarcated by a thin shell of reactive bone (Fig. 20.66). This encystification of a bone infarct can resemble an intraosseous lipoma or even a chondrosarcoma.

Myositis Ossificans

Myositis ossificans is a localized formation of heterotopic bone in the soft tissues that is initiated by trauma. Two types of these lesions have been identified. The first is a well-circumscribed lesion frequently seen adjacent to the cortex of a long tubular or flat bone, so-called juxtacortical myositis ossificans circumscripta; the other is a veil-like lesion that is less delineated. Radiographically, myositis ossificans circumscripta is characterized by a zonal phenomenon—dense, well-organized bone at the periphery of the lesion and less organized, immature bone at the center—and a radiolucent cleft that separates the lesion from the cortex of the adjacent bone (Fig. 20.67; see also Figs. 4.55, 4.56, and 21.27). The appearance of this lesion may mimic a malignant bone tumor such as parosteal or periosteal osteosarcoma (see Figs. 21.24 and 21.25). Most errors in diagnosis occur when a biopsy of the lesion is performed too early in onset, when its histologic appearance may resemble sarcomatous tissue.

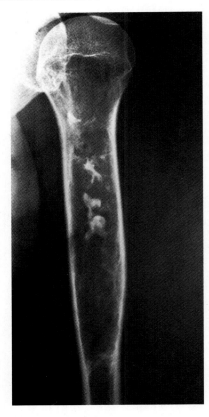

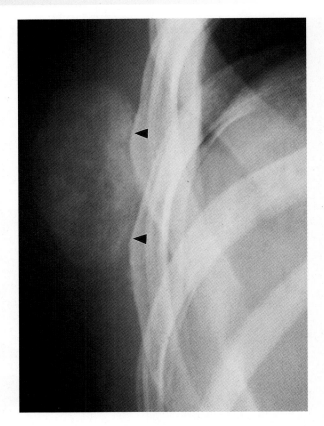

FIGURE 20.66 **Encystified bone infarct.** An expansive, radiolucent lesion in the proximal shaft of the left humerus was an incidental finding in a 31-year-old woman. The lesion exhibits the classic features of an encystified bone infarct: its location in the medullary portion of the bone with central coarse calcifications and a thin rim of reactive sclerosis. Note that although the cortex is thinned and expanded, there is no evidence of a periosteal reaction or soft-tissue mass. (Courtesy of Dr. Alex Norman, New York.)

FIGURE 20.67 **Myositis ossificans.** Characteristic appearance of posttraumatic myositis ossificans circumscripta, adjacent to the right ribs. Note that periphery of the lesion is denser than the center. The *arrowheads* point to the narrow radiolucent cleft that separates the lesion from the cortex of the ribs.

PRACTICAL POINTS TO REMEMBER

[1] SBCs have a predilection for:
  • the proximal diaphysis of the humerus and femur in children and adolescents
  • the pelvis and os calcis in adults.
[2] A SBC is characterized by:
  • its central location in a long bone
  • lack of periosteal reaction in the absence of fracture.
It may be complicated by pathologic fracture, in which case the "fallen fragment" sign is often present and may help in the differential diagnosis.
[3] An ABC, seen almost exclusively in children and adolescents younger than age 20, is characterized by:
  • its eccentric location in a bone
  • a buttress of periosteal reaction
  • its usual containment by a thin shell of periosteum.
[4] An ABC can develop *de novo* or as a result of cystic changes in a preexisting benign (chondroblastoma, osteoblastoma, GCT, fibrous dysplasia) or malignant (osteosarcoma) tumors.
[5] MRI of an ABC usually shows rather characteristic fluid–fluid levels, which represent sedimentation of red blood cells and serum within cystic cavities.
[6] Solid variant of ABC is commonly termed giant cell reparative granuloma. This lesion is seen primarily in craniofacial bones and short tubular bones of the hands and feet.
[7] GCT, seen characteristically at the articular ends of long bones, most often presents as a purely radiolucent lesion without any sclerotic reaction at the periphery. It is impossible to determine radiologically whether a GCT is benign or malignant.

[8] Multifocal GCTs are rare. Most commonly they occur in patients with Paget disease.
[9] Fibrocartilaginous mesenchymoma is a benign lesion composed of two distinct tissues, one cartilaginous, resembling an active growth plate, and one fibrous, resembling a low-grade fibrosarcoma.
[10] Hemangiomas are commonly seen in a vertebral body. Although most frequently asymptomatic, they may produce symptoms if they expand into the spinal canal.
[11] The characteristic MRI appearance of hemangioma includes high signal intensity on T1- and T2-weighted images.
[12] Epithelioid hemangioma represents a variant of conventional hemangioma with predilection for the vertebrae.
[13] Angiomatosis is defined as diffuse involvement of bones by hemangiomatous lesions. When bone is extensively involved, the term cystic angiomatosis is applied.
[14] Gorham disease of bone, also known as massive osteolysis or disappearing bone disease, is characterized by progressive, localized bone resorption, giving rise to a "sucked-candy" appearance.
[15] Intraosseous lipoma frequently presents with central calcification or ossification. The subtrochanteric region of the femur and the calcaneus are common sites for this lesion.
[16] Nonneoplastic conditions frequently mistaken for tumors include:
  • an intraosseous ganglion
  • the brown tumor of hyperparathyroidism
  • LCH (eosinophilic granuloma)
  • Chester-Erdheim disease
  • an encystified medullary bone infarct
  • posttraumatic myositis ossificans.

[17] Intraosseous ganglion resembles a degenerative cyst and has a pre-dilection for the non–weight-bearing segments of the articular end of the long bones.

[18] Brown tumor of hyperparathyroidism appears on the radiographs as a lytic lesion, most commonly in the long and short tubular bones. The name derives from its pathologic appearance: the lesion contains decomposing blood, which gives specimens a brown coloration.

[19] LCH is seen predominantly in children and may be mistaken for Ewing sarcoma.

[20] Chester-Erdheim disease manifests on radiography by extensive medullary sclerosis and cortical thickening, mimicking lymphoma and osteoblastic metastases.

[21] Myositis ossificans is characterized by a zonal phenomenon (well-organized, mature bone at the periphery of the lesion and immature bone at the center), and a radiolucent cleft that separates the lesion from the cortex of adjacent bone.

SUGGESTED READINGS

Adamsbaum C, Leclet H, Kalifa G. Intralesional Ethibloc injections in bone cysts. *Semin Musculoskelet Radiol* 1997;1:310–304.

Adamsbaum C, Mascard E, Guinebretière JM, Kalifa G, Dubousset J. Intralesional Ethibloc injections in primary aneurysmal bone cysts: an efficient and safe treatment. *Skeletal Radiol* 2003;10:559–566.

Alles JU, Schulz A. Immunohistochemical markers (endothelial and histiocytic) and ultrastructure of primary aneurysmal bone cysts. *Hum Pathol* 1986;17:39–45.

Aoki J, Tanikawa H, Ishii K, et al. MR findings indicative of hemosiderin in giant-cell tumor of bone: frequency, cause, and diagnostic significance. *Am J Roentgenol* 1996;166:145–148.

Apaydin A, OzkayTnak C, Yihnaz S, et al. Aneurysmal bone cyst of metacarpal. *Skeletal Radiol* 1996;25:76–78.

Assoun J, Richardi G, Railhac JJ, et al. CT and MRI of massive osteolysis of Gorham. *J Comput Assist Tomogr* 1994;18:981–984.

Athanasou NA, Bliss E, Gatter KC, Heryet A, Woods CG, McGee JO. An immunohistological study of giant-cell tumor of bone: evidence for an osteoclast origin of the giant cells. *J Pathol* 1985;147:153–158.

Bacchini P, Bertoni F, Ruggieri P, Campanacci M. Multicentric giant cell tumor of skeleton. *Skeletal Radiol* 1995;24:371–374.

Backo M, Cindro L, Golouh R. Familial occurrence of infantile myofibromatosis. *Cancer* 1992;69:1294–1299.

Bancroft LW, Kransdorf MJ, Petersson JJ, O'Connor MI. Benign fatty tumors: classification, clinical course, imaging appearance, and treatment. *Skeletal Radiol* 2006;35:719–733.

Baker ND, Greenspan A, Neuwirth M. Symptomatic vertebral hemangiomas: a report of four cases. *Skeletal Radiol* 1986;15:458–463.

Baudrez V, Galant C, Vande Berg BC. Benign vertebral hemangioma: MR-histological correlation. *Skeletal Radiol* 2001;30:442–446.

Beltran J, Simon DC, Levy M, Herman L, Weis L, Mueller CF. Aneurysmal bone cysts: MR imaging at 1.5 T. *Radiology* 1986;158:689–690.

Bergman AG, Rogero GW, Hellman B, Lones MA. Case report 841. *Skeletal cystic angiomatosis*. *Skeletal Radiol* 1994;23:303–305.

Bergstrand A, Hook O, Lidvall H. Vertebral haemangiomas compressing the spinal cord. *Acta Neurol Scand* 1963;39:59–66.

Bertheussen KJ, Holck S, Schiodt T. Giant cell lesion of bone of the hand with particular emphasis on giant cell reparative granuloma. *J Hand Surg [Am]* 1983;8:46–49.

Bertoni F, Bacchini P, Capanna R, et al. Solid variant of aneurysmal bone cyst. *Cancer* 1993;71:729–734.

Bertoni F, Bacchini P, Staals EL. Malignancy in giant cell tumor. *Skeletal Radiol* 2003;32:143–146.

Bertoni F, Present D, Enneking WF. Giant cell tumor of bone with pulmonary metastases. *J Bone Joint Surg [Am]* 1985;67A:890–900.

Bertoni F, Present D, Sudanese A, Baldini N, Bacchini P, Campanacci M. Giant cell tumor of bone with pulmonary metastases: six case reports and a review of the literature. *Clin Orthop* 1988;237:275–285.

Bhaduri A, Deshpande RB. Fibrocartilaginous mesenchymoma versus fibrocartilaginous dysplasia: are these a single entity? *Am J Surg Pathol* 1995;19:1447–1448.

Biesecker JL, Marcove RC, Huvos AG, Mike V. Aneurysmal bone cysts. A clinicopathologic study of 66 cases. *Cancer* 1970;26:615–625.

Blacksin MF, Ende N, Benevenia J. Magnetic resonance imaging of intraosseous lipomas: a radiologic-pathologic correlation. *Skeletal Radiol* 1995;24:37–41.

Bohne WHO, Goldman AB, Bullough P. Case report 96. Chester-Erdheim disease (lipogranulomatosis). *Skeletal Radiol* 1979;4:164–167.

Bonakdarpour A, Levy WM, Aegerter E. Primary and secondary aneurysmal bone cysts: a radiological study of 75 cases. *Radiology* 1978;126:75–83.

Boseker EH, Bickel WH, Dahlin DC. A clinicopathologic study of simple unicameral bone cysts. *Surg Gynecol Obstet* 1968;127:550–560.

Boyle WJ. Cystic angiomatosis of bone. *J Bone Joint Surg [Br]* 1972;54B:626–636.

Bulichova LV, Unni KK, Bertoni F, Beabout JW. Fibrocartilaginous mesenchymoma of bone. *Am J Surg Pathol* 1993;17:830–836.

Bullough PG. *Atlas of orthopedic pathology with clinical and radiologic correlation*, 2nd ed. New York: Gower; 1992:15.12–15.14.

Burmester GR, Winchester RJ, Dimitriu-Bona A, Klein MJ, Steiner G, Sissons HA. Delineation of four cell types comprising the giant cell tumor of bone. *J Clin Invest* 1983;71:1633–1648.

Campanacci M. *Bone and soft tissue tumors*. New York: Springer Verlag; 1986: 345–348.

Campanacci M, Baldini N, Boriani S, Sudanese A. Giant cell tumor of bone. *J Bone Joint Surg [Am]* 1987;69A:106–114.

Campanacci M, Capanna R, Picci P. Unicameral and aneurysmal bone cysts. *Clin Orthop* 1986;204:25–36.

Campanacci M, Giunti A, Olmi R. Giant-cell tumors of bone: a study of 209 cases with long-term follow-up in 130. *Ital J Orthop Traumatol* 1975;1:249–277.

Campbell RSD, Grainger AJ, Mangham DC, Beggs I, Teh J, Davies AM. Intraosseous lipoma: report of 35 new cases and a review of the literature. *Skeletal Radiol* 2003;32:209–222.

Chung EG, Enzinger FM. Infantile myofibromatosis. *Cancer* 1981;48:1807–1818.

Clough JR, Price CH. Aneurysmal bone cyst: pathogenesis and long term results of treatment. *Clin Orthop* 1973;97:52–63.

Cohen J. Etiology of simple bone cyst. *J Bone Joint Surg [Am]* 1970;52A:1493–1497.

Cohen J. Unicameral bone cysts: a current synthesis of reported cases. *Orthop Clin North Am* 1977;8:715–726.

Cohen JW, Weinreb JC, Redman HC. Arteriovenous malformations of the extremities: MR imaging. *Radiology* 1986;158:475–479.

Conway WF, Hayes CW. Miscellaneous lesions of bone. *Radiol Clin North Am* 1993;31:339–358.

Cooper PH. Is histiocytoid hemangioma a specific pathologic entity? *Am J Surg Pathol* 1988;12:815–817.

Dahlin DC. Giant cell tumor of bone: highlights of 407 cases. *Am J Roentgenol* 1985;144:955–960.

Dahlin DC. Giant cell bearing lesions of bone of the hands. *Hand Clin* 1987;3:291–297.

Dahlin DC, Bertoni F, Beabout JW, Campanacci M. Fibrocartilaginous mesenchymoma with low grade malignancy. *Skeletal Radial* 1984;12:263–269.

Dahlin DC, Cupps RE, Johnson EW Jr. Giant cell tumor: a study of 195 cases. *Cancer* 1970;25:1061–1070.

Dahlin DC, McLeod RA. Aneurysmal bone cyst and other nonneoplastic conditions. *Skeletal Radiol* 1982;8:243–250.

Dahlin DC, Unni KK. *Bone tumors: general aspects and data on 8,542 cases*, 4th ed. Springfield: Charles C Thomas; 1986:181–185.

Dumford K, Moore TE, Walker CW, Jaksha J. Multifocal, metachronous, giant cell tumor of the lower limb. *Skeletal Radiol* 2003;32:147–150.

Duncan CP, Morton KS, Arthur JS. Giant cell tumor of bone: its aggressiveness and potential for malignant change. *Can J Surg* 1983;26:475–476.

Egan AJM, Boardman LA, Tazelaar HD, et al. Erdheim-Chester disease. Clinical, radiologic, and histopathologic findings in five patients with lung disease. *Am J Surg Pathol* 1999;23:17–26.

Enzinger FM, Weiss SW. Benign tumors and tumorlike lesions of blood vessels. In: Enzinger FM, Weiss SW, eds. *Soft tissue tumors*, 3rd ed. St. Louis: CV Mosby; 1995.

Fayad L, Hazirolan T, Bluemke D, Mitchell S. Vascular malformations in the extremities: emphasis on MR imaging features that guide treatment options. *Skeletal Radiol* 2006;35:127–137.

Fechner RE, Mills SE. *Tumors of the bones and joints*. Washington, DC: Armed Forces Institute of Pathology; 1993:173–186, 203–209, 253–258.

Francis R, Lewis E. CT demonstration of giant cell tumor complicating Paget disease. *J Comput Assist Tomogr* 1983;7:917–918.

Freeby JA, Reinus WR, Wilson AJ. Quantitative analysis of the plain radiographic appearance of aneurysmal bone cyst. *Invest Radial* 1995;30:433–439.

Friedman DP. Symptomatic vertebral hemangiomas: MR findings. *Am J Roentgenol* 1996;167:359–364.

Garg NK, Carty H, Walsh HPJ, Dorgan JC, Bruce CE. Percutaneous Ethibloc injection in aneurysmal bone cysts. *Skeletal Radiol* 2000;29:211–216.

Glass TA, Mills SE, Fechner RE, Dyer R, Martin W, Armstrong P. Giant-cell reparative granuloma of the hands and feet. *Radiology* 1983;149:65–68.

Goldenberg RR, Campbell CJ, Bonfiglio M. Giant-cell tumor of bone. An analysis of two hundred and eighteen cases. *J Bone Joint Surg [Am]* 1970;52A:619–664.

Gorham UV, Stout AP. Massive osteolysis (acute spontaneous absorption of bone, phantom bone, disappearing bone): its relation to haemangiomatosis. *J Bone Joint Surg [Am]* 1955;37A:985–1004.

Gorham LW, WrightAW, Shultz HH, Mexon FC Jr. Disappearing bones: a rare form of massive osteolysis. *Am J Med* 1954;17:674–682.

Greenfield GB, Arrington JA. *Imaging of bone tumors*. Philadelphia: JB Lippincott; 1995:217–218.

Greenspan A, Jundt G, Remagen W. *Differential diagnosis in orthopaedic oncology*, 2nd ed. Philadelphia: Lippincott Williams & Wilkins; 2007:387–431.

Greenspan A, Klein MJ, Bennett AJ, Lewis MM, Neuwirth M, Camins MB. Case report 242. Hemangioma of the T6 vertebra with a compression fracture, extradural block and spinal cord compression. *Skeletal Radiol* 1978;10:183–188.

Grote HJ, Braun M, Kalinski T, et al. Spontaneous malignant transformation of conventional giant cell tumor. *Skeletal Radiol* 2004;33:169–175.

Han BK, Ryu J-S, Moon DH, Shin MI, Kim YT, Lee HK. Bone SPECT imaging of vertebral hemangioma. Correlations with MR imaging and symptoms. *Clin Nucl Med* 1995;20:916–921.

Hoch B, Hermann G, Klein MJ, Abdelwahab IF, Springfield D. Giant cell tumor complicating Paget disease of long bone. *Skeletal Radiol* 2007;36:973–978.

Hoover KB, Rosenthal DI, Mankin H. Langerhans cell histiocytosis. *Skeletal Radiol* 2007;36:95–104.

Hudson TM. Fluid levels in aneurysmal bone cysts: a CT feature. *Am J Roentgenol* 1984;141:1001–1004.

Hudson TM. Scintigraphy of aneurysmal bone cysts. *Am J Roentgenol* 1984;142:761–765.

Hudson TM. *Radiologic pathologic correlation of musculoskeletal lesions.* Baltimore: Williams & Wilkins; 1987:209–237, 249–252, 261–265.

Hudson TM, Hamlin DJ, Fitzimmons JR. Magnetic resonance imaging of fluid levels in an aneurysmal bone cyst and in anticoagulated human blood. *Skeletal Radiol* 1985;13:267–270.

Hudson TM, Schiebler M, Springfield DS, Enneking WF, Hawkins Jr IF, Spanier SS. Radiology of giant cell tumors of bone: computed tomography, arthrotomography, and scintigraphy. *Skeletal Radiol* 1984;11:85–95.

Hutter RVP, Worcester JN Jr, Francis KC, Foote FW Jr, Stewart FW. Benign and malignant giant cell tumors of bone. A clinicopathological analysis of the natural history of the disease. *Cancer* 1962;15:653–690.

Huvos AG. *Bone tumors: diagnosis, treatment, and prognosis,* 2nd ed. Philadelphia: WB Saunders; 1991:713–743.

Ilaslan H, Sundaram M, Unni KK. Solid variant of aneurysmal bone cysts in long tubular bones: giant cell reparative granuloma. *Am J Roentgenol* 2003;180:1681–1687.

Ishida T, Dorfman HD, Steiner GC, Norman A. Cystic angiomatosis of bone with sclerotic changes, mimicking osteoblastic metastases. *Skeletal Radiol* 1994;23:247–252.

Jacobs JE, Kimmelstiel P. Cystic angiomatosis of the skeletal system. *J Bone Joint Surg [Am]* 1953;35A:409–420.

Jaffe HL. Aneurysmal bone cyst. *Bull Hosp Joint Dis* 1950;11:3–13.

Jaffe HL. Giant-cell reparative granuloma, traumatic bone cyst, and fibrous (fibro-osseous) dysplasia of the jawbones. *Oral Surg* 1953;6:159–175.

Jaffe HL. *Tumors and tumorous conditions of the bones and joints.* Philadelphia: Lea & Febiger; 1958.

Jaffe HL, Lichtenstein L. Solitary unicameral bone cyst with emphasis on the roentgen picture, the pathoogic appearance, and the pathogenesis. *Arch Surg* 1942;44:1004–1025.

Jaffe HL, Lichtenstein L, Perris RB. Giant cell tumor of bone. Its pathologic appearance, grading, supposed variants and treatment. *Arch Pathol* 1940;30:993–1031.

Jordanov MI. The "rising bubble" sign: a new aid in the diagnosis of unicameral bone cysts. *Skeletal Radiol* 2009;38:597–600.

Junghanns H. Lipomas (fatty marrow areas) in the vertebral column. In: *Handbuch de spezielien pathologischen Anatomic and Histologic,* Tome IX/4. Berlin, Germany: Springer-Verlag; 1939:333–334.

Kaplan PA, Murphy M, Greenway G, Resnick D, Sartoris DJ, Harms S. Fluid-fluid levels in giant cell tumors of bone: report of two cases. *Computed Tomogr* 1987;11:151–155.

Keats TE. *Atlas of normal roentgen variants that may simulate disease,* 5th ed. St. Louis: Mosby Year Book; 1992:637–648.

Kohler A, Zimmer EA. *Borderlands of normal and early pathologic findings in skeletal radiography,* 13th ed. Revised by Schmidt H, Freyschmidt J. Stuttgart, Germany: Thieme Verlag; 1993:797–814.

Kransdorf MJ, Sweet DE. Aneurysmal bone cyst: concept, controversy, clinical presentation, and imaging. *Am J Roentgenol* 1995;164:573–580.

Kransdorf MJ, Sweet DE, Buetow PC, Giudici MA, Moser RP Jr. Giant cell tumor in skeletally immature patients. *Radiology* 1992;184:233–237.

Kricun ME. Tumors of the foot. In: Kricun ME, ed. *Imaging of bone tumors.* Philadelphia: WB Saunders; 1993:221–225.

Kricum ME, Kricun R, Haskin ME. Chondroblastoma of the calcaneus: radiographic features with emphasis on location. *Am J Roentgenol* 1977;128:613–616.

Kyriakos M, Hardy D. Malignant transformation of aneurysmal bone cyst, with an analysis of the literature. *Cancer* 1991;68:1770–1780.

Laredo JD, Reizine D, Bard M, Merland JJ. Vertebral hemangiomas: radiologic evaluation. *Radiology* 1986;161:183–189.

Lateur L, Simoens CJ, Gryspeerdt S, Samson I, Mertens V, van Damme B. Skeletal cystic angiomatosis. *Skeletal Radiol* 1996;25:92–95.

Levy WM, Miller AS, Bonakdarpour A, Aegerter E. Aneurysmal bone cyst secondary to other osseous lesions. Report of 5 7 cases. *Am J Clin Pathol* 1975;63:1–8.

Lichtenstein L. Aneurysmal bone cyst. A pathological entity commonly mistaken for giant cell tumor and occasionally for hemangioma and osteogenic sarcoma. *Cancer* 1950;3:279–289.

Lichtenstein L. Aneurysmal bone cyst. Observations on fifty cases. *J Bone Joint Surg [Am]* 1957;39A:873–882.

Lomasney LM, Basu A, Demos TC, Laskin W. Fibrous dysplasia complicated by aneurysmal bone cyst formation affecting multiple cervical vertebrae. *Skeletal Radiol* 2003;32:533–536.

Lomasney LM, Martinez S, Demos TC, Harrelson JM. Multifocal vascular lesions of bone: imaging characteristics. *Skeletal Radiol* 1996;25:255–261.

Lorenzo JC, Dorfman HD. Giant-cell reparative granuloma of short tubular bones of the hands and feet. *Am J Surg Pathol* 1980;4:551–563.

Martinez V, Sissons HA. Aneurysmal bone cyst. A review of 123 cases including primary lesions and those secondary to other bone pathology. *Cancer* 1988;61: 2291–2304.

Marui T, Yamamoto T, Yoshihara H, Kurosaka M, Mizuno K, Akamatsu T. De novo malignant transformation of giant cell tumor of bone. *Skeletal Radiol* 2001;30:104–108.

May DA, Good RB, Smith DK, Parsons TW. MR imaging of musculoskeletal tumors and tumor mimickers with intravenous gadolinium: experience with 242 patients. *Skeletal Radiol* 1997;26:2–15.

McDonald DJ, Sim FH, McLeod RA, Dahlin DC. Giant cell tumor of bone. *J Bone Joint Surg [Am]* 1986;68A:235–242.

McGlynn FJ, Mickelson MR, El-Khoury GY. The fallen fragment sign in unicameral bone cyst. *Clin Orthop* 1981;156:157–159.

McGrath J. Giant-cell tumour of bone: an analysis of fifty-two cases. *J Bone Joint Surg [Br]* 1972;54B:216–229.

Meis JM, Dorfman HD, Nathanson SD, Haggar AM, Wu KK. Primary malignant giant cell tumor of bone: dedifferentiated giant cell tumor. *Mod Pathol* 1989;2:541–546.

Meyer JS, Hoffer FA, Barnes PD, Mulliken JB. Biological classification of soft-tissue vascular anomalies: MR correlation. *Am J Roentgenol* 1991;157:559–564.

Milgram JW. Intraosseous lipoma: radiologic and pathologic manifestations. *Radiology* 1988;167:155–160.

Milgram JW. Intraosseous lipomas. A clinicopathological study of 66 cases. *Clin Orthop* 1988;231:277–302.

Morton KS. The pathogenesis of unicameral bone cyst. *Can J Surg* 1964;7:140–150.

Moukaddam H, Pollak J, Haims AH. MRI characteristics and classification of peripheral vascular malformations and tumors. *Skeletal Radiol* 2009;38:535–547.

Mulder JD, Kroon HM, SchCtte HE, Taconis WK. *Radiologic atlas of bone tumors.* Amsterdam, the Netherlands: Elsevier; 1993:241–254, 507–516, 557–590.

Mulliken JB, Glowacki J. Hemangiomas and vascular malformations in infants and children: a classification based on endothelial characteristics. *Plast Reconstr Surg* 1982;69:412–420.

Mulliken JB, Zetter BR, Folkman J. In vitro characteristics of endothelium from hemangiomas and vascular malformations. *Surgery* 1982;92:348–353.

Murphey MD, Nomikos GC, Flemming DJ, Gannon FH, Temple HT, Kransdorf MJ. From the archives of the AFIP. Imaging of giant cell tumor and giant cell reparative granuloma of bone: radiologic-pathologic correlation. *Radiographics* 2001;21:1283–1309.

Nascimento AG, Huvos AG, Marcove RC. Primary malignant giant cell tumor of bone: a study of eight cases and review of the literature. *Cancer* 1979;44:1393–1402.

Neer CS II, Francis KC, Marcove RC, Tertz J, Carbonara PN. Treatment of unicameral bone cyst. A follow-up study of one hundred seventy-five cases. *J Bone Joint Surg [Am]* 1966;48A:731–745.

Norman A, Schiffman M. Simple bone cyst: factors of age dependency. *Radiology* 1977;124:779–782.

Norman A, Steiner GC. Radiographic and morphological features of cyst formation in idiopathic bone infarction. *Radiology* 1983;146:335–338.

Oda Y, Tsuneyoshi M, Shinohara N. Solid variant of aneurysmal bone cyst (extragnatic giant cell reparative granuloma) in the axial skeleton and long bones: a study of its morphologic spectrum and distinction from allied giant cell lesions. *Cancer* 1992;70:2642–2649.

Peimer CA, Schiller AL, Mankin HJ, Smith RJ. Multicentric giant cell tumor of bone. *J Bone Joint Surg [Am]* 1980;62A:652–656.

Picci P, Baldini N, Sudanese A, Boriani S, Campanacci M. Giant cell reparative granuloma and other giant cell lesions of the bones of the hand and feet. *Skeletal Radiol* 1986;15:415–421.

Picci P, Manfrini M, Zucchi V, et al. Giant cell tumor bone in skeletally immature patients. *J Bone Joint Surg [Am]* 1983;65A:486–490.

Potter HG, Schneider R, Ghelman B, Healey JH, Lane JM. Multiple giant cell tumors and Paget disease of bone: radiographic and clinical correlations. *Radiology* 1991; 180:261–264.

Ratner V, Dorfman HD. Giant-cell reparative granuloma of the hand and foot bones. *Clin Orthop* 1990;260:251–258.

Remagen W. Pathologische Anatomic der Femurkopfnekrose. *Orthopäde* 1990;19: 174–181.

Remagen W, Lampérth BE, Jundt G, Schildt R. Das sogenannte osteolytische Dreieck de Calcaneus. Radiologische and pathoanatomische Befunde. *Osteologie* 1994;3: 275–283.

Resnick D, Kyriakos M, Greenway GD. Tumors and tumor-like lesions of bone: imaging and pathology of specific lesions. In: Resnick D, ed. *Diagnosis of bone and joint disorders,* 3rd ed. Philadelphia: WB Saunders; 1995:3628–3938.

Resnick D, Niwayama J. *Diagnosis of bone and joint disorders.* Philadelphia: WB Saunders; 1988:3782–3786.

Reynolds J. The fallen fragment sign in the diagnosis of unicameral bone cysts. *Radiology* 1969;92:949–953.

Rock MG, Pritchard DJ, Unni KK. Metastases from histologically benign giant-cell tumor of bone. *J Bone Joint Surg [Am]* 1984;66A:269–274.

Rock MG, Sim FH, Unni KK, et al. Secondary malignant giant-cell tumor of bone. Clinicopathological assessment of nineteen patients. *J Bone Joint Surg [Am]* 1986;68A:1073–1079.

Sanerkin NG. Malignancy, aggressiveness and recurrence in giant cell tumor of bone. *Cancer* 1980;46:1641–1649.

Sanerkin NG, Mott MG, Roylance J. An unusual intraosseous lesion with fibromyxoid elements: solid variant of aneurysmal bone cyst. *Cancer* 1983;51:2278–2286.

Schajowicz F. *Tumors and tumorlike lesions of bone: pathology, radiology, and treatment,* 2nd ed. Berlin, Germany: Springer-Verlag; 1994:257–299.

Schajowicz F, Aiello CL, Francone MV, Giannini RE. Cystic angiomatosis (hamartous haemolymphangiomatosis) of bone. *J Bone Joint Surg [Br]* 1978;60B: 100–106.

Schajowicz F, Slullitel J. Giant cell tumor associated with Paget's disease of bone. *J Bone Joint Surg [Am]* 1966;48A:1340–1349.

Schoedel K, Shankman S, Desai P. Intracortical and subperiosteal aneurysmal bone cysts: a report of three cases. *Skeletal Radiol* 1996;25:455–459.

Shankman S, Greenspan A, Klein MJ, Lewis MM. Giant cell tumor of the ischium. A report of two cases and review of the literature. *Skeletal Radial* 1988;17:46–51.

Sim FH, Dahlin DC, Beabout JW. Multicentric giant cell tumors of bone. *J Bone Joint Surg [Am]* 1977;59A:1052–1060.

Sirry A. The pseudo-cystic triangle in the normal os calcis. *Acta Radiol* 1951;36:516–520.

Smith RW, Smith CF. Solitary unicameral bone cyst of the calcaneus. A review of 20 cases. *J Bone Joint Surg [Am]* 1974;56A:49–56.

Soper JR, De Silva M. Infantile myofibromatosis: a radiological review. *Pediatr Radial* 1993;23:189–194.

Spieth ME, Greenspan A, Forrester DM, Ansari AN, Kimura RL, GleasonJordan I. Gorham's disease of the radius: radiographic, scintigraphic, and MRI findings with pathologic correlation. *Skeletal Radiol* 1997;26:659–663.

Spjut HJ, Dorfman HD, Fechner RE, Ackerman LV. *Tumors of bone and cartilage.* Washington, DC: Armed Forces Institute of Pathology; 1971.

Stacy GS, Peabody TD, Dixon LB. Pictorial essay. Mimics on radiography of giant cell tumor of bone. *Am J Roentgenol* 2003;181:1583–1589.

Steiner GC, Ghosh L, Dorfman HD. Ultrastructure of giant cell tumor of bone. *Hum Pathol* 1972;3:569–586.

Struhl S, Edelson C, Pritzker H, Seimon LP, Dorfman HD. Solitary (unicameral) bone cyst. The fallen fragment sign revisited. *Skeletal Radial* 1989;18:261–265.

Taybi H, Lachman RS. *Radiology of syndromes, metabolic disorders, and skeletal dysplasias,* 4th ed. St. Louis: CV Mosby, 1996:580–581.

Tsai JC, Dalinka MK, Fallon MD, Zlatkin MB, Kresel HY. Fluid-fluid level: a nonspecific finding in tumors of bone and soft tissue. *Radiology* 1990;175:779–782.

Tubbs WS, Brown LR, Beabout JW, Rock MG, Unni KK. Benign giant-cell tumor of bone with pulmonary metastases: clinical findings and radiologic appearance of metastases in 13 cases. *Am J Roentgenol* 1992;158:331–334.

Unni KK. *Dublin's bone tumors: general aspects and data on 11,087 cases,* 5th ed. New York: Lippincott-Raven Publishers; 1996.

Vergel De Dios AM, Bond JR, Shives TC, McLeod RA, Unni KK. Aneurysmal bone cyst. A clinicopathologic study of 238 cases. *Cancer* 1992;69:2921–2931.

Vilanova JC, Barceló J, Smirniotopoulos JG, et al. Hemangioma from head to toe: MR imaging with pathologic correlation. *Radiographics* 2004;24:367–385.

Waldron RT, Zeller JA. Diffuse skeletal hemangiomatosis with visceral involvement. *J Can Assoc Radiol* 1969;20:119–123.

Weisel A, Hecht HL. Development of a unicameral bone cyst. *J Bone Joint Surg [Am]* 1980;62A:664–666.

Wenger DE, Wold LE. Benign vascular lesions of bone: radiologic and pathologic features. *Skeletal Radiol* 2000;29:63–74.

Wilner D. *Radiology of bone tumors and allied disorders.* Philadelphia: WB Saunders; 1982:387.

Wold LE, Dobyns JH, Swee RG, Dahlin DC. Giant cell reaction (giant cell reparative granuloma) of the small bones of the hands and feet. *Am J Surg Pathol* 1986;10:491–496.

Wold LE, Swee RG. Giant cell tumor of the small bones of the hands and feet. *Semin Diagn Pathol* 1984;1:173–184.

Wold LE, Swee RG, Sim FH. Vascular lesions of bone. *Pathol Annu* 1985;20/2:101–137.

21

Malignant Bone Tumors I
Osteosarcomas and Chondrosarcomas

Osteosarcomas

Osteosarcoma (osteogenic sarcoma) is one of the most common primary malignant bone tumors, comprising approximately 20% of all primary bone malignancies. There are several types of osteosarcoma (Fig. 21.1), each having distinctive clinical, imaging, and histologic characteristics. The common feature of all types is that the osteoid and bone matrix are formed by malignant cells of connective tissue.

The majority of osteosarcomas are of unknown cause and can therefore be referred to as idiopathic, or *primary*. A smaller number of tumors can be related to known factors predisposing to malignancy, such as Paget disease, fibrous dysplasia, external ionizing irradiation, or ingestion of radioactive substances. These lesions are referred to as *secondary* osteosarcomas. All types of osteosarcomas may be further subdivided by anatomic site into lesions of the appendicular skeleton and axial skeleton. Furthermore, they may be classified on the basis of their location in the bone as central (medullary), intracortical, and juxtacortical. A separate group consists of primary osteosarcoma originating in the soft tissues (so-called extraskeletal or soft-tissue osteosarcomas).

Histopathologically, osteosarcomas can be graded on the basis of their cellularity, nuclear pleomorphism, and degree of mitotic activity. According to Broder's system, the numerical grade (1 to 4) indicates the degree of malignancy (grade 1 indicating the least undifferentiated tumor and grade 4 the most undifferentiated tumor) (Table 21.1). For example, well-differentiated central osteosarcomas and parosteal osteosarcomas are regarded as grade 1 or, rarely, grade 2 tumors; periosteal osteosarcomas and gnathic osteosarcomas as grade 2 or, rarely, grade 3; and conventional osteosarcoma as grade 3 or 4. Telangiectatic osteosarcomas, osteosarcomas developing in pagetic bone, postirradiation osteosarcomas, and multifocal osteosarcomas are usually grade 4 tumors. This grading has clinical, therapeutic, and prognostic importance. Generally speaking, central osteosarcomas are much more frequent than juxtacortical tumors, and they tend to have a higher histologic grade. Although pulmonary metastasis is the most common and most significant complication in high-grade osteosarcoma, it is rare in two subtypes: osteosarcoma of the jaw and multicentric osteosarcoma.

Primary Osteosarcomas

Conventional Osteosarcoma
Conventional osteosarcoma is the most frequent type, having its highest incidence in patients in their second decade and affecting males slightly more often than females. It has a predilection for the knee region (distal femur and proximal tibia), whereas the second most common site is the proximal humerus (Fig. 21.2). Patients usually present with bone pain, occasionally accompanied by a soft-tissue mass or swelling. At times, the first symptoms are related to pathologic fracture.

The distinctive radiologic features of conventional osteosarcoma, as demonstrated by radiography, are medullary and cortical bone destruction, an aggressive periosteal reaction, a soft-tissue mass, and tumor bone either within the destructive lesion or at its periphery, as well as within the soft-tissue mass (Fig. 21.3). In some instances, the type of bone destruction may not be obvious on the conventional studies, but patchy densities representing tumor bone and an aggressive periosteal reaction are clues to the diagnosis (Fig. 21.4).

The degree of radiopacity in the tumor reflects a combination of the amount of tumor bone production, calcified matrix, and osteoid. Tumors may present as purely sclerotic lesions or purely osteolytic lesions, but mostly a combination of both (Fig. 21.5). The borders are usually indistinct, with a wide zone of transition. The type of bone destruction is either moth-eaten or permeative, and only rarely geographic.

The most common types of periosteal response encountered with osteosarcoma are the "sunburst" type and a Codman triangle; the lamellated (onionskin) type of reaction is less frequently seen (Fig. 21.6). In the past, computed tomography (CT) was an indispensable technique for evaluating these tumors (Fig. 21.7). This was particularly important if a limb-salvage procedure was contemplated because extension of the tumor into the medullary cavity is crucial information for effective surgical planning (see Fig. 16.11). Currently, magnetic resonance imaging (MRI) has become a modality of choice for evaluating these tumors, particularly for intraosseous tumor extension and soft-tissue involvement. On T1-weighted images, the solid nonmineralized parts of osteosarcoma generally present as areas of low to intermediate signal intensity. On T2-weighted images, the tumor demonstrates a high signal intensity (Figs. 21.8 to 21.10). Osteosclerotic tumors demonstrate low signal intensity on all imaging sequences (Fig. 21.11). MRI may also effectively demonstrate peritumoral edema. This feature displays an intermediate intensity signal on T1-weighted and a high intensity on T2-weighted images and is seen in the soft tissues surrounding the tumor. CT (see Fig. 16.12) and MRI are also essential in monitoring the results of treatment.

Based on the dominant histologic features, conventional osteosarcoma can be subdivided into three histologic subtypes: osteoblastic, chondroblastic, and fibroblastic. The last may occasionally mimic

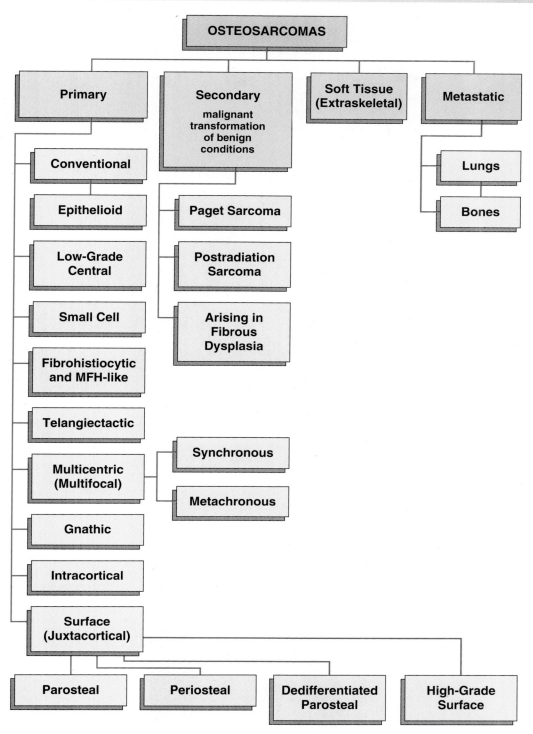

FIGURE 21.1   Classification of the types of osteosarcoma.

TABLE 21.1   Histologic Grading of Osteosarcoma

Grade	Histologic Features	Grade	Histologic Features
1	Cellularity: slightly increased Cytologic atypia: minimal to slight Mitotic activity: low Osteoid matrix: regular	3	Cellularity: increased Cytologic atypia: moderate to marked Mitotic activity: moderate to high Osteoid matrix: irregular
2	Cellularity: moderate Cytologic atypia: mild to moderate Mitotic activity: low to moderate Osteoid matrix: regular	4	Cellularity: markedly increased Cytologic atypia: markedly pleomorphic cells Mitotic activity: high Osteoid matrix: irregular, abundant

According to Unni KK, Dahlin DC, 1984.

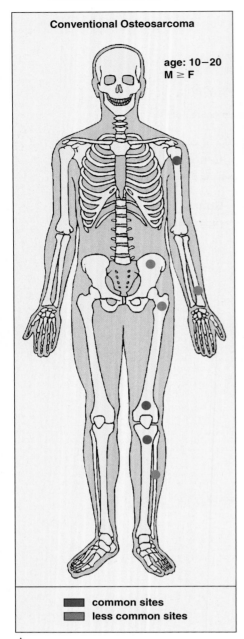

Conventional Osteosarcoma

age: 10–20
M ≥ F

■ common sites
■ less common sites

▲
FIGURE 21.2 Skeletal sites of predilection, peak age range, and male-to-female ratio in conventional osteosarcoma.

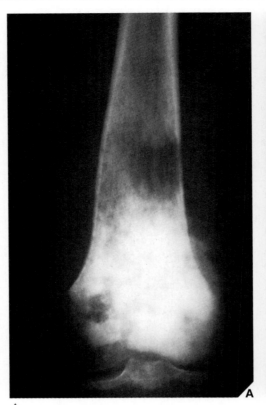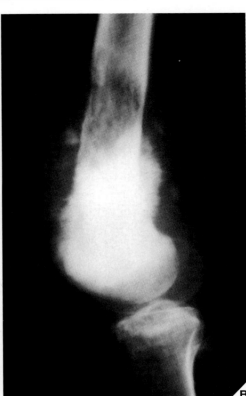

▲
FIGURE 21.3 Osteosarcoma. Anteroposterior (**A**) and lateral (**B**) radiographs demonstrate the typical features of this tumor in the femur of a 19-year-old woman. Medullary and cortical bone destruction can be seen in association with an aggressive periosteal response of the velvet and sunburst types, as well as with a soft-tissue mass containing tumor bone.

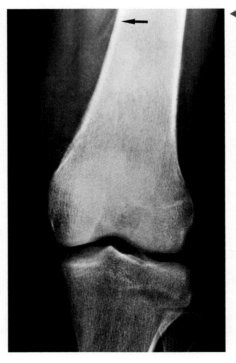

◀ **FIGURE 21.4 Osteosarcoma.** Although there is no gross bone destruction evident in the distal femur of this 16-year-old girl, the patchy densities in the medullary portion of the femur and the sunburst appearance of the periosteal response are clues to the diagnosis of osteosarcoma. Note also the presence of a Codman triangle (*arrow*).

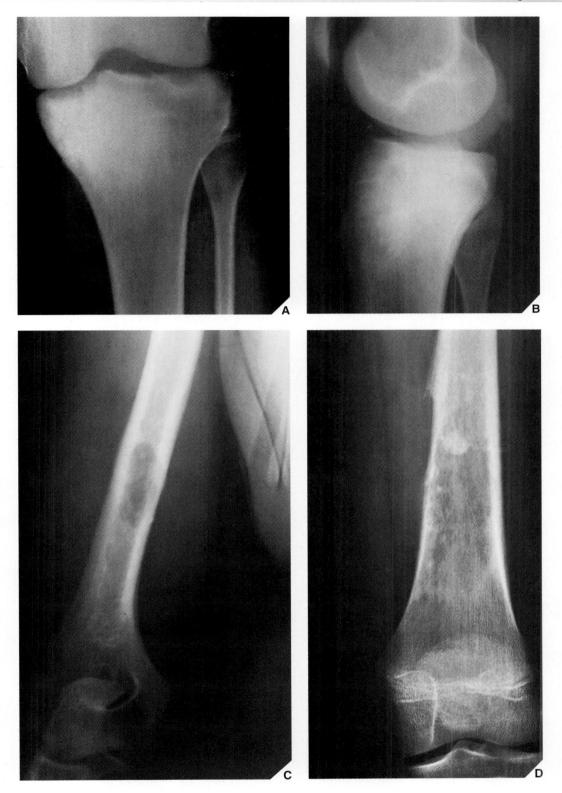

FIGURE 21.5 **Various presentations of a conventional osteosarcoma.** Anteroposterior (**A**) and lateral (**B**) radiographs show sclerotic variant in the proximal tibia. (**C**) Anteroposterior radiograph shows a lytic variant in the distal humerus, which proved to be a fibroblastic osteosarcoma. (**D**) A radiograph of the distal femur shows a mixed variant: areas of bone formation are present within a destructive lytic lesion.

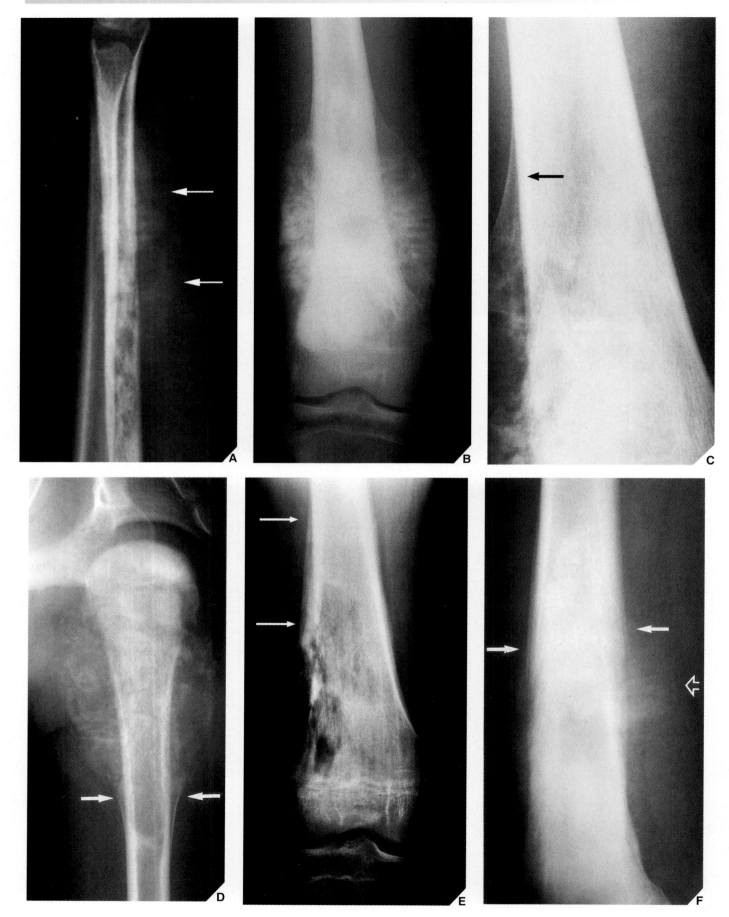

▲
FIGURE 21.6   **Periosteal reaction in osteosarcoma.** Three types of periosteal reaction most commonly accompany osteosarcoma. (**A**) The sunburst or per-pendicular type of periosteal reaction (*arrows*) is seen here on the lateral radiograph of the forearm in an 18-year-old woman with tumor in the radius and (**B**) on the anteroposterior radiograph of the distal femur in a 20-year-old man. (**C**) Codman triangle (*arrow*) may also be encountered, as seen here in a 15-year-old girl with tumor in the femur and (**D**) in an 11-year-old boy with tumor in the humerus (*arrows*). (**E**) The onion skin or lamellated type of periosteal response (*arrows*) is apparent in a 16-year-old girl with tumor in the femur. (**F**) Combination of lamellated (*arrows*) and sunburst (*open arrow*) periosteal reaction is present in a 16-year-old girl with osteosarcoma of the femur.

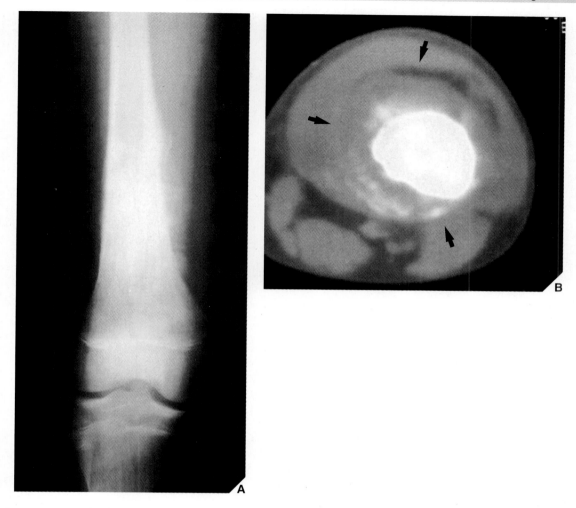

FIGURE 21.7   CT of osteosarcoma. (A) Conventional anteroposterior radiograph reveals a destructive lesion with poorly defined borders extending from the metaphysis of the femur into the diaphysis. Note the aggressive periosteal reaction and the formation of tumor bone. These features are sufficient for making a diagnosis of osteosarcoma in this 14-year-old boy. **(B)** Axial CT section demonstrates the extension of tumor into the soft tissues (*arrows*). The tumor bone in the medullary portion of the bone and in the soft-tissue mass is seen to better advantage.

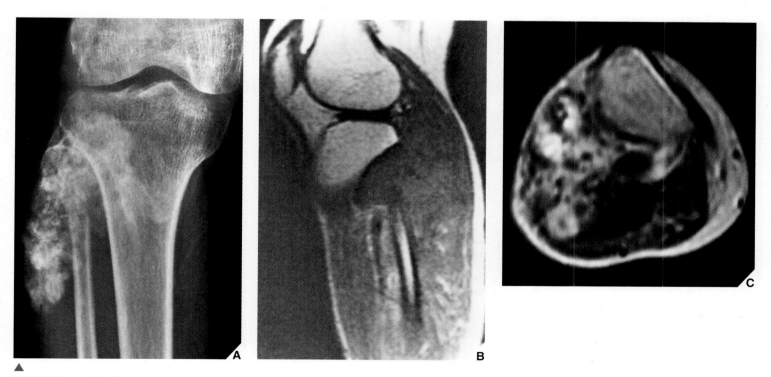

FIGURE 21.8   MRI of osteosarcoma. (A) Conventional radiograph demonstrates involvement of the head of the fibula and extensive soft-tissue infiltration with significant tumor-bone formation in a 20-year-old man. **(B)** Sagittal spin-echo T1-weighted MR image shows that the tumor displays a predominantly intermediate signal, blending with the muscular structures. **(C)** On axial T2-weighted image, the tumor shows high signal intensity in both its intramedullary component and its soft-tissue extension. The foci of tumor-bone formation are imaged as areas of low signal intensity.

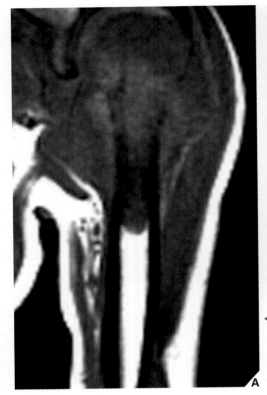

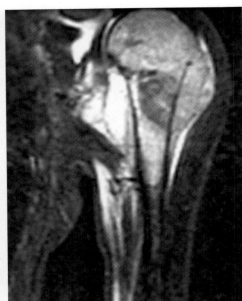

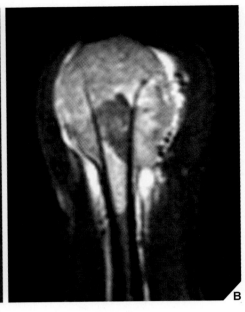

▶ **FIGURE 21.9   MRI of osteosarcoma. (A)** Coronal T1-weighted MR image of the left proximal humerus of a 14-year-old boy shows an intermediate-to-low signal intensity tumor destroying the cortex and extending into the soft tissues. **(B)** Coronal and sagittal T2-weighted fat-suppressed MR images show that the tumor exhibits heterogeneous but mostly high signal. The areas of tumor-bone formation are of low signal intensity.

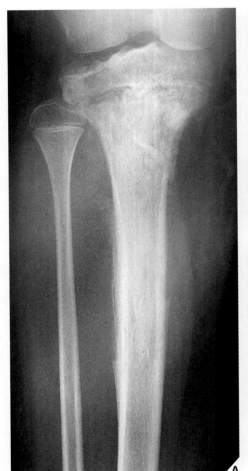

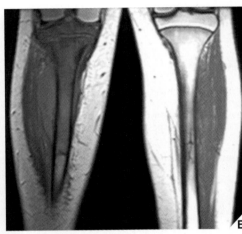

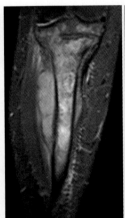

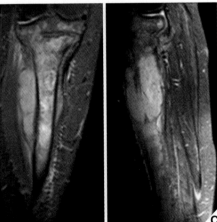

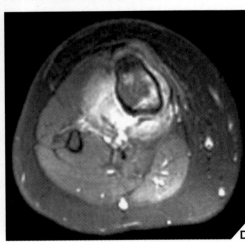

▲

FIGURE 21.10   MRI of osteosarcoma. (A) Anteroposterior radiograph of the right leg of an 11-year-old girl shows an aggressive lesion in the tibial diaphysis, extending to the growth plate. Present is an interrupted periosteal reaction and a soft-tissue mass. **(B)** Coronal T1-weighted MR image shows both the osseous tumor and a soft-tissue mass to be of intermediate signal intensity. **(C)** Coronal and sagittal inversion recovery MR images show heterogeneous character of the tumor that exhibits foci of high signal. **(D)** Axial T1-weighted fat-suppressed MR image obtained after intravenous administration of gadolinium shows marked enhancement of the soft-tissue mass.

malignant fibrous histiocytoma (MFH). At times, the tumor cells may be so undifferentiated that on a purely cytologic basis, it is difficult to tell whether they are sarcomatous or epithelial. This variant of conventional osteosarcoma is sometimes referred to as epithelioid osteosarcoma. The diagnosis usually becomes evident from the patient's age, the production of obvious tumor matrix, and a radiographic appearance typical of osteosarcoma.

Complications and Treatment. The most frequent complications of conventional osteosarcoma are pathologic fracture and the development of pulmonary metastases.

If a limb-salvage procedure is feasible, a course of multidrug chemotherapy is used, followed by wide resection of the bone and insertion of an endoprosthesis (Fig. 21.12). Less frequently, amputation is performed, followed by chemotherapy. Currently, the 5-year survival rate after adequate therapy exceeds 50%.

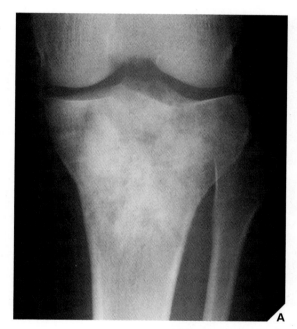

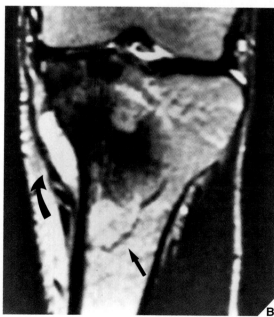

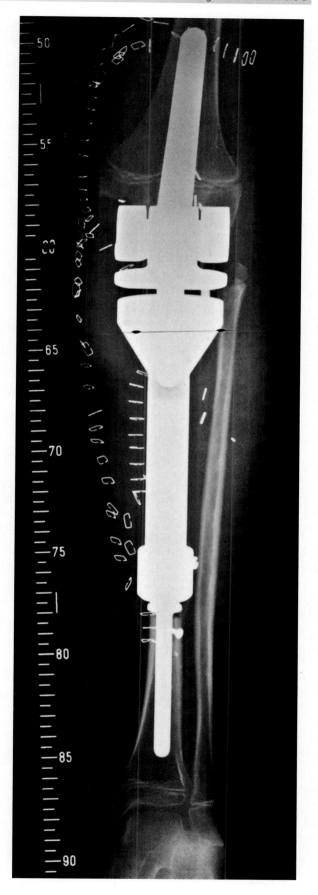

▲
FIGURE 21.11   **MRI of osteosarcoma. (A)** Anteroposterior radiograph demonstrates a predominantly sclerotic tumor extending into the articular end of the left tibia in this 17-year-old boy. **(B)** The sclerotic parts of the lesion display low signal intensity on coronal spin-echo T2-weighted MR image. Distally, a nonmineralized part of the tumor shows high signal intensity (*arrow*). Likewise, the soft-tissue extension of the lesion displays high signal intensity (*curved arrow*).

▲
FIGURE 21.12   **Treatment of osteosarcoma.** An 8-year-old boy underwent a limb-salvage procedure for osteosarcoma in the left tibia. After a full course of chemotherapy, consisting of a combination of methotrexate, doxorubicin hydrochloride, and cisplatin, a wide resection of the proximal tibia was performed and a LEAP metallic spacer inserted. This expandable prosthesis can be adjusted to maintain limb length with the normal contralateral limb as the child grows. (Courtesy of Dr. M.M. Lewis, Santa Barbara, California.)

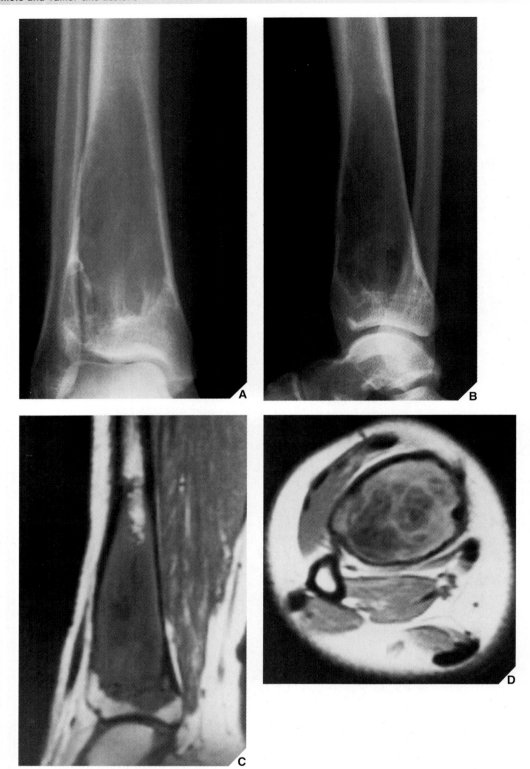

FIGURE 21.13   Low-grade central osteosarcoma. (A) Anteroposterior and **(B)** lateral radiographs of the distal leg in an 18-year-old woman were originally interpreted as showing fibrous dysplasia of the distal tibia. Note a benign-appearing radiolucent lesion exhibiting a geographic type of bone destruction with a narrow zone of transition and no evidence of periosteal reaction. Sagittal **(C)** and axial **(D)** T1-weighted (SE; TR 600/TE 20 msec) MR images demonstrate intermediate to low signal intensity of the lesion and lack of a soft-tissue mass. Biopsy revealed a low-grade central osteosarcoma. (Courtesy of Dr. K.K. Unni, Rochester, Minnesota.)

Low-Grade Central Osteosarcoma

This rare form of osteosarcoma (1% of all osteosarcomas) usually occurs in patients older than those presenting with conventional osteosarcoma, although the sites of predilection are similar. Radiographically, it may be indistinguishable from conventional osteosarcoma, but it grows more slowly and has a better prognosis. At times, its radiographic presentation clearly mimics fibrous dysplasia (Fig. 21.13) or other benign lesion

(Fig. 21.14). Histologic examination typically reveals abundant osteoid and spindle cells with a paucity of cellular atypia and mitotic figures.

Telangiectatic Osteosarcoma

A very aggressive type of osteosarcoma, the telangiectatic variant, also called hemorrhagic osteosarcoma by Campanacci, is twice as common in males than in females and is seen predominantly in patients in their

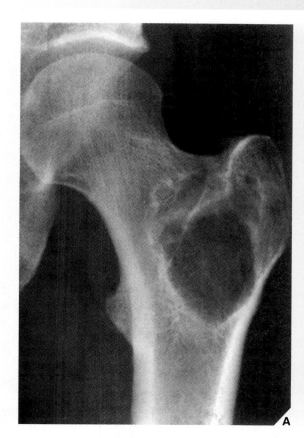
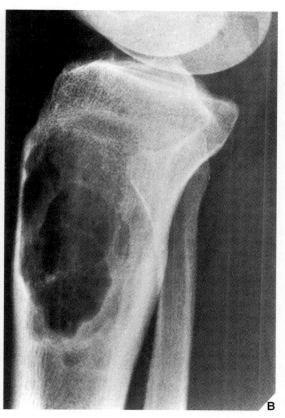

▲
FIGURE 21.14 **Low-grade central osteosarcoma. (A)** A lytic lesion with geographic pattern of bone destruction and a narrow zone of transition is present in the intertrochanteric region of the left femur in a 24-year-old woman. **(B)** Lateral radiograph of the proximal tibia of a 30-year-old woman reveals a lytic lesion with well-defined borders and geographic type of bone destruction. (Reprinted from Greenspan A, Remagen W, 1998, with permission.)

second and third decades of life. It is rare, comprising approximately 3% of all malignant bone tumors. It is characterized by a high degree of vascularity and large cystic spaces filled with blood, which account for its atypical imaging presentation. Most of these tumors arise in the femur and tibia. On radiography, telangiectatic osteosarcoma most commonly presents as an osteolytic destructive lesion with or without matrix mineralization, and with an almost complete absence of sclerotic changes; a soft-tissue mass may also be present (Figs. 21.15 to 21.18). An aggressive periosteal reaction (lamellar, sunburst, or Codman triangle) is present in most patients, reflecting the malignant nature of this tumor, and a pathologic fracture is not uncommon in the case of large lesions. On MRI, telangiectatic osteosarcoma often exhibits areas of high signal intensity on T1-weighted sequences, owing to the presence of methemoglobin. On T2 weighting, signal intensity is commonly heterogeneous. Fluid–fluid levels can occasionally be seen (Fig. 21.19), similar to ones seen in aneurysmal bone cyst.

On gross pathologic examination, the tumor resembles a "bag" of blood and is characterized by blood-filled spaces, necrosis, and hemorrhage. Histologically, it is composed of loculated blood-filled spaces, partially lined by malignant cells producing sparse osteoid tissue. It resembles an aneurysmal bone cyst, both radiologically and pathologically.

Small Cell Osteosarcoma

Described by Sim and associates, small cell osteosarcoma with preferential sites of distal femur, proximal humerus, and proximal tibia, usually occurs as a radiolucent lesion with permeative borders and a large soft-tissue mass. Its radiographic appearance thus mimics that of a round cell bone sarcoma. These lesions usually exhibit small round cells in many histologic fields, much like Ewing sarcoma. The presence, however, of spindled tumor cells, as well as the focal production of osteoid or bone, helps to make a histologic diagnosis of osteosarcoma.

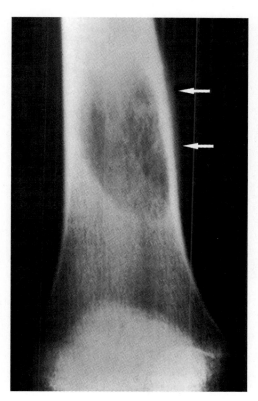

▲
FIGURE 21.15 **Telangiectatic osteosarcoma.** A purely destructive lesion is present in the diaphysis of the femur of this 17-year-old girl. Note the velvet type of periosteal reaction (*arrows*). The sclerotic changes usually seen in osteosarcomas are absent, and there is no radiographic evidence of tumor bone. Biopsy revealed a telangiectatic osteosarcoma, one of the most aggressive types of this tumor. (Courtesy of Dr. M. J. Klein, New York.)

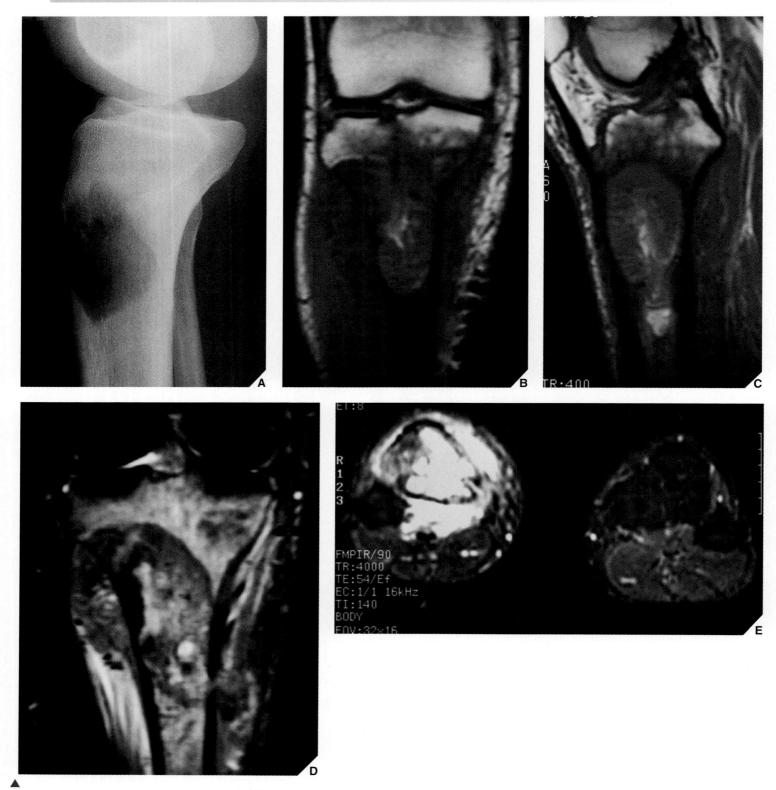

FIGURE 21.16 **MRI of telangiectatic osteosarcoma.** **(A)** Lateral radiograph of the proximal tibia in a 21-year-old man shows a lesion with relatively narrow zone of transition and no visible periosteal reaction. Coronal **(B)** and sagittal **(C)** T1-weighted (SE; TR 400/TE 10 msec) MR images show the tumor to be predominantly of intermediate signal intensity with foci of high signal. No definite soft-tissue mass is demonstrated. Coronal **(D)** and axial **(E)** inversion recovery (FMPIR/90 msec; TR 4000/TE 54/TI 140 msec) images show the extension of the tumor into the soft tissues and presence of peritumoral edema.

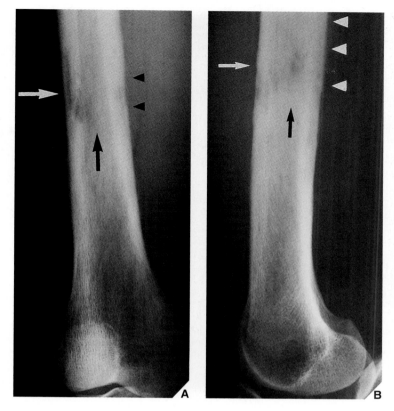

FIGURE 21.17 **Telangiectatic osteosarcoma.** Anteroposterior (**A**) and lateral (**B**) radiographs of the right femur of a 41-year-old man show an ill-defined lesion that exhibits a permeative type of bone destruction (*arrows*). Note the velvet type of aggressive periosteal reaction (*arrowheads*).

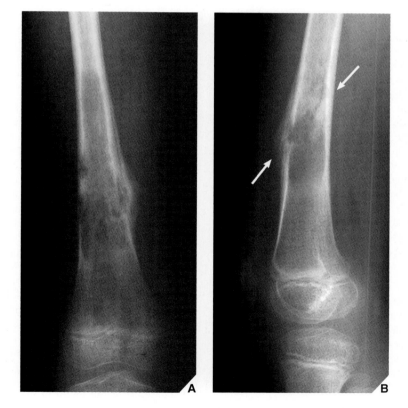

FIGURE 21.18 **Telangiectatic osteosarcoma.** (**A**) A predominantly lytic tumor associated with periosteal reaction is seen in the distal femoral diaphysis of this 6-year-old girl. (**B**) Lateral radiograph demonstrates an oblique pathologic fracture (*arrows*). (Courtesy of Dr. K.K. Unni, Rochester, Minnesota.)

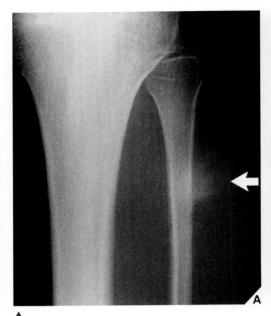
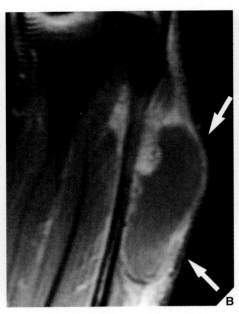
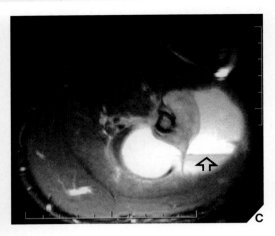

FIGURE 21.19   MRI of telangiectatic osteosarcoma. (A) Conventional radiograph shows permeated focal bone destruction in the proximal fibula associated with bone formation in the soft tissue (*arrow*). **(B)** Coronal T1-weighted fat-suppressed MR image obtained after intravenous administration of gadolinium shows slight enhancement of both the intramedullary tumor and periphery of a large soft-tissue mass (*arrows*). **(C)** Axial T2-weighted fat-suppressed MRI shows fluid–fluid level (*open arrow*). (Reprinted from Greenspan A et al., 2007.)

Fibrohistiocytic Osteosarcoma

Fibrohistiocytic osteosarcoma, which resembles MFH, has recently been described in the literature. It can sometimes be confused with true MFH of bone because both of these tumors tend to arise at a greater age than conventional osteosarcoma, usually after the third decade. Both tend to involve the articular ends of long bones, and less periosteal reaction is typically present than in conventional osteosarcoma. Although on radiography both of these lesions tend to be radiolucent and thus do resemble giant cell tumor and fibrosarcoma, the MFH-like osteosarcoma usually exhibits areas of bone formation resembling cotton balls or cumulus clouds, whereas MFH does not. When such areas are identified on imaging studies, a diligent search should be made for tumor bone in the resected specimen. Histologically, MFH-like osteosarcoma is characterized by pleomorphic spindle cells and giant cells, many of which have bizarre nuclei. This lesion therefore resembles giant cell-rich osteosarcoma. An inflammatory background is not unusual, and the storiform or spiral nebular arrangement, characteristic of MFH, although sometimes a dominant feature, may be less prominent or may be replaced by areas of large pleomorphic cells arranged in diffuse sheets. As in all other subtypes of osteosarcoma, the distinction from other sarcomas depends on the demonstration of osteoid or bone formation by malignant cells in the very typical patterns seen in osteosarcomas.

Intracortical Osteosarcoma

Intracortical osteosarcoma is one of the rarest forms of osteosarcoma. Very few of these tumors have been reported, with an age range of 9 to 43 years (average 24 years) and a male predominance. The presenting symptom is pain, often associated with activity. In some patients, a history of previous trauma has been elicited. The tumor involves the cortex, without extension into the medullary portion of the bone or the soft tissues. The radiographic presentation is that of a radiolucent lesion with surrounding cortical sclerosis. The size of the lesion varies from 1.0 to 4.2 cm. In some instances, the lesion mimics osteoid osteoma or intracortical osteoblastoma.

Gnathic Osteosarcoma

Gnathic osteosarcoma is osteosarcoma arising in the maxilla or mandible. Unlike osteosarcoma arising elsewhere in the skeleton, this tumor occurs in older patients (fourth to sixth decades, with a mean age of 35 years). It is usually a well-differentiated tumor with a low mitotic rate, possessing a predominantly cartilaginous component in a high percentage of cases and with less malignant potential and a better prognosis than for other forms of osteosarcoma.

Multicentric (Multifocal) Osteosarcoma

The simultaneous development of foci of osteosarcoma in multiple bones is a rare occurrence (Figs. 21.20 and 21.21). Whether this entity is truly separate or represents multiple bone metastases from a primary conventional osteosarcoma remains a controversy. This type of osteosarcoma is currently recognized as having two variants: synchronous and metachronous. Multifocal osteosarcoma must be differentiated from osteosarcoma metastasized to other bones.

Surface (Juxtacortical) Osteosarcomas

The term *juxtacortical* is a general designation for a group of osteosarcomas that arise on the bone surface (Fig. 21.22). Usually, these lesions are much rarer and occur a decade later than their intraosseous counterparts. The majority of juxtacortical osteosarcomas are low-grade tumors, although there are moderately and even highly malignant variants.

Parosteal Osteosarcoma. Parosteal tumors are seen largely in patients in their third and fourth decades, with a characteristic site of predilection in the posterior aspect of the distal femur (Fig. 21.23).

Conventional radiography is usually adequate for making a diagnosis of parosteal osteosarcoma. The lesion presents as a dense oval or spherical mass attached to the cortical surface of the bone and sharply demarcated from the surrounding soft tissues (Figs. 21.24 to 21.26). CT (Fig. 21.26B) or MRI (see Fig. 16.21) is often necessary to determine whether the lesion has penetrated the cortex and invaded the medullary region of the bone.

Histologically, the lesion consists of fibrous stroma, probably derived from the outer fibrous periosteal layer. The osseous component is often trabeculated but is at least partially immature, particularly at the periphery of the tumor. This is an important point in differentiating it from the sometimes similar-appearing myositis ossificans, which, however, matures in a centripetal fashion, with its most mature portion outermost.

Differential Diagnosis. Parosteal osteosarcoma must be differentiated from parosteal osteoma (see Fig. 17.4), myositis ossificans, soft-tissue osteosarcoma, parosteal liposarcoma with ossifications, and sessile osteochondroma. Differentiation from myositis ossificans and

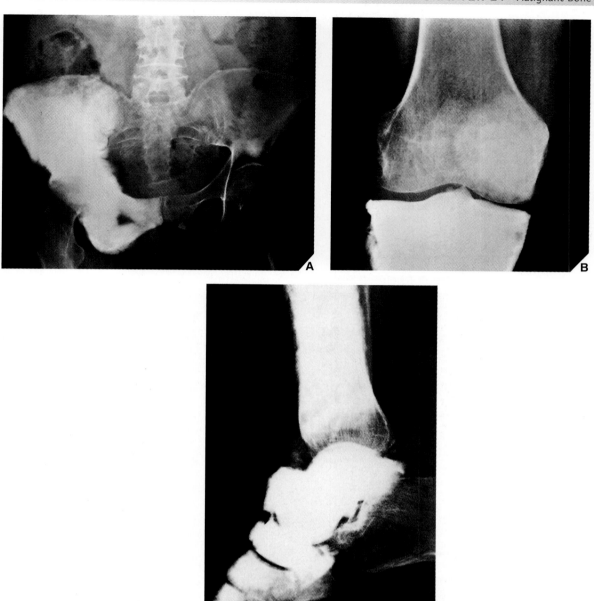

▲
FIGURE 21.20   **Multicentric osteosarcoma.** Multicentric osteosarcoma, a very rare bone tumor, is demonstrated here in the right hemipelvis (**A**), right tibia (**B**), and several bones of the right foot (**C**).

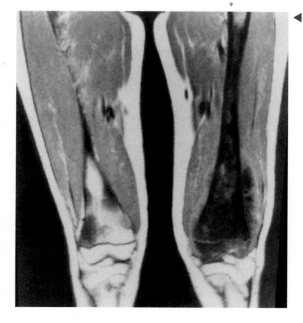

◄ FIGURE 21.21   **MRI of multicentric osteosarcoma.** Coronal T1-weighted image shows multiple low signal intensity lesions in both femora of a 12-year-old girl. (Reprinted from Greenspan A, Remagen W, 1998, with permission.)

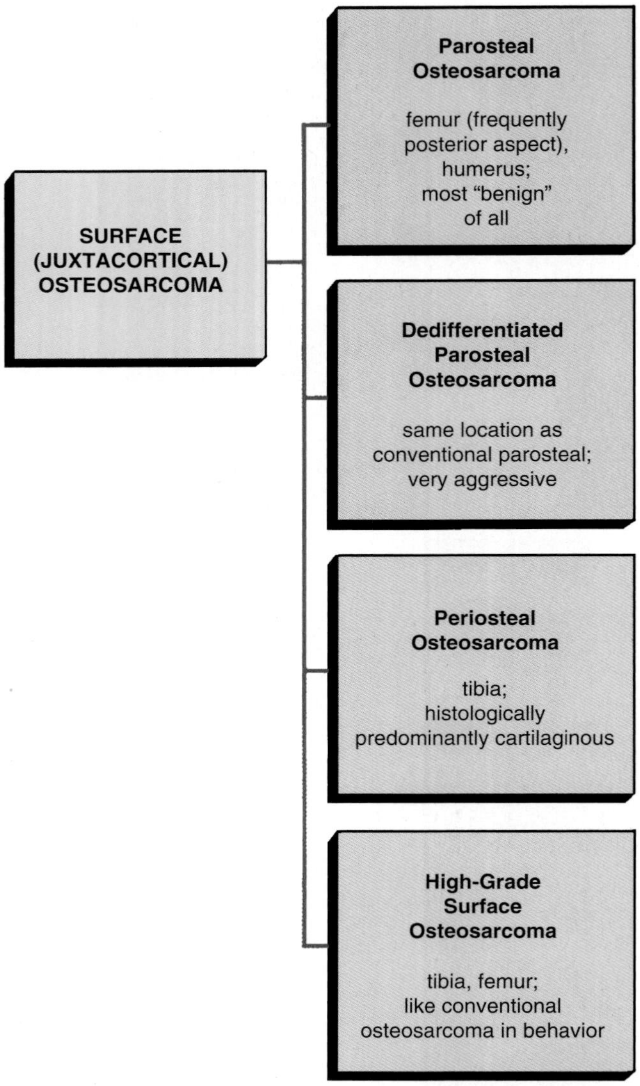

SURFACE
(JUXTACORTICAL)
OSTEOSARCOMA

**Parosteal
Osteosarcoma**

femur (frequently
posterior aspect),
humerus;
most "benign"
of all

**Dedifferentiated
Parosteal
Osteosarcoma**

same location as
conventional parosteal;
very aggressive

**Periosteal
Osteosarcoma**

tibia;
histologically
predominantly cartilaginous

**High-Grade
Surface
Osteosarcoma**

tibia, femur;
like conventional
osteosarcoma in behavior

▲
FIGURE 21.22   Variants of juxtacortical osteosarcoma.

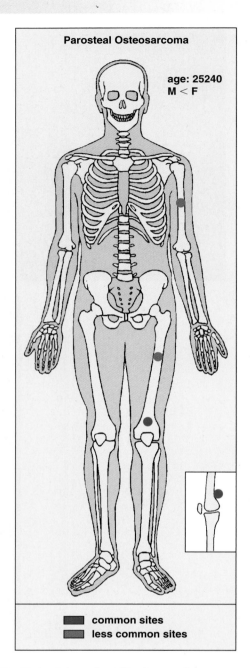

Parosteal Osteosarcoma

age: 25240
M < F

common sites
less common sites

▲
FIGURE 21.23   Skeletal sites of predilection, peak age range, and male-to-
female ratio in parosteal osteosarcoma.

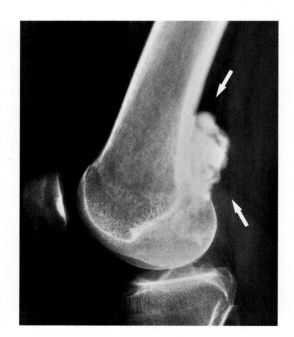

▲
FIGURE 21.24   **Parosteal osteosarcoma.** Typical presentation of this tumor
at the posterior aspect of the distal femur (*arrows*) in a 23-year-old woman.

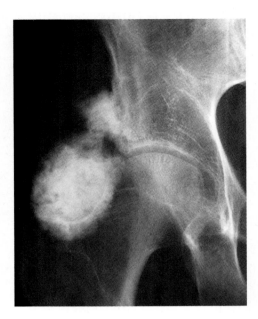

▲
FIGURE 21.25 **Parosteal osteosarcoma.** Anteroposterior radiograph of the right hip shows a large ossific mass attached to the supra-acetabular portion of the ilium. (Reprinted from Greenspan A, Remagen W, 1998, with permission.)

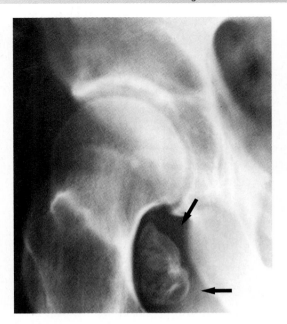

▲
FIGURE 21.27 **Myositis ossificans.** Juxtacortical myositis ossificans, seen here near the medial cortex of the femoral neck (*arrows*), typically presents as a more mature lesion at its periphery, with a center less dense than in parosteal osteosarcoma, and a clear zone representing complete separation of the lesion from the cortex.

osteochondroma is the most frequent source of confusion. Myositis ossificans is distinguished by a zonal phenomenon and by a cleft separating the ossific mass from the cortex (Fig. 21.27; see also Figs. 4.55, 4.56 and 18.28). In sessile osteochondroma, however, the cortex of the lesion merges without interruption into the cortex of the host bone (see Figs. 18.26 and 18.28), a feature not seen in parosteal osteosarcoma. Because the lesion is relatively slow growing and most often involves only the surface of the bone, the prognosis for patients with parosteal osteosarcoma is much better than for those with other types of osteosarcoma. Simple wide resection of the lesion often constitutes sufficient treatment.

Dedifferentiated Parosteal Osteosarcoma. A rare and unusual bone tumor, dedifferentiated parosteal osteosarcoma, was identified by a

group from the Mayo Clinic. Most cases reportedly originate as conventional parosteal osteosarcomas that, after resection and multiple local recurrences, have undergone transformation to histologically high-grade sarcomas. Some cases, however, have presented as primary tumors arising on the cortical surface of a bone *de novo*. Radiographically and histologically, dedifferentiated parosteal osteosarcoma mimics the features of conventional parosteal osteosarcoma. There are, however, some traits of a high-grade sarcoma, such as radiographically identifiable cortical destruction (Fig. 21.28) and histologically identifiable pleomorphic tumor cells with hyperchromatic nuclei and a high mitotic rate. Hence, the prognosis is much worse than that of parosteal osteosarcoma.

Periosteal Osteosarcoma. Most often occurring in adolescence, periosteal osteosarcoma is a very rare tumor (accounting for 1% to 2%

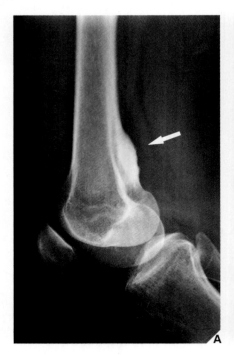
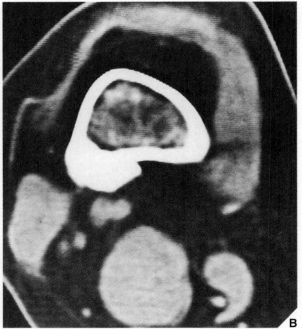

▲
FIGURE 21.26 **CT of parosteal osteosarcoma. (A)** Lateral radiograph of the knee of a 37-year-old woman shows an ossific mass attached to the posterior cortex of the distal femur (*arrow*). Its location and appearance are typical of parosteal osteosarcoma. **(B)** Contrast-enhanced axial CT section demonstrates that the medullary portion of the bone has not been invaded.

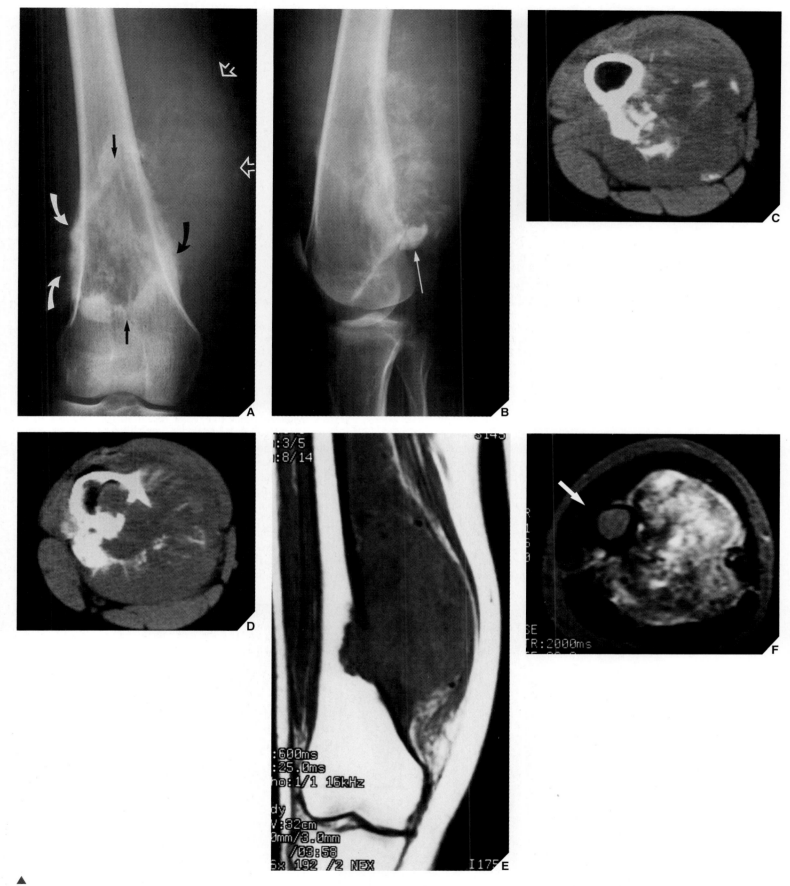

▲
FIGURE 21.28 Dedifferentiated parosteal osteosarcoma. A 24-year-old woman presented with pain and palpable mass above the popliteal fossa of 2 months' duration. Three years before the current symptoms, a parosteal osteosarcoma had been resected from her distal femur. (**A**) Anteroposterior radiograph of the distal femur shows a destructive lesion (*arrows*) associated with an aggressive type of periosteal reaction (*curved arrows*) and a large soft-tissue mass (*open arrows*) with foci of bone formation. (**B**) Lateral radiograph shows in addition the remnants of the previously resected parosteal osteosarcoma (*arrow*). (**C**) The proximal CT section shows a surface tumor exhibiting bone formation and a large soft-tissue mass with foci of tumor-bone. At this level, the bone marrow is not invaded. (**D**) The more distal section reveals in addition the invasion of the medullary cavity, a feature not consistent with a conventional parosteal osteosarcoma. (**E**) Coronal T1-weighted (SE; TR 600/TE 25 msec) MR image demonstrates the extent of both intramedullary invasion and a soft-tissue mass. (**F**) Axial T2-weighted (SE; TR 2000/TE 90 msec) MR image shows heterogeneous signal of a large soft-tissue mass. At the level of this section, the bone marrow is not infiltrated by a tumor (*arrow*).

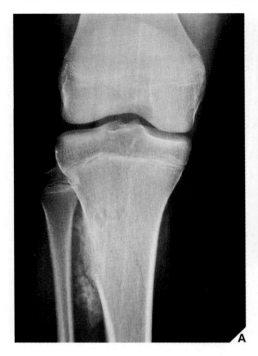

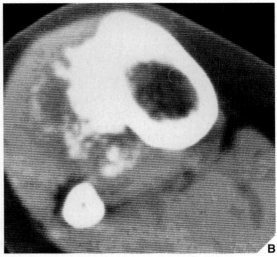

▲
FIGURE 21.29   **Periosteal osteosarcoma. (A)** Anteroposterior radiograph of the right knee of a 12-year-old girl with "discomfort" in the upper leg for 2 months demonstrates poorly defined calcifications and ossifications in a mass attached to the surface of the lateral tibial cortex. There appears to be no bone destruction. **(B)** CT section shows the extent of the soft-tissue mass. Note that the tumor is intimately attached to the cortex, a factor that virtually excludes myositis ossificans.

of all osteosarcomas) that grows on the bone surface, usually at the midshaft of a long bone such as the tibia. The characteristic feature of this tumor, which radiographically may resemble myositis ossificans, is a predominance of cartilaginous tissue (Fig. 21.29). This may lead to an erroneous diagnosis of periosteal chondrosarcoma. The radiologic characteristics of periosteal osteosarcoma were defined by deSantos and colleagues. These include a heterogenous tumor matrix with calcified spiculations interspersed with areas of radiolucency representing uncalcified matrix; occasional periosteal reaction in the form of a Codman triangle (Fig. 21.30); thickening of the periosteal surface of the cortex at the base of the lesion, with sparing of the endosteal surface; extension

of the tumor into the soft tissues; and sparing of the medullary cavity (Fig. 21.31). By microscopy, these tumors have low-grade to medium-grade malignancy and are composed mainly of lobulated chondroid tissue with moderate cellularity. Periosteal osteosarcoma is marked by a better prognosis than the conventional type but a worse one than the parosteal variant.

High-Grade Surface Osteosarcoma. High-grade surface osteosarcoma may exhibit radiographic features similar to those of parosteal or periosteal osteosarcoma (Fig. 21.32). Histologically, this lesion shows elements identical to those of conventional osteosarcoma. It also carries a high potential for metastasis.

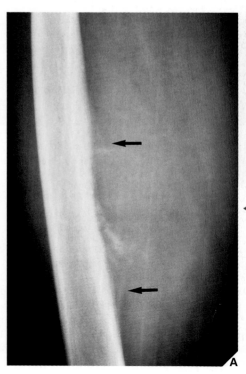

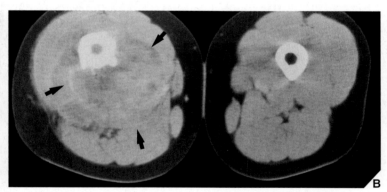

◄ FIGURE 21.30   **Periosteal osteosarcoma. (A)** Anteroposterior radiograph of the right femur of a 16-year-old girl shows a surface lesion affecting the medial cortex, associated with a Codman triangle of periosteal reaction (*arrows*) and a large soft-tissue mass. **(B)** CT shows the soft-tissue component to better advantage (*arrows*). The medullary cavity is not invaded by the tumor; however, an increase in attenuation value, compared with the contralateral marrow cavity, indicates bone marrow edema.

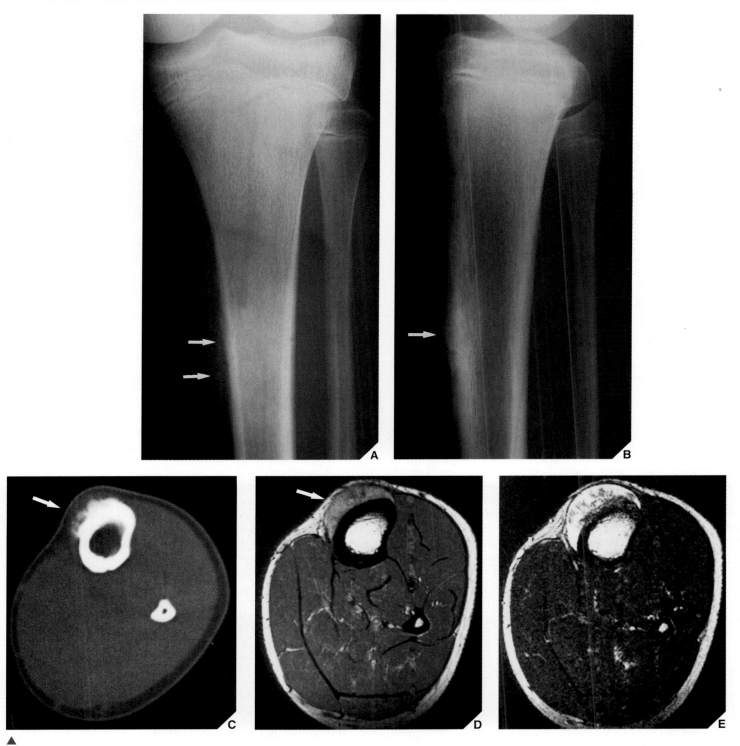

FIGURE 21.31 **Periosteal osteosarcoma.** Anteroposterior (**A**) and lateral (**B**) radiographs of the left leg in a 12-year-old boy show faint ossific densities on the anteromedial surface of the proximal tibia adjacent to the almost indistinct cortical destruction. An aggressive velvet type of periosteal reaction is evident (*arrows*). (**C**) CT section through the tumor shows bone formation on the anterior surface of the tibia (*arrow*) and lack of invasion of the medullary cavity. (**D**) Axial spin-echo T1-weighted MRI shows that tumor displays slightly higher signal than the muscles (*arrow*). Note normal high signal of bone marrow. (**E**) On axial T2-weighted image (SE; TR 2000/TE 80 msec), the mass becomes bright, except for the central areas at which bone formation displays low signal intensity.

Soft-Tissue (Extraskeletal) Osteosarcoma

Osteosarcoma of the soft tissues (extraskeletal, extraosseous) is an uncommon malignant tumor of mesenchymal origin. This tumor possesses the capacity to form neoplastic osteoid, bone, and cartilage. It usually targets middle-aged and elderly individuals, with a mean age at presentation of 54 years. Soft-tissue osteosarcoma is much less common than osteosarcoma of bone, accounting for only 4% of all osteosarcomas. It preferentially affects the lower extremities and buttocks. This lesion may also develop in a number of soft tissues, including breast,

lung, thyroid, renal capsule, urinary bladder, and prostate, and even the pelvic retroperitoneum. A soft-tissue osteosarcoma may rarely arise after radiation therapy.

Patients most commonly present with a slowly enlarging mass that may or may not be accompanied by pain. Radiographic appearance is characterized by a soft-tissue mass with scattered amorphous calcifications and ossifications. The tumor exhibits a disorganized arrangement of osteogenic elements in its center (Fig. 21.33A,B). If the tumor develops close to bone, it may invade the cortex.

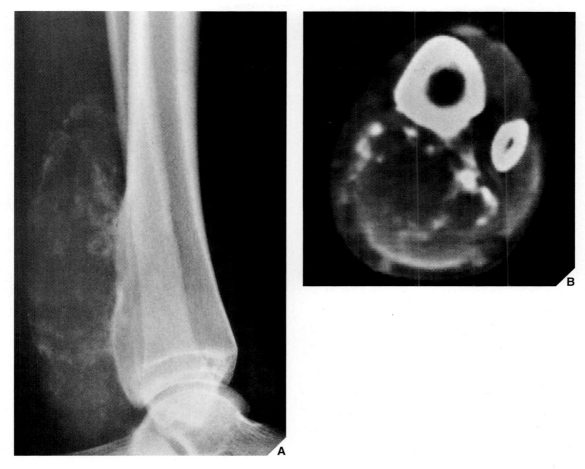

▲
FIGURE 21.32   **High-grade surface osteosarcoma. (A)** Lateral radiograph of the distal leg demonstrates a tumor attached to the posterior cortex of tibia in a 24-year-old man. Poorly defined ossific foci are seen within a large soft-tissue mass. Note the similarity of the tumor to periosteal osteosarcoma (see Figs. 21.29 and 21.30). **(B)** CT section demonstrates the extent of the lesion. Characteristically, the marrow cavity is not affected.

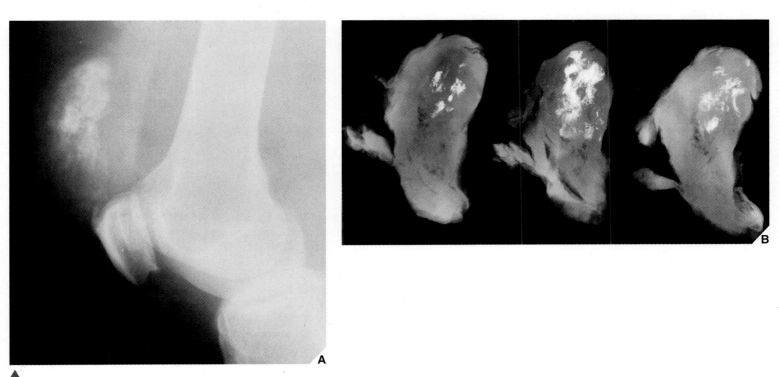

▲
FIGURE 21.33   **Soft-tissue osteosarcoma. (A)** Lateral radiograph of the knee of a 51-year-old woman shows a poorly defined soft-tissue mass above the patella, merging with the quadriceps muscle. The center of the lesion exhibits amorphous calcifications and ossifications. **(B)** Radiograph of the resected specimen of the tumor reveals foci of ossifications in the center of the mass, surrounded by a radiolucent zone at the periphery (so-called reverse zoning). (Reprinted from Greenspan A et al., 1987, with permission.)

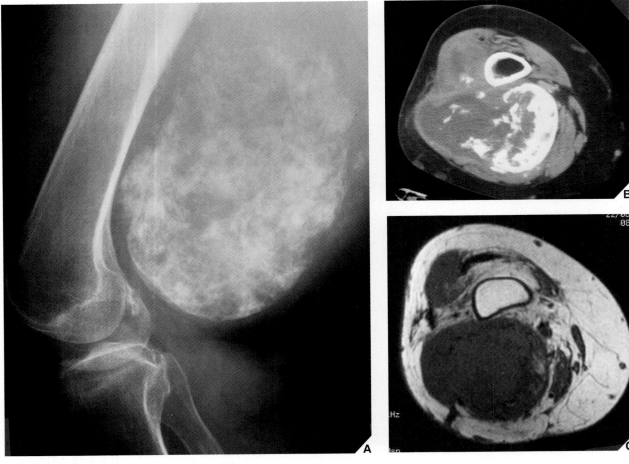

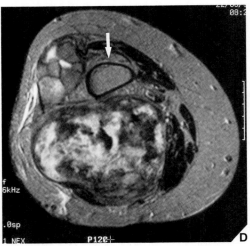

◀ **FIGURE 21.34   CT and MRI of soft-tissue osteosarcoma.** A 68-year-old woman presented with a progressively enlarging soft-tissue mass in the popliteal region of the right knee. (**A**) Lateral radiograph shows a large soft-tissue mass, sharply outlined in its distal extent but poorly delineated at the proximal end. Calcifications and ossifications are present throughout the tumor. (**B**) Axial CT section reveals reverse zoning typical of soft-tissue osteosarcoma. (**C**) Axial T1-weighted MRI shows slightly heterogeneous mass exhibiting low signal intensity. (**D**) Axial T2-weighted MRI reveals marked heterogeneity of the tumor, displaying variation of signals from high to intermediate intensity. Note lack of involvement of femoral bone marrow (*arrow*). (Reprinted from Greenspan A, Remagen W, 1998, with permission.)

On CT, a heavily mineralized soft-tissue mass is usually seen, occasionally with necrotic areas. This technique is often better than radiography at revealing the pattern of central ossification, which is referred to as the "reverse zoning" phenomenon. CT also demonstrates a lack of attachment of the mass to the bone. On MRI, a mass with mixed low signal intensity on T1-weighted images and mixed but predominantly high signal intensity on T2-weighted and inversion recovery sequences is often seen. MRI may also reveal a pseudocapsule of tumor (Fig. 21.34A–D).

The histopathology of soft-tissue osteosarcoma is indistinguishable from that of a conventional osteosarcoma.

Differential Diagnosis. The differential diagnosis of extraskeletal osteosarcoma includes myositis ossificans, tumoral calcinosis, synovial sarcoma, extraskeletal chondrosarcoma, liposarcoma of soft tissues with ossification, and pseudomalignant osseous tumor of soft tissue.

Myositis ossificans is a benign, usually posttraumatic, lesion of the soft tissues that is observed predominantly in adolescents and young adults (see Figs. 4.55, 4.56, and 21.27). The zoning phenomenon reflects the maturation pattern of the lesion. The center of the lesion is undifferentiated and cellular, but increasingly mature ossification is observed toward the periphery constituting the histologic hallmark of this condition. Radiography reveals that the zoning phenomenon of this lesion is characterized by a radiolucent center and a denser and more sclerotic periphery (see Fig. 4.56). The mass is often separated from the adjacent cortex by a radiolucent cleft. The evolution of myositis ossificans can be well correlated with the lapse of time since the trauma.

Synovial sarcoma has a predilection for adolescents and younger adults (13 to 55 years). This tumor is usually located near a joint, especially in the lower extremities and particularly in the area around the knee and foot. Radiography reveals a lobulated mass, and in 25% of cases, amorphous calcifications are present (see Fig. 23.16). Ossification is extremely rare in synovial sarcoma. In approximately 15% to 20% of patients, a periosteal reaction and/or erosion of adjacent bone structures can be observed. There may be osteoporosis of the affected limb secondary to disuse.

Chondrosarcoma of soft tissue is a rare malignant tumor and is much less common than extraskeletal osteosarcoma. It appears as a soft-tissue mass with ring-like or punctate calcifications. Soft-tissue chondrosarcoma can be distinguished from soft-tissue osteosarcoma on imaging studies by the lack of bone formation.

Liposarcoma of soft tissues tends to affect older adults and has a male prevalence. This tumor may closely mimic soft-tissue osteosarcoma, particularly when ossification is present. However, the ossification is usually more organized than that in osteosarcoma of soft tissues, and fatty tissue can usually be identified. This lesion commonly affects the thigh, leg, and gluteal region. Growth of the tumor may proceed very slowly, over many years, and erosion of adjacent bone is common.

Pseudomalignant osseous tumor of soft tissues was first described by Jaffe and later by Fine and Stout. These lesions are rare, are more common in females, and are located in the muscle and subcutaneous tissues. They are probably of infective origin, although this has not been unequivocally confirmed. Some lesions may represent unrecognized foci of myositis ossificans.

Osteosarcomas with Unusual Clinical Presentation

There are numerous genetic disorders, marked by chromosome instability, associated with the development of various tumors including osteosarcomas. Among these rare conditions are Rothmund-Thompson syndrome, Werner syndrome, Li-Fraumeni syndrome, retinoblastoma syndrome, and Bloom syndrome.

The *Rothmund-Thompson syndrome*, also known as congenital poikiloderma, is a hereditary disease with a male predominance of 2:1, appearing in the first year of life, and characterized by erythematous and maculopapular skin lesions with areas of hyperpigmentation. These lesions are associated with a variety of other abnormalities such as sensitivity to light, juvenile cataracts, short stature, growth retardation, premature baldness, hypogonadism, and development of skin malignancies (particularly basal cell and squamous cell carcinoma). Conventional osteosarcoma develops in about 30% of cases (particularly at a younger age), although the presence of multicentric osteosarcoma has also been reported. The syndrome, which is inherited in an autosomal recessive manner, has been attributed to mutations of *RECQL4* gene located at chromosome band 8q24.3, and coding for DNA helicase that unfolds double-stranded DNA into single stranded DNA.

The *Werner syndrome*, also known as adult progeria, is a rare autosomal recessive genetic disorder caused by mutations in the *WRN* gene that has been mapped at chromosome band 8p12-p11. This syndrome is characterized by the premature aging including graying of hair, alopecia, cataracts, scleroderma-like skin changes, osteoarthritis of peripheral joints, short stature, hypogonadism, osteoporosis, diabetes mellitus, and atherosclerotic cardiovascular disease. The patients with this syndrome are also at risk to develop epithelial neoplasms, melanoma, thyroid cancer, and osteosarcoma. Patients with osteosarcoma present at an older age and at atypical sites.

The *Li-Fraumeni syndrome* is a rare autosomal dominant inherited disorder associated with genetic heterozygous germ line R156H, R267Q, and R290H mutation in the *TP53* tumor suppressor gene. The disorder is characterized by multiple primary neoplasms in children and young adults, particularly soft tissue sarcomas, osteosarcomas, breast cancer, brain tumors, and leukemias.

The *retinoblastoma syndrome* consists of the malignant tumor of the retina, originating from the embryonic neural retina. The following dysmorphic abnormalities are associated with this syndrome: microcephaly, broad and prominent nasal bridge, ptosis, protruding upper incisors, micrognathia, short neck, low-set ears, facial asymmetry, genital malformations, and mental retardation. Retinoblastoma is in 60% of patients nonhereditary and unilateral. However, 40% of the cases are inherited in an autosomal dominant manner with almost complete penetrance, and 25% of these patients present with bilateral tumors. The syndrome is caused by a genetic mutation found in the tumor suppressor gene *RB1* located on the long arm of chromosome 13 (13q14.1). Osteosarcoma is the most common secondary malignancy in patients with hereditary

retinoblastoma. Furthermore, these mutations also increase the risk for developing an irradiation-induced secondary osteosarcoma.

The *Bloom syndrome*, also known as Bloom-German syndrome, is an autosomal recessive disorder characterized by congenital telangiectatic erythema of the face resembling lupus erythematosus, dolichocephaly with malar hypoplesia, sensitivity to sunlight, low birth weight and well-proportional dwarfism, immunoglobulin deficiency, limb abnormalities (including syndactyly, polydactyly, and clinodactyly), and propensity for development of malignant tumors, particularly osteosarcoma. This syndrome has been attributed to the functional alteration of DNA-helicase gene *BLM* of the RecQ-family, located on chromosome band 15q26.1.

Secondary Osteosarcomas

In contrast to primary osteosarcomas, secondary lesions occur in an older population. Many of these tumors are responsible for the complications of Paget disease (osteitis deformans) and, characteristically, develop in pagetic bone (Fig. 21.35). The typical radiographic changes in malignant transformation of Paget disease include a destructive lesion

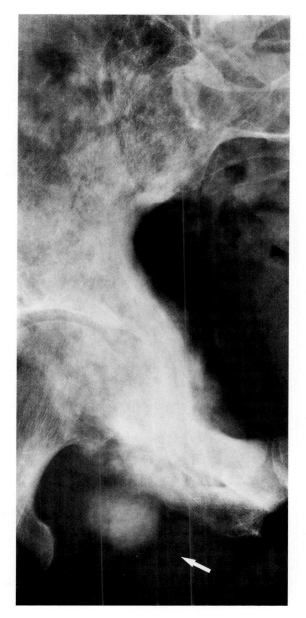

▲

FIGURE 21.35 Secondary osteosarcoma. Radiograph in a 66-year-old man who had extensive skeletal involvement by Paget disease and who had pain in the right hip shows the typical features of osteitis deformans in the right ilium and ischium. There is also destruction of the cortex associated with a soft-tissue mass containing tumor bone (*arrow*)—characteristic features of malignant transformation to osteosarcoma.

in the affected bone, the presence of tumor bone in the lesion, and an associated soft-tissue mass. Osteosarcoma in these patients must be differentiated from metastases to pagetic bone from primary carcinomas elsewhere in the body (most commonly the prostate, breast, and kidney). Secondary osteosarcoma may also develop spontaneously in fibrous dysplasia or after radiation therapy for benign bone lesions such as fibrous dysplasia and giant cell tumor, as well as after irradiation of malignant processes in the soft tissues such as breast carcinoma and lymphoma. (For further discussion of malignant transformation, see the sections in Chapter 22 on Paget disease and radiation-induced sarcoma under the heading Benign Conditions With Malignant Potential.)

Chondrosarcomas

Chondrosarcoma is a malignant bone tumor characterized by the formation of a cartilage matrix by tumor cells. As in osteosarcoma, there are several types of this tumor (Fig. 21.36), each with characteristic clinical, imaging, and pathologic features.

Primary Chondrosarcomas

Conventional Chondrosarcoma
Also known as central or medullary chondrosarcoma, this tumor is seen twice as frequently in males than in females and more commonly in adults, usually in those past their third decade. The most frequent locations are the pelvis and long bones, particularly the femur and humerus (Fig. 21.37). Most conventional chondrosarcomas are slow-growing

tumors, often discovered incidentally. Occasionally, local pain and tenderness may be present.

Radiographically, conventional chondrosarcoma appears as an expansive lesion in the medulla, with thickening of the cortex and characteristic endosteal scalloping; popcorn-like, annular or comma-shaped calcifications are seen in the medullary portion of the bone. A soft-tissue mass may sometimes be present (Figs. 21.38 and 21.39). In typical cases, conventional radiography is sufficient to make a diagnosis (Fig. 21.40). CT and MRI help delineate the extent of intraosseous and soft-tissue involvement (Figs. 21.41 to 21.43).

Histologically, chondrosarcoma is typified by the formation of cartilage by tumor cells. Present are lobules of hyaline cartilage with areas of matrix mineralization in distinctive ring-and-arc–like pattern. The tissue is more cellular and pleomorphic in appearance than enchondroma and contains an appreciable number of plump cells, with large or double nuclei. Mitotic cells are infrequent. The histologic distinction among low-grade, intermediate, and high-grade lesions is based on the cellularity of the tumor tissue, the degree of pleomorphism of the cells and nuclei, and the number of mitoses present. Some invstigators (e.g., Unni) disregard the last feature in grading these tumors (Table 21.2).

Differential Diagnosis. In exceptional cases, particularly in the early stage of development, chondrosarcoma can be indistinguishable from an enchondroma. For this reason, all centrally located cartilage tumors in long bones, particularly in adult patients, should be regarded as malignant until proven otherwise. At the articular ends of the bone, chondrosarcomas frequently lack characteristic calcifications and may mimic a giant cell tumor.

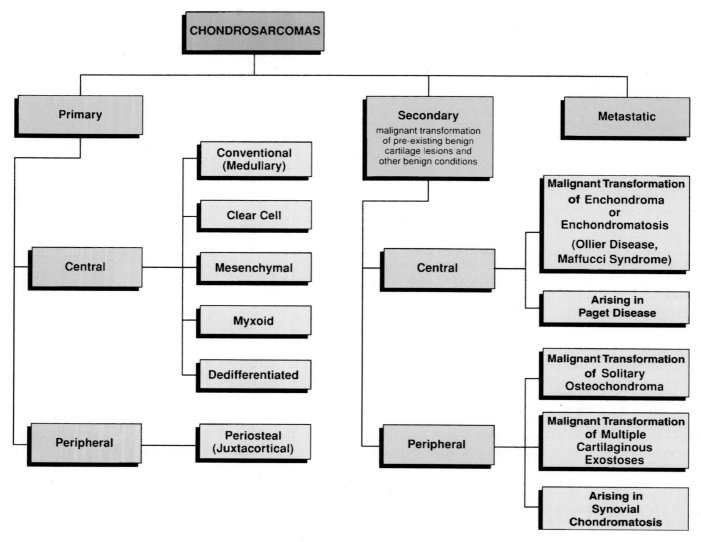

▲
FIGURE 21.36   Classification of the types of chondrosarcoma.

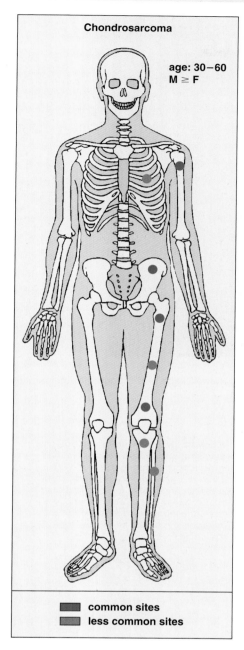

▲
FIGURE 21.37 Skeletal sites of predilection, peak age range, and male-to-female ratio in conventional chondrosarcoma.

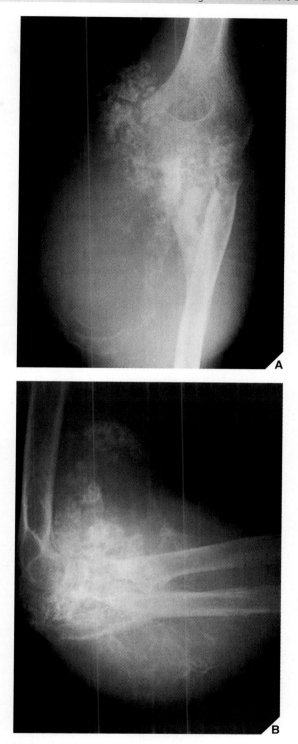

▲
FIGURE 21.38 Chondrosarcoma. Anteroposterior (**A**) and lateral (**B**) radiographs of the right elbow in a 55-year-old man show a tumor arising from the proximal ulna. Note a huge soft-tissue mass containing chondroid calcifications.

Complications and Treatment. Pathologic fractures through conventional chondrosarcomas are rare (Fig. 21.44). Moreover, conventional chondrosarcomas are slow-growing tumors, and only in rare cases do they metastasize to distant areas. Because they are not radiosensitive, surgical resection is the major means of therapy.

Clear Cell Chondrosarcoma

Clear cell chondrosarcoma is a rare (less than 4% of all chondrosarcomas in the Mayo Clinic series) variant of chondrosarcoma. First described by Unni and associates in 1976, it occurs twice as often in males than in females, usually in the third to fifth decades. It is predominantly a lytic

lesion with a sclerotic border, which occasionally may contain calcifications. Many of these lesions resemble chondroblastomas or giant cell tumors, and many involve the proximal end of the humerus and femur (Figs. 21.45 and 21.46). Collins and colleagues reported MRI findings in 34 patients with pathologically documented cases of clear cell chondrosarcoma. The tumors revealed low signal intensity on T1-weighted sequences and moderately to significantly bright signal on T2 weighting. Heterogenic areas seen on T1- and T2-weighted images and on postgadolinium T1-weighted images correlated pathologically to areas of mineralization, intralesional hemorrhage, and cystic changes within the tumor.

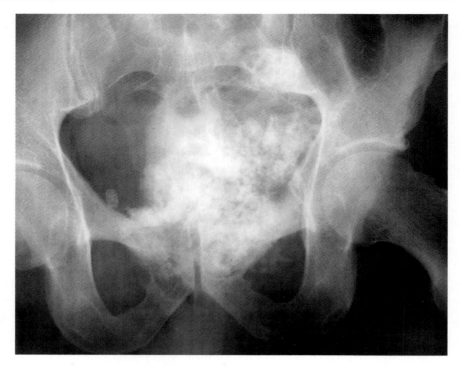

▲
FIGURE 21.39   **Chondrosarcoma.** Anteroposterior radiograph of the pelvis in a 52-year-old man shows a large calcified mass arising from the left pubic bone and extending into the pelvic cavity.

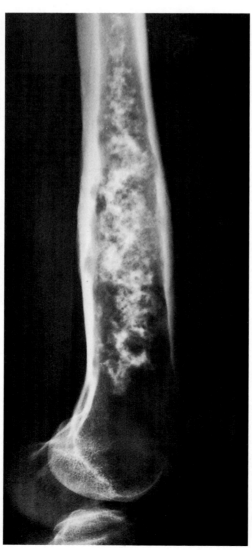

◀ FIGURE 21.40   **Chondrosarcoma.** Lateral radiograph in a 46-year-old man shows the characteristic features of a central chondrosarcoma of the right femur. Within the destructive lesion in the medullary portion of the bone are annular and comma-shaped calcifications. The thickened cortex, which is caused by periosteal new bone formation in response to destruction of the cortex by the chondroblastic tumor, shows the typical deep endosteal scalloping.

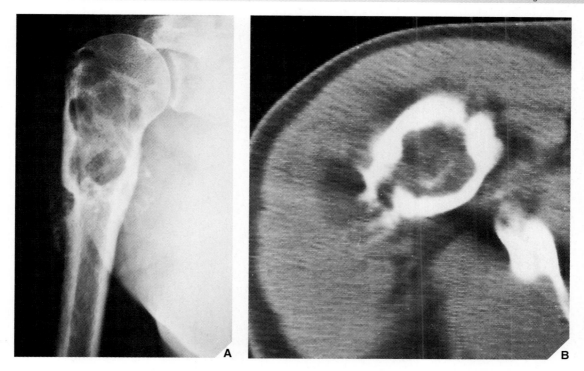

FIGURE 21.41   CT of chondrosarcoma. (A) Anteroposterior radiograph of the right shoulder of a 62-year-old man is not adequate for demonstrating the soft-tissue extension of the chondrosarcoma in the proximal humerus. **(B)** CT section through the lesion demonstrates cortical destruction and a large soft-tissue mass.

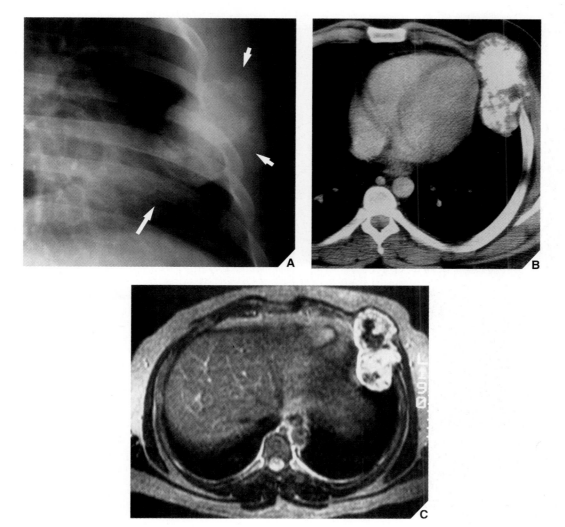

FIGURE 21.42   CT and MRI of chondrosarcoma. (A) A large calcified mass arises from the left anterior sixth rib (*arrows*). **(B)** Axial CT section reveals destruction of the rib and intrathoracic and extrathoracic extension of tumor. **(C)** Axial T2-weighted MRI demonstrates heterogeneity of the tumor. Areas of low-intensity signal represent calcified portions of the mass.

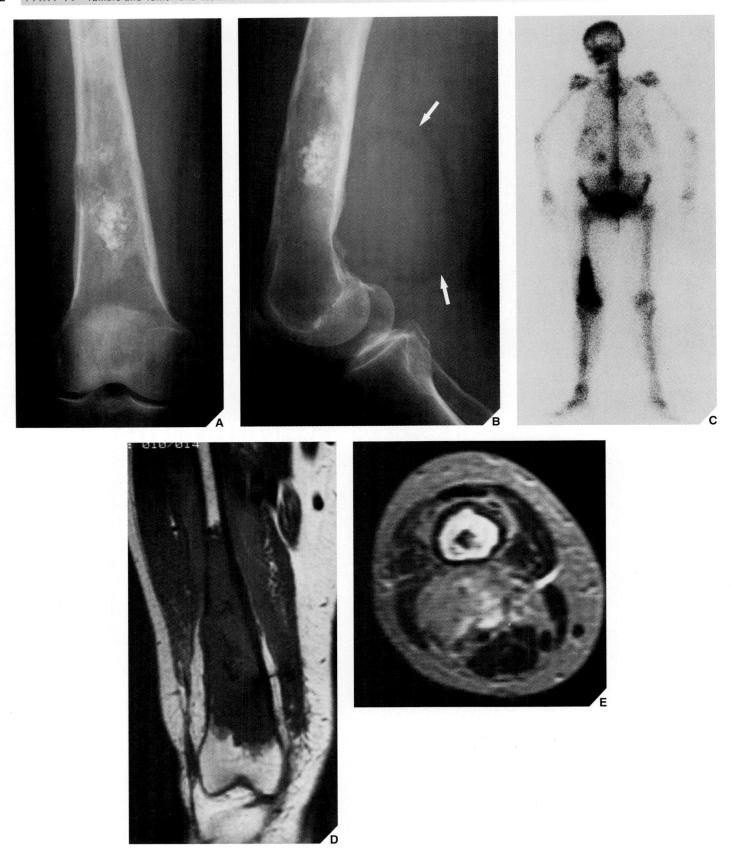

▲
FIGURE 21.43 **Scintigraphy and MRI of chondrosarcoma.** Anteroposterior (**A**) and lateral (**B**) radiographs of the distal femur show typical appearance of central medullary chondrosarcoma. The cortex is destroyed, and there is a large soft-tissue mass projecting posteriorly (*arrows*). (**C**) Radionuclide bone scan obtained after intravenous injection of 15 mCi (555 MBq) of ^{99m}Tc-MDP (technetium-99m-labeled methylene diphosphonate) shows increased uptake of tracer localized to the site of the tumor. (**D**) Coronal T1-weighted (SE; TR 700/TE 20 msec) MR image shows the tumor to be of intermediate-to-low signal intensity. The calcifications display signal void. (**E**) Axial T2-weighted (SE; TR 2000/TE 80 msec) image shows intramedullary tumor displaying a high signal intensity, whereas calcifications are of low signal. The soft-tissue mass shows heterogeneous signal.

TABLE 21.2 **Histologic Grading of Chondrosarcoma**

Grade	Histologic Features
0.5 (borderline)	Histologic features similar to enchondroma, but imaging features more aggressive
1 (low grade)	Cellularity: slightly increased
	Cytologic atypia: slight increase in size and variation in shape of the nuclei; slightly increased hyperchromasia of the nuclei
	Binucleation: few binucleate cells are present
	Stromal myxoid change: may or may not be present
2 (intermediate)	Cellularity: moderately increased
	Cytologic atypia: moderate increase in size and variation in shape of the nuclei; moderately increased hyperchromasia of the nuclei
	Binucleation: large number of double-nucleated and trinucleated cells
	Stromal myxoid change: focally present
3 (high-grade)	Cellularity: markedly increased
	Cytologic atypia: marked enlargement and irregularity of the nuclei; markedly increased hyperchromasia of the nuclei
	Binucleation: large number of double- and multinucleated cells
	Stromal myxoid change: commonly present
	Other: small foci of spindling at the periphery of the lobules of chondrocytes; foci of necrosis present.

Modified from Dahlin DC, Unni KK, 1988.

Histologically, the clear cell variant exhibits larger and more rounded tumor cells than other chondrosarcomas with clear or vacuolated cytoplasm containing large amounts of glycogen. A chondroid matrix, trabeculae of reactive bone, and numerous osteoclast-like giant cells are distinctive features of this tumor.

Treatment. Clear cell chondrosarcoma is considered a low-grade malignancy, although distant metastases have been reported. It has been managed in a variety of ways, from simple observation or curettage to wide resection and even amputation. Although it is a less aggressive tumor than conventional chondrosarcoma, inadequate treatment may lead to recurrence. Therefore, *en bloc* resection with wide surgical margins of bone and soft tissue is the current treatment of choice.

Mesenchymal Chondrosarcoma

Mesenchymal chondrosarcoma is very uncommon (less than 1% of all malignant bone tumors) and tends to occur in the patient's second or third decade. It presents radiographically with the permeative type of bone destruction seen in round cell tumors, and calcifications in the cartilaginous portion of the tumor (Fig. 21.47). It may be indistinguishable from conventional chondrosarcoma and is a highly malignant lesion with a strong capacity for metastases.

Histologically, the mesenchymal variant demonstrates a high degree of malignancy, typified by bimorphic pattern. The tumor is composed of more or less differentiated cartilage, together with highly vascular stroma of mesenchymal tissue containing spindle cells and round cells.

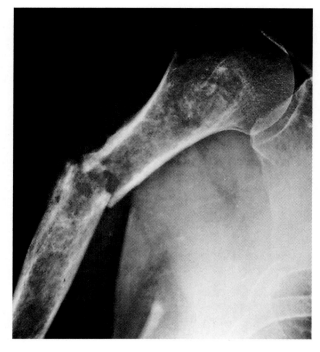

▲
FIGURE 21.44 **Complication of chondrosarcoma.** Pathologic fracture through a tumor, as seen here in the right humerus in a 60-year-old man, is a rare complication of this lesion.

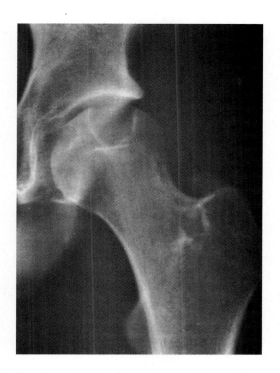

▲
FIGURE 21.45 **Clear cell chondrosarcoma.** A 22-year-old man presented with left hip pain for 3 months. Anteroposterior radiograph demonstrates an osteolytic lesion located in the superolateral aspect of the femoral head and extending into the articular surface. The lesion, which is demarcated by a thin sclerotic border, closely resembles a chondroblastoma. On biopsy, however, it proved to be a clear cell chondrosarcoma.

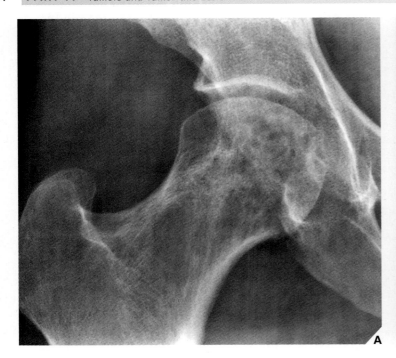
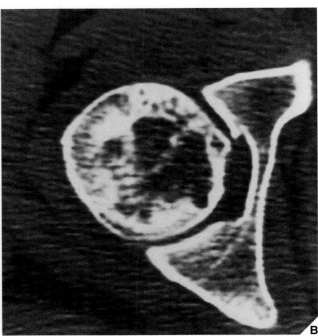

FIGURE 21.46   **Clear cell chondrosarcoma. (A)** Anteroposterior radiograph of the right hip shows a radiolucent lesion with calcifications in the femoral head. **(B)** Axial CT section shows a lytic character of the tumor and central chondroid calcifications. (Reprinted from Greenspan A et al., 2007.)

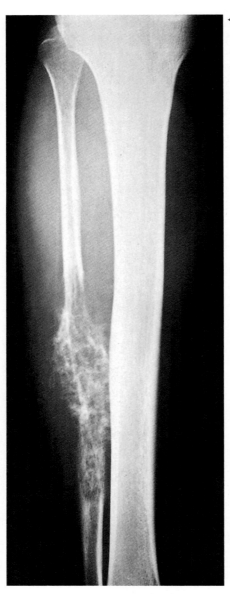

◀ FIGURE 21.47   **Mesenchymal chondrosarcoma.** Antero-posterior radiograph of the right lower leg of a 43-year-old woman with a 6-month history of intermittent pain in the right calf shows a destructive lesion at the midportion of the fibula associated with a large soft-tissue mass. The central portion of the lesion exhibits annular and comma-shaped calcifications typical of a cartilage tumor, but its periphery shows a permeative type of bone destruction characteristic of round cell tumors.

Dedifferentiated Chondrosarcoma

First described by Dahlin and Beabout in 1971, dedifferentiated chondrosarcoma is the most malignant of all chondrosarcomas and consequently carries a very poor prognosis; most patients die from the disease within 2 years of diagnosis. The patient typically has pain of long duration, followed by a more recent onset of rapid swelling and local tenderness. The prolonged pain probably reflects a slow-growing lesion, and the swelling and tenderness may be related to the development of a rapidly growing, more malignant component. The hallmark of this lesion is the appearance of an aggressive sarcoma engrafted on a benign chondral lesion or on a benign-appearing low-grade chondrosarcoma. Although it may radiographically resemble a conventional chondrosarcoma, its histologic composition differs. The dedifferentiated tissue may appear to be a fibrosarcoma, a MFH, or an osteosarcoma.

Radiographically, dedifferentiated chondrosarcomas exhibit calcific foci with aggressive bone destruction and are often accompanied by a large soft-tissue mass (Fig. 21.48). Recently reported by McSweeney and associates, MRI findings of dedifferentiated chondrosarcoma consisted of three distinct patterns. In one group of patients, clear demarcation was seen on T2-weighted images between the low-grade tumor that exhibited high signal intensity and the high-grade tumor that showed relatively reduced signal, a so-called biphasic pattern. In another group of patients, the only MRI evidence of an underlying chondroid lesion was the presence of several areas of signal void corresponding to matrix mineralization identified on the conventional radiography. The third MRI pattern consisted of relatively lower signal intensity of the tumor, accompanied by smaller areas revealing high signal and fluid–fluid levels on T2 weighting, presumably caused by tumor necrosis rather than chondroid tissue.

Histologically, dedifferentiated chondrosarcoma often shows a cartilaginous component of low-grade malignancy combined with highly cellular sarcomatous tissue.

Recently, the validity of the term "dedifferentiation" has been challenged. Studies using electron microscopy and immunohistochemistry indicate that sarcomatous dedifferentiation represents, in fact, the synchronous differentiation of separate clones of cells from a primitive spindle-cell sarcoma to various types of sarcoma.

Periosteal Chondrosarcoma

Generally, periosteal chondrosarcoma has the same imaging and pathologic features as central chondrosarcoma (Fig. 21.49). Because the lesion appears on the bone surface, it must be distinguished from periosteal osteosarcoma. The differentiation of this lesion may create problems for the radiologist and pathologist alike.

Secondary Chondrosarcomas

The most common types of secondary chondrosarcomas are tumors developing in preexisting enchondromas (see Fig. 18.23) or in multiple cartilaginous exostoses (see Figs. 18.33 and 18.40). These tumors develop in a slightly younger age group (age 20 to 40 years) than primary chondrosarcomas and have a more benign course. Because they are usually of low-grade malignancy, the prognosis is more favorable than in conventional chondrosarcoma. Total excision is the treatment of choice. (For further discussion of malignant transformation, see the sections under the heading Benign Conditions With Malignant Potential in Chapter 22.)

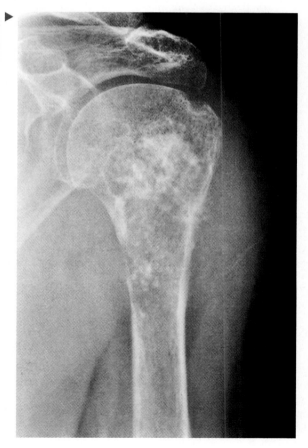

FIGURE 21.48 Dedifferentiated chondrosarcoma. A 70-year-old woman had a destructive lesion in the medullary cavity of the proximal shaft of the left humerus with calcifications typical of a cartilage tumor; there was also a soft-tissue mass. However, although the lesion seen on this film exhibits features typical of medullary chondrosarcoma, biopsy revealed, in addition to typical chondrosarcomatous tissue, elements of a giant cell tumor and MFH, leading to a diagnosis of dedifferentiated chondrosarcoma—the most aggressive of all such tumors.

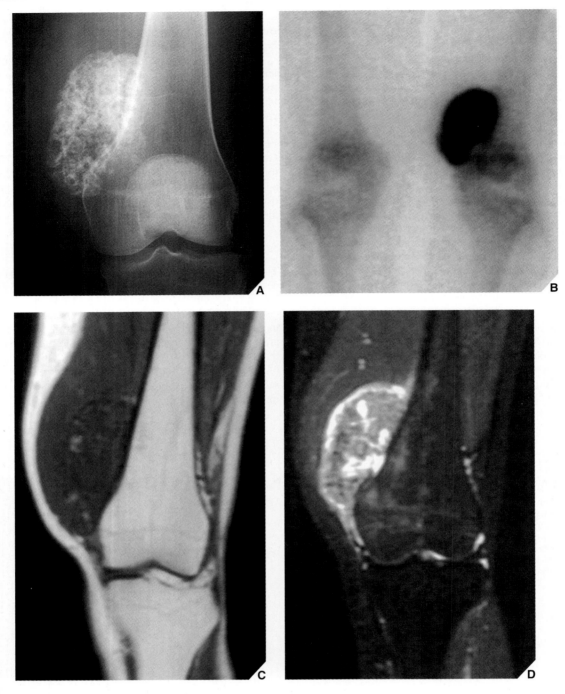

▲
FIGURE 21.49   Periosteal chondrosarcoma. (A) Anteroposterior radiograph of the right knee of a 30-year-old woman shows a parosteal calcified mass at the medial cortex of distal femur, exhibiting chondroid calcifications. **(B)** Radionuclide bone scan obtained after intravenous administration of 15 mCi (555MBq) of ^{99m}Tc-labeled methylene diphosphonate shows markedly increased uptake of radiotracer within the mass. **(C)** Coronal T1-weighted MR image shows the mass to be isointense with surrounding muscles displaying intermediate signal intensity. **(D)** On coronal T2-weighted MRI, the mass becomes bright, but the central calcifications exhibit low signal. (Reprinted from Greenspan A et al., 2007.)

PRACTICAL POINTS TO REMEMBER

Osteosarcoma

[1] Osteosarcoma has the ability to produce osteoid tissue or bone. Its most characteristic radiographic features are:
- the presence of tumor bone in the lesion—the hallmark of this malignancy
- destruction of the medullary portion of the bone or cortex
- an aggressive periosteal reaction—sunburst, lamellated, or Codman triangle
- the presence of a soft-tissue mass.

[2] In the radiologic evaluation of the different types of osteosarcoma—conventional, telangiectatic, multifocal, and juxtacortical:
- Conventional radiography is usually sufficient to identify the radiographic characteristics of each type and make a definitive diagnosis
- CT and MRI are invaluable for defining the extent of the tumor in the bone and soft tissues, and for monitoring the results of presurgical chemotherapy and radiation therapy.

[3] Telangiectatic osteosarcoma, among the most aggressive of osteosarcomas, may present radiographically as a purely osteolytic lesion. It may resemble an aneurysmal bone cyst.

[4] Parosteal osteosarcoma, the least malignant type of osteosarcoma:
- has a predilection for the posterior aspect of the distal femur
- is usually seen attached to the cortex, without invasion of the medullary cavity.

[5] Periosteal osteosarcoma, like parosteal osteosarcoma, is a "surface" lesion. It is, however, more aggressive and contains an excessive amount of cartilaginous tissue. It may resemble periosteal chondrosarcoma and myositis ossificans.

[6] Extraskeletal (soft-tissue) osteosarcoma is a rare malignant tumor of mesenchymal origin, most often affecting middle-aged and elderly individuals. The preferential sites for this neoplasm are lower extremities and buttocks. It may resemble myositis ossificans, tumoral calcinosis, and synovial sarcoma.

[7] The most common form of secondary osteosarcoma is that complicating Paget disease. It is an extremely aggressive lesion; patients usually do not survive beyond 8 months after diagnosis.

Chondrosarcoma

[1] Chondrosarcoma is a malignant bone tumor capable of forming cartilage. Its most characteristic radiographic features are:
- an expansive, destructive lesion in the medullary portion of the bone
- the presence of annular and comma-shaped calcifications within the tumor matrix
- thickening of the cortex and deep endosteal scalloping
- the presence of a soft-tissue mass.

[2] Clear cell chondrosarcoma is characterized radiographically by lytic area occasionally containing calcifications and sclerotic border. It may resemble chondroblastoma.

[3] Mesenchymal chondrosarcoma demonstrates radiographically two different appearances: side-by-side present are areas of permeative type of bone destruction similar to round cell tumors, and areas resembling typical cartilaginous tumor with calcifications.

[4] Dedifferentiated chondrosarcoma, the most aggressive type of all cartilage tumors, carries a poor prognosis. In addition to chondrogenic tissue, it can contain elements of fibrosarcoma, MFH, or osteosarcoma.

[5] Periosteal chondrosarcoma may be indistinguishable from periosteal osteosarcoma.

[6] Secondary chondrosarcoma usually develops in a preexisting benign lesion such as an enchondromatosis or multiple cartilaginous exostoses. At risk are the patients with Ollier disease and Maffucci syndrome.

SUGGESTED READINGS

Abe K, Kumagai K, Hayashi T, et al. High-grade surface osteosarcoma of the hand. *Skeletal Radiol* 2007;36:869–873.

Ackerman LV. Extra-osseous localized non-neoplastic bone and cartilage formation (so-called myositis ossificans). *J Bone Joint Surg [Am]* 1958;40A:279–298.

Ahuja SC, Villacin AB, Smith J, Bullough PG, Huvos AG, Marcove RC. Juxtacortical (parosteal) osteosarcoma: histological grading and prognosis. *J Bone Joint Surg [Am]* 1977;59A:632–647.

Aisen AM, Martel W, Braunstein EM, McMillin KI, Phillips WA, Kling TF. MRI and CT evaluation of primary bone and soft-tissue tumors. *Am J Roentgenol* 1986;146:749–756.

Aizawa T, Okada K, Abe E, Tsuchida S, Shimada Y, Itoi E. Multicentric osteosarcoma with long-term survival. *Skeletal Radiology* 2004;33:41–45.

Allan CJ, Soule EH. Osteogenic sarcoma of the somatic soft tissues. Clinicopathologic study of 26 cases and review of literature. *Cancer* 1971;27:11121–11133.

Alpert LI, Abaci IF, Werthamer S. Radiation-induced extraskeletal osteosarcoma. *Cancer* 1973;31:1359–1363.

Amendola MA, Glazer GM, Adha FP, Francis IR, Weatherbee L, Martel W. Myositis ossificans circumscripta: computed tomographic diagnosis. *Radiology* 1983;149:775–779.

Amstutz HC. Multiple osteogenic sarcomata—metastatic or multicentric? *Cancer* 1969;24:923–931.

Anderson RB, McAlister JA Jr, Wrenn RN. Case report 585. Intracortical osteosarcoma. *Skeletal Radiology* 1989;18:627–630.

Angervall L, Enerback L, Knutson H. Chondrosarcoma of soft tissue origin. *Cancer* 1973;32:507–513.

Angervall L, Stener B, Stener I, Ahren C. Pseudomalignant osseous tumor of soft tissue. A clinical, radiological and pathological study of five cases. *J Bone Joint Surg [Br]* 1969;51B:654–663.

Aoki J, Sone S, Fujioka F, et al. MR of enchondroma and chondrosarcoma: rings and arcs of Gd-DTPA enhancement. *J Comput Assist Tomogr* 1991;15:1011–1016.

Ayala AG, Ro JY, Raymond AK, et al. Small cell osteosarcoma. A clinicopathologic study of 27 cases. *Cancer* 1989;64:2162–2173.

Azura M, Vanel D, Alberghini M, et al. Parosteal osteosarcoma dedifferentiating into telangiectatic osteosarcoma: importance of lytic changes and fluid cavities at imaging. *Skeletal Radiol* 2009;38:685–690.

Bagley L, Kneeland JB, Dalinka MK, Bullough P, Brooks J. Unusual behavior of clear cell chondrosarcoma. *Skeletal Radiol* 1993;22:279–282.

Ballance WA Jr, Mendelsohn G, Carter JR, Abdul-Karim FW, Jacobs G, Makley JT. Osteogenic sarcoma. Malignant fibrous histiocytoma subtype. *Cancer* 1988;62:763–771.

Bane BL, Evans HL, Ro JY, et al. Extra-skeletal osteosarcoma. A clinico-pathologic study of 26 cases. *Cancer* 1990;65:2762–2770.

Bathurst N, Sanerkin N, Watt I. Osteoclast-rich osteosarcoma. *Br J Radiol* 1986;59:667–673.

Berquist TH. Magnetic resonance imaging of primary skeletal neoplasms. *Radiol Clin North Am* 1993;31:411–424.

Bertoni F, Boriani S, Laus M, Campanacci M. Periosteal chondrosarcoma and periosteal osteosarcoma. Two distinct entities. *J Bone Joint Surg [Br]* 1982;64B:370–376.

Bertoni F, Picci P, Bacchini P, et al. Mesenchymal chondrosarcoma of bone and soft tissues. *Cancer* 1983;52:533–541.

Bertoni F, Present D, Bacchini P, et al. Dedifferentiated peripheral chondrosarcomas. A report of seven cases. *Cancer* 1989;63:2054–2059.

Bertoni F, Present D, Bacchini P, Pignatti G, Picci P, Campanacci M. The Instituto Rizzoli experience with small cell osteosarcoma. *Cancer* 1989;64:2591–2599.

Bertoni F, Present DA, Enneking WF. Staging of bone tumors. In: Unni KK, ed. *Bone tumors*. New York: Churchill Livingstone; 1988:47–83.

Bertoni F, Unni KK, Beabout JW, Sim FH. Chondrosarcomas of the synovium. *Cancer* 1991;67:155–162.

Björnsson J, Unni KK, Dahlin DC, Beabout JW, Sim FH. Clear cell chondrosarcoma of bone: observation in 47 cases. *Am J Surg Pathol* 1984;8:223–230.

Blasius S, Link TM, Hillmann A, Rödl R, Edel G, Winkelmann W. Intracortical low grade osteosarcoma. A unique case and review of the literature on intracortical osteosarcoma. *Gen Diagn Pathol* 1996;141:273–278.

Brien EW, Mirra JM, Herr R. Benign and malignant cartilage tumors of bone and joints: their anatomic and theoretical basis with an emphasis on radiology, pathology, and clinical biology. I. The intramedullary cartilage tumors. *Skeletal Radiol* 1997;26:325–353.

Brien EW, Mirra JM, Luck JV Jr. Benign and malignant cartilage tumor of bone and joint: their anatomic and theoretical basis with an emphasis on radiology, pathology and clinical biology. II. Juxtacortical cartilage tumors. *Skeletal Radiol* 1999;28:1–20.

Broders AC. The microscopic grading of cancer. In: Pack CT, Ariel IM, eds. *Treatment of cancer and allied diseases*, vol 1, 2nd ed. New York: Paul B. Hoeber; 1958:55–59.

Burgener FA, Perry P. Solitary renal cell carcinoma metastasis in Paget's disease simulating sarcomatous degeneration. *Am J Roentgenol* 1977;128:835–855.

Campanacci M, Cervellati G. Osteosarcoma: a review of 345 cases. *Ital J Orthop Traumatol* 1975;1:5–22.

Campanacci M, Picci P, Gherlinzoni F, Guerra A, Bertoni F, Nef JR. Parosteal osteosarcoma. *J Bone Joint Surg [Br]* 1984;66B:313–321.

Campanacci M, Pizzoferrato A. Osteosarcoma emorragico. *Chir Organi Mov* 1971;60:409–421.

Cannon CP, Nelson SD, Seeger LL, Eckardt JJ. Clear cell chondrosarcoma mimicking chondroblastoma in a skeletally immature patient. *Skeletal Radiol* 2002;31:369–372.

Capanna R, Bertoni F, Bettelli G, et al. Dedifferentiated chondrosarcoma. *J Bone Joint Surg [Am]* 1988;70A:60–69.

Chung EB, Enzinger FM. Extraskeletal osteosarcoma. *Cancer* 1987;60:1132–1142.

Collins MS, Koyama T, Swee RG, Inwards CY. Clear cell chondrosarcoma: radiographic, computed tomographic, and magnetic resonance findings in 34 patients with pathologic correlation. *Skeletal Radiol* 2003;32:687–694.

Crim JR, Seeger LL. Diagnosis of low-grade chondrosarcoma. *Radiology* 1993;189:503–504.

Dahlin DC. Grading of bone tumors. In: Unni KK, ed. *Bone tumors*. New York: Churchill Livingstone, 1988:35–45.

Dahlin DC, Beabout JW. Dedifferentiation of low-grade chondrosarcomas. *Cancer* 1971;28:461–466.

Dahlin DC, Coventry MB. Osteogenic sarcoma: a study of six hundred cases. *J Bone Joint Surg [Am]* 1967;49A:101–110.

Dahlin DC, Unni KK. Osteosarcoma of bone and its important recognizable varieties. *Am J Surg Pathol* 1977;1:61–72.

Dahlin DC, Unni KK. *Bone tumors: general aspects and data on 8542 cases*, 4th ed. Springfield: Charles C. Thomas; 1986:227–259.

Dahlin DC, Unni KK, Matsuno T. Malignant (fibrous) histiocytoma of bone—fact or fancy? *Cancer* 1977;39:1508–1516.

Dardick I, Schatz JE, Colgan TJ. Osteogenic sarcoma with epithelial differentiation. *Ultrastruct Pathol* 1992;16:463–474.

De Beuckeleer LHL, De Schepper AMA, Ramon F. Magnetic resonance imaging of cartilaginous tumors: retrospective study of 79 patients. *Eur J Radiol* 1995;21: 34–40.

deSantos LA, Murray JA, Finkelstein JB, Spjut HJ, Ayala AG. The radiographic spectrum of periosteal osteosarcoma. *Radiology* 1978;127:123–129.

DeSmet AA, Norris MA, Fisher DR. Magnetic resonance imaging of myositis ossificans: analysis of seven cases. *Skeletal Radiol* 1992;21:503–507.

Edeiken J, Raymond AK, Ayala AG, Benjamin RS, Murray JA, Carrasco HC. Small-cell osteosarcoma. *Skeletal Radiol* 1987;16:621–628.

Ellis JH, Siegel CL, Martel W, Weatherbee L, Dorfman H. Radiologic features of well-differentiated osteosarcoma. *Am J Roentgenol* 1988;151:739–742.

Enzinger F, Weiss S. *Soft tissue tumors*. St. Louis: CV Mosby; 1983.

Enzinger FM, Shiraki M. Extraskeletal myxoid chondrosarcoma—an analysis of 34 cases. *Hum Pathol* 1972;3:421–435.

Enzinger FM, Weiss SW. Cartilaginous tumors and tumorlike lesions of soft tissue. In: Enzinger FM, Weiss SW, eds. *Soft tissue tumors*. St. Louis: Mosby-Year Book; 1988:861–881.

Eustace S, Baker N, Lan H, Wadhwani A, Dorfman D. MR imaging of dedifferentiated chondrosarcoma. *Clin Imaging* 1997;21:170–174.

Farr GH, Huvos AG, Marcove RC, Higinbotham NL, Foote FW Jr. Telangiectatic osteogenic sarcoma: a review of twenty-eight cases. *Cancer* 1974;34:1150–1158.

Fechner RE, Mills SE: *Tumors of the bones and joints*. Washington, DC: Armed Forces Institute of Pathology; 1993.

Fechner RE, Mills SE. Osseous lesions. In: Rosai J, Sobin L, eds. *Atlas of tumor pathology: tumors of the bones and joints*. Washington, DC: Armed Forces Institute of Pathology; 1993:25–77.

Feldman F. Cartilaginous tumors and cartilage-forming tumor-like conditions of the bones and soft tissues. In: Ranniger K, ed. *Bone tumors*. Berlin, Germany: Springer-Verlag; 1977:177–220.

Fine G, Stout AP. Osteogenic sarcoma of the extraskeletal soft tissues. *Cancer* 1956;9:1027–1043.

Frassica FJ, Unni KK, Beabout JW, Sim FH. Dedifferentiated chondrosarcoma. A report of the clinicopathological features and treatment of seventy-eight cases. *J Bone Joint Surg [Am]* 1986;68A:1197–1205.

Garrison RC, Unni KK, McLeod RA, Pritchard DJ, Dahlin DC. Chondrosarcoma arising in osteochondroma. *Cancer* 1981;49:1890–1897.

Geirnaerdt MJA, Bloem JL, Eulderink F, Hogendoorn PCW, Taminiau AHM. Cartilaginous tumors: correlation of gadolinium-enhanced MR imaging and histopathologic findings. *Radiology* 1993;186:813–817.

Geirnaerdt MJA, Bloem JL, van der Woude H-J, Taminiau AHM, Nooy MA, Hogendoorn PCW. Chondroblastic osteosarcoma: characterization by gadolinium-enhanced MR imaging correlated with histopathology. *Skeletal Radiol* 1998;27:145–153.

Geirnaerdt MJA, Hogendoorn PCW, Bloem JL, Taminiau AHM, van der Woude H-J. Cartilaginous tumors: fast contrast-enhanced MR imaging. *Radiology* 2000;214: 539–546.

Gherlinzoni F, Antoci B, Canale V. Multicentric osteosarcomata (osteosarcomatosis). *Skeletal Radiol* 1983;10:281–285.

Gitelis S, Block JA, Inerot SE. Clonal analysis of human chondrosarcoma. The 35th Annual Meeting, Orthopedic Research Society. *Orthop Trans* 1989;13:443.

Glicksman AS, Toker C. Osteogenic sarcoma following radiotherapy for bursitis. *Mt Sinai J Med* 1976;43:163–167.

Goldman AB. Myositis ossificans circumscripta: a benign lesion with a malignant differential diagnosis. *Am J Roentgenol* 1976;126:32–40.

Goldman RL, Lichtenstein L. Synovial chondrosarcoma. *Cancer* 1964;17:1233–1240.

Gomes H, Menanteau B, Gaillard D, Behar C. Telangiectatic osteosarcoma. *Pediatr Radiol* 1986;16:140–143.

Greenfield GB, Arrington JA. *Imaging of bone tumors. A multi-modality approach*. Philadelphia: JB Lippincott; 1955:48–91.

Greenspan A. Tumors of cartilage origin. *Orthop Clin North Am* 1989;20:347–366.

Greenspan A, Jundt G, Remagen W. *Differential diagnosis in orthopaedic oncology*, 2nd ed. Philadelphia: Lippincott Williams & Wilkins; 2007:84–148; 212–249.

Greenspan A, Klein MJ. Osteosarcoma: radiologic imaging, differential diagnosis, and pathological considerations. *Semin Orthop* 1991;6:156–166.

Greenspan A, Steiner G, Norman A, Lewis MM, Matlen JJ. Case report 436. Osteosarcoma of the soft tissues of the distal end of the thigh. *Skeletal Radiol* 1987;16: 489–492.

Griffith JF, Kumta SM, Chow LTC, Leung PC, Metreweli C. Intracortical osteosarcoma. *Skeletal Radiol* 1998;27:228–232.

Hasegawa T, Shimoda T, Yokoyama R, Beppu Y, Hirohashi S, Maeda S. Intracortical osteoblastic osteosarcoma with oncogenic rickets. *Skeletal Radiol* 1999;28:41–45.

Hatano H, Ogose A, Hotta T, Otsuka H, Takahashi HE. Periosteal chondrosarcoma invading the medullary cavity. *Skeletal Radiol* 1997;26:375–378.

Henderson ED, Dahlin DC. Chondrosarcoma of bone: a study of 280 cases. *J Bone Joint Surg [Am]* 1963;45A:1450–1458.

Hermann G, Abdelwahab IF, Kenan S, Lewis MM, Klein MJ. Case report 795. High-grade surface osteosarcoma of the radius. *Skeletal Radiol* 1993;22:383–385.

Hermann G, Klein MJ, Springfield D, Abdelwahab IF, Dan SJ. Intracortical osteosarcoma; two-year delay in diagnosis. *Skeletal Radiol* 2002;31:592–596.

Heul RO van der, Ronnen JR von. Juxtacortical osteosarcoma. Diagnosis, differential diagnosis, treatment, and an analysis of eighty cases. *J Bone Joint Surg [Am]* 1967;49A:415–439.

Hopper KD, Moser RP Jr, Haseman DB, Sweet DE, Madewell JE, Kransdorf MJ. Osteosarcomatosis. *Radiology* 1990;175:233–239.

Hudson TM. Medullary (central) chondrosarcoma. In: Hudson TM, ed. *Radiologic pathologic correlation of musculoskeletal lesions*. Baltimore: Williams & Wilkins; 1987:153–175.

Hudson TM, Chew FS, Manaster BJ. Scintigraphy of benign exostoses and exostotic chondrosarcomas. *Am J Roentgenol* 1983;140:581–586.

Hudson TM, Springfield DS, Spanier SS, Enneking WF, Hamlin DJ. Benign exostoses and exostotic chondrosarcomas: evaluation of cartilage thickness by CT. *Radiology* 1984;152:595–599.

Huvos AG, Rosen G, Bretsky SS, Butler A. Telangiectatic osteosarcoma: a clinicopathologic study of 124 patients. *Cancer* 1982;49:1679–1689.

Ishida T, Dorfman HD, Habermann ET. Dedifferentiated chondrosarcoma of humerus with giant cell tumor-like features. *Skeletal Radiol* 1995;24:76–80.

Ishida T, Yamamoto M, Goto T, Kawano H, Yamamoto A, Machinami R. Clear cell chondrosarcoma of the pelvis in a skeletally immature patient. *Skeletal Radiol* 1999;28:290–293.

Jaffe HL. *Tumors and tumorous conditions of the bones and joints*. Philadelphia: Lea & Febiger; 1968.

Janzen L, Logan PM, O'Connell JX, Connell DG, Munk PL. Intramedullary chondroid tumors of bone: correlation of abnormal peritumoral marrow and soft-tissue MRI signal with tumor type. *Skeletal Radiol* 1997;26:100–106.

Jelinek JS, Murphey MD, Kransdorf MJ, Shmookler BM, Malawer MM, Hur RC. Parosteal osteosarcoma: value of MR imaging and CT in the prediction of histologic grade. *Radiology* 1996;201:837–842.

Johnson S, Tetu B, Ayala AG, Chawla SP. Chondrosarcoma with additional mesenchymal component (dedifferentiated chondrosarcoma). A clinical study of 26 cases. *Cancer* 1986;58:278–286.

Kaim AH, Hügli R, Bonél HM, Jundt G. Chondroblastoma and clear cell chondrosarcoma: radiological and MRI characteristics with histopathological correlation. *Skeletal Radiol* 2002;31:88–95.

Kaufman JH, Cedermark BJ, Parthasarathy KL, Didolkar MS, Bakshi SP. The value of ^{67}Ga scintigraphy in soft-tissue sarcoma and chondrosarcoma. *Radiology* 1977;123:131–134.

Kaufman RA, Towbin RB. Telangiectatic osteosarcoma simulating the appearance of an aneurysmal bone cyst. *Pediatr Radiol* 1981;11:102–104.

Kenan S, Ginat DT, Steiner GC. Dedifferentiated high-grade osteosarcoma originating from low-grade central osteosarcoma of the fibula. *Skeletal Radiol* 2007;36: 347–351.

King JW, Spjut HJ, Fechner RE, Vanderpool DW. Synovial chondrosarcoma of the knee joint. *J Bone Joint Surg [Am]* 1967;49A:1389–1396.

Klein MJ. Chondrosarcoma. *Semin Orthop* 1991;6:167–176.

Klein MJ, Siegal GP. Osteosarcoma: anatomic and histologic variants. *Am J Clin Pathol* 2006;125:555–581

Kramer K, Hicks D, Palis J, et al. Epithelioid osteosarcoma of bone. Immunocytochemical evidence suggesting divergent epithelial and mesenchymal differentiation in a primary osseous neoplasm. *Cancer* 1993;71:2977–2982.

Kransdorf MJ, Meis JM. Extraskeletal osseous and cartilaginous tumors of the extremities. *Radiographics* 1993;13:853–884.

Kransdorf MJ, Meis JM, Jelinek JS. Myositis ossificans: MR appearance with radiologic-pathologic correlation. *Am J Roentgenol* 1991;157:1243–1248.

Kyriakos M, Gilula LA, Besich MJ, Schoeneker PL. Intracortical small cell osteosarcoma. *Clin Orthop* 1992;279:269–280.

Lichtenstein L, Jaffe HL. Chondrosarcoma of the bone. *Am J Pathol* 1943;19:553–589.

Logan PM, Mitchell MJ, Munk PL. Imaging of variant osteosarcomas with an emphasis on CT and MR imaging. *Am J Roentgenol* 1998;171:1531–1537.

Lopez BF, Rodriquez PJL, Gonzalez LJ, Sanchez HS, Sanchez DCM. Intracortical osteosarcoma. A case report. *Clin Orthop* 1991;278:218–222.

Lorigan JG, Lipshitz HI, Peuchot M. Radiation-induced sarcoma of bone: CT findings in 19 cases. *Am J Roentgenol* 1989;153:791–794.

Matsuno T, Unni KK, McLeod RA, Dahlin DC. Telangiectatic osteogenic sarcoma. *Cancer* 1976;38:2538–2547.

McCarthy EF, Dorfman HD. Chondrosarcoma of bone with dedifferentiation: a study of eighteen cases. *Hum Pathol* 1982;13:36–40.

McKenna RJ, Schwinn CP, Soong KY, Higinbotham NL. Osteogenic sarcoma arising in Paget's disease. *Cancer* 1964;17:42–66.

Mercuri M, Picci P, Campanacci M, Rulli E. Dedifferentiated chondrosarcoma. *Skeletal Radiol* 1995;24:409–416.

Mindell ER, Shah NK, Webster JH. Postradiation sarcoma of bone and soft tissues. *Orthop Clin North Am* 1977;8:821–834.

Moore TE, King AR, Kathol MH, El-Khoury GY, Palmer R, Downey PR. Sarcoma in Paget disease of bone: clinical, radiologic, and pathologic features in 22 cases. *Am J Roentgenol* 1991;156:1199–1203.

Moser RP. Cartilaginous tumors of the skeleton. *AFIP atlas of radiologic-pathologic correlation*, vol 2. Philadelphia: Hanley & Belfus; 1990:190–197.

Mulder JD, Schütte HE, Kroon HM, Taconis WK. *Radiologic atlas of bone tumors*. Amsterdam, the Netherlands: Elsevier; 1993:51–76.

Murphey MD, Flemming DJ, Boyea SR, Bojescul JA, Sweet DE, Temple HT. Enchondroma versus chondrosarcoma in the appendicular skeleton: differentiating features. *Radiographics* 1998;18:1213–1237.

Murphey MD, Robbin MR, McRae GA, Flemming DJ, Temple HT, Kransdorf MJ. The many faces of osteosarcoma. *Radiographics* 1997;17:1205–1231.

Murphey MD, Walker EA, Wilson AJ, Kransdorf MJ, Temple HT, Gannon FH. From the archives of the AFIP. Imaging of primary chondrosarcoma: radiologic-pathologic correlation. *Radiographics* 2003;23:1245–1278.

Murphey MD, wan Joavisidha S, Temple HT, Gannon FH, Jelinek JS, Malawer MM. Telangiectatic osteosarcoma: radiologic-pathologic comparison. *Radiology* 2003;229:545–553.

Nakashima Y, Unni KK, Shives TC, Swee RG, Dahlin DC. Mesenchymal chondrosarcoma of bone and soft tissue. A review of 111 cases. *Cancer* 1986;57:2444–2453.

Norman A, Dorfman H. Juxtacortical circumscribed myositis ossificans: evolution and radiographic features. *Radiology* 1970;96:301–306.

Norman A, Sissons HA. Radiographic hallmarks of peripheral chondrosarcoma. *Radiology* 1984;151:589–596.

Nuovo MA, Norman A, Chumas J, Ackerman LV. Myositis ossificans with atypical clinical, radiographic, or pathologic findings: a review of 23 cases. *Skeletal Radiol* 1992;21:87–101.

Okada K, Kubota H, Ebina T, Kobayashi T, Abe E, Sato K. High-grade surface osteosarcoma of the humerus. *Skeletal Radiol* 1995;24:531–534.

Okada K, Unni KK, Swee RG, Sim FH. High grade surface osteosarcoma. A clinicopathologic study of 46 cases. *Cancer* 1999;85:1044–1054.

Onikul E, Fletcher BD, Parham DM, Chen G. Accuracy of MR imaging for estimating intraosseous extent of osteosarcoma. *Am J Roentgenol* 1996;167:1211–1215.

Ontell F, Greenspan A. Chondrosarcoma complicating synovial chondromatosis: findings with magnetic resonance imaging. *Can Assoc Radiol J* 1994;45:318–323.

Park Y-K, Yang MH, Ryu KN, Chung DW. Dedifferentiated chondrosarcoma arising in an osteochondroma. *Skeletal Radiol* 1995;24:617–619.

Partovi S, Logan PM, Janzen DL, O'Connell JX, Connell DG. Low-grade parosteal osteosarcoma of the ulna with dedifferentiation into high-grade osteosarcoma. *Skeletal Radiol* 1996;25:497–500.

Picci P, Gherlinzoni F, Guerra A. Intracortical osteosarcoma: rare entity or early manifestation of classical osteosarcoma? *Skeletal Radiol* 1983;9:255–258.

Price CHG, Goldie W. Paget's sarcoma of bone: a study of eighty cases from the Bristol and Leeds bone tumor registries. *J Bone Joint Surg [Br]* 1969;51B:205–224.

Pritchard DJ, Lunke RJ, Taylor WF, Dahlin DC, Medley BE. Chondrosarcoma: clinicopathologic and statistical analysis. *Cancer* 1980;45:149–157.

Ragsdale BD, Sweet DE, Vinh TN. Radiology as gross pathology in evaluating chondroid lesions. *Hum Pathol* 1989;20:930–951.

Ritts GD, Pritchard DJ, Unni KK, Beabout JW, Eckardt JJ. Periosteal osteosarcoma. *Clin Orthop* 1987;219:299–307.

Ruiter DJ, Cornelisse CJ, van Rijssel TG, van der Velde EA. Aneurysmal bone cyst and telangiectatic osteosarcoma. A histopathological and morphometric study. *Virchows Arch [A]* 1977;373:311–325.

Saito T, Oda Y, Kawaguchi K, et al. Five-year evolution of a telangiectatic osteosarcoma initially managed as an aneurysmal bone cyst. *Skeletal Radiol* 2005;34:290–294.

Salvador AH, Beabout JW, Dahlin DC. Mesenchymal chondrosarcoma—observations on 30 new cases. *Cancer* 1971;28:605–615.

Sanerkin NG. Definitions of osteosarcoma, chondrosarcoma and fibrosarcoma of bone. *Cancer* 1980;46:178–185.

Sanerkin NG. The diagnosis and grading of chondrosarcoma of bone. *Cancer* 1980;45:582–594.

Sanerkin NG, Gallagher P. A review of the behaviour of chondrosarcoma of bone. *J Bone Joint Surg [Br]* 1979;61B:395–400.

Saunders C, Szabo RM, Mora S. Chondrosarcoma of the hand arising in a young patient with multiple hereditary exostoses. *J Hand Surg [Br]* 1997;22B:237–242.

Schajowicz F. *Tumors and tumorlike lesions of bone. Pathology, radiology, and treatment*, 2nd ed. Berlin, Germany: Springer-Verlag; 1994:103–106.

Schajowicz F, Sissons HA, Sobin LH. The World Health Organization's histologic classification of bone tumors. A commentary on the second edition. *Cancer* 1995;75:1208–1214.

Schreiman JS, Crass JR, Wick MR, Maile CW, Thompson RC Jr. Osteosarcoma: role of CT in limb-sparing treatment. *Radiology* 1986;161:485–488.

Sciot R, Samson I, Dal Cin P, et al. Giant cell rich parosteal osteosarcoma. *Histopathology* 1995;27:51–55.

Seeger LL, Farooki S, Yao L, Kabo JM, Eckardt JJ. Custom endoprotheses for limb salvage: a historical perspective and image evaluation. *Am J Roentgenol* 1998;171:1525–1529.

Sheth DS, Yasko AW, Raymond AK, et al. Conventional and dedifferentiated parosteal osteosarcoma: diagnosis, treatment and outcome. *Cancer* 1996;78:2136–2145.

Shuhaibar H, Friedman L. Dedifferentiated parosteal osteosarcoma with high-grade osteoclast-rich osteogenic sarcoma at presentation. *Skeletal Radiol* 1998;27:574–577.

Sim FH, Unni KK, Beabout JW, Dahlin DC. Osteosarcoma with small cells simulating Ewing's tumor. *J Bone Joint Surg [Am]* 1979;61A:207–215.

Sirsat MV, Doctor VM. Benign chondroblastoma of bone. Report of a case of malignant transformation. *J Bone Joint Surg [Br]* 1970;52B:741–745.

Sissons HA, Greenspan A. Paget's disease. In: Taveras JM, Ferrucci JT, eds. *Radiology: diagnosis, imaging, intervention*, vol 5. Philadelphia: JB Lippincott; 1986:1–14.

Sordillo PP, Hajdu SI, Magill GB, Goldbey RB. Extraosseous osteogenic sarcoma. A review of 48 patients. *Cancer* 1983;51:727–734.

Spjut HJ, Dorfman HD, Fechner RE, Ackerman LV. Tumors of bone and cartilage. In: Firminger HI, ed. *Atlas of tumor pathology*, 2nd series, fascicle 5. Washington, DC: Armed Forces Institute of Pathology; 1971.

Stevens GM, Pugh DG. Roentgenographic recognition and differentiation of parosteal osteogenic sarcoma. *Am J Roentgenol* 1957;78:1–12.

Stout AP, Verner EW. Chondrosarcoma of the extraskeletal soft tissues. *Cancer* 1953;6:581–590.

Sun TC, Swee RG, Shives TC, Unni KK. Chondrosarcoma in Maffucci's syndrome. *J Bone Joint Surg [Am]* 1985;67A:1214–1219.

Takeushi K, Morii T, Yabe H, et al. Dedifferentiated parosteal osteosarcoma with well-differentiated metastases. *Skeletal Radiol* 2006;35:778–782.

Tateishi U, Hasegawa T, Nojima T, et al. MR features of extraskeletal myxoid chondrosarcoma. *Skeletal Radiol* 2006;35:27–33.

Tetu B, Ordonez NG, Ayala AG, Mackay B. Chondrosarcoma with additional mesenchymal component (dedifferentiated chondrosarcoma). *Cancer* 1986;58:287–298.

Torres FX, Kyriakos M. Bone infarct-associated osteosarcoma. *Cancer* 1992;70:2418–2430.

Unni KK. *Dahlin's bone tumors: general aspects and data on 11,087 cases*, 5th ed. Philadelphia: Lippincott-Raven; 1996:185–196.

Unni KK. Osteosarcoma of bone. In: Unni KK, ed. *Bone tumors*. New York: Churchill Livingstone; 1988:107–133.

Unni KK, Dahlin DC. Premalignant tumors and conditions of bone. *Am J Surg Pathol* 1979;3:47–60.

Unni KK, Dahlin DC. Grading of bone tumors. *Semin Diagn Pathol* 1984;1:165–172.

Unni KK, Dahlin DC, Beabout JW. Periosteal osteogenic sarcoma. *Cancer* 1976;37:2476–2485.

Unni KK, Dahlin DC, Beabout JW, Ivins JC. Parosteal osteogenic sarcoma. *Cancer* 1976;37:2644–2675.

Unni KK, Dahlin DC, Beabout JW, Sim FH. Chondrosarcoma: clear-cell variant: a report of 16 cases. *J Bone Joint Surg [Am]* 1976;58A:676–683.

Unni KK, Dahlin DC, McLeod RA. Intraosseous well-differentiated osteosarcoma. *Cancer* 1977;40:1337–1347.

Vanel D, De Paolis M, Monti C, Mercuri M, Picci P. Radiological features of 24 periosteal chondrosarcomas. *Skeletal Radiol* 2001;30:208–212.

Vanel D, Picci P, De Paolis M, Mercuri M. Radiological study of 12 high-grade surface osteosarcomas. *Skeletal Radiol* 2001;30:667–671.

Verela-Duran J, Enzinger FM. Calcifying synovial sarcoma. *Cancer* 1982;50:345–352.

West OC, Reinus WR, Wilson AJ. Quantitative analysis of the plain radiographic appearance of central chondrosarcoma of bone. *Invest Radiol* 1995;30:440–447.

Wold LE, Unni KK, Beabout JW, Pritchard DJ. High-grade surface osteosarcomas. *Am J Surg Pathol* 1984;8:181–186.

Wold LE, Unni KK, Beabout JW, Sim FH, Dahlin DC. Dedifferentiated parosteal osteosarcoma. *J Bone Joint Surg [Am]* 1984;66A:53–59.

Malignant Bone Tumors II
Miscellaneous Tumors

Fibrosarcoma and Malignant Fibrous Histiocytoma

Fibrosarcoma and malignant fibrous histiocytoma (MFH) are malignant fibrogenic tumors that have very similar radiographic presentations and histologic patterns. Both typically occur in the third to sixth decades, and both have a predilection for the pelvis, femur, humerus, and tibia (Fig. 22.1).

Because there is no essential difference in the imaging features, clinical behavior, and survival data for these tumors, it is justified to regard them as a single group. Both fibrosarcoma and MFH can be either primary tumors or secondary to a preexisting benign condition, such as Paget disease, fibrous dysplasia, bone infarct, or chronic draining sinuses of osteomyelitis. These lesions may also arise in bones that were previously irradiated. Such lesions are termed secondary fibrosarcomas (or secondary malignant fibrous histiocytomas). Rarely, fibrosarcoma can arise in a periosteal location (periosteal fibrosarcoma). Some investigators postulate, however, that in this location these lesions represent primary soft-tissue tumors abutting the bone and invading the underlying periosteum.

Histologically, fibrosarcoma and MFH are characterized by tumor cells that produce collagen fibers. In fibrosarcoma, however, there is a herringbone pattern of fibrous growth with mild cellular pleomorphism, whereas histiocytic features of a characteristic storiform or pinwheel arrangement of fibrogenic tissue typify MFH. In addition, numerous large bizarre polyhedral cells (histiocytic component) are present. Neither tumor is capable of producing osteoid matrix or bone, a factor distinguishing them from osteosarcoma.

Radiographically, fibrosarcoma and MFH are recognized by an osteolytic area of bone destruction and a wide zone of transition; the lesions are usually eccentrically located close to or in the articular end of the bone. They exhibit little or no reactive sclerosis and in most cases, no periosteal reaction (Figs. 22.2 and 22.3); a soft-tissue mass, however, is frequently present.

On computed tomography (CT) examination, fibrosarcoma and MFH show a predominant density similar to that of normal muscle and exhibit the nonspecific tissue attenuation values of Hounsfield units encountered in most nonmineralized tissues. Hypodense areas reflect areas of necrosis within tumor. Magnetic resonance imaging (MRI) is useful to outline the intraosseous and extraosseous extension of these tumors, but there are no characteristic MRI findings for either one (Fig. 22.4). Some investigators found the signal characteristics comparable to those of other lytic bone tumors. Signal intensity is intermediate to low on T1-weighted images and high on T2 weighting, frequently heterogenous, and varying with the degree of necrosis and hemorrhage within the tumor.

It should be stressed, however, that the entity of MFH has recently fallen out of favor and into disrepute. For example, in the new World Health Organization (WHO) classification of soft-tissue tumors, MFH is considered to represent a small group of undifferentiated pleomorphic sarcomas with no definable line of differentiation, and the term is used with reluctance, although MFH of bone still remains in this classification listed under the heading "fibrohistiocytic tumors."

Differential Diagnosis

Fibrosarcoma and MFH may resemble a giant cell tumor (Fig. 22.5) or telangiectatic osteosarcoma (see Fig. 21.15). They are also often mistaken for metastatic lesions (see Fig. 22.3). Some authorities believe that an almost pathognomonic sign of fibrosarcoma are small sequestrum-like fragments of cortical bone and spongy trabeculae, which may be demonstrated on conventional radiography or CT scan.

Immunohistochemical studies have been helpful in the diagnosis of MFH by demonstrating certain nonspecific markers of histiocytic enzymes such as lysozyme, α_1-antitrypsin, and α_1-antichymotrypsin in the tumor. Other antigens reported to variably stain MFH included vimentin, actin, desmin, and keratin.

Complications and Treatment

Because these tumors do not respond satisfactorily to radiation or chemotherapy, surgical resection is the treatment of choice. Pathologic fracture may occur and, as a palliative measure, internal splinting with a metallic implant may be justified. The tumor has been reported to recur after local excision and may spread to regional lymph nodes. As already stated previously, fibrosarcoma and MFH may complicate benign conditions such as fibrous dysplasia, Paget disease, bone infarction, or chronic draining sinuses of osteomyelitis. They may also arise in bones that were previously irradiated (see the discussion under the heading Benign Conditions with Malignant Potential). The 5-year survival rate after treatment varies according to different studies from 29% to 67%.

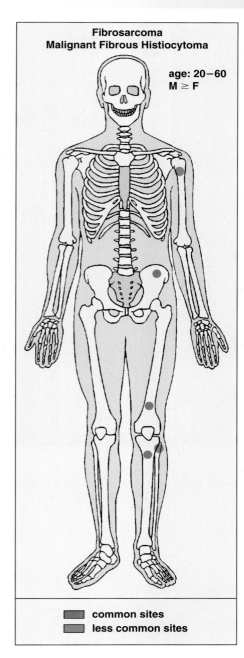

FIGURE 22.1   Skeletal sites of predilection, peak age range, and male-to-female ratio in fibrosarcoma and MFH.

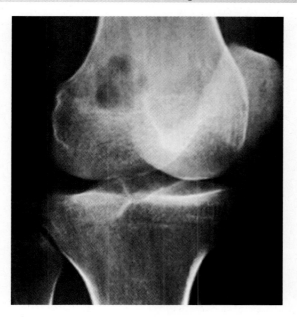

FIGURE 22.2   Fibrosarcoma. Oblique radiograph of the right knee of a 28-year-old woman shows a purely destructive osteolytic lesion in the intercondylar fossa of the distal femur. Note the absence of reactive sclerosis and periosteal response.

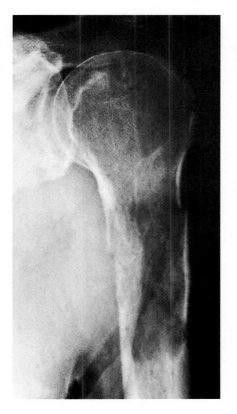

FIGURE 22.3   Fibrosarcoma. A 62-year-old man sustained a pathologic fracture through an osteolytic lesion in the proximal shaft of the left humerus. A metastatic lesion was suspected, but biopsy revealed a primary fibrosarcoma of the bone.

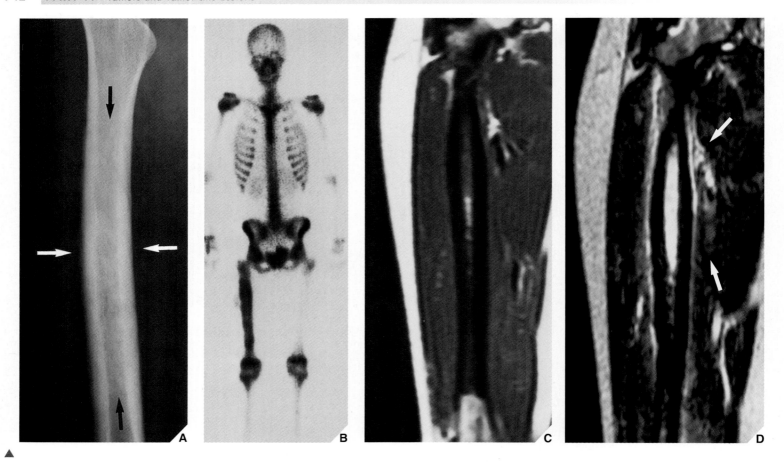

FIGURE 22.4   **Malignant fibrous histiocytoma. (A)** Oblique radiograph of the right femur of a 16-year-old girl shows fusiform thickening of the cortex and permeative type of medullary bone destruction (*arrows*). **(B)** Radionuclide bone scan (⁹⁹ᵐTc-MDP) shows increased uptake of the tracer in the right femur. **(C)** Coronal T1-weighted (SE; TR 500/TE 20 msec) MR image demonstrates the extent of the tumor that involves about 75% of the length of the femur. **(D)** Coronal T2-weighted (SE; TR 2000/TE 80 msec) MR image shows that the tumor exhibits high signal intensity. The soft-tissue extension medially is also accurately depicted (*arrows*).

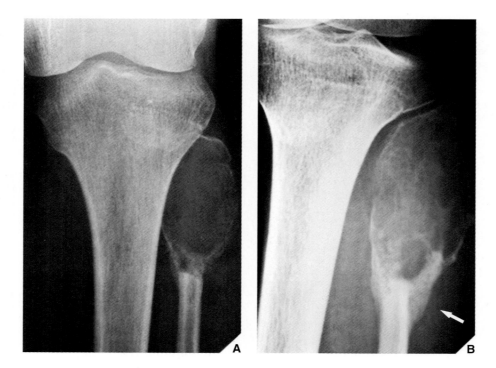

FIGURE 22.5   **Malignant fibrous histiocytoma.** Anteroposterior radiograph of the left knee **(A)** and oblique projection **(B)** demonstrate an expansive, lytic lesion in the proximal end of the fibula in a 13-year-old girl. The cortex has been partially destroyed, and there is a buttress of periosteal new bone formation (*arrow*) secondary to pathologic fracture. The differential diagnosis of this malignancy at this site should include giant cell tumor and aneurysmal bone cyst.

Ewing Sarcoma

Ewing sarcoma, a highly malignant neoplasm predominantly affecting children and adolescents, with decisive male predominance, is representative of the so-called round cell tumors. Its precise histogenesis is unknown, but it is generally thought that Ewing sarcoma originates from bone marrow cells. Some authorities, however, believe that Ewing sarcoma is a neurally derived small round cell malignancy very similar to the so-called primitive neuroectodermal tumor (PNET). Recent studies reveled that all tumors of the Ewing family are characterized by recurrent chromosomal translocations involving chromosomes 11 and 22 [t(11;22)(q24;q12)] or chromosomes 21 and 22 [t(21;22)(q22;q12)] in about 85% and 15% of cases, respectively. In about 20% of cases of Ewing sarcoma, the second most common genetic alteration is the inactivation of the gene *p16* or *INK4A*. In particular, *p16* deletions represent a significant negative predictive factor in Ewing tumor. Approximately 90% of Ewing sarcomas occur before age 25, and the disease is extremely rare in black persons. Ewing sarcoma has a predilection for the diaphysis of the long bones, as well as the ribs and flat bones such as the scapula and pelvis (Fig. 22.6). Clinically, it may present as a localized painful mass or with systemic symptoms such as fever, malaise, weight loss, and an increased erythrocyte sedimentation rate. These systemic symptoms may lead to an erroneous diagnosis of osteomyelitis.

The imaging presentation of this malignancy is usually rather characteristic; the lesion is poorly defined, marked by a permeative or moth-eaten type of bone destruction, and associated with an aggressive periosteal response that has an onion skin (or "onion peel") or, less commonly, a "sunburst" appearance, and a large soft-tissue mass (Fig. 22.7). Occasionally, the bone lesion itself is almost imperceptible, with the soft-tissue mass being the only prominent radiographic finding (Fig. 22.8).

On radionuclide bone scan, Ewing sarcoma shows an intense increase of technetium-99m methylene diphosphonate (^{99m}Tc-MDP) uptake. Gallium-67-citrate (^{67}Ga-citrate) more readily identifies soft-tissue tumor extension. Although scintigraphic findings are nonspecific, this technique provides reliable information concerning the presence of skeletal metastases. CT reveals the pattern of bone destruction, and attenuation values (Hounsfield units) provide information about the medullary extension. In addition, CT may help to delineate extraosseous involvement (see Fig. 22.7). MRI is essential for definite demonstration of the extent of intraosseous and extraosseous involvement by this tumor (Fig. 22.9). In particular, MRI may effectively reveal extension through the epiphyseal plate. T1-weighted images show intermediate to low signal intensity, which becomes bright on T2 weighting. Hypocellular regions and areas of necrosis are of lesser intensity. Imaging after injection of gadolinium-diethylene triamine pentaacetic acid (Gd-DTPA) reveals signal enhancement of the tumor on T1-weighted sequences. Enhancement occurs only in the cellular areas, allowing differentiation of the tumor from the peritumoral edema.

Histologically, Ewing sarcoma consists of a uniform array of small cells with round hyperchromatic nuclei, scant cytoplasm, and poorly defined cell borders. The mitotic rate is high, and necrosis is frequently extensive. Usually, the cytoplasm contains a moderate amount of glycogen, demonstrable with the periodic acid-Schiff (PAS) stain. This PAS-positive material is washed away after digestion with diastase, confirming that, in fact, it represents glycogen. The demonstration of glycogen, which at one time was considered an absolutely distinctive marker for Ewing sarcoma, has fallen into disfavor because in some Ewing sarcoma, glycogen is not found. Moreover, malignant lymphoma and primitive neural tumors may at times contain glycogen. Since the advent of immunohistochemistry, lymphomas are usually differentiated from Ewing sarcomas by demonstrating leukocyte-common antigen, a pathognomic marker for lymphomas, and primitive neural tumors differ from Ewing sarcomas by the fact that they contain neural protein antibodies. Furthermore, immunohistochemistry reveals that almost all Ewing family tumors exhibit a positive membranous and cytoplasmic reaction for CD99 and vimentin, respectively.

Differential Diagnosis

Ewing sarcoma may often mimic metastatic neuroblastoma or osteomyelitis (Fig. 22.10). At times, Ewing sarcoma exhibits a feature once thought to be almost pathognomonic, the "saucerization" of the cortex (Fig. 22.11), which may be related to destruction of the periosteal surface by the tumor combined with the effect of extrinsic pressure by the large soft-tissue mass. Although this sign has recently been reported in other tumors, and even in osteomyelitis, its presence in association with a permeative lesion and a soft-tissue mass favors the diagnosis of Ewing sarcoma. The radiographic distinction of Ewing sarcoma from metastatic neuroblastoma may occasionally be difficult; however, the latter usually occurs in the first 3 years, whereas Ewing sarcoma is uncommon in the first 5 years.

Occasionally, Ewing sarcoma may resemble an osteosarcoma, particularly when the former is accompanied by abundant periosteal new bone formation. Moreover, dystrophic calcifications in the soft-tissue mass may mimic tumor-bone formation in osteosarcoma (Fig. 22.12). Lymphoma must also be included in the differential diagnosis, although

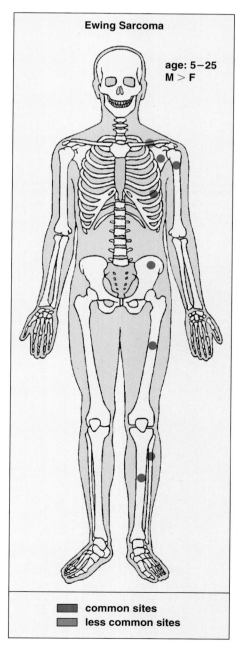

Ewing Sarcoma

age: 5–25
M > F

■ common sites
■ less common sites

FIGURE 22.6 Skeletal sites of predilection, peak age range, and male-to-female ratio in Ewing sarcoma.

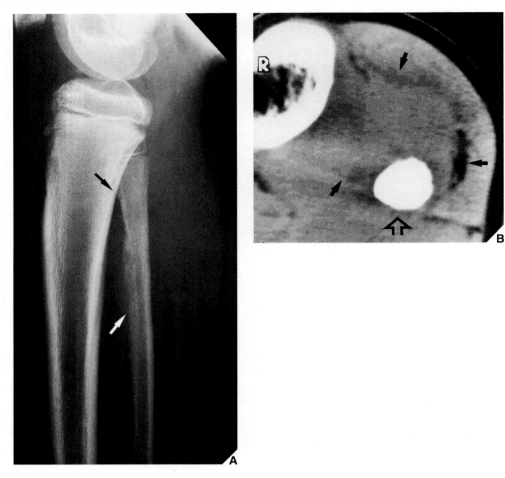

▲
FIGURE 22.7 **Ewing sarcoma. (A)** Lateral radiograph in a 12-year-old boy shows the typical appearance of this tumor in the fibula. The poorly defined lesion exhibits permeative bone destruction associated with an aggressive periosteal reaction (*arrows*). **(B)** CT section through the lesion demonstrates a large soft-tissue mass (*arrows*), which is not clear on the conventional study. Note the complete obliteration of the marrow cavity by tumor (*open arrow*).

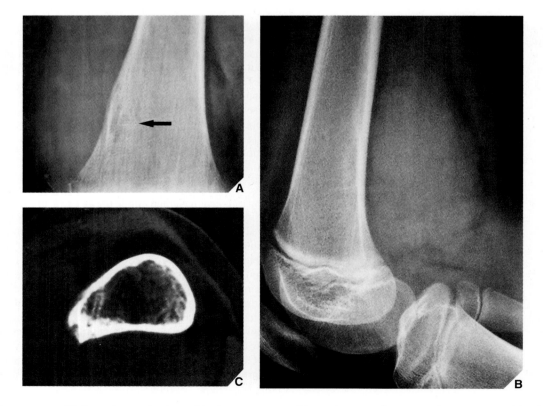

▲
FIGURE 22.8 **Ewing sarcoma. (A)** Bone destruction (*arrow*) is almost imperceptible on this magnification study in a 10-year-old girl with Ewing sarcoma of the distal femoral diaphysis. **(B)** Lateral radiograph of distal femur, however, shows a large soft-tissue mass. **(C)** CT using a bone "window" demonstrates destruction of the medullary portion of the bone, endosteal scalloping, and invasion of the cortex.

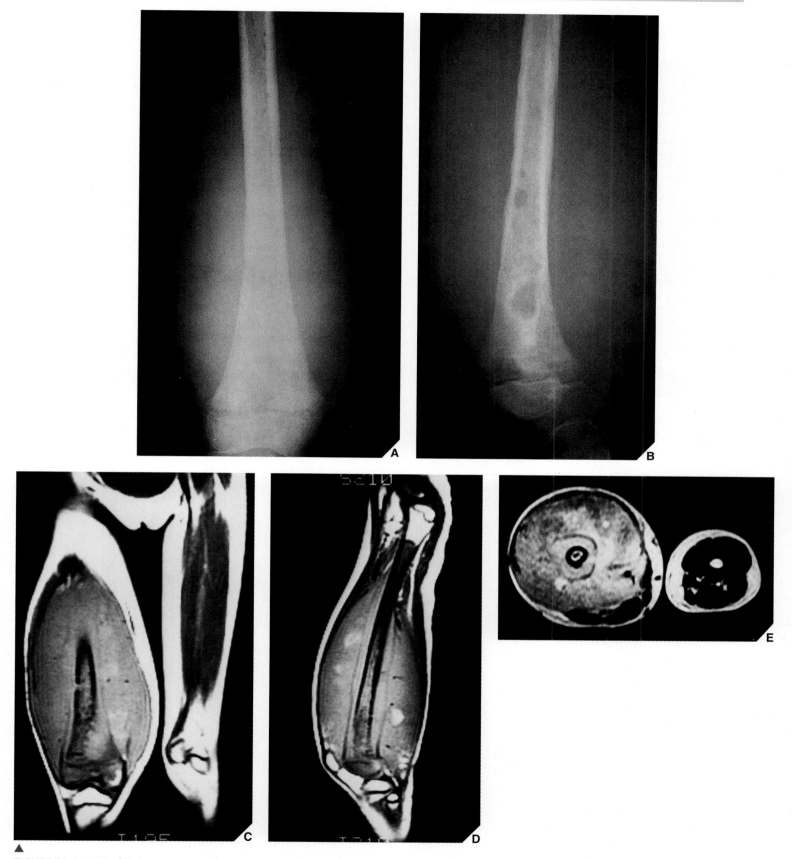

▲
FIGURE 22.9 **MRI of Ewing sarcoma.** Anteroposterior (**A**) and lateral (**B**) radiographs of the right distal femur of a 7-year-old girl show permeative and moth-eaten types of bone destruction in the metaphysis and diaphysis associated with a large soft-tissue mass. Coronal (**C**) and sagittal (**D**) T1-weighted (SE; TR 750/TE 20 msec) MR images demonstrate the intraosseous and extraosseous extent of the tumor. (**E**) Axial T2-weighted (SE; TR 2000/TE 80 msec) MR image shows heterogeneous but mostly high signal intensity of the soft-tissue mass.

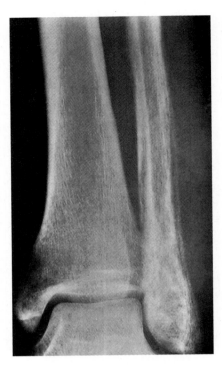

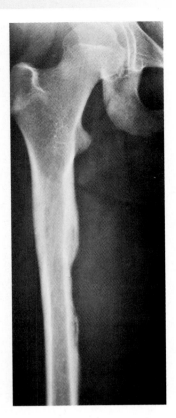

▲
FIGURE 22.10   **Ewing sarcoma.** A 24-year-old man presented with pain and swelling of the left ankle for 8 weeks; he also had a fever. Anteroposterior radiograph of the ankle demonstrates a destructive lesion of the distal fibula exhibiting a permeative type of bone destruction and a lamellated periosteal reaction; a soft-tissue mass is also evident. The appearance is that of infection (osteomyelitis), but biopsy confirmed malignancy.

FIGURE 22.11   **Ewing sarcoma.** Anteroposterior radiograph of the right femur of a 12-year-old girl shows "saucerization" of the medial cortex of the diaphysis, often seen in Ewing sarcoma; there is also an associated soft-tissue mass.

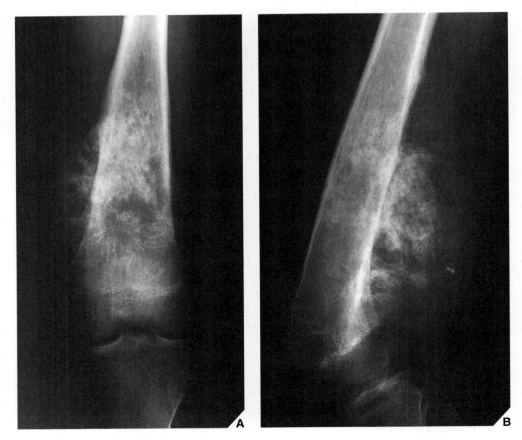

▲
FIGURE 22.12   **Ewing sarcoma.** Anteroposterior (**A**) and lateral (**B**) radiographs of the left femur of a 17-year-old boy show a tumor displaying a significant degree of sclerosis that was originally interpreted as osteosarcoma.

this lesion usually occurs in an older age group. The important radiologic difference is usually the absence of a soft-tissue mass in lymphoma, whereas in Ewing sarcoma a soft-tissue mass is almost invariably present, often being disproportionally large compared with the amount of bone destruction (see Figs. 22.8 and 22.9). The distinction between Ewing sarcoma and PNET cannot be made on the basis of radiography. Differentiation between these two tumors must rely entirely on immuno-histochemistry, electron microscopy, and molecular genetic studies.

Treatment

Ewing sarcoma is usually treated with a preoperative course of chemotherapy, either alone or combined with radiation therapy, to shrink the tumor, followed by wide resection (Fig. 22.13). Sometimes the affected limb can be reconstructed with an endoprosthesis or an allograft.

Malignant Lymphoma

The term *malignant lymphoma* refers to a group of neoplasms that are composed of lymphoid or histiocytic cells of different subtypes in various stages of maturation. Once called "reticulum cell sarcoma," "non-Hodgkin lymphoma," "lymphosarcoma," or "osteolymphoma," bone lymphoma is now known as *large cell* or *histiocytic* lymphoma. According to new WHO classification, malignant lymphomas of bone are subdivided into (a) those that affect one skeletal site with or without involvement of regional lymph nodes; (b) those that affect multiple bones without lymph nodes or visceral involvement; (c) those that present as a primary bone tumor but reveal nodal or visceral lesions; and (d) those occurring in the patients with known lymphoma elsewhere. Groups (a) and (b) are considered primary lymphoma of bone. Primary bone lymphoma is a rare tumor that accounts for less than 5% of all primary bone tumors. It occurs in the second to seventh decades, with a peak age of occurrence from 45 to 75 years; it has a slightly greater prevalence in males. The lesion develops in the long bones, vertebrae, pelvis, and ribs (Fig. 22.14).

Patients may present with local symptoms, such as pain and swelling, or with systemic symptoms, such as fever and weight loss.

Radiographically, histiocytic lymphoma produces a permeative or moth-eaten pattern of bone destruction or is a purely osteolytic lesion with or more commonly without a periosteal reaction (Fig. 22.15). The affected bone can also present with an "ivory" appearance, as is often the case in lesions of the vertebrae or flat bones. Pathologic fractures are occasionally encountered (Fig. 22.16, see also Fig. 22.18). Because lymphoma usually does not evoke significant periosteal new bone formation, this is an important feature in differentiating it from Ewing sarcoma.

Recently, WHO adopted the Revised European-American Classification of Lymphoid Neoplasms (REAL) that originally was proposed by the International Lymphoma Study Group (Table 22.1).

Histologically, lymphomas may be subdivided into non-Hodgkin lymphomas and Hodgkin lymphomas. Although secondary involvement of bones is relatively common in Hodgkin lymphoma, primary Hodgkin bone lymphoma is extremely rare. Non-Hodgkin bone lymphomas are considered primary only if a complete systemic workup reveals no evidence of extraosseous involvement. Histologically, the tumor consists of aggregates of malignant lymphoid cells replacing marrow spaces and osseous trabeculae. The cells contain irregular or even cleaved nuclei. As mentioned in the section on Ewing sarcoma, the most important single procedure used to distinguish lymphoma from the other round cell tumors is the stain for leukocyte-common antigen, because lymphoid cells are the only cells that stain positively with the immunoreaction for CD45, CD20, and CD3 (B-cell and T-cells markers).

Differential Diagnosis

Histiocytic lymphoma must be distinguished from secondary involvement of the skeleton by systemic lymphoma. It may resemble Ewing sarcoma, particularly in younger patients (Fig. 22.17), or Paget disease if the articular end of a bone is involved and there is a mixed sclerotic and osteolytic pattern (Fig. 22.18).

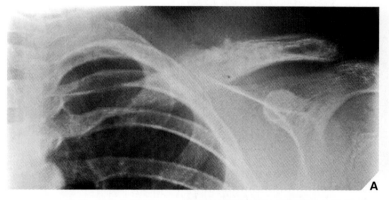
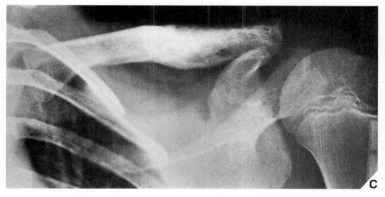

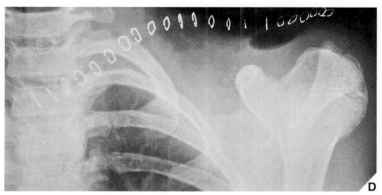

FIGURE 22.13   Treatment of Ewing sarcoma. (A) Radiograph of the shoulder of an 11-year-old boy shows the typical appearance of Ewing sarcoma involving the distal half of the left clavicle. The poorly defined destructive lesion is associated with an aggressive periosteal reaction and a large soft-tissue mass. **(B)** Tomographic cut gives a better picture of the periosteal response and soft-tissue mass. **(C)** After a 4-month course of chemotherapy, the lesion has become sclerotic, the periosteal reaction has disappeared, and the soft-tissue mass has shrunk substantially. **(D)** The clavicle was then removed *en bloc*.

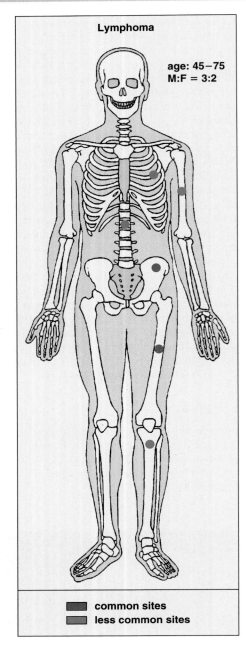

FIGURE 22.14 Skeletal sites of predilection, peak age range, and male-to-female ratio in primary bone lymphoma.

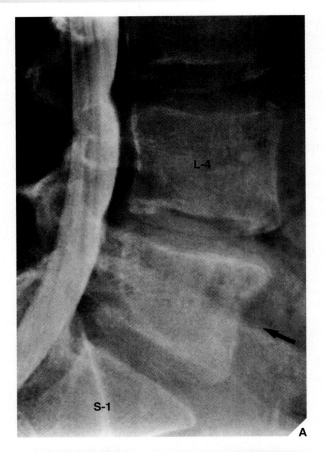

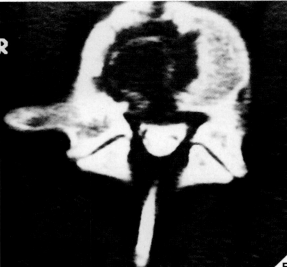

FIGURE 22.15 **Lymphoma.** An 18-year-old woman presented with low-back pain for several months, which was attributed to herniation of an intervertebral disk. (**A**) Myelogram shows that the disk is normal, but the body of L5 (*arrow*) exhibits a mottled appearance and its posterior border is indistinct. (**B**) CT section demonstrates a large, osteolytic lesion extending from the anterior to the posterior margins of the vertebral body.

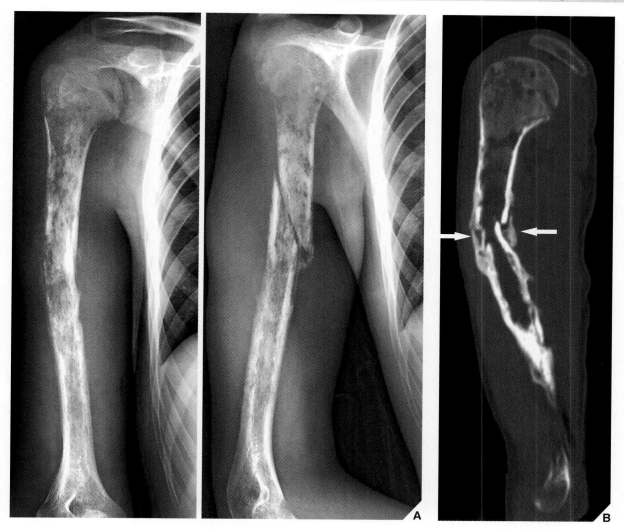

FIGURE 22.16   Lymphoma. (A) Anteroposterior and oblique radiographs of the right humerus of a 20-year-old man show a long lesion exhibiting permeative and moth-eaten type of bone destruction. Periosteal reaction is secondary to the pathologic fracture. **(B)** Sagittal reformatted CT image demonstrates endosteal scalloping and early callus formation at the site of a pathologic fracture (*arrows*).

TABLE 22.1   Revised European-American Lymphoma Classification

B-Cell Lymphomas	T-Cell and Natural Killer Cell Neoplasms	Hodgkin Disease
Precursor B-cell neoplasm • Precursor B-lymphoblastic leukemia or lymphoma Mature B-cell neoplasm • B-cell chronic lymphocytic leukemia, prolymphocytic leukemia, small lymphocytic leukemia • Lymphoplasmacytoid lymphoma • Mantle cell lymphoma • Follicle center lymphoma • Marginal zone B-cell lymphoma • Hairy cell lymphoma • Diffuse large cell B-cell lymphoma • Burkitt lymphoma • High-grade B-cell lymphoma	Precursor T-cell neoplasm • Precursor T-lymphoblastic lymphoma or leukemia Peripheral T-cell and natural killer cell neoplasm • T-cell chronic lymphocytic leukemia • Large granular lymphocyte leukemia • Mycosis fungoides, Sézary syndrome • Peripheral T-cell lymphoma • Angioimmunoblastic T-cell lymphoma • Angiocentric lymphoma • Adult T-cell lymphoma • Anaplastic large cell lymphoma	Nodular lymphocyte predominance (paragranuloma) Nodular sclerosis Mixed cellularity Lymphocyte depletion Lymphocyte-rich classic Hodgkin disease

Modified from Krishnan A et al., 2003, with permission.

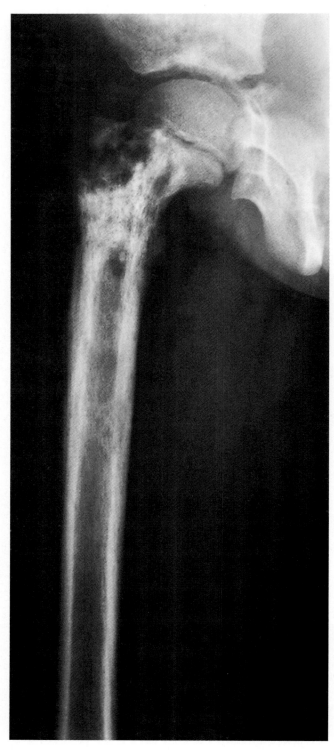

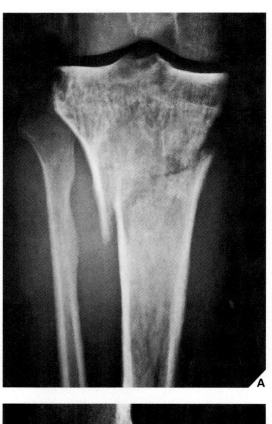

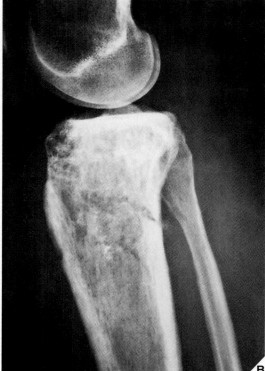

▲
FIGURE 22.17 **Lymphoma.** Conventional radiograph of the right femur of a 7-year-old girl with groin pain and a fever reveals a destructive lesion of the diaphysis extending to the growth plate; there is also a lamellated type of periosteal reaction. Because of the age of the patient, the primary differential diagnosis included Ewing sarcoma, osteomyelitis, and Langerhans cell histiocytosis, all three of which may have a similar radiographic presentation in a long bone. The main factor differentiating these lesions is the duration of the patient's symptoms. In this case, however, biopsy revealed a histiocytic lymphoma.

▲
FIGURE 22.18 **Lymphoma.** Anteroposterior (**A**) and lateral (**B**) radiographs of the right knee of a 47-year-old woman who had knee pain and initially was misdiagnosed with Paget disease, show a destructive lesion of the proximal tibia extending into the articular end of the bone. The mixed sclerotic and osteolytic character of this lesion may resemble the coarse trabecular pattern of Paget disease; however, there is a lack of cortical thickening. There is a pathologic fracture, but only a minimal periosteal response is evident.

Treatment

The treatment for primary bone lymphoma is controversial, and there is no consensus with regard to radiotherapy, although this tumor is radiosensitive. Some cases require chemotherapy as the mainstay and additional adjuvant radiation therapy. The optimal treatment has not been determined and is still being debated.

Myeloma

Myeloma, also known as "multiple myeloma" or "plasma cell myeloma," is a tumor originating in the bone marrow and is the most common primary malignant bone tumor. It accounts for 10% of all hematological malignancies and 1% of all cancers. It is usually seen between the fifth and seventh decades and is more frequent in men than in women. The axial skeleton (skull, spine, ribs, and pelvis) are the most commonly affected sites, but no bone is exempt from involvement (Fig. 22.19).

Rarely, the presentation can be that of a solitary lesion, in which case it is called a *solitary myeloma* or *plasmacytoma*; far more commonly, however, it presents with widespread involvement, in which case the name *multiple myeloma* is applied. Mild and transient pain exacerbated by heavy lifting or other activity is present in approximately 75% of cases and may be the initial symptom. Because of this, in its early course and before diagnosis, the disease may resemble sciatica or intercostal neuralgia. Rarely, a pathologic fracture through the lesion is the first sign of disease. The patient's urine in cases of myeloma contains Bence Jones protein; the serum albumin-to-globulin ratio is reversed and the total serum protein is elevated. Monoclonal γ-globulin is also present, with IgG and IgA peaks demonstrated on serum electrophoresis.

Histologically, the diagnosis is made by finding sheets of atypical plasmacytoid cells replacing the normal marrow spaces. The plasma cell is recognized by the presence of eccentrically situated nucleus within a large amount of cytoplasm that stains either light blue or pink. The neoplastic cells contain double or even multiple nuclei, usually hyperchromatic and enlarged, with prominent nucleoli.

Multiple myeloma may present in a variety of radiographic patterns (Fig. 22.20). Particularly in the spine, it may be seen only as diffuse osteoporosis with no clearly identifiable lesion; multiple compression

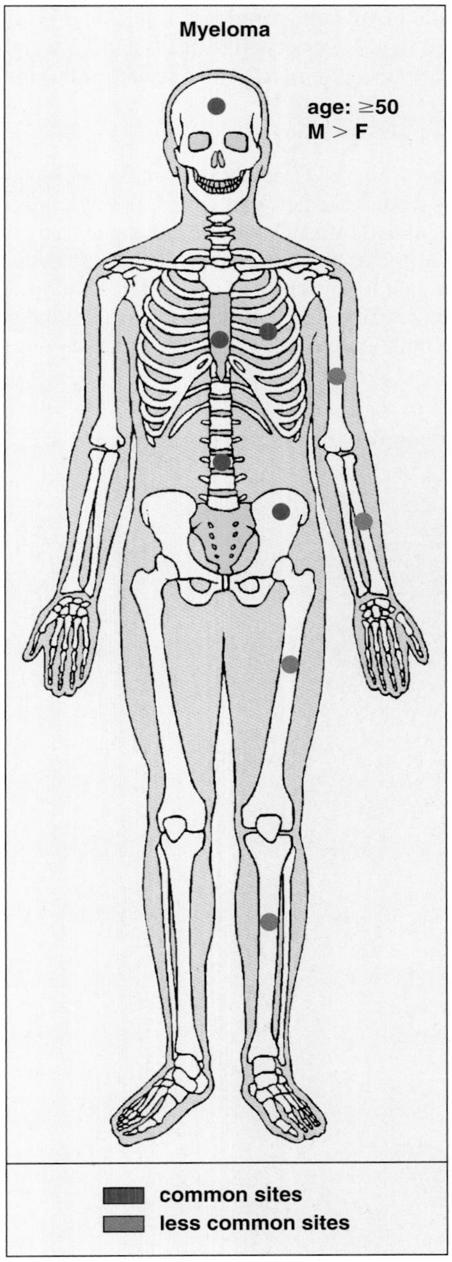

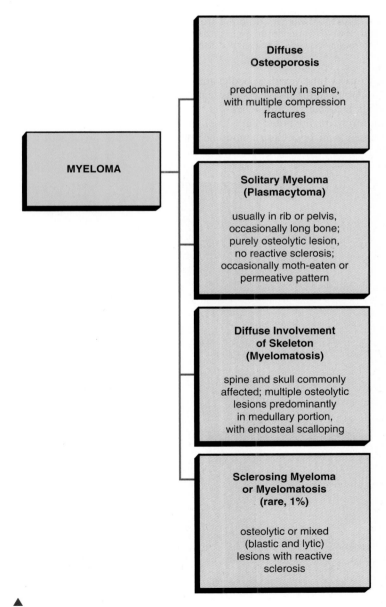

Myeloma

age: ≥50
M > F

common sites
less common sites

▲

FIGURE 22.19   Skeletal sites of predilection, peak age range, and male-to-female ratio in myeloma.

▲

FIGURE 22.20   Variants in the radiographic presentation of myeloma.

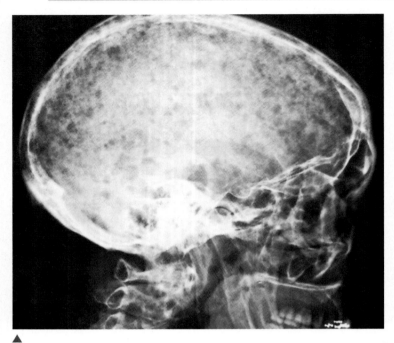

▲
FIGURE 22.21   Multiple myeloma. Involvement of the skull is prominent in this 60-year-old woman. Note the characteristic "punched-out," lytic lesions, most of which are uniform in size and lack sclerotic borders. Occasionally, this pattern may be seen in metastatic disease.

fractures of the vertebral bodies may also be evident. More commonly, it exhibits multiple lytic lesions scattered throughout the skeleton. In the skull, characteristic "punched-out" areas of bone destruction, usually of uniform size, are noted (Fig. 22.21), whereas the ribs may contain lace-like areas of bone destruction and small osteolytic lesions, sometimes

accompanied by adjacent soft-tissue masses. Areas of medullary bone destruction are noted in the flat and long bones, and if these appear about the cortex, they are accompanied by scalloping of the inner cortical margin (Fig. 22.22). Ordinarily, there is no evidence of sclerosis and no periosteal reaction. Fewer than 1% of myelomas may be of a sclerosing type called *sclerosing myelomatosis*.

Whereas in osteolytic myeloma only 3% of patients have polyneuropathy, the incidence of polyneuropathy in the osteosclerotic variant has been reported as 30% to 50%. Compared with classic myeloma, this variant usually occurs in younger individuals and shows fewer plasma cells in the bone marrow, lower levels of monoclonal protein, and a better prognosis.

An interesting variant of sclerosing myeloma is the so-called POEMS syndrome, first described in 1968 but gaining wide acceptance only more recently. It consists of polyneuropathy (P), organomegaly (O), particularly of the liver and the spleen, endocrine disturbances (E) such as amenorrhea and gynecomastia, monoclonal gammopathy (M), and skin changes (S) such as hyperpigmentation and hirsutism. Also known as Crow-Fukase syndrome, Takatsuki syndrome, and PEP (*p*lasma cell dyscrasia, *e*ndocrinopathy, and *p*olyneuropathy) syndrome, this condition represents a clinicopathologic complex of unknown etiology. On radiography and CT, the focal osseous lesions present as either a well-defined or fluffy sclerotic foci, or as a lytic areas with peripheral sclerosis. On MRI, the lesions exhibit decreased signal intensity on both T1- and T2-weighted sequences, and lack of enhancement on postcontrast (gadolinium) images.

Differential Diagnosis

If the spine is involved, as is frequently the case, multiple myeloma must be differentiated from metastatic carcinoma. In this respect, the "vertebral pedicle" sign identified by Jacobson and colleagues may be helpful. They contended that in the early stages of myeloma, the pedicle (which does not contain as much red marrow as the vertebral body) is not involved, whereas even in an early stage of metastatic cancer the pedicle and vertebral body are both affected (Fig. 22.23). In the late stages of multiple

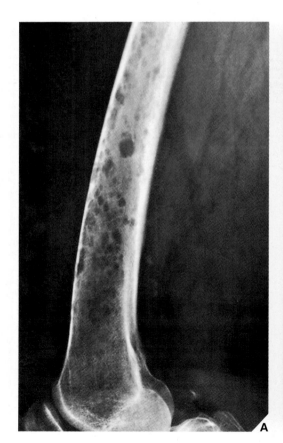

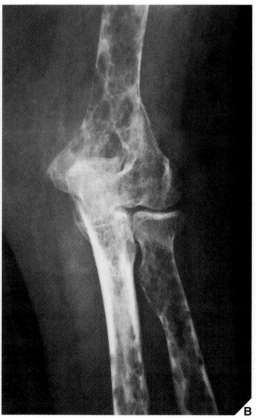

▲
FIGURE 22.22   Multiple myeloma. Lateral radiograph of the distal femur (**A**) and anteroposterior radiograph of the elbow (**B**) in a 65-year-old woman show endosteal scalloping of the cortex typical of diffuse myelomatosis.

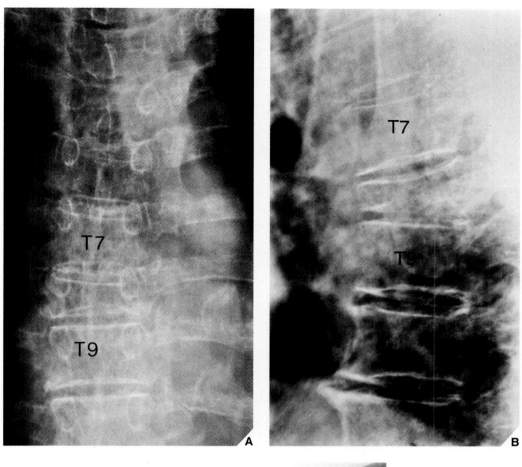

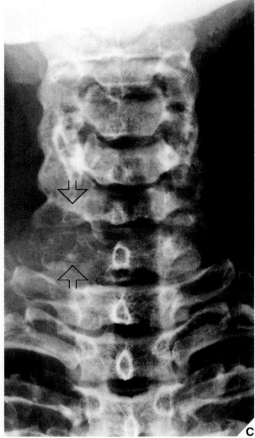

FIGURE 22.23   **Multiple myeloma versus metastatic carcinoma.** Anteroposterior (**A**) and lateral (**B**) radiographs of the spine in a 70-year-old man with multiple myeloma involving both the spine and appendicular skeleton show a compression fracture of the body of T8; several other vertebrae show only osteoporosis. The pedicles are preserved in contrast to metastatic disease of the spine, which usually also affects the pedicles, as seen on this anteroposterior radiograph of the cervical spine (**C**) in a 65-year-old man with colon carcinoma and multiple lytic metastases. Note the involvement of the right pedicle of C7 (*open arrows*).

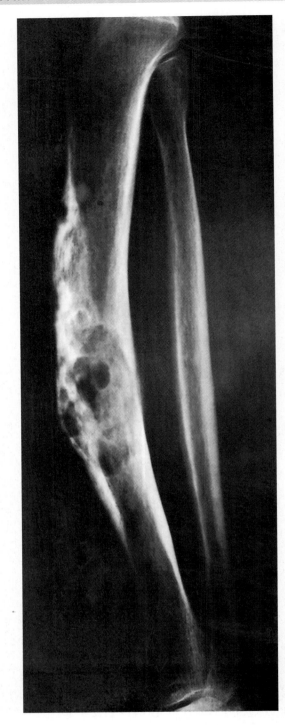

▲
FIGURE 22.24 Adamantinoma. Lateral radiograph of a 64-year-old woman shows a lesion in the midshaft of the left tibia. The destructive lesion is multifocal and slightly expansive, with mixed osteolytic and sclerotic areas creating a "soap-bubble" appearance resembling that of osteofibrous dysplasia (see Fig. 19.40).

Complications and Treatment

A common complication of bone myelomas is pathologic fracture, especially in lesions of the long bones, ribs, sternum, and vertebrae. The development of amyloidosis has also been reported in approximately 15% of patients.

Treatment consists of radiotherapy and systemic chemotherapy. The 5-year survival rate is approximately 10%.

Adamantinoma

Adamantinoma is a rare malignant tumor occurring equally in males and females between the second and fifth decades of life; 90% of cases involve the tibia. Radiographically, the disease is marked by well-defined and elongated osteolytic defects of varying size, separated by areas of sclerotic bone, which occasionally give the lesion a "soap bubble" appearance; ordinarily, there is no periosteal reaction (Fig. 22.24). At times, adamantinoma may affect an entire bone with multiple satellite lesions (Fig. 22.25); "sawtooth" areas of cortical destruction in the tibia are quite distinctive of this tumor.

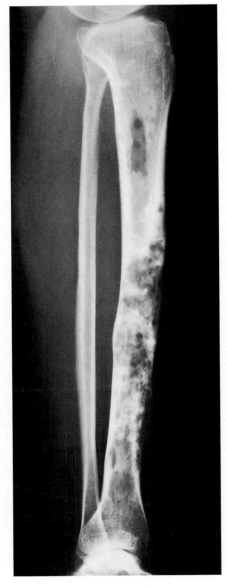

▲
FIGURE 22.25 Adamantinoma. Lateral radiograph of the right leg of a 28-year-old woman shows multiple, confluent lytic lesions involving almost the entire tibia; only the articular ends are spared. The anterior cortex exhibits a predominantly "sawtooth" type of destruction.

myeloma, however, both the pedicle and vertebral body may be destroyed. Radionuclide bone scan can more reliably distinguish these two malignancies at this stage. It is invariably positive in cases of metastatic carcinoma, whereas in most cases of multiple myeloma there is no increased uptake of radiopharmaceutical tracer. This phenomenon appears to reflect the purely lytic nature of most myelomatous lesions and the absence of significant reactive new bone formation in response to the tumor.

A solitary myeloma may create even greater diagnostic difficulty. As a purely osteolytic lesion, it may mimic such other purely destructive processes as the brown tumor of hyperparathyroidism, giant cell tumor, fibrosarcoma, MFH, or a solitary metastatic focus of carcinoma from the kidney, thyroid, gastrointestinal tract, or lung.

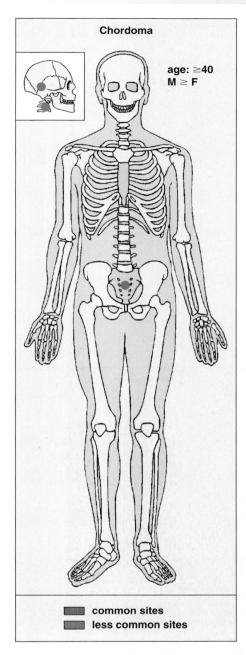

Chordoma

age: ≥40
M ≥ F

common sites
less common sites

▲
FIGURE 22.26 Skeletal sites of predilection, peak age range, and male-to-female ratio in chordoma.

Histologically, the tumor is biphasic and consists of an epithelial component intimately admixed in varying proportions with a fibrous component. Although it has been speculated that adamantinoma represents a form of vascular neoplasm, ultrastructural and immunohistochemical evidence points toward an epithelial derivation.

A relationship of adamantinoma with osteofibrous dysplasia and fibrous dysplasia has been postulated and its coexistence with either of these lesions has been suggested. However, this is still controversial, with some investigators maintaining that the lesions of adamantinoma may contain a fibro-osseous component that can resemble a Kempson-Campanacci lesion or fibrous dysplasia on histopathologic examination. (See also discussion in Chapter 19 in the section on Osteofibrous Dysplasia.)

Treatment

Because adamantinoma is insensitive to radiotherapy, the treatment of choice is *en bloc* surgical resection with application of bone graft. Recurrences have been reported.

Chordoma

A chordoma is a malignant bone tumor arising from developmental remnants of the notochord. Consequently, these tumors occur almost exclusively in the midline of the axial skeleton. Chordomas represent from 1% to 4% of all primary malignant bone tumors. They arise between the fourth and seventh decades and affect men slightly more often than women. The three most common sites for a chordoma are the sacrococcygeal area, the sphenooccipital area, and the C2 vertebra (Fig. 22.26).

The radiographic appearance is that of a highly destructive lesion with irregular scalloped borders; it is sometimes accompanied by calcifications in the matrix, probably as a result of extensive tumor necrosis (Fig. 22.27A). Bone sclerosis has been reported in 64% of cases. Soft-tissue masses are commonly associated with the lesion (Fig. 22.27B). Conventional radiography usually suffices to delineate the tumor (Fig. 22.28), but CT or MRI is required to demonstrate soft-tissue extension (Fig. 22.29) and invasion of the spinal canal. Scintigraphy reveals an increased uptake of radiopharmaceutical tracer around the periphery of the tumor. Areas of abnormally decreased activity due to complete replacement of bone by the tumor may also be observed. Lack of uptake

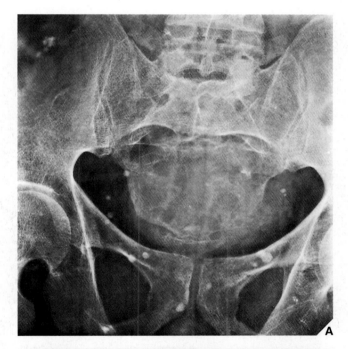

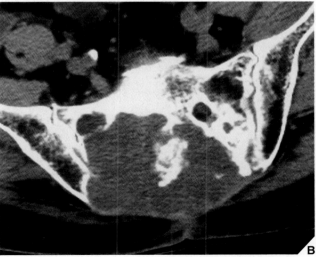

▲
FIGURE 22.27 Chordoma. **(A)** In this destructive lesion in the sacrum of a 60-year-old woman, note its scalloped borders and the amorphous calcifications in the tumor matrix. **(B)** CT shows extensive bone destruction and a large soft-tissue mass.

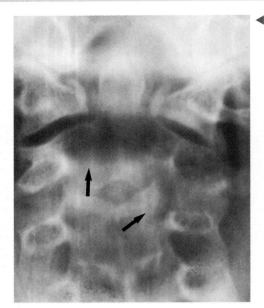

◀ FIGURE 22.28 **Chordoma.** Open-mouth anteroposterior tomogram of the cervical spine of a 52-year-old man demonstrates an osteolytic lesion in the body of C2 (*arrows*).

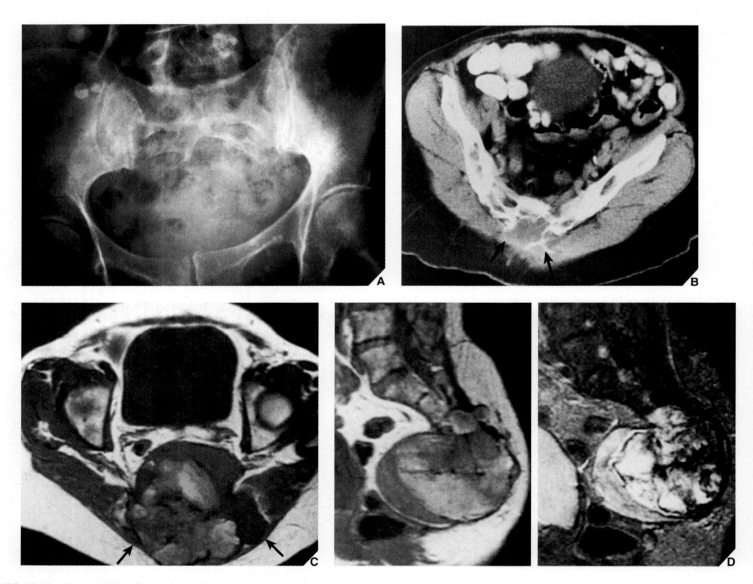

FIGURE 22.29 **CT and MRI of chordoma. (A)** Anteroposterior radiograph of the pelvis of a 68-year-old woman shows a destructive lesion in the lower part of the sacrum, associated with a soft-tissue mass. **(B)** Axial CT section demonstrates the low-attenuation tumor destroying the sacral bone (*arrows*). **(C)** Axial T1-weighted MR image shows a large, heterogeneous tumor mass exhibiting predominantly intermediate signal intensity (*arrows*). **(D)** Sagittal T1- and T2-weighted MR images show the lobulated tumor destroying distal part of the sacrum and coccyx and displaying a heterogeneous signal. (Reprinted from Greenfield GB, Arrington JA, 1995.)

of the tracer within the tumor itself is probably secondary to the absence of vascularity and lack of new bone formation.

Histologically, the tumor consists of loose aggregates of mucoid material separating cord-like arrays and lobules of large polyhedral cells, along with vacuolated cytoplasm and vesicular nuclei referred to as physaliphorous (from Greek for "bubble-bearing") cells.

Complications and Treatment

Invasion of the spinal canal by tumor may cause neurologic complications. Metastases are rare and usually late. The treatment for chordoma consists of complete resection, followed by radiation therapy. Cryosurgery with liquid nitrogen is occasionally used when complete tumor removal proves impossible.

Primary Leiomyosarcoma of Bone

Primary leiomyosarcomas of bone are very rare, with fewer than 150 cases reported in the world literature. More common are skeletal metastases from primary soft-tissue leiomyosarcoma. Therefore, an extraosseous primary tumor, mainly from the gastrointestinal tract or uterus, must be ruled out before a confident diagnosis of primary leiomyosarcoma of bone can be made. Leiomyosarcoma is a malignant, predominantly spindle-cell, neoplasm that exhibits smooth muscle differentiation. Although the patients reported range from 9 to 80 years of age, occurrence before age 20 is uncommon. Males are affected more often than females. The usual clinical presentation is pain of variable intensity and duration. A soft-tissue mass is occasionally observed. The most common sites are the distal femur, proximal tibia, proximal humerus, and iliac bone. Other bones occasionally may be affected, including the clavicle, ribs, and mandible.

Although leiomyosarcoma exhibits no characteristic radiographic features, the tumor most often presents either as a lytic area of geographic bone destruction (Fig. 22.30) or with aggressive-looking, ill-defined borders and a permeative or moth-eaten pattern. Approximately 50% of reported lesions exhibit fine periosteal reaction. On MRI, the lesions are isointense to muscle on T1-weighted sequences, whereas on T2 weighting they exhibit a heterogeneous signal.

Microscopy reveals interlacing fascicles of spindle-shaped cells with eosinophilic cytoplasm, which resemble leiomyosarcoma of soft tissue. The degree of cellularity, nuclear pleomorphism, and necrosis varies from case to case. Rarely, a storiform-like pattern, reminiscent of MFH, is seen. Immunohistochemical staining is positive for vimentin and actin.

Because leiomyosarcoma of bone does not have a characteristic radiologic presentation, several possibilities should be considered in the differential diagnosis. The findings of aggressive bone destruction suggest that fibrosarcoma, MFH, and lymphoma should be considered. In younger patients, Ewing sarcoma is a possibility, as is a solitary metastasis in older patients.

Hemangioendothelioma and Angiosarcoma

These tumors represent the most common malignant vascular lesions. The present nomenclature used to describe malignant vascular tumors is not uniform and is therefore rather confusing. Different terms, including hemangiosarcoma (angiosarcoma), hemangioendothelioma, and hemangioendothelial sarcoma, have been used as synonyms. The tumors have also been classified into different grades, from grade I hemangioendothelioma (well differentiated) to grade III hemangiosarcoma (poorly differentiated). Because of the prevailing confusion, the WHO classification system, although recently revised, continues to categorize these lesions as intermediate or indeterminate (including hemangioendothelioma and hemangiopericytoma) and clearly malignant (angiosarcoma). Unequivocal distinction among these tumors is sometimes difficult.

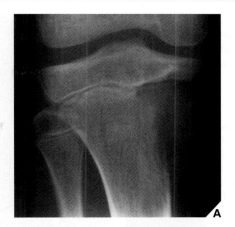

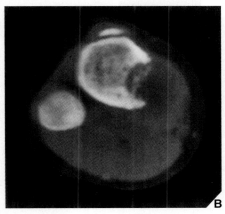

▲ **FIGURE 22.30** Leiomyosarcoma of bone. **(A)** Anteroposterior radiograph of the right knee of a 12-year-old boy reveals an osteolytic lesion in the proximal tibial metaphysis destroying the medial cortex and extending into the soft tissues. **(B)** Axial CT section shows destruction of the medial aspect of the tibia and an associated soft-tissue mass. (From Greenspan A, Remagen W, 1998, with permission.)

Hemangioendothelioma and a recently identified lesion called *epithelioid hemangioendothelioma* are considered to represent true neoplasms because of their independent growth potential, the histopathologic demonstration of nuclear atypia accompanied by occasional mitotic activity, and because they commonly recur after inadequate local excision. They can arise at any age within the range of 10 to 75 years, with a slight predilection for males. The lesion may be solitary or (usually epithelioid variant) multicentric. Patients with multifocal disease are usually 10 years younger than those with a solitary lesion. The most commonly affected sites are the calvaria, spine, and bones of the lower extremities. Clinical symptoms include dull local pain and tenderness. Some swelling and hemorrhagic joint effusion may sometimes be observed.

On radiography, hemangioendothelioma exhibits an osteolytic appearance, either well circumscribed or with a wide zone of transition. Variable degrees of peripheral sclerosis may sharply demarcate the lesion. Occasionally, a soap-bubble appearance with expansion of bone is observed, with extension into the soft tissues. MRI reveals a mixed signal on T1-weighted sequences, with moderately increased signal intensity on T2 weighting (Fig. 22.31). On radiologic studies, it is very difficult to differentiate hemangioendothelioma from other vascular lesions, either benign or malignant. A solitary osteolytic lesion may mimic a metastasis, fibrosarcoma, MFH, plasmacytoma, or lymphoma, and lesions that extend to the articular end of bone can be mistaken for giant cell tumor. Because the radiologic presentation of hemangioendothelioma is usually nonspecific, clinical information may be helpful in narrowing the differential diagnosis.

On histologic examination, hemangioendothelioma reveals markedly pleomorphic endothelial cells with abundant faintly eosinophilic

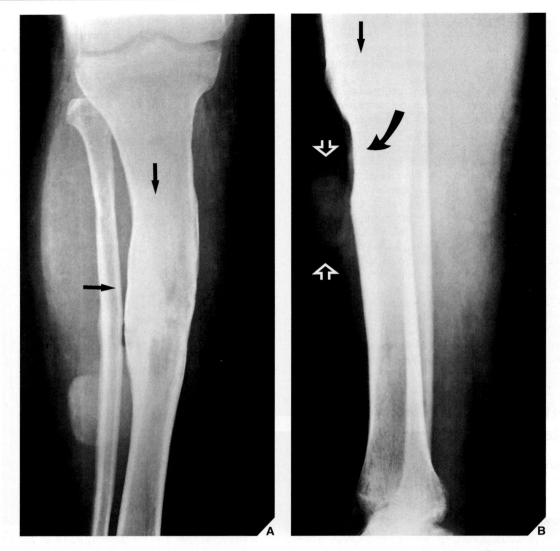

FIGURE 22.34 Squamous cell carcinoma arising in a chronic draining sinus of osteomyelitis. A 59-year-old man was admitted for treatment of an ulcer of the right leg that was present for 5 years. At age 13 years, he had an open fracture of the tibia that became infected, and he developed chronic osteomyelitis. Antero-posterior (**A**) and lateral (**B**) radiographs of the right leg show a large saucerized defect of the anterior cortex of the middle third of the tibia, with dense compact bone lining its base (*curved arrow*). A large sharply circumscribed soft-tissue mass is also evident at this site (*open arrows*). Above the defect, which is postsurgical, are medullary sclerosis and cortical thickening (*arrows*), both characteristic of chronic osteomyelitis. (From Greenspan A et al., 1981, with permission.)

Chronic Draining Sinus Tract of Osteomyelitis

Malignant transformation should be suspected when a long-standing sinus tract of osteomyelitis suddenly becomes painful and discharges purulent, foul material. In most patients with osteomyelitis, the history of the disease dates to childhood, and sinuses draining for more than 20 years are generally the precursors of malignant neoplasms. The development of squamous cell carcinoma is most commonly seen (Fig. 22.34), but fibrosarcoma and osteosarcoma may also be encountered. The incidence of neoplastic transformation, however, is low, ranging from 0.2% to 1.7%. The radiographic features of malignant transformation may occasionally be indistinguishable from those of chronic osteomyelitis, but an increase in the extent of bone destruction usually indicates the onset of sarcoma or carcinoma.

Plexiform Neurofibromatosis

A spectrum of neoplastic disorders is associated with neurofibromatosis as the most serious complication of this disease. Sarcoma of the peripheral nerves and somatic soft tissues is well recognized in neurofibromatosis, with its incidence varying from 3% to 16%. Most such sarcomas are neural in origin, including neurosarcoma, neurofibrosarcoma, and malignant schwannoma; nonneurogenic

sarcomas such as rhabdomyosarcoma and liposarcoma are less common. The precise origin of the sarcomas arising in neurofibromatosis is uncertain; in some instances, the mass clearly originates in a nerve trunk, whereas in others there is no obvious relation to the nerve. The most frequent clinical features of malignant degeneration in a patient with neurofibromatosis are the development of pain, the rapid growth of a preexisting neurofibroma, and a new soft-tissue mass. Radiologically, the diagnosis of sarcomatous transformation is almost certain if abnormal tumor vessels (Fig. 22.35) or a "tumor stain" are demonstrated on arteriography.

Paget Disease

The development of a sarcoma in pagetic bone is a serious complication of Paget disease. Although Paget sarcoma is rare (less than 1%), individuals with Paget disease are 20 times more likely to have a malignant bone tumor develop than are other persons of comparable age. Radiographically, sarcomatous transformation is indicated by the development of a lytic lesion, often with evidence of cortical breakthrough and a soft-tissue mass (Fig. 22.36); a periosteal reaction is uncommon. The bones commonly affected include the pelvis, femur, and humerus. Histologically, the most common type of tumor is osteosarcoma, followed by MFH, fibrosarcoma, and chondrosarcoma,

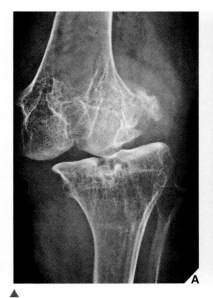
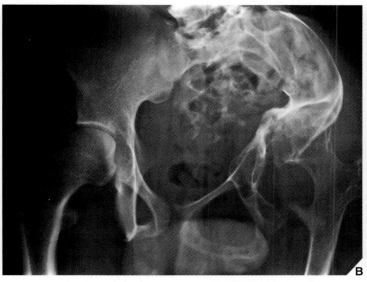
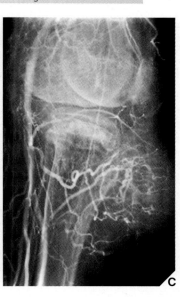

▲ FIGURE 22.35 **Liposarcoma arising in plexiform neurofibromatosis.** An 18-year-old man with known neurofibromatosis since early childhood presented with an enlarging, painful pretibial mass of more than 10 months' duration. (**A**) Anteroposterior radiograph of the left knee shows instability with lateral subluxation. The medial cortex of the medial femoral condyle and the lateral cortex of the lateral femoral condyle are eroded at the site of a soft-tissue mass. (**B**) Anteroposterior radiograph of the pelvis shows asymmetry of the pelvis with a large deformed acetabulum, enlargement of the left obturator foramen, and superolateral subluxation of the left hip—all features typical of neurofibromatosis. (**C**) A femoral arteriogram shows the pretibial mass to be hypervascular, with numerous small tortuous tumor vessels. (From Baker ND, Greenspan A, 1981, with permission.)

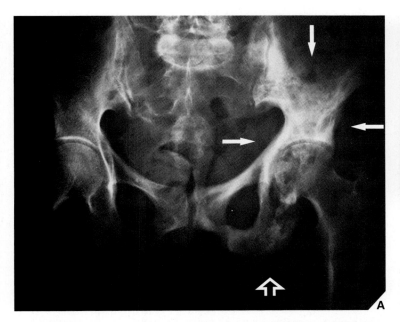
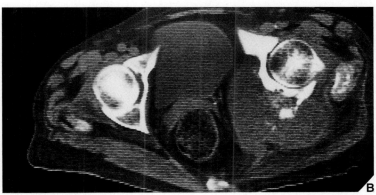
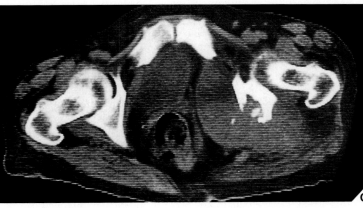
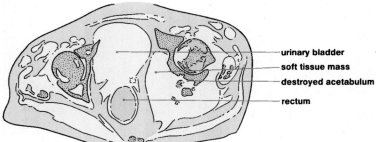

urinary bladder
soft tissue mass
destroyed acetabulum
rectum

◄ FIGURE 22.36 **MFH arising in pagetic bone.** A 66-year-old woman with known Paget disease had pain in the left hip joint radiating to the buttock. (**A**) Anteroposterior radiograph of the pelvis shows extensive involvement of the left hemipelvis by Paget disease (*arrows*). There is also an osteolytic area of bone destruction in the left ischium (*open arrow*). CT sections, one through the femoral heads and acetabula (**B**) and a second through the ischium and pubic symphysis (**C**), demonstrate cortical destruction and a large soft-tissue mass—both signs of malignant transformation to sarcoma. Note the displacement of the rectum and urinary bladder.

in that order. The prognosis for patients with Paget sarcoma is poor; few survive beyond 6 to 8 months.

Radiation-Induced Sarcoma

Radiation-induced sarcomas may arise in areas of normal bone exposed to radiation fields or may be caused by benign conditions treated by irradiation, such as fibrous dysplasia or giant cell tumor. Generally, a sarcoma can develop only if at least 3,000 rads are administered within a 4-week span, although cases have been reported after exposure to only 800 rads. The latency period for radiation-induced tumors varies from 4 to 40 years, with an average of 11 years. Their incidence is rather low, not exceeding 0.5%.

The criteria for diagnosis of postirradiation sarcoma are as follows:
1. The initial lesion and the postirradiation sarcoma must not be of the same histologic type.
2. The site of the new tumor must be within the field of irradiation.
3. At least 3 years must have elapsed since the previous radiation therapy.

Postirradiation osteosarcoma may also develop after the ingestion and intraosseous accumulation of radioisotopes, as has been described in painters of radium watch dials. Regardless of the source of radiation, the most common of such tumors is osteosarcoma, followed by fibrosarcoma and MFH (Fig. 22.37).

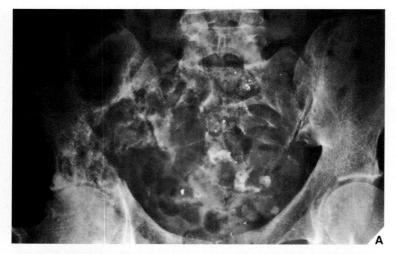

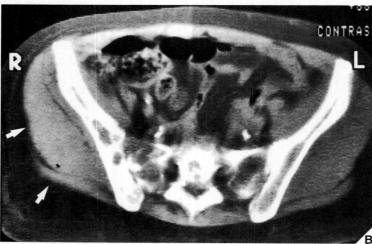

▲
FIGURE 22.37 **Radiation-induced MFH.** A 63-year-old woman had been treated 15 years earlier with radium for carcinoma of the cervix. (**A**) Anteroposterior radiograph of the pelvis shows a large, destructive lesion involving the right ilium and extending into the supra-acetabular region, with destruction of the right wing of the sacral bone. (**B**) CT section, in addition to the changes seen on radiography, demonstrates a soft-tissue mass (*arrows*). Biopsy revealed a MFH. The tumor developed in the ilium that had been exposed to radiation, extending into the soft tissue and invading the sacrum secondarily.

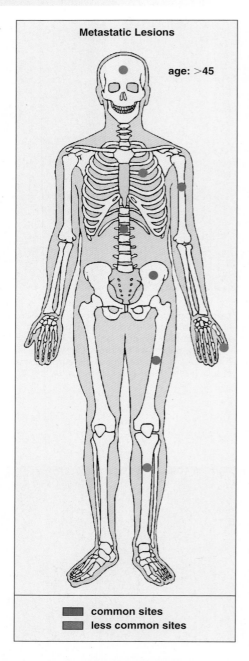

▲
FIGURE 22.38 **Skeletal sites of predilection and peak age range of metastatic lesions.** The occurrence of such lesions distal to the elbow and knee is uncommon, and in those sites a primary malignancy of the breast or lung is usually the origin.

Skeletal Metastases

Skeletal metastases are the most frequent malignant bone tumors and consequently should always be considered in the differential diagnosis of malignant lesions, particularly in older patients. Most metastatic lesions involve the axial skeleton—the skull, spine, and pelvis—as well as the proximal segments of the long bones; only very rarely is a metastasis seen distal to the elbows or knees (Fig. 22.38). These lesions result from the hematogenous spread of a malignancy, the usual mechanism by which a primary neoplasm erodes regional blood vessels, seeding malignant cells to the capillary beds of the lung and liver. Tumor emboli become lodged in the axial skeleton through communication with the vertebral venous plexus.

The incidence of metastases to bone varies with the type of primary neoplasm and the duration of disease. Some malignant tumors have a far greater propensity for osseous metastatic involvement than do others. Because of their frequency, cancers of the breast, lung, and prostate are responsible for the majority of bone metastases, although primary tumors of the kidney, small and large intestines, stomach, and thyroid may also metastasize to bone. Carcinoma of the prostate has been reported to underlie nearly 60% of all bone metastases in men, whereas in women carcinoma of the breast is responsible for nearly 70% of all metastatic skeletal lesions.

Most skeletal metastases are asymptomatic. When metastases are symptomatic, pain is the major clinical symptom, with a pathologic fracture through a lesion only occasionally calling attention to the disease. Metastasis to bone can be solitary or multiple and can be further divided into purely lytic, purely blastic, and mixed lesions. The primary tumors that give rise to purely osteolytic metastases are usually those of the kidney, lung, breast, thyroid, and gastrointestinal tract, although purely lytic lesions may become sclerotic after radiation therapy, chemotherapy, or hormonal therapy. Primary tumors responsible for purely osteoblastic metastases are generally those of the prostate gland, although other primary neoplasms may also be responsible (Fig. 22.39).

The detection of skeletal metastases is not always possible on conventional radiographs, because destruction of the bone may not be visible

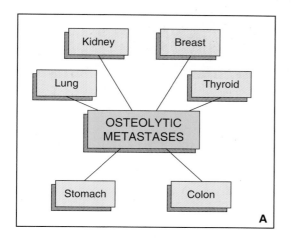

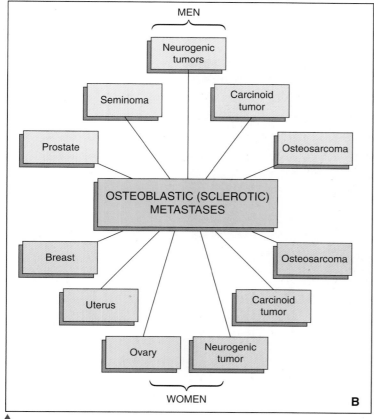

with this technique. Radionuclide bone scan is the best means of screening for early metastatic lesions whether they are lytic or blastic, although recently several investigators have pointed out the usefulness of MRI in detecting metastases, particularly in the spine (Fig. 22.40). The accuracy of MRI in identifying intramedullary lesions and assessing spinal cord and soft-tissue involvement has been demonstrated. Most recent investigations by Daldrup-Link and associates, who compared the diagnostic accuracy of whole-body MRI, skeletal scintigraphy, and 18F-fluorodeoxyglucose (FDG) positron emission tomography (PET) for the detection of bone metastases in children and young adults, suggest the superiority of FDG PET scan (see Fig. 2.31). The latter technique had 90% sensitivity compared with 82% for whole-body MRI and 71% for skeletal scintigraphy.

In general terms, skeletal metastases may appear highly similar, irrespective of their primary source. However, there are instances in which the morphologic appearance, location, and distribution of metastatic lesions may suggest their site of origin. Thus, for instance, 50% of skeletal metastases distal to the elbows and knees—rare sites for metastases—are secondary to breast or bronchogenic carcinomas (Fig. 22.41). Lesions that have an expansive, "blown-out" appearance on radiographs and are highly vascular on arteriography are characteristic of metastatic renal carcinoma (Fig. 22.42). Moreover, Choi and associates recently reported a flow-void sign on MRI, resulting from relatively rapid blood flow through dilated arteries that supply the hypervascular lesion and through dilated veins that drain the lesion, apparently characteristic for osseous metastases from renal cell carcinoma. Multiple round dense foci or diffuse bone density is often seen in metastatic carcinoma of the prostate (Fig. 22.43); in females, sclerotic metastases are usually from breast carcinoma.

Some time ago characteristic cortical metastases have been described as originating from bronchogenic carcinoma; these metastases cause what Resnick has called "cookie bite" or "cookie cutter" lesions of the cortices of the long bones (Fig. 22.44). Because the bulk of metastases that reach the skeleton via hematogenous spread lodge in the bone marrow and in spongy bone, the initial radiographic appearance of metastatic lesions in the skeleton is that of destruction of cancellous bone; only with further growth do such lesions affect the cortex. The anastomosing vascular systems of the cortex, originating in the overlying periosteum, probably serve as the pathway by which malignant cells from the lung reach the compact bone to produce destruction of the cortex. Occasionally, other primary tumors (e.g., breast and kidney) may also metastasize to the cortex.

Single metastatic lesions in a bone must be distinguished from primary malignant and benign bone tumors. A few characteristic features of metastatic lesions may be helpful in making the distinction: (a) metastatic lesions usually present without or with only a small adjacent soft-tissue mass and (b) they usually lack a periosteal reaction unless they have broken through the cortex. The latter feature, however, is not invariably reliable, because in some series more than 30% of metastatic lesions—particularly metastases from carcinoma of the prostate—have been accompanied by a periosteal response. Metastatic lesions to the spine usually destroy the pedicle, a useful feature for distinguishing them from myeloma or neurofibroma invading the vertebra (Fig. 22.45, see also Fig. 22.23).

Histologically, metastatic tumors are easier to diagnose than many primary tumors because of their essential epithelial pattern. Although biopsies of suspected metastases are useful for diagnosis in patients with unknown primary tumors, these procedures are seldom helpful in specifying an exact site of an unknown primary tumor. Occasionally, if gland formation is present, a specific diagnosis of metastatic adenocarcinoma can be made, but rarely will a specific type of the tumor be detected. On occasion, a metastatic lesion may demonstrate a morphologic pattern that strongly suggests the site of a primary tumor, such as the clear cells of renal carcinoma or the pigment production of melanoma.

Complications

Although metastases are themselves complications of a primary malignant process, it must be emphasized that they can cause secondary complications such as pathologic fracture (Fig. 22.46) or, when occurring in the spine, compression of the thecal sac and spinal cord, thus producing neurologic symptoms (Fig. 22.47).

▲ **FIGURE 22.39   Skeletal metastases.** Origin of osteolytic (**A**) and osteoblastic (**B**) metastases. (From Greenspan A, Remagen W, 1998, with permission.)

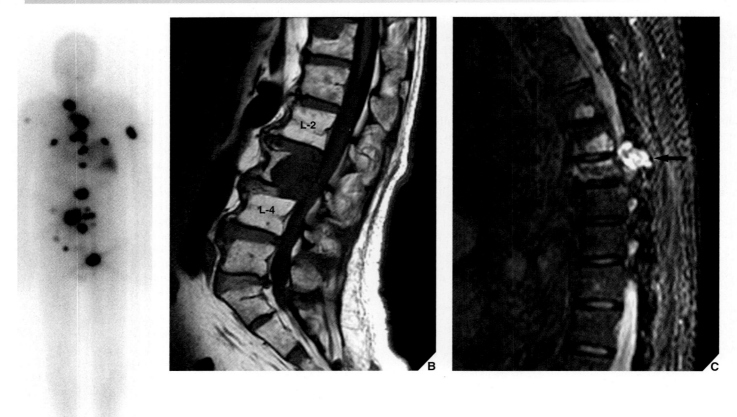

▲

FIGURE 22.40   **Scintigraphy and MRI of metastases.** A 70-year-old man with known follicular thyroid carcinoma presented with severe back pain. (**A**) A total body radionuclide bone scan performed after oral administration of 155mCi ^{131}I sodium iodide shows multiple skeletal metastases. (**B**) Sagittal T1-weighted MR image demonstrates the involvement of T12 and L3 vertebral bodies. (**C**) Sagittal STIR MR image shows extension of metastatic tumor into the spinal canal (*arrow*).

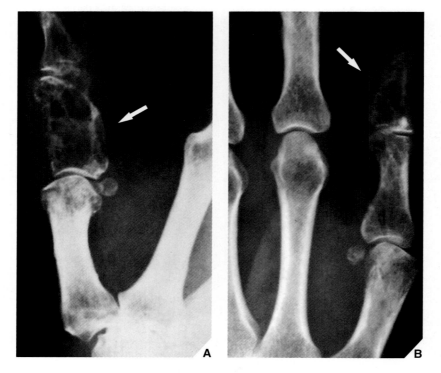

▲

FIGURE 22.41   **Skeletal metastases.** (**A**) A 63-year-old man with bronchogenic carcinoma developed a single metastatic lesion in the proximal phalanx of the left thumb (*arrow*). (**B**) A 50-year-old woman with breast carcinoma had a solitary metastatic lesion in the distal phalanx of the right thumb (*arrow*).

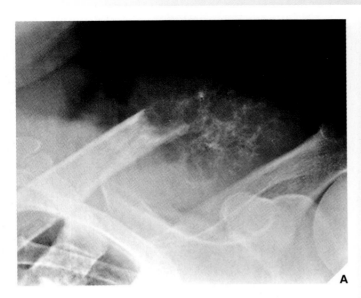
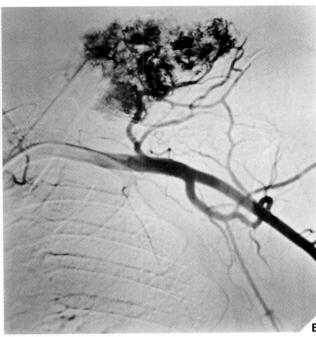

▲
FIGURE 22.42 **Angiography of metastatic lesion.** A 52-year-old man with renal cell carcinoma (hypernephroma) presented with a solitary metastatic lesion in the acromial end of the left clavicle. (**A**) Radiograph shows an expansive "blown-out" lesion associated with a soft-tissue mass destroying the acromial end of the clavicle. (**B**) Subtraction study of a selective left subclavian arteriogram demonstrates hypervascularity of the tumor, a characteristic feature of metastatic hypernephroma.

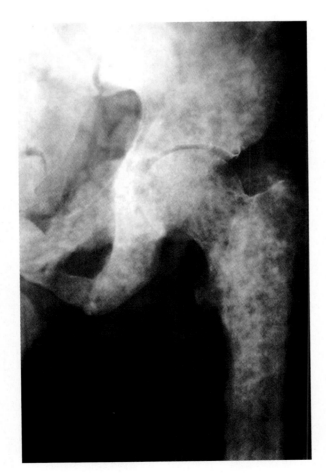

▲
FIGURE 22.43 **Osteoblastic metastases.** Anteroposterior radiograph of the left hemipelvis and proximal femur of a 55-year-old man with carcinoma of the prostate shows extensive blastic skeletal metastases. Multiple sclerotic foci are scattered through the ilium, pubis, ischium, and femur.

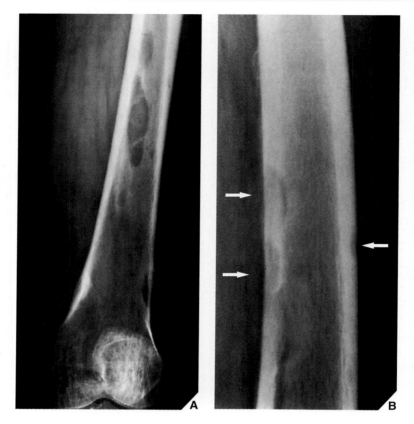

▲
FIGURE 22.44 Cortical metastases. Anteroposterior (**A**) and lateral magnification (**B**) radiographs of the left femur in an 82-year-old man with progressive femoral pain demonstrate multiple sharply marginated osteolytic areas of bone destruction, predominantly affecting the cortical bone. There is no evidence of periosteal reaction. Note the characteristic "cookie bite" appearance of the lesion on the lateral radiograph (*arrows*). On the basis of this feature, attention was focused on the chest, where CT examination (not shown here) demonstrated bronchogenic carcinoma. (From Greenspan A et al., 1984, with permission.)

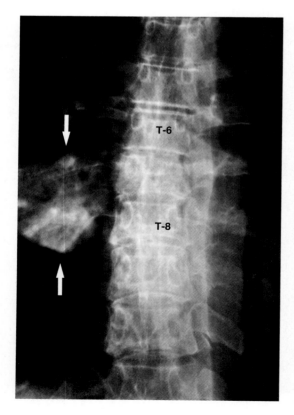

▲
FIGURE 22.45 Vertebral metastasis. Anteroposterior radiograph of the thoracolumbar spine in a 59-year-old woman with bronchogenic carcinoma shows a metastatic lesion in the body of T7. Note the destroyed left pedicle and associated paraspinal mass, features helpful in distinguishing this lesion from myeloma or neurofibroma. The lung tumor is obvious (*arrows*).

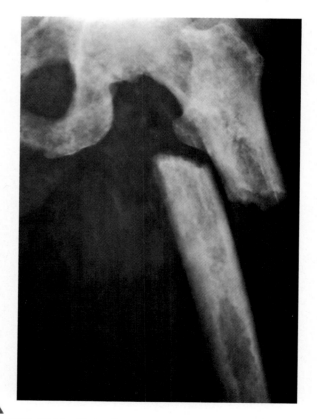

▲
FIGURE 22.46 Skeletal metastases complicated by pathologic fracture. Pathologic fracture may complicate metastatic disease of the skeleton, as seen here in the proximal shaft of the left femur in a 74-year-old man with multiple skeletal metastases from a prostate carcinoma.

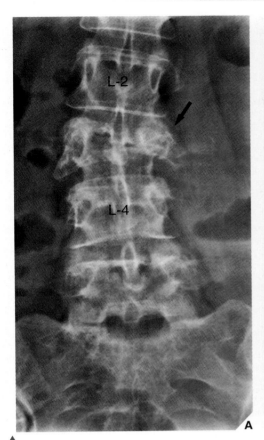
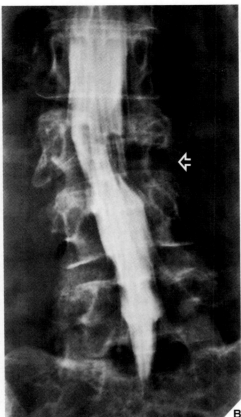
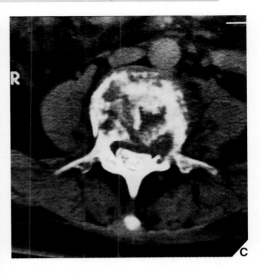

▲
FIGURE 22.47 **Neurologic complication of skeletal metastasis. (A)** Anteroposterior radiograph of the lumbar spine in a 47-year-old woman with breast carcinoma shows destruction of the body of L3 with a pathologic fracture. Note the involvement of the left pedicle (*arrow*). **(B)** A myelogram demonstrates compression of the thecal sac (*open arrow*). **(C)** On CT section, compression fracture of the vertebral body and involvement of the left pedicle are evident; the tumor extends into the soft tissue and compresses the ventral aspect of the thecal sac.

PRACTICAL POINTS TO REMEMBER

[1] Fibrosarcoma and MFH:
- characteristically present as purely osteolytic lesions, frequently in the long bones
- may resemble giant cell tumor, lymphoma, or telangiectatic osteosarcoma
- may develop in certain benign conditions, such as fibrous dysplasia and bone infarct.

[2] Ewing sarcoma, a round cell tumor, usually presents with characteristic radiographic features including:
- a permeative type of bone destruction
- cortical saucerization
- an aggressive periosteal reaction
- a soft-tissue mass.

The diaphysis of long bones, and the pelvis, ribs, and scapula are the most common sites of involvement.

[3] In the differential diagnosis of Ewing sarcoma, osteomyelitis and Langerhans cell histiocytosis should always be considered, as well as metastatic neuroblastoma, particularly in patients in their first decade. The most important distinguishing feature is the duration of symptoms. The amount of bone destruction seen radiographically in patients with Ewing sarcoma reporting symptoms for 4 to 6 months is usually the same as that:
- in patients with osteomyelitis reporting symptoms for 4 to 6 weeks
- in patients with Langerhans cell histiocytosis reporting symptoms for 1 to 2 weeks.

[4] Myeloma, the most common primary malignant bone tumor, has a predilection for the axial skeleton. Four distinctive forms of this lesion can be distinguished radiographically:
- a solitary lesion (plasmacytoma), usually affecting the pelvis or ribs

- diffuse myelomatosis
- diffuse osteoporosis, usually seen in the vertebral column
- sclerosing myeloma, the rarest manifestation of this tumor.

[5] Primary myeloma of the spine can usually be distinguished from radiographically similar metastatic disease by the preservation of the pedicles (vertebral-pedicle sign) in the early stages of the disease.

[6] In myeloma, radionuclide bone scan usually shows no increase in uptake of radiopharmaceutical.

[7] Adamantinoma, a malignant tumor with a strong predilection for the tibia, is characterized radiographically by:
- a "soap-bubble" appearance of the lesion combining lytic and sclerotic areas
- a "sawtooth" appearance of cortical destruction.

[8] Chordoma, which arises from the remnants of the notochord, is located almost exclusively in the midline of the axial skeleton. It tends to arise in the sphenooccipital and sacrococcygeal areas and in the body of C2.

[9] Primary leiomyosarcoma of bone, a rare bone malignancy, exhibits no characteristic radiographic features, although most often presents either as a lytic area of geographic bone destruction or with aggressive-looking, ill-defined borders and permeative or moth-eaten pattern.

[10] Hemangioendothelioma of bone may be solitary or multicentric. The radiographic features include an osteolytic appearance, either well circumscribed or with a wide zone of transition, and occasionally a "soap-bubble" character with extension into the soft tissues.

[11] Angiosarcoma of bone represents the most malignant end of the spectrum of vascular tumors. The radiographic features include a wide zone of transition, cortical permeation, and soft-tissue mass.

[12] Benign conditions with malignant potential include medullary bone infarct, the chronic draining sinus tract of osteomyelitis, plexiform neurofibromatosis, Paget disease, normal tissue undergoing

radiation, enchondroma, osteochondroma, synovial chondromatosis, and fibrous dysplasia.

[13] Prostate carcinoma is the primary tumor most often responsible for blastic metastases to bone. The primary tumors most often responsible for osteolytic skeletal metastases are carcinomas of the kidney, lung, breast, thyroid, and gastrointestinal tract.

[14] Bronchogenic carcinoma frequently produces cortical metastases ("cookie bite" lesions) and is responsible for metastases in sites distal to the elbow, including lesions of the phalanges.

[15] Carcinoma of the kidney usually produces lytic, "blown-out," hypervascular metastatic lesions.

[16] The best technique for mapping metastatic lesions in the skeleton is radionuclide bone scan and FDG PET scan.

SUGGESTED READINGS

Abdelwahab IF, Hermann G, Kenan S, Klein MJ, Lewis MM. Case report 794. Primary leiomyosarcoma of the right femur. *Skeletal Radiol* 1993;22:379–381.

Abdelwahab IF, Kenan S, Hermann G, Klein MJ, Lewis MM. Radiation-induced leiomyosarcoma. *Skeletal Radiol* 1995;24:81–83.

Abrahams TG, Bula W, Jones W. Epithelioid hemangioendothelioma of bone. *Skeletal Radiol* 1992;21:509–513.

Abrams HL. Skeletal metastases in carcinoma. *Radiology* 1950;55:534–538.

Abrams HL, Spiro R, Goldstein N. Metastases in carcinoma. Analysis of 1000 autopsied cases. *Cancer* 1950;3:74–85.

Adler C-P. Case report 587. Adamantinoma of the tibia mimicking osteofibrous dysplasia. *Skeletal Radiol* 1990;19:55–58.

Aggarwal S, Goulatia RK, Sood A, et al. POEMS syndrome: a rare variety of plasma cell dyscrasia. *Am J Roentgenol* 1990;155:339–341.

Algra PR, Bloem JL. Magnetic resonance imaging of metastatic disease and multiple myeloma. In: Bloem JL, Sartoris DJ, eds. *MRI and CT of the musculoskeletal system.* Baltimore: Williams & Wilkins; 1992:218.

Algra PR, Bloem JL, Tissing H, Falke TH, Arndt JW, Verboom LJ. Detection of vertebral metastases: comparison between MR imaging and bone scintigraphy. *Radiographics* 1991;11:219–232.

Algra PR, Heimans JJ, Valk J, Nauta JJ, Lachniet M, Van Kooten B. Do metastases in vertebrae begin in the body or the pedicles? Imaging study in 45 patients. *Am J Roentgenol* 1992;158:1275–1279.

Alquacil-Garcia A, Alonso A, Pettigrew NM. Osteofibrous dysplasia (ossifying fibroma) of the tibia and fibula and adamantinoma. *Am J Clin Pathol* 1984;82:470–474.

Ardran GM. Bone destruction not demonstrable by radiography. *Br J Radiol* 1951;24:107–109.

Avrahami E, Tadmor R, Dally O, Hadar H. Early MR demonstration of spinal metastases in patients with normal radiographs and CT and radionuclide bone scans. *J Comput Assist Tomogr* 1989;13:598–602.

Azzarelli A, Quagliuolo V, Cerasoli S, et al. Chordoma: natural history and treatment results in 33 cases. *J Surg Oncol* 1988;37:185–191.

Bachman AS, Sproul EE. Correlation of radiographic and autopsy findings in suspected metastases in the spine. *Bull NY Acad Med* 1940;44:169–175.

Baker ND, Greenspan A. Case report 172: pleomorphic liposarcoma, grade IV, of the soft tissue, arising in generalized plexiform neurofibromatosis. *Skeletal Radiol* 1981;7:150–153.

Baker PL, Dockerty MD, Coventry MB. Adamantinoma (so-called) of the long bones. *J Bone Joint Surg [Am]* 1954;36A:704–720.

Baraga JJ, Amrani KK, Swee RG, Wold L, Unni KK. Radiographic features of Ewing's sarcoma of the bones of the hands and feet. *Skeletal Radiol* 2001;30:121–126.

Bardwick PA, Zvaifler NJ, Gill GN, Newman D, Greenway GD, Resnick D. Plasma-cell dyscrasia with polyneuropathy, organomegaly, endocrinopathy, M-protein and skin changes: the POEMS syndrome. Report on two cases and review of the literature. *Medicine* 1980;59:311–322.

Bataille R, Chevalier J, Ross M, Sany J. Bone scintigraphy in plasma-cell myeloma. *Radiology* 1982;145:801–804.

Baur A, Stäbler A, Lamerz R, Bartl R, Reiser M. Light chain deposition disease in multiple myeloma: MR imaging features correlated with histopathologic findings. *Skeletal Radiol* 1998;27:173–176.

Beackley MC, Lau BP, King ER. Bone involvement in Hodgkin's disease. *Am J Roentgenol* 1972;114:559–563.

Beaugié JM, Mann CV, Butler ECB. Sacrococcygeal chordoma. *Br J Surg* 1969;56:586–588.

Belza MG, Urich H. Chordoma and malignant fibrous histiocytoma. Evidence of transformation. *Cancer* 1986;589:1082–1087.

Berlin O, Angervall L, Kindblom LG, Berlin IC, Stener B. Primary leiomyosarcoma of bone. A clinical, radiographic, pathologic-anatomic, and prognostic study of 16 cases. *Skeletal Radiol* 1987;16:364–376.

Berrettoni B, Carter JR. Mechanisms of cancer metastasis to bone. *J Bone Joint Surg [Am]* 1986;68A:308–312.

Bertoni F, Bacchini P, Ferruzzi A. Small round-cell malignancies of bone: Ewing's sarcoma, malignant lymphoma, and myeloma. *Semin Orthop* 1991;6:186–195.

Bertoni F, Capanna R, Calderoni P, Bacchini P, Campanacci M. Primary central (medullary) fibrosarcoma of bone. *Semin Diagn Pathol* 1984;1:185–198.

Bessler W, Antonucci F, Stamm B, Stuckmann G, Vollrath T. Case report 646. POEMS syndrome. *Skeletal Radiol* 1991;20:212–215.

Bloom RA, Libson E, Husband JE, Stoker DJ. The periosteal sunburst reaction to bone metastases. A literature review and report of 20 additional cases. *Skeletal Radiol* 1987;16:629–634.

Boland PJ, Huvos AG. Malignant fibrous histiocytoma of bone. *Clin Orthop* 1986;204:130–134.

Boston HC Jr, Dahlin DC, Ivins JC, Cupps RE. Malignant lymphoma (so-called reticulum cell sarcoma) of bone. *Cancer* 1974;34:1131–1137.

Boutin RD, Speath HJ, Mangalic A, Sell JJ. Epithelioid hemagnioendothelioma of bone. *Skeletal Radiol* 1996;25:391–395.

Brandon C, Martel W, Weatherbee L, Capek P. Case report 572. Osteosclerotic myeloma (POEMS syndrome). *Skeletal Radiol* 1989;18:542–546.

Braunstein EM. Hodgkin's disease of bone: radiographic correlation with the histologic classification. *Radiology* 1980;137:643–646.

Breyer III RJ, Mulligan ME, Smith SE, Line BR, Badros AZ. Comparison of imaging with FDG PET/CT with other imaging modalities in myeloma. *Skeletal Radiol* 2006;35:632–640.

Brown B, Laorr A, Greenspan A, Stadalnik R. Negative bone scintigraphy with diffuse osteoblastic breast carcinoma metastases. *Clin Nucl Med* 1994;19:194–196.

Brown TS, Paterson CR. Osteosclerosis in myeloma. *J Bone Joint Surg [Br]* 1973;55B:621–623.

Bullough PG. *Atlas of orthopedic pathology with clinical and radiologic correlations,* 2nd ed. New York: Gower; 1992:17.1–17.29.

Bushnell DL, Kahn D, Huston B, Bevering CG. Utility of SPECT imaging for determination of vertebral metastases in patients with known primary tumors. *Skeletal Radiol* 1995;24:13–16.

Byers PD. A study of histological features distinguishing chordoma from chondrosarcoma. *Br J Cancer* 1981;43:229–232.

Caluser CI, Scott AM, Schnieder J, Macapinlac HA, Yeh SD, Larson SM. Value of lesion location and intensity of uptake in SPECT bone scintigraphy of the spine in patients with malignant tumors. *Radiology* 1992;185(S):315.

Campanacci M. Osteofibrous dysplasia of long bones. A new clinical entity. *Ital J Orthop Traumatol* 1976;2:221–237.

Campanacci M, Laus M, Giunti A, Gitelis S, Bertoni F. Adamantinoma of the long bones. The experience at the Istituto Ortopedico Rizzoli. *Am J Surg Pathol* 1981;5:533–542.

Capanna R, Bertoni F, Bacchini P, Gacci G, Guerra A, Campanacci M. Malignant fibrous histiocytoma of bone: the experience at the Rizzoli Institute. Report of 90 cases. *Cancer* 1984;54:177–187.

Castellino RA. Hodgkin disease: practical concepts for the diagnostic radiologist. *Radiology* 1986;159:305–310.

Cavazzana AO, Miser JS, Jefferson J, Triche TJ. Experimental evidence for a neural origin of Ewing's sarcoma of bone. *Am J Pathol* 1987;127:507–518.

Chan K-W, Rosen G, Miller DR, Tan CTC. Hodgkin's disease in adolescents presenting as a primary bone lesion. A report of four cases and review of the literature. *Am J Pediatr Hematol Oncol* 1982;4:11–17.

Choi J-A, Lee KH, Jun WS, Yi MG, Lee S, Kang HS. Osseous metastasis from renal cell carcinoma: "flow-void" sign at MR imaging. *Radiology* 2003;228:629–634.

Chong ST, Beasley HS, Daffner RH. POEMS syndrome: radiographic appearance with MRI correlation. *Skeletal Radiol* 2006; 35:690–695.

Chu TA. Chondroid chordoma of the sacrococcygeal region. *Arch Pathol Lab Med* 1987;111:861–864.

Citrin DL, Bessent RG, Greig WR. A comparison of the sensitivity and accuracy of the 99m Tc-phosphate bone scan and skeletal radiograph in the diagnosis of bone metastases. *Clin Radiol* 1977;28:107–117.

Clayton F, Butler JJ, Ayala AG, Ro JY, Zornoza J. Non-Hodgkin's lymphoma in bone: pathologic and radiologic features with clinical correlates. *Cancer* 1987;60:2494–2500.

Coerkamp EG, Kroon HM. Cortical bone metastases. *Radiology* 1988;169:525–528.

Coldwell DM, Baron RL, Charnsangavej C. Angiosarcoma: diagnosis and clinical course. *Acta Radiol* 1989;30:627–631.

Coles WC, Schultz MD. Bone involvement in malignant lymphoma. *Radiology* 1948;50:458–462.

Coombs RJ, Zeiss J, McKann K, Phillips E. Multifocal Ewing's tumor of the skeletal system. *Skeletal Radiol* 1986;15:254–257.

Czerniak B, Rojas-Corona RR, Dorfman HD. Morphologic diversity of long bone adamantinoma. The concept of differentiated (regressing) adamantinoma and its relationship to osteofibrous dysplasia. *Cancer* 1989;64:2319–2334.

Dahlin DC. Grading of bone tumors. In: Unni KK, ed. *Bone tumors.* New York: Churchill Livinstone; 1988:35–45.

Dahlin DC, Ivins JC. Fibrosarcoma of bone: a study of 114 cases. *Cancer* 1969;23:35–41.

Dahlin DC, MacCarty CS. Chordoma. A study of fifty-nine cases. *Cancer* 1952;5:1170–1178.

Dahlin DC, Unni KK. *Bone tumors. General aspects and data on 8,542 cases,* 4th ed. Springfield, IL: Charles C. Thomas; 1986:193–336, 208–226, 379–393.

Dahlin DC, Unni KK, Matsuno T. Malignant (fibrous) histiocytoma of bone—fact or fancy? *Cancer* 1977;39:1508–1516.

Daldrup-Link HE, Franzius C, Link TM, et al. Whole-body MR imaging for detection of bone metastases in children and young adults: comparison with skeletal scintigraphy and FDG PET. *Am J Roentgenol* 2001;177:229–236.

Dardick I, Schatz JE, Colgan TJ. Osteogenic sarcoma with epithelial differentiation. *Ultrastruct Pathol* 1992;16:463–474.

Datz FL, Patch GG, Arias JM, Morton KA. *Nuclear medicine. A teaching file*. St. Louis: Mosby Year Book; 1992:28–29.

Dehner LP. Primitive neuroectodermal tumor and Ewing's sarcoma. *Am J Surg Pathol* 1993;17:1–13.

Delbeke D, Powers TA, Sandler MP. Negative scintigraphy with positive magnetic resonance imaging in bone metastases. *Skeletal Radiol* 1990;19:113–116.

Deutsch A, Resnick D. Eccentric cortical metastases to the skeleton from bronchogenic carcinoma. *Radiology* 1980;137:49–52.

Deutsch A, Resnick D, Niwayama G. Case report 145. Bilateral, almost symmetrical skeletal metastases (both femora) from bronchogenic carcinoma. *Skeletal Radiol* 1981;6:144–148.

Dorfman HD, Norman A, Wolff H. Fibrosarcoma complicating bone infarction in a caisson worker: case report. *J Bone Joint Surg [Am]* 1966;48A:528–532.

Enzinger FM, Weiss SW. Hemangioendothelioma: vascular tumors of intermediate malignancy. In: Enzinger FM, Weiss SW, eds. *Soft tissue tumors*, 3rd ed. St. Louis: CV Mosby; 1995.

Enzinger FM, Weiss SW. *Soft tissue tumors*. St. Louis: Mosby; 1988:951–958.

Evison G, Pizey N, Roylance J. Bone formation associated with osseous metastases from bladder carcinoma. *Clin Radiol* 1981;32:303–309.

Fechner RE, Mills SE. *Atlas of tumor pathology. Tumors of the bones and joints*, 3rd series, fascicle 8. Washington, DC: Armed Forces Institute of Pathology; 1993:239–244.

Feldman F, Lattes R. Primary malignant fibrous histiocytoma (fibrous xanthoma) of bone. *Skeletal Radiol* 1977;1:145–160.

Fischer B. Über ein primäres Adamantinom der Tibia. *Frankfurter Z Pathol* 1913;12:422–441.

Fishman EK, Kuhlman JE, Jones RJ. CT of lymphoma: spectrum of disease. *Radiographics* 1991;11:647–669.

Fletcher CD, Unni KK, Mertens F, eds. *World Health Organization classification of tumors. Pathology and genetics of tumours of soft tissue and bone*. Lyon, France: IARC Press; 2002.

Galasko CSB. The anatomy and pathways of skeletal metastases. In: Weiss L, Gilbert H, eds. *Bone Metastasis*. Boston: GK Hall; 1981:49–63.

Galasko CSB. Mechanisms of lytic and blastic metastatic disease of bone. *Clin Orthop* 1982;69:20–27.

Galli SJ, Weintraub HP, Proppe KH. Malignant fibrous histiocytoma and pleomorphic sarcoma in association with medullary bone infarcts. *Cancer* 1978;41:607–619.

Garber CZ. Reactive bone formation in Ewing's sarcoma. *Cancer* 1951;4:839–845.

Ghandur-Mnaymneh L, Broder LE, Mnaymneh WA. Lobular carcinoma of the breast metastatic to bone with unusual clinical, radiologic, and pathologic features mimicking osteopoikilosis. *Cancer* 1984;53:1801–1803.

Gold RH, Mirra JM. Case report 101. Primary Hodgkin disease of humerus. *Skeletal Radiol* 1979;4:233–235.

Gold RI, Seeger LL, Bassett LW, Steckel RJ. An integrated approach to the evaluation of metastatic bone disease. *Radiol Clin North Am* 1990;28:471–483.

Greenfield GB, Arrington JA. *Imaging of bone tumors. A multimodality approach*. Philadelphia: JB Lippincott; 1995.

Greenspan A. Sclerosing bone dysplasias—a target-site approach. *Skeletal Radiol* 1991;20:561–584.

Greenspan A, Gerscovich EO, Szabo RM, Matthews II JG. Condensing osteitis of the clavicle: a rare but frequently misdiagnosed condition. *Am J Roentgenol* 1991;156:1011–1015.

Greenspan A, Klein MJ. Radiology and pathology of bone tumors. In: Lewis MM, ed. *Musculoskeletal oncology. A multidisciplinary approach*. Philadelphia: WB Saunders; 1992:13–72.

Greenspan A, Klein MJ. Giant bone island. *Skeletal Radiol* 1996;25:67–69.

Greenspan A, Klein MJ, Lewis MM. Case report 272. Skeletal cortical metastases in the left femur arising from bronchogenic carcinoma. *Skeletal Radiol* 1984;11:297–301.

Greenspan A, Klein MJ, Lewis MM. Case report 284. Osteolytic cortical metastasis in the femur from bronchogenic carcinoma. *Skeletal Radiol* 1984;12:146–150.

Greenspan A, Norman A. Osteolytic cortical destruction: an unusual pattern of skeletal metastases. *Skeletal Radiol* 1988;17:402–406.

Greenspan A, Remagen W. *Differential diagnosis of tumors and tumor-like lesions of bones and joints*. Philadelphia: Lippincott-Raven; 1998:369–371.

Greenspan A, Stadalnik RC. Bone island: scintigraphic findings and their clinical application. *Can Assoc Radiol J* 1995;46:368–379.

Greenspan A, Steiner G, Knutzon R. Bone island (enostosis): clinical significance and radiologic and histologic correlations. *Skeletal Radiol* 1991;20:85–90.

Grover SB, Dhar A. Imaging spectrum in sclerotic myelomas: an experience in three cases. *Eur Radiol* 2000;10:1828–1831.

Gutzeit A, Doert A, Froehlich JM, et al. Comparison of diffusion-weighted whole body MRI and skeletal scintigraphy for the detection of bone metastases in patients with prostate or breast carcinoma. *Skeletal Radiol* 2010;39:333–343.

Hall FM, Gore SM. Osteosclerotic myeloma variant. *Skeletal Radiol* 1988;17:101–105.

Healey JH, Turnbull AD, Miedema B, Lane JM. Acrometastases. A study of twenty-nine patients with osseous involvement of the hands and feet. *J Bone Joint Surg [Am]* 1986;68A:743–746.

Hendrix RW, Rogers LF, Davis TM Jr. Cortical bone metastases. *Radiology* 1991;181:409–413.

Heyning FH, Kroon HMJA, Hogendoorn PCW, Taminiau AHM, van der Woude H-J. MR imaging characteristics in primary lymphoma of bone with emphasis on non-aggressive appearance. *Skeletal Radiol* 2007;36:937–944.

Higinbotham NL, Phillips RF, Farr HW, Hustu HO. Chordoma. Thirty-five-year study at Memorial Hospital. *Cancer* 1967;20:1841–1850.

Hillemanns M, McLeod RA, Unni KK. Malignant lymphoma. *Skeletal Radiol* 1996;25:73–75.

Hove B, Gyldensted C. Spiculated vertebral metastases from prostatic carcinoma. *Neuroradiology* 1990;32:337–339.

Hudson TM. *Radiologic-pathologic correlation of musculoskeletal lesions*. Baltimore: Williams & Wilkins; 1987:287–303, 359–397, 421–440.

Huvos AG. *Bone tumors: diagnosis, treatment, and prognosis*, 2nd ed. Philadelphia: WB Saunders; 1991:599–624, 695–711.

Huvos AG, Heilweil M, Bretsky SS. The pathology of malignant fibrous histiocytoma of bone. A study of 130 patients. *Am J Surg Pathol* 1985;9:853–871.

Huvos AG, Higinbotham NL. Primary fibrosarcoma of bone: a clinico-pathologic study of 130 patients. *Cancer* 1975;35:837–847.

Huvos AG, Higinbotham NL, Miller TR. Bone sarcomas arising in fibrous dysplasia. *J Bone Joint Surg [Am]* 1972;64A:1047–1056.

Huvos AG, Marcove RC. Adamantinoma of long bones: a clinicopathological study of fourteen cases with vascular origin suggested. *J Bone Joint Surg [Am]* 1975;57A:148–154.

Huvos AG, Woodard HQ, Heilweil M. Postradiation malignant fibrous histiocytoma of bone. A clinicopathologic study of 20 patients. *Am J Surg Pathol* 1986;10:9–18.

Ignacio EA, Palmer KM, Mathur SC, Schwartz AM, Olan WJ. Residents' teaching files. Epithelioid hemangioendothelioma of the lower extremity. *Radiographics* 1999;19:531–537.

Ishida T, Dorfman HD, Steiner GC, Normatz A. Cystic angiomatosis of bone with sclerotic changes mimicking osteoblastic metastases. *Skeletal Radiol* 1994;23:247–252.

Ishida T, Iijima T, Kikuchi F, et al. A clinicopathological and immunohistochemical study of osteofibrous dysplasia, differentiated adamantinoma, and adamantinoma of long bones. *Skeletal Radiol* 1992;21:493–502.

Jacobson HG, Poppel MH, Shapiro JH, Grossberger S. The vertebral pedicle sign: a roentgen finding to differentiate metastatic carcinoma from multiple myeloma. *Am J Roentgenol* 1958;80:817–821.

Jaffe H. Tumors metastatic to the skeleton. In: *Tumors and tumorous conditions of the bones and joints*. Philadelphia: Lea & Febiger; 1958:594–595.

Jaffe HL. *Metabolic, degenerative, and inflammatory diseases of bones and joints*. Philadelphia: Lea & Febiger; 1972:877.

Jundt G, Moll C, Nidecker A, Schilt R, Remagen W. Primary leiomyosarcoma of bone: report of eight cases. *Hum Pathol* 1994;25:1205–1212.

Jundt G, Remberger K, Roessner A, Schulz A, Bohndorf K. Adamantinoma of long bones. A histopathological and immunohistochemical study of 23 cases. *Pathol Res Pract* 1995;191:112–120.

Kahn LB, Webber B, Mills E, Anstey L, Heselson NG. Malignant fibrous histiocytoma (malignant fibrous xanthoma: xanthosarcoma) of bone. *Cancer* 1978;42:640–651.

Kaplan H. *Hodgkin disease*, 2nd ed. Cambridge: Harvard University Press; 1980: 85–92.

Kattapuram SV, Khurana JS, Scott JA, el-Khoury GY. Negative scintigraphy with positive magnetic resonance imaging in bone metastases. *Skeletal Radiol* 1990;19:113–116.

Keeney GL, Unni KK, Beabout JW, Pritchard DJ. Adamantinoma of long bones. A clinicopathologic study of 85 cases. *Cancer* 1989;64:730–737.

Kleer CG, Unni KK, McLeod RA. Epithelioid hemangioendothelioma of bone. *Am J Surg Pathol* 1996;20:1301–1311.

Klein MJ, Rudin BJ, Greenspan A, Posner M, Lewis MM. Hodgkin disease presenting as a lesion in the wrist. *J Bone Joint Surg [Am]* 1987;69A:1246–1249.

Knapp RH, Wick MR, Scheithauer BW, Unni KK. Adamantinoma of bone. An electron microscopic and immunohistochemical study. *Virchows Arch [A]* 1982;398:75–86.

Kramer K, Hicks D, Palis J, et al. Epithelioid osteosarcoma of bone. Immunocytochemical evidence suggesting divergent epithelial and mesenchymal differentiation in a primary osseous neoplasm. *Cancer* 1993;71:2977–2982.

Kumar N, David R, Madewell JE, Lindell MM Jr. Radiographic spectrum of osteogenic sarcoma. *Am J Roentgenol* 1987;148:767–772.

Kyle RA. Diagnostic criteria of multiple myeloma. *Hematol Oncol Clin N Am* 1992;6:347–358.

Lehrer HZ, Maxfield WS, Nice CM. The periosteal sunburst pattern in metastatic bone tumors. *Am J Roentgenol* 1970;108:154–161.

Link TM, Haeussler MD, Poppek S, et al. Malignant fibrous histiocytoma of bone: conventional X-ray and MR imaging features. *Skeletal Radiol* 1998;27:552–558.

Lipshitz HI, Malthouse SR, Cunningham D, MacVicar AD, Husband JE. Multiple myeloma: appearance at MR imaging. *Radiology* 1992;182:833–837.

Llombart-Bosch A, Contesso G, Henry-Amar M, et al. Histopathological predictive factors in Ewing's sarcoma of bone and clinicopathologic correlations. A retrospective study of 261 cases. *Virchows Arch [A]* 1986;409:627–640 (erratum published in *Virchows Arch [A]* 1986;410:263).

Llombart-Bosch A, Lacombe MJ, Peydro-Olaya A, Perez-Bacete M, Contesso G. Malignant peripheral neuroectodermal tumors of bone other than Askin's neoplasm: characterization of 14 new cases with immunohistochemistry and electron microscopy. *Virchows Arch [A]* 1988;412:421–430.

Llombart-Bosch A, Ortuno-Pacheco G. Ultrastructural findings supporting the angioblastic nature of the so-called adamantinoma of the tibia. *Histopathology* 1978;2:189–200.

Lukes RJ, Buttler JJ. Pathology and nomenclature of Hodgkin disease. *Cancer Res* 1966;26:1063–2083.

Markel SF. Ossifying fibroma of long bone. Its distinction from fibrous dysplasia and its association with adamantinoma of long bone. *Am J Clin Pathol* 1978;69:91–97.

Melamed JW, Martinez S, Hoffman CJ. Imaging of primary multifocal osseous lymphoma. *Skeletal Radiol* 1997;26:35–41.

Meyer JE, Schulz MD. "Solitary" myeloma of bone: a review of 12 cases. *Cancer* 1974;34:438–440.

Mirra JM, Bullough PG, Marcove RC, Jacobs B, Huvos AG. Malignant fibrous histiocytoma and osteosarcoma in association with bone infarcts. *J Bone Joint Surg [Am]* 1974;56A:932–940.

Mirra JM, Gold RH, Marafiote R. Malignant (fibrous) histiocytoma arising in association with a bone infarct in sickle-cell disease: coincidence or cause-and-effect? *Cancer* 1977;39:186–194.

Moll RH, Lee I, Gould VE, Berndt R, Roessner A, Franke WW. Immunocytochemical analysis of Ewing's tumors. Patterns of expression of intermediate filaments and desmosomal proteins indicate cell type heterogeneity and pluripotential differentiation. *Am J Pathol* 1987;127:288–304.

Mulder JD, Kroon HM, Schütte HE, Taconis WK. *Radiologic atlas of bone tumors.* Amsterdam, the Netherlands: Elsevier; 1993;267–274, 607–625.

Mulligan ME, Badros AZ. PET/CT and MR imaging in myeloma. *Skeletal Radiol* 2007;36:5–16.

Mulligan ME, Kransdorf MJ. Sequestra in primary lymphoma of bone: prevalence and radiologic features. *Am J Roentgenol* 1993;160:1245–1248.

Mulligan ME, McRae GA, Murphey MD. Imaging features of primary lymphoma of bone. *Am J Roentgenol* 1999;173:1691–1697.

Mulvey RB. Peripheral bone metastases. *Am J Roentgenol* 1964;91:155–160.

Mundy GR, Spiro TP. The mechanisms of bone metastasis and bone destruction by tumor cells. In: Weiss L, Gilbert HA, eds. *Bone metastasis.* Boston: GK Hall; 1981:64–82.

Murphey MD, Gross TM, Rosenthal HG. Musculoskeletal malignant fibrous histiocytoma: radiologic-pathologic correlation. *Radiographics* 1994;14:807–826.

Murray RO, Jacobson HG. *The radiology of bone diseases,* 2nd ed. New York: Churchill Livingstone; 1977:585.

Myers JL, Arocho J, Bernreuter W, Dunham W, Mazur MT. Leiomyosarcoma of bone. A clinicopathologic, immunohistochemical, and ultrastructural study of five cases. *Cancer* 1991;67:1051–1056.

Napoli LD, Hansen HH, Muggia FM, Twigg HL. The incidence of osseous involvement in lung cancer, with special reference to the development of osteoblastic changes. *Radiology* 1973;108:17–21.

Norman A, Ulin R. A comparative study of periosteal new-bone response in metastatic bone tumors (solitary) and primary bone sarcomas. *Radiology* 1969;92:705–708.

Ontell FK, Greenspan A. Blastic osseous metastases in ovarian carcinoma. *Can Assoc Radiol J* 1995;46:231–234.

Ostrowski ML, Unni KK, Banks PM, et al. Malignant lymphoma of bone. *Cancer* 1986;58:2646–2655.

Panchwagh Y, Puri A, Agarwal M, Chinoy R, Jambhekar N. Case report: metastatic adamantinoma of the tibia – an unusual presentation. *Skeletal Radiol* 2006;35:190–193.

Panebianco AC, Kaupp HA. Bilateral thumb metastasis from breast carcinoma. *Arch Surg* 1968;96:216–218.

Powell JM. Metastatic carcinoid of bone. Report of two cases and review of the literature. *Clin Orthop* 1988;230:266–272.

Reinus WR, Kyriakos M, Gilula LA, Brower AC, Merkel K. Plasma cell tumors with calcified amyloid deposition mistaken for chondrosarcoma. *Radiology* 1993;189:505–509.

Resnick D, Greenway GD, Bardwick PA, Zvaifler NJ, Gill GN, Newman DR. Plasma cell dyscrasia with polyneuropathy, organomegaly, endocrinopathy, M-protein, and skin changes: the POEMS syndrome. *Radiology* 1981;140:17–22.

Resnick D, Niwayama G. Skeletal metastases. In: Resnick D, ed. *Diagnosis of bone and joint disorders,* 3rd ed. Philadelphia: WB Saunders; 1995:3991–4065.

Rock MG, Beabout JW, Unni KK, Sim FH. Adamantinoma. *Orthopedics* 1983;6:472–477.

Rosai J. Adamantinoma of the tibia: electron microscopic evidence of its epithelial origin. *Am J Clin Pathol* 1969;51:786–792.

Rosai J, Pinkus GS. Immunohistochemical demonstration of epithelial differentiation in adamantinoma of the tibia. *Am J Surg Pathol* 1982;6:427–434.

Rosenberg AE. Malignant fibrous histiocytoma: past, present, and future. *Skeletal Radiol* 2003;32:613–618.

Ruzek KA, Wenger DE. The multiple faces of lymphoma of the musculoskeletal system. *Skeletal Radiol* 2004;33:1–8.

Schajowicz F. Ewing's sarcoma and reticulum cell sarcoma of bone: with special reference to the histochemical demonstration of glycogen as an aid to differential diagnosis. *J Bone Joint Surg [Am]* 1959;41A:349–356.

Schajowicz F. *Tumors and tumorlike lesions of bone, pathology, radiology, and treatment,* 2nd ed. Berlin, Germany: Springer-Verlag; 1994:301–367, 468–481, 552–566.

Schajowicz F, Santini-Araujo E. Adamantinoma of the tibia masked by fibrous dysplasia. Report of three cases. *Clin Orthop* 1989;238:294–301.

Schajowicz F, Velan O, Santini Araujo E, et al. Metastases of carcinoma in pagetic bone. *Clin Orthop* 1988;228:290–296.

Seiss SW, Enzinger FM. Malignant fibrous histiocytoma: an analysis of 200 cases. *Cancer* 1978;41:2250–2260.

Shih WJ, Riley C, Magoun S, Ryo UY. Paget's disease mimicking skeletal metastases in a patient with coexisting prostatic carcinoma. *Eur J Nucl Med* 1988;15:422–423.

Shirley SK, Gilula LA, Segal GP, Foulkes MA, Kissane JM, Askin FB. Roentgenographic-pathologic correlation of diffuse sclerosis in Ewing's sarcoma of bone. *Skeletal Radiol* 1984;12:69–78.

Sim FH, Frassica FJ. Metastatic bone disease. In: Unni KK, ed. *Bone tumors.* New York: Churchill Livingstone; 1988:226.

Smith J. Radiation-induced sarcoma of bone: clinical and radiographic findings in 43 patients irradiated for soft tissue neoplasms. *Clin Radiol* 1982;33:205–221.

Söderlund V. Radiological diagnosis of skeletal metastases. *Eur Radiol* 1996;6:587–595.

Soule EH, Enriquez P. Atypical fibrous histiocytoma, malignant fibrous histiocytoma, malignant histiocytoma, and epithelioid sarcoma. A comparative study of 65 tumors. *Cancer* 1972;30:128–143.

Spanier SS, Enneking WF, Enriquez P. Primary malignant fibrous histiocytoma of bone. *Cancer* 1975;36:2084–2098.

Spjut HJ, Dorfman HD, Fechner RE, Ackerman LV. *Atlas of tumor pathology. Tumors of bone and cartilage,* 2nd series, fascicle 5. Washington, DC: Armed Forces Institute of Pathology; 1971:347–390.

Springfield DS, Rosenberg AE, Mankin HJ, Mindell ER. Relationship between osteofibrous dysplasia and adamantinoma. *Clin Orthop* 1994;309:234–244.

Stäbler A, Baur A, Bartl R, Munker R, Lamerz R, Reiser MF. Contrast enhancement and quantitative signal analysis in MR imaging of multiple myeloma: assessment of focal and diffuse growth patterns in marrow correlated with biopsies and survival rates. *Am J Roentgenol* 1996;167:1029–1036.

Stein H, Kaiserling E, Lennert K. Evidence for B-cell origin of reticulum cell sarcoma. *Virchows Arch [A]* 1974;A364:51–67.

Steiner GC. Neuroectodermal tumor versus Ewing's sarcoma. Immuno histochemical and electron microscopic observations. *Curr Top Pathol* 1989;80:1–29.

Steiner GC, Matano S, Present D. Ewing's sarcoma of humerus with epithelial differentiation. *Skeletal Radiol* 1995;24:379–382.

Stout AP, Lattes R. Tumors of the soft tissues. In: *Atlas of tumor pathology,* 2nd fascicle, series 1. Washington, DC: Armed Forces Institute of Pathology; 1967.

Sundaram M, Akduman I, White LM, McDonald DJ, Kandel R, Janney C. Primary leiomyosarcoma of bone. *Am J Roentgenol* 1999;172:771–776.

Sundaram M, McLeod RA. MR imaging of tumor and tumorlike lesions of bone and soft tissue. *Am J Roentgenol* 1990;155:817–824.

Sung MS, Lee GK, Kang HS. Sacrococcygeal chordoma: MR imaging in 30 patients. *Skeletal Radiol* 2005;34:87–94.

Sweet DE, Vinh TN, Devaney K. Cortical osteofibrous dysplasia of long bone and its relationship to adamantinoma. A clinicopathologic study of 30 cases. *Am J Surg Pathol* 1992;16:282–290.

Taylor JR. Persistence of the notochondral canal in vertebrae. *J Anat* 1982;11:211–217.

Thrall JH, Ellis BI. Skeletal metastases. *Radiol Clin North Am* 1987;25:1155–1170.

Trias A, Fery A. Cortical circulation of long bones. *J Bone Joint Surg [Am]* 1979;61A:1052–1059.

Triche T, Cavazzana A. Round cell tumors of bone. In: Unni KK, ed. *Bone tumors.* New York: Churchill Livingstone; 1988:199–223.

Triche TJ, Askin FB, Kissane JM. Neuroblastoma, Ewing's sarcoma and the differential diagnosis of small, round blue cell tumors. In: Finegold M, ed. *Pathology of neoplasia in children and adolescents.* Philadelphia: WB Saunders; 1986:145–156.

Ueda Y, Roessner A, Bosse A, Edel G, Bocker W, Wuisman P. Juvenile intracortical adamantinoma of the tibia with predominant osteofibrous dysplasia-like features. *Pathol Res Pract* 1991;187:1039–1043.

Unni KK. Osteosarcoma of bone. In: Unni KK, ed. *Bone tumors.* New York: Churchill Livingstone; 1988:107–133.

Unni KK. Fibrous and fibrohistiocytic lesions of bone. *Semin Orthop* 1991;6:177–186.

Unni KK. *Dahlin's bone tumors: General aspects and data on 11,087 cases,* 5th ed. New York: Lippincott-Raven; 1996.

Unni KK, Dahlin DC, Beabout JW, Ivins JC. Adamantinoma of long bones. *Cancer* 1974;34:1796–1805.

Vilar JL, Lezena AH, Pedrosa CS. Spiculated periosteal reaction in metastatic lesions in bone. *Skeletal Radiol* 1979;3:230–233.

Voss SD, Murphey MD, Hall FM. Solitary osteosclerotic plasmacytoma: association with demyelinating polyneuropathy and amyloid deposition. *Skeletal Radiol* 2001;30:527–529.

Weiss SW. Ultrastructure of the so-called "chordoid sarcoma." Evidence supporting cartilaginous differentiation. *Cancer* 1976;37:300–306.

Weiss SW, Bratthauer GL, Morris PA. Post-radiation malignant fibrous histiocytoma expressing cytokeratin: implications for the immunodiagnosis of sarcomas. *Am J Surg Pathol* 1988;12:554–558.

Weiss SW, Dorfman HD. Adamantinoma of long bone. An analysis of nine new cases with emphasis on metastasizing lesions and fibrous dysplasia-like changes. *Hum Pathol* 1977;8:141–153.

Weiss SW, Enzinger FM. Malignant fibrous histiocytoma: an analysis of 200 cases. *Cancer* 1978;41:2250–2266.

Wenger DE, Wold LE. Malignant vascular lesions of bone: radiologic and pathologic features. *Skeletal Radiol* 2000;29:619–631.

Wippold FJ III, Koeller KK, Smirniotopoulos JG. Clinical and imaging features of cervical chordoma. *Am J Roentgenol* 1999;172:1423–1426.

Wood GS, Beckstead JH, Turner RR, Hendrickson MR, Kempson RL, Warnke RA. Malignant fibrous histiocytoma tumor cells resemble fibroblasts. *Am J Surg Pathol* 1986;10:323–335.

Yochum TR, Rowe LJ. Tumor and tumor-like processes. In: Yochum TR, Rowe LJ, eds. *Essentials of skeletal radiology,* vol. 2. Baltimore: Williams & Wilkins; 1987:699–919.

Yoneyama T, Winter WG, Milsow L. Tibial adamantinoma: its histogenesis from ultrastructural studies. *Cancer* 1977;40:1138–1142.

Zehr RJ, Recht MP, Bauer TW. Adamantinoma. *Skeletal Radiol* 1995;24:553–555.

Tumors and Tumor-like Lesions of the Joints

Benign Lesions

Synovial (Osteo)Chondromatosis

Synovial (osteo)chondromatosis (also known as synovial chondromatosis or synovial chondrometaplasia) is an uncommon benign disorder marked by the metaplastic proliferation of multiple cartilaginous nodules in the synovial membrane of the joints, bursae, or tendon sheaths. It is almost invariably monoarticular; rarely, multiple joints may be affected. The disorder is twice as common in men as in women and is usually discovered in the third to fifth decade. The knee is a preferential site of involvement, with the hip, shoulder, and elbow accounting for most of the remaining cases (Fig. 23.1). Patients usually report pain and swelling. Joint effusion, tenderness, limited motion in the joint, and a soft-tissue mass are common clinical findings.

Three phases of articular disease have been identified: an initial phase, characterized by metaplastic formation of cartilaginous nodules in the synovium; a transitional phase, characterized by detachment of those nodules and formation of free intraarticular bodies; and an inactive phase, in which synovial proliferation has resolved but loose bodies remain in the joint, usually with variable amounts of joint fluid.

The imaging findings depend on the degree of calcification within the cartilaginous bodies, ranging from mere joint effusion to visualization of many radiopaque joint bodies, usually small and uniform in size (Figs. 23.2 and 23.3). The best proof that the bodies are indeed intraarticular is achieved by arthrography or computed tomography (CT) (Fig. 23.4). These modalities can visualize even noncalcified bodies. Magnetic resonance imaging (MRI) may also be helpful, although MRI appearance is variable and depends on the relative preponderance of synovial proliferation, loose bodies formation, and extent of calcification or ossification. Unmineralized hyperplastic synovial masses exhibit high signal intensity on T2-weighted images, whereas calcifications can be seen as signal void against the high–signal-intensity fluid (Figs. 23.5 and 23.6). In addition to revealing loose bodies in the joint, CT and MRI may demonstrate bony erosion.

By microscopy, many cartilaginous nodules are observed as they form beneath the thin layer of cells that line the surface of the synovial membrane. These nodules are highly cellular, and the cells themselves may exhibit a moderate pleomorphism, with occasional plump and double nuclei. The cartilaginous nodules, which often are undergoing calcification and endochondral ossification, may detach and become loose bodies. The loose bodies continue to be viable and may increase in size as they receive nourishment from the synovial fluid.

Differential Diagnosis

Synovial (osteo)chondromatosis should be differentiated from the secondary osteochondromatosis caused by osteoarthritis, particularly in the knee and hip joints, and from synovial chondrosarcoma, either primary (arising *de novo* from the synovial membrane) or secondary (caused by malignant transformation). Distinguishing *primary* from *secondary osteochondromatosis* usually presents no problems. In the latter condition, there is invariably radiographic evidence of osteoarthritis with all of its typical features, such as narrowing of the radiographic joint space, subchondral sclerosis, and, occasionally, periarticular cysts or cyst-like lesions (Fig. 23.7). The loose bodies are fewer, larger, and invariably of different sizes. Conversely, in primary synovial (osteo)chondromatosis the joint is not affected by any degenerative changes. In some cases, however, the bone may show erosions secondary to pressure of the calcified bodies on the outer aspects of the cortex. The intraarticular bodies are numerous, small, and usually of uniform size (see Figs. 23.2 and 23.3).

It is more difficult to distinguish synovial chondromatosis from *synovial chondrosarcoma*. The clinical and radiographic features have not been useful in this differentiation and are equally ineffective in distinguishing a secondary malignant lesion arising in synovial (osteo)chondromatosis. In addition, both entities tend to have a protracted clinical course, and local recurrence is common after synovectomy for synovial chondromatosis or local resection of synovial chondrosarcoma. The presence of frank bone destruction rather than merely erosions, and the association of a soft-tissue mass, should always raise a concern for malignancy (see Fig. 23.18). Although extension beyond the joint capsule should heighten the suspicion of malignancy, some cases of synovial chondromatosis have been reported to have extraarticular extension.

The other conditions that can radiologically mimic synovial chondromatosis include pigmented villonodular synovitis (PVNS), synovial hemangioma, and lipoma arborescens. In *pigmented villonodular synovitis* (discussed in detail later in this chapter), the filling defects in the joint are more confluent and less distinct. MRI may show foci of decreased intensity of the synovium in all sequences because of the paramagnetic effects of deposition of hemosiderin (see Figs. 23.11 and 23.12). *Synovial hemangioma* usually presents as a single soft-tissue mass. On MRI, T1-weighted images show that the lesion is either isointense or

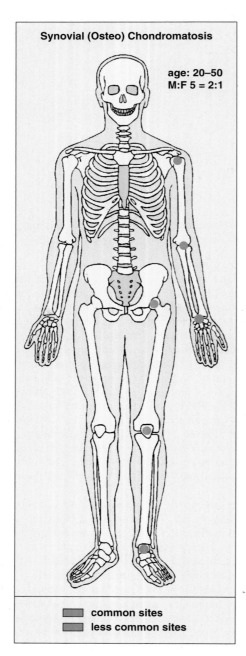

▲
FIGURE 23.1 Synovial (osteo)chondromatosis: skeletal sites of predilection, peak age range, and male-to-female ratio.

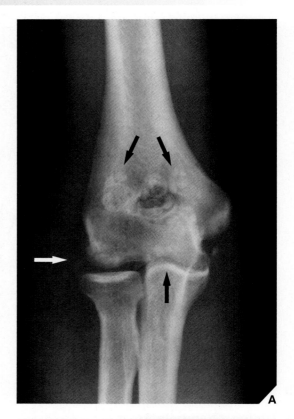

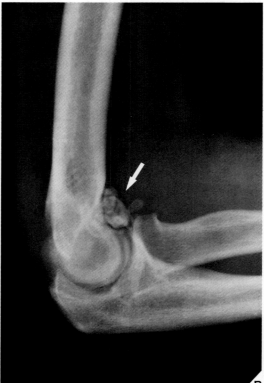

▲
FIGURE 23.2 Synovial chondromatosis. A 23-year-old man reported pain and occasional locking in the elbow joint; he had no history of trauma. Anteroposterior (**A**) and lateral (**B**) radiographs demonstrate multiple osteochondral bodies in the elbow joint (*arrows*), which are regularly shaped and uniform in size.

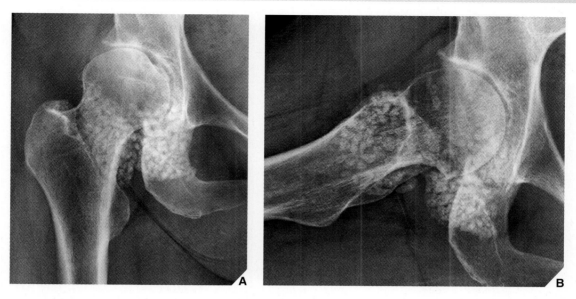

▲
FIGURE 23.3   Synovial chondromatosis. **(A)** Anteroposterior and **(B)** frog lateral radiographs of the right hip of a 59-year-old woman show numerous, uniform in size, intraarticular osteochondral bodies.

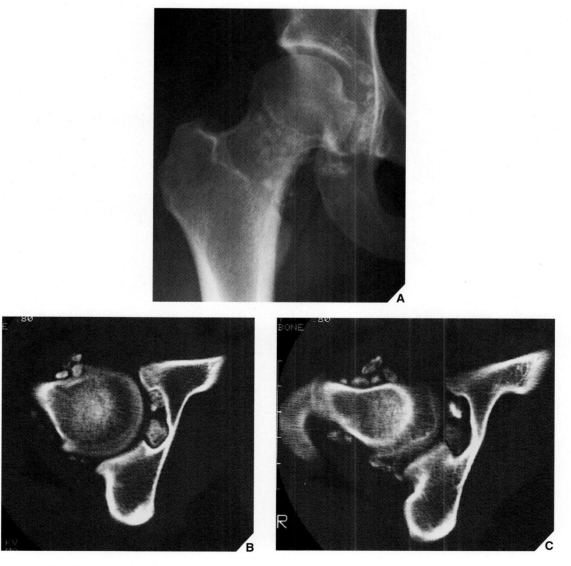

▲
FIGURE 23.4   CT of synovial chondromatosis. **(A)** Anteroposterior radiograph of the right hip of a 27-year-old woman shows multiple osteochondral bodies around the femoral head and neck. Note preservation of the joint space, a characteristic feature of synovial (osteo)chondromatosis. **(B,C)** Two CT sections, one through the femoral head and another through the femoral neck, demonstrate unquestionably the intraarticular location of multiple osteochondral bodies.

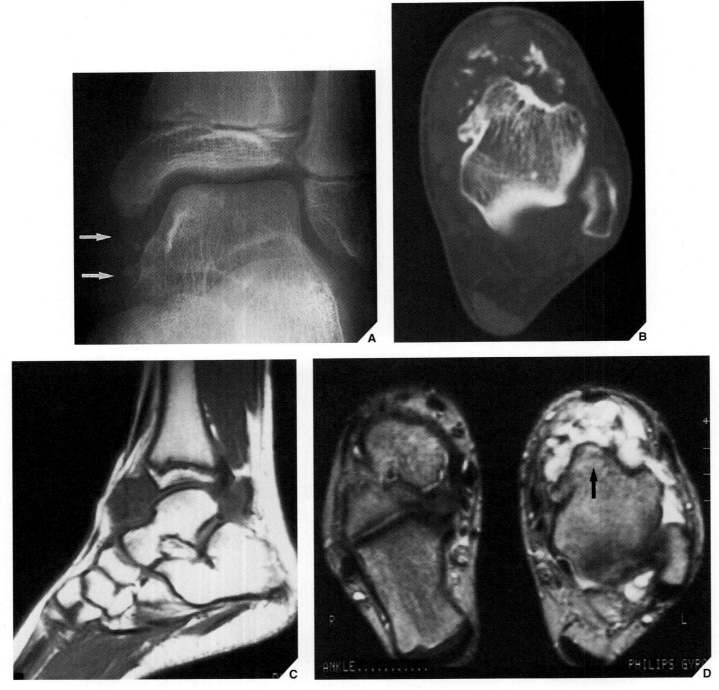

▲
FIGURE 23.5   **MRI of synovial chondromatosis. (A)** Oblique radiograph of the left ankle of a 14-year-old boy shows faint radiopaque foci projecting over the tibiotalar joint (*arrows*). **(B)** CT section shows the location of calcified bodies in the anterior aspect of the joint. **(C)** Sagittal T1-weighted (SE; TR 640/TE 20 msec) MR image shows intermediate signal intensity of the fluid in the ankle joint and dispersed low–signal-intensity osteochondral bodies. **(D)** Coronal T2-weighted (SE; TR 2000/TE 80 msec) MR image of the ankle joint clearly defines low–signal-intensity osteochondral bodies within bright fluid (*arrow*).

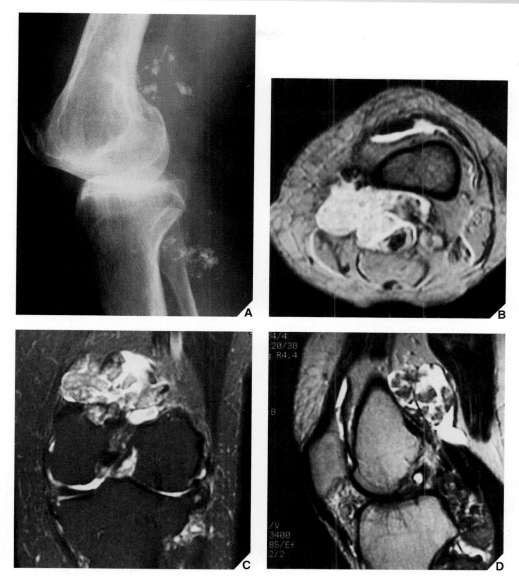

▲
FIGURE 23.6   MRI of synovial chondromatosis. (A) Lateral radiograph of the left knee of a 50-year-old man shows multiple osteochondral bodies in and around the joint. **(B)** Axial T2*-weighted (MPGR; TR 500/TE 20 msec, flip angle 30 degrees) MR image demonstrates high-signal joint effusion and multiple bodies of intermediate signal intensity, primarily located in a large popliteal cyst. Coronal **(C)** fast spin-echo (TR 2400/TE 85 Ef msec) and sagittal **(D)** fast spin-echo (TR 3400/TE 85 Ef msec) MR images show to better advantage the distribution of numerous osteochondral bodies.

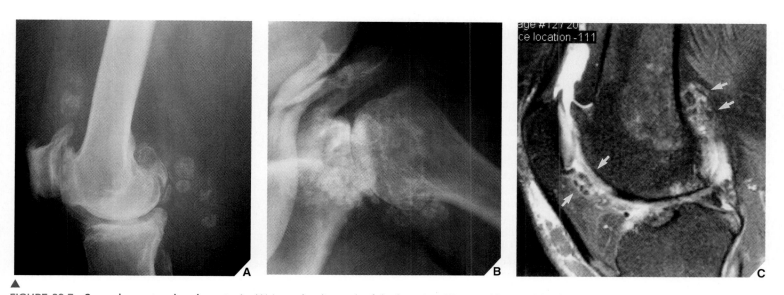

▲
FIGURE 23.7   Secondary osteochondromatosis. (A) Lateral radiograph of the knee in a 58-year-old man with advanced osteoarthritis of the femoropatellar joint compartment shows multiple osteochondral bodies in the suprapatellar bursa and within the popliteal cyst. **(B)** Radiograph of the left shoulder in a 68-year-old woman with osteoarthritis of the glenohumeral joint shows multiple intraarticular osteochondral bodies. **(C)** Sagittal T2-weighted fat-suppressed MRI of the knee in a 54-year-old woman reveals osteoarthritis and numerous, various in size, osteochondral bodies (*arrows*).

slightly higher (brighter) in signal intensity than surrounding muscles, but much lower in intensity than subcutaneous fat. On T2-weighted images, the mass is invariably much brighter than fat (see Fig. 23.14). Phleboliths and fibrofatty septa in the mass are common findings that show low-signal characteristics. *Lipoma arborescens* is a villous lipomatous proliferation of the synovial membrane. This rare condition usually affects the knee joint but has occasionally been reported in other joints, including the wrist and ankle. The disease has been variously reported to have a developmental, traumatic, inflammatory, or neoplastic origin, but its true cause is still unknown. The clinical findings include slowly increasing but painless synovial thickening as well as joint effusion with sporadic exacerbation. Imaging studies reveal a joint effusion occasionally accompanied by various degrees of osteoarthritis (see Fig. 23.15). Histologic examination demonstrates complete replacement of the subsynovial tissue by mature fat cells and the formation of proliferative villous projections (see text below).

Treatment of synovial chondromatosis usually consists of removal of the intraarticular bodies and synovectomy, but local recurrence is not uncommon.

Pigmented Villonodular Synovitis

PVNS is a locally destructive fibrohistiocytic proliferation, characterized by many villous and nodular synovial protrusions, which affects joints, bursae, and tendon sheaths. PVNS was first described by Jaffe, Lichtenstein, and Sutro in 1941, who used this name to identify the lesion because of its yellow–brown, villous, and nodular appearance. The yellow–brown pigmentation is caused by excessive deposits of lipid and hemosiderin. This condition can be diffuse or localized. When the entire synovium of the joint is affected, and when there is a major villous component, the condition is referred to as *diffuse pigmented villonodular synovitis*. When a discrete intraarticular mass is present, the condition is called *localized pigmented villonodular synovitis*. When the process affects the tendon sheaths, it is called *localized giant cell tumor of the tendon sheaths*. The diffuse form usually occurs in the knee, hip, elbow, or wrist and accounts for 23% of cases. The localized nodular form is often regarded as a separate entity. It consists of a single polypoid mass attached to the synovium. Nodular tenosynovitis is most often seen in the fingers and is the second most common soft-tissue tumor of the hand, exceeded only by the ganglion. In the new (2002) revised classification of soft tissue tumors, the World Health Organization (WHO) classifies localized intraarticular and extraarticular lesions as giant cell tumor of tendon sheath, whereas diffuse intraarticular and extraarticular forms are categorized as diffuse-type giant cell tumor (keeping PVNS as a synonym).

Both the diffuse and the localized form of villonodular synovitis usually occur as a single lesion, mainly in young and middle-aged individuals of either sex. One of the most characteristic findings in PVNS is the ability of the hyperplastic synovium to invade the subchondral bone, producing cysts and erosions. Although the cause is unknown and is often controversial, some investigators have suggested an autoimmune pathogenesis. Trauma is also a suspected cause, because similar effects have been produced experimentally in animals by repeated injections of blood into the knee joint. Some investigators have suggested a disturbance in lipid metabolism as a causative factor. It has also been postulated by Jaffe and colleagues that these lesions may represent an inflammatory response to an unknown agent. Ray, Stout, and Lattes contended that they are true benign neoplasms. Although the latter theory was presumed to be supported by pathologic studies indicating that the histiocytes present in PVNS may function as facultative fibroblasts and that foam cells may derive from histiocytes, thus relating PVNS to a benign neoplasm of fibrohistiocytic origin, these findings do not constitute definite proof that PVNS is a true neoplasm. They are rather indicative of a special form of a chronic proliferative inflammation process, as has already been postulated by Jaffe and colleagues.

Clinically, PVNS is a slowly progressive process that manifests as mild pain and joint swelling with limitation of motion. Occasionally, increased skin temperature is noted over the affected joint. The knee

joint is most commonly affected and 66% of patients present with a bloody joint effusion. In fact, the presence of a serosanguinous synovial fluid in the absence of a history of recent trauma should strongly suggest the diagnosis of PVNS. The synovial fluid contains elevated levels of cholesterol, and fluid reaccumulates rapidly after aspiration. Other joints may be affected, including the hip, ankle, wrist, elbow, and shoulder. There is a 2:1 predilection for females. Patients range from 4 to 60 years of age, with a peak incidence in the third and fourth decades (Fig. 23.8). The duration of symptoms can range from 6 months to as long as 25 years.

Although a few "malignant" PVNS have been reported in the literature, this diagnosis is still debatable (see later). Recently attention has been drawn to the extraaticular form of diffuse PVNS, also referred to as *diffuse-type giant cell tumor*. This condition is characterized by the presence of an infiltrate, and extraarticular mass with or without involvement of the adjacent joint. This presentation of PVNS creates a real diagnostic challenge for both radiologist and pathologist because its extraarticular

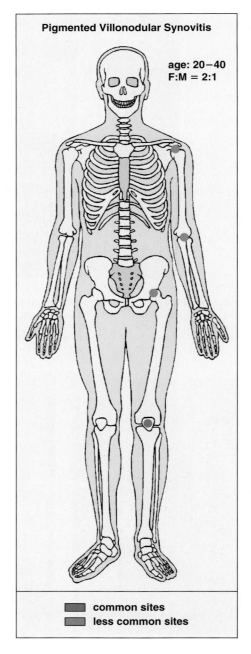

Pigmented Villonodular Synovitis

age: 20–40
F:M = 2:1

common sites
less common sites

▲

FIGURE 23.8 Pigmented villonodular synovitis: sites of predilection, peak age range, and male-to-female ratio.

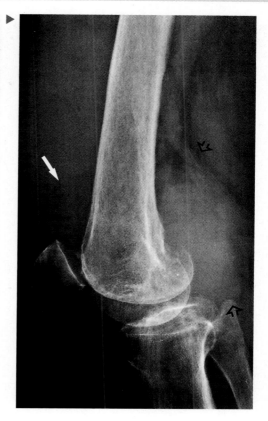

FIGURE 23.9 Pigmented villonodular synovitis. Lateral radiograph of the knee of a 58-year-old man shows a large suprapatellar joint effusion (*arrow*) and a dense, lumpy soft-tissue mass eroding the posterior aspect of the lateral femoral condyle (*open arrows*). These features suggest PVNS. Note that posteriorly the density is greater than that of a suprapatellar fluid.

location, invasion of the osseous structures, and more varied histologic infiltrative pattern may suggest malignancy.

Radiography reveals a soft-tissue density in the affected joint, frequently interpreted as joint effusion. However, the density is greater than that of simple effusion, and it reflects not only a hemorrhagic fluid but also lobulated synovial masses (Fig. 23.9). A marginal, well-defined erosion of subchondral bone with a sclerotic margin may be present (incidence reported from 15% to 50%), usually on both sides of the affected articulation. Narrowing of the joint space has also been reported. In the hip, multiple cyst-like or erosive areas involving non–weight-bearing regions of the acetabulum, as well as the femoral head and neck, are characteristic. Calcifications are encountered only in exceptional cases.

Arthrography reveals multiple lobulated masses with villous projections, which appear as filling defects in the contrast-filled suprapatellar bursa (Fig. 23.10). CT effectively demonstrates the extent of the disease. The increase in iron content of the synovial fluid results in high Hounsfield values, a feature that can help in the differential diagnosis. MRI is extremely useful in making a diagnosis, because on T2-weighted images the intraarticular masses demonstrate a combination of high–signal-intensity areas, representing fluid and congested synovium, interspersed with areas of intermediate to low signal intensity, secondary to random distribution of hemosiderin in the synovium (Fig. 23.11). In general, MRI shows a low signal on T1- and T2-weighted images because of hemosiderin deposition and thick fibrous tissue (Fig. 23.12). In addition, within the mass, signals consistent with fat can be noted, which are caused by clumps of lipid-laden macrophages. Other MRI findings include hyperplastic synovium and occasionally bone erosions. Administration of gadolinium in the form of Gd-DTPA leads to a notable increase in overall heterogeneity, which tends toward an overall increase in signal intensity of the capsule and septae. This enhancement of the synovium allows it to be differentiated from the fluid invariably present, which does not enhance. Apart from its diagnostic effectiveness, MRI is also useful in defining the extent of the disease.

On histologic examination, PVNS reveals a tumor-like proliferation of the synovial tissue. A dense infiltration of mononuclear histiocytes is observed, accompanied by plasma cells, xanthoma cells, lymphocytes,

and variable numbers of giant cells. Long-standing lesions show fibrosis and hyalinization.

Differential Diagnosis

The most common diagnostic possibilities include *hemophilic arthropathy, synovial chondromatosis, synovial hemangioma*, and *synovial sarcoma*. MRI is very effective in distinguishing these entities because it can reveal hemosiderin deposition in PVNS. Although this feature may also be present in *hemophilic arthropathy*, detection of diffuse hemosiderin clumps, synovial irregularity and thickening, and distention of the synovial sac favors the diagnosis of PVNS. In addition, hemophilia, unlike PVNS, commonly affects multiple joints and is associated with growth disturbance at the articular ends of the affected bones. *Synovial chondromatosis* may manifest with pressure erosions of the bone similar to those of PVNS. However, it can be distinguished by the presence of multiple joint bodies, calcified or uncalcified. *Synovial hemangioma* is commonly associated with the formation of phleboliths. *Synovial sarcoma* tends to have a shorter T1 and longer T2 on MRI compared with PVNS, and when calcifications are present the latter diagnosis can be excluded.

Treatment

Treatment usually consists of surgical or arthroscopic synovectomy. Occasionally, intraarticular radiation synovectomy is used when the abnormal synovial tissue is less than 5 mm thick. Recently, reports appeared of postsynovectomy adjuvant treatment with external beam radiation therapy or intraarticular injection of radioactive material such as yttrium-90 (^{90}Y). Local recurrence is not uncommon and is reported in approximately 50% of cases.

Synovial Hemangioma

Synovial hemangioma is a rare benign lesion that most commonly affects the knee joint, usually involving the anterior compartment. This lesion has also been found in the elbow, wrist, and ankle joints, as well as in tendon sheaths. Most cases affect children and adolescents. Almost all patients with synovial hemangioma are symptomatic, frequently presenting with a swollen knee or with mild pain or limitation of movement in the joint. Sometimes patients report a history of recurrent episodes

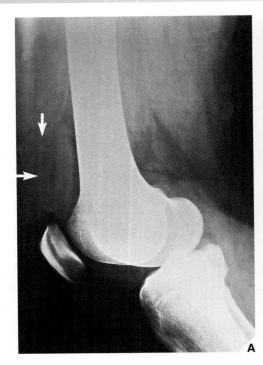
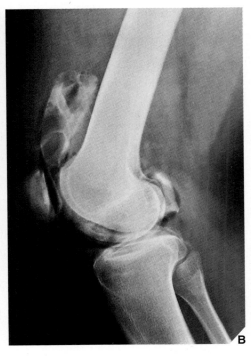

FIGURE 23.10   Arthrography of pigmented villonodular synovitis. (A) Lateral radiograph of another patient shows what appears to be a suprapatellar effusion (*arrows*). The density of the "fluid," however, is increased, and there is some lobulation evident. **(B)** Contrast arthrogram of the knee shows lobulated filling defects in the suprapatellar pouch, representing lumpy synovial masses. Joint puncture yielded thick bloody fluid, which explains the increased density of the soft-tissue mass seen on the radiograph.

of joint swelling and various degrees of pain of several years' duration. Synovial hemangioma is often associated with an adjacent cutaneous or deep soft-tissue hemangioma. For this reason, some investigators classify knee joint lesions as intraarticular, juxta-articular, or intermediate, depending on the extent of involvement. Synovial hemangioma is frequently misdiagnosed. According to one estimate, a correct preoperative diagnosis is made in only 22% of cases.

Until recently, synovial hemangiomas were evaluated by a combination of conventional radiography, arthrography, angiography, and contrast-enhanced CT. Although radiographs appear normal in at least half of the patients, they may reveal soft-tissue swelling, a mass around the joint, joint effusion, or erosions (Fig. 23.13). Phleboliths, periosteal thickening, advanced maturation of the epiphysis, and arthritic changes are also occasionally noted on conventional radiographs. Arthrography

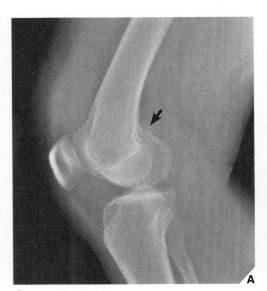
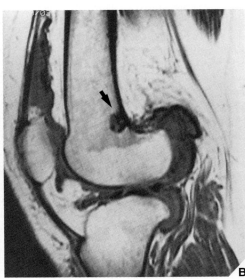
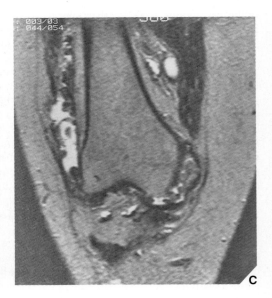

FIGURE 23.11   MRI of pigmented villonodular synovitis. A 22-year-old woman had several episodes of knee pain and swelling. Bloody fluid was aspirated from the knee joint on two occasions. **(A)** Lateral radiograph of the right knee shows fullness in the suprapatellar bursa that was interpreted as "joint effusion." Note also the increased density in the region of the popliteal fossa and subtle erosion of the posterior aspect of the distal femur (*arrow*). **(B)** Sagittal MRI (SE; TR 800/TE 20 msec) shows a lobulated mass in the suprapatellar bursa, extending into the knee joint and invading the infrapatellar fat. Note also the lobulated mass in the posterior aspect of the joint capsule, extending toward the proximal tibia. These masses demonstrate an intermediate to low signal intensity. The erosion at the posterior aspect of the distal femur (supracondylar) is clearly demonstrated by an area of low signal intensity (*arrow*). **(C)** Coronal MRI (SE; TR 1800/TE 80 msec) demonstrates areas of high signal intensity that represent fluid and congested synovium, interspersed with areas of intermediate to low signal intensity, characteristic of hemosiderin deposits.

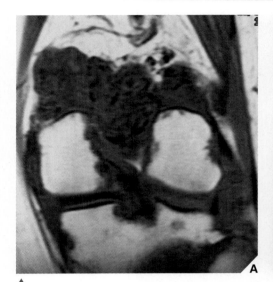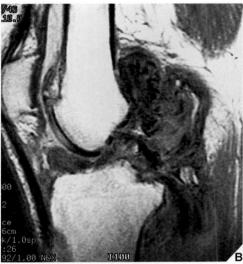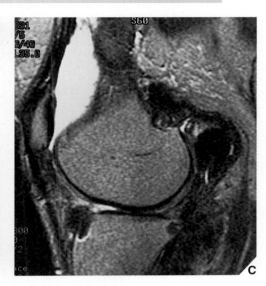

FIGURE 23.12   MRI of pigmented villonodular synovitis. Coronal (**A**) and sagittal (**B**) T1-weighted (SE; TR 600/TE 12 msec) MR images of the knee of a 40-year-old man show lobulated low–signal-intensity masses mainly localized to the popliteal fossa. (**C**) Sagittal T2-weighted (SE; TR 2300/TE 80 msec) MR image shows high-intensity fluid in the suprapatellar bursa. The lobulated masses of PVNS remain of low signal intensity.

usually shows nonspecific filling defects with a villous configuration. Angiograms yield much more specific information than radiography. They can often reveal a vascular lesion and can demonstrate pathognomonic features of hemangioma. Contrast-enhanced CT of the joint typically reveals a heterogeneous-appearing soft-tissue mass that displays tissue attenuation approximating that of skeletal muscle and containing areas of decreased attenuation, some approaching that of fat. CT is effective for demonstrating phleboliths and revealing patchy enhancement around them, as well as enhancement of tubular areas and contrast pooling within the lesion. In some cases, CT reveals enlarged vessels feeding and draining the mass, as well as enlarged adjacent subcutaneous veins.

At present, MRI has become the modality of choice for the evaluation of hemangiomas because with this modality, a presumptive diagnosis can be made. The soft-tissue mass typically exhibits an intermediate signal intensity on T1-weighted sequences, appearing isointense with or slightly brighter than muscle but much less bright than fat. The mass is usually much brighter than subcutaneous fat on T2-weighted images and on fat suppression sequences (Fig. 23.14) and shows thin, often serpentine, low-intensity septa within it. In general, the signal intensity characteristics of hemangiomas appear to be related to a number of factors, including slow flow, thrombosis, vessel occlusion, and increased free water in stagnant blood that pools in larger vessels and dilated sinuses, as well as to the variable amounts of adipose tissue in the lesion. After intravenous injection of gadolinium, there is evidence of enhancement of the hemangioma. In patients with a cavernous hemangioma of the knee, fluid–fluid levels are also observed (Fig. 23.14B), a finding recently reported also in soft-tissue hemangiomas of this type.

Originating in the subsynovial layer mesenchyme of the synovial membrane, synovial hemangioma is a vascular lesion that contains variable amounts of adipose, fibrous, and muscle tissue, as well as thrombi in the vessels. When the lesion is completely intraarticular, it is usually well circumscribed and apparently encapsulated, attached to the synovial membrane by a pedicle of variable size, and adherent to the synovium on one or more surfaces by separable adhesions. Grossly, the tumor is a lobulated soft, brown, doughy mass with overlying villous synovium that is often stained mahogany brown by hemosiderin. On microscopic examination, the lesion exhibits arborizing vascular channels of different sizes and a hyperplastic overlying synovium, which may show abundant iron deposition in chronic cases with repeated hemarthrosis.

Differential Diagnosis

The differential diagnosis of synovial hemangioma includes *PVNS* and *synovial chondromatosis*. All proliferative chronic inflammatory processes, such as rheumatoid arthritis, tuberculous arthritis, and hemophilic

arthropathy, should also be considered in the differential diagnosis, but these conditions, when involving the knee, can usually be distinguished clinically. Because it is extremely uncommon, lipoma arborescens is rarely included in the differential diagnosis. MRI is diagnostic for the latter condition, showing typical frond-like projections of the lesion and fat characteristics (bright on T1- and intermediate on T2-weighted images). In *PVNS*, radiography commonly reveals findings similar to those of synovial hemangioma, such as joint effusion and a mass in the suprapatellar bursa or popliteal fossa region. Radiographs may also demonstrate bone erosions on both sides of the joint. MRI, however, is usually diagnostic for PVNS, demonstrating that the synovium exhibits nodular thickening and masses of heterogeneous signal intensity. Most of the lesion will display a higher signal intensity than muscle on both T1- and T2-weighted sequences, with other portions exhibiting a low signal intensity on all sequences, reflecting the hemosiderin content of the tumor. *Synovial chondromatosis* can be distinguished from synovial hemangioma if radiography shows calcified bodies. Intraarticular osteochondral fragments of uniform size are almost pathognomonic for this condition. CT may be helpful in demonstrating faint calcifications not otherwise seen.

Lipoma Arborescens

Lipoma arborescens, also known as villous lipomatous proliferation of the synovial membranes, is a rare intraarticular disorder characterized by nonneoplastic lipomatous proliferation of the synovium. The term "arborescens" describes the characteristic treelike morphology of this lesion, which resembles a frond-like mass. The condition may be monoarticular or polyarticular. The cause of this condition remains uncertain, although association with osteoarthritis, rheumatoid arthritis, psoriasis, and diabetes mellitus has been postulated. This lesion most commonly affects the knee joint, although involvement of other joints, such as shoulder, hip, wrist, elbow, and ankle, has been sporadically reported by various authors. Occasionally this condition may affect multiple joints. There have been also sporadic reports of bursae involvement. It is more prevalent in males, usually in the fourth and fifth decades. These patients present with slowly increasing but painless joint effusion accompanied by synovial thickening.

Imaging studies, particularly MRI, are very characteristic and allow definite diagnosis of this condition. Joint effusion is invariably present, associated with frond-like masses arising from the synovium that have the signal intensity of fat on all imaging sequences (Fig. 23.15). Occasionally, a chemical shift artifact is present at the fat–fluid interface. Histopathologically, lipoma arborescens is characterized by hyperplasia

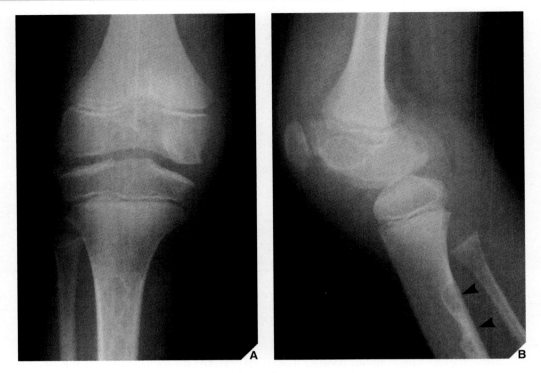

▲
FIGURE 23.13 **Synovial hemangioma.** Anteroposterior (**A**) and lateral (**B**) radiographs of the right knee of a 7-year-old boy show articular erosions at femoropatellar and femorotibial joint compartments. Soft-tissue masses are seen anteriorly and posteriorly. An incidental finding is a nonossifying fibroma in the posterior tibia (*arrowheads*).

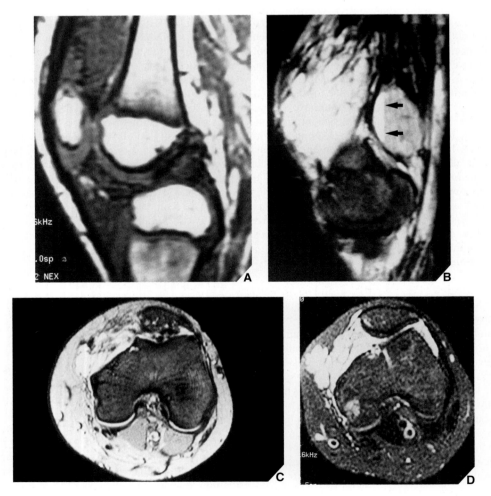

▲
FIGURE 23.14 **MRI of synovial hemangioma.** (**A**) Sagittal T1-weighted (SE; TR 400/TE 11 msec) MR image in a 9-year-old boy shows masses isointense with muscle involving the suprapatellar bursa and infrapatellar Hoffa fat. (**B**) With fat suppression technique, the mass becomes very bright. The fluid–fluid level seen in the popliteal region (*arrows*) is typical for the cavernous type of synovial hemangioma. In another patient, a 16-year-old girl, axial T2*-weighted (MPGR; TR 500/TE 15 msec, flip angle 30 degrees) MR image (**C**) and axial fast-spin echo (TR 5000/TE 85 Ef msec) image with fat suppression technique (**D**) show the size and extent of the synovial hemangioma.

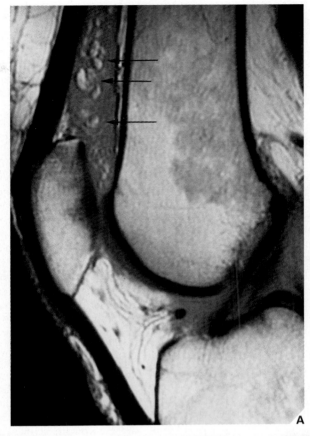

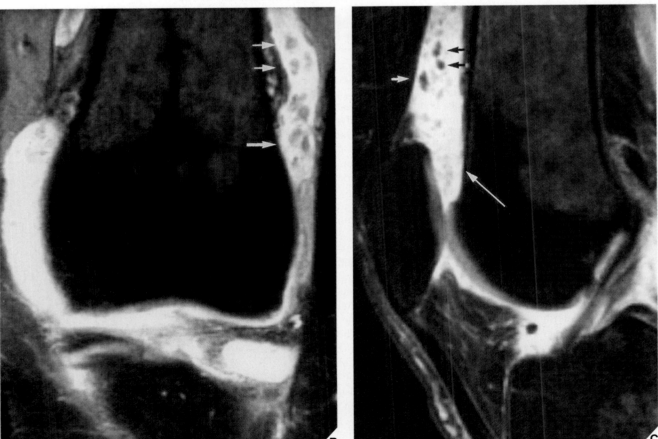

FIGURE 23.15   **MRI of lipoma arborescens.** A 54-year-old woman reports fullness in the left knee for the past 5 months. Conventional radiography (not shown here) revealed knee joint effusion. (**A**) Sagittal proton-density MRI shows numerous structures within suprapatellar bursa exhibiting signal intensity consistent with fat (*arrows*). Coronal (**B**) and sagittal (**C**) T2-weighted fat-suppressed images demonstrate high–signal-intensity joint effusion. Hypertrophic synovial villa (*arrows*) again shows signal consistent with fat.

of subsynovial fat, formation of mature fat cells, and the presence of proliferative villous projections. Osseous and chondroid metaplasia can occur.

Differential diagnosis should include PVNS, synovial chondromatosis, synovial hemangioma, hemophilic arthropathy, and a variety of intraarticular inflammatory conditions.

Treatment usually consists of surgical or arthroscopic synovectomy.

Malignant Tumors

Synovial Sarcoma

Synovial sarcoma (synovioma, synovioblastic sarcoma) is an uncommon mesenchymal neoplasm, comprising approximately 8% to 10% of soft-tissue sarcomas. Despite its name (which was designated because of histologic resemblance of synovial sarcoma to normal synovial tissue), it does not arise from synovium, although it may originate from any other structure, including joint capsules, bursae, and tendon sheaths. The tumor usually occurs before age 50, most commonly between ages 16 and 36 years. There is no sex predilection. The extremities account for 80% to 90% of synovial sarcomas, and the most common sites are around the knee and foot. In exceptional instances, the tumor may be intraarticular. Synovial sarcoma is usually slow growing, with an indolent course, although in late stages it may demonstrate aggressiveness. Metastases to the lung by the hematogenous route and to the soft tissue have been reported. Schajowicz cited a local recurrence rate of more than 50%. The clinical symptoms usually include soft-tissue swelling or a mass and progressive pain. On physical examination, a diffuse or discrete soft-tissue mass is present, usually tender on palpation.

The imaging features of synovial sarcoma include a soft-tissue mass, usually in close proximity to a joint (Fig. 23.16) and occasionally associated with bone invasion. A periosteal reaction may also be observed. The soft-tissue calcifications, usually amorphous in type, are present in approximately 25% to 30% of cases.

CT effectively demonstrates the extent of the soft-tissue mass, calcifications, and bone invasion. MRI shows the tumor to be heterogeneous, multilobulated septated mass of low to intermediate signal intensity with infiltrative margins on T1-weighted sequences, displaying a high signal on T2-weighting (Fig. 23.17), and diffuse enhancement after administration of gadolinium. The most extensive to date MRI study of synovial sarcoma in 34 patients reported by Jones and associates showed that it tends to be deep, large (85% were greater than 5 cm in diameter), and located in the extremities, with epicenter close to the joint. The lesion was usually heterogeneous on T2-weighted images and was clearly delineated from surrounding tissues. Forty-four percent of the cases had a high signal on both T1- and T2-weighted sequences, consistent with hemorrhage within the tumor.

On histopathologic examination, several subtypes of synovial sarcoma have been recognized. Among them are biphasic (fibrous and epithelial), monophasic, and poorly differentiated types. The classical biphasic type exhibits distinct spindle cell and epithelial components arranged in glandular or nest-like patterns. The monophasic synovial sarcoma is composed of interdigitating fascicles and "ball-like" structures formed by the spindle cells. Foci of calcification may also be observed, usually localized in areas of hyalinization within the spindle cell elements of the tumor. A consistent finding, present in about 90% of tumors, is a cytogenetic aberration of translocation involving chromosomes X and 18 [t(x,18) (p11.2;q11.2)], resulting in fusion of *SYT* (also known as *SS18*) to either *SSX1* or *SSX2*. A minority of cases have a gene rearrangement involving *SSX4*.

Treatment includes a wide local resection, followed with adjuvant chemotherapy with combination of adriamycin, cisplatin, vincristine, doxorubicin, and ifosfamide. Postoperative radiation therapy is reserved for the patients in whom surgical intervention was not able to ascertain clear margins of resection. In some cases, amputation of a limb remains a treatment of choice. Local recurrences and metastatic spread of the tumor are common complications.

Synovial Chondrosarcoma

Synovial chondrosarcoma is a rare tumor that originates from the synovial membrane. It may arise as a primary synovial tumor or it may develop as a malignant transformation of synovial (osteo)chondromatosis. The concept of malignant degeneration of synovial chondromatosis is still controversial and the entity is rare, with fewer than 40 well-documented cases on record.

Most synovial chondrosarcomas are located in the knee joint. Rarely, other joints such as the hip, elbow, or ankle are affected. These malignancies show a slight predominance in men, and patients range in age from 25 to 70 years. The symptoms include pain and swelling, with duration in most patients exceeding 12 months. In patients with primary synovial (osteo)chondromatosis, malignant transformation to synovial chondrosarcoma should be clinically suspected if there is development of soft-tissue mass at the site of the affected joint.

Radiologically, the presence of chondroid calcifications within the joint, destruction of the adjacent bones, and a soft-tissue mass are highly suggestive of a synovial chondrosarcoma. In patients with documented primary synovial (osteo)chondromatosis, a soft-tissue mass and destructive changes in the joint should suggest the development of a secondary synovial chondrosarcoma (Fig. 23.18). Note, however, that frequently both uncomplicated synovial chondromatosis and synovial chondrosarcoma may exhibit similar features on radiography and MRI.

The histopathologic distinction between primary synovial chondromatosis and secondary malignancy in synovial chondromatosis has been a matter of dispute. Manivel and associates suggested that histologic features equivalent to those of grade 2 or 3 central chondrosarcoma must be present before chondrosarcoma arising in synovial chondromatosis can be diagnosed. Occasional foci of increased cellularity showing hyperchromatic atypical cells, consistent with grade 1 chondrosarcoma, should not be sufficient evidence for a malignant change in synovial chondromatosis. However, evidence of aggressive growth (invasion) and a lesion's lack of attachment to the synovial lining, combined with hypercellularity and pleomorphisms of the cells, should support the diagnosis of malignancy. Bertoni and coworkers have attempted to develop criteria for making this crucial distinction. They identified several microscopic features indicative of malignancy. The distinguishing features of synovial chondrosarcoma include the following: tumor cells

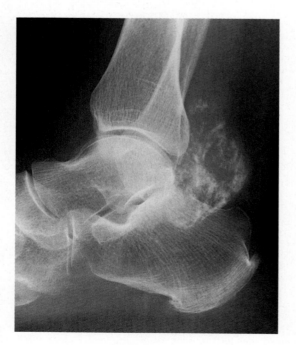

▲
FIGURE 23.16 Synovial sarcoma. Lateral radiograph of the left ankle of a 71-year-old woman shows a large calcified mass located in the soft tissues anteriorly to the Achilles tendon, not affecting the adjacent bones.

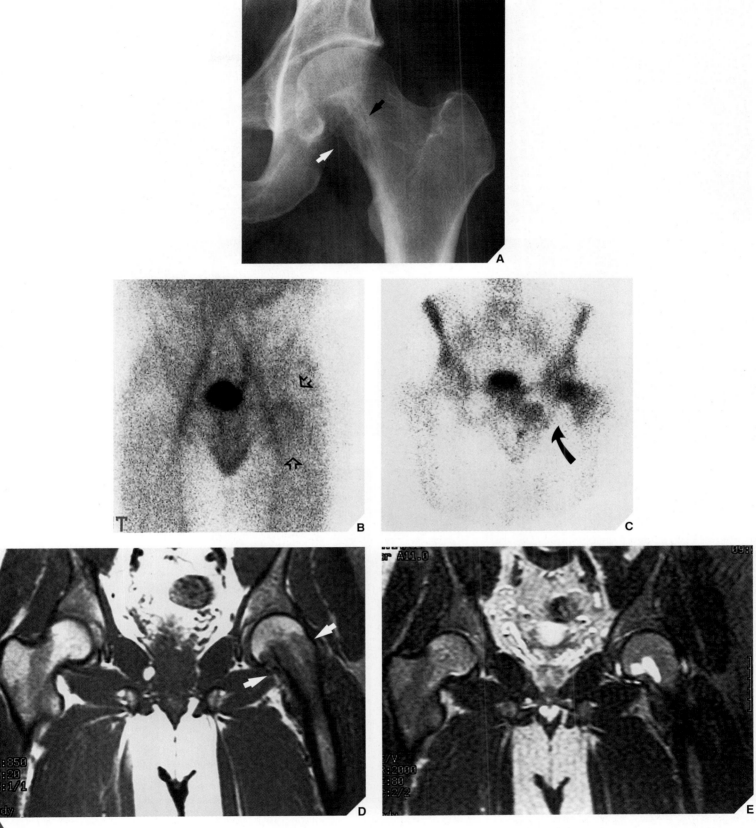

FIGURE 23.17 Scintigraphy and MRI of synovial sarcoma. (A) Anteroposterior radiograph of the left hip of a 37-year-old man shows an osteolytic lesion in the femoral neck bordered laterally by sclerotic margin (*arrows*). **(B)** Scintigraphic (blood pool) examination demonstrates increased vascularity to the left hip joint (*open arrows*). **(C)** Delayed radionuclide bone scan with ⁹⁹ᵐTc methylene diphosphonate (MDP) shows increased uptake of the radiopharmaceutical tracer in the femoral head and neck and around the hip joint (*curved arrow*). **(D)** Coronal T1-weighted (SE; TR 850/TE 20 msec) MR image shows a low–signal-intensity lesion affecting the medial aspect of the left femoral neck (*arrows*). **(E)** Coronal T2-weighted (SE; TR 2000/TE 80 msec) MR image demonstrates increased signal in the femoral neck and in the medial and lateral aspects of the hip joint. Excision biopsy revealed intraarticular synovial sarcoma.

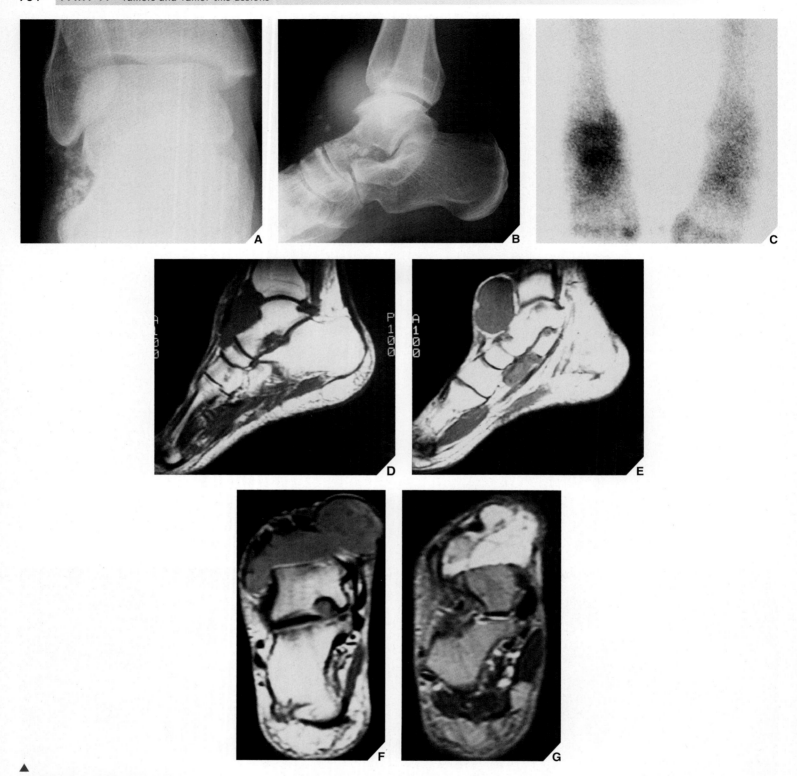

▲

FIGURE 23.18   Malignant transformation of synovial osteochondromatosis to synovial chondrosarcoma. Anteroposterior (**A**) and lateral (**B**) radiographs of the right ankle of a 64-year-old man with a long history of synovial chondromatosis show a large soft-tissue mass on the dorsal aspect of the ankle joint, eroding the talus. Multiple calcifications, uniform in size and shape, are noted laterally. (**C**) After injection of 15 mCi (555 MBq) of ⁹⁹ᵐTc-labeled MDP, there is increased uptake of radiopharmaceutical tracer in the right ankle. (**D**) Sagittal T1-weighted (SE; TR 400/TE 20 msec) MR image shows the mass displaying intermediate signal intensity, isointense with the muscles. (**E**) Parasagittal T1-weighted (SE; TR 400/TE 20 msec) MR image demonstrates the mass to be well encapsulated. (**F**) Coronal proton density (SE; TR 1800/TE 29 msec) MR image shows that the mass is continuous with the ankle joint. (**G**) Coronal T2-weighted (SE; TR 2000/TE 80 msec) MR image demonstrates the mass to be of high signal intensity. Punctated areas of low signal intensity within the mass represent calcifications.

arranged in sheets, myxoid changes in the matrix, hypercellularity with crowding and spindling of nuclei at the periphery, necrosis, and permeation of bone trabeculae. Remarking on the danger of misinterpreting synovial chondromatosis as chondrosarcoma on both radiographic and histopathologic examination, Bertoni and colleagues singled out pulmonary metastases as the only distinguishing feature.

Differential Diagnosis

The main differential diagnosis is between synovial chondrosarcoma and synovial (osteo)chondromatosis. Frequently, the imaging findings in both conditions are similar, although the development of destructive changes around the affected joint favors synovial chondrosarcoma. However, these destructive changes should be differentiated from periarticular erosions occasionally present in synovial chondromatosis. PVNS can usually be excluded without much difficulty, because it does not exhibit calcifications and, in addition, shows rather characteristic MRI features (see previous text).

Malignant PVNS

Recently, Kalil and Unni reported a case of malignancy in PVNS and cited eight other cases from the literature. Enzinger and Weiss defined malignant PVNS as a malignant lesion occurring with concomitant or previously documented benign PVNS at the same location. Bertoni and coworkers documented histologic evolution from benign to malignant PVNS in three cases. The malignancy in PVNS is an extremely rare occurrence, yet this is a controversial issue, mainly because other synovium-centered lesions, such as clear cell sarcoma or epithelioid sarcoma, may be mistaken for malignant PVNS.

PRACTICAL POINTS TO REMEMBER

[1] Characteristic radiographic findings of synovial (osteo)chondromatosis include joint effusion, numerous radiopaque osteochondral bodies (usually small and uniform in size), and bone erosions.

[2] Arthrography, CT, and MRI are effective imaging modalities to demonstrate noncalcified intraarticular bodies.

[3] PVNS is invariably accompanied by serosanguineous synovial fluid. Radiography reveals a soft-tissue density in the affected joint caused by hemorrhagic fluid and lobulated synovial masses.

[4] MRI is very effective in the diagnosis of PVNS because on T2 weighting, the intraarticular masses demonstrate a characteristic combination of high–signal-intensity areas representing fluid and congested synovium, interspersed with areas of intermediate to low signal intensity secondary to the presence of hemosiderin.

[5] Synovial hemangioma is best diagnosed by MRI. Characteristic imaging findings include a soft-tissue mass exhibiting an intermediate signal intensity on T1-weighted images (isointense with or slightly brighter than muscle but not as bright as fat), and high signal on T2 weighting associated with serpentine low-intensity septa.

[6] Lipoma arborescens, a very rare intraarticular disorder, is characterized by nonneoplastic lipomatous proliferation of the synovium. MRI shows joint effusion and frond-like masses arising from the synovium that have the signal intensity of fat on all sequences.

[7] Synovial sarcoma is frequently located in close proximity to the joint. Calcifications and bone erosion are common findings.

[8] Synovial chondrosarcoma, a very rare tumor that originates from the synovial membrane, may be primary lesion or may develop in synovial chondromatosis.

SUGGESTED READINGS

Abdelwahab IF, Kenan S, Steiner GC, Abdul-Quader M. True bursal pigmented villonodular synovitis. *Skeletal Radiol* 2002;31:354–358.

Abrahams TG, Pavlov H, Bansal M, Bullough P. Concentric joint space narrowing of the hip associated with hemosiderotic synovitis (HS) including pigmented villonodular synovitis (PVNS). *Skeletal Radiol* 1988;17:37–45.

Ackerman LV. Extra-osseous localized non-neoplastic bone and cartilage formation (so-called myositis ossificans). Clinical and pathological confusion with malignant neoplasms. *J Bone Joint Surg [Am]* 1958;40A:279–298.

Aglietti P, Di Muria GV, Salvati EA, Stringa G. Pigmented vollonodular synovitis of the hip joint (review of the literature and report of personal case material). *Ital J Orthop Traumatol* 1983;9:487–496.

Armstrong SJ, Watt I. Lipoma arborescens of the knee. *Br J Radiol* 1989;62:178–180.

Atmore WG, Dahlin DC, Ghormley RK. Pigmented villonodular synovitis: a clinical and pathologic study. *Minn Med* 1956;39:196–202.

Baker ND, Klein JD, Weidner N, Weissman BN, Brick GW. Pigmented villonodular synovitis containing coarse calcifications. *Am J Roentgenol* 1989;153:1228–1230.

Balsara ZN, Staiken BF, Martinez AJ. MR image of localized giant cell tumor of the tendon sheath involving the knee. *J Comput Assist Tomogr* 1989;13:159–162.

Bejia I, Younes M, Moussa A, Said M, Touzi M,Bergaoui N. Lipoma arborescens affecting multiple joints. *Skeletal Radiol* 2005;34:536–538.

Bertoni F, Unni KK, Beabout JW, Sim FH. Chondrosarcomas of the synovium. *Cancer* 1991;67:155–162.

Bertoni F, Unni KK, Beabout JW, Sim FH. Malignant giant cell tumor of the tendon sheaths and joints (malignant pigmented villonodular synovitis). *Am J Surg Path* 1997;21:153–163.

Besette PR, Cooley PA, Johnson RP, Czarnecki DJ. Gadolinium-enhanced MRI of pigmented villonodular synovitis of the knee. *J Comput Assist Tomogr* 1992;16: 992–994.

Blacksin MF, Ghelman B, Freiberger RH, Salvata E. Synovial chondromatosis of the hip: evaluation with air computed arthrotomography. *Clin Imaging* 1990;14: 315–318.

Bravo SM, Winalski CS, Weissman BN. Pigmented villonodular synovitis. *Radiol Clin North Am* 1996;34:311–326.

Brodsky AE. Synovial hemangioma of the knee joint. *Bull Hosp Jt Dis Orthop Inst* 1956;17:58–69.

Bullough PG. *Atlas of orthopaedic pathology with clinical and radiologic correlations*, 2nd ed. New York: Gower; 1992:17.25–17.28.

Burnstein MI, Fisher DR, Yandow DR, Hafez GR, DeSmet AA. Case report 502. Intra-articular synovial chondromatosis of shoulder with extra-articular extension. *Skeletal Radiol* 1988;17:458–461.

Cadman NL, Soule EH, Kelly PJ. Synovial sarcoma: an analysis of 134 tumors. *Cancer* 1965;18:613–627.

Campanacci M. *Bone and soft-tissue tumors*. New York: Springer-Verlag; 1990: 998–1012.

Chen DY, Lan JL, Chou SJ. Treatment of pigmented villonodular synovitis with yttrium-90: changes in immunologic features. Tc-99m uptake measurements, and MR imaging of one case. *Clin Rheumatol* 1992;11:280–285.

Cotten A, Flipo R-M, Chastanet P, Desvigne-Noulet M-C, Duquesnoy B, Delcambre B. Pigmented villonodular synovitis of the hip: review of radiographic features in 58 patients. *Skeletal Radiol* 1995;24:1–6.

Cotten A, Flipo RM, Herbaux B, Gougeon F, Lecomte-Houcke M, Chastanet P. Synovial haemangioma of the knee: a frequently misdiagnosed lesion. *Skeletal Radiol* 1995;24:257–261.

Crotty JM, Monu JUV, Pope TL Jr. Synovial osteochondromatosis. *Radiol Clin North Am* 1996;34:327–342.

Dahlin DC, Unni KK. Chondrosarcoma. In: *Bone tumors. General aspects and data on 8,542 cases*, 4th ed. Springfield: Charles C. Thomas; 1986:227–259.

De Beuckeleer L, De Schepper A, De Belder F, et al. Magnetic resonance imaging of localized giant cell tumour of the tendon sheath (MRI of localized GCTTS). *Eur Radiol* 1997;7:198–201.

De St. Aubain Sommerhausen N, Dal Cin P. Giant cell tumour of tendon sheath. In: Fletcher CDM, Unni KK, Mertens F, eds. *World Health Organization classification of tumours. Pathology and genetics. Tumours of soft tissue and bone*. Lyon, France: IARC Press; 2002:110–111.

De St. Aubain Sommerhausen N, Dal Cin P. Diffuse-type giant cell tumour. In: Fletcher CDM, Unni KK, Mertens F, eds. *World Health Organization classification of tumours. Pathology and genetics. Tumours of soft tissue and bone*. Lyon, France: IARC Press; 2002:112–114.

Devaney K, Vinh TN, Sweet DE. Synovial hemangioma: report of 20 cases with differential diagnostic considerations. *Hum Pathol* 1993;24:737–745.

Dorwart RH, Genant HK, Johnston WH, Morris JM. Pigmented villonodular synovitis of synovial joints: clinical, pathologic, and radiologic features. *Am J Roentgenol* 1984;143:877–885.

Doyle AJ, Miller MV, French JG. Lipoma arborescens in the bicipital bursa of the elbow: MRI findings in two cases. *Skeletal Radiol* 2002;31:656–660.

Dunn EJ, McGavran MH, Nelson P, Greer RB III. Synovial chondrosarcoma. Report of a case. *J Bone Joint Surg [Am]* 1974;56A:811–813.

Enzinger FM, Weiss SW. Benign tumors and tumor-like lesions of synovial tissue. In: *Soft tissue tumors*. St. Louis: CV Mosby; 1988:638–658.

Enzinger FM, Weiss SW. *Soft tissue tumors*, 3rd ed. St. Louis: CV Mosby, 1995: 749–751, 757–786.

Eustace SE, Harrison M, Srinivasen U, Stack J. Magnetic resonance imaging in pigmented villonodular synovitis. *Can Assoc Radiol J* 1994;45:283–286.

Evans HL. Synovial sarcoma: a study of 23 biphasic and 17 probably monophasic examples. *Pathol Annu* 1980;15:309–313.

Fechner RE, Mills SE. *Tumors of the bones and joints*. Washington, DC: Armed Forces Institute of Pathology; 1993.

Flanagan AM, Delaney D, O'Donnell P. The benefits of molecular pathology in the diagnosis of musculoskeletal disease. Part I of a two-part review: soft tissue tumors. *Skeletal Radiol* 2010;39:105–115.

Fletcher AG Jr, Horn RC Jr. Giant-cell tumor of tendon sheath origin: a consideration of bone involvement and report of 2 cases with extensive bone destruction. *Ann Surg* 1951;133:374–385.

Georgen TG, Resnick D, Niwayama G. Localized nodular synovitis of the knee: a report of two cases with abnormal arthrograms. *Am J Roentgenol* 1976;126:647–650.

Goldman RL, Lichtenstein L. Synovial chondrosarcoma. *Cancer* 1964;17:1233–1240.

Greenfield GB, Arrington JA, Kudryk BT. MRI of soft tissue tumors. *Skeletal Radiol* 1993;22:77–84.

Greenspan A, Azouz EM, Matthews J II, Décarie J-C. Synovial hemangioma: imaging features in eight histologically proved cases, review of the literature, and differential diagnosis. *Skeletal Radiol* 1995;24:583–590.

Grieten M, Buckwalter KA, Cardinal E, Rougraff B. Case report 873. Lipoma arborescens (villous lipomatous proliferation of the synovial membrane). *Skeletal Radiol* 1994;23:652–655.

Hallel T, Lew S, Bansal M. Villous lipomatous proliferation of the synovial membrane (lipoma arborescens). *J Bone Joint Surg [Am]* 1988;70A:264–270.

Hamilton A, Davis RI, Hayes D, Mollan RA. Chondrosarcoma developing in synovial chondromatosis. A case report. *J Bone Joint Surg [Br]* 1987;69B:137–140.

Hermann G, Abdelwahab IF, Klein MJ, Kenan S, Lewis M. Synovial chondromatosis. *Skeletal Radiol* 1995;24:298–300.

Hermann G, Klein MJ, Abdelwahab IF, Kenan S. Synovial chondrosarcoma arising in synovial chondromatosis of the right hip. *Skeletal Radiol* 1997;26:366–369.

Huang G-S, Lee C-H, Chan WP, Chen C-Y, Yu JS, Resnick D. Localized nodular synovitis of the knee: MR imaging appearance and clinical correlates in 21 patients. *Am J Roentgenol* 2003;181:539–543.

Hughes TH, Sartoris DJ, Schweitzer ME, Resnick DL. Pigmented villonodular synovitis: MRI characteristics. *Skeletal Radiol* 1995;24:7–12.

Ishida T, Iijima T, Moriyama S, Nakamura C, Kitagawa T, Machinami R. Intra-articular calcifying synovial sarcoma mimicking synovial chondromatosis. *Skeletal Radiol* 1996;25:766–769.

Jaffe HL, Lichtenstein L, Sutro CJ. Pigmented villonodular synovitis, bursitis and tenosynovitis. *Arch Pathol Lab Med* 1941;31:731–765.

Jelinek JS, Kransdorf MJ, Shmookler BM, Aboulafia AA, Malawer MM. Giant cell tumor of the tendon sheath: MR findings in nine cases. *Am J Roentgenol* 1994;162:919–922.

Jelinek JS, Kransdorf MJ, Utz JA, et al. Imaging of pigmented villonodular synovitis with emphasis on MR imaging. *Am J Roentgenol* 1989;152:337–342.

Jones BC, Sundaram M, Kransdorf MJ. Synovial sarcoma: MR imaging findings in 34 patients. *Am J Roentgenol* 1993;161:827–830.

Jones FE, Soule EM, Coventry MB. Fibrous xanthoma of synovium (giant-cell tumor of tendon sheath, pigmented nodular synovitis). A study of 118 cases. *J Bone Joint Surg [Am]* 1969;51A:76–86.

Kaiser TE, Ivins JC, Unni KK. Malignant transformation of extra-articular synovial chondromatosis: report of a case. *Skeletal Radiol* 1980;5:223–226.

Kalil RK, Unni KK. Malignancy in pigmented villonodular synovitis. *Skeletal Radiol* 1998;27:392–395.

Kallas KM, Vaughan L, Haghighi P, Resnick D. Pigmented villonodular synovitis of the hip presenting as retroperitoneal mass. *Skeletal Radiol* 2001;30:469–474.

Karasick D, Karasick S. Giant cell tumor of tendon sheath: spectrum of radiologic findings. *Skeletal Radiol* 1992;21:219–224.

Khan S, Neumann CH, Steinback LS, Harrington KD. MRI of giant cell tumor of tendon sheath of the hand: a report of three cases. *Eur Radiol* 1995;5:467–470.

Kindblom LG, Gunterberg B. Pigmented villonodular synovitis involving bone. Case report. *J Bone Joint Surg [Am]* 1978;60A:830–832.

King JW, Spjut HJ, Fechner RE, Vanderpool DW. Synovial chondrosarcoma of the knee joint. *J Bone Joint Surg [Am]* 1967;49A:1389–1396.

Kloen P, Keel SB, Chandler HP, Geiger RH, Zarins B, Rosenberg AE. Lipoma arborescens of the knee. *J Bone Joint Surg [Br]* 1998;80-B:298–301.

Krall RA, Kostinovsky M, Patchefsky AS. Synovial sarcoma: a clinical, pathological, and ultrastructural study of 26 cases supporting the recognition of monophasic variant. *Am J Surg Pathol* 1981;5:137–151.

Kransdorf MJ, Jelinek JS, Moser RP, et al. Soft-tissue masses: diagnosis using MR imaging. *Am J Roentgenol* 1989;153:541–547.

Laorr A, Helms CA. *MRI of musculoskeletal masses: a practical text and atlas.* New York: Igaku-Shoin; 1997.

Laorr A, Peterfy CG, Tirman PF, Rabassa AE. Lipoma arborescens of the shoulder: magnetic resonance imaging findings. *Can Assoc Radiol J* 1995;46:311–313.

Lin J, Jacobson JA, Jamadar DA, Ellis JH. Pigmented villonodular synovitis and related lesions: the spectrum of imaging findings. *Am J Roentgenol* 1999;172:191–197.

Llauger J, Monill JM, Palmer J, Clotet M. Synovial hemangioma of the knee: MRI findings in two cases. *Skeletal Radiol* 1995;24:579–581.

Llauger J, Palmer J, Rosón N, Cremades R, Bagué S. Pigmented villonodular synovitis and giant cell tumors of the tendon sheath: radiologic and pathologic features. *Am J Roentgenol* 1999;172:1087–1091.

Mahajan H, Lorigan JG, Shirkhoda A. Synovial sarcoma: MR imaging. *Magn Reson Imaging* 1989;7:211–216.

McMaster PE. Pigmented villonodular synovitis with invasion of bone. Report of six cases. *J Bone Joint Surg [Am]* 1960;42A:1170–1183.

Miettinen M, Virtanen I. Synovial sarcoma—a misnomer. *Am J Pathol* 1984;117:18–25.

Morton MJ, Berquist TH, McLeod RA, Unni KK, Sim FH. MR imaging of synovial sarcoma. *Am J Roentgenol* 1991;156:337–340.

Mulder JD, Kroon HM, Schütte HE, Taconis WK. *Radiologic atlas of bone tumors.* Amsterdam, the Netherlands: Elsevier; 1993.

Mullins F, Berard CW, Eisenberg SH. Chondrosarcoma following synovial chondromatosis. A case study. *Cancer* 1965;18:1180–1188.

Murphey MD, Gibson MS, Jennings BT, Crespo-Rodriguez AM, Fanburg-Smith J, Gajewski DA. Imaging of synovial sarcoma with radiologic-pathologic correlation. *Radiographics* 2006;26:1543–1565.

Murphey MD, Vidal JA, Fanburg-Smith JC, Gajewski DA. Imaging of synovial chondromatosis with radiologic-pathologic correlation. *Radiographics* 2007;27:1465–1488.

Myers BW, Masi AT. Pigmented villonodular synovitis and tenosynovitis, a clinical epidemiologic study of 166 cases and literature review. *Medicine* 1980;59:224–238.

Nassar WAM, Bassiony AA, Elghazaly HA. Treatment of diffuse pigmented villonodular synovitis of the knee with combined surgical and radiosynovectomy. *Hospital Spec Surg J* 2009;5:19–23.

Norman A, Steiner GC. Bone erosion in synovial chondromatosis. *Radiology* 1986;161:749–752.

Ontell F, Greenspan A. Chondrosarcoma complicating synovial chondromatosis: findings with magnetic resonance imaging. *Can Assoc Radiol J* 1994;45:318–323.

Parsonage S, Mehr A, Davies MD. Lipoma arborescense: a definitive MR imaging diagnosis. *Osteol Közlem* 2001;9:80–82.

Peh WCG, Shek TWH, Davies AM, Wong JWK, Chien EP. Osteochondroma and secondary synovial osteochondromatosis. *Skeletal Radiol* 1999;28:169–174.

Perry BE, McQueen DA, Lin JJ. Synovial chondromatosis with malignant degeneration to chondrosarcoma. Report of a case. *J Bone Joint Surg [Am]* 1988;70A:1259–1261.

Rao AS, Vigorita VJ. Pigmented villonodular synovitis (giant-cell tumor of the tendon sheath and synovial membrane). A review of eighty-one cases. *J Bone Joint Surg [Am]* 1984;66A:76–94.

Resnick D, Oliphant M. Hemophilia-like arthropathy of the knee associated with cutaneous and synovial hemangiomas. *Radiology* 1975;114:323–326.

Rosenthal DI, Aronow S, Murray WT. Iron content of pigmented villonodular synovitis detected by computed tomography. *Radiology* 1979;133:409–411.

Rubin BP. Tenosynovial giant cell tumor and pigmented villonodular synovitis: a proposal for unification of these clinically distinct but histologically and genetically identical lesions. *Skeletal Radiol* 2007;36:267–268.

Ryu KN, Jaovisidha S, Schweitzer M, Motta AO, Resnick D. MR imaging of lipoma aborescens of the knee joint. *Am J Roentgenol* 1996;167:1229–1232.

Sánchez Reyes JM, Alcaraz Mexia M, Quiñones Tapia D, Aramburu JA. Extensively calcified synovial sarcoma. *Skeletal Radiol* 1997;26:671–673.

Schajowicz F. Synovial chondromatosis. In: *Tumors and tumorlike lesions of bones and joints.* New York: Springer-Verlag; 1981:541–545.

Sherry JB, Anderson W. The natural history of pigmented villonodular synovitis of tendon sheath. *J Bone Joint Surg [Am]* 1956;37A:1005–1011.

Sommerhausen NSA, Fletcher CDM. Diffuse-type giant cell tumor. Clinicopathologic and immunohistochemical analysis of 50 cases with extraarticular disease. *Am J Surg Pathol* 2000; 24:479–492.

Soule EH. Synovial sarcoma. *Am J Surg Pathol* 1986;10:78–82.

Stout AP, Lattes R. Tumors of the soft tissue. In: *Atlas of tumor pathology,* 2nd series, fascicle 1. Washington, DC: Armed Forces Institute of Pathology; 1967.

Strickland B, Mackenzie DH. Bone involvement in synovial sarcoma. *J Faculty Radiol* 1959;10:64–72.

Ushijima M, Hashimoto H, Tsuneyoshi M, Enjoji M. Giant cell tumor of the tendon sheath (nodular tenosynovitis). A study of 207 cases to compare the large joint group with the common digit group. *Cancer* 1986;57:875–884.

van Rijswijk CSP, Hogendoorn PCW, Taminiau AHM, Bloem JL. Synovial sarcoma: dynamic contrast-enhanced MR imaging features. *Skeletal Radiol* 2001; 30:25–30.

Wittkop B, Davies AM, Mangham DC. Primary synovial chondromatosis and synovial chondrosarcoma: a pictorial review. *Eur Radiol* 2002;12:2112–2119.

Wright PH, Sim FH, Soule EH, Taylor WF. Synovial sarcoma. *J Bone Joint Surg [Am]* 1982;64A:112–122.

INFECTIONS

Radiologic Evaluation of Musculoskeletal Infections

Musculoskeletal Infections

Infections of the musculoskeletal system can be subdivided into three categories: (a) those involving bones (osteomyelitis); (b) those involving joints (infectious arthritis); and (c) those involving soft tissues (cellulitis). Because of the complexity of the vertebrae and their soft-tissue structures, infectious processes of the spine are considered under a separate heading.

Osteomyelitis

Three basic mechanisms allow an infectious organism—whether bacterium, virus, mycoplasma, rickettsia, or fungus—to reach the bone: (a) *hematogenous spread* via the bloodstream from a remote site of infection, such as the skin, tonsils, gallbladder, or urinary tract; (b) spread from a *contiguous source* of infection, such as from the soft tissues, teeth, or sinuses; and (c) *direct implantation*, such as through a puncture or missile wound or an operative procedure (Fig. 24.1).

Hematogenous spread is common in children, and the usual focus of infection develops in the metaphysis. The metaphyseal location of infection in children is related to an osseous–vascular anatomy that differs in the infant, child, and adult (Fig. 24.2). In the child (ages 1 to 16 years), there is separation of the blood supply to the metaphysis and epiphysis, each having its own source. Moreover, the arteries and capillaries of the metaphysis turn sharply without penetrating the open growth plate; in the region where capillaries become venules, the rate of blood flow is sluggish. Also contributing to the greater incidence of metaphyseal osteomyelitis in children is secondary thrombosis of end arteries with bacteria during transient bacteremia. In the infant (up to 1 year), however, osteomyelitis may sometimes have its focus in the epiphysis because some metaphyseal vessels may penetrate the growth plate and reach the epiphysis (see Fig. 24.2). With obliteration of the growth plate in the adult, there is vascular continuity between the shaft and the articular ends of the bone; hence, the focus of osteomyelitis can develop in any part of a bone.

Contiguous spread and direct implantation are more common in adults. The sites of bone infection via either of these routes are directly related to the focus of soft-tissue infection or the location of the wound.

Infectious Arthritis

An infectious agent may enter the joint by the same basic routes as in osteomyelitis: by direct invasion of the synovial membrane, either secondary to a penetrating wound or after a joint-replacement procedure; from an infection of the adjacent soft tissues; or indirectly via a blood-borne infection. Infectious arthritis may also occur secondary to a focus of osteomyelitis in the adjacent bone (Fig. 24.3).

Cellulitis

Soft-tissue infections most commonly result from a break in the skin leading to direct introduction of an infectious agent. Some patients, such as those with diabetes, are particularly prone to cellulitis caused by a combination of factors, including skin breakdown and local ischemia.

Infections of the Spine

Infections in the spine may be located in a vertebral body, an intervertebral disk, the paravertebral soft tissues, or the epidural compartment; very rarely, an infection may involve the contents of the spinal canal or the spinal cord. The mechanisms of infection are the same as those of osteomyelitis and infectious arthritis. An intervertebral disk infection, for example, may result from a puncture of the canal or of the disk itself during a procedure, as well as from a penetrating injury. It can also spread from a contiguous source of infection such as a paraspinal abscess. Most common, however, is hematogenous spread after surgical procedures such as laminectomy or spinal fusion, or during generalized bacteremia or sepsis (Fig. 24.4). Regardless of the primary location of the infectious process, *Staphylococcus aureus* is responsible for more than 90% of all infections of the spine.

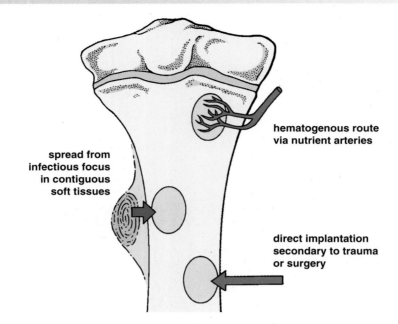

▲
FIGURE 24.1   Entry routes of an infectious organism into a bone. Infectious agents may gain entry to a bone through hematogenous spread, a source of infection in the contiguous soft tissues, or through direct implantation secondary to trauma or surgery.

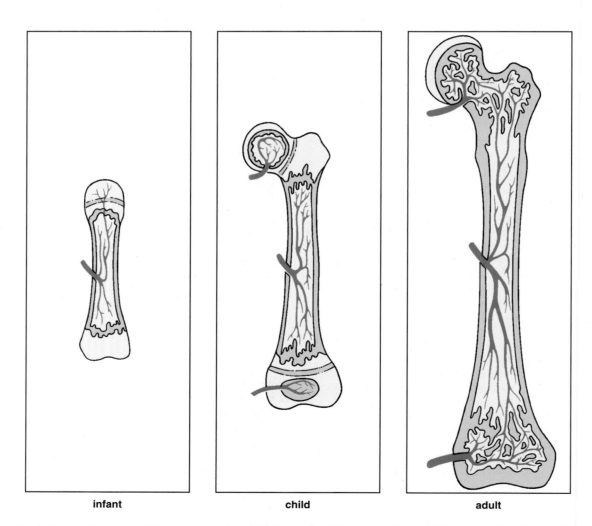

| infant | child | adult |

▲
FIGURE 24.2   Vascular anatomy of long bone. The vascular anatomy of a long bone differs in an infant, a child, and an adult. These differences account for the various locations of infection in each age group. In an infant, nutrient, transphyseal, and foveal arteries are abundant. In a child, the physis becomes avascular when the foveal and transphyseal arteries recede. After the growth plate closes, the foveal arteries and periarticular arteries again become prominent.

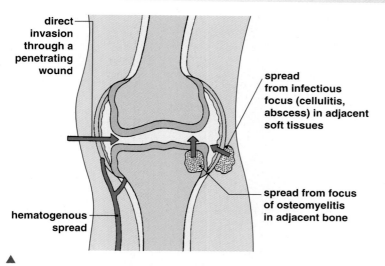

FIGURE 24.3 Entry routes of an infectious organism into a joint. The routes of infection in infectious arthritis are similar to those of osteomyelitis, which itself may be a source of spread.

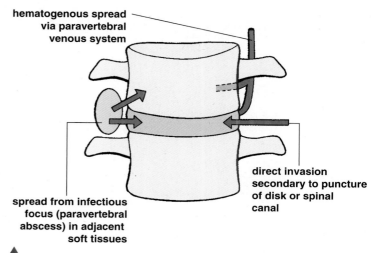

FIGURE 24.4 Entry routes of an infectious organism into a vertebra. The potential routes of infection of a vertebra or an intervertebral disk are direct invasion, hematogenous spread, and extension from a focus of infection in the adjacent soft tissues.

Radiologic Evaluation of Infections

The imaging modalities used to evaluate infections of the musculoskeletal system include the following:

1. Conventional radiography
2. Computed tomography (CT)
3. Arthrography
4. Myelography and diskography
5. Fistulography (sinogram)
6. Arteriography
7. Radionuclide imaging (scintigraphy, bone scan)
8. Ultrasound (US)
9. Magnetic resonance imaging (MRI)
10. Percutaneous aspiration and biopsy (fluoroscopy-guided, CT-guided, or US-guided)

Conventional Radiography and Arthrography

In most instances, radiography is sufficient to demonstrate the pertinent features of a bone or joint infection (Fig. 24.5; see also Figs. 4.50 and 4.51). Magnification radiography used to be helpful in delineating subtle changes representing cortical destruction or periosteal new bone formation (Fig. 24.6), but currently with the advantage of digital radiography and newest technology of PACS (Picture Archive and Communication System) allowing filmless high-resolution image-display format (see Chapter 12), this technique is no longer in practical use. Conventional tomography using multidirectional motion (trispiral tomography) in the past was effective in demonstrating sequestra or subtle sinus tracts in the bone (Fig. 24.7), but at present has been almost completely replaced by CT, which plays a determining role in demonstrating the extent of infection in bones and soft tissues and at times may be very helpful in making a specific diagnosis (Fig. 24.8). Arthrography has rather limited application in the diagnosis of joint infections (see Fig. 25.17B).

Radionuclide Imaging

Scintigraphy has a very prominent role in diagnosing bone and soft-tissue infections. In suspected osteomyelitis, radionuclide bone scan using technetium-99m-labeled (^{99m}Tc) phosphonates is routinely used, because there is an accumulation of tracer in the infected areas. A three- or four-phase technique is particularly useful for distinguishing infected joint tissues from infected periarticular soft tissues if radiography is not diagnostic. With cellulitis, diffuse increased uptake is present in the first two phases, but there is no significant increase in uptake in the bone in the third and fourth delayed phases. Conversely, osteomyelitis causes focally increased uptake in all four phases (Fig. 24.9). In addition, the three-phase bone scan can accurately diagnose osteomyelitis within 3 days of the development of symptoms, much earlier than can be seen with conventional radiography. The three-phase bone scan can also be useful in diagnosing septic arthritis in situ or with extension into the adjacent bone.

Once the bone sustains an injury, such as surgery, fracture, or neuropathic osteoarthropathy, that causes increased bone turnover, routine scintigraphy with technetium-labeled phosphonate becomes less specific for infection. However, radionuclide studies using gallium (a ferric analog) and indium are more specific in these instances. There is still no general agreement on the exact mechanism of gallium localization in infected tissues. After intravenous injections of gallium, more than 99% is bound to various plasma proteins, including transferrin, haptoglobin, lactoferrin, albumin, and ferritin. At least five mechanisms of gallium transfer from the plasma into inflammatory exudates and cells have been suggested. These include direct leukocyte uptake, direct bacteria uptake, the protein-bound tissue uptake, increased vascularity, and increased bone turnover. Because gallium binds to the iron-binding molecule transferrin, the mechanism of gallium uptake in infectious processes is best explained by hyperemia and elevated permeability that increase delivery of the protein-bound tracer transferrin into the area of inflammation. Cells associated with the inflammatory response, particularly polymorphonuclear white cells in which lactoferrin is carried within intracytoplasmic granules, deposit iron-binding proteins extracellularly at the site of inflammation, serving to combat the infection by sequestering needed iron from bacteria. Lactoferrin, which has a high binding affinity for iron, takes the gallium away from the transferrin.

Gallium can also be used to assess the patient's response to therapy. Particularly in osteomyelitis, gallium concentrations enhance the specificity of an abnormal bone scan, and decreased gallium uptake closely follows a good response to therapy.

The other tracer used in infections is indium. Because indium-labeled white blood cells are usually not incorporated into areas of increased bone turnover, scintigraphy with indium-111 (^{111}In) oxine–labeled leukocytes is used as a sensitive and specific test in the general diagnosis of infection of the musculoskeletal system, and in specific instances when infection complicates previous fracture or surgery. Like other imaging procedures in nuclear medicine, this test monitors the internal distribution of a tracer agent to provide diagnostic information. The inherent ability of white blood cells to accumulate at sites of inflammation makes their use in this test particularly effective in the diagnosis of infections. Merkel reported the sensitivity of indium scintigraphy in detecting infections to be 83%, with a specificity of 94% and an accuracy of 88%.

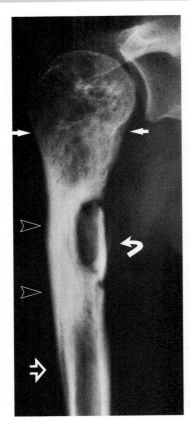

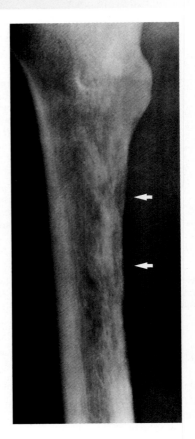

▲
FIGURE 24.5 Chronic osteomyelitis. Anteroposterior radiograph of the right humerus demonstrates the classic features of chronic active osteomyelitis. There is destruction of the medullary portion of the bone (*arrows*), reactive sclerosis (*arrow heads*), and periosteal new bone formation (*open arrow*). Note also a large sequestrum on the medial aspect of the humerus (*curved arrow*), the hallmark of an active infectious process.

▲
FIGURE 24.6 Acute osteomyelitis. Magnification study of the right femur demonstrates subtle changes representative of cortical destruction and formation of periosteal new bone in an early stage of osteomyelitis (*arrows*). These findings were not well delineated on the conventional radiographs.

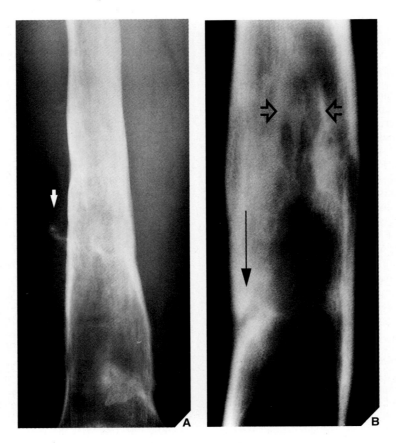

▲
FIGURE 24.7 Tomography of active osteomyelitis. (A) Radiograph of the left femur shows thickening of the cortex, reactive sclerosis, and foci of destruction in the medullary cavity. Faint calcifications in the soft tissue (*arrow*) suggest the presence of a fistula. **(B)** Conventional tomogram enhanced by magnification clearly demonstrates a sequestrum (*open arrows*) and a sinus tract in the cortex (*long arrow*), the characteristic features of active osteomyelitis.

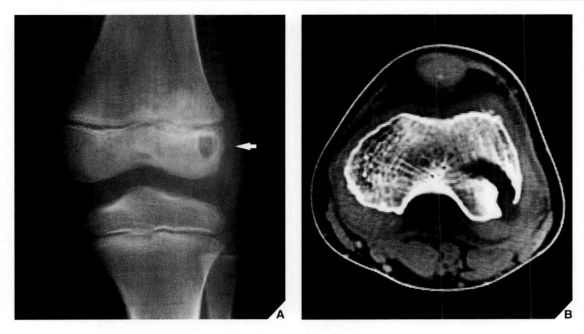

FIGURE 24.8 CT of bone abscess. A 7-year-old boy had intermittent pain in the left knee for 3 weeks; the pain was worse at night and was promptly relieved by salicylates. (**A**) Initial anteroposterior radiograph of the left knee demonstrates a radiolucent lesion with a well-defined, partly sclerotic border in the lateral portion of the distal femoral epiphysis (*arrow*). Osteoid osteoma and chondroblastoma were considered in the differential diagnosis. (**B**) CT examination, however, reveals cortical disruption at the posterolateral aspect of the lateral femoral condyle, a finding not seen on the standard radiographs. The serpentine configuration of the radiolucent tract and its extension into the cartilage prompted a diagnosis of epiphyseal bone abscess, which was confirmed on bone biopsy.

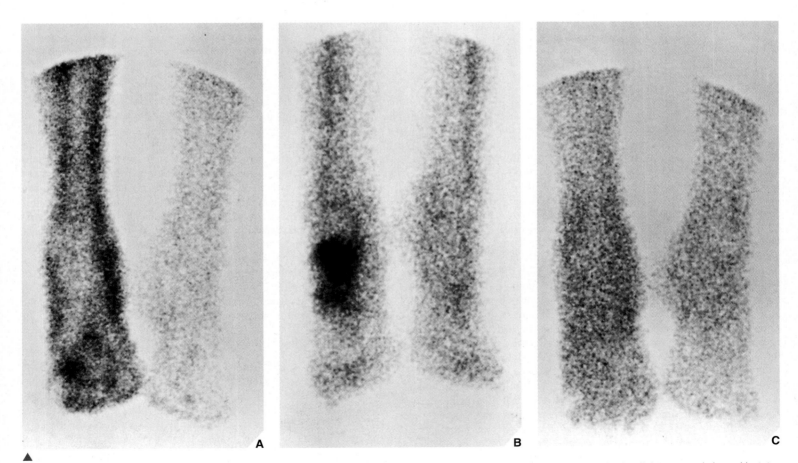

FIGURE 24.9 Application of radionuclide bone scan in infection. A 52-year-old woman with pain in her right ankle had cellulitis around the ankle joint. Although radiographs did not reveal changes in the joint suggestive of infectious arthritis, this possibility could not be ruled out clinically because early changes of infection may not be detected on standard radiographs. A three-phase radionuclide bone scan was performed. (**A**) In the first phase, 1 minute after intravenous injection of a 15 mCi (555 MBq) bolus of ^{99m}Tc-labeled methylene diphosphonate, there is increased activity in the major vessels of the right leg. (**B**) In the second phase, 3 minutes after injection, a blood pool scan demonstrates increased uptake in the area of the infected soft tissues. (**C**) In the third phase, 2 hours after injection, almost complete washout of the radiopharmaceutical agent, with no evidence of localization in the bones on both sides of the joint, excludes the diagnosis of infectious arthritis. (Courtesy of Dr. R. Goldfarb, New York.)

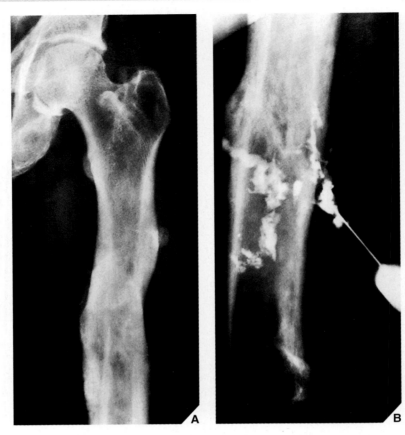

FIGURE 24.10 Fistulography in osteomyelitis. A 48-year-old man who had sustained a fracture of the femur was treated with open reduction and internal fixation using an intramedullary rod. Chronic osteomyelitis developed postoperatively. The rod was removed and the infection was treated with antibiotics. Subsequently, a draining sinus developed. (**A**) Radiograph of the left femur demonstrates changes typical of chronic osteomyelitis. There is focal destruction of the medullary portion of the bone, reactive sclerosis, and a periosteal reaction. (**B**) A sinogram performed to evaluate the extent of the draining fistula demonstrates an intraosseous sinus tract with multiple ramifications.

It must be stressed, however, that because the ^{111}In-labeled leukocytes also accumulate in active bone marrow, the sensitivity for the detection of chronic osteomyelitis is reduced. To improve the diagnostic ability of this technique, a combined ^{99m}Tc-sulfur colloid bone marrow/^{111}In-labeled leukocyte study is advocated. A particularly difficult problem is the patient with diabetic foot neuropathy in whom superimposed infection is suspected. In this circumstance, radiography and even MRI are not very specific. Although soft-tissue infection can be detected by the latter technique, early changes of osteomyelitis may be missed. Often, no single imaging method can provide the correct diagnosis, and a combination of imaging techniques should be used. The traditional sequential use of ^{67}Ga citrate in conjunction with the ^{99m}Tc-methylene diphosphonate (MDP) bone scan as an aid to diagnose osteomyelitis in the diabetic foot has been supplanted in recent years by the use of ^{111}In-labeled leukocytes. The drawback of this technique is that there remain difficulties in differentiating infection in the bone (osteomyelitis) from that in the adjacent tissue (cellulitis). A more recent attempt to improve this situation is the use of a combined ^{99m}Tc-bone scan/^{111}In-labeled leukocyte study to determine whether the leukocyte collection is in the bone or in the soft tissue. A new challenger to ^{111}In leukocyte scanning is the ^{99m}Tc-hexamethylpropylene amino oxine (HMPAO)–labeled leukocyte scan. At the time of this writing, other methods are being tested, namely, isotope-labeled (^{99m}Tc, ^{111}In, or ^{123}I) monoclonal antigranulocyte antibodies, isotope-labeled polyclonal IgG, isotope-labeled monocytes, isotope-labeled chemotactic polypeptide analogs, and isotope-labeled specific antibodies against bacteria.

Arteriography, Myelography, Fistulography, and US

Arteriography is important in the evaluation of the patient's vascular supply, particularly if a reconstructive procedure is planned. Myelography is still useful in evaluating infections within the spinal canal, as well as in vertebral osteomyelitis and disk infection (see Fig. 25.31B). Fistulography (sinogram) is an important examination for outlining sinus tracts in the soft tissues and for evaluating their extension into the bone (Fig. 24.10). US can occasionally be used in diagnosing soft-tissue and joint infections, as well as osteomyelitis. This modality has the advantage of being easily accessible and available at relatively reasonable cost. In addition, this technique does not expose the patient to ionizing radiation. Real-time capability of US is unique in providing a means to evaluate structures under dynamic conditions. In diffuse soft-tissue infection, US may be helpful in distinguishing primary disease from that associated with underlying abscess such as in pyomyositis or osteomyelitis. Furthermore, US plays an important role in the guidance of percutaneous biopsy and aspiration of infectious lesions, as well as the therapeutic drainage of abscesses.

Magnetic Resonance Imaging

At the present time MRI established its place in the evaluation of bone and soft-tissue infections. As several studies have indicated, osteomyelitis, soft-tissue abscesses, joint and tendon sheath effusions, and various forms of cellulitis are well depicted by this modality. MRI is as sensitive as [99m]Tc- MDP in demonstrating osteomyelitis and more sensitive and more specific than other scintigraphic techniques in demonstrating soft-tissue infections, primarily because of its superior spatial resolution. The proper evaluation of musculoskeletal infections with MRI requires both T1- and T2-weighted images in at least two imaging planes. In anatomically complex areas such as the pelvis, spine, foot, and hand, three planes may be necessary. Diagnostic criteria for MRI in diagnosing osteomyelitis are findings of decreased signal intensity in the bone marrow cavity on short spin-echo TR/TE sequences (T1 weighting)

FIGURE 24.11 MRI of osteomyelitis. Sagittal T2-weighted MR image (SE; TR 2000/TE 80 msec) shows a well-defined area of increased signal intensity in the medullary space of the midshaft of the femur (*arrows*), indicating acute hematogenous osteomyelitis in this intravenous drug user. There are soft-tissue inflammatory changes with multiple small abscesses adjacent to the cortex (*arrowheads*). (From Beltran J, 1990, with permission.)

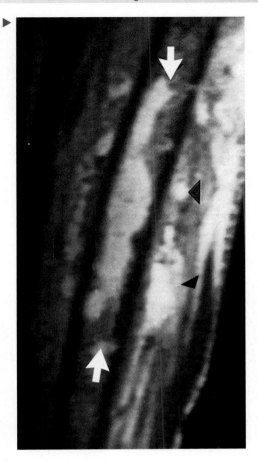

along with increased signal intensity in the bone marrow cavity on long TR/TE sequences (T2 weighting) (Fig. 24.11). Increased signal intensity of the soft tissues on long TR/TE sequences with poorly defined margins is considered indicative of edema and/or nonspecific inflammatory changes. Well-demarcated collections of decreased signal intensity on T1-weighted sequences and increased signal intensity surrounded by zones of decreased signal intensity on T2-weighted images are considered indicative of soft-tissue abscesses (Fig. 24.12). Decreased signal intensity on short TR/TE sequences and increased signal intensity on long TR/TE sequences in the area of the joint capsule or tendon sheath are consistent with synovial effusions and fluid in the tendon sheath.

Contrast enhancement using intravenous injection of gadolinium is routinely used for the diagnosis of musculoskeletal infections. This technique allows the differentiation of osteomyelitis from bone marrow edema or an abscess from cellulites or phlegmon in the soft tissues. The abscess demonstrates high–signal-intensity enhancement of its capsule, whereas the central portion remains of low signal intensity. Conversely, cellulites and phlegmon exhibit diffuse contrast enhancement.

FIGURE 24.12 MRI of soft-tissue abscess. Axial T2-weighted MR image (SE; TR 2000/TE 80 msec) shows high signal intensity of soft-tissue fluid collection anterior to the tibia, with a focus of lower signal intensity in the center, representing the soft-tissue abscess (*arrows*). The abscess is surrounded by a thick low-signal-intensity capsule. Note the high–signal-intensity edema diffusely involving the subcutaneous fat and muscles (*open arrow*). (From Beltran J, 1990, with permission.)

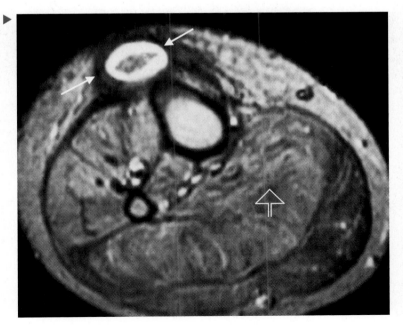

Invasive Procedures

Percutaneous aspiration and US-guided, CT-guided, or fluoroscopy-guided biopsy of a suspected focus of infection may be performed in the radiology suite. It can rapidly confirm a suspected diagnosis of infection and reveal the causative organism.

Monitoring the Treatment and Complications of Infections

Radiology plays an indispensable role in monitoring the treatment of infectious disorders of bone and associated soft tissues (Fig. 24.13). Follow-up radiographs and radionuclide bone scans should be obtained at regular intervals to evaluate the disease state (acute, subacute, chronic, or inactive) (Fig. 24.14) and any complications that may arise (Fig. 24.15). The differentiation of active from inactive osteomyelitis may, however, be extremely difficult by radiologic techniques. The extensive osteosclerotic changes in inactive infection may obscure small foci of osteolytic change signifying reactivation. CT may at times be helpful in delineating fluffy periostitis, poorly marginated areas of osteolysis, or sequestra.

The main complication of osteomyelitis in infants and children is growth disturbance if the focus of infection is in the vicinity of the growth plate (Fig. 24.16). Pathologic fracture is another common complication of osteomyelitis (Fig. 24.17). In adults, the most serious, although rare, complication is the development of a malignant neoplasm in a chronically draining sinus tract (see Fig. 22.34).

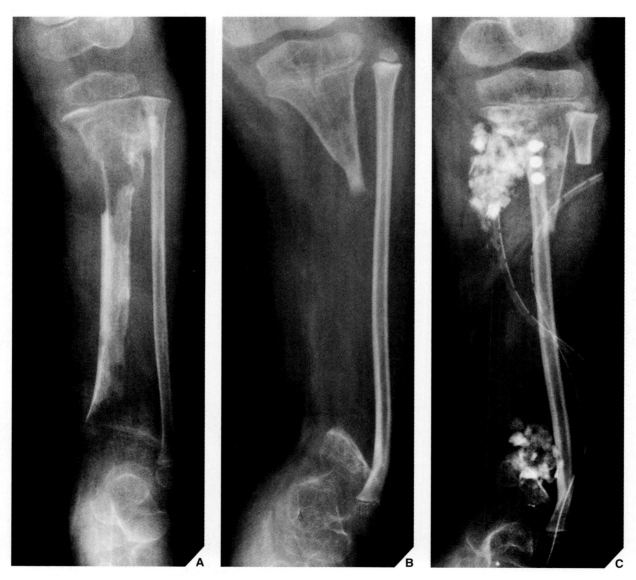

FIGURE 24.13 Treatment of osteomyelitis. A 3-year-old girl had osteomyelitis of the left tibia after chronic tonsillitis. (A) Anteroposterior radiograph of the left leg shows extensive destruction of the tibia with sequestration of the diaphysis. Extensive and long-standing conservative treatment using broad-spectrum antibiotics failed to produce any improvement. (B) One year later, the dead sequestered segment of the tibial diaphysis was resected as a first stage in reconstruction of the limb. (C) Two months later, a fibular graft was attached to the proximal stump of the tibial diaphysis, and bone chips were applied proximally and distally to ensure bony union and stability.

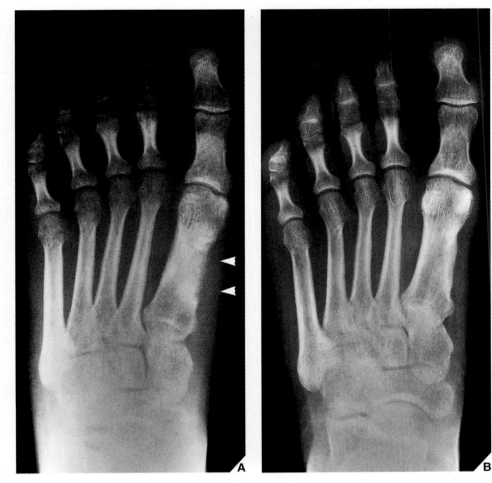

▲
FIGURE 24.14   **Treatment of osteomyelitis.** A 17-year-old girl had an acute pyogenic infection of the first metatarsal bone after a puncture injury of her right foot. (**A**) Anteroposterior radiograph demonstrates changes typical of active osteomyelitis: cortical and medullary bone destruction, a periosteal reaction, and diffuse soft-tissue swelling (*arrowheads*). Note also the significant periarticular osteoporosis. After extensive treatment with antibiotics, a radiograph of the foot (**B**) shows complete healing of the infection, which is in an inactive phase. There is residual endosteal sclerosis, but no destructive changes are evident and the soft-tissue planes are normal.

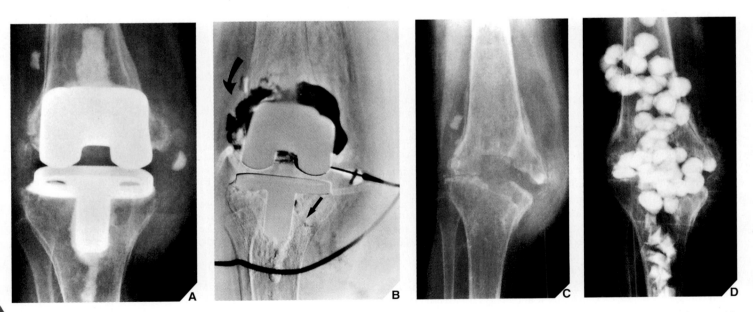

▲
FIGURE 24.15   **Treatment of joint infection after a total knee arthroplasty.** A 62-year-old woman had an infection of the right knee joint after total knee arthroplasty. (**A**) Anteroposterior radiograph shows the joint replacement with a condylar-type cemented prosthesis. Active infection is still evident, as demonstrated by the soft-tissue swelling, joint effusion, and periosteal reaction. Small foci of bone destruction are seen in the proximal tibia. (**B**) An aspiration arthrogram (subtraction study) demonstrates abnormal extension of contrast agent into osteolytic areas of the tibia (*arrow*). The irregular outline on the lateral aspect of the joint (*curved arrow*) is caused by synovitis. Bacteriologic examination of the aspirated material yielded *Staphylococcus aureus*. (**C**) After unsuccessful treatment of the infection with broad-spectrum antibiotics, the prosthesis had to be removed. Note the typical appearance of active osteomyelitis of distal femur and proximal tibia. (**D**) The treatment at this stage consisted of methylmethacrylate cement balls soaked with antibiotics and applied to the infected joint and medullary cavity of the femur and tibia.

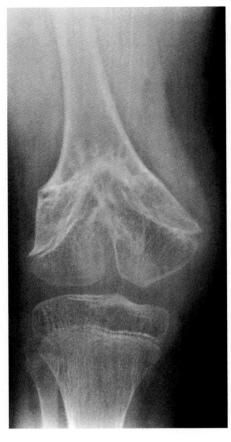

▲

FIGURE 24.16 Complication of osteomyelitis. Anteroposterior radiograph of the right knee of an 8-year-old girl shows a growth disturbance as a sequela of metaphyseal osteomyelitis. Note the hypoplasia of the femur secondary to disuse of the limb and the deformity of the distal epiphysis. The cone-shaped growth plate shows almost complete fusion.

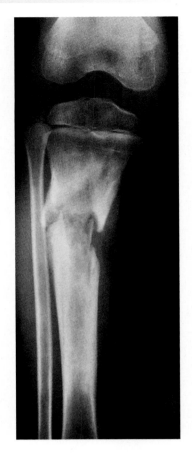

▲

FIGURE 24.17 Complication of osteomyelitis. Radiograph of the right leg of a 6-year-old boy with chronic active osteomyelitis of tibia shows a pathologic fracture, a complication of the infectious process.

PRACTICAL POINTS TO REMEMBER

[1] Three basic mechanisms allow an infectious organism to reach a bone or joint:
   • hematogenous spread
   • spread from a contiguous source
   • direct implantation.

[2] The metaphysis is the most common site of an infectious focus in children, primarily because of the nature of the osseous–vascular anatomy at this stage of development, whereas the shaft of a long bone is a common site of infection in adult patients.

[3] Radionuclide bone scan using ^{99m}Tc-labeled phosphonates is a very useful radiologic modality for distinguishing a joint infection from cellulitis of the periarticular soft tissues.

[4] The scintigraphic radiopharmaceuticals most specific for detection of musculoskeletal infection are gallium-67 citrate and ^{111}In oxine.

[5] MRI is more specific and more sensitive than scintigraphic techniques in demonstrating bone and soft-tissue infections, primarily because of its superior spatial resolution. Both T1- and T2-weighted sequences in at least two imaging planes should be obtained.

[6] Percutaneous aspiration biopsy of a suspected focus of infection is the most direct route for confirming a diagnosis and identifying the causative organism.

SUGGESTED READINGS

Abiri MM, Kirpekar M, Ablow RC. Osteomyelitis: detection with US. *Radiology* 1988;169:795–797.

Alazraki NP. Radionuclide imaging in the evaluation of infectious and inflammatory disease. *Radiol Clin North Am* 1993;31:783–794.

Al-Sheikh W, Sfakianakis GN, Mnaymneh W, et al. Subacute and chronic bone infections: diagnosis using In-111, Ga-67 and Tc-99m MDP bone scintigraphy, and radiography. *Radiology* 1985;155:501–506.

Bassett LW, Gold RH, Webber MM. Radionuclide bone imaging. *Radiol Clin North Am* 1981;19:675–702.

Becker W, Goldenberg DM, Wolf F. The use of monoclonal antibodies and antibody fragments in the imaging of infectious lesions. *Semin Nucl Med* 1994;24:142–153.

Beltran J. *MRI: musculoskeletal system.* Philadelphia: JB Lippincott; 1990.

Beltran J, McGhee RB, Shaffer PB, et al. Experimental infections of the musculoskeletal system: evaluation with MR imaging and Tc-99m MDP and Ga-67 scintigraphy. *Radiology* 1988;161:167–172.

Butalia S, Palda VA, Sargeant RJ, Detsky AS, Mourad O. Does this patient with diabetes has osteomyelitis of the lower extremity? *JAMA* 2008;299:806–813.

Beltran J, Noto AM, McGhee RB, Freedy RM, McCalla MS. Infections of the musculoskeletal system: high field-strength MR imaging. *Radiology* 1987;164:449–454.

Butt WP. The radiology of infection. *Clin Orthop* 1973;96:20–30.

Capitanio MA, Kirkpatrick JA. Early roentgen observations in acute osteomyelitis. *Am J Roentgenol* 1970;108:488–496.

Dagirmanjian A, Schills J, McHenry M, Modic MT. MR imaging of vertebral osteomyelitis revisited. *Am J Roentgenol* 1996;167:1539–1543.

Dangman BC, Hoffer FA, Rand FF, O'Rourke EJ. Osteomyelitis in children: gadolinium-enhanced MR imaging. *Radiology* 1992;182:743–747.

Datz FL. The current status of radionuclide infection imaging. In: Freeman LM, ed. *Nuclear medicine annual*. New York: Raven Press; 1993:47–76.

Datz FL. Indium-111-labeled leukocytes for the detection of infection: current status. *Semin Nucl Med* 1994;24:92–109.

Datz FL, Morton KA. New radiopharmaceuticals for detecting infection. *Invest Radiol* 1993;28:356–365.

Erdman WA, Tamburro F, Jayson HT, Weatherall PT, Ferry KB, Peshock RM. Osteomyelitis: characteristics and pitfalls of diagnosis with MR imaging. *Radiology* 1991;180:533–539.

Fox IN, Zeiger L. Tc-99m-HMPAO leukocyte scintigraphy for the diagnosis of osteomyelitis in diabetic foot infections. *J Foot Ankle Surg* 1993;32:591–594.

Gold RH, Hawkins RA, Katz RD. Bacterial osteomyelitis: findings on plain radiography, CT, MR, and scintigraphy. *Am J Roentgenol* 1991;157:365–370.

Guhlmann A, Brecht-Krauss D, Suger G, et al. Chronic osteomyelitis: detection with FDG PET and correlation with histopathologic findings. *Radiology* 1998;206:749–754.

Harcke HT, Grissom LE. Musculoskeletal ultrasound in pediatrics. *Semin Musculoskel Radiol* 1998;2:321–329.

Hoffer P. Gallium: mechanisms. *J Nucl Med* 1980;21:282–285.

Hopkins KL, Li KCP, Bergman G. Gadolinium-DTPA-enhanced magnetic resonance imaging of musculoskeletal infectious processes. *Skeletal Radiol* 1995;24:325–330.

Howie DW, Savage JP, Wilson TG, Paterson D. The technetium phosphate bone scan in the diagnosis of osteomyelitis in childhood. *J Bone Joint Surg [Am]* 1983;65A:431–437.

Israel O, Gips S, Jerushalmi J, Frenkel A, Front D. Osteomyelitis and soft-tissue infection: Differential diagnosis with 24 hour/4 hour ratios of Tc-99m MDP uptake. *Radiology* 1987;163:725–726.

Jacobson AF, Harley JD, Lipsky BA, Pecoraro RE. Diagnosis of osteomyelitis in the presence of soft-tissue infection and radiologic evidence of osseous abnormalities: value of leukocyte scintigraphy. *Am J Roentgenol* 1991;157:807–812.

Jaramillo D, Treves ST, Kasser JR, Harper M, Sundel R, Laor T. Osteomyelitis and septic arthritis in children: appropriate use of imaging to guide treatment. *Am J Roentgenol* 1995;165:399–403.

Kaim A, Maurer T, Ochsner P, Jundt G, Kirsch E, Mueller-Brandt J. Chronic complicated osteomyelitis of the appendicular skeleton: diagnosis with technetium-99m labelled monoclonal antigranulocyte antibody-immunoscintigraphy. *Eur J Nucl Med* 1997;24:732–738.

King AD, Peters AM, Stuttle AWJ, Lavender JP. Imaging of bone infection with labeled white cells: role of contemporaneous bone marrow imaging. *Eur J Nucl Med* 1990;17:148–151.

Krznaric E, DeRoo M, Verbruggen A, Stuyck J, Mortelmans L. Chronic osteomyelitis: diagnosis with technetium-99m-d, 1-hexamethylpropylene amine oxime labelled leucocytes. *Eur J Nucl Med* 1996;23:792–797.

Lantto T, Kaukonen J-P, Kokkola A, Laitinen R, Vorne M. Tc-99m HMPAO labeled leukocytes superior to bone scan in the detection of osteomyelitis in children. *Clin Nucl Med* 1992;17:7–17.

Lee SK, Suh KJ, Kim YW, et al. Septic arthritis versus transient synovitis at MR imaging: preliminary assessment with signal intensity alterations in bone marrow. *Radiology* 1999;211:459–465.

Lewin JS, Rosenfield NS, Hoffer PB, Downing D. Acute osteomyelitis in children: combined Tc-99m and Ga-67 imaging. *Radiology* 1986;158:795–804.

Lipsky BA. Osteomyelitis of the foot in diabetic patients. *Clin Infect Dis* 1997;25:1318–1326.

McGuinness B, Wilson N, Doyle AJ. The "penumbra" sign on T1-weighted MRI for differentiating musculoskeletal infection from tumour. *Skeletal Radiol* 2007;36:417–421.

Miller TT, Randolph DA Jr, Staron RB, Feldman F, Cushin S. Fat-suppressed MR of musculoskeletal infection: fast T2-weighted techniques versus gadolinium-enhanced T1-weighted images. *Skeletal Radiol* 1997;26:654–658.

Modic MT, Feiglin DH, Piraino DW, et al. Vertebral osteomyelitis: assessment using MR. *Radiology* 1985;157:157–166.

Modic MT, Pflanze W, Feiglin DHI, Belhobek G. Magnetic resonance imaging of musculoskeletal infections. *Radiol Clin North Am* 1986;24:247–258.

Morrison WB, Schweitzer ME, Bock GW, Mitchell DG. Diagnosis of osteomyelitis: utility of fat-suppressed contrast-enhanced MR images. *Radiology* 1993;189:251–257.

Morrison WB, Schweitzer ME, Wapner KL, Hecht PJ, Gannon FH, Behm WR. Osteomyelitis in feet of diabetics: clinical accuracy, surgical utility, and cost-effectiveness of MR imaging. *Radiology* 1995;196:557–564.

Numaguchi Y, Rigamonti D, Rothman MI, Sato S. Spinal epidural abscess: evaluation with gadolinium-enhanced MR imaging. *Radiographics* 1993;13:545–559.

Paajanen H, Grodd W, Revel D, Engelstad B, Brasch RC. Gadolinium-DTPA enhanced MR imaging of intramuscular abscesses. *Magn Reson Imaging* 1987;5:109–115.

Palestro CJ, Love C, Tronco GG, Tomas MB, Rini JN. Combined labeled leukocyte and technetium 99m sulfur colloid bone marrow imaging for diagnosing musculoskeletal infection. *Radiographics* 2006;26:859–870.

Palestro CJ, Roumanas P, Swyer AJ, Kim CK, Goldsmith SJ. Diagnosis of musculoskeletal infection using combined In-111 labeled leukocyte and Tc-99m SC marrow imaging. *Clin Nucl Med* 1992;17:269–273.

Peters AM. The utility of [99mTc] HMPAO-leukocytes for imaging infection. *Semin Nucl Med* 1994;24:110–127.

Schauerwecker DS. The role of nuclear medicine in osteomyelitis. In: Collier BD Jr, Fogelman I, Rosenthall L, eds. *Skeletal nuclear medicine*. St. Louis: CV Mosby; 1996:183–202.

Schauwecker DS. Osteomyelitis: diagnosis with In-111-labeled leukocytes. *Radiology* 1989;171:141–146.

Schauwecker DS. The scintigraphic diagnosis of osteomyelitis. *Am J Roentgenol* 1992;158:9–18.

Seabold JE, Flickinger FW, Kao SCS, et al. Indium-111 leukocyte/technetium-99m-MDP bone and magnetic resonance imaging: difficulty of diagnosing osteomyelitis in patients with neuropathic osteoarthropathy. *J Nucl Med* 1990;31:549–556.

Sorsdahl OA, Goodhart GL, Williams HT, Hanna LJ, Rodriquez J. Quantitative bone gallium scintigraphy in osteomyelitis. *Skeletal Radiol* 1993;22:239–242.

Stöver B, Sigmund G, Langer M, Brandis M. MRI in diagnostic evaluation of osteomyelitis in children. *Eur Radiol* 1994;4:347–352.

Tigges S, Stiles RG, Roberson JR. Appearance of septic hip prostheses on plain radiographs. *Am J Roentgenol* 1994;163:377–380.

Tsan M. Mechanism of gallium-67 accumulation in inflammatory lesions. *J Nucl Med* 1985;26:88–92.

Tumeh SS, Aliabadi P, Weissman BN, McNeil BJ. Chronic osteomyelitis: bone and gallium scan patterns associated with active disease. *Radiology* 1986;158:685–688.

Unger E, Moldofsky P, Gatenby R, Hartz W, Broder G. Diagnosis of osteomyelitis by MR imaging. *Am J Roentgenol* 1988;150:605–610.

Van Holsbeeck M, Introcaso JH. *Musculoskeletal ultrasound*. St. Louis: Mosby-Year Book; 1991:207–229.

Vartanians VM, Karchmer AW, Giurini JM, Rosenthal DI. Is there a role for imaging in the management of patients with diabetic foot? *Skeletal Radiol* 2009;38:633–636.

Wang A, Weinstein D, Greenfield L, et al. MRI and diabetic foot infections. *Magn Reson Imaging* 1990;8:805–809.

Yuh WT, Corson JD, Baraniewski HM, et al. Osteomyelitis of the foot in diabetic patients: evaluation with plain film, 99mTc-MDP bone scintigraphy, and MR imaging. *Am J Roentgenol* 1989;152:795–800.

Zeiger LS, Fox IN. Use of indium-111 labeled white blood cells in the diagnosis of diabetic foot infections. *J Foot Ankle Surg* 1990;29:46–51.

Osteomyelitis, Infectious Arthritis, and Soft-Tissue Infections

Osteomyelitis

Osteomyelitis can generally be divided into pyogenic and nonpyogenic types. The former may be further classified, on the basis of clinical findings, as subacute, acute, or chronic (active and inactive), depending on the intensity of the infectious process and its associated symptoms. From the viewpoint of anatomic pathology, osteomyelitis can be divided into diffuse and localized (focal) forms, with the latter referred to as bone abscesses.

Pyogenic Bone Infections

Acute and Chronic Osteomyelitis

The earliest radiographic signs of bone infection are soft-tissue edema and loss of fascial planes. These are usually encountered within 24 to 48 hours of the onset of infection. The earliest changes in the bone are evidence of a destructive lytic lesion, usually within 7 to 10 days after the onset of infection (Fig. 25.1), and a positive radionuclide bone scan. Within 2 to 6 weeks, there is progressive destruction of cortical and medullary bone, an increased endosteal sclerosis indicating reactive new bone formation, and a periosteal reaction (Fig. 25.2). In 6 to 8 weeks, sequestra indicating areas of necrotic bone usually become apparent; they are surrounded by a dense involucrum, representing a sheath of periosteal new bone (Fig. 25.3). The sequestra, which can be effectively demonstrated with computed tomography (CT) (Fig. 25.4), and involucra develop as the result of an accumulation of inflammatory exudate (pus), which penetrates the cortex and strips it of periosteum, thus stimulating the inner layer to form new bone. The newly formed bone is in turn infected, and the resultant barrier causes the cortex and spongiosa to be deprived of a blood supply and to become necrotic. At this stage, termed *chronic osteomyelitis*, a draining sinus tract often forms (Fig. 25.5; see also Figs. 24.7 and 24.10B). Small sequestra are gradually resorbed, or they may be extruded through the sinus tract.

Subacute Osteomyelitis

Brodie Abscess. This lesion, originally described by Brodie in 1832, represents a subacute localized form of osteomyelitis, commonly caused by *Staphylococcus aureus*. The highest incidence (approximately 40%) is in the second decade. More than 75% of cases occur in male patients. Its onset is often insidious, and systemic manifestations

are generally mild or absent. The abscess, which is usually localized in the metaphysis of the tibia or femur, is typically elongated, with a well-demarcated margin and surrounded by reactive sclerosis. As a rule, sequestra are absent, but a radiolucent tract may be seen extending from the lesion into the growth plate (Fig. 25.6). A bone abscess may often cross the epiphyseal plate, but seldom does an abscess develop in and remain localized to the epiphysis (Fig. 25.7; see also Fig. 24.8).

Nonpyogenic Bone Infections

The most common nonpyogenic bone infections are tuberculosis, syphilis, and fungal infections.

Tuberculous Infections

Tuberculous bone infection usually occurs secondarily as a result of hematogenous spread from a primary focus of infection such as the lung or genitourinary tract. Skeletal tuberculosis represents approximately 3% of all cases of tuberculosis and approximately 30% of all extrapulmonary tuberculous infections. In 10% to 15% of cases, bone involvement without articular disease is encountered. In children, tuberculous osteomyelitis has a predilection for the metaphyseal segment of the long bones; in adults, the joints are more often affected.

In the long and short bones, progressive destruction of the medullary region with abscess formation is apparent on radiography. Typically, there is evidence of osteoporosis but, at least in the early stage of the disease, little or no reactive sclerosis is usually present (Fig. 25.8). Occasionally, destruction in the mid diaphysis of a short tubular bone of the hand or foot (*tuberculous dactylitis*) may produce a fusiform enlargement of the entire diaphysis, a condition known as spina ventosa (Fig. 25.9). The appearance of multiple disseminated lytic lesions in short tubular bones is termed cystic tuberculosis, a form of skeletal tuberculosis seen particularly in children.

Fungal Infections

Fungal bone infections are infrequent, the most common being coccidioidomycosis, blastomycosis, actinomycosis, cryptococcosis, and nocardiosis. The infection is usually low grade, with the formation of an abscess and a draining sinus. The lesion may resemble a tuberculous skeletal infection, because the abscess is usually found in cancellous bone with little or no reactive sclerosis or periosteal response (Fig. 25.10). The location of

FIGURE 25.1   Acute osteomyelitis. A 7-year-old boy ▶ had a fever and a painful knee for 1 week. Anteroposterior radiograph of the left knee demonstrates the earliest radiographic signs of bone infection: a poorly defined osteolytic area of destruction in the metaphyseal segment of the distal femur (*arrow*) and soft-tissue swelling (*open arrows*).

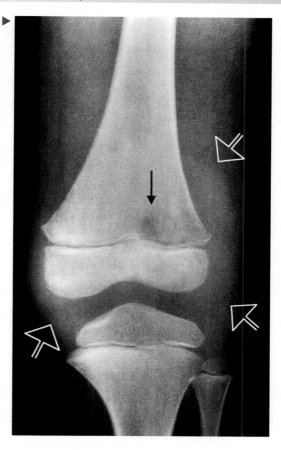

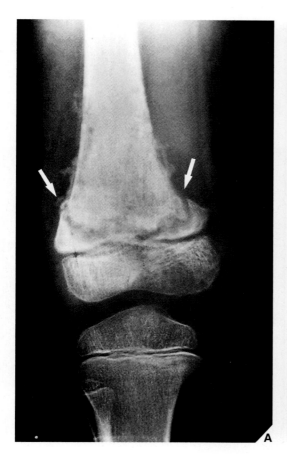

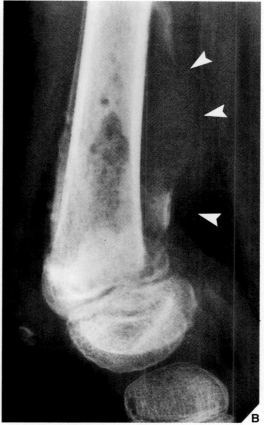

▲

FIGURE 25.2   Acute osteomyelitis. Anteroposterior (**A**) and lateral (**B**) radiographs of the knee of an 8-year-old boy with acute osteomyelitis show widespread destruction of the cortical and medullary portions of the metaphysis and diaphysis of the distal femur, together with periosteal new bone formation. Note the pathologic fracture (*arrows*). On the lateral view, a large subperiosteal abscess is evident (*arrow heads*).

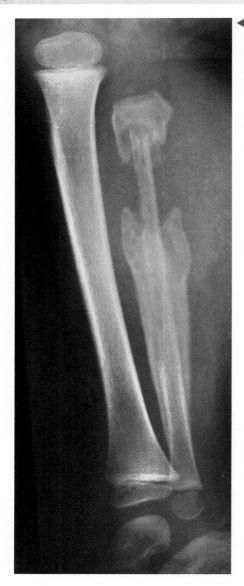

◄ FIGURE 25.3 **Active osteomyelitis.** Sequestra surrounded by involucrum, as seen here in the left fibula of a 2-year-old child, is a feature of advanced osteomyelitis, usually apparent after 6 to 8 weeks of active infection. (Courtesy of Dr. R.H. Gold, Los Angeles, California.)

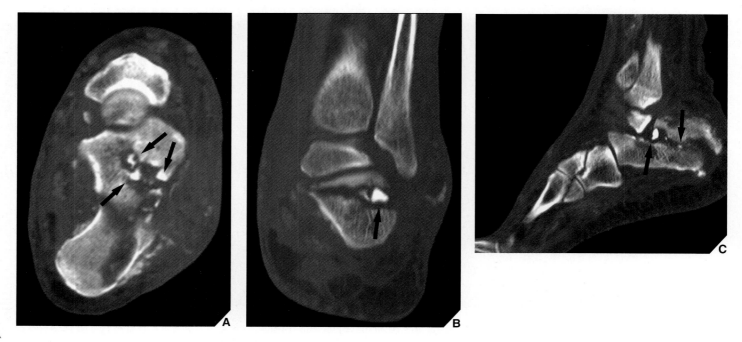

▲

FIGURE 25.4 **CT of active osteomyelitis. (A)** Axial, **(B)** coronal reformatted, and **(C)** sagittal reformatted CT images of the left foot of a 72-year-old diabetic man demonstrate an active osteomyelitis of the calcaneus. Note several high-attenuation osseous fragments representing sequestra (*arrows*).

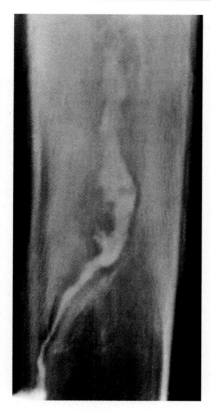

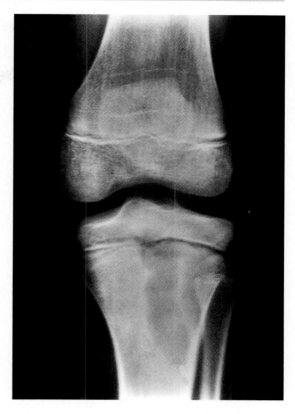

▲
FIGURE 25.5 Chronic osteomyelitis. A 28-year-old man with sickle-cell disease developed osteomyelitis, a frequent complication of this condition. A sinogram shows a draining sinus typical of chronic osteomyelitis. Note the extent of the serpentine tract in the medullary portion of the bone.

▲
FIGURE 25.6 Bone absess. Anteroposterior radiograph of the left knee of an 11-year-old boy with a subacute Brodie abscess in the proximal diaphysis and metaphysis of the tibia shows a radiolucent tract extending into the growth plate.

FIGURE 25.7 Bone abscess. Anteroposterior ▶ radiograph of the left knee of a 13-year-old boy demonstrates a well-defined osteolytic lesion surrounded by reactive sclerosis in the distal epiphysis of the femur (arrow). This is a rare site for a bone abscess.

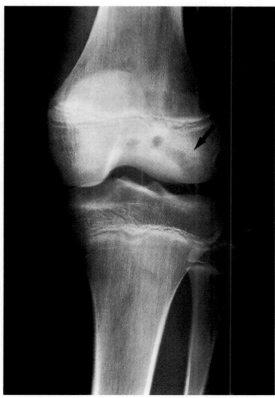

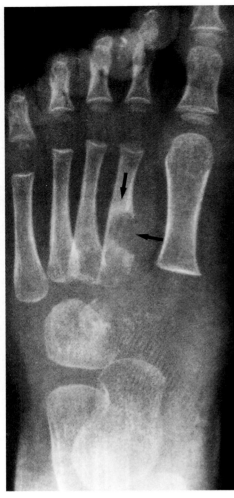

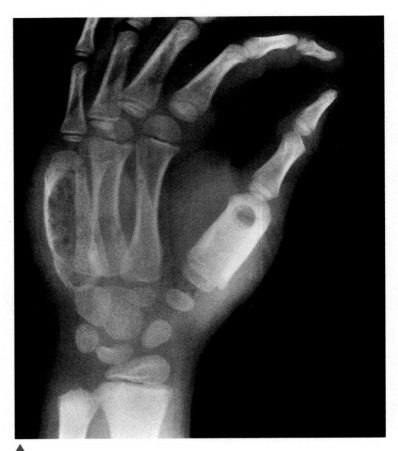

▲

FIGURE 25.8 Tuberculosis of bone. A 20-month-old girl had progressive swelling of the right foot. Anteroposterior radiograph shows a well-defined lytic defect in the medial aspect of the second metatarsal (*arrows*); there is no evidence of reactive sclerosis or periosteal new bone formation, but soft-tissue swelling is apparent. Aspiration of a mass yielded 1 mL of pus-like fluid, which on bacteriologic examination revealed acid-fast bacteria. The causative agent proved to be *Mycobacterium tuberculosis.*

▲

FIGURE 25.9 Tuberculosis of bone. Oblique film of the right hand of a 7-year-old boy shows expansive fusiform lesions of the first and fifth metacarpals associated with soft-tissue swelling; there is no evidence of a periosteal reaction. Such diaphyseal enlargement secondary to tuberculosis is known as spina ventosa.

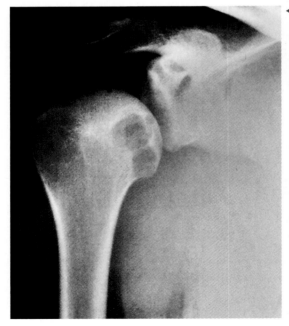

◀ **FIGURE 25.10 Cryptococcosis of bone.** Anteroposterior radiograph of the right shoulder of an 18-year-old man demonstrates a destructive osteolytic lesion in the medial aspect of the humeral head, with minimal sclerosis and no periosteal reaction—the typical appearance of a fungal infection. Aspiration biopsy showed the abscess to be caused by a cryptococcal infection.

a lesion at a point of bony prominence—such as along the edges of the patella, the ends of the clavicles, or in the acromion, coracoid process, olecranon, or styloid process of the radius or ulna—may also suggest a fungal infection. Solitary marginal lesions of the ribs and lesions involving the vertebrae in an indiscriminate fashion, including the body, neural arch, and spinous and transverse processes, also favor fungal infectious process.

Among the fungal infections, coccidioidomycosis is of particular importance, not only because of an increase in the number of these infections in recent years but also because it may closely resemble skeletal tuberculosis. It is a systemic disease caused by the soil fungus *Coccidioides immitis*. This infection is endemic throughout the southwestern United States and the bordering regions of northern Mexico. Infection occurs through inhalation of dust containing the organism. The primary site of infection is the lung, and disease is commonly asymptomatic. Dissemination of coccidioidomycosis is rare, but the incidence is increased in patients with specific risk factors. Those at increased risk include African Americans, Filipinos, Mexicans, males, pregnant women, children younger than 5 years, adults older than 50 years, and immunosuppressed patients. Patients with disseminated coccidioidomycosis usually present during the course of primary pulmonary infection. However, some patients with disseminated disease may have no clinical history or radiographic evidence of pulmonary disease. The skin and subcutaneous tissues are the most common sites of disseminated coccidioidal infection, followed by mediastinal involvement. The skeletal system is the third most common site of dissemination, and osseous manifestations occur in 10% to 50% of patients with disseminated disease.

Radiographic presentation of the lesion of coccidioidomycosis is variable, but it is usually characterized by well-marginated, punched-out osteolytic lesions, typically involving long and flat bones. The lesions are typically unilocular but occasionally may be multiloculated. The other pattern frequently observed is a permeative type of bone destruction, only occasionally accompanied by periosteal reaction. Soft-tissue swelling and osteoporosis are much more common with the permeative pattern than with the punched-out lesions. The third most common pattern is joint involvement (septic arthritis), usually monoarticular and almost invariably associated with osseous involvement. Changes typically seen in joints include periarticular osteoporosis, a permeative/destructive pattern involving both articular surfaces, soft-tissue swelling, and occasional periostitis. Joint involvement in coccidioidomycosis is indistinguishable from that seen with tuberculosis. Involvement of the spine most commonly manifests as vertebral osteomyelitis or rarely as disk space infection (spondylodiskitis). In the former variant, both punched-out and permeative lesions are observed in the vertebral bodies. Cases with almost complete vertebral destruction have also been reported. Coccidioidomycosis often involves the vertebral appendages, and paraspinal soft-tissue extension is common. Disk space narrowing and gibbous deformity, although previously reported, are unusual findings in coccidioidomycosis, whereas both these findings are common in tuberculosis.

Scintigraphy is valuable in the evaluation of patients with disseminated coccidioidomycosis. Radionuclide scans using gallium-67 (^{67}Ga) citrate and technetium-99m (^{99m}Tc) methylene diphosphonate (MDP) have been used to localize disease and can identify disseminated lesions that are clinically unsuspected. No false-negative bone scans have been reported. CT and magnetic resonance imaging (MRI) are helpful in defining bony involvement and in determining the extent of soft-tissue disease (Fig. 25.11). The lesions exhibit low attenuation, often appearing bubbly and expansive. On

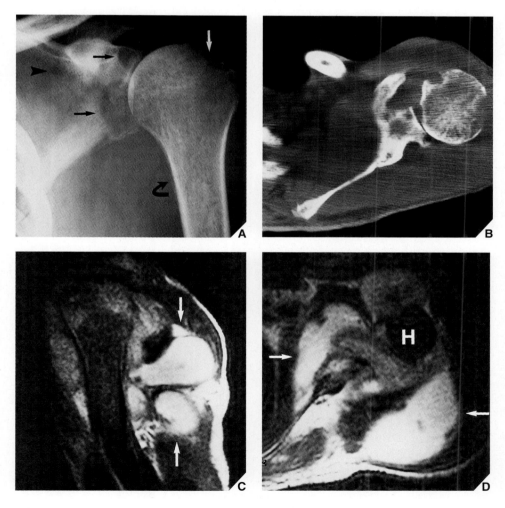

FIGURE 25.11   Coccidioidomycosis of bone. A 42-year-old man presented with a 4-week history of pain and decreased range of motion in the left shoulder. He had been previously hospitalized for pulmonary coccidioidomycosis. (**A**) Anteroposterior radiograph shows several osteolytic lesions affecting the superolateral aspect of the humeral head and glenoid (*arrows*). Small punched-out lesion is noted in the body of the scapula (*arrowhead*). The *curved arrow* points to periosteal reaction along the medial humeral shaft. (**B**) A CT section reveals erosions of the anterior and posterolateral aspects of the humeral head. Also apparent are destruction of the articular surfaces of the humeral head and glenoid and narrowing of the glenohumeral joint. (**C**) Sagittal and (**D**) axial fast-spin echo (TR 4000/TE 102 msec) MR images show multiple, well-defined soft-tissue abscesses displaying high signal intensity (*arrows*). H, humeral head.

MRI, the lesions show decreased signal on T1-weighted images, with a corresponding increase on T2-weighted and gradient-echo sequences.

Recently, osteomyelitis caused by *Nocardia asteroids* has been reported in patients with human immunodeficiency virus (HIV) infection who developed aquired immune deficiency syndrome (AIDS). The clinical and imaging manifestations of this infectious process closely resemble those of tuberculosis. The most cases of *Nocardia* osteomyelitis resulted from direct extension of soft-tissue infection; however, hematogenous dissemination has also been reported.

Syphilitic Infection

Syphilis is a chronic systemic infectious disease caused by a spirochete, *Treponema pallidum*. *Congenital syphilis*, which is transmitted from mother to fetus, may manifest as a chronic osteochondritis, periostitis, or osteitis. The lesions, which most frequently involve the tibia, are characteristically widespread and symmetric in appearance; destructive changes are usually seen in the metaphysis at the junction with the growth plate, producing what is called the Wimberger sign (Fig. 25.12). In the later stages of disease, involvement of the tibia results in a characteristic anterior bowing known as "saber-shin" deformity.

Acquired syphilis may manifest either as a chronic osteitis exhibiting irregular sclerosis of the medullary cavity or as syphilitic abscesses known as gumma (Fig. 25.13). The latter form of the disease may simulate pyogenic osteomyelitis, but the absence of sequestra typically found in bacterial osteomyelitis allows the distinction to be made.

Differential Diagnosis of Osteomyelitis

Usually, the radiographic appearance of osteomyelitis is so characteristic that the diagnosis is easily made with the clinical history, and ancillary radiologic examinations such as scintigraphy, CT, and MRI are rarely needed. Nevertheless, osteomyelitis may at times mimic other conditions. Particularly in its acute form, it may resemble Langerhans cell histiocytosis or Ewing sarcoma (Fig. 25.14). The soft-tissue changes in each of these conditions, however, are characteristic and different. In osteomyelitis, soft-tissue swelling is diffuse, with obliteration of the fascial planes, whereas Langerhans cell histiocytosis, as a rule, is not accompanied by significant soft-tissue swelling or a mass. The extension of a Ewing sarcoma into the soft tissues presents as a well-defined soft-tissue mass with preservation of the fascial planes. The duration of a patient's symptoms also plays an important diagnostic role. It takes a tumor such as a Ewing sarcoma from 4 to 6 months to destroy the bone to the same extent that osteomyelitis does in 4 to 6 weeks and that Langerhans cell histiocytosis does in only 7 to 10 days. Despite these differentiating features, however, the radiographic pattern of bone destruction, periosteal reaction, and location in the bone may be very similar in all three conditions (see Fig. 22.10).

A bone abscess, particularly in the cortex, may closely simulate a nidus of osteoid osteoma (see Fig. 17.18). In the medullary region, however, the presence of a serpentine tract favors the diagnosis of bone abscess over osteoid osteoma (Fig. 25.15).

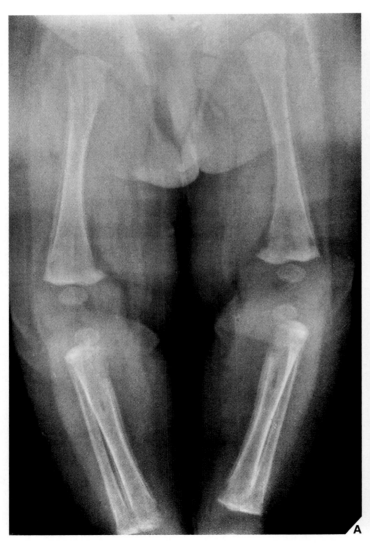
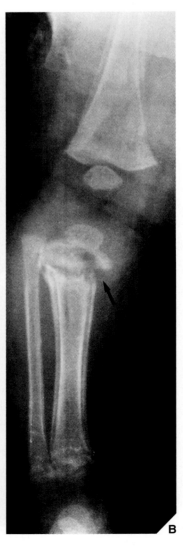

▲
FIGURE 25.12   **Congenital syphilis of bone. (A)** Anteroposterior radiograph of the lower legs of a 7-week-old infant with congenital syphilis demonstrates characteristic periostitis affecting the femora and tibiae. In addition, destructive changes are evident in the medullary portion of the proximal tibiae. **(B)** Two months later, the infectious process has progressed, with destruction of the tibial metaphysis and marked periostitis. The characteristic erosion of the medial surface of the proximal tibial metaphysis is termed the Wimberger sign (*arrow*).

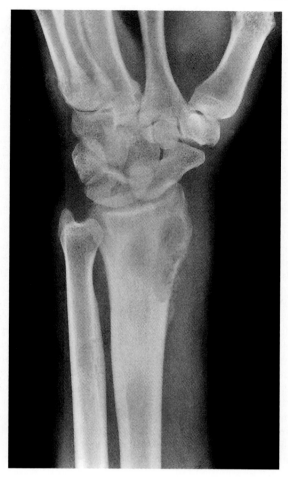

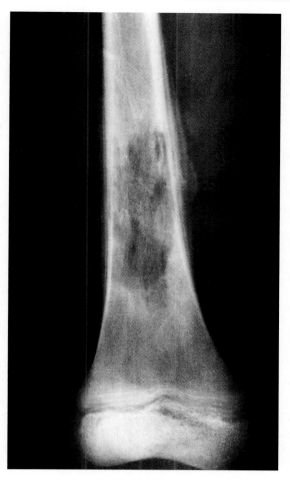

▲

FIGURE 25.13 Acquired syphilis of bone. Oblique radiograph of the distal forearm of a 51-year-old man shows a lytic abscess (gumma) in the lateral aspect of the distal radius.

▲

FIGURE 25.14 Osteomyelitis resembling Ewing sarcoma. A 7-year-old boy presented with pain in his right leg for 3 weeks. Anteroposterior radiograph demonstrates a lesion in the medullary portion of the distal femoral diaphysis with a moth-eaten type of bone destruction, associated with a lamellated periosteal reaction and a small soft-tissue prominence. These radiographic features suggest a diagnosis of Ewing sarcoma. The absence of a definite soft-tissue mass and the short symptomatic period, however, point to the correct diagnosis of osteomyelitis, which was confirmed by biopsy.

FIGURE 25.15 Bone abscess resembling osteoid osteoma. ▶ A 17-year-old boy had a typical history of osteoid osteoma: nocturnal bone pain relieved promptly by salicylates. Anteroposterior radiograph of the distal forearm demonstrates a radiolucent lesion in the distal ulnar diaphysis. The presence of a serpentine tract extending from the radiolucent focus into the growth plate (*arrow heads*) indicates a diagnosis of bone abscess.

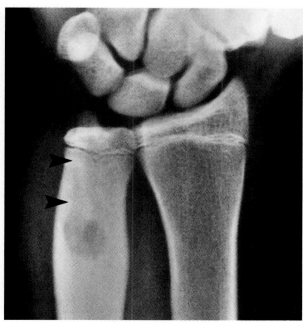

Infectious Arthritides

Most infectious arthritides demonstrate a positive radionuclide bone scan and a very similar radiographic picture, including joint effusion and destruction of cartilage and subchondral bone with consequent joint space narrowing (see Figs. 12.23 and 12.25). However, certain clinical and radiographic features are characteristic of individual infectious processes as demonstrated at various target sites (Table 25.1).

Pyogenic Joint Infections

The clinical signs and symptoms of pyogenic (septic) arthritis depend on the site and extent of involvement as well as the specific infectious organism. Although most cases of septic arthritis are caused by *Staphylococcus aureus* and *Neisseria gonorrhoeae*, other pathogens—including *Pseudomonas aeruginosa*, *Enterobacter cloacae*, *Klebsiella pneumoniae*, *Candida albicans*, and *Serratia marcescens*—are being encountered with increasing frequency in joint infections in drug users caused by the contamination of injected drugs or needles.

Any small or large joint can be affected by septic arthritis, and hematogenous spread in drug addicts is characterized by unusual locations of the lesion, such as the spine (vertebrae and intervertebral disks), sacroiliac joints, sternoclavicular and acromioclavicular articulations, and pubic symphysis.

Conventional radiography usually suffices to demonstrate septic arthritis. Certain characteristic radiographic features may be helpful in arriving at the correct diagnosis. Generally, a single joint is affected, most commonly a weight-bearing joint like the knee or hip. The early stage of joint infection may be seen simply as joint effusion, soft-tissue swelling, and periarticular osteoporosis (Fig. 25.16).

In the later phase of pyogenic arthritis, articular cartilage is destroyed; characteristically, both subarticular plates are involved and the joint space narrows (Fig. 25.17A). Arthrography, which is often performed after aspiration of the joint to obtain a fluid specimen for bacteriologic examination, helps determine the extent of joint destruction and demonstrate the presence of synovitis (Fig. 25.17B). Radionuclide bone scan is often effective in distinguishing a joint infection from a periarticular soft-tissue infection (see Fig. 24.9). It is also useful in monitoring the progress of treatment, although several weeks may be required before the scan demonstrates a completely normal appearance.

Complications

Infectious arthritis of peripheral joints in children may lead to the destruction of the growth plate, with resulting growth arrest (see Fig. 24.16). The infection may also spread to an adjacent bone, causing osteomyelitis. Degenerative arthritis and intraarticular bony ankylosis may also occur.

Nonpyogenic Joint Infections

Tuberculous Arthritis

Tuberculous arthritis represents 1% of all forms of extrapulmonary tuberculosis, although the number of cases has recently been on the rise. The acid-fast tubercle bacilli *Mycobacterium tuberculosis* and *Mycobacterium bovi* are the causative organisms. The infection may be found in all groups, but more frequently in children and young adults. Predisposing factors such as trauma, alcoholism, drug abuse, intraarticular injection of steroids, or prolonged systemic illness are found in most patients with tuberculous arthritis. The joint infection usually is caused by either direct invasion from an adjacent focus of osteomyelitis or hematogenous dissemination of the tubercle bacillus. Large weight-bearing joints such as the hip or knee are most often affected, and monoarticular involvement is the rule.

Conventional radiography is usually sufficient to demonstrate the identifying features of tuberculous arthritis, although its early radiographic appearance is often indistinguishable from that of monoarticular rheumatoid arthritis. However, the involvement of only one joint, as demonstrated by scintigraphy, favors an infectious process (Fig. 25.18). A triad of radiographic abnormalities (Phemister triad), comprised of

TABLE 25.1   **Clinical and Radiographic Hallmarks of Infectious Arthritis at Various Target Sites**

Type	Site	Crucial Abnormalities	Techniques/Projections
*Pyogenic Infections**	Peripheral joints	Periarticular osteoporosis	Radionuclide bone scan (early)
		Joint effusion	Standard views specific for site of involvement
		Destruction of subchondral bone (on both sides of joint)	Aspiration and arthrography
	Spine	Narrowing of disk space	Anteroposterior and lateral views
		Loss of definition of vertebral end plate	
		Paraspinal mass	CT, MRI
		Partial or complete obstruction of intrathecal contrast flow	Myelogram
		Destruction of disk	Diskogram and aspiration
Nonpyogenic Infections			
Tuberculosis	Large joints	Monoarticular involvement (similar to rheumatoid arthritis)	Radionuclide bone scan
		"Kissing" sequestra (knee)	Standard views
		Sclerotic changes in subchondral bone	CT
	Spine	Gibbous formation	Anteroposterior and lateral views
		Lytic lesion in vertebral body	
		Destruction of disk	Diskogram and aspiration
		Paraspinal mass	CT, MRI
		Soft-tissue abscess ("cold" abscess)	
		Obstruction of intrathecal contrast flow	Myelogram
Lyme disease	Knee	Narrowing of femoropatellar compartment	Lateral view
		Edematous changes in infrapatellar fat pad	CT, MRI

*In IV drug users, unusual sites of infection are encountered, including the vertebra; the sacroiliac, sternoclavicular, and acromioclavicular joints; and the pubic symphysis. The radiologic techniques used to evaluate infections at these sites, as well as the crucial radiographic abnormalities, are the same as those for the more common sites.

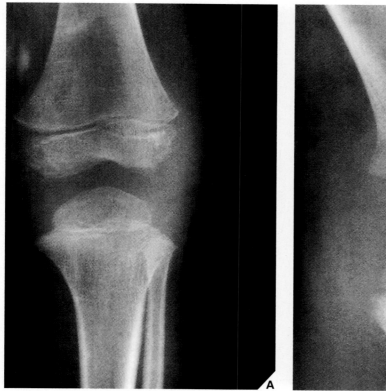
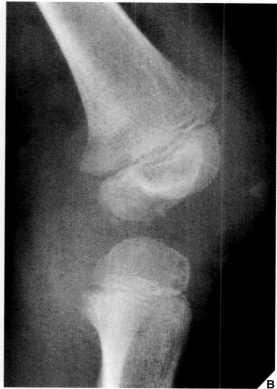

FIGURE 25.16 **Septic arthritis.** Anteroposterior (**A**) and lateral (**B**) radiographs of the left knee of a 4-year-old child demonstrate a significant degree of periarticular osteoporosis and a large joint effusion. Note the small erosions of the distal epiphysis of the femur and the preservation of the joint space. Aspiration revealed hematogenous spread of a staphylococcal urinary tract infection.

periarticular osteoporosis, peripherally located osseous erosions, and gradual diminution of the joint space, should suggest the correct diagnosis; CT examination, however, can be helpful in delineating subtle features (Fig. 25.19). Occasionally, wedge-shaped necrotic foci, so-called kissing sequestra, may be present on both sides of the affected joint, especially in the knee. At a later stage of the disease, there may be complete destruction of the joint, and sclerotic changes in adjacent bones are more frequently encountered (Fig. 25.20).

Other Infectious Arthritides

Less frequently encountered than pyogenic or tuberculous arthritis are joint infections caused by fungi (actinomycosis, cryptococcosis, coccidioidomycosis, histoplasmosis, sporotrichosis, and candidiasis), viruses (smallpox), and spirochetes (syphilis, yaws).

Of interest is *Lyme arthritis*, an infectious articular condition caused by the spirochete *Borrelia burgdorferi*, which is transmitted by the tick *Ixodes dammini* or related ticks such as *Ixodes pacificus* and *Ixodes ricinus*. The illness usually begins in the summer with a characteristic skin lesion (erythema chronicum migrans) at the site of a tick bite, and flu-like symptoms; within weeks to months, a chronic arthritis develops that is characterized by erosions of cartilage and bone. The joint involvement has some similarities to juvenile rheumatoid arthritis and Reiter syndrome. A joint effusion may be present in the early stages of the disease, and characteristic edematous changes of the infrapatellar fat pad may be noted in the knee (Fig. 25.21). MRI may show ribbon-like folds of hypertrophied synovium and frond-like extensions of synovium and synovial fluid into infrapatellar fat pad (Fig. 25.22).

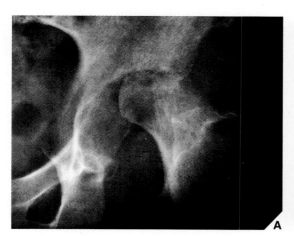
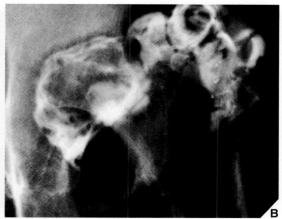

FIGURE 25.17 **Septic arthritis.** A 64-year-old woman had had an upper respiratory infection 6 months before pain developed in her left hip. (**A**) Anteroposterior radiograph of the hip demonstrates complete destruction of the articular cartilage on both sides of the joint and erosion of the femoral head. Note the significant degree of osteoporosis. (**B**) Contrast arthrography was performed primarily to obtain joint fluid for bacteriologic examination, which yielded *S. aureus*. The contrast agent outlines the destroyed joint, showing a synovial irregularity consistent with chronic synovitis.

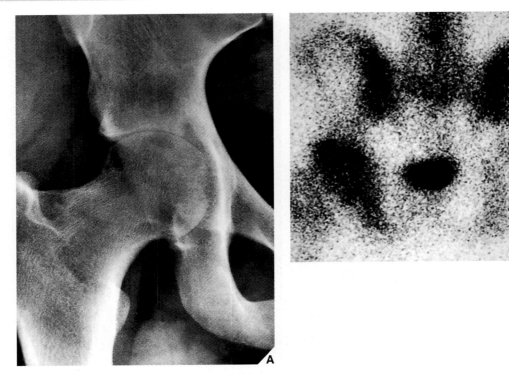

▲
FIGURE 25.18   **Tuberculous arthritis.** A 29-year-old woman with chronic alcoholism presented with right hip pain. (**A**) Anteroposterior radiograph of the hip demonstrates diminution of the joint space, particularly in the weight-bearing region, as well as periarticular osteoporosis. (**B**) Radionuclide bone scan using ^{99m}Tc-labeled diphosphonate demonstrates increased isotope uptake only in the right hip. The increased activity at both sacroiliac joints is a normal finding. The diagnosis of tuberculous arthritis was confirmed by joint aspiration.

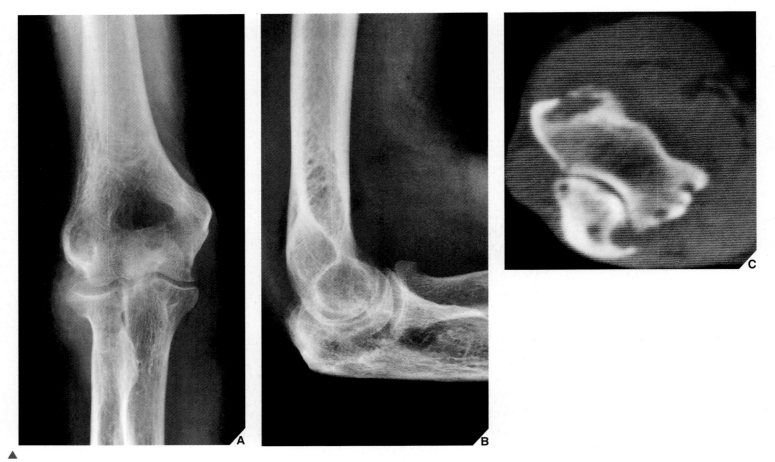

▲
FIGURE 25.19   **Tuberculous arthritis.** A 70-year-old man from India had pain in the left elbow for 4 months. According to his daughter, he had been treated for chronic lung disease. Anteroposterior (**A**) and lateral (**B**) radiographs of the elbow demonstrate a large joint effusion, as indicated by positive anterior and posterior fat pad signs on the lateral projection. Small periarticular erosions are not clear on these views. (**C**) CT section shows narrowing of the joint and peripheral erosions typical of tuberculous infection.

FIGURE 25.20 **Tuberculous arthritis.** Posteroanterior radiograph of the left wrist and hand of a 52-year-old woman with pulmonary tuberculosis shows advanced arthritis involving the left carpus. There is complete destruction of the radiocarpal, midcarpal, and carpometacarpal articulations, as well as whittling and sclerotic changes in the distal radius and ulna. Note the osteoporosis distal to the affected joints and the soft-tissue swelling.

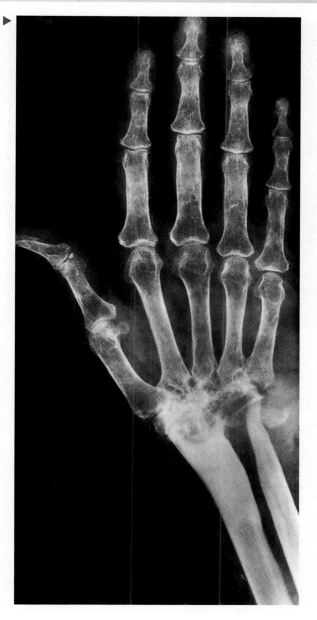

FIGURE 25.21 **Lyme arthritis.** Lateral radiograph of the right knee of a 13-year-old boy, who presented with intermittent soft-tissue swelling and knee effusion for several months, shows periarticular osteoporosis, joint effusion, soft-tissue swelling, and areas of mottled density at the site of infrapatellar fat pad. (Reprinted from Lawson JP et al, 1992, with permission.)

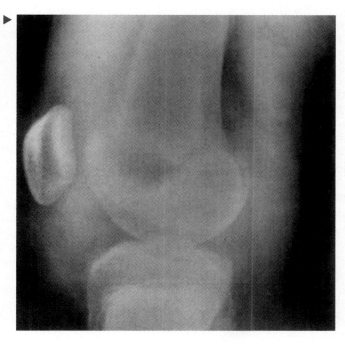

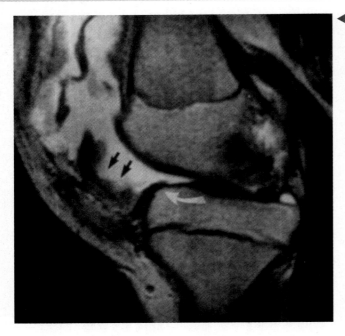

◀ **FIGURE 25.22** MRI of Lyme arthritis. Sagittal T2-weighted MRI of the left knee of a 17-year-old boy, who presented with knee swelling for 7 months, reveals joint effusion that displaced medial meniscus anteriorly (curved *white arrow*). Note ribbon-like folds of hypertrophied synovium and frond-like extensions of synovium and synovial fluid into infrapatellar fat pad (*black arrows*). (Reprinted from Lawson JP et al, 1992, with permission.)

Infections of the Spine

Pyogenic Infections

Infectious organisms may reach the spine by several routes. Hematogenous spread occurs by way of arterial and venous routes (the Batson paravertebral venous system), and the organism lodges in the vertebral body, commonly in the anterior subchondral region. This osteomyelitic focus can spread to the intervertebral disk through perforation of the vertebral end plate, causing disk space infection (diskitis) (Fig. 25.23). Disk space infection can also be induced directly by the implantation of an organism through puncture of the spinal canal, either during spinal surgery or, rarely, by spread from a contiguous site of infection such as a paravertebral abscess (see Fig. 24.4). Disk infection may also occur in children via a hematogenous route because there is still a blood supply to the disk.

Radiographically, disk infection is characterized by narrowing of the disk space, destruction of the adjacent vertebral end plates, and a paraspinal mass. Although most cases are obvious on standard anteroposterior and lateral radiographs of the spine (Fig. 25.24), CT (Fig. 25.25) may yield additional information. Radionuclide bone scan can detect early infection before any changes are noticed radiographically (Fig. 25.26). Occasionally, diskography is performed but, as in the use of arthrography in joint infections, the primary objective is obtaining a specimen for bacteriologic examination. A contrast study, however, may outline the extent of a disk infection (Fig. 25.27).

MRI has become the modality of choice in diagnosing and evaluating infections of the spine. Characteristic findings of disk space narrowing, disk destruction, paraspinal soft-tissue thickening, and edematous changes in the paraspinal musculature are well demonstrated by this technique (Fig. 25.28).

Nonpyogenic Infections

Tuberculosis of the Spine

Infection of the spine by the tubercle bacillus is known as *tuberculous spondylitis* or *Pott disease*. The vertebral body or intervertebral disk may be involved, with the lower thoracic and upper lumbar vertebrae being the preferred sites of infection. The disease constitutes 25% to 50% of all cases of skeletal tuberculosis.

The imaging features of tuberculous infection of the spine are similar to those seen in pyogenic infections. There is disk space narrowing, and the vertebral end plates adjacent to the involved disk show evidence of destruction. A paraspinal mass is common (Fig. 25.29). Rarely, the infectious process may destroy a single vertebra or part of a vertebra (pedicle) without invasion of the disk.

Complications. Tuberculosis of the spine may cause collapse of a partially or completely destroyed vertebra, leading to kyphosis and a gibbous formation. Extension of infection to the adjacent ligaments and soft tissues is also rather frequent; the psoas muscles are often the site of secondary tuberculous infections, commonly called "cold" abscesses (Fig. 25.30). The most common complication of tuberculous spondylitis, however, is compression of the thecal sac and spinal cord with resulting paraplegia. Myelography and MRI are very helpful diagnostically if compression is suspected (Fig. 25.31).

Soft-Tissue Infections

Soft-tissue infections (cellulitis) usually result from direct introduction of organisms through a skin puncture; they are also seen as a complication of systemic disorders such as diabetes. The most frequently encountered organisms are *Staphylococcus aureus, Clostridium novyi*, and *Clostridium perfringens*. These gas-forming organisms may cause an accumulation of gas in the soft tissues that can easily be recognized on plain films as radiolucent bubbles or streaks in the subcutaneous tissues or muscles. This finding usually indicates gangrene caused by anaerobic bacteria. Soft-tissue edema and obliteration of fat and fascial planes are also evident on the standard radiographic examination (Fig. 25.32). CT is effective in this respect, and in addition can differentiate pure cellulitis from that associated with bone infection (Fig. 25.33).

Currently, MRI is considered to be a gold standard to evaluate soft-tissue infection. In particular, soft-tissue abscesses, as well as involvement of tendon sheaths and muscles, are accurately depicted with this modality. Soft-tissue abscesses appear as rounded or elongated—but always well-demarcated—areas of decreased signal intensity on T1-weighted images, changing to increased signal intensity on T2-weighted images (Fig. 25.34). Occasionally, a peripheral band of decreased signal intensity is seen that represents the fibrous capsule surrounding the abscess (see Fig. 24.12). Infected fluid collection within the tendon sheath is always hyperintense on T2 weighting and hypointense on T1 weighting, but this cannot be differentiated from noninfected fluid.

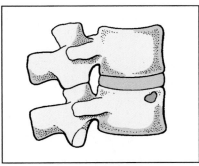

focus of osteomyelitis
in vertebral body

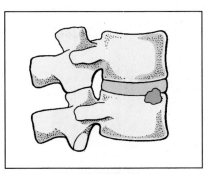

spread of infection
into intervertebral disk
by perforation of
vertebral end plate

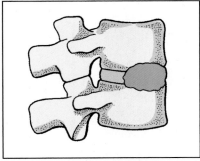

progression of spread
in disk and to adjacent
vertebral body

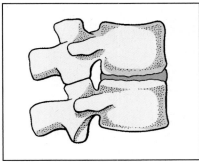

destruction of disk
and narrowing of
intervertebral space

▲
FIGURE 25.23   Sequential stages of involvement of a vertebral body and disk by an infectious process.

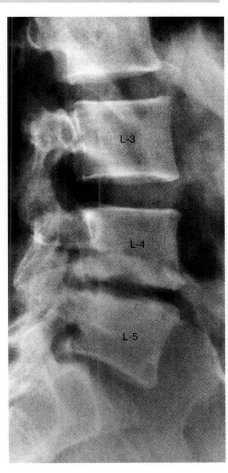

▲
FIGURE 25.24   **Intervertebral disk infection.** Lateral radiograph of the lumbar spine in a 32-year-old man demonstrates the typical radiographic changes of disk infection. There is narrowing of the disk space at L4-5, and the inferior end plate of L4 and superior end plate of L5 are indistinctly outlined. Note the normal end plates at the L3-4 disk space.

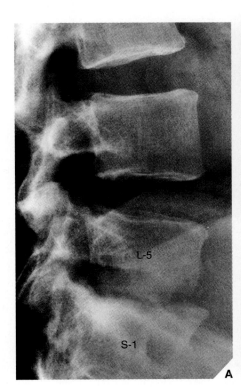
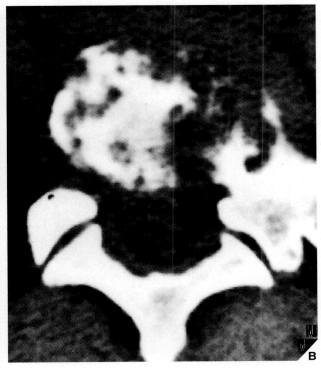

▲
FIGURE 25.25   **CT of intervertebral disk infection.** A 40-year-old man presented with lower back pain for 8 weeks, which he attributed to lifting a heavy object. (**A**) Lateral radiograph of the lumbosacral spine shows narrowing of the L5-S1 disk space and suggests some fuzziness of the adjacent vertebral end plates. (**B**) CT section through the disk space clearly shows destructive changes of the disk and vertebral end plate characteristic of infection.

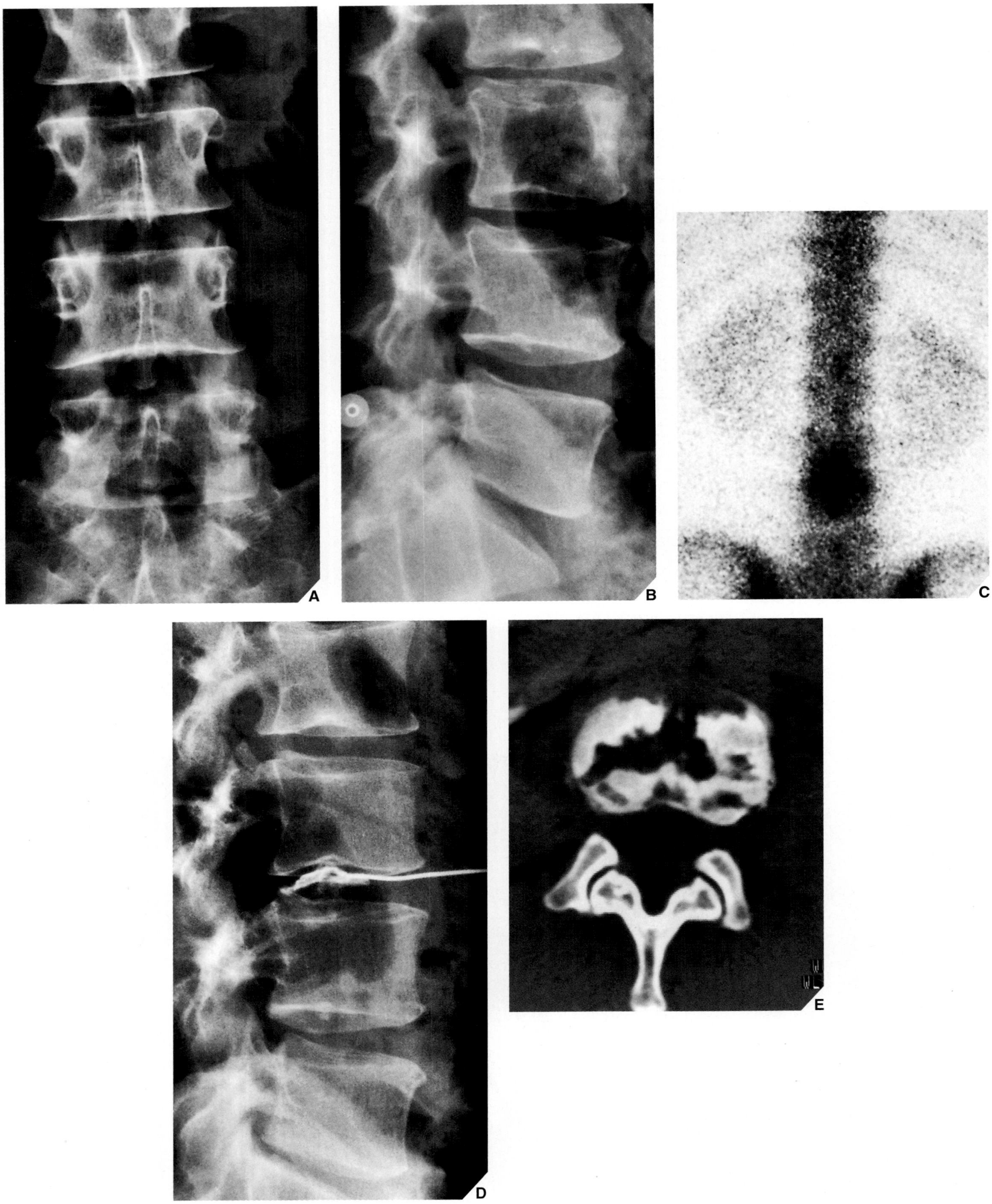

FIGURE 25.26   **Intervertebral disk infection.** Conventional anteroposterior (**A**) and lateral (**B**) radiographs of the lumbar spine of a 40-year-old man who had back pain for 4 weeks show no definite abnormalities. (**C**) Radionuclide bone scan, however, reveals an increased uptake of radiopharmaceutical tracer at the L3-4 level. (**D**) On a subsequent diskogram, using the oblique approach, partial disk destruction is evident. (**E**) The extent of destruction is revealed by CT. Bacteriologic examination of aspirated fluid yielded *Escherichia coli*.

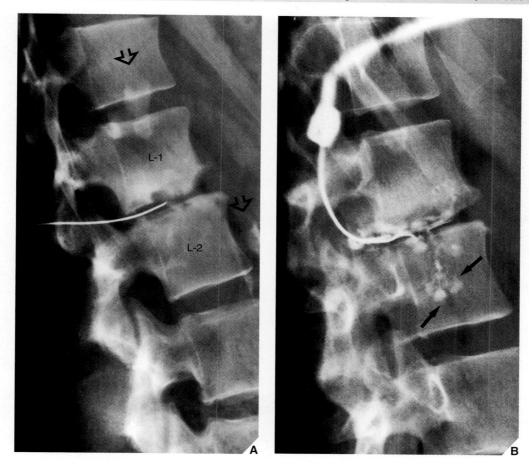

FIGURE 25.27   Disk space infection and vertebral osteomyelitis. A 22-year-old intravenous drug user with back pain for 2 months was diagnosed with an intervertebral disk infection. A diskogram was performed primarily to aspirate fluid for bacteriologic examination, which revealed *Pseudomonas aeruginosa*. Before the puncture, the patient received an intravenous injection of iodine contrast agent to visualize the kidneys, as a precautionary step before spine biopsy at that level. (**A**) Lateral radiograph of the lumbar spine shows narrowing of the disk space at L1-2 and destruction of the adjacent vertebral end plates. The spinal needle is located in the center of the disk. The *open arrows* point to opacified calyces of kidney. (**B**) Lateral radiograph obtained during the injection of metrizamide demonstrates extension of the contrast into the body of L2 (*arrows*), indicating the presence of vertebral osteomyelitis.

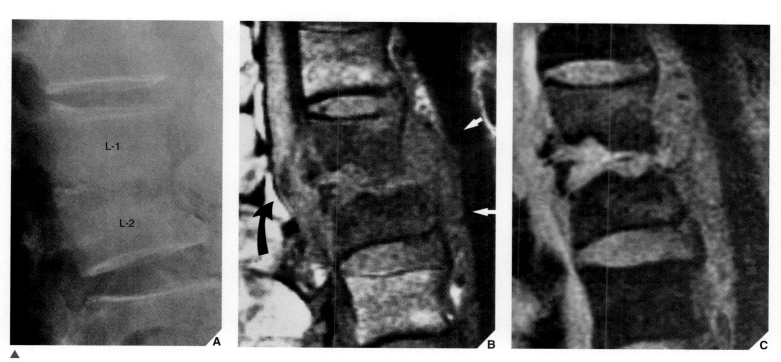

FIGURE 25.28   MRI of disk space infection and vertebral osteomyelitis. A 48-year-old man who is an intravenous drug user developed disk infection at L1-2. (**A**) Lateral radiograph demonstrates classic changes of disk infection: narrowing of the disk space and destruction of the vertebral end plates. (**B**) Sagittal spin-echo T1-weighted MR image (TR 600/TE 20 msec) demonstrates, in addition to the destruction of the disk, a large inflammatory mass extending anteriorly (*arrows*), destroying anterior longitudinal ligament and infiltrating paraspinal soft tissues. Posteriorly, it invades the content of spinal canal (*curved arrow*). (**C**) Sagittal T2*-weighted gradient (MPGR) MR image shows more clearly the fragmentation of the posterior aspect of adjacent vertebral bodies and compression of the thecal sac by a large abscess.

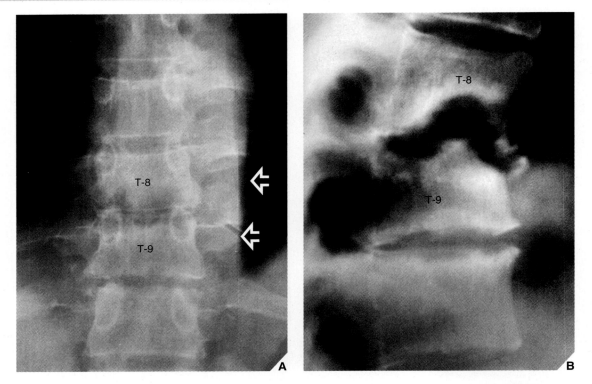

FIGURE 25.29 **Tuberculous spondylitis. (A)** Anteroposterior radiograph of the thoracic spine in a 50-year-old man shows narrowing of the T8-9 disk space, associated with a paraspinal mass on the left side (*open arrows*). **(B)** Lateral tomogram shows destruction of the disk and extensive erosions of the inferior aspect of the body of T8 and the superior end plate of T9.

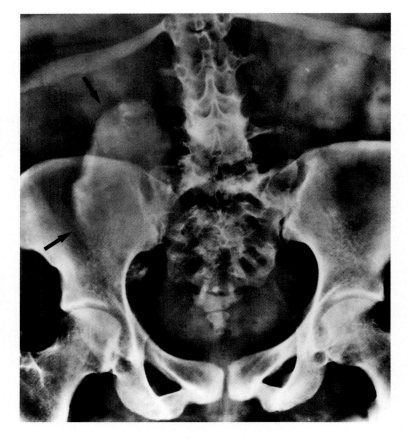

FIGURE 25.30 **Tuberculous "cold" abscess.** Anteroposterior radiograph of the pelvis in a 35-year-old woman with spinal tuberculosis shows an oval radiodense mass with spotted calcifications overlapping the medial part of the ilium and right sacroiliac joint (right psoas muscle) (*arrows*). This is the typical appearance of a "cold" abscess.

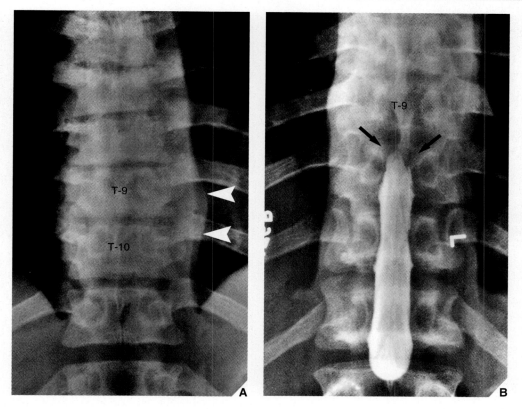

FIGURE 25.31   Tuberculous diskitis. A 39-year-old man with a history of pulmonary tuberculosis had neurologic symptoms of spinal cord compression. (**A**) Anteroposterior radiograph of the lower thoracic spine shows minimal disk space narrowing at T9-10 and a large left paraspinal mass (*arrow heads*). (**B**) A myelogram shows complete obstruction of the flow of contrast in the subarachnoid space at the level of the disk infection (*arrows*).

FIGURE 25.32   Gangrene of soft tissues. Oblique ▶ radiograph of the foot of a 59-year-old man with long-standing diabetes mellitus shows marked soft-tissue swelling and edema, particularly in the region of the fourth and fifth digits. Radiolucent streaks of gas are typical of gangrenous infection.

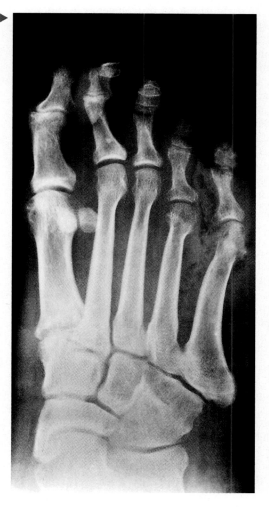

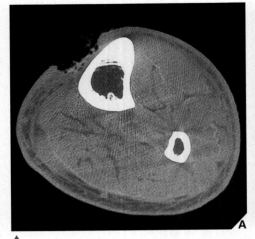 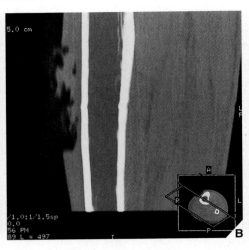

FIGURE 25.33   Soft-tissue abscess. A 26-year-old man had an infection of the anterior aspect of the left lower leg. (**A**) Axial CT section and (**B**) oblique sagittal reformatted image show an abscess and its relation to the tibia. Note that the cortex is not affected.

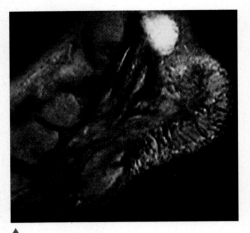

FIGURE 25.34   MRI of soft-tissue abscess. Sagittal spin-echo T2-weighted MR image (TR 2000/TE 80 msec) reveals a high-signal-intensity fluid collection adjacent to the medial malleolus in this diabetic patient with a foot infection. (From Beltran J, 1990, with permission.)

PRACTICAL POINTS TO REMEMBER

Osteomyelitis

[1] The imaging hallmarks of osteomyelitis include:
   • cortical and medullary bone destruction
   • reactive sclerosis and a periosteal reaction
   • the presence of sequestra and involucra.
[2] The metaphysis is a characteristic site of osteomyelitis in children.
[3] Acute osteomyelitis of a long bone frequently mimics Ewing sarcoma and Langerhans cell histiocytosis. The clinical history, especially the duration of symptoms before the discovery of bone changes, usually serves as a clue to the correct diagnosis.
[4] A destructive metaphyseal lesion extending into the epiphysis usually indicates a bone abscess.
[5] A Brodie abscess may clinically and radiographically mimic an osteoid osteoma. In the differential diagnosis, the presence of a radiolucent tract extending from the lesion into the growth plate favors an infectious process.
[6] In congenital syphilis:
   • osteochondritis, periostitis, and osteitis are typical features
   • destruction at the medial aspect of the metaphysis of a long bone (Wimberger sign) is characteristic.

Infectious Arthritis

[1] The characteristic radiographic features of septic arthritis of the peripheral joints include:
   • periarticular osteoporosis, joint effusion, and soft-tissue swelling (early phase)
   • destruction of cartilage and the subchondral plates on both sides of the joint (late phase).
[2] In tuberculosis of a peripheral joint, which usually manifests as a monoarticular disease (strongly resembling rheumatoid arthritis), the Phemister triad of radiographic abnormalities is characteristic and includes:
   • periarticular osteoporosis
   • peripheral osseous erosions
   • gradual narrowing of the joint space.
[3] Lyme arthritis exhibits some similarities to juvenile rheumatoid arthritis and Reiter syndrome. Characteristic edematous changes of the infrapatellar fat pad and folds of hypertrophied synovium are demonstrated on MRI.

Infections of the Spine

[1] In the imaging evaluation of spine infections:
   • radionuclide bone scan can detect disk infection prior to the appearance of any radiographic signs
   • the diskogram is a valid examination performed primarily to obtain aspirate fluid for bacteriologic study
   • MRI is the modality of choice to diagnose and evaluate spine infection.
[2] Pyogenic infection of the spine is recognized radiographically by:
   • narrowing of the disk space
   • destruction of both vertebral end plates adjacent to the involved disk
   • a paraspinal mass.
[3] The radiographic hallmarks of tuberculous infection of an intervertebral disk are:
   • narrowing of the disk space
   • loss of the sharp outline of the adjacent vertebral end plates.
[4] Tuberculous infection of the spine may:
   • destroy the disk and vertebra, leading to kyphosis and a gibbus formation
   • extend into the soft tissues, forming a "cold" abscess.

Soft-Tissue Infections

[1] Cellulitis caused by gas-forming bacteria in soft tissues (gangrene) is recognized radiographically by:
   • soft-tissue edema and swelling
   • radiolucent bubbles or streaks representing accumulations of gas.
[2] Diabetic subjects are particularly prone to soft-tissue infections, the feet being common sites.
[3] Scintigraphy using indium-111–labelled white cells is useful in detecting and localizing the site of infection, whereas MRI is ideal in evaluating the extent of infection in the soft tissues.
[4] MRI using contrast enhancement with gadolinium allows the differentiation of abscess from cellulitis or phlegmon.

SUGGESTED READINGS

Abdelwahab IF, Present DA, Zwass A, Klein MJ, Mazzara J. Tumorlike tuberculosis granulomas of bone. *Am J Roentgenol* 1987;149:1207–1208.
Alexander GH, Mansuy MM. Disseminated bone tuberculosis (so-called multiple cystic tuberculosis). *Radiology* 1950;55:839–842.

Al-Shahed MS, Sharif HS, Haddad MC, Aabed MY, Sammak BM, Mutairi MA. Imaging features of musculoskeletal brucellosis. *Radiographics* 1994;14:333–348.

Armbuster TG, Goergen TG, Resnick D, Catanzaro A. Utility of bone scanning in disseminated coccidioidomycosis: a case report. *J Nucl Med* 1977;18:450–454.

Bayer AS, Guze LB. Fungal arthritis. II. Coccidioidal synovitis: clinical, diagnostic, therapeutic, and prognostic considerations. *Semin Arthritis Rheum* 1979;8: 200–211.

Behrman RE, Masci JR, Nicholas P. Cryptococcal skeletal infections: case report and review. *Rev Infect Dis* 1990;12:181–190.

Beltran J. *MRI: musculoskeletal system*. Philadelphia: JB Lippincott; 1990.

Benninghoven CD, Miller ER. Coccidioidal infection in bone. *Radiology* 1942;38: 663–666.

Birsner JW, Smart S. Osseous coccidioidomycosis: a chronic form of dissemination. *Am J Roentgenol* 1956;76:1052–1060.

Brodie BC. An account of some cases of chronic abscess of the tibia. *Trans Med Chir Soc* 1832;17:238–239.

Bruno MS, Silverberg TN, Goldstein DH. Embolic osteomyelitis of the spine as a complication of infection of the urinary tract. *Am J Med* 1960;29:865–878.

Carter RA. Infectious granulomas of bones and joints, with special reference to coccidioidal granuloma. *Radiology* 1934;23:1–16.

Chelboun J, Sydney N. Skeletal cryptococcosis. *J Bone Joint Surg [Am]* 1977;59A: 509–514.

Cremin BJ, Fisher RM. The lesions of congenital syphilis. *Br J Radiol* 1970;43: 333–341.

Crim JR, Seeger LL. Imaging evaluation of osteomyelitis. *Crit Rev Diagn Imaging* 1994;35:201–256.

Dalinka MK, Greendyke WH. The spinal manifestations of coccidioidomycosis. *J Can Assoc Radiol* 1971;22:93–99.

David R, Barron BJ, Madewell JE. Osteomyelitis, acute and chronic. *Radiol Clin North Am* 1987;25:1171–1201.

Drutz DJ, Catanzaro A. Coccidioidomycosis. Part I. *Am Rev Respir Dis* 1978;117: 559–585.

Drutz DJ, Catanzaro A. Coccidioidomycosis. Part II. *Am Rev Respir Dis* 1978;117: 727–771.

Erdman WA, Tamburro F, Jayson HT, Weatherall PT, Ferry KB, Peshock RM. Osteomyelitis: characteristics and pitfalls of diagnosis with MR imaging. *Radiology* 1991;180:533–539.

Ehrlich I, Kricum ME. Radiographic findings in early acquired syphilis: case report and critical review. *Am J Roentgenol* 1976;127:789–792.

Fletcher BD, Scoles PV, Nelson AD. Osteomyelitis in children: detection by magnetic resonance. *Radiology* 1984;150:57–60.

Gilmour WM. Acute haematogenous osteomyelitis. *J Bone Joint Surg [Br]* 1962; 44B:841–853.

Gold RH, Hawkins RA, Katz RD. Bacterial osteomyelitis: findings on plain radiography, CT, MR, and scintigraphy. *Am J Roentgenol* 1991;157:365–370.

Graves VB, Schreiber MN. Tuberculosis psoas muscle abscess. *J Can Assoc Radiol* 1973;24:268–271.

Guyot DR, Manoli A II, Kling GA. Pyogenic sacroiliitis in IV drug users. *Am J Roentgenol* 1987;149:1209–1211.

Haygood TM, Williamson SL. Radiographic findings of extremity tuberculosis in childhood: back to the future? *Radiographics* 1994;14:561–570.

Hopkins KL, Li KC, Bergman G. Gadolinium-DPTA-enhanced magnetic resonance imaging of musculoskeletal infectious processes. *Skeletal Radiol* 1995;24:325–330.

Jain R, Sawhney S, Berry M. Computed tomography of vertebral tuberculosis: patterns of bone destruction. *Clin Radiol* 1993;47:196–199.

Karchevsky M, Schweitzer ME, Morrison WB, Parellada JA. MRI findings of septic arthritis and associated osteomyelitis in adults. *Am J Roentgenol* 2004;182: 119–122.

Kido D, Bryan D, Halpern M. Hematogeneous osteomyelitis in drug addicts. *Am J Roentgenol* 1973;118:356–363.

Lawson JP, Rahn DW. Lyme disease and radiologic findings in Lyme arthritis. *Am J Roentgenol* 1992;158:1065–1069.

Lawson JP, Steere AC. Lyme arthritis: radiologic findings. *Radiology* 1985;154:37–43.

Lund PJ, Chan KM, Unger EC, Galgiani JN, Pitt MJ. Magnetic resonance imaging in coccidioidal arthritis. *Skeletal Radiol* 1996;25:661–665.

May DA, Disler DG. Case 50: primary coccidioidal synovitis of the knee. *Radiology* 2002;224:665–668.

McGahan JP, Graves DS, Palmer PES. Coccidioidal spondylitis: usual and unusual roentgenographic manifestations. *Radiology* 1980;136:5–9.

McGahan JP, Graves DS, Palmer PES, Stadalnik RC, Dublin AB. Classic and contemporary imaging of coccidioidomycosis. *Am J Roentgenol* 1981;136:393–404.

Modic MT, Feiglin DH, Piriano DW, et al. Vertebral osteomyelitis: assessment using MR. *Radiology* 1985;157:157–166.

Moore SL, Jones S, Lee JL. *Nocardia* osteomyelitis in the setting of previously unknown HIV infection. *Skeletal Radiol* 2005;34:58–60.

Paterson DC. Acute suppurative arthritis in infancy and childhood. *J Bone Joint Surg [Br]* 1970;52B:474–482.

Phemister DB, Hatcher CM. Correlation of pathological and roentgenological findings in the diagnosis of tuberculosis arthritis. *Am J Roentgenol* 1933;29:736–752.

Resnik CS, Ammann AM, Walsh JW. Chronic septic arthritis of the adult hip: computed tomographic features. *Skeletal Radiol* 1987;16:513–516.

Resnick D, Niwayama G. Osteomyelitis, septic arthritis, and soft tissue infection: mechanisms and situations. In: Resnick D, ed. *Diagnosis of bone and joint disorders*, 3rd ed. Philadelphia: Saunders; 1995:2325–2418.

Resnick D, Niwayama G. Osteomyelitis, septic arthritis, and soft tissue infection: organisms. In: Resnick D, ed. *Diagnosis of bone and joint disorders*, 3rd ed. Philadelphia: Saunders, 1995:2448–2558.

Schauwecker D. Osteomyelitis: diagnosis with In-111-labeled leukocytes. *Radiology* 1989;171:141–146.

Stadalnik RC, Goldstein E, Hoeprich PD, dos Santos PA, Lee KK. Diagnostic value of gallium and bone scans in evaluation of extrapulmonary coccidioidal lesions. *Am Rev Respir Dis* 1980;121:673–676.

Theodorou DJ, Theodorou SJ, Kakitsubata Y, Sartoris DJ, Resnick D. Imaging characteristics and epidemiologic features of atypical mycobacterial infections involving the musculoskeletal system. *Am J Roentgenol* 2001;176:341–349.

Trueta J. The three types of acute, haematogenous osteomyelitis. *J Bone Joint Surg [Br]* 1959;41B:671–680.

Young LW. Neonatal and infantile osteomyelitis and septic arthritis. In: Taveras JM, Ferrucci JT, eds. *Radiology—diagnosis, imaging, intervention, vol. 5*. Philadelphia: JB Lippincott; 1986:1–15.

Zeppa MA, Laorr A, Greenspan A, McGahan JP, Steinbach LS. Skeletal coccidioidomycosis: imaging findings in 19 patients. *Skeletal Radiol* 1996;25:337–343.

VI

METABOLIC AND ENDOCRINE DISORDERS

CHAPTER 26

Radiologic Evaluation of Metabolic and Endocrine Disorders

Composition and Production of Bone

Bone tissue consists of two types of material: (a) an extracellular material, which includes *organic matrix* or *osteoid tissue* (collagen fibrils within a mucopolysaccharide ground substance) and an *inorganic crystalline component* (calcium phosphate or hydroxyapatite); and (b) a cellular material, which includes *osteoblasts* (cells that induce bone formation), *osteoclasts* (cells that induce bone resorption), and *osteocytes* (inactive cells).

Bone is a living, dynamic tissue. Old bone is constantly being removed and replaced with new bone. Normally, this continuous process of bone resorption and formation is in balance (Fig. 26.1A), and the mineral content of the bones remains relatively constant. In some abnormal circumstances, however, when the metabolism of the bone is disturbed, this balance may be upset. If, for example, osteoblasts are more active than usual, or if osteoclasts are less active, more bone is produced (a state known as "too much bone") (Fig. 26.1B). If, however, osteoclasts are normal or overactive and osteoblasts underactive, then less bone is produced ("too little bone") (Fig. 26.1C). A generalized reduction in bone mass may also be caused by decreased mineralization of osteoid, with equilibrium in the rate of bone resorption and production (Fig. 26.1D).

The growth and mineralization of bone are influenced by a variety of factors, the most important of which are the levels of growth hormone produced by the pituitary gland, of calcitonin produced by the thyroid gland, and of parathormone produced by the parathyroid glands, along with the dietary intake, intestinal absorption, and urinary excretion of vitamin D, calcium, and phosphorus.

It should be remembered, however, that normal bone density changes with age, increasing from infancy until age 35 to 40, and then progressively decreasing at the rate of 8% per decade in women and 3% in men.

Evaluation of Metabolic and Endocrine Disorders

Most metabolic and endocrine disorders are characterized radiographically by abnormalities in bone density that are generally related to increased bone production, increased bone resorption, or inadequate bone mineralization. The bones affected by these conditions appear abnormally radiolucent (osteopenia) or abnormally radiodense (osteosclerosis) (Table 26.1).

Radiologic Imaging Modalities

The radiologic modalities most often used to evaluate metabolic and endocrine bone disorders are

1. Conventional radiography
2. Computed tomography (CT)
3. Radionuclide imaging (scintigraphy, bone scan)
4. Magnetic resonance imaging (MRI).

Conventional Radiography

Radiography is the simplest and most widely used method of evaluating bone density. This technique can easily detect even very small increases in bone density; however, it generally fails to detect decreases in overall skeletal mineralization unless the reduction reaches at least 30%. It must be pointed out that normal bone can easily acquire an abnormal radiographic appearance as a result of technical errors, such as improper settings for kilovoltage and milliamperage. Overexposure, for instance, creates the appearance of increased bone radiolucency, whereas underexposure creates an artificially increased bone radiodensity.

For these reasons, inspection of a standard radiograph should focus less on apparent increases or decreases in bone density than on the thickness of the bone cortex. Cortical thickness is directly correlated with skeletal mineralization; it can be objectively measured and compared either with a normal standard or with subsequent studies in the same patient. The cortical thickness measurement is obtained by adding the width of the two cortices in the midpoint of a given bone, a sum that should be approximately one half of the overall diameter of the bone; it may also be expressed as an index of bony mass, derived by dividing the combined cortical thickness by the total diameter of the bone (Fig. 26.2). The second or third metacarpal bone is frequently used to obtain these measurements (Fig. 26.3).

A related method for assessing bone density that also uses radiography is the photodensitometry technique. This technique is based on the observation that the photographic density of a bone on a radiographic film is proportional to its mass. Through the use of a photodensitometer, the photographic density of a given bone can be compared with that of known standard wedges, giving an accurate assessment of the degree of bone density.

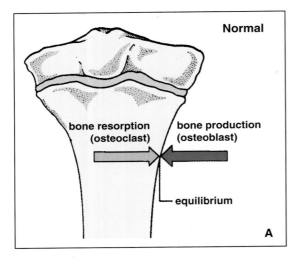
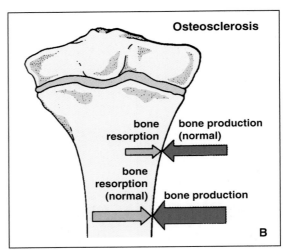
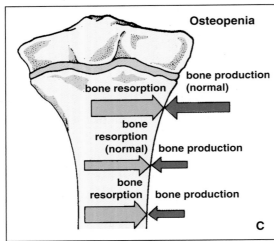
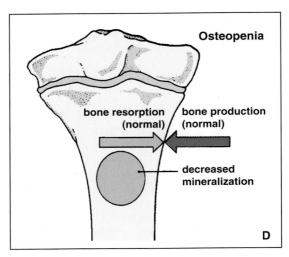

▲
FIGURE 26.1 Bone production and bone resorption. **(A)** In normal bone, the relationship between bone resorption and bone production is in balance. **(B)** One abnormal state ("too much bone") is characterized by decreased bone resorption and normal bone production, or by normal bone resorption and increased bone production. **(C)** The other abnormal state ("too little bone") is characterized by increased bone resorption and normal bone production, by normal bone resorption and decreased bone production, or by increased bone resorption and decreased bone production. **(D)** Too little bone may also be caused by a decrease in bone mineralization, with bone resorption and production in balance.

TABLE 26.1 **Metabolic and Endocrine Disorders Characterized by Abnormalities in Bone Density**

Increased Radiodensity	Increased Radiolucency
Secondary hyperparathyroidism	Osteoporosis
Renal osteodystrophy	Osteomalacia
Hyperphosphatasia	Rickets
Idiopathic hypercalcemia	Scurvy
Paget disease	Primary hyperparathyroidism
Osteopetrosis*	Hypophosphatasia
Pycnodysostosis*	Hypophosphatemia
Melorheostosis*	Acromegaly
Hypothyroidism	Gaucher disease
Mastocytosis	Homocystinuria
Myelofibrosis	Osteogenesis imperfecta*
Gaucher disease (reparative stage)	Fibrogenesis imperfecta
Fluorine poisoning	Cushing syndrome
Intoxication with lead, bismuth, or phosphorus	Ochronosis (alkaptonuria)
	Wilson disease (hepatolenticular degeneration)
Osteonecrosis	Hypogonadism

*These conditions are discussed in Part VII: Congenital and Developmental Anomalies.

Name: NVM	Sex: Female	Height: 63.7 in
Patient ID: 00011	Ethnicity: White	Weight: 161.5 lb
		Age: 69

Referring Physician: 0554

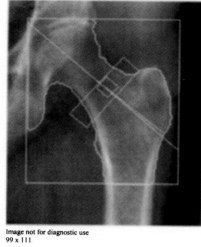

Image not for diagnostic use
99 x 111

Scan Information:

Scan Date: December 19, 2002   ID: K1219020L
Scan Type: a Left Hip
Analysis: December 19, 2002 12:07 Version 11.2
            Left Hip
Operator: DSA
Model: QDR 4500A (S/N 45115)
Comment: 2301

DXA Results Summary:

Region	Area (cm²)	BMC (g)	BMD (g/cm²)	T - Score	PR (%)	Z - Score	AM (%)
Neck	5.07	2.68	0.528	-2.9	62	-1.1	81
Troch	11.31	5.31	0.469	-2.3	67	-1.0	82
Inter	16.59	12.79	0.771	-2.1	70	-0.9	85
Total	**32.96**	**20.77**	**0.630**	**-2.6**	**67**	**-1.1**	**83**
Ward's	1.15	0.38	0.335	-3.4	46	-0.9	76

Total BMD CV 1.0%
WHO Classification: Osteoporosis
Fracture Risk: High

Total

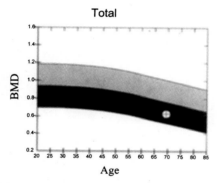

Reference curve and scores matched to White Female

FIGURE 26.11   **DEXA measuring of bone mineral density.** A 69-year-old woman was suspected of developing osteoporosis. DEXA scan of her left hip confirmed this diagnosis, indicating in addition high risk for a fracture.

two energy levels that enable discrimination between bone and surrounding soft tissue. Therefore, an area-based 2D image is generated, and measurements of bone mineral density can be calculated and compared with normal ranges matched for chronological age (Fig. 26.11). Because of the increased flux from an x-ray tube rather than from an isotope source, scanning time and the collimation of the x-ray beam can be decreased. DEXA can be used for spine, hip, and whole-body measurements, enabling patients to be classified as normal, osteopenic, or osteoporotic.

Digital Computer-Assisted X-ray Radiogrammetry. Digital computer-assisted x-ray radiogrammetry (DXR) provides a bone mineral density calculation by a combined computerized radiogrammetric and textural analysis of the three middle metacarpal bones. The involved computer algorithms automatically define regions of interest around the narrowest parts of metacarpals, and subsequently define the outer and inner cortical edges. The mean of the cortical thickness and overall bone cortical thickness are calculated. The acquisition technique and the analysis process itself have high reproducibility values, suggesting a high precision of the DXR method.

Computed Tomography Technique

Quantitative Computed Tomography. Quantitative computed tomography (QCT) is a method for measuring the lumbar spine mineral content

in which the average density values of a region of interest are referenced to that of a calibration material scanned at the same time as the patient. Measurements are performed on a CT scanner and use a mineral standard for simultaneous calibration, a computed radiograph (scout view) for localization, and either single-energy or dual-energy techniques. In quantitative CT scanning, a cross-sectional image of the vertebral body is obtained, allowing differentiation of cortical and trabecular bone. The attenuation, referenced to a mineral equivalent phantom, is expressed as a trabecular bone density in mg/cm³ of calcium hydroxyapatite. The standard examination procedure consists of taking CT scans through the midplane line of three or four adjacent vertebral bodies, usually from T12 to L3 or L1 to L4. Axial images of the vertebral bodies are obtained by scanning the midplane of vertebral bodies while the patient is supine on a standard phantom. The average density from all vertebrae is calculated. The patient's values are compared with the values of bone density calibrated in the phantom (Fig. 26.12). For measuring the spine, QCT has advantages over other methods because of its great sensitivity and precise 3D anatomic localization, its ability to distinguish cancellous bone from cortical bone, and its ability to exclude extraosseous minerals from the measurement. In particular, this method is useful for measurement of spinal bone mineral density in postmenopausal women, in patients with existing osteoporosis, and in patients being treated with corticosteroids.

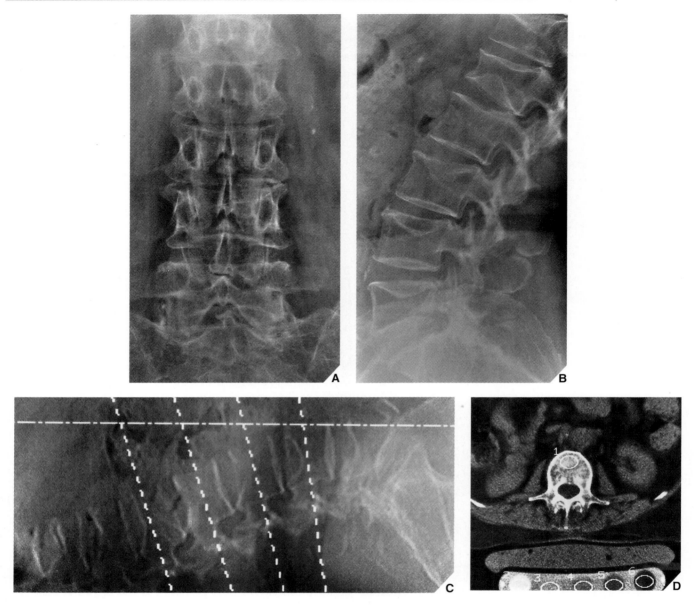

FIGURE 26.12 Quantitative computed tomography. A 62-year-old woman was evaluated for degree of osteoporosis. Anteroposterior (**A**) and lateral (**B**) radiographs of the lumbar spine show diffuse osteopenia with multiple compression fractures. QCT measurements were obtained in the following fashion: The patient was supine on a standard bone mineral calibration phantom. Values were referenced to a translucent calibration phantom scanned with the patient, which contains tubes filled with standard solutions of potassium phosphate (representing minerals), ethanol (representing fat), and water (representing soft tissue). For each axial image, the regions of interest were positioned over the center portion of the phantom calibration compartments, as well as over the central portion of the vertebral body. Transverse (axial) CT scans were made through L1, L2, L3, and L4, with phantom included. Bone density values in mg/cm³ were calculated for each vertebral body using the CT numbers (Hounsfield units) obtained from the calibrated density phantom (**C,D**). Readings are averaged and compared with normal values for given age and sex. Average of readings for vertebral mineral content is also expressed in mg/cm³. In this particular case, the average values of 77.4 mg of mineral/cm³ are below the average values for the patient's age (97.5 mg/cm³), as well as below the levels of fracture threshold (110 mg/cm³).

Quantitative Ultrasound Technique

Ultrasound visualization is based on a mechanical wave vibrating at a frequency range from 20 kHz to 100 MHz. Passage of this wave through bone causes cortex and trabecular component to vibrate on a microscale. The physical and mechanical properties of the bone then progressively alter the shape, intensity, and speed of the propagating wave, which, as Haus et al. pointed out, allows characterization of bone tissue in terms of ultrasound velocity (speed of sound) and broadband ultrasound attenuation. These parameters allow the determination of bone mineral density, predominantly at the calcaneus. Although this method is not as accurate as the methods listed in the previous text, the absence of ionizing radiation with ultrasound, the portability of the equipment, and its cost-effectiveness make ultrasound assessment of bone mineral density an attractive option for screening patients suspected of having osteoporosis.

PRACTICAL POINTS TO REMEMBER

[1] On a standard radiograph, increased bone radiolucency (osteopenia) or increased bone density (osteosclerosis) is related to the process of bone formation and resorption, which under normal circumstances is in equilibrium:
  • If bone resorption exceeds bone production, either because of an increase in osteoclast activity or because of a decrease in osteoblast activity, or if there is insufficient mineral deposition in the matrix, then the result is increased radiolucency of the bone.
  • If bone production surpasses bone resorption, either because of an increase in osteoblast activity or because of a decrease in osteoclast activity, then the result is increased radiodensity of the bone.

[2] Instead of the specific term *osteoporosis*, the nonspecific descriptive term *osteopenia* is used to refer to any generalized or regional

rarefaction of the skeleton, expressed radiographically as increased bone radiolucency, regardless of the specific pathogenesis. The main reason for this usage is that it is usually impossible to distinguish between the various causes of increased bone radiolucency. The term *osteosclerosis* refers to any increase in bone density, again regardless of the cause of the condition.

[3] Osteoporosis is a specific term defining a state in which bone tissue (bone matrix) is reduced but mineralization of the organic matrix is normal. Osteomalacia is a specific term defining a state in which there is insufficient mineralization of osteoid tissue.

[4] The important radiologic techniques used in the evaluation of various metabolic and endocrine conditions include:
- conventional radiography
- CT
- radionuclide imaging (scintigraphy, bone scan)
- MRI

[5] Scintigraphy is a nonspecific but highly sensitive modality to detect bone turnover in various metabolic and endocrine disorders.

[6] MRI provides important information of the status of the bone marrow in such disorders as transient regional osteoporosis, regional migratory osteoporosis, idiopathic juvenile osteoporosis, and reflex sympathetic dystrophy syndrome. This technique is also effective in the evaluation of Gaucher disease and Paget disease.

[7] Several methods have been developed for accurate assessment of mineral content of the bone, including SPA, DPA, DEXA, QCT, and DXR.

[8] At present, DEXA is considered the most effective technique providing measurement of bone mineral density that can be compared with normal ranges matched for chronological age.

[9] QCT is an accurate method for measuring mineral content of cancellous (trabecular) bone of the vertebrae. In this method, the average density of a measured region is referenced to that of a calibration phantom exposed simultaneously with a patient undergoing examination.

SUGGESTED READINGS

Adams JE. Single and dual energy X-ray absorptiometry. *Eur Radiol* 1997;7 (Suppl 2):S20–S31.

Baran DT, Faulkner KG, Genant HK, Miller PD, Pacifici R. Diagnosis and management of osteoporosis: guidelines for the utilization of bone densitometry. *Calcif Tissue Int* 1997;61:433–440.

Cann CE. Quantitative CT applications: comparison of newer CT scanners. *Radiology* 1987;162:257–261.

Cann CE. Quantitative CT for determination of bone mineral density: a review. *Radiology* 1988;166:509–522.

Cann CE, Genant HK. Precise measurement of vertebral mineral content using computed tomography. *J Comput Assist Tomogr* 1980;4:493–500.

Gamble CL. Osteoporosis: making the diagnosis in patients at risk for fracture. *Geriatrics* 1995;50:24–33.

Garn SM, Poznanski AX, Nagy JM. Bone measurement in the differential diagnosis of osteopenia and osteoporosis. *Radiology* 1971;100:509–518.

Genant HK. Current state of bone densitometry for osteoporosis. *Radiographics* 1998;18:913–918.

Genant HK, Glüer C-C, Steiger P, Faulkner KG. Quantitative computed tomography for the assessment of osteoporosis. In: Moss AA, Gamsu G, Genant HK, eds. *Computed tomography of the body with magnetic resonance imaging*, 2nd ed. Philadelphia: WB Saunders; 1992:523–549.

Gramp S, Jergas M, Glüer CC, Lang P, Brastow P, Genant HK. Radiologic diagnosis of osteoporosis: current methods and perspectives. *Radiol Clin North Am* 1993;31:1133–1145.

Gramp S, Steiner E, Imhof H. Radiological diagnosis of osteoporosis. *Eur Radiol* 1997;7(Suppl 2):S11–S19.

Griffith HJ, Zimmerman R, Bailey G, Snider R. The use of photon absorptiometry in the diagnosis of renal osteodystrophy. *Radiology* 1973;109:277–281.

Guglielmi G, Schneider P, Lang TF, Giannatempo GM, Cammisa M, Genant HK. Quantitative computed tomography at the axial and peripheral skeleton. *Eur Radiol* 1997;7(Suppl 2):S32–S42.

Hans D, Fuerst T, Duboeuf F. Quantitative ultrasound bone measurement. *Eur Radiol* 1997;7(Suppl 2):S43–S50.

Hui SL, Slemenda CW, Johnston CC. Age and bone mass as predictors of fracture in a prospective study. *J Clin Invest* 1988;81:1804–1809.

Jergas M, Genant HK. Quantitative bone mineral analysis. In: Resnick D, ed. Diagnosis of bone and joint disorders, 3rd ed. Philadelphia: WB Saunders; 1995:1854–1884.

Jergas M, Glüer C-C. Assessment of fracture risk by bone density measurements. *Semin Nucl Med* 1997;27:261–275.

Kanis JA, Delmas P, Burckhardt P, Cooper C, Torgerson D. Guidelines for diagnosis and management of osteoporosis. *Osteoporosis Int* 1997;7:390–406.

Kanis JA, Melton JL III, Christiansen C, Johnston CC, Khaltaev N. The diagnosis of osteoporosis. *J Bone Miner Res* 1994;9:1137–1141.

Krolner B, Nielsen SP. Measurement of bone mineral contents (BMC) of the lumbar spine, I: Theory and application of a new two-dimensional dual photon attenuation method. *Scand J Clin Lab Invest* 1980;40:653–663.

Lai KC, Goodsitt MM, Murano R, Chesnut CH. A comparison of two dual-energy x-ray absorptiometry systems for spinal bone mineral measurement. *Calcif Tissue Int* 1992;50:203–208.

Lang P, Steiger P, Faulkner K, Glaer C, Genant HK. Osteoporosis. Current techniques and recent developments in quantitative bone densitometry. *Radiol Clin North Am* 1991;29:49–76.

Lenchik L, Rochmis P, Sartoris DJ. Perspective. Optimized interpretation and reporting of dual X-ray absorptiometry (DXA) scans. *Am J Roentgenol* 1998;17:1509–1520.

Lenchik L, Sartoris SJ. Current concepts in osteoporosis. *Am J Roentgenol* 1998;168:905–911.

Lomoschitz FM, Grampp S, Henk CB, et al. Comparison of imaging-guided and non-imaging guided quantitative sonography of the calcaneus with dual X-ray absorptiometry of the spine and femur. *Am J Roentgenol* 2003;180:1111–1116.

Majumdar S, Genant HK. High resolution magnetic resonance imaging of trabecular structure. *Eur Radiol* 1997;7(Suppl 2):S51–S55.

Malich A, Boettcher J, Pfeil A, et al. The impact of technical conditions of X-ray imaging on reproducibility and precision of digital computer-assisted X-ray radiogrammetry (DXR). *Skeletal Radiol* 2004;33:698–703.

Mazess RB. Bone densitometry of the axial skeleton. *Orthop Clin North Am* 1990;21:51–63.

Mazess RB, Barden HS. Measurement of bone by dual-photon absorptiometry (DPA) and dual-energy x-ray absorptiometry (DEXA). *Ann Chir Gynaecol* 1988;77:197–203.

Miller PD, Bonnick SL, Rosen CJ. Consensus of an international panel on the clinical utility of bone mass measurement in the detection of low bone mass in the adult population. *Calcif Tissue Int* 1996;58:207–214.

Nelson DA, Brown EB, Flynn MJ, Cody DD, Shaffer S. Comparison of dual photon and dual energy x-ray bone densitometers in a clinical setting. *Skeletal Radiol* 1991;20:591–595.

Nilas L, Borg J, Gotfredsen A, Christiansen C. Comparison of single- and dual-photon absorptiometry in postmenopausal bone mineral loss. *J Nucl Med* 1985;26:1257–1262.

Passariello R, Albanese CV, Kvasnovà M. Bone densitometry in the clinical practice. *Eur Radiol* 1997;7(Suppl 2):S2–S10.

Pullan BR, Roberts TE. Bone mineral measurement using an EMI scanner and standard methods: a comparative study. *Br J Radiol* 1978;51:24–28.

Reinbold WD, Genant HK, Reiser UJ, Harris ST, Ettinger B. Bone mineral content in early-postmenopausal osteoporotic women and postmenopausal women: comparison of measurement methods. *Radiology* 1986;160:469–478.

Resnick D, Niwayama G. Osteoporosis. In: Resnick D, ed. *Diagnosis of bone and joint disorders*, vol 5, 3rd ed. Philadelphia: WB Saunders; 1995.

Rosenberg AE. The pathology of metabolic bone disease. *Radiol Clin North Am* 1991;29:19–36.

Rupich R, Pacifici R, Delabar C, Susman N, Avidi LV. Lateral dual energy radiography: new technique for the measurement of L3 bone mineral density. *J Bone Miner Res* 1989;4:S194.

Ryan PJ. Overview of role of BMD measurements in managing osteoporosis. *Semin Nucl Med* 1997;27:197–209.

Sartoris DJ. Clinical value of bone densitometry. *Am J Roentgenol* 1994;163:133–135.

Scientific Advisory Board of the Osteoporosis Society of Canada. Clinical practice guidelines for the diagnosis and management of osteoporosis. *Can Med Assoc J* 1996;155:1113–1133.

Slemenda CW, Johnston CC. Bone mass measurement: which site to measure? *Am J Med* 1988;84:643–645.

Slosman DO, Rissoli R, Donath A, Bonjour J-P. Vertebral bone mineral density measured laterally by dual-energy x-ray absorptiometry. *Osteoporosis Int* 1990;1:23–29.

Staron RB, Greenspan R, Miller TT, Bilezikian JP, Shane E, Haramati N. Computerized bone densitometric analysis: operator-dependent errors. *Radiology* 1999;211:467–470.

Svendsen OL, Marslew U, Hassager C, Christiansen C. Measurements of bone mineral density of the proximal femur by two commercially available dual-energy x-ray absorptiometric systems. *Eur J Nucl Med* 1992;19:41–46.

Virtama P, Helelä T. Radiographic measurements of cortical bone: variations in a normal population between 1 and 90 years of age. *Acta Radiol* 1969;7(Suppl):268–293.

Wahner HW, Dunn WL, Brown ML, Morin RL, Riggs BL. Comparison of dual-energy x-ray absorptiometry and dual photon absorptiometry for bone mineral measurements of the lumbar spine. *Mayo Clin Proc* 1988;63:1075–1084.

Wilson CR, Collier BD, Carrera GF, Jacobson DR. Acronym for dual-energy x-ray absorptiometry. *Radiology* 1990;176:875–876.

Osteoporosis, Rickets, and Osteomalacia

Osteoporosis

Osteoporosis is a generalized metabolic bone disease characterized by insufficient formation or increased resorption of bone matrix that results in decreased bone mass and microarchitectural deterioration of bone. Although there is a reduction in the amount of bone tissue, the tissue present is still fully mineralized. In other words, the bone is quantitatively deficient but qualitatively normal.

Osteoporosis has a variety of possible causes and consequently manifests in a number of different forms (Table 27.1). The basic distinction in osteoporosis is between those types that are *generalized* or *diffuse*, involving the entire skeleton, and those that are *localized* to a single region or bone (*regional*) (Fig. 27.1). The basic distinction between possible causes is between those that are *congenital* and those that are *acquired*.

Generalized Osteoporosis

Certain radiographic features are common to virtually all forms of osteoporosis, regardless of their specific cause. There are always some diminution of cortical thickness and decrease in the number and thickness of the spongy bone trabeculae (Fig. 27.2). These changes are more prominent in non–weight-bearing segments and those not subject to stress. The first sites affected by osteoporosis, as well as the ones that are best demonstrated on radiographic study, are the periarticular regions, where the cortex is anatomically thinner (Fig. 27.3). In the long bones, the thickness of the cortices decreases, the bones become brittle, and there is increased clinical incidence of fractures, particularly of the proximal femur (Fig. 27.4), the proximal humerus, the distal radius, and the ribs.

Besides quantitative computed tomography (QCT) and other methods of evaluating osteoporosis (discussed in detail in Chapter 26), some simple methods using conventional radiography have been developed.

The analysis of the trabecular pattern of the bones has been emphasized as an effective method to evaluate osteoporosis, since patterns of trabecular loss correlate well with increasing severity of osteoporosis.

In the femur, these changes may be evaluated using the Singh index, which is based on the trabecular architecture of the proximal femur—namely, the pattern of the principal compressive group of trabeculae, the secondary compressive group of trabeculae, and the principal tensile group of trabeculae (Fig. 27.5 and Table 27.2). The trabecular pattern of the proximal end of the femur is an excellent indicator of the severity of the osteoporosis. Singh has shown that trabecular loss occurs in a predictable sequence that can be used to grade the severity of osteopenia. He recognized that the compressive trabeculae were more essential than the tensile trabeculae, and that the peripherally located trabeculae were more vital than central ones.

Six radiologic grades have been defined according to the trabecular pattern (Fig. 27.6).

In early osteoporosis, both the compressive and tensile trabeculae are accentuated because of initial resorption of the randomly oriented trabeculae, and thus the radiolucency of the Ward triangle becomes more prominent. With increasing severity of osteoporosis, the tensile trabeculae are reduced in number and regress from the medial femoral border to the lateral. When trabecular resorption increases, the outer portion of the principal tensile trabeculae opposite the greater trochanter disappear, opening the Ward triangle laterally. As osteoporosis increases in severity, resorption of all trabeculae occurs, with the exception of those in the principal compressive group. In advanced osteoporosis, the principal compressive component is the last to be involved, a process manifested by a decrease in the number and length of individual trabeculae. Eventually, the upper femur may be completely devoid of all trabecular markings.

The other major area in which osteoporotic changes are evaluated is the axial skeleton, particularly the spine. This is especially true in osteoporosis associated with aging, that is, *involutional* (senescent and postmenopausal) *osteoporosis*, in which the vertebral bodies are particularly vulnerable. Initially, there is a relative increase in the density of the vertebral end plates due to resorption of the spongy bone, causing what is called an "empty box" appearance (Fig. 27.7). Later, there is an overall decrease in density with a loss of any trabecular pattern, creating a "ground glass" appearance. A typical feature of vertebral involvement in osteoporosis is biconcavity of the body, which exhibits a "fish mouth" appearance ("codfish vertebrae") (Fig. 27.8). This presentation results from expansion of the disks, leading to arch-like indentations on both superior and inferior margins of the weakened vertebral bodies. In advanced stages, there is complete collapse of the vertebral body associated with a wedge-shaped deformity. In the thoracic spine, this leads to increased kyphosis.

Of special interest in generalized osteoporosis are the three major varieties of *iatrogenic osteoporosis*. *Heparin-induced osteoporosis* may develop after long-term, high-dose daily heparin treatment (more than 10,000 units). Precisely how this type of osteoporosis is initiated and

TABLE 27.1   Causes of Osteoporosis

Generalized (Diffuse)		Localized (Regional)
Genetic (Congenital)	**Deficiency States**	
Osteogenesis imperfecta	Scurvy	Immobilization (cast)
Gonadal dysgenesis:	Malnutrition	Disuse
Turner syndrome (XO)	Anorexia nervosa	Pain
Klinefelter syndrome	Protein deficiency	Infection
(XXY)	Alcoholism	Reflex sympathetic dystrophy
Hypophosphatasia	Liver disease	syndrome (Sudeck atrophy)
Homocystinuria	**Neoplastic**	Transient regional osteoporosis:
Mucopolysaccharidosis	Myeloma	Transient osteoporosis of the hip
Gaucher disease	Leukemia	Regional migratory osteoporosis
Anemias:	Lymphoma	Idiopathic juvenile osteoporosis
Sickle-cell syndromes	Metastatic disease	Paget disease (hot phase)
Thalassemia	**Steroid-induced**	
Hemophilia	Heparin-induced	
Christmas disease	Dilantin-induced	
Endocrine	Steroid induced	
Hyperthyroidism	**Miscellaneous**	
Hyperparathyroidism	Involutional (senescent/	
Cushing syndrome	postmenopausal)	
Acromegaly	Amyloidosis	
Estrogen deficiency	Ochronosis	
Hypogonadism	Paraplegia	
Diabetes mellitus	Weightlessness	
Pregnancy	Idiopathic	

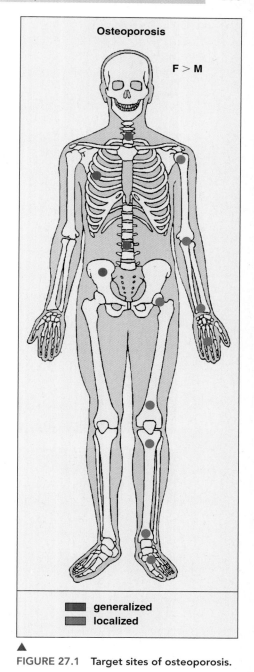

FIGURE 27.1   Target sites of osteoporosis.

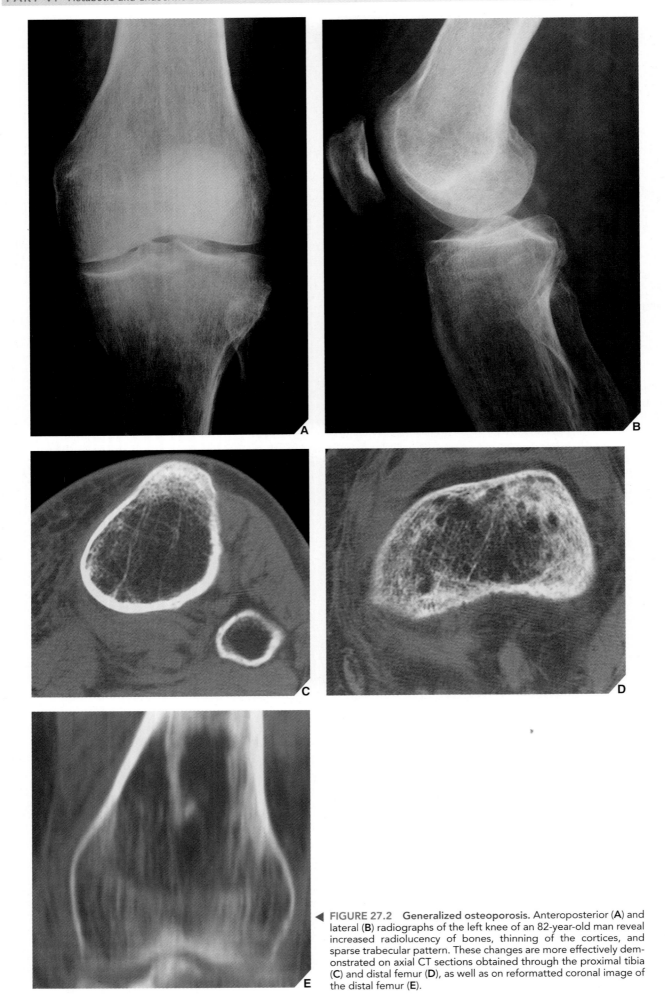

◀ FIGURE 27.2   Generalized osteoporosis. Anteroposterior (A) and lateral (B) radiographs of the left knee of an 82-year-old man reveal increased radiolucency of bones, thinning of the cortices, and sparse trabecular pattern. These changes are more effectively demonstrated on axial CT sections obtained through the proximal tibia (C) and distal femur (D), as well as on reformatted coronal image of the distal femur (E).

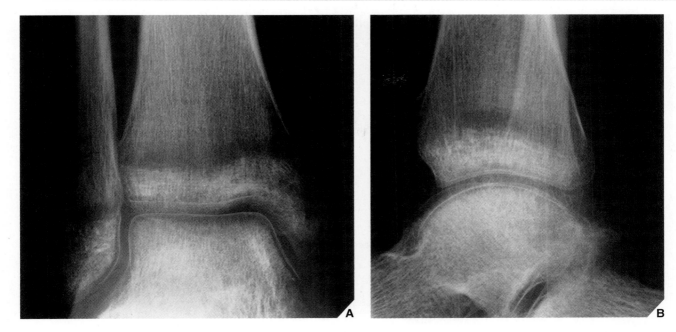

▲
FIGURE 27.3 **Periarticular osteoporosis.** Anteroposterior (**A**) and lateral (**B**) radiographs of an ankle reveal sparse trabecular pattern and increase radiolucency in the subchondral areas.

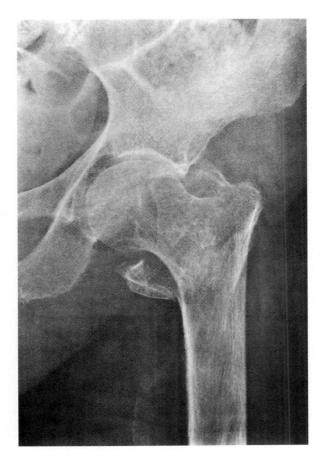

▲
FIGURE 27.4 **Osteoporosis complicated by a fracture.** An 85-year-old woman with advanced postmenopausal osteoporosis sustained an intertrochanteric fracture of the left femur, as seen on this anteroposterior radiograph. Note the thinning of the cortex and the increased radiolucency of the bones.

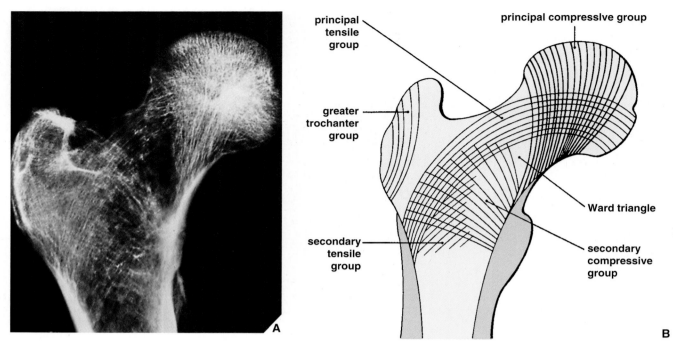

▲
FIGURE 27.5 **The Singh trabecular index. (A)** The trabecular pattern of the proximal end of the femur is an excellent indicator of the severity of the osteoporosis. **(B)** The trabecular arcades are important to the Singh trabecular index. Confluence of principal tensile, principal compressive, and secondary compressive trabeculae in the femoral neck forms a triangular region of radiolucency, the Ward triangle. The principal tensile trabeculae are more important than the secondary trabeculae; the compressive trabeculae are more important than the tensile trabeculae. Bone loss occurs in order of increasing importance. (Modified from Singh M et al., 1970, with permission.)

TABLE 27.2   The Five Major Groups of Trabeculae

1. Principal Compressive Group
   - Extend from medial cortex of femoral neck to superior part of femoral head
   - Major weight-bearing trabeculae
   - In normal femur are the thickest and most densely packed
   - Appear accentuated in osteoporosis
   - Last to be obliterated
2. Secondary Compressive Group
   - Originate at the cortex, near the lesser trochanter
   - Curve upward and laterally toward the greater trochanter and upper femoral neck
   - Characteristically thin and widely separated
3. Principal Tensile Group
   - Originate from the lateral cortex, inferior to the greater trochanter
   - Extend in an arch-like configuration medially, terminating in the inferior portion of the femoral head
4. Secondary Tensile Group
   - Arise from the lateral cortex below the principal tensile group
   - Extend superiorly and medially to terminate after crossing the middle of the femoral neck
5. Greater Trochanter Group
   - Composed of slender and poorly defined tensile trabeculae
   - Arise laterally below the greater trochanter
   - Extend upward to terminate near the greater trochanter's superior surface

SINGH INDEX—RADIOLOGIC GRADES

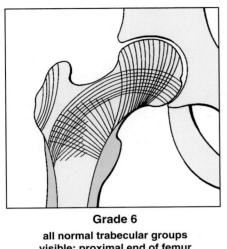

Grade 6
all normal trabecular groups
visible; proximal end of femur
completely occupied by
cancellous bone

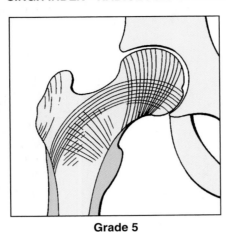

Grade 5
principal tensile and compressive
trabeculae accentuated;
Ward triangle prominent

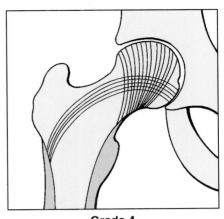

Grade 4
principal tensile and trabeculae
reduced in number but still can
be traced from lateral cortex
to femoral neck

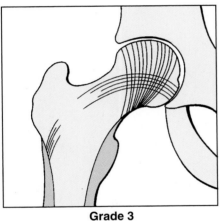

Grade 3
break in continuity of
principal tensile trabeculae
opposite greater trochanter

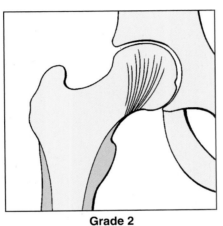

Grade 2
only principal compressive
trabeculae can be seen;
all tensile trabeculae
have been resorbed

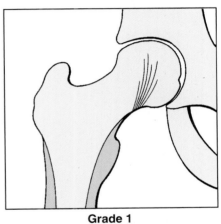

Grade 1
principal compressive trabeculae
markedly reduced in number

▲
FIGURE 27.6 **Singh index—radiologic grades.** (Modified from Singh M et al., 1970, with permission.)

develops is not clearly understood, although osteoclastic stimulation and osteoblastic inhibition with suppressed endochondral ossification have been implicated as potential causes. Spontaneous fractures of the vertebrae, ribs, and femoral neck are noted on radiographic studies. *Dilantin-induced osteoporosis* occasionally develops after prolonged use of phenytoin (Dilantin). The vertebral column and ribs are usually affected, and fractures are a common complication.

Steroid-induced osteoporosis, occurring either during the course of Cushing syndrome or iatrogenically during treatment with various corticosteroids, is characterized by decreased bone formation and increased bone resorption. Although the axial skeleton is most often affected, the appendicular skeleton may also be involved. In the spine, considerable thickening and sclerosis of the vertebral end plates occur without a concomitant change in the anterior and posterior vertebral margins.

Osteoporosis associated with neoplastic processes is discussed in Chapter 16.

Localized Osteoporosis

Transient regional osteoporosis is a collective term for a group of conditions that have one feature in common: rapidly developing

osteoporosis that usually affects the periarticular regions and has no definite etiology like trauma or immobilization. It is a self-limiting and reversible disorder, of which three subtypes have been described. *Transient osteoporosis of the hip* is seen predominantly in pregnant women and in young and middle-aged men. Its primary manifestation is local osteoporosis involving the femoral head and neck and the acetabulum. *Regional migratory osteoporosis*, which affects the knee, the ankle, and the foot, is mainly seen in men in their fourth and fifth decades. This migratory condition is characterized by pain and swelling around the affected joints. It develops rapidly and subsides in about 6 to 9 months; there may be subsequent recurrence and involvement of other joints. *Idiopathic juvenile osteoporosis* is commonly seen during or just before puberty, and typically regresses spontaneously. Skeletal involvement is often symmetrical and is generally juxta-articular in location. It is frequently associated with pain and the presence of vertebral body compression fractures.

Localized osteoporosis secondary to immobilization in a cast or due to disuse of a painful limb is discussed in Chapter 4. Sudeck atrophy (reflex sympathetic dystrophy syndrome) may also occur as a complication of fractures (see Fig. 4.53).

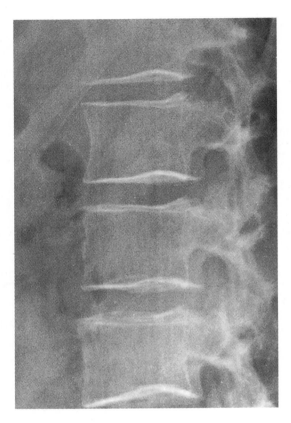

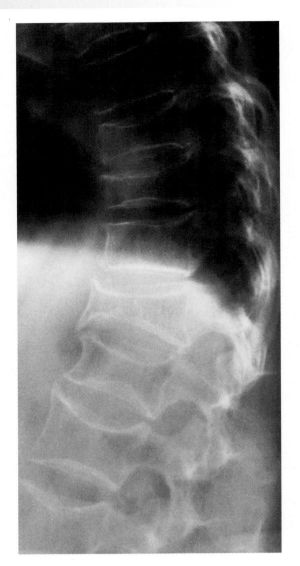

▲ **FIGURE 27.7 Involutional osteoporosis.** Lateral radiograph of the lumbar spine of an 89-year-old woman demonstrates a relative increase in the density of the vertebral end plates and resorption of the trabeculae of spongy bone, creating an "empty box" appearance.

▲ **FIGURE 27.8 Involutional osteoporosis.** Biconcavity, or "codfish vertebrae," seen here on the lateral view of the thoracolumbar spine in an 80-year-old woman, results from weakness of the vertebral end plates and intravertebral expansion of nuclei pulposi.

Rickets and Osteomalacia

Whereas in osteoporosis the fundamental change is decreased bone mass, in rickets (which occurs in children) and osteomalacia (which occurs in adults) the essential bone abnormality is faulty mineralization (calcification) of the bone matrix. If adequate amounts of calcium and phosphorus are not available, proper calcification of osteoid tissue cannot occur.

In the past, the most common cause of rickets (the term evolved from the old English word *wrick*, meaning "to twist") and osteomalacia was *deficient intake* of vitamin D, which is responsible for calcium and phosphorus homeostasis and for maintenance of proper bone mineralization. Now, however, the major causes include *inadequate intestinal absorption*, resulting in the loss of calcium and phosphorus through the gastrointestinal tract in patients who have gastric, biliary, or enteric abnormalities or have undergone gastrectomy or other gastric surgery; *renal tubular disorders* (proximal and/or distal tubular lesions frequently leading to renal tubular acidosis); and *renal osteodystrophy* secondary to renal failure, which results in loss of calcium through the kidneys. Several other conditions associated with osteomalacia have been identified, such as neurofibromatosis, fibrous dysplasia, and Wilson disease, but the exact relationship between the underlying disorder and osteomalacia is still unclear (Table 27.3).

Rickets

Infantile Rickets

Found mainly in infants between 6 and 18 months of age, infantile rickets is characterized by generalized demineralization of the skeleton, which leads to bowing deformities in weight-bearing bones when infants begin to stand and walk. Infants with early rickets are restless and sleep poorly. Closing of the fontanelles is delayed. The earliest physical sign is softening of the cranial vault (craniotabes). Enlargement of the cartilage at the costochondral junction produces a prominence known as "rachitic rosary." The serum values of calcium and phosphorus are low, and that of alkaline phosphatase is increased.

The key radiographic features are observed in the metaphysis and the epiphysis—the regions where growth is most active—particularly at the distal ends of the radius, ulna, and femur, as well as at the proximal ends of the tibia and fibula (Fig. 27.9). Deficient mineralization in the provisional zone of calcification is reflected in widening of the growth plate and cupping and flaring of the metaphysis, which appears disorganized and "frayed" (Figs. 27.10 and 27.11; see also Fig. 26.6). In the secondary ossification centers of the epiphysis, similar changes are seen; the bone becomes radiolucent, with loss of sharpness at the periphery, and bowing deformities frequently occur (Fig. 27.12).

TABLE 27.3 Etiology of Rickets and Osteomalacia

Nutritional Deficiency
Vitamin D
  Dietary
  Insufficient sunlight
  Impaired synthesis
Calcium
Phosphorus
Absorption Abnormalities
Gastric surgery
Intestinal surgery (bypass)
Gastric disorders (obstruction)
Intestinal disorders (sprue)
Biliary diseases
Renal Disorders
Renal tubular disorders
  Proximal tubular lesions (failure of absorption of inorganic
    phosphate, glucose, amino acids)
  Distal tubular lesions (renal tubular acidosis)
  Combined proximal and distal tubular lesions
Renal osteodystrophy
Miscellaneous
Associated with
  Wilson disease
  Fibrogenesis imperfecta
  Fibrous dysplasia
  Neurofibromatosis
  Hypophosphatasia
  Neoplasm

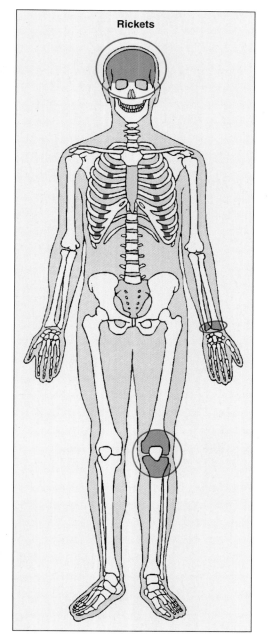

▲
FIGURE 27.9   Target sites of rickets.

Vitamin D–Resistant Rickets

This condition is found in older children (those above 30 months of age), and four distinct types have been reported. *Classic vitamin D–resistant* (or hypophosphatemic) *rickets*, also known as *familial vitamin D–resistant rickets*, is a congenital disorder that is transmitted as a sex-linked dominant trait. Recent studies indicated that hypophosphatemic rickets occur as the result of mutation of *PHEX* gene found on the X-chromosome. This gene normally produces an enzyme zinc-metallopeptidase. Loss of function of this gene results in circulatory clearance of fibroblast growth factor 23 (FGF-23) that acts on the kidneys to increase phosphate excretion and decrease alpha-1 hydroxylase activity. This results in hypophosphatemia, but normal levels of serum calcium. Patients are short, stocky, and bowlegged. Ectopic calcifications and ossifications in the axial and the appendicular skeleton, along with occasional sclerotic changes, are among the identifying radiographic findings. *Vitamin D–resistant rickets with glycosuria* is characterized by an abnormal resorptive mechanism for glucose and inorganic phosphate. *Fanconi syndrome* is characterized by a defect in the proximal renal tubules and deficient resorption of phosphate, glucose, and several amino acids. *Acquired hypophosphatemic syndrome* manifests in late adolescence or early adulthood; it is probably of toxic etiology.

The radiographic findings in all four types of vitamin D–resistant rickets are similar to those in infantile rickets. Bowing of the legs and shortening of the long bones, however, are more pronounced, and occasionally the bones appear sclerotic (Fig. 27.13).

Osteomalacia

Osteomalacia, which results from the same pathomechanism as rickets, occurs only after bone growth has ceased, and hence the term refers to changes in the cortical and trabecular bone of the axial and appendicular skeleton. It is most often caused by faulty absorption of fat-soluble vitamin D from the gastrointestinal tract secondary to malabsorption syndrome. It may also result from dysfunction of the proximal renal tubules, resulting in so-called renal osteomalacia. The most common clinical presentation of this condition is bone pain and muscle weakness.

Histologically, osteomalacia is characterized by excessive quantities of inadequately mineralized bone matrix (osteoid) coating the surfaces of trabeculae in spongy bone and lining the haversian canals in the cortex.

Radiographically, osteomalacia presents with generalized osteopenia, and multiple, bilateral, and often symmetric radiolucent lines are seen in the cortex perpendicular to the long axis of the bone; they are referred to as "pseudofractures" or Looser zones (Fig. 27.14, see also Fig. 26.5). These defects, which represent cortical stress fractures filled with poorly mineralized callus, osteoid, and fibrous tissue, are common along the axillary margins of the scapulae, the inner margin of the femoral neck, the proximal dorsal aspect of the ulnae, the ribs, and the pubic and ischial rami (Fig. 27.15). The condition, described by Milkman and known as *"Milkman syndrome,"* is a mild form of osteomalacia in which the pseudofractures are particularly numerous.

An interesting form of osteomalacia is *oncogenic osteomalacia* (also known as *tumor-induced osteomalacia* [TIO]), a paraneoplastic syndrome characterized by hypophosphatemia, hyperphosphaturia, and low levels

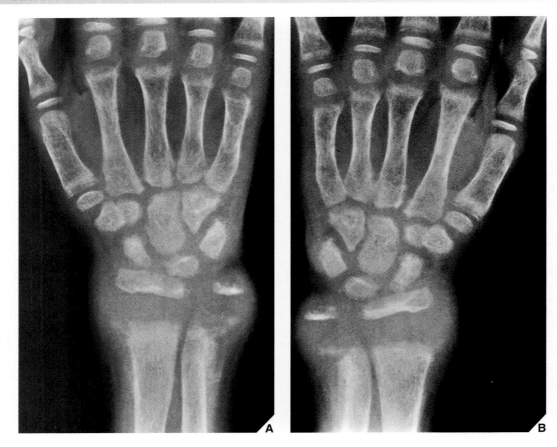

▲
FIGURE 27.10   **Rickets. (A,B)** Anteroposterior radiograph of both hands of an 8-year-old boy with untreated dietary rickets shows osteopenia of the bones, widening of the growth plates of the distal radius and ulna, and flaring of the metaphyses, all typical features of this condition.

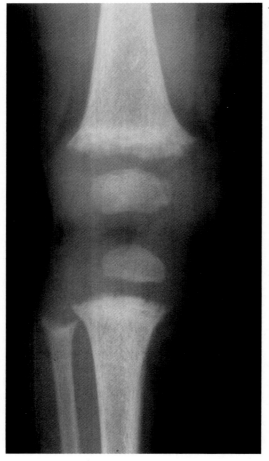

◀ FIGURE 27.11   **Rickets.** Anteroposterior radiograph of the knee in a 4-year-old boy shows widening of the growth plates of the distal femur and proximal tibia secondary to lack of mineralization in the provisional zone of calcification. Note also cupping and flaring of the metaphyses.

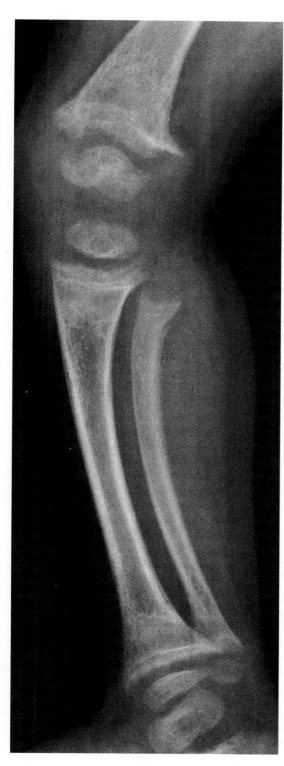

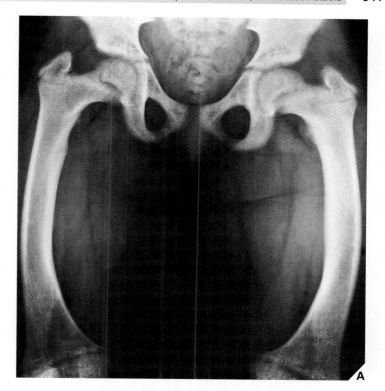

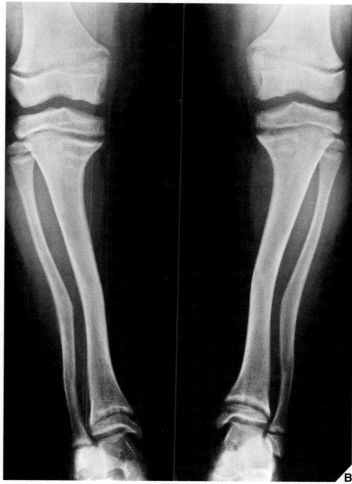

▲
FIGURE 27.12 Rickets. Lateral radiograph of the lower leg of a 3-year-old girl with vitamin D–deficiency rickets shows increased bone radiolucency, widening of the growth plates, cupping and flaring of the metaphyses, and blurring of the outline of the secondary ossification centers, all radiographic hallmarks of this condition. Note also bowing of the tibia and fibula, a frequent feature of rickets.

▲
FIGURE 27.13 Vitamin D–resistant rickets. (A) Anteroposterior radiograph of the femora of a 9-year-old girl with vitamin D–resistant (hypophosphatemic) rickets shows lateral bowing and shortening of both bones. There is also evidence of sclerotic changes, which are occasionally seen in this condition. **(B)** The knees and lower legs of the same patient show a bowing deformity of the tibiae and fibulae, as well as widening and deformity of the growth plates about the knees and the ankles.

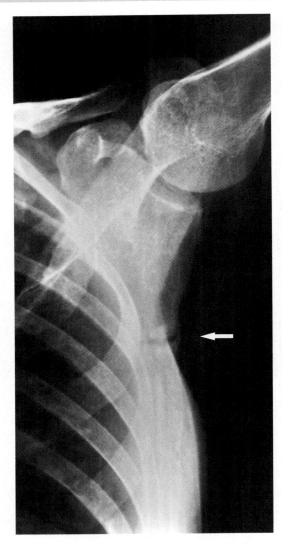

▲
FIGURE 27.14   Osteomalacia. Anteroposterior radiograph of the left shoulder of a 25-year-old woman with osteomalacia caused by malabsorption syndrome shows a radiolucent cleft perpendicular to the cortex of the scapula (*arrow*). Such defects, known as pseudofractures (Looser zones), are almost pathognomonic for osteomalacia (see also Fig. 26.5).

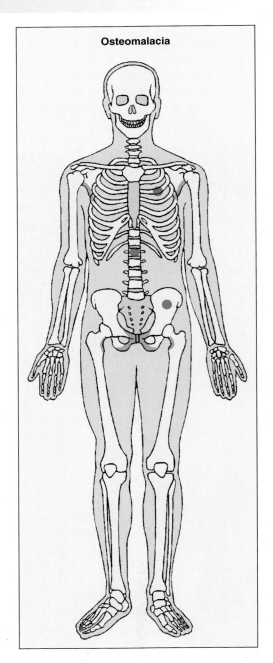

▲
FIGURE 27.15   Target sites of osteomalacia.

of plasma 1,25-dihydroxyvitamin D, caused by a bone and soft-tissue tumors or tumor-like lesions. The tumors commonly responsible for this syndrome are usually benign, slow-growing vascular lesions (such as hemangioma or hemangiopericytoma), osteoblastoma-like lesions, nonossifying fibroma-like lesions, and very rarely some malignant neoplasms. It has been suggested that similar to X-linked hypophosphatemia, mutations in FGF-23 are the etiologic factor in TIO. Tumors producing this syndrome secrete excessive amounts of phosphatonin. The clinical symptoms include muscle weakness, bone pain, and occasionally fractures. The condition is reversed when the inciting lesion is resected.

Renal Osteodystrophy

A skeletal response to long-standing renal disease, renal osteodystrophy (also referred to as "uremic osteopathy") is usually associated with chronic renal failure due to glomerulonephritis or pyelonephritis. The condition is also seen in patients who are on dialysis or who have undergone renal transplantation.

Two main mechanisms, acting in unison but varying in severity and proportion, are responsible for osseous changes associated with this condition: secondary hyperparathyroidism and abnormal vitamin D metabolism. The secondary hyperparathyroidism is provoked by phosphate retention and leads to depression of serum calcium, which in turn stimulates release of parathormone from parathyroid glands. The abnormal vitamin D metabolism is affected by renal insufficiency, since the kidney is the source of an enzyme, 25-OH-D-1 α-hydroxylase, which converts the inactive vitamin D from 25-hydroxyvitamin D (25-OH-D) to active 1,25-dihydroxyvitamin D [1,25 (OH)$_2$D]. Only this most potent, physiologically active form of vitamin D is responsible for calcium and phosphorus homeostasis and for the maintenance of proper bone mineralization.

The major radiographic manifestations of renal osteodystrophy are those associated with rickets, osteomalacia, and secondary hyperparathyroidism. Rickets and osteomalacia secondary to renal osteodystrophy are seldom seen in its pure form; usually there are superimposed changes typical of secondary hyperparathyroidism (Fig. 27.16). Increased bone radiolucency and cortical thinning may be present (Fig. 27.17), but Looser zones are very uncommon. In most patients, some sclerotic changes develop in the bones. Slipped epiphyses may be seen in advanced uremic disease. Soft-tissue calcifications are frequently encountered (Fig. 27.18).

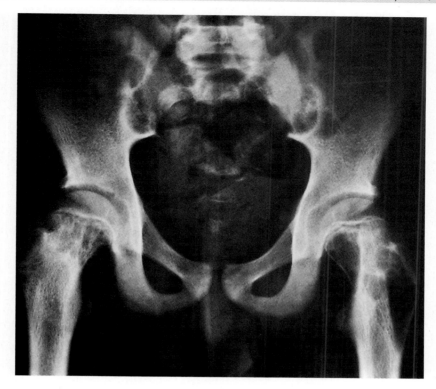

▲

FIGURE 27.16   **Renal osteodystrophy.** A 13-year-old boy with posterior urethral valves and secondary renal failure exhibited radiographic changes typical of renal osteodystrophy, encompassing a mixture of osteomalacia and secondary hyperparathyroidism. Anteroposterior radiograph of the pelvis shows sclerotic changes in the bones and characteristic widening of the sacroiliac joints. The multiple cystic defects in the proximal femora (brown tumors) indicate secondary hyperparathyroidism.

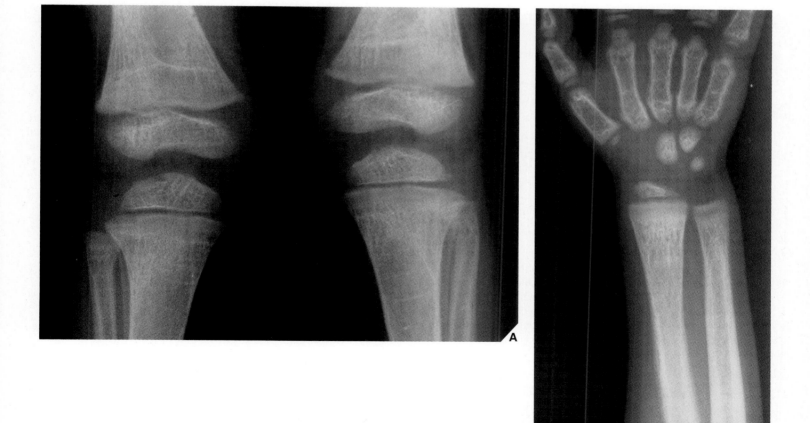

▲

FIGURE 27.17   **Renal osteodystrophy. (A)** Anteroposterior radiograph of the knees and **(B)** dorsovolar radiograph of the wrist of a 6-year-old boy with chronic pyelonephritis reveals osteopenic bones and thin cortices. (Courtesy of Dr. Philip E. S. Palmer, Davis, California.)

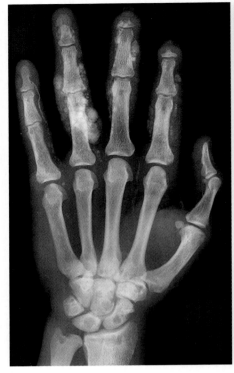 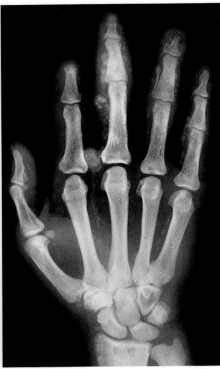

FIGURE 27.18 **Renal osteodystrophy.** Conventional radiographs of the hands of a 45-year-old man on dialysis because of an end-stage renal disease show extensive soft-tissue calcifications and acro-osteolysis of the distal phalanges of the index and middle fingers of the right hand, and the ring finger of the left hand. Note also several brown tumors in the carpal bones.

PRACTICAL POINTS TO REMEMBER

Osteoporosis

[1] Osteoporosis is characterized by:
- insufficient formation or increased resorption of bone matrix, resulting in decreased bone mass
- increased radiolucency of bone and thinning of the cortices on conventional radiography.

[2] The target sites of osteoporotic changes are:
- the axial skeleton (spine and pelvis)
- the periarticular regions of the appendicular skeleton.

[3] The analysis of the trabecular pattern in the proximal end of femur (Singh index) is an effective method of evaluating osteoporosis, since patterns of trabecular loss correlate well with increasing severity of osteoporosis.

[4] In the spine, characteristic radiographic features that indicate the severity of osteoporotic involvement are:
- "empty box" appearance (early stage)
- "codfish vertebrae"
- multiple wedge-shaped fractures (advanced stage).

[5] There are several noninvasive methods available that allow accurate measurements of bone mineral density in patients with osteoporosis. The most effective technique is DEXA, which uses photons produced from a low-dose energy source. The other effective method is QCT for measuring the lumbar spine mineral content.

Rickets and Osteomalacia

[1] Rickets (in children) and osteomalacia (in adults) are the result of faulty mineralization (calcification) of the bone matrix.

[2] On radiographic examination, rickets is characterized by:
- generalized osteopenia
- bowing deformities of the long bones, particularly the femur and tibia
- widening of the growth plate (secondary to deficient mineralization in the provisional zone of calcification) and cupping or flaring of the metaphysis, particularly in the proximal humerus, distal radius and ulna, and distal femur.

[3] The radiographic findings in vitamin D–resistant rickets are similar to those in infantile rickets. Bowing deformities and shortening of the long bones are, however, more pronounced.

[4] Radiographically, osteomalacia is characterized by:
- generalized osteopenia
- symmetric radiolucent lines in the cortex (Looser zones or pseudofractures).

[5] Renal osteodystrophy, usually associated with chronic renal failure due to glomerulonephritis or pyelonephritis, represents a skeletal response to long-standing renal disease. The major radiographic manifestations are those associated with rickets, osteomalacia, and secondary hyperparathyroidism, with predominance of osteosclerosis, bone resorption, and bowing deformities.

SUGGESTED READINGS

Arnstein AR. Regional osteoporosis. *Orthop Clin North Am* 1972;3:585–600.

Beaulieu JG, Razzano D, Levine RB. Transient osteoporosis of the hip in pregnancy. Review of the literature and a case report. *Clin Orthop* 1976;115:165–168.

Briggs AM, Wrigley TV, Tully EA, Adams PE, Greig AM, Bennell KL. Radiographic measures of thoracic kyphosis in osteoporosis: Cobb and vertebral centroid angles. *Skeletal Radiol* 2007;36:761–767.

Carpenter TO. Oncogenic osteomalacia – a complex dance of factors. *New Engl J Med* 2003;348:1705–1708.

Cotton GE, Van Puffelen P. Hypophosphatemic osteomalacia secondary to neoplasia. *J Bone Joint Surg* 1986;68:129–133.

Cumming WA. Idiopathic juvenile osteoporosis. *Can Assoc Radiol J* 1970;21:21–26.

Dunn AW. Senile osteoporosis. *Geriatrics* 1967;22:175–180.

Eggleston DE, Bartold K, Abghari R. Recognition of renal osteodystrophy on bone imaging. *Clin Nucl Med* 1986;11:543–544.

Gillespy T III, Gillespy MP. Osteoporosis. *Radiol Clin North Am* 1991;29:77–84.

Greenfield GB. Roentgen appearance of bone and soft tissue changes in chronic renal disease. *Am J Roentgenol* 1972;116:749–757.

Griffith GC, Nichols G Jr, Asher JD, Flanagan B. Heparin osteoporosis. *JAMA* 1965;193:91–94.

Hesse E, Rosenthal H, Bastian L. Radiofrequency ablation of a tumor causing oncogenic osteomalacia. *New Engl J Med* 2007;357:422–424.

Houang MTW, Brenton DP, Renton P, Shaw DG. Idiopathic juvenile osteoporosis. *Skeletal Radiol* 1978;3:17–23.

Hunder GG, Kelly PJ. Roentgenologic transient osteoporosis of the hip. A clinical syndrome? *Ann Intern Med* 1968;68:539–552.

Jaworski AFG. Pathophysiology, diagnosis, and treatment of osteomalacia. *Orthop Clin North Am* 1972;3:623–652.

Jones G. Radiological appearance of disuse osteoporosis. *Clin Radiol* 1969;20: 345–353.

Jonsson KB, Zahradnik R, Larsson T, et al. Fibroblast growth factor 23 in onco-genic osteomalacia and X-linked hypophosphatemia. *New Engl J Med* 2003;348: 1656–1663.

Kaplan FS. Osteoporosis: pathophysiology and prevention. *Clin Symp* 1987;39:1–32.

Lang P, Steiger P, Faulkner K, Glüer C, Genant H. Osteoporosis: current techniques and recent developments in quantitative bone densitometry. *Radiol Clin North Am* 1991;29:49–76.

Mankin HJ. Rickets, osteomalacia, and renal osteodystrophy—Part I. *J Bone Joint Surg [Am]* 1974;56A:101–128.

Mankin HJ. Rickets, osteomalacia, and renal osteodystrophy—Part II. *J Bone Joint Surg [Am]* 1974;56A:352–386.

Mayo-Smith W, Rosenthal DI. Radiographic appearance of osteopenia. *Radiol Clin North Am* 1991;29:37–47.

McCarthy JT, Kumar R. Behavior of the vitamin D edocrine system in the development of renal osteodystrophy. *Semin Nephrol* 1986;6:21–30.

Milkman LA. Pseudofractures (hunger osteopathy, late rickets, osteomalacia). *Am J Roentgenol* 1930;24:29–37.

Murphey MD, Sartoris DJ, Quale JL, Pathria MN, Martin NL. Musculoskeletal manifestations of chronic renal insufficiency. *Radiographics* 1993;13:357–379.

Parfitt AM. Renal osteodystrophy. *Orthop Clin North Am* 1972;3:681–698.

Parfitt AM, Chir B. Hypophosphatemic vitamin D refractory rickets and osteomalacia. *Orthop Clin North Am* 1971;3:653–680.

Pitt MJ. Rachitic and osteomalacic syndromes. *Radiol Clin North Am* 1981;19:581–598.

Pitt MJ. Rickets and osteomalacia. In Resnick D, ed. *Bone and joint imaging.* Philadelphia: WB Saunders; 1989:589–602.

Pitt MJ. Rickets and osteolamalacia are still around. *Radiol Clin North Am* 1991;29:97–118.

Resnick DL. Fish vertebrae. *Arthritis Rheum* 1982;25:1073–1077.

Resnick D, Deftos LJ, Parthemore JG. Renal osteodystrophy: magnification radiogra-phy of target sites of absorption. *Am J Roentgenol* 1981;136:711–714.

Resnick D, Niwayama G. Subchondral resorption of bone in renal osteodystrophy. *Radiology* 1976;118:315–321.

Riggs BL, Melton JM. Involutional osteoporosis. *N Engl J Med* 1986;314:1676–1686.

Sackler JP, Liu L. Case reports: heparin-induced osteoporosis. *Br J Radiol* 1973;46: 548–550.

Singh M, Nagrath AR, Maini PS. Changes in trabecular pattern of the upper end of the femur as an index of osteoporosis. *J Bone Joint Surg [Am]* 1970;52A:457–467.

Singh M, Riggs BL, Beaubout JW, Jowsey J. Femoral trabecular-pattern index for evalu-ation of spinal osteoporosis. *Ann Intern Med* 1972;77:63–67.

Sundaram M. Metabolic bone disease: what has changed in 30 years? *Skeletal Radiol* 2009;38:841–853.

Walton J. Familial hypophosphatemic rickets: a declination of its subdivisions and pathogenesis. *Clin Pediatr* 1976;15:1007–1012.

Hyperparathyroidism

Pathophysiology

Hyperparathyroidism, also known as generalized osteitis fibrosa cystica or Recklinghausen disease of bone, is the result of overactivity of the parathormone-producing parathyroid glands. Increased production of this hormone is secondary to either gland hyperplasia (9% of cases) or adenoma (90%); only in very rare instances (1%) does hyperparathyroidism occur secondary to parathyroid carcinoma. Excessive secretion of parathormone, which acts on the kidneys and on bone, leads to disturbances in calcium and phosphorus metabolism, resulting in hypercalcemia, hyperphosphaturia, and hypophosphatemia. Renal excretion of calcium and phosphate is increased, and serum levels of calcium are elevated, while those of phosphorus are reduced. Serum levels of alkaline phosphatase are also elevated.

Hyperparathyroidism can be divided into primary, secondary, and tertiary forms. The classic form of the disorder, *primary hyperparathyroidism*, is marked by an increased secretion of parathormone resulting from hyperplasia, adenoma, or carcinoma of the parathyroid glands. Primary hyperparathyroidism is usually associated with hypercalcemia. Women are affected about three times as often as men, and the condition is most often seen in the patient's third to fifth decade. *Secondary hyperparathyroidism* is caused by an increased secretion of parathyroid hormone (PTH) in response to a sustained hypocalcemic state. Usually the fundamental cause of parathyroid gland hyperfunction is impaired renal function. Hyperphosphatemia due to renal failure results in chronic hypocalcemia, which in turn promotes increased parathyroid secretion. Although secondary hyperparathyroidism is usually hypocalcemic, it may be normocalcemic as an adaptive response to the hypocalcemic state. *Tertiary hyperparathyroidism* represents a transformation from a hypocalcemic to a hypercalcemic state. The parathyroid glands "escape" from the regulatory effect of serum calcium levels. Patients in whom this escape occurs are usually receiving kidney hemodialysis; they are considered to have autonomous hyperparathyroidism.

Although primary hyperparathyroidism is traditionally synonymous with the hypercalcemic form of the disorder, some patients nonetheless may have normal or even reduced serum calcium levels. For this reason, Reiss and Canterbury proposed an alternative method of classifying hyperparathyroidism based on serum calcium levels. In this system, hyperparathyroidism is considered either hypercalcemic, normocalcemic, or hypocalcemic.

In order to understand the clinical, pathologic, and imaging manifestations of hyperparathyroidism, knowledge of the interrelated roles of PTH and vitamin D in the metabolism of calcium is essential.

Physiology of Calcium Metabolism

Serum concentrations of calcium are maintained within a narrow normal physiologic range (2.20 to 2.65 mmol/L or 8.8 to 10.6 mg/dL) by the intestines and kidneys, the major sites of classic negative feedback mechanisms that balance calcium intake and excretion. The bones also contribute to preserving calcium homeostasis and, since they represent approximately 99% of elemental calcium in the human body, are considered to be a calcium reservoir. Essential to these mechanisms involving a variety of hormones is the action of PTH, a polypeptide hormone whose secretion is induced by a decrease in the level of calcium in the extracellular fluid. In primary hyperparathyroidism, there is inappropriate oversecretion of PTH in the presence of elevated serum calcium levels, while secondary hyperparathyroidism is marked by appropriate PTH production in response to chronic hypocalcemia.

PTH works to increase serum calcium concentrations by several means. Predominant among these is conserving calcium in the kidneys by promoting both increased reabsorption of calcium and increased excretion of phosphates in the distal renal tubules. PTH also promotes release of calcium and phosphorus from bone by increasing the number and activity of osteoclasts, resulting in bone resorption, although the exact mechanism by which this occurs is not fully understood. Finally, although PTH has been shown to have no direct effect on intestinal calcium absorption, it plays a role in stimulating vitamin D metabolism, with subsequent increased absorption of calcium and phosphorus by the intestines.

Both forms of vitamin D in the human body—ergocalciferol (vitamin D_2), a synthetic compound and frequent food additive; and cholecalciferol (vitamin D_3), formed predominantly in the skin from 7-dehydrocholesterol by the action of ultraviolet light—are metabolized to 25-hydroxyvitamin D in the liver. The critical step in the metabolism of vitamin D occurs in the kidneys, where 25-hydroxyvitamin D undergoes hydroxylation to its most active form, 1,25-dihydroxyvitamin D, and an inactive metabolite, 24,25-dihydroxyvitamin D. This step is catalyzed by the renal enzyme 1-α-hydroxylase, which is synthesized in the kidneys under the stimulation of PTH in the presence of decreased serum calcium and phosphate levels. This gives the kidneys a unique central role in the metabolism of vitamin D. 1,25-dihydroxyvitamin D is the primary mediator of calcium and phosphorus absorption in the small intestine. The kidneys also have the ability to switch between producing the active and inactive forms of vitamin D, yielding a fine control of calcium metabolism.

The symptoms of hyperparathyroidism are related to hypercalcemia, skeletal abnormalities, and renal disease. Hypercalcemia produces weakness, muscular hypotonia, nausea, anorexia, constipation, polyuria, and thirst. The skeletal abnormalities most commonly seen are generalized osteopenia and foci of bone destruction, which are commonly referred to as brown tumors. These pseudotumors represent areas of fibrous scarring in which osteoclasts collect, blood decomposes, and cysts form. The most common sites of involvement are the mandible, clavicle, ribs, pelvis, and femur. Also, subchondral and subperiosteal bone resorption is invariably present. Kidney involvement results in nephrocalcinosis, impairment of renal function, and uremia.

Radiographic Evaluation

The major target sites in the skeletal system for hyperparathyroidism are the shoulder, the hand, the vertebrae, and the skull (Fig. 28.1). Conventional radiography is usually sufficient to demonstrate its characteristic features: generalized osteopenia; subperiosteal, subchondral, and cortical bone resorption; brown tumors; and soft-tissue and cartilage calcifications. Subperiosteal resorption is particularly well demonstrated on radiographs of the hands, where it usually affects the radial aspects of the middle phalanges of the middle and index fingers (Fig. 28.2; see also Figs. 26.7 and 26.9). Commonly, subchondral bone resorption is present resulting in depression of overlying articular cartilage (Fig. 28.3). Also characteristic of this condition is resorption of the acromial ends of the clavicle (Fig. 28.4). Intracortical resorption is manifested by longitudinal striations, a finding known as "tunneling," which can be most clearly appreciated on magnification studies (see Fig. 26.9B). Another characteristic feature is loss of the lamina dura around the tooth socket, which normally is seen as a thin sharp white line surrounding the peridental membrane that attaches the tooth to bone (Fig. 28.5). In the skull, there is a characteristic mottling of the vault, which yields a "salt-and-pepper" appearance (Fig. 28.6). Localized destructive changes in bones affected by hyperparathyroidism take the form of cyst-like lesions of various sizes, commonly referred to as brown tumors. The jaw, pelvis, and femora are the usual sites for these lesions, but they may be found in any part of the skeleton (Fig. 28.7).

In secondary hyperparathyroidism, other characteristic features may be present in addition to the radiographic abnormalities just discussed. A generalized increase in bone density occurs, particularly in younger patients. In the spine, this change is reflected in dense sclerotic bands seen adjacent to the vertebral end plates, giving the vertebrae a sandwich-like appearance. This phenomenon is termed "rugger-jersey" spine because the sclerotic bands form horizontal stripes resembling those of rugby shirts (Fig. 28.8). However, it must be kept in mind in the evaluation of hyperparathyroidism that osteosclerotic changes may also occur as a manifestation of healing, either spontaneously or as a result of treatment. Deposition of calcium in fibrocartilage, articular cartilage, and soft tissue is common, and vascular calcifications are much more frequent in patients with secondary hyperparathyroidism (Fig. 28.9).

Complications

Both primary and secondary hyperparathyroidism may be complicated by pathologic fractures, which usually occur in the ribs and vertebral bodies. Hyperparathyroidism arthropathy, another frequent complication, has been discussed in more detail in Chapter 15. Slipped capital femoral or humeral epiphysis may also be observed on occasion. The involvement of ligaments and tendons results in capsular and ligamentous laxity, which may lead to joint instability. Occasionally, spontaneous tendon avulsion has been observed, a phenomenon attributed to the direct effect of PTH on connective tissue. Even less frequently intraarticular crystal deposition (calcium pyrophosphate dihydrate) in cartilage, capsule, and synovium may occur, which may lead to the pseudogout syndrome.

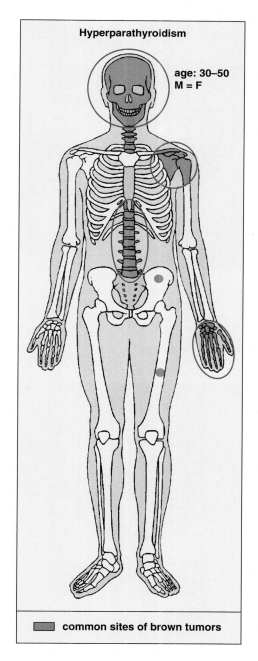

FIGURE 28.1 Major target sites of hyperparathyroidism.

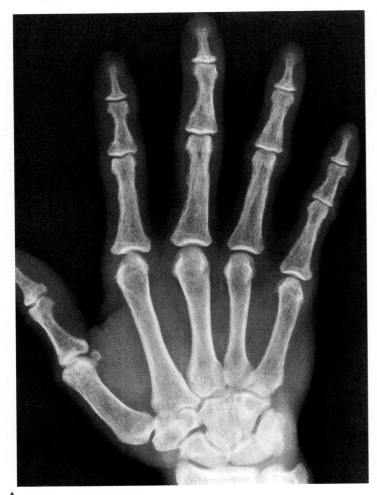

▲ FIGURE 28.2   **Primary hyperparathyroidism.** Dorsovolar radiograph of the left hand of a 42-year-old man with primary hyperparathyroidism caused by hypertrophy of the parathyroid glands shows typical subperiosteal resorption affecting primarily the radial aspects of the middle phalanges of the middle and index fingers.

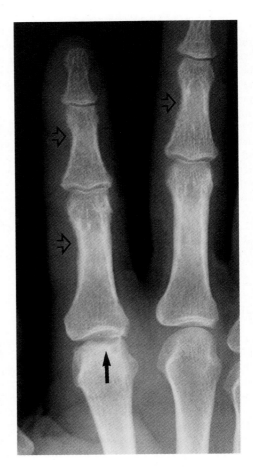

▲ FIGURE 28.3   **Primary hyperparathyroidism.** Subchondral bone resorption is present at the head of the second metacarpal (*arrow*). Note also subperiosteal resorption at the proximal and distal phalanges (*open arrows*).

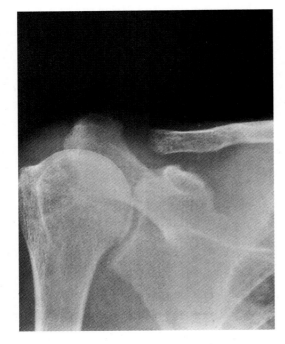

▲ FIGURE 28.4   **Primary hyperparathyroidism.** Anteroposterior radiograph of the shoulder of a 36-year-old woman shows resorption of the acromial end of the right clavicle.

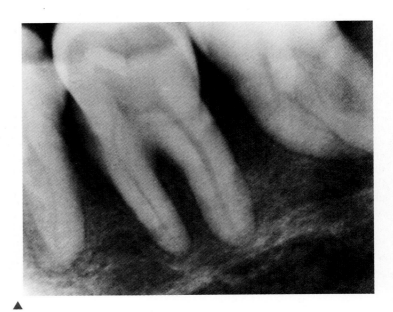

▲ FIGURE 28.5   **Primary hyperparathyroidism.** Radiograph of the lower second molar tooth shows loss of the lamina dura around the tooth socket.

FIGURE 28.6   **Primary hyperparathyroidism.** Lateral radio- ▶
graph of the skull of the patient seen in Figure 28.2 demonstrates a decrease in the overall density of the bone and a
granular appearance of the cranial vault—the so-called salt-
and-pepper skull.

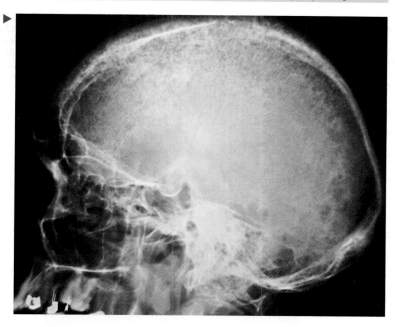

FIGURE 28.7   **Primary hyperparathyroidism.** Anteroposterior ▶
radiograph of the lower legs of the same patient seen in Figure
28.4 shows multiple lytic lesions (brown tumors) in both tibiae.

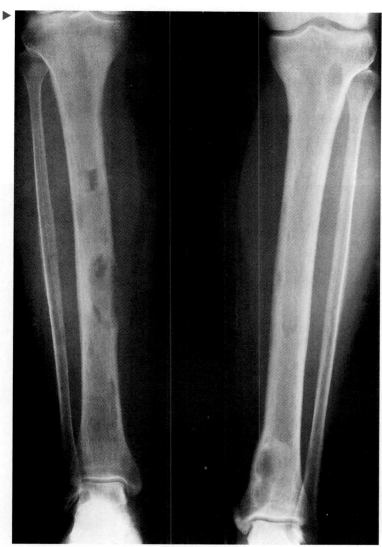

Paget Disease

Pathophysiology

Paget disease, a relatively common bone disorder, is a chronic, progressive disturbance in bone metabolism that primarily affects older persons. It is slightly more common in men than in women (3:2), with an average age of onset between 45 and 55 years, although the disease has been known to occur in young adults. The prevalence of Paget disease varies considerably in different parts of the world, reaching its greatest incidence in Great Britain, Australia, and New Zealand.

The precise nature of Paget disease and its etiology are still debatable. Sir James Paget named the disease *osteitis deformans* in the belief that the basic process was infectious in origin. Other etiologies have also been proposed, such as neoplastic, vascular, endocrinologic, immunologic, traumatic, and hereditary. The hereditary etiology was supported by identification of mutations in the gene encoding sequestosome 1 (SQSTM1/p62) in patients with familial and sporadic Paget disease. Recent ultrastructural studies and the discovery of giant multinucleated osteoclasts containing microfilaments in the affected cytoplasm, as well as intranuclear inclusion bodies, suggest a viral etiology. Some investigators have obtained immunocytologic evidence identifying the particles as analogous to those from the measles group virus material. Other immunologic studies have demonstrated viral antigens in affected cells identical to those from the respiratory syncytial virus. The most recent research indicates a paramyxovirus as an etiologic factor.

Whatever the fundamental cause of Paget disease, its basic pathologic process has to do with the balance between bone resorption and appositional new bone formation. There is disordered and extremely active bone remodeling, secondary to both osteoclastic bone resorption and osteoblastic bone formation in a characteristic mosaic pattern, which is the histologic hallmark of this condition. Biochemically, the increase in osteoblastic activity is reflected in elevated levels of serum alkaline phosphatase, which can rise to extremely high values. Similarly, the increase in osteoclastic bone resorption is reflected in high urinary levels of hydroxyproline, which is formed as a result of collagen breakdown.

The skeletal abnormalities seen in Paget disease are frequently asymptomatic and may be an incidental finding on radiographic examination or at autopsy. When the changes are symptomatic, clinical manifestations are often related to complications of the disease, such as deformity of the long bones, warmth in the involved extremity, periosteal tenderness and bone pain, fractures, secondary osteoarthritis, neural compression, and sarcomatous degeneration. The distribution of a lesion varies from monostotic involvement to widespread disease. The following bones, in order of decreasing frequency, are most often affected: the pelvis, femur, skull, tibia, vertebrae, clavicle, humerus, and ribs (Fig. 29.1). The fibula is involved only in exceptional cases.

Radiologic Evaluation

The radiographic features of Paget disease correspond to the pathologic processes in the bone and depend on the stage of the disorder. In the early phase, the *osteolytic* or *hot phase*, active bone resorption is evident as a radiolucent wedge or an elongated area with sharp borders that destroys both the cortex and cancellous bone as it advances along the shaft. The terms frequently used to describe this phenomenon are "advancing wedge," "candle flame," and "blade of grass" (Fig. 29.2). In flat bones such as the calvarium or the iliac bone, an area of active bone destruction known as osteoporosis circumscripta appears as a purely osteolytic lesion (Fig. 29.3). In the skull, most commonly affected sites are the frontal and occipital bones; both inner and outer calvarial tables are involved, but the former is usually more extensively affected.

In the *intermediate* or *mixed phase*, bone destruction is accompanied by new bone formation, with the latter process tending to predominate. Bone remodeling appears radiographically as thickening of the cortex and coarse trabeculation of cancellous bone (Fig. 29.4). In the pelvis, cortical thickening and sclerosis of the iliopectineal and ischiopubic lines are present. Pubic rami and ischia may enlarge. In the spine, the thin cortex of the vertebral body, which disappears in the hot phase, is later replaced by broad, coarsely trabeculated bone, forming what appears to be a "picture frame" around the body (Fig. 29.5). In the skull, focal patchy densities with a "cotton-ball" appearance are characteristic (Fig. 29.6).

In the *cool* or *sclerotic phase*, a diffuse increase of bone density occurs together with enlargement and widening of the bone and marked cortical thickening, with blurring of the demarcation between cortex and spongiosa (Fig. 29.7). Bowing of long bones may become a striking feature (Fig. 29.8). Similar changes are observed in the skull, where obliteration of the diploic space is also a typical feature (Fig. 29.9).

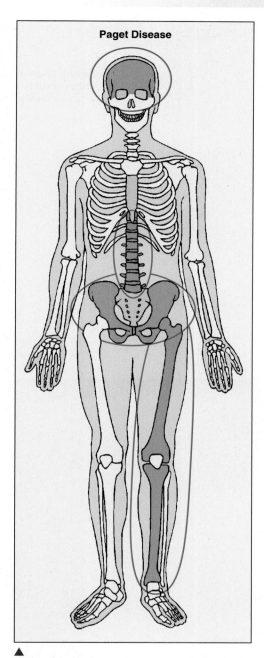

▲
FIGURE 29.1 Major target sites of Paget disease.

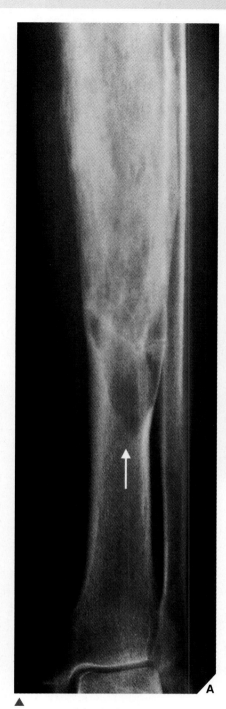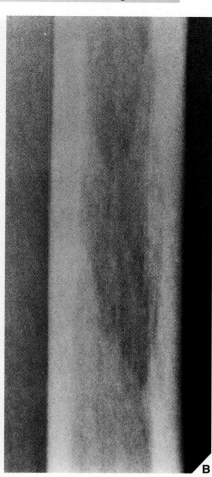

▲
FIGURE 29.2 **Osteolytic phase of Paget disease. (A)** Anteroposterior radiograph of the lower leg of a 68-year-old woman shows an advancing wedge of osteolytic destruction in the midportion of the tibia (*arrow*). **(B)** Magnification study of the midfemur in another patient shows the purely osteolytic phase of Paget disease. In both examples, the lesion resembles a blade of grass or a candle flame. (**A** from Sissons HA, Greenspan A, 1986, with permission.)

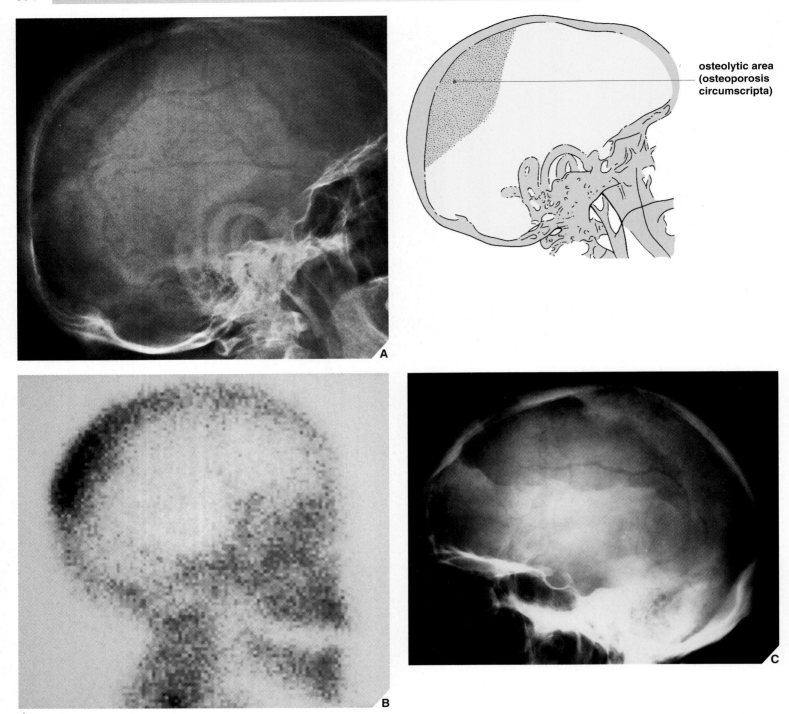

FIGURE 29.3   **Osteolytic phase of Paget disease. (A)** Lateral radiograph of the skull of a 60-year-old man shows an osteolytic lesion in the parieto-occipital area. This sharply demarcated defect, known as osteoporosis circumscripta, represents a hot phase of the disease. **(B)** Radionuclide bone scan shows a characteristic localized increased uptake of the radiopharmaceutical tracer resulting in the appearance of a "yarmulke" sign. **(C)** Lateral radiograph of the skull of a 65-year-old woman reveals osteoporosis circumscripta in the fronto-parietal area.

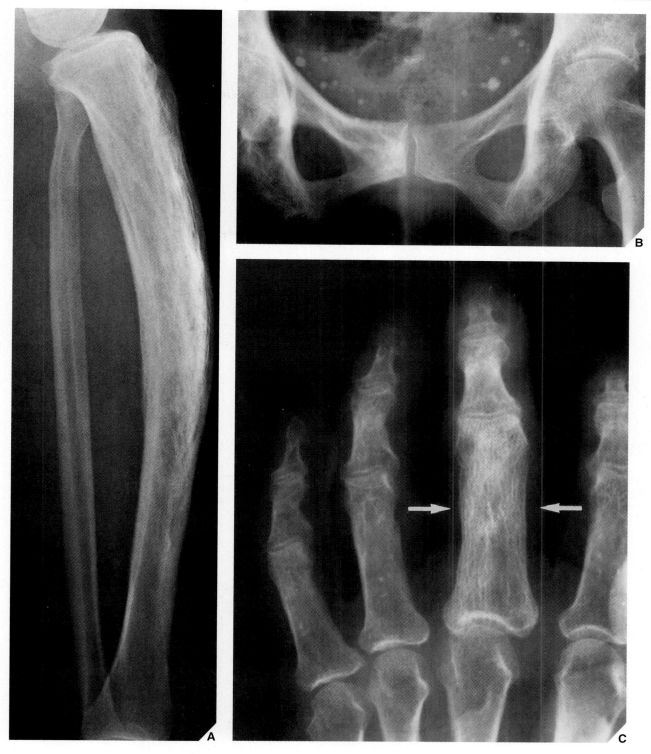

FIGURE 29.4   **Intermediate phase of Paget disease. (A)** In the intermediate phase, seen here affecting the tibia in a 62-year-old woman, thickening of the cortex and a coarse trabecular pattern in the medullary portion of the bone are characteristic features. Note the anterior bowing. **(B)** In another patient, an 81-year-old woman, intermediate phase is seen in the pubic and ischial bones. **(C)** Mixed phase affecting the proximal phalanx of the middle finger (*arrows*) is seen in a 67-year-old woman with monostotic Paget disease.

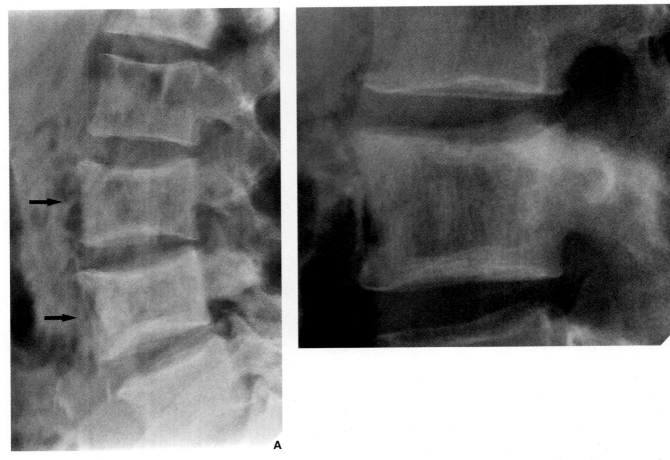

▲

FIGURE 29.5　**Intermediate phase of Paget disease. (A)** Involvement of the lumbar spine in the mixed phase can be recognized by the "picture frame" appearance of the vertebral bodies (*arrows*) created by dense sclerotic bone on the periphery and greater radiolucency in the center. Note the partial replacement of vertebral end plates by coarsely trabeculated bone. **(B)** In another patient, the "picture frame" appearance of the vertebral body of L2 marks the intermediate phase of Paget disease. (**A** from Sissons HA, Greenspan A, 1986, with permission.)

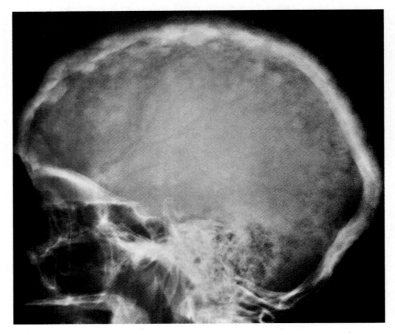

▲

FIGURE 29.6　**Intermediate phase of Paget disease.** Focal patchy densities in the skull, having a "cotton ball" appearance, are typical of the intermediate phase of Paget disease as seen in this radiograph of a 68-year-old woman.

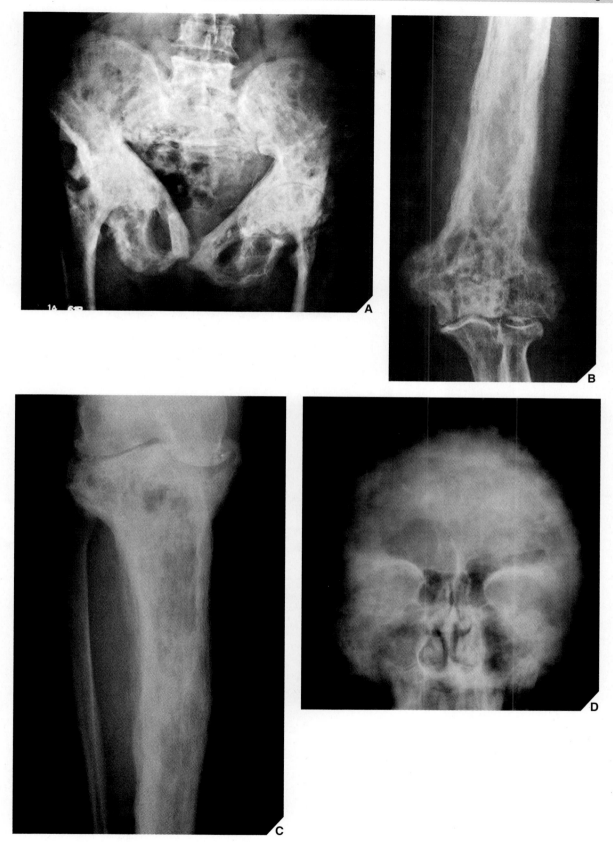

FIGURE 29.7 Cool phase of Paget disease. In the cool phase, there is considerable thickening of the cortex and bone deformity. (**A**) The pelvic cavity, seen here in an 80-year-old woman, may assume a triangular appearance. (**B**) Involvement of a long bone, in this case the distal humerus of a 60-year-old woman, exhibits marked cortical thickening, narrowing of the medullary cavity, and a coarse trabecular pattern. (**C**) Similar changes are present in the tibia in a 72-year-old man. (**D**) Anteroposterior radiograph of the skull of an 82-year-old woman reveals typical changes of the cool phase of Paget disease. (**A** and **B** from Sissons HA, Greenspan A, 1986, with permission.)

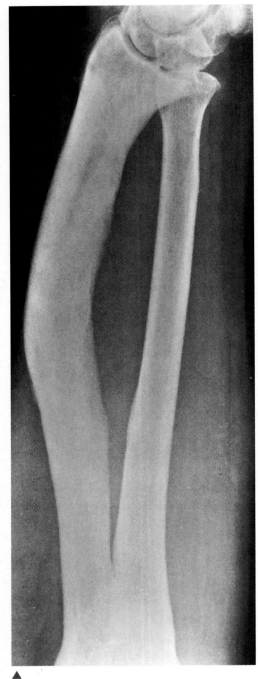

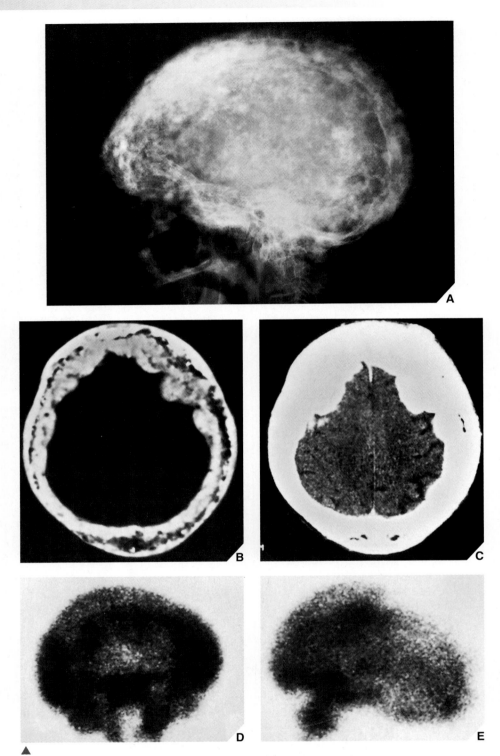

▲
FIGURE 29.8 Cool phase of Paget disease.
Anteroposterior radiograph of the forearm of a
57-year-old man with polyostotic Paget disease
shows enlargement of the left radius with a marked
bowing deformity. Other signs of the cool phase of
the disease are seen in the diffuse sclerotic changes
and the indistinct demarcation between the cortex
and the spongiosa.

▲
FIGURE 29.9   Cool phase of Paget disease. (A) Lateral radiograph of the skull of an 80-year-old
woman demonstrates numerous coalescent densities associated with thickening and sclerosis of
the cranial vault and base of the skull. CT sections clearly demonstrate predominant involvement of
the inner table with marked diminution of the diploic space (B) and thickening of the cranial vault
(C). (D,E) Scintigraphy demonstrates markedly increased uptake of radiopharmaceutical.

It is important to remember that, since in the long bones Paget disease starts at one articular end and advances to the other, all three phases of the disorder may coexist in the same bone (Fig. 29.10A). Likewise, different phases may coexist in the flat bones or in the spine (Fig. 29.10B).

Computed tomography (CT) may demonstrate characteristic features of Paget disease (Fig. 29.11), although it is rarely required. Magnetic resonance imaging (MRI) is occasionally employed to demonstrate cortical and intramedullary involvement better, and to exclude (or confirm) extension of the process into the soft tissues. In general, the pagetic bone exhibits heterogeneous signal intensity. On T1-weighted sequences, intermediate-to-low signal intensity is usually noted. On T2 weighting, the signal may be high, intermediate, or low, depending on the stage of the disease and degree of fibrosis and sclerosis (Figs. 29.12 and 29.13).

Differential Diagnosis

Several conditions may mimic Paget disease, while the disease itself may be mistaken for other pathologic processes; for example, involvement of a single bone can be mistaken for monostotic fibrous dysplasia, and a uniform increase in osseous density may mimic lymphoma or metastatic cancer. The rugger-jersey appearance of the spine in secondary hyperparathyroidism may resemble Paget vertebra (see Fig. 28.8). Vertebral hemangioma also looks very much like Paget vertebra on a radiograph, except that the vertebral body is not enlarged and the vertebral end plates are well outlined (see Fig. 20.46). However, the condition

that bears the most striking resemblance to Paget disease is familial idiopathic hyperphosphatasia, also called "juvenile Paget disease" (see Figs. 30.1 and 30.2). In this condition, unlike Paget disease, the articular ends of the bone may not be affected.

Complications

Pathologic Fractures

Of the numerous complications observed in patients with Paget disease, the most common are pathologic fractures in the long bones. They may resemble partial or incomplete stress fractures, appearing radiographically as multiple short horizontal radiolucent lines on the convex aspect of the cortex (Fig. 29.14). True complete fractures are referred to as "banana-type" because of the horizontal direction of the fracture line as it traverses the affected bone (Fig. 29.15), and they have also been compared with crushed rotten wood or chalk. Fractures are more likely to occur during the osteolytic or hot phase, and they are frequently the main presenting manifestation of Paget disease.

Degenerative Joint Disease

The development of degenerative joint disease is a common complication of Paget disease. This secondary form of osteoarthritis usually occurs in the knee and hip articulations, where the characteristic changes are present, including joint space narrowing and osteophyte formation. Involvement of the acetabulum may be complicated by acetabular protrusio (Fig. 29.16).

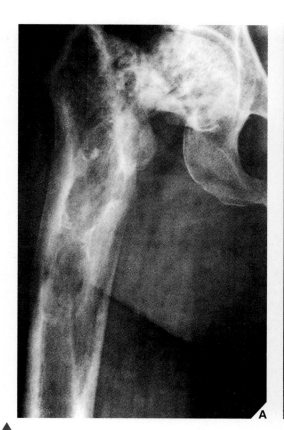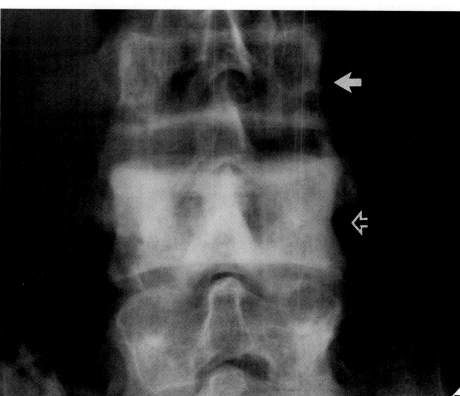

FIGURE 29.10 Coexistence of different phases of Paget disease. (A) Anteroposterior radiograph of the proximal half of the femur of a 77-year-old woman demonstrates all three phases of the disorder. The cool phase is seen in the femoral head, the intermediate phase in the proximal shaft, and the hot phase, represented by an osteolytic wedge of resorption, in the medial cortex more distally. **(B)** In another patient, a 54-year-old man, intermediate phase is seen in the vertebra L3 (*arrow*), whereas the L4 reveals a cool phase (*open arrow*).

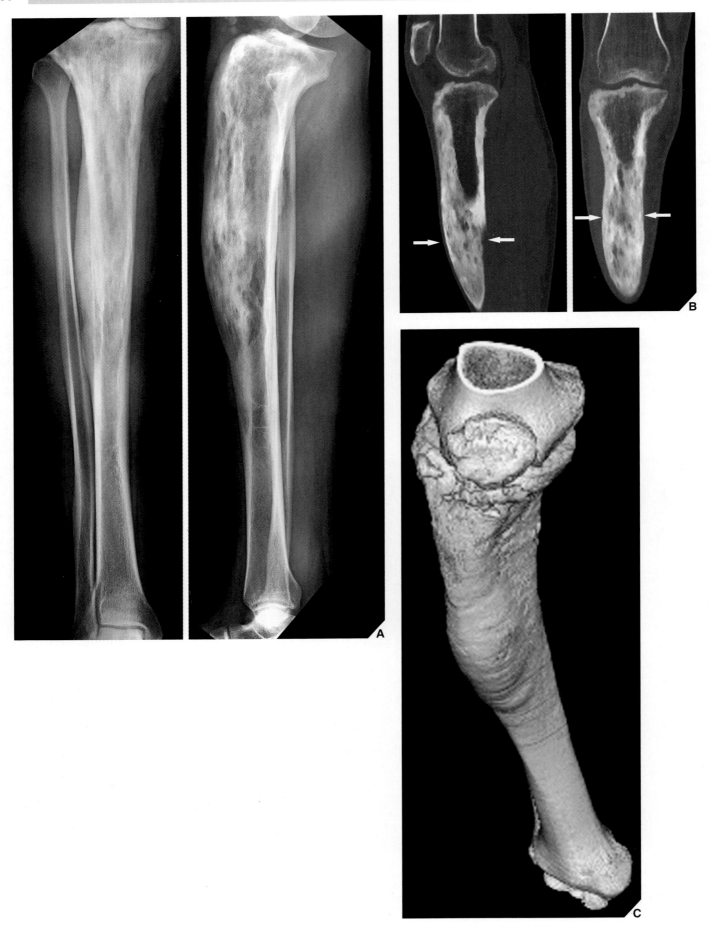

▲
FIGURE 29.11   **CT of Paget disease.** **(A)** Anteroposterior and lateral radiographs of the right leg of a 75-year-old man show thickening of the cortex and a coarse trabeculation of the proximal tibia. **(B)** Sagittal and coronal reformatted CT images demonstrate these abnormalities to the better advantage. Note lack of distinction between the cortex and the spongiosa (*arrows*). **(C)** 3D CT reconstructed image shows deformity of the tibia and anterior bowing.

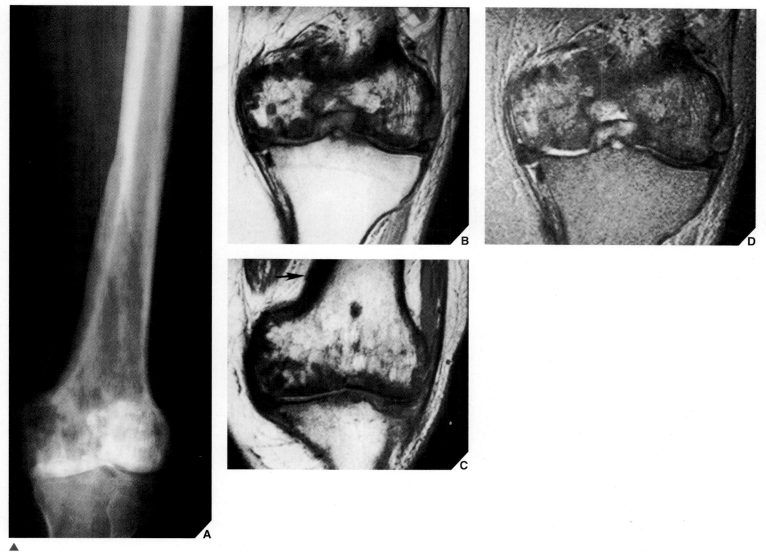

▲
FIGURE 29.12   **MRI of Paget disease. (A)** Anteroposterior radiograph of the left distal femur shows typical appearance of Paget disease: enlargement of the bone, cortical thickening, and sclerosis and coarse trabecular pattern of cancellous bone. **(B,C)** Two coronal T1-weighted (SE; TR 500/TE 20 msec) MR images demonstrate cortical thickening (*arrow*) and low-signal coarse cancellous trabeculae. **(D)** Coronal T2-weighted (SE; TR 2000/TE 80 msec) MRI shows heterogeneous signal in the femoral condyles.

FIGURE 29.13   **MRI of Paget disease.** Sagittal ▶ T1-weighted (SE; TR 500/TE 20 msec) MR image of the lumbar spine shows involvement of the vertebra by Paget disease (*arrow heads*).

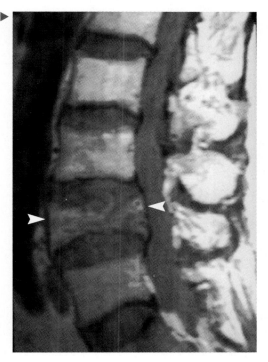

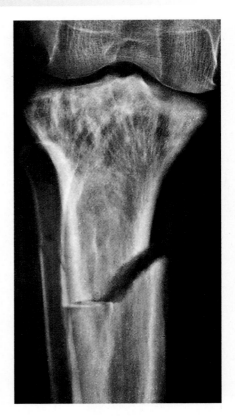

▲
FIGURE 29.15 Pathologic fracture in Paget disease. A 62-year-old man with monostotic Paget disease affecting the right tibia sustained a pathologic fracture. Note that the fracture line traverses the area of active, osteolytic bone destruction. (From Sissons HA, Greenspan A, 1986, with permission.)

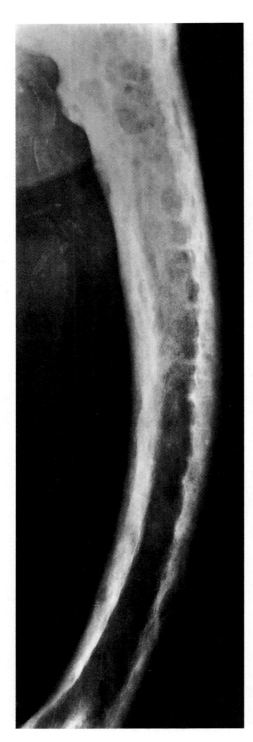

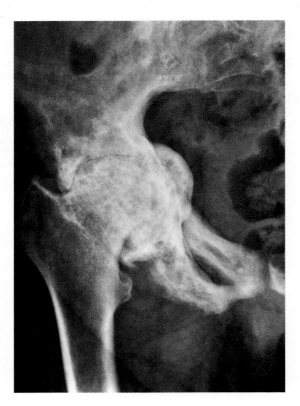

▲
FIGURE 29.14 Stress fractures in Paget disease. Numerous stress fractures, seen in the lateral cortex of the femur in an 80-year-old man with advanced Paget disease, are the most frequent complications of this condition.

▲
FIGURE 29.16 Secondary osteoarthritis in Paget disease. A 75-year-old woman with long-standing polyostotic Paget disease had been reporting progressive pain in her right hip for 1 year. Anteroposterior radiograph demonstrates advanced osteoarthritis and acetabular protrusio. (From Sissons HA, Greenspan A, 1986, with permission.)

Neurologic Complications

The neurologic complications of Paget disease are secondary to involvement of the vertebral column and skull. Collapse of a vertebral body, for example, causes extradural spinal canal block, which may lead to paraplegia (Fig. 29.17). Severe involvement of the bony spinal canal may lead to spinal stenosis, the presence of which can be effectively demonstrated by CT (Fig. 29.18). Basilar invagination due to softening of the skull may lead to encroachment on the foramen magnum and neurologic deficit.

Neoplastic Complications

Benign or malignant giant cell tumors, single or multiple, may complicate Paget disease. The usual sites of these tumors are the calvarium and the iliac bone.

The development of a bone sarcoma is a serious but rare complication of Paget disease; the incidence is less than 1%. Osteosarcoma is by far the most common histologic type (Fig. 29.19), followed by fibrosarcoma, malignant fibrous histiocytoma, chondrosarcoma, and lymphoma, with the pelvis, femur, and humerus at highest risk for the development of malignant transformation. The main radiographic features of this complication are development of a lytic lesion at the site of Paget disease, cortical breakthrough, and formation of a soft-tissue mass (Fig. 29.20); a periosteal reaction is rare. There is often a pathologic fracture as well. The radiographic appearance of Paget sarcoma must be distinguished from that of metastases of a primary carcinoma of the kidney (Fig. 29.21), breast, or prostate. The metastatic deposit may be lodged in either unaffected or pagetic bone. The prognosis for patients with sarcomatous degeneration of Paget disease is poor; the mean survival time usually does not exceed 6 to 8 months. Occasionally, an osteosarcoma in pagetic bone may metastasize to other bones and soft tissues, but metastases to the lung, liver, and adrenals are much more likely.

Orthopedic Management

Because of the variable clinical presentation of Paget disease, decisions regarding therapy must be based on the particular manifestations in each patient. The goal of the medical treatment is the control and relief of pain, rather than restitution of normal bone quality. The role of the orthopedic surgeon in the management of Paget disease is to evaluate and treat the cause of a patient's pain, to assess and manage any deformities, and to provide therapy for pathologic fractures and tumors developing in pagetic bone. The radiologist contributes to these aims by providing essential information. For instance, CT is useful for demonstrating spinal stenosis, which frequently leads to neurologic symptoms in patients with Paget disease (see Fig. 29.18). Radionuclide imaging is also a valuable technique, particularly for determining the skeletal distribution of the disease (see Fig. 26.10).

Medical treatment consists of inhibiting osteoclastic activity by subcutaneous or intramuscular injections of calcitonin, a 32-amino-acid hormone secreted by the C cells of the thyroid gland, and oral administration of biphosphonates, which bind to areas of high bone turnover, decreasing bone resorption. The main action of biphosphonates is decreasing osteoclastic activity. The most frequently used drugs in this group include etidronate, pamidronate, alendronate, residronate, and tiludronate. Recently promising results were achieved with ibandronate and zolendronate. Administration of plicamycin, previously called mithramycin, inhibits RNA synthesis and has a potent cytotoxic effect on osteoclasts. The serum alkaline phosphatase determination and the 24-hour urinary hydroxyproline measurement were the main indicators of the response of the disease to medical treatment; however, the recently developed biochemical markers of bone resorption and formation allow a more accurate assessment of disease activity and response to therapy.

Surgical intervention is indicated for the treatment of pathologic fractures, advanced, disabling arthritis, and extreme bowing deformities

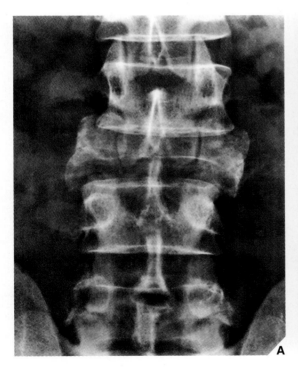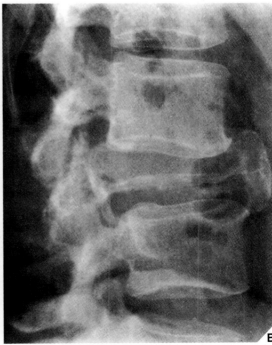

FIGURE 29.17 **Pathologic fracture in Paget disease.** A 60-year-old man with polyostotic Paget disease presented with lower back pain and neurologic symptoms. Anteroposterior (**A**) and lateral (**B**) radiographs of the lumbar spine show a pathologic compression fracture of L3 with encroachment on the spinal canal, which was the source of his symptoms. (From Sissons HA, Greenspan A, 1986, with permission.)

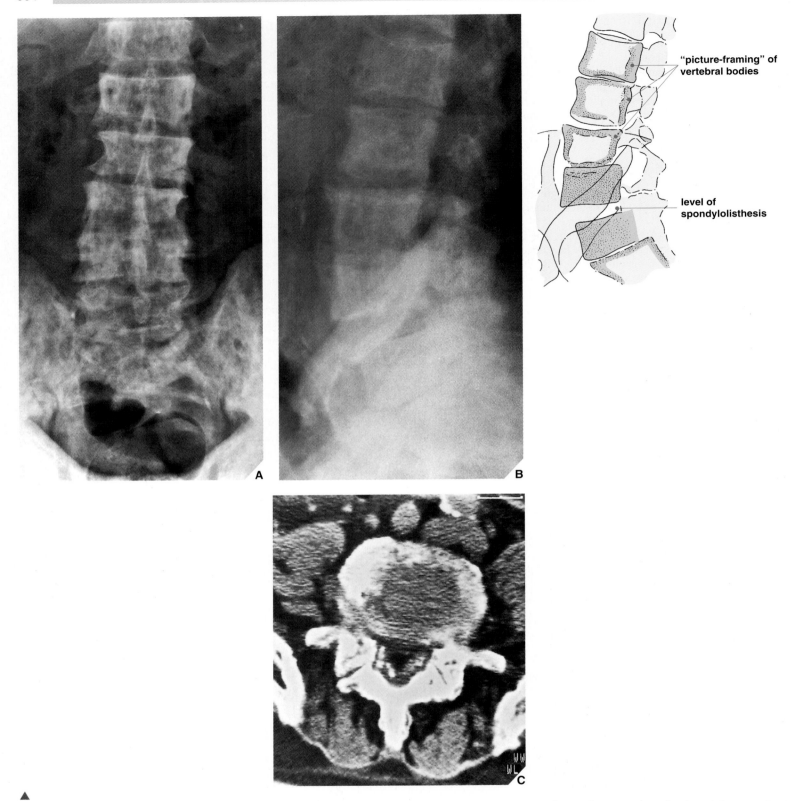

▲
FIGURE 29.18 **Spinal complications in Paget disease.** An 84-year-old man with extensive polyostotic Paget disease for many years developed degenerative spondylolisthesis and spinal stenosis. Anteroposterior (**A**) and lateral (**B**) radiographs of the lumbar spine show Paget disease in the cool phase. Second-degree degenerative spondylolisthesis is seen at the L4-5 level. (**C**) CT section through L5 demonstrates narrowing of the spinal canal characteristic of spinal stenosis, the major cause of most neurologic symptoms in Paget disease.

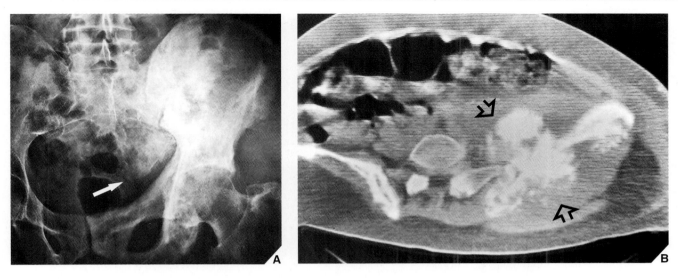

FIGURE 29.19 **Paget sarcoma.** A 70-year-old woman with Paget disease affecting her left hemipelvis had a rare complication, sarcomatous degeneration. (**A**) Radiograph of the pelvis shows extensive involvement of the left ilium, pubis, and ischium by Paget disease. There is also destruction of the cortex and a large soft-tissue mass accompanied by bone formation (*arrow*), typical findings for osteosarcoma. (**B**) CT scan demonstrates the soft-tissue mass more clearly (*open arrows*).

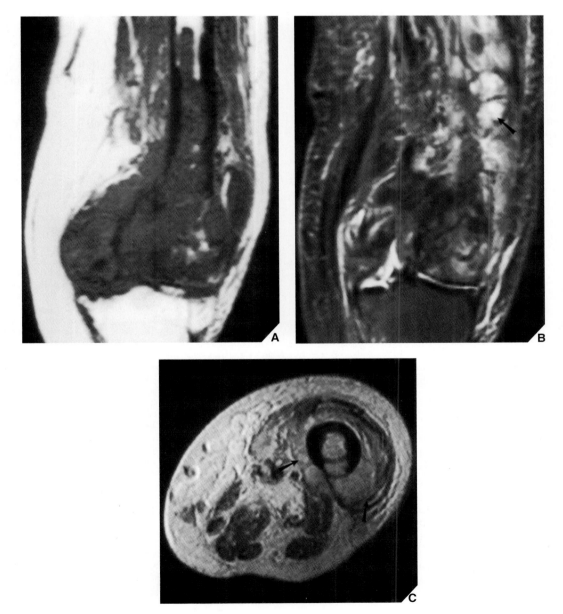

FIGURE 29.20 **MRI of Paget sarcoma.** (**A**) Coronal T1-weighted (SE; TR 500/TE 20 msec) MR image shows Paget disease affecting the distal femur. Destruction of the cortex and soft-tissue mass are well demonstrated. (**B**) Coronal STIR and (**C**) axial T2-weighted sequences confirm the presence of a soft-tissue mass (*arrows*), thus corroborating the diagnosis of malignant transformation.

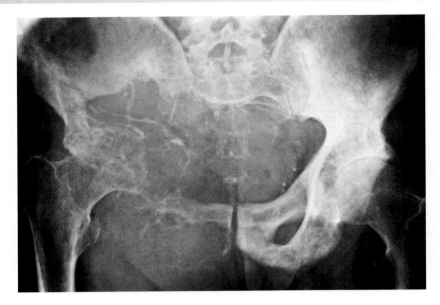

▲
FIGURE 29.21   **Metastases in Paget disease.** Anteroposterior radiograph of the pelvis of a 55-year-old woman with Paget disease for 10 years shows extensive osteolytic destruction of the right ilium, ischium, and pubis secondary to metastatic renal cell carcinoma (hypernephroma). Note the typical involvement of the pelvis by Paget disease. This metastatic lesion should not be mistaken for Paget sarcoma.

of the long bones. Stress or pseudofractures, which occur most often in the tibia and proximal femur, are treated by bracing and protection from weight bearing for a period of several months. Complete fractures are treated either with intramedullary rods or with compression plates and screws. For arthritic complications, which are particularly frequent in the hip and knee articulations, total joint replacement is usually performed.

PRACTICAL POINTS TO REMEMBER

[1] The histologic hallmark of Paget disease is a mosaic pattern of disorderly and active bone remodeling secondary to osteoclastic resorption and osteoblastic formation.
[2] The characteristic radiographic features of Paget disease of bone include:
   • involvement of at least one articular end of a long bone
   • thickening of the cortex and enlargement of the affected bone
   • a coarse trabecular pattern to the spongiosa
   • bowing deformities of the long bones
   • a "picture-frame" appearance of a vertebral body.
[3] Particular radiographic changes in Paget disease are related to the stage of the disorder. In the acute (hot) phase, a radiolucent osteolytic area is seen:
   • in the calvarium or in a flat bone, where it is known as "osteoporosis circumscripta"
   • in a long bone, where it appears as an advancing wedge of active disease, resembling a candle flame or a blade of grass.
[4] Radionuclide bone scan, which invariably shows an increased uptake of the tracer in bones affected by Paget disease, is effective in determining the distribution of the lesion.
[5] The most frequent complication of Paget disease is pathologic fracture, either incomplete stress fractures or "banana-type" complete fractures.
[6] The most serious complication of Paget disease is sarcomatous degeneration. Radiographically, it can be recognized by:
   • osteolytic bone destruction at the site of the pagetic lesion
   • cortical breakthrough
   • a soft-tissue mass.

Malignant transformation must be distinguished from metastatic lesions to pagetic bone from a primary carcinoma of the lung, breast, kidney, gastrointestinal tract, or prostate.
[7] Paget disease must be distinguished from:
   • "juvenile Paget disease" (familial idiopathic hyperphosphatasia)
   • van Buchem disease (hyperostosis corticalis generalisata)
   • vertebral hemangioma
   • rugger-jersey spine seen in secondary hyperparathyroidism
   • lymphoma
   • extensive osteoblastic metastases.

SUGGESTED READINGS

Adkins MC, Sundaram M. Radiologic case study: insufficiency fracture of the acetabular roof in Paget's disease. *Orthopedics* 2001;24:1019–1020.

Altman RD, Bloch DA, Hochberg MC, Murphy WA. Prevalance of pelvic Paget's disease of bone in the United States. *J Bone Miner Res* 2000;15:461–465.

Anderson DC. Paget's disease of bone is characterized by excessive bone resorption coupled with excessive and disorganized bone formation. *Bone* 2001;29:292–293.

Bahk YW, Parh YH, Chung SK, Chi JG. Bone pathologic correlation of multimodality imaging in Paget's disease. *J Nucl Med* 1995;36:1421–1426.

Barry HC. *Paget's disease of bone.* London, UK: Livingstone; 1969.

Basle MF, Chappard D, Rebel A. Viral origin of Paget's disease of bone? *Presse Med* 1996;25:113–118.

Berquist TH. *MRI of the musculoskeletal system*, 3rd ed. Philadelphia: Lippincott-Raven; 1996:920–922.

Birch MA, Taylor W, Fraser WD, Ralston SH, Hart CA, Gallagher JA. Absence of paramyxovirus RNA in cultures of pagetic bone cells and in pagetic bone. *J Bone Miner Res* 1994;9:11–16.

Boutin RD, Spitz DJ, Newman JS, Lenchik L, Steinbach LS. Complications in Paget disease at MR imaging. *Radiology* 1998;209:641–651.

Brandolini F, Bacchini P, Moscato M, Bertoni F. Chondrosarcoma as a complicating factor in Paget's disease of bone. *Skeletal Radiol* 1997;26:497–500.

Brown JP, Chines AA, Myers WR, Eusebio RA, Ritter-Hrncirik C, Hayes CW. Improvement of pagetic bone lesions with risedronate treatment: a radiologic study. *Bone* 2000;26:263–267.

Chapman GK. The diagnosis of Paget's disease of bone. *Aust N Z J Surg* 1992;62:24–32.

Clarke CR, Harrison MJ. Neurological manifestations of Paget's disease. *J Neurol Sci* 1978;38:171–178.

Colarintha P, Fonseca AT, Salgado L, Vieira MR. Diagnosis of malignant change in Paget's disease by T1–201. *Clin Nucl Med* 1996;21:299–301.

Conrad GR, Johnson AW. Solitary adenocarcinoma metastasis mimicking sarcomatous degeneration in Paget's disease. *Clin Nucl Med* 1997;22:300–302.

Delmas PD, Meunier PJ. The management of Paget's disease of bone. *N Engl J Med* 1997;336:558–566.

Edeiken J, Dalinka M, Karasick D. Paget disease (osteitis deformans): metabolic and dystrophic bone disease. In: *Edeiken's roentgen diagnosis of diseases of bone*, vol 2, 4th ed. Baltimore: Williams & Wilkins; 1990:1231–1259.

Fenton P, Resnick D. Metastases to bone affected by Paget's disease: a report of three cases. *Int Orthop* 1991;15:397–399.

Firooznia HF. Paget's disease. In: Firooznia HF, Golimbu C, Rafii M, Rauschning W, Weinreb J, eds. *MRI and CT of the musculoskeletal system*. St. Louis: Mosby-Year Book; 1992:176–181.

Fogelman I. Bone scanning in Paget's disease. In: Freeman LM, ed. *Nuclear medicine annual*. New York: Raven Press; 1991:99–128.

Fogelman I, Carr D. A comparison of bone scanning and radiology in the assessment of patients with symptomatic Paget's disease. *Eur J Nucl Med* 1980;5:417–421.

Fogelman I, Ryan PJ. Bone scanning in Paget's disease. In: Collier BD Jr, Fogelman I, Rosenthall L, eds. *Skeletal nuclear medicine*. St. Louis: CV Mosby; 1996:171–181.

Frame B, Marel GM. Paget's disease: a review of current knowledge. *Radiology* 1981;141:21–24.

Fraser WD. Paget's disease of bone. *Curr Opin Rheumatol* 1997;9:347–354.

Frassica FJ, Sim FH, Frassica DA, Wold LE. Survival and management considerations in postirradiation osteosarcoma and Paget's osteosarcoma. *Clin Orthop* 1991;270:120–127.

Greditzer HG III, McLeod RA, Unni KK, Beabout JW. Bone sarcomas in Paget disease. *Radiology* 1983;146:327–333.

Greenspan A. A review of Paget's disease: radiologic imaging, differential diagnosis, and treatment. *Bull Hosp Jt Dis* 1991;51:22–33.

Greenspan A. Paget's disease: current concept, radiologic imaging, and treatment. *Recent Adv Orthop* 1993;1:32–48.

Greenspan A, Norman A, Sterling AP. Precocious onset of Paget's disease—a report of three cases and review of the literature. *Can Assoc Radiol J* 1977;28:69–72.

Guyer PB, Chamberlain AT. Paget's disease of bone in South Africa. *Clin Radiol* 1988;39:51–52.

Guyer PB, Clough PW. Paget's disease of bone: some observations on the relation of the skeletal distribution to pathogenesis. *Clin Radiol* 1978;29:421–426.

Hadjipavlou A, Lander P, Srolovitz H, Enker IP. Malignant transformation in Paget disease of bone. *Cancer* 1992;70:2802–2808.

Hadjipavlou AG, Gaitanis IN, Kontakis GM. Paget's disease of the bone and its management. *J Bone Joint Surg [Br]* 2002;84B:160–169.

Haibach H, Farrell C, Dittrich FJ. Neoplasms arising in Paget's disease of bone: a study of 82 cases. *Am J Clin Pathol* 1985;83:594–600.

Hosking D, Meunier PJ, Ringe JD, Reginster JY, Gennari C. Paget's disease of bone: diagnosis and management. *Br Med J* 1996;312:491–495.

Hutter RVP, Foote FW Jr, Frazell EL, Francis KC. Giant cell tumors complicating Paget's disease of bone. *Cancer* 1963;16:1044–1056.

Huvos AG, Butler A, Bretsky SS. Osteogenic sarcoma associated with Paget's disease of bone: a clinicopathologic study of 65 patients. *Cancer* 1983;52:1489–1495.

Kaufmann GA, Sundaram M, McDonald DJ. Magnetic resonance imaging in symptomatic Paget's disease. *Skeletal Radiol* 1991;20:413–418.

Kelly JK, Denier JE, Wilner HI, Lazo A, Metes JJ. MR imaging of lytic changes in Paget disease of the calvarium. *J Comput Assist Tomogr* 1989;13:27–29.

Kim CK, Estrada WN, Lorberboym M, Pandit N, Religioso DG, Alaxi A. The "mouse face" appearance of the vertebrae in Paget's disease. *Clin Nucl Med* 1997;22:104–108.

Krane SM. Paget's disease of bone. *Clin Orthop* 1977;127:24–36.

Kumar A, Poon PY, Aggarwal S. Value of CT in diagnosing nonneoplastic osteolysis in paget disease. *J Comput Assist Tomogr* 1993;17:144–146.

Kunin JR, Strouse PJ. The "yarmulke" sign of Paget's disease. *Clin Nucl Med* 1991;16:788–789.

Lander PH, Hadjipavlou AG. A dynamic classification of Paget's disease. *J Bone Joint Surg [Br]* 1986;68B:431–438.

Laurin N, Brown JP, Morisette J, Raymond V. Recurrent mutation of the gene encoding sequestome 1 (SQSTM1/p62) in Paget disease of bone. *Am J Hum Genet* 2002;70:1582–1588.

Lentle BC, Russell AS, Heslip PG, Percy JS. The scintigraphic findings in Paget's disease of bone. *Clin Radiol* 1976;27:129–135.

Maldague B, Malghem J. Dynamic radiological patterns of Paget's disease of bone. *Clin Orthop* 1987;217:126–151.

McKenna RJ, Schwinn CP, Soong KY, Higinbotham NI. Osteogenic sarcoma arising in Paget's disease. *Cancer* 1964;17:42–66.

McKillop JH, Fogelman I, Boyle IT, Greig WR. Bone scan appearance of a Paget's osteosarcoma: failure to concentrate EHDP. *J Nucl Med* 1977;18:1039–1040.

Meunier PJ, Vignot E. Therapeutic strategy in Paget's disease of bone. *Bone* 1995;17:489S–491S.

Milgram JW. Orthopedic management of Paget's disease of bone. *Clin Orthop* 1977;127:63–69.

Milgram JW. Radiographical and pathological assessment of the activity of Paget's disease of bone. *Clin Orthop* 1977;127:43–54.

Miller C, Rao VM. Sarcomatous degeneration of Paget disease in the skull. *Skeletal Radiol* 1983;10:102–106.

Mills BG, Frausto A, Singer FR, Ohsaki Y, Demulder A, Roodman GD. Multinucleated cells formed in vitro from Paget's bone marrows express viral antigens. *Bone* 1994;15:443–448.

Mirra JM. Pathogenesis of Paget's disease based on viral etiology. *Clin Orthop* 1987;217:162–170.

Mirra JM, Brien EW, Tehranzadeh J. Paget's disease of bone: review with emphasis on radiologic features. Part I. *Skeletal Radiol* 1995;24:163–171, 173–184.

Mirra JM, Gold RM. Giant cell tumor containing viral-like intranuclear inclusions, in association with Paget's disease. Case report. *Skeletal Radiol* 1982;8:67–70.

Moore TE, Kathol MH, El-Koury GY, Walker CW, Gendall DW, Whitten CG. Unusual radiologic features of Paget's disease of bone. *Skeletal Radiol* 1994;23:257–260.

Nicholas JJ, Srodes CH, Herbert D, Hoy RJ, Peel RL, Goodman MA. Metastatic cancer in Paget's disease of bone: a case report. *Orthopedics* 1987;10:725–729.

Noor M, Shoback D. Paget's disease of bone: diagnosis and treatment update. *Curr Rheumatol Rep* 2000;2:67–73.

Paget J. On a form of chronic inflammation of bones (osteitis deformans). *Med Chir Trans* 1877;60:37–64.

Pande KC, Ashford RU, Dey A, Kayan K, McCloskey EV, Kanis JA. Atypical familial Paget's disease of bone. *Joint Bone Spine* 2001;68:257–261.

Potter HG, Schneider R, Ghelman B, Healey JH, Lane JM. Multiple giant cell tumors and Paget disease of bone: radiographic and clinical correlations. *Radiology* 1991;180:261–264.

Reid IR. Biphosphonates. *Skeletal Radiol* 2007; 36:711–714.

Resnick D. Paget's disease of bone: current status and a look back to 1943 and earlier. *Am J Roentgenol* 1988;150:249–256.

Resnick D, Niwayama G. Paget's disease. In: Resnick D, ed. *Diagnosis of bone and joint disorders*, 4th ed. Philadelphia: WB Saunders; 2002:1947–2000.

Resnik C. Paget disease of bone: the uncomplicated and the complicated. *Radiologist* 1999;6:1–11.

Roberts MC, Kressel HY, Fallon MD, Zlatkin MB, Dalinka MK. Paget disease: MR imaging findings. *Radiology* 1989;173:341–345.

Rosenbaum HD, Hanson DJ. Geographic variation in the prevalence of Paget's disease of bone. *Radiology* 1969;92:959–963.

Ryan PJ, Fogelman I. Paget's disease—five years follow-up after pamidronate therapy. *Br J Rheumatol* 1994;33:98–99.

Schajowicz F, Santini Araujo E, Berenstein M. Sarcoma complicating Paget's disease of bone: a clinicopathological study of 62 cases. *J Bone Joint Surg [Br]* 1983;65B:299–307.

Serafini AN. Paget's disease of the bone. *Semin Nucl Med* 1976;6:47–58.

Siris ED. Paget's disease of bone. *J Bone Miner Res* 1998;13:1061–1065.

Sissons HA. Epidemiology of Paget's disease. *Clin Orthop* 1966;45:73–79.

Sissons HA, Greenspan A. Paget's disease. In: Taveras JM, Ferrucci JT, eds. *Radiology—imaging, diagnosis, intervention*, vol. 5. Philadelphia: JB Lippincott; 1986:1–14.

Smith J, Botet YF, Yeh SDJ. Bone sarcoma in Paget's disease: a study of 85 patients. *Radiology* 1984;152:583–590.

Smith SE, Murphey MD, Motamedi K, Mulligan ME, Resnik CS, Gannon FH. From the Archives of the AFIP. Radiologic spectrum of Paget disease of bone and its complications with pathologic correlation. *Radiographics* 2002;22:1191–1216.

Som PM, Hermann G, Sacher M, Stollman AL, Moscatello AL, Biller HF. Paget disease of the calvaria and facial bones with an osteosarcoma of the maxilla: CT and MR findings. *J Comput Assist Tomogr* 1987;11:887–890.

Sundaram MG, Khanna G, el-Khoury GY. T1-weighted MR imaging for distinguishing large osteolysis of Paget's disease from sarcomatous degeneration. *Skeletal Radiol* 2001;30:378–383.

Sy WM. *Gamma images in benign and metabolic bone diseases*, vol I. Boca Raton: CRC Press; 1981:58–60.

Tehranzadeh J, Fung Y, Donohue M, Anavim A, Pribram HW. Computed tomography of Paget disease of the skull versus fibrous dysplasia. *Skeletal Radiol* 1998;27:664–672.

Vellenga CJ, Bijvoet OLM, Pauwels EKJ. Bone scintigraphy and radiology in Paget's disease of bone: a review. *Am J Physiol Imaging* 1988;3:154–168.

Wallace E, Wong J, Reid IR. Pamidronate treatment of the neurologic sequelae of pagetic spinal stenosis. *Arch Intern Med* 1995;155:1813–1815.

Waxman AD, McKee D, Siemsen JK, Singer FR. Gallium scanning in Paget's disease of bone: effect of calcitonin. *Am J Roentgenol* 1980;134:303–306.

Wellman HN, Schauwecker D, Robb JA, Khairi MR, Johnston CC. Skeletal scintimaging and radiography in the diagnosis and management of Paget's disease. *Clin Orthop* 1977;127:55–62.

Whyte MP. Paget's disease of bone. *N Engl J Med* 2006;355:593–600.

Wick MR, Siegal GP, Unni KK, McLeod RA, Greditzer HG III. Sarcomas of bone complicating osteitis deformans (Paget's disease): fifty years' experience. *Am J Surg Pathol* 1981;5:47–59.

Wittenberg K. The blade of grass sign. *Radiology* 2001;221:199–200.

Yu T, Squires F, Mammone J, DiMarcangelo M. Lymphoma arising in Paget's disease. *Skeletal Radiol* 1997;26:729–731.

Zlatkin MB, Lander PH, Hadjipavlou AG, Levine JS. Paget disease of the spine: CT with clinical correlation. *Radiology* 1986;160:155–159.

Miscellaneous Metabolic and Endocrine Disorders

Familial Idiopathic Hyperphosphatasia

Familial idiopathic hyperphosphatasia is a rare autosomal-recessive disorder affecting young children, generally within their first 18 months and exhibiting a striking predilection for those of Puerto Rican descent. The condition is associated with progressive bone deformities. Clinically, it is characterized by painful bowing of the limbs, muscular weakness, abnormal gait, pathologic fractures, spinal deformities, loss of vision and hearing, elevation of serum alkaline phosphatase, and an increase in the amount of leucine aminopeptidase.

Imaging Evaluation

Increased turnover of bone and skeletal collagen demonstrated by radionuclide bone scan is a characteristic finding in familial idiopathic hyperphosphatasia. Its radiographic features are typical. Although this disorder has no relationship to classic Paget disease, it is often referred to as "juvenile Paget disease," and it exhibits similar radiographic features. The long bones are increased in size, showing thickening of the cortex and a coarse trabecular pattern (Figs. 30.1 and 30.2). Likewise, bowing deformities are common, as are involvement of the pelvis and skull (Fig. 30.3). However, unlike Paget disease, the epiphyses are usually not affected.

Differential Diagnosis

A few conditions exist similar to familial idiopathic hyperphosphatasia that belong to the general group of endosteal hyperostoses, or hyperostosis corticalis generalisata. In particular, an autosomal-recessive form of these disorders, van Buchem disease, although classified as chronic hyperphosphatasia tarda, is in fact a distinct dysplasia. Its onset is later than that of congenital hyperphosphatasia, and the age of patients ranges from 25 to 50 years. The major radiographic finding is a symmetric thickening of the cortices of the long and short tubular bones. The femora are not bowed, and the articular ends are spared. The cranial bones show marked thickening of the vault and the base. Serum alkaline phosphatase levels are elevated, but calcium and phosphorus levels are normal.

Acromegaly

Increased secretion of growth hormone (somatotropin) by the eosinophilic cells of the anterior lobe of the pituitary gland, as a result of either hyperplasia of the gland or a tumor, leads to acceleration of bone growth. If this condition develops before skeletal maturity (i.e., while the growth plates are still open), then it results in gigantism; development after skeletal maturity results in acromegaly. The onset of symptoms is usually insidious, and the involvement of certain target sites in the skeleton is typical (Fig. 30.4). Gradual enlargement of the hands and feet as well as exaggeration of facial features are the earliest manifestations. The characteristic facial changes result from overgrowth of the frontal sinuses, protrusion of the jaw (prognathism), accentuation of the orbital ridges, enlargement of the nose and lips, and thickening and coarsening of the soft tissues of the face.

Radiographic Evaluation

Radiographic examination reveals a number of characteristic features of this condition. A lateral radiograph of the skull demonstrates thickening of the cranial bones and increased density. The diploë may be obliterated. The sella turcica, which houses the pituitary gland, may or may not be enlarged. The paranasal sinuses become enlarged (Fig. 30.5) and the mastoid cells become overpneumatized. The prognathous jaw, one of the obvious clinical features of this condition, is apparent on the lateral view of the facial bones.

The hands also exhibit revealing radiographic changes. The heads of the metacarpals are enlarged, and irregular bony thickening along the margins, simulating osteophytes, may be seen. Increase in the size of the sesamoid at the metacarpophalangeal joint of the thumb may be helpful in evaluating acromegaly. Values of the sesamoid index (determined by the height and width of this ossicle measured in millimeters) greater than 30 in women and greater than 40 in men suggest acromegaly; however, generally the dividing line between normal and abnormal values is not sharp enough to allow individual borderline cases to be diagnosed on the basis of this index alone. Characteristic changes are also seen in the distal phalanges; their bases enlarge and the terminal tufts form spur-like projections. The joint spaces widen as a result of hypertrophy

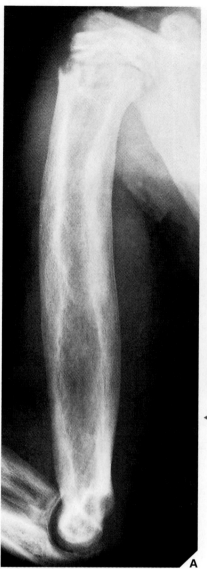

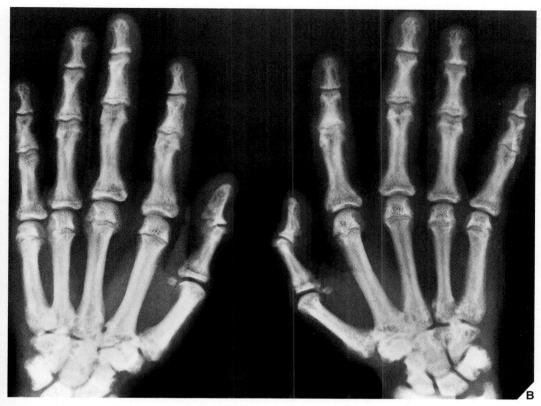

◀ FIGURE 30.1 **Familial idiopathic hyperphosphatasia. (A)** Anteroposterior radiograph of the shoulder and arm of a 12-year-old Puerto Rican boy reveals marked thickening of the cortex of the humerus and coarsening of the bony trabeculae, resembling pagetic bone. **(B)** Radiograph of the hands shows sclerotic changes in the bones and a marked narrowing of the medullary cavity of the metacarpals and phalanges.

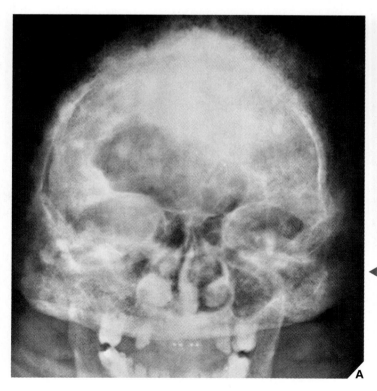

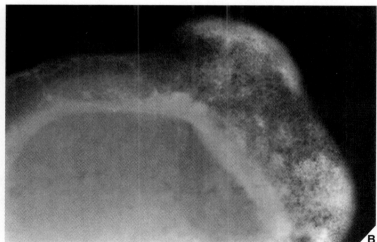

◀ FIGURE 30.2 **Familial idiopathic hyperphosphatasia. (A)** Anteroposterior radiograph of the skull of a 30-year-old man shows calvarial thickening and sclerosis resembling that of Paget disease. **(B)** Magnification study reveals marked thickening of the inner table and widening of the diploë.

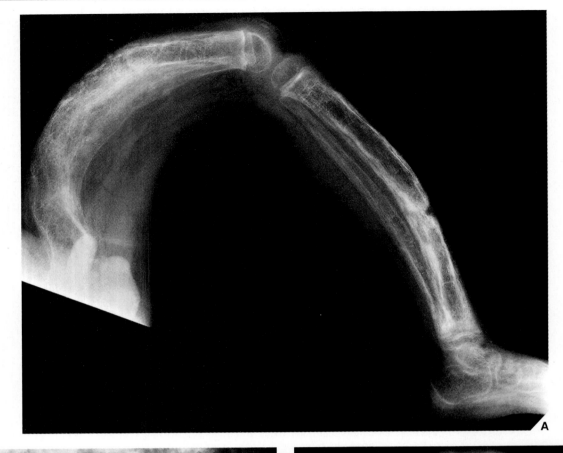

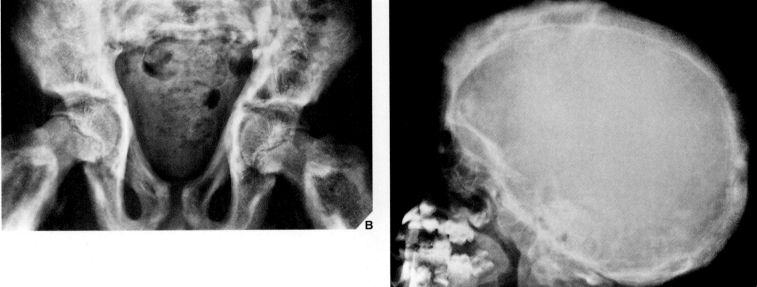

▲
FIGURE 30.3   **Familial idiopathic hyperphosphatasia. (A)** Radiograph of a 4-year-old boy demonstrates marked bowing of the long bones of the lower extremity, a striking feature of this disorder. **(B)** Anteroposterior radiograph of the pelvis shows the coarse trabecular pattern and cortical thickening typical of this condition. Note that the epiphyses are not affected. **(C)** Lateral radiograph of the skull demonstrates thickening of the tables and a "cotton ball" appearance of the cranial vault, similar to that of Paget disease. **(B** from Sissons HA, Greenspan A, 1986, with permission.)

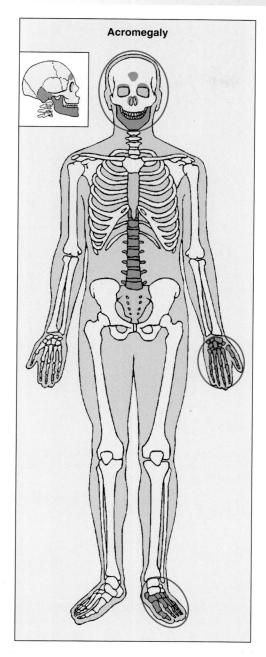

▲
FIGURE 30.4 The most clearly revealing target sites of acromegaly.

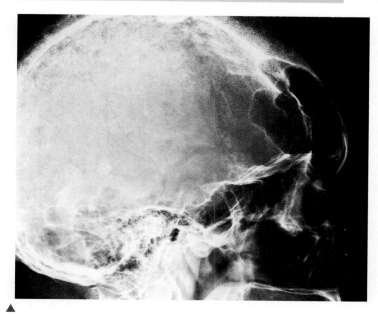

▲
FIGURE 30.5 **Acromegalic skull.** Lateral radiograph of the skull of a 75-year-old woman shows marked enlargement of the frontal sinuses, prominent supraorbital ridges, and thickening of the frontal bones.

been implicated as a potential cause. Other conditions have also been associated with posterior vertebral scalloping (Table 30.1). In addition, thoracic kyphosis is often increased in spinal acromegaly and lumbar lordosis is accentuated. The invertebral disk space may be wider than normal because of overgrowth of the cartilaginous portion of the disk.

of articular cartilage (Fig. 30.6), and hypertrophy of the soft tissues may also occur, leading to the development of square, spade-shaped fingers.

Evaluation of the foot on the lateral view allows an important measurement to be made, the heel-pad thickness. This index is determined by the distance from the posteroinferior surface of the os calcis to the nearest skin surface. In a normal 150-lb subject, the heel-pad thickness should not exceed 22 mm. For each additional 25 lb of body weight, 1 mm can be added to the basic value; thus, 24 mm would be the highest normal value for a 200-lb person. If the heel-pad thickness is greater than the established normal value, then acromegaly is a strong possibility (Fig. 30.7), and determination of growth hormone level by immunoassay is called for.

The spine in acromegaly may also reveal identifying features. A lateral radiograph of the spine may disclose an increase in the anteroposterior diameter of a vertebral body, as well as scalloping or increased concavity of the posterior vertebral margin (Fig. 30.8). Although the exact mechanism of this phenomenon is not known, bone resorption has

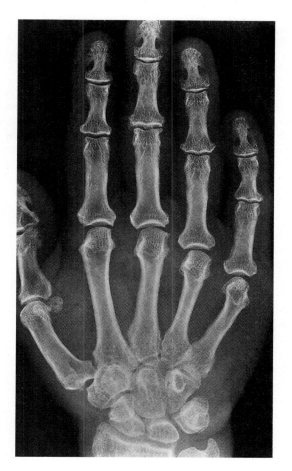

▲
FIGURE 30.6 **Acromegalic hand.** Dorsovolar radiograph of the hand of a 38-year-old woman shows characteristic overgrowth of the terminal tufts and spur-like projections. The bases of the terminal phalanges are also enlarged, and the radiographic joint spaces are widened.

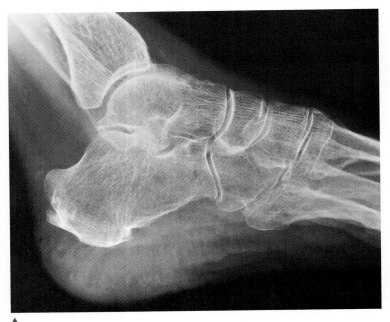

▲
FIGURE 30.7 **Acromegalic foot.** Lateral radiograph of the foot of a 58-year-old man shows a heel-pad thickness of 38 mm, far above normal for this patient who weighs only 140 lb. This measurement corresponds to the shortest distance between the calcaneus and the plantar aspect of the heel.

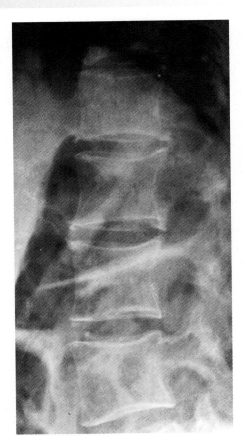

▲
FIGURE 30.8 **Acromegalic spine.** Lateral radiograph of the thoracolumbar spine of a 49-year-old woman demonstrates posterior vertebral scalloping, a phenomenon apparently caused by bone resorption.

The articular abnormalities seen in acromegaly are the result of a frequent complication, degenerative joint disease, which is in turn the result of overgrowth of the articular cartilage and subsequent inadequate nourishment of abnormally thick cartilage. The combination of joint space narrowing, osteophytes, subchondral sclerosis, and formation of cyst-like lesions is similar to the primary osteoarthritic process.

TABLE 30.1 **Causes of Scalloping in Vertebral Bodies**

Increased Intraspinal Pressure
   Intradural neoplasms
   Intraspinal cysts
   Syringomyelia and hydromyelia
   Communicating hydrocephalus
Dural Ectasia
   Marfan syndrome
   Ehlers-Danlos syndrome
   Neurofibromatosis
Bone Resorption
   Acromegaly
Congenital Disorders
   Achondroplasia
   Morquio disease
   Hunter syndrome
   Osteogenesis imperfecta (tarda)
Physiologic Scalloping

From Mitchell GE et al., 1967, with permission.

Gaucher Disease

Classification

Gaucher disease is a familial inherited disturbance of unknown cause transmitted as an autosomal-recessive trait. It is a metabolic disorder characterized by the abnormal deposition of cerebrosides (glycolipids) in the reticuloendothelial cells of the spleen, liver, and bone marrow. These altered macrophages, called *Gaucher cells*, are the histologic hallmark of the disease. The disease results from numerous mutations at the genetic locus encoding the enzyme glucocerebrosidase (glucosylceramidase cerebroside β-glucosidase) that lead to the defective activity of lysosomal hydrolase. It is classified into three distinct categories:

Type I: The *nonneuronopathic*, or *adult type*, is the most common form, occurring mainly in Ashkenazi Jews. Onset is in the patient's first or second decade, and the individuals affected usually live normal life spans. Bone abnormalities and hepatosplenomegaly characterize this form of the disease, although some patients may not show any symptoms.

Type II: The *acute neuronopathic* form is lethal within the patient's 1st year. This type apparently has no predilection for any ethnic group. Hepatosplenomegaly is invariably present, in addition to brain damage and seizure disorder.

Type III: The *subacute juvenile neuronopathic* form, occuring mainly in Swedish nationality from the Norbotten region begins in the latter part of the 1st year and follows a malignant course similar to that of type II. Patients present with hepatosplenomegaly, anemia, respiratory problems, mental retardation, and seizures, and usually die by the end of their second decade of life.

FIGURE 30.9 **Gaucher disease.** Anteroposterior radiograph ▶ of a 12-year-old boy with adult-type of disease shows the Erlenmeyer-flask deformity of both distal femora, secondary to medullary expansion. Note the thinning of the cortex caused by diffuse osteoporosis.

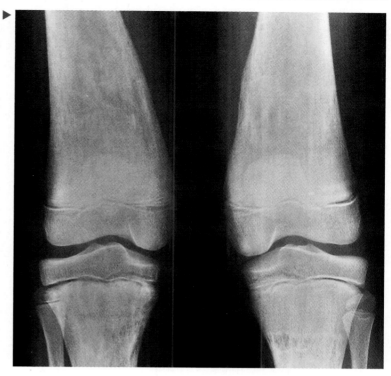

The presenting clinical features of patients depend on the type of disease they have. The adult form of the disorder (type I) is the most common one and typically presents with abdominal distention secondary to splenomegaly. Recurrent bone pain is a sign of skeletal involvement, and acute severe bone pain together with swelling and fever suggests acute pyogenic osteomyelitis. This clinical complex, which is the result of ischemic necrosis of bone, has been called "aseptic osteomyelitis." Pingueculae may be present in the eyes, and the skin may acquire a brown pigmentation. Epistaxis or other hemorrhages caused by thrombocytopenia may occur. The diagnosis is made by demonstrating characteristic Gaucher cells in bone marrow aspirate or in a biopsy specimen from the liver.

Radiologic Evaluation

The radiographic examination in Gaucher disease reveals characteristic findings. There is a diffuse osteoporosis that is frequently associated with medullary expansion. In the ends of the long bones, this phenomenon is referred to as the "Erlenmeyer flask" deformity (Fig. 30.9 and Table 30.2). Localized bone destruction assuming a honeycomb appearance is also typically seen (Fig. 30.10); gross osteolytic destruction is usually limited to the shafts of the long bones. Moreover, sclerotic changes are common, occurring secondary to a repair process or bone infarctions (Fig. 30.11). Medullary bone infarction and a periosteal reaction may lead

TABLE 30.2 **Causes of Erlenmeyer Flask Deformity**

Gaucher disease
Niemann-Pick disease
Fibrous dysplasia
Sickle-cell anemia
Thalassemia
Multiple cartilaginous exostoses
Ollier disease (enchondromatosis)
Albers-Schönberg disease (osteopetrosis)
Engelmann disease (progressive diaphyseal dysplasia)
Pyle disease (metaphyseal dysplasia)
Pycnodysostosis
Lead poisoning

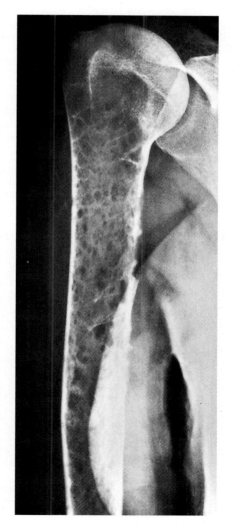

▲ FIGURE 30.10 **Gaucher disease.** Destructive changes, seen here in the proximal right humerus of a 52-year-old woman with the adult form of the disease, may assume a honeycomb appearance.

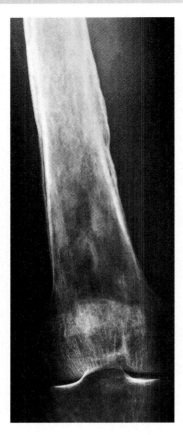

▲

FIGURE 30.11   Gaucher disease. Anteroposterior radiograph of the right distal femur of a 29-year-old man demonstrates medullary infarction of the bone and endosteal and periosteal reactions secondary to reparative processes.

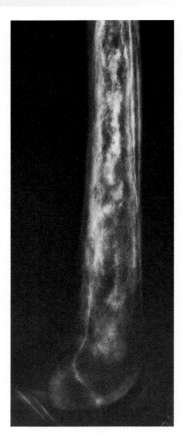

▲

FIGURE 30.12   Gaucher disease. Lateral radiograph of the distal femur in a 28-year-old woman shows extensive medullary infarction and periosteal new bone formation, producing a bone-within-bone appearance.

to a bone-within-bone phenomenon, which may resemble osteomyelitis (Fig. 30.12). Recently, Hermann and associates conducted a study of 29 patients with type I Gaucher disease using MRI to determine the usefulness of this technique in the evaluation of bone marrow involvement. The results of this investigation suggest that MRI is a valuable noninvasive modality in this respect to assess disease activity. Apparently, the patients with decreased signal intensity within bone marrow on both T1-weighted and T2-weighted images, but showing a relative increase in

signal intensity from T1 weighting to T2 weighting can be considered to have an "active process" that correlates well with their symptoms.

Complications

The most common complication of Gaucher disease is osteonecrosis of the femoral head and occasionally of the femoral condyles (Fig. 30.13). Superimposition of degenerative changes is also a frequent finding that

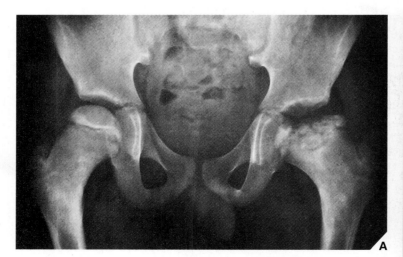

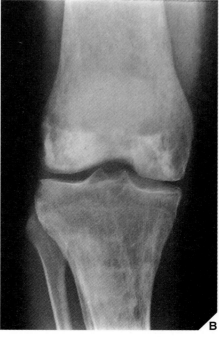

FIGURE 30.13   Gaucher disease complicated by osteonecrosis. (A) Anteroposterior radiograph of the pelvis of an 11-year-old Ashkenazi Jew with non-neuronopathic type of disease shows osteonecrosis of the left femoral head, a common complication of this disorder. **(B)** Anteroposterior radiograph of the right knee of a 25-year-old man with Gaucher disease demonstrates osteonecrotic changes of the medial and lateral femoral condyles. Note also the extensive bone infarction of the proximal tibia.

necessitates surgery. Pathologic fractures are common, and they may involve the long bones as well as the spine. The most serious complication (although fortunately a rare one) is malignant transformation at the site of bone infarcts.

Treatment

Enzyme replacement therapy using placental-derived alglucerase or recombinant (i.e., imiglucerase) preparations has resulted in hematologic improvement and resolution of hepatosplenomegaly. In some patients, signs of skeletal regeneration have been reported. Occasionally, splenectomy is performed. Bone marrow transplantation also have been tried with mixed results.

Tumoral Calcinosis

Pathophysiology

First described by Inclan and coworkers in 1943, tumoral calcinosis is characterized by the presence of single or multiple periarticular lobulated cystic masses containing chalky material. Their formation is the result of the deposition of calcium salt in the soft tissues about the joints—the shoulders (particularly near the scapula), hips, and elbow joints—as well as on the extensile surfaces of the limbs. The masses are painless and usually occur in children and adolescents. Blacks are affected more frequently than other racial groups, with most cases of tumoral calcinosis reported from Africa and New Guinea. Because the cause is unknown, the diagnosis is one of exclusion. Other causes of soft-tissue calcifications, such as secondary hyperparathyroidism, hypervitaminosis D, gout and pseudogout, myositis ossificans, paraarticular chondroma, and calcinosis circumscripta, must be excluded before the diagnosis of tumoral calcinosis can be made. Recent studies have shown that individuals with familial tumoral calcinosis harbor mutations in either the *FGF23* or *GALNT3* genes.

Radiographic Evaluation

Radiographic examination usually reveals well-demarcated and lobulated calcific masses that are circular or oval and located about the joints (Fig. 30.14). They vary in density; some are lacy and amorphous, and others are almost bone-like in appearance. Only in very rare instances is the calcific deposit located within the joint capsule.

Treatment

Surgical excision of the calcified masses is the most effective form of treatment, although attempts to treat this disorder with low-calcium and

FIGURE 30.14 Tumoral calcinosis. A 66-year-old black subject had multiple bumps about the wrists and elbows since childhood. Dorsovolar (**A**) and lateral (**B**) radiographs of the wrists demonstrate calcific masses located on the dorsal aspect just beneath the skin. (**C**) Anteroposterior radiograph of the right elbow shows similar tumoral accumulation of calcium on the anteromedial aspect.

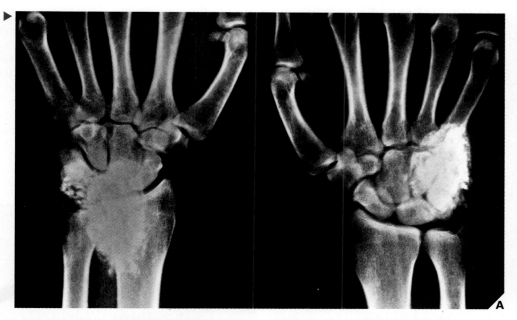

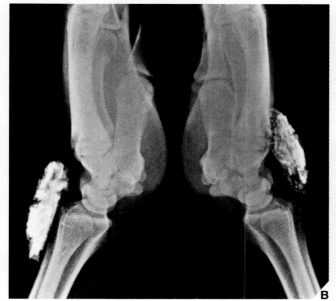

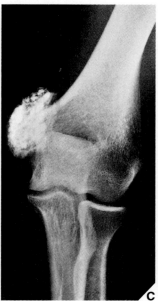

low-phosphate diets and phosphate-combining antacids have had some success.

Hypothyroidism

Pathophysiology

Hypothyroidism is a syndrome encountered in infants and children, resulting from a deficiency of the thyroid hormones thyroxine and tri-iodothyronine, either during fetal life (cretinism) or early childhood (juvenile myxedema or juvenile hypothyroidism). The deficiency may be primary, caused by disease of the thyroid gland, or secondary, caused by lack of thyroid-stimulating hormone (TSH) produced by the pituitary gland. The major target sites are the growth plates and epiphyses, best demonstrated in the hands and the hips (Fig. 30.15). The key symptoms and signs include lethargy, constipation, an enlarged tongue, abdominal distention, and dry skin. The manifestations are typically less severe when the deficiency occurs in early childhood as an acquired disease than when it is congenital.

Radiographic Evaluation

The fundamental radiographic feature in both forms of hypothyroidism is delayed skeletal maturation with stunting of bone growth leading to dwarfism. In particular, the appearance of the secondary ossification centers is greatly delayed, as a dorsovolar radiograph of the hand may demonstrate (Fig. 30.16). Epiphyses ossify from numerous ossification centers, thereby acquiring a fragmented appearance and on occasion appearing abnormally dense (Fig. 30.17). This process may be mistaken for osteonecrosis, as seen in Legg-Calvé-Perthes disease (see Fig. 32.26), or for certain dysplasias, such as dysplasia epiphysealis punctata, also known as Conradi disease. Underpneumatization of the sinuses and mastoids are also typical radiographic findings associated with hypothyroidism.

Complications

One of the common complications of hypothyroidism is the development of slipped femoral capital epiphysis. The radiographic findings of this condition are described in Chapter 32.

Scurvy

Pathophysiology

Barlow disease, as scurvy is also known, results from a deficiency of ascorbic acid (vitamin C). The function of vitamin C is to maintain intracellular substances of mesenchymal derivation, such as connective tissue, osteoid tissue in bones, and dentin in the teeth. In infants, primary deficiency is caused most commonly by failure to supplement the diet with vitamin C, whereas in adults it is usually caused by food idiosyncrasies or an insufficient diet. Deficiency of vitamin C causes a hemorrhagic tendency, leading to subperiosteal bleeding and abnormal function of osteoblasts and chondroblasts. The latter results in defective osteogenesis.

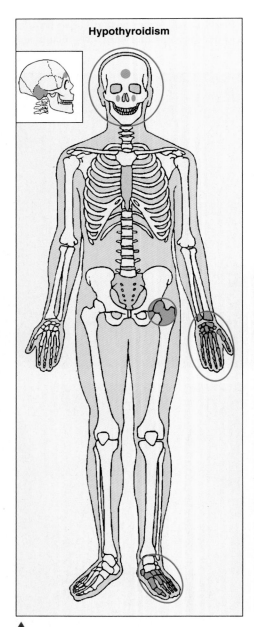

▲ FIGURE 30.15 Target sites of hypothyroidism.

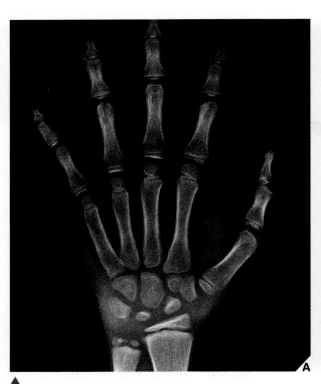
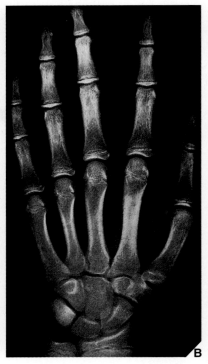

▲ FIGURE 30.16 Juvenile hypothyroidism. **(A)** Dorsovolar radiograph of the right hand of a 13-year-old boy demonstrates skeletal immaturity; the bone age is approximately 8 years. Note the "fragmented" secondary ossification centers of the distal ulna and distal phalanges. In fact, they represent separated foci of ossification. **(B)** The hand of a healthy boy of the same age is shown for comparison.

FIGURE 30.17 Congenital hypothyroidism (cretinism). ▶ Anteroposterior radiograph of the pelvis of a 5-year-old boy shows pseudofragmentation of both capital femoral epiphyses. This process may be mistaken for Legg-Calvé-Perthes disease.

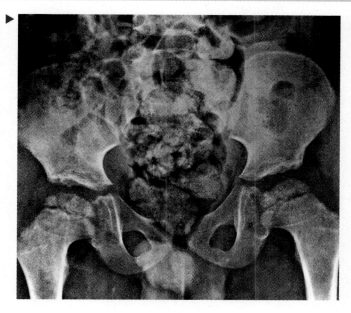

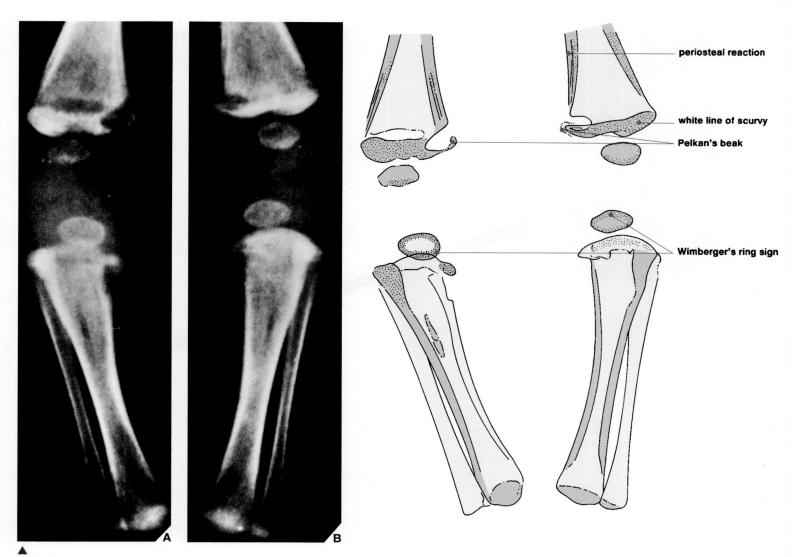

▲
FIGURE 30.18 Scurvy. **(A,B)** Anteroposterior radiographs of the lower legs of an 8-month-old infant shows the typical skeletal changes of scurvy. Note the dense segment adjacent to the growth plate ("white line of scurvy"), the ring of increased density around the secondary ossification centers of the distal femora and proximal tibiae (Wimberger ring sign), and the beaking of the metaphysis of both tibiae (Pelkan beak). A periosteal reaction secondary to subperiosteal bleeding is also noted.

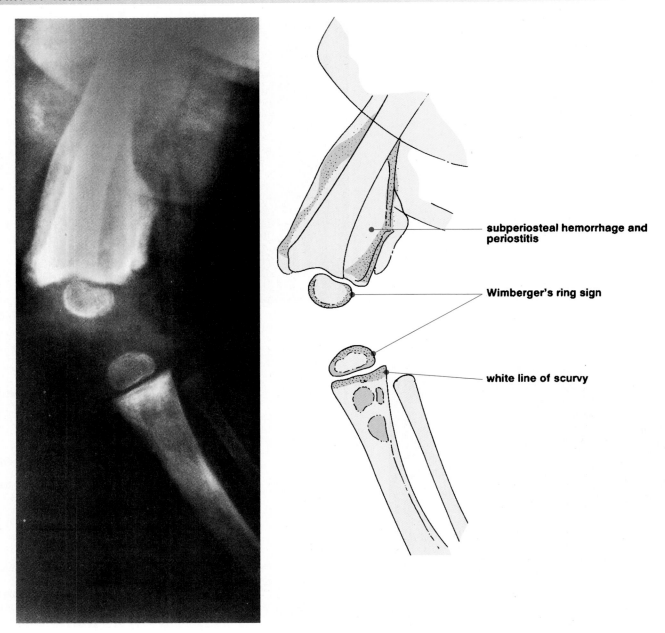

▲
FIGURE 30.19 Scurvy. Lateral radiograph of the right leg of a 10-month-old infant with subperiosteal bleeding secondary to scurvy shows a marked periosteal reaction in the distal femoral diaphysis. A peripheral ring of increased density and central radiolucency, the Wimberger ring sign, is evident in the posteriorly displaced ossification center of the distal femoral epiphysis and in the proximal tibial epiphysis. Note also "white line" in the tibial metaphysis.

Radiographic Evaluation

The characteristic bone lesions of scurvy are caused by cessation of endochondral bone ossification caused by failure of the osteoblasts to form osteoid tissue. Continuing osteoclastic resorption without adequate formation of new bone yields the appearance of osteoporosis, with generalized osteopenia and thinning of the cortices. Deposition of calcium phosphate continues in whatever osteoid tissue is formed, so that an area of increased density develops adjacent to the growth plate. Such areas have been called the "white lines of scurvy" (Fig. 30.18). A ring of increased density is also seen around the secondary centers of ossification, a finding known as a Wimberger ring sign. Fractures of the metaphysis are common, producing a "corner" sign or "Pelkan beak" (see Fig. 30.18).

Increased capillary fragility leads to subperiosteal and soft-tissue bleeding and the formation of hematomas, which may trigger a periosteal reaction (Fig. 30.19). In adults, the bleeding may extend into the joints.

Differential Diagnosis

Scurvy should be differentiated from "battered child syndrome," congenital syphilis, and leukemia. In battered child syndrome, characteristic metaphyseal corner fractures and fractures in different healing stages are characteristic. In congenital syphilis, the epiphyseal centers are normal. In leukemia, radiolucent metaphyseal bands are common, but fractures and epiphysiolysis are not part of the disorder.

PRACTICAL POINTS TO REMEMBER

Familial Idiopathic Hyperphosphatasia

[1] Two conditions of similar radiographic presentation are familial idiopathic hyperphosphatasia ("juvenile Paget disease") and autosomal-recessive form of hyperostosis corticalis generalisata, van Buchem disease. The radiographic features of these disorders, similar to those of Paget disease, are:
 • cortical thickening and a coarse trabecular pattern to the spongiosa
 • sparing of the articular ends of bones (unlike classic Paget disease).

Acromegaly

[1] In the diagnosis and evaluation of acromegaly, the following radiographic projections have specific value:
 • lateral view of the skull to evaluate the thickness of the cranial vault, the size of the paranasal sinuses, and prognathism
 • dorsovolar view of the hands to evaluate the sesamoid index and detect changes of the distal tufts
 • lateral view of the foot to measure the heel-pad thickness
 • lateral view of the spine to evaluate the intervertebral disk spaces and the posterior margins of the vertebral bodies.
[2] One of the frequent complications of acromegaly is degenerative joint disease (osteoarthritis) secondary to undernourished hypertrophied articular cartilage.

Gaucher Disease

[1] Gaucher disease is a metabolic disorder characterized by the abnormal deposition of cerebrosides (glycolipids) in the reticuloendothelial system.
[2] Characteristic radiographic features of Gaucher disease include:
 • Erlenmeyer flask deformity of the distal femora
 • osteonecrosis of the femoral heads
 • medullary bone infarction of the long bones, frequently associated with periosteal reaction
 • generalized osteopenia.
[3] MRI is a noninvasive technique to assess disease activity.

Tumoral Calcinosis

[1] Tumoral calcinosis, a condition seen predominantly in blacks, consists of multiple cystic, calcium-containing masses about the large joints (shoulders, hips, and elbows).
[2] The diagnosis of tumoral calcinosis is one of exclusion: other causes of soft-tissue calcifications, such as secondary hyperparathyroidism, hypervitaminosis D, and juxtacortical myositis ossificans, must be excluded.

Hypothyroidism

[1] The fundamental radiographic feature of hypothyroidism (cretinism and juvenile myxedema) is retarded skeletal maturation, which is best demonstrated on a dorsovolar view of the hand.
[2] Other characteristic radiographic features of hypothyroidism include:
 • a fragmented appearance of the ossification centers of the epiphyses
 • increased density of both epiphyses and metaphyses.
[3] In the femoral heads, these features may mimic osteonecrosis (Legg-Calvé-Perthes disease) or dysplasia epiphysealis punctata (Conradi disease).

Scurvy

[1] The characteristic radiographic changes seen in scurvy (deficiency of vitamin C) include:
 • generalized osteopenia
 • "white lines of scurvy" adjacent to the growth plate
 • Wimberger ring sign, representing increased density around ossification centers

 • the "corner" sign or "Pelkan beak," representing metaphyseal fractures
 • periosteal reaction secondary to subperiosteal bleeding.
[2] Conditions that should be differentiated from scurvy include:
 • battered child syndrome
 • congenital syphilis
 • leukemia.

SUGGESTED READINGS

Albright F. Changes simulating Legg Perthes disease (osteochondritis deformans juvenilis) due to juvenile myxoedema. *J Bone Joint Surg* 1938;20:764–769.
Amstutz HC. The hip in Gaucher's disease. *Clin Orthop* 1973;90:83–89.
Amstutz HC, Carey EJ. Skeletal manifestations and treatment of Gaucher's disease. Review of twenty cases. *J Bone Joint Surg [Am]* 1966;48A:670–679.
Beighton P, Goldblatt J, Sachs S. Bone involvement in Gaucher disease. In: Desnick RJ, Gatt S, Grabowski GA, eds. *Gaucher disease: a century of delineation and research.* New York: Alan R Liss; 1982:107–129.
Beutler E. Gaucher disease. Review article. *N Engl J Med* 1991;325:1354–1360.
Bishop AF, Destovet JM, Murphy WA, Gilula LA. Tumoral calcinosis: case report and review. *Skeletal Radiol* 1982;8:269–274.
Bourke JA, Heslin DJ. Gaucher's disease: roentgenologic changes over 20 years interval. *Am J Roentgenol* 1965;94:621–630.
Cremin BJ, Davey H, Goldblatt J. Skeletal complications of type I Gaucher disease: the magnetic resonance features. *Clin Radiol* 1990;42:244–247.
Desnick RJ. Gaucher disease (1882–1982): centennial perspectives on the most prevalent Jewish genetic disease. *Mt Sinai J Med* 1982;49:443–455.
Detenbeck LC, Tressler HA, O'Duffy JD, Randall RV. Peripheral joint manifestations of acromegaly. *Clin Orthop* 1973;91:119–127.
Duncan TR. Validity of sesamoid index in diagnosis of acromegaly. *Radiology* 1975;115:617–619.
Feldman RH, Lewis MM, Greenspan A, Steiner GC. Tumoral calcinosis in an infant. A case report. *Bull Hosp Jt Dis Orthop Inst* 1983;43:78–83.
Frishberg Y, Topaz O, Bergman R, et al. Identification of a recurrent mutation in GALANT 3 demonstrates that hyperostosis-hyperphosphatemia syndrome and familial tumoral calcinosis are allelic disorders. *J Mol Med* 2005;83:33–38.
Goldblatt J, Sachs S, Beighton P. The orthopedic aspects of Gaucher disease. *Clin Orthop* 1978;137:208–214.
Grabowski GA. Gaucher disease. *Adv Hum Genet* 1993;21:341–377.
Grabowski GA. Phenotype, diagnosis, and treatment of Gaucher's disease. *Lancet* 2008;372:1263–1271.
Grenfield GB. Bone changes in chronic adult Gaucher's disease. *Am J Roentgenol* 1970;110:800–807.
Hermann G. Skeletal manifestation of type 1 Gaucher disease—an uncommon genetic disorder. *Osteol Közlem* 2001;10:141–148.
Hermann G, Goldblatt J, Levy RN, Goldsmith SJ, Grabowski GA. Gaucher's disease type I. Assessment of bone involvement by CT and scintigraphy. *Am J Roentgenol* 1986;147:943–948.
Hermann G, Shapiro RS, Abdelwahab IF, Grabowski G. MR imaging in adults with Gaucher disease type I: evaluation of marrow involvement and disease activity. *Skeletal Radiol* 1993;22:247–251.
Hernandez RJ, Poznanski AK. Distinctive appearance of the distal phalanges in children with primary hypothyroidism. *Radiology* 1979;132:83–84.
Hernandez RJ, Poznanski AW, Hopwood NJ. Size and skeletal maturation of the hand in children with hypothyroidism and hypopituitarism. *Am J Roentgenol* 1979;133:405–408.
Hirsch M, Mogle P, Barkli Y. Neonatal scurvy. *Pediatr Radiol* 1976;4:251–253.
Horev G, Kornreich L, Hadar H, Katz K. Hemorrhage associated with bone crisis in Gaucher disease identified by magnetic resonance imaging. *Skeletal Radiol* 1991;20:479–482.
Inclan A, Leon P, Camejo MG. Tumoral calcinosis. *JAMA* 1943;121:490–495.
Israel O, Jershalmi J, Front D. Scintigraphic findings in Gaucher disease. *J Nucl Med* 1986;27:1557–1563.
Kho KM, Wright AD, Doyle FH. Heel-pad thickness in acromegaly. *Br J Radiol* 1970;43:119–125.
Kinsella RA Jr, Back DK. Thyroid acropachy. *Med Clin North Am* 1968;52:393–398.
Kleinberg DL, Young IS, Kupperman HS. The sesamoid index. An aid in the diagnosis of acromegaly. *Ann Intern Med* 1966;64:1075–1078.
Lacks S, Jacobs RP. Acromegalic arthropathy: a reversible rheumatic disease. *J Rheumatol* 1986;13:634–636.
Lafferty FW, Reynolds ES, Pearson OH. Tumoral calcinosis: a metabolic disease of obscure etiology. *Am J Med* 1965;38:105–118.
Lang EK, Bessler WT. The roentgenologic features of acromegaly. *Am J Roentgenol* 1961;86:321–328.
Lanir A, Hadar H, Cohen I, et al. Gaucher disease: assessment with MR imaging. *Radiology* 1986;161:239–244.
Layton MW, Fudman EJ, Barkan A, Braunstein EM, Fox IH. Acromegalic arthropathy: characteristics and response to therapy. *Arthritis Rheum* 1988;31:1022–1027.

Levin B. Gaucher's disease: clinical and roentgenologic manifestations. *Am J Roentgenol* 1961;85:685–696.

Lin SR, Lee KR. Relative value of some radiographic measurements of the hand in the diagnosis of acromegaly. *Invest Radiol* 1971;6:426–431.

Manaster BJ, Anderson TM Jr. Tumoral calcinosis: serial images to monitor successful dietary therapy. *Skeletal Radiol* 1982;8:123–125.

Mankin HJ, Rosenthal DI, Xavier R. Current concepts review. Gaucher disease–new approaches to an ancient disease. *J Bone Joint Surg [Am]* 2001;83A:748–760.

Mass M, van Kuijk C, Stoker J, Hollak CE, Akkerman EM, Aerts JFMG, den Heeten GJ. Quantification of bone involvement in Gaucher disease: MR imaging bone marrow burden score as an alternative to Dixon quantitative chemical shift MR imaging—initial experience. *Radiology* 2003;229:554–561.

McNulty JF, Pim P. Hyperphosphatasia. Report of a case with a 30-year follow-up. *Am J Roentgenol* 1972;115:614–618.

Melmed S. Acromegaly. *N Engl J Med* 1990;322:966–977.

Mitchell GE, Lourie H, Berne AS. The various causes of scalloped vertebrae and notes on their pathogenesis. *Radiology* 1967;89:67–74.

Nerubay J, Pilderwasser D. Spontaneous bilateral distal femoral physiolysis due to scurvy. *Acta Orthop Scand* 1984;55:18–20.

Palmer PES. Tumor calcinosis. *Br J Radiol* 1966;39:518.

Randall RV. Acromegaly and gigantism. In DeGroot LJ, ed. *Endocrinology*, 2nd ed. Philadelphia: WB Saunders; 1989:330–350.

Riggs BL, Randall RV, Wahner HW, Jowsey J, Kelly PJ, Singh M. The nature of the metabolic bone disorder in acromegaly. *J Clin Endocrinol Metab* 1972;34:911–918.

Rosenthal DI, Scott JA, Barranger J, et al. Evaluation of Gaucher disease using magnetic resonance imaging. *J Bone Joint Surg [Am]* 1986;68A:802–808.

Scanlon GT, Clemett AR. Thyroid acropachy. *Radiology* 1964;83:1039–1042.

Sissons HA, Greenspan A. Paget's disease. In: Taveras JM, Ferrucci JT, eds. *Radiology—imaging, diagnosis, intervention*. Philadelphia: JB Lippincott; 1986:1–14.

Smit GG, Schmaman A. Tumoral calcinosis. *J Bone Joint Surg [Br]* 1967;49B:698–703.

Steinbach HL, Feldman R, Goldberg MG. Acromegaly. *Radiology* 1959;72:535–549.

Steinbach HL, Russell W. Measurement of the heel-pad as an aid to diagnosis of acromegaly. *Radiology* 1964;82:418–423.

Stuberg JL, Palacios E. Vertebral scalloping in acromegaly. *Am J Roentgenol* 1971;112:397–400.

Torres-Reyes E, Staple TW. Roentgenographic appearance of thyroid acropachy. *Clin Radiol* 1970;21:95–100.

Van Buchem FSP, Hadders HN, Hansen JF, Woldring MG. Hyperostosis corticalis generalisata. Report of seven cases. *Am J Med* 1962;33:387–397.

Van Buchem FSP, Hadders HN, Ubbens R. An uncommon familial systemic disease of the skeleton: hyperostosis corticalis generalisata familiaris. *Acta Radiol* 1955;44:109–120.

Zimram A, Gelbart T, Westwood B, Grabowski G, Beutler E. High frequency of the Gaucher disease mutation at nucleotide 1226 among the Ashkenazi Jews. *Am J Hum Genet* 1991;49:855–859.

Zubrow AB, Lane JM, Parks JS. Slipped capital femoral epiphysis occurring during treatment for hypothyroidism. *J Bone Joint Surg [Am]* 1978;60A:256–258.

VII

CONGENITAL AND DEVELOPMENTAL ANOMALIES

TABLE 31.1   **Simplified Classification of Congenital Anomalies of the Skeletal System**

Anomalies of Bone Formation
 Complete failure of formation (agenesis, aplasia)
 Faulty formation
  Decreased number of bones
  Increased number of bones
 Faulty differentiation
  Pseudoarthrosis
  Fusion (synostosis, coalition, syndactyly)
Anomalies of Bone Growth
 Aberrant size
  Undergrowth (hypoplasia, atrophy)
  Overgrowth (hypertrophy, gigantism)
 Aberrant shape (deformed growth)
 Aberrant fit (subluxation, dislocation)

Anomalies of Bone Maturation and Modeling
 Failure of endochondral bone maturation and modeling
 Failure of intramembranous bone maturation and modeling
 Combined failure of endochondral and intramembranous
  bone maturation and modeling
Constitutional Diseases of Bone
 Abnormalities of cartilage and/or bone growth and
  development (osteochondrodysplasias)
 Malformation of individual bones, isolated or in combination
  (dysostoses)
 Idiopathic osteolyses
 Chromosomal aberrations and primary metabolic
  abnormalities

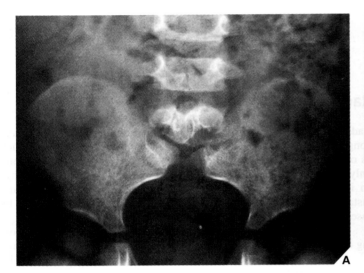

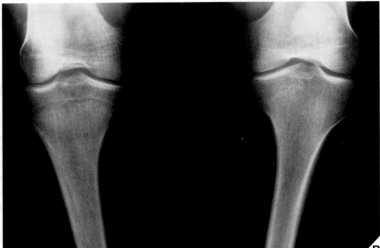

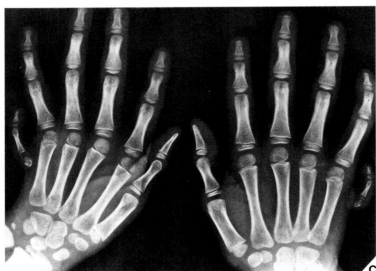

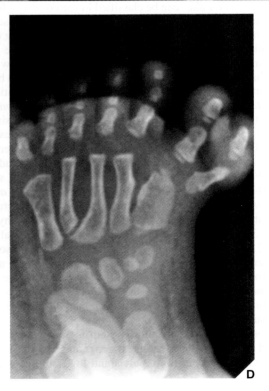

▲
FIGURE 31.1 **Anomalies of bone formation.** Congenital anomalies related to disturbances in bone formation may be seen in the complete failure of a bone to form, as shown on this film in a 1-year-old girl with sacral agenesis (**A**), and in a 26-year-old woman with bilateral agenesis of the fibulae (**B**), or in formation of supernumerary bones, as seen in this 12-year-old boy with polydactyly in both hands (**C**), and in this 3-year-old girl with polydactyly in the right foot (**D**).

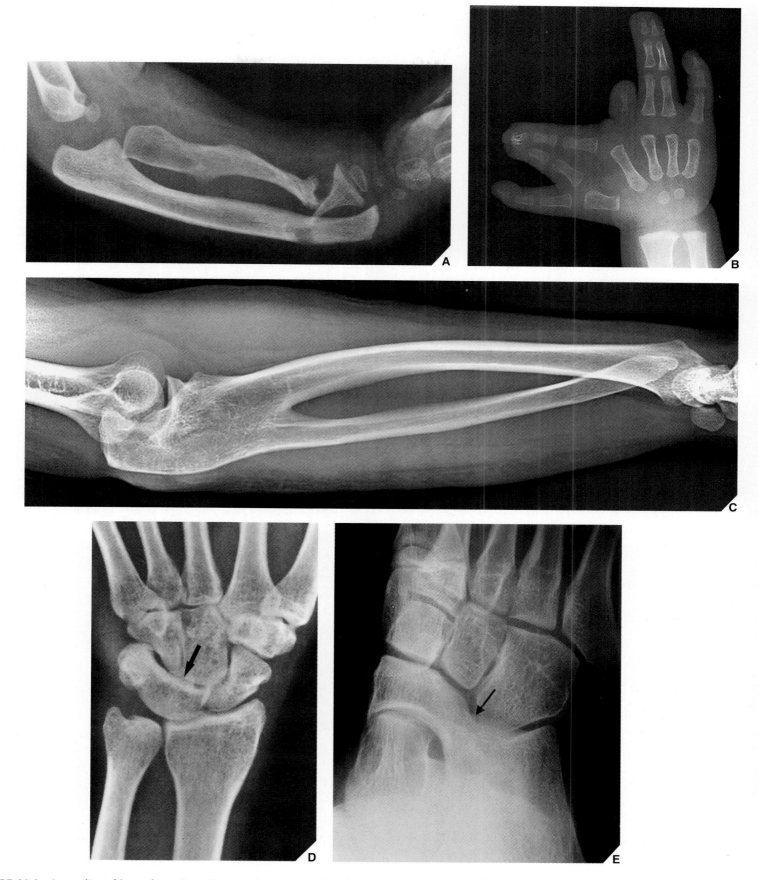

▲
FIGURE 31.2 **Anomalies of bone formation.** Congenital anomalies related to bone division may manifest in congenital pseudoarthrosis, seen here involving the left radius in a 4-year-old boy (**A**); in full fusion of digits (syndactyly), seen here in a 1-year-old boy (**B**) who, in addition, has polydactyly; in partial fusion (synostosis) of two bones, seen here affecting the proximal radius and ulna in a 21-year-old woman (**C**); or in coalition, seen in the complete fusion of the lunate and triquetrum bones (*arrow*) in a 33-year-old man (**D**) and in the fusion of the calcaneus and navicular bones (*arrow*) in a 21-year-old man (**E**).

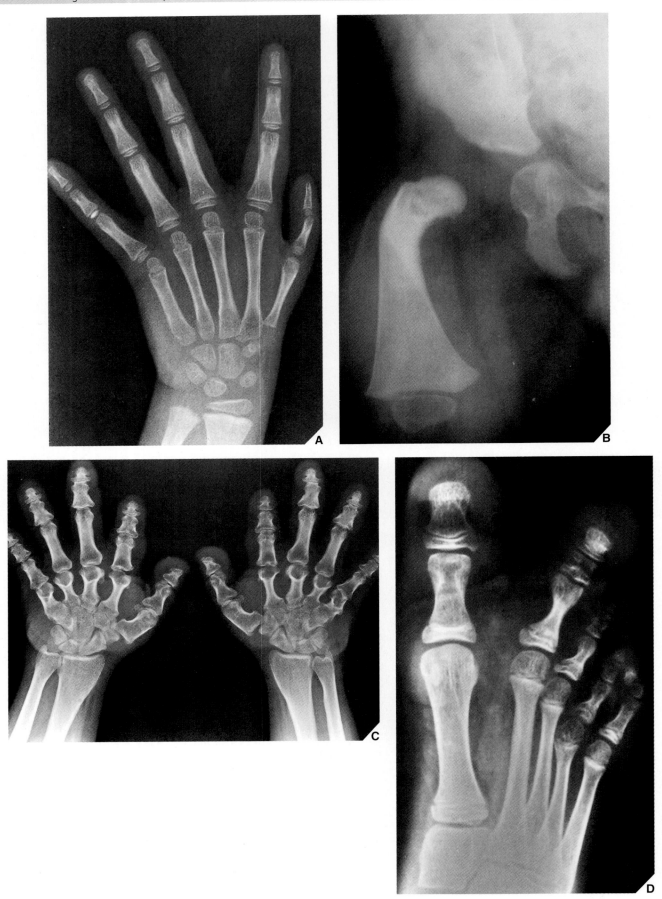

▲

FIGURE 31.3   **Anomalies of bone growth.** Congenital anomalies related to the size of bones may manifest in hypoplasia, as seen here in the right thumb of a 4-year-old girl (**A**), and in the proximal femur of a 7-month-old boy with proximal femoral focal deficiency (**B**), or in congenital brachydactyly, shown here in both hands of a 25-year-old woman (**C**). Overgrowth may also be encountered, as in this case of macrodactyly (megalodactyly) involving the first two digits of the left foot of a 12-year-old girl (**D**).

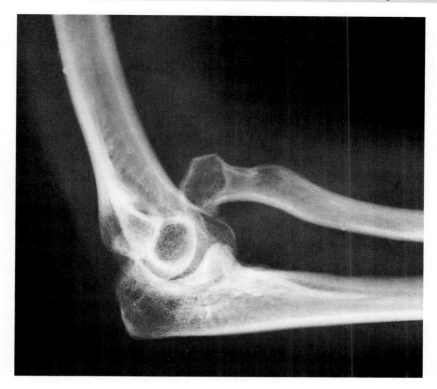

▲
FIGURE 31.4 Anomaly of bone growth. Congenital dislocation of the radial head, seen here in a 35-year-old woman, is an anomaly related to aberrant bone growth leading to a condition affecting the motion of a joint. Note the hypoplasia and abnormal shape of the radial head, an important feature differentiating this condition from traumatic dislocation.

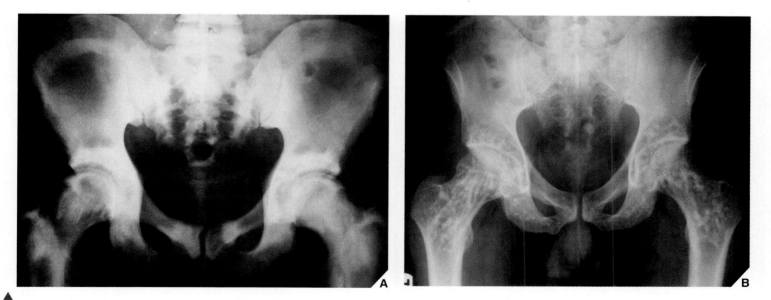

▲
FIGURE 31.5 Anomaly of bone development and maturation. (A) Osteopetrosis (Albers-Schönberg disease), seen here in the spine, pelvis, and both femora of a 28-year-old man, is a congenital anomaly related to the development and maturation of bone. The persistence of immature spongiosa packing the marrow cavity results in the dense marble-like appearance of the bones. **(B)** Osteopoikilosis, seen here affecting the pelvis and proximal femora of a 21-year-old man, is a developmental anomaly of endochondral bone formation, where islands of secondary spongiosa fail to resorb and remodel.

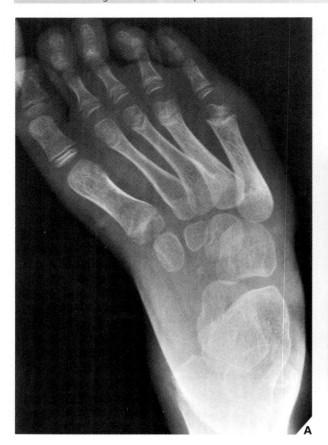

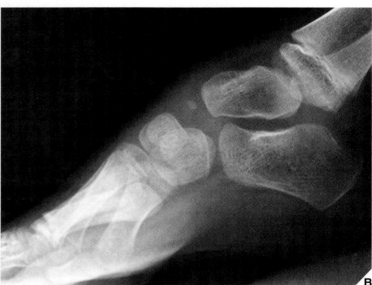

FIGURE 31.6   **Clubfoot deformity.** Dorsoplantar (**A**) and lateral (**B**) radiographs of the foot of a 7-year-old boy are sufficient to demonstrate all the components of congenital equinovarus deformity of the foot (clubfoot), namely, the equinus position of the heel, the varus position of the hindfoot, and the adduction and varus deformity of the forefoot.

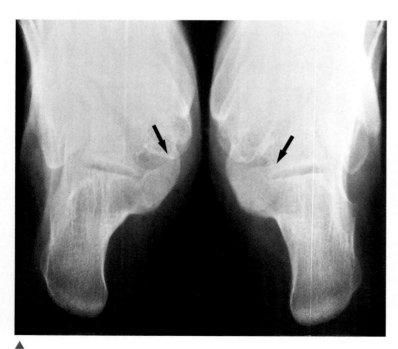

FIGURE 31.7   **Talocalcaneal coalition.** Posterior tangential (Harris-Beath) projection of both calcanei in a 23-year-old woman demonstrates bony fusion at the level of the middle facet of both subtalar joints (*arrows*), a diagnostic feature of a talocalcaneal coalition.

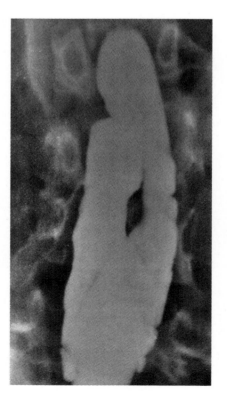

FIGURE 31.8   **Diastematomyelia.** A myelogram of a 9-year-old girl demonstrates a filling defect in the center of the contrast-filled thecal sac, caused by a fibrous spur attached to the vertebral body. This finding is diagnostic of diastematomyelia, a rare congenital anomaly of the vertebrae and spinal cord. Note the associated increase in the interpedicular distances.

FIGURE 31.9 **Congenital hip dislocation. (A)** Standard ▶ anteroposterior radiograph of the right hip of a 7-year-old girl who was treated conservatively demonstrates persistent complete dislocation. **(B)** Arthrography was performed to evaluate the cartilaginous structures of the joint. In addition to a deformed cartilaginous limbus, the ligamentum teres appears thickened and contrast agent has accumulated in the stretched capsule. The thickened ligamentum teres frustrated several previous attempts at closed reduction.

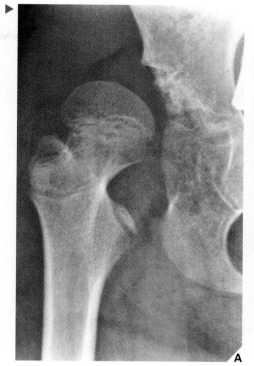
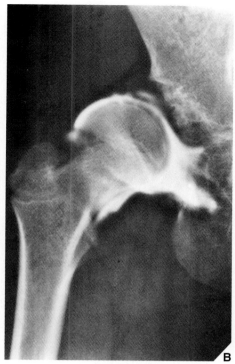

very subtle abnormalities not detected by radiography or arthrography of the hip (Fig. 31.11). A further application of CT is seen in its ability to measure the angle of anteversion of the femoral head, that is, the degree of anterior torsion of the femoral head and neck from the coronal plane (Figs. 31.12 and 31.13). 3D CT reformatted images may be helpful in the global visualization of spinal deformities (Figs. 31.14 and 31.15).

Other ancillary techniques also have important functions in the evaluation of skeletal anomalies. Radionuclide bone scan, for instance, is particularly effective in detecting silent sites of skeletal abnormality in various developmental dysplasias (Fig. 31.16). US has only recently come to be used in the diagnosis of congenital skeletal abnormalities, including hip dysplasia and dislocation. It is effective in assessing the position of the femoral head in the acetabulum, as well as the status of

the cartilaginous acetabular roof and other cartilaginous structures such as the limbus that cannot be demonstrated on the standard radiographs (Fig. 31.17). This technique also offers a noninvasive method of examining the infant hip, which might otherwise require arthrography. In addition, US does not expose the patient to ionizing radiation.

MRI is ideally suited to evaluate congenital and development anomalies of the spine because all structures, including neural components, are shown simultaneously. Because MRI evaluation is mainly an assessment of neuroanatomic development, spin-echo T1-weighted images are usually obtained (Fig. 31.18). However, anomalies affecting the spinal cord and thecal sac are best seen on T2-weighted images because of high contrast of the spinal fluid. These sequences can be quite effective in demonstrating, for example, spinal dysraphism and diastematomyelia (Fig. 31.19).

FIGURE 31.10 **Blount disease. (A)** Antero- ▶ posterior radiograph of the knee of a 4-year-old boy demonstrates congenital tibia vara (Blount disease). **(B)** Double-contrast arthrogram of the knee shows hypertrophy of the medial meniscus and thick nonossified cartilage at the medial aspect of the proximal tibial epiphysis.

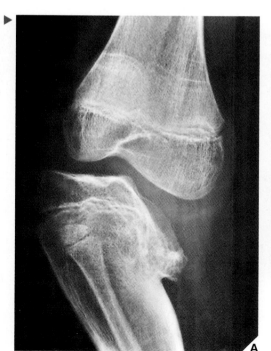
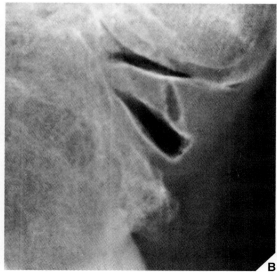

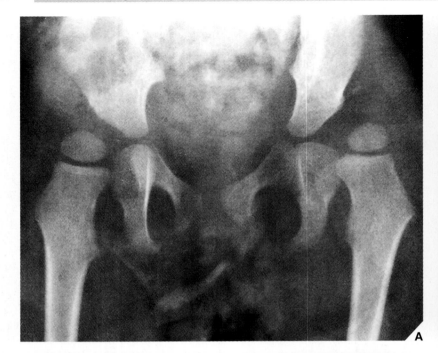
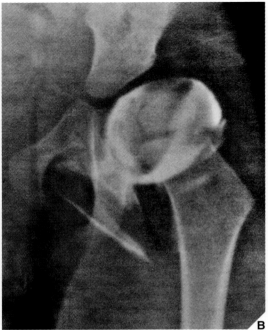
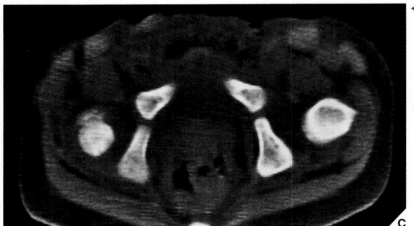

FIGURE 31.11   Congenital hip dislocation. (A) Antero-posterior radiograph of the pelvis in a 1-year-old girl demonstrates congenital dislocation of the left hip. After conservative management with a Pavlik harness, a contrast arthrogram (B) was performed to evaluate the results of treatment. The femoral head appears to be well seated in the acetabulum. Note the smoothness of the Shenton-Menard line (see Fig. 32.8A). (C) CT section, however, demonstrates persistence of posterolateral subluxation.

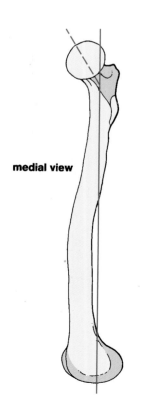
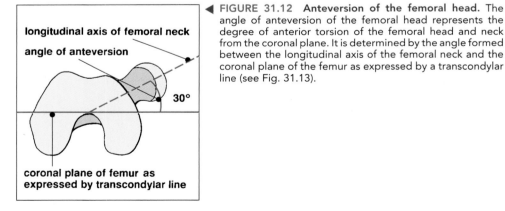

FIGURE 31.12   Anteversion of the femoral head. The angle of anteversion of the femoral head represents the degree of anterior torsion of the femoral head and neck from the coronal plane. It is determined by the angle formed between the longitudinal axis of the femoral neck and the coronal plane of the femur as expressed by a transcondylar line (see Fig. 31.13).

Age (years)	Normal Values of Angle of Anteversion
0–1	30°–50°
1–2	30°
3–5	25°
skeletal maturity	8°–15°

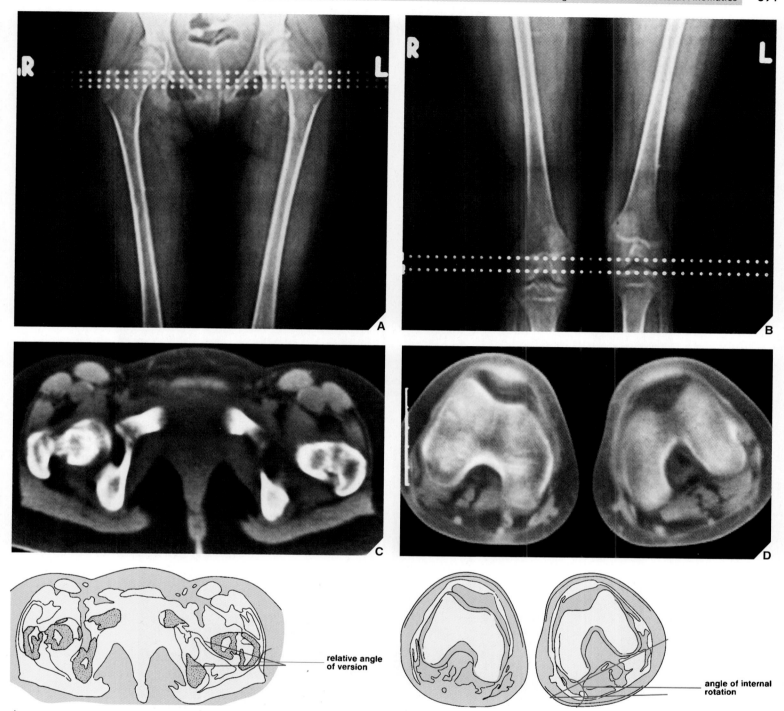

FIGURE 31.13 CT determination of the angle of version of the femoral head. To obtain the angle of version of the femoral head on CT examination, the patient is supine, with the lower extremities in the neutral position, the feet taped together, and the knees taped to the table. Preferably, a single scanogram is obtained that includes both hips and knees on the same film; however, separate films may be obtained (**A,B**) if the patient is too tall. In the latter case, care should be taken not to move the patient between the two takes. On a section through the femoral neck and the upper portion of the greater trochanter (**C**), a line is drawn through the femoral neck, using the femoral head and greater trochanter as guides. The angle that this line forms with the horizontal line (the level of the CT table) determines the *relative* angle of anteversion (or retroversion) of the femoral head. On the CT section through the femoral condyles at the intercondylar notch (**D**), a line is drawn through the posterior margins of the condyles, and the angle formed by this line and the horizontal line determines the degree of internal or external rotation of the extremities. From these two measurements, a *true* angle of version (anteversion or retroversion) is calculated. If the knee is in internal rotation, as in the present case, the sum of both angles yields the degree of anteversion. If the knee is in external rotation, the angle obtained at the knee must be subtracted from the angle at the hip, yielding the degree of version.

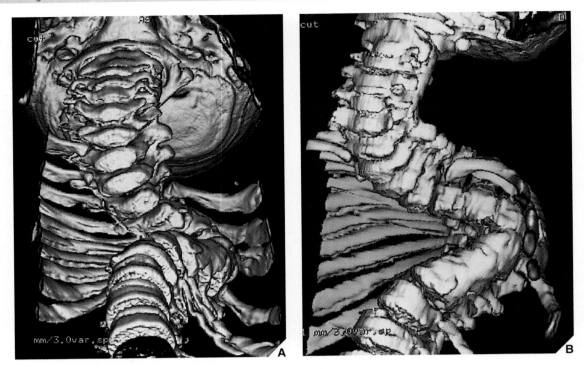

▲
FIGURE 31.14   **3D CT of congenital kyphoscoliosis.** 3D CT reconstructed images of the spine of a 4-year-old boy with congenital kyphoscoliosis in frontal (**A**) and lateral (**B**) orientation are effective in global demonstration of spinal deformity.

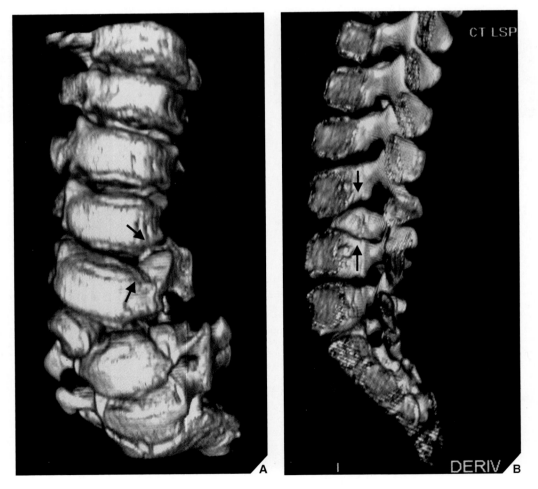

▲
FIGURE 31.15   **3D CT of congenital hemivertebra.** Frontal (**A**) and lateral (**B**) views of 3D CT reconstructed images of the lumbar spine of a 5-year-old girl with congenital dextroscoliosis reveal a hemivertebra (*arrows*) wedged between L3 and L4.

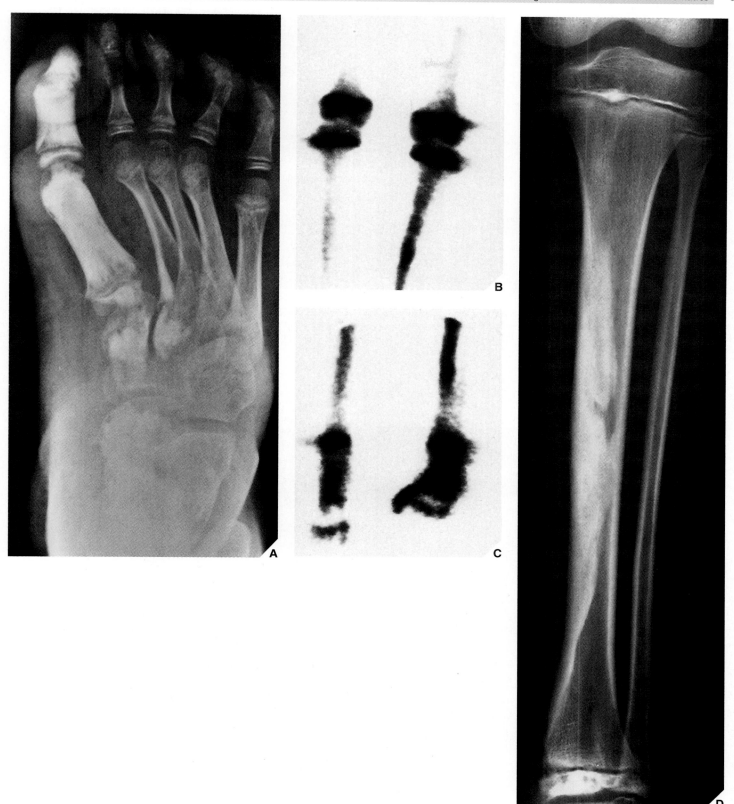

FIGURE 31.16 Scintigraphy of melorheostosis. A 9-year-old boy had a deformity of the left foot since birth, which was diagnosed as a clubfoot. **(A)** Dorsoplantar radiograph of the foot demonstrates the clubfoot deformity, together with sclerotic changes in the phalanges of the great toe, the first and second metatarsals, the first and second cuneiforms, the talus, and the calcaneus. Such changes are typical of melorheostosis, a form of sclerosing dysplasia. **(B,C)** On bone scan, the extent of skeletal involvement is indicated by increased uptake of radiopharmaceutical agent not only in the foot but also in the left tibia, which is confirmed on a subsequent radiograph of the left leg **(D).**

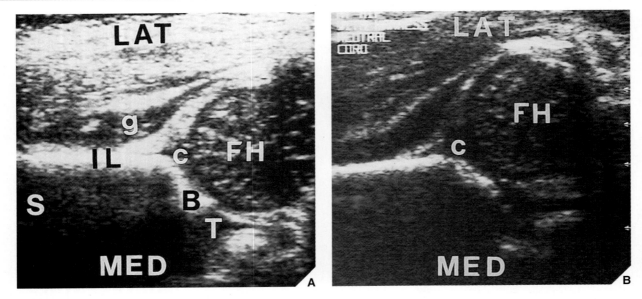

▲
FIGURE 31.17 **US of congenital hip dysplasia. (A)** Coronal ultrasound of the left hip in a newborn boy shows normal relationship of the femoral head and acetabulum. FH, femoral head; c, cartilaginous acetabulum; B, bony acetabulum; T, triradiate cartilage; g, gluteus muscle; IL, ilium; S, superior; LAT, lateral; MED, medial. **(B)** Coronal ultrasound of the left hip in a newborn girl shows dysplastic acetabulum and laterally subluxated femoral head (Courtesy of Dr. E. Gerscovich, Sacramento, California).

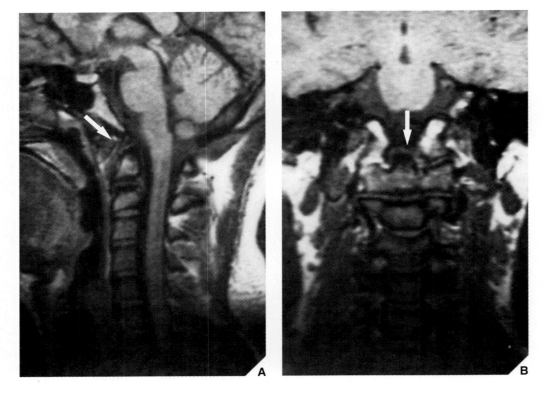

▲
FIGURE 31.18 **MRI of hypoplasia of the odontoid. (A)** Sagittal T1-weighted MR image (SE; TR 800/TE 20 msec) demonstrates a hypoplastic odontoid (*arrow*), which arises from a normal second vertebral body. The anterior arch of the first cervical vertebra is not visualized because of fusion to the occiput. **(B)** Coronal T1-weighted (SE; TR 800/TE 20 msec) MR image confirms that the second cervical vertebral body is normal but only a rudimentary odontoid process has formed (*arrow*). The atlas has fused with the occiput so that there are no occipital condyles (From Beltran J, 1990, with permission).

FIGURE 31.19 MRI of diastematomyelia. (A) Axial ▶
proton density (FSE; TR 5000/TE 16 msec Ef) MR image
in a 17-year-old girl with spina bifida and diastematomyelia shows a split spinal cord at the level of T12. **(B)**
Sagittal T2-weighted (FSE; TR 3000/TE 133 msec Ef)
MR image shows a low-signal fibous septum within a
markedly expanded thecal sac. The spinal fluid exhibits high signal intensity.

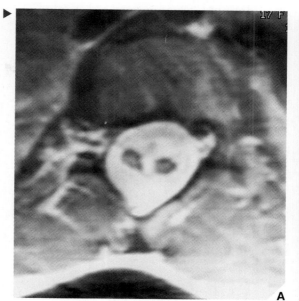

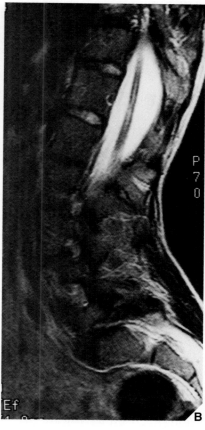

PRACTICAL POINTS TO REMEMBER

[1] Congenital anomalies comprise disturbances in bone formation, bone growth, and bone maturation and modeling.

[2] Although most congenital and developmental anomalies can be diagnosed on standard radiographs, the use of ancillary techniques should be considered, such as:

- radionuclide bone scan, particularly in determining the distribution of sites of involvement in various dysplasias
- CT examination, particularly in the evaluation of congenital hip dislocation and determining the angle of version of the femoral head
- 3D CT, particularly in the evaluation of spinal deformities
- US, particularly in the evaluation of congenital hip dysplasia
- MRI, particularly in the evaluation of abnormalities of the spine, thecal sac, and spinal cord.

[3] Special projections may be required for the evaluation of anomalies of complex structures such as the ankle and foot.

[4] The results and progress of treatment of various congenital disorders, especially congenital hip dislocation, can best be monitored by US and CT examinations.

SUGGESTED READINGS

Bailey JA. *Disproportionate short stature: diagnosis and management.* Philadelphia: WB Saunders; 1973.

Barksy AJ. Macrodactyly. *J Bone Joint Surg [Am]* 1967;49A:1255–1266.

Beighton P, Cremin B, Faure C, et al. International nomenclature of constitutional diseases of bone. *Ann Radiol* 1984;27:275.

Beltran J. *MRI: musculoskeletal system.* Philadelphia: JB Lippincott; 1990.

Berkshire SB, Maxwell EN, Sams BF. Bilateral symmetrical pseudoarthrosis in a newborn. *Radiology* 1970;97:389–390.

Boal DKB, Schwenkter EP. The infant hip: assessment with real-time US. *Radiology* 1985;157:667–672.

Brower JS, Wootton-Gorges SL, Costouros JG, Boakes J, Greenspan A. Congenital diplopodia. *Pediatr Radiol* 2003;33:797–799.

Carlson DH. Coalition of the carpal bones. *Skeletal Radiol* 1981;7:125–127.

Cleveland RH, Gilsanz V, Wilkinson RM. Congenital pseudoarthrosis or the radius. *Am J Roentgenol* 1978;130:955–957.

Eich GF, Babyn P, Giedion A. Pediatiric pelvis: radiographic appearance in various congenital disorders. *Radiographics* 1992;12:467–484.

Gerscovich EO. Infant hip in develomental dysplasia: facts to consider for a successful diagnostic ultrasound examination. *Applied Radiol* 1999;28:18–25.

Graf R. New possibilities for the diagnosis of congenital hip joint dislocation by ultra-sonography. *J Pediatr Orthop* 1983;3:354–359.

Graham CB. Assessment of bone maturation: methods and pitfalls. *Radiol Clin North Am* 1972;10:185–202.

Grissom LE, Harcke HT. Imaging in developmental dysplasia of the hip. *Imaging* 1992;4:79–85.

Hotston S, Carthy H. Lumbosacral agenesis: a report of three new cases and a review of the literature. *Br J Radiol* 1982;55:629–633.

International nomenclature of constitutional diseases of bone. *Am J Roentgenol* 1978;131:352–354.

Kulik SA, Clanfon TO. Tarsal coalition. *Foot Ankle Int* 1996;17:286–296.

Newman JS, Newberg AH. Congenital tarsal coalition: multimodality evaluation with emphasis on CT and MR imaging. *Radiographics* 2000;20:321–332.

O'Rahilly R, Gardner E, Gray DJ. The skeletal development of the hand. *Clin Orthop* 1959;13:42–50.

Page LK, Post MJD. Spinal dysraphism. In Post MJD, ed. *Computed tomography of the spine.* Baltimore: Williams & Wilkins; 1984.

Reed MH, Genez B. Hands. In: Reed MH, ed. *Pediatric skeletal radiology.* Baltimore: Williams & Wilkins; 1992:584–625.

Rubin P. *Dynamic classification of bone dysplasias.* Chicago: Year Book Medical Publishers; 1972.

Sharma BG. Duplication of the clavicle with triplication of the coracoid process. *Skeletal Radiol* 2003;32:661–664.

Smith CF. Current concepts review—tibia vara (Blount's disease). *J Bone Joint Surg [Br]* 1982;64B:630–632.

Walker HS, Lufkin RB, Dietrich RB, Peacock WJ, Flannigan BD, Kangarloo H. Magnetic resonance of the pediatric spine. *Radiographics* 1987;7:1129–1152.

Wechsler RJ, Karasick D, Schweitzer ME. Computed tomography of talocalcaneal coalition: imaging techniques. *Skeletal Radiol* 1992;21:353–358.

Wechsler RJ, Schweitzer ME, Deely DM, Horn BD, Pizzutillo PD. Tarsal coalition: depiction and characterization with CT and MR imgaing. *Radiology* 1994;193:447–452.

Zaleske DJ. Development of the upper limb. *Hand Clin* 1985;1:383–390.

Anomalies of the Upper and Lower Limbs

Anomalies of the Shoulder Girdle and Upper Limbs

Congenital Elevation of the Scapula

Sprengel deformity, as congenital elevation of the scapula is also known, may be unilateral or bilateral. It is marked by the appearance of a scapula that is small, high in position, and rotated with its inferior edge pointing toward the spine—features that are easily identified on an anteroposterior radiograph of the shoulder or chest (Fig. 32.1). The left shoulder is the most commonly affected, and about 75% of all cases are observed in girls. A familial form of the Sprengel deformity is known as Corno disease. The finding of a congenitally elevated scapula is important because of this condition's frequent association with other anomalies, such as congenital scoliosis, fused ribs, spina bifida, and fusion of the cervical or upper thoracic vertebrae, the latter deformity known as Klippel-Feil syndrome (Fig. 32.2). Furthermore, there is sometimes a bony connection between the elevated scapula and one of the vertebrae (usually the C5 or C6 vertebra), creating what is known as the omovertebral bone (Fig. 32.3).

Madelung Deformity

This developmental anomaly of the distal radius and carpus, originally described by the German surgeon Otto Madelung in 1879, usually manifests in adolescent girls presenting with pain in the wrist and decreased range of motion but with no history of previous trauma or infection. Today, the term *Madelung deformity* is often used to describe a variety of conditions in the wrist marked by premature fusion of the distal physis of the radius, with consequent deformity of the distal ulna and wrist. From the etiologic viewpoint, these abnormalities can be divided into posttraumatic deformities, dysplasias, and idiopathic conditions. A genetic cause has also been proposed. Association with mesomelic dwarfism (e.g., Leri-Weill dyschondrosteosis, caused by deletion of the *SHOX* gene) and a mutation on the X chromosome (e.g., Turner syndrome) has also been described. The posttraumatic deformity may occur after repetitive injury or after a single event that disrupts the growth of the distal radius. Among the bone dysplasias associated with Madelung deformity are multiple hereditary cartilaginous exostoses, Ollier disease, achondroplasia, multiple epiphyseal dysplasia, and the mucopolysaccharidoses including Hurler and Morquio syndromes.

On physical examination, the hand is translated volarly to the long axis of the forearm and there is dorsal subluxation of the ulna. A decreased range of motion limits supination, dorsiflexion, and radial deviation, but pronation and palmar flexion are usually preserved.

The radiographic criteria for the diagnosis of Madelung deformity were proposed by Dannenberg and colleagues (Table 32.1). The posteroanterior and lateral projections of the distal forearm and wrist are sufficient to demonstrate any of the abnormalities associated with this deformity (Fig. 32.4).

Surgical treatment of Madelung deformity is indicated for pain relief and cosmetic improvement. A variety of procedures are available. These include ligament release (Vickers physiolysis), wedge osteotomy, Carter-Ezaki dome osteotomy, and radioscaphocapitate arthrodesis. Occasionally, a Darrach or a Suavé-Kapandji procedure is indicated.

Anomalies of the Pelvic Girdle and Hip

An overview of the most effective radiographic projections and radiologic techniques for evaluating the most common anomalies of the pelvic girdle and hip is presented in Table 32.2.

Congenital Hip Dislocation (Developmental Dysplasia of the Hip)

The hip joint is the most frequent site of congenital dislocations. The condition occurs with an incidence of 1.5 per 1,000 births, and eight times more often in girls than in boys. In unilateral dislocation, the left hip is involved twice as often as the right, and bilateral dislocation occurs in more than 25% of affected children. More frequently encountered in white than in black persons, the condition is very common in Mediterranean and Scandinavian countries; it is almost unknown in China, which may be explained in part by the Chinese custom of carrying the infant on the mother's back with its hips flexed and abducted.

The criteria for the diagnosis of congenital dislocation of the hip (CDH) include physical and imaging findings. Certain clinical signs have been identified that are helpful in the evaluation of newborns and infants for possible CDH (Table 32.3).

Radiographic Evaluation

Each of the stages of CDH—dysplasia of the hip, subluxation of the hip, and dislocation of the hip—has a characteristic radiographic

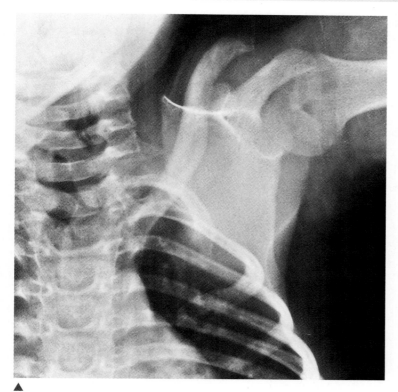

▲
FIGURE 32.1 **Sprengel deformity.** Anteroposterior radiograph of the left shoulder of a 1-year-old boy demonstrates a high position of the left scapula typical of Sprengel deformity.

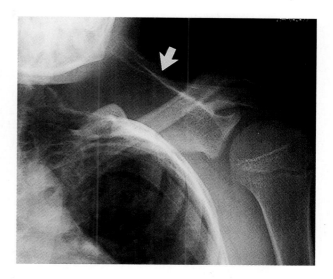

▲
FIGURE 32.2 **Klippel-Feil syndrome and Sprengel deformity.** Anteroposterior radiograph of the left shoulder of a 13-year-old boy with Klippel-Feil syndrome shows an elevated scapula (*arrow*).

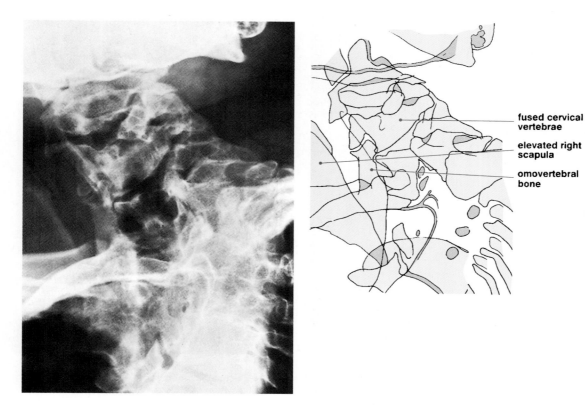

fused cervical vertebrae

elevated right scapula

omovertebral bone

▲
FIGURE 32.3 **Klippel-Feil syndrome and Sprengel deformity.** Posteroanterior radiograph of the cervical and upper thoracic spine in a 37-year-old woman with Sprengel deformity associated with Klippel-Feil syndrome (fusion of the cervical vertebrae) shows the omovertebral bone connecting the elevated right scapula and the C5 vertebra.

TABLE 32.1   **Radiographic Criteria for the Diagnosis of Madelung Deformity**

Changes in the Radius
   Double curvature (medial and dorsal)
   Decrease in bone length
   Triangular shape of the distal epiphysis
   Premature fusion of the medial part of the distal physis, associated with medial and volar angulation of the
      articular surface
   Focal radiolucent areas along the medial border of bone
   Exostosis at the distal medial border
Changes in the Ulna
   Dorsal subluxation
   Increased density (hypercondensation and distortion) of the ulnar head
   Increase in bone length
Changes in the Carpus
   Triangular configuration with the lunate at the apex
   Increase in distance between the distal radius and the ulna
   Decrease in carpal angle

Modified from Dannenberg M et al., 1939, with permission.

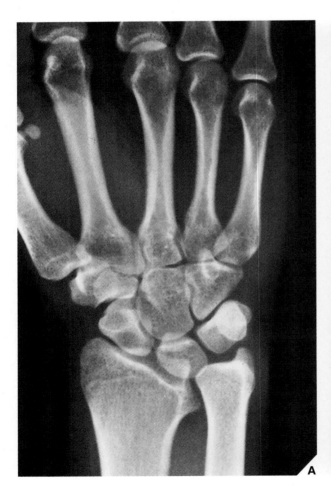 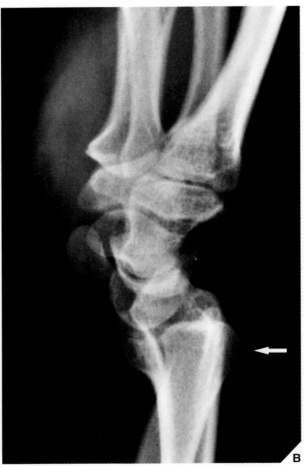

▲
FIGURE 32.4   Madelung deformity. (A) Posteroanterior radiograph of the left wrist of a 21-year-old woman shows a decrease in the length of the radius, the distal end of which has assumed a triangular shape. This is associated with a triangular configuration of the carpus, with the lunate at the apex wedged between the radius and the ulna. **(B)** Lateral radiograph demonstrates dorsal subluxation of the ulna (*arrow*).

TABLE 32.2   **Most Effective Radiographic Projections and Radiologic Techniques for Evaluating Common Anomalies of the Pelvic Girdle and Hip**

Projection/Technique	Crucial Abnormalities
Congenital Hip Dislocation	
Anteroposterior of pelvis and hips	Determination of:
	Hilgenreiner Y-line
	Acetabular index
	Perkins-Ombredanne line
	Shenton-Menard line (arc)
	Center-edge (C-E) angle of Wiberg
	Ossification center of capital femoral epiphysis
	Relations of femoral head and acetabulum
Anteroposterior of hips in abduction and internal rotation	Andrén-von Rosen line
Arthrography	Congruity of the joint
	Status of
	Cartilaginous limbus (limbus thorn)
	Ligamentum teres
	Zona orbicularis
Computed tomography (alone or with arthrography)	Relations of femoral head and acetabulum
	Superior, lateral, or posterior subluxation
Ultrasound	Position of femoral head in acetabulum
	Status of
	Acetabular roof
	Cartilaginous limbus
Developmental Coxa Vara	
Anteroposterior of pelvis and hips	Varus angle of femoral neck and femoral shaft
Proximal Femoral Focal Deficiency	
Anteroposterior of hip and proximal femur	Shortening of femur
	Superior, posterior, and lateral displacement of proximal femoral segment
Arthrography	Nonossified femoral head
Legg-Calvé-Perthes Disease	
Anteroposterior and frog-lateral of hips	Osteonecrosis of femoral head as indicated by crescent sign and subchondral collapse
	Gage sign
	Subluxation of femoral head
	Horizontal orientation of growth plate
	Calcifications lateral to epiphysis
	Cystic changes in metaphysis
Arthrography	Incongruity of hip joint
	Thickness of articular cartilage
Radionuclide bone scan	Decreased uptake of isotope (earliest stage)
	Increased uptake of isotope (late stage)
CT and MRI	Incongruity of hip joint
	Osteonecrosis
Slipped Capital Femoral Epiphysis	
Anteroposterior of hips	Loss of Capener triangle sign
	Periarticular osteoporosis
	Widening and blurring of growth plate
	Decreased height of femoral epiphysis
	Absence of intersection of epiphysis by line tangent to lateral cortex of femoral neck
	Herndon hump
	Chondrolysis (complication)
Frog-lateral of hips	Absence of intersection of epiphysis by line tangent to lateral cortex of femoral neck
	Actual slippage (displacement) of femoral epiphysis
Radionuclide bone scan and MRI	Osteonecrosis (complication)

TABLE 32.3 **Clinical Manifestations of CDH**

Limited abduction of the flexed hip (due to shortening and
  contraction of hip adductors)
Increase in depth or asymmetry of the inguinal or thigh skin folds
Shortening of one leg
Allis or Galeazzi sign*—lower position of knee of affected side
  when knees and hips are flexed (due to location of femoral head
  posterior to acetabulum in this position)
Ortolani "jerk" sign ("clunk of entry" or reduction sign)
Barlow test ("clunk of exit" or dislocation sign)
Telescoping or pistoning action of thighs* (due to lack of
  containment of femoral head within acetabulum)
Trendelenburg test*—dropping of normal hip when child,
  standing on both feet, elevates unaffected limb and bears
  weight on affected side (due to weakness of hip abductors)
Waddling gait*

*This finding can occur in older children.

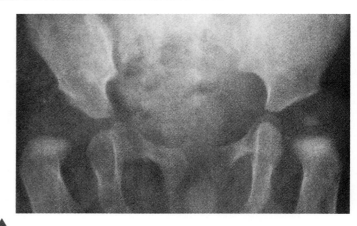

▲
FIGURE 32.5 Congenital hip dysplasia. Anteroposterior radiograph of the pelvis of a 1-year-old boy shows a slightly flattened acetabulum and delayed appearance of the ossification center for the right femoral epiphysis; that of the left epiphysis is normally centered over the triradiate cartilage.

presentation. The term *congenital hip dysplasia*, first introduced by Hilgenreiner in 1925, refers to delayed or defective development of the hip joint leading to a deranged articular relationship between an abnormal acetabulum and a deformed proximal end of the femur (Fig. 32.5). The condition is considered a precursor of subluxation and dislocation of the hip, although some authorities use the term "developmental dysplasia of the hip" (DDH) to denote all stages of CDH. In *congenital subluxation of the hip*, there is an abnormal relationship between the femoral head and the acetabulum, but the two are in contact (Fig. 32.6). *Congenital dislocation of the hip*, however, is marked by the femoral head's complete loss of contact with the acetabular cartilage; the proximal femur is displaced most often superiorly, but lateral, posterior, and posterolateral dislocation may also be seen (Fig. 32.7).

Measurements

In contrast to an adult hip, the relationship between the femoral head and the acetabulum in a newborn's hip cannot be assessed by direct visualization because the femoral head is not ossified, and as a cartilaginous body it is not visible on conventional radiographs. The ossification center first appears between the ages of 3 and 6 months, and a delay in its appearance should be viewed as an indication of congenital hip dysplasia. The neck of the femur must therefore be used for ascertaining this relationship. The anteroposterior radiograph of the pelvis serves as the basis for determining several indirect indicators of the relationship between the femoral head and the acetabulum. To obtain accurate measurements, however, proper positioning of the infant is imperative; the lower extremities should be extended in the neutral position and longitudinally aligned, whereas the central ray should be directed toward the midline, slightly above the pubic symphysis, to ensure the symmetry of both halves of the pelvis. The measurements used to evaluate the relation of the femoral head to the acetabulum are the following (Fig. 32.8):

1. The *Hilgenreiner line* or *Y-line*, which is drawn through the superior part of the triradiate cartilage, is itself a valuable indicator of femoroacetabular relations and serves as the basis for all other indicators.

2. The *acetabular index*, which is an angle formed by a line tangent to the acetabular roof and the Y-line, cannot alone be diagnostic of dislocation, because it can occasionally exceed 30 degrees in normal subjects. Generally, however, values greater than 30 degrees are considered abnormal and indicate impending dislocation. Some investigators propose that only angles in excess of 40 degrees are significant.

3. The *Perkins-Ombredanne line*, which is drawn perpendicular to the Y-line through the most lateral edge of the ossified acetabular cartilage, is helpful in determining subluxation and dislocation

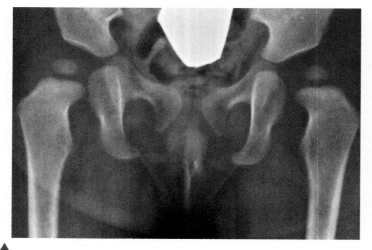

▲
FIGURE 32.6 Congenital hip dysplasia. Anteroposterior radiograph of the pelvis of a 1-year-old girl shows congenital superolateral subluxation of the left hip. Note the slightly smaller size of the left femoral epiphysis.

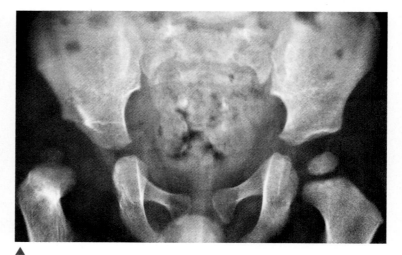

▲
FIGURE 32.7 Congenital hip dislocation. Anteroposterior radiograph of the pelvis of a 2-year-old boy demonstrates complete superolateral dislocation of the right hip. Note the abnormal position of the center of ossification in relation to the acetabulum compared with the normal left hip.

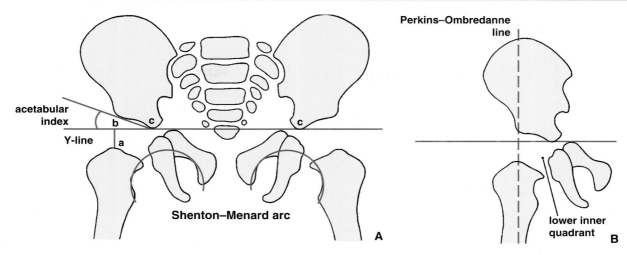

▲
FIGURE 32.8 **Measurements helpful to evaluate the relation of the femoral head to the acetabulum.** **(A)** The *Hilgenreiner line* or *Y-line* is drawn through the superior part of the triradiate cartilage. In normal infants, the distance represented by a line (ab) perpendicular to the Y-line at the most proximal point of the femoral neck should be equal on both sides of the pelvis, as should the distance represented by a line (bc) drawn coincident with the Y-line medially to the acetabular floor. In infants aged 6 to 7 months, the mean value for the distance (ab) has been determined to be 19.3 ± 1.5 mm; the distance for (bc) is 18.2 ± 1.4 mm. The *acetabular index* is an angle formed by a line drawn tangent to the acetabular roof from point (c) at the acetabular floor on the Y-line. The normal value of this angle ranges from 25 to 29 degrees. The *Shenton-Menard line* is an arc running through the medial aspect of the femoral neck and the superior border of the obturator foramen. It should be smooth and unbroken. **(B)** The *Perkins-Ombredanne line* is drawn perpendicular to the Y-line through the most lateral edge of the ossified acetabular cartilage, which actually corresponds to the anteroinferior iliac spine. In normal newborns and infants, the medial aspect of the femoral neck or the ossified capital femoral epiphysis falls in the lower inner quadrant. The appearance of either of these structures in the lower outer or upper outer quadrant indicates subluxation or dislocation of the hip.

of the hip. The intersection of this line with the Y-line creates four quadrants; normally, the medial aspect of the femoral neck or the ossified capital femoral epiphysis falls in the lower medial quadrant.

4. The *Shenton-Menard line*, which forms a smooth arc through the medial aspect of the femoral neck and the superior border of the obturator foramen, may be interrupted in subluxation or dislocation of the hip. Even under normal circumstances, however, the arc may not be smooth if the radiograph is obtained with the hip in external rotation and adduction.

5. The *Andrén–von Rosen line*, which is drawn on a radiograph obtained with the hips abducted 45 degrees and internally rotated, describes the relation of the longitudinal axis of the femoral shaft to the acetabulum (Fig. 32.9). In dislocation or subluxation of the hip, this line bisects or falls above the anterosuperior iliac spine.

After the capital femoral epiphysis achieves full ossification at approximately 4 years of age, a diagnosis of gross displacement can usually be made without difficulty. The evaluation of subtle hip dysplasias, however, can be aided by another parameter of the relation of the femoral head to the acetabulum, the *center-edge (C-E) angle of Wiberg* (Fig. 32.10). Determination of this angle is most useful after full ossification of the femoral head, because its relationship to the acetabulum is then fully established.

Arthrography and Computed Tomography

Aside from conventional radiography, hip arthrography is the most useful technique for evaluating CDH. During the procedure, radiographs are routinely obtained with the hip in the neutral (Fig. 32.11A) and frog-lateral positions (Fig. 32.11B), as well as in abduction, adduction, and internal rotation. In subluxation, the femoral head lies lateral to just below the margin of the acetabular cartilaginous labrum, and the joint capsule is usually loose (Fig. 32.12). In complete dislocation, the femoral head lies superior and lateral to the edge of the labrum (Fig. 32.13). Deformities may also be encountered in the cartilaginous limbus, a structure lying between the femoral head and the acetabulum. In advanced stages, it may be inverted and hypertrophied, thus making

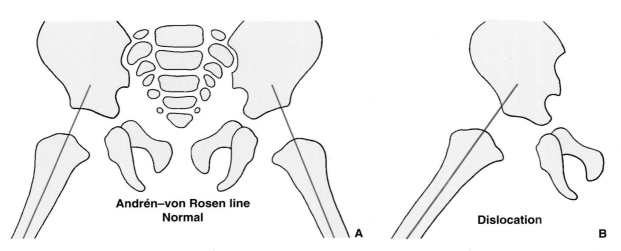

▲
FIGURE 32.9 **The Andrén-von Rosen line.** **(A)** With at least 45 degrees of hip abduction and internal rotation, the line is drawn along the longitudinal axis of the femoral shaft. In normal hips, it intersects the pelvis at the upper edge of the acetabulum. **(B)** In subluxation or dislocation of the hip, the line bisects or falls above the anterosuperior iliac spine.

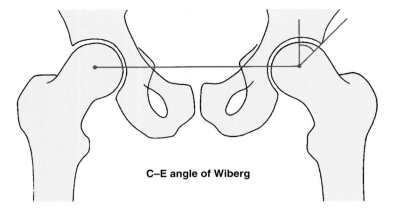

Age (years)	Lowest Normal Value of C–E Angle
5–8	19°
9–12	12°–25°
13–20	26°–30°

C–E angle of Wiberg

▲ FIGURE 32.10 **Angle of Wiberg.** The center-edge (C-E) angle of Wiberg is helpful in evaluating the development of the acetabulum and its relation to the femoral head. A baseline is projected, connecting the centers of the femoral heads. The C-E angle is formed by two lines originating in the center of the femoral head, one drawn perpendicular to the baseline into the acetabulum, and the other connecting the center of the femoral head with the superior acetabular lip. Values below the lowest normal value given for each age group indicate hip dysplasia.

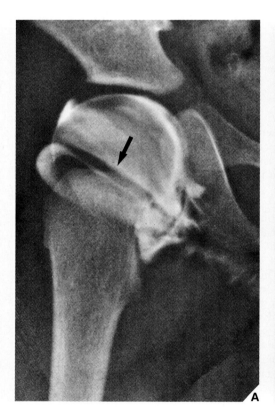

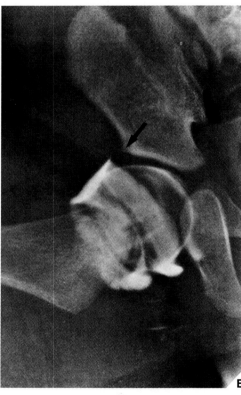

◀ FIGURE 32.11 **Arthrogram of a normal hip.** **(A)** Arthrogram of the right hip in the neural position in a 5-month-old boy shows contrast agent accumulating in the large recesses medial and lateral to the constriction produced by the orbicular ligament (*arrow*). Note the smoothness and even thickness of the cartilage covering the femoral head. **(B)** On the frog-lateral view, contrast is seen outlining the edge of the cartilaginous labrum (*arrow*). The ligamentum teres can be seen medial to the femoral head, extending from the inferior portion of the acetabulum.

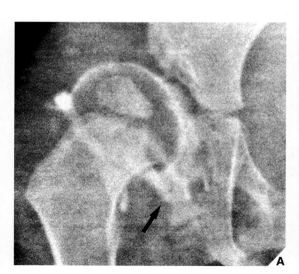

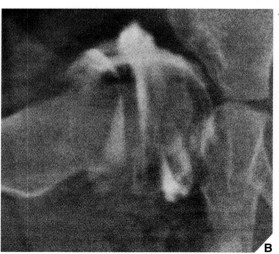

◀ FIGURE 32.12 **Arthrogram of congenital hip dysplasia.** **(A)** Arthrogram of the right hip in the neutral position in a 1-year-old girl with congenital subluxation of the hip shows the typical displacement of the hip lateral to, but below the acetabular labrum. There is accumulation of contrast agent in the stretched capsule (*arrow*), and the ligamentum teres is elongated. **(B)** In the frog-lateral position, the head moves more deeply into the acetabulum, but subluxation is still present.

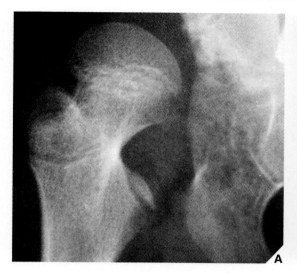
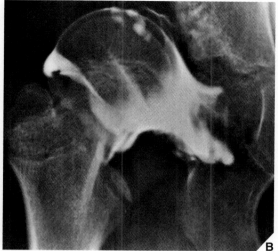

▲
FIGURE 32.13   Arthrogram of congenital hip dislocation. (A) Anteroposterior radiograph of the right hip in an 8-year-old girl demonstrates complete superolateral dislocation of the femoral head. Note the shallow acetabulum. **(B)** Arthrogram of the hip shows a deformed cartilaginous limbus and stretching of the ligamentum teres. The femoral head lies superior and lateral to the edge of the cartilaginous labrum. Note the accumulation of contrast agent in the loose joint capsule.

the reduction impossible. Moreover, the portion of the capsule lying medial to the femoral head is usually constricted to form an isthmus with a "figure-eight" appearance.

Computed tomography (CT), either alone (Fig. 32.14) or with arthrography, is also a frequently used modality in the evaluation of CDH. In subluxation or dislocation, the congruity of the acetabulum and the femoral head, which is normally centered over the triradiate cartilage, is disturbed (Fig. 32.15). CT has proved to be the most accurate technique for determining the degree of subluxation or dislocation. It is also an essential modality for monitoring the progress of CDH treatment.

Ultrasound

In the past decade, ultrasound has become one of the most effective techniques to diagnose and evaluate congenital hip dysplasia. It is performed with the patient at rest, and during motion and stress. A lateral approach is widely used, with the infant supine or in the lateral decubitus position. Scanning is performed in the coronal plane with the hips extended or flexed (see Fig. 31.17). In the axial plane, the thighs are in 90 degrees of flexion, and images are obtained with and without stress. The osseous and cartilaginous components of the hip joint are well demonstrated on the displayed images, and acetabular coverage of the femoral head can be assessed. In addition, the slope of the acetabulum (α-angle) can be measured with respect to the iliac line. An angle of 60 degrees or more is

normal. An angle 50 to 60 degrees is considered physiologic before age 3 months, but needs to be followed up by repeat studies. Values less than 50 degrees are abnormal at any age. A second angle (β-angle) is formed by the iliac line and a line drawn from the labrum to the transition point between the iliac bone and the bony acetabulum. This measurement is indicative of the acetabular cartilaginous roof coverage and is secondary in significance to the α-angle. The smaller the β-angle, the less the cartilaginous coverage because of a better acetabular bony containment of the femoral head. The dynamic study, first described by Harcke in 1984, incorporates the use of real-time ultrasound visualization of the hip joint. The purpose of this technique is to demonstrate the instability. It is performed in the transverse flexion projection and consists of a Barlow maneuver to try to displace, sublux, or dislocate an apparently well-seated femoral head.

Recently, 3D sonographic evaluation of DDH has been attempted. This technique permits evaluation of the osseous and fibrocartilaginous acetabulum and its relationship to the femoral head in a global fashion (*gestalt*) without the need for detailed acetabular angle measurements. The information obtained can be stored for later review, analysis, and additional reconstructions with different parameters. The computer-generated sagittal-plane image offers a unique view of the hip that is unobtainable with conventional sonography (Fig. 32.16). The generated spatial-revolving image likewise yields an informative

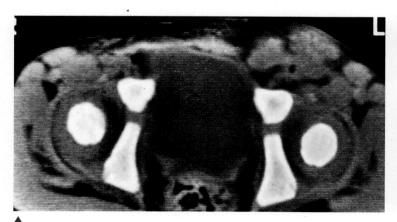

▲
FIGURE 32.14   CT of the normal hips. Axial section of both hips in a 19-month-old infant shows good congruity of the acetabula and femoral heads, which are centered over the triradiate cartilage.

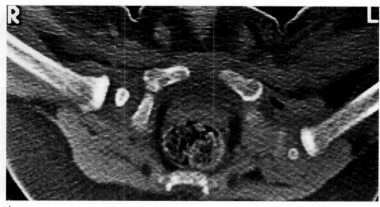

▲
FIGURE 32.15   CT of congenital hip dislocation. Axial section through the proximal femora and hips of a 6-month-old boy shows posterolateral dislocation of the left hip. The right hip is normal.

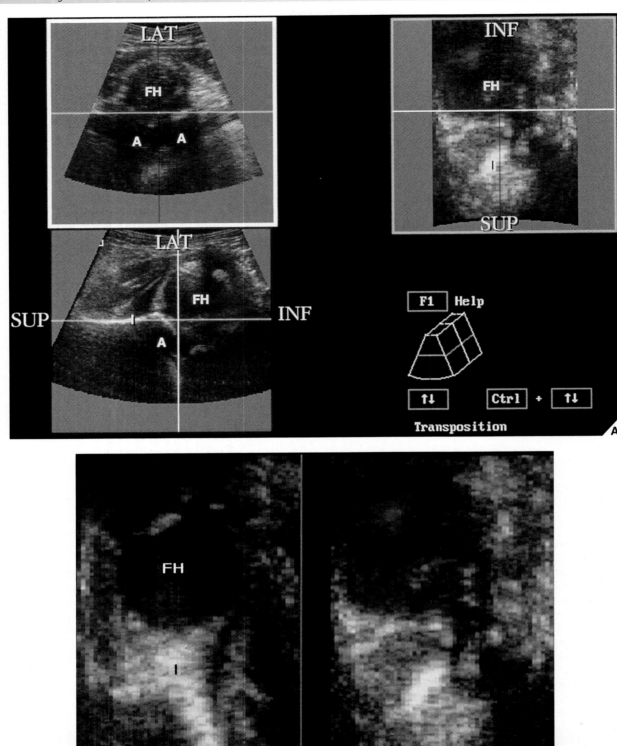

▲
FIGURE 32.16   **Ultrasound of congenital hip dysplasia. (A)** On the coronal 3D ultrasound image of the left hip in a 3-day-old girl (*lower left*) the acetabulum (A) appears shallow, and subluxation of the femoral head can be observed at the intersection of the ilium (I) line with the medial third of the femoral head (FH). On the reconstructed axial image (*upper left*), the femoral head is subluxated but still in contact with the acetabulum. On the sagittal image (*upper right*), only the peripheral segment of femoral head is visualized. **(B)** A sagittal image of a normal left hip (*left*) is shown for comparison. Note that femoral head (FH) is centered over the ilium line (I). A sagittal image of a subluxated head (*right*) clearly shows distortion of femoral head–ilium line relationship. (From Gerscovich EO et al., 1994, with permission.)

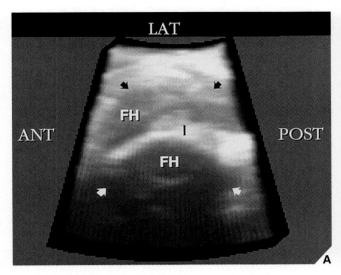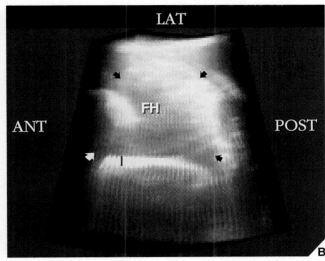

FIGURE 32.17   3D ultrasound of congenital hip dysplasia. (A) Craniocaudal projection (bird's-eye view) of a normal left hip shows the ilium (I) projecting over the midportion of the femoral head (FH) (arrows outline its contour). **(B)** Craniocaudal projection of a subluxated left hip shows that the ilium (I) projects over the medial portion of the femoral head (FH) (arrows outline its contour). The femoral head is laterally displaced. (From Gerscovich EO, et al., 1994, with permission.)

craniocaudal (bird's eye) view of the infant hip (Fig. 32.17). The 3D appearance of the revolving image is enhanced by the transparency of the reconstruction, in contrast to the contour reconstructions available with 3D CT.

Classification

Dunn has proposed a classification of CDH based primarily on the shape of the acetabular margins, the gross contour of the femoral head, and whether there is eversion or inversion of the limbus:

Type I   This is usually seen in neonates. The changes along the acetabular margins are mild. The femoral head, which is anteverted but spherically normal, is not completely covered by acetabular cartilage. This may lead to variable instability, particularly in extension and adduction of the hip. The labrum may also be deformed.

Type II   The hips are subluxed, and the cartilaginous labrum shows eversion. The femoral head is normally anteverted but shows a loss of sphericity. The acetabulum is shallower than in type I, and the failure of the acetabular roof to ossify laterally leads to an increased acetabular angle.

Type III   There is significant deformity of the acetabulum and femoral head, which is posterosuperiorly dislocated, leading to the formation of a false acetabulum by eversion of the labrum. The limbus is hypertrophied, and the ligamentum teres is elongated and pulled, bringing with it the transverse acetabular ligament. This situation compromises the acetabular space, precluding complete reduction.

Treatment

The principle behind conservative treatment is to reduce the dislocation of the femoral head, by means of a flexion-abduction maneuver, for a period sufficient enough to permit proper growth of the head and acetabulum, which in turn ensures a congruent and stable hip joint. This approach is usually taken in the very early stages of CDH and in infants younger than age 2 years; it includes splinting, such as with the Frejka splint or Pavlik harness, as well as various traction procedures (Fig. 32.18). Colonna or buck skin traction is usually used in children 2 months to 12 years of age, with a well-padded spica cast applied simultaneously to the unaffected side. Interval radiographs are obtained to monitor the progress of the traction and the descent of the femoral head. A system for this purpose, composed of various traction "stations," has been described by Gage and Winter (Fig. 32.19). It has been reported that the achievement of "station +2" by means of skeletal traction, before further treatment by open or closed reduction, is associated with a far smaller frequency of osteonecrosis of the femoral head.

When the conservative approach fails, the child is too old for conservative treatment, or the abnormalities are too extensive, then surgical management is indicated. Radiologic assessment of the hip, in which CT examination plays the leading role, is mandatory before surgical intervention because it provides the surgeon with excellent images of the anatomy of the hip, particularly the size of the femoral head, its relation to the acetabulum, and the acetabular configuration. The information regarding these structures may contraindicate the use of certain surgical procedures.

Several surgical techniques are now used for treatment of congenital hip dysplasia. Their common goal is to achieve better coverage of the femoral head. These surgical procedures can be divided into four categories: shelf operations, in which bone grafts are used to extend the acetabular roof; acetabuloplasties, in which the acetabular roof is mobilized and turned down; pelvic osteotomies, in which the acetabulum is redirected; and pelvic displacement osteotomies, in which the femoral head is positioned beneath the displaced bony portion of the pelvis. *Capsulorrhaphy* consists of removal of the excess of the stretched joint capsule, combined with a femoroplasty and/or acetabuloplasty. *Femoral varus derotational osteotomy* is performed to correct an excessive anteversion of the neck and valgus deformity. It involves a varus angulation of the proximal femur, with or without rotation, to redirect the femoral head into the acetabulum. The most popular procedure is the *Salter osteotomy* of the innominate bone, which may be combined with simultaneous derotational varus osteotomy of the femoral neck. It is usually performed in children aged 1 to 6 years. The principle of this technique is to redirect the abnormal orientation of the acetabulum, which in children with CDH faces more anterolaterally, thus rendering the hip stable only in abduction, flexion, and internal rotation. This redirection is accomplished by displacing the entire acetabulum anterolaterally and downward, without changing its shape or capacity, by means of a triangular bone graft (Fig. 32.20). *Pemberton osteotomy* is an incomplete transiliac osteotomy, hinging the anterolateral acetabular roof on the flexible triradiate cartilage. This procedure is indicated when there is an elongated, dysplastic acetabulum; however, it should be performed only in children younger than age 7 years when there is flexibility in the triradiate cartilage and when growth remains for remodeling of the joint surfaces. *Steele triple innominate osteotomy* is usually indicated for children older than age 6 to 8 years who have an immobile symphysis pubis. In addition to Salter osteotomy, osteotomies of the inferior and superior pubic

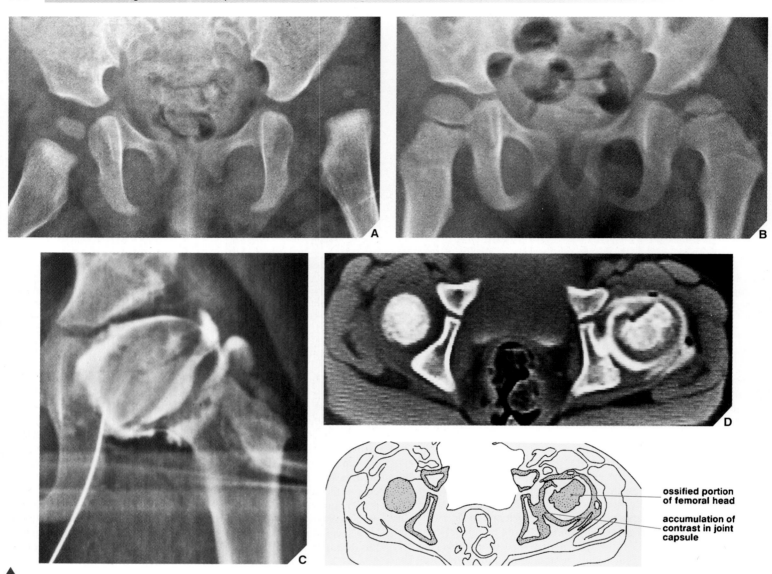

▲
FIGURE 32.18   Treatment of congenital hip dysplasia. (A) Anteroposterior radiograph of the pelvis in a 1-year-old boy demonstrates the typical appearance of congenital dislocation of the left hip. **(B)** After conservative treatment with a Pavlik harness at age 2, there is still subluxation. Note the broken Shenton-Menard arc. At age 3, after further conservative treatment by skin traction and application of a spica cast, there is almost complete reduction of subluxation, as demonstrated by contrast arthrography **(C)**. **(D)** CT scan, however, demonstrates some minimal residual lateral displacement of the femoral head, as evidenced by the medial accumulation of contrast.

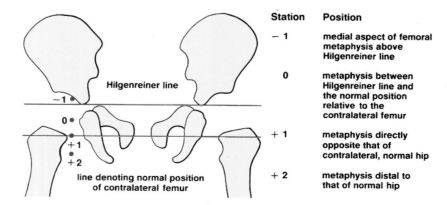

▲
FIGURE 32.19   The Gage and Winter system. This measurement of stations for monitoring the progress of treatment by traction and the descent of the femoral head is based on the position of the proximal femoral metaphysis relative to the ipsilateral acetabulum and the contralateral normal hip.

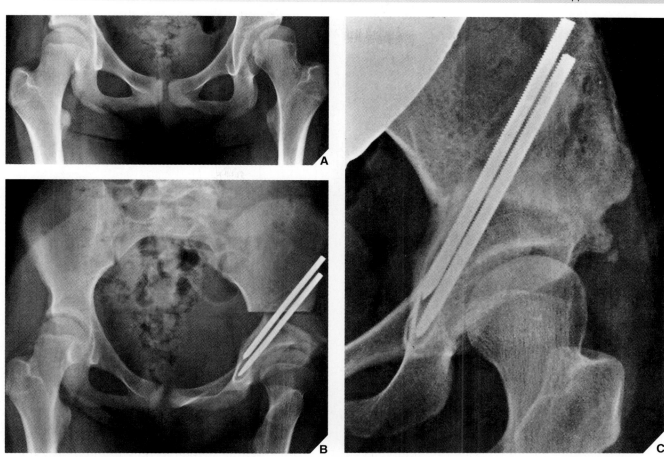

▲
FIGURE 32.20   Salter osteotomy. (A) Anteroposterior radiograph of the pelvis in a 7-year-old girl with CDH shows persistent superolateral subluxation of the left hip following conservative treatment. Note the anterolateral orientation of the acetabulum in comparison with the normal right hip. **(B)** Postoperative film after Salter osteotomy through the supra-acetabular portion of the iliac bone shows the acetabulum displaced anterolaterally and downward; a triangular bone graft, taken from the anterolateral aspect of the ilium, is secured by two Steinmann pins at the site of the osteotomy. **(C)** Four years later, the femoral head is completely covered by the acetabulum. Because of a valgus configuration of the femoral neck, the patient may yet require a varus derotational osteotomy.

rami are performed. The acetabulum is brought forward and rotated in the frontal plane, avoiding external rotation. The *Chiari pelvic osteotomy* is usually reserved for older children. This is a displacement osteotomy that essentially provides a shelf or buttress to limit further proximal subluxation of the femoral head. This procedure displaces the femoral head medially and increases the weight-bearing surface of the head by producing an overhanging superior acetabular ledge. This technique may also be combined with a varus derotational osteotomy of the femoral neck. *Ganz osteotomy*, also known as *Bernese periacetabular osteotomy*, is usually performed in older children and adolescents, and occasionally in adults. The principle behind the procedure is to allow anterior and lateral rotation and medialization of the hip without violation of the posterior column of the hemipelvis. Osteotomies are performed around the acetabulum (complete osteotomy of the pubis and biplanar osteotomy of the ilium); however, the cut through the posterior column of the ischium is incomplete. The acetabular fragment is rotated anteriorly and laterally (maintaining anteversion) and is then medialized. This procedure provides excellent femoral head coverage and acetabular mobility.

Complications

Conservative and surgical management of CDH may be complicated by osteonecrosis of the femoral head, redislocation, infection, sciatic nerve injury, or early fusion of the growth plate caused by prolonged casting. The most frequent late complication of untreated and treated CDH is degenerative joint disease.

Proximal Femoral Focal Deficiency

Proximal femoral focal deficiency (PFFD) is a congenital anomaly characterized by dysgenesis and hypoplasia of variable segments of the proximal femur. The defect ranges in severity from femoral shortening associated with a varus deformity of the neck to the formation of only a small stub of distal femur.

Classification and Radiographic Evaluation

Several classifications of PFFD have been proposed. The one offered by Levinson and colleagues, which is based on the severity of the abnormalities involving the femoral head, femoral segment, and acetabulum, is the most practical from the prognostic point of view:

Type A   The femoral head is present, and the femoral segment is short. There is a varus deformity of the femoral neck. The acetabulum is normal.

Type B   The femoral head is present, but there is an absence of bony connection between it and the short femoral segment. The acetabulum exhibits dysplastic changes.

Type C   The femoral head is absent or represented only by an ossicle. The femoral segment is short and tapered proximally. The acetabulum is severely dysplastic.

Type D   The femoral head and acetabulum are absent. The femoral segment is rudimentary, and the obturator foramen is enlarged.

Conventional radiography is usually sufficient to make a diagnosis of PFFD. The femur is short, and the proximal segment is displaced superior, posterior, and lateral to the iliac crest; ossification of the femoral epiphysis is invariably delayed (Fig. 32.21). Arthrography is useful in the evaluation of this anomaly, particularly in its classification, because early in infancy the nonossified femoral head and acetabulum can be outlined adequately with a positive contrast agent (Fig. 32.21C). This

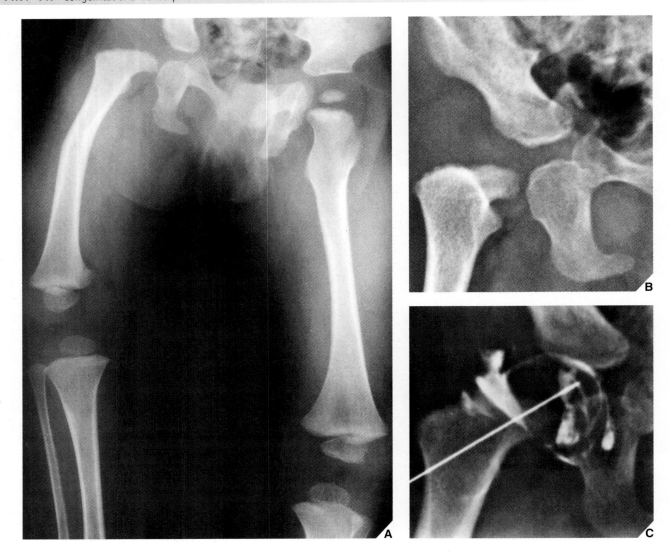

▲
FIGURE 32.21   **Proximal femoral focal deficiency. (A)** Anteroposterior radiograph in an 18-month-old boy who had a short right leg demonstrates a varus configuration at the right hip joint, the absence of an ossification center for the proximal femoral epiphysis, and shortening of the femur—the classic radiographic features of PFFD. **(B)** A coned-down view of the right hip shows superior, posterior, and lateral displacement of the proximal femoral segment in relation to the acetabulum. **(C)** Arthrography was performed to classify the abnormality, and the presence of the femoral head in the acetabulum and the absence of any defect in the femoral neck were found, making this a type A focal deficiency.

technique is also helpful in distinguishing PFFD from the occasionally similar presentations of CDH.

Treatment

Several surgical procedures are used to correct this anomaly, including amputation. One limb-sparing procedure involves conversion of the knee to a hip joint by flexing it 90 degrees and fusing the femur to the pelvis. Another technique, developed by Borggreve in 1930 and called the "turn-about" procedure or "rotation-plasty" after an improvement by Van Nes, converts the foot into the knee joint; the limb is then fitted with a leg prosthesis.

Legg-Calvé-Perthes Disease

Legg-Calvé-Perthes disease, also known as coxa plana, is the name applied to osteonecrosis (ischemic necrosis) of the proximal epiphysis of the femur. Recent genetic studies suggest that beta fibrinogen gene *G-455-A* polymorphism is a risk factor for this condition. The anomaly occurs five times more often in boys than in girls, usually between the ages of 4 and 8 years. Its appearance at an early age is usually associated with a better prognosis. Either hip can be affected, and bilateral involvement, which is successive rather than simultaneous, is seen in approximately 10% of cases (Fig. 32.22). The clinical symptoms consist of pain, limping, and limitation of motion. Not infrequently, the

pain is localized not to the involved hip but to the ipsilateral knee. It is a self-limiting disorder that eventually heals, but because of the progressive deformity it produces in the shape of the femoral head and neck, it often leads to precocious osteoarthritis of the hip joint. The cause of this anomaly has been the subject of debate. Some investigators consider it a type of idiopathic osteonecrosis, but trauma or repeated microtrauma may play a role in compromising the circulation of blood to the femoral capital epiphysis. Trueta has suggested that the blood supply to the femoral head is deficient between the ages of 4 and 8 years, and that this might be a factor in the development of the condition.

Radiologic Evaluation

Radiologic examination is essential for diagnosing Legg-Calvé-Perthes disease and for identifying its prognostic signs. Conventional radiography is adequate for evaluating most of the features of the disease (see Fig. 32.22), whereas arthrography helps in the assessment of acetabular congruity, the thickness of the articular cartilage, and the degree of subluxation (Fig. 32.23). The earliest indication of Legg-Calvé-Perthes disease is demonstrated on radionuclide bone scan by a decreased uptake of tracer in the hips caused by a deficient blood supply. However, with progression of the disease, an increased uptake is seen, which reflects reparative processes.

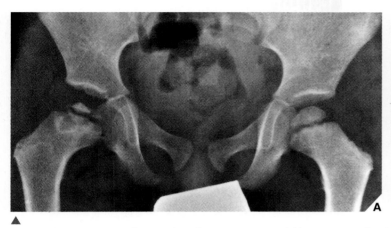
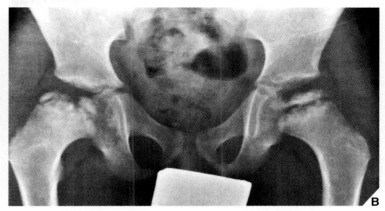

▲
FIGURE 32.22 **Legg-Calvé-Perthes disease.** A 5-year-old boy presented with pain in the right hip for several months. **(A)** Anteroposterior radiograph of the pelvis and hips shows advanced stage of this condition affecting the right hip, where osteonecrosis and collapse of the capital femoral epiphysis are apparent, as are extensive changes in the metaphysis. Note the lateral subluxation in the hip joint. The left hip is normal. **(B)** Three years later, the left hip also became involved. Note the progression of osteonecrotic changes in the right femoral epiphysis.

The earliest radiographic sign of Legg-Calvé-Perthes disease is periarticular osteoporosis and periarticular soft-tissue swelling, with distortion of the pericapsular and iliopsoas fat planes. There may also be a discrepancy in the size of the ossification centers of the capital epiphyses. Later, lateral displacement of the affected ossification center produces widening of the medial aspect of the joint; the presence of the crescent sign (which at times may be detected only on the frog-lateral projection of the hip) (Fig. 32.24), or of radiolucent fissures in the epiphysis, indicates progression of the disease. At a more advanced stage, flattening and sclerosis of the capital epiphysis become apparent and are associated with an increased density of the femoral head secondary to necrosis of the bone, microfractures, and reparative changes known as "creeping substitution." A vacuum phenomenon may occasionally be seen, caused by nitrogen gas released into the fissures in the capital epiphysis. Cystic changes may also be encountered in the metaphyseal segment. Later, there may be broadening of the femoral neck. Throughout the course of the disease, the joint space is remarkably well preserved because the

articular cartilage is not affected. Only in the end stage of Legg-Calvé-Perthes disease, when secondary osteoarthritis develops, does the joint become compromised as in primary degenerative joint disease.

The Moss technique is used to determine the degree of deformity of the femoral head. This consists of overlaying the anteroposterior radiograph of the hip with a template having concentric circles spaced 2 mm apart. If the concentricity of the femoral head deviates by more than two of the 2-mm circles, then the result is rated "poor"; deviation equal to one 2-mm circle is "fair," and no deviation is rated "good." Lateral subluxation can be measured by means of the center-edge angle of Wiberg (see Fig. 32.10). It must be stressed that both measurements do not correlate well with development of secondary osteoarthritis, the main complication of Legg-Calvé-Perthes disease.

Several investigators have recently stressed the applicability of magnetic resonance imaging (MRI) for early detection of Legg-Calvé-Perthes disease and for evaluation of cartilaginous and synovial changes. This technique has also proved valuable for determination of

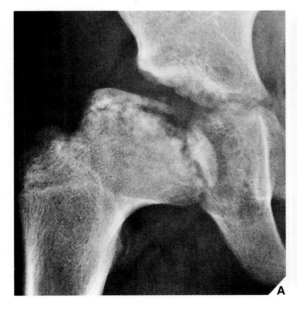
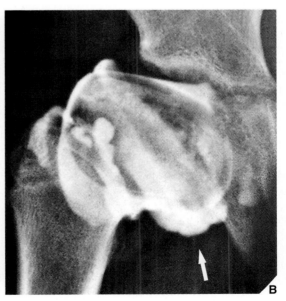

▲
FIGURE 32.23 **Arthrogram of Legg-Calvé-Perthes disease.** A 6-year-old boy presented with progressive pain in the right hip joint and a limp for the previous 8 months. **(A)** Anteroposterior radiograph shows a dense, flattened, and deformed femoral epiphysis, with subchondral collapse and fragmentation, diffuse metaphyseal changes, broadening of the femoral neck, and lateral subluxation. **(B)** Contrast arthrogram demonstrates flattening of the articular cartilage at the lateral aspect of the femoral head and a relatively smooth contour of the cartilage at the anteromedial aspect. The pulling of the contrast medially (*arrow*) indicates lateral subluxation.

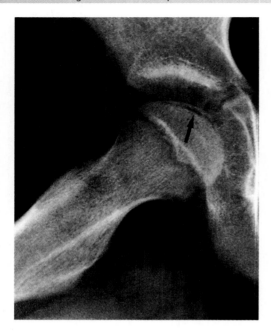

▲
FIGURE 32.24 Legg-Calvé-Perthes disease. Frog-lateral view of the right hip of a 7-year-old girl shows the crescent sign (*arrow*), one of the earliest radiographic features of osteonecrosis.

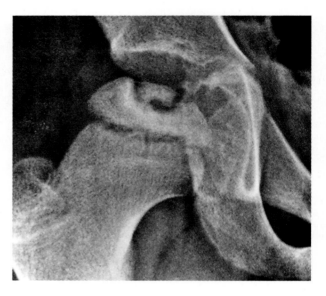

▲
FIGURE 32.25 Legg-Calvé-Perthes disease. Anteroposterior radiograph of the right hip of a 9-year-old boy demonstrates a more advanced stage of disease (Catterall group 2). Note the central defect in the femoral head, with preservation of the lateral and medial buttresses.

the cartilaginous shape of the femoral head. MRI allows preoperative and postoperative assessment of containment of the femoral head and enables its medial aspect to be visualized. The advantages of MRI over arthrography are noninvasiveness, the ability to obtain images in several imaging planes (i.e., axial, coronal, and sagittal), and lack of exposure to the side effects of radiation and injection of intraarticular contrast.

Classification

Several classification systems and prognostic indicators have been developed for the evaluation of Legg-Calvé-Perthes disease. Walderström proposed a three-stage system based on the progression of the osteonecrotic process. The first stage is marked by changes in the blood supply to the femoral epiphysis, with secondary alteration in the shape and density of the femoral head. In the second stage, revascularization takes place, and necrotic bone is replaced by new bone (creeping substitution). The third stage represents a healing phase of the disease in which reconstruction of the femoral epiphysis may result either in congruency of the joint or in incongruency because of deformity of the femoral head (coxa magna), with a predisposition to degenerative changes.

The Catterall classification, which has better prognostic value, divides this anomaly into four groups based on radiographic findings:

Group 1   The anterior portion of the epiphysis is involved; there is no evidence of subarticular collapse or fragmentation of the femoral head. The prognosis is good, and patients do well even without treatment, particularly those younger than age 8 years.

Group 2   The anterior portion of the epiphysis is more severely affected, but the medial and lateral segments are still preserved (Fig. 32.25). Small cystic changes may be seen in the metaphysis. The prognosis is worse than that of patients in group 1, but healing may occur, particularly in children younger than 5 years.

Group 3   The entire epiphysis appears dense, yielding a "head-within-a-head" phenomenon. The changes are more generalized, and the neck becomes widened. The prognosis is poor, and more than 70% of patients require surgical intervention.

Group 4   There is marked flattening and "mushrooming" of the femoral head, eventually leading to its complete collapse; the metaphyseal changes are extensive (Fig. 32.26). The prognosis is much worse than in the previous groups.

Subsequently, Catterall improved this classification by introducing four "head-at-risk" signs that signify a poor prognosis; these features can be demonstrated on an anteroposterior projection of the hip joint:
1. Gage sign—a radiolucent, V-shaped osteoporotic segment in the lateral portion of the femoral head (Fig. 32.27).
2. Calcification lateral to the epiphysis, representing extruded cartilage and indicating pressure on the head from the lateral edge of the acetabulum (see Fig. 32.26).
3. Lateral subluxation of the femoral head (see Fig. 32.26).
4. Horizontal inclination of the growth plate, indicating physeal growth closure (see Fig. 32.22B).
5. Recently, Murphy and Marsh added a fifth sign to this group of indicators—diffuse metaphyseal changes (see Fig. 32.23A).

Patients in any of the four groups who have two or more "head-at-risk" signs have a significantly worsened prognosis. Moreover, the prognosis is poor when the disease is in a late stage at the time of diagnosis and when the patient is older than age 6 years.

Differential Diagnosis

The differential diagnosis of this condition should include other causes of osteonecrosis and fragmentation of the femoral head, which may be seen, for example, in hypothyroidism, Gaucher disease, and sickle-cell anemia.

Treatment

The treatment of Legg-Calvé-Perthes disease is individualized on the basis of the clinical and imaging findings, including the age of onset, the range of motion in the hip joint, the extent of femoral head involvement, and the presence or absence of femoral deformity and lateral subluxation. Although some authorities have suggested eliminating weight bearing to prevent deformity of the femoral head, prevention requires measures that maintain the femoral head within the acetabulum (containment), thereby preventing extrusion and subluxation, as well as obtaining a full range of motion in the hip joint. In this respect, Salter advocates full weight bearing together with containment methods of treatment. To minimize synovitis and its sequelae of pain and stiffness, a combination of non–weight bearing, traction, treatment with nonsteroidal antiinflammatory agents, and gentle range-of-motion exercises is used to enhance molding of the femoral head by the acetabulum. The surgical treatment consists of femoral (varus derotational) or pelvic (innominate bone) osteotomy, aimed at covering the femoral head with the acetabulum.

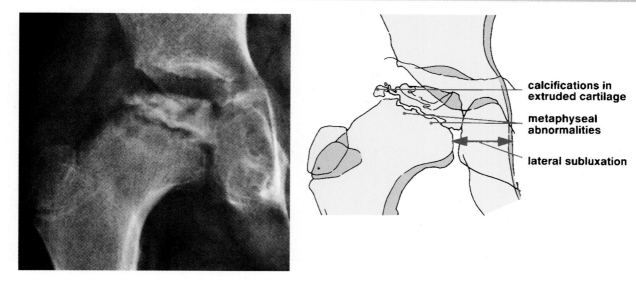

FIGURE 32.26   Legg-Calvé-Perthes disease. Anteroposterior film of the right hip of an 8-year-old girl with advanced disease (Catterall group 4) shows increased density and fragmentation of the entire femoral head. "Head-at-risk" signs are apparent in the metaphyseal changes and the lateral subluxation. Calcifications lateral to the epiphysis represent extruded cartilage and indicate pressure on the head from the lateral edge of the acetabulum.

Slipped Capital Femoral Epiphysis

Slipped capital femoral epiphysis (SCFE) is a disorder of adolescence in which the femoral head gradually slips posteriorly, medially, and inferiorly with respect to the neck. Boys are affected more often than girls are, and children of both sexes with this disorder are often overweight. In boys, the left hip is involved twice as often as the right, whereas in girls both hips are affected with equal frequency. Bilateral involvement occurs in 20% to 40% of patients.

Although the specific cause of SCFE is obscure, its onset, which is usually insidious and without a history of trauma, commonly coincides with the growth spurt at puberty. Studies by Harris have suggested that an imbalance between growth hormone and sex hormones weaken the growth plate, rendering it more vulnerable to the shearing forces of weight bearing and injury.

Regardless of its cause, SCFE represents a Salter-Harris type I fracture (see Fig. 4.30) through the growth plate of the proximal femur. This comes about through posterior, medial, and inferior displacement of the capital epiphysis, resulting in a varus deformity in the hip joint and external rotation and adduction of the femur. Pain in the hip, or occasionally the knee, is often the presenting symptom of this condition, and physical examination may reveal shortening of the involved extremity and limitation of abduction, flexion, and internal rotation in the hip joint.

Radiologic Evaluation

The radiographic abnormalities that may be seen in SCFE depend on the degree of displacement of the capital epiphysis. The anteroposterior radiograph of the hip, supplemented by a frog-lateral view, is usually sufficient to make a correct diagnosis. Several diagnostic indicators of SCFE have been identified on the anteroposterior radiograph of

FIGURE 32.27   Legg-Calvé-Perthes disease. A V-shaped radiolucent defect in the lateral aspect of the physis, a Gage sign *(arrow)*, indicating a "head-at-risk," is demonstrated in this 7-year-old girl.

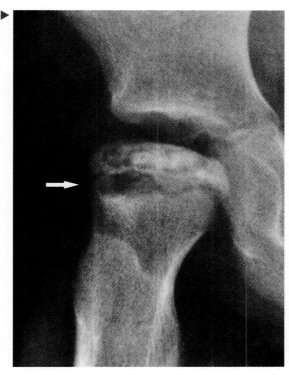

RADIOGRAPHIC FINDINGS IN SLIPPED CAPITAL FEMORAL EPIPHYSIS

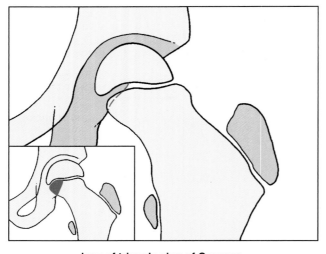

loss of triangle sign of Capener

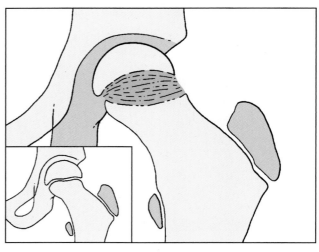

blurring of physis

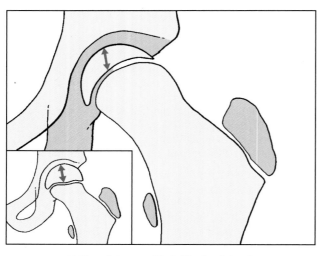

relative decreased height of epiphysis

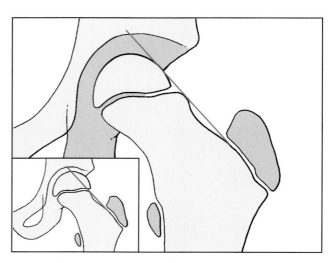

loss of intersection of epiphysis by lateral cortical line of femoral neck

FIGURE 32.28 **Slipped capital femoral epiphysis.** Various radiographic findings have been identified as diagnostic clues to SCFE. The insets show the normal appearance.

the hip (Fig. 32.28). The triangle sign of Capener may be of value in recognizing early SCFE. On conventional radiograph of the normal adolescent hip, an intracapsular area at the medial aspect of the femoral neck is seen overlapping the posterior wall of the acetabulum, creating a dense triangular shadow; in most cases of SCFE, this triangle is lost (Fig. 32.29). In a later stage, periarticular osteoporosis becomes apparent, as do widening and blurring of the physis and a decrease in height of the epiphysis (see Fig. 32.29). Moreover, as the disease progresses, slippage of the capital epiphysis can be identified by the absence of an intersection of the epiphysis with a line drawn tangent to the lateral cortex of the femoral neck (Fig. 32.30). The frog-lateral projection of the hip reveals slippage more readily (Fig. 32.30B), and comparison radiographs of the opposite side are helpful. Chronic stages of this disorder exhibit reactive bone formation along the superolateral aspect of the femoral neck, along with remodeling; this creates a protuberance and broadening of the femoral neck, which gives it a "pistol-grip" appearance known as a Herndon hump (Fig. 32.31). At times, SCFE occurs as a result of acute trauma, in which case it is known as a transepiphyseal fracture (Fig. 32.32).

Occasionally, SCFE is evaluated with MRI. This technique, in addition to findings revealed by radiography, may show a bone marrow edema of the affected femur (Fig. 32.33).

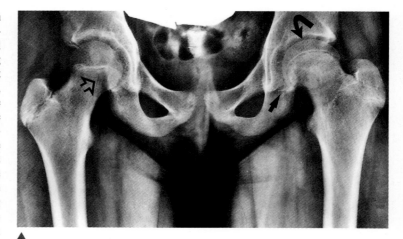

FIGURE 32.29 **Slipped capital femoral epiphysis.** Anteroposterior radiograph of the hips of a 12-year-old girl shows the absence of a triangular density in the area of overlap of the medial segment of the femoral metaphysis with the posterior wall of the acetabulum (Capener sign) (*arrow*). The triangle is clearly seen in the normal right hip (*open arrow*). Note also relative decreased height of left femoral epiphysis (*curved arrow*).

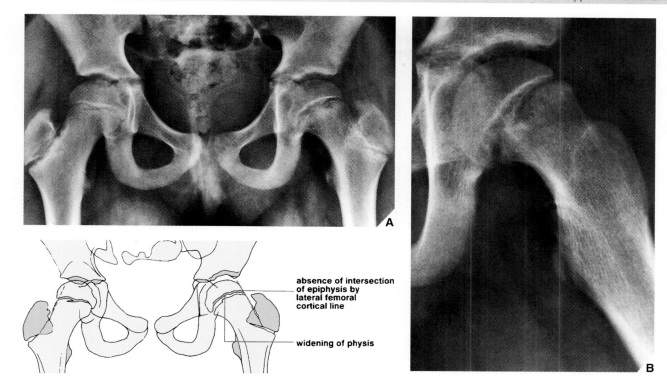

absence of intersection
of epiphysis by
lateral femoral
cortical line

widening of physis

FIGURE 32.30 Slipped capital femoral epiphysis. A 9-year-old girl presented with pain in the left hip and knee for 4 months. On physical examination, there was slight limitation of abduction and internal rotation in the hip joint. **(A)** Anteroposterior radiograph of the pelvis demonstrates a minimal degree of periarticular osteoporosis of the left hip, widening of the growth plate, and a slight decrease in the height of the epiphysis. Note the lack of intersection of the epiphysis by the lateral cortical line of the femoral neck. **(B)** Frog-lateral view of the left hip shows posteromedial slippage of capital epiphysis.

FIGURE 32.31 Slipped capital femoral epiphysis. (A) A 14-year-old boy with a 14-month history of chronic pain in the left hip was examined by a pediatrician because of significant foreshortening of the left leg and a limp. Frog-lateral view of the left hip shows changes typical of chronic SCFE. There is a moderate degree of osteoporosis and a remodeling deformity of the femoral neck, known as a Herndon hump (*arrow*). **(B)** Anteroposterior radiograph of the right hip of a 20-year-old man who had a SCFE treated with pins demonstrates a Herndon hump (*open arrow*) and secondary osteoarthritis.

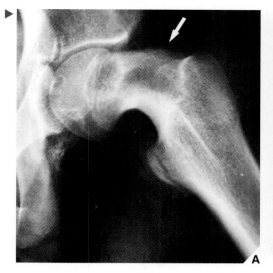

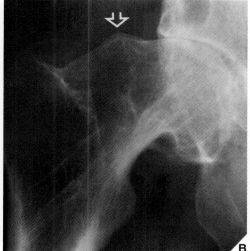

FIGURE 32.32 Slipped capital femoral epiphysis. Anteroposterior radiograph of the left hip of a 13-year-old boy who was thrown from a car in an automobile accident shows acute slippage of the femoral epiphysis. This injury represents a Salter-Harris type I fracture through the growth plate.

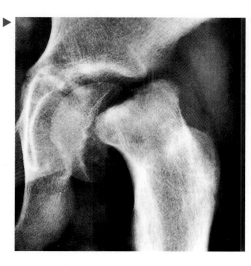

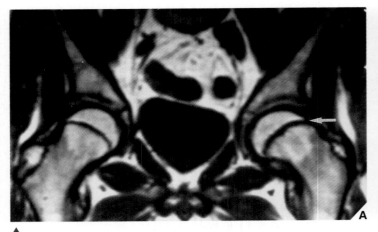
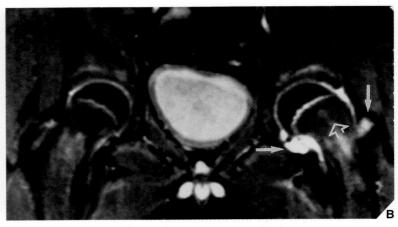

▲
FIGURE 32.33   **MRI of slipped capital femoral epiphysis. (A)** Coronal T1-weighted MRI of the hips in a 14-year-old boy shows slipped femoral epiphysis on the left side (*arrow*). The right hip is normal. **(B)** Coronal T2-weighted fat-suppressed image reveals joint effusion (*arrows*) and marrow edema in the metaphysis (*open arrow*).

Treatment and Complications

SCFE is treated surgically by closed or open reduction of the slippage and internal fixation using various types of nails, wires, and pins to prevent further slippage and to induce closure of the physis. One of the complications of treatment is inadvertent penetration of the articular cartilage of the femoral head by a Knowles pin during placement. Lehman and colleagues have introduced a cannulated pin that prevents this complication by allowing contrast medium to be injected during surgery to determine proper placement of the pin in the femoral head on fluoroscopy. Other complications may be encountered that are not necessarily related to surgical treatment. Chondrolysis is observed in approximately 30% to 35% of patients with SCFE and is much more common in black patients than in white patients. It usually occurs within 1 year of the slippage and may be evident by gradual narrowing of the joint space (Fig. 32.34). Osteonecrosis secondary to the precarious blood supply to the femoral head and the vulnerability of the epiphyseal vessels has been reported in approximately 25% of patients with SCFE (Fig. 32.35). Secondary osteoarthritis may also occur, and it can be recognized by a typical narrowing of the joint space, subchondral sclerosis, and marginal osteophyte formation (Fig. 32.36; see also Fig. 32.31B). A severe varus deformity of the femoral neck, known as coxa vara, may also be encountered.

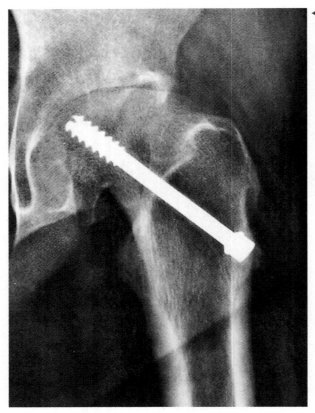

◄ FIGURE 32.34   **Complication of SCFE.** Anteroposterior radiograph of the left hip of a 13-year-old girl who 1 year earlier had been treated for SCFE shows narrowing of the joint secondary to chondrolysis, a complication of this condition.

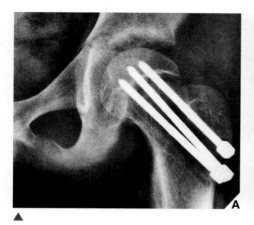
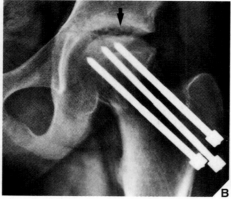
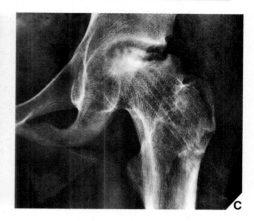

FIGURE 32.35 Complication of SCFE. A 12-year-old boy was treated by the insertion of three Knowles pins into the femoral head (**A**). Six months later, a repeat film (**B**) shows minimal flattening of the weight-bearing segment of the femoral epiphysis (*arrow*), an early sign suggesting osteonecrosis. The pins were removed. (**C**) On a radiograph obtained 1 year later, there is an increase in density of the femoral head together with fragmentation of the epiphysis and subchondral collapse, features of advanced osteonecrosis.

Anomalies of the Lower Limbs

An overview of the most effective radiographic projections and radiologic techniques for evaluating common anomalies of the lower limb and foot is presented in Table 32.4.

Congenital Tibia Vara

Congenital tibia vara, or Blount disease, as this developmental anomaly is also known, predominantly affects the medial portion of the proximal tibial growth plate, as well as the medial segments of the tibial metaphysis and epiphysis, resulting in a varus deformity at the knee joint. The cause of this disorder is unknown. Bateson has demonstrated convincingly that Blount disease and physiologic bowleg deformity are part of the same condition, which is influenced by early weight-bearing and racial factors. On the basis of a study of South African black children, among whom there is an increased incidence of Blount disease (as there is in Jamaica), Bathfield and Beighton have suggested that its cause might be related to the custom of mothers carrying children on their backs. The child's thighs are abducted and flexed, and the flexed knees gripping the mother's waist are forced to assume a varus configuration.

Two forms of Blount disease have been identified: *infantile tibia vara*, which is usually bilateral and affects children younger than age 10 years, with onset most commonly between ages 1 and 3 years; and *adolescent tibia vara*, which is usually unilateral and occurs in children between the ages of 8 and 15 years. The course of the adolescent form of the disease is less severe and its incidence less frequent than in the infantile form. Regardless of its variants, Blount disease must be differentiated from other causes of tibia vara, such as those seen as sequelae to trauma.

Imaging Evaluation and Differential Diagnosis

Radiologically, the early stages of Blount disease are marked by hypertrophy of the nonossified cartilaginous portion of the tibial epiphysis and hypertrophy of the medial meniscus, which represent compensatory changes secondary to growth arrest at the medial aspect of the physis. As the metaphysis and growth plate become depressed, the cartilage decreases in height. In advanced stages of the disease, there is premature fusion of the growth plate on the medial side (Fig. 32.37). The presence of fusion is important information for surgical planning because either resection of the bony bridge or epiphysiodesis (fusion of the physis) would be required in addition to the corrective osteotomy. Double-contrast arthrography is a valuable technique in the radiologic evaluation of Blount disease, because it permits visualization of nonossified cartilage of the medial plateau (Fig. 32.38) and associated abnormalities of the medial meniscus (Fig. 32.39).

In most cases, it is also possible to distinguish Blount disease radiographically, particularly in its advanced stage, from developmental bowing of the legs. In Blount disease, the medial aspect of the tibial metaphysis is characteristically depressed, exhibiting an abrupt angulation and formation of a beak-like prominence, which is associated with cortical thickening of the medial aspect of the tibia. Similar changes are seen in the medial aspect of the tibial epiphysis. Because of the sharp angulation of the metaphysis and adduction of the diaphysis, the tibia assumes a varus configuration (Fig. 32.40). In most instances, the lateral cortex of the tibia remains relatively straight. In developmental bowleg deformity, however, a gentle bilateral bowing is noted in the medial and lateral femoral and tibial cortices; the growth plates appear normal, and depression of the tibial metaphysis with a beak formation is absent (Fig. 32.41). Physiologic bowing resolves to straight alignment without treatment as ambulation increases, with the reversal usually beginning at approximately age 18 months. Both conditions,

FIGURE 32.36 Complication of SCFE. Frog-lateral radiograph of the right hip of a 14-year-old boy who had acute slippage of the capital epiphysis at age 9 demonstrates narrowing of the joint space and osteophytosis (*open arrows*), characteristic features of a secondary osteoarthritic process. Note the presence of a Herndon hump (*arrow*).

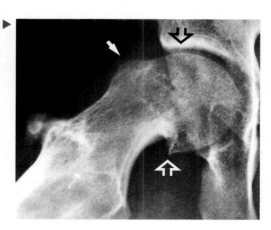

TABLE 32.4 **Most Effective Radiographic Projections and Radiologic Techniques for Evaluating Common Anomalies of the Lower Limb and Foot**

Projection/Technique	Crucial Abnormalities
Cogenital Tibia Vara	
Anteroposterior of knees	Depression of medial tibial metaphysis with beak formation
	Varus deformity of tibia
	Premature fusion of tibial growth plate
Arthrography	Hypertrophy of
	Nonossified portion of epiphysis
	Medial meniscus
Genu Valgum	
Anteroposterior of knees	Valgus deformity
Infantile Pseudoarthrosis of the Tibia	
Anteroposterior and lateral of tibia	Bowing of tibia
	Pseudoarthrosis
Dysplasia Epiphysealis Hemimelica	
Anteroposterior and lateral of ankle (or other affected joint)	Unilateral bulbous deformity of distal tibial (or any affected) epiphysis
Talipes Equinovarus	
Anteroposterior of foot	Varus position of hind foot
	Adduction and varus position of forefoot
	Kite anteroposterior talocalcaneal angle (less than 20 degrees)
	TFM angle (greater than 15 degrees)
	Metatarsal parallelism
Lateral of foot (weight-bearing or with forced dorsiflexion)	Equinous position of the heel
	Talocalcaneal subluxation
	Kite lateral talocalcaneal angle (less than 35 degrees)
Congenital/Developmental Planovalgus Foot	
Anteroposterior of foot	Medial projection of axial line through the talus
Lateral of foot	Flattening of longitudinal arch
Congenital Vertical Talus	
Lateral of foot	Vertical position of talus
	Talonavicular dislocation
	Boat-shaped or Persian-slipper appearance of foot
With forced plantar flexion	Possibility of reduction of dislocation
Anteroposterior of foot	Flat-foot deformity
	Medial displacement of talus
	Abduction of forefoot
Calcaneonavicular Coalition	
Lateral or medial oblique (45 degrees) of foot and CT	Fusion of calcaneus and navicular bone
Talocalcaneal Coalition	
Medial oblique (15 degrees) of foot	Fusion of talus and calcaneus
Lateral of foot	Talar beak
	"C"-sign
	Obliteration of subtalar joint
Posterior tangential of calcaneus and CT	Fusion or deformity of middle facet of subtalar joint
Subtalar arthrography	Cartilaginous or fibrous bridge
Talonavicular Coalition	
Lateral of foot	Anteater nose sign
Computed tomography	Fusion of talus and navicular bone

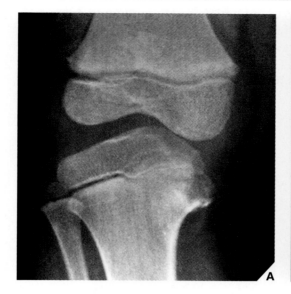
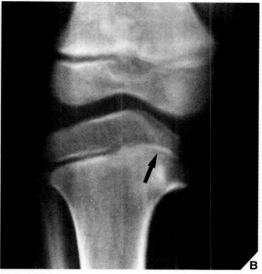

▲

FIGURE 32.37 **Blount disease.** **(A)** Anteroposterior radiograph of the right knee of an 8-year-old girl shows the typical changes of congenital tibia vara. There is, in addition, a possible fusion of the medial portion of the growth plate. **(B)** Conventional tomogram confirms the presence of a bony bridge in the medial aspect of the physis (*arrow*). Treatment of this condition would require either epiphysiodesis or bridge resection in addition to corrective valgus osteotomy of the tibia.

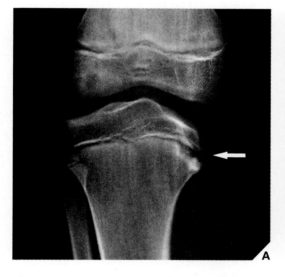
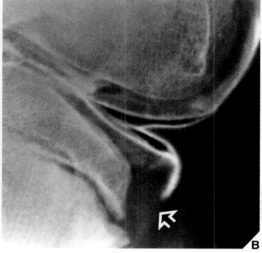

▲

FIGURE 32.38 **Blount disease.** **(A)** Anteroposterior radiograph of the right knee of a 10-year-old boy demonstrates the classic appearance of this condition, as evident in the depression of the medial metaphysis associated with a beak formation and slanting of the medial tibial epiphysis. (*arrow*) **(B)** Spot film of an arthrogram shows contrast outlining the thickened nonossified cartilage of the medial tibial plateau (*open arrow*). In this case, the medial meniscus shows no abnormalities.

FIGURE 32.39 **Blount disease.** Fluoroscopic spot film of a ▶ knee arthrogram in a 4-year-old girl shows hypertrophy of the medial aspect of the proximal tibial cartilage and an enlarged medial meniscus.

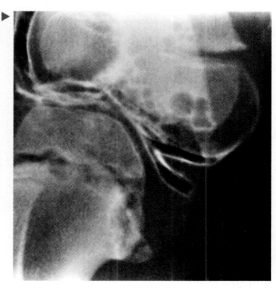

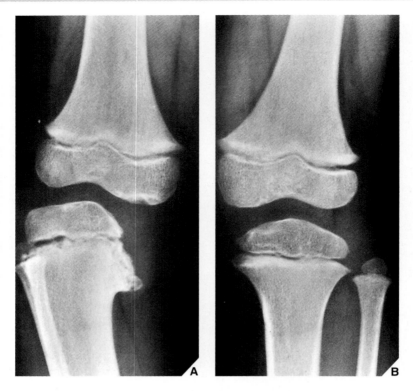

▲
FIGURE 32.40   **Blount disease. (A)** Anteroposterior radiograph of the right knee of a 4-year-old girl with unilateral congenital tibia vara shows depression of the medial tibial metaphysis associated with a beak formation and medial slant of the tibial epiphysis. **(B)** The left knee is normal.

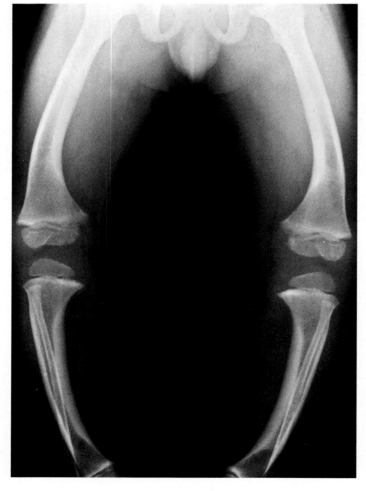

▲
FIGURE 32.41   **Developmental bowleg deformity.** Weight-bearing (standing) anteroposterior film of the legs of a 3-year-old boy demonstrates bowleg deformity of the femora and a varus configuration of the knees. However, there are no signs of Blount disease; both proximal tibial metaphyses and growth plates are normal, although there is associated internal torsion of both tibiae and thickening of the medial femoral and tibial cortices, which is frequently seen in this condition.

however, may be associated with internal tibial torsion. Developmental bowing usually persists for approximately 18 to 24 months, and in most affected children, it decreases progressively, although bowing may occasionally progress with skeletal maturation. Blount disease can be differentiated from rickets on the basis of ossification of the metaphyses and the absence of widening of the growth plate (see Figs. 27.12 and 27.13).

Classification

Based on the progression of radiographic changes in Blount disease, Langeskjöld divided congenital tibia vara into six stages as a guideline for prognosis and treatment:

Stage I   A varus deformity of the tibia, associated with irregularity of the growth plate and a small beak at the medial metaphysis; usually seen in children from 2 to 3 years of age.

Stage II   A definite depression of the medial portion of the metaphysis, associated with slanting of the medial aspect of the epiphysis; usually seen in children from 2 to 4 years of age.

Stage III Progression of the varus deformity and a very prominent beak, with occasional fragmentation of the medial portion of the metaphysis; seen in children between ages 4 and 6 years.

Stage IV   Marked narrowing of the growth plate and severe slanting of the medial aspect of the epiphysis, which shows an irregular border; usually seen in children between ages 5 and 10 years.

Stage V   Marked deformity of the medial epiphysis, which is separated into two parts by a clear band, the distal part having a triangular shape; seen in children between 9 and 11 years of age.

Stage VI   An osseous bridge between the epiphysis and metaphysis and possible fusion of the triangular fragment of the separated medial epiphysis to the metaphysis; seen in children between ages 10 and 13 years.

Stages V and VI represent phases of irreparable structural damage.

Recently, Smith introduced a simplified classification of Blount disease in an attempt to relate the grade of deformity to the need for treatment. His scheme comprises four grades: grade A, potential tibia vara; grade B, mild tibia vara; grade C, advanced tibia vara; and grade D, physeal closure.

Treatment

Blount disease is usually treated conservatively with braces. If the deformity continues to progress despite such treatment, a high valgus tibial osteotomy may be required to achieve normal alignment of the limb; usually, correction of a rotary deformity requires an osteotomy of the proximal fibula as well. Arthrography or MRI may be required before surgery to determine the status of the tibial articular cartilage, information helpful in planning the degree of angular correction necessary to eliminate the deformity.

Dysplasia Epiphysealis Hemimelica

Trevor-Fairbank disease (or tarsoepiphyseal aclasis) is a developmental disorder characterized by asymmetric cartilaginous overgrowth of one or more epiphyses in the lower extremity, with a decided preference for the distal tibial epiphysis and the talus. The lesion is characteristically found on one side of the affected limb, hence the name "hemimelica." Its cause is unknown, and there is no definite familial or hereditary predilection. Males are affected three times as often as females. Pathologically, the lesion shows similarity to an osteochondroma, and for this reason, it is occasionally referred to as "epiphyseal" or "intraarticular osteochondroma." Clinically, there is deformity and restricted motion of the affected joint, and pain, particularly around the ankle, is the most frequent presenting symptom in adults.

Radiographic Evaluation and Treatment

A diagnosis of Trevor-Fairbank disease can be established through radiographic examination. It typically presents with an irregular, bulbous overgrowth of the ossification center or epiphysis on one side,

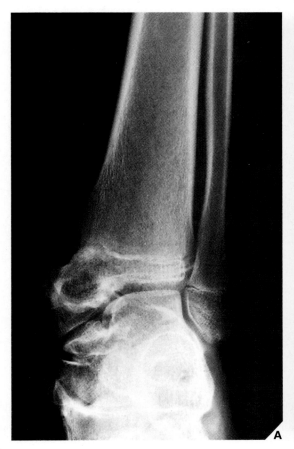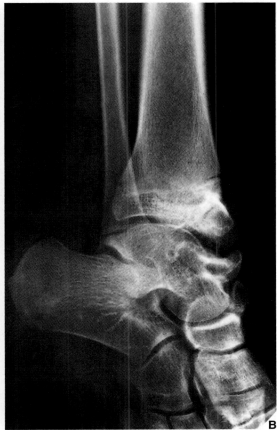

▲
FIGURE 32.42   Trevor-Fairbank disease. A 12-year-old girl presented with pain and limitation of motion in the ankle joint. Anteroposterior (**A**) and lateral (**B**) radiographs of the ankle demonstrate deformity and enlargement of the medial malleolus, talus, and navicular bone, features typical of dysplasia epiphysealis hemimelica. Note that the growth disturbance is limited to the medial side of the ankle and foot. (**A** from Norman A, Greenspan A, 1982, with permission.)

resembling an osteochondroma (Fig. 32.42). Occasionally, the other ossification centers, particularly at the knee, may be similarly affected in the same individual.

Treatment for the condition is individualized according to the amount of deformity and pain; usually, surgical resection of the lesion is required. Recurrence is common.

Talipes Equinovarus

Clubfoot is a congenital deformity comprising four elements: (a) an equinus position of the heel; (b) a varus position of the hindfoot; (c) adduction and a varus deformity of the forefoot; and (d) talonavicular subluxation. Before the ossification of the navicular bone at 2 to 3 years of age, only the first three elements can be verified radiographically.

Measurements and Radiographic Evaluation

A sound knowledge of the anatomy of the foot is essential to understanding and properly describing the various foot abnormalities involved in this disorder (see Fig. 10.2). Certain lines and angles drawn on dorsoplantar and lateral radiographs of the foot are helpful in identifying the deformity. The most useful of these are the Kite angles and the talus-first metatarsal (TFM) angle (Fig. 32.43). In the clubfoot deformity, the Kite anteroposterior talocalcaneal angle is less than 20 degrees, the lateral angle is less than 35 degrees, and the TFM angle is greater than 15 degrees (Fig. 32.44). In addition to these measurements, there are

other alignments in the normal infant's foot that are disrupted in the clubfoot deformity. For example, the anteroposterior view of the normal foot reveals the parallel alignment of the metatarsal bones, which in the clubfoot deformity converge proximally. Likewise, in the determination of the Kite anteroposterior talocalcaneal angle, the lines of the same angle normally intersect the first and fourth metatarsals; in the clubfoot anomaly, these lines fall lateral to the normal points. It is important to note that rendering accurate measurements of these various angles requires a carefully standardized technique for obtaining the anteroposterior and lateral views of the foot, because slight changes in position can alter the relationship of the bones. Whenever possible, both projections should be obtained in weight-bearing positions. With infants in whom this is not possible, an anteroposterior view is obtained with the infant seated and the knees held together; the sagittal plane of the leg must be at a right angle to the radiographic cassette, on which the infant's feet are secured. When a weight-bearing lateral view is not possible, the infant's knee should be held in flexion and the foot should be held in dorsiflexion.

Treatment

Most clubfoot deformities can be corrected with conservative treatment using various manipulations and casts. The necessary degree of correction can be determined from the lines and angles described previously. If complete correction cannot be achieved with conservative treatment,

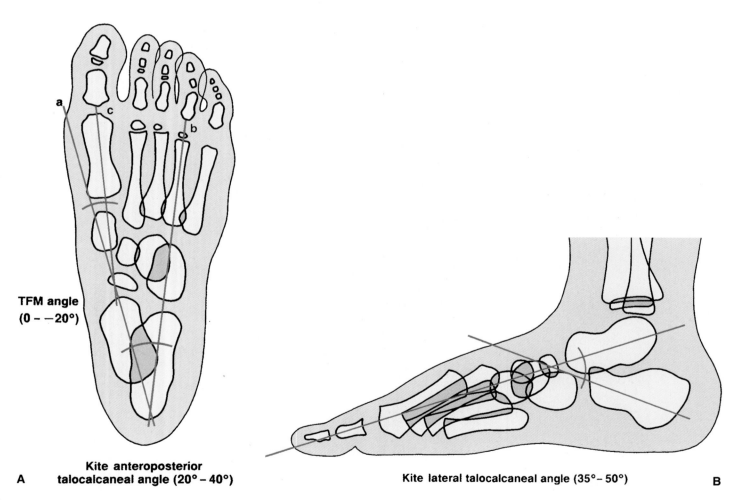

TFM angle (0 – −20°)

A **Kite anteroposterior talocalcaneal angle (20° – 40°)**

Kite lateral talocalcaneal angle (35° – 50°) **B**

FIGURE 32.43 **The Kite measurements. (A)** The Kite anteroposterior talocalcaneal angle and the TFM angle are determined on a weight-bearing dorsoplantar radiograph of the foot. The Kite angle is the intersection of two lines: One line (a) drawn through the longitudinal axis of the talus normally intersects the first metatarsal bone; a second line (b) drawn through the longitudinal axis of the calcaneus usually intersects the fourth metatarsal. The angle of intersection of these lines normally ranges from 20 to 40 degrees; an angle less than 20 degrees indicates a varus position of the hindfoot. The TFM angle is determined on the same radiograph by a line (c) drawn through the longitudinal axis of the first metatarsal and intersecting line (a). The values of this angle normally range between 0 and −20 degrees; positive values indicate adduction of the forefoot. **(B)** The Kite lateral talocalcaneal angle is determined on a weight-bearing lateral radiograph of the ankle and foot by the intersection of lines drawn through the longitudinal axes of the talus and calcaneus (lines parallel to the inferior borders of these two bones). Normally, this angle measures between 35 and 50 degrees; an angle less than 35 degrees indicates an equinus deformity of the heel.

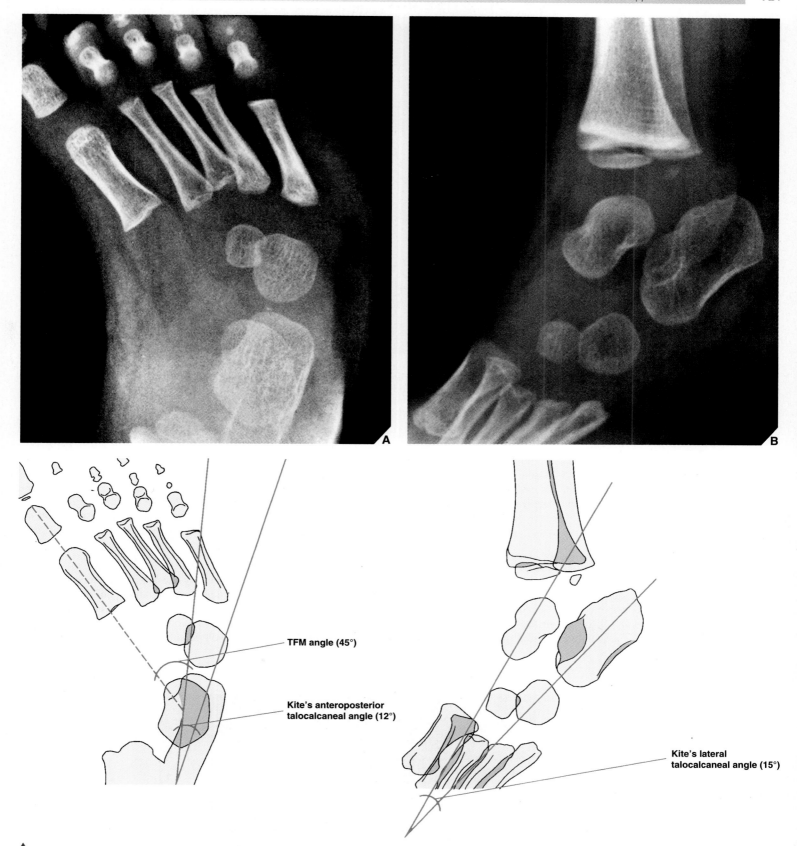

▲
FIGURE 32.44 **Clubfoot deformity. (A)** Dorsoplantar radiograph of the left foot of a 2-year-old boy demonstrates a varus position of the hindfoot, as determined by the Kite anteroposterior talocalcaneal angle, as well as adduction of the forefoot, as indicated by the abnormal values of the TFM angle (see Fig. 32.43A). **(B)** On the lateral projection, an equinus position of the heel is evident from the determination of the Kite lateral talocalcaneal angle (see Fig. 32.43B).

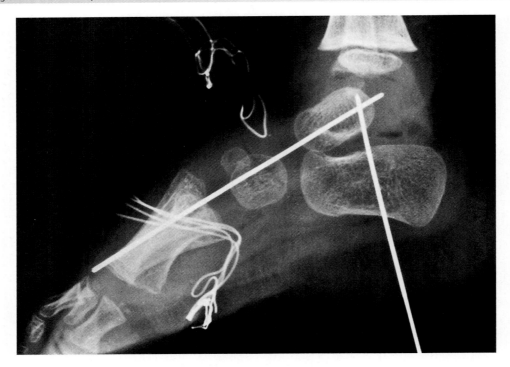

▲
FIGURE 32.45 **Treatment of the clubfoot deformity.** Intraoperative radiograph of the foot of a 2-year-old girl was obtained to verify the degree of correction of a clubfoot. After soft-tissue release (Achilles tendon lengthening and a posterior ankle joint syndesmotomy), two Kirschner wires were passed across the talonavicular and subtalar joints to stabilize the hindfoot. Note the correction of the equinus deformity, as determined by the horizontal position of the calcaneus and the normal value of the Kite lateral talocalcaneal angle (compare with Fig. 32.44B).

then surgical release is usually performed and intraoperative radiography is used to confirm the results (Fig. 32.45). Radiographic evaluation is also essential after surgery to monitor the patient's progress. The most common complication of surgery for a clubfoot is related to overcorrection, which results in a "rocker-bottom" flat-foot deformity.

Congenital Vertical Talus

Congenital vertical talus, as its name denotes, consists of primary dislocations in the talonavicular and talocalcaneal joints, with the talus assuming a vertical position and pointing plantarly and medially. This anomaly, also known as "rocker-bottom foot," occurs more often in males than in females, and is usually diagnosed in the first few weeks after birth. This condition is usually associated with multiple other congenital anomalies and only rarely is an isolated deformity. The reported familial cases are inherited as an autosomal dominat mode with incomplete penetrance. Recent genetic investigations suggest that the mutation in the *HOXD10* gene located in chromosome 2q31 is a causative factor. The foot is usually in dorsiflexion, and a prominent bulge is present on the plantar surface in the midtarsal region. The entire foot may assume a "boat-shaped" or "Persian-slipper" configuration.

Radiographic Evaluation

Radiographic examination, particularly the lateral projection, is diagnostic. The talus is seen in a vertical position, and in children aged 2 to 3 years the fully ossified navicular bone makes talonavicular dislocation obvious (Fig. 32.46). The presence of talonavicular dislocation differentiates this condition from the developmental flat-foot deformity. Before

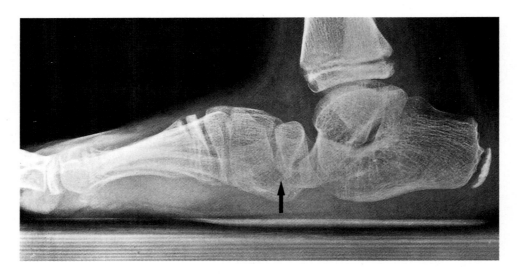

▲
FIGURE 32.46 **Congenital vertical talus.** Lateral radiograph of the foot of a 12-year-old boy shows obvious dislocations in the talonavicular and talocalcaneal articulations. Note the hourglass deformity of the talus and the wedging of the navicular bone (*arrow*).

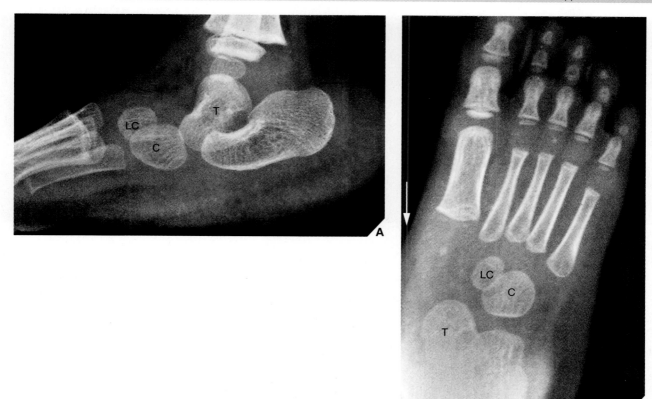

▲
FIGURE 32.47 **Congenital vertical talus. (A)** Lateral radiograph of the foot of a 2-year-old boy demonstrates the vertical position of the talus and the equinus position of the calcaneus. Note the flattening of the longitudinal arch and the alignment of the lateral cuneiform bone with the talar neck. **(B)** Dorsoplantar film shows the talus pointing medially; the navicular bone is not yet ossified. Note the soft-tissue bulge at the medial aspect of the foot (*arrow*). T, talus, C, cuboid; LC, lateral cuneiform.

ossification of the navicular bone occurs, congenital vertical talus can be identified on the lateral radiograph by a slight equinus position of the calcaneus, by widening of the calcaneocuboid joint, and by a valgus position of the forefoot, which is dorsiflexed at the midtarsal joint. The longitudinal arch is reversed, and the entire foot assumes a "rocker-bottom" configuration (Fig. 32.47A). The dorsoplantar projection characteristically reveals medial displacement of the distal talus and abduction of the forefoot (Fig. 32.47B). It is important to obtain a lateral radiograph with the foot in forced plantar flexion to see whether the dislocation can be reduced (Fig. 32.48), because on the basis of this finding, the surgeon can decide not only between conservative and surgical treatment but also on the type of operation to perform.

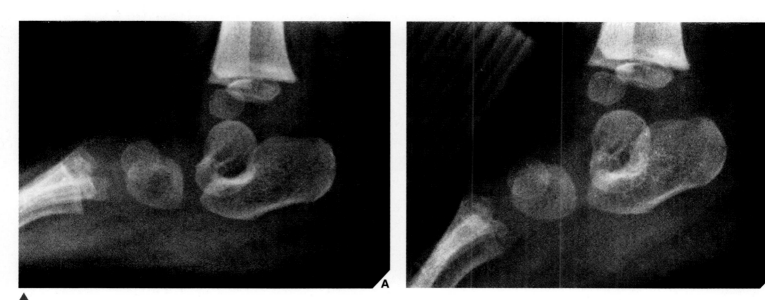

▲
FIGURE 32.48 **Congenital vertical talus. (A)** Lateral radiograph of the foot of a 2-year-old girl shows the vertical orientation of the talus, as well as talonavicular dislocation, although the navicular bone is not ossified. **(B)** Forced plantar flexion of the foot does not reduce the dislocation.

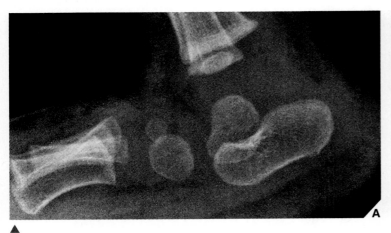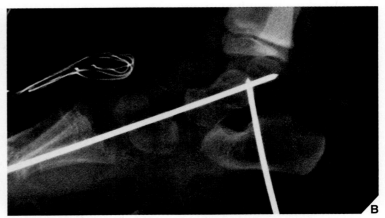

▲
FIGURE 32.49 Congenital vertical talus. **(A)** Preoperative radiograph of the foot of a 2-year-old girl shows the longitudinal axis of the talus in continuity with that of the tibia. **(B)** Intraoperative film demonstrates satisfactory reduction of the talonavicular dislocation.

Treatment

Most cases of congenital vertical talus require surgical correction of the deformity by soft-tissue release, reduction of the dislocation, and pinning of the talus to the navicular bone (Fig. 32.49). In children older than age 6 years, the navicular bone is resected. Radiographic confirmation of the correction is essential.

Tarsal Coalition

Tarsal coalition refers to the fusion of two or more tarsal bones to form a single structure. This fusion may be complete or incomplete, and the bridge may be fibrous (syndesmosis), cartilaginous (synchondrosis), or osseous (synostosis). Various bones may be affected, but most commonly the coalition occurs between the calcaneus and navicular bone, less frequently between the talus and calcaneus, and least often between the talus and navicular and calcaneus and cuboid bones. At times, more

than two bones may be affected. Despite its occurrence at birth, signs and symptoms of tarsal coalition rarely develop before the patient's second or third decade. Pain, particularly associated with prolonged walking or standing, is a typical presenting symptom. On physical examination, peroneal muscular spasm and restricted joint mobility (the so-called peroneal spastic foot) are revealed.

Although the clinical presentation usually suggests the correct diagnosis, radiologic examination is diagnostic. The primary sign of tarsal coalition is evidence of fusion. Secondary signs may also be present, such as dysmorphic sustentaculum tali, nonvisualization of the middle subtalar facet, the talar beak (see Fig. 32.54), shortening of the talar neck, or ball-and-socket ankle joint (see Fig. 32.53), representing adaptive alterations of the affected and adjacent bones and articulations.

Calcaneonavicular Coalition

The best projection for demonstrating this type of fusion is either lateral or a 45-degree medial (internal) oblique view of the foot (Fig. 32.50),

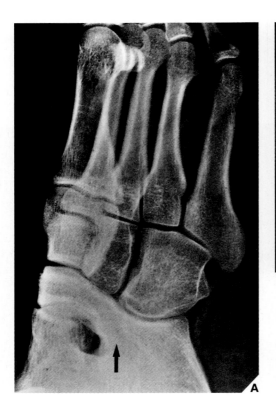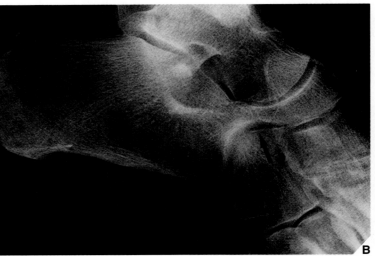

▲
FIGURE 32.50 Calcaneonavicular coalition. **(A)** A 45-degree internal oblique projection of the foot of an 18-year-old man demonstrates solid osseous bridge between the calcaneus and navicular bones (*arrow*). **(B)** In another patient, a lateral view demonstrates a similar osseous fusion of these two bones (*arrow*).

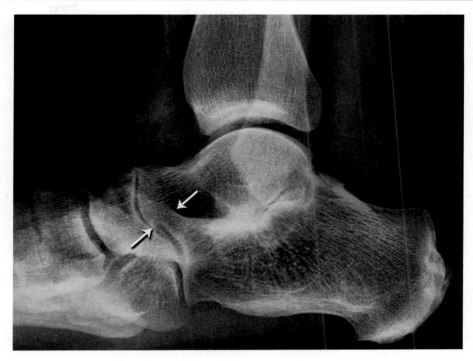

▲
FIGURE 32.51 Calcaneonavicular coalition. Lateral radiograph of the foot of a 27-year-old woman shows characteristic for this anomaly the anteater nose sign (*arrows*).

although CT may at times be useful. The anteater snout (nose) sign is characteristic for this anomaly. This sign, visible on the lateral radiograph of the ankle, is caused by a tubular elongation of the anterior process of the calcaneus that approaches or overlaps the navicular bone and resembles the snout of an anteater (Fig. 32.51). The secondary signs include hypoplasia of the talus head.

Talonavicular Coalition

This rare type of tarsal coalition is best seen on the lateral radiograph of the foot, or on CT and MRI examinations (Figs. 32.52 and 32.53).

Talocalcaneal Coalition

Because osseous fusion of the talus and calcaneus most often occurs at the level of the sustentaculum tali and the middle facet of the subtalar joint, it can effectively be demonstrated on oblique and Harris-Beath (posterior tangential) projections (Fig. 32.54); occasionally, CT examination may also be useful (Figs. 32.55 and 32.56). In suspected cartilaginous or fibrous union that is not readily demonstrated on radiographs, secondary changes should be sought, such as close apposition of the articular surfaces of the middle facet of the subtalar joint, eburnation and sclerosis of the articular margins, and broadening or rounding of

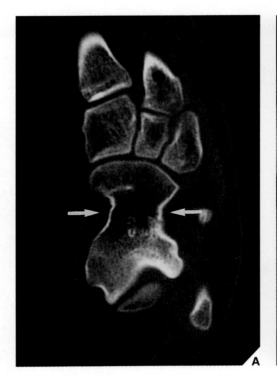
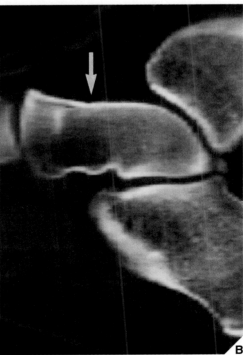

▲
FIGURE 32.52 Talonavicular coalition. Axial (**A**) and reformatted sagittal (**B**) CT sections show a solid osseous fusion of the talus and navicular bones (*arrows*) in a 17-year-old boy.

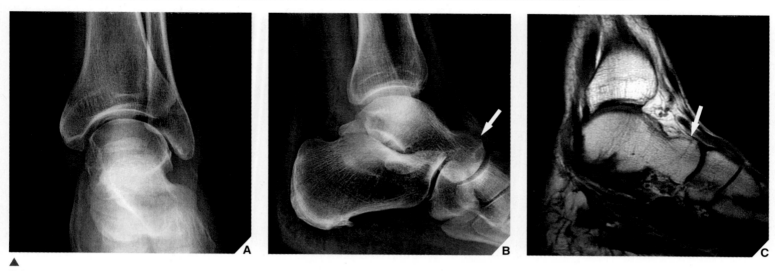

▲
FIGURE 32.53   Talonavicular coalition. (A) Anteroposterior radiograph of a 52-year-old man shows a ball-and-socket deformity of the ankle joint. (B) Lateral radiograph and (C) sagittal T1-weighted MR image show osseous fusion of the talus and navicular bones (*arrows*).

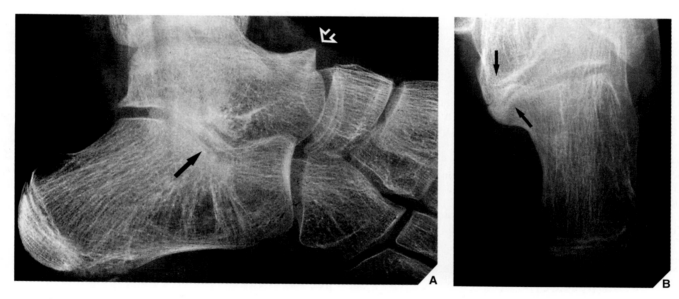

▲
FIGURE 32.54   Talocalcaneal coalition. (A) Oblique radiograph of the hindfoot of a 12-year-old boy shows obliteration of the middle facet of the subtalar joint (*arrow*). Note the prominent talar beak (*open arrow*). (B) A Harris-Beath view confirms the osseous talocalcaneal coalition (*arrows*).

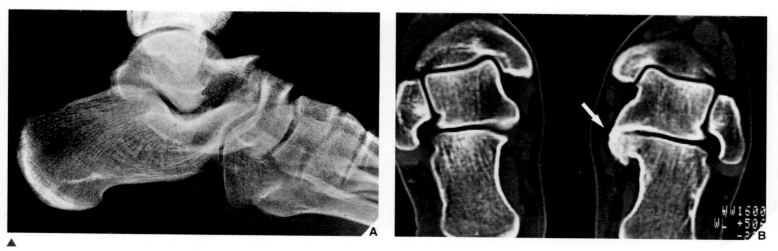

▲
FIGURE 32.55   CT of talocalcaneal coalition. A 25-year-old man presented with pain in his left foot that was particularly pronounced after prolonged walking or standing. (A) Lateral radiograph of the left foot shows sclerotic changes in the middle facet of the subtalar joint, narrowing of the posterior talocalcaneal joint space, and a prominent talar beak—features suggesting tarsal coalition. (B) Coronal CT section clearly demonstrates narrowing of the middle facet joint space and an osseous bridge (*arrow*). The normal right foot is shown for comparison.

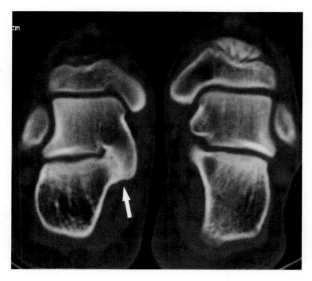

▲ FIGURE 32.56   **CT of talocalcaneal coalition.** A coronal CT scan in a 12-year-old boy with right foot pain shows an osseous talocalcaneal coalition at the site of the middle subtalar facet (*arrow*). The left foot is normal.

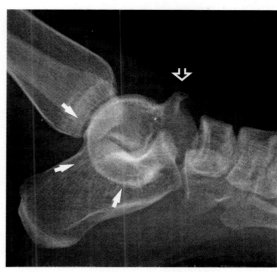

▲ FIGURE 32.57   **Talocalcaneal coalition.** A lateral radiograph of the ankle of a 19-year-old woman shows a prominent anterior talar beak (*open arrow*) and a "C" sign (*arrows*), created by combined shadows of the talar dome and fused middle facet of the subtalar joint.

the lateral process of the talus. Moreover, a C-shaped continuous line extending from the talus to the sustentaculum tali (the so-called C sign, originally described by Lateur et al. in 1994) is visible on lateral radiographs of the ankle (Fig. 32.57). This line is created by the combined shadows of the talar dome and the fused facets of the subtalar joint, together with a prominent inferior outline of the sustentaculum. In addition, the so-called absent middle facet sign, which refers to the lack of visualization of the middle facet of the subtalar joint on standing lateral view of the ankle and originally described by Harris in 1955, may be helpful in diagnosing this anomaly. A common secondary sign of talocalcaneal coalition is an osseous excrescence at the dorsal aspect of the talus, forming what is called a talar beak (see Figs. 32.54A and 32.55A), which is seen in the osseous, chondrus, and fibrous types of coalition. It is important to keep in mind, however, that a similar hypertrophy of the talar ridge may be seen in other conditions as well; for example, it may be related to abnormal capsular and ligamentous traction associated with degenerative changes in the talonavicular joint (Fig. 32.58). Demonstration of nonosseous forms of tarsal coalition may require subtalar arthrography. Similarly, when the clinical presentation is unclear and standard radiographs are equivocal, radionuclide bone scan may help localize the site of coalition by an increased uptake of radiopharmaceutical tracer, although this is a nonspecific finding.

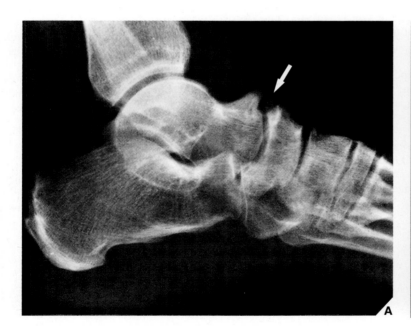

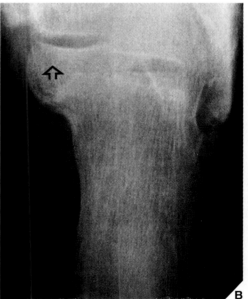

▲ FIGURE 32.58   **Talonavicular osteoarthritis. (A)** Lateral radiograph of the foot of a 61-year-old woman demonstrates a talar beak and degenerative changes in the talonavicular joint (*arrow*). The middle and posterior facets of the subtalar joint appear normal. **(B)** A Harris-Beath view shows normal middle facet of subtalar joint (*open arrow*) and no evidence of tarsal coalition.

PRACTICAL POINTS TO REMEMBER

Anomalies of the Shoulder Girdle and Upper Limbs

[1] Congenital elevation of the scapula (Sprengel deformity) is frequently accompanied by other anomalies, most commonly Klippel-Feil syndrome (fusion of the cervical or upper thoracic vertebrae).

[2] A Madelung deformity can be effectively evaluated on the posteroanterior and lateral radiographs of the distal forearm and wrist. The constant findings include:
  • a decreased radial and an increased ulnar length
  • medial and dorsal bowing of the radius
  • a triangular configuration of the carpal bones with the lunate at the apex.

Anomalies of the Pelvic Girdle and Hip

[1] CDH is bilateral in more than 50% of affected children; therefore, in apparently unilateral cases the unaffected hip should be carefully examined.

[2] Several lines and angles can be drawn on an anteroposterior radiograph of the pelvis and hips to help determine CDH:
  • the Hilgenreiner Y-line
  • the Perkins-Ombredanne line
  • the Andrén-von Rosen line
  • the Shenton-Menard arc
  • the acetabular index
  • the center-edge (C-E) angle of Wiberg.

[3] In addition to conventional radiography, the imaging evaluation of CDH requires arthrography and CT scan, which is particularly valuable in monitoring the results of treatment.

[4] Ultrasound is a highly effective technique to diagnose and evaluate congenital hip dysplasia. The osseous and cartilaginous components of the hip joint are well demonstrated, and acetabular coverage of the femoral head can be assessed.

[5] 3D ultrasound of the infant hip offers a unique image in the sagittal plane and allows evaluation of the joint from the craniocaudal (bird's eye) view.

[6] Before conservative or surgical treatment, skin or skeletal traction is applied to bring the dislocated femoral head to "station +2" to avoid osteonecrosis of the femoral head. The Gage and Winter traction stations are determined by the position of the proximal femoral metaphysis (femoral neck) relative to the ipsilateral acetabulum and contralateral normal hip.

[7] PFFD can mimic congenital hip dislocation. Arthrography is helpful in distinguishing these anomalies by demonstrating:
  • presence of the femoral head in the acetabulum in type A
  • a defect in the femoral neck in type B
  • the absence of the femoral head in types C and D.

[8] Legg-Calvé-Perthes disease (coxa plana) represents osteonecrosis (ischemic necrosis) of the proximal epiphysis of the femur. The imaging evaluation of this condition includes:
  • a radionuclide bone scan, particularly in the early stages
  • conventional radiography
  • contrast arthrography
  • MRI.

[9] The most frequently encountered radiographic findings in Legg-Calvé-Perthes disease include:
  • periarticular osteoporosis
  • increased density and flattening of the capital epiphysis
  • a crescent sign
  • fissuring and fragmentation of the epiphysis
  • cystic changes in the metaphysis and broadening of the femoral neck
  • lateral subluxation in the hip joint.

[10] A femoral "head-at-risk" in Legg-Calvé-Perthes disease is defined by five radiographic signs indicating a poor prognosis:
  • a radiolucent, V-shaped defect in the lateral portion of the femoral head (Gage sign)

  • calcifications lateral to the femoral epiphysis
  • lateral subluxation of the femoral head
  • a horizontal orientation of the growth plate
  • diffuse metaphyseal cystic changes.

[11] A SCFE is a Salter-Harris type I fracture through the physis, which is best demonstrated on the frog-lateral projection. Important diagnostic clues include:
  • loss of the triangle sign of Capener
  • decreased height of the epiphysis
  • widening and blurring of the growth plate
  • lack of intersection of the epiphysis by the lateral cortical line of the femoral neck.

Anomalies of the Lower Limbs

[1] Congenital tibia vara (Blount disease) can be differentiated from developmental bowing of the legs by its characteristic presentation with depression of the medial tibial metaphysis associated with abrupt angulation and the formation of a beak-like prominence on the metaphysis.

[2] Dysplasia epiphysealis hemimelica (Trevor-Fairbank disease) most often affects the ankle joint. The radiographic hallmark of this lesion, which histologically resembles osteochondroma, is an irregular bulbous overgrowth of one side of the ossification center or epiphysis.

[3] The clubfoot deformity is recognized radiographically by:
  • an equinous position of the heel
  • a varus position of the hindfoot
  • adduction and a varus position of the forefoot
  • talonavicular subluxation.

[4] In the evaluation of the clubfoot deformity, certain angles and lines drawn on the anteroposterior and lateral radiographs of the foot are helpful:
  • the Kite anteroposterior and lateral talocalcaneal angles
  • the talus–first metatarsal angle
  • the extension of lines drawn through the longitudinal axis of the talus and the calcaneus.

[5] Proper positioning of the feet is a crucial factor in the radiographic evaluation of infants and small children. Weight-bearing films should be obtained whenever feasible; in small infants, the foot should be pressed against the radiographic cassette.

[6] Congenital vertical talus can be distinguished from developmental flat foot by the presence of dislocation in the talonavicular and talocalcaneal articulations.

[7] In tarsal coalition, the most common cause of the so-called peroneal spastic foot deformity, fusion of the affected bones (usually the talus and calcaneus or calcaneus and navicular bone) may be:
  • fibrous (syndesmosis)
  • cartilaginous (synchondrosis)
  • osseous (synostosis).

[8] The radiologic evaluation of tarsal coalition includes:
  • conventional radiographs in the lateral projection (which reveals the most frequently encountered secondary sign of this condition, the formation of a talar beak), as well as in Harris-Beath and oblique projections
  • computed tomography
  • subtalar arthrography.

SUGGESTED READINGS

Apley AG, Wientrob S. The sagging rope sign in Perthes disease and allied disorders. *J Bone Joint Surg [Br]* 1981;63-B:43–47.

Artz TD, Lim WN, Wilson PD, Levine DB, Salvati EA. Neonatal diagnosis, treatment and related factors of congenital dislocation of the hip. *Clin Orthop* 1975;110: 112–136.

Bahk W-J, Lee H-Y, Kang Y-K, et al. Dysplasia epiphysealis hemimelica: radiographic and magnetic resonance imaging features and clinical outcome of complete and incomplete resection. *Skeletal Radiol* 2010;39:85–90.

Barlow TG. Early diagnosis and treatment of congenital dislocation of the hip. *J Bone Joint Surg [Br]* 1962;44B:292–301.

Barnes JM. Premature epiphysial closure in Perthes' disease. *J Bone Joint Surg [Br]* 1980;62B:432–437.

Bateson EM. Non-rachitic bowleg and knock-knee deformities in young Jamaican children. *Br J Radiol* 1966;39:92.

Bateson EM. The relationship between Blount's disease and bow legs. *Br J Radiol* 1968;41:107–114.

Bathfield CA, Beighton PH. Blount disease. A review of etiological factors in 110 patients. *Clin Orthop* 1978;135:29–33.

Bellyei A, Mike G. Weight bearing in Perthes' disease. *Orthopedics* 1991;14:19–22.

Bennett JT, Mazurek RT, Cash JD. Chiari's osteotomy in the treatment of Perthes' disease. *J Bone Joint Surg [Br]* 1991;73B:225–228.

Bloomberg TJ, Nuttall J, Stocker DJ. Radiology in early slipped femoral capital epiphysis. *Clin Radiol* 1978;29:657–667.

Blount WP. Tibia vara. Osteochondrosis deformans tibiae. *J Bone Joint Surg* 1937;19:1–29.

Boyer DW, Mickelson MR, Ponseti IV. Slipped capital femoral epiphysis—long-term follow-up study of 125 patients. *J Bone Joint Surg [Am]* 1981;63A:85–95.

Brown RR, Rosenberg ZS, Thornhill BA. The C sign: more specific for flatfoot deformity than subtalar coalition. *Skeletal Radiol* 2001;30:84–87.

Caffey J, Ames R, Silverman WA. Contradiction of the congenital dysplasia-predislocation hypothesis of congenital dislocation of the hip through a study of the normal variation in acetabular angles at successive periods in infancy. *Pediatrics* 1956;17:632–641.

Calhoun JD, Pierret G. Infantile coxa vara. *Am J Roentgenol* 1972;115:561–568.

Catterall A. *Legg-Calvé-Perthes' disease.* New York: Churchill Livingstone; 1982.

Catterall A. The natural history of Perthes' disease. *J Bone Joint Surg [Br]* 1971;53B:37–53.

Chapman VM. The anteater-nose sign. *Radiology* 2007;245:604–605.

Cheema JI, Grissom LE, Harcke HT. Radiographic characteristics of lower-extremity bowing in children. *Radiographics* 2003;23:871–880.

Chiari K. Beckenosteotomie zur Pfannendachplastik. *Wien Med Wochenschr* 1953;103:707–714.

Chiari K. Medial displacement osteotomy of the pelvis. *Clin Orthop* 1974;98:55–71.

Clarke NMP, Harcke HT, McHugh R, Lee MS, Borns PF, MacEwen GD. Real-time ultrasound in the diagnosis of congenital dislocation and dysplasia of the hip. *J Bone Joint Surg [Br]* 1985;67B:406–412.

Conway JJ, Cowell HR. Tarsal coalition: clinical significance and roentgenographic demonstration. *Radiology* 1969;92:799–811.

Craig JG, van Holsbeeck M, Zaltz I. The utility of MR in assessing Blount disease. *Skeletal Radiol* 2002;31:208–213.

Crim JR, Kjeldsberg KM. Radiographic diagnosis of tarsal coalition. *Am J Roentgenol* 2004;182:323–328.

Dalinka MK, Coren G, Hensinger R, Irani RN. Arthrography in Blount's disease. *Radiology* 1974;113:161–164.

Dannenberg M, Anton JI, Spiegel MB. Madelung's deformity. Consideration of its roentgenological diagnostic criteria. *Am J Roentgenol* 1939;42:671.

Deutsch AL, Resnick D, Campbell G. Computed tomography and bone scintigraphy in the evaluation of tarsal coalition. *Radiology* 1982;144:137–140.

Dunn PM. The anatomy and pathology of congenital dislocation of the hip. *Clin Orthop* 1976;119:23–27.

Dunn PM. Perinatal observations on the etiology of congenital dislocation of the hip. *Clin Orthop* 1976;119:11–22.

Egund N, Wingstrand H. Legg-Calvé-Perthes disease: imaging with MR. *Radiology* 1991;179:89–92.

Evans IK, Deluca PA, Gage JR. A comparative study of ambulation-abduction bracing and varus derotation osteotomy in the treatment of severe Legg-Calvé-Perthes disease in children over 6 years of age. *J Pediatr Orthop* 1988;8:676–682.

Eyring EJ, Bjornson DR, Peterson CA. Early diagnostic and prognostic signs in Legg-Calvé-Perthes disease. *Am J Roentgenol* 1965;93:382–387.

Fairbank TJ. Dysplasia epiphysealis hemimelica (tarso-epiphysial aclasis). *J Bone Joint Surg [Br]* 1956;38B:237–257.

Felman AH, Kirkpatrick JA Jr. Madelung's deformity: observations in 17 patients. *Radiology* 1969;93:1037–1042.

Freiberger RH, Hersh A, Harrison MO. Roentgen examination of the deformed foot. *Semin Roentgenol* 1970;5:341.

Gage JR, Winter RB. Avascular necrosis of the capital femoral epiphysis as a complication of closed reduction of congenital dislocation of the hip. A critical review of twenty years' experience at Gillette Children's Hospital. *J Bone Joint Surg [Am]* 1972;54A:373–388.

Gallagher JM, Weiner DS, Cook AJ. When is arthrography indicated in Legg-Calvé-Perthes disease? *J Bone Joint Surg [Am]* 1983;65A:900–905.

Ganz R, Klave K, Vinh TS, Mast JW. A new periacetabular osteotomy for the treatment of hip dysplasias. Technique and preliminary results. *Clin Orthop* 1988;232:26–36.

Gerscovich EO. A radiologist's guide to the imaging in the diagnosis and treatment of developmental dysplasia of the hip. I. General considerations, physical examination as applied to real-time sonography and radiology. *Skeletal Radiol* 1997;26:386–397.

Gerscovich EO. A radiologist's guide to the imaging in the diagnosis and treatment of developmental dysplasia of the hip. II. Ultrasonography: anatomy, technique, acetabular angle measurements, acetabular coverage of femoral head, acetabular

cartilage thickness, three-dimensional technique, screening of newborns, study of older children. *Skeletal Radiol* 1997;26:447–456.

Gerscovich EO, Greenspan A, Cronan MS, Karol LA, McGahan JP. Three-dimensional sonographic evaluation of developmental dysplasia of the hip: preliminary findings. *Radiology* 1994;190:407–410.

Goldman AB. Hip arthrography in infants and children. In: Freiberger RH, Kaye JJ, eds. *Arthrography.* New York: Appleton-Century-Crofts; 1979:217–235.

Goldman AB, Schneider R, Martel W. Acute chondrolysis complicating slipped capital femoral epiphysis. *Am J Roentgenol* 1978;130:945–950.

Greenhill BJ, Hugosson C, Jacobsson B, Ellis RD. Magnetic resonance imaging study of acetabular morphology in developmental dysplasia of the hip. *J Pediatr Orthop* 1993;13:314–317.

Harcke HT. Screening newborns for developmental dysplasia of the hip: the role of sonography. *Am J Roentgenol* 1994;162:395–397.

Harcke HT, Kumar SJ. The role of ultrasound in the diagnosis and management of congenital dislocation and dysplasia of the hip. *J Bone Joint Surg [Am]* 1991;73A:622–628.

Harris RI. Rigid valgus foot due to talocalcaneal bridge. *J Bone Joint Surg* 1955;37:169–182.

Harris WR. The endocrine basis for slipping of the upper femoral epiphysis. An experimental study. *J Bone Joint Surg [Br]* 1950;32B:5–11.

Haveson SB. Congenital flatfoot due to talonavicular dislocation (vertical talus). *Radiology* 1959;72:19–25.

Herring JA. Current concepts review. The treatment of Legg-Calvé-Perthes disease. A critical review of the literature. *J Bone Joint Surg [Am]* 1994;76A:448–458.

Herring JA, Neustadt JB, Williams JJ, Early JS, Browne RH. The lateral pillar classification of Legg-Calvé-Perthes disease. *J Pediatr Orthop* 1992;12:143–150.

Herzenberg JE, Goldner JL, Martinez S, Silverman PM. Computerized tomography of talocalcaneal tarsal coalition: a clinical and anatomic study. *Foot Ankle* 1986;6:2730–288.

Hillmann JS, Mesgarzadeh M, Revesz G, Bonakdarpour A, Clancy M, Betz RR. Proximal femoral focal deficiency: radiologic analysis of 49 cases. *Radiology* 1987;165:769–773.

Ito H, Matsuno T, Hirayama T, et al. Three-dimensional computed tomography analysis of non-osteoarthritic adult acetabular dysplasia. *Skeletal Radiol* 2009;38:131–139.

Jones D. An assessment of the value of examination of the hip in the newborn infant. *J Bone Joint Surg [Br]* 1977;59B:318–322.

Kelly FB Jr, Canale ST, Jones RR. Legg-Calvé-Perthes disease. Long-term evaluation of non-containment treatment. *J Bone Joint Surg [Am]* 1980;62A:400–407.

Kettelkamp DB, Campbell CJ, Bonfiglio M. Dysplasia epiphysealis hemimelica. A report of fifteen cases and a review of the literature. *J Bone Joint Surg [Am]* 1966;48A:746–766.

Kim SH. Signs in imaging. The C sign. *Radiology* 2002;223:756–757.

Kite NH. *The clubfoot.* New York: Grune & Stratton; 1964.

Kleiger B, Mankin HJ. A roentgenographic study of the development of the calcaneus by means of the posterior tangential view. *J Bone Joint Surg [Am]* 1961;43A:961–969.

Langeskjöld A. Tibia vara (osteochondrosis deformans tibiae): a survey of seventy-one cases. *Acta Chir Scand* 1952;103:1–22.

Langeskjöld A, Riska EB. Tibia vara (osteochondrosis deformans tibiae). *J Bone Joint Surg [Am]* 1964;46A:1405–1420.

Lateur LM, Van Hoe LR, Van Ghillewe KV, Gryspeerdts SS, Baert AL, Dereymaeker GE. Subtalar coalition: diagnosis with the C sign on lateral radiograph of the ankle. *Radiology* 1994;193:847–851.

Legg AT. An obscure affection of the hip-joint. *Boston Med Surg J* 1910;162:202–204.

Lehman WB, Grant A, Rose D, Pugh J, Norman A. A method of evaluating possible pin penetration in slipped capital femoral epiphysis using a cannulated internal fixation device. *Clin Orthop* 1984;186:65–70.

Levinson ED, Ozonoff MB, Royen PM. Proximal femoral focal deficiency (PFFD). *Radiology* 1977;125:197–203.

Liu PT, Roberts CC, Chivers FS, et al. "Absent middle facet": a sign on unenhanced radiography of subtalar joint coalition. *Am J Roentgenol* 2003;181:1565–1572.

Lloyd-Roberts GC, Catterall A, Salamon PB. A controlled study of the indications for and the results of femoral osteotomy in Perthes disease. *J Bone Joint Surg [Am]* 1976;58B:31–36.

Lowe HG. Necrosis of articular cartilage after slipping of capital femoral epiphysis. Report of six cases with recovery. *J Bone Joint Surg [Br]* 1970;52B:108–118.

Martinez AG, Weinstein SL, Dietz FR. The weight-bearing abduction brace for the treatment of Legg-Perthes disease. *J Bone Joint Surg [Am]* 1992;74A:12–21.

Masciocchi C, D'Archivio C, Barile A, et al. Talocalcaneal coalition: computed tomography and magnetic resonance imaging diagnosis. *Eur J Radiol* 1992;15:22–25.

Maxted MJ, Jackson RK. Innominate osteotomy in Perthes disease: a radiological survey of results. *J Bone Joint Surg [Br]* 1985;67B:399–401.

McClure JG, Raney RB. Anomalies of the scapula. *Clin Orthop* 1975;110:22–31.

McEwan DW, Dunbar JS. Radiologic study of physiologic knock knees in childhood. *J Can Assoc Radiol* 1958;9:59.

Meehan PL, Angel D, Nelson JM. The Scottish Rite abduction orthosis for the treatment of Legg-Perthes disease. A radiographic analysis. *J Bone Joint Surg [Am]* 1992;74A:2–12.

Morin C, Harcke HT, MacEwen GD. The infant hip: real-time US assessment of acetabular development. *Radiology* 1985;157:673–677.

Mose K. Methods of measuring in Legg-Calvé-Perthes disease with special regard to the prognosis. *Clin Orthop* 1980;150:103–109.

Murphy RP, Marsh HO. Incidence and natural history of "head at risk" factors in Perthes' disease. *Clin Orthop* 1978;132:102–107.

Murphy SB, Simon SR, Kijewski PK, Wilkinson RH, Griscom NT. Femoral anteversion. *J Bone Joint Surg [Am]* 1987;69A:1169–1176.

Newman JS, Newberg AH. Congenital tarsal coalition: multimodality evaluation with emphasis on CT and MR imaging. *Radiographics* 2000;20:321–332.

Nielsen JB. Madelung's deformity. A follow-up study of 26 cases and a review of the literature. *Orthop Scand* 1977;48:379–384.

Oestreich AE, Mize WA, Crawford AH, Morgan RC. The "anteater nose": a direct sign of calcaneonavicular coalition on the lateral radiograph. *J Pediatr Orthop* 1987;7:709–711.

Ogden JA, Conlogue GJ, Phillips MS, Bronson ML. Sprengel's deformity. Radiology of the pathologic deformation. *Skeletal Radiol* 1979;4:204–211.

Ogden JA, Moss HL. Pathologic anatomy of congenital hip disease. In: Weill UH, ed. *Progress in orthopaedic surgery*, vol. 2. *Acetabular dysplasia in childhood*. New York: Springer-Verlag; 1978.

Paterson DC, Leitch JM, Foster BK. Results of innominate osteotomy in the treatment of Legg-Calvé-Perthes disease. *Clin Orthop* 1991;266:96–103.

Pavlik A. Die funktionelle Behand-lungmethode mittels Riemenbügel als Prinzip der konservativen Therapie bei angeborenen Hüftgelenks verrenkungen der Säuglinge. *Z Orthop* 1958;8:341–352.

Phillips WE II, Burton EM. Ultrasonography of development displacement of the infant hip. *Appl Radiol* 1995;24:25–32.

Rab GT. Preoperative roentgenographic evaluation for osteotomies about the hip in children. *J Bone Joint Surg [Am]* 1981;63A:306–309.

Rab GT. Surgery for developmental dysplasia of the hip. In: Chapman MW, ed. *Operative orthopaedics*, 2nd ed. Philadelphia: JB Lippincott; 1993:3101–3112.

Resnick D. Talar ridges, osteophytes, and beaks: a radiologic commentary. *Radiology* 1984;151:329–332.

Robbins H. Naviculectomy for congenital vertical talus. *Bull Hosp Jt Dis Orthop Inst* 1976;37:77–97.

Sakellariou A, Sallomi D, Janzen DL, Munk PL, Claridge RJ, Kiri VA. Talocalcaneal coalition: diagnosis with the C-sign on lateral radiographs of the ankle. *J Bone Joint Surg [Br]* 2000;82B:574–578.

Salter RB. Current concepts review. The present status of surgical treatment for Legg-Perthes disease. *J Bone Joint Surg [Am]* 1984;66A:961–966.

Salter RB. Etiology, pathogenesis and possible prevention of congenital dislocation of the hip. *Can Med Assoc J* 1968;98:933–945.

Salter RB. Legg-Perthes disease. The scientific basis for methods of treatment and their indications. *Clin Orthop* 1980;150:8–11.

Salter RB. Role of innominate osteotomy in the treatment of congenital dislocation and subluxation of the hip in the older child. *J Bone Joint Surg [Am]* 1966;48:1413–1439.

Salter RB, Thompson GH. Legg-Calvé-Perthes disease. The prognostic significance of the subchondral fracture and a two-group classification of the femoral head involvement. *J Bone Joint Surg [Am]* 1984;66A:479–489.

Scham SM. The triangular sign in the early diagnosis of slipped capital femoral epiphysis. *Clin Orthop* 1974;103:16–17.

Sellers DS, Sowa DT, Moore JR, Weiland AJ. Congenital pseudoarthrosis of the forearm. *J Hand Surg [Am]* 1988;13A:89–93.

Shingade VU, Song H-R, Lee S-H, et al. The sagging rope sign in achondroplasia – different from Perthes' disease. *Skeletal Radiol* 2006;35:923–928.

Siebenrock KA, Schöll E, Lottenbach M, Ganz R. Bernese periacetabular osteotomy. *Clin Orthop* 1999;363:9–20.

Sohn C, Lenz GP, Thies M. 3-dimensional ultrasound image of the infant hip. *Ultraschall Med* 1990;11:302–305.

Sprengel W. Die angeborne Verschiebung des Schulterblattes nach oben. *Arch Klin Chir* 1891;42:545.

Steel HH. Triple osteotomy of the innominate bone. *J Bone Joint Surg [Am]* 1973;55A:343–350.

Stulberg SD, Cooperman DR, Wallensten R. The natural history of Legg-Calvé-Perthes disease. *J Bone Joint Surg [Am]* 1981;63A:1095–1108.

Sutherland DH, Greenfield R. Double innominate osteotomy. *J Bone Joint Surg [Am]* 1977;59A:1082–1091.

Tachdjian MO. *Congenital dislocation of the hip*. New York: Churchill Livingstone; 1982:20–25.

Takakura Y, Tanaka Y, Kumai T, Sugimoto K. Development of the ball-and-socket ankle as assessed by radiography and arthrography. A long-term follow-up report. *J Bone Joint Surg [Br]* 1999;81B:1001–1004.

Taniguchi A, Tanaka Y, Kadono K, Takakura Y, Kurumatani N. C sign for diagnosis of talocalcaneal coalition. *Radiology* 2003;228:501–505.

Terjesen T, Rundén TO, Johnsen HM. Ultrasound in the diagnosis of congenital dysplasia and dislocation of the hip joints in children older than two years. *Clin Orthop* 1991;262:159–169.

Tillema DA, Golding JSR. Chondrolysis following slipped capital femoral epiphysis in Jamaica. *J Bone Joint Surg [Am]* 1971;53A:1528–1540.

Tönnis D. Normal values of the hip joint for the evaluation of x-rays in children and adults. *Clin Orthop* 1976;119:39–47.

Trevor D. Tarso-epiphyseal aclasis: a congenital error of epiphyseal development. *J Bone Joint Surg [Br]* 1950;32B:204–213.

Trueta J. Normal vascular anatomy of the human femoral head during growth. *J Bone Joint Surg [Br]* 1957;39B:358.

Waldenström H. The first stages of coxa plana. *J Bone Joint Surg* 1938;20:559–566.

Walters R, Simons S. Joint destruction—a sequel of unrecognized pin penetrations in patients with slipped capital femoral epiphysis. In: *The Hip Society: Proceedings of the 8th Open Scientific Meeting*. St. Louis: CV Mosby; 1980:145.

Wechsler RJ, Karasick D, Schweitzer ME. Computed tomography of talocalcaneal coalition: imaging techniques. *Skeletal Radiol* 1992;21:353–358.

Wechsler RJ, Schweitzer ME, Deely DM, et al. Tarsal coalition: depiction and characterization with CT and MR imaging. *Radiology* 1994;193:447–452.

Weinstein SL. Natural history of congenital hip dislocation (CDH) and hip dysplasia. *Clin Orthop* 1987;225:62–76.

Wenger DR, Bomar JD. Human hip dysplasia: evolution of current treatment concepts. *J Orthop Sci* 2003;8:264–271.

Scoliosis and Anomalies with General Affliction of the Skeleton

Scoliosis

Regardless of its cause (Fig. 33.1), scoliosis is defined as a lateral curvature of the spine occurring in the coronal plane. This fact differentiates it from kyphosis, a posterior curvature of the spine in the sagittal plane, and lordosis, an anterior curvature of the spine also in the sagittal plane (Fig. 33.2). If the curve occurs in both coronal and sagittal planes, then the deformity is called kyphoscoliosis. Besides a lateral curvature, scoliosis may also have a rotational component in which vertebrae rotate toward the convexity of the curve.

Idiopathic Scoliosis

Idiopathic scoliosis, which constitutes almost 70% of all scoliotic abnormalities, can be classified into three groups. The *infantile* type, of which there are two variants, occurs in children younger than age 4 years; it is seen predominantly in boys, and the curvature usually occurs in the thoracic segment with its convexity to the left. In the *resolving* (benign) variant, the curve commonly does not increase beyond 30 degrees and resolves spontaneously, requiring no treatment. The *progressive* variant carries a poor prognosis, with the potential for severe deformity unless aggressive treatment is initiated early in the process. *Juvenile idiopathic scoliosis* occurs equally in boys and girls from the ages of 4 to 9 years. By far, the most common type of idiopathic scoliosis, comprising 85% of cases, is the *adolescent* form, seen predominantly in girls from 10 years of age to the time of skeletal maturity. The thoracic or thoracolumbar spine is most often involved, and the convexity of the curve is to the right (Fig. 33.3). Although the cause of this type is unknown, it has been postulated that a genetic factor may be at work and that idiopathic scoliosis is a familial disorder.

Congenital Scoliosis

Congenital scoliosis is responsible for 10% of the cases of this deformity. It may generally be classified into three groups, according to MacEwen (Fig. 33.4): those resulting from a *failure in vertebral formation*, which may be partial or complete (Fig. 33.5); those caused by a *failure in vertebral segmentation*, which may be asymmetric and unilateral or symmetric and bilateral; and those resulting from a *combination* of the first two. The effects of congenital scoliosis on balance and support result in faulty biomechanics throughout the skeletal system.

Miscellaneous Scolioses

Several other forms of scoliosis having a specific cause may develop, including neuromuscular, traumatic, infections, metabolic, and secondary to tumors, among others. Their discussion is beyond the scope of this text.

Radiologic Evaluation

The radiographic examination of scoliosis includes standing anteroposterior and lateral radiographs of the entire spine; a supine anteroposterior film centered over the scoliotic curve (see Figs. 33.3 and 33.5), which is used for the various measurements of spinal curvature and vertebral rotation (discussed below); and anteroposterior radiographs obtained with the patient bending laterally to each side for evaluation of the flexible and structural components of the curve. Care should be taken to include the iliac crests in at least one of these radiographs for a determination of skeletal maturity (see Figs. 33.14 and 33.15).

Ancillary techniques, such as computed tomography (CT), may be required for evaluating congenital lesions such as segmentation failures. Intravenous urography (pyelography, IVP) is essential in congenital scoliosis for evaluating the presence of associated anomalies of the genitourinary tract (Fig. 33.6). Magnetic resonance imaging (MRI) is the technique of choice to evaluate associated abnormalities of the spinal cord and the nerve roots.

An overview of the radiographic projections and radiologic techniques used in the evaluation of scoliosis is presented in Table 33.1.

Measurements

To evaluate the various types of scoliosis, certain terms (Fig. 33.7) and measurements must be introduced. Measurement of the severity of a scoliotic curve has practical application not only in the selection of patients for surgical treatment but also in monitoring the results of corrective therapy. Two widely accepted methods of measuring the curve are the Lippman-Cobb (Fig. 33.8) and Risser-Ferguson techniques (Fig. 33.9). The measurements obtained by these methods, however, are not comparable. The values yielded by the Lippman-Cobb method, which determines the angle of curvature only by the ends of the scoliotic curve, depending solely on the inclination of the end vertebrae, are usually greater than those given by the Risser-Ferguson method. This also applies to the percentages of correction as determined by the two methods; the more favorable correction percentage is obtained by the

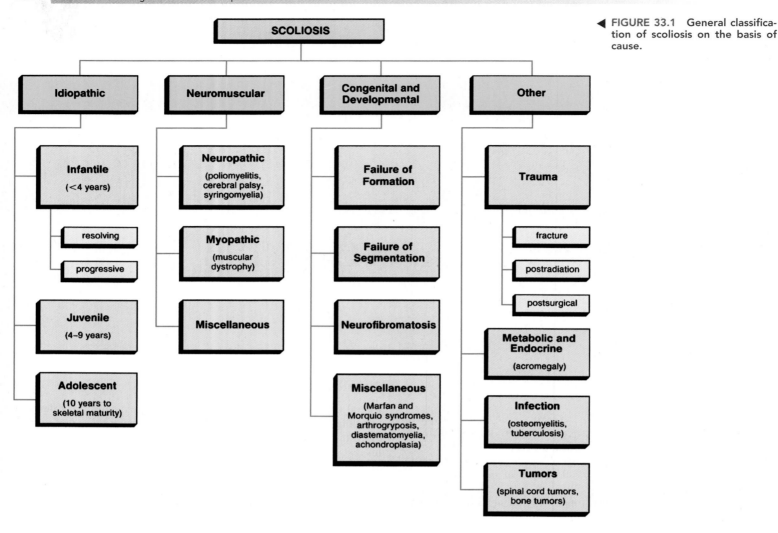

◄ FIGURE 33.1 General classification of scoliosis on the basis of cause.

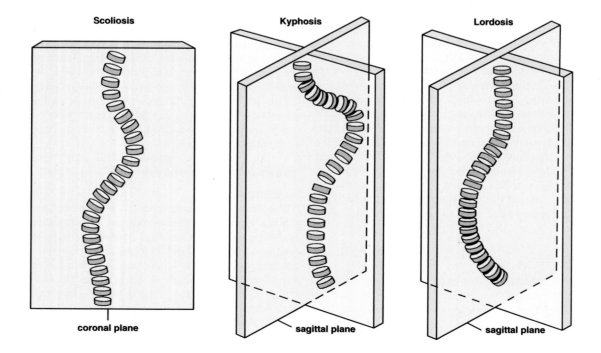

▲

FIGURE 33.2   Definitions. Scoliosis is a lateral curvature of the spine in the coronal (frontal) plane. Kyphosis is a posterior curvature of the spine and lordosis an anterior curvature, both occurring in the sagittal (lateral) plane.

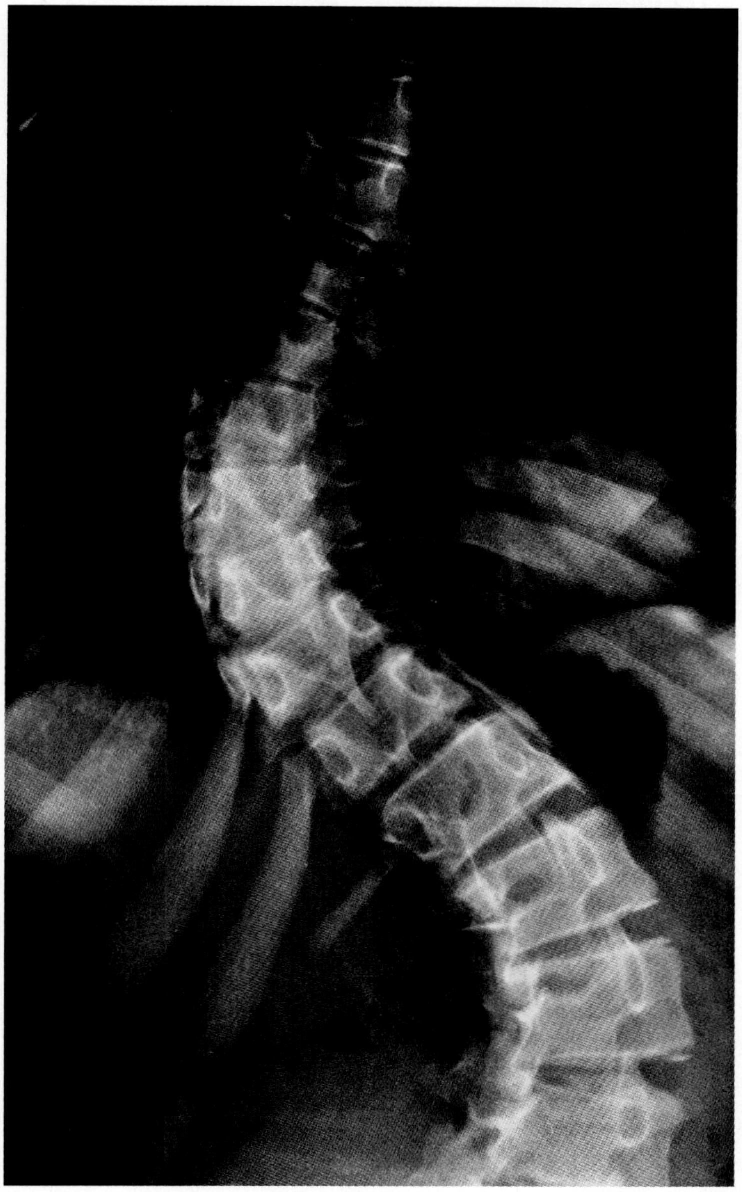

CONGENITAL SCOLIOSIS

Failure of Formation

partial—wedged vertebra   **complete—hemivertebra**

Failure of Segmentation   ### Miscellaneous

unilateral—   **bilateral—**   **combined failures**
unsegmented bar   **block vertebra**   **of formation and**
                                                 segmentation—block
                                                 vertebra associated
                                                 with hemivertebra

FIGURE 33.3 Idiopathic scoliosis. Anteroposterior radiograph of the spine of a 15-year-old girl shows the typical features of idiopathic scoliosis involving the thoracolumbar segment. The convexity of the curve is to the right; a compensatory curve in the lumbar segment has its convexity to the left.

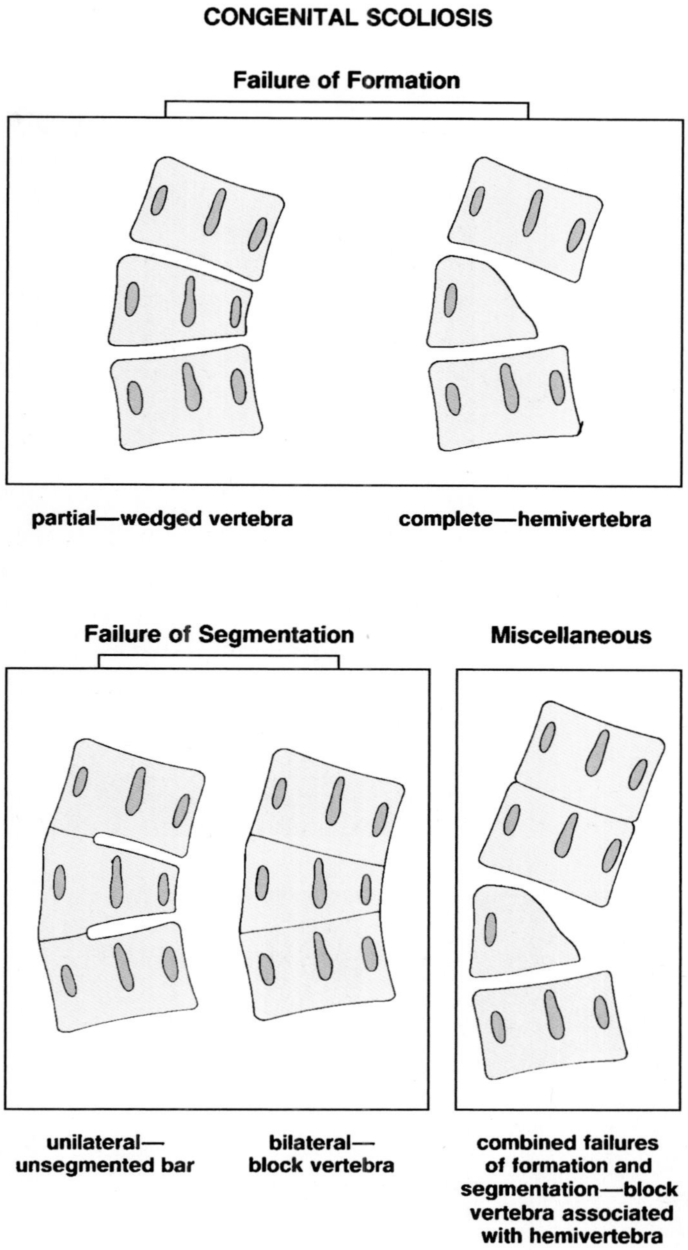

FIGURE 33.4 Classification of congenital scoliosis on the basis of cause. (Modified from MacEwen GD et al., 1968; Winter RB et al., 1968.)

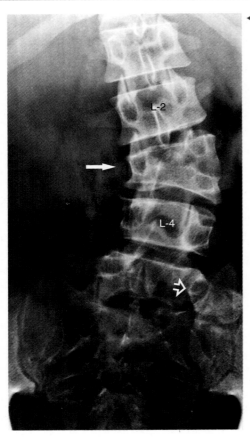

◀ **FIGURE 33.5 Congenital scoliosis.** Anteroposterior radiograph of the lumbosacral spine of a 22-year-old man demonstrates scoliosis caused by hemivertebra, a complete unilateral failure of formation. Note the deformed L3 vertebra (*arrow*) secondary to the faulty fusion of the hemivertebra on the left side, where two pedicles are evident. The resulting scoliosis has its convex border to the left. An associated anomaly is also apparent from the presence of the so-called transitional lumbosacral vertebra (*open arrow*).

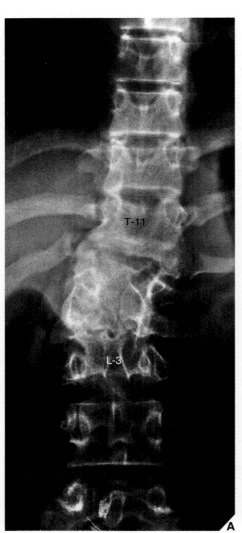
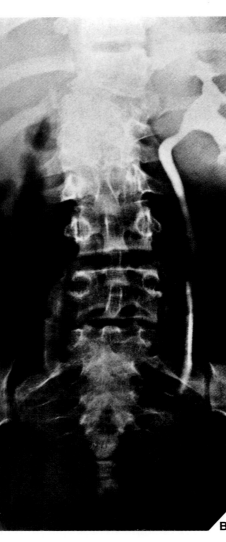

◀ **FIGURE 33.6 Congenital scoliosis. (A)** Supine anteroposterior radiograph of the thoracolumbar spine of a 13-year-old girl shows congenital scoliosis secondary to block vertebrae consisting of a fusion of T12-L2. **(B)** IVP demonstrates only the left kidney, an example of renal agenesis. Congenital scoliosis is frequently associated with urinary tract anomalies.

TABLE 33.1 **Standard Radiographic Projections and Radiologic Techniques for Evaluating Scoliosis**

Projection/Technique	Demostration	Projection/Technique	Demostration
Anteroposterior	Lateral deviation	*Computed Tomography*	Congenital fusion of vertebrae
	Angle of scoliosis (by Risser-Ferguson and Lippman-Cobb methods and scoliotic index)		Hemivertebrae
		Myelography	Tethering of cord
		Magnetic Resonance Imaging	Abnormalities of nerve roots
	Vertebral rotation (by Cobb and Moe methods)		Compression and displacement of thecal sac
of vertebra	Ossification of ring apophysis as determinant of skeletal maturity		Tethering of cord
of pelvis	Ossification of iliac crest apophysis as determinant of skeletal maturity	*Intravenous Urography* *Ultrasound*	Associated anomalies of genitourinary tract (in congenital scoliosis)
lateral bending	Flexibility of curve		
	Amount of reduction of curve		
Lateral	Associated kyphosis and lordosis		

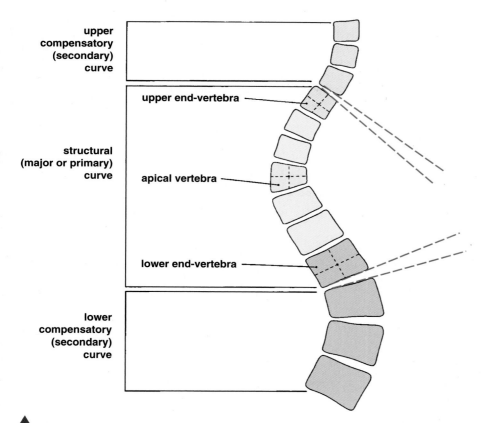

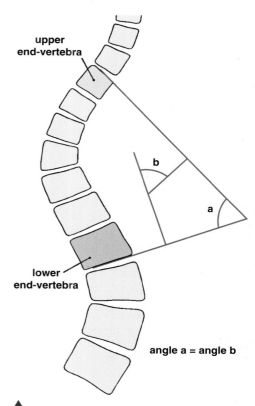

▲

FIGURE 33.7 Terminology used in describing the scoliotic curve. The end vertebrae of the curve are defined as those that tilt maximally into the concavity of the structural curve. The apical vertebra, which shows the most severe rotation and wedging, is the one whose center is most laterally displaced from the central line. The center of the apical vertebra is determined by the intersection of two lines, one drawn from the center of the upper and lower end plates and the other from the center of the lateral margins of the vertebral body. The center should not be determined by diagonal lines through the corners of the vertebral body.

▲

FIGURE 33.8 Lippman-Cobb method. In the Lippman-Cobb method of measuring the degree of scoliotic curvature, two angles are formed by the intersection of two sets of lines. The first set of lines, one drawn tangent to the superior surface of the upper end vertebra and the other tangent to the inferior surface of the lower end vertebra, intersects to form angle (a). The intersection of the other set of lines, each drawn perpendicular to the tangential lines, forms angle (b). These angles are equal, and either may serve as the measurement of the degree of scoliosis.

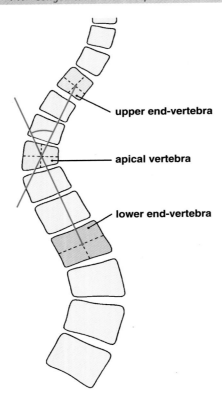

▲
FIGURE 33.9 **Risser-Ferguson method.** In the Risser-Ferguson method, the degree of scoliotic curvature is determined by the angle formed by the intersection of two lines at the center of the apical vertebra, the first line originating at the center of the upper end vertebra and the other at the center of the lower end vertebra.

Lippman-Cobb method. The latter method, which has been adopted and standardized by the Scoliosis Research Society, classifies the severity of scoliotic curvature into seven groups (Table 33.2).

Another technique for measuring the degree of scoliosis, introduced by Greenspan and colleagues in 1978, uses a "scoliotic index." Designed to give a more accurate and comprehensive representation of the scoliotic curve, this technique measures the deviation of each involved vertebra from the vertical spinal line as determined by points at the center of the vertebra immediately above the upper end vertebra of the curve and at the center of the vertebra immediately below the lower end vertebra (Fig. 33.10). Its most valuable feature is that it minimizes the influence of overcorrection of the end vertebrae in the measured angle, a frequent criticism of the Lippman-Cobb technique. Furthermore, short segments or minimal curvatures, often difficult to measure with the currently accepted methods, are easily measurable with this technique.

Recently, computerized methods for measuring and analyzing the scoliotic curve have been introduced. Although more accurate than the

manual methods, they require more sophisticated equipment and are more time consuming than the methods described above.

In addition to the measurement of scoliotic curvature, the radiographic evaluation of scoliosis also requires the determination of other factors. Measurement of the degree of *rotation of the vertebrae* of the involved segment can be obtained by either of two methods currently in use. The Cobb technique for grading rotation uses the position of the spinous process as a point of reference (Fig. 33.11). On the normal anteroposterior radiograph of the spine, the spinous process appears at the center of the vertebral body if there is no rotation. As the degree of rotation increases, the spinous process migrates toward the convexity of the curve. The Moe method, also based on the measurements obtained on the anteroposterior projection of the spine, uses the symmetry of the pedicles as a point of reference, with the migration of the pedicles toward the convexity of the curve determining the degree of vertebral rotation (Fig. 33.12).

The final factor in the evaluation of scoliosis is the determination of *skeletal maturity*. This is important for both the prognosis and treatment of scoliosis, particularly the idiopathic type, because there is a potential for significant progression of the degree of curvature as long as skeletal maturity has not been reached. Skeletal age can be determined by comparison of a radiograph of a patient's hand with the standards for different ages available in radiographic atlases. It can also be assessed by radiographic observation of the ossification of the apophysis of the vertebral ring (Fig. 33.13) or, as is often performed, from the ossification of the iliac apophysis (Figs. 33.14 and 33.15).

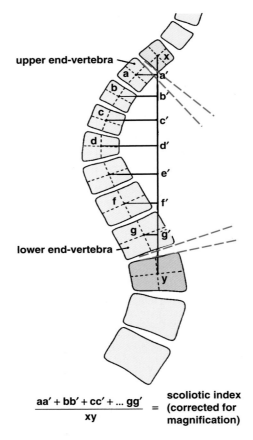

$$\frac{aa' + bb' + cc' + \ldots gg'}{xy} = \begin{array}{l}\text{scoliotic index} \\ \text{(corrected for} \\ \text{magnification)}\end{array}$$

▲
FIGURE 33.10 **Scoliotic index.** In the measurement of scoliosis using the scoliotic index, each vertebra (a–g) is considered an integral part of the curve. A vertical spinal line (xy) is first determined whose endpoints are the centers of the vertebrae immediately above and below the upper and lower end-vertebrae of the curve. Lines are then drawn from the center of each vertebral body perpendicular to the vertical spinal line (aa', bb',... gg'). The values yielded by these lines represent the linear deviation of each vertebra; their sum, divided by the length of the vertical line (xy) to correct for radiographic magnification, yields the scoliotic index. A value of zero denotes a straight spine; the higher the scoliotic index, the more severe the scoliosis.

TABLE 33.2 **Lippman-Cobb Classification of Scoliotic Curvature**

Group	Angle of Curvature (Degrees)
I	<20
II	21–30
III	31–50
IV	51–75
V	76–100
VI	101–125
VII	>125

COBB SPINOUS-PROCESS METHOD FOR DETERMINING VERTEBRAL ROTATION

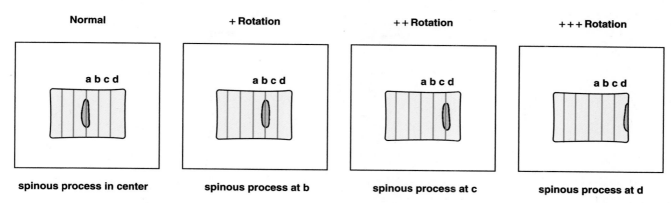

FIGURE 33.11   Cobb spinous-process method. In the Cobb spinous-process method for determining rotation, the vertebra is divided into six equal parts. Normally, the spinous process appears at the center. Its migration to certain points toward the convexity of the curve marks the degree of rotation.

MOE PEDICLE METHOD FOR DETERMINING VERTEBRAL ROTATION

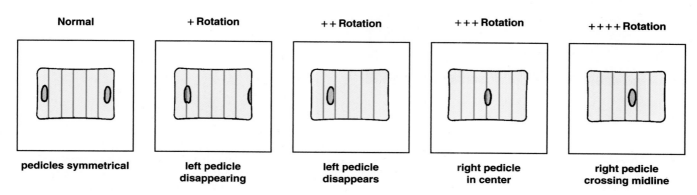

FIGURE 33.12   Moe pedicle method. The Moe pedicle method for determining rotation divides the vertebra into six equal parts. Normally, the pedicles appear in the outer parts. Migration of a pedicle to certain points toward the convexity of the curve determines the degree of rotation.

FIGURE 33.13   Skeletal maturity. Determination ▶ of skeletal maturity from ossification of the vertebral ring apophysis.

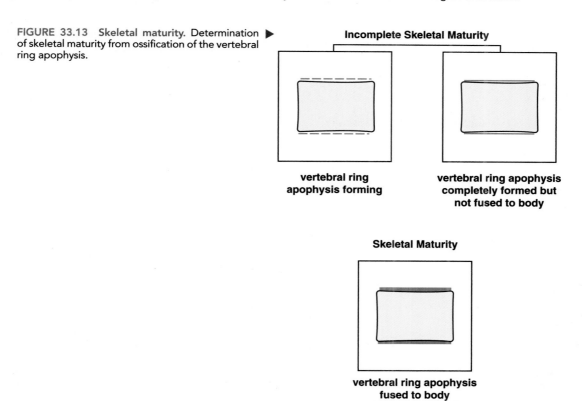

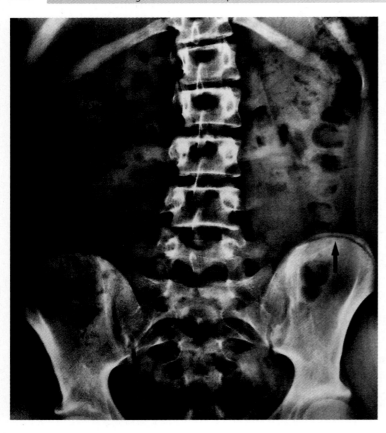

◀ FIGURE 33.14 **Skeletal maturity.** The ossification of the iliac apophysis is helpful in determining skeletal age. Progression of the apophysis in this 14-year-old girl with idiopathic scoliosis has been completed, but the lack of fusion with the iliac crest (*arrows*) indicates continuing skeletal maturation.

Treatment

Various surgical procedures are available for the treatment of scoliosis. The main objective of surgery is to balance and fuse the spine to prevent the deformity from progressing; its secondary objective is to correct the scoliotic curve to the extent of its flexibility. Determining the level of fusion depends on several factors, including the cause of the scoliosis and the age of the patient, as well as the pattern of the scoliotic curve and the extent of vertebral rotation as evaluated during the radiographic examination of the patient.

Spinal fusion is now commonly accompanied by internal fixation of the spine to provide stability. One of the most popular methods for internal fixation is the Harrington-Luque technique (Wisconsin segmental instrumentation), using square-ended distraction rods and wire loops inserted through the bases of the spinous processes and connected to two contoured paravertebral rods (Fig. 33.16). The procedure involves decortication of the laminae and spinous processes, obliteration of the posterior facet joints by removal of the cartilage, and the placement of an autogenous bone graft from the iliac crest along the concave side of the curve. The hooks of the distraction rods are inserted under the laminae at the upper and lower ends of the curve. The prebent stainless-steel paravertebral rods (Luque rods or L-rods) are anchored into the spinous process or pelvis, depending on the location of the curve; wires, passed through the base of the spinous process at each level of the spine to be fused, are

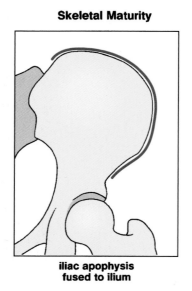

Incomplete Skeletal Maturity   **Skeletal Maturity**

iliac apophysis
progressing medially

iliac apophysis completely
formed but not fused to ilium

iliac apophysis
fused to ilium

▲ FIGURE 33.15 **Skeletal maturity.** Determination of skeletal maturity from the status of ossification of the iliac apophysis.

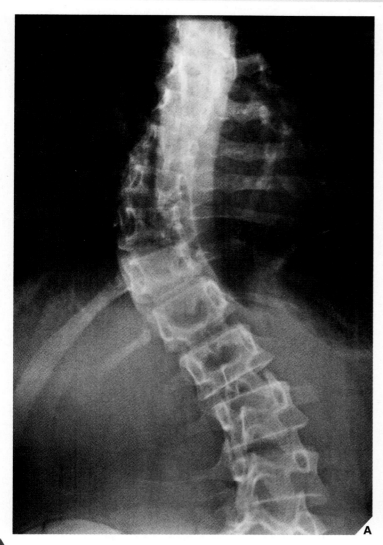
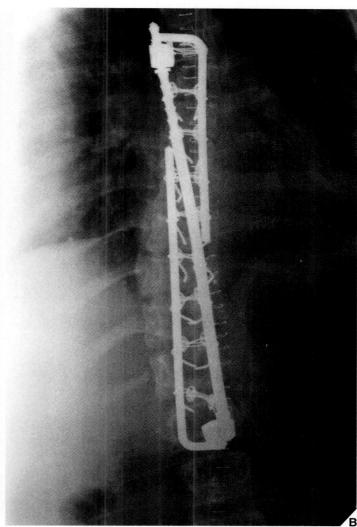

FIGURE 33.16 Treatment of scoliosis. (A) Preoperative anteroposterior radiograph of the lumbar spine in a 15-year-old girl shows idiopathic dextroscoliosis. **(B)** Postoperative film shows the placement of the Harrington distractor and two Luque rods. Note the multiple sublaminar wires fixed into the prebent L-rods.

then fixed to the L-rods. Variations in this technique have been used with L-rod instrumentation alone, which involves the use of sublaminar wires fixed to the rods, or a combination of Harrington distractors and wires fixed to them. Cotrel-Dubousset spinal instrumentation using knurled rods has also gained popularity. Fixation is achieved via pediculotransverse double-hook purchase at several levels. The two knurled rods are additionally stabilized by two transverse traction devices. The Dwyer technique, involving anterior fixation of the spine and obliteration of the intervertebral disks, is also used in the surgical treatment of scoliosis but more often in the paralytic types of the deformity.

The postoperative radiographic evaluation of internal fixation by the Harrington-Luque technique should focus on (a) whether the hooks of the Harrington rod are properly anchored with their brackets on the laminae of the superior and inferior vertebrae of the fused segment; (b) whether a hook has separated or been displaced; and (c) whether the rods and wires are intact. Moreover, evidence of pseudoarthrosis of the fused vertebrae should be sought when the postoperative loss of correction exceeds 10 degrees; a range of 6 to 10 degrees of loss of correction is ordinarily seen. The evaluation of pseudoarthrosis may require CT in addition to the conventional radiography. CT may also be needed within 6 to 9 months after surgery to demonstrate suspected nonunion of the bone engrafted on the concave side of the curve. Union of the graft with the spinal segment should appear solid; tomography may demonstrate radiolucent defects suggesting nonunion. Other complications involving the instrumentation may occur, such as fracture of a distraction rod or of

a wire cable or screw, or excessive bending of the rods. Usually, these are easily demonstrated on conventional radiographs.

Anomalies with General Affliction of the Skeleton

Table 33.3 presents an overview of radiographic projections and radiologic techniques most effective for evaluating congenital and developmental anomalies with general affliction of the skeleton.

Neurofibromatosis

Originally considered a disorder of neurogenic tissue (nerve-trunk tumors), neurofibromatosis (also called von Recklinghausen disease) is now believed to be a hereditary dysplasia that may involve almost every organ system of the body. Neurofibromatosis type 1 is transmitted as an autosomal-dominant trait, with more than 50% of cases reporting a family history. The condition is caused by a mutation or deletion of the *NF1* gene located on the long arm of chromosome 17 (17q11.2) whose product, a protein neurofibromin (a GTPase-activating enzyme), serves as a tumor suppressor. Mutations in the *NF1* gene lead to the production of a nonfunctional version of this protein that cannot regulate the cell growth and division. Sessile or pedunculated skin lesions (mollusca fibrosa) are an almost constant finding, and café-au-lait spots, that may be present at

TABLE 33.3 **Most Effective Radiographic Projections and Radiologic Techniques for Evaluating Common Anomalies with General Affliction of the Skeleton**

Projection/Technique	Crucial Abnormalities	Projection/Technique	Crucial Abnormalities
Arthrogryposis		*Morquio-Brailsford Disease*	
Anteroposterior, lateral, and oblique of affected joints	Multiple subluxations and dislocations Fat-like lucency of soft tissues Cubital and popliteal webbing	Anteroposterior and lateral of spine Anteroposterior of pelvis of hips	Oval or hook-shaped vertebrae with central beak Overconstriction of iliac bodies Wide iliac flaring Dysplasia of proximal femora
Down Syndrome		*Hurler Syndrome*	
Anteroposterior of pelvis and hips of ribs	Hip dysplasia 11 pairs of ribs	Anteroposterior and lateral	Rounding and lower beaking of vertebral bodies
Dorsovolar of both hands	Clinodactyly and hypoplasia of fifth fingers	of spine	Recessed hooked vertebra at apex of kyphoscoliotic curve
Lateral of cervical spine Tomography (lateral) of cervical spine (C1, C2)	Atlantoaxial subluxation Hypoplastic odontoid	of skull	Frontal bossing Synostosis of sagittal and lamdoidal sutures Thickening of calvarium J-shaped sella turcica
Neurofibromatosis		Anteroposterior of pelvis	Flaring of iliac wings
Anteroposterior, lateral, and oblique of long bones	Pit-like erosions Pseudoarthrosis of distal tibia and fibula		Constriction of inferior portion of iliac body Shallow, obliquely oriented acetabula
Anteroposterior of ribs	Rib notching	*Osteopetrosis*	
of lower cervical/upper thoracic spine	Scoliosis Kyphoscoliosis	Anteroposterior and lateral of long bones of spine	Increased density (osteosclerosis) Bone-in-bone appearance "Rugger-jersey" vertebral bodies
Oblique of cervical spine Lateral of thoracic/lumbar spine	Enlarged neural foramina Posterior vertebral scalloping	Anteroposterior of pelvis	Ring-like pattern of normal and abnormal bone in ilium
Myelography	Intraspinal neurofibromas Increased volume of enlarged subarachnoid space Localized dural ectasia	*Pyknodysostosis*	
		Anteroposterior and lateral of long bones	Increased density (osteosclerosis)
Computed tomography	Complications (e.g., sarcomatous	Dorsovolar of hands	Resorption of terminal tufts (acro-osteolysis)
Magnetic resonance imaging	degeneration)	Lateral of skull	Wormian bones Persistence of anterior and posterior fontanelles Obtuse (fetal) angle of mandible
Osteogenesis imperfecta			
Anteroposterior, lateral, and oblique of affected bones	Osteoporosis Bowing deformitites Trumpet-like metaphysis Fractures	*Osteopoikilosis*	
		Anteroposterior of affected bones	Dense spots at the articular ends of long bones
Lateral of skull Anteroposterior and lateral of thoracic/lumbar spine	Wormian bones Kyphoscoliosis	*Osteopathia Striata*	
		Anteroposterior of affected bones	Dense striations, particularly in metaphysis
Achondroplasia		*Progressive Diaphyseal Dysplasia*	
Anteroposterior of upper and lower extremities	Shortening of tubular bones, particularly humeri and femora	Anteroposterior of long bones (particularly lower limbs)	Symmetric fusiform thickening of cortex Sparing of epiphyses
of pelvis	Rounded iliac bones Horizontal orientation of acetabular roofs Small sciatic notches	*Melorheostosis*	
of spine	Narrowing of interpedicular distance	Anteroposterior and lateral of affected bones	Asymmetric, wavy hyperostosis (like dripping candle wax) Ossifications of periarticular soft tissues
Lateral of spine	Short pedicles Posterior scalloping of vertebral bodies		
Dorsovolar of hands	Short, stubby fingers Separation of middle finger ("trident" appearance)		
Computed tomography	Spinal stenosis		

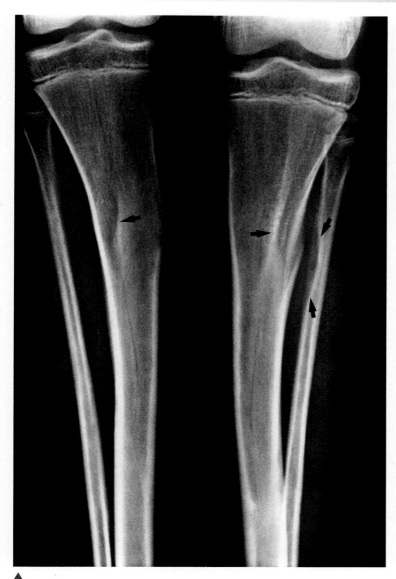

FIGURE 33.17 **Neurofibromatosis.** Anteroposterior radiograph of the lower legs of an 11-year-old girl shows pit-like erosions in the proximal tibiae and fibulae (*arrows*), a common finding in this condition.

(see Fig. 19.6). Whittling of the bones is also a typical feature of neurofibromatosis (Fig. 33.19).

The spine is the second most common site of skeletal abnormalities in neurofibromatosis. Scoliosis or kyphoscoliosis, which characteristically involves a short segment of the vertebral column with acute angulation, commonly occurs in the lower cervical or upper thoracic spine. Widening of the intervertebral foramina in the cervical segment may also occur, resulting from dumbbell-shaped neurofibromas arising in spinal nerve roots (Fig. 33.20). In the thoracic and lumbar segments, scalloping of the posterior border of vertebral bodies is another characteristic feature (Fig. 33.21). Although most of these abnormalities can easily be diagnosed with conventional radiography, some ancillary techniques may be useful. Myelography is particularly valuable for demonstrating the increased volume of the enlarged subarachnoid space and the localized dural ectasia extending into the scalloped defects in the

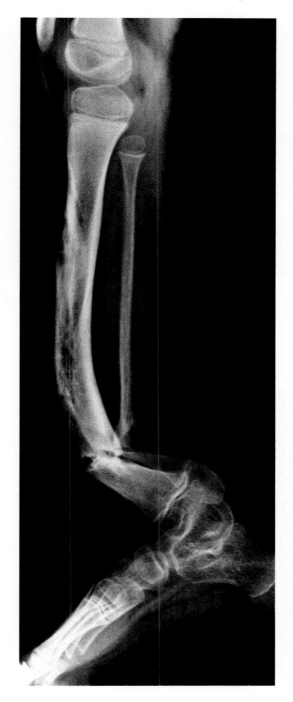

FIGURE 33.18 **Neurofibromatosis.** Lateral radiograph of the right lower leg of an 11-year-old boy with generalized disease demonstrates anterior bowing of the distal tibia and fibula, associated with pseudoarthrosis. Note the pressure erosions in the middle third of the tibial diaphysis.

birth or may appear over time, occur in more than 90% of patients. The latter lesions have a smooth border that has been likened to the coast of California; this distinguishes them from the café-au-lait spots seen in fibrous dysplasia, which have rugged "coast of Maine" borders. These spots increase in size and number as the person grows older. Axillary or inguinal freckles are rare at birth, but appear throughout childhood and adolescence. Plexiform neurofibromatosis is a diffuse involvement of the nerves, associated with elephantoid masses of soft tissue (elephantiasis neuromatosa) and localized or generalized enlargement of a part or all of a limb. Patients with these manifestations are particularly prone to malignant tumors (see Fig. 22.35).

Skeletal abnormalities are often encountered in neurofibromatosis; at least 50% of patients demonstrate some osseous changes, most commonly extrinsic, pit-like cortical erosions resulting from direct pressure by adjacent neurofibromas. This is commonly seen in the long bones (Fig. 33.17) and ribs. The long bones often exhibit bowing deformities, and pseudoarthroses, seen in approximately 10% of cases, most commonly occur in the lower tibia and fibula (Fig. 33.18). This type of false joint formation must be differentiated from congenital pseudoarthrosis. Moreover, the long bones are the site of lesions that were once considered to represent intraosseous neurofibromas; these cyst-like radiolucencies are now regarded as lesions representing fibrous cortical defects and nonossifying fibromas, associated with neurofibromatosis

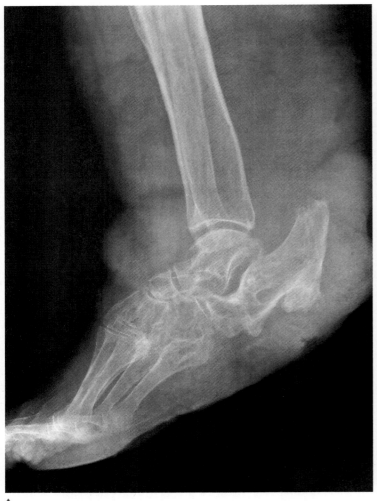

▲

FIGURE 33.19 Plexiform neurofibromatosis. Lateral radiograph of the lower leg and foot of a 37-year-old woman shows whittling of the calcaneus and marked hypertrophy of the soft tissues (elephantiasis).

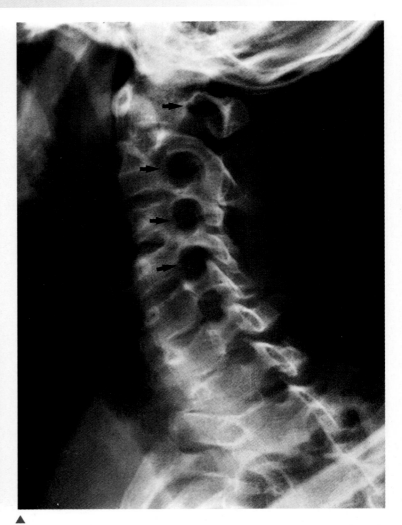

▲

FIGURE 33.20 Neurofibromatosis. Oblique radiograph of the cervical spine of a 26-year-old man demonstrates widening of the upper neural foramina (*arrows*) secondary to "dumbbell" neurofibromas arising in the spinal nerve roots.

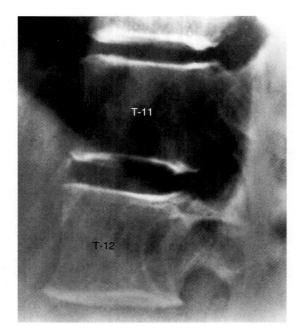

▲

FIGURE 33.21 Neurofibromatosis. Lateral spot-film of the lower thoracic spine in a 29-year-old woman shows scalloping of the posterior border of the T12 vertebra, a common manifestation of this condition.

vertebral bodies; with the introduction of MRI, this modality became more prevalent in investigation of the aforementioned abnormalities.

Neurofibromatosis type 2 is autosomal-dominant disorder with a high penetrance caused by mutation of an *NF2* gene located on the chromosome 22 (22q12.2), which regulates the production of a tumor-suppressor protein merlin (for **m**oezin-**e**zrin-**r**adixin-**li**ke prote**in**), also reffered to as schwannomin. Type 2 of neurofibromatosis is characterized by multiple schwannomas, meningiomas, and ependymomas.

Osteogenesis Imperfecta

Osteogenesis imperfecta (OI), also known as fragilitas ossium, is a congenital, non–sex-linked, hereditary disorder that manifests in the skeleton as a primary defect in the bone matrix. It is characterized by bone fragility resulting from abnormal quality and/or quantity of type I collagen. Depending on the type of OI, the inheritance of the disorder can be autosomal-dominant, autosomal dominant with new mutation, or autosomal recessive. Recently it has been suggested that this disease results from mutations in the genes *COL1A1, COL1A2, CRTAP,* and *LEPRE1.* Looser, in 1906, divided this condition into two forms, "congenita" and "tarda," and suggested that they are expressions of the same disease. OI congenita (Vrolik disease) has been classified as the more severe form, which is evident at birth and marked by bowing of the upper and lower extremities in an infant who is either stillborn or does not survive the neonatal period. The more benign OI tarda (Ekman-Lobstein disease), in which there is a normal life expectancy, may show fractures present at birth, but these more often appear later in infancy. This condition is also associated with other manifestations, such as deformities of the extremities, blue sclerae, laxity of ligaments, and dental abnormalities.

Classification

In general, four major clinical features characterize OI: (a) osteoporosis with abnormal bone fragility; (b) blue sclera; (c) defective dentition (dentinogenesis imperfecta); and (d) presenile onset of hearing impairment. Other clinical features also may be seen, among them ligamentous laxity and hypermobility of joints, short stature, easy bruising, hyperplastic scars, and abnormal temperature regulation. The earlier classification of OI into two types, congenita and tarda, failed to reflect the complexity and heterogenous nature of this disorder. The new classification proposed by Sillence and colleagues in 1979, and later revised, is based on phenotypic features and the mode of inheritance. Currently, four major types of OI and their subtypes are recognized:

Type I   This most common type of the disorder is a relatively mild form, with autosomal-dominant inheritance. Bone fragility is mild to moderate and osteoporosis is invariably present. Sclera are distinctly blue and hearing loss or impairment is a common feature. Stature is normal or near normal. Wormian bones are present. The two subtypes are distinguished by the presence of normal teeth (subtype IA) or dentinogenesis imperfecta (subtype IB).

Type II   This is the fetal or perinatal lethal form of the disorder. This form demonstrates an autosomal-dominant inheritance with new mutation. The very severe nature of generalized osteoporosis, bone fragility, and severe intrauterine growth retardation results in death in the fetal or early perinatal period. Of those infants who survive, 80% to 90% die by 4 weeks of age. All patients in this group have radiologic features typical of OI. In addition, the sclera are blue and the face has a triangle shape caused by soft craniofacial bones and a beaked nose. The calvarium is large relative to the face, and the skull shows a marked lack of mineralization as well as wormian bones. Limbs are short, broad, and angulated. Three subtypes, A, B, and C, are marked by differences in the appearance of the ribs and the long bones. In subtype A, the long bones are broad and crumpled and the ribs are broad, with continuous beading. In subtype B, the long bones also are broad and crumpled, but the ribs show either discontinuous beading or no beading. Subtype C is characterized by thin fractured long bones and ribs that are thin and beaded.

Type III This is a severe progressive form and represents a rare autosomal-dominant inheritance with new mutations. Bone fragility and osteopenia are considerable, leading with age to multiple fractures and severe progressive deformity of the long bones and spine. Bone abnormalities are generally less severe than in type II and more severe than in types I or IV. Sclera are normal, although pale blue or gray at birth, but the color changes through infancy and early childhood until it is normal by adolescence or adulthood. The calvarium is large, thin, and poorly ossified; wormian bones are present.

Type IV   This is also a rare type of OI and is inherited as an autosomal-dominant trait. Characteristically, osteoporosis, bone fragility, and deformity are present, but they are very mild. Sclera are usually normal. The incidence of hearing impairment is low and is even lower than in type I.

Recently, Glorieux and colleagues added two more types, V and VI, and Ward and associates described in details the rarest form of OI, type VII. Type V includes the patients who originally have been classified as type IV, but had a discrete phenotype including heperplastic callus formation without evidence of mutations in type I collagen, and type VI, that includes the patients who sustained more frequent fractures (particularly of the vertebrae) than those with type IV, first documented between 4 and 18 months of age. Sclerae of these patients were white or faintly blue, and dentinogenesis imperfecta was uniformly absent. Serum alkaline phosphatase levels were elevated compared with age-matched patients with OI type IV. The type VII is an autosomal recessive form,

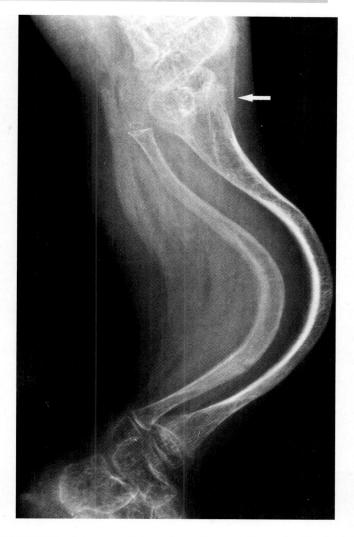

▲ **FIGURE 33.22 Osteogenesis imperfecta.** Lateral radiograph of the leg of a 12-year-old boy with type III disease demonstrates thinning of the cortices and anterior bowing of the tibia and fibula. Note the trumpet-shaped appearance of the tibial metaphysis (*arrow*).

with moderate to severe phenotype, characterized by fractures at birth, blue sclerae, early deformity of the lower extremities, coxa vara, and osteopenia. Rhizomelia is a prominent clinical feature. This form of OI has been localized to chromosome 3p22-24.1, which is outside the loci for type I collagen genes.

Radiologic Evaluation

The radiologic features of OI are easily identified on conventional radiographs. Severe osteoporosis, deformities of the bones, and thinning of the cortices are consistently observed features. The bones are also attenuated and gracile, with a trumpet-shaped appearance to the metaphysis (Fig. 33.22). Other typical skeletal abnormalities are seen in the skull, where wormian bones are a recognizable feature (Fig. 33.23), and in the spine, where severe kyphoscoliosis may develop from a combination of osteoporosis, ligamentous laxity, and posttraumatic deformities (Fig. 33.24). In children with a severe degree of disorder, the metaphyses and epiphyses of the long bones may exhibit numerous scalloped radiolucent areas with sclerotic margins (Fig. 33.25). This appearance is referred to as "popcorn calcifications," and it may be the result of traumatic fragmentation of the growth plate. The pelvis is invariably deformed, and acetabular protrusio is a common finding (Fig. 33.26).

Differential Diagnosis

Occasionally, OI may be misdiagnosed as child abuse and vice versa. Patient and family history, physical examination, diagnostic imaging, and the clinical course of the abnormalities all contribute to the distinction of this condition from child abuse. The keys to distinguishing OI

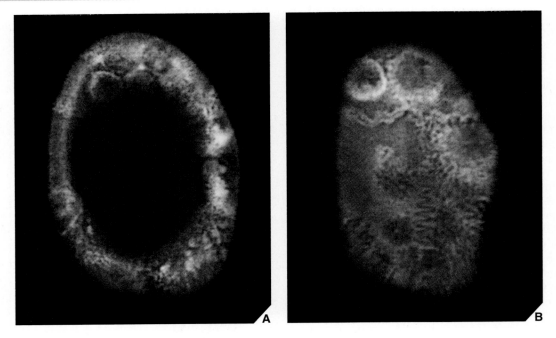

FIGURE 33.23 **CT of osteogenesis imperfecta.** Axial CT sections of the skull (**A**) through the frontal and parietal bones and (**B**) through the vertex show sutural (wormian) bones.

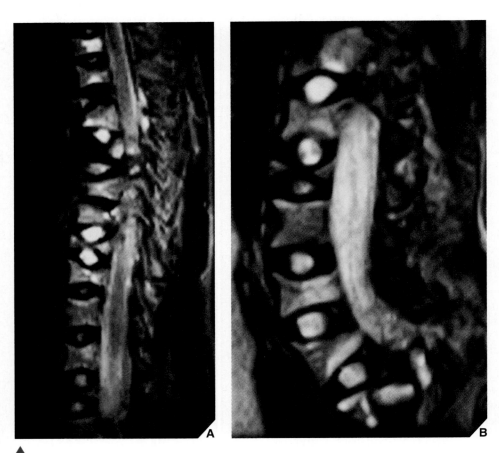

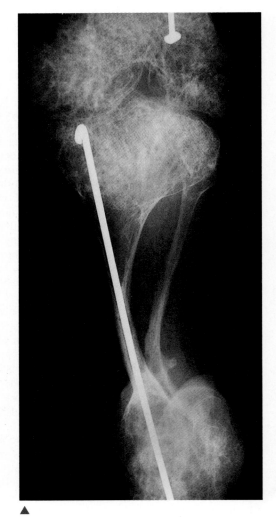

FIGURE 33.24 **MRI of osteogenesis imperfecta. (A)** Sagittal T2-weighted MR image of the thoracic spine of a 13-year-old boy shows compression fractures of several vertebral bodies associated with kyphosis and compression of the spinal cord. (**B**) Sagittal T2-weighted MRI of the lumbar spine demonstrates multiple vertebral fractures and dural ectasia.

FIGURE 33.25 **Osteogenesis imperfecta.** Anteroposterior radiograph of the left leg of a 12-year-old boy with a type III disease shows "popcorn calcifications" at the articular ends of the long bones. A Rush pin has been placed in the tibia because of a pathologic fracture.

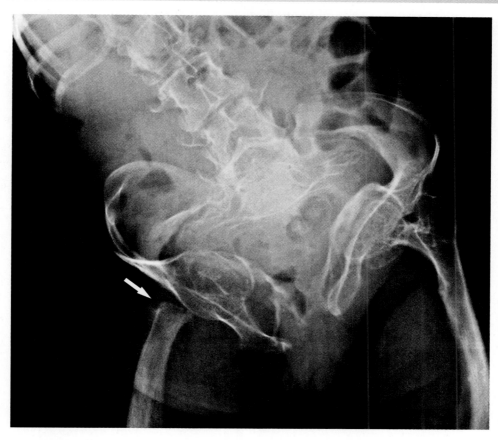

▲
FIGURE 33.26 **Osteogenesis imperfecta.** Marked deformity of the pelvis, seen here in a 27-year-old woman, is a consistent finding in OI tarda. Note the bilateral acetabular protrusio and the pathologic fracture of the right femur (*arrow*).

from a battered child syndrome ("shaken baby syndrome," parent-infant trauma syndrome) are (a) the presence of blue sclera or abnormal teeth in OI; (b) investigation of clinical and family history (invariably positive in OI); (c) physical examination; and (d) radiologic examination for the detection of wormian bones and osteoporosis in OI, and metaphyseal corner fractures and "bucket-handle" fractures that are highly specific and virtually pathognomonic features of child abuse. Several other features are also specific for child abuse, including multiple rib fractures, especially posterior rib fractures near or at the costovertebral junction; multiple fractures and/or multiple fractures showing different stages of healing; and sternal or scapular fractures, especially of the acromion. Transverse, oblique, or spiral fractures of a long bone with normal mineralization in the absence of any previous history, especially in a non-ambulatory infant, are also highly suggestive of child abuse. The key to diagnosis of either condition is the correlation of clinical history, physical examination, family history, and imaging findings.

Treatment

There is no specific treatment for OI other than correction of the deformities it produces and the prevention of fractures. The condition, however, tends to improve spontaneously at puberty, with cessation or a decrease in the number of fractures. Recent reports suggest a gradual increase in bone density after treatment with intravenous infusion of sodium pamidronate. The limb deformities are corrected by various types of osteotomies, with the popular method being the Sofield ("shish kabob") technique, in which the deformed bones are osteotomized in a fragmentation procedure, cut into short segments, and then realigned by threading them onto a rigid or expandable rod (Fig. 33.27). The most common complications of this treatment are rod breakage, refracture of the bone at the end of the metallic device, and pseudoarthrosis.

Achondroplasia

Achondroplasia is a hereditary autosomal-dominant anomaly that begins in utero caused by a failure in endochondral bone formation and affects the growth and development of cartilage. About 80% of cases result from a sporadic mutation in the fibroblast growth factor (FGF) receptor gene encoding *FGFR3*, located on the chromosome 4. Its most prominent effect is short-limb, rhizomelic (disproportional) dwarfism. The hands and feet are short and stubby; the trunk is relatively long, with the chest flattened in the anteroposterior dimension; and the lower limbs are often bowed, producing a characteristic waddling gait. The head is large, with prominent frontal bossing, a depressed nasal bridge, and a "scooped-out" facial appearance.

Radiographically, achondroplasia exhibits distinctive features. As is typical in rhizomelic dwarfism, the tubular bones of the limbs are shortened, with the proximal segments (humeri and femora) more severely affected than the distal portions of the extremities (radius, ulna, tibia, and fibula); the growth plates assume a V-shaped configuration (Fig. 33.28). In the hand, the fingers are short and stubby, with the middle finger separated from the others, giving the hand a "trident" appearance (Fig. 33.29). Identifying features of this disorder may also be encountered in the spine and pelvis. The spine exhibits a characteristic narrowing of the interpedicular distance and short pedicles, which often result in spinal stenosis; scalloping of the posterior aspect of the vertebral bodies is also a common finding (Fig. 33.30). In the pelvis, which is short and broad, the iliac bones are rounded, lacking the normal flaring; the acetabular roofs are horizontally oriented; and the sciatic notches are small. These features together give the hemipelvis the appearance of a ping-pong paddle. The shape of the inner contour of the pelvis has also been likened to a champagne glass (Fig. 33.31).

The most serious complication of achondroplasia is related to the spinal stenosis secondary to the typically short pedicles. Patients with the disease also occasionally have herniation of the nucleus pulposus. CT and MRI are the procedures of choice for confirming these two complications.

It is important to note that there are two other conditions resembling achondroplasia, but they differ from it in the severity of their symptoms and in radiographic presentation. *Hypochondroplasia* is a mild form of osteochondrodystrophy, in which the skeletal abnormalities are less

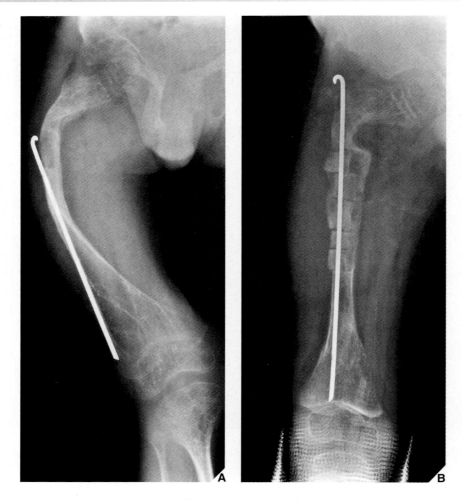

FIGURE 33.27 Treatment of osteogenesis imperfecta. A 10-year-old boy with severe long bone deformities sustained a pathologic fracture of the right femur. **(A)** A single intramedullary Kirschner wire was inserted, and union was achieved. However, there is still marked lateral bowing of the femur. **(B)** Postoperative film after a Sofield osteotomy shows the osseous segments of the femur realigned on a rigid rod.

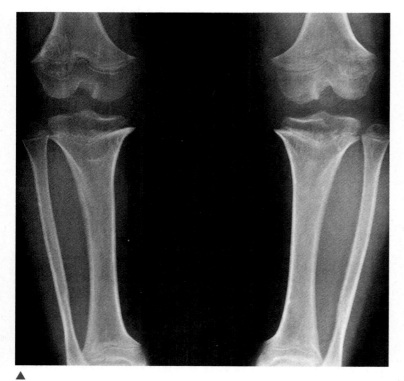

FIGURE 33.28 Achondroplasia. Anteroposterior radiograph of the lower legs of a 12-year-old boy shows the short, broad tibiae characteristic of this disorder; the fibulae are relatively longer. The epiphyses about the knee joints have a V-shaped configuration and appear recessed into the trumpet-like metaphyses. (From Norman A, Greenspan A, 1982, with permission.)

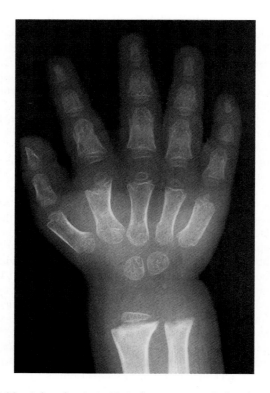

FIGURE 33.29 Achondroplasia. Typical appearance of a hand in a 3-year-old girl. Note short metacarpals and short phalanges of the fingers.

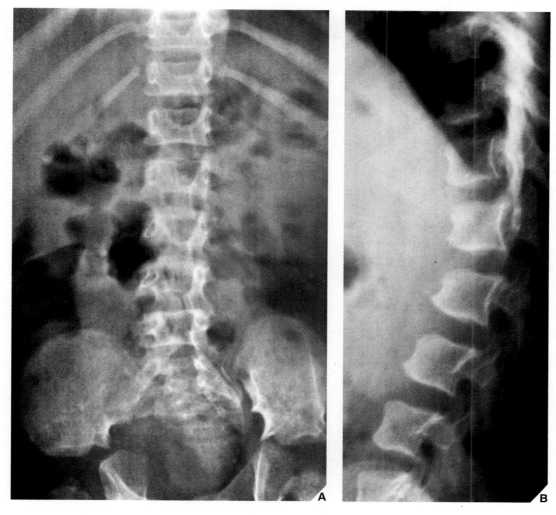

▲
FIGURE 33.30 **Achondroplasia. (A)** Anteroposterior radiograph of the thoracolumbar spine in a 2-year-old boy shows progressive narrowing of the inter-pedicular distance of the lumbar vertebrae in a caudal direction. **(B)** Lateral radiograph reveals the short pedicles and posterior vertebral scalloping.

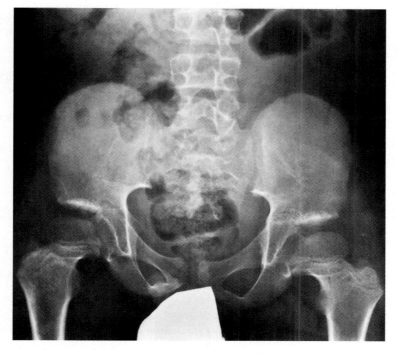

▲
FIGURE 33.31 **Achondroplasia.** Anteroposterior radiograph of the pelvis of a 13-year-old boy shows the classic manifestations of this condition. The iliac bones are rounded, lacking their normal flaring, and the acetabular roofs are horizontal—features rendering the appearance of a ping-pong paddle. Note also the "champagne-glass" inner contour of the pelvic cavity.

severe than in achondroplasia. The skull is unaffected. *Thanatophoric dwarfism*, conversely, is thought to be a severe form of achondroplasia. It is lethal either in utero or within hours to days after birth.

Mucopolysaccharidoses

The mucopolysaccharidoses (MPS) constitute a group of hereditary disorders having in common an excessive accumulation of mucopolysaccharides (glycosaminoglycans) secondary to deficiencies in specific lysosomal enzymes. Although several distinctive types of MPS have been delineated (Table 33.4), each with distinctive clinical and radiologic features, a specific diagnosis of any of these conditions is made on the basis of the patient's age at onset, the level of neurologic stunting, the amount of corneal clouding, and other clinical features. With the exception of Morquio-Brailsford disease, all the MPS are marked by excessive urinary excretion of dermatan and heparan sulfate.

The MPS exhibit common radiographic findings. These include osteoporosis, oval or hook-shaped vertebral bodies, and an abnormal configuration of the pelvis, with overconstriction of the iliac bodies and wide flaring of the iliac wings. The tubular bones are shortened and dysplastic changes are evident in the proximal femoral epiphyses (Fig. 33.32). The MPS, however, do show variations in these radiographic abnormalities; Hurler syndrome, for example, exhibits a characteristic rounding of the vertebral end plates on the lateral projection; the vertebral bodies appear oval in shape but frequently there is a dorsolumbar gibbous with a hypoplastic hook-shaped, recessed vertebral body.

TABLE 33.4 **Classification of the MPS**

Designated Number	Eponym	Genetic and Clinical Characteristics
MPS I-H	Hurler syndrome (gargoylism)	Autosomal-recessive, *IDUA* gene mutations Corneal clouding, mental retardation, micrognathia, hepatosplenomegaly, cardiomegaly Urinary excretion of dermatan and heparan sulfates Deficiency of α-L-iduronidase enzyme
MPS I-S	Scheie syndrome	Autosomal recessive Corneal clouding, retinal degeneration, glaucoma, normal mental development, pigeon chest, short neck, prominent clavicles and scapulae, stiff joints, carpal tunnel syndrome, deformities of hands and feet, flattening of the vertebral bodies, aortic valve disease, inguinal and umbilical hernias
MPS I-H/S	Hurler-Scheie compound syndrome	Moderate mental retardation, short stature, corneal clouding, hearing loss Urinary excretion of same product as in MPS I-H, and same enzyme deficiency
MPS II	Hunter syndrome (mild and severe variants)	Sex-chromosome–linked recessive disorder (males only) Mild mental retardation, absence of corneal clouding Urinary excretion of same product as in MPS I-H Deficiency of iduronate sulfatase
MPS III	Sanfilippo syndrome (A, B, C, and D variants)	Autosomal recessive Progressive mental retardation, motor overactivity, coarse facial features, death by second decade Urinary excretion of heparan sulfate Deficiency of heparan-*N*-sulfatase (A) Deficiency of α-*N*-acetylglucosaminidase (B) Deficiency of acetyl-CoAlpha-glucosaminide acetyltransferase (C) Deficiency of *N*-acetylglucosamine 6-sulfatase (D)
MPS IV	Morquio-Brailsford disease (type A, classic; type B, milder abnormalities)	Autosomal recessive Short-trunk dwarfism, characteristic posture with knock knees, lumbar lordosis, and severe pectus carinatum; corneal opacities; impaired hearing; hepatosplenomegaly Urinary excretion of keratan sulfate Deficiency of *N*-acetylgalactosamine-6-sulfate sulfatase (A) Deficiency of beta-galactosidase (B)
MPS V	Redesignated MPS I-S	
MPS VI	Maroteaux-Lamy syndrome	Autosomal recessive Normal intelligence, short stature, lumbar kyphosis; hepatosplenomegaly, joint contractures, heart defects Urinary excretion of dermatan sulfate Deficiency of *N*-acetylgalactosamine 4-sulfatase
MPS VII	Sly syndrome	Autosomal recessive Growth and mental retardation, hydrocephalus, hepatosplenomegaly, inguinal and umbilical hernia, pulmonary infections, skeletal dysplasia, short stature Urinary excretion of heparan and dermatan sulfates Deficiency of β-glucuronidase
MPS VIII	DiFerrante syndrome	Probably genetic trait Short stature Urinary excretion of keratan and heparan sulfates Deficiency of glucosamine-6-sulfate sulfatase
MPS IX	Natowicz syndrome	Soft-tissue masses around joints, short stature, normal intelligence Deficiency of hyaluronidase

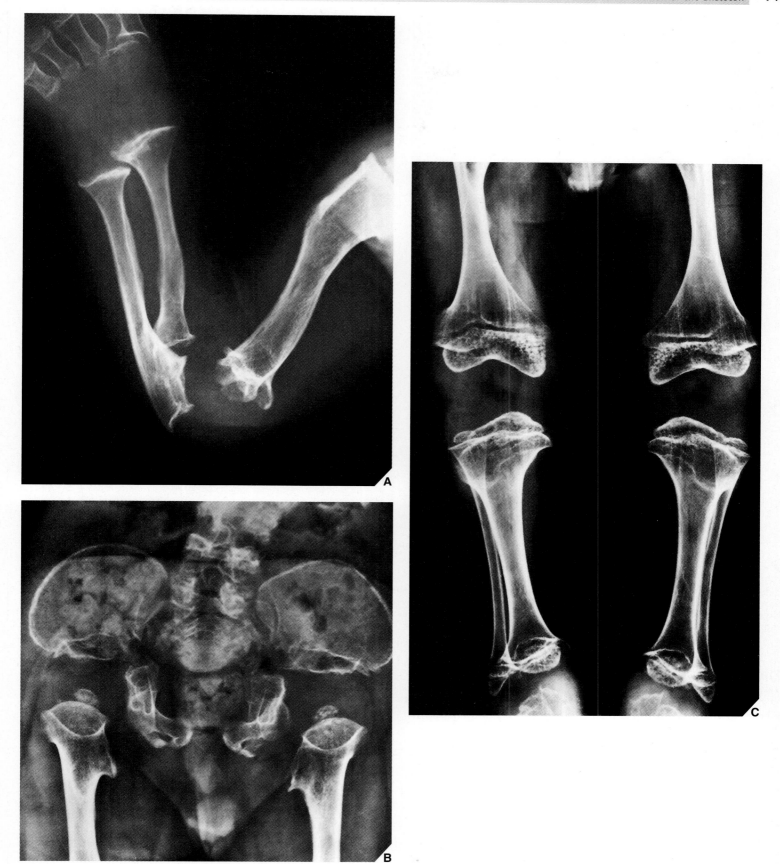

FIGURE 33.32 Morquio-Brailsford disease. The classic features of this disease are present in radiographic studies of a 3-year-old boy. (**A**) Radiograph of the right arm shows foreshortening and deformity of the humerus, radius, and ulna, with an irregular outline of the metaphyses. (**B**) Anteroposterior radiograph of the pelvis and hips shows flaring of the iliac wings and constriction of the iliac bodies. The narrowing of the pelvis at the level of the acetabula, which are distorted, produces a characteristic "wine-glass" appearance. Note the fragmentation of the ossification centers in the femoral heads and the broadening of the femoral necks, with subluxation in the hip joints and a coxa valga deformity. (**C**) The legs show deformities in the epiphyses of the femora and tibiae, as well as foreshortening of these bones. (*continued*)

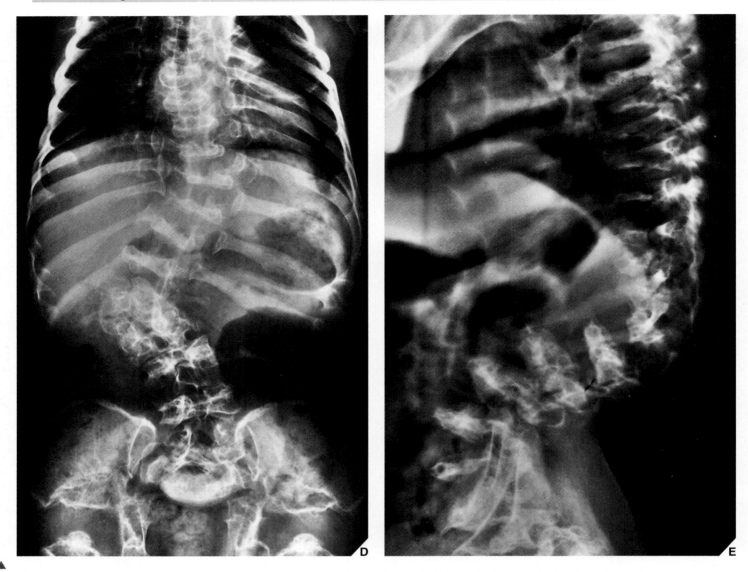

FIGURE 33.32 **Morquio-Brailsford disease.** *Continued.* **(D)** Anteroposterior radiograph of the spine shows marked kyphoscoliosis. The vertebrae are grossly deformed and flat (platyspondylia), and the ribs are wide but with narrow vertebral ends, giving them a characteristic "canoe-paddle" appearance. Note the pronounced osteoporosis. **(E)** Lateral radiograph of the spine demonstrates hyperlordosis in the lumbar segment and kyphosis at the thoracolumbar junction. Note the shape of the vertebral bodies, with the characteristic irregular outline of the end plates and central tongue-like or beak-like projections in the lumbar segment.

Fibrodysplasia Ossificans Progressiva (Myositis Ossificans Progressiva)

Fibrodysplasia ossificans progressiva is a rare systemic autosomal-dominant disorder with variable expressivity and complete penetrance. The responsible *ACVR1* gene has recently been mapped to chromosome 17q21-22, and another study has localized it to chromosome 4q21-31. In most cases, only a single family member is affected. This suggests the involvement of a sporadic mutation.

The primary histopathologic abnormality is in the connective tissues. Most patients are affected early in life (from birth to age 5 years), and there is no sex predominance. The earliest clinical symptom is the appearance of painful nodules and masses in the subcutaneous tissue, particularly around the head and neck, with associated stiffness and limitation of movement. Subsequently, excessive ossification of muscles, ligaments, and fascia occur, with the predominant sites of involvement in the head and neck, the dorsal paraspinal muscles, the shoulder girdles, and the hips. Involvement of intercostal musculature interferes with respiration.

Clinically, the condition progresses from the shoulder girdle to the upper arms, spine, and pelvis. The natural history is one of remissions and exacerbations; death secondary to respiratory failure caused by constriction of the chest wall is an almost inevitable outcome. No effective treatment is known to date.

Radiologic Evaluation

Abnormalities of the thumb and great toe are present at birth and precede the soft-tissue ossification. The characteristic radiologic changes consist of agenesis, microdactyly, or congenital hallux valgus, occasionally with fusion at the metacarpophalangeal or metatarsophalangeal joints (Fig. 33.33A). Short big toes and short thumbs may be associated with clinodactyly of the fifth finger, as well as with brachydactyly. In the soft tissues, extensive ossifications are seen, along with bridging osseous masses in the cervical and thoracic spine, the thorax, and the extremities (Fig. 33.33B). Involvement of the insertions of ligaments and tendons occasionally produces osseous excrescences mimicking exostoses. Joint ankylosis results most often from ossification of the surrounding soft tissue, but a true intraarticular fusion may occur (Fig. 33.33C). CT provides accurate anatomic localization of preosseous lesions. MRI, particularly contrast-enhanced studies, may further characterize soft-tissue abnormalities. Early-stage lesions exhibit low signal intensity on T1-weighted sequences and high signal intensity on T2-weighted images, accompanied by marked homogeneous enhancement on postgadolinium studies.

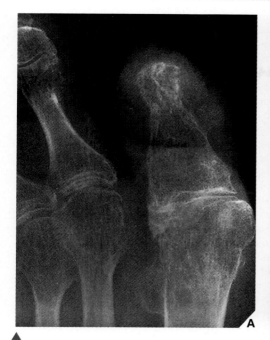
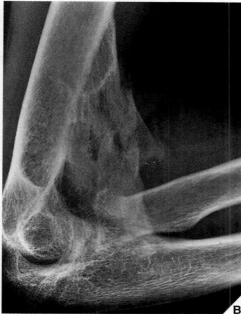
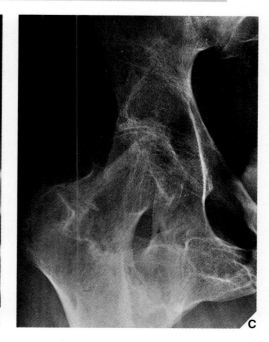

FIGURE 33.33 Myositis ossificans progressiva. A 28-year-old man was diagnosed with fibrodysplasia ossificans progressiva at age 3 years. **(A)** Microdactyly of the great toe is a frequent feature of this disorder. **(B)** Lateral radiograph of the elbow shows extensive ossification in the soft tissues, bridging the distal humerus to the radius and ulna. **(C)** Massive ossification around the hip accompanies the ankylosis of the hip joint.

Histopathology

The pathologic abnormalities are similar to those of myositis ossificans circumscripta, but the zoning phenomenon of centripetal ossification is absent. The earliest histologic changes are edema and inflammatory exudate, followed by mesenchymal proliferation and formation of a large mass of collagen. This collagen is capable of accepting the deposition of calcium salts. Eventually, the lesion is transformed into irregular masses of lamellar and woven bone.

Sclerosing Dysplasias of Bone

The sclerosing bone dysplasias are a group of developmental anomalies that reflect disturbances in the formation and modeling of bone, most commonly as a result of inborn errors in metabolism. A common defect in many of these disorders is reflected in a failure of cartilage and/or bone to resorb during the process of skeletal maturation and remodeling. One defect in many cases involves the resorption capabilities of osteoclasts in the presence of normal osteoblastic activity. In other instances, the defect lies in excessive bone formation by osteoblasts, which may occur in the presence of normal or diminished osteoclastic activity. These basic errors in metabolism most commonly arise during the processes of endochondral and intramembranous ossification. All sclerosing dysplasias share the common feature of excessive bone accumulation resulting in the radiographic appearance of increased bone density. Norman and Greenspan have developed a classification of these disorders based on the site of failure, whether endochondral or intramembranous, in skeletal development and maturation. Recently, Greenspan expanded and modified this classification (Table 33.5). The approach reflected in this classification is focused on target sites of involvement and pathomechanism of these dysplasias.

Osteopetrosis

An inherited disorder, osteopetrosis (also called Albers-Schönberg disease or marble-bone disease), involves a failure in resorption and remodeling of bone formed by endochondral ossification. The result is an excessive accumulation of primary spongiosa (calcified cartilage matrix) in the medullary portion of flat bones and long and short tubular bones, as well as in the vertebrae. Although the etiology of this condition is still debatable, deficiency of the enzyme carbonic anhydrase in

osteoclasts was attributed to the defective bone resorption by these cells. Moreover, mutations of the gene *SLC4A2* in calve and mouse models have recently been reported. Two variants have been described. The infantile "malignant" autosomal-recessive form is recognized at birth or in early childhood, and if not treated by bone marrow transplantation it is frequently fatal because of severe anemia secondary to substantial quantities of cartilage and immature bone packing the marrow cavity. The "benign" autosomal-dominant adult form, which is marked by sclerosis of the skeleton, is compatible with a long lifespan. More recent reports describe what appear to be additional variants of this developmental anomaly, which illustrate the heterogeneity of inheritance of osteopetrosis: intermediate-recessive type and autosomal-recessive type with tubular acidosis.

The radiographic hallmark of this disorder, as of all sclerosing bone dysplasias, is increased bone density. The radiographic examination also reveals a lack of differentiation between the cortex and the medullary cavity and occasionally a bone-in-bone appearance. The long and short tubular bones exhibit a club-like deformity and splaying of their ends secondary to a failure in remodeling (Figs. 33.34 and 33.35). The same failure in the spine results in a characteristic sandwich-like appearance of the vertebral bodies (Fig. 33.36). Osteopetrosis may occur in a cyclic pattern, with intervals of normal growth. This produces alternating bands of normal and abnormal bone in a ring-like pattern, which is particularly well demonstrated in the metaphysis of long bones and in flat bones such as the pelvis and scapula (Fig. 33.37).

Fractures are a frequent complication of osteopetrosis caused by brittle bones.

Pycnodysostosis (Pyknodysostosis)

Pyknodysostosis (Maroteaux-Lamy disease) is an inherited autosomal-recessive disorder caused by mutations in the cathepsin-K gene, whose skeletal manifestations result from a failure of resorption of primary spongiosa. Patients with this disease, like the French painter Toulouse-Lautrec, have a disproportionately short stature, which becomes evident in early childhood. Unlike patients with osteopetrosis, however, those with pyknodysostosis are usually asymptomatic; a pathologic fracture may be the occasion of its discovery.

Radiographically, pyknodysostosis presents with the increased bone density common to all sclerosing bone dysplasias. In addition, in

TABLE 33.5 **Classification of Sclerosing Dysplasias of Bone**

I. *Dysplasias of Endochondral Bone Formation*
  - Affecting primary spongiosa (immature bone)
    Osteopetrosis (Albers-Schönberg disease)
      Autosomal-recessive type (lethal)
      Autosomal-dominant type
      Intermediate-recessive type
      Autosomal-recessive type with tubular acidosis (Sly disease)
    Pycnodysostosis (Maroteaux-Lamy disease)
  - Affecting secondary spongiosa (mature bone)
    Enostosis (bond island)
    Osteopoikilosis (spotted bone disease)
    Osteopathia striata (Voorhoeve disease)
II. *Dysplasias of Intramembranous Bone Formation*
    Progressive diaphyseal dysplasia (Camurati-Engelmann
      disease)
    Hereditary multiple diaphyseal sclerosis (Ribbing disease)
    Endosteal hyperostosis (hyperostosis corticalis generalisata)
      Autosomal-recessive form
        van Buchem disease
        Sclerosteosis (Truswell-Hansen disease)
      Autosomal-dominant form
        Worth disease
        Nakamura disease

III. *Mixed Sclerosing Dysplasias (Affecting Both Endochondral and Intramembranous Ossification)*
  - Affecting predominantly endochondral ossification
    Dysosteosclerosis
    Metaphyseal dysplasia (Pyle disease)
    Metaphyseal dysplasia (Braun-Tinschert type)
    Craniometaphyseal dysplasia
  - Affecting predominantly intramembranous ossification
    Melorheostosis
    Progressive diaphyseal dysplasia with skull base involvement
      (Neuhauser variant)
    Craniodiaphyseal dysplasia
  - Coexistence of two or more sclerosing bone dysplasias
      (overlap syndrome)
        Melorheostosis with osteopoikilosis and osteopathia striata
        Osteopathia striata with cranial sclerosis (Horan-Beighton
          syndrome)
        Osteopathia striata with osteopoikilosis and cranial sclerosis
        Osteopathia striata with generalized cortical hyperostosis
        Osteopathia striata with osteopetrosis
        Osteopoikilosis with progressive diaphyseal dysplasia

Modified from Greenspan A, 1991, with permission.

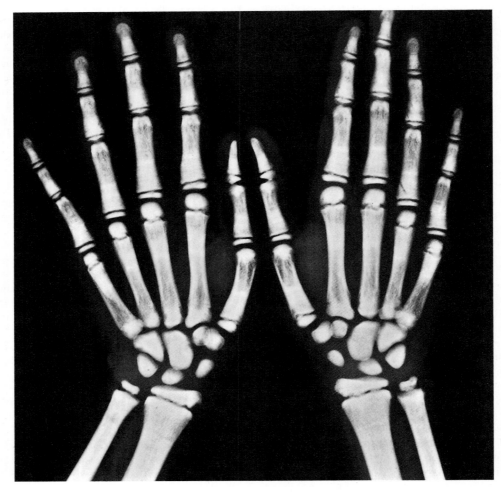

▲
FIGURE 33.34 **Osteopetrosis.** Dorsovolar radiograph of both hands of a 7-year-old boy shows the dense sclerotic bones lacking differentiation between the cortex and medullary cavity that are characteristic of this condition. The metacarpals appear club-like because of a failure in bone remodeling.

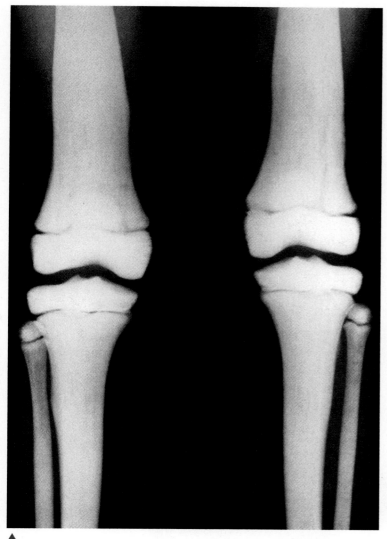

▲

FIGURE 33.35 Osteopetrosis. Anteroposterior radiograph of the legs of a 10-year-old girl shows a uniform increase in bone density in the epiphyses, metaphyses, and diaphyses, with a lack of distinction between the cortical and medullary portions of the bones. The trabecular pattern is completely obliterated by the accumulation of immature bone. Note the splaying deformity of the distal femora and proximal tibiae as a result of remodeling failure.

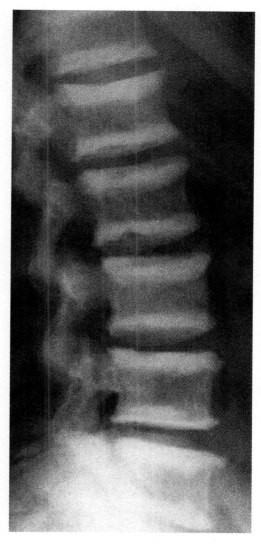

▲

FIGURE 33.36 Osteopetrosis. Lateral radiograph of the thoracolumbar spine in a 14-year-old boy demonstrates the characteristic sandwich-like or "rugger-jersey" appearance seen in this disorder. Note the overall increase in bone density.

the skull, there is persistence of the anterior and posterior fontanelles, wormian bones, and an obtuse angle to the ramus of the mandible (Fig. 33.38). Moreover, there is often a lack of pneumatization as well as hypoplasia of the paranasal sinuses. Spinal abnormalities may also occur: failures in segmentation resulting in block vertebrae are occasionally present, especially in the upper cervical and lumbosacral regions. The features distinguishing this disease from osteopetrosis are hypoplasia of the distal phalanges of the fingers and toes and resorption of the terminal tufts of the distal phalanges (Fig. 33.39). The latter feature, known as acro-osteolysis, may, however, also be seen in a variety of other conditions (see Table 14.3).

Although histologically similar to one another, pyknodysostosis and osteopetrosis exhibit some differences on the microscopic and ultrastructural levels. Most significant among these is evidence of hematopoiesis in pyknodysostosis, because the medullary canal, though narrowed in diameter, is still patent. Both, osteoblastic and osteoclastic activity may be diminished. Electron microscopy of pyknodysostotic bone has identified large cytoplasmic vacuoles filled with bone collagen fibrils in osteoclasts. This finding suggests defective intracellular or extracellular degradation of skeletal collagen, perhaps due to an abnormality in the bone matrix or in the function of osteoclasts.

Enostosis, Osteopoikilosis, and Osteopathia Striata

When endochondral ossification proceeds normally, but mature bony trabeculae coalesce and fail to resorb and remodel, the resulting developmental anomalies are referred to as enostosis (bone island), osteopoikilosis, or osteopathia striata. The exact mode of inheritance of each is not known, but all three are probably transmitted as autosomal-dominant traits. The most common and mildest of the three is *enostosis*, which is asymptomatic; it is important, however, to differentiate this condition from an osteoid osteoma (see Figs. 16.24 and 17.20) and from osteoblastic bone metastasis. Any bone in the skeleton may be affected. On imaging studies, the lesion appears as a homogeneously dense and sclerotic focus of compact bone within the cancellous bone. It may be ovoid, round, or oblong, and is usually oriented with the long axis of the bone parallel to the cortex. In the majority of cases, bone islands measure 1 mm to 2 cm in greatest diameter, although "giant" bone islands (over 2 cm) have been observed, usually exhibiting the same imaging features as their smaller counterparts. A highly characteristic feature of the lesion is a pattern that has been described as "thorny radiation" or "pseudopodia": thickened mature bone trabeculae radiate in streaks through the lesion, aligned with the axes of surrounding uninvolved trabeculae and blending with them in a feathered or

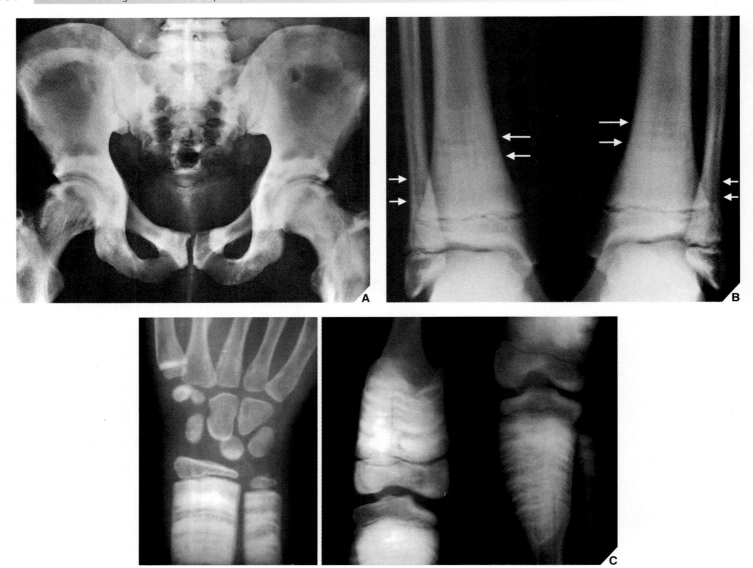

FIGURE 33.37   **Osteopetrosis.** Radiographic examination of a 12-year-old girl demonstrates the cyclic pattern of this dysplasia. In the pelvis (**A**), alternating bands of normal (radiolucent) and abnormal (sclerotic) bone are arranged in a ring-like pattern in both iliac wings. In both legs (**B**), the alternating sclerotic and radiolucent bands are seen in the distal diaphyses and metaphyses of the tibiae and fibulae (*arrows*). (**C**) In another patient, a 3-year-old boy, the alternating sclerotic and radiolucent bands are present in the distal radius and ulna and around the knee joint.

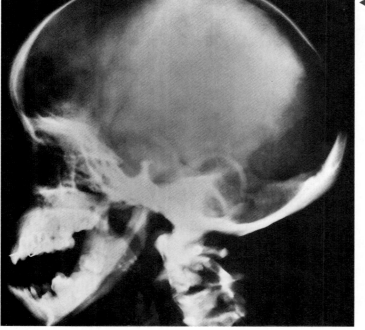

◀ FIGURE 33.38   **Pyknodysostosis.** Lateral radiograph of the skull and facial bones of an 8-year-old boy shows persistence of the anterior and posterior fontanels and the obtuse (fetal) angle of the mandible, common manifestations of this disorder. (Courtesy of Dr. W.E. Berdon, New York.)

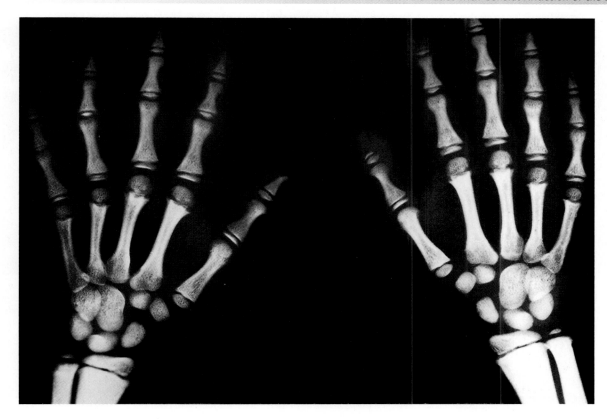

▲
FIGURE 33.39   **Pyknodysostosis.** Dorsovolar radiograph of both hands of a 9-year-old boy shows resorption of the terminal phalangeal tufts (acro-osteolysis), a feature differentiating this condition from osteopetrosis. (Courtesy of Dr. J. Dorst, Baltimore, Maryland.)

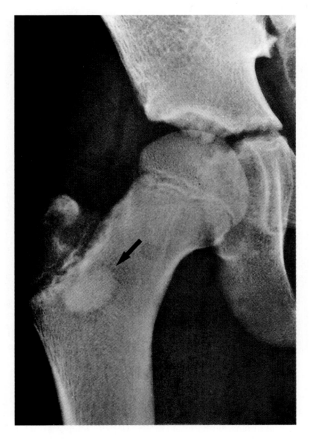

▲
FIGURE 33.40   **Enostosis.** Anteroposterior radiograph of the right hip of a 10-year-old boy who was examined for an injury reveals, as an incidental finding, a giant bone island in the femoral neck (*arrow*), which was completely asymptomatic.

brush-like fashion (Figs. 33.40 and 33.41). Most bone islands represent completed episodes of bone remodeling and thus are not metabolically active. They usually do not grow or demonstrate activity on skeletal scintigraphy, although some may exhibit increased uptake of the radio-pharmaceutical agent. This phenomenon, according to the investigations conducted by Greenspan and colleagues, may be related to osteo-blastic activity and higher degree of bone remodeling in some of the bone islands.

Osteopoikilosis (osteopathia condensans disseminata, or "spotted-bone" disease) is also an asymptomatic disorder, and it is characterized by multiple bone islands symmetrically distributed and clustered near the articular ends of a bone (Fig. 33.42). It is occasionally associated with the hereditary dermatologic condition, dermatofibrosis lenticularis disseminata (Buschke-Ollendorff syndrome), which is marked by the presence of papular fibromas over the back, arms, and thighs. This association suggests that that osteopoikilosis may be a manifestation of a metabolic disorder of connective tissue reflected in a failure in remodeling of mature osseous trabeculae. The imaging studies demonstrate focal condensations of compact lamellar bone in the spongiosa, having characteristic roentgenographic features. They appear as small, symmetrically scattered radiopacities whose appearance at the articular ends of the long bones and in the small carpal and tarsal bone is pathognomic. The lesions may also be present in other areas of articulation, for example around the acetabulum and glenoid; the spine and ribs, although rare, may also be affected. In general, the lesions may exhibit one of three configurations: (1) lenticular-round, oval, or nodular, (2) linear-striated or oblong, and (3) mixture of the two. The last two configurations may not, however, represent the pure entity, but rather the coexistence of osteopoikilosis and osteopathia striata. Although radiography is usually sufficient to make a diagnosis of osteopoikilosis, questionable cases may require radionuclide imaging, which is diagnostic. In osteopoikilosis, a bone scan is relatively normal, unlike in metastatic disease, which invariably shows an increased uptake of radiopharmaceutical. CT

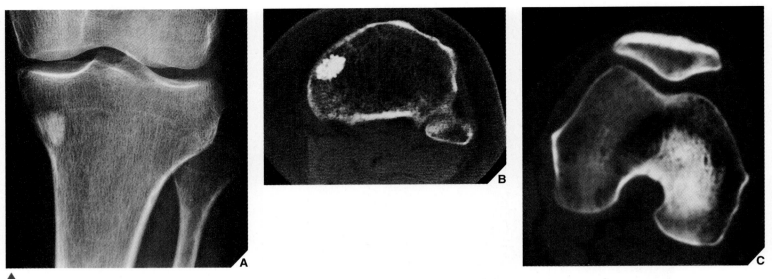

▲
FIGURE 33.41   **CT of enostosis.** Anteroposterior (**A**) radiograph of the knee and CT section (**B**) through the proximal tibia demonstrate a bone island, display-ing characteristic brush border. (**C**) In another patient, CT section through the knee joint shows a giant bone island in the medial femoral condyle.

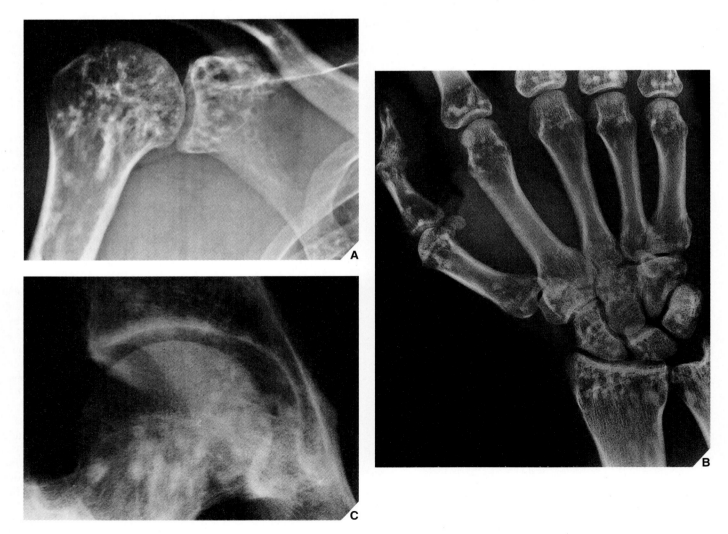

▲
FIGURE 33.42   **Osteopoikilosis.** (**A**) Anteroposterior radiograph of the shoulder of a 34-year-old man who had pain in his right shoulder after an automobile accident shows no fracture or dislocation. However, multiple sclerotic foci representing lesions of osteopoikilosis are apparent, scattered near the articular ends of the scapula and humerus. A subsequent bone survey showed extensive involvement of the skeleton, especially the hands, wrists (**B**), and hips (**C**).

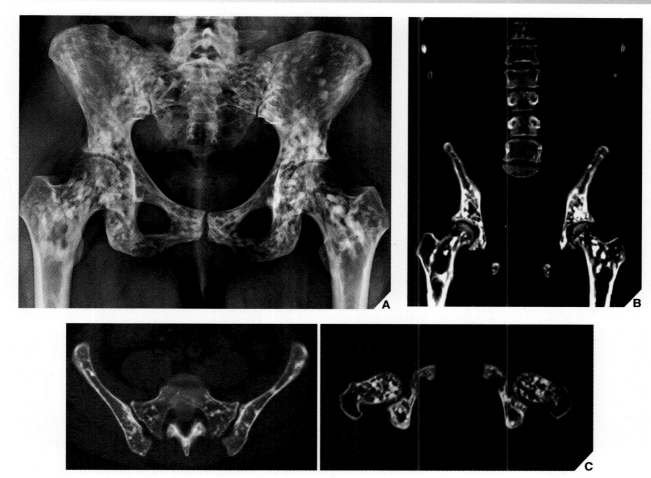

FIGURE 33.43 CT of osteopoikilosis. (A) Anteroposterior radiograph of the pelvis of a 38-year-old woman shows multiple sclerotic lesions in the pelvic bones and proximal femora. **(B)** Coronal CT reformatted image shows involvement of the iliac bones, femora, and several vertebral bodies. **(C)** Axial CT sections obtained through the pelvis and the hip joints show cross-sectional distribution of the lesions.

is rarely required, but it shows cross-sectional distribution of the lesions (Fig.33.43).

Histologically, both enostoses and the lesions of osteopoikilosis are characterized by foci of compact bone scattered in the spongiosa, with prominent cement lines and occasionally haversian systems of nutrient canals. Clinically, osteopoikilosis must be distinguished from more severe disorders such as mastocytosis and tuberous sclerosis, as well as from osteoblastic metastatic lesions.

Osteopathia striata, also an autosomal-dominant disorder, the least common condition in this group, is an asymptomatic lesion marked by fine or coarse linear striations, chiefly in the long bones and at sites of rapid growth such as the knee (Fig. 33.44) and shoulder. Skeletal scintigraphy is invariably normal. Patients with the pure form of this disorder exhibit no known associated physical abnormalities or characteristic laboratory findings. Several authors postulate a relationship between this disorder and osteopoikilosis; some suggest that it is in fact a variant of osteopoikilosis. The association of osteopathia striata with cranial stenosis has been described, and a limited study of individuals with focal dermal hypoplasia (Goltz-Gorlin syndrome) has revealed a high incidence of concomitant osteopathia striata, an association that may be more than coincidental.

Progressive Diaphyseal Dysplasia (Camurati-Engelmann Disease)

Failure of bone resorption and remodeling at the sites of intramembranous ossification (such as the cortex of tubular bones, the vault of the skull, the mandible, or the midsegment of the clavicle) is the abnormality typically noted in progressive diaphyseal dysplasia, also called Camurati-Engelmann disease. The disorder usually manifests itself in the first decade of life, males being more frequently affected than females. Like enostosis, osteopoikilosis, and osteopathia striata, this is an autosomal-dominant disorder with considerable variability of expression. Both sporadic and familial cases have been described. Recent investigations suggest that this disease results from domain-specific mutations in the transforming growth factor-beta-1 gene (*TGFB1*) with locus in the chromosome 19q13.1. Clinically, it is characterized by growth retardation, muscle wasting, pain and weakness in the extremities, and a waddling gait. The level of urinary hydroxyproline is normal, indicating normal bone turnover, and blood chemistry and marrow and peripheral blood elements are normal as well, although occasionally the erythrocyte sedimentation rate may be increased. The condition is self-limiting, and generally resolves by 30 years of age.

Because of its striking tendency toward symmetric involvement of the extremities, with characteristic sparing of the epiphysis and metaphysis (the sites of endochondral ossification), progressive diaphyseal dysplasia is recognized radiographically by symmetric fusiform thickening of the cortices of the long bone shafts, particularly in the lower extremities (Fig. 33.45). The thickening of the cortex, which represents both endosteal and periosteal accretion, progresses along the long axis of the bone both proximally and distally. The external contour of the bone is usually regular. Occasionally, the skull shows hyperostosis of the calvaria, and in some cases described by Neuhauser, there were sclerotic changes at the base of the skull. This latter finding is curious because such changes at the skull base are typical for an error in endochondral ossification. Such a finding invites speculation that perhaps there are two forms of progressive diaphyseal dysplasia, one expressing a pure form of a failure of intramembranous ossification, and the other, a mixed form, showing an endochondral component as well.

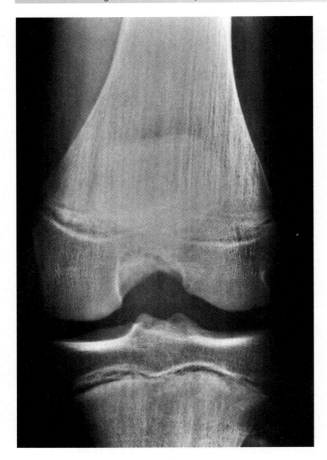

▲
FIGURE 33.44   **Osteopathia striata.** Anteroposterior radiograph of the right knee of a 14-year-old girl who had a history of trauma reveals, as an incidental finding, fine linear striations in the diaphysis and metaphysis of the distal femur and proximal tibia; the epiphyses, however, are spared.

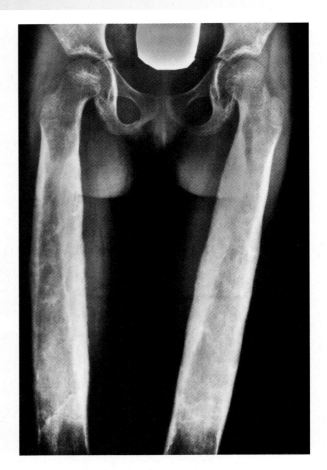

▲
FIGURE 33.45   **Camurati-Engelmann disease.** Anteroposterior radiograph of the hips and upper femora of an 8-year-old boy shows symmetric fusiform thickening of the cortices. Note that only the sites of intramembranous bone formation are affected, whereas the sites of endochondral bone formation are spared. (Courtesy of Dr. W.E. Berdon, New York.)

Hereditary Multiple Diaphyseal Sclerosis (Ribbing Disease)

A familial disorder similar to progressive diaphyseal dysplasia, described by Ribbing and later by Paul, is generally asymptomatic and exhibits limited asymmetric involvement, usually only of the long bones, especially the tibia and the femur. This condition is generally believed to be the same disorder as Camurati-Engelmann disease (Fig. 33.46), although some authors suggest an autosomal-recessive inheritance. Serial studies have shown that lesions may slowly progress over the years, eventually becoming stationary. Radiography reveals focal sclerosis largely caused by the formation of endosteal and periosteal new bone. The medullary portions of the bones are constricted to varying degrees. These findings can be confirmed by CT. Scintigraphy shows an increased uptake of ^{99m}Tc-methylene diphosphonate at the sites of radiographic abnormalities. Histopathologic features are not specific. Reactive cortical thickening is present, with variable formation of woven bone and fibrosis. One study revealed increased numbers of osteocytes per unit area compared with normal bone, as well as focal increases in plump osteoblastic rimming. Haversian systems were normal to markedly reduced in size. In contrast to the histologic evidence of progressive, active bone resorption and new bone apposition in Camurati-Engelmann disease, Ribbing disease shows evidence of only new bone formation. Although they are usually nonspecific, pathologic findings can aid in excluding other diagnoses, for example, infection.

Craniometaphyseal Dysplasia

This mixed sclerosing dysplasia affecting predominantly endochondral ossification, also reffered to as osteochondroplasia or Jackson type of craniometaphyseal dysplasia, is a genetic autosomal-dominant disorder caused by the mutation of *ANKH* gene located on the chromosome 5p15.2-p14.1. Some of the cases may have an autosomal-recessive form of inheritance, in which case a potential locus is chromosome

6q21-q22. It is characterized by metaphyseal widening very similar to Pyle disease, prominent mandible, progressive diffuse hyperostosis of craniofacial bones, resulting in widely spaced eyes, wide nasal bridge, and a "leonine" facial appearance (leontiasis ossea). Progressive thickening of craniofacial bones continues throughout life leading to narrowing of the foramen magnum. Imaging studies reveal thinning of the cortex and radiolucencies of the long bones, club-like flaring and broadening of the metaphyses (Erlenmeyer-flask deformity), and overgrowth of the bones of the skull, facial bones, and mandible (Fig. 33.47).

Melorheostosis

A rare condition of unknown cause, melorheostosis (Leri disease) shows no evidence of hereditary features. It belongs to a group of bone disorders called the mixed sclerosing dysplasias, which combine characteristics of both endochondral and intramembranous failure of ossification. It has been recently postulated that the disease develops due to mutation in *LEMD3* gene. This gene, also known as *MAN1*, encodes for an integral protein of the inner nuclear membrane. Laboratory abnormalities affect osteoblastic specific factor-2 (osf-2), osteonectin, fibronectin, transforming growth factor-beta (TGF-beta), and fibroblast growth factor-23 (FGF-23). The presenting symptom is pain intensified by activity. Limitation of joint motion and stiffness are common, due to contractures, soft-tissue fibrosis, and periarticular bone formation in the soft tissues. The condition may be monostotic (*forme fruste*), affecting only one bone, monomelic, affecting one limb, or polyostotic, with generalized affection of the skeleton. Long bones are most commonly affected, with other sites including the pelvis, and short tubular bones of the hands and feet. The ribs and the bones of the skull are rarely affected. Melorheostosis affecting thoracic vertebrae complicated by involvement of the facet joints has recently been reported.

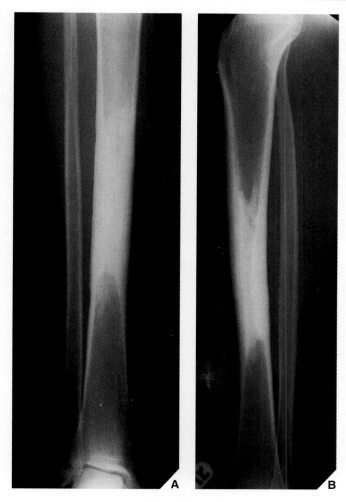

▲
FIGURE 33.46 **Ribbing disease.** Anteroposterior (**A**) and lateral (**B**) radiographs of the right lower leg in an asymptomatic 32-year-old man show features of hereditary multiple diaphyseal sclerosis. Note the slightly irregular circumferential thickening of the cortex of mid-tibia.

Conventional radiography is sufficient to make a diagnosis. The lesion is characterized by a wavy hyperostosis that resembles melted wax dripping down the side of a candle, the feature from which the disease derives its name (Greek *melos*-[member]; *rhein*-[flow]); moreover, only one side of the bone is usually involved (Fig. 33.48). Associated joint abnormalities are also well delineated on standard radiographs. The involvement of soft tissues is not rare, and the ossified masses are often present around the hip and knee joints (Fig. 33.49). CT effectively reveals involvement of the cortex and the medullary cavity, and clear demarcation of normal from abnormal bone (Fig. 33.50A). MRI shows low signal intensity localized to the affected areas on all pulse sequences (Figs. 33.50B,C and 33.51). This technique is also helpful for imaging of soft-tissue involvement. In one study reported by Judkiewicz and associates, soft-tissue masses were heterogeneous on all MRI pulse sequences with signal void in areas corresponding to mineralization on conventional radiographs. Most of the soft-tissue masses exhibited ill-defined margins, were contiguous or adjacent to areas of osseous hyperostosis, and demonstrated enhancement after administration of gadolinium-DTPA. Radionuclide bone scan can determine other sites of skeletal involvement by demonstrating abnormal uptake of radiopharmaceutical tracer (see Fig. 31.16). The factors responsible for increased uptake include the increased mass of the cortex, osteoblastic activity, and local hyperemia. Microscopic examination of melorheostotic specimens reveals nonspecific, hyperostotic periosteal bone formation with thickened trabeculae and fibrotic

changes in the marrow spaces. The bone appears primitive and consists largely of primary haversian systems, particularly on the periosteal surface, that are almost completely obliterated by the deposition of sclerotic, thickened, and somewhat irregular lamellae. Islands of cartilage in periarticular lesions have been described, with evidence of both endochondral and intramembranous bone formation within the cellular fibrous tissue, and osteoblastic activity along the margins of osteons.

Treatment. The disorder is chronic and occasionally debilitating. Conservative treatment with biphosphonate (pamidronate) infusion has been tried occasionally, with mixed results. Surgical treatment consists of soft-tissue procedures such as tendon lengthening, excision of fibrous and osseous tissue, fasciotomy, and capsulotomy. Other procedures include corrective osteotomies, excision of hyperostotic bone, and even amputations in severely affected and painful limbs caused by vascular ischemia. Recurrences are common.

Other Mixed Sclerosing Dysplasias
The most common of the other mixed sclerosing dysplasias is the coexistence of melorheostosis, osteopathia striata, and osteopoikilosis. The radiographic features of this "overlap syndrome" are a combination of each of these three dysplasias (Fig. 33.52), a phenomenon suggesting a common pathogenetic mechanism.

The discussion of other sclerosing dysplasias, listed in Table 33.5, is beyond the scope of this text.

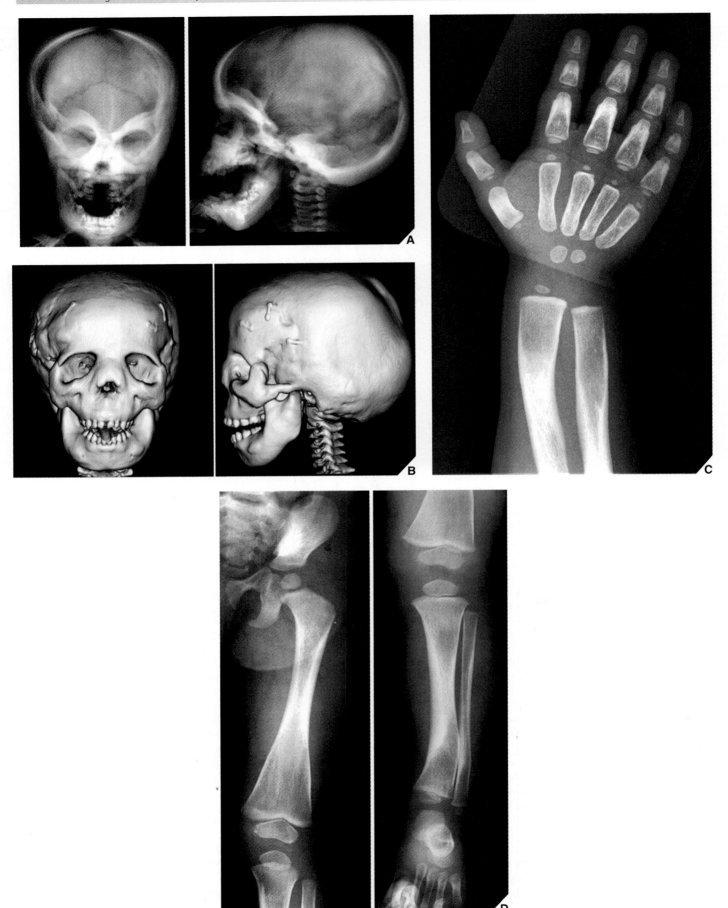

▲
FIGURE 33.47 **Craniometaphyseal dysplasia. (A)** Anteroposterior and lateral radiographs of the skull and **(B)** 3D CT reconstructed images of a 2-year-old girl show hypertrophic changes of the facial bones and calvaria, giving a "leonine" facial appearance. Note mandibular hypertrophy and overgrowth of the zygomatic arches. Radiographs of the hand **(C)** and lower extremity **(D)** show thinning of the cortices, juxtaarticular radiolucency of the bones, and flaring of the metaphyses with Erlenmeyer-flask deformity of the distal femur.

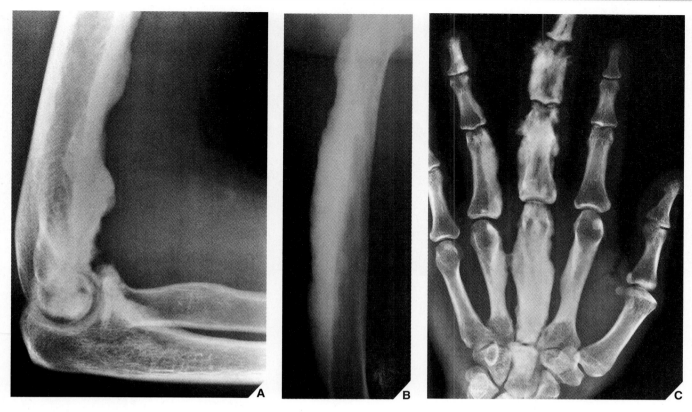

FIGURE 33.48 Melorheostosis. A 28-year-old man presented with pain in the right elbow and an enlargement of the middle finger of his right hand. **(A)** Lateral radiograph of the elbow demonstrates a flowing hyperostosis of the anterior cortex of the distal humerus, typical of melorheostosis. Note the bridging of the joint by the lesion and the involvement of the coronoid process of the ulna. **(B)** The radiograph of the right femur shows involvement of only the anterolateral aspect of the bone. **(C)** Dorsovolar radiograph of the right hand shows marked hypertrophy of the middle digit. The cortices (the sites of intramembranous ossification) are involved, as are the articular ends of the bones (the sites of endochondral ossification). This is characteristic of mixed sclerosing dysplasias.

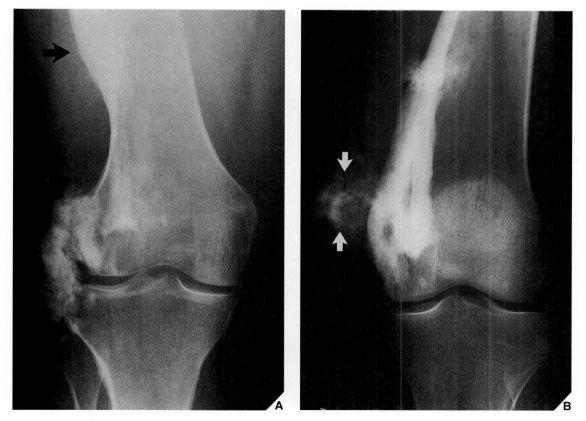

FIGURE 33.49 Melorheostosis. (A) Anteroposterior radiograph of the right knee in a 46-year-old woman shows ossifications of the soft tissues at the lateral aspect of the knee joint. The femoral cortex is also affected (*arrow*). **(B)** A radiograph of the left knee in a 25-year-old woman shows involvement of the medial femoral cortex extending into the soft tissues (*arrows*).

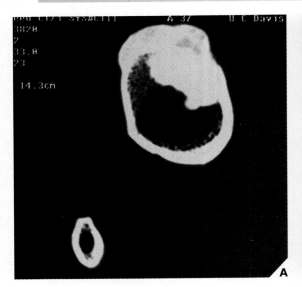

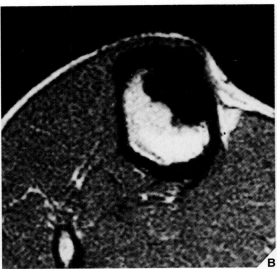

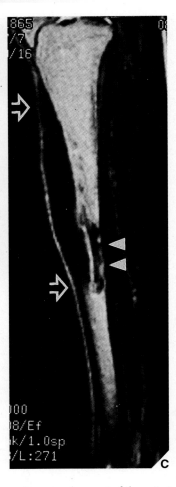

FIGURE 33.50   **CT and MRI of melorheostosis. (A)** CT section through the middle segment of tibia in a 30-year-old woman shows involvement of the anterior cortex and anteromedial portion of medullary cavity. **(B)** An axial T1-weighted (spin-echo, TR 800/TE 16 msec) MRI shows the lesion to be of low signal intensity, which is the same as the cortical bone. The uninvolved bone marrow exhibits high signal similar to the subcutaneous fat. **(C)** A sagittal T2-weighted (fast spin-echo, TR 3000/TE 108 msec Ef) MR image shows that the lesion remains of low signal intensity *(open arrows)*. *Arrow heads* point to the medullary involvement.

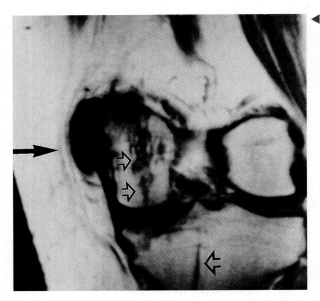

◀ FIGURE 33.51   **MRI of melorheostosis.** A coronal T1-weighted (SE; TR 800/TE 20 msec) MR image of the knee in a 20-year-old man shows decreased signal intensity of the ossific mass attached to the femoral condyle *(arrow)* as well as in the medullary foci of melorheostosis *(open arrows)*.

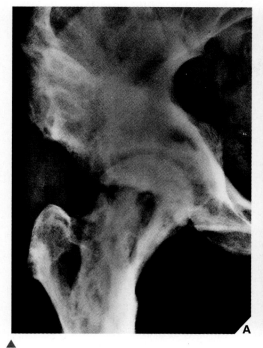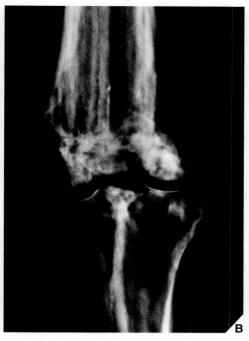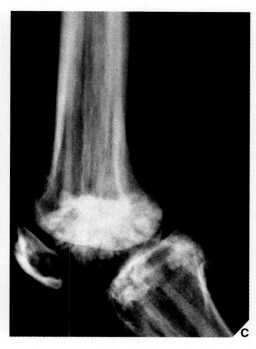

▲
FIGURE 33.52 Mixed sclerosing dysplasia. These radiographic studies in an 18-year-old man demonstrate the coexistence of melorheostosis with osteopoikilosis and osteopathia striata. **(A)** Anteroposterior radiograph of the right hemipelvis and hip shows the wavy hyperostosis typical of melorheostosis affecting the iliac bone and proximal femur. Anteroposterior **(B)** and lateral **(C)** radiographs of the knee demonstrate the linear striations characteristic of osteopathia striata in the distal femur and proximal tibia, as well as the focal densities that are the identifying feature of osteopoikilosis. (From Norman A, Greenspan A, 1986, with permission.

PRACTICAL POINTS TO REMEMBER

Scoliosis

[1] Congenital scoliosis may result from:
  • a failure of vertebral formation, which may be unilateral and partial (wedged vertebra) or unilateral and complete (hemivertebra)
  • a failure of segmentation, which may be unilateral (unsegmented bar) or bilateral (block vertebra)
  • failures of both formation and segmentation.
[2] Idiopathic scoliosis, the most prevalent type of scoliosis (70%), can be divided into infantile (M > F), juvenile (M = F), and adolescent (M < F) categories. In the last type, the structural (major) curve is located in the thoracic or thoracolumbar segment, with its convexity to the right.
[3] In the evaluation of scoliosis, the shape of the curve usually indicates the variant, so that:
  • an S-shaped curve is common in idiopathic scoliosis
  • a C-shaped curve indicates the neuromuscular variant
  • scoliosis marked by a sharply angled short spinal segment is most commonly congenital in origin (e.g., neurofibromatosis, hemivertebra).
[4] The scoliotic curve is described as composed of:
  • a structural (major or primary) curve demarcated by upper and lower (transitional) end vertebrae
  • compensatory (secondary) curves proximal and distal to the transitional vertebrae
  • an apical vertebra showing the most rotation and wedging, and whose center is most displaced from the central spinal line.
[5] Several methods for measuring the scoliotic curve are available:
  • the Lippmann-Cobb method, in which the angle is determined only by the inclination of the end vertebrae of the curve
  • the Risser-Ferguson method, which utilizes three points as determinants of the curve—the centers of the upper and lower end vertebrae and of the apical vertebra
  • the scoliotic index method, which measures the deviation of each vertebra in the scoliotic curve from the central spinal line.

[6] To ensure accuracy in determining the degree of correction of a scoliotic curve, the same measuring points should be used in comparing the pretreatment and posttreatment curvature, even if the end vertebrae have changed their locations.
[7] The rotation of a vertebral body can be evaluated on the anteroposterior radiograph by:
  • the Cobb method, which uses the position of the spinous process as a point of reference
  • the Moe method, which uses the pedicles as points of reference.
[8] The determination of skeletal maturity, an important factor in the prognosis and treatment of congenital scoliosis, may be made by:
  • comparison of a radiograph of a patient's wrist and hand with standards in radiographic atlases
  • evaluation of the ossification of the vertebral ring apophysis or iliac crest apophysis.

Anomalies with General Affliction of the Skeleton

[1] The skeletal abnormalities frequently encountered in neurofibromatosis include:
  • extrinsic cortical erosions
  • pseudoarthroses, particularly in the tibia and fibula
  • short segment kyphoscoliosis marked by acute angulation in the lower cervical and upper thoracic spine
  • enlarged neural foramina and scalloping of the posterior aspect of vertebral bodies.
[2] Malignant transformation to sarcoma is the most serious complication of the plexiform variant of neurofibromatosis.
[3] The radiographic hallmarks of OI, a disorder characterized by excessive fragility of the bones, include:
  • severe osteoporosis
  • thinning of the cortices
  • sutural (Wormian) bones
  • bone deformities, such as trumpet-shaped metaphyses
  • "popcorn calcifications" at the articular ends of long bones
  • kyphoscoliosis
  • multiple fractures.

[4] Radiographically, achondroplasia is characterized by:
- rhizomelic (disproportional) dwarfism
- a configuration of the hemipelves resembling ping-pong paddles and a "champagne-glass" appearance of the inner pelvic contour
- narrowing of the interpedicular distance in the lumbar spine (spinal stenosis)
- scalloping of the posterior aspect of vertebral bodies
- "trident" appearance of the hand.

[5] The various disorders constituting the MPS share common radiographic features:
- osteoporosis
- oval or hook-shaped vertebral bodies
- an abnormal configuration of the pelvis
- shortened tubular bones.

[6] Fibrodysplasia ossificans progressiva (myositis ossificans progressiva) is characterized by extensive ossifications of the muscular structures and subcutaneous tissues, leading to joint ankylosis and constriction of the chest wall. Congenital abnormalities of the thumb and great toe (agenesis, microdactyly, etc.) should alert the radiologist to the possibility of this severely crippling disorder.

[7] The sclerosing bone dysplasias share the radiographic feature of increased bone density.

[8] The radiographic hallmarks of osteopetrosis and pycnodysostosis, disorders related to the failure of endochondral ossification, are:
- a uniformly increased bone density
- the absence of remodeling
- obliteration of the boundary between the medullary cavity and cortex.

Pathologic fractures are common.

[9] The specific changes characteristic of pycnodysostosis include:
- acro-osteolysis
- obtuse angle of the mandible
- persistence of the fontanelles
- wormian (sutural) bones.

[10] Enostosis, osteopoikilosis, and osteopathia striata, conditions also related to a failure of endochondral ossification, are characterized radiographically by:
- foci of sclerotic, mature bone in the medullary cavity (enostosis and osteopoikilosis)
- fine linear striations (osteopathia striata) at sites of rapid bone growth.

[11] Progressive diaphyseal dysplasia and hereditary multiple diaphyseal sclerosis, conditions related to the failure of intramembranous ossification, are recognized radiographically by thickening of the cortices of the long bones. The articular ends of the bones are, as a rule, not affected.

[12] Craniometaphyseal dysplasia is characterized by cranial and facial bones hyperostosis, a "leonine" facial appearance (leontiasis ossea), and "club-like" flaring (Erlenmeyer-flask deformity) of the metaphyses.

[13] Melorheostosis, a mixed sclerosing bone dysplasia marked by failure of endochondral and intramembranous ossification, is recognized radiographically by a flowing hyperostosis ("wax drippings") associated with involvement of the surrounding soft tissues and joint.

SUGGESTED READINGS

Aaro S, Dahlborn M. The longitudinal axis rotation of the apical vertebra, the vertebral, spinal, and rib cage deformity in idiopathic scoliosis studied by computer tomography. *Spine* 1981;6:567–572.

Ablin DS, Greenspan A, Reinhart M, Grix A. Differentiation of child abuse from osteogenesis imperfecta. *Am J Roentgenol* 1990;154:1035–1046.

Abrahamson MN. Disseminated asymptomatic osteosclerosis with features resembling melorheostosis, osteopoikilosis and osteopathia striata. *J Bone Joint Surg [Am]* 1968;50A:991–996.

Andersen PE Jr, Bollerslev J. Heterogeneity of autosomal dominant osteopetrosis. *Radiology* 1987;164:223–225.

Astrom E, Soderhall S. Beneficial effect of long term intravenous biphosphonate treatment of osteogenesis imperfecta. *Arch Disease Childhood* 2002;86:356–364.

Bailey JA II. Orthopedic aspects of achondroplasia. *J Bone Joint Surg [Am]* 1970;52A:1285–1301.

Barnes PD, Brody JD, Jaramillo D, Akbar JU, Emans JB. Atypical idiopathic scoliosis: MR imaging evaluation. *Radiology* 1993;186:73–738.

Bartuseviciene A, Samuilis A, Skucas J. Camurati-Engelmann disease: imaging, clinical features and differential diagnosis. *Skeletal Radiol* 2009;38:1037–1043.

Baser ME. The distribution of constitutional and somatic mutations in the neurofibromatosis 2 gene. *Hum Mutat* 2006;27:297–306.

Bauze RJ, Smith R, Francis JO. A new look at osteogenesis imperfecta. *J Bone Joint Surg [Br]* 1975;57B:2–12.

Beals RK. Endosteal hyperostosis. *J Bone Joint Surg [Am]* 1976;58A:1172–1173.

Beighton P. *Inherited disorders of the skeleton.* Edinburgh, UK: Churchill Livingstone; 1978.

Beighton P, Cremin BJ. *Sclerosing bone dysplasias.* New York: Springer-Verlag; 1984.

Beighton P, Cremin BJ, Hamersma H. The radiology of sclerosteosis. *Br J Radiol* 1976;49:934–939.

Bhullar TPS, Portinaro NMA, Benson MKD. The measurement of angular deformity: an extended role for the "Cobbometer". *J Bone Joint Surg [Br]* 1995;77B:506–507.

Bridges AJ, Hsu K-C, Sing A, Churchill R, Miles J. Fibrodysplasia (myositis) ossificans progressiva. *Semin Arthritis Rheum* 1994;24:155–164.

Bridwell KH. Spinal instrumentation in the management of adolescent scoliosis. *Clin Orthop* 1997;335:64–72.

Brien EW, Mirra JM, Latanza L, Dedenko A, Luck J Jr. Giant bone island of femur. Case report, literature review, and its distinction from low grade osteosarcoma. *Skeletal Radiol* 1995;24:546–550.

Brown RR, Steiner GC, Lehman WB. Melorheostosis: case report with radiologic-pathologic correlation. *Skeletal Radiol* 2000;29:548–552.

Campbell CJ, Papademetriou T, Bonfiglio M. Melorheostosis. A report of the clinical roentgenographic and pathological findings in fourteen cases. *J Bone Joint Surg [Am]* 1968;50A:1281–1304.

Campos-Xavier AB, Saraiva JM, Savarirayan R, et al. Phenotypic variability at the TGF-beta-1 locus in Camurati-Engelmann disease. *Hum Genet* 2001;109:653–658.

Camurati M. Di un raro caso di osteite simmetrica ereditaria degli arti inferiori. *Chir Organi Mov* 1922;6:662–665.

Carlson DH. Osteopathia striata revisited. *J Can Assoc Radiol* 1977;28:190–192.

Caron KH, DiPietro MA, Aisen AM, Heidelberger KP, Phillips WA, Martel W. MR imaging of early fibrodysplasia ossificans progressiva. *J Comput Assist Tomogr* 1990;14:318–321.

Chanchairujira K, Chung CB, Lai YM, Haghighi P, Resnick D. Intramedullary osteosclerosis: imaging features in nine patients. *Radiology* 2001;220:225–230.

Cobb JR. Outline for the study of scoliosis. *AAOS Instr Course Lect* 1948;5:261–275.

Coccia PF, Krivit W, Cervenka J, et al. Successful bone-marrow transplantation for infantile malignant osteopetrosis. *N Engl J Med* 1980;302:701–708.

Connor J, Evans DA. Fibrodysplasia ossificans progressiva: the clinical features and natural history of 34 patients. *J Bone Joint Surg [Br]* 1982;64B:76–83.

Connor J, Evans DA. Genetic aspects of fibrodysplasia ossificans progressiva. *J Med Genet* 1982;19:35–39.

Cremin BJ, Beighton P. Osteopetrosis and other sclerosing bone dysplasias. In: Cremin BJ, Beighton P, eds. *Bone dysplasias of infancy: a radiological atlas.* New York: Springer; 1978:101.

Cremin B, Connor J, Beighton P. The radiological spectrum of fibrodysplasia ossificans progressiva. *Clin Radiol* 1982;33:499–508.

D'Addabbo A, Macarini L, Rubini G, Rubini D, Salzillo F, Lauriero F. Correlation between bone imaging and the clinical picture in two unsuspected cases of progressive diaphyseal dysplasia (Engelmann's disease). *Clin Nucl Med* 1993;18:324–328.

D'Agostino AN, Soule EH, Miller RH. Sarcomas of the peripheral nerves and somatic soft tissues associated with multiple neurofibromatosis (von Recklinghausen's disease). *Cancer* 1963;16:1015–1027.

Davis DC, Syklawer R, Cole RL. Melorheostosis on three-phase bone scintigraphy. Case report. *Clin Nucl Med* 1992;17:561–564.

Deacon P, Flood BM, Dickson RA. Idiopathic scoliosis in three dimensions: a radiographic and morphometric analysis. *J Bone Joint Surg [Br]* 1984;66B:509–512.

Demas PN, Soteranos GC. Facial-skeletal manifestations of Engelmann's disease. *Oral Surg Oral Med Oral Pathol* 1989;68:686–690.

De Vits A, Keymeulen B, Bossugt A, Somers G, Verbruggen LA. Progressive diaphyseal dysplasia (Camurati-Engelmann's disease). Improvement of clinical signs and of bone scintigraphy during pregnancy. *Clin Nucl Med* 1994;19:104–107.

Dickson RA. Early-onset idiopathic scoliosis. In: Weinstein SL, ed. *The pediatric spine: principles and practice.* New York: Raven Press; 1994:421–430.

Donáth J, Poór G, Kiss C, Fornet B, Genant H. Atypical form of active melorheostosis and its treatment with biphosphonate. *Skeletal Radiol* 2002;31:709–713.

Dorst JP. Mucopolysaccharidosis IV. *Semin Roentgenol* 1973;8:218–219.

Drummond DS. Neuromuscular scoliosis: recent concepts. *J Pediatr Orthop* 1996;16:281–283.

Eastman JR, Bixler D. Generalized cortical hyperostosis (van Buchem disease): nosologic considerations. *Radiology* 1977;125:297–304.

Elmore SM. Pycnodysostosis. A review. *J Bone Joint Surg [Am]* 1967;49A:153–158.

Engelmann G. Ein Fall von Osteopathia hyperostotica (sclerotisans) multiplex infantilis. *Fortschr Geb Rontgenstr* 1929;39:1101–1106.

Fairbank HAT. Osteopathia striata. *J Bone Joint Surg [Br]* 1948;30B:117.

Fairbank HAT. Melorheostosis. *J Bone Joint Surg [Br]* 1948;30B:533–543.

Fairbank HAT. Osteopoikilosis. *J Bone Joint Surg [Br]* 1948;30B:544–546.

Fairbank HAT. *An atlas of general affections of the skeleton*. Baltimore: Williams & Wilkins; 1951.

Ferner RE. Neurofibromatosis 1. *Europ J Human Gen* 2007;15:131–138.

Fotiadou A, Arvaniti M, Kiriakou V, Tsitouridis I. Type II autosomal dominant osteopetrosis: radiological features in two families containing five members with asymptomatic and uncomplicated disease. *Skeletal Radiol* 2009;38:1015–1021.

Fujimoto H, Nishimura G, Tsumurai Y, et al. Hyperostosis generalisata with striations of the bones: report of a female case and a review of the literature. *Skeletal Radiol* 1999;28:460–464.

Furia JP, Schwartz HS. Hereditary multiple diaphyseal sclerosis: a tumor simulator. *Orthopedics* 1990;13:1267–1274.

Gehweiler JA, Bland WR, Carden TS Jr, Daffner RH. Osteopathia striata—Voorhoeve's disease: review of the roentgen manifestations. *Am J Roentgenol* 1973;118:450–455.

Gelb BD, Shi GP, Chapman HA, Desnick RJ. Pycnodysostosis, a lysosomal disease caused by cathepsin K deficiency. *Science* 1996;273:1236–1238.

George K, Rippstein JA. A comparative study of the two popular methods of measuring scoliotic deformity of the spine. *J Bone Joint Surg [Am]* 1961;43A:809.

Glorieux FH, Ward LM, Rauch F, Lalic L, Roughley P, Travers R. Osteogenesis imperfecta type VI: a form of brittle bone disease with a mineralization defect. *J Bone Min Res* 2002;17:30–38.

Goldstein LA, Waugh TR. Classification and terminology of scoliosis. *Clin Orthop* 1973;93:10–22.

Green AE, Ellswood WH, Collins JR. Melorheostosis and osteopoikilosis with a review of the literature. *Am J Roentgenol* 1962;87:1096–1111.

Greenspan A. Bone island (enostosis): current concept—a review. *Skeletal Radiol* 1995;24:111–115.

Greenspan A. Sclerosing bone dysplasias—a target-site approach. *Skeletal Radiol* 1991;20:561–583.

Greenspan A, Azouz EM. Bone dysplasia series. Melorheostosis: review and update. *Canad Assoc Radiol J* 1999;50:324–330.

Greenspan A, Pugh JW, Norman A, Norman RS. Scoliotic index: a comparative evaluation of methods for the measurement of scoliosis. *Bull Hosp Jt Dis Orthop Inst* 1978;39:117–125.

Greenspan A, Stadalnik RC. Bone island: scintigraphic findings and their clinical application. *Can Assoc Radiol J* 1995;46:368–379.

Greenspan A, Steiner G, Knutzon R. Bone island (enostosis): clinical significance and radiologic and pathologic correlations. *Skeletal Radiol* 1991;20:85–90.

Greenspan A, Steiner G, Sotelo D, Norman A, Sotelo A, Sotelo-Ortiz F. Mixed sclerosing bone dysplasia coexisting with dysplasia epiphysealis hemimelica (Trevor-Fairbank disease). *Skeletal Radiol* 1986;15:452–454.

Griffiths DL. Engelmann's disease. *J Bone Joint Surg [Br]* 1956;38B:312–326.

Gundry CR, Heithoff KB. Imaging evaluation of patients with spinal deformity. *Orthop Clin North Am* 1994;15:247–264.

Hagiwara H, Aida N, Machida J, Fujita K, Okuzumi S, Nishimura G. Contrast-enhanced MRI of an early preosseous lesion of fibrodysplasia ossificans progressiva in a 21-month-old boy. *Am J Roentgenol* 2003;181:1145–1147.

Hoppenfeld S. *Scoliosis: a manual of concept and treatment*. Philadelphia: JB Lippincott; 1967.

Hopwood JJ, Morris CP. The mucopolysaccharidoses: diagnosis, molecular genetics and treatment. *Mol Biol Med* 1990;7:381–404.

Hundley JD, Wilson FC. Progressive diaphyseal dysplasia. Review of the literature and report of seven cases in one family. *J Bone Joint Surg [Am]* 1973;55A:461–474.

Hurt RL. Osteopathia striata—Voorhoeve's disease: report of a case presenting features of osteopathia striata and osteopetrosis. *J Bone Joint Surg [Br]* 1953;35B:89–96.

Jacobson HG. Dense bone—too much bone: radiological considerations and differential diagnosis. Part I. *Skeletal Radiol* 1985;13:1–20.

Janssens K, Gershoni-Baruch R, Van Hul E, et al. Localisation of the gene causing diaphyseal dysplasia Camurati-Engelmann to chromosome 19q13. *J Med Genet* 2000;37:249–249.

Judkiewisz AM, Murphey MD, Resnik CS, Newberg AH, Temple HT, Smith WS. Advanced imaging of melorheostosis with emphasis on MRI. *Skeletal Radiol* 2001;30:447–453.

Kaftori JK, Kleinhaus U, Naveh Y. Progressive diaphyseal dysplasia (Camurati-Engelmann): radiographic follow-up and CT findings. *Radiology* 1987;164:777–782.

Kaplan FS, McCluskey W, Hahn G, Tabas JA, Muenke M, Zasloff MA. Genetic transmission of fibrodysplasia ossificans progressiva. Report of a family. *J Bone Joint Surg [Am]* 1993;75:1214–1220.

Kaufmann HJ. Classification of the skeletal dysplasias and the radiologic approach to their differentiation. *Clin Orthop* 1976;114:12–17.

Kennedy JG, Donahue JR, Aydin H, Hoang BH, Huvos A, Morris C. Metastatic breast carcinoma to bone disguised by osteopoikilosis. *Skeletal Radiol* 2003;32:240–243.

Kerkeni S, Chapurlat R. Melorheostosis and FGF-23: is there a relationship? *Joint Bone Spine* 2008;75:486–488.

Kim HW, Weinstein SL. Spine update. The management of scoliosis in neurofibromatosis. *Spine* 1997;22:2770–2776.

Klatte EC, Franken EA, Smith JA. The radiographic spectrum in neurofibromatosis. *Semin Roentgenol* 1976;11:17–33.

Kleinman PK. Differentiation of child abuse and osteogenesis imperfecta: medical and legal implications. *Am J Roentgenol* 1990;154:1047–1048.

Kobayashi H, Kotoura Y, Hosono M, Tsuboyama T, Shigeno C, Konishi J. A case of melorheostosis with a 14-year-old follow-up. *Eur Radiol* 1995;5:651–653.

Korovessis PG, Stamatakis MV. Prediction of scoliotic Cobb angle with the use of the scoliometer. *Spine* 1996;21:1661–1666.

Kozlowski K, Nicol R, Hopwood JJ. A clinically mild case of mucopolysaccharidosis type I—Scheie syndrome (case report). *Eur Radiol* 1995;5:561–563.

Kumar B, Murphy WA, Whyte MP. Progressive diaphyseal dysplasia (Engelmann disease): scintigraphic-radiographic-clinical correlations. *Radiology* 1981;140:87–92.

Kumar Jain V, Kumar Arya R, Bharadwaj M, Kumar S. Melorheostosis: clinicopathological features, diagnosis, and management. *Orthopedics* 2009; 32:512–521.

Lagier R, Mbakop A, Bigler A. Osteopoikilosis: a radiological and pathological study. *Skeletal Radiol* 1984;11:161–168.

Langer LO Jr, Baumann PA, Gorlin RJ. Achondroplasia. *Am J Roentgenol* 1967;100:12–26.

Lenke LG, Betz RR, Harms J, et al. Adolescent idiopathic scoliosis. A new classification to determine extent of spinal arthrodesis. *J Bone Joint Surg [Am]* 2001;83A:1169–1181.

Lenke LG, Bridwell KH, Blanke K, Baldus C, Weston J. Radiographic results of arthrodesis with Cotrel-Dubousset instrumentation for the treatment of adolescent idiopathic scoliosis. A five to ten-year follow-up study. *J Bone Joint Surg [Am]* 1998;80:807–814.

Léri A, Joanny J. Une affection non décrite des os. Hyperostose en coulée sur toute la longeur d'un membre ou mélorhéostose. *Bull Mem Soc Med Hop Paris* 1922;46:1141.

MacEwen GD, Conway JJ, Miller WT. Congenital scoliosis with a unilateral bar. *Radiology* 1968;90:711–715.

Mahoney J, Achong DM. Demonstration of increased bone metabolism in melorheostosis by multiphase bone scanning. *Clin Nucl Med* 1991;16:847–848.

Marchesi DG, Transfeldt EE, Bradford DS, Heithoff KB. Changes in intervertebral rotation after Harrington and Luque instrumentation for idiopathic scoliosis. *Spine* 1992;17:775–780.

Maroteaux P, Lamy M. La pycnodysostose. *Presse Med* 1962;70:999–1002.

Maroteaux P, Lamy M. The malady of Toulouse-Lautrec. *JAMA* 1965;191:715–717.

McKusick V. *Hereditary disorders of connective tissue*, 4th ed. St. Louis: CV Mosby; 1972.

Millner PA, Dickson RA. Idiopathic scoliosis: biomechanics and biology. *Eur Spine J* 1996;5:362–373.

Mishra GK, Mishra M, Vernekar J, Tehrai M, Patel BR. Progressive diaphyseal dysplasia: Englemann's disease. *Indian Pediatr* 1987;24:1052–1054.

Moser FG, Mangiardi JR, Kantrowitz AB. Device for accurate localization of vertebrae before spinal surgery. *Am J Roentgenol* 1996;166:626–627.

Murray DW, Bulstrode CJ. The development of adolescent idiopathic scoliosis. *Eur Spine J* 1996;5:251–257.

Murray RO, McCredie J. Melorheostosis and the sclerotomes: a radiological correlation. *Skeletal Radiol* 1979;4:57–71.

Nash CL Jr, Moe JH. A study of vertebral rotation. *J Bone Joint Surg [Am]* 1969;51A:223–229.

Neufeld E, Muenzer J. The mucopolysaccharidoses. In: Scriver CR, Beaudet MC, Sly WS, Valle D, eds. *The metabolic basis of inherited disease*, 6th ed. New York: McGraw-Hill; 1989:1565–1587.

Neuhauser EBD, Schwachman H, Wittenberg M, Cohen J. Progressive diaphyseal dysplasia. *Radiology* 1948;51:11–22.

Norman A. Myositis ossificans and fibrodysplasia ossificans progressiva. In: Taveras JM, Ferrucci JT, eds. *Radiology—diagnosis, imaging, intervention*, vol. 5. Philadelphia: JB Lippincott; 1986.

Norman A, Greenspan A. Bone dysplasias. In: Jahss MH, ed. *Disorders of the foot and ankle: medical and surgical management*, vol. 1, 2nd ed. Philadelphia: WB Saunders; 1991:754–770.

Oestreich AE, Young LW, Poussaint TY. Scoliosis *circa* 2000: radiologic imaging perspective. I. Diagnosis and pretreatment evaluation. *Skeletal Radiol* 1998;27:591–605.

Oestreich AE, Young LW, Poussaint TY. Scoliosis *circa* 2000: radiologic imaging perspective. II. Treatment and follow-up. *Skeletal Radiol* 1998;27:651–656.

Omeroglu H, Ozekin O, Biçimoglu A. Measurement of vertebral rotation in idiopathic scoliosis using the Perdriolle torsionmeter: a clinical study on intraobserver and interobserver error. *Eur Spine J* 1996;5:167–171.

Park HS, Kim JR, Lee SY, Jang KY. Symptomatic giant (10-cm) bone island of the tibia. *Skeletal Radiol* 2005;34:347–350.

Paul LW. Hereditary, multiple diaphyseal sclerosis (Ribbing disease). *Radiology* 1953;60:412–416.

Reichenberger E, Tiziani V, Watanabe S, et al. Autosomal dominant craniometaphyseal dysplasia is caused by mutations in the transmembrane protein ANK. *Am J Hum Genet* 2001;68:1321–1326.

Reinig JW, Hill SC, Fang M, Marini J, Zasloff MA. Fibrodysplasia ossificans progressiva: CT appearance. *Radiology* 1986;159:153–157.

Rhys R, Davies AM, Mangham DC, Grimer RJ. Sclerotome distribution of melorheostosis and multicentric fibromatosis. *Skeletal Radiol* 1998;27:633–636.

Ribbing S. Hereditary, multiple, diaphyseal sclerosis. *Acta Radiol* 1949;31:522–536.

Riccardi VM. Von Recklinghausen's neurofibromatosis. *N Engl J Med* 1981;305:1617–1627.

Rubin P. *Dynamic classification of bone dysplasias*. Chicago: Year Book Medical Publishers; 1964:325–349.

Rutherford EE, Tarplett LJ, Davies EM, Harley JM, King LJ. Lumbar spine fusion and stabilization: hardware, technique, and imaging appearances. *Radiographics* 2007;27:1737–1749.

Scheie HG, Hambrick GW Jr, Barness LA. A newly recognised forme fruste of Hurler's disease (gargoylism): the Sanford R Gifford lecture. *Am J Ophthalmol* 1962;53: 753–769.

Schwartz A, Ramos R. Neurofibromatosis and multiple nonossifying fibromas. *Am J Roentgenol* 1980;135:617–619.

Scott H, Bunge S, Gal A, Clarke L, Morris CP, Hopwood JJ. The molecular genetics of mucopolysaccharidosis type I: diagnostic, clinical and biological implications. *Hum Mutat* 1995;6:288–302.

Seeger LL, Hewel KC, Yao L, et al. Ribbing disease (multiple diaphyseal sclerosis): imaging and differential diagnosis. *Am J Roentgenol* 1996;167:689–694.

Shafritz AB, Shore EM, Gannon FH, et al. Overexpression of an osteogenic morphogen in fibrodysplasia ossificans progressiva. *N Eng J Med* 1996;335:555–561.

Shier CK, Krasicky GA, Ellis IB, Kottamasu SR. Ribbing's disease: radiographic-scintigraphic correlation and comparative analysis with Engelmann's disease. *J Nucl Med* 1987;28:244–248.

Shufflebarger HL, Clark CE. Fusion levels and hook patterns in thoracic scoliosis with Cotrel-Dubousset instrumentation. *Spine* 1990;15:916–920.

Sillence DO. Osteogenesis imperfecta: an expanding panorama of variants. *Clin Orthop* 1981;159:11–25.

Sillence DO, Senn A, Danks DM. Genetic heterogeneity in osteogenesis imperfecta. *J Med Genet* 1979;16:101–116.

Silverman FN. Achondroplasia. *Semin Roentgenol* 1973;8:142–143.

Slone RM, MacMillan M. Montgomery WJ, Heare M. Spinal fixation. 2. Fixation techniques and hardware for the thoracic and lumbar spine. *Radiographics* 1993;13: 521–544.

Sparkes RS, Graham CB. Camurati-Engelmann disease: genetics and clinical manifestations with a review of the literature. *J Med Genet* 1972;9:73–85.

Spieth ME, Greenspan A, Forrester DM, Ansari AN, Kimura RL, Siegel ME. Radionuclide imaging in forme fruste of melorheostosis. *Clin Nucl Med* 1994;19:512–515.

Spranger JW. Mucopolysaccharidosen. In: Schwiegk H, ed. *Handbuch der inneren Medizin.* 5th ed. New York: Springer-Verlag; 1974:212–215.

Spranger JW, Langer LO Jr, Wiederman HR. *Bone dysplasias. An atlas of constitutional disorders of skeletal development.* Philadelphia: WB Saunders; 1974.

Stevenson RE, Howell RR, McKusick VA, et al. The iduronidase-deficient mucopolysaccharidoses: clinical and roentgenographic features. *Pediatrics* 1976;57:111–122.

Stokes IA. Three-dimensional terminology of spinal deformity. *Spine* 1994;19:236–248.

Taitz LS. Child abuse and osteogenesis imperfecta. *Br Med J* 1987;295:1082–1083.

Thompson SB, Eales W. Clinical considerations and comparative measures of assessing curvature of the spine. *J Med Eng Technol* 1994;18:143–147.

Thomsen MN, Schneider U, Weber M, Johannisson R, Niethard FU. Scoliosis and congenital anomalies associated with Klippel-Feil syndrome types I-III. *Spine* 1997;22:396–401.

Urbaniak JR, Schaefer WW, Stalling FH III. Iliac apophyses: prognostic value in idiopathic scoliosis. *Clin Orthop* 1976;116:80–85.

van Buchem FSP. Hyperostosis corticalis generalisata: eight new cases. *Acta Med Scand* 1971;189:257–267.

van Buchem FSP, Hadders HN, Hansen JF, Woldring MG. Hyperostosis corticalis generalisata: report of seven cases. *Am J Med* 1962;33:387–397.

van Buchem FSP, Hadders HN, Ubbens R. An uncommon familial systemic disease of the skeleton: hyperostosis corticalis generalisata familiaris. *Acta Radiol [Diagn]* 1955;44:109–120.

Vanhoenacker FM, Balemans W, Tan GJ, et al. Van Buchem disease: lifetime evolution of radioclinical features. *Skeletal Radiol* 2003;32:708–718.

Van Hul W, Balemans W, Van Hul E, et al. Van Buchem disease (hyperostosis corticalis generalisata) maps to chromosome 17q12-q21. *Am J Hum Genet* 1998;62: 391–399.

Walker GF. Mixed sclerosing bone dystrophies. Two case reports. *J Bone Joint Surg [Br]* 1964;46B:546–552.

Ward LM, Rauch F, Travers R, et al. Osteogenesis imperfecta type VII: an autosomal recessive form of brittle bone disease. *Bone* 2002;31:12–18.

Warkany J. Dwarfs and other little people: an overview. *Semin Roentgenol* 1973;8:135–138.

Weiss IR. Measurement of vertebral rotation: Perdriolle versus Raimondi. *Eur Spine J* 1995;4:34–38.

Whyte MP, Murphy WA, Siegel BA. ^{99m}Tc-pyrophosphate bone imaging in osteopoikilosis, osteopathia striata and melorheostosis. *Radiology* 1978;127:439–443.

Whyte MP, Murphy WA, Fallon MD, Hahn TJ. Mixed-sclerosing-bone-dystrophy: report of a case and review of the literature. *Skeletal Radiol* 1981;6:95–102.

Winter RB. Congenital spine deformity. In: Bradford DS, Lonstein JE, Moe JH, Ogilvie JW, Winter RB, eds. *Moe's textbook of scoliosis and other spinal deformities,* 2nd ed. Philadelphia: WB Saunders; 1987:233–270.

Winter RB, Haven JJ, Moe JH, Lagaard SM. Diastematomyelia and congenital spinal deformities. *J Bone Joint Surg [Am]* 1974;56A:27–39.

Winter RB, Moe JH, Eilers VE. Congenital scoliosis. A study of 234 patients treated and untreated. *J Bone Joint Surg [Am]* 1968;50A:1.

Worth HM, Wollin DG. Hyperostosis corticalis generalisata congenita. *J Can Assoc Radiol* 1966;17:67–74.

Wynne-Davies R, Fairbank TJ. *Fairbank's atlas of general affections of the skeleton,* 2nd ed. New York: Churchill Livingstone; 1976.

Yaghmai I. Spine changes in neurofibromatosis. *Radiographics* 1986;6:261–285.

Ziran N, Hill S, Wright ME, et al. Ribbin disease: radiographic and biochemical characterization, lack of response to pamidronate. *Skeletal Radiol* 2003;31:714–719.

Figure Credits

The following figures were reproduced with permission, in addition to those so indicated in the text.

Figures 7.42, 9.33, 9.47, 29.12, 29.13, and 29.20 from Berquist TH, ed. *MRI of the musculoskeletal system*, 3rd ed. Philadelphia: Lippincott-Raven Publishers; 1997.

Figure 10.14B modified from Berquist TH, ed. *Radiology of the foot and ankle*. New York: Raven Press; 1989.

Figures 9.32, 9.46, 9.77, 9.78, and 13.39 from Bloem JL, Sartoris DJ, eds. *MRI and CT of the musculoskeletal system. A text-atlas*. Baltimore: Williams & Wilkins; 1992.

Figure 11.22B from Chapman MW, Madison M, eds. *Operative orthopaedics*, vol 4, 2nd ed. Philadelphia: JB Lippincott; 1993.

Figures 10.70, 10.71A, and 10.86 from Deutsch AL, Mink JH, Kerr R, eds. *MRI of the foot and ankle*. New York: Raven Press; 1992.

Figures 6.44, 7.31A, 7.106, and 9.65 from Deutsch AL, Mink JH, eds. *MRI of the musculoskeletal system: a teaching file*, 2nd ed. Philadelphia: Lippincott-Raven Publishers; 1997.

Figures 16.26, 16.38, 16.45C, 17.15, 17.18, 21.6B, 22.39, 23.1, 23.13, 23.14, and 23.18 from Greenspan A, Remagen W. *Differential diagnosis of tumors and tumor-like lesions*. Philadelphia: Lippincott-Raven Publishers; 1998.

Figure 7.88A,B from Higgins CB, Hricak H, Helms CA, eds. *Magnetic resonance imaging of the body*, 3rd ed. Philadelphia: Lippincott-Raven Publishers; 1997.

Figures 5.51 and 5.53 from Steinbach LS, Tirman PFJ, Peterfy CG, Feller JF, eds. *Shoulder magnetic resonance imaging*. Philadelphia: Lippincott-Raven Publishers; 1998.

Figures 5.58B,C, 5.63, 5.64, 7.28, 7.105, 9.34, 9.57, 9.79, 9.84, 9.85, 10.59, 10.64, 13.20, 13.22, 13.40, 13.41, and 13.49 from Stoller DW. *MRI in orthopaedics and sports medicine*. Philadelphia: JB Lippincott; 1993.

Index

Page numbers in *italics* denote figures; those followed by a "t" denote tables.